WHO'S WHO
Historical Society

Documenting biographies for history since 1928

Proud publishers of the following reference directories:

International WHO'S WHO of Professionals ™

International WHO'S WHO of Professional Management ™

International WHO'S WHO of Entrepreneurs ™

International WHO'S WHO of Information Technology ™

International WHO'S WHO of Professional Educators ™

International WHO'S WHO of Public Service ™

International WHO'S WHO of Professional Administrators ™

WHO'S WHO in California ™

ISBN: 1-882952-20-0

International WHO'S WHO of Information Technology ™ *is published*
and distributed annually by:
WHO'S WHO Historical Society
1650A Gum Branch Road, P.O. Box 3002
Jacksonville, NC 28541-3002
Phone: (800) ASK-4-WHO
Fax: (910) 455-1937
E-mail: www.whoswhohistoricalsociety.com

The annual edition is available to members only for $369.00.
To order a copy, please call Membership Services at (800) ASK-4-WHO
and give the operator the ISBN number above.
A 10% shipping and handling charge will be calculated for U.S. shipments.
International orders must call for exact rates.
North Carolina residents must add appropriate sales tax.

POSTMASTER send address changes to:
International WHO'S WHO of Information Technology ™
C/O WHO'S WHO Historical Society
1650A Gum Branch Road
Jacksonville, NC 28540

Printed and bound in the United States of America

International
WHO'S WHO
of
Information Technology ™

"Technology is our future, but information is the key... "

Disclaimer

International WHO'S WHO of Information Technology ™ reserves the right to select only the appropriate material deemed to be consistent with the style, standards, and limits of space established. In the unlikely event of errors or omissions in this edition or in any other published materials, the sole responsibility of the publisher will be to correct any such errors in a succeeding edition of that same publication. Such a correction is in lieu of any other remedy. International WHO'S WHO of Information Technology ™ and the WHO'S WHO Historical Society expressly disclaims all other liability or loss or incidental or consequential damage, whether arising from negligence, contract, or any other cause to any party for errors or omissions in publishing. WHO'S WHO Historical Society does not coerce an opinion or any other form of assurance to any party.

No part of this publication may be reproduced or transmitted in any form or by any means, electronic or mechanical, including photocopying, recording, or by any information storage and retrieval system, without permission in writing from International WHO'S WHO of Information Technology ™.

This edition was compiled with the assistance of the following individuals at the WHO'S WHO Historical Society:

Edward A. Bohn
Chairman of the Board

Terrence J. Leifheit
Executive Director

Louann M. Driver
Editor in Chief

Wayne H. Uehara
Publications Manager

Jessica L. Grywalsky
Publications Editor

Travles R. Lane
Editorial Manager

Jennifer L. Wilson
Editor

Yvonne C. Guy
Marketing Director

International WHO'S WHO of Information Technology ™

Published by WHO'S WHO Historical Society

We would like to gratefully acknowledge the willing participation of our Board of Advisors, whose function is to help us maintain the highest standard of membership and provide us with input in regards to world economic, political, industrial, and professional issues. Their voluntary efforts and contributions are greatly appreciated. This edition was compiled with the assistance of the following accomplished individuals who serve on the International WHO'S WHO of Information Technology ™ Board of Advisors:

Daniel D. Reneau, Ph.D.
President
Louisiana Tech University

Edmond J. Blausten
Chief Technical Officer
GTECH WorldServ
GTECH Corporation

Paula K. Singh
Founder, President & CEO
International Academy of
Information Sciences,
Systems & Technologies

Michael A. Marino
President
Carolina Manufacturers
Service, Inc.

Daniel D. Reneau, Ph.D.

President
Louisiana Tech University
Railroad Avenue, Wyly Tower, Room 1620
Ruston, LA 71272
(318) 257-3785
Fax: (318) 257-2928

8221

Business Information: As President, Dr. Reneau is the chief executive administrator responsible for all aspects of academic operations, particularly serving as the University's representative in all outreach and community relations. A full-tenured Professor of Biomedical Engineering, Dr. Reneau continues to conduct research in the field. He was also responsible for the implementation, in 1973, of the Biomedical Engineering Department. Louisiana Tech University is a public-four-year, coed, specialized university with diversified graduate programs. Established in 1894, the University has 407 full-time faculty, 75 part-time faculty, and over 1,100 administrative and support staff. Special programs of study include: Preprofessional programs in Law, Medicine, Veterinary Science, Pharmacy, Dentistry, and Optometry. Six colleges within the University are Engineering, Administration and Business, Education, Life Sciences, Human Ecology, and Graduate School. **Career Highlights:** Louisiana Tech University: President (1988-Present), Vice President of Academic Affairs (1980-87), Professor and Head of the Biomedical Engineering Department (1973-80), Associate Professor and Head of the Biomedical Engineering Department (1972-73). **Associations and Accomplishments:** American Chemical Society; American Institute of chemical Engineers; American Society of Engineering Education; Biomedical Engineering Society; European Society for Microcirculation; International Association for Oxygen Transport Tissue; Louisiana Engineering Society; Louisiana Teachers Association. **Education:** Clemson University, M.S. in Chemical Engineering (1964); Louisiana Tech University, B.S. (1963). **Personal Information:** Married to Linda in 1961. Two children: Dana Reneau Bernhard and John Reneau. Dr. Reneau enjoys reading, fishing, scuba diving, and collecting North Louisiana Indian artifacts.

Edmond J. Blausten

Chief Technical Officer
GTECH WorldServ
GTECH Corporation
P.O. Box 6074
Warwick, RI 02877-6074
(401) 392-7410
Fax: (401) 884-8886
Email: eblausten@gtech.com

7373

Business Information: With over sixteen years of expertise in the communications industry, Mr. Blausten joined GTECH in 1992. Serving as Chief Technical Officer of the Government Services Division, he defines the overall architecture (system and operation) from communication networks to central CPUs. GTECH Corporation is a provider of transaction processing systems and networks for the lottery, welfare, and other government-operated/associated automated programs. GTECH is also moving into the non-gaming side of governmental divisions, having just taken on the Texas Fish and Game Department, and will do licensing by computer, etc. Established in 1982, GTECH reports an annual revenue of $700 million and currently employs more than 4,000 people. **Career Highlights:** Chief Technical Officer, GTECH Corporation (1992-Present); Vice President - TDS, Electronic Data Systems (1992-Present); Director of Research and Development, ITT World Communications, Inc. (1979-85). **Associations and Accomplishments:** International Telecommunications Union; Group Chairman, CCITT; National Association of Radio and Telecommunications Engineers. **Education:** University of Phoenix, M.B.A.; Fairleigh Dickinson, M.S.E.E.; Lehigh University, B.S. **Personal Information:** Married to Toshiko in 1982. Mr. Blausten enjoys showing and breeding dogs.

Paula Kaur Singh

Founder/President/Chief Executive Officer
The International Academy of Information Sciences, Systems, and Technologies
160 West Portola Avenue
Los Altos, CA 94022-1210
(415) 941-8761

8299

Business Information: As Founder, President, and Chief Executive Officer of The International Academy of Information Sciences, Systems, and Technologies, Paula Singh handles all daily activities. She also serves as Chairman of the Board of Directors. A respected professional in her field, she is a member of International WHO'S WHO of Professionals, International WHO'S WHO of Professional Management, International WHO'S WHO of Entrepreneurs, and International WHO'S WHO of Information Technology. Established in 1994, The International Academy of Information Sciences, Systems, and Technologies is an international educational institution for information sciences, systems, and technologies. The International Academy of Information Sciences, Systems, and Technologies strengthens the link between industry and education, promotes breakthroughs by facilitating the transfer of knowledge and technologies, and promotes public awareness of technologies and their impacts. **Career Highlights:** Founder/President/Chief Executive Officer, The International Academy of Information Sciences, Systems, and Technologies (1994–Present); Director of Seminars and Information Services, Mind Matters Seminars, Stanford, California (1993); Founder/President/Chief Executive Officer, Medical Information Management Research and Development (1984–Present). **Associations and Accomplishments:** International Association of Women in Technology; American Association for the Advancement of Sciences; Scientist/Mentor, Boston Museum of Science; Member, Smithsonian Institute; Founding Member, The Library of Congress; Association of Women in Science; American Public Health Association – Forum of Bioethics, Health Education, and Legislative Action Committee; National Association of Female Executives; American Association of University Women; International Federation of University Women; Citizen Ambassador, People to People International. **Education:** Harvard University and Massachusetts Institute of Technology, Senior Executive Education Programs (1997); Stanford University, Executive Education Programs (1996); University of California – Davis, B.S. (1988); Numerous forums, symposiums, and national and international conferences. **Personal:** Ms. Singh enjoys triathlons, white water river guiding, playing the saxophone, singing, photography, and yacht races.

Michael A. Marino

President
Carolina Manufacturers Service, Inc.
2650 Pilgrim Court
Winston-Salem, NC 27104
(910) 631-2867
Fax: (910) 631-2906
mike.marino@cms.inmar-inc.com

8741

Business Information: Incorporating 28 successful years of experience with NYNEX Corporation, a world leading telecommunications conglomeration, Michael Marino's expertise in communications and information technology led him to serve in many key positions. His extensive communications background includes serving as Group Vice President for NYNEX Corporation; Executive Vice President and Chief Operating Officer for NYNEX Mobile Communications Company; Vice President of Strategy and Planning for NYNEX Worldwide Services Group; Executive Vice President and Chief Operating Officer with NYNEX Business Centers; and Vice President of Finance and Administration for NYNEX Business Information Systems Company. Utilizing his vast skills acquired in the telecommunications field, Mr. Marino joined Carolina Manufacturers Service, Inc. as President in 1996. Carolina Manufacturers Service, Inc. leads the North American Market as the longest-standing provider of promotion planning and management services to major consumer product manufacturers and their distribution partners. Currently the largest of three operating subsidiaries of Inmar Enterprises, Inc., Carolina Manufacturers Service, Inc. is headquartered along with them in Winston-Salem, North Carolina. Founded in 1983, the Company employs 2,500 people in North Carolina and in various locations throughout Mexico and Texas. **Associations & Accomplishments:** Alumni Board, Pace University, Lubin Graduate School of Business; Alumni Association, Tufts University; Board of Directors, Wireless Telecom, Inc.; Alumni Association, Beelzebuds of Tufts University; Delta Delta Mu Delta Honorary Society for MBA Graduates; Fundraiser: United Way, Junior Achievement, March of Dimes, Juvenile Diabetes Foundation; Board of Advisors, International WHO'S WHO of Information Technology. **Personal:** Married to Diane in 1988. Two children: Christie and Loryn. Mr. Marino enjoys playing golf, reading, and travel.

International WHO'S WHO of Information Technology ™

On behalf of the WHO'S WHO Historical Society, welcome to the 4th edition of International WHO'S WHO of Information Technology. Your unabbreviated biography in this publication is a milestone in your professional career. Our team of quality writers and editors has clearly and eloquently recorded your life's accomplishments for access by your peers from around the globe. Likewise, your membership in the WHO'S WHO Historical Society entitles you to network with as many successful IT professionals within these pages as you like!

Keeping abreast of the latest trends and technologies is a challenge in and of itself. Let International WHO'S WHO of Information Technology introduce you to the people, who, like you, are interested in maintaining that competitive edge as well as developing the necessary relationships for unlimited growth. Now you can foster those relationships quickly and easily. When you begin contacting your fellow WHO'S WHO colleagues and networking with them, you will undoubtedly soar to new heights, expand your knowledge of various business practices abroad, grow your business into new markets, and make new friends. All you need to do to begin networking is turn the page.

The WHO'S WHO Historical Society further empowers you by equipping you with an online version of this powerful networking tool - Books Online. With Books Online, your comprehensive directory is conveniently accessible to you from your office, home, or laptop computer. International WHO'S WHO of Information Technology is available to members only at www.whoswhohistorical-society.com. For additional information on how you can access to Books Online area of the Web site, simply contact a membership services representative at (800) ASK-4-WHO. He or she will be more than happy to assign you a personalized user name and password.

Your potential for newfound business contacts is virtually unlimited with either the online or hardbound directory. The choice is yours. And each biography has been approved for accuracy and content by the member. This ensures that no matter which version you use, you will access only correct and up-to-date information.

Each biographical entry consists of the following facts, unless withheld by the member:
- Member's Name
- Business Title
- Business Name
- Business Address
- Business Phone and Fax Numbers and Email Address
- Standard Industrial Classification Code
- Business Information
- Career Highlights
- Associations and Accomplishments
- Education
- Personal Information

Your easy-to-understand volume is indexed in several formats to maximize the networking potential for WHO'S WHO Historical Society members.

Section 1 is arranged numerically by Standard Industrial Classification code. Section 2 is an alphabetical index of members by last name. Section 3 is an alphabetical index of members by company name. Section 4 is a geographical index arranged alphabetically by location. Lastly, Section 5 is an alphabetical listing of non-members by last name.

In addition we have included a list of phone codes, to assist you in networking with other IT professionals from around the world. This list is arranged alphabetically by country name to allow you ease in getting in touch with your peers.

For your convenience, our biographies are unabbreviated and contain no confusing jargon. This easy-to-read format is one of the unique characteristics of the WHO'S WHO Historical Society's directories, elevating us above our competitors.

We've compiled a diversified collection of biographies that reflect the unique interests of the world's most accomplished IT professionals. The WHO'S WHO Historical Society enables you to share your experiences as you glean useful strategies from your fellow member and incorporate them into your existing business plans. It is our sincere wish that you will maximize your membership benefits with this unique tool for a lifetime of both professional and personal success.

Afghanistan	93	Cameroon	237	Finland	358
Albania	35	Canada	1	France	33
Algeria	213	Cape Verde Islands	238	French Antilles	590
American Samoa	684	Cayman Islands	345	French Guiana	594
Andorra	376	Central African Republic	236	French Polynesia	689
Angola	244	Chad	235	Gabon	241
Anguilla	809	Channel Islands	44	Gambia	220
Antarctica	672	Chile	56	Georgia	995
Antigua & Barbuda	268	China	86	Germany	49
Argentina	54	Christmas Island	672	Ghana	233
Armenia	376	Cocos Islands	672	Gibraltar	350
Aruba	297	Colombia	57	Greece	30
Ascension	247	Comoros	269	Greenland	299
Australia	61	Congo	242	Grenada and Carriacou	473
Austria	43	Congo, Democratic Republic of	243	Guadeloupe	590
Azerbaijan	994	Cook Islands	682	Guam	671
Bahamas	242	Costa Rica	506	Guatemala	502
Bahrain	973	Croatia	385	Guinea	224
Bangladesh	880	Cuba	53	Guinea-Bissau	245
Barbados	246	Cyprus	357	Guyana	592
Belarus	375	Czech Republic	420	Haiti	509
Belgium	32	Denmark	45	Honduras	504
Belize	501	Djibouti	253	Hong Kong	852
Benin	229	Dominica	767	Hungary	36
Bermuda	441 or 809	Dominican Republic	809	Iceland	354
Bhutan	975	Ecuador	593	India	91
Bolivia	591	Egypt	20	Indonesia	62
Bosnia & Herzegovina	387	El Salvador	503	Iran	98
Botswana	267	Equatorial Guinea	240	Iraq	964
Brazil	55	Eritrea	291	Ireland	353
British Virgin Islands	284	Estonia	372	Isle of Man	44
Brunei	673	Ethiopia	251	Israel	972
Bulgaria	359	Faeroe Islands	298	Italy	39
Burkina Faso	226	Falkland Islands	500	Ivory Coast	225
Burundi	257	Fiji	679	Jamaica	876
Cambodia	855			Japan	81
				Jordan	962

Kazakhstan	7	Myanmar	95	St. Vincent & the Grenadines	784
Kenya	254	Namibia	264	San Marino	378
Kiribati	686	Nauru	674	Sao Tome & Principe	239
Kuwait	965	Nepal	977	Saudi Arabia	966
Kyrgyzstan	996	Netherlands	31	Senegal	221
Laos	856	Netherlands Antilles	599	Seychelles	248
Latvia	371	Nevis	869	Sierra Leone	232
Lebanon	961	New Caledonia	687	Singapore	65
Lesotho	266	New Zealand	64	Slovakia	421
Liberia	231	Nicaragua	505	Slovenia	386
Libya	218	Niger	227	Solomon Islands	677
Liechtenstein	41	Nigeria	234	Somalia	252
Lithuania	370	Niue	683	South Africa	27
Luxembourg	352	Norfolk Island	672	South Korea	82
Macao	853	North Korea	850	Spain	34
Macedonia, Federal Republic of	389	Norway	47	Sri Lanka	94
Madagascar	261	Oman	968	Sudan	249
Malawi	265	Pakistan	92	Suriname	597
Malaysia	60	Palau	680	Swaziland	268
Maldives	960	Panama	507	Sweden	46
Mali	223	Papua New Guinea	675	Switzerland	41
Malta	356	Paraguay	595	Syria	963
Marshall Islands	692	Peru	51	Taiwan	886
Martinique	596	Philippines	63	Tajikistan	7
Mauritania	222	Poland	48	Tanzania	255
Mauritius	230	Portugal	351	Thailand	66
Mayotte	269	Puerto Rico	787	Togo	228
Mexico	52	Qatar	974	Tokelau	690
Micronesia	691	Reunion Island	262	Tonga	676
Midway Islands	808	Romania	40	Trinidad & Tobago	868
Moldova	373	Russia	7	Tunisia	216
Monaco	377	Rwanda	250	Turkey	90
Mongolia	976	St. Helena	290	Turkmenistan	993
Montserrat	664	St. Kitts	869	Turks & Caicos Islands	649
Morocco	212	St. Lucia	758	Tuvalu	688
Mozambique	258	St. Pierre et Miquelon	508	Uganda	256

Country	Code	Country	Code	Country	Code
Ukraine	380	Vanuatu	678	Western Samoa	685
United Arab Emirates	971	Vatican City	39	Yemen	967
United Kingdom	44	Venezuela	58	Yugoslavia	381
United States	1	Vietnam	84	Zaire	243
Uruguay	598	Wake Island	808	Zambia	260
US Virgin Islands	340	Wallis & Futuna Islands	681	Zimbabwe	263
Uzbekistan	7				

Table of Contents

Section 1 - Members Indexed Numerically by Standard Industrial Code..........*1-397*

Section 2 - Members Indexed Alphabetically by Last Name *1-27*

Section 3 - Members Indexed Alphabetically by Company Name...................*1-35*

Section 4 - Members Indexed Alphabetically by Geographic Location.............*1-31*

Section 5 - Non-Members Arranged Alphabetically by Last Name................*1-31*

Members Indexed Numerically by Standard Industrial Code

Section 1

Standard Industrial Code

Table of Contents

0000 – 0999 AGRICULTURE, FORESTRY, and FISHING **1–1**
  0100 Agricultural Production – Crops 1–1
  0200 Agricultural Production – Livestock 1–1
  0900 Fishing, Hunting, and Trapping 1–1

1000 – 1499 MINING **1–1**
  1000 Metal Mining 1–1
  1300 Oil and Gas Extraction 1–2
  1400 Nonmetallic Minerals, Except Fuels 1–3

1500 – 1799 CONSTRUCTION **1–4**
  1500 General Building Contractors 1–4
  1600 Heavy Construction, Ex. Building 1–4
  1700 Special Trade Contractors 1–6

2000 – 3999 MANUFACTURING **1–7**
  2000 Food and Kindred Products 1–7
  2100 Tobacco Products 1–10
  2200 Textile Mill Products 1–11
  2300 Apparel and Other Textile Products 1–11
  2400 Lumber and Wood Products 1–12
  2500 Furniture and Fixtures 1–13
  2600 Paper and Allied Products 1–14
  2700 Printing and Publishing 1–15
  2800 Chemicals and Allied Products 1–22
  2900 Petroleum and Coal Products 1–27
  3000 Rubber and Misc. Plastics Products 1–28
  3100 Leather and Leather Products 1–30
  3200 Stone, Clay, and Glass Products 1–30
  3300 Primary Metal Industries 1–31
  3400 Fabricated Metal Products 1–33
  3500 Industrial Machinery and Equipment 1–35
  3600 Electronic and Other Electric Equipment 1–52
  3700 Transportation Equipment 1–71
  3800 Instruments and Related Products 1–80
  3900 Miscellaneous Manufacturing Industries 1–85

4000 – 4999 TRANSPORTATION AND PUBLIC UTILITIES **1–86**
  4000 Railroad Transportation 1–86
  4100 Local and Interurban Passenger Transit 1–87
  4200 Trucking and Warehousing 1–87
  4300 U.S. Postal Service 1–88
  4400 Water Transportation 1–88
  4500 Transportation By Air 1–89
  4700 Transportation Services 1–91
  4800 Communications 1–91
  4900 Electric, Gas, and Sanitary Services 1–113

5000 – 5199 WHOLESALE TRADE **1–118**
  5000 Wholesale Trade – Durable Goods 1–118
  5100 Wholesale Trade – Nondurable Goods 1–124

5200 – 5999 RETAIL TRADE 1–126
5200 Building Materials and Garden Supplies 1–126
5300 General Merchandise Stores 1–126
5500 Automotive Dealers and Service Stations 1–126
5600 Apparel and Accessory Stores 1–127
5700 Furniture and Homefurnishings Stores 1–127
5800 Eating and Drinking Places 1–129
5900 Miscellaneous Retail 1–130

6000 – 6999 FINANCE, INSURANCE, and REAL ESTATE 1–133
6000 Depository Institutions 1–133
6100 Nondepository Institutions 1–138
6200 Security and Commodity Brokers 1–142
6300 Insurance Carriers 1–148
6400 Insurance Agents, Brokers, and Services 1–156
6500 Real Estate 1–158
6700 Holding and Other Investment Offices 1–160

7000 – 8999 SERVICES 1–162
7000 Hotels and Other Lodging Places 1–162
7200 Personal Services 1–162
7300 Business Services 1–163
7500 Auto Repair, Services, and Parking 1–303
7800 Motion Pictures 1–304
7900 Amusement and Recreation Services 1–305
8000 Health Services 1–306
8100 Legal Services 1–311
8200 Educational Services 1–314
8300 Social Services 1–342
8600 Membership Organizations 1–344
8700 Engineering and Management Services 1–347
8900 Services, Nec 1–370

9100 – 9799 PUBLIC ADMINISTRATION 1–370
9100 Executive, Legislative, and General 1–370
9200 Justice, Public Order, and Safety 1–376
9300 Finance, Taxation, and Monetary Policy 1–379
9400 Administration of Human Resources 1–380
9500 Environmental Quality and Housing 1–386
9600 Administration of Economic Programs 1–389
9700 National Security and International Affairs 1–392

0000 - 0999
AGRICULTURE
FORESTRY
and
FISHING

0100 Agricultural Production-Crops

0111 Wheat
0112 Rice
0115 Corn
0116 Soybeans
0119 Cash grains, nec
0131 Cotton
0132 Tobacco
0133 Sugarcane and sugar beets
0134 Irish potatoes
0139 Field crops, except cash grains, nec
0161 Vegetables and melons
0171 Berry crops
0172 Grapes
0173 Tree nuts
0174 Citrus fruits
0175 Deciduous tree fruits
0179 Fruits and tree nuts, nec
0181 Ornamental nursery products
0182 Food crops grown under cover
0191 General farms, primarily crop

Brett A. Swallow

Senior Information Systems Audit Manager
Archer Daniels Midland Company
4666 East Faries Parkway
Decatur, IL 62526
(217) 424-7423
Fax: (217) 424-7211
swallow@corp.admworld.com

0116

Business Information: Functioning as Senior Information Systems Audit Manager of Archer Daniels Midland Company, Mr. Swallow is responsible for all aspects of auditing to include joint venture and construction auditing. Through a program he adapted, routine audits are performed on the Company-owned bank. All of his auditing is completed from his computer facility. Through the advancements in networking technology, Mr. Swallow is able to travel to all of the offices within the Company and assure that all records are being kept correctly. During his audits, he looks to find any errors that may have been caused either through human error or computer program and brainstorms to create new program additions that would make accounting and auditing more efficient. Mr. Swallow plans to continue with the Company and looks forward to watching its future expansion. Archer Daniels Midland Company is a processor of agricultural commodities. The product line includes beans, corn, cocoa, peanuts, and wheat. Product is grown and cultivated from the extensive acres of farmland owned by the Company. Several products are freeze-dried to maintain their freshness on the marketplace while others are ground and sold to chocolate and flour producing companies. The Company is increasing in size and productivity and through the addition of advertisement on the Internet, annual revenues has made a large jump in profitability. **Career Highlights:** Archer Daniels Midland Company: Senior Information Systems Audit Manager (1999-Present), Department Information Systems Audit Manager (1998-99), Staff Auditor/Senior Auditor/Supervisor (1990-97). **Associations & Accomplishments:** Institute of the Internal Auditors; Information Systems Audit and Control Association; Volunteer Teacher, Junior Achievement of Decatur; Fund Raising, Local Boy Scout Troop; Fund Raising, United Way. **Education:** Eastern Illinois University, Bachelor's degree in Accounting (1990); Richland Community College, Associate's degree in Accounting (1988); Certified Internal Auditor (1994). **Personal Information:** Married to Kelly in 1990. Two children: Ashley and Collin. Mr. Swallow enjoys

intramural sports, travel, personal computers and networking.

0200 Agricultural Production-Livestock

0211 Beef cattle feedlots
0212 Beef cattle, except feedlots
0213 Hogs
0214 Sheep and goats
0219 General livestock, nec
0241 Dairy farms
0251 Broiler, fryer, and roaster chickens
0252 Chicken eggs
0253 Turkeys and turkey eggs
0254 Poultry hatcheries
0259 Poultry and eggs, nec
0271 Fur-bearing animals and rabbits
0272 Horses and other equines
0273 Animal aquaculture
0279 Animal specialties, nec
0291 General farms, primarily animal

Randy M. Black

Network Engineer
Simplot Livestock Company
HC 85
Grand View, ID 83624
(208) 834-2231
Fax: (208) 834-2075
rblack@simplot.com

0211

Business Information: Serving as Network Engineer for Simplot Livestock Company, Mr. Black assumes the responsibility for the Information and Telecommunications of the Company. He maintains a minimum of four Windows® NT□ Enterprise Servers, administrating the local area network in multiple locations and providing support to the wide area network. Offering technical support to the multiple users as well as providing for upwards of 50 to 60 workstations in the Company's various locations. Mr. Black attributes his success to his ability to learn new technology quickly, understand and solve problems, and continuing education. He is currently supporting the implementation of a new feedlot management system, which in turn used correctly, gives Simplot Livestock Company the opportunity to save upwards of $1 million by using the ability to analyze and process data, in turn allowing for better decisions at the management level. Continually striving to improve performance, he works hard to keep his level of expertise at the top. Engaged in the Agriculture industry, Simplot Livestock Company is a large beef producer in the United States. The Company raises approximately 200,000 to 300,000 head of cattle in three separate locations. Simplot Livestock Company employs 200 to 300 dedicated individuals in a variety of positions offered by the Company. **Career Highlights:** Network Engineer, Simplot Livestock Company (1998-Present); Network Engineer, MicroNet Systems, Inc. (1997-98); Technical Support Representative, America OnLine (1996-97). **Education:** MCSE+I certification (In Progress); Certified Careers, Inc., Network Administrator CNA (1997). **Personal Information:** Married to Debra in 1992. Mr. Black enjoys spending time with his wife Debra, motocross racing, snowboarding and reading.

Pamala V. Dover

Manager
Mountaire Farms
Highway 71 South
Lumberbridge, NC 28357
(910) 843-5942
Fax: (910) 843-4058
pamdorer@aol.com

0252

Business Information: Functioning as Manager of Mountaire Farms, Mrs. Dover is responsible for all aspects of day-to-day administration and operational activities of the management information systems infrastructure. As an Oracle Programer, she is accountable for technological advances at all three Company locations. Mrs. Dover, a systems expert, is in charge of LAN/WAN networks, assigning projects, upgrading systems, and troubleshooting and providing solutions. Coordinating resources, time lines, schedules, and budgets also fall within the purview of Mrs. Dover's responsibilities. Her goal is to become more involved in the management aspect of operations. Established in 1996,

Mountaire Farms is a chicken processing company with three locations across North Carolina. More than 1,500 employees coordinate operations in these locations on a daily basis. The Company provides distribution of processed chickens across North Carolina and the surrounding area. **Career Highlights:** Manager, Mountaire Farms (1998-Present); Supervisory Computer Specialist, 4th POG (1994-98); Information Management Specialist, USASOC DCSIM (1990-94); E-5, United States Army (1979-90). **Education:** Campbell University, B.A. (1997). **Personal Information:** Two children: Joshua and Alison. Mrs. Dover enjoys exercising and reading.

0900 Fishing, Hunting, and Trapping

0912 Finfish
0913 Shellfish
0919 Miscellaneous marine products
0921 Fish hatcheries and preserves
0971 Hunting, trapping, game propagation

Joost Van Den Brink

Business Unit Controller
Moore Clark
1350 Kent Avenue SE
Vancouver, British Columbia, Canada V5X 2Y2
(604) 325-0302
Fax: (604) 325-2884
jvandenb@moore-clark.com

0921

Business Information: Mr. Van Den Brink serves as Business Unit Controller with Moore Clark. He is responsible for all aspects of finance and control of day-to-day business functions, including information technology issues. Before joining the More Clark team as Controller, Mr. Van Den Brink was employed as Controller at Trouw Iberica in Madrid, Spain, and Information Technology Manager for BP Nutrition in the Netherlands. Utilizing his extensive academic background, vast business experience, and time as a 3rd Lieutenant in the Dutch Royal Navy, he owns an established track record of producing results in support of business objectives. Mr. Van Den Brink, with the Company for 10 years, also monitors and tracks the Company's profit and loss statements, accounting ledgers, and fiscal year budget. Upgrading and maintaining the systems and network infrastructure is also an integral part of his responsibilities. Remaining and growing with the Company and eventually moving up the corporate hierarchy serves as Mr. Van Den Brink's future goals. Moore Clark engages in fish farming and fish feed production. Established in 1989, the Company is located in Vancouver, British Columbia. Presently, Moor Clark employs a work force of over 200 people who help generate in excess of $150 million in annual revenues. **Career Highlights:** Moore Clark: Business Unit Controller (1997-Present), Controller (1996-97); Controller, Trouw Iberica (1992-95); Information Technology Manager, BP Nutrition (1991). **Associations & Accomplishments:** Dutch Royal Navy, 3rd Lieutenant (1988). **Education:** Eindhover University of Technology, M.Sc. (1987). **Personal Information:** Married to Rebecca in 1988. Three children: Deborah, Christina, and Timothy. Mr. Van Den Brink enjoys sports, music, the piano and church activities.

1000 - 1499
MINING

1000 Metal Mining

1011 Iron ores
1021 Copper ores
1031 Lead and zinc ores
1041 Gold ores
1044 Silver ores
1061 Ferroalloy ores, except vanadium
1081 Metal mining services
1094 Uranium-radium-vanadium ores
1099 Metal ores, nec

Laurence R. Roebke III

Systems Analyst II
Barrick Goldstrike Mines, Inc.
575 11th Street
Elko, NV 89801
(775) 778-8866
Fax: (775) 738-0041
lroebke@bgmi.com

1041

Business Information: As Systems Analyst II of Barrick Goldstrike Mines, Inc., Mr. Roebke also fulfills the responsibility of network domain administrator and SQL database administrator. In his position, he provides support to the Meikle underground operations of 185 computers, 3 NT servers, and 2 SQL servers. Possessing superior talents and an excellent understanding of technology, Mr. Roebke is accountable for systems analysis, installation, modification, configuration, support, and tracking of operating systems, databases, utilities, software, and hardware. One of his most rewarding aspects of his career is planning and installing the NT domains for Barrick Goldstrike Mines. In the future, Mr. Roebke looks forward to continuing with the Corporation and eventually attaining the position of director of information systems. Located in Elko, Nevada, Barrick Goldstrike Mines, Inc. is the world's largest manufacturer of gold. Founded in 1987, the Corporation manufactures approximately 8,000 ounces of gold per day and then sells the gold to contract buyers mainly for technology use and jewelry making processes. Operating internationally, the Corporation is a subsidiary of Barrick, Inc. Presently, the Corporation employs a work force of over 10,000 people who help generate annual revenues in excess of $4 billion. **Career Highlights:** Systems Analyst II, Barrick Goldstrike Mines, Inc. (1997-Present); Management Information Systems Coordinator, Santa Fe Pacific Gold (1996-97); Novell Network Administrator, Wenatchee Valley College North (1993-96). **Associations & Accomplishments:** Member of the Advisory Board, Bureau of Land Management; Boy Scouts of America. **Education:** Wenatchee Valley College, A.A. in Computer Systems (1993); Colorado Mount College, A.A. in Electrical (1978). **Personal Information:** One child: Shea. Mr. Roebke enjoys fishing, hunting and slot car racing with his son. Mr. Roebke also donates hardware, software, and time to daycare centers and pre-schools to give children a head start with computers.

1300 Oil and Gas Extraction

1311 Crude petroleum and natural gas
1321 Natural gas liquids
1381 Drilling oil and gas wells
1382 Oil and gas exploration services
1389 Oil and gas field services, nec

Yingbin "Ian" He, Ph.D.

President
Spur Ventures Inc.
830-789 West Pender Street
Vancouver, British Columbia, Canada V6C 1H2
(604) 689-5564
Fax: (604) 689-7654
spurventures@bc.sympatico.ca

1311

Business Information: With over 16 years of progressive management level experience in the industry, Dr. He joined Spur Ventures Inc. in 1995. At the present moment, he assumes the responsibilities of President. In his role, he develops and implements the Corporation's tactical direction and strategic technology, business, and marketing plans. Dr. He, relying on experience and with a strong academic background, effectively blends management skills with technical expertise in driving the Corporation's overall growth. Aggressively orchestrating expansion into new geographic markets, developing new service offerings, and engaging in strategic alliances and joint ventures also falls within the realm of Dr. He's functions. Weighing technical and human relations implications of decisions, he is skillful in seeking leading edge solutions. He keeps the Corporation at the forefront by staying on top of the latest technologies. Over the next five years, he desires to become more involved in the production side. Dr. He's favorite advice for others in the industry is "be prepared and keep up with technology." Presently, he is coordinating and working on two high visible projects in China. Spur Ventures Inc. operates as a mining and resources entity. Established in 1987, the Corporation has key sites in Vancouver, Canada as well as China. Presently, Spur Ventures Inc. employs a staff of six people. **Career Highlights:** President, Spur Ventures Inc. (1995-Present); Senior Process Metallurgist, Process Research Associates Ltd. (1992-95). **Associations & Accomplishments:** Two research awards from Canadian Institute of Mining, Metallurgy, & Petroleum; One Patent. **Education:** University of British Columbia: Ph.D. (1994), M.A.Sc. (1989); Heilongjing Institute of Mining and Technology, B.Eng. (1982). **Personal Information:** Married to Ying Wang in 1986. Two children: David and Darrick.

Anna L. Jackson

Project Manager
BP Amoco
13001 FM 1764
Sante Fe, TX 77510
(409) 945-1094
Fax: (409) 945-1787
anna_l_jackson@amoco.com

1311

Business Information: Ms. Jackson is Project Manager for BP Amoco's Sante Fe, Texas location. She is responsible for planning and overseeing development and support of software applications, including coordinating resources and schedules for application development projects. Before joining BP Amoco, Ms. Jackson served as Desktop Support of Hardware and Software for Solvay Polymers. She is also Owner and Proprietor of her own massage therapy business. As a four year technology professional with an established track record of producing results, Ms. Jackson is in charge of tracking and monitoring the fiscal year budget and maintaining vendor relations. An expert, she serves as contact with users and systems management. Directing and participating in the analysis, design, configuration, modification, installation, tracking, and support of software applications are also an integral part of Ms. Jackson's responsibilities. Her future goals include continuing to contribute to the growth of the Company. BP Amoco is the world's third largest petrochemicals company in terms of revenues. International in scope, BP Amoco maintains a strong global presence with over 2,000 locations, to include large scale production plants in the United States, United Kingdom, Belgium, France, Germany, and Brazil. Presently, the Company employs more than 2,000 people at the Sante Fe, Texas facility. **Career Highlights:** Project Manager, BP Amoco (1997-Present); Owner/Proprietor, Healing Touch Massage Therapy (1999-Present); Desktop Support of Hardware and Software, Solvay Polymers (1995-97). **Associations & Accomplishments:** Santa Fe Chamber of Commerce; Project Management Institute. **Education:** Northwood University, B.B.A. (1995). **Personal Information:** Married to Charles A. in 1979. Two children: Charles Jr. and Krista.

Jeff Pribich

Project Manager
BP Amoco
150 West Warrenville Road
Naperville, IL 60563-8473
(630) 420-4862
Fax: (630) 961-6947
jeffprib@yahoo.com

1311

Business Information: Mr. Pribich is the Project Manager of BP Amoco. Specializing his services to the information technology department, he assists in managing several projects at a time. He works with teams of two to ten people, helping design new techniques for transmitting information to the Environmental Protection Agency and legislators. He composes and submits proposals to the sponsors and future sponsors of several projects, encouraging their continued support. The highlights of his career include the development of a program distributed to 15,000 international companies, and management of a four year project and never missing a deadline and keeping a very tight budget. In the future, Mr. Pribich hopes to pursue better opportunities and expand his role in e-Commerce and Internet usage. His success is attributed to his affiliation to industry related associations, networking and interacting with other professionals in different fields, as well as determination, luck, and being in the right place at the right time. BP Amoco engages in the exploration of the world's oil and natural gas industries. The Company markets its product around the world through refineries and gas stations. Hosting over 18,000 locations, the Company assists in the testing and development of new government regulations and reporting techniques. **Career Highlights:** Project Manager, BP Amoco (1995-Present); Amoco Corporation: Project Manager (1992-95), Technical Leader (1990-92). **Associations & Accomplishments:** Project Management Institute; President, Homeowner's Association; President, Trustees WWSHS. **Education:** Elmhurst College: B.S. in Computer Science (1989), B.S. (1986). **Personal Information:** Married to Delores in 1976. Two children: Dan and Kimberly.

Raymond Peltz

Software Engineer
TransCanada Energy
532 South 91st Avenue
Omaha, NE 68114
(402) 537-8844

1321

Business Information: Demonstrating his extensive expertise in the technology field, Mr. Peltz assertively serves as a Software Engineer for TransCanada Energy. He is responsible for creating original business applications geared towards the natural gas industry. Before joining TransCanada Energy in 1997, Mr. Peltz served as a Systems Analyst with Physicians Mutual Insurance Company. His background history also includes 11 years of distinguished service as a Captain in the United States Air Force. In his present role, Mr. Peltz also maintains and administrates the LAN for the Company, providing back up and security for the system. Additionally, he maintains the server and individual workstations, providing technical support to the end users. Continually striving to improve his performance and looking forward in assisting the Company achieve its future corporate objectives is cited as Mr. Peltz's future goals. His career success reflects his ability to think outside the box and aggressively take on new challenges. A natural gas broker and dealer, TransCanada Energy markets, transports, and stores natural gas for various companies. Operations employs the services of 50 dedicated individuals. **Career Highlights:** Software Engineer, TransCanada Energy (1997-Present); Systems Analyst, Physician's Mutual Insurance Company (1996-97); Captain, United States Air Force (1985-96). **Education:** Creighton University, M.S.C.S.M. (1996); Pennsylvania State University, B.S. in Meteorology. **Personal Information:** Married to Amy in 1996.

Inder Chawla, P.M.P.

Program Manager
Schlumberger
6363 San Felipe 391
Houston, TX 77057
(713) 350-4556
Fax: (713) 350-4108
chawla@slb.com

1382

Business Information: A savvy veteran in software solution and product development, Mr. Chawla serves as the Program Manager of Schlumberger. Utilizing over a decade of information technology specialization, he manages the life cycle of data management products within the Company's day-to-day operations. An involved process, Mr. Chawla conducts requirement analysis, specification development, design, commercialization, and the initial support of products and services. Operating from the Geoquest Department, he contributes his skill and dedication in the pursuit of a position as the operations manager. His success reflects his hard work ethic, effective leadership, and ability to take on challenges and deliver results. Specifically catering to the international petroleum industry, Schlumberger is a worldwide technical support leader. Employing well over 60,000 professionals hailing from around the world, the Company offers its superior consultation in 100 countries. Focusing its operations on providing integrated solutions for electronic transactions, semiconductor manufacturing, and IP networks, Schlumberger generates more than $10 billion in revenue annually. Now celebrating its 80th anniversary, the Company will continue to enjoy great success in the future, as its strength and leadership in the consulting industry not to be surpassed. **Career Highlights:** Program Manager, Schlumberger (1996-Present); President, Wildcatters Investment (1999-Present); Production Manager, Oil & Natural Gas Corporation (1989-96). **Associations & Accomplishments:** Project Managemet Institute; Society of Petroleum Engineers; American Institute of Chemical Engineers; Published research papers for worldwide annual technical Society of Petroleum Engineers. **Education:** University of Houston, M.B.A. in Marketing and Management Information Systems (2000); Project Management Institute, P.M.P. in Project Management (1999); Texas A&M University, M.S. in Petroleum Engineering (1995); University of Roorkee, B.S. in Chemical Engineering (1989). **Personal Information:** Married to Arvin Sahney in 1994. One child: NavTej. Mr. Chawla enjoys travel, sci-fi movies, computers and reading.

Dean C. Mikkelsen
Consultant
Schlumberger/GeoQuest
15135 Memorial Drive, #4305
Houston, TX 77079
(281) 293-6531
Fax: (281) 293-2015
dmikkelsen@houston.geoquest.sl
dean.c.mikkelsen@usa.conoco.com

1382

Business Information: Mr. Mikkelsen serves as a Consultant for Schlumberger's GeoQuest division. He engages in consulting, software development, and data modelling, and database administration. Before joining GeoQuest, Mr. Mikkelsen's occupational history included stints as a GIS Data Analyst with Veritas DFC and an Independent GIS Consultant. As a technology professional, he assists client companies in improving the efficiency of their information systems architecture through software customization. Working both in-house and on client sites, Mr. Mikkelsen employs and maintains systems and network environments, including Internet and Intranet networks. Ensuring database integrity and security is also in an integral part of his functions. He is also an instructor of Geographic Information Systems, Mapping and Datums, and satellite navigation (GPS) to the oil and gas industry. He has developed several programs that have been used by GeoQuest worldwide to aid in the use and creation of map projection and datum transforms. Moving to the United States from Canada three years ago, his milestone is being the Special Section Editor for the Society of Exploration Geophysicists. Currently learning Spanish and French, Mr. Mikkelsen would like to relocate many times internationally within Schlumberger/GeoQuest and, in the future, pursue a Master's of Science degree in Geodesy Hydrography or GIS. At this time, his focus is on GIS and mapping that is due to be published in the year 2000. Moving up the management hierarchy on the technical side, publishing more, receiving worldwide recognition, and making an impact on the future serve as Mr. Mikkelsen's objectives. A division of Schlumberger, GeoQuest engages in design and development of software for oil and gas exploration and production. International in scale, GeoQuest operates office in over 60 countries around the globe. Established in 1920, the Company's United States headquarters is in Houston, Texas. Presently, GeoQuest employs a workforce of more than 60,000 people who help generate annual revenues in excess of $11 billion. **Career Highlights:** Consultant, Schlumberger/GeoQuest (1996-Present); Data Analyst/GIS, Veritas AFC (1995-96); Independent Consultant/GIS (1994-95); Registered Professional Engineer. **Associations & Accomplishments:** Association of Registered Professional Engineera, Geophysicists, and Geologists of Alberta; Society of Exploration Geophysicists; International Hydrographics Organization; Canadian Association of Petroleum Landmen. **Education:** University of Calgary, B.Sc. in Survey Engineering (1994); Southern Alberta Institute of Technology, Applied Environmental Management Certificate (1995); Mount Royal College, Calgary, Petroleum Land Contract and Administration (1996). **Personal Information:** Mr. Mikkelsen enjoys soaring, mountain biking and down hill skiing.

Alexander Thomas
Engineering Technologist
Alta Mesa Resources
6200 Highway 6 South, Suite 202
Houston, TX 77083
(281) 530-0991
Fax: (281) 530-5278
agni4000@hotmail.com

1382

Business Information: Possessing superior talents and an excellent understanding of technology, Mr. Thomas serves as Alta Meas Resources' Engineering Technologist. In this capacity, he consults with the president on information technology issues concerning the ability to forecast well reserves and economics. Demonstrating technology leadership, Mr. Thomas also provides on-call technical support to all corporate users of the system. Troubleshooting systems difficulties and transfering data in order to maintain efficient operations also fall within the realm of his functions. Currently attending the University of Houston, Mr. Thomas plans to obtain Microsoft Certified Professional certification and attend medical school. Founded in 1990, Alta Mesa Resources engages in oil and gas exploration, acquisition, and development. Incorporating new and innovative technological advancements, the Company develops systems to more efficiently extract and produce oil and gas. Day to day operations in Houston, Texas employs the skills and expertise of 10 personnel. **Career Highlights:** Engineering Technologist, Alta Mesa Resources (1997-Present); Bump Technology Specialist, Texas Instruments (1997); Membership and Member Relations Specialist, American Automobile Association of Texas (1993-96); Assistant Manager, Hollywood Video (1997). **Associations & Accomplishments:** Houston Area Christian Educators; Online Member of Techrepublic; Microsoft's Technet; The "Body" of Christ; Supporter of Feed the

Children and Star of Hope. **Education:** University of Houston, B.S. in Biology (In Progress); Texas A&M University; Southwestern Adventist University. **Personal Information:** Mr. Thomas enjoys walking, reading, learning more about life, science, music, soccer and arts. Mr. Thomas's favorite quotes are Philippians 4:13 "I can do everything through him who gives me strength." and "If a man does not keep pace with his companions, perhaps it is because he hears a different drummer. Let him step to the music he hears, however measured or far away."

Debbie A. Vincent
Oracle Database Administrator
GeoQuest
600 North Dairy Ashford Street, Office 2066
Houston, TX 77079-1100
(281) 293-6133
Fax: (281) 293-2015
debra.a.vincent@asa.conco.com

1382

Business Information: Drawing from previous technical experience, Ms. Vincent currently fulfills the responsibilities of an Oracle Database Administrator for GeoQuest. In this capacity, she creates databases to meet client specifications, installs software, deals with troubleshooting, and monitors use of the database. A leader in the business community, Ms. Vincent also provides user support for customers and develops Sequal and C shell scripts. Always alert to new opportunities, techniques and approaches, she plans on obtaining Oracle 8 certification and continuing to monitor and become more involved in Oracle data. Ms. Vincent attributes her success to her ability to think out-of-the-box, take on challenges, and deliver results on behalf of the Company and its clientele. Founded in 1937, GeoQuest is an established and reputable exploration and production oil service company. The Company provides software support, data management, and information system support for oil and gas corporations. Local operations in Houston, Texas employ the skills and expertise of 54,000 personnel to facilitate every aspect of design, development, and distribution of systems. **Career Highlights:** GeoQuest: Oracle Database Administrator (1998-Present), GeoScientist Information Systems Support (1997-98); Oracle Database Administrator, Unocal (1977-97). **Associations & Accomplishments:** International Oracle Users Group of America; Houston Oracle Users Group; St. Vincent dePaul Soceity. **Education:** Our Lady of Lake University, B.A. (1994). **Personal Information:** Ms. Vincent enjoys music and being a health activist.

Leon J. D'Sylva

Consultant
Hughes Christensen
P.O. Box 6875
Dubai, United Arab Emirates 6875
+971 4837125
Fax: +971 4837477
leon.dsylva@hugheschris.com

1389

Business Information: Mr. D'Sylva works at Hughes Christensen's office in Dubai, and contributes to their success by serving as Consultant. He plans new project possibilities, designs several prototypes, and implements a number of information technology related projects. Mr. D'Sylva controls all Internet and interoffice networking, assisting with the setup of the new Company e-mail system, and joining all of the computers together through one system. Daily, he utilizes his proven problem solving techniques to repair injured computers and restore crashed systems. Before joining Hughes Christensen, he served with Assistant Information Manager with KLM Royal Dutch Airlines and Network Controller for SITA-Telecom. His success reflects his ability to think out-of-the-box and take on new challenges. Looking to the new millennium, Mr. D'Sylva is looking to independently manage a company in the Information Technology field. Introducing their first rotary rock bit in 1909, Hughes Christensen has continued to provide the oil drilling industry with new technology and methods of enhancing their performance. Over the years, the Company has become recognized as one of the leaders in the drill bit manufacturing industry. Salt Lake City, Utah is the base for the Company's headquarters, and branch offices have been established around the globe. One of the many offices world wide is located in Dubai, United Arab Emirates. Established in 1986, the Company's Dubai location hosts 1,000 employees and last year sales were estimated to be at $300 million. **Career Highlights:** Consultant, Hughes Christensen (1996-Present); Assistant Information Manager, KLM Royal Dutch Airlines (1993-96); Network Controller, SITA-Telecom (1990-93). **Education:** University of Hull, M.B.A. (1998). **Personal Information:** Mr. D'Sylva enjoys swimming and working out at the gym.

Susan F. Fry
Systems and Programming Manager
Weatherford International Inc.
1450 Lake Robbins Drive, Suite 500
The Woodlands, TX 77380-1043
(713) 693-4542
Fax: (713) 693-4502
susan.fry@weatherford.com

1389

Business Information: Recruited to Weatherford International Inc. as Systems and Programming Manager in 1997, Mrs. Fry is responsible for overseeing systems operations for one of two software applications utilized by the Corporation. She manages her staff of 10 programmers and analysts in maintaining the existing software as well as monitoring and developing new software improvements. A savvy professional, she is responsible for all high-level jobs because of her ability to work under pressure and deliver results on time. Never missing a deadline, Mrs. Fry attributes her success to never giving up and spending more time listening. Headquartered in Houston, Texas, Weatherford International Inc. is an oil and gas service company. The fourth largest company in its respective field, Weatherford International reports an estimated annual sales of $2.5 billion. The Corporation was established in 1980. **Career Highlights:** Systems and Programming Manager, Weatherford International Inc. (1997-Present); Systems and Program Analyst, Nabors Industries (1994-97); Design Analyst, Sysco Foods (1993-94). **Education:** University of Northern Colorado, B.A. in Business Information Technology (1989); Infinium classes; VB classes; Java classes; IBM Common University. **Personal Information:** Married to Joseph in 1979. Two children: Allison and Andrea. Mrs. Fry enjoys music, the theater, reading and assisting in her husband's store.

1400 Nonmetallic Minerals, Except Fuels

1411 Dimension stone
1422 Crushed and broken limestone
1423 Crushed and broken granite
1429 Crushed and broken stone, nec
1442 Construction sand and gravel
1446 Industrial sand
1455 Kaolin and ball clay
1459 Clay and related minerals, nec
1474 Potash, soda, and borate minerals
1475 Phosphate rock
1479 Chemical and fertilizer mining, nec
1481 Nonmetallic minerals services
1499 Miscellaneous nonmetallic minerals

Elizabeth Rybiski-Joseph
Senior Systems Engineer
Kaiser Aluminum
1111 Airline Highway 61
Gramercy, LA 70052
(225) 869-2320
Fax: (225) 869-2191
betty.joseph@kaiseral.com

1479

Business Information: As Senior Systems Engineer of Kaiser Aluminum, Mrs. Rybiski-Joseph is responsible for computer applications, Oracle database administration, and programming. Drawing from 21 years of technical experience, she is involved in the installation of new systems and applications. Before joining Kaiser, she served as Management Information Systems Manager with Universal Services. Her background history also includes a stint as Information Technology Specialist for Entergy Operation. Presently, Mrs. Rybiski-Joseph is an important contributor to the success of the Company and displays zest and pleasure in her work. She is currently in the process of creating a database for their Jamaican facility. She attributes her success to the ability to communicate well with others and offering a comfort zone to those she teaches and trains. Mrs. Rybiski-Joseph plans to expedite continued promotion through the fulfillment of her responsibilities and her involvement in the advancement of operations. Serving an international client base, Kaiser Aluminum is engaged in the production and sale of aluminum and hydrate chemicals. Also involved in mining, the Company takes raw materials such as red dirt, washes out aluminum, and sells it to other manufacturers to use in their final products. **Career Highlights:** Senior Systems Engineer, Kaiser Aluminum (1996-Present); Management Information Systems Manager, Universal Services (1995-96); Information Technology Specialist, Entergy Operation (1979-95). **Associations & Accomplishments:** AABE; Toastmasters. **Education:** Tulane University, B.S. (1999); Nicholls State University, B.S. (1979). **Personal Information:** Married to Gregory in 1982. Two children: Juan Anthony and Dray

Markus. Mrs. Rybiski-Joseph enjoys reading, jogging, little league coaching and being a mentor.

1500 - 1799
CONSTRUCTION

1500 General Building Contractors

1521 Single-family housing construction
1522 Residential construction, nec
1531 Operative builders
1541 Industrial buildings and warehouses
1542 Nonresidential construction, nec

Nathan D. Reid
Systems Engineer
Pepper Construction
368 Deer Run Drive
Hainesville, IL 60030
(847) 381-2760
Fax: (847) 304-6510
nreid@pepperconstruction.com

1522

Business Information: Mr. Reid serves as Systems Engineer, responsible for all aspects of the network, hardware, and software of Pepper Construction. In this capacity, he evaluates needs by correctly assessing the situation and then purchasing the necessary components. After installation, he maintains the systems including the routers, hubs, switches, and servers in a fully operational condition. Additionally, Mr. Reid works closely with users and systems managers to analyze, specify, and design systems to take advantage of technology. Utilizing his practical work experience, he is currently formulating new ways to improve the Company's Web server and e-mail systems. Internally recognized for his successful implementation of several technological advancements, Mr. Reid is striving to incorporate wireless LAN applications into the Company. Believing that the word "can't" does not exist, he credits his success to ongoing education and a challenging position. Pepper Construction employs over 1,000 people in the Hainesville, Illinois area. The Company provides services to area residents and business that wish to obtain structural improvements or creations. **Career Highlights:** Systems Engineer, Pepper Construction (1999-Present); Systems Engineer, Centegra Health System (1999); Systems Engineer, Kemper Insurance (1996-99); Systems Engineer, United Oil Products (1995-96). **Education:** Northeastern Illinois University, Bachelor's degree (1997); Northwestern Business College, Associate's degree; Bryan Institute, Programming degree. **Personal Information:** Married to Jeannine. Two children. Mr. Reid enjoys flying, racing and learning.

Christopher P. Russell
Application Specialist
Engelberth Construction
463 Mountain View Drive
Colchester, VT 05446
(802) 655-0100
Fax: (802) 655-4882
chrisr@engelberth.com

1522

Business Information: Combining construction knowledge and technical expertise, Mr. Russell serves as the Application Specialist for Engelberth Construction. He is responsible for software administration, installing new applications, and performing routine maintenance. Before joining Engelberth Construction, Mr. Russell served as a Carpenter's Helper and Machinist with Plageman, Kirby, Gagnon & Daughter and Vermont Engine Service. Additionally, he performs hardware installations for the computers and printers. As a five year technology professional, he recently completed a construction degree in Practice and Management. His success reflects his ability to grasp concept methodologies and take on new challenges and responsibilities. Looking to the next millennium, Mr. Russell plans to expand his already extensive technical knowledge, utilizing it to continue to grow with the Company. In operation since 1980, Engelberth Construction performs general contracting for small industrial companies and large commercial firms. Each construction project averages from one million to twenty million dollars. The Company engages the services of more than 230 skilled individuals. **Career Highlights:** Application Specialist, Engelberth Construction (1994-Present); Carpenter's Helper, Plageman, Kirby, Gagnon & Daughter (1993); Machinist, Vermont Engine Service (1992). **Education:** Vermont Technical College, Degree in Construction Practice and Management (1998). **Personal Information:** Mr. Russell is engaged to be married to Ms. Carrie Haselton in the year 2000.

Jim Salter
Information Systems Manager
Patton General Contracting
10740 Dorchester Road
Summerville, SC 29485
(843) 875-6382
Fax: (843) 875-7216
the_shadow@mindspring.com

1522

Business Information: Functioning in the role of Information Systems Manager, Mr. Salter performs multi-level duties for Patton General Contracting. He is responsible for local and remote network administration as well as database and network design. Before joining Patton General Contracting, Mr. Salter served as a Network Administrator for the United States Navy and Desktop Publisher with Talladega Machinery and Supply. An experienced, 10 year veteran, he personally implemented the modernization of information systems for the Company. His goal is to enhance the efficiency of Company operations by utilizing emerging technology. In addition, he owns and operates his own company called JRS Systems Solutions, an information technology consulting firm. Mr. Salter attributes his career success to his initiative and ability to think out-of-the-box, as well as take on new challenges and responsibilities. Established in 1967, Patton General Contracting performs exterior remodeling for commercial and residential customers. Specializing in vinyl siding installation and repair, the Company also offers sunroom design and installation. Employing 76 trained individuals to complete contracted work, annual sales reach more than $15 million. **Career Highlights:** Information Systems Manager, Patton General Contracting (1996-Present); Network Administrator, United States Navy (1990-95); Desktop Publisher, Talladega Machinery and Supply (1989-90). **Associations & Accomplishments:** MENSA. **Education:** Naval Nuclear Power School, diploma (1991); Naval Nuclear Field Electronics Technician (1990). **Personal Information:** Mr. Salter enjoys martial arts, weight lifting and archaeology.

Stephen F. Coyle
Senior Programmer/Analyst
Gilbane
7 Jackson Walkway
Providence, RI 02903
(401) 456-5610
Fax: (401) 456-5650
s_coyle@bigfoot.com

1542

Business Information: Displaying his skills in this highly specialized position, Mr. Coyle assertively serves as Senior Programmer for Gilbane. He is responsible for programming the Company's AS/400 system and designing, developing, and implementing supporting programs. Mr. Coyle maintains the system and performs repairs and troubleshooting as needed. Before joining Gilbane in 1999, he served in the role of Senior Programmer and Analyst for IT Group and Cape Cod/Cricket Lane. He also has over six years of J.D. Edwards experience as well as Microsoft Access and RPGILE. As a savvy, 15-year veteran, he owns an established track record of producing results in support of both technical and business objectives. Keeping abreast of the newest advances in technology by reading trade journals, attending classes, and the Internet, his success reflects his attitude of never giving up, as well as his ability to think out-of-the-box and take on new challenges. Mr. Coyle anticipates his promotion to Project Leader as a result of his continuing efforts to increase his skills through training and professional development activities. Maintaining corporate headquarters in Providence, Rhode Island, Gilbane is a privately owned construction company. The Company first began operations in 1873 and now performs construction projects across the United States, employing the expertise of 2,000 individuals. **Career Highlights:** Senior Programmer, Gilbane (1999-Present); Senior Programmer/Analyst, IT Group (1994-99); Senior Programmer/Analyst, Cape Cod/Cricket Lane (1990-94); Consultant, Self-Employed (1989-90). **Education:** Blue Hills Technical Institute, A.A. (1984). **Personal Information:** Married to Lea in 1994. Mr. Coyle enjoys martial arts, music and sports.

John D. Lord
Vice President
CAS Inc.
620 Fifth Avenue
Pelham, NY 10803
(914) 738-5400
Fax: (914) 738-5934
jlord@componentassembly.com

1542

Business Information: Mr. Lord is a 15 year veteran of the technology field and currently serves as Vice President of CAS Inc. He is responsible for all aspects of day-to-day operation and administration of network and systems design and implementation. As information technology officer, he ensures all business systems run smoothly as well as determines the overall strategic direction and business contribution of the systems function. He oversees and directs all systems installation and troubleshooting functions. Possessing technical savvy, Mr. Lord also develops cutting edge software, linking the Company's network through sophisticated intergrated systems. His future aspirations include growing and expanding the Company's technology to its fullest potential. Founded in 1964, CAS Inc. has been providing commercial construction services to areas surrounding northeast New York, Massachussetts, New Jersey, and Washington D.C. With a work force of 60 indivduals and annual revenue of $78 million, CAS Inc. provides the best quality in construction. The Corporation provides a variety of services to their customers to include contract work and building consturction among other tasks. **Career Highlights:** Vice President, CAS Inc. (1994-Present); Systems Consultant, Self Employed (1993-94); Project Manager, Millbrook Development Corporation (1990-92); Project Engineer, Millbrook Conversion Corporation (1985-89). **Associations & Accomplishments:** MENSA; Aircraft Owners and Pilot Association. **Education:** Rensselaer Polytechnic Institute, B.S. in Mechanical Engineering (1985). **Personal Information:** Married to Manuela in 1999. Mr. Lord enjoys golf, flying planes, scuba diving, rock climbing and reading.

1600 Heavy Construction, Ex. Building

1611 Highway and street construction
1622 Bridge, tunnel, and elevated highway
1623 Water, sewer, and utility lines
1629 Heavy construction, nec

Peter J. Shepard, CPA
Management Information Systems Director
Charles J. Miller, Inc.
3514 Basler Road
Hampstead, MD 21074
(410) 239-8006
Fax: (410) 239-4204

1611

Business Information: Utilizing more than seven years of experience, Mr. Shepard joined Charles J. Miller, Inc. in 1997. In the capacity of Management Information Systems Director, he assumes responsibility for the management of the Corporation's overall computer systems and network infrastructure. He administrates and controls the local area network, monitoring daily activity, installing system applications, and performing software upgrades. Providing a routine back up system to prevent unexpected data loss, he also administers the network security. Mr. Shepard maintains the individual workstations, performing hardware repair or replacement. Troubleshooting any problems that arise, he offers his technical support to the end users. Mr. Shepard is continually formulating new goals and objectives and looks forward to increasing his professional responsibilities within the technology field. Charles J. Miller, Inc. is engaged in a variety of different types of business ventures. The Corporation performs heavy construction and paving services as well as providing various utility services for its commercial and government clientele. Established in 1957, national operations employ more than 400 staff members. Revenue is estimated to be over $60 million a year. **Career Highlights:** Management Information Systems Director, Charles J. Miller, Inc. (1997-Present); Accountant, Tax Accountants of Timonium (1992-97). **Associations & Accomplishments:** Tau Beta Pi; American Society of Mechanical Engineers. **Education:** University of Baltimore, Accounting degree (1997); University of Buffalo, Mechanical Engineering degree (1984); Fredonia College, Physics degree (1982).

John E. Greene, Jr.

Director of Network Operations and Management
Stonehenge Telecom Americas
485 North Keller Road, Suite 450
Maitland, FL 32751
(407) 737-8322
Fax: (407) 737-8482
jgr@stonehenge-telecom.com

1623

Business Information: Mr. Greene is the Director of Network Operations and Management for Stonehenge Telecom Americas. He manages all aspects of Stonehenge Telecom's private IP network in both North and South America. This includes both the installation and provisioning the network and the Network Operations Center in Orlando, Florida. Mr. Greene utilizes his nearly 25 years of telecommunications experience to manage a diverse group of Network Engineers, NOC Operators, Customer Care Representatives, and others. Mr. Greene is also a key member of the global Stonehenge Telecom team working on the next generation of private IP-based transport via Dense Wave Division Multiplexing (DWDM). For the future, Mr. Greene hopes to see the Company successfully bring about an IPO. Stonehenge Telecom is a global telecommunications carrier founded in 1998 that utilizes a private Cisco-powered IP network. Stonehenge Telecom is headquartered in Hoofddorp, the Netherlands, with regional offices in Orlando, Florida and Singapore. **Career Highlights:** Director of Network Operations and Management, Stonehenge Telecom (2000-Present); Technical Manager, Parsons Telecom (1997-2000); Engineering Manager, BellSouth (1994-96); Training Manager, Bellcore (1989-94). **Associations & Accomplishments:** International Electronics and Electrical Engineers. **Personal Information:** Married to Maurita in 1995. Four children: Jonathan, Chelsie, Kimberly, and John III. Mr. Greene enjoys spending time with his family, reading and all outdoor activities.

Matthew K. Reedy

Vice President
J.E. Reedy, Inc.
P.O. Box 1265
Seymour, IN 47274
(812) 497-3380
Fax: (812) 497-3380
adreedy@earthlink.net

1623

Business Information: Serving as the Vice President of J.E. Reedy, Inc., Mr. Reedy is responsible for overseeing major projects. Determining the strategic direction and formulating new business plans, he is accountable for bidding and billing for major projects, attending to customer complaints, coordinating purchase and use of resources and supplies, and enforcing corporate policies. Demonstrating strong leadership and flexibility, Mr. Reedy also implements changes and updates to corporate strategy, ensuring that the Corporation is up to date on the latest legislation in the industry. In the future, Mr. Reedy looks forward to assisting in the expansion of operations and an increase in clientele. His success reflects his ability to take on challenges and new responsibilities and deliver results on behalf of the Corporation and its clientele. Established in 1983, J.E. Reedy, Inc. provides services in the area of underground duct and fiber optics cable placement. Specializing in servcies for the electric and telecommunication market, the Corporation also provides assistance in the areas of splicing and terminations. Headquartered in Seymour, Indiana, the Corporation employs the skills and expertise of 15 personnel. **Career Highlights:** J.E. Reedy, Inc.: Vice President (1997-Present), Foreman (1994-97), Crewman (1990-93). **Associations & Accomplishments:** Church of the Nazarene; PCCA. **Education:** Indiana University (Currently Attending). **Personal Information:** Married to Angela D. in 1993. One child: Bethany Elaine. Mr. Reedy enjoys fishing, family and church youth group.

Charles K. Graham

Senior Programmer
W.H. Linder & Associates
3330 West Esplanade Avenue South
Metairie, LA 70002-3454
(504) 835-2577
graham_c@metairie.whlinder.com

1629

Business Information: As the Senior Programmer for W.H. Linder & Associates, Mr. Graham fulfills the responsibility of information technology manager. Possessing an excellent understanding of his field, he is accountable for engineering applications development. Delegating duties to his technical staff of two employees, he oversees project management, coordinating resources, time lines, and budgets as well as ensuring project completion within both time and budgetary constraints. A visionary who has proven himself on many occasions, Mr. Graham focus is on software applications, e-commerce, and online products. His career highlights include his diversity and being principal within the Firm. Attributing his success to smart work and planning, Mr. Graham's goals are to focus on a broader band of products, serve a wider audience, and attain more leadership responsibilities. W.H. Linder & Associates was founded in 1981. The Firm specializes in offshore development for gas and oil platforms as well as plant and facility work. Reporting an estimated annual revenue in excess of $20 million, the Firm employs over 180 professional, technical, and support staff. Currently, W.H. Linder & Associates is located in Metairie, Louisiana and operates two locations. **Career Highlights:** Senior Programmer, W.H. Linder & Associates (1995-Present); Senior Programmer, Lockheed Martin (1994); Junior Programmer, United States Army Attache Office (1985-93). **Education:** Campbellsville College, B.S. in Business Administration (1984). **Personal Information:** Married to Silvia in 1993. Mr. Graham enjoys stamp and coin collecting.

Dirk Helfenstein, Dipl. Ing.

Project Lead
Kolbstr. 12
Stuttgart, Germany 70180
+49 7111373939
Fax: +49 7116075043
dirk.helfenstein@helpstone.com

1629

Business Information: Possessing superior talents and an excellent understanding of technology, Mr. Helfenstein is a prestigious member of the field and he fulfills a number of duties on behalf of the Company and its clientele. Utilizing years of experience as a software developer, Mr. Helfenstein currently serves as Project Lead of an information technology company, designing, developing, and distributing state-of-the-art software applications to an international clientele. Serving in his role since 1994, he supervises and guides five empolyees in providing a range of services. An innovative leader in his field, Mr. Helfenstein is ambitious about developing and deploying emerging technologies to help the Company and clients remain at the forefront of industry competitors. His success reflects his ability to take on new challenges and deliver results. Regarded as being on of the largest electrical manufacturing companies in the world, the Company is located in Stuttgart, Germany. Established 100 years ago, the Company now operates internationally, constructing power plants, HMI building units, and various other electronic industry services. Presently, the Company employs a global work force of more than 200,000 professional, technical, and support staff. **Career Highlights:** Project Lead (2000-Present); Software Developer (1999-00); Software developer, Self Employed (1994-99). **Education:** University, Dipl. Ing. (1994). **Personal Information:** Mr Helfenstein enjoys space technology.

Charles L. Hodgin

Management Information Systems Director
Crowder Construction
P.O. Box 30007
Charlotte, NC 28230-0007
(704) 348-1307
Fax: (704) 376-3573
chodgin@crowdercc.com

1629

Business Information: Serving as Crowder Construction's Management Information Systems Director, Mr. Hodgin is responsible for all of the Company's systems infrastructure. In this capacity, he is accountable for applications from prospective employees, job listing systems, accounting, payroll, networking, land network to all divisions, purchasing, budgeting, and the leasing of all equipment. A veteran of 18 years with the Company, he manages 3 technical supporters and 250 land network users. Currently, Mr. Hodgin is upgrading the Company's infrastructure and he plans to start a new job costing system in the near future. Crowder Construction is a construction company serving Tennessee, Virginia, North Carolina, South Carolina, and Georgia. Employing approximately 1,000 individuals, the Company has constructed objects such as waste water and raw water treatment facilities, bridges, and asphalt power plants, and has done heavy foundation work. Established in 1947, the Company's annual sales now reach $160 million. **Career Highlights:** Management Information Systems Director, Crowder Construction (1980-Present); Data Processing Director, Johnson Motor Lines (1962-80). **Education:** Kings College (1962). **Personal Information:** Married to Suzie. Five children: Chuck, Cindy, Danny, Chriss, and Lisa. Mr. Hodgin enjoys gardening and outside activites.

Patrick H. Noon

Information Technology Consultant
Saudi Arabian Bechtel Company
c/o Al-Bustan Company Limited, P.O. Box 1868
Al Khobar, Saudi Arabia 31952
+966 38825288
Fax: +966 38825354
phnoon@bechtel.com

1629

Business Information: Mr. Noon functions in the role of Information Technology Consultant for the Saudi Arabian Bechtel Company. Employed with the Company for over 10 years, he provides cutting edge consultation services to all departmental operations. A successful, professional expert, Mr. Noon offers his expertise in the area of data, communication, design, and business expansion. Very proud of his title, he would like to continue in the information technology field and eventually be promoted to higher positions within the corporate structure. Mr. Noon's success reflects his ability to deliver results and aggressively take on challenges and new responsibilities. Operating out of approximately 50 locations, Bechtel was founded in 1898. The Company, headquartered out of the United States with a main office in the United Kingdom, provides services in the areas of power, petro-chemical, industrial, civil, telecom, mining, and metals. A family owned business, Bechtel presently has offices in San Francisco, Gaithersburg, Frederick, Houston, and London in addition to other satellite offices around the world. Operations around the world employ 17,500 individuals. **Career Highlights:** Saudi Arabian Bechtel Company: Information Technology Consultant (1997-Present), Chief Civil/Structural Engineer (1995-98), Project Engineer (1994-97). **Associations & Accomplishments:** European Engineer, FEANI; Chartered Engineer, United Kingdom Engineering Council; United Kingdom Institution of Civil Engineers; Microsoft Certified Systems Engineer. **Education:** Imperial College, London, M.Sc./D.I.C.; Ecole Superieure des Ingenieurs de Beyrouth, B.Sc. in Engineering. **Personal Information:** Married to Rana in 1992. Three children: Tina-Maria, Marc-Henry, and Talia-Lynn. Mr. Noon enjoys music, travel and martial arts.

Dominick Tuzzo

Technical Specialist
BetzDearborn division of Hercules, Inc.
148 Grand Street
Croton On Hudson, NY 10520-2307
(914) 271-4641
Fax: (914) 271-4641
dominick.tuzzo@betzdearborn.com

1629

Business Information: Following 12 years of distinguised service in the United States Navy, Mr. Tuzzo joined Betz Entec division of Betz Laboratories, Inc. in 1996, after five years employed as Utilities Manager and Chief Engineer with Rhone Poulenc and Johns Hopkins Medical Services Corporation. In 1997, Betz Laboratories purchased the Grace-Dearborn water treatment division from W. R. Grace & Co., thus becoming BetzDearborn, Inc. In 1998, Wilmington, Delaware headquartered chemical manufacturer Hercules, Inc. purchased BetzDearborn outright. At present, Mr. Tuzzo serves as a Technical Specialist of the water management group in the NYC metropolitan and surrounding areas. Mr. Tuzzo, owning a consistent record of delivering results through communications, interpersonal skills, and creative problem solving, meets with facilities engineers and executive level decision makers in the NYC vicinity to discuss techniques to reduce their annual operating costs, while simultaneously achieving their environmental objectives. An innovative and high impact technology leader, he increased his territory's annual revenues by $112,000 after only two years on the job. Another career hightlight of Mr. Tuzzo is his achieving the rank of Chief Petty Officer, in only seven short years, while serving with the United States Navy. This distinguished him as being one of the youngest Chiefs in the history of the Navy. His future aspirations include earning his Professional Enginer (P.E.) certification in New York State, and achieving his company's prestigious "Top Gun" and "Eagle" awards. BetzDearborn was established in the early 1900s and operates from locations across the globe. Employing over 2,600 persons, the Corporation specializes in the water treatment of commercial, industrial, and institutional facilities. For fiscal year 1999, parent Hercules, listed over $3 billion in estimated annual revenue. **Career Highlights:** Technical Specialist, BetzDearborn division of Hercules, Inc. (1996-Present); Utilities Manager, Rhone Poulenc (1994-96); Chief Engineer, Johns Hopkins Medical Services Corporation (1991-94); United States Navy: Chief Boiler Technician, Surface Warfare Specialist (1979-91). **Associations & Accomplishments:** Veterans of Foreign Wars; American Institute of Chemical Engineers; American Society of Heating, Refrigeration & Air Condiioning Engineers; Civil Air Patrol, USAF Auxiliary; American Radio Relay League; Westchester Emergency Communications Association; Putnam Emergency Amateur Repeater League; Amateur Radio Emergency Services; Radio Amateur Civil Emergency Services; Putnam/Cortlandt Amateur Radio Association; First Grade Engineer (State of Maryland); Class I Industrial Wastewater Works Operator (State of Maryland);

Commercial Pesticide Applicator (NYSDEP); Journeyman Power Plant Operator, U.S. Department of Labor Certificate; Master of Communications Technology from National Radio Examiners (2000); FCC Licensed Amateur Extra Class and FCC Commercial GROL Licensee. **Education:** Universtiy of the State of New York, Regents College, B.S. Sociology/Marine Enginnering (19913); United States Navy (1979-199l): Senior Enlisted Propulsion Engineering Course (1988), Naval Instructor School (1985), Boilerwater/Feedwater Laboratory Supervisor Course (1984), Main Propulsion Maintenance Supervisor Course (1983), Petroleum Operations Course (1982); Vibration Management & Reduction (1982), Advanced Operators's / Advanced Maintenance Course (1980), Leadership, Management, Education and Training Course (1980), Boiler Technician Class "A" School (1979), Propulsion Engineering Basics and Damage Control School (1979). **Personal Information:** Married to Nereida (Nelly) in 1991. Three children: Jacqueline, Melissa, and Elaine. Mr. Tuzzo enjoys Amateur radio and guitar. Mr. Tuzzo is the Deputy Squadron Commander, Cadet Programs Officer, and Aerospace Education Officer of the Putnam County Composite Squadron, NY Wing, Civil Air Patrol. He further serves as a Trustee and Secretary of the Board at Community Church of Yorktown in Yorktown Heights, NY.

Glenn E. Word
Manager of Engineering Project Support
Kellogg Brown & Root
P.O. Box 3
Houston, TX 77001
(713) 753-5899
Fax: (713) 753-5110
glenn.word@halliburton.com

1629

Business Information: Beginning his association with Brown & Root in 1978, Mr. Word has worked diligently to develop his skills and acquire expertise in his field. He now serves as Manager of Engineering Project Support and provides information technology tools and compatible technical support to execute various projects. A savvy professional, Mr. Word specializes in developing and implementing sophisticated engineering applications for plant design. Presently, he works closely with a staff of 10 in providing IT and CAD support to engineering projects. A business unit of Halliburton Company, Kellogg Brown & Root is an engineering and construction firm. The Firm designs, builds, and maintains petroleum, chemical plants, and pulp and paper mills for a number of international companies. Employing a work force of more than 20,000 personnel, Kellogg Brown & Root maintains offices and project sites around the world, and is headquartered in Houston, Texas. **Career Highlights:** Manager of Engineering Project Support, Kellogg Brown & Root (1999-Present); Brown & Root, Inc: Engineering Systems Manager (1995-98), Engineering Systems Coordinator (1994-95). **Associations & Accomplishments:** Institute of Electrical and Electronics Engineers; Eta Kappa Nu: Electrical Engineering Honor Society; Licensed Professional Engineer in Texas. **Education:** Texas A & M University, B.S. in Electrical Engineering (1978). **Personal Information:** Mr. Word enjoys reading and home improvement projects.

1700 Special Trade Contractors

1711 Plumbing, heating, air-conditioning
1721 Painting and paper hanging
1731 Electrical work
1741 Masonry and other stonework
1742 Plastering, drywall, and insulation
1743 Terrazzo, tile, marble, mosaic work
1751 Carpentry work
1752 Floor laying and floor work, nec
1761 Roofing, siding, and sheet metal work
1771 Concrete work
1781 Water well drilling
1791 Structural steel erection
1793 Glass and glazing work
1794 Excavation work
1795 Wrecking and demolition work
1796 Installing building equipment, nec
1799 Special trade contractors, nec

Jody Nyquist Ziegler
Learning Solutions Development Leader
Honeywell Home & Building Control
P.O. Box 524, MN27-6193
Minneapolis, MN 55440
(612) 951-8867
Fax: (612) 951-8877
jody.ziegler@honeywell.com

1711

Business Information: As Learning Solutions Development Leader of Honeywell Home & Building Control (H&BC) Training Services department, Ms. Ziegler manages technical training developers and project leaders. For more than 23 years, she has diligently performed her duties. Possessing technical savvy, Ms. Ziegler leads a team of seven employees and several outsourced individuals in the design, development, and implementation of proprietary training solutions for the Solutions & Services business of Honeywell Home & Building Control. Her strong resume includes completion of three large-scale systems implementation projects on time and within budgetary constraints. Always moving forward, Ms. Ziegler is currently re-designing and re-engineering the training department to match the ever-changing face of the business due to new developments in the industry. In the near future, Ms. Ziegler plans on staying in her position and implementing a Web-based training management solution for H&BC Solutions & Services employees. Relationship development and technical know how are cited as the main reasons for her success. Honeywell Home & Building Control is one of the world's premier producers and providers of products and services to create efficient, safe, comfortable environments. The business offers controls for heating, ventilating, humidification, and air conditioning equipment; security and fire alarm systems; home comfort products and automation systems; energy-efficient lighting controls; and building management systems and services. Founded over 100 years ago, the Corporation employs over 100,000 individuals globally. Presently, the Corporation's annual revenues exceed $24 billion. **Career Highlights:** Honeywell Home & Building Control: Learning Solutions Development Leader (1996-Present), Field Management Systems Training Manager (1994-96), Total Supply Chain Program Manager (1993-94), Matts Management Systems Project Leader (1986-92). **Associations & Accomplishments:** International Society of Performance Improvement; Society for Applied Learning Technology (SALT); Professional Association for Computer Training (PACT). **Education:** Metropolitan State University, B.A. in Human Resource Management (1986). **Personal Information:** Married. Ms. Ziegler enjoys music, gardening, sewing and powerboating.

Kaye Adkins
Owner
K & R Splicing
2407 Potomac Court
Pekin, IL 61554-1806
(309) 353-7726
Fax: (309) 353-8065
kandrsplicing@msn.com

1731

Business Information: In her role as Partner of K&R Splicing, Ms. Adkins handles a variety of responsiblities on a daily basis. Demonstrating a wide array of knowledge pertaining to the industry, she maintains excellent customer relations by conducting business in a manner that emphasizes quality and service. Recognized for impressive organizational skills and time management abilities, Ms. Adkins keeps clear and concise records to ensure accurate bookkeeping. With creative flair, she designs innovative marketing campaigns that increase visibility of the Company in the industry. Enjoying the challenges of her position, she intends to continue in her current role, initiating growth and expansion plans that will increase clientele. K&R Splicing is engaged in the fiber optical industry. Utilizing modern equipment and state-of-the-art facilities, the Company is able to conduct extensive testing on all fiber optic products. Additionally, the Company splices, repairs, or replaces the cables, many of which are telephone related. **Career Highlights:** Partner, K&R Splicing (1985-Present). **Education:** NT OC48 Op & Mtn, Graduate (1996). **Personal Information:** Married to Richard in 1994. Two children: Victoria Ashley and Joshua Dwayne. Ms. Adkins enjoys golf and driving her Vett.

Glenn J. Darichuk
Project Leader
TAF-TECH Cable Systems
2560 Calais Avenue SW
Calgary, Alberta, Canada T3E 7H8
(403) 243-2280
Fax: (403) 243-2380
glen.darichuk@home.com

1731

Business Information: Mr. Darichuk serves as a Project Leader for TAF-TECH Cable Systems. Working in this capacity since 1993, he performs all network cabling tasks and offers troubleshooting solutions. With experience in data and fiber optic networks, radio, RF, door access systems, and burglary and control systems, Mr. Darichuk continually strives to learn and excel in new technologies and eventually move into a senior position. TAF-TECH Cable Systems is a network data and voice cabling contractor. Specializing in the design, installation, maintenance, and repair of telephone and computer cabling networks, the Company uses twisted pair, coax, and fiber cables for services. Also involved in the sale and installation of NEC phone switches, TAF-TECH Cable Systems currently operates offices located in Calgary and Edmonton and serves various local business interests. Established in 1991, the Company employs 50 people and reports annual revenues of $3.5 million. **Career Highlights:** Project Leader, TAF-TECH Cable Systems (1993-Present); Telecommunications Technologist, AES Technet (1990-93); Technician, T.A.C. Pathfinder (1990); Installation Technician, Tone Communications (1989-90). **Associations & Accomplishments:** Alberta Society of Engineering Technologists (1988-Present); Named to International WHO'S WHO of Information Technology (1998-Present). **Education:** Southern Alberta Institute of Technology, Diploma in Telecommunications Engineering Technology (1989); Alberta Apprenticeship, Certified as Journeyman Communication Electrician (1995); Ortronics, Certified Installer of Ortronics Open System Architecture networking products (1995); Alberta Society of Engineering Technologists, Certified Engineering Technologist (1994). **Personal Information:** Mr. Darichuk enjoys electronics, photography, fitness, cars, motor sports, sports and camping.

James J. Leskody, Jr.
Owner
Systems-Ensync
P.O. Box 93994
Las Vegas, NV 89193
(702) 260-4457
Fax: (702) 260-4457
kody@xts.net

1731

Business Information: As Owner, Mr. Leskody designs information technology and defines utilization for autocad. Drawing upon a strong engineering background, he provides clients with detailed instruction on design and use. He manages administrative responsibilites and strives to project a positive Company image. Highly regarded, he possesses superior talents and an excellent understanding of technology. Mr. Leskody remains abreast of significant changes witihn the information technology industry which effects his level of services to clients. He would like to expand the scope of the Company to build a regional client base, and enhance the Company's overall profitability. His success reflects his ability to aggressively take on challenges and deliver result on behalf of the Company and its clientele. Systems-Ensync is a premier design and construction operation specializing in home theater installation. Established in 1996, the Company operates out of Las Vegas, Nevada, and employs an enthusiastic and highly knowledgeable staff of 80. Systems-Ensync is dedicated to a total quality concept and provides clients with exceptional post delivery and support services. **Career Highlights:** Owner, Systems-Ensync (1996-Present); Convention Services, Park Place Entertainment (1973-Present). **Associations & Accomplishments:** National Rifle Association; CEDA; Microsoft Solutions Provider. **Education:** Information Technology Professional; Microsoft Certified (1997); Microsoft Certified Professional Engineer; Microsoft Certified Solutions Provider. **Personal Information:** Mr. Leskody enjoys computer design and construction of all interiors and exteriors.

Cynthia Sue Peterson
Applications Analyst/Trainer
E&K Companies, Inc.
13324 Chandler Road
Omaha, NE 68138
(402) 896-1614
Fax: (402) 896-4058
c.peterson@e-kco.com

1742

Business Information: Combining technical expertise and a talent for teaching people, Ms. Peterson serves as an Applications Analyst and Trainer for E&K Companies, Inc. She offers her services in a variety of capacities within the Corporation, including writing and editing the Corporation's newsletter and creating training material for employees. A savvy communications specialist, Ms. Peterson trains individuals on the use of software and related applications. In addition, she assists customer service representatives in the help desk and performs computer repair. Responsible for the single-handed conversion of corporate units to Window-based programs, she also provided all training for on its use. Ms. Peterson credits her success to her creativity and resourcefulness. Looking to the future, she intends to one day found her own e-based business. Established in 1956, E&K Companies, Inc. is a specialty contractor, focusing its efforts in interior construction. The Corporation performs commercial work for clients nationwide, offering general services such dry walling and specialized services such as installing accoustical ceilings. Headquartered in Nebraska, the Corporation has nine locations across the country, employing a total of 1,000 construction professionals. **Career Highlights:** Applications Analyst/Trainer, E&K Companies, Inc. (1994-Present); Staff Assistant/Training Specialist, UNMC College of Nursing (1987-94); Trade Show Manager, Peed Corporation (1986-87). **Associations & Accomplishments:** Nebraska/Iowa Computer Training & Support Association; American Society for Training and Development. **Education:** University of Nebraska at Lincoln, B.A.; Mid Plains Community College at North Platte. **Personal Information:** Ms. Peterson enjoys photography.

Jeffrey M. McAndrew
Systems Administrator
Stuart Dean Company
366 10th Avenue
New York, NY 10001
(212) 695-3180
jmcandrew@mail.stuartdean.com

1743

Business Information: Serving as Systems Administrator for the Stuart Dean Company, Mr. McAndrew assumes responsibility for all aspects of the Company's technological needs for 150 users. He presides over the administration of the WAN and LAN networks, application installation, and software upgrades. In charge of telecommunications, he programs the T-1 switches, dial-ins, and phone systems including the cellular phones. Mr. McAndrew credits his success to a thirst for knowledge, whether from colleagues or professors. He states that any new knowledge is welcomed as a challenge to learn more. Committed to further development of the Company, he plans to obtain his MCSE and SYSCO certifications as well as his Master's in Business Administration, enabling him to capitalize on the opportunities provided by the Company. His success reflects his ability to aggressively take on new challenges. Founded in 1939, the Stuart Dean Company maintains a national presence in the United States through its 16 locations. The Company primarily engages in the construction of commercial or public Class A buildings, providing metal, marble, and wood refinishing. Over 500 skilled workers are employed across the nation. Boasting $30 million in annual revenue, the Stuart Dean Company employs national marketing campaigns in an attempt to establish new clients. **Career Highlights:** Systems Administrator, Stuart Dean Company (1997-Present). **Education:** Western Maryland College, B.A. (1992). **Personal Information:** Mr. McAndrew enjoys golf, baseball and surfing.

Bob Luderer
Manager of Accounting and Information Technology
Sloan & Company, Inc.
38 Fairfield Place
West Caldwell, NJ 07006
(973) 227-3555
Fax: (973) 227-6309
bobsied@nji.com

1752

Business Information: Serving as the Accounting and Information Systems Manager for Sloan & Company, Inc. since 1995, Mr. Luderer fulfills a number of duties on behalf of the Corporation and its clientele. He oversees and manages the information systems infrastructure, maintains the functionality of all network systems, supervises his experienced staff of technicians, and analyzes business processes, applying specific technology solutions to streamline these processes. Certified in Timberline, Mr. Luderer is in charge of accounting functions, compiles and organizes business reports, and implements new procedures and policies in order to provide a more efficient and productive business structure. Continually striving for maximum effectiveness, Mr. Luderer focuses on the further development of his professional career with Sloan & Company in order to enable him to capitalize on the opportunities provided by the Corporation. His advice is "Learn as much as you can. Explore!" Engaged in the subcontracting of commercial interiors, Sloan & Company, Inc. was established in 1964. Headquartered in West Caldwell, New Jersey, the Corporation employs a skilled staff of 400 technicians, designers, installers, and administrators providing drywall and carpentry, millwork, and acoustical ceilings and flooring to major clients in the New Jersey and New York locations. Offering consulting services, the Corporation is able to establish future goals and interests in order to provide the best customized services to its continuously expanding client base. **Career Highlights:** Accounting and Information Systems Manager, Sloan & Company, Inc. (1995-Present). **Associations & Accomplishments:** Timberline Certified Trainers; American Guild of Organists. **Education:** Rutgers University, M.B.A. (2000); New York University, B.S. **Personal Information:** Mr. Luderer enjoys playing the organ and piano.

Duane A. Lopes
Network Administrator
Formglas, Inc.
20 Toro Road
Toronto, Ontario, Canada M3J 2A7
(416) 635-8030
Fax: (416) 635-6588
dlopes@formglas.com

1799

Business Information: Mr. Lopes is the Network Administrator for Formglas Inc. He is responsible for maintaining the networking infrastructure in a fully functional and operational status. Utilizing six years of experience in the field, he is also responsible for directing and participating in the analysis, design, evaluation, testing, and deployment of LAN and WAN and Internet/Intranet related computer systems. Programming, installation, modification, confeguration, and support of operating systems and databases also fall within the scope of his functions. Mr. Lopes' focuses on changes that will allow Formglas to take advantage of any leading edge technology to remain flexible, efficient, and profitable in the global industry. Concentrating his efforts on enhancements of international operations, it is his personal goal to promote the services of Formglas Inc. For the future, Mr. Lopes hopes to see the Corporation advance beyond current goals. Success is attributed to his ability to take on challenges and deliver results. Formglas Inc. provides customized interior architectural manufacturing. Established in 1962, the Corporation employs a staff of 300 construction and engineering professionals to provide quality products and service to its clientele. Clients utilize the Corporation's to add a personalized flair of artistic integrity to their home and office. **Career Highlights:** Network Administration, Formglas Inc. (1995-Present); Network Administrator, Atomic Energy; Sales Representative, Radio Shack. **Associations & Accomplishments:** President, Kinsmen Club. **Education:** Sheridan College, degree in Computer Science (1994). **Personal Information:** Married to Tara in 1999. Mr. Lopes enjoys being part of OS/2 user group, Kinsmen and computer games.

2000 - 3999
MANUFACTURING

2000 Food and Kindred Products

2011 Meat packing plants
2013 Sausages and other prepared meats
2015 Poultry slaughtering and processing
2021 Creamery butter
2022 Cheese, natural and processed
2023 Dry, condensed, evaporated products
2024 Ice cream and frozen desserts
2026 Fluid milk
2032 Canned specialties
2033 Canned fruits and vegetables
2034 Dehydrated fruits, vegetables and soups
2035 Pickles, sauces, and salad dressings
2037 Frozen fruits and vegetables
2038 Frozen specialties, nec
2041 Flour and other grain mill products
2043 Cereal breakfast foods
2044 Rice milling
2045 Prepared flour mixes and doughs
2046 Wet corn milling
2047 Dog and cat food
2048 Prepared feeds, nec
2051 Bread, cake, and related products
2052 Cookies and crackers
2053 Frozen bakery products, except bread
2061 Raw cane sugar
2062 Cane sugar refining
2063 Beet sugar
2064 Candy and other confectionery products
2066 Chocolate and cocoa products
2067 Chewing gum
2068 Salted and roasted nuts and seeds
2074 Cottonseed oil mills
2075 Soybean oil mills
2076 Vegetable oil mills, nec
2077 Animal and marine fats and oils
2079 Edible fats and oils, nec
2082 Malt beverages
2083 Malt
2084 Wines, brandy, and brandy spirits
2085 Distilled and blended liquors
2086 Bottled and canned soft drinks
2087 Flavoring extracts and syrups, nec
2091 Canned and cured fish and seafoods
2092 Fresh or frozen prepared fish

2095 Roasted coffee
2096 Potato chips and similar snacks
2097 Manufactured ice
2098 Macaroni and spaghetti
2099 Food preparations, nec

Jeffrey A. House
Senior Project Manager
Campbell Soup Company
One Campbell Place
Camden, NJ 08103
(856) 342-3645
Fax: (856) 968-4304
jeff_house@campbellsoup.com

2032

Business Information: As Senior Project Manager, Mr. House has been providing technical services with Campbell Soup Company for over eight years. An integral member of the Company's information systems group, he is in charge of the centralized business systems infrastructure, overseeing MRP, marketing, and orders. Utilizing his vast experience in business management, he oversees all aspects of project development and manages a staff of programmers who design and maintain the Company's distribution systems. Concentrating his efforts toward building a more efficient and productive business environment, he heads administrative aspects, turning potential into action through preparation and skilled training. The most rewarding aspects of his career include developing the Company's first business and warehouse management systems. Demonstrating expertise in his field with Campbell Soup Company, Mr. House looks to advance in his position and eventually run a department of his own. Campbell Soup Company is an established and reputable food manufacturing and distributing firm established in the 1870s. Headquartered in Camden, New Jersey, the Company employs the skilled services of 25,000 individuals who facilitate every aspect of manufacturing, quality control, and the distribution of products. Producing quality name brand foods including Campbell Soups, Godiva Chocolates, and Pepperidge Farm, the Company generates $6 billion in annual revenues. **Career Highlights:** Campbell Soup Company: Senior Project Manager (1998-Present), Senior Business Systems Analyst (1995-98), Programmer/Analyst (1992-95), Ingredient Planner (1991-92). **Education:** Drexel University, Master's degree (In Progress). **Personal Information:** Married to Linda K. in 1992. Two children: Andrew and Michelle. Mr. House enjoys sports, cars, computers, reading, research and working on his Master's degree.

Greg Fincke

Support Manager
Pasco Inc.
P.O. Box 97
Dade City, FL 33523
(352) 567-5211
Fax: (352) 521-2384
greg.fincke@lykes.com

2033

Business Information: Demonstrating expertise in the technology field, Mr. Fincke has received several promotions since beginning his career with Pasco Inc. and currently serves as Support Manager. He presides over the management of the Management Information Systems Support Center, overseeing the administration of the Corporation's AS/400 and NT networks. New cutting edge program applications and software upgrades are implemented into the systems and individual workstations. Mr. Fincke provides technical support to end users and troubleshoots any problems that arise. Coordinating resources, time lines, schedules, and assignments also fall within the scope of Mr. Fincke's responsibilities. He credits his success to his adaptability and mellow attitude. His future plans include focusing more on his managerial duties and expanding the Corporation's client range. Pasco Inc. is an orange juice manufacturer. The Corporation was founded in the early 1900s and manufactures famous name brand labels such as Sunkist and FloridaGold in addition to others. In the Information Technology Department of the factory, six qualified professionals work diligently to ensure that the computer operations on which the Corporation depends run smoothly. **Career Highlights:** Support Manager, Pasco Inc. (1999-Present); Lykes Data Center: Support Service Consultant (1997-99), Support Supervisor (1995-97). **Education:** M.C.S.E. **Personal Information:** Married to Maggie in 1995. One child: Shea. Mr. Fincke enjoys computers, sports, travel and movies.

Philip M. Borgmann

∙∙∙━━●◎━━∙∙∙

Manager of Systems Development
Aurora Foods
1000 St. Louis Union Station
St. Louis, MO 63103
(314) 613-5515
Fax: (314) 613-5567
phil_borgmann@vdkff.com

2038

Business Information: Mr. Borgmann is the Manager of Systems Development with Aurora Foods. He is responsible for all aspects of systems development. A savvy, 13 year expert, he represents new software programs during their presentation to the Board of Directors where he reports his findings on the program and makes a recommendation. Working on the Internet, he has constant connection with the nationwide network of Company brokers which enables him to make minute by minute updates and proposal ideas. He implemented the data warehousing system that is currently in use at the Company and he is presently doubling as the Project Manager for all technology projects taking place at the St. Louis, Missouri location. Attributing his success to his ability to think outside the box, deliver results, and aggressively take on new challenges, Mr. Borgmann aspires to eventually attain the position of Chief Information Officer. "Find a mentor," is cited as his advice. Aurora Foods engages in the manufacturing and marketing of consumer packaged goods. The Company produces packaged foods for clients across the United States. Since its establishment in 1995, the Company has retained several of its largest clients including Dunkin Heinz, Chief Choice, and Lender's Bagels. Currently hosting a team of 2,000 individuals throughout its facilities, the Company has built its headquarters in San Francisco, California. **Career Highlights:** Manager of Systems Development, Aurora Foods (1996-Present); Systems Analyst, Maritz Inc. (1993-96); Operations Manager, Venture Stores (1989-93); Operations Manager, Wetterau Foods (1985-89). **Associations & Accomplishments:** Chairman, Budget Plus Comshare User Group; Grocery Manufacturers Association; Institute for International Research. **Education:** University of Missouri at St. Louis, B.S. (1986). **Personal Information:** One child: Daniel. Mr. Borgmann enjoys golf and scuba diving.

Martin P. Greenbank

∙∙∙━━●◎━━∙∙∙

Technical Support Manager
Garden Burger
Garden Burger, Inc., Unit A16H Freeport Center
Clearfield, UT 84016
(801) 773-8880
Fax: (801) 773-1955
mgreenbank@gardenburger.com

2038

Business Information: Demonstrating expertise in the technology field, Mr. Greenbank currently serves as the Technical Support Manager of Garden Burger. He assumes responsibility for training the information system support personnel and performing preventive maintenance. Acting as the CMMS Manager and the Spare Parts Coordinator, he orders spare parts and equipment as well as performing equipment maintenance and upgrades. In addition to his duties with Garden Burger, Mr. Greenbank also owns his own business, Swamp Fever, in which he sells rafting accessories. His e-mail for Swamp Fever is: swamp_fever@msn.com. Mr. Greenbank's career milestones include implementing a flexible bag product distribution while with J.R. Simplot; working on a design team at Frito Lay to automate case packer; being in the machine development industry for 20 years; and providing quality services to worldwide clients. He plans to expand his personal business and remain at Garden Burger, striving for improved efficiency and continuing his work in machine design. Garden Burger manufactures frozen vegetable, soy, and oat patties for distribution in the United States and Canada. Nine different flavors are offered. The Company was established in 1986 and has since grown into a $100 million business. Presently, the Company employs a staff of more than 150 individuals. **Career Highlights:** Technical Support Manager, Garden Burger (1997-Present); Owner, Swamp Fever (Present); Maintenance Manager, J.R. Simplot, Caldwell ID (1992-97); Project Manager, Bishop Barn, England (1972-92). **Education:** Birmingham University: Electronic Engineering degree (1972), Mechanical Engineering degree, Electrical Engineering degree. **Personal Information:** Married to Libby in 1997.

Travis Wayne Jennings
Technical Systems Administrator
NCH Corporation
2727 Chemsearch Boulevard, Suite 6-S
Irving, TX 75062-6454
(800) 272-6336
Fax: (972) 438-0959
tjenning@nch.com

2047

Business Information: In his capacity as Technical Systems Administrator of NCH Corporation, Mr. Jennings manages technical aspects of the retail products group. Demonstrating exceptional technical ability, he oversees Web design and development and guarantees sites are user friendly as well as informative. Maintaining LAN and WAN administration, EDI coordination, and help desk support, Mr. Jennings utilizes superior communicative skills to break down complex technical concepts into layman's terms for easy comprehension. As he directs telecommunications operations, he ensures phones and support applications are running smoothly for maximum utilization of resources. Enjoying the challenges of his position, Mr. Jennings intends to continue in his current role as he expands the Corporation's involvement in e-commerce activites and selling products over the Internet. Located in Irving, Texas, the NCH Corporation is engaged in marketing thousands of various products for maintenance, repair, and supply of equipment used by industrial, institutional, and governmental customers. Recent reports estimate sales to exceed $778.2 million for the 70 year old Company; current employee count totals over 10,000. **Career Highlights:** Technical Systems Administrator, NCH Corporation (1998-Present); Information Systems Technician, Air Products and Chemicals, Inc. (1991-98); Airborne Ranger, United States Army (1986-91); Cable Repair Technician, Southwestern Bell Telephone Company (1984-86). **Associations & Accomplishments:** Alpha Sigma Lambda, National Honor Society for Students in Continuing Higher Education; Alpha Chi, National Collegians Honor Scholarship Society; Eagle Scout. **Education:** Dallas Baptist University, B.B.A. (1998). **Personal Information:** Married to Michele in 1995. Mr. Jennings enjoys golf, scuba diving and snow skiing.

Fernando Sandoval
Senior Network Analyst
Rich Products
1 West Ferry Street
Buffalo, NY 14213-1701
(716) 878-8128
Fax: (716) 878-8897
fsandoval@rich.com

2051

Business Information: Mr. Sandoval functions in the role of Senior Network Analyst of Rich Products. He works closely with management and users to analyze, specify, and design new, cutting edge business applications. A savvy, 13 year professional, Mr. Sandoval manages the information technology computing systems at corporate plants and international locations, working with staff associates in leveraging M.R.P., E.R.P., payroll, e-mail, Internet, and data warehousing systems for Company usage. In the future, Mr. Sandoval hopes to become a Senior Business Consultant and become more involved with E.R.P. systems and eCommerce. He owes his career success to his wife who supported him in taking on risks and challenges. Rich Products provides food processing and food services to the consumable industry, functioning as an international manufacturer of non dairy foods, toppings, bakery goods and shrimp desserts. Founded by Hall-of-Fame member Robert Rich, the Company hosts plants in China, Mexico, India, and North Africa. The Company produces $2 billion annually and has a partnership with Sarah Lee. Recognized as one of the top technology companies by Fortune Magazine, the Company has also been recognized for its architectural design by Ernst & Young. **Career Highlights:** Senior Network Analyst, Rich Products (1997-Present); Information Technology Manager, Fantastix Ticketing Company (1996-97); Senior Network Administration, Delaware North Company (1993-96); Senior Systems Engineer, Hughes Aircraft Company (1986-93). **Associations & Accomplishments:** Vice President Operations, Boomers USA, Promotional Apparel Company; Greater Buffalo Partnership; St. James Church of Christ; Council Member, Business Development TLC; Visions for Tomorrow, Buffalo Region, Small Business Council. **Education:** State University of New York, Computer Sciences (In Progress); University of Connecticut; Hewlett-Packard Professional Training; IBM; Digital Equipment Corporation; United States Navy, Computing Architectures (1973-79). **Personal Information:** Married to Katherine in 1989. Three children: Melissa, Jennifer, and Ramon. Mr. Sandoval enjoys golf, basketball, softball and e-commerce studies.

Richard A. Wright
Director of Information Systems
Hazelwood Farms Inc.
8840 Pershall Road
Hazelwood, MO 63042
(314) 595-4790
Fax: (314) 595-4698
richard@inlink.com

2051

Business Information: Mr. Wright is the Director of Information Systems of Hazelwood Farms Inc. He is responsible for setting strategic direction for business systems and business growth through the adaptations and implementations of advance computer hardware and software. He provides administrative and technical support for six plants. Currently working with his staff to ensure Y2K compliancy, Mr. Wright is hoping to develop a cost analysis and proposal database for use on e-commerce. For the future, he is desiring to eventually advance into a position of Vice President or Chief Information Officer. His success reflects his leadership ability to build teams with synergy and technical strength, deliver results, and take on new challenges. Hazelwood Farms Inc. manufactures frozen bread products for commercial and in-store bakeries. A public division of the Pillsbury Company, the Corporation was established in 1985 and has continued to provide first rate frozen bakery goods since then. The products frozen at the facility in Hazelwood, Missouri are packaged and shipped to client businesses around the world. **Career Highlights:** Director of Information Systems, Hazelwood Farms Inc. (1997-Present); Manager of Information Systems, Lincoln Pentair (1988-97); Senior Analyst, St. Louis Shipyard (1981-83). **Associations & Accomplishments:** President, Gateway/400 Group. **Education:** National Lewis University, B.A. in Management Systems (1990); Southern Illinois University, B.A.; Belleville Area College, A.S. **Personal Information:** Two children: Shannon and Courtney. Mr. Wright enjoys Bible study, singing with the gospel choir and playing guitar.

Leo E. Keoghan
Senior Manager for Information Technology Manufacturing Systems
Nabisco
100 Deforest Avenue
East Hanover, NJ 07936
(943) 503-4495
Fax: (732) 462-1018
keoghanl@nabisco.com

2052

Business Information: Mr. Keoghan functions in the role of Senior Manager for Information Technology Manufacturing Systems. In this position, he is a key manager for development and support for manufacturing. An expert with 19 years of academics and occupational experience, Mr. Keoghan determines the overall strategic direction and business contribution of the information systems function. He is responsible for scheduling the shifts of the technical staff, and he manages all payroll issues. On many occasions, Mr. Keoghan discusses labor issues with both his staff and his superiors. Originally joining Nabisco as Assistant Controller of Food Services Division in 1987, he keeps his department functioning in a smooth manner by hiring, training, and retaining skilled individuals, orientating them to all aspects of the Corporation's policy. As for the future, Mr. Keoghan would like to expand his professional role throughout North America. Attributing his career success to his strong desire to succeed, as well as his ability to deliver results and aggressively take on new challenges, Mr. Keoghan's advice is, "Know your client base and be open-minded." Nabisco is a huge multinational corporation. Since 1792, the Corporation has made a reputation out of quality foods and confectionary. Approximately 20,000 people work for Nabisco at multitude of offices, plants, and warehouses located throughout North America. **Career Highlights:** Nabisco: Senior Manager for Information Technology Manufacturing Systems (1996-Present), Manager for Manufacturing Systems (1990-96), Assistant Controller of Food Service Division (1987-90). **Education:** Fairleigh Dickinson University, M.B.A. in Finance (1980); New Jersey University, B.S. in Finance and Accounting. **Personal Information:** Married in 1990. One child: Kate. Mr. Keoghan enjoys fishing.

Daniel K. Lim
Chief Information Officer
Guittard Chocolate Company
10 Guittard Road
Burlingame, CA 94010-2203
(650) 552-2288
Fax: (650) 692-2761
dklim@guittard.com

2066

Business Information: As the Chief Information Officer for Guittard Chocolate Company, Mr. Lim oversees systems applications, software development, networking, and communications for the entire organization. He determines the strategic direction and business contribution of the information systems functions. Dedicated to providing his superior services to the Company, he is also responsible for server support and repair and implementation of strategies. Possessing an excellent understanding of technology, Mr. Lim also formulates marketing and technical plans to keep the Company out in front of competitors in the industry. Coordinating resources, time lines, schedules, and assignments also fall within the realm of his responsibilities. Attributing his success to his ambition and drive, Mr. Lim plans to begin to do more in the e-commerce solution area in the future. Located in Burlingame, California, Guittard Chocolate Company is a manufacturer and producer of chocolate products. The Company supplies products to many major West Coast corporations. Established in 1868, the Company employs more than 300 personnel. **Career Highlights:** Chief Information Officer, Guittard Chocolate Company (1998-Present); Principal Consultant, Oracle Corporation (1995-98); Software Implementation Director, California Pacific Medical Services Organization (1995). **Education:** California State University at Sacramento, B.S. (1986). **Personal Information:** Married to Nancy in 1988. Three children: Amanda, Brandon, and Christopher. Mr. Lim enjoys fishing, skiing and Web development (e-commerce).

Shaun I. O'Donnell

Systems Engineer
Anheuser-Busch, Inc.
3500 Vaidens Court
Lanexa, VA 23089
(757) 253-3826
Fax: (757) 253-3725
shaun.odonnell@anheuser-b

2082

Business Information: As the Systems Engineer for Anheuser-Busch, Inc. in Lanexa, Virginia, Mr. O'Donnell is responsible for the implementation of comprehensive computer programs for inside operations. His other functions include network and database administration and management, management of all AIX, UNIX, Windows NT, and SQL systems, and automation of the production floor. Possessing more than 11 years of experience in the information technology field, Mr. O'Donnell is presently developing strategic plans that are compatible to those of the Corporation including moving to a position in upper management to enhance information technology applications. Anheuser-Busch manufactures, bottles, and distributes alcoholic malt beverages. The Corporation places emphasis on beer packaging and aluminum beverage container recycling. Established in 1852, the Corporation also invests heavily in adventure park entertainment, real estate development, and creative services. Headquartered in St. Louis, Missouri, the Corporation operates out of several international subsidiaries, and generates annual revenues exceeding $13.2 billion. **Career Highlights:** Systems Engineer, Anheuser-Busch, Inc. (1993-Present); Field Engineer, Racal-Datacom (1989-93). **Education:** DeVry Institute, B.S. in Electrical Engineering in Technology (1989). **Personal Information:** Married to Marcia in 2000. One child: Sierra. Mr. O'Donnell enjoys snow skiing and golf.

Sergio Danguillecourt

Director of the Board
Bacardi Ltd.
7724 Fisher Island Drive
Miami, FL 33109-0922
(305) 538-4614
Fax: (305) 672-8837
sergio@sergio.com

2085

Business Information: Mr. Danguillecourt serves in the position of Director of the Board of Bacardi Ltd. He is responsible for a number of duties on behalf of the Company and its clientele. Presently, he is accountable for all aspects of strategic Internet marketing of Company. Possessing superior talents and an excellent understanding of the technology field, Mr. Danguillecourt created the "dot coms" for the Company, to include "bacardi.com" and has also established advertising utilizing the Internet. A savvy, 15 year veteran of the field, Mr. Danguillecourt attributes his success to his ability to think outside the box, take on challenges, and deliver results. His future plans include staying on the cutting edge of technology. Bacardi Ltd. is an international manufacturer of alcoholic beverages currently employing over 6,000 people in 170 nations. Established in 1862, Bacardi reports its annual sales to be in excess of $3 billion. The Company began as a family owned and operated business, and has been passed through six generations, to its current president, Mr. Manuel J. Cutillas. **Career Highlights:** Barcardi Ltd.: Director of the Board (1990-94), Sales Director (1988-90), Sales and Marketing Manager (1985-88). **Associations & Accomplishments:** Director of the Board, Manhattenville College at Purchase, New York. **Education:** Manhattanville College, B.A. **Personal Information:** Married to Beatriz in 1990. Two children: Jorge and Jaime.

E. Anne Lauchlan

Technical Information Manager
United Distillers & Vintners
Brand Technical Center, Menstrie
Clackmannanshire, Scotland, United Kingdom FK11 7ES
+44 1259761481
Fax: +44 1315296807
anne.lauchlan@udv.com

2085

Business Information: Starting out 30 years ago as a scientist for United Distillers & Vintners, Ms. Lauchlan is now the Technical Information Manager responsible for oversight and management of the information systems functions. She works closely with her staff of 100, performing online research, examining data, and consulting. These duties are in preparation of finding a way to make information more available and more up to date. Ms. Lauchlan is in charge of maintaining the database and the only technical resource depratment in the entire Company. She has be an invaluable technical contributor to United Distillers & Vintners and credits her continuing success to her self-motivation and ability to think outside the box, deliver results, and aggressivel take on challenges. United Distillers & Vintners is a company wich includes all aspects of processing alcoholic beverages. The Company is worldwide and is based in London, England. Having recently merged with IDV, Inc., United Distillers & Vintners processes and packages whiskey, gin, and vodka. As part of the entire distilling process, research is done on the characteristics of whiskey and all complaints are handled within the Company. The Scotland plant was established in 1947 where all of the beverages are created, bottled, packaged, and shipped. **Career Highlights:** United Distillers & Vintners: Technical Information Manager (1980-Present), Scientist (1970-80). **Associations & Accomplishments:** National Library Association. **Education:** Napier University, Higher National Certificate with Library and Information Science (1985). **Personal Information:** Ms. Lauchlan enjoys travel, golf and badminton.

Tracy Wentzler

Information Systems Manager
United Distillers
4320 South 94th Street
Omaha, NE 68127
(402) 339-9100
Fax: (402) 597-7289
undi@aol.com

2085

Business Information: As Information Systems Manager of United Distillers, Ms. Wentzler is responsible for all aspects of day-to-day administration and operation of the information systems infrastructure. She supervises two other personnel working with her to maintain the database, PCs, telephony, and NT network of the Company. Through UNIX programming, the team is able to properly manage the employee and clientele files within the computer system. Her team also works to train other employees on the proper and most effective methods to fully utilize the applications and equipment made available to them. Currently, Ms. Wentzler is involved in the implementation of an Internet capability for the Company. Her next project will be the complete upgrade of all computers within the offices to make the equipment operate in a more efficient manner and become a seamless communication environment. Ms. Wentzler's success his attributed to her ability to listen effectively and quickly grasp technical concepts and methodologies. United Distillers is involved in wholesale liquor distribution for the entire state of Nebraska. Established in 1879, the Company hosts a sales force of 35 personnel devoted to complete customer satisfaction from every sale. Altogether the Company has a staff of almost 90 personnel that work to distribute and package products for clients across the state. The Company sells 43 percent of the spirits to markets in Nebraska and offers additional services to clients to ensure their customers are satisfied. Space management and training courses are all available to clients to better educate themselves on the product and learn effective methods of marketing products. **Career Highlights:** Information Systems Manager, United Distillers (1997-Present); Customer Support Representative, Medical Computer Management Inc. (1993-96); SATCOM Technician, United States Air Force (1987-91). **Personal Information:** Married to Peter John Sr. in 1989. Two children: Peter Jr. and Sarah. Ms. Wentzler enjoys music.

Charlie O'Donnell

Project Leader
Pepsi Cola International
1 Pepsi Way
Somers, NY 10589
(914) 767-6975
Fax: (914) 279-7816
charlie_od@msn.com

2086

Business Information: Demonstrating expertise in the technological field, Mr. O'Donnell currently serves as Project Leader of Pepsi Cola International's Information Technology Department. He has developed a number of internal system applications for sales, quality control and data, regional estimates, and execution reports. Providing support for these applications, he acts as the chief technical liaison for users around the world, administering system maintenance, correcting problems, and answering questions. Coordinating resources and schedules and overseeing time lines and assignments also fall within the purview of his responsibilities. Throughout his professional career, Mr. O'Donnell has always struggled to improve the quality of existing systems, streamlining processes, and attempting to obtain a higher degree of reliability. Staying on the cutting edge of his field through personal research, seminars, and tradeshows, he looks forward to becoming a Project Manager, taking on more responsibilities and challenges. Since inception in 1898, Pepsi Cola has become an international leader in soft drink production and sales. Pepsi Cola International maintains global operations from the home office in Somers, New York. The Corporation's international team consists of a staff of 3,000 individuals. **Career Highlights:** Project Leader, Pepsi Cola International (1998-Present); Consultant for Pepsi, Source Services (1993-94); Support Analyst, Gibson, Dunn & Cratcher (1992-93); Computer Analyst, Kraft General Foods (1990-92). **Education:** Rosa State College, B.A. (1991). **Personal Information:** Married to Lynn.

Steve D. Curtis

Information Systems Specialist
The Coffee Beanery Ltd.
3429 Pierson Place
Flushing, MI 48433
(810) 733-1020
Fax: (810) 733-6847
stevec@beanerysupport.com

2095

Business Information: Mr. Curtis serves as an Information Systems Specialist with The Coffee Beanery Ltd. He is responsible for providing technical support for Windows 95, 98, and NT Platforms. Before joining The Coffee Beanery, Mr. Curtis served as Maintenance Specialist at Kith Haven Inc. Quickly establishing his present in the information technology field, he assists in determining the Company's technical direction, and maintaining the functionality and operational status of the computer infrastructure. This includes all system workstations, client servers, and cash register programming, as well as providing technical support to 100 system users. Ensuring all data integrity and reliability, tuning software tools to improve the overall performance, and providing state-of-the-art solutions to system problems also fall within the scope of Mr. Curtis' functions. His success reflects his excellent training and ability to network and interact with colleagues in the field. Conducting some independent consulting on the side, his long range goal is to eventually attain the position of Information Systems Director. The Coffee Beanery Ltd. engages in manufacture and distribution of specialty coffee products. Privately held, the Company is the third largest specialty coffee manufacturer in the United States. Established in the 1970s, The Coffee Beanery operates 148 sites internationally. More than 400 individuals are employed at the Company's headquarters in Flushing, Michigan. **Career Highlights:** Information Systems Specialist, The Coffee Beanery Ltd. (1998-Present); Maintenance Specialist, Kith Haven Inc. (1996-98). **Associations & Accomplishments:** Genesee Baptist Association. **Education:** Genesee Area Skills Center. **Personal Information:** Mr. Curtis enjoys church functions, reading, swimming and physical fitness activities.

Iam Kamese Wamara

Auditor/Manager of Information Technology
Cargill Uganda, Ltd.
P.O. Box 1275
Kampala, Uganda
+25 677403622
Fax: +25 641222612
lankw@hotmail.com

2095

Business Information: As Information Technology Manager and Auditor of Cargill Uganda, Ltd., Mr. Wamara oversees and directs all information technology related activities, such as implementation of computer technology, supervision of the technical support staff, and troubleshooting system difficulties. Possessing an excellent understanding of technology, Mr. Wamara also researches market trends and analyzes data to facilitate growth and expansion. Through the auditing of financial statements, he ensures accurate records and dependable services. Highly regarded in the field, Mr. Wamera has enjoyed substantial success in his present position and looks forward to assisting in the completion of future corporate goals. His professional success reflects his ability to form teams with synergy and technical strength, take on new challenges, and deliver cutting edge results on behalf of the Company and its clientele. Cargill Uganda, Ltd. engages in the processing and export of coffee to countries worldwide. Established in 1995, local operations employ the skilled services of 47 individuals to orchestrate all aspects of manufacture, quality control, and distribution. Headquartered in the United States, the Company maintains operations in

Africa and Uganda, which generate $40 million annually. **Career Highlights:** Cargill Uganda, Ltd.: Information Technology Manager/Auditor (1997–Present), Coffee Trader (1997); Commercial Executive, Picture Group of Industries (1996). **Education:** Washington International University, M.B.A. (1999); Makere University, degree in Business Administration (1996). **Personal Information:** Mr. Wamara enjoys reading and games.

Eduardo D. Benavidez
Network Administrator/Systems Analyst
The Wornick Company - Right Away Division
200 North 1st Street
McAllen, TX 78501
(956) 687-9401
Fax: (956) 687-7028
eddie@wornick.com

2099

Business Information: Mr. Benavidez serves as Network Administrator and Systems Analyst for The Wornick Company - Right Away Division. His major responsibilities include maintaining the local area network as well as designing and implementing other I.T. projects. Projects that include a wide area network connection between the Right Away Division in McAllen, Texas and the Prepared Foods Division in Cincinnati, Ohio. Mr. Benavidez leverages a vast array of unique experiences that allow him to perform many tasks. Strong work ethics and excellent problem solving skills compound his abilities. Mr. Benavidez has had opportunities to field and beta test equipment for various companies and industry leaders including Cisco, V-Con, and Lotus. Mr. Benavidez has also proven himself proficient in other areas as well. The nature of the current position held by Mr. Benavidez requires that he be able to meet the needs of the client by being proactive and innovative in his problem solving approach. The Wornick Company is a global leader in ration manufacturing and it operates two divisions. The Right Away Division is located in McAllen, Texas, and is dedicated to manufacturing, custom contract assembly, packaging, warehousing, and research and development. The Prepared Foods Division is located in Cincinnati, Ohio, and specializes in the production, packaging, and distribution of shelf stable, frozen, and extended shelf life refrigerated foods. **Career Highlights:** Network Administrator/Systems Analyst, The Wornick Company - Right Away Division (1999–Present); Network Administrator, Texas Educational Services Center (1996–99); Computer Proctor, Region One Adult Education C.O.O.P. (1993–96); C.A.D. Home Designer, Karlica Construction (1993). **Education:** University of Texas at Pan American, B.B.A. (1997).

Guillermo Cremerius
Information Technology Manager
Best Foods Brazil
Avenida Paulista 23000, 5º Andar
Sao Paulo, Brazil 01310-300
+55 1131381624
Fax: +55 1131381769
gcremeri@usa.net

2099

Business Information: Displaying advanced technical skills and possessing extensive knowledge of the information technology field, Mr. Cremerius currently serves as Information Technology Manager for Best Foods Brazil. In this capacity since 1998, he is responsible for network administration, maintaining the network infrastructure, and performing daily diagnostic tests. Drawing from his previous occupational experience, Mr. Cremerius adeptly supervises and maintains all applications, while also conducting detailed training for computer technicians. Utilizing new techniques and progressive technology, he develops custom software for the Corporation and is engaged in Web development. Mr. Cremerius looks forward to assisting in the advancement of operations at Best Foods Brazil, and aspires to attain a higher level network administration position within the Corporation. Established in 1929, Best Foods Brazil, a subsidiary of Best Foods North America, is an international manufacturer of food specialties for the consumer market. Located in Sao Paulo, Brazil, the Corporation employs a collective work force of 7,000 administrative, technical, and operational personnel who generate over $1 billion in annual revenue. **Career Highlights:** Information Technology Manager, Best Foods Brazil (1998–Present); Information Technology Manager, CPC International Latin America (1996–98); Project Manager, Best Foods North America (1993–96). **Education:** Fairleigh Dickinson, B.S. Computer Science (1996). **Personal Information:** Married to Andrea in 1984. Two children: Sonia and Lucas. Mr. Cremerius enjoys mountain biking and fly fishing.

Vicente Franco
Information Technology Manager
Nutreco Spain
Ronda Ponlente 9
Madrid, Spain 28760
+34 918075476
v.franco@nutreco.com

2099

Business Information: Mr. Franco serves as Information Technology Manager for Nutreco Spain. In this capacity, he handles over 47 user sites throughout Spain, ensuring all operations run smoothly. Utilizing an extensive knowledge of the industry, he oversees all internal systems as he performs upgrades and maintenance. Offering exceptional customer support, Mr. Franco lends his assistance to instruct clients on technical applications. Additionally, he instructs employees on complicated topics to guarantee all associates are well versed on both hardware and software. Enjoying the challenges of his position, Mr. Franco intends to continue in his current role as he continually updates his education. Nutreco Spain is a food manufacturing company originally part of a Holland-based business, BP Nutrition. Established in 1994, the Company has over 1,500 employees to assist in the completion of daily responsibilities. Annual sales exceed $670 million for the Company, who joined the Amsterdam Stock exchange in 1998. **Career Highlights:** Information Technology Manager, Nutreco Spain (1991–Present); Product Marketing Manager, AT&T/NCR (1998–91); Technical Database Open System Engineer, NCR (1985–88). **Education:** Universidad Politecnica at Madrid, Software Engineering Degree (1985). **Personal Information:** Two children: Sonia and Eduardo. Mr. Franco enjoys music and soccer.

Honore Kamssu
Software Engineer
The Wornick Company
200 North 1st Avenue
McAllen, TX 78501
(956) 687-9401
Fax: (956) 928-7678
hkamssu@netscape.net

2099

Business Information: Recruited to The Wornick Company in 1999, Mr. Kamssu serves in the role of Software Engineer. He is responsible for working with management and users to analyze, specify, and design cutting edge solutions to harness more of the computer's power. Developing customized software, Mr. Kamssu also fulfills the responsibility of Web Developer responsible for design and content of the Company's Web site. Overseeing the Company's programmers, he coordinates resources, schedules, and communications while working as a team lead on several projects. His career highlight is cited as pulling through a project that was two months behind schedule. Mr. Kamssu plans on becoming more involved in project management in the near future. His success is attributed to his ability to tackle new challenges and deliver results. Headquartered in McAllen, Texas, The Wornick Company is an innovator in the food industry. The Company specializes in the production and development of specially packaged and extended life foods such as the MREs used by the military. The Company markets their product all over the world and is 100 percent employee owned. Established in 1978, The Wornic Company operates two divisions and three separate facilities. **Career Highlights:** Software Engineer, The Wornick Company (1999–Present); Software Developer, Objectwave Company (1998–99); Database Administrator, University of Mississippi (1997–98). **Associations & Accomplishments:** Association of Computing Machinery. **Education:** University of Mississippi, M.S. (1999); University of Douala: Master's degree in Finance/Accounting, B.B.A. **Personal Information:** Married to Aurora in 1998. Mr. Kamssu enjoys soccer, football and basketball.

Norman A. Wahn
Telecommunications Manager
Chr. Hansen, Inc.
9015 West Maple Street
Milwaukee, WI 53214
(414) 607-5833
Fax: (414) 607-5859
naw@chr-hansen-us.com

2099

Business Information: Serving in the role of Telecommunications Manager of Chr. Hansen, Inc., Mr. Wahn is responsible for all aspects of telecommunications operations at United States corporate locations. Demonstrating adept technical skills, he accurately evaluates each situation to determine the specific need before making procurement recommendations. After designing customized technical solutions, Mr. Wahn obtains proper equipment and implements necessary hardware or software. Utilizing practical work experience, he successfully integrates voice and phone systems with cellular phones and pagers for billing

purposes and resource maximization. Recognized for his impressive accomplishments, Mr. Wahn is credited with the formulation of several innovative business strategies that have benefited the Corporation through time-saving and cost-cutting techniques. Prior to his role in technology with the Company, Mr. Wahn had extensive experience in the financial areas of Chr. Hansen, Inc. He holds the designation of C.P.A. This experience, combined with technological expertise, makes him a multidimensional player on the corporate team. The Milwaukee, Wisconsin location of Chr. Hansen, Inc., manufactures food ingredients and additives such as flavors and colors. Selling quality, value-priced products to other food producers, the Danish corporation has gained the number one sales position in the industry. Established in 1878, the Corporation generates annual revenues of $200 million and maintains 10 facilities throughout the United States. **Career Highlights:** Chr. Hansen, Inc.: Telecommunications Manager (1997–Present); Taxation Manager (1993–97); Controller (1989–93); Accounting Manager (1985–89). **Associations & Accomplishments:** American Institute of Certified Public Accountants; Wisconsin Institute of Certified Public Accountants. **Education:** University of Wisconsin at Milwaukee, B.B.A. (1980). **Personal Information:** Married to Kim K. in 1976. Three children: Charles, Michael, and David. Mr. Wahn enjoys music, stamps and coin collecting.

2100 Tobacco Products

2111 Cigarettes
2121 Cigars
2131 Chewing and smoking tobacco
2141 Tobacco stemming and redrying

Mark S. Beasley
Administrator
U.S. Tobacco Manufacturing LP
800 Harrison Street
Nashville, TN 37203-3346
(615) 880-4606
Fax: (615) 880-4692
mbeasley@usthq.com

2131

Business Information: Devoting appropriate attention to all responsibilities, Mr. Beasley serves as Administrator for U.S. Tobacco Manufacturing LP. Employed by the Company since 1998, Mr. Beasley is responsible for research and development of all aspects of information systems management. Before joining U.S. Tobacco, Mr. Beasley served as consultant and owner of Edgefield Computing Consultants. His background history also includes a stint as administrator with InterSys, Inc. As a solid, nine-year technology veteran, he effectively utilizes his academic ties and experience in the realm of hardware and software purchase and set-up. Overseeing quality control of technical processes, ensuring all employees are certified to work on specific systems, and directing and controlling all aspects of training also fall within the purview of Mr. Beasley's responsibilities. His success reflects his leadership ability to produce results and aggressively take on new challenges. Moving up the corporate hierarchy into higher management serves as one of his future goals. U.S. Tobacco Manufacturing LP engages in the manufacture of tobacco products. Providing a high number of quality merchandise, its brands include Skoal and Copenhagen. Local operations in Nashville, Tennessee employ the expertise of 500 individuals to orchestrate all activities of research, manufacture, and distribution. The Company was established in 1822. **Career Highlights:** Administrator, U.S. Tobacco Manufacturing LP (1998–Present); Consultant/Owner, Edgefield Computing Consultations (1995–98); Administrator, InterSys, Inc. (1990–95). **Education:** Middle Tennessee State University: M.S. (In Progress); Belmont University, B.S. (1990); Microsoft Certified Systems Engineer (In Progress). **Personal Information:** Mr. Beasley enjoys flying airplanes and reading.

J. West Taylor Jr.
End User Services Manager
DIMON International, Inc.
P.O. Box 650
Farmville, NC 27828
(252) 753-8937
Fax: (252) 753-8426
wtaylor@dimonusa.com

2131

Business Information: Serving as End User Services Manager of DIMON International Inc., Mr. Taylor is responsible for desktop management for the entire North American operation. Utilizing 11 years of experience in technology, he manages help desk functions, provides training for end users, and oversees administration and operations of the Corporation's project offices. Beginning his association with the Corporation as a Project Specialist in 1998, Mr. Taylor is currently deploying Office 2000 related to desk top funtions. Overseeing operations in the United States, his Department is the Central information technology site for client support. Proud of the job he did on the Y2K glitches for his clients, he continually applies his educational background to his vocation. In the future, Mr. Taylor plans on finishing gradute school and moving up the corporate structure to the position of Vice President of Information Technology. DIMON International Inc. is the second largest independent leaf tobacco merchant in the world. Established in 1994, the Corporation engages in purchasing, processing, storing, and selling leaf tobacco. With an estimated annual sales at an astonishing $2 billion, the Corporation employs a work force of more than 19,000 people. **Career Highlights:** DIMON International: End User Services Manager (1999-Present), Project Specialist (1998-99); Senior Customer Service Engineer, Xerox Corporation (1989-98). **Associations & Accomplishments:** Sudan Shrine Club; St. Johns Lodge 4, Ancient Free and Accepted Masons. **Education:** East Carolina University; B.S.B.A. in Management Information Systems (1998); Electronic Computer Programming Institute, Computer Technology II. **Personal Information:** Mr. Taylor enjoys golf.

2200 Textile Mill Products

2211 Broadwoven fabric mills, cotton
2221 Broadwoven fabric mills, manmade
2231 Broadwoven fabric mills, wool
2241 Narrow fabric mills
2251 Women's hosiery, except socks
2252 Hosiery, nec
2253 Knit outerwear mills
2254 Knit underwear mills
2257 Weft knit fabric mills
2258 Lace and warp knit fabric mills
2259 Knitting mills, nec
2261 Finishing plants, cotton
2262 Finishing plants, manmade
2269 Finishing plants, nec
2273 Carpets and rugs
2281 Yarn spinning mills
2282 Throwing and winding mills
2284 Thread mills
2295 Coated fabrics, not rubberized
2296 Tire cord and fabrics
2297 Nonwoven fabrics
2298 Cordage and twine
2299 Textile goods, nec

Stephanie K. Sutherland

Data Translation Specialist
Dan River, Inc.
P.O. Box 261
Danville, VA 24543-0261
(804) 799-7093
Fax: (804) 799-2984
ssutherl@danriver.com

2211

Business Information: Serving as a Data Translation Specialist of Dan River, Inc., Ms. Sutherland works for the electronic data information team that translates data received from the customer to the Corporation's billing programs. Highly regarded and possessing an excellent understanding of technology, Ms. Sutherland is accountable for transferring such data as invoicing and shipping information into billing format. With over six years of professional clerk experience, Ms. Sutherland utilizes her superior knowledge and expertise to devise plans for promotional advancement within the Corporation. Attributing her career success to strong support from her parents and husband, her future plans include advancing into a leadership position and becoming involved as a project analyst. Dan River, Inc. is a textile factory engaged in the manufacturing of sheets, comforters, clothing fabrics, towels, and institutional bedclothes. Established in 1882, the Corporation is headquartered in Danville, Virginia and operates out of several other regional factories and offices. Currently, the Corporation functions under the direction of a work force of more than 8,000 staff who facilitate smooth business operations. **Career Highlights:** Data Translation Specialist, Dan River, Inc. (1998-Present); Account Clerk II, City of Danville (1994); Mail Order Clerk, Dan River, Inc. (1997). **Associations & Accomplishments:** American Business Women's Association. **Education:** Danville Community College. **Personal Information:** Married to Jonathan M. in 1994. Ms. Sutherland enjoys reading, cross stitching and knitting.

Jeffrey B. Kraut

Controller
Associated Textile Converters
295 5th Avenue, Suite 306
New York, NY 10016-7103
(212) 532-8367
Fax: (212) 447-0741
jbkraut@att.net

2231

Business Information: In his role as Controller of Associated Textile Converters, Mr. Kraut is responsible for finances and technology assessment. Demonstrating his versatility and business savvy, he maintains accurate and detailed records and bookkeeping. Meeting with clients, he utilizes exceptional communicative skills as he thoroughly explains product features and handles all aspects of any contracts that are initiated. With technical finesse, Mr. Kraut oversees the information technology areas of operations. He installs software packages to fulfill the needs of the Company, offering support and training to the affected departments. Corporate telephone systems are run by him as well; he conducts ongoing evaluations to ensure all technology is up-to-date within the facility. Credited with the successful creation and implementation of several innovative cost cutting business plans, Mr. Kraut looks forward to continuing in his current position as he aquires additional responsibilities and advance through the corporate structure. Headquartered in New York, New York, Associated Textile Converters produces raw fabric for the textile industry. Established in 1982, the Company employs 165 people to assist in the design, dye, texturization, and sale of the fabrics to wholesalers, manufacturers, and fabric stores. **Career Highlights:** Controller, Associated Textile Converters (1993-Present). **Associations & Accomplishments:** American Institute for Certified Public Accountants; New York State Society of Certified Public Accountants.

Jeff L. Hunt

Data Center Manager
Fruit of the Loom
1 Fruit of the Loom Drive
Bowling Green, KY 42103
(502) 781-6400
Fax: (502) 782-1399
jhunt@fruit.com

2254

Business Information: Serving as Data Center Manager for Fruit of the Loom, Mr. Hunt manages the data center in the Bowling Green, Kentucky headquarters. The Data Center operates IBM, CMOS Mainframe, AS400, SP and RS6000 platforms, with the plant AS400's connected to this central location. An expert, Mr. Hunt ensures that the systems are functioning properly and efficiently in order to provide financial, order processing, manufacturing processs, and forcasting data to the employees. Attributing his success to hard work, dedication, and an eagerness to learn, he has been recognized internally for outstanding performance and nominated for the Lexington's Who's Who. His career success reflects his leadership ability to build teams with synergy and a customer oriented attitude. With an eye on the next millennium, Mr. Hunt is looking forward to taking on more professional responsibilities and anticipates a promotion to the position of Director. A leader in the active wear industry, Fruit of the Loom is one of the major manufacturers of undergarments. Boasting $2.1 billion in annual sales, merchandise is distributed throughout the United States and around the world. Founded in 1926, over 35,000 individuals are employed in international operations. **Career Highlights:** Data Center Manager, Fruit of the Loom (1996-Present); Staff Analyst, Analyst International (1994-96); Production Control Analyst, Henry Ford Hospital (1991-94); Production Control Analyst, Geometric Results, Inc. (1989-91). **Associations & Accomplishments:** Project Management Institute; Air National Guard. **Education:** Detroit College of Business. **Personal Information:** Married to Katherine Marie in 1985. Two children: Jeffrey Allen and Kelli Margaret. Mr. Hunt enjoys golf, running and reading.

Corey Osmer

Manager of Research and Development
Native Textiles
211 Warren Street
Glens Falls, NY 12801
(518) 792-1188
osmer.c@nativetextiles.com

2254

Business Information: As Manager of Research and Development of Native Textiles, Mr. Osmer oversees the design of new fabrics not yet attempted in the textile industry. These new products must meet existing Company regulations and specifications. An expert in this field, Mr. Osmer ensures product quality, value, and selection by overseeing all aspects of new fabric testing. He, in turn, formulates his own conclusions with the help of his staff. Besides the technical aspects of his job, Mr. Osmer supervises the whole staff of researchers. When the need to fill a position arises, he recruits talented new staff members and trained them in the policies and procedures of Native Textiles. Success, Mr. Osmer asserts, is the end product of knowledge and knowing other people. As for the future, he plans to countinue his hard work and advance from within Native Textiles. Since 1934, Native Textiles has manufactured fabric. The Company specializes in single faced wrop knits, which can be found in active wear and intimate apparel. Active wear can be classifed as sports products, the type that Nike and Addidas produce. As for intimate apparel, those items would include hosery and Playtex. Currently, Native Textiles employs 270 people. **Career Highlights:** Manager of Research and Development, Native Textiles (1994-Present). **Education:** State University of New York at Delhi, A.S. (1993); Mayer International School of Textiles, Germany. **Personal Information:** Married to Rebecca in 1998. Mr. Osmer enjoys golf, running and biking.

Zaw W. Oo

IT Manager
Cookson Fibers, Inc.
Highway 52 North
Ansonville, NC 28007
(704) 826-1025
Fax: (704) 826-6159
zawoo@vnet.net

2282

Business Information: Serving as the Information Technology Manager for Cookson Fibers, Inc., Mr. Oo is responsible for the management of two plants in North Carolina, the maintenance of the computer systems, networks, the design of the infrastructure, programming, and ensuring that the Company is Y2K compliant. He has enjoyed substantial success in his career and attributes it to his concentration and focus on the big picture. Mr. Oo continues to grow professionally and hopes to move into networking and pursue his Master's degree. Founded in 1995, Cookson Fibers, Inc. is an established and reputable textile manufacturer, specializing in the manufacture of nylon yarn. Operating from four plants in the United States and one in England, local operations in Ansonville, North Carolina employ the expertise of 250 individuals and reports an estimated annual revenue of $30 million. **Career Highlights:** IT Manager, Cookson Fibers, Inc. (1997-Present); CAD/Test Engineer, Emerson Electronics (1996-97); Plant Engineer Intern, ParkDale Mills, Inc. (1996). **Associations & Accomplishments:** Tau Alpha Phi Engineering Technology Honor Society; Phi Kappa Phi; Omicron Delta Kappa National Leadership Honor Society; Phi Beta Delta National Honor Society for International Scholar; Golden Key National Honor Society. **Education:** University of North Carolina at Charlotte, B.S. in Electronics (1995).

Anthony Ackermann

Information Systems Director
LA Dye & Printworks, Inc.
8321 Canford Street
Pico Rivera, CA 90660-3701
(562) 801-9960

2299

Business Information: As Information Systems Director of LA Dye & Printworks, Inc., Mr. Ackermann coordinates with management and users to determine the overall strategic direction and business contribution of the information systems function. Working as a corporate advisor and information management systems liaison, he is responsible for reviewing operations in order to analyze, specify, and design advanced technical solutions to maintain and enhance the daily operations of the Corporation. Mr. Ackermann was inspired to enter the technology field by attending a high school that was more of a trade school. Highly regarded, he received recognition for integrating several systems which had previously not communicated with each other. His future goals include attaining a position within management and performing duties of a technical consultant. Staying up with emerging technology and learning how it applies to what he does have been contributing factors to Mr. Ackermann's success. Established in 1983, LA Dye & Printworks, Inc. is a textile manufacturing firm. The Corporation currently employs a staff of 1,100 people in its California locations. **Career Highlights:** Information Systems Director, LA Dye & Printworks, Inc. (Present). **Education:** Santa Clara University: M.B.A. (1991), B.S. in Electrical Engineering (1988).

2300 Apparel and Other Textile Products

2311 Men's and boys' suits and coats
2321 Men's and boys' shirts
2322 Men's and boys' underwear and night-wear
2323 Men's and boys' neckwear
2325 Men's and boys' trousers and slacks
2326 Men's and boys' work clothing

2329 Men's and boys' clothing, nec
2331 Women's and misses' blouses and shirts
2335 Women's, juniors', and misses' dresses
2337 Women's and misses' suits and coats
2339 Women's and misses' outerwear, nec
2341 Women's and children's underwear
2342 Bras, girdles and allied garments
2353 Hats, caps, and millinery
2361 Girls' and children's dresses, blouses
2369 Girls' and children's outerwear, nec
2371 Fur goods
2381 Fabric dress and work gloves
2384 Robes and dressing gowns
2385 Waterproof outerwear
2386 Leather and sheep-lined clothing
2387 Apparel belts
2389 Apparel and accessories, nec
2391 Curtains and draperies
2392 Housefurnishings, nec
2393 Textile bags
2394 Canvas and related products
2395 Pleating and stitching
2396 Automotive and apparel trimmings
2397 Schiffli machine embroideries
2399 Fabricated textile products, nec

Ira Anthony Farmer
Systems Operator
Hubbard Company
202 Georgia Avenue North
Bremen, GA 30110
(770) 537-2341

2325

Business Information: Providing technical services, Mr. Farmer holds the position as Systems Operator for the Hubbard Company. He has faithfully served with the Hubbard Company in the technology department since joining the Company in 1983. Focusing on data processing, he concentrates on the analysis of company computer operations. Specifically involved in troubleshooting, Mr. Farmer holds the responsibility of maintaining the Company's database and network system, organizing printed reports, and performing backups. Highly regarded by management, he received various Company awards, to include "Employee of the Quarter." Continuing his growth with the Hubbard Company, Mr. Farmer is committed to growing with the Company and providing excellent systems support in maintaining the functionality of the Company's systems infrastructure. Specializing in the manufacturing of men's slacks, the Hubbard Company, a subsidiary of Tom James Company, was established in 1935. Serving a national client base, the Company is located in Bremen, Georgia. Presently, the Company employs a work force of more than 140 people. **Career Highlights:** Systems Operator, Hubbard Company (Present). **Associations & Accomplishments:** Softball League. **Personal Information:** Married. Two children.

Allen White
Supervisor of Information Technology Operations
Levi Strauss & Co.
8 Campus Circle, Suite 200
Westlake, TX 76262
(817) 262-6351
jwhite4@levi.com

2339

Business Information: Serving as the Supervisor of Information Technology Operations, Mr. White is responsible for maintaining Levi Strauss & Co.'s systems infrastructure at the Westlake, Texas location. He oversees and manages the OS/390 and AS/400 platforms, financial data systems, and all automated and processing equipment for the Company. Drawing from 19 years of hands-on experience in the field, Mr. White supervises a staff of 10 employees in the Department. In the future, he plans to continue working in this capacity, looking forward to new advancement opportunities and the chance to continue to learn and grow. Established in 1850, Levi Strauss & Co. designs, manufactures, and markets clothing. Focusing mainly on denim products such as jeans, the Company distributes products internationally. Headquartered in San Francisco, California, the Company utilizes the latest technological advances in the process of design and manufacture. **Career Highlights:** Supervisor of Information Technology Operations, Levi Strauss & Co. (1994-Present); Operations Shift Manager, Lomas Information Systems (1987-93); Operations Supervisor, Zale Corporation (1979-87). **Personal Information:** Mr. White enjoys reading and computers.

Cindy Davis
Senior Vice President of Retail
Maidenform, Inc.
154 Avenue East
Bayonne, NJ 07002-4596
(201) 436-9200
cdavis@mfww.com

2342

Business Information: Ms. Davis serves as Senior Vice President of Retail for Maidenform, Inc. Beginning her career at Maidenform more than eight years ago, she has received recognition for her diligence and management skills through several promotions to her current position. Reporting directly to the chief executive officer, Ms. Davis supervises the group that runs outlets and e-commerce, closely watching all merchandising, store operations, and real estate sites. Her career highlights include supervising the team that developed the total e-commerce start up for Maidenform in only six months, and working her way through the retail division from manager of Star planning. Ms. Davis' strategic plans for the future include Internet site and retail outlet growth and staying on top of emerging technology. Maidenform, Inc. is an international foundations, panty, and shapewear manufacturing company with outlet retailing and Internet e-commerce. Established in 1922, the Corporation is headquartered in New Jersey with main distribution in Fayetteville, North Carolina. **Career Highlights:** Maidenform, Inc.: Senior Vice President of Retail (Present); Director of Stores, Director of Store Planning.

Razi Ur Rehman
Systems Manager
Poly Products, LLC
St. #7, Rusl Industrial District, P.O. Box 2561
Sultanate, Oman 112
+96 8626044
Fax: +96 8626046
razir@omantel.net.om

2392

Business Information: Utilizing his vast education, Mr. Rehman joined Poly Products, LLC in 1988 as information technology Systems Manager. Responsible for laying out policies and managing the information technology division of the Company, he monitors every aspect of the technology division. Focusing on general administration, strategic planning, and service promotions, Mr. Rehman capitalizes on more than 17 years of solid experience to set up new systems and evaluate software. In addition, he provides on-site technical support. Committed to further development and always alert to new opportunities, techniques, and approaches, Mr. Rehman returned to school in 1999 earning his MSCE certification. Enjoying his prominence with the Company, he plans to remain in his current position and work toward expansion to ensure a bright future for the Company. Established in 1979, Poly Products, LLC engages in the manufacturing of bedding products. Located in Sultanate, Oman, the Company employs 550 highly qualified individuals responsible for administration, gathering data, designing new products and manufacturing processes, marketing merchandise, and sales. An international company in stature, the Company reports annual revenue of $25 million. **Career Highlights:** Systems Manager, Poly Products, LLC (1988-Present); Systems Analyst, ABM Data Systems (1985-88); Systems Analyst, Al-Rashid Microcomputers (1983-85). **Education:** University of Karachi, Bachelor's in Communication; Petromen, Diploma in Computer Science; Microsoft Certified Systems Engineer (1999). **Personal Information:** Married to Rubina Razi in 1993. Mr. Rehman enjoys sports, especially cricket and table tennis.

George W. Henderson, Jr.
Systems Analyst
Unifirst Corporation
2801 Unifirst Drive
Owensboro, KY 42301-0280
(270) 683-5250
Fax: (270) 683-0848
ghenders@unifirst.com

2395

Business Information: Highly skilled in the technology field, Mr. Henderson joined the Unifirst Corporation in 1998 as a Systems Analyst. He has been directly responsible for designing, implementing, and administering several information systems in the corporation's personalization department. Combining knowledge gained through education and experience, he planned and administered systems including Windows NT, Netware, and AS400. Acknowledged for a job well done, Mr. Henderson is enjoying his success and prosperity. Continually striving for maximum effectiveness, he is working on several industry certifications and is planning to return to school this fall to work on a Master's degree in technology. Highly regarded in the industry, he attributes his success to his listening skills and a strong desire to finish what he starts. For the future, Mr. Henderson aspires to a

management role with a focus on software development and database management. Established in 1950, Unifirst Corporation is a leader in the garment industry. The Corporation specializes in emblems and embroidery products. Unifirst recently opened a new plant in Owensboro, Kentucky. The new location employs nearly 300 people responsible for administration, gathering data, designing new products and manufacturing processes, marketing merchandise, and completing sales. Currently supplying products nationally and internationally, the Corporation reports annual income over $480 million. **Career Highlights:** Systems Analyst, Unifirst Corporation (1998-Present); Program Consultant, Daramic Corporation (1995-97); Information Systems Instructor, Owensboro Community College (1997-Present). **Associations & Accomplishments:** Institute of Electronics and Electrical Engineers; Association of Computing Machinery; Owensboro Career Development Association. **Education:** Kentucky Wesleyan College, B.S. in Computer Science (1999); Owensboro Community College: A.S. in Management Information Systems, A.S. in Accounting. **Personal Information:** Married to Audrey in 1967. Two children: George III and Yvonne. Mr. Henderson enjoys mentoring youth, golf, bowling and computer programming.

2400 Lumber and Wood Products

2411 Logging
2421 Sawmills and planing mills, general
2426 Hardwood dimension and flooring mills
2429 Special product sawmills, nec
2431 Millwork
2434 Wood kitchen cabinets
2435 Hardwood veneer and plywood
2436 Softwood veneer and plywood
2439 Structural wood members, nec
2441 Nailed wood boxes and shook
2448 Wood pallets and skids
2449 Wood containers, nec
2451 Mobile homes
2452 Prefabricated wood buildings
2491 Wood preserving
2493 Reconstituted wood products
2499 Wood products, nec

David E. Klein
Management Information Systems Manager
Bertch Cabinet Manufacturing Inc
P.O. Box 2280
Waterloo, IA 50704-2280
(319) 268-2527
Fax: (319) 268-2547
dklein1788@aol.com

2434

Business Information: As Management Information Systems Manager of Bertch Cabinet Manufacturing Inc., Mr. Klein performs all CNC programming, ethernet maintenance, and some electronic maintenance. With two employees under his supervision, he is striving towards complete company system integration and attainment of MCSE. Mr. Klein also utilizes his technical skills in private pursuits, initiating operations of an innovative consulting company. Bertch Cabinet Manufacturing Inc. produces customized wood cabinets, featuring marble tops and mirrors. Established in 1977 and headquartered in Waterloo, Iowa, the Corporation currently employs 850 people. Serving an international clientele, Bertch Cabinet Manufacturing Inc. estimates annual revenues of $70 million. **Career Highlights:** Bertch Cabinet Manufacturing Inc.: Management Information Systems Manager (Present), CNC/Systems Administrator; Computer Repair Technician, United States Air Force (1988-92). **Education:** Keesler Tech Center, Certificate of Training (1989); Electronic Computer and Switching Systems Specialist.

Lee Murray
Senior Database Administrator
Weyerhaeuser Company
P.O. Box 9777, M/S CCB-2C1
Federal Way, WA 98063
(253) 924-7082
Fax: (253) 942-0609
edward.murray@weyerhaeuser.com

2491

Business Information: Mr. Murray is Senior Database Administrator of Weyerhaeuser Company. He is a member of a team responsible for maintaining the functionality and fully operational status of the Oracle database and systems infrastructure. Before joining the Weyerhaeuser Company in 1998, Mr. Murray served in the positions of Database Administrator, Programmer, and Analyst with the Boeing

Company. As an experienced, 22-year technology professional, he owns an established track record of producing results in support of business objectives. Mr. Murray, a recognized expert, is charged with solving technical problems in a timely and systematic manner and maintaining the database for the Company's state-of-the-art commercial door manufacturing system and for other corporate systems. Administering and controlling database resources, ensuring data integrity and security, and tuning software tools to enhance overall performance also fall within the scope of Mr. Murray's functions. Attributing his success to his determination, his career highlights include making a conference presentation on Oracle systems. Obtaining his Doctorate degree and moving to an Internet based system serve as his future endeavors. Weyerhaeuser Company is an international wholesale forest products company. Products include paper and lumber. Headquartered in Federal Way, Washington, the Weyerhaeuser Company recently purchased MacMillan Bloedel, a Canadian forest products company, and maintains a presence in both China and Canada. Established in the 1900s, the Company employs a global workforce of more than 35,800 employees who help generate annual sales in excess of $10.8 billion. **Career Highlights:** Senior Database Administrator, Weyerhaeuser Company (1998-Present); Boeing Company: Database Administrator/Programmer (1995-98), Programmer/Analyst (1990-94). **Associations & Accomplishments:** Digital Equipment Computer Users Society; International Oracle Users Group. **Education:** University of Southern California, M.S. in Systems Management (1987); University of Arizona, B.S. in System Engineering (1977). **Personal Information:** Married to Susan in 1977. Three children: Jennifer, Daniel, and Victoria. Mr. Murray enjoys Web page design, bowling and recreational softball.

Curtis Sutton

Management Information Systems Manager/Mill Analyst
Sierra Pine Adel Division
801 Cook Street
Hahira, GA 31620
Fax: (912) 794-2987

2493

Business Information: As Management Information Systems Manager and Mill Analyst of Sierra Pine Adel Division, Mr. Sutton is concerned with a variety of highly specialized technical processes. Included in his daily schedule are activities that focus on business related technology, such as the monitor of security systems and tracking of computerized orders, shipping, and supplies. Utilizing his impressive knowledge gained through education, practical work experience, and a celebrated military career, Mr. Sutton is able to guide his staff with a proactive leadership style as he incorporates their feedback and input into the creation of strategic operating plans. Enjoying the challenges of his position, Mr. Sutton intends to continue in his current capacity as he assists in the completion of corporate objectives while focusing on the training of other staff. Sierra Pine Adel Division is located in Georgia and employs 144 people at the Hahira facitility. Specializing in the production of particle board, the national company was established in 1968. Recent reports estimate annual revenues to exceed $18 million, proving that the Company's reputation of value and quality has spread throughout the business community. **Career Highlights:** Management Information Systems Manager/Mill Analyst, Sierra Pine Adel Division (1999-Present); Part-time Instructor, Valdosta Technical Institute (Present); Weyerhaeuser: Management Information Systems Manager (1992-99), Mill and Business Analyst (1986-92). **Associations & Accomplishments:** Retired Officers Association; Association of Retired Military Intelligent Officers; Disable American Veteran; Advisory Committee/Board Member, Valdosta Technical Computer Science. **Education:** Valdosta State University, Marketing (1986); M.I.T., Computer Science (1978); Arizona State, Computer Science (1976); Fort Valley State College, Economics (1974); MAXIMO certified (1995); HP-UX certified (1994); Microsoft certified (1994). **Personal Information:** Married to Sharon in 1974. Three children: Curtis Jr., Nikki, and Shawn. Mr. Sutton enjoys golf, fishing and coaching little league.

Derek N. Lipson

Information Systems Manager
SCS, Inc.
1255 Front Street
Fremont, NE 68025-5769
(402) 721-5622
Fax: (402) 721-6170
dlipson@scstruss.inc

2499

Business Information: Since 1998, Mr. Lipson has served as Information Systems Manager for SCS, Inc. He supports LAN and WAN systems for six locations. Mr. Lipson is responsible for all strategic planning, maintenance, upgrading, and troubleshooting of the information database systems which run in the programming languages of Sequel and Access. In addition, he designs and develops Web sites, and maintains all nine servers for seventy client computers. Further, Mr. Lipson facilitates projects as well as maintains the department budget and initiates purchases within budget guidelines. At the same time, Mr. Lipson is a Captain in the Florida Army National Guard and was a Green Beret in the United States Army's Special Forces. Continually striving for maximum effectiveness, he plans to further his technical background to enable him to perpetuate departmental growth. Family owned and operated since 1989, SCS, Inc. employs the services of 300 individuals to facilitate every aspect of design, manufacture, quality assurance and control, and distribution of products. Primarily, the Corporation manufactures wood trusses for the construction industry. To further accomodate clients, SCS has offices and sites in Kansas City; Lincoln; Boone, Louisiana; Des Moines; Minneapolis; and Fremont, and boasts annual sales at $19 million. **Career Highlights:** Information Systems Manager, SCS, Inc. (1998-Present); Chief Executive Officer, Computer Works Plus, Inc. (1996-98). **Associations & Accomplishments:** Chairman of the Board of Christian Education, St. Peter Lutheran Church. **Education:** Midland Lutheran College, B.A. in Journalism (1990). **Personal Information:** Married. Mr. Lipson enjoys reading, war history and family.

2500 Furniture and Fixtures

2511 Wood household furniture
2512 Upholstered household furniture
2514 Metal household furniture
2515 Mattresses and bedsprings
2517 Wood TV and radio cabinets
2519 Household furniture, nec
2521 Wood office furniture
2522 Office furniture, except wood
2531 Public building and related furniture
2541 Wood partitions and fixtures
2542 Partitions and fixtures, except wood
2591 Drapery hardware and blinds and shades
2599 Furniture and fixtures, nec

Jonathan G. Wilson

Personal Computer Specialist
Hickory Springs Manufacturing
235 2nd Avenue NW
Hickory, NC 28601
(828) 328-2201
Fax: (828) 328-5501
jgw@hickorysprings.com

2515

Business Information: Presently entering his third year with Hickory Springs Manufacturing, Mr. Wilson currently fulfills the responsibility of Personal Computer Specialist. In this position, he is accountable for support, maintenance, and update of all personal computers, printers, and portable systems throughout the Company. Possessing an excellent understanding of his field, Mr. Wilson oversees and manages end user software, configuration, modification, and upgrade of in-house software and office products. In the future, he looks forward to designing his own networks and increasing his technical skills. Mr. Wilson attributes his success to education, training, and Novell, CNA 3, CNA 4, and CNE 4 certifications. Hickory Springs Manufacturing is a leading distributor of raw materials for use in the furniture industry. With over 5,000 employees, Hickory Springs Manufacturing has progressed to having international sales. The Company distributes spring, foam, and other building materials, all of which are produced in the United States. **Career Highlights:** Personal Computer Specialist, Hickory Springs Manufacturing (1998-Present); Service Technician, Catawba Valley Computer Service (1997-98); Network Administrator, Wave Communication (1997); Service Manager, Inacom Information Systems (1996-97). **Associations & Accomplishments:** Netware Users International; Starfleet International; Steve Jackson Games. **Education:** Catawba Valley Community College, A.A.S. (1996).

Thomas A. Wysocki

Director
Select Comfort
6105 Trenton Lane North
Plymouth, MN 55442
(612) 551-7046
Fax: (612) 694-3304
wysotx@comfort.com

2515

Business Information: As Director of Select Comfort, Mr. Wysocki is responsible for the network development and maintenance. Overseeing all Oracle applications, he must ensure that the finance, payroll, human resource, and shipping departments are operating successfully at all times. A successful, 26-year veteran of the technology field, Mr. Wysocki is a respected member of the professional technical community; he has been recognized for developing software applications using the Dunn & Bradstreet and Oracle software products as the base architecture. He also works closely with his staff to ensures the Company is current with the technology used in today's progressive society. Enjoying the prominence of his position, Mr. Wysocki intends to continue within the corporate structure while implementing Web based technology into the Company. Established in 1989, Select Comfort specializes in manufacturing air bed matresses. Engaged in the retail sales and distribution of the matresses, the Company strives to satisfy the requests of their target market to consistenly offer them a quality product that is value priced. Proving successful, the estimated annual revenues exceed $300 million. **Career Highlights:** Director, Select Comfort (1996-Present); Project Manager, Fingerhut Inc. (1995-96); Project Manager, Damark International (1990-95). **Associations & Accomplishments:** Oracle Applications User Group. **Education:** Bryant & Stratton Business School, Associate's degree (1968). **Personal Information:** Married to Maryann in 1976. Three children: Teresa, Maria, and Angela. Mr. Wysocki enjoys boating, fishing, golf and coaching softball.

Vonda M. Burroughs

Quality System Coordinator
Hunter Douglas
P.O. Drawer 89
Tupelo, MS 38802
(662) 690-8247
Fax: (662) 690-8255
vonda.burroughs@hunterdouglas.com

2591

Business Information: A certified auditor, Ms. Burroughs serves as Quality System Coordinator for Hunter Douglas. A systems expert in the field, she monitors the Company's quality systems, initiates system improvements, and performs internal quality audits of vendors. Establishing high standards of excellence for other individuals within the industry, Ms. Burroughs attributes her professional success to her ability to motivate other people to the same high standards. Committed to providing continued optimum performance, she anticipates a promotion to a position at the regional level. Her affiliation with the American Society for Auditing enables her to remain current, and allows her to network and interact with her colleagues in different fields. Ms. Burroughs' future endeavors include moving up to the Company's regional level management. A component manufacturing company for window fashions and coverings, Hunter Douglas provides technical and customer services to industry fabricators and warehouse facilities. Beginning operations in 1986, a work force of over 250 individuals are employed. **Career Highlights:** Quality System Coordinator, Hunter Douglas (Present). **Associations & Accomplishments:** American Society for Quality; Alpha Gamma Delta Alumna; Omicron Delta Kappa; Sigma Tau Delta; Gamma Beta Phi; Habitat for Humanity. **Education:** University of North Alabama, B.S. (1997); University of Mississippi, Graduate work; Stat-a-Matrix Institute, Certified Auditor. **Personal Information:** Married to Ken. Ms. Burroughs enjoys gardening and antiques.

Tomm Wisloff

Manager of Application Development
Kinetic Concepts, Inc.
8023 Vantage Drive
San Antonio, TX 78230
(210) 255-6339
Fax: (210) 255-6904
wislofft@kci1.com

2599

Business Information: As the Manager of Application Development for Kinetic Concepts, Inc., Mr. Wisloff fulfills a number of duties on behalf of the Corporation. Possessing an excellent understanding of technology, he manages application development using Oracle software. Capitalizing on his many years of experience, he monitors the productivity of staff, formulating a hands-on management style with an above average aptitude for problem solving. Participating in the analysis, design, evaluation, testing, and deployment of new software into Kinetic Concepts infostructure also fall within the realm of Mr. Wisloff' responsibilities. His focus is on maintaining the Corporation's competitiveness in the market place as well as ensuring the efficiency and profitability of its processes. Always alert to new opportunities, techniques, and approaches, Mr. Wisloff is dedicated to Corporation growth and expansion and looks forward to assisting in the completion of future corporate goals. Kinetic Concepts, Inc. manufactures specialty hospital equipment such as beds and related medical devices. Dedicated to offering patients life-saving care, the Corporation manufactures innovative healing systems, such as specialty support surfaces, mattress replacement systems, and medical devices that address acute and chronic medical difficulties. Established in 1976, the Corporation employs the skilled services of 1,000 individuals to facilitate every aspect of design, manufacture, quality assurance, and distribution of products. The Corporation is headquartered in San Antonio, Texas and distributes products worldwide. **Career Highlights:** Manager of Application Development, Kinetic Concepts, Inc. (1995-Present); Systems Analyst, Bank of Norway (1991-95); Merchandise Analyst, Builders Sqaure, Inc. (1988-91). **Education:** University of Texas at San Antonio, M.B.A. (1988). **Personal Information:** Married to Julie in 1988. Three children: Erik, Heidi, and Lise. Mr. Wisloff enjoys triathlon and children's ministries.

2600 Paper and Allied Products

2611 Pulp mills
2621 Paper mills
2631 Paperboard mills
2652 Setup paperboard boxes
2653 Corrugated and solid fiber boxes
2655 Fiber cans, drums and similar products
2656 Sanitary food containers
2657 Folding paperboard boxes
2671 Paper coated and laminated, packaging
2672 Paper coated and laminated, nec
2673 Bags: plastics, laminated and coated
2674 Bags: uncoated paper and multiwall
2675 Die-cut paper and board
2676 Sanitary paper products
2677 Envelopes
2678 Stationery products
2679 Converted paper products, nec

Almon Allen Jr.

Senior Database Administrator
Bowater Inc.
5300 Cureton Ferry Road
Catawba, SC 29704-7700
(803) 981-8545
Fax: (803) 981-8788
allena@bowater.com

2621

Business Information: As Senior Database Administrator of Bowater, Inc., Mr. Allen is charged with the maintenance of all stored information. He is responsible for daily technical support activities including network troubleshooting, program initiation, and hardware and software development. In this context, he provides data management and design support for the coated paper division. Utilizing his expanded hands on experience and technical background, Mr. Allen continually demonstrate himself to be a valuable and competent Company asset. Maintaining his record of excellence, he plans to climb the corporate ladder to achieve a position as a database project director gaining further recognition as a corporate leader and technical genius. Mr. Allen's success is attributed to his hardwork ethic instilled in him by his father. Bowater Inc. manufactures coated, pulp, and newsprint type paper. Established in 1959, the Corporation has grown to employ 1,100 people who generate a substantial annual revenue. This international company has established itself as a worldwide leader in the manufacturing of specialty paper and paper products, and is currently performing research and development to produce products that will meet the needs of its clients more efficiently. Continuing its excellent product and service record, Bowater plans to expand to overseas locations. **Career Highlights:** Bowater Inc.: Senior Database Administrator (1999-Present), Systems Analyst, MMS (1997-99); Senior Applications Analyst, Bekaert Inc. (1995-97); Senior Programmer Analyst, Healthcare Compare (1994-95). **Associations & Accomplishments:** Ingres Users Group of American; International Oracle Users Group of America; Institute of Electrical and Electronics Society; Big Brothers Association. **Education:** Alabama A&M University, B.S. in Computer Science (1987). **Personal Information:** One child: Steven DeMarcus. Mr. Allen enjoys basketball, billiards, bowling and tennis.

Philip Fiacco

Information Systems Director
Diamond Packaging
111 Commerce Drive
Rochester, NY 14623
(716) 334-8030
Fax: (716) 334-9141
phil@korox.com

2652

Business Information: As Information Systems Director of Diamond Packaging, Mr. Fiacco plans and implements the overall strategic direction and business contribution of the information system function. He oversees and directs all day-to-day administrative activities and operational functions of the Management Information Systems Department, including systems security and reliability and telephony systems. Before coming on board to Diamond Packaging, Mr. Fiacco served as Technology Specialist with Eastman Kodak, and Technology Development Specialist for Harris RF Communications. As a seven year veteran, he is in charge of computer support, technology equipment, and systems and networks; troubleshooting systems difficulties; and evaluating and testing new technology. Mr. Fiacco attributes his success to keeping himself informed, being open and taking advantage to opportunities afforded, and understanding his surroundings. "Learn as much as you can, as fast as you can, so when the next opportunity makes itself available, you are ready," is cited as his advice. A global manufacturer of paper board boxes, Diamond Packaging provides high quality paper board products to include shrink wrap and bubble wrap. A reputable company, Diamond Packaging boast a better turnaround with the capability to change presses in approximately eight hours. Founded in 1961, Diamond Packaging is headquartered in New York and operates a network of two locations. Presently, the Company employs a work force of more than 250 people who help generate annual revenues in excess of $30 million. **Career Highlights:** Information Systems Director, Diamond Packaging (1998-Present); Technology Specialist, Eastman Kodak (1997-98); Technology Development Specialist, Harris RF Communications (1992-97). **Education:** R.I.T., B.A. (In Progress); G.C.C., Associate's degree in Computer Science and Electronic and Electrical Technical. **Personal Information:** Married to Jennifer in 1992. Two children: Alyssa and Shelby.

Sherri Peterson Wynn

Applications Project Manager
Chesapeake Display & Packaging
2900 Lowery Street
Winston-Salem, NC 27101
(336) 650-7613

2653

Business Information: A successful professional, Ms. Wynn serves as the Applications Project Manager for Chesapeake Display & Packaging. She is responsible for management, coordination, and implementation of projects utilizing the JD Edwards software application module. Possessing an excellent understanding of technology, she is also responsible for interfacing with and training system users as well as providing troubleshooting services for the system. Highly regarded, she utilizes 13 years of hands on experience and expertise in all phases of day to day operations. She is an invaluable resource to the Company and her innovative management style encourages Company growth and expansion. Ms. Wynn plans to continue in her present position and looks forward to assisting in the completion of future corporate goals. Her success is attributed to her ambition to succeed and truly loving what she does. Chesapeake Display & Packaging designs specialty corrugated packaging displays and packaging material for customer's products. Headquartered in Winston-Salem, North Carolina, the Company employs an industrious staff of individuals to facilitate every aspect of design, manufacture, quality assurance, and distribution of products. The Company manufactures products for clients internationally, generating annual revenue in excess of $1 billion. **Career Highlights:** Applications Project Manager, Chesapeake Display & Packaging (1999-Present); Manager of JD Edwards Applications, Regent Lighting Corporation (1993-99); Data Processing Manager, Best Distributing Company (1991-93); Coordinator of Computer Operations, Spectrum Glass Products, Inc. (1987-91). **Associations & Accomplishments:** Phi Beta Lambda Professional Division; Who's Who of American High School Students; United Way. **Education:** Sampson Community College: A.A. in Business Administration (1993), A.A. in Business Computer Programming (1987). **Personal Information:** Married to Michael Ray in 1990. Two children: Chandler Michael and Michaela Alexis. Ms. Wynn enjoys reading, sports, travel and family activities.

Jeffrey M. Schuetz

Director of Technology
Sonoco
1 North 2nd Street
Hartsville, SC 29550
(843) 383-7608
Fax: (843) 339-6621
jeffrey.schuetz@sonoco.com

2671

Business Information: Serving as Director of Technology for Sonoco, Mr. Shuetz is in charge of the technology department of the Company's flexible packaging division. In his capacity, he determines the overall strategic direction and vision as well as the business contribution of the information systems functions. Demonstrating strong leadership skills, Mr. Shuetz is responsible for the leading the Company's research and development team of 12 members. Utilizing 17 years of experience, he plans to remain in a technical field, and eventually attain the position of Vice President of a larger business. Highly regarded and an accomplished professional, he currently owns 27 U.S. patents. Mr. Schuetz's career success reflects his ability to think out-of-the-box, take on challenges, and deliver results on behalf of Sonoco. Sonoco is a company that engages in the provision of packaging for a host of client companies in a variety of markets including food, automotive parts, and consumer goods. Established in 1899, the Company offers quality services in order to maintain the reputation of excellence, garner more notoriety, obtain new clients, maintain relationships with existing clients. The Company employs a number of professionals who helps generate annual revenues in excess of $2.5 million. **Career Highlights:** Sonoco: Director of Technology (1999-Present), Technology Manager (1996-99); Research and Operations Manager, Viskase Corporation (1989-96). **Associations & Accomplishments:** Society of Plastics Engineer, Gravure Association of America; Technical Association of Pulp and Paper Industry. **Education:** Purdue University, B.S. in Chemical Engineering (1982). **Personal Information:** Married to Phyllis in 1983. Three children: Greg, Daniel, and Tyler. Mr. Schuetz enjoys golf and boating.

Haluk Yilmaz

Information Technology Supervisor
3M Turkey
Akmerkez B Blok 3K6 Etiler
Istanbul, Turkey 80600
+90 2122822382
Fax: +90 2122821739
haluky@mmm.com

2672

Business Information: Functioning in the capacity of Information Technology Supervisor for 3M Turkey, Mr. Yilmaz assumes the accountability of all information technology operations. A savvy, eight year professional in the field, he ensures the functionality and fully operational status of the information systems function. In addition, Mr. Yilmaz is the Company's Y2K Project team leader. In this context, it is his responsibility to ensure a smooth transition to the new millennium without any systems glitches. A systems expert, he monitors local networks and regional projects to ensure the satisfaction of each client. Mr. Yilmaz was awarded the "Best Employee of the Year" of 1998. He plans to remain with 3M Turkey and eventually move up the corporate hierarchy. His success reflects his ability to think outside the box and aggressively take on new challenges. Established in 1982, 3M Turkey specializes in the production, retail, and marketing of 3M products. The 160 employees construct merchandise and market throughout Turkey and internationally. The retail of products and the superior quality have generated an annual revenue of $5 million. **Career Highlights:** Information Technology Supervisor, 3M Turkey (1997-Present); Application Consultant, EBI (1995-97); Project Engineer, KOG Holding. **Education:** Bilkent University: M.S. in Industrial Engineering (1993), B.S. in Industrial Engineering (1991). **Personal Information:** Mr. Yilmaz enjoys jogging and music.

Jack J. Zhu

Senior Control System Engineer
Avery Dennison, FRNA
726 Sunturn Drive
Fort Wayne, IN 46825
(219) 481-4538
Fax: (219) 481-4596

2672

Business Information: Providing his skilled services as Senior Control System Engineer for Avery Dennison, FRNA, Mr. Zhu is involved in research and development. It is his responsibility to design and develop new machinery for the paper industries that enables companies to enhance their overall production capabilities. Additionally, he maintains the production machines in Avery Dennison, ensuring that each one is running efficiently and that the highest productivity levels are consistently met. Among Mr. Zhu product development accomplishments, are a heart pump that pumps at 3.8 liters per minute and 15 different wheelchair controls that allow the handicapped more convenience with their equipment. As an innovative, 37 year technology professional, his success reflects his ability to think out-of-the-box and aggressively take on new challenges. Continually striving to improve productivity levels, Mr. Zhu is committed to the further development of the Company. Avery Dennison, FRNA provide coating paper services for the printing industry. The Company coats a thin, clear film over phamplets, brochures, and other publications. Established in 1978, national operations employ over 3,000 individuals and yearly sales are reported at $4 billion. **Career Highlights:** Senior Control System Engineer, Avery Dennison, FRNA (1998-Present); Senior Control System Engineer, Kriton Medical Inc. (1995-98); Senior Control System Engineer, Sunrise Medical Inc. (1992-95); Senior Control System Engineer, Innovex Engineering Inc. (1992). **Associations & Accomplishments:** American Men and Women of Science (1998-99); The Most Distinguished Scientists in the United States of America; The Most Distinguished Members; Who's Who Worldwide (1994-95). **Education:** University of Minnesota, Department of Electrical Engineering, Master's degree (1990); Tsinghua University, Department of Automatic Control, China: M.S. (1962), B.S. **Personal Information:** Married to Shannon C. Sun in 1966. One child: Frank Liang. Mr. Zhu enjoys table tennis and swimming.

Eric M. Martin
Information Systems Coordinator
Green Bay Packaging, Inc.
1822 Hogan Lane #2209
Conway, AR 72032
(501) 354-9204
Fax: (501) 328-9992
emartin@conwaycorp.net

2675

Business Information: In his role as Information Systems Coordinator of Green Bay Packaging, Inc., Mr. Martin retains responsibility for a variety of highly specialized technical tasks. Maintaining all information systems and telcommunications, he handles troubleshooting of phones, computers, and application servers, ensuring each is operating at corporate specifications. He demonstrates an extensive knowledge of the industry as he evaluates operational systems and determines upgrades and needed equipment for purchasing. Understanding the importance of customer relations, he designed an informative and user friendly Web site that details the benefits of corporate offerings. Attributing success to a strong motivational drive and unwavering guidance from his mentor, Mr. Martin currently has plans to convert the network to one database by the creation of a new NT server. Returning to school to attain his E.E. and P.E. certifications serves as his future endeavors. Green Bay Packaging, Inc., is located in Conway, Arkansas. Capitalizing on the ever growing logistics needs of expanding international companies and e-commerce business, the Corporation produces paper stock and brown and white boxes. Presently, the Corporation employs a work force of more than 400 who helps generate annual revenues in excess of $40 million. **Career Highlights:** Information Systems Coordinator, Green Bay Packaging, Inc. (1999-Present); Database Programmer, Arkansas Public School Computer Network (1999); Web Developer, University of Central Arkansas (1994-98). **Associations & Accomplishments:** Association of Computing Machinery; Fraternity of Alpha Kappa Lambda. **Education:** University of Central Arkansas, Computer Science degree (1999). **Personal Information:** Mr. Martin enjoys computers, technology, antique automobiles, golf and mechanics.

Isam Salileh
Information Technology Administrator
Lucky Baby Company
P.O. Box 52812
Riyadh, Saudi Arabia 11573
(661) 2651600
Fax: (661) 2650952
isamsal@shamsan-sa.com

2676

Business Information: In his role as Information Technology Administrator of Lucky Baby Company, Mr. Salileh fulfills a variety highly technical responsibilities within the corporate structure. Utilizing his practical work experience and related education, he develops specific software for Company needs as he supports management personnel. Recognized for his impressive technical abilities and productive leadership style, Mr. Salileh lends his insight and guidance at corporate meetings, sharing in management decisions and contributing to project analysis. Mr. Salileh is credited with the successful implementation of several operating processes that maximize the competitiveness of the Company. A well respected member of the professional community, he looks forward to continued advancement within the corporate structure as he prepares for private business ownership. Headquartered in Riyadh, Saudi Arabia, the Lucky Baby Company employs over 600 people. Established in 1975, the Company's extensive product line includes baby and adult diapers, sanitary napkins, tissue paper, and table napkins. Additionally, the Company produces aluminium foil, cling film, and wet wipes, generating annual sales of $46 million. **Career Highlights:** Information Technology Administrator, Lucky Baby Company (1989-Present); Electronic Data Processing Manager, Dar Engineering Contracts Company (1984-89); Project Supervisor, Arab Community College (1983-84). **Education:** Kindy Western University (1986); Arab Community College. **Personal Information:** Married to Hanan Ahamid Na'ami in 1988. Three children: Hanin, Ahmad, and Amjad. Mr. Salileh enjoys working with large manufacturing businesses.

Andrew J. Salisbury II
Network Specialist
SCA Hygiene Products
500 Baldwin Tower Boulevard, Suite 501
Eddystone, PA 19022-1333
(610) 499-3363
andrew.salisbury@hygiene.sca.se

2676

Business Information: As Network Specialist, Mr. Salisbury manages the wide area network for the North American Division. He monitors network activities, and has created new Web sites. Developing network back-up procedures, he is actively involved in building the company's information

systems infrastructure. Possessing business savvy and technical expertise, he is in charge of SCA global network in North America, helping to enhance the WAN/LAN networking environment with over 500 users at 10 sites. Mr. Salisbury is diverse in his professional talents, as he provides critical support for the company's payroll system. He looks forward to new opportunities for growth and exploration in his current position with the Company. SCA Hygiene Products is a paper products manufacturer with offices in Eddystone, Pennsylvania. Created in 1849, the Company produces a wide assortment of hygiene items, including toilet tissue, facial tissue, cotton swabs, and feminine hygiene products. The Company is based in Sweden and employs 32,000 skilled workers, exhibiting tremendous pride in the quality of their work. **Career Highlights:** Network Specialist, SCA Hygiene Products (1996-Present); Network Consultant, Computer Aid (1995-96); LAN Instructor, Computer Learning Center (1995). **Associations & Accomplishments:** Network Professional Association; Institute of Electrical and Electronics Engineers Communications Society; Captain of the Color Guard, Pennsylvania Society of Sons of the Revolution; Military Order of Foreign Wars; St. Andrew's Society at Philidelphia. **Education:** Temple University: M.A. (1980), B.A. **Personal Information:** Married to Mona in 1977. Two children: Andrew and Grace. Mr. Salisbury enjoys BMW motorcycling, sporting clays, Baptiste power yoga and Yoshinkai Aikido.

Barry M. Curcio
Oracle Database Administrator
Lydall, Inc.
One Colonial Road
Manchester, CT 06040
(860) 646-1233
Fax: (860) 646-4917
bcurcio@lydall.com

2678

Business Information: Mr. Curcio is the Oracle Database Administrator of Lydall, Inc. He is also the UNIX Administrator for the programming systems. Mr. Curcio is responsible for maintaining the operation of the system and the effective organization of the database. On a consistent cycle of backing up files, Mr. Curcio has established an efficient file network to secure all of the Corporation's important files and paperwork since his appointment to the position. He is charged with all budgetary responsibilities within his department and for maintaining the operation of all computers in the facility. In the future, Mr. Curcio is working towards obtaining a position in application development with the Corporation. He feels that without his continuing zest for knowledge and attending user group meetings he would not be the success he is. Lydall, Inc. engages in the non computer related manufacturing of paper products. The Corporation hosts over 1,000 employees that strive to maintain an effective production site. All of the machinery is hand monitored and centered around the original methods of production. With clients around the world, the Corporation has established several international locations including a facility in Manchester, Connecticut. **Career Highlights:** Lydall, Inc.: Oracle Database Administrator (1999-Present), UNIX Systems Administrator (1998-99); Senior Research Systems Analyst, Walbro Automotive Corporation (1996-98). **Associations & Accomplishments:** International Oracle Users Group; Oracle Applications Users Group; Network and Systems Professionals Association. **Education:** Middlesex Community College, Associate's degree in Management Information Systems. **Personal Information:** Married to Karen in 1989. Two children: Matthew and Jason. Mr. Curcio enjoys bicycling and skiing.

Christian A. Schmidt
SAP Data Analyst
Mead Corporation
Dayton, OH 45463
(937) 495-4478
Fax: (937) 995-4780
schmidtc@bigfoot.com

2678

Business Information: Utilizing a his extensive academics and occupational experience in technology, Mr. Schmidt is the SAP Data Analyst for the Mead Corporation. In his position, he is responsible for defining the strategy to move data from one place to another. Moreover, he is in charge of gathering all data, entering the information, and clearing the data after use. Highly regarded, Mr. Schmidt possesses superior talents and an excellent understanding of his field. Participating in the analysis, installation, modification, configuration, support, and tracking of the SAP database, server utilities, software, and hardware also fall within the realm of his functions. In the future, Mr. Schmidt looks forward to continuing with the Corporation and moving up the corporate structure. His professional success reflects his ability to think outside the box, take on new challenges, and deliver results on behalf of the Corporation and its clientele. Founded in 1846, Mead Corporation is a manufacturer of paper and forest products. Located in Dayton, Ohio, the Corporation produces more than 1.2 million tons of paper annually for printing and business use. The Corporation also engages in the distribution of paper and packaging supplies to countries around the world. As a

leader in the coated paperboard market, the Corporation is manned by a staff of over 16,000 employees and reports annual revenues in excess of $4 billion. **Career Highlights:** Mead Corporation: SAP Data Analyst (1999-Present), Consultant (1999). **Associations & Accomplishments:** Beta Gamma Sigma Honor Society for AACSD Accredited Business Schools; Philisteria Mercatura Fraternity. **Education:** University of Augsburg: M.A. in Economics (In Progress), B.S. in Business Administration, B.A. in Economics; University of Datyon, M.B.A. (1999).

2700 Printing and Publishing

2711 Newspapers
2721 Periodicals
2731 Book publishing
2732 Book printing
2741 Miscellaneous publishing
2752 Commercial printing, lithographic
2754 Commercial printing, gravure
2759 Commercial printing, nec
2761 Manifold business forms
2771 Greeting cards
2782 Blank books and looseleaf binders
2789 Bookbinding and related work
2791 Typesetting
2796 Platemaking services

Amy L. Gaspardino
Management Information Systems Director
Public Opinion
77 North 3rd Street
Chambersburg, PA 17201
(717) 262-4780
Fax: (717) 262-4791
agaspard@chambers.gannett.com

2711

Business Information: Ms. Gaspardino is the Management Information Systems Director of Public Opinion. She is responsible for all aspects of day-to-day administration and operation of the computer systems function. For approximately four years Ms. Gaspardino used her knowledge and skills in a problem solving capacity, implementing the means of computer technology to meet the needs of the newspaper industry. The Paper heavily relies on the computers to produce its final product and distribute to its customers. Besides overseeing the computer systems, Ms. Gaspardino is involved in formulating policies and procedures, implementing strategies, and marketing plans. She assists the Paper in establishing new business and determining how the best way to market and promote. In the near future Ms. Gaspardino would like to assume a Director's position of a large site. Although she graduated just a few years ago, she has the desire to learn new techniques and is determined to succeed in all her job duties. Public Opinion engages in a daily community newspaper servicing the Chambersburg, Pennsylvania area. Purchased by Gannett Co., Inc. in 1973, the Paper requires a staff of over 100 workers to be able to print a newsworthy paper. **Career Highlights:** Management Information Systems Director, Public Opinion (1999-Present); Systems Specialist, The Burlington Free Press/Gannett (1995-99). **Education:** Trinity College, B.S. (1995).

Frank Schilero
Vice President of Technology
New York Daily News
125 Theodore Conrad Drive
Jersey City, NJ 07305-4615
(212) 210-1748
Fax: (201) 946-7042
fschilero@nydailynews.com

2711

Business Information: Starting in Graphic Arts and having over 20 years of extensive computer experience, Mr. Schilero serves as Vice President of Technology for the New York Daily News. He has numerous corporate duties and responsibilities in his role. Providing management oversight of telecommunications, computer systems, voice communications, and databases as well as desktops and mainframe are his major roles. Utilizing vast, expert knowledge in troubleshooting difficulties, Mr. Schilero implements cutting edge technology to meet organizational needs. He also bears responsibility for designing computer solutions and planning and developing new computer systems. One of his greatest professional accomplishments has been in successfully moving one location into two locations over an 18- hour period without missing any editions of publication. Keeping up with new technology and helping the Newspaper continue to spread circulation into untapped areas serve as his long-term goals. The New York Daily

News, a newspaper with one of the largest circulations in publishing, primarily services New York and sections of New Jersey but has a wide readership throughout the United States. Established in 1918, the Newspaper's featured sections include international, national, and local news; weather; entertainment; sports; comic strips; and syndicated columns. **Career Highlights:** Vice President of Technology, New York Daily News (1983-Present); Director Computer Services, Applied Graphics Technology (1983-91); Director, R R Donnelly & Sons (1981-83). **Associations & Accomplishments:** Piny, Tany, Women in Production; President, Muscular Dystrophy Association, MDA Chapter. **Education:** John Jay College (1970); Programming, Network Communications. **Personal Information:** Married to Christine in 1975. Two children: Stefanie and Joey. Mr. Schilero enjoys softball, baseball, golf, reading and music.

A. J. Thompson

Microcomputer Specialist
The Gazette
1107, 3rd Street
Penrose, CO 81240
(719) 636-0352
thompson@iex.net

2711

Business Information: Serving as the Microcomputer Specialist for The Gazette, Mr. Thompson handles the installation, set up, and configuration of new personal computers. Utilizing extensive technical experience, he accurately and effectively maintains operations including troubleshooting of both hardware and software. He oversees the help desk, guiding the employees with a proactive leadership style. Conducting analysis of customer requests, he is able to pinpoint trouble topics and implement training to ensure each staff member is prepared to handle obscure requests. Recognized as a leader within the organizational structure of the Paper, Mr. Thompson intends to continue in his current position. His success reflects his ability to think outside the box, deliver results, and aggressively take on new challenges. The Gazette is a daily newspaper that serves the residents of Colorado Springs, Colorado. Reporting the events of daily happenings, the Paper strives to keep citizens in touch with the changes within their communities. Businesses from the area contribute to the profitability of the Paper by purchasing advertising space for promotional benefits. **Career Highlights:** Microcomputer Specialist, The Gazette (1986-Present); Instructor, Central Texas College (1984-86); Computer Operator, The Equitable Assurance Society (1978-83). **Associations & Accomplishments:** Rocky Mountain Windows NT Users Group; Micro Certified Professional on Windows NT (1988). **Education:** Pikes Peak Community College. **Personal Information:** Mr. Thompson enjoys hiking and mountain biking.

Dale L. Veach

Corporate Telecommunications Manager
Dispatch Printing Company
34 South 3rd Street
Columbus, OH 43215
(614) 461-5588
Fax: (614) 469-6205
dveach@radar.net

2711

Business Information: Assisting in the advanced services of Dispatch Printing Company, Mr. Veach serves as the Corporate Telecommunications Manager. Utilizing 35 years of hands-on experience and business educational background, he maintains this elite corporate position by overseeing and managing all aspects of the Company's voice network including the integrated equipment, contracts, and vendors. Highly respected, he possesses an excellent understanding of telecommunications technology, and is an expert consultant in regards to Integrated Call Centers and ACD equipment. Seeking a future in telecommunication consulting, Mr. Veach looks forward to new advancements and the introduction of innovative technology in his future. Employing 1,500 people in their Columbus, Ohio location, Dispatch Printing Company provides multi-cultural publishing and broadcasting to service the needs of their regional area. Established in 1928, the Company is engaged in newsprint, television, radio, property investment, publishing, and the venture capital industries through 14 separate and distinct affiliates. Dedicated to providing the most up-to-date, accurate new information to the eastern United States, Dispatch Printing Company strives to maintain the highest performance available from any broadcasting company in the country. **Career Highlights:** Corporate Telccommunictions Manager, Dispatch Printing Company (1998-Present); Manager, Ameritech (1966-96). **Associations & Accomplishments:** Vietnam Veterans of America; Reading Tutor, Columbus Public Schools; St. Peters Catholic Church. **Education:** St. Lukes, Master's degree in Theology (In Progress); Franklin University, B.B.A. (1983). **Personal Information:** Two children: Christian Dale and Kelly Lyn. Mr. Veach enjoys religious study and education.

Harold A. Aris

Director of Information Technology
Vibe Magazine
215 Lexington Avenue, Floor 6
New York, NY 10016
(212) 448-7476
Fax: (212) 448-7400
haris@vibe.com

2721

Business Information: As Director of Information Technology of Vibe Magazine, Mr. Aris handles all networking, Internet, and desktop support for Vibe, Spin, and Blaze Magazine. In his role, he is responsible for all six office's Internet setups, e-mail, servers, all backups, and desktops. Overseeing a 20 server and 250 terminal technology infrastructure, Mr. Aris has taken the Company from old outdated computer systems to installing, designing, and implementing all new servers. Possessing technical savvy and expertise, he has set up cutting edge remote access and mail servers as well as manages the Company's Web site. He is also responsible for all strategic development of technology. A graduate of the New York City Technical College, he is a certified Apple Technician in Laseritus, MacIntosh, OS, and laptops; and specializes in Hewlett Packard printers. In the future, Mr. Aris would like to venture out on his own, providing information technology solutions for advertising and publishing companies. Vibe Magazine is a cultural music magazine based out of New York City. A nationally circulated periodical, the Company has four offices in the United States with 300 employees. Published on a monthly basis, the Magazine focuses on articles about hip-hop and R&B music. **Career Highlights:** Director of Information Technology, Vibe Magazine (1998-Present); Held Desk Manager, YAR Communications (1996-98). **Associations & Accomplishments:** A.I.C.C.S. **Education:** New York City Technical College, B.A. (1996). **Personal Information:** One child: Isaiha. Mr. Aris enjoys real estate investments and carpentry.

Kathleen A. Dernoga

Manager of Acquisitions and Review
American Society for Testing and Materials
100 Barr Harbor Drive
West Conshohocken, PA 19428-2951
(610) 832-9617
Fax: (610) 832-9623
kdernoga@astm.org

2721

Business Information: As Manager of Acquisitions and Review of the American Society for Testing and Materials, or ASTM, Mrs. Dernoga demonstrates her extensive technical knowledge by conducting extensive research programs on topics that are related to books and journals in progress. Securing manuscripts from the authors, Mrs. Dernoga manages experts to review and revise the works, to create a product that is interesting, well-designed, and informative. Handling development of software products, she maintains high standards of workmanship from developers. Mrs. Dernoga has been internally recognized for her impressive acheivements in the industry as she continually creates outstanding products and contributes to the success of the Society. Attributing her accomplishments to the guidance of a mentor who gave her practical advice, she looks forward to assisting in the completion of additional corporate goals as she evolves her position to focus on multimedia products. ASTM develops and publishes technical standards and publications. Founded in 1898, the Society currently employs over 200 people at the headquarters location of West Conshohocken, Pennsylvannia, and has annual revenues exceeding $21 million. Also offering related software products, ASTM is a membership society that offers multimedia services to benefit members. **Career Highlights:** American Society for Testing and Materials: Manager of Acquisitions & Review (1989-Present), Manager, Publications (1983-89). **Associations & Accomplishments:** Society of Scholarly Publishers. **Education:** Villanova University, M.A. in Liberal Arts, cume laude (1993). **Personal Information:** Married to Michael A. in 1991. One child: Melanie Alice. Mrs. Dernoga enjoys Tae Kwon Do and has earned her Brown Belt.

Jono Hardjowirogo

Publisher
Association for Computing
1515 Broadway
New York, NY 10036
(212) 626-0665
Fax: (212) 869-0481
jono@hq.acm.org

2721

Business Information: After 20 years of experience in publishing, Mr. Hardjowirogo followed his fascination of technology into the Association for Computing Machinery or ACM as Publisher. Here, he is responsible for 18 publications on various topics of computing. Mr. Hardjowirogo is proud of having a key role in the first computer books published in the 1980s, on which he worked with authors, such as Peter Norton and Danny Goodman. Through the utilization of computer technology, Mr. Hardjowirogo future plans are to move the publications online. His success reflects his ability to deliver results and aggressively take on challenges and new responsibilities. ACM is a society of computing educators and professionals. Founded in 1947, the Association is the oldest computing society in the world. It publishes transactions and journals. Boasting a 90,000 membership, ACM employs 100 support personnel. **Career Highlights:** Publisher, Association of Computing Machinery (1997-Present); Publishing Director, Berlitz (1994-97); Editorial Director, Bantam Electronic Publishing (1984-94). **Associations & Accomplishments:** Computer Press Association. **Education:** University of California at Los Angeles, M.S. (1972); Long Island University, B.A. (1970). **Personal Information:** Married to Laurie in 1977. Two children: Ariane and Damon. Mr. Hardjowirogo enjoys soccer, tennis and volleyball.

Jane E. Morrill

Editor at Large
Duke Communications Windows 2000 Magazine
221 East 29th Street
Loveland, CO 80538-2769
(970) 203-2762
Fax: (970) 203-2916
jane@win2000mag.com

2721

Business Information: Coupling extensive industry experience with seemingly innate technical knowledge, Ms. Morrill excels in the position of Editor at Large at Duke Communications. The founding editor of Windows 2000 Magazine, she demonstrates adept ability as she handles daily responsibilities, lending eloquence to complex technical terms and concepts. Internally recognized for impressive accomplishments pertaining to her position, she is credited for actively contributing to the development of Custom Publishing capabilities. A savvy, technical professional, Ms. Morrill is credited with compiling interviews from 63 leaders of the industry and putting together a "roundtable" for BYTE Magazine's 15th anniversary. Her awards include the Corporate Achievement Award for Editorial Excellence from McGraw-Hill. Ms. Morrill enjoys the challenges of her position. Duke Communications is recognized throughout the technical industry as a literary leader of progress. Documenting advances and updates, the Company publishes a variety of paper and online magazines that focus on pertinent issues in the information technology field. **Career Highlights:** Duke Communications Windows 2000 Magazine: Editor at Large (1999-Present), Head of Custom Publishing (1996-99), Managing Editor (1995-96); Head of State of the Art Department, McGraw-Hill BYTE Magazine (1988-91). **Education:** Mount Holyoke College, B.A. (1964). **Personal Information:** Ms. Morrill enjoys the mountains, travel and reading.

Cindy Tarte Mullinax

Information Technology Manager
Bobbin Group Publishing
1500 Hampton Street, Suite 150
Columbia, SC 29205
(803) 771-7500
Fax: (803) 799-1461
cmullinax@mfi.com

2721

Business Information: Utilizing over seven years of experience in network administration, Ms. Mullinax serves as the Information Technology Manager for Bobbin Group Publishing. She performs the Company's network administration and provides hardware and software support for the end users. Acting as the Telecommunications Manager, she maintains the phone switch and voice mail. Before joining Bobbin Group Publishing, she served with Bobbin Blenheim as Network Administrator. Her solid career background also includes stints as Executive Support Specialist and Administrative Support Specialist with the State of South Carolina Governor's Office. Ms. Mullinax is also responsible for coordinating resource, time lines, schedules, and assignments; overseeing the technology budget; and tuning software tools to enhance the overall systems performance. Ms. Mullinax credits her success to her love and enjoyment of the technology industry and looks forward to continued professional growth in her current position. A subsidiary of Miller Freeman, Inc., Bobbin Group Publishing publishes English and Spanish speaking versions of magazines relating to the sewn products industry. Beginning operations in 1959, the Company employs the services of 16 individuals. **Career Highlights:** Information Technology Manager, Bobbin Group Publishing (1998-Present); Network Administrator, Bobbin Blenheim (1992-98); State of South Carolina Governor's Office: Executive Support Specialist (1990-92), Administrative Support Specialist (1987-90). **Associations & Accomplishments:** Community

Connection Chair. **Education:** Midlands Technical College, Associate's degree (1982). **Personal Information:** Ms. Mullinax enjoys reading, watching videos, trivia and travel.

Rajesh C. Nana

Graphic and Web Designer
Flexx Magazine
2041 Oakleaf Lane
Lithia Springs, GA 30122-2904
(404) 351-4190
Fax: (404) 351-4190
rajnana@aol.com

2721

Business Information: Putting his scholarly pursuits to work directly after recieving his degree, Mr. Nana is a Graphics and Web Designer for Flexx Magazine. Servicing the entire business' computer infrastructure, he uses his creative imagination and his keen instinct to produce a completely original work of computer based art. In addition to these duties, he also designs the Magazine's Web pages. In the musical aspect of the Magazine, Mr. Nana also designs creative record covers for artists. His future endeavors include staying on top of emerging technologies and establishing himself as a highly effective manager. Success according to Mr. Nana is due to his supportive parents and his ability to think outside the box and deliver results. Established in 1998, Flexx Magazine is a monthly publication that offers its readers the finest in entertainment, sports, education, art, religion, business, money, power, live concerts, and more. Oriented around international music, the Magazine's articles contain meticulously crafted statements by a highly qualified writing staff of 15. Presently, the Magazine is located in Lithia Springs, Georgia. **Career Highlights:** Graphics and Web Designer, Flexx Magazine (1999-Present); Seafood Manager, Winn Dixie (1998-99). **Associations & Accomplishments:** U.S.T.A. **Education:** Georgia State University, B.S. in Computer Science (2000). **Personal Information:** Mr. Nana enjoys tennis and reading.

Nicole M. White Rayner

Design Director
Ziff-Davis
100 Quentin Roosevelt Boulevard, Suite 400
Garden City, NY 11530
(516) 229-3766
Fax: (516) 229-3850

2721

Business Information: Fulfilling a creative spirit, Nicole White is a Design Director for Ziff-Davis. In her capacity, she oversees and directs the design of three publications: "Interactive Week," "Smart Reseller," and "PC Week." Performing her administrative and management duties, Ms. White supervises a staff of 14 talented individuals, four of which are art directors. Possessing unique art and design talent herself, Ms. White is the proud recipient of numerous awards for her innovation. A successful professional, she was also recognized for the design and launch of "Smart Reseller" magazine by the Society of Publication Design. Attributing her success to her ability to listen as well as her empathetic nature, Ms. White's strategic plans include starting publications from scratch, familiarizing herself with Web technology, and redesigning existing publications. Ziff-Davis is one of the largest publishing companies in the United States. Publishing 22 industry magazines, the Company publishes magazines that include "Mac World," "PC Week," "Yahoo! Internet Life," "Computer Shopper," "PC Magazine," and many more. Headquartered in Garden City, New York, Ziff-Davis boasts of 5,000 employees nationwide. **Career Highlights:** Design Director, Ziff-Davis (Present). **Personal Information:** Ms. White Rayner enjoys reading, skiing and travel.

Gene E. Folk

Acting Director of Business Systems
Harcourt, Inc.
6277 Sea Harbor Drive
Orlando, FL 32887
(407) 345-3949
Fax: (407) 345-2799
gfolk@harcourt.com

2731

Business Information: Mr. Folk serves as Acting Driector of Business Systems with Harcourt Inc. Serving the Corporation since 1994, he provides direct support and development of major business systems, order processing, warehouse operations, and sales opportunities. Striving to incorporate the latest technologies, Mr. Folk possesses extensively training and managerial experience in the evaluation and application of computer technology to improve business operations. Highly regarded, he is extremely effective in building and directing technical teams to achieve objectives. Mr. Folk is experienced in long range planning, business applications development, technical training, and technical personnel development techinques. Troubleshooting and maintaining complex networking systems also falls within the realm of his responsibilities. Always alert to new opportunities, techniques, and approaches, Mr. Folk looks to expand his career with a progressive organization in a challenging position that will use hi technical experience and management skills to contribute to the success of the company. Currently, he is coordinating the flow of information over three platforms to the process $100 million of orders for the state of Texas. Located in Orlando Florida, Harcourt, Inc. operates an established and reputable publishing company specializing in the publication and distribution of diversified educational books, tests, and workbooks. Employing qualified personnel, the Corporation specifically publishes and distributes science and medical textbooks, standardized and psycological tests, and high school and elementary textbooks and workbooks to an international clientele. **Career Highlights:** Acting Director of Business Systems, Harcourt, Inc. (1994-Present); Manager of Systems Development, Watkins Motor Lines (1990-94); Manager of Analysis and Design, Travelers/EBS, Inc. (1987-89); Applications Manager, Red Lobster (1982-87). **Education:** Kent State University, Bachelor's degree in Math; Rensselear Polytechnic Institute.

John A. Lawson, III

Systems Specialist
Houghton Mifflin
40 Brook Haven Drive, Apartment 4
Alttleboro, MA 02703
(508) 431-1184
Fax: (508) 431-1184
john_lawson@hmco.com

2731

Business Information: Serving as a Systems Specialist for Houghton Mifflin, Mr. Lawson works with management and users to ensure the functionality and serviceable status of the Company's systems infrastructure. He is responsible for performing systems backups, writing scripts and programs, and ensuring the process is complete. Possessing an excellent understanding of his role, Mr. Lawson contributes a phenomenal amount of insight to the day-to-day running of the Company. Highly regarded, he has helped the Company grow by seven percent in 1999. Continuing his education, Mr. Lawson plans on attending college to obtain his Master's degree in Computer Science and remaining with Houghton Mifflin. Houghton Mifflin is a world leader in publishing. Generating an excess of $920 million in revenues annually, the Publisher produces kindergarten through twelfth grade and college level materials. With levels of high production, the Company has created three subsidiaries: McDougal Littell, Inc., Great Source Education Group, Inc., and Riverside Publishing Company. Houghton Mifflin continues to provide the highest quality products to its customers, ensuring the place as a publishing leader in the 21st century. **Career Highlights:** Systems Specialist, Houghton Mifflin (1996-Present); Supervisor, Northeastern University (1989-99); Co-op, Motorola (1993). **Associations & Accomplishments:** Institute of Electrical and Electronics Engineers; Association for Computing Machinery; Rumford Grange #52, Providence County, Pomona #1; Rising Sun Lodge #30; Temple chapter #3, R.A.M.; Adoniram Council #8 R.S.S.A.M.; Calvary Commandery #13 K.T.; Palestine Shrine; Scottish Rite Valley of Providence; Martha Washington #18 O.E.S. **Education:** Northeastern University, B.S. in Computer Science (1999).

Hakiza Nzabanita

Information Technology Consultant
United Bible Societies
1689 Avenue John Paul II
Lome, Togo BP13472
+22 8261655
Fax: +22 8232129
hakiza@ubs-frsc.org

2731

Business Information: Seeking a scholarship to the United States to further his education in the information technology field, Mr. Nzabanita is the Information Technology Consultant for the United Bible Societies. One of the Society's most skilled and experienced professionals, he develops and implements information technology solutions to increase efficiency of the Society's day-to-day publishing and distribution operations. Highly regarded, Mr. Nzabanita is responsible for maintaining the functionality of the communications, Web site, and systems architectures. His ability to speak fluent English, French, Swahili, and Lingala enables him to oversee and manage the accounting and budgeting functions as well as research new technologies unhindered. Dedicated to utilizing his technical skills for the benefit of others, Mr. Nzabanita also provides consulting services to African businesses to enhance their ability in maintaining a competitive edge in the market place. The most rewarding aspect of his career is helping French speaking companies develop innovative programs for accounting and budgeting systems. Established in 1946, the United Bible Societies publishes and distributes holy scriptures. Operating on a global level, the Society brings scriptures to cultures around the world. Presently, the Society employs a dedicated work force of around 350 professionals, technical, and administrative staff. **Career Highlights:** United Bible Societies: Information Technology Consultant (1999-Present), Information Technician Officer (1997-99), Computer Technical Support Officer (1993-97). **Associations & Accomplishments:** Alexander Hamilton Institute; Institute of Commercial Management; Chartered Institute of Business Administration; Association of Certified Chartered Accountants; Recently completed a feasibility project on the implementation of a videoconferencing system. **Education:** Institute of Commercial Management (ICM) in the United Kingdom, Advanced Diploma in Professional Computing (2000); Ecole Technique Superieure, Graduat en Gestion des Entreprises; Cambridge Tutorial College, Diploma in Computer Appreciation. **Personal Information:** Married to Catherine in 1993. Three children: Dan, Esther, and Ian. Mr. Nzabanita enjoys reading.

James A. Todd

Webmaster/Business Development Mentor
Mcgraw-Hill Higher Education
1333 Burr Ridge Parkway
Burr Ridge, IL 60521
(630) 789-5326
Fax: (630) 789-5218
jim_todd@mcgraw-hill.com

2731

Business Information: Mr. Todd functions in the dual role of Webmaster and Business Development Mentor for Mcgraw-Hill Higher Education. He is responsible for leading the Web development group, maintaining and managing over 500 Web sites, as well as producing various new media titles in the business and economic disciplines. Mr. Todd's career highlight involved the development of a small start up, the first plug-n-play intranet, Web based virtual office. To remain on technology's cutting edge, he keeps educated by reading journals and magazines related to the field. In the future, Mr. Todd hopes to become more involved in integrating e-commerce into the industry. His success is attributed to perseverance and his ability to produce results and take on new challenges. Mcgraw-Hill Higher Education is a college text book publisher. Established in 1909, the Company is regarded as the second largest publishers of college text books. The Company is also involved in publishing kindergarten through twelfth grade and professional books. Headquartered in New York City, the Company has a work force of 600 personnel and markets its completed publications throughout the international clientele it supports. **Career Highlights:** Webmaster/Business Development Mentor, Mcgraw-Hill Higher Education (1997-Present); Database Administrator/Webmaster, Futures Net/NEXTEC Communications (1996-97); Network Administrator/Programmer, Gabriel Laboratories (1990-96); Estimator, Globe Amerada Glass (1987-89). **Education:** Illinois State University, B.S. in Economics (1985). **Personal Information:** Married to Theresa in 1990. One child: Ian. Mr. Todd enjoys wood working, stained glass, fantasy football & baseball and coaching Pop Warner football.

Tajammul H. Awan

Systems Analyst/Management Information Systems Manager
Command Web Offset
100 Castle Road
Secaucus, NJ 07094
(201) 863-8100
Fax: (201) 863-2211
tajawan@yahoo.com

2732

Business Information: Serving in a dual role of Systems Analyst and Management Information Systems Manager of Command Web Offset, Mr. Awan is responsible for hardware and software research and development. Before joining Command Web Offset, Mr. Awan served as Production Planner and estimator with Hamilton Printing Company. His solid background history also includes a stint as Graduate Assistant at Sage Graduate School. Utilizing his extensive academic ties, he supervises and guides his skilled staff of 16 employees in providing technical support to 75 users. As a five year veteran with Command Web Offset, Mr. Awan oversees and directs LAN and WAN operations. Providing systems and network training and performing functions as the chief vendor liaison also fall within the purview of his responsibilities. His future goal is to eventually attain the position of Director with the Company. Mr. Awan's success reflects his ability to build teams with synergy, technical strength, and a customer focused attitude as well as take on new challenges. Command Web Offset operates as a book manufacturing company. Privately held, the Company employs 175 people at a network of six sites located nationally. Currently, the Company is headquartered in Secaucus, New Jersey. **Career Highlights:** Systems Analyst/Management Information Systems Manager, Command Web Offset (1995-Present); Production

Planner/Estimator, Hamilton Printing Company (1990-95); Graduate Assistant, Sage Graduate School (1988-90). **Associations & Accomplishments:** Graphic Arts Technical Foundation. **Education:** Sage Graduate School, M.B.A. in Finance; Glasgow College, B.B.A.; Punjab University, B.A.; Computer Learning Center, Computer Programming (1997); Polytecnic Institute Lahore, Diploma in Associate Engineering. **Personal Information:** Married to Qudsia in 1995. Two children: Marium and Taha. Mr. Awan enjoys computers, tennis, cricket and jogging.

Benedict Jones

West Coast Information Technology Manager
R R Donnelley & Sons
991 Francisco Street
Torrance, CA 90502
(310) 527-7011
Fax: (310) 527-3585
benedict.jones@rrd.com

2732

Business Information: Serving as West Coast Information Technology Manager for R R Donnelley & Sons, Mr. Jones oversees the development and implementation of information technology for 11 sites on the West Coast. He coordinates the reports of 11 employees. A successful, seven year veteran, he maintains the systems to ensure the client documents are secure. Mr. Jones provides user support to eliminate any technical problem areas. He upgrades the current systems to maintain the client's operations on the cutting edge of technology including the utilization of LAN and WAN systems. Mr. Jones has developed a software interface for external clients and restructured the West Coast's infrastructure. In the future, he will expand the department while keeping current with technology advancements through R R Donnelley & Sons. Founded over a hundred years ago, R R Donnelley & Sons engages in financial printing and technology. The printing Company operates five divisions including the printing of books, magazines, yellow pages, multimedia, and a financial division. The employees print financial documents and files these documents with the correct agencies for companies involved with the stock exchange. **Career Highlights:** West Coast Information Technology Manager, R R Donnelley & Sons (1998-Present), Midwest Lead Information Technology Tech (1994-98); Network Administrator, I.I.T. Career Development Center (1992-94). **Associations & Accomplishments:** Pi Kappa Phi Fraternity; Institute of Electronics and Electrical Engineers. **Education:** Illinois State University of Technology, Bachelor's degree in Mathematics (1994), Associate's degree in Physics and Electrical Engineering. **Personal Information:** Mr. Jones enjoys volleyball, soccer, volleyball, drawing and poetry.

Rick Adams

VAX/VMS Systems Administrator
IHS Engineering
31 Lawrence Avenue
Colorado Springs, CO 80909
(303) 858-6099
adamsr2001@hotmail.com

2741

Business Information: Possessing superior talents in the information technology field, Mr. Adams serves as a VAX/VMS Systems Administrator for IHS Engineering. In this capacity since 1999, he utilizes his advanced skills to manage all technical resources for the VAX/VMS computer system used at IHS Engineering. Highly regarded, Mr. Adams is also responsible for performing diagnostic tests, systems upgrades, and equipment reconfigurations. Utilizing new techniques and progressive technology, he uses cutting-edge software to detect anomalies and takes appropriate action to provide a solution. Mr. Adams has enjoyed tremendous success in his current position with IHS Engineering, and he aspires to be promoted to a higher-level management position in the near future. IHS Engineering specializes in international standards consulting for the industrial industry. Established in 1959, the Corporation employs a collective work force of over 3,200 highly trained technicians who support all activities and assist in generating the Corporation's successively high annual revenues. IHS represents the largest, most complete source for industry standards, military specifications, government part listings, electronic component catalogs, and aviation regulations. **Career Highlights:** VAX/VMS Systems Administrator, IHS Engineering (Present); VAX/VMS System Administrator, Sai Software (1999); Senior Field Engineer/Systems Administrator, Stanford Telecom, Inc. (1986-99); Satellite Communications Technician, United States Air Force (1978-86). **Associations & Accomplishments:** American Legion. **Education:**

University of Maryland, A.A. in Management Studies (1996); Georgia Military College, A.A.S. in Applied Science Communications/Electronics Technology (1986). **Personal Information:** Married to Maribeth in 1993. Four children: David, Samantha, Jacob, and Rachel.

Christie Callahan Hale

Production Manager/Art Director/Web Designer
Randol International, Ltd.
13701 West Jewell Avenue, Suite 114
Denver, CO 80228
(303) 986-5579
Fax: (303) 986-5577
christie.hale@att.net

2741

Business Information: Exhibiting expert technology skills as well as displaying adept management abilities, Mrs. Hale serves jointly as Production Manager, Art Director, and Web Designer for Randol International, Ltd. In this capacity, she is responsible for a myriad of administrative and operational duties, to include all production activities, such as scheduling and quality control. Additionally, Mrs. Hale utilizes her artistic talents in graphic design when coordinating publications and oversees print-runs for buyer's guides, mining directories, conference proceedings and agenda booklets. Mrs. Hale is also engaged in Web site maintenance and Web page development. She has enjoyed tremendous success in her current position with Randol International and has future aspirations to venture into entrepreneurship with the establishment of her own Web designing company. Established in 1985 Randol International, Ltd. is a publishing company specializing in publications for the mining industry. Capitalizing on the locale of natural resources, the Company is strategically located in the heart of the Rocky Mountains in Denver, Colorado and employs the talents and expertise of four highly skilled professionals. **Career Highlights:** Production Manager/Art Director/Web Designer, Randol International, Ltd. (1991-Present); Art Director, National Cattlemen's Association (1989-91); Art Director, Graphic Results (1987-89); Art Director, General Communications (1985-87). **Associations & Accomplishments:** Women Helping Others. **Education:** Colorado Institute of Art, Associate's degree in Graphic Design (1984); Louisiana Technological Institute, Interior Design. **Personal Information:** Married to Patrick in 1982. One child: Alexandra Barron Hale. Mrs. Hale enjoys scootering, renovating and gardening.

Mary Jane Cottingham Lehman

Business Systems Manager
Thomson Corporation
5101 Madison Road
Cincinnati, OH 45227-1427
(513) 527-6920
Fax: (951) 426-1996
mary.lehman@itpms.com

2741

Business Information: Mrs. Lehman functions in the role of Business Systems Manager for Thomson Corporation. Fulfilling the functions of information team leader and project manager, she is responsible for leading a team of five expert professional who test, maintain, and support sales and marketing computer systems. In addition, Mrs. Lehman is a program analyst who focuses on developing marketing strategies and ways to enhance the Corporations visibility. Looking to the 21st Century, next millennium, Mrs. Lehman plans to develop and implement a leading edge Sales Force Automation System. Currently, she is proud of her rewrites of the cost system, wich took four teams of programmers to integrate. Mrs. Lehman is striving to improve her technical skills through attendance at seminars and trade shows and reading trade magazines. As for her current success, she attributes it to an innate ability to work with other people. Thomson Corporation generates in excess of $6 billion in annual revenue. The Corporation focuses on informational materials, as it is a publisher for the educational market. Using a devoted work force of 40,000, Thomson Corporation has made a name for itself in the publishing industry. Operating out of Stamford, Connetticut, and Toronto, Canada, the Corporation engages in business on a multinational level. **Career Highlights:** Business Systems Manager, Thomson Corporation (1994-Present); Project Manager, EG&G Mound Applied Technologies (1984-94); Programmer/Analyst, Monsanto Research Corporation (1979-84). **Education:** Park College, B.S. (1996); Clark State University, A.S. in Computing Programming (1978). **Personal Information:**

Married to Paul in 1980. Five children: Robert, Jeremy, Dan, Jennifer, and Jason. Mrs. Lehman enjoys golf.

Vicki Neal Londeree

Financial Systems Analyst
Lexis Publishing
P.O. Box 7887
Charlottesville, VA 22906
(804) 972-7600
Fax: (804) 972-7656
vicki.londeree@lexis-nexis.com

2741

Business Information: Demonstrating an expertise learned over the course of her long career with Lexis Publishing, Ms. Londeree serves as Financial Systems Analyst. She is the Project Lead for the financial system development and its implementation within the Company's network. In charge of system security administration, she ensures that the financial reports and data remain sensitive by maintaining the integrity of the systems infrastructure. Ms. Londeree creates and generates reports for the various areas of Lexis Publishing, enabling the managerial staff to have an overall view of their total operation. A subsidiary of Reed Elsevier, Lexis Publishing specializes in the publication of books and other material relating to the legal field. The Company began operations in the early 1800s and now boasts a total workforce of 7,000 dedicated individuals. **Career Highlights:** Lexis Publishing, Division of Reed Elsevier: Financial Systems Analyst (1995-Present), Accounting Systems Administrator (1990-95), PC Administrator (1989-90). **Associations & Accomplishments:** Charter Member, Rivanna Lions Club; Treasurer, Central Virginia Chapter, National Wild Turkey Federation. **Education:** Mary Baldwin College, B.A. in Business Administration and Computer Science (In Progress); Piedmont Virginia Community College, A.A.S. in Business Management. **Personal Information:** Married to Sherwood in 1982. Ms. Londeree enjoys fishing and travel.

NetMedia International Limited

Ringo Loo

Project Director
NetMedia International Ltd.
5/F, 42 Yee Woo Street, HKSAR
Hong Kong, Hong Kong
+852 25728868
rloo@no1media.com

2741

Business Information: Serving as Project Director, Mr. Loo has been providing his professional management skills with NetMedia International Ltd. since 1997. Overseeing the basic daily operations involved in project development, he is extensively involved in strategic planning, finances, and sales and marketing aspects of the Company. Working closely with his team of technical experts, Mr. Loo directs the necessary funding and materials to developing projects. Possessing an excellent understanding of his field, he is actively involved in the implementation of new technologies to produce a more efficient and reliable product. An accomplished professional, he has been published in numerous newspapers in Hong Kong. Always alert to new opportunities, techniques, and approaches, Mr. Loo is highly regarded and remains committed to the further expansion of the product line with NetMedia International. Engaging in online publishing and selling, NetMedia International Ltd. was established in 1997. Currently holding the responsibility for 20 Web sites, one being the largest healthcare Web site in Hong Kong, the Company designs, develops, and integrates specialized information technologies. Included in the Company's expansive services and products are a diverse set of subsidiaries including Shop No. 1 Ltd., providing online selling; Shop 88 Ltd., providing editorial services; and No. 1 Ltd. Presently, the Company employs a staff of 15 professionals. **Career Highlights:** Project Director, NetMedia International Ltd. (1997-Present); Project Director, Shop No.1 Ltd. (1998-Present); Project Director, No.1 Ltd. (2000-Present). **Education:** Dalhousie University: B.B.A. (1979), 2nd degree in Computer Sceince (1980). **Personal Information:** Married to Anita Lo in 1985. One child: Horson. Mr. Loo enjoys surfing, sports, reading and movies.

Maria Luisa A. Solomon

Technical Support Specialist
Financial Information, Inc.
30 Montgomery Street
Jersey City, NJ 07302-3821
(201) 369-3630
Fax: (201) 369-3664
msolomon@fiinet.com

2741

Business Information: Serving Financial Information, Inc. in the role of Technical Support Specialist, Ms. Solomon is responsible for providing all technical and help desk support as well as user training and systems administration. In her capacity, she is in charge of installing and configuring work stations, implementing software applications, and training and supporting 50 associates. Monitoring and tuning all systems software, peripherals, and networks, Ms. Solomon is accountable for purchasing software, hardware, equipment, and accessories. In addition, manages the equipment account and performs the required maintenance on the infrastructure as well as conducting personnel evaluations and reccommendations. In the future, she plans to advance up the corporate structure and work with larger Fortune 500 companies. Ms. Solomon's success is attributed to her situational awareness and her ability to stay on top of emerging technoloies. Established in the early 1900s, Financial Information, Inc. provides financial information to the securities industries through the use of publications and online services. Headquartered in Jersey City, New Jersey, the Corporation employs 40 individuals to meet the demands of his clientele. **Career Highlights:** Technical Support Specialist, Financial Information, Inc. (1997-Present); Lab Technical Assistant, Jersey City State College (1996-97); Bakery Clerk, Shoprite (1995-98). **Education:** Jersey City State College, B.S. in Computer Science (1998).

Emmanuel Stein

Information Technology Consultant
Elsevier Science
655 Avenue of the Americas
New York, NY 10010
(212) 633-3671
Fax: (212) 633-3880
e.stein@elsevier.com

2741

Business Information: Serving as Elsevier Science's Information Technology Consultant, Mr. Stein fulfills a number of technical duties on behalf of the Company and its clients. He works closely with management and systems users to analyze, specify, design, and implement solutions to enhance the overall capability of information systems functions. Possessing an excellent understanding of his field, Mr. Stein is responsible for deployment of new technologies for the regional sales offices in North and South America. He also creates software and deals with programming, client contact, contract coordination, and technical proposals. In the future, Mr. Stein plans to continue working with the Company, obtaining a position as the Company's Senior Architect. Elsevier Science provides services in the area of Internet publishing. The Company begins with academic content, then publishes a scientific publication, which is then transferred to the Internet in an online format. Information is made available to research labs and universities who utilize the news in daily operations and teaching aspects. A highly sophisticated organizaiton, the Company also provides services in the areas of Internet and Intranet solutions. **Career Highlights:** Information Technology Consultant, Elsevier Science (1999-Present); Systems Engineer, Time Warner/AOL (1999); Associate Manager of Web Development, France Telecom (1997-99); Graduate Research, State University of New York at Albany (1995-97). **Associations & Accomplishments:** Sun Developer Association; Apple Developer Connection; International Computer Security Association. **Education:** State University of New York at Albany, M.A. (1997); New York University, Internet Technologies; Sun Education: Solaris Administration, Java Development; Oracle Corporation, PL/SQL. **Personal Information:** Mr. Stein enjoys time with friends and family and computers.

Brian A Thurogood

e-Business and Information Systems Manager
William Reed
Three Ways Byers Lane
South Gostoden, England, United Kingdom RH9 8JL
+44 1293610202
Fax: +44 1293610382
briant@william-reed.co.uk

2741

Business Information: Demonstrating expertise in the information technology field, Mr. Thurogood currently serves as e-Business and Information Systems Manager for William Reed. He is a specifier and senior analyst for the publishing systems, Web development, and digital integration. Demonstrating sound management skills, he manages 23 employees while implementing new technology and taking advantage of business opportunities for the Company. Beginning his career more than eight years ago, Mr. Thurogood has received recognition for his diligence and management skills through several promotions to his current position. Highly regarded, he attributes his success to having the ability to see opportunities arise and taking advantage of them. Proud of his accomplishments, Mr. Thurogood started his career as a rock musician, writing articles for Rolling Stone and local area newspapesr. His plans are to expedite continued promotion through dedication and the perpetuation of additional growth through more knowledge of the systems and updated technology. William Reed is an established and reputable publishing company providing clients with business-to-business services, contract, trade, business directories, database management, profiling, and on-line services. The Company's customers include food and drink companies that work with fast moving consumer goods. Established in 1863, the Company is located in the United Kingdom and currently employs the skilled services of 300 individuals to acquire business, meet with clients, facilitate projects, and market services. William Reed reports estimated annual sales of £30m. **Career Highlights:** William Reed: e-Business and Information Systems Manager (1992-Present), Systems Consultant (1992); Self-Employed, Systems Consultant (1990-92). **Associations & Accomplishments:** County Councillor Auckland (1981-90). **Education:** Northcote College. **Personal Information:** Married to Melanie J. in 1992. Two children: Amber and Tommy. Mr. Thurogood enjoys being a music journalist, a freelance journalist and tennis.

Nicoledean J. van der Linden

Publisher
Engineering Information, Inc.
1 Castle Point Terrace
Hoboken, NJ 07030-5996
(201) 216-8500

2741

Business Information: A brilliant person with an excellent understanding of his field, Mr. van der Linden is responsible for all Web based products of the Company. His duties include overseeing new product development and managing the database information as well as managing the publication of 15 printed journals. Highly regarded in the publishing field, Mr. van der Linden coordinates the Company's large engineering database and shares this information with other publishers. The final authority in project management, his career highlight is holding the position of Assistant to Chairman responsible for the entire communications network process. He looks forward to managing a larger department here, or mother company, or with one of the subsidiaries. Success, according to Mr. van der Linden, is due to his ability to quickly grasp technical concepts, take on new challenges, and deliver results. Engineering Information, Inc., publishes several electronic databases in the fields of engineering, gas and oil, and paper and pulp. Their mother corporation is Elservier Science. The Corporation is an international company with over 50 employees. Presently, Engineering Information is lcoated in Hoboken, New Jersey. **Career Highlights:** Publisher, Engineering Information, Inc. (1999-Present); Elsevier Sciences: Publisher of Life Sciences (1997-99), Assistant to Chairman (1995-97). **Education:** Rotterdam School of Management, M.B.A. (1992). **Personal Information:** Married.

Derek Werkowitz

Systems Support Manager
O'Neil Associates
425 North Findlay Street
Dayton, OH 45404-2203
(937) 461-1852
Fax: (937) 228-0135
dwerkowitz@oneil.com

2741

Business Information: As Systems Support Manager of O'Neil Associates, Mr. Werkowitz is responsible for a multitude of duties. He is responsible for providing in-house network, installation, and computer support. A savvy, four year veteran, Mr. Werkowitz also assits in maintaining the Help Desk and answering concerns or questions from customers. Keeping abreast with new developments and technologies in the field, Mr. Werkowitz attends professional seminars, conducts training courses, and reads current literature. In the beginning of his career with the Company, Mr. Werkowitz had limited technological knowledge, but with dedication, hard work, and intellect, he acquired greater knowledge and skill and therefore moved to greater positions. The ability to learn and adapt quickly to changing situations are reasons attributed to his professional success. Establsihed in 1948, O'Neil Associates provides electronic publishing, technical documentation, and logistics to clients. This $20 million company presently employs over 200 dedicated and highly skilled employees. **Career Highlights:** Systems Support Manager, O'Neil Associates (1996-Present); Purchasing Coordinator, CCT (1995-96). **Education:** Wright State University.

James D. Wismer

Manager of Current Awareness Products
Institute for Scientific Information (ISI)
3501 Market Street, Floor 1
Philadelphia, PA 19104-3302
(215) 386-0100
james.wismer@isinet.com

2741

Business Information: Demonstrating an extensive knowledge of computer science in the conduct of his daily duties, Mr. Wismer serves as Manager of Current Awareness Products for the ISI or Institute for Scientific Information. He oversees a group of software developers responsible for developing Web-based applications. The six-member staff is presently creating a database with current information for researchers. Mr. Wismer is also in charge of designing new products for the current awareness division of the Institute, developing and implementing new technology through the Internet and Web applications. Overseeing product development through its complete life cycle, Mr. Wismer strives to stay current in the technology field and incorporates his new knowledge into each product that he develops. His professional success is credited to his ability to identify trends in technology and build on these trends as well as setting goals to further his career. One of Mr. Wismer's long-term goals is to offer his services as an independent consultant. Founded in 1958, ISI offers its services as a database publisher. The Institute acts as a secondary publisher for scientific and technical publications numbering more than 16,000. A database is provided, with its bibliographic contents made available to researchers, educators, and the corporate world via Web and CD-ROM applications. ISI is headquartered in Philadelphia, Pennsylvania but maintains offices in Ireland and the United Kingdom. **Career Highlights:** ISI (Institute for Scientific Information): Manager of Current Awareness Products (1998-Present), Programmer/Analyst II (1997-98), Manager of Chemical Product Development (1994-97). **Associations & Accomplishments:** Association of Computer Machinery. **Education:** Drexel University, Master's degree in Computer Science (1995); West Chester University, B.A. in Physics. **Personal Information:** Married to Alice Doosey in 1996. Mr. Wismer enjoys mountaineering and rock climbing.

John Spoon

Lithography Specialist
A&L Lithography
964 Borra Place
Escondido, CA 92029-2011
(760) 743-0051
jbg29@hotmail.com

2752

Business Information: A savvy, 15 year veteran of the technology field, Mr. Spoon offers his services to A&L Lithography while serving as a Ltihography Specialist. In this position, he assumes full responsibility for all day-to-day electronic prepress operations. This includes managing the work flow with computerized printing, meeting with clients to determine what is needed, and ensuring that all equipment is working up to standards. His career highlights include developing the Company's state-of-the-art Web site. Displaying a clear vision of goals, Mr. Spoon would like to become more involved with Web site designs. He credits his success to working smartly and his ability to think outside the box, deliver results, and aggressively take on new challenges. Founded in 1984, A&L Lithography is an established and reputable business. The Company is involved in sheetfed offset lithography printing. The medium sized printing business employs a workstaff of 40 individuals to to facilitate all aspects of design, research and development, distribution, and to meet with customers. There are presently two locations of A&L Lithography for clients within the United States to obtain service. Annual sales are reported at $350,000. **Career Highlights:** Lithography Specialist, A&L Lithography (1985-Present); Graphics Manager, Marfred Paper Company (1981-85); Color Separator, Polen Press (1979-81); Stripper/Carpenter, American Graphics (1975-79). **Associations & Accomplishments:** Cub Scouts and Boy Scouts (15 Years); Recipient, District Award of Merit; Los Angeles County Supervisors Commendation Proclamation. **Education:** Pasadena City College, A.A. (1975); University of Oklahoma, (1960-62); Arizona State University (1964-65). **Personal Information:** Married to Judith Ann in 1964. Eight children: Clay, Butch, Scott, B. J., Sunai, Bill, K. C. , and Jodi. Mr. Spoon enjoys designing Web sites.

Mary Anne Brocious

Telecommunications Manager
Valassis Communications
19975 Victor Parkway
Livonia, MI 48152
(734) 591-4933
Fax: (734) 432-2875
brociousm@valassis.com

2759

Business Information: Functioning in the role of Telecommunications Manager of Valassis Communications, Ms. Brocious is responsible for wide area voice and data management. She has served Valassis Communications in a variety of positions since joining the Company in 1982. In her present capacity, Ms. Brocious works to develop a stable communications network that is extremely cost efficient. Operating a private network, converged network, she provides voice, data, and internet application coordination and networking capabilities to all offices. Working towards a Director's position, Ms. Brocious is planning to eventually attain a Chief Information Officer position. She attributes her success to remaining on the cutting edge of information technology, using good judgement and loyalty to the objectives of the Company. Valassis Communications provides printing and sales promotion services. Established in 1974, the Company has become a major provider of freestanding promotions such as coupons and newspaper inserts. The Company has 15 locations in the U.S., Canada, and Mexico and is ranked as one of the largest printing companies in the United States. Over 1,300 employees staff the various locations, working together to create effective sales promotions for their clients. **Career Highlights:** Valassis Communications: Telecommunications Manager (1995-Present), Facilities Manager (1989-95). **Associations & Accomplishments:** Joint Users of Siemens Technologies; Women's Economic Club of Detroit; Ann Arbor Kennel Club. **Education:** University of Michigan, M.B.A. (In Progress); Pennsylvania State University, B.S. in Business Administration (1971). **Personal Information:** Ms. Brocious enjoys breeding, exhibiting, and judging purebred dogs and community service work.

Teck-Hng Chia

Production Manager
Colour Scan Company Private Limited
Blk 53 Pipit Road, 10-96
Singapore, Singapore 370053
+65 2538888
Fax: +65 7497651
colscan3@singnet.com.sg

2759

Business Information: As the Production Manager of Colour Scan Company Pte. Ltd., Mr. Chia oversees the development and improvement of projects from conception to implementation. As the manager of manpower for the Company, he hires, trains, and excuses qualified individuals. For 12 years, he has been the technology advisor for the Board of Printing Training Advisory Committee of Institute of Technical Education in Singapore, while supervising three operational managers. Mr. Chia is especially proud of his involvement in the development of new products, providing the technological support from ground zero and getting results and customer satisfaction. In the future, he would like to implement new training for his staff, keep up with emergin technology, become involved in the international trade shows, and continue to provide cutting edge support to his clients. Established in 1978, Colour Scan Company Pte. Ltd. is a digital imaging firm. Starting as a reproduction office, they have now upgraded to digital imaging, printing, and post-press. Headquartered in Singapore, the Company boasts an estimated annual sales of $30 million. With two other locations around the world, its clients include Reader's Digest and World Book. ColourScan Company exports over 80 percent of their products. **Career Highlights:** Production Manager, Colour Scan Company Pte. Ltd. (1978-Present). **Associations & Accomplishments:** Institute of Technical Education; London Institute of Printing. **Education:** London College of Printing, Certified in Photolithography (1976); City and Guild (London), Certified in Advanced Craft in Photolithography. **Personal Information:** Married to Yeo Hui Kio in 1979. Two children: Xie Liyi and Xie Liju. Mr. Chia enjoys fishing.

Susan E. Fowler
Director of Information Systems
Nosco Inc.
651 South Utica Street
Waukegan, IL 60085
(847) 336-4200
Fax: (847) 360-4969
sfowler@nosco.com

2759

Business Information: Providing her skilled services as Director of Information Systems of Nosco Inc., Mrs. Fowler is responsible for all data and voice communications and processing. Before joining Nosco, she served as Director of Information Systems with TASC, Inc. Her extensive background history also includes employment as Director of Data Processing for McDougal, Littel & Company and Project Manager at Balcor Company. In her present role, Mrs. Fowler assumes accountability for all aspects of day-to-day administration and operational activities of the Information Systems Department, directly supervising a staff of four employees. As a 14 year technology professional, Mrs. Fowler assists the Corporation determine its overall strategic direction, as well as the business contribution of the information systems function. Coordinating resources, time lines, schedules, assignments, and budgets also fall within the realm of her functions. Consistently achieving quality performance in her field, she anticipates a future promotion to Vice President. Nosco Inc. prints pharmaceutical packing material, specifically that of cartons, roll and cut labels, enclosures, and combinations thereof. Headquartered in Waukegan, Illinois, the Corporation has four separate locations, employing the services of 444 individuals. Nosco Inc. was established in 1906 and is a privately held corporation. **Career Highlights:** Director of Information System, Nosco Inc. (1997-Present); Director of Information System, TASC, Inc. (1994-97); Director of Data Processing, McDougal, Littel & Company (1986-94); Project Manager, Balcor Company (1983-86). **Education:** University of Chicago, M.B.A. (1985); Miami University, B.S. **Personal Information:** Married to David in 1983. One child: Merritt. Mrs. Fowler enjoys golf and assisting with the Girl Scouts.

Kevin Hinson
Group Leader of Electronics Shop
Quebecor World Hawkins
342 Woodland Street
Church Hill, TN 37642-3838
(423) 357-2038
Fax: (423) 357-0706

2759

Business Information: Serving as Group Leader of Electronics Shop for Quebecor World Hawkins, Mr. Hinson maintains all equipment and components throughout the plant. Coupling his education with practical work experience, he is able to effectively maintain operations within his department. Mr. Hinson serves as a liaison between plant employees and the managment staff, and coordinates meetings to discuss procedures that upon implementation, will maximize the productiveness of the entire facility. Handling troubleshooting for all equipment, Mr. Hinson conducts research to formulate cost cutting techniques that continue to focus on quality for the customers. Mr. Hinson credits his success to his ability to work well with all types of people; he strives for advancement within the corporate structure. Established in 1910, Quebecor World Hawkins is one of the world's largest commercial printers with facilities located throughout the United States, Canada, France, and the United Kingdom. With centers in India and Mexico as well, the Company employs over 13,000 people to serve publishing companies such as McGraw-Hill and Random House. Major product categories include inserts and circulars, magazines, books, and newspapers and operations can be done through Web offset, gravure, or sheetfed printing. **Career Highlights:** Group Leader of Electronics Shop, Quebecor World Hawkins (1996-Present); Corrosion Technician, Subcon (1994-96). **Education:** East Tennessee State University, B.S. (1994). **Personal Information:** Married to Janet in 1997. Mr. Hinson enjoys drag racing and streetrod restorations.

Donna R. Longgood
Project Lead
Cox Target Media
8575 Largo Lakes Drive
Largo, FL 33773
(727) 399-3064

2759

Business Information: Demonstrating more than 20 years of experience in the field of information technology, Ms. Longgood serves as the Project Lead for Cox Target Media. She manages the Company's special projects, developing system applications and computer software for five internal networks. In addition, she orders cash testing for the networks and supervises the implementation of the Y2K conversion. Crediting her success to her hunger for knowledge and networking with colleagues, the greatest accomplishment of her professional career is the development of a software application document from start to finish. She looks forward to expanding her managerial responsibilities in the Documentation and Quality Assurance Department. Her success reflects her ability to deliver results and aggressively tackle new challenges. Cox Target Media is engaged in the manufacture and distribution of blue envelope coupons. Serving a regional and international clientele, the Company distributes its coupons from eight strategically placed locations. An approximate work force of 2,500 individuals are employed in overall operations. The Company was founded in 1969. **Career Highlights:** Cox Target Media: Project Lead (1995-Present), Supervisor of Documentation and Quality Control (1994-95); Paradyne Corporation: Manager (1981-88), Senior Technical Writer (1990). **Education:** University of Florida, B.A. (1981); Central Florida Community College, A.S. in Computer Science; Marine Corps Computer Science School, Master Computer Operator and Programmer. **Personal Information:** Ms. Longgood enjoys crosstitch and crochet.

Duc V. Nguyen
Systems Analyst
Moore Business Forms
5903 North Street
Nacogdoches, TX 75961
(409) 564-4683
Fax: (409) 560-2865
dnguyen@netdot.com

2759

Business Information: As Systems Analyst of Moore Business Forms, Mr. Nguyen fulfills a number of functions on behalf of the Company and its clientele. He maintains both the Novell and UNIX systems' functionality and operational status. Possessing an excellent understanding of technology, he provides his expert services to the Company's facilities located in Iowa and Texas. Performing inspections and testing, Mr. Nguyen ensures the proper implementation of new state of the art technologies in order to provide a more productive system. Furthering his advancement with Moore Business Forms, Mr. Nguyan continues to provide top of the line equipment and software in order to promote the further success of the Company. His success reflects his ability to think outside the box, aggressively take on new challenges, and deliver results. Specializing in the printing of official papers, Moore Business Forms was established in 1884. Headquartered in Iowa, the Company has branches throughout the United States and the world. Employing over 1,500 experienced printers and technicians, Moore Business Forms generates an estimated annual sales of $2.4 billion. Specifically printing invoices for their various clients, the Company is continually expanding its business and product line. **Career Highlights:** Moore Business Forms: Systems Analyst (Present), Computer Network Specialist, Electronic Composition. **Education:** Letourneau University, B.S. (1993).

George H. O'Bryant, Jr.
Systems Administrator/Digital Imaging Specialist
Professional Duplicating
33 East State Street
Media, PA 19063
(610) 891-7979
Fax: (610) 565-1522
gob501@yahoo.com

2759

Business Information: Displaying his skills in this highly specialized position, Mr. O'Bryant serves as Systems Administrator and Digital Imaging Specialist for Professional Duplicating. He scans and adjusts photographic material as well as performs maintenance on computer systems infrastructure. Coordinating with various vendors, Mr. O'Bryant ensures a sufficient inventory for plate making and stripping and general project development. Maintaining network systems in two locations, he performs upgrades and troubleshooting incorporating the latest technologies in order to provide a more efficient and productive system. Learning more about scanning technologies, building computer systems, attaining his certifications, and focusing on his further training on systems development, Mr. O'Bryant consistently achieves quality performance in his field. His success is attributed to his supportive family, spiritual life, and communications skills. Ranked 30th nationwide, Professional Duplicating engages in printing and graphic design services for advertising agencies, cooperations, and individuals. Established over 20 years ago, the Company employs the skilled services of 48 individuals to facilitate every aspect of design, development, and the marketing of services. Specifically offering digital output and docutech services, the Company provides its specialized products and services for mainstream corporations, Small Businesses, Advertising Agencies, and Web companies. **Career Highlights:** Systems Administrator/Digital Imaging Specialist, Professional Duplicating (1999-Present); Head, Instructor, Philadelphia School of Printing and Advertising (1987-89); Manager, Minute Man Press (1987-88); Printer, Philadelphia Municipal Services Department (1985-87). **Associations & Accomplishments:** Chairperson, Mount Olivet Seventh-day Adventist School. **Education:** Philadelphia School of Printing and Advertising, Certificate (1997); Pine Forge Academy, Diploma. **Personal Information:** Married to Jacqueline in 1988. One child: Jasmine. Mr. O'Bryant enjoys track and field, computer repair and coaching children.

Joshua S. Reicher
Manager of Internet Systems Service
Advance Business Graphics
3810 Wabash Drive
Mira Loma, CA 91752
(909) 361-7168
Fax: (909) 361-7070
josh.reicher@abgraphics.com

2759

Business Information: As Manager of Internet Systems Service of Advance Business Graphics, Mr. Reicher manages ABG's Internet services team. This added value service promotes customer awareness and also provides a direct link to the Company from the client's office or home. He is responsible for maintaining this link as well as maintaining the files that are transferred into the system. He manages the programmers and directs internal and external applications in the right direction. Mr. Reicher is credited with improving online services and increasing the membership from 10 to 300 active customers. His expanded knowledge of Internet commerce and file mainenance enables him to be an asset to any company with a significant investment in Internet commerce. Mr. Reicher future plans are remain with Advance Business Graphics, and to finish and obtain his MBA. Success is attributed to being in the right place at the right time. Advance Business Graphics provides manufacturing, printing, direct mail, and fulfillment of corporate advertising needs. This international firm is privately held and reports over $46 million in annual sales. By expanding its services to include Internet communication between client and company, the Company has increased its clientele as well as its community recognition. It plans to maintain its customer satisfaction record and continue offering superior printed products to corporate and private customers around the globe. **Career Highlights:** Manager of Internet Systems Service, Advance Business Graphics (1998-Present); Manager of Applications Development, Jaguar Computer Systems, Inc. (1998-98); Systems Specialist, RxLASER, Inc. (1994-98). **Education:** California State Polytechnic University at Pomona, B.S. (1998).

Tony Thelemaque
Director of Information Technology
fp Label
601 Airpark Road
Napa, CA 94558
(707) 259-5075
tonyt@sfo.com

2759

Business Information: As Director of Information Technology of fp Label, Mr. Thelemaque is oversees the information technology and information systems infrastructure for the Company's West Coast operations. Demonstrating an excellent understanding of technology, he is responsible for systems analysis of production management tools; database design, development and implementation; network administration of Ethernet and Twinax; and systems and software administration of 80 nodes spanning a campus of 3 buildings. Highly regarded by his colleagues, Mr. Thelemaque is also in charge of server administration and planning, development, and implementation of corporate Internet/Intranet sites. His major achievements include implementation of corporate Internet access including Cisco router, CSU/DSU and firewall configuration, and designing, constructing, and deploying a campus wide data collection system. Dedicated to the success of fp Label, Mr. Thelemaque plans to remain with the Company and continue to provide cutting edge technology in support of all endeavors. Established in 1936, fp Label is a printing and packaging business located in Napa, California. The Company's main operations are involved in the printing of wine labels and the packaging of wine. Employing 300 personnel, the Company reports annual sales of over $40 million. **Career Highlights:** Director of Information Technology, fp Label (1997-Present); Senior Project Manager, US Web (1997); Systems Manager/Programmer/Analyst, University of California, SF-Repro/Mail Services Department (1994-97); Vice President/General Manager, Dolphin Graphics (1988-94). **Education:** University of North Colorado, B.S. (1983); Microsoft Certified Systems Engineer. **Personal Information:** Married to Tamara Hedges in 1989. Mr. Thelemaque enjoys tennis, skiing, biking, travel and multimedia/video.

Trent S. Wacker
Pre Press Manager
Missourian Publishing
211 East Main
Washington, MO 63909
(573) 439-4161
Fax: (573) 437-1404
twacker@cpcids.com

2759

Business Information: Mr. Wacker is Pre Press Manager for Missourian Publishing. He is responsible for administering networks and quality control. Before joining Missourian Publishing, Mr. Wacker served with Custom Printing Company as E.I. Supervisor and Estimator. At the present time, he fulfills the responsibilities of the Company's pre-press production and quality control, typesetting and formatting page layouts on computer in preparation for printing. In charge of the network's administration, Mr. Wacker oversees all day-to-day operational activities of the systems infrastructure. Maintaining the network's functionality and fully operational status, tuning systems software tools to enhance overall performance, and providing cohesive leadership also fall within the realm of his responsibilities. Possessing a firm academic background and strong problem solving skills, his professional success reflects his ability to aggressively take on new challenges and responsibilities. Continually striving to improve performance, Mr. Wacker would like to increase his involvement with the network administration side of his duties. Missourian Publishing is a small town newspaper publisher. **Career Highlights:** Pre Press Manager, Missourian Publishing (1999-Present); Custom Printing Company: Electronic Imaging Supervisor (1997-99), Estimator (1993-97). **Education:** Central Missouri State University, B.S. (1993). **Personal Information:** Married to Samantha in 1995. Mr. Wacker enjoys fishing and boating.

John D. Glover
Database Administrator
Reynolds & Reynolds
220 Folsom Drive
Dayton, OH 45405
(937) 485-2412

2761

Business Information: Following an extensive occupational history, Mr. Glover is the Database Administrator for Reynolds & Reynolds. He is accountable for the development, implementation, and maintenance of databases for 1,200 dealerships throughout the United States and Canada. Specializing in Sybase databases and relational database management systems, he intends to continue in his current career path with a forward movement into Web based applications. Mr. Glover attributes his success to diligence, hardwork as well as good personal and professional relationships. A publically held company, Reynolds & Reynolds is one of the oldest automotive information management services companies in the United States. Serving an international clientele, the Company has 150 sales offices throughout Canada and the United States, with new offices to be opened overseas in the works, to meet the computer system needs of automotive dealerships. **Career Highlights:** Database Administrator, Reynolds & Reynolds (1999-Present); Senior Systems Engineer, GMAC/EDS (1978-99); Senior Programmer, State Farm Insurance (1970-78). **Education:** Bradley University, M.S. (1975); North Carolina Central University, B.S. in Mathematics. **Personal Information:** Married to Kathleen in 1985. One child: Daphne. Mr. Glover enjoys racquetball and woodworking.

Mark W. Harris
Senior Staff Engineer
Standard Register
120 Campbell Street
Dayton, OH 45408-1973
(937) 221-1609
Fax: (937) 221-1945
mark.harris@standardregister.com

2761

Business Information: Joining Standard Register in 1976, Mr. Harris demonstrates his extensive expertise in the development of technological systems as Senior Staff Engineer. He works closely with management and systems users to analyze, specify, design, and implement advanced solutions in an effort to enhance all areas of operational processes. Concentrating his efforts towards the production of state-of-the-art equipment, Mr. Harris holds the responsibility of engineering research, the development of systems tools and operating systems, and providing technical support. Incorporating the latest technology into production, he is proactively involved in research and development. The most rewarding aspects of his career is designing several Web based programs, such as dynamic Web based sites for

internal use. For the future, Mr. Harris' goal is to facilitate continued Company growth and geographic expansion. Established as the second largest producer of printed business forms, Standard Register was founded in 1912. Located in Dayton, Ohio, the Company specializes in the production of printing systems and equipment including check dispensers, PC based software, Web development, and intelligent printing solutions. Employing the skilled services of 8,000 technicians, designers, and production personnel, the Company generates $1.4 billion in annual sales. **Career Highlights:** Senior Staff Engineer, Standard Register (1976-Present). **Education:** Control Data Institute, Computer Technology Certificate (1975). **Personal Information:** Married to Katherine in 1985. Four children: Mark, Erin, Adem, and Katinka.

Deanne Loy-Tate
Systems Administrator
Reynolds & Reynolds
3909 Northwest 36th Street
Oklahoma City, OK 73112
(800) 654-6768
Fax: (800) 353-2850
dee@southerngrace.com

2761

Business Information: Mrs. Loy-Tate has served with Reynolds & Reynolds in various roles since her arrival in 1995. At present, she fulfills the position of Systems Administrator responsible for the Automotive Division Sales Support Offices in Oklahoma, Los Angeles, San Francisco, and San Diego. Her duties principally involves upgrading computer system infrastructures to include manufacture and installation of technologically advanced software. An expert, Mrs. Loy-Tate provides assistance and advice to users, designs new solutions to harness more of the computer's power, and helps clients leverage their investment in technology, personnel, and processes. Analysis, acquisition, modification, configuration, support, and tracking of operating and networking systems, databases, utilities, software, and hardware also fall within the scope of her responsibilities. Attributing her success to luck and patience, her favorite quote is "he who is afraid of asking is afraid of learning." Among Mrs. Loy-Tate's future goals include involvement in network administration, more training, and M.S.C.E. certification. Reynolds & Reynolds operates as a Fortune 1000 company that produces business forms and computer software for several types of businesses. Additionally, the Company is involved in the sales and service of turn-key minicomputer systems. Founded in 1938, Reynolds & Reynolds employs a work force of 4,500 people generating in excess of $2 billion in annual revenues. **Career Highlights:** Reynolds & Reynolds: Systems Administrator (1997-Present), Sales Assistant (1995-97); Merchandiser, Auto Zone (1995). **Associations & Accomplishments:** Booster, Independent Artists of Oklahoma. **Education:** Rose State College (1995); Microsoft Certified Systems Engineer (In Progress). **Personal Information:** Married to Gary V. in 1998. Mrs. Loy-Tate enjoys computers, animals, art, sports and music.

Dragan Gajic
Director of Technical Operations and Information Systems
E-Greetings
P.O. Box 7501
Santa Cruz, CA 95061-7501
(831) 685-8365

2771

Business Information: Mr. Gajic functions in the capacity of Director of Technical Operations and Information Systems for E-Greetings. He is in charge of all day-to-day technical operations and information systems infrastructure. A savvy, nine year professional, Mr. Gajic manages a large amount of Web sites, ensuring their productivity and success for the client. Coordinating and working closely with clients and investors, he negotiates all contract terms through direct, personal discussions. With an extensive background of bringing businesses to the level of public listing, Mr. Gajic hopes to do the same with E-Greetings and become involved with other businesses. His success reflects his ability to think outside the box, deliver results, and aggressively take on new challenges. He aspires to eventually move into an executive role and do more initial public offerings for other companies. E-Greetings functions within the electronic commerce industry providing an online selection of greetings cards to its clients. Established in 1993, the Company has an extensive array of electronic greeting cards that are able to be delivered to the in-box of any email user's account. Because of the multiple medias the Internet provides access to, the Company has expanded its interaction with an international clientele. **Career Highlights:** Director of Technical Operations and Information Systems, E-Greetings (1999-Present); Manager of Information Technology, Cisco (1996-99); Director of Computer Operations, TAV Software (1995-96). **Associations & Accomplishments:** Association of Computing Machinery; Institute of Electronics and Electrical Engineers; New York Academy of Sciences; MENSA. **Education:** Columbia University: Professional Degree

(1993), M.S. in Electrical Engineering (1990); California Technology University, B.S. in Applied Physics.

Thomas W. Oliver

Web Manager
Furniture City Color
800 Main Street
High Point, NC 27262
(336) 883-7314

2796

Business Information: Utilizing nine years of experience with Furniture City Color, Mr. Oliver now serves as Web Manager for the Company. Providing his skilled services in his role, his duties include supervising the in-house creation of computer files and images that are distributed to furniture manufacturers nationally as well as monitoring cost accounting programs. Posssessing an excellent understanding of technology, Mr. Oliver creates, formats, and organizes all Furniture City Color files on the Internet. His career highlights include fulfilling the responsibility of a Nuclear Chemist while serving with the United States Navy. Continually formulating new goals and objectives, Mr. Oliver hopes to see the expansion of the Company's Internet capabilities, and eventually branch off into his own agency. His success is attributed to his association with high caliber people. Established in 1968, Furniture City Color is a specialty company dedicated to providing film to the printing industries. Image databases, via the Internet, are also supplied to furniture manufacturers and their dealers. Furniture City Color currently employs 32 people in its High Point, North Carolina location, and generates annual revenues in excess of $5 million. **Career Highlights:** Furniture City Color: Web Manager (1999-Present), Color Supervisor/Production Manager (1991-99); Engineering Laboratory Technician, United States Navy (1981-84). **Associations & Accomplishments:** Player, United States Volleyball Association; Young Men's Christian Association: Member, Coach; Elected Church Deacon; Who's Who High School (1977); Top Watch of Radiological Controls, Nuclear Chemistry, Physics, Propulsion, and Personnel Radiation, Aboard the U.S.S. Enterprise, United States Navy. **Education:** United States Navy ELT, Nuclear Chemistry (1981); United States Naval Nuclear Propulsion degree (1980). **Personal Information:** Married to Julie F. in 1985. Two children: Brian R. and Emily D. Mr. Oliver enjoys being a YMCA soccer coach and high school volleyball coach.

2800 Chemicals and Allied Products

2812 Alkalies and chlorine
2813 Industrial gases
2816 Inorganic pigments
2819 Industrial inorganic chemicals, nec
2821 Plastics materials and resins
2822 Synthetic rubber
2823 Cellulosic manmade fibers
2824 Organic fibers, noncellulosic
2833 Medicinals and botanicals
2834 Pharmaceutical preparations
2835 Diagnostic substances
2836 Biological products exc. diagnostic
2841 Soap and other detergents
2842 Polishes and sanitation goods
2843 Surface active agents
2844 Toilet preparations
2851 Paints and allied products
2861 Gum and wood chemicals
2865 Cyclic crudes and intermediates
2869 Industrial organic chemicals, nec
2873 Nitrogenous fertilizers
2874 Phosphatic fertilizers
2875 Fertilizers, mixing only
2879 Agricultural chemicals, nec
2891 Adhesives and sealants
2892 Explosives
2893 Printing ink
2895 Carbon black
2899 Chemical preparations, nec

Mark Kochanowski

Technical Analyst
McWhorter Technologies
99 East Cottage Avenue
Carpentersville, IL 60110
(847) 836-3628
Fax: (847) 551-9763
mkochanowski@hotmail.com

2821

Business Information: Educated in the field of information systems, Mr. Kochanowski brings a wealth of knowledge to McWhorter Technologies in his position as Technical Analyst. In this capacity, he handles personal computer and networking support for the entire Company. Often found at the Help Desk, Mr. Kochanowski is recognized as a progressive, innovative problem solver. Special Projects assigned by the Copmany are frequently delegated to him due to his adept ability to finish a project efficiently and quickly. Mr. Kochanowski also installs upgrades on various systems within the Company. Citing success stemming from his drive to acheive, he is an advocate for higher education. Mr. Kochanowski currently has plans to apply his work experience in the field of consulting. His future goals include professional growth within the Company, excelling in all areas in order to create promotion opportunities. McWhorter Technologies is an internationally based chemical company specializing in the manufacture of resin and latex. Publically held, the Company was established 1994, and also produces various chemical coatings. **Career Highlights:** Technical Analyst, McWhorter Technologies (1998-Present); Consultant, Tek Systems (1997-98); Consultant, ICS Solutions (1996-97). **Associations & Accomplishments:** 3Com User Group. **Education:** DeVry Technical Institute. **Personal Information:** Married to Christine in 1996. One child: Angelica. Mr. Kochanowski enjoys music, gardening, travel and computers.

Lori K. McLaughlin-Nelson

Manager of Information Systems Operations
Advanced Elastomer Systems, L.P.
388 South Main Street
Akron, OH 44311-1064
(330) 849-5000
Fax: (330) 849-5593
lkmcla@aestpe.com

2821

Business Information: Serving in the role of Manager of Information Systems Operations with Advanced Elastomer Systems, L.P. since 1998, Mrs. McLaughlin-Nelson supports the Company's internal information systems functions. She is responsible for all aspects of global telecommunications as well as the Company's information technology infrastructure standards. A savvy, 20-year veteran of the technology field, Mrs. McLaughlin-Nelson engages in strategic development of technologies to include new hardware and software applications. She also develops new solutions primarily for digital and video desktop applications and voice data. Her current projects include updating the company's technology infrastructure from a data-only infrastructure to converging data, voice, and video. Attributing success to strong support from her husband, Mrs. McLaughlin-Nelson aspires to eventually attain the position of chief technology officer. A limited partnership between Exxon and Solutia, Advanced Elastomer Systems, L.P. provides research, development, and manufacture of thermoplastic elastomer products. Serving an international clientele since 1991, the Company employs approximately 700 individuals. **Career Highlights:** Advanced Elastomer Systems, L.P.: Manager of Information Systems Operations (1998-Present), Senior Systems Administrator (1991-98); Scientific Programmer, Goodyear Aerospace (1984-91). **Education:** University of Akron, B.S. in Computer Science (1984). **Personal Information:** Married to Lewis Nelson in 1983. Mrs. McLaughlin-Nelson enjoys motorcycling, outdoor activities and travel.

Racquel D. Caloza

Systems Analyst/Programmer
Merck & Co., Inc
P.O. Box 43
Bridgeport, PA 19405-0043
(215) 652-3965
kingcaloza@hotmail.com

2834

Business Information: As the Systems Analyst and Programmer for Merck & Co., Inc., Ms. Caloza is responsible for systems design and development. In this capacity, she is a developing programmer, integrating processes and survey applications, and is involved with business planning and setting objectives for the Corporation. She keeps technical documents of her daily work, using Oracle and Mircrosoft 2.0, working on projects with systems assembly. Possessing an excellent understanding of technology, Ms. Caloza is certified in Visual Basic 5 and 6, Oracle 8.0, and HTML. Attributing her success to persistence and hard work, Ms. Caloza plans to stay abreast of the technological world, and hopes to go into a business venture of her own, staying in the informational technology environment. Serving an international clientele, Merck & Co., Inc. is engaged in the manufacture and distribution of pharmaceutical products. The Corporation is dedicated to discovering and marketing human and animal health products. Headquartered in New Jersey, Merck & Co., Inc. was established in 1891 and is the third largest pharmaceutical company in the world. **Career Highlights:** Systems Analyst/Programmer, Merck & Co., Inc (Present); Consultant, Bureau of Treasury, Philippines; Programmer, Price Waterhouse, Philippines/Joaquinn Cunanan; Programmer/Technical Operations Engineer, Evolution Services, Inc. **Education:** Ateneo De Manila University, B.S. in Computer Science (1996). **Personal Information:** Ms. Caloza enjoys surfing the Web.

Yuan-Yuan "Chrissie" Chen

Human Resources Information Technology Manager
Genentech
1 DNA Way
South San Francisco, CA 94080
(650) 225-1815
Fax: (650) 225-4152
yyc@gene.com

2834

Business Information: Recruited to Genentech in 1986, Mrs. Chen serves as Human Resources Information Technology Manager, providing information technology support and application services. She is responsible for developing the specific programs that are used by the employees of the Human Resources Department and is in charge of the new project to implement PeopleSoft. Before joining Genentech, Mrs. Chen served as Programmer and Analyst with Compeq, U.S.A. Her solid background history also includes as stint as Teaching Assistant at National Cheng Kung University. Crediting her professional success to constant exposure to the latest technologies and human networking, she has received internal recognition for her services and length of employment. Mrs. Chen anticipates gaining more responsibility as the Company continues to explore more into technology and apply it to its changing strategies. Established in 1976, Genentech utilizes biotechnology to develop and manufacture pharmaceutical drugs. The drugs are distributed globally and are primarily available through Roesch. Approximately 3,600 administrative and scientific personnel are employed in the Company's three California locations. **Career Highlights:** Human Resources Information Technology Manager, Genentech (1986-Present); Programmer/Analyst, Compeq, U.S.A. (1986); Teaching Assistant, National Cheng Kung University (1979-82). **Associations & Accomplishments:** American Rose Society; International Human Resource Information Management. **Education:** University of Wisconsin, M.S. (1985); National Cheng Kung University, B.A. **Personal Information:** Married to Chia Ming in 1983. One child: Andrew W. Mrs. Chen enjoys gardening, ice skating, tennis, reading and spending time with her family.

Eric S. Cofer

Senior Applications Analyst
CN Bioscience
3378 Daley Center Drive #2010
San Diego, CA 92123
(858) 450-5583
ecofer1@san.rr.com

2834

Business Information: Recruited to CN Biosciences as Senior Applications Analyst in 1999, Mr. Cofer oversees and directs a number of technical duties on behalf of the Company. In this context, he is in charge of the development and support of worldwide computer operations, maintenance of the PC network, and designing cutting edge software applications. Highly regarded, Mr. Cofer possesses an excellent understanding of his field. His career highlights include rolling out a proprietory system for a pharmacy chain of 2,400 stores and enjoying a 99 percent success rate. Attributing his success to his family upbringing and integrity, Mr. Cofer believes in working hard. Attaining a role of manager of software department serves as one of his future endeavors. CN Biosciences, established in the 1970s, currently employs 500 people. As manufacturer and distributor of research chemicals, CN Biosciences specializes in selling products to doctors offices, universities, and private labs. All purchasers go through an application process and are qualify by the regulatory department. **Career Highlights:** Senior Applications Analyst, CN Bioscience (1999-Present); Staff Consultant, CSC Consulting (1996-99). **Education:** Bryant College, B.S. in Marketing (1995).

Elsie DaSilva

Director of Application Software
Schein Pharmaceuticals
100 Campus Drive
Florham Park, NJ 07932-1006
(973) 593-5857
Fax: (973) 593-5859
edasilva@schein-rx.com

2834

Business Information: Recruited to Schein Pharmaceuticals in 1993, Mrs. DaSilva has been recognized internally for her outstanding performance through several promotions to her current position of Director of Application Software. She assumes accoutability for four plant sites within the United States, maintaining the computer systems to ensure each one is functioning at optimum levels at all times. Additionally, she is also responsible for the PC applications for the entire Company. Crediting her professional success to her friendly attitude and openmindedness, Mrs. DaSilva is persistent and is able to deal with the industry's continual changes in technology with remarkable proficiency. She is committed to continued growth in the Company, aspiring to the position of Vice President of Information Systems and, eventually, Chief Executive Officer. Headquartered in New Jersey, Schein Pharmaceuticals is an international manufacturer and distributor of generic pharmaceuticals. Currently, the Company maintains five pharmaceutical plants within the United States and one abroad. An approximate work force of 1,500 personnel members is engaged in worldwide operations. Founded in 1990, the Company boasts over $500 million in sales. **Career Highlights:** Schein Pharmaceuticals: Director of Application Software (1999-Present), Manager of Application Software (1997-99), Project Leader (1994-97), Senior PA (1993-94). **Education:** Fairleigh Dickinson University, B.A. in Business Management (In Progress); County College of Morris Computer Science, A.S.; Denville Vo-Tech Computer Programming. **Personal Information:** Married.

Christina K. DeModna

Manager, PKDM Submissions Support Coordinator
Purdue Pharma L.P.
444 Saw Mill River Road
Ardsley, NY 10502
(914) 709-2296
drvet72@aol.com

2834

Business Information: As Manager of the PKDM Submissions Support Group for Purdue Pharma L.P., Ms. DeModna is responsible for coordinating and tracking documents for Investigational New Drug Applications (INDs), New Drug Applications (NDAs) and Abbreviated New Drug Applications (ANDAs) in support of new drug entities to be marketed by Purdue Pharma L.P. She is responsible for establishing the framework necessary for the management and tracking of all technical documentation and database design. Possessing an excellent understanding of her field, her duties include setting up database and government document control. Continually striving for maximum effectiveness, Ms. DeModna plans to take more software courses to stay on the "cutting edge" of technology. She attributes her success to academics and her ability to aggressively take on new challenges and deliver results. Purdue Pharma L.P., established in 1983, is a privately owned manufacturer of pharmaceuticals. The Company employs the services of 200 individuals responsible for administration, data gathering, research, development, manufacture, marketing, and sale of pharmaceuticals. The Company specializes in genetic research. **Career Highlights:** Manager, PKDM Submissions Support Coordinator, Purdue Pharma L.P. (2000-Present); Manager of Technical Writing Group, Par Pharmaceutical, Inc. (1996-00); Analytical Research Technical Writer, Zentih Goldline Pharmaceuticals (1995-96); Lederle Laboratories: Product Support Specialist (1994-95), Technical Writer (1993-94). **Education:** State University of New York at Purchase, B.A. in Chemistry (1988). **Personal Information:** Married to Robert S. in 1996. Ms. DeModna enjoys computers, Macaw parrots and all animals.

Stephanie A. Fiore

WW IS Security Manager
PAREXEL International
900 Chelmsford Street
Lowell, MA 01851
(978) 848-2472
Fax: (978) 275-4263
stephanie.fiore@parexel.com

2834

Business Information: As WW IS Security Manager for PAREXEL International, Ms. Fiore exercises oversight of the Firm's security interests. She became interested in the computer field in the seventh grade and has grown to enjoy the technical challenges presented by the security process. Knowledgeable in the field of computer programming and architecture, Ms. Fiore takes the lead in writing corporate computer security policies and procedures, and providing corporate security awareness. Ms. Fiore's future objective is to become more knowledgeable in the area of firewall management, Internet Security, and overall security of computer system infrastructures. Established in 1983, PAREXEL International provides contract clinical development services worldwide. PAREXEL International employs 4,300 professional, clinical, technical, and support personnel and posts annual revenues of $325 million. **Career Highlights:** WW IS Security Manager, PAREXEL International (1999-Present); Commerce Insurance Company: Information Security Supervisor (1992-99), Project Leader (1989-92); Consultant/Programmer, Key Consultants (1987-89). **Associations & Accomplishments:** Computer Security Institute. **Education:** Montachusett Regional Vocational Technical School, Certificate in Data Processing; Nichols College, Business Courses. **Personal Information:** Ms. Fiore enjoys travel, skiing, music, dancing and outdoor activities.

Tyrone L. Glenn

Managing Principal Database Administrator
Genentech
1 DNA Way
South San Francisco, CA 94080
(650) 225-8519
Fax: (650) 225-6997
glenn.tyrone@gene.com

2834

Business Information: Possessing over 17 years of experience in technology, Mr. Glenn serves as Managing Principal Database Administrator for Genentech. In this capacity, he assumes accountability for the efficient functionality of the Corporation's computer systems and software. Genentech primarily uses Oracle, Informix, and Filemaker Pro database management platform tools in the conduct of complex research involving vast quantities of data on a regular basis. For this reason, Mr. Glenn devotes attention to mainframe utilization and data trafficking and firewall protocols. Relying on his skills and with a strong academic background, he focuses significant attention on network stability, seamless interface implementations, and custom software development. Mr. Glenn owns a consistent record of delivering results in support of business objectives through leadership, use of technology, and creative problem solving. His future interest is to become more involved with information technology management and attain recognition as a solid solutions provider. Genentech, established in 1974, is a biotechnology and pharmaceutical drug development and research company. Approximately 3,000 professional, technical, and support staff are employed by the Corporation which posts annual revenues in excess of $2 billion **Career Highlights:** Managing Principal Database Administrator, Genetech (1994-Present); Systems Analyst/Certified Oracle Database Administrator, Independent Consultant (1992-94); Senior Systems Analyst, Lawrence Livermore National Laboratory (1981-92). **Associations & Accomplishments:** Northern California Oracle Users Group; Drug Information Association. **Education:** Golden Gate University: M.B.A. (1991), B.S.; San Joaquin Delta College, A.A. **Personal Information:** Married to Mary E. Glenn in 1997. Mr. Glenn enjoys the theater, astronomy, aquatics, home improvement, singing and guitar playing.

Deborah L. Graham

Promotions Designer
Astra Zeneca
21700 Oxnard Street #300
Woodland Hills, CA 91367
(800) 995-2173
Fax: (818) 888-0942
deborah.graham@astrapharmaceuticals.com

2834

Business Information: As the Promotions Designer for Astra Zeneca, Ms. Graham produces computer graphics. She is responsible for supporting sales, computer graphics, field promotions, logos, Web design, client logos, and customer needs and ideas and drafting ideas. She enjoys the variety of her duties and took great satisfaction in creating a user friendly asthma management handbook. Her goal is to help the Company develop a Web support network to better serve a growing clientele. Success, according to Ms. Graham, is dependent on staying focused on Company goals and providing a people-oriented environment to keep clients satisfied. At one time separate companies, Astra and Zeneca merged to form Astra Zeneca in June of 1999. The Company engages in pharmaceutical sales and support, targeting a specific sales market of physicians, clinics, HMOs, health plans, and hospitals. Serving international clients, the Company employs over 50,000 individuals. The Company has three different headquarters, the research headquarters in Sweeden, the administrative headquarters in England, and the United States headquarters in Delaware. **Career Highlights:** Promotions Designer, Astra Zeneca (1997-Present); Lead Artist, IVID Communications (1995-96); Computer Graphic Artist, Art Path (1994-97); Flight Attendant, Trans World Airlines (1969-88). **Associations & Accomplishments:** Royal Scottish Country Dancing; Senior Warden, All Souls Episcopal Church in San Diego. **Education:** Platt College, Certificate in Comptuer Graphics (1992); University of Nevada at Reno, B.A. Major in Art, Minor in Biology. **Personal Information:** Two children: Joanna Guy and Gordon Guy. Ms. Graham enjoys playing piano, jogging, reading and dancing.

Joyce L. Hawkins

Associate Director, Human Resources Information Services Group
DuPont Pharmaceuticals Company
P.O. Box 80722
Wilmington, DE 19880
(302) 892-7701
Fax: (302) 992-4919
joyce.l.hawkins@dupontpharma.com

2834

Business Information: Serving as an Associate Director for DuPont Pharmaceuticals Company, Mrs. Hawkins is responsible for management of the human resources department. She is accountable for overseeing information services, systems groups, project management, and generation of reports. Possessing an excellent understanding of her field, Mrs. Hawkins provides the necessary tools for recruiting, payroll, benefits, and training and evaluation. A savy, 20-year professional, she supervises a staff of five employees, overseeing their day-to-day performance and ensuring all duties assigned are completed within time and budgetary constraints. Attributing her success to remaining on the leading edge of technology, Mrs. Hawkins plans to provide Web access to all corporate managers within the Company in the near future. DuPont Pharmaceuticals Company operates facilities in a variety of countries around the globe. Employing 5,000 personnel, the Company reported estimated annual revenue of $3 billion in 1999. Founded in 1991, DuPont Pharmaceuticals is a wholly-owned subsidiary of DuPont which performs research and development into new and innovative medical techniques. The Company is committed to the discovery of new ways of treating currently untreatable diseases. **Career Highlights:** DuPont Pharmaceuticals Company: Associate Director, Human Resources Information Services Group (2000-Present), Project Manager (1998-2000), Programmer (1993-98). **Associations & Accomplishments:** IHRIM; Society for Human Resource Management. **Education:** Goldey Beacom College, Bachelor's degree (1993). **Personal Information:** Married to Ralph T. in 1972. One child: Jennifer Ward. Mrs. Hawkins enjoys fishing, hiking and pet massage.

Jean-Paul Hepp, Ph.D.

Director of Internet Communications
Pharmacia & Upjohn
100 Route 206 North
Peapack, NJ 07977
(908) 901-8589
Fax: (908) 901-8589

2834

Business Information: Dr. Hepp has been employed with Pharmacia & Upjohn for 12 years. He presently offers his services as the Director of Internet Communications. Prior to this position, he was in sales and marketing. Dr. Hepp saw a need for the Internet service within the Company and dedicated himself to creating this for Pharmacia & Upjohn. Utilizing his skills in this dynamic position, Dr. Hepp oversees all aspects of day-to-day Internet research and development. This includes communications, meeting policies and procedures, producing Web sites, and ensuring that the marketing division understands the importance of Internet use within the Company. Developing innovative objectives, Dr. Hepp work in the area of e-commerce, partnerships, automated service, and on-line marketing. His career highlights include heading the Internet project, and helping the Company to be recognized as one of the top five in Internet production and strategies. He credits his success to hard work, creativity, and perseverance. Pharmacia & Upjohn is a global, innovative-driven pharmacueticl company of 30,000 employees operating in more than 100 countries. The Company's core business is the develoment, manufacture, and sale of pharmaceutical products. Annual sales are estimated at $7 billion. **Career Highlights:** Pharmacia & Upjohn: Director of Internet Communications (1998-Present), Project Leader (1997-98); The Upjohn Company: Senior Manager (1995-96), Marketing (1987-95). **Associations & Accomplishments:** Lions Club, Belgium. **Education:** University Antwerp, Ph.D. (1991). **Personal Information:** Married to Van Beveren Lieve in 1977. Two children: Dominik and Eveline. Dr. Hepp enjoys science, philosophy and chess.

James E. Hockman Jr.

Senior Systems Engineer
Merck & Co., Inc.
2778 South East Side Highway, MS Building 42D
Elkton, VA 22827
(540) 298-4000
Fax: (540) 293-4817
james_hockman@merck.com

2834

Business Information: Combining management skills and technical expertise, Mr. Hockman serves as the Senior Systems Engineer for Merck & Co., Inc. As a seven technology professional, he has assertively served with Merck & Co., Inc. in a variety of roles since joining the Corporation as a Telecommunications and Network Engineer in 1992. In his current capacity, Mr. Hockman is the Information Technology Coordinator for the Asia/Pacific region of Merck's Manufacturing Division. Utilizing strategic planning, he acts as the Manufacturing Automation Liaison between corporate headquarters and one of the chemical/pharmaceutical sites in North America. A systems expert, Mr. Hockman attributes his career success to the strong work ethic instilled in him as young child by his parents and unwavering support from his wife Rebecca. Continually striving for maximum effectiveness, he is currently pursuing his M.B.A. degree to enable him to capitalize on the opportunities provided by the Corporation. Merck & Co., Inc. is a chemical and pharmaceutical manufacturer. Corporate headquarters are located in Whitehouse Station, New Jersey. Merck employs over 58,000 qualified individuals and the Corporation reports $26 billion in yearly revenue. **Career Highlights:** Merck & Co., Inc.: Senior Systems Engineer (1999-Present), Information Technology Coordinator, Asia/Pacific Region, Manufacturing Automation Liaison between a site in Ellerton, Virginia and Corporate Headquarters in Whitehouse Station, New Jersey (1999-Present), Integration Services Deployment (1996-98), Senior Telecommunications and Network Engineer (1992-96). **Associations & Accomplishments:** American Management Association; Institute of Electronics and Electrical Engineers. **Education:** James Madison University: M.B.A. (In Progress), B.B.A. in Decision Support Systems (1992); Germanna Community College, Associate's degree in Electrical Engineering. **Personal Information:** Married to Rebecca H. in 1991. Mr. Hockman enjoys farming, raising horses, hiking, travel and music.

Stephane Legault, Ph.D.

Project Leader
Wyeth-Ayerst Canada, Inc.
1025 Boul. Marcel-Laurin
Saint-Laurent, Quebec, Canada H4R 1J6
(514) 748-3632
Fax: (514) 744-9076
legaulst@md.ahp.com

2834

Business Information: Serving with Wyeth-Ayerst Canada, Inc. as Project Leader since 1999, Dr. Leguault lends his experience to the management information systems department. Highly regarded, he possesses an excellent understanding of his field. Charged with the responsibility of administrating the PC side of development for the Corporation, he manages a team of up to six members in upgrading and coordinating the information systems and databases. Coordinating resources, time lines, schedules, and assignments also fall within the realm of his responsibilities. As part of the Corporation's initiative to develop the Internet market, Dr. Leguault is working with technology sites to become more familiar with Web applications. His success is attributed to his ability to think outside the box, aggressively take on challenges, and deliver results. Wyeth-Ayerst Canada, Inc. is a division of Wyeth Ayerst Global Pharmaceuticals which is headquartered in St. Davids, Pennsyvania. A world leader in research, the Corporation is engaged in the development, manufacture, and sale of both perscription and nonperscription drugs. The Corporation also manufactures lifesaving medical devices and equipment. The Canadian division employs a work force of more than 1,500 people and successfully markets their products internationally. **Career Highlights:** Project Leader, Wyeth-Ayerst Canada, Inc. (1999-Present); Teacher, Marianoplis College (1998-99); Vice President Development, In Java Inc. (1996-99). **Associations & Accomplishments:** Society of Actuaries. **Education:** McGill University, Ph.D. (1999); University of Ottawa, B.S. **Personal Information:** Married to Julie Poirier in 1996. Dr. Legault enjoys hockey, curling, cycling, piano, computers and reading.

Jerilee "Jeri" Goodman Levine

Information Systems Director
Andrx
2915 Weston Road
Weston, FL 33331
(954) 217-4791
Fax: (954) 217-4377
jlevine@andrx.com

2834

Business Information: As Information Systems Director of Andrx, Ms. Levine is responsible for day-to-day administration and operational activities of the systems infrastructure. She determines the overall strategic direction and business contribution of the information systems function. Before joining the Corporation, Ms. Levine was employed as Information Systems Director with The Miami Herald. Her background history also includes a stint as Vice President of Information Systems for Burger King Corporation. As a 30 year professional, she maintains the functionality and fully operational status of both voice and data systems. Beginning her association with Andrx two years ago, Ms. Levine has worked diligently to develop her skills and acquire expertise in her field. Working closely with her team of 30 employees, she deploys the qualities that make a manager forceful and effective. She accurately assesses management effectiveness and obtains full commitments throughout the organization. Ms. Levine plans to expedite continued promotion through the fulfillment of her responsibilities and her involvement in the advancement of operations. Established in 1992, Andrx engages in the manufacture and distribution of pharmaceuticals. Employing a staff of 600 individuals, the Corporation reports an estimated annual revenue of $240 million. **Career Highlights:** Information Systems Director, Andrx (1997-Present); Information Systems Director, The Miami Herald (1989-95); Vice President of Information Systems, Burger King Corporation (1981-87). **Education:** Florida International University, M.B.A. (1980); University of Florida, B.S. (1969). **Personal Information:** Married to Marc in 1990. Two children: Michael and Matthew.

Ellen R. Lis, Ph.D.

Principal Database Administrator
Wyeth-Ayerst Research
240 Radnor-Chester Road North
Radnor, PA 19087
(610) 902-1395
eclis@bellatlantic.net

2834

Business Information: Dr. Lis has worked in the information technology field since 1990. She joined the Wyeth-Ayerst Research team of professionals in 1990. Dr. Lis currently assumes the role of Principal Database Administrator responsible for supporting the processing of clinical trial databases and ensuring optimal infrastructure design. She is known for delivery of technical results by communicating effectively, paying close attention to technical details, and solving problems and challenges in a systematic and positive manner. Now an expert in her field, Dr. Lis writes pre-processing routines for the Company. Working with database management systems software, reorganizing and restructuring data to better suit the needs of users, and maintaining the efficiency of the database also fall within the realm of Dr. Lis' functions. Her focus is on helping Wyeth-Ayerst stay flexible, efficient, profitable, and in the forefront of emerging technology. Her career highlights include evaluation and introduction of third party products for clinical data pre-processing, expanding the data mapping capability of a 15 plus member DBA team, writing and executing complex software validations, and combining the functionality of two unrelated applications to generate and load derived data. She successfully provided input of a front-end application properly contoured for third party products. Strong analytical and problem solving abilities have led to her professional success. Engaged in research and manufacturing of ethical and over-the-counter pharmaceuticals, Wyeth-Ayerst Research was established in 1943 and employs more than 3,500 professional, technical, and administrative support personnel. **Career Highlights:** Wyeth-Ayerst Research: Principal Database Administrator (1998-Present), Senior Clinical Database Administrator (1997-98), Clinical Database Administrator (1993-96), Database Assistant (1990-93). **Associations & Accomplishments:** Society for Clinical Data Management. **Education:** Wake Forest University, Ph.D. in Biochemistry (1987). **Personal Information:** Married to Christopher in 1993. Dr. Lis enjoys walking, music, and gardening.

Susan K. McEntyre

Manager
McKesson HBOC
5995 Windward Parkway, MS ATHQ 5200
Alpharetta, GA 30005
(404) 338-3080
Fax: (770) 623-9912
skmcentyre@mindspring.com

2834

Business Information: Combining management skills and technical expertise, Ms. McEntyre fulfills the responsibility of Manager with McKesson HBOC. She has assertively served with McKesson HBOC in a variety of roles since coming on board as a Programmer in 1984. Currently, she supervises a team of individuals across the country who sell implementation services for software products developed by the Company. During her years with the Company, she is proud to have built the tool set used for pricing the implementation services. Consistently achieving quality performance in her field, Ms. McEntyre plans to better her management skills, focusing primarily on dealing with coworkers. Her career success reflects her leadership ability in building strong teams with synergy and technical strength and take on new challenges and responsibilities. McKesson HBOC was formed when McKesson and HBO Company merged. The Company is a pharmaceutical manufacturing company on one side and is an Information Technology business on the other. The Information Technology side develops, implements, and supports healthcare information software for major companies. Software consulting, on-line services, and customer information are available to the Company's clients. **Career Highlights:** McKesson HBOC: Manager (1998-Present), Service Contracting Advisor (1993-98), Project Manager (1991-93), Implementation Analyst (1988-91), Product Development Analyst (1986-88), Programmer/Customer Support Representative (1984-86). **Education:** Texas Tech University, B.B.A. (1978). **Personal Information:** Ms. McEntyre enjoys golf, Bible study and watching sports.

Jeanne Rash

Manager of Customer & Technical Training
Bayer Corporation
511 Benedict Avenue
Tarrytown, NY 10591-5097
(800) 431-1970
Fax: (914) 524-2100
jeanne.rush.b@bayer.com

2834

Business Information: Utilizing more than 25 years of extensive experience in the medical technology field, Ms. Rash assertively serves as Manager of Customer & Technical Training with Bayer Corporation. She has served with Bayer in a variety of roles since joining the team as Manager of Field Service in 1988. Associated with the Diagnostic Sales Division, Ms. Rash assumes responsibility for training the technical field personnel and individual customers on instrumentation sold by the Corporation. Attributing her professional success to patience and the ability to compromise, she keeps abreast of the latest technological advances in medical development by reading trade journals and taking classes. Ms. Rash believes in keeping the door of opportunity open at all times and continues to grow professionally through the fulfillment of her responsibilities. Bayer Corporation is an international, research based chemicals and health care group with major businesses in specialty chemicals, life sciences, and polymers. Worldwide operations employ 120,400 people. A world leader in its sector, annual sales are reported at DM54.9 billion. **Career Highlights:** Bayer Corporation: Manager of Customer & Technical Training (1997-Present), Technical Specialist (1994-97), Manager of Field Service (1988-94). **Associations & Accomplishments:** Medical Technology Licensed, American Society of Clinical Pathologist. **Education:** Fairleigh Dickinson University, B.S. in Medical Technology (1972).

Michael John Skiles

Associate Information Consultant
Eli Lilly and Company
Lilly Corporate Center
Indianapolis, IN 46285
(317) 276-9351
Fax: (317) 279-6569
skiles_michael_j@lilly.com

2834

Business Information: Employed by Eli Lilly and Company since 1995, Mr. Skiles serves as Associate Information Consultant. Combining technical competence with effective communication skills, he devotes his attention to all information technology within the Company. He oversees new projects in the information technology area, conducts research on new software and hardware that would be feasible for the Company, and consults staff members on technical problems. Displaying a clear vision of goals, Mr. Skiles wants to develop more skills in project management. His career success reflects his ability to produce results in support of business objectives and aggressively take on new challenges. Eli Lilly and Company is a research company that specializes in developing pharmaceutical products for the betterment of individuals. The Company contains scientific programs and research partnerships to aid in the further development of products. Presently, Eli Lilly and Company generates annual sales of $6 billion. A work staff of 26,000 highly skilled and educated individuals find the best solutions for certain disease and illness. **Career Highlights:** Associate Information Consultant, Eli Lilly and Company (1995-Present); Manager Customer Support, LBMS (1991-95); Manager Customer Support, Transformlogic/Nastec (1984-91). **Associations & Accomplishments:** Served at Fort Meade, Maryland at NSA. **Education:** Macomb College; United States Army Signal School; Oracle Certified; VMS. **Personal Information:** Married to Debra in 1986. Four children: Deanna, Stephanie, Rachel, and Melissa. Mr. Skiles enjoys baseball card collecting and antique cars.

Caroline Tollenaere

Information Systems and Information Technology Manager
Astrazeneca Belgium
Schaessestraat 15
Destelbergen, Belgium 9070
+32 93534211
Fax: +32 93550964

2834

Business Information: Mrs. Tollenaere is the Information Systems and Information Technology Manager for

Astrazeneca Belgium. She administers and controls the Information Systems and Information Technology Departments where she monitors the equipment to ensure their functionality and fully operational status at all times. Working closely with a staff of 11 technology experts, Mrs. Tollenaere is able to design and implement new programs to better the efficiency of the production line and eliminate the paperwork within the laboratory facilities. With the Company looking at a future merger with another pharmaceuticals leader, Mrs. Tollenaere is currently coordinating several programs to boost the system so it will survive through both merger and the transition to the 21st Century, new millennium, with minimal difficulties. A diversified professional, Mrs. Tollenaere also handles the accounting aspects of her husband's business. Established in 1970, Astrazeneca Belgium is a pharmaceutical company. The Company supports an experimental laboratory facility, production facility, and distributes its medical treatments to businesses around the world. Within its laboratories, new drug treatments and combinations are designed, tested, and explored. The Company employs almost 250 scientists and product specialists at its facilities in Belgium. **Career Highlights:** Astrazeneca Belgium: Information Systems and Information Technology Officer (1997-Present), Information Systems Supervisor (1994-97), Information Systems Programmer (1990-94). **Education:** B.M.E. (1988). **Personal Information:** Married in 1999.

Ngoc-Diem T. Tran

SAP Basic Consultant
Allergan, Inc.
2525 Dupont Drive
Irvine, CA 92612-1599
(714) 246-4910
Fax: (714) 796-3032
tran_diem@allergan.com

2834

Business Information: Operating as SAP Basic Consultant for Allergen, Inc., Mr. Tran offers SAP consulting and systems support. Possessing an excellent understanding of technology, he is responsible for performance tuning of systems and overall health check of the entire systems infrastructure. Maintaining a service level reliability rate of 99.7 percent, he attends to a wide variety of duties including troubleshooting, upgrading, installation, and computer maintenance. With over 13 years of engineering and managerial experience, Mr. Tran is in possession of the knowledge to handle work of the most complex nature. His plans for the future include gaining more knowledge in Web-based areas, such as e-commerce and e-business; and obtaining his M.B.A. A strong motivation to learn has contributed to Mr. Tran's professional success. Allergen, Inc., established in 1950, engages in the manufacturing and distribution of pharmaceuticals. The Corporation specializes in eye care, skin care, and surgical equipment. With the help of 6,000 experienced and dedicated employees, the Corporation provides several types of products for laboratories, clinics, and hospitals. As an important option for health care professionals, systems consulting is provided for all clients. **Career Highlights:** SAP Basic Consultant, Allergan, Inc. (1998-Present); Information Security Consultant, Southern California Gas Company (1997-98); Information Security Manager, Nestle USA (1991-97); Systems Engineer, Computer Task Group. **Education:** University of Cincinnati, B.A. (1987). **Personal Information:** Married to Si Truong in 1987. Two children: Steven and Patrick Truong. Mr. Tran enjoys reading, biking and badminton.

Zoltan Tyeklar, Ph.D.

Director of Management Information Systems
EPIX Medical, Inc.
71 Rogers Street
Cambridge, MA 02142-1118
(617) 250-6130
Fax: (617) 250-6139
ztyeklar@epixmed.com

2834

Business Information: Possessing extensive scientific knowledge and technical expertise, Dr. Tyeklar serves as Director of Management Information Systems for EPIX Medical, Inc. Responsible for overseeing all information technology systems, he orchestrates the efficient transformation of business and scientific data into knowledge. Previously, Dr. Tyeklar served as a chemist with the Corporation. His plans for the future include remaining cognizant of technical innovations and leverage information technology in the pharmaceutical industry. EPIX Medical, Inc. concentrates efforts in the research and development of targeted contrast agents to improve the capability and expand the use of magnetic resonance imaging as a tool for diagnosing diseases. Currently, EPIX Medical, Inc. is developing MS-325, an injectable contrast agent designed for multiple vascular imaging indications which will assist physicians in diagnosing cardiovascular disease. **Career Highlights:** Director of Management Information Systems, EPIX Medical, Inc. (1992-Present); Scientist, Johns Hopkins University; Post Doctoral Fellow, State University of New York at Albany (1985-89). **Associations & Accomplishments:** American Chemical Society; Association for Computing Machinery; Author of a book and more than 40 papers; Secured three patents for his inventions. **Education:** Veszprem University, Ph.D. (1981). **Personal Information:** Two children: Nora and Zoard. Dr. Tyeklar enjoys tennis, music and reading.

Edmond J. Verstraete

Director of Information Management
Janssen Pharmaceuticals
28 Heritage Hills Drive
Washington Crossing, PA 18977-1156
(609) 730-2911
edmond.verstraete@att.worldnet.net

2834

Business Information: As Janssen Pharmaceutica's Director of Information Management, Mr. Verstraete is a successful 18 year professional responsible for the operations of the information management department. He determines the overall strategic direction and business contribution of the information systems fucntions as well as delivers effective solutions, performs research on trends in the market, and oversees workshops. Highly regarded, he possesses an excellent understanding of technology. Attributing his success to always being result focused and wanting to learn from other people, Mr. Verstraete advises that individuals in this field have a strong customer focus in order to be successful. He enjoys his current position and plans to stay within the technology industry and continue to advance his knowledge in the field. Established in 1969, Janssen Pharmaceutica is involved in the sale of prescription and nonprescription drugs. Employing more than 1,000 personnel the Company reports annual revenue of $2 billion. The Company's information management division is responsible for supporting sales and marketing that advertises new drugs by providing information management. **Career Highlights:** Director of Information Management, Janssen Pharmaceutica (1997-Present); Manager of Information Management, Janssen Pharmaceutica Belgium (1992-97); Consultant, Softcore Document Management (1990-92); Project Leader, CFE Belgium (1990). **Associations & Accomplishments:** SIM. **Education:** IHRB Belgium, Engineer degree (1982); Officers Training School. **Personal Information:** Mr. Verstraete enjoys sports and travel.

Michael F. Ward, Ph.D.

Scientific Programmer/Data Analyst
Genentech
1 DNA Way, MS 37
South San Francisco, CA 94080-4990
(650) 255-7046
mward@gene.com

2834

Business Information: Utilizing 15 years of experience, Dr. Ward serves as a Scientific Programmer and Data Analyst for Genentech. As a software engineer in the biocomputing group, he is responsible for the integration of technology with molecular biology research for the scientists. Dr. Ward works with several other staff members to design and develop customized programs utilized by the Company. Before joining Genentech, he served as a Research Scientist for both Harvard and Boston Universities' School of Medicine and Programmer and Analyst with the University of California at Berkeley, where he was involved in functional brain imaging and speech processing. As a systems expert with an established track record of delivering results, Dr. Ward's success reflects his ability to think creatively and cross disciplinary boundaries. Committed to the success of Genentech, he plans to continue in his role of combining academics and industrial software application. Genentech is a biotechnology company focusing on the discovery and manufacture of pharmaceuticals for unmet medical needs. Founded in the 1970s, the Company engages in the development of pharmaceuticals utilizing genetic engineering and processing of human genome information. Presently, Genentech employs a workforce of more than 3,000 people. **Career Highlights:** Scientific Programmer/Analyst, Genentech (1999-Present); Research Scientist, Harvard University School of Medicine (1996-99); Research Scientist, Boston University School of Medicine (1995-99); Programmer/Analyst, University of California at Berkeley (1993-95); Biomedical Engineer, EEG Systems Laboratory (1988-93). **Associations & Accomplishments:** American Psychological Society; International Neuropsychological Society; American Association of Individual Investors. **Education:** Boston University, Ph.D. in Psychology (1999); University of Miami, M.S. in Biomedical Engineering; University of California at Santa Barbara, B.S. in Electrical and Computer Engineering. **Personal Information:** Dr. Ward enjoys bicycling, mountaineering, tennis, wine tasting and travel.

Alvis A. Williams

Information Services Manager
Merck & Co., Inc.
700 Atrium Drive, #FTA-270
Somerset, NJ 08873
(732) 302-5011
Fax: (732) 563-9435
alvis_williams@merck.com

2834

Business Information: Mr. Williams has served with Merck & Co., Inc. in various positions since 1980. At the present time, he fulfills the responsibilities of Information Services Manager. Mr. Williams oversees and directs computer support in an NT server environment, provides information services for internal clients, and manages the systems infrastructure, hardware, and software. He supports a user base of approximately 175 people and is responsible for second level support. Supporting Procurement Training Center and overseeing fiscal year budgets also fall within the purview of his functions. His greatest achievement is being part of a project that provided an automated purchase order system for over 700 internal clients. A systems expert, he has been recognized for outstanding service by being promoted to a managerial position in 1994. Mr. Williams attributes his success to follow-up and perseverance. He has plans to further his education to facilitate promotional opportunities within the Corporation. Merck & Co., Inc. is the world's largest pharmaceutical organization, primarily involved in the health care industry. The Corporation helps treat and irradicate disease and illness for both humans and animals. Serving an international client base, with over 100 locations worldwide, the Corporation employs a total of 40,000 individuals to orchestrate all activities of design, manufacture, testing, and research. Headquartered in White House Station, New Jersey, the Corporation reports an estimated annual revenue of $26.9 billion. **Career Highlights:** Merck & Co., Inc.: Information Services Manager (1993-Present), Associate Manager (1989-93), Senior Programmer Analyst (1984-89); Senior Project Leader (1980-84). **Associations & Accomplishments:** National Association Purchasing Management; Rutgers Alumni Association; Association National Minority Development Purchasing Council. **Education:** University of Phoenix, M.B.A. (In Progress); Rutgers University, degree in Computer Science and Management (1982). **Personal Information:** Married to Diane in 1971. Four children.

Daniel L. Goodhart

Senior Accounting Manager
Procter & Gamble
7786 Meadowcreek Drive
Cincinnati, OH 45244
(513) 626-8826
goodhart.dl@pg.com

2841

Business Information: As Senior Accounting Manager of Procter & Gamble, Mr. Goodhart develops global SAP software in Japan, Latin America, and Canada. Mantaining accounting functionality in United States and Canada, Mr. Goodhart works closely with his staff to develop innovative technical strategies to improve the effectiveness of the departments. Training other employees on various aspects of the financial operating systems, he demonstrates his extensive knowledge of both technical and financial aspects of the Company. Recognized for his impressive abilities, he has worked on a special project that moved the finance and accounting central functions from the headquarters location of Cincinnati, Ohio, to San Jose, Costa Rica. Understanding the importance of adaptability, he looks forward to shifting his career into supporting SAP Solution on a global basis within the Company. Mr. Goodhart credits his success to deeply instilled values that allow him to effectively plan goals. Procter & Gamble is the leading manufacturer of household products and the world's largest advertiser. Operating five main product categories, the Company produces laundry and cleaning supplies, paper goods, beauty care, and foods and beverages. Additionally, the Company offers health care products such as toothpaste and over-the-counter medications. Over half of all sales originate from outside the United States. **Career Highlights:** Procter & Gamble: Senior Accounting Manager (1998-Present), SAP Rollout Team Leader (1995-98), Senior Accounting Manager of General Advertising and Finance (1992-93). **Education:** University of Cincinnati: B.S. in Accounting (1987), B.S. in Information Processing Systems, A.S. in Accounting. **Personal Information:** Married to Jean K. in 1984. Two children: Nathan D. and Chloe J. Mr. Goodhart enjoys travel and is a sports enthusiast.

Allen P. Coniglio

Senior Systems Administrator
Unilever
55 Merritt Boulevard
Trumbull, CT 06611
(203) 381-2776
allen.coniglio@unilever.com

2844

Business Information: Serving as Senior Systems Administrator of Unilever, Mr. Coniglio oversees the installation of operating and database management systems software, monitoring and tuning of systems software, peripherals, and networks, and resolution of systems difficulties. Utilizing 11 years of academics and experience in the field, Mr. Coniglio is the lead manager of Unilever's North American UNIX group. Drawing from his mechanical engineering background, he supervises a team of employees in maintaining the systems infrastructure fully funcational and operational. Eventually attaining the position of Director of Information Technology is cited as one of his many future goals. "Go to college and continue to learn," is serves Mr. Coniglio's advice to others in the industry. Unilever, founded in 1930, was the result of a merger between a Dutch margarine company and a British soap maker. Today, the Company's product line includes Dove, Sunsilk, Magnum, Lipton, and Calve. An international company from its conception, Unilever is expected to satisfy the consumer's needs through brands that have a relatively low environmental impact. Employing over 270,000 people worldwide, the Company has reported an estimated annual sales mark of $60 billion. **Career Highlights:** Senior Systems Administrator, Unilever (1998-Present); Systems Administrator, Hospital of St. Raphaels (1997-98); Senior Mechanical Engineer, Sikorsky Aircraft (1989-97). **Associations & Accomplishments:** Adjunct Professor, Southern Connecticut State University. **Education:** University of New Haven: M.S. in Computer Science (1995), M.B.A. (1992); State University of New York at Stony Brook, Bachelor's degree in Mechanical Engineering (1989).

Shelia LeBeauf

Information Technology Training Coordinator
Equistar Chemicals, LP
1221 McKinney Street, Suite 1600
Houston, TX 77010
(713) 309-7757
Fax: (713) 951-1617
shelia.lebeauf@equistarchem.com

2869

Business Information: Serving as Information Technology Training Coordinator of Equistar Chemicals, Ms. LeBeauf designs and implements information technology training activities and progress for approximately 9,000 employees throughout 36 locations. An expert, she coordinates the high end training for the end users of desktop, Microsoft, SAP, and other related programs, ensuring that every employee is up to date in their knowledge of the latest technological advances used by the Company. Ms. LeBeauf was taught at an early age to always do your best and credits her success to her determination and a passion for her work. Involved in the local community, Ms. LeBeauf was recognized for starting a program providing PCs to disabled children. Looking forward to the new millennium, she would like to add more personnel to the Information Technology Department and play a more active part in developing courseware. Headquartered in Houston, Texas, Equistar Chemicals, LP is a joint venture between Lyondell Chemicals, Millennium Petrochemicals, and Oxychem. It is one of the largest producers of ethylene, propylene, and polyethylene in the world today. The Company is an industry leader committed to being the premier petrochemical and polymer company worldwide. Presently, the Company reports annual revenues in excess of $6.1 billion. **Career Highlights:** Information Technology Training Coordinator, Equistar Chemicals, LP (1997-Present); Data Center Supervisor, Millennium Petrochemicals (1992-97); Senior Programmer Analyst, Quantum Chemicals (1988-92). **Associations & Accomplishments:** American Society for Training and Development; Toastmasters. **Education:** Southern University, B.S. in Computer Science (1981); NATD, Management Training. **Personal Information:** Three children: Nedra, Darrell, and Kascius. Ms. LeBeauf enjoys travel and working with autistic children.

Maurice R. Gates

Senior Telecommunications Engineer
Dow Agrosciences, EDC/LL
9330 Zionsville Road
Indianapolis, IN 46268
(317) 337-4080
Fax: (317) 337-4113
mrgates@dowagro.com

2879

Business Information: Educated in the field of Electrical Engineering, Mr. Gates serves as Senior Telecommunications Engineer for Dow Agrosciences, EDC/LL. He administers the local area and wide area networks for the Company's offices in North America, presiding over both routine maintenance and ongoing upkeep. Before joining Dow Agrosciences in 1995, he assertively served as Senior Telecommunications Engineer and Telecommunications Engineer with Dow Chemical. In his present role, Mr. Gates updates and implements new network systems as necessary, ensuring optimum performance at all times. As a 10 year technology professional, he is especially proud to have single-handedly designed a Token Ring Network used in the Company's mainframe S&A environment. His success reflects his ability to aggressively take on new challenges and responsibilities. Staying attuned to advances in the industry through reading magazines and attending seminars and classes, Mr. Gates plans to continue to advance in the technical aspect of his career. A wholly owned subsidiary of Dow Chemicals, Dow Agrosciences, EDC/LL is an international manufacturer of agricultural products. Founded in 1989, the Company employs 3,500 knowledgeable professionals in the research, testing, and manufacture of chemical and biochemical products. Presently, the Company reports estimated annual revenues in excess of $2 billion. **Career Highlights:** Senior Telecommunications Engineer, Dow Agrosciences, EDC/LL (1995-Present); Dow Chemical: Senior Telecommunications Engineer (1994-95), Telecommunications Engineer (1989-94). **Associations & Accomplishments:** Big Brothers of Indianapolis. **Education:** Lawrence Technological University, B.S. in Electrical Engineering (1989). **Personal Information:** Mr. Gates enjoys golf and basketball.

Patrice Anton

Director of Innovative Technologies
Novacel
27 Rue Du Dr. Bataille
deville Les Rouen, France 76250
+33 232827219
Fax: +33 2357677671
antonpat@aol.com

2891

Business Information: Dr. Anton began his career with Novacell as Engineer of Development in 1980, and has worked his way through the ranks to his current position of Director of Innovative Technologies. He is charged with researching, analyzing, specifying, and designing product enhancements. Possessing superior talents and an excellent understanding of his field, Dr. Anton's emphasis is on 21st century technologies. Highly regarded, he turns potential into action through knowledge and skilled training, therefore establishing high standards of excellence for Novacell. Dr. Anton's future goals include remaining with the Company, developing new adhesive products, and penetrating new markets for additional revenues. Established in 1970, Novacell is an established and reputable international company engaged in the design and manufacturing of adhesives used in surface protection. Distributing to retailers worldwide, the Company employs over 250 skilled individuals to facilitate blueprinting, manufacturing, and distributing of all products as well as office administrative tasks. **Career Highlights:** Novacel: Director for Innovation Technologies (1998-Present), Research and Development Manager (1982-98), Engineer of Development (1980-82). **Associations & Accomplishments:** President, Fencing Association. **Education:** University of Strasseberg, Doctorate degree (1980). **Personal Information:** Two children: Alexandre and Fanny. Dr. Anton enjoys fencing and stamp collecting.

Dewitt Bowens

Software Engineer
AlliedSignal Technical Services
P.O. Box 578
La Plata, MD 20646-0578
(301) 870-3582
Fax: (301) 870-2065
debowens@crosslink.net

2899

Business Information: Serving as Software Engineer of AlliedSignal Technical Services, Mr. Bowens uses SQL and specialty testing software to write and test application programs and add enhancements. He is responsible for defining the specifications for Corporation software and programming. As a 24 year technology professional, Mr. Bowens has served with AlliedSignal in a variety of roles since joining the Corporation as Shift Manager in 1980. Additionally, he creates and maintains ROB databases, providing technical support for its users. Coordinating with users and systems management, he analyzes, specifies, and designs new solutions to harness more of the computer's power, ultimately enhancing overall systems performance. Mr. Bowens states that during his childhood, he was not exposed to much outside influence and this, in turn, has given him a burning desire to experience more as an adult. Committed to the further development of the Corporation, he continually strives to improve performance and looks forward to a obtaining a managerial position within the software department. Allied Signal is an advanced technology and manufacturing company serving customers worldwide with aerospace products, chemicals, fibers, advanced materials, and automotive parts. Headquartered in Morristown, New Jersey, over 10,000 qualified professionals are employed in the Corporation's four technical service centers. **Career Highlights:** Allied Signal Technical Services: Software Engineer (1992-Present), Software Analyst/Applications Programmer (1984-91), Shift Manager (1980-83). **Associations & Accomplishments:** King George Masonic Lodge #314. **Education:** University of Maryland, B.S. in Computer Science (1996); Rappahannock Community College, A.S. in General Studies (1996); DeVry Institute of Technology, A.S. in Electronics Engineering Technology (1975). **Personal Information:** Married to Judy in 1977. Two children: Lawan S. White and Tekeema S. Mr. Bowens enjoys basketball, volleyball, bowling and working out in the gym.

J. Emmett Condon

Senior Systems Analyst
Hercules Inc.
4636 Somerton Road
Tervose, PA 19053
(215) 633-4341
cobol@compuserve.com

2899

Business Information: A performance and results driven information technology professional with over 13 years of experience, Mr. Condon fulfills the responsibilities of Senior Systems Analyst for Hercules Inc. In this position, he directs technical design and development of various leading edge information management systems to facilitate Corporation-wide efforts. Mr. Condon, owning a consistent record of delivering results, oversees all aspects of project planning, staffing, and budgeting. He has led many cross-functional teams through the entire development cycle, from initial needs assessment through specification, development, quality review, and implementation. Mr. Condon is an accomplished professional with highlights that include the design of a "Data Mart" used to expedite corporate profit and loss data collection; and the replacement of obsolete technology with a cutting edge Distributed Approval System expediting product delivering by 50 percent. On promotion's fast track, his goals are to become more involved in management or administration, and at some point, consulting. Mr. Condon, concurrently is an Adjunct Professor at La Salle University, and is Webmaster for the Northeast Central Regional Users Group (NECRUG). His favorite credo is "everything has a price tag." Hercules Inc. manufactures specialty chemicals used in water treatment systems and food products. Established in 1938, the Corporation employs 4,000 people generating in excess of $3 billion in annual revenues. **Career Highlights:** Senior Systems Analyst, Hercules Inc. (1987-Present); Adjunct Professor, La Salle University (1996-Present); Programmer Analyst, Adams - Russel (1985-87); Staff Sergeant, United States Air Force (1981-85). **Associations & Accomplishments:** Board of Directors, Northeast Regional Computer Users Group; International Hewlett-Packard Users Group; Toastmasters International; Institute of Electrical and Electronics Engineers. **Education:** LaSalle University, M.B.A. with focus in Computer Information Systems (1995); Western New England College, B.S. in Business Administration with focus in Computer Information Systems (1987); Delaware County Community College, A.A.S. in Data Processing (1980). **Personal Information:** Mr. Condon enjoys reading, spending time with his girlfriend and their three dogs.

Huy M. Duong

Senior Programmer Analyst
General Chemical Corporation
90 East Halsey Road
Parsippany, NJ 07054
(973) 515-1824
Fax: (718) 457-7742
huyduong@juno.com

2899

Business Information: Functioning in the capacity of Senior Programmer Analyst at General Chemical Corporation, Mr. Duong coordinates with users and management in analyzing, designing, and deploying cutting edge distribution systems. An expert, his strong resume includes a stint as Programmer Analyst with Solar International Shipping prior to joining General Chemical Corporation in 1997. Mr. Duong, utilizing his firm academic ties and experience, is able to deliver state-of-the-art technologies and solve problems and challenges in a highly efficient manner. In addition to leading his team in implementing PeopleSoft software applications, he oversees numerous planning functions to include determining future resource requirements, overseeing time lines, schedules, and assignments, and deploying advanced technologies within General Chemical Corporation. His focus is to help the Corporation stay on the leading edge and stay flexible, efficient, and competitive in the market place. Continue to help General Chemical grow and take the Corporation to the next level serves as Mr. Duong's future endeavors. General Chemical Corporation is engaged in chemical production and distribution. One of the largest chemical providers in the world, General Chemical specializes mainly with performance products. Founded in 1899, the Corporation employs a work force of more than 700 persons who help generate annual revenues in excess of $500 million. **Career Highlights:** Senior Programmer Analyst, General Chemical Corporation (1997-Present); Programmer Analyst, Solar International Shipping (1989-97). **Education:** Hunter College, B.S. (1997). **Personal Information:** Mr. Duong enjoys stock trading.

Ronald Finklestein
Divisional Information Systems Manager
OMNOVA Solutions Inc.
165 South Cleveland Avenue
Mogadore, OH 44260
(330) 628-6601
Fax: (330) 678-6559

2899

Business Information: Utilizing over 24 years of occupational experience, Mr. Finklestein joined the OMNOVA Solutions Inc.'s team of professionals in 1998. Currently serving in the role of Divisional Information Systems Manager, he is responsible for all aspects of the division's hardware, software, and applications functions. He is in charge of day-to-day activities for six plants as well as the strategic planning process of integrating business requirement into technology requirements. A savvy systems expert, Mr. Finklestein provides assistance and advice to users, interpreting problems and providing technical support for hardware, software, and system platforms. His success reflects his ability to think outside the box, deliver results, and take on challenges and new responsibilities. A spin-off of GenCorp Inc. as of October 1999, OMNOVA Solutions Inc. is associated with specialty and performance chemicals. Registering over 2,000 employees, the Corporation estimates annual revenue at $800 million. OMNOVA Solutions is traded on the New York Stock Exchange under the ticker symbol OMN. **Career Highlights:** Divisional Information Systems Manager, OMNOVA Solutions Inc. (1998-Present); Consultant, Bull Worldwide Information Systems (1997-98); Manager, Unisys (1994-97). **Education:** Malone College, B.A. in Business Administration (1990); University of Akron, A.A. in Data Processing (1975). **Personal Information:** Married. Two children: Aaron and Emily. Mr. Finklestein enjoys martial arts.

J. Larry Harvell
Systems Analyst
AlliedSignal
4101 Bermuda Hundred Road
Chester, VA 23836-3245
(804) 530-6137
Fax: (804) 530-6777
jharvell@honeywell.com

2899

Business Information: Utilizing his expertise in the technology field, Mr. Harvell serves in the role of Systems Analyst at AlliedSignal. Capably identifying computer support requirements, he maintains system applications and software that directly pertain to manufacturing, production, warehousing, shipping, and invoicing functions. Ensuring the computers are used to generate meaningful information, Mr. Harvell was instrumental in the integration of software applications for the Oracle database system, and was the subject matter expert for the Company's Y2K project. Keeping abreast of new techniques, he intends to migrate into e-commerce and web development for the Company. Mr. Harvell attributes his success to dedication and knowledge. His advice is "don't be frightened of the speed at which technology changes." Having recently merged with Honeywell, AlliedSignal manufactures diverse products. The main products includes engineering materials, carpet fibers, and industrial nylon for the aerospace and automotive industries. Headquartered in Morristown, New Jersey since 1955, AlliedSignal estimates annual sales at $23 million. Presently, the Chester, Virginia facility is manned by 2,000 employees. **Career Highlights:** AlliedSignal: Systems Analyst (1999-Present), Programmer Analyst (1985-99), Computer Operator (1977-85). **Associations & Accomplishments:** Digital Equipment Corporation Users Society; National Black Data Processing Association; National Black Engineering Association; Prince Hall Free Masons. **Education:** Virginia State University, B.S. in Business (1985); Computer Programming Internation Academy; Lear Siglear Institute. **Personal Information:** Married to Gloria G. in 1972. Two children: John Anthony and Shalin Goodwyn. Mr. Harvell enjoys softball, body building and drag racing.

Sahid Sesay
Chief Technical Officer
Baffin Inc.
1521 Alameda Avenue
Alameda, CA 94501
(510) 769-7856
Fax: (510) 749-6862
eipose@mindspring.com

2899

Business Information: Mr. Sesay functions in the role of Chief Technical Officer for Baffin Inc. He works closely with consulting engineers to design new prototype treatment products, as well as conduct experiments and tests to examine the weaknesses and strengths of each new design. A multi-faceted professional, Mr. Sesay is also in the technical field where he analyzes, specifies, designs, and implements

new, cutting edge business applications. Looking to the 21st Century, he hopes to witness the Corporation's cornering of the chemical market. Attributing his success to his upbringing and values instilled in him by his parents, Mr. Sesay's advice is "Persevere and focus on your target. Know what you want." Baffin Inc. is a research and development facility focusing on waste water treatment processes. Established in 1997, the Corporation designs new chemical combinations that will better aid the treatment and cleansing process of waste water. The Corporation is working to create programs that will make all waste water have the ability to be sanitized and marketed. **Career Highlights:** Chief Technical Officer, Baffin Inc. (1999-Present); Senior Information Security Analyst, VISA International (1997-99); Analyst Programmer, Chicago Board of Options Exchange (1995-96); Analyst Programmer, Australian Bureau of Statistics (1990-92). **Associations & Accomplishments:** S.A.N.S.; United States Telephone Association; U.S.A.E.S.F.S.; Amnesty International; Golden Volunteer, 1996 Summer Olympics hosted in Atlanta, Georgia. **Education:** Australian National University (1988). **Personal Information:** One child: Boi Komeh. Mr. Sesay enjoys tennis, swimming, soccer and community work.

2900 Petroleum and Coal Products

2911 Petroleum refining
2951 Asphalt paving mixtures and blocks
2952 Asphalt felts and coatings
2992 Lubricating oils and greases
2999 Petroleum and coal products, nec

Dale L. Embry
Engineering Principal
Phillips Petroleum Company
269 Geosciences Building
Bartlesville, OK 74004
(918) 661-7783
Fax: (918) 662-1238
dlembry@ppco.com

2911

Business Information: Serving as Engineering Principal of Phillips Petroleum Company, Mr. Embry is charged with the fluid operation of corporate networks. He is responsible for software development process to analyze chemical and physical properties. Possessing an excellent understanding of technology, he is leading his staff in writing codes and developing and implementing mathematical models for economic planning and review. Continuing to demonstrate his paramount communication and leadership skills, Mr. Embry is highly regarded by both technologists and colleagues. A multi-faceted professional, he is co-owner of Quartz Precision Software, LLC, a company that operates as an international software developer in India and Europe. A visionary, Mr. Embry plans to remain with the Company and advance in corporate rank to better support Phillips Petroleum. His success is attributed to taking advantage of opportunities and knowing the right people. Phillips Petroleum Company engages in petroleum processing. This international company was established in 1928, and has grown to employ over 16,000 people who generate annual revenues topping $10 billion. Achieving long-term success, Phillips Petroleum has gained a reputation for quality products and comprehensive customer support. Phillips Petroleum is continuing to maintain an impeccable client record, and plans to further expand its production and distribution sites to gain additional market shares and maximize growth potential. **Career Highlights:** Engineering Principal, Phillips Petroleum Company (1979-Present); Partner, Quartz Precision Software, LLC (Present). **Education:** Texas A&M University: M.S. (1980), B.S. (1977). **Personal Information:** Married to Jane in 1984. One child: Annalee.

Gary Johnson
Senior Security Advisor
Petro-Canada
150 6th Avenue SW
Calgary, Alberta, Canada T2P 3E3
(403) 296-7647
johnson@petro-canada.ca

2911

Business Information: A successful, 27-year veteran of information systems and technology, Mr. Johnson currently serves as Senior Security Advisor at Petro-Canada. Established in 1975, and referred to as "Canada's Gas Station," Petro-Canada is an integrated oil and gas company that provides superior performance through its four core businesses: Grand Banks oil, oil sands, natural gas, and refining and marketing. Mr. Johnson is responsible for protecting the confidentiality, integrity, and availability of corporate information assets. His duties include risk

assessments, secure communications with business partners, information security policy, computer virus infrastructure, client awareness, and recommendation of safeguards for internal and external threats to corporate information systems. Beginning his Petro-Canada career in 1974, he has received recognition for his diligence and skills through several promotions to his current Security position. Continually striving for maximum effectiveness, Mr. Johnson is currently working toward the designation of CISSP, Certified Information Systems Security Professional. Highly regarded by his colleagues, his success is attributed to his family values and being very enthusiastic about everything. **Career Highlights:** Petro-Canada: Senior Security Advisor (1998-Present), SAP Security and Change Control Coordinator (1995-98), Technical Specialist (1974-95). **Associations & Accomplishments:** ISP - Information Systems Professional; Canadian Information Processing Society; SPIE - Security Professional Information Exchange; DRIE - Disaster Recovery Information Exchange; CSI - Computer Security Institute; Citizen of the United States and Canada. **Education:** Atkinson College (1981-83); Control Data Institute, Computer Programming Technology (1973); Kingsway College (1967-71). **Personal Information:** Married to Christine in 1985. Two children: Kasten and Tyler. Mr. Johnson enjoys skiing, 8-ball, woodworking and coaching basketball. Mr. Johnson transferred to Calgary, Alberta from Toronto, Ontario in 1990.

Jeffrey T. Parker
Systems Analyst Buyer
Phillips Petroleum Company
300 West 6th Street
Borger, TX 79007
(806) 275-3298
Fax: (806) 275-3559
jtparke@ppco.com

2911

Business Information: Mr. Parker serves as the Systems Analyst Buyer for Phillips Petroleum Company and is responsible for the upkeep and maintenance of over 2,200 nodes. Purchasing computers, computer components and peripherals, he maintains a private Company stock and is able to setup and deliver computers on demand. An expert, he personally refurbishes and upgrades older computer models for continued use and sets up new models as necessary. His history includes stints as Repair Technician for Amarillo Computer and Squad Leader with the United States Army and National Guard. A savvy, 15 year technology professional, his career success reflects his hard work ethic and his ability to think out-of-the-box, solve system problems in a systematic and efficient manner, and take on new challenges. Mr. Parker anticipates further growth within the Company as an Analyst. Phillips Petroleum Company manufactures and markets refined petroleum, chemical, and plastic products to companies within the United States. Founded in 1933, the Company also engages in the exploration and production of oil and natural gas. With four locations nationwide, Phillips Petroleum consists of a workforce of 17,000 qualified professionals. **Career Highlights:** System Analyst Buyer, Phillips Petroleum Company (1988-Present); Repair Technician, Amarillo Computer (1985-88); Squad Leader, United States Army and National Guard (1981-89). **Associations & Accomplishments:** Deacon, Fair Lanes Baptist Church; Life Member, National Guard Association. **Education:** TSTC, A.A.S. in Computer Science (1985); TSTI, A.A.S. in Computer Electronics (1984); Frank Phillips College, CST Certified; Certified DEC Computer Administrator. **Personal Information:** Married to Denise in 1987. One child: Keshia. Mr. Parker enjoys model railroading.

Jamal Eddine Trache
Senior Contract Engineer
Gasco
P.O. Box 665
Abu Dhabi, United Arab Emirates
+971 6048627

2911

Business Information: Serving with Gasco in various positions since coming on board, Mr. Trache currently serves as the Senior Contract Engineer. Capitalizing on his strengths and expertise in the industry, he is responsible for all technical aspects of the Corporation's gas producing operations. He is accountable for establishing and review the Corporation's dealings with contractors and partners. His extensive employment history with Gasco includes serving in the positions of Planning and Cost Engineer and Area Engineer. Accomplishing great strides, he was recognized for his presentation on environmental national oil. Enjoying substantial success in his field, Mr. Trache plans to continue in his current carrer path with Gasco. His success professional reflects his engineering and leadership ability to take on challenges and deliver results. Headquartered in Abu Dhabi, United Arab Emirates, Gasco operates as a gas processing plant. The Corporation's primary product line includes propane, protane, and butane. Established in 1981, Gasco currently employs more than 800 professional, technical, and support staff to accomplish day-to-day administration and operational functions. **Career Highlights:** Gasco: Senior

Contract Engineer (1999-Present), Planning and Cost Engineer (1993-99), Area Engineer (1990-93). **Education:** Leeds University of England, M.Sc. (1983); University of Bradfore, Bachelor of Technology. **Personal Information:** Mr. Trache enjoys surfing the Internet and all sports.

Andrew Vanover

Senior Information Technology Specialist
Amerada Hess Corporation
54 Wildey Street, Apartment 11
Tarrytown, NY 10591-3119
(212) 536-8265
Fax: (212) 536-8093
dvanover@hess.com

2911

Business Information: As Senior Information Technology Specialist of Amerada Hess Corporation, Mr. Vanover oversees the design and implementation of the networks and infastructures. Facilitating departmental growth through his guidance of the technical staff, he works closely with others to develop innovative strategies that will improve current operating standards. Recognized for impressive achievements within the Corporation, Mr. Vanover is credited with the successful implementation of several procedures that integrate systems and operations, resulting in increased efficiency. Mr. Vanover currently is working on the creation of an information processing system that will become the sole data management system used by all of the corporate sites world wide. Attributing his accomplishments to his love of computers, he utilizes his tenacity to remain competitive in his field, as he aspires to a managment position within the Corporation. Amerada Hess Corporation is engaged in every aspect of the petroleum business, from the exploration of new sites to the production of crude oil and the resale of gasoline and home heating oil. Employing over 8,000 people throughout the United States, the Corporation is also concerned with the transportation and marketing of oil products and maintains an additional facility in Woodbridge, New Jersey. **Career Highlights:** Senior Information Technology Specialist, Amerada Hess Corporation (1999-Present); Manager of Back Office Services, Chase Manhattan Bank (1998-99); Manager, Personal Computer/LAN Support, Neilsen Media Research (1994-98). **Associations & Accomplishments:** United States Tae Kwon Do Union; World Tae Kwon Do Federation; New York Road Runner's Club. **Education:** Western Kentucky University, B.S. (1993). **Personal Information:** Married to Jackie in 1999. Mr. Vanover enjoys rock climbing, running, tae kwon do and hiking.

Shane L. Willerton

Database Analyst
Williams Refining, LLC
P.O. Box 2930
Memphis, TN 38101
(901) 775-8858
shane.willerton@williams.com

2911

Business Information: Serving Williams Refining, LLC as Database Analyst, Mr. Willerton assertively fulfills the responsibilities of applications developer and database administrator. He analyzes, specifies, and designs new data warehousing software and adminsters and control the Company's data resources, ensuring its reliability, security, and integrity. Possessing a superior talent and an excellent understanding of his field, Mr. Willerton also creates reporting tools for the Company's centralized system utilizing Java and Visual Basic. Overseeing SQL Server database management systems also fall within the scope of his responsibilities. His career highlights is cited as LAN implementation for the help desk. Attributing his success to a desire to learn, he plans on learning more about Java and HTML and the development of database application. Established in 1947, Williams Refining, LLC is an oil refinery located in Memphis, Tennessee. Dedicated to making chemicals such as natural gas for resale, the Company distributes petroleum products for home heating and automobile industry. Employing 500 personnel, the Company is also manufactures polyethernal for the plastics industry. **Career Highlights:** Williams Refining, LLC: Database Analyst (1999-Present), Senior Systems Analyst (1997-99); Field Technician, Service Assurance (1997); Technical Services Director, Kiwi Systems, LLC (1996-97). **Education:** Rhodes College. **Personal Information:** Married to Rikki Renee in 1997. Two children: James and Emma. Mr. Willerton enjoys chess and reading.

Karen L. Kemp

Manager of Quality Control
GAF
1361 Alps Road, Building 2
Wayne, NJ 07470
(973) 872-4223
Fax: (973) 628-6387
kkemp@gaf.com

2952

Business Information: As the Manger of Quality Control for GAF, Ms. Kemp displays an effective, productive management style. She oversees production within the information systems department, ensuring proper standards are met and maintained. Highly regarded, she keeps well-informed of new industry technologies and implements policies that will improve production, while still sustaining high-quality products. She encourages and facilitates optimum performance among the staff, thus ensuring all units work together to achive a common goal. Committed to further development of the Company, Ms. Kemp looks forward to assisting in the completion of future Company objectives. GAF manufactures roofing supplies such as shingles. Over 1,000 qualified staff members are employed to meet the demands of a growing clientele. Established in the 1940s, the Company is located in Wayne, New Jersey and reports annual revenue of over $1 billion. **Career Highlights:** Manager of Quality Control, GAF (Present); Director of Education and Training, Education Management Corporation (1998-Present); Senior Consultant, Innovative Consulting (1997-98); Senior Programmer/Trainer, GAFBMC (1995-97). **Associations & Accomplishments:** American Management Association; Society for Software Quality; American Society for Quality. **Education:** Oneonta University, M.S. in Education (1990). **Personal Information:** Ms. Kemp enjoys being a swim coach, biking and tennis.

3000 Rubber and Misc. Plastics Products

3011 Tires and inner tubes
3021 Rubber and plastics footwear
3052 Rubber and plastics hose and belting
3053 Gaskets, packing and sealing devices
3061 Mechanical rubber goods
3069 Fabricated rubber products, nec
3081 Unsupported plastics film and sheet
3082 Unsupported plastics profile shapes
3083 Laminated plastics plate and sheet
3084 Plastics pipe
3085 Plastics bottles
3086 Plastics foam products
3087 Custom compound purchased resins
3088 Plastics plumbing fixtures
3089 Plastics products, nec

Rodney A. Carlton

Network Specialist
Cooper Tire Company
201 Palamino Drive
Texarkana, AR 71854
(870) 779-4320
Fax: (870) 772-2755

3011

Business Information: Offering over a decade of experience and training in technical fields, Mr. Carlton serves as the Network Specialist for Cooper Tire Company. Engaged in the maintenance of all information technology systems utilized by the Company, Mr. Carlton takes on the challenges of sustaining Cooper Tire Company's position as one of the most innovative, state-of-the-art companies in the industry. Seeking the further integration of information technology into his career, Mr. Carlton is currently engaged in the creation of an ASP Department for Cooper Tire Company's Texarkana, Arkansas location. Providing extensive international service, Cooper Tire Company is engaged in the manufacture of replacement tires. Renowned as having the largest facility in the world, the Company produces over 40,000 tires daily. Utilizing the skills of 24,000 professionals located throughout the country, Cooper Tire Company maintains a position ahead of their competition in price, quality, and rate of production. **Career Highlights:** Cooper Tire Company: Network Specialist (1998-Present), Data Communications Specialist (1992-98); Harding University: Computer Repair Technician (1989-92), Systems Programmer (1991-92). **Associations & Accomplishments:** National Honor Society. **Education:** Harding University, B.S. in Computer Science (1992). **Personal Information:** Mr. Carlton enjoys hunting.

Linda S. Cunningham

Business Systems Manager
Michelin
632 Inglesby Parkway
Duncan, SC 29334
(864) 627-5714
Fax: (864) 627-5655
linda.cunningham@us.michelin.com

3011

Business Information: Mrs. Cunningham is Business Systems Manager of Michelin's Duncan, South Carolina location. She concentrates on computer systems for the truck tire retread division. Before joining Michelin, she served as both Operations Manager and Project Leader of Information Systems Research and Development with Uniroyal Goodrich. This, along with her academic ties and managerial and organizational skills, enables Mrs. Cunningham to plan and oversee the design, purchase, installation, management, and support of business computer systems for Michelin's Retread Division. As an 18 year technology professional, she oversees the day-to-day administration and operations of the Information Technology Department. In this realm, she is in charge of monitoring systems to ensure the functionality and fully operational status of Michelin's franchises systems infrastructure. Mrs. Cunningham attributes her career success to Michelin's commitment to excellence and employees. She has held many exciting and challenging positions at Michelin Tire Corporation. Her success reflects her ability to think out-of-the-box and take on new challenges and responsibilities. Mrs. Cunningham's long-term goals include consulting in the information technology and manufacturing arena. In her current position, she concentrates on computer systems for the truck tire retread division of Michelin. **Career Highlights:** Michelin: Business Systems Manager (1997-Present), Production System Development Coordinator (1995-97), Manager of Co-Op Advertising (1990-94); Project Leader, Information Systems, Uniroyal/Goodrich (1986-90). **Associations & Accomplishments:** Professional Woman's Golf Association; West Virginia University Alumni Association. **Education:** West Virginia University, B.S. in Business Administration; Greenville Technical College, Management and Computer Classes. **Personal Information:** Married to Kelly in 1997. One child: Cortney. Mrs. Cunningham enjoys golf, rollerblading, kickboxing, gardening and coaching.

Daniel C. McFarlane

Manager of Business Analysis
Michelin North America
P.O. Box 19001
Greenville, SC 29602
(864) 458-6941
Fax: (864) 458-4543

3011

Business Information: Displaying his skills in this highly specialized position, Mr. McFarlane serves as the Manager of Business Analysis for Michelin North America. He presides over the development and subsequent administration of data warehousing as well as the Company's decision support system. Providing a data structure for the end user to obtain data storage information, he assists the in-house users in their tasks of marketing and selling the Company's products and services. Mr. McFarlane also assists in application development for the database system. He provides training for the managerial personnel on specific software use and is available for technical support by the end users. Dedicated to making Michelin the number one tire manufacturer, he plans to continue with the development and growth of the database project to make the Company the cutting edge user in the industry. Mr. McFarlane credits his professional success to his ability to combine the technical aspects of information technology with business, making it user friendly to nontechnical users. Michelin North America is the second largest tire manufacturer in the United States and around the world. Maintaining North American headquarters in Greenville, South Carolina, the Company employs more than 23,000 skilled individuals in its United States operations. **Career Highlights:** Michelin North America: Manager of Business Analysis (1991-Present), Manager of Brand Forecasting (1989-91); Business Research & Planning, Reliance Electric Company (1984-89). **Associations & Accomplishments:** Treasurer, Foxcroft Homes Association. **Education:** Clemson University: Master's degree in Research and Planning (1977), B.A. (1975). **Personal Information:** Married to Susan in 1974. Three children: Lisa, Adam, and Julie. Mr. McFarlane enjoys soccer, basketball and travel.

Ronald A. Burgess

Manager of Information Systems
IER Industries, Inc.
8271 Bavaria Drive East
Macedonia, OH 44056-2259
(330) 425-7121
Fax: (330) 425-7596
ier@ierindustries.com

3053

Business Information: Mr. Burgess continues to apply his extensive knowledge and expertise in the information technology and engineering fields at IER Industries, Inc. As Manager of Information Systems, he has faithfully served with IER in a variety of capacities since coming on board to the Corporation in 1991. Currently, he is responsible for implementation and management of all data and communications systems. Possessing an excellent understanding of his field, he is in charge of all training, troubleshooting, and project management. Striving for optimal performance, Mr. Burgess intends to gain more knowledge in information systems. His success reflects his managerial ability to aggressively tackle new challenges and responsibilities and deliver results. Established in 1958, IER Industries, Inc. is a manufacturer of precision molded rubber seals. The Corporation currently employs 250 people and serves automotive OEMs and aftermarkets as well as food manufacturing and aerospace industries. Global in scope, the Corporation is presently located in Macedonia, Ohio. **Career Highlights:** IER Industries, Inc.: Manager of Information Systems (1997-Present), Purchasing Production Manager (1995-97), Industrial Engineering Manager (1991-95). **Associations & Accomplishments:** American Production and Inventory Control Society. **Education:** University of Akron, B.S. in Mechanical Engineering (1989); Cuyahoga Community College, AS/400 Operations Management.

Jorge M. Arias

Technical Service Manager
Hules Tecnicos S.A.
Apartado #8-4140/1000
San Jose, Costa Rica
(506) 231-2911
Fax: (506) 231-6523
ariasjo@sol.racsa.co.cr

3069

Business Information: Functioning as Technical Service Manager of Hules Tecnicos S.A., Mr. Arias oversees and directs day-to-day production activities. Before joining Hules Tecnicos in 1993, Mr. Arias served as Industrial Development Manager with CINDE and Technical Manager for Atlas Electrica S.A. In his present position, he ensures effective utilization of manpower and resource, as well as making sure products are lace with quality, value, and selection. As a 17 year engineering professional, Mr. Arias also is in charge of developing strategic and tactical marketing plans, and driving products to market. His success reflects his strong academic background, communicative skills, and his ability to build teams with synergy, technical strength, and a customer oriented focus, in addition to take on new challenges and responsibilities. A Professional Registered Engineer, Mr. Arias' plans are to move up the corporate hierarchy. Hules Tecnicos S.A. engages in the manufacture and distribution of a diverse product line from rubber piping to PCP's. Established in 1980, the Company is local in scope and is located in San Jose, Puerto Rico. Presently, Hules Tecnicos employs a work force of more than 850 people who help generate annual revenues in excess of $36 million. **Career Highlights:** Technical Service Manager, Hules Tecnicos S.A. (Present); Industrial Development Manager, CINDE (1990-93); Technical Manager, Atlas Electrica S.A. (1987-90). **Associations & Accomplishments:** Professional Registered Engineer in Costa Rica. **Education:** Washington University, M.Sc. in Mechanical Engineering (1985); National University, M.B.A. (1989); University of Costa Rica, B.Sc. in Mechanical Engineering (1982). **Personal Information:** Married to Mariella in 1984. Three children: Fernan, Daniella, and Gloriana. Mr. Arias enjoys golf and tennis.

Rob A. Olson

Management Information Systems Manager
Freedom Plastics
1201 Baitinger Court
Sun Prairie, WI 53590
(608) 754-2710
Fax: (608) 754-7583

3084

Business Information: Utilizing more than 25 years of extensive experience in the field of technology, Mr. Olson serves as Management Information Systems Manager for Freedom Plastics. In this capacity, he presides over the networking platform of the Company, performing its administration and maintenance. He ensures that the systems infrastructure is running in an efficient and productive manner and provides a routine backup system and network security to prevent unauthorized access. Mr. Olson is responsible for the Company's technological direction. Continually formulating new goals and objectives, he plans to expedite promotional opportunities through dedication and optimum performance. His success reflects his ability to deliver results and aggressively take on new challenges. Freedom Plastics manufactures residential and commercial PVC pipe and fittings. An approximate work force of 200 skilled factory workers and qualified administrative personnel are employed in the Sun Prairie, Wisconsin location. The Company first began operations in 1976. **Career Highlights:** Management Information System Manager, Freedom Plastics (1997-Present); Programmer/Analyst, APV Crepaco (1991-97); Programmer/Analyst, Thor Enterprises (1988-91); Programmer/Analyst, Quality Systems (1980-88). **Education:** University of Austin, B.S. (1971). **Personal Information:** Married to Trisha in 1978. Two children: Marc. Mr. Olson enjoys skiing and remodeling.

Gary Curry

Software Engineer
Irwin Research and Development
2401 West J Street, Suite A
Yakima, WA 98902-1149
(509) 248-0194
Fax: (509) 452-4909
gcurry@irwinresearch.com

3089

Business Information: Functioning in the capacity of Software Engineer with Irwin Research and Development, Mr. Curry designs and develops systems level software such as machine control and computer user interface. He has served with Irwin Research and Development since coming on board to the Company in 1992. An expert, Mr. Curry works directly with management and users to analzye, design, and specify new, cutting edge software program, as well as monitors and tunes systems software, resolves system debugging problems, and tests all applications. As for the future, Mr. Curry hopes to become involved in animation, graphic design, and Web applications. He lists completing a user language database and a team project as highlights of his career. Irwin Research and Development manufacturers equipment for the plastics industry. Established in 1978, the Company provides jobs to the residents of Yakima, Washington, and the surrounding areas. Currently, the Company employs 350 people. **Career Highlights:** Software Engineer, Irwin Research and Development (1992-Present). **Associations & Accomplishments:** Volunteer Computer Consulting at Church. **Education:** Oregon Institute of Technology, B.S. in Software Engineering (1992). **Personal Information:** Mr. Curry enjoys working with church youth groups and being a church usher.

Daniel W. Gorman

Technical Director, Distance Learning Systems
Nypro, Inc.
101 Union Street
Clinton, MA 01510-2908
(978) 365-8150
Fax: (978) 365-4352
dwgorman@shore.net

3089

Business Information: Serving as Technical Director of Distance Learning Systems for Nypro Inc., Mr. Gorman is responsible for implementing global strategies, and supporting corporate strategic IT objectives. In addition, he performs needs assessments, develops software, and handles troubleshooting. Major accomplishments for him have included the selection of the next generation Real Time GUPTA database Quality Data Analysis System as a global standard, evaluating the existing IBM SNA network and developing a comprehensive strategic plan to deliver new client/server based systems supporting TCP/IP, SNA, and IPX, as well as for designing and implementing router technology to connect all plants to key processing servers (AS-400) through supply partner (MCI) resulting in over $1 million in savings in equipment/software. Nypro, Inc. is engaged in the manufacture of precision plastic components and assemblies. Headquartered in Clinton, Massachusetts, its facility operates with over 90 injection molding machines. Clients include such major companies as Motorola, IBM, Hewlett-Packard, and Johnson & Johnson. Currently employing over 3,000 people, Nypro, Inc. operates 22 facilities in the United States, as well as five overseas branches. **Career Highlights:** Nypro Inc.: Technical Director, Distance Learning Systems (Present), Director of Global Network Technologies (1995), Corporate Manager of Network Technologies/Quality Engineering (1990-95), Quality Engineer (1988-90); Process Engineer Decorating (1983-88). **Associations & Accomplishments:** American Society of Quality Control; Society of Plastics Engineers; Association for Manufacturing Excellence; Former Cub Scout Pack Leader, Boy Scouts of America; Former Pop Wornner Football Coach; Board of Directors, Nypro Chicago, Inc.; Stockholder, Nypro Inc.; Active Blood Donor, Red Cross; Former Life Guard - Rhode Island; Former Red Cross Water Safety Instructor; Rhode Island Governor's Conference; National Plastics Museum; Currently acting as Senior Network Consultant, creating distance learning systems for corporation and University of Massachusetts at Lowel. **Education:** University of Rhode Island, B.S. (1988), M.B.A. program; Nypro Institute Programs; World Management Executive Forum (1990-95); Duke University; Dartmouth College; University of Wisconsin at Madison; University of Limerick, Ireland; Leadership Institute; MRP II. **Personal Information:** Married to Kathleen M. in 1965. Two children: James D. Gorman and Jennifer M. Underwood. Three grandchildren: James Underwood and Jeffery and Joshua Gorman. Mr. Gorman enjoys sailing, golf, playing the guitar and walking with his wife.

Bradley Hedges

Network Engineer
Entegris
102 North Jonathan Boulevard
Chaska, MN 55318-2350
(612) 556-1857
Fax: (612) 556-4077
bhedges@entegris.com

3089

Business Information: Displaying his skills in this highly specialized position, Mr. Hedges serves as a Network Engineer for Entegris. He administrates the corporate network, providing Novell and NT server support and NDS and NT domain structural design and configuration. Before joining Entegris in 1999, Mr. Hedges served as National Technical Support II and Supervisor with DataServ Inc. In his current role, he purchases new hardware and software, installing system applications and software upgrades as needed. Mr. Hedges cites his open-mindedness to new technology as his key to success and stays abreast of advancements in his field by taking classes, specialized training, and reading trade magazines. Presently pursuing additional cross certifications, he is looking forward to entering into the project management arena. Newly formed by a merger between Fluoroware and Empak, Entegris is a manufacturer of plastic components for computers. These components are used in various stages of computer manufacture and are distributed to companies around the world. Boasting $250 million in annual sales, a staff of more than 1,300 skilled workers are employed at the Company's 25 locations. **Career Highlights:** Network Engineer, Entegris (1999-Present); Network Administrator, Fluoroware (1996-99); DataServ, Inc.: National Technical Support II (1994-96), Supervisor (1992-94). **Education:** Brown Institute, Associate's degree (1986); DeVry Institute of Technology. **Personal Information:** Married to Linda in 1985. Two children: Heather and Jessica. Mr. Hedges enjoys softball, tennis and swimming.

Billy D. Torry, Jr.

Sales Engineer
Plaspro (Plastic Provisions Inc.)
3249 Evergreen Road
Sears, MI 49679
(517) 382-7967
Fax: (517) 382-7967
plaspro@earthlink.net

3089

Business Information: Serving as a Sales Engineer for Plaspro, Mr. Torry is responsible for overseeing all day-to-day sales operations. Working out of his home, he visits customers, conducts presentations, indentifies new clients, and fills out purchase orders for the Company. An accomplished professional, Mr. Torry has received recognition for his superior talents in the field of plastics injection molding. In the future, he plans to continue working in his capacity, looking forward to assisting in expansion of the client base. Headquartered in Spring Lane, Michigan, Plaspro sells and distributes products and machinery for the plastics industry. Founded in 1993, the Company sells such items as injection molding machines, robots, part printers, granulators, pad printers, screen printers, screw and barrel components, and mold sprays. International in scope, the Company employs a team of seven professionals. **Career Highlights:** Sales Engineer, Plaspro (1999-Present); Program Manager/Sales Engineer, Pilot Tool, and Die, Inc. (1995-99); Project Engineer, Dott Manufactruing Company (1994-95); Engineer IV, Dow Plastics ETPTS&D (1991-94). **Associations & Accomplishments:** Board of Directors, Mid-Michigan Society of Plastics Engineers; Advisory Board Member, Manufacturing Technology Program; Co-Authored Five Research Publications; Who's Who in Plastics and Polymers; All American Scholar, United States Achievement Academy. **Education:** Ferris State University: B.S. in Plastics Engineering (1991), A.A.S. in Plastics Technology (1990); Certificates: DOE, AUTOCAD, GD&T, Project Management, Plastics Bonding and Leak Testing, Light and Color Measurement, Part Design, APQP, 7 Habits, Effective Negotiating, Internet Marketing, Product Training.

Judi K. Wellnitz

Senior Systems Analyst
Tenneco Packaging
1 Parkway North
Deerfield, IL 60015
(847) 914-1948
Fax: (847) 914-1866
judi_wellnitz@tenneco-packaging.com

3089

Business Information: Providing her skilled services as Senior Systems Analyst of Tenneco Packaging, Ms. Wellnitz assumes responsibility for the Sales and Distribution processes in SAP and other various legacy/external systems. She analyzes business needs, determining which software products can be utilized to its fullest potential within the departmental structure. Designing the programs to be user friendly, she performs its coding, configuration, implementation, and maintenance as well. Striving for quality and demonstrating a love of challenges, her flexibility and diversity in technology and business have always made her an asset to any company or project. She looks forward to increasing her responsibilities in a managerial position, overseeing several project teams. Ms. Wellnitz's success reflects her ability to think outside the box and aggressively tackle new challenges. Founded in 1940, Tenneco is engaged in the manufacture and distribution of packaging and automotive products, both finished and non-finished goods. The Company makes such products as Hefty® brand bags and plates, EZ-Foil® single use aluminum cookware, egg cartons, building products, Monroe® brand shocks and struts, and Walker® brand exhaust systems. Tenneco is in the process of transforming from a conglomerate into two distinct focused, growth-oriented global manufacturing companies-Tenneco Packageing and Tenneco Automotive. Current national operations employ over 50,000 individuals and report $7 billion in annual sales. **Career Highlights:** Tenneco Packaging: Senior Systems Analyst (1999-Present), Systems Analyst (1998-99); Systems/Programmer, Medline Industries (1996-98). **Associations & Accomplishments:** Golden Key National Honor Society; Big Sister Association; Fundraiser, United Way March of Dimes; Fundraiser, Public Broadcasting; Fundraiser, Detroit Museum of Art; Fundraiser, Salvation Army. **Education:** Oakland University, B.S. in Management Information Systems (1994). **Personal Information:** Ms. Wellnitz enjoys travel, billiards, tennis, marathons, dancing and piano.

3100 Leather and Leather Products

3111 Leather tanning and finishing
3131 Footwear cut stock
3142 House slippers
3143 Men's footwear, except athletic
3144 Women's footwear, except athletic
3149 Footwear, except rubber, nec
3151 Leather gloves and mittens
3161 Luggage
3171 Women's handbags and purses
3172 Personal leather goods, nec
3199 Leather goods, nec

Preston K. Tash

Manager of Desktop and Data Communication Services
Dexter Shoe Company
71 Railroad Avenue
Dexter, ME 04930
(207) 924-7341
Fax: (207) 924-7241
tashp@destershoe.com

3144

Business Information: Serving as Manager of Desktop and Data Communication Services of Dexter Shoe Company, Mr. Tash is reponsible for the network infrastructure and personal computer support teams. Possessing an excellent understanding of technology, he oversees his teams in the maintenance of the Company's operating and networking systems functions. A savvy, 18-year veteran, Mr. Tash directed implementation and connectivity of the Microsoft Exchange mail system to all locations. Building networks, e-commerce, implementing SAP, and maintaining Dexter Shoe Company's entire communications infrastructure functionality also fall within the purview of his responsibilities. A visionary who has proven himself on many occasions, his most notable contribution was his role in development of the first T1-based ATM network that won Hannaford Brothers Co. The Smithsonian Award (1998) for technology. Mr. Tash's future endeavors include chasing greater challenges and taking advantage of all opportunities afforded. Operating four locations internationally, Dexter Shoe Company is a major manufacturer of various types of shoes. Specializing in bowling, golf, and men's street shoes, the company's corporate headquarters offices are located in Dexter, Maine. Presently, Dexter Shoe Company employs 1,500 people who are dedicated to providing top quality footwear. **Career Highlights:** Manager of Desktop and Data Communication Services, Dexter Shoe Company (1999-Present); Senior Data Communication Specialist, Hannaford Brothers Company (1990-99); Staff Sergeant, United States Marine Corps (1977-89). **Education:** University of North Carolina, B.S. in Computer Science (1982); North Carolina Community College, A.A. **Personal Information:** Married to Florence in 1998. One child: Bruce. His son Bruce is following in his dad's footsteps, a U.S. Marine stationed in Hawaii.

Jeffrey W. Smith

Principal SAP R/3
Reebok International
549 Wachusett Street
Holden, MA 01520
(508) 849-9081
Fax: (508) 829-7715
jwahlsmith@aol.com

3149

Business Information: As Principal SAP R/3 for Reebok Intenational, Mr. Smith is a SAP R/3, ABAP/4 and BASIS technical consultant responsible for SAP implementation. With a full understanding of all aspects of computer operations and functions, he is able to fulfill his duties in the SAP R/3 technical realm. Mr. Smith assists in discovering the nature of the problem, analyzing the criteria, and making recommendations on a proposed solution. He is able to design new solutions to business, scientific, and data processing systems. His career highlights include working as Chief Technical Architect for the Pentagon in the 1980s, reworking and implementing six major SAP projects around the globe, and becoming certified in two technical areas of SAP. Attributing his success to his adaptability, Mr. Smith's future plans are to stay in his current position and expand his knowledge base. The second largest maker of athletic shoes in the United States, Reebok International specializes in a variety of athletic shoes for everything from basketball and volleyball to aerobics. Headquartered in Stoughton, Massachusetts, Reebok reports annual revenues in excess of $3.6 billion. **Career Highlights:** Principal SAP R/3, Reebok International (1999-Present); SAP R/3 Consultant, IBM Corporation (1998-99); Principal SAP R/3 Consultant, Digital Equipment Corporation (1997-98); SAP Strategic Consultant, Plaut Consulting, Inc. (1996-97); SAP R/3 Basis Consultant, Siemens AG (1995-96). **Associations & Accomplishments:** Great Book Foundation; U.S. Chess Federation; Institute for Certification of Computer Professionals. **Education:** Babson College, M.B.A. (1981); Bentley: B.S. in Computer Science, B.S. in Q.U.; C.M.D., Management Institute; Worchester Polytechnic: C.D.P., C.C.P.; Assumption; I.B.M., I.S.G.C., M.P.C.S.P.; Harvard/Nathan-Tyler; Belllabs, ADP; Carnegie Institute, C.E.S.H.R. **Personal Information:** Mr. Smith enjoys being a Class A chess champion of New England.

3200 Stone, Clay, and Glass Products

3211 Flat glass
3221 Glass containers
3229 Pressed and blown glass, nec
3231 Products of purchased glass
3241 Cement, hydraulic
3251 Brick and structural clay tile
3253 Ceramic wall and floor tile
3255 Clay refractories
3259 Structural clay products, nec
3261 Vitreous plumbing fixtures
3262 Vitreous china table and kitchenware
3263 Semivitreous table and kitchenware
3264 Porcelain electrical supplies
3269 Pottery products, nec
3271 Concrete block and brick
3272 Concrete products, nec
3273 Ready-mixed concrete
3274 Lime
3275 Gypsum products
3281 Cut stone and stone products
3291 Abrasive products
3292 Asbestos products
3295 Minerals, ground or treated
3296 Mineral wool
3297 Nonclay refractories
3299 Nonmetallic mineral products, nec

Jacqulin R. Washington

Information Technology Manager
PPG Industries, Inc.
P.O. Box 2200
Huntsville, AL 35804-2200
(256) 859-8165
Fax: (256) 859-8115
jwashington@ppq.com

3231

Business Information: Ms. Washington serves as Information Technology Manager for PPG Industries, Inc., strategic business unit (SBU) Aircraft Produts, located in Huntsville, Alabama. She is responsible for the overall management of information technology resources for the Aircraft Transparenies business, and for developing information technology solutions to address business opportunities, and provide value added. The transparencies business includes ballistics for amored automobiles and all aircraft, such as helicopters, airplanes, and military aircraft. Ms. Washington functions as an innovator, in leading her SBU in electronic commerce, Internet, Website, electronic credit card, Euro conversion, and LAN and WAN technologies. After Y2K remediation is complete, the goal will be to continue supporting manufacturing and providing support in the expansion of business opportunities with technology. PPG Industries, Inc. is a Fortune 100 company headquartered in Pittsburgh, Pennsylvania with SBU's in North America, Europe, and Australia. Other SBU's are coatings and resins, flat and fiberglass and chemicals plants. PPG was established in 1883, and as a multinational with over 38,000 emplyees world wide, is a leader in manufacturing. **Career Highlights:** Information Technology Manager, PPG Industries, Inc. (1996-Present); Data Center Branch Manager, Oklahoma Department of Mental Health (1994-96); Programmer Analyst, Hertz Corporation (1975-93). **Associations & Accomplishments:** Leadership Oklahoma City; Leadership Huntsville and Madison County; Junior Achievement; Delta Sigma Theta Sorority Inc.; Huntsville Library Volunteer; Past YMCA Board Chairperson; Past Member, Oklahoma Commission on the Status of Women (1990-94); United Way. **Education:** University of Central Oklahoma, M.B.A. (1990); Langston University, B.A. **Personal Information:** Two daughers: Tiannia Washington, an engineering student at Georgia Tech and Regin Tarver, an elementary student. Ms. Washington enjoys history, history and volunteerism.

Taft H. Thomas

Information Systems Technician
Mansfiled Plumbing Products
P.O. Box 472
Kilgore, TX 75662
(903) 984-3525
Fax: (903) 930-3899
tthomas@mansfieldplumbing.com

3261

Business Information: Serving as Mansfiled Plumbing Products' Information Systems Technician since 1998, Mr. Thomas provides support and repair for the computer systems used at two company locations. Demonstrating an extensive technical knowledge, he handles LAN and WAN administration, maintaining optimal operating conditions for both to ensure corporate communications and transmissions are successful. He oversees the database, handling routine maintenance and upgrades to contribute to the effectiveness of the Company. Recgonized for his superior abilities, Mr. Thomas is in charge of telecommunications including video conferencing, alphanumeric pagers, and cellular phones. With a versatility that has long been admired by his superiors, he directs quality control, guiding employees with ease and lending his insight on complex issues to facilitate smooth production. Citing military experience as the firm foundation he has built his career on, Mr. Thomas attributes much of his success to professional contacts in the industry. Looking forward to assisting in the completion of future corporate goals, he aspires to the position of manager of information systems as he continues his education. Established in 1949, Mansfiled Plumbing Products manufactures china products for restrooms such as toilets and sinks. Employing 325 people at the Kilgore, Texas location, the Company maintains five facilities througout the United States. The Company is headquartered in Columbus, Ohio and is recognized throughout the industry as a quality provider of value priced products, that consistently completes commercial contracts accurately and efficiently. **Career Highlights:** Information Systems Technician, Mansfield Plumbing Products (1998-Present); Warranty Repair Manager, Sweeney's Micro Systems (1996-98); Data Systems Technician, United States Navy (1989-95). **Education:** Kilgore College (Currently Attending); Central Texas College; United States Navy Technical Schools. **Personal Information:** Married to Lisa in 1997. One child: Devon. Mr. Thomas enjoys hunting and fishing.

Steve Kalmar

Data Processing Supervisor
Southdown, Inc.
2601 Saturn Street, Suite 200
Brea, CA 92821-6702
(714) 985-4097
Fax: (714) 985-4081
skalmar@southdown.com

3273

Business Information: Mr. Kalmar functions in the capacity of Data Processing Supervisor for Southdown, Inc. He is responsible administering and controlling all aspects of Southdown's data resources. An expert, Mr. Kalmar has faithfully served with the Corporation in a variety of roles since coming on board in 1976. Having over two decades of experience within Southdown, he has advanced to his current position where he monitors the computer activities of the offices, as well as oversees and directs all data processing and communications. Mr. Kalmar is responsible for 12 remote locations of the Corporation and assists 45 users in the operation of their systems. Currently attending classes with Microsoft, Mr. Kalmar is looking forward to obtaining his Microsoft certification. Ensuring data integrity, security, and reliability; eliminating redundancy; and fine tuning system tools to improve data performance also fall within the realm of is responsibilities. His success reflects his dedication to his work and enjoyment of what he does. Southdown, Inc. was founded in 1930 and has grown to become one of the largest companies of its kind. Ranked second in the United States for its size, the Corporation was recently ranked among Fortune 500 businesses. The Corporation has over 1,000 employees with over 100 locations throughout the United States. Involved in the manufacturing of cement and ready-made concrete mixes, the Corporation has several mining locations across the country to extract raw materials such as sand and gravel. **Career Highlights:** Data Processing Supervisor, Southdown, Inc. (1976-Present). **Education:** Fairleigh Dickenson University (1972-76). **Personal Information:** Married to Lillian in 1977. Two children: Jennifer and Stephen Jr. Mr. Kalmar enjoys woodworking and landscaping.

Venkatesha Babu

President
Innosoft Inc.
39 Lavender Drive
Edison, NJ 08820
(908) 757-4116
svenkatesha@hotmail.com

3291

Business Information: Combining management skills and technical expertise, Mr. Babu serves as President of Innosoft Inc. He is responsible for a number of daily functions on behalf of the Corporation and its clientele. In his capacity, he is accountable for consulting services, business promotions, marketing, and sales as well as recruiting of new employees. Drawing from more than seven years of consulting experience, Mr. Babu utilizes his extensive knowledge and expertise to implement policies and procedures that are incorporated into all business operations. His plans for the future include remaining with Innosoft in order to continue taking bold steps toward expansion and growth in the intenational arena. Innosoft Inc. engages in the provision of professional business and technology services to a wide range of vertical businesses including insurance, banking, financial, and telecommunications. The Corporation offers software development, Web design, and consulting. Established in 1996, the Corporation is located in Edison, New Jersey, and functions under the guidance of eight people dedicated to providing quality services for the advancement of business operations. **Career Highlights:** President, Innosoft Inc. (1996-Present); Consultant/Architect, Prudential (1997-Present); Consultant, Dun & Bradstreet (1996-97); Senior Consultant, Sybase Inc. (1993-96). **Education:** Mysore University, Bachelor's degree in Engineering (1980). **Personal Information:** Married to Bhanushree in 1984. Two children: Sneha and Sharath. Mr. Babu enjoys golf, music and television.

3300 Primary Metal Industries

3312 Blast furnaces and steel mills
3313 Electrometallurgical products
3315 Steel wire and related products
3316 Cold finishing of steel shapes
3317 Steel pipe and tubes
3321 Gray and ductile iron foundries
3322 Malleable iron foundries
3324 Steel investment foundries
3325 Steel foundries, nec
3331 Primary copper
3334 Primary aluminum
3339 Primary nonferrous metals, nec
3341 Secondary nonferrous metals
3351 Copper rolling and drawing
3353 Aluminum sheet, plate, and foil
3354 Aluminum extruded products
3355 Aluminum rolling and drawing, nec
3356 Nonferrous rolling and drawing, nec
3357 Nonferrous wiredrawing and insulating
3363 Aluminum die-castings
3364 Nonferrous die-casting exc. aluminum
3365 Aluminum foundries
3366 Copper foundries
3369 Nonferrous foundries, nec
3398 Metal heat treating
3399 Primary metal products, nec

Richard T. Dixon

Manager of Process Control
LTV Steel
3001 Dickey Road
East Chicago, IN 46312
(219) 391-2224
Fax: (219) 391-3367
rtdixon@usa.net

3312

Business Information: Serving as Manager of Process Control for LTV Steel, Mr. Dixon oversees the computer systems and control processes for the Company. He leads the programming and networking staff as well as developing some software programs utilized by the plant. With the Company for more than two decades, Mr. Dixon supervises his staff with a style of management that incorporates employee feedback and respect of fellow employees. In the future, Mr. Dixon plans to remain with the Company and move into an information technology position working more with the technical aspect of operations. Attributing his success to perseverance, his advice is "learn as much as you can, never stop learning." LTV Steel is a manufacturer of rolled steel. Having held strong through two world wars and the great depression, the Company was established in 1859. Today, the Company is the third largest steel producer in the United States. After the merger of LTV and a major tubular producer, it became the largest tubular producer in the world. Serving an international market, the Company employs over 12,000 individuals to carry out operations on a daily basis. **Career Highlights:** LTV Steel: Manager of Process Control (1994-Present), Area Manager of Quality Control (1987-94), Manager of Chemical Labs (1979-87). **Associations & Accomplishments:** Association of Iron and Steel Engineers; American Society of Metals. **Education:** Keller Graduate School of Business (In Progress); University of Pittsburgh, B.S. in Chemistry (1971). **Personal Information:** Married to Jacqueline in 1974. Four children: Jessalyn, Steven, Joell, and Clark. Mr. Dixon enjoys computers and automobile restoration.

John S. Post

LAN Administrator
U.S. Steel-Clairton Works
400 State Street
Clairton, PA 15025
(412) 233-1491
Fax: (412) 233-1813
jspost@uss.com

3312

Business Information: Serving as LAN Administrator for U.S. Steel-Clairton Works, Mr. Post maintains all aspects of the local area network used by the Plant. Offering PC/LAN support to over 300 computers, he utilizes his practical work experience to develop innovative technical solutions for troubleshooting tasks. Recognized for his impressive abilities in the information technology field, Mr. Post has been credited with the success of several LAN projects including upgrades and program implementations. Focusing on the future, Mr. Post relies on his faith in Jesus Christ to help support him throughout his life and his career. U.S. Steel-Clairton Works manufacturers steel and steel products, then distributes them around the United States. Established in 1901, the national Company has successfully maintained a hold on the domestic industry by continually reviewing strategic business planning. **Career Highlights:** LAN Administrator, U.S. Steel-Clairton Works (Present). **Education:** California University of Pennsylvania, B.S. (1992); A+ Certification; Network+ Certification. **Personal Information:** Married to Kathleen in 1994. Two children: Rachel and John Howard. Mr. Post is the son of John H. and Kim Post and the brother of Cameron Post.

Peter Santucci, III

Information Systems Manager
G.O. Carlson Inc.
P.O. Box 526
Thorndale, PA 19372-0526
(610) 383-3420

3312

Business Information: As Manager of Information Systems for G.O. Carlson Inc., Mr. Santucci supervises the daily activities of technical operations while managing new application development. Guiding his staff with personal experience and leadership by example, he implements the plans formulated by the cohesive efforts of his team. Internally recognized for his managerial abilities, Mr. Santucci also serves as a member of the executive committee, helping to make corporate strategic decisions. Attributing professional and academic success to logical problem solving and the proper application of Information Science principles, Mr. Santucci looks forward to guiding the Corporation towards e-commerce activities. He believes the challenge for future application development projects will involve he successful replacement of Legacy applications without interrupting daily operations. Mr. Santucci believes that the following steps are critical to the successful completion of application development projects; formal definition of short term and long term goals, structured application design, managed projects, programmer discipline by adhering to established coding standards, corporate support with funding for staff and training, modular and highly confirmable applications, multiple team member projects, integrated applications and databases to serve all primary corporate departments and processes, proper management of end-user expections and the assignment of developers to functions not entire applications. G.O. Carlson Inc. manufactures stainless steel, nickel alloys, and titanium products. Established in 1936, this national corporation maintains two locations that employ a total of 300 people. **Career Highlights:** Manager of Information Systems, G.O. Carlson Inc. (1998-Present); Project Director, Emtec Inc. (1996-98); Technical Manager, Roy F. Weston Inc. (1985-96). **Education:** Pennsylvania State University, M.S. (1996); Drexel University, B.S. (1985). **Personal Information:** Married to Susan Lehotsky II in 1987. Mr. Santucci enjoys personal computing, history and philosophy.

Kerry G. Farney

Systems Analyst
I/N Tek
30755 Edison Road
New Carlisle, IN 46552
(219) 654-1366
Fax: (219) 654-1536
kgfarn@ibm.net

3316

Business Information: Mr. Farney serves as a Systems Analyst for I/N Tek. He is responsible for all aspects of I/N Tek's business computer infrastructure. Before joining I/N Tek in 1993, Mr. Farney was employed as Assistant Systems Engineer at Dravo Automation Sciences. In his current role, he oversees time lines and schedules, as well as shipping and recording production results. Working with a group of 14 people, Mr. Farney ensures quality products and services. His focus is to ensure products are laced with quality, value, and selection. As a solid, nine year technology professional, he received a promotion in 1996 for working out the "bugs" in a Company-wide system. His career success reflects his overall positive attitude, continuous self-improvement efforts, and never being satisfied with staying the same. Mr. Farney is presently involved in providing cutting edge interfacing and data to a scheduling project. He plans on continuing to play a major role in the Company's growth and expansion nationally and internationally. A joint venture of Ispat Inland and Nippon Steel, I/N Tek manufactures cold rolled steel for the appliance and automotive industries. Located in New Carlisle, Indiana, I/N Tek was established in 1989 and has a sister Company called I/N Kote. Over 500 people are currently employed by I/N Tek. **Career Highlights:** Systems Analyst, I/N Tek (1993-Present); Assistant Systems Engineer, Dravo Astromotion Sciences (1990-93). **Education:** Indiana University Northwest, M.B.A. (In Progress); Purdue University Calumet, B.S. in Electrical Engineering (1990). **Personal Information:** Married to Robin in 1997. Mr. Farney enjoys basketball, chess and computers.

Allen D. Williams

Maintenance Engineer
Ward Manufacturing Inc.
406 Fairway Avenue
Elmira, NY 14904-2404
(570) 638-2131
Fax: (570) 638-2113
alewms@aol.com

3321

Business Information: As Maintenance Engineer of Ward Manufacturing Inc., Mr. Williams oversees a number of engineering duties on behalf of the Company and its clientele. He is responsible for all aspects of support of foundry operations, maintenance on cranes, breathable air, and oven atmosphere systems, CAD drawings, and process improvements. Heading a team of engineers, he enforces Company regulations and standards, oversees workflows, and solves problems to eliminate any negative impact on production. Possessing an excellent understanding of his field, Mr. Williams, is in charge of training seminars and he is also a member of the safety committee. Committed to quality workmanship and client satisfaction, he is involved in troubleshooting and providing efficient solutions to problematic areas. The most rewarding aspect of his career is the development of a test booth for the waterproofing of subway cars. He attributes his success to faith and he believes if it wasn't for God watching out for him, he wouldn't be here. Furthering his growth with the Company, Mr. Williams's goals include attaining the position of information technology manager and publishing a technical paper. A major manufacturer of cast iron pipefittings, Ward Manufacturing Inc. was established in 1924. Dedicated to producing only top quality products, the Company has never experienced failure in its 75-year existence. Employing over 1,000 experienced personnel, Ward Manufacturing offers in-depth training and supervision in order to provide a more efficient work environment. Directly dealing engineering support for various industries, the Company guarantees complete client satisfaction. **Career Highlights:** Maintenance Engineer, Ward Manufacturing Inc. (1995-Present); Production Engineer, ABB Traction (1988-94);

Manufacturing Process Engineer, Sprague Electric (1980-87); Contract Research & Development Engineer, Xerox (1973-79). **Associations & Accomplishments:** Society of Manufacturing Engineers; The Gideons International. **Education:** Rochester Institute of Technology, B.S. in Physics (1973). **Personal Information:** Married to Sharon in 1989.

Joseph D. Vitelli

Information Systems Manager
Howmet Corporation
1 Howmet Drive
Hampton, VA 23661
(757) 825-7972
Fax: (757) 827-1831
jvitelli@howmet.com

3324

Business Information: Mr. Vitelli serves as Information Systems Manager of Howmet Corporation. Demonstrating his extensive technical knowledge of the idustry, he leads his staff with a proactive style of management as he incorporates their feedback and input into the creation of standard operating policies. Working closely with his highly trained team, Mr. Vitelli oversees the programming of automated and robotic computer factory controls. He maintains all computer systems within the Company, handling upgrades and software implementation as well as troubleshooting tasks. Headlining the Y2K project for the past several years, Mr. Vitelli has been credited with several impressive technical achievements within the corporate structure. Attributing his success to his motto to always put the customers first, he looks forward to continual success in his position. Currently, Mr. Vitelli has plans to integrate the Internet and production systems, offering manufactured parts through Web page orders. Headquartered in Connecticut, Howmet Corporation is a manufacturer of investment casting of gas turbine engine parts. Major clients include GE, Pratt Whitney, and Boeing; the Corporation's reputation of value and quality allows high profile clients to be assured of services. The Corporation maintains 20 facilities worldwide; since opening in 1924, the billion dollar company has expanded the corporate roster to include over 10,000 employees. **Career Highlights:** Information Systems Manager, Howmet Corporation (1999-Present); Regional Manager, Goodman Infonology Services (1997-99); Computer Engineer, Tidewater Computer Services (1995-97); Computer Engineer, Tomar Management Services (1993-95). **Associations & Accomplishments:** Hampton Roads Technology Council C-10 Forum. **Education:** St. Leo University, B.A. (1991). **Personal Information:** Married to Janice in 1990. One child: Jessica.

Angela Lynn Barr

Engineering Information Systems Manager
ALCOA Engineered Products
53 Pottsville Street
Cressona, PA 17929-1222
(570) 385-8646
Fax: (570) 385-8804
barral@sf.alumax.com

3341

Business Information: With a Bachelor's degree in Computer Sciences, Ms. Barr utilizes her extensive background in her position as an EIS Manager with a strong background in software engineering. With ALCOA Engineered Products for five years, she is responsible for the design, implementation, and success of computer integrated manufacturing. Her duties include managing a team whose duties include database design and administration, network design and implementation, and application design and implementation. Ms. Barr is currently managing and designing applications on Windows NT and UNIX operating systems and utilizes Oracle and SQL Server databases. Ms. Barr currently manages a technical team of four and hopes to expand ALCOA's technologies through expanded and more diverse applications. ALCOA is the world's leading producer of aluminum and alumina, participating in all major segments of the industry. The company is organized into 21 business units, with 249 operating locations, and 100,000 employees in 30 countries. **Career Highlights:** Engineering Information Systems Manager, ALCOA Engineered Products (1999-Present); Software Engineer, ALCOA Engineered Products (1995-99); Programmer/Analyst, CSIU (1992-95); Systems Administrator Pocono Medical Center (1989-92). **Associations & Accomplishments:** National Female Executive Association; Attendance/Child Accounting Professional Association of Pennsylvania; Technical Advisory Committee, Schuylkill County, Pennsylvania; Technical Advisor Committee, Berks Technical Institute. **Education:** East Stroudsburg Universtiy. B.S. in Computer Science (1992); American Research Group, Certificate in TCP/IP Network Analysis; Extensive Oracle and UNIX training with accompanying certificates. **Personal Information:** Married to Robert in 1996. Ms. Barr enjoys motorcycle racing, archery, golf and racquet ball.

Ryan Leon Hart

Training and Communications Coordinator
Vanalco, Inc.
210 West 41st Street
Vancouver, WA 98660
(360) 696-8651
Fax: (360) 696-8778

3341

Business Information: As the Training and Communications Coordinator for Vanalco, Inc., Mr. Hart fulfills a number of duties on behalf of the Corporation. A successful seven year veteran, he develops classroom and computer based, interactive CD-Rom training programs. Possessing an excellent understanding of his field and communicative skills, Mr. Hart oversees and coordinates all internal communications, such as newsletters, CCTV, and translations. His knowledge of the training process is utilized to enhance employee performance and increase production. In the future, Mr. Hart aspires to a position in human resources management, and he cites as the most rewarding aspect of his career is watching others grow. Vanalco, Inc. specializes in aluminum smelting. The Corporation distributes aluminum to a variety of manufacturers to be used in the production of doors, boats, and cans. Established in 1987, the Corporation employs a work force of 650 employees to orchestrate all activities of design, manufacture, testing, and research. Located in Vancouver, Washington, the Corporation sells its products to a national clientele. **Career Highlights:** Training and Communications Coordinator, Vanalco, Inc. (1995-Present); Field Director, Psi Upsilon International Fraternity (1993-95); Intern, Mosey/Hunt (1993). **Associations & Accomplishments:** Rotary International; Trout Unlimited; American Society for Training and Development Cascadia Chapter; Clark College Worker Retraining Committee; Elected Precinct Committee Officer. **Education:** Oregon State University, M.Ed. (2000); Washington State University, B.A. in Communication (1993). **Personal Information:** Married to Diane in 1999.

M. Parker Finney III

Technical Director
Outokumpu American Brass
P.O. Box 981
Buffalo, NY 14240
(716) 879-6924
Fax: (716) 879-6987
parker.finney@outokumpu.com

3351

Business Information: As the Technical Director of Outokumpu American Brass, Mr. Finney is responsible for a number of duties on behalf of the Company. Supervising metallurgical issues and re-engineering processes, he is charged with maintaining quality in products and services offered by the Company. In this context, he ensures that lab functions are performed according to policy in order to eliminate errors, thus leading to quality products. Mr. Finney's skills and knowledge are utilized in a hands-on management style that instills confidence in his staff and promotes optimum performance. In the future, he plans to continue in his present role, facilitating continued Company growth. His success is attributed to his analytical ability to piece information together. Outokumpu American Brass is a manufacturer of copper and brass sheet and strip for the electronics, automotive, telecommunications, and other industries. The Company maintains three divisions of stainless steel, copper, and metal manufacturers that are used for tubing, ammunition, electronics, and automotive parts. Established in 1906, the Company employs a dedicated staff of individuals to meet the demands of a growing clientele. Headquartered in Finland, Outokumpu American Brass serves clients internationally. **Career Highlights:** Outokumpu American Brass: Technical Director (1999-Present), Senior Metallurgical Engineer (1996-99), Senior Process Engineer (1994-96). **Education:** Lafayette College, B.S. in Metallurgical Engineering (1982). **Personal Information:** Married to Susan in 1982. Two children: Jason and Matthew. Mr. Finney enjoys golf, softball and landscaping.

Patricia A. Shannon

System Analyst
Alcan Aluminum Corporation
390 Griswold Street NE
Warren, OH 44483-2738
(330) 841-3127
Fax: (330) 841-3144
trish.shannon@alcan.com

3354

Business Information: Mrs. Shannon currently serves as a Systems Analyst for the Alcan Aluminum Corporation. Dedicated to the success of the Corporation, she utilizes more than 19 years of experience in the information technology field. She assumes responsibilities for keeping the current Human Resource Package (application) current and up-to-date. She has also been committed to the support of the Accounts Payable Systems throughout the Corporation. Additionally, Mrs. Shannon also oversees the administration of the smaller accounting systems of purchase orders, back up accounts, and the receivable general ledger. She is committed to continued optimum service and looks forward to assisting in the completion of future corporate goals. Her success reflects her ability to think outside the box and deliver results. The Alcan Aluminum Corporation is a publicly traded aluminum manufacturing company. Headquartered in Montreal, Canada, the Corporation produces various aluminum products from numerous plants around the world. An approximate work force of 99,100 workers are employed globally. The Warren, Ohio location serves as a warehouse storage site in addition to its manufacturing operations. **Career Highlights:** Alcan Aluminum Corporation: System Analyst (1988-Present), Computer Operator (1981-88). **Associations & Accomplishments:** Coitsville Township Volunteer Fire Department; Coitsville Township Volunteer Fire Department Ladies Auxillary; Union Township Volunteer Fire Department; Mahoning Township Volunteer Fire Department; Mahoning Valley Fire Fighters Association; Lawrence County Fire Fighters and Fire Chiefs Association. **Education:** Youngstown State University, A.A.S. (1986). **Personal Information:** Married to Dale in 1995. One child: Nicole.

Dimitrios Stathopoulos

RF Design Engineer
Phillips Broad Band Network
141 Avon Road
Syracuse, NY 13206
(315) 682-9105

3357

Business Information: Serving as RF Design Engineer for Phillips Broad Band Networks since 1997, Mr. Stathopoulos designs amplifiers and researches new technology. In addition, he runs simulations on equipment and creates and resolves problems. The most rewarding aspect of his career is receiving full Time Warner acceptance of his customed amplifiers. Possessing an excellent understanding of technology, Mr. Stathopoulos attributes his success to being in the right place to take advantage of an enterprising opportunity. Future plans for Mr. Stathopoulos is to achieve a position of senior engineer with a systems programming department and to update his skills. His success reflects his ability to think outside the box, take on challenges, and deliver results on behalf of the Company. Phillips Broad Band Networks builds custom amplifiers and head end fiber optic receivers for cable television. Established in the 1900s, the Company is headquartered in New York and employs 1,000 skilled technicians, installers, and administrative personnel utilizing their creative skills to generate annual revenues in excess of $230 million. **Career Highlights:** RF Design Engineer, Phillips Broad Band Network (1997-Present). **Associations & Accomplishments:** Triple IE. **Education:** Clarkson University: B.A. (1991), B.S. in Electrical Engineering. **Personal Information:** Mr. Stathopoulos enjoys reading, computers and basketball.

John C. Bennett

Network Administrator
Ravenna Aluminum
5159 South Prospect Street
Ravenna, OH 44266
(330) 296-9053
Fax: (330) 296-1921
jbennett@fsigroup.com

3365

Business Information: Demonstrating expertise in the technology field, Mr. Bennett functions as Network Administrator for Ravenna Aluminum. He assumes responsibility for the network infrastructure, performing systems programming, monitoring daily activities, and providing routine backups. Before joining Ravenna, Mr. Bennett served as Computer Programmer with Nashbar & Associates and Computer Consultant, EMT, and Dispatcher for Pellin EMS Inc. Coordinating future resources, time lines, schedules, and assignments also fall within the scope of his responsibilities. Mr. Bennett was recognized by the Company for designing a state-of-the-art Web site and continues to oversee its development. He believes that the reason for his success is that he enjoys his job and has fun just working and learning. Anticipating an upwards move into management, he eventually intends to own his own consulting firm or computer company. Established in 1949, Ravenna Aluminum is an aluminum casting manufacturer. The castings are sold to automotive manufacturers and are used primarily for the heads and other engine parts. Over $10 billion in sales are reported annually and the factory staff consists of 950 workers. **Career Highlights:** Network Administrator, Ravenna Aluminum (1997-Present); Computer Programmer, Nashbar & Associates (1995-96); Computer Consultant/EMT/Dispatcher, Pellin EMS Inc. (1991-Present). **Associations & Accomplishments:** National Association of EMTS; American Radio Relay League; Amateur Radio Emergency Service; Radio Amateur Civil Emergency Service; Mahoning Valley A.R.A.; National Academy of Emergency Medical Dispatch. **Education:** Youngstown State University, B.S. in Administration (1991). **Personal**

Information: Mr. Bennett enjoys ham radio, severe storm chasing and fire department EMS activities.

3400 Fabricated Metal Products

3411 Metal cans
3412 Metal barrels, drums, and pails
3421 Cutlery
3423 Hand and edge tools, nec
3425 Saw blades and handsaws
3429 Hardware, nec
3431 Metal sanitary ware
3432 Plumbing fixtures fittings and trim
3433 Heating equipment, except electric
3441 Fabricated structural metal
3442 Metal doors, sash and trim
3443 Fabricated plate work (boiler shops)
3444 Sheet metal work
3446 Architectural metal work
3448 Prefabricated metal buildings
3449 Miscellaneous metal work
3451 Screw machine products
3452 Bolts, nuts, rivets, and washers
3462 Iron and steel forgings
3463 Nonferrous forgings
3465 Automotive stampings
3466 Crowns and closures
3469 Metal stampings, nec
3471 Plating and polishing
3479 Metal coating and allied services
3482 Small arms ammunition
3483 Ammunition, exc. for small arms, nec
3484 Small arms
3489 Ordnance and accessories, nec
3491 Industrial valves
3492 Fluid power valves and hose fittings
3493 Steel springs, except wire
3494 Valves and pipe fittings, nec
3495 Wire springs
3496 Misc. fabricated wire products
3497 Metal foil and leaf
3498 Fabricated pipe and fittings
3499 Fabricated metal products, nec

Debra Kraft

Systems Administrator
ABB Alston Power
1755 South Battleground Avenue
Kings Mountain, NC 28086-9237
(704) 739-9513
Fax: (704) 739-3349
debra.a.kraft@us.abb.com

3443

Business Information: Serving in the dual role of Assistant Controller and Information Systems Administrator of ABB Alstom Power, Ms. Kraft is responsible for cost accounting and reconcilliation and reporting financial progress to the financial controller. In addition, she oversees the company's information systems infrastructure, maintaining it in a fully functional and operational status. A savvy systems expert, Ms. Kraft also installs operating systems software, database management systems software, compilers, and utilities. Monitoring and tuning systems software, peripherals, and networks as well as resolving systems difficulties also fall within the scope of her responsibilities. Her accomplishments include upgrading the entire system for the Company and providing user classes. Looking to the future, Ms. Kraft would like to go back to school and become a controller. Her professional success is attributed to her great sense of pride and unwavering dedication. ABB Alstom Power is an international pressure part manufacturer for power plants. The Company specifically produces power boiler components for large electrical utilites. Located in King's Mountain, North Carolina, the Company employs a 150 professional, technical, and administrative support staff. **Career Highlights:** Assistant Controller/Information Systems Administrator, ABB Alstom Power (1997-Present); Plant Accountant, New Cherokee Corporation (1996-97); Accounting Manager, New York Twist Drill (1990-96). **Education:** Hofstra University, B.B.A. (1978). **Personal Information:** Ms. Kraft enjoys golf and bowling.

Raul Ruiz

Lead Manufacturing Engineer
Honeywell-Thermal Systems
510 West Aten Road
Imperial, CA 92251
(760) 355-3587
Fax: (760) 355-3640
raul.ruiz@honeywell.com

3443

Business Information: Mr. Ruiz serves as the Lead Manufacturing Engineer for Honeywell-Thermal Systems. He manages the actual processes optimization and new products introduction to the plant. Possessing an excellent understanding of his field, Mr. Ruiz supervises a staff of seven engineers and guides them in all aspects of daily activities. Demonstrating his organizational skills, he is responsible for compiling and managing project and fiscal budgets. He attributes his success to being a responsible person and his ability to take on new challenges and deliver results on behalf of the Company and its clientele. The most rewarding aspect of his career is reducing the rates for the Company. His plans for the future include attaining the position of manufacturing or product engineering manager at Honeywell-Thermal Systems. Established in 1989, Honeywell-Thermal Systems manufactures aluminum and copper heat exchangers. Recently, the Company started manufacturing cooper nickle heat exchangers. Headquartered in Porrance, California, the Company presently employs 550 skilled individuals. Reported estimated sales for the Company exceed $80 million annually. **Career Highlights:** Honeywell-Thermal Systems: Lead Manufacturing Supervisor (1999-Present), Pre-Production Supervisor (1997-99), Manufacturing Engineer (1995-97), Production Supervisor (1994-95). **Associations & Accomplishments:** Asociacion de Profesionistas Egresados del Cetys. **Education:** Cetys University, B.S. (1993). **Personal Information:** Married to Karla Cardenas in 1997. One child: Ana Paola. Mr. Ruiz enjoys travel, reading and house upgrading.

Steven M. Spiegel

Field Service Engineer
Babcock & Wilcox
12970 Pandora Drive, Suite 203
Dallas, TX 75238
(214) 348-7509
Fax: (214) 221-2565
smspiegel@pgg.mcdermott.com

3443

Business Information: Mr. Spiegel serves in the capacity of Field Service Engineer at Babcock & Wilcox. A savvy professional, he consults with clients, providing services in the field to analyze and resolve problems with boiler systems and related equipment. Mr. Spiegel is also responsible for modifications and upgrades as well as assisting other engineers in maintenance and repairs. Drawing from his expertise in the field, he provides information of the technical aspects of the industries to clients. Remaining with Babcock & Wilcox and moving up the corporate structure is cited as Mr. Spiegel's career goals. His success is attributed to having an open mind and having the ability to deliver results and take on challenges. "Understand the specific industry you are getting into," serves as his advice to others. Since 1867, Babcock & Wilcox has been manufacturing boilers for the industrial and utilities industries. The Company's location in Dallas, Texas provides services to clients in Oklahoma, Texas, Louisiana, and Arkansas. Presently, the Company employs a work force of more than 2,000 individuals to oversee all aspects of day-to-day operations. **Career Highlights:** Field Service Engineer, Babcock & Wilcox (1998-Present); Technical Service, Wyeth Ayerst Pharmaceuticals (1998); Undergraduate Research Assistant, Clarkson University (1997-99). **Associations & Accomplishments:** American Chemical Society. **Education:** Clarkson University, B.S. in Chemical Engineering (1999). **Personal Information:** Mr. Spiegel enjoys ice hockey and music.

Mark G. Langford

Management Information Systems Technician
Southeastern Metals Manufacturing Company
11801 Industry Drive
Jacksonville, FL 32218
(904) 696-2507
Fax: (904) 696-4237
mglangford@semetals.com

3444

Business Information: Demonstrating his expertise in the field of information technology, Mr. Langford serves as Management Information Systems Technician for Southeastern Metals Manufacturing Company. He administers the network for 110 users, maintaining the servers, workstations, and e-mail as well as offering systems usage training. Additionally, he is in charge of the Company's phone systems, performing in house cabling and configuration. Mr. Langford developed an interest in the technology field through his computer games. Always keeping his eyes open for new opportunities, he stays on top of new advancements in the industry by constant reading and networking with colleagues. He is continually striving to improve his performance and looks forward to receiving his MCSE and future business ownership. His success reflects his ability to aggressively take on new challenges. A subsidiary of Gibraltar Steel, Southeastern Metals Manufacturing Company manufactures metal material such as metal sheeting to be used in the construction industry. The Company has eight locations across the country, employing the services of over 750 individuals. Founded in 1964, national operations boast yearly sales of $150 million. **Career Highlights:** Management Information Systems Technician, Southeastern Metals Manufacturing Company (1996-Present); Multilayer Engineer, Source Technology, Inc. (1992-96). **Education:** Draughn's College (1996). **Personal Information:** Mr. Langford enjoys computers, golf, horses and swimming.

Andrew M. Stebenne

Process Engineering/CNC Programmer
Pike Tool & Grinding
4205 High Contry Road, P.O. Box 7729
Colorado Springs, CO 80933
(719) 598-9611
Fax: (719) 598-9614
andy@piketool.com

3444

Business Information: Serving as Pike Tool & Grinding's Process Engineer and CNC Programmer, Mr. Stebenne's main responsibilities are to send and receive files from customers and do layout for N/C punch for CAD Systems. He also serves as a concrete solid designer. A savvy, 15 year technical expert, he is also responsible for manual layouts, flat patterns, prototype parts, plot out prints, software systems, and TWI. Mr. Stebenne has served with the Company in a variety of positions, teaching himself everything he needed to know for the various positions in which he served. In the future, he would like to go to school to receive his B.A. in Drafting so that he will have the opportunity to run the engineering department of the Company. "Stick with it, taking the good with the bad. It'll all happen," is cited as Mr. Stebenne's credo. Pike Tool & Grinding engages in precision sheet metal fabrication including machining plate and paint and assembly. The Company uses lasters to build full service flat pice metal, x-ray cabinets, prototype parts, and provide a very quick turnaround. Established in 1968, the Company employs 150 individuals and reports annual sales of $15 million. **Career Highlights:** Pike Tool & Grining: Process Engineer/CNC Programmer (1990-Present), Inspection (1985-90). **Associations & Accomplishments:** Industry related. **Education:** High School Diploma. **Personal Information:** Mr. Stebenne enjoys being an avid jet skier.

James A. Walker

Systems Manager
WAHLCO Engineered Products, Inc.
29 Lexington Street
Lewiston, ME 04240
(207) 784-2338
Fax: (207) 784-1338
jawalker@wepinc.com

3444

Business Information: Following 17 years of distinguished service in the United States Army, Mr. Walker joined WAHLCO Engineered Products, Inc. in 1991 as Systems Manager. He is responsible for implementing and administrating all computer systems, networks, servers, and telephone systems. Coordinating the activities of his assistants and assigns their projects, Mr. Walker motivates them towards success and is on hand to provide them with the necessary knowledge to complete their tasks. As a 25 year professional, Mr. Walker computerized the Corporation, bringing it from a 12-unit operation to a 60 permanent and 12 laptop computer facility. He is enthusiastic about his career and works to stay abreast of technology through seminars and coursework related to the field. His career success reflects his ability to produce results and aggressively take on new challenges. WAHLCO Engineered Products, Inc. is a manufacturer of pollution control and environmental protection products. Some of these products include gas flow diverters, dampers, metal, and fabric expansion joints. Over 100 employees staff the location in Lewiston, Maine, one of 10 locations across the United States. Dedicated to the design and production of more effective supplies, each employee is devoted to brainstorming activities and team events. Through the combined efforts of the team, the Corporation turns over $16 million every year. **Career Highlights:** Systems Manager, WAHLCO Engineered Products, Inc. (1991-Present); United States Army: Telecommunications NCOIC (1990-91), Telecommunications Supervisor (1974-90). **Associations & Accomplishments:** Association of Systems Manager; Stanton Bird Club. **Education:** Southern Illinois University at Edwardsville: B.S. (1991), Associates degree in Business

(1974). **Personal Information:** Two children: Lynda Preston and Heather Evenson. Mr. Walker enjoys birdwatching and nature photography.

Richard Owrey

Director of Information Systems
Ellwood Group Inc.
800 Commercial Avenue
Ellwood City, PA 16117
(724) 752-3523
Fax: (724) 752-9711
rdo@egi.elwd.com

3462

Business Information: As Director of Information Systems with Ellwood Group Inc., Mr. Owrey determines the overall strategic direction and business contribution of the information systems function. Working at the corporate headquarters, he oversees and directs larger off site divisions and their staff ensuring systems functionality and fully operational status. An information systems professional with 13 years in the industry, Mr. Owrey handles all day-to-day administration and operational activities, including analysis, design, development, implementation, and project management. Coordinating resources, time lines, schedules, assignments, and budgets also are an integral part of his functions. His success reflects his leadership ability to build teams with synergy and aggressively take on new challenges. WAN implementation and updating the Corporation's infrastructure serves as his career highlights. Getting through Y2K, expanding more into Europe, and continuing to grow through mergers and acquisitions is cited as Mr. Owrey's future business objectives. Having a large skilled work force of 900 people, Ellwood Group Inc. is a manufacturing venture related to the steel industry. A parent company, Ellwood Group encompasses seven business units specializing in melting plants, forging, and casting. The products produce are sold to companies in capital equipment and automotive industries. Established in 1910, Ellwood Group generates annual revenues in excess of $280 million. **Career Highlights:** Director of Information Systems, Ellwood Group Inc. (1997-Present); Management Information Systems Manager, Ellwood Engineered Castings (1992-97); Systems Analyst, Ellwood City Forge (1986-92). **Education:** Youngstown State University, M.B.A. (1995); University of Pittsburgh, B.S. in Computer Science. **Personal Information:** Married to Karen in 1991. Two children: Lindsey and Jason. Mr. Owrey enjoys sports and travel.

Ramon G. W. Van Kallen

Managing Director
Continental Forge Company
P.O. Box 4789
Compton, CA 90224-4789
(949) 955-3935
Fax: (310) 898-1074
rvk@cforge.com

3463

Business Information: Relying on strategic leadership skills and extensive technical expertise, Mr. Van Kallen functions in the role of Managing Director for Continental Forge Company. At his post, he oversees and directs all aspects of the day-to-day administration and operational activities of the management information systems department. He determines the overall strategic direction and business contribution of the information systems function. A savvy, 24-year expert in the field, Mr. Van Kallen is responsible for infrastructure development and architecture and is in charge of Web site hosting functions. He ensures that all these aspects of the Company function in a seemless manner, thereby keeping the Company at maximum production. Providing network computing and consulting services also fall within the purview of Mr. Van Kallen's responsibilities. As for the future in the 21st Century, he looks forward to eventually attaining the position of vice president of development in the engineering software realm and becoming more involved with HRIS Systems Management. Success, Mr. Van Kallen asserts, is due to having highly supportive parents. Continental Forge Company forges and casts aluminum for aerospace travel industries. Employing 250 people in the Compton, California area, the Company has gained visibility within the market for its superior services. Since 1968, the Company has seen its profits rise, and currently, Continental Forge Company produces in excess of $25 million in annual revenues. **Career Highlights:** Managing Director, Continental Forge Company (1997-Present); Senior Systems Integrator, Integrated Network Services (1996-97); Network Supervisor, Children's Hospital of Los Angeles (1987-96); Biomedical Engineering Manager, Brotman Medical Center (1979-87). **Associations & Accomplishments:** Masonic Order; Shriners of Los Angeles; Society of Biomedical Engineers; Society for Laser Technology; Chairs the Executive Management Meetings of Continental Forge. **Education:** New York University, B.S. in Biomedical and Computer Science Engineering; New York Community College, A.A.S. in Civil Engineering (1975). **Personal Information:** Three children: Kirsten L., Seane, and Rochelle. Mr. Van Kallen enjoys bicycling, horses, being an equestrian, tennis and voice-over.

Kathleen Fox

Information Systems Manager
Michigan Spring and Stamping
2700 Wickman Drive
Muskegon, MI 48441
(231) 755-1691
Fax: (231) 755-3449
mskathyfox@aol.com

3469

Business Information: Serving as the Information Systems Manager for three years, Mrs. Fox utilizes her vast knowledge of computer management in order to provide professional systems support at Michigan Spring and Stamping. Responsible for governing of help desk operations, she concentrates her efforts towards hardware and ERP software set up, and maintaining the Company's LAN/WAN architecture. Providing systems support for the Company's main computer database, Mrs. Fox also supports information systems of other various divisions of the Company in other states. Offering research and development, she maintains a state-of-the-art system performing upgrades when necessary. Continuing her growth with Michigan Spring and Stamping, Mrs. Fox strives towards gaining the position of Manager over the complete corporate wide system. Specializing in the manufacturing and distribution of coil springs and stampings, Michigan Spring and Stamping was established in 1948. Located in Muskegon, Michigan, the Company employs a knowledgable staff of 150 who focus their production towards meeting the needs of the Company's continuously expanding client base. Implementing new technologies into development and production, the Company remains dedicated to the widening of their product line. **Career Highlights:** Michigan Spring and Stamping: Information Systems Manager (1999-Present), Junior Programmer (1997-99). **Education:** Baker College, Associate's degree (1998); Muskegon Community College. **Personal Information:** Married to William in 1986. Two children: Robert Bultema and Chris Bultema. Mrs. Fox enjoys gardening and wood working.

Robert Bordonaro

Technical Engineer
Sulzer Metco
1101 Prospect Avenue
Westbury, NY 11590-2724
(516) 338-2589
Fax: (516) 338-2558

3479

Business Information: Mr. Bordonaro is a Technical Engineer in the document management department of Sulzer Metco. He provides technical support for engineering and troubleshooting difficulties involving hardware and software. Involved with programming logic controller, he is currently upgrading internal document design software applications as well as conducting product research and development. A savvy, six year veteran of technology, Mr. Bordonaro also has been instrumental in upgrading the Company's ERP system, designing new internal document management software applications, and performing research and development to enhance all equipment available to the Company. His goals include continuing his education in software codes; getting more involved in design work; and gaining more knowledge, thus making himself essential to a growing company. Mr. Bordonaro attributes his career success to being open-minded to suggestions. A global company based in Manhattan, New York, Sulzer Metco was established in the 1940s. The Company's international headquarters is located in Switzerland. Currently, 200 employees man daily operations and help generate annual sales in excess of $350 million. Sulzer Metco specializes in the production of thermal spray coating products used in numerous applications, such as aircraft, jet engines, and bridges. **Career Highlights:** Sulzer Metco: Technical Engineer (1997-Present), Technical Specialist (1996-97); Reprographic Specialist, L.P.S.I. (1994-96). **Associations & Accomplishments:** Society of Manufacturing Engineers. **Education:** State University of New York at Farmingdale: Bachelor of Technology in Manufacturing Engineering (1994), Associate's degree in Mechanical Engineering. **Personal Information:** Mr. Bordonaro enjoys time with his fiancée, outdoor activities, mountain biking and sports.

Vicki Lynn Godsey

PC Support Technician
Royal Ordnance North America
4509 West Stone Drive
Bloomingdale, TN 37660-1048
(423) 578-6165
Fax: (423) 578-6130
godsey_vl@holston-app.com

3489

Business Information: As PC Support Technician for Royal Ordnance North America, Mrs. Godsey is responsible for all computer support functions. A savvy, 19-year veteran of the technology field, she is accountable for the systems infrastructure including hardware, software, and Internet and Intranet support as well as upgrade and maintenance activities. In addition, Mrs. Godsey coordinates the strategic planning of users technical needs and provides training and computer support throughout the Plant. A systems expert, she is A+ certified and is currently working on her Networking + certification. Future implementation of a new MRP system at the Plant will also enable her to focus more on database administration. Originally getting her career start on Telex and mainframe systems, Mrs. Godsey's technical success can be attributed to her ambition and growth opportunities afforded to her by the Company. A British owned firm, with the parent company being BAE Systems, Royal Ordnance North America is a contractor for the Holston Army Ammunition Plant. The Company engages in the manufacture of explosives for the U.S. Army. Established in 1999, the North American location employs approximately 120 individuals. **Career Highlights:** PC Support Technician, Royal Ordnance North America (1999-Present); PC Support Technician, Holston Defense Corporation (1981-99). **Associations & Accomplishments:** Phi Theta Kappa at Northeast State Technical (1991); Named to Who's Who Among American High School Students (1975). **Education:** Northeast State Technical Institute: A.A.S. in Management Information Systems, A.A.S. in Business Management; Computing Technology Industry Association, Certified Service Technician (1998). **Personal Information:** Married to Terry Lynn in 1997.

Nicholas L. Gee

LAN Support Manager
TYCO Valves & Control
650 Spice Islands Drive
Sparks, NV 89431
(775) 359-4100
ngee@tyco-valves.com

3491

Business Information: Serving as LAN Support Manager of Tyco Valves & Control, Mr. Gee monitors the Company's remote sites on the West coast of the United States. He is responsible for systems security and reliability, engineering research and development, and troubleshooting. Possessing an excellent understanding of his field, he also assists in the design and implementation of new, state-of-the-art sites. Mr. Gee recommends purchases of advanced eqiupment and maintains user access as well as user accounts. He has responsibility of five WAN sites and Windows NT and 2000 support. Highly regarded, he began his technology education at the age of 14, when he started to build computers from scratch. In the future, Mr. Gee hopes to venture on his own, building a communications company from scratch, handling a wide variety of tasks. His professional success is attributed to his supportive team, his mentors, and his hardwork ethic. Tyco Valves & Control is a manufacturer of valves and control products to regulate the flow of various liquids and gases. A very large corporation, the Company distributes its product line internationally. Located in Sparks, Nevada, the Company presently employs a work force of more than 135 people. **Career Highlights:** LAN Support Manager, Tyco Valves & Control (2000-Present); Technician Level 1, West Teleservices Corporation (1998-00). **Associations & Accomplishments:** Vocational Industrial Clubs of America; Nevada State Champion for Computer Imaging (1996). **Education:** Glennhare Technical (1993-96). **Personal Information:** Mr. Gee enjoys movies, snowboarding and technology.

Kendra Bender

Information Technology Project Manager
Tipper Tie
2000 Lufkin Road
Apex, NC 27502
(919) 362-8811

3496

Business Information: Starting in public accounting and gravitating to information technology, Ms. Bender serves as Information Technology Project Manager for Tipper Tie. She is responsible for the management of information technology projects and systems strategies. She also has responsibility for integrating e-commerce and technologies with the existing infrastructure. Continually striving for maximum effectiveness, Ms. Bender is currently pursuing her M.B.A. to enable her to capitalize on the opportunities in the IT industry. She attributes her succes to smart outsourcing. Headquartered in Apex, North Carolina, Tipper Tie is a package closure solutions company. As a manufacturer of capital equipment and clips, the Company provides products to a worldwide market. Founded in 1953, and currently staffing 550 individuals, Tipper Tie accomodates their customers by housing companies in Chicago and Germany. **Career Highlights:** Information Technology Project Manager, Tipper Tie (1997-Present); ERP Consultant, Caelus, Inc. (1989-96); Auditor, Coopers & Lybrand (1986-88). **Education:** Gonzaga University, B.A. in Public Accounting (1986). **Personal Information:** Ms. Bender enjoys new technology strategies.

Claudia Kueffel

Technical Sales Manager
Leoni Kabel GmbH & Company KG
Muenchenerstr. 116A
Roth, Germany 91154
+49 9171804115
Fax: +49 403603247387
claudiakueffel@aol.com

3496

Business Information: Highly skilled in the field of technology, Mrs. Kueffel serves as Technical Sales Manager with Leoni Kabel GmbH & Company KG. Holding her current position since 1995, she extends her vast knowledge to overseeing project development operations. In her involvement with the administration, Mrs. Kueffel focuses on turning potential into action through preparation and skilled training. Establishing high standards of excellence for others in the industry, she remains up to date in all current applications of new technologies. Continuing her career with Leoni Kabel GmbH & Company KG, Mrs. Kueffel looks forward to assisting in the achievement of future goals. She also aspires to attain the position of department head or move into one of the Company's foreign offices. Serving an international client base, Leoni Kabel GmbH & Company KG is dedicated to providing a variety of cables and cable networks for the automotive and technology industries. Established in 1917, the Company currently employs a staff of 16,000 qualified personnel to serve the diverse needs of its clientele. Headquartered in Roth, Germany, the Company branches out of 60 operational facilities around the world. **Career Highlights:** Technical Sales Manger, Leoni Kabel GmbH & Company KG (2000-Present); Customer Services Manager, Leonische Drahtwerke AG (1995-2000); Secretary to Marketing Development Services, MSD Sharp & Dohme GmbH (1991-93).**Associations & Accomplishments:** MFC Neustadt e.V. (RC Aircrafts). **Education:** Business degree (2000); Language School, Translator and Interpreter for French and English (1987). **Personal Information:** Mrs. Kueffel enjoys swimming, reading and decorating.

Keith A. Parker

Manager of Information Systems
Inca Metal Products
501 East Purnell Road
Lewisville, TX 75057
(972) 436-5581
Fax: (972) 436-7901
keith@incametals.com

3499

Business Information: Functioning in the capacity of Manager of Information Systems with Inca Metal Products, Mr. Parker is responsible for all of the Company's hardware, software, and acquisition upgrades. Directly supervising one employee, he designs, develops, and implements the software network for 65 users. Before joining Inca Metal Products, Mr. Parker served with Virginia KMP Corporation as an Information Systems Manager. His solid background history also includes stints as Senior Programmer and Analyst for Centrex Oil and Programmer and Analyst at Mercantile Bank of Dallas. A systems expert, Mr. Parker credits his professional success to a well rounded personality, as well as his ability to aggressively take on new challenges. Dedicated to the growth and expansion of the Company, he is planning to increase the Department's staff in the near future. Serving the state of Texas, Inca Metal Products is a manufacturer of industrial rack and shelving. Established in 1980, operations employ the skilled services of 300 personnel. **Career Highlights:** Manager of Information Systems, Inca Metal Products (1997-Present); Information Systems Manager, Virginia KMP Corporation (1987-97); Senior Programmer/Analyst, Centrex Oil (1984-87); Programmer/Analyst, Mercantile Bank Dallas (1980-84). **Education:** Wichita State University, B.B.A. (1976). **Personal Information:** Mr. Parker enjoys music education.

3500 Industrial Machinery and Equipment

3511 Turbines and turbine generator sets
3519 Internal combustion engines, nec
3523 Farm machinery and equipment
3524 Lawn and garden equipment
3531 Construction machinery
3532 Mining machinery
3533 Oil and gas field machinery
3534 Elevators and moving stairways
3535 Conveyors and conveying equipment
3536 Hoists, cranes, and monorails
3537 Industrial trucks and tractors
3541 Machine tools, metal cutting types
3542 Machine tools, metal forming types
3543 Industrial patterns
3544 Special dies, tools, jigs and fixtures
3545 Machine tool accessories
3546 Power-driven hand tools
3547 Rolling mill machinery
3548 Welding apparatus
3549 Metal working machinery, nec
3552 Textile machinery
3553 Woodworking machinery
3554 Paper industries machinery
3555 Printing trades machinery
3556 Food products machinery
3559 Special industry machinery, nec
3561 Pumps and pumping equipment
3562 Ball and roller bearings
3563 Air and gas compressors
3564 Blowers and fans
3565 Packaging machinery
3566 Speed changers, drives, and gears
3567 Industrial furnaces and ovens
3568 Power transmission equipment, nec
3569 General industrial machinery, nec
3571 Electronic computers
3572 Computer storage devices
3575 Computer terminals
3577 Computer peripheral equipment, nec
3578 Calculating and accounting equipment
3579 Office machines, nec
3581 Automatic vending machines
3582 Commercial laundry equipment
3585 Refrigeration and heating equipment
3586 Measuring and dispensing pumps
3589 Service industry machinery, nec
3592 Carburetors, pistons, rings, valves
3593 Fluid power cylinders and actuators
3594 Fluid power pumps and motors
3596 Scales and balances, exc. laboratory
3599 Industrial machinery, nec

Stan J. Schultes

Information Technology Manager
Sun Hydraulic Corporation
1500 West University Parkway
Sarasota, FL 34243
(941) 362-1278
Fax: (734) 448-2957
stans@sunhydraulics.com

3511

Business Information: Mr. Schultes serves as Information Technology Manager of Sun Hydraulic Corporation. He is responsible for the design of the Company's Web site as well as content. Possessing an excellent understanding of his field, he designs and develops data warehouse applications and ensures the functionality and operational status of the manufacturing system infrastructure. A visionary, Mr. Schultes' highlights include publishing columns for Visual Basic Programmer Journal; and being selected as head of a product strategy task force, modyfing business to integrate supply chain management technology. He attributes his career success to chasing and pushing all technological advances, and experimenting with new ideas. His future plans are to use the Web for advertising and marketing data warehousing technology, attracting potential clients to the Company. Established in 1970, Sun Hydraulic Corporation is a hydraulic component manufacturer. The Corporation manufactures hydraulic screw cartridge valves and hydraulic manifolds for use in hydraulic power applications for example, forklifts and logging equipment. The products are distributed to customers nationally. Sun Hydraulic Corporation is located in Sarasota, Florida and employs 800 skilled technicians. Presently, the Corporation reports annual revenues in excess of $80 million. **Career Highlights:** Information Technology Manager, Sun Hydraulics Corporation (1999-Present); Technical Manager, SunOpTech, Ltd. (1995-99); Project Engineer, Corning, Inc. (1981-95). **Associations & Accomplishments:** Microsoft Certified Professional in Visual Basic. **Education:** Purdue University, B.S. in Computer Engineering (1981). **Personal Information:** Married to Laurie in 1980. Two children: Tyler and Erik. Mr. Schultes enjoys high adventure sports.

James German

WAN Administrator
Wartsila NSD Corporation
201 Defense Highway, Suite 100
Annapolis, MD 21401
(410) 573-2150
Fax: (410) 573-2200
james.german@wartsila.nsd.com

3519

Business Information: Serving as the WAN Administrator of Wartsila NSD Corporation, Mr. German is responsible for all LAN and WAN networks throughout the Western Hemisphere. Installating and maintaining hardware and software, he administers and controls seven WANs in North America, South America, the Caribbean, and Guam. Possessing an excellent understanding of network technology, Mr. German manages information traffic, audits, and new LANs as well as provides assistance to technical support personnel. Troubleshooting network usage and computer peripherals, performing backups and recovery operations, and resolving WAN communications problems also fall within the scope of Mr. German's responsibilities. Attributing his success to a desire to learn and his good work ethics, he plans to continue working in this capacity. Wartsila NSD Corporation manufactures and provides service and maintenance of diesel engines. The Corporation provides products to power plants and cruise lines. Engines are used as backup power for large industrial organizations. Employing over 1,300 personnel, the Corporation reports estimated annual revenue of $1.7 billion. **Career Highlights:** WAN Administrator, Wartsila NSD Corporation (1998-Present); Network Specialist, ATG, Inc. (1997-98); Consultant, Predators (1994-97); United States Army (1989-94). **Associations & Accomplishments:** Parent Teachers Association. **Education:** Westminster High School, Diploma (1989). **Personal Information:** Married to Kary in 1997. One child: Austin. Mr. German enjoys spelunking, hiking and rock climbing.

Galen C. Blankers

Engineer
Dethmers Manufacturing Company
4010 320th Street
Boyden, IA 51234
(712) 725-2311
Fax: (712) 725-2446
galen.blankers@demco-products.com

3523

Business Information: Displaying his skills in this highly specialized position, Mr. Blankers serves as an Engineer for Dethmers Manufacturing Company. He has been a key member of the Company since 1983, and is currently responsible for installation and maintenance of the Company's computer based network, including associated peripherals. As a savvy, 16 year professional, Mr. Blankers effectively applies his extensive skills in performing electrical work, training personnel, teaching classes, and assisting the computer aided design operators. Working with users and management, he analyzes and designs new solutions to harness more of the computer's power, and helps Dethmers Manufacturing remain at the forefront in the industry. His professional success reflects his ability to think out-of-the-box and aggressively take on new challenges and responsibilities. Continue moving forward in the information technology and engineering realms serves as Mr. Blankers' future endeavors. Dethmers Manufacturing Company manufactures a full line of agriculture products, car trailers, wagons, appliance carts, field sprayers, and tow bars. Established in 1950, the Company employs the skilled services of 250 individuals who orchestrate design, manufacture, quality control, and the distribution of products. **Career Highlights:** Engineer, Dethmers Manufacturing Company (1983-Present); Emergency Medical Services Instructor, Northwest Iowa Community College (1995-Present). **Associations & Accomplishments:** Boyden Iowa Area Fire, Ambulance, and Rescue; Matlock Iowa Fire and Emergency Medical Services. **Education:** Northwest Iowa Community College, E.M.T. (1992); A.S. Manufacturing Engineer Technology; Presently working on M.C.S.E certification. **Personal Information:** Married to Denise in 1984. Three children: Elizabeth, Craig, and Christopher.

Nathan J. Misirian

Manager of Information System Training
Case Corporation
5729 Washington Avenue
Racine, WI 53406
(414) 636-7108
Fax: (414) 636-7776
nmisirian@casecorp.com

3523

Business Information: Mr. Misirian functions in the role of Manager of Information System Training for Case Corporation. He is responsible for all of the Corporation's PC and information technical computer training in North America and Ireland. Quickly establishing his presence in the technology field, Mr. Misirian has served with Case in a variety of positions since coming on board as Information Systems Technical Education Strategist in 1997. A systems expert, he is involved in designing the curculum, implementing new training systems, and upgrading the present training curricula. Mr. Misirian spoke at a national conference on how to implement computer based training for global companies. Remaining within the training realm and becoming a leader in Web based training serves as his future objectives. His success is attributed to his practical experiences, technical certifications, and higher education, as well as his ability to deliver results and take on new challenges. Serving an international client base, Case Corporation was founded in 1883. The Corporation is engaged in the manufacture of agricultural and construction equipment such as tractors and combines, in addition to financial services and loans for various business industries. There is presently a work force of 17,000 employees that are hired to orchestrate all activities of design, manufacture, and the distribution of products to clients all over the world. Annual sales are reported at $6 billion. Headquarters are located in Racine, Washington. **Career Highlights:** Case Corporation: Manager of Information

Systems Training (1999-Present), Information Systems Technical Education Strategist (1997-99); Management Information Systems Director, Shepherds Home (1995-97). **Associations & Accomplishments:** National Member, American Society for Training & Development; Education & Technical Guidance to Racine School Board, Community Technical Advisor Committee; Education Committee, Racine Area Manufacturer & Commerce Association. **Education:** University of Wisconsin at Milwaukee, M.S. in Management Information Systems (In Progress); Cedarville College, B.A. in Education; Certified Network Engineer, Novell Education. **Personal Information:** Married to Julie in 1994. Mr. Misirian enjoys sailing, travel, consulting to small business on technology needs, water skiing and reading.

Stephen C. Quist

Information Technology Analyst
John Deere Company
*11145 Thompson Avenue
Lenexa, KS 66219
(913) 310-8614
Fax: (913) 310-8348
quiststephenc@jdcorp.deer*

3523

Business Information: Demonstrating expertise in the technology field, Mr. Quist serves as Information Technology Analyst for the John Deere Company and he is responsible for a wide variety of duties involving technical support. Highly regarded, his primary functions include managing accounts, access requirements, proper user audits, departmental access, and documentation of NAAMC security procedures. With more than 30 years of technological experience, Mr. Quist utilizes his superior intellect and professional talents to pave his way to a position in upper management. His success reflects his ability to take on challenges and deliver results on behalf of the Company and its international clientele. John Deere Company engages in the manufacturing, marketing, and sale of large agricultural equipment, such as lawnmowers, garden tractors, mulchers, and other farming vehicles. Established in 1846, the Company is headquartered in Illinois, and operates out of a number of international subsidiaries. The Company functions under the direct guidance and expertise of more than 1,250 highly skilled professionals at the Lenexa, Kansas facility. **Career Highlights:** John Deere Company: Information Technology Analyst (1998-Present), Online Systems Coordinator (1981-88), Senior Computer Operator (1974-81); Computer Operations Supervisor, Nation Car Rental (1967-74). **Associations & Accomplishments:** Association for Systems Management; Association for Couples Marriage Enrichment; Foundation for Fathers; Chemical Dependancy Facilitator. **Education:** University of Minnesota (1970). **Personal Information:** Married to Glenna in 1981. Three children: Natalie, Heather, and Kirstin. Mr. Quist enjoys neighborhood computer assistance, bowling, cards and chuch activities.

Alan R. Fedele

Management Information Systems Manager
Zagar Inc.
*24000 Lakeland Boulevard
Euclid, OH 44132-2646
(216) 731-0500
regal@lakestream.net*

3546

Business Information: As Management Information Systems Manager of Zagar Inc., Mr. Fedele is responsible for hardware and software installation and maintenance for the AS400 operating system. He oversees all day-to-day administration and operational activities of the systems infrastructure. Currently, Mr. Fedele is involved in the applications necessary to complete the system upgrade to a PC based, NT system. He also serves as a vendor liaison for design, development, and implementation. Mr. Fedele credits his career successes to his perseverance throughout life, and that plays a key role in the training of his staff personnel. Perseverance has provided him with patience and willingness to achieve his goals. In the future, Mr. Fedele is striving to become a Consultant within the Corporation and further his education within the Industry. The Corporation was established in the midst of the Great Depression, in 1936, and survived that global economic catastrophe to employ 85 personnel since expanding business operations. Zagar Inc. is located in Euclid, Ohio, a suburb that is home to more than 55,000 people in the northeastern Cleveland metropolitan area. The Corporation concentrates on the designing, manufacturing, and shipping of unique tools for customers Internationally. The largest sales item for the Corporation is their manufactured multi-head spindle drills. **Career Highlights:** Management Information Systems Manager, Zagar Inc. (1991-Present); Supply Corps, United States Navy (1965-91). **Education:** Temple University, M.S. in Business Administration; Lakeland Community College, certified in LAN, C/C++, RPG (1998). **Personal Information:** Married to Deborah M. in 1984. One child: Regina. Mr. Fedele enjoys golf and playing bridge.

Jason A. Pryor

Webmaster
Greenlee Textron
*4455 Boeing Drive
Rockford, IL 61109
(815) 397-7070
Fax: (815) 397-8289
jpryor@greenlee.textron.com*

3546

Business Information: Educated in the field of computer science, Mr. Pryor serves as Webmaster for Greenlee Textron. In this capacity, he assumes responsibility for the design, development, and maintenance for the Web sites of the Company's four divisions, Greenlee, Klauke, Fairmont, and Datacom, the Corporate Intranet and Extranet, as well as the E-Commerce. Directly supervising four employees, coordinating resources, time lines, schedules, assignments, and strategic planning also fall within the purview of his responsibilities. Before joining Greenlee Textron in 1998, he served as Internet Consultant with Digicom Global. Mr. Pryor enjoys his job as a Webmaster and feels that enjoyment of one's work is the key to professional success. He anticipates his promotion to Director of E-Commerce as a result of his continuing efforts to increase his skills through training and professional development activities. Greenlee Textron was founded in 1862 and is an electrical tool manufacturer. A subsidiary of Textron, the Company employs a workforce of 4,200 people. Last year, annual earnings were reported to be upwards of $250 million. **Career Highlights:** Webmaster, Greenlee Textron (1998-Present); Internet Consultant, Digicom Global (1994-98). **Associations & Accomplishments:** Microsoft Beta Tester; Planet IT Contributor; CMP Advisory Board; HTML Writers Guild; Strategic Enterprises Knowledge Center Foundation. **Education:** Rockford College, B.S.in Computer Science (1999); Rockvalley College; Cardinal Stritch University; Net Guru Technologies: Certified Internet Webmaster Professional Administrator, Microsoft and Novel Certifications. **Personal Information:** Mr. Pryor enjoys spending time with kids, golf, tennis and running.

Vincent W. Kwan, Ph.D.

Staff Chemist
Marconi Data Systems, Inc.
*326 Inverrary Lane
Deerfield, IL 60015
(630) 860-7300
Fax: (630) 616-3622
kwan_vincent@marconidata.com*

3555

Business Information: Serving as Staff Chemist of Marconi Data Systems, Inc., Dr. Kwan joined the Corporation in 1995 and is responsible for research and development of new cutting edge technology. Producing ink formulations by combining various chemicals and testing, he is extensively involved in the implementation of new technologies in product development. Coordinating with various suppliers, Dr. Kwan maintains a proper supply of materials necessary for all aspects of research and production. Utilizing over 12 years of experience in chemistry and 5 years in inkjet production, Dr. Kwan remains an invaluable asset to Marconi Data Systems. Highly regarded by his colleagues, he currently owns four patents. Looking to the future, Dr. Kwan aspires to eventually become manager of the chemistry department and take inkjet technology to a new level. A leading manufacturer of Novel inkjet printers and accessories, Marconi Data Systems, Inc. has been serving an international client base since its opening in 1975. Headquartered in Deerfield, Illinois, the Corporation employs 1,300 expert designers and technicians devoted towards providing specialized products to major accounts in the industrial area. **Career Highlights:** Staff Chemist, Marconi Data Systems, Inc. (1995-Present). **Associations & Accomplishments:** American Chemical Society; Society for Image Display. **Education:** University of Minnesota, Ph.D. (1992); University of Hong Kong, B.S. with Honors. **Personal Information:** Dr. Kwan enjoys reading.

Hans-Bernd Boettger, Ph.D.

Manager
Battenfeld Extlenrusionstechnik GmbH
*Bromberger Str. #8
Bad-Muender, Germany 31848
+49 5731242271
Fax: +49 5731242571
boettger.h@bex.battenfeld.com*

3559

Business Information: Serving as Manager for Battenfeld Extlenrusionstechnik GmbH, Dr. Boettger presides over the completion of all information technology administration and operational tasks. He helps develop the strategic direction and formulate business plans to keep the Company on the cutting edge and out-front of competitors. A highly successful, 26-year professional, Dr. Boettger oversees and directs information systems activities at three locations in Germany. A key player in the Company, he reports directly to the head of commercial affairs, keeping top management informed on all adverse trends. Satisfied with his current position, Dr. Boettger plans to remain with the Company, continuing efforts to increase his skills through training and professional development activities. His success reflects his leadership ability to aggressively take on challenges and deliver results. Battenfeld Extlenrusiontechnik GmbH is a mechanical engineering company specializing in extrusion systems. Established in 1980, the Company builds machines for extrusion of plastic pipes and profiles. With three locations throughout Germany, the Company employs 450 staff members to facilitate every aspect of design, manufacture, quality assurance, and distribution of products. Serving an international clientele, the Company reports $85 million in annual sales. **Career Highlights:** Manager, Battenfeld Extlenrusionstechnik GmbH (1991-Present); Head of Technical Calc. & EDP., Damp Herzeugerbau (1986-91); Collaborator, Academy of Sciences of GDR (1974-82); Collaborator, Polish Academy of Science (1975-79). **Associations & Accomplishments:** Deutsch-Polnische Gesellschaft der Bundesrepublich Deutschland e.v.; Deutsch-Japanische Gesellschaft Hannover-Chado-Kai e.V. **Education:** Technical Sciences, Institute of Fund, Ph.D.; University of Lublin, M.Sc. in Math (1974); Technological Problems of Polish Academy of Sciences. **Personal Information:** Married to Alicja Dziedzic in 1973. One child: Kora. Dr. Boettger enjoys tea and astronomy.

Cathy N. Riley, C.N.E., M.C.P., A.S.E.

Management Information Systems Manager
SPX Corporation
*8001 Angling Road
Portage, MI 49024
(616) 329-7844
Fax: (616) 324-7541
criley@spxateg.com*

3559

Business Information: Ms. Riley serves as the Management Information Systems Manager of the SPX Corporation. As the technical services leader, she manages the Kalamazoo and Wayland, Michigan and Montpelier, Ohio divisions of SPX. Relying on the help of her staff, she oversees the telecommunications, network, Intranet, Internet, e-commerce infrastructures, and supports over 500 users throughout the United States and Canada. Possessing systems savvy and expertise, Ms. Riley is responsible for over 15 remote access servers. She also handles the administrative end of her division, taking care of database support and the enterprise resource planning system, Boan. Having dedicated herself to the SPX Corporation, Ms. Riley intends to get involved in the sales and consulting sectors of SPX. Her aspirations include obtaining her Master's degree and eventually holding a chief information officer's position. The SPX Corporation is an automotive diagnostic and test equipment manufacturer. All products manufactured are distributed to automotive dealerships and maintenance garages worldwide. The Portage, Michigan division of the Corporation specializes in service solutions and amplitude modulation tool and equipment. A combined staff of over 5,000 members contribute their knowledge and experience to assist the SPX Corporation in maintaining an annual revenue in excess of $2.5 billion. **Career Highlights:** Management Information Systems Manager, SPX Corporation (1999-Present); Technical Services Specialist, Secant Technologies (1993-98). **Associations & Accomplishments:** National Associaiton for Female Executives. **Education:** Western Michigan University, Bachelor's degree (1995); Certified Netware Engineer, Novell; Microsoft Certified Professional; Accredited Systems Engineer, Compaq.

Chris Rosivach

Senior Designer
Davis Standard/HES
*11 Extrusion Drive
Paucatuck, CT 06379
(860) 599-1756
Fax: (860) 599-8893
crisuvach@davis-standard.com*

3559

Business Information: As Senior Designer of Davis Standard/HES, Mr. Rosivach creates hardware and software for machine control systems. Working with two product lines, he oversees all electronic components in addition to providing field support. He is adept at analyzing problem situations, troubleshooting any problems with ease. Credited with the development of a unique algorithm for the creation of bump tubing, he provided an accurate, cost effiecient way to produce materials. Mr. Rosivach feels that his success stems from his hard work and skills; he aspires to a management role within the corporate structure. Davis Standard/HES is an original equipment manufacturer of plastic processing equipment for the plastics industry. With the recent acquisition of Killion Extruders, the international Company now employs over 400 people. Established in 1945, Davis Sandard/HES is headquartered in Paucatuck, Connecticut and has annual revenues of $650 million. **Career Highlights:** Senior Designer, Davis Standard/HES (1999-Present); Senior Electrical Engineer, Killion Extruders (1989-99); Draftsman/Designer, Waage Electric (1986-89). **Associations & Accomplishments:** Knights of Columbus, Council 2859. **Education:** Rutgers Univesity, B.S. in Electrical Engineering (1989). **Personal Information:** Married to René in 1991. Two children: Morgan and Katherine. Mr. Rosivach enjoys golf.

Richard A. Yarussi

Senior Optical Engineer
Nanometrics, Inc.
310 Deguigne Drive
Sunnyvale, CA 94086
(408) 746-1600
Fax: (408) 720-0196
ryarussi@nanometrics.com

3559

Business Information: Holding the position of Senior Optical Engineer, Mr. Yarussi provides professional product development with Nanometrics, Inc. Highly recruited to Nanometrics in 1997, Mr. Yarussi fulfills a number of technical duties on behalf of the Company and its clientele. Responsible for optical systems design, he is extensively involved in project research and development, implementing new technologies in order to produce a more effective product. Directing the analysis, design, evaluation, testing, and implementation of advanced technologies within Nanometrics also fall within the realm of his responsibilities. His focus is on maintaining the Corporation's competitiveness in the market place. Utilizing his expansive knowledge in the field of information technology, Mr. Yarussi continues to provide excellent technical services with Nanometrics. Established in 1975, Nanometrics, Inc. provides metrology equipment for the semiconductor industry. Headquartered in Sunnyvale, California, the Corporation employs 125 technical experts who focus on the development of flat panel displays and a wide range of semiconductor products. Distributing their specialized products to an international client base, the Corporation generates $30 million in annual sales. **Career Highlights:** Senior Optical Engineer, Nanometrics, Inc. (1997-Present); Optical Engineer, Penn State University (1994-97). **Education:** University of Rochester, M.S. (1994); Penn State University, B.S. (1993).

James C. Fleming

Director of Design and Development
T&T Pump Company, Inc.
Route 8, Box 343
Fairmont, WV 26554
(304) 363-7474
Fax: (304) 363-7474
jfleming12@compuserve.com

3561

Business Information: Serving as the Director of Design and Development for T&T Pump Company, Inc., Mr. Fleming is responsible for supervising the headquarters plant. He works as a pump engineer, troubleshooting new desings, working on conceptual desings and computer programming. A dedicated and determined individual, Mr. Fleming also travels and conducts seminars on how to operate pumps. Attributing his success to perseverance, he notes the highlight of his career as the development of a pure water pump. In the future, Mr. Fleming plans to continue working in this capacity, staying open to new opportunities that may come his way. Mr. Fleming founded DocuPrep, a multimedia company in 1991. Founded in 1964, T&T Pump Company, Inc. is a manufacturer of industrial water pumps used in reverse osmosis to purify water. International in scope, the Corporation sells to companies of all sizes from small businesses to large industries. Headquartered in Fairmont, West Virginia, the Corporation employs 40 personnel to fulfill all aspects of operation. **Career Highlights:** Director of Design and Development, T&T Pump Company, Inc. (1995-Present); T&T Pump, Inc.: Director (1995), Plant Supervisor (1974), Purchasing Agent (1971); Founder/Owner, DocuPrep (1991-Present). **Education:** Fairmont State College, B.A. (2000); Computer Science Courses. **Personal Information:** Married to Amy A. in 1969. Three children: Christy, James, Jr., and Misty. Mr. Fleming enjoys playing the guitar and music. A proactive entrepreneur, Mr. Fleming founded DocuPrep, a multimedia company, in 1991.

Alice Kim

Web Site Administrator
Gast Manufacturing
2550 Middlebrook Road
Benton Harbor, MI 49023
(616) 927-5763
Fax: (616) 925-8288
webmaster@gastmfg.com

3561

Business Information: Serving as Web Site Administrator of Gast Manufacturing, Ms. Kim oversees maintenance of the corporate Web site and offers techncial support for Internet based programs. Demonstrating an extensive knowledge gained from her education and practical work experience, Ms. Kim develops e-commerce solutions for e-commerce businesses that are interested in creative, innovatice technical solutions. Attributing her success to a motivational drive and intense interest in the information technology field, she is credited with the successul implementation of Internet operating procedures now in use by the Company. Looking forward to continuing her career with the Company, Ms. Kim currently has plans to make the corporate Web site more user friendly and informative. Gast Manufacturing specializes in the production of neumatic components for air compressors and vacuum pumps for the industrial manufacturing field. Established in 1921, the Company is headquartered in Benton Harbor, Michigan and employs 600 dedicated people. There are five international locations to serve clients throughout the world. **Career Highlights:** Web Site Administrator, Gast Manufacturing (1997-Present); Library Assistant, University of California at Berkeley, Main Library (1993-95). **Associations & Accomplishments:** HTML Writers Guild. **Education:** University of California at Berkeley, B.A. (1993). **Personal Information:** Married to Tony Clark in 1995.

Mark A. Ludwig

NT Server and Microsoft Exchange Administrator
AW Chesterton Company
45 Grand Street
Canton, MA 02021-1809
(781) 481-2365
Fax: (801) 382-0930
markludwig@msn.com

3561

Business Information: Mr. Ludwig is the NT Server and Microsoft Exchange Administrator of AW Chesterton Company. Responsible for all day-to-day administration and operations, he is in charge of all NT server functions and directs the analysis, design, evaluation, testing, and deployment of firewall technology. A savvy, 12-year professional, Mr. Ludwig is also responsible for system backups, troubleshooting, and upgrading as well as all Y2K projects. Overseeing mail servers, logs, mailboxes, and NT Exchange issues also fall within the purview of his administrator's functions. For the future, he hopes to gain more knowledge as he works towards additional Microsoft certifications. Eventually, Mr. Ludwig would like to start a career in information technology consulting, specializing in NT Infrastructure and Firewall protection. His key to success is the diligence he put into achieving his goal of becoming an I.S. professional and the dedication and hardwork he puts into his career on a daily basis. AW Chesterton Company manufactures hydraulic sealing devices, pump systems, and technical products. The Company has been dedicated to the advancement of plumbing technology around the world through an ever-expanding clientele and product line. **Career Highlights:** NT Server and Microsoft Exchange Administrator, AW Chesterton Company (1999-Present); Systems Engineer, Entex Information Services (1998-99); Systems Engineer, Stream International Inc. (1997-98). **Education:** Westfield State College, B.S. (1988). **Personal Information:** Married to Jacqueline in 1990. One child: Bridget K.

William Wayne Ferrier

Associate
Dresser-Rand Company
5710 South Garnett Road
Tulsa, OK 74146
(918) 254-4099
Fax: (918) 252-9055

3563

Business Information: Possessing superior talents in the information technology field, Mr. Ferrier joined Dresser-Rand Company in 1995 as an Associate. In his position, he manages the information systems functions. He also fulfills the capacity of network engineer and design drafter of machine parts. Possessing an excellent understanding of technology, he oversees the design of parts for engineering and stays up to date on current technology. The most rewarding aspects of his career is owning his is own businesses, Computer Aided Concepts and Draftek, Inc. In the future, Mr. Ferrier's plans include becoming a network engineer as well as develop and expand upon his knowledge base. His success reflects his ability to think outside the box, take on challenges, and deliver results on behalf of the Company and its clientele. Dresser-Rand Company is a worldwide manufacturer of energy equipment. The Company constructs oil and gas compressors, turbines, and generators. Established in 1926, the Company is located in Tulsa, Oklahoma and employs 8,500 individuals to facilitate every aspect of design, manufacture, quality assurance, and distribution of products as well as generating extensive amounts of revenue. **Career Highlights:** Associate, Dresser-Rand Company (1995-Present); President/Owner, Computer Aided Concepts (1993-95); President/Owner, Draftek, Inc. (1985-93). **Education:** Associate's degree in Design Drafting (1982); Continuous education in network engineering and related topics. **Personal Information:** Married to Alice in 1999. Five children: Jennifer Ferrier, Kyle Ferrier, Rikki Ferrier, Austin Barrett, and Joshua Barrett. Mr. Ferrier enjoys sports, camping, spelunking and sciences.

Gunilla Beard

Regional Support Center Manager
Tetra Pak Americas, Inc.
1100 Peachtree Street NE, Floor 19
Atlanta, GA 30309-4501
(404) 815-3393
gunilla.beard@tetrapak.com

3565

Business Information: Serving as the Regional Support Center Manager for Tetra Pak Americas, Inc., Ms. Beard is also the director of information systems within the Corporation. She is responsible for internal information systems support for approximately 2,000 systems users located at 12 manufacturing facilities throughout North, Central, and South America. Possessing an excellent undestanding of her role, Ms. Beard is also accountable for all software applications, change management, and conducting the Corporation's needs analysis. The most rewarding aspect of her career is overcoming the cultural and language barriers. In the future, she plans on remaining with Corporation and eventually moving up to a higher position in the realm of project management and development. Located in Atlanta, Georgia, Tetra Pak Americas, Inc. is a multinational company that is headquartered in Sweden. Founded in 1950, the Corporation produces liquid beverages for clients globally. Servicing North, Central, and South America, the Georgia location engages in the manufacturing of processing and packaging equipment for the food industry. Presently, the Corporation employs a work force of more than 17,000 people. **Career Highlights:** Tetra Pak Americas, Inc.: Regional Support Center Manager (2000-Present), Manager of Information Systems Support (1998-99), Systems Analyst (1993-98). **Education:** University of Lund, B.S. (1991). **Personal Information:** Married to Mike in 1999.

Peter D. Nicholson

Technical Development Manager
CCL Label
4083 East Airport Drive
Ontario, CA 91761
(909) 605-8235
Fax: (909) 605-6203
pnicholson@ccllabel.com

3565

Business Information: Serving as CCL Label's Technical Development Manager, Mr. Nicholson fulfills a number of activities on behalf of the Company. He oversees new product development, manages the information systems functions, develops technical strategies, and directs operational support. With an excellent understanding of technology, Mr. Nicholson also deals hands-on with technical machines and he is responsible for ensuring the efficiency of all day-to-day technical operations. The most rewarding aspects of his career is the design and development of a labeling machine that is now used around the world. Mr. Nicholson's plans include continuing his work with the Company. Highly regarded, his professional success reflects his ability to think outside the box, aggressively take on challenges, and deliver results. CCL Label is involved in the manufacture of standard and custom label application equipment. Employing the skills and expertise of 100 personnel, the Company designs and builds all labels. Striving for continued customer satisfaction, CCL Label ensures quality products and services. **Career Highlights:** CCL Label: Technical Development Manager (1998-Present), Engineering Manager (1996-98); Engineering Manager, Avery Dennison USA (1989-96); Engineering Supervisor, Avery Dennison Canada (1984-89). **Associations & Accomplishments:** International Society of Pharmaceutical Engineers; Civil Air Patrol. **Education:** University of Waterloo, B.S. in Mechanical Engineering (1982). **Personal Information:** Married to Jennifer in 1989.

Mr. Nicholson enjoys private pilot and competitive shooting sports.

Sharon A. Nourse

Systems Administrator
Packaging Technologies
807 West Kimberly Road
Davenport, IA 52806
(319) 391-1100
Fax: (319) 391-4951

3565

Business Information: Serving as Systems Administrator of Packaging Technologies, Ms. Nourse utilizes her education and extensive practical work experience to handle complex technical challenges with ease. Demonstrating exceptional communicative skills, she is able to effectively work with her team to design and implement innovative strategies for the improvement of networking. Troubleshooting, hardware and software upgrades, and LAN and WAN administration are just a few of the specialized tasks she completes on a daily basis. Recognized for adept ability and skill, she is credited with the successful formulation of comprehensive support systems for the sales force's laptop equipment. Ms. Nourse cites the support she receives from colleagues, mentors, and employers as the keys to her success, and intends to continue in her role as she shifts her career focus to include network architecture. Her advice is "get education, use the Internet as a tool, and network with others." Packaging Technologies is a manufacturing firm that produces machines to bundle and package items such a food or pharmaceuticals. Clients are found in all corners of the globe, in industries as diverse as the countries they represent. Established in 1944 by a corporation located in Germany, the Company currently employs 250 people at the Davenport, Iowa location. **Career Highlights:** Systems Administrator, Packaging Technologies (1999-Present); Local Area Network Administrator, MCI WorldCom Conferencing (1997-99); Local Area Network Administrator, The Rock Island Bank (1993-97); Systems Administrator, Bityminous Insurance Company (1992-93). **Associations & Accomplishments:** Membership Chairman, Association of Information Technical Professionals; Program Chairman, Novell Users Group. **Education:** Northern Illinois University, Microsoft Certified Systems Engineer (In Progress), Certified Novell Administration (In Progress); Black Hawk College, A.A. in Computer Programming (1991). **Personal Information:** Married to Larry in 1973. Two children: Heather and Nicholas. Ms. Nourse enjoys shooting sporting clays.

Franklin J. Highland

Mechanical Design Engineer
L.T.G. Technologies, Inc.
7631 West Holmes Avenue
Greenfield, WI 53220
(414) 672-7700
Fax: (414) 423-2589

3567

Business Information: Mr. Highland got involved in technology while in high school and attributes his success to scientific curiosity. At present, he serves as Mechanical Design Engineer with Industrial Heat Enterprises International. In this capacity, he is responsible for product design, related calculations, and developing specifications. As Computer Systems Administrator, Mr. Highland exercises oversight and control of the Company's Unix operating platform. He utilizes computer-aided drawing technology to draft new products and help make dreams into reality. Directing the analysis, acquisition, installation, modification, and support of databases and utilities also fall within Mr. Highland's functions. His career highlights include maintaining and performing safety analyses of nuclear power plants. His future goals include growing and improving at what he does. His motto is "Keep up with technology and have fun with it." Industrial Heat Enterprises International is engaged in the manufacture of industrial ovens, washers, conveyors, and coolers as well as paint finishing systems. Established in 1978, the Company operates a network of three production plants generating $35 million in annual revenue. The local operation in Franklin is manned by a work force of more than 150 people. **Career Highlights:** Mechanical Design Engineer, Industrial Heat Enterprises International (1996-Present); Senior Mechanical Engineer, Fauske & Associates, Inc. (1986-94); Senior Engineer, Commonwealth Edison Company (1973-86). **Associations & Accomplishments:** American Society of Mechanical Engineers. **Education:** General Motors Institute, B.S. in Mechanical Engineering (1972). **Personal Information:** One child: Amy. Mr. Highland enjoys golf and volunteer driver for Disabled American Veterans.

Duane E. Tipton Jr.

Technical Manual Coordinator
Aeroglide Corporation
100 Aeroglide Drive
Cary, NC 27511-6900
(919) 851-2000
Fax: (919) 851-6029
dtipton@aeroglide.com

3567

Business Information: Mr. Tipton joined the Aeroglide Corporation team of professionals as Technical Manual Coordinator in 1997. Relying on seven years of extensive academics, business experience, and technical expertise, Mr. Tipton is charged with oversight of writing and editing technical owner's manuals for industrial dryers and coolers. His present role principally involves working closely with systems engineers, gathering technical knowledge on products and services, and then synthesizing and translating the technical data into an understandable format for users. An expert at what he does, Mr. Tipton works primarily with Microsoft tools. He owns a consistent record of delivering product results by communicating effectively both in written and oral formats. Mr. Tipton attributes his professional success to strong persistence. "Learning as much as you can and keep going. Find your niche and focus on that," is cited as Mr. Tipton's advice to others in the industry. Aeroglide Corporation designs and builds industrial driers and coolers. Targeting Fortune 500 companies, the Corporation also exports products to Mexico, China, South America, and Canada as well as a location in Europe. With the only manufacturing site in Raleigh, North Carolina, Aeroglide was founded n 1940 and presently employs 151 professional and technical personnel. **Career Highlights:** Technical Manual Coordinator, Aeroglide Corporation (1997-Present); Assistant Manager, Pizza Hut (1991-95). **Associations & Accomplishments:** Beta Gamma Chi; Los Angeles Marathon Volunteer (1987-91). **Education:** Point Loma Nazarene College, B.A. in Business (1991). **Personal Information:** Mr. Tipton enjoys golf.

Brian J. Perkins

Manager of Computer Systems
Sumitomo Machinery Corporation of America
4200 Holland Boulevard
Chesapeake, VA 23323
(757) 485-3355
Fax: (757) 485-7190
bperkins@suminet.com

3568

Business Information: With extensive experience in the field of information technology, Mr. Perkins serves as Manager of Computer Systems for the Sumitomo Machinery Corporation of America. He supervises the administration of the LAN/WAN networks, HP/UNIX operating systems, and T1 communication frame relay for the corporate headquarters and six remote sites. Handling the responsibilities of vendor liaison, he purchases the hardware equipment and software for the various workstations and computer systems. Mr. Perkins is assisted in his duties by six departmental staff members. Dedicated to the success of the Corporation, he looks forward to a future promotion to Chief Information Officer. A subsidiary of Sumitomo Industries, the Sumitomo Machinery Corporation of America is a leading manufacturer of non-automotive transmissions. The Corporation has several locations around the globe, including nine plants in the United States and two in Mexico. Founded in 1968, operations employ the services of 250 skilled individuals. **Career Highlights:** Manager of Computer Systems, Sumitomo Machinery Corporation of America (1994-Present); Computer Consultant, Origin Technology (1991-94). **Education:** State University of New York at Cortland, B.S. in Economics and Management Science (1988). **Personal Information:** Mr. Perkins enjoys travel with his family.

Ricardo R. Matos

Mechanical Engineer
Parkson Corporation
2727 North West 62nd
Fort Lauderdale, FL 33340-8399
(954) 974-6610
Fax: (954) 974-6182
rmatos@parkson.com

3569

Business Information: Functioning in the role of Mechanical Engineer for Parkson Corporation, Mr. Matos is involved in design, manufacture, and distribution of various products. He plans and designs tools, engines, machines, and other mechanical equipment. A savvy, nine year professional, he specializies in applied mechanics, design engineering, heat transfer, power plant engineering, pressure vessels and piping, and underwater technologies. Mr. Matos designs tools needed by other engineers for their work. Beginning his association with Parkson Corporation in 1999, Mr. Matos has quickly established himself as a vital contributor to the success of the Corporation. He attributes his success to seizing the opportunity when it knocked. Mr. Matos' goal is to eventually establish his own retail business. His advice is "Stick to it and don't give up." Parkson Corporation is engaged in the manufacture of equipment used in the water treatment process for plant, city, and commercial use. Located in Fort Lauderdale, Florida, the Corporation employs a work force of more than 125 people. Established in 1979, Parkson Corporation presently reports annual revenues in excess of $17 million. **Career Highlights:** Mechanical Engineer, Parkson Corporation (1999-Present); CAD Designer, Combustion Tec (1998-99); Restaurant Development Manager, Food System (1995); Fermaton Manufacturer, Ray Metro N Association (1990). **Education:** ITT Technical Institute, Designer.

Joe Guadalupe Rios

Project Engineer
Peerless Manufacturing Company
2819 Walnut Hill Lane
Dallas, TX 75229-5711
(214) 353-5580
Fax: (214) 351-0194

3569

Business Information: A savvy, seven year veteran of technology, Mr. Rios serves as Project Engineer of the Peerless Manufactuing Company. He plans and oversees design, development, and support of entire SCR systems for the Company. Working closely with management and users, he handles everything from sales to production. Coordinating resources, schedules, assignments, time lines, and project budgets, Mr. Rios' ensures projects are completed in a timely manner and within budgetary constraints. Utilizing his academics and industry experience, his career highlights include designing reactors for power plants in California and Arizona. He looks forward to remaining with Peerless Manufacturing and eventually moving up the corporate structure. His success is attributed to his persistence, dedication, and networking with his colleagues in different fields. Established in 1933, Peerless Manufacturing Company produces power generation environmental products such as pressure vessels, filtration products and moisture septic systems. As the largest producer of SCR systems, the Company is internationally known and presently employs a staff 250 professional, techncal, and support personnel. The Company primarily serves the oil, gas, and power industries. **Career Highlights:** Peerless Manufacturing Company: Project Engineer (1999-Present), Research Assistant (1997-99); Computer Technician, United States Department of Agriculture (1993-97). **Associations & Accomplishments:** American Society of Mechanical Engineers. **Education:** Texas A&M University, B.S. (1999). **Personal Information:** Married to Connie in 1999. Mr. Rios enjoys Tae Kwon Do and mountain biking.

Alan Maurice Wamsley

Show Manager/Applications Engineer
Chiron America, Inc.
14201 South Lakes Drive
Charlotte, NC 28273
(704) 587-9526
Fax: (704) 587-0485
cncaian@aol.com

3569

Business Information: A savvy, seven year professional, Mr. Wamsley serves as Show Manager and Applications Engineer of Chiron America, Inc. In his capacity, he organizes and coordinates sales presentations at conventions and marketing expos as well as identifies new markets and avenues for additional revenues. Possessing superior talents and an excellent understanding of technology, Mr. Wamsley is also in charge of working closely with management and users to analyze, specify, and design new machiery and tooling equipment. His many responsibilities include overseeing the sales staff, managing logistical networks, and ensuring order fulfillment. Mr. Wamsley applies his extensive experience in machine technology to completely meet the needs of his clients, thereby guaranteeing customer satisfaction. Plans for the future include staying with the Corporation and assisting in its growth and expansion. His success reflects his ability to communicate effectively, tackle new challenges, and deliver results. Chiron America, Inc. engages in the manufacturing of fabrication machines. At its inception in 1993, the Corporation was located in Phoenix, Arizona and was moved to Charlotte, North Carolina in 1997. Currently staffed by 75 industrious and enterprising employees, the Corporation generates an annual revenue of over $65 Million. With extensive experince in electrical, mechanical and software systems, Chiron America is a commanding force in the industry. **Career Highlights:** Show Manager/Applications Engineer, Chiron American, Inc. (1995-Present); CNC Machinist, Estul Tool and Manufacturing Company (1994-95); Core Technician, Schrader Automotive (1993-94). **Associations & Accomplishments:** Phi Theta Kappa Honor Society; Society of Manufacturing Engineers; CPCC. **Education:** Central Piedmont Community College: Associate's degree in Machine Technology (2000), Diploma in Machine Technology. **Personal Information:** Married to Karla in 1993. Two children: Christopher and Nicole. Mr. Wamsley enjoys coaching soccer.

Katty Almeida-Coffron
Functional Manager
Hewlett-Packard Company
3495 Deer Creek Road
Palo Alto, CA 94304-1393
(650) 857-3082
katty_almeida@np.com
3571

Business Information: Ms. Almeida-Coffron has served with Hewlett-Packard Company in a variety of roles since joining the Company as Research and Development Engineer in 1987. In her current position of Functional Manager, Ms. Almeida-Coffron is responsible development and support of leading edge financial applications software. A savvy, 13 year veteran of technology, she manages the support team and fiscal budgets as well as interfaces with other divisions to obtain their requirements for enhancing existing software. Determining the strategy, obtaining research and development data, and overseeing certain aspects of project management also fall within the realm of Ms. Almeida-Coffron's responsibilities. Possessing common sense and good decision making capabilities enables her to meet all goals. Ms. Almeida-Coffron plans to continue developing her skill set and establishing a better network. Her advice is "get education and look for opportunities that spark your interest." Hewlett-Packard is a manufacturer of computers, printers, and peripheral products. Functioning on a corporate level, the Company maintains locations around the globe, used to manufacture and retail computers and related technology. Headquartered in Palo Alto, California, the Company is recognized throughout the technology industry as a leader in systems design and implementation. **Career Highlights:** Hewlett-Packard Company: Functional Manager (1997-Present), Research and Development Project Manager (1995-97), Technical Education Consultant (1994-94), Research and Development Engineer (1987-93). **Associations & Accomplishments:** Project Management Institute; American Management Association; National Association for Female Executives. **Education:** University of California at Davis, B.S. in Computer Systems Engineering (1989). **Personal Information:** Married.

Michael Benedict
Webmaster
Telxon Corporation
3330 West Market Street
Akron, OH 44333-3352
(330) 664-4635
Fax: (330) 664-2058
mbene@telxon.com
3571

Business Information: A successful, 16 year veteran of the technology field, Mr. Benedict serves in the role of Webmaster of Telxon Corporation. He is responsible administering and controlling the Corporation's intricate and diverse Web site environment. Utilizing his academics and occupational experience, he maintains and updates the current content of a 400 to 700 page Web site. Providing internal and external support and ensuring the functionality and operational status of the Internet and Intranet infrastructure, Mr. Benedict is presently involved with redesigning Telxon's Web sites, keeping them on the cutting edge of technology and user friendly. His awards include the "Award of Excellence" while employed by Allen Bradley. There, he single-handedly redesigned their Internet and Intranet systems. Enjoying his role as a Webmaster, Mr. Benedict plans to mentor a large staff and lead larger projects. Success have been attributed to his honesty and integrity. An international technology company, Telxon Corporation operates as a mobile computer hardware manufacturer. The Corporation offers a wide range of wireless solutions. Headquartered in Akron, Ohio, Telxon currently employs a 1,100 professional, technical, and administrative support staff. Telxon Corporation was established in 1984. **Career Highlights:** Webmaster, Telxon Corporation (1994-Present). **Associations & Accomplishments:** N.I.C.E.T.; A.S.C.E.T. **Education:** Cleveland State University, B.S. in Electronic Technology (1984); A.S.E.E.T. **Personal Information:** Married to Paula in 1999. Four children: Thomas, Ashley, amanda, and Bryan. Mr. Benedict enjoys bowling, camping, boating, fishing and hunting.

Dennis R. Bradley
Senior Information Technology Specialist
IBM Corporation
590 Madison Avenue
New York, NY 10022-2524
(212) 745-4110
Fax: (718) 527-1305
drbradl@us.ibm.com
3571

Business Information: As the Senior Information Technology Specialist for IBM Corporation, Mr. Bradley maintains the functionality and operational status of the information systems infrastructure as well as determines the business contribution of the systems functions. Possessing an excellent understanding of technology, he installs software and configures Cisco routers and Microsoft operating systems. Mr. Bradley is also responsible for the analysis, acquisition, installation, modification, configuration, support, and tracking of operating systems, databases, server utilities, software, and hardware. His focus is on the discovery, investigation, and deployment of advanced technolgies within IBM. Dedicated to the success of the Corporation, Mr. Bradley plans to continue his work, while obtaining more professional certifications in his field. His success reflects his ability to think outside the box, take on challenges, and deliver results. IBM is one of the world's leading developers and manufacturers of electronic equipment and computer peripheral devices. The Corporation is a developer, manufacturer, and marketer of advanced information processing products including computers and microelectric techonolgy software, networking systems, and information technology. The Corporation's enterprise management division provides various information technology consulting to corporations. **Career Highlights:** IBM Corporation: Senior Information Technology Specialist (1998-Present), Advisory Information Technology Specialist (1997-98), Information Technology Specialist (1996-97). **Education:** DeVry Technical Institute; Fordham University. **Personal Information:** Married to Donna in 1997. Four children: Dennis, Tamika, Sukara, and Kimara. Mr. Bradley enjoys sports and family time.

Genelle R. Braggs
Open Systems Manager
IBM Corporation
1500 Riveredge Parkway NW
Atlanta, GA 30328
(770) 858-7720
Fax: (770) 858-2800
bgraggs@us.ibm.com
3571

Business Information: Mrs. Braggs functions in the role of Open Systems Manager with IBM Corporation. She is responsible for all aspects of open system technical support for the Global Services Division. An expert in the field, Mrs. Braggs has served with IBM in a variety of capacities since joining IBM as Resource Manager in 1985. She effectively supervises a technical support staff of 17 professional and technical people. In addition, Mrs. Braggs manages personnel issues, such as staffing, recruiting, and training of new workers. Possessing a customer oriented attitude, she motivates and coaches her staff in providing quality solutions in dealing with all customer service issues. As for the future, Mrs. Braggs' goals include broading her professional horizons within the management realm. She attributes her success to her strong faith in God and her ability to build teams with synergy and technical strength, as well as produce results and aggressively take on new challenges. IBM Corporation is an undisputed, international leader in computer technology. In existence years before the advent of the personal computer, the Corporation has developed and manufactured everything from typewriters to super-computers for the Department of Defense. The Global Services Division is a technical support wing of IBM. This Division employs 17 people, all of which assist customers either over the telephone or sending somebody to meet with the customer. **Career Highlights:** IBM Corporation: Open Systems Manager (Present), Support Manager, Field Manager, Resource Manager. **Associations & Accomplishments:** A.I.M. Committee at Church. **Education:** Georgia State; Mortgage Loan Processor; Manicurist License. **Personal Information:** Married to Tony in 1996. Mrs. Braggs enjoys golf, basketball, tennis and reading.

Peter Bufford
Project Manager
Solectron Corporation
311 Cutter Street
Foster City, CA 94404
(408) 956-6479
peterbufford@ca.slr.com
3571

Business Information: Mr. Bufford is in the position of Project Manager for strategic business systems at Solectron Corporation. He is currently accountable for the roll out of a new MRP system to Solectron California. In this context, he is responsible for defining the project, coordinating resources, and driving the successful implementation. Possessing an excellent understanding of his field, Mr. Bufford works closely with management and systems users to identify gaps between system capabilities and user requirements, analyze and specify changes needed, and ensure the delivery of the necessary business solutions. Mr. Bufford has served with the Corporation in a variety of positions since joining Solectron in 1992. His career highlights include the execution of all key elements of the MRP implementation as planned and a presentation of this project of the board of directors. He attributes his success to hard work, education, and his ability to work as a team player. Established in 1977, Solectron Corporation is the world's largest electronics services manufacturing company offering a full range of integrated supply-chain solutions for leading original equipment manufacturers. Integrated technology solutions, materials, manufacturing, and services provide customers advanced manufacturing technologies, shortened product launch cycles, more effective asset utilization and reduced total cost of ownership. The California site, located in Milpitas and Fremont, California, employs 1,200 professional, technical, and support staff, and reports annual revenues in excess of $2.5 billion. Solectron has received more than 210 quality and service awards from its customers in addition to the 1997 and 1991 Malcolm Baldrige National Quality awards. **Career Highlights:** Solectron Corporation: Project Manager (1998-Present), Manager of New Business Development (1996-97), Warehouse Manager (1994); Retired, United States Army Reserves. **Associations & Accomplishments:** United States Army Reserves (retired). **Education:** University of California at Berkeley, M.B.A. (1983); Georgia Institute of Technology, B.S. in Industrial Management. **Personal Information:** Married to Norma Simpson in 1984. Three children: Laura, Carolyn, and Teresa. Mr. Bufford enjoys skiing, tennis and biking.

Carrie D. Buzby
Computer Security Specialist/Project Manager
IBM Corporation
11900 Pecos Street
Denver, CO 80234
(305) 538-5799
Fax: (303) 538-7971
rabbit@lucent.com
3571

Business Information: Utilizing technical knowledge and skills learned over the course of her professional career, Ms. Buzby serves as Computer Security Specialist and Project Manager for IBM Corporation. In her capacity, she assumes responsibility for two of the Company's data centers, providing systems maintenance, upgrades, and systems security for highly sensitive industry data. Before joining IBM as Systems Administrator and Migration Specialist in 1995, Ms. Buzby also served with Lucent Technologies in the same positions. Her background history also includes a stint with AT&T as Database Administrator, Database Developer, and GUI Applications Developer. Ms. Buzby is highly skilled in both computer and telephone technology. Dedicated to IBM's success, she anticipates a promotion to Director of the Information Systems Security Department. IBM Corporation provides professional information technology services to businesses internationally. Services in computer systems, software, networking systems, storage devices, and microelectronics are offered. **Career Highlights:** IBM Corporation: Computer Security Specialist/Project Manager (1998-Present), Lead Systems Administrator (1998); Systems Administrator/Migration Specialist, IBM Corporation/Lucent Technologies (1995-98); Database Administrator/Database Developer/GUI Applications Developer, AT&T (1986-95). **Associations & Accomplishments:** Shepherd of Love Fellowship; Has done work for Telephone Pioneers, WILL, and numerous animal rescue organizations. **Education:** Numerous Professional courses from companies such as AT&T, IBM Corporation, Lucent Technologies, Oracle, SUN Microsystems, Microsoft, and Visual Basics. **Personal Information:** Married to Jeff in 1992. One child: Morgen T. Van Esselstine. Ms. Buzby enjoys gold panning, designing, creating tile and gold panning.

Joao Roberto Monteiro Cerqueira
Consulting Manager
Hewlett-Packard Company
R. Guiratinga 500-Apto. 101
Sao Paulo, Brazil 04141
+55 1172978475
joao_cerqueira@hp.com
3571

Business Information: Serving as the Consulting Manager, Mr. Cerqueira has been providing exceptional client services for over five years as a member of the Hewlett-Packard Company team of professionals. Involved in project management, he directs funds and materials to the necessary areas of development. Concentrating his efforts towards project strategy, Mr. Cerqueira focuses his attention towards implementing new technologies and ideas in production. Presiding over all aspects of project management, he develops cutting edge products and processes to enhance his clients' information technology environment. Continuing his career with Hewlett-Packard, Mr. Cerqueira remains committed to providing excellent services in product development. His goals include consolidating his leadership positions. Established in 1939, Hewlett-Packard specializes in the manufacturing and distribution of computers, peripherals, and accessories. Located in Sao Paulo, Brazil, the Company provides sales and services throughout the world. Employing over 89,000 specialized technicians and developers, the Company concentrates its efforts towards implementing new technologies in order to produce a more efficient and cost worthy product. Generating an estimated $39 billion in annual sales, Hewlett-Packard remains one of the premier leaders in the technology industry. **Career Highlights:** Consulting Manager, Hewlett-Packard Company (1995-Present); Project Manager, CPM (1993-95); Project Manager, JMA (1991-93). **Associations & Accomplishments:** Project Management Institute. **Education:** FMU, M.B.A. (1992); FEI, Electronic Engineering degree. **Personal Information:** Married to Tania M. I. de Azevedo. Mr. Cerqueira enjoys reading science fiction books and basketball.

Vito De Cesare

Product Manager
Solectron Technology Company
6800 Solectron Drive
Charlotte, NC 28262
(204) 509-8541
Fax: (786) 513-0293
vitodecesare@nc.slr.com

3571

Business Information: Serving as Product Manager of Solectron Technology, Mr. De Cesare has been providing professional operational direction for Solectron Technology since 1998. Maintaining quotations for the North American division, he focuses his efforts towards production and distribution on the East Coast. Enforcing state mandatory procedures and policies in manufacturing, Mr. De Cesare maintains a safe and efficient work environment. Utilizing his 18 years of experience in the field of technologies, he manages international communications with the Company's major clients. Continuing his career with Solectron Technology, Mr. De Cesare focuses his attention towards the increase of international clients. In the future, he aspires to eventually attain the position of Global Project Manager. A world leader in electrical manufacturing, Solectron Technology provides excellent contract manufacturing and consulting services to an international client base. Headquartered in California, the Company employs over 4,300 experienced technicians, engineers, and consultants who establish confidential relationships with large PC companies. The Company creates PC and computer equipment for consumer purchase. Concentrating their efforts towards expanding their client base, Solectron Technology continues to strive in excellence in the computer technology field. **Career Highlights:** Product Manager, Solectron Technology (1998-Present). **Education:** Stevens Institute of Technology, B.S. (1982); Syracuse University, Master's degree.

Tony J. Edwards

Manager of Technical Services
Telxon Corporation
12005 Ford Road, Suite 510
Dallas, TX 75234
(972) 443-1217
Fax: (972) 443-1250
tedwa@telxon.com

3571

Business Information: Functioning in the capacity of Manager of Technical Services for Telxon Corporation, Mr. Edwards manages a five state region within the Southwest area of the United States. He is responsible for all pre- and post-sales technical support. Before joining Telxon, he served as Senior Information Technology Consultant with IBM Corporation. His background history also includes a stint as Senior Information Technology Consultant at FCG. With over 16 years experience, Mr. Edwards is highly qualified to lead a group of eight engineers and eight account representatives to enhance the success of the Corporation. He ensures all departments are efficiently producing and that customers are completely satisfied. Mr. Edwards hopes to attain the position of Regional Vice President in the near future. In this new position, he obtain greater responsibility, monitor productivity of staff, and acquire more valuable knowledge about the field. His success reflects his ability to think outside the box, deliver results, and aggressively take on new challenges. Headquartered in Akron, Ohio, Telxon specializes in wireless RF computing equipment manufacturing. This $500 million Corporation provides services internationally. **Career Highlights:** Manager of Technical Services, Telxon Corporation (1998-Present); Senior Consultant, IBM Corporation (1996-98); Senior Information Technology Consultant, FCG (1994-96). **Education:** DeVry Institute of Technology, Associate's degree (1984). **Personal Information:** Married to Kendra D. in 1991. Three children: Naomi Nicole, Savannah Rae, and Alex Wood. Mr. Edwards enjoys golf, softball and coaching soccer.

Abe Elfadel, Ph.D.

Research Staff Member
IBM Corporation
Taconic Parkway, Route 134, Room 33-133
Yorktown, NY 10598
(914) 945-2278
Fax: (914) 945-4469
elfadel@us.ibm.com

3571

Business Information: As a Research Staff Member of IBM Corporation, Dr. Elfadel engages in research and development for this Department. He is a team leader involved in project scheduling and management and communications. Possessing superior talents and an excellent understanding of technology, Dr. Elfadel works closely with management and users to analyze, specify, and design new technology solutions. Directing and participating in the evaluation, testing, implementation of advanced technologies within IBM is also and integral part of his functions. His focus is on changes that will allow IBM and customers to take advantage any newly developed technical solutions to remain flexible, efficient, and profitable in the Information Technology Age. Attributing his success to his creativity, Dr. Elfadel plans to move into management or stay on the technical track to become an IBM Fellow. IBM Corporation designs, manufactures and markets high-tech products globally including information systems products and services, computers, semi-conductors, networking hardware and software, computer hardware and software as well as outsourcing services and consulting. Established in 1924, the Corporation maintains a design automation department that develops cutting edge tools for the microprocessor designers. **Career Highlights:** Research Staff Member, IBM Corporation (1996-Present); Adjunct Associate Professor, Columbia University (2000-Present); Visiting Scientist, Massachusetts Institute of Technology (1995-96). **Associations & Accomplishments:** Institute of Electrical and Electronics Engineers; Association of Computing Machinery. **Education:** Massachusetts Institute of Technology, Ph.D.

Allan D. Ellis

Manager of Technical Services
Telxon Corporation
911 Western Avenue, Suite 401
Seattle, WA 98104-1031
(206) 340-6763
Fax: (360) 613-1863
adellis@email.msn.com

3571

Business Information: Mr. Ellis is Manager of Technical Services for the Telxon Corporation. He is responsible for the combined management of his division and is focused on providing technical support to clients within his particular region. Mr. Ellis is an expert troubleshooter who strives to quickly respond to the various situations that may arise because of difficulties in the programming or usage of the scanners. He integrates all new technology into the Corporation's computer systems and maintains the LAN and WAN networking services. An accomplished professional, he worked on creating the first non-IBM device for Motorola as the team's design manager. For the future, Mr. Ellis is working to establish a mobile work force that has unlimited capabilities to service customer's needs. He would also like to advance the current networking capabilities of the Corporation to accommodate e-commerce and Internet interfacing. Reading trade journals, working more sophisticated projects, and being open-minded has contributed to his success. Telxon Corporation is a wireless data terminal device manufacturing company. Established in 1972, the Corporation has made the change from the retail grocery industry into the technology industry through the innovation of new products for the data collections field. The Corporation creates hand held scanning devices and communicators to collect information in a timely matter during inventories and audits. The Corporation has a staff of 1,500 personnel designing, producing, marketing, and demonstrating the newest items in the product line. **Career Highlights:** Manager of Technical Services, Telxon Corporation (1987-Present); Manager of Management Information Systems, Galvin Supply (1985-87); Manager of Management Information Systems, Chain Gear (1982-85). **Associations & Accomplishments:** American Management Association; Washington State Youth Soccer. **Education:** University of Pudget Sound, M.B.A. (1982); University of Washington, B.A. **Personal Information:** Married to Melinda in 1972. Three children: Brent, Bryan, and Amanda. Mr. Ellis enjoys being a licensed soccer coach and referee and reading trade journals.

Michael W. Garner

Senior Software Developer
IBM Corporation
2614 Grande Valley Circle
Cary, NC 27513-3142
(919) 543-1921
garnerm@us.ibm.com

3571

Business Information: Possessing business savvy and 14 years of experience in the technology field, Mr. Garner serves as the Senior Software Developer of IBM Corporation. Joining the IBM team as Technical Support Lead in 1993, he currently works in the unannounced products division. In this context, Mr. Garner functions as team lead in the development of cutting network operating systems and Netfinity server. An respected expert in systems development, he was in charge of the IBM team overseeing and maintaining the operating and networking infrastructure at the 1996 Olympics in Atlanta, Georgia. Working closely with management and systems users to analyze, specify, and design new technical solutions also fall within the purview of Mr. Garner's responsibilities. His future goals include remaining with IBM and designing new technology to the benefit of consumers around the globe. One of the world's largest information technology solutions provider, IBM engages in developing, manufacturing, and marketing new computer hardware, software, and related peripheral equipment. From over 1,000 locations around the world, consumers can recieve consulting, technical support, and outsourcing services to compliment their office machinery. **Career Highlights:** IBM Corporation: Senior Software Developer (1996-Present), Advisory Software Engineer (1993-96), Technical Support Lead (1993). **Education:** University of Texas at Dallas (1993); North Carolina State University (1991-92); University of Texas at Arlington (1986-91). **Personal Information:** Married to Nonie in 1991. One child: Megan. Mr. Garner enjoys reading, software development, hockey and football.

Alexander Gelfenbain

Architect
Sun Microsystems, Inc.
901 San Antonio Road
Palo Alto, CA 94303
(650) 786-9047
gelf@acm.org

3571

Business Information: A prominent and respectful technology professional, Mr. Gelfenbain is dedicated to the success of Sun Microsystems, Inc. and applies his knowledge and expertise in the field of computer technology in serving as Architect. Possessing an excellent understanding of technology, he is charged with the design and implementation of software as well as facilitating corporate proposals in accordance with schedules. Mr. Gelfenbain establishes high standards of excellence for other individuals in the industry, and continues to produce innovative software, delegating Sun Microsystems as a pilot in the industrial world. The most rewarding aspect of his career is the design and implementation of font downloading software for Solaris. His success is attributed to good education and lots of luck. Serving an international client base, Sun Microsystems operates as a manufacturer of computers as well as a software designer for UNIX and Solaris systems. Founded in 1982, the Corporation employs a team of skilled individuals to research, design, and develop technological systems and their components. The Corporation continues to design innovative and contemporary computer systems and software, making it a leader in this fast-growing, competitive market. **Career Highlights:** Architect, Sun Microsystems, Inc. (1994-Present); Localization Manager, Jet Infosystems (1992-94); Software Engineer, Intermicro (1991-92). **Associations & Accomplishments:** Association of Computing Machinery. **Education:** Moscow State University, M.S. (1991).

Orazio Granato

European Services Delivery Program Manager
Hewlett-Packard Company
Via Don Luigi, Palazzolo 67
Bergamo, Italy 24122
+39 035503410
Fax: +39 035503998
orazio_grawad@hp.com

3571

Business Information: Serving as Hewlett-Packard Company's European Services Delivery Program Manager since 1997, Mr. Granato works with the service group from the Software Support division. By focusing his attention on the logistics of deliveries from an engineering viewpoint, Mr. Granato is able to develop strategic business plans to improve the accuracy of the Company's shipping. Internally recognized for his innovative implementation of several creative prodcedures, Mr. Granato is a valuable assest the the

Company. Always alert to new technologies and approaches, he currently is expanding his knowledge of the technical industry so that he may better utilize his education and practical work experience. His advice is "come everyday to your desk and make sure what you left yesterday will be different today." Hewlett-Packard is a leading manufacturer of computer hardware, ranging from personal computers to high end corporate systems. Additionally, they produce various printer models such as laser and ink jet. Offering quality customer support and trained technician, Hewlett-Packard is one of the most successful information technology companies in operation. **Career Highlights:** Hewlett-Packard Company: European Services Delivery Program Manager (1997-Present), Business Process Manager (1996-97), Architect Technical Manager (1995-96), Research and Development Manager (1994-95). **Associations & Accomplishments:** President, Associazione Volontari Italiani del Sangue. **Education:** SDA Bocconi of Milan, M.B.A. (1998); Pisa University, Computer Science. **Personal Information:** Married to Marcella in 1994. One child: Anastasia. Mr. Granato enjoys gardening, soccer, attending the theater and spending time with his four month old daughter.

Anis S. Hasan

Systems Administrator
Sun Microsystems, Inc.
2nd Floor, Petroleum Building, P.O. Box 31685
Khobar, Saudi Arabia 31952
+966 38748719
Fax: +966 38766013
anis.hasan@sun.com

3571

Business Information: Combining leadership skills and vast technical experience, Mr. Hasan serves as Systems Administrator for Sun Microsystems, Inc.'s Khobar, Saudi Arabia facility. He is responsible for maintaining all inner office technical functions, such as adminstering and controlling support for the systems infrastructure, monitoring system performance, and maintaining smooth operations for unaltered business functions. Joining the Corporation in 1999, Mr. Hasan superior talents and possesses an excellent understanding of technology. Monitoring and tuning systems software, peripherals, and networks as well as resolving systems difficulties also fall within the realm of his responsibilities. His future plans include staying with the Corporation and exceling in his personal area of expertise. "Read a lot about UNIX," is cited as Mr. Hasan's advice. Offering a variety of quality services, Sun Microsystems, Inc. is recognized as the number one company in the United Arab Emirates that provides enterprise computing solutions. Catering to the oil and gas industry, the Corporation's services include auditing, program management, and professional consulting. Established in 1982, the Corporation is headquartered in California and operates out of several international subsidiaries. The Corporation functions under the direct guidance and talents of 65,000 professionals who help generate global revenues in excess of $6.7 billion annually. **Career Highlights:** Systems Administrator, Sun Microsystems, Inc. (1999-Present); Technical Support Manager, Abdulla Fouad Company (1993-99); Technical Support Consultant, Reuters (Pakistan), Ltd. (1992-93). **Associations & Accomplishments:** Founding Member, Shipowners College Science Club. **Education:** Karachi University, B.S. (1985). **Personal Information:** Married to Zahida in 1990. Three children: Salman, Nabeel, and Ali. Mr. Hasan enjoys reading, karate and electronics.

Derek P. Hill

Development Environment Manager
Hewlett-Packard Company
5301 Stevens Creek Boulevard, Maildrop 55-34
Santa Clara, CA 95051
(408) 345-8987
Fax: (408) 553-6260
derek_hill@hp.com

3571

Business Information: Functioning as Development Environment Manager with Hewlett-Packard, Mr. Hill is a project member for vantive and point deployment. Before joining Hewlett-Packard Company as a Systems Support Technician in 1995, Mr. Hill served as an Automobile Technician at Wilson Mortors. As a four year professional with an established track record of delivering results, he creates cutting edge database software from scratch, including coding and providing users support. His career success reflects his ability to think out-of-the-box and aggressively take on new challenges and responsibilities. Administering and controlling data resources, ensuring data integrity and security, and monitoring and tuning software tools to enhance performance also fall within the purview of Mr. Hill's responsibilities. He attributes his success to his excellent people and troubleshooting skills. Going into consulting in strategic implementation serves as one of his future goals. Mr. Hill's favorite quotable quote is "None of the above." One of the world's largest computer manufacturers, Hewlett-Packard Company is also a producer of test and measurement equipment. A Fortune 500 company, Hewlett-Packard maintains a presence in over 120 countries around the globe. Established in 1939, the Company is headquartered in Palo Alto, California. Presently, Hewlett-Packard employs a work force of more than 120,000 people who help generate annual revenues in excess of $47 billion. **Career Highlights:** Hewlett-Packard Company: Development Environment Manager (1998-Present), System Support Technician (1995-98); Automobile Technician, Wilson Motors (1992-95). **Associations & Accomplishments:** Desert Storm Veteran. **Education:** Oregon State University, B.A. in Management Information Systems (1997); Linn Benton Community College, A.S. in Business Administration. **Personal Information:** Mr. Hill enjoys skiing, scuba diving and soccer.

Kevin L. Hinkston

Business Consultant/Project Manager
Hewlett-Packard Company
3000 Hanover Street
Palo Alto, CA 94304-1112
(650) 857-2822
Fax: (650) 857-4586
kevinh5748@aol.com

3571

Business Information: Serving as Business Consultant and Project Manager for Hewlett-Packard Company, Mr. Hinkston serves the Information Technology Department as an advisor to educational teams. He instructs world wide groups of students regarding software application and hardware maintenance. To further employee knowledge, he coordinates instructional courses from vendors to lecture and teach hands-on application seminars. In the future, Mr. Hinkston would like to expand his role in project management while continuing to develop his skills and provide additional training to staff members. As an enterprising professional, he serves on the Board of Directors for several start-up companies. Personally, he believes, "volunteerism is the rent we pay to stay on this earth." Mr. Hinkston founded several community programs, including instructing high school students about computer skills and corporate etiquette. A business leader in the community, he has also started intern, scholarship, and mentoring programs. A Fortune 500 company, Hewlett-Packard is primarily involved in the creation and manufacture of computers, peripherals, and other computer-related services. The second ranked provider of servers and peripherals, and the third ranked supplier of PCs, Hewlett-Packard is expanding into the forum of cable television products, document copying, and digital photography. Established in 1939, Hewlett-Packard currently depends upon a skilled international staff of 120,000 professionals and technicians to create an annual revenue in excess of $50 billion. **Career Highlights:** Hewlett-Packard Company: Business Consultant/Project Manager (1998-Present), Information Technology Consultant (1996-98), Project Manager/Consultant (1995-96); Consultant, IBM (1991-95). **Associations & Accomplishments:** President, Boda IT Thought Leaders, San Francisco Bay Area Chapter; U.S. Black Engineer Award for Technical Contributions; Small Business Association, Minority Business Advocate of the Year Nominee. **Education:** University of Santa Clara, B.S. in Electrical Engineering. **Personal Information:** Married to Ulanda in 1992. Three children: Alana, Adrienne, and Kevin Jr. Mr. Hinkston enjoys volunteering and mentoring.

Brent M. Hoey

Principal
IBM Corporation
2323 Harper Drive
Orange, VA 22960
(412) 237-2885
hoeyb@us.ibm.com

3571

Business Information: Mr. Hoey has been active in the information technology arena since 1980. He joined the IBM Corporation in 1985, and has served in a variety of capacities in IBM. Currently, Mr. Hoey serves as a Principal for all aspects of establishing and delivering enterprise resource planning engagements. He is a certified IBM professional. His present role principally involves strategic planning and implementation of state-of-the-art solutions and innovations for IBM's clients. Mr. Hoey has a long track record of delivering creative results by effectively using emerging technologies and addressing challenges in a systematic and efficient manner. An expert in his field, he is well versed on Oracle platforms. Maintaining IBM's excellent reputation in global services, Mr. Hoey is focused on deploying advanced technologies with IBM clients. His objectives are to help clients stay on the leading edge, remain flexible, efficient, competitive, and profitable in the 21st century. Penetrating new markets and overseeing schedules, scope, cost, and resources fall within the purview of his responsibilities. Looking toward the 21st century, Mr. Hoey's affiliation with industry associations such as Project Management Institute, Association of Computing Machinery, and IEEE enables him to stay up-to-date, and allows him to interact with professionals in different fields. Growing with IBM and helping to take it to higher levels continues to serve as his goals. IBM Corporation, founded in 1920, is the worlds largest provider of professional services and one of the world's leading manufacturers of computer technology. Presently, IBM employs a global work force of more than 250,000 people who contribute to an annual generation of revenues in excess of $67 billion. **Career Highlights:** Principal, IBM Corporation (1985-Present). **Associations & Accomplishments:** Project Management Institute; Association of Computing Machinery; Institute Electronics and Electrical Engineers; American Motorcycle Association. **Education:** Trinity University, B.A. (1978). **Personal Information:** Married. One child. Mr. Hoey enjoys motorcycles and golf.

Jennifer L. Jones

Information Technology Transition Manager
Hewlett-Packard Company
467 Saratoga Avenue #801
San Jose, CA 95129-1326
(650) 236-2377
Fax: (650) 857-4586
jennifer_jones@hp.com

3571

Business Information: Ms. Jones, who has been a member of the Hewlett-Packard Company team since 1995, is an Information Technology Finance Transition Manager. She works on special projects involving the realignment of Hewlett-Packard and Agilent Technologies. In addition, she manages Information Technology crantracts and finance. Ms. Jones attributes success to her sense of perserverence and the desire to complete all objectives. As for the future, she hopes to be actively involved in more joint ventures and mergers. Beside her current occupation with Hewlett-Packard, Ms. Jones is also an Attorney at Law. Her success reflects her ability to think outside the box, deliver results, and aggressively take on new challenges. Hewlett-Packard is a leading manufacturer of computers, peripheral hardware, and medical equipment. The personal computers are geared towards Microsoft's Windows Operating system. With the help of 10,000 workers, the Company has become a leader in the industry, which is illustrated by a $47 billion estimated annual revenue. **Career Highlights:** Hewlett-Packard Company: Information Technology Transition Manager (1999-Present), Strategic Alliance Manager (1997-99), Real Estate Finance Manager (1995-97). **Associations & Accomplishments:** State Bar of California; State Bar of Nevada; Association of High Tech Acquisition Professionals. **Education:** Santa Clara University School of Law, J.D. (1991); Santa Clara University Leavey School of Business, M.B.A. (1991); University of California at San Diego, B.A. (1987). **Personal Information:** Married to Jim Friedl in 1997. Ms. Jones enjoys snowboarding and concerts.

Shirley J. Kaltenbach

Project Manager
Compaq Computer Corporation
110 Spit Brook Road
Nashua, NH 03062-2711
(603) 884-1099
Fax: (603) 884-0575
shirley.kaltenbach@compaq.com

3571

Business Information: Ms. Kaltenbach utilizes her superior talents in technology by serving as a Project Manager with Compaq Computer Corporation. Joining Compaq's team of professionals in 1998, she is recognized for her elite managerial skills in leading a group of performance consultants and instructional designers in developing advanced computer hardware and software. Ms. Kaltenbach also manages project budgets and recommends new purchases. Working closely with her team of 12 employees, she uses a management style that incorporates input and feedback from all staff members. The most rewarding aspects of her career is obtaining her Master's in Computer Science and working on various successful projects. Committed to the further development of the Corporation, Ms. Kaltenbach coordinates strategic planning to ensure continued success for Compaq. Established in 1957, Compaq Computer Corporation has grown to be one of the world's leading manufacturers of personal computers. Headquartered in Houston, Texas, the Corporation serve an international clientele, and maintains offices worldwide. The Corporation employs over 55,000 individuals who facilitate the design, manufacture, distribution, and sales of computers as well as hardware and software. Reporting annual revenues in excess of $24 million, Compaq continues to pilot the market with innovation, reliability, and efficiency, maintaining the Corporation's status as a Fortune 500 company. **Career Highlights:** Project Manager, Compaq Computer Corporation (1998-Present); Project Manager, Digital Equipment Corporation (1995-98); Resource Coach, Digital Equipment Corporation (1993-95). **Education:** Rivier College, M.S. in Computer Science (1987); Westmont College, B.A. in History (1971). **Personal Information:** Ms. Kaltenbach enjoys tennis.

Kathy L. Khalifa

Advisory Software Engineer
IBM Corporation
1005 Brittley Way
Apex, NC 27502-6424
(919) 254-4464
Fax: (919) 254-6430
khalifa@us.ibm.com

3571

Business Information: Highly proficient in the technology field, Ms. Khalifa serves as Advisory Software Engineer for the IBM Corporation's Research Triangle Park (RTP), North Carolina division. A recognized expert in Java, C++, and GUI, she designs and develops cutting edge software. Currently, Ms. Khalifa is working on web transcoding technology for pervasive devices and holds three patents for technological systems. Effectively developing individual, departmental, and organizational goals, she looks forward to expanding the Web applications development arena within the RTP facility. Ms. Khalifa attributes her professional success to persistence and enjoying what she does, as well as her ability to deliver results and aggressively take on challenges. A highly reputable international technology company, IBM Corporation manufactures and distributes software and hardware products. The Corporation was established in 1940 and maintains offices worldwide. The IBM North Carolina division employs 15,000 individuals. **Career Highlights:** Advisory Software Engineer, IBM Corporation (1983-Present). **Associations & Accomplishments:** Institute of Electrical and Electronics Engineers. **Education:** Georgia State University, B.S. (1985). **Personal Information:** Married to Ahmed in 1993. Two children: Jessica Pryor and Maria Karunuñgan. Ms. Khalifa enjoys music, art, riding horseback and her job.

Marc Kindermans

Business Development Manager
Hewlett-Packard Belgium
Elzenbroek Straat 13
Oud Haverlee, Belgium 3053
+32 7783638
Fax: +32 27783315
marc_kindermans@hp.com

3571

Business Information: Joining Hewlett-Packard Belgium as an Information Technology Consultant in 1993, Mr. Kindermans now serves as Business Development Manager for the Company. Drawing upon an extensive background, he is responsible for overseeing all of new business developments and joint ventures in the communications industry. Posssessing an excellent understanding of technology, Mr. Kindermans performs research for new markets, maintains client relationships, and provides individual services to each client. Moreover, he supervises a staff of employees who are dedicated to their work and report to him direclty. In the future, he looks forward to continuing with the Company in his current position. Mr. Kindermans attributes his success to his speed and degree of learning and observing others in the work environment. Located in Oud Heverlee, Belgium, Hewlett-Packard Belgium engages in the design and manufacture of computational devices and systems. Founded in 1939, the Company develops cutting edge systems used in business, health care, and education as well as a variety of other global industries. Furthermore, the Company distributes the information technology hardware, software, and services to an international clientele. With a work force of over 93,000 employees worldwide, the Company reports an estimated annual revenue of $43 billion. **Career Highlights:** Hewlett-Packard Belgium: Business Development Manager (1999-Present), Principal Consultant (1997-99), Information Technology Consultant (1993-97). **Education:** Leuven University, Master's degree in Computer Science; INSEAD, Bachelor's degree in Engineering and Electronics (2000). **Personal Information:** Married to Kristel in 1990. Four children: Daan, Johanna, Charlotte, and Elizabeth. Mr. Kindermans enjoys family time and church choir.

Keith S. Klemba

Chief Technology Advisor
Hewlett-Packard Company
100 Mayfield Avenue
Mountain View, CA 94043
(650) 691-3051
Fax: (650) 691-3047
keith_klemba@hp.com

3571

Business Information: Motivated to stay at the forefront of all modern technology, Mr. Klemba serves as the Chief Technology Advisor of Hewlett-Packard Company. Presently operating from the Company's headquarters in Palo Alto, California, Mr. Klemba conducts new business consultation and design. Specializing in new business strategy, he introduces innovative structures, and performs evaluations of new technologies that may be utilized by client companies. Recently offering outreach programs for his large client base, Mr. Klemba goes directly to the new business sites, and conducts evaluations of business partners and operational situations. The most rewarding aspect of his career is working on a radio during the early days of the Internet and doing work internationally. His success is attributed to his ability to think outside the box, take on challenges, and deliver results. Ranked among the five largest and highest quality PC providers, Hewlett-Packard Company has established a new class of computers, their services and products are available around the globe in the competitive computer market. Engaged in the manufacture of computers, peripherals, and computer related equipment as well as test and measurement of medical electronic equipment, Hewlett-Packard Company generates an incredible $40 billion in annual revenue. A major employer of over 100,000 information technology professionals worldwide, the Company is situated at the center of the corporate world. **Career Highlights:** Chief Technology Advisor, Hewlett-Packard Company (1987-Present); Product Engineering Manager, Vitalink (1984-87); Principle Investigator, SRI International (1969-84). **Personal Information:** Married to Lynda Alexander.

Kenneth O. Larson

Senior Consultant
Compaq Computer Corporation
1124 Tower Road
Schaumburg, IL 60713
(847) 781-6820
Fax: (847) 781-6507
ken.larson@compaq.com

3571

Business Information: Serving as Senior Consultant, Mr. Larson has been providing professional services on behalf of Compaq Computer Corporation since 1987. Establishing and maintaining major client relationships, he is extensively involved in pre-sale and post-sale operations and the negotiation of contracts. Managing projects with up to 20 employees, he provides architecture solutions and turns potential into action. Highly regarded, Mr. Larson also serves as project manager of enterprise systems, with a focus on e-business services. Managing the budget and initiating specific purchases of materials needed also fall within the realm of his responsibilities. Always alert to new opportunities, techniques, and approaches, Mr. Larson strives to incorporate the latest technologies into systems development with an emphasis on his potential for further advancement. A Fortune 500 company, Compaq Computer Corporation is the third largest computer company of its kind in world. Established in 1982, the Corporation manufactures and distributes computer systems to an international client base. Employing over 50,000 skilled technicians, engineers, and designers, the Corporation is known for excellent sales and services. Also involved in systems integration, the Corporation remains committed to servicing the specific needs of its expanding clientele. **Career Highlights:** Senior Consultant, Digital Equipment Corporation/Compaq Computer Corporation [acquired Digital Equipment Corporation in 1997] (1987-Present); Section Leader/Designer, Sargent & Lundy Engineers (1975-87). **Associations & Accomplishments:** American Society of Mechanical Engineers; Association of Internet Professionals; Past Chairman, St. John's School. **Education:** Illinois Institute of Technology, B.S. in Engineering Graphics (1975). **Personal Information:** Married to Kathleen in 1975. Three children: Coreen, David, and Allen. Mr. Larson enjoys computer sciences, genealogy and home remodeling.

Myungho Lee, Ph.D.

Senior Performance Technologist
Sun Microsystems, Inc.
901 San Antonio Road, MS SUN03-311
Palo Alto, CA 94303-4900
(408) 616-5571
Fax: (408) 774-8154
myungh.lee@eng.sun.com

3571

Business Information: Drawing upon his extensive education and experience, Dr. Lee generates ideas in the area of analysis to improve compiler, hardware, and processor performance. A savvy veteran of technology, he is a lead developer of leading edge applications software targeted specifically towards the SPARC (tm) processor. Dr. Lee plans to continue providing full and concrete analysis, facilitating the success of the SPARC (tm) processor, and advancing within the Corporation's hierarchy. He became interested in both parallel and high performance computing technology upon completion of his Ph.D. program which led him to his current position. Dr. Lee has enjoyed substantial success based upon being open-minded and his ability to explore new areas of change within the field. Sun Microsystems, Inc. based in the Bay Area of California, manufactures and distributes high performance computers on an international scale, providing leading edge technology and solutions for companies in the communication age. The Corporation also produces and distributes proprietary software and hardware for it's trademark SPARC processors. **Career Highlights:** Senior Performance Technologist, Sun Mircrosystems, Inc. (1999-Present); Graduate Research Assistant, University of Southern California (1997-99). **Associations & Accomplishments:** Institute of Electrical and Electronics Engineers; Association of Computing Machinery; Past Member/Current Cooperator, Legion of Mary; Cooperator, Opus Dei. **Education:** University of Southern California: Ph.D. (1999), M.S.; Seoul National University, B.S. **Personal Information:** Married to Won-Hye Doh in 1997. One child: Richard Lee. Dr. Lee enjoys reading and music.

Gilles Leveque

Information Systems Manager
Hewlett-Packard Company
#58 5 Avenue Raymond Chanas-Eybens
Grenoble Cedex 9, France 38053
+33 476141741
Fax: +33 476146505
gilles_leveque@hp.com

3571

Business Information: Serving as Hewlett-Packard Company's Information Systems Manager since 1998, Mr. Leveque is responsible for the networking and upgrades of the European distribution center computer product group. Focusing his attention on hardware and software support, he is an advocate for open communication between employees of the Company, realizing the unified sense of teamwork that can develop. Mr. Leveque supervises the staff of the information technology department, manufacturing division center, marketing center, and the distribution center, completing evaluations and training for them as well. Mr. Leveque intends to continue in his current capacity, seeking advancement opportunities within the corporate structure. Hewlett-Packard is an international controller and communications manufacturer of technical hardware for businesses and individuals. As a service provider, the Company focus on the support of products distributed, by offering outstanding customer service. Established in 1989, Hewlett-Packard's estimated annual global revenue exceeds $3 billion. **Career Highlights:** Hewlett-Packard Company: Information Systems Manager (1998-Present), Inbound Logistics Manager (1993-98); Consultant/Project Manager, Anderson Consulting (1988-92). **Associations & Accomplishments:** Loger Phone Acres; Re-Activ. **Education:** INSA Lyon, Engineering degree (1988). **Personal Information:** Married to Isabelle in 1994. Two children: Lisa and Thomas. Mr. Leveque enjoys sports, jogging, swimming, cycling and rugby.

Maria Levin

Mail and Messaging Consultant
Compaq Computer Corporation
945 Riverside Drive, Apartment 29A
Methuen, MA 01844-6741
(978) 725-8298
maria_levin@yahoo.com

3571

Business Information: Utilizing several years of experience in the technology field, Ms. Levin serves as Mail and Messaging Consultant for the Compaq Computer Corporation. Before joining Compaq, she assertively worked as a Technical Support Specialist with Digital Equipment Corporation. In her current role, Ms. Levin is Microsoft Certified and acts as the Microsoft Exchange Agent between Fortune 500 companies and the Corporation. Attributing her success to focus, dedication, and setting goals, she keeps abreast of technological advancements by reading trade journals and networking with peers. Quickly establishing her presence in the technical field, Ms. Levin looks forward to assisting in achieving future corporate goals and moving up within the consulting world. The Compaq Computer Corporation is a name easily recognized by anyone familiar with the computer industry. Best known for its sale of the popular desktop computers, the Corporation sells servers to the business sector as well. Desktop support and other professional computer related services are offered to businesses and individuals. Compaq Computer Corporation was established in 1965 and employs over 20,000 personnel worldwide. **Career Highlights:** Mail and Messaging Consultant, Compaq Computer Corporation (1998-Present); Technical Support Specialist, Digital Equipment Corporation (1996-98). **Education:** State University of New York at Albany, B.S. (1996). **Personal Information:** Ms. Levin enjoys tennis and volleyball.

Mark A. Livingston, Ph.D.

Research Programmer
Hewlett-Packard Labs
1501 Page Mill Road
Palo Alto, CA 94304-1126
(650) 236-2414
Fax: (650) 852-3791
mark_livingston@hpl.hp.com

3571

Business Information: Conducting research on computer graphics and computer vision of Hewlett-Packard Labs, Dr. Livingston serves in the position of Research Programmer. In his role, he utilizes his extensive expertise to reconstruct geometric properties, assist in consumer applications for display on the Web, and conduct independent research on computer graphics. Possessing extensive technical expertise, Dr. Livingston cites as his career highlights his dissertation on systems for tracking user and vitual environment as well as developing a real time system used in medical and surgical operations. Keeping abreast of new developments in the field, Dr. Livingston incorporates pertinent information into daily activities. Future plans include contributing to the overlay of computer graphics over video. His success reflects his ability to think out-of-the-box and deliver results. Hewlett-Packard Labs, interantionally recognized, specializes in computer systems and peripherals. Established in 1939, a staff of 78,000 dedicated professionals lend their expertise in various aspects of Hewlett-Packard operations. Headquartered in California, the Company strives to meet the demanding technological needs of its consumers. **Career Highlights:** Research Programmer, Hewlett-Packard Labs (1998-Present). **Associations & Accomplishments:** Association of Computing Machinery; SIGGRAPH; Institute of Electical and Electronics Engineers; Golden Key National Honor Society; Eagle Scout, Boy Scouts of America. **Education:** University of North Carolina at Chapel Hill: Ph.D. (1998), M.S. (1996); Duke University, A.B. (1993). **Personal Information:** Dr. Livingston enjoys tennis, running, and contract bridge.

Michael LuVisi

Information Technology Architect
IBM Corporation
3300 East Spring Street, Mail stop DK54-215
Long Beach, CA 90806-2428
(562) 988-4357
Fax: (562) 988-4042
michael.luvisi@iname.com

3571

Business Information: Recruited to IBM Corporation in 1993, Mr. LuVisi currently serves as Information Technology Architect. He is responsible developing complex information systems solutions and resolving technical implementation issues to optimize performance. A systems expert, he also plans, organizes, designs, installs, operates, and maintains UNIX operating systems within the Corporation. Highlights of Mr. LuVisi's career include obtaining three professional certifications, finishing his B.S. Degree, and participating in transition management on the Boeing aircraft contract. All this was accomplished in only one year. For the future, he plans to further his education and complete his M.B.A. Mr. LuVisi attributes his success in the industry to his parents and his girlfriend Billie. The IBM Corporation is a recognized leader in the computer and information technology arena. Functioning to enhance the technology era through the implementation of state-of-the-art, affordable technology solutions, IBM's focus is to improve the typical business workplace. Maintaining a global presence, the Corporation presently employs a work force of more than 292,000 professional, technical, and support staf f. **Career Highlights:** IBM Corporation: Information Technology Architect (1996-Present), Information Technology Specialist, Systems Management Integration (1993-96); Senior Staff, Information Systems Support Analyst, McDonnell Douglas Company (1991-93). **Associations & Accomplishments:** Eagle Scout, Boy Scouts of America; USA Roller Skating. **Education:** University of Phoenix, Southern California Campus, B.S. in Business/Information Systems (1999); Learning Tree, Client/Server Systems Certified Professional (1998); Internetworking Certified Professional (1998); Internet/Intranet Certified Professional (1998); Golden West Junior College, C.C. (1975). **Personal Information:** Two children: Sheree L. and Thomas W. L. Mr. LuVisi enjoys scuba diving, snow skiing, roller skating, horseback riding and amateur radio.

Shamun Mahmud

Staff Consultant
Amdahl Corporation
5335 Wisconsin Avenue NW, Suite 500
Washington, DC 20015
(202) 895-4439
Fax: (202) 966-9047
shahmud@amdahl.com

3571

Business Information: As the Staff Consultant of Amdahl Corporation, Mr. Mahmud fulfills a number of consulting duties on behalf of the Corporation and its clientele. He works closely with management and systems users to analyze, specify, design, and implement advanced technological solutions to enhance operations at the Corporation and client sites. Highly regarded, MR. Mahmud offers superior technical support to regional customers. He demonstrates his skills and knowledge through his hands-on management and his above average aptitude for problem solving. Alert to new challenges and opportunities, Mr. Mahmud's future goals include attain a position in sales, encouraging further corporate growth and expansion. Amdahl Corporation, a subsidiary of Fujitsu Ltd., develops and implements systems, services, and support for the world's most computer-intensive corporations and governments. Established in 1974, the Corporation has stayed on the cutting-edge of computer innovation, developing the Intranet in 1994, and offering top-notch software to clients internationally. Amdahl employs a staff of more than 10,000 individuals to serve the diverse needs of clients and generates annual revenue of approximately $40 billion. **Career Highlights:** Amdahl Corporation: Staff Consultant (1999-Present), Senior Staff Marketing Engineer (1998-99); UNIX Consultant, BSG/Alliance IT (1997). **Associations & Accomplishments:** Institute of Electrical and Electronics Engineers Computer Society. **Education:** James Madison University, M.B.A. (1993); George Mason University (1991); Northern Virginia Community College (1989). **Personal Information:** Mr. Mahmud enjoys researching on the Web, reading and surfing the Internet.

Michael A. Maimbourg

Production Engineer
Solectron Corporation
1403 Baldridge Drive
Gatesville, TX 76528-1120
(512) 425-6600
sooner@sage.net

3571

Business Information: Mr. Maimbourg is the Production Engineer for Solectron Corporation. He is the liaison between internal customers and external customers, advising on testing, building, placements, and quotes. It is very important for Mr. Maimbourg to pay close attention to the details of his job, since every thing must be documented for presentation during business meetings. His superior drive and determination are major contributors to his success, alongside his enjoyment in what he does. Mr. Maimbourg's interest in the profession of technology was sparked by his grandfathers employment with Southwestern Bell. He has pride in his ability to provide services to his customers. Therefore, he intends to stay with the Corporation and move higher up so that he may provide even better services. Established in 1977, Solectron Corporation provides supply chain solutions for the world's top manufacturers of original electronic equipment. With more than 43,000 associates in 40 locations around the world, the Corporation reports annual revenues in excess of $10 billion. Solectron's target industries are in computer, computer peripheral, networking, telecommunications, and others. **Career Highlights:** Production Engineer, Solectron Corporation (1995-Present); Product Engineer, Texas Instruments (1989-95). **Associations & Accomplishments:** International Society of Certified Electrical Technician/Engineer; Who's Who Among American High School Students (1982-84); Who's Who Among American College Students (1985-89). **Education:** Central Texas College, A.A.S. (1989). **Personal Information:** Mr. Maimbourg enjoys computer related hobbies and HTML programming.

Violet E. Markowski

Data Management & Business Intelligence Sales Associate
IBM Corporation
114 Varnum Street
Arlington, MA 02474
(781) 895-2820
Fax: (781) 895-2659

3571

Business Information: Miss Markowski assumes responsibility for two separate roles within IBM Corporation. Serving in Business Intelligence Sales, she supervises two sales partners and is responsible for business intelligence solutions which are engineered towards American clients and sold to enterprise, small, and medium business accounts. In her role in Data Management, she works with sales representatives to sell integrated products to clients. Additionally, she assists in the management of a sales pipeline worth in excess of $40 million. As a four year professional, Miss Markowski attributes her career success to a policy of open communication, follow through, and providing clients with the capability to provide solutions to their customers. Her major accomplishments include receiving Summit Award nomination while employed by Lotus Development. Dedicated to the success of the Corporation, she plans to continue taking an active part in the sales of IBM products and services. Headquartered in Armonch, New York, IBM Corporation is the leader in development and manufacture of computers and other related technological accessories. Established in 1911, approximately 300,000 skilled individuals are employed at the Corporation's large network of locations internationally. **Career Highlights:** Data Management Business Intelligence Sales Associate, IBM Corporation (1998-Present); Central Regional Sales Associate, Lotus Development (1996-98); Project Developer/Sales and Marketing Associate, Information Access Company (1995-96). **Associations & Accomplishments:** Junior League of Boston; Simmons College Alumnae Resources Committee; League of Women Voters of Boston. **Education:** Simmons College, B.A. in Management and Marketing (1995). **Personal Information:** Miss Markowski enjoys tennis and running.

Yukie Masuda

Advisory Education Specialist
IBM Japan
I-53 Nisshincho Kawasaki-Ku Kawasaki-Shi
Kanagawa, Japan 210-0024
+81 442015084
Fax: +81 442009043
yukiem@jp.ibm.com

3571

Business Information: Working as an Advisory Education Specialist with IBM Japan for over five years, Ms. Masuda, educates IBM's internal workers by implementing the Corporation's learning systems and instructing employees in current technologies. Also responsible for the long-distance education of employees, Ms. Masuda maintains high educational standards for employees who are attending seminars over the Internet. With this technology, she enables the employees to better serve their clients worldwide by providing customer service and quality software. In the future, Ms. Masuda plans to use her vast experience to move into infrastructure design and internal corporate consultation. She attributes her success to hard work, patience, and team work. IBM Japan, an international subsidiary of IBM, manufactures computers for personal and commercial use. Specializing in peripheral devices for those computers, the Corporation manufactures software and networking systems as well as offering services and consultations in information technology. Established in 1985, IBM Japan maintains an international base of clients with over 18,000 employees who provide software support and technical support solutions to numerous customers the world over. **Career Highlights:** Advisory Education Specialist, IBM Japan (1994-Present). **Associations & Accomplishments:** Japanese Board on Books for Young People. **Education:** Keio University, Bachelor's degree in Economics (1985). **Personal Information:** Ms. Masuda enjoys Japanese traditional tea, non traditional theater plays and hand crafts.

James L. Meyerson

Senior Technical Consultant
Hewlett-Packard Company
19111 Pruneridge Avenue
Cupertino, CA 95014
(408) 447-2000
Fax: (408) 447-1053

3571

Business Information: As a Senior Technical Consultant with Hewlett-Packard Company, Mr. Meyerson is primarily responsible for designing large databases and solutions to meet the needs of client companies. Mr. Meyerson has led multi-organization teams in developing high-end OLTP applications and very large Data Warehouse implementations. Possessing an excellent understanding of both technology and the relationship of business process to technology, he currently directs business intelligence and e-commerce efforts for Hewlett-Packard, working to provide quality solutions for a reasonable price. Highly regarded, Mr. Meyerson was recruited to the Company in 1996. With more than 23 years of experience in the computer industry, he is currently working to expand the industrial client base. Mr. Meyerson's future plans include continued involvement in high-end e-commerce and business intelligence technology, as well as expansion into next wave e-Service technology. Founded in 1939, Hewlett-Packard is the second largest computer manufacturer in the world. With a staff of 88,000 and annual sales currently exceeding $44 billion, the Company creates hardware, software, and operates as a systems solution provider. Corporate headquarters are in Palo Alto, California, and subsidiaries are located in 120 countries around the world. Hewlett-Packard is listed in the top 20 of

Fortune 500 companies. **Career Highlights:** Senior Technical Consultant, Hewlett-Packard Company (1996-Present); Tandem Computers: Senior Advisory Analyst (1992-95), Senior Instructor (1987-92). **Associations & Accomplishments:** Data Warehousing Institute; Tau Beta Pi; Eta Kappa Nu; multiple oustanding employee awards (STAR, TOPS). **Education:** Arizona State University, M.S. in Engineering (1979); Purdue University, B.S. in Electrical Engineering (1977). **Personal Information:** Married in 1984. Mr. Meyerson enjoys running, bridge, reading and Web research.

Walkiria Monteiro

Systems Manager
Compaq Computer Corporation
R.D. Campinas Mogi-Miram, Jagyarauna
Sao Paulo, Brazil 13130-596
+55 1938677163
Fax: +55 1938677062
walkiria.monteiro@compaq.com

3571

Business Information: As the Systems Manager for Compaq Computer Corporation, Mrs. Monteiro oversees and directs a number of duties on behalf of the Corporation and its clientele. She is responsible for all systems related to manufacturing and the shop floor control. Utilizing more than 10 years of experience in the computer industry, she deals with systems maintenance and oversees nine personnel within three shifts. The most rewarding aspects of her career is her work in the U.S. on several projects with industry giants, such as Compaq and IBM. Assertively working with the Corporation since coming on board as Systems Supervisor in 1994, Mrs. Monteiro plans to continue in her position with Compaq and is looking forward to assisting in the completion of future corporate goals. Serving an international clientele, Compaq is one of the world's premier manufacturer and distributor of PCs for different segments including consumer environment and commercial for small and medium accounts and enterprise for large accounts. Products include desktops and portable computers, software, and hardware. Headquartered in Houston, Texas, the Corporation maintains a global presence. Presently, the operational plant in Sao Paulo, Brazil is manned by a large work force. **Career Highlights:** Compaq Computer Corporation: Systems Manager (1997-Present), Systems Supervisor (1994-97); Consultant, DBM Brazil (1991-94). **Education:** BUCC University at Campinas, Bachelor's degree in Computer Science (1996). **Personal Information:** Married to Paulo R. F. in 1996. Two children: Paulo Henrique and Gabriel Henrique. Mrs. Monteiro enjoys walking on the beach, smiling and joking with his kids.

Ellen M. Moser

Project Executive
IBM Corporation
128 Nevada Street
Redwood City, CA 94062-2134
(650) 369-0333
Fax: (650) 568-9191
e-moser@pacbell.net

3571

Business Information: A successful, 18 year veteran of IBM Corporation, Mrs. Moser serves as Project Executive for the Redwood City, California office. She is responsible for providing project management expertise to external clients for their information technology projects as well as managing IBM teams in solutions delivery. Possessing strong business savvy and expertise, Mrs. Moser meets with clients and executives to analyze, specify, design, and implement her clients' specific business needs. She is also in charge of providing, reviewing, and approving all progress reports. Accountable for profits at customer's sites, she mentors her teams consisting of 5 to 200 people, and provides planning and direction of projects worth from $30 million to $100 million. Most of her projects last approximately seven months. Her career highlights include managing her first project in 1987 and competitively beating Oracle; and working on large projects bringing in an additional $32 million to IBM. A supportive family, dedication and hard work, and being at the right place at the right time are reasons for Mrs. Moser's professional success. Her goals are to continue to learn and eventually start up her own business. IBM is one of the world's largest provider of technical solutions and technolog project management and consulting services. Headquartered in Chicago, Illinois, the Corporation is known for manufacturing products such as computers, servers, and refurbished equipment. Services offered include e-business, systems integration, and network consulting. The Corporation reports annual revenues in excess of $81 billion. **Career Highlights:** IBM Corporation: Project Executive (1995-Present), Principal of Information Systems Management Practice (1993-95), Consulting Services Manager (1990-93). **Associations & Accomplishments:** Project Management Institute; A.S.P.C.A.; KQED-San Francisco. **Education:** Rochester Institute of Technology, M.S. (1981); Northampton Community College, A.A. (1978). **Personal Information:** Married to Jerry in 1986. Mrs. Moser enjoys sports, scuba diving and music.

Sheldon Mundle

Senior Consultant
IBM Corporation
1704 Chanson Place
Marietta, GA 30062

3571

Business Information: Serving as Senior Consultant for IBM Corporation since 1997, Mr. Mundle's primary responsibility is working on Lawson software. This replaces a company's home Human Resources Department, payrolls, and benefits to allow for outsourcing. Working with Fortune 500 companies, he administers projects, installing and implementing systems. Before joining IBM in 1997, he served as a Consultant with Cap Gemini Consultant. Mr. Mundle recently completed an 18 month project in Chicago in which he demonstrated his mainframe client server and project management skills. An engineer major in college, Mr. Mundle found himself spending more and more time with computer people and a career was born. He stays in touch with his peers in the technology field and reads trade journals to keep up with changes in the technology industry. Persistence has enabled him to be successful. His success reflects his ability to think out-of-the-box and aggressively take on new challenges and responsibilities. Looking to the future, Mr. Mundle plans to grow and work with e-business applications. Incorporated in 1911, IBM is the world's leading information technology company. The Corporation creates, develops, and manufactures products such as computer systems, software, storage devices, and microelectronics. More than 250,000 skilled and knowledgeable professionals provide expertise in consulting services, systems integration, solution development, and technical support. **Career Highlights:** Senior Consultant, IBM Corporation (1997-Present); Consultant, Cap Gemini Consultant (1996-97). **Education:** Drexel University, Bachelor's degree in Science (1996).

James W. Pringle

Senior Solution Architect
Compaq Computer Corporation
3743 Churn Creek Road
Redding, CA 96002
(530) 224-1637
Fax: (530) 224-1557
james.pringle@compaq.com

3571

Business Information: Providing extensive technological solution services, Mr. Pringle functions in the position of Senior Solution Architect for Compaq Computer Corporation. He designs state-of-the-art system infrastructures and implements enterprise networking and messaging solutions for Fortune 100 companies. To maintain sharp skills, he stays on the cutting edge of technology by reading manuals and performing hands-on solutions. An expert in the field, Mr. Pringle has published two books, served as editing author of Monitoring Microsoft Exchange, and functioned as contributing author to LAN Times Guide to Interoperability. One of his greatest professional accomplishments is implementation of a networking system in California which had approximately 220,000 users. As a long-term goal, he would like to continue to grow and keep up with technology. Mr. Pringle's credo for success is the expression, "He who throws dirt, loses ground." Compaq Computer Corporation assesses, designs, and implements networking and messaging solutions for Fortune 100 companies. The Corporation primarily sells computers and provides consultation services on software. The second largest manufacturing company in the world, Compaq Computer Corporation recently purchased Digital Equipment Corporation. Established in 1958, the Corporation employs a work force of 110,000 people generating in excess of $35 billion in annual revenue **Career Highlights:** Senior Solution Architect, Compaq Computer Corporation (1996-Present); Technical Site Manager, Weyerhauser Company (1995-96); Senior Consulting Engineer, CompuCom Systems (1994-95); Network Manager, Wall Data Inc. (1991-94). **Associations & Accomplishments:** Networking Professional Association; Sigma Alpha Epsilom; MCSE; MCP; Novell CNE; Certified Network Expert (Cethernet)(CNX). **Education:** City University (1995); Chico State University, B.S. in Computer Science with a minor in Business Administration; Shasta College, Redding, California, A.A. in Information Systems and General Education. **Personal Information:** Married to Laurel in 1990. Five children: Tamara, Loren, Christopher, Andrew, and James III. Mr. Pringle enjoys racquetball, computers and strategic games.

Luis E. Rosado

Senior Consultant
Sun Microsystems, Inc.
1918 Cresson Drive
Southlake, TX 76092
(817) 875-7931
Fax: (817) 416-1452
rosados@swbell.net

3571

Business Information: A successful, 14 year veteran of technology, Mr. Rosado serves as the Senior Consultant of Sun Microsystems, Inc. He oversees and directs the infrastructure of high availability systems integration. Working closely with management and users, he guides his team of 15 employees in analyzing, specifying, and designing state-of-the-art enterprise data systems. Possessing an excellent understanding of technology, 90 percent of Mr. Rosado's time is spent sharing his knowledge with others in the field. In this context, his focus is on expanding and growing the Corporation and mentoring his staff to avoid mistakes. The analysis, design, evaluation, testing, and implementation of operating and networking systems, databases, utilities, software, and hardware also fall within the realm of his responsibilities. Contributing his professional success to his willingness to share information, he plans to continue teaching and growing with technology. Founded in 1986, Sun Microsystems is a computer consulting company. An independent software and hardware vendor, the Corporation is engaged in the manufacture of high end work stations. Sun Microsystems is also involved in systems integration services and design of data centers. Presently, the Corporation employs 150 professional and technical experts at the Southlake, Texas facility. **Career Highlights:** Senior Consultant, Sun Mircrosystems, Inc. (2000-Present); Senior Consultant, ISCC (1998-00); Senior Systems Integrator Consultant, COMMS People (1997-98); Systems Integrator IV, Sprint (1995-97). **Education:** U.P.R.-R.U.M., B.S. in Computer Engineering (1986). **Personal Information:** Married.

Linda L. Rose

Environmental Health and Safety Specialist
Hewlett-Packard Company
2411 Southeast 183rd Loop
Vancouver, WA 98683
(360) 212-4861
linda_rose@hp.com

3571

Business Information: Ms. Rose is the Environmental Health and Safety (EHS) Specialist for Hewlett-Packard Company, working at its location in Vancouver, Washington. She manages the injury and illness database records for employees worldwide. Boasting strong managerial talents, she has been appointed as the information technology project leader for the EHS systems implementation. Her background history includes employment as Research Associate with Oregon Health Sciences University and Nursing Supervisor at Sun Health Corporation. Working closely with Dr. William Hersh, Ms. Rose developed her Master's thesis, "Factors that influence successful information retrieval from nurse practitioner students." Her major accomplishment to date is presenting her research for her thesis at a Occupational Health Nurse Conference. After dedicating five years to Hewlett-Packard, Ms. Rose is looking forward to continuing with the Company and advancing her education through the opportunities made available to her. Her success reflects her passion for technology as well as her ability to think outside the box, deliver results, and aggressively take on new challenges. Hewlett-Packard Company was established in 1953 and has continued to rise as one of the leading producers of computer hardware and software in the world. The Company has multiple locations throughout the world including several manufacturing sites, distribution centers, and sales offices. With thousands of employees and acess to the most cutting edge technology in the industry, Hewlett-Packard has a strong network to stand behind every product and work with every customer to ensure their complete satisfaction. **Career Highlights:** Environmental Health and Safety Specialist, Hewlett-Packard Company (1994-Present); Research Associate, Oregon Health Sciences University (1996-98); Nursing Supervisor, Sun Health Corporation (1989-91). **Associations & Accomplishments:** Sigma Theta Tau, Nursing Honor Society; Association of Occupational Helath Nurses. **Education:** Oregon Health Sciences University, M.S. (1998); Grand Canyon University, B.S. in Nursing. **Personal Information:** Two children: Roxanne Berryman and Tammy Thomas. Ms. Rose enjoys information retrieval research.

Steven W. Sachs

Director of Retail Systems Integration
Telxon Corporation
8302 New Trails Drive
The Woodlands, TX 77381
(281) 719-1774
Fax: (281) 719-1746
ssach@telxon.com

3571

Business Information: Mr. Sachs is the Director of Retail Systems Integration at Telxon Corporation. He designs and implements cuttting edge mobile and RF LAN computing solutions for retailers, including Walmart, Macy's, and Kroger Company. A 17-year veteran in retail systems design, Mr. Sachs is responsible for ensuring that all products fit the needs and solve the business problems of the retailing industry. Assisting in the hiring and training of new engineering and marketing employees is also an integral part of his responsibilities. In collaboration with other executives, Mr. Sachs helps Telxon to formulate policies and procedures, develop goals, and implement strategies. His main objective is to see the Corporation grow, and expand its technological influence in the world marketplace. An expert in retail systems design and implementation, he is proud to have participated in several retail systems "firsts," including the first entirely RDBMS based POS system at Mervyn's Department Stores in 1991 while with POST Software International. This retail data model was used as the basis of the Association for Retail Technology Standards model. Another was the first supermarket-style, full scanning system implemented at a college bookstore for California State University at Northridge in 1985. Mr. Sachs attributes his success to his father who taught him how to analyze problems objectively from multiple aspects and design the appropriate solutions. Telxon Corporation, originally established in 1969 as Electronic Laboratories, Inc., is a leading global designer and manufacturer of wireless and mobile information systems for vertical markets. Telxon has over 1,400 employees in more than 40 offices in the United States and offices, subsidiaries, and distributors in over 60 countries. **Career Highlights:** Director of Retail Systems Integration, Telxon Corporation (1993-Present); Project Leader/Staff Programmer, POST Software International (1990-93); Senior Software Engineer, Citicorp POS (1989-90); Programmer, Carter Hawley Hale Stores IS (1987-89). **Associations & Accomplishments:** JavaPOS (TM) Standards Committee. **Education:** L.A. Pierce College, A.A. (1982); Control Data Institute (1983). **Personal Information:** Married to Lou Ann B. in 1986. Mr. Sachs enjoys golf, flying and poker.

Antonio Ernesto Schettino

Hardware Design Manager
Kb/TEL
Insurgentes Sur 3500, Torre Telmax, 4th Floor
Mexico City, Mexico 14060
+5252440693
Fax: +5252440671
aschettino@kbtel.com

3571

Business Information: As the Hardware Design Manager, Mr. Schettino has been providing professional services to Kb/TEL for over nine years. Supervising a knowledgable staff of highly experienced designers, they are responsible for developing the electronic equipment used in the various devices produced. Specifically designing the systems themselves, he then assigns it to his team in order for them to implement them into the necessary project. Continueing the development of his managerial skills, Mr. Schettino is utilizing his experience with the Company in order to start his own. Specializing in the development and distribution of wireless telecommunications, Kb/TEL was establishedi n 1989. Providing specific communications equipment for point to point data networking, they distribute their products throughout Latin America. Included in their variety of products are networking, wireless services used for internet access, and wireless connections for cash machines and bank branches. Headquartered in Mexico City, Mexico, over 150 employees dedicate their work towards the development of new products in order to service their clientel in a more efficient manor. **Career Highlights:** Kb/TEL: Hardware Design Manager (1998-Present), Senior Hardware Designer (1995-98), Hardware Designer (1992-95). **Associations & Accomplishments:** Institute of Electrical and Electronics Engineering; Sociedad de Exalumnos de la Facultad de Ingenieria. **Education:** King's College University of London, M.S. in Communications Engineering (1994); Facultad de Ingenieria Universidad Autonoma de Mexico, B.S. in Electrical Engineering (1993). **Personal Information:** Married to Nuria Gonzalez in 1995. Mr. Schettino enjoys jazz music and tennis.

Barry Price Scott

Support Manager
Sun Microsystems, Inc.
10951 Edgemont Drive
San Jose, CA 95127-1740
(510) 574-9573
Fax: (408) 251-1749
barry.scott@sun.com

3571

Business Information: Mr. Scott serves as Support Manager of Sun Microsystems, Inc. He is responsible for 1st level support of Sun's e-commerce and e-business clientele. Possessing an excellent understanding of technology, he supports direct and indirect sales and maintains the servers as well as all network functions. A successful, 28 year professional, Mr. Scott is in charge of troubleshooting systems difficulties. Well versed in all aspects of UNIX systems, he is highly regarded in the industry. He has received numerous internal awards at Sun Microsystems. Career success, according to Mr. Scott, is due to his determination and ability to tackle new challenges and deliver results. His advice is "step up to the leading edge and master new technology." Sun Microsystems is a UNIX based workstation and server manufacturer. Specializing in Solaris operating systems and Web equipment, the Corporation's targeted clientele include manufactures and e-businesses. International in scope, Sun Microsystems employs 30,000 professional, technical, and support staff who help generate in excess of $11 billion in annual revenues. The Corporation was established in 1982. **Career Highlights:** Support Manager, Sun Microsystems, Inc. (1999-Present); Senior Technical Support Specialist, Oracle Corporation (1999); Sun Microsystems, Inc.: Quality Assurance Manager (1997-99), Senior Software Technical Analyst (1990-97). **Education:** University of Santa Clara, M.B.A. (1972); Oregon State University, B.S. **Personal Information:** Married to Judith in 1966. One child: Peter Soo Woon. Mr. Scott enjoys flying, fishing and computers.

Stewart A. Skomra

Senior Director of Product Marketing
Telxon Corporation
8302 New Trails Drive
The Woodlands, TX 77381
(281) 719-1870
sskom@telxon.com

3571

Business Information: As Senior Director of Product Marketing of Telxon Corporation, Mr. Skomra is responsible for product line, to include software, hardware, and wireless equipment and accessories. A brilliant technologist with an excellent understanding of his field, Mr. Skomra is considered a visionary who has provent himself correct on many occasions. Highly regarded in the wireless LAN industry by both colleagues and the customers he serves, he strives to implement the latest technological advancements for high performance products. Showcasing his perseverance, Mr. Skomra manages business case formulations and product progression from infancy through development and implementation. The highlights of his career include working for IBC for seven years; being a previous co-owner of a software company, delivering network integration and cutting edge technologies. A credit to the Corporation, Mr. Skomra hopes to eventually start up his own wireless company. Established in 1970, the Telxon Corporation designs, develops, and manufactures, wireless communication systems. Headquartered in Akron, Ohio, Telxon proudly serves a vast corporate clientele in offices around the globe. The Corporation specializes in mobile information systems and wireless LAN, with quality installation and ongoing technical support. Concentrating efforts on the creation of portable computers and applications, Telxon strives to maintain a competitive edge in an ever evolving information industry. **Career Highlights:** Senior Director of Product Marketing, Telxon Corporation (1994-Present).

Savitha Srinivasan

Advisory Programmer
IBM Corporation
7190 Silver Lode Lane
San Jose, CA 95120-3340
(408) 927-1430
rssrinivasan@hotmail.com

3571

Business Information: Ms. Srinivasan has served with IBM Corporation in a variety of roles since joining the Corporation in 1989. Recently promoted to the position of Advisory Programmer, Ms. Srinivasan works in the research division, responsible for prototype testing and finding new applications. She believes that by understanding the positive and negative aspects of a product, improvements are able to be made. She is currently personally responsible for two new products in speech recognition. Keeping on the leading edge, Ms. Srinivasan keeps up to date by reading trade journals and conferencing with fellow team members and colleagues. In the future, she plans to keep developing new software that is useful to the public. IBM Corporation is a software development company. Always an innovator in the field of computer technology, IBM is currently working on such projects as speech recognition, video processing, data forum creation, and video media creation. Their research division has three separate research centers. Maintaining a global presence, IBM presently employs a work force of more than 300,000 professional, technical, and support staff. **Career Highlights:** Advisory Programmer, IBM Corporation (Present). **Associations & Accomplishments:** Association of Computing Machinery; Institute of Electrical and Electronics Engineers. **Education:** Pace University, M.S. (1988); Bachelor's degree in Engineering. **Personal Information:** Married.

Michael W. Studer

Software Engineer
Sun Microsystems, Inc.
6249 Quartz Place
Newark, CA 94560
(510) 574-9538
michael.studer@sun.com

3571

Business Information: Mr. Studer has been with Sun Microsystems, Inc. since 1996 and currently serves in the capacity of Software Engineer. Responsible for applications development, he oversees specific projects from conception to design retaining sole accountability for the finished product. He focuses time on extensive research and lab testing, where he demonstrates his stellar technical knowledge as he solves challenges and removes flaws to result in superior software. Utilizing his extensive education and practical work experience, Mr. Studer writes codes for programming and is involved in the development of JAVA browser applications. Crediting success to his interpersonal relationships, Mr. Studer looks forward to assisting in the completion of future coporate goals. Headquartered in Mountain View, California, Sun Microsystems, Inc. manufactures high-performance computer systems including workstations, servers, central processing units, and operating system software. With a diverse clientele including educational, engineering, and technical industries, the international company also offers Internet usage to customers. With over 60,000 employees worldwide, annual sales exceed $1.5 billion proving that the Corporation has built a firm foundation in a progressive field. **Career Highlights:** Sun Microsystems, Inc.: Software Engineer (1999-Present), Kernel Technical Support (1997-99), UNIX Technical Support (1996-97). **Associations & Accomplishments:** Retired Navy Petty Officer. **Education:** Broome Community College; College of the Sequoyas. **Personal Information:** Married to Lorina in 1985. Two children: Kimberly and Ashley. Mr. Studer enjoys ham radio and being a pilot.

DeAnnaKay Swetzig

Product Manager
Hewlett-Packard Company
700 71st Avenue, OEM
Greeley, CO 80634
(970) 350-4292
Fax: (970) 350-5688
deannakay_swetzig@hp.com

3571

Business Information: Possessing an excellent understanding of technology, Ms. Swetzig serves as Product Manager of Hewlett-Packard Company responsible for product marketing functions for the automation storage section of an original equipment manufacturer business unit. She is specifically responsible for the pricing, forecasting, business planning, and positioning of Hewlett-Packard storage products and services to various industries. For over 20 years, she has exemplified a professional record, originating in engineering. Enjoying the fact that her position has afforded her the opportunity to travel the globe for business, Ms. Swetzig attributes her success to her perseverance and her ability to recognize customer needs. In the future, she hopes to become more reliant on the Internet, business-to-business, and e-commerce. Hewlett-Packard is ranked among the top five manufacturers of personal computers, servers, peripherals, and services such as system integration and storage systems. Recently allied with information technology giants Intel and Microsoft, the Company is revitalizing its computer business and is using this as a step towards other markets and services. **Career Highlights:** Product Manager, Hewlett-Packard Company (1980-Present). **Associations & Accomplishments:** Dai Nippon Shimpu-kai Karate Nidan Black Belt; Advisory Board, Union Colony Civic Center; National Advisory Council/Ambassador, Miss Rodeo America; Miss Rodeo Colorado. **Education:** University of Northern Colorado, B.S. in Information Science (1977). **Personal Information:** Married to Scott T. Perkins in 1987. One child: Jordan Robert. Ms. Swetzig enjoys travel.

Wendy E. Taylor

Management Information Systems Manager
Fullarton Computer Industries Inc.
810 South Church Street
Winterville, NC 28590
(252) 355-3443
Fax: (252) 355-0049

3571

Business Information: Possessing several years of experience in the technology field, Mrs. Taylor serves as the Management Information Systems Manager for Fullarton Computer Industries Inc. Before joining Fullarton Computer, Mrs. Taylor served as a Network Consultant with McGladrey & Pullen, LLP and Network Assistant for Craven Community College. In her present capacity, she is responsible for maintaining all communications within the Corporation's two locations. Traveling frequently, she performs the LAN, WAN, and telephone administration for Fullarton Computer. A systems expert, Mrs. Taylor also offers technical advice to the systems' users and troubleshoots problems as they arise. She continues to grow professionally through the fulfillment of her responsibilities and looks forward to advancing into a higher level information technology position. Fullarton Computer Industries Inc. is a manufacturer of IBM servers and desktop model computers. The Corporation employs over 1,500 skilled professionals to design and equip all computer aspects for IBM from the rough draft to production. **Career Highlights:** Management Information Systems Manager, Fullarton Computer Industries Inc. (1998-Present); Network Consultant, McGladrey & Fullen, LLP (1993-98); Network Consultant, Craven Community College (1993). **Associations & Accomplishments:** Data Processing Management Association. **Education:** Craven Community College, A.A.S. in Microcomputer System Technology (1993); Certified Netware Engineer. **Personal Information:** Married to Randy in 1983. Two children: Jason and Emily.

Ralph Thomas Wilson, Jr.

Senior Enterprise Consultant
Compaq Computer Corporation
30 Apple Blossom Lane
Newtown, CT 06470-2202
(203) 426-9447
Fax: (203) 426-4259
tom@quietstorm.com

3571

Business Information: With past management and technology experiences with major corporations, Mr. Wilson functions as Senior Enterprise Consultant. In this position, he works primarily with lucrative accounts of some of the largest companies in the world. Development and implementation of cutting edge software technology fall under his realm of responsibilities. Providing companies with enterprise solutions, mass configurations, and problem solving techniques are his other responsibilities. Also, Mr. Wilson spearheads all technical support efforts of the Corporation. An acknowledged expert, his greatest professional accomplishment was re-engineering and the re-architecture of Dannon's infrastructure in communications, human resources, desktop, sales, automation, and finance. Providing test environment so that customers can observe the testing of products first-hand serves as his major responsibility. Compaq Computer Corporation serves as the leading computer company in the world. Compaq provides computers, servers, network, disk drives, and various other computer products. Established in 1982, Compaq has over 80,000 employees and produces $26 billion in annual sales. **Career Highlights:** Senior Enterprise Consultant, Compaq Computer Corporation (1996-Present); Director of Information Systems, The Dannon Company (1994-96); Product Marketing Manager, Dataswitch (1991-92); Manager of Network Solutions, General Electric Consulting Services (1989-91). **Associations & Accomplishments:** I.C.C.P. **Education:** University of Delaware, B.A. in Management Information Systems (1984); University of Virginia, B.A. in English Literature (1982). **Personal Information:** Married to Louise in 1988. Mr. Wilson enjoys being a triathlete and sports.

Randy L. Wolf

RF Engineer
IBM Corporation
100 River Road, Mail Stop 862G
Essex Junction, VT 05452
(802) 769-0816
Fax: (802) 769-7509
randyw8498@aol.com

3571

Business Information: Drawing upon an extensive knowledge in information technology, Mr. Wolf is the RF Engineer for the RF Development Division of IBM Corporation. He is responsible for designing the RF circuits and fixtures which allow accurate testing of RF "system on chip" modules. By achieving this, he is able to test the prototypes and production precisely, enabling him to better help the entire Corporation. Moreover, Mr. Wolf designs the test boards for the modules and provides support and supervision to several employees daily. In the future, he looks forward to continuing with the Division in IC development and working to make it function better. He attributes his success to the love and support of his wife. Located in Essex Junction, Vermont, IBM Corporation is one of the leading computer and information technology companies worldwide. Within the Corporation, several divisions work in various areas to ensure quality and customer satisfaction. The RF development division engages in developing tests to characterize parts, design manufacture, and test frequency ICs. The Division administers the testing by using SiGe technology to provide effective results. With a staff of over 100,000 employees globally, the Corporation, as a whole, reports a substantial annual revenue. **Career Highlights:** RF Engineer, IBM Corporation (1999-Present); RF Development Engineer, Telecom Analysis Systems (1997-99). **Associations & Accomplishments:** Tau Beta Pi; Eta Kappa Nu; Golden Key National Honor Society. **Education:** Drexel University, B.S. in Electrical Engineering (1997). **Personal Information:** Married to Belinda in 1993. Mr. Wolf enjoys reading, astronomy and running.

Guogen Zhang, Ph.D.

Advisory Software Engineer
IBM Santa Teresa Lab
555 Bailey Avenue
San Jose, CA 95141
(408) 463-2012
Fax: (408) 463-3834
gzhang@us.ibm.com

3571

Business Information: Operating as Advisory Software Engineer for Database Technology Institute for System/390 (DBTI/390) since 1998, Dr. Zhang focuses on research and development of query processing for Business Intelligence. His additional responsibilities include query optimization and performance and object extensions to relational databases. Also, he conducts research on object normalization. Dr. Zhang identifies problems and provides solutions in areas of star queries, summary tables, and global query optimization. Using his expert knowledge and skills in a problem solving capacity, Dr. Zhang implements the means for the database to meet the customers' needs. Before joining IBM, Dr. Zhang was a graduate student at Computer Science Department of University of California at Los Angeles, where he carried out research on query formulation and dialogue. **Career Highlights:** Advisory Software Engineer, IBM Santa Teresa Lab (1998-Present); Researcher, University of California at Los Angeles, CoBase Research Laboratory (1994-98); Assistant Professor, Jinan University (1989-92); Certified Systems Analyst of P.R. China (1991); Software Engineer, Lucky Computer Systems (1988). **Associations & Accomplishments:** Association of Computing Machinery; Institute of Electrical and Electronics Engineers Computer Society; Institute of Electrical and Electronics Engineers Technical Committees on Data Engineering, Distributed Processing, Software Engineering, and YUFORIC. **Education:** University of California Los Angeles, Ph.D. (1998); University of Kansas, M.S. in Computer Science; Zhongshan University and Jinan University, M.S. in Computer Science; Hangzhou University, B.S. **Personal Information:** Married to Qian Chen in 1992. Two children: Jeffrey and Alice. Dr. Zhang enjoys Chinese cuisine, playing bridge, tennis, fishing and surfing the Internet.

Keith J. Hubbard

Equipment Support Technician
Seagate Technology
7801 Computer Avenue
Minneapolis, MN 55435
(612) 844-7208
mena@uswest.net

3572

Business Information: Demonstrating his expertise in the field of technology, Mr. Hubbard serves as the Equipment Support Technician for Seagate Technology in its Minneapolis, Minnesota location. He is responsible for the maintenance and repair of the various equipment utilized for the manufacture of hard drive products. Mr. Hubbard also offers wafer support for the Company's chip making operations. Attributing his success to a solid education and his people skills, he looks forward to an eventual promotion to Senior Technician as a result of his dedication and superior job performance. Created in 1990, Seagate Technology is one of the leading manufacturers of computer hard drives in the United States. The Company performs continual research in an effort to supply the rapidly changing technology industry with cutting edge equipment. An approximate work force of 2,000 skilled professionals are engaged in national operations. Corporate headquarters are maintained in Silicon Valley, California. **Career Highlights:** Equipment Support Technician, Seagate Technology (1991-Present); Copier Technician, Copy Duplicating Products (1988-91); Custodial Engineer, Independent School District #255 (1985-88); Maintenance Technician, Gauthier Industries (1980-85). **Associations & Accomplishments:** Children's International. **Education:** Brown Institute, Electronics degree (1986); Rochester Technical Institute, Surgical Technology degree (1982); Inter American University, A.S. (1978). **Personal Information:** Married to Myrtha in 1975. Three children: Jennifer, Michael, and Ryan. Mr. Hubbard enjoys sports, hiking, camping, history, art and music.

Zdzislaw "Jess" Jaworski

Chairman
B.R.M.
Landmark House, Station Road, Horsham
West Sussex, England, United Kingdom RH16 1TD
+44 1403262616
Fax: +44 1403268552
jess_jaworski@brm.easynet.co.uk

3572

Business Information: Utilizing over 20 years of experience in the informantion technology recruitment industry, Mr. Jaworski is currently serving as the Chairman of B.R.M. He oversees a variety of responsibilities on a daily basis. He directs the board and sensor management team, ensuring that activities are being carried out in accordance to corporate policy. By offering his input at departmental meetings, Mr. Jaworski is directly involved in the development of strategic planning. Additionally, he negotiates contracts with clients to secure agreements that are suited to the best interests of both parties. Through his membership in several professional organizations, he is able to stay abreast of changes and new technologies within his industry. Th those entering the informantion technology recruitment field, Mr. Jaworski advises, "What is impossible today, is possible tomorrow." Mr. Jaworski is pleased to announce the acquisiton of an information technology recruitement company using e-commerce; this will allow B.R.M. to produce three new products based on the resouces the company has to offer. B.R.M. is a software house specializing in tape and disk storage performance software. Established in 1991, the Company employs 14 talented people to help assist customers with their technological choices. A major client for B.R.M. is Storage House, in the Untied States. **Career Highlights:** Chairman, B.R.M. (1998-Present); Director of Strategic Systems, Spring I.T. Personnel Plc. (1997-98); Managing Director/Founder, Intertech Computer Consultants Ltd. (1985-97). **Associations & Accomplishments:** Chairman, Computing Division (1992-95), Federation of Recruitment and Employment Services; Fellow (1989-Present), F.Inst.D; Institute of Directors. **Education:** Exeter University, B.S. with honors (1971). **Personal Information:** Married. Mr. Jaworski enjoys skiing and reading science fiction books.

Keith J. Kavanaugh

Systems Engineer
StorageTek
12200 Tech Road
Silver Spring, MD 20904
(301) 680-1378
Fax: (301) 622-7857
keith_kavanaugh@storagetek.com

3572

Business Information: Mr. Kavanaugh has served with StorageTek in various technical positions since his recruitment in 1977. At the present time, he fulfills the responsibilities of Systems Engineer. He works directly with the Company's marketing representatives to assist them in answering clients' pre and post sales technical questions and concerns. Mr. Kavanaugh assists marketing representatives to respond to client problems with hardware, software, mainframe, and network business solutions. His thirst for knowledge keeps him on a continual quest for additional knowledge and he credits his professional success to a burning desire to achieve. "Look at the bigger picture and strive to see the forest, not just the trees," he states. A publicly traded company, StorageTek is engaged in the manufacture, sales, and service of a wide range of computer equipment. The Company's products are distributed to an international client base, employing the services of over 10,000 individuals. Founded in 1969, operations currently boast $2.4 billion a year in revenue. **Career Highlights:** StorageTek: Systems Engineer (1994-Present), Software Support Representative (1990-94), Customer Service Engineer (1977-90). **Associations & Accomplishments:** Armed Forces Communication and Electronics Association; National Association of Student Personnel Administration. **Personal Information:** Married to Colleen in 1974. Two children: Keith Jr. and Kelly Dawn. Mr. Kavanaugh enjoys woodworking.

Richard Lyle

Support Engineer
StorageTek
2324 Ridgepoint Drive, Suite F
Austin, TX 78754
(512) 926-3690
Fax: (512) 926-9614
richard_lyle @storagetek.com

3572

Business Information: Mr. Lyle is a Support Engineer for the StorageTek's Austin, Texas location. He assumes responsibility for several large customer accounts in Austin and provides computer support and system administration. Working with customers in open systems and mainframe environments, he helps customers resolve performance and technical issues. Continuing efforts to increase his skills through training and professional development, he has benefited StorageTek and its customers. StorageTek manufactures tape, disk, and storage area networks (SANS) equipment for mainframe and open systems environments. Established in 1972, the Company employs the skilled services of 800 individuals to facilitate all aspects of operation. Headquartered in Colorado, the Company maintains sales and support for 9,000 worldwide computer and network systems, generating annual revenue of $1.5 billion. **Career Highlights:** Support Engineer, StorageTek (1994-Present); Technical Specialist, Amperif Corporation (1984-94); Customer Service Engineer, StorageTek (1982-84). **Associations & Accomplishments:** Microsoft Certified Professional Association. **Education:** United States Air Force, A.S. (1977); Microsoft Certified Professional; Sun Solaris Administration; Network Systems Extension Course; Fiber Channel Disk; StorageTek Networking Courses. **Personal Information:** Married to Deborah in 1984. Two children: Lindsey and Jacob. Mr. Lyle enjoys golf and travel.

John J. Nutter

Senior Firmware Engineer
Quantum Corporation
333 South Street
Shrewsbury, MA 01545-4171
(508) 770-5639
Fax: (508) 770-5920
nutter@shrsonata.tdh.qntm.com

3572

Business Information: Mr. Nutter serves as Senior Firmware Engineer for Quantum Corporation. In this capacity, he designs the architectural infrastructure for the fibre channel interface process on the disk drive. He also leads a development team of three employees, dedicated to the creation of innovative process to enhance drive performance. Relying on his education and receptiveness to new concepts, Mr. Nutter has achieved considerable success in his field. Quantum Corporation designs high capacity, high performance disk drives for installation in personal computers and large systems. During 18 years of operation, the Corporation has expanded to encompass a workforce in excess of 7,500 people and currently generates annual revenue near $5.3 billion. **Career Highlights:** Senior Firmware Engineer, Quantum Corporation (1995-Present); Data General Corporation: Principal Engineer (1991-95), Section Manager (1990-91). **Associations & Accomplishments:** Institute of Electrical and Electronics Engineers; NICET; Attends numerous conferences. **Education:** Wentworth Institute of Technology, B.S. in Engineering Technology (1981); Franklin Institute of Technology, Associate's degree in Engineering. **Personal Information:** Married to Karen in 1983. Two children: Lauren and Edward. Mr. Nutter enjoys computers and woodworking.

Russell A. Schaeffer

Senior Director
Seagate Technology
2505 Trade Center Avenue
Longmont, CO 80503
(303) 684-1793
Fax: (303) 499-3989

3572

Business Information: Mr. Schaeffer serves as Senior Director of Seagate Technology. He is responsible for over $800 million in annual electronic component procurement. As a 16 year technology professional, Mr. Schaeffer has served with Seagate in a variety of roles since joining the team as Director of Strategic Commodity Management for Semiconductors. Before being promoted to his present position in 1998, he filled the role of Director of Electrical Procurement. His expertise centers around commodity procurement and supply chain management. Overseeing daily electrical commodity management, Mr. Schaeffer supervises and mentors a team of six employees, as well as 17 indirectly. His background history also includes stints with major companies, such as Conner Peripherals, Hughes, and TRW. An accomplished professional, he was much sought after by Cyprus Seminar to conduct training on the hard disk drive business realm. In addition, he recently completed a symposium for 35 summer interns on commodity management. His success reflects his persistence and willingness to change, as well as his ability to analyze and design solutions to meet his client's specific needs. Combining electrical commodities and supply chain management into a single function serves as one of Mr. Schaeffer's future endeavors. Seagate Technology engages in design and manufacture of hard disk drives. Established in 1982, Seagate presently employs an international work force of more than 80,000 professional, technical, and support personnel. At present, the Company reports annual revenues in excess of $8 billion. **Career Highlights:** Seagate Technology: Senior Director (1998-Present), Director of Electrical Procurement (1996-98), Director of Strategic Commodity Management for Semiconductors (1994-96). **Associations & Accomplishments:** Past Member, Institute of Electronics and Electrical Engineers; Past Member, Big Brothers. **Education:** California Institute of Technology, certificate in Engineering Management (1999); University of Arizona, B.S. in Electrical Engineering (1983). **Personal Information:** Married to Nitaya Podhipleux in 1998. Mr. Schaeffer enjoys rock climbing, weight lifting, volleyball and jogging.

Daniel Shields

Senior Director, Information Technology EMEA
Seagate Technology
62 bis Avenue André Morizet, Boulogne-Billancourt
Paris, France 92643
+33 141861042
daniel_p_shields@notes.seagate.com

3572

Business Information: As Senior Director of Information Technology, Europe for Seagate Technology, Mr. Shields determines the overall strategic direction and business of the information systems function. A 16-year veteran of technology, he has assertively served with Seagate in a variety of capacities since joining the Company in 1988. He oversees and controls all day-to-day administration and operational information technology functions. His present scope encompasses oversight of an Oracle ERP system operating on Sun Microsystems platform, in addition to Microsoft applications utilized on most desktop equipment. Mr. Shields, combining extensive management skills and strategic systems expertise, leads his staff of approximately 30 people in providing technical support to over 2,000 users at Company sites in Holland, Scotland, England, Germany, Sweden, Ireland, and France. In addition, he handles numerous resource-planning functions that include people development, new technology evaluation, and determining future requirements to accommodate change in business climate. Mr. Shields' other responsibilities include oversight of LAN and WAN, enterprise servers, software, video conferencing, and telephony. He is based in the Company's European headquarters in Paris and speaks fluent French and English. A recognized professional, interviews with Mr. Shields on topics such as technology, telephony, and long-distance networked telephone systems have been published in international trade publications. Developing the Company's e-commerce capability and participating with vendors and customers to streamline the supply chain are among Mr. Shields' future goals. Seagate Technology (symbol SEG on the New York Stock Exchange) is a leading provider of technology and products enabling people to store, access, and manage information. Seagate is the world's largest manufacturer of disc drives, magnetic discs and read-write heads, an innovator in tape drives, and a leading developer of Enterprise Information Management software. Seagate can be found around the globe and on the World Wide Web at www.seagate.com. **Career Highlights:** Seagate Technology: Senior Director, Information Technology EMEA (1999-Present), Director of Information Technology Europe (1995-99), Manger of Applications Development (1992-95), Senior Programmer/Analyst (1988-92); Financial Analyst, Victor Technologies (1983-87). **Associations & Accomplishments:** American Management Association; American Management Center Europe; International Internet Society; American Club of Paris; Société des Amis du Louvre. **Education:** Monterey Institute of International Studies, M.B.A. (1983); Miami University, B.A. (1978); Practical Certificate in Commercial and Economic French, CCIP Paris (1983).

Sunnie Tsai

Consultant
Seagate Technology Inc.
1294 Sierra Court
San Jose, CA 95132
(831) 439-2469
Fax: (408) 267-2386
tsai707@yahoo.com

3572

Business Information: Serving as Consultant of Seagate Technology Inc., Miss Tsai leads the Corporation in establishing higher standards in technological advancements. Serving with the Corporation for over five years, she focuses on maintaining an organized corporate structure. Heading all day to day international sales operations for Asia and Europe, Miss Tsai concentrates on business strategy and implementing technologies to improve efficiency. Overseeing administrative aspects, she is responsible for recruiting new individuals, compiling benefits packages and salary agreements, and developing skilled training programs. Committed to the increase of profit, Miss Tsai dedicates her time to the managing the annual budget, and directing all sales and revenues to necessary areas. She has received three customer awards and four company awards. Advancing in her career with Seagate Technology, Miss Tsai devotes her attention to running a global department, focusing on networks and storage. Engaged in the manufacturing and distribution of computer components, Seagate Technology Inc. was established over 20 years ago. Located in San Jose, California, the Corporation employs the skilled services of more than 180,000 technicians, engineers, and technical administrators to facilitate every aspect of design, manufacture, and the distribution of products. Specifically producing computer storage products, Seagate Technology strives to incorporate the latest technologies, ensuring state of the art products with emphasis on quality, value, and reliability. **Career Highlights:** Consultant, Seagate Technology Inc. (1994-Present); Conner Peripherals: Assistant Senior Vice President of International Sales Operation (1990-94), Account Specialist (1989-90); Purchasing Consultant, American Metac Corporation (1988-89). **Personal Information:** Miss Tsai enjoys reading.

Barbara Wheeler

Lead Developer/Manager of Software Tools
ECCS
One Shiela Drive, Building 6A
Tinton Falls, NJ 07724
(732) 747-6995
Fax: (732) 741-6945
tnee99@hotmail.com

3572

Business Information: Ms. Wheeler serves in the dual capacity of Lead Developer and Manager of Software Tools for ECCS. She is responsible for interface products the Company provides, advising her staff on the technical detail design. Supervising three employees, she conducts reviews and training while mentoring her staff to attain higher positions. A savvy, 19 year professional, Ms. Wheeler works in developing layout architecture and coordinating the paperwork within her department. Looking to the next millennium, Ms. Wheeler hopes to stay within the development aren and remain competitive in the industry through the opening of her own business. Her success is attributed to her ability to quickly grasp technical concepts and methodologies as well as her extensive knowledge. Established in 1987, ECCS manufactures storage subsystems and network attached storage. With an intensive innovative department, the Company has designed some of the most intricate hardware protection units and software systems. The Company has focused its attention towards database development and the protection of all information stored within a computer. **Career Highlights:** Lead Developer/Manager of Software Tools, ECCS (1998-Present); Software Engineer, Bellsouth Wireless Data (1998); Lead Developer/Manager of Software Tools, ECCS (1996-98); Senior Software Engineer, National Information Bureau (1995-1996). **Associations & Accomplishments:** Microsoft Developers Network. **Education:** Brookdale Community College, A.A. in Liberal Arts (1980). **Personal Information:** Ms. Wheeler enjoys woodworking and software design.

Shreyas S. Phatak

Programmer/Analyst
Micronpc.com
1800 North Cole Road, Apartment B104
Boise, ID 83704
(208) 898-1344
redspider@netscape.net

3575

Business Information: Higly recruited to Micronpc.com as Programmer and Analyst in 1998, Mr. Phatak is a successful eight year professional who possesses an excellent understanding of technology. In his capacity, he works with closely with management and users in order to model, implement, and support supply chain product line, to include software applications. Demonstrating his resourcefulness, Mr. Phatak follows the supply chain products by maintaining all warehouse levels and department contacts and trasferring products on a timely basis as well as performing inventory on a regular basis. In the future, Mr. Phatak aspires to move up within the Company's hierarchy and obtain his Master's degree in Computer Science. Established in 1995, Micronpc.com is a manufacturer of computers, peripherals, and accessories. Located in Boise, Idaho, the Company also produces servers and business and personal software. The Company's products are distributed to individual retailers on an international level. With a work force of more than 2,700 professional, technical, and support staff, the Company reports annual revenues in excess of $2 billion. **Career Highlights:** Programmer/Analyst, Micronpc.com (1998-Present); Senior Consultant, Encodex Technologies (1997-98); Senior Specialist, Digital Equipment Corporation (1996-97). **Education:** Walchand Institute of Technology, B.S. in Computer Science (1992). **Personal Information:** Married to Abha Bhagwat in 2000. Mr. Phatak enjoys whollyball, health issues, soccer, chess and cricket.

Hasan Akhtar
Customer Quality Engineer
Innovex
One Precision Drive
Litchfield, MN 55355
(320) 693-2891
Fax: (320) 693-4406
hasan66@hotmail.com

3577

Business Information: As Customer Quality Engineer for Innovex, Mr. Akhtar is responsible for such duties as acting as liaison between customers and engineers, while overseeing work, quality control, and indulging in problem solving. He demonstrates the ability to recognize problems and develop new, improved, and comprehensive solutions for the well being of all employees and clients. With more than six years of experience, Mr. Akhtar communicates with other companies, and performs extensive research in order to better understand customer needs and provide better services. Highly regarded, he possesses an excellent understanding of technology. His plans include gaining more experience and eventually attaining the position of engineering manager. Innovex was established in 1975 to manufacturing, market, and sell flexible circuits which are used in such items as hard disk drives and various medical devices. With a work force consisting of 360 professional technicians, the Company provides the circuits which allow various devices to perform a wide variety of functions daily. The Company helps clients to understand the purpose and functions of the curcuits, while giving them the knowledge of how to maintain them. With a growing clientele bracket, the Company now enjoys annual sales of more than $100 million. **Career Highlights:** Innovex: Customer Quality Engineer (1999-Present), Manufacturing Applications Engineer (1996-99); Felxible Circuitry Engineer, LPC (1994-96). **Associations & Accomplishments:** IPC. **Education:** Minnesota State University, M.S. in Manufacturing (1998); Mankato State University, B.S. in Mechanical Engineering. **Personal Information:** Mr. Akhtar enjoys Internet, reading and travel.

Anne Ashford
Senior Web Business Analyst/Webmaster
NEC Technologies, Inc.
305 Foster Street
Littleton, MA 01460-2004
(978) 742-8183
Fax: (978) 742-8557
aashford@netech.com

3577

Business Information: Highly skilled in the information technology field, Ms. Ashford serves as Senior Web Business Analyst and Webmaster for NEC Technologies, Inc. Providing support for the users of strategic systems, she determines electronic business processing needs, develops on line data processing tools, and oversees all corporate electronic commerce communications. Additionally, Ms. Ashford is responsible for staff technical training and Web site maintenance. Concurrent to her position, she is writing a computer book for children. Serving NEC Technologies, Inc. since 1990, Ms. Ashford would like to continue creating innovative Web sites for the Corporation in the future. Founded in 1989, NEC Technologies, Inc., a subsidiary of NEC USA and operating in affiliation with NEC Corporation, is a manufacturer of computer peripherals. Products include CD Roms, hard drives, monitors, printers, projectors, and presentation equipment. Also engaged in the production of anti-lock and air bag release technology for the automotive industry, NEC Technologies, Inc. develops automated fingerprint identification equipment. Operating six facilities in the United States and Mexico, the Itasca, Illinois based Corporation currently employs 1,100 people. **Career Highlights:** NEC Technologies, Inc.: Senior Web Business Analyst/Webmaster (1994-Present), Communications Specialist (1993-94), Desktop Technical Support (1990-93). **Associations & Accomplishments:** Webmaster's Guild; Association of Internet Professionals; Association for Interactive Media; Toastmaster's International; Junior League of Boston. **Education:** Northeastern University, Webmaster Certification; Bridgewater State College, B.S.; Lesley College; London University. **Personal Information:** Married to Jonathan Ashford in 1988. Three children: Sarah, Amy, and Todd. Ms. Ashford enjoys theatre, cooking, skiing, hiking, sailing and the Investment Club.

Chephren Chua
Information Technology Manager
Digital Scanning Corporation
Block 66, Toa Tawoh Lor 4, 07-307
Singapore, Singapore 310066
+65 6657500
Fax: +65 657522
chephren@dsc.com.sg

3577

Business Information: Possessing superior talents and an excellent understanding of technology, Mr. Chua joined Digital Scanning Corporation in 1999 as Information Technology Manager. In this capacity, he is responsible for overseeing the administration of network and operating systems. He is also in charge of project management, coordinating resources, time lines, and assignments, and systems implementation. Demonstrating strong leadership, Mr. Chua provides follow up on sales and supervises a staff of two engineers and technicians, ensuring that all technical operations within his department are functional and running smoothly. A very prominent and respected professional, Mr. Chua plans to follow his entrepreneurial spirit and eventually start up his own company. His success reflects his ability to think outside the box, take on challenges, and deliver results on behalf of the Corporation and its clientele. Founded in 1994, Digital Scanning Corporation specializes in bar code, RFID, and data collection services. Serving an international clientele, the Corporation is headquartered in Singapore. Employing 20 personnel, the Corporation reports estimated annual revenue exceeding $3 million. **Career Highlights:** Information Technology Manager, Digital Scanning Corporation (Present); Web Master, RAC Technologies; Technical Manager, Tri Tech Systems Ent.; Technical Officer, Ngee Ann Polytechnic. **Personal Information:** Mr. Chua enjoys computers and books.

Donald F. Felix
General Manager/Vice President of Sales and Marketing
CBM Business Machines Inc.
110 Clinton Street
Johnstown, PA 15901
(814) 536-5356

3577

Business Information: Following four years of distinguished service in the United States Army's Medical Corp., Mr. Felix joined the CBM Business Machines Inc. team in 1994. In that same year, he was promoted and currently fulfills a dual role of General Manager and Vice President of Sales and Marketing. Mr. Felix, relying on his extensive business experience, is charged with oversight of all sales and marketing activities. He is also a stock holder in the Corporation. Mr. Felix leverages his management skills in developing both strategic and tactical marketing plans and orchestrating aggressive expansion into new markets. Responsible for taking a leading role in driving growth, he determines and penetrates new markets to meet market demand and fiscal responsibility for bringing bottom line profits to meet objectives. Mr. Felix, in addition to supervising his staff of seven sales people, oversees all day-to-day administration and operational activities of the Corporation. Designing and deploying advertising and media campaigns and managing contract negotiations and incentive programs also fall within the purview of his responsibilities. A well rounded professional, with no college background, Mr. Felix attributes his success to a strong supportive family. His future goals include continuing to build sales and take care of his team. "You take care of your people and they'll take care of you," is cited as Mr. Felix's credo. CBM Business Machine Inc. is engaged in sales of business equipment. Targeting Fortune 500 companies in southern and western Pennsylvania, the Corporation specializes in network and software support as well as machines to include personal computers, copiers, faxes, digital equipment, and other traditional and nontraditional machines. CBM Business Machines, national and regional in scope, was established in 1964 and presently employs a staff of more than 20 persons. **Career Highlights:** CBM Business Machines Inc.: General Manager/Vice President of Sales and Marketing (1994-Present), Sales Manager (1994); Medical Specialist, United States Army Medical Corp. (1990-94).

Arthur E. Garverick
Management Information Systems Director
Labor Ready, Inc.
30841 52nd Avenue South
Auburn, WA 98001-2727
(253) 382-3955

3577

Business Information: Utilizing 25 years of diversified experience with emphasis on general management, financial margin, and operational performance, in addition to a vast educational background, Mr. Garverick serves as Management Information Systems Director for Labor Ready, Inc. In his position, he manages and establishes the technology direction and strategy in the area of operations and network support. His responsibilities include the implementation of an 850 international node wide area network, developing an in-house expertise for technical solutions, and creating operations and support programs that meet the long-term business needs of the IS organization. In addition, Mr. Garverick is in charge of standardization and vendor selection, voice and data contract negotiation, and providing visibility for the Corporation's technical capabilities through presentations, publications, and budget reviews. Strong planning and implementation abilities with a proven track record in working with and through others to achieve results has contributed to his career success. Mr. Garverick's proven past accomplishments provides a strong background for future endeavors. Founded in 1989, Labor Ready, Inc. specializes in providing temporary workers for manual day labor. The Corporation, based in Auburn, Washington, has offices in Puerto Rico, Canada, and the United Kingdom. Operating nearly 850 dispatch offices, the Corporation attracts workers for short-term, unskilled jobs on behalf of more than 250,000 customers in fields like landscaping, construction, freight handling, and light industrial. **Career Highlights:** Management Information Systems Director, Labor Ready, Inc. (2000-Present); Digital Equipment Corporation/Compaq Computer Corporation: Customer Service Manager (1998-00), Business Manager (1996-98), Service Delivery Manager (1981-96). **Associations & Accomplishments:** Adjunct Faculty Professor, City University Bellevue, Washington; Chairperson, Bates Vocational Technical Institute. **Education:** Seattle University, M.B.A. with concentrations in Law, International Business and Management Strategy (1991); City University, B.S. in Business Administration (1988).

Michael Greene
e-Business Development Manager
3Com
5400 Bayfront Plaza MS 8314
Santa Clara, CA 95052
(408) 326-3621
Fax: (408) 326-6832
michael_greene@3com.com

3577

Business Information: Mr. Greene serves as the e-Business Development Manager for 3Com. He is responsible for network designs and product configurations for the assembly of Web usage tools. Before joining the Company in 1996, Mr. Greene was employed as Art Director for NETG. A savvy, eight year professional, Mr. Greene is involved in developing of cutting edge sales applications and migrating the Company's systems, network, and databases to the new infrastructures. Striving to stay abreast of changes in the industry, he reads several trade journals to stay on the bleeding edge of e-business technology. Mr. Greene's success reflects his ability to think outside the box and finding new approaches to solve technological problems, as well as produce results and aggressively tackle new challenges. 3Com engages in networking. Established in 1979, the Company has expanded its service to 180 locations in the United States and 146 locations in other countries. The Company employs 13,000 competent personnel to facilitate those locations and strives to remain on the cutting edge of technology to enhance services to its clients. **Career Highlights:** e-Business Development Manager, 3Com (1996-Present); Art Director, NETG (1995-96). **Associations & Accomplishments:** Rosetta Net. **Education:** PSF, Bachelor's degree in Fine Art (1993); Marchutz, Bachelor's degree in Fine Art (1991). **Personal Information:** Married to Marie-Laure in 1995. One child: Chloe Morgan. Mr. Greene enjoys rock climbing, sailing and scuba diving.

Robert Duane Hatch
Senior Technical Training Manager
Iomega Corporation
429 South Joshua Drive
Kaysville, UT 84037
(801) 332-5036
Fax: (801) 332-4870
rhatch@enol.com

3577

Business Information: Mr. Hatch presently serves as Senior Manager of Technical Training with Iomega Corporation. He is responsible for all aspects of employee training and development. Utilizing 13 years of technical savvy and experience, he effectively deploys training programs as well as monitors progress of employees during all phases of employment. An innovative leader, he provides instructor-led courses and Internet-based instruction. His focus is on changes that will allow the Corporation to take advantage of new technology to remain flexible, efficient, and profitable in the markets. Mr. Hatch became the first to create online training systems at his previous position with WordPerfect Corporation, and in the future, hopes to have a major influence on applications over the Internet. His success is attributed to being creative and technical at the same time. The Iomega Corporation manufactures and distributes removable storage units for computers. Striving to impact the information technology industry, the Corporation produces cutting-edge zip drives and disks to more effectively store data, clik drives and disks to enhance product performance, and jazz drives and disks. Founded in 1980 at the start of the Internet age, the Corporation is headquartered in Roy, Utah and operates throughout the world. Presently, Iomega employs a work force of 4,200 people who help generate in excess of $1.7 million annually. **Career Highlights:** Senior Manager of Technical Training, Iomega Corporation (1998-Present); Program Manager, Novell, Inc. (1996-98); Team Manager, Wordperfect Corporation. **Education:** Brigham Young University, B.S. (1987). **Personal Information:** Married to Diana in 1982. Four children. Mr. Hatch enjoys astronomy, collecting rare books, drawing, graphic design, internet and software development.

Melanie Hudson

Account Manager/Marketing Analyst
Lexmark
740 West New Circle Road
Lexington, KY 40550-0001
(606) 232-1421
Fax: (606) 232-6078
mdpowers@lexmark.com

3577

Business Information: As Account Manager and Marketing Analyst of Lexmark, Mrs. Hudson fulfills a multitude of varied responsibilities within the business printers division. Demonstrating exceptional time managment and organizational skills as she effectively handles her dual roles, Mrs. Hudson maintains open communication between all of herself and the staff. She conducts accurate forecasting of the market, analyzing trends to develop strategic business plans. With exceptional communicative abilities, she meets with customers to discuss available services as she serves as an outstanding representative of the Company. Recognized for her contributions towards the completion of corporate goals, Mrs. Hudson looks forward to continued success as she advances to a higher marketing or purchasing position. Lexmark is a developer, manufacturer, and supplier of printing solutions and products. Heaquartered in Kentucky, the $3 billion company has an extensive product line that includes laser, inkjet, and dot matrix printers and associated supplies. Founded in 1991, the Company employs 10,000 people who fulfill responsiblities from sales to service within the corporate structure. **Career Highlights:** Lexmark: Account Manager/Marketing Analyst (1999-Present), Account Manager (1995-Present), Logistics Analyst (1993-95). **Associations & Accomplishments:** American Production and Inventory Control Society; Toastmasters. **Education:** Xavier University, M.B.A. (1998); CPIM Certified (1996); Eastern Kentucky University, B.A. (1993). **Personal Information:** Married to Daniel in 1995. Mrs. Hudson enjoys reading.

Huy T. Khong

Automation Specialist
HMT Technology
843 Auburn Court
Fremont, CA 94538
(510) 770-3032
Fax: (510) 438-0324
hkhong@hmtt.com

3577

Business Information: As the Automation Specialist at HMT Technology, Mr. Khong oversees robot and PLCs programming. Specializing in robots from manufacturers such as Adept, Kawasaki, Motoman, and Staubli, he demonstrates a superior ability in the technical industry. He designs creative products, quickly and effectively working through challenges to achieve an end result of a superior, quality product. In addition to his electro-mechanical and automation skills, Mr. Khong has developed impressive Web sites that are appealingly user friendly. The Web site features the online documents and online manuals to help maintenance technicians in real time troubleshooting. Keeping his goals consistent with the objectives of the Company, he looks forward to assisting in the completion of future corporate goals. Founded in 1989, HMT Technology manufactures hard disk media. Headquartered in the heart of Silicon Valley, California, the $200 million company also maintains one other location in Oregon and employs a total of 1,000 employees corporate wide. **Career Highlights:** Automation Specialist, HMT Technology (1995-Present); Equipment Engineer, Valance Technology (1992); Equipment Engineer, Altus Corporation (1983). **Education:** San Jose State University (Currently Attending). **Personal Information:** Mr. Khong enjoys working with computers.

James J. Quinn

Director, Research & Development
Newbridge Networks
15036 Conference Center Road
Chantilly, VA 20151
(703) 679-5910
Fax: (703) 679-5995
iquinn@newbridge.com

3577

Business Information: Combining strategic management skills and engineering expertise, Mr. Quinn within Newbridge Networks from Northchurch Communications (a startup acquired by Newbridge), was promoted from the Director of Quality to the Director of Research & Development in Chantilly, Virginia. In his current capacity, Mr. Quinn is responsible for the development and verification of the IP routing software for all of the Newbridge Network platforms. He attributes his career success to conducting the research needed to remain current. Mr. Quinn owns a consistent record of delivering results in support of business objectives through leadership, use of technology, and creative problem solving. In addition, Mr. Quinn relies on the web to keep track of new services and technical services. Over the next five years, he desires to become involve in consulting and design and deploy large scale networks. His advice for others in the industry is "proactively plan your network." Newbridge Networks, established in 1986, is a world leading provider of network equipment for the carrier marketplace. The Company headquarters are located in Kanata, Canada with several engineering sites worldwide, including Andover, Massachusetts and Chantilly, Virginia. **Career Highlights:** Director, Research & Development, Newbridge Networks (2000-Present); Director of Quality, North Church Communications (1998-00); Technical Director, DNPG (Cabletron - 1998) (Digital - 1993-98); Digital various groups (1978-93). **Associations & Accomplishments:** Institute of Electrical and Electronics Engineers. **Education:** St. Mary's Halifax at Nova Scotia, B.Sc. (1967). **Personal Information:** Married to Teresa A. in 1971. Two children: Ian and Colin.

Amy Renner, D.Pharm.

Product Information Coordinator
Clinical Pharmacologic Research Communications
P.O Box 464
Morgantown, WV 26504
(800) 843-9915
Fax: (800) 843-9916

3577

Business Information: As Product Information Coordinator for Clinic Pharmacologic Research Communications, Dr. Renner is responsible for reviewing all forms, while also answering inquiries, conducting presentations, and managing the activities of 14 employees. She is also charged with the obligation to enter cell counts into the Company's database. High regarded, Dr. Renner is a member of the quality assurance committee. With several years of technical experience, she utilizes her superior knowledge and expertise to devise plans for helping the Company in expansion maneuvers, Clinical Pharmacologic Research Communications engages in a host of activities for the Midland Pharmaceutical Company. The Company offers such services as systems monitoring for the research of white blood cell diseases that require constant counts of the white blood cells. Established in 1999, the Company functions under a host of professionals who facilitate smooth business operations. **Career Highlights:** Product Information Coordinator, Clinical Pharmacologic Research Communications (Present); Pharmacist, CVS (Present). **Associations & Accomplishments:** American Pharmaceutical Association; American Study of Health System Pharmacists. **Education:** West Virginia Univeristy School of Pharmacy: D.Pharm. (1999), B.S. in Pharmacy (1998).

John C. Trainor

Manager of Information Technology
Epson Electronics America Inc.
1960 East Grand Avenue, Floor 2
El Segundo, CA 90245-5060
(310) 955-5341
Fax: (310) 955-5441
jtrainor@eea.epson.com

3577

Business Information: Mr. Trainor is the Manager of Information Technology of Epson Electronics America Inc. With 16 years of experience under his belt, there is not a technology project out there that he would not feel equipped to handle. Functioning as a leader to newcomers in the information technology industry, he strives to provide optimistic support and guidance. Always having been involved in technology and a love for this field, Mr. Trainor remains on the very leading edge. He was a member of the Epson's project team that redesigned and built a 13,000 square feet data center, and converting from a Hewlett-Packard mainframe to an IBM mainframe. In 1998, when Epson spun off its own company, Mr. Trainor did the complete set up of the information technology department. For the future, he hopes to become heavily, heavily involved with the world of the Internet. He feels that outstanding work ethics and a strong desire to be in the information technology industry have led to his success. Epson Electronics America Inc. provides sales and marketing support for Epson and Seiko Epson computer products. The Corporation advises its clients on making appropriate technology choices for their business or home office. Founded in 1998, the Corporation was created to better manage the overflow of customers within Epson and provide new clients with a more personalized and friendly computer-buying experience. **Career Highlights:** Epson Electronics America Inc.: Manager of Information Technology (1998-Present), Data Communications Specialist (1995-98); Data Center Supervisor (1989-95); Data Center Leader, Northrop (1984-89). **Education:** University of Phoenix, B.S. in Information Technologies (1999). **Personal Information:** Married to Colette in 1997. One child: Stephen. Mr. Trainor enjoys family activities.

Raymond E. Wilson

WAN Manager
Viewsonic
381 Brea Canyon Road
Walnut, CA 91789
(909) 444-8895

3577

Business Information: A proven veteran of technology, Mr. Wilson serves as Worldwide Network Manager of Viewsonic. He is responsible for overseeing and directing all aspects of day-to-day administration and operations of 14 global networks. An experienced expert in his field, Mr. Wilson is also in charge of designing cutting edge networks and ensuring their functionality and operational status. His career highlights include his ability to search and hire high level staff to oversee daily operations. Implementing cutting edge technology, his success is attributed to his negotiating skills and his persistence in delivering quality products. Looking to the future, Mr. Wilson plans to use his skills to establish his own business in the technical industry. Viewsonic is an international monitor manufacturer based in Walnut, California. With 14 locations globally, the Company offers quality service and products to a diverse clientele. Established in 1994, the Company employs a professional staff to assist in various aspects of the operation. **Career Highlights:** Worldwide Network Manager, Viewsonic (Present). **Education:** Pasadena City College, Associate's degree; Technical College of Los Angeles, Diploma. **Personal Information:** Three children: LeRaya, Jamila, and Jamaah. Mr. Wilson enjoys being an internet investor.

Bill Abu-Zahra

Business Manager
MICROS Systems, Inc. - Southern California Region
6 Rex Court
Aliso Viejo, CA 90920
(714) 816-3411
Fax: (714) 827-9069
babu-zahra@micros.com

3578

Business Information: Mr. Abu-Zahra performs the duties of Business Manager for MICROS Systems, Inc. Operations, budgeting, and strategic planning are segments of his responsibilities. Other duties assigned to him are development and implementation of measures that ensure growth and expansion of all aspects of the business. This includes monitoring profit and loss statements, developing new business, and training employees on the technical side of the business. Future professional aspirations for Mr. Abu-Zahra include becoming Senior Vice President. Headquartered in the state of Maryland, MICROS Systems, Inc. is dedicated to the market and distribution for point of sales systems such as UNIX and NT 95. There are 11 operating locations in the Corporation's network for customers to buy these systems. Established in 1985, the Corporation employs 45 people in the Southern California region generating in excess of $8 million in annual revenues. **Career Highlights:** Business Manager, MICROS Systems, Inc. - Southern California Region (1996-Present); Project Manager, ISSC Division of Integration (1988-96); Point of Sale and Information Systems Director, Family Restaurants, Inc. (1986-88). **Associations & Accomplishments:** Institute of Electrical and Electronics Engineers; National Restaurant and Hotel Association; Arizona State University Alumni Associations; OC Engineers. **Education:** Arizona State University, B.S. in Electrical and Computer Engineering (1986); Wayne State University (1982); Bir-Zeit University-Israel, B.S. in Math and Physics (1980). **Personal Information:** Mr. Abu-Zahra enjoys volleyball, volleyball, basketball, real estate, stock investments and travel.

Jennifer D. Terwey

Implementation Consultant
MICROS Systems, Inc.
46 North Park Avenue #1
Chicago, IL 60148
(847) 439-5006
Fax: (847) 439-5003
jennifer_terwey@hotmail.com

3578

Business Information: Ms. Terwey was recruited to MICROS Systems, Inc. as the Implementation Consultant in 2000. In her role, she is responsible for standardizing, training, and supporting the implementation department. Possessing an excellent understanding of the technology field, she effectively assists the sales and management team with technical specifications. A successful, five year professional, Ms. Terwey also provides product, customer, and inhouse training events as well as performs troubleshooting and maintenance of systems. Her career highlight was the development of a point-of-sale system for the Mirage in Las Vegas. Her success is attributed to her interpersonal and people skills. Moving forward in her career and eventually attaining the position of department head serve as Ms. Terwey's goals. A national technology company, MICROS Systems, Inc. operates as a hospitality management software and hardware company. Operating eight offices in the United States, the Corporation specializes in point-of-sale and property management systems. The Corporation also offers custom programming and technical support. Established in 1970, the Corporation employs more than 2,000 professional, technical, and administrative support staff. **Career Highlights:** Implementation Consultant, MICROS Systems, Inc. (2000-Present); Open Systems Consultant, SSA Inc. (1999-00); Systems Administrator, Cloud Corporation (1998-99). **Education:** University of Nevada of Las Vegas, Bachelor's degree in Management Information Systems (1995). **Personal Information:** Ms. Terway enjoys snowboarding, golf, camping and boating.

Philippe M. Bourdon

UNIX System Administrator
IKON Office Solutions
755 Winding Brook Drive
Glastonbury, CT 06033
(860) 659-6431
Fax: (860) 657-4888
pbourdon@ikon.com

3579

Business Information: Utilizing several years of extensive experience in the technology field, Mr. Bourdon serves as the UNIX System Administrator for IKON Office Solutions. Entrusted with the care of the UNIX system for the Northeast District of the Company, he monitors the daily activity, provides security for industry sensitive data, and provides a daily back up systems to prevent data loss. A systems expert, Mr. Bourdon maintains the hardware and software of the individual workstations, providing upgrades and repair as necessary. Coordinating resources, time lines, schedules, and assignments; tuning systems software to improve overall performance; and providing cohesive leadership also fall within the realm of Mr. Bourdon's responsibilities. Continually striving to improve performance, he looks forward to assisting the Company achieve future goals and anticipates a promotion to Director. Boasting $6 million in annual revenue, IKON Office Solutions is one of the world's leading office technology providers. The Company offers copier and printing services, mailroom and copy center management, overflow duplicating, and computer networking services. Established in 1995, international operations employ over 40,000 personnel. **Career Highlights:** UNIX System Administrator, IKON Office Solutions (1999-Present); Production Analyst, ITDS (1996-99). **Education:** University of Pittsburgh, M.A. in International Affairs (1996). **Personal Information:** Married to Andrea in 1989. Mr. Bourdon enjoys scuba diving, basketball and working out.

Brian Douglas Dix

Project Manager V
NCR Corporation
200 Highway 74 South
Peachtree City, GA 30269-0205
(770) 487-7000
Fax: (770) 487-7150
bd128420@ncr.com

3579

Business Information: Joining NCR Corporation or National Cash Register as Software Engineer in 1992, Mr. Dix serves as Project Manager V for the Corporation. Possessing years of business savvy and expertise in the technology field, he effectively deploys information technology and professional services solutions worldwide. Presently, Mr. Dix he is in charge of deploying a cutting edge Global Customer Service Management System into NCR's locations in Canada, the Caribbean, and Latin America. Developing project schedules and assigning tasks, perfoming both systems analysis and programming, serving as chief liaison with users and systems management, and managing project budgets also fall within the purview of Mr. Dix's management responsibilities. The highlights of his career includes development and implementation of a global billing system in Puerto Rico. Keeping NCR out-front of competitors, he facilitate the management of new processes. Having enjoyed substantial success in his career, Mr. Dix future endeavor is to develop an advanced electronic interface to enhance Web technology. Success is due to his tenacity. A leading manufacturer of ATMs, NCR Corporation provides information technology solutions that enable businesses to capture and analyze data. In addition, the Corporation specializes in helping clients maximize customer acqusition, retention, and profitability. Reporting annual sales in excess of $7 billion, NCR currently employs the skilled services of 33,000 professional, technical, and support staff. NCR was established in 1884. **Career Highlights:** NCR Corporation: Project Manager V (1998-Presnet), Deployer (1995-98), Software Engineer (1992-95). **Associations & Accomplishments:** Professional Management Institute. **Personal Information:** Married to Marie-Daniele C. Mr. Dix enjoys snow skiing, water skiing and mountain biking.

David W. Geer

Program Manager
NCR Corporation
487 Severnside Drive
Severna Park, MD 21146-2215
(301) 212-5060
Fax: (410) 987-2718
dgeer@bellatlantic.net

3579

Business Information: Demonstrating technical expertise and managerial skills in the technology field, Mr. Geer was recruited to NCR Corporation in 1997. At the present time, he fulfills the responsibilities of Program Manager. In this capacity, he is actively involved in the discovery, investigation, and initial deployment of advanced technologies within NCR Corporation. Relying on over 22 years of technology experience and a strong academic background, he exercises oversight of all management aspects of new software development as well as hardware technology and control system applications. Directing and participating in the analysis, acquisition, installation, modification, configuration, and support and tracking of operating systems, databases, utilities, and software and hardware also falls within the realm of Mr. Geer's responsibilities. Continuously searching for new technology, he is working closely with the United States Navy on a leading edge damage control system application. Founded in 1895, NCR Corporation is engaged in development of software and control system applications to help businesses move beyond the box and build a long lasting relationship with the customers. A leading provider of technology and scalable data warehousing-based solutions, the Corporation is manned by a work force of more than 55,000 professional, technical, and support personnel. **Career Highlights:** Program Manager, NCR Corporation (1997-Present); Product Manager, CAE Electronics (1992-96); Senior Program Manager, NKF Engineering, Inc. (1990-92). **Associations & Accomplishments:** American Society of Naval Engineers; Life Member/Founding Member, Surface Navy Association. **Education:** Navy Post Graduate, B.S. in Operations Research (1966); Naval Academy, Marine Engineering. **Personal Information:** Married to Virginia in 1960. Four children: Joseph, Kelly, Thomas, and David. Mr. Geer enjoys spending time with his family.

Mark R. Hilton

Executive Vice President of European Operations and Worldwide Quality Assurance
NCR Corporation
2651 Satellite Boulevard
Duluth, GA 30096
(770) 623-7842
Fax: (770) 623-7010
hilton@exchange.ailantaga.ncr.com

3579

Business Information: As the Executive Vice President of European Operations and Worldwide Quality Assurance for the NCR Corporation, Mr. Hilton is responsible for worldwide quality assurance and Europe, Middle East, and Africa logistics, operations, and manufacturing. He works to ensure customer satisfaction throughout their entire interaction with the Corporation. He supports a $400 million budget, providing reports on the future expectations and current investments of the Corporation's revenue. Utilizing over 10 years of experience and service with the Corporation, Mr. Hilton works to motivate his staff through stories of his past lessons in hopes that they will learn from them and use them during their current negotiations. He is striving to master the skills required to fully operate the Corporation and is looking towards a position as chief executive officer. Mr. Hilton also aspires to write a book. His advice is, "Focus on cultural and best practices process within the company." NCR Corporation does data warehousing for hard drive and software to include retail and store solutions within the financial means of a client. Established in 1887, the Corporation began assisting clients in restructuring their bookkeeping and has advanced into the computer era through the advancement of its information technology division and is now completely focused on technology consulting. The Corporation's 3,800 employees are working to build the largest data warehouse in the world, currently functioning with 101 teradatabytes. Working with offices in 130 countries, the Corporation has divided its services into two core divisions: financial and retail. Presently, NCR reports annual revenues in excess of $1.8 billion. **Career Highlights:** Executive Vice President of European Operations and Worldwide Quality Assurance, NCR Corporation (1995-Present); Assistant Vice President of Quality, Tandy Electronics/AST (1990-94); Senior Director of Operations and Quality, Space Shuttle Program (1987-90); Program Director, Northrope Corporation (1984-87). **Associations & Accomplishments:** Regional Director, American Society for Quality Control; Chair, Regional Software Council for CMM; Co-Chair, Reliability Institution at Arizona State University; Georgia 100, Sponsoring Mentoring Senior Female Professionals in Atlanta Area. **Education:** Southern Illinois University, B.S. (1984); Riverside School of Aeronautics, Associate's degree in Engineering. **Personal Information:** Married to Debbie in 1976. Two children: Jayme and Sandy. Mr. Hilton enjoys boating, golf and camping.

Tameen Khan

Software Engineer
Siemens Electrocom LP
2910 Avenue F
Arlington, TX 76011
(817) 695-5537
Fax: (817) 695-3165
tameen.khan@arl.siemens.com

3579

Business Information: Dedicated to the success of Siemens Electrocom LP, Mr. Khan applies his knowledge and expertise in the field of software design in serving as Software Engineer. He is responsible for all aspects of software design and implementation, from simple tools to the actual automation production line, used to automate the United States postal environment. Before joining Siemens Electrocom in 1998, Mr. Khan served as Assistant LAN Administrator with the University of North Texas. His success reflects is ability to think out-of-the-box and take on new challenges. Continually striving for maximum effectiveness, Mr. Khan is currently pursuing his Master's degree in Business Administration to enable him to capitalize on the opportunities provided by the Company. He plans on remaining and growing with Siemens Electrocom, as well as staying on the the cutting edge. Siemens Electrocom LP is a manufacturer of postal automation machines. A work force of over 2,000 staff members are employed in the design and creation of the machines which are used to date, stamp, and process mail, ensuring proper delivery. **Career Highlights:** Software Engineer, Siemens Electrocom LP (1998-Present); Assistant LAN Administrator, University of North Texas (1994-98). **Associations & Accomplishments:** Golden Key Honor Society. **Education:** University of Texas at Dallas, M.B.A. (In Progress); University of North Texas, B.S. with Honors (1998).

James M. Mancini

Executive Vice President of Service & Support
IKON Technology Services
16715 Von Karmen Avenue, Suite 210
Irvine, CA 92606
(949) 399-3311
jmancini@ikon.com

3579

Business Information: Demonstrating expertise in computer engineering, Mr. Mancini currently serves as Executive Vice President of Service & Support with IKON Technology Services. He manages the field engineering effort and assumes accountability for all professional services, including network design and project management functions. Before joining IKON Technology Services, he served as Product Marketing Engineer with Cisco Systems, Inc. and Senior Systems Engineer for Newport Systems Solutions, Inc. Combining his management skills and extensive experience, he sets the overall strategic direction of the Company, coordinates resources and schedules, oversees time lines and assignments, and takes a leading role in driving product and service offerings to market. Establishing goals that are compatible with those of the Company, he hopes to establish a nationwide organization of network integration experts under the IKON brand name. Crediting his professional success to his continued diligence, Mr. Mancini's success reflects his ability to take on new challenges and responsibilities. Created in 1994, Virtual Networks is a computer network developer that was acquired in 1997 as part of IKON Technology Services' expansion into the internetworking market. The Company employs a staff of over 150 knowledgeable professionals to design and implement various types of networks including LAN/WAN, campus, and global networks. Last year the Company boasted annual revenue in excess of $5 billion. **Career Highlights:** Executive Vice President of Service & Support, IKON Technology Services (1995-Present); Product Marketing Engineer, Cisco System, Inc. (1994-95); Senior Systems Engineer, Newport Systems Solutions, Inc. (1993-94). **Education:** Cisco Certified Internetworking Expert; Cisco Certified Design Professional; Security and Voice/Data Integration Specialist.

Kevin Nuwer

UNIX Core Developer
Xerox
122 Deehearst Lane, Apartment 2
Webster, NY 14580-2708
(716) 231-8393
kevin.nuwer@usa.xerox.com

3579

Business Information: Serving as the UNIX Core Developer for Xerox, Mr. Nuwer fulfills a number of technical duties on behalf of the Corporation and its clientele. He has faithfully served with Xerox in a variety of positions since joining the Corporation as Network Printer Technical Focal in 1998.

Possessing superior talents and an excellent understanding of his field, Mr. Nuwer is responsible for designing and developing printer drivers and utilities for the UNIX/Linux platforms. He creates tools that assist in the management and application of programs as well as provides driver and administrative support for copiers and printers. Mr. Nuwer's innovative skills are fundamental to the Corporation's continued success. He continues to enjoy immense satisfaction in his current position and aspires to attain more responsibility in engineering development. Xerox develops, manufactures, and services information processing products, such as copiers, scanners, printing systems, and personal computers. Headquartered in Stamford, Connecticut, the Corporation employs an enterprising staff to meet the demands of a growing clientele. Xerox distributes its products worldwide, and focuses on quality products and business solutions. **Career Highlights:** Xerox: UNIX Core Developer (2000-Present), Network Printer Technical Focal (1998-00). **Education:** State University of New York at Brockport, B.S. in Computer Science (1997). **Personal Information:** Mr. Nuwer enjoys hiking, camping and canoeing.

James O. Ownby

Southeast District Network Manager
IKON Education Services
1001 Keys Drive
Greenville, SC 29615
(864) 415-1071
Fax: (864) 286-5000
jownby@ikon.com

3579

Business Information: As the Southeast District Network Manager for IKON Technology Services, Mr. Ownby assumes a number of responsibilities, such as supervising the network, hardware, and WAN connections for eight locations. Supervising a staff of eight people, he also researches and implements new technologies that will improve systems functions. His hands-on management style encourages and facilitates optimum performance among the staff and ensures that all units work together to achieve a common goal. Mr. Ownby has enjoyed substantial success and looks forward to assisting the Company in future growth and expansion. IKON Technology Services is an industry leader in new office technologies, such as imaging and digital networking, outsourcing and facilities management, and systems integration and technical education. The Company provides services that improve office information management, workflow, and competitiveness in virtually any office environment in any industry. Established in 1982, the Company employs a skilled staff of 114 personnel to meet the diverse needs of a growing clientele. The Company is headquartered in Pennsylvania, maintains 40 offices nationwide, and generates annual revenue of approximately $17 million. **Career Highlights:** IKON Education Services: District Network Manager (1989-Present), Microsoft Certified Trainer (1988-89); Systems Engineer, MEMC Electronic Materials (1986-88); Electronic Technician, MEMC (1986-87). **Education:** DeVry Institute of Technology, Associate's degree (1987). **Personal Information:** Married to Leah in 1990. Two children: Chance and Chandler. Mr. Ownby enjoys spending time with his family and remodeling.

Carlos Manuel Perez Munguia

Operations Manager
NCR de Mexico S.A. de C.V.
Col. Lomas de Chapultepec
Mexico City, Mexico 11000
+52 52023977
Fax: +52 52029659
carlos.perez@mexico.ncr.com

3579

Business Information: Mr. Perez Munguia serves as Operations Manager of NCR de Mexico S.A. de C.V. Fulfilling his duties, he assists in determining the strategic direction and operational business plans to keep NCR de Mexico out-front of competitors in the industry. Concentrating his extensive talents within the Company's Mexican area of operations, he effectively monitors import and export distribution activities. Managing the operational budget and coordiating resources, time lines, schedules, and assignments also fall within the realm of Mr. Perez Munguia's functions with the Company. In the future, he plans on advancing to the highest level of management possible, attaining the position of general manager, and having the authority to make all of the decisions. NCR de Mexico S.A. de C.V. is a leading developer of software and hardware. Headquartered in Ohio, the Company has been operating within the information technology industry for over 100 years, consulting with clients and supplying them with products necessary to successfully operate within today's market place. The Company's clientele spans from large businesses such as banks and international retailers to locally operated private companies. Presently, the Company employs a work force of 300 professional, technical, and support staff. **Career Highlights:** Operations Manager, NCR de Mexico S.A. de C.V. (1991-Present); International Traffic Supervisor, Grupo IDESA (1988-91); Import/Export Assistant, Sweda (1984-88). **Associations & Accomplishments:** Instituto Mexicano de Ejecutivos en Comerico Exterior; Normalizacion y Certificacion Electronica; Camara Nacional de la Industria Electronica, Telecomunicaciones & Informatica. **Education:** EBC, Master's degree in Business (In Progress). **Personal Information:** Married to Norma Buenrustro in 1988. Two children: Carlos Eduardo and Mario Fernande.

John A. Private

Documentation Specialist
Zebra Technologies Corporation
333 Corporate Woods Parkway
Vernon Hills, IL 60061
(847) 793-2715
Fax: (847) 821-1492
japrivat@zebra.com

3579

Business Information: Displaying his skills in this highly specialized position, Mr. Private serves as Documentation Specialist for Zebra Technologies Corporation. Developing software installation instructions for bar code printers, he is responsible for writing the maintenance manuals in a language easily understood by the layman. A systems expert, Mr. Private administers training courses for technicians new to the industry and those wanting to improve their skills. Additionally, he repairs and refurbishes machines sent back to the factory. A technical writer for 20 years, he recently developed a Talking Interactive Maintenance Manual that is available on video and CD-rom. His success reflects his ability to take on new challenges and responsibilities. Dedicated to the success of the Corporation, Mr. Private anticipates a promotion to Manager of the Technical Media Department within the next two to three years. He aspires to one day retire and start up his own consulting and contracting company. Privately owned, Zebra Technologies Corporation is an international manufacturer of bar code printers. The Corporation manufactures and distributes bar code printers, smart cards, and related supplies as well as developing the software installed in each machine. Established in 1974, the Corporation presently employs a work force of more than 1,400 individuals. **Career Highlights:** Documentation Specialist, Zebra Technologies Corporation (1997-Present); Technical Writer/Training Coordinator, Vapor Corporation (1985-95); Senior Technical Writer, A.B. Dick Company (1972-85). **Education:** Oakton Community College. **Personal Information:** Mr. Private enjoys designing Web pages.

Jesse H. Zepeda

Director of Engineering
IKON
13231 Addington Street
Whittier, CA 90602
(949) 399-3300
Fax: (562) 464-9416
jzepeda@ikon.com

3579

Business Information: Exhibiting expert technical skills and advanced knowledge of the information technology field, Mr. Zepeda serves as Director of Engineering for IKON. In this capacity since 1996, he is responsible for all network administration including network design, network infrastructure, maintenance, and diagnostic testing. With the notable ability to understand complex problems and communicate solutions to both the client and internal staff, Mr. Zepeda directs pre-sale customer support and meets regularly with clients. He also assumes oversight of 20 Cisco certified system engineers, providing them with training, guidance, and comprehensive direction as they endeavor to meet departmental needs. Highly regarded, Mr. Zepeda enjoys tremendous success in his current position with IKON and aspires to attain a higher-level management position in the future. Established in 1994, IKON, a Cisco Systems Gold Partner, designs, sells, installs, and implements networking using Cisco equipment. Located in Whittier, California, the Company employs a collective work force of 50 highly trained technicians who generate annual revenues in excess of $30 million. **Career Highlights:** Director of Engineering, IKON (1996-Present); Systems Engineer, Virtual Networks (1994-96); Network Engineer, Southern California Bank (1994-96). **Education:** DeVry Institute, B.S. (1994) **Personal Information:** Married to Jessica in 1996. One child: Jezelle. Mr. Zepeda enjoys sports, music and reading.

Daniel L. Budd

Software Engineer
Control Systems International
4920 Grant Street
Merriam, KS 66203-1774
(913) 599-5010
dbudd@worldnet.att.net

3585

Business Information: Drawing upon nine years of practical experience in the information technology field, Mr. Budd serves as a Software Engineer for Control Systems International. Recruited to the Company in 1994, he designs and develops new software, performs coding functions, and debugs new programs to ensure effective, efficient finalized products. Demonstrating a love for his work that has contributed significantly to his current success, he plans to continue in his present capacity with the Company. He advises others entering the software engineering field, "Find a job and sick with it. Don't jump ship when you hit a bump." Mr. Budd stays abreast of the latest developments in the industry by reading trade magazines and through his association with several professional organizations. Mr. Budd believes education is a very important factor in determining a person's success in his field. Headquartered in Merriam, Kansas, Control Systems International offers its quality products to an ever-increasing global clientele. The Company specializes in developing industrial control software utilized for product tracking and accounting functions, among others. The software division of the Company also produces fuel distribution software. An approximate workforce of 150 skilled individuals is employed in all aspects of operations. **Career Highlights:** Software Engineer, Control Systems International (1994-Present); Software Engineer, CIM Software (1990-94). **Associations & Accomplishments:** Institute of Electrical and Electronics Engineers; Association of Computing Machinery; KC Cares Volunteer Organization. **Education:** University of Missouri at Columbia, B.S.E.C.E. (1989). **Personal Information:** Mr. Budd enjoys backpacking, biking, camping and water and snow skiing.

Doug McCandless

Network Analyst
International Comfort Products
4164 Old State Road
Hampshire, TN 38461
(931) 270-4157
Fax: (931) 285-2275
doug.mccandless@icpusa.com

3585

Business Information: Possessing unique talent in the systems engineering field, Mr. McCandless joined International Comfort Products in 1998 as a Network Analyst. In this capacity, he assumes responsibility for the administration of the Company's entire network inclusive of 32 servers and over 800 individual users. Before joining International Comfort Products, Mr. McCandless served as Senior Systems Analyst with Laidlaw Environmental Corporation. His solid background history also includes stints as Systems Programmer for Advanced Engineering and Senior Systems Engineer at Inacom Inc. Additionally, he performs system and application setup, installs software upgrades, and troubleshoots problems as needed. His success reflects his ability to think out-of-the-box and take on new challenges and responsibilities. Looking to the next millennium, Mr. McCandless anticipates entering into a management role with the Oracle databases. International Comfort Products manufacturers HVAC units for residential and commercial use. Created in 1985, operations now employ 3,000 dedicated individuals. **Career Highlights:** Network Analyst, International Comfort Products (1998-Present); Senior System Analyst, Laidlaw Environmental Corporation (1996-98); Systems Programmer, Advanced Engineering (1998-99); Senior Systems Engineer, Inacom Inc. (1994-96). **Education:** Columbia State College, Associate's degree (1976). **Personal Information:** Married to Marilyn in 1973. One child: Eric. Mr. McCandless enjoys gardening.

Julie Tauche

Technology Services Manager
Knetico Inc.
10845 Kinsman Road
Newbury, OH 44065
(440) 564-9111
Fax: (440) 564-9541

3589

Business Information: As Technology Services Manager of Knetico Inc., Ms. Tauche is responsible for the telecommunications infrastructure, including a AS/400 platform, Novell and LAN network, and J.D. Edwards financial moduals. Joining the Corporation in 1991, she oversees and directs update and maintenance of application and software decisions, as well as systems troubleshooting and help desk operations. Retrieving, storing, and updating information, PCs, and mainframes; overseeing time lines, schedules, and budgets; and providing cohesive leadership also fall within the purview of her functions. Working at the headquarters location, Ms. Tauche attributes her success to her determination and ability to aggressively take on new challenges. Her career highlights include implementing 15 moduals in just 18 months. Continually striving for maximum effectiveness, Ms. Tauche is currently pursuing her Master's degree in Management to enable her to capitalize on the opportunities provided by Knetico. Knetico Inc. is a manufacturer of water quality devises such as water filters. Established in 1974, the Corporation installs water quality devises in residential homes turning well or hard water into soft water and undrinkable into drinkable. Their devises are used commercially also for restaurants and car washes to prevent water spots, and by communities or town water drums in order to filter tanked water. The Company employs a staff of 350 individuals to help meet the needs of a growing clientele. **Career Highlights:** Technology Services Manager, Knetico Inc. (Present). **Associations & Accomplishments:** Township Clerk, Paris Township. **Education:** Hiram College, Bachelor's degree in Management (In Progress); Kent State University. **Personal Information:** One child: Thom J. Ms. Tauche enjoys her work.

Alex Grigoryev

Programmer
ATS
3134 Normandy Woods Drive, Apartment F
Ellicott City, MD 21043
(703) 506-0088
Fax: (703) 903-0416
alex_grigoryev@hud.gov

3599

Business Information: Serving as a Programmer for ATS, Mr. Grigoryev fulfills a number of duties on behalf of the Company and its clientele. Responsible for the development and maintenance of cutting-edge applications, he utilizes PowerBuilder 6.5 to design and implement programs used by the U.S. Department of Housing and Urban Development. Working in the computer industry for a number of years, Mr. Grigoryev has gained a great deal of knowledge in the area and excels in developing visionary strategies for the Company. Attributing his success to academics and family support, he looks forward to the opportunity to obtain the position of president of the Company. Established in 1992, ATS is a computer company that develops programs for HUD. The Company deals in object oriented development and design of data processing applications. Local operations in Ellicot City, Maryland employs the skills of 1,000 personnel to fulfill all aspects of daily operation. **Career Highlights:** Programmer, ATS (1999-Present); Programmer, The Logistics Company (1998-99); Analyst/Programmer, Wang Federal (1998). **Associations & Accomplishments:** Engineer Constructor; Instructor in Building Construction; Certified PowerBuilder Programmer from Tekmetrics, world's largest provider of high-quality, structured, skills certification exams on the Internet (July 9, 1999); Bronze Medal Reward, USSR Government (August 1982). **Education:** Polytechnic University, B.S. (1975); Goal Training Center, Certification of PowerBuilder Programmer, Tekmetrics (1999); Certification of Programming (1996); Computer Center in Ukraine, Certification of Programming. **Personal Information:** Married to Tatyana in 1998. Three children: Aleksandr, Olga, and Olesya. Mr. Grigoryev enjoys sports, music, reading and computing.

Thomas P. Linfante

Programmer
Jerry's Precision Company
52A Richboynton Road
Dover, NJ 07801
(973) 366-5005

3599

Business Information: Drawing from his wealth of technical experience learned through on the job training, Mr. Linfante serves as a Programmer for Jerry's Precision Company. A C&C programming expert, he is responsible for maintaining the functionality and operational status of the Company's information systems and networking infrastructure. Highly regarded, Mr. Linfante is actively involved in the analysis, acquisition, installation, modification, configuration, support, and tracking of all systems, databases, utilities, software, and hardware. Attributing his success to being good with his hands and his math skills, Mr. Linfante anticipates his promotion to manager as a result of his continuing efforts to increase his skills through training and professional development activities. Jerry's Precision Company operates as a machine shop and general manufacturing shop. Local in scope, the Company is located in Dover, New Jersey and employs a work force of seven skilled machinist and administrative personnel utilizing their professional skills to generate annual revenues in excess of $14 million. **Career Highlights:** Programmer, Jerry's Precision Company (Present); Manager of Manufacturing, Picket Sales. **Associations & Accomplishments:** Bar Association **Education:** On the job training. **Personal Information:** Mr. Linfante enjoys reading, online research and surfing the Internet.

3600 Electronic and Other Electric Equipment

3612 Transformers, except electronic
3613 Switchgear and switchboard apparatus
3621 Motors and generators
3624 Carbon and graphite products
3625 Relays and industrial controls
3629 Electrical industrial apparatus, nec
3631 Household cooking equipment
3632 Household refrigerators and freezers
3633 Household laundry equipment
3634 Electric housewares and fans
3635 Household vacuum cleaners
3639 Household appliances, nec
3641 Electric lamps
3643 Current-carrying wiring devices
3644 Noncurrent-carrying wiring devices
3645 Residential lighting fixtures
3646 Commercial lighting fixtures
3647 Vehicular lighting equipment
3648 Lighting equipment, nec
3651 Household audio and video equipment
3642 Prerecorded records and tapes
3661 Telephone and telegraph apparatus
3663 Radio and TV communications equipment
3669 Communications equipment, nec
3671 Electron tubes
3672 Printed circuit boards
3674 Semiconductors and related devices
3675 Electronic capacitors
3676 Electronic resistors
3677 Electronic coils and transformers
3678 Electronic connectors
3679 Electronic components, nec
3691 Storage batteries
3692 Primary batteries, dry and wet
3694 Engine electrical equipment
3695 Magnetic and optical recording media
3699 Electrical equipment and supplies, nec

Thomas S. Brown III

Analytics Manager
Square D Company
1010 Airpark Center Drive
Nashville, TN 37217
(615) 844-8713
Fax: (615) 844-8703
browniit@squared.com

3612

Business Information: An expert in the his field, Mr. Brown serves as Analytics Manager with Square D Company. He is credited with the introduction and support of advanced engineering technologies, which are utilized by product development teams in the Company's design centers located throughout North America. Possessing an excellent understanding of his role, Mr. Brown provides superior engineer analysis and assistance to his surrounding peers. Having received several recognitions for his accomplishments within the Company, Mr. Brown is placed in a leadership role, where he sets the direction, implements advanced engineering tools and upgrades, evaluates software, and deploys simulation tools as well as fields and executes analysis tasks. Taking pride in his work, Mr. Brown plans on moving into product development, where he can fully integrate his talents and hands-on skills in the operations and success of the Company. A subsidiary of Snyder Electric, Square D Company serves as an electric power distributor and a manufacturer of control products for industrial and residential settings. Leading the industry in design, manufacture, and sales, the Company generates in excess of $2.75 billion annually. Headquartered in Chicago, Illinois, Square D Company is one of the City's foundations, employing an incredibly large staff of 17,000 people from the surrounding community. Currently nearing their 100th year anniversary, Square D Company was founded in 1903, and still remains a leader in the electric industry. **Career Highlights:** Analytics Manager, Square D Company (1997-Present); Various positions, McDermott Babcock & Wilcox (1984-96); Applications Development Staff Engineer, Celanese (1978-84); Engineering Teacher, University of Akron. **Associations & Accomplishments:** Church Councilman, Church Committees. **Education:** University of Missouri at Rolla, M.S. in Civil Engineering (1973); Lehigh Univesity, B.S. in Civil Engineering (1969). **Personal Information:** Married to Lee N. in 1970. Two children: Daryl and Heather. Mr. Brown enjoys tennis and wood working.

Margaret M. Nickele

Computer Graphic Specialist
S&C Electric Company
6601 North Ridge
Chicago, IL 60626
(773) 338-1000
Fax: (847) 583-9718
mnickele@sanc.com

3613

Business Information: Combining her technical knowledge with artistic talent and a flair for the written word, Ms. Nickele serves as the Computer Graphic Specialist for S&C Electric Company. She is in charge of the creation of all presentations and multimedia used internally by the Company for various functions including training and informational. Ms. Nickele personally creates the multimedia slide shows and visuals used by the president of the Company at international trade shows and slide shows utilized for training sales people. Receiving personal recognition for her work from others in the Company, Ms. Nickele believes her professional success can be attributed to her dedication and a supportive husband. Her advice to others entering the field is "absorb everything you can about your focus in technology." Ms. Nickele is looking forward to the new challenge of creating an interactive CD for sales representatives and plans to continue her education, striving toward obtaining her Master's degree. The S&C Electric Company is an international manufacturer of high voltage switching equipment for various electric companies around the world. Currently, the Company has manufacturing plants in Toronto, China, Brazil, and the United States, with a total of six locations. Corporate headquarters is maintained in Chicago, Illinois, employing more than 1,600 dedicated individuals. **Career Highlights:** Computer Graphic Specialist, S&C Electric Company (1989-Present); Art Director, American Foundrymen Society (1983-88); Art Director, ADCOMM Advertising (1981-83). **Education:** Quincy University, B.F.A. (1980). **Personal Information:** Married to Peter J. Sitkowski in 1981. Ms. Nickele enjoys embroidery, golf and stain glass work.

Bruno R. F. Reyntjens

Senior Control Systems Engineer
In Controls Inc.
P.O. Box 179
Hurricane, WV 25526
(304) 757-4228
Fax: (304) 562-2476
reyntjens@hotmail.com

3625

Business Information: Mr. Reyntjens is the Senior Control Systems Engineer for In Controls Inc. He works within the Engineering Department to control the environment and ensure the productivity of the staff. Managing major projects, he assigns the various tasks and creates the schedules for the projects. An expert, Mr. Reyntjens negotiates contracts for the Corporation and is involved in business and marketing strategic plans for his department. He advises a staff of four engineers and works to maintain the established budgets. Mr. Reyntjens' objective is to grow to a management position in a large organization. His success reflects his ability to deliver results and he aggressively takes on new challenges. In Controls Inc. specializes in industrial automation by refurbishing and servicing existing equipment. The Corporation aids in designing new automated systems and creating hardware and software processes. Integrating control systems, the three-year old Corporation is involved in automotive, water and waste control, coal, and chemistry companies. **Career Highlights:** Senior Control Systems Engineer, In Controls Inc. (1997-Present); Electrical Engineer, Rhone-Poulenc Chemicals (1996-97). **Associations & Accomplishments:** Scout Member (1982-96). **Education:** Belgium, Leuven, degree in Electrical Engineering (1996); Financial and Business Management (1996); Special Year Advanced Mathematics. **Personal Information:** Mr. Reyntjens enjoys travel, rollerblading, sailing, hiking, running, biking, snowboarding and surfing.

Johnny Kim Garza

Network Manager
DACOR
950 South Raymond Avenue
Pasadena, CA 91109
(626) 403-3148
Fax: (626) 441-9632
jgarza@dacorworld.com

3631

Business Information: As Network Manager of DACOR, Mr. Garza engages in systems integration for the entire Company. Handling all networking responsibilities, he oversees the WAN, LAN, and phone systems integration. As department manager, Mr. Garza supervises a staff of four employees using a direct and efficient style of management. With innovative strategic planning, he assisted in the development of a world class phone system for the Company. Credited with expanding sales 40 percent each year and shifting the departmental focus to fiber optics, Mr. Garza worked hands on with AT&T introducing a VPN in 1997. A dedicated employee, he continually seeks advancement opportunities within the corporate structure, aspiring to Director of Management Information Systems and Information Technology. Mr. Garza's advice is "be patient thinking in the box." DACOR is a manufacturing company that produces high end kitchen appliances such as stell overns. The family owned and operated business employs 300 full time and 200 part time people. With new product lines leaning towards the housewares line, the Company is a modern member of the industry. **Career Highlights:** Network Manager, DACOR (1997-Present); Senior Technical Advisor III, Earthlink Network (ISP) (1997); Systems Integration Analyst, Unisys Corporation (1992); Systems Liaison Officer, U.S. Fiberline (1989). **Associations & Accomplishments:** Volunteer,

Sierra Madre Public Library; Co Founder, O.Y.K.B. San Clemente (1984-Present). **Education:** University of California at San Diego, Bachelor's degree (1989); Visual Arts degree; Urban Studies and Planning degree. **Personal Information:** Married to Lori in 1995. One child: Jessica Anne Kim. Mr. Garza enjoys golf.

Michael J. Juettner

Information Technology Manager
AEG/Electrolux
Bodelschwinghstr 1
Rothenburg Bay, Germany 91541
Fax: +49 9861694492
mjuettner@hotmail.com

3635

Business Information: Functioning in the role of Information Technology Manager for AEG/Electrolux, Mr. Juettner exercises oversight of network design, training, and technical documentation. His responsibilities involve many aspects in maintaining highly advanced computer operations companywide. Additionally, he strives to develop open lines of communication between his employees to facilitate an environment that is conducive to teamwork. Foucusing on quality, Mr. Juettner directs his team to provide efficient, accurate internal service to ensure the smooth operations of all departments. He has been recognized by the Company for his ability to successfully improvise in situations most employees would view as challenges. In the future, Mr. Juettner would like to continue to help the Company grow and expand into other regions. AEG/Electrolux was established in 1900, and is a leading manufacturer of household machines. Employing more than 7,000 people throughout the world, the Company has a reputation of quality and value. **Career Highlights:** AEG/Electrolux: Information Technology Manager (1997-Present), Information Technology Administrator (1986-97). **Personal Information:** Mr. Juettner enjoys golf.

Ashley Aubrey Boyd

Network Administrator
Rheem Manufacturing Company
P.O. Box 244020
Montgomery, AL 36124
(334) 260-1581
Fax: (334) 260-1439
aboyd@rheem.com

3639

Business Information: Demonstrating his expertise in the field of technology, Mr. Boyd currently serves Rheem Manufacturing Company as Network Administrator. Beginning his career more than three years ago, he has received recognition for his diligence and management skills through his promotion to his current position. Utilizing his expansive knowledge of technologies, Mr. Boyd concentrates his efforts toward the set up of complex networks, performance of troubleshooting, and providing problematic solutions. The most rewarding aspect of his career is obtaining his Microsoft Certified Professional certification. Continuing his career with Rheem Manufacturing Company, Mr. Boyd strives to incorporate the latest technologies into manufacturing, producing a more state-of-the-art product. Established in the early 1900s, Rheem Manufacturing Company is dedicated to providing the manufacturing and maintenance of water heaters and air conditioner units. Headquartered in Montgomery, Alabama, the Company employs the skilled services of 2,000 professionals to facilitate every aspect of design, manufacture, quality assurance, and the distribution of products. Serving an international client base, the Company generates $350 million in annual revenues. **Career Highlights:** Rheem Manufacturing Company: Network Administrator (1999-Present), Network Technician (1997-99). **Education:** JP Technical College, Associate's degree in Computer Science (1996); Microsoft Certified Professional. **Personal Information:** Married to Susanne in 1997. One child: Abigail Frances.

Jeffrey Dale Enlow

PC Technician/Network Administrator
Sunbeam Outdoor Products
4101 Howard Bush Drive
Neosho, MO 64580-9164
(800) 641-4500
Fax: (417) 451-8499
jenlow@earthlink.net

3639

Business Information: Demonstrating his expertise in the field of information technology, Mr. Enlow serves as PC Technician and Network Administrator. He presides over the administration of the LAN/WAN networks and computer systems, performing routine maintenance tasks and providing a back up system to prevent data loss. In charge of the purchase of software programs and hardware equipment, he is responsible for the set up and training of users in six regional locations. Continually striving for maximum effectiveness, Mr. Enlow is currently pursuing his Bachelor's degree in Computer Science in preparation for his Master's to enable him to capitalize on the opportunities provided by the Company. He attributes his success thus far to a solid educational background and was actively involved in switching the LAN servers from a Novell to a Windows NT based environment. Serving an international clientele, Sunbeam Outdoor Products manufactures and distributes several well-known name brand products through its 117 globally placed plant locations. Subsidiaries of the Company include, First Alert, Oaster, Health-O-Meter, Mr. Coffee, East Pack, Grill Master, and Pulzar. The Neosho, Missouri plant manufactures Grill Master, Pulzar, and Sunbeam products. **Career Highlights:** PC Technician/Network Administrator, Sunbeam Outdoor Products (1998-Present); Programmer/Analyst/PC Specialist, CARMAR Group, Inc. (1996-98); Accounts Manager, CARMAR Freezers, Inc. (1993-96). **Education:** Missouri Southern State College, B.S. in Computer Science (In Progress); Northwest Arkansas Community College (1996-97); Northwest Technical Institute, diploma in Microcomputer for Business and Programmer/Analyst (1996). **Personal Information:** Married to Jerry in 1997. Mr. Enlow enjoys coin collecting.

Shyam Ramachandran

Systems Administrator/Management Information Systems Supervisor
Viking Range Corporation
111 West Front Street
Greenwood, MS 38930-4442
(662) 451-4342

3639

Business Information: In his role as Systems Administrator and Management Information Systems Supervisor, Mr. Ramachandran is responsible for all aspects of networking issues as well as the installation of hardware and software. Demonstrating extensive knowledge of the field, he guides his staff with a proactive leadership style as he incorporates their feedback and input into the development of strategic operating procedures. On a regular basis, he handles troubleshooting challenges and upgrading tasks, evaluating current systems to determine optimal solutions. Aspiring to an executive management position within the Corporation, Mr. Ramachandran intends to continue in the field, gaining valuable experience as he completes post-graduate studies. He believes in having a sincere attitude towards work and fellow employees, and helping in anyway he can. Viking Range Corporation is engaged in the manufacture of high-end, professional home appliances. Product lines are diverse, and include items such as trash compactors, dishwashers, and range tops. Recent reports estimate annual sales to exceed $140 million. The international corporation was founded in 1985 and currently employs 650 people. **Career Highlights:** Systems Administrator/Management Information Systems Supervisor, Viking Range Corporation (1994-Present). **Associations & Accomplishments:** National Computer Security Association; Institute of Electrical and Electronics Engineers. **Education:** Mississippi State University, M.S. in Electrical Engineering (1994); Madras Institute of Technology, Master's degree in Technology; Annamalai University, Bachelor's degree in Electronics & Instrumentation. **Personal Information:** Married to Dr. Veena Ammal in 1995. Mr. Ramachandran enjoys reading, working out, watching movies and playing tennis and badminton.

Gerald L. Wolf

Director of Management Information Systems
Kalas Manufacturing Inc.
25 Main Street
Denver, PA 17517-1609
(717) 335-0131
Fax: (717) 336-4248
glwolf@kalaswire.com

3643

Business Information: Originally interested in mathematics and physics, Mr. Wolf started in the technological arena 28 years ago. Possessing extensive technical skills, he joined Kalas Manufacturing Inc. in 1993. At the present time, Mr. Wolf fulfills the responsibilities of Director of Management Information Systems. In that capacity, he oversees all aspects of day-to-day operations of the Information Systems Department and controls and directs all information infrastructure resources to include LAN and WAN. A staff level position, Mr. Wolf reports directly to the President of the Corporation on technology issues. He is also responsible for reorganizing and restructuring systems to better suit the needs of the users. Maintaining the efficiency of the infrastructure, system security, and design of new technology solutions also falls under the realm of Mr. Wolf's responsibilities. He has over 20 years experience working with companies domestically and globally to implement the concepts of "ERP" and "MRP." A recognized authority in the field, he has been a presenter at both the APICS International Convention and the APICS Congress for Progress. His presentations have been published in the APICS annual reviews. He attributes his success to his ability to organize, coordinate, and work with people as well as strong support from his family. Becoming more involved in enterprise communications training with a focus on network information procedures serves as Mr. Wolf's long-term goal. Kalas Manufacturing Inc. is engaged in the manufacture and distribution of copper based wire and cable products. A privately owned company, the Corporation is headquartered in Denver, Pennsylvania and operates three network facilities in Central Pennsylvania. National in scope, the Corporation was established in 1958 and employs a work force of 300 people generating in excess of $80 million in annual revenues. **Career Highlights:** Director of Management Information Systems, Kalas Manufacturing Inc. (1993-Present); Manager of Systems and Programmers, First Data Resource (1988-93); Senior Analyst, Easco (1987-88); Senior Analyst/Programmer Manager, Black & Decker (1983-87). **Associations & Accomplishments:** American Production and Inventory Society; MENSA; Association of the Institute for Certification of Computer Professionals. **Education:** York College, B.S. (1990). **Personal Information:** Married to Linda in 1970. One child: Christine Knaub. Mr. Wolf enjoys spending time with his family, golf, restoring classic cars and model trains.

Jose I. Arpide Jr.

Assistant Analyst
Osram Sylvania
71 Cherry Hill Drive
Beverly, MA 01915
(978) 750-1733
jarpide@bigfoot.com

3645

Business Information: Serving as Assistant Analyst of Osram Sylvania, Mr. Arpide fulfills the responsibility of client server systems developer and database administrator. Possessing an excellent understanding of technology, he programs new software utilizing the PowerBuilder applications development system. A technical expert, Mr. Arpide maintains applications and adds enhancements to existing programs. In addition, he conducts research to add new ports to the Internet as well as analyzes, specifies, and designs solutions for systems difficulties. A visionary who have proven himself correct on many occasions, Mr. Arpide's future strategic plans are to move more into Internet development of Web based programs. Established in 1993, Osram Sylvania specializes in lighting research and development. The Company, headquartered in Denverst, Massachusetts, employs 10,000 people at their 8 locations worldwide. Osram Sylvania strives to provide quality lighting fixtures for area residential and business use. Always seeking new concepts, the Company keeps its clients as top priority. **Career Highlights:** Assistant Analyst, Osram Sylvania (1997-Present); Client/Server Developer/Contractor, Ciber, Inc. (1993-97); Client/Server Developer/Systems Analyst, Cyrk, Inc. (1997-99). **Education:** Worcester State College, B.S. (1992). **Personal Information:** Married to Jennifer in 1994. Two children: Elizabeth and Daniel. Mr. Arpide enjoys woodworking.

Elizabeth Charpentier

Acting Manager of Management Information Systems
Wasco Products Inc.
26 Pioneer Avenue
Sanford, ME 04073
(207) 657-8090
Fax: (207) 324-9005
echarpentier@wascoproducts.com

3645

Business Information: Miss Charpentier is the Acting Manager of Management Information Systems for Wasco Products Inc. She is responsible for networking, hardware and software, maintenance, phone systems, and the Internet exchange. With the Corporation for the last two years, she determines the overall strategic direction and business contribution of the information systems function. Miss Charpentier also assists in developing goals, formulating policies, and implementing strategies. Her dedication to the Corporation has made her an invaluable resource. One of her biggest achievements was building Wasco's networking environment from the ground up. In the future, Miss Charpentier aspires to eventually attain the position of Network Administrator. Continuous reading keeps her abreast on key issues and new technology advancements. Miss Charpentier attributes her professional success to her high school networking administrator. Wasco Products Inc. manufactures and sells skylights and patio dome lights for residential and commercial customers. Established in 1983, the Corporation provides services through one location in Maine. Presently, Wasco Products is manned by a work force or more than 150 dedicated personnel. **Career Highlights:** Wasco Products Inc.: Acting Manager of Management Information Systems (1999-Present), Manager of Information Systems Intern (1997-99); Crew, McDonalds (1995-97). **Education:** York County Technical College, Computer Application Technology (In Progress). **Personal Information:** One child: Trevor Scott Merrill.

Frank Little

Safety and Environmental Manager
Design Fabricators
555 Aspen Ridge Drive
Lafayette, CO 80026
(303) 661-9800
Fax: (303) 661-9814
flittle@designfab.com

3646

Business Information: Serving as the Safety & Environmental Manager for Design Fabricators, Mr. Little fulfills a number of day to day duties on behalf of the Company and its clientele. A savvy, 14 year professional, he is responsible for designing, implementing, and enforcing all work area safety programs. Utilizing ten years of experience in his field and four years as a member of the United States Air Force, Mr. Little also deals with environmental programs and workers compensation claims for both of the Company's locations. In the future, he looks forward to continuing to growing and excelling in his current position. His success reflects his ability to take on challenges and new responsibilities and deliver the appropriate results. Established in 1988, Design Fabricators manufactures commercial store lighting fixtures. Employing 340 personnel, the Company reports estimated annual revenue in excess of $33 million. Headquartered in Lafayette, Colorado, the Company creates specialty designs made to fit clients specific needs. **Career Highlights:** Safety and Environmental Manager, Design Fabricators (1998-Present); Veterans Employment Representative, State of Nevada (1996-98); Electronic Engineer/Technical Writer, LORALI Aerospace Corporation (1986-95). **Education:** Community College of the Air Force, A.A.S. in Avionics Technology (1986). **Personal Information:** Married to Jacqueline in 1966. Two children: Paige and Patty. Mr. Little enjoys woodworking, softball and golf.

Masood Hussain

Management Information Systems Manager
Saudi Lighting Company
P.O. Box 25609
Riyadh, Saudi Arabia 11476
+966 12651010
Fax: +966 12652194
masdh@yahoo.com

3648

Business Information: Recruited to Saudi Lighting Company in 1991, Mr. Hussain serves as Management Information Systems Manager. In his capacity, he is responsible for designing, implementing, and managing the Company's and client's voice and data networks. A leader in the telecommunications community, he directly contributes to the development of creative and high impact technology and business strategies. Drawing from over 15 years of occupational experience, Mr. Hussain does consultant work part time, and as a visionary his goals include expansion of the Company on an international level. His professional success is due to his knowledge of the industry and keeping abreast of changes and developments. Saudi Lighting Company, established in 1980, manufactures state-of-the-art indoor and outdoor lighting for residential and commercial customers for Persian Gulf countries. The Company employs 540 individuals responsible for administration, gathering data, designing new products and manufacturing processes, marketing merchandise, and sales. Located in Riyadh, Saudi Arabia, the Company reports annual revenue of $200 million. **Career Highlights:** Management Information Systems Manager, Saudi Lighting Company (1991-Present); Data Processing Manager, Saudi Continental Insurance Company (1988-91); Data Processing Manager, YIT & MABCO Joint Venture (1985-88). **Education:** M.S. in Mathematics (1977). **Personal Information:** Married to Andaleeb in 1984. Three children: Sundus, Samir, and Shizza.

Gary Fadely

Technical Trainer
Thomson Consumer Electronics
7225 Winton Drive
Indianapolis, IN 46268
(317) 415-2139
Fax: (317) 587-9443
fadelyg@tce.com

3651

Business Information: A savvy, 27 year veteram in technology, Mr. Fadely serves in the role of Technical Engineer of Thomson Consumer Electronics, carrying out his daily responsibilities for program development for field services operations. With extensive experience as a technical engineer, he develops all field training programs for multimedia and installation of DSS. Mr. Fadely also implements Chilton manuals into his training courses. His career achievements include being part of the first plant to install an automated warehouse system at General Motors, being hired by Thomson Consumer Electronics, and being involved in the DSS rollout and HDT startup. Mr. Fadely plans to continue with the Company, obtain his Bachelor's degree, become more involved in programming, and receive CD Rom and HDT training. His success reflects his ability to think outside the box, take on challenges, and deliver results. Thomson Consumer Electronics began with the purchase of RCA and G.E. 1987. The Company currently manufactures RCA, G.E., and Proscan consumer and commercial electronic products. The Company specializes in audio, visual, DSs, engineering, and other electronics such asd VCRs, televisions, and stereos. International in scope, Thomson Consumer Electronics is headquartered in Indianapolis, Indiana and employs a global work force of more than 45,000. **Career Highlights:** Thomson Consumer Electronics: Technical Engineer (1994-Present), Consumer Relations (1992-94); Engineering Suppot Technician, 3M (1992). **Associations & Accomplishments:** Vocational Industria Clubs of America; Board Member, Church Federation of Greater Indianapolis; Vestry, St. Alban's Episcopal Church. **Education:** ITT Technical Institute, Associate's degree (1973). **Personal Information:** Married to Teresa in 1980. Three children: Andrew, Jessica, and Joni. Mr. Fadely enjoys golf, model railroading, community volunteerism and faith-based activities.

Joel S. Teller

Director of Quality Audio Products
Thomas Consumer Electronics
101 West 103rd Street
Indianapolis, IN 46290
(317) 587-5378
tellerj@tce.com

3651

Business Information: As the Director of Quality Audio Products for Thomson Consumer Electronics, Mr. Teller oversees the manufacture of stereo, speaker, and sound components. Possessing an excellent understanding of his field, he researches product lines, compares the quality of competitors, and implements policies that will ensure higher quality for the Company. He also directs the manufacturing processes to guarantee that all components are produced according to Company standards. His years of experience with notable companies such as IBM have instilled a dedication to consistently achieve quality performance. In the next three to five years, Mr. Teller plans to continue in his present position, thus ensuring future Company success. Thomson Consumer Electronics manufactures electronic components for companies, such as RCA, General Electric, and Pro Scan. Located in Indianapolis, Indiana, the Company distributes products to clients in the United States and across the globe. The Company's enterprising and industrious staff is dedicated to producing the finest in electronic components. **Career Highlights:** Director of Quality Audio Products, Thomson Consumer Electronics (1995-Present); Tech Operations Manager for Portable Computer, IBM (1989-95); **Associations & Accomplishments:** American Society for Quality Control. **Education:** Southeastern Massachusetts, B.S. in Electrical Engineering (1981), B.S. in Civil Engineering (1981). **Personal Information:** Married to Robyn in 1973. One child: Marc. Mr. Teller enjoys gourmet cooking and fishing.

Michael R. Warmelink

Senior Systems Analyst
Thomson Consumer Electronics
10330 North Meridian Street
Indianapolis, IN 46290-1024
(317) 587-5082
Fax: (317) 587-6755
warmelim@tce.com

3651

Business Information: Utilizing over six years of experience, Mr. Warmelink was a consultant until May 2000. Then he went to work for Thomson Consumer Electronics. Highly skilled in his field, he develops cutting edge systems in Oracle, UNIX, and Informatica for Thomson Consumer Electronics. Mr. Warmelink's responsibilities include scripting, data warehouse support, and evaluation of partnerships and products. One of many career highlights, the greatest is being part of a United States Air Force team that developed a system from scratch, rewriting the entire program in just eight months and earning the Air Force's Achievement Medal for being integral in this accomplishment. Always alert to new opportunities, techniques, and approaches, his goals include becoming technical lead manager with the Corporation. Highly regarded, Mr. Warmelink's success is due to his ability to work well with others as well as communicate effectively with peers and upper management. In 1892, the merger of Thomson-Houston and Edison General electric companies created General Electric, which is the original company that has evolved today into Thomson Consumer Electronics. Thomson Consumer Electronics manufactures the RCA, GE, and Proscan brand of consumer electronics. **Career Highlights:** Senior Systems Analyst, Thomson Consumer Electronics (May 2000-Present); Senior Information Technology Consultant, ONEX, Inc. (Aug. 1998-May 2000); Consultant, Ambassador Consulting, Inc. (June 1998-Aug. 1998); Information Systems Programmer, United States Air Force (Aug. 1994-May 1998). **Associations & Accomplishments:** Midwest Oracle Users Group; Midwest Informatica Users Group; Indiana Oracle Users Group; United States Air Force's Achievement Medal; United Way Local Area Charities. **Education:** Troy State Univeristy (1997); Indiana University Northwest (1992-94). **Personal Information:** Married to Molly in 1996. One child: Michael. Mr. Warmelink enjoys volleyball and basketball.

Jean-Marc Allain

Systems Engineer
New Bridge Technology
3040 Post Oak Boulevard, Suite 1215
Houston, TX 77056
(713) 280-3600
Fax: (713) 280-3650

3661

Business Information: Displaying his expertise in this highly specialized position, Mr. Allain serves as the Systems Engineer for New Bridge Technology. He is a consultant to the Company's clients. Communicating technical terms in a language the layman can understand, he explains different types of systems function and gives his expert advice on the one most beneficial to the individual client. Before joining New Bridge, he served as Support Manager with Castleton Network Systems. His background history also include a stint as President for A&G International. In his present role, Mr. Allain designs each network system to the client's exact specifications and performs installation as well. Technical support is provided after the installation. Committed to the success of the Company, Mr. Allain looks forward to increasing his responsibilities in a management role and anticipates obtaining a position as Senior Engineer. A systems expert, his success reflects his ability to think outside the box and aggressively tackle new challenges. New Bridge Technology is an international telecommunication and network equipment provider. Publicly traded, the Company maintains United States headquarters in Herndon, Virginia. Global headquarters are located in Canada. New Bridge Technology was established in 1986 and employs approximately 6,600 skilled professionals worldwide. Annual sales were reported to be $1.9 billion for the last fiscal year. **Career Highlights:** Systems Engineer, New Bridge Technology (1997-Present); Support Manager, Castleton Network Systems (1996-97); President, A&G International (1993-96). **Associations & Accomplishments:** Coach, Minor League Baseball. **Education:** SHL Systemshouse: Network Analyst (1996), Systems Engineer (1996). **Personal Information:** Married to Chantel in 1994. One child: Alexandre. Mr. Allain enjoys reading.

NORTEL NETWORKS

Richard Austin

Director of Information Services and Real Estate Systems
Nortel Networks
8200 Dixie Road
Brampton, Ontario, Canada L6T 5P6
(905) 863-7280
Fax: (905) 863-8006
richaus@nortelnetworks.com

3661

Business Information: As Director of Information Services and Real Estate Systems for Nortel Networks, Mr. Austin oversees a $6 million operating budget and a virtual team of 50 technical and professional staff throughout North America, Europe, and Asia. Responsible for legal, real estate, and customer value systems, he oversees Web site development, business process automation, and technology solutions. With more than 15 years of professional experience in information technology, Mr. Austin continues to grow professionally through the fulfillment of his responsibilities and his involvement in the advancement of Nortel Networks operations. Consistently achieving quality performance in his field, Mr. Austin attributes his success to his decision making, organizational, and leadership skills as well as his versatility. One of the leading multinational telecommunications manufacturers, Nortel Networks provides a variety of equipment for local and international companies. The Company offers such products as telephone switches, wireless and optical network, and hardware products. Established in the early 1900s, the Company is headquartered in Toronto, Canada and operates out of a number of international subsidiaries. Combined, the

Company employs more than 85,000 professionals who assist in the generation of annual revenues in excess of $24 billion. **Career Highlights:** Nortel Networks: Director of Information Services and Real Estate Systems (1999-Present), Senior Manager (1997-99), Manager (1995-97). **Associations & Accomplishments:** International Development Research Council. **Education:** Concordia University, Master's degree in Educational Technology (1985); McGill University, B.A. in Educational Technology (1985). **Personal Information:** Mr. Austin enjoys painting and contemporary art. Visit www.torontopainter.com to see his art, which has been exhibited and sold internationally.

Wilhelm Bogner
Information Technology Security Administrator
Frequentis
Laurenzgasse 3-1-15
Vienna, Austria 1050
+43 678181150
Fax: +43 18115077 Ext. 1556
willy.bogner@usa.net

3661

Business Information: Serving as Information Technology Security Administrator, Mr. Bogner provides his expert services on behalf of Frequentis and its clients. Joining the Company in 1999, he is responsible for controlling systems access, implementing firewalls, designing antivirus strategies, and conducting encryption. Highly regarded, he is currently working on a project that will enable the Company's staff to access and disable security programs by the use of a specific type of card. Concentrating his attention towards the newly developing security card project, Mr. Bogner continues to provide excellent services in information technology management. The most rewarding aspect of his career is implementing management controls, restrictions, and security for the Company. Providing voice and data communication systems, Frequentis provides its specialized services and products for the air traffic control field. Established in 1947, the Company is located in Vienna, Austria and serves an international clientele base primarily in Austria, Canada, and East Asia. Employing 500 technical experts and administrators, the Company generates ATS1 billion in annual revenues. **Career Highlights:** Information Technology Security Administrator, Frequentis (1996-Present); Information Technology Consultant/Owner, WSM Software Management (1992-96); Network Administrator, Funworld A.G. (1990-92). **Education:** Joh. Kepler University (Currently Attending). **Personal Information:** Married to Christina in 1996. Two children: Tobias and Eva-Maria. Mr. Bogner enjoys snooker, music, computers, walking with family and wine hill walking.

Rae Ann Bruno
• • • ◉ • • •

Director of Information Systems Customer Service
Siemens Energy and Automation
3333 Old Milton Parkway
Cumming, GA 30041
(770) 751-4936
Fax: (678) 297-8086
raeann.bruno@sea.siemens.com

3661

Business Information: As Director of Information Systems Customer Service, Mrs. Bruno creates, constructs, and supervises the technical groups and products. Reporting directly to the Chief Information Officer, she assists her staff of 30 with troubleshooting and operating procedures for various projects. A dedicated and capable employee, her most recognized achievement was the successful implementation by the Company of her customer service and training program, resulting in the creation of her current position. Always looking towards the future, Mrs. Bruno is continually seeking opportunities for advancement within the corporate structure. Attributing her success to keeping in tune to people, having the big picture, and knowing the customers needs, Mrs. Burno plans on training Company personnel in multi-media software and products. With 10,000 employees worldwide, the Siemens Energy and Automation group is recognized as being a leader in the electrical components industry. The Company manufactures products such as breakers, breaker boxes, and MCCs. **Career Highlights:** Director of Information Systems Customer Service, Siemens Energy and Automation (1997-Present); Cutler-Hammer: Staff Manager, Enterprise Support (1996-97), Manager, Training/Documentation (1995-96). **Associations & Accomplishments:** International Customer Service Association; National Association for Female Executives; Georgia 100 Mentor Exchange; Help Desk Institute; Help Desk 2000. **Education:** Bowling Green State University, B.A. in Communications (1985). **Personal Information:** Married to Jeffrey A. in 1996. One child: Trent.

Christopher Allen Bunt
Internal Business Manager for Dallas
Nortel Networks
P.O. Box 833805
Richardson, TX 75083-3805
(972) 685-1753
Fax: (972) 842-8347
cbunt@bigfoot.com

3661

Business Information: As Internal Business Manager for Dallas with Nortel Networks, Mr. Bunt is responsible for supporting, maintaining, and managing internally driven e-commerce tools. Bringing with him valuable experience as a technical consultant, he has faithfully served with Nortel Networks since coming on board to the Company in 1996. He is credited with developing a cutting edge time tracking tool for Nortel. Aspiring to see Nortel Networks at it's fullest potential, Mr. Bunt plans to bring the Company to a global level servicing companies internationally. A firm believer in hard work, he attributes his success to finding ways to be more effective as an employee as well as having a supportive family. Established as Nortel Networks in 1975, the Company provides network and telecommunication services for such clients as MCI and Sprint. Currently employing over 70,000 people, Nortel creates an estimated annual revenue in excess of $16 billion. Headquartered in Georgia, the Company provides broad band, wireless, public network, and enterprise network services. **Career Highlights:** Internal Business Manager for Dallas, Nortel Networks (1997-Present); Technical Consultant, Comsys Technical (1996-97); Consultant, BCI Protocol (1996). **Associations & Accomplishments:** Promise Keepers; Former Volunteer Fireman. **Education:** Richland College, A.A.S. (1998); Microsoft Certified Professional. **Personal Information:** Two children: Ariel Follbaum and Bryan.

Philip D. Darby
Senior Information Security Analyst
Siemens Energy and Automation
Atlanta, GA 30341
(770) 751-4902
Fax: (770) 751-4332

3661

Business Information: As a Senior Information Security Analyst, Mr. Darby aids the information security department in making sure the corporate information infrastructure is conducting secure practices. In his capacity, he advises other departments on trends and changes in the information security market. A very hard working and dedicated professional, Mr. Darby can be given credit for his automation abilities in this area. A prominent professional who believes hard work and consistency pays off, Mr. Darby intends to increase his knowledge and career opportunities and advancements by obtaining the following certifications: CLP, CCNA, and CNA. Mr. Darby will currently obtain his MCSE and MCP+I. Mr. Darby is currently employed by Siemens Energy and Automation. **Career Highlights:** Senior Information Security Analyst, Siemens Energy and Automation (1998-Present); Site Technology Manager, Precision Response Corporation (1997-98); Advanced Technician Level II, PriceWaterhouse LLP (Mia) (1995-97). **Education:** American Technology Institute, A.S. in Electrical Engineering (1991). **Personal Information:** Married to Martine in 1995. Mr. Darby enjoys exercise, gym activities, reading, music and studying.

Minh-Kha Do
Verification Engineer
Nortel Networks
2351 Alfred-Nobel Boulevard
Saint-Laurent, Quebec, Canada H4S 2A9
(514) 818-1010
Fax: (514) 818-4902
mkado@yahoo.com

3661

Business Information: Serving as Verification Engineer for Nortel Networks, Mr. Do fulfills a number of duties in the performance of his job on behalf of the Company and clients. He is responsible for desk plans, systems optical carriers, and software regression testing. Possessing superior talents and an excellent understanding of technology and troubleshooting software applications, Mr. Do works on software programs which have been modified to ensure that the original operations remain functional and without any systems glitches. In the future, he looks forward to advancing within the Company's corporate structure to a team leader position. His success reflects his ability to tackle challenges and deliver results. Founded in 1990, Nortel Networks provides services in data communication and optical networks. Serving a global clientele, the Company's networks are capable of transferring applications internationally. This allows Company clients to work with businesses around the globe and communicate with

customers. **Career Highlights:** Verification Engineer, Nortel Networks (1997-Present); Quality Assurance Reliability Engineer, Harris Farinon (1993-97); Verification Engineer, Philips Electronics Ltd. (1988-93). **Associations & Accomplishments:** Ordre Aes Ingenisurs Du Quebec; American Society Quality Software and Reliability. **Education:** University of Montreal, Bachelor's degree in Engineering (1986). **Personal Information:** Mr. Do enjoys tennis and computers.

Travis M. Farral
Senior Project Manager
Nokia, Inc.
6000 Connection Drive
Irving, TX 75039
(972) 894-5195
Fax: (817) 490-7359
travis.farral@nokia.com

3661

Business Information: As Senior Project Manager of Nokia, Inc., Mr. Farral plans and oversees the development and support of information technology related applications and functional areas. An experience, four year technology veteran, he joined the Nokia, Inc. team in 1995. He has assertively served in a variety of capacities since his arrival to the Corporation. Mr. Farral, at the present time, is responsible for large projects relating to Nokia's internal data and voice network and server infrastructure. Combining his extensive management skills and strategic systems expertise, he oversees installation and maintenance of equipment and networks at 34 sites. Coordinating resources, developing project schedules and assigning tasks, performing both systems analysis and programming, and serving as contact with users and systems management also fall within the purview of Mr. Farral's responsibilities. He attributes his success to studying outside of work and investing in self-improvement. Moving into other areas, staying hands on, continuing to obtain certifications, and remaining open to new ideas serve as Mr. Farral's future endeavors. An international telecommunications company, Nokia, Inc. is involved in design and development of telecommunications and other digital technologies that include mobile planes, telecommunications networks, wireless data solutions, and multimedia terminals. Founded in 1865, Nokia's headquarters is located in Finland, and United States headquarters in Irving, Texas. Presently, the Corporation employs a work force of more than 47,000 persons who help generate in excess of $15 billion in annual revenues. **Career Highlights:** Nokia, Inc.: Senior Project Manager (1998-Present), Systems Administrator (1997-98), Industrial Engineer Technician (1995-96). **Associations & Accomplishments:** Microsoft Certified Professional; Radio Amateur Civil Emergency Service. **Education:** DeVry Institute of Technology. **Personal Information:** Married to Lisa Y. in 1996. Four children: Thomas, Gary, Heidi, and Courtney. Mr. Farral enjoys playing hockey, reading and HAM radio.

Alan W. Jackson
WAN/LAN Manager
Nortel Networks
155 Smith Avenue
Stoughton, MA 02072-3938
(978) 375-1956
ajackson@nortelnetworks.com

3661

Business Information: Serving as the WAN/LAN Manager for Nortel Networks, Mr. Jackson is responsible for the remote access group. Possessing an excellent understanding of technology, he effectively manages the WAN/LAN systems architecture for the Company's Stoughton, Massachusetts location. He supervises project teams, providing strategic planning and project management direction as well as oversees maintenance and troubleshooting activities. Utilizing 12 years of experience in the field, Mr. Jackson displays an effective, productive management style and is aware of potential contributions of the department. In the future, he plans to obtain a position as the Manager or Vice President of Information Services. Established in 1990, Nortel Networks provides services in data communication and optical networks. Serving an international clientele, the Company's networks are capable of transferring applications throughout the world. Employing more than 10,000 personnel, the Company reports annual revenues in excess of $21 billion. **Career Highlights:** WAN/LAN Manager, Nortel Networks (Present); Lab Manager, Bay Networks; Hardware/Software Lab Technician, Xylogics. **Associations & Accomplishments:** President, Little League Baseball. **Education:** Northeastern University, B.S. in Engineering Technology (1988). **Personal Information:** Married to Mary in 1990. Mr. Jackson enjoys softball.

Billy R. Jones, II

Quality Assurance Technician
Siemens Energy and Automation
601 Sixth Avenue
Bristol, TN 37620
(423) 461-2704
billy.jones@sea.siemens.com

3661

Business Information: Combining communication skills with technological expertise, Mr. Jones began his career with Siemens Energy and Automation in 1992 as a Manufacturing Technician. Working his way through the ranks to his current position of Quality Assurance Technician, he is charged with ensuring all products meet standardized testing and answering customer queries as well as cross-referencing the warranty database. Mr. Jones anticipates his promotion to Program Manager as a result of his continued efforts to increase quality while operating on schedule. His professional success reflects his ability to think outside the box, take on challenges, and deliver results on behalf of the Company. Siemens Energy and Automation is an established and reputable company engaged in the development, manufacturing, and marketing of fiber optic cables, ancillary hardware, and connectors as well as specialized copper wiring utilized in voice, data, and video communication applications. Siemens Energy and Automation employs the skilled services of over 900 personnel to meet the demands of a growing, international clientele, and is recognized as a leader in the field of telecommunications technology. **Career Highlights:** Quality Assurance Technician, Siemens Energy and Automation (1995-Present); Manufacturing Technician, Siemens Industrial Automation (1992-95); Line Technician, Texas Instruments (1989-92). **Associations & Accomplishments:** Board of Supervisors, Bristol Federal Credit Union. **Education:** Milligan College, B.A. (In Progress); Northeast State Technical Community College, Associate's degree in Electronic Engineering Technology (1989). **Personal Information:** Married to Jennifer C. in 1996. One child: Christian Reeves. Mr. Jones enjoys the stock market, researching, historic renovation and antiques.

David R. Leitzel

Senior Systems Engineer
Unisphere Solutions
5445 DTC Parkway, Penthouse 4
Englewood, CO 80111
(303) 488-3450
Fax: (253) 830-0969
dleitzel@unispheresolutions.com

3661

Business Information: Serving as the Senior Systems Engineer for Unisphere Solutions, Mr. Leitzel is responsible for testing and integrations. He monitors and tracks pre- and post-sales, ensuring that products sold are fully functional and serviceable, thus living up to the Company's reputation for excellence. Dedicated to the Company's success, he has assertively worked in the technology industry for more than 18 years and he continues to grow professionally through the fulfillment of his responsibilities. Mr. Leitzel looks forward to remaining with the Company and continuing to assist in the completion of future corporate goals. Established in 1997, Unisphere Solutions is involved in voice and data switching hardware sales. With a presence in more than 160 countries, the Company's products are designed to provide for the needs of service providers. Reporting annual revenues of $150 million, the Company's products are designed to build great networks for consumers. Operations in Englewood, Colorado employ the skills and expertise of 500 personnel. **Career Highlights:** Senior Systems Engineer, Unisphere Solutions (1999-Present); Senior Systems Engineer, Fore Systems Inc. (1997-99); Senoir Systems Engineer, First Data Corporation (1995-96); Senior Systems Engineer, Apollo Communications (1996-97). **Education:** Lincoln Technical Institute, Associate's degree (1982). **Personal Information:** Married to Dana in 1983. One child: Derek. Mr. Leitzel enjoys fly fishing.

Pam McElvy

A/R Supervisor/Commissions Administrator
InterVoice-Brite, Inc.
17811 Waterview Parkway
Dallas, TX 75252-8027
(972) 454-8752
Fax: (972) 454-8098

3661

Business Information: Mrs. McElvy functions as A/R Supervisor and Commissions Administrator of InterVoice-Brite, Inc. She is responsible for all aspects of daily administration of the Corporation. As a 17 year veteran in her field, Mrs. McElvy has assertively served with InterVoice, Inc. in a variety of capacities since joining the team as A/R Clerk for Commissions in 1986. In her present role, she compiles and synthesizes large quantities of data to determine commissions for the Corporation's sales force. Mrs. McElvy, in addition, manages a staff of two employees who handles all administration activities for the Corporation. Conducting personnel evaluations; overseeing administrative resources, time lines, and schedules; and ensuring data accuracy and integrity also fall within the purview of her responsibilities. Mrs. McElvy's career success reflects her dedication and commitment and ability to aggressively take on new challenges and responsibilities. Recently merging with Brite Voice Systems, InterVoice-Brite, Inc. designs, develops, manufactures, and distributes state-of-the-art voice response systems and call automation solutions. Established in 1983, InterVoice is a premier and leading supplier of inbound and outbound call automation and interactive systems. Presently, the Corporation is manned a skilled staff of over 750 professional, technical, and support personnel. **Career Highlights:** InterVoice-Brite, Inc.: A/R Supervisor/Commissions Administrator (1997-Present), A/R Clerk for Commissions (1986-97). **Education:** Midwestern State University, B.B.A. (1982). **Personal Information:** Married to David in 1990. Two children: Brandon and Nicholas.

Scott C. Neal

Network Engineer
Nortel Networks
9225 Indian Creek Parkway, Suite 120
Overland Park, KS 66210
(913) 706-0250

3661

Business Information: Mr. Neal functions in the role of Network Engineer for Nortel Networks. He is responsible for the design, implementation, and support of telecommunication networks for businesses in the Midwest. Before joining Nortel Networks, Mr. Neal served as Senior Technical Services Engineer for Datatec Systems, Inc. His solid technical background history also includes a stint as Network Engineer with Sprint. As a five year expert in the field, he is involved in the pre-sale design of customer networks as well as post-sale support for equipment. Working with users and systems management to analyze, specify, and design new technical solutions to eliminate difficulties and improve overall system functions also fall within the purview of Mr. Neal's responsibilities. His success reflects his perseverance and his ability to think out-of-the-box and take on new challenges. Ultimately attaining the position of Regional Director for Nortel serves as one of Mr. Neal's future endeavors. Nortel Networks is a leading telecommunications equipment and solutions provider. Established in the 1860s, the Company employs an international work force of more than 75,000 professional, technical, and support personnel. Providing network and telecommunications equipment and related services, Nortel reports consolidated annual sales in excess of $17.6 billion. **Career Highlights:** Network Engineer, Nortel Networks (1999-Present); Network Engineer/Senior Technical Services Engineer, Datatec Systems, Inc. (1999); Network Engineer, Technology Planning & Integration Department, Sprint (1995-99). **Education:** Institute of Technology, degree in Computer Information Systems (1995); University of Missouri at Kansas City, M.B.A (1993); University of Missouri at Columbia, B.S. in Business Administration (1990). **Personal Information:** Married to Donna in 1991. Two children: Michael and Katherine. Mr. Neal enjoys golf, boating, fishing and sports.

Abraham Omran

Design Engineer
Cyras Systems, Inc.
46832 Lakeview Boulevard
Fremont, CA 94538

3661

Business Information: Utilizing extensive experience in the communications industry, Mr. Omran serves as Design Engineer for Cyras Systems, Inc. He works closely with a team of staff members on the board level of the Engineering Department, designing and implementing new company communication products. Obtaining his Master's degree in Electrical Engineering while working full-time, Mr. Omran has been recognized several times by his employers and past client companies for his outstanding job performance. He attributes his professional success to years of experience and patience, as well as his ability to think out-of-the-box and aggressively take on new challenges. Founded in 1998, Cyras Systems is privately funded, and aims to be the frontrunner in complete multi-service-over-optics carrier solutions. Mr. Omran's past client companies sell communication products, voice, and data services, serving primarily a national clientele with the addition of some selected international accounts. **Career Highlights:** Design Engineer, Cyras Systems, Inc. (1999-Present); Design Engineer, EAS Solutions/Raychem (1994-99); Design Consultant, ESL, Subsidiary of TRW (1993-94); Senior Hardware Design Engineer, Alcatel Network Systems (1991-93); Senior Design Engineer, DSC Communications (1986-91). **Associations & Accomplishments:** Certified Professional Engineer in California; Institute of Electrical and Electronics Engineers; National Society of Professional Engineers; California Society of Professional Engineers; Life Member, University of California Alumni Association; Berkeley Engineering Alumni Society. **Education:** Santa Clara University, M.S. in Electrical Engineering (1996); University of California at Berkley, B.S. in Electrical Engineering (1977); Registered Professional Engineering License, #E15005. **Personal Information:** Mr. Omran enjoys soccer and chess.

Richard K. Wright, D.Sc.

Senior Member of Technical Staff
Siemens Microelectronics, OptoElectronics Division
19000 Homestead Road
Cupertino, CA 95014-0712
(408) 725-3441
Fax: (408) 725-3413
rich.wright@smi.siemens.com

3661

Business Information: Utilizing more than 25 years of experience in the engineering field, Dr. Wright serves as Senior Member of the Technical Staff for Siemens. He orchestrates assembly development processes of prototypes and conducts materials research. Dr. Wright's plans for the future include remaining cognizant of advances in technology and concentrating efforts on the development of more efficient diagnostic tools for the Company. Siemens, one of the largest electrical engineering and electronics companies in the world, is divided into five industrial operating groups. As a production site for the microelectronics division, the Cupertino, California facility designs and manufactures semiconductors, optoelectronics, and passive components. Serving the communications, computer peripherals, and automotive markets, Siemens Microelectronics Division employs more than 200 personnel and generates estimated annual revenue of more than $300 million. **Career Highlights:** Senior Member of Technical Staff, Siemens (1994-Present); Self Employed (1989-94); Senior Systems Design Engineer, Amdahl Corporation (1983-89); Process Engineer, Tektronix Corporation (1977-82); Process Engineer, Motorola (1973-77). **Associations & Accomplishments:** Society for Information Display; Former Member, American Association for the Advancement of Science; Former Member, Materials Research Society; American Physical Society. **Education:** EuroTechnical Research University, D.Sc. in Physics (1989); Arizona State University, B.S. in Physics (1975). **Personal Information:** Married to Judie in 1969. Four children: Kimberlee, Jamie, Ashlee, and Lindsay. Dr. Wright enjoys hunting, fishing and hunting. He is a licensed private pilot.

Olumide A. Ademidun

Information Technology Manager
Spar Aerospace
46 Saka Tinubu V/Island, Lagos P.O. Box 50716
Ikey Lagos, Nigeria
+23 412624700
oademidun@hotmail.com

3663

Business Information: Recruited to Spar Aerospace as Information Technology Manager in 1997, Mr. Ademidun administers, controls, and maintains the functionality of the company's operating infrastructure. A savvy, technical expert, he installs operating and database management systems software, compilers, and utilities. Responsible for running the company's entire network computer infrastructure in Nigeria and Canada, Mr. Ademidun takes pride in the challenging projects that he works on, sharing new methodology concepts with the Company, and working with leading consulting agencies. His focus is on changes that will allow Spar Aerospace to take advantage of new, cutting edge technology to remain flexible, efficient, and profitable in the Information Technology Age. He is inspired by the challenges of a very fast-paced industry that requires a continued knowledge in the field. According to Mr. Ademidun, his success is attributed to his ability to think outside the box, take on new challenges and responsibilities, and deliver positive results. Created in 1985, Spar Aerospace engages in space telecommunications. An international service provider, the Company is headquartered in Canada and provides advanced informational technology services to clients such as Chevron, Texaco, Exxon, and Citibank. The Company reports annual sales of approximately $4 million. Local operations in Jkoy J, Nigeria, employs 100 professional and technical staff to meet the needs of a growing and diverse clientele. **Career Highlights:** Information Technology Manager, Spar Aerospace (1997-Present); General Manager Operations, Mark Burton & Company (1995-97); General Manager, DivAccess, Ltd. (1993-95). **Associations & Accomplishments:** British Computer Society; Office Development Advisory Panel, Microsoft Redmond. **Education:** Strategic Management Centre, Ogun State University, M.B.A. (2000); University of Lagos, B.Sc. in Computer Science with Honors (1992); Microsoft Certified Professional; Certified Lotus Professional. **Personal Information:** Married to Aramide in 1996. Two children: Oreoluwatomiwa and Oreoluwakitan. Mr. Ademidun enjoys reading, golf and family outings.

Clifton J. Barber

Director
Oki Network Technologies
70 Crestridge Drive, Suite 150
Suwanee, GA 30024
(678) 482-2669
Fax: (678) 482-9946
cbarber@okitele.com
3663

Business Information: Representing Oki Network Technolgies at industry trade shows worldwide, Mr. Barber serves as Director and specializes in wireless technology and the related markets. Focusing his directing activity within the North American Research Center, Mr. Barber promotes the development of new technologies and features in the cellular communication industry, supporting their widespread usage throughout the Oki Network Technologies. Demonstrating strong leadership skills, Mr. Barber determines the overall strategic direction and formulates and implements business development plans. His objective is to keep the Company at the indutry's leading edge and maintaining the efficiency and profitability of the Company. An accomplished professional, Mr. Barber owns three U.S. patents with four other patents now pending. His future endeavors include remaining with the Company, prepare third generation activities, and becoming involved establishing new marketing strategies. Providing innovative global service to countries around the world, Oki Network Technologies is engaged in the design, development, and manufacture of cellular telephone products. One of the most established companies of their kind, Oki Network Technologies was founded in 1978, and now employs over 300 communication specialists. Centrally operated from the Company headquarters in Milpitas, California, Oki Network Technologies is currently seeking the latest trends and advances to provide the best service to their customers. **Career Highlights:** Director, Oki Network Technologies (2000-Present); Oki Telecom, Inc.: Director of Wireless Technologies and Markets (1998-00), Product Manager for Digital Platforms (1995-98), Program Manager for Automotive Products (1990-95), Director of OEM Products (1988-90). **Associations & Accomplishments:** Chair Emeritus, Jomandi Productions, Inc. **Education:** Georgia State University, M.B.A. (1980); Illinois Institute of Technology, B.S. in Electrical Engineering (1973). **Personal Information:** Married to Deborah in 1979. Three children: Carla Harper, Kashaka Byrdsong, and Jekonni. Mr. Barber enjoys theater and sports.

Keith F. Childs

RF/Microwave Engineer
Inmet Corporation
300 Dino Drive
Ann Arbor, MI 48103
(734) 426-5553
keith_childs@hotmail.com
3663

Business Information: As an RF/Microwave Engineer of Inmet Corporation, Mr. Childs is responsible for engineering prototype of new products and manufacturing support. Possessing superior talents and an excellent understanding of the engineering field, he also engages in troubleshooting and testing of new products prior to their launch. Drawing from his previous engineering experience in research and development, Mr. Childs performs daily tasks with outstanding proficiency and accuracy. In the future, he hopes to design prototypes which can maximize the efficiency in higher frequencies. His success reflects his ability to aggressively tackle new challenges and deliver results on behalf of the Corporation and its clientele. Founded in 1975, Inmet Corporations operates in the communications industry. Providing RF and microwave communications, the Corporation employs 66 individuals of various professional degrees. Headquartered in Ann Arbor, Michigan, the Corporation reports an estimated $11 million in annual revenue. **Career Highlights:** RF/Microwave Engineer, Inmet Corporations (2000-Present); Research and Development Enineer, Advanced Modular Power Systems, Inc. (1996-99); Medical Researcher, University of Michigan Medical School (1987-96). **Associations & Accomplishments:** American Chemical Society. **Education:** Eastern Michigan University, B.S. **Personal Information:** Married to Sandy in 1992. Two children: Amanda and Megan. Mr. Childs enjoys golf, surfing the Internet and investing.

Darlene Love

Industrial Engineer
Motorola
1313 East Algonquin Road
Schaumburg, IL 60196
(847) 576-7547
Fax: (847) 576-3476
d.love@motorola.com
3663

Business Information: Ms. Love serves as an Industrial Engineer for Motorola in the Aftermarket Products Division. The Division employs approximately 5,000 employees. She is assigned to manage projects, test equipment and new products, and perform timed-motion studies to determine operational efficiencies. Ms. Love's efforts are directed at finding new ways to improve efficiencies and decrease costs. In her capacity as a Project Engineer, she makes purchases on behalf of her department and ensures budgetary compliance. The Motorola's Aftermarket Products Division oversees the distribution of parts to all products made by the Company to vendors and customers worldwide. In monitoring these transactions, the Company is able to assess durability and predict product lifespans. Ms. Love's plan for the future includes achieveing a full Project Manager or a Sales and Marketing position with the Company. Motorola is one of the world's leading providers of wireless communications, semiconductors, and advanced electronic systems, components, and services. The Company maintains sales, service, and manufacturing facilities throughout the world, and conducts business on six continents. Motorola employs more than 150,000 people worldwide. Established in 1928, the Company posts annual revenues of $30 billion. **Career Highlights:** Motorola: Industrial Engineer (1997-Present), Supervisor (1995-96); Substitute Teacher, Board of Education of Chicago (1994-96). **Associations & Accomplishments:** Institute of Industrial Engineers; Rainbow Coalition/Operation PUSH; National Society of Black Engineers. **Education:** Purdue University, B.S. in Industrial Engineering (1989). **Personal Information:** Ms. Love enjoys skating, bowling, tennis and reading.

Maung Nyeu

Computer Scientist
Odetics, Inc.
P.O. Box 5037
Irvine, CA 92616
(714) 780-7930
Fax: (714) 780-7696
mnyen@home.com
3663

Business Information: Highly skilled in the field of computer electronics, Mr. Nyeu has been a Computer Scientist with Odetics, Inc. since 1997. An expert, he concentrates his efforts on the research, design, and development of high speed Space products that will expedite the analysis of critical satellite transmittal data for U.S. defense and national security purposes. Since the age of 18, Mr. Nyeu has dedicated his life to computer science and engineering to find innovative ways to invent and apply technology to improve quality of life. His Bachelor's, Master's, and Ph.D. program all in the field of Electrical and Computer Engineering have prepared him to focus on high-speed computer networks. In the future, Mr. Nyeu plans to continue his scientific endeavor in the design and development of faster, better, and more affordable technology. An industry leader in computer and electronic engineering products, Odetics, Inc. specializes in the manufacturing and distribution of computer networking hardware and software products. The Corporation also has been a supplier of solid state recorders for government Space programs, specifically NASA since 1969. Adeos-1, Hubble telescope, Gallileo Space, Radarsat Satellite, Magellan, and the Space Shuttle Discovery all carry Odetics sophisticated data gathering and transmittal products. Located in Irvine, California, the Corporation was established in 1969 and employs over 565 expert computer technicians, designers, and support personnel. Generating $120 million in annual revenues, the Corporation remains committed to providing excellent services. **Career Highlights:** Computer Scientist, Odetics, Inc. (1997-Present); Principal Engineer, Standard Microsystems (1997); Senior Engineer, FileNet Corporation (1995-99). **Associations & Accomplishments:** Chair, Institute of Electrical and Electronics Engineers Computer Society, Orange County; Institute of Electrical and Electronics Engineers; Member of Advisory Committee, International Conference Multimedia Applications Technology Conference; Fellow, Institute for the Advancment of Engineering; Former Vice-Chair, Executive Committee, Institute of Electrical and Electronics Engineers Communications Society; Former Vice Chair, Executive Committee, Institute of Electrical and Electronics Engineers Signal Processing Society; Research Fellowship, Swiss Scientific and Computing Center, Switzerland; **Education:** University of Hawaii, M.S. (1991); Enignereing University, B.U.E.T., B.S. (1987). **Personal Information:** Mr. Nyeu enjoys technology.

Matthew S. Sabin

Telecommunications Supervisor
Radio Frequency Systems
200 Pondview Drive
Meriden, CT 06450
(203) 630-3311
Fax: (203) 634-2010
matthew.sabin@rfsworld.com
3663

Business Information: As the Telecommunications Supervisor for Radio Frequency Systems in Meriden, Connecticut, Mr. Sabin oversees and directs all telecommunications service use. Possessing an excellent understanding of technology, he ensures all telephone, wireless, voice, and paging systems are working at optimum levels, guaranteeing satisfied clients and facilitating repeat business. His goal is to deploy advanced technologies within the Company, maintaining its competitiveness in the global market place. Mr. Sabin's goal is to encourage continued Company growth and geographic expansion. He aspires to the position of Chief Information Officer with Radio Frequency Systems or with another company. Remaining on the cutting edge through researching new technologies and reading, Mr. Sabin attributes his success to his curiosity and his ability to form teams with synergy and technical strength and deliver results on behalf of the Company. Radio Frequency Systems is a telecommunication systems sub-components manufacturing company. Headquartered in Charlotte, North Carolina, the Company operates 12 additional locations providing services for clients worldwide. Employing a skilled staff of 800 qualified personnel to orchestrate all activites, Radio Frequency Systems generates annual revenue of approximately $210 million. **Career Highlights:** Radio Frequency Systems: Telecommunications Supervisor (2000-Present), Network Administrator (1996-00). **Education:** Kennedy Western University (Currently Attending); Whitman College; Rutgers University. **Personal Information:** Married to Ann in 1990. One child: Beryl M.

Michael Tringali

Technical Supervisor
Dolby Laboratories
100 Potrero Avenue
San Francisco, CA 94103
(415) 558-0798
Fax: (415) 863-1373
mzt@dolby.com
3663

Business Information: One of the most highly renowned and influential Technical Supervisor ever employed by Dolby Laboratories, Mr. Tringali leads the licensing, collection of royalties from manufacturers, and the review of submitted consumer related products. Utilizing 26 years of experience in the field, he has been honored with such recognition as "Employee of the Month," among various other achievements. Looking to further extend his responsibilities, Mr. Tringali plans on attaining a position of Manager in the maintenance of technical support. Established in 1965, Dolby Laboratories offers technological licensing of audio and consumer electronics to corporate and residential customers. Providing service internationally, the Company employs the skills of eight professionals who specializes in the audio technical industry. Dolby Laboratories, currently generating sales in excess of $100 million, maintains a leading position among its competitors. **Career Highlights:** Technical Supervisor, Dolby Laboratories (1998-Present); Electronics Supervisor, Meyer Sound Labs Inc. (1987-98); Technical Supervisor, Sequential Circuits Inc. (1981-87). **Education:** Ohlone Junior College, A.A. in Liberal Arts (1976). **Personal Information:** Married to Barbara in 1982. Two children: Dallas and Brittley. Mr. Tringali enjoys being a wrestling coach and music.

Michael Wise

Technology Manager
Mitsubishi Wireless Communications Inc.
3805 Crestwood Parkway NW, Suite 350
Duluth, GA 30096
(770) 638-2100
Fax: (770) 921-4522
mwise@mwci.mea.com
3663

Business Information: Serving in the position of Technology Manager for Mitsubishi Wireless Communications Inc., Mr. Wise is extensively involved in technology research, keeping an organized record of all technology that can be applied for the production of new telecommunication products. Holding his position with Corporation for over a year, Mr. Wise initiates recommendations within the marketing capacity to engineering groups in order to further expand the product line. Utilizing his technical expertise in the development of new telecommunicative products and services, Mr. Wise remains committed to the further successes of Mitsubishi Wireless Communications. His future plans include developing a link for technology and research sharing within the Corporation. "Get involved at a standard activity level within your chosen field," is cited as Mr. Wise's advice. Engaging in the manufacture and distribution of wireless telecommunications equipment, Mitsubishi Wireless Communications Inc. was established in the early 1980s. A subsidiary of the Mitsubishi Corporation located in Japan, the Corporation is headquartered in Duluth, Georgia servicing customers in their cellular and PCS area. Focusing on the engineering, designing, sales, and marketing of the Corporation's products, the Corporation strives towards providing complete customer satisfaction. **Career Highlights:** Technology Manager, Mitsubishi Wireless Communications Inc. (1999-Present). **Personal Information:** Mr. Wise enjoys wood working, making furniture, swimming, golf and inline skating.

Lydia M. Bandong

Customer Operations Specialist
Arris Interactive
3871 Lakefield Drive, Suite 300
Suwanee, GA 30024
(770) 622-8688
Fax: (770) 622-8476
lydia.bandong@arris-i.com

3669

Business Information: Possessing unique talent in the technology industry, Ms. Bandong serves as the Customer Operations Specialist for Arris Interactive. Before joining Arris, she served as Systems Engineer with Purvis Systems Inc. In her present role, Ms. Bandong interfaces with new and existing customers in an effort to increase product development and service revenue through market development. Additionally, she devotes considerable attention to improving the MSO technical operations of the Company. Ms. Bandong travels extensively, offering technical support to clients and attending industry trade shows. Crediting her success to family support, she aspires to a managerial position and looks forward to increasing her professional responsibilities. Serving an international clientele, Arris Interactive is engaged in the design and production of telephony and data solutions for the cable and telecommunications industry. Approximately 700 skilled and knowledgeable professionals are employed in the Company's Suwanee and Atlanta corporate office locations. The Company is privately owned and was created in 1997. **Career Highlights:** Customer Operations Specialist, Arris Interactive (1997-Present); Systems Engineer, Purvis Systems, Inc. (1995-97). **Education:** Drexel University, B.S. in Electrical Engineering (1994). **Personal Information:** Ms. Bandong enjoys photography.

Krikor Batmazian

CAD Applications Engineer
Cisco Systems, Inc.
540 Mansion Park Drive, Apartment #109
Santa Clara, CA 95054
(408) 527-8549
Fax: (408) 527-0840
krikorb@cisco.com

3669

Business Information: As co-owner of Cisco Systems, Inc., Mr. Batmazian serves as CAD Applications Engineer responsible for research and development of cutting edge software applications. Also serving as design manager, he works closely with management and users to analyze, specify, and design technical solutions to harness more of the computer's power. A successful, 33 year professional with an excellent understanding of his field, Mr. Batmazian also writes applications to support the Corporation's inhouse tools. Directing and participating in the analysis, evaluation, testing, and implementation of advanced CAD software also fall within the realm of his responsibilities. His focus is on changes that will allow clients to remain flexible, efficient, and profitable in the Information Technology Age. He plans to stay with Cisco and work to continue developing contemporary tools for support engineering endeavors. Success, according to Mr. Batmazian, is due to his love for the industry and what he does as well as being open-minded. Cisco Systems, Inc. engages in software engineering. The Corporation specializes in CAMTEC and CAD/CAM software engineering. Located in Santa Clara, California, Cisco Systems also engages in designing innovative software and hardware, and Internet support devices such as routers and switches. Cisco Systems was established in 1987, and the Santa Clara office employs 3 professionals who generate annual earnings in excess of $100,000. **Career Highlights:** CAD Applications Engineer, Cisco Systems, Inc. (1996-Present); Senior Systems Programmer, Zygo Corporation (1995-96); Software Consultant, Intergraph Corporation (1991-95). **Associations & Accomplishments:** Association of Mathematicians; Association of PCB Designers; Association of Software Engineering. **Education:** University of Sofia, Master's degree in Math; Helsinki University of Technology, Master's degree in Computer Science. **Personal Information:** Married to Boriana in 1991. Two children: Emma and Dimitar. Mr. Batmazian enjoys tennis, swimming and carpenting.

Kirby R. Bradford

Director of Information Systems Operations
Lucent Technologies
1701 Harbor Bay Parkway
Alameda, CA 94502
(510) 747-2516
Fax: (510) 747-2616
kbradford@asend.com

3669

Business Information: As Director of Information Systems Operations of Lucent Technologies, Mr. Bradford manages Lucent's global management information systems operations. Also hiring staff and overseeing production systems and networks, Mr. Bradford displays an effective and efficient, productive management style. Before joining Lucent, he served as Managing Consultant for International Network Services and Information Systems Manager with Brobeck, Phleger & Harrison. In addition to supervising a staff of 28 employees, Mr. Bradford handles numerous resource planning functions, including personnel evaluations, determining future resource requirements, and overseeing time lines, schedules, and assignments. As a 24 year professional, he owns an established track record of delivering results in support of Lucent's global business and bottom line objectives. Determining the overall strategic plans and business contribution of the information systems function also fall within the scope of Mr. Bradford's functions. He plans to expedite continued promotion through the fulfillment of his responsibilities and his involvement in the advancement of operations. Established in 1989, Lucent Technologies is a diverse company offering Internet services and manufacturing computer hardware. Serving an international client base, the Company is headquartered out of Morristown, New Jersey. With a work force of 3,500 people, the Company reports an estimated annual revenue of $1.5 billion. **Career Highlights:** Director of Information Systems Operations, Lucent Technologies (1996-Present); Managing Consultant, International Network Services (1992-96); Information Services Manager, Brobeck Phleger & Harrison (1991-92). **Education:** John F. Kennedy School of Law, Juris Doctorate (1994); Texas Wesleyan University, B.S. (1975). **Personal Information:** Mr. Bradford enjoys camping and fishing.

Darrell R. Brauner

Information Systems and Information Technology Controller
Ericsson, Inc.
7001 Development Drive
Research Triangle Park, NC 27709
(919) 472-6951
Fax: (919) 472-6045

3669

Business Information: Displaying his expertise in this highly specialized position, Mr. Brauner serves as the Information Systems and Information Technology Controller for Ericsson, Inc. He controls the entire information systems and information technology budgets for the overall Americas Region. Collaborating with other global IS/IT controllers, they determine the Corporation's overall global product focus and allocate funds accordingly to each region. Mr. Brauner oversees the distribution of departmental funds within the Americas Region and ensures that the latest in the Corporation's products and services are made available to the sales and technical professionals employed. Establishing goals that are compatible with those of Ericsson, Inc., he looks forward to continuing to grow with the Corporation. His success reflects his ability to produce results and aggressively tackle new challenges. World renowned, Ericsson, Inc. is a leading supplier of telecommunication equipment, producing advanced systems and products for wired and wireless communications networks. The Corporation specializes in the manufacture of wireless mobile phones and has a strong international presence in 130 countries. Approximately 3,000 individuals are employed in the Americas Region and the Corporation has 110,000 employees worldwide. **Career Highlights:** Information Systems and Information Technology Controller, Ericsson, Inc. (1997-Present); Product Manager, Levi, Ray & Shoup, Inc. (1996-97); Business Systems Analyst, Central Illinois Public Service Company (1992-96); Business Systems Analyst, Enron Corporation (1989-92). **Associations & Accomplishments:** American Management Association. **Education:** Stephen F. Austin State University, B.B.A. (1988). **Personal Information:** Married. Two children.

David W. Chang

Technical Leader
Cisco Systems, Inc.
170 West Tasman Drive
San Jose, CA 95134
(408) 525-4330
Fax: (408) 525-9156
dwchang@cisco.com

3669

Business Information: As Technical Leader of Cisco Systems, Inc., Mr. Chang develops state-of-the-art layer 2/3/4 wire speed gigabit Ethernet switches with ATM and SONET capability. He plans and oversees all phases of development, to include installation and implementation stages. As a topnotch, 17 year consulting and engineering professional, Mr. Chang owns an established track record of delivering results. His career success reflects his ability to think out-of-the-box and take on new challenges and responsibilities. Before joining Cisco Systems in 1998, he served as a Senior Principal Engineer with Hitachi Internetworking. His solid occupational history also includes serving as a Senior Consultant Engineer with J Frank Consult and a Senior Staff Engineer at Amdahl Corporation. A patent on communications messenger which is still pending, and receiving the 1990 and 1991 Director's Award from Amdahl Corporation is cited as Mr. Chang's significant achievements. His new inspiration is to change daily life in the technology arena for homes. The global leader in providing internetworking solutions, Cisco Systems, Inc. sells and distributes cutting edge product and service offerings to customers in approximately 115 countries. Established in 1983, Cisco is Headquartered in San Jose, California. Presently, the Corporation employs an international work force of more than 18,500 people who help generate revenues in excess of $9 billion annually. **Career Highlights:** Technical Leader, Cisco Systems, Inc. (1998-Present); Senior Principal Engineer, Hitachi Internetworking (1995-98); Senior Consultant Engineer, J Frank Consult (1991-95); Senior Staff Engineer, Amdahl Corporation (1987-91). **Associations & Accomplishments:** Institute of Electrical and Electronics Engineers, Inc. **Education:** University of Oregon, M.S. in Computer Science (1982); Chang-Yen University, B.S. in Physics. **Personal Information:** Married to Yuan-Sheng in 1987. Two children: Jenny and Michael. Mr. Chang enjoys computer networking, tennis and reading.

Srinivas P. Doddapaneni

Technical Staff
Lucent Technologies
404 Eagle Drive
Emmaus, PA 18049-1927
(610) 712-2473
srid@lucent.com

3669

Business Information: Mr. Doddapaneni serves as a Member of the Technical Staff of Lucent Technologies, responsible for the research and design of cutting edge software development tools and applications. Demonstrating an extensive knowledge of the industry, he engineers virus detection programs, then conducts rigorous testing trials. After perfecting each model, he successfully implements it into operating systems, preparing for production. Internally recognized for impressive accomplishments pertaining to the design of innovative embedded signal digital programs, Mr. Doddapaneni attributes success to a genuine love of the industry coupled with unwavering dedication. Owning four patents, he cites his Ph.D. research work on dial up frame programs as his career highlight. His research in this area of technology led to new ideas in Internet process and real time collaboration. Mr. Doddapaneni looks forward to increasing his responsibilities within the corporate structure, aspiring to a position that will better utilize his abilities. Formerly a division of AT&T, Lucent Technologies began independent operations in 1996 and has already reached estimated annual sales of $38 billion. Headquartered in New Jersey, the Company operates facilities throughout the United States, employing over 150,000 people. **Career Highlights:** Member of Technical Staff, Lucent Technologies (1998-Present); Advisory Software Engineer, IBM T.J. Watson Research Center (1996-98). **Associations & Accomplishments:** Association of Computing Machinery. **Education:** Georgia Institute of Technology, Ph.D. (1997); Indian Institute of Technology, Bachelor's degree in Technology with honors (1986). **Personal Information:** Married to Mythili in 1997. One child: Venkat.

Marino A. Fernandez

Hardware Design Engineer
Cisco Systems, Inc.
250 Apollo Drive
Chelmsford, MA 01824
(978) 244-8102
Fax: (978) 244-8039
fernandm@cisco.com

3669

Business Information: Mr. Fernandez functions in the capacity of Hardware Design Engineer for Cisco Systems, Inc. He is responsible for all aspects of hardware design and implementation. Dedicated to the success of Cisco, Mr. Fernandez joined the Corporation in 1997 after serving as Hardware Design Engineer at Dagaz Technologies, Inc. His background history also includes a stint as Hardware Engineer with Ford Motor Corporation. Working closely with a team of professionals, Mr. Fernandez is actively involved in planning and implementing new designs and working with research and development to create quality hardware merchandise. He credits his success to his educational and occupational experience and his ability to produce results and take on new challenges. His goals include eventually attaining the position of Director. Cisco Systems was established in 1989. The Corporation is engaged in the manufacture of various types of computer networking equipment for residential or commercial use. Worldwide Cisco operations employ more than 10,000 professional, technical, and support personnel who help in the design, manufacture, distribution, and promotion of products. **Career Highlights:** Hardware Design Engineer, Cisco Systems, Inc. (1997-Present); Hardware Design Engineer, Dagaz Technologies, Inc. (1966-97); Hardware Engineer, Ford Motor Company (1992-96). **Associations & Accomplishments:** Institute of Electronics and Electrical Engineers. **Education:** The John Hopkins University, M.S. in Electrical Engineering (1992); The

City University of New York, B.S. in Electrical Engineering (1987).

Mark A. Gaither

Business Development Manager
Cisco Systems, Inc.
175 West Tasman Drive, Mail Stop 1-2
San Jose, CA 95134
(408) 527-6075
Fax: (408) 525-5662
magaith@msg.pacbell.com

3669

Business Information: Serving as Senior Contract Manager for SBC/Pacific Bell, Mr. Gaither negotiates data communications contracts for ADSL, VPN, Web hosting, and e-commerce with small and medium sized businesses. Before joining Pacific Bell, he served as a Law Clerk for both Law Offices of Roger S. Gaither and Chevron. Mr. Gaither is presently working with four other teams to create a generic data communications package for smaller businesses. This package will offer the same dependability and advantages as is offered to larger companies and corporations. Continually formulating new goals and objectives, Mr. Gaither is looking forward to focusing his attention on business planning after the completion of the new project. He attributes his success to his extensive knowledge of all aspects of company operations including contracts, business, legal, and technical. SBC/Pacific Bell was created in 1986 by a buyout of Pacific Bell by SBC. While the Company still operates as a regional Bell operating company, this buyout expanded its regional operating area and allowed it to offer a larger variety of telecommunication services. SBC/Pacific Bell offers data communications such as Internet access, high speed traffic, and virtual private networking to small and medium sized businesses. Approximately 130,000 individuals are employed and the Company reports $4,8 billion in annual revenue. **Career Highlights:** Business Development Manager, Cisco Systems, Inc. (1999-Present); SBC/Pacific Bell: Senior Contract Manager (1997-99), Contract Manager (1997); Law Clerk, Law Offices of Roger S. Gaither (1996-97); Law Clerk, Chevron (1989-95). **Associations & Accomplishments:** California State Bar; American Bar Association; Deacon, Missouri, First Baptist Church Castro Valley, California; ADSL Forum Member. **Education:** J.F. Kennedy University, Juris Doctorate (1995); Biola University, B.S. (1988). **Personal Information:** Married to Kathryn in 1989. Four children: Evan, Jordan, Breanna, and Victoria. Mr. Gaither enjoys skiing, ski diving, scuba diving and rock climbing.

Jeffrey L. Gardner

Senior Product Manager
Ericsson
2737 South Cypress Circle
Plano, TX 75075
(972) 583-3192
Fax: (972) 583-1832
jgardn01@airmail.net

3669

Business Information: Possessing unique talent in the telecommunications field, Mr. Gardner joined Ericsson in 1996 as Senior Product Manager. His job is to improve service and reduce the cost of communication services. Before joining Ericsson, he served as Director of Communications with Electronic Data Systems. His background history also includes as stint with the United States Air Force as an Information Systems Control Technician. Mr. Gardner accomplishes his present mission by constantly upgrading the Company's products and remaining on the absolute cutting edge of the industry's new technological advances. As new products are designed and existing ones improved, Mr. Gardner troubleshoots any arising problems. Continually striving for maximum effectiveness, he is currently pursuing his Master's degree in Business Administration to enable him to capitalize on the opportunities provided by the Company. Ericsson engages in the business of telecommunications and offers its customers a full range of services from Internet to teleconferencing. Established in 1876, Ericsson boasts $20 billion in annual sales and employs approximately 100,000 professionals around the globe. **Career Highlights:** Senior Product Manager, Ericsson (1996-Present); Director of Communications, Electronic Data Systems (1987-96); Information Systems Control Technician, United States Air Force (1982-87). **Education:** LeTourneau University, M.B.A. (In Progress), B.S. in Business Management; University of Maryland; Community College of the Air Force; University of Nebraska-Lincoln. **Personal Information:** Married to Veronica in 1995. One child: Belicia. Mr. Gardner enjoys travel, hiking, photography and Internet computing.

Arun Garg

Solutions Project Manager
Cisco Systems, Inc.
170 West Tasman Drive
San Jose, CA 95131-1409
(408) 853-6134
Fax: (408) 527-1713
arung@cisco.com

3669

Business Information: As Solutions Project Manager at Cisco Systems, Inc., Mr. Garg develops and implements engineering development plans for leading total market space network solutions. A 15 year veteran of information technology, he joined the Corporation in 1999, after years of hands on as Director, Senior Manager, Assistant General Manager, and Manager with startups like Duet Technologies and giants such as Hughes Software Systems, Usha-Matra and Texas Instruments. Responsible for taking a lead role in driving growth, Mr. Garg is charged with providing leadership to project and functional managers associated with individual products, which comprise the total solution space. He manages large, cross Business Unit, engineering development programs, and works with customers, account teams, engineering, marketing, partners and many other internal and external organizations associated with producing products. Mr. Garg has authored technical articles, spoken at conferences and has been recognized with various internal awards in the companies that he has worked. The worldwide leader in networking for the Internet, Cisco Systems, Inc. provides end-to-end networking solutions that customers use to build a unified information infrastructure of their own, or to connect to one's network. Since shipping its first product in 1986, Cisco has grown into a global market leader that holds #1 or #2 market share in virtually every market segment in which it participates. Cisco Systems, Inc.'s (NASDAQ: CSCO) web site www.cisco.com provides more information about the company. **Career Highlights:** Solutions Project Manager, Cisco Systems, Inc. (1999-Present); Director of Marketing, Duet Technologies, Inc. (1996-99); Senior Manager, Hughes Software Systems (1994-96); Assistant General Manager, Usha-Matra (1991-94); Manager, Texas Instruments (1985-91). **Associations & Accomplishments:** Indian Institute of Technology, Kanpur, Alumni Association. **Education:** Indian Institute of Technology, Kanpur, Bachelor's degree in Technology in Electrical Engineering (1985). **Personal Information:** Married to Natasha in 1993. Two children: Namrata and Aanchal. Mr. Garg enjoys badminton.

Youhong Wade Gong

Senior Engineer
Cisco Systems, Inc.
1 Burlington Woods
Burlington, MA 01803-4503
(781) 852-2212
Fax: (781) 272-9989
wadegong@cisco.com

3669

Business Information: Serving as Senior Software Engineer for Cisco Systems, Inc., Mr. Gong oversees all technical research and development. He works closely with management and systems users to analyze, specify, and design new software to harness more of the computer's power. A successful, 18 year professional in technology, he directs research in the right direction by providing valuable insight gained by his expanded hands on experience. By effectively managing his department, Mr. Gong has earned the reputation for attention to detail and results driven action. His superior communication skills and management style promote a workplace condusive to constructive criticism and employee feedback. His career highlights include assisting in the design of Cisco's Customer Interaction Suite and development of the historical database for the manufacturing executive system. Attributing his success to beinging open-minded, Mr. Gong's plans are to become more involved in Internet and Java Enterprise technologies. Cisco Systems produces telecommunications and computer equipment. This international company is firmly established in the technology industry and employs over 26,000 people, and generates an annual revenue of over $16 billion. Cisco Systems plans to continue gaining global respect as a quality component manufacturer, and to expand operations on a larger international basis. The Corporation has become the leader in computer and telecommunications component manufacturing by providing superior quality and complete client technical support. **Career Highlights:** Senior Engineer, Cisco Systems, Inc. (1999-Present); Senior Software Engineer, Webline Communications (1997-99); Senior Software Engineer, FASTech Communications (1994-97); Senior Software Engineer, Applicon/Schlumberger (1992-94). **Education:** Massachusetts Institute of Technology, Master's degree (1992); Shanghai Jiao Tong University: Master's degree (1984), Bachelor's degree (1982). **Personal Information:** Married to Xiaoyan in 1988. Two children: Jennifer and James. Mr. Gong enjoys reading novels and bridge.

Frank E. Gordon

Customer Support Manager
Quad Systems Corporation
2405 Maryland Road
Willow Grove, PA 19090
(215) 706-3902
Fax: (215) 657-6356
fgordon@quad.sys.com

3669

Business Information: Serving as the Customer Support Manager of Quad Systems Corporation, Mr. Gordon presides over the entire customer service team and field service engineers. Additionally, he manages over the phone support group and ensures that Company employees receive 24 hour, 7 day a week technical service. Mr. Gordon administers all of the technical assistance, dispatching technicians and maintaining the help desk. Beginning his career in 1976 by simply building mechanical components, he feels he owes his professional success to his wife's determination. Mr. Gordon's career highlight includes setting up a complete automated system in 1983, encompassing 40 pieces of equipment. His success reflects his ability to think out-of-the-box and take on new challenges and responsibilities. He anticipates a promotion to a higher management position and looks forward to assisting in the completion of future corporate goals. Distributing products to companies around the world, Quad Systems Corporation manufactures surface mount equipment, otherwise known as pick and place machines. The Corporation began operations in 1981 and presently consists of a workforce of over 200 staff members in at the Willow Grove, Pennsylvania headquarters. **Career Highlights:** Quad Systems Corporation: Customer Support Manager (1997-Present), Production Manager (1997); Clean Room Manager COB, Valtronic USA (1991-97); Field Service Engineer, Kulicke & Soffa Industries (1976-90). **Education:** Pennco Tech, Technology degree. **Personal Information:** Married to Joy in 1970. Three children: Frank II, David, and Samantha. Mr. Gordon enjoys autos and boats.

Ivory J. Griskell

Senior Manager of Information Technology
Lucent Technologies
9333 South John Young Parkway
Orlando, FL 32819-8698
(407) 371-6120
Fax: (407) 371-3120
griskell@lucent.com

3669

Business Information: Mr. Griskell seves in the position of Senior Manager of Information Technology at Lucent Technologies' Orlando, Florida operation. Managing a skilled staff of 25 software developers and support programmers, he plans and oversees the research, evaluation, development, and integration of new technology systems development methodologies, capacity planning, and technical support functions. A savvy, technical expert, Mr. Griskell is involved in the discovery, investigation, and deployment of advanced technologies within Lucent Technologies. Building his team from the bottom up, he has instilled in them synergy and techincal strength, and together his team has developed over 500 new applications. His advice to others is "keep yourself surrounded with positive people." A reputable technology company, Lucent Technologies is recognized throughout the world for its advancements in technology. At the location in Orlando, Florida, the Company manufactures integrated circuits, modem boards, and circuit boards. Having recently merged, the Company is a standoff business from AT&T. International in scope, Lucent operates over eight locations around the globe. **Career Highlights:** Senior Manager of Information Technology, Lucent Technologies (1988-Present). **Education:** Auburn University, M.S. (1991); Stillman College, B.S. (1988). **Personal Information:** Married to Gwendolyn in 1989. Four children: Ivory II, Alexander, Chanteliese, and Ashanta.

Sheena Gu

Principal Software Engineer
Lucent Technologies
1 Robbins Road
Westford, MA 01886
(978) 952-1559
Fax: (978) 952-7734
sheena.gu@ascend.com

3669

Business Information: Demonstrating expertise in the engineering field, Ms. Gu serves as Principal Software Engineer for Lucent Technologies. She is responsible for design and development of cutting edge software applications for the networking environment. Before joining Lucent Technologies, Ms. Gu served as the Principal Software Engineer with Ascend Communications. Her history also includes stints as Senior Software Engineer for Megapulse and Software Engineer at Virtual Prototypes. In her current position, she is the Project Leader responsible for coordinating resources and schedules and overseeing time lines and assignments. As a 17 year technology expert, she also provides infrastructure and backup support. Always alert to new opportunities, techniques, and approaches, Ms. Gu would like to enhance her technical knowledge and continue to set high standards of excellence for others in the information technology field to follow. Lucent Technologies is one of the largest manufacturers of telecommunications equipment in the United States. Products include wireless networks, business communication systems, and switching and transmission equipment. Operations currently employ the skilled services of 2,000 individuals who help generate annual sales in excess of $1 billion. Established in 1989, headquarters for the Corporation is located in Murray Hill, New Jersey. **Career Highlights:** Principal Software Engineer, Lucent Technologies (Present); Principal Software Engineer, Ascend Communications (1995); Senior Software Engineer, Megapulse (1993-95); Software Engineer, Virtual Prototypes (1991-93). **Associations & Accomplishments:** New England Chinese Information Network Associate; The Greater Boston of the American Computing Machinery. **Education:** University of Massachusetts at Boston, M.S. (1989); Shanghai University, B.S. (1982). **Personal Information:** Married to Yibin Xiang in 1985. Two children: David and Elaine. Ms. Gu enjoys line dancing and swimming.

David M. Hershfield

Director of Technical Communications
Lucent Technologies
1701 Harbor Bay Parkway
Alameda, CA 94502
(510) 747-2719
Fax: (510) 747-3838
dh37@lucent.com

3669

Business Information: Serving as Director of Technical Communications for Lucent Technologies, Mr. Hershfield is responsible for managing the technical communications group of 28 individuals. In this capacity, he oversees Web sites, writing of product documentation, departmental budgets, provides software engineering training, localizes documents into multiple languages, and works with the engineering and marketing departments. Attributing his professional success to good communication skills and the ability to form teams with synergy and technical strength, Mr. Hershfield plans to continue working with Lucent, building up his group. Lucent Technologies is involved in the design, manufacture, and sale of a wide variety of communications products. Founded in 1996, the Company provides products which are capable of handling voice, image, and data communications across an international telephone network. Employing more than 150,000 personnel, the Company reports annual revenues exceeding $35 billion. **Career Highlights:** Director of Technical Communications, Lucent Technologies/Ascend Communications (1995-Present); Lead Information Specialist, Attacamate/DCA (1990-95); Senior Technical Writer, Racal Data Comm (1988-90). **Associations & Accomplishments:** Big Brothers/Big Sisters; STC. **Education:** University of California at Berkeley, B.A. (1983). **Personal Information:** Married to Edie in 1996. One child: Madison. Mr. Hershfield enjoys golf and reading.

Geoffrey D. Hill

Business Analyst
Lucent Technologies LTCP
13 Dogwood Drive
Chester, NJ 07930
(973) 581-3943
Fax: (973) 581-3743
ghill@pcc.lucent.com

3669

Business Information: As Business Analyst of Lucent Technologies LTCP, Mr. Hill is charged with maintaining fluid operation of the Company. As business analyst for the distribution area, he oversees the supply chain, ensuring that all orders are proccessed accurately and efficiently. Mr. Hill plans to complete current projects then advance to a position on the operations side of the business, becoming a facilitator between technical and operations. His career highlights include helping to start four distribution facilities from the ground up as well as receiving two achievement awards from Lucent Technologies. He has demonstrated his ability to effectively manage his staff by illustrating strong leadership and communication skills. Success, according to Mr. Hill, is due to his interest and love in what he does. Lucent Technologies LTCP engages in design, manufacture, and sale of consumer communications products. This Division is responsible for systems infrastructure support for all consumer products. This corporate spin-off of AT&T was established in 1997, and has grown to employ over 2,500 people who generate a multi-million dollar annual revenue. Lucent Technologies controls numerous manufacturing and distribution centers worldwide, and plans to continue further expansion to accommodate increased consumer demand. This international Company has become a leader in telecommunication technology by providing quality products and complete customer service. **Career Highlights:** Business Analyst, Lucent Technologies LTCP (1996-97); Systems Analyst, AT&T (1988-96); Systems Analyst, Hartz Mountain (1986-88). **Associations & Accomplishments:** American Production and Inventory Control Society; CPIM; CIRM. **Education:** Chubb, Programming Certificate (1984); University of New Hampshire.

Tom Hutson

Program Manager
United Defense
3058 Cedar Ridge Court
San Jose, CA 95148
(408) 289-4615
tom_hutson@udip.com

3669

Business Information: Serving in a highly specialized and vital position, Mr. Hutson serves as the Program Manager for United Defense. Managing several multi-faceted activities including terms on specific projects and new assignments to develop corporate e-commerce portals, Mr. Hutson has gained the respect and admiration of his peers on an international level. Associating with a team of coders on specific technological advances, he designs and launches new products, tests software, and retails spare parts and training products. Seeking out further advancement within United Defense, Mr. Hutson plans on attaining the role of Director of E-Commerce Division when the Company reaches their current goal of $60 million in retail revenue annually. Providing systems integration of complex defense equipment for virtually all of the military branches, United Defense operates under an annual budget of $1.3 billion. Founded in the 1940s, the Company utilizes software and hardware advances, and is engaged in the innovative field of implementing digital technology for mapping. Now recognized as one of the largest companies in the country, United Defense employs a staff in excess of 6,000, operating year round to produce high quality defense equipment. **Career Highlights:** United Defense: Program Manager (1999-Present), Acting Director of Advanced Programs (1997-98), Corporate Information Technology Council (1997-Present). **Associations & Accomplishments:** Board of Directors, Guadalyne River Park & Garden Corporation; National Defense Industrial Association; Association of the United States Army. **Education:** University of Arizona, B.S. (1968); Stanford University, Continuing Education. **Personal Information:** Mr. Hutson enjoys golf, fishing and Web publishing.

José A. Justicia

President/Chief Executive Officer
Justice Communications
2170 Fourth Avenue, Suite 100
San Diego, CA 92101
(619) 470-8608
Fax: (619) 470-7949
justice_comm@earth-link.net

3669

Business Information: As Owner of Justice Communications, Mr. Justicia serves as President and Chief Executive Officer. He is responsible for determining the overall strategic direction and business contribution of the information systems function. As a 28 year professional, Mr. Justicia handles administration and service to the customers. In addition, he oversees day-to-day operations such as staffing, ensuring that the Company operates smoothly. To increase profit margins, Mr. Justicia spearheads the development of strategic plans and the incentives to meet all goals. He coordinates efforts to stay within the annual budget, and he supervises the marketing of telecommunications equipment. Success, Mr. Justicia asserts, is the final product of his ability to provide high quality service. Since its inception in 1993, Justice Communications operates as a telecommunications equipment vendor. The Company, besides selling CBX & PBX systems, digital key systems, auto attendant/voice mail processors, CTI integration, modems, and fax machines, is also a computer and networking provider. Operating out of a headquarters in San Diego, California, Justice Communications maintains business on an international level. **Career Highlights:** President/Chief Executive Officer, Justice Communications (1993-Present); Senior Technician, SciComm (1990-93); Telecommunications Instructor, Associated Technical College of San Diego (1987); Field Service Technician, Revcom, Inc. (1986); Special Services Field Technician, Rolm Corporation (1983-86); Special Services Installer, General Telephony Co. (1978-83); Field Service Technician, Volt Telecom (1976-78); Special Services Field Technician, Puerto Rico Telephone Co. (1971-76). **Associations & Accomplishments:** Elder, New Covenant Tabernacle Church (1992-Present); Minister and Pastor, Church in Mexico-Tijuana Tabernaculo del Nuevo Pacto, Colonia Simon Bolivar (1993-Present); Dean of Students, Word Bible College, National City Campus (1995-97). **Education:** Graduated from the Evangelical Church Alliance School of Theology (1994); Completed Certification on Comdial, Mitel Siemens, Toshiba, Panasonic, Vodavi, Rohm, and other systems; Associate's degree in Electronics, Technological Institute of Puerto Rico (1971); Graduated from Gabriela Mistral High School in Puerto Rico (1969). **Personal Information:** Married to Balbina Garcia in 1989. Three children: José A. Jr. III, Jezzabelle M., Jennifer, and Melody. Mr. Justicia enjoys mission work. Mr. Justicia finds meaning in spreading the love and Gospel of the Lord Jesus Christ.

Carolyn R. Keaton-Culp

Member of the Technical Staff
Lucent Technologies
2000 North Naperville Wheaton Road
Naperville, IL 60563
(630) 979-6316
Fax: (630) 979-4613
ckeaton@lucent.com

3669

Business Information: As a Member of the Technical Staff of Lucent Technologies, Ms. Keaton-Culp works closely with systems management and users to analyze, specify, and design technical solutions to harness more of the computers power. Utilizing six years of academics and technical experience, she is responsible for training Company employees on the utilization of new products, consulting with the Company on new product technology, and providing all aspects of technical support. She directs and participates in the analysis, acquisition, installation, modification, configuration, support and tracking operating and database systems, utilities, and software and hardware. As an expert systems engineer, Ms. Keaton-Culp is involved in the discovery, investigation, and initial deployment of advanced technologies within Lucent Technologies. She originally began her association with the Lucent team of professionals as Software Developer in 1996. Looking forward to taking advantage of opportunities afforded, Ms. Keaton-Culp's goal is to move up into positions of greater scope and responsibility within the corporate structure. Lucent Technologies, a spin-off of AT&T, develops, manufactures, markets, and services advanced voice and data communications solutions for clients around the world. Headquartered in Murray Hill, New Jersey, the Company presently employs a global work force of more than 130,000 people helping to generate revenues in excess of $30 billion annually. **Career Highlights:** Lucent Technologies, Inc.: Member of the Technical Staff (1999-Present), Software Developer (1996-99). **Associations & Accomplishments:** DuPage AME; Volunteer Tutor, Quad County Urban League. **Education:** Tennessee State University, M.S. in Electrical Engineering (1996); Morgan State University, B.S. in Electrical Engineering (1994). **Personal Information:** Married to DeWayne in 1999.

Christopher K. Kislow

Senior Programmer/Analyst
DI
600 West Duerer Street
Egg Harbor City, NJ 08215-3737
(609) 485-5820
Fax: (609) 485-8200

3669

Business Information: Serving as a Senior Programmer and Analyst for DI, Mr. Kislow is responsible for maintaining a system called MASS, which logs activity from airport radars and any other equipment the airport would like to keep a watch on. New technology developed by Mr. Kislow is done in Visual C++ and Basic. Duties include rewriting, design coding, and testing. He would like to attribute his success to having family support and time working with computers. **Career Highlights:** Senior Programmer/Analyst, DI (1999-Present); Senior Programmer, HTSC (1997-99); Programmer/Analyst, HTSX (1993-97). **Associations & Accomplishments:** Germania Volunteer Fire Company. **Education:** Monmouth University, M.S.; Stockton State College, B.S.; Atlantic Community College, A.S. **Personal Information:** Mr. Kislow enjoys golf.

J. Christopher Landes

Market Development Manager
Lucent Technologies
211 Mount Airy Road, Room 1W427
Basking Ridge, NJ 07920
(908) 953-8680
Fax: (908) 953-2105
jclandes@lucent.com

3669

Business Information: A leading expert in financial transaction networks, intelligent networks, and mobile and IP Communications services and their role in various market segments, Mr. Landes serves as Market Development Manager for Lucent Technologies. He manages the positioning, product development, and offer segmentation of Lucent's Internet Call Center, MMCX, and other IP Communications offers. A 10 year systems expert, Mr. Landes also advises customers regarding IP

Communications deployments and strategies. His solid background history includes stints with TeleChoice, Inc. where he managed integrated services studies within the Local and Long Distance Practice, and AT&T where he held various high-level strategic planning positions working with product management and business unit directors on critical market trends and emerging strategies. Mr. Landes has been widely quoted in the national and regional press and has appeared on CNNfn, CNBC, NBC News, CBS Radio 880, and has published several articles in the trade press. Committed to further development of the Company, he continues to coordinate strategic planning to ensure a bright future for a position as Vice President. Publicly owned, Lucent Technologies is a telecommunication network solutions provider. The Company designs, builds, and delivers a wide range of public and private networks, systems, software, and components. Approximately 130,000 skilled professionals are employed internationally. Boasting $35 billion in sales, the Company was founded in 1996. **Career Highlights:** Market Development Manager, Lucent Technologies (1998-Present); Consultant, TeleChoice, Inc. (1996-98); Analyst, AT&T Consumer Communication Services (1989-96). **Associations & Accomplishments:** Rotary International; Booz Allen and Hamilton Alumni Association; Nazareth Chamber of Commerce; Yankee Group One Network Conference; Public Speaker, PBX 2000 Conference; Public Speaker, jBand2 Conference; Public Speaker (1997), Community Conference. **Education:** Columbia University, M.S. (1986); Moravian College, B.A. (1981). **Personal Information:** One child: Kathleen Dee. Mr. Landes enjoys photography, biking, hiking and volunteering.

R. Scott Lewis

Systems Manager
Ericsson Messaging Systems
145 Crossways Park Drive West
Woodbury, NY 11797
(516) 677-1103
Fax: (516) 677-1111
scott.lewis@ericsson.com

3669

Business Information: Mr. Lewis is Systems Manager of Ericsson Messaging Systems. He is responsible for future development of systems software, hardware, firmware, and documentation in departmental matrix reporting structure. Before joining Ericsson in 1995, Mr. Lewis served as Member of the Technical Staff with NYNEX Science & Technology. As a 14 year technology expert, he prepares strategies and tactics for the board of directors that emphasize and explain object oriented technologies. He performs technical evaluations on both the internal and external components of MXE or Multimedia Messaging Exchange, a product he is currently developing. Creating prototypes and working to identify patents, and troubleshooting current product line also fall within the purview of Mr. Lewis' responsibilities. He is well versed in a wide range of hardware, compilers and tools, middleware, operating systems, configuration management, PC application software, and statistical packages. Eventually attaining the role of Vice President of the Company is cited as one of his future endeavors. A subsidiary of Ericsson Company, Ericsson Messaging Systems is a wireless electronic messaging solutions provider. Ericsson Company was founded in 1890, and maintains a presence in 140 countries around the globe. Presently, Ericsson employs a global workforce of more than 90,000 people who help generate annual revenues in excess of $22 billion. **Career Highlights:** Systems Manager, Ericsson Messaging Systems (1995-Present); Technical Staff, NYNEX Science and Technology (1991-95); Acting Staff Director, Telesector Research Group (1988-91); Business Information Systems: Marketing Support Manager (1988), Project Manager (1985-87), Systems Engineer (1985-86). **Associations & Accomplishments:** Former Vice President/Treasurer, Old Harbour Green Association; Former Director, Data Processing Management Association; Former Charter Member, Sigma Phi Epsilon National Fraternity; Former President, Engineering Society at SUNY Fredonia. **Education:** Dowling College, M.B.A. (1997); State University College at Fredonia, B.S. in Computers and Economics; State University of New York at Stony Brook; Dale Carnegie Institute for Public Speaking. **Personal Information:** Married. One child: Samantha Noelle. Mr. Lewis enjoys the piano, tennis, skiing and climbing.

Ramez H. Mallouk

Project Manager
Nokia
P.O. Box 321 Valimotie 9, Fin-00380
Helsinki, Finland 00045
ramezm@usa.net

3669

Business Information: As a Project Manager for Nokia, Mr. Mallouk supervises work teams and coordinates overseas timetables, ensuring seamless service for customers. Possessing an excellent understanding of technology, he provides powerful, commonsense leadership thus guaranteeing that all units work together to ahcieve a common goal. His 10 years of educational and employment experience is vital to the Company's continuing success. Continually striving for maximum effectiveness, Mr. Mallouk is currently pursuing his Ph.D. to enable him to capitalize on the opportunities provided by Nokia and to assist in the completion of future Company goals. His success is attributed to a close friend, his attitude as a person, his management activities, and his ability to absord knowledge and perform and excel in his field. Nokia is the world's largest supplier of mobile phones, telecommunications networks, and wireless data solutions. Established in 1865, the Company employs a skilled staff of approximately 47,000 who maintain over 100 locations worldwide. Headquartered in Helsinki, Finland, the Company distributes products internationally, generating annual revenue of approximately $15 billion. **Career Highlights:** Project Manager, Nokia (2000-Present); Information Technology Expert, Forward Project (1994-00); Technical Manager, Cats (1993-00); Senior Programmer, Abla Ayoub Est. (1992-93). **Associations & Accomplishments:** Jordan Computer Society. **Education:** B.Sc. in Computer Science (1993); Christian College; Jordan University. **Personal Information:** Mr. Mallouk enjoys soccer, football and group games.

John V. Matthews, Jr.

Member of Technical Staff
Lucent Technologies
6200 East Broad Street, Room 4d05-1m
Columbus, OH 43213-1530
(614) 860-4333
Fax: (614) 860-5161
jvmatthews@lucent.com

3669

Business Information: As Member of Technical Staff with Lucent Technologies, Mr. Matthews manages the hardware laboratory to ensure all products and activities are accounted for. Included in his daily schedule are such activities as set-up of test equipment, maintenance of projects, and detailed inventory counts. Demonstrating productive workmanship, Mr. Matthews lends his knowledge of the industry to lab engineers as he supports them through product trials and testing challenges. Recognized for his technical abilities and creative problem solving techniques, he is credited with the creation of an improved broadband system in which he increased quality and cut costs. As he looks forward to the future, Mr. Matthews intneds to continue with the Company as he provides hardware integration support for cellular and digital products. Lucent Technologies manufactures telecommunication and networking equipment such as semiconductors and wireless cellular products. Employing over 153,000 people worldwide, the Company is concerned with the research and development of technology and progressive professional services. Established in 1869, the Company is headquartered in New Jersey and has annual revenues of over $30 billion. **Career Highlights:** Member of Technical Staff, Lucent Technologies (1983-Present); Research Associate, Ohio University Avionics Engineering Center (1981-83); Research/Engineering Coop, General Dynamics (1977-79). **Associations & Accomplishments:** Board of Directors of Information Technology Director, Lighthouse Counseling. **Education:** Ohio University, M.S. (1983); Georgia Technical College, Bachelor's degree in Electrical Engineering (1981). **Personal Information:** Married to Karleen in 1993. Four children: Lindsey, Natalie, Wesley, and Kelsey. Mr. Matthews enjoys computers, music, saxophone and video.

Dennis Joseph Mills

Programmer Analyst
Comsearch
2002 Edmund Halley Drive
Reston, VA 20191
(703) 620-6300
dmills@comsearch.com

3669

Business Information: As a Programmer Analyst for Comsearch, Mr. Mills implements solutions for microwave engineering, land-based point-to-point terrestrial communication, and satellite antenna systems. This is achieved by designing engineering models using software programs and the latest in computer languages and technologies. Comsearch is a leading provider of consulting, engineering services, and software products to the wireless and telecommunications industry. Comsearch is a subsidiary of The Allen Telecom, Inc. which employs 146 people with revenues of $31 million. **Career Highlights:** Comsearch: Programmer Analyst (1994-Present); Programmer I, II, III (1987-94); Frequency Coordinator, Associate Frequency Coordinator (1983-86); earned 5, 10, and 15 year service awards. **Associations & Accomplishments:** Institute of Electrical and Electronics Engineers, Inc. **Education:** George Mason University, B.S. in Computer Science (1990); Northern Virginia Community College, A.A.S.; 2 year Engineering (1983). **Personal Information:** Mr. Mills is a Volkswagon enthusiast, admiring cars from the 1950s and 1960s, and a music collector from 1950s to the present. He is a firm believer in the protection of animals from harmful action. Mr. Mills collects lighthouse prints and enjoys attending antique, arts and crafts shows.

Andie Molnar

Product Manager
Lucent Technologies
168 Christol Street
Metuchen, NJ 08840
(908) 953-6491
Fax: (908) 953-6491
amolnar@lucent.com

3669

Business Information: Serving Lucent Technologies since 1996, Ms. Molnar, a pioneer woman PBX installer, has received recognition for her diligence and management skills through several promotions to her current position of Product Manager. In this capacity, Ms. Molnar coordinates a staff of technical experts involved in security systems management ensuring systems reliability and integrity. In addition, she is responsible for developing state-of-the-art security solutions and securing and negotiating contracts. A recognized professional, Ms. Molnar won Gold and Silver Presidential Awards for team exellence and a Partner of Choice Award. Through self training and study, she hopes to attain a technical role within the Company's optical networking group. Ms. Molnar attributes her career success to innovative thinking, a positive outlook, and her ability to deliver results. Formerly AT&T Network Systems, Lucent Technologies is a voice and data communications provider. The Company provides switching, transmission, fiber-optic cable, wireless systems, and operations systems to meet the needs of communication service companies. Lucent Technologies is international in scope. **Career Highlights:** Lucent Technologies: Product Manager (1998-Present), Technology Sales Manager (1996-98). **Associations & Accomplishments:** Friends of The Metuchen Library; Silver Bell Labs Award (1999); Gold Presidential Award (1999); Partner of Choice Award (1997). **Education:** Rio Hondo College, Liberal Arts (1975). **Personal Information:** Ms. Molnar enjoys archery and bridge.

Mark Neal Nachlis

Senior Manager of Support Services Market
Cisco Systems, Inc.
2720 Sequoia Way
Belmont, CA 94002
(408) 525-0997
mnachlis@cisco.com

3669

Business Information: As Senior Manager of Support Services Market of Cisco Systems, Inc., Mr. Nachlis manages the marketing communications for the service and support division. In this capacity, he deals with advertising, customer relations, Web sites, brochures, CD-ROMs, video, collateral, strategic seminars, interview trade shows, and magazine articles. Mr. Nachlis is responsible for 12 direct and 18 indirect employees. He plans to stay with the Corporation, advancing to either managing a market organization, running a technical observation or becoming a field engineer. His highlights include producing an award winining sales tool that explained all services and support offered; bringing team from three people to forty in just two years; and increasing revenues to two billion dollars. Mr. Nachlis attributes his success to his incredible desire to prosper in his field. The second largest corporation in the world, Cisco Systems, Inc. connects the Internet to the world. The Corporation deals with support and professional services including customer, technical assistance, engineering, warranty, installation, and paint design. Established in 1986, the Corporation employs over 17,000 individuals and reports annual sales of $15 billion. **Career Highlights:** Senior Manager of Support Services Market, Cisco Systems, Inc. (1998-Present); Vice President, Pentagon Partners (1996-98); Senior Manager, MCI Telecommunications (1991-96); Manager, General Electric (1987-91). **Associations & Accomplishments:** Jewish Federation for Young Adults; High Tech Society Silicon Valley. **Education:** Polytechnical University, M.S. (1996); Widener University, B.S. **Personal Information:** Married to Michelle Corbett in 1999. Mr. Nachlis enjoys auto racing, yacht racing and golf.

Senthil Kumar Nagarajan

Web Architect
Cisco Systems, Inc.
33 Union Square, Apartment 831
Union City, CA 94587
(510) 475-1830
trichy_nsk@hotmail.com

3669

Business Information: Serving as a web architect for on-line automation tools project at Cisco Systems, Inc. Areas of responsibility include web development including application design, development and architecture. Mr. Nagarajan concentrates his work efforts on enterprise web applications. Possessing an excellent understanding of his field, he is responsible for all aspects of project planning and software architecture for his modules. His success reflects his ability to take on challenges and deliver results on behalf of the corporation and its clientele. In the future Mr. Nagarajan hopes to work on complex web based assignments providing original and creative technical solutions. Cisco Systems, Inc. is the world's leading provider of internetworking solutions. Prior to this position, Mr. Nagarajan served as a project leader for Oracle Corporation, headquartered in Redwood Shores, California. **Career Highlights:** Web Architect, Cisco Systems, Inc. (2000-Present); Project Leader, Oracle Corporation (1998-2000); Senior Member of Technical Staff, Butler Technology Solutions (1997-98). **Associations & Accomplishments:** Golden Key Honor Society. **Education:** RMIT University, M.S. in Engineering Information Technology (1996); University of Mysore India, M.S. in Computer Science (1990). **Personal Information:** Married to Kalpana in 1997. Mr. Nagarajan enjoys reading materials on Eastern philosophy and astrology.

Sonali Rao

Senior Marketing
Arris Interactive
3871 Lakefield Drive, Suite 300
Suwanee, GA 30024-1242
7706228400
Fax: 7706228725
sonali.rao@arris-i.com

3669

Business Information: Serving as the Senior Marketing Specialist for Arris Interactive, Mr. Rao is responsible for all European clients. This includes new product announcement, tracking trails and demonstrations, forecasting, scheduling deliveries, introducing new programs, implementing new feature requests, dealing with weekly conference calls, and troubleshooting. Possessing an excellent understanding of his field, Mr. Rao performs a great deal of research within the area, providing results to upper management and promoting new and innovative marketing techniques. Attributing his success to his education, he looks forward to continuing his work with the Company and performing more work in the data area. Specializing in cable telephony, Arris Interactive is a combination of ANTEC Corporation and Nortel Network, forming a competitive edge for the communications companies. Established in 1996, the Company provides products that deliver voice and data services over hybrid fiber coax networks. Employing the skills and expertise of 350 personnel, the Company's world headquarters is in Suwanee, Georgia, with a development and test lab at this location. **Career Highlights:** Arris Interactive: Senior Marketing Specialist (2000-Present), Senior Customs Operators Specialist (1996-00); Senior Software Engineer, BNR (1992-96). **Associations & Accomplishments:** Maharashita Mandal of Aranta; Recycling Committee of BNR; United Way Campaign at BNR; Women's Engineers Teaching High School Girls Math and Science. **Education:** Georgia State University, M.B.A. (1998). **Personal Information:** Married to Arvind Benegal in 1989. One child: Minoti. Mr. Rao enjoys travel, pottery, reading, music and travel.

Frank P. Saladis

Global Project Management Advocate
Cisco Systems, Inc.
97 Mountainview Avenue
Staten Island, NY 10314
(718) 698-0965
Fax: (718) 698-6891
fsaladis@cisco.com

3669

Business Information: A topnotch, 29 year veteran of information technology, Mr. Saladis joined Cisco Systems, Inc. December 1999 as a Global Project Management Advocate. He is currently responsible for training, mentoring, and coaching project managers and developing practitioner training courses in project management. After spending his entire career with AT&T, Mr. Saladis joined the International Institute for Learning, Inc. as Senior Instructor and Consultant in 1998. Putting his system skills and technical expertise to use, he travels extensively across the United States to teach and share tested and proven principles of Project Management. In this context, Mr. Saladis develops introductory and executive level course curricula using state-of-the-art technologies. His active affiliation with the Project Management Institute enables him to stay up-to-date, and allows him to personally interact with the many professionals in different fields. Operating, coordinating, and offering professional communication courses; supporting and mentoring new instructors; and overseeing time lines, schedules, and assignments also fall within the purview of Mr. Saladis' responsibilities. He attributes his success to a combination of creativity, seeking out what needs to be done, overcoming obstacles, and pushing forward to accomplish objectives and goals. Becoming well known in Project Management serves as one of Mr. Saladis' future goals. The largest internetworking vendor for equipment and networking management, Cisco Systems, Inc. maintains a global presence generating revenues in excess of $12.2 billion in fiscal 1999. Presently, Cisco Systems is headquartered in San Jose, California. **Career Highlights:** Global Project Management Advocate, Cisco Systems, Inc. (1999-Present); Senior Instructor/Consultant, International Institute for Learning Inc. (1998-99); National Project Manager, AT&T (1990-98). **Associations & Accomplishments:** Project Management Institute: President of New York City Chapter (1991-99), President of Assembly of Chapter (1998-99). **Education:** George Washington University, Project Management Professional Certification (1992); Master's Certificate in Commercial Project Management; Certification as PMP (1998). **Personal Information:** Married in 1972. Mr. Saladis enjoys guitar, music, art and song writing.

Reba Shackelford

Training Consultant
Lucent Technologies
2413 Country Valley Road
Garland, TX 75041
(972) 745-5853
Fax: (972) 745-5856
cr4690@gte.net

3669

Business Information: Ms. Shackelford is Training Consultant with Lucent Technologies. She is responsible for providing on-site training for corporate clients. Before joining Lucent, she served as Contract Trainer with Apac Teleservices and Course Administrator for AT&T. As a four year technology training professional, Ms. Shackelford travels extensively to the client's sites to train systems administrators in the proper utilization and maintenance of Lucent products. In addition, she effectively teaches Lucent employees on how to program and properly use the Company's state-of-the-art equipment. Providing technical and training support and problem resolutions for 22 sales associates also fall within the purview of her functions. An expert, Ms. Shackelford has received many internal awards recognizing her diligences and teaching talent. One of her many accomplishments include bringing in $100,000 worth of business for the Company. Attributing her success to her strong faith, her future goal is to start her own computer consulting and training company. With division headquarters in Copell, Texas, Lucent Technologies offers telecommunications services to customers around the world through hundreds of international branch locations. Lucent specializes in the manufacture and distribution of telephony equipment to businesses and call centers internationally. **Career Highlights:** Training Consultant, Lucent Technologies (1999-Present); Contract Trainer, Apac Teleservices (1997-98); Course Administrator, AT&T (1995-97). **Associations & Accomplishments:** American Management Association; American Society for Training and Development. **Education:** Computer Learning Center, MCSE certification (1999). **Personal Information:** Married to Cliffton in 1990. Two children: LaQuita Michelson and Clarence Cheatham. Ms. Shackelford enjoys spending quality time with her family and her grandchildren.

Sandeep Shukla

Global Operations Manager
Lucent Technologies
478 East Altamonte Drive, Suite 108, #171
Altamonte Springs, FL 32701
(407) 767-2711
Fax: (815) 366-1368
sandeepshukla@angelfire.com

3669

Business Information: Recruited to Lucent Technologies in 1996, Mr. Shukla presently serves in the position of Global Operations Manager. He is responsible for a variety of tasks, which includes managing the daily operations, maintaining the wireless networks, and providing operational support to various international projects. Highly regarded, he possesses an excellent understanding of the technology field and his role. Mr. Shukla is involved in business case development and staffing for the network operations. In addition, he oversees the integration and testing of the networks. In his previous assignment with Lucent Technologies, he was responsible for providing engineering training on wireless products. Mr. Shukla performs public relations, to include interfacing with customers, conducting presentations, and ensuring customers are satisfied. In the future, he plans on moving into a senior management position. Lucent manufacturers and markets voice information processing systems and provides long distance and wireless services. The Company's wireless services include cellular and paging packages as well as telephones. With locations worldwide, the Company operates several subsidiaries manned by a global work force of more than 170,000 people. **Career Highlights:** Global Operations Manager, Lucent Technologies (1996-Present); Assistant Professor, DeVry Institute of Technology (1992-96); Assistant Engineer of Maintenance, Veenu Constructions Ltd. (1985, 1989-90); Electrical Engineer, Plastics Article Factory (1984-85); Electrical Engineer Trainee, Hindustan Aeronautics Ltd. (1983). **Associations & Accomplishments:** Institute of Engineers, Australia; Institute of Electrical Engineers, United Kingdom; Institute of Electrical and Electronics Engineers, United States; Recipient, Gold Medal for First Position in Bachelor's Program; Recipient, Teaching Excellence Award. **Education:** Ohio University: M.A. in Telecommunications (1991), M.S. in Electrical and Computer Engineering (1988), M.A. in International Affairs (1987); Kamla Nehru Institute of Science & Technology, Bachelor's degree of Technology in Electrical Engineering (1984); Institute of Engineers of Australia, Certified Professional Engineer (1990); Various technical and management courses. **Personal Information:** Mr. Shukla enjoys travel.

Rebecca L. Smith

Documentation Services Manager
Nokia Networks
6000 Connection Drive
Irving, TX 75039
(972) 894-5894
Fax: (972) 894-5874

3669

Business Information: Serving as the Documentation Services Manager, Ms. Smith currently works within the business unit of Radio Access Systems for Nokia Networks. She and her skilled team of 10 qualified technical professionals work diligently to perform all of the documenting functions for the Company at its Irving, Texas location. Ms. Smith is also actively involved in an international council dedicated to the implementation of a global strategy for documentation. The highlight of her professional career came when she planned a three-day conference for Nokia Networks documentation professionals from around the world. Her success reflects her ability to deliver results and aggressively take on new challenges. Internationally renowned, Nokia Networks has built one of the leading cellular infrastructures used in the world today. Providing cellular services since the 1970s, the Company actually got its start in the telecommunications industry when it manufactured field telephones for the military. At the present time, more than 38,000 individuals are employed in operations worldwide. **Career Highlights:** Documentation Services Manager, Nokia Networks (1996-Present); Documentation Specialist, Nokia Mobile Phones (1995-96); Technical Writer, Tandy Corporation (1992-94). **Associations & Accomplishments:** Society of Technical Communications; Published author of several articles in trade publications. **Education:** West Texas A&M University, B.A. (1985); Texas Tech University.

Normand A. Terault

Principal Database Administrator
Simplex Time Recorder
100 Simplex Drive
West Minster, MA 01441-0001
(978) 874-8638
Fax: (978) 874-8833
teraultn@simplexnet.com

3669

Business Information: Charged with maintenance of the vital ERP system, Mr. Terault currently serves as the Principal Database Administrator for Simplex Time Recorder. Taking on the challenging lead role of designing, creating, and managing the content of the database warehouse, Mr. Terault has been recognized for his accomplishemnts and dedication within the Company's operations. Currently maintaining the oversight of thirty individual database systems and three of database personnel, Mr. Terault is credited with the creation of the entire database warehouse system, from the conceptual ideas to the present fully integrated operation. His future aspiration includes moving up the corporate hierarchy into top management. Serving an extensive client portfolio of major commercial companies and organizations on an international basis, Simplex Time Recorder manufactures fire and security detection systems as well as nurse call and time management systems. Renowned for the quality and reliability of their products, the Company has experienced record growth as of recent, resulting in annual revenues in excess of $800 million. An established and reputable company, the Simplex Time Recorder was founded in 1898, and employs over 6,000 people nationwide. **Career Highlights:** Simplex Time Recorder: Principal Database Administrator (2000-Present), Data Warehouse Architect (1997-99); Information Systems Consultant, Allmerica Financial (1994-97). **Associations & Accomplishments:** International Datawarehouse Association. **Personal Information:** Married to Ann in 1983.

Felice Tinelli

Regional Director
Lucent Technologies
13630 Northwest 8th Street
Sun Rise, FL 33325
(954) 835-2945
Fax: (954) 389-3261
ftinelli@aol.com

3669

Business Information: Possessing unique talent in the telecommunications field, Mr. Tinelli joined Lucent Technologies in 1995 as Regional Director. In this capacity, he is the Business Manager for Latin America and assumes responsibility for the entire spectrum of operational and administrative functions from sales through distribution. Before joining Lucent, Mr. Tinelli served as Account Manager with AT&T and Field Service Engineer for KLA. As a solid, 30 year technology professional, he supervises a staff of five employees in coordinating resources, time lines, schedules, and assignments. Compiling and synthesizing large quantities of data into management reports, overseeing the fiscal year budget, driving products and services to market, and providing cohesive leadership also fall within the realm of Mr. Tinelli's functions. Dedicated to further development of the Company, Mr. Tinelli anticipates a promotion to Vice President due to his dedication and the perpetuation of additional growth through increased sales. Lucent Technologies is a publicly owned company providing communication and networking services to companies and corporations. Beginning operations in 1992, the Company boasts $200 million in yearly sales. **Career Highlights:** Regional Director, Lucent Technologies (1995-Present); Account Manager, AT&T (1992); Field Service Engineer, KLA (1990). **Education:** University, Marketing degree (1989). **Personal Information:** Married to Nilda in 1990. Two children: Yuri and Danae. Mr. Tinelli enjoys skiing, tennis, golf, theatre and travel.

Dick Walter
President/Founder
Laser Wireless Inc.
2145 Lincoln Plaza
Lancaster, PA 17603
(877) 527-3757
Fax: (717) 394-7833
sales@laserwireless.com

3669

Business Information: Functioning in the dual role of President and Founder of Laser Wireless Inc., Mr. Walter oversees all day-to-day administration and operations. He sets the technical direction and vision, as well as develops innovative marketing and business strategies. Excited about the recent merger with Hyperion Technologies Inc., Mr. Walter feels together, they can create dynamic new product and service offerings to capture a significant niche in the wireless communication market nationally and internationally. A savvy, 43 year veteran of technology, he engages in all aspects of sales and marketing and takes a leading role in driving products to market. His solid, resume includes extensive experience with networks to include troubleshooting network usage and computer peripherals and resolving operational problems for his clients. Directing research, evaluation, and integration of new technologies, determining future resource requirements, and overseeing time lines, schedules, assignments, and budgets are also an integral part of Mr. Walter's responsibilities. A hard charging professional, he was inspired to start Laser Wireless because it was something he always wanted to do, and was tired of time going by without trying. Attaining the $20 million mark in revenue serves as his short term target. "Just work hard," is cited as is advice. Recently acquired by Hyperion Technologies Inc., Laser Wireless Inc. operates in the optical communications field. The Corporation specializes in development of wireless optical atmospheric communications systems used to transmit voice, video, telephone, and data on a beam of light. Located in Lancaster, Pennsylvania, Laser Wireless employs a staff of 12 professional and technical experts who help generate in excess of $15 million annually. **Career Highlights:** President/Founder, Laser Wireless Inc. (1983-Present); Senior Manager, RCA Corporation (1956-83). **Associations & Accomplishments:** Past Master (1977), Masonic Lodge. **Education:** B.S. (1956). **Personal Information:** Married to Judy in 1983. Five children: Glenn, Lynn, Doug, Laurie, and Mark. Mr. Walter enjoys classic cars.

Revell Wheeler
National Technical Network Manager
ACT Teleconferencing, Inc.
275 West Campbell Road, Suite 501
Richardson, TX 75080-8017
(972) 354-6400
Fax: (972) 354-6404
rwheller@dhc.net

3669

Business Information: As the National Technical Network Manager of ACT Teleconferencing, Inc., Mr. Wheeler handles all technical aspects of the operation. He is involved in all network applications, from personal computers to video interfacing, and is responsible for the development of power alternatives. Working closely with his team of four employees, Mr. Wheeler displays the managerial qualities that make a manager both forceful and effective. A savvy, 22 year veteran of the field, he attributes his substantial success to endurance and persistence, as well as his ability to deliver results and aggressively take on new challenges. Mr. Wheeler hopes to expedite continued promotion, enabling him to better serve his clientele. Founded in 1999, ACT Teleconferencing, Inc. is an up and coming video conference bridge service. Employing a staff of 20 individuals, the Corporation offers international video and audio conferencing bridges for locations worldwide. The Corporation currently reports an estimated annual revenue of $1.5 million. **Career Highlights:** National Technical Network Manager, ACT Teleconferencing, Inc.

(1999-Present); Senior Support Engineer, NEC (1996-99); Senior Engineer, CLI (1989-96); Network Manager, Honeywell Inc. (1981-89). **Education:** Bishop College: B.S. (1977), M.S., A.S. **Personal Information:** Married to Beverly in 1975. Two children: Rachelle and Dee. Mr. Wheeler enjoys photography.

Joseph A. Terrell
Systems Administrator
Clinton Electronics Corporation
6701 Clinton Road
Loves Park, IL 61111
(815) 633-1444
Fax: (815) 633-8712
admarlj@inwave.com

3671

Business Information: Mr. Terrell is the Systems Administrator for Clinton Electronics Corporation. He is responsible for overseeing or carrying out all aspects of information management. A six year professional, he networks two buildings, one research laboratory, and one production plant in Taiwan. He updates and maintains the current systems while working to develop and install new hardware and software programs to advance the technology for the Corporation. A local expert in the technology field, Mr. Terrell also teaches at the local community colleges reaching almost 2,000 students every year. He instructs Internet applications and programs as well as beginning networking. In the future, Mr. Terrell is looking to receive a more focused role within a larger company that would better accentuate his management and networking capabilities while allowing him to maintain a part-time teaching position. His success is attributed to a strong faith in God and a quality education which he received with the support of his parents. Clinton Electronics Corporation manufactures high-end monochrome CRTs and monitors. The Corporation sells its bare bulbs and monitors to international clients such as Hewlett-Packard and IBM. Established in 1965, the largest portion of its product is sold through another name, however, the Corporation does sell a portion of its monitors under the same name. **Career Highlights:** Systems Administrator, Clinton Electronics Corporation (1997-Present); Instructor, Rock Valley College (1996-99); Department Coordinator, Christian Life Center Schools (1993-97). **Associations & Accomplishments:** Association of Information Technology Professionals. **Education:** Rockford College: M.B.A. (In Progress), B.S. (1996). **Personal Information:** Mr. Terrell enjoys political activism.

Abhijit Bandyopadhyay, Ph.D.
Staff Engineer
Cypress Semiconductor Corporation
19400 Sorenson Avenue, Apartment 133
Cupertine, CA 95014
(408) 544-1698
Fax: (408) 922-0833
iba@cypress.com

3672

Business Information: As a Staff Engineer of Cypress Semiconductor Corporation, Dr. Bandyopadhyay is responsible for the development of radio frequency products for the next generation of digital wirless communication. With more than 12 years of technical experience, he has dedicated three years of his talented career with IC Works/Cypress Semiconductor Corporation, demonstrating his abilities to perform work of the most complex nature. The most rewarding aspect of his career is working for a research company in Singapore and developing an integrated microphone for hearing aids and RFIC technology. Continually striving to improve performance, Dr. Bandyopadhyay plans ro remain with the Corporation in order to continue engineering excellence in wireless communication. His success is attributed to determination and the values instilled in him by his parents. Cypress Semiconductor manufactures integrated circuits and semiconductor chips for a host of client companies that produce products, such as computers and cellular phones. The Corporation focuses diligently on research and development of products of the best quality. Established in 1982, the Corporation is headquartered in San Jose, California, and functions under the direct guidance and expertise of approximately 3,000 professionals who help generate annual revenues in excess of $700 million. **Career Highlights:** Staff Engineer, IC Works Inc./Cypress Semiconductor Corporation (1997-Present); Technical Staff Member, IME Singapore (1994-97); Manager, SCL (1982-94). **Associations & Accomplishments:** Institute of Electrical and Electronics Engineers; Reference Asia, Asia's Who's Who of Men & Women of Achievement; Associate Member, IETE. **Education:** IIT Delhi, Ph.D. in Electrical Engineering (1991); IIT Kharagpur, M.S. in Electrical Engineering; University of Calcutta, B.S. in Electrical Engineering. **Personal Information:** Married to Adity in 1987.

One child: Reeti. Dr. Bandyopadhyay enjoys reading, photography, outing and listening to music.

Michael Yearwood
Information Technology Manager
Coretec, Inc.
2020 Ellesmere Road
Toronto, Ontario, Canada M1H 2Z8
(416) 439-2000
Fax: (416) 739-8846
mayearwo@coretec-inc.com

3672

Business Information: As Information Technology Manager for Coretec, Inc., Mr. Yearwood is responsible for the professional oversight of all daily information technology activities including administration, production, and distribution. He coordinates resources, schedules, assignments, and various aspects of communications for project development. Utilizing 10 years of skills and knowledge attained through an extensive employment and educational history, Mr. Yearwood capitalizes on his experience in all phases of operation, and monitors the productivity of his six-member staff, while formulating a hands-on management style with an above average aptitude for problem solving. Committed to the growth and expansion of the Company, Mr. Yearwood hopes to earn a senior level position within its operations in the near future. Coretec, Inc. is manufacturing firm that produces state of the art technology in the form of printed circuit boards for marketing and distribution to a host of computer manufactures. Established in 1983, the Corporation is headquartered in Toronto, Canada and employs the skills and full support of more than 360 professionals. A growing firm in the information technology community, Coretec, Inc. generates annual revenues in excess of $62 million. **Career Highlights:** Information Technology Manager, Coretec, Inc. (1998-Present); Consultant, Praegitzer Asia (1998); Management Information Systems Manager, Rexcan Circuits (1991-98). **Education:** Loyalist College, Electronic Engineering Technologist (1990). **Personal Information:** Married to Heather in 1991. Two children: Alexander and Madison. Mr. Yearwood enjoys mountain biking, scuba diving, electronic repair, reading, press releases and sports.

Murtaza Ali, Ph.D.
Senior Member of Technical Staff
Texas Instruments
P.O. Box 660199, MS8653
Dallas, TX 75266-0199
(214) 480-4532
Fax: (972) 761-6987
mali@ti.com

3674

Business Information: Drawing on years of extensive academics and experience in the technical field, Dr. Ali serves as Senior Member of Technical Staff of Texas Instruments. He plans and oversees the research, evaluation, and integration of new technology and systems development methodologies. In this context, he is responsible for research and development of algorithms; systems for communication systems, such as DSL, V.90, and home networking; and software applications to run on them. Working closely with systems management and users to analyze, specify, and design new software, Dr. Ali directs the planning and development and support of a specific application or functional area. Coordinating resources, time lines, and communications for new projects also fall within the scope of his responsibilities. A respected professional, Dr. Ali has assertively served with Texas Instruments in variety of positions since joining the Company as Member of the Technical Staff and Research Scientist in 1995. Becoming more involved in management of communications projects is cited as his future endeavor. His success is attributed to his education and ability to read and grasp technical concepts quickly. An international technology company, Texas Instruments engages in manufacturing and selling semiconductors. The Company specializes in developing digital signal processors (DSP) and mixed signal processors (MSP), as well as solutions based on DSP and MSP. Headquartered in Dallas, Texas, the Company was established in the 1950s and presently employs a global workforce of over 38,000 professional, technical, and administrative support staff. **Career Highlights:** Texas Instruments: Senior Member of Technical Staff (1997-Present), Member of Technical Staff/Research Scientist (1995-97). **Associations & Accomplishments:** Institute of Electrical and Electronics Engineers: Signal Processing Society, Communications Society, Information Theory Society; Home Phoneline Networking Alliance. **Education:** University of Minnesota: Ph.D., M.S. in Electrical Engineering (1995); Bangladesh University of Engineering and Technology, B.Sc. **Personal Information:** Married to Tanzia Amreen in 1991. One child: Afeef. Dr. Ali enjoys reading, comparative religion and study of society.

Isidro Alvarez

Software Engineer
Motorola
8000 West Sunrise
Fort Lauderdale, FL 33322
(954) 723-6329
i1a001@email.mot.com

3674

Business Information: Mr. Alvarez, possessing an extensive background in software engineer, joined the Motorola team in 1997. A 19 year veteran, he assumes the role of Software Engineer responsible for raise and pre-raise Firmware development. In addition to his duties, Mr. Alvarez handles numerous resource planning functions to include determining resource requirements, project management, and assuming responsibility for the integrity and quality of assigned projects. Providing advice to users, designing new solutions to harness more of technology's power, and implementing the means for technology to meet the specific needs of the organization also fall within the scope of Mr. Alvarez's responsibilities. His professional highlight is moving to the United States, not knowing English, and becoming a success in his chosen career path. Mr. Alvarez's affiliation with industry associations such as IEEE Computer Society enables him to remain technologically up to date, and allows him to interact with other professionals in the field. Keeping on top of emerging technologies, becoming more known in the field, and completing his M.B.A. in Marketing serves as his future goals. Motorola is a communications enterprise offering consumers and businesses two way radio and paging system technologies. Founded in the 1940s, Motorola employs a work force of more than 50,000 professional, technical, and support personnel. The Corporation is headquartered in Illinois. **Career Highlights:** Software Engineer, Motorola (1997-Present); Software Engineer, Racal-Datacom, Inc. (1994-97); Research Engineer/Professor, "Jose A. Echeverria" Higher Polytechnic Institute at Havana (1982-88). **Associations & Accomplishments:** Institute of Electrical and Electronics Engineers; Communication and Computer Society; Order of Engineers. **Education:** University of Miami, M.B.A. in Marketing (In Progress); Florida International University, M.S. in Computer Engineering (1990-96); "Jose A. Echeverria" Higher Polytechnic Institute at Havana, B.S. in Electrical Engineering (1982). **Personal Information:** Mr. Alvarez enjoys raquetball and raquetball.

Kelley P. Archer

Information Technology Security Manager
FSI International
322 Lake Hazeltine Drive
Chaska, MN 55318-1096
(952) 361-8594
Fax: (952) 361-7476
karcher@fsi-intl.com

3674

Business Information: As the Information Technology Security Manager for FSI International, Mr. Archer is responsible for establishing policies and procedures, while conducting security awareness programs for all employees. His other obligations include reviewing new projects, making recommendations, and purchasing new security equipment, such as firewalls. With more than 15 years of security experience, Mr. Archer ensures that all company assets are protected at all times. His plans for his career include encouraging people to become more aware of Internet security. Mr. Archer's success reflects his ability to think outside-the-box, take on new challenges, and deliver results. FSI International is a leading global supplier of processing equipment used at key production steps to manufacture microelectronics. The Company develops, manufactures, markets, and supports products used in the technology areas of microlithography, surface conditioning, and spin-on dielectrics. FSI International's customers include microelectronics manufacturers located throughout North American, Europe, Japan, and the Asia-Pacific region. The Company operates out of several locations under the dedication and talents of more than 850 professionals who facilitate standard procedures for quality products. **Career Highlights:** Information Technology Security Manager, FSI International (1997-Present); Information Systems Security Manager, General Dynamics-I.S. (1995-97); Lockheed Martin Missiles & Space: Computer Security Analyst (1987-95), Program Security Representative (1987-92). **Associations & Accomplishments:** Sponsor, James Ferguson I.T. Security Scholarship; ISSA; Minnesota Industrial Security Awareness Council; High School Varsity Girls Hockey Coach. **Education:** University of San Fransisco, B.S. in Organizational Behavior (1990); Certified Information Systems Security Representative. **Personal Information:** Married to Sharon in 1975. Two children: Colleen and Kathryn. Mr. Archer enjoys racing stock cars, being a professional Santa, writing and photography. Mr. Archer has been a professional Santa for over 30 years. He is currently writing a book about all his wonderful to strange experiences while doing this, and is looking for it to get published.

Lawrence Azar

President
ppb, Inc.
30 Arapahoe Court
Portola Valley, CA 94028
(650) 851-4387
Fax: (650) 851-4388
azar@megasonics.com

3674

Business Information: Serving as President, Mr. Azar is the owner and founder of ppb, Inc. He is responsible for all day-to-day administration and operational activities. As a five year engineering professional, he is able to determine the overall strategic direction, as well as drive products and services to market through formulation of creative sales and marketing plans. An expert, Mr. Azar provides broad organizational support for all areas of the Corporation, including research and development, specification, and production. In addition to supervising his staff, he monitors the overall well-being of the Corporation financially and physically to make sure that the Corporation is providing services that customers need. Coordinating resources and schedules, overseeing time lines and assignments, and calculating and managing the fiscal year budget also fall within the purview of his functions. Displaying a clear vision for the 21st Century, Mr. Azar wants to the triple the size and take the Corporation to the next level. Offering a variety of quality services, ppb, Inc. manufactures instruments that detect energy in ultrasonic cleaning tanks used in the semiconductor, disk drive, medical, electronics, and aerospace industries. The instruments can also used to put pieces of products together in a manufacturing plant. Established in 1998, the Corporation reports annual sales of $300,000. **Career Highlights:** President, ppb, Inc. (1998-Present). **Associations & Accomplishments:** Associate Member, Massachusetts Institute of Technology; Sigma Xu; Scientific Research Society; Habitat for Humanity. **Education:** Massachusetts Institute of Technology, M.S. in Civil Engineering (1996); University of California at Berkeley, B.S. in Civil Engineering. **Personal Information:** Married to Pilar in 1996. Mr. Azar enjoys tennis, sailing and swimming.

John A. Cochran

Solutions Architect
DuPont Photomasks, Inc.
131 Old Settlers Boulevard
Round Rock, TX 78664
(512) 310-6384
Fax: (512) 310-6086
john.cochran@photomask.com

3674

Business Information: Providing his skilled services to DuPont Photomasks, Inc. as Solutions Analyst, Mr. Cochran works in the Information Technology Department of the Corporation. He is responsible for network and system engineering as well as developing technical IT systems, handling ERP systems, and related applications. Before joining DuPont Photomasks, he served as a Systems Manager for both Power Computing and Ocean Drilling Program. Currently working with Oracle on a project that will be the world's first to support multi-currencies, Mr. Cochran credits his success to hard work, continuing self-education, and being surrounded by topnotch technical professionals. Looking forward to the next millennium, he plans to expand the IT Department and venture into new technological endeavors. The largest of its kind in the world, DuPont Photomasks, Inc. engages in the manufacture of semiconductors and chips for such companies as Motorola, IBM, and Texas Instruments. Publicly owned, the Corporation spun off from its parent company, El DuPont, in 1997. Operations employ 1,500 individuals in the Corporation's 12 plants and annual revenue is reported at $270 million. **Career Highlights:** Solutions Architect, DuPont Photomasks, Inc. (1997-Present); Systems Manager, Power Computing (1997); Systems Manager, Ocean Drilling Program (1992-97). **Associations & Accomplishments:** Oracle Applications User Group. **Education:** Texas A&M University, Associate's degree (1994). **Personal Information:** Mr. Cochran enjoys home improvements and antique cars.

James A. Crawford, III

Manager of Manufacturing Engineering
Schneider Electric
15 Shelly Drive
Westford, MA 01886
(978) 975-9210
Fax: (978) 978-2968
james.crawford@modicon.com

3674

Business Information: Possessing unique talent in manufacturing engineering, Mr. Crawford joined Schneider Electric in 1995 as the Manager of Manufacturing Engineering. Mr. Crawford presides over a wide range of responsibilities such as new product introduction, process development, capital planning and implementation, and cost reduction programs. Additionally, he creates and maintains all process documentation and all of the machine maintenance functions. Mr. Crawford's history includes serving as Director of Business Development with Bull Electronics and Manager of Industrial Engineering for Honeywell Information Systems. His career success reflects is leadership ability to build strong teams with synergy and technical strength and take on new challenges and responsibilities. Consistently achieving quality performance in his field, he looks forward to assisting in the completion of future Company goals. With the fire of enterperneurship burning bright, Mr. Crawford eventually plans to participate in a start-up opportunity. Schneider Electric is a manufacturer of programmable logic controllers. Essentially little brains inside machines, these controllers direct all control aspects of different types of machinery and industrial processes. Employing a work force of 75,000 skilled individuals, the Company reports annual revenues in excess of $8 billion. **Career Highlights:** Manager of Manufacturing Engineering, Schneider Electric (1995-Present); Director of Business Development, Bull Electronics (1991-95); Manager of Industrial Engineering, Honeywell Information Systems (1980-91). **Education:** University of Massachusetts, B.S. in Information Technology (1977). **Personal Information:** Married to Michele Pitoniak-Crawford in 1984. Three children: Connor, Sean, and Ryan. Mr. Crawford enjoys golf, ice hockey, home improvements and travel.

Ernest G. DeNigris

President/Chief Executive Officer
Actel
15 Colville Drive
Mendham, NJ 07945
(973) 543-1081
Fax: (973) 543-2559
egdenigris@worldnet.att.net

3674

Business Information: Mr. DeNigris presently holds the demanding positions of President and Chief Executive Officer of Actel. He assists in developing the business plan and oversees all aspects of technical effort and design. Utilizing his network skills, Mr. DeNigris promotes the services of the Corporation while establishing new business and relationships. He also formulates policies and procedures, directs activities, develops goals, and implements strategies to achieve proposed goals. Mr. DeNigris plans to stay involved in the field of communications, focusing on development and expanding into other markets. His advice is "establish a network with professionals and companies and provide yourself with a challenging project." Mr. DeNigris' success is attributed to his ability to get along with other people, his love of challenges, and his willingness to do what it takes to get the job done. Established in 1997, Actel provides telecommunications services in Africa using geosync satellite technology. The Corporation, currently in its developmental stage, employs approximately five highly skilled employes to assist in various duties. Services are provided internationally. **Career Highlights:** President/Chief Executive Officer, Actel (1997-Present); AT&T: General Manager (1992-97), Director (1984-92), Division Manager (1981-84). **Education:** Massachusetts Institute of Technology, M.S. in Mechanical Engineering (1967); University of Notre Dame, B.S. in Mechanical Engineering (1966). **Personal Information:** Married to Catherine.

David L. Dinsmore

Field Applications Engineer
Linear Technology Corporation
17000 Dallas Parkway, Suite 219
Dallas, TX 75248
(972) 733-3071
Fax: (972) 380-5138
dldins@mindspring.com

3674

Business Information: As a Field Applications Engineer of the Linear Technology Corporation, Mr. Dinsmore is responsible for a number of engineering design and management duties on behalf of the Company. Recruited to the Corporation in 1986, he possesses an excellent understanding of his field. Utilizing his academics and 20 years of engineering experience, Mr. Dinsmore works closely with management and systems users to analyze, specify, and design advanced, customized applications, and standard products. Working primarily on-site, he is actively involved in developing state-of-the-art engineering solutions as well as designing new circuits. His career highlights include assisting the Company triple in size in 1994. Attributing his success to his integrity and honesty, Mr. Dinsmore plans to design customized home automation after his retirement. provides analog semiconductors. Linear Technology Corporation is a global manufacturer of linear and mixed signal circuits. Established in 1981, Linear Technology's purpose is to bridge the world of analog to the digital computer world. With annual sales in excess of $650 million, the Company provides new technologies for the computer, telecommunications, military, space, and industrial fields. Headquartered in Milpitas, California, Linear Technology Corporation is manned by 750 professional, technical, and support staff. **Career Highlights:** Field Applications Engineer, Linear Technology Corporation (1986-Present); Design Engineer, Boehringer Mannheim GmbH (1984-86); Design Engineer, Texas Instruments (1980-84). **Education:** West Virginia University Technical Institute at Montgomery, B.S. in Electrical Engineering (1980). **Personal Information:** Married to Donna in 1986. Three children: Dana, Darbianna, and Dawson. Mr. Dinsmore enjoys vintage auto racing.

Phillip K. Doan

Senior Systems Administrator
Marvell
645 Almanor Avenue
Sunnyvale, CA 94086
(408) 222-2560
Fax: (408) 281-3919
pdoan@marvell.com

3674

Business Information: As Senior Systems Administrator of Marvell Semiconductor, Inc., Mr. Doan is responsible for the planning, implementation, design, maintenance, and support of all Company networking. He is involved in systems networking and local and wide area networking. Beginning his career more than three years ago, Mr. Doan has developed the skills needed to maintain the highest standards of professional excellence. He attributes his substantial success to always taking a challenge. He has plans to pursue his Ph.D. and hopes to expedite continued promotion within his field. Marvell Semiconductor, Inc. is engaged in the manufacture of computer chips and conductors. Established in 1995, the Company currently offers read channel and datacom services and employs a staff of 160 individuals dedicated to serving the needs of a growing clientele. **Career Highlights:** Senior Systems Administrator, Marvell (1998-Present); Systems Administrator, Xilinx (1996-98); Systems Administrator, I.M.I. (1996). **Associations & Accomplishments:** Vietnamese Soccer. **Education:** National University, M.S. (1999); San Jose State University, B.S. in Management Information Systems & Computer Science. **Personal Information:** Mr. Doan enjoys telecommunications books and soccer.

Bettina Rice Ensor

Management Information Systems Manager of North American Region
Applied Materials
2703 Telecom Parkway, Suite 190A
Richardson, TX 75082
(972) 761-4358
bettina_ensor@amat.com

3674

Business Information: Offering her valuable services in North America, Mrs. Ensor serves Applied Materials in the role of Management Information Systems Manager of the North American Region. Employed with Applied Materials since 1995, she oversees all aspects of day-to-day administration and operations of the information systems infrastructure. In addition to devoting her attention to ensuring the functionality and maintenance of servers, desktops, PBX, and security of systems for clients, Mrs. Ensor supervises 12 employees as well as manages all resources, time lines, schedules, and budgets. Her accomplishments include earning Team of the Quarter award and having the most key performance indexex in the Company. Strategic goals for Mrs. Ensor include attaining the position of Chief Infomation Officer for this Company or a different company. A benchmark for providing technical support, she credits her success to listening to the customer, knowing what will solve the problem, producing results, and aggressively taking on new challenges. Applied Materials is engaged in the manufacture of water and semiconductor materials. Providing custom made products, clients include IBM, Motorola, Texas Instruments, Intel, and Micron. Operations in Richardson, Texas presently employs 15,000 qualified and skilled individuals to orchestrate all aspects of manufacture, distribution, and research and development. Reporting annual sales of $4 billion, Applied Materials is the world leader within the industry. **Career Highlights:** Management Information Systems Manager of North American Region, Applied Materials (1995-Present); Project Manager/Regional Analyst, Centex (1993-95); Technical Support Specialist, Edisto Resources Corporation (1990-93). **Associations & Accomplishments:** First Baptist Church of Richardson. **Education:** University of Kentucky, B.B.A. (1987); Transylvania University; University of Texas; Prestonburg Community College; Certifications: Video Conferencing, Window95, NT Novell, AT&T. **Personal Information:** Married to Charles in 1988. One child: Matthew Alexander Rice Ensor. Mrs. Ensor enjoys arts and craft, interior design and genealogy.

Gianantonio Ercolani

Manager
Intel Corporation
Naupliaallee, 3
Ottobrunn, Germany 85521
+49 8999143258
Fax: +49 8999143420
gianni.ercolani@intel.com

3674

Business Information: As the Manager of EMEA ISRG for Intel Corporation in Feldkirchen, Germany, Mr. Ercolani supervises a field unit that manages the relationship with Internet solutions developers. Possessing an excellent understanding of his field, he also assists in promoting new technology, thus creating new business opportunities. Capitalizing on over 18 years of experience in all phases of operation, he monitors staff productivity, formulating an innovative management style that encourages optimum performance. Mr. Ercolani plans to continue in his present position, fostering corporation growth and aspires to obtain a position with the Corporation in the United States or Europe. Intel is one of the largest semiconductor manufacturers in the world, however, the Corporation also supplies the computer and communications industries with the "ingredients" of computers, servers, chips, boards, systems, software, networking, and communications products. Intel's mission is to be the preeminent building block supplier to the worldwide Internet economy. Established in 1968, the Corporation is headquartered in Santa Clara, California and maintains facilities worldwide. Intel employs a skilled staff of 70,000 and generates annual income of approximately $30 billion. **Career Highlights:** Intel Corporation: Manager (1997-Present), Olivetti District Manager (1991-97), OEM Sales Manager (1985-90). **Education:** University of Pisa, Degree in Computer Science (1975). **Personal Information:** One child: Isabella. Mr. Ercolani enjoys skiing, sailing and reading history.

Jesse Fang, Ph.D.

Engineer Manager
Intel Corporation
2200 Mission College Boulevard
Santa Clara, CA 95054
(408) 765-5871
Fax: (408) 725-0722
jesse.z.fang@intel.com

3674

Business Information: Serving as Manager of Engineers for Intel Corporation, Dr. Fang manages system compilers and the Java Research Laboratory. Utilizing his strong academic ties and systems expertise, he develops enabling technologies to promote Intel hardware platform sales. On the leading edge of the technological spear, he researches and identifies innovative ways to enhance the unprecedented Intel chips. Dr. Fang is also developing a high end software package that translates program language to machines. Respected as a leader, he is a sponsor representative for Intel at seminars and conferences. According to Dr. Fang, he has achieved the American dream. After coming from China 19 years ago, he has fulfilled his dream of "being the best he can be" by attaining a position with Intel Corporation. Attributing his career success to his supportive wife, Dr. Fang hopes to continue in his current role and help Intel maintain its competitive edge in the market. The World's leading manufacturer of microprocessors, Intel owns over 90 percent of the microprocessing market. One of the largest manufacturer of semiconductors in the world, additional products include supercomputers, video technology software, multimedia hardware, PC enhancement products, and mircocomputer components. The Company markets its products directly to original computer equipment companies for incorporation into their systems. **Career Highlights:** Manager of Engineers, Intel Corporation (1995-Present); Project Manager, Hewlett-Packard Labs (1991-95); Program Manager, Convex Coporation (1988-91). **Associations & Accomplishments:** Institute of Electrical and Electronics Engineers; Association of Computing Machinery; Chinese Software Association. **Education:** University of Illinois, Post Ph.D. (1985); University of Nebraska at Lincoln, Ph.D. in Computer Science (1984). **Personal Information:** Married to Kerry Hsieh in 1990. One child: Joshua. Dr. Fang enjoys playing bridge, mountain walking and tennis.

Kiminori Fujisaku

General Manager
Fujitsu Microelectronics, Inc.
3545 North First Street
San Jose, CA 95134-1804
(408) 922-9507
Fax: (408) 922-8975
kfujisak@ibm.net

3674

Business Information: A prominent and respected professional, Mr. Fujisaku serves as General Manager for Fujitsu Microelectronics, Inc. Utilizing more than 20 years of practical experience in his field, he is responsible for the system-on-a-chip design methodology development for the Fujitsu Semiconductor Group worldwide. In addition, he conducts interviews of potential employees, hiring professionals with experience and devoting attention to their initial training. A faithful and assertive professional, Mr. Fujisaku has served with Fujitsu Microelectronics in a variety of roles since joining the Corporation as Director of ASSP Development in 1993. In order to be successful, Mr. Fujisaku states, "you need the experience in system design and the ability to stay up to date with new technology." Committed to the success of the Corporation, Mr. Fujisaku plans to remain with Fujitsu Microelectronics, continuing to work with methodology systems and grow in knowledge. His success reflects his ability to think outside the box and aggressively tackle new challenges and responsibilities. The largest computer company in Japan and one of the largest in the United States, Fujitsu Microelectronics, Inc. produces semiconductors for companies around the world. Examples of the Corporation's products include switching systems and network systems. **Career Highlights:** Fujitsu Microelectronics, Inc.: General Manager (1998-Present), Director of Strategic Marketing (1995-98), Director of ASSP Development (1993-95). **Education:** Keio University, M.S.I.E. (1977). **Personal Information:** Married to Kaoru in 1978. Two children: Keiko and Takayuki. Mr. Fujisaku enjoys skiing and spending time with his family.

Chris D. Gardner

Systems Manager
Micron Technology
3345 South Holden Avenue
Boise, ID 83706
(208) 368-1163
cdgardner@worldnet.att.net

3674

Business Information: Mr. Gardner has assertively served with Micron Technology in a variety of positions since joining the team of professionals as Simulation Programmer in 1995. In 1999, he received a promotion to his current position of Systems Manager. In his capacity, Mr. Gardner is responsible for managing layered applications in a multi-operating system environment. Possessing an excellent understanding of technology, he is in charge of installing third party applications for customers within Micron Technology, to include all UNIX and document management systems. Highly regarded by his colleagues, Mr. Gardner troubleshoots systems malfunctions and is able to work on multiple projects simultaneously. His strategic plans include remaining with the Corporation and becoming involved in wireless communications technology. Established in 1978, Micron Technology manufactures memory chips. Specializing D-RAM chips, the Corporation also engages in Micron PC sales and Internet services as well as manufacturing memory modules. Employing over 12,000 professional, technical, and support staff, the Corporation markets its products directly to users. With eight locations throughout the Northwest, the Corporation's headquarters is located in Boise, Idaho. **Career Highlights:** Micron Technology: Systems Manager (1999-Present), Simulation Programmer (1994-99); Fire Direction Specialist, United States Army (1983-92). **Associations & Accomplishments:** National Foresic League. **Education:** Technology related. **Personal Information:** Mr. Gardner enjoys AI/Fuzzy logic programming, study of ancient history and study of religion.

Dennis R. Goggins

Manager of Information Systems
National Semiconductor
1111 West Bardin Road, E Stop
Arlington, TX 76017
(817) 557-7632
Fax: (817) 468-6431
dgoggins@gte.net

3674

Business Information: A respected professional, Mr. Goggins serves as the Information Systems Manager for National Semiconductor. He oversees the factory automation and technology infrastructure and is responsible for the IT FAB processes, desktop support, and automated turnkey systems. In addition, he supervises the Windows Frame and NT server support. A staff of six professionals reports directly to him in the performance of their duties. Mr. Goggins formed a mentoring program within the Company in an effort to improve the effectiveness of the technicians and their promotional opportunities. Two employees have since been promoted due in part to the program's assistance. Mr. Goggins has been focusing on switching the help desk and desktop to new operating systems to reduce the number of technicians needed to maintain it. Continuing to advance professionally, he looks forward to becoming the information systems director of a small to mid-size company. Serving a national clientele, National Semiconductor is a renowned semiconductor manufacturer. The Company specializes in the manufacture of digital and analog circuits, distributing its products to other semiconductor manufacturing companies. Client companies are primarily aircraft, power circuits, cell phone, and digital component manufacturers. With locations across the country, the Company's Arlington, Texas facility focuses on semiconductor wafer-computer boards. A work force of 1,200 skilled professionals is employed at this location. Established in the 1970s, yearly turnover is estimated at $1 billion. **Career Highlights:** Manager of Information Systems, National Semiconductor (1995-Present); Account Manager, Digital Equipment (1995); Field Service Engineer, CAS Systems. **Associations & Accomplishments:** Council Member, City of Justin (1990-96). **Education:** DeVry Institute, Associate's degree (1982). **Personal Information:** Married to Kim in 1985. Three children: Adam, Mark, and David. Mr. Goggins enjoys camping and computers.

Rich Hering

Manager of Telecommunications
ADP Marshall, a Fluor Daniel Company
7415 East Orion Circle
Mesa, AZ 85207
(520) 795-0017
Fax: (480) 832-6421
rich.hering@adpmarshall.com

3674

Business Information: As Manager of Telecommunications for ADP Marshall, a Fluor Daniel Company Mr. Hering is responsible for interfacing with clients as well as traveling to different sites. Utilizing a vast knowledge of many technical skills, he works on new technical development practices, develops plans for e-business, and coordinates contracts with marketing groups, trying to blend emerging technology with existing technology. Mr. Hering's areas of expertise include telecommunications design; complete systems integration including planning, design, and implementation; and construction and project management for telecommunications to include budget planning, analysis, and tracking. He has been or is currently involved with projects for Intel, IBM Fishkill and Burlington, ST Semiconductors, Wafer Technologies Malaysia, dominion Semiconductor, and Level 3. Mr. Hering enjoys staying on the cutting edge by reading and taking classes that will enable him to capitalize on the opportunities provided by the Company. Obtaining his LAN specialist certification from BISCI, adding to his ratings, developing outsourcing strategies, and designing new e-commerce products serve as Mr. Hering's future endeavors. Established in the 1940s, ADP Marshall is involved in the construction of high-tech, semiconductor manufacturing buildings. The Company manufactures components for the technical industry and designs all types of networks that go into the buildings. Serving an international client base, the Company builds interfaces for tooling inside clean rooms to ERP, CIM, and BAS systems infrastructure. **Career Highlights:** Manager of Telecommunications, ADP Marshall, a Fluor Daniel Company (1999-Present); Senior Designer, Industrial Design Corporation (1996-99); Principal Engineering Technician, New York State Department of Transportation (1990-96). **Associations & Accomplishments:** Building Industry Consulting Standards International; Network and Systems Professionals Organization. **Education:** Clarkson College of Technology; University of Phoenix; Certifications: IBM PS/2, IBM LAN, IBM Mainframe Connectivity, IBM Sales and Management, Novell Advanced LAN Manager, Novell Network, 3Com Network, Apple Network, Apple Macintosh, Apple Mainframe Connectivity Digital Equipment Sales and Service, Compaq, Hewlett-Packard Sales and Service, Epson Sales and Service, NEC Sales and Service, Commodore Service, MicroSoft University Training, Lotus, Dbase, Aldus Pagemaker, Wordperfect, MicroStation Training, MicroSoft Office. **Personal Information:** Married to Jill in 1981. Two children: Tabitha and Richard III. Mr. Hering enjoys cars, skiing, boating, travel and hiking.

Stephen G. Hume

Senior Member Technical Staff, Test Systems Development
Maxim Integrated Products, Inc.
14320 Southwest Jenkins Road
Beaverton, OR 97005
(503) 641-3737
Fax: (503) 644-9929
shume@pacifier.com

3674

Business Information: Utilizing more than 10 years of extensive experience in the field of information technology, Mr. Hume functions in the role of Senior Member of the Technical Staff in the Test Systems Development Department of Maxim Integrated Products, Inc. He assumes responsibility for developing the software and hardware used in the production testing of high performance analog integrated circuits. His staff of four employees assist him in the completion of his duties. Attributing his success to his God-given talents, he looks forward to performing software and hardware research and development. A solid veteran in the technology field, Mr. Hume's objectives include remaining on the leading edge of technology. Based in Sunnyvale, California, Maxim Integrated Products, Inc. is a publicly traded integrated circuits manufacturing corporation. The Corporation supplies equipment manufacturers in numerous markets with analog integrated circuits with applications to be used in a variety of systems including data conversion, portable computing, and fiber and wireless communications. Established in 1983, Maxim Integrated Products employs over 3,000 skilled individuals to serve its international clientele. **Career Highlights:** Maxim Integrated Products, Inc.: Senior Member Technical Staff, Test Systems Development (1997-Present), Member Technical Staff, Test Systems Development (1994-97); Software and Hardware Engineer II, Tektronix, Inc. (1992-94). **Education:** University of Portland, B.S. in Electrical Engineering (1988). **Personal Information:** Married to Lorraine in 1989. Three children: S. Andrew, A. Lee, and Janey E. Mr. Hume enjoys photography, gardening, hiking and church activities.

Kristen A. Jensen

Instructional Designer
Intel Corporation
1740 Northwest Murray Road
Portland, OR 97279
(503) 696-8080
krismus@snap.com

3674

Business Information: Ms. Jensen serves in the position of Instructional Designer for Intel Corporation. Joining the Corporation's team of professionals in 1997, she designs and implements training opportunities including needs analysis, video production, multimedia, and Web based training. Overseeing knowledge management for the Corporation also falls within the realm of her responsibilities. Highly regarded, Ms. Jensen possesses superior talents and an excellent understanding of the technology field. She has enjoyed substantial success in her role and finds her work greatly rewarding. Committed to further development of the Corporation, she coordinates strategic planning and detemines the business contribution of the systems functions to ensure a bright future for Intel Corporation. Intel Corporation is a manufacturer of microprocessor and software design. The Corporation is the worlds number one maker of microprocessors, with 90 percent of the market. Intel's microprocessors, including the Pentium have been providing the brains for IBM-compatible personal computers since 1981. Established in the 1900s, the Corporation is located in Oregon and employs 70,000 staff members to facilitate every aspect of design, manufacture, quality assurance, and distribution of products. **Career Highlights:** Instructional Designer, Intel Corporation (1997-Present); Database Manager, La Follette Institute (1995-97); Instructional Designer, Center for Cooperatives (1994-95). **Associations & Accomplishments:** Oregon Media Production Association. **Education:** University of Wisconsin at Madison, M.S. in Educational Technology (1997); University of Michigan, M.A. in History (1993); Rutgers University, B.A. in History and Spanish. **Personal Information:** Ms. Jensen enjoys hiking and cross country skiing.

Emil Lambrache

Senior Staff Design Engineer
Atmel Corporation
1054 South Winchester Boulevard, Apartment 15
San Jose, CA 95128
(408) 436-4289
emil@atmel.com

3674

Business Information: As Senior Staff Design Engineer of Atmel Corporation, Mr. Lambrache oversees design and development of state-of-the-art systems level software such as operating systems, network management, and database management software. A tested and proven, 14 year veteran of information technology, he came on board to the Atmel Corporation team in 1993. Mr. Lambrache, relying on his academic ties, business experience, and technical expertise, is specifically in charge of systems integration of technical computers using advanced semiconductor technology. An expert who delivers results in support of product enhancement, Mr. Lambrache currently owns four patents which includes memory design and system-on-a-chip innovations. Concurrently fulfilling the role of product manager, he is also responsible for determining future resource requirements; overseeing time lines, schedules, assignments, and budgets; and ensuring product and service offerings are lace with quality, value, and selection. He really enjoys what he does. Mr. Lambrache's future goals include obtaining his Ph.D. and remaining up to date in the technology arena. A billion dollar company, Atmel Corporation is engaged in semiconductor integrated circuit design and manufacturer, specifically nonvolatile memory and ASIC products. An international company, Atmel operates a network of plants in Colorado, France, and Germany as well as design centers in Finland and Japan. Founded in 1984, Atmel employs a global work force of more than 5,000 persons. **Career Highlights:** Senior Staff Design Engineer, Atmel Corporation (1993-Present); Senior Design Engineer, National Semiconductor (1992-93); Design Engineer, Seeq Technology (1991-92). **Associations & Accomplishments:** Institute of Electrical and Electronics Engineers. **Education:** Politechnica University, M.S. in Electrical Engineering (1985).

Dale R. Lindner

Project Manager of Corporate Development
Texas Instruments
7839 Churchhill Way
Dallas, TX 75251
(972) 917-7361
Fax: (972) 917-3804
dlindner@ti.com

3674

Business Information: In his role as Project Manager of Corporate Development for Texas Instruments, Inc., Mr. Lindner works closely with business unit managers and department heads to develop strategic operational policies as he oversees the completion of specific corporate projects. Evaluating the needs of each assignment on an individual basis, he is able to effectively formulate action plans that aid in the timely attainment of production goals. Additionally, he assists in the design of contracts for mergers and acquisitions, lending knowledge gained from hands on experience to executive management members. Mr. Lindner attributes his success to excellent listening and interpersonal skills, and looks forward to continued prosperity within his position. His advice is "have enthusiasm." Texas Instruments Inc. is a global manufacturer of semiconductors, leading the industry in technology and achievement. The Corporation supplies companies such as cellular phone and computer disk drive manufacturers with electrical and technical components that are essential to the proper design of their products. Originally established in 1930, the Corporation employs 36,000 people throughout the world, generating estimated annual revenues of $8.8 billion. **Career Highlights:** Texas Instruments Inc.: Project Manager of Corporate Development (1995-Present), Financial Planning Manager, ITGC (1990-95), Financial Planning Superintendent, DSEG (1985-90). **Associations & Accomplishments:** Board of Directors, Lewisville Lake Symphony. **Education:** Albright College, B.S. (1979). **Personal Information:** Married to Therese K. in 1972. One child: Matthew D.

Chen Liu

Speech Technologist
Motorola
55 Shuman Boulevard, Suite 600
Naperville, IL 60563
(630) 305-4514
Fax: (630) 305-4585
liu@casd.mot.com

3674

Business Information: Mr. Liu is a Speech Technologist for Motorola. Working out of the Company's offices in Naperville, Illinois, he is involved in the research and development of speech recognition and speech signal processing programs. He designs new systems to accommodate the technology needs in voice recognition. The programs provide a means to enable people to interactively use Internet-based applications via vioce, such as accessing valuable information and controlling remote machines. The benefits are enormous to anyone who does not have an Internet-connected computer at hand but a telephone or a cellular phone and especially to handicapped persons who have difficulty using a keyboard. He encourages aspiring professionals to obtain a strong educational background and believes that knowledge, together with perseverance have made him a success in his business life. In the future, Mr. Liu hopes to devote his time in studying robust speech processing. His success reflects his ability to think outside the box, deliver results, and aggressively take on new challenges. Motorola is a global leader in providing integrated communications solutions and embedded electronic solutions. Established in 1920, the Company turns over $30 billion each year through sales of telecommunications and electronic technology. The Company has offices around the world and hosts over 140,000 employees. These employees assist customers in locating the necessary products to facilitate their residential or corporate networking needs. **Career Highlights:** Speech Technologist, Motorola (1998-Present); Visiting Assistant Professor, Department of ECE, University of Illinois at Urbana-Champaign (1998); Beckman Fellow, Beckman Institute, University of Illinois at Urbana-Champaign (1996-98). **Associations & Accomplishments:** Acoustical Society of America; Institute of Electrical and Electronics Engineers; Audio Engineering Society; American Association for the Advancement of Science. **Education:** Technion-Israel Institute of Technology, D.Sc. (1995); Tianjin University, China, M.Sc. (1990). **Personal Information:** Married to Qing Qi in 1992. One child: William R. Mr. Liu enjoys travel, reading and listening to music.

Tiffany Olney

Application Analyst
American Microsystems Inc
2300 West Buckskin Road
Pocatello, ID 83201-2798
(208) 234-6029
Fax: (208) 234-6795
tolney@poci.amis.com

3674

Business Information: As Application Analyst for American Microsystems Inc., Ms. Olney specializes in applications for the Oracle Financial program. Acting as a liaison between software users and the developers of financial systems as well as the project leader of such programs, Ms. Olney demonstrates her superior communication skills and leadership initiative. Looking to start up an independent consulting firm and eventually progressing into a management position with American Microsystems Inc., Ms. Olney is leading the software industry to new levels of achievement and record success. A savvy, three year technology professional, her success is attributed to her academics, a combination of her accounting and technology degrees. A private company headquartered in San Diego, California, American Microsystems Inc. specializes in the manufacture and production of semiconductors. Providing service internationally to their very extensive client base of major corporations and independent customers, the Corporation employs over 1,600 personnel to meet the demand of their product. **Career Highlights:** American Microsystems Inc: Application Anlayst (1999-Present), Financial Analyst (1997-99); Financial Systems Assistant, Idaho State University Financial Services (1995-97). **Associations & Accomplishments:** Institute of Management Accountants. **Education:** Idaho State University: M.B.A. (1997), B.B.A. **Personal Information:** Ms. Olney enjoys photography, crafts and hiking.

Kenneth W. Pearson

Firmware Architect and Developer
Zilog
1303 Roadrunner Drive
Cedar Park, TX 78613
(512) 838-1418
Fax: (512) 249-1952
kpearson@austin.rr.com

3674

Business Information: Demonstrating his excellent skills in computer technology, Mr. Pearson serves as a Firmware Architect and Developer with Zilog at the Cedar Park, Texas location. Extensively involved in the design and architecture of individual computer chips, he is committed to the design and development of specialized techonologies. Utilizing his experience in the computer field, Mr. Pearson implements his acquired knowledge in order to produce a more complex and efficient product. Continuing his growth with Zilog, he remains dedicated to the Company's further expansion and growth in computer technology. His future endeavors doing the same type of work in a different industry, such as the biomedical field. Specializing in the design and distribution of computer components, Zilog was established in 1989. Specifically providing advanced RISC 6000 servers, the Company focuses on implementing new technologies in order to produce a more expansive and efficient product line. Headquartered in California, the Company extends its excellent sales and services to an international client base. Employing 4,000 expert computer techinicians and designers at their Texas facility, the Company remains focused towards supplying thier numerous consumers with specialized computer parts and services. **Career Highlights:** Firmware Architect and Developer, Ziglog (2000-Present); IBM: Firmware Developer (1998-00), Firmware Team Lead/Developer (1993-98), RISC 6000 Test Lead (1989-93). **Associations & Accomplishments:** Tau Beta Pi Association; Eta Kappa Nu Association. **Education:** University of Kentucky, B.S. in Electrical Engineering (1989). **Personal Information:** Married to Betty Schuyler in 1996. Mr. Pearson enjoys rock climbing, mountain biking and photography.

Thomas L. Petroski

Software Engineer
Motorola
566 Clark School Road
De Soto, IL 62924-3461
petnuc@yahoo.com

3674

Business Information: Highly regarded in the wireless sector of the technology field, Mr. Petroski serves as Software Engineer. He is responsible for software development and testing programs. He joined Motorola in 1999 after serving six years in United States Navy as a Nuclear Reactor Operator. Tested and proven, he now oversees testing programs that simulate the hand-over process and code injections. Utilizing the advantages he learned in the military, Mr. Petroski is a team player with solid work ethics and who has the ability to aggressively take on challenges and responsibilities and deliver results. His future goals are to get into a stable environment, own a home, and work toward to management position within the Corporation. Success is attributed to a supportive family and his upbringing and ethics instilled in him by his parents. Founded in the 1930s, Motorola is the world's leader in analog cellular phone sales. The Corporation is divided into seven sectors: automotive, energy and components, cellular networks and space, cellular subscriber, land mobile products, motorola computer group, messaging, information and media, and semiconductor. The Corporation offers a myriad of consumer and infrastructure communications products. Also, the Corporation provides semiconductors including the Power PC microprocessor used in cars and consumer electronics. Other products include computers, electronic components and systems, lighting, navagation, modems, and routers. **Career Highlights:** Software Engineer, Motorola (1999-Present); Nuclear Reactor Operator, United States Navy (1991-97). **Associations & Accomplishments:** Association of Computing Machinery. **Education:** Sothern Illinois University, B.S. (In Progress). **Personal Information:** Married to Cheri in 1992. Mr. Petroski enjoys reading.

Richard J. Sachen, Jr.

Senior Production Supervisor
KLA-Tencor
160 Rio Robles
San Jose, CA 95134
(408) 875-5737
Fax: (408) 875-6511
rsachen@netscape.net

3674

Business Information: Mr. Sachen functions in the capacity of Senior Production Supervisor for KLA-Tencor. He is responsible for managing a multidisciplinary team in the production of data computers and performance of PCBA repair and testing. Before joining KLA-Tencor, Mr. Sachen served as both Master Scheduler and Planner for Varian Associates. In his present role, he coordinates all resources and schedules for the production process. He also trains employees in the department and provides technical support and problem resolution when required. Mr. Sachen has been recognized for his achievements that includes the implementation of DFT, a production marketing tool. A seven year veteran, he hopes to move into a managerial or executive position in the future, acquiring greater responsibilities. Preparation and education and his leadership ability to produce results and take on new challenges have contributed to Mr. Sachen's career successes. KLA-Tencor manufactures semiconductor equipment. Providing services since 1972, approximately 4,000 people are currently employed to assist in various duties. After recently merging together, KLA and Tencor has become the largest manfacturer of semiconductor equipment. Presently, KLA-Tencor generates annual revenues in excess of $800 million. **Career Highlights:** Senior Production Supervisor, KLA-Tencor (1996-Present); Master Scheduler, KLA Instruments (1995-96); Varian Associates: Master Scheduler (1994-95), Planner (1991-94). **Associations & Accomplishments:** American Management Association; National Association of Purchasing Management. **Education:** Santa Clara University, M.B.A. (1995); Cal Poly at San Luis Obispo, B.S. in Construction Management (1987); Certified in Production and Inventory Management by APIC. **Personal Information:** Married. One child.

Dane C. Scott

Chief Engineer
Emcore
394 Elizabeth Avenue
Somerset, NJ 08873
(732) 271-9090
Fax: (732) 271-9686
dane@emcore.com

3674

Business Information: Extensive experiences as Engineering Program Manager, Internal Engineering Consultant, and Vice President of Engineering for several major technology companies have laid the foundation for Mr. Scott's current position with Emcore. At the present time, he fulfills the responsibilities of Chief Engineer. In his role, he oversees all aspects of design and manufacture of state-of-the-art robotic automation systems. Using raw technical engineering skills, Mr. Scott also performs design work on Flare Craft and is concurrently Vice President of a small start-up company. An accomplished authority in the field, he presently holds four patents on design of liquid delivery systems with two pending approval. He is listed in Stratmore's famous WHO's WHO. Attributing his success to being in the right place at the right, Mr. Scott's long-range strategies are to apply more automation technology. Founded in 1984, Emcore manufactures equipment and operates foundries for the growth of epitaxy layers for III-V semiconductors (MOCVD) as well as growing layers on wafers for the III-V market. Products include high-bright LED lasers, chips for high-end mobile phones, solar cells for satellites, and wafers for General Motor's crankshafts. Headquartered in New Jersey, the Company operates a network of branch offices in Europe, Japan, Taiwan, and Singapore. Presently, Emcore is manned by a staff of 300 employees generating in excess of $60 million in annual revenues. **Career Highlights:** Chief Engineer, Emcore (1994-Present); Engineer Program Manager, Assembly Technologies (1989-94); Internal Engineering Consultant, Qualcorp Division Penn-Central (1987-89); Vice President of Engineering, Forox Corporation (1985-87). **Associations & Accomplishments:** American Vacuum Society; SEMI; Patents: two Semiconductor Liquid Delivery Systems patents and one pending patent, two Semiconductor Silver-Glass Paste Applicator patents, one pending Modular EPI flow flange patent. **Education:** University of Pennsylvania, M.S. in Mechanical Engineering (1968); Northwestern University, Certificate in Industrial Radiography; Kodak, Certificate in Industrial Radiography. **Personal Information:** Married to Jeri in 1967. Two children: Heather and Hillary. Mr. Scott enjoys sailing.

Mike Spence

Program Manager
Texas Instruments
P.O. Box 660199
Dallas, TX 75266-0199
(214) 480-2856
Fax: (214) 480-2611
m-spence@ti.com

3674

Business Information: Serving as a Program Manager for Texas Instruments since 1996, Mr. Spence oversees hardware and software development, manages the departmental budget, and manages the Company's micro-chip improvement teams. Beginning his professional career with Texas Instruments as the Marketing Manager in 1993, Mr. Spence has rapidly ascended through the Company's hierarchy, and he is viewed as a key factor in the success of the department and its consistently high productivity rate. Possessing superior talents and an excellent understanding of his field, he is accountable for quality assurance and diagnostic tests to ensure that each digital sound processor properly converts sounds and light into corresponding digital signals. By continually developing strategies to remain on top of the ever-changing world of digital processing, Mr. Spence is leading Texas Instruments to new levels of prosperity and growth. He attributes his occupational success to strong work ethics and his faith in God. Established in 1935, Texas Instruments is a world leader, designer, and manufacturer of digital signal processors for programmable devices such as VCRs, camcorders, cellular phones, and automotive equipment. Based in Dallas, Texas, Texas Instruments employs over 20,000 highly trained professionals who are instrumental in generating the Company's successively high annual revenues. The Company continues to remain a worldwide leader in the technology market and is perpetually in motion to be one step ahead of the worlds future digital needs. **Career Highlights:** Texas Instruments: Program Manager (1996-Present), Marketing Manager (1993-96); Principle, Adamson Consulting (1991-93). **Associations & Accomplishments:** Fellowship Bible Church. **Education:** University of North Texas, M.B.A. (1984); Texas Christian University. **Personal Information:** Married to Helen in 1979. Mr. Spence enjoys reading and racing.

David L. Standley, Ph.D.

Technical Lead Designer
Biomophic VLSI
563 Hampshire Road, Apartment 165G
Thousand Oaks, CA 91361-2204
(805) 497-9055

3674

Business Information: Serving as Technical Lead Designer for Biomorphic VLSI, Dr. Standley is charged with guiding research and development. He handles the VLSI design conception phase, providing valuable insight on current manufacturing and development needs. Dr. Standley specializes in analog design and product mask geometry, illustrating his technical background and expanded hands on experience. His career highlights include starting Biomorphic VLSI and contributing to the success of Rockwell's Science Center. Enjoying the challenges of the technical world, Dr. Standley has established himself as a productive supervisor by demonstrating innovative and creative design methods, in addition to superior communication skills. His key to success is having a balanced work and social life as well as being open-minded to new methodologies. Biomorphic VLSI researches, developes, and manufactures circuits that are utilized in many technical and industrial capacities. The Company produces CMOS integrated circuits for image sensing in commercial products such as digital cameras and video camcorders. Established in 1997, this international business has grown to employ over 30 employees, who will generate a projected multimillion annual revenue. Currently expanding its operational capacity, Biomorphic VLSI is beginning construction to accomodate its increasing manufacturing and shipping demands. **Career Highlights:** Technical Lead Designer, Biomorphic VLSI (1997-Present); Member of Technical Staff, Rockwell International Science

Center (1991-97). **Associations & Accomplishments:** Institute of Electrical and Electronics Engineers. **Education:** Massachusetts Institute of Technology: Ph.D. in Electrical Engineering (1991), M.S. (1986); Rensselaer Polytechnic Institute (1984).

Sunyo L. Suhaimi

Director, IT Infrastructure
Integrated Device Technology, Inc.
2975 Stender Way, M/S C4-40
Santa Clara, CA 95054
(408) 492-8417
Fax: (408) 492-8629
sunyo.suhaimi@idt.com

3674

Business Information: Maintaining a position as one of the leading business professionals in the information technology industry, Mr. Suhaimi serves as Director of IT Infrastructure at Integrated Device Technology, Inc. Highly educated and qualified for his current role, Mr. Suhaimi oversees the worldwide IT infrastructure. Currently focusing his talents on the IT infrastructure aspects of Company operations, he is developing strategy to establish a "no down-time" policy. Attributing his success to remaining on the cutting-edge of the industry knowledge, Mr. Suhaimi dedicates his personal time to reading and researching the field to find the newest innovations available. Engaging in semiconductor manufacturing, Integrated Device Technology, Inc. operates from many locations worldwide, creating the opportunity to work with new industrial developments from two very diverse markets. Headquartered in Santa Clara, California, the Company is in its 21st year of operation and reports annual revenues in excess of $700 million. Having expanded to encompass an international client base, the Company employs a staff of 4,800 to meet the demands of its superior services. **Career Highlights:** Director, IT Infrastructure, Integrated Device Technology, Inc. (1998-Present); Manager, WebTV Networks (1997-98); Self Employed Consultant (1993-98). **Education:** University of California at Santa Cruz, B.A. (1989). **Personal Information:** Married to Caroline Wiboub in 1996. Two children: Joceline Claudia and Joshua Christopher. Mr. Suhaimi enjoys photography.

Sebastian Thalanany

Lead Software Engineer/Wireless Network Architect
Motorola
1506 Quaker Hollow Court North
Buffalo Grove, IL 60089
(847) 435-9296
sebastn@attglobal.net

3674

Business Information: As a Lead Software Engineer and Wireless Network Architect for Motorola, Mr. Thalanany serves the Corporation in a number of different capacities. He is a computer engineer and software developer dealing with cellular infrastructure, design software, network architecture, and wireless Internet access. The high points of Mr. Thanlanany's career have been numerous and include developing patents for phone unit subscribers, reducing overhead on the technical side, researching avenues to be more effective, leading technical teams, and making presentations at seminars. Mr. Thanlanany attributes his success to his ability to analyze a problem and take an analytical approach to problem solving. Developing new applications and techniques serves as his future endeavors. Established in 1928, Motorola engages in wireless networks. The Corporatio deals with infrastructure, subscribers, microprocesses, semiconductors, government electronics, satelite communications, and multimedia business. Employing a global work force of over 150,000 personnel, the Corporation reports annual revenues in excess of $30 billion. **Career Highlights:** Motorola: Lead Software Engineer/Wireless Network Architect (1997-Present), Lead Software Engineer (1995-97), Senior Software Engineer (1992-95). **Associations & Accomplishments:** Institute of Electrical and Electronics Engineers. **Education:** Oklahoma State University, M.S. in Electrical Engineering (1985); Arizona State University. **Personal Information:** Married to Rosemary in 1981. Two children: Kevin and Elizabeth. Mr. Thalanany enjoys photography, soccer and travel.

Sekar Udayamurthy

Senior Technical Analyst
Texas Instruments
6606 Maple Shade Lane, #19F
Dallas, TX 75252
(972) 917-2654
sudayamurthy@ti.com

3674

Business Information: Functioning in the capacity of Senior Technical Analyst with Texas Instruments, Mr. Udayamurthy evaluates and implements state-of-the-art business solutions. Performing market analysis and public interest observation, he designs and deploys the most effective product development and marketing strategies for the best financial return. Before joining Texas Instrument in 1998, Mr. Udayamurthy served as Systems Analyst for both Nucleus Software Inc. and Rane Brake Linings. As an experienced, nine year technology professional, he provides strategic direction to ERP vendors concerning Company products and services. Directing and participating in the analysis, design, implementation, configuration, maintenance, support, and tracking of operating systems, database software, client server utility programs, software, and hardware also fall within the purview of Mr. Udayamurthy's functions. His success reflects his ability to think out-of-the-box and take on new challenges. Growing with Texas Instruments, helping to take the Company to the next level, and moving up the corporate hierarchy serves as his future endeavors. Texas Instruments is a designer and manufacturer of electronic chips for digital products and educational and productivity solutions. International in scope, the Company employs a work force of more than 500 professional, technical, and administrative support people. Presently, Texas Instruments reports estimated annual revenues in excess of $500 million. **Career Highlights:** Senior Technical Analyst, Texas Instruments (1998-Present); Systems Analyst, Nucleus Software Inc. (1995-96); Systems Analyst, Rane Brake Linings (1990-95). **Education:** Birla Institute of Technology and Science at Pilani, B.S. in Information Systems (1996); University of Madras, B.S. in Chemistry; National Computing Centre, Diploma in Computer Studies; Annamalai University, diploma in System Analysis and Data Processing. **Personal Information:** Married to Shashi Rekha Sekar in 1992. Two children: Rishabh and Karthik. Mr. Udayamurthy enjoys tennis and listening to music.

Camilo E. Villamil

Business Development Manager
Motorola
5900 North Andrews Avenue, Suite 500
Fort Lauderdale, FL 33309-2370
(954) 489-2103
Fax: (703) 991-5529
camilo.villamil@motorola.com

3674

Business Information: As Business Development Manager of the Latino Branch of Motorola, Mr. Villamil handles a multitude of responsibilities within the corporate structure. Demonstrating an extensive knowledge of the field gained through education and practical work experience, he leads his staff through the completion of daily activities with a proactive management style. Incorporating staff feedback and input into the development of strategic business development, Mr. Villamil is able to formulate innovative campaigns to aid the markets of Peru, Venezula, Mexico, and Columbia. Recognized for his creative problem solving approach, Mr. Villamil is credited with the successful integration of several different procedures and policies that have contributed to the overall effectiveness of the Company in the global market. Motorola is a global leader in the manufacture of consumer and commercial cellular, computer, pager, and other related telecommunications equipment. The Company also manufactures wireless communications and and technical quality standards for cellular products and services. Established in 1920, the Company currently employs 150,000 people throughout the world. Recent reports estimate annual revenues to exceed $30 billion; the Company's reputation of quality standards in products and applications continues to add to this figure. **Career Highlights:** Motorola: Business Development Manager (1999-Present), Program Manager (1998-99), Systems Engineer (1996-98). **Associations & Accomplishments:** PM Institute. **Education:** University of Miami, M.B.A. (In Progress); Univesidad Santo Tomas, degree in Electronic Engineering. **Personal Information:** Married to Liliana Hurtado in 1998. Mr. Villamil enjoys sports.

Hong Wang, Ph.D.

Section Manager
Siliconix, Inc.
2201 Laurelwood Road
Santa Clara, CA 95054
(408) 567-8115
Fax: (408) 567-8941
hongwang@iname.com

3674

Business Information: Serving as Section Manager for Siliconix, Inc., Dr. Wang supervises process integration for old and new products. He is responsible for research and development, support, marketing, and process modification of new product enhancements. Before joining Siliconix in 1995, Dr. Wang served as a Research Assistant with Brookhaven National Laboratory. Always alert to new opportunities, techniques, and apporaches, he plans to continue with the Corporation hoping obtain further promotion and new challenges. Dr. Wang attributes his professional success to his dedication and ability to solve complex problems in research and development projects. Siliconix, Inc. provides research and development, process modification, manufacture, and support of semiconductor fabrication. Employing 1,700 people, the Corporation was established in 1963 and reports estimated annual sales of $350 million. The Santa Clara, California location is a Class 1, six inch wafer fab facility. Patents are held by the Corporation for products such as Power ICs, analog switches, multiplexers, and Power MOSFETs, all of which route analog signals in video and multimedia systems such as cell phones and computers. The Corporation is traded on NASDAQ. **Career Highlights:** Section Head, Siliconix, Inc. (1995-Present); Research Associate, Brookhaven National Lab (1993-95). **Associations & Accomplishments:** Institute of Electrical and Electronics Engineers. **Education:** Florida Atlantic University, Ph.D. (1993). **Personal Information:** Married to Yan Liu in 1983. One child: Paul X. Dr. Wang enjoys music and ping pong.

Teresa M. Hope

Product Specialist
Lemo USA, Inc.
335 Tesconi Circle
Santa Rosa, CA 95401
(707) 578-8811
Fax: (707) 578-0869

3678

Business Information: Functioning in the role of Product Specialist for Lemo USA, Inc., Ms. Hope deals directly with Corporation clients to design customized connectors to fit their machines. She fields calls from primarily engineers and designs connectors from their specifications or sends a Corporation representative to the client site to obtain the correct specifications needed to complete the design. Before joining Lemo USA, Ms. Hope distinguishly served as an Aviation Machinist Mate with the United States Navy. She has achieved substantial success in her field and plans to eventually expand her responsibilities by working with fiber optic connectors and cameras. Ms. Hope's success is attributed to her ability to produce results and aggressively tackle new challenges. Headquartered in Ceubles, Switzerland, Lemo USA, Inc. is an international manufacturer and distributor of electronic connectors such as quick-connect, DIS-connect, and circular connectors. The Corporation distributes its connectors to original equipment manufacturers in the medical, aviation, and oil industries as well as the military. Founded in 1946, 60 skilled staff members are employed in the Santa Rosa, California plant operations. **Career Highlights:** Lemo USA, Inc.: Product Specialist (1993-Present), Shipping Clerk (1991-93); Aviation Machinist Mate, United States Navy (1985-97). **Associations & Accomplishments:** American Legion, Post 21; American Legion Auxiliary Unit 21; Inducted into the Baseball Junior College of Fame (1998). **Education:** Santa Rosa Junior College, Business Management Certificate Program (In Progress); A.S. (1983). **Personal Information:** Ms. Hope enjoys baseball, softball, Tai Chi, the Church retreat program and is an avid fan of the New York Giants.

Hans Burg

Electronic Data Processing and Information Technology Manager
ALPS Electric Europa GmbH
Hansaallee 203
Duesseldorf NRW, Germany 40549
+49 21159770
Fax: +49 2115977146
hans.burg@alps-europe.com

3679

Business Information: Mr. Burg functions in the dual role of Electronic Data Processing and Information Technology Manager of ALPS Electric Europa GmbH. He is responsible for determining the overall strategic direction and business contribution of the information systems function. A smart, nine year professional in the technology field, Mr. Burg tackles all data processing and networking environment issues that may arise on a day-to-day basis. He has faithfully served with ALPS Electric Europe since coming on board to the Company as a Sales Engineer in 1990. Mr. Burg, looking to the next millennium, plans on implementing advanced technology within the Company. In this context, his goals include providing the Company the capability to make orders on the Internet as well as move the forward in the e-commerce realm. His success reflects his ability to think outside the box, deliver results, and aggressively take on new challenges and responsibilities. ALPS Electric Europa GmbH is a Japanese company which sells its products around the world. Established in 1979, the Company has developed subsidiaries throughout the globe. The Company designs passive components, switches, encoders, and computer accessories that are manufactured at locations throughout Europe. The Company is also involved in the exploration and development of digital television technology and high frequency products. **Career Highlights:** ALPS Electric Europa GmbH: Electronic Data Processing and Information Technology Manager (1998-Present), Sales Engineer (1990-98). **Personal Information:** Married in 1990. One child: Thomas. Mr. Burg enjoys Web design and travel.

Gary A. Cobb

Program Office Manager
Corning Inc.
310 North College Road
Wilmington, NC 28405
(910) 395-7353
Fax: (910) 395-7255
cobbga@corning.com

3679

Business Information: Mr. Cobb joined the Corning Inc. team in 1985. A loyal team player, he currently serves as Program Office Manager. Mr. Cobb is responsible for the oversight and execution of an IT "Renewal" strategy designed to create a more responsive and cost effective IT organization that is tightly linked to the business. His responsibilities include working with key business leaders to confirm strategic business requirements; development of the business case and financial justification for Renewal projects; facilitation of an IT leadership team through the development and deployment of an overall IT architecture; dissemination of project management methodology best practices; and management of the Renewal Program Office for oversight of the IT project portfolio that will construct the final IT architecture. Phase 1 of the $20 million deployment plan is currently in progress with good results and strong customer particiapation. Prototyping for phase 2 efforts is also underway. In addition to the technical deployment, this effort is also implementing for the first time legacy application outsourcing, a comprehensive IT metrics program based on the Balanced Scorecard approach, and use of the Software Engineering Institute (SEI) Capability Maturity Model (CMM). Mr. Cobb aspires to become Chief Information Officer. A Fortune 500 company, Corning Inc. is known worldwide as a technology leader in glass, ceramics, optics, and photonics. Headquartered in New York, Corning Inc. employs a work force of 20,000 people. Established in the 1840s, the Corporation generates $5 billion in annual revenue. **Career Highlights:** Corning Inc.: Program Office Manager (1998-Present), Systems Engineering Supervisor (1991-98), Project Leader (1994-96), Senior Project Engineer (1990-91), Digital Control Engineer (1985-90). **Associations & Accomplishments:** American Management Association. **Education:** University of North Carolina, M.B.A. (1991); Clemson University, B.S. in Computer Engineering (1985). **Personal Information:** Married to Marla in 1988. Two children: Stephanie and Brittany. Mr. Cobb enjoys boating.

Jeremy B. Coullard

Information Technology Manager
Barco, Inc.
30 South Satellite Road
South Windsor, CT 06074
(860) 291-7043
Fax: (860) 291-7001
chad.coullard@barco.com

3679

Business Information: Mr. Coullard serves as Information Technology Manager of Barco, Inc. He is responsible for engineering, acquiring, installing, and maintaining all necessary hardware and software. Mr. Coullard has in excess of 30 years of hands-on experience, giving him complete knowledge of midrange computers, network managment, applications programming, and voice communications. An accomplished professional, he worked on the first computerized typesetting system and several highly successful ERP implementations. Remaining in the field and changing with technology, Mr. Coullard attributes his success to his ability to "cut to the chase" and look at things from a different angle. He plans to lead his staff into the new millennium designing and implementing the newest technology, then distributing it to the global market. Barco, Inc. is a Belgium-based company that manufactures satellite communications electronics, electronics tooling systems, projection systems, and printer systems for graphic arts applications. The Corporation was founded in 1932, building its ranks to over 2,000 highly motivated personnel. The Corporation has provided the international market with the technology that made today's information superhighway possible. **Career Highlights:** Information Technology Manager, Barco, Inc. (1998-Present); Gerber Scientific, Inc.: Special Projects Coordinator (1990-98), Management Information Systems (1986-90), Database and Technical Support Manager (1979-86). **Associations & Accomplishments:** Association of Computing Machinery. **Education:** Nichols College, M.B.A. (1986); Syracuse University, B.S. in Mathematics (1969). **Personal Information:** Mr. Coullard enjoys golf and bowling.

Leigh C. Dubnicka

Change Analyst
Philips Medical Systems
710 Bridgeport Avenue
Shelton, CT 06484
(203) 926-7192
Fax: (203) 929-6099

3679

Business Information: Serving as the Change Analyst for Philips Medical Systems, Mrs. Dubnicka assumes the responsibility for a wide range of duties within the Company. She presides over the general operations of the Shelton, Connecticut location and provides third level helpdesk support. As a 10 year technology professional, Mrs. Dubnicka has faithfully served with Philips Medical Systems in a variety of roles since coming on board to the Company as Logistics Supervisor in 1995. In charge of the mainframe and SAP change management at Philips Medical, she coordinates the mainframe schedules and time lines. Citing her people skills as the reason for her success, Mrs. Dubnicka reads trade magazines to keep her on the cutting edge of technology. She is continually striving to improve performance and would like to expand her helpdesk management duties. Philips Medical Systems specializes in the manufacture and distribution of medical imaging equipment for the healthcare industries. The Company also provides the clientele with equipment servicing after the sale. A subsidiary of the Dutch owned Philips Electronics, United States operations employ more than 1,600 qualified personnel members. **Career Highlights:** Philips Medical Systems: Change Analyst (1998-Present), Logistics Supervisor (1995-98); Helpdesk Manager, Ann Taylor Inc. (1989-95). **Associations & Accomplishments:** Image of Excellence Award (1996). **Education:** Rodger Williams College (1985-89). **Personal Information:** Married to Paul in 1994. One child: Mara. Mrs. Dubnicka enjoys gardening, oil painting, travel and spending time with her family.

Jon M. Hilton, Jr.

Manager of Information Technology
Vishay-Sprague
678 Main Street
Sanford, ME 04073
(207) 490-7285
Fax: (207) 490-7241
jon@hilton.org

3679

Business Information: Functioning in the capacity of Manager of Information Technology with Vishay-Sprague, Mr. Hilton is responsible for all data processing functions and assets. Before coming on board to Vishay-Sprague, he served as Network Administrator for Shawnee Mission Schools. His background also included a stint as Operations Manager with B.I.D. Financial. In his present role, he monitors Internet activities and wide and local area networks for three geographically separated sites. A systems expert Mr. Hilton began his career following four years of distinguished service as an Intelligence Analyst in the United States Army. He is dedicated to facilitating technology to meet the manufacturing needs of the Company. He attributes his substantial success to recognizing trends and staying on top of his field by reading and attending seminars. Mr. Hilton looks forward to supporting global operations by facilitating voice over frame relays on wide area networks. Founded in 1926, Vishay-Sprague is engaged in the manufacture of electronic components. Specializing in tantulum compassitors, the Company's products are used in cellular phones, lap top computers, and more. Employing more than 800 individuals, the Company reports an estimated annual revenue of $200 million. **Career Highlights:** Manager of Information Technology, Vishay-Sprague (1997-Present); Network Administrator, Shawnee Mission Schools (1995-97); Operations Manager, B.I.D. Financial (1993-95); Intelligence Analyst, United States Army (1989-93). **Education:** Regents College, B.S. in Sociology (1993). **Personal Information:** Mr. Hilton enjoys flying, travel and reading.

Rick Kilbashian

Director of Management Information Systems
Fishman Transducers
340-D Fordham Road
Wilmington, MA 01887
(978) 988-9199
Fax: (978) 988-0770
skillet@fishman.com

3679

Business Information: Recruited to Fishman Transducers in 1989, Mr. Kilbashian currently fulfills the responsibilities of Director of Management Information Systems. He presides over all aspects of the Corporation, from product manufacturing to the accounting department. Directly supervising three staff members at headquarters and one staff member at the factory site, he implements system and user training, LAN maintenance, and software and hardware updates. Mr. Kilbashian's ability to come up with solutions in new information technology has contributed greatly to his professional success. Fishman Transducers is currently pursuing several acquisitions within the industry and Mr. Kilbashian will assume responsibility for constructing the WAN that will connect the various sites. He is committed to providing quality performance and looks forward to a future position as Vice President. Privately held, Fishman Transducers manufactures and distributes high end electronics for the music industry. Established in 1979, the Corporation has grown from 12 employees to a strong work force of 170 individuals and is considered to be one of the global leaders in music accessories. Currently, Fishman reports annual sales in excess of $8 million. **Career Highlights:** Director of Management Information Systems, Fishman Transducers (1989-Present). **Associations & Accomplishments:** Network Users International. **Education:** Netware Certified Novell Administrator; Microsoft Certified Systems Engineer. **Personal Information:** Married to Maria in 1985. Two children: Caitlin and Matthew. Mr. Kilbashian enjoys biking, camping and music.

David J. McFarlin

Director of Operations
Barco, Inc.
30 South Satellite Road
South Windsor, CT 06074
(860) 291-7010
Fax: (860) 291-7001
dave.mcfarlin@barco.co

3679

Business Information: Mr. McFarlin has served with Barco, Inc. in various positions since 1993. At the present time, he fulfills the responsibilities of Director of Operations. In that capacity, he oversees all aspects of operations, manufacturing, material control, and quality assurance. Additionally, he is responsible for purchases and facilities as well as filling the position of ISO 9001 management representative. Always wanting to be in technology, Mr. McFarlin uses the Internet to keep pace with new technology. Becoming the Vice President of Operations serves as his long-term goal. Barco, Inc. is a world leader in laser imaging systems design and manufacturing. The Company's focus is on supporting printed circuit board fabrication and the graphic arts industries with laser imaging and CAM and CAD software, capital, and equipment. Employing 150 people, the Company was established in 1970 and reports estimated annual revenues in excess of $35 million. **Career Highlights:** Barco, Inc.: Director of Operations (1997-Present), Director of Marketing (1996-97), Production Manager (1994-95); Materials Manager, PTR Precision Technology (1987-91). **Associations & Accomplishments:** American Production and Inventory Control Society. **Education:** Worcester Polytechnic Institute, B.S. in Industrial Engineering (1983). **Personal Information:** Married to Lynn in 1998. Mr. McFarlin enjoys boating.

Steven M. McGary

Information Technology Manager
Corning Inc. Science Division Products
45 Nagog Park
Acton, MA 01720-3413
(978) 635-2212
Fax: (978) 635-2488
mcgarysm@corning.com

3679

Business Information: Serving as Corning Inc. Science Products Division's Information Technology Manager at the division level, Mr. McGary oversees daily technical operations. Responsible for supply chain organization, he utilizes innovative business plans to create impressive results for challenges on a regular basis. Incorporating employee feedback and input into his productive management style, Mr. McGary effectively motivates his staff to approach responsibilities with a positive attitude. Overseeing the sales and marketing teams, he develops and implements support systems, then provides maintenance and support. Aspiring to a senior level management position within the Corporation, Mr. McGary looks forward to continual career advancement. Corning Inc. is a leader in the technical industry of today's global economy. A provider of various products such as high performance glass, optical fibers, ceramic substrates, and specialized polymers, the Corporation retains ownership of 50 percent or less in 50 affiliated companies in 16 countries. Corning Inc. Science Division Products manufactures life science and biotechnical products; the parent corporation employs over 15,000 people worldwide. **Career Highlights:** Corning Inc. Science Division Products: Information Technology Manager (1999-Present); Information Technology Leader for Supply Chain (1997-99); Information Technology Leader for Samco Location (1995-97). **Associations & Accomplishments:** United States Tennis Association; Kappa Alpha Psi Fraternity; Boston Fellows; National Association for the Advancement of Colored People. **Education:** Howard University, M.B.A. (1992); Chapman

College, B.S. in Computer Information Systems. **Personal Information:** Married to Tonya in 1995. Mr. McGary enjoys tennis and time with family.

Karen Schoenung

Information Technology Manager
Duni Corporation
West 165 North 5830 Ridgewood Drive
Menomonee Falls, WI 53051
(414) 252-7700
Fax: (414) 252-7710
karen.schoenung.@duni.com

3679

Business Information: Dedicated to the success of Duni Corporation, Mrs. Schoenung serves as Information Technology Manager. She has assertively served Duni since joining the Corporation as Accounts Receivable Manager in 1995. As a 13 year technology professional, Mrs. Schoenung fulfills the responsibilities of NT Network Administrator for the Corporation, providing set up and maintenance of the computer system infrastructure. Troubleshooting problems, she maintains a system backup to prevent data loss in the event of an emergency and provides technical support to system users. Coordinating resources, time lines, schedules, and assignments; reviewing technology and expenses; and providing cohesive leadership also fall within the realm of her responsibilities. Continually striving to improve performance, Mrs. Schoenung looks forward to assisting in the completion of future corporate goals. As a division of Duni AB, Duni Corporation is a manufacturer of high-quality, disposable tabletop products. Innovation, atmosphere, and inspiration are key concepts embraced by Duni Corporation for future product development. **Career Highlights:** Duni Corporation: Information Technology Manager (1999-Present), Accounts Receivable (1995-98); Accounts Receivable, Metz Baking Company (1988-95). **Associations & Accomplishments:** Volunteer, Wings for Wishes, Ltd. (A non-profit organization that fulfills the wishes of terminally ill adults for Southeastern Wisconsin at present and hoping to expand as funds are available). **Education:** Waukesha County Technical College, Microsoft Certified System Engineer (In Progress); Milwaukee Area Technical College, Associate's degree in Business Data Processing (1986). **Personal Information:** Married to Philip in 1991. One child: Anthony. Mrs. Schoenung enjoys crafts, computers and motorcycle riding.

Michael W. Sobolewski, Ph.D.

Senior Computer Scientist
GE
1 Research Circle K1 5C 14A
Schenectady, NY 12309
(518) 385-2211

3679

Business Information: Dr. Sobolewski is the Senior Computer Specialist for GE's CRD. He joined the Company in August 1994 and his credited with leading GE's successful CAMnet project, developing tools and methodology to deliver manufacturing and engineering services via the World Wide Web. Expert in the field, Dr. Sobolewski, along with researchers and developers, designs, develops, and implements projects. He also created tools that allowed enablers to build Web-based workbooks and record books. An authority, he has over 70 publications in journals, conferences, and books in the areas of AI, knowledge representation, expert systems, object oriented programming, and concurrent engineering. Clearly establishing goals to achieve a productive, significant impact, Dr. Sobolewski would like to achieve technical excellence and stay informed on technology. An experienced, 28 year technology professional, Dr. Sobolewski credits his success to having a technical background and utilizing his experience in solving difficult problems. Headquartered in Connecticut, GE's CRD assumes the responsibility of providing the research and development for General Electric Company. GE's CRD is engaged in the distribution of cutting services by way of the World Wide Web. **Career Highlights:** Senior Computer Scientist, GE (1994-Present); Senior Technical Manager, Citicorp North America, Inc. (1989-94); Polish Academy of Sciences: Head of Picture Recognition and Processing Department, Head of Expert Systems Laboratory (1976-94). **Associations & Accomplishments:** American Association for Artificial Intelligence; Institute of Electrical and Electronics Engineers; Association of Computing Machinery; I.S.P.E.; Who's Who Registry of Business Leaders (1997-99); GE Managerial Award (1996,1998); International Society for Productivity Leadership Award (1996); Award, Outstanding Service as the Program Chairman for the First, Second, and Third International Conference on Concurrent Engineering (1991-96). **Education:** Computer Science Institute of Computer Science, Polish Academy of Sciences, Ph.D. (1978); Gdansk Technical University, Poland and Leninghrad Electrotechnical Institute, M.S. in Computer Engineering (1971). **Personal Information:** Dr. Sobolewski enjoys lecturing. Also, Dr. Sobolewski has served as a visiting professor, lecturer, and consultant in Sweden, Finland, Italy, Switzerland, Germany, Hungary, Czechslovakia, Poland, Russia, and the United States.

Stephen Wong, Ph.D., P.E.

Chief Architect/Development Director, ICS
Philips Medical Systems
2171 Langings Drive
Mountain View, CA 94043-0837
(650) 426-2506
Fax: (650) 426-2525
swong@lri.ucsf.edu

3679

Business Information: Dr. Wong currently serves as Chief Architect and Development Director for ICS, Philips Medical Systems. He manages product development for medical imaging information technologies and is at the leading edge of advancing technologies in biomedical imaging. Dr. Wong has 18 years of experience in his field and is considered a pioneer in image infomatics. As a faculty member of UCSF and UC Berkeley and a teacher at Stanford University, Dr. Wong has written articles about his research work including more than 150 technical papers and has edited four journals, all of which have been published. He is the author of a published book and holds five patents for his creations. He is currently involved in the development of large-scale biomedical imaging IT projects and wants to be the first to create a digital hospital. Philips Medical Systems, is a core, multi-billion dollar business unit of Philips Electronics, N.V. and has over 100 years of establishment. The Company's local operation in Mountain View, California, employs a staff of 100 people. **Career Highlights:** Chief Architect/Development Director, ICS, Philips Medical Systems (1997-Present); Assistant Professor of Radiology, Neurology, Bioengineering, and Medical Infomatics, University of California at San Francisco (1993-Present); Senior Researcher, MITI - Fifth Generation Computer Project (1991-93); Senior Member of Technical Staff, AT&T Bell Laboratories (1985-87); Head, Factory Automation, AT&T Microelectronics in Asia (1985-87). **Associations & Accomplishments:** Institute of Electrical and Electronics Engineers; American Computing Machinery; Association of American Physicists in Medicine; Healthcare Management Information System Society; Life Science Advisor, Technical Museum of Innovation San Jose; Scientific Review Panels, NIH and NSF. **Education:** Lehigh University: Ph.D. in Computer Sciences (1991), M.Sc. in Computer Sciences (1989); University of Western Australia, Bachelor's degree in Electrical Engineering (1983). **Personal Information:** Married to Sandie Ho in 1991. Two children: Solomon and Gabriella. Dr. Wong enjoys squash, tennis and classical music. He is involved in the PTA, teaches Sunday School, and is studying theology.

Kelvin K. Ho

Sales Manager
YKE International Inc.
45-03 Junction Boulevard
Corona, NY 11368
(718) 699-0707
Fax: (718) 699-2685
kelvinho@yke.com

3695

Business Information: Combining technical sales expertise and management skills, Mr. Ho serves as the Sales Manager for YKE International Inc. He is in charge of the marketing and advertising functions for the Corporation's import and export operations. E-commerce is utilized to a great extent to promote product awareness and increase business. A large number of sales is performed on the Internet through the corporate Web site. Mr. Ho also supervises all aspects of the sales department's telecommunications. Crediting his success to a great opportunity realized, he is currently developing more hubs in an efforts to increase the Corporation's networking capabilities. Founded in 1986, YKE International Inc. is engaged in the manufacture of computer hardware. The Corporation distributes its wide range of multimedia products to wholesale companies around the world. Employing the services of 15 sales personnel members, operations boast approximately $13 million in annual sales. **Career Highlights:** Sales Manager, YKE International Inc. (1997-Present); Sales Executive, Aspect Computer Corporations (1996-97); Central Purchasing, Ramapo College of New Jersey (1994-96); Sales Executive, Met Life Insurance (1993-94). **Associations & Accomplishments:** National Associates of Business Association, New Jersey Chapter (1995-97); National Dean's List (1991-92); Named to Who's Who Executives and Professionals (1999); Named to Who's Who Among Students in American Junior Colleges (1992-93). **Education:** Ramapo College of New Jersey, B.S. (1995); Rockland Community College of the State University of New York, Associate's Degree in Applied Sciences.

Shariff Al Hadad

Engineer
Golden Enterprises
250 Perimeter Center, 4450 West Eau Gallie Boulevard
Melbourne, FL 32936
(407) 259-0854
shariff@jahque.com

3699

Business Information: Mr. Al Hadad functions in the role of Engineer for Golden Enterprises. Involved in the programming and hardware engineering divisions, he utilizes his creative talents to design and produce personalized programs for clients around the world. Specializing in systems integration and configuration, he travels throughout Florida to set up new computer networks into the offices of the leading businesses of the area. In the future, Mr. Al Hadad hopes to become more involved in vertical marketing and assist the Company in keep pace with new computer technology. Golden Enterprises engages in the development of communications equipment. Established in 1974, the Company hosts detailed innovation laboratories where new designs are tested and explored for possible implementation into the industry. The Company turns over $4 million annually and is expecting a boost in its revenue within the next few years due to its research into the voice data field. **Career Highlights:** Engineer, Golden Enterprises (1998-Present); Technical Director, DMC (1997-98); Programmer, Paper Chase Inc. (1994-97). **Education:** Florida Tech, M.S. (1996).

John A. Fee

Fellow
MCI Corporation
2209 Red Oak Lane
Richardson, TX 75082
(972) 729-7503
Fax: (972) 729-6017
john.fee@wcom.com

3699

Business Information: After 19 years of work in the optical fiber cable and networking industry, Mr. Fee helped establish Avanex Corporation, a successful publically traded corporation, in 1998. As Co-Founder, he fulfilled the role of Chief Technology Officer responsible for corporate technology development, Intellectual Property, strategic direction and standards activities, and the Advanced Technology Demonstration Center. Mr. Fee's credentials include previous positions at MCI as Director or Executive Staff Member. He was responsible for MCI's participation in development of the 10, 11, and 12 submarine systems and providing the entire network design for the Avantel Mexico transmission, multiplexer, and digital cross-connect network. For over 10 years, he represented MCI's interest in domestic and global standards forums. Mr. Fee possesses a long-track record of delivering results. His accomplishments include personally being responsible for MCI standards and international acceptance of the Optical Fiber ITU-T Grid Wavelength Channel Plan, pioneering the OC-48/OC-192 SONET systems and networking business, writing the technical specifications and assisting in the implementation of a SONET Voice Switch System, directing the development of LS and next generation optical fiber, founding the MCI Optical Amplifier Systems Business, providing leadership in the Dispersion Compensation area, driving Single Mode Fiber Development for the industry in 1982, starting the Optical Fiber Ground Wire business at MCI, establishing the MCI National OTDR Database, and providing leadership in the study and analysis of fiber nonlinear effects. Mr. Fee, a recognized authority, is credited with authoring over 20 publications in addition to owning the rights to 15 patents. An international optical fiber optical processor company, Avanex Corporation provides solutions for submarines and digital networks. Presently, the Corporation employs a staff of more than 50 professional and technical personnel. **Career Highlights:** Fellow, WCOM, consultant to Richardson-based startup company (Present); Vice President/Chief Technology Officer, Avanex Corporation (1998-Present); Director of Executive Staff, MCI (1987-98); Senior Manager, General Cable (1982-87); Engineer, Corning (1980-82). **Associations & Accomplishments:** Optical Amplifier Conference Committee and Advisory Board; Institute of Electrical and Electronics Engineers; Amateur Radio Operator; OSA; 15 Patents. **Education:** University of Tennessee: M.S. in Industrial Engineering, B.S. in Electrical Engineering. **Personal Information:** Married to Valerie in 1995. Two children: Alex and Jonathon. Mr. Fee enjoys tennis, golf, music, building speakers, real estate and investments.

Darryl W. Gilley

Manager of Business Development
Marconi Services Corporation
557 Mary Esther Cut-Off
Fort Walton Beach, FL 32548
(850) 244-7506
Fax: (850) 244-7590
gilleyd@aol.com

3699

Business Information: As Manager of Business Development for Marconi Services Corporation in Fort Walton Beach, Florida, Mr. Gilley directs and manages business development efforts including marketing and proposals. Mr. Gilley also performs at local public speaking engagements and publishes technical articles through industry journals. Headquartered in Fort Walton Beach, Florida, Marconi Services Corporation is a major technology service company, completing projects around the globe. Concurrently, Mr. Gilley co-owns Suncoast Scientific Inc. of Shalimor, Florida. **Career Highlights:** Manager of Business Development, Marconi Services Corporation (Present); Manager of Business Development, Tracor (1997-Present); Program/Proposal Manager, Manufacturing Technology, Inc. (1994-97); Research Engineer II, ERIM (1990-94); Associate Staff Member, BDM International, Inc. (1988-90); Industrial Engineer GS-12, United States Air Force Civil Service (1984-88). **Associations & Accomplishments:** Association of Old Crows; American Tae Kwon Do Association; American Defense Preparedness Association; United States Naval Institute. **Education:** University of Alabama, B.S. in Chemical Engineering (1982). **Personal Information:** Mr. Gilley enjoys Tae Kwon Do, deep sea fishing, golf and arranging music.

Charles L. Howard

Site Manager
Pulau Electronics Corporation
3655 El Morro Road, Lot A106
Colorado Springs, CO 80910
(719) 579-9232
Fax: (719) 579-9232
clh5240@aol.com

3699

Business Information: Demonstrating a remarkable proficiency in the electronics field, Mr. Howard serves as Site Manager for the Pulau Electronics Corporation's location in Colorado Springs, Colorado. He supervises the overall operation and maintenance of the corporate computer systems, ensuring that the more than 75 systems are functioning properly at all times. Utilizing over 35 years of experience in the performance of his duties, he credits his professional success to his parents and high school teacher, as well as his ability to think outside the box, produce results, and aggressively take on new challenges. Mr. Howard plans to remain with Palau Electronics and continue to upgrade its computer systems. A world renowned electronics corporation, the Pulau Electronics Corporation has been providing quality information technology products for more than 55 years. The Military Division of the Corporation produces computer systems for military war exercises and games for various governments' armed forces. In addition to software, Pulau Electronics manufactures simulators and hardware as well as providing maintenance for its computer systems and equipment. **Career Highlights:** Site Manager, Pulau Electronics Corporation (1997-Present); Owner/President, CLH Enterprises (1990-97); Operations Manager, CPR Electronics (1987-90). **Education:** Foothill College, degree in Electrical Engineering (1964); J. Perry Institute; Yakima Valley College. **Personal Information:** Two children: Christopher and Charles. Mr. Howard enjoys politics, camping and golf.

3700 Transportation Equipment

3711 Motor vehicles and car bodies
3713 Truck and bus bodies
3714 Motor vehicle parts and accessories
3715 Truck trailers
3716 Motor homes
3721 Aircraft
3724 Aircraft engines and engine parts
3728 Aircraft parts and equipment, nec
3731 Ship building and repairing
3732 Boat building and repairing
3743 Railroad equipment
3751 Motorcycles, bicycles, and parts
3761 Guided missiles and space vehicles
3764 Space propulsion units and parts
3769 Space vehicle equipment, nec
3792 Travel trailers and campers
3795 Tanks and tank components
3799 Transportation equipment, nec

Linda Marie Foster Carter

System Analyst/Process Consultant
Ford Motor Company
18849 Middlesex Avenue
Lathrup, MI 48076
(313) 322-9965
lmfcarter@aol.com

3711

Business Information: Mrs. Foster Carter serves as System Analyst and Process Consultant for Ford Motor Company, Lathrup Village, Michigan location. Her responsibilities include various aspects of the maintenance of highly technical operations for a globally recognized company. Demonstrating her extensive knowledge of the industry, Mrs. Foster Carter works closely with clients to identify needs, then implements innovative solutions to improve production and services. Troubleshooting the corporate network, she handles all areas of information technology systems including hardware, software applications, and upgrades. Crediting her parents for the ethics and morals they instilled into her, Mrs. Foster Carter places value on hands-on experience, coupled with the educational process. Keeping her goals consistent with the objectives of the Company, she intends to shift her career focus to front-end analysis. The Ford Motor Company is widely known throughout the manufacturing industry as one of the Big Three, meaning it is one of the top three automobile manufacturers in the world. In 1903, Henry Ford created the first horseless carriage, now known as the automobile. Today, his invention supports a company that has 300,000 global employees and is still headquartered in Detroit, "Motortown" Michigan where Mr. Ford first began his quest into the industry. **Career Highlights:** System Analyst/Process Consultant, Ford Motor Company (1990-Present); System Analyst, Ford Motor Credit (1968). **Associations & Accomplishments:** Alpha Kappa Alpha Sorority, Inc.; The Drifters Inc.; National Association of Parliamentarians. **Education:** Central Michigan University, M.S.A. (1990); Dillard University at New Orleans, B.A. (1968). **Personal Information:** Married to Pierre in 1971. Two children: Pierre Sharif and Reginald Lamar. Mrs. Foster Carter enjoys reading and working with graphic design.

Luis Marcial Hernández González

Project Engineer
General Motors
1140 South Val Vista Drive, Apartment 2029
Mesa, AZ 85204
luismh@cs.unm.edu

3711

Business Information: Utilizing a strong background in engineering and computer science, Mr. Hernández González serves as the Project Engineer for General Motors' Mesa, Arizona location. In his position, he is responsible for the programming of instrumentation for the test automobiles. Moreover, he is charged with exploring all parts of the Corporation, implementing new ideas, and providing support to co-workers. The most rewarding aspect of his career according to Mr. Hernández González has been helping people solve their computer-related problems while in a technical support role. Highly regarded in the industry, he looks forward to continuing to take classes to stay on the cutting edge of technology. Located in Mesa, Arizona, General Motors engages in the design and manufacture of automobiles. Founded in 1899 and serving an international clientele, the Corporation is headquartered in Detroit, Michigan and is one of the world's largest full-line vehicle manufacturers. The Corporation has an abundance of locations worldwide, many contributing subsidiaries, and a staff of hard working employees who are dedicated to providing durable, high quality vehicles. Presently, the Corporation's facility in Mesa is staff by a work force of 1,000 people. **Career Highlights:** Project Engineer, General Motors (2000-Present); System Administrator, University of New Mexico Computer Science Department (1999-00); Software Engineer, General Motors (1999); Computer Lab Manager, University of New Mexico Department of Computer Information Resources Technology (1996-99). **Associations & Accomplishments:** Association of Computing Machinery; National Society of Professional Engineers; Golden Key National Honor Society; American Civil Liberties Union. **Education:** University of New Mexico, B.S. in Computer Science with minor in Mathematics (2000). **Personal Information:** Mr. Hernández González enjoys camping, ballroom dancing and backpacking.

Scott M. Herrmann

Chief Manufacturing Engineer
Edelbrock Corporation
2700 California Street
Torrance, CA 90503
(310) 781-2222 Ext. 2714
Fax: (310) 328-4814
sherrmann@edelbrock.com

3711

Business Information: Mr. Herrmann is Chief Manufacturing Engineer of Edelbrock Corporation. He is responsible for management and oversight of four manufacturing plants. Ranked as the number two person in charge of all corporation manufacturing facilities, Mr. Herrmann supervises and directs over 30 employees in performing day-to-day administration and operational activities. As a 17 year engineering and technology professional with an established track record of delivering results, Mr. Herrmann's career success reflects his extensive knowledge of his field, as well as his ability to take on new challenges and responsibilities. Coordinating resources, schedules, time lines, and assignments also fall within the realm of his functions. Looking toward the next millennium, Mr. Herrmann's future endeavors include eventually attaining the position of Vice President. Edelbrock Corporation engages in the manufacture and distribution of automotive engine components. Established in 1938, the Corporation is international in scope. Presently, Edelbrock Corporation employs a work force of more than 550 people who generate revenues in excess of $100 million annually. **Career Highlights:** Chief Manufacturing Engineer, Edelbrock Corporation (1984-Present). **Associations & Accomplishments:** Society of Mechanical Engineers; Computer and Automated Systems Association. **Education:** El Camino College (1994); Northrop University, B.S. in Airframe and Powerplant (1982). **Personal Information:** Married to Vania in 1995. Mr. Herrmann enjoys racing cars and boats.

Desmond Hunt

Warranty Operations Manager
Habberstad Nissan
17833 134th Avenue
Jamaica, NY 11434-4007
(516) 439-7062

3711

Business Information: Mr. Hunt serves as Warranty Operations Manager of Habberstad Nissan. He is charged with overseeing the warranty department, processing warranty claims, training new employees on the computer system, maintaining and supporting the computer network, and disposing and analyzing reports for all departments. Mr. Hunt's computer expertise enables him to become a vital part of the Company, producing quality reports and upgrading software applications. He plans to stay focused, fulfilling his dream of working for a major corporation as a Network Administrator or Technical Support Coordinator in the near future. Success, according to Mar. Hunt, is due to his commitment to excellence as well as his ability to aggressively tackle new challenges and deliver results. Habberstad Nissan serves as a Nissan distributor, marketing, selling, and maintaining Nissan automobiles. Leading the region in sales and customer satisfaction, this Dealership was established in 1975 and employs 85 people dedicated to excellence. Habberstad Nissan utilized the newest technology to market its products, receive customer input, maintain Company records, and perform product repairs. **Career Highlights:** Warranty Operations Manager, Habberstad Nissan (1986-Present); Network Specialist, Kellman Computing (1998-Present). **Associations & Accomplishments:** Long Island Videographics Association; Hunt Productions; Animator/Videographer; Youth Counselor; Business Manager, Lindennaires Concert Chorale; Computer Concultant, Linden School, New York; Finance Committee, Linden SDA Church. **Education:** Computer Career Center, Network Specialist (1999); Atlantic Union College in South Lancaster: M.A., B.S. in Computer Science (1985), B.S. in Business Administration (1985). **Personal Information:** Married to Brenda in 1989. Two children: Briana and Brian. Mr. Hunt enjoys videography, photography and computer animation.

Michael Stuart Rofe

Senior Project Manager
e-GM
Deer Court, San Ban Kan 302, 1231 Horinouchi
Omiya City, Japan 330-0204
+81 354242687
Fax: +81 486462855
mike.rofe@gol.com

3711

Business Information: As the Senior Project Manager for e-GM, Mr. Rofe is responsible for management of the Company's e-direct strategy. He stays well informed of new technological advances that may be utilized to advance day to day e-business activities. Possessing an excellent understanding of technology, Mr. Rofe also oversees employee productivity, manages the fiscal budget, and presides over the completion of administrative tasks. Highly regarded, he implements policies and procedures that optimizes performance, thus assisting in maximizing the Company's global Internet business. In the future, Mr. Rofe plans to encourage continued Company growth and bring e-GM to its fullest potential in the development of its global e-business activities and business-to-business and business-to-consumer operation. e-GM is a part of General Motors, the world's largest industrial manufacturer of automobiles. Established in 1908, General Motors employs the skilled services of over 680,000 individuals to serve the diverse needs of clientele. Headquartered in Detroit, Michigan, General Motors serves clients internationally, generating annual revenue of more than $200 billion. e-GM is one of the many divisions of General Motors, purposely designed to accelerate the evolution of e-business within the Company. **Career Highlights:** Senior Project Manager, e-GM (2000-Present); Technical Planning Manager, DirecTV Japan (1997-00); Technical Director, Reuters Japan (1994-97); Engineer Broadcast Division, Sony (1981-94). **Associations & Accomplishments:** Society of Motion Pictures & Television Engineers; Royal Television Society; British Kinematographic Sound & Television Society. **Education:** BBC Woodnorton, HND Broadcast Engineering (1979): South Trafford College, OND Technology with Commendation (1977). **Personal Information:** Married to Minako in 1989. Three children: Alex, Andrew, and Julian. Mr. Rofe enjoys motorcycles, paragliding, horseback riding, swimming and ice skating.

Lisa Lenchner Rosenbaum

GMPT
General Motors
4640 Pickering Road
Bloomfield, MI 48301
(248) 857-0342
Fax: (248) 857-6565
lisa.rosenbaum@ogm.com

3711

Business Information: Recently promoted to the position of GMPT at General Motors, Mrs. Rosenbaum oversees all aspects of information technology application databases. Included in her daily schedule are activites such as meetings with senior managmement staff, departmental strategy devleopment, and technical need analysis. Demonstrating an extensive knowledge gained from education and practical work experience, Mrs. Rosenbaum implements hardware and software she feels will contribute to the efficiency of the department. A dedicated employee, she attributes her success to her persistance; she is recognized within the Company as a valuable asset. Currently striving to move up in the corporate structure, Mrs. Rosenbaum aspires to a position that will allow for increased responsibility. Her advice is "Keep digging and learning. Finish what you start and never give up." General Motors specializes in automotive manufacturing, information systems, services, and General Motors power train. **Career Highlights:** General Motors: GMPT (1998-Present), Manager of Information Systems and International Economics Marketing Analysis (1997-98), Research and Development Advanced Technician of Portfolio (1993-96), Research and Development of Biomedical Sciences (1980-93). **Associations & Accomplishments:** American Chemical Society; Project Management Institute; Professional Ski Instructors of America. **Education:** University of Michigan, M.B.A. (1992); Michigan State University, B.S. in Biochemistry (1978). **Personal Information:** Married to Richard A. in 1994. Two children: Jared Scott and Eric Marc. Mrs. Rosenbaum enjoys snow skiing, biking and reading.

Robert Stewen

Information Technology Coordinator
Mercedes-Benz USA, Inc.
7700 Wisconsin Avenue, Suite 1010
Bethesda, MD 20814-3578
(301) 718-3888
Fax: (301) 718-3889
stewen@mbusa.com

3711

Business Information: Joining the Mercedes-Benz USA, Inc.'s Bethesda, Maryland office over nine years ago, Mr. Stewen has held his current position of Information Technology Coordinator for the past five years. In this capacity, he coordinates all activities of the regional helpdesk for three facilities, maintains computer and telephony systems, troubleshoots, and oversees the 26 field laptops. Additionally, Mr. Stewen upgrades hardware, software, and related peripheral equipment. Analyzing and solving systems difficulties also fall within the scope of his responsibilities. Possessing 17 years of business savvy and expertise, he created a system that is utilized by retailers today. Enjoying success in the technology field, Mr. Stewen plans on attaining his M.B.A. which will enable him to capitalize on professsional opportunities. "Mercedes-Benz" is known all over the world as the byword for both tradition and innovation. Mercedes-Benz USA, Inc. is a wholly owned sudsidiary of DaimlerCrysler AG. Headquartered in New Jersey, the Bethesda, Maryland division provides all marketing aspects for the Company. **Career Highlights:** Mercedes-Benz USA, Inc.: Information Technology Coordinator (1995-Present), Senior Programmer/Analyst (1990-95); Senior Programmer/Analyst, Nielsen & Bainbridge (1988-90). **Education:** Ramapo College, B.S. in Computer Science (1983); Stevens Institute of Technology. **Personal Information:** Mr. Stewen enjoys jigsaw puzzles, mountain biking and golf.

Terri W. Anderson

Database Administrator
Breed Technologies
5300 Allan K Breed Highway
Lakeland, FL 33807
(813) 672-3402

3714

Business Information: Serving as Database Administrator of Breed Technologies, Ms. Anderson handles the shipping and supplies financial manufacturing systems. Ms. Anderson directly supervises two staff members, dealing with migration, upgrades, and systems maintenance. Before joining Breed Technologies, Ms. Anderson served as Member of Technical Staff 1 with GTE, Database Engineer for LCC, and Technical Specialist for HFSI. Currently, she is converting the financial manufacturing systems of each of the Corporation's locations to Oracle. Administering and controlling data resources and ensuring data integrity, reliability, and security also fall within the purview of Ms. Anderson's functions. During her time with Breed Technologies, she is proud to have converted its Home Grow system to a financial one. As an experienced, 14 year technology professional, she owns an established track record of producing results in support of business and technical objectives. Ms. Anderson enjoys her work and plans to continue to successfully migrate the Corporation's systems to Oracle. Founded in 1987, Breed Technologies designs, develops, and manufactures full automotive occupant restraint systems and components. Among the top three occupant safety suppliers in the world, the Corporation employs a staff of approximately 16,000 people. The Corporation has experienced dynamic growth in recent years and boasts annual sales of $1.3 billion. **Career Highlights:** Database Administrator, Breed Technologies (Present); Member of Technical Staff 1, GTE (1997-98); Database Engineer, LCC (1994-98); Technical Specialist, HFSI (1985-94). **Associations & Accomplishments:** International Oracle User Group. **Education:** Strayer (Currently Attending).

Richard Bechard

Reliability Technologist
Siemens Canada
118 Burton Avenue
Chatham, Ontario, Canada N7M 4Z5
(519) 436-3894
Fax: (519) 436-3790

3714

Business Information: Serving in the position of Reliability Technologist for Siemens Canada, Mr. Bechard heads the electronic product division and focuses his efforts on research, design, development, and manufacture of pollution control devices. He assumes oversight of all staff members, providing them with guidance and comprehensive direction as they strive to carry out their many responsibilities. Accountable for a variety of duties, Mr. Bechard introduces new materials to incorporate into the development of new products, approves devices, and conducts statistical testing. With over three decades of occupational experience in the industry, Mr. Bechard is viewed as a key factor in the success of the department and its consistently high productivity rate. Highly regarded, he is currently engineering new testing devices, thereby leading the Company to new levels of prosperity and ensuring his personal satisfaction and occupational success. Established in 1993 Siemens Canada, a subsidiary of Siemens Automotive, is a leading manufacturer of vehicular parts for the automotive industry. Currently employing over 150 qualified personnel, the Company estimates millions in annual revenue. Located in Ontario, Canada, the Company exports products worldwide to automotive moguls such as General Motors Corporation. With current plans to expand its facilities and develop new products, Siemens Canada displays a strong commitment to continue its course as a leader in manufacturing products for the automotive industry. **Career Highlights:** Reliability Technologist, Siemens Canada (Present). **Personal Information:** Married to Mary Jane in 1970.

Georg Berner

Head of Information & Communications Innovation Field
Siemens AG
Otto Hahn Ring 6
Munich, Germany 81730
+49 8963648045
Fax: +49 8963640440
georg.berner@mchp.siemens.de

3714

Business Information: Mr. Berner is the Head of Information and Communications Innovation Field. He is responsible for defining and realizing new businesses with high revenues and high profits for the Company. Before joining Siemens as Vice President of Strategic Planning and Mergers and Acquisitions in 1994, he served as in the dual role of Sales Manager and Accounts Manager with Texas Instruments. Mr. Berner's history includes: Chief Financial Officer for FENWIS Corporation, a start up business; author of several books to include "Management Basics" due to be released in the year 2000; and speeches and published articles in magazines on topics such as strategy, marketing, portfolio management, sales, innovations, and I&C future 2025. As a 15 year professional with an established track record of producing results, his success as a leader reflects his ability to deliver products and services to improve living standards and benefit humankind around the world. A global powerhouse in electrical engineering and electronics, Siemens AG engages in research and development by harnessing innovative technologies. The Company currently ranks third in the industry worldwide and has customers in over 190 countries and more than 500 manufacturing locations worldwide. Siemens AG is active in six business segments: Energy, Industry, Information and Communications, Transportation, Healthcare, and Lighting. Presently, Siemens AG reports annual net sales approaching DM 120 billion and employs more than 416,000 people. **Career Highlights:** Head of Information & Communications Innovation Field, Siemens AG (1997-Present); Vice President of Marketing, Siemens Nixdorf IT-Networks (1996-97); Vice President of Planning and M&A, Siemens Group Network Systems (1994-96); Sales Manager/Account Manager, Texas Instruments (1990-93). **Associations & Accomplishments:** Chief Financial Officer, FENWIS Corporation. **Education:** Technical University Munich, Diploma (1984). **Personal Information:** Married to Petra Agnes in 1983. Three children: Patricia, Tobias, and Andreas. Mr. Berner enjoys any keyboards, skiing, tennis and repairing his children's toys.

Luiz Henrique Cauzzo

Information Technology and Purchasing Manager
Filtros Mann, Ltda.
Al Filtros Mann, 555-jd Tropical-cp 210
Indaiatuba, Brazil 13330-970
+55 1938949360
Fax: +55 1938949478
luiz.cauzzo@mannhummel.com.br

3714

Business Information: As Information Technology and Purchasing Manager of Filtro Mann, Ltda., Mr. Cauzzo fulfills a number of functions on behalf of the Company and its clientele. Overseeing product management, he maintains the computer and data processing activities for all projects. Supervising his staff of eight technicians, he is also responsible for nonproductive purchasing and implementation of new technologies in order to produce a more cost efficient product. Committed to the further success of the Company, Mr. Cauzzo remains devoted to quality service and products. His future endeavors include obtaining his M.B.A., completing a joint venture project with Ohio University, and eventually attaining the position of director Specializing in the manufacturing of parts and services in the automotive industry, Filtros Mann, Ltda. was established in 1941. Located in Brazil, the Company is partnered with another located in Germany and branches out to 21 subsidiaries worldwide. Employing over 5,000 machinists, technicians and mechanics, Filtros Mann concentrates its efforts towards providing efficient and quality automotive parts specifically the Mann Filter. Committed to the furthering expansion of its product line, the Company generates over $70 million in annual sales. Continuing its expansion worldwide, Filtros Mann, Ltda. remains focused towards supplying goods and services suited to their clients specific needs. **Career Highlights:** Information Technology and Purchasing Manager, Filtros Mann, Ltda. (1995-Present); Gruro Eucatex: System Manager (1993-94), Private Consultant (1991-92); Information Technology Manager, Gruro D. Paschoal (1987-91). **Associations & Accomplishments:** America's SAP User's Group. **Education:** University of Sao Paulo, Post Graduate degree (1992); DUCCAM, Computer Science degree. **Personal Information:** Married to Denise Correa in 1990. Two children: Felipe Correa and Carolina Correa. Mr. Cauzzo enjoys volleyball, reading and volunteer work.

David W. Cox

Information Systems Manager
Dana Corporation
P.O. Box 750
Fort Wayne, IN 46801
(219) 481-3502
Fax: (219) 481-3403
dave.cox@dana.com

3714

Business Information: As Information Systems Manager for Dana Corporation, Mr. Cox manages the Corporation's LAN network which consists of 60 terminal users, 236 personal computers, and 65 thin clients. In addition, he exercises oversight of data collection, analysis, and storage, as well as barcoding implementations and shop floor systems. Mr. Cox's greatest achievement during his tenure with Dana has been the construction, installation, and implementation of a complete NT network across the shop floor at Dana's Fort Wayne plant, which is the largest facility operated by the Corporation. He plans to keep abreast of technological changes in the industry by reading technical literature and attending workshops and seminars. He also hopes to continue his rise through the management hierarchy. Founded in 1904, Dana Corporation is one of the world's largest, independent suppliers of automotive parts, operating 270 major facilities in 33 countries. The Corporation manufactures and markets a wide variety of automotive equipment, including axles, drive trains, suspension systems, and numerous other components, which are used on more than 95 percent of the world's 650 million motor vehicles. Headquartered in Toledo, Ohio, the Corporation employs around 79,000 professional, technical, and support staff, and posted pro forma sales of $11.9 billion in 1997. **Career Highlights:** Information Systems Manager, Dana Corporation (1995-Present); Senior Programmer/Analyst, Magnavox (1989-95); Manager, Compusystems (1984-89). **Education:** Purdue University, B.S. in Computer Technology (1985). **Personal Information:** Married to Polly in 1987. Three children: Tiffany, Nicole, and David. Mr. Cox enjoys coaching his daughter's baseball team.

Jen Crawford

Systems Administrator
Royal Oak Boring
4800 South Lapeer Road
Lake Orion, MI 48359
(248) 340-9200
Fax: (248) 340-9277
jen.crawford@roi-1.com

3714

Business Information: Ms. Crawford is the Systems Administrator for Royal Oak Boring. Displaying her skills in this highly specialized position, she oversees all aspects of the technical department. She monitors servers, works with research and development to keep abreast on the latest technological developments, and presides over the planning over all new programs and activities within the technical department. Ms. Crawford also maintains and upgrades present systems, supervises employees, as well as offers troubleshooting support. Starting in this position from scratch, she woud like to continue with Royal Oak Boring, gain experience, grow with technology, and obtain her Microsoft Certified Systems Engineer certification. Ms. Crawford's success is attributed to her multitasking abilities and ability to pick up things quickly. Royal Oak Boring began operations in 1981. The Company, located in Lake Orion, Michigan, is engaged in the manufacture of powertrain componets. Serving clients located only in Michigan, products are mainly used for Caterpillar and Detroit Diesel equipments and machines. A workstaff of 250 individuals are employed with Royal Oak Boring in several positions including manufacture, distribution, and product marketing. The Company presently owns and operates out of five locations. **Career Highlights:** Systems Administrator, Royal Oak Boring (1998-Present); Computer Consultant, Central Michigan University (1997-98). **Education:** Cleary College, B.S. (1999); Central Michigan University. **Personal Information:** Ms. Crawford enjoys computer repair, orchestra and musical instrument repair.

Jerry L. Crowl

Network Administrator
Michigan Production Machining, Inc.
21165 Claudette Drive
Macomb, MI 48044
(810) 228-9700
Fax: (810) 228-7347
jcrowl@michpro.com

3714

Business Information: Recruited to Michigan Production Machining, Inc. as Mechanical Engineer in 1997, Mr. Crowl currently serves as the Corporation's Network Administrator. He maintains the networking infrastructure's functionality and operational status as well as peforms system backups and data recovery. A savvy, five year veteran of technology, he oversees a Windows NT network and all mechanical engineering for production part drawings. Interfacing with his customers, he is responsible for monitoring and tuning the network software, peripherals, and equipment and resolving technical difficulties. Designing a $6 million, state-of-the-art machining facility for Colmach, Inc. and taking over the network for Michigan Production Machining is cited as Mr. Crowl's career highlights. In the near future, he hopes to continue with computers and obtain his Microsoft certifications. Michigan Production Machining, Inc. provides high production machining of automotive transmission and drive train components. The Corporation supplies merchandise for the three leading automobile manufacturers around the world and delivers results through its subsidiaries in Michigan, New York, Indiana, and Mexico. **Career Highlights:** Michigan Production Machining, Inc.: Network Administrator (1999-Present), Mechanical Engineer (1997-99); Facility Engineer, Colmach, Inc. (1991-96). **Associations & Accomplishments:** Volunteer Fire Fighter. **Education:** Stark State College, A..A.S. in Mechanical Engineering Technology (1995). **Personal Information:** Married to Joyce in 1985. Three children: Michelle, Shawn, and Aaron. Mr. Crowl enjoys scuba diving.

Angela M. Fisher

Management Information Systems Manager
Lear Corporation
1905 Beard Street
Port Huron, MI 48060
(810) 989-2295
Fax: (810) 987-8085
afisher@lear.com

3714

Business Information: Ms. Fisher serves as Management Information Systems Manager of Lear Corporation, overseeing the daily activities of the Corporation's technical aspects. Recognized for her creative ability to resolve problems, she is responsible for installation, troubleshooting, and maintenance of all hardware and software used throughout the plant. Ms. Fisher, additionally, directs telecommunications to ensure that proper upgrades are being implemented. Utilizing her practical work experience, she is able to effectively coordinate all projects within her department and frequently acts as a liasion between senior management and her staff. Ms. Fisher is credited with the development and successful implementation of the Management Information Systems Department within the Corporation as well as the introduction of the EDI system. Attributing her success to a positive attitude and current education, Ms. Fisher is continually attending seminars and training courses in addition to her personal research. Keeping her goals consistent with the objectives of the Corporation, she currently is working to make the plant technology more user friendly. Lear Coporation is a leading producer of automotive headliners for the majority of the auto industry. Employing nearly 500 people, the Corporation has changed greatly since opening in 1914 when the main focus was the manufacture of automobiles. **Career Highlights:** Management Information Systems Manager, Lear Corporation (1998-Present); United Technologies Automotive: Business System Coordinator (1992-98), Computer Operator (1989-92). **Education:** Baker College, A.A.S. (In Progress); Grand Rapids School of the Bible and Music; Pontiac Business Institute; St. Clair County Community College.

Andrew R. Koluch

User Support Analyst
Federal-Mogul
6565 Wells Avenue
St. Louis, MO 63133
(314) 512-8115
Fax: (314) 512-8130
mcsemo@earthlink.net

3714

Business Information: Writing his first computer program in 1978, Mr. Koluch works on the Federal-Mogul Information and Technology Department Helpdesk. As a Helpdesk Representative, he provides telephone technical support and incident tracking for the Corporation's various business systems including Intel-Based Personal Computers, IBM AS/400, IBM Mainframe, Citrix Winframe, Windows NT, Novell Intranetware, and SAP. Concurrently, he is a Webmaster for the United States Army Reserve's 388th Chemical Company. Mr. Koluch looks forward to registering his own domain and developing and hosting Web pages. Celebrating its 100th birthday this year, Federal-Mogul manufactures parts for the automotive industries. Its products include Champion Spark Plugs, Anco Windshield Wipers, Moog Ball Joints, Fel-Pro, and many others. Known for its manufacturing mastery, Federal-Mogul had sales last year of $4.4 billion. **Career Highlights:** User Support Analyst, Federal Mogul and Cooper Automotive (1997-Present); Webmaster, United States Army Reserves, 388 Chemical Company (1999-Present). **Associations & Accomplishments:** Novell Users International; St. Louis Internet Users Group; Newsletter Publishing Officer, St. Louis Netware Users Group; United States Air Force Communication Electronics Honor Award (1991); United States Army Chemical Corps Regimental Association (1999). **Education:** Rhode Island College, B.S. in Management (1982); Community College of the Air Force, Associates of Applied Science in Electronics Technology (1996); CDI, Career Development Institute Honor Graduate in Computer Technology (1992); Microsoft Certified Professional; Microsoft Certified Systems Engineer; Microsoft Certified Professional Internet; Certified Netware Administrator. **Personal Information:** One child: Emily. Mr. Koluch enjoys travel and meeting new people. NIC Registered Domain name: www.freconomix.com.

Michael J. Lane

Skill Trade Technician
Toyota Motor Manufacturing of Kentucky
1001 Cherry Blossom Way
Georgetown, KY 40324
(502) 868-4388
(502) 868-2000
mlane@mis.net

3714

Business Information: Utilizing more than 20 years of experience in the automotive industry, Mr. Lane serves as the Skill Trade Technician for Toyota Motor Manufacturing of Kentucky. He maintains the systems, troubleshoots problems, and designs improvements for the process equipment and conveyors of the auto manufacturing assembly. Additionally, he performs PLC programming for the process control applications. His background history includes stints as Tool & Die Repair with Norris Industries and Automotive Technician for Morley's Wheel Service. Crediting his success to honesty and dedication, Mr. Lane keeps up to date with technological advancements by reading industry publications and attending classes. He anticipates his promotion to a management position as a result of his continuing efforts to increase his skills through training and professional development activities. Since inception in 1937, Toyota Motor Manufacturing of Kentucky has become an internationally recognized company in the automotive industry. Operations consist of over 6,000 employees in the two major manufacturing plants in Kentucky from which three lines of Toyota vehicles are produced. **Career Highlights:** Toyota Motor Manufacturing of Kentucky: Skill Trade Technician (1999-Present), Maintenance Technician (1988-99); Tool & Die Repair, Norris Industries (1985-88); Automotive Technician, Morley's Wheel Service (1978-85). **Associations & Accomplishments:** Toyota Motors Activities Association. **Education:** Toyota Motors Skilled Trades Program, Graduate (1995); Central Kentucky Technical School, degree in Machine Technology (1988); Garrard County Vocational School, Auto Mechanics Graduate (1978). **Personal Information:** Mr. Lane enjoys car restoration.

Hector Jose Lozano

Consultant
Francisco Benitez 78 Casa 7
San Jeronimo, Mexico 01080
+52 52704715
evangaythor@mexis.com

3714

Business Information: Years of experience and success in the technology field motivated Mr. Lozano to venture out on his own and establish his own business. He currently offers consulting services in an effort to assist other businesses in cutting edge developing information technology. Serving as a Consultant in information technology, Mr. Lozano keeps on top of new developments in order to provide his clientele with the most up-to-date services possible. Possessing strong business savvy and expertise, he helps his clients formulate innovative, short- and long-term strategies to keep them out-front of competitors. He promotes and generates revenue through signing software develpment contracts, implementing new ideas and products, and ensuring all operations comply with set standards. A sharp, 10 year veteran of technology, he aspires to start a new cycle where he can grow. Future plans include becoming recognized as a reputable consultant in the information technology and achieve professional success abroad in the United States and Central America. Proud of his commitment and contributions, Mr. Lozano's reasons for success is attributed to his dedication, his knowledge in information technology, and his continuing research to improve and remain current in the Information Technology Age. **Career Highlights:** Consultant, Self-employed (1989-Present). **Education:** Universidad Iberoamericana (Currently Attending). **Personal Information:** Married in 1999. Mr. Lozano enjoys music, rock climbing and go-karts.

Julio Cesar Mendoza
Information Technology Director
Lear Seating Inespo Comercial
Av. Piraporinha, 1210
Diadema Sp, Brazil 09950
+55 1140668005
Fax: +55 1140666960
jmendoza@learsp.com.br

3714

Business Information: Utilizing more than 10 years of experience in the industry, Mr. Mendoza serves as the Information Technology Director for the Lear Corporation, overseeing all of the South American operations in Brazil, Argentina, and Venezuela. He assumes responsibility for the control, management, and planning of all systems activities. Directly supervising 18 staff members, he takes care of administrative communications within the internal corporate networks, purchases supplies, reviews product information communications, and writes the departmental budgets. Mr. Mendoza recently implemented a new system within the Corporation, integrating the ERP software with the BBCS system. This enables the Corporation to keep track of its manufacturing, accounting, shipping, and quality systems in one overall system. Mr. Mendoza's education and experience has contributed to his current success and he advises others to keep moving in their careers. "You never know what tomorrow will bring." The Lear Corporation is an internationally renowned first tier supplier of interior automotive parts. Established in 1995 in South America, the Corporation manufactures and distributes all types of interior automotive parts to original equipment vehicle manufacturers. Parts such as headliners, seats, carpet, dashboards, and door panels are sold to a worldwide client base. Approximately 1,500 individuals are employed in the Corporation's Brazilian location, generating annual revenue of $380 million. **Career Highlights:** Information Technology Director, Lear Corporation (1994-Present); Systems Manager, Interprotección S.C. (1992-94); Owner/Systems Manager, Apsys Computación (1989-92). **Education:** Instituto Technológico de Monterrey, Engineering and Electronic Systems (1985). **Personal Information:** Married to Veronica in 1994. Two children: Sylvia and Paulina. Mr. Mendoza enjoys time with his family.

David A. Muehlius
Information Systems Manager
E.C. Styberg Engineering Company
P.O. Box 788
Racine, WI 53401
(262) 637-9301
Fax: (262) 637-1319
dmuehlius@styberg.com

3714

Business Information: As Information Systems Manager of E.C. Styberg Engineering Company, Mr. Muehlius supervises the development of software applications. Maintaining all aspects of the hardware and software used throughout the Company, he demonstrates his adept technical abilities as he handles UNIX administration. Working closely with serveral clients in varying industries, he also supports DBA tasks by implementing innovative technical solutions developed through team efforts at departmental meetings. Mr. Muehlius credits success to his ability to be a team player, facilitating departmental growth. A respected member of the professional community, he aspires to a managerial position within the industry. E.C. Styberg Engineering Company manufactures various components for the automotive industry such as metal brakes, clutches, and transmission parts. Handling several government contracts, the 33 year old company employs over 190 people at the headquarters location in Racine, Wisconsin. **Career Highlights:** Information Systems Manager, E.C. Styberg Engineering Company (1995-Present); Programmer/Analyst, Arandell Corporation (1993-95); Programmer, Wisconsin Centrifugal (1988-93). **Associations & Accomplishments:** EDI Users Group. **Education:** University of Wisconsin at Oshkosh, B.B.A. (1988). **Personal Information:** Married to Julie in 1991. One child: Jacob. Mr. Muehlius enjoys baseball, hunting and fishing.

Clifford R. Newton
Consultant
Delphi Saginaw Steering Systems
3900 East Holland Road
Saginaw, MI 48601
(517) 757-1164
Fax: (517) 757-1176
cliffn@bigfoot.com

3714

Business Information: As a Consultant of Delphi Saginaw Steering Systems, Mr. Newton works primarily with Professional Technologies Services, Inc. He offers consulting and development services regarding systems administrations, systems development, and systems implementation of various world wide maintenance management computer systems. Beginning his association with the Company in 1969 as an Electrician, Mr. Newton has received recognition for his diligence and management skills through several promotions to his current position. Mr. Newton attributes his substantial success to his ability to think logically. He continues to grow professionally and hopes to continue in the consulting field. Established in the 1920s, Delphi Saginaw Steering Systems is engaged in the manufacture of automotive components. Serving an international client base, the Company employs a staff of 7,000 plus individuals dedicated to serving the growing needs of their clientele. **Career Highlights:** Delphi Saginaw Steering Systems: Consultant (1998-Present), Leader/Planner (1996-98), Electrician Leader (1986-96), Electrician (1969-86); Owner/Manager, Apsolut International, LLC (1997); Instructor, Delta Community College Corporate Service (1985-95). **Education:** Saginaw Valley University (1989). **Personal Information:** Three children: Trina, Michelle, and Jeffery.

Cynthia L. Schultz
Information Systems Supervisor
Bosch Automation Technology
7505 Durand Avenue
Racine, WI 53406
(262) 598-2375
Fax: (262) 554-6039
cindy.schultz@us.bosch.com

3714

Business Information: A successful 10-year professional, Mrs. Schultz serves as Information Systems Supervisor for Bosch Automation Technology. In her role, she oversees and directs all technical and programming operations of the Division. She works closely with management and systems users to analyze, specify, and design new solutions to harness more of the computer's power. Highly regarded, Mrs. Schultz possesses superior talents and an excellent understanding of technology. Her focus is on implementing changes that will allow Bosch Automation Technology to maintain its competitiveness in the market place as well as remain flexible, efficient, and profitable in the information technology age. In the future, Mrs. Schultz plans to continue deploying new manufacturer packages. Bosch Automation Technology's division located in Racine, Wisconsin was established in 1988. The Company engages in the manufacture of pumps, valves, manifolds, power units, and other pneumatic devices. Employing approximately 300 individuals of various professional degrees, the Company was founded in 1886. **Career Highlights:** Information Systems Supervisor, Bosch Automation Technology (1998-Present); Programmer/Analyst, E.R. Wagner Manufacturing Company (1995-98); Programmer, Signicast Corporation (1989-95). **Education:** Cardinal Stritch University, B.B.A. (1997); Straton College, Associate's degree in Computer Data Processing (1990). **Personal Information:** Married to James in 1991. One child: Leah.

Karen E. Spencer
Network Specialist
Aisin USA
1700 East 4th Street Road
Seymour, IN 47274-4309
(812) 523-1969
Fax: (812) 523-1984
k-spencer@aisinusa.com

3714

Business Information: Ms. Spencer is the Network Specialist of Aisin USA. She maintains the entire Windows NT network within the Company's Indiana location. To better facilitate the computer needs of other employees, she conducts user training courses where staff members can explore the opportunities available to them through their computers. Planning to remain with the Company in the future, she is coordinating a return to school so she can enhance her education within her field. Aisin USA engages in the manufacture of auto parts with the team effort of 1,500 employees throughout its locations. Established in 1987, the Company has provided parts and accessories to the leading retail shops and dealerships around the world. Headquartered in Japan, the Company has a total of 20 international locations and 13 locations in the United States. **Career Highlights:** Network Specialist, Aisin USA (1997-Present); Peer Consultant, Turning Point (1992). **Associations & Accomplishments:** Steering Committee Member/Volunteer, Youth for Christ; Youth Sponsor/Teacher, Seymour Christian Church; Developer/Instructor, Scholarship Career Program. **Education:** Indiana University (Currently Attending). **Personal Information:** Ms. Spencer enjoys reading and working with youth.

Sarah Lee Springer
Business Systems Analyst
AEMP Corporation
2404 Doctor F.E. Wright Drive
Jackson, TN 38305-7503
(901) 424-0400
Fax: (901) 424-2210
sarah_plunk@aemp.com

3714

Business Information: As Business Systems Analyst of AEMP Corporation, Ms. Springer provides insights into the effectiveness of the Corporation's daily operations and production processes. She also serves as systems and database administrator and programmer. In this context, she is responsible for programming software and hardware for the business system and production database as well as providing technical support to management and users. Compiling management reports, transferring data, performing backups, and resolving systems and network technical difficulties also fall within the realm of Ms. Springer's responsibilities. She has faithfully stood by the Corporation before they were employee-owned and has seen it through downsizing and corporate buyouts. Getting more involved in management on the business side of operations is cited as Ms. Springer's strategic plan. AEMP Corporation is a national manufacturer of aluminum automobile parts through a special process known as semi-solid forging. The Corporation was established in 1985 and currently employs a quality work force of more than 400 people. AEMP Corporation is located in Jackson, Tennessee. **Career Highlights:** Business Systems Analyst, AEMP Corporation (Present). **Associations & Accomplishments:** Club ICP for Informix Certified Professional; Church of Christ. **Education:** Freed Hardeman University, B.S. in Computer Science and Business (1995); Informix 7.x Database Specialist Certification (1999); Informix 7.x Database Administrator Certification (1999). **Personal Information:** Ms. Springer enjoys outdoor activities.

Roger St. Aubin
Space Management Specialist/Webmaster
Atlantiques Promotions
770 Guimond Boulevard
Longueuil, Quebec, Canada J4G 1V6
(450) 646-2025
staubin@sympatico.ca

3714

Business Information: Providing his skilled services as Space Management Specialist and Webmaster, Mr. St. Aubin has been with Atlantiques Promotion since 1993. Capitalizing on more than six years of extensive experience in all phases of marketing, he displays an effective and productive creative style. Concentrating his efforts on marketing strategies, Mr. St. Aubin forms proposals for store displays and digital picture advertising projects. Coordinating all aspects of Web design, he continually upgrades Web sites and creates cutting edge screen savers. Managing an annual budget, he initiates all purchases within budgetary guidelines. Mr. St. Aubin continues to grow professionally through the fulfillment of his responsibilities and his involvement in the advancement of operations with Atlantiques Promotions. Attributing his success to never giving up and always looking for more challenges, Mr. St. Aubin's goals include moving up the corporate structure and becoming involved in e-commerce. Established in 1965, Atlantiques Promotions is dedicated to providing the marketing and distribution of kitchen tools and automotive accessories. Serving an international clientele, the Company employs the skilled services of 150 individuals to acquire business, meet with clients, facilitate projects, and market services. Generating $50 million in annual sales, the Company continues to strive towards establishing higher standards of excellence for others in the industry. **Career Highlights:** Atlantiques Promotions: Space Management Specialist (1996-Present), Webmaster (1999-Present); Space Management Specialist, Club Biz (1994-95). **Associations & Accomplishments:** Eccnet Planograming Committee. **Education:** University, Bachelor's degree (1992); Teaching Certificate. **Personal Information:** Mr. St. Aubin enjoys travel, biking and the Internet.

Claudio Suárez del Real
Information Systems Manager
Valvu las Keystone de Mexico
Calle Serpentario 3787, Apartment 4, Jalisco
Zatopan, Mexico 45070
+52 36684060
Fax: +52 48140235
claudio.suarez@alliedsignal.com

3714

Business Information: Utilizing 12 years years experience in information systems, Mr. Suárez del Real was recruited to Valvu las Keystone de Mexico as Information Systems Manager in 1998. In his position, he is responsible for a number of day-to-day technology related tasks. A sucessful professional, he is accountable for the LAN/WAN and ERP Glovia. Mr. Suárez del Real is also responsible for ensuring the functionality and fully operational status of the systems infrastructure, to include software, hardware, applications, and file servers. Possessing expertise in the information systems field, he looks forward to helping to grow and expand the Company and eventually move up within the Company to a higher position. His success reflects his ability to take on challenges and deliver results in support of all endeavors. Established in 1993, Valvu las Keystone de Mexico sells valves to various companies specializing in the manufacturing and sale of automotive environmental catalysts for catalytic converters. Located in Zatopan, Mexico, the Company employs a work force of 85 hardworking employees. Presently, Valvu las Keystone de Mexico reports annual revenues in excess of $60 million. **Career Highlights:** Information Systems Manager, Valvu las Keystone de Mexico (1998-Present); Information Systems Manager, Allied Signal Environmental Catalysts (1995-98); Project Leader, Cumins, S.A. de C.V. (1991-95); Systems Analyst, Banco del Centro, SNC (1989-90); Junior Systems Administrator, SARH (1988). **Education:** M.B.A. in Finance (In Progress); Instituto Technologico de San Luis, B.S. (1990). **Personal Information:** Mr. Suárez del Real enjoys dancing, reading and music.

Ergin Altan
Senior Programmer
Turkish Aerospace Industries
Tai Lojmanlari BL A 4-9 Akinci
Ankara, Turkey 0936
+90 3128111800
Fax: +90 3124407125
ealtan@tai.com.tr

3721

Business Information: Devoted to the success of Turkish Aerospace Industries, Mr. Altan applies his knowledge and expertise in the field of mechanical programing by serving as the Company's Senior Programmer. He is responsible for designing and creating programs for CNC milling machines, deterimining tool requirements, and maintaining all systems functions. Analyzing, specifying, and developing advanced solutions to harness more of the computer's power also fall within the realm of his responsibilities. Utilizing more than 14 years of hands on engineering experience, Mr. Altan has received various commendations for his diligence and mechanical skills through several promotions to his current position. His plans for his career include remaining with the Company in order to continue providing comprehensive services. Mr. Altan's success reflects his ability to take on challenges and deliver results. Turkish Aerospace Industries engages in the manufacturing of various types of aircraft, such as F16s, Casa CN235s, and Cougars. The Company also provides parts and components for various building projects and subcontracts. Established in 1984, the Company is headquartered in Andara, Turkey and operates out of several other international locations. Presently, the Company is manned by more than 2,000 professionals who facilitate smooth business operations. **Career Highlights:** Turkish Aerospace Industries: Senior Programmer (1993-Present), Production Specialist (1989-93); Aeronautical Engineer, Eskisehir Air Supply and Maintenance Center (1987-87). **Associations & Accomplishments:** Turkish Society of Mechanical Engineers. **Education:** Istanbul Technical University, B.S. (1986). **Personal Information:** Married to Tuläy in 1992. One child: Eray. Mr. Altan enjoys homemade computer controlled mechanical devices, bridge, chess and electronics.

Ramon F. Baez
Director of Software Engineering
Northrop Grumman
P.O. Box 655907
Dallas, TX 75265-5907
(972) 946-4045
Fax: (972) 946-5679
baezra@mail.northgrum.com

3721

Business Information: Serving as Director of Software Engineering of Northrop Grumman, Mr. Baez directs the development and maintenance of all business and scientific systems. Controlling the design, building, and delivery of products, he plots the strategy of future planning, develops solutions to technical problems, and implements various state-of-the-art systems. Possessing an excellent understanding of his field, he deploys three different enterprise resource planning systems. Among his accomplishments, Mr. Baez assisted in software development of the B-2 bomber. In the future, he hopes to gain a business leadership position within the Corporation. Established in 1939, Northrop Grumman is a leader in the aerospace and defense industries. The Corporation is divided into three divisions: aerospace, electronics, and information technology. Such technological masterpieces as the B-2 stealth bomber and the Joint Stars battlefield surveillance systems are credited to the Corporation's defense division. The electronics division has seen an equal amount of success, producing radar-jamming equipment, missile systems, and computer systems. The information technology department's specific area of expertise is communications and intelligence, training and simulation, and high

performance computing. The Corporation also performs its own research and development, to stay on the cutting edge of the industry. **Career Highlights:** Northrop Grumman: Director of Software Engineering (1999-Present), Division Chief Information Officer (1994-99), B-2 Program Office Manager (1985-98). **Associations & Accomplishments:** Calvary Chapel; Southwest Baptist Church, Texas. **Education:** University of LaVerne, B.S. (1995). **Personal Information:** Married to Kelly in 1998. Three children: Angeline Nicole, Ramon VIII, and Ryan Kearns. Mr. Baez enjoys golf.

Ali Bahrami, Ph.D.
Chief Architect
The Boeing Company
P.O. Box 3707
Seattle, WA 98124
(425) 865-6316
Fax: (425) 865-2964
abahrami@yahoo.com

3721

Business Information: Dr. Bahrami serves as the Chief Architect of The Boeing Company's Human Resource DSS/DW Project. He performs research and participates in the design, development, and transfer of leading edge technologies. Highly regarded by his colleagues, Dr. Bahrami possesses superior talents and an excellent understanding of technology. Prior to joining the Boeing team of professionals, he served as an Associate Professor with Rhode Island College. Dr. Bahrami is also the Founder of Process@work.com. His active membership in industry-related associations enables him to stay on top of emerging technology, as well as network and interact with professional in many different fields. Demonstrating his innovativeness, Dr. Bahrami plans on developing a building tool to integrate business processes and networks. His success is attributed to his ability to think out-of-the-box, take on challenges, and deliver results on behalf of the Company. The Boeing Company operates as an aerospace company conducting research and looking at technologies five years into the future. Established in 1920, the Company has grown to enormous proportions, and currenlty employs a global work force of more than 200,000 people. Presently, Boeing reports annual revenues in excess of $56.2 billion. **Career Highlights:** Chief Architect, The Boeing Company (1997-Present); Founder, Process@work.com (2000-Present); Associate Professor, Rhode Island College (1992-97). **Associations & Accomplishments:** Institute of Electronics and Electrical Engineers Computer Society; Decision Science Institute; The International Neural Networks Society; The Society of Manufacturing Engineers; Northeast Decision Sciences Institute; Society of Manufacturing Engineers; Association of Computing Machinery. **Education:** University of Missouri at Rolla, Ph.D. (1992); University of Nebraska at Lincoln, M.S. in Computer Science (1985), MCRP (1983); Wesleyan University, B.S. in Mathematics (1980). **Personal Information:** Married to Soheila in 1983. Two children: Ava and Lili. Dr. Bahrami enjoys photography, playing santour, tennis and travel.

Charles Caster
Senior Database Analyst
Gulfstream Aerospace
P.O. Box 2206, M/S-A-05
Savannah, GA 31402-2206
(912) 965-4629
Fax: (912) 965-3820
charles.caster@gulfaero.com

3721

Business Information: As Senior Database Analyst at Gulfstream Aerospace, Mr. Caster is in charge of installation, administration, technical support, and recovery for database systems. He also provides technical expertise to the application development staff for in-house training, design reviews, and application problem resolution. Mr. Caster demonstrates an uncanny ability to recognize opportunities for technical improvement within his department, thereby producing comprehensive solutions to be utilized for better business development. He is co-author of a 200-page book, defining a comprehensive system development life cycle. Mr. Caster plans on staying with the Company, possibly moving into a management position, and continuing his work to enhance company operations. Established in 1958, Gulfstream Aerospace, a wholly owned subsidiary of General Dynamics, is widely known as the world leader in business aviation. The Company's flagship products, the Gulfstream IV-SP and the Gulfstream V, are the world's most technologically advanced business aircraft. Headquartered in Savannah, Georgia, Gulfstream employs over 8,200 highly skilled and dedicated individuals at 8 locations to help maintain the high standards of the business, and generate a total annual revenue over $3 billion. **Career Highlights:** Senior Database Analyst, Gulfstream Aerospace (1987-Present); Memorial Medical Center: Technical Support Supervisor (1986-87), Systems Programmer (1979-86). **Education:** Armstrong State College, B.S. (1981); Georgia Southern College, M.S.T. (1973); Earlham College,

B.A. (1971). **Personal Information:** Married to Rev. G. Lois Caster in 1986. Two children: William and Michael.

Robin S. Dalton
Computer Security Specialist
The Boeing Company
800 Southwest 39th Street
Seattle, WA 98124
(253) 657-9327
Fax: (253) 657-9477
robin.s.dalton@boeing.com

3721

Business Information: As a Computing Security Specialist for The Boeing Company, Ms. Dalton is responsible for creating policies and procedures for the design of state-of-the-art telecommunications systems. These innovative systems are implemented globally from corporate offices to personal residences. Utilizing the experience of 20 dedicated years with Boeing, Ms. Dalton owns an established track record of producing results in support of all business objective. Her success reflects are ability to ensure Company standards are met and or exceeded, as well as take on new challenges and responsibilities. Ms. Dalton has enjoyed many years of dedicated service with Boeing Company and plans to continue her success in the future. Looking toward the next millennium, her goal is to maintain her current position with added responsibilities. The Boeing Company, a multi billion dollar company, is the largest designer and manufacturer of commercial jet aircraft in the world. Established in 1917, the Company recently began the acquisition of a network of telecommunications satellites. Soon, Boeing will provide telecommunications through the agency Teledesic, of which Boeing owns 10 percent. With 200,000 employees, the Company is still primarily an aircraft producer. **Career Highlights:** The Boeing Company: Computer Security Specialist (1991-Present), Functional Analyst (1990-91), Configuration Management (1985-89), Programmer/Analyst (1979-84). **Associations & Accomplishments:** Computer Technology Investigators Northwest; Usenix. **Education:** North Seattle Community College, Certificate in Data Processing (1979); Mount Diablo Community College, A.A.; University of California. **Personal Information:** Ms. Dalton enjoys boating, travel and dogs.

Darren L. Fowler
Senior Systems Developer
Raytheon Travel Air
101 South Webb
Wichita, KS 67201
(316) 676-3718
darren_fowler@raytheon.com

3721

Business Information: Functioning as Senior Systems Developer for Raytheon Travel Air, Mr. Fowler is responsible for design, development, and deployment of software applications. An expert, he effectively supervises and guides 11 employees in development of advanced operating and networking environments for users of Raytheon Travel Air, be it hardware or software. Before joining Raytheon Travel Air, Mr. Fowler served as a Programmer with Via Christi Hospitals. As a four year programming professional, he coordinates resources and schedules, oversees time lines and assignments, ensures the functionality and fully operational status of the systems infrastructure, and designs new technical solutions to harness more of the computer's power. God's blessings have made him increasingly successful throughout all of his life. Mr. Fowler, aspiring to become an Engineer, enhances Raytheon Travel Air's performance by attending seminars and schools to remain on the cutting edge for the industry. His professional success reflects his ability to think out-of-the-box and take on new challenges. Established in 1997, Raytheon Travel Air is a division of Raytheon Aircraft. The Company specializes in offering fractional-ownership programs for aircraft sales. International in scope, the Raytheon Travel Air presently employs a staff of more than 275 professional, technical, and administrative support personnel. **Career Highlights:** Raytheon Travel Air: Senior Systems Developer (1998-Present), Programmer (1997-98); Programmer, Via Christi Hospitals (1995-97). **Associations & Accomplishments:** Aircraft Owners and Pilots Association. **Education:** Wichita State University. **Personal Information:** Married to Angela in 1998. Mr. Fowler enjoys golf, water sports and being a private pilot.

Roxanne M. Jordan
Systems Administrator
Rockwell
1100 West Hibiscus Boulevard
Melbourne, FL 32901
(321) 953-1816
mjordan@collins.rockwell.com

3721

Business Information: A successful, technology professional, Ms. Jordan currently serves with Rockwell

Collins as Systems Administrator. She is responsible for installing operating systems software as well as monitoring and tuning systems software, peripherals, and networks. In this context, she provides technical support to the personal computer and networking infrastructure that includes printers and servers. Utilizing more than 12 years of technical savvy and expertise, Ms. Jordan is charged with ensuring the functionality and fully operational status of the operating and networking environments. One of many career accomplishments, her greatest is receiving a promotion to the information technology department. Future goals include attaining her Bachelor's degree in Telecommunications and working up the corporate ladder into a higher management position. Ambition, motivation, and drive have contributed to Ms. Jordan's success. Her advice to others is "get involved." An aerospace company, Rockwell Collins engages in the design and development of aviation jet aircraft. Headquartered in Iowa, the Company operates a satellite network of several facilities in the United States, including the Melbourne, Florida location. **Career Highlights:** Systems Administrator, Rockwell Collins (Present). **Personal Information:** Married. Ms. Jordan enjoys music, reading mystery books, pool and bowling.

Stephen D. Liguori

Software Engineer
Northrop Grumman
South Oyster Bay Road
Bethpage, NY 11714
(516) 346-7583
Fax: (516) 346-7625
dksb@erols.com

3721

Business Information: Utilizing more than 25 years of experience in the industry, Mr. Liguori serves as Software Engineer of Northrop Grumman. Acting as a Project Leader, he works with a team of skilled and knowledgeable professionals to encode existing air defense systems for the Department of Defense. To keep the Corporation in the forefront of airspace technology systems, Mr. Liguori designs, develops, and implements new systems, as well as provides technical support to users and management. He stays on the cutting edge of new technology through the discipline of self education. His career success reflects his ability to think out-of-the-box and aggressively take on new challenges. Continually achieving quality performance in his field, Mr. Liguori looks forward to assisting in the completion of future corporate goals and anticipates a promotion to Director. Northrop Grumman is a publicly traded company specializing in defense electronics programs, commercial aerostructures, airspace management systems, and information technology systems and solutions. Employing a work force of around 20,000 qualified professionals, the Corporation reports estimated annual sales in the billions of dollars. **Career Highlights:** Software Engineer, Northrop Grumman (1977-Present); Manager, Davis Aircraft (1977). **Education:** Queens College, B.S. (1971). **Personal Information:** Married to Dawn in 1984. Four children: Kaitlin, Bryan, Dennis, and Dawn. Mr. Liguori enjoys handball, reading scientific journals and camping.

Christophe Loustaudaudine

Project Manager
CAC Systèmes
29 Rue de la Vallée du Loir
Areines, France 41100
+33 254526568
lstdne@club-internet.fr

3721

Business Information: As a Project Manager for CAC Systèmes, Mr. Loustaudaudine is responsible for automatic pilots for airplanes and helicopters. In this capacity, he develops software for stability, piloting, and navigation and is overall responsible for the installation and testing of new software. Coordinating resources, time lines, and assignments also fall within the realm of his functions. Mr. Loustaudaudine has earned an extensive education in electronics and automation and is continuing to work towards his Ph.D. degree. In the future, he plans to expedite continued promotion through dedication and the perpetuation of additional growth through proper management styles. His success reflects his leadership ability to take on challenges and deliver results. CAC Systèmes provides target and U.V.A. (Unmanned Air Vehicles) systems technologies. The Company manufactures of airplanes with automatic pilots used by the military for targets and surveillance. Serving an international clientele, the Company also performs research in an attempt to discover new ways in which to manufacture more advanced products. **Career Highlights:** Project Manager, CAC Systèmes (1993-Present); Doctorate Research, Robosoft (1989-93). **Education:** Laboratorie de Robotique de Paris; University of Paris 6, Master's degree in Electronics and Automation. **Personal Information:** Married to Nathalie in 1989. Three children: Emilie, Antoine, and Arégoire. Mr. Loustaudaudine enjoys model airplanes.

Phyllis J. Michaelides

Director/Chief Technologist
Textron, Inc.
40 Westminster Street
Providence, RI 02903
(401) 457-3165
Fax: (401) 457-3546
pmichaelides@textron.com

3721

Business Information: Serving in the dual role of Director and Chief Technologists of Textron, Inc., Ms. Michaelides determines the strategic direction and business contribution of the information systems function. Joining Textron in January 2000, she is responsible for integrating the corporations activities with e-business, networking technology, hand held devices, and PCs. Providing oversight of the corporate information management infrastructure, she is working on gaining additional information on the Corporation's structure with plans on having a bigger impact on the global market place. Before joining Textron, Ms. Michaelides served as Manager of Technology Architecture for AlliedSignal/Honeywell. Her background also includes stints with Deere & Company as a Project Manager and John Deer Waterloo Works as Team Leader. Enhancing Textron's overall mainframe and network environments serves as Ms. Michaelides' strategic plans. Her success reflects her leaderhips ability to build teams with synergy and technical strenght and deliver results. Textron, Inc. is a diversified conglomerate with over 30 separate companies in three primary areas: aerospace and defense technology, financial services, and communications. The Corporation also manufactures quality auto parts. Established in 1923, Textron reports annual revenues in excess of $11.5 billion. Currently, the Corporation employs a global work force of more than 64,000. **Career Highlights:** Director/Chief Technologist, Textron, Inc. (2000-Present); Technology Strategy/Architecture Manager, Allied Signal/Honeywell (1996-00); Project Manager, Deere & Company (1996); Team Leader, John Deere Waterloo Works (1993-96). **Education:** Oberlin College, B.A. (1956). **Personal Information:** One child: Christopher. In addition, she is very creative and musically inclined.

Richard Stroud

Systems Administrator
BAE Systems
1601 Research Boulavard
Rockville, MD 20850
(301) 231-1640
Fax: (301) 231-1233
richard_stroud@baesystems.com

3721

Business Information: A savvy, 11 year veteran of the technology field, Mr. Stroud serves as the Systems Administrator of BAE Systems. In his capacity, he administers and controls all systems tools and computer resources, ensuring the system remains functional and operational. Possessing an excellent understanding of technology, Mr. Stroud is responsible for overseeing database management systems software, monitoring all software programs, performing troubleshooting, and resolving systems problems. Moreover, he is charged with conducting network configuration as well as ensuring the integrity, security, and reliability of the systems functions In the future, Mr. Stroud looks forward to continuing with the Company in his current position and obtain additional certifications. Located in Rockville, Maryland, BAE Systems is a defense contractor. Founded in 1950, the Company is owned by Great Britain and works mainly with government agencies around Rockville. Operating on a regional level, the Company has a work force of over 5,000 employees who are dedicated to providing quality services. **Career Highlights:** Systems Administrator, BAE Systems (1989-Present); Work Study Programmer, GE (1987-89). **Education:** University of North Carolina at Wilmington, B.S. (1989); Microsoft Certified Systems Engineer. **Personal Information:** Married to Stephanie in 1988. Mr. Stroud enjoys wood working, racing, astronomy and computers.

Chris West

Mechanical Designer
Northrop Grumman-Canada Ltd.
777, Walkers Line
Burlington, Ontario, Canada L7N 2G1
(905) 333-6000
Fax: (905) 333-6053
chrisw@ngcan.com

3721

Business Information: Currently holding the position of Mechanical Designer for Northrop Grumman-Canada Ltd., Mr. West has been employed by the Corporation for over 16 years. Possessing an excellent understanding of his field, he has previously served as a mechanical designer with Spar Aerospace and Northern Telecommunications. In his current role, he brings with him invaluable experience as well as knowledge and skill in the industry. A savvy professional, Mr. West is in charge of designing systems for steel work, developing printed circuit boards, coordinating projects and metal work, and building prototypes. Highly regarded, he takes pride in his accomplishments and thoroughly enjoys working on computer terminals. Mr. West attributes his success to being an adaptive learner and being practical. Enjoying his position, he plans to continue designing new equipment and technologies for the airline industry. Founded in 1996 and staffing 186 employees, Northrop Grumman-Canada Ltd. designs and builds electronic media for the government and large industries. The Corporation creates self-service computer terminal kiosks for the airline industry, sonar equipment for military, and light tracing equipment for the cutting of sheet steel. **Career Highlights:** Mechanical Designer, Northrop Grumman-Canada Ltd. (1984-Present); Mechanical Designer, Spar Aerospace (1983-84); Mechanical Designer, Northern Telecommunications (1981-83); Rolls-Royce Ltd. in England (1964-80). **Education:** Peoples College, Higher National Diploma. **Personal Information:** Mr. West enjoys scuba diving, dancing and golf.

Gregory P. Chapman

Systems Analyst
EFTC
2113 Arrowhead Circle
Olathe, KS 66062
(785) 229-3929
Fax: (785) 242-4950
greg-chapman@eftc.com

3724

Business Information: Serving as a Systems Analyst of EFTC, Mr. Chapman integrates years of U.S. Army experience with CNE certification to satisfy his current demands of planning, designing, and upgrading the entire LAN and telephone systems within EFTC. Dedicating his services to this innovative Company since coming on board in 1999, Mr. Chapman ranks among the highest qualified experts in the fields of user support and help desk administration. Drawing great satisfaction from his service with EFTC, he is continuing his efforts, focusing his knowledge and skill in areas of technical consulting to promote his career to a position as Management Information Systems Director. His success reflects his ability to think outside the box, take on challenges, and deliver results on behalf of the Company and its clientele. Established in 1988 as a manufacturer of aviation equipment, EFTC has become one of the world's largest production companies, the scope of their client base extending on an international level. Specializing in contract manufacturing, the Midwest office of the Company focuses on board level, general aviation products, specifically designed for Honeywell. Employing 360 people in their offices nationwide, EFTC operates year round to produce the highest quality goods available on the market, resulting in the generation of $45 million annually. **Career Highlights:** Systems Analyst, EFTC (1999-Present); Systems Analyst, Garmin International (1995-99); LAN Administrator, Clark, Richardson, & Biskup (1995); LAN Administrator, Robert D. O'Byrne & Associates (1991-94). **Education:** Kansas State University, B.S. in Agriculture (1979). **Personal Information:** Mr. Chapman enjoys hunting and fishing.

Arif A. Dar

Manager of Affiliates Y2K Program
General Electric Company
4300 Wildwood Parkway, 2-14C-05
Atlanta, GA 30339
(770) 859-6504
Fax: (770) 859-6953
arif.dar@ps.ge.com

3724

Business Information: Serving as Manager of Affiliates Y2K Program for General Electric Company, Mr. Dar assumes responsibility for the Y2K remediation and conversion of over 100 General Electric facilities and joint venture partners across the globe. One hundred individuals report directly to him. Before joining General Electric, Mr. Dar served as Director of Technical Investment Group for Groome Capital Advisory, Canada. His solid history also includes a stint as Manager of Communications Systems with National Grid, United Kingdom. Additionally, he is the Information Group Manager for General Electric and handles the Company's business development regarding new technological advances. Utilizing his extensive academic ties, Mr. Dar stays on the cutting edge utilizing one simple means, study, study, study. Establishing goals that are compatible with those of the Company, he is looking forward to a promotion to Program Manager. Publicly owned, General Electric Company is the fifth-largest United States corporation. The manufacturing divisions produce a variety of products such as aircraft engines and kitchen appliances. Presently employing a work force of more than 10,000 people, General Electric boasts $100 billion in annual revenue. **Career Highlights:** Manager of Affiliates Y2K Program, General Electric Company (1998-Present); Director of Technical Investment Group,

Groome Capital Advisory, Canada (1997); Manager of Communications Systems, National Grid, United Kingdom (1993-95). **Associations & Accomplishments:** Institute of Electrical and Electronics Engineers; Associate Member, Institute of Electrical Engineers, United Kingdom; Certified Management Consultants of Canada; Pakistan Engineering Council. **Education:** Richard Ivey School of Business, M.B.A. (1998); University of London, Master's degree in Engineering; University of Engineering and Technology, Bachelor's degree in Engineering. **Personal Information:** Married to Nageen in 1998. Mr. Dar enjoys squash, coin collecting and home building.

Hui Gao

Computer Scientist
General Electric Company
1 Research Circle, GECRD
Schenectady, NY 12301
(518) 387-4076
Fax: (518) 387-4187
gaohu@crd.ge.com

3724

Business Information: Proficient in all areas of information technology, Mrs. Gao began her career with General Electric Company as a Computer Scientist in 1998. She fulfills a number of duties on behalf of the Company and its clientele and is responsible for working closely with management and users to analyze, specify, and design solutions to enhance the Company's line of products and services. A successful, 12 year professional, Mrs. Gao is in charged of the design and implementation of customer blueprinted software and Internet consulting and Web research and development. A recipient of the "GE Management Award," Mrs. Gao plans to remain with the Company, establishing innovative designs and goals that are compatible with General Electric as well as becoming Chief Technology Officer of a next generation company. An industrial giant, General Electric Company operates a wide array of businesses internationally. The Company employs a global work force of more than 340,000 people. Founded in 1892, the Company's wide range of services include technology, manufacturing, and telecommunications and electronics consulting. The Company is moving towards e-commerce and supporting client companies via the Internet. Presently, General Electric reports annual revenues in excess of $11.5 billion. **Career Highlights:** Computer Scientist, General Electric Company (1998-Present); Software Consultant, R&I 1 (1996-98); Computer Scientist, University of 1, Super Computing Center for Research & Development (1990-94). **Associations & Accomplishments:** Society for Industrial and Applied Mathematics; American Matehmatical Society. **Education:** Union College at New York, M.B.A. (In Progress); University of Illinois at Urbana, M.S. (1988); Xian Jiaotong University, B.S. in Computer Science. **Personal Information:** Married to Xiang Li Chen in 1994. Two children: Victoria Huiyu Chen and Angela Huixu Chen. Mrs. Gao enjoys tennis and bridge.

Mark J. Grindle

Information Technology Manager
General Electric
1 Research Center, P.O. Box 8
Schenectady, NY 12309
(518) 387-7381
Fax: (518) 387-6560
mark.grindle@crd.ge.com

3724

Business Information: Mr. Grindle has served with General Electric in various positions since 1994. At the present time he fulfills the responsibilities of Information Technology Manager responsible for maintaining the entire systems infrastructure in a fully functional and operational status. Possessing an excellent understanding of his role, he supports the global implementation of advanced information technologies and voice and network infrastructures. In addition, Mr. Grindle is responsible for starting up remote operations at international sites. Looking to the future, his goals include attaining the position of Chief Information Officer with General Electric as a result of his continuing efforts to increase his skills through training and professional development activities. General Electric provides research and development and operates a wide array of businesses. The fifth largest U.S. corporation, General Electric produces aircraft engines, electronic appliances, industrial products and systems, and materials such as plastics. Established in 1900, General Electric is an global company located in New York. Currently 4,000 people are employed at the Schenectady, New York location to facilitate every aspect of design, manufacture, quality assurance, and distribution. **Career Highlights:** General Electric: Information Technology Manager (1999-Present), Service Quality Manager (1997-99), Products and Security Manager (1996-97), Business Manager (1994-96). **Education:** Bentley College, B.S. (1982). **Personal Information:** Mr. Grindle enjoys golf and travel.

Paul R. Holland, III

Deputy Director
Logicon, Inc.
1301 Mason Mill Court
Herndon, VA 20170-5738
(703) 318-1074
Fax: (703) 318-1098
pholland@logicon.com

3724

Business Information: With a desire to succeed and move ahead, Mr. Holland has served with Logicon, Inc. in various positions since 1991. At the present time, he fulfills the responsibilities of Deputy Director. In his capacity, he manages all aspects of systems engineering, keeps track of all engineering tasks, and monitors a budget in excess of $45 million. He also is in charge of developing and deploying creative and high-powered marketing strategies. Concurrently, Mr. Holland is a partner in Vision Technology, a company that provides oral presentation coaching for contract proposals submitted to federal agencies. His career milestones includes the development of a joint task force tactical communications architecture in 1998, and being an integral member of a cutting edge team who developed a joint tactical communications interoperability architecture for LAN defense of the continental United States. Mr. Holland's motto is "Keep abreast of leading edge technology." Founded in 1986, Logicon, Inc. conducts telecommunications interoperability work for the government and U.S. Department of Defense. Based out of Virginia, the Corporation operates three satellite locations manned by 9,000 individuals generating $682 million in annual revenues. **Career Highlights:** Deputy Director, Logicon, Inc. (1991-Present); Principal Staff, BDM International (1986-91); Operations Research Analyst, U.S. Army (1983-86). **Associations & Accomplishments:** Armed Forces Communications and Electronics Association; Military Operations Research Society; Coach, National Capital Soccer League Boys Travel Soccer Team. **Education:** University of Southern California, M.S. in Information Systems (1987); University of Baltimore, M.S. in Criminal Justice (1979); Washington & Lee University, B.A. in Political Science (1974). **Personal Information:** Married to Laurie in 1975. Four children: Cyndi, Jennifer, Matthew, and Meghan. Mr. Holland enjoys coaching soccer.

Kevin J. Kao, Ph.D.

Staff Engineer
General Electric (GE) Corporate Research and Development
Building K-1, Room 3A59B, One Research Circle
Niskayuna, NY 12309
(518) 387-6287
Fax: (518) 387-5459
kao@crd.ge.com

3724

Business Information: Serving as Staff Engineer of General Electric (GE) Corporate Research and Development, Dr. Kao is responsible for designing a distributed software environment, offering web-based services to provide a truly concurrent engineering design process. Lapping existing and advanced technology, he reduces design cycle time and improves the in-house applications tools. Utilizing his acute undertstanding of customer requirements, Dr. Kao also executes and implements communications with other sites' engineers. His future plans are threefold, apply technology in the business unit, organize workshops, and advertise to other companies. Career highlights include his involvement with professional organizations and presenting GE as a leader in technology. A savvy, six and a half-year veteran, Dr. Kao's success is attributed to working smartly, communication skills, working in a great environment, and not being afraid. Headquartered in Fairfield, Conneticut, General Electric is the fifth largest corporation in the United States. Involved in many industries from electronic appliances to aircraft engines to capital services, the facility in Niskayuna, New York provides technical leadership, advanced innovations, and technical expertise to assist GE businesses in developing products and processes. **Career Highlights:** Staff Engineer, GE Corporate Research & Development (1999-Present); Research Assistant, Stanford University (1995-99); Research Assistant, Carnegie Mellon University (1994-95). **Associations & Accomplishments:** American Society of Mechanical Engineers; Institute of Electrical and Electronics Engineers Computer Society. **Education:** Stanford University, Ph.D. (1999); Carnegie Mellon University, M.S. (1995). **Personal Information:** Married to Heidi H. Su in 1996. Dr. Kao enjoys piano and harmonica.

Aaron P. Yim

Information Technology Manager
General Electric
217 Natchez Drive
Jonesboro, AR 72404
(870) 933-3206

3724

Business Information: As Information Technology Manager for the Jonesboro, Arkansas location of General Electric, Mr. Yim reports directly to the Chief Technical Officer as he completes a variety of techncial activities within the corporate structure. Utilizing his adept abilities within his role, he handles upgrades, maintenance, and development of new software applications that will assist in both production and sales. Striving to create strategic, innovative programs, Mr. Yim is directly involved in the formulation of policy that will contribute to the overall effectiveness of the Company by lowering overhead and raising quality and quantity of production. Recognized for his impressive abilities within his field, Mr. Yim is credited with several programs currently in use by the Company such as "internship awareness." Currently, he is striving to become Chief Information Officer of the Company as he continually exceeds expectations within his department. General Electric manufactures a vairety of electrical equipment. Emloying hundreds of thousands of people throughout the world, the Company focuses much time and resources on the development of aircraft engines, appliances, broadcasting, and indsustrial electrical distribution. In addition, the Company is concerend with the manufacture of ABS resins, power systems, technical products, and other materials. The Jonesboro, Arkansas location specializes in the production of motors and other parts for appliances. **Career Highlights:** Information Technology Manager, General Electric (Present).

Joseph Nassani

Systems Administrator
ITT Avionics
100 Kingsland Road
Clifton, NJ 07014
(973) 284-5095
Fax: (973) 284-3294
jnassani@avionics.itt.com

3728

Business Information: As Systems Administrator of ITT Avionics, Mr. Nassani is involved in virtually every area of design. He is responsible for designing, installing, monitoring, troubleshooting, and analyzing NT servers, SQL databases, and WEB servers. Mr. Nassani has served with ITT Avionics in various positions since 1988. Coordinating resources, schedules, time lines, and assignments; serving as contact with users and systems management; and overseeing integration of new technology, training, and technical support also fall within the purview of Mr. Nassani's responsibilities. Drawing from an extensive education and previous occupational experience, he fosters a strong sense of teamwork and purpose among others in the Company. He plans to expedite continued promotion through the fulfillment of his responsibilities and his involvement in the advancement of operations. ITT Avionics provides aerospace and avionics equipment for the U.S. and international governments. In addition, the Company provides personal contracts for independent companies. Operations employ the expertise of 1,100 individuals to orchestrate all activities of design, manufacture, testing, and research. **Career Highlights:** ITT Avionics: Systems Administrator (1995-Present), Systems Engineer (1988-95). **Education:** Hofstra University, B.S. in Electrical Engineering (1988); Track On, Certified Novell Administrator; Global Knowledge Network, Microsoft Certified Systems Engineer. **Personal Information:** Married to Cathy in 1988. Three children: Adam, Sararose, and Annalise. Mr. Nassani enjoys biking and hiking.

Angela E. Picariello

Information Technology Staff
Rockwell Collins
1100 West Hibiscus Boulevard
Melbourne, FL 32901
(321) 768-7247
Fax: (321) 953-1825
aepicari@collins.rockwell.com

3728

Business Information: A respected professional, Ms. Picariello serves as a Senior Programmer Analyst for Rockwell Collins. In this capacity, she is the group leader for the network desktop support team and directly supervises a staff of 10 people. Along with her team of professionals, she provides client support on the network infrastructures, desktops, servers, operating systems, and its various applications. Ms. Picariello provides the oversight and supervision of the department which ensures its smooth operation. Beginning her career originally as a Secretary with the Harris Corporation, she soon switched to the MIS division of the corporation, demonstrating a talent for the technical field. Citing prior experience in competitions as a child and teenager as the reason for her success, she learned to fight for herself and has continued to practice that in a professional manner throughout her career. Ms. Picariello looks forward to working in new e-commerce and telephony development with the Company, and plans to begin working toward her certification as a CNA. Rockwell Collins, a division of Rockwell, serves as the communication division for numerous types of transportation. One type of transportation in which the Company specializes is avionics manufacturing. The Company manufactures cockpit communication systems that are utilized for land-to-air communication and OPS systems. These systems are sold to companies and corporations worldwide within the avionics industry. **Career Highlights:** Senior Programmer Analyst, Rockwell Collins (1995-Present); Information Technology Staff, Harris Corporation (1984-95). **Associations & Accomplishments:** Past Director, Project Whiz Kids; Past Member, Rotary International. **Education:** Barry University, B.S. in Professional Studies (1993). **Personal Information:** Ms. Picariello enjoys reading and music.

Michael A. Rolenz

Systems Engineer
The Aerospace Corporation
26333 Senator Avenue
Harbor City, CA 90710
(310) 336-0722

3728

Business Information: Serving as a Systems Engineer for The Aerospace Corporation, Mr. Rolenz works with management and clients to analyze, specify, and design new cutting edge systems. He is responsible for daily design development of technical aeronautic and space exploration equipment. Currently working on contracted projects for government and private agencies, Mr. Rolenz is leading the Corporation to new levels of technology design and implementation. Utilizing his extensive expertise of flight control systems and navigation databases, he has established himself as a competent and valuable asset. Continuing his high productivity and excellent work record, Mr. Rolenz plans to remain with The Aerospace Corporation to promote its best interests, thereby achieving personal satisfaction and occupational success. The Aerospace Corporation engages in aerospace systems engineering. Established in 1960, the Corporation has grown to employ over 3,000 people who generate over $300 million in annual revenues. Specializing in the design, development, and implementation of high tech navigation, control and stabilitzation, object recognition, and communication systems, The Aerospace Corporation has established itself as an international leader in a complex and competitive industry. Maintaining its level of development, the Corporation plans to expand its spectrum of services to additonal countries throughout the world. **Career Highlights:** The Aerospace Corporation: Systems Engineer (1996-Present), Prject Engineer (1993-96); Software Reliability Analyst II, Sonicraft Inc. (1983-84). **Associations & Accomplishments:** Society of Industrial and Applied Mathematics; American Statistical Association. **Education:** Rutgers, M.S. (1982); Kent State University, B.S. **Personal Information:** Mr. Rolenz enjoys collecting books and stamps, cooking, fine wines, photography, reading and colecting.

Keith A. King

Architect
Puget Sound Naval Shipyard
1400 Farragut Avenue
Bremerton, WA 98314-5001
(360) 476-7990
Fax: (360) 476-2741
kingk@psns.navy.mil

3731

Business Information: With extensive professional experience in architecture dating back to 1985, Mr. King functions as Architect for Puget Sound Naval Shipyard. In this capacity, Mr. King's responsibilities include supervising all phases of architecture and having oversight of design support functions for construction. These diverse functions include departmental CAD, document management, implementation of major applications, and participation in Pacific Northwest Public Works Regionalization efforts. An accomplished expert in his field, Mr. King has been recognized with various professional and educational awards. Earning a Master's degree in Architecture in 1998, Mr. King would like to continue to be actively involved with technology by implementing new ideas from this realm into the facilities management or architectural arena. Coming under the direction of the United States Navy, the Puget Sound Naval Shipyard executes ship maintenance services. The variety of services provided includes planning, engineering projects, repairing, modernizing, and recycling. The Public Works Department maintains the facilities to support this overall effort. Established in 1891, approximately 11,800 active duty personnel and 9,500 civilians support the Shipyard's efforts. **Career Highlights:** Architect, Puget Sound Naval Shipyard (1991-Present); Lead Architect, Naval Facilities Engineering Command (1989-91); Architect, Design Manager, Naval Facilities Engineering Command South Dakota (1985-89). **Associations & Accomplishments:** Chair, Property Management Committee at the First Lutheran Church of Port Orchard Washington. **Education:** California Poly State University, M.S. in Architecture (1998); Virginia Polytechnic Institute and State University, Bachelor's degree in Architecture (1984). **Personal Information:** Married to Jerri O. in 1986. Two children: Hannah E. and Zachary E. Mr. King enjoys church softball league activities, basketball, yard work, gardening, computer graphics and spending time with his family.

Adrienne Hughes

Senior Systems Analyst
Sea Ray Boats, Inc.
2600 Sea Ray Drive, Building 2
Knoxville, TN 37914
(865) 971-6561
Fax: (865) 971-6456
ahughes@searay.com

3732

Business Information: Serving as Senior Systems Analyst, Mrs. Hughes has been providing professional technical services for Sea Ray Boats, Inc. since 1997. Specifically leading in the development of programs for A/S400 and UNIX systems in RPG and Oracle, she focuses on promoting products and services for the corporation as well as maintaining the Corporation's Web site. Mrs. Hughes is also involved in Web reporting. Utilizing her vast knowledge of the computer field, she uses 13 years of experience in providing new technologies and ensuring a more efficient and productive work environment. Continuing her career with Sea Ray Boats, Mrs. Hughes remains committed to the furthering success of the Corporation. Her success reflects her desire to succeed and her ability to think outside the box, take on challenges, and deliver results on behalf of the Corporation and its clientele. Specializing in the manufacturing of leisure boats and motor boats, Sea Ray Boats, Inc. was established in 1967. Located in Knoxville, Tennessee, the Corporation employs over 3,000 production personnel, administrative staff, and managerial staff. Offering sales and services in 11 locations throughout the United States, Sea Ray Boats remains committed to providing excellent boating machinery and equipment. **Career Highlights:** Senior Systems Analyst, Sea Ray Boats, Inc. (1997-Present); Programmer/Analyst, House Hassom Hardware (1995-97); Programmer, Mahle, Inc. (1988-94). **Associations & Accomplishments:** Oracle Developer Users Group; United States Navy Veteran. **Education:** Walters State Community College, A.S. (1987). **Personal Information:** Married to Leonard in 1997. Three children: Travis, Jessica, and Amirina. Mrs. Hughes enjoys swimming, reading and bike riding.

Salvatore D. Magnotta

Computer Programmer
Union Switch and Signal
265 Waynesburg Road
Washington, PA 15301
(412) 638-2555
sdm@pulsenet.com

3743

Business Information: A successful, 11-year veteran of information technology, Mr. Magnotta serves as a Computer Programmer for Union Switch and Signal. He plays a vital role in the day-to-day operation and maintenance of the systems architecture and tools. Charged with overseeing the development and maintenance of the Company's software products, Mr. Magnotta incorporates his gained knowledge and natural insight into Windows 95 and NT, and Microsoft software applications. As a Project Manager with the AISE, he has been recognized for his major contributions to the Company. His effort is responsible for the incredible utilization of high technology equipment within the Company. Mr. Magnotta's future goals include attaining the position of project leader and eventually starting up his own software company. Established in 1881, Union Switch and Signal has been a world leader in the design and manufacture of railway signaling and control systems and equipment. Since its founding by George Westinghouse, Union Switch and Signal has developed control technology that has made railroad and transit operations safer, more reliable, and more efficient. **Career Highlights:** Computer Programmer, Union Switch and Signal (2000-Present); Project Leader, Association of Iron and Steel Engineers (1999-00); Computer Programmer, Retail Control Systems (1998-99); Computer Programmer/Software Engineer, Sensus Technologies (1996-98). **Associations & Accomplishments:** Association of Iron and Steel Engineers. **Education:** Rochester Institute of Technology, M.S. (1993); Washington and Jefferson College, B.A. (1989). **Personal Information:** Married to Mary S. Redd in 1991. Mr. Magnotta enjoys computer, video games and automobiles.

Kimberly L. Crockett

Y2K Specialist
NASA's Sounding Rocket Operations Contract
P.O. Box 1045
Chincoteague Island, VA 23336

3761

Business Information: Ms. Crockett is the Y2K Specialist for NASA's Sounding Rocket Operations Contract. She tests, repairs, configures, and purchases date-related or processor-driven equipment to ensure Y2K compliance. With 10 years of experience in the computer and space exploration industry, she functions as a contractor for Interim through Litton PRC. In 1998 she published "Solution 2000-A Practical Step-by-Step Approach to Identifying and Solving your Company's Year 2000 Problems," while chairing Y2K training seminars for NetTek, LLC. In 1997, she worked with the Naval Exchange Command to change their systems from Novell 3.12 to Novell 4.11, networking over 30 servers and 3,500 Web users. In the future, Ms. Crockett plans to remain with the Company and she would like to obtain her MCSE and Cisco certifications. Her success is attributed to perseverance. NASA's Sounding Rocket Operations Contract designs, develops, manufactures, and launches sub-orbital sounding rockets used for experimental and educational studies. A smaller division of NASA's aeronautical exploration division, the Company hosts over 200 employees who are continuously designing and testing new products and supplies to better the space exploration program of the United States. **Career Highlights:** Desktop Administrator/NT Administrator/Y2K Specialist, NASA's Sounding Rocket Operations Contract (1998-Present); Training Coordinator, NetTek, LLC (1998); Network Administrator, Nexcom (1997-98); Network Administrator, Jackson Hewitt, Inc. (1993-97). **Associations & Accomplishments:** Planetary Society; National Space Society; American Legion Auxiliary; Chincoteaque Town Council Bicycle Committee (1999-2000). **Education:** Tidewater Community College, A.A.S. in Computer Science (1995).

David Hedgley, Ph.D.

Mathematician
NASA-DFRC
MS-D-2701
Edwards, CA 93523-0273
(661) 258-3552
dhedgley@aol.com

3761

Business Information: As a Mathematician at NASA' DFRC or Dryden Flight Research Center, Dr. Hedgley engages in research work in applied mathematics, computer science, mechanical engineering, and aeronautics. He has been a successful member of the Dryden Flight Research Center for over 34 years, focusing on problem solving for computer graphics. Highly regarded, he gained national recognition and commendation by former President Ronald Reagan for solving a computer problem in computer graphics. He is planning to retire form his position soon, in order to create written works on philosophy, or to work as a consultant. Success, according to Dr. Hedgley, is attributed to his ability to think out-of-the-box, aggressively take on challenges, and deliver results. DFRC stands proud as NASA's primary Facility for aeronautical research. The Center engages in computer science, mechanical engineering, and aeronautical research. The Center originally began operations during the pioneering days following World War II, with the first attempts by a group of pilots, technicians, and engineers to break the sound barrier in the infamous X-1. Since then, the Center has remained on the cutting edge of aeronautics and space technology. **Career Highlights:** Mathematician, NASA-DFRC (1966-Present). **Education:** Somerset University, Ph.D. (1988); California State University, M.S. in Mathematics; Michigan State University, B.S. in Mathematics; Virginia Union University, B.S. in Biology/Chemistry. **Personal Information:** Two children: Andrea Hethery and Angela Garber. Dr. Hedgley enjoys bridge, chess, music and sports.

Omar Young Spaulding

Management Information Systems Consultant
NASA
300 East Street SW, Code YF
Washington, DC 20024
(203) 358-0777
ospauldi@hqnasa.gov

3761

Business Information: As a Management Information Systems Consultant for NASA, Mr. Spaulding works closely with the technology and commercial industries, helping companies develop new, leading edge technology. Utilizing over 20 years of hands on experience and knowledge gained from an extensive educational background, he is responsible for designing advanced information systems for high performance computing. Highly regarded, Mr. Spaulding is also accountable for small business development, research and development for new line of products, and monitoring the environment. Demonstrating strong leadership, he instills confidence in his staff, encouraging open lines of communications and fostering a strong sense of teamwork and purpose among others in the office. In the future, Mr. Spaulding's goals include expanding and "building bridges" internationally as well as bringing technology into underdeveloped countries. NASA is a U.S. government agency that conducts research on flight within and beyond the earth's atmosphere. NASA employs approximately 21,000 scientists, engineers, and technicians at 10 different installations across the country. Established in 1958, the Agency's primary focus is on research and development for several departments. **Career Highlights:** Management Information Systems Consultant, NASA (Present); President of Technology Team, Federal Aviation Administration; President of Technology Team, Internal Revenue Service. **Education:** Momith College, M.S. in Computer Science (1979); Fargo North Dakota College, B.S. in Electrical and Electronic Engineering (1975). **Personal Information:** Married. One child. Mr. Spaulding enjoys volunteer work.

Frank "Rusty" Timberlake

Senior Network Administrator
Orbital Sciences Corporation
21700 Atlantic Boulevard
Sterling, VA 20166-6801
(703) 406-5091
Fax: (703) 406-3506
timberlake.rusty@orbital.com

3761

Business Information: Self educated and highly motivated to succeed, Mr. Timberlake operates as Senior Network Administrator for Orbital Sciences Corporation. Possessing no formal degree, he has been with the Corporation for more than six years. Primarily, Mr. Timberlake establishes infrastructures, LAN/WAN, and desktop systems. In addition, he works on phone switches and data systems. Using his expert knowledge and skills in a problem solving capacity, he implements and deploys the means for telecommunications and networking to meet the needs of Orbital Sciences Corporation. One of his greatest professional accomplishments was working in Spain where he built a network to support satellite launches. As a long-term goal, Mr. Timberlake desires to remain with the Corporation to experience professional growth. Working in the aerospace industry, Orbital Sciences Corporation provides both satellites and launch vehicles. Headquartered in Virginia, Orbital Sciences Corporation has locations in the United States and various international sites. Established in 1983, the Corporation is manned by over 4,000 employees. **Career Highlights:** Senior Network Administrator, Orbital Sciences Corporation (1996-Present); Network Administrator, Computer Sciences Corporation (1995-96); Network Administrator, Orbital Sciences Corporation (1992-95). **Personal Information:** Married to Kelli in 1990. Two children: Tyler and Todd. Mr. Timberlake enjoys sound engineering and playing drums.

Sandra Kay Young

Senior Software Engineer
Microcosm
2377 Crenshaw #350
Torrance, CA 90501
(888) 619-3555
skyoung_11@yahoo.com

3761

Business Information: Ms. Young is the Senior Software Engineer of Microcosm, responsible for a variety of duties. Her primary responsibilty is to design software for the Scorpius Project. Since 1983, Ms. Young has coded, designed, tested, and implemented various projects for the Company. Utilizing years of experience in the field, she is capable of leading the department in research and development of software. She also assists in implementing policies and procedures, developing goals, implementing strategies to achieve those goals, and ensuring all aspects of the operation run within the framework of the Company's overall plan. Ms. Young strives to do her best work on every project and to complete her job in an alotted time and within budgetary constraints. In the future, Ms. Young hopes to utilize new technology and help Microcosm in its growth, development, and expansion. Professional success can be attributed to her faith in God and various people who have given her support throughout her career. Established in 1984, Microcosm specializes in launch vehicles for satellites. Rockets and other vehicles for space are distributed to NASA and related companies in the field. Approximatelty 55 highly knowledgeable and trained individuals presently work for the Company, assisting in a variety of duties. **Career Highlights:** Senior Software Engineer, Microcosm (1999-Present); Senior Software Engineer, IVS, Inc. (1998-99); Senior Software Engineer, Ericsson (1998). **Education:** University of California at Los Angeles, B.S. in Computer Engineering (1983). **Personal Information:** One child: Devin C. Fields. Ms. Young enjoys the theatre and sports.

Claire Billings

Computer-Based Training (CBT) Team Lead
Lockheed Martin
700 North Frederick Avenue, Building 181, Room 2Y30
Gaithersburg, MD 20879
(301) 240-4087
Fax: (301) 240-5326
claire.billings@lmco.com

3769

Business Information: Mrs. Billings is the Computer-Based Training (CBT) Team Lead at Lockheed Martin. She works with customers, engineers, and software developers to understand the user's needs and system to develop multimedia computer-based training courses for the customer. A savvy, nine-year veteran, she develops courses and has taught several classes to enhance the education of clients on a particular system or technology. During her nine years with IBM/Loral/Lockheed Martin, she has developed a breadth of experience in systems engineering, proposal writing, software development, test, and training. Her success is attributed to her mother's advice, "Do the best job you can." Lockheed Martin is a governmentally contracted business dedicated to the technological enhancement of government systems for the United States. The Company specializes in programs that satisfy the needs for technology within the nation's highest branches of legislative government as well as the Department of Defense. **Career Highlights:** Lockheed Martin: Computer-Based Training (CBT) Team Lead (1997-Present), Training Systems Engineer/Instructor (1996-97); End User Systems Engineer, Loral (1994-96); Software Engineer, IBM (1990-94). **Associations & Accomplishments:** Reiki Master; Women of Color Technology Certificate of Merit (1999). **Education:** University of Maryland at College Park, B.S. in Computer Science with a Minor in Studio Art; Dundalk Community College, certificate in Retail Floristry. **Personal Information:** Married to Doug in 1994. Mrs. Billings enjoys travel, studying and practicing energy healing. She is working on her certification as a Healing Touch Practitioner.

Charlton E. Corson

Systems Administrator and Integrator
Lockheed Martin Enterprise Information Systems
P.O. Box 179 MS DC5670
Denver, CO 80201-0179
charlton.e.corson@lmco.com

3769

Business Information: As a Systems Administratror and Integrator for Lockheed Martin Enterprise Information Systems EIS, Mr. Corson leverages his extensive computer and electrical engineering skills while proving sustaining engineering support for Enterprise wide projects. In this capacity, he assists in the management of the Enterprise directory service using X.500 and LDAP protocols for the e-mail system, and future Windows 2000 active directory implementations. Along with this responsiblity, he also provides systems testing of NT, Windows 2000, and UNIX support for EIS, and administration of configuration management Web based document control systems. He owns a record of delivering results through effective problem solving, configuring of user rights and permissions, updating software and hardware, and implementing network settings. Now an expert, Mr. Corson also performed operating systems re-installations and training and mentoring information technology interns. Mr. Corson's career accomplishments include completing the projects such as, "Projectile Motion" software simulation and demonstration and "Improved Short Wave Radio." Additionally, he was awarded first prize in the IEEE programming contest for the entry "Physics Analysis and Simulation" C++ program. His affiliation with relevant industry organizations such as the IEEE enables him to stay technologically up-to-date and allows for interaction with the many professionals in the field. He attributes his success to dedication. Mr. Corson's advice to others in the industry is "always find time to keep up-to-date on technology, use effective troubleshooting methodologies, and have a positive calm attitude." Attaining the position of Chief Information Officer of Information Technology serves as his future goal. EIS is part of Lockheed Martin's Information and Services business unit, which provides support for both internal and commercial IT projects and systems. **Career Highlights:** Systems Administrator and Integrator, Lockheed Martin Enterprise Information Systems (1999-Present); Metropolitan State College of Denver: Systems Administrator (1998), Electronic and Network Assistant (1995-98); Automobile Parts Clerk, Checkers Automobile (1991-92). **Associations & Accomplishments:** Institute of Electrical and Electronics Engineers Professional Branch; Phi Theta Kappa; Channel 9 Health Fair Blood Screening Section. **Education:** Metropolitan State College of Denver, B.S. in Electrical Engineering Technology with minor in Computer Science (1998). **Personal Information:** Mr. Corson enjoys working on older automobiles and collecting antiques.

Winston E. Lewis

Systems Engineer
Lockheed Martin
803 Whitney Street
Los Banos, CA 93635-5130
(408) 756-5758
winjack12@yahoo.com

3769

Business Information: Serving as a Systems Engineer for Lockheed Martin, Mr. Lewis fulfills the duties of systems architect for the system of systems portion of the SBIRS (Space Based Infrared System) program. Responsible for system architecture, he participates in the design, development, and deployment of advanced hardware and software. Working closely with management and users, Mr. Lewis draws from his 20 years of related experience in defense systems to provide the Department of Defense with the most up-to-date and cost effective defense systems available. Continuing his education in information technology and software, he is negotiating with the Company to get more involved with mission management software. He attributes his success to his ability to plan and being in the right place at the right time. Lockheed Martin specializes in aerospace engineering and systems integration. The Company engages in the manufacturing of satellites and missiles for the U.S. Department of Defense. The Company is headquartered in Bethesda, Maryland and operates from 939 facilities in 57 cities in 45 states, and internationally in 56 nations and territories. The Company currently functions under the direction of more than 147,000 professionals who facilitate smooth business operations. Presently, Lockheed Martin reports annual revenues in excess of $25.35 billion. **Career Highlights:** Systems Engineer, Lockheed Martin (1999-Present); Logistics Team Leader, Harris Sunnyvale (1996-98); Logistics Systems Analyst, TRW/ESL (1992-96); Intelligence Analyst, United States Air Force (1978-99). **Associations & Accomplishments:** Association of Old Crows; Recipient of Military Awards: Joint Service Meritorious Service Award, Air Force Commendation Medal. **Education:** College of Notre Dame, M.S. in Systems Management (1999); Wayland Baptist University, Honolulu Campus, B.S; Community College of the Air Force, A.A. in Radio Communications Processing Management. **Personal Information:** Married to Jackie Bronson in 1980.

Edward Longstrom

Enterprise Network Engineer
Lockheed Martin
1801 State Route17C, MD220
Owego, NY 13827-3998
(607) 751-7122
Fax: (607) 751-5775
ed.longstrom@lmco.com

3769

Business Information: As an Enterprise Network Engineer for Lockheed Martin, Mr. Longstrom is responsible for large scale systems architecture, information and network security, and LINUX development. Before joining Lockheed Martin in 1998, he served as Director of Information Technology with Spectra.Net. His background history also includes a stint as Lead Architect at Resource Recycling Technologies. Mr. Longstrom, drawing from extensive educational ties and occupational experience, is a key contributor to the success of his department. He works and coordinates with users and systems management to analyze, specify, and design new technologically advanced solutions. His performance continuously exceeds job requirements and he displays industriousness, conscientiousness, and diligence in performing all tasks. He attributes his career success to his communication skills and ability to work in a team environment. Mr. Longstrom's future objective goals include becoming more involved in all aspects of operations. He also plans to expedite continued promotion through his involvement in the advancement of operations. Lockheed Martin is a publicly owned company engaged in the manufacture of commercial systems for the Department of Defence and the aerospace industry. Headquartered in Maryland, the Company serves an international client base. The Company employs the expertise of 165,000 individuals and reports an estimated annual revenue in excess of $6.19 billion. **Career Highlights:** Enterprise Network Engineer, Lockheed Martin (1998-Present); Director of Information Technology, Spectra.Net (1994-98); Lead Architect, Resource Recycling Technologies (1990-93). **Education:** Binghamton University, B.S. (1994). **Personal Information:** Mr. Longstrom enjoys reading, camping, mountain biking and hockey.

Iris Lynn Moore-Fore

Information Security Engineer
Lockheed Martin
401 M Street SW
Washington, DC 20460
(202) 260-6421
Fax: (202) 260-6636
irislmf@hotmail.com

3769

Business Information: As Information Security Engineer for Lockheed Martin, Ms. Moore-Fore is responsible for personnel, computer, information, and physical security. Before joining Lockheed in 1998, Ms. Moore-Fore served as Security Administrator with Booz Allen & Hamilton. Drawing from more than 20 years of experience in the security field, she establishes and deploys procedures to ensure infrastructure integrity, reliability, and security. Coordinating resources, schedules, time lines, and assignments also fall within the realm of his responsibilities. Ms. Moore-Fore attributes her professional success to her supportive mother and husband. She remains in the forefront of the security field by reading security and trade journals, attending trade shows, and searching the Internet. Ms. Moore-Fore plans to expedite continued promotion through the fulfillment of her responsibilities and her involvement in the advancement of operations. Serving an international client base, Lockheed Martin is one of the leading government contractors in the United States. The Company specializes in aerospace engineering, as well as software development in the areas of aerospace and defense technology. Established in 1996, Lockheed Martin employs a work force of 347 individuals to meet with clients, facilitate scheduling, and address customer queries. **Career Highlights:** Information Security Engineer, Lockheed Martin (1998-Present); Security Administrator, Booz Allen & Hamilton (1989-98). **Education:** National Louis University, B.A. (1995); Central Texas College, Electrical Engineering Certificate. **Personal Information:** Married. to Michael in 1982. Three children: Ashanti, Adia, and Shaka. Ms. Moore-Fore enjoys sewing, aerobics and weight training.

Loren Mark Walker

Senior Systems Engineer
Lockheed Martin
755 Dividing Road
Severna Park, MD 21146-4305
(410) 796-3478
loren.walker@mciworldcom.net

3769

Business Information: Offering his extensive systems engineering expertise, Mr. Walker serves as the Senior Systems Engineer for Lockheed Martin. Specializing in communication systems, he designs, develops, and deploys systems. Working in both a technical and managerial position, Mr. Walker possesses a seat on the systems engineering steering committee which works to improve the overall engineering processes. As a prominent figure for over 30 years, he delivers many presentations at seminars including this past summer's presentation on "System Prospective of Y2K" in Brighten, England. A sharp professional, Mr. Walker looks forward to authoring an article on "System Infrastructure for Large Complex Systems" as well as being session chairman for presentations at the regional conference in Washington, D.C. on "Applied Systems Engineering Methods in Diverse Context." Mr. Walker attributes his success to his initiative and implementing personal goals that enable him to capitalize on vast opportunities afforded in the industry. Lockheed Martin performs systems development in the areas of commercial, aerospace, and defense technology. Merged in 1995 with Martin Marietta, the Corporation specializes in the design, manufacture, integration, operation, and maintenance of systems and products in the fields of aeronautics, electronics, energy and environment, information and technology services, and space and missiles. Presently, the Corporation employs a work force of more than 40,000 professional, technical, and support personnel. **Career Highlights:** Lockheed Martin: Senior Systems Engineer (1999-Present), Senior Systems Engineer/Manager (1996-99); Senior Systems Engineer, TASC (1994-96); Systems Engineer, Department of Defense (1967-94). **Associations & Accomplishments:** President of the Maryland Chapter (Present, 1995), International Council on Systems Engineering; Past Member, Institute of Electrical and Electronics Engineers; President (1985-86), Manhattan Beach Civic Association. **Education:** University of Southern California, M.S. in Systems Management (1974); Bucknell University, B.S. in Electrical Engineering (1967). **Personal Information:** Married One child. Mr. Walker enjoys astronomy and Boy Scout activities. He is an Assistant Scoutmaster with the Boy Scouts of America.

3800 Instruments and Related Products

3812 Search and navigation equipment
3821 Laboratory apparatus and furniture
3822 Environmental controls
3823 Process control instruments
3824 Fluid meters and counting devices
3825 Instruments to measure electricity
3826 Analytical instruments
3827 Optical instruments and lenses
3829 Measuring and controlling devices, nec
3841 Surgical and medical instruments
3842 Surgical appliances and supplies
3843 Dental equipment and supplies
3844 X-ray apparatus and tubes
3845 Electromedical equipment
3851 Ophthalmic goods
3861 Photographic equipment and supplies
3873 Watches, clocks, watchcases and parts

Antonio C. Gellineau

Senior Software Engineer II
Raytheon
106 Lanthorn Circle
Madison, AL 35758-7433
(256) 722-4442
agellineau@mindspring.com

3812

Business Information: As a Level II Senior Software Engineer of Raytheon, Mr. Gellineau is responsible for maintaining and increasing the level of technology and productivity that is achieved by a staff of over 250 systems engineers. With over 25 years in the Industry, and posessing over three degrees in information technology, he is well qualified to work on proposals and make bids to win government and civilian contracts. Mr. Gellineau also directs the research and development of prototypes that will bring the Company to the forefront of the international defense electronics industry. Strategic plans include getting more involved on the technical side and project management, and leading a technical team of 50 to 100 engineers in the delivery of leading edge defense systems. His success reflects his consistency and desire to grow as well as his ability to establish realistic and attainable goals. Raytheon specializes in the development and implementation of defense electronics. This electronics company employs over 100,000 people and has contracts with the government, and other civilian clientele to design software in the aviation recognition arena. These systems have been designed for and installed in the patriot missiles batteries as well as other military and civilian applications. **Career Highlights:** Senior Software Engineer II, Raytheon (1990-Present); Staff Specialist, Data General (1987-89); Project Engineer, Schlumberger (1982-86). **Education:** University of Texas at Austin, M.A. in Computer Science (1986); Massachusetts Institute of Technology: M.S. in Computer Science (1976), M.S. in Electrical Engineering (1976), B.S. in Electrical Engineering (1974). **Personal Information:** Married to Anne Martyne in 1997. One child: Hendryck Antonio. Mr. Gellineau enjoys chess and family time. Mr. Gellineau was an international chess player.

Michael George

Software Engineer
Lockheed Martin Federal Systems
1801 State Route 17C
Owego, NY 13827
(607) 751-4539
Fax: (607) 757-3170
mikegeorge@stny.rr.com

3812

Business Information: Mr. George began his association with Lockheed Martin Federal Systems in 1999, and currently serves as a Sofeware Engineer. He works closely with Department of Defense and systems management and users to analyze, specify, and design software solutions for new and existing weapon systems. Demonstrating systems knowledge and expertise, Mr. George is presently involved with software integration for the United States Navy's SH-60R helicopter upgrades. In this context, he develops life cycle codes and flight tests for on board computer systems that will help the Navy keep the competitive edge in combat scenarios. Future endeavors for Mr. George include staying with Lockheed Martin and continuing the upgrade and development of new versions of software. His success is attributed to support of his family and friends as well as his adaptability and flexibility. Lockheed Martin Federal Systems operates as an international corporation specializing in defense contracts and systems integration. Established in 1996, the Corporation is based out of Owego, New York. Presently, Lockheed Martin Federal Systems employs a 4,000 professional, technical, and administrative support staff who help generate annual earnings in excess of $1 billion **Career Highlights:** Software Engineer, Lockheed Martin Federal Systems (Present). **Associations & Accomplishments:** Association for Computing Machinery; Boy Scouts of America. **Education:** State University of New York at Binghamton, B.S. (1999).

M. Melissa Losson

Senior Principal Software Engineer
Raytheon Company
1428 Pheasant Court
Fullerton, CA 92833
(714) 446-3710
mloss@aol.com

3812

Business Information: As the Senior Principal of Software Engineering of the Raytheon Company, Ms. Losson is a highly respected software systems technical lead and manager of a U.S. air navigation system. Responsible for incorporating Company policies and procedures in the engineering department, she supervises her staff of eight employees. Utilizing over 16 years of software engineering experience, Ms. Losson manages project budgets, oversees toll systems, and works on various projects designing, testing, coding, and developing cutting edge software. Purchasing required supplies and coordinating resources, time lines, and assignments also fall within the realm of Ms. Losson's responsibilities. An accomplished professional, she has received several superior performance awards. Attributing her success to her training and experience, she plans to continue developing new technology as she aspires to move up in the Company's corporate management ladder. The Raytheon Company manufactures hardware and develops software for air traffic control and navigation, military systems, and commercial applications. Established in 1960, the Company is headquartered in Fullerton, California, and operates out of several national subsidiaries. The Company currently employs the skills and professional talents of more than 90,000 individuals who facilitate smooth business operations. **Career Highlights:** Senior Principal Software Engineer, Raytheon Company (1997-Present); Software Systems Engineer, Hughes Aircraft Company (1984-97). **Associations & Accomplishments:** Vice President, Peppermill Run Homeowners Association. **Education:** University of Southern California, M.S. in Computer Engineering (1987); Western Kentucky University, B.S. in Computer Science (1984). **Personal Information:** Ms. Losson enjoys reading, golf and home improvement projects.

William Shih

Engineer
Raytheon Systems
651 West Grondahl Street
Covina, CA 91722
wshih@usc.edu

3812

Business Information: As an Engineer with Raytheon Systems, Mr. Shih fulfills a number of functions on behalf of the Company and its government clientele. He works with management and users to analyze, specify, and design new solutions to enhance overall computer operations. Responsible for product support, he coordinates resouces, time lines, schedules, and assignments during all phases of project management. Utilizing his expansive knowledge in the computer field, Mr. Shih concentrates his efforts towards the design and development of new software and hardware systems. Involved in corperate training, he ensures the proper education of the engineers in roder to produce qualty systems. Continuing his growth with Raytheon Systems, Mr. Shih remains committed towards products laced with quality, value, and realiability. His success reflects his ability to think outside the box, aggressively take on new challenges, and deliver results. Specializing in software engineering, Raytheon Systems was established as a consulting agency for the federal government. Located in Covina, California, the Company performs a wide range of services within the field of information technology nationwide. Developing software and databases designed to suit the purchasers individual needs and desires, Raytheon Systems focuses on implementing state-of-the-art technologies in order to produce a more efficeint and effective product. **Career Highlights:** Engineer, Raytheon Systems (Present); Product Support Specialist, Office of Advanced Analytical Tools (1999); Technical Support Specialist, Office of Support Services (1998); Web Master, University of Southern California (1997-98). **Associations & Accomplishments:** Tau Beta Pi; Eta Kuppa Nu; Upsilon Pi Epsilon. **Education:** University of Southern California, B.S. in Computer Engineering (2000). **Personal Information:** Mr. Shih enjoys building solar cars and tennis.

Kerry Spangler

Principal Technical Support and Training Development Specialist
Raytheon
1001 Boston Post Road East
Marlborough, MA 01752
(508) 490-3133
Fax: (508) 490-3466
kspdng8393@aol.com

3812

Business Information: Displaying his expertise in this highly specialized field, Mr. Spangler serves as Principal Technical Support and Training Development Specialist with Raytheon, providing computer based and classroom training programs for individuals involved in the research and development of the Company's diverse product line. Keeping well informed of new legislation affecting the work place, Mr. Spangler incorporates specific procedures and policies to enhance productivity, quality, value, and integrity of the product line. Focusing on the market strategies, he provides promotional plans for the development of new products and training services. The most rewarding aspects of his career include development of a computer based training for the Australian defense air traffic controllers. Mr. Spangler continues to grow professionally through the fulfillment of his responsibilities and his involvement in the advancement of operations. His success is attributed to his experience, exposure, ability to learn quickly, and the opportunities afforded to him. The third largest defense contractor, Raytheon is an established and reputable manufacturer of complex defense mechanisms and devises founded in 1986. Located in Marlborough, Massachusetts, the Company employs the expertise of a number of qualified personnel to facilitate all aspects of research and development, testing, and distribution of missiles, aircrafts, radar and survailance equipment, and automations for military installations. Serving an international clientele, the Company strives to implement the latest technologies into the production and distribution of international and domestic air traffic control systems. **Career Highlights:** Principal Technical Support and Training Development Specialist, Raytheon (1998-Present); United States Air Force: Training Development Manager (1994-98), Logistics Superintendent (1991-94). **Associations & Accomplishments:** American Society of Training Developers; International Society of Logistics Engineers. **Education:** Community College of the Air Force, Associate's Degree (1995). **Personal Information:** Married to Sarah in 1987. Two children: Amy and Brenden. Mr. Spangler enjoys golf.

Michael D. Tsengouras

Project Manager
Navigation Technology
953 Mallard Circle
Schaumburg, IL 60193
(847) 699-6500
Fax: (847) 437-7731
tseggy@ix.netcom.com

3812

Business Information: As Project Manager of Navigation Technology, Mr. Tsengouras leads the ARC/information development team. With 10 years of field experience, Mr. Tsengouras offers insightful management to the development group, emphasizing the use of ARC information, the creation of innovative tools, and geographic information systems. After he has achieved a stabilized production level, Mr. Tsengouras would like to assume a more instrumental role in client interactions to improve the quality of the data. Navigation Technology builds and maintains databases utilized in in-vehicle navigation systems. The privately funded Company provides worldwide mapping, amassing navigational capabilities for door to door directions. Established in 1985, the Company employs 800 people throughout three production facilities and six offices. **Career Highlights:** Project Manager, Navigation Technology (1995-Present); Senior Systems Engineer, OCS Technologies (1993-95); Senior Systems Engineer, GTE Government Information Services (1989-93); Technical Manager - ARC/Info, GTE Infotech (1988-89).

Jackie D. Wilkins

Senior Electrical Design Engineer
Raytheon/TI Systems Company
401 West Jefferson
Van Alstyne, TX 75495
(972) 462-2116
Fax: (972) 462-3375
a0458171@rtxmail.rsc.raytheon.com

3812

Business Information: Mr. Wilkins is Senior Electrical Design Engineer for Raytheon/TI Systems Company. He is responsible for designing board and system level electronics for prototype and ATE systems. Before joining Raytheon Systems Company in 1996, Mr. Wilkins served as Project Engineer with Campbell Soup Company. His background history also includes a stint as Project and Electrical Design Engineer with McDonald & Associates. A savvy, technology professional with 14 years in the field, he is experienced in all aspects of analysis, design, development, implementation, and project management. His affiliation with industry related associations enables him to remain current and allows him to network and interact with his colleagues in the different fields. Moving into mid management serves as one of Mr. Wilkins' future goals. Raytheon/TI Systems Company engages in research and development of cutting edge defense system electronics for the Department of Defense. Established in 1922, the Company employs more than 6,000 professional, technical, and support personnel who help generate in excess of $15 billion annually. **Career Highlights:** Senior Electrical Design Engineer, Raytheon/TI Systems Company (1996-Present); Project Engineer, Campbell Soup Company (1992-96); Project/Electrical Design Engineer, McDonald & Associates (1991-92). **Associations & Accomplishments:** Texas Society of Professional Engineers; Southwest Officials Association; Phi Beta Sigma Fraternity Inc.; Institute of Electronics and Electrical Engineers. **Education:** Prairie View A&M, B.S. in Electrical Engineering (1985). **Personal Information:** Married to Donna F. in 1987. Three children: Brandon Jarrell, Jaclyn Denise, and Olivia Nicole. Mr. Wilkins enjoys being a football referee and baseball umpire.

Tara Lyn Nylese

Technical Sales Manager
EDAX Inc.
12880 Vista Pine Circle
Fort Myers, FL 33913
(941) 561-5311
Fax: (941) 561-5310
tnylese@edax.com

3821

Business Information: A successful five year veteran, Ms. Nylese serves as Technical Sales Manager of EDAX Inc. Joining the team of professionals 1996, she currently manages the Corporation's sales region, providing engineering, support, and software services. Possessing an excellent understanding of her field, Ms. Nylese has many tasks within the Company, to include coordinating resources, schedules, and assignments ensuring smooth operations. Ms. Nylese also administers software checks to keep her sales region's computer network current and manages existing client accounts. Attributing her success to her good personality and positive attitude, her future plans include growing technically, keeping up with sales, and becoming more involved in product or research development. Headquartered in New Jersey and employing 180 people, EDAX Inc. strives to manufacture the best lab equipment. Founded in 1962, the Corporation is a leader in the medical equipment industry. EDAX focuses on building machinery for X-ray microanalysis, which is similar to a microscope. The product is used in many types of research as well as in the semiconductor and forensics industries. **Career Highlights:** EDAX Inc.: Technical Sales Manager (1996-Present), Applications Engineer (1996); Laboratory Specialist, Hoechst Celanese (1995-96). **Associations & Accomplishments:** Volunteer, Lee County Soup Kitchen; Big Sisters/Big Brothers; Big Sisters of America; Past President, Best Buddies International; Beta Beta Beta Science Honor Society; Phi Eta Sigma Honor Society; Alpha Phi Fraternity; Ronald McDonald House Havana Cup 2000 Participant. **Education:** University of Richmond, B.S. (1995). **Personal Information:** Married to Gerald in 1999. Ms. Nylese enjoys sailing.

Rafael Benavides

Information Technology Manager
Fisher-Rosemount
9 Founders Boulevard, Suite C
El Paso, TX 79906-4965
(915) 772-4112
Fax: +52 14197010
rafaelb@micromotion.com

3823

Business Information: Mr. Benavides began his career with Fisher-Rosemount in 1997, and presently assumes the title and responsibilities of Information Technology Manager at the Company's El Paso facility. Through the past few years, he has acquired an in-depth knowledge of all aspects of the business activities and is able to resolve current issues or porblems that may directly affect the future of the Company. The position requires Mr. Benavides to oversee all internal networking and communication aspects of the business as well as assist in maintaining software and telecommunication systems in a fully functional and operational status. Utilizing his expereince and expertise in the technology field, he supervises a team of four employees and ensures all aspects of the operation run according to plan and comply with set regulations. Mr. Benavides plans to continue in his position of Information Technology Manager at Fisher-Rosemont and complete a Master's program. Fisher-Rosemount is a manufacturing company of flow/mass meters and sensors. Established in 1995, this Minnesota-based company employs a staff of 200 skilled and knowledgeable individuals to assist in various aspects of the Texas location operation. A division of Emerson Electric, this international businesss strives to provide quality and professional services to clients. **Career Highlights:** Information Technology Manager, Fisher-Rosemount (1997-Present); Project Leader, UPS Worldwide Logistics (1996-97); Operations Supervision, Electronic Data Systems (1994-96). **Education:** Chihuahua Technical Institute, degree in Electrical Engineering (1991). **Personal Information:** Married to Jacqueline Grajeda in 1994. One child: Rafael. Mr. Benavides enjoys surfing the Internet, music, tennis and computing.

Peter N. Nguyen

Principal Engineer
Furon FHP
3340 East La Palma Avenue
Anaheim, CA 92806
(714) 238-1350
Fax: (714) 666-8461
pnnguyen@earthlink.net

3823

Business Information: Utilizing seven years of experience in the mechanical engineering field, Mr. Nguyen functions in the role of Principal Engineer for Furon FHP. He is responsible for new product design for the teflon fluid handling products and oversees its development from conception to manufacture. Feasibility testing is performed and product quality assurance is ensured. Mr. Nguyen also assists on formulating sales and marketing plans for the completed product to the industries in which it is utilized. Passionate about his work, he always remains alert to new opportunities, techniques, and approaches. He entertains the dream of owning his own business in the future. Mr. Nguyen's success reflects his ability to think outside the box, produce results, and aggressively tackle new challenges. Established in 1969, Furon FHP produces a variety of teflon fluid handling products for a large international clientele. The publicly traded company employs approximately 350 dedicated staff members in its Anaheim, California location. Reporting yearly revenues in upwards of $470 million, Furon is headquartered in Laguna Nequel, California. **Career Highlights:** Principal Engineer, Furon FHP (1994-Present); Design Engineer, Hydrospin, Inc. (1993-94); Consultant Engineer, T11 Technical Education Systems (1992-93); Research Assistant, CSUF Mechanical Engineering Department (1992). **Associations & Accomplishments:** American Society of Mechanical Engineers. **Education:** CSUF, B.S. in Mechanical Engineering (1994). **Personal Information:** Married to Eliza in 1995. Two children: Lizette and Colette. Mr. Nguyen enjoys computers and RC helicopters.

Laurence Picherot

Manager Data Services Europe
Honeywell
80 Route des Lucioles BP 159
Sophia Antipolis, France 06903
+33 492941526
Fax: +33 492941521
laurence.picherot@honeywell.com

3823

Business Information: A successful professional in the technology field, Ms. Picherot serves as Manager Data Services Europe wtih Honeywell. Naturally skilled in the information technology industry, she has mastered the challenging duty of managing all aspects of databases and Internet mobility services for Honeywell. Highly recognized, Ms. Picherot has received rewards, such as the "Premier Achievement Award" in 1996, the "Productivity Growth Award" and "Euro Quest Participation Award" in 1998, and the "Sigma Award for Outstanding Productivity Project" in 1999. The most rewarding aspect of her career is completing a large project on time and within budget. Presently involved in the construction of an advanced company networking system, Ms. Picherot is evaluating and consolidating operations to enhance the efficiency of day-to-day activities as well as creating additional services to broaden the horizons of Honeywell in the European market. One of the largest industrial companies in the world, Honeywell engages in the development and production of control solutions for major corporations, which in turn results in the benefit of customers. Striving for improved productivity, competitiveness, enhanced comfort, increased safety, environmental protection, and energy conservation, Honeywell maintains goals of perfecting the operations of successful companies. Serving a large portion of its client portfolio in the automotive, aerospace, chemical, and building construction industries, the Company generates an incredible $25 billion in annual revenue. Positioned in a leading role after the merger of Honeywell with AlliedSignal in December, the combined has resulted in the increased staffing to over 100,000 employees. **Career Highlights:** Manager Data Services Europe, Honeywell (2000-Present); AlliedSignal: Manager of Enterprise Wide Network (1997-99), Project Manager for Networks (1995-97). **Education:** Degree in Engineering (1991). **Personal Information:** One child: Iris Briand. Ms. Picherot enjoys sports and rollerblading.

Stephen E. Sayian

Training Group Manager
Teradyne Inc.
321 Harrison Avenue
Boston, MA 02118-2238
(617) 422-2681
Fax: (617) 422-2867
stephen.sayian@teradyne.com

3825

Business Information: In his role as Product Support Training Manager of Teradyne, Inc., Mr. Sayian focuses time and attention on the policies of industrial customer support. He has been involved in the technical training arena for the last 14 years. Demonstrating adept technical ability, he is able to develop computer based instructional programs such as CD-Rom training and documentation. With exceptional communicative skills, he incorporates student feedback into the design of new curriculum, customized for the diverse needs of East and/or West Coast clients. Enjoying the challenges of his position, Mr. Sayian intends to continue in his current role as he initiates the formulation of comprehensive training programs. Teradyne Inc. specializes in the manufacture of large scale test equipment for the semiconductor industry. Recognized as the international leader of the market, the Corporation produces equipment that tests computer chips and wafers for all industry areas including automotive and medical wireless. Headquartered in Boston, Massachusetts, the Corporation employs 7,000 highly trained employees who assist in the annual generation of $1.6 billion. **Career Highlights:** Teradyne Inc: Product Support Training Manager (Present), Training Group Manager (1998); Training Group Leader, Raytheon Company (1985-98); Trainer, Avco Systems Division (1984-85); Logistics Specialist, United States Civil Service, Department of United States Air Force (1973-84). **Associations & Accomplishments:** American Society of Training and Development; South Shore Yacht Club: Board of Directors, Corporate Officer. **Education:** Northeastern University, B.S. in Management Information Systems (1996); Massasoit Community College, A.S. in Computer Science (1986). **Personal Information:** Married to Gwendolyn in 1982. Two children: Grant and Adrienne. Mr. Sayian enjoys sailing and golf.

George E. Oulundsen, Jr.

Sales Engineer
Millipore Corporation
80 Ashby Road
Bedford, MA 01730
(800) 221-1975
Fax: (603) 880-4822
george_oulundsen@millipore.com

3826

Business Information: Displaying his excellent skills in this highly specialized position, Mr. Oulundsen serves as Sales Engineer with Millipore Corporation, dedicating his attention towards the research and development of the Corporation's specialized products and services. Forming new clients within the pharmaceutical industry, Mr. Oulundsen presents all newly discovered products and their specific uses in the complex areas of medical technologies. Providing training programs, he implements specific procedures and policies pertaining to the development of products. An accomplished professional, Mr. Oulundsen owns a patent that optimizes the removal of plasma in products. He is also the author of several publications on use of membranes to remove virus, such as "Vox Songa." The most rewarding aspects of his career include developing an innovative management training program that is now utilized worldwide. In the future, Mr. Oulundsen looks forward to the introduction of a virus removal and cross flow filtration tool prior to his retirement. Specializing in separation sciences for the life sciences and biological technology industries, Millipore Corporation was established in 1954. Providing micro-electronics and research and development in the purification process, the Corporation employs the expertise of 4500 individuals to orchestrate all activities of research and development, testing, and distribution of products to an international clientele. In 1999, the Corporation generated an estimated annual revenue of $800 million and remains committed to serving the diverse needs of a growing client base.. **Career Highlights:** Millipore Corporation: Sales Engineer (1985-Present), Process Sales (1980-85), Production Manager (1973-80). **Associations & Accomplishments:** Sigma Xi; Scientific Research Society; American Association for the Advancement of Science; Board of Directors, Home Health and Hospice Care; Mashua NIT; Reserve Officers Association; Chairman, Solid Waste Committee. **Education:** University of Connecticut: M.S. in Bio-Chemistry (1968), M.S. in Bacteriology (1969); Providence College, Associate's Degree in Business (1961); Brown University (1957-59). **Personal Information:** Married to Elaine in 1985. Two children: George III and Nils Ole. Mr. Oulundsen enjoys woodworking, gardening, hiking, biking and photography.

Alan P. Su, Ph.D.

Software Design Engineer
Agilent Technologies, Inc.
5601 Lindero Canyon Road
Westlake Village, CA 91362-6493
(818) 879-6344
Fax: (818) 879-6394
alan_su@agilent.com

3826

Business Information: Years of extensive education and hands on experience in the field has enabled Dr. Su to achieve the position of Software Design Engineer of Agilent Technologies, Inc. Utilizing his expertise in the field, he designs and implements electronic design automation tools specifically for digital signal processing applications. A 14 year veteran of technology, he conducts independent research, analyzes information, and assists in developing computer application solutions. Dr. Su plans on developing innovative tools that will have a great impact on society and assist in future technology. Working with a dynamic group of professionals and experts and the ability to interact and share ideas have contributed to Dr. Su's overall success in all career endeavors. Agilent Technologies, Inc. is a $8.9 billion operation specializing in the test and measurement technologies. A total staff of 42,000 skilled and trained employees assist in various aspects of the operation, striving to achieve goals set by the Corporation. A spin off of Hewlitt-Packard, the business is known for keeping abreast on new developments in the field and providing quality and professional services. **Career Highlights:** Software Design Engineer, Agilent Technologies, Inc. (1999-Present); Software Design Engineer, Hewlett-Packard Company (1998-99); Instructor, University of California at Riverside (1994-98). **Associations & Accomplishments:** Association of Computing Machinery. **Education:** University of California at Riverside, Ph.D. (1998); University of Missouri at Rolla, M.S. (1994); Chung Yuan Christian University, B.S. (1986). **Personal Information:** Married to Ingfang Tsai in 1989. Three children: Joey, Ryan, and Helen. Dr. Su enjoys fishing and travel.

Julie-Anne Walker

E-Business Manager
Agilent Technologies, Inc.
2 Robbins Road
Westford, MA 01886-4113
(978) 266-3521
Fax: (978) 266-3537
julie_walker@agilent.com

3826

Business Information: As E-Business Manager of Agilent Technologies, Inc., Ms. Walker is responsible for a number of e-commerce duties on behalf of the Company. Possessing an excellent understanding of his field, she is in charge with the development of innovative e-business programs to drive revenue growth through e-commerce, Internet enablement, and e-services. A savvy, nine year professional in technology, Ms. Walker joined Agilent in 1999 after serving with Hewlett-Packard in a variety of positions. Her focus is on changes that will allow Agilent Technologies and its clients to take advantage of any newly developed e-services to remain in the forefront of the industry, as well as to remain flexible, efficient, and profitable in the Information Technology Age. Future endeavors for Ms. Walker include continuing to excel in the industry and eventually start her own nonprofit organization for gifted children. An international technology company, Agilent Technologies is an independent measurement company composed of test and measurement components, chemical analysis and medical businesses, and a computing and imaging company that includes all of Hewlett Packards computing, printing and imaging businesses. The Company provides quality measurement tools and components for manufacturers and service providers in the communications industry. Presently, Agilent employs a work force of more than 40,000 professional, technical, and support staff. **Career Highlights:** E-Business Manager, Agilent Technologies, Inc. (1999-Present); Hewlett-Packard: Internet Strategy Manager (1997-99), Senior Account Representative, Australia (1996-97), Marketing Communications Manager, Australia (1994-96). **Associations & Accomplishments:** National Association of Female Executives; President, Alleshree Children's Fund. **Education:** University of Melbourne, Bachelor's degree of Engineering in Electronics (1991). **Personal Information:** Ms. Walker enjoys singing and musical theater.

John S. Brown

Network Engineer
Optical Coating Laboratory
2789 Northpoint Parkway
Santa Rosa, CA 95407
(707) 525-7143
Fax: (707) 525-7410

3827

Business Information: Displaying his expertise in this specialized position, Mr. Brown serves as the Network Engineer for Optical Coating Laboratory. He assumes responsibility for the efficient functioning of the local area network and the wide area network infrastructures for the Corporation. Working in a team oriented environment, he also oversees the file and application servers that operate the programs on which the Corporation depends. Mr. Brown has been recognized for his work within the technology industry and has been published in the LAN times. Crediting his professional success to God, he looks forward to entering into a managerial position in the near future. His success reflects his ability to produce results and aggressively take on new challenges. Publicly owned, Optical Coating Laboratory is engaged in the high tech manufacturing of optically variable vacuum deposited thin film coatings. The coatings are used in a wide range of markets within the United States and around the world. Founded in 1951, the Corporation employs the skilled services of over 1,600 employees. Annual sales are boasted to be upwards of $255 million. **Career Highlights:** Network Engineer, Optical Coating Laboratory (1973-Present). **Associations & Accomplishments:** Certified NetWare Engineer; Ordained Pastor, Christian and Missionary Alliance in the Cambodian District; District Secretary, Cambodian District of C&MA. **Education:** University of California at Berkeley: B.A. in Math (1972), Secondary Teaching Credential (1973); C&MA, Theological Education by Extension (1994). **Personal Information:** Married to Judy in 1983. Five children: Rosemary, Zachary, Vorn, Tony, and Sarot. Mr. Brown enjoys running, cycling, speed skating and is self-taught in the Khmer language.

Michael J. Wilcox, Ph.D.

Chief Executive Officer
Hyperacuity Systems
6555 Delmonico Drive, Apartment 212
Colorado Springs, CO 80919-4014
(719) 333-6002
Fax: (719) 333-2420
mike.wilcox@usafa.af.mil

3827

Business Information: Serving a company engaged in research for the United States Navy, Dr. Wilcox works with Hyperacuity Systems. As the Chief Executive Officer he oversees day to day operations and conducts electrical recording of nerve cells. Possessing an excellent understanding of technology, Dr. Wilcox also produces computer simulations that tests VLSI circuitry, designed to emulate nervous functions. In addition to the production of these simulations, Dr. Wilcox also manufactures and conducts testing of the final devices and products. Widely recognized and accomplished in his field, Dr. Wilcox is the recipient of the1999 Science Engineer Award from the United States Air Force, and has been featured in the "Journal of Glaucoma" for his development of a patented device to treat glaucoma as well as the "IEEE Transactions of Neutral Networks." Established in 1996, Hyperacuity Systems was founded to conduct visual system prototypes and analog information processing. Presently the Company is engaged in the design of artificial eyes for robots and other prototypes for the United States Navy. Also credited with discovering major medical breakthroughs in recent years, the Company conducts research and development of human diseases. **Career Highlights:** Chief Executive Officer, Hyperacuity Systems (1996-Present); Research Professor, United State Air Force Academy (1997-Present); Research Associate Professor, University of New Mexico. **Associations & Accomplishments:** Biology Honorary; Beta-Beta-Beta; Physics Honorary, Sigma Pi Sigma; Sigma X; Institute of Electrical and Electronics Engineers; SPIE; American Association for the Advancement of Science; National Geographic. **Education:** Purdue University: Ph.D. (1979), M.S., B.S. **Personal Information:** Married to Claudie in 1980. Two children: Christopher and Marc.

Georgiy R. Minasyan, Ph.D.

Senior Scientist
Astro-Med, Inc.
2042 Spring Mill Road
Lafayette Hill, PA 19444-2110
(610) 397-0293
minasyan@ieee.org

3829

Business Information: Dr. Minasyan brings 14 years of experience in the area of signal processing and computer modeling to his current position as Senior Scientist with Astro-Med, Inc. Currently working in the gzass-telefactor division, he is directly involved in research and development of epilepsy monitoring and neurology software and is a key player in new equipment design, analysis, and implementation. An accomplished professional, he was directly responsible for the development of seizure detection equipment that is now being used extensively in hospitals worldwide. He intends to continue his research into implementing new technology aimed towards a more complete understanding of epilepsy. Dr. Minasyan attributes his success to his dedication to keeping himself up to date by reading pertinent articles, attending various seminars, and participating in meetings with his peers. Astro-Med, Inc. is a neurophysiological instrumentation company founded in 1970, currently employing 365 specialists. The Corporation has three separate divisions that produce neurological testing and measurement equipment, specifically targeted towards the treatment and better understanding of epilepsy. **Career Highlights:** Senior Scientist, Astro-Med, Inc. (1999-Present); Senior Scientist,Telefactor Corporation (1997-99); Senior Scientist, Acoustics Institute, Moscow, Russia (1986-99). **Associations & Accomplishments:** Institute of Electronics and Electrical Engineers; E.M.B.S.; I.N.N.S.; Signal Processing Society; Institute of Electronics and Electrical Engineers Computer Society; Acoustical Society of America; New York Academy of Sciences. **Education:** Acoustics Institute, Ph.D. (1994); Moscow Institute of Ragioengineering, Electronics and Automation, M.S. (1986). **Personal Information:** One child: Anna. Dr. Minasyan enjoys chess, music and travel.

John K. Nebel

Software Engineer
Schenck Turner Inc.
100 Kay Industrial Drive
Orion, MI 48359
(248) 377-2100
Fax: (248) 377-2743
rebeljk@schenck-turner.com

3829

Business Information: Providing special services in programming and testing, Mr. Nebel holds the position of Software Engineer for Schenck Turner Inc. Utilizing his vast knowledge of software application, he oversees the diagnostic testing of all systems including measurements and the creating of databases and hardware. Providing training for new employees, Mr. Nebel ensures accurate and efficient products. Furthering his growth with the Corporation, he continues to obtain more experience in the software engineering field by attending training sessions, seminars, and being actively involved in research. Attributing his success to his supportive parents and his wife, Mr. Nebel's goals include eventually attaining the position of software department manager and overseeing all systems. Established in 1950, Schenck Turner Inc. provides excellent services in the testing and balancing of equipment for the automotive and electrical industries. Specifically, the Corporation provides reliable balancing techniques for any type of equipment that rotates or is supported in bearings. Located in Orion, Michigan, Schenck Turner is the largest internationally recognized manufacturer of balancing equipment. Presently, the Corporation offers over 200 machines and instruments to choose from. **Career Highlights:** Software Engineer, Schenck Turner Inc. (1995-Present); Senior Engineer, Allied Signal Inc. (1989-94); Senior Software Engineer, ARD Corporation (1987-89). **Education:** John Hopkin's University, Master's degree (1994); Northern Michigan University, B.S. (1987). **Personal Information:** Married to Linda in 1985. One child: Lauren. Mr. Nebel enjoys activities, gardening and outdoor sports.

Cody Doan

Product Review Board Coordinator
S 304
1905 Stevens Avenue
Minneapolis, MN 55403-3871
doan0011@mail.com

3841

Business Information: Mr. Doan serves in the role of Product Review Board Coordinator for a 40-year-old, international medical technology manufacturer based in Minneapolis, Minneapolis. He is responsible for quality control and assurance of all products. In this context, he Mr. Doan ensures the medical products are made under strict specifications as well as determines whether the products are worthy to be shipped. In addition, he is responsible for enforcing shipping regulations. Always seeking self-improvement, Mr. Doan's future goals obtaining his Master's degree in Mechanical Engineering. His career success reflects his ability to take on new challenges and deliver positive results. Established in 1960, this Minnesota based corporation currently employs a work force of over 13,000 people. The Corporation's chief product line includes medical components, such as heart defibrillators and pacemakers. Presently, the Corporation reports annual revenues in excess of $2.3 billion. **Career Highlights:** Product Review Board Coordinator (Present). **Education:** Master's degree in Mechanical Engineering (In Progress). **Personal Information:** Mr. Doan enjoys playing ice hockey, snow boarding and skate boarding.

Daniel J. Hines

Senior Technical Analyst
Baxter Healthcare Corporation
5602 Tinder Drive #3
Rolling Meadows, IL 60008
(847) 270-4491
Fax: (847) 270-4414
dan_hines@Baxter.com

3841

Business Information: Utilizing more than 15 years of experience, Mr. Hines serves as the Senior Technical Analyst for Baxter Healthcare Corporation. His primary function is the administration and troubleshooting of the local area network consisting of four servers. He also assumes responsibility for the wide area network. Handling the ISDN line support, he offers desktop support for the end users as well. Mr. Hines is often able to perform his duties through RAS, or remote access away from the office. Committed to providing continued optimum service, he looks forward to assisting in the completion of future corporate goals. His success reflects his ability to think outside the box, produce results, and aggressively take on new challenges. A research and development company, Baxter Healthcare performs research for the nation's healthcare industry. The Corporation employs a work force of more than 18,000 knowledgeable personnel members to develop healthcare policies. **Career Highlights:** Senior Technical Analyst, Baxter Healthcare Corporation (1996-Present); Local Area Network Design/Support, Wilton Industries (1996); Information Systems Manager, City of Evanston (1993-96); Field Engineer, Compunet (1992-93). **Education:** Baton Rouge School of Computers, Associates degree in Civil Engineering (1985); Certified Novell Engineer Training; HP9000 UNIX Basics; Winframe Training. **Personal Information:** Married to Susan in 1996. Mr. Hines enjoys photography, hiking and skiing.

Paul R. Kuczerepa

Senior Technical Consultant
Baxter Healthcare Corporation
Baxter Technology Park
Round Lake, IL 60073
(847) 270-5488
Fax: (847) 270-5559
paul_kuczerepa@baxter.com

3841

Business Information: In his position as Senior Technical Consultant for Baxter Healthcare, Mr. Kuczerepa is accountable for the efficiency and operation of computer systems and applications. A graduate of Loyola University of Chicago, he strives to maintain quality operations for the Company. After several years practical business experience, Mr. Kuczerepa concentrates on clinical research and development activities as well as network support, financial management, and budgeting. Founded in 1930, Baxter Healthcare Corporation is an international manufacturing company. With a global workforce of 35,000 people, the Company engineers, produces, and distributes biomedical products and services to hospitals, nursing homes, and health care facilities globally. Additionally, Baxter Healthcare specializes in research and development operations, and is considered a forerunner in biomedical engineering. **Career Highlights:** Senior Technical Consultant, Baxter Healthcare (1988-Present); Medical Technologist, Gottlieb Memorial Hospital (1985-88); Medical Technologist, St. Mary of Nazareth Medical Center (1978-85). **Associations & Accomplishments:** American Association of Clinical Chemistry; American Society of Clinical Pathologists; National Creditation Agency. **Education:** Loyola University, B.S. (1983); St. Mary of Nazareth School of Medical Technology. **Personal Information:** Married to Cheryl in 1987. Three children: Jadwiga, Aubrey, and Shannon. Mr. Kuczerepa enjoys water skiing, snow skiing and sailing.

Alexander Salinas

Information Technology Manager
Perclose, Inc.
400 Saginaw Drive
Redwood City, CA 94063-4749
(650) 474-3115

3841

Business Information: As Information Technology Manager for Perclose, Inc. Mr. Salinas fulfills a number of technical duties on behalf of the Corporation and its international clientele. He works closely with users to ensure the functionality and operational status of the technology infrastructure. In coordination with top management, he determines the strategic direction and business contributions of the information systems functions. Highly regarded and possessing an excellent understanding of technology, he oversees and manages the information technology department with regard to design of infrastructures, policies, procedures, and telecommunications. Capitalizing on many years of experience, Mr. Salinas also monitors the productivity of a four man staff, formulating a hands-on management style with an above average aptitute for problem solving. Attributing his career success to his creativity and logic as well as his ability to tackle new challenges and deliver results, Mr. Salinas' future endeavors include attaining the position of director. He also aspires to become a chief information officer of a start up company. Established in 1994, Perclose, Inc. engages in the manufacturing, distribution, and selling of medical devices such as pacemakers for the heart and products used in intensive care units, emergency rooms, and physicians' offices. Located in Redwood City, California, the Company employees 400 qualified individuals responsible for administration, gathering data, designing new products and manufacturing processes, marketing merchandise, and sales. The Company reports annual revenues in excess of $50 million. **Career Highlights:** Information Technology Manager, Perclose, Inc. (1998-Present); Senior Network Engineer, Corio, Inc. (1998); Information Systems Manager, Wolfe Engineering (1997-98); Information Systems Manager, Simons & Susslin Manufacturing (1996-97). **Education:** Gilroy High School, Diploma (1983). **Personal Information:** Married to Berenice in 1995. One child: Michael A. Mr. Salinas enjoys bicycling, photography and reading.

Joel A. Cox

Manager of ERP Technical Services
Hollister Inc.
2000 Hollister Drive
Libertyville, IL 60048
(847) 918-5828
Fax: (847) 918-5858
joel.cox@hollister.com

3842

Business Information: Serving as the Manager of ERP Technical Services for Hollister Inc., Mr. Cox assumes responsibility for development and technical support as it relates to the SAP R/3 and BW systems. He supervises his staff employees, facilitates logistics through strategic planning, and manages administrative duties such as the budget for the department. Possessing an excellent understanding of technology, Mr. Cox ensures that his staff is providing the highest quality of technical support, communicating problems and solutions effectively. In the future, Mr. Cox would like to build on his present success by assuming a larger managerial role. His success reflects his ability to keep up with technology and deliver results on behalf of the Corporation and its clientele. Hollister Inc. is a medical products manufacturer producing and distributing disposable items for wound care, obstetrics, identification, continence, and ostomy. Established in 1921, the Corporation employs the skilled services of 2,300 individuals to facilitate every aspect of design, manufacture, quality control, and distribution of products. The Corporation is located in Libertyville, Illinois and distributes merchandise to customers internationally. **Career Highlights:** Hollister Inc: Manager of ERP Technical Services (1999-Present), ERP Technical Project Lead (1998-99), Computer Services Manager (1991-97). **Education:** Post Secondary; Various technical courses. **Personal Information:** Married to Julie-Anne in 1991. Mr. Cox enjoys water sports and Bible education.

Phil A. Hersey

Engineer
Dentsply International
570 West College Avenue
York, PA 17404
(717) 849-4436
Fax: (717) 849-4765
phil.hersey@gte.net

3843

Business Information: Mr. Hersey functions in the capacity of Engineer with Dentsply International. He is responsible for peforming life testing of products and mechanical design, as well as 3-D CAD design and process improvements. Before joining the Dentsply team, Mr. Hersey served as a Teacher at York County Adult Education. His background also includes a stint as Manager for United Artist Theaters. Primarily involved in the prototyping of new products, creating computer databases on the product, and designing a testing system to ensure the security of the product, Mr. Hersey hopes to eventually advance in solid modeling and prototyping. An expert in his field, he attributes his success to his parents and good upbringing, in addition to his ability to deliver results and aggressively take on new challenges. "Listen, formulate, and do," is cited as Mr. Hersey's motto. Dentsply International is the largest manufacturer of artificial teeth in the world. Established in 1898, the Company has successfully created a business with over 100 years of satisfied customers and strong work ethics. The Company designs a mouthpiece to the specifications of the client and delivers the finished product to their home. **Career Highlights:** Engineer, Dentsply International (1981-Present); Teacher, York County Adult Education (1998-Present); Manager, United Artist Theaters (1983-98). **Associations & Accomplishments:** Save the Bay Association; United States Power Squadron. **Education:** Williamsport Area Community College. **Personal Information:** Married to Cindy in 1974. One child: Rich. Mr. Hersey enjoys sailing, photography, old car restoration and cooking.

M. D. Paka Antle

Director of Information Technology
DRS Optronics
1063 Egret Lake Way
Viera, FL 32940
(321) 494-5932
antle@prodigy.net

3845

Business Information: Mr. Antle was recently recruited to the firm of DRS Optronics in the role of Director of Information Technology. Utilizing practical education and related work experience, he handles a variety of specialized tasks on a daily basis including staff leadership and systems interfacing. Evaluating technical needs, he is able to design and implement strategic technical plans that aid in the effectiveness of the Company as a whole. He ensures that troubleshooting, maintenance, and upgrades are all handled with accuracy and efficiency. With a forte in networking and satellite communications, he is able to master the operations of LAN and WAN situations with ease. Employing his business savvy and technical expertise, he concurrently provides consulting services to the Defense Intelligence Agency via CTI. Enjoying the challenges of the industry, Mr. Antle intends to continue gathering information and valuable experience in his current position as he prepares to seek the role of chief information officer. Founded in 1979, DRS Optronics is a progressive technical firm that lends cutting edge technology to businesses and government agencies. Over 250 highly trained employees assist in the completion of corporate activities, generating annual revenues of over $55 million. **Career Highlights:** Director of Information Technology, DRS Optronics (2000-Present); Engineer, CTI/SAIC (1997-00); Lead Engineer, Northrop Grumman (1995-97); Systems Engineer, Harris Corporation (1992-95). **Associations & Accomplishments:** Armed Forces Communication and Electronics Association. **Education:** B.Sc. in Computer Science. **Personal Information:** Married to Deborah in 1995. Two children: Mark and Lauren. Mr. Antle enjoys optics and lasers. Also, Mr. Antle enjoys the study of all enhanced communications technologies.

Dean R. Fink

Lead Technical Writer
ATL Ultrasound
P.O. Box 3003
Bothell, WA 98041
(425) 487-7907

3845

Business Information: Utilizing over 20 years of aca demics and occupational experience, Mr. Fink serves as the Lead Technical Writer for ATL Ultrasound. He is responsible for writing and updating the service and operations manuals and transferring the manuals to CD-ROM and Internet Web pages. Possessing superior talents and an excellent understanding of his position, he conveys how to install, use, and repair the equipment to customers and employees. Highly regarded, Mr. Fink has won various writers awards from the Society for Technical Communication for his work with the Company. In the future, he looks forward to continuing with the Company and possibly move to a higher position. Success, according to Mr. Fink, is due to his work ethic and values instilled in him by his parents. Founded in 1969, ATL Ultrasound is a m anufacturer of medical ultrasound equipment. The equipment is used to diagnose cardiac, abdominal, vascular, and obstetric issues for hospitals, clinics, and veterinarians around the world. Located in Bothell, Washington, the Company is a division of Philips Medical Systems and employs a work force of over 2,200 employees. **Career Highlights:** Lead Technical Writer, ATL Ultrasound (1988-Present); Technical Writer, Milmanco, Inc. (1985-88). **Associations & Accomplishments:** Society for Technical Communication. **Education:** Gonzaga University, B.S. in Biology and History (1980). **Personal Information:** Mr. Fink enjoys biking, hiking, making wood-strip boats and running.

Lucy J. Johnson

Technical Consultant
Alcon Laboratories
6201 South Freeway
Fort Worth, TX 76134
(817) 551-8440
lucy.johnson@alconlabs.com

3851

Business Information: As a Technical Consultant for Alcon Laboratoies, Ms. Johnson is responsible for Oracle development programs that support the Company's test results entry system. Highly regarded, she possesses superior talents and excellent understanding of the Oracle database applications field. Her experience with such companies as General Dynamics makes her uniquely qualified to implement new and innovative technical solutions in the quality assurance, manufacturing, and research and development fields. In the next three to five years, Ms. Johnson aspires to continue in her present position and expand her knowledge of Web and Oracle database applications, thus ensuring future Company success. Alcon Laboratories is a pharmaceutical company that specializes in the manufacture of eyecare products. Established in 1952, the Company employs an industrious and enterprising staff of 8,000 who are dedicated to providing the finest products available. Located in Fort Worth, Texas, the Company reports annual revenue of $2 billion. **Career Highlights:** Technical Consultant, Alcon Laboratories (1990-Present); General Dynamics: Oracle Datebase Administrator and Developer (1987-90), ADA Programmer/Teacher (1980-87). **Associations & Accomplishments:** Association of Systems Management; Conference Chair, Perkin Elmer Informatics-LIMS; Treasurer, "Kids Who Care" Acting Group; Board Member, Parent Teacher Association; Former President/Newsletter Editor, South Central Oracle Users Group; Former Editor, General Dynamics "Ada Gazette" Newsletter; PEI SAL'LIMS Listserver Group; President, PE Informatics Users Group LIMS; Editor, International Oracle Users Journals, 2, 3, 4. **Education:** Stephen F. Austin State University, B.A. (1979). **Personal Information:** Married to Reggie Whitehead in 1979. Two children: Hillary and Hayley. Ms. Johnson enjoys tennis, acting and golf.

Francisco Pollock

Senior Information Specialist
Alcon Laboratories
Burleson, TX 76028
(817) 551-6912
Fax: (817) 551-7550
fpollock@sprintmail.com

3851

Business Information: Serving as the Senior Information Specialist for Alcon Laboratories, Mr. Pollock fulfills a number of duites on behalf of the Company. Possessing superior talents and an excellent understanding of technology, he provides international and local server systems support. Maintaining the functionality and serviceability of 130 servers in the Texas facility, Mr. Pollock is responsible for planning, implementing, operating, and maintaining systems. Demonstrating his expertise, he also is in charge of setup and installation, upgrading and troubleshooting, and managing utilization of all systems. Project management also fall within the scope of his responsibilities. In the future, Mr. Pollock's goals include attaining the position of Manager through tailored training management. His success is attributed to a combination of praying, studying, and working hard as well as his ability to think out-of-the-box, aggressively take on challenges, and deliver result. Established in 1945, Alcon Laboratories is a pharmaceutical company involved in the development and manufacturing of opthalmic products. The Company manufactures and distributes medical instruments for eye care and performs research in on-site laboratories. Employing more than 10,000 personnel, the Company reports annual revenue of $2 billion. **Career Highlights:** Senior Information Specialist, Alcon Laboratories (1996-Present); Communications Specialist, Alcon-Puerto Rico, Inc (1993-96); Systems Analyst, The Wyatt Company (1991-93). **Associations & Accomplishments:** Seventh-day Adventist Church. **Education:** Interamerican University, B.S. (1986); Army Signal School, Computer Programming. **Personal Information:** Married to Adyanez in 1998. One child: Leilani. Mr. Pollock enjoys swimming, camping and jogging.

Mark Gulling

Assistant Chief Information Officer
Eastman Kodak Company
343 State Street
Rochester, NY 14650-1245
(716) 781-9606
Fax: (716) 781-7779
mgulling@kodak.com

3861

Business Information: Mr. Gulling is the Assistant Chief Information Officer for Eastman Kodak Company. He has been with the Company for 25 years, holding a variety of positions in many of Kodak's business and functional areas. In his highly specialized position, Mr. Gulling currently serves as the program manager for ERP global implementation. He works with the business to develop strategy, outline ERP rollout plans, and oversee the design and implementation of new business processes and systems. He manages an organization of over 600 people. His goal is to eventually attain the position of Chief Information Officer or run a business unit. Mr. Gulling credits his success to his listening skills and his ability to think outside the box, deliver results, and aggressively take on new challenges. Headquartered in Rochester, New York, Eastman Kodak Company is engaged in the manufacture of imaging materials and photographic equipment. Products produced that generate annual revenues in excess of $14 billion include cameras, scanners, paper, x-ray films, professional photography products, microfilm, and motion picture films. Serving an international client base, Eastman Kodak offers products and services to commercial and individual customers. There are presently 80,000 individuals employed with the Company in over 100 locations. **Career Highlights:** Eastman Kodak Company: Assistant Chief Information Officer (1998-Present), Director of ERP Program (1996-98), Director of Office Imaging Information Systems (1993-96). **Associations & Accomplishments:** Past Member, Society of Infomation Managers. **Education:** Ashland University, B.S. (1974). **Personal Information:** Married to Kathryn in 1974. Two children: Kelly and Gregory. Mr. Gulling enjoys sports, military history, travel and spending time with his family.

David C. Nemchick

Senior Systems Analyst
Eastman Kodak Company
1100 Ridgeway Avenue
Rochester, NY 14652-6266
(716) 477-5248
Fax: (716) 722-6637
dnemchck@kodak.com

3861

Business Information: As Senior Systems Analyst at Eastman Kodak Company, Mr. Nemchick provides information systems support to the Health, Safety, and Environment Laboratories of Eastman Kodak. His duties range from Project Management responsibilities for implementation of purchased software packages, to developing and implementing custom database applications. Mr. Nemchick's experience also includes development and implementation of validation plans for software applications running in regulated environments. He has worked on platforms ranging from mid range systems, such as VAXes, to PCs in the client server environment. Mr. Nemchick has also been heavily involved in Quality Improvement efforts for his division, achieving Level 2 of the Capability Maturity Model. With 20 years of dedicated service to Eastman Kodak, Mr. Nemchick keeps his skills sharp by attending at least 40 hours of training courses each year. This training enables him to maintain his professional certification as Certified Computing Professional (CCP). He became involved in computer technology while working with early PCs as part of his previous job at the University of Rochester. Originally a Biological Sciences major, Mr. Nemchick has found that his current position supporting health and environmental applications is a good way to combine his biology training with his knowledge and experience with computers. Mr. Nemchick's success reflects his ability to think out-of-the-box and take on new challenges. With the change of technology taking place, he sees himself moving more toward the Web based and client server market. The Eastman Kodak Company was established in 1890 and specializes in design, manufacture, and distribution of a variety of photographic and imaging products. The most known and widely used products by far are Kodak's range of personal cameras and films. **Career Highlights:** Eastman Kodak Company: Senior Systems Analyst (1998-Present), Systems Developer (1981-98), Research Technician, University of Rochester (1974-81); Medical Lab Technician, Ideal Hospital (1971-74). **Associations & Accomplishments:** Certified Computing Professional (CCP) awarded by Institute for Certification of Computing Professionals; Past Member, St. Lawrence School Board, Rochester, New York. **Education:** State University College at Brockport, B.A. (1971), Post Graduate Work (1971-81); Broome Community College A.A. (1969); Rochester Institute of Technology (1974-81). **Personal Information:** Married to Joyce in 1974. Two children: Laura and Adam. In his spare time, Mr. Nemchick enjoys flying radio control planes with his son, as well as gardening, woodworking, and do-it-yourself projects.

3900 Miscellaneous Manufacturing Industries

3911 Jewelry, precious metal
3914 Silverware and plated ware
3915 Jewelers' materials and lapidary work
3931 Musical instruments
3942 Dolls and stuffed toys
3944 Games, toys, and children's vehicles
3949 Sporting and athletic goods, nec
3951 Pens and mechanical pencils
3952 Lead pencils and art goods
3953 Marking devices
3955 Carbon paper and inked ribbons
3961 Costume jewelry
3965 Fasteners, buttons, needles, and pins
3991 Brooms and brushes
3993 Signs and advertising specialties
3995 Burial caskets
3996 Hard surface floor coverings, nec
3999 Manufacturing industries, nec

Sang H. Im
Director of Information Systems
Kurgan & Cheviot
5340 Alla Road
Los Angeles, CA 90066
(310) 574-3400
Fax: (310) 574-3401
sim@kurgan-cheviot.com

3911

Business Information: As Director of Information Systems of Kurgan & Cheviot, Mr. Im is responsible for planning, implementing and maintaining all information systems for the Company. In addition, Mr. Im presides over all projects, equipment, and services. Working closely with his team of four employees, he also assumes accountability for all local and wide area networking. Beginning his association with the Company in 1995 as a Programmer, Mr. Im has received recognition for his diligence and management skills through a promotion to his current position. He continues to grow professionally and hopes to become more involved in Web based systems. His success reflects his optimistic character. Established in 1986, Kurgan & Cheviot is engaged in the manufacture of jewelry. Serving an international client base, the Company employs a work force of more than 150 people who help generate annual revenues in excess of $100 million. **Career Highlights:** Kurgan & Cheviot: Director of Information Systems (1995-Present), Programmer (1995); Software Engineer, GARJAK Research, Inc. (1987). **Education:** University of California at San Diego, B.S. (1991). **Personal Information:** Married to Rachel in 1992. Mr. Im enjoys golf, travel and swimming.

George A. Thomas
Director of Information Technology
Retro Studios
12505 Stapp Court
Austin, TX 78732
(512) 751-5660
Fax: (512) 493-4602
gthomas@texas.net

3944

Business Information: Displaying his expertise in this highly specialized position, Mr. Thomas serves as the Director of Information Technology for Retro Studios. He presides over all aspects of the Company's telecommunications functions, including the T-1 and PBX system setup, configuration, and its subsequent management. Equally as important, he is in charge of the data systems as well. His duties entail administrating the LAN/WAN networks, user e-mail and Internet access, and providing a secure firewall against hackers. Mr. Thomas also assists in the design of various game platforms. He has enjoyed several professional successes in his information technology career such as designing the Cheyenne Mountain upgrade, a United States Air Force Space Command LAN Data Center which supports 5,000 users. Citing teamwork as the secret of his success, he plans to continue to learn and grow within his chosen profession. Created in 1998 in response to the almost phenomenal demand for computer games, Retro Studios is engaged in the high tech development of such games for both the PC and console platforms. The Company is currently designing a 3-D motion capture studio download to disc for the well known Nintendo corporation. Approximately, 60 administrative, programming, and support personnel are employed. **Career Highlights:** Director of Information

Technology, Retro Studios (1998-Present); Information Technology Director of Acclaim Studios, Acclaim Entertainment (1996-98); Systems Specialist, Cyber Crews (1995-96); Space Command Systems Director, United States Air Force (1992-95). **Education:** Colorado Tech (1995); Park College, B.S. in Management (1988); Community College of United States Air Force: A.S. in Communications Systems (1980), A.S. in Electronics (1980). **Personal Information:** Married to Alesia in 1984. One child: Andrew. Mr. Thomas enjoys sailing, golf and skiing.

Jim VanMeter
CAD Administrator
The Little Tikes Company
2810 Barlow Road
Hudson, OH 44236-4199
(330) 650-3882
Fax: (330) 650-3322
jim.vanmeter@littletikes.com

3944

Business Information: Possessing advanced technical skills and adept management capabilities, Mr. VanMeter serves as CAD Administrator for The Little Tikes Company. In this capacity since 1996, he is responsible for all network administration including implementation of hardware and software as well as supervising the DOS, UNIX, and Windows operating environment. Highly regarded and possessing an excellent understanding technology, Mr. VanMeter assumes oversight of a 30-member staff, providing them with guidance, comprehensive direction, and technical training. Mr. VanMeter is also responsible for server upkeep, upgrading the system network, and purchasing software, hardware, and new technology for the Corporation. He enjoys tremendous success in his current position and looks forward to assisting in the advancement of corporate operations. Established in 1970, The Little Tike Company is a renowned manufacturer of children's toys. Headquarters are located just outside of Cleveland, Ohio in Hudson, where the Corporation employs a collective work force of over 1,500 administrative, technical, and operational personnel who generate annual revenue in excess of $435 million. The Corporation currently operates several international plants as well as operation throughout the continental United States **Career Highlights:** CAD Administrator, The Little Tike Company (1996-Present); Systems Administrator, Hunt Machine & Manufacturing Company (1993-96); Engineering Manager, Soundwich, Inc. (1991-93). **Associations & Accomplishments:** Society of Manufacturing Engineers; Ohio Youth Wrestling. **Education:** University of Akron, B.S. in Mechanical Engineering (1991); Stark Technical College; Embry Rydell University. **Personal Information:** One child: Steven. Mr. VanMeter enjoys reading, computers and playing golf.

Michael W. Crawford
Director of Information Systems
United Titanium Inc.
3450 Old Airport Road
Wooster, OH 44691
(330) 264-2111
Fax: (330) 265-1336
mikec@unitedtitanium.com

3965

Business Information: Serving as United Titanium Inc.'s Director of Information Systesms, Mr. Crawford oversees technical operations on a daily basis. Demonstrating his expertise in the information technology field, he evaluates the technical needs of each department then implements solutions to increase the overall effectiveness of the Corporation. He maintains all systems including hardware and software; he is responsible for upgrades and purchasing of new equipment. Credited with the creation of an inventory managment system in JAVA, Mr. Crawford utilized his education and practical work experience to develop a point of sale program to increase efficiency in the logistics area. Enjoying his current position with the Corporation, Mr. Crawford looks forward to assisting in the completion of future corporate goals. United Titanium Inc. manufactures fasteners for the industrial field such as bolts, screws, and nuts. Established in 1972, the international company focuses on the production of titanium items, though other exotic metals are used as well. Over 100 employees at the Wooster, Ohio location strive to uphold the reputation of quality built by excellent service and value priced products. **Career Highlights:** Director of Information Systems, United Titanium Inc. (1999-Present); Senior Project Manager, Camelot Music, Inc. (1995-99); Senior Programmer and Analyst, Cleveland Clinic Foundation (1994-95); Systems Consultant, Logica, Inc. (1991-94). **Education:** Muskingum College, B.S. (1986). **Personal Information:** Married to Lisa in 1993. Four children: Jamie, Danielle, Emily, and Theadore. Mr. Crawford enjoys reading, water skiing and being in the outdoors.

Dale Cox
Systems Manager
Integrated Systems Engineering
1850 North 600 West
Logan, UT 84321-1738
(435) 753-2224
Fax: (435) 752-8513
dalec@utah.uswest.net

3993

Business Information: Effectively combining management skills with technical expertise, Mr. Cox serves as Systems Manager of Integrated Systems Engineering. He monitors and maintains the business' computers and local area network and serves as a consultant for the production department. In the future, he would like to keep abreast of innovations in technology and acquire an administrative position. Integrated Systems Engineering is a manufacturer of electronic message center displays, including sports scoreboard equipment and billboards. Established in 1972, the Logan, Utah manufacturing facility currently employs 95 professionals and is a subsidiary of the Trans-Lux Corporation with headquarters in Norwalk, Connecticut. **Career Highlights:** Integrated Systems Engineering: Systems Manager (1988-Present), Electronic Technician (1978-88). **Associations & Accomplishments:** Eagle Scout. **Education:** Ricks College (1975); Utah State University, Classes in Microprocessors; Bridgerland Applied Technology Center, Classes in Personal Computer Repair and Networking; National Institute for Certification in Engineering Technologies, Associate Engineering Technician. **Personal Information:** Married to Laura in 1978. Mr. Cox enjoys spending time with his family, travel, camping and Ham radio.

Michael Phillip Corsello
Information Systems Operations Manager
The Upper Deck Company, LLC
5909 Sea Otter Place
Carlsbad, CA 92008
(760) 929-3431
Fax: (760) 929-6531
mike_corsello@upperdeck.com

3999

Business Information: Serving as Information Systems Operations Manager of The Upper Deck Company, LLC, Mr. Corsello oversees the information systems and network infrastructures and determines the business contributions of the systems functions. In this context, he is in charge of computer and telecommunications systems and human resources management. Utilizing seven years experience of the field of technology, Mr. Corsello maintains Internet connectivity, provides help desk support, and directs and participates in the analysis, design, evaluation, testing, and implementation of LAN and WAN and Internet/Intranet related computer systems. His background includes six years in the United States Marine Corps. He is self-taught and is MCSE certified. Attributing his success to tenacity, he plans on increasing his knowledge base, keeping pace with technology. "Find something you enjoy," is cited as Mr. Corsello's advice. The Upper Deck Company, LLC is a trading card manufacturer. The Company manufactures sports, music, and games trading cards as well as trading cards for companies such as Disney. An international company with only one location in Carlsbad, California, the Company employs over 250 people. Established in 1986, The Upper Deck Company reports annual sales in excess of $200 million. **Career Highlights:** Information Systems Operations Manager, The Upper Deck Company, LLC (1997-Present); Systems Operations Manager, The Plug Connection (1993-97); Noncommissioned Officer in Charge, United States Marine Corps (1991-92). **Education:** Eisenhower Senior High School, diploma (1986). **Personal Information:** Married to Chandra in 1992. Three children: Cody, Samantha, and Sarah. Mr. Corsello enjoys family time.

John F. Eckert, Jr.
Network Administrator/Computer Specialist
Insulgard Corporation
5133 Lawerence Place
Hyattsville, MD 20781
(301) 927-8855
Fax: (301) 927-4531

3999

Business Information: Mr. Eckert was recruited to the Insulgard Corporation as Network Administrator and Computer Specialist in 1994. In his position, he is responsible for running the entire in-house network, troubleshooting, and designing solutions to fix and/or eliminate systems difficulties. He administers and controls all network tools and infrastructure as well as ensures the functionality and operational status of all systems functions. Possessing an excellent understanding of technology, Mr. Eckert is involved in the analysis, acquisition, installation, modification, configuration, support, and tracking of operating and networking systems, hardware, e-mail server, and utilities. The most rewarding aspect of his career is establishing

Insulgard's network from scratch. In the future, Mr. Eckert plans to continue with the Corporation in his current position. Located in Hyattsville, Maryland, Insulgard Corporation is a manufacturer of bullet resistant windows and doors. Founded in 1974, the Corporation supplies these products to businesses, sheriffs' and police departments, government offices, and other business entities. Operating on an international basis, the Corporation employs a staff of 25 employees at the Maryland location. Presently, Insulgard reports annual revenues in excess of $15 million. **Career Highlights:** Network Administrator/Computer Specialist, Insulgard Corporation (1994-Present); Network Administrator, AMPSKO (1990-94). **Personal Information:** Married to Tracy in 1992. Three children: Daniel, Shannon, and Rachel. Mr. Eckert enjoys crafts, gardening and working with local food bank.

Chandler R. Grunstad

Business Support Specialist
Pentacon Industry Group, Inc.
3010 Independence Drive
Fort Wayne, IN 46808
(219) 482-3671
Fax: (219) 484-1502
chandler.grunstad@maumleind.com

3999

Business Information: A system administrator and network technician, Mr. Grunstad serves as Business Support Specialist for the Pentacon Industry Group, Inc. He is in the process of establishing a worldwide network for the Corporation, implementing new technology in an effort to increase staff productivity. Additionally, he provides telecommunication secure data lines for the transfer of sensitive data between locations. Mr. Grunstad built his first computer when he was in the first grade. Since that time, he has received several awards for his work including the "Custom Made Software 98" award and the "Sisk to Disk Platform J.D. Edwards Software" award. Crediting his success to knowledge and education, he stays on the cutting edge of technology through continuous self education. Mr. Grunstad plans to become a System and Network Administrator and continue producing creative work for the Corporation. Founded in 1978, the Pentacon Industry Group, Inc. is a small parts and fastener supplier for original equipment manufacturers. The Corporation's Quality Control Department is QS-9000 certified and offers Job Instruction Training services. Operations employ 350 qualified workers and annual sales are reported to be over $350 million. **Career Highlights:** Business Support Specialist, Pentacon Industry Group, Inc. (1992-Present); Dangerous Good Specialist, Burlington Air Express (1988-92). **Associations & Accomplishments:** Mercedes Benz Club of America. **Education:** Purdue University (Currently Attending). **Personal Information:** Mr. Grunstad enjoys mountain biking, white water rafting and hiking.

Warren L. Schmitt

Systems Network Manager
Newport
5480 Nathan Lane North
Minneapolis, MN 55442
(612) 593-0722

3999

Business Information: Proficient in all areas of technology, Mr. Schmitt serves as the Systems Network Engineer for Newport. He presides over the Management Information Systems Department of the Minneapolis, Minnesota branch, administering the LAN network and telecommunications aspects. Additionally, he oversees the facility security infrastructure to prevent unauthorized corporate entrance and data access. Before joining Newport, Mr. Schmitt served as Computer Analyst for GRACO Corporation. His background history also includes a stint as Application Specialist for Norwest/Wells Fargo. An expert, Mr. Schmitt personally ensures that the systems infrastructure on which the Corporation depend are functioning efficiently by monitoring daily activity and performing routine maintenance. Continually formulating new goals and objectives, Mr. Schmitt looks forward to increasing his professional responsibilities and anticipates a promotion to a managerial position. His success reflects his ability to produce results and aggressively tackle new challenges. Newport is a manufacturer of computer related and non-related stages. Established in 1983, the Corporation is capable of manufacturing stages down to the ½ micron level. Boasting sales of $150 million, products are distributed internationally from six locations. The Corporation employs a total work force of 1,100 skilled personnel. **Career Highlights:** Systems Network Manager, Newport (1996-Present); Computer Analyst, GRACO Corporation (1987-96); Application Specialist, Norwest/Wells Fargo (1979-85). **Associations & Accomplishments:** Novell Users Group; Network Professionals Association; Netware Users International; NT Users Group. **Education:** ACREW, M.C.S.E. Certification; Metro State University; University of Minnesota. **Personal Information:** Married to Gayle in 1996. Mr. Schmitt enjoys real estate, stock investing, lumberjacking, sailing and photography.

Larry Snyder

Software Engineer
Control Contractors, Inc.
1128 Poplar Place South
Seattle, WA 98144-2897
(206) 328-1730
Fax: (206) 328-0829
larrys@controlcontractor.com

3999

Business Information: Following a distinguished career with the Department of the Navy, Mr. Snyder joined Control Contractors, Inc. in 1999 as Software Engineer. His duties include programming for control systems, engineering specifications development, controlling software, troubleshooting, and maintaining systems. Responsible for providing training, Mr. Snyder works closely with his team of associates. Continually striving for maximum effectiveness, his goal is to keep up with new technology to enable him to capitalize on promotional opportunities provided by the Company. Mr. Snyder attributes his success to a willingness to learn, being open-minded, and having a sense of humor. Established in 1975, Control Contractors, Inc. is a specialist provider of programming for heat and vent controls used for engergy optimization. Targeting the industrial facilities market, the Company develops, manufactures, and sells systems and graphics. A subsidiary of Invensys of Chicago, Illinois, Control Contractors, Inc. is located in Seattle, Washington. **Career Highlights:** Software Engineer, Control Contractors, Inc. (Present); Department of the Navy: Electronic Controls Technician (1993-99), Electrician (1984-93), Electrician Apprentice (1980-84). **Associations & Accomplishments:** Explorer Search and Rescue; Boy Scouts of America. **Education:** Olympic College. **Personal Information:** Married to Cheryl in 1991. Four children: Sharissa, Julie, Lori, and Jennifer.

4000 - 4999

TRANSPORTATION AND PUBLIC UTILITIES

4000 Railroad Transportation

4011 Railroads, line-haul operating
4013 Switching and terminal services

Michael E. Gililland

Senior Systems Developer I
Burlington Northern Santa Fe Railway
7525 Teakwood Court
Fort Worth, TX 76180-2807
(817) 333-2263
Fax: (817) 333-7833
michael.gililland@bnsf.com

4013

Business Information: Mr. Gililland began his career with Burlington Northern Santa Fe Railway in 1997, and presently assumes the title and responsibilities of Senior Systems Developer I. In this context, he is the lead developer for the Railway's rate price management system, a pricing system for customer and way bills. Over the past few years, he has acquired an in-depth knowledge of all aspects of the operation and is able to assist in various projects. In collaboration with end users, Mr. Gililland works to improve current software programs and solve relevant problems. With over five years of experience in the field and dedicated to keeping abreast on new developments, he has become a great asset to Burlington Northern Santa Fe Railway. Mr. Gililland has been recognized numerous times for his skills and contibutions to the Company and plans to continue in his career, seeking new and larger opportunities. Taking full advantage of opportunities afforded and his faith in God is cited as reasons for his success. Established in 1995, Burlington Northern Santa Fe Railway is a railroad company engaged in transporation services. A work force of 45,000 plus skilled workers assist in various aspects of day-to-day operations. The Railway's information systems department is primarily involved in developing rate price management systems. **Career Highlights:** Senior Systems Developer I, Burlington Northern Santa Fe Railway (1997-Present); Rauscher Pierce Refsnes: Software Engineer (1996-97), Computer Analyst (1993-96). **Associations & Accomplishments:** Midtown Church of Christ. **Education:** University of Texas at Arlington, B.S. in Information Systems (1994). **Personal Information:** Married to Karen in 1992. Two children: Lindsey and Corban. Mr. Gililland enjoys gymnastics, church activities, piano and music.

Lettie K. Haynes

Information Systems Services Director
Burlington Northern Santa Fe Railway
777 Main Street, Suite 600
Fort Worth, TX 76102
(817) 333-7538

4013

Business Information: As a Information Systems Services (ISS) Director of Burlington Northern Santa Fe Railway (BNSF), Ms. Haynes is responsible for several key areas within the ISS organization. Ms. Haynes joined BNSF in 1993 as a Project Lead. She has quickly moved up the corporate hierarchy to her current position. With over 15 years experience in I T, she is well prepared to be accountable for Data Warehousing, Measurements & Profitability Systems, Corporate Reference Files along with ISS Development Tools. Ms. Haynes joined BSNF with the intent to automate the RR (railroad) and she has been a key player in this effort. She co-managed a major implementation of an application which is responsible for managing the equipment across the BNSF network. BNSF is the largest grain hauling railroad in USA. BNSF hauls 90 percent of the coal in the US A. Staying on the cutting edge, she is ready to take on more challenges. She is responsible for forging the new distributed environment including Java and Web solutions at BNSF. Ms. Haynes attributes her success to the ability to work with others. Teamwork is the key! Presently, a professional and technical staff of 50 persons man day-to-day operations in the ISS Department. **Career Highlights:** Burlington Northern Santa Fe Railway: Information Systems Services Director (1999-Present), Manager/Project Lead (1993-99); Supervisor, Policy Management Systems (1987-93). **Education:** Texas Christian University, M.B.A. (In Progress); North Texas State University, B.S. in Computer Science (1982). **Personal Information:** Married. One child. Ms. Haynes enjoys reading and listening to gospel and jazz.

Sheldon C. Larson, CISA

Senior Audit Specialist of Information Technology
Canadian Pacific Railway
P.O. Box 530, Suite 420
Minneapolis, MN 55440
(612) 337-7539

4013

Business Information: As Senior Audit Specialist of Canadian Pacific Railway, Mr. Larson is responsible for providing independent reviews, assessments, and recommendations for systems of control over the Company's information technology. Focusing on the reliability, integrity, and accuracy of information, he strives to ensure the adequacy of internal controls, safeguarding of Company informational and physical assets, and compliance with Company policies, procedures, and government regulations. Canadian Pacific Railway has an audit staff of 20 people, with Mr. Larson being the only one in the United States. He frequently coordinates all aspects of application system audits and consults on control issues for systems under development. Mr. Larson recently completed a SAP systems infrastructure audit and is in the process of reviewing the Company's telecommunications network controls, moving on to join a team reviewing e-business controls. Further, during the 10 years Mr. Larson was at Canadian Pacific Limited and Railway, he continued to develop his knowledge and expertise in mainframe, midrange, client-server, and personal computers. Canadian Pacific has utilized his information technology and audit experience in successfully completing audits and risk assessments of their subsidiary companies in Forest Product, Trucking, Hotels and Resorts, Shipping, Coal Mining, and Railroads. Mr. Larson's career success is attributed to his ability to quickly learn and understand new concepts, methodologies, corporate structure, and politics to deliver efficient and cost effective results. Founded in 1887, Canadian Pacific Railway provides high quality customer service in transporting freight for its domestic and international customers. A North American railway company with transcontinental service across Canada and service in the Midwest and Northeast United States. The Railway employs 19,000 individuals with estimated annual revenue of $3.5 billion CDN. **Career Highlights:** Senior Audit Specialist of Information Technology, Canadian Pacific Railway (1989-Present); Regional Director of EDP, United States Department of Justice - INS (1984-89); Manager of Systems and Programming, Northrup King Company (1978-84); Manager of Information Systems, Horton Manufacturing (1974-78). **Associations & Accomplishments:** Informations Systems Audit and Control Association; Soo Line Credit Union Supervisory Committee. **Education:** University of Minnesota, B.A. (1974); Certified Information Systems Auditor; Various courses in auditing and information technology. **Personal Information:** Married to Patricia. One child: Marinda. Mr. Larson enjoys horses, wood working and exploring the Internet.

James L. Thorpe

Information Technology Project Manager
Rail Inc.
7001 Weston Parkway
Cary, NC 05713
(919) 651-5058
Fax: (919) 553-8052
thorpeentc@aol.com

4013

Business Information: Displaying his skills in this highly specialized position, Mr. Thorpe serves as the Information Technology Project Manager for Rail Inc. He utilizes more than 20 years of practical experience in the performance of his duties, assuming the responsibility for leading a group of 10 senior and junior programmers in various information technology projects such as the Y2K program. Crediting his professional success to his single minded determination, he keeps abreast of advancements in the computer industry by attending classes and reading trade journals. Mr. Thorpe continues to grow professionally through the fulfillment of his responsibilities and his involvement in the advancement of operations. Continually formulating new goals and objectives, he looks forward to realizing his entrepreneurial dream of owning his own company. Serving an international client base, Rail Inc. offers specialized information technology services to railroads. The Corporation services all of the railroad companies across the United States as well as throughout Canada and Mexico. A staff of 150 skilled professionals are engaged in daily operations. **Career Highlights:** Information Technology Project Manager, Rail Inc. (1998-Present); Senior Technical Analyst, Blue Cross Blue Shield (1994-98); Senior Technical Analyst, Aetna Life & Casualty (1977-94). **Education:** CPI, Operations degree (1981). **Personal Information:** Married to Dolores in 1979. Mr. Thorpe enjoys gardening, home repairs and car repairs.

4100 Local and Interurban Passenger Transit

4111 Local and suburban transit
4119 Local passenger transportation, nec
4121 Taxicabs
4131 Intercity and rural bus transportation
4141 Local bus charter service
4142 Bus charter service, except local
4151 School buses
4173 Bus terminal and service facilities

Allan Balkema

Network Systems Administrator
Regional Transportation District
1900 31st Street
Denver, CO 80216
(303) 299-6135
Fax: (303) 299-6191
allan.balkema@rtd-denver.com

4111

Business Information: Serving in the role of Network Systems Administrator of Regional Transportation District or RTD, Mr. Balkema maintains the functionality and operational status of the District's network infrastructure. In his capacity, he supervises all users desktops, supports all systems software, and keeps the hardware and software up to date. With an excellent understanding of his field, he oversees 12 servers and networks. He maintains good vendor relationships, approves purchases, and mentors his staff of five people. Highly regarded in the industry, Mr. Balkema enjoys his job and is ready to install Windows 2000 into the Company's structure. Obtaining Microsoft Certified Systems Engineer certification is cited as his next goal. Success, according to Mr. Balkema is his ability to aggressively tackle new challenges and deliver results. RTD is a public transportation system, providing rapid public transportation services in a 20 mile service area around Denver and Boulder. The Agency also provides light rail services to about 1.5 million people. Currently possessing over 600 buses and 20 trains, RTD plans on expanding to the Southwest corridor. **Career Highlights:** Network Systems Administrator, Regional Transportation District (1996-Present).

Dorina George

Information Technology Project Manager
PSEG Services Corporation
7000 Kennedy Boulevard East
West New York, NJ 07093-4818
(973) 430-5068
Fax: (201) 868-1674
dgeorge000@aol.com

4111

Business Information: Serving as Information Technology Project Manager of PSEG Services Corporation, Ms. George is charged with supplying clients with project specifications. She is responsible for all daily business affairs including resource scheduling, budgeting, and workload distribution to ensure project completion in a timely and cost efficient manner. Managing client projects to ensure quality, Ms. George supervises project workers and vendors, prepares expense reports, and discusses project modifications with clients and project engineers. Demonstrating her expanded hands on experience and technology background, Ms. George has established herself as a competent and valuable asset. Maintaining her reputation of attention to detail and perseverance, she plans to develope, implement, and manage new technologies to support the Corporation as it strives to provide better service and customer satisfaction. PSEG Services Corporation is a utility company providing gas and electric resources. Established over a century ago, the Corporation employs over 11,000 people who generate substantial annual revenues. By providing superior customer service and maintenance schedules, PSEG Services has established itself as a national leader in utility provision for regulated and unregulated businesses and residences. Sustaining its impeccable service record, the Corporation plans to expand its service area to neighboring regions to gain consumer recognition and to maximize earnings potential. **Career Highlights:** Information Technology Project Manager, PSEG Services Corporation (1997-Present); Network Administrator, Mitshubishi International Corporation (1992-97); Promotion and Sales Manager, Nathan & Company, Inc. (1988-90); Financial Analyst, ELM Secruities, Inc. (1986-88). **Education:** New York University Stern School, M.B.A. (In Progess); Columbia College, Columbia University, B.A. in Economics and Philosophy. **Personal Information:** Ms. George enjoys volleyball, travel and reading.

Gerald J. McLennan

Director of Information Technology
OC Transpo
1645 Tupello Way
Orleans, Ontario, Canada K4A 1V3
(613) 841-7186
Fax: (613) 741-7359
gmcl01@magma.ca

4111

Business Information: As Director of Information Technology of OC Transpo, Mr. McLennan is responsible for providing support and leadership to the information technology department. He determines the overall strategic direction and business contribution of the information systems functions. Demonstrating strong leadership and technical expertise, Mr. McLennan's duties include hardware and software support, strategic planning, and software development. He also applies himself in the areas of technological research and attends to all aspects of the telecommunications infostructure. Attributing his success to his ability to take a business approach to technology, Mr. McLennan's future goal is to eventually attain the position of chief information officer in a larger corporation. OC Transpo engages in the daily transport of citizens to various location in and around the Ottawa, Canada area. The Company provides such forms of transportation as buses, trains, and paratransit, which caters to the handicapped citizens of the city. Established in 1909, the Company is operates several locations manned by over 2,300 professionals who apply expertise and dedication to transporting citizens in a timely and cost efficient manner. The Company, with the utilization of various vehicular services, enjoys annual revenues exceeding $200 million. **Career Highlights:** Director of Information Technology, OC Transpo (1997-Present); Weld Wood of Canada: Manager of Applications (1994-97), Finance and Sales Systems Manager (1992-94). **Education:** B.C.I.T., National diploma (1982). **Personal Information:** Mr. McLennan enjoys woodworking.

Avelino Mark A. Valonzo Jr.

Management Information Systems Manager
Atlantic Express
7 North Street
Staten Island, NY 10302-1205
(718) 442-7000
Fax: (718) 448-7624
mvalonzo@atlanticexpress.com

4111

Business Information: Mr. Valonzo is the Management Information Systems Manager of Atlantic Express. He monitors the activities of all of the computer technology used within the Company's Staten Island, New York location. Networking with the remaining 37 locations, he is in constant contact with his counterparts around the country and together they create a successful and operable system. He is responsible for the integration of the local area and wide area networking hardware and is trained in reprogramming basic software to fully utilize its accessories in the office setting. In the future, Mr. Valonzo hopes to stay within the transportation industry and is currently involved in enhancement planning for the betterment of the Company as it strives to become number one. He attributes his career success to love and passion for what he's doing and his academic foundation. Atlantic Express is the second largest transportation provider in the United States. Established in 1972, the Company offers clients assistance during their travels around the country through its extensive fleet of transportation mobiles. Its primary method of transportation is via the automobile and the Company turns over $400 million annually. **Career Highlights:** Management Information Systems Manager, Atlantic Express (1996-Present); Computer Consultant, Salomon Smith Barney (1995-96); Computer Consultant, Citicorp New York (1994-95); Computer Consultant, Morgan Stanley (1993-94). **Associations & Accomplishments:** Philippine American Civic & Cultural Community of Staten Island; Staten Island Philippine Athletic Group. **Education:** Columbia University, M.B.A. (1993); Fordham University: B.S. in Computer Science, B.S. in Computer Engineering. **Personal Information:** Married to Cristy in 1994. Two children: Demelina and Gerolyn.

Isiah Taylor

Computer Administrator
New York City Transit Authority
130 Livingston Street, Room 149
Brooklyn, NY 11201
(718) 694-1024
Fax: (718) 694-4610
itaylor@gowebway.com

4131

Business Information: Mr. Taylor is Computer Administrator for New York City Transit Authority. He has faithfully served with the Transit Authority in a variety of roles since coming on board as Associate Staff Analyst in 1989. As a 22 year professional, Mr. Taylor is responsible for computer LAN administration for facilities management operations, such as bus and train stations, repair shops, and general administration offices. Utilizing his extensive educational and occupational experience, he provides systems back up and technical support for all aspects of the systems infrastructure. Coordinating resources, time lines, schedules, and assignments also fall within the purview of his functions. In the future, Mr. Taylor is hoping to move to larger systems with greater responsibilities at the New York City Transit Authority. His success reflects his ability to produce results and aggressively take on new challenges. New York City Transit Authority was established in 1950 and maintains buses, trains, and subways in New York City. Grossing $1 billion annually, the Authority employs over 44,000 personnel to work in all areas of the industry from automobile repairs and track maintenance to chauferring and piloting each mode of transportation. **Career Highlights:** New York City Transit Authority: Computer Administrator (1994-Present), Mailroom Specialist (1991-94), Associate Staff Analyst (1989-91). **Associations & Accomplishments:** Former Member, American Society of Public Administration. **Education:** City University of New York, Baruch College M.P.A. (1984); City University of New York, Queens College, B.A. in Math and Economy (1977). **Personal Information:** Married to Gloria in 1987. One child: Naomi. Mr. Taylor enjoys spending time with his family.

4200 Trucking and Warehousing

4212 Local trucking, without storage
4213 Trucking, except local
4214 Local trucking with storage
4215 Courier services, except by air
4221 Farm product warehousing and storage
4222 Refrigerated warehousing and storage
4225 General warehousing and storage

4226 Special warehousing and storage, nec
4231 Trucking terminal facilities

Stephen Jones

Information Systems Manager
Als Cartage Ltd.
190 Goodrich Drive
Kitchener, Ontario, Canada N2C 2L3
(519) 893-6660
Fax: (519) 893-6050
stepjone@alscartage.com

4213

Business Information: Serving as the Information Systems Manager for Als Cartage Ltd., Mr. Jones fulfills the responsibilities of systems administrator, programmer, database administrator, and systems analyst. In these capacities, he is in charge of the computer systems infrastructure and custom development of the Company's information systems functions. An extremely smart individual, Mr. Jones wrote his first computer program at age 11, and since this time has enjoyed working in the industry. Attributing his success to a dedication and love for what he does, Mr. Jones plans to be more involved with the Internet and e-commerce in the future. Als Cartage Ltd. is a transportation company headquartered in Kitchener, Ontario, Canada. The Company is involved in the transportation of freight throughout Southern Ontario and is dedicated to ensuring that all clients receive products in an efficient and timely manner. **Career Highlights:** Information Systems Manager, Als Cartage Ltd. (1995-Present); Self-Employed, Consulting and Programming (1994-Present); Systems Programmer, Holstein Association of Canada (1994-95). **Associations & Accomplishments:** Lions International Royal City Lions. **Education:** Connestoga College, Computer Programmer/Analyst (1993). **Personal Information:** Married to Brenda in 1997. Mr. Jones enjoys reading, curling, camping, golf and archery.

Andreas Köhler

Information Technology Manager
LKW Walter AG
Alszeile 17-7
Vienna, Austria 1170
+43 22366062620
Fax: +43 223660652620
koehler@lkw-walter.com

4213

Business Information: As Information Technology Manager of LKW Walter AG, Mr. Köhler oversees and directs many technical duties on behalf of the Company. In this context, he is responsible for maintaining the functionality and operational status of the company's operating system and network infrastructure. Possessing an excellent understanding of technology, Mr. Köhler oversees and manages the company PC network as well as all telecommunications including fax and e-mail. Assisting the Company maintain its flexibility, efficiency, and profitability, Mr. Köhler is also involved in the analysis, acquisition, installation, support, deployment, and tracking of new technologies within LKW Walter AG. Helping the Company in its success, he intends to strive for a higher performance and eventually attain a higher position within the technology infrastructure. Established in 1924, LKW Walter AG is a transport and freight company. Utilizing its large fleet of over 5,000 trucks, the Company employs a work force of more than 1,000 people. Crossing international boundaries, the Company operates two locations serving clients in Middle and Eastern Europe. **Career Highlights:** Information Technology Manager, LKW Walter AG (1997-Present); Project Manager, LST (1992-97); Consultant, Cure (1996-97). **Education:** University, MAG (1997).

Terry Seebo

Network Systems Administrator
May Logistics Services, Inc.
5650 Dolly Avenue
Buena Park, CA 90621-1872
(714) 994-0821
Fax: (714) 523-0544
tseebo@servicecraft.com

4213

Business Information: Dedicated to the success of May Logistics Services, Inc., Mr. Seebo applies his knowledge and expertise in the field of network management in serving as the Network Systems Administrator. Before joining May Logistics, he served as Warehouse Manager with Servicecraft Corporation. His background history also includes a stint as General Manager for Kellers Delivery Services. In his current capacity, he designs and develops customized systems for the Corporation, implementing software system integration of the existing system with the new one. Acting as the vendor liaison and consultant for software and hardware purchases, Mr. Seebo performs his duties with the assistance of two dedicated staff members. He credits his success to stubbornness, reading, industry research, and aggressively tackling new challenges. Continually striving for optimum effectiveness, Mr. Seebo anticipates a promotion to Director. May Logistics Services, Inc. specializes in providing third party logistics and distribution services to companies and corporations. Employing the skilled services of 600 knowledgeable professionals throughout five locations across the country, headquarters are located in Buena Park, California. The Corporation was established in 1964. **Career Highlights:** Network Systems Administrator, May Logistics Services, Inc. (1993-Present); Warehouse Manager, Servicecraft Corporation (1983-93); General Manager, Kellers Delivery Service (1970-83). **Education:** Novell Networks; Motorola Routers. **Personal Information:** Three children: Rob, Jodie, and Shelly. Mr. Seebo enjoys reading, fishing and surfing the Internet.

Peter W. Kessler, Jr.

Network Analyst
Saddle Creek Corporation
440 Joe Tamplin Industrial Boulevard
Macon, GA 31217-7607
(912) 752-6309
Fax: (912) 746-8311
peterk@saddlecrk.com

4225

Business Information: As a Network Analyst for Saddle Creek Corporation, Mr. Kessler works with management and users to analyze, specify, and design cutting edge solutions to harness more of the computer's power. Possessing superior talents and an excellent understanding of technology, he is involved in database management and network infrastructure support and analysis. In this capacity, he is responsible for watching network overhead, providing network management, handling ODCB connections, administration tasks, client server management, and attending to PL Sequel requests. Acquisition, installation, modification, configuration, support, and tracking operating systems, databases, utilities, software, and hardware also fall within the realm of his responsibilities. Highly regarded, Mr. Kessler is dedicated to his work and hopes to eventually obtain a trainer or instructor position with the Corporation. Established in 1966, Saddle Creek Corporation is a third party logistics firm providing warehousing and distribution. Employing 500 personnel, the Corporation reports annual revenue of $60 million. A leading provider of warehousing, transportation, and integrated logistics services, the Corporation's mission is provide first class third party logistics solutions and services for customers utilizing whatever methods it might take. Headquartered in Lakeland, Florida, the Corporation's operations concentrate mainly on food, non-food grocery, tobacoo, and similar boxed goods items. **Career Highlights:** Network Analyst, Saddle Creek Corporation (1998-Present); Computer Support Analyst, USDA-APHIS-VS (1994-97). **Education:** University of Florida, B.S. (1996). **Personal Information:** Mr. Kessler enjoys database information design and Web based development.

Maryanne T. Muhlstadt

Manager of Special Projects
K-mart Distribution Center
333 South Spruce Street
Manteno, IL 60950-3244
(815) 468-3426
Fax: (815) 468-2543
mmuhlsta@manteno.kmart.com

4226

Business Information: Serving as Manager of Special Projects for the K-mart Distribution Center, Ms. Muhlstadt coordinates the warehouse management systems responsible for controlling tables. She assumes the responsibility of the implementation and debugging of the new inventory system customized for the Center's exclusive use. As a seven year veteran in the technology field, she has served with K-mart in a variety of roles since coming on board to the Company as Project Manager of Systems Implementation in 1992. In her current role, Ms. Muhlstadt presides over any special projects and offers technical support to users and systems management. A self-motivated person, she demonstrates a willingness to achieve and a curiosity that keeps her on the cutting edge of technology. Establishing goals that are compatible with those of the Center, Ms. Muhlstadt plans to continue in her present capacity as Manager of Special Projects and obtain her Master's degree. Her success reflects her ability to aggressively tackle new challenges. The K-mart Distribution Center performs the distribution logistics for the giant K-mart retail chain. Employing a work force of over 700 dedicated individuals, over 200 stores in the Midwest region of the United States receive their merchandise through this Center. **Career Highlights:** K-mart Distribution Center: Manager of Special Projects (1998-Present), Inventory Control and Quality Assurance Manager (1995-98), Second Shift Manager (1994-95), Project Manager of Systems Implementation (1992-94). **Associations & Accomplishments:** Women in Business; Branch of River Valley Chamber of Commerce; United Service Organization (1969-79). **Education:** Governor State University, B.A. (1992); Kankakee Community College: A.A. in Business Management, A.A. in Accounting. **Personal Information:** Ms. Muhlstadt enjoys travel, photography and horticulture.

4300 U.S. Postal Service

4311 U. S. Postal Service

Lawrence A. Callaway

Information Technology Specialist
United States Postal Service
8409 Lee Highway
Merrifield, VA 22081
(703) 698-6679
Fax: (703) 207-3694
lacallawa@email.usps.gov

4311

Business Information: As Information Technology Specialist for the United States Postal Service, Mr. Callaway fulfills a number of duties on behalf of the Agency. Serving as a network administrator, he is responsible for the functionality and operational status of seven LAN sites located throughout Virginia. Possessing superior talents and an excellent understanding of technology, Mr. Callaway provides help desk and technical support to over 1,200 users and manages all aspects of user accounts. Troubleshooting difficulties, providing e-mail administration, rebuilding stations, and participating in the configuration of networking environments also fall within the realm of Mr. Callaway's responsibilities. The most rewarding aspects of his career has been his role in developing and implementing the Agency's Y2K program. Looking to the future, he plans on establishing his own consulting business and attaining Cisco and Novell certifications. An agency of the federal government, the United States Postal Service provides timely delivery of letters and parcels. The Agency offers a wide variety of services including packaging, express mail, and home delivery of letters and parcels. Operating out of locations across the United States, the Agency employs 1,000 people at the Merrifield, Virginia location to facilitate smooth day to day administration and operational activities. **Career Highlights:** United States Postal Service: Information Technology Specialist (1995-Present), Mail Processor (1986-95). **Education:** Wave Technologies, Inc., Microsoft Certified Systems Engineer+Internet (1997). **Personal Information:** Married in 1991.

4400 Water Transportation

4412 Deep sea foreign trans. of freight
4424 Deep sea domestic trans. of freight
4432 Freight trans. on the Great Lakes
4449 Water transportation of freight, nec
4481 Deep sea passenger trans, ex. ferry
4482 Ferries
4489 Water passenger transportation, nec
4491 Marine cargo handling
4492 Towing and tugboat service
4493 Marinas
4499 Water transportation services, nec

Gerhard H. Ostermann

Project Manager
Panalpina Inc.
1776 On-The-Green, 67 Park Place
Morristown, NJ 07960-7103
(973) 683-9000
Fax: (973) 451-2639
gerhard.ostermann@mbl.panmail.com

4412

Business Information: Serving as Project Manager of Panalpina Inc., Mr. Ostermann is responsible for the information technology group, analysis and design of applications, e-commerce, and coordinating electronic data information. Involved in worldwide effort, he is assigned to a team in the United States to implement/roll out a new Freight Forwarding System with the purpose of meeting and serving the Corporation's business for the 21st Century. This involves ongoing coordination and development of necessary projects required for the U.S. in the form of new local business applications and provides the necessary EDI interface extentions. Beginning his career more than 14 years ago, he has worked diligently to enhance his skills and acquire expertise in his field. Mr. Ostermann's future goals are to continue to perform and function in his role with the Company as Business Systems Integrator and to maintain customer oriented focus in areas such as CRM and E-Commerce Projects, and promote use of XML transparant transaction level message exchange between the web applications and core business applications. Based in Switzerland, Panalpina Inc. specializes in international freight forwarding and transportation as well as the development and design of new procedures. **Career Highlights:** Project Manager, Panalpina Inc. (1985-Present). **Education:** St. John's University, B.S. in Computer Science (1985). **Personal Information:** Married to Ruth in 1989. Two children: Andrea and Matthew. Mr. Ostermann enjoys participating in sports activities.

Joe Chan
Technical Analyst
Orient Overseas Container Line, Ltd.

31/F Harbour Centre, 25 Harbour Road
Wanchai, Hong Kong
+852 28333664
Fax: +852 25318250
joecool@alumni.cuhk.edu.hk

4449

Business Information: As a Technical Analyst of Orient Overseas Container Line, Ltd., Mr. Chan is a member of the e-commerce products team. He helps to formulate the Company's EDI service strategy, ship e-commerce products, and manage the sales-systems reengineering project. Possessing superior talents and an excellent understanding of technology, Mr. Chan also administers the company's diversified, global Intranet environment. Highly regarded by his peers, he is proud of administering the Intranet project for all 160 offices. Continuing to work in the company's e-commerce arena, Mr. Chan plans on taking advantage of opportunities on the Web side of the business. Established in 1969, Orient Overseas Container Line, Ltd. offers global container transportation. Internationally, the Company covers east to west shipping corridors. Offering complementary operations such as container management, freight forwarding, and cargo consolidation, the Company owns and operates container vessels and terminals in order to provide their clients with outstanding support and service. Operating 160 offices in 50 countries, the Company employs a work force of 4,000 people. Clients can visit the company's Web site and book via the Internet. **Career Highlights:** Orient Overseas Container Line, Ltd.: Technical Analyst (1999-Present), Assistant Technical Analyst (1997-99). **Associations & Accomplishments:** Sir Edward Youde Scholar Association (1997-Present). **Education:** The Chinese University of Hong Kong, B.S. in Mathematics (1997). **Personal Information:** Mr. Chan enjoys Western calligraphy, reading and cooking.

Greg J. Vurdela
Information Technology Director
BCMEA

300-349 Railway Street
Vancouver, British Columbia, Canada V6A 1A4
(604) 688-1155
Fax: (604) 684-2397
gvurdela@bcmea.com

4449

Business Information: Mr. Vurdela has served with BCMEA in a variety of positions since coming on board to the Company as manager of information technology in 1990. Receiving a promotion in 1994, he now fulfills the obligations of Director of Information Technology for all aspects of daily technical operations of BCMEA. Mr. Vurdela determines the strategic direction and business contribution of the information systems functions. He is also responsible for planning new software applications, managing the fiscal budget, and setting Internet strategies as well as overseeing benefits administration. In the future, Mr. Vurdela hopes to take on larger challenges within the Company. Established in 1965, BCMEA engages in the logistics and transportation industry. Specifically, the Company maintains a presence in the Port of Vancouver and all British Columbia ports. Employing 27 individuals within the IT Department, the Company is a worldwide organization. With over 70 members, BCMEA deals with federal and municipal governments transportation needs. **Career Highlights:** BCMEA: Director of Information Technology (1994-Present), Manager of Information Technology (1990-94); Programmer/Analyst, WEBC (1986-90). **Associations & Accomplishments:** World Wide Information Technology Council; CIOABC; Education and Training Society of British Columbia. **Education:** S.F.U., Management Certificate (1996); British Columbia Institute of Technology, Systems Technology Diploma (1986).

Inigo Thomas, Ph.D.
Director of Management Information Systems
Diamond State Port Corporation

1 Hausel Road
Wilmington, DE 19801
(302) 472-7846
Fax: (302) 571-4646
ithomas@port.state.de.us

4491

Business Information: As Director of Management Information Systems of Diamond State Port Corporation, Dr. Thomas determines both strategic and tactical direction and business contribution of the Corporation's information systems functions. He came on board to Diamond State Port in 1997 as a Consultant, and within two years was elevated to his current position. In addition to supervising and mentoring his staff of three persons, Dr. Thomas handles numerous resource planning functions to include personnel evaluations; determining future resource requirements; and overseeing project time lines, schedules, assignments, and budgets. He is in charge of maintaining an online radio based inventory system that he implemented. Operating on an Oracle database, he fulfills all inventory and billing functions. Dr. Thomas, concurrently, functions as Systems Administrator responsible for all aspects of day-to-day technology processing. In this context, installation, modification, configuration, support, and tracking operating systems software, database management systems software, compilers, and client server utilities also fall under the scope of Dr. Thomas' responsibilities. He has published articles on robotics and computer vision in various journals. Modernizing the Corporation through implementation of advanced technology serves as one of his future endeavors. An international agricultural port on the East coast, Diamond State Port Corporation maintains the largest dock storage facility for importation of bananas and fruits, automobiles such as Volkswagons, and export of GM and Ford automobiles as well as other bulk commodities. State run since 1996, the Port was originally founded in 1923 and presently employs a work force of more than 350 people. The Corporation reports annual revenues exceeding $16 million. **Career Highlights:** Director of Management Information Systems, Diamond State Port Corporation (Present); Director of Software Development, Clearview Software (1995-97); Post Doctoral Fellow, University of Pennsylvania (1993-95); Graduate Assistant, University of Massachusetts (1987-93). **Associations & Accomplishments:** Institute of Electrical and Electronics Engineers. **Education:** University of Massachusetts: Ph.D. in Computer and Information Sciences (1993), M.S. in Computer and Information Sciences; Anna University, Bachelor's degree in Computer Science and Engineering (1987). **Personal Information:** Married to Anne in 1990. One child: Anne. Dr. Thomas enjoys ping pong and travel.

4500 Transportation By Air

4512 Air transportation, scheduled
4513 Air courier services
4522 Air transportation, nonscheduled
4581 Airports, flying fields and services

Pamela J. Buchner
Management Information Systems Analyst/Instructor
Alaska Airlines

P.O. Box 68900
Seattle, WA 98166
(206) 433-3399
Fax: (206) 431-5081
pam.buchner@alaskaair.com

4512

Business Information: Ms. Buchner is Management Information Systems Analyst and Instructor of Alaska Airlines. She is responsible for technical support of hardware and software for 300 plus computers in a production base hangar. Before joining Alaska Airlines in 1997, she served as Registration Software Instructor and Application Analyst with Hamot Medical Center. As a nine year technology professional, Ms. Buchner tracks systems and all documentation and is in charge of systems analysis. Her work primarily deals with parts, work orders, and synthesizing and compiling reports required by the Federal Aviation Administration. Currently, she is revamping the infrastructure from Macintosh to PC units. Recommending and ordering software and providing training to employees also fall within the realm of her responsibilities. Getting the new PC units up to speed and training the Company's personnel serves as her future goals. Ms. Buchner remains on the cutting edge of technology by attending Microsoft courses, reading, networking, and surfing the Interne. Alaska Airlines provides commercial air travel between Alaska and the West Coast, Canada to Mexico, and as far east as Las Vegas, Nevada. A

self sufficient operation, the Company's maintenance department is located in the hangar area of the production office. Aircraft maintenance includes light and minor repairs to major repairs, as well as replacement of major aircraft components. Founded in 1932, Alaska Airlines employs a work force of more than 10,000 professional, technical, and support personnel. **Career Highlights:** Management Information Systems Analyst/Instructor, Alaska Airlines (1997-Present); Hamot Medical Center: Registration Software Instructor (1996-97), Application Analyst (1990-96). **Associations & Accomplishments:** National Member, Harley Owner Group, Ladies of Harley; Institute of Management Accountants; Pennsylvania Association of Notaries. **Education:** Mercyhurst College: B.S. (1997), B.S. in Accounting and Marketing (1982). **Personal Information:** Ms. Buchner enjoys motorcycling, running, volleyball and backpacking.

Martha J. Knotts
Senior Analyst of Electronic Product Development
Continental Airlines

1600 Smith Street
Houston, TX 77002
(713) 324-3488
Fax: (713) 324-2715
mknott@coair.com

4512

Business Information: As the Senior Analyst of Electronic Product Development for Continental Airlines, Ms. Knotts develops and integrates new electronic offerings which provide value to end users. Through her duties in electronic product development, Ms. Knotts provides valuable data to the Airline leading to new electronic products which contribute to increased revenue to the Corporation. She possesses many years of educational and industry experience valuable to Continental Airlines. Continually striving for maximum effectiveness, Ms. Knotts is currently pursuing her second Master's degree to enable her to capitalize on the opportunities provided by the Airlines. Continental Airlines is one of the largest airlines in the United States, offering daily flights to 137 domestic and 57 international locations. Employing over 50,000 individuals, the Airline provides valuable service to commercial and leisure flights across the globe. Continental Airlines was established in 1934 and is rated twenty-third in the JD Powers "100 Best Companies to Work For." Operating from its headquarters in Houston, Texas, where Ms. Knotts is employed, the Company generates annual revenue of over $8.6 million. **Career Highlights:** Senior Analyst of Electronic Production Development, Continental Airlines (1999-Present); Instructional Technologist, Amadeus GTD (1996-99); Senior Instructor, System One/Amadeus (1986-99); Senior Representative, One Pass, Continental Airlines (1984-86); Public School Teacher (1972-79). **Associations & Accomplishments:** American Society for Training and Development. **Education:** University of Houston, M.S. in Occupational Technology (In Progress); Sam Houston University: Master's degree in Education, Bachelor's degree in Music Education. **Personal Information:** Ms. Knotts enjoys singing in concert choirs, teaching piano and desktop publishing.

Reiulf Lindberg
Administration Manager
Scandinavian Airlines

Department OSLMH
Oslo, Norway 0080
+47 64818171
Fax: +47 64816011
reiulf.lindberg@sas.no

4512

Business Information: In his position as Administration Manager for Scandinavian Airlines, Mr. Lindberg oversees and directs a number of administrative tasks on behalf of the Company and its clientele. He is responsible for supervising business controls, the information technology department, and administrative services within the technical division. Possessing an excellent understanding of technology, Mr. Lindberg also maintains the functionality and operational status of the information technology infrastructure to facilitate a seamless operation. A successful, 14 year professional, he fosters a strong sense of teamwork and purpose among office staff, ensuring that all employees work together to achieve a common goal. Mr. Lindberg has enjoyed substantial success in his present position and continues to grow professionally through the fulfillment of his responsibilites and his involvement in the advancement of operations. Moving up the corporate hierarchy either within Scadinavian Airlines or with another company serves as Mr. Lindberg's future goal. Scandinavian Airlines provides air transport for commercial and leisure travelers. Established in 1946, the Company employs the skilled services of more than 25,000 to facilitate all aspects of day to day operations. Headquartered in Oslo, Norway, the Company operates internationally and generates annual revenues in of $5.2 billion. **Career Highlights:** Scandinavian Airlines: Administration Manager (1996-Present), Information Technology Manager (1992-96), Business Controller (1989-91), Manager of Systems Development (1986-89). **Associations &**

Accomplishments: Odd Fellow. **Education:** B.I. of Olso, degree in Business Administration. **Personal Information:** Married to Mette in 1979. Two children: Camilla and Elisabeth. Mr. Lindberg enjoys family, friends and motor cars.

Shirley S. Payne

Communication Center Supervisor/Computer Specialist
Tri-Cities Regional Airport
P.O. Box 1055
Blountville, TN 37617-1055
(423) 325-6344
Fax: (423) 325-6335
spayne@triflight.com

4512

Business Information: Mrs. Payne functions in the dual role of Communication Center Supervisor and Computer Specialist with Tri-Cities Regional Airport. She is responsible for management of the Telecommunications Ddepartment and monitors the entire computer network infrastructure at the Airport. As Computer Specialist, she provides technical support for the Airport's software and hardware system. She works with vendors and the creators of networking systems to ensure the functionality and fully operational status of the systems. An expert, she utilizes her creativity to design computer systems and security systems. In the future, Mrs. Payne plans to channel her knowledge into a specified educational path. Her success reflects her aggressiveness and determination, as well as her ability to produce results and take on new challenges. Tri-Cities Regional Airport provides international transportation opportunities to the surrounding area of Blountville, Tennessee. Established in 1938, the Airport provides direct transportation to Virginia and Tennessee where they are able to connect with the leading airlines of the country and transport themselves anywhere in the world. **Career Highlights:** Supervisor, Tri-Cities Regional Airport (1992-Present); Self-employed Upholsterer (1978-92). **Associations & Accomplishments:** A.P.C.O. **Education:** St. Leo University, B.S. in Computer Science (In Progress); NSTCC, A.A.S. (1996). **Personal Information:** Married to Paul in 1969. One child: Niki Payne Wyatt. Mrs. Payne enjoys fishing, computers, painting, sewing and reading.

Teressa S. Chambers

Lead Technical Specialist
United Parcel Service
911 Grade Lane
Louisville, KY 40213
(502) 359-6181
Fax: (502) 359-7399
app1tls@air.ups.com

4513

Business Information: Serving in the capacity of Lead Technical Specialist of United Parcel Service, Ms. Chambers technical innovations keeps UPS on the leading edge in the packaging and delivery industry. As the technical lead, she is responsible for all aspects of designing, programming, and implementing new software applications to better monitor and track deliveries worldwide. Directing and participating in the analysis, acquisistion, installation, modification, evaluation, and testing of operating and database management systems, utilities, and software and hardware also fall within the technical scope of Ms. Chambers' responsibilities. Before joining UPS in 1988, she served as a Consultant with ICMS. A savvy, 15 year veteran of technology, she attributes her success to her perseverance and personal integrity as well as her ability to tackle challenges and deliver results. United Parcel Service, established in 1907, is an international company specializing in package delivery services worldwide. Currently, 350,000 employees man daily operations and help generate annual revenues in excess of $17 billion. The Company has been accredited Fortune 500 honors, and was named the most admired package delivery company in the world. **Career Highlights:** Lead Technical Specialist, United Parcel Service (1988-Present); Consultant, ICMS (1985-88). **Education:** University of Louisville, B.S. (1985). **Personal Information:** Married to Tony in 1989. Two children.

Jennifer L. Fischer

Business Analyst
UPS Information Services
334 New York Avenue
Jersey City, NJ 07307
(201) 828-2810
jfischer@tigger.jvnc.net

4513

Business Information: Ms. Fischer works within the subsidiary support groups in the position of Business Analyst of UPS Information Services. Prior to her current position, she worked in the analysis of document services and technology which enabled her to acquire relevant skills and knowledge useful to her present job description. Possessing extensive business savvy and technical expertise, Ms. Fischer is able to assist in various areas of the operation. Duties include overseeing the architectural design of UPS subsidiaries, ensuring all Company buildings comply with set regulations and policies. An invaluable asset, she plans on pursuing her Ph.D. and evolving into areas of knowledge management and decision support systems. Looking to the future in the 21st century, Ms. Fischer finds herself more heavily involved in teaching and consulting professionally. UPS Information Services is the information technology division of transportation, logistics, e-business. A division of UPS, the Company supports various groups within UPS from a corporate administrative aspect and operations as well as packaging facilities throughout the country. There are presently five facilities available throughout the United States with a staff of 400 empoyees, lending their expertise in day-to-day operations. **Career Highlights:** Business Analyst, UPS Information Services (1998-Present); Performance Engineer, Logical Design Solutions (1997-98); Managing Editor, Prentice Hall (1991-97) **Associations & Accomplishments:** American Association of University Women; Association of Computing Machinery; American Society for Information Science; International Communication Association; Institute of Electrical and Electronics Engineers Computer Society; National Association for Female Executives. **Education:** Drew University, P.D. (In Progress); The New School for Social Research, M.A. in Communications (1997); William Patterson University, B.A. in English (1992). **Personal Information:** Ms. Fischer enjoys study of world myths, legends, folklores and antique shopping.

Marion Hilliard

Technical Recruiter
Federal Express
1925 West John Carpenter Freeway, Suite 1000
Irving, TX 75063
(972) 444-6270

4513

Business Information: Serving as Technical Recruiter for Federal Express, Mr. Hilliard has the responsibility of filling positions within the Information Technology division. He is a team leader, and demonstrates an effective, productive style of managment as he works closely with his staff to implement strategic plans developed from collective efforts. Using media forms such as the Internet and newspapers, Mr. Hilliard also relies on employee referrals and job fairs to scout new talent for the Company. Attending techncial formus and seminars, he is able to remain current on modern issues. Keeping his goals consistent with the advancement of corporate objectives, Mr. Hilliard aspires to a management position within the Company. Federal Express is an international transporter of packages and letters and is headquartered in Memphis, Tennessee. With nearly 30,000 employees worldwide, the Company strives to uphold the reputation of accuracy and efficiency acheived through consistent performance. **Career Highlights:** Senior Technical Recruiter, Federal Express (1979-Present). **Associations & Accomplishments:** American Management Association; CUBY Certification; Managing Personal Growth Certification. **Education:** University of Phoenix, Master's degree (In Progess); Lehi University, Bachelor's degree.

Bruce K. Klatt

Management Information Systems Director
Corporate Air
P.O. Box 30998
Billings, MT 59107-0998
(406) 247-3131
Fax: (406) 247-3154
bkklatt@aol.com

4513

Business Information: Utilizing 10 years of experience with Corporate Air, Mr. Klatt is currently the Management Information Systems Director, in charge of corporate computer systems and workstations. He monitors the installation and maintenance of all hardware and software, as well as writes and implements customized system programs. Additionally, Mr. Klatt is accountable for the management of a help desk providing technical support to 120 end users. In the future, he is hoping to advance to the position of Chief Information Officer. Established in 1981, Corporate Air fulfills contracts with United Parcel Service, the United States Postal Service, Federal Express, and related courier services for the air transportation of freight. Headquartered in Billings, Montana, the Corporation currently operates 13 facilities in the United States and one facility in Manila. Corporate Air generates annual funds near $35 million. **Career Highlights:** Corporate Air: Management Information Systems Director (1989-Present), Accountant (1987-89); Meat Market Assistant Manager, Buttrey Foods (1983-86); Produce Assistant Manager, Safeway (1976-81). **Education:** Montana State University, B.S. in Business Administration (1987); Miles Community College, Associate's degree in Electronics. **Personal Information:** Married to Sally Anne in 1983. Two children: Jordan and Alex. Mr. Klatt enjoys woodworking, bike riding, hiking and fishing.

Samuel Spurlock

Senior Programmer Analyst
FedEx, ITD/Finance in Legal Systems
60 Fedex Parkway, First Floor Horizontal
Collierville, TN 38017-990
(901) 921-9150
Fax: (901) 922-5045

4513

Business Information: Mr. Spurlock first began with FedEx, or Federal Express Corporation, in 1997 as System Analyst for the Payroll Department. Since that time, his responsibilities have grown and he now serves as the Senior Programmer Analyst. He presides over the design, development, and implementation of software programs for the Corporation's payroll, finance, and legal departments. Program training and technical support is also provided by Mr. Spurlock. Staying on the cutting edge of the technology field by reading industry publications and other self-educational efforts, he attributes his success to his diverse professional background. Mr. Spurlock consistently achieves quality performance in his field and looks forward to a future promotion to Director of his division. Headquartered in Memphis, Tennessee, FedEx is world renowned for its package shipping operations. The Corporation was formed in 1978 in response to America's growing package shipping needs. With offices in major cities around the world, over 147,000 personnel members are now employed in international operations. **Career Highlights:** FedEx, ITD/Finance in Legal Systems: Senior Programmer Analyst (1999-Present), System Analyst Payroll (1997-99); EDP Auditor, First Tennessee National Bank (1995-97). **Associations & Accomplishments:** Association of American Military Engineers; Black Data Processors Association; American Engineer Association; Kappa Alpha Psi Fraternity Inc. **Education:** Mississippi Valley State University, B.S. (1992); Engineer Diploma; Advanced Engineer Officer Diploma. **Personal Information:** Married to Sheronda in 1999. Mr. Spurlock enjoys golf, chess, swimming, basketball, computers and reading.

James Ashford Wallace, Jr.

Recruiter
FedEx
50 Fed Ex Parkway, 3rd Floor
Collierville, TN 38017
(901) 263-8719
Fax: (910) 263-8716
jawallace@fedex.com

4513

Business Information: As a Recruiter for FedEx, Mr. Wallace serves as the Manager of all global information technology recruitment. He is responsible for locating programmers, business analysts, and more. Working closely with a team of 20 recruiters, Mr. Wallace utilizes a management style that incorporates both input and feedback from all staff members. He attributes his substantial success to his mentors, networking, and staying up to date by attending seminars and reading. Mr. Wallace has plans to pursue his Master's degree and hopes to continue working in the information technology recruiting field. Founded in 1973, FedEx is ranked as the largest express transportation company in the world. Employing a staff of 175,000 individuals in 211 countries around the world, the Company ships time sensitive documents and packages. Serving an international client base, the Company currently reports an estimated annual revenue of $18 billion. **Career Highlights:** Recruiter, FedEx (1984-Present); Director of Human Resources, Federated Department Stores (1977-84); President, Common Market Company (1975-77). **Associations & Accomplishments:** Society of Human Resources Management; American Society for Training and Development; Leadership Collierville; Germantown Chamber of Commerce. **Education:** University of Tennessee, M.S. (1975); Southern Methodist University, B.A. **Personal Information:** Married to Nancy in 1985. Three children: Katherine, Lauren, and Ann. Mr. Wallace enjoys photography, tennis and coaching.

Wyatt H. Miler

Vice President
George Miler, Inc.
5205 Sand Lake Drive
Melbourne, FL 32934
(407) 254-8726
Fax: (407) 254-3799
wmiler@nyx.net

4581

Business Information: Mr. Miler holds the title of Vice President of George Miler, Inc. He is responsible for formulating policies and procedures, developing goals, and implementing strategies to enhance the efficiency of the Corporation. Hiring and training employees, planning budgets, and establishing new business and partnerships are additional duties. As the Chief Technician, Mr. Miler is charged with maintaining technical equipment at airports which facilitates pilots in landings and taking off. He also manages and guides three employees in maintaining the functionality and serviceability of the computer network infrastructure and Automated Weather Observation Systems. For close to a decade, Mr. Miler has overseen all aspects of the Corporation. In the future, he hopes to attain the position of President and assist the Corporation in its growth and development. George Miler, Inc. is a navigation aid maintenance (ILS systems) business. The Corporation, established in 1970, provides air traffic maintenance and manufacturing. Headquartered in Greenville, South Carolina, there are currently three locations. **Career Highlights:** George Miler, Inc.: Vice President (1991-Present), Technician (1987-91). **Associations & Accomplishments:** Association for Computing Machinery; International Television Association; South Carolina Aviation Association; Student Council Representative, Video Department Savannah College of Art & Design. **Education:** Savannah College of Art & Design, B.A. (1996); Federal Aviation Administration Academy, Instrument Landing Systems Concepts; Greenville Technical College, A.S. (1992). **Personal Information:** Mr. Miler enjoys water skiing, swimming, reading, sailing and computers.

4700 Transportation Services

4724 Travel agencies
4725 Tour operators
4729 Passenger transport arrangement, nec
4731 Freight transportation arrangement
4741 Rental of railroad cars
4783 Packing and crating
4785 Inspection and fixed facilities
4789 Transportation services, nec

Joseph E. Green

Senior Network Administrator
American Express One
500 Atrium Way
Mount Laurel, NJ 08054
(856) 222-3900
Fax: (856) 722-0091
joe.e.green@aexp.com

4724

Business Information: As Senior Network Administrator of American Express One, Mr. Green maintains the integrity of systems and technical operations. Demonstrating an exceptional knowledge of his position, he handles all aspects of security administration as he oversees protection of data transmittals and security breaches. A gifted systems architect, Mr. Green has successfully developed and implemented several innovative applications that have aided in the overall effectiveness of the Company. With superior communicative skills, he leads the customer support staff through quality issues to ensure each user feels comfortable with their systems and services. Recognized for countless accomplishments and achievements within the Company, Mr. Green intends to continue in his current capacity as he furthers his involvement in corporate expansion. American Express One is a business travel agency that employs 3,500 people throughout the world. Established in 1999 when American Express Credit Corporation acquired a travel service bureau, the Company has grown to generate annual revenues of $3.5 billion. Headquartered in New York, the Company operates over 400 locations worldwide. **Career Highlights:** Senior Network Administrator, American Express One (1998-Present); Senior Personal Computer Technician, Check Point Systems Inc. (1998); Personal Computer and Network Technician, Sensar Inc. (1996-98). **Education:** Hiram College, B.A. (1996); Penn State, UNIX, C, C++. **Personal Information:** Mr. Green enjoys computers, music and outdoor activities.

Jeffrey W. Mason

Director of Information Services
Sundance Travel International
8687 Research Dirve
Irvine, CA 92618
(949) 453-8687
Fax: (949) 453-9551
jmason@sundancetravel.com

4724

Business Information: Providing his skilled services as Director of Information Systems of Sundance Travel International, Mr. Mason is responsible for the accurate booking of corporate and leisure travel arrangements. Before joining Sundance Travel International, he served as Network Administrator for Associated Travel. In his present role, he oversees all network operations, monitoring daily server and end user activity, administering booking program software upgrades, and providing a routine backup system. In addition to supervising his staff, Mr. Mason determines the overall technical direction and vision of the Company, as well as formulates the business contribution of the information systems function. Coordinating resources, time lines, schedules, and assignments also fall within the realm of his functions. Mr. Mason greatly enjoys his work in the travel industry which enables him to combine his dual loves of technology and travel. He sees his work as a way of providing dream visions for people. His success reflects his leadership ability to build teams with synergy, technical strength, and a customer oriented attitude; think out-of-the-box; and take on new challenges. Since inception in 1980, Sundance Travel International has provided individual and corporate clients with superb travel arrangements customized to each clients needs. Currently, operations employ 150 staff members and annual revenue is reported at more than $150 million. **Career Highlights:** Director of Information Systems, Sundance Travel International (1997-Present); Network Administrator, Associated Travel (1997). **Education:** Perris Union, Honor Graduate (1988); Pacific Travel School. **Personal Information:** One child: Taylor. Mr. Mason enjoys fun in the sun and any activity that involves the outdoors.

Mohammed Noortheen

Systems Analyst
Net Tours & Travel
P.O. Box 50777
Dubai, United Arab Emirates
+971 42666655
Fax: +971 42699694
mohd.noor@usa.net

4725

Business Information: Charged with maintaining the functionality of Net Tours & Travel's computer and network infrastructure, Mr. Noortheen serves as Systems Analyst. He is responsible for the database management systems and implementation of comprehensive programs ensuring seamless day to day operations. Possessing superior talents and an excellent understanding of technology, Mr. Noortheen also serves as manager and is accountable for supervises a work force of 151 employees. With over eight years of hands on experience, Mr. Noortheen utilizes his leadership skills to incorporate e-commerce into the Agency's marketing strategies. His future goals include increase utilization of both e-commerce and Internet technologies to assist the Agency in penetrating new markets and avenues for additional revenues. One of the leading tourist agencies in the Gulf region, Net Tours & Travel engages in the provision of information, guide, airline ticketing, and temporary lodging to tourists from all over the world. Founded in 1980, the Agency employs the skilled services of several individuals to promote services, facilitate scheduling, and address customer queries. The Agency currently operates out of several national locations for the convenience and benefit of all clients. **Career Highlights:** Systems Analyst, Net Tours & Travel (1996-Present); Systems Manager, Ministry of the Interior (1992-96). **Education:** Indian Council for Labor Management, H.R.D. and Quality Control (1998); College of Professional Management, Computer in Modern Management (1991). **Personal Information:** Married to Meharunnisha in 1997. One child: Ms. Marzuka Khannam. Mr. Noortheen enjoys travel and reading.

My Tien Van

Chief Information Officer
Livingston International
300-405 The West Mall
Etobicoke, Ontario, Canada M9C 5K7
(416) 626-2800

4731

Business Information: Serving as the Chief Information Officer for Livingston International, Ms. Van is responsible for information technology on a strategic level. She oversees the telecommunications data center, marketing and service of Company software, and daily internal administration and technical operations. Possessing an excellent understanding of technology, Ms. Van implements policies and procedures to ensure seamless operations, thus guaranteeing client satisfaction. Working closely with her team of associates and uses, she utilizes a managment style that incorporates input and feedback from staff members, thereby encouraging optimum performance among the staff. Ms. Van's goal is to facilitate continued Company growth and she looks forward to assissting in the completion of future corporate achievements. "Be open and truthful to what you think. Listen well!" is cited as her advice. Livingston International provides services to people who trade from the United States and Canada. Services also include custom brokerage as well as tax and duty transportation. Established in 1950, the Company employs an industrious staff of 1,600 individuals to acquire business, meet with clients, facilitate projects, and market services. The Company is located in Ontario, Canada and provides services to clients internationally. **Career Highlights:** Livingston International: Chief Information Officer (1998), Vice President of Software Factory (1996); Project Director, CIBC (1995). **Education:** McGill University: M.B.A. (1986), Bachelor's degree in Communications; Harvard, Executive Development Program. **Personal Information:** Ms. Van enjoys hiking, painting, gardening, the outdoors, music and art.

Corlis Yvette Dunston

Information Systems Security Officer
Fleet & Industrial Supply Center
1968 Gilbert Street, Suite 600, Code 80.1
Norfolk, VA 23511-3392
(757) 443-1529
Fax: (757) 443-1526
corlis_y_dunston@nor.fisc.navy.mil

4789

Business Information: As Information Systems Security Officer of Fleet & Industrial Supply Center, Mrs. Dunston provides direct input to the Information Technology Director to ensure that the information systems security program follow technical policies and guidelines. Lending her knowledge, she provides support for both hardware and software as she relies on her practical education and work experience. Mrs. Dunston evaluates the security needs of the users and network in order to remain secure. Crediting her career success to her strong determination and the positive environment in which she grew up in, Mrs. Dunston aspires to a management position as she prepares herself for a political role within the United States Congress. Her advice is, "Keep at it, be determined." Fleet & Industrial Supply Center provides logistics and support services to fleet units and shore commands. Established in 1919, the Center employs over 1,000 people and is known throughout the region as a provider of quality, cost-effective supply and support. **Career Highlights:** Information Systems Security Officer, Fleet & Industrial Supply Center (1997-Present); Accountant, U.S. Army Corps of Engineer (1989-97); Budget Analyst, Department of Transportation (1997). **Associations & Accomplishments:** Federal Information Systems Security Educator's Association; Level I and II Acquisition Certification in Communications-Computer Systems, Navy Acquisition Intern (1997); Summer Aide, Internal Revenue Service; Student Aide, Department of the Army. **Education:** Troy State University, M.P.A. (1996); Norfolk State University, B.S. in Business and Marketing (1991); Old Domunion University; Tidwater Community College. **Personal Information:** Married to Anthony in 1992. Two children: Mahogany and Toni. Mrs. Dunston enjoys writing poetry, writing short stories and attending the theater.

4800 Communications

4812 Radiotelephone communications
4813 Telephone communications, exc. radio
4822 Telegraph and other communications
4832 Radio broadcasting stations
4833 Television broadcasting stations
4841 Cable and other pay TV services
4899 Communications services, nec

Nabil Isa Al-Nimri

Telex Exchange Engineer
JTC
P.O. Box 6238
Amman, Jordan 1118
+962 64637733

4812

Business Information: Beginning his association with the Jordanian Telecommunications Company or JTC in 1996, Mr. Al-Nimri is responsible oversees daily telecommunications operations. Serving in the capacity of Engineer, he is in charge of maintaining the exchange's functionality and operational status. A successful, 18 year veteran in the field and with a wealth of experience, Mr. Al-Nimri supervises his staff of nine technical experts as well as ensures all work is accomplished within governmental guidelines and regulations. Looking to the future in the 21st century, Mr. Al-Nimri anticipates ownership of a business that provides construction and sale of cutting edge telecommunications devices. His success reflects his ability to take on challenges and deliver the desired results. Established in 1967, JTC is a government owned telecommunications company. Headquartered in Amman, Jordan, the Company provides excellent mobile phone and Internet services to consumers in the local area. Presently, JTC employs nine professional, technical, and support staff to oversee day-to-day administration and operations. **Career Highlights:** Engineer, Jordanian Telecommunications Company (1996-Present). **Associations & Accomplishments:** Jordanian Engineers Associations.

Education: Irbid High School, diploma (1982). **Personal Information:** Mr. Al-Nimri enjoys swimming, walking and reading.

Barbara A. Bass

Senior Manager
Pagemart Wireless
5646 Milton Street
Dallas, TX 75206-3907
(214) 765-3443
Fax: (214) 765-4983
bbass@pagemart.com

4812

Business Information: Mrs. Bass has been employed with Pagemart Wireless in several positions since joining the team of professionals as Market Support Manager. In her current position as Senior Manager, she assumes many responsibilities within the course of a day. Mrs. Bass supervises the work activities of a total of 90 customer service representatives, coordinates continuous training programs for employees, answers client questions, as well as presides over the preparation of profit and loss statements. Mrs. Bass also assumes responsibility for the collection of money, inventory fulfillment, and cash administration. Her career highlight includes the design and implementation of a central operations center that helped reduce fiscal operating cost by $500,000. Displaying a clear vison of goals, Mrs. Bass would like to become the Vice President of Pagemart Wireless. She credits her success to her mentor, Fran Hopkins. Pagemart Wireless is a division of Pagemart Inc. The Company, founded in 1989, offers wireless communication services to clients located in Dallas, Texas and the areas surrounding it. Pagemart Wireless is also a provider of digital paging as well as Internet services. Employing a qualified and skilled workstaff of 2,500 personnel, the Company is the number one network in the country. **Career Highlights:** Pagemart Wireless: Senior Manager (Present), Regional Quality Manager, Market Support Manager. **Personal Information:** Married to Matthew in 1997. Mrs. Bass enjoys watching football, reading and cooking.

Ken H. Cerda

Senior Systems Analyst
Verizon Wireless
3420 Country Square Drive, Apartment 1709
Carrollton, TX 75006-6778
(214) 922-8010
kcerda@yahoo.com

4812

Business Information: Joining the staff at Verizon Wireless in 1998, Mr. Cerda works closely with management and systems users to analyze, specify, and design new solutions to enhance the systems infrastructure as well as maintain the its functionality. Utilizing many years in the technology field, he oversees and supports over 350 Window Servers, ensuring all installations are done prompty and correctly. Possessing an excellent understanding of technology, Mr. Cerda is also responsible for developing strategies to ensure the smooth transition of the recent merger. His plans for the future includes faciliating growth for Verizon Wireless, remain hands on and move into management. Success, according to Mr. Cerda, is due to his aptitude and his ability to stay out-front of technology and deliver results. Verizon Wireless, established in 1986, is the world's leader in wireless communication. Recently merging with major companies, such as Bell Atlantic, GTE, Air Touch, and Primco, the Corporation employs over 500 people who manage accounts all over the country, ensuring that their clientele has the lastest in the world's cellular technology. Verizon Wireless continues to expand, facilitating resource and technology and keeping their customers up to date on new advances. **Career Highlights:** Senior Systems Analyst, Verizon Wireless (1998-Present); Consultant, Modis Solutions (1998-Present); Network Administrator, Summit Acceptance Corporation (1997-98); Network Administrator, Duck Ventures, Inc. (1991-97). **Education:** University of Houston (1983); Houston Community College. **Personal Information:** Married to Kim in 1998. Mr. Cerda enjoys music.

Michael K. Craft

Professional Skills Curriculum Developer
Sprint PCS
4800 Main Street, Suite 132
Kansas City, MO 64112
(816) 559-5140
Fax: (816) 559-1291
mcraft01@sprintspectrum.com

4812

Business Information: Mr. Craft is Professional Skills Curriculum Developer of Sprint PCS. He is responsible for all design and development aspects of the retail training curriculum. Mr. Craft has assertively served with Sprint PCS in a variety of roles since coming on board to Sprint PCS as Retail Sales Representative in 1996. With a solid track record of producing results, he was elevated to Special Event Leader in 1997, then in 1999, Mr. Craft was promoted to his current position. An expert, he oversees and conducts need assessments and analyzes, creates, and delivers retail curriculum training packages for the sales channels and management teams in the field. He works directly with systems analyst and programmers to write and edit the training curriculum and systems documentation, training courses, and procedures. Mr. Craft thoroughly loves his work and attributes his professional success to his father. His credo is "good things come to those who wait, but it's usually left-overs from those who hustle," a quote from Abraham Lincoln. Eventually attaining the positions of Assistant Vice President and Vice President of Sales Distribution serves as his future goals. The world's leading wireless communications provider, Sprint PCS specializes in CDMA technology. Using a nationwide CDMA network, Sprint PCS provides customers with CDMA digital communications solutions laced with sound quality, reliability, security, and capacity. Established in 1996, Sprint PCS employs a domestic workforce of more than 35,000 professional, technical, and administrative support personnel. **Career Highlights:** Sprint PCS: Professional Skills Curriculum Developer (1999-Present), Special Event Leader (1997-Present), Retail Sales Representative (1996-Present). **Associations & Accomplishments:** Kansas City Missouri Chamber of Commerce. **Education:** Fort Hays State University, B.A. (1996); Hutchinson Community College: B.A. in Education, A.A. in Psychology.

Dennis Enos

Account Manager for the Information Technology National Support Services Team
AT&T Wireless Services
12150 Research Parkway
Orlando, FL 32826
(407) 514-5082
Fax: (407) 514-6091
dennis.enos@attws.com

4812

Business Information: As a pioneer in wireless communications, Mr. Enos serves as the Account Manager for the Information Technology National Support Services Team of AT&T Wireless Services. Supporting operational systems, Mr. Enos manages a team of employees to ensure that communications and information services meet the quality and standard needs of individual and corporate clients. Utilizing 10 years of experience in the communication industry, Mr. Enos is highly recognized at AT&T Wireless Services for his problem solving techniques and his ability to communicate effectively with team members. Attributing his success to his flexibility, the most rewarding aspect of his career is helping to develop and coordinate a diversity awareness program for the Company. Continually formulating new goals and objectives, Mr. Enos plans to pursue his entrepreneurial ambitions and open his own consulting company. His advice is "be ready to change." Internationally recognized, AT&T Wireless Services is a provider of wireless telecommunication products and services. The Company specializes in providing cellular phones, pagers, Internet access, and voice mail. With local operations in Orlando, Florida, the Company employs the skilled services of 210,000 individuals who assist in selling products and services to hundreds of clients internationally. **Career Highlights:** AT&T Wireless Services: Account Manager for the Information Technology National Support Services Team (2000-Present), Area Development Manager, Project Manager, User Support Center Manager. **Associations & Accomplishments:** Board of Directors, Civic Theatres of Central Florida. **Education:** University of Connecticut, Associate's degree (1972).

Wu-Chang Feng, Ph.D.

Senior Architect
Puma Technology
5801 Christie Avenue, Suite 300
Emeryville, CA 94608
(510) 923-9175
wuchang@eecs.umich.edu

4812

Business Information: As Senior Architect for Puma Technology, Dr. Feng is in charge of the design and architecture of Internet services and software. He possess an excellent understanding of technology and its potential. Utilizing vast education and experience, he is responsible for technical evaluations, deployment, performance evaluations, and programming support for a large number of users of their hardware and software. While obtaining his Ph.D., Dr. Feng wrote his thesis on "Core Networking" and his plans for the future include gaining more knowledge of this immense program. Puma Technology is a wireless infrastructure provider for Internet services. The Company focuses on wireless solutions and building services such as POAs, cellphones, and pagers. Having six locations in the United States, the Company is also international. The Company is headquarterd in San Jose, California. **Career Highlights:** Senior Architect, Puma Technology (1999-Present). **Associations & Accomplishments:** Institute of Electrical and Electronics Engineers; Association of Computing Machinery; Golden Key National Honor Society. **Education:** University of Michigan: Ph.D. (1999), M.S. in Engineering (1994); Pennsylvania State University, B.S. (1992). **Personal Information:** Dr. Feng enjoys Ultimate Frisbee and technology.

Matthew Geary

Software Engineer II/Application Administrator
Sprint PCS
1300 Corporate Avenue
Lenexa, KS 66219-1374
(913) 307-3532
Fax: (913) 307-3535
mgeary02@sprintspectrum.com

4812

Business Information: Recruited to Sprint PCS as Software Engineer II and Applications Administrator, Mr. Geary works in the information technology division, maintaining Sprint's point-of-sale and e-business applications. A savvy business and technical expert, his responsibilities include maintaining fully functional and operational communication lines, processes, and servers at all times. Troubleshooting difficulties and developing new program methods, procedures, and preventative maintenance programs are also an integral part of Mr. Geary's functions. Key to his success are his academic ties and hard work. Advancing in a management role and working with systems integration and database management serve as his future endeavors. Sprint PCS provides global long-distance, voice, data, and video products and services. The Company also provides local telephone services in 19 states. The only all digital, all PCS cellular phone service provider in the Northwest, the Company was established in 1995. Presently, Sprint PCS generates an annual revenue of $15 billion and employs a work force of 20,000 trained technicians and staff to keep networks and telephone systems operational. **Career Highlights:** Software Engineer II/Application Administrator, Sprint PCS (1999-Present); Reference Librarian, Oklahoma State University Library (1994-99). **Education:** Oklahoma State University: M.B.A. (1999), B.S. in Psychology (1997). **Personal Information:** Mr. Geary enjoys sailing, woodworking and being a stock trading analyst.

Peter H. Gregory

Information Technology Manager
AT&T Wireless Services
P.O. Box 97059
Redmond, WA 98073-9759
(425) 702-2836
Fax: (425) 702-2568
peter.gregory@attws.com

4812

Business Information: Serving as Information Technology Manager of AT&T Wireless Services, Mr. Gregory, as Architect and Network Manager, is responsible for computing infrastructure for the Strategic Technology Group, a Research and Development Arm of AT&T Wireless. Mr. Gregory attributes his success to skillful decision making and the ability to look at entire situations in relation to the end result. Established in 1994, AT&T Wireless Services is a division of AT&T, one of the world's leading telecommunication providers. The Division delivers state of the art wireless communication services to businesses and individuals around the world, utilizing cellular and satellite communication technologies. **Career Highlights:** Information Technology Manager, AT&T Wireless Services (1994-Present): Consulting Manager, ASIX Inc. (1993-96); Systems Architect, World Vision U.S. (1990-93); Software Engineer, Bally Manufacturing (1986-90). **Associations & Accomplishments:** Usenix Association; Technical Reviewer, Prentice-Hall Publishing. **Education:** Columbia Pacific University; University of Nevada at Reno. **Personal Information:** Married to Corinne in 1992. One child: Alana Noelle. Mr. Gregory enjoys landscape gardening and photography.

Adam Holland

Information Security Manager
Verizon Wireless
5175 Emerald Parkway
Dublin, OH 43017-1063
(614) 560-2767
Fax: (614) 560-2719
adam.holland@airtouch.com

4812

Business Information: Possessing over 10 solid years of experience in technology, Mr. Holland joined the Airtouch Cellular team in 1994. Serving in various positions with the Corporation, he currently assumes the responsibilities of Business Systems Analyst. In this capacity, he assists in the management of a variety of information security and business continuity projects throughout the western half of the U.S. Mr.

Holland, relying on his skills and firm academic background, leads an enterprise-wide Information Security and Business Continuity Education Awareness effort. His other areas of responsibility are that of Virus Information and Support and Desktop/Laptop Security. Mr. Holland is involved in strategic budgetary planning activities for the Corporation. Looking forward to the developments and opportunities in the 21st Century, Mr. Holland's future objectives include becoming an Information Technology Leader. He attributes his career success to the education he received from the DeVry Institute of Technology. Verizon Wireless is a Joint Venture between Vodafone Airtouch and Bell Atlantic. Mr. Holland is located at one of the three main data centers in Dublin, Ohio. **Career Highlights:** Information Security Manager, Verizon Wireless (1999-Present); Airtouch Cellular: Business Systems Analyst (1998-99), Technical Support Specialist (1994-98); Systems Engineer, Sarcom, Inc. (1993-94); PC Analyst, St. Ann's Hospital (1990-93). **Education:** Franklin University, M.B.A. (December 2000 graduate); DeVry Institute Technology, B.S. in Electronic Engineering Technology (1992); Erie Institute of Technology, Associate's degree in Electronic Engineering. (1988). **Personal Information:** Married to Amee in 1997. One child: Hunter Adam. Mr. Holland enjoys golf and snowmobiling.

Marvin P. Keenan

Senior Project Manager
Air Touch
713 Tonstad Place
Pleasant Hill, CA 94523
(925) 279-6803
Fax: (925) 279-6081
marv.keenan@airtouch.com

4812

Business Information: A savvy, 27 year veteran of the technology field, Mr. Keenan serves as Senior Project Manager for the Pleasant Hill, California location of Air Touch. His position involves making cutting edge improvements to desktop adminstration features, while developing new features for customers as well. He is responsible for all aspects of project management to include coordinating resources, time lines, schedules, assignments, and budgets. Serving in a human resources role within the Company, Mr. Keenan handles the interviewing and hiring of employees for his department. Working closely with a staff of eight capable people, Mr. Keenan strives for accurate completion of projects. His three year plan includes retiring and starting his own consulting and freelancing business in technology and data communications. Attributing his success to his leadership ability to deliver results and take on new challenges, Mr. Keenan's advice is "keep open-minded to change and diversify your background." Air Touch is a wireless service provider for most of the United States. Established in 1988, the Company has over 100 users and 13,000 employees staffing centers throughout the United States. International in scope, Air Touch's corporate office is located in San Francisco, California. **Career Highlights:** Air Touch: Senior Project Manager (1999-Present), Manager Network Engineer (1970), Manager Network Projects (1995-98). **Education:** Harbor College, Electronics (1975); United States Air Force, Telecommunication (1969).

Clinton F. McCusker

Systems Integration Architect
Lightbridge Inc.
67 South Bedford Street
Burlington, MA 01803
(781) 359-4877
Fax: (781) 359-4500
cmcusker@mediaone.net

4812

Business Information: Serving as a Systems Integration Architect, Mr. McCusker has been providing his professional services to the industry since 1979. Utilizing his extensive hands on experience in the field of information technology, he focuses his efforts on the design, development, and integration of customized networks and databases. Responsible for maintaining the functionality of existing systems, he implements new technologies into the upgrade of these systems, ensuring a more state-of-the-art product. Heading all on-line volume, he works specifically with Web design and Internet hosting. Furthering his career, Mr. McCusker continues to grow professionally through the fulfillment of his responsibilities and his active involvement in the advancement of operations. The highlight of his career is the developing an online presence for First Mutual Insurance, providing them the capability to sell commercial insurance on the Internet. His future endeavors include attaining the position of Manager of Technical Support. A telecommunications service provider, Lightbridge Inc. was established in 1989. Headquartered in Burlington, Massachusetts, the Corporation employs a skilled staff of 700 technicians, engineers, and technical administrator operating out of eight branches nationwide. Providing their specialized sales and services for major telecommunication companies, such as Nextel, AT&T, and Sprint, the Corporation generates an estimated $100 million in annual sales. **Career Highlights:** Systems Integration Architect, Lightbridge Inc. (1999-Present); Systems Integration Specialist, Children's Hospital (1998-99); Senior Systems Manager, Putnam Investments (1997-98); Senior Systems Manager, Atlantic Companies (1988-97). **Associations & Accomplishments:** Phi Beta Kappa; Association of Internet Professional; DECUS; Institute Electrical and Electronics Engineers Computer Society; Oracle Development Tools User Group; The Internet Society; Natural Resource Defense Council. **Education:** Virgnia Western, A.A.S. (1997); Hunter College, B.A. in English (1979); New York Univerisity, M.S. in Computer System Design (1979). **Personal Information:** Married to Katherine in 1984. Two children: Katrina and Daniel. Mr. McCusker enjoys theology, music, art and literature.

Curtis W. O'Keefe

Director of Product Marketing
Winstar
7799 Leesburg Pike, Suite 700S
Falls Church, VA 22043-2413
(703) 917-9117
Fax: (703) 905-9169
cokeefe@winstar.com

4812

Business Information: Mr. O'Keefe is the Director of Product Marketing for Winstar. Accordingly, he defines, develops, and manages the Company's full suite of local, long distance, and data products. Mr. O'Keefe hopes to continue working with the software side of the industry and he would like to enhance his involvement in e-Commerce and Internet service providers arena. Winstar is a global provider of local and long distance telephone, Internet, and data services. Established in 1994, the Company has worked to remain a leader within all aspects of worldwide telecommunications. The Company currently employs a staff of over 3,000 personnel. **Career Highlights:** Director of Product Marketing, Winstar (1996-Present); NOS Communications, Inc.: Vice President of Operations (1994-96), Director of Operations (1993-94). **Associations & Accomplishments:** City of Rockville Telecom Action Team. **Education:** West Virginia University, B.S. (1992). **Personal Information:** Mr. O'Keefe enjoys tennis and running.

Agnes C. Oakeley

Systems Engineer
Inter-tel Technologies, Inc.
2701 Pan American Freeway, Suite C
Albuquerque, NM 87107
(888) 234-7166
Fax: (505) 345-2817
agnes_oakelely@inter-tel.com

4812

Business Information: Following six years of distinquished service in the United States Army, Mrs. Oakeley now serves as Systems Engineer for Inter-tel Technologies, Inc. In her role, she designs cutting edge networking and systems environments for the Company's Albuquerque, New Mexico location. An systems expert, Mrs. Oakeley is also engaged in design and development of new wireless communication, cable systems, and paging technologies. Dedicated to whatever she is part of, Mrs. Oakeley was recepient of the U.S. Army's 1994 "Soldier of the Year" award. Looking to the year 2000 and beyond, Mrs. Oakeley plans on becoming M.C.S.E. certified and gain more experience within the Company and technology industry. Her quote is "telephones and computers will be one by the year 2001." Inter-tel is involved in the wireless communications industry. Employing a staff of 300 employees, the Company counsels its clients on establishing a communications system of wireless telephones, paging systems, and cable systems. The Company has an international system of operation where digital and cellular telecommunications products are provided for the clients. **Career Highlights:** Systems Engineer, Inter-tel Technologies, Inc. (1997-Present); Management Information Systems Coordinator, Santa Fe County (1996-97); Database Manager, United States Army (1989-95); Mathematics Teacher, Taos Junior High School (1986-89). **Education:** Webster University, M.A. (1995); New Mexico Highlands University, B.A. **Personal Information:** Married to Patrick in 1997.

Lonnie J. Pate

Direct Sales Manager
Southern Linc
401 Mall Boulevard Suite, 201A
Savannah, GA 31406
(912) 691-5274

4812

Business Information: In his role as Direct Sales Manager of Southern Linc, Mr. Pate handles account acquisition. Utilizing a proactive management style, he meets with his staff to develop strategic business plans. Understanding the importance of empowerment and teamwork, he incorporates employee feedback into daily operations, ensuring that staff input and suggestions are given due attention. Mr. Pate leads the sales team to continual success, excelling in all areas of customer relations. Consistently achieving maximum results when completing corporate objectives, he is recognized for his contributions to the structure and integrity of the Company. Attributing success to his communicative abilities and exceptional people skills, he remains current in his field by attending seminars and reading trade journals. Mr. Pate intends to continue in his current capacity as he expands his role within the corporate structure. Southern Linc specializes in digital communication services and products. Established in 1996, the Company employs 16 people to assist in the completion of daily responsibilities. Headquartered in Savannah, Georgia, the Company has experienced rapid growth as reputation of quality, value, and outstanding customer support services spread throughout the region. **Career Highlights:** Direct Sales Manager, Southern Linc (1996-Present); Sales Manager, Savannah Communications (1991-96); Account Executive, Motorola (1990-91). **Associations & Accomplishments:** Home Builders Association; First Baptist Church Choir. **Education:** Georgia College & State University, B.B.A. (1990). **Personal Information:** Married to Kristin in 1992. One child: Chandler. Mr. Pate enjoys sports and singing.

Vincent Cheng-Kun Peng

Senior Engineer
Taiwan Cellular Corporation
3rd Floor, #2A-609, Section 5, Chung Shin Road, San Chung
Taipei, Taiwan 241
+88 6222782222
Fax: +88 6222783535
vincentpeng@podc.com.tw

4812

Business Information: As the Senior Engineer for Taiwan Cellular Corporation, Mr. Peng is responsible for the enforcement of regional rules and regulations that govern all internal and external business operations. Throughout his daily routine, he is charged with the obligation to monitor all network performance, while also optimizing the network, analyzing traffic, and tracking performance control. Beginning his information technology career three years ago, Mr. Peng has received recognition for his diligence and management skill through several promotions to his current position. He continues to grow professionally through the fulfillment of his responsibilities and his involvement in the advancement of operations. Highly regarded, Mr. Peng's plans for his career include remaining with the Corporation, obtaining more knowledge and expertise in his chosen profession, and moving up the corporate structure. Taiwan Cellular Corporation is the largest operator of mobile networks in Taiwan. The Corporation offers a wide variety of mobile services to private and corporate clients through various offers of GSM cellular communications that utilize more than 1800 megahertz. In association with Suretone Communications Corporation, Taiwan Cellular is headquartered in Taipei, Taiwan and functions under the direction of 500 professionals, technical, and administrative support staff. Currently, the Corporation reports annual revenues in excess of $1.5 billion. **Career Highlights:** Senior Engineer, Taiwan Cellular Corporation (2000-Present); Senior Engineer, Suretone Communication Corporation (1997). **Education:** Yuan-Ze Institute of Technology, Master's degree in Electrical Engineering (1997).

Douglas Pittas

Information Systems Director
Alltech Data Systems
855 Busse Highway
Bensenville, IL 60106-1219
(630) 595-5055
Fax: (630) 595-5056
douglasp@alltechdata.com

4812

Business Information: Mr. Pittas is the Information Systems Director for Alltech Data Systems. He is responsible for determining the overall strategic direction and business contribution of the information systems function. An expert in the field, Mr. Pittas assumed accountability for the technology infrastructure and Internet connectivity in over six offices throughout the United States. Looking to the next millennium, he has been slated to oversee five to ten other locations throughout the West Coast. In addition, he hopes to remain as a key figure in developing the voiceover IP and video conferencing. Current success, Mr. Pittas asserts, is the end product of his patience and relying on his staff of professionals and experts. Alltech Data Systems is a communications company. Engaged in wide area networking, LAN implementation, design, and troubleshooting, the Company has kept abreast of the ever-changing currents in contemporary technology. Established in 1993, Alltech Data Systems has averaged an annual revenue figure of $60 million. With the technical skills of 250 talented individuals, the Company is able to conduct business on both a local and global scale. **Career Highlights:** Information Systems Director, Alltech Data Systems (1997-Present); WAN Manager, Fimat Facilities Management; Information System Manager, Follett Software. **Associations &**

Accomplishments: Boy Scouts of America. **Personal Information:** Married to Dina in 1998.

Channasandra Ravishankar, Ph.D.

Senior Principal Engineer
Hughes Network Systems
11717 Exploration Lane
Germantown, MD 20876
(240) 453-2141
Fax: (240) 453-2201
cravishankar@hns.com

4812

Business Information: A prominent and respected professional, Dr. Ravishankar serves as the Senior Principal Engineer for Hughes Network Systems. In this capacity, he assumes the responsibility for the systems design for the Company's voice, fax, and data services. He develops new technological advancements within the fields to improve current operations and offer new services to increase the efficiency of business operations for Company clients. Citing a solid education and his peers as the reason for his professional success, Dr. Ravishankar stays on the cutting edge of technology by patenting his ideas and reading technical journals. Dr. Ravishankar currently serves as Editor for Speech Proccessing for IEEE transactions on communications. He is committed to the success of Hughes Network Systems and looks forward to leading its system design group in the wireless domain. Hughes Network Systems is engaged in the manufacture of various types of telecommunications equipment including satellite and wireless systems. Headquartered in Maryland, the Company has development and manufacturing facilities across the United States and abroad, employing the skilled services of approximately 3,000 knowledgeable professionals. The Company boasts $1 billion in sales each year. **Career Highlights:** Senior Principal Engineer, Hughes Network Systems (1995-Present); Member Technical Staff, Comsat Laboratories (1991-95). **Associations & Accomplishments:** Institute of Electrical and Electronics Engineers; Eta Kappa Nu. **Education:** Purdue University, Ph.D. (1991); Indian Institute of Technology, India, M-Tech (1987). **Personal Information:** Married to Jayshri in 1992. One child: Veda. Dr. Ravishankar enjoys travel and reading.

Chad D. Rhine

Member of Technical Staff
Hughes Network Systems
11717 Exploration Lane
Germantown, MD 20876
(301) 212-7978
Fax: (301) 548-1272
crhine@hns.com

4812

Business Information: Mr. Rhine, an innovative leader in the technology field, joined the Hughes Network Systems team as Member of Technical Staff in 1998. At present, he is an invaluable team member of the Web Technology Group within Software Technology. Relying on extensive academics and training, Mr. Rhine's role principally involves design and development of state-of-the-art Web-based applications. He leverages his technical skills in researching and finding new innovations and solutions. Mr. Rhine owns a consistent record of delivering technical results by communicating effectively and solving problems and challenges in a systematic and efficient manner. A recognized expert, he is responsible for training scenarios and making presentations to internal customers, which include Vice Presidents. He attributes his professional success to a strong faith in God, values instilled in him by his parents, and his leadership experience. Mr. Rhine's advice to others following the same career path is "Be honest in everything you do. If you're not true to yourself, then you can't be successful." Attaining the role of Project Lead on a project starting from scratch, moving up the management hierarchy, and gathering additional technical skills serves as Mr. Rhine's future goal. Hughes Network Systems is a world leader in telecommunications, satellite, digital cellular, and enterprise network technologies. The Company is a subsidiary of Hughes Electronics and General Motors. Founded in 1972, the Company presently employs a staff of more than 3,000 professional, technical, and support staff. **Career Highlights:** Member of Technical Staff, Hughes Network Systems (1998-Present); Software Technology Intern, Hughes Network Systems (1997-98); Teaching Assistant, Purdue University (1996-98); Computer Information Systems Intern, The Timken Company (1996). **Associations & Accomplishments:** Upsilon Pi Epsilon; Association of Computing Machinery; Omicron Delta Kappa; Golden Key; Phi Eta Sigma; Sigma Phi Epsilon; Phi Sigma Pi; Boy Scouts of America; Order of the Arrow; American Red Cross; Word of Life; University of Pittsburgh Senior of the Year Finalist. **Education:** Purdue University, M.S. in Computer Science (1998); University of Pittsburgh: B.S. in Computer Science (1996), B.S. in Math (1996). **Personal Information:** Married to Christina M. in 1998. Mr. Rhine enjoys being active in Church ministries, studying the Bible, spending time with his wife, leadership and sports.

Lisa S. Romish

Senior Product Manager
Sprint PCS
4717 Grand Street, 4th Floor
Kansas City, MO 64112
(816) 559-3618
Fax: (816) 559-1514
lromis01@mail.sprintpcs.com

4812

Business Information: As Senior Product Manager of Sprint PCS at the headquarters location in Kansa City, Missouri, Ms. Romish oversees the technical support of phones. Demonstrating a productive style of management, she works closely with her staff to development new products as she implements their feedback and input. Establishing a geniune rapport with various manufacturing representatives, she acts a liaison for the field representatives to handle software releases and solve product problems. Ms. Romish handles hiring and reviews for the staff of her department, conducting evaluations and making promotion recommendations when necessary. Ms. Romish stays up-to-date on current technology by reading trade magazines, researching on the Internet, and attending vender meetings. Crediting her success to the support she receives from her family and friends, she believes her faith in God has helped to overcome many challenges. Keeping her goals consistent with corporate objectives, Ms. Romish looks foward to continuing in her current role. Offering complete wireless service to millions of individuals, Sprint PCS is the United State's largest CDM provider. The Company was established in 1995, and currently serves over 95 percent of all cellular customers in the United States. Employing over 7,000 nationwide, the Company strives to maintain market shares through continually providing excellent products, services, and customer support. **Career Highlights:** Sprint PCS: Senior Product Manager (1999-Present), Product Manager (1996-99); Senior Project Manager, Novell (1994-95); International Editor, Word Perfect (1990-94). **Associations & Accomplishments:** Women in Wireless Telecommunications; Thunderbird Alumni Group. **Education:** American Graduate School of International Management, M.I.M. (1995); BYU, B.S. in Business Management. **Personal Information:** Ms. Romish enjoys travel, cooking and reading.

Terri J. Spencer

Technical Manager, Data Warehousing
Providian Financial
5060 Crandallwood Drive
Fremont, CA 94555
(925) 227-2658
Fax: (925) 227-2622

4812

Business Information: Responsible for several implementations of Data Warehouses, Ms. Spencer is currently the Technical Manager of Data Warehousing at Providian Financial. She is in charge of the Data Warehouse management for the Company and is also responsible for the creation of the Corporate Information Factory (CIF). The CIF includes implementing the following infrastructure: Data Marts, Operation Data Stores (ODS), the data mining environment, exploration environment, Internet access and updates to the environment, e-commerce, and Internet, client server access, and implementation of linear storage access and storage. She is also currently responsible for implementing and maintaining the current Data Warehouse which involves installing software applications, front end tools, data quality, managing budgets, managing vendor relationships, creating proposals, and performing presentations to top management. These tasks are performed to support the Company and internal clients at the Company's Pleasanton, California location. Ms. Spencer attributes her professional success to her adaptability to new situations, and her flexibility, recieving internal recognition and accolades for her outstanding performance in many previous positions. Committed to the success of the Company, she plans to remain in Data Warehouse management but intends to focus more on larger corporation factory infrastructures. Ms. Spencer's success reflects her ability to deliver results and aggressively tackle new challenges. From numerous locations in the United States and the United Kingdom, Providian Financial offers a full line of financial services and provides secured and unsecured credit cards as well as mortgage loans. The Company was founded in 1992 and is the sixth largest credit card company with its headquarters residing in San Francisco, California. **Career Highlights:** Technical Manager, Data Warehousing, Providian Financial (1999-Present); Technical Manager for Data Warehouse, Pacific Bell Wireless (1996-99); Project and Technical Lead II, Nestle Beverage Company (1991-96). **Associations & Accomplishments:** International Data Management Association; The Data Warehouse Institute; Outstanding Young Women of America. **Education:** Howard University, Master's degree; Fisk University, B.A. (1982). **Personal Information:** Ms. Spencer enjoys skiing, painting, travel and meeting new people.

John Anthony Veguilla, III

Senior Technical Consultant
Winstar Telecommunication
50 Fremont, Suite 1900
San Francisco, CA 94105
(415) 625-9847
Fax: (415) 625-9902
jveguilla@winstar.com

4812

Business Information: In his role as Senior Technical Consultant of Winstar Telecommunications, Mr. Veguilla handles a variety of administrative and information technology responsibilities on a daily basis. He demonstrates his exceptional knowledge of the industry as he meets with clients at their locations to assess their needs, then designs action plans that may include ecomonic models such as return on investment anaylsis or Internet development for e-commerce activities. Well versed in both technical and economic aspects of his position, Mr. Veguilla is recognized for lending support to sales and marketing divisions of Fortune 100 and 500 companies. Realizing that technology is constantly changing and growing in today's progressive society, he keeps abreast of changes through seminars, conferences, and by reading trade journals. Credited with the successful implementation of several innovative procedures and creative technical marketing plans, Mr. Veguilla currently is completing his post graduate studies; he aspires to an executive management role to better utilize his abilities. Winstar Telecommunications is a national provider of wireless services for local networks. Specializing in ISDN, Internet, broadbands, ATM, and broad relay services, the Company has a diverse clientele that ranges from financial institutions and commerical companies to private individuals. Widely traded on NASDAQ as WCII, the 10 year old company has received numerous praises when reviewed by industry experts. **Career Highlights:** Senior Technical Consultant, Winstar Telecommunications (1998-Present); Regional Manager, Advance Fibre Communication (1997-98); Technical Manager, MCI (1992-97). **Education:** Master's in E-Commerce (In Progress); Golden Gate University, M.S. (1996); University of Maryland, B.S. **Personal Information:** Married to Un-Chu in 1981. Two children. Mr. Veguilla enjoys chess and astronomy.

Dennis H. Watts

Manager of Information Technology Web Development
Weblink Wireless
3333 Lee Parkway, Information Technology Department
Dallas, TX 75219
(214) 765-3397
Fax: (214) 765-4901
dennis.watts@weblinkwireless.com

4812

Business Information: Demonstrating his extensive expertise in his field, Mr. Watts serves as the Manager of Information Technology Web Development for Weblink Wireless. Holding the position for three years, he manages 12 members within his department and guides them in the implementation of new technologies, strategies, and techniques in order to build and maintain more efficient technological systems, to include software paging systems. Utilizing his expansive knowledge in technology development, Mr. Watts concentrates his efforts towards the building of inhouse networking systems, and is proactively involved with launching e-commerce initiatives. Forecasting, scheduling, and project management and tracking also fall within the realm of his responsibilities. With continuing dedication to his position, Mr. Watts remains committed to providing excellent project development and management. Established in 1990, Weblink Wireless is dedicated to providing excellent sales and services in wireless communications. Headquartered in Texas, the Company provides its specialized services to an international client base. Professional administration are employed to facilitate every aspect of daily operations including the distribution of wireless telecommunication devices, e-mail services, paging, Web development, and software design. **Career Highlights:** Weblink Wireless: Manager of Information Technology Web Development (1998-Present), Lead Senior Analyst (1997-98); Lead Systems Analyst, Texas Instruments (1986-97). **Associations & Accomplishments:** Housing Standards Board; International Association of Business Communicators. **Education:** Tarleton State University, B.B.A. in Marketing and Management (1984). **Personal Information:** Married to Dana Kay in 1990. Two children: Kirsten Danielle and Erika Nicole. Mr. Watts enjoys guitar, snow skiing and scuba diving.

Edward S. Abramczyk

Manager Network Management Systems
Concert
11440 Commerce Park Drive
Reston, VA 20191
(703) 716-8944
Fax: (703) 716-8888
ed.abramczyk@concert.com

4813

Business Information: As Manager of Network Management Systems for Concert, Mr. Abramczyk handles a multitude of highly specialized technical activities. Leading his staff with a proactive attitude, he ensures each employee comprehends their role in the corporate structure and can fully apply procedures and policies to their tasks. By lending his insight and guidance at departmental meetings, he is directly involved in the development of strategic technical planning. Internally recognized for impressive achievements in his position, he is credited with such accomplishments as the formulation of tools for performance fault software, and the creation of southwest routers and switches. He gathers data and statistics from users regarding operational procedures and couples it with independently generated information to accurately forecast needs and trends. Citing the keys to his success as teamwork and strong motivation, Mr. Abramczyk intends to shift his career focus to the global market place so that he may assist in the design of regulatory rules and regualtions for the industry. Concert is an international telecommunications company that provides technical support to businesses in the Reston, Virginia area. Servicing companies and corporations from the Fortune 500 listing, the Company provides installation and maintenance of networking systems and hardware to ensure smooth completion of daily responsibilities. **Career Highlights:** Manager of Network Management Systems, Concert (1999-Present); Systems Engineering Manager, PRC, Inc. (1988-99). **Education:** American University, Master's degree in Public Administration (1987); Clarion University, B.S. (1985). **Personal Information:** Married to Debra in 1990. Two children: Alison and Jordan. Mr. Abramczyk enjoys football and is a avid Cleveland Browns fan.

Steve E. Aden

Information Systems Manager
ITS Communications
2212 Madison Avenue SE
Grand Rapids, MI 49507
(616) 456-0614
saden@itscommunications.com

4813

Business Information: Displaying his skills in this highly specialized position, Mr. Aden serves as the ITS Communications as Information Systems Manager. In this capacity, he provides internal information systems management and is responsible for servers, networks, and client computers. He ensures systems are backed up and that recovery systems are available, maintaining the Corporation's entire internal network architecture. A dedicated and determined individual, Mr. Aden hopes to acheive a position as the Chief Information Officer by keeping up on technological news and developments in the area of networking. Headquartered in Grand Rapids, Michigan, ITS Communcations provides voice and data communications services. A wireless Nextel dealership, the Corporation offers voice circuits and hardware for phone systems, and WAN systems and monitoring. A group of 115 professionals with an extensive and proven track record in the industry are employed to fulfill all aspects of operation. **Career Highlights:** Information Systems Manager, ITS Communications (1999-Present); NT Operator, Dow Chemical (1996-99). **Education:** Central Michigan University, B.S. (1995); Michigan Technological University. **Personal Information:** Mr. Aden enjoys auto repair.

Shakir Ahmed

Building Management Systems and Security Operations Specialist
ETISALAT
P.O. Box 14
Fujairah, United Arab Emirates
+971 92022333
shakir14@emirates.net.ae

4813

Business Information: Proficient in all areas of the engineering and technology fields, Mr. Ahmed was recruited to ETISALAT in 1995. Serving as a Building Management Systems and Security Operations Specialist, he is responsible for implementing and reinforcing professional integrity in such areas as hi-rise building management systems. His focus is on monitoring all systems and maintaining the functionality of all electrical mechanical equipment. With more than 18 years of technical experience, Mr. Ahmed attributes his success to hard work and convenient opportunities that allows him to demonstrate his ability to perform work of the most complex nature. Highly regarded, he possesses an excellent understanding of his field. In the process of devising definite plans to remain with the Company, Mr. Ahmed aspires for enhanced professional growth by attaining a position in upper management. Serving an international client base, ETISALAT operates as a telecommunicationa and Internet service provider for the United Arab Emirates and surrounding countries. The focus of the Company is to offer comprehensive programs and devises to individuals and corporations who utilize Internet, mobile phones, and regular phone services. Established in 1972, the Company is headquartered in Fujairah, United Arab Emirates and operates out of several subsidiaries, functioning under the expertise and talents of over 5,000 of highly skilled professionals. **Career Highlights:** Building Management Systems and Security Operations Specialist, ETISALAT (1995-Present); Site Engineer, Breezer (1990-95); Foreman, UTS Carrier (1986-90). **Associations & Accomplishments:** Association of Diploma of Associate Engineers-Pakistan. **Education:** Government College of Technology, Associate's degree in Engineering (1982). **Personal Information:** Married to Maryam in 1986. Three children. Mr. Ahmed enjoys reading, computering and playing cricket.

Ijaz Ul Haq Badar

Engineer
Emirates Telecom Corporation
P.O. Box 3838-5WD
Abu Dhabi, United Arab Emirates
+971 26184671
Fax: +971 26218899
ihbadr@emirates.net.ae

4813

Business Information: Utilizing more than 20 years of practical experience in the highly specialized field of telecommunications, Mr. Badar has been providing professional technical services with Emirates Telecom Corporation since 1991 while serving as an Engineer. Incorporating the latest technologies, he is proactively involved in the upgrading of the Corporation's complex database system and providing technical support and monitoring of the Corporation's network. Continually striving for maximum effectiveness, Mr. Badar is currently pursuing his M.B.A. to enable him to capitalize on the opportunities afforded by the Corporation. Serving an international client base, Emirates Telecom Corporation is dedicated to providing the distribution of quality telecommunications products and services, generating $1 billion in annual revenues. Headquartered in Abu Dhabi, United Arab Emirates, the Corporation employs the skilled services of 5,000 professional technicians, engineers, and customer support representatives to promote services, facilitate projects, and address customer queries. **Career Highlights:** Engineer, Emirates Telecom Corporation (1991-Present); Engineer, Pakistan Telecommunications Company (1983-91); Sales Engineer, Philips Pakistan (1982). **Associations & Accomplishments:** Pakistan Engineering Council. **Education:** Engineering University of Lahore, B.S. in Electrical Engineering (1981). **Personal Information:** Married to Sadia in 1987. Three children: Ahmaed, Samia, and Ali. Mr. Badar enjoys reading and time with family.

Ayananshu Banerjee

Senior Analyst
SBC Communications Inc.
4485 Barat Hall Drive, Apartment B3
St. Louis, MO 63108-2532
(314) 235-6470
Fax: (314) 235-0162
ab2246@momail.sbc.com

4813

Business Information: Serving as the Senior Analyst for SBC Communications Inc., Mr. Banerjee works closely with management and end-users to analyze, specify, design, develop, and deploy new software applications used by external LSP, ISP, and IXC, business customers and internal employees. Possessing an excellent understanding of technology, he is responsible for maintaining the systems functionality, ensuring the proper operation of infrastructure and application software. Continually striving for maximum effectiveness, Mr. Banerjee is currently pursuing his M.B.A., which will enable him to capitalize on the opportunities provided by the dynamic communications industry and eventually become a successful manager in information technology. Established in 1984, SBC Communications Inc. is a leading telecommunication company. Providing services and products worldwide, the Corporation utilizes a global network to ensure proper operation of each location. A group of more than 200,000 talented professionals are employed to fulfill all aspects of the business. **Career Highlights:** SBC Communications Inc.: Senior Analyst (2000-Present), Process Specialist (1996-99); Research Associate Staff, Washington University (1996). **Associations & Accomplishments:** General Secretary, Bengali Association; National Scholar and Recipient of Governor's Medal, India. **Education:** Washington University, M.S. (1996); Indian Institute of Technology, Kharagpur, India, Bachelor's degree in Technology (1994). **Personal Information:** Married to Shyama in 1998. Mr. Banerjee enjoys sports, music and books.

Linda M. Berg

Internet and Technical Support Administrator
West Wisconsin Telecom Cooperative, Inc.
912 Crescent Street
Menomonie, WI 54751
(715) 235-1692
Fax: (715) 235-1898
bergl@wwt.net

4813

Business Information: Demonstrating technological expertise, Mrs. Berg was recruited to West Wisconsin Telecom Cooperative in 1997. At the present time, she assumes the responsibilities of Internet and Technical Support Administrator. In her capacity, she exercises oversight of all management aspects of day-to-day technical support administration. Drawing from several years of experience and educational history, she manages intra-network upgrades, maintains the intra-network operating at optimum efficiency, troubleshoots system difficulties, and teaches and assists customers in use of Internet and other services. Directing and participating in the analysis, design, evaluation, testing, and implementation of Internet and Intranet-related computer systems also falls within the realm of her responsibilities. Mrs. Berg has received several public speaking awards and is also sought after to speak at local high schools on technology issues. She attributes her success to a strong faith in God. "Never give up, always strive ahead," is Mrs. Berg's favorite motto. Attaining MCSE certification and moving up the hierarchy to the position of Chief Information Officer serves as her future goals. Incorporated in 1954, West Wisconsin Telecom Cooperative, Inc. is a small independent, local telephone company owned by members. Serving several counties, the Corporation is manned by 25 employees and growing. Services provided include Internet, cellular, digital, satellite, paging, phone, and voice mail as well as installation and technical services. **Career Highlights:** Internet and Technical Support Administrator, West Wisconsin Telecom Cooperative, Inc. (1997-Present); Technical Instructor, Cray Research, Inc. (1976-94). **Associations & Accomplishments:** Chippewa Falls Chamber of Commerce; Notre Dame Catholic Church. **Education:** University of Wisconsin, Stout, B.S. in Industrial Technology in Telecommunications (1994-97); CVTC, Supervisory Management (1993-94). **Personal Information:** Married to Richard H. in 1971. Two children: Wade and Jason. Mrs. Berg enjoys walking, crocheting, computing, four-wheeling, hunting and teaching 8th grade religion class. Her son Wade is married to Pam and they have two children named Jordan and Jacob.

Barbara D. Bonner

District Manager
AT&T
55 Corporate Drive, Room 33A69
Bridgewater, NJ 08807-1265
(908) 658-6315
Fax: (215) 699-0292
b.bonner@att.net

4813

Business Information: Ms. Bonner, equipped with 20 years of technological experience, is a District Manager with AT&T. She supports new product development through the deployment of billing and operational systems and process design. Utilizing her business savvy and technical expertise in the field, she is primarily responsible for developing new systems and assisting in their implementation. Ms. Bonner, a great asset to AT&T, offers advice and instructions on the use of particular programs and resolves current problems or issues. Her career highlights include launching a cutting edge billing platform and building a loyalty program. Attending professional seminars, reading current literature, and networking with other professionals in the field enables Ms. Bonner to keep abreast of new developments in the field and incorporate pertinent information into daily activities. Remaining on top of emerging technology and supporting companies in the communications area serves as her career goal. AT&T is a well-established telecommunications company and Internet service provider. Offering quality services since 1878, this reputable Company employs over 200,000 professionals to assist in various aspects of its global operation. Keeping abreast of new developments in the field, the Company is one of the premier leaders in telecommunications. **Career Highlights:** AT&T: District Manager (1996-Present), Manager of Operational Planning (1993-96), Manager of Billing Strategy (1991-93), Sales/Network Services & Phone Systems Manager (1980-91). **Associations & Accomplishments:** Philadelphia Folk Festival (fundraiser for Philadelphia Folksong Society, proceeds for music therapy programs). **Education:** Drexel University, B.S. in Management (1988); University of Pennsylvania/Wharton, Master's certificate in

Business Management; AT&T School of Business. **Personal Information:** Married to Noel Squitieri in 1996. Ms. Bonner enjoys genealogy and travel.

Douglas E. Brammer

Senior Specialist for Strategic Planning
Bell Atlantic
13100 Columbia Pike
Silver Spring, MD 20904
(301) 236-2704
douglas.e.brammer@bellatlantic.com

4813

Business Information: Mr. Brammer, having extensive experience in sales and strategic planning, is currently a Senior Specialist of Strategic Planning for Bell Atlantic's Wholesale Services business unit. He assesses the impact of technological, regulatory, industry, and competitive developments on the Wholesale Services market. Additional responsibilities include the identification of revenue growth potential and new market opportunities. His primary focus is to develop recommendations and establish the strategic direction for the $6 billion business unit. Additionally, Bell Atlantic's Vice President of Advanced Technology selected Mr. Brammer to assist in the development of an e-Business strategy for the network services organization. Independent of his work at Bell Atlantic, Mr. Brammer's future plans include directing the worldwide expansion of an e-Eommerce web site he helped launch in September 1999. Bell Atlantic is a premier provider of advanced wireline voice and data services, a market leader in wireless services, and the world's largest publisher of directory information. Bell Atlantic is also one of the world's largest investors in high-growth global communications markets with operations and investments in 23 countries. **Career Highlights:** Bell Atlantic: Senior Specialist for Strategic Planning (1997-Present), Strategic Planning of Public Communications (1996-97), Strategic Planning of Large Business (1995-96). **Associations & Accomplishments:** Past Member of Board of Director, Lynchburg College Alumni Association; Past Member of Board of Director, Bell Atlantic Credit Union; Past Member of Board of Director, University Christian Church; Big Brothers and Big Sisters: Vice President, Board of Directors; Outstanding Young Men of America; Past Chairman, Bell Atlantic Community Relations Team; Phi Kappa Phi National Honor Society; Who's Who in American Colleges and Universities. **Education:** University of Maryland, Master's degree (1995); Lynchburg College, B.A.; Broward Community College, A.A. **Personal Information:** Married to Elise in 1988. Two children. Mr. Brammer enjoys outdoor activities, spending time with his family, hiking and camping. Mr. Brammer enjoys spending as much time as possible with his two children.

D. Dean Brickerd, Jr.

Director
Orbcomm
21700 Atlantic Boulevard
Sterling, VA 20166
(703) 406-5000
Fax: (703) 404-8092
brikerd.dean@orbcomm.com

4813

Business Information: As Director of Orbcomm, Mr. Brickerd supervises the devleopment of customer interface systems. Utilizing his extensive education and work expereince, he maintains the subscriber communication systems including vendor managmement. Working closely with his staff of trained employees, Mr. Brickerd formulates innovative technical solutions to assist in troubleshooting of software applications and hardware maintenance. He acts as a representative for FCC licensing of internal equipment, demonstrating his communication skills and statistical knowledge, gained by research. Credited with the initial devleopment of the communication devices used by the Company, Mr. Brickerd is recognized for his role in the GTE Space Net G Star 3 satellite program. Looking forward to technical advances in the future, he currently has impressive growth plans for the Company, which include going public. Orbcomm provides two way data communications systems, specializing in worldwide remote monitoring systems. Currently, the Company has over 35 satellites in orbit, and employs over 450 people to supervise the daily activites of the communication, which occurs via the satellites. **Career Highlights:** Director, Orbcomm (1992-Present); Engineer, GTE Spacenet (1989-92); Consultant, Booz, Allen to Hamilton (1988-89). **Education:** George Mason University, M.S. (1996); North Carolina State University, B.S. in Computer Engineering (1988); Purdue University, B.S. in Biology (1981). **Personal Information:** Married to Teresa in 1989. Two children: Mallory and Kyle. Mr. Brickerd enjoys mountain biking, skiing, running and squash.

Tom Bryant

Senior Manager of Operations
RCN Corporation
956 Massachusetts Avenue
Arlington, MA 02476
(781) 316-8885
Fax: (781) 316-8899
tom.bryant@rcn.net

4813

Business Information: Utilizing nearly a decade of service to the telecommunications industry, Mr. Bryant currently serves as Senior Manager of Operations with RCN Corporation. Responsible for managing the staff of 120 technicians, installers, and 5 managers, he directs and participates in the installation, troubleshooting, supporting, and tracking of telecommunications networks, peripherals, and equipment for a clientele numbering over 38,000. Attributing his professional success to his natural leadership and communication skills, Mr. Bryant remains on the leading edge of technology by reading and attending training seminars and conferences. His future endeavors include tripling the size of the Corporation, expanding the services area and clientele, and establishing the Corporation as one of the premier telecommunications provider. Providing telecommunications services from Boston to Washington, and San Francisco to Seattle, RCN Corporation is one of the leading service providers in the country. Headquartered in Princton, New Jersey, RCN offers high speed data connections, telephone, CATV, and long distance services. Established in 1994, the Corporation has experienced widespread, phenomenal growth and incorporates 120 employees into their operation, meeting the demands of a growing client population. **Career Highlights:** Senior Manager of Operations, RCN Corporation (1994-Present); Director of Operations, Cablevision of Boston (1984-94); Supervisor, Antennae Works (1983-84). **Associations & Accomplishments:** Scoiety of Cable Television Engineers. **Education:** Emerson College (1988); Bradford College, Associate's degree. **Personal Information:** Married to Patricia in 1990. One child: Sean. Mr. Bryant enjoys skiing, golf and carpentry.

Flavian M. Castelino

Manager of Data Communications
National Telephone Services
P.O. Box 2786, Ruwi, PC 112
Muscat, Oman 112
+968 709281
Fax: +968 709284
flavian@ieee.org

4813

Business Information: As Manager of Data Communications for National Telephone Services, Mr. Castelino oversees all major operations of the Company including design, project testing, inventory, and the supervision of approximately 15 dedicated individuals. Beginning as a customer support representative, he is proud of his accomplishments and he attributes his success to his deep desire to excel in all endeavors. With over 15 years of professional experience, Mr. Castelino wishes to continue providing guidance and leadership to all of his fellow employees, while obtaining his CCIE certification. Established in 1985, National Telephone Services engages in the provision of support for all forms of telecommunications including offers of convenient features to consumers and corporations. With the help of over 150 highly skilled professionals, the Company acts as a contractor and carrier of local and long distance services, which are offered by large companies within the telecommunications industry, such as AT&T, Sprint, and BellSouth. Presently on the rise, the Company enjoys an annual turnover of more than $10 million. **Career Highlights:** National Telephone Services: Manager of Data Communications (1996-Present), Customer Support Manager (1991-96); Customer Support Manager, Phillips NV (1987-91). **Associations & Accomplishments:** Institute of Electrical and Electronics Engineers; National Geographic Society. **Education:** University of Mysore, Bachelor's in Engineering (1987); Cisco Certified Network Professional; Cisco Certified Design Professional; Microsoft Certified Professional. **Personal Information:** Married in 1993. Mr. Castelino enjoys gardening and sports, especially hockey.

Gregory S. Catalone

Network Engineer
Sprint
12490 Sunrise Valley Drive
Reston, VA 20196
(703) 689-7910
Fax: (703) 478-5471
catalone@sprint.net

4813

Business Information: A person who is always looking to learn something new each day, Mr. Catalone opted for a career in the field of computers. Involved in the retrieval of information for the past 10 years, he currently serves as Network Engineer for Sprint. In this capacity Mr. Catalone is responsible for the maintenance of the Sprint Internet network. He provides support to Internet customers in the areas of diagnosis of individual problems in information retrieval, configuration changes, and troubleshooting of every day and unusual problems when they occur. He attributes his success to enjoying what he does. Becoming a Senior Engineer and getting more involved in design work serves as Mr. Catalone's long-term goals. Established in 1899, Sprint is one of the world's leading providers of local and long distance, wireless communications, and information transfer services. A consistent leader in the use of the "information superhighway," Sprint employs a global work force of 48,000 people generating $14 billion in annual revenues. **Career Highlights:** Network Engineer, Sprint (1997-Present); Senior Technician, Mindspring Inc. (1996-97); Assistant Manager, PSINet Inc. (1995-96); Systems Engineer, Information Delivery Systems (1990-95). **Education:** Computer Learning Center, Certificate (1985); Harrisburg Area Community College. **Personal Information:** Married to Deena L. in 1995. One child: Gregory S. Jr. Mr. Catalone enjoys the study of Medieval European history. He also enjoys keeping up-to-date on news and events from around the world.

Carol Y. Chui

Test Engineer
Sprint
1350 Old Bay Shore, Suite 470
Burlingame, CA 94010
(650) 685-5012
Fax: (650) 685-5050
carol.y.chui@mail.sprint.com

4813

Business Information: Ms. Chui is Test Engineer of Sprint. She is responsible for interacting with users and systems management to analyze, develop, and implement software solutions, including designing test plans and testing new feature's functionality. Recruited to Sprint right out of the University of Oklahoma in 1996, Ms. Chui owns an established track record of producing results. Her success reflects her ability to think out-of-the-box and aggressively take on new challenges. In addition to supervising and directing her staff of three engineers, she manages numerous technical operations such as testing software and network applications developed in-house. Planning and overseeing evaluation and integration of new technology, systems development methodologies, capacity planning, and technical support also fall within the realm of Ms. Chui's responsibilities. She keeps at the bleeding edge of technology by reading trade journals and taking classes. Her self motivation to succeed has contributed to her professional success. Eventually attaining the position of Senior Testing Engineer serves as one of Ms. Chui's future goals. Sprint is a global provider of a wide range of voice and data telecommunications products and services. Headquartered in Kansas City, Missouri, Sprint employs more than 50,000 people worldwide and generates estimated annual revenues of $14 billion. **Career Highlights:** Test Engineer, Sprint (1996-Present). **Associations & Accomplishments:** Malaysian Professional & Business Association; Leo Club of San Francisco; Delta Sigma Pi. **Education:** University of Oklahoma, B.B.A. in Information Systems (1996); Inti College. **Personal Information:** Ms. Chui enjoys reading, playing keyboard and outdoor activities.

Jean Clan

Project Manager
AT&T
3400 Ashwood Circle
La Grange, KY 40031-9350
(502) 429-1140
Fax: (502) 429-1108
jeanclan@att.com

4813

Business Information: Recruited to AT&T as Project Manager in 1999, Mrs. Clan is responsible for the implementation of AT&T's larger business projects. Charged with management and oversight of telecommunications and data communications, she supports the Company's post sales activities and ensures all frame relays and private lines are functional and fully operational. Possessing an excellent understanding of his field, Mrs. Clan is also responsible for all aspects of project management, from the coordination of resources and time lines to delivery. Working closely with management and users, she conducts weekly conference calls keeping clients informed of project status. Attributing her success to a positive attitude, Mrs. Clan's personal goals include pursuing MCSE and Cisco certifications and eventually become a freelance consultant. AT&T is the international leader in the provision of telecommunications services. Services include voice, data, Internet, and Web intergration. Also, the Company works closely with partners and other industries to provide outsourcing services. Founded over 100 years ago, AT&T works hard to ensure that customers and clients receive the best in data and telecommunications. **Career Highlights:** Project Manager, AT&T (1999-Present); Business Consultant, Micro Computer Solutions (1998-99); Technical Consultant, Espire Communications (1997-98); Sales Engineer/Project

Manager, Common Data (1992-97). **Associations & Accomplishments:** Treasurer, High School Reunion Committee. **Education:** Louisville Technical Institute, Associate's degree (1992); Cosmo Casablance Talent and Modeling Agency, Professional Modeling. **Personal Information:** Married to Mel in 1975. Mrs. Clan enjoys gardening, cooking, reading and exercising.

Kerry Keith Clements

Operations Manager
U S WEST
931 14th Street, Room 510
Denver, CO 80202
(303) 787-4688
Fax: (303) 624-7027
kkcleme@uswest.com

4813

Business Information: As Operations Manager of U S WEST, Mr. Clements handles midrange computing and technical support. He manages an infrastructure comprising of 1,400 systems and well over 4,000 applications. Mr. Clements directs all toubleshooting, networking, telecommunications, and desktop issues maintaining minimal down time and ensuring total customer satisfaction. He is directly responsible for saving the Company over $10 million by designing and installing new systems himself. His self taught expertise ensures that Mr. Clements is a valuable systems administrator to any company. Long range plans include managing other areas of this highly successful Company or attaining the position of Director or Vice President. Success is attributed ot his ability to build teams with synergy and technical strength, tackle challenges, and deliver results. U S WEST is engaged in telecommunications and information technology. The Company provides a 14 state region with local telephone and Internet services. Specializing in networking and data solutions, U S WEST has become recognized as a leader in today's highly competitive information technology market. **Career Highlights:** U S WEST: Operations Manager (1999-Present), Member of Technical Staff (1991-98), Supervisor (1985-90). **Personal Information:** Married to Jerri in 1994. Two children: Shiloh Michelle and Taylor McKenzie. Mr. Clements enjoys art and coaching youth sports.

John J. Colaianne

Project Manager
Crown Communications Inc.
375 Southpointe Boulevard
Canonsburg, PA 15317
(724) 416-2228
Fax: (724) 416-4228
jcolaianne@aol.com

4813

Business Information: Utilizing his extensive skills in this highly specialized position, Mr. Colaianne serves as Project Manager for Crown Communications Inc. He assumes responsibility for the Corporation's financial systems, developing and supporting key computer based processes for building towers and for the Corporation's accounting functions at all levels. Before joining Crown Communications Inc. in 1998, Mr. Colaianne served as Director of Management Information Systems with Premier Refractories, and IBM Operations Supervisor for Equitable Resources Inc. Working with a team of highly trained technical professionals, Mr. Colaianne directly supervises eight staff members. Coordinating resources and schedules, overseeing time lines and assignments, and managing project budgets also fall within the purview of his responsibilities. Mr. Colaianne attributes his success to his knowledge of software gained through years of experience. Establishing goals that are compatible with the Corporation, he anticipates a promotion to Director. Founded in 1983, Crown Communications Inc. is a premier company in the wireless telecommunications industry. A subsidiary of Crown Castle International, the Corporation builds large towers used by companies around the world for wireless communications technology. Boasting annual sales of $2 billion, more than 1,500 skilled individuals are employed worldwide. **Career Highlights:** Project Manager, Crown Communications Inc. (1998-Present); Director of Management Information Systems, Premier Refractories (1997-98); IBM Operations Supervisor, Equitable Resources Inc. (1988-97). **Associations & Accomplishments:** J.D. Edwards International User Group; Adult Leader, Order of DeMolay; Freemasonry of Pennsylvania; The Syria Shrine; Youth Leader/Assistant Organist, Episcapol Church; Past Officer, Knight Templar Royal Arch Masonry; Junior Warden, Verona Lodge #548. **Education:** Robert Morris College, B.S. (In Progress); Forbes Road Area Vocational Technical School. **Personal Information:** Married to Bonnie in 1980. Two children: Adam and Sara. Mr. Colaianne enjoys coaching soccer, music and computer programming and repair.

Patrick Neal Cowan

Manager of Corporate Disaster Recovery
Qwest Communications
555 17th Street, 9th Floor, Disaster Recovery
Denver, CO 80202
(303) 992-4134
Fax: (303) 992-1729
patrick.cowan@qwest.com

4813

Business Information: Mr. Cowan was recruited from AT&T to Manager of the Disaster Recovery Program at Qwest in May of 2000. Recruited to Teleport Communications Group (TCG) in 1997, Mr. Cowan assumed the responsibility for corporate disaster recovery. In his role as manager of corporate disaster recovery, he exercises oversight, development, and implementation of contigency plans in the event of any communication or business interruption. Drawing from 20 years of progressively increasing responsibility both internationally and within the continental United States, as well as four years with the Federal Emergency Management Agency (FEMA), Mr. Cowan is responsible for providing responsive, informative training of personnel in safety, systems continuity and, in the event of disaster, complete recovery. He was instrumental in the development and deployment of the Local AT&T Network Y2K Program, as he helped to ensure continuity of service during the millennium transition. An accomplished professional in his field, he has received FEMA's "Disaster Recovery Service Award" and "Outstanding Support Award" for his work in the Midwest floods of 1993 and the Northridge, California earthquake. Additionally, he shares his knowledge of business continuity and disaster preparedness with businesses and individual families through his involvement with the "Disaster Preparedness Corps," a not for profit corporate dedicated to the survivability of everyone for the first 72 hours of disaster. Ultimately making business continuity a daily routine and part of doing business within AT&T Qwest Communications and its customers is Mr. Cowan's long range plan. As one of the world's leading telecommunications providers, Qwest Communications offers local, Internet, voice and high speed data services using cutting-edge fiber technology. Headquartered in Denver, Colorado, Qwest Communications and its business units, along with joint venture partner, KPN Qwest, operate within both the Continental United States and Europe. **Career Highlights:** Manager of Disaster Recovery, Qwest Communications (1998-Present); Manager of Corporate Disaster Recovery, Teleport Communications Group (1997-98); Consultant/Owner, Cowan & Company (1987-97); Mission Assignment Coordinator/Financial Manager, FEMA (1992-96). **Associations & Accomplishments:** Disaster Preparedness Corps; Civil Air Patrol; Toastmasters International; Host and Technical Advisor, "The Open Water Experience," An Introduction to Scuba Diving; Multi-Engine Instrument Pilot; Instructor Trainer, Scuba Diving; Mixed Gas Saturation Diver. **Education:** Jacksonville University, B.B.A. (1988). **Personal Information:** Two children: Tiffany and Victoria. Mr. Cowan enjoys flying, mountain biking, scuba diving, sky diving, motorcycles, racquetball, photography and horseback riding. His less adventerous pursuits are reading, military history, and woodworking.

Lowell V. Dickman

AEII
ITC Delta Com
4451 N.E.C.R. 337
Bronson, FL 32621
(352) 387-2612
Fax: (352) 486-2085
lowellvernon@msn.com

4813

Business Information: As AEII of ITC Delta Com, Mr. Dickman is responsible for the sale of telecomm services to small and medium sized businesses. He also oversees sales of Internet and wireless communications services. A successful professional, Mr. Dickman believes his success can be attributed to knowing the right people. With the Company since 1999, he utilizes his knowledge of the industry for the benefit of his customers and fellow employees. His greatest accomplishment to date is receiving a $10,000 commission of the sale of services to the second largest paging company in the United States. In the future, Mr. Dickman looks forward to obtaining a management position with the Company and continuing the success he has achieved. ITC Delta Com specializes in telephony. Established in 1896, the Company provides the sale of long-distance and local telecom services, Internet services, as well as trade on NASDAQ. Headquartered in Alabama, the Company averages an annual revenue of $170 million. Serving a national market, ITC Delta Com is dedicated to customer satisfaction and return business. **Career Highlights:** AEII, ITC Delta Com (1999-Present).

Christian Fällberg

Technical Coordinator
Telia AB
Bergstigen 25
Stocksund, Sweden 182 78
+46 87132986
Fax: +46 86240027
christian.p.fallberg@telia.se

4813

Business Information: Serving as the Technical Coordinator for Telia A.B., Mr. Fällberg oversees a number of duties on behalf of the Company and its clientele. Possessing an excellent understanding of the telecommunications and technology industries, he is responsible for coordinating the Company's new Intranet portal. Supervising a work force of 80 professional and technical staff, Mr. Fällberg ensures that all day to day operations within his department remain functional and operational at all times. A multi-faceted professional, he is also the owner of a Web agency consultancy, a business for which he is solely responsible. Attributing his success to an interest in his work, Mr. Fällberg plans to improve both internal and external Web coordination for Telia AB. The largest telecommunications company in Sweden, Telia AB was established in 1911. Providing telecommunications, Internet service, mobile Internet, and wireless communications, the Company employs more than 32,000 personnel worldwide. Presently, the Company is located in Stocksund, Sweden. **Career Highlights:** Technical Coordinator, Telia AB (1999-Present); Owner/Partner, Eyesite Stockholm AB (1999-Present); Creative Director/Head of Web Section, Think Twice Interactive A.B. (1998-99); Consultant, Infomedia Interactive (1998). **Associations & Accomplishments:** Dataföreningen Svenge; Several computer related organizations. **Education:** Tålje Gymnasium (1989). **Personal Information:** Mr. Fällberg enjoys fencing and is currently ranked number five in Sweden as a junior.

Helder Flavio Ferrao

Operations Manager
Netstream Telecom
Rua Rafael Correa Sampaio, 977-91
Sao Caetano Du Sol, Brazil 09541
+55 1133651511
Fax: +55 133651504
helder.ferrao@bol.com.br

4813

Business Information: Highly recruited to Netstream Telecom in 1999, Mr. Ferrao serves as Operations Manager for Netstream Telecom. Utilizing over 15 years of experience in his field of work, he is responsible for overseeing all of the services that are offered, managing the network infrastructure, and maintaining quality services in all areas of operations. Moreover, Mr. Ferrao ensures that there are no glitches with any of the services and emphasizes customer satisfaction. He recently had an article published about him and his work in 1999 in a magazine called "Info." The most rewarding aspects of his career was working for Citibank for 13 years and J.P. Morgan for 2 years. In the future, Mr. Ferrao looks forward to establishing an ATM network for Brazil and becoming the leading IP network in the country. Located in Sao Caetano Du Sul, Brazil, Netstream Telecom operates as a telecommunications firm. Operating on a national level, the Company focuses on fiber optics, transmissions, Internet access, and data and voice communications. Recenty acquired by AT&T, Netstream will soon be changing their name. With a staff of approximately 200 employees, the Company is in the process of extending business to 35 other cities and adding a few more facilities. **Career Highlights:** Operations Manager, Netstream Telecom (1999-Present); Technology Director, J.P. Morgan (1998-99); Operations Manager, Citibank N.A. (1984-98). **Education:** Graduated University, Business Administrator (1999). **Personal Information:** Married to Ana Rita in 1996. Mr. Ferrao enjoys music, travel, games, basketball and football.

Jeanette Fielden

Manager of Internet Services
U S WEST Interprise Networking Services
1999 Broadway
Denver, CO 80202
(303) 541-4000
jfield@uswest.com

4813

Business Information: Ms. Fielden is the Manager of Internet Services of U S WEST Interprise Networking Services. Talented in the technology field, she focuses her role on content acquisition and managing content across all U S West Internet platforms, Web, wireless data, handhelds, and broadband. A successful, 12 year professional in the field, Ms. Fielden she is responsible for wireless and broadband technologies as well as negotiating and implementation phases of new network services. An expert in wireless communications, she enhances the networking services of U

S WEST throughout the United States. Her future goals include joining a hi-tech corporation currently in acquisition and merger process. Career highlight for Ms. Fielden is building the first Web server. Success is attributed to her strong academics, knowledge power, and enjoyment of what she does. U S WEST Interprise Networking Services provides networking services to a 14-state region. Founded in 1994, the Company has expanded its operations to incorporate a 1,600 member strong staff. The Company focuses its services on wireless communications, product development, and network design. **Career Highlights:** Manager of Internet Services, U S WEST Interprise Networking Services (1999-Present); Member of Technical Staff, U S WEST Advanced Technologies (1993-99); Internet Consultant, State of Colorado (1995-96); Research Assistant, Laboratory for Atmospheric & Space Physics (1988-93). **Associations & Accomplishments:** Association for Colorado Telecommunication Professionals; Internet Chamber of Commerce; Boulder Community Network. **Education:** University of Colorado: M.S. in Telecommunications (1997), B.S. in Computer Science (1992).

Christy S. Forquer

Communications Director/Alliance Liaison
US Telecom - PhoneMaster Division
211 Main Street, Suite 401
Joplin, MO 64801
(417) 781-7000
Fax: (417) 623-2963
christyf@usti.com

4813

Business Information: As the Communications Director and Alliance Liasion of US Telecom's PhoneMaster Division, Ms. Forquer is responsible for the creation of all sales and marketing literature, establishing third party vendor relationships, and overseeing efforts of the marketing team. The Company relies on Ms. Forquer's expertise in the field to promote services and products to the education market nationwide. Understanding the importance of promoting and marketing, she networks to establish new business relationships. Dedicated to the success of the PhoneMaster Division and US Telecom as a whole, Ms. Forquer keeps abreast of new developments in the education field and incorporates pertinent information into her daily duties. She plans to assist US Telecom as it expands into new markets, as well as establish a broader client base. Ms. Forquer attributes success to knowing the market place, putting the customer first, and staying ahead of the competition. PhoneMaster, a division of US Telecom, is a voice telephony software company. Services provided include an auto-dialing system complete with voice mail and IVR applications, used by schools nationwide to alert parents of important information regarding their child's activity and progress in school. US Telecom was established in 1983. **Career Highlights:** US Telecom - PhoneMaster Division: Communications Director/Alliance Liasion (1998-Present), PhoneMaster Sales Representative (1995-98); Sales and Service Representative, Hallmark Cards, Inc. (1991-95); Advertising Account Executive, KCCV Radio (1988-91); Sales Service Supervisor, KTVO-TV (1986-88). **Associations & Accomplishments:** Dale Carnegie Sales course graduate; Republican Precinct Committeewoman Olathe, Kansas; Young Life Volunteer; Active member of Christ Community Church in Leawood, Kansas. **Education:** Truman State University, formerly Northeast Missouri State Univeristy, B.S. (1986).

Pinkley Francis

ISP Manager/Head of Information Technology and Data Services
Cable & Wireless
P.O. Box 111
Castries Bwi, St. Lucia
(758) 453-9294
Fax: (758) 453-9766
francisp@candw.lc

4813

Business Information: Serving in dual capacity of ISP Manager and Head of the Information Technology and Data Services of Cable & Wireless, Mr. Francis is responsible for all ISP and data services at the St. Lucia location. Possessing an excellent understanding of his field, he manages Web sites internally and assures clients that all services are online. Highly regarded in the wireless and cable industry, Mr. Francis anticipates his promotion to Regional Head of Information Technology for the Caribbean as a result of his continuing efforts to increase his skills thorugh training and professional development activities. His success reflects his ability to aggressively take on new challenges and deliver results. Serving an international client base and with locations worldwide, Cable & Wireless operates as a telecommunications company. With headquarters located in the United Kingdom, the Company deals with general phone service and Internet access and recently merged with MCI's Internet service. The Company employs 80,000 individuals across the globe, 380 of which are located in St. Lucia. Established in 1921, the Company works to provide customers with quality phone service and Internet access, always aware that the customer is the basis for the business. **Career Highlights:** Cable & Wireless: ISP Manager/Head of Information Technology and Data Services (1999-Present), Multimedia Services Manager (1997-99). **Associations & Accomplishments:** Institute of Electrical and Electronics Engineers. **Education:** Sheffield University, M.S. (1996). **Personal Information:** Mr. Francis enjoys reading and politics.

Mac Gardner Jr.

Systems Engineer
Bell Atlantic
610 Seabury Drive
Wilmington, DE 19810
(215) 466-3770
Fax: (215) 466-3770
macgard@aol.com

4813

Business Information: Utilizing several years of experience in technology, Mr. Gardner is the Systems Engineer with Bell Atlantic. Fulfilling responsibility of project manager, he modifies UNIX systems as well as plans, coordinates, and excecutes project management. Possessing an excellent understanding of his field, he is in charge of new server information, support for Internet applications, and overseeing installation of advanced technology. Mr. Gardner also works with the Company's hardware deployment team, ensuring systems functionality and operational status. He first got involved in the information technology field while working in the research department at the University of Pennsylvania. He received large funding from the Department of Defense for his research while and the University. Highly regarded, Mr. Gardner is credited with implementing the core Interent services at Bell Atlantic. In th future, he plans on remaining with the Company, training for his MCSE and Cisco certification, and becoming project manager. Located in Wilmington, Delaware, Bell Atlantic is a leading provider of local telecommunication services. The Company provides services within Delaware, Pennsylvania, New Jersey, and New York. As a leader in the telecommunications field, the Company provides advance voice and data services as well as wireless communications to customers at a cost efficient rate. Additionally, the Company provides paging services, computer services, and training programs. Headquartered in New York, New York, the Company as a whole employs a work force of 140,000 professional, technical, and support staff. **Career Highlights:** Systems Engineer, Bell Atlantic (1998-Present); Laboratory Manager, University of Pennsylvania (1996-98); Department Head, Graduate Hospital (1996-97); Office Manager, Dr. Mark Watkins (1986-91). **Associations & Accomplishments:** Aquatic Exercise Association; Choral Arts Society; Secretary, Philadelphia Museum of Art. **Education:** University of Delaware (1996); Newmann College. **Personal Information:** Mr. Gardner enjoys aerobics instructing, fishing and the outdoors.

Rajiv Garg

Data Consultant
U S WEST/Global Crossing
100 South Washington, Suite 1135
Minneapolis, MN 55401
(612) 316-4700
Fax: (612) 667-2579
rajiv@uswestmail.com

4813

Business Information: An integral part of the operations of U S WEST/Global Crossing, Mr. Garg serves in the role of Data Consultant. He offers consulting services to Fortune 1000 companies in the areas of data applications and leading edge technology. He serves in an aspect of human resources by keeping all employees updated as to technical changes and upgrades. Before joining U S West, Mr. Garg served as Regional Systems Engineer with Anixter International and Manager of Technical Service for Lansystems. As an 11 year technology professional, he owns an established track record of producing results in support of business objectives. His success reflects his ability to think out-of-the-box and aggressively take on new challenges and responsibilities. Eventually, Mr. Garg desires to move up to the position of Director of New Applications. U S WEST/Global Crossing functions as a telecommunications company with several divisions. A full range of connectivity solutions are offered to more than 25 million business, government, and residential customers in 14 Western and Midwestern states. **Career Highlights:** Data Consultant, U S West (1994-Present); Regional Systems Engineer, Anixter International (1993-94); Manager of Technical Services, Lansystems (1989-93). **Associations & Accomplishments:** Asian Pacific Roundtable. **Education:** Executive M.B.A. (In Progress); University of Minnesota, B.A. in Computer Science (1988). **Personal Information:** Married to Sangeeta in 1988. Three children: Priya, Sonali, and Sonya. Mr. Garg enjoys travel, reading, family time and theater.

Sukumar Ghosh

Software Systems Engineer
MCI WorldCom, Inc.
6929 North Lakewood Avenue, M.S. 3.2-111H
Tulsa, OK 74117
(918) 590-6473
Fax: (918) 590-0499
sukumar.ghosh@wcom.com

4813

Business Information: As Software Systems Engineer of MCI WorldCom, Inc., Mr. Ghosh lends his insight and guidance to the development of various application development activities. Utilizing his varied and extensive work and educational experience, he handles project management activities with ease as he works with peers and seniors with a proactive leadership style. Currently involved in various stages of the Software Development Life Cycle of multi-platform, Object Oriented, mission critical Telecommunications Systems, he is recognized for his contributions in technical and organizational areas that aid in the overall success of the Department. He derives his rich work experience from the successful technical and managerial positions he's held so far in his career. Attributing his success to commitment, initiative, thoroughness, adaptability, and leadership style, Mr. Ghosh's strategic plans are to quickly move over to the managerial path to subsequently head a IT department that works towards adding value to an organization's operations, thereby increasing customer satisfaction and company profits. Enjoying the challenges of his position, Mr. Ghosh looks forward to continued success and prosperity as he receives increased responsibilities within the corporate structure. Established in 1983, MCI WorldCom is a global provider of Local, Long Distance, International, and Internet services. The Corporation employs 80,000 people throughout the world and is recognized as a leader in the Telecommunications industry. **Career Highlights:** Software Systems Engineer, MCI WorldCom, Inc. (1998-Present); DHL Worldwide Express, India: Assistant Manager of Quality Assurance (1995), Branch Manager (1994-95). **Associations & Accomplishments:** Association of Information Technology Professionals; Sigma Iota Epsilon; Star Performers in Operations and Technology award, MCI Worldcom; Named to National Dean's List (1998), Texas Tech University. **Education:** Texas Tech University, M.S. in Management Information Systems (1998); Institute for Technology & Management, M.B.A. in Marketing; St. Xavier's College, University of Bombay, B.S. in Physics. **Personal Information:** Married to Sohini in 1999. Mr. Ghosh enjoys travel, music, reading, camping and rock climbing.

Jim Gibbons

Chief Information Officer
National Rural Telecommunications Cooperative
2121 Cooperative Way, Suite 500
Herndon, VA 20171-3024
(703) 787-7297
Fax: (703) 787-7297
jgibbons@nrtc.org

4813

Business Information: Mr. Gibbons is the Chief Information Officer for the National Rural Telecommunications Cooperative. In this capacity, he handles all business application activities, networks, mainframes, and related computer technologies for the Cooperative. The National Rural Telecommunications Cooperative provides advanced satellite services to rural areas for telecommunications needs. Currently, the NRTC operates C-Ban TV and Direct TV. Presently, NRTC is active in eight million American households. Established in 1987, the Corporation employs 180 people. **Career Highlights:** National Rural Telecommunications Cooperative: Chief Information Officer (1999-Present), Vice President of Information Technology (1994-99); Director - Project Management, Net Express (1992-94); United States Air Force (1972-92). **Associations & Accomplishments:** A.F.A.; American Legion; Veterans of Foreign Wars. **Education:** University of Northern Colorado, M.A. (1978); Rutgers College, A.B. (1971). **Personal Information:** Married to Marlene in 1971. Mr. Gibbons enjoys photography.

John P. Gorney

Vice President/General Manager
Teaco Inc.
P.O. Box 472261
Tulsa, OK 74147-2261
(918) 628-1206
Fax: (918) 628-1207

4813

Business Information: Recruited to Teaco Inc. in 1991, Mr. Gorney currently serves as Vice President and General Manager. He exercises oversight of sales and marketing of Teaco's products and services as well as determining and penetrating new markets. Accumulating over 21 years of experience and with a strong academic history, Mr. Gorney facilitates the formulation of the Corporation's vision and development of powerful marketing, sales, and business strategies. Prior to joining the Teaco team, he gained a wealth of experience and technical skills while working as Major and National Account Executive for American Communications Inc., Commercial Electronics of Tulsa, Cellular One of Tulsa, AT&T, and Southwestern Bell. His diversified background has proven invaluable to the Corporation, as Mr. Gorney is involved in design and management of multi-media presentations and proposals, personnel management, major account management, project management, and purchasing. One of many accomplishments, the greatest is increasing sales by over 40 percent during three consecutive years, while increasing profitability by 14.5 percent. Mr. Gorney attributes his success to his ability to build unique teams to meet market demand and fiscal responsibility, and ensuring bottom line profits meet objectives. Teaco Inc. is a provider of world-class communication systems such as data, voice, and video systems. Based in Tulsa, the Corporation is a leading supplier of services, solutions, and products that meet today's business needs and tomorrow's business goals. **Career Highlights:** Vice President/General Manager, Teaco Inc. (1991-Present); Major National Account Executive, American Communications Inc.; Major National Account Executive, Commercial Electronics Inc.; Major National Account Executive, AT&T and Southwestern Bell Telephone Company. **Associations & Accomplishments:** Member of Board of Trustees, local church; Member of Show Committee, The Great Plains Housing Institute; Former Company Chairman, Tulsa Area Community Chest; Co-Founder/Administrator, Nimitz Junior High Wrestling Program; Assistant Coach, Thomas A. Edison Junior High Football Program; Founder/Vice President/Director, B.M.G.R. Rod and Gun Club. **Education:** University of Oklahoma, Degree in Business Administration with Minor in Finance and Insurance; Tulsa Junior College, Computer Design and Programming; Massachusetts Institute of Technology, Interprocess Communication and UNIX Programming Language.

William F. Greene IV

Network Engineer I
Sprint
6100 Sprint Parkway
Overland Park, KS 66212
(913) 315-3577
Fax: (913) 315-3934

4813

Business Information: Mr. Greene functions in the capacity of Network Engineer I with Sprint. He is responsible for network equipment and nationwide roll-outs of advanced technologies, as well as assisting other employees in achieving a better understanding of the technology they work with. Before coming on board to Sprint in 1999, Mr. Greene served as an Installation and Service Technician with Muzak. His highlights include being able to provide excellent customer service, and graduating from DeVry Institute of Technology with Honor and a 4.0 GPA, while working full time and being a father to his four children. In the future, he hopes to advance into the designing side of the telecommunications industry. Sprint is a long distance service within the telecommunications industry. Established in 1899, the Company has continued to provide top quality customer service for over a century. The Company focuses its service to the telephone industry, however, it also features Internet, cellular, and digital communication services. **Career Highlights:** Network Engineer I, Network Equipment Databasing Group, Sprint (1999-Present); Installation and Service Technician, Muzak (1985-99); Meat Cutter, Red-X (1984-85). **Education:** DeVry Institute of Technology, B.S. (1999). **Personal Information:** Married to Gina in 1984. Four children: Benjamin, Nicholas, Samuel, and Tyler. Mr. Greene enjoys tae kwon do and choir.

Lianne H. Griffin, PMP

Program Manager
BellSouth
675 West Peachtree Street NE, Room 19U85 BellSouth Center
Atlanta, GA 30375
(404) 927-7060
Fax: (404) 927-7488
lianne.griffin@bridge.bellsouth.com

4813

Business Information: Beginning her association in 1980 with Southern Bell as an Engineer, Ms. Griffin has received recognition for her diligence and management skills through several promotions to her current position as Program Manager. In her capacity, she coordinates resources, time lines, schedules, and budgets. As a member of the Information Technology Solutions Group, Ms. Griffin develops mechanized service ordering systems for XDSL products. Further, she oversees all program management of software developers and technical staff. She looks forward to managing a group of project managers. Her advice is, "Be flexible because technology is constantly changing. Stay current with the industry and market place as well as develop your skills." Headquartered in Atlanta, Georgia, and established in 1983, BellSouth serves the South and Southeastern region of the United States. With the aid of 86,000 individuals, the Corporation serves the telecommunications industry, providing wireless and wireline services, Internet, Yellow pages, publishing, and telecommunications services to customers. **Career Highlights:** BellSouth: Program Manager (1999-Present), Operations Center Manager (1998-99), Engineer Staff Manager (1996-98), Engineering Specialist (1980-96). **Associations & Accomplishments:** Project Management Institute, National Chapter; Project Management Institute, Atlanta Chapter; Girl Scout Council of Northwest Georgia; Boy Scouts of America, Atlanta Area Council; BellSouth/Georgia Tech Club; Girl Scout Council of Northwest Georgia Awards: Outstanding Leader, Outstanding Volunteer, and Lighthouse; Volunteer Service Grants (1995-98), BellSouth; Project Management Institute, Project Management Professional (1998). **Education:** Georgia Tech, B.S. in Industrial Management (1980); George Washington University, Master's certificate in Project Management (1997). **Personal Information:** Married to R. Mark in 1980. Two children: Jennifer and Branden. Ms. Griffin enjoys Girl Scouts, Boy Scouts, stained glass and gardening.

Andrew G. Guald

Technical Consultant
AT&T
307 Middletown Lincroft Road, Room 3N213
Lincroft, NJ 07738
(732) 576-5594
Fax: (732) 576-4473
andrew.gauld@at&t.com

4813

Business Information: Highly proficient in all areas of information technology field, Mr. Gauld was recruited to AT&T in 1982. Fulfilling a number of duties as a Technical Consultant, he is responsible for advising a host of clients in the areas of software development, systems upgrade, and client relations. With several years of information technology experience, Mr. Gauld utilizes his extensive knowledge in his profession to provide useful programs and comprehensive information for all systems. His future plans include remaining with AT&T and moving more into voice over IP and Internet related materials. Success is attributed to his ability to take on challenges and deliver results. AT&T firmly stands as the world's number one cable and long distance carrier that provides local phone, wireless, and Internet services. The Company caters to an international clientele, offering a host of specialty services for business and private use. Established in 1956, the Company maintains a global presence, and functions under the guidance and expertise of professionals who facilitate smooth business operations on a daily basis. **Career Highlights:** Technical Consultant, AT&T (1984-Present). **Education:** Ruftones, Master's degree in Computer Science; University of Maryland, B.S. in Electrical Engineering. **Personal Information:** Mr. Guald enjoys swimming, skiing and family activities.

Michael R. Hall

Design Engineer
State Government of Illinois Telecommunications
120 West Jefferson
Springfield, IL 62702
(217) 785-9050
Fax: (217) 524-0755
mike_hall@ccmailgw.state.il.us

4813

Business Information: As Design Engineer for State government of Illinois Telecommunications, Mr. Hall supervises three junior engineers in the design of communication systems. Having mastered the implementation of private networks instead of multiple circuits, Mr. Hall would like to advance to Head of Design and initiate the use of transport video to desktop applications. State Government of Illinois Telecommunications provides telephone system administration as well as networking capabilities to government offices in the state of Illinois. The Agency operates out of Springfield and employs 300 professionals in the field. **Career Highlights:** State Government of Illinois Telecommunications: Design Engineer (1990-Present), Network Consultant (1985-90), Network Operations Manager (1980-85). **Associations & Accomplishments:** Association of Information Technology Professionals. **Education:** University of Illinois, Associate's degree (1980). **Personal Information:** Married in 1978. Mr. Hall enjoys antique automobiles and steam traction engines.

Byron Dean Hart

Information Technology Engineer III
Excel Communications
P.O. Box 805
Howe, TX 75459-0805
(972) 738-1313
vfcbdh@airmail.net

4813

Business Information: Mr. Hart is the Information Technology Engineer III of Excel Communications. He is responsible for assuring the computer networking system is fully operational, in addition to supervising the automation, scheduling, and invoice research groups. Before joining Excel Communications as Operations Analyst in 1996, Mr. Hart served as the Production Control Analyst at Affiliated Computer Systems and Oryx Energy Company. As an experienced, 11 year technology professional, he is constantly employing new technology to improve the current system. Mr. Hart's career highlights include earning certifications and successfully migrating an entire data center after the center became outdated. His other functions include working with users and management to analyze, specify, and design systems level software and applications to improve overall systems performance. Monitoring and maintaining network operations and troubleshooting all hardware, software, and transmission problems also fall within the realm of Mr. Hart's responsibilities. His success reflects his ability to think out-of-the-box and take on new challenges and responsibilities. Established in 1988, Excel Communications is a privately owned telecommunications company. The Company employs over 3,000 personnel to maintain customer relations and proper service throughout the world. Providing long distance telephone service around the globe, Excel offers services to residential and industrial clients with opportunities available to enhance their long distance services. **Career Highlights:** Excel Communications: Information Technology Engineer III (1999-Present), Operations Analyst (1996-98); Production Control Analyst, Affiliated Computer Systems (1996); Production Control Analyst, Oryx Energy Company (1988-96). **Education:** University of Texas at Arlington. **Personal Information:** Mr. Hart enjoys reading and attending concerts.

Abdulla K. E. Hassan

Senior Technical Officer
Bahrain Telecommunications Company
Bahrain-Manama, P.O. BO14_BX12
Manama, Bahrain
+973 885885
Fax: +973 536699
akehassan@batelco.com.bh

4813

Business Information: As the Senior Technical Officer for Bahrain Telecommunications Company, Mr. Hassan is head of the diplomatic area. Responsible for 20 employees, he oversees lines, small private and government exchanges, and bank maintenance. Displaying an effective, productive management style, he also installs all new systems and digital lines. The Company is currently restructuring and Mr. Hassan is committed to providing continued optimum service to Bahrain Telecommunications Company. He continues to grow professionally through the fulfillment of his responsibilities and his involvement in the advancment of operations. Mr. Hassan's success reflects his ability to aggressively take on new challenges and deliver results. Bahrain Telecommunications Company is an established and reputable telecommunications company which engages in the installation and maintenance of all types of PABX. Established in 1980, the Company employs over 2,000 individuals. As the first and only telecommunications company in Bahrain, the Company has many locations throughout the country. Local operations in Manama, Bahrain employ the skilled services of 25 personnel to operate and maintain the location. **Career Highlights:** Bahrain Telecommuncations Company: Senior Technical Officer (1981-Present), Technician (1981); Lab Technician, Ministry of Education (1980-81). **Associations & Accomplishments:** Manager, Samahij Club. **Personal Information:** Married to Fahima in 1981. Four children: Hani, Abbas, Yasser, and Mohammed. Mr. Hassan enjoys football, sports and reading.

Wallace L. Hattenhauer

Data Systems Engineer
SBC Communications Inc.
210 Northeast 3rd
Bryant, AR 72022
(501) 257-9878

4813

Business Information: Mr. Hattenhauer served as chief information officer of Northeast Arkansas Clinic, and in that capacity he fulfilled a variety of roles. Utilizing extensive technical training and education, he served as Information Systems Director, Y2K Coordinator, and Network

Administrator. He conducted extensive reviews and evaluations of current hardware and software, recommending purchases and developing cost analysis of operations. Responsible for the transition of data storage from paper to computerized form, Mr. Hattenhauer is credited with the development of time saving, accurate techniques that contribute to the overall efficiency of operations. Crediting success to his patience and strong self-improvement desires, he looks forward to advancing his career by adding certifications to his achievements. Located in Jonesboro, Arkansas, Northeast Arkansas Clinic is a multi-specialty medical facility that serves a population of 60,000 residents in various cities and towns. Several offices are located strategically throughout the region, employing a total of 400 professionals. The Clinic was originally established in 1977 and operates with a budget of $60 million, providing unparalleled medical services to individuals in need. Recently, Mr. Hattenhauer accepted a position with SBC Communications Inc. as a Data Systems Engineer. He is now responsible for a variety of technical tasks, such as network design, configuration, implementation, and overall network integrity. His new position involves him with hundreds of business accounts all over the state of Arkansas. Mr. Hattenhauer recently gained Cisco Systems CCNA certification and is currently pursuing CCNP certification. **Career Highlights:** Data Systems Engineer, SBC Communications Inc. (2000-Present); Chief Information Officer, Northeast Arkansas Clinic (1998-00); Officer,Office Manager/Technician, Alltech Computers (1995-98). **Associations & Accomplishments:** Cisco Systems Certified Network Associate; Association of Information Technology Professionals; Teaching Teachers, Volunteer Computer Training; Y2K Council of Arkansas; Sigma Pi Fraternity. **Education:** Arkansas State University, Bachelor's degree in Management Information Systems (1999). **Personal Information:** Mr. Hattenhauer enjoys swimming, mountain biking, kayaking and exercise.

Michael J. Hickman

Project Engineer
GTE
1 GTE Place
Thousand Oaks, CA 91362-3813
(805) 372-6653
Fax: (805) 372-8200
michael.hickman@telops.gte.com

4813

Business Information: Mr. Hickman has been a member of the GTE team since 1996. Employed as a Project Engineer for service products, as well as data and video services for customer networks. In addition, he has assumed responsibility for the budget within his sphere of influence, and he has been involved in troubleshooting and problem solving. As for the next three to five years, Mr. Hickman hopes to advance from within GTE and see his career blossom further. As for the current time, he keeps abreast of all technological advancements through reading professional literature and attending training sessions. He attributes his success to persistence and his ability to deliver results and aggressively take on new challenges. GTE provides telecommunication services. As a long distance provider of video, voice, and data, the Corporation has averaged an estimated annual revenue of $1 billion. Engaged in business on a global scale, the Corporation operates from a headquarters in Dallas, Texas and has rivaled other corporations such as MCI and AT&T. Founded in 1918, GTE employs 15,000 technically skilled individuals. **Career Highlights:** GTE: Project Engineer (1997-Present), Senior Engineer (1996-97); Test Engineer, AG Communication Systems (1991-96). **Associations & Accomplishments:** Toastmasters. **Education:** California Lutheran University, B.A. in Business Administration (1991). **Personal Information:** Mr. Hickman enjoys sports and reading.

Steve Hobbs

Technical Director
Cable & Wireless Global Mobile
26 Redlions Square
London, England, United Kingdom WC1R 4HQ
+44 1713156353
Fax: +44 1753156316
steve.hobbs@plc.cwplc.com

4813

Business Information: Following 12 years of distinguished service in the British Royal Navy, Mr. Hobbs found his way into the commercial wireless communication industry in 1977 when he joined Cable & Wireless. Since then, he has been a key member of its mobile technical team, from deploying the world's first moden cellular network starting a commerical service in 1978 until the present 3G developments. He was inaugural chief engineer when C & W started its Global Mobile business unit in 1991, moving to head up mobile operations in Asia in 1996 when the Company opened it's regional headquarters in Singapore. Returning to the United Kingdom in 1998, he was appointed as Technical Director of the Global Mobile Group, handling all aspects of cellular and wireless technology within an expanded business unit. In this highly skilled position, Mr. Hobbs assumes responsibility for the network design and technical oversight of corporate cellular operations worldwide. In addition, he has technical responsibility for the development of wireless data business and evolution to wireless IP and internet applications within C & W's new Global Operations unit. Displaying a clear vision of goals, Mr. Hobbs would like to become more involved with all aspects of cellular companies as they enter into the mainstream date arena. His success reflects his ability to think outside the box, deliver results, and aggressivley take on new challenges and responsibilities. Serving an international client base, Cable & Wireless Global Mobile was formed in 1991, and incorporated within its Global Operations Group in 1999. From its headquarters in London, the Company offers a variety of quality communications services worldwide. Cable & Wireless has major operating companies in the United States, Europe, Carribbean, Asia, Japan, and Australia, employing circa 40,000 people. Most recently through an aggressive program of build and acquisition C & W has deployed the largest global IP network. **Career Highlights:** Cable & Wireless Global Mobile: Technical Director (1998-Present), Head of Operations, Asia (1996-98), Chief Engineer (1991-96). **Personal Information:** Married to Mary Elizabeth in 1972. Four children: Tifaine, Miriam, Thomas, and John.

Edward C. Hooke

Manager of Switching Control
Southern New England Telephone
84 Deerfield Lane
Meriden, CT 06450
(203) 420-7140
Fax: (203) 235-5707
edward.c.hooke@snet.com

4813

Business Information: Mr. Hooke functions in the role of Manager of Switching Control with Southern New England Telephone. He monitors the 142 switching offices within the Connecticut facilities and works with over 70 employees. Securing the completion of every phone call and the successful provision of calling features have been his responsibilities for over two decades. Before coming on board to Southern New England Telephone as Network Technician in 1996, he served with Executive Information Systems as Service Technician and Coordinator. In the future, Mr. Hooke hopes to learn more about the telecommunications industry and he would like to move to the district level in three years. A local hero, he has been recognized by the Federal Bureau of Investigation for his assistance in locating a kidnapped child. His success reflects his ability to produce results and aggressively tackle new challenges and responsibilities. Southern New England Telephone is a telecommunications company, providing telephone service to the state of Connecticut. Established in 1870, the Company provides its clients with connection services to their local and long distance telephone connections and has evolved with the rest of the country to incorporate the world of the Internet. Just recently, the Company was purchased by SBC in Texas and has achieved the highest goals imaginable for a telecommunications company. **Career Highlights:** Southern New England Telephone: Manager of Switching Control (1998-Present), Network Technician (1996-98); Executive Information Systems: Service Technician (1994-96), Service Coordinator (1993-94). **Associations & Accomplishments:** Southern New England Telephone Foremans Club; Licensed Foster Parent, State of Connecticut. **Education:** University of Connecticut at Bridgeport (1977); Lucent Technologies-5 ESS; Siemens Switch Theory and Architecture. **Personal Information:** Married to Marie in 1990. Three children: Rose, Nicholas, and Draceena. Mr. Hooke enjoys sharing time with family, motorcycle riding and snow skiing.

Kyunam Hwang

Senior Network Engineer
oCen Communications
4900 Rivergrade Road, Suite C110
Irwindale, CA 91706
(626) 338-6611
Fax: (626) 338-8995
knhwang@ocen.com

4813

Business Information: As Senior Network Engineer of oCen Communcations, Mr. Hwang is responsible for the VOIP network design and engineering as well as business development. He utilizes his extensive experience to conduct the activities of his position. As one of the first developers to design the ISDN switch and CDMA switch for wireless use, Mr. Hwang is an accomplished and invaluable resource to the Company. He believes his success has come from his ablility to get along with others and incorporate hands on training into his job. Mr. Hwang would like to become more involved in the design and planning side of the Company. Founded in 1997, oCen Communications is a leading Internet communication service provider (ICSP) focused on North American and Asian markets. oCen provides IP telephony and other real-time enhanced IP communications services to its customers - consumers, carriers, and corporations in the United States and Asia over managed IP networks. **Career Highlights:** Senior Network Engineer, oCen Communications (1998-Present); Manager of Business Development, Naray Telecom (1997-98); Assistant Manager of Strategy Planning, Naray Mobile Telecommunication (1995-97); Research Engineer, LG Information & Communications (1991-95). **Education:** Yonsei University, B.S. (1991). **Personal Information:** Married to Young Hee in 1993. One child: Seouk Hyan.

Jeffrey M. Jones

Lead Project Manager
Pacific Bell
2600 Camino Ramon, Room 3e250i
San Ramon, CA 95624
(925) 901-8879
Fax: (925) 355-1984
jmjone6@pacbell.com

4813

Business Information: Providing his skilled services as Lead Project Manager, Mr. Jones assumes responsibility for Pacific Bell's SBC Services. He manages multiple Web sites and data-driven Web application development projects as well as database design. Mr. Jones previously worked for Pacific Bell as a Systems Analyst in 1992, moving on to IBM Consulting Group as Information Technology Specialist in 1995, then rejoined Pacific Bell in 1996. Additionally, he performs business and requirements analysis and establishes policies and standards for the department's developmental processes. Mr. Jones cites his tenacity and his ability to deliver results and aggressively tackle new challenges as the secrets to his professional success. Establishing goals that are compatible with those of the Company, he anticipates a promotion to a Director's position. A subsidiary of Southwestern Bell, Pacific Bell is a telecommunications provider. The Company provides voice, data, and special services to consumers and commercial clients in California. Regional operations employ a work force of over 63,000 skilled workers. **Career Highlights:** Lead Project Manager, Pacific Bell (1996-Present); Information Technology Specialist, IBM Consulting Group (1995-96); Systems Analyst, Pacific Bell (1994-95). **Associations & Accomplishments:** University of California at Davis Alumni Association; National Society of Black Engineers; Black Engineering Association; National Association for the Advancement of Colored People; Air Force Association. **Education:** Golden Gate University, Master's degree in Management Information Systems (In Progress); University of California at Davis, B.S. in Computer Science and Engineering (1995); Solano Community College, A.A. in Mathematics (1991); Community College of the United States Air Force, A.S. in Applied Science (1990). **Personal Information:** Married to Cynthia in 1989. Two children: Brandon and Donovan. Mr. Jones enjoys golf, weightlifting and listening to Jazz music.

Jay K. Kantaria

Technical Lead Engineer
Nextlink
2700 Summit Avenue
Plano, TX 75074-3700
(972) 516-5349
jkantaria@nextlink.com

4813

Business Information: Serving as Technical Lead Engineer of Nextlink, Mr. Kantaria is charged with research and development. He guides a team of five engineers to design and implement new technologies that benefit wireless, corporate networks, and software configurations. Continuing to utilize his expanded technical knowledge and superior communication skills, Mr. Kantaria has led his department to the forefront of technology design within the telecommunications industry. Career highlights include completing his Master's degree while working full time. He moved to the United States 12 years ago and has been a catalyst in the technology sector for the last 4 years. Advancing to the position of Developer or Technical Manager to achieve personal and occupational success, Mr. Kantaria attributes his career success to his supportive parents. Nextlink is a national telecommunications provider. This highly successful company specializes in the sales, installation, and maintenance of telecommunication hardware and software. Established in 1994, the Company has grown to employ over 3,500 people who generate a substantial annual revenue. Nextlink has become a national leader in the telecommunications industry, and plans to expand to foreign markets to gain global market shares and maximize growth potential. **Career Highlights:** Technical Lead Engineer, Nextlink (2000-Present); Configuration Management Engineer, Sprint Long Distance (1998-99); Software Developer, D.S.C. Communication (1997-98); Scientist, Johnson & Jonson (1996). **Associations & Accomplishments:** Southern Methodist University Alumni; Cal State Hayward Alumni. **Education:** Southern Methodist University, M.S. in Software Engineering (1999); Cal State Hayward, B.S.; Ohlone College, A.S. **Personal Information:**

Married to Kajal in 1998. Mr. Kantaria enjoys technology network, investing and engineering.

William Michael Kirkland
Systems Designer II
BellSouth Business Systems
301 West Bay Street, BellSouth Tower, Suite 19KK2
Jacksonville, FL 32202
(904) 359-7228
Fax: (904) 359-7290
mike_kirkland@bbs.bellsouth.com

4813

Business Information: Serving as Systems Designer II for BellSouth Business Systems, Mr. Kirkland designs, prices, presents, and implements complex telecommunications networks and services for large Fortune 500 companies. As a savvy, 28-year technology professional, he administers and offers technical support to multi-state accounts. Working with users and management to analyze, specify, and design new solutions; ensuring systems functionality, reliability, and integrity; and coordinating resources, schedules, and time lines also fall within the realm of his functions. Mr. Kirkland greatly enjoys his work in programming and attributes his professional success to his belief in treating people as people. Continually striving for maximum effectiveness, he is looking forward to becoming a third level Design Engineer. BellSouth Business Systems was created in 1992 as a business unit of Bell South, Inc. established in 1880, and is an international provider of a variety of telecommunication products and services. Approximately 83,000 personnel members are employed around the world to provide individuals and corporations with voice, data, video, and Internet services. The Company also provides corporate clients with wireless data and cellular services as well as network management. **Career Highlights:** Systems Designer II, BellSouth Business Systems (1989-Present); Adjunct Instructor, Florida Community College at Jacksonville (Present); Adjunct Instructor, Webster University, Jacksonville Campus (1997-Present); Communication Systems Representative, BellSouth Advanced Systems (1983-89); Technician Maintenance, Southern Bell Telephone & Telegraph (1971-82). **Associations & Accomplishments:** Adjunct Professor, Computer Science and Telecommunications, Webster University Graduate Studies Program; Association of Information Technology Professionals; Alpha Chi Collegiate Honor Society; Stafford Caldwell Masonic Lodge; Morocco Temple; White Paper Publication, "Leadership and the Process." (1999). **Education:** Nova Southeastern University: M.B.A. (1997), Undergraduate degree in Professional Management (1995); Hill & Associates, DataLeap I/500 Series Certification; BellSouth Certified Data/Voice Training; Nortel Systems Data/Voice Certifications; University of North Florida, Certificate of Completion for Trainer Techniques. **Personal Information:** Married in 1977. Mr. Kirkland enjoys woodworking, gardening, teaching and freshwater fly fishing.

James E. Kleinschmidt
Communications Engineer
Gulf Telephone
116 North Alston Street
Foley, AL 36535
(334) 952-5401
Fax: (334) 943-5400
bigfoot@gulftel.com

4813

Business Information: Beginning his association with Gulf Telephone as a Communications Supervisor in 1979, Mr. Kleinschmidt received recognition for his diligence and management skills through several promotions to his current position of Communications Engineer. In this role, he is responsible for developing and researching new telecommunications features for new offices as well as elaborating on upcoming call platforms. Possessing business savvy and extensive technical expertise, Mr. Kleinschmidt's career highlights include converting Gulf Telephone to the digital platform. In the future, he plans on becoming more focused catering to the customers' specific needs and getting involved in the CLEC business. His success is attributed to his hard work eithic and staying on the leading edge of technology. Founded in 1929, Gulf Telephone provides various services to the community. The Company is an independent local and long distance phone and Internet service provider. Regional in scope, the Company also has a payphone access subsidiary and is a partial owner for wireless services. The Company provides services to more than 51,000 subscribers. Gulf Telephone also recently merged with Madison River in September 1999. **Career Highlights:** Gulf Telephone: Communications Engineer (1986-Present), Communications Supervisor (1979-86). **Associations & Accomplishments:** Certified 1st Class Engineer (1988-Present), NARTE; Leader (1985-Present), Boy Scouts of America; General FCC License. **Education:** Veteran Administration, Engineering Training. **Personal Information:** Married to Virginia in 1978. Two children: James and John. Mr. Kleinschmidt enjoys fishing, woodworking and yard work.

Mendy Kupfer
Voice Engineer
Destia
1450 37th Street
Brooklyn, NY 11218-3716
(718) 686-5656
Fax: (801) 409-7058
mkupfer@econo.com

4813

Business Information: Mr. Kupfer functions in the role of Voice Engineer for Destia. He provides dialtones for all employees within the Company and assists them in maintaining their operability within the workplace. A savvy, three year professional, Mr. Kupfer meticulously monitors several call centers within Destia as well as assists the staff in responding to the questions of clients. Working closely with both users and systems management, Mr. Kupfer analyzes, specifies, designs, and updates help desk operations, voice technology, and systems applications. Looking to the new millennium, Mr. Kupfer plans to continue within a similar role as he remains on the cutting edge of technology. His success is attributed to his supportive family and his ability to think outside the box, tackle challenges and new responsibilities, and deliver results. Destia is a telecommunications service provider for an international and nationally based clientele. Headquartered in New Jersey, the Company has established several locations around the United States to facilitate the requests and demands of an ever expanding clientele. Established in 1990, the Company has introduced a private business that provides long distance services, Internet adaptable modem lines, and unique toll-free calling services. **Career Highlights:** Voice Engineer, Destia (1998-Present); Telecommunications Engineer, ACSS (1998); Telecommunications Engineer, Time Warner (1997-98); Telecommunications Engineer, BLC (1996-97). **Associations & Accomplishments:** N.E.C. **Education:** B.S. in Computer Information Systems; New York University; New York Institute of Technology; Brooklyn College.

Rachael LaBounty
Director of Information Technical Services
Sprint
600 New Century Parkway
New Century, KS 66031
(913) 768-5574
Fax: (913) 768-5585
rachael.labounty@mail.sprint.com

4813

Business Information: As Director of Information Technical Services at Sprint, Mrs. LaBounty is responsible for 7x24x365 operation on a national scale. She determines the overall technical services direction and business contribution of the information systems function. Mrs. LaBounty has served with Sprint in a variety of roles since joining the Corporation as Director of Revenues for the state of Missouri in 1989. As a solid, 14 year veteran of the technology field, she oversees and directs the call center and internal help desk. In this context, Mrs. LaBounty provides users and management with training, technical support, and problem resolution. Coordinating resources, schedules, time lines, and assignments; monitoring system resources and response time for operational problems; and tracking and compiling financial reports also fall within the realm of her functions. Looking toward the next millennium, Mrs. LaBounty plans to stay with Sprint and grow from within. Sprint is one of the largest telecommunications corporations in the world. While offering voice, video, and data services, Sprint is most widely known as an efficient, cost effective, long distance communications service. Those functions include, but is not limited to residential long distance, toll free telephone numbers, and voice mail communications. Established in 1995, the New Century, Kansas facility employs a staff of 125 individuals. **Career Highlights:** Sprint: Director Information Technical Services (1997-Present), Director of Operations NE/WY (1992-97), Director of Revenues MO (1989-92). **Associations & Accomplishments:** President, Graduate School Alumni-Park College; President (1994-96), WY Tele Association; Western Commissioner for NE Governor's Info Tech Task Force (1995-97); Chamber of Commerce. **Education:** Park College, M.P.A. (1988); St. Louis University. **Personal Information:** Married to David in 1985. Two children: Andrew and Seth. Mrs. LaBounty enjoys reading.

Wing Lam
Senior Business Development Manager
HK Net Company, Ltd.
14-F, Flat 1, 313 Nathan Road
Kowloon, Hong Kong
+852 21104099
Fax: +852 23844445
winglam@hknetmail.com

4813

Business Information: As Senior Business Development Manager for HK Net Company, Ltd., Mr. Lam is responsible for project management worldwide. Including the development of new products and services, he focuses on implementing new technologies in order to provide a more efficient and cost effective product. Committed to the widening of the product line, he is deeply involved in the marketing aspects of the Company. In this context, he formulates strategies and new business and marketing plans to keep the Company at the forefront. He strives towards meeting the specific needs of his clients. Continuing his career with HK Net Company, Mr. Lam remains focused on the goals and furthering success of the Company. His success reflects his ability to think outside the box, take on challenges, and deliver results on behalf of the Company and its clientele. A telecommunications firm, HK Net Company, Ltd. remains one of the largest in their industry since their opening in 1995. Providing ESP, IDD, e-commerce, broadband, wireless, and fixed networks, the Company remains dedicated to complete customer satisfaction. Headquartered in Kowloom, Hong Kong, the Company expands their reputable business throughout the world. Employing over 200 administrative staff, experienced technicians, designers and engineers, the Company concentrates it's efforts towards the expansion of services. **Career Highlights:** Senior Business Development Manager, HK Net Company, Ltd. (1999-Present); Marketing Development Manager, UNIFI Communication HK, Ltd. (1996-99); Account Manager, Telegroup (1995-96). **Education:** University of Canberra of Australia, M.B.A. in Ecommerce (2000); Macquaine University, Bachelor's in Commerce. **Personal Information:** Mr. Lam enjoys soccer and sports.

Danny Lavardera
Implementation Engineer
SITA
55 Orville Drive
Bohemia, NY 11716
(516) 503-4866

4813

Business Information: Demonstrating expertise in the technology field, Mr. Lavardera serves as the Implementation Engineer for SITA. He primarily performs research and development for networking topologies in the Microsoft NT and Novell Netware environments. Before joining SITA, Mr. Lavardera served as Systems Engineer at ATEC Group. His background history also includes a stint as LAN/WAN Administrator for IBM Corporation. Working with a team of other professionals at SITA, he implements the newly manufactured systems designed to replace or complement previously existing systems. Mr. Lavardera attributes his success in the industry to his education, family support, the knowledge learned from other professionals, and aggressively tackling new challenges. Consistently achieving quality performance, he anticipates a promotion to a managerial position with the Company. An international telecommunications provider for the airport industry, SITA also specializes in the research and development of networking topologies. Established in 1949, the Company is headquartered in Belgium. A publicly traded company, SITA employs the services of 8,000 qualified professionals in its worldwide operations. **Career Highlights:** Implementation Engineer, SITA (1996-Present); Systems Engineer, ATEC Group (1998-99); LAN/WAN Administrator, IBM Corporation (1995-98). **Associations & Accomplishments:** Long Island NUI Group for Novell; Long Island Board of Realtors. **Education:** New York Institute of Technology, B.S. in Management (1992); Nassau Community College, A.S. in Management; LANOP -Novell C.N.S.; Productivity Point, M.C.S.E. **Personal Information:** Mr. Lavardera enjoys sports and computers.

Kevin H. Liu, Ph.D.
Research Scientist
Bellcore
331 Newman Spring Road
Red Bank, NJ 07701
(732) 758-3340
Fax: (732) 758-4372
liuke@research.bellcore.com

4813

Business Information: Recruited to Bellcore as a Research Scientist in 1998, Dr. Liu coordinates with systems management and users to analyze, specify, and design new solutions to harness more of the computer's power. Proactively involved in cutting-edge research and development, he focuses on computer communications and networking technologies. Drawing from a strong academic base and years of hands-on experience, Dr. Liu participates in the discovery, investigation, and initial deployment of advanced technologies within Bellcore. He focuses on changes that will allow the Company as well as its customers to remain flexible, efficient, and profitable in the information technology age. The most rewarding aspects of Dr. Liu's career are participating in optical network research and several multi-million U.S. government funded projects. Looking to the future, he plans on remaining with the Company and helping Bellcore maintain the networking research optical leadership in the industry. Headquartered in Morristown, New Jersey, Bellcore is a telecommunications company. Founded in 1984, the Company is involved with major contracts as well as the Internet. Operating on an international level, the

Company provides Internet services to a large client base and is committed to producing quality services. With a staff of more than 7,000 employees globally, the Company reports annual revenues in excess of $2 billion. **Career Highlights:** Research Scientist, Bellcore (1998-Present); Research Faculty, Rutgers University (1997-98); Lecturer, Victoria University of Technology at Melbourne (1996-97). **Associations & Accomplishments:** Institute of Electrical and Electronics Engineers; Association of Computing Machinery. **Education:** School of Communication & Informatics, Ph.D. in Computer Science (1997); Victoria University of Technology at Melbourne.

Thomas E. Massey

Senior Software Engineer
PageNet
6688 North Central Expressway, #306E
Dallas, TX 75206
(972) 801-8410
Fax: (972) 801-0711
tom_massey@pagenet.com

4813

Business Information: Displaying his skills in this highly specialized position, Mr. Massey serves as Senior Software Engineer for PageNet. He assumes responsibility for designing the programs on which the Company networks run. Additionally, he installs new software and upgrades existing software to ensure that the network is operating at its optimum level. Mr. Massey performs system support for the end users and troubleshoots problems as they occurs. His solid background history includes stints as Developer with USAA and Technical Developer for Chevron. His success reflects his ability to take on new challenges and responsibilities. Continually formulating new goals and objectives, Mr. Massey plans to remain on the cutting edge of technology and looks forward to assisting in the completion of future corporate goals. The leading provider of wireless messaging and information, PageNet has more than 10 million subscribers in the United States, Canada, and Spain. In addition to offering a full range of paging and messaging services, the Company also develops integrated wireless solutions for major corporations. Employing a work force of over 5,000 people, PageNet reports annual revenues in excess of $968 million. **Career Highlights:** Senior Software Engineer, PageNet (1998-Present); Developer, USAA (1997-98); Technical Developer, Chevron (1996-97). **Associations & Accomplishments:** Volunteer Fire Fighter, Shoreacres, Texas. **Education:** University of Texas at El Paso, B.S. in Computer Science (1991).

Clarissa R. McIntosh

Software Development Engineer
Alcatel USA
1000 Coit Road, M/S PB2-1150
Plano, TX 75075
(972) 519-2454
Fax: (205) 791-1286
rissamc@juno.com

4813

Business Information: A rising star in the technology industry, Ms. McIntosh functions as Software Development Engineer of Alcatel USA. In that capacity, she develops and customizes software tools and works closely with application developers and provides user-level support. Currently, Ms. McIntosh is involved with database design, production, and maintenance used to operate network switches. Ms. McIntosh got involved in technology because her uncles (former employees of IBM) introduced her to the field, in order to apply what she had learned in school. As a long-term goal, Ms. McIntosh desires to attain her Master's degree in Computer Science. Designing, developing, manufacturing, and marketing a variety of technical products, Alcatel USA was established in 1998 upon the merger of DSC with Alcatel. Among the products and services provided include digital switching, transmission, access, and private network system products for worldwide telecommunications. Located in Texas, the Corporation employs an international work force of approximately 6,000 people to provide a variety of services. **Career Highlights:** Software Development Engineer, Alcatel USA (1998-Present); Academic Tutor, TRIO Academic Services, The University of Alabama at Birmingham (1997-98); Research Intern of Materials Laboratory, Pennsylvania State University (1996 Summer); Temporary Receptionist, Five Points Temporary Services (1994-96). **Associations & Accomplishments:** Association for Computing Machinery National Chapter; Golden Key National Honor Society; Omicron Delta Kappa National Honor Society; Phi Kappa Phi National Honor Society; Who's Who Among Students in American Colleges and Universities; National Collegiate Computer Science Award; All American Scholar Achievement Award; National Dean's List Multiple Year Award. **Education:** University of Alabama at Birmingham, B.S. Computer Science (1998). **Personal Information:** Ms. McIntosh enjoys reading, playing the piano, exercising, cooking and skating.

Jorma Mellin

Development Manager
Telia Finland Ltd.
Myyrmaentie 2, P.O. Box 24
Vantaa, Finland 01600
+35 83039941
Fax: +35 8303994700
jorma.meelin@telia.fi

4813

Business Information: Utilizing more than 20 years in the telecommunications industry, Mr. Mellin serves as the Development Manager for Telia Finland Ltd. He is responsible for the Company's datacom and high tech network development. Designing new technological innovations using the Internet as a tool, Mr. Mellin also develops other types of technology products and concepts. Before joining Telia Finland, he faithfully served as a Technical Advisor with Mikrolog Ltd. Mr. Mellin strives to remain at the cutting edge of technology in the datacom area and continues to grow professionally through the fulfillment of his responsibilities and his involvement in the advancement of operations. His success reflects his ability to think outside the box, produce results, and aggressively tackle new challenges. Striving to provide customers with reliable and efficient service, Telia Finland Ltd. is one of the largest telecom companies in the Nordic countries. A variety of telecommunication services are provided to businesses and individuals. A subsidiary of a Swedish based entity, the Company was established in 1994 and has quickly grown into a $100 million business. Approximately 550 skilled professionals are employed in the Vantaa, Finland location. **Career Highlights:** Development Manager, Telia Finland Ltd. (1995-Present); Technical Advisor, Mikrolog Ltd. (1988-95). **Associations & Accomplishments:** Internet Society; ISOC AC; Ministry of Communication and Telecom Administration Centre; Member of various governmental bodies in Finland. **Education:** Helsinki Professional School, Telecom Professional (1981); Cisco Systems CCIE #4185 (1998). **Personal Information:** Married in 1999. Mr. Mellin enjoys sailing, travel and sports. He is fluent in three languages: English, Finnish, and Swedish.

Daniel A. Mixon

Large Account Manager
AT&T
P.O. Box 3249
Fort Smith, AR 72913
(501) 782-7950
Fax: (501) 782-7925
dmixon@att.com

4813

Business Information: Serving as Large Account Manager of AT&T's Large Account Department, Mr. Mixon assumes responsibility for bringing in new business, winning back previous clients, and maintaining existing accounts. He presides over the Department's customer service, monitoring quality control and often visiting client sites to correct any existing problems. Mr. Mixon has been recognized several times by the Company for top performance and attributes his success to persistence, a strong career focus, and customer dedication. As a savvy, technology professional, his career success reflects his ability to solve problems systematically and aggressively take on new challenges. He advises newcomers to the industry to continuously train and stay active within the field. Constantly striving to improve performance, Mr. Mixon plans to continue serving in the same position, but gain recognition once again for top service and revenues. Internationally recognized, AT&T is a telecommunication sales and services company. New to the Company, the Large Account Department was created in 1999. The Department is based out of Little Rock, Arkansas and Dallas, Texas and primarily works locally to maintain services and gain new business. **Career Highlights:** Large Account Manager, AT&T (1999-Present); Account Executive, Messaging/Metro Call (1997-99); Account Executive, AT&T (1994-97). **Personal Information:** One child: Taylor Danielle. Mr. Mixon enjoys spending time with his daughter, going to the park, working out and golf.

Srinivasa S. Munukut

Senior Systems Administrator
AT&T
2608 Rivendell Way
Edison, NJ 08817
(973) 564-2684

4813

Business Information: Utilizing seven years of occupational experience, Mr. Munukut serves as the Senior Systems Administrator for AT&T's Edison, New Jersey office. He troubleshoots software and hardware as well as the network infrastructure. A systems expert, Mr. Munukut works closely with both users and management to develop and coordinate all aspect of strategic planning and long-term goals. Utilizing his strengths in technology, he was instrumental in planning and execution of the Y2K compliance program for the Edison facility. Continually striving for knowledge, Mr. Munukut intends to enhance personal and professional educational and occupational growth. He attributes success to good relationships with his colleagues. His advice is "there is no limit to the industry, keep current and up-to-date." One of the largest, major long-distance telecommunications provider, AT&T provides domestic and international voice and data communications, management services, telecommunications products, and leasing and financial services. The Edison, New Jersey office is responsible for the local market. **Career Highlights:** Senior Systems Administrator, AT&T (1998-Present). **Associations & Accomplishments:** Institute of Electrical and Electronics Engineers Computer Society. **Education:** NJID, Master's in Management Information Systems (1992). **Personal Information:** Mr. Munukutla enjoys body building.

George E. Murphy, Jr.

Director of Network Operations
Premiere Conferencing
2221 East Bigou, Suite 100
Colorado Springs, CO 80920
(719) 457-2796
Fax: (719) 457-2820
george.murphy@premconf.com

4813

Business Information: As Director of Network Operations of Premiere Conferencing, Mr. Murphy manages all telecommunications and data communications systems for the Company. He sets the overall strategic direction and business contribution of the information systems function. Mr. Murphy ensures that the circuits and systems are functioning properly and handles all upgrades to systems and servers. In addition, he deals with clients relating to the data aspects of the Company. Coordinating resources and schedules, overseeing time lines and assignments, and calculating and managing the operations budget also fall within the realm of his functions. As an experienced, 14 year technology professional with an established track record of producing results, Mr. Murphy's success reflects his strong ability to build teams with synergy and take on new challenges and responsibilities. He anticipates his promotion to Chief Information Officer as a result of his continuing efforts to increase his skills through training and professional development activities. Created in 1984, Premiere Conferencing is a telecommunications and teleconferencing company. Providing telecommunication and data communication equipment to major companies throughout the world, the Company employs a work force of over 600 individuals in two locations. The Company boasts an annual revenue of $55 million. **Career Highlights:** Director of Network Operations, Premiere Conferencing (1997-Present); Network Manager, United States Marine Corps (1985-97). **Associations & Accomplishments:** Colorado Springs CISCO Users Group. **Personal Information:** Three children: Patrick, Ashley, and Delaney. Mr. Murphy enjoys playing golf.

Stephen A. Oliva, P.E., Ph.D.

Manager of Transport Planning
Sprint
9985 Hemlock Drive
Overland Park, KS 66212
(913) 534-5584
Fax: (913) 534-2086
steve.oliva@mail.sprint.com

4813

Business Information: Planning, designing, and maintaining the core network for a progressive telecommunications company such as Sprint is a challenging process. This challenge is one that Dr. Oliva readily accepts on a daily basis. Functioning as Manager of Transportation Planning, he is responsible all aspects of day-to-day transport layer planning activities of the network planning and design department of Sprint's long distance division. He ensures the success of the network through initiating deployment of upgrades and implementation of new equipment. His goals include providing the highest quality network while ensuring the lowest unit cost for each type of transport equipment. Dr. Oliva's advice is, "Use continuing education to enhance your telecommunications skills." His stubborn perseverance in ensuring each project meets current strategic technology and price goals has contributed to his professional success. Past research interests include methods for connection admission control in ATM networks and the biological effects of electromagnetic radiation. His current employer, Sprint, is the third largest long-distance provider in the United States, providing telecommunications solutions to businesses and individuals worldwide. Originally established in 1899, Sprint currently employs over 60,000 people and generates over $17 billion in annual revenue. **Career Highlights:** Sprint: Manager of Transport Planning (1999-Present), Operations Manager (1988-96); Communications Officer, United States Army Signal Corps (1967-88); Assistant Professor of Electrical Engineering, United States Military Academy (1979-82). **Associations & Accomplishments:** Institute of Electrical and Electronics Engineers; 1600 Communications Association; Society of the First Infantry Division; Veterans of

Foreign Wars; Two patent applications; Sixteen published papers in the areas of telecommunications and biological effects of electromagnetic radiation. **Education:** University of Kansas, Ph.D. in Electrical Engineering (1999); Rutgers University, M.S. in Electrical Engineering (1974); University of Rhode Island, B.S. in Electrical Engineering (1967); United States Army Command & General Staff College, M.M.A.S. (1979); Licensed Professional Engineer in Virginia. **Personal Information:** Married to Marianne in 1970. Four children: Mary Ellen, Ruth, Michael, and Amy. Dr. Oliva enjoys reading, hunting, trap and skeet shooting and coin collecting. He is also an amateur radio operator and a computer hobbyist.

William W. Olsen
Network Analyst
Madison River Communications
P.O. Box 253
Manito, IL 61546
(309) 477-0303
Fax: (309) 347-0999
dsenw@gallatinriver.com

4813

Business Information: Possessing superior talents and an excellent understanding of the information technology field, Mr. Olsen joined Madison River Communications as a Network Analyst in 2000. He oversees the provisioning of circuits for the Company's new CLEC customers and monitoring of critical equipment. Utilizing 12 years of experience in his field, Mr. Olsen continues to assist the Company in the completion of corporate goals. He anticipates his promotion to management as a result of his continuing efforts to increase his skills through training and professional development activities at Madison River Communications. His success reflects his ability to take on challenges and deliver results on behalf of the Company and its clients. Madison River Communications is a telecommunications company. The Company provides basic local services and dial tone data services, repair, and customer service for their clientele. Established in 1996, the Company is located in Manito, Illinois and employs 10 qualified personnel to serve the diverse needs of their customers. **Career Highlights:** Network Analyst, Madison River Communications (2000-Present); Systems Analyst, Centracom Microelectronics (1997-00); Communications Coordinator, Morrison Kneldsen Corporation (1998-99); Electronics Tech, United States Marine Corps (1986-90). **Education:** Illinois Central College, Microsoft Certification (1999); Certificate Microsoft Certified Professional; Harris Network Management Administrator; Nortel Network DMS Training. **Personal Information:** Married to Julie in 1997. Two children: Shayla and Chase.

Janet Paddock
Management Information Systems Director
Alaska Power & Telephone Company
P.O. Box 222
Port Townsend, WA 98368
(360) 385-1733
Fax: (360) 385-5177
dpapt@olympus.net

4813

Business Information: As Management Information Systems Director of Alaska Power & Telephone Company, Ms. Paddock is in charge of computer systems, hardware, software, and communications software. Experienced in installing NT networks, servers, and frame relays, Ms. Paddock is currently responsible for data processing, getting systems up and running, the HP 3000, customer power and telephone systems, monitoring systems, billing, customer service, and troubleshooting. A smart, 19 year professional expert, Ms. Paddock attributes her substantial success to her learning ability, persistence, a good memory, and logic, as well as her ability to deliver results and aggressively take on new challenges. Ms. Paddock continues to grow professionally and plans on remaining in the computer industry. Established in 1957, Alaska Power & Telephone Company is a power and telephone company offering both local and long distance phone service and hydro electric services. Operating from 15 service centers, the Company currently employs a staff of 140 individuals and is in the process of adding GTE exchanges. **Career Highlights:** Management Information Systems Director, Alaska Power & Telephone Company (1993-Present); Instructional Technician, Peninsula College (198-93); Moorage Manager, Port of Port Townsend (1980-89). **Personal Information:** Married to Daryl in 1980. Two children: Amber and Joe. Ms. Paddock enjoys horses, hiking and reading.

Barry A. Parker
Manager of Product Strategy & Development
AT&T
295 North Maple, Room 6111F3
Basking Ridge, NJ 07920
(908) 221-7642
baparker@att.com

4813

Business Information: Rapidly ascending through the Company's hierarchy in his years with AT&T, Mr. Parker currently serves as the Manager of Product Strategy & Development. He assumes responsibility for the product development and market launch of new communications services for consumers. Keeping abreast of new technological advances in the telecommunications industry by attending seminars, trade classes, and reading, he is continually on the lookout for ideas that will lead to the development of new products. Mr. Parker credits his professional success to his ability to work with different people and his adaptability to various situations. He aspires to obtain a higher level of responsibility within the Company. His success reflects his ability to think outside the box and aggressively tackle new challenges. Founded in the 1885, AT&T is a communications service provider. The Company provides the traditional local and long distance services and is beginning to expand its business outreach by investing into the cable business. **Career Highlights:** AT&T: Manager of Product Strategy and Development (1996-Present), Product Manager of Automated Operator Services (1993-96), Lead Analyst of Revenue Forecasting and Analysis (1990-93). **Associations & Accomplishments:** Played a role in the development of speech processing, co-inventor of idea. **Education:** Olivet Nazarene University, B.S. in Business Administration (1981); University of Houston; University of Central Florida. **Personal Information:** Married to Christine in 1996. One child: Jarod. Mr. Parker enjoys skiing, biking, golf and family time.

Mitool M. Patel
Director of Database and Information Services
Z-Tel
3340 Peachtree Road NE, Suite 2900
Atlanta, GA 30326
(404) 504-7393
mpatel@z-tel.com

4813

Business Information: Serving as the Director of Database and Information Services for Z-Tel, Mr. Patel oversees the Company's data and information architecture. He administers and controls data resources and tools and ensures data reliability, availability, serviceability, and sealability. Possessing superior talents and an excellent understanding of technology, Mr. Patel determines the overall strategic direction and business contribution of the database infrastructure. He is also accountable for compiling data and translating information into management reports for upper level management to keep them abreast of any adverse trends. The most rewarding aspect of his career is getting into the technology field. Mr. Patel got involved in the field after receiving his degree in computer science in London, England. He has since worked as a consultant, systems architect, and lead systems architect. His enjoyment of what he does keeps him on the cutting edge. Attributing his success to his family's encouragement, Mr. Patel's plans for the foreseeable future include providing high-end scalable database architectures in support of the company's goals and objectives. National in scale, Z-Tel is a telecommunications and Web communication services provider. Established in 1998, the Company is headquartered in Tampa, Florida. Employing the skills and expertise of 1,000 personnel at the Atlanta, Georgia location, the Company provides services such as dial tone and enhanced communication services encompassing major metropolitan markets. **Career Highlights:** Director of Database and Information Services, Z-Tel (1998-Present); Lead Systems Architect, Metamorph Enterprises (1996-98); Systems Architect, Turner Broadcasting (1996); Advisory Systems Consultant, Merrill Lynch (1993-96). **Associations & Accomplishments:** International Oracle User Group. **Education:** University of Westminster, B.S. (1988). **Personal Information:** Married to Manisha in 1988. Mr. Patel enjoys volleyball, tennis, travel, soccer and investing.

Ollie C. Patterson
Senior Manager
MCI WorldCom, Inc.
6 Concourse Parkway
Atlanta, GA 30328
(770) 284-3611
Fax: (770) 284-5984
ollie.patterson@wcom.com

4813

Business Information: Combining management skills and technical expertise, Mr. Patterson serves as the Senior Manager over a large wholesale customer service department for MCI WorldCom, Inc. He presides over highly automated processes used to input data into mainframe computers which determine features as well as for the billing for each client. Mr. Patterson was the first to introduce desktop automation several years ago, which is now used on a widespread basis throughout the Corporation. He attributes the success of his organization to hiring talented individuals, and providing aggressive training opportunities which keep his team on the cutting edge. Along with automating order entry processes, he presides over the development and implementation of a highly sophisticated reporting mechanism capable of delivering critical metrics information near real time. Committed to the success of the Corporation, he looks forward and continually accepts challenging assignments and takes on more professional responsibilities. MCI WorldCom is a global telecommunications company. It has one of the leading long-distance and Internet market shares, local facilities in more than 100 markets and an international presence in more than 200 countries. The Corporation reported 1H99 revenues of approximately $16.6 billion **Career Highlights:** Senior Manager, MCI WorldCom, Inc. (1984-Present); President, Patterson & Associates (1983-84). **Education:** University of Texas at El Paso (1975). **Personal Information:** Married to Anna in 1982. Four children: Aaron, Daniel, Tamrah, and Nathan. Mr. Patterson enjoys music and ping pong.

Gregory Peterson
Principal Technical Staff Member
AT&T Labs
307 Middletown Lincroft Road, Room #IK216
Lincroft, NJ 07738-1526
(732) 576-5594
Fax: (732) 576-2332
gregp@att.com

4813

Business Information: Mr. Peterson is Principal Technical Staff Member of AT&T Labs. He is responsible for leading market trials and proof of methodology concepts, including research, design, and development of advanced communications technology. Before joining AT&T Labs in 1989, Mr. Peterson has assertively served as Senior Technical Support Member with Noble Loundes Actuaries, and Systems Programmer at Dunn & Bradstreet. As a solid, 12 year technology professional with an established track record of producing results, he is charged with formulating the technical direction and development strategies. Providing technical support to applications programmers, monitoring and maintaining communications network operations, and troubleshooting infrastructure hardware, software, and transmission problems are also an integral part of Mr. Peterson's responsibilities. Eventually attaining the position of Lead Technical Contact serves as one of his short term goals. His success reflects his ability to build teams with synergy and technical strength, think out-of-the-box, and take on new challenges and responsibilities. The research and development arm of AT&T, the world's largest telecommunications provider, AT&T Labs creates and develops the cutting edge technology architectures required to achieve AT&T's vision. Formed in 1996, AT&T Labs is located in Lincroft, New Jersey. Presently, AT&T employs more than 100,000 people worldwide, while at the same time employing over 2,000 individuals at AT&T Labs. **Career Highlights:** Principal Technical Staff Member, AT&T Labs (1989-Present); Senior Technical Support, Noble Loundes Actuaries (1988-89); Systems Programmer, Dunn & Bradstreet (1987-88). **Associations & Accomplishments:** Basketball Coach, CYO; Visiting Lecturer, William Paterson University. **Education:** New Jersey Institute of Technology, M.S. in Computer Sciences (1993); William Paterson University, B.S. in Computer Sciences (1987). **Personal Information:** Married to Carolyn in 1990. Mr. Peterson enjoys fly fishing.

Douglas R. Rampley
Systems Integrator
Sprint
1500 East Rochelle Boulevard
Irving, TX 75039-4307
(972) 405-1335
Fax: (972) 405-1767
doug.rampley@mail.sprint.com

4813

Business Information: Mr. Rampley, a Systems Integrator with the Sprint, provides network design and installation services of high end data communication equipment for the data center. He is also involved in troubleshooting, analysis of networks, and related activities. Sprint is a long distance and local area telecommunications provider. Established in 1980, it is an international corporation employing over 20,000 people, and has an estimated annual revenue in excess of $15 billion. **Career Highlights:** Sprint: Systems Integrator (1999-Present), Technology Analyst (1993-99); General Manager - Mexican Operations, Betacom Industries (1990-93); Telecommunication Analyst, General Dynamics Corporation (1989-90). **Education:** Has over 28 years experience in the communication industry. **Personal**

Information: Married to Lisa in 1996. Three children: Ricky, Brandon, and Charles. Mr. Rampley enjoys bowling, fishing and camping. The Rampley family recently welcomed Felicia into their home, a baby girl they adopted.

Dana E. Reed

• • • ━━◖◉◗━━ • • •

Manager of Systems Deployment
Sprint
1310 East 104th Street
Kansas City, MO 64131
(816) 501-6004
Fax: (816) 501-6767
dana.reed@mail.sprint.com

4813

Business Information: Mr. Reed serves as Manager of Systems Deployment for Sprint and has been in this position since 1998. He is responsible for NT and UNIX standards and deployment as well as UNIX database management and software acquisition. Possessing leadership talents and an excellent understanding of technology, he manages five software coordinators, ensures the deployment of correct software and hardware equipment, and oversees server, software, and hardware inventory. Utilizing 24 years experience in the information technology field, Mr. Reed also oversees database management and assigns technical support functions to his staff. Future plans for Mr. Reed include making the Company more automated and creating a depot to cut back a "manpowered process" to ensure a brighter future for Sprint. Sprint is a telecommunications firm that oversees all external networking and information systems servers for client telephone companies. The Company provides services for both residential and business customers. Established in 1898, the Company is headquartered in Kansas City, Missouri, and employs 70,000 skilled engineers, contractors, customer service, accounting, and administrative staff. **Career Highlights:** Sprint: Manager of Systems Deployment (1998-Present), Desktop Systems Integration Manager (1995-98), VM Systems Manager (1988-95); Senior Systems Programmer, UCCEL Corporation. **Associations & Accomplishments:** Boy Scouts of America; American Payroll Association; P.D.G.A. **Education:** York College. **Personal Information:** Married to Bianca in 1993. Four children: Jason, Justin, Dalen, and Taryn. Mr. Reed enjoys golf, billiards, fishing and canoeing.

Teresa G. Reynolds

EDI Manager for Order Management
Alcatel USA
1000 Coit Road, MS-ORDM1
Plano, TX 75075-5813
(972) 519-2953
Fax: (972) 519-4152
teresa.reynolds@usa.alcatel.com

4813

Business Information: Functioning in the role of EDI Manager of Order Management at Alcatel USA, Mrs. Reynolds is a crucial part of the electronic data interchange management team. Before joining Alcatel, Mrs. Reynolds served as Order Administration for Intecom. Her background history also includes a stint as Office Manager at Reynolds Electric. In her present position, she supervises two employees who assists in providing technical support to the Company and maintaining the system database to ensure its functionality and fully operational status. Her success stems from the continuous dedication and encouragement of her family and her commitment to the Lord. For the future of her career, Mrs. Reynolds is working towards her advancement within the Company. Alcatel USA provides telecommunications solutions to the domestic market. Operating out of Texas, the Company was established in 1991, and aquired Rockwell's telecommunication activities. The Company employs in excess of 10,000 people at locations across the United States. Alcatel USA is devoted to providing clients with top-of-the-line technology in the communications field for their homes and businesses. With 1998 sales of approximately $3.5 billion, the Company produces a strong market standing in the industry and has expanded services to include the global Internet interest and digital telecommunications advancements. **Career Highlights:** EDI Manager of Order Management, Alcatel USA (1993-Present); Order Administration, Intecom (1985-92); Office Manager, Reynolds Electric (1973-85). **Associations & Accomplishments:** National Management Association; Telecommunications Industry Forum. **Education:** Amber University, B.B.A. (In Progress); Grayson City College, Associate's degree in General Business; Cheyne Estimating. **Personal Information:** Married to Danny in 1974. One child: Dena. Mrs. Reynolds enjoys floral designing.

Angelo Romano

Vice President of Operations
Tritec Communications Inc.
296 State West Route 10
East Hanover, NJ 07936
(973) 428-0505
Fax: (973) 428-0454
triteccom@aol.com

4813

Business Information: Mr. Romano is Vice President of Operations with Tritec Communications Inc. He is responsible for all day-to-day administration and operational activities. As co-founder, he assists in determining the overall strategic direction and business contribution of the communications function. Before joining Tritec Communications, Mr. Romano served as Sales Engineer with TSM. His history also includes stints as Operations Manager for Total Communications and Service Manager at Aim Telephones. An experienced technology professional with an established track record of delivering excellent results in support of all business objectives, Mr. Romano's reflects his ability to take on new challenges and responsibilities. Looking to the 21st Century, Mr. Romano's strategic gaols include doubling the size of the Corporation, as well as increasing bottom line profits. Tritec Communications Inc. provides telephone, voice mail systems, data and voice cabling, and overhead paging services. Located in East Hanover, New Jersey, the Corporation was established in 1996. Presently, Tritec Communications employs a staff of five professional and technical experts. **Career Highlights:** Vice President of Operations, Tritec Communications Inc. (Present); Sales Engineer, TSM; Operations Manager, Total Communications; Service Manager, Aim Telephones. **Personal Information:** Married to Diane in 1992. One child: Aleksandra. Mr. Romano enjoys motorcycles and fishing.

Cynthia L. Rook

Systems Technologist
BellSouth Communications Systems
500 North Orange Avenue, Room 534
Orlando, FL 32801
(407) 245-2090
Fax: (407) 245-2002
crook1@bellsouth.net

4813

Business Information: As Systems Technologist of BellSouth Communications Systems, Ms. Rook acts as a Project Manager and System Administrator on PBX and provides user support on various programs that are used such as Microsoft NT and Microsoft Office. She is responsible for troubleshooting, local area networking administration, and upgrade configurations. Before joining BellSouth, Ms. Rook was Owner and Operator of Cynthia's Temp Service. Her background history also includes a stint as Systems Administrator with Florida National Bank. A systems expert, she attributes the substantial success she has achieved in her career to the work ethics instilled in her by her parents. Ms. Rook plans to expedite continued promotion through continued dedication and the demonstration of high standards of professional conduct. She aspires to eventually attain the position of Project Manager. Established in 1986, BellSouth Communications Systems is involved in telecommunications and corporate data services providing installation and programming of key systems, SL-1PBX, and local area networking support and hardware. The Company employs a staff of 100 individuals to orchestrate every aspect of the day-to-day operations. **Career Highlights:** Systems Technologist, BellSouth Communications Systems (1986-Present); Owner/Operator, Cynthia's Temp Service (1984-86); Systems Administrator, Florida National Bank (1983-84). **Associations & Accomplishments:** Communications of America. **Education:** Seminole Communication College (1997). **Personal Information:** Ms. Rook enjoys spending time at the beach and reading.

Soren Schafft

Director of Business Development
Telenor, Inc.
12369-B Sunrise Valley Drive
Reston, VA 20191-3415
(703) 234-5010
Fax: (703) 251-0705
sorens@norcom.net

4813

Business Information: Mr. Schafft is the Director of Business Development for Telenor, Inc., the United States representative office for Norwegian State PTT, Telenor A.S. Concentrating on the North American region, he primarily provides development support services for the Company's business areas expanding into the region. He is responsible for analyzing the marketplace to ensure proper development, establishing relationships between Telenor and the United States and Canadian strategic entities, and developing business opportunities. For the future, he hopes to help establish a more significant North American presence for Telenor, especially in the areas of Internet and wireless data. As of November 1998, Telenor A.S. has merged with Telia AB, the Swedish State PTT. The combined entity will be the sixth largest telecommunications group in Europe with annual revenues of US $10.1 billion and approximately 51,000 employees. **Career Highlights:** Business Development Manager, Telenor, Inc. (1999-Present); Deputy Information Technology Director, Pannon GSM RT (1994-99); Senior Consultant, KPMG (1993-94). **Associations & Accomplishments:** SAP T-SIG; Several Hungarian associations focused on project management, Y2K issues, and information technology. **Education:** London School of Economics, M.S. in Economics (1992); University of Maryland, B.A. (1990); University of Vienna (1988-89). **Personal Information:** Married to Annamaria Benke in 1997. One child: Emese Janka. Mr. Schafft enjoys reading, basketball and travel.

Bret Daniel Snouffer

Instructor of Retail Markets
GTE
1300 Columbus Sandusky Road North
Marion, OH 43302-8578
(740) 382-7767
Fax: (740) 382-5498

4813

Business Information: Mr. Snouffer is an Instructor of Retail Markets at GTE's location in Marion, Ohio. He is in charge of retail markets, training consumers within the residential market. As a past detective in the narcotics unit, he recognized the risks he was taking and the pressures he was placing on his family. Wanting a more stable environment for his loved ones and made the dramatic career change into the telecommunications industry. In just seven months, he proved his expertise and advanced into a management role. For the future, Mr. Snouffer is celebrating his new career and plans to return to school and obtain his Master's degree in Guidance Counseling. Attributing his success to a positive attitude, networking, and effectively utilizing resources, Mr. Snouffer's quote is "anything is possible through today's technology." GTE specializes in providing telecommunications services to its clients around the world. Established in 1960, the Company is recognized as one of the leading communication provider in the industry. The Company has remained on the cutting edge of technology within the industry, advancing its equipment and facilities along with the market. Producing $23 billion every year, the Company supports the assistance of 65,000 employees. **Career Highlights:** Instructor of Retail Markets, GTE (1996-Present); Detective/Patrol Officer/Dare Officer, Marion Police Department (1991-96); Instructor, Marion Technical College Police Academy (1993-96); Detective/Patrol Officer/Dare Officer, Burgrus Police Department (1987-91). **Associations & Accomplishments:** Midwest Gang Investigators Association; National Dare Officer's Association; Ohio Dare Officer's Association. **Education:** Cedarville College, B.A. (1982). **Personal Information:** Two children: Kristie and Brian. Mr. Snouffer enjoys spending time with his children, flying and being an ultra light pilot.

Matts Sporre, Ph.D.

Senior Advisor and Strategist
Telia Mobile
Augustendalsvägen 7
Nacka Strand, Sweden 13186
+46 0706013050
Fax: +46 086017268
matts.c.sporre@telia.se

4813

Business Information: As the Senior Advisor and Strategist for Telia Moblie, Dr. Sporre coordinates the UMTS acitivities within the Company's business area. Possessing superior talents and an excellent understanding of technology, he fulfills a number of duties on behalf of the Company and its clientele. He prioritizes operating strategy for the system in order to provide the most consistent and efficient service, ensuring satisfied customers and Company growth. An expert, his years of practical experience make him an invaluable asset to Telia Mobile. Continually striving to improve performance, Dr. Sporre plans to firmly establish the Company's UMTS units, thus guaranteeing future growth and expansion. His career success reflects his ability to think outside the box, take on challenges, and deliver results. Telia Mobile provides 3rd generation mobile systems preparation and services, such as licensing, test systems, and procurement. Established in the early 1950s, the Company employs a skilled staff of approximately 2,000 qualified personnel to meet the diverse needs of its clientele. The Company maintains headquarters in Nacka Strand, Sweden and provides service to about three million subscribers in over forty countries internationally. Generating annual revenue of Skr 10 billion, Telia Mobile possesses the distinction of being the first mobile system ever established. **Career Highlights:** Senior Advisor and Strategist, Telia Mobile (2000-Present); Programme Manager, Telia Research A.B. (1997-00); Project Leader, Ericsson Radio A.B. (1995-97); Post Doctoral

Fellow, Niels Bohr Institute (1993–95). **Education:** Stockholm University, Ph.D. (1993); Sussex University; State University of New York at Stony Brook. **Personal Information:** Married to Eva in 1998. Two children: Daniel and Emil. Dr. Sporre enjoys squash, soccer and reading.

Matthew C. Sprouse
Software Engineer
Bell Atlantic
13100 Columbia Pike
Silver Spring, MD 20904
(301) 989-5101
Fax: (301) 989-5110
matthew.c.sprouse@bellatlantic.com

4813

Business Information: Possessing a strong background in the technology field, Mr. Sprouse was recruited to Bell Atlantic in 1996. At the present time, he fulfills the responsibilities of Courseware Track Manager and Technical Instructor for all UNIX and C programming courses. In his roles, he oversees all aspects of technical training development, coordination, delivery, and client follow-up for his curriculum areas. A key member of a small, highly dynamic training organization, Mr. Sprouse is in charge of all courses relating to UNIX or C programming taught at Bell Atlantic. While employed by Comdial, he was one of two technology specialists who put together a cutting-edge applicaiton called "Inntouch Concierge" that provided hotels and motels the capability to perform all "front desk" functionality via the telephone switching system. In addition, one of his college research projects was published both nationally and internationally. Always interested in the field, Mr. Sprouse stays abreast of new technology by reading trade magazines and attending trade shows and seminars. A respected expert, he attributes his success to networking. Becoming a manager of a group of programmers and attaining his Master's degree in Computer Science serves as his long-term goals. Bell Atlantic is a diversified and global telecommunications company providing voice, data, and video conferencing services and related products. Founded in 1984, the Corporation employs an international work force of 120,000 people generating in excess of $30 billion in annual revenues. **Career Highlights:** Specialist, Bell Atlantic (1996–Present); Software Engineer, Comdial Corporation (1995–96); Officer, United States Navy (1991–94). **Education:** Virginia Military Institute: B.S. in Mathematics (1991), B.S. in Computer Science (1991).

Cary A. Svendsen
Manager
BellSouth
675 West Peachtree Street NE, Room 32L65
Atlanta, GA 30375
(404) 529-6749
Fax: (404) 614-1246
cary.svendsen1@bridge.bellsouth.com

4813

Business Information: Mr. Svendsen is a Manager for BellSouth. He is responsible for managing and directing new consumer product rollouts. Mr. Svendsen has assertively served with BellSouth in a variety of roles since coming on board as Assistant Force Manager in 1993. With 11 solid years of service to the telecommunications industry, he possesses an established track record of delivering results in support of business and communications objectives. In addition to supervising a staff of 11 employees, Mr. Svendsen is in charge of numerous resource planning functions to include personnel evaluations, coordinating resources and schedules, overseeing time lines and assignments, and taking a lead role in driving products and services to market. He attributes his career success to taking advantage of hands on training, attending classes, reading trade journals, and his firm faith in God. BellSouth, located in Atlanta, Georgia, is the parent company of a multi-billion dollar operation. The Company provides local telephone service for 9 Southeastern states, and is at the top in cellular service, responsible for more than 3.5 million customers in the United States. With a great concentration in Latin America, BellSouth telecommunications service customers are at one million strong. Presently, BellSouth reports estimated annual revenues in excess of $30 billion. **Career Highlights:** BellSouth: Manager (1998–Present), Program Manager (1996–98), Assistant Force Manager (1993–96). **Associations & Accomplishments:** Board of Directors: Beach United Methodist Church, Cannon United Methodist Church, Talico, Inc. **Education:** University of Florida, B.S. in Business Administration (1988). **Personal Information:** Married to Lou Ann in 1991. Three children: Daniel, Kelly, and Haley. Mr. Svendsen enjoys golf, reading, music and teaching adult Sunday school.

Ivory L. Thomas
Project Manager
Avantel
1715 Lordsburg Drive
Garland, TX 75040-3827
(972) 918-7815

4813

Business Information: Serving with the United States Army for 20 years, Mr. Thomas gained extensive knowledge in all inner and outer workings of the communications industry. Utilizing various equipment in numerous telephonic applications, he joined MCI in 1988 as a Network Engineer. Currently with Avantel as a Project Manager, he is responsible for project planning, organization, supervision and completion. Managing the implementation of eight international projects in Mexico City, Monterrey, and Guadalajara, Mr. Thomas also maintains, analyzes, and interprets project cost tracking reports, prepares budget studies, and handles other related duties. Attributing his success to enjoying his career, he hopes to continue in his professional path. Avantel, an affiliate of MCI Communications, is a long distance network offering telecommunications services throughout Mexico. **Career Highlights:** Project Manager, Avantel Communications (1996–Present); Lead Engineer, MCI Telecommunications (1988–96); Senior Manager, United States Army Signal Corps (1968–88). **Education:** Dallas Baptist University. **Personal Information:** Married to Martha M. Adams in 1972. Two children: Ivory Lawrence and Martha Corrine. Mr. Thomas enjoys woodworking.

Ralph Tritt
Senior Systems Programmer/Administrator
AT&T
412 Mount Kemble Avenue
Morristown, NJ 07960-6617
(973) 644-7283
tritt@j51.com

4813

Business Information: Recruited to AT&T in 1993, Mr. Tritt serves as the Senior Systems Programmer and Administrator who is responsible for a number of duties on behalf of the Corporation and its clientele. Utilizing his extensive background and academic ties, he develops server plans, oversees project management, and performs troubleshooting on the Corporation's large systems infrastructure. Highly regarded, Mr. Tritt possesses superior talents and an excellent understanding of the telecommunications industry. He also adminsters and controls and operating and database management systems ensuring its integrity, reliability, and security. To keep up with the ever changing technology, Mr. Tritt intends to become Windows 2000 certified and eventually obtain a higher position within the technology department. Attributing his success to his ability to organize multiple projects and keep them running efficiently, his advice for others is "continue to learn." Established in 1887, AT&T is a telecommunication company currently employing a global work force of more than 100,000 professional, technical, and support people. A $53 billion corporation, AT&T employs an entire technology department responsible for managing servers, troubleshooting, and performing systems maintenance. **Career Highlights:** Senior Systems Programmer/Administrator, AT&T (1993–Present); Consultant (1992–93); Systems Expert/Instructor, United States Air Force (1971–92). **Associations & Accomplishments:** Role Playing Gaming Association; Rockland County PC Users Group. **Education:** Florida Institute of Technology, B.S. in Astronautics (1970); Microsoft Certified Professiona (1998); Microsoft Certified Professional+Internet (1998); Microsoft Certified Systems Engineer (1998). **Personal Information:** Married to Suellen in 1999. Three children: Teresa, Gelawon, and Michael. Mr. Tritt enjoys computer gaming.

Michael Tuttle
Lead Technician
Intermedia Communications
3625 Queen Palm Drive
Tampa, FL 33619-1309
(813) 829-2969
Fax: (813) 829-2747
mftuttle@intermedia.com

4813

Business Information: Utilizing almost 30 years of extensive experience in the telecommunications industry, Mr. Tuttle serves as Lead Technician for Intermedia Communications. Before joining Intermedia, he assertively served as Field Operations Technician with MediaOne. His solid background history also includes stints as NOC Technician for British Telecom and Lead Technician at ITT Federal Electric. Overseeing and directing day-to-day administration and operations of Company's Network Operations Center, he offers technical support to other technicians, delegates work flow, and acts as the chief liaison with other communication

carriers. Through his work with the Center, Mr. Tuttle is able to correct customer problems using remote testing and working with his contacts in other carriers. Coordinating technical resources, schedules, time lines, and assignments also fall within the purview of his responsibilities. A systems expert, Mr. Tuttle is continually striving to improve performance, and anticipates a promotion to a higher management position. He feels he owes his present professional success to the caliber of managers he has worked for in the past. Intermedia Communications is a telecommunications firm providing voice and data services for customers across LATA boundaries. Over 200 locations allow the Company to offer several types of communications programs to companies across the country utilizing technology such as relay voice, ATM, and Dart fiber. Established in 1987, the Company presently employs a work force of more than 4,000 individuals. **Career Highlights:** Lead Technician, Intermedia Communications (1997–Present); Field Operations Technician, MediaOne (1996–97); NOC Technician, British Telecom (1993–96); Lead Technician, ITT Federal Electric (1989–93). **Personal Information:** Mr. Tuttle enjoys playing the drums.

James J. "Jack" Urban
Senior Engineer
U S WEST
1201 Farnam Street, Room 400
Omaha, NE 68102-1837
(402) 422-4386
Fax: (402) 422-4279
jjurban@uswest.com

4813

Business Information: Mr. Urban has served with U S WEST since 1976. At the present time, he fulfills the position of Senior Engineer and is responsible for coding and implementing automated operations and products to support the Information Technologies Department. He deals with main automation tools and handles BMC'S COMMAND/Post product for the enterprise events which monitors all systems in one tool. Mr. Urban played a significant part in automating the Company's UNIX base and writing the management scripts for the Amdahl UTS® environment. He now acts as a go between for applications and hardware. Establishing goals that are compatible with that of the U S WEST, Mr. Urban desires to improve system management to reduce outages and wants to bring architecture to a higher level. A recognized professional, he and his team received the Boole & Babbage (now BMC) "Best Practices Award" for 1999. His success reflects his ability to think out-of-the-box and take on new challenges. Created in 1984, U S WEST was put together as a result of the AT&T Bell System divestiture from the companies known as Mountain Bell, Northwestern Bell, and Pacific Bell. The Company employs approximately 55,000 people providing basic telephone service, wireless service, and internet access to businesses and individuals in 14 states. Last year, U S WEST boasted annual revenue of $12 billion. **Career Highlights:** Senior Engineer, U S WEST (1999–Present); Technical Staff, U S WEST Communications (1983–99). **Associations & Accomplishments:** Boole & Babbage Best Practices Award 1999. **Education:** University of Nebraska at Omaha: M.S. in Computer Science (1998), B.S. in Computer Science (1982). **Personal Information:** Mr. Urban enjoys trap shooting and driving his Corvette.

Soumahoro Vassidiki
Consultant
Cote D'Ivoire Telecom
17 B.P. 275
Abidjan, Ivory Coast (Cote d'Ivoire) 17
+22 5344501
Fax: +22 5344502

4813

Business Information: Mr. Vassidiki has served with Cote D'Ivoire Telecom in various positions since 1991. At the present time, he fulfills the responsibilities of Consultant. In his role, Mr. Vassidiki is in charge of assessing all matters related to communications and networking. A respected and proven expert in the field, he is also the Acting Director when the Director is away. Mr. Vassidiki assumes accountability for formulating policies and directing the operations of the Company as well as directing individual departmental activities. Utilizing strong interpersonal skills and human resource expertise, he is responsible for assessing the need for services, personnel management, and recommending purchase of technology equipment. Established in 1991, Cote D'Ivoire Telecom is a national company specializing in telecommunication operations. The Company provides services to 80 geographically separated locations in Côte d'Tvoire. Operations employ the expertise of 3,000 individuals to market services and assist clients. **Career Highlights:** Cote D'Ivoire Telecom: Consultant (1995–Present), Inspector (1995), Director of Planning (1992), Chief of Installation Department (1991). **Associations & Accomplishments:** Rotary Club Abidjan Deux-Plateaux. **Education:** INCT Paris, degree in Engineering (1976); University Pierre and Marie Curie Paris; University Paul Sabatier Toulouse; ENSTP; Lycee Technique; Lycee Municipal Bouake. **Personal Information:** Married to Mariame in 1992. Four children: Sarah, Ibrahim-Khalil,

Daouda Abdoul-Aziz, and Cheick Abdoul-Kader. Mr. Vassidiki enjoys walking, swimming, reading and African art.

Barbara E. Venz, CDP

••• ━━━◉━━━ •••

Senior Manager
MCI Telecommunications
111 Shenandoah Loop, P.O. Box 638
McCormick, SC 29835
(770) 623-1836
Fax: (770) 280-5232
barbara.venz@mci.com

4813

Business Information: Ms. Venz serves as Senior Manager of MCI Telecommunications, providing management for systems development for new product billing to the market. She also participates in marketing and systems development as well as the supervision of over 50 staff members. MCI Telecommunications is one the world's three leading telecommunications providers of services and products. Established in 1968, the Company remains ahead of innovative technologies, making additions to the list of products and services when they become available. Telephony, value added, and satellite related products and services are among the most recent additions. Current annual revenues of the entire operation are estimated at $18 billion. **Career Highlights:** Senior Manager, MCI Telecommunications (1988-Present); Systems Analyst, Crawford & Company (1985-88); Professor of Computer Information Systems, William Woods College (1978-85). **Associations & Accomplishments:** Association of Information Technology Professionals; Information Technology Advisory Committee for Gwinnett Technical College; Computer Information Curriculum Redesign Committee for Georgia State Department of Technical Education; Original Committee Member of Computer Information Systems Curriculum. **Education:** University of Missouri at Columbia, Master of Vocational Technical Education (1976); Southern Missouri State University, B.S. in Education (1963). **Personal Information:** Married to Gary J. in 1962. Two children: Susan and Steven. Ms. Venz enjoys raising and growing orchids.

Virginia A. Vertetis, PMP

••• ━━━◉━━━ •••

Senior Project Manager
AT&T
500 Atrium Drive
Somerset, NJ 08873-4104
(732) 805-5129
Fax: (732) 805-5588
vvertetis@att.com

4813

Business Information: Serving as Senior Project Manager of AT&T, Ms. Vertetis is a visionary who has proven herself correct on many occasions. She is responsible for delivery of systems software on schedule, within budgetary constraints, and with the utmost quality. In addition to her systems project management responsibilities, Ms. Vertetis performs all administrative duties including personnel management, policy and procedure enforcement, and budget allocations. Possessing an excellent understanding of her field, she has established herself as an effective manager by illustrating leadership skills and an expanded knowledge of information technology solutions. A great support system and having great parents who helped her build a strong foundation have contributed to Ms. Vertetis' professional success. AT&T provides telecommunication services for residential, corporate, and international applications. This international company has grown to employ over 151,000 people who generate an annual revenue in excess of $53 billion. Ms. Vertetis' specific branch of AT&T specializes in the development of customer care center software and hardware system design and implementation. By providing quality services and superior customer satisfaction, AT&T has established itself as an international leader in the fields of telecommunication and information technology solutions. **Career Highlights:** AT&T: Senior Project Manager (1998-Present), Manager of Project Management (1995-98), Project Manager (1994-95). **Associations & Accomplishments:** Project Management Institute-New Jersey Chapter; Certified Project Management Professional; AT&T Cares; Parishoner/School Substitute, St. Michaels Church; Swim Instructor, Young Women's Christian Association. **Education:** College of St. Elizabeth, M.S. in Management with an emphasis in Organziational Change; Upsala College, B.S. in Computer Information Systems; Project Management Institute, PMP Certification. **Personal Information:** Married to Scott Robert in 1990. Two children: Kellie Elizabeth and William Scott. Ms. Vertetis enjoys exercise and reading.

Christopher W. Walsh

Director of Y2K Program
RCN Corporation
214 Carnegie Center
Princeton, NJ 08540
(609) 734-3872
Fax: (617) 670-3223
chrisw@ultranet.com

4813

Business Information: As Director of Y2K Program for RCN Corporation, Mr. Walsh operates the year 2000 compliance program, handling all technical and enterprise aspects. Coupling his work experience with knowledge of the technical industry, he is able to develop innovative strategies for the remedy of systems throughout the Corporation's various locations. He is currently 95 percent complete with the project, which was assigned to him specifically based on his motivation and dedicated work ethics. Realizing a large part of his success stems from his ability to accurately delegate tasks to his staff, then offer organized work loads for completion, Mr. Walsh intends to move to the Internet based side of business. In doing so, he will manage software design groups that focus attention on Internet applications. RCN Corporation is a full service telecommunications firm, offering cable television, telephone, and Internet services. Established in 1997, the Corporation employs over 3,500 people and has estimated annual revenues of $350 million. **Career Highlights:** Director of Y2K Program, RCN Corporation (1998-Present); Information Technology and Engineering Director, UltraNet Communications (1995-98); Principal Software Engineer, Digital Equipment Corporation (1981-95). **Education:** Michigan State University, B.S. in Computer Science (1979). **Personal Information:** Married to Lynne C. in 1981. Two children: Jonathan and James.

Charlie Wancio

Software Engineer
Alcatel USA
1000 Coit Road
Plano, TX 75075
(972) 519-3117
Fax: (972) 519-4830
charlie.wancio@usa.alcatel.com

4813

Business Information: Recruited to Alcatel USA as a Software Engineer, Mr. Wancio is a successful 11 year professional of the information technology field. He is currently responsible for designing the Extranet site to accommodate their clients' needs. Heading a knowledgable team of technicians and engineers, his focus is on design, development, and deployment of systems where the customer can view and purchase available products on-line. His project his due for completion in July and August 2000 time frame. Possessing superior talents and an excellent understanding of technology, Mr. Wancio is credited for writing and developing two shop floor tracking systems currently in use by the Company. Committed to the further expansion of the product line, Mr. Wancio's plans to continue learning and eventually attaining a management level position. He attributes his success to his creativity and logical thinking. Specializing in the manufacturing of telecommunications products, Alcatel USA was established in 1974. Headquartered in Plano, Texas, the Company serves millions of customers nationwide. Employing over 6,000 dedicated service workers and administrative staff, the Company ensures complete customer service and satisfaction, and holds accounts with major clients such as MCI, Sprint, and AT&T. Alcatel focuses on the implementation of new technologies in order to increase sales and services for their clientele. **Career Highlights:** Software Engineer, Alcatel USA (1994-Present); Software Engineer, Solectron Inc. (1992-94). **Education:** East Tennessee State University, B.S. in Computer Science (1989). **Personal Information:** Mr. Wancio enjoys sports.

Richard S. Whitt, J.D.

Senior Policy Counsel
MCI WorldCom, Inc.
1801 Pennsylvania Avenue NW #416
Washington, DC 20006-3606
(202) 887-3845
Fax: (202) 887-3866
richard.whitt@wcom.com

4813

Business Information: Mr. Whitt, who has worked for MCI WorldCom, Inc. since 1998, now serves as Senior Policy Counsel. He fulfills duties of an advocacy representative to the Federal Communications Commision and Department of Commerce. In addition, he has served as an advisor and lobbyist at the Whitehouse and Capitol Hill. Within MCI, Mr. Whitt has assisted in the creation of policy regarding the Internet and data services. As for the future, he plans to become more involved with the Internet, data, and voice technologies. Mr. Whitt attributes his success to good mentors, education, and leadership, as well as his ability to deliver results and take on new challenges. MCI WorldCom, Inc. is the second largest global telecommunications corporation. Since 1968, the Corporation has offered long distance telecommunications, as well as region-specific services. A work force numbering 75,000 has assisted the Corporation in reaching its current success. Per year, MCI WorldCom has averaged an estimated revenue of $38 billion. **Career Highlights:** MCI WorldCom, Inc.: Senior Policy Counsel (1998-Present), Director of Federal Affairs (1995-98); Regulatory Counsel, IDB WorldCom (1994-95); Associate Attorney, Sutherland, Asbill & Brennan (1990-94). **Associations & Accomplishments:** Federal Communications Bar Association; FCBA Foundation; District of Columbia Bar. **Education:** Georgetown University Law Center, Juris Doctorate Cum Laude (1988); James Madison University, B.S. (1984). **Personal Information:** Married to Cathy J. in 1995. Mr. Whitt enjoys tennis and travel.

Thomas R. Woolverton

Area Technical Coordinator
IXC Communications
38029 Schoolcraft Road
Livonia, MI 48150-1065
(330) 342-1671
Fax: (330) 342-3698
twoolverton@broadwing.com

4813

Business Information: Recruited to Broadwing Communications in 1977, Mr. Woolverton serves as Area Technical Coordinator for Great Lakes Region in U.S. He oversees approximately 23 staff members who provide technical support, inner department coordination, and systems analysis. Drawing from over 24 years of extensive business savvy and technical expertise, Mr. Woolverton effectively coordinates daily resources, time lines, schedules, assignments, and budgets. A recognized expert in his field, he instituted the first 8-lamda and 16-lamda fiber optics system in the United States. Taking advantage of opportunities afforded to him, Mr. Woolverton's goals are to attain the position of Operations or Technical Support Manager within the corporate structure. His success is attributed to staying on top of emerging technology. Headquartered in Austin, Texas, Broadwing Communications operates as a fiber optic transmission provider. Established in 1978, the Company maintains an global presence with over 800 locations both in the United States and internationally. Presently, the Company employs a work force of more than 5,000 professional, technical, and support personnel. **Career Highlights:** Area Technical Coordinator for Great Lakes Region of U.S., Broadwing Communications (1997-Present); COE Specialist of Operations, Poxa Lambro TCI (1995-97); Technician of OSP Construction, Southwestern Bell (1977-95); Systems Technician, Big Spring Cable (1976-77). **Associations & Accomplishments:** Morris Animal Foundation; American Red Cross; National Geneological Society; Society of Creative Anachronism. **Education:** Howard College (1995); Josephinum College. **Personal Information:** Three children: Shawn, Brad, and Ashley. Mr. Woolverton enjoys woodcarving and historical studies.

David K. C. Yan

Director of Information Systems/Information Technology
AmTelecom Group, Inc.
245 Britannia Road Inc. East
Mississauga, Ontario, Canada L4Z 2Y7
(905) 890-4004
Fax: (905) 890-4507
dyan@ics-canada.net

4813

Business Information: Serving as Director of Information Systems and Information Technology for AmTelecom Group, Inc., Mr. Yan is responsible for a number of activities on behalf of the Corporation and its clientele. In his capacity, he ensures the functionality and operational status of the entire information systems infrastructure. Possessing strong leadership skills and an excellent understanding of technology, Mr. Yan determines the strategic direction and business contributions of the information systems functions. Directing and participating in the analysis, design, evaluation, testing, and implementation of related computer systems also fall within the realm of his responsibilities. The most rewarding aspects of his career were working with interns on Project Gold and establishing the technology department from scratch. Mr. Yan plans to help the Corporation become more involved in the Internet. His success reflects his ability to aggressively tackle new challenges and responsibilities and deliver results. AmTelecom Group, Inc. is a telecommunications company. Established in 1907, the Corporation's 2,000 talented professionals have an extensive and proven track record in the telecommunications and transportation area. The Corporation is an independent telephone company providing Internet cable television services. Presently, the Corporation reports annual sales of $130 million. **Career Highlights:** Director of Information Systems/Information Technology, AmTelecom Group, Inc. (1998-Present); Manager of Information Systems and Information Technology, Amtelecom Business Services (1998); International Project Leader, OTIS Elevator (1986). **Education:** Manchester Polytechnics, B.Sc. in Engineering with Honors (1983). **Personal Information:** Married to Magdalene in 1985. One child: Chrisanna.

Ning Yang

Senior Member of Technical Staff
GTE Laboratories, Inc.
40 Sylvan Road
Waltham, MA 02451
(781) 466-3286
Fax: (781) 466-5846

4813

Business Information: Mr. Yang is Senior Member of Technical Staff at GTE Laboratories, Inc. He has been doing research and development in telecommunication field. He is doing modeling, simulation, performance analysis, and system design of communication systems. His research interests include broadband communication networks, error control coding, CDMA spread spectrum technology, interference cancellation, adaptive signal processing, and digital signal processing. GTE Laboratories, Inc. traces its roots back to 1943 and is a research and development firm in the telecommunications industry. **Career Highlights:** Senior Member of Technical Staff, GTE Laboratories, Inc. (1995-Present); Research Assistant, Mobile and Portable Radio Research Group, Virginia Tech (1994-95). **Associations & Accomplishments:** Senior Member, Institute of Electronics and Electrical Engineers; Honor Society, Tau Beta Pi; Honor Society, Eta Kappa Nu. **Education:** Virginia Polytechnic Institute and State University, M.S in Electrical Engineering (1995); Tianjin University, B.S. in Instrumentation and Electrical Engineering (1989). **Personal Information:** Mr. Yang enjoys playing tennis.

Tsutomu Yoneyama

Senior Engineer
Livedoor, Inc.
New River Residence 1001, 1-6-11, Shinkawa, Chuo-Ku
Tokyo, Japan 104-0033
+81 355422306
Fax: +81 355422307
yoneyama@livedoor.net

4813

Business Information: Serving with Livedoor, Inc. since its establishment in 1999, Mr. Yoneyama fulfills the responsibility of the Corporation's Senior Engineer. In this capacity, he is accountable for all aspects of technical project management, network engineering, and online advertisement management. Possessing superior talents and an excellent understanding of technology, Mr. Yoneyama ensures the functionality and operational status of the Corporation's operating and network infrastructure as well as its peripherals and accessories. Directing and participating in the analysis, design, evaluation, testing, and implementation of LAN/WAN and Internet/Intranet related computer technology also fall within the realm of Mr. Yoneyama's responsibilities. Dedicated to Livedoor's success, he looks forward to assisting in the completion of future corporate goals. His success reflects his ability to take on challenges and deliver results on behalf of the Corporation and its clientele. Established in 1999, Livedoor, Inc. is Japan's first provider of free Internet access. The Corporation is currently the fastest growing Internet service provider in Japan and is ranked among the country's top ten. Employing a work force of more than 40 professional, technical, and support staff, the Corporation provides users free access to international locations via the Internet. **Career Highlights:** Senior Engineer, Livedoor, Inc. (1999-Present); Project Manager, Tomen Corporation (1993). **Associations & Accomplishments:** Japan's Venture Business Community. **Education:** Osaka Prefecture University, B.A. in Industrial Engineering (1993).

Thomas Holzeisen

Webmaster/Application Programmer
Musipl@y GmbH
Ringberstr 27
Bad Wiessee, Germany 83707
+49 8938007192
webmaster@freeonweb.com

4832

Business Information: Serving as Webmaster and Application Programmer, Mr. Holzeisen engages in developing applications and Web sites for Musicpl@y GmbH, a newly founded company. Possessing an excellent understanding of technology, he is able to learn the base of a program language in approximately four days by reading existing source codes. Utilizing his expertise and hands on experience in understanding the complexities of technology, he directs the programming of hardware devices up to the development of visual components for Windows applications. Mr. Holzeisen's focus is on the creation of cutting edge database applications and Web sites. In his last project, he developed an automatic software installation system, enabling the installation of Microsoft Windows and all software in a very short time and fully automatic. The Company, Musicpl@y GmbH, is the first mp3 radio station which broadcasts digital music in the mp3 audio format by using the videotext bandwidth of a European television station. This new technology allows a very high download speed without online costs, and attracts a lot of customers for the e-commerce part of the Company. **Career Highlights:** Webmaster/Application Programmer, Musicpl@y GmbH (2000-Present); GE CompuNet: Systems Engineer (1999-00), Group Leader (1998). **Education:** Electrical Engineering degree. **Personal Information:** Mr. Holzeisen enjoys books, music, billards and creating Web sites.

Wayne N. Braithwaite

Information Systems Engineer
Bonneville International Corporation
55 North 300 West
Salt Lake City, UT 84103
(801) 575-7592
Fax: (801) 575-7544
wbraithwaite@bonnint.com

4833

Business Information: Mr. Braithwaite is an Information Systems Engineer for Bonneville International Corporation. In this capacity, he presides over all local and wide area networks utilized by the Corporation, work stations, and end user applications. Bonneville International Corporation owns and operates television and radio broadcasting facilities. Established in 1950, the Corporation currently operates 18 facilities across the United States in affiliation with the Church of Jesus Christ of Latter Day Saints. **Career Highlights:** Information Systems Engineer, Bonneville International Corporation (1995-Present); Systems Engineer, Random Access (1994-95); Graphics Engineer, Access Software (1992-94); Network Manager, Unibase (1990-92). **Associations & Accomplishments:** Cisco Certified Network Associate; Certified Network Engineer; CNA - Novell; MCP/MCPS Microsoft; Teacher, CNE courses for LDS Business College. **Personal Information:** Married to Jennifer in 1992. Two children: Laura and Ashley. Mr. Braithwaite enjoys computer games, using the Internet and fishing.

Scott W. Erickson

Senior Network Engineer
CBS
524 West 57th Street, Room 3800
New York, NY 10019-2924
(212) 975-7866
Fax: (212) 975-9288
swerickson@cbs.com

4833

Business Information: Demonstrating his expertise in this highly specialized position, Mr. Erickson serves as a Senior Network Engineer for CBS. He assumes responsibility for the design and continuous support of the LAN/WAN network infrastructure and consolidation for four regional locations. Additionally, he administrates the NT, Novell, Notes, and SQL servers in each of the sites. Mr. Erickson performs the budget presentation at the internal assembly of infrastructure and was in charge of the migration project that switched CBS from a desktop and server standard to a Windows NT operating environment. Attributing his professional success to the support of his parents and his wife, he is currently involved in the content providing Wink TV feeding in the Company's television service. Currently the largest media company in the world, CBS recently orchestrated a merger with Viacom to strengthen its global marketing position in the industry. CBS is renowned for its television broadcasting services, which still serves as its main core operation. A work force of more than 10,000 qualified individuals are employed worldwide. **Career Highlights:** Senior Network Engineer, CBS (1996-Present); LAN Manager, Chemical Bank (1994-96); Senior Computer Technician, Computers Unlimited (1990-94). **Education:** State University of New York at Old Westubury, B.A. (1991). **Personal Information:** Married to Jennifer in 1996. Mr. Erickson enjoys skiing, hiking and mountain biking.

Gennadiy Borisov

Director, Digital Media Platform
MTVi Group
770 Broadway
New York, NY 10003
(212) 654-9884
gmb@iname.com

4841

Business Information: Demonstrating his experience in the information technology field, Mr. Borisov serves as a Director of the Digital Media Platform for the MTVi Group. He oversees and directs Digital Media Services and Research for the entire MTVi Group and partners in order to deliver products and services to the multitude of online and offline properties worldwide. Capitalizing on more than 12 years of extensive cross-industry experience, Mr. Borisov monitors the progress of deliverables and productivity of staff, formulating a hands-on management style with an above average aptitude for problem solving. Presently, Mr. Borisov is building products and services for MTV.com, VH1.com, Sonicnet.com, and more than 25 international properties of the MTVi Group as well as conducting research in the areas of Media Delivery Networks, Interactive Media Creation, and Next Generation Media Delivery Platforms. In the future, he anticipates his promotion to Senior Vice President or CTO of the MTVi Group, as a result of his continuing efforts to increase his skills through training and professional development activities. His success reflects his leadership ability to form teams with synergy and deliver results. MTVi Group is the world's leading Internet music content company, with dozens of music Web site destinations around the world, including MTV.com., VH1.com, and SonicNet.com. The MTVi Group is a unit of MTV Networks, which is owned by Viacom Inc. Headquartered in downtown New York City, the MTVi Group has satellite offices in San Francisco, California. Established in 1999, the Company currently employs a staff of 300 qualified professionals to serve the diverse needs of its clientele. **Career Highlights:** Director, Digital Media Platform, MTVi Group (1999-Present); Development Lead and Manager, Williams Communications (1998-99); Engineering Manager, Wave Systems (1997-98); Senior Analyst, CEM Corporation (1992-95); Senior Developer, National Technical University of Ukraine, Kiev, Ukraine (1988-92). **Associations & Accomplishments:** Vice Chair of the Content and Applications Group, Broadband Content Delivery Forum (2000); New York New Media Association (NYNMA) (1999-Present); Association of Internet Professionals (1999-Present); Information Technology Talent Association (1999-Present); Publication Review Team for WROX Publishing (1997-Present). **Education:** Thomas A. Edison State College, B.S. in Applied Science and Technology (1995); National Technical University of Ukraine, Kiev, Ukraine, B.S. in Computer Science and Technology (1992). **Personal Information:** Mr. Borisov enjoys travel, reading, boating and martial arts.

Kelly K. Hunt

Operations Manager
Time Warner Communications
1266 Dublin Road
Columbus, OH 43215
(614) 481-5257
kelly.hunt@twcable.com

4841

Business Information: A prominent and respected business professional, Ms. Hunt serves as Operations Manager for the Road Runner project division of Time Warner Communications. She assumes accountability for the entire spectrum of the Division's operational and administrative functions, providing technical support for internal technicians and customers alike. Utilizing five years of experience in this field, she developed her current position and managed the installation team responsible for the implementation of the UUNET operating platform. She plans to continue in her present position, looking forward to further expanding the Road Runner division. Ms. Hunt's success reflects her ability to deliver results and aggressively tackle new challenges. Founded in 1977, Time Warner Communications provides multimedia services to businesses and individuals across the United States. The Company's most recent service, the Road Runner, was introduced in 1997 and offers high speed data access via cable. Approximately 600 skilled professionals are employed in the department. **Career Highlights:** Operations Manager, Time Warner Communications (1999-Present); UUNET, an MCI WorldCom Company: Shift and Project Manager (1998-99), Applications Analysis (1996-98). **Associations & Accomplishments:** National Association of Female Executives; Women in Cable and Telecommunications. **Education:** Ohio State University, Bachelor's degree (1989); Certified Netware Administrator.

Patrick Knorr

Datavision Manager
Sunflower Cablevision
644 New Hampshire Street
Lawrence, KS 66044
(785) 830-1177
Fax: (785) 830-1175
pknorr@sunflower.com

4841

Business Information: Mr. Knorr serves as Datavision Manager with Sunflower Cablevision. He is responsible for setting strategic policies, goals, and objectives to grow and broaden the Company's Internet and Telecommunication Divisions. Before joining Sunflower Cablevision in 1998, Mr. Knorr assertively served as General Manager for JC Onramp Internet. His background history also includes stints as Consultant with Netspace Internet and Chief Executive Officer for Global Storefronts. In his current role, Mr. Knorr is in charge of all database aspects of day-to-day operations. Providing backups, ensuring data integrity and reliability, and tuning software tools to enhance overall performance also fall within the realm of his responsibilities. A solid, seven year professional, he is looking forward to growing Sunflower's operations through the Internet and taking it to the next level of success. His professional success reflects his ability to take on new challenges and responsibilities. Founded in 1971, Sunflower Cablevision is a provider of cable television, broadcasting, telecommunications, and Internet services. Located in Lawrence, Kansas City, the Company presently employs a work force of more than 100 professional, technical, and support personnel. **Career Highlights:** Datavision Manager, Sunflower Cablevision (1998-Present); General Manager/Chief Operations Officer, JC Onramp Internet (1997-98); Consultant, Netspace Internet (1996-97); Chief Executive Officer, Global Storefronts (1995-96). **Associations & Accomplishments:** CTAM; Society of Cable Telecommunications Engineers; KISPA; City of Lawrence Y2K Committee; Junction City Chamber of Commerce; Junction City Rotary International. **Education:** Kansas State University, B.S. (1998); Manhattan Technical College, Marketing degree (1991); **Personal Information:** Married to Kerri in 1995. One child: Thomas. Mr. Knorr enjoys sailing and history.

David L. Lorenzi

Director of Network Engineering
Comcast
200 Cresson Boulevard
Oaks, PA 19456
(610) 650-3034
Fax: (610) 650-1011

4841

Business Information: Possessing extensive experience in the information technology field, Mr. Lorenzi serves as Director of Network Engineering for Comcast. Since joining the Company in 1999, he fulfills a number to technical duties on behalf of the Company and its clientele. Highly regarded, he manages all outside cable plants, supervises six employees directly, oversees the budget, and recommends and approves purchases. Reflecting a strong leadership ability, Mr. Lorenzi also maintains the functionality of the networks, oversees the reliability and integrity of the cable, travels to different Company branches, and directs all day to day operations of the entire division. Proud of his achievements, Mr. Lorenzi received the "Excellence in Engineering Award" from Comcast. He plans to expedite continued promotion through dedication and the perpetuation of additional growth of Comcast. Comcast is the third largest cable television company in the country. The Company provides telecommunications services, such as Internet access. Founded in 1962, Comcast is located in Pennsylvania and employs the skilled services of 10,000 individuals to acquire business, meet with clients, facilitate projects, and market services. Estimated annual revenue for the Company is in excess of $4 billion. **Career Highlights:** Comcast: Director of Network Engineering (1999-Present), Regional Project Manager (1994-99), Construction Manager (1985-94). **Associations & Accomplishments:** Society of Cable Telecommunications Engieners. **Education:** Providence College, B.S. in Management (1979). **Personal Information:** Married to Kathleen in 1985.

Kevin W. Manning

Manager of Web Services
MediaOne Group
9785 South Maroon Circle
Englewood, CO 80112-5919
(303) 925-2526
Fax: (303) 925-2577
kevmanning@mediaone.com

4841

Business Information: Serving as Manager of Web Services of MediaOne Group, Mr. Manning is responsible for the development, implementation, and maintenance of Intranet and Internet systems. Utilizing his extensive technical knowledge to include advances in the World Wide Web, he has participated in developing an award winning web site for the Company. By attending technical classes, seminars, and leadership classes, and reading trade publications, Mr. Manning is prepared to implement changes that are continuously occuring in the industry. Crediting his success to his excellent communications and relational skills, he currently is working to make the Intranet more user friendly while focusing on his abilities as a team player. Recently purchased by AT&T, MediaOne Group is one of the world's largest broadband communications companies. The national company is headquartered in Englewood, Colorado, where services such as cable television, wireless communications, and internet features are provided. **Career Highlights:** Manager of Web Services, MediaOne Group (1999-Present); Manager of Systems Integration (1998-99); Consulting Services Manager, Digital Equipment Corporation (1987-98). **Associations & Accomplishments:** Microsoft Webmasters. **Education:** United States Navy, Data Processing Schools. **Personal Information:** Married to Joan in 1996. Five children: Jennifer, Allison, Bo, Joe, and Whitney. Mr. Manning enjoys golf and boating.

Andrew H. Snyder

Technical Manager
Time Warner
75 Rockefeller Plaza, Office 2-23
New York, NY 10019
(212) 484-8753
Fax: (212) 405-5108
andrew.snyder@twi.com

4841

Business Information: Recruited to Time Warner in 1998, Mr. Snyder serves in the role of Technical Manager for global network operations. He is responsible for the computer network in the Services Delivery Department and oversees the network operations and monitoring tools. Designing and adapting technology to the Company's needs, he has implemented new systems to improve the efficiency of operations. A systems expert, Mr. Snyder stays current with the technological industry through periodicals, networking through Web sites, and colleagues in the industry. Crediting his success to hard work, perseverance, and a positive attitude, he has received previous internal recognition and a publisher's award for his innovative work in programming. Continually striving for maximum effectiveness, Mr. Snyder is currently completing his undergraduate degree and plans to increase his professional responsibilities and move upwards into a technical management position. A Fortune 200 company, Time Warner is world-renowned for movie and film productions. Founded in 1989, the Company has expanded business ventures to include the cable industry, broadcasting, news media, and over 50 publications of books and periodicals. Through an international presence in over 30 countries, estimated revenue stands at $13 billion annually. **Career Highlights:** Technical Manager, Time Warner (1998-Present); Senior Technical Support Analyst, Becton Dickinson; Systems Administrator, Ernst & Young; Programmer/Analyst, The New York Times. **Education:** New Jersey Institute of Technology, B.S. in Electrical Engineering and Technology (In Progress); County College of Morris, A.A.S. in Electrical Engineering and Technology. **Personal Information:** Married to Jutta in 1991. Mr. Snyder enjoys kendo.

Anthony Williams

Management Information Systems Manager
KSLA TV
1812 Fairfield Avenue
Shreveport, LA 71101
(318) 222-1212

4841

Business Information: Displaying his expertise in the field of information technology, Mr. Williams serves as the Management Information Systems Manager of KSLA TV at its Shreveport, Alabama location. He assumes accountablity for the Station's various computer systems, including the PC network system, the AS/400, and the local area network. Mr. Williams adminstrates each individual system, performing maintenace tasks, monitoring daily activity, and providing back up system to prevent data loss. Network security is also provided to guard against viruses and unauthorized access. Attributing his professional success to his good communication skills, he looks forward to future position as the Management Information Systems Director of KSLA TV. A subsidiary of Raycom Media, KSLA TV is a CBS affiliate and provides local television coverage. The Station is based in Montgomery, Alabama and has several television stations in the Southeastern part of the United States. Approximately 150 qualified personnel members are employed in local operations at the station in Shreveport, Alabama. **Career Highlights:** Management Information Systems Manager, KSLA TV (1998-Present); Management Information Systems Manager, Parish of Caddo (1993-98). **Associations & Accomplishments:** M.S.C.E. **Education:** Grambling State, B.S. in Design Engineering (1993); Microsoft Systems Certified Engineer. **Personal Information:** Mr. Williams enjoys computer gaming, sports and gaming.

Peyman Azizi

Senior Internet Engineer
Loral Cyberstar
2440 Research Boulevard, Suite 400
Rocksville, MD 20850
(301) 670-6576
Fax: (301) 590-7401
pazizi@lorallorion.com

4899

Business Information: Mr. Azizi is the Senior Internet Engineer for Loral Cyberstar. Centering his services around network design and software development, he creates new programs and technologies to facilitate the needs of a particular client. He pioneered the video braodcasting division of the Company which was an exciting challenge to him and continues to provide interesting situations as it continues to develop. In the future, Mr. Azizi hopes to become more involved in research and development with cutting edge technologies in the field. Attributing his success to enjoying what he does, his advice is "be dedicated, committed, and have the knowledge." Loral Cyberstar is an Internet and access service provider to Eastern Europe, Asia, and South America. Focusing on providing service over a satellite link, the Company also conducts video broadcasting. The Company turns over an annual revenue of $100 million and has assisted in networking several of the leading businesses in the area. **Career Highlights:** Senior Internet Engineer, Loral Cyberstar (1997-Present); Senior Network Project Engineer, e.Spire Comm. Inc. (1992-97); Network Engineer, Hughes Network Systems (1985-93). **Associations & Accomplishments:** A.R.I.N.; R.I.P.E.; Institute of Electrical and Electronics Engineers; A.P.N.I.C.; Board of Trustees, Montgomery County Churchill Association. **Education:** University of South Carolina, B.S. (1983); Johns Hopkins University, Cisco. **Personal Information:** Married to Flora Tajalli in 1989. Mr. Azizi enjoys golf, skiing and scuba diving.

Edward Bradish, Jr.

Field Engineer
Channel Communications
P.O. Box 105
Wyano, PA 15695
(412) 812-1791
lzrdkng@nb.net

4899

Business Information: Dedicated to the success of Channel Communications, Mr. Bradish functions in the capacity of Field Engineer for Channel Communications. In this positon, Mr. Bradish assumes many responsibilities. He serves as a sweep engineer, coordinates system testing, and performs troubleshooting activities. Mr. Bradish is presently working on a new cable project which involves dense wave division, multiplexing two fiber optical signals at two frequencies on one fiber. Mr. Bradish continues to grow professionally and looks forward to continuing to run the system within the Company. His success reflects his ability to think outside the box, produce results, and take on new challenges. Taking pride in his work and with a wealth of technical knowledge, Mr. Bradish's quote is, "Possibilities are endless in technology." Channel Communications was established in 1978. A CATV contracting company, Channel Communications builds turnkey projects and cable networks, as well as enabling Internet access. Local operations in Ohio, Illinois, West Virginia, Pennsylvania, and Georgia employ 100 individuals to meet with clients, facilitate projects, and market services. Services are provided to new businesses in addition to the individual client. Channel Communications was bought by a larger company in 1998, Orius Corporation Large Capacity. **Career Highlights:** Field Engineer, Channel Communications (1987-Present); CATV Splicer, Rybarik CATV Inc. (1994). **Education:** Cleveland Institute of Electronics; Henkels & McKoy CATV Training. **Personal Information:** Married to Marlene in 1986. One child: Eric. Mr. Bradish enjoys jet boat building, hunting and fishing.

Kevin Calderbank

President/Chief Executive Officer
Southern Internet
3931 RCA Boulevard, Suite 3122
Palm Beach Gardens, FL 33410-4215
(561) 627-7227
Fax: (561) 691-1655
kevin@southernet.net

4899

Business Information: As the President and Chief Executive Officer of Southern Internet, Mr. Calderbank is also one of the founders of the Company. He is responsible for overseeing the day-to-day operations within the Company, formulating all new business developments and strategic planning, and developing and implementing all Company policies and procedures. Mr. Calderbank attributes his substantial success to surrounding himself with smart individuals. He continues to grow professionally and hopes to build Southern Internet into a billion dollar company. Established in 1995, Southern Internet is an up and coming Internet service provider. Headquartered in Palm Beach Gardens, Florida, the

Company operates from 10 locations and provides Internet services to the entire Eastern seaboard. Southern Internet currently employs the expertise of 15 individuals dedicated to providing quality services to a growing clientele. **Career Highlights:** Southern Internet: President/Chief Executive Officer (1999-Present), Chief Operating Officer (1997-99), Vice President of Marketing (1995-97). **Education:** Florida State University, B.S. (1981); Davidson College; University of Florida. **Personal Information:** Mr. Calderbank enjoys scuba diving and skiing.

André A. de Freitas

Senior Engineer
Vital Network Services
42 Broadway
New York, NY 10004
(718) 694-3002
Fax: (718) 694-4305
andre.defreitas@vitalnetsvc.com

4899

Business Information: As Senior Engineer of Vital Network Services, Mr. de Freitas fulfills the capacity of on-site communications consultant at the New York City Transit. He is responsible for installation and maintenance of General DataComm's on-site equipment, as well as other equipment on contract. Before joining Vital Network Services, Mr. de Freitas assertively served as Data Communications Engineer with United Bank in Trinidad. His history also includes filling the role of Technician with Manufacturers Hanover Trust. An expert, he works with users and management to analyze, specify, design, and implement advanced wide area network and ATM technologies. The research, evaluation, test, and deployment of computer networking architecture also fall within the realm of Mr. de Freitas' responsibilities. He credits his success to his parents and grandparents. Owning his own consulting firm serves as one of his future endeavors. A communications service provider, Vital Network Services is a wholly owned subsidiary of General DataComm. The services and development arm, Vital Network specializes in wide area networks and ATMs. Currently, the Company owns 80 percent of the ATM market in Europe. Headquartered in Middlebury, Connecticut, Vital Network Services was established in 1969. Presently, the Company is manned by over 1,400 people who help generate revenues in excess of $100 million. **Career Highlights:** Senior Engineer, Vital Network Services (1987-Present); DataComm Engineer, United Bank (1982-87); Technician, Manufacturers Hanover Trust (1979-82). **Associations & Accomplishments:** Public Television for Quality Programming; Four Time Winner of General Datacomm's "Employee of the Quarter Award." **Education:** Brooklyn College, B.A. in Economics (1990); Technical Career Institute, A.A.S. in Electronics Engineering Technology (1980); Certified Nortel Networks Router Specialist (1999). **Personal Information:** Mr. de Freitas enjoys taking classes, reading journals and taking classes.

Lorli Dima-Ala Villanueva

Marketing Manager
Sequel Communications
316 East 49th Street, Apartment 3E
New York, NY 10017
(908) 668-5300
girlashda@aol.com

4899

Business Information: As Marketing Manager of Sequel Communications, Ms. Dima-Ala Villanueva oversees advertising, updating, training, and marketing strategies. She also meets with clients, attends conventions, writes press releases, and is engaged in networking. Also the President/CEO of an advertising agency in the Phillipines, Ms. Dima-Ala Villanueva has received numerous awards. She has received awards for acting and directing, and has received scholastic recognition, and is a founding member of the National Theater. She also ran a cable station in Chicago, Illinois and implemented various ethnic programs, which she considers a career milestone and attributes her success to her faith in God and her preparedness. Ms. Dima-Ala Villanueva plans to expedite continued promotion through her involvement in the advancement of operations and take her company in the Philippines international. Her favorite quotable quote is, "The first thing you sell is yourself." Sequel Communications is the largest communications company in the United States. The Company provides strong phone card services such as disposable and rechargeable cards. Sequel Communications is also the parent company for Sequel Concepts, a consulting service, and Sequel Destinations, a travel service. Founded in 1989, the Company is international in scope and operates a network of four locations. **Career Highlights:** Marketing Manager, Sequel Communications (1999-Present); President/Chief Executive Officer, Emmaus Enterprises (1991-Present); Vice President for Academic Affairs, Pamantasaan ng Lungsod ng Pasay (1995-96) **Associations & Accomplishments:** Fulbright Hay Scholars Association; Rotary Club of Quezon City **Education:** Northern Illinois University, M.A. in Communication Studies (1982); Baguio Colleges, B.A. in English and Education; University of the Philippines, Second Year Law. **Personal Information:** Four children: Sybil, Denden, Donnah, and Girlie. Ms. Dima-Ala Villanueva enjoys singing, dancing and acting.

Anthony M. Donato

Webmaster
ASCOT Communications
729 Jersey Avenue
Greenwood Lake, NY 10925
(888) 914-2337
Fax: (914) 477-9304
websites@ascotcom.com

4899

Business Information: Demonstrating an exceptional mastery of information technology skills, Mr. Donato assertively serves as Webmaster for ASCOT Communications. He is responsible for all day-to-day administrative support, development of the Corporation's online presence, and troubleshooting systems problems. Before joining ASCOT in 1998, Mr. Donato served as Webmaster with Magic Carpet Technologies. A systems expert, he also designs Intranet and Internet Web sites which includes graphic design, e-commerce, and multimedia communications. His success reflects his ability to think out-of-the-box and take on new challenges and responsibilities. Displaying a clear vision of goals, Mr. Donato would like to continue his work with ASCOT Communications and receive his Microsoft Certified Systems Engineer certification. A wholly owned subsidiary of Communications Corporation of America, ASCOT Communications is an established and reputable corporation. Different communication services are offered by the Corporation. Services include e-commerce integration, voice technologies, Web site development, network development, wireless communications, and information technology solutions. Founded in 1986, operations employ over 40 qualified personnel to generate annual sales of $4 million. **Career Highlights:** Webmaster, ASCOT Communications (1998-Present); Webmaster, Magic Carpet Technologies (1996-98). **Associations & Accomplishments:** Greenwood Lake Volunteer Fire Department; Membership Chairman, Greenwood Lake Chamber of Commerce. **Personal Information:** Married to Tara in 1986. Two children: Christopher and Anthony. Mr. Donato enjoys youth football coaching and teaching Web site design.

Scott Walter Eshelman

Engineering Manager
1-800-VIDEO-ON
4001 Discovery Drive, Suite 270
Boulder, CO 80303
(303) 448-7822
Fax: (303) 415-3540

4899

Business Information: Presently assuming the title and responsibilty of Engineering Manager, Mr. Eshelman oversees and directs a multitude of duties. He effectivley maintains telephone networks, video bridges, and hardware and software support. A savvy, five-year professional, Mr. Eshelman designs and maintains telecommunication networks. In collaboration with other managers, he ensures that all aspects of the operation run within the framework of the Companys' overall plan. Mr. Eshelman aids in developing goals, implementing strategies to achieve proposed goals, and directing activities of his department. His career highlights include building a communications system between his carriers such as AT&T, MCI, and Sprint. A conferencing expert, he plans to implement internet conferencing for his Company. Keeping abreast with new developments in the field, Mr. Eshelman attends professional seminars, trade shows, and reads current literature. 1-800-VIDEO-ON is a video teleconferencing company established in 1996. Headquartered in Chicago, the Company presently employs approximately 75 people to assist in the completion of various duties. There are currently two locations available to offer both ISDN and Internet-based multipoint conferencing. **Career Highlights:** Engineering Manager, 1-800-VIDEO-ON (1996-Pressent); Quality Assurance Manager, Mammoth Micro Productions (1994-96). **Education:** California University, B.S. in Electrical Engineering (1994). **Personal Information:** Mr. Eshelman enjoys hiking, fishing, backpacking, skiiing and white water rafting.

Rafael Manuel Fernandez

President
Infosinergia, S.A.
7801 Northwest 37th Street, EPS-I-5777
Miami, FL 33166
(809) 531-3403
Fax: (809) 531-3507
mfernandez@aguaita.com

4899

Business Information: Combining technical expertise and management knowledge, Mr. Fernandez serves as the President of Infosinergia, S.A. His primary responsibility is to develop innovative products and services designed to enhance and expand the Company's business operations. He designs and implements new software programs and hardware equipment for various companies and corporations. Mr. Fernandez also performs strategic planning and facilitates promotional activities on behalf of the Company. Citing his ability to meet and exceed client demands as the secret to his success, he is looking forward to taking Infosinergia, S.A. public in the near future. Coming online for the first time in 1998, Infosinergia, S.A. provides businesses and individuals in the Dominican Republic with Internet searching services. Geared to the primarily Spanish-speaking population, these information services are provided entirely in Spanish. Four skilled professionals work diligently to advance operations in this growing field. **Career Highlights:** President, Infosinergia, S.A. (1998-Present); Information Technology Consultant, United Nations Development Program (1990-Present); Co-Founder/Partner, Sistemas & Techologia (1987-Present). **Associations & Accomplishments:** Association of Computer Machinery; Dominican Researchers Network. **Education:** American University, M.S. in Management Information Systems (1990); Universidad Catolica Madre Y Maestra, Systems Engineer (1987). **Personal Information:** Married to Miguelina in 1988. Two children: Pamela and Anamelia. Mr. Fernandez enjoys basketball.

John T. Fraze

Sales Manager
Verio, Inc.
8005 South Chester Street, Suite 200
Englewood, CO 80112
(303) 708-2233
Fax: (303) 792-0082
jfraze@verio.net

4899

Business Information: Utilizing more than 15 years of extensive experience, Mr. Fraze serves as Sales Manager for Verio, Inc. He presides over a six person sales team responsible for sales in the state of Colorado. Mr. Fraze sells the Corporation's services to businesses and individuals, visiting client sites, explaining each of the Internet services, and giving advice on the best option for them or their business. In receipt of numerous internal awards such as the "Top Sales Person" of the Corporation, he credits this success to his ability to communicate extraordinarily well and aggressively take on new challenges. Mr. Fraze is committed to the success of Verio and looks forward to continuing to move up the corporate ladder into higher managerial positions. Verio, Inc. is an Internet solutions company, focusing on bringing businesses and individuals together on the Internet as well as hosting Web sites for clients. Established in 1996, the Corporation employs approximately 1,300 employees in over 50 locations across the country. Headquartered in Denver, Colorado, plans are in the works to expand operations outside of the United States. Sales are reported at $250 million a year. **Career Highlights:** Sales Manager, Verio, Inc. (1996-Present); Account Executive, Advanced Systems Group (1995-96); Account Executive, Texas Instruments (1994-95); Account Executive, Digital Equipment (1984-94). **Associations & Accomplishments:** Denver Metro Chamber of Commerce; Southeast Metro Chamber of Commerce; Internet Metro Chamber of Commerce; Denver Telcom Professionals. **Education:** Colby College, B.A.; Adelphi University. **Personal Information:** Two children: John Jr. and Harley. Mr. Fraze enjoys golf, tennis, skiing and bicycling.

Kingson Gunawan

Software Engineer
Excite@Home
4617 Fallstone Court
San Jose, CA 95124
(650) 569-2071
kingson@geocities.com

4899

Business Information: Demonstrating expertise in the information technology field, Mr. Gunawan serves as Software Engineer with Excite@Home. He is responsible for many aspects of product architecture and implementation. Mr. Gunawan is adept at understanding the complex issues encompassing the technical industry and communicates the solutions through effective product design. In a rapidly changing field, Mr. Gunawan focuses attention on regularly evaluating the performance of current products and services to ensure that the needs of his customers are being met. A leader in his field, he also offers consultations to other software engineers and colleagues. One of his most notable accomplishments was the development and successful implementation of an Internet-based search engine. Always alert to new opportunities, techniques, and approaches, Mr. Gunawan plans to create customized products in his field and continue advancement within the corporate structure. Established in 1995, Excite@Home is a subscription based Internet portal company, providing Internet access to an internationally based clientele. Approximately 1,900 people are employed at the Redwood City, California location which also serves as the global Company's headquarters. **Career Highlights:** Software Engineer, Excite@Home (1996-Present); Systems Software Engineer, Intel

(1995-96); Test Engineer, National Semiconductor (1992-95). **Associations & Accomplishments:** Eta Kappa Nu; Tau Beta Pi; Who's Who Worldwide (1994-95). **Education:** San Jose State University, M.B.A. (1993); University of Illinois at Champaign-Urbana: M.S. in Electrical Engineering (1991), B.S. in Electrical Engineering (1990).

Margaret Harmon
••• ◉ •••

Traffic Manager
America Online Inc.
22070 Broderick Drive
Sterling, VA 20166
(703) 265-2234
peggyharmon@aol.com

4899

Business Information: Functioning in the role of Traffic Manager with America Online Inc., Mrs. Harmon manages all aspect of internal information systems for a studio of approximately one hundred employees. She is responsible for and directs resource allocation to better provide cilents with needed services. Before joining AOL as Production Manager of the Enterprise Division in 1995, Mrs. Harmon served with the Army Times Publishing Company as both Online Services Technician and Office Manager. An expert in the field, she effectively utilizes a project system that tracks all of the creative technologies for America Online, as well as deciphers the supply and demand of AOL's client companies. Her accomplishments include pushing the integration of over 12 e-commerce initiatives. In the future, Ms. Harmon plans to manage American Online's integration system. "Have a good understanding of technology," is cited as her advice. Her success reflects her dedication and her ability to think outside the box, produce results, and tackle new challenges. America Online Inc. provides Internet services worldwide. Established in 1985, over 10,000 employees develop and perfect Web pages, interactive chat rooms, messenger services, and search engines for the personal and corporate use of clientele. The rendering of superior services has generated an annual revenue of$2 billion. Currently, America Online Inc. is expanding their European market. **Career Highlights:** America Online Inc.: Traffic Manager (1997-Present), Production Manager for the Enterprise Division (1995-97); Army Times Publishing Company: Online Services Tecnician (1994-95), Office Manager (1992-94). **Education:** George Mason University, B.S. (1993). **Personal Information:** Married to Larry in 1988. Mrs. Harmon enjoys reading.

Andy Jimeno
Systems Administrator
Lincoln County Technology Group
220 West 6th Street
Libby, MT 59923-1855
(406) 293-3534
Fax: (406) 293-4235
andy@libby.org

4899

Business Information: Mr. Jimeno serves as Systems Administrator for the Lincoln County Technology Group. He installs operatintg systems software, database management systems software, compilers, and utilities. A savvy, seven year professional, Mr. Jimeno monitors and maintains systems software, peripherals, and networks, as well as hardware ensuring the complete functionality and fully operational status of the entire infrastructure. As a member of the board of directors, he oversees help desk operations, providing support to customers and is involved in all aspects of technical decision-making, new purchases, pesonnel management, and finances. Planning to attend Microsoft and Cisco certification coursework, Mr. Jimeno has future aspirations of eventually working for a larger company. His success is attributed to strong family support and his ability to think outside the box, deliver results, and aggressively tackle new challenges. Lincoln County Technology Group is an Internet service provider for Lincoln County, Montana. A non-profit organization, the Group was established in 1994 to develop an outreach program that would bring the world of the Internet to the surrounding area. The Group operates from a $360,000 annual budget and has successfully marketed its services across the region. **Career Highlights:** Systems Administrator, Lincoln County Technology Group (1998-Present); Systems Solutions, Inc.: Vice President (1996-98), Internet Support (1995-96). **Associations & Accomplishments:** United States Army Reserve (1987-Present). **Education:** Montana State University, B.S. (1992). **Personal Information:** Married to Tawny in 1996. One child: Logen. Mr. Jimeno enjoys sports, reading and travel.

Melissa C. Johnsen
••• ◉ •••

Chief Technology Officer
Netstock Direct Corporation
1000 124th Avenue NE
Bellevue, WA 98005
(425) 467-7374
melissaj@netstock.com

4899

Business Information: Providing her skilled services as the Chief Technology Officer, Ms. Johnsen joined Netstock Direct Corporation in early 2000. She oversees all aspects of the Information Technology Department at Netstock. This includes all Internet, and Intranet application design and development, as well as the day to day maintenance of all back office applications that support the business of Netstock. Ms. Johnsen also assumes the oversight responsibility for the Company's corporate help desk, data center operations, systems and application security, the WAN/LAN, and general applications and infrastructure architecture. She plans to continue to raise the performance bar for the IT organization, implementing new processes, organization, and strategic technology to facilitate the growth of the business. "Always be able to look in the mirror everyday and know that you did the right thing for the company," she states. Very diverse in her technical knowledge, Ms. Johnsen performs various speaking arrangements each year. Netstock Direct, founded in 1996, is the leading Internet company in direct stock purchases (NetstockDirect.com) and dollar-based investment versus shared-based (ShareBuilder.com) investment services. **Career Highlights:** Chief Technology Officer, Netstock Direct Corporation (2000-Present); Starbucks Coffee Company: Vice President of Production Services (1998-00), Director of Technical Architecture (1998); Director of Presentation Services, Nationwide Financial Services (1995-98). **Associations & Accomplishments:** University of Washington MBA Mentor Program; Advisory Board Member, Bates Technical Institute (focus on Reentry workers); Advisory Board Member, Puget Sound Technology Institute (focus on inner city and minority students); WITI (Women in Technology International). **Education:** University of California at Davis, B.A. in History (1979). **Personal Information:** Married to John Malloy in 1996. Ms. Johnsen enjoys golf, antique collection and reading.

Christopher Laforet
President
Netpath, Inc.
2260 South Church Street, Suite 601
Burlington, NC 27215
(910) 226-0425
Fax: (910) 226-1688
laforet@netpath.net

4899

Business Information: Utilizing his vast experience in the computer field, Christopher Laforet founded Netpath, Inc., in 1995 in order to provide a quality service to clients. As President, he is responsible for overall direction, marketing and business development, public relations, and strategic planning. Mr. Laforet attributes his success to his commitment as a Christian and having a good team with which to work. Netpath, Inc. is an Internet service provider, including Web site dialup access, T-1 customer dedicated lines, and development of their own software. Netpath offers services to a two-country area. The Company focuses on two areas: one is a one-stop shop for Internet connection, and the other is a support arm, developing bulletproof software for Internet providers. **Career Highlights:** President, Netpath, Inc. (1995-Present); Proprietor/Development Head, Chris Laforet Software (1988-Present); Programmer/Developer, Dave Neathery Software (1987-88); Quality Control Technician, Roche Biomedical Labs, Inc. (1986-87). **Education:** Campbell University, B.S. (1984). **Personal Information:** Married to Sherry in 1985. One child: Rebekah Leigh. Mr. Laforet enjoys motorcycle touring and writing.

Irene Lauda
Technical Support Technician
Speed Link Inc.
53 1/2 West Huron Street, Suite 211
Pontiac, MI 48342-2121
(248) 334-5492
Fax: (248) 334-1159
ilauda@speedlink.net

4899

Business Information: Serving as Technical Support Technician for Speed Link Inc., Mrs. Lauda maintains various aspects of specialized operations on a daily basis. Offering customer service to residential and commercial clients, she performs troubleshooting tasks to provide maximum efficiency of services rendered. Handling all contract records, Mrs. Lauda evaluates client satisfaction and any noted problems to create operating procedures that amplify corporate benefits. Mrs. Lauda demonstrates her technical abilities by creating Web pages that are creative and user friendly and guiding challenging projects from start to completion. Enjoying the responsibilities of her current position, Mrs. Lauda intends to continue in this capacity with the Corporation. Providing fast and efficient Internet access service for southeast Michigan, Speed Link Inc. operates 33 branches across the state. Employing five people at the headquarters location in Pontiac, the four year old company has established a reputation of quality services. **Career Highlights:** Technical Support Technician, Speed Link Inc. (1998-Present); PC Technician, EDS/Teksystems (1998-98); Network Administrator, Royal Oak School District (1997-98). **Associations & Accomplishments:** N.U.G.I. **Education:** Control Data Institute, C.M.T. (1989); The Computer Classroom, Shell Scripting, and Systems Administration. **Personal Information:** Married to Peter in 1997. Three children: Dan, Jon, and Jen.

Wolfgang Lauffher
Network Designer
T-Online International AG
Postfach 101152
Darmstadt, Germany 64211
+49 6151680551
Fax: +49 6151680519
wolfgang@lauffher.de

4899

Business Information: Demonstrating superior talents and an excellent understanding of the technology field, Mr. Lauffher serves as the Network Designer of T-Online International AG. In his capacity, he is charged with the responsibility of designing and updating all aspects of the Company's network infrastructure as well as managing the Company's data center. With more than 10 years of professional scientific experience, Mr. Lauffher utilizes his knowledge and expertise to work directly with his fellow employees, creating the most professional network for European clients. An accomplished professional, he has published two research papers. His plans for the future include obtaining a position in upper management and providing customers more comprehensive services. The largest European Internet service provider, T-Online International AG engages in the provision of a full line of services for Internet users worldwide. The Company offers services, such as e-mail, access to various Web sites, and expedient search directories. Established in 1996, the Company operates out of several international locations for fast, comprehensive services to a host of private users and corporate clients. The Company currently functions under the direction and expertise of more than 1,300 professionals who facilitate smooth business operations. **Career Highlights:** Network Designer, T-Online International AG (1999-Present); Scientist, Fgan/FFR (1997-99). **Associations & Accomplishments:** Industry related. **Education:** Kathe-Kollwitz-Gymnasium, Abitur (1990); University of Osnabruck (1996). **Personal Information:** Mr. Lauffher enjoys reading, badminton, sports and swimming.

Gregory D. Leung
Director of Global Systems Integration Alliances
EC Cubed
29 Rolling Hills Drive
Nesconset, NY 11767
(516) 428-3894
Fax: (516) 863-1702
gregleung@prodigy.net

4899

Business Information: Serving as the Director of Global Systems Integration Alliances for EC Cubed, Mr. Leung is responsible for the development and implementation of the Company's global systems integration alliance program designed to create e-commerce solutions for Fortune 2000 companies. He is currently focusing on Asia for business expansion with future plans to expand to South America, Europe, and further into North America. A delivery service model is used to accomplish these goals. EC Cubed is striving to become the marketing leader and a major software solutions provider for the e-commerce industry. Mr. Leung plans to assist the Company achieve its goal of global expansion through systems integration alliances by developing a strong core strategy. A e-commerce software solutions provider, EC Cubed specializes in joining several software applications together to make components technology solutions. The Company focuses on Fortune 2000 companies, aiming to stay ahead of the curve by developing a core solution able to be passed down as an accepted market platform for small to mid-sized companies. EC Cubed was established in 1996 and employs the skilled services of 100 professionals. **Career Highlights:** Director of Global Systems Integration Alliances, EC Cubed (1999-Present); Vice President of Business Development, Computer Associates (1998-99); Vice President of Sales-Americas, Cheyenne Software, Division of Computer Associates (1996-98); Global Sales Manager, Cheyenne Software (1993-96). **Education:** Hofstra University, B.B.A. in Banking and Finance (1989). **Personal Information:** Married to Lisa in 1993. Mr. Leung enjoys scuba diving, rock climbing, mountain biking and skiing.

Jeffrey Jessey Limon

General Manager
J.L. Communications
3301 Conflans Road, Suite 305
Irving, TX 75061
(972) 554-8789
Fax: (972) 986-5584
jlimon@ticnet.com

4899

Business Information: Mr. Limon is the General Manager of J.L. Communications. He is responsible for engineering new techniques and negotiating through bids and quotes with the client. With 16 years of experience in the industry, he was a valuable addition to the J.L. Communications team and in four years he has dramatically impacted the success of the Company. His largest achievement with the Company has been his acquisition of the regional H&R Block contract. In the future, he hopes to finish several of his certification programs to better his service to the clientele. J.L. Communications provides voice and data cabling systems for businesses needing an advanced, more sophisticated method of communication. Established in 1987, the Company strives to upgrade the telephone and data peripheral systems to enhance the performance of an older system through simple cabling and rewiring techniques. The Company turns over $900,000 annually and operates from a staff of nine employees within Irving, Texas. **Career Highlights:** General Manager, J.L. Communications (1996-Present). **Associations & Accomplishments:** Dallas Hispanic Chamber of Commerce; Alpha Phi Omega National Service Fraternity. **Education:** Texas Technical University; University of Texas; Cisco Certified Network Analyst. **Personal Information:** Married to Terri in 1998. Mr. Limon enjoys electronics and computers.

Barbara E. Monson

Manager of Information Technology
Carlson Hospitality Worldwide
4747 Oceanside Boulevard, Suite C
Oceanside, CA 92056
(760) 631-2023
Fax: (760) 631-0807
bmonson@carlson.com

4899

Business Information: Ms. Monson serves as Manager of Information Technology for Carlson Hospitality Worldwide. As such, she is responsible for the analysis, design, coding, and installation of software used at the Reservation Center. She also manages three programmers. Developing easier and more efficient ways to service customers, Ms. Monson responds, maintains, and enhances the "Curtis-C" program. This program is involved in the delivery of reservations to hotels, and acts as a customer interface with agents and hotels. Additionally, Ms. Monson has received a patent for a travel agent program "Look to Book." This is an incentive program for travel agents that offers prizes and bonus points for travel bookings. A fully automated system, "Look to Book" tracks points and prizes received on a national level. Attributing her success to her love of computers, Ms. Monson is heavily involved in all facets of the computer field, from brainstorming ideas, to developing, writing, and installing programs. Carlson Hospitality Worldwide provides toll free reservation services for Carlson brands, including Radisson, Country, and Regent Hotels. Privately owned by Curtis Carlson, the Company works hand in hand with travel agents in providing complete travel plans to customers. Headquartered in Omaha, Nebraska, Carlson Hospitality Worldwide operates through a network of affiliates throughout the world. **Career Highlights:** Manager of Information Technology, Carlson Hospitality Worldwide (1990-Present); Programmer Analyst, Radisson Hospitality Worldwide (1989-90); Programmer, Action Software (1988-89). **Associations & Accomplishments:** Inventor of Patent #5483444 for Radisson - system for awarding credits to persons who book travel-related reservations; TT&L Industry Representative for ASC X12 - participated in development of standard Edifact messages for TT&L. **Education:** Control Data Institute, Associate's degree in Computer Science (1988); Palomar College, Associate's degree in Liberal Arts and Sciences; Certificates in Power Builder, Oracle, SQL, PL/SQL, Data Modeling. **Personal Information:** Married to Thomas in 1992.

Darius J. Munshi

Software Engineer
Houston Associates
4601 North Fairfax Drive
Arlington, VA 22203
(703) 284-8065
Fax: (703) 284-8018
djmunshi@yahoo.com

4899

Business Information: Functioning in the role of Software Engineer with Houston Associates, Mr. Munshi handles the weighty task of developing state-of-the-art PC based solutions used to control and communicate with graphic servers during emergency response simulations. Before joining Houston Associates, Mr. Munshi served as Applications Engineer for Claritas, Inc. and Software Engineer with Xerox Corporation. Additionally, he presides over all application development for the network services provided to the Company's corporate clients. Participating in the analysis, design, implementation, configuration, test, evaluation, support, and tracking of networks, databases, client server utility programs, software, and hardware also fall within the purview of his functions. Mr. Munshi is continually striving to improve performance and is committed to doing his part in taking the Company to the next level of success. His success reflects his ability to aggressively take on new challenges. Founded in 1982, Houston Associates is a network and wireless communication solutions provider for government agencies and private sector companies. Utilizing a staff of 350 qualified professionals, the Company also administers graphical simulations used to train emergency response personnel. Houston Associates boasts annual sales of $75 million. **Career Highlights:** Software Engineer, Houston Associates (1998-Present); Applications Engineer, Claritas, Inc. (1997-98); Software Engineer, Xerox (1996-97). **Education:** Monroe Community College, Associate's degree in Computer Science (1996); Rochester Institute of Technology. **Personal Information:** Mr. Munshi enjoys biking, swimming and reading.

Hyun Park

Associate
Starmedia Network, Inc.
200 Riverside Boulevard, Apartment 25E
New York, NY 10069
(212) 520-6451
Fax: (212) 548-9654
hyun@starmedia.net

4899

Business Information: Mr. Park functions as an Associate with for Starmedia Network, Inc. Beginning employment with the Company in 1999, he is dedicated to providing efficient and effective service to each customer. Mr. Park's responsibility is to find unique and innvative ideas to use on the online Web site. By doing this, individuals become attracted and then want to become involved within the Corporation. Mr. Park is also involved with meeting clients and negotiating contracts with them. Displaying a clear plan of goals, he would like to continue with Starmedia Network and eventually attain a higher position. Mr. Park credits his success to his parents and his ability to enhance systems by thinking outside the box, produce cutting edge results, and aggressively tackle new challenges. His quote is "jump on it, don't be afraid." Offering a variety of services, Starmedia Network, Inc. is an Internet portal and service provider. A young business, the Corporation was established in 1996. Starmedia Network offers services to Spanish speaking countries within Latin America and is the largest mulitimedia corporation within the these countries. Annual sales are reported at $11 million. **Career Highlights:** Associate, Starmedia Network, Inc. (1999-Present); Analyst, Morgan Stanley Dean Witter (1997-99). **Education:** Yale University, B.A. (1997); Milton Academy.

Charles Paul

President
Rise Communications, Inc.
P.O. Box 321
Jacksonville, TX 75766
(903) 939-8300
Fax: (903) 586-9188
cpaul@risecom.net

4899

Business Information: Serving as President of Rise Communications, Inc., Mr. Paul assumes responsibility for the Corporation's administration, personnel, finances, and future growth. He personally oversees the technical aspects of the Corporation, ensuring that his clients receive the best service and equipment possible. Determining and coordinating resources and schedules, overseeing time lines and assignments, and taking the lead role in driving products and services to market also fall within the purview of his functions. Mr. Paul has been in the technology industry for 10 years and credits his success thus far to persistence and having good people around him. Staying on the cutting edge of technology by attending conferences, reading trade journals, and keeping updated through the Internet, he intends to transform Rise Communications into a national corporation by utilizing strategic planning. Founded in 1998, Rise Communications, Inc. is a communications corporation providing Internet access to customers in the eastern region of the state of Texas. Reporting $500,000 in annual sales for the first year of business, the Corporation sells pagers, prepaid cellular phones, and is an authorized re-saler of Gateway and DTK computers. **Career Highlights:** President, Rise Communications, Inc. (1998-Present); President, E-Tex Internet, Inc. (1995-98); System Administrator, Lon Morris College (1993-95). **Associations & Accomplishments:** Deputy Grand Knight, Knights of Columbus. **Education:** Singapore Polytechnic University, Diploma (1987); Lon Morris College, A.A.

Michael A. Pease

Network Specialist
Equinix
21711 Filigree Court, Suite C
Ashburn, VA 20147
(703) 723-2300
Fax: (703) 421-0819

4899

Business Information: Drawing on five years of technical skills and expertise, Mr. Pease functions in the role of Network Specialist with Equinix. He is responsible for cable and fiber installations and termination routers. Also, he has been a central factor in server installation, configuration, and day-to-day network operations, maintaining the functionality and fully operational status of the systems infrastructure. Before joining the Equinix's team of professionals, Mr. Pease served as Systems Engineer with Klein Technologies, Inc. His background also includes stints as Network Administrator for Reliable Software Technologies, and a Firefighter where he got his start in technology by reparing computers and building his first NT network. Looking to the 21st Century, Mr. Pease plans on focusing on more on telecommunications technologies. As for his current success, he attributes it to a "never quit" attitude. Founded in 1998, Equinix is a start up business specializing in Internet connections. In this regard, the Company serves the general public, but offering a local network free of server crashes. Presently, the Company employs a work force of more than 60 professional, technical, and support personnel. **Career Highlights:** Network Specialist, Equinix (1999-Present); Systems Engineer, Klein Technologies, Inc. (1998-99); Network Administrator, Reliable Software Technologies (1995-98). **Associations & Accomplishments:** Association of Windows NT Professionals; Institute of Electrical and Electronics Engineers Computer Society. **Education:** Northern Virginia Community College (1999); Microsoft Certified Professional; Commscope Designing the Data Infrastructure; Ascend Max; Pipeline; Max TNT; Navis Access. **Personal Information:** Married to Cheryl in 1995. Mr. Pease enjoys being a search and rescue volunteer, being a dog handler, Harley Davidsons and camping.

Alex Petrov, Ph.D.

Project Manager
DirectNet Telecommunications
4400 MacArthur Boulevard, Suite 410
Newport Beach, CA 92660
(714) 892-4504
Fax: (949) 474-1078
apetrov@directnet.com

4899

Business Information: Dr. Petrov joined the DirectNet Telecommunications in 1997. His scope of responsibilities include strategic planning, management of on-going projects, and coordination between international projects. Dr. Petrov is also accountable for the strategic development of the Company's technology based products, systems, and services. An accomplished professional, he received an "Outstanding Teaching Award" while a Graduate Assistant at Pennsylvania State University. DirectNet Telecommunications is engaged in providing global telecommunication services. Founded in 1992, the Company specializes in voice and data communications, and employs more than 100 professional, technical, and administrative support personnel worldwide. **Career Highlights:** Project Manager, DirectNet Telecommunications (1997-Present); Graduate Assistant, Pennsylvania State University (1995-97). **Education:** Pennsylvania State University, Ph.D. in Electrical Engineering (1997); Bauman Moscow State Technical University, Optical Engineering (1993).

K. B. Reddy

President/Chief Executive Officer
Digiquest
1700 Iowa Avenue, Suite 100
Riverside, CA 92507
(909) 686-3090
Fax: (909) 686-5406

4899

Business Information: Functioning in the dual role of President and Chief Executive Officer of Digiquest Corporation, Mr. Reddy advises his staff throughout the day-to-day operations of the offices. He is involved in new business development with entreprenuerial clients and in the marketing of the Corporation. As an 18 year professional veteran of the technology field, Mr. Reddy supervises advertisement campaigns and strives to maintain the high reputation of the Corporation. One of his primary duties is that of contract negotiations with vendors, clients, and suppliers. Mr. Reddy is working to increase the revenue of the Corporation and would like to move on to a new joint venture. Success, he feels, came from his strong ability to think outside the box, deliver results, and aggressively take on new challenges. Digiquest Corporation provides information technology consulting and technical support. Established in 1995, the Corporation was originally created from its home office in Illinois. The Corporation's subsidiary in Riverside, California facilitates the needs of private and business clients within the local area. Clients are counseled on new systems and are advised on the technological future of their business. Through the combined efforts of all subsidiaries, the Corporation produces $6 million annually. **Career Highlights:** President/Chief Executive Officer, Digiquest Corporation (1995-Present); Marketing Manager, CDEC Corporation (1992-94); Plant Manager, AE Staley (1990-92); Plant Production Manager, McCain Citrus (1989-90). **Associations & Accomplishments:** GITA Member; IFT Professional; Asian American Chamber of Social; America Telugu Association; Indian American Friendship Council; International Relations Committee Chamber of Commerce City of Riverside. **Education:** University of Arkansas, M.S. (1981); Japan America Institute of Management Sciences; Japan Management Program degree; Andhra Pradesh Agricultural University, B.S. in Agricultural Sciences. **Personal Information:** Married to Kishori in 1978. Two children: Divya and Dushyanta. Mr. Reddy enjoys golf, horse riding and collecting rare coins and prints.

Johnson Regalado
Head of Sales and Marketing
Mabuhay Philippine Satellite Corporation
Suite 308, FMSG Building, 3rd Street Corner Balete Drive
New Manila, Philippines 1112
+63 2 8875788
Fax: +63 2 4166666
jregalado@mabuhaysat.com

4899

Business Information: As the Head of Sales and Marketing Department, Mr. Regalado focuses on strategic planning and is responsible for the entire region in opening up new markets. He is currently involved in establishing partnerships with four satellite teleport operators and internet gateway operators in Asia Pacific and Hawaii, each capable of Internet broadband and multimedia broadcasting, along with technology providers and integrators. Utilizing his education and capitalizing on more than 16 years of solid experience in satellite communications and telecommunications integration, he helps develop new products and new technologies with regard to broadcasting Internet over satellite communications. Mr. Regalado has always been a visionary and ahead of his time. He helps to open up new opportunities like in Hawaii, long before it was needed, now it is one of the biggest United States satellite gateway stations. Mabuhay Philippine Satellite Corporation, established in 1998, offers a wide range of satellite-based services such as Internet-over satellite, video and data transmission, broadcasting and bandwidth-on-demand. Non-traditional services such as network design/planning and consultancy are also offered. MPSC's services reach an estimated population of over two billion people. Operating and maintaining the very powerful Agila II Satellite, the Company's Ku-band coverage includes the Philippines, Taiwan, Hanoi, Hongkong, and China while its C-band coverage spans the Asia Pacific region, the Indian subcontinent and Hawaii. The last, farther extending Agila II's reaches to include the United States mainland. **Career Highlights:** Head of Sales and Marketing, Mabuhay Philippine Satellite Corporation (1999-Present); General Manager, Telecommunications Integrator Corporation (1996-99); Sales Manager, AT&T, Network Wireless Systems (1989-96); Project Coordinator, WESA/ATT&T (1986-89); Earth Station Engineer, Philippine Communications Satellite Corporation (1984-86). **Associations & Accomplishments:**

Director, Vocational Services, Rotary International. **Education:** Pamantasan Ng Lungsod Ng Maynila, M.B.A., Executive Program Candidate; St. Louis University, B.S. in Electronics and Electrical Engineering (1984). **Personal Information:** Married to Aurelia Carolyn Torres in 1980. Two children: Neil Albert and Raisa Victoria.

Chrystiana Sailer
Director of Technology
RoseTel Systems
10390 Willshire Boulevard
Los Angeles, CA 90024
(619) 565-6494

4899

Business Information: Functioning as Director of Technology for RoseTel Systems, Ms. Sailer is responsible for setting up San Diego with the world's first video dial-up phone system. Overseeing a staff of ten individuals, she recognizes the important roles of responsibility, authority, and accountability, and shows those qualities that make a manager forceful and effective. Concurrently, she fulfills the positions of Director of Technology Development with Lightning Corporation and President and Chief Executive Officer for Artists Montage, Inc. Coordinating resources, time lines, schedules, assignments, and budgets also fall within the purview of her responsibilities. Ms. Sailer attributes the substantial success she has achieved in her career to her integrity and ability to build teams with synergy and technical strength, as well as aggressively take on new challenges. Her goal is to lead RoseTel Systems into the international arena and have most United States cities wired for the video dial-up phone system within the year. RoseTel Systems offers a new, plug-in, state of the art, videophone, and video conferencing solution, combined with video program delivery and data transmission services. The services are economically provided via a revolutionary technology that runs from desktop to globally switched broadband telephones. **Career Highlights:** Director of Technology, RoseTel Systems (Present); Director of Technology Development, Lightning Corporation (Present); President/Chief Executive Officer, Artists Montage, Inc. (Present). **Associations & Accomplishments:** California Communications Alliance; Women in Business; Women in Film. **Education:** San Diego State University, B.A. (1986); Kaimuki College, Hawaii; Grossmount Community College, A.A. **Personal Information:** Ms. Sailer enjoys fishing, sailing, softball, surfing, playing guitar and art.

Eric R. Schaetzlein
Partner/Manager of Domain Services
Schlund + Partner AG
Erbprinzenstr. 4-12
Karlsruhe, Germany 76133
+49 72191374510
Fax: +49 72191374215
eric@schaetzlein.de

4899

Business Information: As a co-founder of Schlund + Partner AG, Mr. Schaetzlein serves as Partner and Manager of Domain Services. Supervising six professional experts in technology, he is responsible for DNS services, domain registration, and new business development. Possessing superior talents and an excellent understanding of technology, Mr. Schaetzlein is involved in strategy planning and formulating innovative marketing plans on behalf of the Company and its clients. His focus is on keeping the Company and clients out-front of competitors in the market place. Planning its initial public offering in the near future, Mr. Schaetzlein's future objectives include growth and expansion on an international scale, spreading across Europe in the year 2000. Established in 1995 and based out of Karlsruhe, Germany, Schlund + Partner is an Internet service and applications provider. The Company provides customers with Web space, e-mail, unified messaging, and domain registration. International in scope, the Company also offers solutions and sevices in e-commerce and hosting for individuals, families, and businesses. Schlund + Partner's parent company is 1&1 Internet AG, a subsidiary of The United Internet Group. **Career Highlights:** Partner/Manager of Domain Services, Schlund + Partner AG (1998-Present); Partner, 1&1 Internet AG (Present); Co-Founder, RWS GbR (1995-98); Software Developer, Gerkhardt Software GmbH (1992-94). **Associations & Accomplishments:** Internet Society (ISOC). **Education:** University of Karlsruhe, Vordiplom (1996); Eleonoreu-Gymnasium; Worms; Abitur. **Personal Information:** Mr. Schaetzlein enjoys going to the gym, fitness and competitive ballroom dancing. Mr. Schaetzlein participated in the Latin Ballroom Dance Comptetition in Rheinland.

Steven R. Simkins

Chief Technology Officer
MTA Solutions
619 East Ship Creek Avenue, Suite 241
Anchorage, AK 99502
(907) 793-4141
Fax: (907) 793-4122

4899

Business Information: Functioning in the role of Chief Technology Officer with MTA Solutions, Mr. Simkins supervises all aspects of day-to-day technical projects. Applying crucial engineering knowledge and expertise, he works closely with clients to develop technical enhancements which meet individual needs. He supplies constructive direction to personnel, ensuring all safety and quality standards are strictly enforced. A born innnovator, Mr. Simkins consistently strives to produce cutting edge solutions which positively impact business productivity. His primary career objectives include doubling the Company's size and implementing new training criteria for associates. He attributes his accomplishments to drive and ambition, as well as his leadership ability to form teams with synergy, technical strength, and a customer oriented attitude. MTA Solutions engages in integration of data, voice, and video technologies. A relatively new venture formed in 1998, the Company reports an annual turnover of $3 million. The Company provides specifically designed internetworking solutions comparable to the harsh environments of Alaska. Top quality solutions are produced for satellite usages, telemedicine, distance education, and other information mediums. Qualified professionals possess technical expertise in WAN, LAN, video, and Internet technologies. **Career Highlights:** Chief Technology Officer, MTA Solutions (1998-Present); Vice President of Engineering, Troika Technologies (1996-98); Director of Technology, Digitech Solutions (1995-96); Senior Engineer, Alascom, Inc. (1992-95). **Education:** University of Alaska (1987). **Personal Information:** Married to Barbara in 1991. Two children: Adam and Katherine. Mr. Simkins enjoys science.

Rod Vandenbos
Executive Vice President
Digital Internet Services Corporation
74-785 Highway 111, Suite 103
Indian Wells, CA 92210
(760) 776-0800
Fax: (760) 776-0076
rod@dis.net

4899

Business Information: Mr. Vandenbos is Executive Vice President and a co-founder of Digital Internet Services Corporation. He is responsible for strategic alliances and oversees business development, including investments and acquisitions. Before joining Digital Internet Services, he served as Technology and Strategic Business Alliance Consultant to Electronic Vision Technology Inc. after spending two years as President of etravel (TM), one of the pioneering companies in interactive Internet travel and information services. Mr. Vandenbos was promoted Executive Vice President of the Vacation Channel Online, Inc., a parent organization of etravel (TM). His solid history includes: Director New Technologies for Creative Film & Television at Universal Studios Florida, Team Strategist and Business Alliance Coordinator for Media Management Group, Inc., and Creative Director at Destiny Motion Pictures Corporation at Universal Studios Florida. A savvy, 10 year Internet and media professional with an established track record of producing consistent results, Mr. Vandenbos' career success as a leader reflects his ability to build strong teams, think out-of-the-box, and aggressively take on new challenges. Ultimately attaining the position of Chief Executive Officer or President of the Corporation serves as his future goal. Digital Internet Services Corporation is an Internet service provider. Located in Indian Wells, California, the Corporation operates a network of three other locations across the United States. Presently, Digital Internet Services employs a staff of more than 19 at the Corporation's headquarters. **Career Highlights:** Executive Vice President, Digital Internet Services Corporation (1997-Present); Executive Vice President, Electronic Vision Technology, Inc. (1996-97); President, etravel (TM) (1994-96); Vice President, The Vacation Channel Online, Inc. (1993-94). **Associations & Accomplishments:** Council for National Policy; Academy of Motion Pictures, Arts, and Science; National Association of Television, Arts, and Science; National Association of Television Programming Executives. **Education:** Trinity Western University, B.A. (1986); University of British Columbia; Pacific College; Sony Institute of America; University of Southern California. **Personal Information:** Mr. Vandenbos enjoys emerging technology, scuba, competitive shooting and motorcycle riding.

Joel S. Wright
President/Vice President Marketing and Business Development
DigitalXpress
2550 University Avenue
St. Paul, MN 55114
(651) 647-5211
joelwright@att.net

4899

Business Information: Serving as President and Vice President of Marketing and Business Development, Mr. Wright oversees and directs a number of functions on behalf of the Company and its clientele. Providing the Company professional promotional skills since coming on board to the Company in 1997, he focuses on cutting edge marketing and sales strategies and branding products and services guaranteeing an increase in profits. Concentrating his efforts towards the expansion of the client base, he strives to implement new marketing concepts into sales procedures. Organizing programs and services designed for the clients' particular needs and maintaining client relationships, Mr. Wright remains committed to the further development of the Company. Remaining with DigitalXpress, he attributes his professional success to his ability to think outside the box, take on challenges and push products to market, and deliver excellent results on behalf of the Company and its clientele. Specializing in broadcast communications, DigitalXpress was established in 1995. The Company provides services in broadband IP multicasting, satellite digital services, and television streamed on corporate LANs. Located in St. Paul, Minnesota, the Company employs a number of experienced technicians and engineers providing professional services in the production of specialized products. Committed to the furthering advancement in their product line, DigitalXpress focuses on implementing new technologies in order to provide a more efficient product. **Career Highlights:** President/Vice President Marketing and Business Development, DigitalXpress (1997-Present); Manager, Business Development, The Boeing Company (1985-97). **Associations & Accomplishments:** International Television Association; USDLA. **Education:** Western Baptist College, B.S. (1981). **Personal Information:** Married to Diane in 1979. Three children: Robert, Sara, and Jacob. Mr. Wright enjoys coaching youth sports, camping and outdoor activities.

4900 Electric, Gas, and Sanitary Services

- 4911 Electric services
- 4922 Natural gas transmission
- 4923 Gas transmission and distribution
- 4924 Natural gas distribution
- 4925 Gas production and/or distribution
- 4931 Electric and other services combined
- 4932 Gas and other services combined
- 4939 Combination utilities, nec
- 4941 Water supply
- 4952 Sewerage systems
- 4953 Refuse systems
- 4959 Sanitary services, nec
- 4961 Steam and air-conditioning supply
- 4971 Irrigation systems

Bruce N. Anderson
Manager of Technology Planning and Application Services
Duke Energy Corporation
526 South Church Street, P.O. Box 1006
Charlotte, NC 28202
(704) 382-4355
Fax: (704) 382-4545
bnanders@duke-energy.com

4911

Business Information: Mr. Anderson currently holds the demanding position of Manager of Technology Planning and Application Services with Duke Energy Corporation. He coordinates and leads technology planning for both the enterprise and diverse business units. Additionally, he is in charge of strategic and technical planning and application support. The Corporation is facing a number of challenges in the months ahead. As an example of the diverse expansion of energy services, Duke is building and/or acquiring power generation plants worldwide and expanding gas gathering and pipelines throughout the United States, Canada, South America, and Australia. An example is the Corporation's efforts to establish pipelines in Australia to connect Sydney for the 2000 Olympics. It is critical that the Corporation completes the job correctly and efficiently. Duke Energy Corporation has other projects currently in process including the gas processing plants in Peru. Mr. Anderson has high expectations for the future of the Corporation. He hopes to see Duke Energy become the leading energy company in North America to use nuclear energy, fossil fuels, and natural gases. Mr. Anderson holds an extensive background in the energy

field and has the knowledge, dedication, and determination to assist the Corporation in its expansion and development. Duke Energy Corporation is an energy service business providing a variety of services including gas pipeline, gas gathering, energy trading, electric generation, and distribution. The Corporation's clients are located in South America, Europe, and the Pacific. Over 25,000 natural gas wells are used to assist this international Corporation in providing services. Established in 1904, Duke Energy presently reports annual revenues in excess of $17.6 billion. **Career Highlights:** Manager of Technology Planning and Application Services, Duke Energy Corporation (1995-Present); Manager of Application Delivery, Carolina Power & Light (1991-95); Senior Manager, Price Waterhouse (1984-91). **Associations & Accomplishments:** Society of Information Management; Information Technology Complexity Reduction Work Group; Instructor, Master of Business Administration, University of North Carolina at Charlotte. **Education:** Cleveland State University, M.B.A. (1980); Bowling Green State University, B.S. in Economics (1971); Harvard University; John F. Kennedy School of Government (1983). **Personal Information:** Married to Flor in 1974. Three children: Jessica, Victoria, and Cristina. Mr. Anderson enjoys photography, bike riding, golf and motorcycles.

Larry J. Bailey
Technical Specialist/Scientist
Southern California Edison
2255 Walnut Grove
Rosemead, CA 91770
(626) 302-5070
Fax: (909) 242-8470
baileyL@sce.com

4911

Business Information: Recruited to Southern California Edison in 1997, Mr. Bailey serves in a dual role of Technical Specialist and Scientist. He presides over the administration of the Oracle Database, assisting with application development, performing routine maintenance functions, and troubleshooting problems as necessary. Mr. Bailey also works with other Company databases, utilizing more than 15 years of experience in the performance of his duties. His ability to resolve complex situations rapidly has contributed greatly to his professional success. Continually striving to improve performance, he anticipates a promotion to a higher level managerial position within the Company's database arena. Mr. Bailey's success reflects his ability to think outside the box, deliver results, and take on new challenges. An innovative leader in the electrical utility industry, Southern California Edison has been offering customers with quality services since 1886. The Company provides electricity to millions of customers in Southern California with the help of a 13,000 member work force. Southern California Edison has expanded operations internationally throughout its more than 100 year history and now serves individuals and businesses alike around the world. **Career Highlights:** Technical Specialist/Scientist, Southern California Edison (1997-Present); Senior Technical Consultant, Sanwa Bank California (1990-97); Software Engineer, Sterling Software, Inc. (1987-90). **Associations & Accomplishments:** Ordained Minister of the Gospel. **Education:** Riverside City College, A.S. (1995). **Personal Information:** Married to Phyllis in 1973. Two children: Larry Jr. and Shelli. Mr. Bailey enjoys tennis and fishing.

Donald A. Barrows
IS/GIS Coordinator
Lassen Municipal Utility
P.O. Box 2341
Susanville, CA 96130-2341
(530) 257-6932
Fax: (530) 257-4554
dbarrows@psln.com

4911

Business Information: Mr. Barrows functions in the role of IS/GIS Coordinator for Lassen Municipal Utility. He is responsible for coordinating information systems and GIS resources and projects. Before coming on board to Lassen Municipal Utility in 1993, Mr. Barrows served as Hydrographer with Gahagan & Bryant Associates. His background also includes stints as Field Engineer for Morrison Knudsen, Inc. and Land Surveyor with Escatech Corporation. A 26-year professional, Mr. Barrows is also involved in GIS development, network administration, and systems integration, as well as providing PC support. In this context, he sets up the geographic information system, mapping database, and LAN network. In the future, Mr. Barrows plans to remain with the Company and eventually move into a higher position that involves more decision-making. Lassen Municipal Utility provides electric utilities to the surrounding community of Susanville, California. Established in 1988, the Company offers electrical services to facilitate the needs of several clients within the area. A nonprofit organization, the Company manages the effective distribution of electricity between 12,000 meters. **Career Highlights:** IS/GIS Coordinator, Lassen Municipal Utility (1993-Present); Hydrographer, Gahagan & Bryant Associates (1988-93);

Field Engineer, Morrison Knudsen, Inc. (1983-88); Land Surveyor, Escatech Corporation (1978-83). **Associations & Accomplishments:** Geospatial Information and Technology Association. **Education:** Dakota Wesleyan University, B.A. (1973). **Personal Information:** Married to Linda in 1993. Mr. Barrows enjoys travel, art glass, jewelry design, cooking and photography.

Michael Bouwma
UNIX Team Leader
Alliant Energy
222 West Washington Avenue
Madison, WI 53703-2719
(608) 252-0456
Fax: (608) 283-6933
mikebouwma@alliant-energy.com

4911

Business Information: In his position as UNIX Team Leader for Alliant Energy, Mr. Bouwma supervises UNIX system operations. He monitors staff productivity, facilitating and encouraging optimum performance and ensuring that all employees work together to achieve a common goal. His knowledge and skills are utilized in technology management, and he excels in using information technology to reduce costs. Highly regarded, Mr. Bouwma continues to grow professionally through the fulfillment of his responsibilities and his involvement in the advancement of operations. Alliant Energy provides electric, water, and gas utility services for more than one million customers. Established in 1915, the Corporation employs a skilled staff to facilitate all aspects of operation, such as business acquisition, maintenance and repair, and addressing customer queries. The Corporation is located in Madison, Wisconsin and is a vital part of the community. Presently, the Corporation employs a work force of more than 6,000 people. **Career Highlights:** UNIX Team Leader, Alliant Energy (1994-Present); UNIX Administrator, Madison Kipp Corporation (1993-94); UNIX Administrator, Custom Products Corporation (1989-93). **Associations & Accomplishments:** Interex. **Education:** Technology related. **Personal Information:** Married to Peggy in 1982. Mr. Bouwma enjoys horses and computer games.

Ziad E. Chbeir
General Manager
If and Then
32 High Street
Croton On Hudson, NY 10520
(212) 627-6079
Fax: (212) 658-9356
zchbeir@if-then.com

4911

Business Information: In his position as General Manager of If and Then, Mr. Chbeir oversees and directs day to day operations in the New York region. A co-owner, he demonstrates strong leadership and organizational skills in maintaining the fiscal budget, acquiring new business, and presiding over the completion of administrative duties. In addition, Mr. Chbeir is in charge of computer systems maintenance to ensure flawless operation. His skills and knowledge are vital to Company's development, and he plans to build on past achievements to encourage future Company expansion. His success reflects his leadership ability to form teams with synergy and technical strength and deliver results on behalf of the Company and its clientele. In and Then provides virtual chief information officer services to manage information technology from a strategic planning and business goals perspective. The Company also offers e-Commerce development, enterprise resource planning, and customer relationship management. Established in 1999, the Company employs an enterprising staff to facilitate all aspects of operation. If and Then is headquartered in Croton on Hudson, New York and provides service to clients internationally. **Career Highlights:** General Manager, If and Then (1999-Present); Principal Consultant, Inacom (1999-00); Managing Consultant, Software Spectrum (1996-99). **Associations & Accomplishments:** Tau Beta Pi; Polytechnic Alumni. **Education:** Polytechnical University: M.S. in Electrical Engineering (1995), B.S. in Computer Engineering. **Personal Information:** Married to Janet in 1996. One child: Kristin. Mr. Chbeir enjoys wind surfing, skiing, horseback riding and travel.

Rohdonda R. Hardin
Information Technology Training Specialist
American Electric Power Company
1 Riverside Plaza, Floor 8
Columbus, OH 43215
(614) 223-3183
Fax: (614) 223-3737
rrhardin@aep.com

4911

Business Information: Ms. Hardin serves as Information Technology Training Coordinator for American Electric Power Company. Utilizing strong knowledge of the information technology field, she is one of twelve team members who provide training to customer service employees for working on computers. Highly regarded, Ms. Hardin coordinates training courses, provides all necessary tools needed for the training, and offers assistance to employees if they have any questions or concerns. A successful two-year professional, she was recruited to the Company in 1998 to oversee all aspects of training in an effort to help keep the Company on the leading edge of customer service and support. In the future, she looks forward to completing her Master's degree and moving up to a higher position within the Company's corporate structure. Ms. Hardin's success is due to her ability to communicate effectively, tackle all challenges, and deliver results on behalf of American Electric Power and its clientele. Founded in 1917, the American Electric Power Company provides customers with a large variety of electrical services. Located in Columbus, Ohio, the Company has a customer base of residential and business customers within a seven-state radius. With over 18,000 employees, the Company is committed to providing quality services and efficient hookups and troubleshooting methods **Career Highlights:** Information Technology Training Coordinator, American Electric Power Company (1998-Present). **Education:** Franklin University, M.B.A. (In Progress); Ohio University, M.S. in Education (1994). **Personal Information:** One child: Alex. Ms. Hardin enjoys reading and travel.

Angela D. Hare

Information Technology Specialist
Central Electric
128 Wilson Road
Sanford, NC 27330
(919) 774-4131
Fax: (919) 774-1860
angela.hare@central.ncemcs.com

4911

Business Information: With several years educational and occupational experience, Mrs. Hare began her career with Central Electric in 1999. As Information Technology Specialist, she is responsible for maintaining all 15 systems within the Company as well as ensuring all software programs are running efficiently. Additional duties include management and oversight of all automated systems and Windows NT administration. Currently attending classes to obtain her Microsoft Certified Systems Engineer certification, Mrs. Hare strives to incorporate her skill and knowledge into the field of networking administration. Established in 1940, Central Electric is a member owned company that provides electrical and natural gas services to five counties in central North Carolina. From their headquarters in Sanford, North Carolina, the Company employs the skilled services of 59 personnel to provide and maintain electrical and natural gas services to customers. Central Electric has more than 50 years experience in the industry, and will continue to provide optimal service to the residents of central North Carolina. **Career Highlights:** Information Technology Specialist, Central Electric (1999-Present); Software Analyst, Applied Computer Technologies (1997-99). **Associations & Accomplishments:** Microsoft Technet; 4-H Honor Club. **Education:** Central Carolina Community College, A.S. in Micro Computer Systems Technology (1997); Microsoft Certified Systems Engineer (In Progress). **Personal Information:** Married to Dewayne in 1997. One child: Cassidy Marie. Mrs. Hare enjoys gardening, fishing, horseback riding and cooking.

Pat E. Howard

Director of Information Services
Commonwealth Energy
15991 Red Hill Avenue
Tustin, CA 92780-7320
(714) 259-2511
Fax: (714) 259-2599
phoward@powersavers.com

4911

Business Information: Mrs. Howard serves in the role of Director of Information Services of Commonwealth Energy. She directs all functions of the information services and data processing departments. A savvy, 13 year professional in her field, she oversees all aspects of programming, network support, data entry, data research, equipment evaluation, and purchasing. Mrs. Howard utilizes her extensive experience and expertise in planning and overseeing projects, and working with senior management to determine systems development strategies and standards. Her success is attributed to her work ethic instilled in her by her mother. Future endeavors for Mrs. Howard include making changes in the EDI process and Web based activity environment as well as eventually attaining the position of Chief Information Officer. Commonwealth Energy is an energy services provider. Established in 1997, the Company is dedicated to providing continuous electrical power to each resident within the area. A team of 250 professional, technical, and support personnel work together to enhance customer service and provide new alternatives and processes to increase productivity and efficiency. **Career Highlights:** Commonwealth Energy Corporation: Director of Information Services (1999-Present), Data Processing Manager (1998-99); Data Processing/Office Manager, National Sanitary Supply Company (1998). **Associations & Accomplishments:** American Business Woman's Association; ABWA Impact Council; Chapman University Women History Week Committee; Oshmans Women and Sports Recognition Day; Race for the Cure; Remarkable Woman Among Us NAWBO; Anaheim Children Art Festival; Campus Crusade for Christ. **Education:** University of Redlands, B.A. (1978); Long Beach City College, A.A. (1977). **Personal Information:** Married to Keith L. in 1960. Three children: Richard, Elaine, and Beth.

Rieko Ikeda-Hayes

Programmer Analyst
Omaha Public Power District
315 Elk Ridge Drive
Papillion, NE 68046-4368
(402) 533-7335
Fax: (402) 597-6210
rikeda-hayes@oppd.com

4911

Business Information: Serving as Programmer Analyst of Omaha Public Power District, Ms. Ikeda-Hayes is responsible for working closely with systems users and management to analyze, specify, and design business applications to keep the Company on the industry's leading edge. Possessing academics and expertise in the technology field, Ms. Ikeda-Hayes is charged with programming applications, developing Web sites, and taking care of all troubleshooting functions. As the Company's Webmaster, she manages two internal and one external Web sites, as well as oversees the Company's Intranet with over 5,000 users. Ms. Ikeda-Hayes is also trained and certified in both UNIX and Oracle. Working for an outstanding Company, she plans to remain with the Company and eventually attain the position of Systems Manager. A supportive family and her extensive academic ties are key reasons for Ms. Ikeda-Hayes' professional success. Omaha Public Power District engages in production of electricity in a nuclear power station and distribution to the community. The largest of its kind in the state of Nebraska, the Omaha Public Power District employs a work force of more than 5,000 professional, technical, and support staff to oversee all aspects of day-to-day operations. The Power District was established in 1948. **Career Highlights:** Programmer Analyst, Omaha Public Power District (1995-Present); Laboratory Assistant, Dana College (1992-95); Science Teacher, Fukushima Private School (1990-91). **Education:** Bellevue University, M.S. in Computer Science (2000); Dana College, B.A. in Chemistry and Mathematics. **Personal Information:** Married to Alexis N. in 1995. Ms. Ikeda-Hayes enjoys travel, investments, music and arts applications.

Barney McCauley

Principal Information Technology Specialist
SMUD
6001 South Street
Sacramento, CA 95817-1825
(916) 932-5186

4911

Business Information: Mr. McCauley has served with SMUD in a variety of roles since joining the Company in 1996. Promoted to the position of Principal Information Technology Specialist in 1997, Mr. McCauley is responsible for coordinating all aspects of project management requirements. In this context, he coordinates resources, schedules, communication links, and budgets. He is accountable for completing information technology projects on time and within budget as well as assisting in the design and development of state-of-the-art software solutions, garnering more of the computer's power. A savvy, 25 year veteran of technology, Mr. McCauley also teaches information technology and management courses to undergraduate and graduate students at the University of Phoenix. He has been teaching for 14 years. Attributing his success to keeping on top of technology, Mr. McCauley plans on retirement in the near future. SMUD is an electric utility business serving the needs of the Sacramento, California area. Established in 1947, the Company has supported the city since the implementation of a publicly owned facility to govern electricity was created. **Career Highlights:** SMUD: Principal Information Technology Specialist (1997-Present), Supervisor Software Administrators (1996-97). **Associations & Accomplishments:** Professor, University of Phoenix. **Education:** Sacramento State University, M.S. (1979). **Personal Information:** Married to Eilean in 1975. Four children: Katie, Scott, Kevin, and Jamie.

Gary D. Muller

Senior Customer Support Officer
Eskom
P.O. Box 2100
Bellville, South Africa 7535
+27 219152851
Fax: +27 219152763
gary.muller@eskom.co.za

4911

Business Information: Displaying his expertise in the field of information technology, Mr. Muller serves as the Senior Customer Support Officer for Eskom. He assumes responsibility for the Company's mainframe and netware support administration throughout the country. Additionally, he handles and maintains software, hardware, and some programs within the Management Information Systems Department. A systems expert, he performs routine maintenace, monitors the daily activity, provides back up systems, and ensures the complete network security, reliability, and integrity. Consistently achieving quality performance, Mr. Muller looks forward to increasing his professional responsibilities and aspires to a managerial position. His success reflects his ability to think outside the box, produce cutting edge solutions, and aggressively tackle new challenges. Eskom is an electricity supplier for South Africa. The Company was established in 1923 and provides services to residents and businesses in all areas of the country. More than 10,000 administrative, engineering, and support personnel are employed in all areas of operation. Eskom reports R500 million each year in annual revenue. **Career Highlights:** Senior Customer Support Officer, Eskom (1996-Present); Programmer, Sweet-Orr & Lybro (1995-96); Creditors Clerk, Foschini (1994-95). **Associations & Accomplishments:** Computer Society of South Africa. **Education:** Peninsula Technikon, received three diplomas in Information Technology (1993-95). **Personal Information:** Mr. Muller enjoys reading, movies, camping and going to the gym.

Corey D. Ramey

Information Systems Engineer
Tennessee Valley Authority
400 West Summit Hill Drive
Knoxville, TN 37902
(865) 632-2016
Fax: (865) 632-7170
coreydramey@yahoo.com

4911

Business Information: Concentrating his efforts on anit-virus protection, executive support, and networking, Mr. Ramey serves as Information System Engineer for the Tennessee Valley Authority. Utilizing his four years of experience in the field of technology, he focuses his attention on the development of cutting edge products and systems including home security systems and Internet security systems. Alert to changes in technologies and technical approaches, Mr. Ramey implements procedures and policies in order to produce a more effective product gaurunteeing higher levels of efficiency and productivity. Maintaining the department budget, he initiates the purchases of hardware and software for the building of complex networks within budget guidelines. Committed to his career with the Tennessee Valley Authority, Mr. Ramey continues to grow professionally through the fulfillment of his responsibilities and his involvement in the advancement of operations. A diversified division of the federal government, Tennessee Valley Authority is an electrical utility department established in 1933. Located in Knoxville, Tennessee, the Company employs a skilled staff of 13,000 expert electricians, and administrators who facilitate every aspect of design, manufacture, quality control, and distribution of services. The largest power supplier in the United States, the Company serves a seven state region. **Career Highlights:** Tennessee Valley Authority: Information Systems Engineer (1999-Present), Computer Specialist (1999); Graduate Teaching Assistant, University of Tennessee at Knoxville (1997-99). **Associations & Accomplishments:** Association of Computing Machinery; Alpha Phi Alpha Fraternity, Inc.; Who's Who Among American Colleges and Universities. **Education:** University of Tennessee at Knoxville: Ph.D. (In Progress), M.S. in Computer Science (1998), B.S. in Computer Science (1996). **Personal Information:** Mr. Ramey enjoys computer animation, Web publishing, drawing, basketball and volunteering.

Kathleen K. Shumway

Supervisor of Software Development
Niagara Mohawk Power Corporation
P.O. Box 63, Lake Road
Lycoming, NY 13093
(315) 349-1048
Fax: (315) 349-7661
shumwayk@nimo.com

4911

Business Information: As Supervisor of Software Development at the Nine Mile Point Nuclear Station, Ms.

Shumway oversees all the implementation of software systems at the Site. She is accountable for the update of all existing systems as well as the integration of new ones as needed. An experienced 14-year computer science professional, Ms. Shumway contributes to the strategic direction and vision of information management at the Site. Coordinating resources and schedules, overseeing timelines and assignments, and ensuring the integrity, security, and reliability of the systems function fall within the purview of Ms. Shumway's responsibilities. Her professional success reflects her ability to think out-of-the-box and take on new challenges and responsibilities. Ms. Shumway's goal is to become more involved in project management. Amergen recently purchased the nuclear division of Niagara Mohawk Power Corporation. Final turnover is scheduled for first quarter 2000. The 1,350 permanent personnel at the Site operate the two nuclear plants 24 hours a day, 7 days a week to generate electricity. Safety is the prime goal of all employees at the Plant. **Career Highlights:** Niagara Mohawk Power Corporation: Supervisor of Software Development (1998-Present), Project Manager/Information Management (1996-98), Systems Analyst/Software Development (1994-96). **Associations & Accomplishments:** Phi Kappa Phi National Honor Society; Delta Mu Delta National Honor Society. **Education:** State University of New York at Oswego: M.B.A (1997), M.S. (1995), B.A. in Computer Science (1985). **Personal Information:** Married to Donald in 1971. Two children: Jeremy and Renee. Ms. Shumway enjoys horseback riding, caring for her dogs and gardening.

Rebecca M. Wingenroth

Director of Business Development
GPU Energy
2800 Pottsville Pike
Reading, PA 19605
(610) 921-6451
Fax: (610) 921-6526
ewingenroth@gpu.com

4911

Business Information: As Director of Business Development of GPU Energy, Ms. Wingenroth is accountable for all business growth. With the offer of providing location services at no cost, Ms. Wingenroth attracts and retains corporations from throughout the world to locate in the Company's franchise territory. She establishes business set ups for clients and recruits new businesses. Working closely with her team of 16 employees, she ensures customer satisfaction and resolves all employee conflicts. Ms. Wingenroth has been published in Site Selection Magazine regarding questions, comments, and regulations, and is involved in public speaking. She continues to grow professionally and hopes to expedite continued promotion through the fulfillment of her responsibilities and continued Company growth. A division of GPU Inc., GPU Energy is the largest electric utility infrastructure company in the nation. Located in Pennsylvania and New Jersey, the Company provides transmissions and distribution of electric services throughout the world. Established in 1905, local operations in Reading, Pennsylvania employ 10,000 individuals and report an estimated annual revenue of $4 billion. **Career Highlights:** Director of Business Development, GPU Energy (1996-Present); Director, Customer Services, Met-Ed/Penelec (1994-96); Manager of Rates, Metropolitan Edison Company (1989-94). **Associations & Accomplishments:** Investor Owned Utilities Economic Development Association; D-21 International Utility Economic Development Organization; PA Economy League; Board of Governor's; Berks County March of Dimes, Board Member and Public Affairs Chairman; Elizabethtown College; United Kingdom Board Member, American Chamber of Commerce. **Education:** Purdue Krannert, M.S.M. (1992). **Personal Information:** Ms. Wingenroth enjoys sports, reading and gardening.

Wayne J. Gautreaux

UNIX Systems Administrator
El Paso Energy
4 East Greenway Plaza
Houston, TX 77046-0400
(713) 940-6961
Fax: (713) 402-4516
wgautreaux@sonat.com

4922

Business Information: Mr. Gautreaux functions in the role of UNIX Systems Administrator with El Paso Energy. In his capacity, he manages, upgrades, installs, and improves both workstation and server environments for the entire Company. A savvy, 15 year expert in the technology field, Mr. Gautreaux assisted in the implementation of several cutting edge programs including a new software interface and Windows NT. Looking to the new millennium, Mr. Gautreaux hopes to keep up with emerging technology and increase his education within UNIX technology so he can further the Company's database system. His success is attributed to his parents and his ability to think outside the box, deliver results, and aggressively take on challenges and new responsibilities. El Paso Energy is a petroleum and gas exploration company. Recognized as the largest gas line facility in the United States, the Company has been strengthening its standing in the industry for over 40 years. Headquartered in Houston, Texas, the Company focuses on providing effective gas programs and exploration for the industry. **Career Highlights:** UNIX Systems Administrator, El Paso Energy (1997-Present); UNIX Systems Administrator, Zilkha Energy Company (1996-97); UNIX Systems Administrator, Landmark Graphics Inc. (1991-96). **Education:** Stephen F. Austin State University, Master's degree in Geology (1991); Nicholls State University, Bachelor's degree in Geology (1984). **Personal Information:** Mr. Gautreaux enjoys reading, computer games and fishing.

Domingo Llagostera

Senior Engineering Systems Analyst
El Paso Energy Corporation
15634 Rosewood Hill Court
Sugar Land, TX 77478
(713) 420-3761
Fax: (713) 420-5037
mllagost@ev1.net

4922

Business Information: Possessing advanced analytical skills and technical expertise, Mr. Llagostera has received recognition for his diligence and management skills through several promotions to his current position of Senior Engineering Systems Analyst for El Paso Energy Corporation. Drawing from over two decades of occupational experience, he adeptly supervises and maintains engineering applications, manages the network infrastructure, and performs daily diagnostic testing. Utilizing new techniques and progressive technology, he also develops software for the Corporation and is engaged in Web design. Mr. Llagostera has enjoyed tremendous success in his current position with the Corporation, and he aspires embark on his own business venture as an independent consultant. Established in 1928, El Paso Energy Corporation is engaged in natural gas transmission, gas gathering and processing, gas and oil production, power generation, merchant energy services, international project development and telecommunications. El Paso Energy spans North America with over 40,000 miles of the best-run, safest, most reliable natural gas transmission pipeline in the business. The Corporation, located in the metropolis of Houston, Texas, employs a collective work force of over 3,000 administrative, technical, and operational personnel. **Career Highlights:** Senior Engineering Systems Analyst, El Paso Energy Corporation (1998-Present); Systems Analyst/CAD Coordinator, Tenneco Energy/TGP (1990-98); Drafter/Systems Coordinator, Tenneco Corporation (1979-90). **Associations & Accomplishments:** School District Parent Teacher Association; St. Theresa Catholic Church Parish; Intelliquest Technology Panel. **Education:** University of Houston/Houston Community College, Associate's degree in Pre-Engineering (1986). **Personal Information:** Married to Maria Mercedes in 1980. Three children: Domingo M., Alejandro D., and Brittany M. Mr. Llagostera enjoys travel, fishing, golf and softball.

Jeffrey W. Carter

Manager of Systems
Consolidated Natural Gas
625 Liberty Avenue
Pittsburgh, PA 15222
(412) 690-1285
Fax: (412) 690-7602
jcarter@corp.cng.com

4923

Business Information: As Manager of Systems Administration for Consolidated Natural Gas, Mr. Carter is responsible for the hardware and software maintenance of 115 midrange applications data servers. These servers include human resources, financial, and the Internet. An expert, he also oversees the gas flow and nomination, help desk, electronic commerce, and electronic data interchange. Determining future resource requirements and schedules, overseeing time lines and assignments, and maintaining system functionality and fully operational status also fall within the purview of Mr. Carter's responsibilities. Supervising 11 employees, he maintains his extensive knowledge in the industry through frequent attendance at seminars and courses pertaining to his field. In the future, Mr. Carter is looking to expand his present position and obtain recognition as the Director or Vice-President within his Department. Consolidated Natural Gas is recognized as one of the largest companies specializing in the production, transportation, distribution, and marketing of natural gas in the United States. The customer base is primarily centered in New York, Ohio, Pennsylvania, Virginia, and West Virginia, with sparse locations throughout the Northeast and Mid-Atlantic. With such a broad base, the Company provides natural gas service to nearly two million clients throughout the nation. **Career Highlights:** Manager of Systems Administration, Consolidated Natural Gas (1997-Present); Thrift Drug: Manager Teca Support (1991-97), Project Manager (1988-91). **Associations & Accomplishments:** Treasurer, Youth Baseball Organization. **Education:** Waynesburg College. **Personal Information:** Married to Barbara in 1982. Two children: Sean and Nicole. Mr. Carter enjoys golf, bowling and managing baseball.

Gary S. Merritt

Information Technology Manager
Greeley Gas Company
1301 Pennsylvania Street, Suite 800
Denver, CO 80203
(303) 831-5675
Fax: (303) 837-9549
gary.merritt@greeleygas.com

4924

Business Information: Displaying his skills in this highly specialized position, Mr. Merritt serves as Information Technology Manager with Greeley Gas Company. He provides the maintenance of all mobile terminals, customer support, and troubleshooting. Managing all telecommunication vendors, Mr. Merritt oversees the implementation of the latest technology, gauranteeing complete client satisfaction. Supervising the production of two employees, he incorporates skilled training programs to enhance customer service and project management. Focused on the further progression of the Company, Mr. Merritt played a major role in the design and development of the Company's Web site. He plans to further his education by obtaining his master's and bachelor's degrees to facilitate promotional opportunities within Greeley Gas Company. Mr. Merritt attributes his success to his relationship with Jesus Christ. Established in 1932, Greeley Gas Company is an established and reputable natural gas utility company providing coverage for the Kansas and Colorado regions. Headquartered in Denver, Colorado, the Company employs the expertise of 300 qualified personnel to meet the demands of a growing clientele. Specifically offering services in energy utility for residential and commercial homes and offices, the Company generates $250 million in annual revenue. **Career Highlights:** Information Technology Manager, Greeley Gas Company (1999-Present); United Cities Gas Company: Information Technology Coordinator (1997-99), Assistant Manager of Management Information Technology (1995-97), Information Technologyf Systems Analyst (1990-95). **Associations & Accomplishments:** Charter Member, Kiwanis Club; Chartered Pack 14, Cub Scout Pack 1989; Alderman/Vice Mayor of Spring Hill, Tennesee. **Education:** Regents University, B.S. in Management Information Systems (In Progress); University of South Dakota (1977). **Personal Information:** Married. Six children: Nathaniel, Joel, Michael, Evie, Benjamin, and Laura. Mr. Merritt enjoys walking, biking and reading.

Joshua Batiste

Applications Manager
Reliant Energy HL&P
12301 Kurland Drive
Houston, TX 77034
(713) 945-7656
Fax: (713) 945-7399
joshua-batiste@reliantenergy.com

4931

Business Information: As Applications Manager of Reliant Energy HL&P, Mr. Batiste manages the development of several computer applications. He designed and deployed cutting edge monitoring tools used at electrical power plants. Mr. Batiste serves as an international liaison providing tool creation assistance for increasing overseas production, service time, and work management systems. Because Mr. Batiste services regulated and deregulated plants, he has had to learn to process them separately. One of his goals for the future involves the complete deregulation of the facilities hopefully within the next two years. At all of the electrical facilities within the Company, Mr. Batiste also handles all computer applications, software and hardware installations, and repairs. His career highlights include serving as Lead Program Instructor at a technical institute, and supporting the entire construction life cycle of a power plant from start to finish. In the future, he is looking to expand his role within the Company by becoming more involved with the international plants. Mr. Batiste is also aspiring to become a specialist internationally. Established in 1895, Reliant Energy HL&P provides electric utilities for many residents in the Houston, Texas area. The Company is a subsidiary of Reliant Energy Corporation, a Fortune 500 energy company. Reliant Energy HL&P generates and transmits electric and gas power for consumption worldwide. International in scope, the Company employs 11,000 personnel to assist in repairs, connections, and customer services. **Career Highlights:** Applications Manager, Reliant Energy HL&P (1980-Present); Programming Director, Control Data Corporation (1978-79); Computer Analyst, Computer Sciences (1976-78). **Associations & Accomplishments:** Phi Beta Sigma Fraternity; Junior Achievement; Volunteer, Mason City of Hope; Volunteer, Juvenile Diabetes Foundation; Volunteer, Houston International Festival; Volunteer, Power of Houston. **Education:** Southern University, B.S. (1974); College of the Mainland; University of Houston. **Personal Information:** Mr. Batiste enjoys gardening, genealogy, aerobics and fishing.

Michael J. Chohrach

Manager, SAP Applications Production Support
Reliant Energy
6161 Rothway
Houston, TX 77040
(713) 934-5273
Fax: (713) 934-5339
michael-chohrach@reliantenergy.com

4931

Business Information: Presently serving as the Manager of SAP Applications Production Support for Reliant Energy, Mr. Chohrach is responsible for all enhancements and corrections to the SAP production system. He is also responsible for consulting with clients in order to prioritize needs based on business impact. Possessing advanced technical abilities, Mr. Chohrach enjoys his work and would like to continue serving the Corporation in the future. Established in 1982, Houston Industries, Inc. merged with NorAm Energy in 1997 to form Reliant Energy. Providing natural gas and electric services to residential, commercial, and industrial customers throughout a six state region, the Houston, Texas based Corporation currently employs 15,000 personnel members throughout sevral facilities. **Career Highlights:** Manager, SAP Applications Production Support, Reliant Energy (1999-Present); Information Technology Lead - SAP Materials Management Functional Implementation Team, Houston Industries, Inc. (1997-98); Entex, A Noram Energy Company: Senior Programmer Analyst (1996-97), Programmer Analyst (1993-96). **Associations & Accomplishments:** Institute for Certification of Computing Professionals; Certified Computing Professional. **Education:** Texas A&M University, B.B.A. (1985). **Personal Information:** Married to Karen in 1996. Mr. Chohrach enjoys golf, reading, computers and woodworking.

David J. Horn

Video Services Product Line Manager
Entergy Services
200 Westbank Expressway
Gretna, LA 70053-5615
(504) 364-7683
Fax: (504) 364-7765
dhorn@entergy.com

4931

Business Information: As Video Services Product Line Manager with Entergy Services Inc, a unit of Entergy Corporation, Mr. Horn manages 30 video conferencing sites, is responsible for health and quality of the video conferencing network, supports Satellite uplinks and down links and other video related services. Mr. Horn consults with other business entities within Entergy Corporation as well as other companies and provides direct support as needed. Entergy Corporation (NYSE:ETR), headquartered in New Orleans, Louisiana, is a major energy company with global power production and distribution operations, plus related diversified services. Entergy provides retail energy services to about 4.8 million customers, about half of whom reside in the Company's United States service area which includes portions of Arkansas, Louisiana, Mississippi, Texas, and New England. Entergy also provides power marketing services, sells electricity wholesale, and offers a broad range of energy management, security monitoring, and telecommunications services. **Career Highlights:** Video Services Product Line Manager, Entergy Services (1995-Present); Hughes Aircraft Company: Staff Management Systems Analyst (1990-95), Telecommunications Analyst (1979-90), Facility Manager and Analyst (1974-79). **Associations & Accomplishments:** International Telecommunications Association - Los Angeles Chapter: Former President, Former Member of Board of Directors; USSF Registered Referee. **Education:** West Coast University, B.S. in Business Administration (1980). **Personal Information:** Married to Joyce in 1980. Two children: Samantha and John. Mr. Horn enjoys being a USSF registered referee.

Mike W. Leary

Supervisor of Gas Drafting
The Montana Power Company
40 East Broadway Street
Butte, MT 59701-9394
(406) 497-2298
Fax: (406) 497-2126

4931

Business Information: Mr. Leary has served with The Montana Power Company in various positions since 1974. At the present time, he fulfills the responsibilities of Supervisor of Gas Drafting. In his capacity, he presides over all aspects of the Gas Drafting Department that provides construction drawings for gas transmission. Utilizing several years of solid experience, Mr. Leary supervises a staff of six people who oversee land and photography developments, along with plant design drawings for compressor stations, gate stations, and any other piping design requirements. A prominent and respected professional, he is currently working on expanding operations using today's technology, which includes the use of GPS for planning and as-built surveys of gas transmission pipelines. Mr. Leary's goals are to continue his career progression and to move up the corporate ladder. Established in 1912, The Montana Power Company operates as an electric and gas transmission company. Located in Butte, Montana, the Company provides two-thirds of the state of Montana with electric and gas services. Presently, the Company is divided into eight divisions and serves 228,000 electric customers and 123,000 gas customers. The Company's strategic goals are to continue providing quality services and to continue growing and expanding operations and technologies. **Career Highlights:** The Montana Power Company: Supervisor of Gas Drafting (1984-Present), Assistant Supervisor (1980-84), Design Draftsman (1978-80). **Associations & Accomplishments:** American Design Drafting Association; Terra Verde Volunteer Fire Department; Recipient of 1997 Outstanding Alumni Award from Montana Tech College of Technology. **Education:** Butte Vo Tech (1974). **Personal Information:** Married to Debbie in 1982. Two children: Abby and McKenna. Mr. Leary enjoys camping, fishing, skiing and sporting events.

John T. Lombardini, Jr.

Public Affairs Manager
Public Service/Electric & Gas
80 Park Plaza T10
Newark, NJ 07102
(973) 430-5785
Fax: (973) 643-8069
john.lombardini@pseg.com

4931

Business Information: As Public Affairs Manager of Public Service/Electric & Gas, Mr. Lombardini supports the entire Company through his maintenance of databases and Intranet management. Utilizing extensive education and practical work experience, he oversees databases concerned with information technology, human resources, municipal and contributions, and economic development. With a proactive leadership style, Mr. Lombardini lends knowledge and insight as staff members strive to develop innovative, strategic action plans. Coupling his marketing and technical experience, he demonstrates adept ability in all roles he serves within the corporate structure, be it in Public Affairs, Account Management, or Website Design. Mr. Lombardini attributes his success to excellent communicative skills and his ability to easily comprehend technical aspects of business operations. Public Service/Electric & Gas of New Jersey is the regulated parent company of various utility subsidiaries. Established in 1903, the Company currently has the largest distribution in the state as they hold 80 percent of services for the population and employ over 100,000 people. **Career Highlights:** Public Service/Electric & Gas: Public Affairs Manager (1996-Present), Strategic Account Manager (1995-96), Director of Information Technology (1994-95). **Education:** Fairleigh Dickinson University, M.B.A. (1985); New Jersey Institute of Technology, B.S. in Civil Engineering (1975).

Ianthe Helen McCrea

Senior Vice President of Information Technology/Chief Information Officer
Reliant Energy, Inc.
P.O. Box 1700
Houston, TX 77251-1700
(713) 207-7010

4931

Business Information: Serving as Senior Vice President of Information Technology and Chief Information Officer for Reliant Energy, Inc., Ms. McCrea directs the activities of the Corporation's Information Technology organization. She oversees all aspects of IT: strategy, architecture, business consulting, applications development, and maintenance as well as responsibilities of the IT infrastructure. This includes data and voice networks, data center operations, and distributed computing. Focus has been on implementing an ERP system for the Corporation, overseeing major changes through acquisitions, divestitures, and industry deregulation and innovations in the E-Business arena. Reliant Energy, Inc. is a publicly held establishment engaged in providing gas and electric energy to businesses in the retail, commerical, and industrial markets. Established in 1882, the Corporation employs 13,000 people in over 300 facilities located throughout the world. **Career Highlights:** Senior Vice President of Information Technology/Chief Information Officer, Reliant Energy, Inc. (1997-Present); Executive Vice President of Information Systems, Banc One (1992-97); Senior Vice President of Commercial and Corporate Systems, Security Pacific National Bank (1983-92); Date Officer, Texas Commerce Bank (1980-83); Systems Manager, Occidental Petroleum Corporation (1973-80). **Associations & Accomplishments:** Energy and Utility CIO Advisory Board; IBM; Hugh O'Brien Youth Foundation; National Association of Female Executives. **Education:** University of Texas at Arlington; Harvard School of Business; Business of Banking School, Cornell University; University of Virginia Darden Business School. **Personal Information:** Ms. McCrea enjoys collecting art, travel, collecting antique glass and playing the piano.

Alan Rizzuto

Applications Lead/Y2K Project Manager
Colorado Springs Utilities
30 South Nevada
Colorado Springs, CO 80903
(719) 661-1112
arizzuto@csu.org

4931

Business Information: Mr. Rizzuto, fulfilling the responsibilites of Applications Lead and Y2K Project Manager, handles the development of Web based applications and the integration of Legacy computer systems. Utiliizing his strong educational background and practical experience in the information technology industry, he also directs the Y2K compliance project to ensure the Company is able to make a smooth transition into the millenium. One of his most notable accomplishments was the creation of process automation control systems for nuclear power and gas corporations. Mr. Rizzuto is able to keep abreast of changes and new technologies within his industry through his attendance at conferences and seminars and attributes his professional success to studying. Always alert to new opportunities, techniques, and approaches, Mr. Rizzuto plans to increase his involvement in Web development. Colorado Springs Utilities provides water resources and power to over 500,000 residents of the Colorado Springs, Colorado area. Established in 1880, the Company employs 1,200 people to perform such tasks as overseeing the functions of equipment to completing service calls at homes or businesses. **Career Highlights:** Colorado Springs Utilities: Applications Lead/Y2K Project Manager (1998-Present), Senior Program Analyst (1997-98); Senior Field Service Engineer, Texas Institute (1971-97). **Associations & Accomplishments:** Institute of Electronics and Electrical Engineers. **Education:** Colorado Technical University, M.S. in Computer Science (1996); Regis University, B.S. in Computer Science (1992); Pennsylvania State University, Electronics and Electric Technology. **Personal Information:** Married to Lynnea in 1971. Five children: Shane, Chad, Jeremy, Lauren, and Lindsay. Mr. Rizzuto enjoys being a Ham radio operator.

Charles P. Bates

Information Technology Account Manager
Northeast Utilities
107 Selden Street
Berlin, CT 06037
(860) 665-4824
Fax: (860) 665-3324
batescp@nu.com

4939

Business Information: Demonstrating a broad knowledge of technology products and processes, Mr. Bates is an Information Technology Account Manager for Northeast Utilities. A successful, 27-year professional, he assumes responsibility for identifying opportunities to address business needs within Corporate Center departments and for gaining project approval for implementation. Mr. Bates oversees nine employees, provides desktop troubleshooting support, works on identifying technology solutions, as well as carries out the various administrative duties these functions entail. Mr. Bates' goals include broadening his information technology role and gaining expertise in project management and infrastructure. His success is attributed to his ability to think analytically as well as an understanding of technology and systems from a business viewpoint. Mr. Bates' advice is, "Keep your education as diversified as possible, especially concerning the different aspects of technology. And by all means, make sure you enjoy your work." Northeast Utilities is a full service public utility located in Berlin, Connecticut. Created from the merger of several companies in 1967, the Company provides electric and gas services to Connecticut, Massachusetts, and New Hampshire. A workstaff of more than 9,000 individuals provides electric and gas services to more than one million customers. Annual revenues are more than $3 billion. **Career Highlights:** Northeast Utilities: Information Technology Account Manager (1997-Present), Supervisor of Accounting Information Systems (1992-97), Supervisor of Regulatory Relations Information Systems (1980-92). **Education:** University of Hartford, B.S. in Business Administration (1971). **Personal Information:** Married to Elaine M. in 1976. Two children: Jonathan A. and Benjamin A. Mr. Bates enjoys jogging, singing, jazz and church.

Dana A. Boyles

Senior Computer Analyst
SRP
1600 North Priest Drvie #Isb104
Tempe, AZ 85281-1202
(602) 236-2815
Fax: (602) 683-3232
daboyles@srpnet.com

4939

Business Information: Demonstrating his expertise in the information technology field, Mr. Boyles serves as the Senior Computer Analyst for SRP. He handles the administration of several Company projects relating to the research and development of various software programs and hardware equipment. Mr. Boyles is responsible for the software and hardware testing and evaluation and distributes software programs via Tivoli. Offering technical support to the Company's multitude of users as the Desktop Manager, he also troubleshoots and repairs users' workstations as necessary. He is responsible for the implementation of several projects and attributes his success to self-discipline and maintaining an awareness of changes in the technology field. Mr. Boyles is currently pursuing his MCSC and Network + certifications to enable him to capitalize on the opportunities presented by the Company. Established in the 1800s, SRP is one of the oldest water and power utility plants in the United States. The Company serves 650,000 individuals in the Phoenix Metropolitan Area in the state of Arizona. Approximately 3,500 skilled and knowledgeable professionals are employed in all phases of operation. **Career Highlights:** Senior Computer Analyst, SRP (1993-Present); Senior Computer Operator, McDonnell Dougals Helicopter Company (1989-93). **Associations & Accomplishments:** A+ Certified. **Education:** DeVry Institute of Technology, B.S. in Computer Information Systems (1986). **Personal Information:** One child: Letricia. Mr. Boyles enjoys stock car racing.

Barbara D. Lawson

Information Technology Technician
Baltimore Gas & Electric
1650 Calvert Cliffs Parkway
Lusby, MD 20657-4700
(410) 495-2108
Fax: (410) 495-2187

4939

Business Information: Displaying her skills in this highly specialized position, Ms. Lawson serves as the Information Technology Technician for the Baltimore Gas & Electric Company. She is in charge of the UNIX system administration for one of the Company's power plants. A mid-range systems administrator, she handles the plant maintenance records and administrates the office operation systems and servers. The highlight of her career came when she configured the mid-range system for the Company which resolved the Y2K problems and challenges. Establishing goals that are compatible with those of the Company, Ms. Lawson anticipates obtaining a position as Team Leader, offering more of a project oriented opportunity. Baltimore Gas & Electric is an electric and gas utility company. Established in 1994, the Company has two nuclear power plants and one corporate office. The Information Technology Department is spread out amongst the three locations. Presently, the Company employs a work force of more than 500 professional, technical, and support personnel. **Career Highlights:** Baltimore Gas & Electric: Information Technology Technician (1995-Present), Associate Systems Analyst (1989-95); Technician, Personnel Resources (1988-89). **Associations & Accomplishments:** Business and Professional Women Club, Inc; 4-H Club of America; 4-H All Star; United Methodists Women; Alpha Phi Omega National Fraternity; Mu Tau Chapter; Recipient of a Service Key award for outstanding performance. **Education:** West Virginia Institute of Technology, degree in Computer Management and Data Processing (1988). **Personal Information:** Married to James T. in 1988. Two children: William P. and James H.

George A. McQuillister, III

Mobile Computing Product Manager
Pacific Gas & Electric
3450 Malcolm Avenue
Oakland, CA 94605
(510) 568-6297
Fax: (510) 568-7612
mobilemcq@aol.com

4939

Business Information: Mr. McQuillister is currently the Mobile Computing Product Manager for the Computer and Telecommunications services Department of Pacific Gas & Electric. He has been an employee of the Company for nearly 20 years and has help positions for diverse capacities, such as Meter Reader, Accounting Clerk, Computer Production and Systems Operator, and Mainframe Supervisor. Mr. McQuillister's primary responsibilities involve providing consulting services to internal clients who employ or are considering adopting mobile technologies to meet their business needs. He also monitors industry trends and networks with other professionals, sharing information, and exchanging ideas. As an enthusiastic proponent of the use of technologies for applicable business solutions, Mr. McQuillister is considering diving into a consulting business. Founded in 1905, Pacific Gas & Electric utility services to 8 million customers in a 70,000 square mile region of Northern and Central California with the support of 21,000 member work force. Customers include residential and commercial establishments and yield $9 billion in estimated annual returns. **Career Highlights:** Pacific Gas & Electic: Mobile Computing Product Manager (1995-Present), Learning Consultant (1994-95), Distance Learning Specialist (1993-94). **Associations & Accomplishments:** AM/FM International; Associantion of Computing Machinery; Bay Area Distance Learning Forum; Black Employees Association of P.G. & E.; Open Users Recommended Solutions, Personal Digital Assistant Industry Association; Utility Industry Hand-Held & PDA Forum Advisory Board. **Education:** St. Mary's of California, B.A. in Business Management (2000). **Personal Information:** Married to Pat in 1991. Three children: Stephanie, Erica, and George IV. Mr. McQuillister enjoys family, reading, listening to music, watching old films, golf, fishing and spectator sports.

Richard Peterson

Supervisor of Technical Support Services
Illinois Power Company
370 South Main Street
Decatur, IL 62523-1479
(217) 424-6946

4939

Business Information: Mr. Peterson functions in the role of Supervisor of Technical Support Services for Illinois Power Company. He is responsible for supervising eight systems programmers who ensure the functionality and fully operational status of the Company's OS390 mainframe operating system. A savvy, 27 year veteran and systems expert, Mr. Peterson has faithfully served with Illinois Power since he came on board as Senior Technical Analyst. In addition, he and his team of experts monitor the operation of the database infrastructure, ensuring its productivity, accessibility, reliability, and security. A recognized leader in the Company, Mr. Peterson is also an integral member of the the applications review committee. His career highlight includes maintaining systems availability at 99.6 percent. In the future, he hopes to move into application development where he would provide Internet services to clients within Illinois. Mr. Peterson's success reflects his leadership ability to form teams with synergy, technical strength, and a customer oriented attitude, as well as produce results and aggressively tackle new challenges. Illinois Power Company provides gas and electric utilities to the state of Illinois. With individualized subsidiaries in each county of the state, the Company is better able to accommodate for the supply needs of its clients. Presently, the Company supports over 50 percent of the gas and electric customers within Illinois. **Career Highlights:** Illinois Power Company: Supervisor of Technical Support Services (1998-Present), Senior Technical Consultant (1996-98), Senior Technical Analysis (1992-96). **Associations & Accomplishments:** National Parks and Conservation Association; Nature Conservancy; Study Circles for Race Relations; S.H.A.R.E. **Education:** Millikin, M.A. (1972). **Personal Information:** Married to Frances C. in 1967. Two children: Kristin and Erika. Mr. Peterson enjoys wildlife and home repair.

Carlos P. Saldana

Senior Communications Electrician
Los Angeles Department of Water and Power
1141 West 2nd Steet
Los Angeles, CA 90012-2093
(213) 367-5880
Fax: (213) 367-5906
carlossadlana@juno.com

4939

Business Information: As Senior Communications Electrician of the Los Angeles Department of Water and Power, Mr. Saldana handles all aspects of communication systems used within the Department. Utilizing his knowledge of the electronical industry, he oversees the installation, maintenance, and repair from system level to component level. Working closely with his staff of journeymen, Mr. Saldana supervises the mobile communication shop which handles radio repair. Recognized for his technical abilities he is credited with the installation of a 900 megahurtz system, greatly improving communcations in the Department. Attributing his success to his determination to acheive, he stays up-to-date in his progressive field by reading publications and attending conventions. Enjoying his position within the Department, Mr. Saldana intends to continue in his current capacity. Los Angeles is located on the Pacific Coast in southern California, about half way between the Mexican border and San Francisco. A racially, ethnically, and socially diverse city, Los Angeles attracts millions of tourists every year to the countless beaches and entertainment events. Providing utlities for all 10 million metropolitian residents is the Los Angeles Department of Water and Power. Employing over 150 people, the public utility company strives to offer dependable service to the City's ever-growing population. **Career Highlights:** Senior Communications Electrician, Los Angeles Department of Water and Power (1981-Present); Teacher, Los Angeles Electrical Training Trust (1996-Present); Electronic Technician, Los Angeles Unified School District (1981). **Associations & Accomplishments:** International Brotherhood of Electrical Workers. **Education:** Columbia State University, B.S. in Electrical Engineering (1996); United States Marine Corps Electronic Communications School (1977). **Personal Information:** Married to Alicia Garcia in 1982. Four children: Carlos, Robert, David, and Cindy. Mr. Saldana enjoys teaching, electronics, mathematics, martial arts and music.

Edward J. Simko Jr.

Network Engineer
Prudentual Reality and Relocation Services
17-3 Steven Drive
Ossining, NY 10562
(203) 614-5207
Fax: (914) 944-0362
esimko@bestweb.net

4939

Business Information: Providing his skilled services as Network Engineer of Prudentual Reality and Relocation Services, Mr. Simko is the Team Leader for the LAN and the technology client server data network. Four employees report directly to him and he supervises programming of the switches and routers regulating the Company's critical operations. Mr. Simko's most basic responsibility is to ensure that all networks are functioning at its optimum level and prevent interruptions of operations by providing a series of backup measures. Coordinating resources, time lines, schedules, and assignments also fall within the purview of his responsibilities. His success reflects his ability to take on new challenges and responsibilities. Continually formulating new goals and objectives, he looks forward to assisting in the completion of future corporate goals. Prudentual Reality and Relocation Services is a publicly owned company providing utility and communication services across 26 states. Founded in 1960, operations employ a work force of approximately 8,000 skilled professionals nationwide. **Career Highlights:** Network Engineer, Prudentual Reality and Relocation Services (1999-Present); Network Engineer, Citizens Utilities (1997-99); County of Westchester: Manager of Network Design (1996-97), Data Communication Analyst (1985-96). **Associations & Accomplishments:** Eagle Scout; Scout Master, Boy Scout Troop 4. **Education:** Manhattan College, B.S. in Business (1981); Lehman College, Certificate in Computer Technology. **Personal Information:** Mr. Simko enjoys the outdoors, hiking, camping, biking and golf.

William "Sandy" E. Warrington

Instructor/Database Administrator
EG&G Defense Materials
11600 Stark Road
Toole, UT 84074
(435) 882-5883
Fax: (435) 882-8085
swarrington@egg.com

4953

Business Information: Serving as an Instructor and Database Administrator of EG&G Defense Materials, Mr. Warrington teaches operations, safety, and environmental compliance to all employees. As a database administrator, he designs, developes, and implements training databases to track employee training. Before joining EG&G Defense Materials, he served as Principal Specialist of General Physics Corporation. His background also includes a stint as Principal Specialist with Continental Can Company. His personal motivation is to be an instructor, thereby being able to "give back what he has learned." Mr. Warrington's goal is to become an Information Systems Manager and ultimately become Chief Information Officer. He attributes his success to being thorough and analytical. His personal credo is "Never give up on education!" Established in 1989, EG&G Defense Materials, a subsidiary of EG&G Inc., is contracted to the United States Army to dispose of 42 percent of this nation's lethal chemical weapons. Started by several former Secretary of Defense, the Company currently has approximately 650 employees who help generate in excess of $100 million. **Career Highlights:** Instructor/Database Administrator, EG&G Defense Materials (1991-Present); Principal Specialist, General Physics Corporation (1980-90); Production Supervisor, Continental Can Company (1974-80). **Associations & Accomplishments:** National Model Railroad Association. **Education:** University of Phoenix: M.S. in Computer Information Systems (1999), B.S. in Business and Information Systems (1997). **Personal Information:**

Married to C. J. in 1988. Mr. Warrington enjoys model railroading and family time.

5000 - 5199
WHOLESALE TRADE

5000 Wholesale Trade - Durable Goods

5012 Automobiles and other motor vehicles
5013 Motor vehicle supplies and new parts
5014 Tires and tubes
5015 Motor vehicle parts, used
5021 Furniture
5023 Homefurnishings
5031 Lumber, plywood, and millwork
5032 Brick, stone, and related materials
5033 Roofing, siding, and insulation
5039 Construction materials, nec
5043 Photographic equipment and supplies
5044 Office equipment
5045 Computers, peripherals and software
5046 Commercial equipment, nec
5047 Medical and hospital equipment
5048 Ophthalmic goods
5049 Professional equipment, nec
5051 Metals service centers and offices
5052 Coal and other minerals and ores
5063 Electrical apparatus and equipment
5064 Electrical appliances, TV and radios
5065 Electronic parts and equipment
5072 Hardware
5074 Plumbing and hydronic heating supplies
5075 Warm air heating and air-conditioning
5078 Refrigeration equipment and supplies
5082 Construction and mining machinery
5083 Farm and garden machinery
5084 Industrial machinery and equipment
5085 Industrial supplies
5087 Service establishment equipment
5088 Transportation equipment and supplies
5091 Sporting and recreational goods
5092 Toys and hobby goods and supplies
5093 Scrap and waste materials
5094 Jewelry and precious stones
5099 Durable goods, nec

Michael Glen Mirau

Chief Information Officer
eLogo.com Encorporation
300 Cressent Court, Suite 350
Dallas, TX 75201
(214) 756-6235
Fax: (214) 756-6230
mirau@att.net

5013

Business Information: Mr. Mirau serves as Director of External Services for Interstate Batteries, performing technical services for account and distribution centers, major account holders, EDI Relationship Vendors, and truck account routing systems. He created and presented the concept for hand held computers for the distribution personnel. His endeavors in the project facilitated route management and resulted in the current operation of 1,000 hand held computers and a significant rise in productivity. Mr. Mirau is presently focusing on local and wide area network development for global marketing in relation to the leverage provided by power Internet activities. Established in 1955, Interstate Batteries has become the largest wholesaler of replacement batteries in the world. With 300 regional distributors and 210,000 dealers, the Dallas based Company reports estimated annual sales in excess of $500 million. **Career Highlights:** Chief Information Officer, eLogo.com Encorporation (1999-Present); Interstate Batteries: Director of External Services (1997-99), Vice President of Information Services (1996-97), Director of Information Services (1985-96); Systems Analyst, J.C. Penney Co. (1984-85). **Associations & Accomplishments:** Deacon, Forest Meadow Baptist Church; American Management Association; Society of Information Management; Microsoft Advisory Council; Curriculum Advisory Committee; Society of Information Management; Data Processing Management Association; Featured in Computer World and Executrain magazines. **Education:** Texas A & M University - Commerce, B.S. in Human Resources and Computer Science (1984). **Personal Information:** Married to Tammy in 1981. One child: Staci. Mr. Mirau enjoys surfing the Internet, golf and reading.

Mark Philip Roden

Algorithm Engineer
Delphi Automotive
217 West Rockwell Street
Fenton, MI 48430-2078
(810) 494-4775
Fax: (810) 494-4456
markroden@hotmail.com

5013

Business Information: A key team member of the Chassis Division, Mr. Roden serves in the role of Algorithm Engineer for Delphi Automotive. In his position, he is responsible for the design and development of prototype algorithms for the design of chassis systems used in the automotive industry. Utilizing his expertise in the computer simulation field, Mr. Roden develops advanced, high-tech programs and software. Vehicle testing and calibration is also part of his scope of responsibilities. A recognized technical expert, he was the recipient of the "Team Contribution Award." Looking to the 21st century, Mr. Roden anticipates continual professional growth that will enable him to move more towards the advanced side of the Company. He attributes his professional success to people and marketing skills as well as his ability to think "out-of-the-box," deliver results, and take on challenges. Originating in 1888, Delphi Automotive is the biggest auto supplier in the world. The Company provides products for brake control and hardware. Employing an enormous staff of 201,000 individuals, Delphi Automotive boasts an annual revenue of $28.5 billion. **Career Highlights:** Delphi Automotive: Algorithm Engineer (1999-Present), Algorithm Cooperative Engineer (1998-99), Electrical Systems Design Cooperative Engineer (1997-98), Algorithm Cooperative Engineer (1995-97). **Associations & Accomplishments:** Society of Automotive Engineers. **Education:** Kettering University, Electrical Engineering (1999). **Personal Information:** Mr. Roden enjoys home repair and renovation, bowling, sports and writing.

N. Diana Swanson

Systems Administrator
Aceomatic Recon
6550 Hamilton Avenue
Pittsburgh, PA 15206-4170
(412) 441-7353
Fax: (412) 441-4242

5013

Business Information: Providing her skilled services as Systems Administrator of Aceomatic Recon, Ms. Swanson presides over the management of the Information Systems Department. In this capacity, she assumes responsibility for the Company's networking functions over a Sco UNIX server and a Novell Network environment. These systems support the accounting system, the local area network for the Pittsburgh office, and the wide area network which connects the office to four branch offices in four states. Ms. Swanson provides technical hardware support to the approximate 75 users and is in charge of all of the telecommunication functions of the Company as well. Striving for maximum effectiveness, she is pursuing her certification in the UNIX operating system to enable her to capitalize on the opportunities presented by the Company. She attributes her professional success thus far to her hard work and flexibility. A leading wholesale parts supplier, Aceomatic Recon provides its products to all transmission shops on the East coast of the continental United States. The Company has approximately 28,000 different parts from various manufacturers available to its clients. Aceomatic Recon was established in 1968. **Career Highlights:** Aceomatic Recon: Systems Administrator (1993-Present), A/P Manager (1989-93). **Associations & Accomplishments:** Jehovah's Witness; Alumni Member, Future Business Leaders of America. **Education:** University of Pittsburgh; New Horizon Learning Center: Networking Fundamentals, Windows NT Certification. **Personal Information:** Ms. Swanson enjoys inline skating, running, biking, computers and playing with her dog.

Vincent A. VanDoorne

Systems Director/Chief Information Officer
Ford Power Products
28333 Telegraph Road, Suite 300
Southfield, MI 48034
(248) 945-4510
Fax: (248) 945-4511
vvandoor@ford.com

5013

Business Information: Utilizing 15 years of experience in the industry, as well as 12 years of service with Ford Power Products, Mr. VanDoorne oversees all internal system activities as Systems Director and Chief Information Officer. Supervising the four main divisions of the Company's operations, Mr. VanDoorne maintains a leading role within the strategy, planning, and budgeting group, enterprise resource planning, system administration, and the change of control computer group. As chief liaison between two additional Ford entities, he conducts planning and ERP support. Remaining at the forefront of the Company's increasing growth, Mr. VanDoorne strives to maintain the utilization of cutting edge technology. An accomplished professional, he has spoken at many user groups. Promoting and increasing business services is cited as one of Mr. VanDoorne's future endeavors. Ford Power Products, founded in 1947, is a sales and distribution center that re-engineers products manufactured by Ford to be sold to non-automotive markets. Reporting yearly sales in excess of $150 million, the Company employs 130 professionals who carry out the trade on an international basis. Offering the full support and guarentee of their product, Ford Power Products provides engineering services, warranty, training, service manuals, parts, and installation. Headquartered in Southfield, Michigan, the Company has incorporated two targeted markets, the industrial OEMs and contract sales. **Career Highlights:** Systems Director/Chief Information Officer, Ford Power Products (1996-Present); Development Manager, Geometric Results (1992); Branch Manager, Automated Business Systems and Service (1987). **Education:** Walsh College, B.A. in Computer Information Systems (1985). **Personal Information:** Married to Barbara Jean in 1988. Three children: Leah, Carol and Alyssa. Mr. VanDoorne enjoys family time.

George A. Percifield, Jr.

Director of Management Information Systems
Raymond Building Supply
7751 Bayshore Road
North Fort Myers, FL 33917-3506
(941) 731-8300
Fax: (941) 731-3299
gap@rbsc.net

5031

Business Information: A veteran of the technology field with 18 years of experience, Mr. Percifield currently serves as Director of Management Information Systems of Raymond Building Supply. He plans the strategic direction and oversees the entire information systems infrastructure as well as determines the business contributions of the systems functions. In this context, Mr. Percifield is responsible for management and maintenance of all copiers, faxes, telephones, cellular phones, computers, LAN/WAN connectivity, servers, and printers. Utilizing his business savvy and expertise, he is in charge of purchasing and transferring equipment and supplies, troubleshooting systems difficulties, providing training on software usage, and coordinating with all vendors. Future goals for Mr. Percifield includes enhancing software and tools for the Company, turning the operation into a paperless activity by depending more on e-mail, Internet, and Intranet technologies, as well as bridging the gap between all divisions within the Company through technology. His attributes his professional success to his strong faith and belief in God. Raymond Building Supply is a local supplier of building materials such as doors, lumber, trusses, architectural hardware, windows, and millwork. Established in 1957, the Company is based in North Fort Myers, Florida and operates three locations. Presently, the Company employs a staff of 365 people. **Career Highlights:** Raymond Building Supply: Director of Management Information Systems (1998-Present), Designer (1989-98); Designer, Wickes Lumber (1985-89); Designer, Mack Industry (1982-85). **Associations & Accomplishments:** Former Church Trustee; Former School CRA Chairman; Former Member, Truss Association. **Personal Information:** Married to Brenda in 1975. Two children: George and Kyle. Mr. Percifield enjoys wood working.

Dwayne Wells

Director of Information Technology
Long Fence & Home
6811 Kenilworth Avenue, Floor 6
Riverdale, MD 20737
(301) 209-2700
Fax: (301) 209-2762
dwayne@longfenceandhome.com

5039

Business Information: Functioning in the role of Director of Information Technology for Long Fence & Home, Mr. Wells oversees and directs all aspects of day-to-day administration and operational activities of the systems infrastructure. Before joining Long Fence & Home, Mr. Wells served as Vice President for both Robert Plan Corporation and Infomedia Corporation. His solid history also includes a stint as Director for PM Consulting. In his current capacity, he is in charge of all hardware, software, database, and client server utility programs, and compiling all information requests. A systems expert, he guides five employees in managing and running call center operations, as well as three NT 4.0 networks, a telecommunication network, and PBX and T1 lines. His success reflects his ability to build teams with synergy and a customer oriented attitude and take on new challenges. Solidifying the corporate offices connectivity, utilizing

Internet-interactive Web technology serves as one of Mr. Wells' future endeavors. A home improvement company, Long Fence & Home is one of the largest providers of windows, doors, and siding for home owners in the Mid-Atlantic region of the United States. Offering lifetime warranty on products and services, the Company specializes in sales, installation, and service work. Established in 1996 and regional in scope, Long Fence & Home employs a work force of 100 people who help generate in excess of $12 million annually. **Career Highlights:** Director of Information Technology, Long Fence & Home (1996-Present); Vice President, Robert Plan Corporation (1991-96); Vice President, Infomedia Corporation (1985-91); Director, PM Consulting (1982-83). **Associations & Accomplishments:** Association of Information Technology Professionals. **Education:** B.S. (1984). **Personal Information:** Married to Germaine in 1988. Two children: Jessica and Rebecca. Mr. Wells enjoys all kinds of athletics.

Donald Schmidt

Service Manager
Karl Williams Inc.
2920 South MacArthur Boulevard
Springfield, IL 62704
(217) 528-6873
Fax: (217) 528-0827
ryobidon@aol.com

5044

Business Information: Mr. Schmidt has been the Service Manager for Karl Williams Inc. since 1992. In this capacity, he represents the Corporation as he travels to various client locations demonstrating a vast product knowledge to install, service, and train individuals on the operation of Ryobi printing presses and other equipment related to the printing industry. Mr. Schmidt is a self-directed employee who is motivated, and takes it upon himself to learn techniques that will amplify the effectiveness of his services as he works closely with clients. Technically inclined, he is credited with the creation of the Corporation's Web site which is informative, visually appealing, and user friendly. Keeping his skills current with the ever-changing technology in today's progressive society, Mr. Schmidt looks forward to continual advancement within the corporate structure. Karl Williams provides services for the printing industry such as equipment sales, supplies, and service. Established in 1978, the Corporation employs seven people at the headquarters location of Springfield, Illinois. Recognized for outstanding service and support, the national company incorporates extensive customer satisfaction techniques into its operating policy. **Career Highlights:** Service Manager, Karl Williams Inc. (1992-Present); Printing Department Manager, Foster & Gallagher (1983-92). **Associations & Accomplishments:** Illinois Audubon Society; Emiquon Audubon Society. **Personal Information:** Mr. Schmidt enjoys photography, bird watching and travel.

David Chien

President
Atima Technology Inc.
PMB 772, 39120 Argonaut Way
Fremont, CA 94538
(510) 475-9088
Fax: (510) 475-9020

5045

Business Information: Functioning in the capacity of President of Atima Technology Inc., Mr. Chien oversees and directs day-to-day administration and operational activities. He is responsible for establishing the overall strategic direction, and formulating marketing and business planning strategies. Prior to his current role, Mr. Chien served as Vice President and Managing Director for DTK Computer Inc., as well as Vice President with J-Bond Computer Inc. Drawing from his vast technical and managerial skills, he provides product educational and training packages to Atima's consultants. Mr. Chien's thorough knowledge of competitors and markets enables him to effectively develop sales strategies and drive products to market. As a solid, 21 year professional, he determines future resource requirements; oversees time lines, assignments, and schedules; and calculates and manages the fiscal year budget. Mr. Chien's career success reflects his ability to build teams with synergy and technical strength and take on new challenges. Growing with the Atima Technology and taking the Corporation to the next level serves as his future objectives. A domestic, PC mainboard distributor, Atima Technology Inc. designs, manufacture, and distributes high tech products to wholesale distributors at retail prices. Established in 1993, the Corporation employs a staff of six people who help generate in excess of $5 million annually. **Career Highlights:** President, Atima Technology Inc. (1999-Present); DTK Computer Inc.: Vice President (1988), Managing Director (1991); Vice President, J-Bond Computer Inc. (1992). **Education:** Nihhon University (1978). **Personal Information:** Married to Li-Ing in 1985.

Bruce A. Clark

Director of Customer Service
Cal-Pak Systems
761 Kearney Avenue
Modesto, CA 95350
(209) 342-5210
Fax: (209) 342-5212

5045

Business Information: Demonstrating more than 18 years of experience in the field of technology, Mr. Clark serves as the Director of Customer Service for Cal-Pak Systems. He offers his services as technical support to company clients, answering their questions, assisting them in simple technical tasks, and recommending quality solutions for larger scale problems. In charge of quality assurance, he strives to ensure that every client is happy with the services offered by the Company. Mr. Clark also oversees all the technical writing tasks for the Company. Citing his willingness to excel as the reason for his success, he anticipates a future promotion to Vice President of Customer Support. A subsidiary of MTC Distributing, Cal-Pak Systems offers the sales and service of software applications and hardware equipment to various wholesale distributors. Operations employ the skilled services of over 200 employees and boasts $124 million in sales each year. MTC Distributing was established in 1921. **Career Highlights:** Director of Customer Service, Cal-Pak Systems (1998-Present); Triad Systems Corporation: Senior Programmer Analyst (1989-98), Supervisor (1985-89), Programmer Analyst (1981-85). **Education:** Chico State University, B.S. (1981). **Personal Information:** Married to Kathy in 1980. Two children: Kindra and Bradley. Mr. Clark enjoys snow skiing, bike riding and computers. Mr. Clark is also very involved in his church, overseeing AWANA Clubs and sitting on the Elder Board.

Donald N. Davis

Advanced Systems Analyst 3
MicroAge
910 West Redondo Drive
Gilbert, AZ 85233
(480) 366-7239
ddavis@microage.com

5045

Business Information: Mr. Davis functions in the capacity of Advanced Systems Analyst 3 with MicroAge. He is responsible for all aspects of technical support assistance provided to e-commerce applications. With the highlight of his time with the Company being the completion of his college degree, Mr. Davis has contributed three years of service to the department and looks forward to remaining with the Company in the future. He hopes to advance to a managerial position somewhere within the wireless telecommunications industry. An expert, Mr. Davis encourages future members of the industry to review trade magazines, surf the Internet, and talk to peers and mentors regularly. His success reflects his determinination and drive to get it right and get it right the first time. MicroAge provides computer infrastructure services to a nationwide clientele. Established in 1978, the Company assists its clients in establishing a successful network of computers to link their offices with their associates around the world. The Company provides constant repair services and a 24-hour technical support line clients to ensure their satisfaction and guarantee their return, producing $1.5 billion annually. **Career Highlights:** Advancec Systems Analyst 3, MicroAge (1997-Present); Computer Technician, Honeywell (1996-97); Accounts Payable Technician, Tri-Star Computer Insight Enterprises (1992-96). **Education:** Western International University, B.S. (1996).

Gabrielle Ivey

Manager Business Systems Support
Lexmark International, Inc.
740 West New Circle Road
Lexington, KY 40511-1876
(606) 232-1122
Fax: (606) 224-0500
givey1@gte.net

5045

Business Information: Drawing from a wealth of technical experience in the technology field, Ms. Ivey currently serves as Manager of Business Systems Support with Lexmark International Inc. She is responsible for technical training, skills assessments, and Web based training strategies. A technical expert, she provides technical solutions and tools to meet the specific needs of her corporate clients. In this context, she works closely with outside vendors, finding and implementing new technology. Ms. Ivey also conducts international conferences to provide sales managers from Asia, Europe, and the Pacific with technical information and details of the Corporation's product line. Future plans include moving to the education side of the Corporation, teaching a broader view of technology. One of many accomplishments, Ms. Ivey's greatest is the creation of a benchmark study, helping grow Lexmark International's e-commerce sector. A reputable technology solutions provider, Lexmark International Inc. is a global developer, manufacturer, and supplier of printing solutions and products. Products include laser, inkjet, and dot matrix printers and supplies. Established in 1991, the Corporation presently employs a 8,000 professional, technical, and support staff who help generate in excess of $3 billion annually. **Career Highlights:** Lexmark International Inc.: Manager of Business Systems Support (1999-Present), Manager of Sales Education (1997-99); Director of Corporate Education, Chubb Computer Services (1993-97); President, P.C. Help! Inc. (199-93). **Associations & Accomplishments:** Board of Directors, Bluegrass Community Foundation; Executive Board, Steering Committee, YMCA Black Achievers; Citizen Rview Panel for Child Protective Services; Volunteer, United Way. **Education:** Midway College, B.A. in Organizational Management (2000); Community College of the Air Force, A.S. in Data Processing (1983). **Personal Information:** Ms. Ivey enjoys running.

Kunwar Jain

Vice President
Express Computer Supply
4867 Mercury Street
San Diego, CA 92111-2104
(858) 565-6100
Fax: (858) 565-6194

5045

Business Information: Mr. Jain founded Express Computer Society in 1986. Since then the Company has rapidly grown under his leadership and is now recognized as one of the leading distributors of computer supplies and accessories in North and South America. Express Computer Supply is the wholesale distributor for over 60 major manufacturers of computer supplies and sells primarily to computer dealers, VARS, wholesalers, and strategic alliance accounts. The Company projects sales of approximately $60 million for the current year. While overseeing the daily operations, Mr. Jain also presides over the design and execution of the marketing campaigns and the negotiation of sales contracts. His vision and entrepreneurship have primarily contributed to the tremendous success of the Company in a highly competitive industry. **Career Highlights:** President, Express Computer Supply (1987-Present). **Associations & Accomplishments:** Recently featured among the top ten Chief Executive Officers of Asian Indian Origin in the United States by India Abroad, an Indian weekly newspaper published in the United States, and the prestigious Economic Times of India, not to mention the "rite up" in San Diego leading newspaper (Union Tribune) and Business Journal. **Education:** College. **Personal Information:** Married to Vipin in 1980. Two children: Mukul and Komal. Mr. Jain enjoys karate, golf and tennis.

Jeremy Kaufman

Integration Service Manager
Cranel Inc.
8999 Gemini Parkway
Columbus, OH 43240-2010
(614) 431-8000

5045

Business Information: Possessing expertise in the computer field, Mr. Kaufman performs as the Integration Service Manager for Cranel Inc. A technical expert on products sold by Cranel, he configures and builds computer systems, upgrades scanners and mass storage units, and maintains the functionality and fully operational status of all systems. Pretesting and providing technical support during the pre-sale process also fall within the scope of his responsibilities. Continually looking for new educational and occupational opportunities, Mr. Kaufman intends to take advantage of all opportunities offered. He attributes his success to his talents and skills in troubleshooting as well as his mechanical ability. Established in 1985, Cranel Inc. operates as a technology reseller and distribution company. Focussing on mass storage devices for computer networks and imaging scanners, the Corporation is devoted to offering clients with the most up-to-day, cutting edge products laced with quality, value, and reliability. Headquartered in Columbus, Ohio, Cranel Inc was established in 1985. Operating a network of four locations nationwide, the Corporation presently employs a 170 professional, technical, and support staff. **Career Highlights:** Integration Service Manager, Cranel Inc. (1999-Present). **Education:** Ohio State

University, B.S. (1997). **Personal Information:** Married to Tamara in 1999. Mr. Kaufman enjoys bike riding.

Christopher M. Kozlov

Network Administrator
Arlington Industries
1001 Technology Way
Libertyville, IL 60048
(847) 362-1001
Fax: (847) 362-3773
whoswho@kozlov.net

5045

Business Information: Mr. Kozlov functions in the role of Network Administrator for Arlington Industries. He is responsible for installing operating systems and database management software, compilers, and utilities, as well as build up and design entire networking system infrastructures. Monitoring and tuning systems software, peripherals, and networks; and resolving systems problems also fall within the realm of Mr. Kozlov's responsibilities. In the future, he hopes to become involved with larger projects in the technology field. He encourages all newcomers to the industry to investigate the industry thoroughly to determine if it is really something they really want to do. Mr. Kozlov's success is attributed to his family values and his ability to deliver results and take on new challenges. His advice is "investigate the industry to see if it is really something that you really want to do and do a lot of reading." Arlington Industries is an imaging wholesaler of imaging products to major distributors throughout the world. Established in 1972, the Company distributes its products around the United States from its locations in Libertyville, Illinois. The Company turns over $110 million each year and supports a staff of 150 employees. **Career Highlights:** Network Administrator, Arlington Industries (1997-Present); LAN Administrator, Elek-Tek, Inc. (1997); Information Technology Level 2-Team Leader, Dean Witter, Discover & Company (1996-97); Information Systems Specialist, Follett Campus Resources (1995-96). **Associations & Accomplishments:** President, Housing Corporation; Lambda Gamma Chapter, Sigma Nu International Fraternity. **Education:** Eastern Illinois University, B.A. in Economics (1994).

George A. Passantino, Jr.

Systems Administrator
Manchester Equipment
160 Oser Avenue
Hauppauge, NY 11788
(631) 951-7896
gpastino@mecnet.com

5045

Business Information: Following one year of distinguished service with the United States Army, Mr. Passantino has earned three years of experience in the technology industry. Serving with Manchester Equipment as Systems Administrator, he is responsible for management and oversight of the Company's Citrix system infrastructure. Possessing an excellent understanding of technology, Mr. Passantino ensures all users and accounts are properly maintained and guarantees that the system functional and operational at all times. In the future, he plans to continue working for the Company, hoping to move into presales engineering and create a new network. Founded in 1973, Manchester Equipment is a value added reseller and service provider of computer equipment. Employing 400 personnel, the Company buys old computers which are then refurbished and upgraded. In 1999, the Company reported estimated annual revenue in excess of $200 million. **Career Highlights:** Systems Administrator, Manchester Equipment (1998-Present); Parts Manager/Technician, Peradata Technology Coproration (1997-98); Infantry, United States Army (1996-97). **Education:** New Horizons Learning Center, Microsoft Certified Professional, Microsoft Ceritifed Systems Engineer. **Personal Information:** Mr. Passantino enjoys paintball games and automotive racing.

Howard C. Phillips, B.A.

Application Architect
Lexmark International, Inc.
740 New Circle Road NW
Lexington, KY 40550
(606) 232-2974
Fax: (606) 281-9912

5045

Business Information: Displaying his skills in this highly specialized position, Mr. Phillips serves as Application Architect for Lexmark International, Inc. He is the Global

Architect for all of the Corporation's manufacturing, financial, and Web based systems, defining the application architecture for Lexmark. As a solid, 33 year technology professional, Mr. Phillips has served with Lexmark International in a variety of role since joining the team in 1966. Working closely with the Information Technology Department, he evaluates and recommends software packages for purchase by the Department. Mr. Smith demonstrates considerable pride in his computer science degree, having returned to school at age 40 to achieve it. He credits his professional success to working for a very supportive company and the self motivation to continue to gain knowledge through the Internet, trade journals, and other sources. Consistently achieving quality performance, Mr. Smith looks forward to assisting in the completion of corporate goals. A publicly traded corporation, Lexmark International, Inc. engages in the manufacture, sales, and distribution of laser printers, inkjet printers, and related supplies. The Corporation was formed in the 1990 when IBM sold the former division to an outside interest. Boasting $3 billion in gross sales, a work force of 7,000 is employed in international operations. **Career Highlights:** Lexmark International, Inc.: Application Architect (1997-Present), Advisory System Analyst (1991-97), Application Development Manager (1990-91). **Associations & Accomplishments:** Board of Directors, J.D. Edwards Quest User Group; Common AS400 User Group; Deacon, Alton Baptist Church. **Education:** Transylvania University, B.A. (1990). **Personal Information:** Married to Opal in 1966. Two children: Darrin and Jaime. Mr. Phillips enjoys golf and fishing.

Victoria Rexford-Husko

Reginal Sales Manager
ASAP Software Express
3355 Lenox Road, Suite 750
Atlanta, GA 30326
(847) 465-3700
Fax: (847) 465-3277
vrexford@asapsofware.com

5045

Business Information: Ms. Rexford-Husko has assertively served with ASAP Software Express in a variety of positions since joining the Company as a Sales Representative in 1992. Rapidly ascending the Company's hierarchy, she now fills the role of Regional Sales Manager for the Southeast region. She is accountable for advising a large group of outside sales representatives. Her hands on experience in designing and managing multi-media presentations and proposals, personnel management, project management, and purchasing have made her an invaluable asset to ASAP Software Express. Developing sales promotions and strategies as well as determining and penetrating new markets and avenues for additional revenues also fall within the realm of Ms. Rexford-Husko's responsibilities. Noted for her hard work and organizational skills, she is considered one of the top managers in the Company. ASAP Software Express was established in 1983 and currently employs more than 200 people. A software provider, ASAP is considered by many to be a leader in the computer industry. As a distribution center, the Company focuses on selling their clients desktop applications that fit their business plans. Headquartered in Chicago, the Company caters to Fortune 500 companies with 200 PCs or more. These companies use ASAP as a service provider, as well as buying bulk software from them. A focused company with qualified personnel, ASAP will be at the top of the computer industry for years to come. **Career Highlights:** ASAP Software Express: Regional Sales Manager (1999-Present), District Sales Manager (1998-99), Sales Representative (1992-98). **Associations & Accomplishments:** American Management Association; Northern Illinois Business Association. **Personal Information:** Ms. Rexford enjoys sports and house renovation.

Simon P. Yu

President
M-Plus
46701 Fremont Boulevard
Fremont, CA 94538-6539
(510) 440-8588
Fax: (510) 440-9797
mplus@slipnet.com

5045

Business Information: Mr. Yu serves as President of M-Plus. As a co-founder of the Company, he provides strategic planning advice for long and short term plans, as well as formulates marketing and business strategies to keep the Company on the cutting edge of technology. Talented in the business sector, Mr. Yu devotes his time to the finance control and purchasing, assisting and advising the staff on successful bookkeeping tactics to maintain within the office. Looking to the next millennium, Mr. Yu hopes to remain on the leading edge and plans to keep his eyes open for new opportunities within the Company. His success reflects his ability to set realistic goals, deliver results, and aggressively take on new challenges. M-Plus is a wholesale computer hardware and software resaler. Established in 1992, the Company

coordinates networking systems for educational and application uses within the personal or business office. The largest portion of its clientele are from the small to medium sized computer manufacturers. The Company turns over $8 million annually. **Career Highlights:** President, M-Plus (1995-Present); Material Control Manager, Apaq System Inc. (1992-95); Manufacturing Manager, Elite Group (1991-92). **Education:** Colorado State University, M.S. (1990). **Personal Information:** Married to Aileen Jin in 1985. Two children: Nelson and Dianna.

Garfield W. Tresidder

Management Information Systems Officer
Tri State Hospital Supply Corporation
3310 South Main Street, Suite A
Salisbury, NC 28147
(704) 638-0424
Fax: (704) 636-9546
garfield@salisbury.net

5047

Business Information: Serving as the Management Information Systems Officer for the Tri State Hospital Supply Corporation, Mr. Tresidder is the MIS Department's sole employee. As a result, he assumes responsibility for every aspect of the Corporation's network and individual work stations. He maintains, repairs, and updates all computer related equipment from the phones and e-mail to the sterilization departmental equipment. As a 10 year computer technology expert, Mr. Tresidder keeps the PC work stations in top condition and performs administration of the AS/400 system. Complementing his duties as a MIS Coordinator, he works on his own with handicapped and computer challenged individuals offering PC training and advice on computer purchases. Mr. Tresidder is currently working on his MSCE and Internet certifications. He looks forward to one day owning his own consulting business. A leading medical supplier, Tri State Hospital Supply Corporation provides a wide range of medical kits and supplies. Everything from surgical kits for everyday operations to surgical tools and equipment is offered. The Corporation supplies hospitals across the country. Presently, the Corporation employs over 120 individuals. **Career Highlights:** Management Information Systems Officer, Tri State Hospital Supply Corporation (1997-Present); Instructor, Salisbury Business College (1997); Owner/President, CareerChangers, Unlimited (1992-97). **Associations & Accomplishments:** Wildlife Instructor, North Carolina Wildlife Federation. **Education:** Catawba College, B.A. in Business Administration with a major in General Business Management (1995); West Union Training School, Assistant Repeater Chief. **Personal Information:** Mr. Tresidder enjoys his work as a freelance systems instructor.

Kimberly A. Bosworth

Technical Services Manager
Minibar Systems
7340 Westmore Road
Rockville, MD 20850-1260
(301) 309-1100
Fax: (301) 309-1115
kimble.bosworth@minibarna.com

5049

Business Information: Demonstrating remarkable expertise in the technology industry, Mrs. Bosworth serves as the Senior Account Manager for Minibar Systems. In this capacity, she assumes the overall responsibility for the five member technical support staff and two help desk personnel. She has faithfully served with Minibar Systems in a variety of roles since joining the Company as Regional Account Manager in 1994. An expert, she coordinates two satellite systems, provides new employees with technical training on the computer systems, and assigns the databases to be installed in the hotels. Attributing her success to continual self-education, she developed a new software program that is currently being utilized by the Company. Consistently achieving quality performance, Mrs. Bosworth aspires to a future promotion to Vice President of Information Technology within the Company. Focusing on the hotel and hospitality industry, Minibar Systems is engaged in the manufacture and distribution of minibars and in-room safes. The Company provides computeriezed posting and monitoring solutions for capture and reporting of Minibar revenues. Four different types of computer systems are available according to the different needs and size of the hotel. Established in 1979, the Company currently employs 30 qualified staff members. **Career Highlights:** Minibar Systems: Technical Services Manager (1999-Present), Senior Accounts Manager (1997-99), Regional Accounts Manager (1994-97); Sales Manager, Tropical Nut & Fruit (1992-94). **Education:** Vanderbilt University, B.S. (1989). **Personal Information:** Married to Christopher in 1997.

Vrajesh Thakkar
Account Executive for Sales
AMS Inc.
521 East 14th Street, Apartment 7H, Stuyvesant Town
New York, NY 10009-2925
(212) 254-7456
Fax: (212) 254-7456
invowthank7@aol.com

5049

Business Information: Combining sales expertise and technical skills, Mr. Thakkar serves in the position of Account Executive for Sales with AMS Inc. He travels to client sites to conduct sales presentations for the Corporation's debit and credit card software programs. Keeping abreast of advancements in the technology industry by attending seminars, he attributes his professional success to having a sincere interest in the industry and the ability to think outside the box, produce results, and take on new challenges. Mr. Thakkar continues to grow professionally through the fulfillment of his responsibilities and his involvement in the advancement of operations. Since its inception in 1959, AMS Inc. has developed specialized software for businesses within the local area. Today, the Corporation produces debit and credit card systems for companies in the New York and New Jersey metropolitan areas. An approximate workforce of 50 dedicated employees work diligently to develop the programs and ensure the security of sensitive personal data. **Career Highlights:** Account Executive for Sales, AMS Inc. (1987-Present); Senior Field Service Engineer, Raytheon Data System (1976-87); Field Service Engineer, Kybe Corporation, Sycore Inc., Incoterm Corporation; International Account Coordinator, Memorex Telex Corporation. **Associations & Accomplishments:** American Management Association. **Education:** RCA Institutes, Inc.: degree in Electronics Engineering Technology T-3 (1971), degree in Electronics Technology (1968); Bombay University (1967). **Personal Information:** Married to Patricia in 1976. Two children: Neil and Natalie. Mr. Thakkar enjoys travel, chess and tennis.

James B. Keane, Jr.
Information Technology Administrator
Northstar Steel & Aluminum, Inc.
205 Bouchard Street
Manchester, NH 03108-4886
(603) 668-3600
Fax: (603) 629-9943
jkeanejr1@cs.com

5051

Business Information: Joining the Northstar Steel & Aluminum, Inc. team of professionals as purchasing assistant in 1995, Mr. Keane was recently promoted to his current position of Information Technology Administrator. He oversees the Corporation's systems infrastructure and determines the business contribution of the information systems functions. In his position, he is responsible for a variety of tasks including inventory control, providing software support, conducting data analysis, and troubleshooting. In the future, Mr. Keane looks forward to continuing with the Corporation and getting more involved with Web design and publishing. Located in Manchester, New Hampshire, Northstar Steel & Aluminum, Inc. engages in the distribution of aluminum and stainless steel products. The Corporation processes the material at an in-house production factory and then ships the products to companies and industries throughout the New England area. With a staff of 70 dedicated employees, the Corporation looks forward to continued growth and success in the years to come. **Career Highlights:** Northstar Steel & Aluminum, Inc.: Information Technology Administrator (1999-Present), Purchasing Assistant (1995-99); Administrative Assistant, Hussey Disposal Company (1991-99); Data Entry, TAC/Temps - United Parcel Service (1993-94). **Education:** Powerpoint 97 Certification (2000); Web Site Development & Design Certification (2000); Advanced PC Troubleshooting Certification (1999); Troubleshooting, Maintaining, and Upgrading PCs Certification (1999); Intermediate Windows 95 Certification (1997); Reiki Master Therapist Certification (1997); AS/400 Query Certification (1996); Supervisory Headache Certification (1996); Peachtree Software Certification (1994); Londonderry High School (1988).

Cheryl L. Duay
e-Commerce Project Leader
GE Supply
2 Corporate Drive, 10th Floor
Shelton, CT 06484
(203) 944-3444
Fax: (203) 944-2925
cheryl.duay@supply.ge.com

5063

Business Information: Recruited to GE Supply in 1997, Mrs. Duay now serves as the e-Commerce Project Leader. She has served with GE Supply in a variety of roles since coming on board through one of GE's selective management training programs in 1997. In her current capacity, Mrs. Duay leads one of the Company's e-Commerce initiatives from the design of the Internet offering through the development and deployment of the Website. Coordinating resources, time lines, and assignments to meet aggressive deadlines also fall within the realm of her functions. Working hard, Mrs. Duay performs in a manner that is sure to bring commendation and recognition. Her career success reflects her ability to think out-of-the-box and aggressively take on new challenges and responsibilities. Mrs. Duay plans to expedite continued promotion through dedication and quality performance. GE Supply, an electrical distribution business, distributes over 100,000 electrical products through domestic and international sales. Founded in 1929, the Company consists of a work force of more than 2,500 employees and boasts in excess of $2 billion in annual sales. **Career Highlights:** GE Supply: e-Commerce Project Leader (1999-Present), Special Assignment, Mergers and Acquisitions (1998-99); Management Training Program, Distribution and Sales (1997-98). **Associations & Accomplishments:** General Electric Elfun Society; General Electric Women's Network; Meals on Wheels; Green Peace; Habitat for Humanity; Read Aloud for Children; MS115 Bike Tour For a Cure. **Education:** University of Pittsburgh: B.S. in Business Administration (1997), B.S. in Psychology (1997). **Personal Information:** Married to Federico in 1997. Mrs. Duay enjoys biking, rock-climbing, snowboarding, backpacking, exercise, travel, piano and Spanish language study.

Kin Wing Horace Cheng
• • •◄══════◉══════►• • •

Field Application Engineer
Atek Electronics Company Ltd.
Unit 5, 8th Floor, Fu Hang Industrial Building, #1 Hok Yuen Street East
Kowloon, Hong Kong
+852 91757658
horacecg@hutchcity.com

5065

Business Information: Joining Atek Electronics Company Ltd. in November 1999, Mr. Cheng currently serves as the Field Application Engineer. Drawing on several years of service in engineering positions, as well as an extensive education in scientific engineering, Mr. Cheng maintains a role as one of the leading experts in the industry. In addition to his researching activity, Mr. Cheng offers client support to assist in technical integration. Dedicated to the success and future growth of the Company, he takes part in identifying modern technology trends to promote the introduction of these innovations to Atek Electronics Company's operation Located in Hong Kong, Atek Electronics Company Ltd. is one of the world's leading distributors of Texas Instruments semiconductor devices. Playing an integral role in this industry, Atek Electronics Company Ltd. provides leading retailers and manufacturers with electronic components. Distributing primarily throughout Hong Kong, the Company exports only 5 percent of their product for international use. Operating two major locations to produce their goods, Atek Electronics Company Ltd. employs twenty professionals in Hong Kong and thirteen in China. **Career Highlights:** Field Application Engineer, Atek Electronics Company Ltd. (1999-Present); Application Engineer, Comet Electronics Ltd. (1999-Present); Sales Engineer, Simmon's Electronic Products Ltd.(1999). **Associations & Accomplishments:** Institute of Electronic Engineers; Institute of Electronics and Electrical Engineers; Association of Computing Machinery; The New York Academy of Sciences. **Education:** University of Leeds, M.S. in Engineering (1992); Heriot-Watt University, Diploma Information Technology (1990); University of Leeds, Bachelor's degree in Engineering (1986). **Personal Information:** Mr. Cheng enjoys walking, photography and music.

Ryan A. DeMent
PC Technician
Tyco Packaging Systems
30962 Santana Street
Hayward, CA 94541
(510) 476-5606
lumbyl@jps.net

5065

Business Information: Mr. DeMent is PC Technician with Tyco Packaging Systems. He is responsible for the day-to-day maintenance and repair of Tyco's computers and systems infrastructure. Before joining Tyco Packaging Systems, Mr. DeMent served as PC Technician for SSE Telecom. Quickly establishing his presence in the technology field, he oversees and handles all systems functions at the Hayward, California facility. In this context, Mr. DeMent participants in the analysis, design, configuration, upgrade, installation, maintenance, support, and tracking of systems and networks, client server utility programs, software, and hardware. Looking forward to the next millennium, he plans to expedite continued promotion through the fulfillment of his responsibilities and his involvement in the advancement of operations. His aspirations are to become a Systems Administrator, and eventually start his own computer consulting company. Mr. DeMent attributes his career success to his ability to quickly grasp new concept methodologies and emerging technologies. Serving a national and international client base, Tyco Packaging Systems is a publicly owned company specializing in back plane assembly. Headquartered in Pennsylvania, the Company employs a work force of 70 qualified individuals to provide for the diverse needs of Tyco's clientele. **Career Highlights:** PC Technician, Tyco Packaging Systems (1998-Present); PC Technician, SSE Telecom (1997-98). **Education:** Chabot College; Heald Business College. **Personal Information:** Mr. DeMent enjoys Web pages and video games.

Trade Winds on Extranet-21
Twx-21

Hiroyuki Kitajima
Technology Director
Hitachi, Ltd.
890 Kashimada Saiwai, Kawasaki
Kanagawa, Japan 212-8567
+81 445491246
Fax: +81 445491274
hkitaji@system.hitachi.co.jp

5065

Business Information: A successful 30 year veteran of technology, Mr. Kitajima is the Technology Director for Hitachi, Ltd.'s business-to-business e-commerce service provider named TWX-21, Trade Winds on extranet in the 21st century. He leads research and development, defines the business model, and constructs systems architectures. Demonstrating strong leadership, Mr. Kitajima determines the strategic direction and business contribution of the systems functions. Additionally, he supervises all maintenance, ensuring flawless system operations. His skills and knowledge are utilized in design application and implementation. Mr. Kitajima has enjoyed substantial success in his present position and looks forward to assisting in the completion of future Company goals. His success is attributed to his networking, perseverance, and his knowledge and expertise. Hitachi, Ltd. is well known for its products and services provided internationally. Established in 1910, the Company employs 60,000 individuals to facilitate all aspects of operation. Headquartered in Tokyo, Japan, the Company maintains many diversified interests throughout the world, such as home appliances, information systems, and industrial components. Presently, the Company generates about ¥4 trillion ($40 billion) annually. **Career Highlights:** Hitachi, Ltd.: Technology Director (1997-Present), e-Commerce Research Director (1995-97), Research Department Manager (1991-95). **Associations & Accomplishments:** Institute of Electrical Engineers of Japan; Japan Information Processing Society; Institute of Electrical and Electronics Engineers. **Education:** University of Tokyo, M.S. (1971); University of California at Los Angeles, Master's degree in Engineering (1979). **Personal Information:** Married to Michiko in 1970. Two children: Tatsuya and Shimpei. Mr. Kitajima enjoys golf, classical music and playing the clarinet and flute.

Kuet Leong Lam
Chief Application Engineer
Kyoei Electronics (S) Pte. Ltd.
Block 607, Senja Road, #02-06
Singapore, Singapore 670607
+65 4721566
kllam@singnet.com.sg

5065

Business Information: Demonstrating expertise in the information technology field, Mr. Lam serves as Chief Application Engineer for Kyoei Electronics (S) Pte. Ltd. Responsible for maintaining all technical operations, he designs and develops software applications for semiconductors used in consumer electronic products. Highly regarded, he possesses superior talents and an excellent understanding of his field. By staying abreast of the latest innovations, Mr. Lam is able to ensure optimal technical efficiency for all day to day operations at the Company. He is currently pursuing his Master's degree in Business Administration that will enable him to capitalize on the opportunities provided by the Company. **Career Highlights:** Chief Application Engineer, Kyoei Electronics (S) Pte. Ltd. (1994-Present). **Associations & Accomplishments:** Institute of Electrical and Electronics Engineers. **Education:** Strathclyde Graduate Business School, M.B.A. (In Progress); National University of Singapore, Bachelor's degree in Engineering (1994). **Personal Information:** Mr. Lam enjoys reading and painting.

Martin P. Registe, Jr.

Network Specialist
Cellstar
1728 Briercroft Court Road
Carrollton, TX 75006
(972) 466-5284
Fax: (972) 323-4507
mregiste@cellstar.com

5065

Business Information: As Network Specialist of Cellstar, Mr. Registe handles a variety of technical responsibilities including development, testing, and production of new products. Demonstrating an extensive knowledge of the industry gained through related education and practical work experience, Mr. Registe evaluates current systems to ensure maximum resources are being utilized. Handling troubleshooting of the network, LAN, and WAN, he is able to offer guidance and support for current production. He excercises exceptional communication skills as he works closely with colleagues, striving to devleop cutting edge procedures that will lower overhead and raise both quality and quantity. Attributing success to a positive attitude and a willingness to go the extra mile, Mr. Registe currently is preparing for the position of Chief Information Officer of Cellstar or another telecommunication company. Established in 1981, Cellstar became a public company in 1992. The largest provider of cellphones and wireless products in the nation, the Company manufactures products for Nokia, NEC, Quacom, and Global Star. Keeping pace with progressive technology changes, the Company has recently begun distributing satellites. **Career Highlights:** Cellstar: Network Specialist (1999-Present), Technical Services Supervisor (1998-99), Network Technician (1997-98). **Education:** Ambassador University: B.S. in Management Information Information Systems (1996), B.S. in Business Administration (1996). **Personal Information:** Mr. Registe enjoys soccer, basketball and football.

Roseann M. Tiseo

Human Resource Information Systems Computer Programmer 2
Arrow Electronics
25 Hub Drive
Melville, NY 11747
(516) 391-4268
rtiseo@arrow.com

5065

Business Information: Miss Tiseo has been employed with Arrow Electronics for several years, and currently serves in the capacity of Human Resource Information Systems Computer Programmer. In this capacity, she fulfills a multitude of technical functions including software development. Demonstrating an extensive knowledge of the industry as she provides software support, Miss Tiseo lends her expertise to the Corporation as she implements solutions to technical challenges. Recognized for her impressive acheivements, she is proud to have acquired her skills through self-taught courses and practical experience. Miss Tiseo credits her success to her intelligence and motivations, and strives to advance within the corporate structure as she continues her education and dedicated work practices. Headquartered in Melville, New York, Arrow Electronics is an international distributor of electrical components, systems, and related items through an extensive customer network in North America, Europe, and Asia. Operating over 150 marketing facilities and 10 primary distribution centers, the Corporation employs a workforce of more than 6,600 individuals. **Career Highlights:** Arrow Electronics, Inc.: Human Resource Information Systems Computer Programmer 2 (1999-Present), Management Information Systems Programmer 1 (1997-99), Management Information Systems Programmer/Associate (1996-97). **Education:** Dowling College: M.B.A. (1996), B.B.A. (1994). **Personal Information:** Miss Tiseo enjoys tennis, fitness and Barbie collecting.

David M. Schartel

Managed Information Systems Director
Thomas Hardware
1001 Rockland Street
Reading, PA 19604
(610) 921-3558
Fax: (610) 921-9794
dschartel@ptd.net

5072

Business Information: Utilizing years of experience in network administration and programming, Mr. Schartel serves as Managed Information Systems Director for Thomas Hardware. He is responsible for planning, organizing, and administering all aspects of the Company's computer and telecommunications systems. Mr. Schartel develops the Company's Technology and E-Commerce Plans, manages outsourced/contracted services and projects, develops the Company's Technology Policies, and the Company's Disaster Recovery Plan. Keeping abreast of technology, he analyzes and improves business processes by introducing new technology. Thomas Hardware is a nationwide industrial hardware distributor. A workforce of 50 qualified individuals is employed in daily operations throughout the Company's four strategically located distribution centers. Annual sales are boasted at an estimated $20 million. **Career Highlights:** Management Information Systems Director, Thomas Hardware (1998-Present); Management Information Systems Director, Singer Equipment (1997-98); Senior Systems Administration/Programmer, Reading Body Works (1994-97). **Education:** Albright College, B.S. in Computer Science (1994). **Personal Information:** Married to Denise A. in 1985. Two children: Aubrey and Jennifer. Mr. Schartel enjoys volleyball and softball.

Brenda K. Angle

Systems Engineer
A. Louis Supply Company
5610 Main Avenue
Ashtabula, OH 44004
(440) 993-1074
Fax: (440) 992-5165
bangle@interplaced.net

5074

Business Information: Ms. Angle, providing her skilled services as Systems Engineer, is responsible for computer conversions for the Y2K system. As Data Center Manager, she is in charge of networking, documentation, and training as well as research conversion and forecasting hardware requirements. Concurrently, Ms. Angle is coordinator for electronic data interchange and the engineering steering committee. In her capacities, she provides management of title systems engineering and integrating solutions for new networks and platforms. A leader in the business community, Ms. Angle is also the curator of A. Louis Supply's information technology's history museum. Always alert to new opportunities, her goal is to help the Company keep pace with cutting edge technology. Serving a local clientele, A. Louis Supply Company operates as an industrial wholesale company. Privately held, the Company specializes in electrical, industrial, waterworks, pipe, valve, and fittings, tools, plumbing, heating, hardware, and municipal supplies. Being a large and diversified wholesaler, A. Louis Supply Company stocks well over 40,000 line items and also has the capability to perform special orders. The Company is located in Ashtabula, Ohio and serves customers within a 50 mile radius. Presently employing a work staff of 30 people, the A. Louis Information Center has been in existence since 1967. A. Louis Supply Company was one of the first in the industry and the area to implement a mainframe environment to better service their business and customer needs. Recognized and published in the "Supply House Times" in 1969. **Career Highlights:** Systems Engineer, A. Louis Supply Company (1971-Present); Independent Consultant, University Hospital of Cleveland (1996); Trained Facilitator (AT&T School of Business) Advanced Certificate. **Associations & Accomplishments:** Chapter President/Region Vice President, Association of Info Tech Professionals; Advisory Committee, Data Processing for Ashtabula County Vocational School; Advisory Board Committee Member, Ashtabula Kent State University; Advisory Board Member, Data Processing Review Committee; AS-400 Users Group; Published article in Lupus Magazine (1998); Interviewed for Computer World; AITP Committee; AITP Leadership Committee; Operates a "Helpline" for two Lupus Support Groups; Facilitator for the Northern Ohio Lupus of America Foundation Support Groups. **Education:** Vocational Education, degree (1972); Continuing Education, IBM, AITP Conferences. **Personal Information:** Ms. Angle enjoys Investment Club activities, dancing, writing technical articles, philosophy, public speaking for professional groups and school and collecting music. Ms. Angle is a Mary Kay cosmetic consultant.

Jeffrey J. Gilbeaux

Systems Manager
Trane
9603 Deerec Road
Timonium, MD 21093
(410) 252-8100
Fax: (410) 252-7330
jjgx1@yahoo.com

5075

Business Information: As Systems Manager of Trane, Mr. Gilbeaux is responsible for building systems, controlling equipment, sales, installations, and reporting revenue. In his current capacity, he oversees and directs the work flow for three engineers, two programmers, and seven technicians. Utilizing his knowledge in the air conditioning industry, Mr. Gilbeaux evaluates equipment, meets with building owners and contractors on a daily basis, and attends to local and area networks. During his employment with Trane, his long list of accomplishments includes installation of the chiller plant at St. Francis Hospital, the automation system at Independence Hall, the controls at QVC Studio, and the equipment and controls at Temple Shriners Hospital. Highly regarded, Mr. Gilbeaux helped Trane grow from a $467,000 to a $2.5 million Company. His success reflects his ability to take on challenges and deliver results on behalf of the Company and its satisfied clientele. Established in 1885, Trane is a reputable, Fortune 500 company specializing in heating, air conditioning, and ventilation control systems as well as automation. Currently operating with a staff of 65, Trane's Timonium, Maryland's location is run by American Standard. **Career Highlights:** Systems Manager, Trane (1998-Present); Project Manager, Johnson Controls, Inc. (1996-98); Project Manager, DVY, Inc. (1988-96). **Associations & Accomplishments:** American Society of Human Resource Associate Executives; National Society of Professional Engineers; PSPE; American Statistical Society; MENSA. **Education:** Pennsylvania State University, M.S. in Engineering (1999); Drexel University.

Kenneth S. Jathanna

Information Technology Manager
Carrier Saudi Arabia
P. O. Box 9784
Riyadh, Saudi Arabia 11423
+966 14911333
Fax: +966 14915325
kenneth@jathanna.com

5075

Business Information: Possessing unique talent in the technology field, Mr. Jathanna joined Carrier Saudi Arabia in 1996 as Information Technology Manager. He oversees and directs all daily administration and operational activities of the information systems infrastructure. As a 12-year technology professional, Mr. Jathanna coordinates system upgrades, software implementation, and routine maintenance and backup. Coordinating resources and schedules, overseeing time lines and assignments, and tuning tools to improve overall system performance also fall within the realm of Mr. Jathanna's functions. Diligent and dedicated, he has received several company awards recognizing his outstanding service. He believes that his hard work ethic and good luck are the reasons for his career success. Committed to continued optimum performance, Mr. Jathanna is currently developing a computer program that will allow the Company to better serve an international clientele. Carrier Saudi Arabia provides sales, distribution, and after sales service of heating, ventilation, and air conditioning equipment. Established in 1980, the Company employs a work force of 230 staff members and is the sole distributor and service provider of HVAC equipment in Saudi Arabia. **Career Highlights:** Information Technology Manager, Carrier Saudi Arabia (1996-Present). **Associations & Accomplishments:** Internal Quality Award (1993 & 1995); Outstanding Service Award (1996). **Education:** Ravishankar University, B.S. (1987); National Institute of Informational Technology, Diploma in Systems Analysis. **Personal Information:** Married to Angeline Stella in 1997. One child: Andrea Kristin. Mr. Jathanna enjoys listening to music and watching cartoons.

Kathy Lynn Koehn

Communications Manager
Midwest Cooperative
202 Grove Street
Quinter, KS 67752-0366
(785) 754-3348
Fax: (785) 754-3826
kathy@midwestcoop.net

5083

Business Information: Mrs. Koehn serves in the role of Communications Director for the Midwest Cooperative, a position which entails a multitude of technical responsibilities on a daily basis. Utilizing formal training and education, she maintains systems and networking capabilities as she guides her staff with a proactive leadership style. As Web site manager, she handles e-commerce activities and engineers the corporate site to be informative, attractive, and user friendly. With a creative approach, Mrs. Koehn designs marketing campaigns that are innovative as she strive to increase visibility of the Co-Op within the agricultural community. Enjoying the challenges of her position, she intends to continue in her current role as she assists in the advancements of the Co-Op in the next decade. Midwest Cooperative is a jointly owned enterprise, engaged in the production and distribution of goods and the supplying of services, operated by a group of farmers for mutual benefit. Agriculturally based, the Co-Op is equipped with grain elevators, gas stations, feed distributors, and fertilizers to ensure smooth operations in the farming and home center. Located in the great plains of Kansas, the Co-Op was founded in 1945 and currently employs 75 people. **Career Highlights:** Midwest Cooperative: Communications Manager (1998-Present), Elevator Scale Operator (1996-98); Telephone Computer Consultant, Sykes Enterprises, Inc. (1996). **Associations & Accomplishments:** Boy Scouts of America; Girl Scouts of America; United Methodist Church; Chamber of Commerce. **Education:** Kansas City Technical College, B.S. in Engineering (1974). **Personal Information:** Married to Ronald in 1974. Three children: Dean, Lynn, and

Renee. Mrs. Koehn enjoys bowhunting for deer, computers, gardening, reading and Beanie Babies.

Gregory Alexander Clements

Electronic Data Interchange Manager
W.W. Grainger
45 Charles Court
Vernon Hills, IL 60061
(847) 535-3103
Fax: (847) 535-3095
clements@grainger.com

5084

Business Information: As Electronic Data Interchange Manager for W.W. Grainger, Mr. Clements oversees and directs data interchange operations. He utilizes his skills and knowledge to ensure flawless operation of the summary billing statement system, thereby allowing the Corporation to conduct business without interruption. Mr. Clements is committed to providing continued optimum service to the Corporation and aspires to an expanded role in project management as a result of his dedication and his involvement in the advancement of operations. W.W. Grainger is one of the distributors of equipment, components and maintenance supplies. Headquartered in Vernon Hills, Illinois, the Corporation distributes over 600,000 products from more than 560 branches in the United States, Canada, Mexico, and Puerto Rico. The Corporation employs a dedicated staff to facilitate all aspects of operation and through its determined efforts has earned the distinction of becoming one of the nation's Fortune 500 companies. **Career Highlights:** W.W. Grainger: Electronic Data Interchange Manager (1999-Present), Manager of Sales Compliance and Reporting Systems (1997-98), Technical Analyst (1992-97). **Associations & Accomplishments:** Data Interchange Standards Association; XML/EDI Organization. **Education:** LF Graduate School of Management, M.B.A. (1999); University of Wisconsin, B.B.A. in Management Information Systems (1984). **Personal Information:** Married to Charlene in 1992. One child: Kathryn. Mr. Clements enjoys reading, fishing and time with family.

Leon L. Richmond

Manager of Logistics Information Systems
Applied Industrial Technologies
1 Applied Plaza
Cleveland, OH 44115-5044
(216) 426-4647
Fax: (216) 426-4820
lrichmon@apz-applied.com

5084

Business Information: Serving as Manager of Logistics Information Systems for Applied Industrial Technologies, Mr. Richmond is responsible for managing an information systems department that supports the Logistics Group at Applied. The supported technology base includes Corporate systems for inventory management, automated replenishment, purchasing, and four distributed Warehouse Management systems. The paperless WMS utilizes Radio Frequency terminals and communicates with the Corporate systems in an automated near real time communications environment. As the Information Systems adjunct to the staff of the Vice President of Logistics, he ensures that the department staff of six and the local WMS administrators maintain the operation of the logistics function as a competitive advantage within the framework of the Corporation's overall plan. A combination of years of technological experience, education, and work experiences that includes distribution line management positions has enabled Mr. Richmond to acquire the necessary skills and knowledge that establishes a high level of professional credibility. Dedicated to the growth and development of Applied Industrial Technologies, Mr. Richmond keeps abreast of new developments in the information technologies and supply chain methodologies and incorporates pertinent information into his daily duties. He hopes to obtain a higher management position, gaining greater authority and responsibility. Applied Industrial Technologies is an industrial distributor of MRO items and technologies. Established in the 1920s, the Corporation maintains its headquarters in Cleveland, Ohio and with an associate base of 4,500 operates a network of 450 service centers and seven distribution centers. **Career Highlights:** Manager of Logistics Information Systems, Applied Industrial Technologies (1992-Present); Senior Technical Support Analyst, UNISYS (1980-92); Internal Operations Auditor, White Motor (1977-80); After Market Parts Manager, Baker Material Handling (1975-77). **Associations & Accomplishments:** Council of Logistics Management. **Education:** Baldwin-Wallace College, M.B.A. (1975); Miami University, B.S. (1967). **Personal Information:** Married.

Charles K. Rightmer

Project Manager
Entech Sales & Service Inc.
10139 Metropolitan Drive
Austin, TX 78758-4942
(512) 719-5191
Fax: (512) 719-5192
crightmer@entechsales.com

5084

Business Information: Serving as Project Manager of Entech Sales & Service Inc., Mr. Rightmer manages a team of skilled programmers, engineers, and installation personnel. He awards and supervises subcontracts for each job that is contracted by the Corporation. It is his responsibility to oversee field operations and resources as well as purchasing and billing for each contracted job. As a topnotch, 13 year technology professional, Mr. Rightmer has advanced steadily in his professional career due in large part to his refusal to take no for an answer. The highlight of his career came when he designed an access control installation for Trilogy Development Group. Committed to the further success of Entech Sales & Service, Mr. Rightmer plans to expedite continued promotion through dedication and quality performance. Providing mechanical services for commercial and industrial buildings, Entech Sales & Service Inc. is actually several cohesive business groups working together. Each group specializes in a different area such as HVAC, access, and process controls as well as building automation, security, and closed circuit television. Established in 1982, the Corporation has grown to encompass a work force of more than 300 qualified individuals. **Career Highlights:** Entech Sales & Service Inc.: Project Manager (1998-Present), Project Engineer (1998), Software Engineer (1997-98); Systems Analyst, University of Texas at Austin, Department of Utilities (1992-97). **Associations & Accomplishments:** Director/Finance Officer/Board of Directors (1996-98), Austin Municipal Utilities District #2. **Education:** Texas Lutheran College, B.A. (1986); Certified Andover Controls Network and System Administrator. **Personal Information:** Married to Karen in 1989. Three children: Jessica, Kelsey, and Caleb. Mr. Rightmer enjoys tennis and golf.

Lois G. Hammons

Computer Coordinator
Rubber Products Distributors
2725 Tobey Drive
Indianapolis, IN 46219
(317) 898-2511
Fax: (317) 898-0772
lhammons@rubbergrommets.com

5085

Business Information: Since 1987, Ms. Hammons has been the Computer Coordinator for Rubber Products Distributors. She is the administrator of a RS/6000, which runs custom software, and also an NT server that runs other programs within the Company. Possessing an excellent understanding of technology, she is responsible for keeping the programs up and running smoothly and recommending and negotiating new software programs. Additionally, Ms. Hammons custom designs software systems for the Company and implements all recommended systems. A savvy technical expert, she looks forward to continuing with Rubber Products Distributors and eventually attaining the position of vice president. Her success is attributed to her leadership and flexibility. Founded in 1987, Rubber Products Distributors is a distributor of rubber and plastic products. Located in Indianapolis, Indiana, the Company began as a J.I.T. supplier and vendor consolidation company and has grown into a successful international company. The Company is an authorized 3M distributor of rubber products and a master distributor for Heyco Products Inc. Presently, 36 employees man Company operations. **Career Highlights:** Computer Coordinator, Rubber Products Distributors (1987-Present); Administrative Manager, Pictorial Inc. (1984-87); Secretary to Associate Provost, Ball State University (1982-87). **Associations & Accomplishments:** Local Church Administrative Board. **Education:** Indiana Wesleyan University, B.A. (1967). **Personal Information:** Three children: William L., Geoffrey T., and Richard A. Ms. Hammons enjoys reading.

C. Allen Thornhill

Manager
US Filter Distribution
1820 Metcalf Avenue
Thomasville, GA 31792-6845
(912) 227-8659
Fax: (912) 227-8833
thornhilla@usfilter.com

5085

Business Information: As Manager of US Filter Distribution, Mr. Thornhill is oversees and directs 1,700 employees in ensuring the serviceability and functionality of underground parts, such as pipes, valves, and fire hydrants. He is responsible for keeping employees up to date on new technology and leads them though problem solving scenarios. Possessing an excellent understanding of technology, Mr. Thornhill administers and controls the help desk software that connects all Company terminals throughout the country. During his career with US Filter Distribution, Mr. Thornhill is credited with developing software improvements and authoring the 95-page manual. This cutting edge software is still widely used. Attributing his successful career to his parents, he plans on remaining in technology and merging his technical expertise with his marketing skills. Mr. Thornhill's credo is "Give a man a fish and he eats for a day. Teach him to fish and he eats for a life time." Established in 1938, US Filter Distribution operates with 7 divisions and 1,700 employees. Headquartered in Paris, France this 1.2 billion dollar company handles everything involved with industrial and commercial water filtration. Operating internationally, US Filter Distribution operates 150 locations in the United States alone with domestic headquarters in California. **Career Highlights:** US Filter Distribution: Manager (1999-Present), Y2K Coordinator (1998-00); Graduate Assistant, Georgia Southern University (1996-98). **Associations & Accomplishments:** Phi Kappa Phi National Honor Society; Golden Key National Honor Society; Beta Gamma Sigma Honor Society for Collegiate Business Schools; USGA. **Education:** Georgia Southern University, M.B.A. (1998), B.B.A. in Marketing. **Personal Information:** Mr. Thornhill enjoys exercising, golf, running, travel and Web surfing.

Steven M. Boegeman

Systems Administrator
Ashten Racks, Inc.
15 Chrysler
Irvine, CA 92618
(800) 543-7083
steveb@ashtenracks.com

5094

Business Information: Holding the position of Systems Administrator, Mr. Boegeman has been with Ashten Racks, Inc. since 1999. He administers and controls all systems tools and ensures the integrity, reliability, and security of the systems infrastructure. Primarily responsible for the maintaining and upgrading of the Company's network system and database, he focuses on implementing new technologies in order to provide a more effective system. Managing three sites, he directs necessary software and computer equipment to the development of new computer systems. Mr. Boegeman concentrates his efforts toward specializing in database administration with Ashten Racks, Inc. His success reflects his ability to take on challenges and deliver results on behalf of the Company and its clients. Engaging in the distribution of retail products, Ashten Racks, Inc. was established in 1997. Holding 30,000 accounts in North America, the Company generates $60 million in annual revenues. Ashten Racks, Inc. remains dedicated to providing excellent sales and services to its continuing expanding clientele. **Career Highlights:** Systems Administrator, Ashten Racks, Inc. (1999-Present); Retail Manager, CompUSA (1994-98). **Education:** Saddleback College; Microsoft Certified Systems Engineer (MCSE); Microsoft Certified Database Administrator (MCDBA); Microsoft Certified Professional (MCP). **Personal Information:** Mr. Boegeman enjoys web networking.

Tung S. Chu

Vice President of Operations
Ever Glitter International Ltd.
57 West 38th Street
New York, NY 10018
(212) 768-3388
Fax: (212) 768-4939

5099

Business Information: A 25 year veteran of information technology, Mr. Chu demonstrates strategic management skills and technology expertise serving as Vice President of Operations of Ever Glitter International Ltd. In this position, he exercises oversight of all aspects of day-to-day operations and information technology activities. Mr. Chu, an innovative and focused information technology leader, is charged with overseeing financial statements; determining future resource requirements to meet changes in business climate; developing schedules, budgets, policies and procedures to improve asset management; and providing cohesive leadership and reports to senior management and staff regarding the status and successful implementation of new technologies. With a proven record of delivering results in support of business operations, Mr. Chu is responsible for the maximum utilization of technologies as it impacts the operations, sales, and trading segments of the Company. His focus is on helping Ever Glitter Internation leverage the investments in technology, personnel, and processes to remain flexible, efficient, and profitable in the global market place. His career highlight is setting up and training the staff on a new, advanced computer system infrastructure for the Company. He attributes his success to dedication and being a loyal team player. Mr. Chu's future goals include staying on top of emerging technologies, and keeping the Company out-front in the industry. Ever Glitter International Ltd. operates as an export trading firm. Global in scope, the Company specializes in scrape metal. Established in 1973, the Company is headquartered in New York and presently employs a staff of 25 people. **Career Highlights:** Vice

President of Operations, Ever Glitter International Ltd. (1990–Present); Senior Engineer/Placement Manager, Ammann & Whitney Inc. (1983–90); Senior Engineer, Canatom (1980–83); Project Engineer, Deminion Bridge (1974–80). **Associations & Accomplishments:** Order of Engineers of Quebec. **Education:** McGill University, Master's degree in Engineering (1974). **Personal Information:** Married.

5100 Wholesale Trade - Nondurable Goods

5111 Printing and writing paper
5112 Stationery and office supplies
5113 Industrial and personal service paper
5122 Drugs, proprietaries, and sundries
5131 Piece goods and notions
5136 Men's and boys' clothing
5137 Women's and children's clothing
5139 Footwear
5141 Groceries, general line
5142 Packaged frozen foods
5143 Dairy products, exc. dried or canned
5144 Poultry and poultry products
5145 Confectionery
5146 Fish and seafoods
5147 Meats and meat products
5148 Fresh fruits and vegetables
5149 Groceries and related products, nec
5153 Grain and field beans
5154 Livestock
5159 Farm-product raw materials, nec
5162 Plastics materials and basic shapes
5169 Chemicals and allied products, nec
5171 Petroleum bulk stations and terminals
5172 Petroleum products, nec
5181 Beer and ale
5182 Wine and distilled beverages
5191 Farm supplies
5192 Books, periodicals, and newspapers
5193 Flowers and florists' supplies
5194 Tobacco and tobacco products
5198 Paints, varnishes, and supplies
5199 Nondurable goods, nec

Guy Lefebvre

Network Administrator
Graphic Resources
345 Passmore Avenue
Scarborough, Ontario, Canada M1V 3N8
(416) 412-9231
Fax: (416) 412-9246
pcman@graphic-resources.com

5111

Business Information: A successful, six year veteran of the information technology field, Mr. Lefebvre was recruited to Graphic Resources and now serves as Network Administrator. He is responsible maintaining the functionality and operational status of the Company's information systems and networking infrastructure. Utilizing his business savvy and technical expertise, Mr. Lefebvre ensures all Company servers are operational and provides cutting edge support and troubleshooting in the event of systems' failure. In his present role, he is accountable for all aspects of programming and installing the AS400 and maintaining backups as necessary. A systems expert, Mr. Lefebvre oversees and maintains a PC infrastructure of 350 users. He cites as his career highlight setting up the entire Company network to include installing, implementing, and programming. Success is attributed to his perseverance in coming up with the right solution and never giving up. His plans for the future is to do more local area networking through Web and Intranet technologies. A reputable division of Rolland Inc., Graphic Resources operates as an international paper wholesale distributor. Based out of Canada, the Company was established in 1890, and continues to provide quality and value in all their products. Presently, Graphic Resources employs a work force of more than 500 people who help generate high annual revenues. **Career Highlights:** Cambrian Network Administrator, Graphic Resources (1995–Present); Customer Support Manager, Health Canada (1994). **Education:** Cambrian College (1994). **Personal Information:** Mr. Lefebvre enjoys hockey and baseball.

Rolf Karlsen
Information Technology Manager
Gulius Maske
Ladem K. Alle 2
Trondheim, Norway 7042
+47 73892908
Fax: +47 73892800
rolfkar@online.no

5112

Business Information: Functioning in the role of Information Technology Manager of Gulius Maske, Mr. Karlsen is responsible for all information technology activities within the Company. He continuously updates the software databases within the Company and replaces hardware equipment as it becomes out-dated. As a 25 year technology professional, Mr. Karlsen is currently negotiating with the Board of Executives within the Company concerning the need for Internet technology, and its ultimate benefits for expanding the revenue of the Company. In the future, Mr. Karlsen would like to be given the opportunity to completely network the Company's current facility and hopes to advance the systems within the next few years. His success reflects his ability to think outside the box, deliver results, and aggressively tackle new challenges. Gulius Maske is involved in the wholesale distribution of several products. Established in 1858, the Company's primary source of revenue stems from the sale and redistribution of paper. Other revenue for the Company is gained through the selling of computer parts and accessories. The Company employs over 200 personnel to induct, market, sell, and redistribute products throughout its Norwegian market. **Career Highlights:** Information Technology Manager, Gulius Maske (1990–Present); Information Technology Manager, Elag, A/L (1982–90); Systems Manager, Aspelin Strombull, A/S (1977–81); Systems Manager, Datasaab, A.S. (1974–76). **Associations & Accomplishments:** Norwegian Society for Electronic Data Processing. **Personal Information:** Mr. Karlsen enjoys music, fishing and walking in the mountains.

Michele Holder
Information Systems Manager
Madison International Sales
695 East Main Street
Stamford, CT 06904
(203) 324-8714
Fax: (203) 359-2539
michele.holder@madpaper.com

5113

Business Information: Serving as Information Systems Manager of Madison International Sales, Ms. Holder is responsible for the technological aspects for the sales infrastructure. Before joining Madison International Sales, Ms. Holder served as Support Specialist with Unilever and Help Desk Supervisor at G.E. Capital. Acting as the Company's chief liaison with vendors, she purchases the offices' hardware and software, administers the LAN and WAN networks, and oversees the telecommunications acquisitions. Occasionally, she contracts outside consultants on an as needed basis. Determining the overall strategic direction and business contribution of the information systems function, and ensuring the reliability, security, and integrity of the systems and network infrastructure also fall within the purview of Ms. Holder's responsibilities. She remains at the cutting edge of technology by reading trade journals and attending classes. Owing her success to perseverance and a deep sense of responsibility to finish what she has started, Ms. Holder possesses an established track record of delivering results. Establishing goals that are compatible with the Company, attaining the position of Chief Information Officer serves as one of her future goals. Wholly owned by New York Times and Melsa-Serla, Madison International Sales is a wholesale paper company, selling a wide range of products from paper mills to printers. Established in 1996, the Company employs more than 500 dedicated individuals and maintains corporate headquarters in Stanford, Connecticut. **Career Highlights:** Information Systems Manager, Madison International Sales (Present); Support Specialist, Unilever (1996); Help Desk Supervisor, G.E. Capital. **Education:** Computer Programming Institute, A.E. in Mechanical Engineers (1987). **Personal Information:** Two children: John Jr. Mayton and Daniel Mayton. Ms. Holder enjoys Web and interior design.

Lorraine M. Korber
ISO 9000 Coordinator/Quality Analyst
Henry Schein, Inc.
35 Terrace Avenue
Stevens, PA 17578
(717) 335-7230
Fax: (717) 335-7240
shandy@supernet.com

5122

Business Information: As ISO 9000 Coordinator and Quality Analyst for the Denver, Pennsylvania branch of Henry Schein, Inc., Miss Korber controls and oversees all training and development of the ISO 9000 system, performs administrative duties, and is responsible for direct interfacing with all corporate distribution areas. In addition, she maintains the central document repository, performs diagnostic system tests, and serves as a consumer support liaison for external affairs. Drawing from an extensive education and previous occupational experience, Miss Korber is leading Henry Schein, Inc. to new levels of prosperity, thereby ensuring corporate longevity and her occupational success. Her success reflects reflects her ability to take on challenges and deliver results on behalf of the Corporation. Established about 1950, Henry Schein, Inc. is an international and domestic distributor of health care products and equipment for all practices in the medical field. The Corporation operates four distribution centers across the continental United States, and is headquartered in Melville, New York; Indiana, Texas, and Nevada, and corresponding location in Pennsylvania. Currently, the Corporation employs the skilled services of more than 3,000 professionals to acquire business, meet with clients, facilitate production operations, and market products. **Career Highlights:** Henry Schein, Inc.: ISO 9000 Coordinator/Quality Analyst (1996–Present), Executive Assistant to the Director of Operations. **Associations & Accomplishments:** Who's Who in US Executives; Who's Who in Female Executives; International WHO'S WHO of Professionals; National Association of Female Executives; National Organization of Women. **Education:** Dorothea B. Lane Home Study Course, Certificate in Progress Accounting and Bookkeeping; C.W. Post, degree in Business Management Administration; Nassau Community College.

Johannes Reinert

Head of Information Technology
kohlpharma GmbH
Bahnhofstr. 4-6
Perl Saarland, Germany 66706
+49 68679203507
Fax: +49 68679201018
jreinert@kohlpharma.com

5122

Business Information: As Head of Information Technology of kohlpharma GmbH, Mr. Reinert oversees and directs all aspects of the information technology infrastructure, including retailing systems and various other applications. Working closely with his team of 24 professionals and experts, Mr. Reinert utilizes a management style that incorporates both input and feedback from all staff members. He continues to grow professionally and hopes to become involved in hardware consolidation which would allow for a more advanced retailing system and implementation of quality control. Mr. Reinert is proud of the key role he played in increasing his Department's staff from four to twenty four employees, as well as the viable training program that he personally implemented. His success reflects his ability to form teams with synergy, technical strength, and a customer oriented attitude. kohlpharma GmbH is engaged in the import of drugs from countries within the European Union for sale to pharmaceutical wholesalers and pharmacies within Germany. Established in 1979, the Company currently employs a staff of 650 individuals and reports an estimated annual revenue of $213 million. **Career Highlights:** Head of Information Technology, kohlpharma GmbH (1996–Present); Teamleader of Software Development, Dacos Software GmbH (1991–96); Help of Professorship, University of Saarbrücken (1985–91). **Associations & Accomplishments:** Gesellschaft fur Informatik; Regional Shooters Society; Communal Political Organization. **Education:** University of Saarbrücken, Diploma in Informatikes (1991). **Personal Information:** Married to Sabine Görgen in 1986. Two children: Ramona and Manuel. Mr. Reinert enjoys shooting, reading and political activities.

Sandra K. Weaver
Order Support for Management Information Systems
Roundy's Ohio Division
1100 Prosperity Road, Box 510
Lima, OH 45801
(419) 228-3141
Fax: (419) 995-2054
sweaver@roundys.com

5141

Business Information: Ms. Weaver has served in various positions throughout her career with Roundy's Ohio Division since 1973. At present, she fulfills the responsibilities of Order Support for Management Information Systems. An expert, Ms. Weaver maintains and updates the customer order machines as well as the DottCom which processes the in house sales orders. She maintains the System Output Archival and Retrieval and SIA system; Ms. Weaver also performs maintenance on the Company's EPIC, the tape backup system. Coordinating resources, time lines, schedules, and assignments also fall within the purview of her functions. Ms. Weaver is proud to note that she was promoted to her current position due to her strong work ethic and self education efforts. She stays abreast of new technological developments through classes, workshops, seminars, and reading. Dedicated to the success of the Company, she is looking forward to new challenges and plans to continue to advance and gain in responsibilities. Beginning operations in 1959, Roundy's Ohio Division is a retail grocery warehouse, suppling grocery stores with their brand name items. Purchasing products from vendors, the Company sells these items to small and large grocery stores that wish to add additional stock to its shelves. Presently, Roundy's Ohio Division employs a staff of more than 600 people. **Career Highlights:** Roundy's Ohio Division: Order Support for Management Information Systems (Present), Computer Operations Specialist; Shift Supervisor; Data Entry, Roundy's/Scot Lad. **Education:** Wayne Chicago Illinois, Diploma (1973). **Personal Information:** Married to Marvin in 1974. Three children: Nicholas, Joshua, and Maria. Ms. Weaver enjoys golf and reading.

Gary L. Sill

• • •〓◉〓• • •

Information Systems Manager
Peirone Produce
524 Trent Avenue
Spokane, WA 99202
(509) 838-3515
Fax: (509) 838-3916
gsill@icehouse.net

5148

Business Information: Serving as the Information Systems Manager since 1991, Mr. Sill provides systems support to the network and database for Peirone Produce. Demonstrating his expansive knowledge in computer systems technology, he manages an A/S 400 with a NT network front end, as well as a WAN architecture that includes three companies in three states. Supervising a team of technical experts, Mr. Sill provides systems maintenance and upgrades, and is extensively involved in project management. Utilizing his experience in the computer field, Mr. Sill plans on moving to a larger company, while remaining in the information systems field. Established in 1945, Peirone Produce specializes in the wholesale and distribution of fresh produce. Located in Spokane, Washington, the Company employs 140 experienced manufacturers and distributors including drivers of long haul trucks with routes in four states across the nation. Forming major client relations, the Company is dedicated towards providing complete customer satisfaction in their specialized sales and services. **Career Highlights:** Information Systems Manager, Peirone Produce (1994-Present). **Associations & Accomplishments:** A/S400 Users Group; Italian American Club. **Education:** SCC, A.A. (2000). **Personal Information:** Married to Nancy in 2000. Mr. Sill enjoys skiing and scuba diving.

West McKillip
RORC Support Specialist
AFI
5103 Peterson Road
Amarillo, TX 79118-3222
(806) 345-7741
Fax: (806) 622-8419
west@amaonline.com

5149

Business Information: Functioning in the capacity of RORC Support Specialist for AFI or Affiliated Foods, Inc., Mr. McKillip provides hardware and software support within a five state area. He is responsible for 24x7x365 on call maintenance support that involves systems configuration, set up, and implementation, as well as provides training on new specialized systems. Before joining AFI, Mr. McKillip served as Computer Technician and Operator for Whitney Russell Printers. As a six year technology professional, he is involved in all aspects of systems support functions and is charged with making recommendations for purchase of new hardware and software products. Mr. McKillip keeps on top of emerging technologies by constantly working with new products. Future endeavors include gaining Microsoft and Novell certifications. His success reflects his ability to think outside the box, deliver results, and aggressively take on new challenges and responsibilities. AFI is a wholesale grocery distributor. Established in 1949, the Corporation distributes grocery to several hundred stores in a six state area. Targeting grocery chains and convenient stores, AFI is regional in scope and employs a work force of more than 1,000 people. **Career Highlights:** RORC Support Specialist, AFI (1995-Present); Computer Technician/Operator, Whitney Russell Printers (1992-95). **Associations & Accomplishments:** Data Processing Managers Association; OEA; CMA; Who's Who Among American High School Students. **Education:** West Texas A&M University: B.S. (1993), B.S. in Customer Service and Accounting. **Personal Information:** Married to Jo Ann in

1994. Two children: Reece and Jordan. Mr. McKillip enjoys the Internet, camping and fishing.

David B. Leach
Technology Manager of Control Strategies
Air Products & Chemicals, Inc., GEGE Process Controls A32H2
7201 Hamilton Boulevard, A32H2
Allentown, PA 18195-1501
(610) 481-8693

5169

Business Information: Serving as Technology Manager of Control Strategies for the Gases and Equipment Group of Air Products & Chemicals, Inc., Mr. Leach performs needs analysis, evaluates new process control technologies, specifies and installs plant automation systems, and performs applications consulting in the areas of advanced process control, plant information management, and process dynamics analysis and simulation. Mr. Leach is also responsible for the training of control and process engineers and supervises newly recruited employees. In the future, he would like to move into product development as well as other areas of technology management. Air Products & Chemicals, Inc., is a major global supplier of industrial gases and related equipment and services, and selected chemicals. Established in 1940, the Corporation generates annual revenues of $5 billion, operates hundreds of facilities worldwide and employs over 15,000 people. Corporate headquarters are in eastern Pennsylvania's Lehigh Valley, near Allentown. **Career Highlights:** Technology Manager of Control Strategies, Air Products & Chemicals, Inc. (1980-Present); Process/Control Engineer, Stauffer Chemical Company (1974-80); Production Supervisor, Union Carbide Corporation (1970-73). **Associations & Accomplishments:** Senior Member, Instrument Society of America; Past Member, South Charleston, West Virginia Jaycees; Former Junior Achievement Counselor; Top 100 Contributors Member, United Way of Lehigh Valley; Published several articles and provided presentations on supervisory computer control and batch control, Chilton's Instruments and Control Systems, Chemical Engineering, Chemical Processing; Organized and Conducted a Batch Control Seminar, Control Engineering Magazine's Control Expo (1987); Presented 15 papers for technical meetings and seminars on various process control topics, including advanced control, dynamics analysis tools, batch control, and distillation control; Received Air Products' highest corporate technical award twice for innovation using process control and simulation technologies; Received Chemicals Group highest technical award three times for similar innovations; Invited Guest Lecturer on distributed process control systems, Lehigh University (1990). **Education:** Bucknell University, B.S. in Chemical Engineering (1970). **Personal Information:** Mr. Leach enjoys running, camping, hiking, nature and wildlife photography and riding motorcycles.

Mark M. Booth
Manager of Systems and Integration
Southern Wine & Spirits
1600 Northwest 163rd Street
Miami, FL 33169
(305) 625-4171
markbooth@southernwine.com

5182

Business Information: A 13 year veteran of Southern Wine & Spirits, Mr. Booth serves as Manager of Systems and Integration. He oversees all strategic and tactical planning of ERP systems and implementation as the Company moves to IBM AS400s from outdated mainframes. Mr. Booth's responsibilities also include the technical implementation of a seven million dollar SAP R/3 System. In part, he is also responsible for hiring, firing, and conducting performance evaluations for his staff. Owning a consistent record of delivering results, he formulates the Company's strategic direction in addition to research and evaluation of business partners and vendors. Mr. Booth facilitates decision-making and communication between multiple departments in forecasting, calculating, and managing the management information systems budget. A skilled and creative problem solver, he turns chaos into order by establishing disaster recovery procedures, standards, and training packages utilizing state-of-the-art technologies. Being able to motivate people and possessing excellent skills in organizing large projects has attributed to Mr. Booth's success. His future objectives include implementation of a successful plan and eventually attaining the position of Chief Information Officer. Southern Wine & Spirits, established in 1968, is a wholesale distributor of liquor, wine, and beer. The largest distributor in the United States, the Company operates in nine states and sells beverage products to hotels, groceries, restaurants, and the transportation industry. Headquartered in Florida, the

Company employs 5,200 people generating in excess of $3.1 billion in annual revenues. **Career Highlights:** Southern Wine & Spirits: Manager of Systems and Integration (2000-Present), Manager of Disaster Recovery Planning (1999-00), Director of Operations (1998-99), Director of Warehouse Information Technology (1997), Director of Information Systems (1988-96). **Associations & Accomplishments:** AOPA.

Binglin "Bing" Yang
Corporate I/T Customer Relationship Manager
Cargill, Inc.
6000 Clearwater Drive
Minnetonka, MN 55343
(612) 984-5530
Fax: (612) 742-7917
bing-lin_yang@cargill.com
bing-lin_yang@cargill.com

5191

Business Information: Mr. Yang is a 15-year veteran of the information technology field. He was recruited to Cargill in 1993 and served a two-year duty in China s Country Information Technology Manager. Mr. Yang now serves as Cargill Corporate I/T Customer Relationship Manager for Asia, Europe, and Latin America as well as Steel, Salt, Juice, and Cocoa divisions in North America. His position principally involved customer interfacing and services between business units and I/T technologies and telecommunications. He exhibits a cross-cultural approach to business operations, as he understands different cultures. Mr. Yang's favorite credo is "constantly improve yourself in today's challenges 'small' global village environment. Knowing differences between cultures and business practices is critical to success of business ventures." His success has been attributed to the combination of technical and business expertise as well as extensive international experience. The world's largest privately held company, Cargill, Inc. is involved in over 50 lines of business. The Corporation has 130 years of service and international expertise in commodity trading, handling, transporting, processing, and risk management. Cargill primarily trades grains and oil seeds as well as markets other agricultural and nonagricultural commodities. A complex network of rail and road systems is utilized to transport goods and services. Presently, Cargill employs a global work force of more than 80,000 people generating in excess of $60 billion in annual revenues. **Career Highlights:** Cargill, Inc.: Corporate I/T Customer Relationship Manager (1999-Present), International Telecommunications Manager (1997-99); Country Information Technology Manager, Cargill China, Ltd. (1995-97). **Associations & Accomplishments:** Telecom Group, AT&T. **Education:** Georgia State University, M.S. in Computer Science (1992); Montana Tech, M.S. in Petroleum Engineering; Jilin University, B.S. in Physics. **Personal Information:** Married to Laural in 1986. Two children: Diane and Sarah. Mr. Yang enjoys socials, table tennis, soccer, music and surfing the Internet.

Anthony P. Costa
Information Technology Manager
Sher Distributing
891 Leonardville Avenue
Leonardo, NJ 07737
(973) 256-4050
tony.costa@usa.net

5192

Business Information: Mr. Costa, serving as Information Technology Manager of Sher Distributing, oversees all aspects of the information systems department. He is responsible for supporting multiple systems including Web sites and e-commerce. Possessing an excellent understanding of his field, Mr. Costa plans and executes all plans and marketing strategies. He also performs troubleshooting and purchasing, manages the Internet based business, monitors backup systems, and ensures quality customer support. Highly regarded, Mr. Costa manages the Company's relationship with their Internet service provider. Among his many achievements, he managed and supported a 3,000 user e-mail network connected to the Internet. Users included Cornell Medical School and five hospitals. In the future, Mr. Costa hopes to learn more about IX and get more involved with different projects at the Company. Sher Distributing is a book distribution company. Founded in 1955, the Company distributes paperback and hardcover book, mainly to retail stores. The Company's services include field servicing accounts, warehousing, inventory, and in-house marketing. Reporting an estimated annual sales of $150 million, the Company distributes its product nationally, and employs 1,700 individuals. **Career Highlights:** Information Technology Manager, Sher Distributing (1999-Present); Team Leader, New York Presbyterian Hospital (1996-99); New York Hospital: Senior Systems Engineer (1994-96), Systems Engineer (1991-94). **Education:** The Cettone Institute, Certificate (1987). **Personal Information:** Married to Susan in 1988. Three children: Lindsey, Kristen, and Antonia. Mr. Costa enjoys skiing and fishing.

5200 - 5999

RETAIL TRADE

5200 Building Materials and Garden Supplies

5211 Lumber and other building materials
5231 Paint, glass, and wallpaper stores
5251 Hardware stores
5261 Retail nurseries and garden stores
5271 Mobile home dealers

Dana Milner

Director of Information Services
Home Depot
2455 Paces Ferry Road C-7
Atlanta, GA 30339
(770) 384-5024
Fax: (770) 384-4973
dana_milner@homedepot.com

5211

Business Information: As Director of Information Services for Home Depot, Mr. Milner is in charge of the extensive Internet service the Company provides to its clients. He is responsible for determining the overall strategic direction and business contribution of the information systems function. Before joining Home Deport, Mr. Milner served as President of Dana Milner & Associates. His background history also includes a stint as Manager of Recruiting for Ernst & Young. Motivating and controlling the actions of his dedicated team members and tackling any human resources needs within Home Depot also fall within the realm of his responsibilities. As a 29 year professional, Mr. Milner oversees and directs activities of the Company's information systems shops throughout the country, negotiating any legal issues that may arise. He hopes to expand his department's services and would like to teach more indepth courses on Internet and Intranet usage and capabilities. Home Depot is a home improvement warehouse. Established in 1979, The Company provides customers with everything from garage door openers to kitchen sinks. Almost 200,000 employees work at the multiple locations across the United States. Customers are able to have assistance in determining their product needs and supply necessities to complete their home-based projects. Nationwide, the Company turns over $37 billion through its sales and first class customer service. **Career Highlights:** Director of Information Services, Home Depot (1997-Present); President, Dana Milner & Associates (1990-97); Manager of Recruiting, Ernst & Young (1987-90). **Associations & Accomplishments:** Southeast Employment Network; Colorado Technical Recruiters Network; Habitat for Humanity; Trustee, Lanier Technical Institute; Regional Advisory Council for Atlanta with Department Industry Tourism and Trade. **Education:** North Georgia College, B.S. (1970); Art Institute Atlanta Photography. **Personal Information:** Two children: Lindsay and Amanda. Mr. Milner enjoys golf, photography and backpacking.

5300 General Merchandise Stores

5311 Department stores
5331 Variety stores
5399 Misc. general merchandise stores

Juliann M. Fiorito

Lead Programmer/Analyst
May Department Stores
4217 Westminster Drive
Lorain, OH 44053
(440) 233-7162
Fax: (440) 233-3434

5311

Business Information: Serving in various positions with May Department Stores since 1973, Ms. Fiorito currently serves as Lead Programmer and Analyst for the Data Processing Center within the Company. An information systems professional with 26 years experience in the industry, Ms. Fiorito is experienced in all aspects of analysis, design, development, implementation, and project management. She directly supervises two skilled staff members and is responsible for writing the technical specifications for internal program changes. Testing the new system changes to ensure its efficiency and functionality, she installs the updated programs and trains employees on its correct usage. Coordinating resources, schedules, and assignments also fall within the realm of her responsibilities. Ms. Fiorito credits her success to her people skills and looks forward to a long career as a Departmental Manager. May Department Stores is a publicly traded company with a string of retail outlets across the country. Although the Company's primary function is the sale of clothing, household goods, and other related products for the average consumer, it also maintains a data processing center for the corporate client. **Career Highlights:** May Department Stores: Lead Programmer/Analyst (1999-Present), Various Positions (1973-99). **Associations & Accomplishments:** Big Brothers Big Sisters of Lorain County: Board Member (1998-Present), Volunteer (1996-Present). **Education:** Lorain County Community College; Youngstown State University. **Personal Information:** Ms. Fiorito enjoys cross stitch, reading, sports and working with children.

Don R. Standford

DIS Supervisor
Target
1448 82nd Avenue
Oakland, CA 94621
(510) 918-2279

5331

Business Information: Recruited to Target in 1995, Mr. Stanford utilizes his extensive knowledge as an electrical engineer in serving as DIS Supervisor. A systems expert in his field, he travels to the Company's regional stores, performing PC programming, software and hardware installations, and PC repair as necessary. Additionally, he maintains the central network that allows the individual stores to communicate to one another and administrates the closed circuit television cameras and network. Coordinating resources, time lines, schedules, and assignments also fall within the purview of Mr. Standford's responsibilities. Committed to Target's further development, Mr. Standford coordinates strategic planning to ensure a bright future for a position as Area Manager. His success reflects his ability to thing out-of-the-box and aggressively take on new challenges. Competing against such retail giants as Wal-Mart and K-Mart, Target is a retail store selling a wide range of consumer items from clothing to hardware. The Company has a chain of stores across the country and continues to expand its geographical area. Target opened its first outlet in 1968. **Career Highlights:** DIS Supervisor, Target (1995-Present); Director of Maintenance, Roundsville Rehabilitation (1982-95); Senior Engineer, United Airling (1971-81). **Education:** Stanford University, Electrical Engineering (1973).

Robin L. Hoggard

Management Information Systems Director
Beasley Enterprises
P.O. Box 1386
Ahoskie, NC 27910-1386
(252) 332-5021
Fax: (252) 332-8161
hoggardr@coastalnet.com

5399

Business Information: Recruited to Beasley Enterprises in 1996, Ms. Hoggard serves as the Management Information Systems Director. She oversees the administration of the corporate headquarters local area network, as well as the wide area network that connects all of the separate business entities to the main office. Acting as the Company's technological vender liaison, she purchases hardware and software for the various network systems and individual workstations. Ms. Hoggard trains new users on the systems and provides technical support. Staying on the cutting edge of technology by attending seminars and reading industry publications, she looks forward to assisting the Company in the completion of future goals. Her success reflects her ability to aggressively tackle new challenges. Headquartered in Ahoskie, North Carolina, Beasley Enterprises is the owner and operator of several different business entities. The Company owns 38 Red Apple Market convenient stores, 8 oil plants, and a fuel transport company. Additionally, Beasley Enterprises operates several farms and an environmental company. Established in 1920, operations employ the dedicated services of 550 individuals. **Career Highlights:** Management Information Systems Director, Beasley Enterprises (1996-Present); Roanoke-Chowan Community College: Information Systems Instructor (1992-97), Computer Lab Assistant (1991-92). **Education:** East Carolina University, Master's degree in Instructional Technology Computer Specialist (1996); Elizabeth City State University, B.S. in Computer Science with minor in Business Administration; Roanoke-Chowan Community College, A.A.S. in Business Computer Programming. **Personal Information:** Two children: Randy and Michelle. Ms. Hoggard enjoys travel, reading and cooking.

5500 Automotive Dealers and Service Stations

5511 New and used car dealers
5521 Used car dealers
5531 Auto and home supply stores
5541 Gasoline service stations
5551 Boat dealers
5561 Recreational vehicle dealers
5571 Motorcycle dealers
5599 Automotive dealers, nec

Brian D. Ferraro

Internet Manager
C&C Ford Sales Inc.
1100 Easton Road
Horsham, PA 19044
(215) 674-3600
Fax: (215) 672-4367
cancford1@aol.com

5511

Business Information: In his capacity of Internet Manager, Mr. Ferraro oversees and manages Internet sales for C&C Ford Sales Inc. Working closely with his team, he facilitates the development of the e-commerce department and presides over all Internet sales functions. Among his management responsibilities, Mr. Ferraro is Chairman of the STARZ Committee, identifying potential challenges for the dealership and creating solutions to those challenges. Always alert to new opportunities, techniques and approaches, he intends to establish the e-commerce Internet services for the other eight dealerships. Mr. Ferraro attributes his success to a supportative family and his honesty and dedication. C&C Ford Sales Inc. is a Ford car and truck dealership that is part of the Chapman Group, and eight other dealerships. Established in 1959, the Corporation serves a local clientele. Being a self contained facility C&C Ford offers a multitude of services. The dealership facilitates conveniences for customers by having a personal body shop, and a 24 hour parts and service department. The Corporation presently employs 125 staff members to meet the demands of a growing clientele. **Career Highlights:** C&C Ford Sales Inc.: Internet Manager (1999-Present), F&I Manager (1998-99), Sales Manager (1997-98). **Associations & Accomplishments:** Pennsylvania State Alumni Association; Burlington County Board of Realtors. **Education:** Bucks County Technical School (1973). **Personal Information:** Married to JoAnn in 1975. Two children: Cristina and Douglas. Mr. Ferraro enjoys music, electronics and motorcycles.

Dennis R. Lynk

Director of Programs
Benedict Corporation
P.O. Box 350
Norwich, NY 13815
(607) 334-2224
Fax: (607) 334-4456
dennislynk@hotmail.com

5511

Business Information: Working for Benedict Corporation for more than six years, Mr. Lynk currently fulfills a number of duties as the Director of Programs. He is responsible for new and used car sales and inventory management. Possessing an excellent understanding of technology, he manages the Web site and contents and serves as an Internet sales manager and title clerk. Mr. Lynk is also responsible the computer network administration and G.M. access as well as warehouse and stock inventory. Concurrently, he is the Owner of Dennis Lynk Enterprises. In the future, Mr. Lynk looks forward to obtaining a computer based position, dealing solely with Internet sales. His success reflects his ability to take on challenges and deliver the cutting edge results. Established in 1905, the Benedict Corporation is a new and used car dealership. Selling Pontiac, Cadillac, GMC, Oldsmobile, and

Subaru vehicles, the Dealership is dedicated to finding dependable, reliable used cars to offer clients. Employing 35 personnel, the Dealership offers parts and service on these vehicles, and ensures that each client is able to find a loan to fit their needs. **Career Highlights:** Director of Programs, Benedict Corporation (1994–Present); Owner, Dennis Lynk Enterprises (1992–Present); Owner, Pure Springs Enterprises (1972–92). **Associations & Accomplishments:** Charter Member, Norwich Lions Club; George Rider Hook & Ladder Fire Company; United States Army (1966–69). **Education:** State University of New York at Morrisville, A.A.S. in Accounting and Business Management (1978). **Personal Information:** Married to Diana in 1981. Two children: Christopher and Randy. Mr. Lynk enjoys travel.

Michael A. Maher
Management Information Systems Manager
Weber Chevrolet
P.O. Box 419009
St. Louis, MO 63141-9009
(314) 567-3300
Fax: (314) 567-1745
maher19@mvp.net

5511

Business Information: Serving as Management Information Systems Manager of Weber Chevrolet, Mr. Maher is responsible for the company's system and operating infrastructure, including Internet, voice mail, and Web site maintenance. He helps determine the strategic direction and business contribution of the information systems function. The Company depends on Mr. Maher to keep the system fully functional and operating smoothly to ensure an effective and efficient operation. Additionally, he is in charge of the procurement of equipment and supplies and the e-commerce sector for business marketing online. In the future, he hopes to expand the company's e-commerce division and continue being a pro-active problem solver. Success, according to Mr. Maher, is due to his ability to think outside the box, take on challenges, and deliver results. Weber Chevrolet operates as a new and used car dealership. Offering the latest models from the production line, the Company also services vehicles. Located in the midwestern metropolis of St. Louis, Missouri, Weber Chevrolet is headquartered in Creve Coeur, Missouri. Founded in 1902, the Company employs a team of 300 professional, technical, and support staff. **Career Highlights:** Management Information Systems Manager, Weber Chevrolet (1981–Present); Manager, Feld Chevrolet (1975–81). **Associations & Accomplishments:** Soccer Club Official. **Personal Information:** Married to Patricia in 1971. Two children: Brian and Holly. Mr. Maher enjoys hunting, fishing, camping and boating.

Belinda J. Mathis
Human Resource Information Systems Specialist
Mercedes Benz U.S. International
P.O. Box 100
Tuscaloosa, AL 35403
(205) 507-2640
Fax: (205) 507-3301

5511

Business Information: With extensive experience in the technology field, Ms. Mathis serves as the Human Resource Information Systems Specialist for Mercedes Benz U.S. International. She fulfills the dual role of Project Leader and Systems Administrator for the Human Resources Department's information systems. Evaluating the internal infrastructure and network service Web page, she trains end users and makes hardware and software recommendations for the Department. Coordinating resources, time lines, schedules, and assignments also fall within the purview of her responsibilities. Ms. Mathis is continually striving for maximum effectiveness and anticipates a promotion to Manager. She credits her success to God, family support, and a solid education, as well as her ability to aggressively take on new challenges. Headquartered in Vance, Alabama, Mercedes Benz U.S. International is a publicly owned automotive manufacturer. The Company manufactures and distributes the Mercedes Benz M Class, world famous for its quality and style. Presently, the Company employs a work force of more than 1,900 people. **Career Highlights:** Human Resource Information Systems Specialist, Mercedes Benz U.S. International (1996–Present); Bristol-Myers Squibb: Sales Information Analyst (1998–96), Manager of Payroll (1993–95), Business Development Associate (1988–93). **Associations & Accomplishments:** Delta Sigma Theta Sorority; Society for Human Resources Management; National Black M.B.A. Association; Jack and Jill of America; Leadership Tuscaloosa; Leadership Class (1998–99). **Education:** State University at New York, M.B.A. (1996); Rochester Institute Technology: B.S. in Business

Administration, A.S. in Accounting. **Personal Information:** One child: Amani Kendra Salih. Ms. Mathis enjoys travel.

5600 Apparel and Accessory Stores

    5611 Men's and boys' clothing stores
    5621 Women's clothing stores
    5632 Women's accessory and specialty stores
    5641 Children's and infants' wear stores
    5651 Family clothing stores
    5661 Shoe stores
    5699 Misc. apparel and accessory stores

Lynn A. Bowen
Manager of Database Administration
Talbot's
4300 West Cypress Street
Tampa, FL 33607
(813) 829-6009
Fax: (813) 829-6218
lynn.bowen@talbots.com

5621

Business Information: As Manager of Database Administrator of Talbot's, Ms. Bowen fulfills a number of duties on behalf of the Company and its clientele. She is responsible for day to day technical and managerial activities, such as data entry, workload distribution, employee supervision, and sales forecasting. Also performing administrative duties, Ms. Bowen conducts contract negotiations, technical guidance, policy and procedure development, personnel management, and strategic business planning. Possessing an excellent understanding of her field, she leads a staff of 10 employees in attending to IMS, DVZ, Oracle, and PeopleSoft support. Continuing to lead Talbot's to new levels of prosperity, Ms. Bowen plans to promote the Company's best interests in her current capacity; thereby achieving personal satisfaction and occupational success. Talbot's markets women's and children's clothing. Established in 1947, the Company has grown to employ 9,000 people who generate substantial revenues from an international market. Specializing in the distribution and retail of high quality apparel, Talbot's has become a global leader in the fashion industry. Maintaining an impeccable service and product record, the Company is expanding operations to additional cities and countries throughout the world, gaining profit potential and consumer recognition. **Career Highlights:** Manager of Database Administration, Talbot's (1998–Present); Volvo Information Technology: Senior Project Leader (1997–98), Manager of Information Systems Administration (1989–97); Systems Programmer, Mellon Bank (1987–89). **Education:** Indiana University of Pennsylvania, B.S. (1983); Westmoreland County Community College, A.A.S. **Personal Information:** Married to Phil D'Jernes in 1994. One child: Mackenzie Delacour.

Berthil Sorstedt

Information Technology Manager
Lindex AB
Lindex
Alingsas, Sweden 44184
+46 32277900
Fax: +46 32274600
berthil.sorstedt@lindex.se

5621

Business Information: Mr. Sorstedt functions in the capacity of Information Technology Manager of Lindex AB. He concurrently fulfills the role of the Chief Informations Officer, responsible for planning and developing the overall strategic direction and business contribution of the information systems function. Through his innovative ideas and techniques, the Company utilizes state-of-the-art technologies to monitor the shipment and inventory of all of products, as well as all employee records and store databases. In the future, Mr. Sorstedt goals are to eventually attain the position of Managing Director and implement and make use of all new technologies. His ability to speak Swedish, English, and some French and German enables his to operate in the global market place unhindered. Lindex AB is a Swedish retail chain focusing its product line on lady's wear and lingerie and children's wear. Established in 1954, the Company is dedicated to the superior quality of each article of clothing placed on the racks within its stores. The Company turns over $450 million annually and supports a staff of 3,000 employees. **Career Highlights:** Information Technology Manager, Lindex AB (1999–Present); Information Technology Manager, Ellos AB (1995–98); Information Technology Consultant, Guide AB

(1989–94). **Education:** IHM Business School, Master's Controller degree (1996); Chalmers University, Master's degree in Electronics Engineering **Personal Information:** Married to Kerstin in 1979. Three children: Arik, Elin, and Emelie. Mr. Sorstedt enjoys tennis and classical music.

James W. Johnston
Computer Operations Manager
Shoe Carnival
8233 Baumgart Road
Evansville, IN 47725
(812) 867-4215
Fax: (812) 867-3625
jaydog@scvl.com

5661

Business Information: Educated in the field of electrical engineering, Mr. Johnston serves as Computer Operations Manager for Shoe Carnival. In his capacity, he assumes responsibility for all technical aspects of the Corporation's 40 locations across the nation. Before joining Shoe Carnival, Mr. Johnston served with ITT Technical Institute as Electronics and Math Professor. His background history also includes a stint with Primus as an Electronic Technician. In his present role, he administers and maintains all servers, LANs, WANs, and hardware and software, as well as offers technical support for its users. Coordinating resources, time lines, schedules, and assignments; tuning software tools to improve overall performance; and providing cohesive leadership also fall within the purview of his responsibilities. Dedicated to the success of the Corporation, Mr. Johnston anticipates a promotion to Director of the Information Systems Department. A retail footwear company, Shoe Carnival sells shoes for both adults and children. National operations employ over 5,000 individuals. Sales for the 1998 annual fiscal year were reported upwards of $280 million. **Career Highlights:** Computer Operations Manager, Shoe Carnival (1996–Present); Electronics and Math Professor, ITT Technical Institute (1996–97); Electronic Technician, Primus (1995–96). **Associations & Accomplishments:** National Vocational Honor Society. **Education:** ITT Tech: B.S. in Electrical Technology (1996), Associate's degree in Electrical Engineering. **Personal Information:** Married to Leslie in 1995. One child: Danielle. Mr. Johnston enjoys fishing and sports.

David M. McIntyre II
Senior Analyst
The Shoe Show of Rocky Mount
776 Florence Street
Concord, NC 28027-5922
(704) 782-4143
dmcinii@bellsouth.net

5661

Business Information: Mr. McIntyre is Senior Analyst for The Shoe Show of Rocky Mount. He is responsible for all aspects of network administration, program maintenance, and systems and network design and development. Before joining The Shoe Show of Rocky Mount, Mr. McIntyre served as Senior Programmer of Lyles Data Systems and Computer Instructor with Robeson Community College. As a 14 year technology professional, he owns an established record of producing results. Working with users and management to analyze, specify, and design systems to harness more of the computer's power; maintaining and upgrading the systems infrastructure; and tuning software tools to enhance overall systems performance also fall within the realm of Mr. McIntyre's responsibilities. Originally an accounting teacher, he became involved in technology after taking computer classes. Attributing his success to his wife and family, he received Lyes Data Systems' "Premier Performer" in 1993, 1996, and 1997. One of his future goals include rewriting the entire retail system for The Shoe Show in the client server area. A retail shoe corporation, The Shoe Show of Rocky Mount is located in Concord, North Carolina. The Company was established in 1960. **Career Highlights:** Senior Analyst, The Shoe Show of Rocky Mountain (1997–Present); Senior Programmer, Lyles Data Systems (1990–97); Instructor, Robeson Community College (1985–90). **Education:** Florence Darlington Technical College, A.S. (1985); Presbyterian College, B.S. (1983). **Personal Information:** Married to Melva G. in 1989. Two children: David III and Alec.

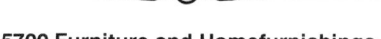

5700 Furniture and Homefurnishings Stores

    5712 Furniture stores
    5713 Floor covering stores
    5714 Drapery and upholstery stores
    5719 Misc. homefurnishings stores
    5722 Household appliance stores
    5731 Radio, TV, and electronic stores
    5734 Computer and software stores

5735 Record and prerecorded tape stores
5736 Musical instrument stores

Rick Sutter

President
SutterTel.Com
1827 South Washington Street
Kennewick, WA 99337
(509) 585-1900
Fax: (509) 585-2601
rick@suttertel.com

5731

Business Information: Mr. Sutter is President of SutterTel.Com. He oversees day-to-day administration and operational activities, including development of sales and marketing strategies, purchasing, and Web site design and maintenance. Before starting SutterTel.Com with his wife and business partner, Deby, Mr. Sutter served as Management Consultant of Sutter Associates, Quality Assurance Manager at IT Corporation, and Project Management Specialist with Kaiser Engineers. As a nine year technology professional, he is responsible for product and Web site promotion, identifying manufacturers and distributors for new products, and taking a lead role in the development of creative advertisements and driving products to market. Analyzing, supporting, and monitoring communications network operations and troubleshooting systems hardware, software, and transmission problems also fall within the realm of Mr. Sutter's responsibilities. He attributes his success to calculated risk taking. Expanding sales and increasing revenues and clientele serve as his strategic objectives. An online store, SutterTel.Com provides consumer electronics and telecommunications services. The Store specializes in sales and marketing of electronics to homes, small businesses, universities, and commercial production companies. Established in 1995, SutterTel.Com is 100 percent e-commerce capable. National in scope, the Store presently employs six people who generate revenues in excess of $1.5 million annually. **Career Highlights:** President, SutterTel.Com (1995-Present); Management Consultant, Sutter Associates (1994-96); Quality Assurance Manager, IT Corporation (1992-94); Project Management Specialist, Kaiber Engineers (1990-92). **Education:** University of Phoenix, M.A. in Organization Management (1996); University of New York, B.S. (1992). **Personal Information:** Married to Deby in 1993. Four children: John, Nichelle, Nicholle, and Noelle. Mr. Sutter enjoys Internet commerce and music.

Lisa Abbott

Senior Manager of Distributed Logistics Systems
Office Depot
2200 Germantown Road
Delray Beach, FL 33445-8299
(561) 438-3560
Fax: (561) 438-2369
labbott@officedepot.com

5734

Business Information: Serving as Senior Manager of Distributed Logistics Sysetms at the headquarters location of Office Depot in Delray Beach, Florida, Mrs. Abbott handles a variety of specialized tasks that pertain to technical operations. With personable ease, she directs her staff as they accomplish daily objectives, working closely with them to offer insight and guidance. She demonstrates her financial expertise as she allocates corporate budget funds for the completion of departmental activities and technical research. Demonstrating impressive skill in the areas of information technology and management information systems, Mrs. Abbott evaluates current corporate policies and programs then makes decisions for improvements and changes based on her professional opinion. Enjoying the challenges of her position, she intends to continue in this role as she shift the focus of technical activities towards e-business. Office Depot is a mass merchadiser of office supplies and furnitures, computers and accessories, and various small electronic devices such as telephones, calculators, and day planners. Additionally, the Company offers services to the general public and to local businesses such as sending and receiving faxes, copying documents, and digital scanning of photgraphs and papers. Established in 1987, the Company has nearly 1,000 employees worldwide with estimated annual revenues of $10 billion. **Career Highlights:** Office Depot: Senior Manager of Distributed Logistics Systems (1997-Present), Senior Manager of Store Systems (1995-97); Staff Programmer/International, IBM Corporation (1988-95). **Education:** Rutgers University, Bachelor's degree (1987). **Personal Information:** Married to Richard in 1993. One child: Ronnie. Mrs. Abbott enjoys kayaking and piano.

Harry C. Athey

Information Technology Manager
Philips P.C. Peripherals
4435 Arrowswest Drive
Colorado Springs, CO 80907-3445
(719) 593-4237
Fax: (719) 593-4211
harry.c.athey@philips.com

5734

Business Information: Educated in the field of computer science, Mr. Athey serves as the Information Technology Manager for Philips P.C. Peripherals. He assumes the responsibility for overseeing the information technology functions for the Company's North American operations. In this capacity, he coordinates the LAN and WAN administration, computer repair, and systems maintenance. A staff of 35 qualified professionals assist him in the completion of his daily duties. Mr. Athey recently developed a Logistic Management System which tracks the product inventory, allowing the Company to monitor inventory levels and destinations more efficiently. He attributes his success to knowing the right people and being able to communicate with everyone in their own language. Continually striving to improve performance, Mr. Athey long term goal is to become Chief Information Officer. Founded in 1985, Philips P.C. Peripherals is one of the top, leading providers of personal computer peripherals. The Company sells add on computer equipment such as cameras and monitors to large computer original equipment manufacturers. Annual sales are estimated to be $1 billion for the next fiscal year. **Career Highlights:** Information Technology Manager, Philips P.C. Peripherals (1995-Present); Systems Engineer, Summit Consulting (1994-95). **Associations & Accomplishments:** Association of Computing Machinery; TAV ALPHA PIE. **Education:** Colorado Technical University, M.S. (1999), B.S. in Computer Science (1997). **Personal Information:** Mr. Athey enjoys scuba diving, rock climbing and boating.

Alan L. Boyles

Network Engineer
AAA Business Machines
2715 North Drake Street
Fayetteville, AR 72703
(501) 442-4185
Fax: (501) 442-0342
aboyles@aaabm.com

5734

Business Information: As Network Engineer for AAA Business Machines, Mr. Boyles handles all aspects of network engineering for the Company. He is responsible for the repair of computer systems for clients, the internal installation and maintenance of computer systems for the Company, and the maintenance of all networks. Beginning his association with the Company more than five years ago, Mr. Boyles has received recognition for his diligence and expertise. He attributes his success to staying up-to-date in technology, possessing hands on experience, and reading. Mr. Boyles hopes to keep up with technology and has plans to continue his education. Established in 1979, AAA Business Machines is engaged in the resale of computer systems. A locally owned company, AAA Business Machines employs a staff of 54 qualified individuals dedicated to providing quality office equipment and supplies to clients in northwestern Arkansas. **Career Highlights:** Network Engineer, AAA Business Machines (1994-Present). **Education:** Northwest Arkansas Community College, Programming degree (1999).

Greg Darmenio

Director of Systems Development and Production
Chain Store Guide
3922 Coconut Palm Drive
Tampa, FL 33619
(813) 627-6840
Fax: (813) 627-7002
gdarmenio@aol.com

5734

Business Information: As Director of Systems Development and Production for Chain Store Guide, Mr. Darmenio is responsible for all aspects of information technology. Utilizing his managerial experience and practical education, he demonstrates an in-depth knowledge of the industry as he works closely with his departmental teams to develop innovative business solutions that maximize customer service, support, and value. Overseeing the production of informational compact disks, Mr. Darmenio formulates creative plans that allow the Company to maintain low overhead while manufacturing more efficiently. Credited for several cost cutting techniques that have been implemented throughout the Compnay, Mr. Darmenio believes his success stems from his ability to visualize goals, then form concrete plans to create tangible results. Looking forward to assisting in the further completion of corporate goals, he intends to shift departmental focus to Web based technologies. Established in 1935, Chain Store Guide is engaged in the sale of commercial intelligence to various industries. Employing over 250 people at the Tampa, Florida location, the international company reaps sales of $11 million. As society becomes more technically focused, the Company easily follows the lead, offering directories on CD-Rom versus book form and developing Web site for convenient customer purchasing. **Career Highlights:** Director of Systems Development and Production, Chain Store Guide (1998-Present); Financial Systems Manager, Lykes Steamship Company (1995-98); Principal Consultant, Darmenio & Associates (1992-95); Bureau Chief of Development, City of Orlando (1984-92). **Associations & Accomplishments:** Toastmasters; Lake Magdelen Parent Teacher Association; American Legion; American Catholic Church; Data Processing Managers Association. **Education:** Orlando College, M.B.A. (1986); Columbia College, B.A. (1975). **Personal Information:** Married to Suzanne L. in 1998.

Charles E. Derrick

Area Manager
Revacomp Inc.
8369 Montgomery Run Road, Suite A
Ellicott City, MD 21043
(410) 203-9756
Fax: (410) 203-9757
love2plaay@aol.com

5734

Business Information: Possessing unique talent in the computer industry, Mr. Derrick joined Revacomp Inc. in 1992 as an Area Manager. He assumes responsibility for overseeing the management of the Mid Atlantic and Southeast United States regional offices. Marketing the Corporation to increase its business, he visits client sites, responding to any sales and service concerns. Mr. Derrick has received internal recognition for his job performance and was just promoted to handle the logistics of the Prime Computer Merger in Europe. Known by his coworkers for his "no problem" attitude, he has the ability to solve and provide solutions to any difficulties. As technology continues to change, he plans to watch the trends and take an active part in the industry. Revacomp Inc. provides computer sales and servicing to small and medium sized businesses across the nation from 20 strategically placed locations. Established in 1982, the Corporation is currently in the process of forming several strategic alliances with other maintenance corporations, allowing it to expand its markets within the computer industry. Presently, Revacomp employs a skilled staff of 15 people. **Career Highlights:** Area Manager, Revacomp Inc. (1992-Present); National Inventory Central Manager, Prime Computer (1990-91); Buyout Transition Manager, Prime Computer/Computer Vision (1988-90). **Associations & Accomplishments:** Masonic Lodge; Porsche Club; Shriners. **Education:** Cal State Poly Technique, Marketing (1991); Microsoft Certified Systems Engineer. **Personal Information:** Four children: David, Matthew, Nicholas, and Adam. Mr. Derrick enjoys autocross, sports car racing and camping.

Christian Poupart

Systems Integrator
Buscom MKS
850-1450 City Councillors
Montreal, Quebec, Canada H3A 2E5
(514) 848-1110
Fax: (514) 848-1879
cpoupart@buscom.com

5734

Business Information: Serving Buscom MKS in the position of Systems Integrator, Mr. Poupart has been providing cutting edge technical services since joining the Company's team of professionals over seven years ago. Assessing the diverse needs of a growing clientele, he is specifically involved in the management of document and integration solutions that provides a more efficient and productive network system. Heading all administrative aspects, Mr. Poupart turns potential into action through preparation and skilled training programs. Overseeing project development, he strives to incorporate the latest technologies and superior technical support gauranteeing complete client satisfaction. Committed to his career with Buscom MKS, Mr. Poupart utilizes his vast knowledge in order to expand the product line. "Never let go of goals," is cited as his credo. Established in 1984, Buscom MKS is a software reseller of optimal CAD solutions and autodesk. Headquartered in Quebec Canada, the Company employs the skilled services of 50 qualified technical personnel to orchestrate all activities of design, manufacture, distribution, and integration to major companies in the engineering, architectual, and manufacturing industries internationally. Presently, the Company reports annual sales in excess of $10 million. **Career Highlights:** Buscom MKS: Systems Integrator (1998-Present), Service Manager (1995-98). **Associations & Accomplishments:** Up With People International Alumni Association. **Education:** College Huntsic, degree in Electronics (1993). **Personal Information:** Married to Lyne Pelletier in 1994. Two children: Jean-Michel and Vincent. Mr. Poupart enjoys scale modeling, RC modeling and computers.

Steven J. Walden
Vice President
Pace/Butler Corporation
13900 North Harvey Avenue
Edmond, OK 73013
(405) 755-3131
Fax: (405) 755-1114
swalden@pace-butler.com

5734

Business Information: In his position as Vice President of Pace/Butler Corporation, Mr. Walden oversees all computer systems, maintains inventory, and presides over the completion of all administrative tasks. He oversees all budgetary aspects, reviews all client contracts, and facilitates promotional projects. Additionally, he researches market trends in order to keep abreast of the latest technology and provide corporate direction. Mr. Walden has enjoyed substantial success in his present position and he looks forward to assisting in the completion of future corporate goals. His strategic plans include growing with the Corporation, increasing products and opportunities for clients, and gaining more knowledge. Pace/Butler Corporation engages in the purchase and resale of computer equipment, parts, and peripherals. The Corporation also manages all aspects of information technology for client companies. The Corporation is also a partner of IBM Business and Microsoft Solution. Established in 1987, the Corporation employs the skilled services of 51 individuals to facilitate all aspects of daily operation. The Corporation is headquartered in Edmond, Oklahoma and provides services to customers internationally, generating $10 million in annual revenue. **Career Highlights:** Pace/Butler Corporation: Vice President (1999-Present), Sales Manager (1998-99), Parts Manager (1991-98). **Associations & Accomplishments:** Christian Men's Network; Promise Keepers; Oklahoma Runners Club. **Education:** Oklahoma State University. **Personal Information:** Married to Kim. Five children: Tiffany, Stacy, James, Cassie, and April. Mr. Walden enjoys writing, running, travel, cars, skiing and reading.

Juanita D. Woodworth
Applications Engineer
CVIS
4630 West Jacquelyn Avenue, Suite 100
Coarsegold, CA 93722-6431
(559) 277-1000
arch@cvis.com

5734

Business Information: Serving as an Applications Engineer for CVIS or Central Visual Information Systems, Mrs. Woodworth fulfills a number of technical duties on behalf of the Company and its clientele. Demonstrating experties in her field, she provides state of the art training for architects and CAD managers. In this capacity, she assists clients in understanding state-of-the-art programs developed by the Autodesk, such as 3D Studio Viz, Architectural Desktop, and other Autocad programs. Attributing her success to being positive and having a good upbringing, Mrs. Woodworth plans to continue working in this capacity, looking forward to staying in touch with new technological advances. Her credo is "he who has faith has everthing." Located in Fresno, California, CVIS is one of the top professional consulting firms West of the Mississippi River. The Company provides services in the area of design, implementation, integration, and deployment of computer services. Employing 30 personnel, the Company provides services mainly to architects, civil engineers and land surveyors. **Career Highlights:** Applications Engineer, CVIS (1999-Present); Electral Drafter/Designer, 2H Engineer (1996-99); Customer Service Representative, Bank of America (1995-96). **Associations & Accomplishments:** A Chapter of The American Institute of Architects, AIA San Francisco; Yosemite Lakes Park Community Church. **Education:** Fresno City College, Certificate of Architecture (1998); Certified: Autocad 2000, Architectural Desktop R2, 3D Studio VIZ, and Autocad Map 2000. **Personal Information:** Married to Steven in 1999. Four children: Olivia Montes, Jevon, Brandy Preston, and Cordero Garza. Mrs. Woodworth enjoys martial arts, fishing, camping, designing and gardening.

5800 Eating and Drinking Places

5812 Eating places
5813 Drinking places

Randy E. Frye
Systems Coordinator
Country Oven, Inc.
300 North Mountain Road
Harrisburg, PA 17112-2656
(717) 652-0500
Fax: (717) 541-8991
randyfrye@afo.net

5812

Business Information: Ensuring that the computer systems of Country Oven, Inc. remain functional and fully operational to produce essential data reports, Mr. Frye functions as the Systems Coordinator. He has involvement with setup, maintenance and training. An expert, he also participates in the integration of electronic systems that offer back office accounting. Handling systems upgrades, he produces payroll reports and accounting and profit and loss statements. In addition to supervising two employees, Mr. Frye handles numerous resource planning functions to include personnel evaluations, coordinating resources and schedules, and taking charge of hardware and software acquisition. Serving as chief liaison between the Country Oven and vendors also fall within the purview of his functions. His success reflects his ability to aggressively take on new challenges and responsibilities. Eventually, Mr. Frye would like to attain the position of Chief Information Officer. Country Oven, Inc. operates as a restaurant that seats 380 people and has gained a regional reputation for its American cuisine, including delectable Prime Rib and mouth-watering Maryland style crab cakes. The chain's popularity is evidenced by revenues exceeding $2.5 million annually. Established in 1978, the Corporation employs a work force of 100 people. **Career Highlights:** Systems Coordinator, Country Oven, Inc. (1994-Present); Sales Associate, Silo (1993-94). **Education:** Pennsylvania State University, Electrical Engineering (1991). **Personal Information:** Mr. Frye enjoys fishing and camping.

Shirley B. McCraw
Senior Systems Programmer
SYSCO Corporation
1390 Enclave Parkway
Houston, TX 77077-2099
(281) 584-1172
mccraw.shirley.r000@sysco.com

5812

Business Information: As a Senior Systems Programmer of SYSCO Corporation, Ms. McCraw works closely with management and users to analyze, specify, develop and implement new solutions and programs within the Corporation. Her focus is on maintaining the Corporation's competitive edge in the food industry. Possessing superior talents in her field, she manages UNIX systems and maintains the functionality and serviceability status of the distribution infrastructure by installing, upgrading, monitoring, and resolving system problems. With the desire to remain on top, she continually reads technical journals and networks with business contacts. Among Ms. McCraw's many professional achievements, she developed and implemented a program for a university that displayed three-dimensional images and prepared mission critical systems for the year 2000. In the future, she hopes to continue to keep up with technological advances and be committed to life-long learning. Established in 1969, the SYSCO Corporation is the nation's largest food distributor and second largest of overall wholesalers. Providing an inventory list of over 200,000 products, the Corporation is headquartered in Houston, Texas. Reporting an estimated $18 billion in annual sales, SYSCO distributes products to over 270,000 restaurants, schools, hotels, and health care facilities. **Career Highlights:** Senior Systems Programmer, SYSCO Corporation (1998-Present); Senior UNIX Specialist, Administaff (1996-98); Systems Manager, EPIC Geophysical (1993-96); Systems Analyst, University of Houston (1982-92). **Associations & Accomplishments:** Association of Computing Machinery; Institute for Electrical and Electronics Engineers Computer Society. **Education:** Our Lady of the Lake University, B.S. in Computer Information Systems. **Personal Information:** Ms. McCraw enjoys family activities.

Nancy Rubin
Vice President
Camp Cuisine
5851 Holmberg Road, #1614
Parkland, NY 33067
(954) 227-7672

5812

Business Information: Possessing vast experience in providing food services to summer camps, Mrs. Rubin functions as Vice President for Camp Cuisine. In this capacity, she oversees all aspects of daily management operations. In addition, Mrs. Rubin ensures operations are efficient and profitable and selection of cost efficient food items and supplies. Achieving consistent quality in food preparation and service is another of her major roles. A recognized professional expert, Mrs. Rubin also attends to various administrative duties including inventory and profit and loss statements. Of utmost importance to the Company is the recruiting, training, and supervising of staff members. Mrs. Rubin's sound management skills have led to overwhelming successful results in these areas. The major attributes for her success include having good people skills and the fact that the Company has a solid database. Getting her Master's degree in Information Systems and establishing the Company's web page serve as Mrs. Rubin's long-term goals. Camp Cuisine provides food services management for summer camps. A seasonal business which primarily operates during the summer months, the Company works with European culinary students and has several interim contacts. **Career Highlights:** Vice President, Camp Cuisine (1994-Present); Assistant Director, Camp Chipinaw (1986-94). **Associations & Accomplishments:** Association of Computing Machinery. **Education:** Marist College, M.S. in Information Systems; Syracuse University, B.S. in Marketing. **Personal Information:** Married to David in 1986. Mrs. Rubin enjoys tennis, walking and the outdoors.

James F. Schaefer
Director of Information Systems Technology
Eat 'N Park Restaurants
100 Park Manor Drive
Pittsburgh, PA 15205
(412) 788-1600
Fax: (412) 787-1771
schaefer@cheerful.com

5812

Business Information: As the Director of Information System Technology of Eat 'N Park Restaurants, Mr. Schaefer manages the local area network and wide area network and oversees all information system operations. Responsible for all information systems technology, Mr. Schaefer leads his staff of three employees in overseeing functions of a 40 desktop computer infrastructure. Beginning his association with the Restarurant more than 19 years ago, Mr. Schaefer has established himself as a vital contributor to the success of Eat 'N Park. He attributes his success to his continuing education as well as his ability to tackle challenges and new responsibilities and deliver results. Looking to the Year 2000 and beyong, Mr. Schaefer hopes to continue to grow, learn new technology, and stay current. Founded in 1949, Eat 'N Park Restaurants is an established and reputable restaurant chain consisting of 75 restaurants nationwide. The Restaurant currently employs a staff of 7,500 individuals around the country dedicated to serving the dining needs of their customers. **Career Highlights:** Director of Information Systems Technology, Eat 'N Park Restaurants (1980-Present); Senior Programmer/Analyst, Contraves Goerz Corporation (1975-80). **Associations & Accomplishments:** Board of Trustee, Western Allegheny Community Library; Cub Scouts Den Leader; North Payette Athletic Association. **Education:** Alliance College, B.S. in Mathematics (1975). **Personal Information:** Married to Judy in 1988. Four children: Nicole, Robert, Jaclyn, and Gregory. Mr. Schaefer enjoys golf and time with family.

Sheryl A. Wilson
Systems Administrator
Desert De Oro Foods Inc.
1449 Mustang Springs Road
Kingman, AZ 86401
(520) 753-3344
Fax: (520) 753-3399
Alt. Ph.: (520) 757-2238
sherylw@ctaz.com

5812

Business Information: As Systems Administrator of Desert De Oro Foods Inc., Ms. Wilson has primary responsibility for administration and operations of the systems infrastructure including NT 4.0 Domains, MS Exchange Server, and regional intranet with 35 administrative users and 10 managers accessing Exchange from laptops via RAS. She is also responsible for point-of-sale/polling system computers in the 49 Taco Bell stores and 4 full-service restaurants. She maintains data integrity, creates and distributes analysis reports, and resolves accounting problems. She handles the purchasing of all computer equipment enterprisewide. Before joining Desert do Oro Foods, Inc. in 1997, Ms. Wilson served as Systems Administrator with The Meadows/Wickenburg, overseeing and directing daily operations of a Novell 4.11 server with 25 administrative and 10 laptop users accessing the network via DUNS. Prior to joining The Meadows, Ms. Wilson was an independent Accounting Software Consultant for 13 years, providing support, training, and sales for RealWorld accounting software. During 1991 through 1993, she worked for SCINET Inc. in Scottsdale, Arizona, an Information Technology company specializing in Medical Management Systems, performing training and support on RealWorld and Solomon III on UNIX platforms, as well as handling the internal accounting. It is noteworthy that The Meadows and Desert de Oro Foods were previous clients that hired her on the basis of her skills and her integrity. As a 20-year technology professional, who had her introduction to PCs on a NorthStar Horizon running two 5.25 floppies on CPM, Ms. Wilson has progressed with the changes in technology. She has overseen the conversion and implementation of over 100 new or upgraded accounting systems. Her strengths in accounting are consistently utilized to assist in daily accounting operations, programming of Financial Statements, and auditing accounting reports from RealWorld, MAS90, and F9. Ms. Wilson has establish ed a record of delivering results, her success reflects her ability to build strong teams with synergy, technical strength, and a customer oriented focus; and tackle new challenges and responsibilities with enthusiasm. She looks forward to the new challenges as Web master of the Intranet, and adding Web and MS Access programming to her repertoire. Desert De Oro Foods Inc. restaurant operations are regional in scope and located in Kingman, Arizona. Established in 1983, Desert De Oro Foods and its related enterprises employ a workforce of more than 2,000 people. **Career Highlights:** Systems Administrator, Desert De Oro Foods Inc. (1997-Present); Income Tax Preparation (1978-Present); Systems Administrator, The Meadows, Wickenburg (1996-97); Independent Accounting Software Consultant (1984-96); Accounting Software Consultant, SCINET Inc. (1991-93); Full Charge Accounting, BPI (ACCPAC) (1982-84); Full Charge Accounting, CPM System, Reprographics, Inc. **Associations & Accomplishments:** Sierra Club; Museum of Northern Arizona; National Honor Society, High School. **Education:** Phoenix College (1982); Maricopa Community College: NT 4.0, Novell 4.11 Administration. **Personal Information:** Two children: Smauel P. Martinez and Aaron R. Martinez. Ms. Wilson enjoys travel, hiking, photography, reading, music and movies.

5900 Miscellaneous Retail

5912 Drug stores and proprietary stores
5921 Liquor stores
5932 Used merchandise stores
5941 Sporting goods and bicycle shops
5942 Book stores
5943 Stationery stores
5944 Jewelry stores
5945 Hobby, toy, and game shops
5946 Camera and photographic supply stores
5947 Gift, novelty, and souvenir shops
5948 Luggage and leather goods stores
5949 Sewing, needlework, and piece goods
5961 Catalog and mail-order houses
5962 Merchandising machine operators
5963 Direct selling establishments
5983 Fuel oil dealers
5984 Liquefied petroleum gas dealers
5989 Fuel dealers, nec
5992 Florists
5993 Tobacco stores and stands
5994 News dealers and newsstands
5995 Optical goods stores
5999 Miscellaneous retail stores, nec

J. Max Daugherty

Director of Strategic Clinical Services Information Systems
PharMerica
2503 Pecan Grove Court
Pearland, TX 77584
(713) 680-1325
Fax: (713) 680-8279
(800) 627-7351
mdaugherty@pdg.net

5912

Business Information: Serving as Director of Strategic Clinical Services Information Systems, Mr. Daugherty supervises technical activities on a daily basis. He works closely with his staff, utilizing a productive form of management that incorporates employee input and feedback. As a team, they strive to develop innovative technical strategies that will increase the effectiveness of the department. Demonstrating his extensive knowledge, he integrates software applications and hardware, specializing in data processing. Mr. Daugherty believes success cannot come to those who do not keep up-to-date in their field and is therefore continually maintaining his education through seminars and courses. Relying on his wife's support to help guide him, he aspires to a position within the corporate structure that will increase his responsibilities. PharMerica is a national firm that owns pharmacies all over the world. The Firm strives to attain large quantities of over-the-counter drugs and prescription medications to pass the value savings on to the customers. **Career Highlights:** PharMerica: Director of Strategic Clinical Services Information Systems (1997-Present), Management Information System Coordinator for Clinical Services (1997); Pharmacy Corporation of America: Information Technology Project Manager (1996-97), Consult Ware Project Lead (1995-96). **Associations & Accomplishments:** American Society of Consultant Pharmacists; TPA Section of Consultant Pharmacists; Harris County Pharmacy Association; Elder/Chairman of the Board of Elders/Lead Information Technology Committee, Ephiphany Lutheran Church. **Education:** University of Houston College of Pharmacy, B.S. in Pharmacy (1984). **Personal Information:** Married to Karen in 1979. Two children: Matt and Jared. Mr. Daugherty enjoys golf and wood working.

Laura Fritz

Director of Product Systems
Hastings Entertainment, Inc.
3601 Plains Boulevard
Amarillo, TX 79102
(806) 351-2300
Fax: (806) 351-2727
laura.fritz@hastings-ent.com

5942

Business Information: Begining her association with Hastings Entertainment, Inc. as a clerk, Mrs. Fritz has worked diligently to develop her skills and acquire expertise in her field. At the present time, she fulfills the responsibility of the Director of Product Systems. In this capacity, she directs the development and maintenance of information systems related to product purchasing, distribution, and advertising. Mrs. Fritz attributes her success to the management of the Corporation and its ability to help people develop in this profession. Her goal is to facilitate continued corporate growth and geographic expansion while gaining more responsibilities. Established in 1968, Hastings Entertainment, Inc. is dedicated to providing customers quality music, books, videos, video games, and software products. The Corporation is the corporate headquarters for Hastings Books, Music and Video, and a chain of 150 retail stores located in 22 states. Employing approximately 5,000 people, the Corporation reports annual sales of $500 million. **Career Highlights:** Hastings Entertainment, Inc.: Director of Product Systems (1997-Present), Information Systems Project Manager (1994-97), Video Operations Manager (1992-94). **Associations & Accomplishments:** Project Management Institute. **Education:** Project Management Institute, Project Management Professional (1999); University of Texas at San Antonio (1986-89). **Personal Information:** Married to James in 1998. Three children: Ryan, Kevin, and Austin. Mrs. Fritz enjoys water sports, dancing and travel.

John L. Rosano

Application Developer
barnesandnoble.com
250 West 15th Street, Apartment 6A
New York, NY 10011
(212) 414-6244
johnrosano@hotmail.com

5942

Business Information: Mr. Rosano works for barnesandnoble.com as Application Developer. Functioning within the information technology industry, he strives to update the Company's Web site and design new features to make it more attractive and appealing to the audience. He is involved with debugging the error messages or complications that may become apparent and maintaining the extensive database of language codes used during the programming process. Specializing in the interpretation of the codes, Mr. Rosano is currently experimenting with new, more secure codes. For the future, he hopes to remain in Web development. After obtaining his M.B.A., Mr. Rosano is planning to increase his role in voice activation programming and is also an aspiring entrepreneur. His success reflects his ability to think outside the box, deliver results, and aggressively tackle new challenges. barnesandnoble.com is involved in expanding the literary world of every reader across the United States. Featuring several bookstore locations throughout the nation, barnesandnoble has an extensive library featuring everything from children's books to research manuals. The Company has also increased its profitability and world-spread recognition through its addition of a Web site. On the Web site, readers can browse through book selections, chat with other readers through online book clubs, and even order new releases to be delivered directly to their home or office. **Career Highlights:** barnesandnoble.com: Application Developer (1998-Present), Web Developer and Produce (1997-98); Online Manager and Production, hachette filipacchi new m (1996-97). **Education:** Columbia University, C.T.A. (In Progress). **Personal Information:** Mr. Rosano enjoys skiing, snowboarding and soccer.

Lennart Rudstrom

Information Technology Manager
Disney Consumer Products
49 Boulevard D'alsace
Cannes, France 06400
+39 0229085216
lrudstrom@disney.com

5947

Business Information: Proficient in all areas of technology, Mr. Rudstrom serves Disney Consumer Products as Information Technology Manager, overseeing the complex systems integration involved in publishing and consumer products. Beginning his career in this highly specialized position with the Company in 1998, he now focuses on all information technology systems in the regional location of Italy, restructuring their design and implementing advanced technologies in the upgrading to Oracle systems. Overseeing the Italy re-foundation project, Mr. Rudstrom plans to incorporate his attained knowledge and skills towards his further advancement to the management of international projects specifically those in the United States with Disney Consumer Products. Licensing the "Walt Disney" name including characters, visual and literary products, is the division of Walt Disney known as Disney Consumer Products which was established in 1932. Within this division of Walt Disney are four other more diverse divisions including Merchandising Licensing, The Disney Store, Disney Publishing, Walt Disney Art Classics, and Disney Interactive, all engaged in the presentation and promotion of the reputable Company's products including books and magazines, audio and computer software, and film and video merchandise. Employing the skilled services of over 10,000 globally, Disney Consumer Products generated an estimated $3. billion in annual revenues in 1999. **Career Highlights:** Information Technology Manager, Disney Consumer Products (1998-Present); Communication Services Engineer, Atos (1996-97); Project Manager, Bull (1991-96). **Education:** Paris Graduate School of Management, Master's degree in Management (1996); Stockholm Institute at Technology, M.S. **Personal Information:** Mr. Rudstrom enjoys tennis, skiing, sailing and kayaking.

Jeffrey M. Adkins

Data Center Manager
Coldwater Creek
100 Coldwater Creek Drive
Mineral Wells, WV 26120
(304) 420-0625
Fax: (304) 420-0611
jeffreyadkins@wv.freei.net

5961

Business Information: Mr. Adkins is the Data Center Manager of Coldwater Creek. He is responsible for all aspects of mechanical and technical support as well as day-to-day computer administration and operational activities. Ten people within the Data Center report to Mr. Adkins. Before joining the Company, he served as a Technical Support Analyst with General Electric Plastics. His background history also includes a stint as Computer Specialist at the U.S. Treasury Department, Bureau of Public Debt. In his current role, he ensures information services are produced correctly and efficiently, delivered with quality, and that customers are satisfied. Mr. Adkins hopes to eventually attain a position in senior executive management. He credits his professional success to education, an innate desire to succeed, and his ability to produce results and aggressively tackle new challenges. Coldwater Creek is a direct catalog retailer with two distribution centers, two call centers, and 12 retail stores. The Company, established in 1984, employs more than 2,000 professionals who help generate in excess of $300 million annually. **Career Highlights:** Data Center Manager, Coldwater Creek (1998-Present); Technical Support Analyst, General Electric Plastics (1997-98); Computer Specialist, U.S. Treasury Department, Bureau of Public Debt (1988-97). **Associations & Accomplishments:** Network and Systems Professionals Association. **Education:** DeVry Institute of Technology, B.S. in Computer Information Systems (1988). **Personal Information:** Married to Kimberly in 1985. Mr. Adkins enjoys music, automobiles, computers, sports, hunting and fishing.

Martin Beukhof

Director of Systems Management Group
Fingerhut
6150 Trenton Lane North
Plymouth, MN 55442-3240
(612) 519-4007
Fax: (612) 519-4797
martin.beukhof@fingerhut.com

5961

Business Information: Functioning in the role of Director of Systems Management Group at Fingerhut, Mr. Beukhof is responsible for the support and enhancement of all production applications. He has served with Fingerhut since his arrival to the Company as Project Manager in 1979. As a solid, 23 year technology professional, Mr. Beukhof owns an established track record of producing results. His success reflects his leadership ability to build teams with synergy and a customer focused attitude, think out-of-the-box, and take on new challenges. In his present position, Mr. Beukhof oversees and maintains the support of production application systems ensuring the functionality and fully operational status. In addition to supervising his staff of 106 employees, he handles numerous planning and personnel functions to include personnel evaluations, coordinating future resources and schedules, overseeing time lines and assignments, and managing the Information Systems Management Group's fiscal year budget. Fingerhut is one of the nation's largest direct marketing companies selling goods and services through catalogs, telemarketing, and the Internet. Established in 1948, Fingerhut employs a workforce of more than 10,000 people who help generate revenues in excess of $1.8 billion annually. **Career Highlights:** Fingerhut: Director of Systems Management Group (1995-Present), Group Manager (1983-95), Project Manager (1982-83). **Associations & Accomplishments:** Project Management Institute; Project Management Professional. **Education:** Southwest Minnesota State, B.A. in Mathematics and Physics (1974). **Personal Information:** Married to Janet in 1975. Three children: Christine, Stacy, and Tom. Mr. Beukhof enjoys being part of his local church leadership and attending his children's school/sporting events.

Terry M. Glenn

Manager of Applications Development
Eddie Bauer, Inc.
P.O. Box 97000
Redmond, WA 98073
(425) 861-4894
Fax: (425) 556-7225
tglenn@gte.net

5961

Business Information: As Manager of Applications Development of Eddie Bauer, Inc., Mr. Glenn directs the activities of technical teams. Utilizing a productive style of management, he works closely with his staff incorporating feedback and input to foster a sense of teamwork in the workplace. Demonstrating his extensive technical knowledge of highly specialized operations, he is recognized for his abilities to develop innovative applications for internal use. Mr. Glenn focuses time and attention on the formulation of cost-cutting techniques for critical areas such as distribution and logistics, striving to implement procedures that allow for maximum quality with minimum overhead. Internally recognized for his successful integration of warehouse management procedure improvements, Mr. Glenn credits his achievements to his balanced lifestyle and education. Enjoying the challenges of his position, he looks forward to continued advancement within the corporate structure as he incorporates Internet based technologies into daily operations. Eddie Bauer, Inc. was established in 1920 and is a division of Spiegel, Inc. Headquartered in Redmond, Washington, the multi-unit, private label retailer and catalog company offers apparrel for men, women, and children. Additionally, the Corporation offers accessories and home goods and employs nearly 10,000 throughout the United States. Estimated annual sales exceed $1.5 billion, proving the traditionally styled, casual products fill a growing need in the lives of today's busy working generations. **Career Highlights:** Manager of Applications Development, Eddie Bauer, Inc. (1993-Present); Senior Application Analyst, Nike, Inc. (1989-93); Application Analyst, AutoZone, Inc. (1988-89). **Education:** Arizona State University (1987). **Personal Information:** Married to Maria in 1994. Mr. Glenn enjoys boating.

Ray D. Liming

Systems Analyst
Merck-Medco Rx
700 West Third Avenue
Columbus, OH 43212
(614) 421-8217
Fax: (614) 421-8262
ray_liming@merck.com

5961

Business Information: As Systems Analyst of Merck-Medco Rx, Mr. Liming is responsible for programming and maintaining databases. He oversees all upgrading, troubleshooting, and support of the system infrastructure. Utilizing 19 years of extensive experience in his field, Mr. Liming continues to assist the Company in the completion of corporate goals. Coordinating resources, schedules, time lines and assignments; synthesizing large quantities of data into monthly reports; and designing new solutions to harness more of the computer's power also fall within the realm of his functions. He has enjoyed substantial success as a Systems Analyst and finds his work greatly rewarding. Mr. Liming plans to expedite continued promotion through the fulfillment of his responsibilities and his involvement in the advancement of operations. Merck-Medco Rx is a mail order pharmacy. Consisting of a call center for different companies, the Company offers mail order drugs for clients who are confined to their homes or just want the added convenience. Established in 1993, the Company has become a valuable part of the industry. Merck-Medco Rx, at the Ohio facility, employs a staff of 600 individuals to meet the needs of a growing clientele. **Career Highlights:** Systems Analyst, Merck-Medco Rx (1995-Present); Consultant, Software Engineering (1980-95); Analyst, Nielsen (1975-80). **Associations & Accomplishments:** Power Builder Association; Franklin County Heart Association. **Education:** Franklin University, B.S. in Computer Science (1993); degree in Microcomputing; Aspect Custom View Editor Advanced Programmer. **Personal Information:** Married to Dana in 1984. One child: Zachery. Mr. Liming enjoys fishing and PC games.

Mark C. Rucker

Database Administrator
Service Merchandise
7100 Service Merchandise Drive
Brentwood, TN 37027
(615) 660-4356
Fax: (615) 660-4321

5961

Business Information: Functioning as Database Administrator for Service Merchandise, Mr. Rucker assumes responsibility for the DBMS that controls the inventory, replenishment, merchandising, and purchase orders. Information entered into these systems by customers or internal personnel are transferred to the databases of the Company's warehouses which ship the ordered products. Mr. Rucker was responsible for the implementation of the current database system in 1991. He was also part of the team for the Company's software migration project. Dedicated to the further development of the Company, he plans to continue to ensure that the database network runs efficiently and smoothly. Mr. Rucker's success reflects his ability to deliver results and aggressively take on new challenges. Established in 1960, Service Merchandise sells various types of products such as homewares, jewelry, and electronics. Products are distributed through different distribution channels, retail stores, catalogs, and the Internet. In retail stores, stock is made available on the shelf in order to reduce the length of lines and waiting time for customers. The Company's merchandise catalogs have been made into a smaller and cutdown version in an effort to highlight or specialize products. Tremendous response has greeted the new addition of Internet sales as a distribution channel. Several million in sales has already been produced. Service Merchandise is increasing marketing efforts and making customer service its number one priority. **Career Highlights:** Database Administrator, Service Merchandise (1988-Present); Adjunct Instructor, Nashville State Technical Institute (1999-Present). **Associations & Accomplishments:** Network and Systems Professionals Association; Alpha Beta Gamma National Business Honor Society. **Education:** Nashville State Technical Institute, degree in Business Data Processing (1989); Hinds Junior College, A.S. (1988). **Personal Information:** Married to Melissa in 1996. One child: Lindsey. Mr. Rucker enjoys writing music and reading.

David M. Sherman

Director of Telecommunications and Cell Center Technology
J Crew Group, Inc.
770 Broadway, Floor 11
New York, NY 10003
(212) 209-8665
Fax: (212) 209-8400
dsherman@jcrew.com

5961

Business Information: As Director of Telecommunications and Call Center Technology of J Crew Group Inc., Mr. Sherman is responsible for the advancement of the Corporations communication activities. He is a key player in the development of multiple plans for the strategic enhancement of the networking abilities of the Corporation. He unites departments within the Corporation through the implementation of new products. As a director, he also strives to create positive career paths for the employees he works with. For the future, Mr. Sherman hopes to continue his work with J Crew and hopes to expand his role in the systems infrastructure side of the Corporation. J Crew Group Inc. specializes in catalogue mail order and e-commerce business within the clothing industry. Recognized for its designer merchandise, J Crew has risen among today's teenagers and college age students as a leader in wardrobe design. The rise in sales has been the result of a culmination of activities within the marketing department and the launch of an extensive array of merchandising campaigns, catalog advertisements, and the opening of the Corporation's Web site where customers can order and view items online. **Career Highlights:** Director of Telecommunications and Cell Center Technology, J Crew Group Inc. (1997-Present); Manager of Telecommunications, Liz Claiborne Inc. (1988-97); Communications Manager, Stern's Division, Allied Stores Corporation (1984-88). **Associations & Accomplishments:** Technology Managers Forum; Communications Managers Association; Telecommunications Committee, Indug; NRF. **Education:** Computer Processing Institute, degree in Computer Programming (1984); Boston University, B.S. in Business Administration. **Personal Information:** Married to Annette in 1990. Five children: Allison, Jillian, Davis, Aidan, and Rebecca.

Peter Simonsen

Manager of System Services
Amazon.com
1516 2nd Avenue
Seattle, WA 98101
(206) 834-7168

5961

Business Information: Serving as the Manager of System Services for Amazon.com, Mr. Simonsen provides change and configuration management implementation and availability and business impact measurements. He maintains the Company's systems, ensuring its efficient operation at all times. Presiding over technical projects, he performs project planning and real time exclamations with the assistance of his team of 20 professionals. Coordinating resources, time lines, schedules, and assignments also fall within the purview of his responsibilities. Mr. Simonsen has received internal recognition for his implementation projects and attributes his success to his ability to work well with others, his understanding of technology, and his ability to apply that knowledge to the business world. An expert, he plans to continue to introduce new technology to the Company, thus impacting its business end. Providing a viable alternative to traditional retail shopping, Amazon.com is a wholly-based Internet retailer. The Company has become the leader in the Internet retail business through its use of virtual business marvels. Headquartered in Seattle, Washington, Amazon.com has three locations and employs the services of 2,900 qualified individuals. **Career Highlights:** Manager of System Services, Amazon.com (1998-Present); McKinsey & Company: Technology Manager (1993-98), European Infrastructure Manager (1987-93). **Education:** Danish Business School, B.S. **Personal Information:** Married to Diana. Mr. Simonsen enjoys fly fishing.

Robert F. Usiak, Jr.

Associate Telecom Engineer - Data
Home Shopping Network
One HSN Drive
St. Petersburg, FL 33729
(727) 872-4516
Fax: (727) 872-6616
usiakb@hsn.net

5961

Business Information: As an Associate Telecom Engineer for the Home Shopping Network, Mr. Usiak installs and maintains the networking components and the network architecture in a fully functional mode. Also, within the Network Engineering realm, he researches and implements appropriate upgrades, ensuring accurate and reliable communications. Utilizing more than 20 years practical experience gained from his service in the United States Marine Corps as well as his work with the Home Shopping Network, he is continually striving to improve performance. Highly regarded, he has been named "Employee of the Month" three times, including "Top Gun" for Outstanding Performance. In the future, Mr. Usiak plans to continue in his present position, fostering company growth and expansion. The Home Shopping Network is an electronic retailing company that sells products via television and e-commerce. The Company employs the skilled services of over 5,000 individuals nationwide to acquire business, facilitate projects, and market services. Established in 1977, the Company is headquartered in St. Petersburg, Florida and markets products worldwide. **Career Highlights:** Associate Telecom Engineer - Data, Home Shopping Network (1986-Present); United States Marine Corps Reserve (1986-93); United States Military, United States Marine Corps (1978-86). **Associations & Accomplishments:** Non-Commissioned Officers Association; Operation DESERT STORM Veteran. **Personal Information:** Mr. Usiak enjoys sports, fitness, music, reading and memorabilia collection.

Charles X. Yang, Ph.D.

Chief Executive Officer/President
USHarbor.com, Inc.
2500 Hospital Drive #1
Mountain View, CA 94040
(650) 964-1855
Fax: (650) 964-1165
charlesyang@usharbor.com

5961

Business Information: Dr. Charles Yang is the founder, Chairman, and Chief Executive Officer of USHarbor.com, Inc. USHarbor.com provides international goods trading services on the web, helping small to medium-size retail and online stores to maintain competitive by importing best value products directly from manufacturers around the world. Dr. Yang is extremely knowledgeable on Internet Commerce, multimedia technologies, digital cameras, and scanners. He is a great technical and visionary leader, for who engineers love to work with. He motivates them and challenges them without over stressing them. Dr. Yang is very capable of managing the whole life cycle of a commercial Internet and Intranet Web site development. He has successfully managed the recruiting, planning, designing, architecture, prototyping, and developing of several highly regarded Web sites: www.gap.com; www.babygap.com; www.gapkids.com; www.usa.canon.com; www.pixera.com. As the Director of Gap Online, Dr. Yang has architected and overseen the whole Gap online Web development. Under his technical and visionary leadership, Gap Online has been recognized as the online stare leader in the apparel industry. Based on the MSN, Yahoo, and AOL survey, Gap Online has been consistently ranked one of the most popular online stores. **Career Highlights:** Chief Executive Officer/President, USHarbor.com, Inc. (1999-Present); Director, Gap Online (1998-Present); Manager, Canon, Inc. (1996-98); Senior Research Scientist, FMRC (1992-95). **Associations & Accomplishments:** United States Information Technology Delegation to China; Commerce Net; Association of Computing Machinery; Institution for Electrical and Electronics Engineers. **Education:** University of California: Ph.D. (1989), M.S. (1987); Xian Jiaotong University, M.S. (1985), B.S. (1982). **Personal Information:** Married to Betty Weng in 1985. One child: Carolyn W. Dr. Yang enjoys classic and popular music and reading.

Sylvain Casabon

Director of Information Systems
Groupe Cantrex, Inc.
4445 Rue Garand
Saint-Laurent, Quebec, Canada H4R 2H9
(514) 335-0260
Fax: (514) 745-1741
casabons@centrex.com

5999

Business Information: Serving as Director of Information Systems for Groupe Cantrex, Inc., Mr. Casabon oversees and directs all daily operations of systems infrastructure. He determines the overall strategic direction and business contribution of the the information systems functions. Managing the technology budget, Mr. Casabon is responsible for the serviceability of all equipment and peripherals as well as the functionality of the systems infrastructure. Possessing superiror leadership and an excellent understanding of technology, he supervises and guides his staff of 16 employees in the management of applications, Internet, e-mail, and other tasked related issues. Designing databases and software applications and maintaining quality control and systems support for the Corporation's networking and operating environments also fall within the realm of Mr. Casabon's responsibilities. Concentrating his efforts towards integrating supply chain dealers and extending Web site development, Mr. Casabon plans to take Groupe Cantrex national. Specializing in retail purchasing, Groupe Cantrex, Inc. was established in Quebec, Canada. Employing a staff of 325 people, the Corporation extends its sales and services throughout Canada and the United States including Montreal, Washington D.C., and Richmond, Virginia. Specifically offering its specialized services in electronics, photography, floor covering, houseware appliances and furniture, the Corporation works closely with 500 suppliers and 1,200 dealers. Committed towards furthering its expansion, Groupe Cantrex continues to widen its client base and product line. **Career Highlights:** Director of Information Systems, Groupe Cantrex, Inc. (1999-Present); Adventure Electronic, Inc.: Director of Information Systems (1996-99), Analyst/Programmer (1990-96); Analyst/Programmer, Atlantic Video & Sound (1987-90). **Education:** University of Quebec, Bachelor's degree (1985). **Personal Information:** Three children: Sophie, Matthieu, and Daniel.

Valdonna Greenlaw

Senior Director
edu.com
125 Lincoln Street
Boston, MA 02111
(408) 247-7175
Fax: (408) 247-7175
valg@hypersurf.com

5999

Business Information: Possessing a superior educational and occupational background in technology, Ms. Greenlaw was highly recruited to edu.com as Senior Director in 2000. She is responsible for fulfilling a number of technical duties on behalf of the Company, and determining marketing plans and business contribution of the information systems functions. Demonstrating superior leadership and technical expertise, Ms. Greenlaw is charged with designing and implementing business proposals, comprising the annual budget and operational plans, and managing and mentoring the Company's staff. She also travels extensively to meet with executives at universities to assist in systems implementation and recruit new clients. The most rewarding aspect of her career is increasing annual revenues while employed at Apple Computer, Inc. Attributing her success to great mentors, Ms. Greenlaw aspires to attain the position of Vice President of Marketing and Sales. Established in 1998, edu.com operates as an educational tool accessible through the Internet for college students all over the world to purchase books and materials at an affordable rate. The Company employs the skilled services of 100 individuals to promote services, facilitate packaging and distribution, as well as answer customer queries. The Company continues to provide students excellent learning materials at affordable prices, piloting edu.com as an educational partnership for universities. **Career Highlights:** Senior Director, edu.com (2000-Present); Director, Apple Computer, Inc. (1998-99); Director, Silicon Graphics, Inc. (1987-97); Product Manager, Hewlett-Packard, Inc. (1979-87). **Education:** Virginia Tech, B.S. in Computer Science (1979). **Personal Information:** Ms. Greenlaw enjoys fly fishing.

Ron D. Johnson

Enterprise Architect
SciQuest.com
5151 McCrimmon Parkway
Morrisville, NC 27560
(919) 659-2389
Fax: (954) 827-0795
rjohnson@sciquest.com

5999

Business Information: As the Enterprise Architect for SciQuest.com, Mr. Johnson is responsible for providing the planning and development expertise. He links an enterprise's plans with the data architecture, enterprise application architecture, and enterprise technical architecture. Possessing an excellent understanding of his role, Mr. Johnson also monitors new enterprise developments as well as all engineering standards required for successful launch and implementation of state-of-the-art enterprise architectures. In addition, he supervises the analysis, installation, modification, and configuration of systems architecture to ensure quality, integrity, and reliability. Mr. Johnson looks forward to remaining with SciQuest.com and excelling in the industry. Founded in 1996, SciQuest.com is a leading business-to-business e-marketplace for scientific products used by pharmaceutical, chemical, biotechnology, industrial, and educational organizations worldwide. By leveraging its extensive laboratory products and supply chain management expertise with its exclusive supplier relationships and robust portfolio of e-procurement solutions, SciQuest.com reduces customers' procurement costs and increases researchers' productivity. Additionally, SciQuest.com provides suppliers cost-effective sales and marketing channel. The Company's e-marketplace is distributor-neutral and can be customized and seamlessly integrated with its customers' enterprise systems. SciQuest.com is headquartered in Research Triangle Park, North Carolina, with offices in Mountain View, California, and Plainview, New York. For more information about SciQuest.com, please visit www.sciquest.com or call 919-659-2100. **Career Highlights:** Enterprise Architect, SciQuest.com (2000-Present); Independent Consultant & System Contractor (1995-2000); Senior Director/Co-founder, Applied System Engineering & Development Corporation (1982-94); Business Owner, Integrated Systems Technology Corporation (1979-82); Director of System Engineering, Digital Equipment Corporation (1974-79); Computer Scientist, National Bureau of Standards (1969-74). **Associations & Accomplishments:** Institute of Electrical and Electronics Engineers; IAMS; ISACF; Registered Data Professional; Data Managment Society; ISO Working Group; CICA; Working Member, Computerized Information System; Electronic Commerce Research Foundation. **Education:** University of Maryland (1974). **Personal Information:** Married to Jan in 1974. Three children: Kristina, Suzanne, and Aimee. Mr. Johnson enjoys golf and fishing.

Renee McCown

Systems Manager
Polo Ralph Lauren
9 Polito Avenue
Lyndhurst, NJ 07071
(201) 531-6155
Fax: (201) 531-6010
rmccown@poloralphlauren.com

5999

Business Information: Demonstrating expertise in the information technology field, Ms. McCown currently serves as Systems Manager with Polo Ralph Lauren. She manages 12 employees, oversees the budget and finances, performs human resources duties, and evaluates systems tools. In addition, Ms. McCown reviews and develops software applications, maintains and oversees the maintenance of applications, recommends software, and performs research and development. Beginning her association with the Company in 1996 as a Business Analyst, Ms. McCown has worked diligently to develop her skills and acquire expertise in her field. Proud of her accomplishments, she developed the datawarehouse for Polo Ralph Lauren. Future plans for Ms. McCown are to become more involved in database development, achieve a higher position within the Company's corporate structure, and start up her own consulting group. Polo Ralph Lauren is a manufacturer of men's, women's, and children's apparel. The Company provides retail and wholesale services. Established in 1967, Polo Ralph Lauren is an international company with locations worldwide. Local operations in Lyndhurst, New Jersey employs the expertise of 4,000 individuals to facilitate every aspect of design, manufacture, quality assurance, and distribution of products. The Company reports an annual revenues in excess of $47 billion. **Career Highlights:** Polo Ralph Lauren: Systems Manager (Present), Business Analyst (1996), Data Analyst (1996), Data Analyst. **Associations & Accomplishments:** Minorities in Technology, New York City Computer Club. **Education:** City University of New York (1994); University of North Carolina at Chapel Hill, B.A. in Science (1983). **Personal Information:** Ms. McCown enjoys scuba diving and dancing.

Michael P. Morris

Chief Information Officer
Vitamin Shoppe Industries, Inc.
4700 Westside Avenue
North Bergen, NJ 07047
(201) 210-3009
mmorris@vitamin.shoppe.com

5999

Business Information: Combining 20 years of technological expertise and consumer products retailing experience, Mr. Morris serves as Chief Information Officer for Vitamin Shoppe Industries, Inc. Supervising a staff of 20 skilled professionals, he oversees and manages the information systems infrastructure and voice and data communication systems. Delegating responsibilities to his staff, Mr. Morris monitors applications development, WAN/LAN administration, automation warehouse management, program logistics, and data warehousing management. Additionally, he performs escalated troubleshooting for the Corporation's systems. An authority, his history includes nine years on Wall Street, as well as prior employment with giants such as AT&T and Arthur Andersen Consulting Division. His career highlights include implementation of a retail Web site for the J. Crew Group and creation of a new backoffice infrastructure for Leslie Fay. Mr. Morris is committed to assisting the Corporation attain future goals and is working to make the e-tail.com subsidiary the premier place to shop for vitamins on the Web. One of the nations largest retailer of health and wellness products, Vitamin Shoppe Industries, Inc. sells vitamins, nutritional supplements, neutraceuticals, and other related products. Reporting $200 million in annual revenue, the Corporation distributes products lines through three distinct distribution channels: direct mail, brick and mortar retail stores, and e-tailer through the Corporation's wholly owned subsidiary, VitaminShoppe.com. Established in 1977, the Corporation employs a staff of more than 600 individuals. **Career Highlights:** Chief Information Officer, Vitamin Shoppe Industries, Inc. (1999-Present); Chief Information Officer, J. Crew Group, Inc. (1996-99); Vice President of Management Information Systems, Leslie Fay/Kasper ASL (1993-96); Director of Business Systems Development, Sandoz Pharmaceutical (1990-93). **Associations & Accomplishments:** Society of Information Management; National Retail Federation, Information Technology Council; United Jewish Appeal. **Education:** New York University, M.B.A. (1980); University of Bridgeport, B.A. (1978). **Personal Information:** Married to Lauren in 1985. Two children: Ari Chaim and Ertan Yitzchak. Mr. Morris enjoys baseball, hockey, bike riding, golf, reading and spending time with his family. Mr. Morris also enjoys participating in community functions, including teaching at the local synagogue.

Jake Smith
Vice President of Information Technology Strategy
Zydeco.com
801 1st Avenue South
Seattle, WA 98134
(206) 903-6444
Fax: (206) 903-6006
jake@zydeco.com

5999

Business Information: Drawing upon an extensive background in computer science, Mr. Smith serve as the Vice President of Information Technology Strategy for Zydeco.com. In his position, he is responsible for developing long lasting relations with client companies including industry giants, such as IBM and Oracle. Utilizing a personable attitude, Mr. Smith also develops strong consumer based relations, while keeping in mind who is buying the products, profiling, and examining the consumers' behavior. Moreover, he creates associations and database for each consumer to be categorized under, depending on his research findings. In the future, Mr. Smith looks forward to staying on top of technology and growing and expanding business operations. A start up company, founded in 2000, Zydeco.com is a e-retail company. Located in Seattle, Washington, the Company engages in specialty products and appeals mainly to small and medium sized businesses. With products representing over 500 manufacturers, the Company's main goal is to provide high quality items. Operating on an international level, the Seattle location employs a staff of 25 hard working people. **Career Highlights:** Vice President of Information Technology Strategy, Zydeco.com (2000-Present); Business Development Manager, IBM (1999-00); Channels Strategy Manager, Sequent Computer Systems (1996-99). **Education:** Lewis and Clark College, B.A. (1993). **Personal Information:** Married to Jennifer in 1993.

6000 - 6999

FINANCE

INSURANCE

and

REAL ESTATE

6000 Depository Institutions

6011 Federal reserve banks
6019 Central reserve depository, nec
6021 National commercial banks
6022 State commercial banks
6029 Commercial banks, nec
6035 Federal savings institutions
6036 Savings institutions, except federal
6061 Federal credit unions
6062 State credit unions
6081 Foreign bank and branches and agencies
6082 Foreign trade and international banks
6091 Nondeposit trust facilities
6099 Functions related to deposit banking

Lisa Marie Yrizarry
Technical Specialist
Federal Reserve Bank
P.O. Box 3436
Portland, OR 97208-3436
(503) 221-5975
lisa.yrizarry@sf.frb.org

6011

Business Information: Combining her business administration expertise and technical talent, Ms. Yrizarry serves as a Technical Specialist for the Federal Reserve Bank. In this capacity, she assumes responsibility for the local area network administration and computer users' support. She provides users with software and system application training and makes herself available to answer questions and solve any problems that arise. Ms. Yrizarry is also in charge of maintaining the Bank's Web Site. In an effort to stay on the cutting edge of technology, she performs independent research and attends industry conferences and seminars. She attributes her professional success to her determination, her ability to establish goals, and her single-minded focus. Continuously striving to improve her performance, Ms. Yrizarry looks forward to taking on a more managerial role as well as leading more projects and directing department staff and activities. The Federal Reserve Bank is the United States central bank. It is an arm of the Treasury Department anf functions as a quasi-governmental agency. The Bank performs several functions including processing checks, and has regional offices throughout the country. The Branch in Portland, Oregon employs a qualified staff of 150 knowledgeable individuals. **Career Highlights:** Technical Specialist, Federal Reserve Bank(1995-Present); Computer Programmer/Analyst, Ponce Bank, Puerto Rico (1992-94); Financial Systems Analyst Intern, New England Power, Westboro, Massachusetts (1990). **Education:** Northeastern University, M.B.A. (1991); Baylor University, B.B.A. (1986). **Personal Information:** Ms. Yrizarry enjoys foreign and domestic travel, learning new cultures and learning new cultures and working with children.

George E. Dritsas
Senior Systems Engineer
Wells Fargo Bank
1535 Roberts Avenue, Unit 2
Whiting, IN 46394
(612) 316-4761
gdritsas@yahoo.com

6021

Business Information: Serving with Wells Fargo Bank since 1998, Mr. Dritsas currently fulfills the responsibilites of the Senior Systems Engineer. In this capacity, he serves as a UNIX system administrator, troubleshooting and maintaining the operating system. One of the highlights of his career was when he was able to marry the Internet with banking, assisting the Bank in efforts to provide 24-hour services by offering clients online access to accounts. Attributing his success to his education in physics, Mr. Dritsas stays on top of the industry by subscribing to technical magizines and doing a lot of networking for the Bank. He enjoys his current position and plans to remain with the Bank, moving up the corporate structure. Wells Fargo Bank is an international financial institution providing personal, responsive service by connecting customers to essential financial services 24-hours a day. This is done through the use of ATMs, phone or personal computer, and a growing network of traditional and supermarket branches. Employing more than 80,000 personnel, the Bank provides services such as checking and savings accounts, credit cards, home equity loans, and home mortgages, all of which are offered to customers worldwide. **Career Highlights:** Senior Systems Engineer, Wells Fargo Bank (1998-Present). **Associations & Accomplishments:** Society of Physics Students. **Education:** Chicago State University, B.S. in Physics (1998). **Personal Information:** Married to Leslie in 1999. Mr. Dritsas enjoys rollerblading.

Kevin B. Eggleston
Senior Vice President
Bank of America
9000 Southside Boulevard, MC-FL9-100-05-06
Jacksonville, FL 32256-0793
(904) 464-6286
Fax: (904) 987-8450
kevin.eggleston@bankofamerica.com

6021

Business Information: As the Senior Vice President of Bank of America, Mr. Eggleston, leading a group of developers and analysts, manages the implementation of technology-based and operational projects. Utilizing his technological expertise, Mr. Eggleston is involved in improving systems with new hardware and software to provide customers with the best possible service on site. Demonstrating his managerial skills, he is in charge of budget and resource negotiation. Highly regarded, he possesses superior talents and an excellent understanding of technology as it applies to the financial industry. Concurrently, Mr. Eggleston owns a bed and breakfast business with his wife called "The Fig Tree Inn." His goals for the future include being involved in a startup technology company. One of the world's largest banking institutions, Bank of America provides full service banking to both national and international customers. Viewing business relationships as partnerships, the Bank works personally with clients to provide the best solutions in order to realize financial goals. Located in Jacksonville, Florida, the Bank employs the services of 28 in their information technology department responsible for developing cutting edge brokerage systems and investment services for the clients. **Career Highlights:** Senior Vice President, Bank of America (1999-Present); Vice President, Nations Bank (1997-99); Systems Manager, Barnett Bank (1983-97). **Education:** Union College (1982); Albany Business College, A.S. (1976). **Personal Information:** Married to Dawn in 1976. Two children: Jennifer and Kerr. Mr. Eggleston enjoys Girl Scout activities.

Michael P. Hussey
Information Technology Manager
Wells Fargo
525 Market Street
San Francisco, CA 94105
(415) 396-0243
mpoh@msn.com

6021

Business Information: Serving Wells Fargo as the Information Technology Manager, Mr. Hussey has been with the Company for two years. He supervises a staff of 14 employees in overseeing the application engineering group and providing a common platform for private client services. Concentrating his attention towards project development, he strives to incorporate the latest technologies in order to provide a more efficient and effective product. Heading all administrative aspects, Mr. Hussey focuses on turning potential into action through preparation and skilled training. He is also responsible for personnel and budget management, interfacing with regional offices, and supplying products and services to end users. Capitalizing on more than five years of extensive experience in this highly technical field, he monitors productivity, formulating a hands-on management style with an above average aptitude for problem solving. Dedicating his expertise towards the further expansion of the user base, Mr. Hussey looks forward to his promotion with Wells Fargo. An established and reputable investment management and brokerage firm, Wells Fargo was founded in 1852. The Company is the fourth largest in its industry. Located in San Francisco, California, the Company employs the skilled services of 102,000 individuals to acquire business, meet with clients, facilitate projects, and market services. Providing excellent services in investment, financial advising, and private, commercial, and retail banking, the Company serves an international client base. **Career Highlights:** Information Technology Manager, Wells Fargo (1999-Present); Senior Systems Analyst, Cirrus Logic (1998-99); LAN Manager, Loma Linda University (1995-98). **Associations & Accomplishments:** Toastmasters International; San Francisco NT Users Group; Microsoft Certified Trainer. **Education:** Loma Linda University, M.S. (1997); University College at Galway, B.S. **Personal Information:** Married to Sheila in 1990. Two children: Cian and Niamh. Mr. Hussey enjoys reading, photography and electronics.

Jonathan R. Mathes
Help Desk Manager
U.S. Bank
3108 Bryant Avenue South, Suite 1
Minneapolis, MN 55408
(612) 342-8780
Fax: (612) 342-1076
jmathes@pjc.com

6021

Business Information: Serving in the role of Help Desk Manager, Mr. Mathes provides computer support to U.S. Bancorp Pifer Jaffray, the brokerage division of U.S. Bank. In his position, he designs, develops, and implements project strategies, oversees employee relations, coordinates training sessions, orchestrates divisional and company-wide project reviews, and directs the roll out of new software technology. Due to his dedicated efforts in training and building long-term employee relations, Mr. Mathes was instrumental in the promotion of 10 associates. Recently, he successfully completed a project involving the testing of workstations and the enhancement of U.S. Bank's computer speed that saves the Bank $2 million annually. Mr. Mathes attributes his success to continuing professional improvement. He looks forward to obtaining a position that enables him to manage more than one group of people. U.S. Bancorp Piper Jaffray of U.S. Bank is the brokerage division that provides financial and investment solutions. Offering 120 brokerage branches, U.S. Bank acquired the brokerage division two years ago and is now the 11th largest brokerage company in the United States. Established in 1870, U.S. Bank currently employs the services of 33,000 individuals. **Career Highlights:** Help Desk Manager, U.S. Bank (1998-Present); Information Systems Manager, Damark International (1997-98); Information System Support Analyst, Dayton Hudsopn Corporation-Target (1995-98). **Associations & Accomplishments:** Board of Directors (1996), Stevens Square Association. **Education:** St. Thomas University, Business and Computer Science degree (Currently Attending); St. John's University (1990-92). **Personal Information:** Mr. Mathes enjoys voice, keyboard, reading, exercise, biking, horticulture and flute.

Maria J. Rueger

Assistant Vice President
Bank of America
10550-526 Bay Meadows Road
Jacksonville, FL 32256
(904) 987-3519
Fax: (888) 453-0837
mjrueger@prodigy.net

6021

Business Information: Mrs. Rueger functions in the capacity of Assistant Vice President for Bank of America's branch office in Jacksonville, Florida. She oversees and directs all aspects of day-to-day administration and operations of the Bank, working to ensure an attractive and effective facility exists to encourage the customers to invest in Bank of America. Before joining the Bank as Developer and Data Modeler in 1998, Mrs. Rueger served as Computer Systems Analyst for Artel, Inc. Her background also includes a stint as Account Clerk and Tax Specialist for Fairfax County Government. Currently, she is heavily involved in meetings and is continuously working on large projects. Assisting in the development of the Bank, she is responsible for modeling data and is a titled data architect. In the future, Mrs. Rueger hopes to advance into the role of Vice President of the Bank. "Work hard," is cited as her advice. Bank of America has recently expanded its international recognition through its acquisition of NationsBank. The Bank has locations throughout the United States and has branched itself internationally in recent years. A financial institution, the Bank provides financial advice and financing opportunities to all of its clients. Clients are also able to invest in savings and checking accounts while enhancing the value of their invested dollar. **Career Highlights:** Assistant Vice President, Bank of America (1999-Present); Assistant Vice President, NationsBank/Bank of America (1998-99); Computer Systems Analyst, Artel, Inc. (1998); Account Clerk/Tax Specialist, Fairfax County Government (1987-98). **Associations & Accomplishments:** Institute of Electronics and Electrical Engineers Computer Society. **Education:** Strayer University: B.S. in Computer Science and Computer Information Systems (1999), A.S. in Computer Information Systems (1997); Z.D.U. University; Magellan University. **Personal Information:** Married to Walter C. in 1978. One child: Jeremy A. Mrs. Rueger enjoys reading, collecting sea shells and developing websites.

Loren M. Schweitzer

Associate Vice President
Bank of America
1201 Main Street, 31st Floor
Dallas, TX 75202
(214) 508-8473
loren.schweitzer@bankofamerica.com

6021

Business Information: Functioning in the capacity of Associate Vice President of Bank of America, Mr. Schweitzer designs, develops, and implements cutting edge software. Streamlining his efforts to the various needs of Bank of America, he is responsible for testing software and working out bugs and flaws. Before joining the Bank, Mr. Schweitzer served as Database Programmer for Blockbuster. His background history also includes stints as Database Programmer with Daily Data Inc. and Account Executive at National Asset Placement Corporation. A systems expert with four years experience in the field, Mr. Schweitzer responsibilities centers around programming client server database applications. As for the future, Mr. Schweitzer plans to assist in the growth of Bank of America and eventually advance to the position of Vice President of Development. Bank of America is an international financial institution. Offering loans, checking accounts, saving accounts, and a variety of investment opportunities, the Bank offers services of great benefit to all their customers. Covered by Federal Deposit Insurance Corporation, all customers of the Bank have the satisfaction of knowing their money is secured against loss. **Career Highlights:** Database Programmer, Bank of America (1999-Present); Database Programmer, Blockbuster (1998-99); Database Programmer, Daily Data Inc. (1996-98); Account Executive, National Asset Placement (1993-96). **Associations & Accomplishments:** Delphi Developers of Dallas. **Education:** University of Texas at Austin, B.A. (1989). **Personal Information:** Mr. Schweitzer enjoys cycling and reading the written Word.

David M. Trice

Vice President of Receivables Services
Bank of America
6000 Feldwood Road
College Park, GA 30349
(770) 774-6244
Fax: (770) 774-6290
david@trices.com

6021

Business Information: Utilizing more than 25 years of experience in the information technology industry, Mr. Trice serves as the Vice President of Receivable Services in Atlanta, Georgia for Bank of America. He manages the implementation of new accounts and performs contingency planning in both the operations and technology departments. Beginning his career with NationsBank 15 years ago as a programmer, he has worked his way up the corporate hierarchy to his present position. Mr. Trice believes that his professional success can be attributed to people and by helping and focusing his attention on the needs of his employees. Representing the Bank at the TAWPI conference in 1999, he lectured on the implementation of imaging in the banking industry. Constantly striving to improve his performance, he plans to take on a more global role with the Bank, increasing his responsibilities in strategic development and the management of technology. Bank of America is a reputable financial institution. The Bank continues to offer its customers a variety of personal and commercial services from branches spread throughout the nation from the East Coast to the West Coast. Corporate headquarters are located in Charlotte, North Carolina, however, the majority of the accounts receivable work is performed in the Atlanta, Georgia facility. The workforce of approximately 1,500 staff members at the College Park, Georgia location performs bookkeeping, statement, and accounts receivable functions for the Bank. **Career Highlights:** Vice President of Receivables Services, Bank of America (1998-Present); NationsBank: Manager of Application Development Lock Box (1996-98), Manager of Application Development Deposit System (1990-96); Senior Service Analyst, C&S Bank (1986-90). **Education:** University of Georgia, B.B.A. (1974). **Personal Information:** Married to Brenda in 1977. Two children: Jessica and Maggie. Mr. Trice enjoys hunting, gardening, golf and sports.

Khoa Van Huynh

Lead Developer
First Union National Bank
1639 Bonnie Lane
Charlotte, NC 28213
(704) 590-3176
Fax: (704) 590-0342
khuynh@perigee.net

6021

Business Information: Utilizing several years of experience in the computer technology field, Mr. Van Huynh joined the First Union National Bank in 1997. In the capacity of Lead Developer, he assumes responsibility for the development of the Bank's Internet banking application. Before joining First Union National Bank, Mr. Van Huynh served as Software Engineer with IBM Corporation. A system expert, he is currently working to make available personal and commercial banking information through the Internet for the client. Committed to providing continued optimum performance, Mr. Van Huynh looks forward to assisting in the completion of future corporate goals. His career success reflects his ability to thing out-of-the-box and aggressively take on new challenges and responsibilities. First Union National Bank is a full service banking institution. The Bank provides services on all financial matters from mortgages to personal checking for corporations and individuals. **Career Highlights:** Lead Developer, First Union National Bank (1997-Present); Software Engineer, IBM Corporation (1995-97). **Education:** University of North Carolina at Charlotte, B.S. in Computer Science (1997); Catawba Community College, Associate's degree.

Philip A. Curto

Technical Support Manager/Assistant Vice President
KBC Bank New York N.V.
125 West 55th Street
New York, NY 10019-5369
(212) 541-0620
Fax: (212) 541-0785
philip.curto@kb.be

6022

Business Information: As the Technical Support Manager for KBC Bank New York N.V.'s Information Technology department, Mr. Curto is responsible for the New York office as well as Atlanta, Los Angeles, and the disaster recovery site. His duties include administration of all transactional systems across all platforms, LAN, WAN, PBX voice recording, telecommunications, and data center technical support staff. The Data Center provides technical analysis and support of Trading, Corporate, and Investment bank sectors, as well as Operations and Financial Control. KBC Bank New York N.V. is an international corporate and investment bank operating out of New York, with representative offices also located in Los Angeles and Atlanta. Headquartered in Brussels, Belgium, U.S. operations were established in 1977, and currently employ 190 people. **Career Highlights:** Officer and Manager of Technical Support and Communications Systems Network Engineer, KBC Bank NV (1995-Present); Consultant, Canadian Imperial Bank of Commerce Supporting the Trading Floor (1993-94); Computer Network Technician, Flexible Business Systems (1992-93). **Education:** Grumman Data Systems Institute, Electrical Engineering and Computer Science Technology (1993). **Personal Information:** Mr. Curto enjoys video and audio editing, exercising and fishing.

Patricia J. Fitzgerald

Project Manager
Bank Boston
2 Morrissey Boulevard, MACPK 09-03-03
Boston, MA 02125
(617) 533-6432
Fax: (617) 533-3092

6022

Business Information: Mrs. Fitzgerald serves as Project Manager for the Bank Boston. She is responsible for maintaining technology software tools. A savvy, 22 year veteran of the technology field, Mrs. Fitzgerald specializes in the development and implementation of new cutting edge software and hardware into the existing financial tracking system. She has faithfully served with Bank Boston in a variety of positions as Business Technical Consultant. Working with a team of 50 professionals and experts, Mrs. Fitzgerald utilizes her extensive experience to accommodate the troubleshooting needs of the Bank. In the 21st Century, she hopes to continue working with Bank Boston and helping the Bank achieve success. Her advice is, "Try hard not to focus on one technology." Mrs. Fitzerald attributes her initiation to her late husband, David Fitzgerald. Bank Boston is a banking facility accomodating the financial planning and savings needs of customers within Massachusettes. A multi-service, commercial and residential bank, the Bank recently merged into Fleet Financial and is able to better serve the financing needs of its clients. Employing over 40,000 personnel, the Bank ensures the satisfaction of its clientele through its expert team of financial advisors and support teams. **Career Highlights:** Bank Boston: Project Manager (1997-Present), Manager (1995-97), Business Technical Consultant. **Education:** Suffolk University, B.S. (1989). **Personal Information:** Two children: Julianne and Irene. Mrs. Fitzgerald enjoys Disney collectables and community volunteering.

Paul R. Lambert, III

Database Administrator
PFF Bank & Trust
399 North Garey Avenue
Pomona, CA 91769
(888) 733-5465
lambert3@mcipnet.com

6022

Business Information: As Database Administrator of PFF Bank & Trust, Mr. Lambert is responsible for management information systems reporting and analysis for banking operations and branch administration. He handles all financial management issues within the Bank such as dababase analysis for all departments and branch administration. The highlights of his career are holding the title of Project Coordinator for Staff Modulating SW system, and handling database access and checking systems. Mr. Lambert was a small business consultant through college and through demonstrating his skills and knowledge in the field, quickly advanced to his present position. He plans to increase his knowledge in the database management and work more on data warehousing. Success can be attributed to creativity, devotion, and taking into consideration the needs of those who work for and with him. PFF Bank & Trust is a regional full-service community bank established in 1896. Approximately 500 highly trained people work at the Bank to assist in a variety of duties. The Bank has close to $3 billion in assets and 25 branches to provide services. Headquartered in Ponoma, the Bank offers its service to the community. **Career Highlights:** PFF Bank & Trust: Database Administrator (1999-Present), User Analyst (1998-99); Commercial Banking Relationship Associate, Wells Fargo Bank (1996-98). **Associations & Accomplishments:** Volunteer Staff Leader, Outdoor Recreation Program-Casa Colina Centers for Rehabilitation; Eagle Scouts. **Education:** Arizona State University, B.S. (1994). **Personal Information:** Mr. Lambert enjoys hiking, boating and camping.

Neal D. Fraser

Network Systems Administrator
South Bay Bank
2200 Sepulveda Boulevard
Torrance, CA 90501-5301
(310) 784-3059

6029

Business Information: Mr. Fraser, as the Network Systems Administrator for South Bay Bank, locates wiring contractors, performs software design and development, and installs hardware for the wide area network utilized by the Bank. Established in 1982, South Bay Bank is a commercial lending institution with a hundred million dollar network that services the business needs of Torrance, California. The Bank employs 45 financial professionals and is renowned for being community oriented, gaining insight in and trust from local vendors and corporations. **Career Highlights:** Network Systems Administrator, South Bay Bank (1995-Present); Integrated Marketing Coordinator, Resolution Trust Corporation (1992-95); Asset Technician, Resolution Trust Corporation (1990-92); Independent Stock Broker

(1989-90). **Associations & Accomplishments:** National Association of Securities Dealers. **Education:** University of Phoenix, M.B.A. (1997); Indiana University, B.S. **Personal Information:** Mr. Fraser enjoys home remodeling.

Chene W. Godsey

Lead Systems Administrator
Standard Federal Bank
2600 West Big Beaver Road
Troy, MI 48084
(800) 466-3000
Fax: (248) 637-2778
chene.godsey@abnamro.com

6029

Business Information: As Lead Systems Administrator of Standard Federal Bank, Mr. Godsey has been providing professional information technology direction since coming on board to the Bank as a computer technician in 1997. He administers and controls all system tools and resources, ensuring its functionality and operational status. Managing a server team of three technicians, he concentrates his efforts toward design, development, configuration, support, and implementation of NT Enterprises. Merging the latest technologies into the Banks's financial systems, he provides an efficient and effective network environment. Highly regarded, he possesses superior talents and an excellent understanding of technololgy. Mr. Godsey has plans to further his education by obtaining his Bachelor's degree and Microsoft certifications in order to facilitate promotional opportunities within Standard Federal Bank. His advice is "Find an internship and determine what you enjoy. Continue your education." A subsidiary of ABN AMRO North America, Standard Federal Bank is an established and reputable financial institution offering commercial and personal banking services. Located in Troy, Michigan, the Bank employs the expertise of more than 4,000 professional, technical, and financial administration staff to promote banking services, facilitate scheduling, and address customer queries. Headquartered in Troy, Michigan, the Bank services the diverse financial needs of a regional client base. **Career Highlights:** Standard Federal Bank: Lead Systems Administrator (2000-Present), Systems Administrator (1999-00), Server Operator (1998-99), Computer Technician (1998). **Education:** Oakland University (Currently Attending). **Personal Information:** Mr. Godsey enjoys surfing the Internet, computers, hockey, theme parks and rollerblading.

Clinton W. Hamner

Project Administrator
Charter One Bank
7848 Normandie Boulevard, Apartment L2
Middleburg Heights, OH 44130
(216) 579-1881
Fax: (216) 781-8445
chamner@charterone.com

6029

Business Information: As Project Administrator for Charter One Bank, Mr. Hamner is responsible for supplying such attributes as support and leadership to both clients and employees, as his duties include maintaining a host of in-office projects. His primary projects include everything from marketing consumer information files and the Bank's Web page. Highly regarded, Mr. Hamner also speeks to peers about new technology, while creating new projects and showing job opportunities. The most rewarding aspect of his career is creating and publishing forms for 400 branch offices and overseeing the database for customer information, securities, and funds. Mr. Hamner's plans for the future include establishing his own consulting firm to help small businesses. His success reflects his leadership ability to form teams with synergy, tackle new challenges, and deliver results on behalf of the Bank and its clientele. Charter One Bank engages in the provision of financial management for both consumer and corporate clients. The Bank offers such services as savings and checking accounts and home loans. Established in 1989, the Bank is operated out of several locations throughout the United States, while functioning under the talents and expertise of over 7,000 professionals, to include accountants, loan officers, and other financial managers. The Bank presently enjoys annual assets of more than $32 billion dollars. **Career Highlights:** Project Administrator, Charter One Bank (Present). **Education:** Kent State University, degree in Business Administration (1999). **Personal Information:** Married to Monica in 1999. Mr. Hamner enjoys golf, fishing and camping.

Marianne L. Kerry

Vice President, Strategic Marketing
SSB-City
7 World Trade Center, 39th Floor
New York, NY 10048
(212) 783-6475
Fax: (212) 783-1168
mik1000@aol.com

6029

Business Information: Coupling financial savvy with extensive experience her field, Ms. Kerry serves as Vice President of Strategic Marketing of SSB City, overseeing the North American sales market. Actively participating in the development of quantitative planning, she demonstrates a proactive style of leadership, and incorporates staff input and feedback into policies and procedures. Conducting thorough research, she is able to accurately forecast market trends and prepare analytical strategies and action plans. Recognized throughout the industry as a gifted industry mogul, she carries out her tasks with savior-faire, acting as a mentor and role model for others in her department. Citing adaptability and interpersonal skills as the keys to her success, Ms. Kerry intends to continue in her current role. She enjoys the challenges of her position and looks forward to further advancement within the corporate structure. The business philosophy of SSB-City clearly states implementation of high quality standards, coordination of marketing and relationship management for ease of transactions, and the creation of economies of scale to increase efficiency as the cornerstones of successful financial relationships. By combining the resources of dynamic financial powerhouses, investors in local, regional, and global markets reap benefits of quality and excellence and continually entrust the Group with their assets, currently resulting in a total of $351 billion. **Career Highlights:** Vice President, Strategic Marketing, SSB-City (1998-Present); Citibank SLC Division: Marketing Director (1996-98), Research and Development Director (1992-98), Quality Director (1990-92). **Education:** University of Rochester, M.B.A. (1986); Chestnut Hill College, B.A. (1977); New York University-School of Continuing Education, Portfolio Management Certificate (1999). **Personal Information:** Ms. Kerry enjoys tennis and gardening.

Henry M. Mui

Database Designer/Information System Developer
Chase Manhattan Bank
270 Park Avenue, Floor 36
New York, NY 10017
(212) 270-3076
Fax: (212) 270-1645
henry.mui@chase.com

6029

Business Information: Educated in database design and systems administration, Mr. Mui has served in the dual role of Database Designer and Information Systems Developer for Chase Manhattan Bank since 1997. He performs the information system development and database design, providing a database management system allowing the Bank to create files, query and update information, and print reports. Administering the nostral systems, he ensures its proper and efficient functioning for application and employee support. Mr. Mui is committed to the success of the Bank and looks forward in assisting in the completion of future corporate goals. His success reflects his ability to think outside the box and aggressively take on new challenges. He aspires to become more involved in a managerial position. One of the oldest banks in the United States, Chase Manhattan Bank was established in 1799. The Bank is engaged in correspondence banking and offers a full line of financial services to its individual and commercial clients. Through its numerous locations across the country, national operations employ a work force of more than 77,000 qualified personnel. **Career Highlights:** Database Designer/Information Systems Developer, Chase Manhattan Bank (1997-Present). **Education:** Rutgers University, B.A. (1997).

Reynaldo D. Padilla

Senior Technical Analyst
The Bank of Nova Scotia
888 Birchmount Road
Scarborough, Ontario, Canada M1K 5L1
(416) 288-4048
Fax: (416) 288-4792
rey.padilla@scotiabank.com

6029

Business Information: Mr. Padilla is the Senior Technical Analyst for The Bank of Nova Scotia. Working out of the Toronto corporate office, his responsibilities include ensuring the connectivity of desktops to LAN from cabling to installation of software. He is accountable for all aspects of maintaining the functionality and operational statud of the Bank's information and networking infrastructure. In addition to his network maintenance responsibilities, Mr. Padilla also reccomends the purchase of advanced software and hardware technologies. Among his many accomplishments, the greatest is rennovation and restructuring of the entire department of approximately 4,000 users. In the future, he hopes to eventually attain the position of project leader. Success, according to Mr. Padilla, is attributed to his supportive family and his spirituality. Established in 1831, The Bank of Nova Scotia is a full service retail bank. Providing checking, savings, mutual funds, and insurance, the Bank also provides retail banking for the international market. Headquartered in Toronto, Canada, the Bank employs 36,000 people. **Career Highlights:** The Bank of Scotia Bank: Senior Technical Analyst (1995-Present), Network Support (1990-95); Customer Systems Engineer, Bell Canada (1979-81). **Associations & Accomplishments:** Fellow, Institute of Canadian Bankers; B.L.D. Covenant Community. **Education:** U of T/York University, F.I.C.B. (1979); Philippine School of Business Administration, B.Sc. **Personal Information:** Married to Rosario in 1972. One child: Abigail Marie. Mr. Padilla enjoys community leading.

Randy Peterson

Technical Engineer
Citicorp International Communications Inc.
701 East 60th Street North
Sioux Falls, SD 57104
(605) 331-2675
Fax: (605) 563-2804
rapeter@byelectric.com

6029

Business Information: Functioning in the role of Technical Engineer with Citicorp International Communications Inc., Mr. Peterson is responsible for all aspects of daily network support of the Corporation's infrastructure. Before joining Citicorp International Communications in 1989, Mr. Peterson served as Installation Technician with A.C. Neilsen Company. A savvy, 14 year technology professional, he oversees and directs telephony, LAN and WAN, data and SNA, and all credit card operations. His career highlights include the implementation of two G3 PBX and the complete change out of the phone systems. Mr. Peterson's career success reflects his perseverance and his ability to take on new challenges. Becoming more involved on the engineering and network side of the industry and eventually attaining the position of Senior Engineer serves as his future endeavors. He remains up to date in emerging technology by reading trade magazines and attending classes and seminars. A subsidiary of Citicorp, Citicorp International Communications Inc. offers a wide range of banking and financial services. Established in 1984, Citicorp International Communications presently employs a work force of 3,200 professional, technical, and support personnel. International in scope, the Corporation is currently headquartered in New York. **Career Highlights:** Technical Engineer, Citicorp International Communications Inc. (1989-99); Installation Technician, A.C. Neilsen Company (1985-1989). **Education:** Southeast Area VoTech, Associate's degree (1985). **Personal Information:** Married to Debra in 1979. Two children: Wyatt and Matthew. Mr. Peterson enjoys farming.

Mario J. Recchioni

Vice President of Data Center
Citigroup, Inc.
8725 West Sahara Avenue
Las Vegas, NV 89164
(702) 797-4283
Fax: (702) 341-8353
mjr172@msn.com

6029

Business Information: Rapidly ascending through the Corporation's hierarchy in his years with Citigroup, Inc., Mr. Recchioni now occupies the position of Vice President of the Data Center. The Data Processing Command Center handles all of Citibanks' credit cards worldwide. Mr. Recchioni assumes accountability for daily operations, resolving any problems that arise, ensuring that the Center runs smoothly and efficiently. Four shift supervisors report directly to him and he coordinates the maintenance of the customer service on-line databank system. As a solid, 14 year professional with an established track record of delivering results, Mr. Recchioni's leadership reflects his ability to build strong teams with synergy and technical strength, think out-of-the-box, and take on new challenges and responsibilities. Looking to the future, one of his goal is to eventually attain the position of Director. Citigroup, Inc. was created in 1987 by the merger of Citicorp and Travels Group. Specializing in banking and bank cards, the Corporation offers all types of financial services for commercial and personal use. Headquartered in New York, Citigroup, Inc. employs 36 professional, technical, and support personnel within the Data Center. **Career Highlights:** Citigroup, Inc.: Vice President of Data Center (1997-Present), Assistant Vice President (1987-97). **Associations & Accomplishments:** Volunteer, Christmas in

April Program. **Education:** Mattatuck Community College, A.S. (1975); IBM, Data Processing Operations Certification. **Personal Information:** Married to Darlene in 1999. Four children: Joe, Jared, Shelley, and Lisa. Mr. Recchioni enjoys golf, swimming and working on home personal computer.

Marwan Samadi
Information Technology Manager
National Bank of Kuwait
P.O. Box 11-5727
Beirut, Lebanon
+96 11741111
Fax: +96 11747846
msamadi@cyberia.net.lb

6029

Business Information: Serving as Information Technology Manager, Mr. Samadi maintains technical integrity for the National Bank of Kuwait at Lebanon. The Beirut location boasts an advanced data center which is supervised by Mr. Samadi, who also oversees the LAN and WAN network. Further demonstrating exceptional talent in the industry, he handles all operating systems. Troubleshooting, maintenance, upgrades: these are all tasks he completes on a regular basis. Achieving maximum results through positive actions, he understands the importance of flexibility and patience while working in a technical environment. Mr. Samadi enjoys the challenges of his position and intends to continue in his current capacity as he implements progressive technology into the Bank. National Bank of Kuwait has a major location in Beirut, Lebanon, that was established in 1959. Offering a variety of features for both private individuals and businesses in the area, the Bank provides retail and traditional services. Operating with state-of-the-art equipment and modern systems, the "best small bank in the world" maintains 10 branches throughout Lebanon. Profits last year exceeded $250 million; the Bank was the only financial institution to survive the Kuwaiti invasion. **Career Highlights:** Information Technology Manager, National Bank of Kuwait-Lebanon (1992-Present); Information Technology Assistant Manager, Lebanon and Gulf Bank (1990). **Associations & Accomplishments:** Beirut Lions Club. **Education:** Lebanese American University, M.S. in Computer Science (1997). **Personal Information:** Married to Maya Moukahal in 1994. Mr. Samadi enjoys music.

Sue L. Shreffler
Computer Programmer Analyst
Federal Home Loan Bank
2 Townsite Plaza
Topeka, KS 66603
(785) 232-0507
suesheffler@fhlbtopeka.com

6029

Business Information: Miss Shreffler serves as Computer Programmer Analyst of Federal Home Loan Bank. She is responsible for installing and maintaining operating systems, and providing technical support to other programmers. Before joining Federal Home Loan Bank in 1996, Miss Shreffler served as a Physical Therapy Assistant at both Kansas Rehabilitation Hospital and Walter Crum RPT. Her present position primarily involves programming software, ensuring the functionality and fully operational status of the Legacy programs, and maintaining and upgrading mainframe and PC infrastructure as changes occur. Quickly establishing her presence in the field, Miss Shreffler performs troubleshooting of both software and hardware to ensure their efficiency and integrity. Analyzing and supporting computer operations for internal and external clients, as well as assisting in Web page design are also an integral part of her responsibilities. One of her major accomplishments was the recent design of her first Web page. She attributes her career success to her mother who taught her to accept responsibility and finish what she starts. "Be open to new suggestions and have a desire to learn," is cited as Miss Shreffler's advice. Becoming more involved within the Internet arena and object oriented languages, and continuing her education in those areas serve as her future endeavors. Federal Home Loan Bank operates as a wholesale bank responsible for loaning money to banks under a government mandate. Regulated by the Federal Housing Finance Board in Washington, D.C., the Institution is part of a network of 12 locations across the United States. National in scope, the Institution was founded in 1932. Presently, 150 employees man the Topeka, Kansas location. **Career Highlights:** Computer Programmer Analyst, Federal Home Loan Bank (1996-Present); Physical Therapy Assistant, Kansas Rehabilitation Hospital (1989-96); Physical Therapy Assistant, Walter Crum RPT (1985-89). **Associations & Accomplishments:** American Physical Therapy Association; Kansas Physical Therapy Association. **Education:** Washburn University: B.A. (1999), A.A. (1985); Wichita State University, B.S. (1979). **Personal Information:** Miss Shreffler enjoys team sports, reading, computers and dogs.

Steve Watkins
Assistant Vice President/Director of Information Technology
Summit National Bank
4360 Chamblee-Dunwwody Road, Suite 300
Atlanta, GA 30341
(770) 454-0400
Fax: (770) 458-7818
swatkins@btnc.net

6029

Business Information: Combining his strategic technical skills and management expertise, Mr. Watkins serves as Assistant Vice President and Director of Information Technology for the Summit National Bank. He presides over all of the Bank's data communication operations and determines its technological direction. Supervising a staff of skilled professionals, he ensures that the various networks and computer systems on which the Bank's critical operations depend is functioning efficiently and productively. Mr. Watkins was responsible for implementing the new Internet access and e-mail systems. Citing his love of technology as the key to his success, he looks forward to expanding his professional responsibilities, aspiring to a role as Chief Information Officer. The Summit National Bank offers commercial banking services to small and medium sized companies and corporations. A full line of financial services is also provided to the Bank's individual clients. Founded in 1987, the Bank boasts more than $300 million in annual revenue. The Atlanta, Georgia and San Jose, California locations employs the services of 125 administrative, financial, and support personnel. Summit National Bank provides six strategically placed locations from which its banking services are offered. **Career Highlights:** Assistant Vice President/Director of Information Technology, Summit National Bank (1999-Present); Information Technology Manager, Esquire Communications, Ltd. (1998-99); Information Technology Director, Calder, Watkins & McWilliam, PLLC (1991-98). **Education:** Campbell University, Juris Doctor (1993); Carson-Newman College, B.A. (1987). **Personal Information:** Married to Kay in 1996. Mr. Watkins enjoys golf, church, travel and baseball.

Adrian U. Chee
Management Information Systems Manager
International Savings
225 Queen Street, 5th Floor
Honolulu, HI 96813
(808) 535-3641
Fax: (808) 535-3638
achee@cb-hi.net

6036

Business Information: For the past 14 years, Mrs. Chee has been a highly regarded employee of International Savings. Serving as Management Information Systems Manager since 1992, she oversees all network and hardware used by the Bank. Additionally, she is responsible for 11 employees within the department. On a daily basis, she handles troubleshooting and maintenance issues as well as upgrades. Utilizing an informative, concise approach, Mrs. Chee effectively communicates reccomendations for software and hardware after thrououghly evaluating the need. Citing good work ethics and excellent education as the main factors in her success, Mrs. Chee keeps informed of current technological issues by continuing education, reading periodicals, and networking with other professionals. Looking towards the 21st Century, she plans to keep her department moving towards Web based technology so that the Bank may remain competitive. A subdivision of CB Bank Shares Inc., International Savings is a sister of City Bank. With more than 350 employees and 11 branches, the Bank is an expanding financial institution in Hawaii. **Career Highlights:** International Savings: Management Information Systems Manager (1999-Present); Network Administrator (1988-92), Administrative Assistant II (1986-88). **Associations & Accomplishments:** Hawaii Telecommunications Association. **Education:** Hawaii Pacific University, B.S. in Computer Science (1992); Certified Novell Engineer; M.C.N.A. **Personal Information:** Married to Curtis K. K. W. in 1992. Two children: Kapena and Keanu.

David J. Hill
Assistant Director of Marketing/Webmaster
Power FCU
P.O. Box 1297
Syracuse, NY 13201
(315) 474-1226
Fax: (315) 474-1754
dhill1@twcny.rr.com

6061

Business Information: Mr. Hill functions in the dual role of Assistant Director of Marketing and Webmaster with Power FCU. He is responsible for cutting edge Web site design, management, and marketing research. Before joining Power FCU, Mr. Hill served as a Marketing Specialist for First Teachers FCU. His background history also includes a three year stint as a Lead Designer in the AD services department with the "Schenectedy Daily Gazette." A six year professional, he develops updates and programs the Web site, oversees project management, and develops and administers marketing promotions and schedules. Always interested in computers, Mr. Hill is an expert on HTML and Java Scripting and does professional freelance work for local and national companies. Attributing his success to his wife, a stable home, and hard work, he plans on increasing his involvement in marketing projects and web design and graphic design. Power FCU is a federal credit union accommodating the fiscal needs of residents within Central New York. Established in 1939, the non-profit Credit Union is regarded as one of the largest in central New York offering a full range of financial services. The Credit Union offers Internet banking, savings and checking accounts, and financial investment opportunities to provide a secure environment for money to grow. **Career Highlights:** Assistant Director of Marketing/Webmaster, Power FCU (1998-Present); Professional Freelance Designer (1993-Present); Marketing Specialist, First Teachers FCU (1996-98); Ad Services, The Daily Gazette (1993-96). **Associations & Accomplishments:** Security on the Internet Certified. **Education:** College of St. Rose, B.S. in Graphic Designs (1989-93); Certification in Security on the Internet. **Personal Information:** Married to Kim in 1994. Mr. Hill enjoys being a musician, golf and online gaming.

Douglas M. Graham
Manager of Information Systems
Commonwealth Credit Union
417 High Street
Frankfort, KY 40601-2112
(502) 564-4775
Fax: (502) 564-5911
dgraham@cwcu.org

6062

Business Information: As a Certified Network Engineer, Mr. Graham serves as Manager of Information Systems for the Commonwealth Credit Union. Presiding over the Information Systems Department, he manages the departmental budget, delegates LAN and WAN administration duties, and acts as chief liaison to vendors responsible for recommending and approving new technology. As a systems expert, he effectively monitors the Institution's on-line banking products activities and ATM networks, as well as implements state-of-the-art touch screen technology. Coordinating resources, schedules, time lines, and assignments also fall within the realm of his responsibilities. Committed to further development of the Institution, Mr. Graham coordinates strategic planning to ensure a bright future as Chief Information Officer. A financial institution, the Commonwealth Credit Union maintains three locations from which to serve an international clientele. Providing checking, savings, loan, and related financial services, the Institution was established in 1958. Presently, the Institution employs a staff of 180 individuals. **Career Highlights:** Manager of Information Systems, Commonwealth Credit Union (1996-Present); Senior Systems Analyst, University of Kentucky (1995-96); Network Engineer, Data Stream (1994-95). **Education:** University of Kentucky; Certified Network Engineer. **Personal Information:** Married to Joan in 1986. Two children: Cassidy and Mea. Mr. Graham enjoys listening to music.

Mary Ann Hughes
Director of Computer Operations
Arizona Central Credit Union
3611 North Black Canyon Highway
Phoenix, AZ 85015-5498
(602) 798-7169
Fax: (602) 631-4280
blogik@aol.com

6062

Business Information: Ms. Hughes functions in the role of Director of Computer Operations for Arizona Central Credit Union. She is responsible for the entire network, LAN/WAN administration, and data processing system within the Credit Union, while also taking care of the purchasing needs for the systems. She advises the Board on the most productive and cost-effective programs to obtain that will still meet the needs of the Credit Union. For the future, Ms. Hughes hopes to complete her M.B.A. in Technology Management and advance her role within the Credit Union into a Vice President position. Her success is attributed to her mother's push to be and do her best. Arizona Central Credit Union is a non-profit, state chartered, financial institution. With a staff of 150 employees, the Credit Union offers its members an extensive variety of financing and investing needs. The Credit Union offers savings opportunities and investment advice to all patrons wanting to better their financial situations. **Career Highlights:** Arizona Central Credit Union: Director of Computer Operations (1998-Present), Computer Operator II (1997-98), Computer Operator (1993-97). **Education:** University of Phoenix, M.B.A. in Technology Management (In Progress); Arizona State University, B.A. in English (1998). **Personal Information:** Ms. Hughes enjoys dancing, working with dogs and travel.

Anissa M. Lomax

Data Processing Manager
Seaboard Credit Union
4230 Southpoint Parkway
Jacksonville, FL 32216
(904) 332-4201
Fax: (904) 332-9305
aml@southeast.net

6062

Business Information: Mrs. Lomax functions in the capacity of Data Processing Manager for Seaboard Credit Union. She is responsible for maintaining both hardware and software for the Credit Union's information systems infrastructure. Establishing her presence in the field, she was promoted to her current position six months after coming on board to Seaboard Credit Union in 1996. Mrs. Lomax, a savvy professional, monitors the computer databases of the Credit Union and ensures the continuous network accessibility from each machine on the system. For the future, she plans on implementing more advanced technology within Seaboard Credit Union and specialize her career in network hardware administration. Her ability to learn has kept Mrs. Lomax at the head of her field. Success is attributed to attending training seminars and surfing the Internet, as well as her ability to produce results and aggressively take on new challenges. Seaboard Credit Union is a non-profit financial institute serving the citizens of Jacksonville, Florida. Established in 1929, the Credit Union is able to better serve the financial needs of its customers by focusing entirely on customer service without having to meet a plethora of goals and profit margins. Presently, Seaboard Credit Union employs a staff of 55 people. **Career Highlights:** Data Processing Manager, Seaboard Credit Union (Present). **Personal Information:** Married.

David D. Rogers

Information Systems Manager
San Gabriel Valley Credit Union
11024 Concert Street
El Monte, CA 91731
(626) 443-6013
Fax: (626) 443-7346
davidrog@pacbell.net

6062

Business Information: Mr. Rogers serves as Information Systems Manager of San Gabriel Valley Credit Union. He is responsible for maintaining the systems infrastructure functional and operational. Possessing an excellent understanding of his field, he works with upper management and users to research, design, and develop new solutions to harness more of the computer's power. The analysis, acquisition, installation, modification, configuration, support, and tracking of operating systems, databases, utilities, software, and hardware also fall within the scope of his responsibilities. Mr. Rogers' career highlights include his recruitment by the Credit Union to fill his present position and the implementation of a "Member Advantage Program." Attaining his B.B.A. degree and the position of manager or vice president of data processing is cited as his future endeavors. Success, according to Mr. Rogers, is due to his desire to succeed and ability to deliver results. San Gabriel Valley Credit Union was established in 1966 and is located in El Monte, California. The Credit Union specializes in CDs, interest and noninterest checking accounts, loans, savings accounts, and equity lines of credit. San Gabriel Valley Credit Union currently employs a staff of 25. The Credit Union and has approximately 15,000 members. **Career Highlights:** Information Systems Manager, San Gabriel Valley Credit Union (1998-Present); Owner, D&J Computers (1998-Present); Owner, D.R. Marketing (1996-98); Assembler, Scala Electronic Corporation (1995-97). **Education:** Citrus Community College (Currently Attending); Universal Technical Institute, Certificate. **Personal Information:** Married to Jean in 1999. Three children: Hethyr, Sarah, and Dakota. Mr. Rogers enjoys building computers, building models, reading and science fiction.

Pamela T. Allen

Project Manager
ABN AMRO Bank
181 West Madison Street
Chicago, IL 60602
(312) 904-1047
Fax: (312) 904-4006
pamela.allen@abnamro.com

6081

Business Information: Mrs. Allen is Project Manager of ABN AMRO Bank. She is responsible for the ABN AMRO's Information Technology Group. Before joining the Bank in 1997, Mrs. Allen served as Lead Programmer and Analyst with Blue Cross Blue Shield. Her strong, 21 year history includes: Senior Team Leader at Kemper Financial Services and Senior Programmer and Analyst with Continental Bank. In her present position, Mrs. Allen is the chief liaison between business clients and systems management. She helps by overseeing and working different project initiatives and coordinating all project related tasks. Determination and perseverance has contributed to her career success. Her success reflects her ability to think out-of-the-box and take on new challenges and responsibilities. "Get as much education as possible and formulate a path to go as far as your career goes," is cited as Mrs. Allen's advice. A Dutch owned financial institution, ABN AMRO Bank is ranked as the world's 15th largest bank. A full service banking institution, ABN AMRO's services include securities trading and brokerage. The Bank maintains a strong presence in Europe, Asia, South America, Canada, and the United States. With corporate headquarters in Amsterdam, The Netherlands, ABN AMRO Bank employs a global work force of more than 5,000 professional, technical, and administrative support personnel. **Career Highlights:** Project Manager, ABN AMRO Bank (1997-Present); Lead Programmer/Analyst, Blue Cross Blue Shield (1988-97); Senior Team Leader, Kemper Financial Services (1986-88); Senior Programmer/Analyst, Continental Bank (1978-85). **Associations & Accomplishments:** American Tae Kwon Do Association; Parent Teachers Organization; Pallen Partners. **Education:** Chicago State University, B.S. in Information Systems (1978). **Personal Information:** Married to Sylvester Jr. in 1982. Two children: Marcus Thomas and Malcolm Taylor. Mrs. Allen enjoys mentoring and martial arts and gardening.

Michel Fries

Information Technology Manager
Dexia Bank International in Luxembourg
67 Rue Mühlenberg
Athus, Belgium 6791
+352 45902005
Fax: +352 45902952
friesm@bigfoot.com

6081

Business Information: Devoted to the managerial operations of Dexia Bank International in Luxembourg, Mr. Fries holds the position of Information Technology Manager for the Bank. He detemines the strategic direction and business contribution of the information systems functions. Possessing an excellent understanding of his field, Mr. Fries formulates technical and marketing plans to enhance the Bank's operations, thereby maintaining a competitive edge in the financial industry. He is responsible for implementing various new technology systems to ensures an efficient, flexible, and profitable operation. Specifically handling the security aspects of critical data, he oversees funds management and various other financial matters. Involved in the development of several support products, Mr. Fries is moving the Bank towards a more direct banking system using asset management and the Internet. His success reflects his ability to take on challenges and deliver results on behalf of the Bank and its clientele. Headquartered in Athus, Belgium, Dexia Bank International in Luxembourg specializes in a variety of banking services. Employing over 3,500, the Bank provides private banking services, such as checking and savings accounts, loan programs. and retirement programs. Also dealing with retail banking with local branches, the Bank is dedicated to providing efficient services and funds for the surrounding banks. Managing the funds of financial institutions worldwide, the Bank is a major supplier of money and information technology integration. **Career Highlights:** Dexia Bank International in Luxembourg: Information Technology Manager (1999-Present), Database Applications Manager (1990-99), Applications Operations (1984-90). **Associations & Accomplishments:** President, Radio Amateur Association, Section South Luxembourg. **Education:** I.T.S. Jemelles, Graduate (1984). **Personal Information:** Married to Katty in 1989. One child: Allyson. Mr. Fries enjoys reading and stock trading.

Mohamed Ahmed Mohamed

Information Technology Director
Cairo Barclay's Bank
P.O. Box 110, Garden City Maglis El Shaab
Cairo, Egypt
+20 23662808
Fax: +20 23662810
mam@eis.com.eg

6081

Business Information: As Information Technology Director of Cairo Barclay's Bank, Mr. Mohamed is responsible for all information technology development and management. Included in his daily schedule are activities that include the maintenance of hardware, troubleshooting of software and equipment, and systems upgrades. He demonstrates his extensive knowledge of technical systems by developing training programs that highlight main areas of interest and point out common concerns. Believing in the value of an ongoing education, Mr. Mohamed looks forward to continual advancement within the Bank and intends to conclude his career serving as a Board Member. Established in 1976, Cairo Barclay's Bank is the result of a venture between Barkleys' Bank of the United Kingdom and Bank Cairo of Egypt. Focusing on corporate accounts, roughly two-thirds of the Bank is geared towards business clients although they maintain superior services for retail banking as well. Currently, all four Cairo branches are introducing personal banking and premiere accounts. **Career Highlights:** Cairo Barclay's Bank: Information Technology Director (1999-Present), Senior Manager of Computer (1995-99), Manager of Computer Department (1992-95). **Associations & Accomplishments:** Technical Information Technology Committee, Banks Association of Egypt. **Education:** Ain Shams University, Bachelor's degree in Commerce (1979); American University at Cairo, Computer Science Diploma (1979). **Personal Information:** Married to Laila Abdel Salam in 1986. Two children: Alia and Rana. Mr. Mohamed enjoys football, music and reading.

Joanna M. Riopelle

Senior Vice President
ABN AMRO
135 South LaSalle, Suite 640
Chicago, IL 60603
(312) 904-2955
jmrpw@aol.com

6081

Business Information: As Senior Vice President of ABN AMRO, Ms. Riopelle is responsible for the development and implementation of policies and procedures that are the heart of every successful effort within the Bank. Throughout daily routines, she is held accountable for a number of strategic duties. Among them are such activities as business development, administration, loan portfolio management, and origination of credit and treasury products for media and telecommunications companies. Known for her outstanding performance and superior management and team work ethic, Ms. Riopelle is also possesses the ability to understand complex problems and communicate solutions to both clients and internal staff. She focuses her attention on developing new policies and procedures that ensures that all units work together to achieve one common goal. Ms. Riopelle serves in a number of other positions, such as senior banker and team leader for the Midwest Division of the Media and Telecommunications Group. Always alert to new opportunities, techniques, and approaches, she continues to grow professionally through the fulfillment of her responsibilities and her involvement in the advancement of operations. Establishing goals that are compatible with those of the Bank, Ms. Riopelle is currently striving to obtain the position of chief financial officer, while also considering running a division with another investment firm. ABN AMRO is a full service banking institution. The Bank specializes in financing telecommunications companies, to include wireless, satellite, cable and equipment manufacturing. Maintaining a strong capital base with a respectable position in international markets, the Bank caters to a wide array of private and corporate clients. Headquartered in the Netherlands, the Bank also operates out of several international locations, including 3,500 offices in 76 countries and territories. Established in 1825, the Bank functions under the direction of more than 70,000 individuals, to include senior bankers, loan officers, consultants, and professional auditors. The Bank currently maintains annual assets exceeding $30 million and loan commitments worth over $3.5 billion. **Career Highlights:** ABN AMRO: Senior Vice President (1998-Present), Group Vice President (1994-98), Vice President (1993-94): Vice President, First Chicago (1984-93). **Associations & Accomplishments:** Treasurer, Imagine Chicago; Consultant, World Bank; Chicago Council of Foreign Relations; Center for Neighborhood Technology. **Education:** University of Wisconsin, M.B.A. (1984); St. Norbert College, B.A. in Communications. **Personal Information:** Married. Ms. Riopelle enjoys being an opera singer and performing publically.

Doug J. Tignor

Network Specialist
Swiss Bank Corporation
4225 Naperville Road, Suite 250
Lisle, IL 60532-3659
(630) 955-4947
tignord@wdr.com

6081

Business Information: Utilizing more than five years of experience in the field of information technology, Mr. Tignor serves as Network Specialist for the Swiss Bank Corporation. In this capacity, he assumes responsibility for the wide area network for the UBS in 100 countries. He provides timeplex support to other network technicians and handles the day routers, ensuring that the Corporation's sensitive data is routed efficiently and to the correct final location. An accomplished troubleshooter, he travels frequently to various sites around the world. Mr. Tignor attributes his professional success to his ability to learn quickly and he is continually striving to increase his knowledge. Currently, he is pursuing several technical certifications to enable him to capitalize on the opportunities presented by the Corporation. Swiss Bank Corporation is a full service financial institution serving businesses and individuals in several countries around the globe. The largest bank in Switzerland, worldwide operations employ a work force of more than 10,000 qualified staff members. Tracing its roots back to the 1500s, the Corporation is one of the oldest of its kind. **Career Highlights:** Network Specialist, Swiss Bank Corporation (1995-Present); Student, Ball State University (1995); Manufacture Supervisor, Milgard Manufacturing (1987-93). **Associations & Accomplishments:** Leader, Boy Scouts of America; Run Itasca Food Pantry Every 5th Month for Church. **Education:** Ball State University, M.S. in Information Sciences (1995); Ohio University, B.S. in Communication Systems Management; Moorpark College, A.S. in Business Management (1984-85). **Personal Information:** Married to Karen in 1986. Three children: Jessica, Shawn, and Tyler. Mr. Tignor enjoys motorcross riding, camping, travel and fishing.

William A. Blaylock

Director of Management Information Systems
Checkfast
5181 Amelia Earhart Drive
Salt Lake City, UT 84116
(801) 364-8200
Fax: (801) 401-4094
will@checkfast.com

6099

Business Information: Possessing unique talents in the information technology field, Mr. Blaylock joined Checkfast as the Director of Management Information Systems in 1999. Utilizing several years of experience in the computer software industry, Mr. Blaylock is in charge of the networking and operating systems infrastructure as well as software development and compiling management reports for Checkfast's top management. A successful technical professiona, he determines the strategic direction and business contribution of the information systems functions. Maintaining the functionality and operational status of the systems infrastructure and Web server, Mr. Blaylock is continually seeking new opportunities and responsibilities in the field. In the near future, he would like to work for a larger company performing similar tasks, where he will be able to interact with Internet groups and become more involved with design and development of Web pages. Checkfast is a merchant service company that provides NSF check clearing, point of sales, and credit credit verification services to a large retail clientele, to include RadioShack and Candies. Established in 1995, the Company is national in scope and headquartered in Salt Lake City, Utah. Presently, the Company employs a staff of 50 people who oversee all aspect of day-to-day business operations. **Career Highlights:** Director of Management Information Systems, Checkfast (1999-Present); Owner, Comfortable Software (1981-Present). **Associations & Accomplishments:** Chief Information Officer, Tech Guild Professionals; Borland Users Group; Utah Linux Club. **Education:** Weber State University: Chef (1984), degree in Compute Science (1982); University of Utah. **Personal Information:** Married to Valerie in 1989. Mr. Blaylock enjoys photography, cooking and genealogy.

Shannon McLemore

Management Information Systems Manager
Continuous Forms & Checks, Inc.
400 West Park Court
Peachtree City, GA 30269
(770) 631-6070
Fax: (770) 631-6188
smclemore@cfcmail.com

6099

Business Information: Serving as Management Information Systems Manager of Continuous Forms & Checks, Inc., Mr. McLemore oversees every facet of each of the computer systems utilized by the Corporation. He administers the network, providing network security, as well as supports upgrades and setups. Performing system maintenance, Mr. McLemore monitors daily activity and provides for routine backups. Before joining Continuous Forms & Checks, he served as Network Engineer with McCollough Sherrill and Help Desk Support Technician at Georgia State University. Quickly establishing his presence in the field, Mr. McLemore's success reflects his ability to solve system problems in a systematic and efficient manner and aggressively take on new challenges. Keeping abreast of the latest advances in technology by reading industry publications and attending seminars, he anticipates moving upwards within the Corporation into a management position. Continuous Forms & Checks, Inc. is a manufacturer of forms and checks for financial institutions. Founded in 1982, the Corporation employs a work force of 400 staff members to facilitate every aspect of design, manufacture, quality assurance and control, and distribution of products. **Career Highlights:** Management Information Systems Manager, Continuous Forms & Checks, Inc. (1998-Present); Network Engineer, McCollough Sherrill (1997-98); Help Desk Support Technician, Georgia State University (1997). **Education:** Georgia State University, B.B.A. (1997); Certified Novell Engineer; Microsoft Certified System Engineer; A+ Certified Technician.

6100 Nondepository Institutions

6111 Federal and federally sponsored credit
6141 Personal credit institutions
6153 Short-term business credit
6159 Misc. business credit institutions
6162 Mortgage bankers and correspondents
6163 Loan brokers

Judith Colclough Bennett

Manager of Computer Services
North Carolina State Education Assistance Authority
P.O. Box 14103
Research Triangle Park, NC 27709
(919) 549-8614
Fax: (919) 248-6635
judester@ncseaa.edu

6111

Business Information: Serving as Manager of Computer Services for the North Carolina State Education Assistance Authority, Mrs. Colclough Bennett manages and directs all information technology services for the Agency. With the responsibility of a network of 90 users in the Microsoft Exchange system, she is directly accountable for the actions of nine technicians. Performing maintenance and database conversion on an AS/400, she is also responsible for Microsoft NT LAN/WAN networks, telephony system, and building security. Recipient of IBM's most prestigious "Rally" award, she has converted $437 million to the AS/400 system. Highly regarded, Mrs. Colclough Bennett lives by the motto "work like you don't need the money, love like you've never been hurt, and dance like no one is watching." The North Carolina State Education Assistance Authority was founded in 1965. A guarantor of federal and state generated student assistance monies, the Authority offers student loans, grants, and scholarships. Employing 75 individuals, the Authority provides these services for residents of North Carolina, and is affiliated with the University of North Carolina General Administration. **Career Highlights:** Manager of Computer Services, North Carolina State Education Assistance Authority (1992-Present); Lead Product Specialist, IBM (1993-99); Assistant Claims Manager, N.A.S.I. Welfare Fund (1991-92); Plan Administrator, Infinet, Inc. (1988-91). **Associations & Accomplishments:** Watts Street Baptist Church; Phi Beta Kappa. **Education:** University of North Carolina at Chapel Hill, B.A. (1986). **Personal Information:** Married to Jerry in 1999. One child: Abby. Mrs. Colclough Bennett enjoys aerobics, dancing, music and running.

Edwin C. Hermann, Jr.

Systems/Operations Analyst of the Investment Recovery Division
CitiFinancial
11436 Cronhill Drive, Suite H
Owings Mills, MD 21117
(410) 581-6868
Fax: (410) 581-6893
hermanne@citifinancial.com

6141

Business Information: In his position as Systems and Operations Analyst of the Investment Recovery Division of CitiFinancial, Mr. Hermann assumes a number of responsibilities on behalf of the Institution and its clientele, to include administering and controlling systems tools and resources. He determines which computer hardware and software is needed to establish new systems or incorporate system changes, and coordinates research and tests to ensure optimal performance thus eliminating system errors. Demonstrating an excellent understanding of technology, Mr. Hermann utilizes 30 years of experience in a problem solving capacity, implementing state-of-the-art computer technology to meet the individual needs of the Institution. Tunning systems software, ensuring the integrity and security of data, and resolving systems difficulties also fall within the realm of his responsibilities. Mr. Hermann has enjoyed substantial success and plans to continue in his present position. CitiFinancial offers financial services for more than 2.5 million individuals across the United States and Canada. Established in 1912, the Institution provides home equity loans, personal loans, and debt consolidation through its 1,200 offices. The Institution employs the skilled services of 4,000 personnel to meet the diverse needs of its clientele and generates over $1 billion annually. **Career Highlights:** Systems/Operations Analyst of the Investment Recovery Division, CitiFinancial (1989-Present); Vice President, Commercial Credit International Banking Corporation (1979-88); International Operations Executive, First National Bank of Maryland (1970-79). **Education:** Western Maryland College, B.A. in Economics cum laude (1970). **Personal Information:** Married to Susan B. in 1988. Mr. Hermann enjoys investing and surfing the Internet.

Donald R. B. "Donn" Howard

Manager of Technology Asset Management
American General Finance
601 Northwest 2nd Street, P.O. Box 59 TAMMT4
Evansville, IN 47701-0059
(812) 468-5741
Fax: (812) 468-5018
dhoward@agfinance.com

6141

Business Information: Drawing from 15 years of experience in the technology field, Mr. Howard is Manager of Technology Asset Management. He controls all computer assets, while monitoring hardware for 1,350 locations and 9,000 users around the United States and the Caribbean. Throughout his sphere of influence, Mr. Howard is also accountable for project management, purchasing, contract management, leasing, expense management, and budgetary issues. Current success, he asserts, is a product of finding oppurtunities. As for the future, he foresees that he will continue finding opportunities, accomplishing them, and advancing through the ranks of information technology. Mr. Howard works for the consumer finance division of American General Financial Group. American General is a market leader in retirement services, life insurance, and consumer loans, serving the financial security needs of more than 12 million customers. American General common stock is listed on the New York, Pacific, London, and Swiss stock exchanges. **Career Highlights:** American General Finance: Manager of Technology Asset Management (1996-Present), Business Systems Analyst (1994-96); American General Life Insurance Company: Management Consultant (1992-94), Information Center Consultant (1988-91). **Associations & Accomplishments:** Cub Master/Assistant Scout Master/Committee Chairman/Den Leader, Boy Scouts of America; Charter President, Newburgh Optimist Club. **Education:** Main Event Management Institute (1992, 1993); University of Houston (1989); Texas Tech University (1984). **Personal Information:** Married to Lynnette in 1983. Four children: Seth, Owen, Grant, and Trevor. Mr. Howard enjoys scouting, cars and singing.

Mindy L. Kirkpatrick

Vice President of Global Intranet
Visa International
P.O. Box 8999
San Francisco, CA 94158-8999
(650) 432-1865
mkirkpat@visa.com

6141

Business Information: Ms. Kirkpatrick serves in the position of Vice President of Global Intranet for Visa International. Working out of the office in San Francisco, California, she strives to guarantee the continuity and internal maintenance of the Company's Intranet structures. Providing direct assistance to the team, she oversees the development of the Web site for Visa. Determining the strategic direction, attending meetings, and motivating the Company's 5,500 employees to aggressively push Visa's products and services into the markets also fall within the realm of Ms. Kirkpatrick's evangelist activities. The highlight of her professional career was her implementation of the Visa Intranet system, making it a primary source of information. Very passionate of what she does, Ms. Kirkpatrick hopes to continue in her pursuit of knowledge for online, e-business, and e-commerce functions. Visa International provides financial services for the credit card industry. One of the largest credit card businesses in the world, the Company works with corporate and private clients to support businesses as well as private citizens. Presently, Visa International is located in San Francisco, California. **Career Highlights:** Visa International: Vice President of Global Intranet (1997-Present), Vice President of Information Policy (1996-97); Vice President of ATM Marketing, Bank of America (1994-96). **Associations & Accomplishments:** Leadership Midpeninsula. **Education:** University of California at Santa Cruz, B.A. in Psychology (1989). **Personal Information:** Married to John in 1992.

Brooke Manino

Vice President of Information Technology
American Express - TRS
67 Beech Avenue
Berkeley Heights, NJ 07922-1608
(212) 640-1337

6141

Business Information: A valued employee of American Express - TRS since 1988, Mrs. Manino fulfills the responsibilities of Vice President of Information Technology.

Utilizing powerful, effective management skills and a strong educational history, she provides direct oversight of the global information technology team of 175 people. Additionally, Mrs. Manino ensures that new business partner applications operate properly. Her greatest professional accomplishment was four-years spent in Japan for American Express and participating on the management team there. Serving as the main credit and travel division of American Express, the Company is located in New York and has also begun to make international inroads in the global markets. **Career Highlights:** American Express - TRS: Vice President of Information Technology (1995-Present), Director of Information Technology (1993-94); Director of Finance, American Express International - Japan (1991-93). **Associations & Accomplishments:** Oxford Alumni Association of New York. **Education:** American Graduate School of International Management, Master's degree in International Management (1984); William Jewell College (1983); Regents Park College; Oxford University.

Ronaldo Pereiras Marques

Head of Production Control
American Express
19640 North 31st Avenue, Floor 1
Phoenix, AZ 85027-3905
(602) 766-1479
rmarques@uswest.net

6141

Business Information: As Head of Production Control at American Express, Mr. Marques is responsible for the proper completion of all technically related projects at the Australia, Latin America, Brazil, and Argentina locations. He retains the same responsiblity at locations throughout Europe and Japan, demonstrating his superior knowledge of information systems. Working closely with several teams from various production departments, Mr. Marques devleops creative solutions to manufacturing challenges, resulting in superior quality and value products. Recognized as a vital asset, he is credited with the formulation and implementation of cutting edge programs that have helped increase the effectiveness of the Corporation in a fiercely competitive market. Looking forward to assisting in the completion of future corporate goals, Mr. Marques intends to continue his work while seeking advancement within the corporate structure. American Express is a diversified provider of travel and financial services on an international scale. Operating in 160 companies around the world, the Corporation employs over 70,000 people to offer services such as trip reservations, expenditure management, and investment advisory to a diverse clientele. **Career Highlights:** American Express: Head of Production Control (1997-Present), Supervisor of the Data Center (1989-97); Supervisor of the Data Center, ITAU Bank (1975-89). **Education:** F.M.U. College, Business Administration (1982). **Personal Information:** Married to Isaura C. P. in 1989. Two children: Denis C. and Igor C. Mr. Marques enjoys basketball, soccer and tennis.

Conrad O. Menezes

Lead Network Engineer
American Express Company
200 Vesey Street
New York, NY 10285
(212) 640-4509
Fax: (212) 640-4509
conrad.menezes@aexp.com

6141

Business Information: As Lead Network Engineer at American Express Company, Mr. Menezes is involved in the design, implementation, and maintenance of the global company enterprise wide local, metropolitan, and wide area network connectivity. Beginning his career more than 10 years ago, Mr. Menezes has worked diligently to enhance his skills and acquire expertise in his field. He has enjoyed substantial success in his career including having written several articles for publication. A 10-year professional, he hopes to expedite continued promotion through his involvement in the continued success and advancement of operations. Established in 1850, American Express is one of the United States' largest financial services companies and the world's largest corporate travel agency. In addition to offering charge cards, credit cards, Travelers cheques, and stored value products, the Company also offers financial planning, brokerage services, mutual funds, insurance, and other investment products. Employing a staff of over 70,000 individuals worldwide, the Company reports an estimated annual revenue of $2.14 billion. **Career Highlights:** Lead Network Engineer, American Express Company (1996-Present); Enterprise Project Engineer, Vanstar Corporation (1995-96); Senior LAN Engineer, IDP Computer Services, Inc. (1992-95); Computer Consultant, University of Toledo Computer Services (1991-92); Associate Customer Engineer, CMS Computer Serices Pvt. Ltd. (1988-89). **Associations & Accomplishments:** Institute of Electrical and Electronics Engineers; Ohio Academy of Science; University of Toledo Alumni; Don Bosco Alumni; Technical Advisory Group for Remote Access Products, Cisco Inc. Networkers (1997); American Express Technologies Employee Recognition Award (1996); Session Co-Chair, 35th Midwest Symposium on Circuits and Systems (1992); Graduate Research presented and published in the proceedings of the IEEE 35th Midwest Symposium on Circuits and Systems; the 13th Annual Sigma Xi Graduate Research Symposium proceedings; the 101st Annual Meeting of the Ohio Academy of Science - the Ohio Journal of Science. **Education:** University of Toledo, M.S. in Electrical Engineering (1992); Jawaharlal Nehru Engineering College India, B.S. in Electronics and Telecommunications (1988); S.I.E.S. College of Arts, Science, and Commerce India, H.S.C. (1983). **Personal Information:** Married to Benedicta in 1993. Mr. Menezes enjoys philately, numismatics, leading edge computer technology and travel.

Sherry Reyes

Programmer Analyst II
American Express
3200 East Camelback Road
Phoenix, AZ 85018
(602) 766-7874
Fax: (602) 766-7298
tarma@iname.com

6141

Business Information: Educated in the field of computer programming, Mrs. Reyes was recruited to American Express in 1997. Serving as a Programmer Analyst II, she assists the Company's various divisions in coding. She designs codes, assists in existing code changing, and performs interface testing. To date, Mrs. Reyes has assisted 15 interfaces to go to production. She believes that her sunny disposition and great outlook on life is an asset to her professional career. Quickly establishing herself in the field, her success reflects her ability to think out-of-the-box, solve system problems in an efficient manner, and take on new challenges. Continually formulating new goals and objectives, she is striving to increase her knowledge of her chosen profession through various means such as attending classes, reading industry publications, and speaking with fellow colleagues. Most famous for credit cards, American Express is a publicly owned company offering a variety of financial services to private individuals and large corporations alike. Established in 1850, the Company maintains corporate headquarters in New York and provides such services as charge cards, credit cards, and car rental insurance. Presently, American Express employs a work force in excess of 2,000 people at the Phoenix, Arizona location. **Career Highlights:** American Express: Programmer Analyst II (1998-Present), Programmer Entry (1997-98). **Associations & Accomplishments:** Girl Scouts of America. **Education:** DeVry Phoenix, B.S. in Computer Information Systems. (1997). **Personal Information:** Married to Jose in 1998. Mrs. Reyes enjoys reading and volunteering with the Girl Scouts of America.

John P. Manges

Technical Specialist
Primerica Financial Services
3120 Breckinridge Boulevard
Duluth, GA 30099
(770) 564-5385
seapldoc@aol.com

6159

Business Information: Mr. Manges holds the position of Technical Specialist with Primerica Financial Services. He is responsible for many technical duties on behalf of the Company. Possessing an excellent understanding of his field, he single-handedly designs, builds, installs, and supports a variety of turnkey financial computer systems. He is extremely well-versed in a rare programming language called APL, which he has used for over 25 years. Highly regarded as a unique professional by his colleagues, Mr. Manges has written over 60 applications while at Primerica. Attributing his success to perseverance and a strong engineering background, Mr. Manges' future plans include working in robotics and artificial intelligence. Established in the late 1980s, Primerica Financial Services provides financial services for the parent corporation, Citigroup. The Company provides financial services, mutual funds, home mortgages, and life insurance to clients and businesses. Primerica Financial Services helps customers with their financial needs. Located in Duluth, the Company employs 1,600 skilled individuals. **Career Highlights:** Technical Specialist, Primerica Financial Services (1987-Present); Product Manager, HBO & Company (1983-87); Systems Specialist, The UpJohn Company (1980-83); Programmer, DASD Corporation (1979-80); Programmer, Mark Controls Corporation (1978-79); Programmer, American Hospital Supply Corporation (1977-78); Programmer, A.S. Hansen, Inc. (1976-77). **Associations & Accomplishments:** President, South East APL Users' Group; Editor, "The APL Planet"; Columnist, Association of Computing Machinery/SIGAPL. **Education:** Tri State University, B.S. (1976). **Personal Information:** Married to Jackie in 1983. Two children: Michelle and Sandra. Mr. Manges enjoys robotics, gardening and billiards. His nickname is "Doc."

Zaina Nasser

Computer Manager
Oman Development Bank
P.O. Box 309
Muscat, Oman 113
(968) 737281
Fax: (968) 736903
006be@omantol.net.om

6159

Business Information: As Computer Manager of Oman Development Bank, Ms. Nasser has sole responsibility of the information technology department. Working closely with her staff of 28 people, she is continually upgrading and integrating the networks of the Bank. Additionally, she is developing computerized banking services for some branches that have never before had modern technology capabilities. An entreprenuer by nature, Ms. Nasser also founded both a bridal wear shop, where she designs many of the gowns, and a computer consulting firm. Attributing her success to her patient abilities, she offers the advice of starting at the bottom, and working your way up to the top. Enjoying her prominence as a respected member of the professional community, she intends to continue in her current roles, while completing on-going education for the advanced field she works in. Oman Development Bank offers a variety of banking and credit services to industrial and agricultural businesses and individuals. Established in 1980, the Bank was the result of the economic improvement Oman saw after oil was discovered in 1964 and exporting brought revenues to the southeastern Arabian country. Headquartered in the capital city of Muscat, the Bank employs 150 hard working individuals at 10 branches who strive to offer the best in customer service. **Career Highlights:** Computer Manager, Oman Development Bank (1998-Present); Oman Agriculture Bank: Computer Manager (1985-98), Computer Programmer (1983-85). **Education:** Computer Science Undergraduate (1989). **Personal Information:** Married to Yahta Seif in 1984. Three children: Salah, Aziza, and Aziz. Ms. Nasser enjoys travel and swimming.

Leonard Randazzo

Senior Partner
Dwarf Holdings, LLC
2 Tuve Lane
South Hackensack, NJ 07606-1631
(212) 903-4301
Mobile: (201) 410-3590

6159

Business Information: Mr. Randazzo possesses a decade of high-level business and technical expertise in building and managing e-commerce applications, re-engineering business processes, and piloting the identification and implementation of business critical solutions. He started his career as an independent management consultant while earning his Master's degree in Management from Stevens Institute of Technology and completing his degree with a perfect 4.0 GPA. Brandishing an exceptionally eclectic resume, Mr. Randazzo's industry experience spans medical, retail, electronics, financial, and e-commerce. Presently, Mr. Randazzo displays his proficiency in the field of information technology serving as a Senior Partner with Dwarf Holdings, LLC. An established e-commerce expert, he assists clients with business developmental strategies, e-commerce counsel, and systems execution. To satisfy this role, he maintains proficiency in utilizing key strategic alignment methodologies, expertise in implementing e-commerce technologies, and in-depth knowledge in the subjects of product distribution and fulfillment. Moreover, he assumes the responsibility for developing critical Company partnerships and alliances. Attributing his rapid success to self-discipline and a sense of balance in his life, Mr. Randazzo plans to complete his doctoral level studies and aspires to the position of Managing Partner. Founded in 1999, Dwarf Holdings, LLC is an Internet incubator whose primary business driver is firmly rooted in the concept of "Value Based Contracting," the shared risk-reward between the incubation firm and the innovative entrepreneur. The Company is a catalyst for Internet based entrepreneurs in bringing their concept to market quickly and successfully. In exchange for a flexible compensation structure, Dwarf provides emerging Internet companies with business planning, access to investment capital, executive infrastructure building, public and investor relations, project management, and e-commerce systems implementation. **Career Highlights:** Senior Partner, Dwarf Holdings, LLC (1999-Present); Integrations Manager, Genesis Direct, Inc. (1998-99); Systems Development Specialist, Sharp Electronics Corporation of America (1997-98); Isys/Biovation (1995-97); Management Consultant (1992-95). **Associations & Accomplishments:** Charter Member, World War II Memorial; National Space Society; Planetary Society. **Education:** Stevens Institute of Technology, M.S. in Management (1997); Montclair State College, B.A. in Economics; Microsoft Certified Professional. **Personal Information:** Mr. Randazzo enjoys music, and is a jazz standards fan, a financial markets enthusiast and is fluent in Italian.

Stephen T. Benson

Director of Network Operations
GMAC Commercial Mortgage
650 Dresher Road
Horsham, PA 19044-2204
(215) 328-3935
Fax: (215) 328-3812
sbenson@gmaccm.com

6162

Business Information: As Director of Network Operations of GMAC Commercial Mortgage, Mr. Benson administers and controls all aspects of the day-to-day network infrastructure. He is responsible for installing and maintaining hardware and software, troubleshooting network usage, and resolving network difficulties when they occur. A savvy, six year professional, Mr. Benson determines the technical strategy by conducting strategy meetings with business users. Maintaining vendor relations, ensuring all support functions are operating smoothly, managing network operations teams, and monitoring network security and reliability also fall within the scope of Mr. Benson's responsibilities. His future goals include assuming the role of Technology Officer or another strategic position, enabling the Company to become one of the premier ecommerce company. GMAC Commercial Mortgage is a leading commercial mortgage finance company. They originate loans in all areas of real estate. Established in1995, GMAC Commercial Mortgage's parent company is GMAC Holding Company. Presently, GMAC Commercial Mortgage employs a work force of over 1,500 people. Headquarters is currently located in Horsham, Pennsylvania. **Career Highlights:** GMAC Commercial Mortgage: Director of Network Operations (1997-Present), Network Manager (1996-97), Network Engineer (1995-96). **Associations & Accomplishments:** Global Technology Assessment Board. **Education:** LaSalle University, B.S. in Computer Science (1994). **Personal Information:** Married to Grace in 1996. One child: Kaitlyn. Mr. Benson enjoys hunting, fishing, golf and boating.

Sharon M. Brown

Team Leader
GMAC Commercial Mortgage
650 Dresher Road
Horsham, PA 19044
(215) 328-1940
Fax: (215) 328-3810
sharon_brown@gmaccm.com

6162

Business Information: Joining GMAC Commercial Mortgage in 1997 as Team Leader, Miss Brown develops software for the Information Technology Department. In her capacity, she leads a team of software development technicians, creating, designing, and developing software for loan origination systems. Miss Brown writes computer and programming codes for applications used by 600 people in the Corporation's new loan division. Assuring quality and integrity of software programs and apex control, she works closely with clients to solve problems and to make sure that technical requirements are being met through programming. Miss Brown attributes her career successes to mentors. GMAC Commercial Mortgage offers a broad array of mortgage banking, real estate loans, and other financing services through the General Motors Corporation. The Corporation employs 3,300 people at numerous locations nationwide. **Career Highlights:** Team Leader, GMAC Commercial Mortgage (1997-Present). **Associations & Accomplishments:** Association for Computing Machinery. **Education:** La Salle University, B.A. in Computer Science (1998). **Personal Information:** Miss Brown enjoys reading, music, theatre, poetry, gardening, walking, bowling and crafts.

Jack Y. Cheng

Information Technology Administrator
Infoloan
1800 Stokes Street, Apartment 168
San Jose, CA 95126
(408) 573-0802
Fax: (408) 292-3462
yjcheng@hotmail.com

6162

Business Information: Mr. Cheng has recently joined the team at Infoloan as Information Technology Administrator. Possesing several years of education and experience in this industry, he exercises oversight of the Company's Web site. Previously, Mr. Cheng was employed by General Electric Corporation where his most notable acheivment was the design and physical implementation of a database management system to ease the data collection process. Currently, Mr. Cheng is responsible for online marketing of Infoloan, developing opportunities to obtain a greater percentage of the target market. Working closely with five assistants in his department, he ensures efficient networking capabilities for all clientele. Mr. Cheng's future endeavors include attaining the position of Project Manager and becoming more involved in network installation. Infoloan is an Internet based mortgage company licensed by the California Department of Real Estate. Offering on-line, no fee, 24 hour loan status and mortgage tools such as loan calculators, pre-qualification, and pre-approval, the Company is the lending institution of the millennium. Competitive rates and plentiful portfolio features add to the desirability of Infoloan as a lender. **Career Highlights:** Information Technology Administrator, Infoloan (1999-Present); Database Specialist, General Electric (1999); Networking Technician, Jonesboro Public School (1998). **Associations & Accomplishments:** Director of Technical Support, Committee of Association of Information; Vice President, Malaysian Student Association. **Education:** Arkansas State University, Master's degree in Information Systems, Minor in Computer Science (1996). **Personal Information:** Mr. Cheng enjoys reading, surfing the Internet and studying.

H. James Collier, Jr.

Director
Advanta Corporation
Welsh & Mckean Road, P.O. Box 918
Spring House, PA 19477
(215) 323-3428
Fax: (215) 444-5524
jcollier@advant.com

6162

Business Information: Recruited to Advanta Corporation in 1999, Mr. Collier serves as Director. He is responsible for all aspects of data warehouse design and research. Operating from the Corporation's location in Springhouse, Pennsylvania, he delegates responsibilities to one person and helps design new processes for the transfer of data. Directing and participating in the analysis, design, evaluation, testing, and implementation of cutting edge data warehouses also fall within the realm of Mr. Collier's functions. For the future, he plans to stay with the Corporation and transfer Advanta Corporation's information online using the Internet. His career highlights include staying on the bleeding edge of technology, working with data process projects, and developing a data process inhouse system with three people in 1982 through 1984. His success, according to Mr. Collier, is attributed to being open minded to new ideas and having creativity. The Advanta Corporation is a financial services company. Established in 1954, the Corporation has locations throughout the United States to assist its clients in purchasing homes and creating a strong foundation for a new business. Employing 1,100 personnel, the Corporation is devoted to the enhancement of its available services and strives to utilize the latest technologies to better serve its clietns. **Career Highlights:** Director, Advanta Corporation (1999-Present); Manager of Programming, Dechert, Price & Rhoades (1998-99); Consultant, IBM Corporation (1996-98); Senior Information Architect, Vanguard (1994-96). **Associations & Accomplishments:** Data Warehouse Institute. **Education:** LaSalle College, B.S. (1976). **Personal Information:** Married to Janice in 1969. One child: Brian.

D. David Fraedrich

Director of Information Technology
Home Mortgage Inc.
6245 North 24th Parkway 200
Phoenix, AZ 85016
(602) 295-5982
d_fraedrich@homemortgageinc.net

6162

Business Information: Having recently moved to Home Mortgage Inc., Mr. Fraedrich is the Director of Information Technology. He assumes accountability for the management of the WAN system and telecommunications infrastructure as well as applications software. In addition, Mr. Fraedich maintains and implements hardware and software, supervises daily computer operations, and manages the Web server. Always alert to new techniques and approaches, he coordinates strategic and tactical planning and implements new technology. A formidable professional, Mr. Fraedich often speaks at conferences. His most recent presentation was in 1998 for the Cardiff Company on the implementation of the DCR applications. In recognition for his career success and dedication, he has attained several awards that includes "Application of the Year" by Cardiff. Mr. Fraedich anticipates promotion opportunities into strategic capacities such as Vice President and Chief Informations Officer for Home Mortgage Inc. Home Mortgage Inc. is a nationwide mortgage company. A growing company, the Corporation has a total of 20 offices spread throughout twelve states. **Career Highlights:** Director of Information Technology, Home Mortgage Inc. (1999-Present); Director of Application Support, Prison Fellowship Ministries (1997-99); EG&G WASC, Inc.: Manager of PC and Network Development (1992-97), Systems Manager/Development Manager (1986-92). **Education:** Old Dominion University (1980). **Personal Information:** Two children: Michael Aaron and Peter Christian. Mr. Fraedrich enjoys assisting at church with plays and programs.

Phillip K. Gosnell

Microcomputer Systems Administrator
Regions Financial Corporation
106 St. Francis Street
Mobile, AL 36602
(334) 690-1256
Fax: (334) 690-1581
pgosnell@regionsbank.com

6162

Business Information: Mr. Gosnell serves as Microcomputer Systems Administrator for the Mobile, Alabama, location of Regions Financial Corporation. Providing all back office support, he maintains the personal workstations, LAN, WAN, and software applications used by associates throughout the various branches. Working closely with his team, he troubleshoots problems then develops and implements technical solutions. Recognized for his superior abilities, Mr. Gosnell was given sole responsibility for the Y2K project in which he leads the technical staff to solve programming and coding challenges. Credited with the successful intergration of the WAN into all 900 branches of the Corporation, he attributes his impressive endeavors to his current education. Regions Financial Corporation is a full service financial institution serving individuals and businesses. Offering mortgages, leasing, commercial banking, and securities brokerage, the Corporation also provides credit life insurance to customers. Based in the Southern region of the United States, the headquarters are located in Birminham, Alabama. The Corporation employs over 13,000 people nationwide in capacities such as accountants, bank managers, production managers, and computer programmers. **Career Highlights:** Microcomputer Systems Administrator, Regions Financial Corporation (1998-Present); Information Technology Manager, Continental Grain (1996-98); Sales Manager, Lanier Micro (1994-96); Sales Manager, Curtis Mathis (1985-94). **Associations & Accomplishments:** United Way Leadership Club. **Education:** Gainesville College, Computer Science degree (1997). **Personal Information:** Married to Michelle in 1980. One child: Ryan. Mr. Gosnell enjoys sports.

deAnna A. Harper

Systems Producer
Capital Thinking, Inc.
52 Vanderbilt Avenue, 8th Floor
New York, NY 10017
(212) 692-4018
Fax: (212) 972-1666
dharper@capitalthinking.com

6162

Business Information: Demonstrating expertise in the technology field, Ms. Harper serves as Systems Producer for Capital Thinking, Inc. Working closely with her team of associates, she utilizes a management style that incorporates input and feedback from all staff members and is responsible for all technical requirements in the technical form, bug tracking and analysis, quality assurance, and data testing. In this capacity, she writes programs, tests software, and handles the design of artificial intelligence. Ms. Harper's goals for the future include keeping on the cutting edge of technology in order to design, consult, publish, and speak regarding Web sites. She attributes her success to her flexibility and ability to take on challenges and deliver results on behalf of the Corporation and its clientele. Capital Thinking, Inc., established in 1999, is an online commercial mortgage marketplace providing a variety of quality financial services. Located in New York, New York, the Corporation employs 45 highly trained individuals who aim at promoting competition and diversity in the market by specializing in matching mortgage borrowers and brokers. **Career Highlights:** Systems Producer, Capital Thinking, Inc. (1999-Present); Web Project Manager, Silicon Alley Festival (1999); Web Project Manager, MerCon, Inc. (1994-99). **Associations & Accomplishments:** Management Information Systems Society of USF; Alumni Society of University of South Florida. **Education:** University of South Florida, B.A. in Management Information Systems (1999); St. Petersburg Junior College, A.A. with high Honors. **Personal Information:** Ms. Harper enjoys reading, being a seamstress and paper sculpture.

Kevin Hoggard

Computer Department Manager
City Mortgage Corporation
121 West Fireweed Lane, Suite 120
Anchorage, AK 99503
(907) 263-0703
Fax: (907) 263-0799
hoggardk@citymortgagealaska.com

6162

Business Information: Demonstrating expertise in the technological field, Mr. Hoggard serves as the Computer Department Manager for City Mortgage Corporation. Providing database management, he converted the original eight standard databases into the current single system utilized by the Corporation. He presides over the network and desktop systems, administering upgrades and equipment replacements as needed. Mr. Hoggard completed the Y2K conversion that enabled City Mortgage to remain up and running. He also serves as the secondary marketing liaison for the purpose of maintaining good investor relations. Keeping current with trade journals, industry publications, and the Internet, he believes that he owes success in his professional career completely to God. Establishing goals that are compatible with those of the Corporation, Mr. Hoggard intends to increase his role in the database structure and anticipates a future promotion to Information Technology Manager. City Mortgage Corporation is a privately owned mortgage financing company. Established in 1989, the Corporation provides mortgage banking services to home owners at eight branch locations in the state of Alaska. Presently, the Corporation employs a staff of more than 45 professionals. **Career Highlights:** Computer Department Manager, City Mortgage Corporation (1998-Present); Mortgage Originator, Alaska Home Mortgage (1995-98); First National Bank of Anchorage: Mortgage Originator (1993-95), Management Trainee (1992-93). **Associations & Accomplishments:** Hillcrest Church of the Nazarine. **Education:** University of Alaska at Anchorage, B.A. in Finance (1992); Florida College, A.A. in Business Administration (1989). **Personal Information:** Married to Paige in 1998. Mr. Hoggard enjoys computers, church activities, biking, cross country skiing and hiking.

Morten Irve

Systems Engineer
BRF Kredit a/s
Klampenborgvei 205
Lyngby, Denmark 2800
+45 45262947
miv@brf.dk

6162

Business Information: Possessing unique talent in the field of technology, Mr. Irve serves as the Systems Engineer for BRF Kredit a/s. In this capacity, he assumes responsibility for the research and development of new information technology products on a commercial level. These products are designed to bring new business to the Company and increase recognition for its services. Before joining BRF Kredit, Mr. Irve served as Systems Engineer with Maersk Data a/s. An information technology expert, he plans to continue to develop his professional skills in an effort to increase his job responsibilities and expedite promotional opportunities within the Company. His success reflects his ability to think out-of-the-box, deliver results, and aggressively take on new challenges and responsibilities. BRF Kredit a/s is a full service financial institution serving consumers and commercial clients throughout Denmark. Beginning operations in 1959, the Company specializes in providing mortgage loans to the clientele. Approximately 610 qualified professionals are dedicated to providing the very best in service to each individual client of BRF Kredit. **Career Highlights:** Systems Engineer, BRF Kredit a/s (Present); System Engineer, Maersk Data a/s (1997). **Education:** Microsoft Systems Engineer (1998); Electronic Engineer. **Personal Information:** Mr. Irve enjoys computer programming, travel and family.

Sanjiv Kalkar

Systems Administration
National Standard Mortgage
150 White Plains Road, Suite 108
Tarrytown, NY 10591
(914) 631-6060
Fax: (914) 631-9172
smk421@yahoo.com

6162

Business Information: Serving as Systems Administration of National Standard Mortgage, Mr. Kalkar provides systems analysis and integration as he maintains day-to-day operations from a technical standpoint. Coupling practical work experience with his education, he is able to effectively administer database applications development. He oversees all aspects of network installation, from evaluation of need to design of the systems. After formulating a technical action plan, Mr. Kalkar purchases hardware and software then implements the equipment into the current operating system. Recognized for his impressive acheivements within the Corporation, he looks forward continual advancement within the corporate structure. His advice is "get a mentor and listen." National Standard Mortgage handles banking services that pertain to the initiation and maintenance of mortgages. A technically progressive company, daily operations are completed through the use of Windows NT and Novell Shop. Information is stored in an Oracle database to allow for easy retrieval. The national company is headquartered in Tarrytown, New York and has established a reputation of quality services throughout the industry. **Career Highlights:** Systems Administration, National Standard Mortgage (1999-Present); Systems Analyst, Columbia Equines Ltd. (1997-99); Program Analyst, National Standard Mortgage (1994-97). **Education:** Brooklyn College, B.S. (1995).

Keith S. Lufkin

Systems Administrator
Southern Trust Mortgage
9030 Stony Point Parkway, Suite 530
Richmond, VA 23235
(804) 330-5925
Fax: (804) 330-5786
keithl@southerntrust.com

6162

Business Information: As Systems Administrator of Southern Trust Mortgage, Mr. Lufkin handles all technical system operations for the Company. Overseeing the network infastructure, he directs every aspect of the department's activities, from hardware and software installation and maintenance to planning and execution of technical strategies. Mr. Lufkin demonstrates an adept ability in the creation of operating systems, and was credited with the successful opening of three functional offices in one month resulting in fully automated services. To keep up-to-date with current issues in today's technologically progresssive society, Mr. Lufkin reads pertinent literature and searches the Internet. Attributing success to support from his family, he looks forward to assisting in the further development of the corporate Web site. Southern Trust Mortgage offers mortgage banking services in the Mid-Atlantic region. Though most clients are residential, the Company is experienced in handling investor property mortgages as well. Established in 1997, 125 people are employed at the Company's headquarters in Richmond, Virginia to serve the regional community. **Career Highlights:** Systems Administrator, Southern Trust Mortgage (1999-Present); Mid-Atlantic Financial Group: Assistant Vice President of Technology Based Mortgages (1997-99), Technical Coordinator (1993-97). **Associations & Accomplishments:** Alpha Eta Rito Aviation Fraternity; Deacon, Three Chopt Presbyterian Church; Science Museum of Virginia. **Education:** State University of New York at Farmingdale, A.A.S. in Aerospace (1973); Federal Airframe and Power Plant Technician (1979). **Personal Information:** Married to Heather in 1982. One child: Hilary. Mr. Lufkin enjoys golf and hiking.

Del R. Newberry

Systems Analyst
First Horizon Home Loans
2910 Geneva Drive
Garland, TX 75040
(972) 969-6042
Fax: (630) 604-8365
delnew@aol.com

6162

Business Information: Serving as First Horizon Home Loans' Systems Analyst since 1990, Mr. Newberry creates and analyzes financial and servicing reports. In this context, he is responsible for providing reports and ordering systems for the Company. A savvy, 15 year professional, he oversees the automation needs of the Company and services the loans after the sale. His career highlights include making the Company Y2K compliant and converting the computer system from a ten digit loan number to a seven digit loan number. Mr. Newberry would like to learn more about PCs and personal workstations. His success is attributed to his integrity. First Horizon Home Loans was established in 1864 and engages in selling and servicing mortgage loans. In addition, the Company specializes in escrow accounts, taxes, and targets mostly residential and small business markets. There is currently 10,000 skilled employees working at First Horizon Home Loans. **Career Highlights:** Systems Analyst, First Horizon Home Loans (1990-Present); Senior Technical Analyst, Sunbelt Savings (1987-90); Senior Programmer/Analyst, Systematics, Inc. (1985-87). **Education:** LeTourneau University, B.S. in Business Management (1992). **Personal Information:** Married to Kim in 1982. Two children: Melinda and Charis. Mr. Newberry enjoys church activities.

Ricky Lee Rinker

Banking Officer
Legacy Bank of Texas
P.O. Box 869111
Plano, TX 75086-9111
(972) 461-1472
Fax: (972) 461-1581
rickyr@legacytexas.com

6162

Business Information: As Banking Officer of the Legacy Bank of Texas, Mr. Rinker manages and operates the information systems infrastructure. He ensures the functionality and operational status of the AS400 system as well as determines the banking contributions of the information systems functions. Drawing from 11 years of academics and occupational experience, Mr. Rinker is responsible for all day-to-day operations including statement processing, maintenance, and systems upgrades. He supervises a staff of eight employees. Always interested in technology, he actually found his start in the industry through a job with a bank. He attributes his success to the encouragement and support from family and friends. In the future, Mr. Rinker would like to learn more functions and move into the networking area. For over 10 years, the Legacy Bank of Texas has been providing banking services to clients in the city of Plano, Texas. Services provided include checking, savings, and loans. Presently, the Legacy Bank of Texas operates nine branches manned by a work force of more than 130 professional, technical, and support staff. **Career Highlights:** Legacy Bank of Texas: Banking Officer (1999-Present), Operations Manager (1998-99); Customer Support Manager, Peerless Group (1995-98); Computer Operator, Compass Bank (1989-95). **Associations & Accomplishments:** Kappa Kappa Psi National Music Fraternity. **Education:** Angelo State University. **Personal Information:** Mr. Rinker enjoys woodworking, volleyball, softball and golf.

Richard M. Tramontana

Senior Technical Officer
Chase Manhattan Mortgage Corporation
343 Thornall Street
Edison, NJ 08837
(732) 205-0898
Fax: (732) 205-0906
dick_tramontana@chase

6162

Business Information: Mr. Tramontana functions in the role of Senior Technical Officer for Chase Manhattan Mortgage Corporation. He oversees and directs all aspects of day-to-day operations of the systems infrastructure. In addition, he assertively fulfills the responsibility of Risk Management Program, providing program support to loan officers and managers. Before joining Chase Manhattan Mortgage Corporation, Mr. Tramontana served as Treasurer for ACR Inc. His extensive background also includes employment as the Systems Development Manager for Caltex Petroleum Corporation and Customer Service Manager with Chase Manhattan Bank. In his role, he determines the overall strategic direction as well as business contributions of the information systems function. He recently advanced from his role in the information technology department to undertake the enormous task of managing the entire Internet involvement of the Corporation. An expert, he monitors and designs cutting edge client and server programs and Web sites. For his next project, Mr. Tramontama is working to create a loan oriented computer system to better track borrowers and limit the Corporation's loss margin. His advice to others is "learn business database information." Chase Manhattan Mortgage Corporation was established in 1980 to facilitate the home mortgage needs of Chase Manhattan Bank customers. The full service mortgage institute is able to accommodate the financing needs of clients around the world through its network of 1,000 employees. The Corporation produces $10 billion annually and has continued to provide customer service excellence during the entire business relation between the client and their Corporation representative. **Career Highlights:** Senior Technical Officer, Chase Manhattan Mortgage Corporation (1985-Present); Treasurer, ACR Inc. (1982-85); Systems Development Manager, Caltex Petroleum Corporation (1972-82); Customer Service Manager, Chase Manhattan Bank (1966-72). **Associations & Accomplishments:** Tasters Guild. **Education:** University of New York at Buffalo, B.S. in Accounting and Economics (1962). **Personal Information:** Married to Viviah in 1971. Mr. Tramontana enjoys jazz, theatre, opera, gourmet cooking, wine tasting, cooking and dining.

Mark W. Wyss

Manger of Networking Technologies
Bentley Management Corporation
7995 East Hampden Avenue, Suite 200
Denver, CO 80231
(303) 306-3244
Fax: (303) 306-3248
mark.wyss@bentleycorp.com

6162

Business Information: Possessing unique talent in the technology field, Mr. Wyss serves as Manager of Networking Technologies for the Bentley Management Corporation. He is essentially in charge of all technological aspects of the Corporation, presiding over the administration of both the voice and data communication networks. Mr. Wyss ensures that back up systems are provided for the computer and telephone systems to prevent data loss and maintains a state of the art security system to protect the sensitive personal information of individual customers. Technical support is offered to network users. Always striving to improve his performance, Mr. Wyss looks forward to continued promotions within the Corporation. His success reflects his ability to produce results and aggressively tackle new challenges. The Bentley Management Corporation supplies indirect lending services to members of several different credit unions. Loans are offered for mortgages, automobiles, and personal use. Founded in 1986, operations employ the qualified services of 125 staff members. The Corporation reports an estimated

$672 million in revenue each year. **Career Highlights:** Manger of Networking Technologies, Bentley Management Corporation (1998-Present); Senior Network Consultant, Born Information Services (1997-98); Team Lead of the Network Department, JCIT Institute of Technology (1996-97); Client Support Analyst, Sprint Communications (1987-96). **Education:** University of Phoenix (Currently Attending); Microsoft Certified Professional; Microsoft Certified Systems Engineer. **Personal Information:** Married to Deborah in 1994.

6200 Security and Commodity Brokers

6211 Security brokers and dealers
6221 Commodity contracts brokers, dealers
6231 Security and commodity exchanges
6282 Investment advice
6289 Security and commodity services, nec

Douglas J. Brickley
Vice President
De Bellas & Co.
2 Northpoint Drive, Suite 230
Houston, TX 77060-3242
(281) 448-5252
Fax: (281) 448-5264
doug@debellas.com

6211

Business Information: As a Vice President of De Bellas & Co., Mr. Brickley provides expert representation to companies providing information technology services whose owners wish to achieve maximum value in the sale of their businesses. As a recognized specialist in the industry, Mr. Brickley's knowledge of the information technology services sector, including the current market dynamics and the most strategic acquirers, assists these owners in achieving the best possible outcome. Mr. Brickley also provides expert representation to leading information technology services companies wishing to expand existing practices or to develop new lines of business through acquisition or strategic business combination transactions. He has been published a number of times in leading industry publications, and attributes his success to ambition, drive, and the determination to succeed. Mr. Brickley plans to continue his career in investment banking and to strive to strike a perfect balance between job requirements and outside personal needs. Prior to joining De Bellas & Co. in 1998, he spent three years in the New York Investment Banking Department of Janney Montgomery Scott Inc., where he was involved in numerous investment banking transactions which included public and private debt and equity offerings, mergers and acquisitions, fairness and valuation opinions, and several strategic financial advisory assignments for middle market, emerging growth, and special situation companies. Mr. Brickley began his career in the Management Consulting Services group of Price Waterhouse where he gained extensive experience serving as a team leader on management information systems consulting and change integration engagements for Fortune 100 clients. Mr. Brickley is a graduate of Price Waterhouse's Management Consulting Services Information Technology Individual Study program where he learned multiple programming languages and was exposed to all stages of system development. Mr. Brickley is also a certifie Established in 1983, De Bellas & Co. is a specialty investment banking firm that provides Merger & Acquisition, Valuation, Financial Advisory, and Strategic Planning Services to businesses specializing in Information Technology Services and Staffing. As merger and acquisition specialists to middle market companies, De Bellas & Co. has consummated well over 100 transactions and has one of the largest and fastest growing practices dedicated to information technology staffing, solutions, and consulting in the country. **Career Highlights:** Vice President, De Bellas & Co. (1998-Present); Vice President, Janney Montgomery Scott Inc. (1995-98); Senior Consultant, Price Waterhouse (1992-95). **Associations & Accomplishments:** Beta Gamma Sigma; Omicron Delta Epsilon; Financial Management Association National Honor Society; Pi Kappa Phi Fraternity; Bible Study Fellowship International; Certified SAP R/3 Consultant. **Education:** Baylor University, M.B.A. in Finance (1992); Texas A&M University, B.S. in Political Science (1990). **Personal Information:** Married to Kathleen in 1995. Mr. Brickley enjoys golf.

Ali Coplu
Analyst/Developer
Goldman Sachs & Company
276 Willow Avenue
Lyndhurst, NJ 07071-1831
(212) 855-0935
Fax: (212) 428-1053
coplu@usa.net

6211

Business Information: Serving as an Analyst and Developer for Goldman Sachs & Company, Mr. Coplu is in charge of servicing the portfolios of wealthy clients for the purpose of maintaining account information. Possessing an excellent understanding of technology, he handles quality assurance, testing, and business development. He was inspired to go into his field because of the opportunities for growth. Mr. Coplu became interested in how the information was used, and took advantage of his situation and his professional strengths. His plans are to remain with the Company in order to implement new systems and obtain his MBA. Success, according to Mr. Coplu, his due to his ability to think outside the box and deliver results. Goldman Sachs & Company stands as the largest investment bank in the world and functions as the leader in mergers and acquisitions. The Company provides various forms of financial management for both local and international corporations. Services provided by the Company include managing portfolios, consulting on mergers and acquisitions, and investment supervision. Established in 1869, the Company incorporates the professionalism of over 13,000 individuals into the $14 billion day-to-day operation. **Career Highlights:** Analyst/Developer, Goldman Sachs & Company (1999-Present); Software Quality Assurance Engineer, D.E. Shaw & Company (1998-99); Software Engineer, SyncSort Inc. (1996-98). **Associations & Accomplishments:** Association of Computing Machinery; Institute of Electronics and Electrical Engineers. **Education:** New York University, M.B.A. (In Progress); University of Pennsylvania, M.S. (1996). **Personal Information:** Married to Elif in 1998. Mr. Coplu and his wife are expecting their first child.

Ronelle De Shazer
Manager of Information Systems
Code Hennessy & Simmons
10 South Wacker Drive, Suite 3175
Chicago, IL 60606
(312) 876-2690
Fax: (312) 876-3854
rdeshaz@chsonline.com

6211

Business Information: Combining management skills with technical expertise, Mr. De Shazer currently serves as Code Hennessy & Simmons' Manager of Information Systems. In this capacity, he manages the entire infrastructure, purchases software and hardware, trains employees on applications, and formulates the budget. A prominent and respected professional, Mr. De Shazer plans to continue working in this capacity, striving to obtain a position as the Vice President or Director of Information Systems. Founded in 1988, Code Hennessy & Simmons provides services in the area of private equity. Headquartered in Chicago, Illinois, the Firm obtains majority ownership of other companies, and then provides support and representation of these organizations. Employing 60 personnel, the Firm represents such companies as Ace Products, Inc., American Reprographics Company, and Beacon Sales Company, Inc. **Career Highlights:** Manager of Information Systems, Code Hennessy & Simmons (2000-Present); Technical Manager, Best Buy, Inc. (1999-00); Software Suppor Specialist, Nicer Gas (1996-99). **Associations & Accomplishments:** Microsoft Certified Professional. **Education:** Benedictine University, B.B.A. (1998). **Personal Information:** Mr. De Shazer enjoys swimming, basketball and golf.

Mark Ely
Manager of Information Systems and Information Technology
Dreher & Associates, Inc.
One Oakbrook Terrace, Suite 708
Oakbrook Terrace, IL 60181
(630) 932-5697
Fax: (630) 916-8585
docely@mindspring.com

6211

Business Information: Functioning in the capacity of Manager of Information Systems and Information Technology with Dreher & Associates, Inc., Mr. Ely determines the overall strategic direction and vision of the Corporation and business contribution of the information systems function. He oversees daily administration of the infrastructure and ensures systems functionality and fully operational status at all times. A seven year technology professional, Mr. Ely manages and develops all programs used to properly track, monitor, and assists associates sell securities and mutual funds. His career success reflects his ability to think out-of-the-box and aggressively take on new challenges and responsibilities. Concurrently, Mr. Ely, along with his partner Jeremy, owns and operates a company called GIM Productions, that specializes in cutting edge Web development and video production using Java Script and HTML. Remaining with Dreher & Associates and doing more integration work, as well as home schooling and virtual reality. A financial broker and dealer, Dreher & Associates, Inc. provides financial planning services as well as rapid stock and bond order transactions, and access to all options and securities exchanges. Established in 1980, the Corporation is international in scope and operates a network of 256 financial advisors across the globe. **Career Highlights:** Manager of Information Systems and Information Technology, Dreher & Associates, Inc. (1998-Present); Medical Technician, Smithkline Beacham; President, G.I.M. Productions. **Associations & Accomplishments:** Phi Sigma Ioda Honor Society; Microsoft Certified Professional. **Education:** Webster, M.B.A., H.S.M. (1999); U.M.R., B.S. in Life Science (1996), B.S. in Chemistry (1996); C.C.A.F., Associates degree in Technical Engineering (1992). **Personal Information:** Married to Linda in 1998. Five children: Paul, Rachel, Zachery, Josuha, and Dorinda. Mr. Ely enjoys weight lifting, camping and church.

Joanne C. Gallegos
Senior Project Coordinator
Charles Schwab
22 Franciscan Court
Danville, CA 94526
(415) 667-9773
Fax: (415) 667-0245
joanne.gallegos@schwab.com

6211

Business Information: Serving as Senior Project Coordinator of Charles Schwab for the past year, Mrs. Gallegos is in charge of all aspects of daily project management. Possessing an excellent understanding of technology, she is responsible for implementation, process flow design, and performing data analysis. A successful, seven-year professional, Mrs. Gallegos coordinates resources, schedules, and communications with employees and customers as well as serves as the chief liaison with user groups and systems management. Highly regarded by her colleagues, she established a 12-member team who deploy information technology projects worldwide. Aggressively looking to the future, Mrs. Gallegos would like to lead a group at a higher level. Her success reflects her leadership ability to form teams with synergy and technical strength, take on challenges, and deliver results. Established in 1974, Charles Schwab specializes in investments, brokerage house, and on-line trading. Serving an international clientele, the Firm was the first of its kind to offer on-line trading to customers. Focusing mainly on the small investor, the Firm employs 14,000 professional, technical, and support staff. **Career Highlights:** Senior Project Coordinator, Charles Schwab (1999-Present); Pacific Bell: Senior Systems Analyst (1997-99), Quality Assurance, Quality Control, and Implementation Manager (1993-97). **Education:** University of Phoenix, B.S. in Computer Information Systems (1998). **Personal Information:** Married to Mark in 1987. Two children: Mark and Chelsea. Mrs. Gallegos enjoys soccer, skiing, cooking, biking and baseball.

Sunil George

Webmaster
Merrill Lynch
P.O. Box 9083
Princeton, NJ 08543-9083
(609) 282-6507
Fax: (609) 282-6896
sunil.george@ml.com

6211

Business Information: Displaying technical expertise, Mr. George serves as Webmaster of Merrill Lynch. He assumes accountability for designing, developing, and maintaining the Web sites. Additionally, Mr. George is responsible for all technical issues and providing technical support of three marketing departments. Currently, he is creating a web site for the Marketing division which will replace each of the Marketing departments' web sites. Merrill Lynch is a leading financial services provider for individuals, businesses, and government agencies worldwide. Services include personal financial planning, trading and brokering, securities underwriting, and investment banking and advisory services. Headquartered in New York, the Company operates in 43 countries throughout six continents. **Career Highlights:** Webmaster, Merrill Lynch (1989-Present); Assistant Manager, Photos in a Hour

(1988-89); Various Temporary Jobs (1984-88). **Education:** Susquehanna University, Economics studies (1984). **Personal Information:** Married to Rachel in 1997. Mr. George enjoys photography and family time.

Ashok S. Jha

Senior Programmer Analyst
Goldman Sachs & Company
1 New York Plaza, 46th Floor
New York, NY 10004
(212) 902-7477
Fax: (212) 902-4731
ashok.jha@gs.com

6211

Business Information: Mr. Jha is Senior Programmer Analyst of Goldman Sachs & Company in New York. He is responsible for the Research Department's information technology infrastructure. His focus is ensuring the functionality and fully operational status of operating and network systems. As a five year technology professional, Mr. Jha fulfills the role of Project Leader for financials systems. Utilizing his firm expertise and academic ties, he is in charge of designing systems and network strategies, in addition to implementing and testing the strategies. In addition to supervising and mentoring his staff of six employees, Mr. Jha handles numerous resource planning functions to include determining future resource requirements, overseeing time lines and schedules, and providing cohesive leadership. His success reflects his ability to learn fast, think out-of-the-box, and aggressively take on new challenges and responsibilities. Growing day-to-day operations, deploying advanced technology within Goldman Sachs, and implementing artificial intelligence serves as Mr. Jha's future endeavors. Goldman Sachs & Company is a leader in investment, banking, finance, research, and mergers and acquisitions. A global investment bank and securities firm, Goldman Sachs & Company is headquartered in New York, and operates three regional headquarters in Hong Kong, London, and Tokyo. Established in 1876, the Company employs a global work force of over 12,000 people who help generate in excess of $2.9 billion annually. **Career Highlights:** Senior Programmer Analyst, Goldman Sachs & Company (1996-Present); Assistant Project Manager, CEI System & Engineering (1995-96); Programming Officer, Bhart Petroleum Corporation, Ltd. (1993-95). **Associations & Accomplishments:** Computer Society of India. **Education:** V.R.E.C., Bachelor's degree in Engineering (1990-93); diploma in Industrial Electronics. **Personal Information:** Married to Geeta Menghani in 1998. Mr. Jha enjoys astrophysics.

William A. Levine

Information Technology Director
First Continental Trading
150 South Wacker Drive, Suite 805
Chicago, IL 60606-4102
(312) 424-3048
wlevine@interaccess.com

6211

Business Information: Demonstrating his business savvy and technical expertise as Director of Information Technology of First Continental Trading, Mr. Levine determines the overall strategic direction and business contribution of the information technology functions. Possessing leadership skills, he oversees a 13 technical and support staff responsible for developing cutting edge software and maintaining the Company's worldwide systems infrastructure. Excelling in his field, Mr. Levine developed and imlemented the side background software transmission system for a major lock box of a large Chicago bank, as well as designed and deployed the Company's screen trading technology. Enjoying tremendous success, Mr. Levine intends to stay on top of new technology, enabling him to promote the Company's technical competitiveness. Possessing a strong interest in the technology field and his ability to tackle challenges and deliver results have contributed to Mr. Levine's success. Specializing in proprietary futures and options trading, First Continental Trading operates numerous branch offices around the globe. Currently First Continential Trading employs more than 120 brokers, technical, and support staff at the United States headquarters in Chicago, Illinois. Established in 1984, the Company's international headquarters is located in London, England. **Career Highlights:** First Continental Trading: Director of Information Technology (1997-Present), Senior Software Developer (1995-97); Assistant Vice President of Communications Software, Harris Trust & Savings Bank (1991-95). **Associations & Accomplishments:** Board Member/Vice President (1996-99), Lake Shore Symphony Orchestra. **Education:** University of Chicago: M.A. (1976), B.A. (1974). **Personal Information:** Mr. Levine enjoys cello, music, and reading.

Alen Lo Kar Ming

Information Technology Audit Manager
HSBC
Flat 708 Block 18
Heng Fa Chuen, Hong Kong
+852 26297855
Fax: +852 29561634

6211

Business Information: As an Information Technology Audit Manager for HSBC, Mr. Lo is responsible for the audit and security of all computer systems. Capitalizing on more than 10 years of extensive experience in all phases of operation, he monitors the productivity of the staff, formulating a hands-on management style with an above-average aptitude for problem solving. In addition to his expertise in his field, he also speaks fluent English, Mandarin, and Cantonese. Continually striving for maximum effectiveness, Mr. Lo has completed his M.B.A. to enable him to capitalize on the opportunities provided by the Institution. His career success reflects his ability to think out-of-the-box and aggressively take on new challenges and responsibilities. He aspires to eventually become head of general audit functions and become regionally recognized. Established in 1857, HSBC is a global banking corporation engaged in retail and corporate banking. The Institution also offers investment banking and insurance and financial services. Ranked as one of the top 10 global banks in the world, the Institution employs a staff of 55,000 individuals worldwide. Local operations in Hong Kong employ a staff of 13,000 to serve the needs of the Asia-Pacific area. **Career Highlights:** Information Technology Audit Manager, HSBC (1999-Present); Sub-Manager/Senior Information Technology Auditor, Wing Hang Bank, Ltd. (1989-99); Part-time Instructor, ABRS International, Ltd. (1995-Present). **Associations & Accomplishments:** Information Systems Audit & Control Association; Quality Assurance Institute, Orlando; Institute for Certification of Computer Professionals; Established the Information Technology Audit Function in Wing Hang Bank; Developed various audit and control technologies, leading to zero external audit finding in 1998. **Education:** The Chinese University of Hong Kong, M.B.A. (1999); University of Hong Kong, B.S. with honors in Mathematics and Computer Science (1989). **Personal Information:** Married to Tam Mei Han in 1993. Mr. Lo enjoys reading, driving and swimming.

James Lombardi

Information Technology Manager
Robertson Stephens
64 North Road
Bronxville, NY 10708
(212) 407-0952
jim_lombardi@rsco.com

6211

Business Information: As Information Technology Manager for Robertson Stephens, Mr. Lombardi oversees and direct a number of technical duties on behalf of the Firm. He ensures the functionality and operational status of the systems and network functions at the Bronxville, New York office. Throughout daily activities, Mr. Lombardi provides technical assistance to users, maintains vendor relationships, and implements support procedures and policies. With over four years of hands-on technology experience, Mr. Lombardi's plans include getting more involved in e-commerce activities, while also working in with information technology products and sales. "Be flexible and be able to learn new technologies," is cited as his advice. Robertson Stephens is an investment bank that offers a variety of investment services to corporate clients. Established in 1987, the Firm specializes in the financial management needs of technology companies, and builds innovative options through its parent, Fleet. Headquartered in San Francisco, California, the Firm employs a work force of more than 1,500 professionals who facilitate smooth business operations on a daily basis. Presently, the Firm reports annual revenues in excess of $1 billion. **Career Highlights:** Information Technology Manager, Robertson Stephens (1999-Present); Technical Project Manager, Goldman Snacks (1998-99); Deskstop Support Manager, JP Morgan (1996-98). **Education:** Polytechnic University of New York, M.O.T. (1998); Columbia University, Master's of Public Health; Fordham University, B.S. **Personal Information:** Married to Stella Guarnieri in 1991. Mr. Lombardi enjoys travel, sports and theatre.

Neil A. Matthews

Information Technology Specialist
CIBC Offshore Banking Services Corporation
CIBC Corporate Centre, 4th Floor Warrens
St. Michael, Barbados
(246) 367-2405
neil.matthews@cibc.ca

6211

Business Information: Serving as Information Technology Specialist of CIBC Offshore Banking Services Corporation, Mr. Matthews is responsible for aligning the overall information technology objectives with business goals and communicating this to the management committee. In addition, he creates innovative systems strategies and plans as well as evaluates new technologies. Utilizing his business and technical experience, he oversees all aspects of project management and planning, provides technical support, develops the staff, and implements training programs. Mr. Matthews is further dedicating his time to starting a technical society in Barbados. His advice is "one must always learn with the constant change going on in information technology." Mr. Matthews' strategic plans include developing the information technology more in the offshore sector, making it more functional. His professional success reflects his ability to take on challenges and deliver results. CIBC Offshore Banking Services Corporation engages in global financial services and investment management. Established in 1996, the international corporation is located in Barbados and reports directly to CIBC Toronto. Referred to as a "Banker's Bank," the Corporation employs 25 professionals possessing advanced banking experience. **Career Highlights:** Information Technology Specialist, CIBC Offshore Banking Services Corporation (1997-Present); Technical Analyst, CIBC Caribbean Ltd. (1997); Assistant Manager, Mutual Financial Group (1997). **Associations & Accomplishments:** Network Professional Association; Institute of Network Professionals.

Khanh Nguyen

Managing Director of Information Technology
Nova Bancorp Group, Ltd.
1700-1200 Avenue McGill College
Montreal, Quebec, Canada H3B 4G7
(514) 908-3227
Fax: (514) 940-3511
knguyen@novabancorp.com

6211

Business Information: As Managing Director of Information Technology for Nova Bancorp Group, Ltd., Mr. Nguyen oversees and directs a number of duties on behalf of the Company and its clientele. He determines the overall technical direction and business contribution of the information systems functions. Demonstrating strong leadership, Mr. Nguyen's responsibilities include managing all aspects of communications, network environments, and technical support. With more than seven years of hands on experience, he utilizes his superior talents and excellent understanding of his field to keep the Company on the financial industry's leading edge. In the future, Mr. Nguyen plans to move up the corporate hierarchy as the Company expands internationally. Nova Bancorp Group, Ltd. engages in the provision of currency management for individuals and client companies. The Company conducts business in the forms of mutual funds, portfolio management, and full service banking in accounts and loans. Established in 1982, the Company is located in several convenient locations. Moreover, the Montreal, Canada location functions under the talents and expertise of more than 50 professionals, including accountants, loan officers, and auditors. **Career Highlights:** Managing Director of Information Technology, Nova Bancorp Group, Ltd. (1999-Present); Senior Counselor, National Bank of Canada (1999); Senior Analyst, Bombardier Transportation (1998); Senior Chief of Information Technology, Television Quatre Saisons (1993-97). **Education:** Sherbrooke University, B.S. (1993); Microsoft Certified Systems Engineer. **Personal Information:** Married to Thu-Suong in 1994. Mr. Nguyen enjoys ballroom dancing.

Russell H. Ross

Manager, System Security
E Trade
4500 Bohannon Drive
Menlo Park, CA 94025
(650) 331-5315

6211

Business Information: As Manager of Systems Security of E Trade, Mr. Ross oversees the operations of the security department and employees. Utilizing an effective style of management, he incorporates employee feedback and input into standard operating procedures to create a feeling of empowerment among his staff. Together, they strive to develop innovative methods of security to protect sensitive information that is transmitted on the Internet from the Company's Web site to the server. Demonstrating skill and expertise, Mr. Ross monitors the systems and implements successful applications that exceed current security requirements. Aspiring to an executive management postion within the Company, he expresses a desire to continue his education and training to remain current in today's technically progressive society. E Trade specializes in on-line financial services such as banking and trading. Established in 1994, the Company employs over 1,800 people worldwide and reaps annual revenues that exceed $1 billion. Headquartered in Menlo Park, California, the Company offers stock trading and options as well. **Career Highlights:** Manager of System Security, E Trade (1997-Present); Manager of System Security, Viking Freight (1995-97); Network Security Manager, Lockheed (1991-95). **Associations & Accomplishments:** ISC□-CISSP Certificate #4897;

International Securities Services Association, Silicon Valley Chapter; HTCIA, Silicon Valley Chapter; Computer Security Institute; System Administrative Networking and Security Association; Harley Owners Group, Fremont Chapter. **Education:** University of Phoenix, B.S. in Information Technology (In Progress); Ohlone College, A.A. in Business Management (1990). **Personal Information:** Married to Beth in 1981. Three children: Ashley, Mike, and Kristy. Mr. Ross enjoys surfing, golf and riding Harley's.

Ivan NJ Santhumayor
Database Administrator
Goldman Sachs & Company
10 Hanover Square, 15th Floor
New York, NY 10005
(212) 902-4171
ivan.southumayor@gr.com

6211

Business Information: Displaying his skills in this highly specialized position, Mr. Santhumayor serves as Database Administrator for Goldman Sachs & Company. In administering and controlling the Company's database resources, he works frequently with Cybase, UNIX, Windows NT, and Microsoft's Sequel server, designing and implementing new software exclusive to Goldman Sachs. His primary role is the support of and maintenance of the day-to-day operations of the database system. Before joining Goldman Sachs & Company, Mr. Santhumayor served as Systems Analyst with Sonata, India, and Programmer Analyst for Dart, India. As a seven year technology professional, his success reflects his ability to think out-of-the-box and take on new challenges. Mr. Santhumayor stays on the cutting edge of technology by reading and studying the industry's trade journals. Establishing goals that are compatible with those of the Company, he sees himself entering into project management. Goldman Sachs & Company is a publicly traded Wall Street brokerage company providing services in investments, finance and research, as well as mergers and acquisitions. Headquartered in New York City, New York, the Company has offices throughout the Americas, Europe, and the Asia-Pacific region. Goldman Sachs is a member of the major securities and commodities exchanges world wide, including the New York Stock Exchange, Tokyo Stock Exchange, and the London Stock Exchange. Founded in 1869, the Company employs a global work force of more than 15,000 individuals **Career Highlights:** Database Administrator, Goldman Sachs & Company (1995-Present); Systems Analyst, Sonata (1994-95); Programmer Analyst, Dart (1993-94). **Education:** National Institute of Engineering, B.S. (1992). **Personal Information:** Married to Priya in 1995. One child: Brandon. Mr. Santhumayor enjoys travel, reading and sports.

Khayyam Siddiqui
Information Technology Specialist
Goldman Sachs & Company
184 Davey Street, Apartment D
Bloomfield, NJ 07003
(212) 855-0703
Fax: (212) 902-1384
khayyam.siddiqui@gs.com

6211

Business Information: As Information Technology Specialist with Goldman Sachs & Company, Mr. Siddiqui is responsible for all information technology aspects of day-to-day operations. In this capacity, he develops financial software, maintains the management information systems, intiates reporting of OLAP, assesses under management gathering, as well as coordinates revenue accrual and payment reconciliation. Possessing expertise and technican savvy, Mr. Siddiqui also troubleshoots and develops applications for the accounting department. Anticipating the future position of Senior Manager, he intends to maximize profits of long-term projects, however, he also looks forward to owning a financial trading business on the Web. Since 1870, Goldman Sachs & Company has served as a global asset management investment firm. Employing 15,000 individuals, the Company provides services to an international clientele in Japan, Hong Kong, and London, and the United States. Currently, Goldman Sachs & Company registers annual revenues in excess of $215 billion. **Career Highlights:** Information Technology Specialist, Goldman Sachs & Company (1998-Present); Information Technology Consultant, Prudential Securities (1997-98); Analyst/Developer, Lombard Odier (1994-97). **Associations & Accomplishments:** Association of Computing Machinery; Institute of Electrical and Electronics Engineers; Microsoft Certified Professional; B.C.S. **Education:** Cardiff University, M.S. in Electronic Engineering (1993). **Personal Information:** Mr. Siddiqui enjoys cricket, golf, skiing and rugby.

Kenneth L. Stanley
Manager of Electronic Development and Technology
American Century Investments
4500 Main Street
Kansas City, MO 64111-1834
(816) 340-4822
Fax: (816) 340-7616
ken_stanley@americancentury.com

6211

Business Information: Mr. Stanley has served with American Century Investments in various positions since 1993. At the present moment, he serves as Manager of Electronic Development and Technology. In this capacity, he exercises oversight of design and development of cutting edge electronic commerce technology. Mr. Stanley is responsible for maintaining all aspects of the corporate Intranet, annual budgeting, and making and approving new technology purchases. He is in charge of formulating the Company's creative vision and developing powerful technology and marketing strategies. Coaching and guiding his staff of eight, Mr. Stanley deals with vendors and clients, coordinates all training, and is a member of the Company's Internet council. Directing and participating in the analysis, design, evaluation, and testing as well as implementation of LAN, WAN, Internet, and Intranet-related computer systems also falls within the realm of his responsibilities. Mr. Stanley's focus is on changes that will allow his clients to take advantage of new technology to remain flexible, efficient, and profitable in the global Information Age. He attributes his success to his curiosity. Attaining the position of Chief Information Officer serves as his future goal. The fifth largest mutual fund in the United States, American Century Investments is engaged in selling mutual funds. With $100 billion in assets under management, the Company employs a staff of more than 2,500 professional, technical, and support personnel. **Career Highlights:** American Century Investments: Manager of Electronics Development and Technology (1997-Present), Manager of Digital Technologies (1993-97); Manager of Marketing Printing, American Nurses Association (1988-93). **Associations & Accomplishments:** Technology Boards, Silicon Prairie Technology Association. **Education:** Millikin University, B.F.A.; Northern Illinois University, Grad School; Johnson County Community College, Technology. **Personal Information:** Married to Diane in 1973. Mr. Stanley enjoys golf, drawing, painting and history.

Nagesh B. Sudula, Ph.D.
Vice President
Merrill Lynch
800 Scudders Mill Road
Plainsboro, NJ 08536
(609) 282-8728
Fax: (609) 282-0920
nagesh_sudula@ml.com

6211

Business Information: Serving as Vice President of Merrill Lynch, Dr. Sudula oversees day-to-day database administration and operations of the Funds Department. He has assertively served with Merrill Lynch in a variety of roles since joining the Company as Project Manager in 1994. On a daily basis, Dr. Sudula directs the external processing, to include pricing of funds and ensuring financial institution records are balanced. His effort makes regular client updates possible. In his time with Merrill Lynch, he has taken the Funds Department database group from a staff of one to a staff of four and the database instances were increased manifold from a couple of instances to more than twenty-five. Dr. Sudula began his career as an Image Processing Scientist. Upon coming to the United States, he joined the Merrill Lynch team and was quickly recognized for his dedication and quest for knowledge. He has ascended through the corporate hierarchy and looks forward to the continued success and growth of the Company. His success reflects his ability to build strong teams with synergy and technical strength and take on new challenges and responsibilities. Dr. Sudula plans to look into the possibility of entering the consulting field. Merrill Lynch is a finance and brokerage firm and a leading brokerage firm in the international investment market. The Company offers other lines of services, including government bonds and insurance. With offices across the world, Merrill Lynch employs over 50,000 personnel to plan, invest, and manage client funds. Revenue is estimated at over $37 million a year. **Career Highlights:** Merrill Lynch: Vice President (1997-Present), Manager/Database Administrator (1995-97), Project Manager (1994-95). **Associations & Accomplishments:** International Oracle Users Group. **Education:** Indian Institute of Technology: Ph.D. (1992), M.S. (1984); College of Engineering, B.S. **Personal Information:** Married to Vijaya in 1989. Two children: Susruta and Urjita. Dr. Sudula enjoys reading and games.

Shamya M. Ullah
Associate
Goldman Sachs
125 Broad Street, 37th Floor
New York, NY 10004
(212) 357-3030

6211

Business Information: Serving as an Associate of Goldman Sachs since 1997, Ms. Ullah assumes a number of financial duties on behalf of the Firm and its clientele. Possessing an excellent in understanding of the financial sector, she is responsible for developing new e-commerce strategies with an emphasis on maintaining the Firm's competitive edge in the markets. Applying innovative applications and methods to Internet design, Ms. Ullah is always alert to new opportunities, techniques, and approaches. Remaining with Goldman Sachs, she finds comfort in achieving personal satisfaction and occupational success in her area of expertise. In the future, Ms. Ullah aspires to start up her own consulting company. Her success reflects her drive, motivation, and ability to work with other people. Goldman Sachs is a leading global investment banking firm. Established in 1869, the Firm is one of the oldest, largest, and most reputable banking firms on Wall Street. Headquartered in New York City, Goldman Sachs employs 10,000 highly skilled individuals to acquire business, meet with clients, facilitate projects, and market services. Serving an international client base, the Firm provides a full range of investing, advisory, and financial services to private and corporate clientele. **Career Highlights:** Associate, Goldman Sachs (1997-Present). **Education:** Columbia University: B.A., B.S. (1997). **Personal Information:** Ms. Ullah enjoys music.

Sajini Sara Varghese
Director of Research Development
Instinet
850 3rd Avenue
New York, NY 10022
(212) 310-7294
Fax: (212) 421-9582
sajini_varghese@instinet.com

6211

Business Information: Drawing from 10 years of extensive academic ties and professional experience, Ms. Varghese serves as Director of Research Development for Instinet. Instinet is the world's largest agency brokerage firm and a wholly-owned subsidiary of Reuters Group PLC trading daily in over 40 global markets and a member of 18 exchanges in North America, Europe, and Asia. In her capacity, Ms. Varghese is responsible for defining and managing the execution of critical e-commerce initiatives for Instinet's Equities Division. Some of Ms. Varghese's career highlights include managing the EMU project for Merrill Lynch's Foreign Exchange Systems globally, implementing a distributed credit risk simulation system for Sumitomo Bank Capital Markets, and leading the development of resource management software for IBM's SP line of supercomputers. She is excited about the potential of the Internet to provide opportunities for talented entrepreneurs in developing countries such as India previously limited in this regard by their country's infrastructure. She would like to be able to facilitate such efforts in the future. Ms. Varghese's advice is, "People in technology should fully understand the technologies of the day as well as the fundamental needs and vision of their customers, since that will make them design truly effective and pertinent solutions." **Career Highlights:** Director of Research Development, Instinet (1999-Present); Vice President, Merrill Lynch and Co. (1996-99); Assistant Vice President, Sumitomo Bank Capital Markets (1994-96); Senior Associate Programmer, IBM Corporation (1990-94). **Education:** Syracuse University, M.S. in Computer and Information Science (1990); Regional Engineering College, India, B.E. in Computer Science and Engineering (1988). **Personal Information:** Ms. Varghese enjoys playing the piano, reading extensively, traveling to a different country every year and social and classical dancing.

Edward Gartin
Systems Manager
The Pezrow Companies Inc.
535 East Crescent Avenue
Ramsey, NJ 07746
(201) 825-9400
Fax: (201) 825-8556
egartin@pezrow.com

6221

Business Information: Demonstrating expertise in the technology field, Mr. Gartin serves as Systems Manager for The Pezrow Companies Inc. In this capacity, he administers the Corporation's wide area network, and is involved in an ongoing process to link all corporate locations via Windows NT system capabilities. Directing the analysis, design, evaluation, testing, and implementation of leading edge messaging environments, directory services, security, and server-based services to support a computer network environment also falls within the realm of his responsibilities.

Mr. Gartin stays at the leading edge of computer technologies by reading voraciously and by attending seminars and training courses. He attributes his success to understanding the market place and accomplishing the Corporation's goals. His future objective is to learn more about solutions for the Year 2000 computer dilemma and obtain his MCSE, MCP, and CISCO certifications. Mr. Gartin hopes to continue his rise through the Corporation's management hierarchy. Established in 1949, The Pezrow Companies Inc. brokers food products throughout the Northeastern United States. Approximately 1,500 professional, technical, and support staff are employed by the Corporation that is headquartered in Ramsey, New Jersey. **Career Highlights:** Systems Manager, The Pezrow Companies Inc. (1996-Present); Database Specialist, Office of Ombudsmen (1996); Database Specialist, DeVry Institute of Technology (1996). **Associations & Accomplishments:** Phi Theta Kappa Society; Data Processing Managers Association. **Education:** DeVry Technical Institute, A.S. in Computer Information Systems (1996). **Personal Information:** Mr. Gartin enjoys golf and travel.

Joseph M. Betty

Technical Support Supervisor
The Vanguard Group
P.O. Box 2900
Valley Forge, PA 19482
(610) 669-0477
Fax: (610) 669-1714
joe_betty@vanguard.com

6282

Business Information: Functioning in the capacity of Technical Support Supervisor of The Vanguard Group, Mr. Betty provides technical improvement services to the Group's LAN Administration system, as well as evaluates, determines, and implements automation mechanisms. Before joining The Vanguard Group, Mr. Betty served as an Advanced Network Engineer with Compucom and LAN Administrator for The Score Board, Inc. As a solid, 10 year technology professional, he owns a track record of producing results. In his present role, he oversees and manages the Macintosh support network, creates support tools, and designs and develops cutting edge Web and systems software applications. Analyzing and supporting computer operations, monitoring systems resources and response time, and providing state-of-the-art solutions for operational problems also fall within the realm of Mr. Betty's responsibilities. His success is attributed to his personal initiative and his determination and willingness to learn. Eventually attaining the position of Web Development Manager serves as one of his future goals. As the world's largest no-load mutual fund service provider, The Vanguard Group offers a wide variety of technical and financial careers in its endeavor to help clients manage their funds and portfolios. Established in 1974, Vanguard employs a domestic work force of more than 12,000 professionals who help manage over $500 billion in assets. **Career Highlights:** Technical Support Supervisor, The Vanguard Group (1997-Present); Advanced Network Engineer, Compucon (1997); LAN Administrator, The Score Board, Inc. (1994-97). **Associations & Accomplishments:** Handyman Club of America. **Education:** Apple Certified Training, Systems Engineer; PTS Learning Systems, Microsoft TC/IP and Windows NT Core Technologies; Lotus Notes Development. **Personal Information:** Married to Patricia L. in 1996. Mr. Betty enjoys programming and electronic technology.

Alex F. Dalal, Ph.D.

Project Manager
The Vanguard Group
115 Acorn Way
Honey Brook, PA 19344
(610) 503-6010
Fax: (302) 369-5430
(610) 857-4855
alexdala@worldnet.att.net

6282

Business Information: As the Project Manager for The Vanguard Group since 1999, Dr. Dalal is responsible for a number of Technical projects in the Defined Benefits group. The current projects include Data Modeling, BenXL Calculator for calculating benefits for retired employees, and Web development. He is responsible for budgeting, hiring, organizing, planning, and leading the day-to-day technical and business activities of the projects. Activities include the following: identifying necessary project tasks, allocating available team members and consultants, running core team meetings on a day-to-day basis, verifying the completion of tasks, insuring the quality of products, interacting with OEM vendors, and maintaining project plans and schedules. In his past employment with Agfa Incorporated, Dr. Dalal was responsible for all aspects of multi-million dollar (2,500+ node, $5 million budget, 35+ people) DuPont LINX networking, NT Workstations, Archives and Client (PowerBuilder) - Server (Sybase) hardware and software projects from conception to completion. Attributing his success to his knowledge and people skills, Dr. Dalal's plans for the future include attaining upper level management roles in Software and Hardware Application Development and Systems Integration in Information Technology. Located in Malvern, Pennsylvania, The Vanguard Group is an international mutual funds firm. As one of the largest companies in the world, the Company has 10,000 employees worldwide and reports annual revenues in excess of $540 million. **Career Highlights:** Project Manager, The Vanguard Group (1999-Present); Project Manager, Agfa Inc. (1997-99); Project Manager Spartan Mills (1996-97). **Education:** Case Western Reserve University, Ph.D. (1986); Rutgers University, Courses in Management and Finance. **Personal Information:** Married to Nina in 1987. Dr. Dalal enjoys swimming, table tennis and walking.

Felice R. Gabardi III

Assistant Vice President of Infrastructure
MFS Investment Management
11 Martin Drive
Raynham, MA 02767
(617) 954-5642
Fax: (617) 954-6619
frg@mfs.com

6282

Business Information: As Assistant Vice President of Infrastructure of Massachusetts Financial Services, Mr. Gabardi presides over the design and implementation of global voice and data networks. In addition, he has cognizance over daily operations, systems maintenance tools, remote access, and has extensive design responsibilities in support of the company's services. His desire is to become even more influential in the Company's business decisions and how newly developing technology will influence its decisions. A savvy, 14-year professional and a five-year veteran of the Company, he is also actively pursuing the convergence of all data and voice network functions within the Company. Mr. Gabardi attributes his success primarily to the unwavering support of his family and working within a Company that utilizes his special abilities to their fullest. Massachusetts Financial Services, founded in 1924, is a subsidiary of Sun-Life Canada. Staffed by more than 2,700 professionals, the Company is the oldest mutual fund organization in America. The Company offers customers financial management, share holding, mutual fund administration, investment research, and retirement services. Global in scope, Massachusetts Financial Services is located in Boston, Massachusetts. **Career Highlights:** Assistant Vice President of Infrastructure, Massachusetts Financial Services (1994-Present); Senior Network Analyst, Faxon (1992-94); Network Analyst, GTECH Corporation (1990-91). **Education:** University of Lowell, B.S. in Electrical Engineering (1991). **Personal Information:** Married to Kelly in 1991. Two children: Rudy and Hanna. Mr. Gabardi enjoys snow mobiling, motorcycles and boating.

Kyle Gerstner

Senior Systems Analyst
IBEX Capital Markets
60 State Street, Suite 950
Boston, MA 02109
(617) 305-4252
Fax: (617) 305-4230
kgertstner@ibexboston.com

6282

Business Information: As Senior Systems Analyst of IBEX Capital Markets, Mr. Gerstner is in charge of all technical aspects of the networking systems. Demonstrating an extensive knowledge of the field, he fulfills the requirements of a highly specialized position by conducting research to develop specific solutions to daily technical challenges. Overseeing the departmental budget, he ensures each project has proper funding by carefully researching valid needs for equipment and supplies. Mr. Gerstner maintains the corporate Web site, striving to implement information and creativity that will foster positive responses of the Company. Understanding that the majority of his success stems from an in-depth knowledge of technical business practices, Mr. Gerstner currently has plans to continue his education as he aspires to advancement within the corporate structure. IBEX Capital Markets is a structured financial firm, focusing attention on the banking and finance industries. Founded in 1996, the Firm operates effectively and efficiently with 10 trained employees. Serving as a CDO vehicle for commerical paper customers, the Firm coordinates assets, loans, and United States bonds to ensure portfolios are in order. **Career Highlights:** Senior Systems Analyst, IBEX Capital Markets (1998-Present); Database Administrator, Fidelity Investments (1996-98); Webmaster, MCI (1995-96); Software Developer, Bernhard, Eisenbraun & Associates (1991-94). **Associations & Accomplishments:** Microsoft Certified Professional. **Education:** Brown University, B.A. (1990). **Personal Information:** Mr. Gerstner enjoys soccer, chess, motorcycling and book clubs.

John D. Glenn

Programming Analyst I
Van Kampen Funds
2800 Post Oak Boulevard, Floor 43
Houston, TX 77056
(713) 438-4770
glennj@vankampen.com

6282

Business Information: Specializing his expertise and skill as the Programming Analyst I for Van Kampen Funds, Mr. Glenn acts as the liaison between the information technology departments and service departments for the Firm. Providing cutting edge assistance and consultation regarding mutual funds for major companies, Mr. Glenn hosts such clients as the Investor Service departments. Especially skilled in areas of technological work, he performs application testing, problem reacting services, and works in cooperation with software vendors. Extending his responsibilities beyond the current boundaries of his service, Mr. Glenn will begin project management and delegation in the near future, his professional career emphasized by extensive research in the financial fields. His success reflects his ability to take on challenges and deliver results on behalf of the Firm and its clientele. Headquartered in Houston, Texas, Van Kampen Funds is one of the largest mutual fund firms in the country, employing 1,500 accountants, financial professionals, and consultants. Offering specialized services to influential corporate clientele and major companies worldwide, Van Kampen Funds provides assistance in selecting appropriate funds and investment directions for individual customer needs. **Career Highlights:** Van Kampen Funds: Programming Analyst I (2000-Present), Service Systems Analyst (1999-00); Disc Jockey, Complete Music (1997-98). **Associations & Accomplishments:** Miss Southeast Texas Scholarship Pageant. **Education:** North Harris Community College, A.S. (1998). **Personal Information:** Married to Joanna in 1997. Mr. Glenn enjoys being a professional magician and golf.

Andrew H. Grilk

Senior Software Engineer
Thomson Financial Securities Data
2 Gateway Center
Newark, NJ 07102-5003
(973) 645-9678
Fax: (973) 622-1421
andrew.grilk@tfn.com

6282

Business Information: As Senior Softwarwe Engineer of Thomson Financial Securities Data, Mr Grilk creates the searching and reporting software enabling clients to access the Company's financial database by way of desktop, browser applications, and interfaces. He has served in his current positon since 1994, bringing with him a very broad knowledge base and extensive experience in the software developement field. Some of his notable accomplishments include the public release of his software and the restructuring of his current team of co-workers. Mr. Grilk is working towards integrating the Company's databases into a Web based interface. He attributes his success to his technical expertise as well as his ability to build teams with synergy and technical strength, tackle new challenges, and deliver results in behalf of his clientele. Thomson Financial Securites Data, founded in 1985, is currently manned by approximately 500 highy skilled professionals. The Company is the world's premier provider of authoritative financial data and high quality business research on companies, industries, and markets worldwide. Currently, the Company is located in Newark, New Jersey. **Career Highlights:** Senior Software Engineer, Thomson Financial Securities Data (1994-Present); Consultant, Williams, Alexander & Associates (1995-Present). **Education:** Ramapo College, B.S. in Computer Science with a minor in Mathematics (1994). **Personal Information:** Married to Michelle in 1999. Mr. Grilk enjoys basketball, hunting and the Hawthorne Caballeros.

Brian K. Guild

Systems Administrator
Bridgewater Associates
2 Cobblestone Road
Greenwich, CT 06831-4212
(203) 226-3030
bguild@iname.com

6282

Business Information: As Systems Administrator of Bridgewater Associates, Mr. Guild handles a myriad of responsibilities within the corporate structure. Demonstrating adept technical abilities, he maintains a 15 server, 90 client WindowsNT ethernet network. Utilizing his education and practical work experience, he ensures operating efficiency through the implementation of strategically designed business plans. With exceptional communicative abilities, he meets with clients to discuss technical needs and negotiates details of any contracts that may initiate. Enjoying the challenges of his position, Mr. Guild currently aspires to a higher management plan as he focuses on networking advancements. Bridgewater Associates provides financial consultancy services to businesses in the Greenwich, Connecticut area. Established in 1975, the Company employs 90 people to assist in money management services. **Career Highlights:** Systems Administrator, Bridgewater Associates (1999-Present); Systems Support Consultant, GE Capital Corporation (1998-99); Senior Lab Technician, Data General Corporation (1996-98). **Associations & Accomplishments:** Connecticut Computer Users Group Association; Connecticut Small Business Association. **Education:** Worcester Polytechnic Institute; Microsoft Certified Systems Engineer. **Personal Information:** Mr. Guild enjoys tennis, drag racing and building computers.

Barry David Johnston

Director of Information Technology Systems
Scudder Investments
1 South Place
London, England, United Kingdom EC2M 2ZS
+44 1715391150
Fax: +44 2076618420
barry.johnston@scudder.co.uk

6282

Business Information: Mr. Johnston functions in the role of Director of Information Technology Systems for Scudder Investments. A successful, 23 year veteran, he is responsible for maintaining the operable status of all computer networks and personal hardware throughout all facilities of the Company. Mr. Johnston determines the overall information technology strategy and and business contribution of the information systems function. Additionally, he is a member of the Company's global strategy team. Meeting with users and management advisors, he provides his input and advice regarding the development of the telecommunications equipment. Originally from Australia, Mr. Johnston got into the information techology field because of the vast opportunities afforded. Looking to the next millennium and beyond, he hopes to advance the Company to a more global level where he can see the Company operate on a more networked system. Scudder Investments is a management business concentrating on corporate investments. Established in 1909, the Company assists major businesses of the area appropriately invest their funds into secure accounts and opportunities. Headquartered in Zurich, the Company works with clients around the world, dealing with pension investments of no less than $10 million. **Career Highlights:** Director of Information Technology Systems, Scudder Investments (1996-Present); Director of Technology, Clever Communications Ltd. (1984-96); Research and Development Manager, J. Hempstead Associates Ltd. (1980-84); Communications Consultant, Pactel (1977-80). **Associations & Accomplishments:** Institute of Directors. **Education:** Box Hill Tafe. of Melbourne, Australia, Technology (1976). **Personal Information:** Married to Judith in 1992. Three children: Angus, Gavin, and Callum. Mr. Johnston enjoys skiing, golf and do-it-yourself projects.

Timothy R. Maholm

Manager of Technology Training
McDonald Investments
800 Superior Avenue
Cleveland, OH 44114
(216) 443-3992
Fax: (216) 563-2191
tmaholm@mcdinvest.com

6282

Business Information: Demonstrating his ability to effectively communicate ideas and problem soving techniques to his staff, Mr. Maholm serves as Manager of Technology Training of McDonald Investments. In this capacity, he directs the training department and coordinates practical learning classes for all staff, sales force, and adminstrative personnel. Additionally, Mr. Maholm develops distance learning and Internet-interactive programs for these same employees. Recognizing the long-run cost effectiveness of these innovative programs, the Company allowed him free reign when designing and supporting the recently implemented training programs. The results were well received, and the entire staff was quickly up-to-date. Citing the different mentors he has had throughout his career as a large contributor to his success, Mr. Maholm looks forward to advancement within the corporate structure. McDonald Investments deals with institutional and private investments and banking. A Key Corporation Company, they have 71 investment centers and over 250 branches. The Company specializes in investment trading, stocks and bonds, and corporate consumer lending. **Career Highlights:** Manager of Technology Training, McDonald Investments (1998-Present); Training Manager, Macola Software (1998); Quality Training Manager, Pioneer Standard Electronics (1996-97); Associate Director, Ernst & Young (1987-96). **Associations & Accomplishments:** North East Ohio International Society of Performance Improvement: Former President, Vice President of Communications, Board of Directors; North Olmsted, Soccer Coach. **Education:** Indiana University: M.S. in Education (1985), B.S. in Business (1981). **Personal Information:** Two children: Ryan and Dylan. Mr. Maholm enjoys outdoors, photography and collecting knives.

Sean F. Plumb

Project Manager III
Schwab Institutional
4500 Cherry Creek Corporate Center
Denver, CO 80246
(303) 639-2416
Fax: (303) 639-2636

6282

Business Information: Providing his skilled services as Project Manager III, Mr. Plumb is a member of the strategic planning and development group. He performs contingency planning and is responsible for coordinating the Company's Y2K project for the vendors' infrastructure, ensuring their compliance with the necessary changes. As a 17 year professional, Mr. Plumb has served with Schwab International in a variety of roles since joining the team as Electronic Mutual Fund Trading Manager in 1997. Additionally, he serves as a Golf Club Design Owner for Wicked Styx. Utilizing his strong academic ties and extensive experience, Mr. Plumb coordinates resources, time lines, schedules, and assignments; ensures services are laced with quality, value, and selection; and provides cohesive leadership. Establishing goals that are compatible with those of Schwab Institutional, Mr. Plumb plans to continue to grow within the Company and take it to the next level of success. Schwab Institutional is the premier full service financial service company, providing services to Top Money and Investment Manages. The Company was established in 1974. **Career Highlights:** Schwab Institutional: Project Manager III (1998-Present), Electronic Mutual Fund Trading Manager (1997-98); Wicked Styx Golf Club Design Owner, Wicked Styx (1996-Present). **Associations & Accomplishments:** Mayor's Office of Arts Culture and Film; Volunteer, Arts Street Youth Employment Project; Steering Committee; Marketing and Public Relations Committee. **Education:** University of Denver: M.B.A. (In Progress), Master's degree in Music Theory and Composition (1984); Webster State College of Colorado, B.A. in Music Theory and Composition (1982); University of Southern California, B.A. in Art (1982). **Personal Information:** Married to Karen in 1987. Two children: Jessica and Max. Mr. Plumb enjoys golf, music, art and investing.

Sornkawee Puranachoti

Executive Director of Information Technology
KGI Securities One Public Company, Ltd.
United Center Building, 25th Floor, Silom Road
Bangkok, Thailand 10500
+66 22311111
Fax: +66 26322793
sornkawee@securities-one.com

6282

Business Information: As the Executive Director of Information Technology of KGI Securities One Public Company, Ltd., Mr. Puranachoti detemines the overall strategic direction and business contribution of the information systems function. He is responsible for planing and overseeing the research, evaluation, and integration of advanced technology within the Company. A successful 18 year professional, Mr. Puranachoti administers performance appraisals, salaries, hiring, and budgets for his department. He also coordinates resouces, schedules, and communications, with a focus on technical changes that will help the Company and its clientele to remain flexible, efficient, and profitable in the information technology age. A member of industry related associations, Mr. Puranachoti stays current on emerging technology and is able to network and interact with the many technology professionals in different fields. His success reflects his leadership ability to form teams with synergy and technical strengths, take on challenges, and deliver results on behalf of the Company and clients. KGI Securities One Public Company, Ltd. was established in 1987 as an investment and securities bank handling pension funds for clients worldwide. Fully operational with 400 employees, Security One Public Company is a subsiday of Hong Kong KGI with locations in the Philipines, Taiwan, and Korea. **Career Highlights:** Executive Director of Information Technology, KGI Securities One Public Company, Ltd. (1987-Present); EDP Manager, Vibhavadi General Hospital (1982-87). **Associations & Accomplishments:** Network Professional Association in the United States; Director, Information Technology Club for Securities Business in Thailand **Education:** Assumption University, M.S. in Computer Information Systems (1995). **Personal Information:** Married to Pavinee in 1991. One child: Chatchapon. Mr. Puranachoti enjoys golf, reading and stamp collecting.

Al Quint

Systems Analyst
Cal PERS
400 P Street
Sacramento, CA 95814
(916) 231-7792
Fax: (916) 231-7900
al_quint@calpers.ca.gov

6282

Business Information: Providing his skilled services as a Systems Analyst for Cal PER, Mr. Quint acts as the General Ledger Module Functional Lead for the PeopleSoft Financial Accounting System. He provides system upgrades, tests to ensure smooth performance, and troubleshoots problems as necessary. A Certified Public Accountant, he utilizes more than 27 years of experience in the performance of his duties. Attributing his success to the quality of people he has worked with, Mr. Quint is continually striving to improve his performance. He looks forward to increasing his professional responsibilities and becoming the Manager of all of the PeopleSoft Accounting Systems in the state of California. Providing general ledger maintenace of retirement funds for various companies, Cal PERS is the largest in the United States and the second largest in the world. The Company has several field offices, providing quality computer systems to organize the data and train professionals to maintain the systems. Created in 1949, operations employ the services of more than 1,000 personnel members. **Career Highlights:** Systems Analyst, Cal PERS (1998-Present); State Controller-CA: PC Analyst/Technician (1996-98), Governmental Auditor (1992-95), Accounting Systems Analyst (1981-92). **Associations & Accomplishments:** Association of Governmental Auditors; Sacramento PC Users Group. **Education:** California State University in Sacramento, B.S. in Business Administration with a concentration in Auditing (1988); American River College, A.A. **Personal Information:** Married to Sherri in 1981. One child: Matt. Mr. Quint enjoys skiing, music and working on computers.

Heidi Schlabs

Director of Business Services
Marketing Specialists
2445 Gateway Drive, Suite 100
Irving, TX 75063
(972) 753-1722
Fax: (972) 753-1763
hschlabs@mssc.com

6282

Business Information: Mrs. Schlabs began with Marketing Specialists as Operations Manager in 1997 and now serves as Director of Business Services. In this capacity, she presides over the EDI Department, overseeing supervisors of the database and managing the EDI team and trainers. Representing Marketing Specialists, she attends EDI conferences in an effort to raise awareness of the Company within the industry. Before joining Marketing Specialists, Mrs. Schlabs served as Human Resources Manager for Quantum Plus and both Customer Services and Human Resources Manager with Target Stores. Watching trends and the budget, Mrs. Schlabs examines various computer systems to determine the best system for the Company's future needs. Coordinating resources and schedules, overseeing time lines and assignments, maintaining customer relations, and identifying new clients also fall within the purview of Mrs. Schlabs' responsibilities. Attributing her success to determination and perseverance, she tells newcomers to the field to set high standards and goals, attaining them no matter what it takes. The largest food broker in the nation, Marketing Specialists represents many food manufacturers and distributes some nonfood products such as health and beauty aids. Presently, the Company is orchestrating a merger with a publically held company that will make Marketing Specialists the only publicly traded food brokerage company in the country. Established in 1978, the Company can trace its beginnings to 1892. Manned by 3,000 people, the Company is currently in 33 states and making plans to expand operations. **Career Highlights:** Marketing Specialists: Director of Business Services (1999-Present), Operations Manager (1997-99); Human Resources Manager, Quantum Plus (1996-97); Customer Services and Human Resources Manager, Target Stores (1993-96). **Associations & Accomplishments:** Society of Human Resources Management. **Education:** Century University, B.S. in Business Administration (1999); Target Business College. **Personal Information:** Married to Craig in 1996. Mrs. Schlabs enjoys sewing, crafts and reading.

David L. Scott

•••━━■◉■━━•••

Director of Information Technology
Public Financial Management
2 Logan Square, Suite 1600
Philadelphia, PA 19103-2707
(215) 567-6100
Fax: (215) 567-4180
scottd@publicfin.com

6282

Business Information: Utilizing a strong academic and occupational background in information technology, Mr. Scott is the Director of Information Technology for Public Financial Management. In his position, he is responsible for overseeing and controlling the LAN/WAN network architecture, conducting upgrades on the Firm's Intranet, and managing the Web development as well as Internet access capabilities. Moreover, Mr. Scott is charged with supervising the information technology department and the employees who report directly to him with any problems or concerns. Highly regarded, he possesses an excellent understanding of technology. In the future, Mr. Scott looks forward to continuing with the Firm and enhancing the e-commerce capabilities. Located in Philadelphia, Pennsylvania, Public Financial Management is a public financial firm. Founded in 1976, the Firm engages in providing financial advisory services to public entities such as city governments. With a staff of approximately 200 employees, the Firm reports substantial annual revenue. **Career Highlights:** Director of Information Technology, Public Financial Management (1996-Present); Manager of Technology, Nova Care, Inc. (1991-96); Manager of Technical Services, Amkor Electronics (1988-91); Network Manager, Boeing Computer Services (1985-88). **Associations & Accomplishments:** Delaware Computer Users Group; Delaware Valley Computer Users Group; American Medical Association; Juvenille Diabetes Foundation. **Education:** Pennsylvania State University, M.S. (1994); Ohio State University, B.S. (1979). **Personal Information:** Married to Mary in 1981. Four children: Bridget, Christina, Mary, and Jennifer. Mr. Scott enjoys fitness, travel and history.

David S. Tanigawa

Senior Systems Administrator
Thomson Financial
22 Thomson Place
Boston, MA 02210
(617) 856-1772
Fax: (617) 261-5499
david.tanigawa@tfn.com

6282

Business Information: Utilizing several years of extensive experience in systems administration, Mr. Tanigawa serves as the Senior Systems Administrator for Thomson Financial. He has served with Thomson Financial in a variety of roles since joining the team of professionals as UNIX Systems Administrator in 1997. In this current capacity, he is responsible for building, maintaining, and administering SUN and Hewlett-Packard hardware. Additionally, he is responsible for the installation, administration, and maintenance of the Solaris and SCO openserver operating systems. Mr. Tanigawa continues to grow professionally through the fulfillment of his responsibilities and his involvement in the advancement of operations. As a nine year technology professional, his success reflects his ability to think out-of-the-box and aggressively take on new challenges and responsibilities. A leading provider of quality financial information, Thomson Financial researches, analyzes, and develops software products to the world wide investment and corporate communities. Established in 1980, approximately 7,000 knowledgeable individuals are employed nationwide. Annual sales are boasted at $960 million. **Career Highlights:** Thomson Financial: Senior Systems Administrator (1999-Present), UNIX Systems Administrator (1997-99); Supervisor and Technical Support, Salie Mae (1996-97). **Associations & Accomplishments:** USENIX. **Education:** Gordon College, B.A. (1990). **Personal Information:** Married to Alyssa in 1998. One child: Victoria Houle. Mr. Tanigawa enjoys photography and music.

Steven M. Alsedek

Systems Administrator/OTC Trader
Coastal Securities LP
700 North Pearl Street, Suite 900
Dallas, TX 75201
(214) 979-0660
Fax: (214) 720-4461
salsedek@nationwide.net

6289

Business Information: Combining his unique talents in network administration and market trading, Mr. Alsedek serves as the Systems Administrator and OTC Trader for Coastal Securities LP. During the time period when the stock market is open, his main focus in on trading and he stands ready to buy or sell commodities. At the close of the market, Mr. Alsedek switches to his role as Systems Administrator. He presides over the administration and maintenance of five networks and 170 computers for 32 traders. Responsible for bringing the Firm up to speed with the latest technology, he has received internal recognition for his outstanding performance. Mr. Alsedek attributes his success to his ability to stay current in technology, think outside the box, and aggressively tackle new challenges. A Nasdaq market maker, Coastal Securities LP is unique from other firms in the industry. The Firm is without customers of any sort, instead focusing solely on market trading. Headquartered in Houston, Texas, this location is the investment arm of the limited partnership. Other locations include El Paso, Austin, Chicago, and Boca Raton. Presently, the Firm employs 35 professionals at Houston to keep tabs on the nation's stock market. **Career Highlights:** Systems Administrator/OTC Trader, Coastal Securities LP (1998-Present); Consultant, Cardinal America Consultant (1997-98); Technical Recruiter, CFS Inc. (1996-97). **Associations & Accomplishments:** Lambdi Chi Alpha Fraternity. **Education:** Drury College, M.B.A. (1993); Shepherd College, B.S.; United States Army Command and General Staff College; Combined Arm Services Staff School; Military Intelligence Officer Advanced Course; Military Intelligence Officer Basic Course. **Personal Information:** Mr. Alsedek enjoys travel.

Eileen Rose Campbell

Business Writer
Merallis Company
70 Inwood Road
Rocky Hill, CT 06067
(860) 257-0010
Fax: (860) 257-1660
eileencampbell@merallis.net

6289

Business Information: As a Business Writer for the Merallis Company, Ms. Campbell fulfills a number of technical duties on behalf of the Company and its clientele. She writes business specifications, maps payers specifications to the Company's internal systems, and works with payers to establish connections. Interacting with HMOs, such as Blue Cross Blue Shield and Medicaid, Ms. Campbell attends to unit and vial testing and working with management, users, and programmers to establish efficient and effective business systems through timely upgrades. Conducting meetings and training opportunities and coodinating projects also fall within the purview of her responsibilities. Most rewarding aspects of Ms. Campbell's career is upgrading systems in a short time period and completing a conversion project, migrating from a tape to electronic system. In the future, Ms. Campbell would like to become more oriented, and learn more standards. She credits her success to a supportive family and good supervisors and her willingness to learn more. Established in 1993, the Merallis Company engages in the interchange of electronic data within the medical industry. Employing the talents of 70 individuals, the Company completes transactions electronically, specifically for physicians. Presently, the Company is located in Rocky Hill, Connecticut. **Career Highlights:** Business Writer, Merallis Company (1999-Present); EDI Business Analyst, ENVOY (1997-99); EDI Specialist, Aetna US Healthcare (1987-97). **Associations & Accomplishments:** United States Junior Chamber of Commerce. **Education:** Asnuntuck Community College, Associate's degree (1984).

David R. Lembke

Network Services Manager
Investors Fiduciary Trust
801 Pennsylvania Avenue
Kansas City, MO 64105-1307
(816) 871-9529
Fax: (816) 871-9641
drlembke@iftc.com

6289

Business Information: Serving with distinction in the realm of network administration and services for close to 10 years, Mr. Lembke operates as Network Services Manager for Investors Fiduciary Trust. In his capacity, he functions in numerous capacities and has various roles and responsibilities. Whenever difficulties arise in LAN and WAN networks, he provides solutions to difficulties. A respected professional, Mr. Lembke is also involved in research and development for WAN firewall and design of electronic commerce, internet, intranet, and remote access infrastructures. Continually on the cutting edge of technology, he is preparing the Company for the Y2K compliance and developing a contingency plan for system recovery in the event of a disaster. With the construction of the Company's new state-of-the-art building, Mr. Lembke is responsible for working on the designs using gigabyte and ATM technology. His future goal is keeping pace with new technology. A subdivision of the State Bank of Boston, Investors Fiduciary Trust deals primarily with mutual funds and custodial accounts. Incorporated in the late 1880s, the State Bank of Boston has locations throughout the United States. Established in 1985, Investors Fiduciary Trust's office in Kansas City employs a staff of 600 people. **Career Highlights:** Network Services Manager, Investors Fiduciary Trust (1996-Present); Network Manger, Gardere & Wynne, L.L.P. (1995-96); Network Administration, Final Oil & Chemical (1990-95). **Education:** University of Kansas, B.S. in Business Administration and Accounting (1984). **Personal Information:** Two children: Erika and Kurt. Mr. Lembke enjoys hunting, fishing, golf and travel.

Dino D. Moler

Director of Business Development
The National Transportation Exchange, Inc.
1400 Opus Place, Suite 800
Downers Grove, IL 60515-5709
(630) 724-8610
Fax: (630) 963-2790
dmoler@nte.net

6289

Business Information: Highly skilled in the logistics field, Mr. Moler serves as the Director of Business Development for The National Transportation Exchange, Inc. Mr. Moler owns a vertical segment that focuses on 3PL and 4PL to offer the best service to the Corporation's members. He is responsible for determining the overall business direction, as well as formulating new strategic and tactical business development plans. Before joining The National Transportation Exchange, Inc. in 1997, Mr. Moler served as Director of Business Development with Ryder Integrated Logistics. Utilizing extensive knowledge gained through 15 years of experience, he concentrates his efforts on business development and strategy for the growth of the Corporation. Attributing his success to networking with colleagues, industry involvement, and the high quality of people he works with, Mr. Moler is dedicated to the success of The National Transportation Exchange. He plans to strengthen his position with alliances and work towards connecting the portal capability. Created in 1993, The National Transportation Exchange, Inc. is an Internet logistics business. The National Transportation Exchange offers the Corporation's shipper and carrier membership a Real-Time Trading Exchange or RTX for the industry. Presently, more than 35 people are employed by the Corporation. **Career Highlights:** Director of Business Development, The National Transportation Exchange, Inc. (1997-Present); Director of Business Development, Ryder Integrated Logistics (1985-97). **Associations & Accomplishments:** Council of Logistics Management. **Education:** Indiana University, B.A. (1985). **Personal Information:** Married to Christine in 1988. Two children: Matthew and Alexander. Mr. Moler enjoys sports, travel and collecting.

David A. Schultz

Senior Network Administrator
Bank of New York Clearing Services
111 East Kilbourn Avenue
Milwaukee, WI 53202
(414) 225-4721
Fax: (414) 225-4876
dschultz@bnyclearing.com

6289

Business Information: As Senior Network Administrator of Bank of New York Clearing Services, Mr. Schultz maintains computer networks. He draws on nine years of experience in the information technology field, using his technical knowledge to repair and administer host servers and hardware. In addition, to keep the Company to date with ever shifting patterns within the technological boom, Mr. Schultz designs new systems to help process work in more efficient manners. To this end, he is a central figure in systems management, configuration, and installation. As for the future, Mr. Schultz plans to pursue graduate school and broaden his professional perspective into management. Current acheivment, he asserts, has been a product of his education thus far. Bank of New York Clearing Services provides finance-specific services on the Internet. Involved in Web hosting and online trading for correspondent firms, the Company has utilized existing technologies to turn a profit. The Company's main concern is clearing and processing electronic stock transactions. Established in 1998, the Company has benefited from the technical skills of a 500 person workforce. **Career Highlights:** Senior Network Administrator, Bank of New York Clearing Services (1998-Present); Network Analyst, Everen Securities Inc. (1996-98); Management Information Systems Coordinator, Beloit Beverage Company Inc. (1995-96). **Education:** Keller Graduate School of Management, Master's degree in Information Systems Management (In Progress); Milwaukee School of Engineering, Bachelor's degree in Management Information Systems (1993); Moraine Park Technical College,

Associate's degree in Computer Integrated Manufacturing (1998).

6300 Insurance Carriers

6311 Life insurance
6321 Accident and health insurance
6324 Hospital and medical service plans
6331 Fire, marine, and casualty insurance
6351 Surety insurance
6361 Title insurance
6371 Pension, health, and welfare funds
6399 Insurance carriers, nec

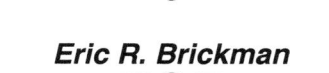

Eric R. Brickman

Director
Prudential
751 Broad Street, Floor 12
Newark, NJ 07102
(973) 802-9626
Fax: (973) 645-1712
ebrickman@prudential.com

6311

Business Information: In his role as Director of Prudential's eCommerce Group, headquartered in Newark, New Jersey, Mr. Brickman is responsible for formulating the strategic direction for this new business. Coupling his knowledge of the industry with a proactive leadership style, he is able to foster a sense of unity and empowerment among his staff as he manages the Group's strategy, marketing, product development, competitive research, and partner negotiations. With adept technical ability, he is credited with the development of an innovative, e-commerce-based financial planning capability, resulting in the increase of market share, sales, and customer satisfaction. The recipient of several prestigous awards doled out by industry officials, Mr. Brickman intends to remain in his current capacity, continually focusing on the formulation of advanced e-commerce business and capabilites. Prudential is recognized throughout the professional community as a leading provider of broad-based financial services to businessess and individuals. Popular services include insurance, annuities, mutal funds, financial planning, employee benefits, and investment, brokerage, and asset management services. Founded in 1875, the Company maintains facilities throughout the world. **Career Highlights:** Prudential: Director (1998-Present), Manager, Service Strategy and Customer Management (1997), Manager of Corporate Information Technology (1996); Manager, Field Operations (1995), Project Manager (1991). **Associations & Accomplishments:** Technology Forum Award of Excellence; American Society for Training and Development Leader's Award; Masie Center for Learning Technologies; Society for Applied Learning Technologies. **Education:** Seton Hall University, Institute of International Business: M.B.A. (1995), Advanced Certificate in International Management (1995); Muhlenberg College, B.A. (1991). **Personal Information:** Mr. Brickman enjoys drumming, music, world travel, running and attending the theater. Mr. Brickman is looking forward to his upcoming marriage to his fiancée, Ms. Gail Ratzker.

Stephen D'Amico

Senior Database Administrator
Aegon Equity Group
232 Millstone Drive
Palm Harbor, FL 34683
(727) 299-1800
sdamico@aegonusa.com

6311

Business Information: The Senior Database Administrator for Aegon Equity Group, Mr. D'Amico assumes responsibility for all data processing applications. He adminsters and controls database tools and systems ensuring its functionality and operational status. Possessing an excellent understanding of the DMBS, Mr. D'Amico is able to supply information to different insurance tables, thus leading to a seamless Company operation. In his current position since 1995, Mr. D'Amico relies on 15 years of hands on experience in overseeing the systems infrastructure and ensuring data integrity, security, and reliability. In the future, Mr. D'Amico plans include taking on new challenges, managing a larger group, and becoming involved in Web based products. Aegon Equity Group offers life insurance policies for business and personal use. Established in 1980, local operations in Palm Harbor, Florida employ the skilled services of 1,300 individuals to meet with clients, facilitate scheduling, and promote services. The Company is headquartered in The Netherlands and operates facilities internationally. **Career Highlights:** Senior Database Administrator, Aegon Equity Group (1994-Present); Senior Analyst/Designer, Martin Marietta (1990-94); Senior Analyst, GTE Data Services (1988-90); Senior Programmer/Analyst, Neilson Media Research (1985-88). **Associations & Accomplishments:** Biography in Who's Who in the East; MCN of Achievement. **Education:** University of Scranton, degree in Computer Science (1975). **Personal Information:** Married to Judith in 1976. Two children: Jason and Christina. Mr. D'Amico enjoys racquetball, volleyball, softball and science fiction.

Flo Fallacara

Associate Business Systems Analyst
MetLife
501 U.S. Highway 22
Bridgewater, NJ 08807
(908) 253-2477
Fax: (908) 253-1472
ffallacara@metlife.com

6311

Business Information: Ms. Fallacara began her career with MetLife as Training Coordinator in 1995, and now assertively serves as an Associate Business Systems Analyst. She is responsible for analyzing business operations, developing general systems solutions, and providing insights into an operation with a focus on making process improvements. In this context, Ms. Fallacara writes the system specifications for group packages and Company procedures. All of the written specifications are first tested before being sent to the Greenville, South Carolina office and input into the Company's network. In charge of 20 locations, Ms. Fallacara also performs investigative analysis. She states, "It is very demanding and takes a lot of time to be a successful professional but it is very rewarding." Her success reflects her ability to think out-of-the-box and aggressively take on new challenges and responsibilities. Ms. Fallacara enjoys working in the technology field and looks forward to obtaining her bachelor's degree. A world renowned life insurance company, MetLife offers clients a variety of insurance services including home and automobile. Special packages are offered to employees of commercial clients in which payments may be deducted automatically from an employee's checking account or paycheck. Presently, MetLife employs a work force of more than 5,000 professional, technical, and support personnel. **Career Highlights:** MetLife: Associate Business Systems Analyst (Present), Training Coordinator (1995); Administrator, Ortho McNeil Pharmacy (1993). **Associations & Accomplishments:** All Star Cheerleading Association. **Personal Information:** Married to Vito in 1977. Four children: Arthur, Jennifer, Dana, and Nicole. Ms. Fallacara enjoys sewing, computers, cheerleading and gymnastics.

Jack Dyer Hillman

Information Technology Process Manager
Amica
25 Amica Way
Lincoln, RI 02865-1165
(401) 334-6000
Fax: (401) 334-1634
jhillman@amica.com

6311

Business Information: Serving as Information Technology Process Manager of Amica, Mr. Hillman oversees the efforts of the SEPG group to develop, monitor, measure, and implement process improvements for the Company's information technology development. He is the original leader of the new process project and heads up its computer information systems efforts to install information technology processes by establishing and documenting the processes to follow for each project. Mr. Hillman also oversees the JAD team and the Package Software Solutions process, directing the team in the input and installation of software. Committed to the success of the Company, he looks forward to assisting in its development by making it mature at all levels of processes and delivery in information technology. Founded in 1907, Amica provides every type of insurance for individuals and residences. Approximately half a million households are currently insured by the Company. Headquartered in Rhode Island, 3,300 qualified personnel are employed nationwide. **Career Highlights:** Amica: Information Technology Process Manager (1998-Present), Applications Programming Manager (1997-98), Applications Programming Assistant Manager (1992-97). **Associations & Accomplishments:** Boston Software Process Improvement Network; Software Engineering Institute; Project Management Institute; Vice President of Administration/Board of Directors, Rhode Island Project Management Institute Chapter. **Education:** Bryantt & Stratton, Scientific Data Processing (1972). **Personal Information:** Married to Barbara in 1976.

Izett M. E. McCalla, III

Director of Computer Environment
Island Life Insurance Company
4-6 St. Lucia Avenue
Kingston, Jamaica 5
(876) 926-1470
Fax: (876) 926-2679
infotech@islandlife_ja.com.jm

6311

Business Information: Demonstrating expertise in the information technology field, Mr. McCalla serves as Director for Island Life Insurance. Overseeing the computer environment, he is responsible for maintaining all day to day technical operations, to include the functionality and operational status of the systems infrastructure. He conducts daily network testing, designs and develops software applications, and conducts systems diagnostic reviews. With over 15 years of work related experience, Mr. McCalla brings to the Company an adept ability to recommend and implement new technology improvements by keeping abreast of the latest innovations. He is leading Island Life Insurance to new heights, thereby ensuring corporate longevity and his personal occupational success. Established in 1971, Island Life Insurance is a full service life insurance company located in Kingston, Jamaica. Island Life Insurance specializes in providing clients with individual or and business life insurance, annuities, mutual funds, and group benefit programs. Currently employing more than 200 skilled professionals, Island Life Insurance generates revenues in excess of $12 million annually. **Career Highlights:** Director, Island Life Insurance (1994-Present); Fiscal Services EDP Ltd.: Director of Data Centre (1990-94), Senior Systems Analyst (1987-90); Accounting and Auditing Specialist, Agricultural Credit Bank (1986-87). **Associations & Accomplishments:** Jamaica Computer Society. **Education:** University of West Indies, M.Sc. in Management Information Systems (1998); University of the West Indies, B.Sc. in Management. **Personal Information:** Mr. McCalla enjoys soccer, motor racing and cricket.

Debi C. McKinney

Team Lead
Nationwide Insurance
1 Nationwide Plaza 3-15-02
Columbus, OH 43215-2239
(614) 677-2360
Fax: (614) 677-0146
mckinnd1@nationwide.com

6311

Business Information: Serving in the role of Team Lead at Nationwide Insurance, Ms. McKinney is responsible for information systems and Web development for data warehousing applications. As a proven team leader for Web development, Ms. McKinney guides a team of professionals in design, development, and employment of cutting edge Intranet and Internet technology. Her hard work is focused on improving the networking capabilities and maintaining the existing environment functional and fully operational. Looking to the new millennium, Ms. McKinney plans to pursue a degree in Computer Science, and afterwards, she hopes to advance within the corporate structure. Nationwide Insurance is one of the largest financial and insurance services provider in the United States. Providing auto, business, and homeowner's insurance, the Company maintains a presence in 37 countries overseeing and managing $100 billion in assets. Presently, Nationwide Insurance employs an international work force of more than 35,000 employees. **Career Highlights:** Team Lead, Nationwide Insurance (1997-Present); Financial Advisor, University of Arkansas (1996-97). **Associations & Accomplishments:** Phi Theta Kappa; Outstanding Student for Behavioral Sciences; Phi Kappa Phi; National Dean's List; Chancellor's List; Epsilon Sigma Alpha; Dean's List; A.P.S.A.C. **Education:** Franklin University, Computer Science degree (In Progress); University of Arkansas, B.A. in Psychology (1997); University of Arkansas at Little Rock, B.A. in Liberal Arts (1996). **Personal Information:** Ms. McKinney enjoys Shar-Pei dogs, skiing and public speaking.

K. C. Morrison

Systems Programmer
Principal Financial Group
711 High Street
Des Moines, IA 50392-0002
(813) 414-9300
Fax: (515) 248-3719
morrison.kc@principal.com

6311

Business Information: Displaying his expertise in the technology industry, Mr. Morrison serves as a Systems Programmer for the Principal Financial Group. He works with the Company's mainframe automation monitoring system, providing support and troubleshooting to the vendor software on which the system is based. Sharing the responsibility for the system with other capable programmers through job scheduling, he works in a team environment. Citing his long memory and previous mentors as the reason for his success, Mr. Morrison stays on the cutting edge of technology by reading industry publications and performing research. He is dedicated to the further development of the Company and aspires to a future position in project management. Established in 1879, the Principal Financial Group is a financial services provider. The Company maintains an international presence where life, health, and mortgage services are offered to individuals in several countries. Approximately 16,000 staff members are employed. **Career Highlights:** Systems Programmer, Principal Financial Group (1997-Present); Programmer, The HON Company (1996-97); Call Center Analyst, Amoco Motor Club (1994-96). **Education:** Grand View College: B.A. (1996), A.A.; Des Moines Area Community College, A.A. **Personal Information:** One child: Kennon Richard. Mr. Morrison enjoys real estate.

Beth Ouellette

Systems Director
Prudential Insurance
80 Livingston Avenue, Mailstop 2NE90
Roseland, NJ 07068
(973) 716-1195
Fax: (973) 716-1242
beth.ouellette@prudential.com

6311

Business Information: Ms. Ouellette is the Systems Director for Prudential Insurance. Part of her responsibilities include her career doubling as the Professional Project Manager for the regional office's Information Systems Department. In her role, she oversees and directs all aspects of project development undertaken by the Department and strives to ensure their success. Responsible for channeling all information to the Chief Executive Officer, Ms. Ouellette works towards budget adherence and is determined to complete every project on time and in a cost effective manner. Scheduling and ensuring quality in all services and products are also an integral part of her responsibilities. Through her Department, the Company's entire networking systems are adapted, updated, and supervised. In the future, Ms. Ouellette aspires to become known as an expert in Project Management, as well as perform public speaking at conferences and seminars. Prudential Insurance was established in 1900 and provides reassurance solutions for clients desiring to insure valuable possessions. The Company advises clients on effective ways to invest their financial savings. Located across the United States, Prudential employs over 40,000 personnel and has become a leader in the insurance and financial planning industry. **Career Highlights:** Prudential Insurance: Systems Director (1998-Present), Systems Director/Quality Marketing Manager (1995-1998). **Associations & Accomplishments:** Project Management Institute; Quality Assurance Institute. **Education:** New York University at Stern, M.B.A. in Finance (1994); Eastern Michigan University, B.S.; Greenville Technical College, degree in Programming; Baptist College, degree in Elementary Education. **Personal Information:** Ms. Ouellette enjoys reading and networking.

Gina L. Pierson

PC/LAN Specialist
Prudential Insurance Company of America
63 Mudcut Road
Lafayette, NJ 07848
(973) 579-7034
glp@interactive.net

6311

Business Information: Serving as a PC/LAN Specialist of Prudential Insurance Company of America, Ms. Pierson monitors and troubleshoots enterprise NT and UNIX servers from the company's operations command center. She ensures the company's systems infrastructure is fully functional and operational throughout all aspects of its daily worldwide operations. Overseeing the local area networking service, she guides the information technology staff through successful upgrade services and works with members of a team to troubleshoot all difficulties that may arise. In the future, Ms. Pierson plans on becoming more involved in network engineering as well as gaining more exposure and training. Her career success reflects her ability to take on challenges and deliver results. One of the leaders in the insurance industry within the United States, the Prudential Insurance Company of America strives to effectively communicate insurance coverage options to its clients. Offering life, casualty, automobile, and related insurances, the Company specializes in its financial consulting advice. With locations around the world, the Company utilizes the talents from a staff of 60,000 employees who guide, counsel, and support each client to reach their highest level of success. **Career Highlights:** PC/LAN Specialist, Prudential Insurance Company of America (1997-Present); Computer Operator, United States Army (1991-97). **Education:** Thomas Edison State University, B.S.A.S.T. (In Progress).

Sharon L. Richards

Database Administrator
Safeco Life Insurance
5069 154th Place NE
Redmond, WA 98052
(425) 558-5008
Fax: (425) 867-8288
sricha@safeco.com

6311

Business Information: Ms. Richards functions in the capacity of Database Administrator for Safeco Life Insurance. She is responsible for administering and controlling DB2 and Sequel servers, ensuring their functionality and fully operational status. Before coming on board to Safeco in 1997, Ms. Richards served as Technical Services Specialist for Blue Cross of Idaho. Her background also includes stints as IMS Database Administrator and Technical Services Specialist with West One Bank, and Technical Services Specialist at The Benjamin Franklin Savings & Loan. An expert identifier of trouble spots, she analyzes each file and program to safeguard her systems against viruses. She conducts consultations with the staff regarding the operation of the system and creates new programs to ease the use of the database, as well as recover corrupted data and tuning software tools to improve database performance. Looking the next millennium, Ms. Richards hopes to fully utilize her speaking talents by opening a consulting firm and conducting speaking seminars. Her keys to success include her positive attitude and keeping on top of emerging technologies through reading and training. Safeco Life Insurance is a life, home, and automobile insurance business. Established in 1920, the Firm hosts a long standing tradition for excellence and expertise in the industry built from the life-long support of many clients. The Firm has also involved itself in financial investing through advising its clients on proper investments, annuities, and funds to expand the fiscal future. **Career Highlights:** Database Administrator, Safeco Life Insurance (1997-Present); Technical Services Specialist, Blue Cross of Idaho (1996-97); IMS Database Administrator/Technical Services Specialist, West One Bank (1991-96); Technical Services Specialist, The Benjamin Franklin Savings & Loan (1984-91). **Associations & Accomplishments:** Vice President, D.R.M.A.; N.A.S.P. **Education:** Portland State University; Whitman College. **Personal Information:** One child: Catherine. Ms. Richards enjoys baking, golf and gardening.

Bruce A. Smith

Project Consultant
Metropolitan Life
2201 North Forest Trail
Dunwoody, GA 30338-5829
(678) 319-2271
bruceandrew@mindspring.com

6311

Business Information: Mr. Smith has served with Metropolitan Life in various positions since 1987. At the present time, he assumes the responsibilities of Project Consultant. In his capacity, he exercises oversight of programming and security performance application. Drawing from 14 years of experience as programmer and analyst, he maintains all data systems and programs used to monitor and track investment premiums. Analysis, acquisition, installation, modification, configuration, and support and tracking of operating systems, databases, utilities, and software and hardware also falls within the realm of his responsibilities. Keeping up with technology by reading trade magazines and networking, Mr. Smith attributes his success to hard work and his ability to quickly grasp technical concepts. Learning more about client server technology and keeping pace and staying hands on with technology serves as his long-term goals. Metropolitan Life operates as a life and group insurance company. The second largest asset holding insurance company in the United State, the Company was founded in 1868 and is currently manned by more than 710,000 associates. **Career Highlights:** Metropolitan Life: Project Consultant (1995-Present), Senior Programmer Analyst (1991-95), Systems Analyst (1989-91), Programmer (1987-89); Coopers & Lybrand: Systems Analyst (1986-87), Programmer (1984-87). **Education:** Fairleigh Dickinson University, M.B.A. in Finance (1991); Rensselaer Polytechnic Institute, B.S. in Computer Information Systems (1984).

Lawrence J. Bechtel

Technical Trainer
Blue Cross & Blue Shield of Louisiana
5525 Reitz Avenue
Baton Rouge, LA 70809
(225) 298-3098
Fax: (225) 295-2082
lbectel@excite.com

6321

Business Information: As Technical Trainer for Blue Cross & Blue Shield of Louisiana, Mr. Bechtel handles employee instruction on the corporate level. Considered to be an expert in the field of technical computer training and programming, he utilizes an informative style of management that is direct, incorporating specific student concerns into his lectures and demonstrations. The Company requires his services on a regular basis, when employees desire training for career advancement, technical updates, and new employee education. Internally recognized for his impressive accomplishments within the corporate structure, Mr. Bechtel credits his eagerness to learn as a contributing factor in his success. In the future, he looks forward to assisting to the completion of corporate goals as he continues his education. His advice to others is "learn as much as possible, if there appears a new opportunity or opportunities, then take them." Established in 1946, Blue Cross & Blue Shield provides healthcare insurance to individuals through policies that are usually obtained through employers. With each of the 50 United States in possession of a license to operate their own branch of the insurance company, the nationwide employee totals reach 1,500 and reap estimated revenues of $56 million. The Louisiana division is headquartered in Baton Rouge, and has acheived a reputation outstanding customer support. **Career Highlights:** Technical Trainer, Blue Cross & Blue Shield of Louisiana (1999-Present); Instructor, Ascension College (1998-99); Consultant, Bechtel Enterprises (1997-98). **Associations & Accomplishments:** Block Captain of Bernard Terrace Civic Association; American Society of Training and Development; Toastmaster; President, Bluesmasters. **Education:** University of Phoenix, Bachelor's degree in Information Systems Design Engineering (In Progress); University of St. Thomas: Master's degree in Liberal Arts (1996), Bachelor's degree in Liberal Arts (1994). **Personal Information:** Mr. Bechtel enjoys computers, raising his two dogs, cooking and electronics.

Dennis G. Boland

Technology Consultant
American Family Insurance Company
6000 American Parkway
Madison, WI 53783
(608) 242-4100
Fax: (608) 243-4926
dboland@amfam.com

6321

Business Information: Mr. Boland is Technology Consultant for American Family Insurance Company. He is responsible for design, implementation, and support of storage solutions for corporate distributed systems. Before joining American Family Insurance, Mr. Boland served as Information Systems Consultant and Systems Engineer for IBM Corporation. As a savvy, 13 year technology professional, Mr. Boland is charged with development and implementation of state-of-the-art methodologies to keep all of the back up files for the Company in a safe location, and at the same time maintaining file functionality, accessibility, and integrity. Investigating new, emerging architecture for the distributed storage management system also fall within the realm of his responsibilities. Looking toward the next millennium, Mr. Boland's future objectives include continuing to design and develop distributed storage management systems. American Family Insurance Company is an insurance provider. The Company provides casualty, life, health, and liability insurance in 13 states throughout the United States. Opportunities are available to clients on an individual basis, or as an entire company to obtain any combination of the several forms of insurance offered. The Madison office acts as the corporate headquarters for the state of Wisconsin. Presently, the Company employs several thousand representatives that either work from the headquarters building or have private offices in various cities throughout the region to cover a broader range of clients on a more personal level. **Career Highlights:** Technology Consultant, American Family Insurance Company (1995-Present); IBM Corporation: Information Systems Consultant (1991-95), Systems Engineer (1986-91). **Associations & Accomplishments:** Network and Systems Professionals Association. **Education:** Edgewood College, B.S. in Business (1993); University of Wisconsin at Madison; Madison Area Technical College. **Personal Information:** Married to Ann. Two children: Erin and Beth. Mr. Boland enjoys fishing and golf.

Cel Giannotta
Vice President of Information Technology
Liberty Health
3500 Steeles Avenue East
Markham, Ontario, Canada L3R 0X4
(905) 946-4380
Fax: (905) 946-4449
cel.giannotta@health.lmig.ca

6321

Business Information: A successful 20 year professional with a wealth of knowledge of technology and the heathcare industry, Mr. Giannotta currently serves as Vice President of Information Technology with Liberty Health. He oversees and directs the technology department and he is responsible for the overall technology and data management for the Company. Highly regarded in the industry, Mr. Giannotta determines the strategic direction and business contribution of the information systems functions. As the custodian for all aspect of information technology, he is tasked with introducing new technology to the Company and managing its products. His focus is on deploying advanced technology into Liberty Health's operating and networking environments to help the Company stay flexible, efficient, and profitable and maintain the competitive edge in the industry. A health insurance company, Liberty Health is a large health insurance firm located in Ontario, Canada. Offering an array of services to its client base, the Company employs a staff of over 500 trained consultants and professionals in their regional locations. **Career Highlights:** Liberty Health: Vice President of Information Technology (1998-Present); Director of Systems Development (1997-98); Manager of Applications, Ontario Blue Cross (1993-97). **Education:** Humber College, degree in Computer Sciences (1980); Queen's University. **Personal Information:** Married to Anne in 1987. Five children: Nik, Alannah, Cori, Kailee, and Tomas.

Jason Howard

Systems Consultant
Blue Cross & Blue Shield of Alabama
450 Riverchase Parkway East
Birmingham, AL 35244
(205) 444-6203
Fax: (205) 733-7255
jhoward@bcbsal.org

6321

Business Information: Displaying his expertise in the field of technology, Mr. Howard serves as Systems Consultant for the Blue Cross & Blue Shield of Alabama. He presides over the administration of the Company's Novell, NT, and UNIX operating systems. Mr. Howard performs system maintenance, monitors daily activity, handles network security, and provides a routine back up system for the various operating systems. Additionally, he provides technical support to the Company's many users. During his career, Mr. Howard has worked for two companies as a Systems Administrator, integrating systems to increase its versatility through a newfound ease of use while at the same time decreasing system training costs. Looking forward, he anticipates increasing his networking responsibilities and plans to obtain his CISCO and CCIE certifications. The Blue Cross & Blue Shield of Alabama provides quality health insurance coverage services to its clients within the state of Alabama. Blue Cross & Blue Shield of Alabama presently employs a work force of more than 3,000 qualified personnel. Each Blue Cross & Blue Shield is independently operated and follows a specified guideline to conduct business. **Career Highlights:** Blue Cross & Blue Shield of Alabama: Systems Consultant (1999-Present), LAN Administrator (1997-99); EDI Administrator, Bruno's, Inc. (1995-97). **Associations & Accomplishments:** Birmingham NT User Group. **Education:** Herzing College, Associate's degree (1996); Microsoft Certified System Engineer; Microsoft Certified Professional+Internet; Certified Novell Engineer; CCNA. **Personal Information:** Married to Melissa in 1996.

Patricia J. Jablonske

Manager of Information Systems
Blue Cross & Blue Shield of Minnesota
P.O. Box 64560
St. Paul, MN 55164-0560
(651) 662-2227
patricia_j_jablonske@bluecrossmn.com

6321

Business Information: Ms. Jablonske serves as Manager of Information Systems of Blue Cross & Blue Shied of Minnesota. She oversees programmers in the applications division. In her capacity, she handles staffing and other administrative duties for the enhancement of business development. Possessing an excellent understanding of the technology field, Ms. Jablonske is responsible for application delivery and project management work, tracking items for scheduling, and implementing various levels of expertise into every aspect of day-to-day operations. Future endeavors for Ms. Jablonske include completing her M.B.A. in management information systems, and expanding her area of accountabilities within the information systems division. Her success is attributed to her people skills and her ability to deliver results. Established in 1933, Blue Cross & Blue Shield of Minnesota provides various forms of health insurance to Minnesota service members. The Company started with Blue Cross, which merged with Blue Shield in 1972, forming the oldest health plan in Minnesota. This nationally acclaimed Firm offers various options of coverage, including HMO and PMO for life, dental, and disability. The Company also provides dependable services for the provision of ways to manage the costs of workers' compensation and other health expenses for Minnesota-based companies throughout the country, merging with other Blue plans to provide more comprehensive service. **Career Highlights:** Blue Cross & Blue Shield of Minnesota: Manager of Information Systems (1997-Present), Programmer (1991-97). **Associations & Accomplishments:** Business Association; Association of Computing Machinery. **Education:** University of St. Thomas, M.B.A. in Management Information Systems (In Progress); University of Wisconsin at River Falls: B.S. in Business (1991), B.S. in Computer Science (1991). **Personal Information:** Ms. Jablonske enjoys golf and rollerblading.

Russell W. Jones, Jr.
Project Manager
Healthcare Management
100 East Penn Square, Wanamaker Building, Floor 9
Philadelphia, PA 19107-3322
(215) 832-4737
Fax: (215) 832-4632
rjones8349@aol.com

6321

Business Information: Mr. Jones is Project Manager of Healthcare Management. He is responsible for managing large corporate projects and planning technical strategies, and fulfilling the role of information systems outsource liaison. Before joining Healthcare Management, Mr. Jones assertively served as Program Manager with First Union, formerly Core States Bank. His occupational history includes Project Manager and Strategic Planner for Keane, and Senior Consultant at AJIOLON. As a solid, 27 year technology professional with an established track record of delivering results, Mr. Jones is charged with starting up large projects and overseeing these turnkey operations to completion. Providing information technology training for management using state-of-the-art technologies also fall within the purview of his responsibilities. He credits his professional career success to good mentors, hard work ethic, and being a change agent. Eventually attaining the role of Chief Information Officer serves as one of Mr. Jones' future goals. A Medicaid heath maintenance organization, Healthcare Management provides health care services to the Medicaid population. The Organization offers physician sponsored network and managed care development and management services. A subsidiary of AmeriChoice, Healthcare Management is located in Philadelphia, Pennsylvania, and employs a staff of over 160 professional, Healthcare, administrative support personnel. **Career Highlights:** Project Manager, Healthcare Management (1997-Present); Program Manager, First Union (1994-97); Senior Consultant, AJIOLON (1992-94); Project Manager/Strategic Planner, Keane (1985-92). **Associations & Accomplishments:** Project Management Institute; Educational Society for Resource Management; Black Data Processing Associates. **Education:** Drexel University (1985); Community College of Philadelphia, A.A.S. (1973). **Personal Information:** Married to Gloria in 1996. One child: Russell. Mr. Jones enjoys photography.

Colette M. L'Heureux
Senior Systems Integrator
Standard Insurance
1100 Southwest 6th Avenue, M.S. P8A
Portland, OR 97207
(503) 321-8181
Fax: (503) 321-7290
unixwomen@yahoo.com

6321

Business Information: With a strong background in Unix systems as Systems Administrator, Ms. L'Heureux was recruited to Standard Insurance in 1998. At the present time, she assumes responsibilities of Senior Systems Integrator. In that capacity, she manages and maintains more than 30 Sun Microsystems Unix machines in fully operational status. A member of the elite Unix expert community, she possesses extensive experience in business and corporate applications in Unix systems. Drawing from years of experience, Ms. L'Heureux designs and creates the Company's electronic communications and data collection and retrieval systems including data warehousing and LAN and WAN networks. Establishing and maintaining fire walls and finding new ways to harness more of the computer's power also falls within the realm of her responsibilities. Standard Insurance is a national leader in offering long-term and short-term insurance, disability, and retirement planning services. The Company has an old and long-respected name recognition in the industry, and continues to grow its market share through advanced technological applications. Founded in 1905, the Company employs 1,700 people. **Career Highlights:** Senior Systems Integrator, Standard Insurance (1998-Present); Lead Unix System Administrator, Nationwide Insurance (1997-98); Unix System Administrator, Sun Microsystems Inc. (1995-97); Unix System Administrator, DHL Airways Inc. (1992-94). **Education:** Portland State University (1998); Golden Gate University (1997); University of California at Santa Cruz Extension, Certificate of Unix System Administration/Management; Drake/Pro Metrix Solaris, 2.X Unix System Administration Certification.

Carolyn W. Luther
Senior Director of Managed Care Systems
Independence Blue Cross
1901 Market Street
Philadelphia, PA 19103
(215) 241-2031
Fax: (215) 241-2283
carolyn.luther@ibx.com

6321

Business Information: Ms. Luther is the Senior Director of Managed Care Systems of Independence Blue Cross. She implements software applications for the Company that will better serve the managed healthcare systems. Her programs define and highlight the most usable programs within the systems and she trains her staff and fellow co-workers on the proper maintenance and techniques to make better use of the technology made available to them. With 17 years of information technology experience, Ms. Luther is able to successfully coordinate the projects within her department. She has worked with the Company for ten years and plans to eventually attain the position of Vice President. Her success reflects her ability to enhance operations by being able to thinking outside the box, deliver results, and aggressively take on new challenges. Independence Blue Cross specializes in healthcare insurance for residents of Pennsylvania. The Company has almost 30 representatives operating within its Philadelphia location to successfully accommodate the medical coverage needs of their clients. Clients are able to select the specific packages that would best facilitate their particular needs. **Career Highlights:** Senior Director of Managed Care Systems, Independence Blue Cross (1990-Present); Director of Application Development, Hospital of the University of Pennsylvania (1986-90); Manager of Software Implementation, Sanchez Computer Association (1985-86). **Associations & Accomplishments:** Alumni, Leadership Inc.; Daughters of the American Revolution. **Personal Information:** Married to Scott in 1986. Ms. Luther enjoys horseback riding, golf and tennis.

Anthony L. Niel
Manager of Network Engineering
Kaiser Permanente
711 Kapiolani Boulevard
Honolulu, HI 96813
(808) 597-5420
Fax: (808) 597-5293
tony.niel@kp.org

6321

Business Information: Mr. Niel is Manager of Network Engineering. He is responsible for providing network connectivity and telephony services to 22 facilities across the state of Hawaii. As an 11 year technology veteran, Mr. Niel has served with Kaiser Permanente in a variety of capacities since joining the Company as Telecommunications Manager in 1992. A systems expert, he designs, installs, implements, and maintains LAN/WAN hardware and software, as well as troubleshoots network and system usage and resolves LAN communications problems. Coordinating future resources, schedules, time lines, and assignments also fall within the realm of Mr. Niel's responsibilities. With an established track record of delivering results, his success reflects his ability to think out-of-the-box and take on new challenges. Looking toward the next millennium, Mr. Niel plans on remaining and growing with the Company. Kaiser Permanente provides health care and insurance in a variety of settings. Serving both hospitals and clinics, the Company covers both inpatient and outpatient services. Established in 1958, the Kaiser Permanente employs a staff of more than 3,000 people. **Career Highlights:** Kaiser Permanente: Manager of Network Engineering (1997-Present), Network Planning Manager (1996-97), Telecommunications Manager (1992-96). **Associations & Accomplishments:** Honolulu Telecommunications Association. **Education:** Roosevelt University, Bachelor's in General Studies and Computer Science (1988). **Personal Information:** Married in 1985. Mr. Niel enjoys swimming, golf and personal computing.

Kenneth O. Ohaeri

Senior Information Systems Manager
Blue Cross & Blue Shield
3535 Blue Cross Road
St. Paul, MN 55122
(651) 662-6260
Fax: (651) 662-1199
ohaerik@yahoo.com

6321

Business Information: Mr. Ohaeri has been in the position of Senior Information Systems Manager for Blue Cross & Blue Shield for five years. He is responsible for information systems technology management which includes enterprising computing networks, managing the database, and e-commerce. Mr. Ohaeri delegates duties to 15 skilled individuals. He manages corporation claims and develops market and research strategies for the Company. Mr. Ohaeri attributes his success to his childhood and attending the best schools. He has been in the technology field for 15 years and research keeps him up-to-date with emgerging technology. Mr. Ohaeri would like more management responsibilities with the Company in the future. Established in 1960, Blue Cross & Blue Shield provides information systems management for health maintenance organizations, health insurance, and employee benefits. The Company operates corporatewide and provides computer networks, data management, and e-commerce strategies. Blue Cross & Blue Shield is a national company headquartered in Illinois and employs 4,000 skilled individuals. The Company reports annual earnings in excess of $2.1 million. **Career Highlights:** Senior Information Systems Manager, Blue Cross & Blue Shield (1994-Present); Senior Project Manager, GMAC, Residential Funding Corporation (1992-94); Database Administrator, ITT Finance (1988-92). **Associations & Accomplishments:** International Systems Dynamics Group; International Data Management Association. **Education:** Metropolitan State University, M.B.A. (1990); Minnesota State University, B.S. (1985). **Personal Information:** Married to Nagwa in 1994. Two children: Rebecca and Jessica. Mr. Ohaeri enjoys tennis, jogging and soccer.

Brian J. Pardy

Programmer
Oxford Health Plans
23 Laurel Street, 3rd Floor
Branford, CT 06405
(203) 459-6960
posterkid.@psnw.com

6321

Business Information: As Programmer of Oxford Health Plans, Mr. Pardy creates new electronic data interchange software. Possessing an excellent understanding of technology, he troubleshoots difficulties and develops cutting edge electronic data transfer software. Working on a myriad of projects, he also maintains and functionality and operational status of company's core systems. The analysis, modification, configuration, support, and tracking of operating systems, databases, utilities, software, and hardware also fall within the scope of his responsibilities. In his position for only one year, Mr. Pardy has displayed an exemplary record of achievement. His accomplishments include helping the Company improve its data intake. A visionary who has proven himself correct on many occasions, Mr. Pardy's goals include performing his programming wizardry for an Internet company. A health maintenance organization, Oxford Health Plans was founded in 1984. Providing health insurance to large companies for their employees, the Company is headquartered in Trumbull, Connecticut. The Firm's area of operations includes the states of New York, New Jersey, and Connecticut. Additionally, the Company provides Medicare benefits and employs 4,500 individuals total. **Career Highlights:** Programmer, Oxford Health Plans (1999-Present); Programmer, Guardian Industries (1996-99). **Education:** College of the Sequoias at Visalia (1999).

Sonya B. Piazza

Manager of Corporate Quality Assurance
Blue Cross & Blue Shield of Alabama
450 Riverchase Parkway E
Helena, AL 35080-3923
(205) 733-7775
Fax: (205) 733-7367

6321

Business Information: Mrs. Piazza functions in the role of Manager of Corporate Quality Assurance for Blue Cross & Blue Shield of Alabama. The sphere of her influence rests mainly in Web design and software implementation. On many occasions, Mrs. Piazza inspects Web sites, programs, and the individuals operating computers to ensure that all customers of Blue Cross & Blue Shield of Alabama receive service of only the highest quality. In addition, she implements stress testing, making sure that computer systems can withstand large data loads and prolonged usage. Success, Mrs. Piazza asserts, is the end product of her education and experience. Blue Cross & Blue Shield of Alabama provides medical and dental coverages to many of the citizens of Alabama. Providing insurance coverage, Blue Cross & Blue Shield has often been used by employers as part of a worker's benefit package. Since 1938, people have turned to the Company for assistance when it comes to medical services. The Company, in addition, utilizes the efforts of 2,500 workers to ensure the smooth and efficient operation. **Career Highlights:** Blue Cross & Blue Shield of Alabama: Manager of Corporate Quality Assurance (1999-Present), Database Administrator (1999), Systems Analyst (1997-99). **Associations & Accomplishments:** National Management Association. **Education:** Jacksonville State University, B.S. in Computer Information Systems (1992). **Personal Information:** Married to Michael in 1995. Mrs. Piazza enjoys instructing aerobics and fitness.

Kenneth T. Rolfsmeyer

Network Technology Analyst
American Family Insurance
2218 Luann Lane, Apartment 104
Madison, WI 53713
(608) 242-4100
Fax: (608) 243-4726
krolfsme@amfam.com

6321

Business Information: As American Family Insurance's Network Technology Analyst, Mr. Rolfsmeyer designs, implements, and supports management solutions for client server networks. He is responsible for supporting different technology and new solutions for systems management, performing such tasks as monitoring Web server applications and troublshooting any system problems. He works with several different systems including UNIX, Windows NT, Hewlett-Packard, and Novell. Mr. Rolfsmeyer notes the highlights of his career as the time he managed a multimillion dollar project with complete success; being involved with converting 3,400 AIX systems to Windows NT, replacing 9,000 systems within eight months. He is currently attending Lakeland College, pursuing a degree to further his technological knowledge. Success, according to Mr. Rolfsmeyer, is attributed to his ability to learn quickly and absord information. The 11th largest insurance company in the United States, American Family Insurance is dedicated to providing employees of both private and commercial industries with high quality health insurance. Established in 1924, the Company employs more than 15,000 customer service representatives, administrative, and sales personnel. The Company's goal is to ensure that customer's claims are given the highest consideration in order to bring the high cost of health care down to a more reasonable and affordable price. **Career Highlights:** Network Technology Analyst, American Family Insurance (1997-Present); Systems Engineer, Modern Business Technology (1996-97); Technical Support Specialist, Exton Technology Group (1995-96). **Education:** Lakeland College (Currently Enrolled); A+ Certification; Microsoft Certified Systems Engineer. **Personal Information:** Mr. Rolfsmeyer enjoys exercising, playing pool, travel and reading.

Laura A. Starr

Systems Manager
Independent Health
511 Farber Lakes Drive
Williamsville, NY 14221
(716) 635-3557
Fax: (716) 929-1027
lstar@independanthealth.com

6321

Business Information: Serving as the Systems Manager, Mrs. Starr has faithfully served with Independant Health since coming on board to the Company's team of professionals in 1997. Supervising a staff of eight programmers, she is responsible for maintaining the functionality and operational status of the systems infrastructure in order to keep lines of communications open between healthcare providers and their clients. Demonstrating strong leadership, Mrs. Starr concentrates her attention towards the maintenance of the Company's database, distribution of work assignments, and enforcement of mandatory procedures and policies. Utilizing her 13 years of experience in the technology field, she aspires to attain the position of director and expand her knowledge through continuous education as well as completing her Bachelor's degree. A major leader in providing healthcare coverage, Independant Health was established in 1980. Located in Williamsville, New York, the Company employs over 750 experienced administrative personnel who work in diversified departments, such as claims processing, physician assistance, customer service, and financial consulting. Working with over 2,500 healthcare providers, the Company gaurantees a full line of health coverage for their continuously expanding membership base. **Career Highlights:** Independent Health: Systems Manager (1997-Present), Programmer/Analyst (1993-97); Programmer/Analyst, Empire of America RCC (1988-93). **Education:** Bryant and Stratton, A.A.S. (1986). **Personal Information:** Married to Neil C. in 1986. One child: Emily R. Mrs. Starr enjoys crafts, family time and bowling.

R. Brent Tolman

Information Technology Team Leader
Premera Blue Cross
13005 West Charles Road
Nine Mile Falls, WA 99026
(509) 536-4688
btolman@ekomkey.com

6321

Business Information: Serving as an Information Technology Team Leader for Premera Blue Cross, Mr. Tolman is responsible for maintaining the Agency's software and maintaining the functionality of the operating and networking architecture. This includes creating possible problems and implementing solutions, working with a team of 12 individuals to ensure systems are properly maintained. Possessing an excellent understanding of technology, Mr. Tolman is currently concentrating on a systems program named "Interplan" for the Agency. A recipient of a number of information technology awards, he plans to continue working with the Agency, while building up his company, "e-comkey," to an e-commerce business. Established in 1933, Premera Blue Cross is a health insurance agency. An affiliate of Blue Cross Blue Shield, the Agency is a non-profit organization that provides insurance coverage for hospital visits to individuals and groups. The Agency also offers coverage for visits to doctors, dentists, and other medical professionals. Located in Nine Mile Falls, Washington, the Agency employs 2,000 people and reports estimated annual revenue of $1 billion. **Career Highlights:** Information Technology Team Leader, Premera Blue Cross (1996-Present); Medical Service Corporation: Supervisor of Technology Systems (1991-96), Supervisor of Business Systems (1986-91). **Associations & Accomplishments:** Association of Computing Machinery; HIMSS; MSHUG; Boy Scouts of America; Vice President, Credit Union Board. **Education:** Eastern Washington University: B.S. in Information Science (1985), B.A. in Business (1984), B.A. in Humanities (1984). **Personal Information:** Married to Cherie in 1989. Two children: Adrian and Hillary. Mr. Tolman enjoys chess, history, backpacking, camping and geology.

Robert A. Tuttle, Jr.

Senior National Manager for National Web Services
Kaiser Permanente
2101 Webster, 20th Floor
Oakland, CA 94612
(510) 627-2297
Fax: (707) 763-7327
tuttlebo@aol.com

6321

Business Information: Mr. Tuttle is Senior National Manager for National Web Services at Kaiser Permanente. He is responsible managing a national group of Web professional and technical experts in the deployment of a national Intranet architecture. As a solid, 23 year veteran of the technology field, Mr. Tuttle has assertively served with Kaiser Permanente in a variety of roles since the Company as Manager of Strategic Technology in 1990. Concurrently serving as the Senior Technical Consultant, he oversees the networking infrastructure, including Intranet, Internet, and Extranet. In this context, he provides Kaiser with a state-of-the-art, integrated program for physicians to share and consolidate information. Mr. Tuttle attributes his success to his service oriented and Christian lifestyle. "Learn something new everyday," is cited as his advice. Retiring in three years, obtaining his Ph.D., and becoming involved in writing, videography, teaching, and consulting serves as his future endeavors. Kaiser Permanente is the largest healthcare maintenance organization in the United States. A $7 billion company, Kaiser offers a wide range of services, including family practice, pediatrics, obstetrics and gynecology, and behavior health care. Maintaining a presence in 13 to 15 states, the Company employs a work force of more than 80,000 people. Established in 1942, Kaiser Permanente is currently headquartered in Oakland, California. **Career Highlights:** Kaiser Permanente: Senior National Manager for National Web Services (1999-Present), National Project Manager/Senior Technical Consultant (1997-99), Manager of Distributed Computer Infrastructure (1995-97), Manager of Strategic Technology (1990-95). **Associations & Accomplishments:** Institute of Electrical and Electronics Engineers; Rotary International; Gideons International. **Education:** Golden Gate University, M.B.A. (1992); University of Phoenix, B.S. in Business Administration; Diablo Valley Junior College, A.S. in Electrical Engineering. **Personal Information:** Married to Marilyn in 1966. Four children: David, Diana, James, and Melissa. Mr. Tuttle enjoys ranching, music, art, gardening, computers and writing.

Usha Vargas

Operations and Database Manager
Palm Beach County Health Care District
324 Datura Street, Suite 401
West Palm Beach, FL 33401-5417
(561) 659-1270
Fax: (561) 659-1628
uvargas@pbchcd.state.fl.us

6321

Business Information: Functioning in the dual role of Operations and Database Manager of Palm Beach County Health Care District, Ms. Vargas is responsible for day-to-day telecommunications and server operations. Before joining Palm Beach County Health Care District, Ms. Vargas served as Project Leader of Financial Systems with In Phynet Medical Management, Inc. Her history also includes a stint as Systems Analyst for St. Thomas University. As a 12 year technology professional, she also fulfills the position of Oracle Database Administrator. Combining her academic foundation and technical skills, Ms. Vargas leads a team of seven employees in maintaining the systems infrastructure. Performing as the chief hardware and software vendor liaison, coordinating resources and schedules, and overseeing time lines and assignments also fall within the realm of her responsibilities. Crediting her success to her people skills, Ms. Vargas keeps on top of technology through online management and trade journals. Eventually attaining the position of Chief Information Officer serves as one of her future goals. Palm Beach County Health Care District operates as a separate taxing district of the county that provides trauma services to Palm Beach, as well as free health care to the indigent population. Established 1989, the Agency employs a work force of more than 525 health care professional, technical, and administrative support personnel. **Career Highlights:** Operations and Database Manager, Palm Beach County Health Care District (1995-Present); Project Leader of Financial Systems, In Phynet Medical Management, Inc. (1993-95); Systems Analyst, St. Thomas University (1988-93). **Associations & Accomplishments:** International Oracle Users Group. **Education:** St. Thomas University: M.S. in Management Information Systems (1989), Bachelor's degree in Computer Science (1987). **Personal Information:** Married to Joseph in 1995. One child: Ravi Joseph. Ms. Vargas enjoys reading, being a mother and playing chess.

Monte Tak Ho Chan

Programmer/Analyst
MVP Health Plan
111 Liberty Street
Schenectady, NY 12305-1892
(518) 357-5332
mchan@mvphealthplan.com

6324

Business Information: Utilizing several years of experience in the technology industry, Mr. Chan joined MVP Health Plan in 1998. As a Programmer and Analyst, he designs and developments software programs for internal use by the Company as well as use by various clients. He performs the implementation of his customized systems, training users and providing technical support after the implementation. Mr. Chan works with a team of other skilled programmers in the performance of his duties. In addition, he also performs Web site management for the Company's Web site. Crediting his success to working smart, he remains current with changes in his field by reading industry publications and networking with other professionals on the Internet. He looks forward to a future position in project management. MVP Health Plan is a health management organization designed to reduce overall medical costs by promoting preventive health habits and prevent the excessive use of health specialists by utilizing a primary physician. Founded in 1980, approximately 1,000 individuals are employed across the nation. **Career Highlights:** Programmer/Analyst, MVP Health Plan (1998-Present); Programmer, Ebeling Associates (1997-98). **Education:** New York University at Albany: B.S. in Mathematics, B.S. in Computer Science with Applied Mathematics (1997). **Personal Information:** Mr. Chan enjoys cooking, knitting, making ice cream and bridge puzzles.

Ginger M. Chugg

Assistant Director information Services
Inland Northwest Health Services
P.O. Box 248
Spokane, WA 99210-0248
(509) 473-6766
Fax: (509) 473-6183
chugg@inhs.org

6324

Business Information: Utilizing more than 15 years of experience in the field of information technology, Ms. Chugg serves as the Assistant Director of Information Services. She supervises a staff of 15 professionals, directing the client/server and contract services in implementing LAN and WAN systems at the regional, affiliate, and rural healthcare partners' offices. These systems interface with the Company's system for the Foundation Meditech HIS System. Ms. Chugg is also involved in the strategic planning and development of technology from network integration to software implementation. As a member of the INHS executive team, she credits her current career success to being flexible, listening, and her analytical skills. She is continually striving to advance to higher positions of managerial responsibility. She is diligently working to become the information system director in the short-term and a chief information officer in the long-term. Inland Northwest Health Services is engaged in the growing industry of healthcare management. The Company is the result of a collaborative healthcare effort between two hospitals, Sacred Heart Medical Center, a Sister's of Providence organization, and Empire Health Services. Each of the two hospitals, a 823-bed facility and a 350-bed facility respectively, is managed independently and is very competitive with the other as well as 28 rural hospitals and 41 clinics. A staff of 1,100 administrative and medical personnel is employed to attend to all aspects of operations for INHS. INHS was established in 1994. **Career Highlights:** Inland Northwest Health Services: Assistant Director of Information Services (1999-Present), Team Manager (1996-99); Regional Director of information Systems, Healthtrust, Inc. (1990-92); Operator/Programmer, Bannock Hospital (1986-90). **Associations & Accomplishments:** Association For Domestic Violence Crisis Hotline; Big Brothers, Big Sisters; National Association of Female Executives; Data Processing Managers Association. **Education:** Idaho State University, Master's degree in Computer Information Systems (In Progress), B.S. (1989).

Terrance J. Farris

Project Manager
OSF Healthcare Systems
800 Northeast Glen Oak Avenue
Peoria, IL 61603-3200
(309) 655-4816
terry.farris@osfhealthcare.org

6324

Business Information: Mr. Farris was recruited to OSF Healthcare Systems as Information Systems Consultant in 1989. After serving in various positions, he was promoted to the position of Project Manager in 1996. Currently, he is responsible for selecting and implementing complex computer systems throughout the Company. In his capacity, Mr. Farris is assigned to Hipaa legislation. In addition to providing status reports and budget analysis, he also worked hard to prepare the systems infrastructure for the year 2000 conversion. A savvy technical expert, he also manages all outside consulting. Highlights for Mr. Farris include making the Company Y2K compliant and his growth within the OSF Healthcare Systems' hierarchy. His success is attributed to his team's commitment to excellence, the opportunities afforded to him by the Company, and his supportive wife. OSF Healthcare Systems provides quality healthcare through their six accute care hospitals. In addition, they also provide continuous care services, in home nursing, and medical equipment sales and rentals. They have an HMO division and a medical group division. With 200 physicians they are able to provide excellent primary care and services for their patients. Established in 1876, OSF Healthcare Systems employs a staff of over 10,000 healthcare providers and administrators. **Career Highlights:** OSF Healthcare Systems: Project Manager (1996-Present), Senior Information Systems Consultant (1993-96), Information Systems Consultant (1989-93). **Associations & Accomplishments:** Healthcare Financial Management Association. **Education:** Illinois State University, B.S. (1987). **Personal Information:** Married to Nancy in 1998. Two children: T. J. and Tyler.

Karen E. Henry

UNIX Administrator
Eastern Health System, Inc.
50 Medical Park East Drive
Birmingham, AL 35235-3335
(205) 838-6320
kraybur@bellsouth.net

6324

Business Information: Serving as UNIX Administrator of Eastern Health System, Inc., Mrs. Henry is responsible for all management aspects of day-to-day UNIX administration. At the present moment, she exercises oversight of system services and ensures networks remain functional and fully operational. Accumulating 10 years of experience and with a strong educational background, Mrs. Henry manages upgrade and troubleshooting services for financial and clinical systems and databases. Directing and participating in the analysis, acquisition, installation, modification, configuration, support, and tracking of operating systems, databases, utilities, software, and hardware also falls within the realm of Mrs. Henry's responsibilities. Her long-term goals include achieving her MIS Certification, attaining her B.S. in Psychology, and moving into upper level management as Chief Information Officer. Mrs. Henry's greatest professional accomplishment centers on her work at Eastern Health System, Inc. Eastern Health System, Inc. provides an extensive array of health care services to patients. The Corporation services three hospitals, a variety of nursing homes, and 300 doctors' offices. Established in 1960, Eastern Health System, Inc. employs over 2,000 personnel. **Career Highlights:** UNIX Administrator, Eastern Health System, Inc. (Present); Consultant Enterprise Services, HBOC (1998); Clinical System Specialist, Eastern Health Systems, Inc. (1995-98); Registered Nurse, Medical Center East (1993-95); WC/EMT, DePaul Hospital (1988-92). **Associations & Accomplishments:** Home Healthcare, University of Alabama; National Association of Orthopedic Nurses; System Redesign Teams to include Documentation, Automation & Technology, Implementation, and Steering Committee (1995-98); Member of the Project Management Institute. **Education:** University of St. Francis, M.B.A. (In Progress); University of New York, B.S. (1999); Regents College, B.S. in Nursing (1999); Jefferson State University, A.S. (1993); Laramie County Community College: Practical Nursing Certificate (1992), Associate's degree in Criminal Justice (1986); Auburn University, Project Management Certification (2000); State of Wyoming, Emergency Medical Technician Certification; PICC Certification; BLS Instructor Certification. **Personal Information:** Mrs. Henry enjoys studying, reading and participating in online courses over the Internet.

Craig M. Hunter

Manager of Information Systems
Vancouver/Richmond Health Port
1060 8th Avenue West
Vancouver, British Columbia, Canada V6H 1C4
(604) 730-7614
Fax: (604) 734-7897
chunter@urhb.bc.ca

6324

Business Information: Serving as Manager of Information Systems of Vancouver/Richmond Health Port, Mr. Hunter is charged with maintaining all computer network systems within this large Hospital. He is responsible for all computer needs including diagnostics, setup, upgrades, and maintenance. Specializing in systems infrastructure, Mr. Hunter is recognized for designing, installing, and implementing the current high speed Hospital network. This network is designed to optimize organizational processes and patient record accuracy. Mr. Hunter plans to complete three current integration projects, then initiate the design and construction of system upgrades for future infrastructure expansion. His career success is attributed to his ability to listen and learn as well as tackle new challenges and deliver results. "Make sure you understand how the business works," is cited as his advice. Vancouver/Richmond Health Port provides health care from a hospital servicing the community of Vancouver, British Columbia. This health care facility specializes in long term care for HMO patients as well as emergency, trauma, oncology, and dialysis services. Establishing itself as an esteemed medical facility since its founding, Vancouver/Richmond Health Port is continuing to provide top quality diagnostic and treatment services, and plans to expand its facilities to accomodate increased patient influx and technological advances. **Career Highlights:** Manager of Information Systems, Vancouver/Richmond Health Port (1996-Present); Manager of Development, MDS-Metro (1993-96); Manager of Management Information Systems, Rlutow (1987-93); Manager of Systems Program, Woodwards (1984-87). **Associations & Accomplishments:** C.I.P.S. **Education:** City University, M.B.A. (1993); University of British Columbia, B.Sc. (1976). **Personal Information:** Married in 1978.

Michael R. McGuire

Senior Software Developer
Kaiser Health Plan
25 North Via Monte, #LN2N
Walnut Creek, CA 94598-2599
(925) 926-3210
Fax: (925) 926-3890
michael.mcguire@kp.org

6324

Business Information: Mr. McGuire serves in the position of Senior Software Developer of Kaiser Health Plan. He works directly with management and users to analyze, specify, design, and develop state-of-the-art patient care software applications. A savvy, 33 year professional, he is also the principal designer of patient related operating and database management systems software. Programming and conducing business and systems analysis, design, evaluation, testing, and implementation of patient automated processes also fall within the realm of Mr. McGuire's responsibilities. His career highlights include development of an advanced automated system for patient appointments. Attributing his success to his supportive family and friends, Mr. McGuire's future goals include automating patient medical records and becoming certified in Web IP. Being open minded and having interest in different areas are keys to his success. Kaiser Health Plan is a health maintenance organization specializing in medical care. The largest nonprofit business of its kind in the United States, Kaiser strives to guarantee the most effective medical coverage for every patient. Created 45 years ago, the Company was designed to protect undercovered patrons of society by providing the necessary medical coverage. **Career Highlights:** Senior Software Developer, Kaiser Health Plan (1982-Present); Software Engineer, Systems Development Corporation (1974-80); Technical Consultant, MITRE Corporation (1971-74). **Associations & Accomplishments:** Association of Computing Machinery; Institute of Electrical and Electronics Engineers. **Education:** University of California at Santa Cruz; Pennsylvania State University, M.S. in Computer Science (1970); University of California at Davis, B.A. (1967). **Personal Information:** Married to Bonnie Chin. Mr. McGuire enjoys automating medical records and universal patient records.

Debora L. Meier
Senior Programmer/Analyst
Family Health Systems
2941 Fish Hatchery Road #120
Madison, WI 53713-3155
(608) 251-4156
deb_meier@ghc-hmo.com

6324

Business Information: As the Senior Programmer and Analyst for the Family Health Services, Ms. Meier works with management and users to analyze, specify, and design cutting edge solutions for the family health technical system. Possessing an excellent understanding of technology, Ms. Meier is responsible for all aspects of computer programming and data analysis as well as teaching programming skills and updating systems programs. Directing and participating in the analysis, design, evaluation, testing, implementation, and support of operating systems, LAN/WAN, and Internet/Intranet related computer systems also fall within the realm of Ms. Meier's responsibilities. Beginning with the Company as a programmer and analyst in 1987, she has exhibited exemplary effort and skill in his field. In the future, Ms. Meier would like to continue in the health care industry and grow with the Company. Established in 1976, the Family Health Systems operates as a health maintenance organization. Located in Madison, Wisconsin, Family Health Systems is manned by over 550 health care professionals and administrators. The Family Health Systems specifically performs administrative work for its clientele. **Career Highlights:** Family Health Systems: Senior Programmer/Analyst (1996-Present), Programmer/Analyst (1987-96); Programmer/Analyst, Foremost Guaranty (1985-87). **Associations & Accomplishments:** Madison AS/400 User's Group. **Education:** Northern Wisconsin Technical College at Green Bay, Associate's degree (1976). **Personal Information:** Ms. Meier enjoys collecting stamps, crafts, reading and walking.

Leo H. Meyer
Senior Consulting Systems Programmer
Humana Inc.
708 Magazine Steet
Louisville, KY 40203-2043
(502) 580-4062
Fax: (502) 491-9356
lmeyer@humana.com

6324

Business Information: Continually to learn new, emerging technologies, Mr. Meyer currently serves as Senior Consulting Systems Programmer for Humana Inc. In his capacity, he is the chief liaison between technical servers and 480 developers. He is responsible for all monitors, systems compatibility and tuning, and maintaining the systems infrastructure's functionality and operational status. A successful, 22 year veteran and technical lead, Mr. Meyer heads the front end of major projects and provides cutting edge methodologies and recommendations. An expert architecture in systems analysis, he is credited with the development of the automated overhead conveyor program for IBM, the request respond server which bridged Honeywell and IBM systems, and the network compression for special needs at GE reducing the network traffic by 87 percent. Mr. Meyer looks forward to remaining in his current position and staying on top of technology. Created in 1965, Humana Inc. is in the insurance arena. Specializing in health insurance and HMOs, the Corporation is currently developing a health business via the Internet, with hopes of reaching a more national market. Employing 17,000 individuals, Humana Inc. estimates annual revenues at $8 billion. **Career Highlights:** Senior Consulting Systems Programmer, Humana Inc. (1990-Present); Systems Programmer/Project Manager, General Electric (1986-90); Project Manager, IBM (1984-86). **Associations & Accomplishments:** Computer Measurement Group; St. Barnabas Church; Louisville Ski Club; Derby Parrot Heads (Jimmy Buffet Fan Club). **Education:** University of Louisanna-Speed Scientific (1978). **Personal Information:** Married to Cheryl in 1994. Six children: Tricia, Thomas, Shannon, Jacob, Katie, and Paul.

Mr. Meyer enjoys boating, snow boarding, snow skiing and water sports.

David E. Rose
Manager of Network Services
Physicians Health Plan
8101 West Jefferson Boulevard
Fort Wayne, IN 46804
(219) 432-6690
Fax: (219) 432-0493
drose@phpni.com

6324

Business Information: Demonstrating strong leadership qualities and expertise in the information technology field, Mr. Rose serves as Manager of Network Services for Physicians Health Plan. Utilizing over 22 years of occupational experience, he is responsible for the management and maintenance of systems software for the Institution. Concurrently he maintains systems performance, table files, queries data, and reports on request. In addition, Mr. Rose is tasked with performing diagnostic tests and performs system upgrades when needed. He has enjoyed tremendous occupational success in his current position with Physicians Health Plan, and aspires to attain the position of Management Information Systems Director in the future. Physicians Health Plan is a managed health-care organization serving the northeast region of Indiana. Centrally located in the city of Fort Wayne, the Organization provides affordable, quality healthcare to over 60,000 healthcare plan members through emergency and trauma centers, a heart center, home services, and other specialized facilities. Currently employing 110 healthcare professionals, the Organization plans to continue offering the best quality care possible to patients. **Career Highlights:** Manager of Network Services, Physicians Health Plan (1998-Present); Hardware and Software Support Specialist, PHD, Inc. (1992-98); DEC Systems Administrator, Tokheim Corporation (1988-92); Customer Service Engineer, Schlumberger Technologies (1985-88). **Education:** ITT Technical Institute, Associate's Degree (1978). **Personal Information:** Married to Cynthia A. in 1980. Two children: Shannon E. and Braden E. Mr. Rose enjoys reading.

Ron R. Sutton
Information Technology Manager
Lifemark Corporation
1 Virginia Avenue #350
Indianapolis, IN 46204
(317) 359-7501

6324

Business Information: In his role as Information Techology Manager of Lifemark Corporation, Mr. Sutton handles a variety of responsibilities and technical tasks. Maintaining all computers and telephones, he demonstrates adept ability as he solves challenging situations with a creative approach. He supervises the employees within four different divisions: data analysis, developmental group, support group, and telecommunications, lending his knowledge and insight to the development of improved operational policies and procedures. Internally recognized for impressive achievements while in his position, Mr. Sutton cites the secret to his success as his associations with committed, smart, and goal oriented people. Enjoying the challenges of the industry, he aspires to the position of Chief Information Officer. His advice is "do a self assessment to see if you'll be happy with your choice." Lifemark Corporation is the largest managed health care provider in Indiana. Headquartered in Phoenix, Arizona, the Corporation employs 125 people at the Indianapolis, Indiana location. Recent reports estimate annual revenues to exceed $10 million for the Corporation that was voted "best managed care provider in the state" by benefit recipients. **Career Highlights:** Information Technology Manager, Lifemark Corporation (1996-Present); LAN Administrator/Analyst, Sensormatic Electronics (1985-96); Computer Manager, Jenn-Air Corporation (1978-85). **Associations & Accomplishments:** Association for System Management of Central Indiana. **Education:** Indiana University, B.A. (1971); Georgia Institute of Technology. **Personal Information:** Mr. Sutton enjoys radio news and sports.

Crissy M. Willis
Systems Analyst
Commonwealth Health Corporation
800 Park Street
Bowling Green, KY 42101
(270) 796-3524
Fax: (270) 796-2107
cmwillis@chc.net

6324

Business Information: As Systems Analyst of Commonwealth Health Corporation, Mrs. Willis handles various technical aspects of daily operations. On a regular

basis, she investigates and evaluates current systems, then designs solutions and purchases necessary equipment. Coordinating technical procedures with overall operations, she implements, installs, and maintains new software packages for the Corporation. Lending her impressive knowledge and guidance to staff, she offers instruction and guidance on the operation of systems. Mrs. Willis uses information technology to improve the business processes of the Corporation, believing her passion for the field is what drives her to succeed. She currently has plans to build up the department by hiring more staff. Commonwealth Health Corporation is the parent company of the subsidary, Center Care. Center Care contracts with physicans throughout Kentucky and Tennessee to join various networks, then works with employers to utilize these networks. Headquartered in Bowling Green, Kentucky, the Corporation employs 2,500 people. Commonwealth Health Corporation is the parent company of the subsidary center care contracts with physicians throughout Kentucky and Tennessee to join various networks and works with employers to utilize these networks. Headquartered in Bowling Green, Kentucky, the Corporation employs 2,500 people. **Career Highlights:** Systems Analyst, Commonwealth Health Corporation (1997-Present); Computer Instructor, GM Corvette Plant (1997); Testing Specialist, West Telemarketing (1989-91). **Associations & Accomplishments:** Association of Information Technology Professionals; Beta Gamma Sigma Honor Society; Golden Key Honor Society. **Education:** Western Kentucky University, B.S. (1997). **Personal Information:** Married to Kevin in 1997. Three children: Lindsay, Luke, and Logan. Mrs. Willis enjoys being a missionary leader at church, golf and family time.

P. Peter Anniko
Programmer/Analyst
Fidelity & Deposit Company of Maryland
3800 Erdman Avenue
Baltimore, MD 21213-2026
(410) 659-3759
proosit@yahoo.com

6331

Business Information: Mr. Anniko serves the role of Programmer/Analyst at the Fidelity and Deposit Company of Maryland. Utilizing his extensive education and practical work experience, he handles programming for both mainframe operating systems and personal computers. On a regular basis, he must evaluate current systems and maintain or modify equipment, platforms, and/or applications as he sees fit. He is responsible for the design of a database that increases the efficiency and accuracy of processing of customer information for insurance claims and policies. Citing persistence as the key to his success, Mr. Anniko intends to continue in his current role as he shifts his career focus to include the design and engineer of software applications. The Fidelity and Deposit Company of Maryland was established in 1896 and is currently a subsidiary of the Zurich Insurance Company. Headquartered in Baltimore, Maryland, the national company maintains facilities throughout the United States offering many lines of commercial insurance. **Career Highlights:** Programmer/Analyst, Fidelity & Deposit Company of Maryland (1997-Present); Programmer/Analyst, CheckFree Corporation (1994-97); Senior Programmer/Analyst, VIPS Inc. (1988-94). **Associations & Accomplishments:** Association of Computing Machinery. **Education:** Towson University, B.S. in Computer Science (1998). **Personal Information:** Mr. Anniko enjoys computer security, virology and cryptozoology.

Brian E. Clark
Director of Enterprise Network Services
The Zenith
1390 Main Street
Sarasota, FL 34236-5687
(941) 906-5326
Fax: (941) 362-6034
bclark@thezenith.com

6331

Business Information: Serving in the position of Director of Enterprise Network Services of The Zenith, Mr. Clark oversees the Company's networking environment and LAN/WAN. A savvy, 14 year technology expert, he maintains the entire systems infrastructure to include servers, workstations, and Internet access for the entire Company. Ensuring the efficiency of 28 employees placed in his charge, Mr. Clark utilizes his hands on experience in the field to keeping the networks fully functional and operational. Proud of his ability to build networks from the ground up, he has accomplished this feat of for three companies. Satified at The Zenith, Mr. Clark would like to remain in his current position and take the Company to the next level. Attributing his success to dedication and his ability to think outside the box and deliver results, Mr. Clark's advice is "take all the free training you can." An insurance company headquartered in Los Angeles, California, The Zenith was established in 1983. Dealing mainly with workers' compensation, the Company has locations in 25 states of the United States. Processing applications for insurance, accepting/denying, reviewing cases and ordering investigations in questionable cases, and payout of policies are functions of The Zenith. Presently, the Company employs a 1,500 professional, technical, and administrative support staff. **Career Highlights:** Director of Enterprise Network Services, The Zenith (1994-Present); Network Manager, FCCI Insurance (1989-94); Field Service Engineer, American PC Services (1987-89). **Associations & Accomplishments:** Nortel User Group. **Education:** Electronic Technical Institute, B.S. in Electronic Engineering (1986). **Personal Information:** Married to Carrie in 1994. One child: Hunter. Mr. Clark enjoys hunting, fishing and woodworking.

Ken W. Gilliam
Technical Analyst
State Farm Insurance
Rural Route 3, Box 312
Bloomington, IL 61604
(309) 735-5490
marino13@davesworld.net

6331

Business Information: As Technical Analyst of State Farm Insurance, Mr. Gilliam provides support for network services. Monitoring the Enterprise system, he lends his expertise to the maintenance of the WAN used by the Company. On a regular basis, he must evaluate the needs of the telecommunications capabilities and determine which changes, uprgrades, or improvements must be made to continue optimal performance. Continually attending technical seminars and courses and reading magazines, Mr. Gilliam is up-to-date on all aspects of his position and the advances within his industry. Crediting his success to his ability to take planned risks, he intends to continue in his current capacity while facilitating company growth. State Farm Insurance provides all lines of insurance to residential and commercial customers throughout the United States and Canada. Established in 1922, the Company employs over 76,500 trained employees to serve their diverse clientele. **Career Highlights:** Technical Analyst, State Farm Insurance (1999-Present); Network Administrator, Ruppman (1997-99); Systems Analyst, Chestut Health Systems. **Education:** Southern Illinois University at Carbondale, B.S. in Business Administration with minor in Computer Science (1994); Microsoft Certified Systems Engineer. **Personal Information:** Married to Cindy in 1995.

Thomas John Kosco
Director
American Reinsurance
555 College Road East
Princeton, NJ 08540-4784
(609) 243-4784
Fax: (609) 951-8288
tkosco@amre.com

6331

Business Information: Serving as American Reinsurance's Director, Mr. Kosco is in charge of the technical group of American Reinsurance Brokers and the Client Services Technical Account Manager for Munich American Global Services. In this capacity, he acts as a representative between the companies and the IT Division. Demonstrating his knowledge of the industry, Mr. Kosco evaluates technical needs, and develops and implements solutions in a timely, effective manner. Directing employees, he strives to create open lines of communications to foster a sense of teamwork among his staff. Internally recognized for his accomplishments and vision in many information technology projects involving company mergers, Y2K projects, system conversions, evaluation of support services, application rennovations, and EDI, he also assumed responsibility for a technical department a short time after starting with the Company. In the future, Mr. Kosco aspires to be entrusted with the supervision of additional departments to better utilize his ongoing education. A member of the Munich Re Group, American Reinsurance is one of the leading writers of property and casualty reinsurance in the United States. Established in 1917, the Company provides treaty facultative reinsurance and related services to other insurance companies. Concerned with domestic and international business, American Reinsurance employs over 2,000 nationwide. **Career Highlights:** American Reinsurance: Director (1998-Present), Technical Manager (1988-98); Electronic Associates, Inc.: Manager of MIS (1986-87), Technical Manager (1984-86). **Associations & Accomplishments:** COMMON User Group; Delaware Valley Computer Users Group; IBM PartnerWorld for Developers; Explorer Advisor, Boy Scouts of America. **Education:** Trenton State University, B.S., Summa Cum Laude (1983). **Personal Information:** Married to Anna Arrambide in 1975. Two children: Jaclyn and Carolyn. Mr. Kosco enjoys wood working, gardening and wine making.

Brian Pulcine
Oracle Database Administrator
Parkway Insurance
12 Sapphire Lane
Franklin Park, NJ 08823
(908) 704-9751
Fax: (908) 429-3856
bpulcine@parkway.com

6331

Business Information: As Oracle Database Administrator for Parkway Insurance, Mr. Pulcine is responsible for the administration of the Agency's network infrastructure, database design and administration, and Web site design and creation. Possessing an excellent understanding of technology, Mr. Pulcine maintains the functionality of the NT/Unix administration systems and provides management and support for the network operations department. Controlling data resources, using tools to fine tune computers, peripherals, and accessories, and resolving technical difficulties as well as ensuring data security and integrity also fall within the realm of Mr. Pulcine's responsibilities. With more than seven years of technology experience, Mr. Pulcine utilizes his superior knowledge and talents to take the steps necessary to obtain his Oracle certification, while simultaneously working to attain his M.B.A. degree. Parkway Insurance engages in the provision of auto insurance for New Jersey residents. Also, the Agency offers other services for rental and homeowners insurance. Established in 1991, the Agency operates out of a number of regional locations and functions under the direction and full support of more than 90 professionals who facilitate smooth business operations. **Career Highlights:** Database Administrator, Parkway Insurance (1996-Present); Systems Technician, Information Incorporated (1994-96). **Associations & Accomplishments:** New Jersey Linux Users Group; New Jersey Oracle Users Group. **Education:** New Jersey Institute of Technology, B.S. in Computer Science (1993). **Personal Information:** Married to Alicia in 1998. One child: Olivia. Mr. Pulcine enjoys fitness and motorcycles.

Alvina C. Rogers
Network Administrator
American Agrisurance
535 West Broadway
Council Bluffs, IA 51503
(712) 325-5323
Fax: (712) 325-5359
arogers@amag.com

6331

Business Information: Providing her skilled services as Network Administrator for American Agrisurance, Ms. Rogers is an integral part of the Company's Information Technology Systems team. In her capacity, she is in charge of hardware and software installation and maintenance as well as administrating the local area network and the wide area network, consisting of 35 servers. Overseeing the individual user network setup, she administrates their e-mail functions as well. As a 10 year information technology professional, Ms. Rogers offers her technical expertise to internal staff, insurance agents, and local underwriters. She also provides group training for inhouse users. Citing her drive and extensive knowledge as the reason for her success, she looks forward to gaining her certification as a Microsoft Systems Certified Engineer+Internet. Ms. Rogers' success reflects her ability to think outside the box, produce results, and aggressively tackle new challenges. Affiliated with the international Acceptance Insurance Companies, American Agrisurance is the third largest crop insurance company in the world today. The Company insures farmers throughout the United States and have developed several insurance lines which have been approved by the federal government. **Career Highlights:** American Agrisurance: Network Administrator (1998-Present), Systems Technician (1994-98); Systems Manager, Panhandle Corporation (1988-94). **Associations & Accomplishments:** Christian Motorcycles Association. **Education:** Laraine County Community College, A.A. (1988).

Jeffrey Lawrence Romel
Consultant
The Hartford
1 Hartford Plaza NP-5-5
Hartford, CT 06115-1707
(860) 547-6667
Fax: (860) 547-5083
jromel@thehartford.com

6331

Business Information: Mr. Romel has worked in the information technology field since 1979. He has been a Systems Analyst and Senior Systems Analyst/Consultant for The Hartford Financial Services Company since 1986. He now consults for The Hartford Technology Services Company, LLC, a wholly owned IT subsidiary of The Hartford. He previously worked for the Travelers Insurance Companies and for the State of Connecticut. Mr. Romel possesses a long track record of delivering results by communicating effectively,

paying close attention to technical details, and solving problems and challenges with a positive, can-do attitude. His present position principally involves the design, development, and support of a sophisticated Smalltalk server application that handles complex insurance transactions via the Internet. Having worked extensively with object oriented technologies since 1995, he is able to effectively deploy leading edge enhancements to the applications he supports. His future consulting goals include continuing to mentor others, modernizing and developing applications and eventually attaining the position of Architect. Founded in 1810 as a fire insurer, The Hartford has become one of the most trusted financial services companies in the world. Operating on an international level, the Company specializes in providing financial services and building investment portfolios for individuals, organizations, and major corporations. The Company is located in Hartford, Connecticut and employs over 20,000 persons globally. **Career Highlights:** Consultant, The Hartford (1995-Present); ITT Hartford: Senior Systems Analyst (1990), Systems Analyst (1986). **Associations & Accomplishments:** Connecticut OO Users Group; Former member of the Focus Users Group of New England; Supporter of Connecticut Public Television and Radio. **Education:** Management degree program (In Progress); Manchester Community College, A.S. in Data Processing; Computer Processing Institute, Certificate in COBOL Programming; Dozens of OJT courses and seminars; Continuous Learning. **Personal Information:** Mr. Romel enjoys family and friends, most outdoor activities, camping, reading, music, augmenting his career skills and his dog and cat.

Robert Stanley Urbanowicz
Help Desk/Assistant to Network Administrator
Parkway Insurance
P.O. Box 6880, 1200 East Route 22
Bridgewater, NJ 08807
(908) 725-1400
rurbanou@earthlink.net

6331

Business Information: Highly recruited to Parkway Insurance in August 1999, Mr. Urbanowicz serves in a dual role of Help Desk and Assistant to Network Administrator. He works with users and management to analyze, specify, and design solutions to solve systems problems and harness more of the computer's power. Before joining Parkway Insurance, Mr. Urbanowicz served as Sale Support Specialist for R H Macy's/Macy's East. He concurrently fills the role of Consultant for both Bristol Meyers Squibb and Woodrow Wilson Fellowship Foundation. In addition to his new duties with Parkway, Mr. Urbanowicz has been an entrepreneur since the age of 18 and provides consulting in database development on the side. Eventually attaining the position of Network Administrator and moving to a higher management level in the information technology realm serves as his future endeavors. Mr. Urbanowicz's success reflects his positive attitude and his resiliency. **Career Highlights:** Help Desk/Assistant to Network Administrator, Parkway Insurance (1999-Present); Sales Support, R H Macy's/Macy's East (1993-99); Consultant, Bristol Meyers Squibb (1999-Present); Consultant, Woodrow Wilson Fellowship Foundation (1999-Present). **Associations & Accomplishments:** Association of Internet Professionals; Kappa Delta Rho Alumni Association; Livingston College Alumni Association. **Education:** Rutgers University, B.A. (In Progress) (1999); Raritan Valley Community College: A.S.in Management Information Systems, A.A.S. in Computer Networking. **Personal Information:** Mr. Urbanowicz enjoys rock climbing and radio control racing and being a Tamiya enthusiast.

Terry Lanier Williams
Data Processing Specialist
Palisades Safety & Insurance Management
5 Marine View Plaza, Suite 102
Hoboken, NJ 07030-5722
(201) 217-7926

6331

Business Information: As Data Processing Specialist of Palisades Safety & Insurance Management, Mr. Williams is responsible for data processing including installation, upgrades, maintenance, and repairs of all personal computers. He conducts inventory, troubleshoots hardware and software, and assists in e-mail migration. Years of experience in the technological field has enabled Mr. Williams to effectively fulfill his job obligations and assist top management in resolving technical problems that may effect the profitability of Palisades Safety and Insurance Management. His position requires that he oversee various areas of the business from systems integration to small business implementation of networks. Mr. Williams plans to become MCSE certified and have the ability to become more involved in network implementation. His fundamental goal is to utilize his experience in the field to establish his own consulting business. Palisades Safety & Insurance Management is an automobile insurance provider established in 1992. A staff of 200 skilled individuals lend their expertise in various areas of the business and keep abreast on new developments in the field. The Company currently provides services to drivers of the state of Massachusetts and New Jersey. **Career Highlights:** Data Processing Specialist, Palisades Safety & Insurance Management (1999-Present); Systems Engineer, Brisbane Management (1997-99). **Education:** Chubb Institute, Diploma (1998); Lincoln University. **Personal Information:** Mr. Williams enjoys bowling, softball and track and field.

Edward Alton Wilson

Technical Analyst 3
State of Connecticut Workers Compensation
21 Oak Street, Floor 4
Hartford, CT 06106
(860) 493-1528
Fax: (860) 247-1361
edward.wilson@po.state.ct.us

6331

Business Information: Serving as Technical Analyst 3 for the State of Connecticut Workers Compensation, Mr. Wilson oversees database administration (Sybase), network management (Novell 5.0), and WAN and Internet support (Cisco systems). With a full understanding of technological issues and years of education and experience, Mr. Wilson has acquired the skills necessary to effectively fulfill his job obligations. Dedicated to the success of State of Connecticut Workers Compensation, he keeps abreast of new developments in the field and incorporates pertinent information into his daily duties. A successful, 13 year veteran, Mr. Wilson believes that the key to success is to never stop learning. State of Connecticut Workers Compensation is an oversight commission functioning as a judiciary between claimants and the insurance industry. Approximately 220 people lend their expertise in various areas of the operation. There are nine locations available to provide assistance. **Career Highlights:** Technical Analyst 3, State of Connecticut Workers Compensation (1990-Present); Programmer Analyst, SCAN Optics Inc. (1988-89); Senior Programmer, Sigma Software Inc. (1986-87); Systems Analyst, Bank of Hartford (1983-85). **Associations & Accomplishments:** Glastonbury Yacht Club. **Education:** Computer Processing Institute: Associate's degree in Programming (1990), Computer Operations degree (1983). **Personal Information:** Married to Charlotte E. in 1995. Mr. Wilson enjoys music and is a musician.

Pedro P. Perez

Project Manager
Cross Country Home Service
7256 Northwest 61st Terrace
Parkland, FL 33067
(954) 845-2356
Fax: (954) 845-2264
pperez@cchs.com

6351

Business Information: Mr. Perez serves as the Project Manager of Cross Country Home Services. In his role, he is responsible for the development and deployment of cutting edge business applications, data warehouse software, and systems infrastructure hardware. Possessing an excellent understanding of his field, Mr. Perez also works closely with management and systems users to analyze, specify, and design solutions and requirements for the enhancement of the systems functions. Coordinating strategic resources, time lines, schedules, and assignments as well as performing maintenance and upgrades, teaching and training employees and staff, and deployment of new technologies also fall within the scope of Mr. Perez's responsibilities. Maintaining a competitive edge, he plans on designing new business applications, such as an employment investment system; and becoming a speaker for the Oracle user groups. "Ensure you have a good background in systems management and always look for the cause of a problem," is cited as his advice. Established in 1980, Cross Country Home Services is a provider of service for home warranties. The Company honors home service contracts and home assistance programs. Over 250 skilled technicians and engineers work with the Company to generate annual sales of more than $60 million. **Career Highlights:** Project Manager, Cross Country Home Service (1999-Present); Team Leader, NCCJ (1994-99); Senior Programmer, Prudential Health Care (1997). **Education:** Florida Atlantic University, M.B.A. (1999); University of Simon Bolivar, Computer Engineer (1987). **Personal Information:** One child: Diana. Mr. Perez enjoys tennis.

Robert W. Brown

Manager of Data Services
Employers Unity
7903 Allison Way
Arvada, CO 80005
(303) 424-7004
Fax: (303) 423-4374
b.brown@empunity.com

6371

Business Information: As Manager of Data Services, Mr. Brown has been servicing the technological needs of Employers Unity since joining the Company in 1999. Incorporating the latest technologies, he manages specialized imaging, data entry, and PC maintenance departments. Responsible for the organization of analytic reports, he performs complete evaluations of his department implementing specific procedures and policies where needed. Highly regarded, he posssesses superior talents and an excellent understanding of technology. Mr. Brown anticipates his promotion to Vice President as a result of his continuing efforts to increase his skills through training and professional development activities. Established in 1977, Employers Unity is dedicated to providing unemployment benefits to businesses, and representation of clients at hearings. Located in Arvada, Colorado, the Company offers specialized cost analysis and tax rates to a national client base. Branching out from 14 offices across the country, the Company is dedicated to servicing the needs of a continually expanding clientele. **Career Highlights:** Manager of Data Services, Employers Unity (1996-Present); Office Manager, Sacramento Denta Centers (1995-96); United States Air Force: Dental Superintendent, McClellan Air Force Base (1990-95), Dental Superintendent, Okinawa, Japan (1986-90). **Associations & Accomplishments:** Air Force Sergeants Association; Rocky Mountain Oldsmobile Club. **Education:** Executrain, Microsoft Certified Systems Engineer Certification (1999); Community College of the Air Force, Associate's degree in Dental Assisting (1986). **Personal Information:** Two children: Rick and Irene. Mr. Brown enjoys restoring old Oldsmobiles.

Bill Burchfield

Development Manager
Police and Firemen's Disability
140 East Town Street
Columbus, OH 43215-5125
(614) 628-8242
Fax: (614) 564-1545
wburchfield@pfdpf.org

6371

Business Information: Mr. Burchfield functions as Development Manager for Police and Firemen's Disability. He plans and oversees research, evaluation, and integration of new technology into the existing systems infrastructure. Befor joining the Agency, Mr. Burchfield served as a Consultant with Affiliated Resource Group. His background also includes a stint with Liqui-Box as both Senior Programmer and Programmer. An eight year expert, he works closely with users and management to analyze, specify, and design business applications, harnessing more of the computer's power. Responsible for development of software programs, he designs new programs to assist in tracking payments and maintain an extensive database of personal files. Mr. Burchfield's highlight is the development of a cutting edge contribution processing system. Looking to the 21st Century, he plans to advance his Windows development skills and convert all computers within the the Agency's office to Windows. Police and Firemen's Disability provides financial services to the police officers and firefighters across the United States. Established in 1969, the Ohio branch of the Agency monitors the dispersement and allocation of payments for the retired and injured-on-the-job workers. Over 140 employees work together to control the funds and ensure every customer receives the payments they are elligible for. **Career Highlights:** Development Manager, Police and Firemen's Disability (1995-Present); Consultant, Affiliated Resource Group (1995); Liqui-Box: Senior Programmer (1994-94), Programmer (1992-93). **Associations & Accomplishments:** Ohio State University Alumni Association; Homeless Family Foundation. **Education:** Ohio State University, B.S. in Business Administration (1991). **Personal Information:** Married to Elaine in 1995. Mr. Burchfield enjoys home improvement.

Dave P. Luiz

System Software Specialist 1
Health & Welfare Agency
1651 Alhambra Boulevard
Sacramento, CA 95816-7092
(916) 739-7703
Fax: (916) 739-7771
dluiz@hwdc.state.ca.us

6371

Business Information: Functioning in the role of System Software Specialist 1 with the Health & Welfare Agency, Mr. Luiz is responsible for application programming, UNIX system administration, network management, and DNS administration. Before joining the Health & Welfare Agency as a Programmer, Mr. Luiz served as a Programmer for the Department of Health Services. As a technology professional, he is in charge of design, development, and implementation of advanced software applications, as well as tuning software tools to improve systems and network performance. Working on a team of twenty-five professional and technical experts, Mr. Luiz supervises and guides two employees in conducting research and development of new cutting edge applications. Crediting his success to his mother, his success reflects his ability to think out-of-the-box and take on new challenges. His goals include becoming a Consultant and Application Developer in Web design. Owned by the state of California, Health & Welfare Agency is the largest information technology data collection center in the United States. Regional in scope, the Agency operates over 2,800 office locations in the region. Established in 1977, the Health & Welfare Agency employs a staff of more than 500 people. **Career Highlights:** Health & Welfare Agency: System Software Specialist 1 (1996-Present), Programmer; Programmer, Department of Health Services. **Associations & Accomplishments:** Management of Information System Association; Golden Key National Honor Society; California State University, Sacramento Alumni Association. **Education:** California State University, B.S. in Business Administration and Management Information System (1999). **Personal Information:** Married to Tami in 1984. Two children: Bryan and Danielle. Mr. Luiz enjoys computers, hot rod and motorsports.

Peter V. Tamas

Trade Floor System Engineer
Barclays Global Investors
P.O. Box 7101
San Francisco, CA 94120-7101
(415) 908-7677
peter.tamas@bglobal.com

6371

Business Information: Providing his skilled services as Trade Floor System Engineer of Barclays Global Investors, Mr. Tamas presides over the system administration, providing technical support and acting as a troubleshooter when necessary. He performs software installations, upgrades, and configurations for the Company's 20 UNIX servers and 50 desktop computers. In charge of a three person staff, Mr. Tamas manages special projects and provides input for the yearly budget. He has standardized all the Company's UNIX systems, enabling the employees to work together efficiently. Coordinating resources and schedules and overseeing time lines and assignments also fall within the purview of his functions. Looking to the future, Mr. Tamas desires to perform more project management and advance from his current position. His success reflects his ability to think out-of-the-box and take on new challenges and responsibilities. Established in 1974, Barclays Global Investors performs management for pension funds, index funds, and portfolios. The Company has seven locations and is a subsidiary of Barclays Bank. Serving people and business worldwide, Barclays Global Investors guarantees average stock prices for Company clients. **Career Highlights:** Trade Floor System Engineer, Barclays Global Investors (1997-Present); Computer Consultant, Owner (1989-94). **Education:** Temple University: M.B.A. (1987), B.A. in Economics (1983). **Personal Information:** Mr. Tamas enjoys being a Scout leader and the Principal of a weekend Hungarian school.

Ann C. Burgoyne

Operations Manager of Financial Services
Berwanger Overmyer Associates
2245 Northbank Drive
Columbus, OH 43220
(614) 326-4931
Fax: (614) 326-7493
aburgoyne@boa-ins.com

6399

Business Information: Recruited to Berwanger Overmyer Associates in 1998, Mrs. Burgoyne serves as the Operations Manager of Financial Services. Recently, the Professional Association Department was put underneath her management and she now directly supervises a staff of 10 individuals. Mrs. Burgoyne developed and maintains the automated client/policy information system used by the Financial Services Department, enabling the employees to access a client's data quickly. Always looking for a challenge, she has more than 15 years of experience in the industry and credits her success to her persistence. "Never take no for an answer," she states. Mrs. Burgoyne is looking forward to completely automating the Agency and anticipates a promotion to a position which allows her a larger role in decision-making processes. Noted as one of the top 20 agencies nationwide, Berwanger Overmyer Associates is the largest independent insurance agency in the state of Ohio. The Agency offers commercial and personal property and casualty insurance, financial services, employee benefits, pension benefits, and third party administration. Boasting annual revenue upwards of $20 million, Berwanger Overmyer Associates employs a staff of 180 personnel to administer to its clients insurance and financial needs. **Career Highlights:** Operations Manager of Financial Services, Berwanger Overmyer Associates (1998-Present); Paul Revere: Brokerage Representative (1992-93), Sales Specialist (1988-92). **Associations & Accomplishments:** Columbus Life Underwriters Association. **Education:** Ohio State University; Northwestern Business College, Associate's degree. **Personal Information:** Married to Michael in 1984. Three children: Andrew, Shane, and Alex. Mrs. Burgoyne enjoys travel, gardening and music.

Karen Ann Estelle Dzhidzhora

Tele-Education Systems Administrator
Mortgage Guaranty Insurance Corporation
270 East Kilbourn Avenue
Milwaukee, WI 53202
(414) 347-6954

6399

Business Information: Serving as Tele-Education Systems Administrator for Mortgage Guaranty Insurance Corporation, Mrs. Dzhidzhora administers corporate contracts and provides educational services to people buying homes. A systems expert, she supervises six employees and is responsible for computer operations, distributing new software upgrades, installing new system applications, and providing network security to ensure that operations continue at optimum levels. Coordinating resources, schedules, time lines, and assignments, as well as assisting in formulating the strategic direction and contribution of the systems function to the overall corporate strategy also fall within the purview of her responsibilities. As a five year professional, her career success reflects her ability to work smartly, think out-of-the-box, and take on new challenges and responsibilities. Mrs. Dzhidzhora plans to expedite continued promotion through dedication and quality performance. Based in Wisconsin, the Mortgage Guaranty Insurance Corporation is a publicly held mortgage insurance corporation. Providing insurance to mortgage companies around the world, the Corporation first began operations in the 1960's. Presently, Mortgage Guaranty Insurance employs a staff of more than 1,200 individuals. **Career Highlights:** Tele-Education Systems Administrator, Mortgage Guaranty Insurance Corporation (1996-Present). **Education:** St. Norbert College, B.A. (1994). **Personal Information:** Married to Oleg G. in 1994. Mrs. Dzhidzhora enjoys sewing, teaching and tennis.

Ginger F. Edwards

Accountant/Systems Administrator
McInturff Miligan & Brooks
P.O. Box 1600
Greeneville, TN 37744
(423) 639-5171
Fax: (423) 639-7129
coolroy@xtn.net

6399

Business Information: Responsible for performing dual roles within McInturff Miligan & Brooks, Ms. Edwards serves as the Accountant and Systems Administrator. She performs the accounts payable and receivable functions for the Agency as well as reconciling customer accounts. In her role as Systems Administrator, she maintains the local area network and provides technical support to the staff. Ms. Edwards performs system upgrades, monitors daily activity, and provides network security. Citing perseverance as the key to her success, she plans to increase her involvement in the technical field. She states that the highlight of her professional career was the ownership of her own company. An independent insurance agency, McInturff Miligan & Brooks serves the regional area surrounding Greeneville, Tennessee and offers a variety of commercial and personal insurance lines such as life, health, group, and automobile. Fifteen staff members are dedicated to upholding the Agency's 80 year policy of providing quality customer service to their clients. **Career Highlights:** Accountant/Systems Administrator, McInturff Miligan & Brooks (1998-Present); Accounts Receivable, Marsh Petroleum (1996-98). **Education:** Milligan College, B.S. in Business Management (1990); Northeast State Technical, A.S. in Computer Science (1984). **Personal Information:** Ms. Edwards enjoys personal computing, reading science fiction and gardening.

John F. Franz III

President
V.I.P.S.
1776 North Pine Island Road
Plantation, FL 33322
(954) 577-0073
Fax: (954) 472-1633
jfranz@vipscorp.com

6399

Business Information: Mr. Franz developes software and is the President of V.I.P.S. or Virtual Insurance Processing System. In this capacity, he thoroughly tested all programs and has weeded out glitches and bugs. In addition, he has ensured that all bases are covered for infrastructure and assumed accountability for networks and SAN systems. Besides the technical aspects, Mr. Franz fulfills all adminstrative duties that are part of being a president of a company. He implements his own personal vision to keep the Company out-front of competitors. To acheive this end, he has formulated strategic plans and the methods needed to reach established objectives. In the next three to five years, Mr. Franz hopes to seen the Company grow larger at a quicker pace. Planning to reach this goal by using more fiber optic cables to increase communications potential, Mr. Franz's advice is "have fun." His success is attributed to his faith in God and Jesus Christ. Founded in 1999, V.I.P.S. has made a business out of going head to head with the rest of the industry. The Company has reengineered policy processes into thousands in a fraction of less time, and they have used the Internet as the backbone of their internal servers. As a result, the Company has enabled contact between themselves and their customers to happen in a swifter, more efficient manner. Currently, the revenue, for a Company with only three employees, has climbed to $350,000. **Career Highlights:** President, V.I.P.S. (1999-Present); Director of Corporate Telecommunications, US Diagnostic (1999); Information Systems Analyst 3, Broward County Mass Transit (1998); Network Manager, Parsongs Brinckeroff Construction Services(1993-96). **Associations & Accomplishments:** Network. **Education:** Broward County Community College. **Personal Information:** Mr. Franz enjoys travel, sailing, scuba diving and hiking.

Nicolas Santoli

Management Information Systems Director
Campania Management Company Inc.
111 Berry Street SE
Vienna, VA 22180-4806
(703) 242-9224
Fax: (703) 242-3815
nsantoli@erols.com

6399

Business Information: Mr. Santoli has served with Campania Management Company Inc. in various positions since 1992. At the present time, he fulfills the role of Management Information Systems Director responsible for determining the overall strategic direction and business contribution of the information systems function. Performing research on existing hardware and software on the market, Mr. Santoli designs and implements system applications customized specifically for the Campania Management Company. A systems expert, he administers and directs systems maintenance, trains end users, and provides technical support to the Company systems infrastructure. As an eight year veteran, Mr. Santoli credits his professional success to his creativity and ability to think out-of-the-box and take on new challenges. Mr. Santoli is looking toward to the 21st Century and eventually owning his own technology consulting firm. Headquartered in Vienna, Virginia, Campania Management Company Inc. offers a variety of insurance services to companies and individuals across the nation from six strategically located branches. The Company was created in 1992 and is a subsidiary of Campania Holding. Presently, the Company is manned by more than 35 individuals. **Career Highlights:** Campania Management Company Inc.: Management Information Systems Director (1997-Present), Network Administrator (1995-97), Technician (1994-95), Clerk (1992-94). **Education:** George Mason University, degree in Accounting and Management Information Systems (In Progress). **Personal Information:** Mr. Santoli enjoys the fine arts, music and literature.

Mary F. Tyler

Senior Systems Manager
The New England
501 Boylston Street
Boston, MA 02117
(617) 578-4067
mtyler@nef.com

6399

Business Information: As Senior Systems Manager of The New England's Boston Office, Ms. Tyler is in charge of the administration of project, product, and individual insurance systems. She installs systems, designs applications, initiates network use, and purchases equipment. Ms. Tyler also performs troubleshooting and conducts systems maintenance when necessary. Eager to improve her career skills, Ms. Tyler would like to further her knowledge in the technical field. Founded in the early 1950s, The New England provides clients with insurance and investment services. Private consumers, commercial businesses, school, and related organizations patronize the Firm as a broker of mutual funds, IRA accounts, and all types of insurance coverage. The Firm currently employs 1,500 representatives at locations throughout the United States. **Career Highlights:** The New England: Senior Systems Manager (1994-Present), Systems Manager (1990-94). **Education:** Livingstone College, B.S. (1978); Boston University, Certificate in Client Server Development. **Personal Information:** Married to Milliken in 1981. Two children: Milliken Jamar and Bryant. Ms. Tyler enjoys reading, working with children and teaching others how to use computers.

Timothy J. Wilkie, Sr.

Senior Network Administrator
Republic Mortgage Insurance Company
190 Oak Plaza Boulevard
Winston-Salem, NC 27105
(336) 661-4050
Fax: (336) 661-2276
tim_wilkie@rmic.com

6399

Business Information: Utilizing his extensive educational background and experience in the computer engineering field, Mr. Wilkie presently serves as Senior Network Administrator for Republic Mortgage Insurance Company. Providing analysis of personal computers and network functions, Mr. Wilkie administers Company networks and the help desk to ensure the efficient operations of all computer systems. He also installs all software and trains staff concerning each new program to another. Responsible for the management of all user accounts, Mr. Wilkie also controls corporate backups to prevent any long term computer problems. In addition to his work with the Company, he also serves as the Co-Owner and Vice President of Design and Development of Wilkie Associate's nationwide and remaining cognizant of innovations in technology. Specializing in mortgage insurance, Republic Mortgage Insurance Company provides private home mortgage insurance to lending institutions nationwide. Established in 1972, the Company employs 496 staff members in directing the sales and service of mortgage insurance for residential areas through participating banking institutions. Serving a national market, the Company's home office is in Winston-Salem, North Carolina. **Career Highlights:** Senior Network Administrator, Republic Mortgage Insurance Company (1996-Present); Vice President of Design and Development, Wilkie Associate's (1995-Present); Support Services, Microsoft/Rhotech (1995-96); Network Integrator, Deer Park Computers (1993-95). **Associations & Accomplishments:** Moose Lodge Chapter 2019; Legion of the Moose, Tarheel Lodge; Microsoft Certified Professionals Users Group; Microsoft Site Builders Network; National Information Technology Contractors Association. **Education:** Engineering Institute of America, Bachelor's degree in Engineering Management (1985); Microsoft Beta Support Certificate (In Progress). **Personal Information:** Married to LeaAnn in 1993. Three children: T.J., Elynanne, and Robert. Mr. Wilkie enjoys Web page development and collecting baseball cards.

6400 Insurance Agents, Brokers, and Services

6411 Insurance agents, brokers, and service

James E. Bearce

Network Engineer
Copeland Associates, Inc.
2 Tower Center Boulevard
East Brunswick, NJ 08816
(732) 514-2555
Fax: (732) 514-2416
jbearce@copeland.com

6411

Business Information: Serving with Copeland Associates, Inc. in several positions since 1995, Mr. Bearce currently fulfills the responsibilities of Network Engineer. In his capacity, he oversees all aspects of network engineering and new technology research. Relying on a depth of experience and technical expertise, Mr. Bearce helps design and support networks as well as participates in some programming functions. He performs coding and tests, maintains system functionality, troubleshoots, and installs and upgrades. An expert in the field, Mr. Bearce recommends purchases and works at the helps desk for the purpose of providing technical support. Server maintenance, software distribution, project standardization, and budget calculation and input also falls within the realm of Mr. Bearce's responsibilities. His strategic long-term goals include earning his CNE, MCSE, and becoming more involved in networking. He primarily desires to work as a Technical Lead person. Copeland Associates, Inc. operates as a retirement planning and insurance business. The Corporation works in collaboration with Smith

Barney and provides 401K programs, life insurance, and other retirement services. The Corporation primarily works with government, education, and private sector clients. Operating a network of 38 offices nationally, the Corporation employs 1,500 professional, technical, and support staff. **Career Highlights:** Network Engineer, Copeland Associates, Inc. (1997-Present); Computer Network Analyst, Halo Network Management (1996-97); PC Support Specialist, Copeland Associates, Inc. (1995-96). **Associations & Accomplishments:** Aircraft Owner and Pilots Association; Civil Air Patrol. **Education:** Lehigh University. **Personal Information:** Mr. Bearce enjoys general aviation, music, boating and being a volunteer emergency medical technician.

Glenn L. Davison

Information Technology Manager
Maxson Young Associates, Inc.
1 Sansome Street, Suite 950
San Francisco, CA 94104-4429
(415) 392-6034
Fax: (415) 392-6503
glenn.davison@maxsonyoung.com

6411

Business Information: Mr. Davision, the present Information Technology Manager of Maxson Young Associates, Inc., oversees a multitude of duties. He has accumulated eight years of experience in the field and over time has acquired a working knowledge of all aspects of the business. Utilizing his business savvy and expertise in the technological field, Mr. Davison maintains the Internet structure, evaluates business strategies, and assists in monitoring unit support. Keeping abreast of new development, integrating customer relations in day-to-day operations, and managing Extranets and Web based technologies serves as his strategic goals. An invaluable asset to the Corporation, he attributes his success to his strong work ethics and ability to think outside the box and take on challenges. Maxson Young Associates, Inc. is a company specializing in insurance adjusting services. Establsihed in 1993, the Corporation employs a staff consisting of 160 skilled professionals who lend their expertise in various aspects of the operation. The Corporation's main responsibility is to act as the international adjuster for self-insured groups. **Career Highlights:** Information Technology Manager, Maxson Young Associates, Inc. (1992-Present); Controller/Management Information Systems Manager, Four Star Maintenance (1985-92). **Education:** Metropolitan State College, B.S. (1984). **Personal Information:** Married to Traci in 1997. One child: Keith. Mr. Davison enjoys carpentry, photography, cycling and backpacking.

Luis R. Feliz

Information Systems Manager
KRM Risk Management and Insurance Services, Inc.
4270 West Richert Avenue, Suite 101
Fresno, CA 937252-6366
(559) 277-4800
Fax: (559) 277-4950
lou@feliz.net

6411

Business Information: As Information Systems Manager, Mr. Feliz presides over all Information Systems operations throughout the organization consisting of operations in California; Atlanta, Georgia; Nashville, Tennessee; and Tallahassee, Florida. He is in charge of coordinating all information systems projects, determines equipment acquisitions, and manages the wide area network for the organization. KRM Risk Management is a Managing General Underwriter for Workers' Compensation Insurance. Founded in 1993, KRM Risk Management processes premiums in excess of $90 million. Mr. Feliz transitioned into his current position from Van Beurden Insurance, a major stakeholder in the KRM Risk Management, in mid 1998. **Career Highlights:** Information Systems Manger, KRM Risk Management and Insurance Services, Inc. (1998-Present); Management Information Systems Manager, Van Beurden Insurance (1993-98); Programmer Analyst, Goodweather America (1987-93). **Education:** Sid Craig School of Business, California State University at Fresno, M.B.A. (In Progress); New York Institute of Technology, B.S. in Computer Science (1990). **Personal Information:** Mr. Feliz enjoys golf, cycling, reading and computers.

Pamela D. Hale

Manager of Client Server Development
AdminaStar Federal
9901 Linn Station Road, Suite 600
Louisville, KY 40223
(502) 339-5470
Fax: (502) 327-5243
pam_hale@aici.com

6411

Business Information: Functioning in the role of Manager of Client Server Development at AdminaStar Federal, Mrs. Hale is responsible for a team of employees in charge of the development of computer applications using VB/SQL, Internet, and Intranet services. Focusing primarily on the operational arena of the Company, Mrs. Hale assists in the automation of manual tasks, development of visual basics, and tracking of accuracy in order to save the Company money. A 19 year professional, her goals include contributing to the growth and success of AdminaStar Federal, putting 23 applications in production, and establishing the Company as one of the top two contractors for Health Care Financing Administration. Established in 1963, AdminaStar Federal is engaged in the processing of Medicare claims in accordance with various government contracts throughout the United States. Following strict performance standards and regulations set forth by the Health Care Financing Administration, the Company consists of many departments involved in dealing with pre and post claims for Medicare. Ranked as one of the Top 5 companies based on the number of claims processed, AdminaStar Federal currently employs more than 1,400 individuals nationwide. **Career Highlights:** AdminaStar Federal: Manager of Client Server Development (1997-Present), Local Area Network Team Manager (1996-97), Local Area Network Team Leader (1995-96). **Associations & Accomplishments:** Business and Professional Women of River City; Troop 1782 Leader, Girl Scouts of America; Volunteer, Junior Achievement. **Education:** Sullivan College of Business (1980). **Personal Information:** Married to Hansford Lee in 1991. Two children: Pamela Joyce and Jessica Susanne. Mrs. Hale enjoys reading, skating and family.

Timothy J. Humphreys

Senior Director of Business Information Systems
USI Prescription Benefits
675 Foxon Road, Suite 204
East Haven, CT 06513
(203) 468-8367
Fax: (203) 468-8723

6411

Business Information: As Senior Director of Business Information Systems at USI Prescription Benefits, Mr. Humphreys directs all day-to-day operations of the information systems and technology infrastructure. By managing the network systems, he designs strategic development plans to ensure proper operation of the data system desktop and data warehouse as well as develops cutting edge business software development strategies. At the same time, Mr. Humphreys serves on the technical board which started the Company. Focusing on the medical process side of the Company, he cites as one of his career accomplishments as the development and implementation of the reporting department. In the 21st century, Mr. Humphreys looks forward to utilizing more technology and facilitating educational growth. USI Prescription Benefits manages and processes pharmacy benefits for employers, associations, and other groups. Created in 1995, the Company currently employs the skilled services of 25 individuals. Through continued efforts of convenience, USI Prescription Benefits operates 10 locations. **Career Highlights:** Senior Director of Business Information Systems, USI Prescription Benefits (1999-Present); Manager of Business Information Systems, Yale New Haven Health-MCD (1997-99); Team Leader, York Prescription Benefits (1995-97); United States Marine Corps. **Associations & Accomplishments:** National Council for Prescription Drug Programs. **Education:** University of Connecticut: M.B.A. (In Progress), B.A. (1989). **Personal Information:** Married in 1993. Mr. Humphreys enjoys travel, photography and reading.

Lophney H. Knight

Assistant Vice President
Marsh USA, Inc.
1 World Trade Center, 95th Floor
New York, NY 10048
(212) 345-4375
Fax: (212) 948-4375
lophney.h.knight@marshmc.com

6411

Business Information: Serving as Assistant Vice President of the server management group within Marsh USA, Inc., Mr. Knight conducts a number of managerial activities of the U.S. based Intel server infrastructure including Web site and server maintenance and corrective monitoring. High regarded, he possesses superior talents and an excellent understanding of technology and his position with Marsh USA. Credited with implementing the Time Keeper System for the very influential New York Port Authority, Mr. Knight has taken part in the most vital operations Marsh USA, Inc. has to offer. Microsoft certified, he has received various recognition for is outstanding services. His success reflects his ability to think outside the box, take on new challenges and responsibilities, and deliver results on behalf of the Corporation and its clientele. Founded in the 1870s Marsh USA, Inc. is one of the most established and well respected insurance brokerage agencies in the United States. Located in the World Trade Center Building, New York, the Agency utilizes over 54,000 employees to serve the global corporate world and elite private sector. Presently generating $9.4 billion in annual revenue, Marsh USA, Inc. attributes their success to being customer oriented, providing a unique personal approach to their services. **Career Highlights:** Assistant Vice President, Marsh USA, Inc. (1996-Present); Systems Integration/Designer, Port Authority of New York and New Jersey (1986-96). **Education:** College of Staten Island, A.A.S. (1985). **Personal Information:** Married to Teresa in 1988. One child: Elissa. Mr. Knight enjoys volleyball.

Ryan M. Peters

Desktop Support Manager
Windsor Group
1300 Parkwood Circle
Atlanta, GA 30339
(770) 951-5599
rmpeters@windsorgroup.com

6411

Business Information: Fulfilling the responsibilities of Desktop Support Manager, Mr. Peters supports the computer systems throughout the Company. Supervising special group projects for the Company, he monitors the activities of five employees working under him. One of his greatest professional accomplishments has been to roll out Windows NT in the entire company. Windsor Group is a full service insurance family of five companies providing property and casualty coverage for personal automobiles and light commercial vehicles. The Group currently sells policies in 33 states through more than 14,000 independent agents. Headquartered in Atlanta, Georgia, Windsor Group operates branch offices in Oklahoma, Arizona, Florida, Missouri, Oregon, and Texas. Windsor Group's companies include American Deposit Insurance Company, Coventry Insurance Company, Regal Insurance Company, Windsor Insurance Company, and Texas Windsor Group. Operating since 1949, the Group employs over 1,000 insurance professionals. **Career Highlights:** Desktop Support Manager, Windsor Group (1996-Present); Internet Programmer, Harmony Leland Elementary School (1997-Present). **Associations & Accomplishments:** Phi Mu Alpha Professional Music Fraternity; Information System Employee Recognition Program Award (1998-99). **Education:** University of South Carolina, B.S. in Computer Information Systems (1996). **Personal Information:** Married to Crystal in 1996. Mr. Peters enjoys playing the French Horn, Disc golf, developing web pages and fishing.

Eugene M. Rotondo

Software Quality Assurance Manager
MIB Inc.
160 University Avenue
Westwood, MA 02090-2336
(781) 751-6371
Fax: (781) 329-3379
erotondo@mib.com

6411

Business Information: As Software Quality Assurance Manager for MIB Inc., Mr. Rotondo fulfills a number of duties on behalf of the Corporation. He is responsible for all quality assurance activities on software produced by MIB. Such actions include performing quality assurance tests, while implementing new processes for software design and development. With more than 20 years of hands on experience and expertise, Mr. Rotondo possesses superior talens and an excellent understanding of his field. Ensuring software and systems security, integrity, reliability, and value also fall within the realm of his responsibilities. His future plans include remaining with MIB and helping the Corporation grow and expand geographically. "Perseverance and the ability to think outside the box and deliver results," is attributed to Mr. Rotondo's success. MIB Inc. is an insurance service support agency that specializes in fraud detection. The objective of the Corporation is to ensure that all claims are factual and complete. Established in 1897, MIB Inc. is located in Westwood, Massachusetts and functions under the direction of over 180 professionals who facilitate smooth business operations on a daily basis. **Career Highlights:** Software Quality Assurance Manager, MIB Inc. (1999-Present); Software Quality Assurance Manager, Aguidneck Management (1996-99); Software Quality Assurance and IV&V Manager, Aguidneck Data Company (1979-96). **Associations & Accomplishments:** American Society for

Quality; Certified Quality Analyst, Quality Assurance Institute; ISO 9000 Lead Auditor Certificate. **Education:** Bryant College, M.B.A. Program; University of Rhode Island, M.B.A. Program; Roger Williams University, B.A. (1971). **Personal Information:** Married to Florence in 1969. Two children: Jennifer and Joseph. Mr. Rotondo enjoys writing, music, running and sports.

William W. Tomlinson

Director of Technology
Willis North America, Inc.
26 Century Boulevard
Nashville, TN 37214-3685
(615) 872-6105
Fax: (615) 872-6241
tomlinson_bi@willis.com

6411

Business Information: Demonstrating leadership skills and superior talents in the information technology field, Mr. Tomlinson joined Willis North America, Inc. in 1998 as a Director of Technology. He directs the technology research and development efforts to help keep the Corporation up to date, and oversees the adoption and implementation of new, cutting edge technology trends in the market. In addition, Mr. Tomlinson identifies new technical processes to improve day to day business activities. Determining the overall strategic direction and business contribution of the systems functions also fall within the realm of his responsibilities. Highly regarded, Mr. Tomlinson anticipates his promotion to Chief Information Officer with Willis North America, Inc. as a result of his continuing efforts to increase his skills through training and professional development activities. Willis North America, Inc. is the third largest risk management and insurance brokerage in the world. The Corporation is a licensed brokerage and serves as a risk management consulting firm that assesses the clients needs and facilitates planning strategies. Established in 1937, Willis North America is an international company headquartered in Nashville, Tennessee. The Corporation employs the expertise of 2,000 agents and 10,000 individuals to promote services, facilitate scheduling, and answer customer questions. **Career Highlights:** Director of Technology, Willis North America, Inc. (1998-Present); Management Information Systems Director, Intessera LLP/a TCI Company (1995-98); Technical Advisor, Federal Express Corporation (1985-95). **Associations & Accomplishments:** Boy Scouts of America; Association for Information and Image Management International. **Education:** University of Phoenix, B.S. in Business Administration (1990). **Personal Information:** Married to Mary in 1977. Mr. Tomlinson enjoys woodworking.

6500 Real Estate

6512 Nonresidential building operators
6513 Apartment building operators
6514 Dwelling operators, exc. apartments
6515 Mobile home site operators
6517 Railroad property lessors
6519 Real property lessors, nec
6531 Real estate agents and managers
6541 Title abstract offices
6552 Subdividers and developers, nec
6553 Cemetery subdividers and developers

Dr. Dong-Keun Shin

Independent Researcher
Hwa Shin Building
Building Management/CS Lab, 7th Floor, 705-22 Yuksam-dong, Kangnam-gu
Seoul, South Korea 135-080
+82 25657972
Fax: +82 25657907
www.dkshin.com

6512

Business Information: Dr. Shin conducts independent research in computer science, trying to complete his theories and practices. His research interests include computer science theory and database systems. He received his education in computer science from the University of California at Berkeley and from the George Washington University. Dr. Shin worked for the EECS Department at University of California at Berkeley and lectured on computer software and hardware at George Washington University. As an engineer, an analyst, or a programmer, he has worked at several companies, including British Telecommunications, Xerox, CBSI, SRA, and Samsung Electronics. With more than 15 years of experience in computer science, Dr. Shin has published papers in computer science journals. While surveying hash functions for his doctoral dissertation, he verified for the first time that there is no distinguishable difference between the performance of one relatively good and data independent hash function and that of another. He coined the term "phenomenon of relatively good (RG) solutions" in reference to the verification. Based on the first verification of the kind, he has developed the hypothesis that the phenomenon of RG solutions is present in each group of polynomial time solutions for complex problems that basically require exponential time algorithms as solutions. He is preparing to verify the hypothesis for other complex problems. He has also made significant contributions to computer science by discovering and proposing best algorithms in the areas of sorting, hash functions, massive cross-referencing or the join database operation, and polygon clipping. Dr. Shin's papers show that his algorithm for massive cross-referencing or the join, with its several versions, is the best algorithm of its kind to date and that Dr. Shin's (mapping) hash function is the best hash method. In early 1997, Dr. Shin offered a challenge to the world's academic communities and computer scientists to refute the legitimacy of his verification and discoveries as well as his claim to having made the greatest contribution to computer science. ured computer-based systems for an introductory course at the University of Maryland Asian Division. He is also involved in managing his family owned Hwa Shin Building in Downtown Seoul. He plans to continue conducting computer science research and publishing his theories and ideas in the computer science and engineering fields. At that time, he sent letters to one or two highest leaders, the minister of education or equivalent one, chairman of UNESCO, and head of major universities and colleges in each of approximately 170 countries to gain leadership of the world's computer science academia. The total number of schools to which he sent his letters asking for a challenge was over 4,300. He has not encountered any serious challenge yet. Moreover, on July 3, 1998, he discovered a new sorting algorithm; Shin sort, named after his last name, is the best solution to the problem of sorting and searching. The new sorting and searching method that Dr. Shin found seems to secure his victory in his battle for the world leadership in computer science. He is currently designing and implementing a prototype of his sorting and searching software. From the prototype, his software will eventually develop into a Shin sort and search database management system entitled (i.e., S3DBMS). S3DBMS creates Shin's trees in main memory or local memory for fast text/image/sound data retrievals. Dr. Shin's press release in April 1999 shows that his sorting and searching scheme that traverses Shin's tree will replace current sorting and searching algorithms, hashing schemes and hash tables, and most trees including B-trees due to Shin sort/search algorithm's theoretical superiority. Dr. Shin believes that Shin sort will be used in most database systems and computer-based systems in the future. For further investigation on Dr. Shin's achievements, one may acquire his research collection entitled "A Collection of Research Processes for Genealogy and Proofs," currently 30 volumes, which have been submitted to the Chairperson of the EECS Department at the University of California at Berkeley, Berkeley, California 94720, USA. **Career Highlights:** Independent Researcher, Hwa Shin Building (1997-Present); Chief Scientist, Samsung Electronics (1992-97); Software Engineer, Xerox Corporation (1988); Academic Computing Coordinator, Electrical Engineering and Computer Sciences Department, University of California at Berkeley (1981-83). **Associations & Accomplishments:** Association for Computing Machinery; Institute of Electrical and Electronics Engineers Computer Society; Lecturer, Computer-based Systems, University of Maryland, Asian Division, Korea. **Education:** George Washington University: Doctor of Science in Computer Science (1991), M.S. in Computer Science; University of California at Berkeley, B.A. in Computer Science (1983). **Personal Information:** Married to Helen Chang in 1991. Two children: Paul J. and Lucas J. Dr. Shin enjoys collecting stones, playing piano and playing guitar.

Patrick A. Beaumont

Systems Administrator
Housing Fiscal Services
495 Broadway
New York, NY 10012
(212) 651-0612
Fax: (212) 431-6228
bap9510@aol.com

6513

Business Information: As Systems Administrator of Housing Fiscal Services, Mr. Beaumont focuses his attention on the technical needs of the Agency. Acting as a data program manager, he upgrades the operating systems and applications used by the employees. Offering both hardware and sofware support, he often fills the capacity of liasion between the Agency and software consultants. Mr. Beaumont also serves as Manager of Accounts Receivable, where he maintains accurate records and prepares financial reports for accounting purposes. He also supports "We Magazine" computers for the publishing department. "We Magazine" is a magazine for people with disabilities. Looking to the future, he currently has plans to help the Agency evolve into a web based business by creating a Web site and foucusing on Internet advantages. Housing Fiscal Services is a real estate agency that manages and owns low income housing throughout New York City. The Agency must rent and maintain the housing units and collect rent and payments due from the tenants. **Career Highlights:** Systems Administrator, Housing Fiscal Services (1989-Present); Computer Consultant, Acadia Travel (1982-89); Senior Program Analyst, Yonkers General Hospital (1980-82). **Associations & Accomplishments:** Institute of Electrical and Electronics Engineers, Inc. **Education:** New York University, (1999); Bernard Baruch College, B.A. in Business Administration (1995); Laguardia Community College, A.S. in Computer Science (1989). **Personal Information:** Married to Gladis Terrazas de Beaumont in 1988. Mr. Beaumont enjoys gardening, dancing and computer technology.

Gilbert S. Almeda

Regional Supervisor of Central Region
Grubb & Ellis Company
2215 Sanders Road, Suite 400
Northbrook, IL 60062
(847) 753-7556
Fax: (847) 753-9854
gilbert.almeda@grubb-ellis.com

6531

Business Information: Serving as the Regional Supervisor of Central Region for Grubb & Ellis Company, Mr. Almeda engages in technical support management, network administration, engineering, and technology project management. He is responsible for supplying DSL Internet access to the proper employees and working closely with vendors to enhance overall efficiency and production of the Company. Dedicated to the success of the Company, he monitors and manages all networks, ensuring that employee have access to the proper areas of the system and that the systems functions are operational at all times. In the future, Mr. Almeda's goals are to obtain more responsibility including management of the Company's regional managers. His success reflects his leadership ability to form teams with synergy and technical strength and deliver the appropriate results on behalf of the Company and its clientele. A real estate agency, Grubb & Ellis Company specializing in commercial real estate. Founded in 1980, the Company is headquartered in Northbrook, Illinois. Presently, Grubb & Ellis employs a work force of over 4,000 personnel to fulfill all aspects of client representation. **Career Highlights:** Grubb & Ellis Company: Regional Supervisor of Central Region (1999-Present), Senior Analyst (1997), Lead Technology Analyst (1997). **Associations & Accomplishments:** Microsoft Certified Professional+Internet; Microsoft Certified Systems Engineer **Education:** Roosevelt University; Northwestern University; University of Illinois. **Personal Information:** Married to Cecille in 1990. One child: Danica. Mr. Almeda enjoys seminars, reading, reasearch, basketball, softball, tennis and bowling.

Dennis J. Brown

Technical Services Manager
Grubb & Ellis Company
2215 Sanders Road, Suite 400
Northbrook, IL 60062
(847) 753-7616
Fax: (847) 919-5822
dennis.brown@grubb.ellis.com

6531

Business Information: Holding a prestigious management position among the Grubb & Ellis Company's 4,400 employees, Mr. Brown serves as the Technical Services Manager. Supervising the voice and data system services corporate wide, he negotiates all local and long distance voice service contracts, while simultaneously overseeing the activity of five team analysts. A recognized leader in his field, Mr. Brown contributes his expertise to construct project teams, with which he contributes knowledge gained from continuous education and attendance at industry seminars. Attributing his success to awareness in his field, and the ability to make quick decisions, Mr. Brown will continue on his current path with Grubb & Ellis Company, incorporating video and voice data integration to their operations in the near future. The third largest public related company in the industry, Grubb & Ellis Company specializes in commercial real estate transaction and management services. A unique company in the applications of their software and quality of their services, Grubb & Ellis Company operates with Quest Communications, Nortell Networking, and IBM which maintains a position as their largest accounts. Providing services to an international client base, the Company in their 42nd year of business has experienced unparalleled growth and expansion in the industry, currently generating $300 million in revenues annually. **Career Highlights:** Technical Services Manager, Grubb & Ellis Company (1997-Present); Network Engineer, Apollo Travel Services (1996-97); Network Analyst, White Cap Inc. (1994-96). **Associations & Accomplishments:** United States Navy: four letters of commendation, Sailor of the Quarter, Navy League Award for special merit, numerous letters of appreciation. **Education:** Indiana Vocational Technical College, Technical Certificate (1984); United States Navy (1985-90). **Personal Information:** One child: Jessica Lynn. Mr. Brown enjoys metal detecting, golf and bowling.

Ginger B. Duggins

Manager of Information Systems
Prudential Carolinas Realty
301 South Elm Street, Suite 214
Greensboro, NC 27401
(336) 478-0203
Fax: (336) 478-0201
gduggins@prudentialcarolinas.com

6531

Business Information: Serving as Manager of Information Systems for Prudential Carolinas Realty, Ms. Duggins is responsible for wide area network operations at 21 offices within the region. Throughout daily routines, she is accountable for quality maintenance of 400 nodes and 16 servers based on Microsoft Terminal Server and Citrix Metaframe. A savvy, seven-year veteran of technology, Ms. Duggins possesses superior talents and an excellent understanding of her field. The most rewarding aspects of her career include obtaining her Microsoft certifications. For the future, she plans on remaining with the Firm and obtaining her Microsoft Certified Systems Engineer certification. Her success reflects her ability to think outside the box, take on challenges, and deliver results. Prudential Carolinas Realty specializes in the buying and selling of residential and commercial real estate. Offering mortgage services and title insurance, the Firm's central office in located in Greensboro, Noth Carolina. Presently, the Firm employs a work force of more than 1,200 professional, technical, and administrative support personnel. **Career Highlights:** Manager of Information Systems, Prudential Carolinas Realty (1997–Present); Service Manager, Computer Clinic of the Triad (1993–97). **Education:** Guilford County Technical Community College (1995); Microsoft Certified Professional; A+ Hardware Certified; Hewlett-Packard Certified. **Personal Information:** One child: Ariel Paige. Ms. Duggins enjoys swimming and dancing.

Chris L. Hale

Operations Director
Russellville Realty
1310 West Main Street
Russellville, AR 72801–2816
(501) 968-1430
Fax: (501) 968-1763
chale@cswnet.com

6531

Business Information: Mr. Hale has served as Operations Director of Russellville Realty since 1997. In his present role, he determines the overall strategic direction and business contribution of the information systems function. He is responsible for coordinating property leases and contracting maintenance companies to maintain individual properties under the Company's care. Fulfilling responsibilities of a computer administrator, Mr. Hale manages the Company's computer system and all day-to-day administration and operations. He assumes accountability for the life cycle of information technology hardware and software and performs the purchasing of the hardware and software necessary for each computer and the server. As a technology professional, he owns an established track record of producing results in support of business goals and objectives. Mr. Hale contributes his success to internal motivation. His success reflects his ability to think out-of-the-box and aggressively take on new challenges and responsibilities. He looks forward to becoming General Manager and eventually desires to open his own business. Russellville Realty offers property management and rental property services to the city of Russellville and the surrounding areas. The Company was founded in 1963 and currently employs 26 individuals. **Career Highlights:** Operations Director, Russellville Realty (1997–Present); Route Manager, CM Vending Company (1997). **Associations & Accomplishments:** Arkansas Board of Realtors. **Personal Information:** Married to Terra in 1994. Three children: Robert Daniel, Conlee, and Maebee. Mr. Hale enjoys golf, computers and the Internet.

Elmer S. B. Pang

Rental Agent/Programmer
Kazuo Totoki Ltd.
705 South King Street, Suite 208
Honolulu, HI 96813–3029
(808) 531-0221
Fax: (808) 538-3027

6531

Business Information: Mr. Pang has served as Rental Agent and Programmer with Kazuo Totoki Ltd. since 1986. His diverse duties include inspection of properties prior to move-in by tenants, to ensure the apartment is in top shape; and after their departure, to protect the interest of KTL in assessing damages prior to deposit refunds. He assumes accountability for scheduling repair and maintenance on properties, and tracks all costs and incomes related to all units. Talented, Mr. Pang monitors three separate database programs, which are used by various staff members throughout the Company. His dedicated efforts have resulted in accurate data entry and effective backup scheduling. An expert in the field, he provides technical support and training to staff members in the event of upgrades and new software implementations. Mr. Pang also performs D-Base and Fox-Pro programming to facilitate recordkeeping and computational capabilities within the Company. As an internal consultant, he works closely with management to stay ahead of anticipated shifting in business operations. Mr. Pang keeps up with changes in technologies employed by Kazuo Totoki by reading magazines and technical literature and by surfing the internet. He hopes to continue his rise through the management hierarchy. In Honolulu, Hawaii, Kazuo Totoki Ltd., focuses on property management. Kazuo Totoki handles administrative and management tasks for five residential properties with a staff of eight. **Career Highlights:** Rental Agent/Programmer, Kazuo Totoki Ltd. (1997–Present); Programmer/Data Entry, Homesite, Inc. (1989–97). **Education:** University of Hawaii, B.S. in Computer Science (1985). **Personal Information:** Mr. Pang enjoys computer games, walking and ice skating.

Stuart Reicher

Management Information Systems Manager
Sure Air Ltd.
333 Ludlow Street
Stamford, NY 06902
(203) 323-9800
Fax: (203) 323-9791
sreicher@smeari.com

6531

Business Information: Recruited to Sure Air Ltd. in 1985, Mr. Reicher serves as Management Information Systems Manager. When he first began with the Company, there was a single PC. Since that time, Mr. Reicher has increased the number of computers to 110 and created a call logging program that enables employees to input client information and receive almost instantaneous feedback as to the closest repair company able to respond. Extremely knowledgeable in computer and telephone technology, he maintains the telephony and mainframe database systems' functionality and fully operational status at all times. Dedicated to the success of the Company, Mr. Reicher anticipates a promotion to a Head Information Technology position once the department expands. He is planning to educate himself more on Web design and is looking forward to designing the Company's Web site. Since inception in 1966, Sure Air Ltd. has specialized in providing air conditioning repair services to retail store chains. In 1987, the Company expanded services to electrical repairs, plumbing repairs, site management, and help desk assistance. An expert staff of 90 individuals engage the services of over 4,000 subcontractors to fulfill the Company's obligations. Last year, Sure Air Ltd. boasted annual revenue upwards of $32 million. **Career Highlights:** Management Information Systems Manager, Sure Air Ltd. (1985–Present). **Associations & Accomplishments:** WABC; Partners, Professional Association Golfers. **Education:** Mercy College, B.S. (1985). **Personal Information:** Married to Virginia in 1987. One child: Cameron James. Mr. Reicher enjoys bowling, golf, fishing and gardening.

Jeffrey A. Sharp

Sales and Marketing Representative
Indy Residential Services
P.O. Box 20353
Indianapolis, IN 46220
(317) 466-0712
Fax: (317) 254-1658
sharp1ja@juno.com

6531

Business Information: In his position as a Sales and Marketing Representative for Indy Residential Services, Mr. Sharp performs a variety of functions. A graduate of Indiana University, he helps first-time home buyers and counsels people with ownership problems and distress situations. Mr. Sharp enjoys working with others and providing creative solutions. In the future, he plans to utilize his computer experience to bring increased technology to the Company. Established in 1991, Indy Residential Services is a residential real estate investment operation. The Company acquires, repairs, markets, and sells starter homes, executive homes, and investment properties. They specialize in offering sellers fast, customized solutions for any situation. For buyers, they offer flexible purchase plans, often with minimal bank involvement. Currently, Indy Residential Services employs two people full time as well as a number of independent contractors for repairs and decorating. **Career Highlights:** Sales and Marketing Representative, Indy Residential Services (1995–Present); Computer Analyst, Indianapolis Power and Light Company (1989–95); Programmer Analyst, The Limited (1988–89); Programmer Analyst, Ball Corporation (1985–88). **Associations & Accomplishments:** National Association of Realtors; Indiana Association of Realtors; Indianapolis Real Estate Investors; Toastmasters International. **Education:** Indiana University, B.A. in Computer Science (1985); Indiana Vocational Technical College, Vocational Electricity; Various computer, professional, sales, marketing and real estate seminars attended. **Personal Information:** Married to Anne in 1987. Mr. Sharp enjoys sailing.

John Anthony Sherwood

Information Technology Director
Synermark
5929 Balcones Drive, Suite 100
Austin, TX 78731
(512) 483-3819
Fax: (512) 454-3100
jsherwood@synermark.com

6531

Business Information: Mr. Sherwood functions in the capacity of Information Technology Director for Synermark. He oversees all daily administration and operational activities of the systems infrastructure, in addition to determining the overall strategic direction and vision and business contribution of the information systems function. Before joining the Synermark team in 1998, Mr. Sherwood served in the United States Air Force in various roles, including Systems Manager, Network Administrator, and Combat Crew Leader. An information systems professional with 10 years of experience, he is in charge of recommending and purchasing all hardware and software; developing, overseeing, and directing operations; and managing servers, protocols, desktop servers, routers, switches, and hubs. One of his many career accomplishments includes the data migration from a 60 bit AS400 to a Window NT platform. Mr. Sherwood attributes his success to his self motivation and determination. Eventually attaining the role of Regional Director serves as one of his future endeavors. Synermark engages in commercial real estate sales, leasing, and management. Headquartered in Austin, Texas, the Company operates offices in Albuquerque, New Mexico, Tulsa, Oklahoma, and three cities in Texas: San Antonio, Dallas, and Houston. Established in 1995, Synermark presently employs a work force of more than 150 professional, technical, and support personnel. **Career Highlights:** Information Technology Director, Synermark (1998–Present); United States Air Force: Systems Manager (1994–98), Network Administrator (1992–94), Combat Crew Leader (1988–92). **Associations & Accomplishments:** Air Force Association (1984). **Education:** St. Edwards University, M.B.A. in Management Information System (In Progress); Embry Riddle Aeronautical University, B.S. (1994). **Personal Information:** Married to Eunice Su-Ai in 1998. Mr. Sherwood enjoys playing the drums, big band and jazz.

Jean-Luc Valente

Chief of Marketing and Operations
Homebid.com
8700 North Gainey Center Drive #150
Scottsdale, AZ 85258–2104
(480) 609-4627
Fax: (480) 309-4646
jl@homebid.com

6531

Business Information: Mr. Valente fulfills the accountability of Chief of Marketing and Operations with Homebid.com. He is responsible for all aspects of day-to-day business operations, including formulating technology, sales, and marketing strategies. A savvy, 17-year veteran, Mr. Valente is involved in business development, e-commerce activities, customer service, project management, corporate development, and administration. Besides supervising a team of 30 executives, managers, and employees, he coordinates resources, time lines, schedules, assignments, and budgets, as well as demonstrates the successful promotion of a business run entirely through the Internet. His career highlights include building successful IT business domestically and abroad for Computer Associates, Viasoft, and Homebid.com. Looking to the next millennium, Mr. Valente hopes to become the Chief Executive Officer of an e-commerce or Internet business. His success reflects his innovative ideas, energy, and integrity. Homebid.com is an online real estate broker. Created in 1998, the Company became the first Internet real estate firm to successfully run an Internet auction of residential properties, selling 137 homes out of 196 over a three-day period. The Company received $25 million from major East and West Coast venture capital firms. Over the past six months, Homebid has become a recognized leader in the e-commerce and real estate fields. **Career Highlights:** Chief of Marketing and Operations, Homebid.com (1998–Present); Senior Vice President of Marketing, Viasoft (1996–98); Vice President of Strategic Marketing, Computer Associates International (1987–96). **Education:** E.F.R.E.I. at Paris, Master's degree in Electrical Engineering (1982). **Personal Information:** Married to Marie-Anne in 1981.

Jennifer Faith Fidelman

Marketing Manager
Playa Vista
12555 West Jefferson Boulevard
Los Angeles, CA 90066
(310) 448-4606
jfidelman@playavista.com

6552

Business Information: Ms. Fideleman serves as the Marketing Manager for Playa Vista. Recruited to the Company in 1997, he strives to promote the Company, In this context, he oversees and directs advertising, public relations, and Web site development. Managing a professional team of builders and electronic mediums, she is responsible for placing teams of workers and contractors to various job sites. Utilizing her public relations skills, she organizes and executes advertising campaigns for the further promotion of Playa Vista. Considering the Internet as a main source of advertisement, Ms. Fidelman created the Company's Web site in order to increase the clientele. Continuing to grow with the Company, she is constantly searching for new concepts to further the success of Playa Vista. Since 1997, Playa Vista has been specializing in large community planning for the surrounding Los Angelos, California area. The Company provides not only commercial planning, but also residential and habitat restoration. Analyzing a location and drawing up specific plans, Playa Vista is capable of developing communities, considerating traffic flow and building development. Working directly with the community, the Company learns what is important and necessary in the development of their town. Presently, Playa Vista is manned by a work force of 65 people. **Career Highlights:** Marketing Manager, Playa Vista (1997-Present); Marketing Events Coordinator, Desk Talk Systems (1996-97); Marketing and Program Manager, Online Expo (1995-96); Marketing Coordinator, Fred Sands (1994). **Associations & Accomplishments:** Sales and Marketing Council, Building Industry Association; National Association of Female Executives; Volunteer, Free Arts for Abused Children. **Education:** Pepperdine University: B.A. (1993), Law School. **Personal Information:** Ms. Fidelman enjoys rollerblading and ice skating.

Danny E. Gonzalez

Director of Data Administration
Fairfield Communities, Inc.
6400 North Andrews Avenue
Fort Lauderdale, FL 33309-2172
(954) 351-8500
danny.gonzalez@fair-field.com

6552

Business Information: As Director of Data Administration for Fairfield Communities, Inc., Mr. Gonzalez is responsible for the coordination of data warehousing, analysis, and the creation of summary tables. WIth more than six years of data experience, he is also accountable for organizing and storing all Corporation information into one location to be accessed by all subsidiaries. Mr. Gonzalez oversees the production databases and coordinates and fulfills both data processing and data entry. His plans for the future include advancement within the Corporation, and to continue working to develop more efficient data warehousing. Fairfield Communities was founded in 1966 for the provision of real estate development and establishment of timeshare resorts. Utilizing the experience and knowledge of over 5,000 individuals, the Corporation also offers these resorts as additions to vacation packages to tourists from all around the world who wish to discover the more scenic areas of the United States. Recently, the Corporation has reported the annual revenues in excess of $500 million. **Career Highlights:** Fairfield Communities, Inc.: Director of Data Administration (1998-Present), Senior Programmer Analyst (1997-98); Senior Data Warehouse Administration, Department of Information Systems (1995-97); Programmer Analyst, Arkansas Blue Cross Blue Shield (1994-95). **Associations & Accomplishments:** Data Warehousing Institute; Microsoft Developers Network. **Education:** University of Arkansas at Little Rock, B.S. in Construction Engineering (1995). **Personal Information:** Married to Dustye in 1995. One child: Elliot. Mr. Gonzalez enjoys tennis.

Jacqueline R. Guzzetta

Information Systems Manager
Macklowe Properties
142 West 57th Street, 15th Floor
New York, NY 10019
(212) 265-5900
Fax: (212) 554-5860

6552

Business Information: As Information Systems Manager for Macklowe Properties, one of the leaders in New York City's fast-paced real estate development marketplace, Ms. Guzzetta maintains the Company's overall systems infrastructure. She assists in the design, acquisition, installation, implementation, and troubleshooting of new software and hardware applications for the Company, which owns an extensive portfolio of Class A commercial and residential buildings, and several major development sites throughout New York City. Ms. Guzzetta provides ongoing technical assistance to the Company's staff and deals with a wide variety of telecommunications providers in an effort to continually upgrade the Company's productivity. By utilizing her excellent communication skills and superior multi-tasking capabilties, Ms. Guzzetta hopes, in addition to her daily tasks, to acquire a better understanding of the telecommunications and network administration facets of her current assignment. On the lighter side, Ms. Guzzetta attributes her professional success to divine intervention. **Career Highlights:** Information Systems Manager, Macklowe Properties (1998-Present); Network Administrator, Board of Education (1998-93). **Education:** Marymount Manhattan, B.A. (1997).

Jeffrey T. Miller

Vice President of Information Systems
Simpson Housing Ltd. Partnership
3201 South Tamarac Drive
Denver, CO 80231-4361
(303) 306-4162
Fax: (303) 338-5978
millerj@simpsonhousing.com

6552

Business Information: Serving as Vice President of Information Systems of Simpson Housing Ltd. Partnership, Mr. Miller fulfills the role of director of informations systems, responsible for all personal computer and network operations and designs. Possessing strong business savvy and expertise, Mr. Miller provides oversight and management of a 600 node computer infrastructure. Learning from his four year tour as an information systems specialist with United States Marine Corps, he remains focused and continuously seeks improvement in all areas of his responsibilities. His future plans include becoming a chief information officer with a large information technology company and eventually becoming an independent, starting his own consulting business. Mr. Miller's success reflects his ability to form teams with synergy and technical strength and tackle challenges and deliver results. A subsidiary of Great West Management, the Simpson Housing Ltd. Partnership engages in muti-family housing development and management. Established in 1975, the Partnership is involved in building and developing apartment complexes throughout the United States. Presently, the Partnership employs a team of 10 professional, technical, and support staff. **Career Highlights:** Vice President of Information Systems, Simpson Housing Ltd. Partnership (1988-Present); United States Marine Corp. (1982-86). **Personal Information:** Married to Tanya in 1991.

Bill Nicholson

Director of Information Services
Catellus Development Corporation
201 Mission Street
San Francisco, CA 94105-1831
(415) 974-4523
Fax: (415) 974-4646

6552

Business Information: Displaying his strategic skills in this highly specialized position, Mr. Nicholson serves as Director of Information Services for the Catellus Development Corporation. In this capacity, he is in charge all of the technological aspects and direction of the Corporation. He presides over the property management systems and administrates the LAN and WAN networks, as well as Internet, Intranet, and Extranet infrastructure. Performing the routine maintenance of the various systems, he provides network security against unauthorized access and vandalism and a back up system to guard against data loss. A systems expert, Mr. Nicholson is committed to providing continued optimum service and looks forward to assisting in the completion of corporate goals. His success reflects his ability to deliver results and aggressively tackle new challenges. Created in 1990, the Catellus Development Corporation is involved in various aspects of real estate including property management, property development, and residential construction. The Corporation serves clients at the local, state, and national level through its numerous locations. Boasting $1 billion in annual revenue, operations employ the services of over 500 skilled workers. **Career Highlights:** Director of Information Services, Catellus Development Corporation (1999-Present); Network Manager, Singerton, Inc. (1991-99). **Education:** University of San Francisco. **Personal Information:** Three children. Mr. Nicholson enjoys reading and spending time with his family.

Leigh Irish Young

Assistant Database Administrator
Cooper Communities, Inc.
1801 Forest Hills Boulevard
Bella Vista, AR 72714
(501) 855-5307
Fax: (501) 855-5310
leigh@ccias.com

6552

Business Information: A 10 year veteran of information technology, Ms. Young has assertively served with Cooper Communities, Inc. since joining the Corporation as Operations Coordinator and Operator in 1989. In 1997, Ms. Young was elevated to Assistant Database Administrator. Her history includes a four year stint as a Hospital Corpsman while serving with the United States Navy. In her present position, she oversees a multitude of tasks, including the operation of several Sequel server databases. An expert, she performs maintenance and backups, as well as ensures the functionality and fully operational status of the systems infrastructure. Administering and controlling the Corporation's data resources, ensuring data security and reliability, and tuning software tools to enhance database performance also fall within the purview of Ms. Young's functions. She attributes her career success to her dedication and being cautious about doing new things. Ms. Young believes it is vital to ask questions and expand knowledge through hands on experience regardless of your field. She looks forward to continued success with Cooper Communities. Cooper Communities, Inc. was established in 1954. Its attention is on community development. Among the various projects undertaken include building vacation and recreational communities, homes, businesses, and timeshare properties. Cooper Communities, Inc. has developments in four states. The Corporation and its subsidiaries are headquartered in Arkansas and employ a staff of more than 500. **Career Highlights:** Assistant Database Administrator, Cooper Communities, Inc. (1997-Present); United States Navy Reserves (1988-Present); Operations Coordinator/Operator, Cooper Communications, Inc. (1989-97); Hospital Corpsman, United States Navy (1983-87). **Education:** University of Arkansas.

6700 Holding and Other Investment Offices

6712 Bank holding companies
6719 Holding companies, nec
6722 Management investment, open-end
6726 Investment offices, nec
6732 Educational, religious, etc. trusts
6733 Trusts, nec
6792 Oil royalty traders
6794 Patent owners and lessors
6798 Real estate investment trusts
6799 Investors, nec

Theodore J. Layne

Vice President for Information Technology Services
FT Mortgage Companies
4000 Horizon Way
Irving, TX 75063
(317) 951-4110
Fax: (317) 951-4160
tlayne@ftmortgage.com

6712

Business Information: As Vice President for Information Technology Services for FT Mortgage Companies, Mr. Layne determines the overall strategic IT direction and business contribution of the information systems function. He formulates new IT strategies and plans to keep FT Mortgage out-front of industry competitors in the market. A successful and proven professional in the field, Mr. Layne manages the database, UNIX, and security groups, while overseeing a staff of 30 employees. Coordinating all aspects of day-to-day activities of all groups, Mr. Layne is currently building the security group and working on enhancing the overall operation through process improvements. Being one of the principal founders of the Enterprise Mortgage Banking Division of Cybertek and taking the division from $1 million to $20 million in revenues in just three years is highlighted as one of his career accomplishments. Attributing his professional success to his strong and effective leadership, Mr. Layne's goals include eventually attaining the position of Chief Information Officer for a mid size mortgage company or possibly obtaining a senior technical role with a start up. National in scope, FT Mortgage Companies is the 10th largest mortgage holding company in the United States. Currently holding services for seven different companies, FT Mortgage reports annual revenues in excess of $15 billion in originations, and has experienced a 100 percent growth within the last three years. **Career Highlights:** Vice President for Information

Technology Services, FT Mortgage Companies (1999-Present); Cybertek Corporation: Mid West Regional Services Manager (1998-99), Director of Technical Services (1996-98); Assistant Vice President of Data Architecture, Banc One Mortgage Corporation (1995-96). **Associations & Accomplishments:** Mortgage Bankers Association; International Oracle Users Group. **Education:** Midwestern State University, M.S. in Computer Science (1995); Chapman University, B.S. in Computer Science. **Personal Information:** Married to Annette in 1978. Three children: Charlene, Rachel, and Rebecca. Mr. Layne enjoys wood working and golf.

Stephen A. Wineteer

Systems Architect
1st National Bank of Omaha
P.O. Box 1452
Bellevue, NE 68005
(402) 633-7017
Fax: (402) 292-5115
wineteer@probe.net

6712

Business Information: As a Systems Architect of 1st National Bank of Omaha, Mr. Wineteer is responsible for data processing projects, IBM assembly, and language programming, among other duties. In the technology age, the Bank depends on its computers to carry out a wide array of financial services with speed and accuracy. The systems infrastructure, in turn, depend on Mr. Wineteer for servicing, upgrading, and programming new software solutions. Begining his information technology career in 1968 with an IBM1130, computers are in his bloodline, as two of his sons are computer programmers also. Concurrent to his present role, Mr. Wineteer also teaches computer programming at a local community college. His career highlights include development of a totally automated banking system, and deploying a Java application for an inventory management system. In the future, he plans on remaining with the Bank and get a Linux education. His advice is "stay in school." Over a century old, 1st National Bank of Omaha is the oldest financial institution west of the Mississippi River. With locations in Nebraska, Colorado, Kansas, Missouri, and South Dakota, the Bank is a financial institution that engages in a wide range of commercial and financial services. With over 5,000 employees, the Bank also engages in lending and loan practices to qualified individuals. **Career Highlights:** Systems Architect, 1st National Bank of Omaha (2000-Present); Director of Systems Engineering, First Data Resources (1989-00); Manager of IBM Systems Programming, 1st National Bank of Omaha (1983-89). **Associations & Accomplishments:** Vice President, Czech Cultural Club of Omaha; Part Time Instructor, Iowa Western Community College (1980-Present); Faculty Advisory Committee, IWCC (1985-Present). **Education:** San Diego State University, B.S. in Microbiology (1963). **Personal Information:** Married to Geraldine in 1989. Five children: Stephen Jr., Paul Buschkemper, Michael, Stephanie Dickey, and Teresa Laird. Mr. Wineteer enjoys stamp collecting.

Marwan Y. Besiso, Ph.D.

Consultant
Al Zamil Group of Companies
P.O. Box 10081
Riyadh, Saudi Arabia 11433
+966 14767794
Fax: +966 14762587
nibham@zamilu.com

6719

Business Information: Dr. Besiso is the Economic and Management Consultant for the Al-Zamil Group of Companies. Operating from the headquarters location, he is responsible for the reporting of economic statistics to the Board of Directors. He evaluates the current status of the productivity of the Group and its effect on the local and international economies. A successful, 12-year professional, he joined the management team in 1995 and has continued to work towards the enhancement of the economic development of the area through his position with the Group. Currently putting the finishing touches on his own book, Dr. Besiso is also coordinating plans for the establishment of his own business. Al-Zamil Group of Companies is the largest combined group of businesses in the Middle East. The Group specializes in a variety of industrial works and has provided superior talent in the market since 1972. Headquartered in Riyadh, Saudi Arabia, the Group supports a total of 20 locations throughout the region. **Career Highlights:** Consultant, Al Zamil Group of Companies (1996-Present); General Manager, EASY COM for Communication (1993-96); General Manager, Fast Food Marketers (1990-93). **Associations & Accomplishments:** International Marketing Association of Bahrain; American Marketing Association; American Business Group of Riyadh. **Education:** Tulsa University: Ph.D. (1987), M.B.A. (1978); Certified Public Accountant Review Course (1979). **Personal Information:** Married to Ghada in 1980. Four children: Najia, Dina, Dawood, and Omar. Dr. Besiso enjoys writing articles and books.

Jeffrey W. Fox

Systems and Network Manager
Pacific Investment Management Company
840 Newport Center Drive
Newport Beach, CA 92660
(949) 720-6305
Fax: (949) 719-2428
onyxsolutions@mindspring.com

6722

Business Information: Mr. Fox is the Systems and Network Manager for Pacific Investment Managenment Company. In his position, he oversees and directs all activities associated with the systems and network environment. Mr. Fox presides over employees, provides technical support to all departments, as well as oversees the development of data systems and applications. A savvy, 16 year professional, he also works in research and development to keep abreast of the latest technology and does presentations to Company executives. In the future, Mr. Fox would like to work more in the area of network engineering. He credits his success to professional associations, reading, conferences, and vendors. Pacific Investment Management Company is an established and reputable financial services firm located in Newport Beach, California. Founded in 1970, the Company provides services to clients in the area of financial and portfolio management with specific concentration in fixed income investments. There are 1,200 professional peopel working within Pacific Investment Management Company advising each client on the best use of finances, answering client queries, and promoting activities throughout the community. **Career Highlights:** Systems and Network Manager, Pacific Investment Management Company (1997-Present); Senior Systems Engineer, Professional Computing Inc. (1996-97); Senior Systems Engineer, Network Support Services (1995-96); Network Engineer, Chrysler Corporation (1987-95). **Associations & Accomplishments:** Network Professionals Association. **Education:** Madonna College, B.S. (1983); Central Texas College; Control Data Institute; Microsoft Certified Systems Engineer; Cisco Certified Network Associate. **Personal Information:** Married to Debra in 1999.

Yehuda Stuart Frager, Ph.D., OCP-DBA

Senior Staff Associate
T. Rowe Price Associates
6209 Western Run Drive
Baltimore, MD 21209
(410) 345-8134
Fax: (410) 345-3360
yehuda_frager@troweprice.com

6726

Business Information: Dr. Frager is a Senior Staff Associate and Technical Research Consultant for T. Rowe Price Associates. He is the Data Management specialist for Infrastructure Planning and Development within the Production Services department, an interdisciplinary team of IT professionals. Before joining T. Rowe Price Associates in 1999, Dr. Frager served as Senior Database Consultant with the Maxim Group. His background history also includes employment as Assistant Director, Information Technology for the Regional Economics Studies Institute at Towson University and Senior Project Manager for Smith, Abbott and Company, all companies located in Baltimore, Maryland. Prior to this employment history, Dr. Frager served as a database, systems integration, and management consultant to private and public sector organizations for 15 years. An experienced, 23-year IT professional, Dr. Frager is involved in evaluating new enterprise technologies, special project management, and production support services. He provides a technical leadership role in assisting the Company with formulating goals, developing policies and procedures, and implementing strategies pertaining to enterprise data management. He is involved in the hiring and mentoring of technical staff in his interdisciplinary team and aspires to become more involved in technical management for the future. Established in 1939, T. Rowe Price Associates provides mutual fund sales and services, retirement planning, and other financial services. The Company buys stocks, securities and bonds, and has almost $200 billion in assets and nearly 4,000 employees. **Career Highlights:** Senior Staff Associate, T. Rowe Price Associates (1999-Present); Senior Database Consultant, Maxim Group (1997-99); Assistant Director, Information Technology, Regional Economics Studies Institute at Towson University (1996-97); Senior Project Manager, Smith, Abbot and Company (1993-96). **Associations & Accomplishments:** International Oracle User Group; Oracle Certified Professional-Database Administration; Oracle Masters Certification; Institute for Operational and Management Science; Part-time Rabbi and Cantor; Volunteer Secondary School Computer Instructor; Adjunct/Visiting Professor; Outstanding Young American (1978); BSA Eagle Scout. **Education:** University of Maryland, Ph.D. in Information Systems (1996), dissertation on "Model Management in Decision Support Systems for Dynamic Policy"; The Johns Hopkins University, M.S. in Computer Science (1980); Ner Israel Rabbinical College, B.A. in Talmudical Law (1977). **Personal Information:** Married to Tzipora C. Shuvalsky in 1977. Six children: Sora, Rafael, Mordecai, Jonathan, Ezra, and Jacob. One granddaughter, Rena. Dr. Frager enjoys music, playing guitar, piano and keyboards, Talmudic and religious studies, martial arts and chess.

C. Millard Stephens

Consultant/Systems Analyst
Fidelity Investments
P.O. Box 650078
Dallas, TX 75265-0078
(972) 584-5181
Fax: (972) 756-0531
millard.stephens@fmr.com

6726

Business Information: Mr. Stephens has worked in the information technology field since 1987. Joining Fidelity Investments in 1996, after nine years employed by Mobil Oil as both an MVS Performance Analyst and Hardware Configuration Analyst, Mr. Stephens fulfills the role of Consultant Systems Analyst. His position principally involves MVS and UNIX capacity planning and workload management. Mr. Stephens owns a record of delivering results by communicating effectively, paying close attention to technical details, and solving problems and challenges in systematic and positive fashion. Now an expert in the field, he conducts process assessments and applications analysis. Looking for future trends and forecasts, Mr. Stephens' focus is on advanced technologies to help Fidelity leverage and maximize its investments in technology and processes. He desires to continue to work in various areas of capacity planning. One of his greatest professional accomplishments occurred in 1998 as he implemented a performance and capacity data storage warehouse for several hundred UNIX servers. His new innovation enabled quick and accurate access to data which was previously unavailable. Fidelity Investments functions as a financial service providing mutual fund management, brokerage services, and 401K and 403B plans as well as employer payroll and benefits services. Fidelity presently employs a global staff of more than 30,000 people. **Career Highlights:** Consultant/Systems Analyst, Fidelity Investments (1996-Present); Mobil Oil Corporation: MVS Performance Analyst (1994-96), Hardware Configuration Analyst (1987-93). **Associations & Accomplishments:** Computer Measurement Group; The Honor Society of Phi Kappa Phi; Lay Speaker, United Methodist Church. **Education:** Texas A&M University: M.B.A. (1987), B.S. in Computer Science (1985). **Personal Information:** Married to Dawn in 1989. Two children: Adam and Daniel. Mr. Stephens enjoys golf, travel, being involved in church and city league sports.

Diane J. Crincoli

Vice President of LAN Administration
Bank of New York Trust Company
4403 Hanover Park Drive
Jacksonville, FL 32224-8604
dcroncoli@aol.com

6733

Business Information: As Vice President of LAN Administration at the Bank of New York Trust Company, Ms. Crincoli is responsible for the information systems infrastructure for the Company's eastern region that includes all states east of the Mississippi River and Texas. A sharp, 10-year veteran of the technology field, Ms. Crincoli lends her extensive expertise to manage the computer and telephone systems in a multi-location, multi-platform nationwide environment. As chief liaison between system users and development staff, she initiates, motivates, and manages medium to large projects and project teams from planning to implementation, training, and signoff. Many of Ms. Crincoli's career highlights involve taking companies from dumb terminal infrastructures to sophisticated midrange and computer infrastructure with integrated world class enterprise resource planning applications such as Lawson Software and BPCS. Preferring a tried and true software system, Ms. Crincoli's plans include a more seamless software environment that enables the users to jump to different platforms through continued Lotus Notes development of the front end software systems. The Bank of New York Trust Company is the United States' largest trust company in market share, number of issues, and proceeds as well as one of the world's leading financial institutions. The Bank of New York, founded by Alexander Hamilton in 1784, is not only the oldest bank in New York but is one of the oldest banks in the world. The Bank provides comprehensive financial services to individuals, small and mid-sized businesses, multinational corporations, financial institutions, governments, and public agencies worldwide. **Career Highlights:** Vice President of LAN Administration, Bank of New York Trust Company (1999-Present); Vice President of Professional Services,

MACPRO (1996-99); Information Systems Manager, Huron Machine Products (1993-96). **Associations & Accomplishments:** Institute of Electrical and Electronics Engineers; Association of Computing Machinery. **Education:** Florida Altantic University: Master's degree (In Progress), B.S. in Computer Science (1990); University of Florida, B.A. in Animal Science. **Personal Information:** Ms. Crincoli enjoys emerging technologies and surfing the Internet.

7000 - 8999

SERVICES

7000 Hotels and Other Lodging Places

7011 Hotels and motels
7021 Rooming and boarding houses
7032 Sporting and recreational camps
7033 Trailer parks and campsites
7041 Membership-basis organization hotels

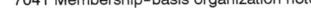

Brian J. Brady

Information Systems Director
Crown American Hotels Company
1 Pasquerilla Plaza
Johnstown, PA 15901-1999
(814) 536-9515
Fax: (814) 533-4688
brianbr@crownam.com

7011

Business Information: Mr. Brady has served in several different positions since he began his career with the Crown American Hotels Company. At the present time, he fulfills the responsibilities of Information Systems Director. Assuming responsibility for the planning and implementation of all corporate and property specific information systems, he performs systems integration through the assistance of third parties. He handles the hardware and software procurement and is the Company's chief liaison with technology vendors. Performing company-wide strategic planning, Mr. Brady ensures that the hotels have the most efficient technological tools with which to perform their functions in a timely manner. His goal is to continue to grow within the Company in the area of information technology systems. The Crown American Hotels Company is a hotel owners and management company with 27 hotels across the United States. Privately owned and operated, national operations employ the skilled services of 2,000 dedicated individuals. Since its inception in 1950, the Company has grown in size and locations and currently reports over $100 million in yearly revenues. **Career Highlights:** Crown American Hotels Company: Information Systems Director (1999-Present), Hotel Acquisition Analyst (1996-99), Associate Director of Hotel Operations (1992-96), General Manager (1990-92). **Associations & Accomplishments:** Hospitality Financial and Technology Professionals; Certified Hospitality Technology Professional; Naval Reserve Association. **Education:** Bristol University, M.B.A. (1992); Pennsylvania State University, B.S. in Accounting (1985). **Personal Information:** Married to Tammy in 1990. One child: Brian J. Jr. Mr. Brady enjoys golf, antiques and books.

Cindy Koubek

Management Information Systems Manager
Fairmont Hotel
123 Baronne Street
New Orleans, LA 70112-2355
(504) 529-4760
Fax: (504) 529-4869
ckoubek@fairmont.com

7011

Business Information: Serving in the role of Management Information Systems Manager for Fairmont Hotel, Ms. Koubek oversees and directs all aspects of day-to-day administration and operations of the systems infrastructure. She also determines strategies and business contributions of the systems functions. Accordingly, she maintains LAN connectivity and PCs, provides hardware and software support, operates the Hotel's help desk, and develops the end user training curriculum. She has faithfully served with Fairmont in a variety of positions since coming on board in 1994. Believing in the Bible verse "I can do all things through Christ who strengthens me," Ms. Koubek continues to enjoy substantial success and plans to remain in her chosen career path. With constant attention to detail, the Fairmont Hotel serves the most discriminating needs of today's guest and meeting planner. Attaining the Fairmont name in 1907, the Hotel approaches the 21st century with the mission of being recognized as the most innovative, personalized and distinctive luxury hotels and resorts worldwide. **Career Highlights:** Fairmont Hotel: Management Information Systems Manager (1998-Present), Staff Accountant (1994-98). **Education:** Jefferson Davis Junior College. **Personal Information:** Ms. Koubek enjoys music, creating databases and commercial art.

Joseph A. Maio

Senior Manager
Hilton Hotels Corporation
1170 Spring Street
Elizabeth, NJ 07201
(908) 820-2938
Fax: (908) 351-3952
joe_maio@hilton.com

7011

Business Information: Senior Manager of the Information Technology Department within the Hilton Hotels Corporation, Mr. Maio utilizes his proficiency in the industry to support computer networks and servers at all Hilton Hotel locations, reservation centers, and sales offices. In the supervision of 12 employees, Mr. Maio is charged with the software development and network design while gaining membership with HFTP or Hospitality, Finance, & Technical Professionals. Committed to the future development and success of the Hilton Corporation, Mr. Maio is centralizing all hotel systems and is working closely with the Hotel's management and systems users in the developemnt of innovative systems to allow more efficient operation. Consistently achieving superb performance in his field, Mr. Maio is working towards a position of Vice President of Operational Systems where he will be able to fully utilize his abilities. The Hilton Hotels Corporation is a major hotel and hospitality chain established in 1919. Operating with over 220 hotels internationally, the Corporation is renowned for their high profile locations and superior accommodations. Manned by 12 technical experts, the Corporations's information technology department maintains the entire systems infrastrucuture. **Career Highlights:** Hilton Hotels Corporation, Information Technology Division: Senior Manager (1999-Present), Project Manager (1996-99), Manager of Installation and Training of Hotel Systems (1994-96). **Education:** University of Houston, B.S. (1989); Paul Smiths College, A.A.S. **Personal Information:** Mr. Maio enjoys golf and skiing.

Marjorie Nial

Information Technology Technical and Administrative Assistant
SCIT
7070 East Broadway Road
Mount Pleasant, MI 48858
(517) 775-0170
Fax: (517) 775-0154
mnial@sagchip.org

7011

Business Information: As an Information Technology Technical and Administrative Assistant with SCIT, Ms. Nial is responsible for maintaining, reviewing, and correlating the Information Technology Department's annual budget of $4 million. Ms. Nial has also designed SCIT's database, and maintains the database infrastructure, continually performing systems upgrades as needed. Exercising her administrative capabilities, Ms. Nial facilitates office operations by trafficking files, processing crucial paperwork, and regulating the Departmental inventory. Continually formulating new goals and objectives, Ms. Nial plans to pursue more training in information technology, thereby, ensuring SCIT's longevity and personal occupational success. SCIT is a casino and resort, providing full-scale lodging and dining facilities to tourists in Mount Pleasant, Michigan. Established in 1994, the Resort currently employs more than 7,000 trained professional who aid in generating the Department's high annual revenues. Dedicated to customer satisfaction, SCIT is noted for its high-end service and remains a top resort for travelers in the Northeast region. **Career Highlights:** Information Technology Technical and Administrative Assistant, SCIT (Present). **Associations & Accomplishments:** National Association of Executive Females. **Education:** Mid Michigan Community College, General Technology and Medical Science (In Progress); University of Maryland, degree in Business. **Personal Information:** Married to Anthony Maynard in 2000. Ms. Nial enjoys tennis and painting.

Linda L. Shoemaker

Management Informations Systems Director
Frontier Hotel Gambling
3120 Las Vegas Boulevard South
Las Vegas, NV 89109
(702) 794-8424
Fax: (702) 794-8401
shoemaklin@aol.com

7011

Business Information: As Management Informations Systems Director of Frontier Hotel Gambling, Ms. Shoemaker oversees the entire systems infrastructure and ensures its functionality and operational status. Maintaining systems security and reliability are other important aspects of her responsibilities. A successful systems expert, Ms. Shoemaker provides proper backups and disaster relief systems. Handling all aspects of AS400 platform and LAN networks, she is also responsible for developing access listings, designing and implementing advanced technology, and purchasing new equipment and accessories. Her highlight was surviving Y2K. Ms. Shoemaker says the key to her success is persistence. She plans to increase her technical skills and take advantage of new opportunities afforded to her by the Hotel. One of the oldest establishments in Las Vegas, Nevada, the Frontier Hotel Gambling was the first establishment in Las Vegas to book Elvis Presley and the first to feature Sigfried and Roy. The Hotel houses 984 rooms and features a full service gambling casino. **Career Highlights:** Management Information Systems Director, Frontier Hotel Gambling (1998-Present); Information Systems Support, Primm Valley Resorts (1992-96); Computer Operations, Harrah's Hotel & Casino (1979-95). **Personal Information:** Two children: Ralph L. and Laurie Dawn.

7200 Personal Services

7211 Power laundries, family and commercial
7212 Garment pressing and cleaners' agents
7213 Linen supply
7215 Coin-operated laundries and cleaning
7216 Drycleaning plants, except rug
7217 Carpet and upholstery cleaning
7218 Industrial launderers
7219 Laundry and garment services, nec
7221 Photographic studios, portrait
7231 Beauty shops
7241 Barber shops
7251 Shoe repair and shoeshine parlors
7261 Funeral service and crematories
7291 Tax return preparation services
7299 Miscellaneous personal services, nec

Vickey A. Kjelvik

Help Desk Analyst/Department Web Editor
Transamerica Tax Service
1201 Elm Street, Suite 400
Dallas, TX 75270
(214) 571-2853
Fax: (214) 571-2329

7291

Business Information: Serving as Help Desk Analyst and Department Web Editor of Transamerica Tax Service, Ms. Kjelvik provides technical support to the approximate 1,500 internal onsite, remote, and external customers. As a part of a four person Help Desk team, she troubleshoots problems, works with field representatives, and internal departments. A systems expert, Ms. Kjelvik created her department's Web site and developed its entire training program. Currently working to obtain her A+ certification, she looks forward to taking a more active part in the Internet and assisting in designing the Web site for the entire service department. Ms. Kjelvik credits her success to her ability to think out-of-the-box and aggressively take on new challenges. Transamerica Tax Service is a real estate tax service provider. The Company performs tax tracking services for businesses, researching and maintaining tax information for clients. Established in 1928, Transamerica Tax Service employs 1,500 service and research professionals nationwide. On July 21, 1999, Transamerica merged with Aegon. **Career Highlights:** Help Desk Analyst/Department Web Editor, Transamerica Tax Service (1994-Present); Manager, Conoco (1992-94). **Education:** M.T.S.U. (1994). **Personal Information:** Ms. Kjelvik enjoys martial arts and Renaissance festivals. Ms. Kjelvik is engaged to Robert Beaver.

Elizabeth D. Moosman

Executive Assistant
Equitable Tax Service
2500 North 300 East, Trailer 12
Logan, UT 84341-5734
(435) 755-9827
Fax: (435) 755-9827

7291

Business Information: Ms. Moosman functions as the an Executive Assistant for Equitable Tax Service. She runs computer programs and often meets with the customers as she attempts to save them money. A successful professional in the technology field, Ms. Moosman assists the Owner of the Company in completing various day-to-day tasks. The highlight of her career has been earning a scholarship to medical school, and being the first woman to win this scholarship award. As for the future, she plans to be self-supportive and grow on the leading edge of technical email. Her advice is "make business home-based and save on tax deductions." Current success, she states, has been the direct result of spousal support and her ability to deliver results and take on challenges and new responsibilities. Founded in 1986, Equitable Tax Service helps clients pay all their taxes. To do so, the two full-time employees meet with prospective customers and tailors their services to client's needs. In addition, the Company helps others prepare for audits. On many occasions, Equitable Tax Service has represented their clients and met with IRS officials. **Career Highlights:** Executive Assistant, Equitable Tax Service (1986-Present). **Associations & Accomplishments:** Secretary/Treasurer, City Business Association; Cache Handicap Action Council; White House Conference in Handicapped Persons; National Association of Tax Practitioners; National Association of Enrolled Agents. **Education:** Utah State University (1992); University of Utah, B.S. **Personal Information:** One child: Shannon Taelon Moosman Perkins. Ms. Moosman enjoys travel, painting and music.

7300 Business Services

7311 Advertising agencies
7312 Outdoor advertising services
7313 Radio, TV, publisher representatives
7319 Advertising, nec
7322 Adjustment and collection services
7323 Credit reporting services
7331 Direct mail advertising services
7334 Photocopying and duplicating services
7335 Commercial photography
7336 Commercial art and graphic design
7338 Secretarial and court reporting
7342 Disinfecting and pest control services
7349 Building maintenance services, nec
7352 Medical equipment rental
7353 Heavy construction equipment rental
7359 Equipment rental and leasing, nec
7361 Employment agencies
7363 Help supply services
7371 Computer programming services
7372 Prepackaged software
7373 Computer integrated systems design
7374 Data processing and preparation
7375 Information retrieval services
7376 Computer facilities management
7377 Computer rental and leasing
7378 Computer maintenance and repair
7379 Computer related services, nec
7381 Detective and armored car services
7382 Security systems services
7383 News syndicates
7384 Photofinishing laboratories
7389 Business services, nec

Rudy Barrow Jr.

Director of Information Technologies
DMB&B Advertising
6500 Wilshire Boulevard, Suite 1000
Los Angeles, CA 90048
(323) 658-4518
Fax: (323) 658-4102
rudy_barrow@dmbb.com

7311

Business Information: Mr. Barrow is the Director of Information Technologies for DMB&B Advertising. He oversees all technical aspects of the Agency. A five year veteran of the technology field, he also fulfills the accountability of Senior Instructor. Understanding all services of the operation, Mr. Barrow manages the infrastructure hardware, e-mail administration, staff support, and proactive telecommunications systems. DMB&B Advertising Agency depends on technology to complete high tech projects correctly and efficiently. He devotes much of his time to clearly defining the goals of the system and understanding the individual steps used. Mr. Barrow has a team helping to direct information technologies. He hopes to lead a larger group, possibly moving into an administrative role. But, he wants to keep his skills sharp and stay ahead in technology. Mr. Barrow has received numerous recognitions as well as monetary bonuses for creations and ideas he has implemented. His professional success has been achieved due to the ability and desire to learn. DMB&B Advertising is an advertising agency owned by the MacManus Group. Headquartered in New York, this full-service agency has approximately 150 locations worldwide to assist in providing a variety of services. Clients include Coca Cola, Burger King, the Australian Tourist Commission, and General Motors. Presently, the Los Angeles office employs a work force of more than 100 people. **Career Highlights:** Director of Information Technologies, DMB&B Advertising (1998-Present); Development Manager, G&J USA Publishing (1997-98); Senior Support Analyst, Saatchi & Saatchi Advertising (1994-96). **Personal Information:** Mr. Barrow enjoys music, sports, outdoors, travel and good comedy.

Manoj S. Bhandary

Software Development Manager
Annuncio
342 Greendale Way #2
San Jose, CA 95129
(650) 314-6182
bhandarym@aol.com

7311

Business Information: Drawing upon eight years of software management experience, Mr. Bhandary is the Sofware Development Manager for Annuncio. He works closely with management and users to analyze, specify, and design cutting edge software to harness more of the computer's power. In his capacity, he ensures that all of the products are of the highest quality and shipped to their destinations in a timely manner. Moreover, Mr. Bhandary guarantees that the Corporation's products are laced with quality, value, and reliability as well as shipped to the correct location. In the future, he looks forward to continuing with the Corporation and conducting more business to business solutions. He attributes his success to having role models such as political leaders in his life. Founded in 1997, Annuncio is an Internet based firm. Located in San Jose, California, the Corporation produces marketing campaigns for a variety of businesses and industries around the United States. With a staff of 104 employees, the Corporation reports an estimated annual revenue of $192 million. **Career Highlights:** Software Development Manager, Annuncio (2000-Present); Software Engineering Manager, Informix Soft, Inc. (1992-00). **Associations & Accomplishments:** Institute of Electrical and Electronics Engineers Association. **Education:** Santa Clara University, M.S. in Engineering Management (1999); University of Bombay, B.S. in Computer Science. **Personal Information:** Married to Mallika in 1995. One child: Mayur M. Mr. Bhandary enjoys tennis and reading.

Maynard S. Clark

Executive Director
Vegetarian Resource Center
P.O. Box 38-1068
Cambridge, MA 02238-1068
(617) 625-3790
Fax: (815) 346-1306
vrc@tiac.ngt

7311

Business Information: Serving as Executive Director of the Vegetarian Resource Center, Mr. Clark oversees and directs all daily administration and operations on behalf of the Center and its clients. He is responsible for aspects of quality, control of information, design and development of new resources and tools, supervision of data delivery, and filling the position of event organizer and publicist. An active member of industry related associations enables Mr. Clark to remain current on new technology as well as network and interact with other professionals in different fields. Highly regarded in his field and by his colleagues, he possesses superior talents and an excellent understanding of technology. His success is attributed to his ability to think outside the box, aggressively take on new challenges, and deliver results. Established in 1993, the Vegetarian Resource Center offers services in telecommunications and resource networking to help advance the latest trend in plant-based diets. Currently operating with four partners, the Center is continuously supplying materials on at home and dining out meals via the Internet. Anticipating further growth for the Vegetarian Resource Center, Mr. Clark would like to expand with yet another service offering information in the area. **Career Highlights:** Executive Director, Vegetarian Resource Center (Present). **Associations & Accomplishments:** Lifetime Member, International Vegetarian Union; Lifetime Member, Vegetarian Union of North America; Past Vice President, North American Vegetarian Society. **Education:** Harvard Divinity School; Software Council Fellowship Program (1998-99); Tufts University; California State University at Hayward; Wheaton College.

Fred H. DeCarlo

Director
Bozell Group
40 West 23rd Street
New York, NY 10010
(212) 727-5530

7311

Business Information: As a partner of the Bozell Group, Mr. DeCarlo serves as the Director responsible for overseeing all Agency endeavors involving information technologies. Possessing superior talents and an excellent understanding of technology, he supervises Web development projects, as well as database and infrastructure development for the Agency. Lending his expertise to project management, Mr. DeCarlo is incorporating the Internet and its advanced capabilities to enhance existing and new business relationships. His success is attributed to education and drive. Located in New York, New York, the Bozell Group is a subsidiary of True North, one of the largest advertising agencies in the world. Some of the Agency's better known accounts are Datek On-line, MassMutual, and Bank of America. The Agency is also well known for the Milk Mustache advertising campaign. With the current trend in marketing, the Agency is also involved in producing e-commerce advertising campaigns. **Career Highlights:** Director, Bozell Group (1998-Present). **Associations & Accomplishments:** CCNA. **Education:** William Patterson College of New Jersey, B.A. (1991); Microsoft Certified System Engineer+Internet.

Lynn R. Hafen

IBM AS400 Systems Administrator
MarkeStar
2475 Washington Boulevard
Odgen, UT 84401-2315
(801) 622-9788
Fax: (801) 393-4115
lhafen@mktstar.com

7311

Business Information: Serving as IBM AS400 Systems Administrator of MarketStar, Mr. Hafen installs operating systems software. Database management systems software, compilers, and utilities. In this context, he monitors and fine tunes systems software, peripherals, and networks. Administering and controlling IBM AS400 operations, Mr. Hafen is responsible for the maintenance and functionality of the systems infrastructure. Demonstrating exceptional command of computer upgrades and installation, he also lends his expertise in the area of software implementation. In the future, he would like to broaden his skills by learning other operating systems at an enterprise level within the Company. His continued success is a product of solid computer training and strong problem-solving skills. Operating as one of the largest companies in the United States, MarketStar is a product and service marketing agency. Formed in 1988, the Company employs the talents and professional expertise of 4,000 individuals to provide positive representation of MarketStar. The Company creates innovative marketing concepts and strategies designed to attract new clients and strengthen ties with existing clientele. **Career Highlights:** IBM AS400 Systems Administrator, MarketStar (1998-Present); IBM AS400 Administrator, First Security Bank (1997-96); Systems Specialist, Bordon Meadow Gold (1995-96); Sales Manager/Operator, Swire Coca-Cola (1980-95). **Associations & Accomplishments:** National Rifle Association; American Wildlife Resources; ALWA. **Education:** UVCC (1989). **Personal Information:** Married to Kathleen in 1993. Mr. Hafen enjoys shooting guns, skiing, hunting, ATVs, painting, photography and art.

Dan A. Mastroianni

Manager of Systems and Programming
MBI Inc.
677 Connecticut Avenue
Norwalk, CT 06854
(203) 854-9400
Fax: (203) 866-6943
dmastroianni@mbi-inc.com

7311

Business Information: Serving as the Manager of Systems and Programming for MBI Inc., Mr. Mastroianni is responsible for the operation of the A/S400 platform. He oversees and manages the departmental budget, programming details, and maintenance of all computer systems. Capitalizing on more than 15 years of experience, he has honed his considerable knowledge and skills, demonstrating a comprehensive knowledge of his field. An accomplished professional, he wrote and developed a distribution package for a previous employer. Mr. Mastroianni continues to grow professionally through the fulfillment of his responsiblities and his involvement in the advancement of operations. Attributing his success to his ability to see the big systems' picture, he looks forward to assisting in the completion of future corporate goals. MBI Inc. advertises and sells collectors' items, such as books, stamps, and porcelain. Established in 1969, the Corporation employs the skilled services of 400 individuals to market services, address customer queries, and facilitate projects. Located in Norwalk, Connecticut, the Corporation sells products to clients internationally. **Career Highlights:** Manager of Systems and Programming, MBI Inc. (1992-Present); Senior Program Analyst, ASCOM/Hasler (1986-92). **Education:** University of Bridgeport, B.A. (1984). **Personal Information:** Married to Anne McKenzie in 1986. Three children: Danielle McKenzie, Thomas McKenzie Mastroianni, and William McKenzie Mastroianni. Mr. Mastroianni enjoys tennis and music. Recording, composing, and performing professionally, Mr. Mastroianni considers music his second profession.

Greg O'Brien

President
G&L Enterprises
P.O. Box 11
Pearisburg, VA 24134
(540) 921-3193
Fax: (540) 921-3150
mrgregob@aol.com

7311

Business Information: Venturing out into the entrepreneurial world with his fiancée, Mr. O'Brien is founder and co-partner of G&L Enterprises. Serving as President, he determines the overall strategic direction and vision as well as formulates business ventures and marketing plans to propel the Company to the forefront of the industry. Possessing an excellent understanding of his field, he maintains the company's Web site, researches new business, and does all the promotions. Maintaining close client relations enables Mr. O'Brien to analyze, specify, design, and execute cutting edge promotional solutions. Concurrently, he serves as a software specialist for Castle Rock Insurance, where he maintains the functionality and operational status of the company's systems infrastructure. He attributes his professional success to his drive and determination to succeed. Mr. O'Brien's strategic goal is to find new members and new businesses to represent. A very reputable and dependable business, G&L Enterprises operates in the Internet market, representing both small and large businesses. Established in 1999, the Company provides cutting edge promotion solutions. Located in Pearisburg, Virginia, the Company is owned and operated by Mr. O'Brien and his fiancée. **Career Highlights:** President, G&L Enterprises (1999-Present); Software Specialist, Castle Rock Insurance (1994-Present); Veterinary Assistant, Animal Care Center (1988-92). **Associations & Accomplishments:** International Association of Webmasters and Designers; Heritage Foundation; Mentor, Providence United Methodist Church; New River Community College Alumni Association. **Education:** New River Community College, A.A.S. (1997). **Personal Information:** Mr. O'Brien enjoys reading, movies, outdoor activities, dogs, and computers.

Kevin M. Parker

Information Technology Support Engineer
McKinney & Silver
P.O. Box 1918
Raleigh, NC 27602-1918
(919) 821-6493
Fax: (919) 821-5122
kparker@mckinney-silver.com

7311

Business Information: Providing his skilled services as Information Technology Support Engineer, Mr. Parker presides over all aspects of the information technology operations for McKinney & Silver. He ensures that the networks and computer systems are functioning at optimum levels, utilizing marketing data to keep the Company on the forefront of its industry's technological advancements. Mr. Parker has the ability to incorporate his technical and business knowledge together to provide overall sound strategies for the Company's future technological direction. Consistently achieving quality performance, he aspires to a more people orientated managerial position. Mr. Parker's success reflects his ability to think outside the box, produce results, and aggressively take on new challenges and responsibilities. Owned by US WEB/CKS, McKinney & Silver is an Internet advertising and technical consulting firm. The Company performs advertising, marketing consultancy, strategic business, and e-commerce consulting for its various business clients. Founded in 1979, McKinney & Silver has 30 locations across the country. Approximately 180 knowledgeable individuals are employed in the Raleigh, North Carolina office. **Career Highlights:** Information Technology Support Engineer, McKinney & Silver (1999-Present); Consultant, Robert Half Consulting (1998-99); Network Engineer, Compucom, Inc. (1998); Network Engineer, Apex Systems (1997-98). **Education:** Elon College, B.S. (1994). **Personal**

Information: Married to Caroline in 1996. Mr. Parker enjoys computers, information technology, fishing, camping and the Internet.

Kevin M. Parker

Information Technology Support Engineer
McKinney & Silver
P.O. Box 1918
Raleigh, NC 27602-1918
(919) 821-6493
Fax: (919) 821-5122
kparker@mckinney-silver.com

7311

Business Information: Providing his skilled services as Information Technology Support Engineer, Mr. Parker presides over all aspects of the information technology operations for McKinney & Silver. He ensures that the networks and computer systems are functioning at optimum levels, utilizing marketing data to keep the Company on the forefront of its industry's technological advancements. Mr. Parker has the ability to incorporate his technical and business knowledge together to provide overall sound strategies for the Company's future technological direction. Consistently achieving quality performance, he aspires to a more people orientated managerial position. Mr. Parker's success reflects his ability to think outside the box, produce results, and aggressively take on new challenges and responsibilities. Owned by US WEB/CKS, McKinney & Silver is an Internet advertising and technical consulting firm. The Company performs advertising, marketing consultancy, strategic business, and e-commerce consulting for its various business clients. Founded in 1979, McKinney & Silver has 30 locations across the country. Approximately 180 knowledgeable individuals are employed in the Raleigh, North Carolina office. **Career Highlights:** Information Technology Support Engineer, McKinney & Silver (1999-Present); Consultant, Robert Half Consulting (1998-99); Network Engineer, Compucom, Inc. (1998); Network Engineer, Apex Systems (1997-98). **Education:** Elon College, B.S. (1994). **Personal Information:** Married to Caroline in 1996. Mr. Parker enjoys computers, information technology, fishing, camping and the Internet.

Michael Springer

Director Information Systems and Operations
Tecmark LLC
9403 Preserve Trail
Woodbury, MN 55125-7500
(651) 683-4770
Fax: (651) 452-9196
mspringe@isd.net

7311

Business Information: Mr. Springer is the Director of Information Systems and Operations of Tecmark LLC. He determines the strategic direction and business contribution of the information systems function. A savvy, 18 year professional, he oversees all day-to-day operations, such as mailings and systems software and hardware support. He is responsible for purchasing, installing, and troubleshooting all computer systems. Together with his staff, he guarantees the functionality and operational success of the networking environment. Working with vendors and clients on new deployments also fall within the purview of his responsibilities. Attaining Master's degree in March 2000, Mr. Springer's goals include becoming more involved in e-commerce on the Web and developing a voice response system. Working on his MCSE+I certification, he plans on being more creative on the Web. Tecmark LLC provides loyalty marketing services. Founded in 1990, the Company's clientele primarily stem from the hotel industry. A team of 20 individuals work to most effectively advertise the success and opportunities available through every client. Headquartered in Mindora Heights, Minnesota, the Company is working with the latest in technology to enhance their advertisement capabilities. **Career Highlights:** Director of Information Systems and Operations, Tecmark LLC (1999-Present); Senior Systems Administrator, Metris Companies (1997-99); Senior Network Analyst, Response Inc./Mayo Medical Center (1996-97); Senior Systems Administrator, Northwest Airlines Inc. (1987-96). **Associations & Accomplishments:** Microsoft Certified Systems Engineer; FCC License. **Education:** Kennedy Western University, Master's degree in Telecommunication Information Services (2000); Northwestern Electronics College, A.A. in Electronics Technology (1984); North Central College, B.S. in Behavioral Science (1982). **Personal Information:** Mr. Springer enjoys dancing and sports.

Wim Vincken, Ph.D.

Research and Development Manager
Coovi.com
Moshe Sharet 12/12
Bat Yam, Israel 5995
+972 54559824
Fax: +972 35075170
wim@dotcom2001.com

7311

Business Information: Serving as the Research and Development Manager for Coovi.com and possessing superior talents and an excellent understanding of systems technology, Dr. Vincken oversees all research projects and analyzes resulting data. Capitalizing on over 20 years of employment and educational experience, he implements innovative ideas that fosters Company growth and expansion. An accomplished professional, Dr. Vincken has published over 100 articles and 12 books as well as 2 books that were published internationally. Highly regarded, he also has delivered information technology seminars in Tel Aviv, and was a weekly guest speaker for IBM Corporation. His career success is attributed to his ability to think outside the box, take on challenges, and deliver results. Coovi is developing infrastructure for cross media hybrid promotional advertising campaigns. Established in 1999, the Company employs an industrious staff of 20 individuals to orchestrate all facets of design, research, and implementation. The Company is located in Jerusalem, Israel and provides services to customers worldwide. **Career Highlights:** Research and Development Manager, Coovi.com (1999-Present); Research and Development Manager, Delta Three (1999); Software Manager, IRT (1997); Consultant, Optimedia (1996). **Associations & Accomplishments:** Israeli Programmers Association. **Education:** University of Amsterdam, Ph.D. (1983); HTS Eindhoven, B.S. in Mathematics and Database Management. **Personal Information:** Married to Helena in 1993. Two children: Michael and Ashley. Dr. Vincken enjoys tennis, science fiction and writing manuals.

Bryan T. Walczak

Director of Management Information Systems
Arian Lowe & Travis
343 West Erie, Suite 520
Chicago, IL 60610
(312) 787-3300
Fax: (312) 787-3599
bryan@altadv.com

7311

Business Information: Mr. Walczak is Director of Management Information Systems for Arian Lowe & Travis. He is responsible for all aspects of day-to-day administration and operational functions. Quickly establishing his presence in the field, Mr. Walczak joined Arian Lowe & Travis in 1998 right out of Loyola University of Chicago. In his present role, he displays superior executive leadership in coordinating crucial data for other departments. Utilizing his expertise and communication skills, he determines the overall strategic direction and business contribution of the information systems function. Overseeing network concepts, desktop PCs, Macintosh PBXs, and audio visual technologies also fall within the scope of his responsibilities. Attending seminars and conducting Internet research, Mr. Walczak has a marked edge in the information technology field. Attributing his success to discipline, he is currently involved in the development of a new color scanner and copier. He aspires to one day open his own information technology company. Arian Lowe & Travis is a full service advertising agency. Staffed with 80 highly skilled employees, the Company specializes in print, radio, and television advertising packages. Utilizing advanced technology, coupled with state of the art equipment, Arian Lowe & Travis provides professional quality services. **Career Highlights:** Director of Management Information Systems, Arian Lowe & Travis (1998-Present). **Education:** Loyola University of Chicago, degree in Computer Systems (1998). **Personal Information:** Mr. Walczak enjoys baseball, volleyball, basketball and in-line skating.

Bruce Wang

Help Desk Supervisor
Draft Worldwide
114 Chirstopher Street, Apartment 20
New York, NY 10014
(212) 546-8354
Fax: (212) 546-7812
bwang@draftnet.com

7311

Business Information: Mr. Wang functions in the role of Help Desk Supervisor for Draft Worldwide. In his position, Mr. Wang oversees and directs all aspects of day-to-day activities associated within his department. Utilizing previous employment and education, Mr. Wang evaluates, installs, and supports PCs, Macs, and associated peripherals. He tests computers and software, keeps update on new hardware and software programs through research and development, and obtains funds to acquire new computers. Before joining Draft Worldwide in 1998, Mr. Wang served as Associate Account Manager for CompuServe Network Services. Developing realistic goals and looking to the next millennium, Mr. Wang plans on attaining the position of Manager of Information Systems Department at Draft Worldwide. "Play with all new technology," is cited as his advice to others. Offering a variety of quality services, Draft Worldwide is an established advertising firm. Founded in 1985, the Company offers services to business clients in the advertising area of direct mail, marketing, and commercials. Serving an international client base, Draft Worldwide employs 400 creative-minded individuals in the area of marketing, sales, graphic arts, and public relations. Headquarters for Draft Worldwide is located in Chicago. **Career Highlights:** Supervisor, Help Desk, Draft Worldwide (1998-Present); Associate Account Manager, CompuServe Network Services (1996-98). **Education:** University of Southern California, B.S. (1993).

Brad W. Aldridge

SQL Server Administrator
Radio Advertising Bureau
4030 Valley View Lane, Apartment 203
Dallas, TX 75244-5027
(972) 753-6756
brada@rab.com

7313

Business Information: Mr. Aldridge functions in the role of SQL Server Administrator for the Radio Advertising Bureau. He administers and controls a 15,000 record database, as well as manages, updates, querries information, and creates new fields and screens as necessary for the on-line promotion of its activities. Establishing himself in the field, Mr. Aldridge smartly utilizes software packages to ensure data integrity and security, recover corrupted data, eliminate redundancy, and tunning tools to enhance the database performance. His future endeavors include gaining more knowledge within the industry and fully utilizing his talents within the server administration sector. Career success is attributed to his persistance and ability to deliver results and aggressively take on new challenges. Radio Advertising Bureau provides radio station sales teams with the training, co-op advertising, and materials they need to effectively sell radio advertisement time. Established in 1954, the Bureau has created several instructional programs that have assisted hundreds of account executives in creating their motivational platform for advancement into the management sectors of the sales industry. **Career Highlights:** SQL Server Administrator, Radio Advertising Bureau (1999-Present). **Associations & Accomplishments:** Phi Theta Kappa. **Education:** Brookhaven College, A.A.S. in Computer Information Systems (1999); Northlake College; University of North Texas.

Kevin D. White

Senior Technologist
EURO RSCG DSW Partners
4 Triad Center
Salt Lake City, UT 84180-1411
(801) 366-1125
Fax: (801) 536-7350
kevin.white@dsw.com

7313

Business Information: As Senior Technologist of EURO RSCG DSW Partners, Mr. White oversees one of the small groups of technogists that directs and manages all interactive and World Wide Web production. On a daily basis, he must interact with employees as well as clients to determine the best course of action to meet their specific needs. Demonstrating a managment style that incorporates employee feedback and input, Mr. White works closely with his staff to formulate strategic business plans to improve current departmental policies. Internally recognized for his impressive accomplishments while serving as a member of project and technology management, he remains up-to-date on current subjects by devoting two hours of his busy daily schedule to technical research. Mr. White believes his success stems from his love for the field he is in. For the next millennium, he looks forward to advancement within the corporate structure. EURO RSCG DSW Partners is a brand communications and advertising agency. The largest company of it's kind in the inter-mountain area of the Western United States, the headquarters are located in New York. Specializing in interactive mediums, print, television, and radio, the Company employs over 250 people with revenues in excess of $300 million. **Career Highlights:** Senior Technologist, EURO RSCG DSW Partners (1999-Present); Director, Technology, Kelltech Internet Services (1998-99); Senior Developer, BVC (1998); Computational Geneticist, CWRU (1997-98). **Associations & Accomplishments:** Sierra Club; Zeta Psi Fraternity; Republican Party; HTML Author's Guild. **Education:** CWRU, B.A. in Economics (1996). **Personal Information:** Mr. White enjoys extreme outdoor activities.

Christopher A. Bates

Manager of Store Systems
Catalina Marketing
10308 Seabridge Way
Tampa, FL 33626-1838
(727) 579-5277
Fax: (727) 570-8507
cbates1@tampabay.rr.com

7319

Business Information: Mr. Bates is the Manager of Store Systems of Catalina Marketing. He manages a development group responsible for the manufacturing and enhancing of store side software used to evaluate purchases and print incentives. Recruited to the Company in 1998, Mr. Bates supervises a staff of 12 professional and technical experts who ensures the store wide system remains functional and operational. A multi-faceted professional, he also oversees all day-to-day operations, including personnel management and compiling and monitoring the budget and expenditures. Looking to the future in the new millennium, Mr. Bates goals include attaining the position of vice president of a software development company. His career success is attributed to his persistence and self motivation. Catalina Marketing provides a multi-functional communications network that offers targeted incentives, including sampling, in-store instant win games, advertising messages and loyalty programs to more than 152 million customers in over 13,000 retailers each week. International in scope, the Company is headquartered in Tampa, Florida, and presently employs a staff of 700 people who help generate annual revenues in excess of $250 million. **Career Highlights:** Manager of Store Systems, Catalina Marketing (1998-Present); Vice President of Software Development, Automated Technologys Systems (1997-98); Software Engineer, Concurrent Technologies Corporation (1991-97). **Associations & Accomplishments:** Association of Computing Machinery; International Brotherhood of Magicians; Who's Who in American High School Students. **Education:** California University of Pennsylvania: B.S. in Applied Computer Science (1990), A.S. **Personal Information:** Married to Polly Ann in 1990. Mr. Bates enjoys animals, music and magic.

Kent Brown

WAN Engineer
Donovan Data Systems
115 West 18th Street
New York, NY 10011
(212) 633-5120
Fax: (212) 633-5515
kent.brown@donovandata.com

7319

Business Information: Recently recruited to Donovan Data Systems, Mr. Brown serves as WAN Engineer. He assumes responsibility for network design and implementation, network control center operations, and performs second level data support. Maintaining the database and connectivity for the internal frame relay network, he monitors operations and administers program installations and upgrades for the network's eight nodes. Mr. Brown is proud to claim responsibility for implementing the National Science Foundation (NSF NET) network and the Prodigy Data Communications network while employed at MCI-Worldcom. As an eight year technology professional with an established record of producing results, Mr. Brown's success reflects his ability to think out-of-the-box and take on new challenges. Looking to the future, he plans to expand his horizon of experience by entering into the client server and e-commerce environments. Maintaining two locations in London and New York City, Donovan Data Systems is a mainframe information provider for the advertising industry. The Company specializes in advertising industry database management, information storage and retrieval, and installation and facilities management. Established in 1968, operations employ the skilled services of 600 individuals to acquire business, meet with clients, facilitate projects, and market services. The Company boasts annual sales of $100 million. **Career Highlights:** WAN Engineer, Donovan Data Systems (1999-Present); Network Analyst, Automatic Data Processing (1995-99); Senior Network Engineer, New York City Transit Authority (1991-95); Network/Systems Engineer, MCI Telecommunications (1987-91). **Associations & Accomplishments:** Network and Systems Professionals Association; Trailblazers; National Association of Telecommunications Professionals. **Education:** John Jay College (1997); Old Dominion University. **Personal Information:** Mr. Brown enjoys basketball and bowling.

Sharron L. Ball

Information Systems Manager
Jon Barry & Associates, Inc.
216 LePhillip Court
Conord, NC 28025
(704) 723-4204
Fax: (704) 723-4213
sball@jbarry.com

7322

Business Information: Having dedicated her time with Jon Barry & Associates, Inc. for five years, Mrs. Ball serves as the Information Systems Manager. In her capacity, she oversees all of the computer systems, networking, software, and hardware within the Corporation's infrastructure. Maintaining six systems, she is responsible for making sure the systems run smoothly and operate in an efficient manner. Managing a staff of four highly skilled individuals, Mrs. Ball has contributed to the growth of the Corporation through creating an information systems department. Looking toward the future for the Corporation, Mrs. Ball plans on helping the Corporation expand its networking and frame relay capabilities, as well as getting more involved with automated systems and the Web page. She also plans on obtaining more knowledge about technology. Jon Barry & Associates, Inc. was founded on the basis of contributing its services to the heathcare industry. Established in 1987, the Corporation serves as a collection agency and extended business office, specifically for the healthcare industry. In addition, they also conduct follow ups for the insurance companies. While employing the skilled service of nearly 85 people, the Corporation reports an annual revenue of $3.8 million. **Career Highlights:** Information Systems Manager, Jon Barry & Associates, Inc. (1995-Present); Database Programmer/Consultant, Information Technology Ma (1993-95); ACH/ATM/EFT Clerk, First City Texas Bank (1986-91). **Associations & Accomplishments:** Upe Society of Lamar University; Church Choir. **Education:** Lamar University, B.S. in Computer and Information Sciences (1994). **Personal Information:** Married to John in 1979. Two children: Stephanie and Jennifer. Mrs. Ball enjoys sewing, crafts, programming and time with her children.

David J. Lalone II

Management Information Systems Manager
Vengroff, Williams & Associates
3808 North Tamiami Trail
Sarasota, FL 34234
(941) 355-5900
Fax: (941) 355-4700
vwafla@aol.com

7322

Business Information: A savvy, eight year professional, Mr. Lalone was recruited to Vengroff, Williams & Associates as Management Information Systems Manager in 19998. In his position, he controls all computers, set up to networking, running all computer lines for networking and maintenance of computers. Possessing an excellent understanding of his field, Mr. Lalone monitors the networking environment, provides toubleshooting, and administers the phone grouping. He looks forward to continuing with the Company in the technical field and possibly moving to a higher position. A creative visionary who has proven himself correct on many occasions, Mr. Lalone's professional success reflects his technical ability to tackle challenges and deliver results. Established in 1965, Vengroff, Williams & Associates is the second largest national collection agency in the United States. The Company handles past due accounts for client companies. Located in Sarasota, Florida, the Company currently has a staff of 145 employees. Presently, the Company reports annual revenues in excess of $3 million. **Career Highlights:** Management Information Systems Manager, Vengroff, Williams & Associates (1998-Present); General Manager, Buccaneer Inn of Lomgboat Key (1996-98); Chef Apprentise, Cedars Cafe (1995-96); General Manager, Alez-Teco (1993-95). **Education:** Mississippi State University, degree in Hotel and Restaurant Management (1992). **Personal Information:** Mr. Lalone enjoys computer design, web publishing and power point presentations.

Ariane M. Eisman

Management Information Systems Director
Fala Direct Marketing, Inc.
70 Marcus Drive
Melville, NY 11747
(631) 694-1919
Fax: (631) 249-8550
aeisman@fala.com

7331

Business Information: Serving as a Director of Management Information Systems for Fala Direct Marketing, Inc., Ms. Eisman manages all client/server, network, and Web-based systems. Reporting directly to the chief financial officer, he maintains and develops projects. Possessing an excellent understanding of technology, Ms. Eisman also oversees data warehousing and e-commerce services. Dedicated to the success of the Corporation, she plans to continue to work with the Corporation for a number of years to come. The most rewarding aspects of her career is rebuilding a network in just six months. Ms. Eisman's success is attributed to his ability to think outside the box, take on new challenges, and deliver results. Fala Direct Marketing, Inc. provides services as a marketing firm. Established in 1926, the Corporation deals with a large direct mail market and a PC network of 250 systems. With three locations on Long Island, New York, the Corporation employs more than 600 personnel. **Career Highlights:** Director Management Information Systems, Fala Direct Marketing, Inc. (1998-Present); Independent Consultant, AME Consulting (1996-98); DIS Research: Director of Network Technology (1994-96), Senior Analyst (1992-94). **Associations & Accomplishments:** Long Island Software & Technology Network; Society of Women Engineers. **Education:** Columbia University, B.S. in Electrical Engineering (1990); Queens College, B.A. in Physical Sciences (1990). **Personal Information:** Married to Robert in 1989. Three children: Jason Elliot, Alec Jonah, and Emily Florence. Ms. Eisman enjoys piano and music.

Charel Margison-Evans
Technical Department Manager
Triplex Director Marketing Corporation
20 Leveroni Court
Novato, CA 94949
(415) 382-7136
Fax: (415) 382-7170
charelme@hotmail.com

7331

Business Information: Serving as Technical Department Manager for Triplex Director Marketing Corporation, Ms. Margison-Evans oversees and directs all daily technical operations on behalf of the Corporation. She is responsible for ensuring the efficiency and effectiveness of her department and resolving all technical difficulties and issues. Demonstrating her leadership skills, Ms. Margison-Evans supervises a staff of 14 employees, and is responsible for all personnel management that includes interviewing, hiring, staff reviews, and coordination of work load. Her professional success is attributed to her ability to inspire others, think logically, grasp the overall "Big Picture", and deliver results. Established in 1975, Triplex Director Marketing Corporation provides services dealing with direct mail computer services. The Corporation eliminates invalid and duplicate addresses and sorts for postal discounts for more cost-effective mailings. Local operations in Novato, California employ the expertise of 150 individuals to promote services, facilitate scheduling, and address customer queries. **Career Highlights:** Technical Department Manager, Triplex Director Marketing Corporation (1999-Present). **Education:** Strathclyde University, B.A. (1987). **Personal Information:** Ms. Margison-Evans enjoys reading.

Carolyn B. Tang
Web Coordinator
PointStar.com
1375 East Woodfield Road, Suite 300
Schaumburg, IL 60173
catango@hotmail.com

7331

Business Information: One of the leading experts in the marketing industry, Ms. Tang has ventured into the Internet aspects of global business marketing, introducing a new wave of client interaction where customers are offered the freedom and comfort of home travel via the Internet. Serving Pointstar.com as Web Coordinator, Ms Tang draws on her excellent understanding of technology and natural marketing ability to fulfill the responsibility of Web producer and Web advertising coordinator. Promoting special client offers and researching new innovative ways to attract people to the Web site are the most vital aspects of her daily activities. The highlight of her career is helping to increase the number of client merchants on the Web from 50 to 250. Presently studying Internet marketing strategies, Ms. Tang is searching for new ways of making the e-commerc experience more user friendly and more readily accessed to the public. PointStar.com, currently in their fourth year of operation, is an incentive direct marketing company whose service is specialized in areas on on-line shopping. Driven to raise the current merchant portfolio 250 percent, Pointstar.com has taken the necessary steps to ensure a successful career. **Career Highlights:** Web Coordinator, PointStar.com (2000-Present); Senior Producer of Online Broadcasts for KnowledgeSpace, Arthur Andersen KnowledgeSpace (1997-00); Freelance Copywriter, Hammacher Schlemmer (1997); Writer, Radio Free Europe/Radio Liberty (1996-97). **Associations & Accomplishments:** Chinese Mutual Aid Association (1998-Present); Medill. Graduate Editorial Council (1996); Web Girls International. **Education:** Northwestern University, Medill School of Journalism, M.S. in Journalism (1996); University of California at Berkeley, B.A. (1995). **Personal Information:** Ms. Tang enjoys travel, gardening, photography, biking, creative writing and tennis.

Brad J. Steven
Information Technology Manager
Print Tech, Inc.
6800 Jackson Road
Ann Arbor, MI 48103-9565
(734) 996-2345
Fax: (734) 996-2340
pt@printtechinc.com

7334

Business Information: Presently serving as Information Technology Manager for Print Tech, Inc., Mr. Steven is responsible for ensuring the efficient and effective operation of information technology equipment and systems throughout the Corporation. Directing the maintenance and upgrading of servers, digital files, and approximately 25 work stations, Mr. Steven also trains employees concerning the usage of office equipment. He is credited for his efforts in implementing additional technological systems for the Corporation. Attributing his success to his education and experience, Mr. Steven plans to become a Certified Netware Engineer and Certified Network Administrator in the near future. Established in 1981, Print Tech, Inc. is a full service printing company which provides one to four color offset printing, digital printing, and document management services for clients throughout the Ann Arbor, Michigan area. The Corporation also offers desktop publishing, binding, and digital graphics services. Currently employing 30 staff members, Print Tech, Inc. reports $3.2 million in estimated annual revenue and plans to continue providing excellent printing services while acquiring a larger customer base. **Career Highlights:** Information Technology Manager, Print Tech, Inc. (1996-Present). **Education:** University of Michigan, Bachelor's degree (1996). **Personal Information:** Mr. Steven enjoys travel and being an audiophile.

Donna R. Chabrier
Principal/Account Manager
Reactor
196 Castro Street, Floor 2
Mountain View, CA 94041
(650) 625-8660
Fax: (650) 625-8662
donnac@reactr.com

7336

Business Information: Ms. Chabrier serves in the dual role of Principal and Account Manager of Reactor. She is responsible for new business development, strategic planning, and marketing. Possessing business savvy and expertise, Ms. Chabrier performs as the financial comptroller who monitors financial and profit and loss statements as well as the fiscal budget. Maintenance of client relationships and meeting with vendors and referrals also fall within the purview of her responsibilities. She enjoys getting to know her clients on a professional and personal level, in order to really understand their needs. Her two busines partners of Reactor are Michael and Leon. In the future, Ms. Chabrier would like to implement a high-tech arena to be in a position to add additional staff members, and double the Company's annual sales. "Do it, have a plan and follow it," is cited as her credo. Reactor is a high-tech marketing firm. Established in 1999, the Company is manned by 4 employees who help generate in excess of $1 million in annual sales. The Company markets communication graphics design as well as assists clients in the development of logo branding messages, web banners, trade shows, and Web site design. **Career Highlights:** Principal/Account Manager, Reactor (1998-Present); Owner/President, On Campus Marketing (1995-98); Sales Executive, Net Manage (1994-95); Regional Sales Manager, STAT, Inc. (1991-94). **Associations & Accomplishments:** Business Marketing Association; American Marketing Association; Volunteer Participant, Friends of Inn Vision. **Education:** University of Phoenix, B.S. in Business Administration (1992). **Personal Information:** Married to James A. in 1990. Two children: Warren and Monroe. Ms. Chabrier enjoys musical theater, volunteer activities and being a teacher's aide.

Jonathan Harlap
Director of Multimedia Design
Reel Film Festival, Inc.
17 Cote St. Catherine, Suite 4
Montreal, Quebec, Canada H2V 1Z7
(514) 948-0489
jon@reelfilmfestival.com

7336

Business Information: Charged with all of the Web site and print design aspects of Reel Film Festival, Inc., Mr. Harlap serves as the Director of Multimedia Design. He is responsible for maintaining the functionality and operational status of the Corporation's Web site. Dedicated to creating and maintaining a corporate Web site and individual publications for viewing persons outside of the Festival's activity, he contributes his extensive education and experience to create the most state-of-the-art productions. Renowned among his peers for having the best work in the country, Mr. Harlap will

continue to expand his network of contacts, further ensuring the future success of the Festival. Attributing his success to drive and detemination, his advice is "never stop learning." Striving to create a forum for artists and film makers, Reel Film Festival, Inc. offers the opportunity for recognition and networking with professionals in the industry. Catering to the needs of students and independent artists, the Reel Film Festival employs a staff of six at their Montreal, Canada location. Established in 1999, Reel Film Festival stands by their goal of gaining an international audience, while their additional exposure will make way for the introduction of new actors and film makers. Reel Film Festival can be corresponded with at P.O. Box 444, Postal Station B, Montreal, Quebec, H3B 3J7. **Career Highlights:** Director of Multimedia Design, Reel Film Festival, Inc. (1999-Present); Web Design and 3D Animator, Freelance (1996-99); Computer Technician, Freelance (1993-97). **Education:** McGill University (1997). **Personal Information:** Mr. Harlap enjoys 3D animation, music, poetry and short fiction novels.

Beth E. Jones
Marketing Strategist
Scott Hull Associates
68 East Franklin Street
Dayton, OH 45459
(937) 433-8383
Fax: (937) 433-0434
sabriel25@aol.com

7336

Business Information: Providing her skilled services as Marketing Strategist for Scott Hull Associates, Ms. Jones' primary responsibility is to perform market research in order to develop new ways to sell the artists' work. In addition, she develops innovative campaign names and public relations promotions. Assisting Scott Hull Associates to enter new markets, Ms. Jones created and maintains the Company's Web site. With a thorough knowledge of markets and competitors, she designs powerful marketing strategies that drive the artists' work to market. Concurrent to her present role with Scott Hull Associates, Ms. Jones serves as President of Executive Internet Imaging and Film Critic for the Clarion Newspaper, a local Ohio newspaper. Establishing goals that are compatible with those of the Company, she commits to providing continued optimum performance. Scott Hull Associates represents artists in the commercial illustration industry, acting as an agent between the illustrator and potential buyer. Currently representing more than 20 artists, the Company, created in 1981, boasts $3 million in annual revenue. **Career Highlights:** Marketing Strategist, Scott Hull Associates (1998-Present); President, Executive Internet Imaging (1998-Present); Film Critic, Clarion Newspaper (1994-Present). **Associations & Accomplishments:** Sinclair Community College Alumni Association's Executive Council; Director of Special Events/Communications, Ohio Fellows Leadership Development Program; Youth Counselor, YMCA. **Education:** University of Dayton, B.A. in Classical Literature (In Progress); Sinclair Community College: A.A. in English (1998), A.S. in Business Administration (1997). **Personal Information:** One child: Gabrielle Kirsten. Ms. Jones enjoys reading, hosting the local television show, reading and Web design and development.

Aik W. Tan
Systems Manager
Colorscope, Inc.
1100 Corporate Center Drive
Monterey Park, CA 91754
(323) 266-1111
aik@colorscope.com

7336

Business Information: Recruited to Colorscope, Inc as Systems Manager in 1996, Mr. Tan is in charge of all technology dealing with machines, presses, software, and files base. A savvy business professional and technical expert, he has been recognized for his diligence and skills, and is now responsible for troubleshooting, output devises, and high end profiling systems. The only systems manager in Colorscope, Mr. Tan has brought new technologies to the Corporation. His future strategic goals include delivering Internet access to clients and providing them a faster turnaround and access to online images. In addition, he wants to provide Web site consulting services as well. Dedicated to the idea of bringing more technology to the Corporation, Mr. Tan has always been interested in computers and is very willing to spend the extra time in order to succeed. Established in 1977, Colorscope, Inc. is engaged in the business of prepress services. The Corporation employs 19 highly skilled individuals who specialize in color correction, graphic stagework, and retouch. The objective of the Corporation is to provide their customers with reliable and efficient prepress services. **Career Highlights:** Systems Manager, Colorscope, Inc. (1996-Present). **Associations & Accomplishments:** Network/Website Volunteer, Buddhist Tzu-Chi Free Clinic. **Education:** California State University at Los Angeles, B.S. (1997).

William Langley

Operations and Information Systems Director
Medscribe Information Systems, Inc.
3325 Hendricks Avenue, Suite A
Jacksonville, FL 32207
(904) 398-0068
Fax: (904) 398-8401
bill@med-scribe.com

7338

Business Information: Mr. Langley is the Operations and Information Systems Director of Medscribe Information Systems, Inc. He assists in the designing and developing stages of all new software programs, testing them for durability and virus suceptibility. Available 24 hours a day, he ensures the productivity of the computer system that is operating within the Corporation's offices in Jacksonville, Florida. He also conducts orientation seminars to train all new transcriptors on the accessories and usage of the computer network. In the future, Mr. Langley hopes to hire new and young developers to advance the Corporation's capabilities even further. His success reflects his ability to quickly grasp new concepts and methodologies. Medscribe Information Systems, Inc. is a medical transcription service provider. Established in 1992, the Corporation works across the United States to assist emerging businesses in translating their medical records for computer databases. The Corporation develops specialized equipment for use during hospital registration that will maintain a patients entire profile for several years on a computerized data system. **Career Highlights:** Operations and Information Systems Director, Medscribe Information Systems, Inc. (1993-Present); Lead Mechanical Engineer, Naval Aviation Depot, United States Navy (1986-93). **Associations & Accomplishments:** American Association of Medical Transcriptionist; American Society for Testing and Materials; American Society of Mechanical Engineers. **Education:** University of Florida, B.S. in Mechanical Engineering (1986). **Personal Information:** Married to Tracy in 1990. Two children: Melissa and Caroline. Mr. Langley enjoys woodworking and water skiing.

Charles L. Savage

Management Information Systems Director
Atkinson-Baker, Inc.
330 North Brand Boulevard, Suite 250
Glendale, CA 91203
(818) 551-7310
Fax: (818) 551-7330
csavage@depo.com

7338

Business Information: Providing his skilled services as Management Information Systems Director of Atkinson-Baker Inc., Mr. Savage was responsible for the design of the current computer network and manages its administration and maintenance. He develops and implements software and related applications for court reporting within the network. Before joining Atkinson-Baker, he served as Master Technician for the 3M Company and Service Manager at Top Music. Additionally, Mr. Savage manages the office suites. Coordinating resources, acquisitions, schedules, time lines, and assignments also fall within the purview of his responsibilities. Committed to further development of the Corporation, Mr. Savage orchestrates both strategic and tactical planning to ensure a bright future as Chief Information Officer. Atkinson-Baker Inc. is a privately owned court reporting agency. Corporate headquarters are in Glendale, California and national operations employ 81 persons. Reporting $15 million in annual revenue, the Corporation was founded in 1985. **Career Highlights:** Management Information Systems Director, Atkinson-Baker Inc. (1989-Present); Master Technician, 3M Company (1979-89); Service Manager, Top Music (1975-79). **Associations & Accomplishments:** Los Angeles County Museum of Art; Cult Awareness Network; RIGPA; Citizens Commission on Human Rights; Los Angeles Jazz Society; The HTML Writers Guild. **Education:** Washington University of St. Louis (1972). **Personal Information:** Married to Catherine in 1974. Two children: Mollie and Nora. Mr. Savage enjoys dining out, movies, travel and sailing.

William F. Ference

Project Manager
Golden Eagle Credit Corporation
90 Grove Street
Ridgefield, CT 06877
(203) 438-0700
Fax: (203) 438-0702
wfjr@aol.com

7359

Business Information: Dedicated to the success of Golden Eagle Credit Corporation, Mr. Ference applies his knowledge and expertise in the field of system administration in serving as Project Manager. One of his current projects includes preparing the Corporation for transition to the year 2000. In this context, Mr. Ference ensures systems functionality and readiness by performing and directing Y2K remediation and conversion. Presiding over the Management Information Systems Department, he manages the network infrastructure and delegates network administration responsibilities to departmental technicians. Coordinating resources, schedules, time lines, and assignments also fall within the scope of his functions. Mr. Ference's continuing education enables him to stay current with technology and advance in his professional career. Establishing goals that are compatible with that of the Corporation, he plans to develop a large database, diversified from finance to information technology. Beginning operations in 1987, Golden Eagle Credit Corporation provides equipment leasing services to other companies. A variety of technological equipment is offered, including Skytel pagers with e-mail, Palm Pilots, and Microtickets. Presently, the Corporation employs a staff of 80 individuals. **Career Highlights:** Project Manager, Golden Eagle Credit Corporation (1997-Present); Manager of Operations, Computer Systems (1995-97); Director of Finance and Management Information Systems, The Picower Institute (1995); Director of Finance, Cendant Mobility (1981-94). **Associations & Accomplishments:** Danbury Area Computer Society. **Education:** Fairfield University, Certificate of Advanced Study (1998); Sacred Heart University, M.B.A. (1984), B.S. (1978). **Personal Information:** Married to Joyce in 1979. Three children: William, Brian, and Robert. Mr. Ference enjoys family time and scouting activities. Mr. Ference is a Scout Master for Boy Scout Troop 90 in Fairfield, Connecticut.

Bill L. Barto

Information Technologies Division Head
RWJ & Associates
5909 Northwest Expressway, Suite 150
Oklahoma City, OK 73132
(405) 720-4616
Fax: (405) 717-8392
bbarto@rwj.com

7361

Business Information: Beginning his career with RWJ & Associates as Information Technology Recruiter in 1997, Mr. Barto has worked his way through the ranks and now serves as Information Technologies Division Head. Working closely with his team of four associates, he is responsible for ensuring all prospective candidates are adequately screened for placement as well as formulating the divisional budget. Ranked as the second recruiter in RWJ & Associates, Mr. Barto's goal is to expand his division regionally, and looks forward to assisting in future Company goals. He attributes his professional success to sticking with it and never giving up. Founded in 1983, RWJ & Associates is an established and reputable firm engaged in the recruitment of qualified personnel for corporate clientele nationwide. The Firm currently employs the skilled services of a team of associates to recruit and interview prospective individuals as well as assess skills for placement. RWJ & Associates continues to be a leader in recruiting qualified staffing for corporate clients. **Career Highlights:** RWJ & Associates: Information Technologies Division Head (2000-Present), Information Technologies Recruiter (1997-00); Sales Respresentative, Sprint PCS (1996-97). **Associations & Accomplishments:** Church Sponsor; A.F.T.P. **Education:** University of Oklahoma, B.A. (1994). **Personal Information:** Married to Genny in 1998. Mr. Barto enjoys golf and camping.

Gary D. Causey

Consultant
Comforce Info Tech
Rural Route 2, Box 135
Dike, TX 75437
(972) 583-8029
Fax: (972) 583-7814
gusgycy@am1.ericson.se

7361

Business Information: Serving as Consultant with Comforce Info Tech, Mr. Causey offers specialized services in several areas. Highly regarded, he has experienced a very exciting career. His many accomplishments include design and development of image processing systems from conceptual ideas and a leading-edge missile systems simulator. Possessing superior talents and an excellent understanding of his position, he uses Oracle to analyze and design processes to enhance drilling operations. Currently, Mr. Causey heads Oracle Financials implementations, equipment ordering, and inventory tracking. To continue his career in the forefront of the industry, he has taken Java courses to become involved with the rapidly growing field of e-commerce. His success reflects his ability to think outside-the-box, take on challenges, and deliver results on behalf of the Company and its clientele. One of the largest and fastest growing companies in the industry, Comforce Info Tech specializes in staffing and consulting services in the information technology, professional, technical, and financial fields. By maintaining a database of 8,000 professionals, Comforce staffs its 2,000 international clients with skilled professionals. Currently operating with 63 offices in the United States, Comforce provides the most efficient and cost effective services worldwide. **Career Highlights:** Consultant, Comforce Info Tech (1998-Present); Consultant, Ericsson, Inc. (1998-Present); Consultant, Digital Switch Corporation (1994-96): Consultant, Arco Oil & Gas Company (1988-93). **Education:** Collin County Community College (1996-99); East Texas State University: M.S., B.A. with High Honors. **Personal Information:** Mr. Causey enjoys photography.

John L. Channell

Information Technology Manager
Resource Technologies Corporation
431 Stephenson Highway
Troy, MI 48083
(248) 585-4750
Fax: (248) 585-7157
john@rtc-employment.com

7361

Business Information: Serving as Resource Technologies Corporation's Information Technology Manager, Mr. Channell directs the information technology staffing team. Striving to diversify the Corporation's reserve of applicants, Mr. Channell works closely with the members of his staff to recruit technologically knowledgeable individuals. Internally recognized as an exemplary employee of the Corporation, he has received numerous awards for his performance, namely he acheived the number one supplier position to DiamlerChrysler as senior account manager. Drawing on his practical work experience, he is currently expanding his business department to allow for a more varied array of services. Attributing his professional success to supportive co-workers, friends, and family members, Mr. Channell keeps abreast of changes and new technologies within his field through networking with others and attending numerous roundtables and seminars. Resource Technologies Corporation provides professional staffing and recruitment for technical and engineering companies. Through networking and refferals, the Corporation is able to locate qualified, capable employees to fit the needs of the customer. Founded over 30 years ago in 1968, the Corporation employs 400 people who strive to fill the customer needs as quickly as possible. **Career Highlights:** Resource Technologies Corporation: Information Technology Manager (1999-Present), Recruiter (1996-99); Sales, Tri-Chem Corporation (1984-96). **Associations & Accomplishments:** Elks Club; Elder Presbyterian Church. **Education:** Oakland Community College (1994); New England College (1980). **Personal Information:** Married to Kathy in 1984. Two children: Anthony and Tyler. Mr. Channell enjoys golf, soccer and cooking.

Donna M. Connell

Consultant
Comforce Company
2480 Woodland Hills Drive
Cumming, GA 30040-7130
(404) 303-4285
dconnell@bellsouth.net

7361

Business Information: Drawing from an extensive academic background and occupational experience, Mrs. Connell joined Comforce Company as a Consultant in 1996. Proficient in telecommunications and possessing the ability to design, specify, and develop software systems, she is an invaluable asset to Comforce, lending her expertise to her clients. Mrs. Connell is very innovative and is constantly introducing new ideas to different organizations. Her career highlights include accomplishing a complete overhaul of the financial system while employed at HomeBanc Mortgage Corporation. Being an entrepreneur at heart, she aspires to start her own business someday providing technical information to clients. Mrs. Connell's career success reflects her ability to take on challenges and deliver results. Comforce Company is a consulting firm that introduces consultants to vendors. The Company's parent is Uniforce. Comforce provides solutions to vendor problems by designing a better system of control over inventories and expenses and assisting in planning relocations. These are just two of the many organizational problems that consultants help solve. International in scope, Comforce is located in Cummings, Georgia. **Career Highlights:** Consultant, Comforce Company (1996-Present); Senior Program Manager, Independant Contractor (1996); Senior Consultant, The Systems Group (1994-96); Program Manager, Digital Equipment Corporation (1979-94). **Education:** Boston University Graduate School of Management, Executive M.B.A. (1989); Emmanual College, B.S. in Chemistry and Math (1972). **Personal Information:** Married to James A. in 1994.

Andrew Duda
Principal Consultant
AM Search Consulting, Inc.
1801 Research Boulevard, Suite 602
Rockville, MD 20850-3152
(301) 315-9030
Fax: (301) 315-9036
aduda@amsearch.com

7361

Business Information: Functioning in the role of Principal Consultant for AM Search Consulting, Inc., Mr. Duda is instrumental in filling key positions available in Fortune 500 companies. Managing AM Search Consulting, he is actively involved in the entire recruitment process. Displaying his sharp organizational and communicative skills, he provides critical start up assistance for new companies. In an effort to establish lasting client relationships, Mr. Duda regularly consults wih businesses to assess their specific needs. His first position out of college and one of the top billers of the Corporation, Mr. Duda plans to continue providing hs clients with quality, value, and selection. Success is attributed to his personal honesty and his not stopping until everything is completed attitude. AM Search Consulting, Inc. is an executive management consulting firm located in Rockville, Maryland. Created in 1993, the Corporation is a relatively new venture, but already reports an annual turnover of $3 million. The Corporation provides recruitment services for Fortune 500 companies in search of accomplished professionals. Individuals possessing specialized skills and training are among the list of potential candidates. **Career Highlights:** Principal Consultant, AM Search Consulting, Inc. (1998-Present). **Associations & Accomplishments:** City Java Forum; ERP Forum; CRM Forum. **Education:** Central Michigan University, B.A. in Organizational Communications (1998). **Personal Information:** Mr. Duda enjoys fishing, skiing and technology.

Burt Israel
Executive Director
National Search Associates
2035 Corte Del Nogal
Carlsbad, CA 92009-1411
(760) 431-1750
Fax: (760) 431-7078
burt@nsasearch.com

7361

Business Information: Mr. Israel manages the Hardware and Telecommunications Division of National Search Associates. He is responsible for a staff of recruiters who place engineers and managers in high tech companies ranging from Fortune 100 firms to start-ups. His focus is on developing business relationships and new clients throughout the United States. And then recruiting professionals to fill senior level positions. His background, spanning over 35 years in high tech and computer related industries, makes him universally qualified to deal with executives at all levels. NSA, founded in 1992, is one of the largest search firms in California. **Career Highlights:** Executive Director, National Search Associates (1992-Present); Regional Manager, Robert Half Personnel (1979-91); Director, Aetna Insurance (1974-79); IBM (1964-74). **Education:** University of Hartford, M.B.A. (1967); Carnegie Mellon University, B.S. in Mechanical Engineering. **Personal Information:** Married to Frances. Three children: Kenneth, Karen, and Rena. Mr. Israel enjoys golf, travel, hiking and reading.

CorDell R. Larkin
Senior Consultant
David Gomez & Associates, Inc.
20 North Clark Street, Suite 3535
Chicago, IL 60602-5086
(312) 346-5525
Fax: (312) 346-1438
clarkin@dgai.com

7361

Business Information: As Senior Consultant, Mr. Larkin oversees a group of five consultants responsible for all aspects of client management. A seasoned veteran, he orchestrates strategic planning for the enhancement of business development. Coordinating candidate sourcing and delivery, Mr. Larkin conducts extensive interviews with applicants. His development and implementation of employee training results in the mobilization of a polished team of consultants. Mr. Larkin is the Corporation's top producer this year, having set a record for being promoted to senior consultant faster than any other employee. His proficiency and dedication have afforded him the opportunity to handle the Corporation's largest account. Possessing aspirations of being a Partner, he strives to improve upon his expertise. Ultimately, he would like to open offices in New York

and San Francisco. Mr. Larkin attributes his success to knowledge, and the support of friends and associates. David Gomez & Associates, Inc. provides executive recruiting for information technology professionals in e-commerce, manufacturing, healthcare, and management consulting. Established in 1977, the Corporation consists of 35 knowledgeable professionals, providing outstanding services for their clients. The retainer based executive search Corporation, operates a marketing and advertising department as well as financial and accounting departments. Twenty-seven consultants and a 10 member support staff comprise the second largest corporation of its kind in the Chicago area. One of Inc. 500's fastest growing companies, the Corporation has an annual turnover of $6 million. **Career Highlights:** Senior Consultant, David Gomez & Associates, Inc. (1997-Present). **Associations & Accomplishments:** Council of Logistics Management; Association of Productions and Inventory Control Society; J.D. Edwards User Group "Quest;" Computer Security Institute; Disaster Recovery Institute; Alumni Mentor, Lake Forest College Graduates/Students. **Education:** Lake Forest College, B.A. (1997).

Philip M. Mingin, C.P.M.
Assistant Vice President, Procurement
Olsten Corporation
175 Broad Hollow Road
Melville, NY 11747
(516) 844-7309
Fax: (516) 844-7331
www.olsten.com
phil.mingin@olsten.com

7361

Business Information: As Assistant Vice President of Procurement with Olsten Corporation, Mr. Mingin presides over the sourcing and purchasing of all goods and services for the Corporation. He is responsible for the strategic supply chain managment process, the direct supervision of eight employees, and the execution of various technical duties. Mr. Mingin develops new strategies regarding sourcing and has written an article for various internal publications. Olsten Corporation is a world leader in staffing services and North America's largest provider of home health care and related services. With 1,400 locations, the Corporation generates annual revenue near $5.2 billion from the placement of professionals in a variety of industries, including healthcare, accounting, legal, and clerical. Olsten Corporation is presently focusing on the implementation of centralized purchasing through an Intranet based front end with an oracle back. **Career Highlights:** Assistant Vice President, Procurement, Olsten Corporation (1997-Present); The New York Times Company, Director of Purchasing (1995-97); The New York Times Newspaper, Purchasing Manager (1991-95); Manager of Material Systems, Loral Fairchild Systems (1985-91). **Associations & Accomplishments:** First Vice President, National Association of Purchasing Management-New York and Long Island; National Contract Management Association; New York City Partner in Education; Matron Business Travel Association; ACTE. **Education:** Hofstra University, B.B.A. (1990). **Personal Information:** Married to Valerie in 1982. Mr. Mingin enjoys fishing, skiing and golf.

Suresh Peram, Ph.D.
Chief Executive Officer
JobsMadeEasy.com
1950 Spectrum Circle, Suite 400
Marietta, GA 30067
(770) 857-4442
Fax: (770) 857-4446
speram@hotmail.com

7361

Business Information: Serving as JobsMadeEasy.com's Chief Executive Officer, Dr. Peram is still developing and designing Web sites. In addition to his tnformation technology duties, he is responsible for accounting, contacting clients, and ensuring the proper legal protection has been accounted for. Focusing on development and release of information, Dr. Peram has formed strategic partnerships with other Web-based companies. Among his many technological accolades, he served as the project leader on client server project for Delta Airlines. His strategic plans for the future are to be with Internet based companies in various different capacities. Success, according to Dr. Peram, is attributed to his ability to think out-of-the-box, aggressively tackle new challenges, and deliver results. JobsMadeEasy.com is a fresh faced online based business. Established in 1996, the Company provides Internet based job sites and job search services. The Company is headquartered in Georgia. Providing interaction between recruiters and potential employees, JobsMadeEasy.com is still under development. Reporting an annual sales mark of $150,000, the Company is a fast growing e-commerce business. **Career Highlights:**

Chief Executive Officer, JobsMadeEasy.com (1999-Present); Senior Architect, Platinum Technology (1998-99); Chief Executive Officer, Object Connections, Inc. (1996-98). **Associations & Accomplishments:** Association of Computing Machinery; Institute of Electronics and Electrical Engineers. **Education:** Texas A&M University, Ph.D. (1994); Indiana Institute of Technology at Madras. **Personal Information:** Married to Olga in 1998. One child: Nikolai. Dr. Peram enjoys movies, languages and science fiction.

Christopher M. Petsche
Vice President of Management Information Systems
Cooperative Resource Services
5875 Landerbrook Drive, Suite 200
Cleveland, OH 44124-4069
(440) 684-5354
Fax: (440) 684-5526
chrisp@crscms.com

7361

Business Information: Possessing eight years of extensive experience with Cooperative Resource Services, Mr. Petsche serves as Vice President of Management Information Systems. He applies unique coding, manages personal computer applications, maintains telephones, and oversees all technological functions. Mr. Petsche also assumes responsibility for monitoring fax machines, computer servers, writes purchase plans, and formulates program development. Effectively using contemporary management concepts, he provides corporate managers with valid and reliable information for human resources planning. Envisioning future goals, Mr. Petsche has recently re-tooled Cooperative Resource Services' infostructure to a NT Shop format and oversaw the rewrites of all three legacy systems. Established in 1982, Cooperative Resource Services is a national company that specializes in relocation of corporate executives. This includes selection of locations to live in rural areas, selecting adequate school districts, and marketing to assess homes. The Company pre-selects top-selling real estate agents to negotiate contracts. Cooperative Resource Services' sister company offers loan mortgages and bids on houses. Local operation in Cleveland, Ohio employs the services of 300 skilled individuals to provide all services, facilitate projects, meet with clients, and perform administrative tasks. Presently, the Company generates in excess of $15 million in annual revenues. **Career Highlights:** Vice President of Management Information Systems, Cooperative Resource Services (1992-Present); Manager Management Information Systems, United States Postal Service (1981-92). **Associations & Accomplishments:** Data Processing Management Association. **Education:** University of Akron, Data Processing (1981). **Personal Information:** Married to Lisa in 1983. Two children: Jason and Jessica. Mr. Petsche enjoys golf, camping and spending time with family.

Pamela Plambeck
Account Manager
Hall Kinion
1880 Arapahoe Street, #2203
Denver, CO 80202-1908
(303) 741-9900
Fax: (303) 741-9986
pamelaplambeck@hotmail.com

7361

Business Information: Recruited to Hall Kinion in 1999 as an Account Manager, Ms. Plambeck acts as the Company's business to business liaison responsible for all aspects of client accounts, ensuring an accurate database is maintained. With over 17 years of business savvy and experience, she travels to clients' sites to learn and determine their specific staffing needs. Compiling and analyzing the information gathered, Ms. Plambeck then conducts a thorough search to find the best possible candidate taking into account the clients' current projects and expertise required to complete the job. Before joining the Company, she served in the positions of team leader and account representative with Sprint. While at Sprint, Ms. Plambeck received the prestigious "Mentor Award" for her hard work in developing and harnessing the potential of employees. Starting up her own consulting business in graphic design and Web site development is cited as her future endeavors. Her advice to others is, "Make a commitment to education and share your knowledge with your peers." An international information technology staffing agency, Hall Kinion specializes in Internet and e-commerce talent outsourcing to businesses and companies needing its services. Presently, the Company operates 30 offices in the United States and 2 in the United Kingdom. Founded in 1987, Hall Kinion reports annual revenues exceeding $200 million. **Career Highlights:** Account Manager, Hall Kinion (1999-Present); Sprint: Team Leader (1999), Account Representative (1998-99). **Education:** Stephens College, B.A. (1983). **Personal Information:** Ms. Plambeck enjoys dancing and acting.

Chris A. Quintanilla

General Manager
Intellisource
1341 North Delaware Avenue
Philadelphia, PA 19125-4300
(215) 739-7112
Fax: (215) 739-7125
chrisqu@usa.net
7361

Business Information: Serving as General Manager of Intellisource, Mr. Quintanilla is responsible for the operations and fiscal management of the Philadelphia office. He is charged with personnel managment, profit and loss analysis, recruiting of technical specialists, and job placement of employees. Coordinating resources, time lines, schedules, assignments, and fiscal operating budgets also fall within the realm of his responsibilities. Mr. Quintanilla's extensive information technology background provides him with the knowledge and problem solving abilities to handle the most complex network and software difficulties. With a background in network administration, Mr. Quintanilla was originally hired to Intellisource as the Senior Network Engineer. He plans to attain a Chief Information Officer's position of a mid to large company or to start his own company providing technical solutions. His success is attributed to this ability to think outside the box, tackle new challenges, and deliver results. Intellisource is an information technology outsourcing agency. This Company was established in 1998 to help soften the impact of government cutbacks and military base closures. Providing temporary civilian professionals to government agencies, such as FAA, NASA, and DoD. Intellisource also provides technical assistance to clients in the city of Philadelphia through outstanding customer service and reliable personnel. Presently, the Company employs a skilled staff of 25 who help generate annual revenues in excess of $2 million. **Career Highlights:** General Manager, Intellisource (1998-Present); Network Manager, IBM Corporation (1996-98). **Associations & Accomplishments:** Network Professionals Association; Institute of Networking Professionals; Philadelphia Chamber of Commerce. **Education:** Embry-Riddle Aeronautical University, degree in Computer Science (1994). **Personal Information:** Mr. Quintanilla enjoys photography, computer programming and writing.

Lisa S. Russell, C.P.C.

Chief Operating Officer
Key Staff
600 Univeristy Street, Suite 1720
Seattle, WA 98101
(206) 667-8911
Fax: (206) 867-8981
lisa@keystaff.com
7361

Business Information: As Key Staff's Chief Operating Officer, Ms. Russell is responsible for managing the sales and day-to-day operations of the sales staff. A co-owner of the Company, she is responsible for determining the strategic direction and business contribution of the information systems functions. Possessing an excellent understanding of the needs of the technology industry, Ms. Russell is actively involved in the recruitment of technical personnel to fill positions within client companies. Noting her professional highlights as gaining the ability to interact and communicate with different people, she attributes her success to her ability to network and interact with other professionals. Ms. Russell plans to continue her work with the Company and form a strategic partnership to promote growth and expansion. Established in 1996, Key Staff is an executive recruiting agency. The Company provides clients with qualified personnel to fill positions in information technology and finance. A group of 33 talented professionals are employed to assist the Company in generating annual revenues in excess of $2.9 million. **Career Highlights:** Chief Operating Officer, Key Staff (1995-Present); Microsoft: Technical Recruiter (1994-95), Marketing Manager (1993-94). **Associations & Accomplishments:** Seattle Chamber; Washington Software Alliance; NW Recruiters Association; Forum of jWomen Entrepreneurs; National Association of Personnel Services; National Technical Services Association. **Education:** University of Oklahoma, B.A. (1993). **Personal Information:** Ms. Russell enjoys hiking and climbing Mount Rainer.

Angelito H. Sandiego

Systems Integration Specialist
Perot Systems
1600 Heritage Drive, Apartment 1025
McKinney, TX 25069
litosandiego@hotmail.com
7361

Business Information: Serving as a Systems Integrations Specialist of Perot Systems, Mr. Sandiego is responsible for combining the knowledge of multiple information systems and packaged software to create solutions to specific business requirements. In this context, he supports new applications programming using visual information. A savvy, five year veteran of the field, Mr. Sandiego is one of the pioneers who installed a sub-system for Allied Informations Services. Analyzing, upgrading, programming, installing, and maintaining information systems operating and networking environments also fall within the realm of Mr. Sandiego's responsibilities. Staying on top of emerging technology is cited as the reason for his success. In the future, he aspires to remain on the cutting edge, become more involved as a consultant, attain a management role, and be in charge of turnkey operations. Perot Systems provides outsourcing services support. Established in 1993, the Company is an information technology services provider specializing in network analysis, security, and enterprise solutions. Employing over 8,000 professional individuals, Perot Systems enjoys a global reputation of excellence. **Career Highlights:** Systems Integration Specialist, Perot Systems (1999-Present); Senior Systems Analyst, IMR Global (1999-99); Senior Systems Engineer, Allied Information Services of the Philadelphia (1996-98). **Education:** Mapua Institute of Technology, B.S.E.C.E. (1995); Certificate in COBOL Programming; Systems Technology Institute, Business Systems. **Personal Information:** Two children: Angelo and Vincent. Mr. Sandiego enjoys chess and online games.

Robert A. Sarkes

Director of Information Technology
Epronet
2600 Campus Drive, Suite 200
San Mateo, CA 94403
(650) 356-2819
Fax: (408) 287-6211
rsarkes@mindsteps.com
7361

Business Information: As Information Technology Director, Mr. Sarkes holds the responsibility of maintaining Epronet's computer network and Internet operations. Utilizing over eight years of skills and knowledge attained through an extensive education and employment history, he is proactively involved in building the Company's infostructure, and maintaining server activity. Managing within an organized annual budget, he oversees purchasing of materials used in the design of the network. Heading administrative tasks, he turns potential into action through preparation and skilled training. He also conducts information technology consulting on the side. Continuing his advancement with Epronet, Mr. Sarkes anticipates his promotion to Chief Information Officer as a result of his continuing efforts to increase his skills through training and professional development. Engaging in online services, Epronet was established in 1996. Located in San Mateo, California, the Company employs the skilled services of 38 professional computer technicians, engineers, and designers to facilitate all Web site activities. Operating as an online executive recruiting service, the Company provides online employment opportunities for alumni of top 21 leading universities. Generating $5 million in annual revenues, the Company remains committed to the development of services for its expanding member base. **Career Highlights:** Information Technology Director, Epronet (1998-Present); Information Systems Manager, Micromodule Systems, Inc. (1996-98); Information Systems Administrator/Senior Programmer, Elantec Semiconductor, Inc. (1994-96). **Associations & Accomplishments:** Lambda Chapter of Phi theta Kappa National Honor Society; Merit Scholarship (1980-81), Sears, Roebuck & Company; Scholastic Achievement Award (1985), Who's Who in American Colleges. **Education:** AMA College, M.S. in Computer Science (1992); B.S. in Computer Science. **Personal Information:** Mr. Sarkes enjoys personal computing, power boating and reading.

Audrey J. Stetson

Office Manager/Systems Administrator
Newport Strategic Search LLC
3088 Pio Pico Drive, Suite 203
Carlsbad, CA 92008-1965
(760) 434-9894
Fax: (760) 434-9896
audrey@newportsearch.com
7361

Business Information: A successful 27-year professional of technology, Ms. Stetson was recruited to Newport Strategic Search LLC as Office Manager and Systems Administrator in 1998. In her capacity, she fulfills a number of administrative and technical functions on behalf of the Company and its clientele. She is responsible for accounts payable, recruiting, and maintenance of systems infrastructure and LAN/WAN network environments. A systems expert, Ms. Stetson also serves as Webmaster with oversight of the Company's Web site and content. Dedicated to the success of Newport Strategic Search, she consistently performs high quality work and possesses the ability to take on challenges and deliver results. In the future, Ms. Stetson plans to remain working with the Company and looks forward to obtaining her Microsoft Certified Systems Engineer certification. Established in 1987, Newport Strategic Search LLC engages in telecom and data communications recruiting. Working with clients throughout the United States, the Company is dedicated to providing clients with qualified personnel for information technology positions. Employing the skills and talent of 12 individuals, the Company reports annual revenues in excess of $1 million. **Career Highlights:** Office Manager/Systems Administrator, Newport Strategic Search LLC (1998-Present); Administrative Assistant, J.K. Williams News Distribution (1982-98); Classified Employee, Vista Unified School District (1986-97). **Associations & Accomplishments:** National Genealogy Association; Stetson Kindred Association; New Mexico Genealogy Society; San Diego Computer Genealogy Association; Published Family History Research, New Mexico Genealogy Society; Helping Hand Volunteer Award, Boy Scouts of America; Voted Outstanding School District Volunteer. **Education:** Fulton Montgomery Community College, A.S (1973); Gemological Institute of America, Colored Stone Appraisal and Diamond Appraisal Certificates. **Personal Information:** Married to Robert in 1974. Two children: Christopher and Matthew. Ms. Stetson enjoys scouting, piano, computers, bowling and genealogy research.

Theresa J. Tober

Data Processing Coordinator
Job Service North Dakota
1000 East Divide Avenue
Bismarck, ND 58506
(701) 328-1684
7361

Business Information: Ms. Tober is Data Processing Coordinator for Job Service North Dakota. She is responsible for maintaining the functionality and operational status of the data processing infrastructure. Ms. Tober has served with Job Service North Dakota in a variety of positions since coming on board as Word Processing Supervisor in 1981. In 1996, she moved up into the position of OAU Forms Designer and Troubleshooter. In her current capacity, Ms. Tober serves as the chief liaison between her department and data processing mainframe, and is in charge of troubleshooting software and hardware problems. Ensuring users have correct access to all screens and providing training packages utilizing state-of-the-art technologies also fall within the realm of her responsibilities. Concurrent to her present role, Ms. Tober works part time with an insurance company. Her success reflects her flexibility and her ability to aggressively take on new challenges and responsibilities. She is very content with what she does, but wants to become more involved on the network side of day-to-day operations. "Nothing is impossible," serves as her credo. A state agency, Job Service North Dakota administers, controls, and disburses disaster and unemployment and layoff payments. Established in 1939, the Agency also provides training to assist people who have lost their jobs get back in the work force. Local in scope, the Agency presently employs a staff of more than 446 people. **Career Highlights:** Job Service North Dakota: Data Processing Coordinator (1998-Present), OAU Forms Designer/Troubleshooter (1996-98), Word Processing Supervisor (1981-96). **Associations & Accomplishments:** Secretary, International Association of Personnel in Employment Security; National/International Wildlife Federation; Whale Adoption Project. **Personal Information:** Ms. Tober enjoys crafts, reading, gardening, Beanie Babies, walking and Indian pottery.

Laurie J. Weinberg

Account Manager
Management Recruiters International
4 Clearview Road
Springfield, NJ 07081
(908) 725-2595
Fax: (908) 725-0439
weinberg@mrbridgewater.com
7361

Business Information: Ms. Weinberg functions under the corporate title of Account Manager for Management Recruiters International. She specializes in the placement of information technology professionals within her personal client companies. Ms. Weinberg works closely with her associates who are dedicated to recruiting top candidates for placement with their clients. Ensuring prospects are dependable and capable of handling high-paced activities and who can maintain professional appearance and composure, Ms. Weinberg is responsible for interviewing, training, and qualifying all candidates. Highly regarded in the industry, she has been devoted to making sure that her selections and placements are nothing short of the best. Ms. Weinberg plans to remain in the industry and better herself by attending seminars and conferences as well as networking with her many colleagues in different fields. Her credo is "knowledge is power." Management Recruiters International is the largest staffing firm in the United States, specializing in search and recruitment for information technology corporation around the world. The Compnay is extremely selective, in that an outstanding staff works diligently to accept applications, test, and train highly intellectual individuals to be placed in such positions as secretarial, administrative, management, and executive. Presently, a staff of 22 people are employed by the Company. **Career Highlights:** Account Manager, Management Recruiters International (1999-Present); Information Technology Technical Recruiter, RCM Technologies (1998-99); Marketing and Sales Associate, Trans Travel Inc. (1996-98). **Associations & Accomplishments:** Class Agent for Moravian College Alumni Association. **Education:** Moravion College, B.A. (1997). **Personal Information:** Ms. Weinberg enjoys travel.

M. Susan Zwickel

Owner/President
Snelling Personnel Services
363 Route 46 West
Fairfield, NJ 07004
(973) 276-0166
Fax: (973) 276-0173

7361

Business Information: As Owner and Executive Recruiter of Snelling Personnel Services, Ms. Zwickel performs all managerial aspects of the Company with the support of six employees. She also participates in the recruitment of qualified individuals for clients and interacts with other companies in need of additional personnel. Established in 1979, Snelling Personnel Services is a full-service job placement agency, specializing in the permanent job placement. The Company offers permanent and temporary placement as well as professional consulting. Although Ms. Zwickel specilizes in placing IS/IT Professionals, her office also places people in office services positions. Headquartered in Fairfield, New Jersey, the Company has grown to 300 offices worldwide and over $500 million in revenue. **Career Highlights:** Owner/President, Snelling Personnel Services (1997-Present); Computron Software Inc.: Vice President of Worldwide Corporate Contracts (1996-97), Director of Corporate Contracts (1994-96); Director of Corporate Contacts, Information Builders (1991-94). **Associations & Accomplishments:** National Associations of Female Executives; Executive Women of New Jersey. **Personal Information:** Married to Jay in 1967. Three children: Alan, Erica, and Richard. Ms. Zwickel enjoys gardening, antiquing and decorating.

Ron A. Lynch

Branch Manager
Tekmark Global Solutions
993 Old Eagle School Road
Wayne, PA 19087
(610) 687-9510
Fax: (610) 687-9512
ron@tekmarkinc.com

7363

Business Information: Mr. Lynch is the Branch Manager of Tekmark Global Solution's Philadelphia and Virginia sites. Duties for this position include assessing the technical and business requirements of each customer. In addition, he determines solutions for clients curious about fixed prices and implements all binding regulations. For quality assurance, Mr. Lynch often supervises staff members and monitors their activities. As for the next three to five years, he plans to grow from the Virginia office by making salient use of e-commerce. He also hopes to countinue managing both of his current regional branches. Success, Mr. Lynch asserts, is the final produce of perseverance, respecting others, and being responsible and dependendable through objective thinking. His advice is "listen to others." Tekmark Global Solutions provides information technology staffing solutions throughout the United States. Placing competent professionals in long and short term assignments, Tekmark Global Solutions has been an invaluable partner to businesses with personnel shortages. Established in 1979, the Company has embarked on a path of success. Currently, that has lead to a $100 million annual revenue figure. Tekmark Global Solution employs 950 people. **Career Highlights:** Branch Manager, Tekmark Global Solutions (1992-Present); Branch and Division Manager, Day & Zimmerman-HL Yoh Company (1989-92); Technical Specialist, Technical Placement, Inc. (1985-89); Technical Recruiter, Main Line (1983-85). **Associations & Accomplishments:** Past Member, Technology Council of Eastern Pennsylvania. **Education:** Cabrini College, B.A. in Psychology (1983). **Personal Information:** One child: Lindsay M. Mr. Lynch enjoys cars, literature and the internet.

David S. Mohammed

Information Technology Division Manager
Connection Staffing, Inc.
4300 West Cypress Street, Suite 100
Tampa, FL 33607
(813) 879-2212
Fax: (813) 879-2320
dmohammed@connectionstaffing.com

7363

Business Information: Possessing elite skills in the field of information technology, Mr. Mohammed was recruited to Connection Staffing, Inc. as Information Technology Division Manager. He oversees and directs the day to day operations of the information technology department at two branches and is responsible for 11 employees. Highly regarded, he also determines the business contribution of the information systems functions. Mr. Mohammed is also accountable for designing innovative marketing strategies, in addition to developing and maintaining the departmental fiscal budget. Attributing his success to his knowledge, his future goals include helping facilitate continued Agency growth as well as take the Agency public and expand its information technology division. Established in 1995, Connection Staffing, Inc. is a temporary employment agency. Employing the skilled services of 30 individuals, the Agency fulfills employment needs of businesses around the country by providing skilled temporary personnel to administer positions ranging from clerical, accounting, and information technology. Reporting over $10 million in gross revenue, Connection Staffing continues to charter skilled individuals to rewarding careers. **Career Highlights:** Information Technology Division Manager, Connection Staffing, Inc. (1999-Present); Director of Recruiting, National Computers (1998-99); Resoruce Director, Arcuss Staffing Resources (1996-98); Executive Recruiter, Lloyd Prescott & Associates (1994-96). **Associations & Accomplishments:** Board of Fellows. **Education:** University of Hartford, M.B.A. (1991); New England College, Bachelor's degree in Accounting (1989). **Personal Information:** Mr. Mohammed enjoys tennis and stamp and coin collecting.

Richard D. Abercrombie

Staff Systems Programmer
Datapoint Corporation
8410 Datapoint Drive
San Antonio, TX 78229
(210) 593-7108
Fax: (210) 593-7920

7371

Business Information: Utilizing over 15 years of extensive experience in the technology field, Mr. Abercrombie serves as Staff Systems Programmer for Datapoint Corporation. He has served with Datapoint in a variety of roles since coming on board as Senior Systems Consultant in 1992. In his current capacity, he works with three other programmers, designing, developing, and implementing software systems support and technical products. Before joining Datapoint Corporation, Mr. Abercrombie served as Consultant for JES, Inc. His background history also includes a stint as Vice President of Data Processing with Central Distributing Company. Dedicated to the success of Datapoint Corporation, Mr. Abercrombie recently attained his certification as a Microsoft Certified System Engineer. He continues to grow professionally through the fulfillment of his responsibilities and his involvement in the advancement of operations. Expanding the staff and remaining on the leading edge of technology are cited as his future goals. Datapoint Corporation is a publicly owned corporation providing networking, voice, data, and video technology services. The Corporation was established in 1970 and operations employ the skilled services of 200 professionals. **Career Highlights:** Datapoint Corporation: Staff Systems Programmer (1996-Present), Senior Systems Consultant (1992-96); Consultant, JES, Inc. (1989-92); Vice President of Data Processing, Central Distributing Company (1982-89). **Associations & Accomplishments:** SAADUG; ANSI PL/B (J15). **Education:** Southwest Texas State University, B.B.A. (1982); Microsoft Certified System Engineer (1999). **Personal Information:** Married to Sharon in 1978. Two children: Teri and Tracey. Mr. Abercrombie enjoys soccer and the outdoors.

Sharon K. Adams

Technical Support Coordinator
Process Software Corporation
100 Apollo Drive
Chelmsford, MA 01824
(508) 879-6994
Fax: (508) 879-0042
imzadhi.tiac.net

7371

Business Information: Displaying his skills in this highly specialized position, Ms. Adams serves as the Technical Support Coordinator for the Process Software Corporation. She coordinates the technical calls received through the Corporation's automated call system and distribution center, assigning staff professionals to troubleshoot problems or answer client questions. In her role as Corporate Support Webmaster, she provides support to the corporate Web site and was responsible for the development and implementation of the Corporation's customer service survey through the Internet. Ms. Adams is committed to providing continued optimum service and looks forward to assisting in the completion of future corporate goals. Based in Framingham, Massachusetts, the Process Software Corporation is engaged in various types of software development. The Corporation specializes in Virtual Memory System (VMS) applications for use on the VAX computer equipment and TCP/IP, the communications protocol that allows people to route data transmissions. Operations employ the services of approximately 100 skilled professionals. **Career Highlights:** Technical Support Coordinator, Process Software Corporation (1998-Present); Information Systems Administrator, JWG Associates, Inc. (1997-98); Consultant Trainer/City of Boston, EDP Contract Services (1996-97). **Associations & Accomplishments:** World Organization of Webmasters. **Personal Information:** Married to Tony in 1985. Three children: Robert, Samantha, and Amber. Ms. Adams enjoys Web design, horseback riding and quilt making.

Vivek S. Adesh

Chief Executive Officer
Starternet
9465 Highway 5, Suite 203
Douglasville, GA 30135-1501
(770) 920-6744
Fax: (770) 920-6743
vic@starternet.net

7371

Business Information: As Chief Executive Officer of Starternet, Mr. Adesh oversees all daily administration and operations. Possessing an excellent understanding of his field, he provides cutting edge knowledge for the development of new products and services. Determining the strategic direction and vision of the Company, Mr. Adesh's responsibilities include client searches, program analysis, and design and development of data warehousing software. To better serve his clientele, he employs consultants who are considered experts in the medical field. This strategy enables Starternet to design advance software programs for clients in the health and medical industry. His highlights include his ability to touch and speak software, and his certification in data warehousing. Attributing his success to luck and education, Mr. Adesh's goals are to expand Company operations and focus strictly on the medical field. Established in 1998, Starternet engages in custom programming all aspects of PCs. Also offering training in hard and software, the Company also provides technical support for end users. The Company facilitates information technology for the health care and medical industry. Headquartered in Douglasville, Georgia, Startnet distributes serves a clientele in the United States and Canada. Presently, seven professional and technical experts man day-to-day operations. **Career Highlights:** Chief Executive Officer, Starternet (1998-Present). **Associations & Accomplishments:** Alpha Beta Kappa. **Education:** Florida Metropolitan University, B.S. (1997); Bharatyiya Vidya Sansthhaan, B.I. Mus. **Personal Information:** Married to Kadambari in 1982. Two children: Sameeksha and Pragati.

Marjorie Aguero Blanco

Computer Programmer
DaimlerChrysler Aerospace Orbital Systems Inc.
1020 Bay Area Boulevard
Houston, TX 77058
(281) 461-8409
margeblanc@mindspring.com

7371

Business Information: Serving as a Computer Programmer for DaimlerChrysler Aerospace Orbital Systems Inc., Mrs. Aguero Blanco works with management and systems users to analyze, specify, design, and deploy new cutting edge software solutions. Throughout daily activities, she is held accountable for database Oracle modifications, qualifying software to ensure that it is bug free, and time sheets. Possessing an excellent understanding of her field, Mrs. Aguero Blanco is also responsible for internal Web page updates, functionality of the Web server and Internet, and calculations of Oracle tables and database management system. Personal involvement in building the international space station, troubleshooting, and working with Pearl and JavaScript also fall within the realm of Mrs. Aguero Blanco's functions. Attributing her success to her supportive parents, she plans on obtaining her MCP and MCSE certifications as well as Master's in Cmputer Science degree. DaimlerChresler Aerospace Orbital Systems Inc. is a software firm specializing in the modifications and enhancements of software used in the international space station. Catering to such agencies as NASA and Boeing, the Corporation offers UNIX platforms for all client companies. Presently, the Corporation functions under the direction and guidance of professionals who facilitate smooth day to day operations. **Career Highlights:** Computer Programmer, DaimlerChrysler Aerospace Orbital Systems Inc. (2000-Present); Computer Programmer, Crystal Communications (1990-Present); Software Consultant, Best Drivers Resources (1999-Present); Management Information Systems Coordinator, F&S Corporate Advisors (1999). **Associations & Accomplishments:** Outstanding Officer, Phi Eta Sigma and Honors College Society; Howard E. Moore Outstanding Lower Division, Omicron Delta Kappa Student Leadership Award; Florida Depratment of Education Gold Seal Endorsement; Dean's List (1997-98). **Education:** Florida International University, B.S. in Computer Science (1999). **Personal Information:** Married to Carlos in 1999.

Israel D. Anandan

Manager of Database Team
IMS HEALTH Strategic Technologies
3398-F Chelsea Park Lane
Norcross, GA 30092
(404) 841-5284
Fax: (404) 841-4115
sowkki@yahoo.com

7371

Business Information: Serving as Manager of Database Team of IMS HEALTH Strategic Technologies, Mr. Anandan fulfills a number of technical activities in the performance of his duties on behalf of the Company. In his role, he oversees 10 database administrators, and he is the primary technical resource for all database management systems as well as support of applications support. Rapidly ascending through the Company's hierarchy, he has proven himself to be a invaluable asset. Highly regarded, Mr. Anadan has enjoyed considerable success as he looks forward to assisting in the completion of future Company goals. Mr. Anandan's goals include obtaining a management level role and taking on more responsibilities. IMS HEALTH Strategic Technologies engages in the development of software and support services to assist in the marketing of pharmaceutical products. Established in 1983, the Company employs the skilled services of 1,000 individuals to acquire business, facilitate projects, and market services. The Company is located in Norcross, Georgia and provides a vital service to its growing clientele. **Career Highlights:** IMS HEALTH Strategic Technologies: Manager of Database Team (1999-Present), Senior Database Administrator (1997-99), Senior Software Engineer (1996-97). **Associations & Accomplishments:** International Oracle Users Group; Oracle Replication Special Interest Group **Education:** Maudurain Kamary University, B.S. (1990). **Personal Information:** Married to Bhanani in 1997. One child: Sachit. Mr. Anandan enjoys reading.

Maribeth Anderson

Chief Information Officer
First Chicago/Mercantile Services
525 West Monroe Street, Suite 0925
Chicago, IL 60661-3629
(312) 441-4015
Fax: (312) 441-4099
manderson@fcmservices.com

7371

Business Information: Serving as Chief Information Officer of First Chicago/Mercantile Services, Ms. Anderson oversees all technical operations. Utilizing technical expertise, she plans, programs, and executes solutions. In the future, Ms. Anderson plans to expand the Firm's Internet services. First Chicago/Mercantile Services is a software development firm specializing in customized electronic payment and information services. Providing solutions to government and private organizations, the Company is recognized for developing, implementing, and operating EFTPS, the largest electronic payment collection system in the world. Established in 1994 through the joint venture of First Chicago NBD Corporation and Bancorporation Inc, First Chicago/Mercantile Services currently employs 80 information technology professionals. **Career Highlights:** First Chicago/Mercantile Services: Chief Information Officer (1994-Present), Business Reengineering Architect (1991-94), Manager of Eight Regional Offices (1988-91), Manager of Quality Systems Implementation (1986-88). **Associations & Accomplishments:** Women in Management; Quoted in articles of technical magazines; Recipient of the Best in Banking Award, Microbanker. **Education:** Loyola University, M.B.A. (1986); Northern Illinois University, B.S. in Computer Science. **Personal Information:** Married to James in 1991. Three children: Nicole, Ryan, and Kyle. Ms. Anderson enjoys travel.

Michael E. Anderson

Chief Scientist
Integrated Chipware
1861 Wiehle Avenue, Suite 300
Reston, VA 20190
(703) 736-3504
Fax: (703) 736-3556
mike@chipware.com

7371

Business Information: As Chief Scientist of Integrated Chipware, Mr. Anderson is responsible for technical evaluations, fulfillment of customer base requirements, and development and teaching of courseware, and ensuring applications are compatible with the product line. He has enjoyed substantial success in his field by having received recognition for a patent with three other people in a Video Backup and Real Time Data Acquisition problem. He attributes his success to the ability to know where technology is headed and in being at the right place at the right time when the technology arrives. Mr. Anderson enjoys his current field and plans to expedite continued promotion through dedication and consistent superior service. Integrated Chipware is engaged in real time and embedded systems development. Established in 1995, the Company is a venture capitol funded system with two main divisions: required tracibility tools and real time operating systems builders. Employing a staff of 75 individuals, the Company reports an estimated annual revenue in excess of $8 million. **Career Highlights:** Chief Scientist, Integrated Chipware (1999-Present); Chief Engineer, Sparta, Inc. (1987-99); System Integration Analyst, Analytic Services, Inc. (1986-87); System Integration, The Stonehouse Group (1982-86). **Education:** George Mason University, M.S. in Computer Science (1991); University of South Florida, B.A. in Mathematics (1981). **Personal Information:** Married to Christine G. in 1986. One child: Melanie A. Mr. Anderson enjoys martial arts and spending time with his family. He is a Ta'i Chi and Kung Fu instructor and is YMAA-certified in the art of Chin Na.

Daniel A. Bachrach

Senior Network Administrator
BEST! Software, Inc.
888 Executive Center Drive
St. Petersburg, FL 33702
(727) 579-1111
dbachrac@ij.net

7371

Business Information: Dedicated to the success of BEST! Software, Inc., Mr. Bachrach applies his extensive knowledge and expertise in serving as Senior Network Administrator. In this capacity, he presides over the network administration and management for the St. Petersburg, Florida location. Before joining BEST! Software, he served as Site Manager for Computer Generated Solutions. His background history also includes a stint as Instructor and Network Manager with Sun Coast Learning Center. In his present role, Mr. Bachrach assumes the responsibility for the operation maintenance and exchange connection between corporate sites. Crediting his success to his education and stubbornness, he stays current with technology by reading industry publications and attending trade shows. Continually striving for maximum effectiveness, Mr. Bachrach is completing his Microsoft Internet Certification and plans to pursue his Master's degree in Business Administration. He anticipates a future promotion to Chief Information Officer. BEST! Software, Inc. is engaged in software development and specializes in Human Relations and Fixed Asset programs. Employing a work force of 500 qualified individuals, the Corporation has four locations worldwide and serves approximately 100,000 customers. Annual revenue is estimated in excess of $150 million. **Career Highlights:** Senior Network Administrator, BEST! Software, Inc. (1999-Present); Site Manager, Computer Generated Solutions (1996-98); Instructor/Network Manager, Sun Coast Learning Center (1996). **Associations & Accomplishments:** Microsoft Certified Professionals; Marine Corps Reservist. **Education:** University of South Florida, B.A. in International Studies (1995). **Personal Information:** Married to Erika B. in 1999. Mr. Bachrach enjoys flying, scuba diving, sailing, computing, building models and competitive hunting.

Robert Baukman

Computer Programmer I
Mynd
1005 Old Isaac Road
Eastover, SC 29044
(803) 333-5142
rbaukma@hotmail.com

7371

Business Information: Serving as Computer Programmer I, Mr. Baukman was recruited to Mynd's professional team in 1999. Concentrating his skills on the development and maintenance of Web pages, he offers technical support and troubleshooting, ensuring a functional and quality system. With an extensive background in computer programming, Mr. Baukman utilizes new techniques and approaches towards the creation of promotional Web sites and various other Internet capabilities. Highly regarded and possessing an excellent understanding of technology, he writes COBOL codes for 1-Tier AS/400 and 3-Tier Windows NT as well as develops ASP pages. Committed to his career with Mynd, Mr. Baukman continues to grow professionally through the fulfillment of his responsibilities and his involvement in the advancement of operations. His future goal is to eventually attain the position of Technology Manager or Database Administrator. Established in 1968, Mynd specializes in the development of Web pages and various other business logic used in the insurance industry. Located in Eastover, South Carolina, the Company employs the technical expertise of 7,000 individuals to facilitate all aspects of design, development, and integration. Striving to incorporate the latest technology, the Company is dedicated to meeting the diverse needs of an expanding client base generating $100 million in annual revenues. **Career Highlights:** Computer Programmer I, Mynd (1999-Present); Graduate Assistant, Clemson University (1994-97); Test Engineer, NCR Corporation (1989-94). **Associations & Accomplishments:** Tau Beta Pi; Eta Kappa Nu; Institute or Electrical and Electronics Engineers; PEER; Golden Key; National Association for the Advancement of Colored People; Habitat for Humanity; Explorer Scouts; National Society of Black Engineers; National Society of Professional Engineers. **Education:** Midlands Tech, Computer Technology Diploma (2000); Clemson University, degree in Electrical Engineering; Midlands Tech Special Schools, Graduate degree. **Personal Information:** Mr. Baukman enjoys reading and arcade games.

Andrew D. Becker

Chief Financial Officer
DNA Systems Inc.
1278 Millstone River Road
Somerville, NJ 08876
(908) 431-1799
Fax: (908) 281-1939
andrew_becker@bmc.com

7371

Business Information: Possessing exceptional technical skills, Mr. Becker began his career in the information technology field at the age of 13 when he created the arcade game Centipede, licensed by Atari. Currently, Mr. Becker serves as Chief Financial Officer of DNA Systems, Inc. He oversees all financial transactions of the Company, including invoices, client statements, and accounts payable and receivable. In the future, Mr. Becker would like to keep abreast of innovations in technology and continue acquiring more responsibilities with the Company. DNA Systems Inc. is a systems integrator, combining network administration and system analysis. DNA Systems Inc. has been operating since 1985 and employs 12 information technology professionals and generates approximately $1 million in estimated annual revenue. **Career Highlights:** Chief Financial Officer, DNA Systems Inc. (1995-Present); Software Consultant, BMC Software (1993-95); Disaster Recovery Improvement Manager, AT&T Solutions(1996-97); Project Leader, HP (1996); Unix Administrator, Hiserv. N.A. Inc. (1987-97). **Associations & Accomplishments:** Data Processing Management Association. **Education:** American University, B.S. in Business Administration (1989); AT&T Corporate Training, Certificate of Unix Administration. **Personal Information:** Married to Phyllis J. in 1993. Mr. Becker enjoys enjoys raising dogs.

David H. Beebe

Principal Information Engineer
Automation Research Systems, Limited
4480 King Street, Suite 600
Alexandria, VA 22302
(703) 914-8430
Fax: (703) 914-8500
dbeebe1@csc.com

7371

Business Information: Displaying expertise in the field of database administration, Mr. Beebe serves as Principal Information Engineer of Automation Research Systems, Limited. He has oversight of five servers in the areas of development and production. Designing a variety of database systems, Mr. Beebe provides assistance to five international sites. He is currently working on building a "Joint Total Asset Visibility System" (JTAV). An expert, he functions as the point-of-contact for any problems that may occur. His greatest professional highlight to date has been through his service as the original designer of the database system that is the heart of JTAV. He has remained on the cutting edge through subscribing to such periodicals as Oracle Magazine and Exploring Oracle Journal, being involved in Web site discussion groups, and attending various courses. Becoming an Oracle Certified Professional by the Automation Research Systems, Limited before the year 2000 serves as one of Mr. Beebe's goals. Automation Research Systems, Limited functions as an information technology company that works with clients on a contractual basis. Currently subcontracted to Computer Sciences Corporation, the Company primarily works with those in the government and commercial industries. Automation Research Systems, Limited is the number one provider for Cisco router hardware and training. Established in 1982, the Company has multiple offices throughout the United States employing more than 400 people. **Career Highlights:** Principal Information Engineer, Automation Research Systems, Limited (1994-Present); Naval Officer, United States Navy (1976-94). **Associations & Accomplishments:** Association of Computing Machinery; Institute of Electronics and Electrical Engineers. **Education:** United States Naval Post Graduate School, M.S. in Computer Science (1989); Western Michigan University, B.A. in Mathematics (1975). **Personal Information:** Married to Janet M. in 1986. Two children: Ruth and Deanna. Mr. Beebe enjoys music.

Michael W. Brown

Developer
RIA - Research Institute of America
2395 Midway Road
Carrollton, TX 75006
(972) 250-8334
mikeb@anet-dfw.com

7371

Business Information: Recruited to Research Institute of America (RIA), formerly Computer Language Research, in 1997, Mr. Brown currently serves as Developer. Utilizing his extensive occupational experience and firm academic foundation, Mr. Brown is responsible for designing and testing commercial software solutions for clients and other corporate businesses. In addition, he provides troubleshooting solutions should difficulties arise and has the ability to train others on the proper use and function of software. Committed to further development of RIA, Mr. Brown was very instrumental in upgrading the Company's DOS program with Windows front end. Coding software, developing and researching, fixing and adding features, and debugging are other responsibilities which Mr. Brown possesses. Alert to new opportunities, his long-term goals are keeping an eye on the horizon and staying on top of new technology. RIA functions as a computer consulting and software development company. The Company primarily works with those in the accounting field. Bearing responsibility for making the Fast Tax programs, providing computer consulting on software packages and development, and providing assistance in fixed asset management serve as the Company's other functions. **Career Highlights:** Developer, RIA - Research Institute of America (formerly Computer Language Research) (1997-Present); Developer, Howard Systems International (1996-97); Developer, Trammel Crow (1995-96). **Associations & Accomplishments:** Association of Computing Machinery; American Association for Artificial Intelligence; Deming Study Group of Dallas. **Education:** Southern Methodist University, M.L.A. (1984); University of Maryland, B.S. in Math (1972); Georgia Tech, Certificate in Knowledge Engineering; Anne Arundel Community College, A.A (1969). **Personal Information:** Mr. Brown enjoys football, opera, lacrosse, ballet and travel.

Perry Leon Bullied

Systems Analyst
Information Retrieval
209 Hampton Lee Court, Apartment 2A
Cary, NC 27513
(919) 460-7447
Fax: (919) 677-1897
bullied@ibm.net

7371

Business Information: In his position as Systems Analyst for Information Retrieval, Mr. Bullied is responsible for installing programs and designing and modifying computer systems. Highly regarded, he is accountable for project management and coordinating resources, time lines, and assignments. His 20 years of extensive experience are utilized in training new employees, monitoring support calls, and developing state of the art systems infrastructures. Mr. Bullied continues to grow professionally through the fulfillment of his responsibilities and he aspires to an expanded position in project management. His success reflects his ability to think out-of-the-box, tackle new challenges, and deliver results on behalf of the Company and its clientele. Information Retrieval engages in the development and installation of mainframe, server, and client software. The Company also configures systems network architecture, transmission control and Internet protocols for use in business and personal computers. Established in 1988, the Company employs 40 individuals to facilitate all aspects of operation. Information Retrieval is located in Cary, North Carolina and provides service to clients internationally. **Career Highlights:** Systems Analyst, Information Retrieval (1995-Present); Systems Analyst, Visa International (1991-94); Programmer, Bank of Montreal (1976-91). **Education:** Web Design University (Currently Attending); York University, B.Sc. **Personal Information:** Mr. Bullied enjoys travel, hiking and reading.

Elizabeth J. Burns

Senior Database Administrator/Architect
ProcureNet, Inc.
99 Holcomb Hill Road
New Hartford, CT 06057
(860) 676-4574
Fax: (860) 677-7157
beth_burns@hotmail.com

7371

Business Information: As the Senior Database Administrator and Architect for ProcureNet, Inc., Mrs. Burns supports all database technology for both internal and external customers. She is responsible for all database technical support, maintenance and upgrades to the database infrastructure, and conducting DBA conference calls with the other office sites once a week. Mrs. Burns manages Oracle, DB2, Informix, Sybase, and Microsoft SQL Server databases and keeps on the cutting edge of the business by researching, testing, and rolling out new database releases, getting feedback and information from the Internet, taking the appropriate DBA Administration classes, reading a lot of technical manuals and doing a lot of networking with other DBA's in the field. Possessing an excellent knowledge of computer technology, she also administers and controls all data resources and ensures their security and integrity. She got involved in computers after realizing how much potential there was for growth and advancement within the field. Mrs. Burns attributes her success to doing the very best she possibly can in her work and she plans to continue to strive for success with the Corporation she is currently with. ProcureNet, Inc. designs and implements procurement software that is state-of-the-art. Located in Avon, Connecticut; Fairfield, New Jersey; Pittsburgh, Pennsylvania; and Houston, Texas, the Corporation writes software and distributes it to the clientele. Dedicated to customer satisfaction, the Corporation works to ensure that each client is provided with cutting edge technology in a timely and cost-efficient manner. **Career Highlights:** Senior Database Administrator/Architect, ProcureNet, Inc. (1999-Present); Senior Database Architect, AMS Services (1997-99); Oracle Database Administrator, The Hartford, Simsbury, Connecticut (1996-97); Lead Database Administrator, Connecticut Natural Gas (1995-96); Programmer/Database Administrator, The Travelers (1983-93). **Associations & Accomplishments:** Australian Consulate of New York; Shares Program. **Education:** Manchester Community Technical College, Associate's Degree (1986). **Personal Information:** Married to Sean in 1993. One child. Mrs. Burns enjoys semi-professional tap dancing, hip-hop and boating.

Gerard W. Callahan

Chief Executive Officer
I Connection Inc.
2504 Washington Street, Suite 502
Waukegan, IL 60085-4998
(847) 662-0877
Fax: (847) 662-0325
jerry@iconnect.net

7371

Business Information: The Owner and Founder of I Connection, Mr. Callahan serves as the Chief Executive Officer. In this capacity, he assumes responsibility for the entire spectrum of operational and administrative functions. A savvy, 17 year professional, Mr. Callahan determines the overall strategic direction and business contribution of the information systems function. His extensive background includes stints as President of Midwest Software Development, Inc. and Vice President of Midwest Software Ltd. He firmly believes in going the extra mile to ensure customer satisfaction and support. This tenet is one of the secrets behind his success. His success is also attributed to his ability to think outside the box, produce results, and aggressively take on new challenges. Continually formulating new goals and objectives, Mr. Callahan has plans to begin a foray into the DSL field. He looks forward to continued growth and hopes to expand the Corporation with several new locations. I Connection Inc. is one of the more recent additions to the growing list of Internet service providers. Established in 1995, the Corporation provides Internet access to businesses and individuals in the state of Illinois. Web site development and host services are also provided. Currently, the Corporation boasts annual revenue of $500,000. The two person staff is dedicated to offering quality services and rapid Internet access to their clients. **Career Highlights:** Chief Executive Officer, I Connection Inc. (1995-Present); President, Midwest Software Development, Inc. (1992-95); Vice President, Midwest Software Ltd. (1982-92). **Associations & Accomplishments:** Lake County Chamber of Commerce. **Personal Information:** Married to Aree in 1984. Mr. Callahan enjoys chess.

Chris A. Campbell

Art Director
BsG Inc.
Rural Route 2, Box 393A
Dallas, PA 18612-9584
(570) 283-5000
Fax: (570) 674-6028
kris@bsg-inc.com

7371

Business Information: Mr. Campbell serves as Art Director for BsG Inc. Also fulfilling the role of network administrator, he ensures projects are completed to client satisfaction and in a timely manner as well as oversees the creative process. He keeps abreast of the latest technology, which he utilizes in the design process. Highly regarded, Mr. Campbell focuses on the financial aspects, implementing new policies, maintaining the budget, and ensuring accurate records. Always alert to new opportunities, Mr. Campbell is currently pursuing his Bachelor's degree in Commercial Arts and Internet, expanding networking potential, and becoming more involved in new technology. His emphasis is to capitalize on the opportunities provided by the Corporation. BsG Inc. provides Web site design for clients internationally. Established in 1995, the Corporation primarily builds Web sites for music bands, maintaining headquarters in Lehman, Pennsylvania. Local operations employ the skilled services of four individuals to facilitate all aspects of design, business acquisition, and customer service. **Career Highlights:** Art Director, BsG Inc. (1995-Present); Webmaster, Global Infonet (1998-Present); Art Director/Webmaster, Wheels America Advertising (1999-Present). **Associations & Accomplishments:** HTML Writers Guild; Mentor for High School students learning HTML in school. **Education:** Luzerne Community College: Associate's degree in Computer Graphics (1995), Associate's degree in Graphic Design (1995). **Personal Information:** Mr. Campbell enjoys snowboarding, rollerblading, mountain biking, reading, frisbee and hiking.

Jamie A. Chaikin

Principal Performance Engineer
Telcordia Technologies
Room 4E 233, 444 Hoes Lane
Piscataway, NJ 08854
(732) 699-6314
Fax: (732) 336-3594
jchaikin@telcordia.com

7371

Business Information: As Principal Performance Engineer for Telecordia Technologies, Mrs. Chaikin analyzes architecture, design, performance of networks, and makes recommendations for improvement. It is her responsibility to see that products run efficiently and additionally, she is in charge of recruiting new employees from City College. Utilizing many years of education and experience in her field, Mrs. Chaikin joined the Company in 1995 and since that time has been recognized for her diligence and skills, receiving an award from Women in Industry in 1999. Always alert to new techniques and approaches, it is Mrs. Chaikin's goal to continue to learn about new technology in order to facilitate advancement of the Company. Telecordia Technologies, established in 1998, is a telecommunications company specializing in the development of advanced network systems. Headquartered in Morristown, New Jersey and operating from four different locations, the international company employs 6,000 individuals to develop software solutions for voice and data networks. A subsidiary of SAIC, the Company is famous for its "next generation" networks. **Career Highlights:** Principal Performance Engineer, Telcordia Technologies (1995-Present); Database Specialist, Bellcore (1986-95); Systems Programmer, Bell Labs (1976-86). **Associations & Accomplishments:** Technical Recruiter, Community College of New York; Manager, Franklin Township Superstars; Recipient, Women in Industry Award 1999. **Education:** Stevens Institute, M.S. in Computer Science (1978); Cornell Univeristy, B.S. in Operations Research (1975). **Personal Information:** Married to Bill in 1988. Two children: Otto and Scotty.

John A. Christly

Chief Technology Officer
The Golf Network, Inc.
4361 West McNab Road, #27
Pompano Beach, FL 33069
(954) 979-9327
Fax: (954) 974-6760
jachristly@aol.com

7371

Business Information: Displaying his skills in this highly specialized position, Mr. Christly assumes both a technical and executive role at The Golf Network, Inc. He is the overall technical "guru" with responsibilities ranging from building state-of-the-art application servers to high powered web, e-mail, and Ecommerce systems. Presiding over the Corporation's application development functions, he supervises a team of contract programmers, as well as a group of engineers and technical support individuals. Mr. Christly is responsible for making the majority of decisions regarding how the Corporation will choose to implement cutting-edge technology, reporting directly to the Corporation's owners. Coordinating resources, time lines, schedules, assignments, and budgets also fall into the purview of his responsibilities. His professional success reflects his leadership ability to build strong teams with synergy, technical strength, and a customer oriented attitude as well as deliver results and aggressively take on new challenges. **Career Highlights:** Chief Technology Officer, The Golf Network, Inc. (1998-Present); Owner, NCSC (1993-Present); Army National Guard (1991-93); Member, International Executive Guild (1999). **Associations & Accomplishments:** Industry related. **Education:** B.S. in Information Systems (In Progress); A.S.B. in Business Management (In Progress); Certification: Network Administration, Programming, Project Management. **Personal Information:** Mr. Christly enjoys mountain biking, swimming, travel, rollerblading and music.

Scott Churetta

Software Design Engineer
Accu Sort Systems Inc.
511 School of House Road
Telford, PA 18969-1196
(215) 996-8155
Fax: (215) 996-8181
smchure@accusort.com

7371

Business Information: A savvy, 13 year professional of the technology field, Mr. Churetta serves as Software Design Engineer of Accu Sort Systems Inc. Working closely with systems management and users, he analyzes, specifies, and designs and develops software for single and multiple application systems. In this context, Mr. Churetta uses his technical expertise in designing specific software for bar coding systems. He implements software that helps the computers determine destinations of packages and items. Upon determination, items are moved to specific warehouse locations using the conveyor belt system. The discovery, investigation, and initial deployment of advanced scanning technologies within Accu Sort Systems is also an integral part of Mr. Churetta's responsibilities. His future endeavors include enhancing his already vast technical skills and remaining on the leading edge. Success is attributed to his ability to think outside the box, take on new challenges, and deliver results. Established in 1971, Accu Sort Systems Inc. is an international provider of bar code technology. Specializing in the design, development, and distribution of bar code scanning devices, the Corporation is located in Telford, Pennsylvania. Presently, the Corporation employs a work force of more than 550 professional, technical, and support personnel. **Career Highlights:** Software Design Engineer, Accu Sort Systems Inc. (1996-Present); Computer Operator, Bethlehem Area School District (1987-96). **Education:** Lehigh University, Bachelor's degree in Computer Science (1995). **Personal Information:** Married to Debra in 1990.

Karen L. Ciarlette

Project Manager
Computer Associates
1815 South Meyers Road
Oakbrook Terrace, IL 60181
(630) 481-4797
Fax: (630) 481-4150
karen.ciarlette@cai.com

7371

Business Information: Utilizing education and several years of experience, Ms. Ciarlette joined Computer Associates in 1999 as Project Manager for the Benefits Department. Responsible for projects revolving around human resources and benefits, she facilitates online enrollment, outsourcing, and employee relations. Being resourceful, Ms. Ciarlette stays on top of new benefit packages and is the main contact and support for employees of the Company, providing them with the latest updated information. Ms. Ciarlette enjoys her position with the Company and intends to remain in the field. Computer Associates, established in 1976, develops, markets, and sells software. Specializing in providing mission critical software solutions, the Company is the leading developer of client server and distributed computer software. International in stature, the Company is headquartered in New York. Employing 800 employess at the branch in Illinois, the Company has over 20,000 qualified individuals to facilitate daily operations. **Career Highlights:** Project Manager, Computer Associates (1999-Present); Platinum Technology Inc.: Benefits Services Manager (1998-99), Senior Systems Analyst (1996-98); Senior Programmer/Analyst, Federal Reserve Bank of Chicago (1991-1996). **Associations & Accomplishments:** American Compensation Association; Society for Human Resource Management. **Education:** University of St. Francis: M.B.A. (1997), B.A. (1994). **Personal Information:** Married to Timothy in 1996.

Michael A. Cole

Consultant
Analysts International
3805 Bee Tree Lane
Fort Worth, TX 76133
(817) 333-7425
malancol@flash.net

7371

Business Information: As a brilliant Consultant with Analysts International at the Dallas, Texas location, Mr. Cole is currently assigned to IBM, providing consultations on AIX/SP planning, integration, and administration. Possessing an excellent understanding of his field, Mr. Cole utilizes 11 years of consulting experience in dealing with mainframes, PCs, point of sales, RS/6000s, RS/6000 SPs, and all AIX services. Highly regarded in the industry, he is especially proud of being able to have the opportunity to install the SPs on the IBM project. He looks forward to going to a full-time position with Burlington Northern Santa Fe and aspires to become an Information Technology Architect. A savvy, 12-year professional, Mr. Cole attributes his success to his inquisitiveness and his ability to aggressively take on challenges and deliver results. Established in 1966, Analysts International is a global computer consulting firm. The Corporation assists clients in analyzing, designing, and developing systems using different programming languages and software. Headquartered in Minneapolis, Minnesota, the Corporation reports an annual revenue in excess of $600 million. Presently, the Corporation employs a staff of over 4,000 professional, technical, and support staff. **Career Highlights:** Consultant, Analysts International (1996-Present); Retail Technical Supervisor, Winn Dixie of Fort Worth (1985-96). **Associations & Accomplishments:** DFW Unix Users Group. **Education:** Tarrant County Junior College, Associate's degree in Business (1988). **Personal Information:** Married to Melinda in 1991. One child: Laura. Mr. Cole enjoys reading and music.

Ruth Cordle

Technical Advisor
Anteon Corporation
2770-H Gunter Park Drive East
Montgomery, AL 36109
(334) 277-2005
Fax: (334) 277-2331
rcordle@anteon.com

7371

Business Information: Mrs. Cordle is Technical Advisor of Anteon Corporation. She is responsible for information management systems development and project management, and is currently managing a systems project. Before joining Anteon Corporation, Mrs. Cordle served as a Consultant with Oracle Corporation, Technical Lead and Senior Software Engineer for Harris Technical Services Corporation, and Project Leader and Software Engineer at Naval Undersea Warfare Center. Managing a department of 21 professional and technical experts, she oversees commercial adventures by serving as the technical lead for each project, provides technical assistance in problem solving with clients and employees, and redesigns and implements projects and schedules. Remaining with Anteon, staying abreast of new technology, and continuing to provide quality service. "You have to have self discipline and stay on top of technology," is cited as Mrs. Cordle's advice. A full service software development company, Anteon Corporation provides information systems technology, systems engineering, network systems, and logistics management support to government and commercial customers. An international company, Anteon was established in 1977, and presently employs a global work force of more than 2,500 people. **Career Highlights:** Technical Advisor, Anteon Corporation (1997-Present); Consultant, Oracle Corporation (1996-97); Technical Lead/Senior Software Engineer, Hams Technical Services Corporation (1993-96); Project Leader/Software Engineer, Naval Undersea Warfare Center (1985-92). **Associations & Accomplishments:** International Oracle Users Group. **Education:** Rensselear Polytechnic Institute, M.S. in Computer Science (1990); University of Georgia, B.S. in Computer Science (1985); Oracle Certified Application Developer (1998). **Personal Information:** Married to Vance in 1985. One child: Christopher. Mrs. Cordle enjoys music and concerts, attending her son's activities and spending time with her family.

Nickolaos C. Costis

Information Technology Manager
Eurisko S.A.
1st Constantinoupoleos Str., Kalamaki-Athens
Attica, Greece 17455
+30 13533362
info@locomotion.gr

7371

Business Information: Possessing an excellent understanding of technology, Mr. Costis serves as Information Technology Manager of Eurisko S.A. He is responsible for the information technology department and is head of the five-member research and development team. Utilizing his technical expertise, Mr. Costis works closely with users to analyze, specify, and design solutions to meet their specific needs. In this context, he oversees project management and time tables; and writes scripts that the Company uses to fulfill the communications needs of clients. Highly regarded, Mr. Costis was nominated twice as "Best Information Technologist" in Sweden. He is proud of his ability to apply his knowledge and to combine this with his work. In the future, he hopes to have an more significant role in information technology. Established in 1999, Eurisko S.A. is involved In internet technologies. In this capacity, the Company engages in e-commerce, portal development, Internet advertising, Web site construction, and multmedia services. The Company employs seven individuals who work to ensure customer satisfaction with all services provided. **Career Highlights:** Information Technology Manager, Eurisko S.A. (1999-Present); Head of Research & Development, Foundation of Hellenic World (1998-Present); Founder/Research & Development Manager, The Locomotion Team (1997); New Technologies Manager, Epimeleia S.A. (1996). **Associations & Accomplishments:** The Greek Experts Association; Virtual Think Tank. **Education:** Technological University, Bachelor's degree (1992); Sivitanideios Technical Institute, B.A. in Hard Automation. **Personal Information:** Mr. Costis enjoys the guitar and Tai Chi.

Rick Cothern

Co-Owner
Cothern Computer Systems, Inc.
3760 Interstate 55 North, Floor 2
Jackson, MS 39211
(601) 969-1155
Fax: (601) 989-1184
rickco@eesliwa.com

7371

Business Information: Dedicated to the success of Cothern Computer Systems, Inc. Mr. Cothern actively leads the Corporation as its founder and Co-Owner. Establishing and maintaining major client relationships, he focuses his attention towards providing telephony and e-business solutions in order for the further progression of their business. Overseeing all aspects of daily operations, Mr. Cothern maintains an organized corporate structure with a concentration on marketing management and promotional strategy. Continuing in his committment with Cothern Computer Systems, Mr. Cothern's goal is to facilitate continued corporate growth and geographical expansion. "Select a technology in early stages and develop products and services around that," is cited as his advice. Founded in 1981, Cothern Computer Systems became an IBM business partner in 1983. Providing specialty services in computer technologies consulting, the Corporation is divided into three parts specializing in computer telephony that provides turnkey solutions to call centers. With nationwide operations out of Jackson, Mississippi and an expert staff of 26, the Corporation is extensively involved in the design and production of software development, custom made to fit the diverse needs of their continuously expanding client base. **Career Highlights:** Co-Owner, Cothern Computer Systems, Inc. (1981-Present); Systems Analyst, Currie-White Associates (1980-81); Systems and Office Manager, Clinical Pathology Labs (1976-80). **Associations & Accomplishments:** IBM Systems User Group. **Education:** Mississippi College, B.S. (1975); HJC, Associate's Degree (1972). **Personal Information:** Married to Carol in 1973. Two children: Jennifer and Paul. Mr. Cothern enjoys golf.

Benjamin Bryan Cox

Customer Support Manager
Micro Technology Unlimited
405 Thyme Place
Raleigh, NC 27609-3309
(919) 870-0344
bry21317@aol.com

7371

Business Information: As Customer Support Manager of Micro Technology Unlimited, Mr. Cox utilizes an extensive knowledge of technical practices as he works with clients on-site and on the phone to solve their technical challenges. Recognized for his talent and adept ability, he is engaged in Web page design and updates and the maintenance and/or implementation of hardware and software. Working closely with customers, Mr. Cox is able to incorporate their feedback and input into the formulation of strategic operational procedures and policies. He attributes his success to guidance he has received from his father and other family members. Mr. Cox currently is preparing himself for future ownership of the business by attending technical classes and attaining various certifications. Located in the bustling city center of Raleigh, North Carolina, Micro Technology, Unlimited specializes in the development of software and applications. Producing DSP boards for digital and audio workstations, the family owned company has established a solid reputation of quality and value since opening in 1977. **Career Highlights:** Customer Support Manager, Micro Technology Unlimited (1998-Present). **Education:** Wake Technical Community College, B.B.A. (In Progress); Barton College; North Carolina State University. **Personal Information:** Mr. Cox enjoys computers, boating, snow/water skiing, helping clients and motorcycling.

Brett Craven

Consultant
Ciber Custom Solutions Group
12980 Metcalf, Suite 150
Overland Park, KS 66213
(816) 767-7307
bcraven@swbell.net

7371

Business Information: Utilizing 10 years of tested and proven experience in the technology field, Mr. Craven serves as a Consultant with the Ciber Custom Solutions Group. He works closely with users and management to analyze business processes and design solutions that enhance client's efficiency and cost effectiveness. Currently developing the imaging and workflow division, Mr. Craven oversees the implementation and upgrade of new systems and maintains vendor relationships. Displaying an intense desire and determination, he intends to continue with the development of the imaging and workflow practice while working to obtain his Master's degree in information systems management. Attributing his success to enthusiasm and delivering results, Mr. Craven's advice to others is, "Don't be afraid to make the first move." Ciber Custom Solutions Group is a computer systems consulting, implementation, and integration service provider. The Company provides e-commerce solutions to businesses worldwide through application solutions, Web hosting, and the development of Web sites. Headquartered in Englewood, Colorado, Ciber Custom Solutions Group meets the demands of an international clientele. **Career Highlights:** Consultant, Ciber Custom Solutions Group (1999-Present); Project Manager, Computer Sciences Corporation. **Education:** William Jewell College, Business and Management degree (1989). **Personal Information:** Married to Lori in 1994. One child: Quinlin. Mr. Craven enjoys golf and bicycling.

Lori Ann DeSantis

President
ASAP II
960 Northwest 36th Street
Oakland Park, FL 33309-5909
(954) 630-2303
Fax: (954) 630-2033

7371

Business Information: Working in the capacity of President of ASAP II, Ms. DeSantis directs all aspects of daily administratoin and operations. As a highly regarded software developer and marketing representative, she has an excellent understanding of her field. Starting in a male dominated industry, she has had to work harder to gain respect, which in turn made her a battle tested consultant. Utilizing 15 years of experience as a self employed consultant, Ms. DeSantis wanted complete control of the company, and she also wanted to grow. For years she patiently waited for the oppurtunity to put her expertise in the information technology field to the test. With the encouragement of her parents, she has become a success story in the industry. Her background includes working on IBM mid-frame and PC networks. A visionary who has proven herself correct on many occasions, Ms. DeSantis' accolades include the installation of a mainframe for 30 companies. Her strategic plans for the Company are to double the existing client base, and continue to provide a quality product. Established in 1999, ASAP II is a software development company. Providing services for the general aviation industry, the Company employs three individuals. Currently, ASAP II is located in Oakland Park, Florida. **Career Highlights:** President, ASAP II (1999-Present); Software Developer/Consultant, ASAP (1985-98); Management Information Systems Manager, Profile Industries (1984-85). **Associations & Accomplishments:** SNUG Computer Users Group. **Education:** Ohio State University, B.S. in Math (1984). **Personal Information:** One child: Theresa. Ms. DeSantis enjoys boating.

Dennis Desroches

Support Analyst
Radian International Software
1000 Louisiana, Suite 1975
Houston, TX 77284
(713) 276-3240
dennis_desroches@radian.com

7371

Business Information: Functioning in the capacity of Support Analyst of Radian International Software, Mr. Desroches analyzes environmental, health, and safety functional areas and develops solutions to enhance overall performance. Before coming on board to Radian in 1998, Mr. Desroches served as Principal Support Analyst with Atrion. As a technology professional with an established record of delivering results, his career success reflects his ability to take on new challenges and responsibilities. In his present position, he is primarily involved with environmental applications, and answering questions dealing with database applications for internal and external clients. Utilizing his skills, Mr. Desroches identifies new and potential customers, analyzes their needs, proposes business solutions, and oversees the implementation of these solutions. Maintaining database applications and developing strategic and tactical sales plans also fall within the realm of his functions. Mr. Desroches' future objective is to achieve a senior management position. Recently bought by a Canadian company, Radian International Software engages in software design and development focused on environment, health, and safety. The Company offers advanced Oracle database applications for the following: emissions standards for the EPA, and training regulations for health and safety issues for the petro chemical and manufacturing industries. Established in 1995, Radian International Software employs a work force of more than 45 people. **Career Highlights:** Support Analyst, Radian International Software (1998-Present); Principal Support Analyst, Atrion (1999). **Education:** University of Phoenix, B.S. in Business Administration. **Personal Information:** Married to Dawn in 1998. Four children: Erica, Daniel, Megan, and Devon.

Jon Dodge

Senior Systems Architect
Lotus Development Corporation
6404 Maryview Street
Alexandria, VA 22310
(703) 851-7407
jon_dodge@lotus.com

7371

Business Information: Drawing from eight years of extensive educational ties and previous occupational experience, Mr. Dodge is functions in the capacity of Senior Systems Architect for Lotus Development Corporation. He is responsible for providing architectural integration services. Primarily, Mr. Dodge oversees and directs the development and implementation of infrastructure integration and software development and implementation. Mr. Dodge is proud of his accomplishment of developing a state-of-the-art deployable information system platform for the United States Navy, providing services to over 20,000 users at 130 sites in 13 countries around the globe. Continually striving for maximum effectiveness, Mr. Dodge is currently pursuing his Ph.D. to enable him to capitalize on the opportunities provided by Lotus Development. Mr. Dodge attributes his success to his tenacity and a belief that you must expect to work harder than you think. Obtained by IBM in 1996, Lotus Development Corporation engages in collabrative systems development. Serving an international clientele, the Corporation specializes in large scale value chain systems architecture development and systems planning. In addition to consulting, support, and educational services, the Corporation produces products such as Lotus Domino and Smart Suite. **Career Highlights:** Senior Systems Architect, Lotus Development (1997-Present); Director of Collabrative Systems, CACI, International (1994-97). **Education:** Santa Clara University, Master's degree in Computer Science (1994). **Personal Information:** Married to Diane L. Brown in 1998. Three children: Aaron Liszewski, Rebecca Liszewski, and Jilyan. Mr. Dodge enjoys wood working, testing new products and reading trade publications.

Michael Eblowitz

Chief Executive Officer
MacroSoft
28983 Glenrock Place
Highland, CA 92346
(909) 863-9169
Fax: (909) 863-9168
meblowitz@linkline.com

7371

Business Information: Serving as Chief Executive Officer of MacroSoft, Mr. Eblowitz supervises the Company's programmers and handles product sales, attending trade shows and offering live demonstrations. He determines the strategic direction and business contribution of the information systems function. As a 20 year technology professional, Mr. Eblowitz personally offers technical support to clients and assists them in learning to use the programs. Mr. Eblowitz became the Chief Executive Officer of MacroSoft in 1990 and enjoys the freedom and flexibility his current position offers him. Crediting his career success simply to seeing his clients' needs before they know they have them, he plans to continue to focusing his efforts on his current clients, providing quality products and services. A recognized leader in the field, Mr. Eblowitz is recipient of a 1999 "Hot Product of the Year" award from Modern Steel Construction Magazine. Created in 1990, MacroSoft is dedicated to writing software for the construction industry. Programs are geared towards structural steel detailing, shop drawings for steel plans, and shop fabrication of steel. Based in Highland, California, the Company distributes its software to construction firms around the world. **Career Highlights:** Chief Executive Officer, MacroSoft (1990-Present); Vice President, Geometric Data Flow (1979-90). **Associations & Accomplishments:** American Institute of Steel Construction; University of California at Los Angeles Alumni. **Education:** University of California at Los Angeles, B.S. (1982). **Personal Information:** Mr. Eblowitz enjoys boating, jet skiing and walking.

Srikanth Elaprolu

Developer
USI
14585 Avion Parkway
Chantilly, VA 20151
(703) 222-2866
Fax: (703) 222-0543
srikanth_elaprolu@usiva.com

7371

Business Information: Utilizing several years of experience in software development, Mr. Elaprolu serves as a Developer for USI. He works directly with the client company to develop customized software for its individualized needs. Implementing the specialized software, he will provide technical support and training on its use. Additionally, Mr. Elaprolu installs the standard products of the Company or simply provides his skilled services as a trainer. He performs all aspects of USI services according to each client's needs. Crediting his success to his ability to take charge of any project presented to him from scratch, he is able to follow through without hesitation and complete it with quality and efficiency. Mr. Elaprolu anticipates a promotion as the Project Management Team Leader due to his diligence and quality performance. USI is a computer software development company. Created in 1988, the Company develops documentation measuring and documentation management systems for businesses of all sizes. USI performs the installation and customization of its systems, providing end user training and technical support. Over 500 skilled professionals are employed in the Company's international operations. **Career Highlights:** Developer, USI (1999-Present); Developer, ADI (1997-99); Systems Analyst, University of Mississippi (1996-97). **Associations & Accomplishments:** Society of Automotive Engineers; Society of Mechanical Engineers; Mississippi Academy of Science. **Education:** Virginia Polytechnic & State University, M.B. A. (In Progress); University of Mississippi, M.S. (1997); Karnatakn University, India, B.S. (1995). **Personal Information:** Mr. Elaprolu enjoys computer games, reading and music.

L. Daniel Elkin

Senior Consultant
Macrophage International
8113 Moores Lane, Suite 1900, PMB 252
Brentwood, TN 37027
(615) 352-1155
Fax: (615) 376-4665
info@macrophage.net

7371

Business Information: As the Senior Consultant for Macrophage International, Mr. Elkin is responsible for software development. He concentrates on providing sales and consulting services to the vertical market sales. Working closely with management and systems users, he is accountable for the analysis, design, evaluation, testing, and implementation of cutting edge software applications. Highly regarded in the technology field, Mr. Elkin plans to continue growing professionally through the fulfillment of his responsibilities and involvement in the advancement of operations. Dedicated to the success of Macrophage International, he effectively utilizes his expertise, as he works with his clients during all technical phases of software development. In the future, Mr. Elkin looks forward to assisting in the completion of future corporate goals. Established in 1999, Macrophage International is an applications software provider. The Company offers Internet software developing, mainly for the legal market. Employing six personnel, the Company works with clients to develop software to meet specific business needs. Presently, the Company is located in Brentwood, Tennessee. **Career Highlights:** Senior Consultant, Macrophage International (1999-Present); Owner, Rivergate ADS Inc. (1987-99). **Personal Information:** Married to Lisa in 1994. Four children: Lilly, Midred, Michael, and Gabriel. Mr. Elkin enjoys going to church.

Thomas J. Engvall

Web Developer
RLI Corporation
9025 North Lindbergh Drive
Peoria, IL 61615-1499
(309) 692-1000
tom.engvall@rlicorp.com

7371

Business Information: A lifelong love of technology has motivated Mr. Engvall to pursue a career in the technological field. He currently assumes the title and responsibility of Web Developer at RLI Corporation, overseeing a multitude of daily duties. A savvy, 20-year veteran, he utilizes his extensive knowledge of Visual Basic and other languages to develop and implement effective Web pages. Maintaining client relations, Mr. Engvall monitors and updates the various Web sites as necessary. His accomplishments include a Web program that allows brokers to rate earthquake policies with net based policy printing and archival. For a previous employer, he wrote a program to monitor missile safety at the United States Army's Pacific Missile Range. He plans on improving his technological skills, staying focused in the use of Microsoft tools, and becoming MCSD certified. A positive attitude is one reason for his career success. RLI Corporation is a business designed to provide insurance and electronic commerce services to an international client base. Selling property insurance and specialty marketing is also RLI's forte. Founded in 1963, this reputable Corporation employs a professional staff of approximately 500 people to assist in various aspects of the operation. The main objective of the Corporation is to develop Web pages for brokers. **Career Highlights:** Web Developer, RLI Corporation

(1998-Present); Information Technology Consultant, Renaissance Worldwide (1996-98); Range Safety Digital Engineer, Raytheon, RSI (1988-96); Senior Engineer, Digivision Inc. (1986-87). **Associations & Accomplishments:** President (1980), Eta Kappa Nu. **Education:** San Diego State University, B.S. in Electrical Engineering (1980). **Personal Information:** Married to Marilyn in 1990. Two children: April and Coleen. Mr. Engvall enjoys antique restoration and wheels of time museum.

Timur Fanshteyn

Senior Developer
CDS Inc.
270 Lafayette Street, Suite 1002
New York, NY 10012-3327
(212) 965-1193
Fax: (212) 965-1218
tim@cds-ny.com

7371

Business Information: Serving as Senior Developer of CDS Inc., Mr. Fanshteyn handles all aspects of highly technical processes and activities. Working closely with his team, he demonstrates an extensive education gained through practical work experience and related schooling. Utilizing a productive style of management, Mr. Fanshteyn incorporates staff feedback and input to create innovative technical solutions and standard operating procedures. He maintains the overall infastructure of the network including the LAN and WAN as he contributes to the development of new software. Conducting extensive research projects, Mr. Fanshteyn is able to effectively forecast market trends and style thereby formulating products that are applicable. Attributing success to a strong interest and love of the industry, Mr. Fanshteyn looks forward to continually progressing into Web integration. Established in 1994, CDS Inc. offers software solutions to the fashion industry. Developing software and related applications, the 10 employee company is able to assist in the organization of modeling and talent scheduling for agencies and clothing houses. Located in New York, New York, the international corporation caters to elite members of the style-conscious industry. **Career Highlights:** Senior Developer, CDS Inc. (1996-Present); Associate Developer, CIBC World Market (1998-99). **Education:** New York University, B.S. (1997). **Personal Information:** Mr. Fanshteyn enjoys swimming, skiing and browsing the Web.

Eugenia Fey
Senior Software Architect
Crystallize
5832 Naneva Court
West Bloomfield, MI 48322
(734) 761-1631
Fax: (248) 538-9207
jfey@crystallizes.com

7371

Business Information: As the Senior Software Architect for Crystallize, Ms. Fey works closely with management and systems users to analyze, develop, and implement new generation software. Possessing superior talents and an excellent understanding of technology, she researches client needs and designs computer software that assists in building their business. She also tests and provides solutions when necessary. A successful, 18 year professional, Ms. Fey has recieved special recognition for the implementation of certification systems. Her skills and knowledge are utilized in the supervision of employees and she encourages open communication to facilitate optimum working conditions. In the future, Ms. Fey plans to pursue a position in Web design. A start up software developer, Crystallize engages in designing cutting edge software specializing in automating merges of enterprise resource systems. Established in 1998, the Company employs a skilled staff of 80 individuals to facilitate all aspects of operation. Located in West Bloomfield, Michigan, the Company distributes products and serves to an international clientele. **Career Highlights:** Senior Software Architect, Crystallize (1999-Present); Project Leader, Gabe Group (1997-99); Project Leader, Society of Manufacturing Engineers (1995-97). **Associations & Accomplishments:** International Oracle Users Group; Oracle Development Text Users Group. **Education:** Azerbaijom Oil and Chemistry University, Master's degree in Applied Math (1991). **Personal Information:** Married to Victor in 1984. Two children: Tanya and Ida. Ms. Fey enjoys travel and reading.

Susan B. Fig
Director
HNC Software, Inc.
5935 Cornerstone Court West
San Diego, CA 92121-3711
(858) 799-8171
Fax: (858) 799-8048
sbf@hnc.com

7371

Business Information: Serving as Director of HNC Software, Inc., Ms. Fig is responsible for a wide array of duties on behalf of the Corporation. She oversees and manages a number of accounts as well as training, documentation, and product support. Possessing an excellent understanding of her field, Ms. Fig attends user group meetings, while creating innovative Web sites and increasing customer satisfaction. Drawing from 17 years of industry experience, Ms. Fig utilizes her leadership talents in managing all aspects of post-sales customer relationships. Her plans for the future include remaining with the Corporation in order to continue excelling in her field of expertise. Success, according to Ms. Fig, is due to her ability to form teams with synergy and technical strength, take on challenges, and deliver cutting edge results. HNC Software, Inc. engages in the provision of predictive software solutions that help service industry companies maintain more profitable customer relationships on an individually professional basis. The Corporation offers services in a wide variety of interests including e-commerce, insurance, and telecommunications. Established in 1986, the Corporation is headquartered in San Diego, California. Functioning under the direct guidance and expertise of more than 1,000 professionals, the Corporation enjoys annual revenues of more than $54.6 million. **Career Highlights:** HNC Software, Inc.: Director (1999-Present); Senior Partner/Manager (1998-99); Senior Accounts Manager (1995-99). **Associations & Accomplishments:** Parents and Teachers Association; Education Committee. **Education:** University of Missouri, B.S. (1983). **Personal Information:** One child: Nicole. Ms. Fig enjoys writing children's self-help books, golf, tennis and reading historial novels.

Terrance Fisher
Development Support Analyst
Horizon Healthware, Inc.
266 West Millbrook Road, Suite B
Raleigh, NC 27609
(919) 676-8090
Fax: (507) 262-0401
kefall92@yahoo.com

7371

Business Information: Serving as Development Support Analyst of Horizon Healthware, Inc., Mr. Fisher is tasked with software development and support. Demonstrating outstanding technical expertise, he orchestrates programming and cutting edge applications development. Highly regarded, he forms and monitors the Corporation's Web site, and takes an innovative approach to client Web site design. Mr. Fisher is currently collaborating with his partner on a book about software for database applications and hopes to eventually start his own software company. A visionary who has proven himself correct on many occasions, Mr. Fisher credits his accomplishments to his mother's unwaivering support. Horizon Healthware, Inc. is a software application vendor for small home health and hospice agencies. Created in 1984, the Corporation supplies customized software and organizational systems for enhanced business operations. Horizon Healthware provides state regulated billing documents, cost effective applications, training, and on going technical support for their clients. Presently, the Corporation is staffed by four technical experts. **Career Highlights:** Development Support Analyst, Horizon Healthware, Inc. (1998-Present); General Ledger Support Analyst, IVIS International, Inc. (1996-98); Quality Assistant Analyst, SAS Institute, Inc. (1994-96). **Education:** St. Augustine's College, B.S. (1994). **Personal Information:** One child: Terrance II.

David A. Frackman
Chief Technical Officer/President
Madscience
150 Lafayette 9F
New York, NY 10013
(212) 472-8586
Fax: (212) 898-0129
ven_whoswho@madscience.com

7371

Business Information: As Chief Technology Officer and President of Madscience, Mr. Frackman oversees the basic operations of the Company. Heading all administrative and financial aspects of the Company, he ensures proper funding and staffing of each particular project. Presiding over all client relationships, he is responsible for maintaining their goals and interests in regards to creating specific Web sites used to achieve higher levels of success. Involved in the marketing aspects of the Company, Mr. Frackman concentrates his efforts towards the promotion of new software developed and services offered. Committed to the further success of Madscience, Mr. Frackman remains focused on the widening of the client base and the expansion of the product line. Specializing in Web software development, Madscience was established in 1998. Forming reliable and confidential client relationships, Web sites are designed specifically for their individual purposes. Designing Web sites according to the client's specific needs, the Company's products are not available through software retailers. Coordinating efforts with their numerous clients, the Company is capable of completing complex projects in six weeks or less. Specifically obtaining accounts with Gateway clients, the Company maintains accounts nationally. Utilizing state-of-the-art equipment and systems, Madscience is dedicated towards providing top of the line Web-site creations. **Career Highlights:** Chief Technical Officer/President, Madscience (1999-Present); Consultant, Paltalk (1999); Technical Director, Young & Rubicam New Tech (1997-98); Technical Director, Web Partners (1995-96). **Associations & Accomplishments:** Institute of Electrical and Electronics Engineers; Association of Computing Machinery; USENIX: SAGE. **Education:** State University of New York at Purchase, B.A. (1994).

Robert T. Frangieh
Customer Support Manager
elcom.com, Inc.
60 Dinsmore Avenue, Apartment 112
Framingham, MA 01702
(781) 407-5070
rfrangieh@hotmail.com

7371

Business Information: Dedicated to the success of elcom.com, Inc., a subsidiary of elcom International, Mr. Frangieh applies his knowledge and expertise in the field of consumer relations in serving as Customer Support Manager. Responsible for managing the Corporation's call center, Mr. Frangieh is held accountable for daily operational activities, ensuring all client issues are handled with immediate proficiency. Currently heading the customer support team that develops up-to-date e-business solutions and strategies, Mr. Frangieh is leading elcom.com, Inc. to new levels of prosperity, thereby ensuring corporate longevity and his personal occupational success. His future goals include attaining the position of Chief Information Officer by continually working hard and maintaining certifications current. Established in 1991, elcom International is a leading Internet firm engaged in corporate consulting and e-commerce solutions. Specializing in new media, the Corporation provides comprehensive state-of-the-art software and new technology consultation around the clock. Currently elcom.com, Inc. is comprised of over 600 highly skilled technicians who generate revenues in excess of $200 million annually. With the growing demand for information technology experts, elcom.com is one of the fastest growing firms of its kind in the industry, and is leading the globe in new media solutions. **Career Highlights:** Customer Support Manager, elcom.com, Inc. (1999-Present); Network Engineer, Trellis Network Services (1998-99); Northeast Account Executive, Professional Support, Inc. (1991-98). **Education:** American University of Beirut, M.B.A (1987); Microsoft Certified Systems Engineer (1999). **Personal Information:** Mr. Frangieh enjoys squash, reading, tennis and hiking.

Douglas N. Franklin
Team Leader
McKesson HBOC
5995 Windward Parkway, Mail Stop ATHQ 2303
Alpharetta, GA 30005
(404) 338-2523
franklin@america.net

7371

Business Information: A successful, 13 year veteran of technology, Mr. Franklin serves as a Team Leader of McKesson HBOC. Possessing an excellent understanding of architecture, he designs and develops cutting edge document imaging products. A pioneer in the industry, he also serves a mentor responsible for 20 to 40 employees at any given time. Fully aware of his surroundings, Mr. Franklin remains on top of emerging technologies. Attributing his success to the continuation of his learning experiences, he hopes to achieve the position of Chief Architect and bring in new concept methodologies. McKesson HBOC was established in 1833. Reporting an estimated annual sales at a staggering $20 billion, the Company employs about 20,000 individuals. Headquartered in north Atlanta, Georgia, McKesson HBOC provides information systems and technology to the health care industry. With its primary product being "Pathways 2000," the Company also offers outsourcing services. Included in these are strategic information, systems planning, data center operations, receivables management, and major systems conversions. **Career Highlights:** Team Leader, McKesson HBOC (1999-Present); Group Leader of Development, IMNET Systems, Inc. (1993-98); Director of Imaging Peripheral Development, Summit Software

(1987-93). **Associations & Accomplishments:** Life Member, National Rifle Association; Life Member, North American Hunting Club. **Education:** Georgia Institute of Technology, B.S.I.C.S. (1987). **Personal Information:** Mr. Franklin enjoys photography, remote control cars, firearms, military history, auto racing and science fiction.

Cynthia French

Assistant Management Information Systems Director
Ahlers & Associates
1710 Washington Avenue
Waco, TX 76701-1195
(254) 756-1836
Fax: (254) 755-0267
cfintexas@yahoo.com

7371

Business Information: Utilizing her extensive skills and knowledge of computers, Ms. French serves as Assistant Management Information Systems Director with Ahlers & Associates. She assumes accountablility for all computer programming. In addition, Ms. French supervises her department, maintains internal support of customers as well as maintains computer hardware. Proficient in the field of computers, she designed the software system "Debug" for Ahlers & Associates which is still in use today. Through the study of technical journals, research on the Internet, and networking, Ms. French intends to acquire more knowledge of e-commerce to further advance the Company. She attributes her success to the support of family and friends as well as flexibility and creativity. Established in 1979, Ahlers & Associates provides data collection and software for non-profit organizations. Employing 30 individuals, the Company services 500 clients nationwide. **Career Highlights:** Assistant Management Information Systems Director, Ahlers & Associates (1999-Present). **Education:** Texas State Technical College, A.A.S. (1994). **Personal Information:** One child: Brianna. Ms. French enjoys reading, crafts, NASCAR and church.

Darren K. Gabriel

Senior Applications Analyst
ERDAS, Inc.
2801 Buford Highway NE, Suite 300
Atlanta, GA 30329
(404) 248-9000
Fax: (404) 248-9400
gabriel@erdas.com

7371

Business Information: Displaying his skills in this highly specialized position, Mr. Gabriel serves as the Senior Applications Analyst for ERDAS, Inc. He consults with clients, analyzing their Applications to determine their specific needs, and working with them to design a customized work flow. Providing training and consulting to end users on newly implemented systems, he offers technical support and troubleshoots problems long after the sale. Before joining ERDAS, Inc., he served as GIS Analyst and Forester for Hammon, Jensen, Waller & Associates, Inc. Mr. Gabriel's solid background history also includes a stint as Research Assistant with Texas A&M University. Consistently achieving quality performance in his field, Mr. Gabriel attributes his success to an outstanding education, a supportive family, and being employed by the World's premier Geographic Imaging firm. He looks forward to obtaining a management position. ERDAS, Inc. designs and distributes remote sensing software and solutions to Academic, Military/Intelligence, Natural Resource, Telecommunications, and other service oriented organizations. Employing a staff of 150 skilled individuals, the Corporation was founded in 1978 and boasts nearly $18 million in annual sales. **Career Highlights:** Senior Applications Analyst, ERDAS, Inc. (1994-Present); GIS Analyst/Forester, Hammon, Jensen, Waller & Associates, Inc. (1992-94); Research Assistant, Texas A&M University (1987-92). **Associations & Accomplishments:** Gualala Municipal Advisory Committee; Society of American Foresters; Board of Directors, St. Paul's United Methodist Church; Board Member, American Society for Photogrammetry and Remote Sensing; St. Paul's United Methodist Church; Youth Mentor, Hopewell United Methodist Church. **Education:** Texas A&M University: M.S. in Forest Service (1994), B.S. in Forest Management (1989), B.S. in Urban Forestry (1989). **Personal Information:** Married to Ann S. in 1992. One child: Taylor Cline. Mr. Gabriel enjoys church choir, fishing, landscaping, hunting and physical fitness.

Ravi Gaddam

Senior Database Administrator
Analysts International
5329 East Morning Glory Place
Littleton, CO 80126
(303) 896-1476
Fax: (720) 344-2523
rgaddam@uswest.com

7371

Business Information: Possessing unique talents in the information technology field, Mr. Gaddam joined Analysts International in as the Senior Database Administrator in 1998. He is responsible for administering and controlling data resources, tuning data tools to enhance overall operations, and ensuring the integrity and security of the database. Possessing an excellent understanding of technology, Mr. Gaddam also provides consulting services to clients and updates the computer systems. Overseeing the installation of Oracle hardware and software products also fall within the realm of his responsibilities. He attributes his success to his listening power, understanding requirements, and his leadership qualities. In the future, Mr. Gaddam anticipates his promotion to Lead Database Administrator with Analysts International as a result of his continuing efforts to increase his skills through training and professional development activities. Analysts International is a $400 million turnover company specializing in consulting and project development. Established in 1963, the Corporation is headquartered in Minneapolis and maintains corporate offices worldwide. Presently, Analysts International employs the skilled services of 4,600 individuals to acquire business, meet with clients, facilitate projects, and market services to generate vast sums of annual revenues. **Career Highlights:** Senior Database Administrator, Analysts International (1998-Present); Database Administrator, ITC Infotech (1997-98); Senior Programmer/Analyst, Datacons Pvt. Ltd. (1994-97). **Associations & Accomplishments:** Oracle Users Group; Oracle Technology Network; Intraware Membership. **Education:** Master's degree in Computer Application (1995); Oracle Certification for Database Administration. **Personal Information:** Married to Kranthi Tallui in 1999. Mr. Gaddam enjoys reading and games.

Dramise D. Gates

Software Quality Assurance Manager
Sonic Foundry, Inc.
754 Williamson Street
Madison, WI 53703
(608) 256-3133
dramiseg@sonicfoundry.com

7371

Business Information: Serving with Sonic Foundry, Inc. since coming on board in 1998, Mrs. Gates fulfills the responsibility of the Software Quality Assurance Manager. Possessing superior talents and an excellent understanding of technology, she ensures products and services are laced with quality, reliability, and value. Demonstrating her management skills, Mrs. Gates supervises a staff of 21 employees in areas that include project management, teaching, and training. Dedicated to the success of the Corporation, she ensures quality practices are designed and implemented. In the future, she plans on remaining with the Corporation in a technical position. Her advice is "Do an internship first and don't focus on just one thing." Established in 1991, Sonic Foundry, Inc. is a software development company that manufactures digital editing tools for music. The Corporation performs a great deal of research into new and innovative techniques in which to edit sound. Recently, the Corporation began offering premium solutions for delivering audio and video content online. Over 300 employees man day-to-day operations. **Career Highlights:** Software Quality Assurance Manager, Sonic Foundry, Inc. (1998-Present); Senior Software Quality Assurance Engineer, Databeam Corporation (1995-98); Senior Software Quality Assurance Engineer, Compuware (1995). **Associations & Accomplishments:** The American Society for Quality. **Education:** University of Maryland, B.S. in Computer Science and Information Systems (1993). **Personal Information:** Married to Tom in 1987. Three children: Tyler, Brandon, and Jessie. Mrs. Gates enjoys outdoor sports.

Donna F. Gaul

Director of Information Technology
Regional Network Communications, Inc.
190 Brodhead Road, Suite 300
Bethlehem, PA 18017
(610) 865-6500
dgaul@rnci.com

7371

Business Information: As an experienced, 19 year professional, Mrs. Gaul serves as Director of Information Technology for Regional Network Communications, Inc. She determines the strategic direction of the Corporation as well as business contribution of the information systems functions. Before joining Regional Network Communications, she served as Secretary and Treasurer for Ominus Systems, Inc. and Senior Principal Information Technology Specialist with Air Products & Chemicals. Her present position involves management of the Corporation's development teams. In this context, she provides sound leadership for both aspects of operations, including development and Web site design. Mrs. Gaul specializes in designing dynamic sites that have appealed to customers and have had a direct impact on the Corporation's growth. Under her technological guidance a series of programs on the virtual community have been developed. She attributes her success to the mentor that has directed her life since the age of 22. Mrs. Gaul's plans are focused on remaining with the Company where she is very content. Regional Network Communications, Inc. has developed plans to expand the realm of services offered. Currently, the Corporation functions include: dynamic, Web site design and development of virtual community online programs. Established in 1995, a core group of 50 employees handle a variety of technology functions. **Career Highlights:** Director of Information Technology, Regional Network Communications, Inc. (1998-Present); Secretary/Treasurer, Ominus Systems, Inc. (1998-Present); Senior Principal Information Technologist Specialist, Air Products & Chemicals (1980-98). **Education:** Bloomsburg University, B.S. (1980). **Personal Information:** Married to Stephen E. Jr. in 1997. Two children: Drew and Jacob. Mrs. Gaul enjoys motorcycle riding, sewing, the piano and gardening.

Lorraine Leandra Gauvin

Corporate Recruitment Manager
Havas Interactive, Inc.
3380 146th Place SE
Bellevue, WA 98007
(425) 649-9800
Fax: (425) 401-4925
lorraine.gauvin@havasint.com

7371

Business Information: Ms. Gauvin functions in the role of Corporate Recruitment Manager for Havas Interactive, Inc. She is involved in locating and acquiring new business contacts and future employees. Before joining Havas Interactive, Ms. Gauvin served as Divisional Human Resources Manager for Sierra On-line. Her background also includes a stint as Regional Human Resources Manager for RPS, Inc. In her present capacity, she strives to positively demonstrate the uses of various software programs during a brief period of time to both investors and realtors in the industry. Her career highlights include reducing the turnover rate by 100 percent with a previous employer, and establishing a centralized recruiting system with her current employer. Looking to the 21st Century, Ms. Gauvin plans to remain with the Corporation and assist it in the strategic planning for its own future. Her success reflects her ability to build relationships with customers and co-workers, as well as her ability to think outside the box, deliver results, and take on new challenges. Havas Interactive, Inc. designs and distributes software for entertainment and educational products. Established in 1999, this unique twist to the entertainment and computer video games industries has sparked a new market for online, virtual simulation games. **Career Highlights:** Corporate Recruitment Manager, Havas Interactive, Inc. (1998-Present); Divisional Human Resources Manager, Sierra OnLine (1998-99); Regional Human Resources Manager, RPS Inc. (1995-98). **Associations & Accomplishments:** Washington Software Alliance; Lake Washington Human Resource Association; Society of Human Resources Management. **Education:** Golden Gate University, M.S. (1998); California State University at Sacremento, B.A. **Personal Information:** Ms. Gauvin enjoys kayaking, outdoor activities, hiking and skiing.

Mira E. Genser

Worldwide Marketing Manager
InfoRay, Inc.
One Canal Park
Cambridge, MA 02141
(617) 250-1406
Fax: (617) 250-1451
m.genser@inforay.com

7371

Business Information: Utilizing eight years of experience, Ms. Genser serves as Worldwide Marketing Manage of InfoRay, Inc. In this capacity, she fulfills the responsibilities of worldwide marketing. She is responsible maintaining customer relations, product marketing, organizing special demonstrations of newly developed software, and collateral writing. Her seven person international marketing team conducts research and surveys of companies to better determine future corporate needs. An accomplished professional, Ms. Genser has auhored key articles in top journals such as Business Week and Wall Street. In addition, she has received several internal and client awards. The success she brings to the Corporation ensures that InfoRay will be a public company in the near future. Success is attributed to her great mentors in the industry and long hours she has put into her work. "Be a quick learner," is cited as Ms. Genser's advice. InfoRay, Inc. is an internet software developer for Fortune 1000 companies. It specializes in finance, telecommunications, and logistics software to maximize its clients' efficiency and capabilities. This international company was founded in 1994, and has expanded to employ over 80 motivated personnel who respond to clients' needs by developing customized software to fit any application. **Career Highlights:** Worldwide Marketing Manager, InfoRay Inc. (1999-Present); Public Relations, Programart Corporation (1998-99); Marketing Manager, Psion Computers (1997-98); Senior Account Executive, Brodeur Worldwide (1993-97). **Associations & Accomplishments:** Business Marketing Association; Public Relations Society of America; Publicity Club; Ad Club. **Education:** University of Vermont, B.S. (1992). **Personal Information:** Ms. Genser enjoys golf, running and skiing.

Joshua A. Gerlick

President
Obsidian Corporation
3511 Woolley Road
Oswego, IL 60543
jgerlick@obsidiancorporation.com

7371

Business Information: Serving as President, Mr. Gerlick is the founder of Real Science CD-Rom. He acts as a liaison between the administration and employees. A member of the administrative board, he takes part in the decision-making aspects of the Company. Mr. Gerlick is making plans to expand to the surrounding five states and wants to increase distribution to 5,000 magazines from the current 1,000 copies. He is working on a national program to incorporate all state guidelines and standards into the magazine, and wants to expand marketing to science museums to enable individuals access to the service. Mr. Gerlick built Real Science CD-Rom from the ground up and enjoys being able to offer a positive influence to students and teachers in Illinois. Concurrently, he serves as a Webmaster with Illinois Mathematics and Science Academy. His success reflects his leadership ability to communicate effectively and take on new challenges and responsibilities. Established in 1998, Real Science CD-Rom produces and distributes educational multimedia CD-Rom magazines for third through fifth grade students and teachers in Illinois. It is designed to supplement the existing standard science curriculum. The CD-Rom magazine is two-part, providing teachers with a forum to share experiences with colleges and giving students the opportunity to study a project or idea through all areas of science. Presently, the Company employs five people. **Career Highlights:** President, Real Science CD-Rom (1998-Present); Illinois Mathematics and Science Academy: Technical Coordinator (1998), Webmaster (1997-Present); Safety Engineer, Dekalb County Forest Preserve (1998). **Associations & Accomplishments:** Eagle Scout; Order of the Arrow Brotherhood. **Education:** Illinois Mathematics and Science Academy, Diploma.

Paul H. Glaeser

Software Engineer
CSI Maximus, Inc.
998 Old Eagle School Road
Wayne, PA 19087
(610) 687-9202
Fax: (610) 971-9447

7371

Business Information: With extensive experiences in the technical field, Mr. Glaeser was recruited to CSI Maximus, Inc. in 1999 and now functions as Software Engineer. In this capacity, he codes and maintains the open road part of the Fleet management application to include C modules. An acknowledged expert in the industry, Mr. Glaeser is highly proficient in C and SQL programming. Utilizing years of experience and a firm academic base, he works on creating software, software applications, and debugging of software. In addition, Mr. Glaeser maintains the Oracle and Ingres databases in a fully operating mode. Using his vast knowledge to solve problems, Mr. Glaeser implements technology to meet the Corporation's needs. Also, he designs new, cutting-edge solutions and plans and develops new computer systems. Learning programming languages to include C++ and Java serve as his long-term goals. A success in the field, Mr. Glaeser attributes professional success to being persistent and not giving up. CSI Maximus, Inc. specializes in fleet management software. This particular software application operates on multiple hardware platforms. Headquartered in Wayne, Pennsylvania, the Corporation operates a satellite facility in Minneapolis, Minnesota and employs a staff of 100 people corporation-wide. **Career Highlights:** Software Engineer, CSI Maximus, Inc. (1999-Present); Senior Programmer/Analyst, Control Software, Inc. (1998-99); Senior Programmer/Analyst, CTDI, Inc. (1996-98); Programmer/Analyst/Consultant, Fastech, Inc. (1996); Programmer/Analyst, GMIS, Inc. (1994-95). **Associations & Accomplishments:** Institute of Electronics and Electrical Engineers Computer Society; Association of Computing Machinery. **Education:** Polytechnic University, B.S. in Electrical Engineering (1988). **Personal Information:** Married to Elizabeth in 1993. Two children: Jennifer and Angelica. Mr. Glaeser enjoys reading and home repair.

Raphael D. Goins

Systems/Network Administrator
Flexon
130 7th Street
Pittsburgh, PA 15222
(412) 749-0400
Fax: (412) 749-0410
(800) 365-3667
rdg@flexonic.com

7371

Business Information: Mr. Goins functions in the role of Systems/Network Administrator with Flexon. He is responsible for all aspects of advising, supporting, installing, and repairing Symix, ERP, and MRP Systems, including computer networks, and Windows NT and UNIX systems. Before joining the Flexon's team of professionals in 1997, Mr. Goins served as a Network Switching Systems Supervisor for the Pennsylvania Army National Guard. Also, he continues to serve as a Weather Analyst with the Pennsylvania Air National Guard. As a 12 year professional, he is tasked with supporting all levels of networking and technology such as Microsoft, Novell, and special applications. He is also involved in both telephony and onsite client network support by performing network evaluations and designing solutions to eliminate difficulties and improve overall systems performance. Mr. Goins attributes his success to his people and communication skills and his ability to help others understand new technology. Becoming more involved in a managerial role in technology serves as one of his future endeavors. Flexon operates as a national technology reseller specializing in ERP software. The Corporation also offers a full range of technical support and programming services. Targeting mainly small manufacturing companies, Flexon was established in 1977. Presently, the Corporation is manned by over 35 people who help generate in excess of $1.5 million annually. Headquartered in Pittsburgh, Pennsylvania, Flexon operates a network of three offices across the country. **Career Highlights:** Systems/Network Administrator, Flexon (1997-Present); Weather Analyst, Pennsylvania Air National Guard (1996-Present); Network Switching Systems Supervisor, Pennsylvania Army National Guard (1987-94). **Education:** Robert Morris College, B.S. in Management Information Systems (1998). **Personal Information:** Married to Laura A. Frobe in 1997. One child: Ryan E.

Nancy A. Gorgen

Operations Director
Soft Ad
4 Parklane Boulevard, Suite 355
Dearborn, MI 48126
(313) 253-3654
Fax: (313) 441-2408
ngorgen@softad.com

7371

Business Information: Providing her skilled services as Operations Director to Soft Ad, Ms. Gorgen assumes accountability for the smooth and efficient running of operations. She oversees the project management, supervising the creative departmental staff and concentrating her efforts on quality assurance. Ultimately, she is responsible for the overall profit and loss of the Company. Coordinating resources, schedules, time lines, and assignments also fall within the purview of Ms. Gorgen's responsibilities. Her solid background history includes stints as Intranet Webmaster with GM Truck and Powertrain Webmaster for Ford Motor Company. Crediting her success to her professionalism and a passion for the field of information technology, Ms. Gorgen is currently pursuing her Master's degree in Business Administration. She looks forward to a promotion to the position of Vice President. Soft Ad provides Internet applications development and professional services to an international clientele. Privately owned, the Company boasts $12 million in annual revenue and employs a work force of 60 staff members. **Career Highlights:** Operations Director, Soft Ad (1998-Present); Intranet Webmaster, GM Truck (1997-98); Powertrain Webmaster, Ford Motor Company (1995-97). **Education:** University of Michigan, M.B.A. (In Progress); Oakland University, B.S. in Management Information System (1987); Macomb College, Associates degree in Data Processing (1985). **Personal Information:** Married to William in 1998. Two children: Eric and Emily. Ms. Gorgen enjoys downhill skiing and gardening.

Sebastian Graf

Chief Operating Officer
PROMATIS Corporation
3223 Crow Canyon Road, Suite 310
San Ramon, CA 94583
(925) 904-0380
Fax: (925) 904-0385
sebastian.graf@promatis.com

7371

Business Information: Utilizing an extensive knowledge in information technology, Mr. Graf is the Chief Operating Officer for the PROMATIS Corporation. In his position, he is responsible for overseeing all of the operations throughout each day including product development. Moreover, he is charged with managing all of the technology within the Corporation and supervising a staff of employees who report directly to him with any problems or issues. Drawing upon a strong background in this field, Mr. Graf has become an asset to the Corporation and looks forward to continuing with the Corporation, and eventually transferring to a real product company. The most rewarding aspect of his short career is attaining his present position with PROMATIS. He attributes his success to being with the right company and his education. Mr. Graf ensures quality in each product and is dedicated to his work. Located in San Ramon, California, the PROMATIS Corporation engages in software development and consulting services. Founded in 1999, the Corporation, headquartered in Carlsbad, Germany, is currently partnering with Oracle. Presently, PROMATIS employs a staff of 15 hard working technical experts. **Career Highlights:** Chief Operating Officer, PROMATIS Corporation (1999-Present); PROMATIS AG: Head of Development (1997-99), Consultant (1995-97). **Education:** University of Karlsruhe, M.S. in Computer Science (1994). **Personal Information:** Mr. Graf enjoys travel abroad.

Andrea M. Griffiths

Technical Trainer
Analytical Graphics
4291 State Road
Phoenixville, PA 19460
(610) 578-1072
Fax: (610) 578-1001
andrea@stk.com

7371

Business Information: Serving as a Technical Trainer for Analytical Graphics, Mrs. Griffiths leads the software test group in performing the astrodynamics validation and verification for the Company's specialized products. She directly supervises three capable staff members who assist her in the routing of software bugs and feature requests. Mrs. Griffiths previously served as the team leader for NASA's shuttle program software updates and states that her former position as a software trainer with Analytical Graphics was the highlight of her career. Crediting her professional success to being in the right place at the right time, she looks forward to increasing her involvement in more Web based applications. Established in 1987, Analytical Graphics specializes in the development of a Satellite Tool Kit. This software tool is sold and distributed for use in mission planning, design, and flight operations for those businesses with satellites and aircraft. Approximately 150 skilled professionals are employed in national operations. **Career Highlights:** Technical Trainer, Analytical Graphics (1997-Present); Engineer, Rockwell Space Operations Company (1987-97). **Associations & Accomplishments:** American Society for Training Development. **Education:** Parks College of St. Louis University, B.S. in Aerospace Engineering (1986). **Personal Information:** Married to Timothy in 1994. Two children: Byrce and James. Mrs. Griffiths enjoys reading, sewing, children's crafts and sports.

Ju Guo, Ph.D.

Principal Engineer
MediaFair
6932 Rosemead Boulevard, #20
San Gabriel, CA 91775-1423
(323) 981-1702
juguo@mediafair.com

7371

Business Information: The semantic video object extraction system designed by Dr. Guo is considered a truly innovative system to solve a difficult problem. Dr. Guo applies low level features to interpret the semantic homogeneity, and adaptively processing the signals. The system can perform at real time with pixel-wise accuracy. Dr. Guo's work has been recognized internationally, and his work is going to be published by KLUWER ACADEMIC PUBLISHERS. Dr. Guo joined MediaFair as a senior engineer in 1999. Currently, Dr. Guo is leading a small talent technique team to develop next generation video processing softwares as well as global internet applications. He was a researcher at integrated media and systems center (IMSC) at University of Southern

California (USC) since 1997. Dr. Guo made a significant contribution in the digital video processing area. **Career Highlights:** Senior Engineer, MediaFair (1999-Present); Researcher, IMSC, University of Southern California (1997-99). **Education:** University of Southern California, Ph.D. (1999). **Personal Information:** Married.

Thomas C. Guyton Jr.
Data and Voice Account Manager
Carlyle, Inc.
6801 South 180th Street
Seattle, WA 98188-4807
(425) 656-5680
Fax: (425) 251-8826
tomguyton@carlyle-inc.com

7371

Business Information: Combining management skills with technical expertise, Mr. Guyton serves Carlyle Inc. as a Data and Voice Account Manager. In this position, he designs various products concerning LAN and WAN upgrades. After determining which product or service would be best for the client, Mr. Guyton implements it into their current system. Assuming the responsibility of a $3 million account base, he is credited with the acquisition and retention of a new client such as COSTCO. Mr. Guyton is continually striving for excellence in his field and is currently pursuing his Registered Communications Distribution Designer and Cisco Certified Design Professional certifications to further enhance his skills. His success reflects his ability to deliver results and aggressively take on new challenges. Headquartered in Seattle, Washington, since 1970, the Corporation employs over 200 people. With annual sales totaling an estimated $30 million, Carlyle Inc. is recognized as the leading value added reseller of hardware, racks, routers, and hubs. Also dealing with several hundred other products and supplies such as cable assemblies, test equipment, and fiber optic cables, the Corporation specializes in LAN and WAN design and network upgrades. **Career Highlights:** Data and Voice Account Manager, Carlyle, Inc. (1998-Present); Senior Account Executive, MCI WorldCom (1997-98); Account Consultant, AT&T (1994-96). **Associations & Accomplishments:** Building Industries Consulting Services International; Big Brothers Association; Missouri Division of Social Services; Certified Cisco Design Associate; Certified Cisco Sales Expert, Small Businesses; Certified Cisco Sales Expert, Executive Businesses; Certified Design Architect, The Siemon Co. **Education:** Denison University, B.A. in Psychology (1987); University of Washington, Certification Data Communications. **Personal Information:** Married to Makiko Takamatsu in 1996. Mr. Guyton enjoys travel, reading and golf.

Jeffrey D. Halaut
••• ◉ •••

Senior Systems Engineer
Radian Inc.
5845 Richmond Highway
Alexandria, VA 22303
(703) 329-9311
Fax: (703) 462-1768
jdhalaut@aol.com

7371

Business Information: Serving as the Senior Systems Engineer for Radian, Inc., Mr. Halaut fulfills a number of duties on behalf of the Corporation. Working closely with management and systems users, he is responsible for the development, design and implemention of cutting-edge security systems at client sites. Possessing an excellent understanding of his field, Mr. Halaut is also responsible for computerized badging, intrusion detection, access control, and CCTV monitoring system. Attributing his success to Dennis Drews, who taught him everything he knows, he remains on the leading edge of technology by training and reading. In the future, Mr. Halaut looks forward to attaining the position of program director within his division. Radian, Inc. provides asset protection through security systems. Serving an international clientele, the Corporation is headquartered in Alexandria, Virginia and serves as an access control security integrator, linking systems together. **Career Highlights:** Senior Systems Engineer, Radian, Inc. (1996-Present); Computer Engineer, Unlimited Vision (1993-96); Owner/President, Old South Construction (1989-93). **Education:** Clarion University; Learning Tree International (1998); American Magnetics Systems Training 350/450/550; Unlimited Vision Instructor, UNIX 1088, 1088++, QuickPic. **Personal Information:** Married to Rhonda in 1988. Three children: Doug, Spencer, and Andrew.

Nader Hamzei
Director of Software Development
Internet Solution Group
2535 Townsgate Road
West Lake Village, CA 91361
(805) 446-2222
Fax: (805) 446-2244
lordnader@earthlink.net

7371

Business Information: In his position as Director of Software Development for Internet Solution Group, Mr. Hamzei analyzes, specifies, and designs new programs for his clientele. From inception through installation, he oversees each phase of software development and implementation, ensuring quality and customer satisfaction. Possessing an excellent understanding of technology, Mr. Hamzei instructs trainers, monitors management teams, and provides specifications for the team of engineers. Through the recruitment and training of new engineers, he guarantees the highest quality software. Mr. Hamzei attributes his substantial success to his knowledge, perseverance, and a championship mentality. His future plans include starting up his own company and growing his current business called "Net Insured." Internet Solution Group engages in the development of large scale Internet and Windows Web based programs. Specializing in the creation of programs for insurance companies, the Group was established in 1999. Presently, the Group employs the skilled services of more than 100 individuals to facilitate every aspect of design, test, and implementation of programs. Located in West Lake Village, California, the Group serves an international clientele and generates in excess of $80 million in annual revenues. **Career Highlights:** Director of Software Development, Internet Solution Group (2000-Present); Senior Software Developer, DVD Express (1998-00); Lead Engineer, Bowne Global Solutions (1996-98); Senior Software Architect, Seti Consultants (1991-97). **Associations & Accomplishments:** Co-Founder, One Tribe; Marine Environment Preservation Society; Passion and Dreams Funding Inc. **Education:** University of California Los Angeles. **Personal Information:** Mr. Hamzei enjoys sky diving, scuba diving and archery.

Andrew G. Hargreave, III
Enterprise Technology Architect
Geneer, Inc.
1400 East Touhy Avenue
Des Plaines, IL 60018
(847) 294-0300
Fax: (847) 294-0358
agh3@agh3.com

7371

Business Information: Possessing a high level of technical knowledge, Mr. Hargreave utilizes his skills as Enterprise Technology Architect for Geneer, Inc., a leading eServices development firm. Mr. Hargreave uses his experience in building Intranets/Internets in helping design their client's systems. Working in the Geneer Labs division, he also works with the latest technology to help ensure that Geneer's technology experts have access to the latest and greatest tools and technology. He enjoys the challenges of the IT industry, the Intenet, and how technology can be used to streamline processes. Established in 1984, Geneer partners with clients creating just the right services to give their clients a competitive edge. Geneer is based in suburban Chicago. **Career Highlights:** Enterprise Technology Architect, Geneer, Inc. (1989-Present); Assistant Regional Computer Coordinator, Ecology & Environment (1988-89); Management Information Systems Manager, Compass Health Care Plans (1987-88). **Education:** DeVry Institute of Technology, B.S. in Computer Information Science (1987). **Personal Information:** Married to Leigh Ann in 1987. Three children: Drew, Noah, and Jordan. Mr. Hargreave enjoys computers, reading and spending time with his family.

Dana B. Harris
Chairman of the Board/Chief Information Officer
Systems Made Simple, Inc.
One Northern Concourse
Syracuse, NY 13212
(315) 455-3200
Fax: (315) 455-3120
dana.harris@sms-mail.com

7371

Business Information: Mr. Harris serves as Chairman of the Board and Chief Information Officer of Systems Made Simple, Inc., responsible for all information technology planning. As a Founder of the Corporation, Mr. Harris guides the direction of the Corporation and utilizes his technical skills as the Chief Scientist. He continues to keep his skills up to date, sharing his knowledge and expertise in publications such as Defense Science and IEEE Software. Established in 1991, Systems Made Simple, Inc. provides custom software application development services. The Corporation creates business

---

specific software application, which are implemented to facilitate business processes. Systems Made Simple, Inc. also produces Internet applications, front end Window interface, and products for retail sale. The total operation yields annual funds in excess of $3 million. **Career Highlights:** Systems Made Simple, Inc.: Chairman of the Board/Chief Information Officer (1994-Present), President (1991-94); Senior Computer Scientist, Computer Sciences Corporation (1992-94); Program Manager, Presearch Inc. (1984-92); Computer Sciences Corporation (1983-84); E-Systems, Inc. (1981-83). **Associations & Accomplishments:** Association of Computing Machinery; Institute of Electrical and Electronics Engineers; Who's Who in Finance and Industry (1997); Who's Who in Science and Engineering (1996/1997); Who's Who in America (1997, 1998); Who's Who in the World (1996); Who's Who in the East (1995/1996). **Education:** University of New York at Potsdam: B.A. in Computer Science (1981), B.A. in Physics (1980). **Personal Information:** Married to Tammy in 1983. Three children: Danielle, Brittany, and Zachery. Mr. Harris enjoys building computers, reading science fiction, skiing, watching football and making tacos for his family.

Dave F. Harty
Director Research and Development
Acsis, Inc.
3000 Lincoln Drive East
Marlton, NJ 08053-1561
(856) 489-4914
Fax: (856) 489-1007
dharty@acsisinc.com

7371

Business Information: As Director Research and Development of Acsis, Inc., Mr. Harty directs all research and development activities, evaluates new technologies, and determines new product potentials. Over 15 years of experience in the field has enabled him to effectively fulfill his job obligations and become a great asset to the business. Utilizing his expertise in the field, Mr. Harty assists top management in the areas of research and development and has lectured at well known universities such as Yale. He currently holds four patents and is continually learning and growing and keeping abreast of new developments in the field. Mr. Harty's strategic plans are to bring technology to the masses and make it easier for the average person to grasp. Attributing his success to perseverance, his advice to others is "not be afraid of technology, but to learn more about the field." Acsis, Inc. is a software development and data collection systems integration company specializing in RFIDs and ERPs. Established in 1968, this $30 million company employs a staff of over 100 people to assist in various aspects of the operation. A leader in the field, the Company works with clients internationally. **Career Highlights:** Director of Research and Development, Acsis, Inc. (1996-Present); President, B.C.I. (1993-96); Vice President, EIS (1991-93). **Associations & Accomplishments:** Girls Basketball Coach. **Education:** St. Joseph's University, B.S. (1989). **Personal Information:** Married to Kathleen in 1989. Two children: Krista and Colin. Mr. Harty enjoys travel.

Dawn M. Haynes
Product Manager
Rational Software
20 Maguire Road
Lexington, MA 02421-3104
(781) 676-7584
Fax: (781) 676-2460
dhaynes@world.std.com

7371

Business Information: As Product Manager, Ms. Haynes is a member of the Education and Training Group of Rational Software's university. Applying her extensive engineering expertise, she conducts performance testing. She develops training courses and provides technical input and direction throughout the production phase of software tools. Ms. Haynes credits her success to seeking out opportunities, surrounding herself with good mentors, setting goals, and possessing endless drive. She plans to pursue additional certification to enhance her professional expertise, and to start a training organization. Her advice is "to have stamina to learn a lot, find your niche, and be resourceful and tenacious." Rational Software is a vending company specializing in software tools utilized by software development groups. Established in 1985, the Company is headquartered in Cooperfino, California and possesses five distinct charters. Highly skilled technicians develop innovative concepts in processing, methodology, design time, tooling, configuration, source control, and tool testing. International in scope, the Lexington, Massachusetts location employs a considerable work force of 2,000 and generates $450 million in annual sales. **Career Highlights:** Rational Software: Product Manager (1998-Present), Sales Engineer (1996-98); Technical Support/Porting Engineer, Xerox Imaging Systems (1991-96). **Associations & Accomplishments:** Notary Public. **Education:** Northeastern University, B.S. in Business Administration (1995). **Personal Information:** Ms. Haynes enjoys skiing, figure skating, bass guitar, keyboard and knitting.

Judy A. Hedenberg

Software Support Specialist
Medical Manager West
16461 Sherman Way, Suite 180
Van Nuys, CA 91406-3808
(818) 373-7425
Fax: (818) 373-7435
judyh@mdmgr.com

7371

Business Information: A savvy veteran of information technology, Ms. Hedenberg was recruited to Medical Manager West as a Software Support Specialist in 1997. She is responsible for providing technical support new design and development of new, cutting edge medical office and administration software. An expert, she supports 51 clients through help desk and on-site technical support as well as providing training on existing and new software. The analysis, installation, modification, configuration, support, and tracking of operating systems, utilities, software, and hardware also fall within the realm of his responsibilities. Career highlights include working for Medical Manager West and regaining clients confidence in her capabilities. Attributing success to people skills, Ms. Hedenberg intends to continue in her role with the Company and looks forward to continued promotions and prosperity. Medical Manager West provides state-of-the-art medical management software for doctor offices, hospitals, and clinics. Organized in 1985, the Company employs more than 175 professionals and technical experts who lead out in acquiring new clients, meetig with customers, facilitating projects, and marketing services and products. Dedicated, the Company provides clients the latest in software technology. **Career Highlights:** Software Support Specialist, Medical Manager West (1997-Present); Medical Office Billing/Collections, National Staff Network (1992-97); Trust Services, California Federal Bank (1977-91). **Education:** University of California at Irvine, B.A. (1976); Concorde Career College, degree in Medical Office Management (1991); Learning Tree, Medical Transcription (1996). **Personal Information:** Ms. Hedenberg enjoys tai chi, martial arts, tap dancing and travel.

David J. Hedtke

Manager of Information Systems Development
Birch Telecom, Inc.
2020 Baltimore Avenue
Kansas City, MO 64108
(816) 300-3394
Fax: (816) 300-3293
dhedtke@birch.com

7371

Business Information: Educated in systems design, Mr. Hedtke serves as Manager of Information Systems Development for Birch Telecom, Inc. He is in charge of the Information Systems Department, supervising the team of software engineers responsible for application programming. Participating in the hands on software development, he designs and documents specific telecommunication applications. Before joining Birch Telecom, he served as a Systems Engineer for both Information Industries, Inc. and TEKsystems. Mr. Hedtke continues to grow professionally through the fulfillment of his responsibilities and his involvement in the advancement of operations. His success reflects his ability to think out-of-the-box and take on new challenges and responsibilities. He looks forward to moving upwards into a position with middle management. Birch Telecom, Inc. engages in enterprise and OSS application design for the telecommunications industry. Created in 1997, a work force of more than 450 knowledgeable professionals are employed. **Career Highlights:** Manager of Information Systems Development, Birch Telecom, Inc. (1998-Present); Systems Engineer, Information Industries, Inc. (1997-98); Systems Engineer, TEKsystems (1997). **Associations & Accomplishments:** UNIX Administrators Association. **Education:** Friend's University, B.S. in Computer Information Systems (1999). **Personal Information:** Married to Kerstin in 1988. Three children: Alicia, Paige, and Christopher.

Kristine M. Herron

Software Developer
Chain Link Technologies Inc.
1314 Chesapeake Terrace
Sunnyvale, CA 94083
(408) 543-4486
kherron@clti.com

7371

Business Information: As a Software Developer of Chain Link Technologies Inc., Ms. Herron provides a number of technology services on behalf of the Corporation and its clientele. Working closely with management and systems users, she designs and develops integrated software systems. Maintaining current developments and the update of software, Ms. Herron implements new technologies in order to provide a more efficient product. Providing cutting-edge support to her clients, she assists in the installation, configuration, and support of operating and network systems, server utilities, and software. Continuing her advancement within Chain Link Technologies' corporate structure, Ms. Herron remains committed toward the design, development, and deployment of advanced technology. Specializing in software design and development, Chain Link Technologies Inc. was established in 1995. Located in Sunnyvale, California, the Corporation employs 170 experienced technicians and engineers. **Career Highlights:** Software Developer, Chain Link Technologies Inc. (1999-Present); Technical Consultant, Andersen Consulting (1997-99). **Education:** Brown University, B.A. in Computer Science (1997). **Personal Information:** Ms. Herron enjoys swimming, running, listening to classical music, opera and reading.

Jack D. Hidary

President/Chief Executive Officer
EarthWeb, Inc.
3 Park Avenue, 33rd Floor
New York, NY 10016
(212) 725-6550
Fax: (212) 725-6559
jack1@earthweb.com

7371

Business Information: Jack D. Hidary and his co-workers formed a bold vision to reshape the information technology (IT) industry by providing a unique set of targeted online services. Under Mr. Hidary's leadership of EarthWeb (Nasdaq: EWBX) as President and Chief Executive Officer, the Corporation secured two rounds of funding from Warburg Pincus Ventures, completed a record-braking initial public offering, and closed a secondary pubic offering. The Corporation also recruited a world-class management team, expanded services internationally, and achieved record revenues. As a result, EarthWeb has become the leading provider of business-to-business online services to the global IT industry. Today, Mr. Hidary's responsibilities include developing the Corporation's strategic vision and leadership as well as managing the Corporation's executive team worldwide. Under his stewardship, EarthWeb has earned the prestigious Business Week Info Tech 100 award, and was named the third fastest growing IT company in the Info Tech 100. Mr. Hidary has received several industry and community awards including the Einstein Technology Medal from Israel's High-Tech Mission and New York Magazine's "New York Cyber Sixty." He has also presented at the Smithsonian, SIIA, Red Herring, SIGS Java and Bear Stearns Internet Conferences. In addition, he has been a guest lecturer at such business schools as Harvard and Columbia. **Career Highlights:** President/Chief Executive Officer, EarthWeb, Inc. (1994-Present); Stanley Fellow in Neurosciences, National Institutes of Health (1991-94). **Associations & Accomplishments:** Board of Directors at TrickleUp, an international nonprofit organization that helps low-income people start small businesses and help themselves out of poverty. **Education:** Columbia University (1991). **Personal Information:** Mr. Hidary enjoys sculling.

Dan J. Hobbs

Manager
Mylex
39 Park Warren Place
San Jose, CA 95136
(510) 608-2367
Fax: (510) 608-2407
danh@mylex.com

7371

Business Information: Displaying his skills in this highly specialized position, Mr. Hobbs serves as Manager for Mylex. He directly supervises a staff of five and is fully responsible for the Corporation's network infrastructure from the desktop to the client server utility program. Performing network and system maintenance, Mr. Hobbs ensures its efficient functioning and provides routine system backup. In addition, he provides technical support to the users. Coordinating resources, schedules, time lines, and assignments; building a team with synergy and technical strength; and managing the technology budget also fall within the realm of Mr. Hobbs' responsibilities. As a 29 year technology professional, he attributes his success to tenacity and keeping abreast of new technology by performing Web research and taking courses. Mr. Hobbs is committed to further development of Mylex and coordinates strategic planning to ensure a future position as a Director. Headquartered in Fremont, California, Mylex is a publicly owned subsidiary of IBM Corporation. The Corporation designs and sells RAID controllers as well as providing network services to an international clientele. Reporting $200 million in yearly sales, a work force of approximately 500 persons are employed. **Career Highlights:** Manager, Mylex (1996-Present); Value Added Reseller (1989-96). **Education:** Golden Gate University, B.S. (1972). **Personal Information:** Married to Susan in 1968. Three children: Jeffrey, Andrea, and Gregory. Mr. Hobbs enjoys backpacking, bicycling and woodworking.

Akbar G. Jaffer

Manager, Sustaining and Performance Engineering
Snapfish.com
799 Market Street, 6th Floor
San Francisco, CA 94103
(415) 820-3867
Fax: (415) 820-0570
akbar@thejaffers.net

7371

Business Information: Mr. Jaffer is currently serving as the Manager of Sustaining and Performance Engineering at Snapfish.com. He is responsible for performance and sustaining of Snapfish.com software. A savvy professional, Mr. Jaffer owned his own consulting firm for five years while attending college. He believes, "The more important a project is, the more time one should spend planning," and encourages individuals to "Learn the technology the right way and to get a solid education in Computer Science." Continually striving for optimum results, Mr. Jaffer is proud of playing a key role in the early stages of Search QA group at Inktomi Corporation and now at Snapfish.com. Being at Inktomi helped him better understand the business aspects of a high tech company. His success is attributed to his determination, desire to learn, and networking with colleagues. Snapfish.com is a start-up company in San Francisco, which is helping to redefine the digital and film-based consumer photography market by providing complete on-line services for free. **Career Highlights:** Manager, Sustaining and Performance Engineering, Snapfish.com (2000-Present); Software Engineer, Inktomi Corporation (1998-00); Software Engineer, HAL Computer Systems (1996-98). **Associations & Accomplishments:** Board of Trustees, College of Dupage Illinois District 502; Bay Area Chapter of Association of Computing Machinery; USENIX Association; Stanford Savovards Theater Company; San Jose Lyric Theater. **Education:** Stanford University, M.Sc. in Computer Science (In Progress); University of Illinois at Urbana-Champaign. **Personal Information:** Married to Christine in 1997. Mr. Jaffer enjoys volunteer work, off-roading Jeeps, comedy, film, theatre, music and travel. Although he does not have children at this time, the Jaffers have two horses, four goldfish, and two dogs.

Tamie Joeckel

Partner
Catalyst Software Evaluation Centers Inc.
1501 LBJ Freeway, Suite 150
Dallas, TX 75234-6029
(972) 620-1997
Fax: (972) 620-7447
tamie@catalysteval.com

7371

Business Information: With over 20 years of extensive experience in the accounting and technology fields, Ms. Joeckel is a Partner of Catalyst Software Evaluation Centers Inc. Serving as Chief Financial Officer, she manages the technical consulting divisions of the Company and privides the vision strategies as the Company diversifies into the e-Commerce and ASP markets. The Company's primary line of business is the sale and implementation of SWL-based ERP systgmes with specialization in e-Commerce, manufacturing, and distribution industries. Ms. Joeckel develooped the requirements assessment and implementation methodologies necessary to assist clients in the evaluation, selection, and implementation of mission critical applicationssupported by a Microsoft technology platform. Ms. Joeckel continues to remain involved in key professional organizations. Her awards and certifications include: NASBA certified CPE speaker and instructor; National Advisory Council member of Epicor Software, Sage Software and Great Plains Software; Reseller of the Year for Sage Software, Epicor Software; Fastest Growing SQL VAR in North America for Epicor Software; Accounting Today's Technology Pacesetter Award (1998-99). Continually pushiing forward, Ms. Joeckel's goals are to expand Catalyst operations nationally. Founded in 1997, Catalyst is a successor corporation to Aquita Integrated Management Systems which was founded in 1986 in Hartford, Connecticut. Catalyst functions as a Microsoft systems integrator with a foucus on medium and large companies. Specializing in ERP systems, Catalyst was the first comany to obtain the licesnses to sell asll the leading SQL Server financial systmes on the market. Headquartered in Texas, the Corporation currently has four locations and generates einexcess of $10 million in annual revenues. **Career Highlights:** Partner, Catalyst Software Evaluation Centers Inc. (1997-Present); Partner, Aquila IMS (1992-97); Manager, IBM (1988-92); Manager, Arthur Andersen & Co. (1986-88); Chief Financial Officer, Gregory Enterprises (1982-86). **Associations & Accomplishments:** National Association of Accounting; Women in Technology; Team Leader, United Way; Oklahoma Executive Foundation Board; Who's Who; Leadership Oklahoma. **Education:** Florida Atlantic University, M.B.A. (1992); East Central State University: B.A. in Computer Science, B.A. in Accounting. **Personal Information:** Married to Peter in 1992. Three children: Tanna, Trent, and Trey. Ms. Joeckel enjoys lacrosse, football, boating and golf.

Werner B. Joerg

President/Chief Technical Officer
Netessence
6246 Rodeo Lane
Salt Lake City, UT 84121-2035
(801) 277-8697
Fax: (801) 277-0692
wjoerg@netessence.com

7371

Business Information: Mr. Joerg founded Netessence in 1996 as a service company, emphasizing a philosophy of quality, accuracy, and comprehensive assistance to all customers. He couples this same philosophy with business savvy as he serves in the position of President and Chief Techncial Officer. Guiding his staff with a proactive leadership style, he incorporates employee feedback and input into the generation of innovative technical solutions. Clients enjoy personal attention they receive from Mr. Joerg, and appreciate his creative approach to solving challenges. Conducting extensive research and testing trials, he is able to accurately forecast industry trends, designing essential products devoted to education and information gathering. Recognized as an industry leader, Mr. Joerg looks forward to the expansion of business to business relations. He attributes his success to hardwork and persistence. Netessence capitalizes on the needs of busy computer users who cannot fit time consuming research into their full schedules by providing software and applications to conduct Internet searches. The Company uses knowledge mining technology to develop these tools, and is engaged in the distribution and on-line deployment of them as well. Though the term "knowledge mining" may seem obscure, it refers to the search and automatic classification of information from the Internet. **Career Highlights:** President/Chief Technical Officer, Netessence (1998-Present); Professor, University of Alberta (1984-98); Software Engineer, Landis 7 Guy Corporation (1971-83). **Associations & Accomplishments:** Association of Computing Machinery; Institute of Electrical and Electronics Engineers. **Education:** ETH-Z Switzerland, diploma in Math (1971). **Personal Information:** Married to Charlotte in 1995. Mr. Joerg enjoys golf and skiing.

Janet Lee Johnson

Lead Programmer Analyst
SCT
1733 Harrodsburg Road, Suite 100
Lexington, KY 40504
(606) 277-1500
Fax: (606) 277-2300
jajohnso@sctcorp.com

7371

Business Information: Demonstrating expertise in software programming, Mrs. Johnson serves as the Lead Programmer Analyst for SCT. She assumes responsibility for the analysis, design, development, and implementation of new programs and software. Mrs. Johnson provides customer support, systems maintenance, and program modification services. Coordinating resources, time lines, schedules, and assignments; serving as contact between users and systems management; and resolving systems problems also fall within the purview of her responsibilities. Attributing her success to a supportive family and a strong educational background, she aspires to the position of Project Leader. Serving an international clientele, SCT develops software to fit the specific needs of each client. The Company provides client server network, mission-critical, enterprise software, and a series of other related information technological services for clients such as governments, manufacturing and distribution companies, and universities. Presently, SCT employs a workforce of more than 3,600 people. **Career Highlights:** Lead Programmer Analyst, SCT (1997-Present). **Education:** University of Kentucky, M.B.A. (1995); Morehead State University, B.B.A. **Personal Information:** Married to Brian in 1992. One child: Casey Danielle. Mrs. Johnson enjoys gardening and flowers.

Patricio Johnson

Executive Director
Cyberweb Telecommunications
763 Ruiz De Castilla
Quito, Ecuador
+59 39708991
Fax: +59 32229634
patricio@cybw.net

7371

Business Information: After spending 25 years in several managerial positions with Pinturas Condor, Mr. Johnson decided to venture out on his own and establish Cyberweb Telecommunications. At the present time, he assumes the responsibilities of Executive Director. In his capacity, he formulates the Company's vision and policies and develops creative marketing and technology strategies. Drawing from years of managerial experience and a firm academic foundation, Mr. Johnson is also responsible for the Company's bottom line. Personnel management, profit and loss statements, accounting and finance, new business development, and property management also falls within the realm of Mr. Johnson's responsibilities. Growing operations from the ground up and providing the best corporate web design in the international markets serves as his long-term goals. An international web site and design company established in 1998, Cyberweb Telecommunications specializes in corporate web sites. Based in Quito, Ecuador, the Company is manned by one technology expert. **Career Highlights:** Executive Director, Cyberweb Telecommunications (1998-Present); General Manager, Pinturas Condor (1990-98); Commercial Manager, Pinturas Condor (1972-90). **Associations & Accomplishments:** Board of Trustees, Universidad San Fracisco De Quito; Vice President, Universidad Del Sur, Quito; Executive Committee Member, Pichincha's Chamber of Industry; President, South of Quito Enterprenurs Association. **Education:** Universidad Central, Economist (1972); University of Texas, Linguistics (1968). **Personal Information:** Married to Jenny in 1972. Two children: Frank and Melanie. Mr. Johnson enjoys tennis.

Toby L. Joplin

Accounting Division Manager
TaascFORCE
6914 South Yorktown Avenue
Tulsa, OK 74136
(918) 493-6500
Fax: (918) 493-6189
tjoplin@tasscforce.com

7371

Business Information: Serving as Division Manager over Accounting Software products at TaascFORCE, Mr. Joplin supervises 50 employees in three departments, and is responsible for help desk/call center, technical communications and user training, and product Q/A functions. TaascFORCE designs, develops, and markets financial software, including accounting and tax applications. Established in 1980, the Company employs 250 professionals and caters to 14,000 accountants and small businesses nationwide. **Career Highlights:** Accounting Division Manager, TaascFORCE (1993-Present); Senior Tax Accountant, Guest & Company (1991-93); Certified Public Accountant, Sartain Fischbien (1988-91). **Associations & Accomplishments:** American Institute of Certified Public Accountants; Oklahoma Society of Certified Public Accountants; Help Desk Institute; Owasso Historical Society; Owasso Education Foundation; First Christian Church of Owasso; Leadership Owasso; Kansas City Barbecue Society; Kansas City Blues Society; Tulsa Blues Club; National Barbecue Association. **Education:** Oklahoma State University: M.B.A. (in progress), B.S. in Accounting (1986). **Personal Information:** Married to Katherine in 1981. Two children: Heather and Jeremiah. Mr. Joplin enjoys blues music, basketball and barbecue.

Cindy M. Jutras

Vice President of Production Strategy
InterBiz of Computer Associates
1 Tech Drive, Suite 201
Andover, MA 01810
(978) 691-4276
Fax: (978) 686-3295
cindy.jutras@cai.com

7371

Business Information: In her role as Vice President of Product Strategies of InterBiz of Computer Associates, Ms. Jutras is responsible for the organization and marketing of technical trends. Demonstrating extensive knowledge of the industry, she oversees the development of new products and tools, guiding the engineering and production staff with a proactive style of leadership. Noted as an authority within her field, she is frequently asked to speak at civic assemblies and conferences. She excels in application technology, solving complex challenges with a creative approach. Her career highlight includes pushing several innovative products to markets representing the constant change in technology. Ms. Jutras attributes hard work and persistence as the keys to her career success, and she intends to continue in her current role as she implements technical changes and upgrades. She plans on staying ahead of new technology, enabling her to solve e-business problems in real time. InterBiz of Computer Associates is a leading provider of technical support services. Employing over 10,000 people in the state of California alone, the international company offers all aspects of software services including consulting. **Career Highlights:** Vice President of Production Strategies, InterBiz of Computer Associates (1994-Present); Manager of Manufacturing Consulting, The Ask Group (1984-94); Manager of Production Management, Interactive Management Systems (1978-83); Project Analyst, ADL Systems (1977-78). **Education:** Boston University, M.A.S. (1978); Merrimack College, B.A. (1975). **Personal Information:** Married to B. Glenn in 1977. Ms. Jutras enjoys time with family, skiing, gardening and sumie painting. Ms. Jutras holds black belts in three different styles of martial arts.

Kathleen Kitts Malik

Ergonomics Coordinator
SAS Institute
105 Anvil Court
Cary, NC 27513
(919) 677-8000
Fax: (919) 677-4444
kathleen.kitts@sas.com

7371

Business Information: Beginning her career with SAS Institute in 1990 as Wellness Coordinator, Ms. Kitts Malik has received recognition for her diligence and technology skills through a promotion to Ergonomics Coordinator. Utilizing years of education and experience, she is responsible for equipment design and implementation. Along with these duties, Ms. Kitts Malik strives to create more efficient workflow and teach safe work habits to the staff. Continually striving for maximum effectiveness, she keeps up with current technology to enable her to capitalize on the opportunities provided by the Institute. A savvy, 13 year professional, her success is attributed to her power to think positively as well as her ability to tackle new challenges and deliver results. Established in 1975, SAS Institute is a large privately owned software company. Located in Cary, North Carolina, the Institute employs over 5,000 individuals responsible for research, development, marketing, sales, and support. The Institute provides software for video games and business solutions and reports annual revenue of $1 billion. **Career Highlights:** SAS Institute: Ergonomics Coordinator (1998-Present), Wellness Coordinator (1990-98); Cardiac Catheterization, Duke University Medical Center (1989-90); Wellness Assistant, University of North Carolina at Chapel Hill (1987-89). **Associations & Accomplishments:** American Council of Exercise, Instructor; American College of Sports Medicine Exercise Test Technologist. **Education:** University of North Carolina at Chapel Hill, M.A. (1989). **Personal Information:** Ms. Kitts Malik enjoys snow skiing, scuba diving, camping, hiking and animals.

John V. Kleinman

LAN Administrator
SCT Corporation
1 East Main Street
Fort Wayne, IN 46802-1815
(219) 427-1152
Fax: (219) 427-1394
jvkleinman@hotmail.com

7371

Business Information: Functioning as LAN Administrator for SCT Corporation, Mr. Kleinman is responsible for all aspects of day-to-day operations of the information systems infrastructure. Before joining SCT as Micro Computer Specialist in 1996, Mr. Kleinman served as Night Supervisor of Open Computer Laboratory for Ivy Technical State College. In his present capacity, he provides support for PCs and applications and networks. Working closely with users and systems management, Mr. Kleinman analyzes, specifies, and designs applications to his clients' specific requirements. Currently, he is outsourced to the Board of Health. "Don't be afraid to try new things," is cited as his advice to others following the same career path. His future endeavors include remaining in his position and staying current with new technology. Mr. Kleinman's success reflects his ability to deliver results and aggressively take on new challenges. SCT Corporation engages in information systems and information technology outsourcing. Established in 1968, the Corporation specializes in creating application software for manufacturers and colleges, as well as managing the clientele's data department. Regional in scope, over 3,400 professionals are employed by SCT Corporation. **Career Highlights:** SCT Corporation: LAN Administrator (1999-Present), Micro Computer Specialist (1996-99); Night Supervisor of Open Computer Lab, Ivy Tech State College (1994-96). **Education:** Ivy Tech State College, A.A.S. in Computer Information Systems (1996); Certified Novell Administrator. **Personal Information:** Two children: Caleb and Jacob. Mr. Kleinman enjoys collecting old computers and setting up home networks.

James Brian Knotts

Senior Architect
SCT
4 Country View
Malvern, PA 19355
(610) 578-7207
bknotts@sctcomp.com

7371

Business Information: Mr. Knotts functions in the capacity of Senior Architect for SCT or Systems and Computers Technology. He fulfills the responsibility of project manager, architect, and researcher enabling him to have a key role in all steps of the production process. He primarily focuses within the research and development of particular projects while utilizing his architectural talents in designing more adaptable equipment for the Company. With a United States patent pending, Mr. Knotts' greatest accomplishment with the

Company has been his development of a natural language interface that correlates with relational database systems. In the future, he plans to follow along the technical wave to whatever height it takes him. His key to success is strong listening skills and being very analytical and getting to the real problem. SCT manufactures administration software for use in various industries. Established in 1968, the Company has concentrated its services within the higher education, government, utilities, and manufacturing industries. The Company employs more than 3,500 professional, technical, and support personnel who help generate in excess of $500 million annually. **Career Highlights:** Senior Architect, SCT (1985-Present); Director of Global Information Systems, IBAH (1998). **Associations & Accomplishments:** Patent Pending on Simplified Data Access. **Education:** Pennsylvania State University, B.S. (In Progress). **Personal Information:** Married to Deborah in 1990. Three children: Megan, Leah, and James.

Daune C. Kramer

Product/Consulting Competency Manager
Clarus Software
170 Indian Hills Court
Marietta, GA 30068-3900
(770) 291-5352
Fax: (770) 973-7188
daunek999@aol.com

7371

Business Information: As Product and Consulting Competency Manager at Clarus Software, Mr. Kramer is responsible for managing consulting, product development, methodology, consulting on partner certification, alpha testing, and releasing software. He is heavily involved with software development from conception. A successful, 10 year veteran in the tehcnology field, Mr. Kramer manages the software controlled release through methodical testing. He focuses on discovering problem areas and eliminating this area through the implementation of new programming. Through internal training development, Mr. Kramer increases the knowledge of present and oncoming employees to adhere to Company goals and policies. He constructs and conducts training for certification levels. An expert, he constructed the OLAP software. Within three months, Mr. Kramer had the OLAP application solidified and completed a four city tour in one week to give consultations concerning the application projects for the next year. While he was an independent consultant, Mr. Kramer completed 45 implementations in two and a half years. Looking to the next millennium and beyond, he will continue focusing on the overall picture and begin to predict trends for Clarus Software. Established in 1992, Clarus Software is a Web based commerce software development company. The 180 employees develop electronic commerce software with Web-based programming. The Company produces software such as "E-Procurement" which connects business with catalogue and Clarus View concepts. The Company supports the developed software programs especially the "Fusion" program. The services are provided throughout the United States. The success of rendered services has generated an annual revenue of $40 million. **Career Highlights:** Product/Consulting Competency Manager, Clarus Software (1998-Present); Systems Consultant, Independent (1997-99); System Development Manager, Scotty's, Inc. (1993-97). **Associations & Accomplishments:** Board of Directors, Georgia Writers, Inc.; Mensa International; Certified Public Accountant. **Education:** University of South Florida, B.S. (1989). **Personal Information:** Married to Alicia in 1990. Mr. Kramer enjoys writing and tennis.

Bryan M. Kreft

Intern of Strategy and Strategic Alliances Marketing Team
Silicon Graphics
500 El Camino Real, Suite 3193
Santa Clara, CA 95053
(650) 933-4558
bmkreft@scu.edu

7371

Business Information: Mr. Kreft is an Intern of Strategy and Strategic Alliances Marketing Team of Silicon Graphics, where he works in conjunction with a trained staff on the development of marketing strategy. As he forms a strong alliance among the employees, he demonstrates a strong ability in the field as he designs effective action plans to solve challenges. Addressing a host of technical issues on a daily basis, Mr. Kreft proves to be a reliable and dedicated employee as he successfully handles negotiations and contract discussions. Internally recognized for his impressive acheivements as a protège, he credits his drive and dedication as motivating factors in the completion of corporate and personal goals. Aspiring to a position with a legal team of a major corporation, Mr. Kreft is contemplating a future in politics. Established in 1986, Silicon Graphics manufactures high-performance computing hardware and software. Producing technical solutions for a progressive society, the Company has a diverse clientele, representing a variety of industries. Headquartered in Mountain View, California, the Company employs nearly 10,000 people throughout the United States and has annual revenues that total $2.7 billion. **Career Highlights:** Intern of Strategy and Strategic Alliances Marketing Team, Silicon Graphics (1999-Present). **Associations & Accomplishments:** Works with local drum and bugle corps and marching band drum majors. **Education:** Santa Clara University: J.D., M.B.A.; University of California at Los Angeles, B.A. **Personal Information:** Mr. Kreft enjoys drum corps, marching band, rock climbing, golf and volleyball.

Lori A. Krell

Design Coordinator
Pixel Magic Imaging
2600 Gracy Farms Lane, Apartment 718
Austin, TX 78758
(512) 396-7251
Fax: (512) 396-8767
lorik@pxlmagic.com

7371

Business Information: Miss Krell functions as a Design Coordinator for Pixel Magic Imaging. She is responsible for all technical writing, Web development, software analysis, graphic design, advertising, and tradeshow design. Before joining Pixel Magic Imaging, Miss Krell served as Operator II and Graduate Research Assistant with Southwest Texas State University. She concurrently is a freelance Graphic and Web Designer and Developer for Southwest Texas State University and Texicana Cafe in Financial City. Supervising a team of four employees, Miss Krell is also a Webmaster who coordinates and provides a wide range of technical support. She credits her success to her extensive computer skills and hands on learning experiences. Her career milestones include design and implementation of new software for a large account that was successfully completed in about one year. Moving into more of a design and administrative role in Web coordination and software design serves as her future endeavors. A spin off of EPS Photographic, Pixel Magic Imaging creates state-of-the-art retail and professional computer systems for digital mini-labs and studios and for photographic use. Large accounts include Eckerd and K-Mart. International in scope, the Company was established in 1996 and is located in San Marcos, Texas manned by a domestic work force of over 60 professional, technical, and administrative support personnel. **Career Highlights:** Design Coordinator, Pixel Magic Imaging (Present); Graphic and Web Design, Freelance for Southwest Texas State University (1995-Present); Web Development, Freelance for Financial City's Texican Cafe (1998-Present); Operator II/Grand Research Assistant, Computing Services, Southwest Texas State University (1994-98). **Associations & Accomplishments:** Sigma Tau Delta, International English Honor Society; Golden Key National Honor Society. **Education:** Southwest Texas State University: M.A. in English and Technical Communications (1999), B.A. in English (1997). **Personal Information:** Miss Krell enjoys reading, writing, Web and graphic design, drawing and painting.

Monica B. Kropp

Software Engineer
EER Systems, Inc.
P.O. Box 7127
Fort Gordon, GA 30905
(706) 791-8299
Fax: (706) 791-8300
kroppm@emh.gordon.army.mil

7371

Business Information: Ms. Kropp is Software Engineer with EER Systems, Inc. She is responsible for development, maintenance, and support of software for the Department of Defense. In this context, she oversees Y2K remediation, database administration, and hardware and software integration. Before joining EER Systems, Ms. Kropp served as Electrical Engineer with Thermo King Corporation and Application Engineer at Johnson Controls, Inc. As a four year technology professional, she works with users and management to analyze, specify, design, and implement advanced solutions in which to harness more of the computer's power. The analysis, configuration, test, evaluation, support, and tracking of operating systems, database, client server utility programs, software, and hardware also fall within the purview of Ms. Kropp's responsibilities. Her future short term goals include attaining the position of Project Leader, responsible for coordinating resources, schedules, and communications for application development programs. Possessing the capability to take on new challenges and responsibilities reflects Ms. Kropp's technical and leadership ability. EER Systems, Inc. is located in Fort Gordon, Georgia, with headquarters in Maryland. The Corporation utilizes innovative resources to create competitive technological software systems and applications for the Department of Defense. **Career Highlights:** Software Engineer, EER Systems, Inc. (1997-Present); Electrical Engineer, Thermo King Corporation (1996-97); Application Engineer, Johnson Controls, Inc. (1995). **Education:** Michigan State University, B.S. in Electrical Engineering (1996). **Personal Information:** Married to Wayne in 1998. Ms. Kropp enjoys tennis and arts and crafts.

Palmer V. LaGrange

Principal Programmer Analyst
CBSI - Computer Based Systems, Inc., An AverStar Company
2750 Prosperity Avenue, Suite 300
Fairfax, VA 22031
(703) 816-4445

7371

Business Information: Accumulating over 44 years in the computer science field, Mr. LaGrange joined the CBSI team in 1998. At the present time, he assumes responsibilities of Principal Programmer Analyst. In this capacity, Mr. LaGrange is involved in quality assurance and testing of Oracle client server systems. He directs and participates in the analysis, acquisition, installation, modification, configuration, support, and tracking of Oracle operating platforms, databases, utilities, software, and hardware. Writing applications and conducting Beta testing on new software applications also falls within the realm of his responsibilities. Currently, Mr. LaGrange is working on-site for the EPA. He is focused on converting existing systems to enhance the EPA's capability to compile and summarize reports for industries. With a strong educational history in computers and programming, Mr. LaGrange attributes his success to enjoying his work, his passion for learning, and keeping pace with technology. One of many professional accomplishments, the greatest is working on weapon software for the B-52 bomber missile system. Completing his Master's and B.S. in Mathematics and becoming more involved in the simulation process serves as his future goals. CBSI or Computer Based Systems, Inc. designs, develops, tests and installs systems for various government agencies using Oracle database client server systems. National in scope, the Corporation is headquartered in Fairfax and presently employs a staff of more than 600 professional, technical, and support personnel. **Career Highlights:** Principal Programmer Analyst, CBSI - Computer Based Systems, Inc., An AverStar Company (1998-Present); Software Engineer, E-OIR Measurements, Inc. (1997-98); System Analyst, Statistica, Inc. (1997); Software Specialist, Science Applications International, Inc. (1995-97). **Associations & Accomplishments:** Armed Forces Communications Electronics Association; Association of Computing Machinery; American Mathematical Society; MENSA; Dean's List at University of Maryland. **Education:** University of Maryland University College: B.S. in Mathematics (In Progress), B.S. in Computer Science (1994); Johns Hopkins University, Graduate Studies of Math (In Progress). **Personal Information:** Married to Beaulah in 1958. Five children: Patricia Lynda, Elizabeth Rugh, James Matthew, Margaret Rose, and John Christopher. Mr. LaGrange enjoys reading and collecting books.

Robert R. Lang, Jr.

Manager
GE Harris Railway
633 North Orange Avenue
Orlando, FL 32801
(321) 752-3454
blang@orlanfosentinel.com

7371

Business Information: Serving as Manager of GE Harris Railway, Mr. Lang is responsible for maintaining the functionality and operational status of the Company's systems infrastructure as well as determining the business functions of the information systems function. Highly regarded, Mr. Lang possesses an excellent understanding of technology as evident by his prior employment with The Orlando Sentinel in a variety of computer related positions for seven years. He is responsible for maintaining UNIX servers, providing PC support to over 1,500 users, and attending to DNS software and the NIS naming service. Among his many professional achievements, he has created a user system for Microsoft Exchange. His success reflects his ability to take on challenges and deliver results on behalf of the Company and its clients. Mr. Lang's future goals include eventually attaining the position of information technology manager for another company. GE Harris Railway is a developer of software and hardware. Located in Orlando, Florida, the Company specializes in the design and manufacture of railway electronics products and accessories as well as programming software to operate critical real time systems. **Career Highlights:** Manager, GE Harris Railway (2000-Present); The Orlando Sentinel: PC Support Manager (1997-00), UNIX Programmer (1995-97), Senior Electronic Technician (1993-95). **Education:** Attended numerous schools during 19 years in the Navy: Oracle, IBM AIX, Sun Solaris Training. **Personal Information:** Married to Christine in 1974. Two children: Jason and Matthew. Mr. Lang enjoys scuba diving and automobile restoration.

Jon E. Lapp
Programmer
Plantrol Systems, Ltd.
100 Bourne Street
Westfield, NY 14787
(716) 326-4900
Fax: (716) 326-6503
jon@plantrol.com

7371

Business Information: As Programmer of Plantrol Systems, Ltd., Mr. Lapp primarily offers hardware, operating system, and third party technical support. As a 10 year technology professional, he assumes responsibility for the NT Sequel server, configures the document management system, performs maintenance on 17 routers, and performs Visual Basic programming. Before joining Plantrol Systems, Mr. Lapp served as a Auxiliary Operator with Niagara Mohawk Power Corporation. To keep abreast of technological advances, he reads trade journals and surfs the Internet. His success reflects his ability to think out-of-the-box and aggressively take on new challenges and responsibilities. Mr. Lapp is committed to the further development of Plantrol Systems and coordinates strategic planning to ensure a bright future for a promotion to Project Manager. A privately held company, Plantrol Systems, Ltd. serves the business forms industry, providing software, hardware, and document management solutions. The Company began operations in 1978 and employs a work force of more than 35 qualified individuals. **Career Highlights:** Programmer, Plantrol Systems, Ltd. (1997-Present); Auxiliary Operator, Niagara Monawk Power Corporation (1989-97). **Education:** Jamestown Community College: A.S. in Computer Science (1997), A.A.S. in Computer Information Systems (1997). **Personal Information:** Married to Lucinda in 1991. One child: Justin D. Mr. Lapp enjoys wood working, snow mobiling and cooking.

Tami M. Lasky
Senior Project Manager
Stratum New Media
1534 Plantation Lakes Circle
Chesapeake, VA 23320-8114
(757) 626-0222
Fax: (757) 626-0333
tasky@hotmail.com

7371

Business Information: Serving as the Senior Project Manager, Mrs. Lasky provides professional direction and vision on behalf of Stratum New Media. Focusing her attention towards project development, she oversees consultants and technicians, ensuring project completion and client satisfaction. Forming reliable client relationships, she provides sufficient staffing, materials, and funding to each project. Managing an experienced crew, Mrs. Lasky offers training programs and develops strategic planning in order to maintain an efficient work force. Continuing in her career with Stratum New Media, Mrs. Lasky devotes her attention towards the betterment of her department in order to increase productivity and effectiveness. Specializing in interactive media, Stratum New Media was established in 1995. Located in Chesapeake, Virginia, the Company employs eight expert technicians and integrators who are extensively involved in Web development and design, the creation of CD-ROMS, and the traditional print and audio components of the computer. Implementing new technologies, the Company continues to strive towards supplying a more state-of-the-art product. **Career Highlights:** Senior Project Manager, Statrum New Media (1999-Present); Senior Web Developer, Sandiego.com (1997-99); Customer Care Manager, Public Online (1996-97). **Education:** University of Washington, B.A. (1993). **Personal Information:** Married to Joshua in 1994. Concerned about her community, Mrs. Lasky volunteers at a youth crisis center locally.

Pascal Le Melinaire, Ph.D.
• • • —■—◉—● • • •

Project Leader
Landmark Graphics
220 Foremost Drive
Austin, TX 78745
(512) 329-2276
Fax: (512) 292-2220
plemelinaire@lgc.com

7371

Business Information: As Project Leader of Landmark Graphics, Dr. Le Melinaire oversees and directs all day-to-day research and development activities. Also responsible for the design, development, and implementation setup at trade shows, Dr. Le Melinaire works closely with his team of nine technical experts to ensure that all units work together to achieve a common goal. Coordinating resources, time lines, schedules, and assignments also fall within the realm of Dr. Le Melinaire's functions. His career success is attributed to his supportive parents and good networking, as well as reflects his ability to think out-of-the-box and aggressively take on new challenges and responsibilities. Dr. Le Melinaire plans to expedite continued promotion through the fulfillment of his responsibilities and his involvement in the advancement of operations. One of his future goals is to eventually attain the position of Director of Technology. Landmark Graphics is a publicly owned software provider for the oil and gas industry. Established in 1980, the Company employs a staff of 1,000 qualified individuals to acquire business, meet with clients, facilitate projects, and market services. Serving an international client base, the Company is a subsidiary of Halliburton Inc. **Career Highlights:** Project Leader, Landmark Graphics (1995-Present); Consultant, Sisie (1994-95); Professional Sportsman, La Poste (1992-94); Engineer, Chevron Oil (1992). **Education:** INPL, Ph.D. (1992); University of Texas at Austin, M.B.A.; ENSG, Engineer. **Personal Information:** Dr. Le Melinaire enjoys sailing, flying and playing the piano.

Donna M. LeFaive
Product Manager
Trinary Systems Inc.
5715 126th Avenue
Fennville, MI 49408
(616) 561-6103
Fax: (801) 340-4399
dlefaive@accn.org

7371

Business Information: Serving as Product Manager of Trinary Systems Inc., Ms. LeFaive is responsible for the design, marketing, and overall specifications of the Corporation's software. She is further responsible for developing and coordinating all activities associated with the software development program. Instrumental in every aspect of Internet based research, Ms. LeFaive is currently developing new solutions to more efficiently and effectively track suppliers. Further implementing XTML technology and striving to increase e-business to make people's jobs easier, Ms. LeFaive showcases her project management skills in coordinating resources, time lines, schedules, and assignments. Some of her personal achievements include receiving the Automotive Industry Action Group's "Outstanding Achievement Award" in 1999. In the future, Ms. LeFaive plans on completing her Master's degree in Systems Management, pursuing an active role in the marketing of high-tech equipment, and providing consulting services. Staffed by 60 highly trained technicians, Trinary Systems Inc. develops computer software. The Corporation specializes in e-commerce and business-to-business communications software solutions. Clients of the Corporation include the automotive industry. Presently, the Corporation is located in Fennville, Michigan. **Career Highlights:** Trinary Systems Inc.: Product Manager (1999-Present), Product Development (1998-99); Prince Corporation: Supply Chain Engineer (1998), Business Analyst (1991-98). **Associations & Accomplishments:** Automotive Industry Action Group, Awarded Outstanding Achievement Award (1999); Vice-Chairman, Discovery Elementary School Board of Education; Downtown Development Authority; Co-Chair, Materials Management Project Team of Automotive Industry Action Group; Co-Chair, Material System Guideline Development Work Group; Co-Chair, Modeling Methodologies Work Group. **Education:** Denver University, M.S. in Systems Management (1990); Susquehanna University, B.A. in Math and Computer Science. **Personal Information:** Two children: Brendon and Adam.

Suzanne L. Lechner
Vice President/Consultant
CCW
W5128 East Division Street
Fond du Lac, WI 54935-4672
(920) 922-2820
Fax: (920) 922-6911
ccw@ccwkeepaccount.com

7371

Business Information: Ms. Lechner serves as Vice President and Consultant with CCW. As such, she handles systems analysis, programming, policy and procedure consulting, user training, and project coordination. She attributes her success to recognizing opportunity and to the support and encouragement of her friends and family. Established in 1985, CCW specializes in computer software development and consulting. Working in the field of corrections, CCW is an international company. **Career Highlights:** Vice President/Consultant, CCW (1987-Present); Medical Technologist, Fond du Lac Clinic S.C. (1972-80). **Associations & Accomplishments:** Registered Member, American Society of Clinical Pathologists; Board Member, Fond du Lac Soccer Association Inc.; Association of Information Technology Professionals. **Education:** Moraine Park Technical College, Associate's degree in Computer Operations and Programming (1985); University of Wisconsin - Oshkosh, B.S. in Medical Technology (1972). **Personal Information:** Married in 1972. Two children: Matthew and Rachel. Ms.

Lechner enjoys computers, hiking, biking, reading and soccer.

Francisco Lewis A.
Creative Lead
Plural
25 Broad Street, Apartment 4A
New York, NY 10004-2518
(212) 233-9890
Fax: (212) 233-9897
lewispma@li.net

7371

Business Information: Recruited to Plural as Creative Lead in 1999, Mr. Lewis A. is the Company's engagement point person for all aspects of day-to-day software development activities. Possessing an excellent understanding of technology, he leads a 40 person team in working with management and clients to analyze, specify, and design software solutions to harness more of the computer's power. A visionary who has proven himself correct on many occasions, Mr. Lewis A. develops the Company's overall vision and assures all aspects of project management remain on course. The highlights of his career include working for Forbes.com and designing and generating innovative ads for his clients. Attributing his success to his tenacity and people skills, Mr. Lewis A.'s goal is to develop broad ban vision. The number one Microsoft partner, Plural engages development of e-commerce software for Fortune companies. The Company specializes in fulfillment engines and multi threaded coding for large corporations and public sector online accounts. Established in 1988, Plural employs a work force of 1,200 professional, technical, and support staff who help generate annual revenues in excess of $2 billion. **Career Highlights:** Creative Lead, Plural (1999-Present); Creative Director, Forbes.com/Forbes Magazine (1997-99); Creative Director, Earthweb (1995-97); Senior Art Director, CMP Media (1992-95). **Associations & Accomplishments:** Yale Club. **Education:** Hunter College/Yale University, Master's degree in Fine Arts (1991). **Personal Information:** Mr. Lewis A. enjoys snowboarding.

Karen G. Littman
President/Owner
Morphonix
94 Windsor Avenue
San Rafael, CA 94901-1068
(415) 456-2561
Fax: (415) 456-1433

7371

Business Information: As President and Owner of Morphonix, Ms. Littman delegates assignments, assists programmers, artists and writers, and approves program production. Ms. Littman also assumes responsibility to generate financial support, oversee marketing efforts, and interface with government officials to obtain grants. Ms. Littman is in the process of introducing the Company to the International market through increased public exposure. Established in 1990, Morphonix develops CD-ROM and multimedia programs for children. The Company also conducts educational research and creates innovative applications using new technology. One of the Company's most successful programs, "Journey Into the Brain," an interactive story-based game for children, was a 1999 finalist for the Educational Title of the Year from the Academy of Interactive Arts and Sciences. Another program, "Interview," a CD-ROM that assists in interviewing children about possible sexual abuse, has also been very successful for the Company. **Career Highlights:** President/Owner, Morphonix (1990-Present); President, Boulder Productions, Inc. (1983-90); President, Handicapped Information Service for the Motion Picture and Television Industry (1979-90). **Associations & Accomplishments:** Computer Game Developer Association; Northbay Multimedia Association. **Education:** George Washington University, M.A. (1973); New York State University at Buffalo, B.S. (1970). **Personal Information:** Ms. Littman enjoys walking, singing and playing the piano.

Ningsheng Liu
Senior Software Engineer
Experian
5670 Greenwood Plaza
Englewood, CO 80111
(720) 528-5533
ningsheng.liu@experian.com

7371

Business Information: An experienced, 15 year technology professional, Mr. Liu serves as Senior Software Engineer of Experian. He is responsible for presiding over data warehouse design and modeling. Before joining Experian, he served as Senior Software Engineer with Evolving Systems Inc. His history include filling the roles of Senior Systems Analyst for Cable System Group and Associate Professor at Nanjing Normal University in China. He is deeply involved in the high level design of different company projects and engages in the start ups requirement gatherings. Mr. Liu credits his success to the knowledge he has gained through the years and keeps current in his field by training, surfing the Internet, and reading books and articles. He advises others to gain experience first. Continually striving to improve performance, Mr. Liu intends to focus on Relational Database and obtain his Ph.D. Head quartered in California, Experian provides data warehousing services to clients in Europe and the United States. The branch of the Company located in Englewood, Colorado employs 300 skilled individuals to develop software for campaign management and build customized data warehouse databases for customers. Experian has over 10,000 employees world wide. **Career Highlights:** Senior Software Engineer, Experian (1999-Present); Senior Software Engineer, Evolving Systems, Inc. (1995-99); Senior System Analyst, Cable System Group (1994); Associate Professor, Nanjing Normal University (1984-90). **Associations & Accomplishments:** Mr. Liu is author and co-author of three books and more than 50 papers in natural language analysis and processing, information, and cognition. **Education:** University of Denver, M.A. in Computer Science (1996); University of Colorado at Boulder, M.A. in Cognitive Studies (1994); Nanjing Normal University: M.A. in Linguistics (1984), B.A. in Chinese (1982). **Personal Information:** Married to Jun Cai in 1982. One child: Kathy. Mr. Liu enjoys reading and classic music.

Cheryl C. Long
Manager of Information Development
Ross Systems
1100 Johnson Ferry Road NE
Atlanta, GA 30342
(770) 351-9600
Fax: (404) 843-8371
cheryl_long@rossinc.com

7371

Business Information: Serving as Ross System's Manager of Information Development, Ms. Long oversees all technical activities on daily basis. Concerned with the direction of her staff, she implements procedures into her management style that foster a sense of unity and teamwork within the department. In a human resources role, Ms. Long is responsible for scheduling, hiring, and evaluating her staff. Working closely with senior management, she is directly involved in the development of strategic business planning by offering her insight and guidance on several topics and issues. Concurrent to her present position, Ms. Long also serves as an Adjunct Professor at Mercer University, teaching two communications courses per semester. One of her accomplishments is being named "Outstanding Student of the Year" at Southern Polytechnic State University. Crediting her success to strong internal motivation, she is aspiring to a role within the Company that will allow increased responsibility within the communication department. Ross Systems specializes in the development of software technology. Established in 1972, the Company employs 500 technically trained people to assist in the creation of enterprise resource planning and e-commerce systems. **Career Highlights:** Manager of Information Development, Ross Systems (1996-Present); Adjunct Professor, Mercer University (Present); Executive Administrator, Old Castle (CRH) (1996); International Development Analyst, Georgia-Pacific (1992-96). **Associations & Accomplishments:** Society of Technical Communication; Alpha Sigma Lamba National Honor Society. **Education:** Southern Polytechnic State University, M.S. in Technical and Professional Communication (1998); Mercer University, B.A. in Communication (1996). **Personal Information:** Two children: Sarah C. and Christopher R. Ms. Long enjoys writing creative nonfiction and poetry and landscape painting.

John R. Maltais
Senior Consultant
CBSI
16 Lenn Road
Springfield, MA 01118
(413) 782-8715

7371

Business Information: Utilizing his extensive experience in the field of information technology, Mr. Maltais serves as the Senior Consultant for CBSI. In this capacity, he consults with various companies, analyzing operating systems in an effort to offer a customized business solution which allows the companies to gain a competitive edge over others within its respective market. Before joining CBSI, Mr. Maltais served as Senior Programmer and Analyst for Westvaco. His background history also include a stint as Programmer with Massachusetts Mutual. In his present role with CBSI, he provides the latest in today's technological advancements in system upgrades and mainframe applications to each client in response to individual business needs. Committed to the success of the Company, Mr. Maltais is continually striving to improve his performance. His success reflects his ability to

think outside the box, deliver results, and aggressively tackle new challenges and responsibilities. CBSI is a consultancy firm, specializing in providing a wide range of business solutions to commercial clients in an effort to better enhance their corporate image and increase their marketability. Approximately 4,000 professionals consultants work with companies and corporations across the country to provide innovative and up to date technological solutions. The Company was established in 1985. **Career Highlights:** Senior Consultant, CBSI (1998-Present); Senior Programmer/Analyst, Westvaco (1987-98); Programmer, Massachusetts Mutual (1984-87). **Education:** Western New England, M.S. in Information Systems (1995); Westfield State College, B.S. in Computer Science; American International College, B.A. in Liberal Studies. **Personal Information:** Married. Mr. Maltais enjoys singing.

Ryan H. Marinoff
Field Technician
DynaLink
5201 Richmond Road
Cleveland, OH 44146
(216) 595-0007
Fax: (216) 464-3317
ryan_marinoff@hotmail.com

7371

Business Information: Serving as Field Technician for DynaLink, Mr. Marinoff travels to the client sites and handles the installation, configuration, and troubleshooting of company workstations and servers using Microsoft operating systems. He currently works on a team of three persons and has received verbal recognition for his work from corporate superiors. Crediting his career success to his dedication and an enjoyment of his job, he performs a great deal of networking in his home and reads industry publications to keep updated on changes in his field. Mr. Marinoff plans to continue his studies and move up within the Corporation, possibly focusing on computer security. His success reflects his ability to work well with others and aggressively take on new challenges. DynaLink provides data networking computer systems in local area networks and wide area networks as well as telephone services and troubleshooting. Offered internationally, these services are primarily for new companies building their first business sites and old companies in need of establishing system networking. Presently, the Corporation employs a staff of 100 individuals. **Career Highlights:** Field Technician, DynaLink (1998-Present); Internship, Pittsburgh Technical (1998). **Associations & Accomplishments:** Senior DeMolay, Order of DeMolay. **Education:** Pittsburgh Tech Institute, Associate's degree (1996-98). **Personal Information:** One child: Alexandria Moon Wright-Marinoff. Mr. Marinoff enjoys computer gaming, role playing and collecting.

Candace C. Marton
Y2K Project Manager
ProxyMed, Inc.
9553 Everglades
Boca Raton, FL 33428
(954) 851-7180
Fax: (954) 473-2341
cmarton@proxymed.com

7371

Business Information: Serving as Y2K Project Manager of ProxyMed, Inc., Mrs. Marton oversees Year 2000 planning, testing, and compliance for the entire Corporation. Recognizing the importance of Year 2000 issues, Mrs. Marton's job is to ensure that the Corporation's software products, connectivity services, subsidiaries, and divisions' products and services, along with the internal infrastructure systems will work accordingly at the turn of the century. She manages the inventory, assessment, remediation, and testing of all company hardware and software products, and connectivity services; oversees and assigns various projects for employees under her supervision; and ascertains third party/vendor compliance for corporate, subsidiaries, divisions, and acquisitions. She is also responsible for all customer and client communication concerning Year 2000 issues. Mrs. Marton attributes her success to being in the right place at the right time, and never backing away from a challenge. The leader in healthcare connectivity, ProxyMed, Inc., develops healthcare desktop software, pre-formatted printers, and provides electronic data interchange services for clinics, labs, doctors, pharmacies, insurance, and governmental agencies. The Corporation, registered on NASDAQ, employs more than 200 qualified individuals to assist in clinical and financial EDI services and support. **Career Highlights:** Y2K Project Manager, ProxyMed, Inc. (1998-Present); EDI Coordinator/Y2K Project Manager, S&H Fabricating and Engineering (1998); EDI Consultant, CMarton Consulting (1996-98); Management Information System Department Head, Iron Horse Bicycles Company (1995-98). **Associations & Accomplishments:** Volunteer House Manager, Little Palm Family Theater; Congregation

B'nai Israel, School Board Member; Member of various committees. **Education:** Ramapo College of New Jersey. **Personal Information:** Married to Steven in 1980. Three children: Heather, Rebecca, and Seth. Mrs. Marton enjoys spending time with her family and reading.

Sameer Mathur
Engineering Team Leader
Phoenix Technologies Ltd.
411 East Plumeria Drive
San Jose, CA 95134
(408) 570-1122
Fax: (408) 570-1324
sameer_mathur@phoenix.com

7371

Business Information: Recruited to Phoenix Technologies Ltd. in 1996, Mr. Mathur currently serves as the Engineering Team Leader. Involved in first level engineering management, he is in charge of product design and manages several teams of skilled engineers in the development and coding of new software products. Coordinating resources, schedules, time lines, and assignments also fall within the realm of his responsibilities. Utilizing more than 10 years of engineering experience working with international companies, Mr. Mathur has several patents pending for personal product designs. Committed to the success of the Company, he coordinates strategic planning to ensure a bright future for a managerial position in a larger department. Established in 1979, Phoenix Technologies Ltd. engages in the development of BIOS, networking, and Internet enabling software. Although the Company specializes in software development, hardware enabling products are available also. Presently, more than 680 professional, technical, and support personnel are employed by Phoenix Technologies. **Career Highlights:** Engineering Team Leader, Phoenix Technologies Ltd. (1996-Present); Senior Engineer, OEC Japan (1995-96); Senior Engineer, IBM Japan (1994-95). **Associations & Accomplishments:** Solid State Floppy Disk; Smartmedia Forum. **Education:** L.D. College of Engineering, B.S. (1991).

Haywood McDowell
Owner/Chief Executive Officer
The Stock Market Reference Desk
2395 Hunters Square Court
Reston, VA 20191
(703) 464-6011
Fax: (413) 674-7210

7371

Business Information: As Owner of The Stock Market Reference Desk, Mr. McDowell serves as its Chief Executive Officer. He determines the overall strategic direction and formulates powerful business and marketing strategies to keep the Company out front of its competitors. He has devoted his career to further exploration of the Internet and its capabilities. A financial genius, he combined his two talents and created his own business. Today, this business has geared itself towards the private investor and caters to their home office needs to successfully monitor their finances without having to strain for research. Becoming a $20 million company and remaining on the cutting edge serves as Mr. McDowell's future objectives. Established in 1998, The Stock Market Reference Desk is the entrepreneurial adventure of Mr. McDowell. Located on the Internet at <www.investment.web.com>, the Company features a variety of links to portfolio tracking, real-time quotes, research, commentary, and charts and news headlines. The Company provides access to a Stock Market, DOW, and NASDAQ ticker and, through a partnership with Edgar Online Inc., clients are also able to browse through links with initial public offering listings. Mr. McDowell also works as a Help Desk Analyst at Concert Inc., where he provides prompt solutions to PC and LAN difficulties and maintains the complete functionality and operational status of the network. These include Novell and Microsoft Windows NT administration, reporting LAN/WAN outages, resolving call issues, and dispatching other team members as appropriate. Concert provides global end to end managed products, offering customers voice, managed data, and bandwidth services. Over the course of one year, Concert is able to turn over $3 billion in revenue and its profitability continues to increase over the years. **Career Highlights:** Owner/Chief Executive Officer, The Stock Market Reference Desk (1997-Present); Help Desk Analyst, Concert Inc. (Present); Manager of Help Desk, PPG Inc. (1997-99); Project Manager, America Online Inc. (1990-97). **Associations & Accomplishments:** District of Columbia Young Professionals; Air and Space Smithsonian; Library of Congress; Professional Association of Diving Instructors; National Association of Underwater Instructors. **Education:** Strayer University, degree in Computer Information Systems (1990). **Personal Information:** Married to Lisa D. in 1994. Two children: Chelisa D. and Evan Haywood.

Hope Eyre Meckley

E-Business Strategy Manager
SAP
1171 Arborvista Drive
Atlanta, GA 30329
(404) 943-3016
Fax: (404) 943-2957
hope.meckley@sap.com

7371

Business Information: As E-Business Solution Architect of SAP, Mrs. Meckley is responsible for Internet business strategy and the design of applications. Lending her impressive knowledge to the architectural staff, she assists in the extension of enterprise resource planning applications to the Internet to allow clients easier access. With exceptional communicative skills, Mrs. Meckley works closely with clients from large process manufacturing firms. Meeting with corporate representatives, she analyzes the business to develop an action plan, then brings resources together to generate solutions. Mrs. Meckley is credited with the successful implementation of several complex policies, including strategy formulation. She attributes her accomplishments to her ability to do a job she loves well; as her role within the Company expands, she intends to incorporate more Internet based products into corporate procedures. Mrs. Meckley's credo is "there is no substitute for a complete understanding of the industry." SAP is recognized as the largest provider of enterprise resource planning software in the world. The German based company employs 18,000 people throughout the world, generating annual revenue of $5 billion. Established in 1974, the Company produces software that is sold to Global Enterprise companies. **Career Highlights:** E-Business Solution Architect, SAP (1999-Present); Human Resources Strategy, Coca-Cola Company 1998-99); Information Designer, Dun & Bradstreet Software (1990-97). **Associations & Accomplishments:** Board of Editors, Life Sciences. **Education:** Emory University, M.B.A. (1999); Purdue University, B.A. (1987). **Personal Information:** Married to John in 1987. Mrs. Meckley enjoys scalling, reading and skiing.

Alexander P. Messes

Interactive Developer
The Allied Group Inc.
628 Hebron Avenue, Building 2
Glastonbury, CT 06033
(860) 815-0055
Fax: (860) 815-0008
alex-messes@thealliedgroup.com

7371

Business Information: Serving as Interactive Developer for The Allied Group Inc., Mr. Messes develops Internet based computer software and performs enterprise-wide system integration for Fortune 1000 companies. A certified Java expert, the majority of his work is done in Java development. Mr. Messes works closely with each individual client to ascertain their needs and deliver the best service. A savvy, 22 year technology professional, he owns an established track record of producing results. His success reflects his ability to think out-of-the-box and take on new challenges. Committed to providing continued optimum service to the Corporation, his next goal is to become a Java Systems Architect. One of the fastest growing companies in the United States, The Allied Group Inc. performs software research and development for Fortune 500 and 1000 companies. The only authorized Java center in Connecticut, the Corporation is also a Netscape partner and Oracle center. Since inception in 1989, the Corporation has become a $100 million company employing a work force of 90 skilled professionals. **Career Highlights:** Interactive Developer, The Allied Group Inc. (1999-Present); Webmaster, National Physicians Datasource, LLC (1997-99); Management Information Systems Director, PenMedica Systems, Inc. (1994-97). **Associations & Accomplishments:** Institute of Electronics and Electrical Engineers Computer Society; Java Lobby. **Education:** Polytechnical University, Master's degree (1977); Java certification from Sun Microsystems, Inc. (1999). **Personal Information:** Married to Nadia in 1983. One child: Dmitry. Mr. Messes enjoys photography.

Jason P. Meszaros

Information Technology Manager
Retek Information System
801 Nicollet Mall
Minneapolis, MN 55402
(612) 630-5635
Fax: (612) 630-5710
jason.meszaros@retek.com

7371

Business Information: Displaying exceptional technological skills, Mr. Meszaros serves as Information Technology Manager for Retek Information System. In this capacity, he is responsible for myriad of operational responsibilities to include computer and software purchasing, network management, and technical support. Highly regarded, Mr. Meszaros also conducts all technical support training, and has received awards for his innovative programs. In addition, he assumes oversight of an eight member staff of technicians, providing them with guidance and comprehensive direction as they endeavor to meet departmental needs. Continually striving for maximum effectiveness, Mr. Meszaros is currently pursuing his Master's degree in Information Technology and has aspirations to move up to higher level management positions within the Corporation. He attributes his success to being in the right place at the right time, networking, and his self motivation. Retek Information System specializes in software development for the retail industry. Headquartered in Minneapolis, Minnesota current operations utilize a collective work force of over 700 highly trained technicians who expedite all activities and assist in generating the Corporation's successively high annual revenues. Retek Information System offers a multitude of software including merchandise tracking, data warehousing, and data forecasting. The Corporation also operates business-to-business e-commerce, such as retail.com, an online supply chain portal, and is currently setting the pace for progression in the dot.com world. **Career Highlights:** Information Technology Manager, Retek Information System (1998-Present); Office Automation Specialist, RAM, Inc. (1997-98); Database Manager, Universe Technologies (1997). **Associations & Accomplishments:** Help Desk 2000; Microsoft Certified Professional; Dell Certified Technician; Former United States Army Intelligence Officer; Psychological Operations Officer. **Education:** Winona State University, B.S. in Marketing (1994); University of St. Thomas, Mini M.B.A. Program; University of Wisconsin at La Crosse, M.S. in Sports Administration. **Personal Information:** Married to Karen in 1999. Mr. Meszaros enjoys volleyball.

Patrick J. Meyer, II

Information Systems Manager
Information Graphics Systems Inc.
5777 Central Avenue, Suite 200
Boulder, CO 80301
(303) 448-3666
Fax: (303) 444-6143

7371

Business Information: Providing his skilled services as Information Systems Manager for Information Graphics Systems Inc., Mr. Meyer presides over the corporate voice and data networks for the production and development environments of the Corporation. In this capacity, he ensures that the system developers have licensed software and adequate equipment to perform their jobs. Over 100 servers are utilized for development purposes and in daily operations. Mr. Meyer also performs network administration and deskside support, and is responsible for all of the Corporation's telecommunications functions. Crediting his success to diligence and an eagerness to take on new challenges, he has received internal recognition for his accomplishments. He is currently pursuing his M.C.S.E. and Bachelor's degree in Information Systems to enable him to capitalize on the many opportunities provided by the Corporation. Founded in 1987, Information Graphics Systems Inc. specializes in software development for the telecommunications and e-commerce industries. Additional preferred services are middleware, database integration, and Web development. The Corporation serves a primarily national clientele but does have some international accounts. Boasting $20 million in annual sales, operations employ 165 qualified professionals. **Career Highlights:** Information Systems Manager, Information Graphics Systems Inc. (1999-Present); Technical Support Engineer/Systems Administrator, Lucent Technologies (1998-99); Technical Support Engineer, IBM for Lucent Technologies (1996-98); Service Manager, Rocky Mountain SysPro, Inc. (1995-96). **Education:** University of Phoenix, B.S. in Information Systems (In Progress); Microsoft Certified Professional in System Architecture and Network Design. **Personal Information:** Married to Marilyn M. in 1996. Three children: Maggie, John, and Charlie. Mr. Meyer enjoys down hill skiing, softball, roller blading, camping and fishing.

Noohu Mohamed

Software Engineer
2GoTrade.com
21/F, The Broadway, Lockhart Road
Wanchai, Hong Kong
+85 223220301
Fax: (914) 678-0802
noohu@netscape.net

7371

Business Information: Affiliated with 2GoTrade.com since their foundation in March 2000, Mr. Mohamed serves as the leading Software Engineer. Engaged in the multi-faceted challenges of database development, maintenance, and administration, Mr. Mohamed utilizes several years of experience in the database industry as well as a technological degree for the field. One of the most highly renowned software developers in the world, Mr. Mohamed specializes his creations in areas of e-commerce to support new industries engaged in the Internet market. His success reflects his ability to think out-of-the-box, take on challenges, and deliver results. A subsidiary of Epro Systems, 2GoTrade.com is one of the leading software and hardware development companies in all of Hong Kong. Employing a staff of 12 people, 2GoTrade.com is currently involved with the introduction of a new product line, which will be made available for purchase in August 2000. **Career Highlights:** Software Engineer, 2GoTrade.com (2000-Present); Service Manager, R&H Systems (1997-98); Analytical Engineer, Enviropace Ltd. (1993-97). **Associations & Accomplishments:** Instrument Society of America. **Education:** Bharathiar University, Bachelor's degree in Technology (1993). **Personal Information:** Married to Payal Sharma in 2000. Mr. Mohamed enjoys windsurfing, canoeing and football.

Patrick H. Moles

Owner/Operator
Integrated Solutions Group
3 Encinal
Foothill Ranch, CA 92610-1860
(949) 460-9525
patrick@isgcom.com

7371

Business Information: As Owner and Operator of Integrated Solutions Group, Mr. Moles oversees and directs the development and implemention of technology. He is an independent contractor providing networking for all core programming databases. Years of extensive education and experience in the technology field has enabled Mr. Moles to acquire the necessary skill to effectively complete his job duties and lead Integrated Solutions Group in its growth, development, and ultimate success. He would like to expand the Company to eight people and attain a greater and diverse client base. His professional success is attributed to his excellent mentors who demonstrated the importance of hard work ethic. Mr. Moles' advice is, "Have confidence and experience." Established in 1997, Integrated Solutions Group engages in technology services, offering Web integration and consulting. A staff of two individuals oversees all aspects of the operation. The Company designs and develops e-business solutions for businesses such as financial and manufacturing institutions. **Career Highlights:** Owner/Operator, Integrated Solutions Group (1997-Present); Director Information Technology, New Century Financial (1996). **Associations & Accomplishments:** Orange County Visual Basic User Group; Novell Developer Net Group. **Education:** Stephen F. Austin State, B.A. in Computer Science (1986). **Personal Information:** Married to Shellie May in 1993. One child: Hannah Lyvone. Mr. Moles enjoys softball, flag football and Web development.

Benoit Montreuil, Ph.D.

Chief Technology Officer
SET Technologies, Inc.
3950 Chaudiere, Suite 105
Sainte-Foy, Quebec, Canada G1X 4M8
(418) 659-4922
benoit.montreuil@set.qc.ca

7371

Business Information: Dr. Montreuil, as Chief Technolgy Officer of SET Technologies, Inc., maintains a very demanding role in that he is also the founder. Internationally recognized, he coordinates various strategies for product development, catering full office solutions to customers. A savvy technical expert, he makes decisions as to what services have the greatest potential for survival and growth, such as networking, Internet, and control systems. In addition, he determines the overall strategic direction and formulates both tactical and strategic marketing and new business plans to keep SET Technologies out-front of competitors. In the future, Dr. Montreuil's plans include expansion and becoming a major consultancy for large businesses. As the mastermind behind new plans, he will continue to study all projects which relate to all developments and offers in the years to come. He also plans on making the Corporation the worldwide leader in domain. Vision and education as well as his leadership ability to form teams with synergy and technical strength has contributed to Dr. Montreuil's success. SET Technologies, Inc., established in 1989, was created to help other companies develop better business practices. The Corporation provides advanced business planning, implementing state of the art software. The products are marketed to a broad spectrum of clients around the world. With the skillful assistance of 20 professionals, the Corporation is growing at an impressive rate and is aiming its products toward leading edge manufacturing companies who are serious about their future. **Career Highlights:** Chief Technology Officer, SET Technologies, Inc. (Present); Professor, Université Laval (1988-Present); President, Systemes Espace Temps, Inc. (1989-96); Codirector, CENTOR, Université Laval (1998-Present). **Associations & Accomplishments:** Professional Engineer, Quebec; Institute of Industrial Engineers; INFORMS. **Education:** Georgia Institute of Technology: Ph.D. in Industrial Engineering (1982), M.S. in Industrial Engineering (1980); Université Du Quebec A Trois

Riveieres, Bachelor's degree in Engineering (1978). **Personal Information:** Married to Johanne in 1979. Four children: Christelle, Geneviève, Anthony, and Zachary. Dr. Montreuil enjoys skiing, snowboarding, trekking and camping.

Michael F. Mulleady

Software Project Manager
Kay Elemetrics Corporation
2 Bridgewater Lane
Lincoln, NJ 07035
(973) 628-6200
mikemulleady@mindspring.com

7371

Business Information: Mr. Mulleady functions in the role of Software Project Manager with Kay Elemetrics Corporation. He is responsible for developing systems, evaluating technical projects, and writing software. His focus is on working with users in the medical field to analyze, specify, and design new solutions to improve equipment performance in detecting cancer. An information systems professional with 12 years in the industry, Mr. Mulleady is experienced in all aspects of analysis, design, development, implementation, and project management. He has served with Kay Elemetrics in a variety of capacities since joining the team as Project Leader in 1994. Coordinating all resources, time lines, schedules, assignments, and budgets also fall within the realm of Mr. Mulleady's functions. He attributes his success to listening, not having an ego, and treating people as an individual. Transtioning from a desktop environment to Internet access serves as one of his future goals. He remains on the leading edge of technology by reading and attending Microsoft seminars. Kay Elemetrics Corporation engages in design, development, and distribution of medical imaging equipment. The Corporation delivers cutting edge imaging technology used to detect ear, nose, and throat cancer. Established in 1947, Kay Elemetrics employs a work force of 50 people who help generate annual revenues in excess of $10 million. **Career Highlights:** Kay Elemetrics Corporation: Software Project Manager (1996-Present), Project Leader (1994-96). **Education:** Dublin City University, B.S. (1987). **Personal Information:** Married to Catherine in 1991. Mr. Mulleady enjoys running, golf, physical fitness, reading and current affairs.

Frank L. Mullen

Consultant
SMA Inc.
19506 Highway 59 North
Humble, TX 77338
(281) 446-5000
Fax: (281) 446-7492
frank_mullen@ev1.net

7371

Business Information: Drawing upon a strong technical background and expertise, Mr. Mullen serves as a Consultant with SMA Inc. In his position, he is responsible for all aspects of quality assurance testing, software installation, and employee training on the correct usage of systems programs. Possessing an excellent understanding of technology, Mr. Mullen is charged with identifying areas within the systems infrastructure, troubleshooting, and developing solutions to fix and eliminate all difficulies. Highly regarded, he also provides consulting services for the Corporation's clientele. In the future, Mr. Mullen looks forward to continuing with the Corporation in his current position. Located in Humble, Texas, SMA Inc engages in software development of mainframe systems. Established in 1981, the Corporation operates on an international level with locations in several countries including France, Korea, and Canada as well as many offices throughout the United States. With a staff of 40 employees at the Texas location, the Company reports a substantial annual revenue. **Career Highlights:** Consultant, SMA Inc. (1985-Present); Operator, Louisville Bedding Company (1988-95); Telecommunications Control Operator, United States Army (1983-87). **Associations & Accomplishments:** University of Louisville Alumni Association. **Education:** University of Louisville, B.S. in Business Administration (1994). **Personal Information:** Mr. Mullen enjoys travel, golf and coin collecting.

John Mulligan

Senior Account Manager
Bureau of Translation Services Inc.
30 Washington Avenue
Haddonfield, NJ 08033
(609) 795-8669
Fax: (609) 795-8737
jmulligan@btsinc.com

7371

Business Information: Mr. Mulligan is Senior Account Manager for Bureau of Translation Services Inc. He is responsible for overseeing and handling all corporate client accounts within the Corporation's Sales Division. Before joining Bureau of Translation Services in 1997, Mr. Mulligan served as Inventory Control Supervisor with Office Depot Inc. His history also includes a stint as Computer Service Consultant for State University of New York College at Brockport. He prides himself in staying informed on all department activities and being able to research and identify where the Corporation's assets would be best utilized. Identifying new customers, analyzing their specific business needs, proposing solutions, and negotiating contracts, as well as implementing proposals and ensuring a smooth running operation also fall within the scope of Mr. Mulligan's functions. A tested and proven professional, he has received numerous internal recognition and letters of commendation, and been asked to make presentations at conferences and seminars. He attributes his success to his research ability and his very supportive wife. Remaining and growing with the Corporation, and eventually starting up his own consulting company serves as his future endeavors. "Stay in the practice, keep active in a focused area," is cited as Mr. Mulligan's advice. A subsidiary of Translation Group, Bureau of Translation Services Inc. engages in translating and localizing software to a wide variety of different international languages. The Corporation also provides cutting edge Internet services and multilingual information and support programs. Global in scope, Bureau of Translation Services operates network office world wide. Established in 1982, the Corporation employs a work force of 100 throughout the Company. Presently, the Corporation reports estimated annual revenues in excess of $5 million. **Career Highlights:** Senior Account Manager, Bureau of Translation Services Inc. (1997-Present); Inventory Control Supervisor, Office Depot Inc. (1995-97); Computer Service Consultant, State University of New York College at Brockport (1994-95). **Associations & Accomplishments:** Director/Founder, Cephas New Jersey; Deacon, First Presbyterian Church. **Education:** State University of New York College at Brockport. **Personal Information:** Married to Sandra in 1996. One child: Evan. Mr. Mulligan enjoys golf, fishing and computer repair.

Michael G. Mychalczuk, MCSE, MCP+I, MCP, CNA

Product Manager, Knowledge Products
Mission Critical Software
13939 Northwest Freeway
Houston, TX 77040
(713) 548-1873
Fax: (713) 548-1771
mike.mychalczuk@missioncritical.com

7371

Business Information: Mr. Mychalczuk functions in the capacity of Product Manager for Mission Critical Software. He is responsible for conducting competitive and comparative analysis as well as systems integration for technical products in the customer environments. A systems expert, Mr. Mychalczuk oversees and directs all aspects of program writing for systems integrations. He also reviews tech-evaluations and does various subject matter presentations on subjects ranging from information technology infrastructures and products to future product direction. Supervising a staff of talented computer experts, Mr. Mychalczuk's plans to pursue greater challanges while staying with the Company. As a whole, he looks forward to a broadening of his professional horizons. As for his current success, he attributes it to his very supportive wife and children, and his ability to think outside the box, produce results, and aggressively take on new challenges. Established in 1995, Mission Critical Software is a software development copmany. The Company employs 178 professional, technical, and support people. Currently, Mission Critical Software is in fast pursuit of creating software suites for NT4.0 and NT2000, specializing in system event management and administration. **Career Highlights:** Product Manager, Knowledge Products, Mission Critical Software (Present); Systems Integrator/Project Manager, Sprint (1996-99); Production and Facilities Engineer, Central Missouri State University (1991-96); Online Editor, Welsh National Opera's Splott Cinderella video production (1994); Production Lighting Technician, Hunt Midwest Entertainment (1988-91). **Associations & Accomplishments:** Broadcast Educators Association (1996); Society of Broadcast Engineers (1994-98); National Broadcasting Society (1992-98); Named to International WHO'S WHO of Entrepreneurs (1997); Technical Consultant/Advisor, Fine Arts Department, North Kansas City School District High School (1991-99). **Education:** Central Missouri State University, B.S.ed Integrated Communications (1996); International Studies at the University of Glamorgan, and the Wesh College of Music and Drama (1993); Post Graduate work at Keller Graduate School of Management while in pursuit of Masters in Telecommunications Management. **Personal Information:** Married to Karen in 1995. Two children: Kyrie and Andrew. Mr. Mychalczuk enjoys music and being involved in church activities.

Tony H. Nguyen

Network Administrator
Chicago Title & Trust
20525 Nordhoff Street
Chatsworth, CA 91311
(818) 773-7148
Fax: (818) 773-7191
nguyent@ctt.com

7371

Business Information: Utilizing more than 10 years of experience, Mr. Nguyen serves as the Network Administrator for Chicago Title & Trust. He assumes accountability for the smooth functioning of the primary LAN and manages the Company's network infrastructure. Before joining Chicago Title & Trust, he served as Network Specialist with Compu Cal and Systems Specialist at American Group. In his present position, Mr. Nguyen provides network security and integrity, installs applications and software upgrades, and monitors daily activity. Providing a storage management program, he performs routine backups. Directing and participating in the analysis, design, configuration, test, support, and tracking of networking systems, client server utility programs, software, and hardware also fall within the purview of Mr. Nguyen's functions. He attributes his career success to his education. His success reflects his ability to think out-of-the-box and take on new challenges and responsibilities. Mr. Nguyen continues to grow professionally through the fulfillment of his responsibilities and his involvement in the advancement of operations. Chicago Title & Trust is a title insurance company which creates title software and information systems. Established in the 1980s, the Company now employs over 5,000 professionals nationwide. **Career Highlights:** Network Administrator, Chicago Title & Trust (1998-Present); Network Specialist, Compu Cal (1993-98); Systems Specialist, Americal Group (1989-93). **Associations & Accomplishments:** Eagle Scout, Explorer; The VECNH of San Fernando Valley. **Education:** University of California at Los Angeles, B.S. (1989); MCSE (1995); CNE (1994). **Personal Information:** Married to Kathy in 1988. Two children: Theodore and Joshua. Mr. Nguyen enjoys sports, fishing and golf.

David S. Oglensky

Sales Consultant/Sales Engineer
Data Management Services
185 Ridgedale Avenue
Cedar Knolls, NJ 07927
(973) 829-0505
Fax: (973) 829-7193
dso@dms2.com

7371

Business Information: As Sales Consultant and Sales Engineer for Data Management Services, Mr. Oglensky evaluates and selects technologies and solutions to be sold. His primary responsibility lies within single-source solution development; he creates and sells information technology strategies to the mid-market, as well as manages vendor relationships. Working closely with clients, he evaluates their technical needs then formulates plans that maximize their productiveness. Crediting his success to a strong focus on technological changes in the industry, Mr. Oglensky has followed his mother's professional example throughout his career, as they are in the same industry. Keeping his goals consistent with the objectives of the Company, he looks forward to advancement within the corporate structure. Data Management Services engages in enterprise resource planning counsulting and implementation. Established in 1885, the Company handles all aspects of network planning, integration, and applications development for a wide array of clients. Offering e-commerce consulting as well, the Company has successfully gained a well deserved reputation for full service and quality. **Career Highlights:** Sales Consultant/Sales Engineer, Data Management Services (1998-Present); Account Manager, Premio Computers (1997-98); Account Manager, Fountain Technologies (1995-97). **Associations & Accomplishments:** Microsoft Usability Research Panel; Morris County College Technology Advisory Committee; American Management Association; AFSMI; Intelliquest Research Panel; Tally Group Research Panel; NPD On-line Research Panel; CMP Research Panel; Gartner Interactive. **Education:** Thomas Edison State University, M.S. (In Progress); University of Hartford, B.A. in Business Administration (1995). **Personal Information:** Mr. Oglensky enjoys guitar and sports.

William Walter Page

Manager
E-Citi
12731 West Jefferson Boulevard
Los Angeles, CA 90066
(310) 302-3316
Fax: (310) 302-4100
page@cdcla.com
7371

Business Information: Serving as E-Citi's Manager since 1980, Mr. Page is responsible for deployment of leading edge financial software applications. In this context, he ensures all software requirements as well as quality, value, and reliability are included in the software package prior to implementation. Possessing an excellent understanding of technology, Mr. Page is involved in the discovery, investigation, and initial deployment of advanced technologies within E-Citi. His focus is on changes that will allow E-Citi and customers to take advantage of to remain flexible, efficient, and profitable in the Information Technology Age. Training technical personnel on new software is also an integral part of his responsibilities. Honesty and the ability to tackle challenges and deliver results have contributed immensely to Mr. Page's success within the corporate structure. Gearing up for retirement in five years, his adivce is "make sure your life is rich and full." Established in 1972, E-Citi is the technical arm of Citibank. The Company specializes in research and development of financial software and investment banking. E-Citi focuses on home banking, ATMs, and related services. Headquartered in Los Angeles, California, E-Citi currently employs 400 skilled individuals. **Career Highlights:** Manager, E-Citi (1980-Present); Systems Engineer, Jet Propulsion Lab (1974-79). **Associations & Accomplishments:** Chairman of the Board of Directors (1989-90), L.A.C.A.N. **Education:** University of Southern California: M.S. in Management (1976), M.S. in Computer Science (1972); University of New Hampshire, B.S. in Math (1969). **Personal Information:** Married to Isabel in 1990. Two children: Nicholas and Timothy. Mr. Page enjoys golf and magic.

Jeffrey M. Pagliei

Technical Support Analyst
ESPS, Inc.
1300 Virginia Drive
Fort Washington, PA 19034
(215) 619-6280
Fax: (610) 544-9846
oraclexy@aol.com
7371

Business Information: Mr. Pagliei serves as Technical Support Analyst of ESPS, Inc. He is part of the global technical team that troubleshoots and solves software issues with West Coast clients. In his position, he conducts testing on software components which enables him to pinpoint the specific problem areas and devise a solution to fix the problem. Additionally, Mr. Pagliei provides the Corporation with creative ideas for troubleshooting and also for solutions to problems. In the future, he looks forward to continuing with ESPS and helping the Corporation grow and expand operationsl. His success reflects his ability to tackle new challenges and deliver results on behalf of the Corporation and its clientele. Founded in 1994, ESPS, Inc is a software manufacturer that makes high volume publishing software for major corporations. Located in Fort Washington, Pennsylvania, the Corporation produces quality products for clients located throughout the United States. With a work force of 250 employees, the Corporation reports annual revenues in excess of $14 million. **Career Highlights:** Technical Support Analyst, ESPS, Inc. (1999-Present); Y2K Implementor, West Chester University (1999); PowerPoint Specialist, SAP America (1997-98); Hardware and Software Technician, West Chester University (1995-97). **Education:** West Chester University, Bachelor of Fine Arts (1999). **Personal Information:** Mr. Pagliei enjoys art, computers, graphic design, music and photography.

Kerry Parker

Web Design Developer
SalesSupport.com
5932 Golden Gate Drive
Dallas, TX 75241-5221
(817) 685-5647
Fax: (972) 225-8917
kparke19@idt.net
7371

Business Information: Possessing a wealth of knowledge in the technology field, Mr. Parker was recruited to SalesSupport.com in 1999, and currently serves as Web Designer and Developer. Responsible for the Web development team, he designs graphics for in-house and external Web sites. A savvy, eight year veteran, Mr. Parker is tasked with assisting major server commerce and Web projects using Visual Interdev, SQL, Photoshop, and ASP. SalesSupport.com relies on his expertise to provide the Company' clients with customized Web sites with innovative graphics and multi-media content. One of many accomplishments, his greatest is his ability to work with the Company and his professional colleagues in delivering cutting edge solutions. Attributing his career success to his parents, Mr. Parker's goals include obtaining his degree in information technology and master's in e-commerce. A reputable, technology services company, SalesSupport.com provides complex, computer based, high quality marketing and sales support to the business community. Services include e-commerce development and hosting; and sales and marketing. Established in the 1980s, SalesSupport.com presently employs a 400 professional, technical, and administrative support staff. **Career Highlights:** Web Designer/Developer, SalesSupport.com (1999-Present); Web Designer/Developer, KerryParker.com (1998-Present); Computer Operator, Tandy Corporation (1992-99). **Associations & Accomplishments:** HTML Writers Guild; National Association of Photoshop Professionals; Oracle Technology Network; IBM Solution Developer Program; Dallas Museum of Fine Arts; International Freelance Photographers Organization; Amateur Photographers Association; Texas Photographic Society; Cross Country Club of Dallas; The American Running Association. **Education:** College, degree in Information Technology (In Progress); SMU Meadows School of Art; Cedar Valley Junior College; Columbus College of Arts and Design; Capstone.com, Web Development; Digital.com, Digital Training; NewHorozin.com, Web Development; Rockhurst College, Publishing Training. **Personal Information:** Mr. Parker enjoys art, marathons, photography, physical fitness and movies.

Brian P. Parrish

Software Engineer
J.C. Solutions, LLC
1000 Technology Drive, Suite 3320
Fairmont, WV 26554
(304) 368-4143
Fax: (304) 367-1759
parrish@jc-solutions.com
7371

Business Information: As a Software Engineer with J.C. Solutions, LLC, Mr. Parrish works closely with management and users to analyze, specify, design, and deploy solutions and enhancements to systems and network architectures. A systems expert with years of experience, to include four years as a AWACS Programmer and Analyst with the United States Air Force, Mr. Parrish designs, codes, tests, and implements database Web integration solutions in order to improve productivity and efficiency of his client's database management systems. Always alert to new opportunities, techniques, and approaches, Mr. Parrish continues to provide optimum technical services. Attributing his success to adaptability, self-discipline, and determination, he remains on the cutting edge of technology through research and reading technical journals. His future endeavors include attaining the position of Project Manager. Established in 1997, J.C. Solutions is dedicated to providing excellent software engineering services, primarily contracting to the military. Headquartered in Morgantown, West Virginia, the Company employs five expert computer technicians, and administrator who engages in development and implementation of Web sites and database services for an international clientele. Continually striving towards higher standards of excellence in computer technology, the Company remains committed to providing optimum products and services. **Career Highlights:** Software Engineer, J.C. Solutions, LLC (1998-Present); Software Engineer, Mantech Corporation (1998); Software Engineer, DSD Laboratories, Inc. (1997-98); AWACS Programmer/Analyst, United States Air Force (1994-97). **Associations & Accomplishments:** Affiliate Member, West Virginia High Tech Consortium. **Education:** Fairmont State College. **Personal Information:** Married in 1999. Mr. Parrish enjoys being an avid golfer.

Richard R. Parrish

Owner/Operator
Randy's Professional Web Site Design
312 North Main Street
Winnsboro, TX 75494-2524
(903) 342-0020
Fax: (903) 342-5264
randy@rpwsd.com
7371

Business Information: A computer geniuse, Mr. Parrish, the Owner and Operator of Randy's Professional Web Site Design is a devoted follower of innovative information technology advancements. He created the Company to fulfill his lifetime dream of owning his own business and has been celebrating his freedom and success since its first day in the market. He builds Web sites for his clients and is also involved in constructing complete computer networks for area businesses and private residences. For the future, Mr. Parrish looks forward to continued success and he hopes to further his knowledge in the leading technology fields and latest innovative designs. Randy's Professional Web Site Design caters to the personalization needs of its clients in successfully creating globally accessible Web site for its clientele. Established in 1998, the Company has brainstormed several of the most innovative and user-friendly Web sites to assist its clientele in demonstrating their products through a computer. The Company features a staff of two computer geniuses who are not afraid to tackle large projects and attempt the seemingly impossible tasks. **Career Highlights:** Owner/Operator, Randy's Professional Web Site Design (1998-Present); Technician, Network Technologies (1998-Present); Technical Support, LCI (1998-99); Technician, Hearthside Communications (1998); Technician, Micro Techniques (1997-98).

Suzanne Sacek Pattock

Senior Oracle Database Administrator
CIBER Enterprise Application Services
40 East Mall Plaza, Suite 202
Carnegie, PA 15106
(412) 279-7111
Fax: (412) 279-8001
pattock.suzanne@summitgroup.com
7371

Business Information: As Senior Oracle Database Administrator of CIBER Enterprise Application Services, Mrs. Pattock oversees and directs day-to-day Oracle administration and operations. She is responsible for controlling all data resources and ensuring data integrity and reliability. Before joining The Summit Group, Inc., now known as CIBER EAS, in 1999, she served as Oracle Database Administrator with Paragon Solutions and Computer Analyst at Intell Rx. As a 10 year technology professional with an established record of producing results, Mrs. Pattock maintains the Oracle database functionality and fully operational status. Overseeing software installation and implementation, troubleshooting systems difficulties, tuning software tools to enhance overall performance, and coordinating resources and schedules are also an integral part of her functions. Mrs. Pattock credits her professional success to her supportive parents. "Be the best you can be," is cited as her advice. Her strategic plans include eventually attaining the position of Manager of Oracle. CIBER Enterprise Application Services turns opportunities into reality. The Company's experience cuts across a multitude of industries and business applications. CIBER EAS's Consulting and System Selection Services provide the knowledge and expertise to combine a strategic Corporate vision with the implementation services that brings that vision to life. CIBER EAS is the one source for Software and Hardware. Partnership's with industry-leading providers of Enterprise Resource Planning software, including Baan, Lawson, Oracle, and J.D. Edwards, give the Company an in-depth understanding of the best applications available. CIBER EAS is also closely involved in developing software upgrades, as well as defining future software needs. An authorized remarketer of IBM and Hewlett Packard hardware, the Company helps select and configure the most appropriate hardware for the customers' environments. Optimizing warehouse and transportation capabilities is a key element in building efficiency. A product of CIBER EAS, Logistics Pro, combines all warehouse and transportation functions into one cohesive system. Established in the 1970s, the Company now operates a network of more than 80 nationwide locations, and employs a domestic workforce of more than 7,500 professional, technical, and support personnel. **Career Highlights:** Senior Oracle Database Administrator, CIBER Enterprise Application Services (1999-Present); Senior Oracle Database Administrator, CIBER, presenty, The Summit Group, Inc., Senior Oracle Database Administrator (1999-99); Oracle Database Administrator, Paragon Solutions (1997-99); Computer Analyst, Intell Rx (1995-97). **Education:** Duquesne University: M.B.A. (1997), M.S. in Management Information Systems (1995); Pennsylvania State University, B.S. in Science (1989). **Personal Information:** Married to James in 1995. Two children: James Jr. and Audrey. Mrs. Pattock enjoys antique shopping, the outdoors and NASCAR.

Kathleen A. Perras

Health and Human Services Director
Dynamics Research Corporation
60 Frontage Road
Andover, MA 01810
(978) 475-9090
Fax: (978) 475-9090 Ext. 2114
kperras@drc.com
7371

Business Information: Ms. Perras serves as Health and Human Services Director for Dynamics Research Corporation. With the assistance of over 150 staff members, Ms. Perras seeks out potential business clients while maintaining relations with existing clients who include the states of Colorado, New Hampshire, and Arkansas. Within the next year, she plans to expand her customer base within existing state governments and add an additional state customer. She also hopes to continue to strive for consistent on time delivery in her department. Dynamics Research Corporation provides information technology solutions through custom software development, tailoring, and re-engineering services. Established in 1955, the Corporation is headquartered in Andover, Massachusetts and employs over 1,500 people. Annual revenues generated from the fulfillment of service contracts have most recently been reported at $182 million, growing the health and human services business from $4 million in 1996 to $40 million in 1998. **Career Highlights:** Dynamics Research Corporation: Health and Human Services Director (1996-Present): TICARRS Test Director (1994-96), AMP Program Manager (1991-94). **Education:** Union College: M.S. in Computer Science (1975), B.S. in Computer Science (1975). **Personal Information:** Married to John in 1975. Two children: Christopher and Devin. Ms. Perras enjoys gardening, racquetball and indoor soccer.

Billie Peterson

Human Resources Information Systems Specialist
Pervasive Software Inc.
12365 Riata Trace Parkway, Building 2
Austin, TX 78727
(512) 231-6066
Fax: (512) 231-6095
billie.peterson@pervasive.com

7371

Business Information: Utilizing six years of practical work experience, Mrs. Peterson has successfully evolved the Human Resources Department at Pervasive Software Inc. into an efficient working environment. Monitoring the Corporation's internal Web site as Human Resources Information Systems Specialist, she handles support within the boundaries of the office. By superivising the development of the external Web site, she lends her expertise to create a product that potential clients are continually impressed with. Mrs. Peterson regularly works on recovery projects which involve the Corporation's databases, working to rebuild them to current standards. Looking forward to advancement opportunities within the corporate structure, Mrs. Peterson is working on the completion of courses to become a Microsoft Certified Professional. Pervasive Software Inc. designs Web-based applications to assist in the creation of Web sites and e-commerce. The international company was established in 1982 and employs over 400 people worldwide. With competitors such as Microsoft's Sequel Server, the Company is continually striving to develop innovative products for the progressive market. **Career Highlights:** Human Resources Information Systems Specialist, Pervasive Software Inc. (1998-Present); Human Resource Information Systems Analyst, Cirrus Logic (1993-98). **Associations & Accomplishments:** American Business Women's Association; Austin Junior Forum; Laguna Gloria Fiesta. **Education:** University of Arkansas, B.S. (1987). **Personal Information:** Married to Scott in 1993. One child: Colton Lee. Mrs. Peterson enjoys gardening, skiing and cooking.

Christopher J. Potowski

Product Developer
SBPA Systems, Inc.
10777 Westheimer Road, Suite 125
Houston, TX 77042
(713) 974-7272
Fax: (713) 974-3544
chris.potowski@prodigy.net

7371

Business Information: As Product Developer for SBPA Systems, Inc., Mr. Potowski is engaged in programming and development reporting packages for OLAP and ad hoc reporting tools as well as their deployment to clients. He is also responsible for designing data dictionary software and a series of dynamic corporate reports published daily on the Intranet. A systems expert, Mr. Potowski is well versed in Visual Basic, DEC Basic, SQL, ODBC utilities, Impromptu, and Quiz programs. Drawing from an extensive education and previous occupational experience, Mr. Potowski establishes high standards of excellence for other individuals in the industry. He remains on the cutting edge by attending seminars, evaluating new products, reading trade journals, and networking with colleagues in the field. Mr. Potowski plans to expedite continued promotion through the fulfillment of his responsibilities and his involvement in the advancement of operations. He aspires to eventually attain the position of Project Manager. Established in 1976, SBPA Systems, Inc. is an established and reputable software company in the industry. The Corporation is involved in the development of healthcare information systems. Operations employ the expertise of 50 qualified individuals to help meet the diverse needs of its clientele. **Career Highlights:** Product Developer, SBPA Systems, Inc. (1997-Present); Intern, State University of New York (1996); Manager, Electronics Boutique (1993-95). **Associations & Accomplishments:** National Honor Society, Alpha Chi; Presidential Scholar-Dowling College; New York State Teaching Certification - Mathematics. **Education:** State University of New York at Stony Brook, Master's degree (1996); Dowling College: B.A. in Mathematics (1993), 24 graduate credits in Education and Math. **Personal Information:** Mr. Potowski enjoys computers, creative writing, sports, outdoor activities and reading.

Kathryn L. Ramsey

Manager of Technical Publications/Webmaster
Eclipse Inc.
1909 26th Street
Boulder, CO 80302-5701
(303) 938-8801
klramsey@aol.com

7371

Business Information: Mrs. Ramsey serves as Manager of Technical Publications and Webmaster for software manufacturer Eclipse Inc. The focus of her position is to manage the documentation department and to help write new content for the Web site, eclipseinc.com. She specifically deals with all aspects of corporate communication and coordinates and writes press releases. In this capacity, she gathers the necessary information and presents it in a way that presents the Corporation in a positive light. Her dealings with the media also include writing newspaper articles to build a professional image of the Corporation within the community. She constantly updates the Eclipse's Web site and ensures that it contains verified facts and information. Mrs. Ramsey's greatest accomplishments include her volunteer work for the Society of Technical Communications and writing a user's guide that received "Best of Show Award." Learning more about SGML and XML as well as working more with Internet technology, on-line help, and JavaHelp serves as her long-term goals. Established in 1991, Eclipse Inc. publishes specialized computer software for hard goods distributors around the world. Headquartered in Shelton, Connecticut, the Corporation operates offices in the United States, Canada, and Mexico. The 110 employees of the Boulder branch combine efforts to expand the Corporation and meet the needs of the existing customers. **Career Highlights:** Manager of Technical Publications/Webmaster, Eclipse Inc. (1998-Present); Senior Technical Writer, Xilinx, Inc. (1996-98); Senior Technical Writer, XVT Software (1994-96); Senior Technical Writer, Resource Solutions, Inc. (1993-94). **Associations & Accomplishments:** Senior Member, Society for Technical Communications; Boulder Writer's Alliance; Rocky Mountain Internet Users Group. **Education:** Colorado State University, B.S. in Electrical Engineering (1978). **Personal Information:** Married to Neil H. in 1987. Two children: Cynthia and Greg. Mrs. Ramsey enjoys gardening, cooking, jewelry making and church related activities.

Daniel A. Rawsthorne, Ph.D.

Director of Program Management/Development Practices/Chief Architect
Access
3131 Western Avenue, Suite 530
Seattle, WA 98121-1028
(206) 285-4994
Fax: (206) 285-1807
drawstho@acm.org

7371

Business Information: In his role as Director of Program Management and Development and Chief Architect of Access, Dr. Rawsthorne demonstrates adept technical ability as he completes specialized tasks pertaining to the research, development, and design of customized software. Utilizing his extensive education and related work experience, he oversees production and testing as he implements quality assurance standards. Recognized for his talents, he developed aircraft tracking algorithms currently in use at a military test range for an Air Traffic Control System. A celebrated author, Dr. Rawsthorne intends to continue in his position as he participates in continued company growth. He plans to shift his career focus to methological product software in the future. Being a conservative and a realist have contributed to Dr. Rawsthorne's success. In today's progressive society, many businesses seek technical assistance from Access, a leading provider of software and graphic art applications for corporations such as Walgreens and Sears. Located in Seattle, Washington, the Company employs 20 people who generate sales of over $2 million annually. **Career Highlights:** Director of Program Management and Development Practices/Chief Architect (1999-Present); OO Instructor/Mentor, Iconix Software (1998-99); Chief Methodologist/Architect, Odyssey Software (1997-98); Development Manager, BDM (1987-97). **Associations & Accomplishments:** Association of Computing Machinery; Institute of Electronics and Electrical Engineers. **Education:** University of Illinois, Ph.D. (1980); Harvey Mudd College, B.S. (1975). **Personal Information:** Married to Grace in 1975. Two children: Derek and Catherine. Dr. Rawsthorne enjoys bowling.

James A. Renard

Founder/Engineer
JWR Systems
7829 193rd Place SW
Edmonds, WA 98026
(425) 778-0441
jrenard@jwrsys.com

7371

Business Information: The Founder of JWR Systems, Mr. Renard utilizes more than 20 years of practical experience in serving as its Engineer. He assumes accountability for the entire spectrum of the Company's daily operational and administrative functions. Working with the sale and installation of media retrieval systems, he develops various customized software programs. Mr. Renard creates specialty controls for business clients and devotes attention to restaurant and park themes. Additionally, he is involved in Web design and CD entertainment. His goal is to produce a system with TITV that will function with the latest technology. He believes his greatest professional achievement has been the founding of JWR Systems. Dedicated to the further development of the Company, Mr. Renard credits his current success to his honesty, knowing the right people, and being in the right place at the right time. Utilizing standard PC components, JWR Systems specializes in providing custom programming solutions for the control of audio and video systems. The Company was created in 1991 and has enjoyed a great deal of success offering its services to international businesses. A growing company, currently staffed by three talented individuals, provide quality custom programming. **Career Highlights:** Founder/Engineer, JWR Systems (1999-Present); Audio Video Design Engineer, AEI Music Network, Inc. (1994-99); Electrical and Video Engineer, Rank Video Services (1989-93); Electrical and Video Engineer, Technicolor (1983-89). **Education:** North American Technical Institute, A.S. in Electrical Engineering (1978). **Personal Information:** Mr. Renard enjoys musical composition and flying.

Carl W. Reynolds

Owner/Operator
Hyperbole Software, Unlimited
9383 East Tate Ridge Road
Madison, IN 47250-8754
(812) 839-6635
hyperbole@wolfscratch.com

7371

Business Information: As Owner and Operator of Hyperbole Software, Unlimited, Mr. Reynolds is actively involved in software development as well as Web page, graphics, and computer program design and implementation. While consulting for such companies as IBM, NUNES, and General Electric, he has done robotic and computer grpahics research. He has published five articles relating to computer graphics and robitics and was selected for inclusion in Who's Who in Computer Graphics from 1984 through 1986. Mr. Reynolds is looking forward to development of more Web projects and further development in the Internet community. Having served for 10 years in the United States Navy, he has a wide array of knowledge directly relating to his current vocation. A savvy technical expert, he Mr. Reynolds attributes his success to his high level of dedication to customer satisfaction and his innate ability to treat all people with the utmost respect. Hyperbole Software, Unlimited, founded in 1983, provides software design consulting services, Web page design, computer graphic services as well as scientific and engineering programs including both physics and robotics. Based in Madison, Indiana, the Company reports annual revenues in excess of $75,000. **Career Highlights:** Owner/Operator, Hyperbole Software, Unlimited (1983-Present); Principal Grpahics Specialist, NYNEX Information Resources (1992-1995); Graphics Consultant, IBM, Research (1987-1989); Robotics Research. **Associations & Accomplishments:** Bahai Faith. **Education:** New York Institute of Technology, M.A. in Computer Graphics (1995); University of Idaho, B.S. in Physics (1979). **Personal Information:** Married to Anita in 1980. Five children: Amy, Megan, Chaun, Christopher, and Chase.

Nicholas J. Ricciardelli

President/Chief Executive Officer
ICC International
7944 East Beck Lane, Suite 210
Scottsdale, AZ 85260-1774
(480) 367-1313
Fax: (480) 367-1312
nick@iccjobs.com

7371

Business Information: The President of ICC International, Mr. Ricciardelli also serves as its Chief Executive Officer.

Presiding over the day-to-day operations and administration, he assumes the responsibility of determining the business direction of the Company. He facilitates promotional activities on behalf of ICC International to develop new business and increase sales. Mr. Ricciardelli directly supervises a staff of 30 qualified professionals and acts as the liaison for clients. Citing his determination and will to succeed as the key to his professional success, he states that knowledge is power and service is paramount. Always alert to new opportunities, techniques, and approaches, Mr. Ricciardelli is committed to the further development and expansion of the Company. His success reflects his ability to think outside the box and aggressively take on new challenges. ICC International is a privately held information technology services company. Headquartered in Scottsdale, Arizona, the Company offers software engineering and computer programming to companies and corporations across the globe. **Career Highlights:** President/Chief Executive Officer, ICC International (Present). **Personal Information:** Mr. Ricciardelli enjoys golf.

Susan E. Richardson
Systems Administrator
Wang Healthcare
Hudson, NH 03051
(978) 439-1970
Fax: (978) 670-1291
susan.richardson@wang.com

7371

Business Information: Ms. Richardson serves as the Systems Administrator for Wang Healthcare. In her capacity, she conducts management and support of a host of network servers, workstations, and Web servers. Administering and controlling systems tools, she is currently the only information systems professional employed by the Company. Possessing a superior understanding of technology, Ms. Richardson is responsible for all aspects of networking, rebuilding machines, and maintaining Web sites. Attributing her career success to her peers, mentors, and supervisors, she plans to continue working for the Company in this capacity. Looking forward to assisting in the completion of future corporate goals, Ms. Richardson's ability to take on challenges and deliver results has enabled her to maintain the functionality and operational status of the information systems functions. Established in 1997, Wang Healthcare is a start-up company which produces emergency medical record software for clinics and doctors offices. Headquartered in Billerica, Massachusetts, the Company employs 50 personnel. **Career Highlights:** Systems Administrator, Wang Healthcare (1999-Present); Management Information Systems Manager, Barlo Signs (1998-99); NT Support Specialist, Borden Global Packaging (1991-98). **Education:** New Hampshire College, B.S. (1995); Learningtree Institute: WindowsNT 4.0 Certification, PC Support and Troubleshooting Certification. **Personal Information:** One child: Keith.

Marck R. Robinson
President
Power Data Corporation
500 108th Avenue NE, Suite 960
Bellevue, WA 98004
(425) 637-9960
Fax: (425) 637-9971
marck@powerdata.com

7371

Business Information: Functioning as President of Power Data Corporation, Mr. Robinson coordinates all design for new accounts. He is responsible for determining the overall strategic direction and business contribution of the information systems function. Before forming Power Data Corporation, Mr. Robinson served as Software Engineering Manager with ESCA Corporation. An experienced, 13 year technology professional, he is vocal in the development of programs for each and every client. With an extensive electronics background, he establishes high standards for others in the industry to follow. His career success reflects his leadership ability to build strong teams with synergy and technical strength, think out-of-the-box, and take on new challenges. Mr. Robinson's strategic objective is to see the growth and expansion of the Corporation within the industry. Power Data Corporation provides the service of software development. Created in 1990, the operation now utilizes a staff of 10 to oversee the daily office operations. Offering the design, implementation, and management of original software, makes Power Data Corporation appealing to clientele with unique products and ventures. **Career Highlights:** President, Power Data Corporation (1990-Present); Software Engineering Manager, ESCA Corporation (1987-90). **Associations & Accomplishments:** Washington Software Alliance; Institute of Electronics and Electrical Engineers. **Education:** Washington State University, B.S in Computer Science (1986). **Personal Information:** Mr. Robinson enjoys skiing and scuba diving.

Robert "Rob" Romano
Director
BarPoint.com
1 East Broward Boulevard
Fort Lauderdale, FL 33301
(305) 742-5099
rob@planconnect.com

7371

Business Information: As Director of Sales for BarPoint.com, Mr. Romano is responsible for the creation of advertising strategies for wireless e-commerce partners and digital marketing projects. Recruited out of college to work for economist and current Federal Reserve chairman Alan Greenspan, Mr. Romano is also the founder of Work Comp Solutions. Drawing from his extensive technical expertise and proven hands-on experience, he develops and executes high-powered marketing strategies for his clients. In the future, Mr. Romano hopes to expand the digital publishing field and the international wireless industry as well as open an office in the European market. His professional success is attributed to his intellect and honesty in dealing with his clients. Founded in 1998, BarPoint.com is on the consumers' edge of Internet-based commerce. Using the universal product codes that appear on millions of products, consumers can instantly obtain specific product information on the Internet or via wireless devices. Additionally, the Company has a unique, patent-pending search engine. Presently, BarPoint.com employs 55 professional and technical experts. **Career Highlights:** Director of Sales, Barpoint.com (1999-Present); Vice President, KMGI.com (1998-99); Chief Operating Officer, Work Comp Solutions (1991-97). **Education:** Pace University, M.B.A. (1986); State University of New York at Stonybrook, B.A. in Economics. **Personal Information:** Married to Consuelo in 1986.

Jerry D. Russ
Senior Computer Technician
Walls Computers Etc.
615 Park Avenue, Apartment 3
Hot Springs, AR 71901
(501) 525-8484
jruss@ipa.net

7371

Business Information: Functioning in the role of Senior Computer Technician with Walls Computers Etc., Mr. Russ is responsible for building computer units and performing major repairs. Beginning his association with the Company more than four years ago, he custom creates systems and upgrades in order to keep clients on the cutting edge of technology. Coordinating resources, time lines, schedules, assignments, and budgets also fall within the purview of Mr. Russ' responsibilities. He performs with unusual accuracy, thoroughness, and effectiveness, as well as achieves the highest standard of excellence. Quickly establishing his presence in the field, Mr. Russ' future goal is to continue to expedite continued promotion through his involvement in the advancement of operations. His career success reflects his ability to think outside the box and aggressively take on new challenges. Walls Computers Etc. provides a variety of quality technology services. The Company resells computers that they have built or rebuilt as well as provides Internet services. Established in 1995, Walls Computers Etc. employs a staff of seven committed individuals to help meet the diverse needs of its clientele. **Career Highlights:** Senior Computer Technician, Walls Computers Etc. (1995-Present). **Education:** Garland County Community College, A.A.S. in Data Processing (1995). **Personal Information:** Mr. Russ enjoys computer gaming.

Michael Safford
Manager of Desktop Technologies
Autodesk, Inc.
24 Morrison Road
Windham, NH 03087
(603) 621-3103
Fax: (603) 621-3381
mike.safford@autodesk.com

7371

Business Information: Functioning in the capacity of Manager of Desktop Technologies for Autodesk, Inc., Mr. Safford advises the information technology desktop technicians working within the Corporation's network offices in America. He supervises a staff of 28 people individually directed towards a specific portion of each program. His highest accomplishment while with the Corporation has been his work in designing an integrating program to unite two companies through software adaptations made to their computer databases. In the future, Mr. Safford would like to start his own consulting firm. Testing, evaluating, and being an instructor has kept him on the bleeding edge of technology. His professional success is attributed to being in the right place at the right time and his ability to produce results and aggressively take on new challenges. Autodesk, Inc. is the fourth largest software company in the world. Founded in 1984, the Corporation has specialized its software development to concentrate on CAD engineering software programs. A team of 2,600 employees brainstorm more effective techniques and user-friendly tasks that are possibilities for added features to current programs. Altogether, the internationally spread Corporation produces $500 million annually through the sales and marketing of its product. **Career Highlights:** Manager of Desktop Technologies, Autodesk, Inc. (1996-Present); Information Technology Manager, Softdesk Inc. (1992-95); Manager of Technical Services, Concord Hospital (1990-92); Senior Systems Integrator, Versyss Inc. (1985-90). **Associations & Accomplishments:** Eagle Boy Scout; Alpha Beta Kappa Society; New Hampshire Job Training Council. **Education:** A.A. (1985); Rhode Island School of Electronics; E/TAC Technical School. **Personal Information:** Married to Loriann Four children: Kevin, Benjamin, Samual, and Lydia. Mr. Safford enjoys time with his family.

Timothy R. Salaver
• • • ◉ • • •

President/Chief Executive Officer
Cornerstone Systems Solutions, Inc.
3960 Howard Hughes Parkway, 5th Floor
Las Vegas, NV 89109
(702) 990-3877
Fax: (702) 990-3501
tsalavar@cornerstone-solutions.com

7371

Business Information: Mr. Salaver is President and Chief Executive Officer of Cornerstone Systems Solutions, Inc. He is responsible for the strategic direction and corporate vision, including client relations, systems and solutions design and development, human resources, sales and marketing, and logistical network. Before starting Cornerstone Systems Solutions, Mr. Salaver served as Financial Systems Manager with National Information Group and Implementation Manager for Lawson Software. His history includes fulfilling the role of Member of Board of Directors of Accent Teller Services, Inc. As a 12 year technology professional, Mr. Salaver owns an established record of delivering results. His success in the technology field reflects his ability to build teams with synergy, technical strengths, and a customer oriented attitude as well as think out-of-the-box and take on new challenges and responsibilities. In 1995, he won a Grammy with the San Francisco Symphony Chorus. "Surround yourself with people who are smarter than you," is cited as Mr. Salaver's advice. His strategic plans include increasing e-commerce business and developing Internet products. A systems integration and consulting company, Cornerstone Systems Solutions, Inc. services the needs of fast growing startups and established Fortune 1000 companies. The Corporation provides business-to-business solutions, e-commerce, Internet access, and electronic publishing with a core focus on ERP and supply chain management. National in scope, Cornerstone Systems Solutions was established in 1998. Headquartered in Las Vegas, Nevada, the Corporation operates a network of offices in Indianapolis, Indiana and Dallas, Texas. Presently, Cornerstone Systems Solutions employs 10 people at the Las Vegas office who help generate revenues in excess of $1.5 million annually. **Career Highlights:** President/Chief Executive Officer, Cornerstone Systems Solutions, Inc. (1998-Present); Financial Systems Manager, National Information Group (1997-98); Implementation Manager, Lawson Software (1996). **Associations & Accomplishments:** Member of the Board of Directors, Accent Teller Services, Inc. **Education:** Golden Gate University: B.Sc. (1987), A.A. degree in Business Administration. **Personal Information:** Two children: Malorie and Trevor.

Tim A. Sander
Senior Technical Advisor
Applied Systems, Inc
200 Applied Parkway
University Park, IL 60466-4131
(708) 534-5575
Fax: (708) 534-3286
tsander@appliedsystems.com

7371

Business Information: Utilizing several years of service with Applied Systems, Inc., Mr. Sander contributes his talents and expertise as the Senior Technical Advisor of the Corporation, performing varied sales engineering, troubleshooting, and training functions as well as acting Advisor to the Board of Directors. A certified Microsoft Trainer, Mr. Sander is equipped to mentor professionals in the technological industry including corporate board employees, customers, and international employees. Continuing his years of commitment to the Corporation, Mr. Sander intends to remain in the information technology industry, gaining satisfaction from its several challenging qualities. A multi-million dollar corporate leader, Applied Systems, Inc. engages in the development of software for the insurance industry, offering services to major brokers and agencies around the world. Employing the skills of 900 professionally trained information technology specialists, Applied Systems draws on 17 years of service to satisfy the diverse needs of their extensive client base. Recently experiencing phenomenal growth within the industry, the Corporation has developed into one of the largest software developers in the country, reporting annual revenues in excess of $86 million. **Career Highlights:** Applied Systems, Inc: Senior Technical Advisor (1997-Present), Director of Technical Services (1994-96), Manager of Network Administration (1993-94). **Associations & Accomplishments:** Lowell Volunteer Fire Department; FFII; EMT; Eagle Scout. **Education:** SSC (1989). **Personal Information:** Married to Leisa in 1995. One child: Robert. Mr. Sander enjoys water sports, hiking and biking.

Raul Jose Santos
General Manager
Informatica Asociada
Fuente de Piramides 1650A
Tecamachalco, Mexico 54300
(525) 520-4099
Fax: (525) 520-4099
ia@acm.org

7371

Business Information: Mr. Santos, relying on his extensive academic ties, business experience, and management skills, jump started Informatica Asociada in 1993. As owner, he fulfills the role of General Manager responsible for all day-to-day administration and operational activities. He sets the technical and business direction and vision, and formulates both strategic and tactical marketing plans. Mr. Santos, well versed in technology, is principally involved in design and development of state-of-the-art software applications. In addition to supervising and mentoring three employees, he handles numerous resource planning functions to include personnel staffing and management; overseeing time lines, schedules, and assignments; negotiating contracts; and maintaining good client relationships. He is very proud of the quality work that is performed on the customer's behalf. Working with users to analyze, specify, and design business applications, providing technical and analytical advice and assistance during the development phase, and planning and overseeing evaluation and integration of new technology systems development methodologies, data administration, capacity planning, training, and technical support also fall within the scope of Mr. Santos' responsibilities. His plans for the future include expanding software development operations nationally and internationally. Informatica Asociada, established in 1993, is engaged in development of software and hardware as well as performing maintenance on systems architectures. The Company is manned by four persons who provide customized technical services. Currently, Informatica Asociada is located in Tecamachalco, Mexico. **Career Highlights:** General Manager, Informatica Asociada (1993-Present); Consultant, Loteria Nacional Para Assist. Pub. (1992-93). **Associations & Accomplishments:** Associate Member, Institute of Electrical and Electronics Engineers, Inc.; Association of Computing Machinery; CLP Notes Principals Application Developer R4; CLP Notes System Administrator R4. **Education:** Georgia Institute of Technology, M.Sc. in Information and Computer Science (1992), M.Sc. in Industrial Engineering in Manufacturing Systems (1992); University of Lancaster, M.A. in Systems Management (1985); Itesm Estado de Mexico, Industrial and System Engineers (1984). **Personal Information:** Mr. Santos enjoys chess.

William Anthony Schubert
Software Architect
Unlimited Solutions Inc.
400 Venture Drive
Columbus, OH 43035
(614) 840-1400

7371

Business Information: Mr. Schubert serves as a Software Architect for Unlimited Solutions Inc. He designs and creates tools and prototype new designs for systems. While performing his post, Mr. Schubert was instrumental in acquiring a multi-million dollar contract with the Burton Group. The Burton Group International is one of several clients utilizing the Company's services. Unlimited Solutions Inc provides point of sale systems software compatible with Windows NT. Established in 1992, USI has become competitive in the global market and employs over 100 professionals in the field. **Career Highlights:** Software Architect, Unlimited Solutions Inc. (1995-Present); Consultant, JTS - Huntington Bank (1994-95); Software Developer, Out of State Lotto Network Inc. (1993-94). **Associations & Accomplishments:** Microsoft Certified Professional; National Audubon Society. **Education:** Edinboro University of Pennsylvania, B.A. in Mathematics (1990). **Personal Information:** Mr. Schubert enjoys travel.

Felix A. Schupp
Vice President of Software Engineering
MMT Corporation
50 Airport Parkway, Suite 104
San Jose, CA 95110
(408) 437-7725
Fax: (403) 437-4987
fschupp@acm.org

7371

Business Information: As the Vice President of Software Engineering of MMT Corporation, Mr. Schupp oversees and directs all aspects of software engineering. In this context, he supervises a team of software engineers in the architecture and design of cutting-edge software solutions. Possessing an excellent understanding of technology, Mr. Schupp is also engaged in systems integration implementation. Establishing an international presence, his focus is on the discovery, investigation, and deployment of emerging technologies, helping his clientele maintain flexibility, efficiency, and profitability in the information technology age. Deriving great pride from being published in a prestigious German technology magazine dealing with "Real Time Operations System", Mr. Schupp is also proud of his integration of streaming media. Attributing his success to being in the right place at the right time, he hopes to eventually attain his Ph.D. Established in 1997, MMT Corporation is a computer basesd solutions provider. Also developing streaming media applications for information appliance, the Corporation is engaged in the development and production of multimedia enabled network solutions for embedded systems. Presently, the Corporation employs a technical and professional staff of 12 experts. **Career Highlights:** Vice President of Software Engineering, MMT Corporation (2000-Present); Director of Strategic Management, Software Service LLC (1997-99). **Associations & Accomplishments:** Association of Computing Machinery; Institute of Electrical and Electronics Engineers; Phi Kappa Phi; Golden Key National Honor Society; Usenix; SAGE; Senator of Student Government, Gold Gate University. **Education:** San Jose State University, B.S. in Engineering (2000). **Personal Information:** Mr. Schupp enjoys diving, sailing and snowboarding.

Richard Schweitzer
President
Savvy Data
3201 West Commercial Boulevard, #118
Pompano Beach, FL 33309
(954) 486-2600
Fax: (954) 486-7086
r.schweitzer@savvydata.com

7371

Business Information: Serving as the President of Savvy Data, Mr. Schweitzer oversees and directs all aspects of day to day administration and operational activities. He determines the strategic direction and formulates innovative marketing and business plans to enhance the Company's standing in the market place. Possessing an excellent understanding of his field, Mr. Schweitzer is in charge of acquisitions, coordinating with consultants, researching and indentifying new markets, and assessing the needs of clients. The most rewarding aspect of his career is starting up his own pulishing company in 1983, and producing Better Business Bureau Consumer Resource Books. Attributing his success to 25 years of management experience, determination, and networking, Mr. Schweitzer plans to continue pursuing the advancement of operations. Founded in 1997, Savvy Data is an information provider and software developer. The Company's software is developed to provide access to sensitive reports, such as criminal records, credit information, and driving records. Serving a clientele across the United States, the Company employs 25 personnel and supplies software to institutions, to include police departments, human resources departments, and courts. **Career Highlights:** Savvy Data: President (1999-Present), Chief Operating Officer (1998-99), Vice President Sales (1998). **Education:** Chabot College (1969). **Personal Information:** Married to Linda in 1993. Two children: Scott and Shannon. Mr. Schweitzer enjoys softball and bowling.

Thomas R. Seney
Manager of Software Development
RTC Technologies, Inc.
8338 Washington Avenue, Suite 114
Racine, WI 53406-3770
(262) 884-4488
Fax: (262) 884-4499
tseney@rtctech.com

7371

Business Information: Serving as Manager of Software Development, Mr. Seney has been providing his expert services with RTC Technologies, Inc. since 2000. He coordinates project management, serves as the chief liaison for clients, oversees business details, and creates custom software. Utilizing 22 years of experience in the computer field, he continues to assist the Corporation in the completion

of corporate goals. Capitalizing on his extensive experience in all phases of operation, he monitors the productivity of the staff, formulating a hands-on management style with an above average aptitude for problem solving. Always alert to new opportunities in the technology field, Mr. Seney continues to grow professionally through the fulfillment of his responsibilities and his involvement in the advancement of operations. Engaging in the application of computer systems into business actions, RTC Technologies, Inc. was established in 1990. Located in Racine, Wisconsin, the Corporation employs the skilled services of 25 individuals who assist in the design, development, and integration of the Corporation's specialized services and products. Analyzing the client's business structure, software is custom designed in order to improve efficiency and productivity. **Career Highlights:** Manager of Software Development, RTC Technologies, Inc. (2000-Present); Computer Consultant, IBS, Inc. (1994-2000); Computer Consultant, Omni Resources, Inc. (1989-94). **Associations & Accomplishments:** South Milwaukee Lions International; City of South Milwaukee Alderman; City of South Milwaukee School Board Member; Letter of Accommodation, S.C. Johnson Wax (1993); Associated System Management Award (1990). **Education:** University of Wisconsin at Parkside, B.B.A. (1981). **Personal Information:** Married to Ramona M. in 1978. Three children: Jason, Stephanie, and Samantha. Mr. Seney enjoys sports.

Azmat Bilal Shami
Account Manager
Cressoft Inc.
6860 South Yosemite Court, Suite 2000
Englewood, CO 80112
(303) 488-2134
Fax: (303) 488-2127
azmat@aol.com

7371

Business Information: As Account Manager of Cressoft Inc., Mr. Shami supervises the daily activities of his 10 person staff. In this capacity, he approves project design and coordinates customer systems offering impressive customer services to clients. Utilizing his education and practical work experience, Mr. Shami formulates marketing campaigns for the airline industry that incorporates fresh ideas to maintain the Company's competitive edge. Serving as a representative of the Company while meeting with clients to discuss satisfaction evaluations, Mr. Shami maintains corporate standards while symbolizing the positive image Cressoft Inc. strives for. Enjoying the challenges of his current position, he aspires to advancement within the corporate structure as he remains abreast of technology changes. Cressoft Inc. specializes in the development of custom software applications for the telecommunications and e-commerce industries. Offering consulting services, the Corporation also serves many clients in the financial and airline industries. Established in 1994, the $6 million company employs 40 people at the Englewood, Colorado location which is one of five international business centers. **Career Highlights:** Cressoft Inc.: Account Manager (1998-Present), Senior Software Engineer (1996-98); Crescent Software Products: Principal Software Engineer (1995-96), Senior Software Engineer (1992-94). **Associations & Accomplishments:** Lawrence College Old Gallians Association; Foundation for Advancement of Science and Technology Alumni. **Education:** ICS-Karachi University, B.S. in Computer Science (1991). **Personal Information:** Married to Komal in 1999. Mr. Shami enjoys golf, travel, dining, ping pong and fishing.

M. Lea Shaw
Manager of Customer Educational Services
Carleton Corporation
700 Technology Park Drive
Billerica, MA 01821-4134
(978) 667-1110
Fax: (978) 439-9229
leas@carleton.com

7371

Business Information: After taking a management information systems course as an undergraduate based on her husband's advice, Ms. Shaw fell in love with information technologies. Currently serving as Manager of Customer Educational Services with Carleton Corporation, Ms. Shaw is responsible for all documentation and training aspects of the Corporation. Working closely with a group of technical writers, she is involved in the production of manuals and online help manuals for various products produced by the Corporation. Drawing from 18 years of extensive practical occupational experience, she successfully manages and motivates her group of trainers and technical writers. Ms. Shaw attributes her success to her tenacity and problem solving skills and aspires to attain the position of Director. Carleton Corporation is engaged in the development of software providing datamart, data warehouse software in the customer relationship management arena. Established in 1982, the Corporation is a public company employing the expertise of 90 individuals dedicated to customer relations management. Headquartered in Minnetonka, Minnesota, the Corporation reports an estimated annual revenue of $8 million. **Career Highlights:** Manager of Customer Educational Services,

Carleton Corporation (1998-Present); Senior Trainer, American International Group (1992-98); Manager of Training, Computer Assistance (1989-92); Senior Programmer/Analyst, Associate Gorvers of Nebreska, Inc. (1983-89). **Associations & Accomplishments:** President, New Hampshire Parent Head Club; Editor, New Hampshire Parrot DISE Pages. **Education:** Rivier College: M.B.A. (1991), B.A. **Personal Information:** Married to Steven W. in 1976. Ms. Shaw enjoys music, travel, stained glass and charitable works.

John E. Simmons

Vice President of Product Design
InAir
18221 Edison Avenue
Chesterfield, MO 63005
(314) 406-2744
jsimmons@inair.com

7371

Business Information: Dedicated to the successs of InAir, Mr. Simmons applies his knowledge and expertise in the field of information technology by serving as Vice President of Product Design. In this capacity, he is charged with the responsibility to meet with a variety of Company members and clients to develop new developmental methods and implement them into the customer's infrastructure. The state of the art systems are utilized to track inspections, upgrades, and component replacements. Capitalizing on more than 11 years of hands on experience, Mr. Simmons conducts presentations on the Company's new technical solutions. He is certified in systems engineering and database administration, and is currently working on his application developer certification. His plans for his career include either becoming Chief Information Officer of InAir or Vice President and Chief Information Officer of an airline or aviation company. InAir is a manufacturing firm that develops, distributes, and installs software for maintenance and engineering clients. The Company caters to the aviation industry through the manufacuring of various flight operations components. Established in 1996, the Company is located in Chesterfield, Missouri and functions under the direction of more than 125 professionals who facilitate smooth business operations. The Company currently generates annual revenues exceeding $25 million. **Career Highlights:** Vice President of Product Design, InAir (1998-Present); Senior Director of Management Information Systems, Sabre Decision Technologists (1993-98); Senior Director of Planning and Management Information Systems, Lockhead Commercial Aircraft (1990-93); Senior Director of Planning, Dee Howard (1989-90). **Associations & Accomplishments:** Institute of Industrial Engineers; Council of Logistic Management. **Education:** Southern Illinois University, M.B.A. (1986); Maryville University, B.S. in Mathematics (1978). **Personal Information:** Married to Michelle in 1994. One child: Matthew. Mr. Simmons enjoys golf.

Jagdeep Singh

Senior Analyst
Envision Financial System, Inc.
3701 Parkview lane, Suite 8D
Irvine, CA 92612
(714) 247-0030
Fax: (714) 247-0029
jag-deep@hotmail.com

7371

Business Information: As the Senior Analyst for Envision Financial System, Inc., Mr. Singh performs Internet and C/S software design and development. He is in charge of two products, the Power Agent and the Power Agent Administrator. Possessing an excellent understanding of technology, he continues to grow professionally through the fulfillment of his responsibilities and his involvement in the advancement of operations. Dedicated to the success of the Company, Mr. Singh plans to continue to work in this position, staying involved in the growth and expansion of the Company. His success reflects his ability to take on challenges and deliver results on behalf of the Company and its clients. Established in 1996, Envision Financial System, Inc. specializes in software development and applications software. Employing 25 personnel, the Company manufactures seven products in the financial industry. The Company reports annual sales of $1.8 million and is dedicated to providing all customer with a high quality product. **Career Highlights:** Senior Analyst, Envision Financial System, Inc. (1999-Present); Senior System Analyst, Cendent Mortgage (1999); Systems Analyst, CSX Transportion (1998); Programmer, Southern California Edison (1998). **Education:** Thapar University, Master of Computer Application (1995); Delhi Productivity Council, M.B.A. (1992); New Delhi University, B.S. in Computer Science (1991). **Personal Information:** Married to Kamal J. Kaur in 1999. Mr. Singh enjoys music, soccer and tennis.

Christi L. Sink

Marketer
Latent Technology
5646 Milton Street, Suite 329
Dallas, TX 75206
(214) 987-2227
Fax: (214) 987-1455
christi@latent.com

7371

Business Information: Serving as a Marketer for Latent Technology, Ms. Sink is responsible for the promotion of customers' Web sites. In this capacity, she directs promotion programs, combining advertising with purchase incentives to increase sales of products and services. She assists clients in developing closer contact with purchasers and providing purchase incentives such as discounts, samples, gifts, rebates, coupons, and sweepstakes. Dedicated to the success of Latent Technology, Ms. Sink plans to continue in her line of work and assist in the completion of future corporate goals. Established in 1997, Latent Technology is a Web site development firm. The Company concentrates on e-commerce solutions for small to medium sized businesses as well as provides services to other businesses. Local in scope, the Dallas, Texas operation employs the expertise of a work force of 16 professional, technical, and support staff. **Career Highlights:** Marketer, Latent Technology (1998-Present). **Education:** Arkansas State University, Associate's degree in History. **Personal Information:** Ms. Sink enjoys sports.

Wolfgang Sitterberg

Group Manager
Citrix System, Inc.
6400 Northwest 6th Way
Fort Lauderdale, FL 33309
(954) 267-3000
wolfgang.sitterberg@citrix.com

7371

Business Information: Utilizing an extensive managerial and technical background, Mr. Sitterberg is the Senior Manager of Citrix System, Inc. In his position, he is responsible for overseeing and directing worldwide sales and i-business operations. Moreover, he is charged with managing the information business ASP market and conducting review of all programs. Mr. Sitterberg supervises a staff of employees who report directly to him with any problems or mishaps that may arise. Highly regarded, he possesses an excellent understanding of his field and strong leadership skills. In the future, Mr. Sitterberg looks forward to continuing with the Corporation in his current position and assisting in the growth of business. Located in Fort Lauderdale, Florida, Citrix System, Inc. is an Internet and networking software server based manufacturing company. Founded in 1989, the Corporation operates on a national level, employing over 1,200 dedicated workers. Furthermore, the Corporation is committed to providing quality services and achieving extreme customer satisfaction. **Career Highlights:** Senior Manager, Citrix System, Inc. (Present); Chief Operating Officer, Interactive Network Solutions (1996); Engagement Manager of Business Solutions, AMDAHL Germany (1994-96); Engineering Services Manager, AEG/Modcomp (1984-94). **Education:** University of Konstanz, B.A. (1984). **Personal Information:** Married in 1988. Mr. Sitterberg enjoys golf, petangue and travel.

Jennifer M. Smith

Consultant
SS&C Technologies
30 West Monroe, Suite 1700
Chicago, IL 60603
(312) 443-7681
Fax: (312) 443-1279
jensmith@sscinc.com

7371

Business Information: Ms. Smith functions in the capacity of a Consultant with SS&C Technologies. She is responsible for implementing trading front-end software, installation, sets up, and report writing. Working closely together with her clients, she determines their needs and evaluates the situation in order to make an appropriate recommendation regarding the updating needs of the client. Looking to the 21st Century, Ms. Smith hopes to increase her knowledge in the industry and continue working in the industry, increasing her background and experience. Her success is attributed to her upbringing by her parents, academic ties, and knowledge obtained through reading. SS&C Technologies specializes in software development for investment firms. The Firm creates specifically designed programs to promote the success of its clients through the user friendly software it provides. The Firm hosts five United States and five international locations, with its headquarters operating out of Connecticut. **Career Highlights:** Consultant, SS&C Technologies (1998-Present); Accounting & Finance Associate, Citadel Investment Group (1997-98); Senior Auditor, Chicago Board of Trade (1994-97). **Associations & Accomplishments:** Volunteer, March of Dimes; Volunteer, Starlight Foundation; Alpha Phi Sorority Alumni. **Education:** Miami University of Ohio, B.S. in Finance & Accounting (1994). **Personal Information:** Ms. Smith enjoys travel, reading, physical fitness and spending time with her friends.

Leo V. Snetsinger

Information Technology Manager
ROI Systems
5701 Kentucky Avenue North
Minneapolis, MN 55408
(612) 797-5541
Fax: (612) 595-9450
lvs@online-ontime.com

7371

Business Information: As Information Technology Manager of ROI Systems, Mr. Snetsinger demonstrates an ability to recognize management problems and develop clear and concise solutions for the enhancement of technical support. He is charged with the responsibility of maintaining the functionality of computer operations and assisting on support help lines. Mr. Snetsinger also ensures that all technical employees are able to make full use of software capabilities by continually upgrading Web sites and effectively managing corpoarte Internal and Intranet networks. A dedicated and remarkable asset to ROI Systems, Mr. Snetsinger wishes to continue his education in order to obtain a position at Microsoft, while operating and developing his own consulting company. His success reflects his ability to think outside the box, aggressively take on challenges, and deliver results. ROI Systems is one of the largest software developers for ERP solutions in the United States. Established in 1985, the Company utilizes the combined talents of global business partners and operates through offices throughout the world. Clients consists of large corporations who are serious about the development of their companies. Presently, ROI Systems employs a work force of 250 dependable and highly skilled people who work hard to assist companies in find solutions. **Career Highlights:** ROI Systems: Information Technology Manager (1997-Present), Information Systems Manager (1996-97), Help Line Technician (1995-96). **Associations & Accomplishments:** Network Professional Association. **Education:** Bridge Data, Microsoft Certified Systems Engineer..

Michael P. Songy

Software Engineering Manager
Creative Labs, Inc.
1655 McCarthy Boulevard
Milpitas, CA 95035
(408) 546-6457
Fax: (408) 954-1260
msongy@creaf.com

7371

Business Information: Serving as Software Engineering Manager at Creative Labs, Inc., Mr. Songy is responsible for the development of software and some hardware. Focusing primarily on graphics, Mr. Songy draws from over three years of practical occupational experience in the field. He has developed the skills needed to maintain the highest standards of professional excellence and attributes his success to perseverance and believing that if you set your mind to something, you can do it. A successful systems expert, he hopes to continue working with graphics and establish a business of his own in the future. Mr. Songy's advice is "keep studying and learning and staying on top of technology." Creative Labs, Inc. is engaged in the development of multimedia and personal digital entertainment hardware and software. Headquartered in Singapore, local operations in Milpitas, California are also involved in the development of graphics and speakers. **Career Highlights:** Software Engineering Manager, Creative Labs, Inc. (1998-Present); Senior Software Engineer, Quantum 3D (1997-98); Software Engineer, Holy Grail Productions, Inc. (1997). **Associations & Accomplishments:** Computer Game Developers Association. **Education:** University of Texas (1988-93). **Personal Information:** Mr. Songy enjoys computer gaming, graphics programing and skiing.

Daniel E. Stalker, Jr.

Systems Administrator
Augmentix, Inc.
5151 East Broadway Boulevard, Suite 600
Tucson, AZ 85711
(520) 547-6544
Fax: (520) 790-3034
stalker-daniel@augmentix.com

7371

Business Information: In his position as Systems Administrator for Augmentix, Inc., Mr. Stalker is responsible for engineering and administering all Internet, Intranet, and

Extranet servers, and ensuring the systems infrastructure is functional and operational. Additionally, he provides top-tier support to service teams, supervises systems availability, and ensures all security measures are in place. Utilizing more than 15 years of extensive experience in his field, Mr. Stalker encourages and facilitates optimum performance among the staff and ensures that all employees work together to achieve a common goal. He has enjoyed substantial success in his present position and looks forward to assisting in the completion of future Company goals. "Do your homework," is cited as Mr. Stalker's advice. Augmentix, Inc. engages in the design, implementation, and support of world-class technologies that augment business performance by coordinating, motivating, and focusing on human talents. Established in 1993, the Corporation employs the skilled services of 25 individuals to facilitate all aspects of operation. Originally, the Corporation developed hospital software and paging systems, and has since delved into the world of consulting and the coordination of management teams. Presently, the Corporation reports annual revenues in excess of $3 million. **Career Highlights:** Systems Administrator, Augementix, Inc. (1997-Present); Data Specialist, The Way International Bookstore (1989-94); Consultant, C&W Computers (1986-89). **Associations & Accomplishments:** Coordinator, The Way International (1975-Present). **Education:** Cleveland State University, B.S. in Computer Information Systems (1986); The Way College of Emporia, Bachelor's degree in Biblical Studies (1986). **Personal Information:** Married to Sheryl Hope. Mr. Stalker enjoys ministry, teaching classes and skin diving.

Amy E. Stephens

Director of Customer Service
Fascor
1014 Vine Street, Suite 1700
Cincinnati, OH 45202-1179
(513) 421-1777
Fax: (513) 421-1191
stephens5@prodigy.net

7371

Business Information: As Director of Customer Service at Fascor, Ms. Stephens oversees operations of various departments to ensure quality service to customers. Monitoring the help desk and technical support teams, she implements procedures designed to maximize the client experience with the Company. Negotiating contracts, she utiltizes her customer service relations skills to present all aspects and benefits of the agreement to various company representatives. Ms. Stephens has been recognized for the development of the customer service department; she has worked in the technical field for several years. Attributing her success to her faith in God, she intends to continue in her current capacity while creating a certification program for the employees. Established in 1979, Fascor is a software developer that creates custom applications for various industries. Specializing in warehouse management, the Company provides innovative packages to direct staff, monitor inventory, and optimize logistics. Employing 35 people, the Company strives to offer quality services at value prices. **Career Highlights:** Director of Customer Service, Fascor (1994-Present). **Associations & Accomplishments:** Help Desk Institute; Red Cross; Children's Home Guild. **Education:** Northern Kentucky University, B.S. in I.F.S. (1994). **Personal Information:** Ms. Stephens enjoys gardening and cooking.

Laura Baker Stocker

Director of Account Services
Pipeline Interactive
815 Cumberland Street, 5th Floor
Lebanon, PA 17042
(717) 273-5665
Fax: (717) 273-5266
laura@pipelineinteractive.net

7371

Business Information: In her role as Director of Account Services for Pipeline Interactive, Ms. Stocker handles all aspects of new business development and client service. Demonstrating exceptional communicative skills, she prepares presentations for clients that explain web services offered and available programs. Ms. Stocker develops personalized strategic business plans to fulfill the needs of clients, ensuring they receive maximum attention. Ms. Stocker has supervised the development of web sites and multimedia projects for companies as diverse as Westinghouse, Elf Atochem, and Carlisle SynTec. Pipeline Interactive develops and implements multimedia and web-based solutions that make it easier to do business. From strategic consulting to online commerce, Pipeline Interactive offers comprehensive e-business solutions. Established in 1999 in Lebanon, Pennsylvania, the Company offers cutting-edge technology for the e-commerce industry. **Career Highlights:** Director of Account Services, Pipeline Interactive (1999-Present); Account Executive, Godfrey Interactive (1996-99); Advertising Manager, The Daily News (1995-96); Events Marketing Manager, Hersheypark (1988-95). **Associations & Accomplishments:** Annville Community Theatre. **Education:** Temple University, B.A. (1988). **Personal Information:** Married to Brad Stocker in 1993. Ms. Stocker enjoys community theatre.

Walter Stucki

Development Manager
NCI
Ave Des Baumes 7
La Tour De Peilz, Switzerland 1814
+41 219442822
walter.stucki@bluewin.ch

7371

Business Information: Utilizing more than 30 years of extensive experience in the field of information technology, Mr. Stucki functions in the role of Development Manager for NCI. In this capacity, he assumes responsibility for information surveys, architecture designs, and actual development of the Company's applications. A systems expert in the field, he also develops leading edge routines. Fluent in four languages, including English, French, German, and Albanian, Mr. Stucki has been the reciepient of several internal awards for his outstanding job performance. He is committed to continued optimum performance and strives towards the admirable goal of improving the general economy through application development. Mr. Stucki's success reflects his leadership ability to form teams with synergy and technical strength, as well as produce cutting edge results and aggressively tackle new challenges. Specializing in systems application development, NCI serves a broad clientele of various government bodies and large international companies. In addition to the customized applications developed, the Company sets up local area networks and creates wide area networks for its clients. Based in Albania, operations employ the talents of 24 skilled professionals. NCI was founded in 1996. **Career Highlights:** Development Manager, NCI (1996-Present); Education Manager, AT&T (1991-95); Education Manager, NCR (1986-90); Database Specialist, Sperry UniVac (1969-85). **Education:** Western Michigan University, M.A. in Audio Visual Media (1967); Lausanne University, M.B.A. (1965). **Personal Information:** Married to Zhaneta in 1998. One child: Patricia. Mr. Stucki enjoys skiing, swimming and being a Judo trainer.

Richard A. Sundell

Software Developer
Tone Software Corporation
1735 South Brookhurst
Anaheim, CA 90204
(714) 991-9460
Fax: (714) 991-0719
rs@tonesoft.com

7371

Business Information: As Software Developer of Tone Software Corporation, Mr. Sundell's creates new software that will enable end users to improve the ease and efficiency of using software programs. He plans, designs, develops, and implements new products in addition to working on resolutions and enhancements required by individual customers. Before joining Tone Software, he served as Senior Systems Administrator for the Boeing Company and O/S Advisor with Rockwell International. Mr. Sundell attributes his success to previous mentors and being in the right place at the right time. His career success reflects his ability to think out-of-the-box and aggressively take on new challenges. He keeps current with advancements in his field by attending classes and conferences and reading trade journals. Consistently achieving quality performance in his field, Mr. Sundell anticipates attaining the position of Developer Manager. Tone Software Corporation is an Industry Standard Architecture writer and software developer for IBM mainframe and UNIX environment operating systems. Created in 1975, the Corporation employs a staff of 60 qualified professionals and serves an international clientele. **Career Highlights:** Software Developer, Tone Software Corporation (1998-Present); Senior Systems Administrator, Boeing Company (1996-98); O/S Advisor, Rockwell International (1982-96). **Associations & Accomplishments:** National Management Association; Share; USENIX; Beta Gamma Sigma; Sigma Iota Epsilon. **Education:** United States International University, Database Administrator (1999); California State University at Long Beach: M.B.A., B.S. **Personal Information:** Married to Dianna in 1976. Two children: Jennifer and Kathryn. Mr. Sundell enjoys soccer, surfing and working with the Girl Scouts of America.

Martin H. Swafford

ASQ Certified Software Quality Engineer and Quality Auditor
Compuware Corporation
15305 Dallas Parkway, Suite 900
Addison, TX 75001
(972) 960-0960
Fax: (972) 960-8489
martin.swafford@compuware.com

7371

Business Information: Utilizing more than 14 years of extensive experience in software engineering, Mr. Swafford serves as a Chief Information Architect for Compuware Corporation. He leads a team of Information Engineers in the QASolutions group of the professional services solutions division to manage and develop software quality assurance and testing methodologies. He is the co-developer of the patent-pending software testing methodology, QualityPoint (SM). His background also includes stints with Autotester, Inc. as the director of information engineering and a business unit of Teledyne Brown Engineering as the quality manager. Mr. Swafford enjoys his work with the Corporation and looks forward to assisting in the completion of high-value and cost-effective solutions for the customers. Compuware is a worldwide provider of quality software products and services designed to increase productivity. Practical solutions are created to meet customers needs and surpass their expectations. Headquartered in Detroit, Michigan and founded in 1973, Compuware has helped people transform their information technology investments into business assets. Compuware employs more than 15,000 people with a skilled professional services staff of over 11,000 employees. **Career Highlights:** Compuware Corporation, Chief Information Architect (1999-Present); Autotester, Inc., Director of Information Engineering (1998-99); Lead Services Developer (1997-98); Teledyne Brown Engineering, Quality Manager (1993-96); Teledyne Geotech, Software Configuration Manager (1989-92); R.A.M. Inc., Branch Chief (1986-89). **Associations & Accomplishments:** RAB Certified ISO Assessor, Internaitonal Quality System Standard; Certified Quality Auditor/Software Quality Engineer, American Society for Quality; Software Division's Southwest Region (14) Counselor, American Society for Quality; West Point Society of North Texas. **Education:** Webster University, M.A. (1990); United States Military Academy at West Point, B.S. (1980). **Personal Information:** Mr. Swafford enjoys running.

Brian J. Taylor

Director of Technical Operations
Skymall Inc.
16220 North 61st Avenue
Glendale, AZ 85306
(602) 528-3264
Fax: (602) 744-6069
btaylor@skymall.com

7371

Business Information: Serving as Skymall Inc.'s Director of Technical Operations, Mr. Taylor handles the management of all hardware, software, and technical aspects of operations. Maintaining Web sites, he develops and implements network infrastructure design, utilizing his education and practical work experience. Supervising the call center, he provides outstanding customer services and support based on techniques devleoped at departmental meetings. Keeping his goals consistent with the objectives of the Company, Mr. Taylor looks forward to advancement within the corporate structure while aspiring to private business ownership. Skymall Inc., engages in e-commerce by developing Web sites for products. In doing so, the Corporation allows potential consumers to browse through information for the products, thereby increasing visibility and sales prospects. Established in 1989, the Corporation employs 350 people at the Phoenix, Arizona location. **Career Highlights:** Director of Technical Operations, Skymall Inc. (1998-Present); Management Information System Director, CCI-Tempe (1997-98); Management Information System Manager, Celwave-Phx (1995-97); Senior Program Analyst, Latric Labs (1994-95). **Education:** DeVry at Phoenix, B.S. in Computer Information System (1993); Certified Management Analyst. **Personal Information:** Married to Melanie in 1985. Three children: Katie, Brandon, and Courtney. Mr. Taylor enjoys motorcycles, fishing, hunting, computers and playing the guitar.

TheresaMarie Temple

Senior Consultant
Entology, Inc.
1 Crossroads Drive
Bedminister, NJ 07921-2688
(908) 833-2315
Fax: (908) 238-1692
mrs_temple@yahoo.com

7371

Business Information: As the Senior Consultant at Entology, Inc., Mrs. Temple is responsible for creating e-business solutions, while also maintaining excellent rapport with Entology's clientele. As a senior level developer, she designs Web sites, manages projects, maintains codes, and assists in administering database management systems. One of the most rewarding aspect of her professional career was having the opportunity of owning and operating two of her own consultant companies: Intelligent Technology, Inc. and SportsSoft Inc. She has also copyright protected her own software package. Utilizing more than eight years of experience, Mrs. Temple is currently devising plans to continue her education and certification goals in Oracle, Microsoft, ColdFusion, and computer hardware (A+). Entology, Inc. is one of the largest custom software development companies on the East Coast of the United States. The Company caters to a host of client companies, both domestic and international, specializing in e-business solutions. Established in 1997, the company is located in Bedminster, New Jersey, and functions under the direction of 45 individuals who facilitate smooth operations. **Career Highlights:** Senior Consultant, Entology, Inc. (1998-Present); Senior Systems Engineer II, KSM, Inc. (1997-98); President, Sportsoft, Inc. (1996); President, Intelligent Technology, Inc. (1996); Systems Integrator, The Prudential (1993-96). **Associations & Accomplishments:** Microsoft Certified Professional (1999); Executive Womens Golf Association; MS-150 Participant; Cycling for Red Cross; New Jersey Womens Sports Association; Division One National Collegiate Athletic Association Soccer Player (1988). **Education:** The Chubb Institute: Diploma in Client/Server Application Development (1996), Diploma in Computer Programming; University of Massachusetts, B.S. in Retail Marketing with Marketing concentration (1992). **Personal Information:** Married to Rory Allan Sr. in 1998. One child: Rorya Allan Jr. Mrs. Temple enjoys soccer, cycling, building computers and her new baby boy.

Bradford Thelin

Network Operations Center Specialist
Connect South
9600 Great Hills Trail
Austin, TX 78759
bthelin@csouth.net

7371

Business Information: Utilizing a strong background in information technology, Mr. Thelin serves as the Network Operations Center Specialist for Connect South. In his position, he is responsible for traveling on-site to clients' offices and troubleshooting and resolving systems difficulties as well as providing support services for network environments. Moreover, Mr. Thelin offers instruction to management and users and supervises a staff of employees in the performance of systems analysis, installation, configuration, modification, support, and tracking functions. In the future, he looks forward to continuing with the Company, while working in a challenging environment and designing advanced network technologies. Established in 1994, Connect South is a start up company which is a provider of DSL programs. Located in Austin, Texas, the Company targets mainly small businesses in the Southern United States, operating on a regional level. With a staff of 500 employees, the Company reports a substantial annual revenue. **Career Highlights:** Network Operations Center Specialist, Connect South (2000-Present); Corporate Network Engineer, Insurance Holdings of America, Inc. (1998-00); Technical Support Analyst, PSDI (1997-98). **Associations & Accomplishments:** BCR. **Education:** University of Montana, B.S. in Resource Conservation (1996). **Personal Information:** Mr. Thelin enjoys sports, camping, biking and routers.

Doyce E. Tomlin

President
Micro Revisions Inc.
4102 Way Out West Drive, #J1
Houston, TX 77092
(713) 690-6676
Fax: (713) 690-5669
detomlin@flash.net

7371

Business Information: As President of Micro Revisions Inc., Mr. Tomlin oversees all day-to-day administration and operations. He is responsible for developing and implementing the overall strategic direction and business contribution of the information systems function. With a strong entrepreneurial spirit, Mr. Tomlin ventured into the corporate world in 1983 to start Micro Revisions. As a 29 year professional with an established track record of delivering results, his success reflects his ability to form teams with synergy and technical strength. As chief executive of the Corporation, Mr. Tomlin oversees and directs computer services for 150 different companies, as well as computer, software, and network installation and upgrades. Planning strategic alliances, joint ventures, business development, and investments, and tracking and monitoring fiscal responsibility and bottom line profits also fall within the purview of his executive responsibilities. He credits his success to his ability to quickly learn complex technical concepts and methodologies. Mr. Tomlin is very content with the Company and plans on continuing to lead and expand operations. Micro Revisions Inc. engages in computer hardware and software installation and programming. Established in 1983, Micro Revisions is local in scope and presently employs three professional and technical experts. **Career Highlights:** President, Micro Revisions Inc. (1983-Present). **Education:** University of Texas at Austin, B.A. in Mathematics (1971). **Personal Information:** Mr. Tomlin enjoys golf.

Theodore T. Tsung

Chief Technology Officer
Digitrade Inc.
55 Broadway, Floor 6
New York, NY 10006
(212) 271-2048
Fax: (212) 271-3222

7371

Business Information: The Founder of Digitrade Inc., Mr. Tsung sold the Corporation to Thompson Financial in 1998. At the present time, he fulfills the responsibilities of Chief Technology Officer. Before venturing out to start Digitrade, Mr. Tsung served as President for Unitask Enterprise Corporation. In his current capacity, he sets the technological direction of the Corporation, ensures that contracts are performed in a timely manner, and oversees the outsourcing operations. Attributing his success to knowledge of technology, business, and the marketplace, Mr. Tsung states that you have to make sure that your business vision will fit the marketplace you are aiming at. He plans to remain at the helm of the Corporation, expanding operations to an international level and venturing into brokerage insurance. Digitrade Inc. is a service bureau and software development house, specializing in the manufacturing and management of information technology systems in retail trading for the financial and brokerage industries. The first Corporation to perform this type of service, Digitrade Inc. is now a subsidiary of Thompson Financial. Established in 1994, operations employ a work force of 35 qualified professionals and boast $15 million in annual revenue. **Career Highlights:** Chief Technology Officer, Digitrade Inc. (1994-Present); President, Unitask Enterprise Corporation (1990-94). **Education:** Columbia University: M.S. in Electrical Engineering (1983), B.S. in Electrical Engineering (1982). **Personal Information:** Married to Jennifer in 1987. One child: Anthony. Mr. Tsung enjoys tennis, golf and other sports.

Paul W. Wagner

President/Chief Executive Officer/3D Artist
Squeal Media Arts
800 North Smith Avenue, #Y35
Bloomington, IN 47408
(812) 336-3000
pww@squeal.net

7371

Business Information: As President of one of the most innovative and dynamic companies to ever enter the world of multimedia design, Mr. Wagner conducts the three-dimensional design and animation of Web sites for Squeal Media Arts. He also serves as Chief Executive Officer and 3D Artist for the Company. Individually crafting award winning Web designs for the custom specifications of his clients, Mr. Wagner utilizes a degree from Indiana University to support his natural artistic and creative talents. Looking to extend upon the boundaries of the services of Squeal Media Arts, Mr. Wagner is expanding the production of his Web sites, paving the way for expansion and growth. Headquartered in Bloomington, Indiana, Squeal Media Arts is engaged in the multi-faceted aspects of Web design, from content development to the creation of "webisodes." Recently established in 1999, the Company maintains their rank as one of the most rapidly growing companies on the forefront of Internet art and Web site development. **Career Highlights:** President/Chief Executive Officer/3D Artist, Squeal Media Arts (1999-Present); Systems Administrator, Teletron, Inc. (1998-00). **Education:** Indiana University, B.A. (1998). **Personal Information:** Mr. Wagner enjoys water sports, photography, flying and model railroads.

Kwok Wai-Hung

Project Manager
Nexcel Limited
Flat A 24th Floor, Lai Kwan Court 40038, Castle Peak Road
Kowloon, Hong Kong
+852 21945861
Fax: +852 27841255
thomas@nexcel.net

7371

Business Information: Supervising a team of 10 within Nexcel Limited, Mr. Wai-Hung serves as the Project Manager. A successful professiona, he is charged with making the most vital and influential decisions necessary to the Company, he utilizes his degree in the field to perform the most educated evaluations of any given situation, and develop appropriate judgements and actions. Coordinating resources, time lines, assignments, and project budgets also fall within the realm of Mr. Wai-Hung's responsibilities. Highly regarded, he possesses superior technical abilities and an excellent understanding of technology. Possibly making a career change to further his executive management capabilities in the near future, Mr. Wai-Hung is ensuring the future of his professional career in the software industry. His success reflects his ability to think out-of-the-box, take on challenges, and deliver results on behalf of the Company and its clientele. Serving the local area of Kowloon, Hong Kong, Nexcel Limited offers Internet software development to their client portfolio inclusive of corporate, business, and independent customers. Established in 1997, the Company has now grown to incorporate the skills of 15 professionals who have dedicated their careers to developing the latest technologies and software available in the industry. **Career Highlights:** Project Manager, Nexcel Limited (1998-Present); Assistant Computer Officer, The Chinese Univeristy of Hong Kong (1997-98). **Education:** The Chinese University of Hong Kong: Master's degree in Philosophy (1997), Bachelor's degree in Information Engineering (1995). **Personal Information:** Mr. Wai-Hung enjoys travel, tennis and sports.

Laura H. Williams

Director of Product Architecture
Resource Information Management Systems, Inc.
500 Technology Drive
Naperville, IL 60566
(630) 428-5403
lwilliams@rims.com

7371

Business Information: Utilizing more than 15 years of extensive experience in software design, Ms. Williams serves as the Director of Product Architecture for Resource Information Management Systems, Inc. She assumes accountability for developing the Java product architecture for the Corporation's technology based software products. Managing the project teams, she oversees all phases of software development and supervises the installation process at the client sites. Ms. Williams also offers job training and troubleshoots any problems that arise during the software implementation. She is proud to have singlehandedly developed a new corporate product and personally marketed it successfully. Dedicated to the success of the Corporation, she is developing e-commerce solutions for clients to assist them in providing quality customer service to the general public. Nationally renowned, Resource Information Management Systems, Inc. develops software and provides technical solutions services to the health insurance industry. Boasting $40 million in annual sales, the Corporation was created in 1981 and employs a work force of 365 skilled individuals to fulfill its clients' demands. **Career Highlights:** Director of Product Architecture, Resource Information Management Systems, Inc. (1994-Present); Programming Supervisor, Policy Management Systems Corporation (1990-94); Design Supervisor, Advanced System Applications (1985-90). **Associations & Accomplishments:** Institute of Electronics and Electrical Engineers. **Education:** Illinois State University, B.S. in Applied Computer Science (1985). **Personal Information:** Ms. Williams enjoys swimming and skiing.

Alex L. Wilsdon

Internet Strategist
Leopard Communications
6230 Lookout Road
Boulder, CO 80301-3319
(303) 527-5147
Fax: (303) 530-3480
awilsdon@stanfordalumni.org

7371

Business Information: Mr. Wilsdon serves in the role of Internet Strategist with Leopard Communications, handling a variety of highly specialized tasks on a daily basis. Coupling impressive technical ability with superior communicative skills, he meets with clients to discuss their needs regarding operational procedures. After conducting thorough analysis, Mr. Wilsdon is able to design innovative technical solutions that consistently exceed client expectations. Additionally, he prepares business plans and conducts industry research to ensure the Company remains competitive in the field. Recognized for his stellar ability to lead information technology classes with a proactive style, Mr. Wildson attributes success to his ability to bridge the gap between technology and business. Leopard Communications provides marketing and communications consulting services to businesses in the Boulder, Colorado area. Employing 100 technically inclined individuals, the Company is able to offer superior e-business solution building, and assist clients in the development of on-line brands. **Career Highlights:** Leopard Communications: Internet Strategist (1999-Present), Manager of Technical Services (1997-99); Productivity Point Trainer: Microsoft Certified Trainer, Technical Instructor, Consultant (1994-97). **Associations & Accomplishments:**

Rocky Mountain Internet Users Group; Windows NT Users Group; Microsoft Certified Trainer; Microsoft Certified Systems Engineer. **Education:** Stanford University, B.A. (1980). **Personal Information:** Married to Ann Stewart in 1991.

James B. Winklesky

Website Developer/Database Administrator/Server Administrator
O'Brien Interactive
5189 Lupine Lane NW
Acworth, GA 30102
(770) 792-8100
Fax: (770) 792-8118
winkjb@hotmail.com

7371

Business Information: Drawing from an extensive educational and occupational experience, Mr. Winklesky is the Website Developer and Database and Server Administrator for the Company. A savvy and respected expert in the field, he is responsible for numerous activities including, programming, creation of active server pages, and Website design and development. Currently attending military flight school, Mr. Winklesky looks forward to graduation so as to become a helicopter pilot for the United States Army Reserve. He will also be working in the information technology field while serving in the military. He attributes his success to discipline and initiative. Mr. Winklesky's advice is "get started and get as much knowledge as you can." Established in 1997 by an AT&T contractor, O'Brien Interactive is a provider of Internet technologies. Utilizing the skilled services of six individuals, the Company provides Website development, hosting, and reporting of graphics production. Located in NW Acworth, Georgia, O'Brien Interactive provides services in the states of Georgia, New Jersey, and Virginia. **Career Highlights:** Website Developer/Database Administrator/Server Administrator, O'Brien Interactive (1998-Present); Information Management Officer, United States Army Reserves, 335th TSC (1997-Present); Technical Support, Georgia State University (1997-98). **Associations & Accomplishments:** Phi Theta Kappa; Association of Computing Machinery; Association of the United States Army; Scabbard & Blade. **Education:** Emory University, B.S. (1999); Marion Military Institute, A.A.

Willmer B. Wonsang

Systems Engineer
CommVault System
8105 Yacht Street
Frisco, TX 75035
(972) 705-8850
Fax: (972) 994-4321
wwonsang@mail.com

7371

Business Information: Combining strong management skills and technological expertise, Mr. Wonsang joined CommVault System in 1999. Serving as Systems Engineer with the Company, he draws from his academic and occupational experience in directing and participating in the analysis, design, evaluation, testing, and implementation of ComVault's storage management products. He is also charged with product technical support at existing customer sites as well as providing technical training seminars on new product development. Attributing his success to surrounding himself with intelligent people, Mr. Wongsang presides over the completion of all technological tasks. Enjoying what he does, his future goals include assuming more of a consulting role with the Company. Established in 1996, CommVault System is a data manufacturing company that facilitates the design and manufacturing of software as well as creating system back ups and restoring damaged systems. Headquartered in Ocean Port, New Jersey, the Company employs the expertise of 300 personnel to blueprint and assemble new software implementing them into existing systems, consult on systems support, and provide disaster restoration. **Career Highlights:** Systems Engineer, CommVault System (1999-Present); Network Engineer, EDS (1994-99); Management Information Systems Manager, Sunrise Energy (1990-94). **Education:** Midwestern State University (1987); Desert Palms Springs College, Associate's degree in Electronic Technology. **Personal Information:** Married to Gay L. in 1990. Two children: Willmer "Kye" and Scout Alexis. Mr. Wonsang enjoys weight lifting and coaching soccer.

Jason Woodlee

Chief Executive Officer
CTech
106 Conforti Avenue
West Orange, NJ 07052
(973) 324-0088
Fax: (973) 324-0522
jwoodlee@ctechcentral.com

7371

Business Information: The Owner of CTech, Mr. Woodlee founded the Corporation in 1997 and currently serves as its Chief Executive Officer. He oversees and directs all aspects of day-to-day administration and operational activities. Before starting CTech, Mr. Woodlee served as Vice President of Engineering with both Inergy Inc. and www.malls-ltd.com. Educated in the field of computer engineering, he designs and implements programs for his clients and devotes attention to developing strong client relationships. Coordinating resources, schedules, time lines, and assignments; building a team with synergy and technical strength; and calculating and managing the fiscal year budget also fall within the purview of Mr. Woodlee's executive responsibilities. He believes he owes his professional success to his flexibility and states that one should always be prepared to change. Mr. Woodlee is utilizing strategic planning to expand his business and grab a larger share of the available market. He looks forward to the day when he can go public with the Corporation. Specializing in Web application design, CTech provides companies and individuals with e-commerce, Internet, information database, and network services. **Career Highlights:** Chief Executive Officer, CTech (1997-Present); Vice President of Engineering, Inergy, Inc. (1995-97); Vice President of Engineering, www.malls-ltd.com (1994-95). **Associations & Accomplishments:** Chamber of Commerce; Society of Electrical Engineers. **Education:** Boston University, B.S. in Computer Engineering (1996). **Personal Information:** Married to Elaine in 1999. Mr. Woodlee enjoys scuba diving, sky diving, horses and racing.

Ian Y. Xie

President/Chief Executive Officer
Medio Systems, Inc.
2107 North First Street, Suite 530
San Jose, CA 95131
(408) 452-5500
Fax: (408) 452-5522
ianxie@mediosys.com

7371

Business Information: Mr. Xie is the President and Chief Executive Officer of Medio Systems, Inc. Serving with the Company since 1998, Mr. Xie manages the finances and budget, creates policies and procedures, and oversees sales and marketing as well as determines the strategic direction and vision. In addition, he is in charge of fund raising activities and utilizes strategic planning to increase business and establish new client relationships. Mr. Xie attributes his success to having the desire to make a difference and his ability to form teams with synergy and technical strength, take on challenges, and deliver results. Future plans for Mr. Xie are to continue to develop new technology for Medio Systems Inc. and to stay ahead of industry competitors. Medio Systems, Inc. specializes in software research and development. The Corporation provides video compresent on the Internet. Established in 1998, the Corporation is headquartered in San Jose, and employs 20 skilled technicians, programmers, and administrative personnel providing their creative services to promote vast sums of revenue. **Career Highlights:** President/Chief Executive Officer, Medio Systems, Inc. (1998-Present). **Education:** The University of Texas at Austin, M.S. (1991). **Personal Information:** Married to Amy in 1992. Mr. Xie enjoys tennis, bicycling, skiing and reading.

Travis Yates

Chief Executive Officer
Remington Agency
2130 Northwest 54th Terrace
Gainesville, FL 32605
(352) 375-9089
Fax: (352) 374-7994
tyates@remingtonagency.com

7371

Business Information: Functioning in the role of Chief Executive Officer for Remington Agency, Mr. Yates oversees and directs all aspects of day-to-day administration and operational activities. He determines the overall strategic and tactical direction and business contribution of the information systems function. Mr. Yates is concurrently fulfills the responsibilities of Webmaster, artist, and designer. Following 12 years of distinguished service with the United States Navy, Mr. Yates began his association with Remington in 1994. In his capacity, he is responsible for consulting, sales and marketing, writing articles, presenting lectures, and overseeing the graphic and Web art areas of the Company. He continues to grow professionally and hopes to continue to develop and integrate his skills by moving into a more delegation role. Attributing his success to his faith in God, Mr. Yates' advice is "learn as much as you can before you start." Founded in 1974, Remington Agency is a full service design advertising and marketing firm offering various services to clients including Web development and Web design. The Company currently employs a staff of five individuals to orchestrate every aspect of the operation. **Career Highlights:** Chief Executive Officer, Remington Agency (1994-Present); Medical Public Relations Liaison, United States Navy (1982-94). **Associations & Accomplishments:** Director, Web Development Services Legal Technology Institute, Levin College of Law, University of Florida; Web Masters Association; Veterans Association. **Education:** Santa Fe Community College, A.A. (1998); Rutgers University; William Paterson State University; Morris County Community College; E. Stroudsburg State University. **Personal Information:** Married to Ann in 1976. Three children: Melissa, Travis, and Amy. Mr. Yates enjoys music, theater, sports and wine.

Gregg L. Zepp, II

Account Executive
Infinite Wisdom Web Designs
5 Rumsford Court
Reisterstown, MD 21136
(410) 409-7024
Fax: (410) 288-3719
gzepp@iwisdom.com

7371

Business Information: Mr. Zepp serves as an Account Executive of Infinite Wisdom Web Designs. A consultant to his clients, he performs Web site development and design. Possessing strong business savvy and technical expertise, he is also a technical consultant to the Maryland Republican Party. Also, Mr. Zepp is the founder of "Tech Talks," which is an association for the local information technology professionals and currently has a membership of 20 individuals. It was formed to keep the IT professionals informed on current affairs in the industry. His plans are to grow Infinite Wisdom Web Designs and become more administratively involved in all day-to-day operations. A certified Web Specialist, he is also member of the Maryland Young Republicans, where he is the treasurer. Success is attributed to Mr. Zepp's ability to think out-of-the-box and tackle new challenges and deliver results. A technology company, Infinite Wisdom Web Designs, established in 1998, is a Web development solutions provider in database and real time. The Company offers innovative Web site development to primarily the educational and political sectors. Infinite Wisdom Web Designs is presently located in Reisterstown, Maryland. **Career Highlights:** Account Executive, Infinite Wisdom Web Designs (Present); Sales and Technology Center Manager, Staples, Inc. (Present); Assistant Manager/Systems Trainer, Wal-Mart (1996-98). **Associations & Accomplishments:** Board Member, Northwest Republican Club; Treasurer, Greater Baltimore Young Republicans; Moderator, Tech Talks Discussion Group for Information Technology Professionals in the Greater Baltimore area; HTML Writers Guild; Microsoft Developer Network. **Education:** Pennsylvania State University, Double Bachelor's degrees (1996); Univerity of Maryland, Web Systems Specialist I & II Certification; Computer Learning Institute, working towards MCSE/A+ Certificiations. **Personal Information:** Mr. Zepp enjoys Web site construction, hardware, political orientation, financial management and organizational management. He also enjoys financial and organizational management books.

Eric Yanguang Zhao, Ph.D.

Software Architect
Solution Soft Systems, Inc.
20422 Via Napoli
Cupertino, CA 95014-6306
(408) 346-1405
Fax: (408) 996-9518
ericzhao@yahoo.com

7371

Business Information: A successful, 15 year veteran of the technology field, Dr. Zhao serves as Software Architect of Solution Soft Systems, Inc. He is responsible for design and development of innovative systems level software. Working directly with systems managers and users, he analyzes, specifies, designs, and implements new business solutions as well as enhance existing products such as data structures and testing software. Before his recruitment to Solution Soft Systems, Dr. Zhao served as Staff Engineer with Synopsys Systems, Inc. His extensive background also includes employment as Member of Technical Staff at Viewlogic Systems, Inc. One of many accomplishments, Dr. Zhao's greatest is his 10 year stay in the EDA industry working on semiconductor chips for simulator manufacturers. His success is attributed to being in the right place at the right time. Staying in design, Dr. Zhao plans on delivering global networks and compress transfer data technology in a faster and more cost effective manner. A technology company, Solution Soft Systems, Inc. engages in computer software development. The Corporation's product line includes time machines, compression solutions, and velocity FTPs. Based in California, the Corporation employs a 50 professional, technical, and support staff who help generate annual revenues in excess of $10 million. Solution Soft Systems, Inc. was established in 1993. **Career Highlights:** Software Architect, Solution Soft Systems, Inc. (1998-Present); Staff Engineer, Synopsys Sytems, Inc. (1997-98); Member of Technical Staff, Viewlogic Systems, Inc. (1994-97). **Associations & Accomplishments:** Association of Computing Machinery; Institute of Electrical and Electronics Engineers. **Education:** University of California at Santa Cruz, Ph.D. (1985). **Personal Information:** Married to Mee Y. Cheung in 1991. Three children: Lin, Shan, and Erica. Dr. Zhao enjoys swimming.

Brigit Ananya, Ph.D.

President
Ananya Systems, Inc.
15732 Los Gatos Boulevard, #500
Los Gatos, CA 95032
(408) 353-3555
info@ananya.com

7372

Business Information: As the Owner and President of Ananya Systems, Inc., Dr. Ananya is responsible for managing the entire business. Her main responsibilities are developing and programming the Company's software product line, which provides new computer graphics software solutions. She also manages employees, oversees negotiations on all contracts, and oversees all finances. Established in 1998, Ananya Systems specializes in computer graphics software programs, written in Java 2, that enable the user to draw curves with greater ease, more precision and more speed than previously possible. Currently, the Company has patents pending for this technology that will be licensed to computer graphics software and CAD companies. Dr. Ananya has plans to expand the Company's product line. She feels that her mathematical background helps her to find new solutions, and she advises that others in the field acquire a good mathematical background. **Career Highlights:** President, Ananya Systems (1998-Present); Senior Engineer/Scientist, Apple Computer (1994-97); Senior Member of Advanced Technology, Sun Microsystems (1987-90); Senior Engineer in Graphics Applications, Xerox Corporation (1983-87). **Associations & Accomplishments:** Association for Computing Machinery (ACM); Institute of Electrical and Electronics Engineers (IEEE); Society of Industrial and Applied Mathematics (SIAM); Prize from E.T.H. Zurich for Ph.D. thesis, which gives a broad generalization of the funamental theorem of differential geometry. **Education:** E.T.H. (Swiss Federal Institute of Technology) Zurich, Switzerland, Ph.D. in Mathematics (1978). **Personal Information:** Married to Michael Gluckman in 2000. Dr. Ananya enjoys creating geometric art, playing the piano, aikido and the teaching of nonduality.

Jay Armstrong

Project Manager
Tivoli Systems
9442 Capital of Texas Highway North
Austin, TX 78759
(512) 436-8839
Fax: (512) 436-1994
jay.armstrong@tivoli.com

7372

Business Information: With extensive operational, implementation, and consulting experience in the IT Services field, Mr. Armstrong was recruited to the Tivoli Systems team in 1999. At the present moment, he serves the role of Project Manager for Tivoli Support Strategy and Planning. Currently, he is working on new support offerings and documenting the Tivoli support process. Mr. Armstrong's favorite advice to others in the industry is "Give the customer what they ask for through diligent review of their requirements, accurately assessing the current operations, tenaciously delivering on time and within budget, and finally relentlessly communicating with the customer throughout the entire process." He attributes his success to communicative skills that helped him to communicate effectively with various levels within the organization. His strategic goals include continuing to provide quality services, help companies understand strategic goals, and show them how IT services can fulfill these goals. To date, Mr. Armstrong's professional highlight is designing and implementing a new On-Site Support organization for IBM's EMEA (Europe, Middle East, Africa) organization. Through his hard work, he brought several different technologies, as well as cultures together to complete the project on time and within budget. This project resulted in a 30 percent cost savings across the EMEA OSS organization while improving service levels in all countries. Tivoli Systems Inc., an IBM company, provides the industry's leading open, highly scalable, and cross-platform management solutions that span networks, systems, applications, and business-to-business commerce. Tivoli is a global company dedicated to providing products, services, and programs that enable companies of any size to manage their networked PCs and distributed systems from a single location. Since its inception in 1989, Tivoli has helped leading companies around the world reduce the cost and complexity of managing networks, systems, databases, and applications. Tivoli products, services, and partner programs transform IT management into a business advantage maximizing the benefit of repaid deployment and ROI. Tivoli Enterprise products are the industry's first end-to-end solutions to make it easy to manage hundreds of thousands of separate devices without sacrificing productivity, security, or performance. Tivoli also provides a variety of solutions for small and mid-sized businesses, aimed at IT management of specific mission-critical processes. Tivoli's partner association, Team Tivoli, is dedicated to providing customers with premium enterprise systems management services, allowing customers to choose the provider and selection of services that best meet their needs. It is a further expression of Tivoli's celebrated "openness" commitment, which is central to the Tivoli philosophy. Headquartered in Austin, Texas, Tivoli distributes its products worldwide through a network of global sales offices, systems integrators, resellers, and IBM sales channels. **Career Highlights:** Project Manager, Tivoli Systems (1999-Present); Business Consultant, CTG (1995-99); Senior Programmer, IBM (1994-95); Manager of Operations, CSC (1990-94). **Education:** Texas A&M University, B.B.A. in Management Information Systems. **Personal Information:** Married to Beata. Mr. Armstrong enjoys travel, motor sports, golf, basketball, racquetball, gourmet foods and time with family and friends.

Paul L. Ashford

Senior Applications Developer
Software Consulting Services
3162 Bath Pike
Nazareth, PA 18064
(610) 837-8484
pashford@nscn.fast.net

7372

Business Information: Utilizing education and practical work experience, Mr. Ashford serves as Senior Applications Developer of Software Consulting Services. This position includes a variety of responsibilities, including that of developer and programmer of software solutions. Mr. Ashford applies his experitse in solving technical difficulties within the Company, fulfilling the capacity of support specialist. An efficient and productive employee, he also has proven successful in the Sales Department, consistently exceeding goals the Company has set for him. Recgonizing his ability to acheive, the senior management appointed Mr. Ashford as a part time manager. Overseeing 50 employees throughout the Company, he delegates tasks, handles conflict resolution, and deals with customer service issues. Attributing his success to his personality and getting along with people, Mr. Ashford's advice is "keep up with technology so you don't get lost." Established in 1974, Software Consulting Services develops program applications for the publication industry. The global company has clients in Europe, Canada, and South and North America. **Career Highlights:** Software Consulting Services: Senior Applications Developer (1997-Present), Junior Applications Developer (1996-97). **Education:** University of Pittsburgh at Johnstown, B.S. in Computer Science and minor in Mathematics (1995). **Personal Information:** Mr. Ashford enjoys skiing, kayaking, mountain biking, hiking and yoga.

Brian C. Blake

Senior Consultant
VERITAS Software
37 Deborah Lane
Buffalo, NY 14225
(716) 706-0155
Fax: (716) 681-3157
brian.blake@veritas.com

7372

Business Information: Mr. Blake functions in the role of Senior Consultant with VERITAS Software. A key member of the Consulting Services Group, he is responsible for all aspects of post-sales configuration, customization, and training. Before joining Veritas Software in 1997, Mr. Blake served as a Technical Analyst with Sprint Paranet. His solid background history also includes a stint as Software Engineer for Gilbarco, Inc. A four year technology expert, he works with users and management in making assessments of the client's environment and recommending the best solution to eliminate difficulties and improve the overall systems performance. Designing and producing a wide range of backup products is also an integral part of Mr. Blake's functions. His career milestones include being Project Manager for a product controlling off site vault management. Remaining in the storage management industry serves as one of his future endeavors. VERITAS Software engages in manufacturing end to end storage management software for enterprise server environments. Hardware independent and neutral, the Corporation targets hardware Fortune 2000 companies. Established in 1990, VERITAS employs more than 1,100 professional, technical, and administrative support personnel. Presently, the Corporation reports estimated revenues in excess of $250 million annually. **Career Highlights:** Senior Consultant, VERITAS Software (1997-Present); Technical Analyst, Sprint Paranet (1996-97); Software Engineer, Gilbarco, Inc. (1995-96). **Associations & Accomplishments:** Association of Computer Machinery; Institute of Electronics and Electrical Engineers Computer Science; International Brotherhood of Magicians; Society of American Magicians. **Education:** State University of New York at Buffalo, B.S. (1995). **Personal Information:** Mr. Blake enjoys magic, boating and hiking.

Chris N. Brown

Technology Specialist/Manager
Sybase, Inc.
8400 East Crescent Parkway, Suite 400
Greenwood Village, CO 80111
(303) 486-7761
Fax: (303) 486-7730
chris.n.brown@sybase.com

7372

Business Information: As Technology Specialist and Manager of Sybase, Inc., Mr. Brown also fulfills the responsibility of pre-sales consultant. Overseeing sales, consulting, technical resources, client calls, presentations, on-site work, problem solving, installation, and training, Mr. Brown has proven to be an invaluable asset and has proven himself to be a visionary on many occasions. To remain at the forefront of the industry, Mr. Brown reads, experiments with products, and participates in ongoing research. He is most proud of being recognized for increasing the Corporation's business base, and saving several large deals while working for PLATINUM technology. Remaining with Sybase serves as Mr. Brown's future endeavors. Sybase, Inc. is a database vending firm, offering information services to some of the largest companies and corporations worldwide. Integrating database systems into companies provides their clients access to customer and vendor information with the touch of a button. Established in 1984, Sybase currently serves the most respected and influential corporations globally. Sybase serves 70 of the 100 leading banks in the world, all 20 of the largest life insurance companies, the top 125 telecommunication and media corporations, all 5 of the best managed healthcare organizations, and 32 Blue Cross Blue Shield plans. Generating annual sales of 871.6 million dollars annually, Sybase, Inc. employs 5,000 trained professionals at their Connecticut headquarters. **Career Highlights:** Technology Specialist/Manager, Sybase, Inc. (1999-Present); Product Specialist, PLATINUM technology (1998-99); Database Administrator, Koch Industries (1997-98); Database Administrator, MCI/World Com (1994-97). **Education:** University of Oklahoma, B.B.A. (1993). **Personal Information:** Mr. Brown enjoys cars, golf, skiing and snow boarding.

Thomas K. Brown

Technical Consultant
Resource Systems, Inc.
6 East 45th Street, Room 1800
New York, NY 10017
(212) 599-5561
Fax: (212) 559-6151
tombrown@ressysinc.com

7372

Business Information: Serving as Technical Consultant of Resource Systems, Inc., Mr. Brown oversees internal networking issues. He handles troubleshooting of hardware and software and also deals with maintenance of hardware and software such as installation. Utilizing his education and practical work experience, he is able to assist with sales and marketing as he demonstrates an extensive knowledge of the industry. Mr. Brown has obtained numerous technical certifications, making him a versatile member of the professional staff of the Company. He is currently working towards his Microsoft SQL Server 7 certification exam to finish his requirements for attaining MCSE status. Resource Systems is a consulting firm and accounting software reseller, focusing on technical solutions. Established in 1996 in the United States and 1981 in Europe, the Company employs four people at the New York City, New York location which serves clients who are operating on small to mid-size platforms. **Career Highlights:** Technical Consultant, Resource Systems, Inc. (1998-Present); Accountant, HSBC Investment Banking (1994-98). **Education:** Hunter College (1976); Microsoft Certified Professional in Windows NT 4.0 and TCP/IP; Sun Systems Certified. **Personal Information:** Married to Rosa in 1999.

Isaac Brumley

Senior Consultant
Attachmate Corporation
134 Broad Street
Bremerton, WA 98312-3122
(360) 731-7799
Fax: (360) 839-7186
ibrumley@krl.org
7372

Business Information: Possessing over 15 years of experience in the technological field, Mr. Brumley serves as Senior Consultant and Owner for Neophyte Computer Systems. His principal focus is the area of server setup, installation, configuration, and management of Novell, Windows NT, and UNIX platforms. He provides troubleshooting services for new users and trains administrators in recommended network management processes. Directing the analysis, acquisition, installation, modification, configuration, support, and tracking of operating systems, databases, utilities, software, and hardware also falls within the realm of his responsibilities. Established in 1990, Neophyte Computer Systems specializes in providing consulting services to medium to large corporations while still providing services to the small business and home users alike.. **Career Highlights:** Systems Engineer, Microsoft Corp. (1999-Present); Senior Network Engineer, Attachmate Corporation (1995-99); United States Department of Defense: Network Administrator (1992-95), COmputer Specialist (1988-92). **Associations & Accomplishments:** Netware Users International; Association of Windows NT Systems Professionals; Life Member, Veterans of Foreign Wars, Life Member Disabled American Veterans. **Education:** New York Regents, B.S. (1998); Certified Novell Administrator; Certified Novell Engineer; Microsoft Certified Systems Engineer; A+ Service Technician Certified. **Personal Information:** Married to Geraldine in 1992. One child: Samuel. Mr. Brumley enjoys gardening.

Nicolas A. Bucchino

Senior Direct Response Manager
VERITAS Software
1600 Plymouth Street
Mountain View, CA 94043-1232
(650) 526-2832
Fax: (520) 396-6435
nickb@veritas.com
7372

Business Information: Serving in the capacity of the Senior Direct Response Manager of VERITAS Software, Mr. Bucchino is in charge of global direct response campaigns for the Corporation. Specifically the North American market, he is also responsible for the coordination with various agencies to provide developmental peace. Dealing with the internal sales representatives, he then conducts follow-up procedures. He is specifically in charge of 400 employees, including field representatives and internal sales groups. In addition to all of these responsibilities, he also perfoms the strategic planning for the Corporation. Looking to the future, Mr. Bucchino hopes to be on the product management team. VERITAS Software is a multi faceted company. Established in 1979, the Corporation provides enterprise storage management solutions. With offices around the globe, Veritas deals with high profile clients, such as Oracle and Boeing. The Corporation's mission is to back up existing data, protect access management to ensure the data contained is under tight security to stop database intrusions. Presently, VERITAS Software reports and estimated annual sales mark of $6.7 million. **Career Highlights:** Senior Direct Response Manager, VERITAS Software (1998-Present); Field Marketing Specialist, Microsoft Software (1998); Project Manager, IBM Corporation (1996-98); Customer Marketing Manager, Hall Mark Computer Products (1996). **Associations & Accomplishments:** Direct Marketing Association. **Education:** Emerson College, M.A. (1994); Boston University, B.S. (1991). **Personal Information:** Mr. Bucchino enjoys sailing and Tae Kwon Do.

Ahmed R. Chami

General Manager
Microsoft Corporation - North West Africa
Twin Center, Tour A, 15ème étage, Boulevard Zerktouni - Maârif
Casablanca, Morocco 20100
+971 4513888
Fax: +971 4527444
ahmedc@microsoft.com
7372

Business Information: Mr. Chami is the General Manager for the North West African interests of the Microsoft Corporation. He is responsible for 23 countries on the African continent. In the past, he has been the General Manager for Morocco and then for the Middle East. Mr. Chami has been affiliated with Microsoft for six years. He also ensures all customer satisfaction, reseller channel development, establishment of large accounts, and consulting services. As a spokesman for the Corporation, he is involved in the consolidation of the Microsoft image throughout the region. He is credited for developing new territories in the Middle East and North African region as well as founding Distrisoft, a Microsoft distributor in Morocco. Microsoft Corporation - North West Africa, a branch of the American operation, is a sales and support corporation for all clients utilizing the Microsoft network and hardware and software services. The subsidiary is one of the 56 satellite offices worldwide. **Career Highlights:** Microsoft Corporation: General Manager, North West Africa (1997-Present), General Manager, Middle East (1996-97), General Manager, North Africa (1993-96); General Manager, Distrisoft - Morocco (1991-93); General Manager, Sais Lait (1989-91). **Associations & Accomplishments:** Association des Anciens Elevés de l'Ecole Centrale de Paris; Association Maroc 2020; Featured in Business Press, Trade Press, and Gulf News. **Education:** University of California at Los Angeles, M.B.A. (1989); Ecole Centrale de Paris, Master's degree in Engineering (1985). **Personal Information:** Married to Soumiya Regragui in 1998. Three children: Mohamed, Kamil, and Ghita. Mr. Chami enjoys soccer and movies.

Rodney W. Chan

BIOS Engineer
American Megatrends Inc.
6145-F Northbelt Parkway
Norcross, GA 30071
(770) 246-8600
Fax: (770) 326-9135
rodneyC@omi.com
7372

Business Information: As BIOS Engineer for American Megatrends Inc., Mr. Chan works closely with management and systems users to analyze, specify, and design new solutions to enhance computer operations. He attends to programming, customizing, and customer service as well as performing research and creating databases, new technology, software, and hardware. Highly regarded, he possesses superior talents and an excellent understanding of technology. Offering hands on experience and expertise, Mr. Chan has served with American Megatrends since May 1999. Taking great pride in the assembly of all things he creates, he continues to research and find innovative ideas. Mr. Chan believes that the key to success is having an interest in your field. Continuing to learn new things and better himself is cited as part of his future endeavors. American Megatrends, founded in 1985, specializes in creating RAID controllers, motherboards, storage area network solutions, remote network assistants, and systems management utilities. Currently employing a solid work force of more than 500 professional, technical, and support staff, American Megatrends operates out of the Company's headquarters in Norcross, Georgia. **Career Highlights:** BIOS Engineer, American Megatrends Inc. (1999-Present). **Associations & Accomplishments:** Institute of Electrical and Electronics Engineers. **Education:** Univeristy of Tennessee, degree Electrical Engineering (1999). **Personal Information:** Mr. Chan enjoys research and reading.

Tracy J. Clarke, MCSE

Senior Systems Engineer
Symantec Corporation
230 Anderson Street, Room 2H
Hackensack, NJ 07601
(201) 489-1321
Fax: (201) 489-3673
tclarke@symantec.com
7372

Business Information: Displaying his unique talents in technology engineering, Mr. Clarke actively serves Symantec Corporation as Senior Systems Engineer. Concentrating his efforts toward incorporating the latest technologies into systems security solutions, he provides technical support and guidance to major corporate customers in the mid-Atlantic region of the United States. Implementing a hands-on managment style, Mr. Clarke coordinates efforts directly with the sales personnel during pre-sales evalutions, providing troubleshooting and maintenance of the complex systems. In the future, Mr. Clarke plans to further his education by attaining CISSP certification, in addition to MCSE, in order to facilitate promotional opportunities within the Corporation. "Get some type of professional certification," serves as his advice. Symantec Corporation is an established and reputable software vendor and world leader of Internet security technology. Founded in 1982, the Corporation is dedicated to providing a broad range of content and network security, aiming its products and services to both consumer and corporate markets. Headquartered in Cupertino, California, the Corporation extends its excellent sales and services to an international client base. Employing the expertise of 2,500 qualified personnel to acquire business, meet with clients, facilitate projects, and market services, the Corporation generates over $700 million in annual revenues. **Career Highlights:** Symantec Corporation: Senior Systems Engineer (2000-Present), Systems Engineer (1998-00); Product Support Analyst (1994-98); Technician, Spectra-Physics Scanning Systems (1993). **Education:** University of Oregon: B.S. in Computer and Information Sciences (1996), B.S. in Mathematics and Physics (1991).

Larry Clements

Vice President of Operations
Viquity
1161 North Fair Oaks Avenue
Sunnyvale, CA 94089-2102
(408) 747-5570
Fax: (408) 747-5586
larry@larryclements.com
7372

Business Information: Mr. Clements is the Vice President of Operations for Viquity. In this position since early June 2000, he has made great strides in developing Viquity's operations strategy and developing a world-class data center operation. Reporting to Chris Grejtak, Viquity's Chief Executive Officer, Mr. Clements oversees the development of both Viquity's data center and information technology operations. He also assumes responsibility for the overall quality, scalability, and integration of Viquity's operational infrastructure and initiatives. Working with a fast growing staff, Mr. Clements oversees all data center operations, web and call strategies, and internal IT to ensure the successful rollout of the Viquity Dynamic Commerce Network (DCN) service to its growing client base. Aggressively taking on challenges, Mr. Clements' team is providing a proactive approach, contiuously monitoring and assessing the health of both the system's components as well as the overall performance of DCN. This approach is assuring the Viquity's uptime is at levels well above industry benchmarks. Under his leadership, Viquity has quickly scaled an operation and infrastructure that provides 24x7 support. With more than 20 years of IT and management experience, Mr. Clements previously served as Director of Oracle's Headquarter Data Center responsible for maintaining Oracle's production servers. He also headed Oracle's worldwide server consolidation, and was responsible for Oracle's Network Control Center. The emerging leader for secure Internet infrastructure services and software, Viquity provides secure, OLTP-class e-business infrastructure for actionable business documents. A privately held, venture backed company, Viquity was founded in 1998 and is currently located in Sunnyvale, California. The Viquity Dynamic Commerce Network enables business clients of all sizes to deploy internet-based trading networks that incorporates transactional integrity, reliability, and availability. **Career Highlights:** Vice President of Operations, Viquity (2000-Present); Senior Manager of Data Center Operations, Oracle Corporation (1996-2000); Configuration Manager, Wind River Systems (1995-96); Configuration Manager, Personal Library Software (1993-95); Configuration/Data Manager, GTE Government Systems (1991-93); Project Manager, Evaluation Research Corporation (1990-91); President, Xanadu Computer Training and Support, Inc. (1989-90). **Associations & Accomplishments:** President, ClearCase International Users Group (1995-98). **Education:** Huntington College; Faulkner University; Palm Beach Junior College. **Personal Information:** Married to a Chinese-American named Shawnee. One child: Jim. Mr. Clements enjoys reading, helicopters and Star Trek.

Clarence B. Defiesta

Application Developer Consultant
Microsoft Corporation
One Microsoft Way
Redmond, WA 98052
(425) 704-3293
Fax: (425) 936-7329
clared@microsoft.com
7372

Business Information: Possessing expertise in the computer programming field, Mr. Defiesta performs as a Application Developer Consultant for the Microsoft Corporation. He assists programming on Web servers which entails providing consultant solutions, guidelines, and samples of code to developers specifically in active server pages. At the same time, Mr. Defiesta serves as an Instructor at Bellevue Community College where he teaches mastering Web development through Visual InterDev, a specific Microsoft application. He got his start in computers while in high school. Starting in programming, Mr. Defiesta has experience in hardware configuration, networking, database solutions, and design. A systems analyst, he is also versed in most computer languages such as Visual Basic, Visual C++, and HTML. Enjoying substantial success in his career choice, Mr. Defiesta looks forward to becoming more involved in e-commerce development, and enhancing his knowledge and skills in the marketing of cutting edge technology. Originating in 1975, Microsoft Corporation is one of the leading software creation companies. Employing 30,000 individuals, the Corporation primarily provides software for personal computer users. **Career Highlights:** Microsoft Corporation: Application Developer Consultant (2000-Present), Support Engineer (1999-00); Instructor, Bellevue Community College (1999-Present); Contractor, Select Group (1998-99); Senior Analyst/Programmer, Anteon Corporation (1996-98). **Associations &**

Accomplishments: Affiliate, Institute of Electrical and Electronics Engineers Computer Society; Association of Computing Machinery; Society of Amerian Military Engineers; Life Member, Reserve Officers Association. **Education:** University of Hawaii, B.S. in Computer Science (1995). **Personal Information:** Mr. Defiesta enjoys Latin and ballroom dancing.

Leasa M. Di Luna
Senior Data Architect
S1 Corporation
119 Russel Street
Littleton, MA 01460
(978) 985-6101
Fax: (508) 529-6684
leasa.diluna@s1.com

7372

Business Information: Having joined S1 Corporation in January 2000, Mrs. Di Luna serves in the position of Senior Data Architect. In this capacity, she manages the definition and development of architecture features and coordinates and plans the functionality included in architecture releases. With an excellent understanding of her field, Mrs. Di Luna works with object and data modeling, completes infrastructure analysis and design, and develops distribution standards and guidelines. Highly regarded by her colleagues, she is involved in the mentoring of engineers, conducting reviews, and coordinating with other architects. The key to success, according to Mrs. Di Luna, is her ability to tackle challenges and deliver results. S1 Corporation is a leading provider of online financial services solutions for the banking, brokerage, and insurance industries. Employing 1,700 individuals, and with global offices in 11 countries on 5 continents, S1 reports revenues of $92.9 million. The Company was established in 1995 as the first Internet bank, and has since narrowed its focus on offering the world's leading financial institutions the software and services necessary to build an effective transactional Internet presence. S1 works with global customers such as Bank of America, Citigroup, and Zurich Financial Services. **Career Highlights:** Senior Data Architect, S1 Corporation (2000-Present); Senior Design and Development Software Engineer, Raytheon Systems (1997-00); Software Engineer/Technical Leader, TMM, USA. **Associations & Accomplishments:** Raytheon Professional Software Engineering Association; Women in Technology. **Education:** University of Massachusetts. **Personal Information:** Married to F. Anthony in 1996. Two children: Justin and Lisa. Mrs. Di Luna enjoys coaching children's soccer, swimming, skiing and hiking.

Hai Thanh Do
Software Release Engineer
Electronics Arts
2027 Shellback Place
San Jose, CA 95133
(650) 628-7670
hdo@ea.com

7372

Business Information: Possessing an excellent understanding of the technology field, Mr. Do serves in the position of Software Release Engineer of Electronic Arts. As a savvy version control administrator, he is responsible for building and releasing software. Highly regarded in the industry, Mr. Do creates the software control management processes to effectively track and monitor software defects. He is also an Intranet developer. A visionary who has proven himself, Mr. Do goals include becoming a major software developer for Electonic Arts. His success reflects his ability to think outside the box, aggressively tackle challenges and new responsibilitie, and deliver results. Electronic Arts is a recognized leader in the video game industry. The Company creates video games and video game products. Currently, the Company is in the process of starting an Internet site so people can play online. Clients include Playstation and Nintendo. Established in 1982, Electronic Arts employs over 1,500 professional, technical, and support staff. **Career Highlights:** Software Release Engineer, Electronic Arts (1999-Present); Systems Administrator, KML/Vector Fabrication (1999); Software Release Engineer, Actel Corporation (1997-98); Computer Lab Assistant, California State University at Hayward (1997). **Associations & Accomplishments:** Director of Planning/Research (1997-Present), Casdai Youth Association; President (1994-95), Vietnamese Student Association. **Education:** California State University at Hayward, B.S. in Computer Science (1998). **Personal Information:** Mr. Do enjoys playing soccer and computers.

Gregory J. Dorman
Vice President of Research and Development
Information Builders Inc.
1250 Broadway, 38th Floor
New York, NY 10001-3701
(212) 736-4433

7372

Business Information: As Vice President, Mr. Dorman is responsible for the research and development of software programs for computers. Information Builders Inc., one of the oldest software companies in the United States, is a privately-held business software company. Products include: Focus (decision support), EVASQL (market leaders and client server), and a new product to be released serving Fortune 500 and 1000 companies worldwide. Established in 1975, Information Builders, Inc. reports annual revenue of $250 million and currently employs 1,500 people. **Career Highlights:** Information Builders Inc.: Vice President of Research and Development (1990-Present), Vice President of Development (1987-90), Director of Programming (1985-87). **Education:** Columbia University, M.S. (1982). **Personal Information:** Mr. Dorman enjoys ancient languages, sky diving, reading and travel.

Thomas S. Dunlap
Co-Founder/Senior Systems Advisor
Themis, Inc.
5173 Longrifle Road
Westerville, OH 43081-4459
(908) 233-8900
Fax: (614) 899-7333
tomd@themisinc.com

7372

Business Information: Possessing 30 solid years of experience in the technology field, Mr. Dunlap serves as Co-Founder and Senior Systems Advisor of Themis, Inc. In these capacities, he exercises oversight of development and large system performance management. He oversees onsite consulting, tunes the infrastructure, and finds solutions for DB2 databases and MQ series. Mr. Dunlap manages leading edge software development as well as coding and testing operations. Responsible for taking a leading role in driving growth, he develops and implements strategic and tactical technology, business, and marketing plans. He is also responsible for project management. Calculating and managing the budget, sales forecast, client-specific marketing programs, purchases, technical support, and training also falls within the realm of Mr. Dunlap's responsibilities. His extensive analytical skills have contributed to his career success. Becoming a Product Manager and eventually Chief Technology Officer or Chief Information Officer serves as his future goals. Themis, Inc. provides software development and consulting services. The Corporation resolves systems related problems and conducts capacity planning, systems integration, training, and education. In addition, Themis, Inc. helps tune systems and solves problems while serving as an IBM solution partner. Established in 1991, the Corporation has 18 well-trained technology professionals. **Career Highlights:** Co-Founder/Senior Systems Advisor, Themis, Inc. (1991-Present); Consultant, Online Software (1989-91); Product Manager, Morino Associates (1984-89). **Education:** Akron University, M.S. in Computer Science (1974); Kent State University, B.S. in Computer Science (1968). **Personal Information:** Married to Pamela in 1973. One child: Dawn Maria. Mr. Dunlap enjoys wine collecting, historical activities, Renaissance fairs and music.

Chris Hughes
Senior Director of Development
Micrografx
505 Millennium Drive
Allen, TX 75013
(214) 495-4230
Fax: (214) 495-4073
(214) 495-4000
chrish@micrografx.com

7372

Business Information: Mr. Hughes is the Senior Director of Development for Micrografx. He supervises three teams, a total of 35 employees, involved in software engineering, quality assurance, and documentation procedure for the Development Department. The teams design and test new software programs and author the explanatory manuals behind the new program. Responsible for all aspects of the production of his teams, he pays careful attention to the budget guidelines and strictly enforces the regulations. In the future, Mr. Hughes hopes to become the Vice President of Research and Development. His success is attributed to working effectively with a variety of people, with a focus on quality and cooperation. Micrografx manufactures prepackaged software for graphic-oriented businesses. Established in 1981, the Company prepares graphic titles for personal computer use in diagramming, 3-D designing, or photoediting. The Company processes the improvements of

each program and demonstrates their capabilities. Producing $50 million annually, the Company's largest buyers come from the automotive, aerospace, and defense industries. **Career Highlights:** Micrografx: Senior Director of Development (1998-Present), Director of International Development (1995-98); Manager of Software Development, A.C. Nielsen (1985-95). **Associations & Accomplishments:** Usability Professional Association; Localization International Standards Association. **Education:** University of Dallas, M.B.A. (1995); University of Vermont, B.S. (1985). **Personal Information:** Married. Two children.

Henry D. Jay
Product Manager, Siebel Call Center
Siebel Systems, Inc.
1855 South Grant Street
San Mateo, CA 94402
(650) 295-5366
Fax: (650) 295-5114
hjay@siebel.com

7372

Business Information: Mr. Jay functions in the capacity of Product Manager for Siebel Systems, Inc. Aggressively working within the design stages of the Siebel CTI and Siebel Call Center products, he strives to ensure the marketability, value, and quality of every product. Before joining the Siebel Systems team of professionals, Mr. Jay faithfully served in the positions of Advisory Product Manager, Technical Planner, and Staff Engineer and Scientist for Siemens. A savvy, 13 plus year expert in the technology field, Mr. Jay also meets with the creation team to guarantee the functionality and content of every product meets customer needs and requirements. Looking to the new millennium, he hopes to advance his position and expand his responsibilities. Mr. Jay's success is attributed to his mentors and his ability to think outside the box, deliver results, and tackle challenges and new responsibilities. Siebel Systems designs, develops, and markets enterprise front office customer relationship management software systems. Established in 1993, the Company develops and manufactures front office software products for businesses around the world. A staff of 2,500 plus employees focuses on customer success and satisfaction in all aspects of the Company. **Career Highlights:** Product Manager, Siebel Call Center, Siebel Systems, Inc. (1997-Present); Siemens: Advisory Product Manager, Global Call Center Products (1996-98), Technical Planner, Network Management Systems (1994-96), Staff Engineer/Scientist (1991-94). **Education:** California Polytechnic State University, B.S. in Computer Science (1986). **Personal Information:** Married.

Deke Andrew Johnson

Electronic Sales Manager
Oracle Corporation
500 Oracle Parkway OPL-4
Redwood Shores, CA 94065
(650) 633-4269
Fax: (650) 506-7126

7372

Business Information: Combining technical skills and management expertise, Mr. Johnson serves as an Electronic Sales Manager for Oracle Corporation. He governs the DMD sales force and assumes the ultimate accountability for all of the Corporation's DMD sales. Responsible for setting the vision and voice to improve e-business as we know it, he is determined to make Oracle the foremost leader and expert in e-commerce. Born with good business sense, he credits his current professional success to his drive, solid work ethic, and ability to "work smart." Mr. Johnson is committed to further development of the Corporation, coordinating strategic planning to ensure a bright future as a Director. Oracle Corporation, most famous for its operating program of the same name, specializes in the design and development of software and e-commerce solutions. The Corporation has grown rapidly since its inception, becoming a leader in the software industry. Operations employ the skilled services of 40,000 professionals and boasts more than $8 billion a year in sales. **Career Highlights:** Oracle Corporation: Electronic Sales Manager (1999-Present), Account Manager (1997-99); Sales/Operations Director, FAI (1994-97). **Associations & Accomplishments:** Toastmasters. **Education:** State University of New York at Albany, B.S. in Marketing, Management, and Economics. **Personal Information:** Mr. Johnson enjoys softball and tennis.

Sean R. Kenney
Client Engagement Manager
Commerce One
8042 Iglesia Drive
Dublin, CA 94568
(650) 465-9851
sean.kenney@commerceone.com

7372

Business Information: Tasked with building a consulting group in the engineering department to engage commerce customers, Mr. Kenney has several managers helping to deliver solutions to his customers as well as a number of engagement leads. Commerce One is a leader in the B2B e-commerce space leading the way to bring businesses together on the Internet. The Company is an international company delivering solutions around the world. **Career Highlights:** Client Engagement Manager, Commerce One (2000-Present); Magenic Technologies: Managing Director (1997-00), Computer Consultant (1995-97); Senior Consultant, Analsys International (1994-95); Senior Software Engineer, The Wyatt Company (1993-94). **Associations & Accomplishments:** Microsoft Certified Solutions Developer. **Education:** Regis University, B., divingS. (1991); Pikes Peak Community College, A.A. (1989). **Personal Information:** Married to Teri in 1983. Two children: Ann and Sean II. Mr. Kenney enjoys skiing and sailing.

Gregory J. Kittredge

NT Systems Administrator
Gamesville
1049 Belmont Street
Watertown, MA 02472-1022
(617) 673-1588
Fax: (617) 673-1199
gkittredge@gamesville.com

7372

Business Information: Mr. Kittredge got involved in the technology industry due to his interest in the field and by chance. Prior to his association with Gamesville as NT Systems Administrator, he installed LAN and software for his parents' mortgage company, Kittredge Mortgage Corporation, increasing the corporation's potential by 200 percent. In his current role, he installs operating systems and database management software, monitors and tunes systems software, peripherals, and networks, as well as resolving systems problems. He attributes his success to being given the "freedom to do." His primary goal is to remain with Gamesville. Mr. Kittredge's intention is to remain on the cutting edge of the technology field by resourcing, experimentation, staying ahead, and additional training. His professional success reflects his ability think outside the box, take on challenges and deliver results. An international company established in 1991, Gamesville develops and hosts interactive video games for the Internet, specifically for the Lycos domain. Presently, the Company is located in Watertown, Massachusetts, and employs a staff of 900 people who help generate in excess of $5 billion annually. **Career Highlights:** NT Systems Administrator, Gamesville (1999-Present); Technical Consultant, Mass Financial Services (1998-99); NT Systems Administrator, Kittredge Mortgage Corporation (1989-98). **Associations & Accomplishments:** Guilford Hounds; Mational Aeronautical Association; PADI; National Rifle Association. **Education:** Castleton State College, B.S. (1995); Microsoft Certified Systems Engineer. **Personal Information:** Mr. Kittredge enjoys scuba diving, being a private pilot and MFH of foxhunting.

Shawn B. Landrigan

Senior Account Executive
Novell, Inc.
2323 Horsepen Road
Herndon, VA 20171
(703) 713-3506
slandrigan@novell.com

7372

Business Information: Serving as Senior Account Executive for Novell, Inc., Mr. Landrigan is charged with selling technology to the Department of Defense and other large companies. Possessing an excellent understanding of his field, he handles account consultation, software maintenance, client appointments, and contract negotiations. Mr. Landrigan frequently travels to ensure customer support and contract closure. He has established himself as a prominant business leader, securing a position in a world class company. Highly regarded by his colleagues, Mr. Landrigan demonstrates his keen business sense and attention to detail to achieve record sales and fluid corporate operations. Novell, Inc. is the world's largest networking software and hardware manufacturer and distibutor. International in scope, Novell provides components for networks and systems functions. Established in 1985, Novell has gained rapid success providing technology to the Department of Defense and other government agencies. By maintaining a multi-million dollar annual revenue, this company employs over 5,000 people in over 100 manufacturing, distribution, and administrative sites. Novell plans to expand operations to additional offshore locations, allowing for further international recognition and corporate profit potential. **Career Highlights:** Senior Account Executive, Novell, Inc. (1998-Present); Business Development Manager, CACI (1992-98); Account Manager, Digital Equipment Corporation (1987-97). **Associations & Accomplishments:** AFCEA; Sierra Club; Special Olympics. **Education:** Plymouth State College, Bachelor's degree in

Business with minor in Marketing (1984). **Personal Information:** Married to Julia in 1996. One child: Alexandra.

Lubomir Litchev

Senior Software Engineer
Symantec Corporation
20300 Stevens Creek Boulevard
Cupertino, CA 95014
(408) 864-2941
Fax: (408) 253-4593
llitchev@symantec.com

7372

Business Information: Rapidly ascending through the ranks of Symantec Corporation, Mr. Litchev exhibits traits and knowledge necessary for success as the Senior Software Engineer of a major corporation. His extensive work background, education, and willingness to adapt to new and emerging technologies sets him apart as a leader in his field. As the Senior Software Engineer, he helped design and implement seamless debugging systems for Java based software. Utilizing Visual Café, Mr. Litchev instructed and aided his team in the development of the Debug Engine. In addition, he worked on EROT, a debugging system which works on a multiple WAN system. In his position, he also heads the Internet Development Division and oversees all Web development and design. Siting technology as the driving force in his life, Mr. Litchev wants to stay technically oriented, continue working on current projects, and also begin more exciting and innovative projects as well. Symantec Corporation develops tools in order to protect and safeguard most computer systems. The Corporation deals mainly with three divisions: Utilities, Internet, and Windows. Each division is responsible for the research and design of techniques that will enhance profitability and productivity for Symantec's clients. Established in 1982, the Corporation currently estimates annual revenue in excess of $600 million and employs more than 2,400 qualified professional, technical, and support staff. **Career Highlights:** Symantec Corporation - Internet Tools Division: Senior Software Engineer (1998-Present), Software Engineer (1997-98); SQA Engineer/Automation Lead, Symantec Corporation - Contact Management Division (1996-97). **Associations & Accomplishments:** Local Committee President/Founder, AIESEC (Student Association at the University of Gabrovo in Bulgaria). **Education:** Technical University of Gabrovo, Master's degree in Computer Science (1994). **Personal Information:** Mr. Litchev enjoys the outdoors, hiking and horseback riding.

Gary Lyng

General Manager of Consumer Products
VERITAS Software
1600 Plymouth Street
Mountain View, CA 94043
(650) 526-2604
Fax: (650) 526-2733
glyng@veritas.com

7372

Business Information: Serving as General Manager of Consumer Products of VERITAS Software, Mr. Lyng provides direction for the VERITAS Products Group. He determines the strategic direction of the Group and formulates product and marketing plans to keep Veritas out-front in the industry. Utilizing his leadership and systems expertise, he conducts extensive market research to determine what prospective clients want and expect from products. Mr. Lyng closely monitors product testing, develops innovative PC solutions, and strives to increase the Corporation's sales. Enjoying taking complex issues and making them easier, his highlights include writing a midware program for Aston-Tate, and taking an engineering business and turning it into a multi-tier oriented business. He plans to remain with VERITAS Software, as he continues to project a positive business image, and render outstanding customer services. Operating as the third largest software company in the world, VERITAS Software is based in Mountain View, California. Veritas is a leading international provider of enterprise class application storage management systems. Listed as one of Forbes Magazine's 200 best small companies, Veritas was formed in 1982. The Corporation is ranked first worldwide in cross platform storage management software solutions, and generates an annual turnover of $10.4 billion. The Mountain View, California location produces $680 million in sales, with the assistance of 2,700 enthusiastic representatives. **Career Highlights:** General Manager of Consumer Products, VERITAS Software (1997-Present); Director of Marketing, Visioneer; Director of Marketing, Checkpoint Software; Director of Marketing, Gupta Corporation. **Education:** degree in Computer Science. **Personal Information:** Married to Gina Marie in 1994. One child: Daniella Marie.

Judith L. Marcus

Senior Consultant
Oracle Corporation
245 East 40th Street
New York, NY 10016-1730
(212) 949-0713
jlmarcos@worldnet.att.net

7372

Business Information: Ms. Marcus serves as Senior Consultant for Oracle Corporation. Operating out of the New York office, she is responsible for the implementation and documentation of new systems. Her work focuses on the use of the product and she concentrates on creating effective training programs and user manuals for new programs. A savvy, 12 year professional expert, Ms. Marcus also monitors each program to ensure it meets the expectations of all clients. Looking the Year 2000 and beyong, she hopes to become more involved in the World Wide Web applications and, feeling she was born to teach, she plans to enhance her role with training seminars and tutorials within the Corporation. Oracle Corporation is one of the world's most reputable computer consulting service providers. Headquartered in California, the Corporation operates locations around the globe to support the diverse clientele and their requests. The most popular service Oracle offers is its financial application development, within the program, all aspects of system development and implementation are covered to ensure the satisfaction of each client. Established in the early 1980s, Oracle continues to be a leading force in the information technology age and has developed several of the most state-of-the-art technologies for its clients. **Career Highlights:** Senior Consultant, Oracle Corporation (1998-Present); Assistant Manager of Financial Systems, Insurance Services Office, Inc. (1987-98). **Education:** Pace University; Marymount Manhattan College; Brooklyn College. **Personal Information:** Ms. Marcus enjoys swimming, gourmet foods, jazz and shows.

Don H. Marshall

Technical Advisor
Attachmate Corporation
3617 131st Avenue SE
Bellevue, WA 98006
(425) 649-6452
Fax: (425) 474-9924
donna@attachmate.com

7372

Business Information: Serving as a Technical Advisor at Attachmate Corporation, Mr. Marshall provides high-end data communications and network consulting and training services to customer support operations. After evaluating the business impact of new technologies, Mr. Marshall develops appropriate learning tools and determines efficient delivery mechanisms. In addition, Mr. Marshall provides advanced technical consulting to the customer support, systems engineering, and software development staff. Established in 1984, Attachmate Corporation has become the leading provider of host communication and terminal emulation software and services. With 14 years of experience in the market, Attachmate Corporation has expanded to include a 2,000 member workforce and has reached an annual revenue of over $400 million. As a Consulting Systems Engineer at GRID Systems Corporation, Mr. Marshall provided telephone support, onsite assistance and training to corporate and government clients. Mr. Marshall gained Novell CNE and CNI status and managed a Novell Authorized Education Center (NAEC). He also helped design his multidisciplinary degree in Business Computer Instruction from Western Washington University that he received in 1984. **Career Highlights:** Technical Advisor, Attachmate Corporation (1993-Present); Senior Consulting Engineer, Grid Systems Corporation (1989-93); Systems Engineer/Computer Instructor, Tandy Corporation (1985-89). **Associations & Accomplishments:** Data Processing Management Association; Network Professional Association; Puget Sound Novell User Group; Technical Support Advisory Committee, Bellevue Community College. **Education:** Western Washington University, B.A. in Business Computer Instruction (1984); Novell Certified Network Engineer/Certified Novell Instructor. **Personal Information:** Mr. Marshall enjoys mountain biking, camping, skiing and photography.

Lars E. Martinsson

Senior Applications Architect
Oracle Corporation
500 Oracle Parkway 6 op 9
Redwood City, CA 94065
(650) 506-1982
lmartins@us.oracle.com

7372

Business Information: Mr. Martinsson serves in the role of Senior Applications Architect in product development at Oracle Corporation. His responsibilities include overall architecture responsibility for all Sales, Marketing, and BIS product families. These product families represent a major part of the Customer Relationship Management solution Oracle offers and includes products like iMarketing, iStore,

Field Sales, Telesales, Marketing intelligence, Customer intelligence, Sales intelligence, Sales Compensation, and Marketing Encyclopedia System. As a savvy five-year veteran of the information technology field, Mr. Martinsson has served with Oracle in a variety of roles since joining the team as Consultant in 1994. Mr. Martinsson is also a member of Oracle's Architecture Review Group that resolves major cross-product issues for the entire Corporation. **Career Highlights:** Oracle Corporation United States: Senior Applications Architect (1999-Present), Project Leader (1998-99), Senior Applications Developer (1997-98); Senior Consultant, Oracle Corporation New Zealand (1995-97); Consultant, Oracle Corporation Sweden (1994-95). **Education:** University of Stockholm, Sweden, M.Sc. (1994); University of Umea, Sweden, B.Sc. (1993). **Personal Information:** Mr. Martinsson enjoys hunting, fishing, travel, squash, cross-country skiing and running. Mr. Martinsson is fluent in English and Swedish as well as speaks some Norwegian and Danish.

Felicity F. McGourty
Director of Product Management Strategy
Tivoli Systems
9442 North Capital of Texas Highway
Austin, TX 78759
(512) 436-8709
Fax: (512) 436-1191

7372

Business Information: Ms. McGourty serves as Director of Product Management Strategy of Tivoli Systems. She determines the overall strategic direction and future requirements for advanced technology in the markets. A savvy, 19 year professional, she devotes countless hours to studying and examining investment strategies and analyzing possible alternatives for new technologies. She is also responsible for developing, building, and delivering new products on schedule and within budgetary constraints. Her involvement in the discovery, investigation, and deployment of leading edge technologies within Tivoli Systems demonstrates her leadership ability and technical skills. In the future, Ms. McGourty's plans on attaining the position of Vice President, enabling her to drive the market and establish Tivoli Systems as the model for ebusiness. Her advice is "keep every day a challenge." Operating from Austin, Texas, Tivoli Systems provides system management assistance to its clients within the information technology aspects of their daily operations. A subsidiary of IBM, the Company oversees the availability, distribution, and management of all information technology related tools. The Company strives to anticipate technology changes and evolutions throughout its daily procedures and works to implement the next wave of future technology into the market place. Presently, the Company employs a work force of more than 4,000 professional, technical, and support staff. **Career Highlights:** Director of Product Management Strategy, Tivoli Systems (1997-Present); Director of Product Management, Bode & Babbage (1992-97); Sales Executive, IBM Corporation (1982-91). **Education:** University of Pretoria, B.S. (1981); University of Potchefstrom, degree in Management Information Systems; University of Witwatosrand, degree in Business Management. **Personal Information:** Married to Gerald in 1997.

Laura Anne Michael
Senior Manager of Publications, Localization and Usability
Attachmate Corporation
P.O. Box 90026
Bellevue, WA 98009
(425) 849-6615
Fax: (425) 649-6048
laura@attachmate.com

7372

Business Information: Ms. Michael serves as Senior Manager at Attachmate Corporation. She oversees the writing of software, its usability, and the documentation localization process. To that end, she is in charge of a team of technical writers producing software documentation for high-end users and front-end users. Performing document management and strategy analysis, Ms. Michael checks for vendor's relations language stipulation and usability by testing software in its early stages, redesigning it if necessary. Beginning her career in 1980, she started as a prospectus writer for the legal department and has since worked her way into technical writing and up to her current position. Ms. Michael attributes her professional success solely to her determination and her desire to succeed. She plans to become more involved with e-commerce relations, striving toward the ultimate goal of the localization and globalization of clients' needs. Established in 1982, Attachmate Corporation is a privately held software company. The Corporation specializes in providing Web-to-enterprise, desktop-to-host, host-to-Web, and Web-to-host solutions for the access and management of business information. Directing its services toward Fortune 500 companies, the Corporation's main client bases are those businesses with IBM applications and mainframe systems in various industries. A staff of approximately 1,900 skilled individuals is employed to attend to all aspects of operations. **Career**

Highlights: Attachmate Corporation: Senior Manager of Publications, Localization and Usability (1999-Present), Manager of Publications (1989-98), Technical Writing (1988). **Associations & Accomplishments:** Advisory Board, University of Washington, Technical Writing and Editing Certificate Program.

Aleksey Moiseyev, Ph.D.
Software Engineer
Parametric Technology Corporation
128 Technology Drive
Waltham, MA 02154
(781) 398-5235
amoisseev@ptc.com

7372

Business Information: With extensive education and experience in the field of information technology, Dr. Moiseyev serves as a Software Engineer for Parametric Technology Corporation. In this capacity, he works within the department of research and development, providing his expertise in designing new software products for sale and distribution by the Corporation. Dr. Moiseyev has been recognized for his contributions to the computer science industry, publishing 50 articles in various magazines and publications. He is also the author of two books, one of which is used frequently by leaders in the information technology industry in Russia. Demonstrating a love and talent for his work, Dr. Moiseyev continues to develop innovative products and strives to achieve a higher level of professional success in software research and development. Parametric Technology Corporation is one of the five largest software companies in the world. The Corporation focuses its efforts on the design, development, and production of programming software, catering to corporate clients internationally. Best known for its computer aided designs, the Corporation's products are used in the manufacturing industry by such business giants as Toyota and Siemens. Parametric Technology Corporation maintains its headquarters in the United States, but utilizes the talents of individuals from across the globe. **Career Highlights:** Software Engineer, Parametric Technology Corporation (1999-Present); Senior Engineer, Joint Stock HGS Center (1996-99); Assistant Professor, MIIT (1991-96). **Education:** MIIT, Moscow, Russia, Ph.D. (1991). **Personal Information:** Married to Tatyana in 1997. Dr. Moiseyev enjoys reading.

Nina M. Moorehouse
Consultant
Novell, Inc.
2205 Erin Way
Bel Air, MD 21015
(800) 714-1700
Fax: (954) 697-8392
nmoorehouse@novell.com

7372

Business Information: Mrs. Moorehouse was the first female systems engineer at GE Capital. Currently, however, she functions as a Consultant for Novell, Inc. Her duties include speaking with customers and potential clients of Novell about their products and networking technologies and capabilities. Enterprise and information systems environments are also major areas of Mrs. Moorehouse's concern. On many occasions, she travels and meets with clients personally, reporting special projects for Novell and how they would meet their special needs. The key to success, Mrs. Moorehouse states, is her personal drive and a very supportive husband. As for her future, she foresees staying with the Corporation and advancing upwards. Established in 1983, Novell, Inc. is headquartered in Provo, Utah. The Corporation is a leader in the development and implementation of networking software. In addition, the Corporation produce complimentary software. In a world of changing technologies, Novell, Inc. has remained the second largest manufacturer of networking software. This has lead to an estimated annual sales figure of $1.3 billion. The Corporation employs 4,700 skilled individuals. **Career Highlights:** Consultant, Novell, Inc. (1999-Present); Senior Systems Engineer, GE Capital, Information Technologies Solutions (1994-99); Information Center Analyst, Michigan Senate (1992-94); Software Instructor, Automation Resource Corporation (1989-92). **Education:** Michigan State University, M.A. in Educational Systems Development (1995); Milwaukee School of Engineering, B.S. in Technical Communication (1989). **Personal Information:** Married to David in 1989. Mrs. Moorehouse enjoys roller blading and motorcycle dirt bike riding.

Erhan Odok
Senior Consulting Specialist
Oracle Corporation
5955 TG Lee Boulevard
Orlando, FL 32822-4427
(407) 458-1123
Fax: (407) 458-4813
eodok@us.oracle.com

7372

Business Information: Holding the position of Senior Consulting Specialist, Mr. Odok has been providing professional services for the Oracle Corporation for over six years. Specializing in the creation and delivery of information software suited for the particular purposes the client establishes, he forms confidential and reliable relationships in order to provide value added and premium services in training and sales escalations. Managing project development, Mr. Odok utilizes his vast knowledge in the field of information technology to produce high quality and dependable software. Continuing his growth with Oracle, he remains committed to the furthering advancement of the Corporation and eventually attaining the role of high end technical architect. Established in 1977, Oracle Corporation is the world's second largest independent supplier of software for information management. Divided into several levels of information technology development, the division Center of Expertise specializes in high level training and escalation services. Performing architectural reviews and performance for Oracle's top 50 clients, consultants involve themselves in site visits in order to produce efficient software programs designed to promote productivity and further expansion. Adding value to their client's businesses, Oracle remains committed to providing optimal information management assistance. **Career Highlights:** Senior Consulting Specialist, Oracle Corporation (1997-Present); Technical Support Manager, Oracle Turkey (1994-97); Technical Support Analyst, IBM Solution Partner Turkey (1990-94). **Education:** Bogazici University, B.S. in Computer Engineering (1988). **Personal Information:** Married to Miné in 1990. Two children: Selim and Ebru.

Philippe Parot
President
Sarl Cyberjet
12 Avenue 8 Mai 45
Etampes, France 91150
+33 164947502

7372

Business Information: Displaying strong management and leadership skills, Mr. Parot functions as President of Sarl Cyberjet. Some of his major accomplishments with the Company have included increasing the staff, helping profits double, and building an alliance with other airlines. Mr. Parot serves as a powerful asset to the organization and effectively applies sound management principles. Very goal oriented, he excels in planning, forecasting, setting objectives, and determining courses of action. As 98 percent owner of the Company, he exercises control of sales, marketing, and negotiations as well as project management and financial strategies. Mr. Parot projects self-confidence, authority, and enthusiasm. He strives to make more meaningful and challenging contributions for the betterment of the Company. A visionary, he ensures that Sarl Cyberjet's vision and mission are clearly articulated. Sarl Cyberjet develops software for air transport companies. Additionally, the Company produces airline software, air ground data link communications, and distribution agreements with larger companies. **Career Highlights:** President, Sarl Cyberjet (1997-Present); Marketing Manager Ground Datalink, Rockwell Collins, United Kingdom (1994-97); Vice President, SATOA (1989-94); Flight Operations Manager, Europe Aero Service (1987-89); IT Manager, Air Caledonie (1984-87). **Associations & Accomplishments:** City Mayor Assistant. **Education:** ENAC, Engineering degree (1981); French Civil Aviation University, Air Transport Engineering degree. **Personal Information:** Married to Marie-Laure in 1984. Three children.

Ashutosh Patil
Project Lead
Oracle Corporation
60PD608-500 Oracle Parkway
Redwood Shores, CA 94065
(650) 506-0891
Fax: (650) 654-6212
arpatil@us.oracle.com

7372

Business Information: Possessing over six years of experience in software development, Mr. Patil serves as Project Lead of the Oracle Corporation. Acting as Lead Developer, he diagnoses problems in existing software, resolves the problems, and develops new versions of the same programs. Mr. Patil works with a team of three or four engineers, to perform the software analysis, development, and new specifications. He advises others to be technology savvy, understand the terminology, have an awareness of the industry and where the trends are heading. Coordinating resources and schedules, overseeing time lines and assignments, calculating and managing budgets, and providing cohesive leadership also fall within the realm of Mr. Patil's responsibilities. Crediting his success to hard work and fortuitous events, he plans to enter into management, taking on more responsibility and dealing less with the technical issues. Mr. Patil's success reflects his ability to think out-of-the-box and take on new challenges. Established in 1980, the Oracle Corporation develops software for an international clientele and maintains corporate headquarters in Redwood Shores, California. Approximately 25 to 30 skilled professionals are employed in the Software Division where the majority of business is from Fortune 500 companies. The Division primarily develops promotional and financial accounts software and performs software defects diagnosis. Presently, Oracle reports annual revenues in excess of $7 billion. **Career Highlights:** Project Lead, Oracle Corporation (1997-Present); Software Engineer, Information Technology Solutions (1996); Systems Officer, Telco-Pune (1993). **Education:** University of California at Berkeley, M.B.A. (1999); College of Engineering, University of Pune, Bachelor's degree in Mechanical Engineering (1993).

Bowie J. Poag

Founder/Project Manager
Propaganda
3250 East Fort Lowell Road, Apartment 114
Tucson, AZ 85716
(520) 327-5259
Fax: (520) 420-7759
poag@u.arizona.edu

7372

Business Information: Displaying his leadership skills in this demanding position, Mr. Poag serves as Founder and Project Manager of Propaganda. Utilizing more than seven years of extensive educational and employment experience, he focuses on implementing specific procedures and policies to produce the best possible system and graphics package available on the market. Coordinating with vendors and managing annual budgets, Mr. Poag is responsible for directing funds and materials to various projects. Involved in consulting, he utilizes expert communications techniques in negotiating contracts and establishing reliable and confidential client accounts. Implementing attained skills and knowledge in his field, Mr. Poag dedicates his attention towards the design and development of the Company's Web site. Dedicated to the commercializing of the Company, his goal is to facilitate continued Company growth and geographic expansion. Founded in 1998, Propaganda specializes in the production and distribution of the multi-volume series of desktop enhancement graphics packages used in Linux and various other operating systems and industries. Located in Tucson, Arizona, the Company employs the technical expertise of 11 qualified individuals to orchestrate all activities of design, manufacture, testing, and distribution. Establishing high standards of excellence for others in the industry, the Company remains committed to the incorporation of the latest technologies ensuring an expansion in their client base. **Career Highlights:** Founder/Project Manager, Propaganda (1998-Present); UNIX Network Manager, University of Arizona, Department of Chemistry (1998-99); Senior Lab Coordinator, Business and Professional Institute (1994-96); Student Aide, Seton Computing Center (1993-94). **Associations & Accomplishments:** Tucson Free UNIX Group; Project Manager and Founder of System IZ; IPO Invitations; Red Hat Software; VA LINUX Systems. **Education:** University of Arizona, Bachelor's Degree (In Progress); College of DuPage, A.S. (1996).

Peter J. Robson

Product Manager
Oracle Corporation
1191 Alameda, Apartment 21
Belmont, CA 94002
(650) 506-1204
Fax: (650) 506-7615
probson@us.oracle.com

7372

Business Information: As Product Manager at Oracle Corporation, Mr. Robson is a member of the Enterprise Managerial Division and the Systems Product Management Group. He arranges customer visits, conducts presentations,and creates marketing materials. Drawing upon his extensive technical expertise, Mr. Robson coordinates all strategic sessions and other activities to provide direction in the development of GUI tools for databases. Mr. Robson oversees quality assurance to guarantee all products meet maximum specifications. His goal is to expand his expertise and interests in a broader field, concentrating his energies in marketing. Mr. Robson attributes his accomplishments to possessing motivation and enthusiasm. Success is attributed to his motivation and enthusiasm. Oracle Corporation engages in the development of database software and end user tools for small to large companies. Established in 1978, the Corporation creates software suitable for storing and accessing all applications data. Skilled technicians and engineers employ the latest technological advancements to provide individualized information systems. International in scope, the Corporation is comprised of a considerable workforce of 40,000. **Career Highlights:** Oracle Corporation: Product Manager (1999-Present), Senior Curriculum Developer (1998-99), Technical Specialist/Instructor (1996-98); Database Administrator, Canberra Institute of Technology (1992-96). **Associations & Accomplishments:** Northern California Oracle Users Group; Boys Brigade; Salvation Army/Red Cross. **Education:** University of Canberra, Bachelor's degree in Engineering (1996); Phillip College. **Personal Information:** Mr. Robson enjoys travel and gardening.

Sergey Shindnes

Senior Programmer
Information Builders Inc.
Farmington, CT 06032
(860) 339-5863
Fax: (860) 674-9085
sshind@ix.netcom.com

7372

Business Information: Using extensive skills and expertise in computer and database systems, Mr. Shindnes functions in the capacity of Senior Programmer with Information Builders Inc. He is responsible for developing state-of-the-art software used as both tools and applications. Before coming on board to the Information Builders' team of professionals in 1997, Mr. Shindnes faithfully served as Software Developer with new Dimension Software. His background also includes stints as Programmer at SURECOMP Development and Software Engineer and Team Lead for All - Union Research Institute. In addition, he has played a key role in developing and implementing enterprise data security for the Windows NT platform. In 1992, Mr. Shindnes won the "Borland Information Award." He believes that success comes from a postive mixture of education and experience. As for the future, the next millennium, he plans to remain in his current position and help the Corporation to prosper and expand operations. Founded in 1985, Information Builders Inc. engages in consulting and software development. As information builders, the Corporation specializes in design and development of cutting edge database infrastructures. Information Builders utilizes the efforts of more than 240 professional, technical, and support personnel to conduct all aspects of day-to-day operations. **Career Highlights:** Senior Programmer, Information Builders Inc. (1997-Present); Software Developer, New Dimension Software (1995-97); Programmer, SURECOMP Development (1992-95); Software Engineer/Team Lead, All Union Research Institute (1985-91). **Associations & Accomplishments:** Institute of Electronics and Electrical Engineers. **Education:** M.S. degree in Applied Math (1988). **Personal Information:** Married to Olga in 1985. Two children: Alexander and Gabriel. Mr. Shindnes enjoys tennis, skiing, reading, photography and listening to music.

Keith R. Slater

Director of Clinical Implementations
Medic Computer Systems
8601 Six Forks Road, Suite 300
Raleigh, NC 27615-5276
(800) 877-5678
Fax: (919) 846-4006
keiths@medcmp.com

7372

Business Information: Mr. Slater serves as Director of Clinical Implementations of Medic Computer Systems. A savvy, eight year veteran, he is in charge of training the staff who travel to deal directly with clients, thereby catering to a higher level of expectations from Medic Computer Systems customers. Mr. Slater is also responsible for important duties such as projecting revenues, personnel staffing, and determining and implementing strategic objectives. Managing a staff of 25 experts, he ensures all clients are able to make full use of the Company's software capabilities. A recognized expert, Mr. Slater intends on staying abreast of emerging technology and continuing to provide the best service possible. His highlights include being successful at implementing at wide range of products, taking non-profit divisions to profit in 12 months, and building teams with synergy and technical strength. Success, according to Mr. Slater, is due to his ability to interact with people as well as his analytical skills. Medic Computer Systems, established in1982, engages in the sales and marketing of software for medical administrative programs, acting as a vendor of such products as electronic scanners, systems for scheduling, scheduling, collections, and electronically filed records. All programs created are sold to a variety of medical facilities like doctor's offices, clinics, and hospitals. Over 1,600 highly intelligent and dedicated professionals work together to ensure that the medical field is provided with the best software for high-paced working environments. **Career Highlights:** Medic Computer Systems: Director of Clinical Implementations (1998-Present), Custom Programming Manager (1998), Regional Field Manager (1995-98); Physician Services Manager, Forum Health Care (1990-95). **Education:** Youngstown State University, Bachelor's degree in Computer Information Systems (1992). **Personal Information:** Mr. Slater enjoys physical fitness.

Daniel J. Smith

Quality Assurance Database Administrator
BMC
10431 Morado Circle
Austin, TX 78759
(512) 340-6413
Fax: (512) 996-6514
daniel_smith@bmc.com

7372

Business Information: Currently working in the Quality Assurance Department of BMC, Mr. Smith serves as Quality Assurance Database Administrator. He primarily deals with end to end quality assurance testing of enterprise data processing for mainframe and client-server databases. The Corporation's core set of products relate to migrating from a mainframe to a client-server based environment. Utilizing 18 years of experience, Mr. Smith has personally set up Sybase on client-server platforms, set up the target test environment, and mapped out test cases. Throughout his career, he is proud to have bridged Powerbuilding to IDMS on a mainframe, combined client-server processing with mainframe processing, and written interface messages for Tandem. Mr. Smith is dedicated to the success of the Corporation and plans to add additional target platforms to help make the Enterprise Data Processing Division a success, taking mainframe to client-server integration in new directions. Created in 1980, BMC is a member of the Forbes 500 and S&P 500. Based in Houston, Texas, the Corporation engages in software development with a focus on database administration software tools. The Corporation consists of a work force of 6,000 qualified professionals and boasts $1.3 billion in yearly sales. **Career Highlights:** Quality Assurance Database Administrator, BMC (1999-Present); Litton Enterprise Solutions: Principal Engineer (1998-99), Database Consultant (1996-98), Senior Technical Consultant (1995-96). **Associations & Accomplishments:** AICCP. **Education:** Austin College, B.A. in Mathematics (1981). **Personal Information:** Mr. Smith enjoys reading, renaissance festivals and listening to music.

Steven E. Smith

Director of Information Technology
Corepoint Technologies
9025 River Road
Indianapolis, IN 46240
(317) 554-7700
Fax: (317) 554-7955

7372

Business Information: An innovative, focused, and high-impact information technology leader, Mr. Smith was recruited to the Corepoint Technologies team in 1998. At present, he assumes the responsibilities of Director of Information Technology with oversight of all aspects of day-to-day administrative and operational activities. Mr. Smith, demonstrating strategic systems and technical expertise, controls and manages the Company's global infrastructure. He is responsible for formulating powerful strategic and tactical acquisition and transition, business, and marketing plans. Owning a consistent record of delivering results through leadership and communication and interpersonal skills, Mr. Smith supports the Company's worldwide network infrastructure, internal ADPS's, and hardware. Aligning the information technology goals with the Company's overall objectives also fall within the realm of his responsibilities. His career highlights include development of the infrastructure at Corepoint. Mr. Smith's success is attributed to understanding the Company and being a people's person. His future aspiration is to become a Chief Information Officer of a technology company. A software developer, Corepoint Technologies generates in excess of $350 million in annual revenues. As a division of IBM, the Company also features customer relationship management. Established in 1998, Corepoint Technologies employs a work force of more than 554 professional, technical, and support personnel. **Career Highlights:** Director of Information Technology, Corepoint Technologies (1998-Present); Midwest Regional Information Technology Manager, Tivoli Systems (1997-98); Manager of Information Technology, Software Artistic (1996-97); Technical Support Manager, Sigma Micro Corporation (1992-96). **Education:** Purdue University: B.S. (1992), A.A.S. **Personal Information:** Married to Victoria L. in 1992. Two children: Allison and Noha. Mr. Smith enjoys spending time with his family.

Michael S. Vedda

Information Technology Director
S1 Corporation
2840 San Tomas Expressway
Santa Clara, CA 95051
(408) 982-2000
Fax: (408) 928-9957
mikev@edify.com

7372

Business Information: Mr. Vedda demonstrates extensive understanding of the technical field as he maintains operations of the Asia Pacific and Western United States regions of S1 Corporation's targeted area. In this capacity, he oversees the maintenance, upgrade, and implementation of hardware and software as well as infastructure planning. Directly involved in the devleopment of strategic business planning through his contributions to design and integration of practical application, Mr. Vedda administers tasks effectively to his staff as they strive to complete corporate goals. The proud recipient of several internal and community wide awards, Mr. Vedda attributes success to focus and dedication within the industry. Edify Corporation merged with S1 in September 1999 to form S1 Corporation. Currently one of the most powerful Internet based banking industries in the world, the Corporation also hosts international data centers. **Career Highlights:** Information Technology Director, S1 Corporation (1996-Present); LAN Administrator, Safeway (1985-96). **Associations & Accomplishments:** Microsoft; Novell; NPA. **Education:** Golden Gate University, M.B.A. (1999); San Jose State University, B.S. in Accounting. **Personal Information:** Mr. Vedda enjoys teaching, biking and outdoor activities.

Lee M. Vermont

Raid Test Engineer
American Megatrends Inc.
6145-F Northbelt Parkway
Norcross, GA 30071
(770) 246-8600
lvermont@mindspring.com

7372

Business Information: Proficient in all areas of technology, Mr. Vermont displays his skills in his highly specialized position of RAID Test Engineer with American Megatreds Inc. Beginning his association with the Corporation in 1998, he effectively utilizes his knowledge of systems development and management in order to provide a more functional and efficient systems infrastructure. Capitalizing on more than three years of practical experience in the field of technology, Mr. Vermont implements specific procedures and policies into the developmental process with an emphasis on improving production, distribution, and the further expansion of the product line. With a notable ability to understand complex problems and communicate them to both client and internal staff, he provides troubleshooting and system support for the many clients and their businesses. Continuing his growth professionally through the fulfillment of his responsibilities and his involvement in the advancement of operations, Mr. Vermont anticipates his promotion to Head of Testing Department or to extending his focus on networking with American Megatreds Inc. Serving an international clientele, American Megatreds Inc. was established in 1995 and is dedicated to providing quality computer technology services in the development of motherboards, RAID controllers, computer BIOS, and software utility systems. Headquartered in Norcross, Georgia, the Corporation employs the expertise of over 500 qualified technical personnel to facilitate all aspects of design, test, manufacture, and distribution and integration of products and systems. Establishing high standards of excellence for other individuals in the industry, the Corporation remains committed to serving the diverse needs of a growing client base. **Career Highlights:** Raid Test Engineer, American Megatrends Inc. (1998-Present); Technical Support Representative, Mindspring Enterprises (1997-98). **Associations & Accomplishments:** Jamaica Pegasus Hotel Tennis Club. **Education:** University of the West Indies, degree in Accounting (1997). **Personal Information:** Mr. Vermont enjoys tennis and digital video editing.

Narayanan Viswanathan

Solutions Architect
i2 Technologies
1204 Hidden Ridge, Apartment 1011
Irving, TX 75038
(214) 860-7577
harayanan-viswanathan@i2.com

7372

Business Information: As a Solutions Architect for i2 Technologies, Mr. Viswanathan fulfills a number of technical functions on behalf of the Company and its clientele. He works closely with management and users to analyze, specify, and design creative software solutions for the automobile industry. Possessing an excellent understanding of technology, Mr. Viswanathan also designs management solutions. Deploying project teams, he is able to analyze and define client's needs, compose solutions, and implement new software to enhance systems performance. In the future, Mr. Viswanathan aspires to the position of senior solutions architect. His success is attributed to his ability to think outside the box and deliver results. i2 Technologies provides business to business software for industries and corporate information systems. Optimizing business through the creation of solutions software, the Company helps maintain high levels of production for industry as well as management. Established in 1988, the Company employs an industrious and enterprising staff of 3,000 who helps generate annual revenues in excess of $700 million. Presently, the Company is headquartered in Dallas, Texas. **Career Highlights:** Solutions Architect, i2 Technologies (1999-Present). **Education:** University of Wisconsion at Madison, M.S. (1998); Indian Institute of Technology, Bachelor's degree in Mechanical Engineering. **Personal Information:** Mr. Viswanathan enjoys travel, books and music.

Julian W. Waits Sr.

Director of Emerging Technologies
BMC Software
2101 Citywest Boulevard
Houston, TX 77042
(713) 918-5026
jwaits@bmc.com

7372

Business Information: Serving as Director of Emerging Technologies for BMC Software, Mr. Waits performs strategic business planning for the Mergers and Acquisitions Division. He utilizes Enterprise Storage Management, searching for ways to optimize increased intelligent storage systems for the Company. Keeping abreast of current technology through conferences, seminars, and industry publications, Mr. Waits actually forecasts technological advancements in reference to his Company, in effect pushing him to research information. Mr. Waits became successful in his present career through hands on experience and self education without the benefit of a degree. He considers this to be one of his most significant achievements. Looking to the future, he plans to become more involved in the operations side of BMC Software. His success reflects his ability to aggressively take on new challenges. A management software manufacturer, BMC Software produces application and database management systems and systems management software. These "Data Availability" programs are major platforms for corporations during mergers and acquisitions. Boasting a client base of primarily Fortune 500 companies or large corporations, the Company employs a work force of over 4,000 skilled professionals. **Career Highlights:** Director of Emerging Technologies, BMC Software (Present); Senior Systems Engineer, Banyan Systems; Senior Systems Engineer, Compaq Computer Corporation. **Associations & Accomplishments:** Advisory Director, Houston Technology Center. **Education:** Loyola University at New Orleans. **Personal Information:** Married to Tahirah in 1988. Two children: Julian II and Taylor. Mr. Waits enjoys playing golf and performing and listening to jazz and gospel music.

Kimberly A. White

Technical Manager
Commerce One
23 Risa Court
Orinda, CA 94563

7372

Business Information: Utilizing extensive experience in the information technology field, Mrs. White recently joined Commerce One as Technical Manager of the services department. Demonstrating her managerial skills, she oversees two employees in analysis, programming, systems testing, systems installation, and systems support services. Mrs. White addresses technical concerns, creates plausible solutions, and assumes accountability for hardware and software upgrades. Highly regarded, she possesses superior talents and an excellent understanding of technology. She attributes her success to good teamwork. Mrs. White's professional goals include becoming more knowledgeable on cutting edge technology, leading larger projects, and acquiring more responsibilities. Commerce One is an international developer of performance management solutions, providing software network support and personal computer administration. The Company employs 28,000 information technology professionals and generates more than $8 billion in estimated annual revenue. **Career Highlights:** Technical Manager, Commerce One (2000-Present); Sun Microsystems: Database and Technology Manager (1996-00), Business Analyst (1995-96); Information Systems Analyst, Farallon Computing (1992-95). **Education:** Western University, B.S. in Computer Science (1983). **Personal Information:** Married to Dan. Mrs. White enjoys reading.

Cathy D. Whittington

Consultant
Novell, Inc.
301 East Germantown Pike
East Norriton, PA 19401
(610) 278-1300
Fax: (610) 278-1399
cwhittington@novell.com

7372

Business Information: Ms. Whittington is a Consultant for Novell, Inc. Primarily focused on customers needing on-site assistance, she concentrates on software installation. She has become an expert at troubleshooting for computer errors and networking difficulties while out in the field. Ms. Whittington is often hired by organizations and businesses to instruct brief tutorials and courses overviewing the recently installed programs or upgrade changes to the employees and software users. When not at the office, Ms. Whittington is a paramedic for the area emergency and rescue medical services. In the future, she is working to establish her own clientele base and hopes to operate as an individual consultant. Her success reflects her ability to think outside the box and aggressively take on new challenges. Novell, Inc. offers software development and technical support for business networks. Established in 1983, the Corporation has strived to provide continual expertise to its clients in the information technology industry. Hosting over 10,000 employees throughout its multiple locations, the Corporation has built a firm reputation for its product and excellence in 26 countries around the globe. **Career Highlights:** Consultant, Novell, Inc. (1998-Present); Process Specialist H&A Engineering (1996-97); Research Associate, Scott Paper International, (1984-96). **Associations & Accomplishments:** Parkridge Fire Company Vol. 1, Paramedic; Smithsonian Institute Associate; Sterling Who's Who. **Education:** Widener University, B.A. (1996); Chubb Institute Network on Data Communications. **Personal Information:** Ms. Whittington enjoys walking, building home networks, reading, training and working on the Internet.

Piotr Winkler

System Network Engineer
Uproar, Inc.
20-26 Himrod Street
Ridgewood, NY 11385
(917) 416-3832
piotr@winklenet.com

7372

Business Information: Serving in the capacity of System Network Engineer for Uproar, Inc., Mr. Winkler is in charge of network operations and technical support. Demonstrating an extensive working knowledge of the Internet, software applications, and technical hardware, he handles troubleshooting and maintenance in addition to system upgrades. Monitoring the antivirus system, he is continually revising standard operating procedures for the improvement of the department. Mr. Winkler works closely with his staff to develop creative strategies, maximizing employee effectiveness. He plans on obtaining Cisco and MCSE certifications and gaining additional knowledge in HTML, programming, and database technologies. Looking forward to assiting in the completion of future corporate goals, Mr. Winkler intends to continue in his current capacity. Uproar, Inc., engages in the development and implementation of free games on the Internet. Established in 1999 as the result of a merger between Opera USA and Price Point, the Corporation employs over 200 people in the Ridgewood, New York area. **Career Highlights:** System Network Engineer, Uproar, Inc. (1999-Present); Systems Network Engineer, Multiplan, Inc. (1999); Network Systems Engineer, CompUSA (1997-99); Systems Network Engineer, IRC, Inc. (1994-97). **Education:** University of Gdansk, degree in Robots and Machine System (1989). **Personal Information:** Married to Ewa in 1997. Mr. Winkler enjoys skiing, sailing, tennis and tourism.

Matthew Winship

Consultant
Washburn & Associates, Inc.
6901 Shawnee Mission Parkway, Suite 217
Overland Park, KS 66202
(913) 432-0100
Fax: (913) 432-0440
mwinship@teamwashburn.com

7372

Business Information: Drawing from his educational background, Mr. Winship was recruited to Washburn & Associates, Inc. as a Consultant. He works closely with management and users to analyze, specify, design, and deploy new solution to enhance the operations of the clients' systems and networking architectures. A systems expert, he installs, sets up, supports, and tracks accounting software for client companies. Maintaining training opportunities for new and existing employees also fall within the realm of his responsibilities. A successful six year veteran, Mr. Winship's aspirations include attaining the position of Senior Project Manager. Washburn & Associates, Inc. engages in the provision of consulting for midsized client companies in such areas as accounting software. The Corporation offers a variety of consulting services including software and business development, marketing, and financial auditing. Established in 1988, the Corporation operates out of Overland Park, Kansas. Presently, the Corporation employs a staff of 12 professionals who facilitate smooth business operations. **Career Highlights:** Consultant, Washburn & Associates, Inc. (1998-Present). **Education:** University of Tulsa, Bachelor's degree in Accounting (1998). **Personal Information:** Mr. Winship enjoys playing and coaching sports.

Shelby M. Wuosmaa
Project Manager
Cambar Software
4975 Lacross Road
Charleston, SC 29406
(843) 740-6014
Fax: (843) 554-2970
swuosmaa@cambarsoft.com

7372

Business Information: Functioning in the capacity of Project Manager for Cambar Software, Ms. Wuosmaa handles technical and administrative duties connected with the establishment of various projects. An expert, she leads the Livingston Canada dedicated support and modification team. Before joining the Cambar Software team, she served as Software Analyst with Black & Veatch. In addition to supervising a core group of 9 to 20 people, Ms. Wuosmaa coordinates resources and schedules, oversees time lines and assignments, and performs personnel evaluations. By providing quick, efficient troubleshooting services, Ms. Wuosmaa has helped Cambar Software build solid business relationships with the Company's clientele. Her long term goals are focused on becoming a better manager and maintaining the latest skills in information technology. Her professional success reflects her leadership ability to build strong teams with synergy and technical strength, think out-of-the-box, and take on new challenges and responsibilities. Ms. Wuosmaa fully credits success to her family. Cambar Software is an employee owned warehousing and order management software company. The Company assesses and consults with businesses and determines the best available software to meet client needs. Software applications are implemented and troubleshooting functions applied. Established in 1980, Cambar Software features a core group of 120 people. **Career Highlights:** Project Manager, Cambar Software (1997-Present); Software Analyst, Black & Veatch (1995-97). **Education:** St. Mary College, B.S. (1995). **Personal Information:** Married to David in 1997. One child: Christian.

Melvin Baker
Senior Training Analyst
PROSOFT
21 Enterprise Parkway, Suite 400
Hampton, VA 23666
(757) 896-9700
Fax: (757) 896-0900
bakm@nn.prosoft-eng.com

7373

Business Information: As a Senior Training Analyst at PROSOFT, Mr. Baker handles a variety of educational and training administrative tasks. Utilizing his knowledge of the industry, he designs, develops, and instructs distance learning courses to ensure students receive maximum instruction at locations that are convenient to their schedules. Recognized for his technical abilities and exceptional communicative skills, Mr. Baker was given the added positions of Site Coordinator and Technician for the corporate executive video conferencing suite. Preparing customized projects for clients such as the U.S. Military, local universities, and other IT companies, he is credited with the successful development of several impressive distance learning training programs. Enjoying the challenges of his position, Mr. Baker intends to continue in his current role as he increases his distance learning knowledge and skills to focus on changing delivery methods. PROSOFT is a professional technical services company with a full array of communications integration, training development, and instructional services. Established in 1984, the Company employs over 280 personnel supporting various government contracts and related services around the world. A quality Company, with quality people, that equals quality results. **Career Highlights:** PROSOFT: Senior Training Analyst (1997-Present), Training Analyst (1995-97); Program Director, United States Army Training Support Center (1993). **Associations & Accomplishments:** USDLA; President, VADLA; American Technology Honor Society; Board Member/Past President, Williamsburg Bluffs Homeowners Association. **Education:** Nova Southwestern University, Ed.D. in Instructional Technology and Distance Education (2002); Embry-Riddle Aeronautical University, Master's degree in Aeronautical Science; Appalachian State University, Bachelor's degree in Technology; Catawba Valley Community College, A.S.; King's College, A.S. **Personal Information:** Married to Leslie in 1968. Two children: Kerri and Emily. Mr. Baker enjoys exercising, travel and distance learning.

Kapil Bansal
Software Engineer
Sapient Corporation
100 Manhattan Avenue, Apartment 318
Union City, NJ 07087
(201) 521-5305
kbansal@sapient.com

7373

Business Information: As a Software Engineer for Sapient Corporation, Mr. Bansal fulfills a number of functions on behalf of the Corporation and its clientele. Working closely with management and users, he is responsible for software analysis, design, and development. His software applications are used by clients that provides a more customer friendly e-commerce environment. Utilizing his extensive education, Mr. Bansal assisted in the development of the e-commerce Internet digital wave. In the future, he looks forward to continuing in this line of work with Sapient Corporation, hoping to facilitate continued corporate growth and geographic expansion. Mr. Bansal also aspires to become engaged in architectural design work at a higher level. Established in 1991, Sapient Corporation provides e-commerce consulting services. Located in Union City, New Jersey, the Corporation employs more than 2,400 personnel. The Corporation offers services, such as Web page design and upkeep and assists new clients in transitioning their business to e-commerce. **Career Highlights:** Software Engineer, Sapient Corporation (1999-Present); Lecturer, Rutgers University (1997-99). **Associations & Accomplishments:** Rutgers University Alumni. **Education:** Rutgers University, M.S. (1999); JNE College, Bachelor's degree in Engineering. **Personal Information:** Married to Charu in 2000. Mr. Bansal enjoys reading fiction, music and cooking.

Katrina Belousov
LAN Administrator
CSC Consulting Firm
4936 Strathmore Drive, Apartment 10
Cincinnati, OH 45227-4602
(513) 381-4440
Fax: (513) 763-3222
kbelouso@csc.com

7373

Business Information: Serving with CSC Consulting Firm as LAN Administrator, Ms. Belousov installs and maintains LAN hardware and software as well as troubleshooting network usage and peripherals. Possessing an excellent understanding of technology, she provides technical support, performs back ups, integrates systems, and resolves LAN problems. Utilizing her extensive resources, Ms. Belousov provides all level of network support in the particular area needed. Overseeing the various servers, databases, networks, and systems and handling VM and phone lines, she ensures the functionality and operational status of the network infrastructure. Looking to the future, Ms. Belousov's goals include working for the federal government in the computer crimes unit for the FBI. Established in 1959, CSC Consulting Firm is a reputable source of information technology. Dealing directly with clients in the commercial and government industries, CSC offers a variety of services in order to help thier clients businesses become more efficient and productive. Specifically offering consulting in the financial area, CSC is able to provide changes in business strategy, operation, and management. CSC offers a wide range of outsourcing services, custom made databases, and networking operations as well as consulting in strategic and operational planning and systems integration. CSC is dedicated to problem solving utilizing information technology. Presently, the Firm employ a work force of more than 47,000 professional, technical, and support staff. **Career Highlights:** LAN Administrator, CSC Consulting Firm (1999-Present); Lab Consultant, Xavier University (1996-99). **Associations & Accomplishments:** Association of Computing Machinery. **Education:** Xavier University, B.S. in CSCI (1999). **Personal Information:** Ms. Belousov enjoys computer security and law enforcement.

Marc G. Boffardi
Real-Time Systems Engineer
Factset Research Systems
1 Greenwich Plaza
Greenwich, CT 06830
(203) 863-1500
Fax: (203) 863-5766
mboffardi@factset.com

7373

Business Information: Demonstrating his expertise in the software engineering field, Mr. Boffardi serves as the Real-Time Systems Engineer for Factset Research Systems. He is responsible for the design, implementation, and support of real-time data feed handlers for a variety of types of financial data. His programs enable data to be processed immediately and distributed to appropriate clients in an efficient and expedient manner. Before joining Factset Research, Mr. Boffardi served as Software Engineer with the

NASDAQ Stock Market. In addition to working with a team of three experts in the field, he coordinates resources, time lines, schedules, and assignments; oversees project budgets; and takes a leading role in driving products and services to market. Giving 200 percent, Mr. Boffardi is working hard to gain the technical, political, and financial knowledge he needs to attain a position as a Senior Engineer within the Company. Created in 1979, Factset Research Systems provides real-time financial data to its clients. The Company combines and stores multiple large scale financial databases into a single coherent mainframe computer information system which is accessible from clients' individual workstations within their offices. Earning $103 million in yearly revenue, operations employ approximately 300 dedicated staff members. **Career Highlights:** Real-Time Systems Engineer, Factset Research Systems (1997-Present); Software Engineer, NASDAQ Stock Market (1995-97). **Associations & Accomplishments:** USENIX Association; Volunteer Firefighter/E.M.T., New Fairfield. **Education:** State University of New York at New Paltz, B.S. in Computer Science (1995); Dutchess Community College, A.S. in Computer Science. **Personal Information:** Married to Nicole in 1998. Mr. Boffardi enjoys reading, history, science fiction and computers.

Steven H. Bullock
Director
Computer Sciences Corporation
15245 Shady Grove Road
Rockville, MD 20850
(301) 921-3404
Fax: (301) 921-0985
sbulloc1@csc.com

7373

Business Information: Combining strategic technical skills and management expertise, Mr. Bullock serves as a Director at Computer Sciences Corporation. In this capacity, he assumes responsibility for the overall organization and operations of major business capture activities. He identifies and generates new business markets for the Corporation to target in order to expand business operations. A hardcharging professional, he assisted in capturing new business opportunities with contract values in excess of $500 million since 1995. Consulting with clients, he assists them to achieve their business goals through the use of information technology. Continually striving for higher performance, Mr. Bullock looks forward to a future position as Vice President. His success reflects his ability to build teams with synergy, technical strength, and a customer oriented attitude. Computer Sciences Corporation provides software and systems development, consulting services, and professional outsourcing to companies and governments around the globe. Established in 1959, international operations employ a workforce of over 52,000 knowledgeable professionals. The Corporation's total sales are $9.4 billion a year. **Career Highlights:** Computer Sciences Corporation: Director (1997-Present), Senior Manager (1990-97). **Associations & Accomplishments:** Armed Forces Communications and Electronics Association; Society of Satellite Professionals; Contributing Member, Smithsonian Institution; National Geographic Society; Reserve Officers Association. **Education:** VPI, B.S. (1968); United States Army, Command and General Staff College. **Personal Information:** Two children: Steven Jr. and Caitlin. Mr. Bullock enjoys sailing and old cars. Mr. Bullock is a retired Lieutenant Colonel of Field Artillery.

Melody D. Byrd
Consultant
IDX
One East 22nd Street
Lombard, IL 60148
(630) 495-2600
mel.byrd@excite.com

7373

Business Information: With extensive experience in the healthcare field, Ms. Byrd serves as a Consultant for IDX. She is assigned different clients within her service region and must travel to the clients' sites, consulting with them to determine the type of setup that would best meet their business' needs. After installing the necessary healthcare software, Ms. Byrd provides training to the end users and additional support as needed. Before joining IDX, she served as Manager and Provider with FHP Healthcare. Her history includes stints as Patient Services Relations Coordinator and Concurrent Coordinator with American Healthcare Providers and Health Care Compare. As a solid, 11 year veteran with an established track record of delivering results, she attributes her career success to good role models and a healthy upbringing. Her advice, "Don't let others tell you what you can or cannot do. Do your own research and find out what you are interested in and want to do." Continually striving to improve performance, Ms. Byrd plans to attain her Master's degree in Project Management. Affiliated with some of the most prestigious healthcare organizations in the nation, IDX sells healthcare related software. The Company employs a staff of approximately 1,000 knowledgeable professionals to develop, market, sell, and install software solutions. The software is designed so that it integrates well with software sold by other companies. From IDX's beginnings in 1969, the Company has grown to a nationally with seven regional offices. **Career Highlights:** Consultant, IDX (1997-Present); Manager/Provider, FHP Healthcare (1992-97); Patient Services Relations Coordinator, American Health Care Providers (1991-92); Concurrent Coordinator, Health Care Compare (1989-91). **Associations & Accomplishments:** Vice President, Zeta Phi Beta Sorority, Inc.; Zeta Tau Zeta Chapter, Chicago; American College of Health Care Executives; Black Data Processor of America. **Education:** University of Illinois at Champaign-Urbana, B.S. (1988).

Michael P. K. Cheng

Owner/Technical Consultant
11108 West Valley Boulevard, Unit #4A
Alhambra, CA 91702
(213) 400-4004
Fax: (626) 280-5200
mcheng@mcconsulting.org

7373

Business Information: Since 1994, Mr. Cheng has assumed the title and responsibilties of Owner and Technical Consultant. He owns an international network consulting firm for small and medium sized businesses. Presently there are approximately 200 users and 50 clients. Mr. Cheng provides consulting services, usually on a contract basis, wherby a company solicits consulting from the Company. He defines the nature and extent of the problem, analyzes the data, and observes the operation. Utilizing years of experience in the field, Mr. Cheng is capable fo developing solutions to problems and report his findings and recommendations to clients. He is professionally certified in Microsoft and Novell. Mr. Cheng hopes to assist his Company in its growth, development, and expansion and become a successful enterprise. His advice is, "Start out slow and grow through dedication and education." Branching to Internet toward e-commerce serves as Mr. Cheng's strategic plans. **Career Highlights:** Owner/Technical Consultant (1997-Present).

Donald Thomas Cherry

Computer Scientist
Computer Sciences Corporation
71 Deerfield Lane
Meriden, CT 36450
(203) 317-5051
wildcherr@aol.com

7373

Business Information: Highly recruited to Computer Sciences Corporation or CSC in 1988, Mr. Cherry utilizes more than 15 years of extensive experience in serving as Computer Scientist. He assumes all accountability for the smooth operation and maintenance of the computers and peripherals within the Educational Department. Before joining CSC, Mr. Cherry was employed as Quality Assurance Manager for Autotote Lottery. His background history also includes a stint as Communications Specialist with Ensign Bickford Industrial. Providing solid technical support to departmental employees, he is also responsible for their hiring and quality job performance. Establishing goals that are compatible with those of the Company, Mr. Cherry looks forward to increasing his responsibilities and aspires to a higher managerial position. His professional success reflects his ability to deliver results and aggressively take on new challenges. CSC is an outsourcing company, providing a variety of information technology contracting to companies and corporations. Depending on the individual client needs, CSC recruits qualified professionals for AS/400 systems to SAP. Last year, the Company reported in excess of $2 billion in annual revenue. **Career Highlights:** Computer Scientist, Computer Sciences Corporation (1988-Present); Quality Assurance Manager, Autotote Lottery; Ensign Bickford: Communications Specialist, Office Automations Consultant, Computer Supervisor, Computer Supervisor Night Shift, Computer Supervisor Second Shift. **Associations & Accomplishments:** Massachusetts Mason; Massachusetts Shriners. **Education:** Springfield Technical Community, A.S. (1992). **Personal Information:** Married to Marilyn in 1994. Mr. Cherry enjoys golf, football and computers.

Robert L. Childs Jr.

Training Manager
Sapient Corporation
1 Memorial Drive
Cambridge, MA 02142
(617) 374-0387
Fax: (617) 738-0514
rchilds@sapient.com

7373

Business Information: Combining technical knowledge and human relations expertise, Mr. Childs serves as Training Manager for the Sapient Corporation. He performs design development and internal staff training for the Corporation's learning on-line. In addition, he acts as a corporate performance consultant for personnel members. A trainer for vendor negotiations of contracts, he handles all of the external training in vendor relations. Citing networking with colleagues as a large part of his current success, he states that one also needs to adapt, be flexible, and take the initiative in order to achieve success. Mr. Childs is committed to continued optimum performance and plans to expand the creative department within the Corporation. The highlight of his professional career thus far came when he had the opportunity to run the entire Internet machine operations for the show of the National Director of Conference Services for the Blackhawks. A professional service firm, Sapient Corporation focuses on Internet solutions for start-ups or previously existing companies. Total end-to-end solutions are offered and the Corporation assists its international clientele with branding, business strategies, systems integration, and creative designs. Founded in 1991, approximately 2,000 skilled professionals are employed in the Cambridge, Massachusetts location. In 1998, the Corporation reported yearly earnings of $10.3 million. **Career Highlights:** Training Manager, Sapient Corporation (1998-Present); Midwest Regional General Manager, Aaron Rents & Sells (1997-98); Blackhawk Convention Services: National Director of Convention Services (1997-98), Director of Operations (1996-98). **Associations & Accomplishments:** National Political Science Association; Phi Sigma Alpha; National Political Science Fraternity. **Education:** Emerson College, M.A. in Communications (In Progress); University of Massachusetts in Dartmouth, B.A. in Political Science, Minor in English Writing and Communications. **Personal Information:** Mr. Childs enjoys lacrosse, playing the guitar, mountain biking, adventure racing, writing and fundraising.

Joseph J. Chizmarik

Founder
The Knowledge Sculptors
79 North Passaic Avenue
Chatham, NJ 07928-2526
(800) 635-7703
Fax: (973) 635-8949
bjthecyberdj@earthlink.net

7373

Business Information: Utilizing over 20 years of experience in information technology and expertise in various industries and computer platforms, Mr. Chizmarik serves as President of The Knowledge Sculptors. He performs in an administrative and technical capacity for the Firm. In addition to his consulting activities, Mr. Chizmarik, as BJ The Cyber DJ, hosts a radio talk show, discussing the Internet and its social ramifications with callers and industry level guests. His plans for the future include writing a book designed to assist individuals and businesses in succeeding in an increasingly Internet augmented society. Established in 1988, The Knowledge Sculptors is an information technology consultancy. The Firm provides services in the areas of Internet and Intranet technologies, consulting, systems integration, maintenance, production support, Y2K, management and reengineering issues. Using tools such as Java, virtual reality, broadcasting, and intelligent agents, The Knowledge Sculptors can create an Intranet environment leveraging both the clients' legacy systems and existing business knowledge. With a goal of guiding business into the 21st century, the Firm serves companies in the areas of manufacturing, distribution, sales, insurance, finance, and communications. **Career Highlights:** President, The Knowledge Sculptors (1988-Present); Talk Show Host of Cyber On! America!, KFNX 1100 AM (Phoenix, AZ) and WALE 990 AM (Providence, RI) (Present); New York Law School; New York Power Authority; Bell Laboratories; American Electric Power (1976-82). **Associations & Accomplishments:** Stevens Institute of Technology Alumni Association; Association for Computing Machinery; Institute of Electrical and Electronics Engineers; New York Personal Computer Users Group; C++/Java SIG of NYPC; Object Developers Group; Business Initiatives in Java's Online Universe; NY Java SIG; Association of Computer Support Specialists; Technology Managers Forum International; New York New Media Association; Participated in numerous information technology trade shows featuring companies from

around the world; Unix Expo (1995), Internet Business Expo (1997), IT Forum (1997), New York, New York. **Education:** Stevens Institute of Technology: M.S. in Mathematics (1976), B.S. (1973). **Personal Information:** Married to Linda in 1976. Mr. Chizmarik enjoys sports, reading, music, the theater and collecting. He welcomes business inquires, comments, and well-wishes from all individuals and organizations.

Thomas Chow

Data Center Manager
Computer Curriculum Corporation
1287 Lawrence Staton Road
Sunnyvale, CA 94089
(408) 541-3260
Fax: (408) 745-1766
tom.chow@cccpp.com

7373

Business Information: As the Data Center Manager of Computer Curriculum Corporation, Mr. Chow oversees the operation of the data center that includes 22 NT servers and two HP3000s. Supervising a staff of five employees, he ensures a flawless 7x24 operation of the systems infrastructure, to include applications software and hardware. Capitalizing on years of experience in all phases of operation, he monitors the productivity of the staff, formulating a hands-on management style with an above average aptitude for problem solving. Mr. Chow has enjoyed substantial success and finds his work greatly rewarding. His future goals include attaining the position of senior operations manager or director with the Corporation. Computer Curriculum Corporation develops education software for teachers and students in grades kindergarten through twelfth grade. The Company also provides online activities at the Web site, CCCnet.com. As part of CCC's ongoing initiative to provide the best online student learning and teacher support materials, CCC will be succeeded by SuccessMaker Internet. Established in 1970, the Corporation employs a skilled staff of 640 people. Headquartered in Sunnyvale, California, the Corporation reports annual revenues in excess of $100 million. **Career Highlights:** Data Center Manager, Computer Curriculum Corporation (1999-Present); Lead Technical Support Engineer, Tivoli - IBM (1997-99); Data Center Operations Manager, Applied Materials (1995-96); Data Center Operations Manager, Ultratech Stepper Lithography Lasers (1993-95). **Education:** United States Navy; A.S. in Computer Science; Various management and technical courses at IBM and Hewlett-Packard. **Personal Information:** Married to Lena in 1985. Two children: Thomas and Raymond. Mr. Chow enjoys travel, school activities and vacationing.

Marquis R. Coleman

President
Advanced Web Design
18222 Ashton Avenue
Detroit, MI 48219
(313) 541-4861
marquis@futureshockent.com

7373

Business Information: Leading Advanced Web Design, Mr. Coleman has actively held the position of President for the Company since 1986. A team leader in project management, he focuses his attention towards implementing new technologies in order to produce a more state-of-the-art system and widen the product line. Extensively involved in formulating marketing and business strategies, he maintains community contacts and concentrates his efforts towards expanding the clientele base. Heading all administrative issues, Mr. Coleman maintains sufficient staffing and enforces specific procedures and policies. Continuing in his career with Advanced Web Design, Mr. Coleman remains committed to its further expansion and being recognized as "Entrepreneur of the Year." Established as a software development company, Advanced Web Design was founded in 1984. Located in Detroit, Michigan, the Company employs eight experienced software designers and technicians. Specializing in computer software integration, the Company is extensively involved in the custom Web design and networking systems for their numerous clients. Offering excellent sales and services in their specialized computer assessments, Advanced Web Design provides individual attention in installation and systems support in order to maintain a satisfied client base. **Career Highlights:** President, Advanced Web Design (1986-Present); Building Engineer, Detroit Public Schools (1984-Present). **Education:** University of Detroit, degree in Mechanical Engineering; Local 547 Stationary Engineer Education Center, Stationary Engineer. **Personal Information:** Married to Brenda in 1992. Two children: Marquis II and William. Mr. Coleman enjoys spending time with family and reading.

Douglas G. Crane, Jr.

Technical Services and Project Manager
Kent Datacomm
1321 Rutherford Lane, Suite 200
Austin, TX 78753
(512) 835-1152
Fax: (512) 339-7613
dcrane@kentelec.com

7373

Business Information: Drawing from 11 years of experience in the technology field, Mr. Crane serves as the Technical Services and Project Manager for Kent Datacomm, having remained with the Company in his present position after it purchased SabreData Inc., his previous employer. He is charged with attending to all customer contracts including bidding and ensuring that they are handled with the speed and efficiency that clientele have come to expect from the Company. Possessing superior talents, Mr. Crane als oensures that all purchase ordering is accomplished in an expedient manner so that all contracts can be filled within the time frame set. Committed to further development of the Company, Mr. Crane coordinates strategic planning to ensure a prosperous future for Kent Datacomm. The highlight of his career is attaining A+ certification and being promoted to his present position. Attibuting his success to his upbringing, his goals include helping the Company experience a 40 percent growth and eventually obtain the role of regional service manager. Kent Datacomm is an established and reputable company dedicated to the installation and set-up of service networks. Maintaining 15 locations and employing 750 highly efficient personnel, the Company expedites the integration of networking environments, in addition to repairing computer hardware. Kent Datacomm continues to persevere in a highly competitive market, maintaining high standards. **Career Highlights:** Technical Services and Project Manager, Kent Datacomm (1999-Present); Computer Technician, SabreData Inc., recently acquired by Kent Datacomm (1989-99). **Associations & Accomplishments:** Rockdale Fair Association. **Education:** T.S.T.I, Associate's degree (1989). **Personal Information:** Married to Audrea in 1993. Mr. Crane enjoys working in yard and travel.

David C. Croswell

PeopleSoft Consultant
Majestic Systems Integration
27771 Desert Place
Castaic, CA 91384-4511
david_croswell@yahoo.com

7373

Business Information: An independent contractor for Majestic Systems Integration, Mr. Croswell serves in the capacity of PeopleSoft Consultant. He provides extensive technical skills and knowledge in the design and development of PeopleSoft software applications. Mr. Croswell works closely with management and systems users to examine and analyze client company's resources, and specify and design new cutting-edge software that will fill current needs as well as allow for business growth. His extensive experience with such companies as PeopleTek and Future Technology Personnel make him uniquely qualified to detect and solve software difficulties. In the future, Mr. Croswell plans to continue in his present position, thus ensuring future personal and business success. Majestic Systems Integration is an independent contracting company that consults clients in business application software. Established in 1997, the Company employs an industrious staff of 27 and is located in Castaic, California. **Career Highlights:** PeopleSoft Consultant, Majestic Systems Integration (1999-Present); Senior PeopleSoft Consultant, Future Technology Personnel (1999); Senior PeopleSoft Consultant, PeopleTek (1999). **Associations & Accomplishments:** Toastmasters. **Education:** University of Southern California, B.S. in Biology (1981); Computer Learning Center (1982). **Personal Information:** Married to Beverly A. in 1979. One child: Ryan C. Mr. Croswell enjoys RC modeling and surfing the Internet.

Lupe Delgado-Lopez

Senior Business Analyst
Computer Sciences Corporation
9500 Arboretum Boulevard
Austin, TX 78759-6336
(512) 340-4898
lopez1101@prodigy.net

7373

Business Information: In her position as Senior Business Analyst of Computer Sciences Corporation or CSC, Ms. Delgado-Lopez is responsible for the development and maintenance of client relationships. Utilizing her education and extensive practical work experience, she meets with her clients to discuss their business needs, effectively gathering their information and presenting corporate services. After ascertaining the clients' situation, Ms. Delgado-Lopez is able to formulate customized business and technical strategies that exceed the expectations of their clients. Demonstrating a thorough knowledge of the technical field, she is in charge of technical writing and preparation of reports. Being a mentor, sharing processes, and teaching others are cited as Ms. Delgado-Lopez's career highlights. Enjoying the challenges her position represents, she intends to continue in her current capacity as she advances through the corporate structure. CSC is a software development firm that caters to the financial service industry. Headquartered in Austin, Texas, the international company employs 54,000 trained professionals in areas such as engineering, networking, accounting, and production.. **Career Highlights:** Senior Business Analyst, Computer Sciences Corporation (1998-Present); Insurance Professional, Financial Industries Corporation; Assistant to Dean of Instruction, El Centro College. **Associations & Accomplishments:** El Centro College, Professional Support Staff Employee of the Year; Financial Industries Corporation, Special Achievement Award. **Education:** University of Texas College of Communications, B.A. in Advertising (1980). **Personal Information:** Married to Jose Gerardo. Two children: Monica and Rene. Ms. Delgado-Lopez enjoys current events and reading.

Albert L. Edwards, Jr.

Program Manager
Computer Sciences Corporation
4045 Hancock Street
San Diego, CA 92110-5107
(619) 225-2487
Fax: (619) 226-0462
aedward2@csc.com

7373

Business Information: Mr. Edwards has spent three years with Computer Sciences Corporation and currently functions as a Program Manager. He manages tasks associated with the United States' government contracts. An expert in his field, he is involved with the marketing and new business development and is a key player in proposal development, staffing, and key strategic decisions. He attends trade shows in order to promote CSC. Mr. Edwards' background in the information technology industry came from serving over 25 years with the United States Marine Corps. There, he learned key management philosophy, work-place communications, ethics, and motivational factors related to managing a focus-oriented organization. His success reflects his leadership ability to build teams with synergy and technical strength, as well as produce results and aggressively tackle new challenges. Computer Sciences Corporation is a Fortune 250 information technology company. Established in 1959, the Corporation has risen to be recognized as one of the world's leading information technology services provider. WIth a staff of over 52,000 employees operating around the world, Computer Sciences Corporation provides information technology services to both government and commercial clients. **Career Highlights:** Program Manager, Computer Sciences Corporation (1996-Present); Major LDO, United States Marine Corps (1971-96) **Associations & Accomplishments:** Who's Who of American Colleges and Universities (1989); Sigma Chi National Honors Society (1989); Delta Mu Delta Honors Society (1989); Armed Forces Communications and Electronics Association (1996-Present); Marine Corps Counterintelligence Association (MCIA); National Defense Industrial Association (NDIA). **Education:** Hawaii Pacific University, B.S. in Management (1989). **Personal Information:** Married to Minnie in 1980. Mr. Edwards enjoys power boating.

Kelli A. Ernst

Curriculum Specialist
Computer Curriculum Corporation
5810 Kingstowne Center, #120-746
Alexandria, VA 22315
(513) 235-0701
Fax: (703) 566-4389
kelli-ernst@cccpp.com

7373

Business Information: Providing her skilled services as a Curriculum Specialist for Computer Curriculum Corporations, Ms. Ernst fulfills a number of duties on behalf of the Corporation and its clientele. In her capacity, she is responsible for focusing on large scale implementations and presentations. This includes developing techniques in which to present the capabilities of newly developed systems and ensuring that clients are well informed of systems' uses. A prominent and respected professional, Ms. Ernst plans to continue working in this capacity, looking forward to assisting in the completion of future corporate goals. Her success reflects her ability to think out-of-the-box and take on challenges and new responsibilities. Founded in 1967, Computer Curriculum Corporation is a multimedia software firm. Focused on advancing learning and enriching the lives of students in kindergarten through twelfth grades, the Corporation incorporates the use of technology with the learning potential which it obtains. Employing 200 personnel, the Corporation reports estimated annual revenue exceeding $1 billion. **Career Highlights:** Computer Curriculum Corporation: Curriculum Solutions Specialist (2000-Present), Senior Improvement Specialist (1996-00); Special Needs Teacher, Dayton Public Schools (1993-96). **Education:** Kent State University, M.Ed. (1996); University of Dayton, B.S. in Education of Handicapped. **Personal Information:** Ms. Ernst enjoys working with people with disabilities and dancing.

Roberta J. Fox

President/Chief Executive Officer
Roberta Fox Group Inc.
146 Laird Drive, Suite 303
Toronto, Ontario, Canada M4G 3V7
(905) 472-1094
Fax: (905) 472-7728
robertafox@robertafoxgroup.com

7373

Business Information: Dedicated to the success of the Roberta Fox Group Inc., Ms. Fox applies her knowledge and expertise in the technology field by serving as President and Chief Executive Officer. She leads the consulting and integration practice and delivers technology and strategy consulting integration services to her clients. Possessing superior talents and an excellent understanding of her field, Ms. Fox oversees all daily e-commerce and multi-media call centre business, technology consulting, and integration services. A successful, 18-year professional, she travels internationally to create solutions for clients, such as Jones Apparel Group and RBC Dominion Securities. Recognized for her efforts, Ms. Fox and her clients have received numerous awards including "E-Commerce of the Year Solutions 1999." Her home offices were recently nominated for CTV's most-wired house in Canada for its innovative use of wired and wireless voice and data communications. Future endeavors include building up her strategy consulting company, Fox-Hoey Consulting Inc. to 35 people as well as continuing to expand Roberta Fox Group as a leading think-tank integration firm. Her success is attributed to her customer service attitude, extensive corporate IT experience, being flexible, and working with client teams. The Roberta Fox Group Inc. engages in the provision of technology integration solutions, which involve hardware and software solutions for the Web enabled e-commerce solutions. The Corporation also partners with Fox-Hoey Consulting Inc., which focuses on strategy and management consulting for the telecommunications and technology industry. Established in 1999, the Corporation operates out of several locations for the provision of international services, strategies and market focus under the direct guidance of a number of experienced telecommunication professionals who bring over 200 years of experience. **Career Highlights:** President/Chief Executive Officer, Roberta Fox Group Inc. (1999-Present); President/Senior Partner, Fox-Hoey Consulting Inc. (Present); Director, AT&T Solutions (1998); Senior Manager, Deloitte Consulting (1996-98); Network Manager, Hewlett-Packard Canada Ltd. (1991-96); Telecommunications Manager, Citibank Canada (1989-91); Systems Engineer Ungermann-Bass (1988-89); Field Service Engineer, Develcon Electronics & Datamex Ltd. (1982-88). **Associations & Accomplishments:** Ms. Fox is a sought-after speaker for leading industry conferences on technology trends, multi-media call centers and e-commerce solutions. She has appeared on numerous radio and television shows and is known for her ability to translate complex technology into understandable concepts for all walks of life; Canadian Telecommunications Consultants Association; Canadian Women in Communications; Board of Director, Canadian Telework Association; Women's Executive Network; Past Chair, Telecommunications Council and Information Highway Task Force for Information Technology Association of Canada; Past Board of Director/Vice Chair, Canadian Business Telecommunications Alliance; Women in Science in Technology; Founding Chair/Member, Canadian Association of Home-Based Business. **Education:** Fanshawe College, Degree in Electronic Engineering and Business Administration (1983). **Personal Information:** Married to Stephen Lawson in 1991.

Philip H. Francis

Managing Partner
Mascon Information Technologies
1515 East Woodfield Road, Suite 450
Schaumburg, IL 60173
(847) 240-2444
Fax: (847) 240-2480
philip@masconit.com

7373

Business Information: Demonstrating strategic management skills and consulting expertise, Mr. Francis joined the Mascon Information Technologies team of professionals in 1997. He serves as Managing Partner responsible for oversight of the Company's worldwide consulting service offerings. He owns a consistent record of delivering results in support of business objectives and goals through leadership, communication and interpersonal skills, use of technology, and creative problem solving. Mr. Francis, relying on over 30 years of experience and with strong academic ties, is responsible developing strategic and tactical sales and marketing as well as management consulting plans. With a thorough knowledge of service offerings, markets, and competitors, he is able to identify new service and market opportunities that will support the annual growth target. Directing the analysis, design, evaluation, testing, and implementation of operating and networking systems, databases, utilities, software, and hardware also falls within the realm of Mr. Francis' responsibilities. An accomplished professional, he has authored four books and written over 70 articles. His future objective is to establish Mascon as a premier global technology consulting leader. Established in 1980, Mascon specializes in system design and integration, ERP products, management consulting, and software development. A global manufacturer of technology, the Company's targets the manufacturing, financial, transportation, and other industries. Presently, 1,000 professional, technical, and support personnel staff Company operations. **Career Highlights:** Managing Partner, Mascon Information Technologies (1997-Present); Client Partner, AT&T Solutions (1995-96); Vice President/Chief Technical Officer, Square D/Group Schneider (1988-94); Director, Motorola (1986-88). **Associations & Accomplishments:** Fellow, American Society of Mechanical Engineers; Industrial Research Institute. **Education:** St. Mary's University, M.B.A. (1972); University of Iowa: Ph.D. (1965), M.S. (1960); California Polytechnic, B.S. (1959). **Personal Information:** Married to Diana V. in 1972. Four children: P. Scott, Edward P., Mary A., and Kenneth J.

Richard E. Friend

Senior Infosec Engineer
Computer Sciences Corporation
500 Lethbridge Court
Millersville, MD 21108
(410) 684-6434
Fax: (410) 684-2049
rfriend@csc.com

7373

Business Information: As Senior Information Security Engineer of Computer Sciences Corporation, Mr. Friend is responsible for various aspects of evaluation of client technical security systems. Demonstrating an impressive knowledge of the industry, he meets with customers to discuss their needs, expectations, and current operations, then formulates a security solution that exceeds the industry standards. He is internally recognized for his creative problem solving approaches that have consistently earned the Corporation praises from prestigious customers. Attributing his success to an established network of colleagues, Mr. Friend stays up-to-date on current technical issues in today's progressive society by focusing on client needs. Enjoying the challenges of his position, he intends to continue in this role and looks forward to assisting in the completion of future corporate goals. His advice is "Don't give up! Focus on what you want." Computer Sciences Corporation is one of the largest independent providers of information technology consulting, outsourcing, and systems integration in the world. Originally one of the first providers of computer software and related services, the Corporation has expanded since opening in 1954 and now also conducts extensive research programs that allow for the strategic use of information resources and the design, engineering, installation, and operation of computer-based communications systems. With over 55,000 employees worldwide, the $11 billion Corporation has become ingrained into nearly every major industry and government. **Career Highlights:** Computer Sciences Corporation: Senior Information Security Engineer (1999-Present), Security Engineer (1999), Computer Scientist (1997-99). **Associations & Accomplishments:** National Association of Student Personnel Administration; C.S.I. **Education:** University of Maryland University College, B.S. (1997); United States Government, Infosec Assessment Methology.

Phillip D. Garinger

Project Manager
Microman, Inc.
1514 Miami Trace Road SE
Washington Central Heights, OH 43160
(614) 792-0645
Fax: (614) 792-6868
phil@microman.com

7373

Business Information: Mr. Garinger servers as Project Manager for Microman, Inc. and handles many aspects of highly technical programs on a muli-platform level. Lending his knowledge and expertise to the department, he works closely with his staff to assist in the development of strategic business plans. He demonstrates financial expertise planning budget allocations for special projects and handling the logistics of scheduling to ensure sufficient production and delivery times. Realizing the role genuine integrity plays in the success of his career, Mr. Garingner believes his practical work experience has greatly contributed to his professional accomplishments. Looking forward to assisting in the completion of future corporate goals, he plans to shift the corporate focus to small business integrations. His quote is "Get the experience!" Headquartered in central Ohio, Microman, Inc. handles sales and services of computer hardware, telephones, cables, and equipment. Additionally, the technically progressive company offers networking solutions and consulting to various businesses who struggle with the organization of telecommunication systems. Founded in 1987, the growing company looks forward to continued expansion opportunities throughout the next serveral decades. **Career Highlights:** Project Manager, Micorman, Inc. (1995-Present); Owner, Garinger Computerizes Office Systems (1988-95); Senior Personal Computer Specialist, Battelle Memorial Institute (1985-88). **Associations & Accomplishments:** Former Rotarian; President, Local Soccer Association; Director, Local Royal Rangers Youth Outpost; New Breath Assembly of God Church. **Education:** Ohio State University (1984-85); Certified Netware Engineer; Master Certified Netware Engineer; Microsoft Certified Professional. **Personal Information:** Married to Carla in 1995. Three children: Timothy, Kimberly, and Daniel. Mr. Garinger enjoys camping, singing and family.

Victor Gaspar

Managing Director
DIS-Process S.L.
Alda Recalde 64 Bis Epta. Dcha.
Bilbao, Spain 48010
+94 4435365
Fax: +94 4430864
100013.634@compuserve.com

7373

Business Information: In his role as Managing Director of DIS-Process S.L., Mr. Gaspar oversees the direction of operations. Demonstrating a proactive style of management he incorporates the input and feedback of his executive staff, fostering a sense of teamwork and empowerment among the staff. Concerned with the status of financial progress, Mr. Gaspar maintains accurate bookkeeping, approves procurement activities, and monitors profit and loss statements. An original founder of the Company, he currently retains the responsibilities of Managing Director and co-partner. Internally recognized as a valuable asset to the competitive nature of the Company, Mr. Gaspar intends to continue in his current role as he initiates expansion plans. DIS-Process S.L. is specifically involved in the integration and maintenance of network systems on Intel platforms. Offering custom programming for management and engineering applications, the Company has established a reputation of quality and value since being established in 1989. Currently, the Company employs five people to assist in the completion of daily tasks; annual revenues exceed $300,000. **Career Highlights:** Managing Director, DIS-Process S.L. (Present); Systems Manager, Editisa (1983-90); Technical Advisor, Bunge Cía (1980-83); Computer Systems Teacher, St. George's School (1983-Present). **Associations & Accomplishments:** President, European Association of Autodesk User Groups; Chairman, Autodesk User Group of Spain; Autocad Developers Group; Experimental Aircraft Association. **Education:** Escuela De Quimica Y Electronica, Electronic Engineering Degree (1985); St. George's English School (1968-82). **Personal Information:** Married to Estibaliz Moncalian in 1995. One child: Marina V. Mr. Gaspar enjoys skiing, reading, classical and opera music and flying. He has a private pilot's license.

Cary W. Gilmore

Systems Support Specialist
Black & Veatch
11401 Lamar Avenue
Overland Park, KS 66211
(913) 458-7049
Fax: (913) 458-4994
gilmorec@bvsg.com

7373

Business Information: Originally hired by Black & Veatch as a Manual Drafter in 1979, Mr. Gilmore has served in several information technology positions since 1992. At the present time, he fulfills the responsibilities of Systems Support Specialist. Providing system set-up, application upgrades, and system back-up, he presides over the NT server management for two of the Company's departments. He works with the systems' end users, offering them technical support. Continually striving for maximum effectiveness, Mr. Gilmore is currently pursuing his Associate's degree in the Occupational Studies of Microprocessors and Telecommunications to enable him to capitalize on the opportunities provided by the Company. He is anticipating moving upwards into a managerial role within B&V Solutions Group. Employing a workforce of more than 500 knowledgeable staff members, B&V Solutions Group is an integration and information technology provider. The Company provides up-to-date information technology services to client companies in an effort to better assist their business operations. In addition, technical services designed to enhance businesses are offered as well. **Career Highlights:** Black & Veatch: Systems Support Specialist, B&V Solutions Group (1997-Present), Network Supervisor, E&T Division (1994-97), PC Support, E&T Division (1992-94); Drafter/CAD Operator (1979-92). **Education:** Electronics Institute, A.S. in Occupational Studies-Microprocessors/Telecommunications (In Progress). **Personal Information:** Married to Nora C. Bowdish in 1999. Mr. Gilmore enjoys playing Native American flutes at retirement homes.

Bryan Gorby

Information Technology Manager
Equant
1495 Seaspray Lane
Dunedin, FL 34698
(727) 533-3691
Fax: (727) 533-3711
bgorby@techforce.com

7373

Business Information: As Information Technology Manager of Equant, formerly TechForce Corporation, Mr. Gorby fulfills a number of duties on behalf of the Company and its clientele. Overseeing the integration of systems across North America, he manages three different call centers' voice and data services. Concentrating his efforts in the implementation of new technologies, Mr. Gorby ensures state-of-the-art equipment and materials are used in systems integration. The most rewarding aspects of his career are migrating about 450 to 500 users from a Mircosoft Exchange environment to Lotus, and moving a corporate office to another builiding with no down time. He attributes his success to his personality and networking as well as staying on top of leading edge companies. Continually advancing the Company into the Information Technology Age, he remains focused on the furthering of his career and eventually attaining the position of Director. Recently enhancing its operations with the acquisition of TechForce Corporation, Equant is a global commercial enterprise that engages in network and systems integration. The Company also provides support, and maintenance from PC-hubs/switches-routers-CSU/DSU-Channel Extension. Equant is divided into three sectors--network systems for major airlines, network applications for a variety of businesses, and integration that offers PC warranty and service and project management. Dedicated to providing quality customer service, the Company employs over 380 people who design and install systems according to the clients particular needs. **Career Highlights:** Information Technology Manager, Equant (2000-Present); TechForce Corporation: Information Technology Manager (1998-00), System Analyst (1997-98), Systems Engineer (1995-97). **Education:** National Institute of Technology, A.A. (1986). **Personal Information:** Married to Melanie in 1995. Two children: Emily and Rebekah. Mr. Gorby enjoys computers, golf and rocketry.

Darrell R. Hix

Senior Network Consultant/Project Manager
Electronic Systems, Inc.
361 South Port Circle
Virginia Beach, VA 23452-1144
(757) 497-8000
Fax: (757) 497-2095
darrellh@mail.esi.net

7373

Business Information: Fulfilling the duel responsibilities of Senior Network Consultant and Project Manager for Electronic Systems, Inc., Mr. Hix fills a variety of needs throughout the Corporation. Working closely with his eight person staff, he performs troubleshooting tasks, site surveys, and consulting services. Displaying an effective management style, Mr. Hix is an advocate for open communication, fostering a strong sense of teamwork among the members of his staff. One of his most notable accomplishments was the network upgrade for Tarmac, consisting of the integration of corporate offices in five states. Mr. Hix is also responsible for formulating new goals and objectives. Mr. Hix is able to stay abreast of changes and new technologies within his field through his membership in several professioinal organizations as well as attending seminars and reading trade journals and industry related magazines. Attributing his success to being in the right place at the right time, he is striving to provide customers the best service possible by offering solutions instead of products. Electronic Systems, Inc. is an integrator of Novell, Microsoft and Sun systems. Established in 1984, the Corporation also focuses on office automation such as printers, copiers, and networking. **Career Highlights:** Senior Network Consultant/Project Manager, Electronic Systems, Inc. (1996-Present); United States Navy: Network Engineer (1993-96), Computer Supervisor (1989-93). **Associations & Accomplishments:** Network and Systems Professional Association; Hampton Roads Professional Netware Association; Netware Users International. **Education:** Central Texas College (1991). **Personal Information:** Married to Teresa in 1991. Mr. Hix enjoys offshore saltwater fishing, computers, bicycling and the theatre.

John M. Jamieson III

Staff Engineer
Chesapeake Sciences
1127 Benfield Boulevard
Millersville, MD 21108
(410) 923-1300
Fax: (410) 280-2640
jamieson@csciences.com

7373

Business Information: Mr. Jamieson is a Staff Engineer for Chesapeake Sciences, working in the corporate office in Maryland. He interacts with customers and provides internal assistance in financial management, network administration for the local area network, and maintenance for two servers. Mr. Jamieson also performs technical configurations and disaster recoveries as needed by various departments. Employing 30 people, Chesapeake Sciences is engaged in the development of high resolution data acquisition and processing systems, such as data storage and retrieval systems. Established in 1991, the Company focuses on generating clients in the oil industry and in government. Operating from three locations, Chesapeake Sciences also develops hardware and components, as well as offers systems integration services for customers in five countries. **Career Highlights:** Staff Engineer, Chesapeake Sciences (1995-Present); Director, U.S. Design (1992-95); Chief Staff Engineer, Smart House, L.P. (1987-92); Project Engineer, Gould Info Systems (1982-87). **Associations & Accomplishments:** ATM Forum. **Education:** Johns Hopkins University, M.S. in Information and Telecommunications Systems (1997). **Personal Information:** Married to Lori in 1990. Two children: Joshua and Zachary. Mr. Jamieson enjoys golf, boating and spending time with his family.

Steven M. Jimmo

President
Genesys Computing Technologies
1783 Memorial Drive
Chicopee, MA 01013
(413) 536-5529

7373

Business Information: Establishing Genesys Computing Technologies in 1994, Mr. Jimmo serves as President and is responsible for all aspects of operations. In addition, he directs strategic planning, as well as the design and implementation of systems for clients. Mr. Jimmo also ensures customer satisfaction and oversees all customer relations aspects. Genesys Computing Technologies is engaged in computer consulting, as well as the design and development of client server systems. The Company also performs network design and systems integration. Serving clients nationally, from Maine to California, future plans for the Company include targeting Canadian and European markets. **Career Highlights:** President, Genesys Computing Technologies (1994-Present); Technical Director, Epsilon Data Management (1990-93); Senior Systems Analyst, United States Army (1974-90). **Associations & Accomplishments:** Who's Who World Wide; Sterlings Who's Who; American Legion. **Education:** University of Maryland, Business Management (1982). **Personal Information:** Married to Sandra T. in 1980. Two children: George and Michael. Mr. Jimmo enjoys scuba diving.

Ginger Sears Johnson

Chemicals Control Engineer
Dean Oliver International
1 Herons Nest
Savannah, GA 31410
(912) 236-4565
Fax: (912) 236-4048
gingerjo@mindspring.com

7373

Business Information: Possessing 15 solid years of engineering experience, Ms. Johnson arrived to Dean Oliver International in 1995. Relying on strong academics, business experience, and technical expertise, Ms. Johnson fulfills the role of Process Control Engineer. She leverages these skills in providing configuration services and maintaining control systems in a fully operational status. Ms. Johnson is charged with modifications and upgrades of operating systems as well as oversight of new projects. Tracking and monitoring technology processes, she ensures the integrity and quality of products and services provided by Dean Olvier International and other vendors. One of many career accomplishments, Ms. Johnson's greatest involved the programming and installation of the first DCS System while employed by International Paper Company. She attributes her success to persistence and endurance. Dedicated to providing for the needs of the customers, Ms. Johnson's advice to others in the industry is "pay attention to details." To be with an engineering firm performing a combination of process and control work, and becoming involved in EIT testing as well as earning her Professional Engineering degree serves as her future goals. Dean Oliver International is a multi-discipline engineering firm. Established in 1982, the Company is privately held and employs a staff of 150 people. Currently, Dean Olvier International is headquartered in Atlanta, Georgia. **Career Highlights:** Chemical Controls Engineer, Dean Oliver International 1995-Present); Power Engineer, Union Camp Corporation (1988-94); International Paper Company (1982-88). **Associations & Accomplishments:** American Institute of Chemical Engineers; Technical Association of the Pulp and Paper Industry; Instrument Society of America. **Education:** Georgia Southern University, M.H.S. (1995); Vanderbilt University, B.S. in Chemical Engineering (1982). **Personal Information:** Married to Jim in 1992.

Anthony Joseph Kaskoun

Lead Engineer
Proconex
321 Surrey Lane
Hatboro, PA 19040
(610) 337-4660
Fax: (610) 337-4610
tony.kaskoun@frco.com

7373

Business Information: Mr. Kaskoun serves as Lead Engineer for Proconex; in this capacity he handles the distribution of control systems. Heading up the chemical and pharmaceutical teams, he works closely with his staff to develop applicable technical strategies to assist in the client service industry. He directs his team through an agressive startup for each project taken on, thereby increasing motivation and enthusiasm among the employees. Mr. Kaskoun credits his success to his faith in God; looking towards the future, he intends to implement NT based applications into his work. Proconex is a systems integration company, located in Hatboro, Pennsylvannia. Employing nearly 110 employees, the 51 year old Company also handles control and PLC systems for local businesses. Offering installation and maintenance, as well as technical support the Company has proven to be a full service systems supplier. **Career Highlights:** Lead Engineer, Proconex (1997-Present); Systems Engineer, C.B. Ives (1992-97); Systems Application Engineer, Fischer & Porter Company (1990-92). **Associations & Accomplishments:** Instrument Society of America; International Society of Pharmaceutical Engineers; Gideons International. **Education:** Spring Garden College, B.S. in Computer Science (1988); Drexel University, B.S. in Commerce & Engineering (1981). **Personal Information:** Married to Susan in 1985. Two children: Christopher and Daniel.

Gregory Kawasaki

Principal Consultant
CSC Consulting
266 Second Avenue
Waltham, MA 02154
(781) 906-2765
Fax: (626) 358-3490
gkawasak@csc.com

7373

Business Information: Possessing nearly 18 years of engineering and information technology experience, Mr. Kawasaki was recruited to CSC Consulting in 1998. At the present time, he assumes the responsibilities of Principal Consultant. In this capacity, he presides over all aspects of information architecture and performance engineering projects. Drawing from practical experience and professionals conductiong design work from Washington, D.C. to Los Angeles, he leads a crew of 14 technology professionals. A tested and proven authority, Mr. Kawasaki's concentrated area of work centers around imporving integrated system performance. Current efforts include increasing the overall Web performance of financial clients in on-line trading and electronic commerce. One of his career accomplishments includes successfully re-engineering the logistics operation of the Express Mail Delivery system for the United States Postal Service. He attributes his success to strong support from his family and professional colleagues. Continuing in his role and working on his Ph.D. serves as his long-term goals. Mr. Kawasaki's favorite credo is "Keep both eyes opened and both feet on the ground." CSC, established in 1963, operates as a global technology and information consulting and outsourcing firm. Based in Massachusetts and California, the Company specializes in software integration for government and commercial clients. The Company is manned by a workforce of 30,000 professionals generating in excess of $2.6 billion in annual revenues. **Career Highlights:** CSC Consulting: Principal Consultant (1999-Present), Senior Consultant (1998-99); Senior Consultant, AT&T (1997-98); AUNET Inc.: Vice President of Engineering (1989), Technical Marketing Director (1983). **Education:** California State Polytechnic University at Pomona, B.S. in Information Systems (1981). **Personal Information:** Married to Pamela in 1989. Two children: Brandon and Alysha. Mr. Kawasaki enjoys photography, travel, cooking, woodworking and remodeling.

Kyle "Ki Jong" Kim

Director
SDS America
One Exeter Plaza, 9th Floor
Boston, MA 02116
(617) 638-0113
Fax: (617) 638-0111
kyle@pretzel.com

7373

Business Information: As Director of SDS America, Mr. Kim directs all aspects of operations. Overseeing strategic development of marketing and business planning, he has direct involvement in the creation of policies and procedures. In a human resources role, he handles the recruitment of employees from all over the world, focusing on Korea. With an emphasis on sales and marketing, he initiates customer relations and contracts, then maintains any agreements that may be in force. Mr. Kim demonstrates his superior abilities by assisting the Company in the development of e-commerce. Keeping his goals consistent with the objectives of the Company, Mr. Kim looks forward to continual advancement within the corporate structure. SDS America is a division of Samsung SDS, the largest electronics manufacturer in Korea, with revenues exceeding $1 billion. Producing mainly cellular phones and televisions, the Company performs systems integration based on e-infra. Established in 1997, the Company employs 30 people in the American endeavor, which brings over $8 million in revenue to the parent company. **Career Highlights:** Director, SDS America (1999-Present); Strategic Planning, CSR Worldwide (1998-99); SDS Korea: Oversea Business (1997-98), SAP Business Team (1995-97). **Associations & Accomplishments:** SAP Partnership in Korea; MS Partnership in Korea. **Education:** University of Bridgeport: M. S. (1986), B. S. (1984). **Personal Information:** Married to Kyung Ae Lee in 1986. Three children: Seoung Yeon, Jung Yeon, and Thomas Jaeho. Mr. Kim enjoys golf and chatting.

Jeffrey A. Kolber

System Architect
Computer Sciences Corporation
300 Executive Drive
West Orange, NJ 07052
(973) 243-0023
Fax: (973) 243-7580
jkolber@home.com

7373

Business Information: Mr. Kolber has worked in the IT and MIS arena since 1976 and is experienced in Client-Server, Internet, and divergent Technologies, working in such industries as: Government, Banking, Retail, Healthcare, Manufacturing, and Financial News. Mr. Kolber currently serves as System Architect of Computer Sciences Corporation. He participates in the SDLC from Requirements thru Implementation. Mr. Kolber is responsible as Project Leader on major projects and is considered a subject matter expert on Middleware solutions for his Division. He has performed such services as: Y2K and infrastructure assessments; package selection; development of architecture models; migration planning; project management; application development, and database administration. In addition to his career accomplishments, he has written articles for Data Communication Magazine, Data Management Review, and is currently writing a book about the life in the computer world. In the future, he would like to acquire a senior executive position. Computer Sciences Corporation is a world leader in the science of information technology. With annual revenues of $6.3 billion and nearly 44,000 employees in more than 500 offices worldwide, CSC provides clients with a wide range of professional services including management consulting, information systems consulting and integration, and operations support. **Career Highlights:** System Architect, Computer Sciences Corporation (1996-Present); Senior Consultant, Coopers & Lybrand (1993-96); Director, FlexSys Technology (1989-92). **Associations & Accomplishments:** President, Homeowners Association of Plainsboro; Keynote Speaker, Dallas Technology Conference (1997); Session Instructor, NY Chapter of ACM. **Education:** Bernard M. Baruch School of Business, M.B.A.; Hofstra University, B.B.A. **Personal Information:** Married to Linda. Four children. Mr. Kolber enjoys being President of a local homeowners association, health and fitness and movies. In addition, Mr. Kolber has three grandchildren.

James E. Lawlor

Manager of Information Systems Development
TASC, Inc.
55 Walkers Brook Drive
Reading, MA 01867
(781) 942-2000
Fax: (781) 944-3653
jelawlor@tasc.com
7373

Business Information: The distinguished position of Manager of Information Systems Development for TASC, Inc., currently held by Mr. Lawlor, requires the capacity to handle many responsibilities. He is in charge of large complex decision support systems, staffing, project implementation, financial budgets, and developing future goals of the Corporation. Additional duties include customer relations and establishing new business and partnerships. Dedicated to the growth and success of Tasc Inc., Mr. Lawlor has been a member of the Corporation for 26 years. He has made great advancements throughout his years including being the Program Manager of a team who was responsible for developing a large scale logistics system for the United States Air Force. Mr. Lawlor is strategically planning to move the Corporation to a client server Web enabled system. Years of success can be attributed to Mr. Lawlor's extremely supportive family. Established in 1966, this $500 million a year Corporation provides services with the assistance of over 2,800 employees. The government and large companies are main business clients of TASC, Inc. **Career Highlights:** TASC, Inc.: Manager of Information Systems Development (1983-Present), Department Manager (1993-96), Logistics Analyst (1973-83). **Education:** Northeastern University, M.S. in Research (1979); Salem State University, B.A. in Mathematics (1971). **Personal Information:** Married to Maureen in 1970. Two children: Elizabeth and Kathleen. Mr. Lawlor enjoys fast pitch softball, history and travel.

Gregory W. Legutki

Technology Mentor
CTAP
601 North East Street
San Bernardino, CA 92410
(909) 387-3137
glegutki@rims.k12.ca.us
7373

Business Information: Serving as Technology Mentor for CTAP, Mr. Legutki is responsible for instructing educators. He works with personnel who educate students in kindergarten through twelfth grade, informing them on the best way to effectively integrate technology into classroom curriculum. Utilizing skills gained through an extensive education and a background in technology, Mr. Legutki provides a number of seminars as well as works one on one with teachers in the classroom. Dedicated to spreading the knowledge of technological resources, Mr. Legutki plans to continue this type of work for the Organization. His success reflects his ability to communicate, take on challenges, and deliver results. Funded by the California Department of Education, CTAP is an organization which trains teachers in the area of technology education. The Organization provides a four county region with information on the integration of technology into the classroom. **Career Highlights:** Technology Mentor, CTAP (Present). **Associations & Accomplishments:** Association of California School Administrators. **Education:** California State University at Santa Barbara, M.A. (1994); University of California at Los Angeles, B.A. (1978). **Personal Information:** Two children: Matthew and Jeffrey. Mr. Legutki enjoys geneaology.

Dinah B. Little

Manager of Professional Services
Computer Curriculum Corporation
1407 Lehman Court
Annapolis, MD 21401-5483
(410) 349-9612
Fax: (410) 349-9612
dinah_little@cccpp.com
7373

Business Information: As Manager of Professional Services of Computer Curriculum Corporation, Ms. Little manages delivery of goods and services to schools thereby enhancing technology and curriculum integration. Working closely with her staff of 10 highly trained people, she demonstrates a proactive style of management as she incorporates employee feedback and input into the creation of innovative technical strategies. With superior communicative skills, Ms. Little meets with clients to discuss needs and expectations of systems architecture as he designs customized plans. Attributing her success to a strong vision of accomplishment and acheivement, Ms. Little looks foward to continued development of educational technology. Her advice is "set goals and have a plan to achieve them." Computer Curriculum Corporation engages in technology curriculum integration. The educational software engineering firm works closely with teachers and other educators to promote the professional development and technological integration of the companies and institutions. Since opening in 1967, the Company has gained recognition as the number one provider of educational software in the world. **Career Highlights:** Computer Curriculum Corporation: Manager of Professional Services (1994-Present), Senior Educational Consultant (1992-94); Classroom Teacher, Anne Arundel County Board of Education (1968-87). **Associations & Accomplishments:** Maryland Affiliate, American Society for Training & Development; Maryland Affiliate, Association for Supervision and Curriculum Development. **Education:** Johns Hopkins University, M.L.A. (1979). **Personal Information:** Ms. Little enjoys amateur theatre.

Erich Karl Loechner

Senior Systems Engineer
Computer Land
4373 View Ridge Avenue
San Diego, CA 92123
(619) 492-1400
Fax: (619) 492-1416
erich@clandsd.com
7373

Business Information: Serving as Senior Systems Engineer at Computer Land, Mr. Loechner works closely with his staff to ensure the entire department is run with accuracy and efficiency. On a regular basis, he must evaluate each aspect of a job that needs to be completed, and then successfully complete the assignment. Demonstrating his productive style of management and his open, direct style of communication, he is able to effectively place employees in positions within the department that will best utilize their individual abilities. Mr. Loechner also handles the installation and troubleshooting of equipment owned by customers and the Company. Always alert to new opportunities, approaches, and techniques, Mr. Loechner is looking forward to continual advancement within the corporate structure. His success reflects his ability to think outside-the-box, deliver results, and take on challenges and new responsibilities. Computer Land is a value added reseller and systems integrator of technical hardware and software. Offering troubleshooting services to the public, the Company also repairs equipment. Established in 1976, the Company has made the successful transition into the modern technological society by providing services customers request, and hiring well trained staff. **Career Highlights:** Senior Systems Engineer, Computer Land (1997-Present); EMA, Raytheon (1991-93); United States Navy HT, United States Navy (1983-91). **Associations & Accomplishments:** Certified Novell Engineers; San Diego Neware Users Association. **Education:** Coleman College, Certificate Computer Applications and Networking (1996-97); Netware 411 Certified Network Engineer; Netware 5 Certified Network Engineer; IBM Professional Server Expert; Microsoft Certified Systems Engineer; A+ Certified; Compaq ASE 3.12 CNA; HP Star Certification; Microsoft Certified Professional; Dell Certified. **Personal Information:** Married to Wanda in 1997. Three children: Jonathan, Erich, and Alexandra. Mr. Loechner enjoys motorcycles and sports.

Barbara Anne Long

Computer Programmer/Analyst
Computer Sciences Corporation
2361 Jefferson Davis Highway
Crystal City, VA 22202
(703) 413-7316
blong53343@aol.com
7373

Business Information: As a Computer Programmer and Analyst at Computer Sciences Corporation or CSC, Ms. Long has been a member of the Corporation's work staff since 1995. In that timeframe, she has fulfilled a list of serious duties. Ms. Long develops and maintains individualized software for different clients. To accomplish this feat, she often meets and conferences with all of her customers, where she discusses the software. Based on that interview, Ms. Long is able to revise the programs based on what works and what needs to be streamlined. Currently, she is working on a database application for the United States Patent and Trademark Office. Ms. Long believes that her success is deeply rooted in her ability to work well in team oriented environments. As for her future, she hopes to become more involved with Web based Internet applications. CSC provides computer software to clients. Focused mainly on databasing solutions, the Corporation has held contracts with governmental agencies and commercial companies. The Corporation uses the talents of 50,000 employees, and that large work force has played an important role in increasing CSC's profit margins. Established in 1959, the Corporation has satisfied customers on an international level. **Career Highlights:** Computer Programmer/Analyst, Computer Sciences Corporation (1995-Present); Computer Programmer/Analyst, VSE (1990-95); Computer Programmer/Analyst, Vanguard Technologies, Inc. (1989). **Education:** George Washington University, B.S. (1983); Certificate, 2 Oracle Applications Courses (1994). **Personal Information:** Ms. Long enjoys writing poetry and short stories. Ms. Long received the Hammer Award for her work with the U.S. Department of Defense.

Victor C. Louie

Technical Sales and Support Representative
IKOS Systems
17 East Emerson Street
Arlington Heights, IL 60005
(630) 717-2930
vlouie@yahoo.com
7373

Business Information: Demonstrating expertise in the information technology field, Mr. Louie currently serves as Technical Sales and Support Representative with IKOS Systems. He oversees pre-post sales for the Midwest region. In addition, he ensures customer satisfaction with the products and provides sales training, customer presentations, and on-site technical support. Respected and trusted by his clients, Mr. Louie utilizes strategic planning to increase business and bottom line results. IKOS Systems specializes in the design of computer hardware and software, and the marketing of products. Established in 1984, IKOS Systems is headquartered in Cupertino, California with offices throughout the world. It currently employs 350 personnel to facilitate every aspect of design, manufacture, quality assurance, and distribution of products. **Career Highlights:** Technical Sales and Support Representative, IKOS Systems (1999-Present); Design Manager, LSI Logic (1991-99); Project Manager, Fujitsu (1989-91). **Associations & Accomplishments:** Tan Beth Pi; Eda Kappa Nu; Institute of Electrical and Electronics Engineers. **Education:** University of Chicago, M.B.A. (1997); University of Illinois at Urbana Champaign, B.S. in Electrical Engineering (1982). **Personal Information:** Married to Waiyi W. in 1987. Three children: Janice, Jireh, and Naomi. Mr. Louie enjoys travel, investing, reading and seminars.

Charles J. Luman

Managing Consultant
MCI Systemhouse
5500 Wayzata Boulevard
Minneapolis, MN 55416
(612) 545-4100
Fax: (612) 542-7400
cluman@shl.com
7373

Business Information: As Managing Consultant of MCI Systemhouse, Mr. Luman is in charge of project management. He is responsible for generating new business and building solid relations between the Company and its clients. Mr. Luman manages and directs his projects, normally administering two or three at a time. Before joining MCI Systemhouse, he served as Manufacturing Systems Consultant with Ernst & Whinney and Industrial Engineering Manager for 3M. Coordinating resources and schedules and overseeing time lines and assignments also fall within the purview of Mr. Luman's responsibilities. Attributing his success to his educational knowledge and keeping abreast of technology, he maintains that one should always strive to keep current. His success reflects his ability to think out-of-the-box and take on new challenges and responsibilities. Mr. Luman is presently taking courses on-line for his Masters degree in Computer Science. Eventually, he hopes to open his own business. Founded in Canada in 1983, MCI Systemhouse develops computer based systems for businesses worldwide. The Systems Integration Division provides enterprise to enterprise integration within a vertical market. With 60 locations in 15 countries, the Company employs over 9,000 individuals who help generate revenues in excess of $2 billion annually. **Career Highlights:** Managing Consultant, MCI Systemhouse (1996-Present); Manufacturing Systems Consultant, Ernst & Whinney (1975-84); Industrial Engineering Manager, 3M (1962-70). **Associations & Accomplishments:** Grand Master, Masons in Minnesota; Fellow, American Production and Inventory Control Society; Certified in Systems Integration by the Institute of Industrial Engineers. **Education:** University of Illinois, B.S. in Engineering (1957); American Graduate School of International Management, Executive Management. **Personal Information:** Married to Libby in 1960. Three children: Charles, Anne, and Susan.

Scott Maley

Senior Software Engineer
TASC, Inc.
1342 South Douglas Boulevard
Midwest City, OK 73130
(405) 737-3300
7373

Business Information: Serving as Senior Engineer, Emerging Technology with TASC, Inc., Mr. Maley is involved in software engineering, simulations, and design aspects. He also mentors employee training and systems analysis and integration aspects. Mr. Maley attributes his success to tenacity and dedication to this work. TASC provides information technology consulting and system integration services to businesses internationally. Programs offered include set up, training, system design, and analysis. Established in 1969, the Corporation employs approximately 2,500 people and reports annual revenues of $500 million. **Career Highlights:** Senior Software Engineer, TASC, Inc. (1986-Present); Principal Software Engineer, Martin Marietta Data Systems (1984-86); Senior Software Engineer, Martin Marietta Aerospace (1981-84); MTS, Rockwell - Space Transportation (1974-81). **Associations & Accomplishments:** Oregon Institute of Science and Medicine; Free Soul; High Frontier; Heritage Foundation; Carpathia Society; H.S.L.; Boy Scouts, Order of the Arrow. **Education:** Oregon State University, B.S. (1973). **Personal Information:** Mr. Maley enjoys reading and travel.

T. Steve Matsumoto
Systems Administrator
Computer Sciences Corporation
114 Regina Drive
Sterling, VA 20165-5830
(703) 471-3105
Fax: (703) 406-1296

7373

Business Information: Mr. Matsumoto functions in the role of Systems Administrator for Computer Sciences Corporation. He is responsible for coordinating and working with the federal sector, concentrating on local area networks and their connectivity. He also maintains the file server which monitors the user log-ins to the system. A savvy, nine year professional, Mr. Matsumoto also runs and maintains backup systems to ensure reliability and security of databases. One of his many career highlights was being a member of the United States Marine Corps. In the future, he hopes to obtain his Associate's degree in Computer Information Technology. His success is attributed to his faith in God and reading technical magazines, as well as his ability to deliver results and take on new challenges. Computer Sciences Corporation is a technical service provider assisting residents of Sterling, Washington and the surrounding communities. An Internet service provider for the area, the Corporation assists clients in logging on to the World Wide Web for the frst time and helps them get connected to the wealth of opportunities available to them through its services. **Career Highlights:** Systems Administrator, Computer Sciences Corporation (1997-Present); Desktop Support Specialist, Future Technologies (1995-97); Office Administrator, Food and Drug Administration (1993-95); Computer Specialist/World Wide Marine Corps Community Services Operator, United States Marine Corps (1990-92). **Associations & Accomplishments:** Japanese-American Citizens League; Disabled American Veterans. **Education:** North Virginia Community College, A.S. in Information System Technology (In Progress). **Personal Information:** Married to Cynthia in 1993. One child: Virginia.

Thomas C. Michales
Senior Project Manager
Af Associates
100 Stonehurst Court
Northvale, NJ 07647
(201) 750-3039
Fax: (201) 784-8637
tmichales@earthlink.net

7373

Business Information: As the Senior Project Manager of Af Associates, Mr. Michales retains full authority over all projects, from the start of the design until completion. He works closely with engineers, insulators, architects, and clients to ensure the project is completed according to specifications. Beginning his career more than 12 years ago, Mr. Michales has developed the skills needed to maintain the highest standards of professional excellence. He attributes his success to his thirst for knowledge and wanting to learn more. Mr. Michales hopes to continue in the information technology field, whereever it is heading. His advice is "definitely get the education, but don't forget hands on experience is also important to success." Af Associates is an established and reputable systems integrator focusing on the broadcasting industry. Founded in 1968, the Company employs a staff of 50 individuals dedicated to working with operators of mobile products. Currently, Af Associates reports an estimated annual revenue of $25 million. **Career Highlights:** Senior Project Manager, Af Associates (1997-Present); Sony Electronics Inc.: Senior Systems Engineer (1994-97), Senior Product Superintendent Engineer (1989-94), Product Superintendent Engineer (1987-89). **Associations & Accomplishments:** Institute of Electronics and Electrical Engineers; S.M.P.T.E.; S.I.D; Professional Management Institution; Volunteer, F.S.E.A. (1993-97). **Education:** Fairleigh Dickinson University, B.S. in Electrical Engineering Technology (1987); University of California at Santa Cruz, diploma in Project Management; Devry Technical Institute, Engineering Technology diploma (1983). **Personal Information:** Married to Delilah in 1989. Two children: Evan and Jillian. Mr. Michales enjoys architecture, photography, model trains and cinema.

Larry J. Morrow
Chief Technical Officer
Newnan Technologies, Inc.
41 Jefferson Street
Newnan, GA 30263
(770) 252-3473
Fax: (770) 252-4230
larry@a-plus.net

7373

Business Information: Demonstrating extensive knowledge in the field of technology, Mr. Morrow joined Newnan Technologies, Inc. as Chief Technical Officer in 1999. In charge of all technical aspects of the Corporation, he provides telephone services, builds servers contracted by clients, and supervises the technical staff. Mr. Morrow is responsible for establishing goals aimed at enhancing the Corporation's business development and growth. Before joining Newnan Technologies, Inc., Mr. Morrow served as Southeast Regional Director for Newlink Global Engineer. His occupational history also includes stints as Research Scientist with Georgia Tech Research Institute and Counterintelligence Analyst for the United States Army. Dedicated to the success of Newnan Technologies, he is working towards taking the Corporation to a higher level of technology. Mr. Morrow's success reflects his leadership ability to build teams with synergy, technical strength, and a customer oriented attitude and take on new challenges. Newnan Technologies, Inc. is an IP service integration company offering Web site hosting, information technology outsourcing services, and consultations on service automation. Established in 1998, the Corporation has 6 full-time employees and already reports annual earnings of $300,000. **Career Highlights:** Chief Technical Officer, Newnan Technologies, Inc. (1999-Present); Southeast Regional Director, Newlink Global Engineering (1994-99); Research Scientist, Georgia Tech Research Institute (1992-94); Counterintelligence Analyst, United States Army (1976-92). **Associations & Accomplishments:** Coweta Association for the Advancement of Technology; Association of Old Crows; BICSI; Armed Forces Communication and Electronics Association; ISBE. **Education:** University of Arizona, M.S.S.E. (1995); Georgia Technical College, B.S. in Electrical Engineering (1994); State University of New York, B.S.S.E. (1994). **Personal Information:** Married to Cheryl in 1992. One child: Shayna. Mr. Morrow enjoys basketball, softball and cycling.

Greg D. Moxley
Senior Manager
Computer Sciences Corporation
3217 North Armistead Avenue, Suite G
Hampton, VA 23666
(757) 865-0226

7373

Business Information: In his role as Senior Manager at Computer Sciences Corporation or CSC, Mr. Moxley is responsible for the operations and successful completion of specific projects for prestigious clients. Currently working with the United States Air Force's Air Combat Command, he retains accountability for the design and specifications of their contracts. With accuracy and efficiency, he gathers data to prepare status reports for executive management members as well as for clients. Internally recognized for his contributions to the growth and expansion of the Corporation, Mr. Moxley intends to continue in his current capacity. Attributing his accomplishments to divine intervention and reasonable goal setting, he looks forward to the evolution of new technology. CSC provides information technology support to various companies and agencies on an international basis. Headquartered in California, the Corporation offers services such as software and systems engineering, stock control, and data analysis to clients such as the United States Department of Defense as well as many other companies and civil government organizations. **Career Highlights:** Computer Sciences Corporation: Senior Manager (1997-Present), Staff Officer, Headquarters ACC/SC (1996-97), Consultant supporting United States Air Force at SM-ALC (1995-96). **Associations & Accomplishments:** NASA Langley Toastmasters. **Education:** Embry-Riddle Aeronautical University (Currently Attending); California State University at Sacramento, B.S. in Electrical and Electronic Engineering (1986). **Personal Information:** Mr. Moxley enjoys riding bicycles and restoring old cars.

Michael R. Murawaski
Director of Desktop and Distributed Systems
Computer Sciences Corporation
30849 Moroso Drive
Warren, MI 48093-3276
(810) 825-8650
Fax: (810) 825-8764
mmukawsk@.csc.com

7373

Business Information: Serving as Director of Desktop and Distributed Systems, Mr. Murawaski provides experienced

technical engineering at Computer Sciences Corporation or CSC. Coordinating on a personal basis with the clientele, he implements new projects in computer integration to establish a more productive and efficient business. Possessing an excellent understanding of technology, he oversees desktop and distributed systems and implementation as well as project management. Managing the development of software and hardware, Mr. Murawaski focuses on creating advanced computer technology in order to establish and meet the specific goals of a global client base. Continuing his advancement within CSC's corporate structure, Mr. Murawaski remains committed to the furthering expansion of the clientele base and bottom line. His success reflects his ability to think outside-the-box, take on challenges, and deliver results. Specializing in computer programming, CSC's outsourcing contract was established in Sterling Heights, Michigan in l992. Offering services in hardware and software development, networking, and facilities management operations, CSC employs 185 experienced technicians, engineers and system supporters at the Sterling Heights facility. Leading in the computer industry, the Corporation forms client relations in the consulting and implementing of new technologies in computer networking and database development. International in scope, CSC is dedicated towards the development of new products and services and remains committed to the furthering expansion of their product line. **Career Highlights:** Computer Sciences Corporation: Director of Desktop and Distributed Systems (Present), Project Manager. **Associations & Accomplishments:** Industry related. **Education:** Northwood University, B.A. (1993). **Personal Information:** Married to Patricia.

Teresa M. Newsome
Website Administrator
TASC, Inc.
4801 Stonecraft Boulevard
Chantilly, VA 20151
(703) 633-8300
Fax: (703) 449-3400
tmnewsome@tasc.com

7373

Business Information: In her role as Website Administrator for TASC, Inc., Ms. Newsome assumes numerous responsibilities on behalf of the Corporation. She maintains Web sites for the government, updating, replicating data, and troubleshooting in order to preserve quality and reliable sites. Her varied experience has greatly contributed to her present success and she utilizes her knowledge and skills to supervise employees, encouraging and facilitating optimum performance among the staff. With the notable ability to understand complex problems and communicate solutions to both the client and internal staff, she implements policies that will maintain a high level of accuracy and customer satisfaction. In the future, Ms. Newsome plans to further her education to facilitate promotional opportunities within the Corporation. TASC is a government contractor that maintains locations all throughout the United States. Headquartered in Washington, D.C., the Corporation employs over 3000 skilled individuals to facilitate all aspects of day to day operations. **Career Highlights:** Website Administrator, TASC, Inc. (1997-Present); Technical Writer, QuesTech, Inc. (1997); Office Automation Clerk, Intelligence and Electronic Warfare Directorate (1996-97). **Education:** NOVA.

Sigward Nilsson
Owner
CS Cybernetic Systems AB
Nyhagavdgen 13
Vallentuna, Sweden 18642
+46 851172080
Fax: +46 8347817

7373

Business Information: As Owner of CS Cybernetic Systems AB, Dr. Nilsson exercises oversight of cybernetic pedagogics, or feedback and learning through utilization of world wide web knowledge banks. At the core of his responsibilities is formulation and maintenance of methods of collaboration through utilization of the Principia Cybernetica Project (PCP). He assists in project organization issues in the development of the PCP and its various node knowledge bases. In addition, he devotes attention to creating methods of contributing to the PCP, its mailing lists, bibliographies, journals, and dictionaries. Dr. Nilsson's primary role as a facilitator of PCP information is to distribute results to universities and colleges. He serves as a pivotal "explorer" directing inquiries from scientific and educational researchers to appropriate areas of the massive PCP web, and responding to the inquirer with an appropriate set of answers or current knowledge resources. He has published more than 135 articles and four books on a variety of topics within his field, and is widely known as an expert in cybernetics. CS Cybernetic Systems works with the Principia Cybernetica Project (PCP) to collaboratively develop a computer-supported evolutionary-systemic philosophy, in the context of the transdisciplinary academic fields of systems science and cybernetics. PCP is one of the oldest, best organized, and largest, fully connected hypertexts on the Internet. **Career Highlights:** Owner, CS Cybernetic Systems AB (1980-Present); Assistant Professor, Stockholm University (1962-92). **Associations & Accomplishments:**

Swedish Association of Distance Education; Gesellschaft für Pedagogik und Information, Berlin, Germany; Swedish Physical Society; Principia Cybernetica Project, Brussels, Belgium. **Education:** Uppsala University, Ph.D. (1958). **Personal Information:** Married to Kerstin in 1946. Two children: Katarina and Petra.

Amanda Noble

Technical Project Manager
CSC
110 South 7th Street
Richmond, VA 23219-3931
(804) 782-8378
Fax: (804) 782-8431
amott@csc.com
7373

Business Information: As Technical Project Manager of Computer Sciences Corporation (CSC), Ms. Noble has directed the activities of the Y2K readiness project. Working closely with four seperate project teams, she supervises the development and implementation of technical solutions into the standard operating procedures of the Company. In an administrative capacity, Ms. Noble handles the budgeting and procurement activities of the teams she supervises. Additionally, she does all the hiring, scheduling, and evaluations of her staff. Earlier in her career, she was recognized for her contribution, development, and implementation of an Electronic Consumer Help Online System. Focusing her attention on open communication with her staff and the constant evolution of the networking systems, Ms. Noble looks forward to advancement within the corporate structure. CSC is a global company providing technical solutions through out-sourcing. Established in 1959, the Corporation employs 52,000 people throughout the United States, acheiving sales that exceed $8 billion. **Career Highlights:** Year 2000 Technical Project Manager, CSC (1995-Present); Tech Lead, Mutual of New York (1994-95); Tech Analyst/Programmer, Niagara Mohawk (1991-93). **Associations & Accomplishments:** Year 2000 Users Group. **Education:** State University of New York at Morrisville, A.A.S. (1980); Syracuse University, Client Server Certification. **Personal Information:** Two children: Jenna and Michael. Ms. Noble enjoys swimming and gardening.

Mohamed El-Sayed Nofal, Ph.D.

Managing Director
High Technology Systems Ltd. (Hitechnofal)
28 Mohgeldin Abouelezz Street, Mohandesin
Cairo, Egypt 12655
+20 27491051
Fax: +20 23486278
genfile@hightechnofal.com
7373

Business Information: A successful 38 year professional, Dr. Nofal serves in the position of Managing Director for High Technology Systems Ltd. or Hitechnofal. He oversees and directs all daily administration and operations. Demonstrating strong leadership, he determines the overall strategic direction and formulates new business and marketing plans with a focus on keeping the Company out-front and on the leading edge. A proud founder of the Company, Dr. Nofal concentration is onmarketing activities and establishing strong business relations with suppliers. He also attends to financial issues, such as purchases and profit and loss statements and fiscal budgeting activities. Coordinating resources, time lines, schedules, and assignments also fall within the purview of Dr. Nofal's functions. He continues to grow professionally through the fulfillment of his management responsibilities and his involvement in the advancement of operations. In the future, he plans to continue to grow in the industry, hoping to have the number one systems integration business in the region within the next few years. Dr. Nofal's success reflects his leadership ability to form teams with synergy and technical strength, aggessively take on new challenges, and deliver results. An international technology company, High Technology Systems Ltd. was established in 1987. The Company provides a wide range of services, to include systems integration. Highly reputable, Hitechnofal is ISO 9001 certified and offers multimedia services to clients. Supported by both assembly and distribution units, the Company is dedicated to ensuring that clients are completely satisfied with products and services. Headquartered in Cairo, Egypt, the Company employs a work force of 76 professional, technical, and administrative support staff to fulfill all aspects of day to day operations. Presently, the Company reports annual revenues in excess of $17 million. **Career Highlights:** Managing Director, High Technology Systems Ltd. (Hitechnofal) (1986-Present); Middle East Regional Manager, Rolychem Corporation (1980-86); Business Development Manager, Arab Organization for Industries (1974-79); Head of Division, Military Technical College (1962-73). **Associations & Accomplishments:** American Chamber of Commerce in Egypt; Egyptian HiTec Association; European Association for Economic Development; International Economic Forum. **Education:** Bruno University, Ph.D. in Engineering (1972); Faculty of Engienering, B.Sc. in Electrical Engineering (1962); American University in Cairo, Management of International Business Administration (1978); Xerox Sales and Marketing Diploma (1983). **Personal Information:** Married to Sahar Mohamed Sallab in 1978. Two children: Karim M. and Hatem M. Dr. Nofal enjoys reading, jogging, billiard and golf.

Nicholas N. Noor

President/Owner
International Online Relations
15 Brook Hollow Drive
New Windsor, NY 12553-8626
(914) 534-5820
7373

Business Information: As President and Owner of International Online Relations, Mr. Noor is responsible for daily activities, development, and implementation of technical support features. Demonstrating his extensive knowledge of the industry, he develops strategic business plans that accentuate the benefits of corporate services for the Company that he formed. An advocate for open communication, Mr. Noor implements employee feeback and input into standard operating procedures to foster a sense of teamwork among the staff. Attributing his success to a diversified knowledge of the industry, he recognizes patience as an essential trait when working in this industry. In the future, Mr. Noor would like to shift the focus of his Company more on the e-commerce side of the field, offering technical solutions and business plans to companies around the world. Established in 1996, International Online Relations provides human resources systems integration, software development, and Web commerce integration for companies on a national and international scale. Employing four people at the headquarters location of New Windsor, New York, the Company has annual revenues of $80,000 and maintains one other office. **Career Highlights:** President/Owner, International Online Relations (Present); Unix Administrator, OM Tech (Present); Network Engineer, Citicorp (1996-99). **Associations & Accomplishments:** Industry related. **Education:** Columbia University, CTA Certificate (1997); Pace University, M.S.; New College, M.A. (1982). **Personal Information:** Mr. Noor enjoys running and being a musician.

Kevin W. Norwood

Internet and Data Management Technology Practice Leader
Premier Systems Integrators
5715 Manchester Drive
Richardson, TX 75082-2863
(214) 202-5658
Fax: (972) 699-8397
Alt. Fax: (972) 501-1750
knorwood@norwoodss.com
7373

Business Information: Drawing from his 15 years of educational and occupational experience in the information technology field, Mr. Norwood holds the position of Internet and Data Management Technology Practice Leader of Premier Systems Integrators. Deeply involved in the strategic planning and specific software development, he deals directly with the clientele. Utilizing data access technologies, he specifically focuses on creating designs of large-scale Internet technology sites. Overseeing personnel within the Company, he ensures the proper staffing for the particular jobs. Contracting out specific personnel needed, he is able to efficiently meet the needs of a developing project. Continuing his career with Premier Systems Integrators, Mr. Norwood is dedicated to providing complete and quality services. His key to success is staying current of emerging technology. Specializing in consultant services pertaining to information technology, Premier Systems Integrators is a reputable company established in 1992. Specifically dealing in the integration of network systems, the Company commands a bold national presence as a total IT solutions implementor, providing professional services ranging from enterprise infrastructure implementation to Internet technology and electronic commerce. Analyzing the various future goals and interests of the clientele, Premier Systems Integrators evaluates their business and provides efficient problematic solutions. Employing over 300 experienced IT professionals, the Company offers services throughout the United States. **Career Highlights:** Internet and Data Management Technology Practice Leader, Premier Systems Integrators (1999-Present); Owner/Consultant, Norwood System Solutions (1998-99); Project Manager, Southwest Airlines (1995-98); Application Developer, DSC Communications; Database Administrator, Pagenet Corporation; Systems Analyst, Lockheed Corporation. **Associations & Accomplishments:** International Oracle Users Group; Oracle Users Group; Texas Wesleyan Alumni Association. **Education:** Texas Wesleyan University, B.S. in Computer Science (1993); Oklahoma State University, A.S. in Electrical Engineering (1984). **Personal Information:** Married to Laretha in 1989. Three children: Keyonna, Kalyn, and Nia. Mr. Norwood enjoys video engineering, reading, jogging, sailing and deep sea fishing.

Ahmet V. Orhon

Manager/Owner
Siskon Electronic Company
Ataturk Cad 132
Izmir, Turkey 35210
+90 2324834887
Fax: +90 2324839075
aorhon@efes.net.tr
7373

Business Information: As the Manager and Owner of Siskon Electronic Company, Mr. Orhon oversees and directs all daily operations. He supervises employees, ensuring quality production and satisfied clients. Possessing an excellent understanding of technology, he also maintains the budget, procures supplies, and presides over the completion of additional administrative tasks. His many years of educational and employment history are vital to the Company's continued success. Highly regarded, Mr. Orhon plans to encourage further expansion into e-commerce, Web TV, and consulting on an international basis. Siskon Electronic Company engages in the development of system integration and networking systems, focusing on the design of large database programs, such as Oracle and UNIX, many of which are made especially for use in Turkey. Established in 1993, the Company employs the skilled services of 11 individuals to orchestrate all facets of design, research, testing, and implementation. Headquartered in Izmir, Turkey, the Company's systems are used throughout the country, generating annual revenue of approximately $250,000. **Career Highlights:** Manager/Owner, Siskon Electronic Company (1991-Present); Technical Director, Raks Elektronik (1986-91). **Associations & Accomplishments:** Institute for Electrical and Electronics Engineers; N.Y.A.S.; American Association for the Advancement of Science. **Education:** Technical University of Istanbul, B.S. in Electronic and Communications Engineering (1975); Cranfield Institue of Technology, M.C.I.T. **Personal Information:** Married to Huylya in 1985. Three children: Sulide, Bureu, and Halil. Mr. Orhon enjoys computers and cars.

Robert L. Phenicie Jr.

2614 William Short Circle #102
Herndon, VA 20171-4454
(703) 561-2577
rphenicie@comtechniologie.com
7373

Business Information: Mr. Phenicie's current assignment involve writing white papers used to assess network technologies pertinent to the customer's mission. Previously, Mr. Phenicie served with Communication Technologies, Inc. or Comtec, Inc. as Project Manager of a wireless inventory control system program. He possesses extensive occupational and project management experience in the network and communications industry. A highly diversified and prominent resident expert, Mr. Phenicie has successfully completed all integration and testing of wireless barcode systems and terminals. Attributing his previous successes to his strong ability to solve highly complex technical issues, Mr. Phenicie's personal goal is to continue working as a network engineer. Comtec, Inc. is an established and experienced 8(a) certified small business administration, telecommunications, and information systems integrator with high level program management expertise. Established in 1990, Comtec, Inc. presently employs a work force of 120 highly qualified professionals. **Career Highlights:** Communication Technologies, Inc. (1996-97); Senior Information Systems Specialist, Northrop Grumman Technical Services (1995-96); Associate Systems Engineer, Vector Data Systems (1993-95); Senior Engineer of Design, McDonnell Douglas Space Systems (1992). **Associations & Accomplishments:** Air Force Communications and Electronics Association; The Institute of Electrical and Electronic Engineers, Inc. **Education:** Northeastern University (In Progress); Florida Institute of Technology: M.S. in Electrical Engineering (1991), B.S. in Electrical Engineering (1983). **Personal Information:** Mr. Phenicie enjoys surfing the internet, biking, golf and fishing.

Anthony A. Rios

Chief Information Officer
Accelerated Imaging, Inc.
15661 Red Hill Avenue, Suite 120
Tustin, CA 92780-7328
(714) 566-9166
Fax: (714) 566-9166
anthony@aimaging.com
7373

Business Information: Mr. Rios serves as Chief Information Officer of Accelerated Imaging Inc. He exercises direct oversight of project data processing, imaging, and storage, and is charged with ensuring the quality and integrity of all files, transport media, and archives. Mr. Ross monitors operational and security activities regularly, and evaluates the performance factors of all systems and peripherals in accordance with parameters established by management. His efforts provide support to the Company's 15 technical and support staff, who drive the scanning and conversion processes. Mr. Rios performs analysis of system utility rates and ensures access and system availability as needed. A significant portion of his time is devoted to researching current technologies, and evaluating their potential for integration into the existing systems. He presents recommendations to the Corporation's management and takes charge of installation, function-merging, and training required to effectively utilize the additions. Accelerated Imaging Inc., based in Tustin, is a document imaging conversion specialist offering turn-key document management services and solutions. Clients include commercial businesses, healthcare facilities, professional practices, and government agencies. Principal services offered include data entry, OCR, and SGML conversions, custom coding, and hypertext linking. A variety of scanning options are also offered for paper, film-based documents, page composition, copy editing, and indexing provisions. Presently, the Corporation reports $2.5 million in annual sales. **Career Highlights:** Chief Information Officer, Accelerated Imaging, Inc. (1994-Present); International Engineer, Kofax Image Products (1990-94). **Associations & Accomplishments:** Association for Information and Image Management International. **Education:** ITT Technical Institute, B.S. in Electrical Engineering (1992). **Personal Information:** Married to Betty in 1989. Three children: Jonathan, Anthony, and Austin. Mr. Rios enjoys tennis and soccer.

Louis F. Rodriguez

President/Senior Consultant
Techware Solutions, Inc.
160 Highview Drive
West Paterson, NJ 07424
(609) 282-5029
Fax: (973) 742-4821
techware@is.netcom.com

7373

Business Information: Serving as President and Senior Consultant of Techware Solutions, Inc., Mr. Rodriguez is involved in all operational and administrative aspects of the business. He performs the Corporation's marketing and sales, as well as systems design and programming. For larger projects, he utilizes the services of subcontractors to ensure optimum quality service. Mr. Rodriguez began this business from scratch and has seen it grow at an incredible rate. His history includes stints as Senior Network Engineer with Ing Barings, Senior PC and LAN Analyst for Bear Stearns & Company, Project Manager and Systems Engineer at Star Com Solution, and Programmer and Analyst of AT&T. As a 10 year professional in Information Technology, his success reflects his ability to thing out-of-the-box and take on new challenges. His strategic plans for the future are to expand Techware Solutions further by taking on larger projects and increase his staff by hiring more qualified consultants. Created in 1997, Techware Solutions, Inc. offers a wide range of information technology services to its Fortune 500 clientele. The Corporation offers systems integration, information systems consulting, end user training, and is a hardware and software reseller. Employing a staff of two qualified professionals, each one is skilled and knowledgeable in the use of the latest technology. **Career Highlights:** President/Senior Consultant, Techware Solutions, Inc. (1997-Present); Senior Network Engineer, Ing Barings (1996-97); Senior PC/LAN Analyst, Bear Stearns & Company (1995-96); Project Manager/Systems Engineer, Star Com Solution (1992-95); Programmer/Analyst, AT&T (1990-92). **Associations & Accomplishments:** American Association of Individual Investors; NT Pro-Association. **Education:** Fairleigh Dickinson University, B.S. in Electrical Engineering Technology (1989); Certified NetWare Engineer; Microsoft Certified Systems Engineer. **Personal Information:** Married to Kathy in 1989. Mr. Rodriguez enjoys tennis, snorkeling, scuba diving, travel, sports and performance cars.

John H. Rogers

Vice President of Operations/Partner
Total Technology Services
743 Broadway
South Portland, ME 04106
(207) 799-6580
Fax: (207) 741-2577
johnr@totalts.com

7373

Business Information: Serving as Vice President of Operations and Partner of Total Technology Services, Mr. Rogers conducts operations from the main office in South Portland, Maine. He oversees and directs all aspects of daily administration and operations, such as coordinating resources, time lines, and assignments. Possessing an excellent understanding of technology, he helps orchestrate the overall technology direction and formulate new business and marketing strategies. Utilizing a technical degree combined with years of experience in the industry, Mr. Rogers provides network design, full service Web development, and engineering and migration consulting. Within the near future, he will move out of the operations arena, and begin a career focusing more intensely on high technology consulting with the Company. Engaging in the integration of computer systems and business technology consulting, Total Technology Services offers a diverse range of operations for their clients. Founded in 1997, the Company employs a staff of nine professional technology consultants, all educated in areas of systems design and engineering, focusing their ability on Internet/Intranet and Extranet services for major corporate customers. Currently generating $1 million in annual revenues, Total Technology Services has developed into a well known and respected consulting authority. **Career Highlights:** Vice President of Operations/Partner, Total Technology Services (1999-Present); Partner, New England Techworks (1998-99). **Associations & Accomplishments:** ITS Portland Partner. **Education:** V Tec, Microsoft Certified Systems Engineer (1999); Syracuse University; Hartford Camerata Conservatory of Music, Vocal degree.

Eric C. Rosenquist

LAN Administrator
Internet of Lawton
29 Southwest E Avenue
Lawton, OK 73501
(580) 248-5289
Fax: (580) 248-5283
eric@lawtonok.net

7373

Business Information: Functioning in the role of LAN Administrator for Internet of Lawton, Mr. Rosenquist is responsible for the design and maintenance of network infrastructures. Before becoming an integral part of Internet of Lawton, he served as a Technician with LawtonNet Internet Promotions. His background history also includes a stint as a Student Worker, Network at the University of Oklahoma, Office Systems. A five year technology professional, Mr. Rosenquist administers and controls the LAN, provides technical assistance, troubleshoots network usage and computer peripherals, performs system backups and data recovery, and resolves LAN communications problems. Quickly establishing himself as an expert, Mr. Rosenquist's future endeavors include starting a new Internet service company for rural areas. His success reflects his ability to think outside the box, deliver results in support of business objectives, and aggressively tackle new challenges. Internet of Lawton is an Internet service provider. Established in 1997, the Company specializes in LAN/WAN integration, Web construction and hosting, and e-commerce. Internet of Lawton provides local and regional services and is manned by a staff of five professional and technical personnel. **Career Highlights:** LAN Administrator, Internet of Lawton (1997-Present); Technician, LawtonNet Internet Promotions (1997); Student Worker, Network, University of Oklahoma Office Systems (1995). **Associations & Accomplishments:** Who's Who Among American High School Students (1993-95); Eagle Scout Award (1995), Boy Scouts of America. **Education:** University of Oklahoma. **Personal Information:** Mr. Rosenquist enjoys camping, hiking, backpacking and figuring out what makes things tick.

Ronald G. Schall

Director of Corporate Sales
Professional Communications Systems
5426 Beaumong Center Boulevard, Suite 350
Tampa, FL 33594
(813) 888-5353
Fax: (813) 684-6649
rschall@pcomsys.com

7373

Business Information: As Director of Corporate Sales at Professional Communications Systems, Mr. Schall handles the day-to-day responsibilities of the department. He demonstrates his extensive technical product knowledge on a regular basis as he works with clients to negotiate contracts. An advocate for open communication, Mr. Schall utilizes his personal relation skills to aid in his successful navigation of the industry, excelling in all customer related areas. Realizing the importance of higher education in today's technically progressive society, he stays a step ahead of the competition by attending seminars and courses geared towards his field. Aspiring to a visible position within the audio and video industry as a recognized expert, Mr. Schall looks forward to advancement within the corporate structure. Specializing in telecommunications, Professional Communications Systems employs 50 people to assist local businesses in audio and video systems intergration. Established in 1985, the Company has developed a reputation of quality services and dependable workmanship by offering outstanding customer support. **Career Highlights:** Director of Corporate Sales, Professional Communications Systems (1998-Present); Chief Executive Officer, Harney Manufacturing (1996-98); Regional Sales Manager, Pujitsu (1992-96). **Associations & Accomplishments:** Vice President, Programs, American Society of Training and Development; Deacon, First Baptist Church. **Education:** Southern Illinois University, B.S. (1981); International Communications Industry Association, CTS Certification. **Personal Information:** Married to Beth in 1987. One child: Ronald II. Mr. Schall enjoys golf, Internet surfing and family time.

Paul A. Schomaker

Program Manager
Database Technologies
4530 Blue Lake Drive
Boca Raton, FL 33431
(561) 982-5000
Fax: (561) 982-5966
paul@dbt.net

7373

Business Information: Utilizing his technical expertise as Program Manager at Database Technologies, Mr. Schomaker oversees and directs the daily administration and operational functions of the Programming Department. Before joining the Company in 1994, Mr. Schomaker served as a Quality Assurance Engineer with Topspeed Corporation. His background history also includes a stint as Systems Programmer for NDL Products Inc. In his present capacity, he is charged with online interface and data integration, as well as synthesizing and compiling reports. In addition to supervising and mentoring his staff of seven employees, Mr. Schomaker oversees online application programs, time lines, schedules, assignments, and budgets. Two of his future goals include becoming more involved in research and development and doubling his staff. His success reflects his leadership ability to produce results and aggressively take on new challenges. Database Technologies provides access to public record databases for investigations. The Company offers a continuously updated database system allowing law enforcement agencies and private investigators the opportunity to conduct research through one directory that will link them to several sources around the world. **Career Highlights:** Program Manager, Database Technologies (1994-Present); Quality Assurance Engineer, Topspeed Corporation (1990-94); Systems Programmer, NDL Products Inc. (1987-90). **Education:** Indiana University, B.S. (1982). **Personal Information:** Mr. Schomaker enjoys brewing beer.

Chris V. Sees

Systems Engineer
Micro Technology Groupe
49 East 8th Street
Pennsburg, PA 18073
(215) 245-8144
csees@fast.net

7373

Business Information: Serving as a Systems Engineer for Micro Technology Groupe, Mr. Sees works closely with management and users to analzye, specify, and design new solutions to enhance the computer's power. In his position, he provides school district clients technical services, to include fixing crashes to installing new software to fixing systems and network problems. Highly regarded and possessing an excellent understanding of technology, Mr. Sees is also responsible for the acquisition, modification, configuration, and tracking of operating systems, databases, server utilities, software, and hardware. Attributing his success to a passion for the job, Mr. Sees is currently attending school in hopes of receiving his CCNP and obtaining his Cisco Certified Internetwork Expert certification in order to better serve the Group. Established in 1990, Micro Technology Groupe is a systems integrator. The Group provides a wide variety of high tech systems to companies within a three states area. Located in Pennsburg, Pennsylvania, the Group serves both corporations and educational clients with products for everything from the desktop to servers. **Career Highlights:** Systems Engineer, Micro Technology Groupe (1999-Present); MCC Integration; Alphanet Solutions. **Education:** Penn State University, B.S. in Operations Management (1994); Computer Learning Center (1997). **Personal Information:** Mr. Sees enjoys guitar, hockey, skiing and rollerblading.

Joshua D. Smith

Industry Solutions Architect
Acxiom RTC, Inc.
1025 West Hillgrove Avenue
La Grange, IL 60525-5824
(630) 719-0466
Fax: (520) 447-1211
joshua_smith@juno.com

7373

Business Information: Serving as Industry Solutions Architect for Acxiom RTC, Inc., Mr. Smith is in possession of the knowledge to perform work of the most complex nature, as he is responsible for all aspects of daily technical operations. Possessing an excellent understanding of his field, he is held accountable for creating new ways to separate large systems, designing, creating large databases and enterprise solutions designed to avoid maintenance, and providing innovative ways for databases to communicate. Inspired by the fact that he possesses superior talents and an excellent understanding of technology, Mr. Smith is heavily involved in the implementation of new cutting edge computer solutions. His future goals include becoming a business consultant and become more involved in the technology upgrade. "Pursue what you want and set your goals and just do it," is cited as his advice. Established in 1969, Acxion RTC, Inc. engages in the processing, warehousing, and integration of data for implementation into large information systems. Operating out of several locations to serve a growing international clientele bracket, the Corporation functions under the guidance of more than 6,000 professional, technical, and support staff. Presently, the Corporation reports annual sales revenues in excess of $700 million. **Career Highlights:** Industry Solutions Architect, Acxiom RTC, Inc. (2000-Present); Lead Database Architect, Nextec Communications (1998-00); Consultant, New Login, Inc. (1997-98); Consultant, Spectrum Group (1996-97). **Education:** Kent Career Technical Center, Associates (1994); Oracle Masters in Data Warehousing. **Personal Information:** Married to Christine M. in 1998. Mr. Smith enjoys reading scientific journals and studying neurology.

Richard D. Smith

Technical Writer

TRW

12904 Fork Road
Baldwin, MD 21013
(301) 507-5917
richsd@erols.com

7373

Business Information: Successful 25 year professional in the technical field, Mr. Smith serves as a Technical Writer for TRW. He is responsible for the writing of technical manuals and user guides for government contracts. Before joining the TRW team of professionals, he served as a Logistics Engineer with Augmentation. His background history also includes a stint with Computer Science Corporation as a Logistics Engineer. Possessing superior talents and an excellent understanding of technology, Mr. Smith helped developa the e-dot user guide for NASA systems. His focus is helping TRW and defense clients to take advantage of new, advanced technology to remain on the leading edge of defense technology. Highly regarded, he enjoys programming in C, C++, Java, and Visual Basics. Mr. Smith's success reflects his ability to think outside the box, aggressively take on challenges, and deliver results on behalf of the Corporation and its clientele. TRW is a contract company with EDOS, a NASA contractor, at the Greenbelt location in Maryland. Established decades ago, the Corporation is headquartered in Ohio and employs 30,000 individuals to provide technical support, administration, and other positions implementing their expert skills to create vast revenues. **Career Highlights:** Technical Writer, TRW (1996-Present); Logistics Engineer, Augmentation (1994-96); Logistics Engineer, CSC (1993-94). **Associations & Accomplishments:** Society of Logistics Engineer. **Education:** New York Institute of Technology, B.S. (1975); Cleveland Institute of Electronics, Electronics Technology (1995). **Personal Information:** Married to Anita Queen in 1984. One child: Ambre. Mr. Smith enjoys visual basic programming.

Russell Thomas

President/Chief Executive Officer

Review Technology Group

6051 Crestway Drive
Brookville, OH 45309
(888) 677-2378
Fax: (888) 677-2378
russellt@reviewtechnologygroup.com

7373

Business Information: Mr. Thomas currently holds the prestigious position of President and Chief Executive Officer of Review Technology Group. Responsible for overseeing a multitude of duties, he keeps abreast of new developments in the field in an effort to effectively fulfill his job obligations. Mr. Thomas develops and implements programs and keeps on top of technical issues and new technology, introducing technology into the field through seminars. In collaboration with his staff of professionals, Mr. Thomas resolves problems; develops and implements business, technical, and marketing strategies; establishes goals and objectives; and ensures quality products and services. When not working in his role as President, he hosts a radio talk show discussing the latest in computer technology; writes a column for "IT Review," a magazine published by his company; and provides consultation to clients introducing new technologies such as Microsoft Windows 2000. Mr. Thomas networks with other professionals in the field in an effort to establish new business relationships and contacts in the technology industry. He is in the process of opening offices in various cities including Indianapolis, Cincinnati, Columbus, and Dayton. Mr. Thomas believes that everyone has the ability to succeed. Review Technology Group specializes in high-end network maintenance, consultation, and support, providing certified training. Established in 1999, this $500,000 company offers servcies nationally. In an effort to meet the demanding needs of clients, the Company employs a staff of 12 skilled and trained individuals to assist in various aspects fo the operation. **Career Highlights:** President/Chief Executive Officer, Review Technology Group (1999-Present); Managing Partner/Director of Operations, Certified PC, Ltd. (1999-Present); Lead Instructor/Courseware Developer, Zife-Davis University (1997-Present); Certified Trainer, Edison College (1997-Present). **Associations & Accomplishments:** Americorps (1997-98); Microsoft Certified Professional+Internet; Microsoft Certified Software Engineer; MCT; A+ Certified Instructor. **Education:** Franklin University, B.A. (In Progress). **Personal Information:** Married to Leslie Schwartz in 1986. Three children: Jason, Nathaniel, and Connor. Mr. Thomas enjoys travel, reading and time with family.

Anthony J. Tocco

Consultant

Compsat Technology

27901 Manhattan
St. Clair, MI 48081
(248) 223-1020
Fax: (248) 223-1026
ttocco@compsat.com

7373

Business Information: As a Consultant for Compsat Technologies, Mr. Tocco deals directly with companies such as General Motors, Ford, and Mead to create disaster and recovery plans. Demonstrating efficient techniques, Mr. Tocco also implements and trains others in SAN technology. One of 25 employees, Compsat Technology has earned premier status in the IBM Business Partner Software Program. Prior to this position, Mr. Tocco was a Network Administrator at Woodward FST responsible for implementing, maintaining, and supporting all LAN/WAN networking activities. He also was accountable for all security, disaster, and recovery of exchange servers. Mr. Tocco believes in himself and his abilities, giving substance to his advice that one should not let other people be discouraging factors. His career success is attributed to his "go-getter" attitude. As a premier information storage technology, the Company provides leading international companies with customized data storage solutions. These storage solutions protect critical information, improve performance of business applications, and help to manage data growth. Located in Southfield, Mighigan, the Company assists in the improvement of the overall availability and accessibility of information, providing investment protection and configuration. **Career Highlights:** Consultant, Compsat Technology (2000-Present); Network Administrator, Woodward FST (1997-00); Network Engineer, Detroit Medical Center (1996-97); Network Engineer, EMP Division of ALCOA (1996). **Education:** NIT, Diploma in Electrical Engineering (1994). **Personal Information:** Mr. Tocco enjoys all outdoor activities.

P. Trivedy

Managing Director

Multicom Business Systems Ltd.

45 Scarle Road, Middlesex
Wembley, England, United Kingdom HA0 4SR
+44 817950563
Fax: +44 817950563
multicom@rmplc.co.uk

7373

Business Information: In his role as Managing Director of Multicom Business Systems Ltd., Mr. Trivedy oversees all aspects of daily operations. Demonstrating exceptional ability in his position, he is actively involved in technical consulting activities, meeting with clients to discuss their needs and expectations before designing customized action plans. On a regular basis, he assists in the installation of hardware and software at off-site locations. Overseeing project management, Mr. Trivedy ensures every aspect of each job is handled with the utmost care. Recognized for the formulation of several innovative business plans, Mr. Trivedy intends to continue in his current role as he prepares for corporate expansion into the European and African markets. Multicom Business Systems Ltd., is a value-added reseller of technical equipment, located in Wembley, England. The Company is recognized as a leading systems integrator for personal computer systems, continually implementing technology changes into standard operating procedures to develop the best networking capabilities possible. Established in 1992, the Company has quickly become a cornerstone in the professional community and currently generates annual revenue of £700,000. **Career Highlights:** Managing Director, Multicom Business Systems (1992-Present); London Borough of Brent: Technical Support Manager (1991-92), Support Officer (1989-91); Technology Office, Royal Air Force, Ministry of Defense (1986-89). **Associations & Accomplishments:** Associate Member, Institute of Electrical and Electronics Engineers (Fellowship Pending); Certified Netware Engineer. **Education:** University of Essex, B.Sc. in Electronic Engineering with Honors (1986). **Personal Information:** Married to Marshida in 1990. Mr. Trivedy enjoys football, technical and religious reading, Western and Asian music, travel, and wildlife conservation.He also enjoys watching historical, geographic, and nature documentaries.

James E. Tyler

Systems Administrator

Premier Systems Integrators

5747 Legacy Circle
Charlotte, NC 28277
(704) 969-2234
Fax: (704) 321-2323
jim.tyler@premier-systems.net

7373

Business Information: As Systems Administrator of Premier Systems Integrators, Mr. Tyler installs HP client servers, operating systems software, compiler software, and utility programs. He oversees and directs administration and operational activities of the infrastructure. A first rate, 33 year veteran of the field, Mr. Tyler provides UNIX systems administration and performs UNIX system management training using state-of-the-art technologies. His solid resume includes 30 years as a Systems Engineer with GTE. Monitoring and tuning systems software, peripherals, and networks, ensuring the integrity, reliability, and security of the infrastructure, and working closely with management and users to provide upgrades and new solutions to enhance systems performance also fall within the purview of Mr. Tyler's responsibilities. Remaining with the Company and eventually attaining the role of Technical Lead or Director serves as his short term goals. Premier Systems Integrators operates as a value added reseller and integrator of systems, software, and hardware to include IBM, Cisco, EMC, and Sun Microsystems platforms and Oracle, Informix, and PeopleSoft software. Established in 1992, the Company employs a work force of more than 125 persons who help generate revenues in excess of $90 million annually. **Career Highlights:** Systems Administrator, Premier Systems Integrations (1997-Present); Systems Engineer, GTE (1966-97). **Associations & Accomplishments:** Sunday School Teacher, River at Tampa Bay Christian Church; Information Management Advisor for L.A. Urban League; Youth Advisor, Local Church. **Education:** University of Phoenix, B.S. in Business Administration (1986), A.A. in Business Administration (1976). **Personal Information:** Married to Robbie C. in 1969. Two children: Jennifer Autumn and Erica Winter. Mr. Tyler enjoys reading, woodworking crafts and homeless shelter volunteer work.

Kari R. Ujanen

Chief Executive Officer/Principal Consultant

Ujanen

695 5th Street
San Francisco, CA 94107
(415) 348-9613
Fax: (650) 462-9311

7373

Business Information: Functioning in the dual role of Chief Executive Officer and Principal Consultant at Ujanen, Mr. Ujanen oversees all day-to-day administration and operations. He creates the vision of the Company, and determines the overall strategic direction and business contributions of the information systems function. A solid, 20 year veteran of technology, Mr. Ujanen owns a consistent record of delivering results in support of business and technical objectives. As Principal Consultant, he farms out financial work using strategic alliances and joint ventures, and works with other companies to design and develop customized, technical solutions. He works with management and users to analyze, specify, and design business applications. Combining multiple platforms and applications to create low cost solutions, assisting clients establish operational procedures, and redefining work flows are also an integral part of his responsibilities. He attributes his success to his knowledge and experience in the industry. "Get a good education and get to work immediately and stick to it. Keep current," is cited as Mr. Ujanen's advice. A distributed management consulting firm, Ujanen provides systems integration and design and consulting services to Fortune 500 companies. Established in 1998, the Company presently employs a staff of five people. International in scope and headquartered in Palo Alto, California, Ujanen operates two locations in San Francisco and Palo Alto. The Company's strategic plans include increasing the number of employees to 30 by the end of the year. **Career Highlights:** Chief Executive Officer/Principal Consultant, Ujanen (1998-Present); Amdahl: Principal Consultant (1990-98), Staff Engineer (1986-90); Field Engineer, Control Data (1980-86). **Education:** University of Toronto: M.B.A. (1993), B.Sc. (1991). **Personal Information:** Married to Evelyn.

Ronald Martin Vallon

Senior Consultant
CSC Consulting & Systems Integration
E-Business Development Center, 266 2nd Avenue
Waltham, MA 02052
(781) 869-2079
vrmj@msn.com
7373

Business Information: Mr. Vallon is a Senior Consultant of CSC Consulting. He has been responsible for assembler language renovations in the formerly named Year 2000 National Practice Center in the United States. As the sole resource for Y2K readiness of assembler, he has also analyzed other mainframe COBOL Code on a UNIX platform for readiness inspection. Client-Server certified, his success as a professional reflects his analytical ability and technical strength. He now faces new interesting challenges in e-business development and data warehousing. Established in 1959, CSC (Computer Sciences Corporation) Consulting specializes in computer consulting and systems integration throughout the United States and Europe. Headquartered in El Segundo, California, the Corporation is manned by over 50,000 people who help generate revenues in excess of $9 billion. **Career Highlights:** Senior Consultant, CSC Consulting & Systems Integration (1997-Present); Staff Analyst, Boston Edison Company (1987-97); Research Consultant, Massachusetts Department of Health (1980-87). **Associations & Accomplishments:** Holy Cross Club of Boston; Boston College Graduate School of Social Work Alumni Association. **Education:** Boston College, Master's degree in Social Work with a major in Research (1979); College of the Holy Cross, A.B. in Sociology (1969); Clark University, Certificate in Client/Server Development (1996); Assembler Training, Worcester Polytechnic Institute (1974). **Personal Information:** Married to Kathryn in 1972. Two children: Erica and Jordan.

George W. Velez

Senior Network Engineer
CSC
614 Winterberry Boulevard
Jackson, NJ 08527
(212) 235-1283
gvdepot@cs.com
7373

Business Information: Providing his skills and dedicated services to CSC since 1997, Mr. Velez currently serves as the Senior Network Engineer and Project Manager, taking on the challenges of overseeing the Lab Group. In his specified division of CSC, Mr. Velez and his energetic associates are directly involved with e-commerce for JP Morgan. Highly respected by his colleagues, he possesses an excellent understanding of emerging techology. Utilizing his superior leadership and communication ability, Mr. Velez supervises the technology group, engaging in providing solutions to end-user problems and supporting technical consulting to CSC's client base. "You have to stay up to date with new technology," is cited as his advice. His future goals include becoming more involved in the networking side of the industry. Employing over 10,000 financial professionals nationwide, CSC is one of the largest financial companies in the world. Operating as the parent company for such major corporations as Pinnacle Alliance, AT&T, and Bani, CSC provides international services through headquarters in California and Virginia. Maintaining the superior operations of multi-million dollar operations throughout the world, CSC holds a leading role among their peers in the financial industry. **Career Highlights:** Senior Network Engineer, CSC (1997-Present); Network Engineer, Perot (1996-97); Project Manager, Swiss Bank Corporation (1993-95). **Education:** University of Phoenix, B.S. in Information Technology (In Progress); Cisco Certified Network Administrator (2000); Microsoft Certified Systems Engineer (1999). **Personal Information:** Married to Herlinda T. in 1995. Mr. Velez enjoys golf.

Michael A. Verna

Professional Services Manager
Inacom
485 East Route 1 South
Iselin, NJ 08830
(732) 404-2033
Fax: (732) 404-2030
mverna@inacom.com
7373

Business Information: Mr. Verna serves as Professional Services Manager for Inacom's Iselin, New Jersey facility. He is responsible for developing and implementing strategic plans to generate new business. Before joining Inacom in 1998, Mr. Verna served as Enterprise Engineer with Vanstar. As a solid, 15 year professional, he oversees, directs, and delivers large scale projects; serves as chief client liaison; manages the engineering staff personal; and develops and maintains customer relations. In addition to supervising a staff of 20 employees with various skills at different levels, Mr. Verna is in charge of resource planning functions that includes personnel evaluations; coordinating resources, time lines, schedules, and assignments; and compiling and synthesizing large quantities of data in management reports. An expert, he attributes his success to his father who directed him in the right path. Mr. Verna, looking toward the new millennium, plans on attaining the position of Area Director or Manager of Consultants. Inacom operates as a third party computer integrator and professional services provider. International in scope, the Company is headquartered in Omaha, Nebraska. Founded in 1986, Inacom presently employs a skilled work force of more than 7,000 professional, technical, and support personnel. **Career Highlights:** Professional Services Manager, Inacom (1998-Present); Enterprise Engineer, Vanstar (1996-98). **Associations & Accomplishments:** Knights of Columbus. **Education:** Dale Carnegie, Bachelor's degree in Technology (1999); Microsoft Certified System Engineer; A+ Technician; HP Star. **Personal Information:** Married to Donna in 1992. One child: Anthony Michael. Mr. Verna enjoys collecting hess trucks and die cast cars.

Georgette F. Walls

Senior Consultant
CSC Consulting
300 Excecutive Drive, Suite 300
West Orange, NJ 07052
(973) 243-7725
Fax: (973) 243-7540
gwalls1@csc.com
7373

Business Information: Serving as Senior Consultant of CSC Consulting, Ms. Walls oversees and directs the work activities of 350 plus field consultants. Possessing 11 years of business savvy and field experience, she provides high level mentoring, basically career counseling and development. Dedicated and committed to the success of the Corporation, Ms. Walls provides consultants with innovative training opportunities as well as attendance at high powered seminars and conferences. A reputable expert in her field, she received the Spring 1999 "Outstanding Employee Awardl." Always moving forward, Ms. Walls plans to get back into the field and become involved in international projects. Networking with her colleagues in different fields is cited as her reason for success. "You have to be devoted," serves as her advice for others. With a work force of 54,000 worldwide, CSC Consulting was established in 1972 and has grown to be one of the major computer companies internationally. This Corporation provides a large variety of services to their clientele to include management and computer consulting to name a few. Most of the Corporation's clientele are large corporations seeking to improve their departments. **Career Highlights:** Senior Consultant, CSC Consulting (1996-Present); Consultant, ICM (1993-96); Software Instructor, OBS (1990-93). **Education:** Drexel University, B.S. (1999). **Personal Information:** Ms. Walls enjoys photography, tennis and golf.

Michael R. Weigand

Vice President
Master Automation, Inc.
10437 Briar Hill Drive
Kirtland, OH 44049-9463
(440) 729-4480
Fax: (216) 462-0220
mrweigand@acm.org
7373

Business Information: Serving as Vice President of Master Automation, Inc., Mr. Weigand oversees all operations. Retaining accountability for the success or failure of the business, he enures all aspects of the Corporation run according to plan and comply with set regulations. Possessing business savvy and expertise, he helps in determining the overall strategic direction and formulating plans to keep the Corporation out-front of competitors in the industry. Mr. Weigand's management and organizational skills enables him to effectively oversee sales and promotion, marketing, product development, and quality control. He is also able to resolve various issues or concerns having an impact of the Corporation. In an effort to achieve professional success, Mr. Weigand plans to stay on top of emerging technology and continually evaluate current tools and resources. His success is attributed to his attention to detail and his ability to deliver results. Based in Kirtland, Ohio, Master Automation, Inc. offers automated testing systems as well as factory automated and system integrated software. Founded in 1997, this $750,000 company employs a small, yet knowledgebale, staff of three individuals. Top mangement of the business keep abreast on new developments in the field in an effort to meet the needs of clients. **Career Highlights:** Vice President, Master Automation, Inc. (1997-Present); Senior Systems Engineer, WM Associates Inc. (1986-97); Systems Engineer, Allen Bradley I.A.S. Division (1984-86). **Associations & Accomplishments:** Institute of Electrical and Electronics Engineers; Association of Computing Machinery. **Education:** University of Akron, B.S. of Electrical Engineering (1984). **Personal Information:** Married to Katherine in 1984. Two children: Steven and William.

Robert S. Wood

Senior Software Engineer
Auto Gas Systems Inc.
1000 North Walnut, Suite 201
New Braunfels, TX 78130
(830) 620-6252
scott.wood@acm.org
7373

Business Information: With extensive experience in software development, Mr. Wood serves as Senior Software Engineer for Auto Gas Systems Inc. Bearing responsibility for the architecture of systems, he uses his knowledge to solve problems and implement technology to meet organizational needs of the Corporation. In addition, he plans and develops new computer systems, and designs hardware and software as needed. Diversified, Mr. Wood predominately functions as a designer but also works as a developer. He is the leader of a 10-person team of engineering developers. Utilizing his ingenuity, Mr. Wood designs and creates point of sale products for retail businesses such as convenient stores and large retail outlets. Within the next five years, he would like to eventually move up to a technical management position and stay on the cutting edge of technology. Auto Gas Systems Inc. provides island automation for the convenience store gasoline industry. The Corporation manufactures, designs, and develops machines used in retail businesses such as credit card and debit machines. Established in 1987, Auto Gas Systems Inc. generates $15 million annually and has 120 employees. **Career Highlights:** Senior Software Engineer, Auto Gas Systems Inc. (1995-Present); Software Developer, Milsoft Integrated Solutions (1991-95); Software Developer, Credit Verification Corporation (1987-91). **Associations & Accomplishments:** Association for Computing Machinery. **Education:** Abilene Christian University, B.S. in Computer Science (1986). **Personal Information:** One child: John Hunter. Mr. Wood enjoys lifestyle sports, kayaking, skiing, and rock climbing.

Aaron C. Young

Internal Technology Manager
AppliedTheory
125 Elwood Davis Road
Syracuse, NY 13217
(315) 453-2912
Fax: (315) 453-3052
acyoung@appliedtheory.com
7373

Business Information: As Internal Technology Manager of AppliedTheory, Mr. Young provides all the technology services that enables the Corporation to function. Working closely with his team of nine employees, Mr. Young is responsible for UNIX, Novell server, NT, telephony, and desk top support. Coordinating resources, time lines, schedules, and assignments also fall within the realm of his functions. Beginning his career in this field more than 15 years ago, Mr. Young recognizes the important roles of responsibility, authority, and accountability and displays those qualities that make a manager forceful and effective. He respects both employee rights and management prerogatives and achieves high productive output while maintaining high morale. An expert, Mr. Young attributes his success to his clear thinking ability and plans to expedite continued promotion through dedication and the fulfillment of his responsibilities. Eventually attaining the position of Director serves as one of his future goals. Established in 1984, AppliedTheory is an Internet service provider. Employing a staff of 200 individuals, the Corporation reports an estimated annual revenue of $30 million. **Career Highlights:** Internal Technology Manager, AppliedTheory (1995-Present); Systems Administrator, NYSENET, Inc. (1994-95); Systems Administrator, Syracuse University (1990-94); Satellite Network Controller, United States Army (1984-88). **Associations & Accomplishments:** Institute of Electronics and Electrical Engineers. **Education:** Syracuse University, M.S. in I.R.M. (1999); Syracuse University, B.S. in Computer Engineering; Onondaga Community College, A.S. in Computer Science. **Personal Information:** Married to Melanie C. in 1995. Two children: Holden and Keegan. Mr. Young enjoys parachuting, running and motorcycling.

Sergey Goldman, Ph.D.

Software Developer
ADP
2525 Southwest 1st Avenue
Portland, OR 97201
(503) 402-3645
sgoldman@prodigy.net
7374

Business Information: Dr. Goldman functions in the role of Software Developer for ADP. He is responsible for all aspects of software research and development. Before joining ADP in 1996, Dr. Goldman served as a Research Scientist for Oregon Graduate Institute. His background history also includes a stint as Researcher for Argoprigor. In his current position, Dr. Goldman uses his extensive academic ties and technical experience in designing and developing financial circulation software for his clientele. A 20 year technology professional, he is responsible for setting up new techniques and processes to help client companies' financial departments operate with efficiency and effectiveness. Dr. Goldman attributes his success to working well with people, thinking outside the box, producing results, and aggressively tackling new challenges. His strategic plans include improving his overall computer skills and eventually becoming a Software Architect. "Continue your education and enjoy it," is cited as his advice to others. A Fortune 500 company, ADP engages in software research and development, as well as provides a wide range of technological services. Established in 1974, the Company is located in Portland, Oregon. Presently, ADP employs a work force of more than 600 professional and technical experts to meet the demand of its clientele. **Career Highlights:** Software Developer, ADP (1996-Present); Research Scientist, Oregon Graduate Institute (1990-94); Researcher, Argoprigor (1979-90). **Associations & Accomplishments:** American Association for the Advancement of Science. **Education:** Saraton State University: Ph.D. in Physics, M.S. in Physics, B.S. in Physics and Computer Science; OGI, M.S. **Personal Information:** Married to Lilia in 1991. Two children: Mirian and Joseph. Dr. Goldman enjoys collecting Mickey mouse small toys.

Brian P. Hollands
Client Operations Analyst
ADP Hayes Ligon
12917 Prestwick Drive
Riverview, FL 33569
(813) 672-4408
bholland@hayes.ds.adp.com

7374

Business Information: Displaying advanced analytical and interpersonal skills; Mr. Hollands was recruited by ADP Hayes Ligon Product Manager in 1996. Since then, he has received recognition for his diligence and adept management skills through several promotions to his current position of Client Operations Analyst. In this capacity since 1998, he is responsible for providing North America after-sales product support, where he ascertains new methods to improve training materials in an effort to make products as user friendly as possible. Evangelizing, he also conducts training for all personnel chartered to create and spread product philosophy to users via group presentations, one on one training, and interactive television. Mr. Hollands has enjoyed tremendous occupational success in his current position and looks forward to attaining a higher-level management position within the Corporation. "Keep your eyes and ears open," is cited as his advice. Established in 1949, ADP Hayes Ligon is a international supplier of interactive software and hardware, such as electronic service pricing guides utilized by automotive dealerships to offer direct price quotes to consumers. Located in Riverview, Florida, the Corporation employs a collective work force of 29,000 administrative, technical, and operational personnel who generate millions in annual revenue. The Corporation currently operates four divisions across the globe and operates a satellite-training program used by automotive manufacturers worldwide. **Career Highlights:** ADP Hayes Ligon: Client Operations Analyst (1998-Present), Product Administrator (1997-98), Product Manager (1996-97); Researcher, Automotive Service Consultants (1993-95). **Education:** St. Lawrence University, B.S. (1989). **Personal Information:** Married to Bonnie in 1997. Mr. Hollands enjoys ice hockey and automobile restoration.

Braden P. Jeunesse
PC Coordinator
ADP
8100 Cedar Avenue
Minneapolis, IN 55425-1802
(952) 854-1700
Fax: (952) 853-1374
braden_jeunesse@es.adp.com

7374

Business Information: As the PC Coordinator for ADP or Automatic Data Processing, Mr. Jeunesse monitors and maintains the computer infrastructure. Possessing a superior talent and an excellent understanding of his field, he installs and troubleshoots ADP's payroll and human resources systems' using SQL Base and Oracle databases. A multifaceted professional, Mr. Jeunesse also serves as the assistant LAN administrator. In this context, he maintains and LAN hardware and software and troubleshoots network usage and computer peripherals. Highly regarded by his peers, Mr. Jeunesse also is involved in project management, testing systems, and training employees in documenting standards and systems implementation. An accomplished professional, he conducts seminars and lectures to educate users on new technology. Becoming more involved in Internet and Intranet related networks serves as his future endeavors. Established in 1949, ADP provides outsourcing payroll and human resources solutions and tax services. Regional in scope, the Company employs 30,000 professional, technical, and

support staff who provides services to mid to large sized companies, such as IBM. Headquartered in Roseland, New Jersey, the Company operates satellite locations throughout the regional and providies superior services to its clientele. **Career Highlights:** PC Coordinator, ADP (Present). **Education:** University of Minnesota, B.A. (1995).

Gary V. Roll
Supervisor
ADP Dealer Services
1950 Hassell Road
Hoffman Estates, IL 60195
(847) 397-8628
Fax: (847) 885-0627
rollg@hoffman.ds.adp.com

7374

Business Information: As Supervisor of ADP's Dealer Services Division, Mr. Roll is responsible for supervising tier one and two internal support teams. His responsibilities include hiring, training, and supervising help desk personnel. Most recently, Mr. Roll was instrumental in the transition from Unix-based host support to new client/server platform application support. Before joining ADP, he served as Director of Technical Support with Advanced Retail Technologies. Beginning his association with the Company in 1991, as a Client Support Representative, he has received recognition for his diligence and managements skills through several promotions to his current position. Coordinating resources, time lines, schedules, assignments, and budgets also fall within the realm of his responsibilities. As a 14 year technology professional, Mr. Roll continues to grow professionally and plans to accept greater management responsibilities as a key player in ADP's transition to new technologies. ADP Dealer Services is a leading provider of integrated computing solutions to automotive and truck manufacturers and dealers. As one of the largest independent computing services firms in the world, Automatic Data Processing, Inc. (NYSE:AUD) is a $5 billion international corporation serving more than 425,000 clients. **Career Highlights:** ADP Dealer Services: Supervisor (1999-Present), Regional Support Technician (1995-99), Client Support Representative (1991-95); Director of Technical Support, Advanced Retail Technologies (1989-91). **Associations & Accomplishments:** First United Methodist Church. **Education:** University of Illinois, B.S. (1985). **Personal Information:** Married to Kathy Schaeffer in 1996. Mr. Roll enjoys concerts, novels, photography, biking, skiing and volunteer activities.

John A. Winquist
Repair Supervisor
ADP Dealer Services
5743 Northeast Columbia Boulevard
Portland, OR 97218
(503) 402-3703
Fax: (503) 280-8266
jwinquist@go.huskies.com

7374

Business Information: Beginning his career with ADP Dealer Services more than 10 years ago, Mr. Winquist currently serves as Repair Supervisor. He is responsible for supervising the repair technicians and performing database design for the Company. Additionally, he assumes accountability for the implementation of the new Oracle system within the internal network. Staying abreast of technological advancements by surfing the Internet and membership in access user groups, Mr. Winquist attributes his success to perseverance and a sense of humor. His most memorable quote is, "Failing to prepare is preparing to fail; there is a method to the madness." Committed to the success of the Company, he has plans to completely redesign the repair process and increase its efficiency. Mr. Winquist anticipates a promotion to Process Manager. Founded in 1946, ADP Dealer Services engages in the sale of software to the automotive industry. The Company also provides computer hardware repair, offering the services of one of its 250 field engineers. Approximately 36,000 qualified individuals are employed in overall operations. **Career Highlights:** ADP Dealer Services: Repair Supervisor (1997-Present), Repair Group Lead (1994-97), Repair Technician (1988-94). **Education:** City University, M.B.A. (1993); ITT Technical Institute: Bachelor of Applied Science, A.A.S. **Personal Information:** Mr. Winquist enjoys golf, photography, music, travel and beer brewing.

Dmitri Baliakhov
Software Systems Architect
EMC Corporation
171 South Street
Hopkinton, MA 01748
(508) 435-1000
Fax: (508) 497-8012
dimal@emc.com

7375

Business Information: Always interested in technology and remaining on the leading edge of software development, Mr. Baliakhov was recruited to EMC Corporation in 1997. At the present time, he assumes the responsibilities of Software Systems Architect. In his capacity, he is actively involved in software development for mass storage technology and systems support of Unix, Windows, OS/2 embedded applications. Utilizing his expert technical skills, Mr. Baliakhov keeps all software, hardware, and databases up-to-date with evolving technology. Additionally, he provides assistance and advice to users, interpreting problems and providing technical support, and helps organizations realize the maximum benefit from the monies investment in equipment, personnel, and processes. Getting into technology to be successful, Mr. Baliakhov keeps pace with emerging technology through research and reading. One of his career accomplishments include building a new architecture for a company in Russia. Maintaining his extensive technical expertise in computer architecture and making a difference in the corporate world serves as Mr. Baliakhov's long-range strategic plans. Based in Massachusetts, EMC Corporation is a world leader in supplying intelligent enterprise storage and retrieval technology. Traded on the New York Stock Exchange and a member of the S&P 500 Index, the Corporation employs 8,000 worldwide and reports annual revenues in excess of $2.9 billion. **Career Highlights:** Software Systems Architect, EMC Corporation (1997-Present); Senior Software Developer, SoftJoys (1995-97); Software and Hardware Designer, Nienschanz (1992-95). **Education:** Leningrad State University, M.Sc. in Physics (1984). **Personal Information:** Married to Elena in 1983. One child: Sofia.

David Hui-Wen Cheng, Ph.D.
Editor in hief
TrustMed.com
11th Floor, #102, Section 2, Roosevelt Road
Taipei, Taiwan 110
+886 223686171
Fax: +886 223640169
dhwcheng@trustmed.com.tw

7375

Business Information: Serving as the Editor in Chief of TrustMed.com, Dr. Cheng is responsible for the content of published articles. He is also a shareholder of the Company. Possessing superior talents and an excellent understanding of his field, he oversees all translations from English to Chinese, and write articles for publishing online. An accomplished professional, he has published four books. Attributing his success to innovation and caring for the health of the community, Dr. Cheng is proud of his part in the growth of the Company. In the future, he plans to establish other branches and have patents approved. Headquartered in Taipei, Taiwan, TrustMed.com is an Internet content provider focusing on the medical industry. Having started out as a nonprofit organization in 1998, the Company became a for profit organization in 2000. The Company provides health information for the Chinese market in Chinese format, catering to 1.5 billion people. **Career Highlights:** Editor in Chief, TrustMed.com (1998-Present); Professor, Taipei Medical College (1992-00); Researcher, Sola/Barnes Hind (1988-92); Associate Researcher, Cetus, Inc. (1987-88). **Associations & Accomplishments:** Health Care Association. **Education:** University of California at San Francisco, Ph.D. (1985). **Personal Information:** Married. Dr. Cheng enjoys exercising and running.

Robert W. Dossett
Director
TerraComm, Inc.
3711 North Atlantic
Spokane, WA 99205
(509) 327-2008
rwd@terracomm-inc.com

7375

Business Information: Utilizing several years of experience, Mr. Dossett is the Director for TerraComm, Inc. In his position, he is responsible for managing all of the network and Web servers throughout the Corporation. Moreover, he is charged with providing hardware and technical support to employees and ensuring that all of the bills are paid on time and correctly. In addition to his current position, Mr. Dossett works as technical support specialist for Microsoft in order for them to fund this Corporation. In the future, he looks forward to continuing with the Corporation and offering high speed access to the entire United States, specifically in rural areas. He attributes his success to confidence and an abundance of ideas. Established in 1999, TerraComm, Inc. is an Internet service provider. Located in Spokane, Washington, the Corporation takes ideas and develops them into business plans enabling the employees to assist entreprenuers in start up businesses. The Corporation provides quality plans and solutions for the business owners to build successful companies. With a staff of four employees at present, the Corporation reports an estimated annual revenue of $1 million. **Career Highlights:** Director, TerraComm Inc. (1999-Present); Technical Support, Microsoft (1999-Present); Computer Lab Consultant, Eastern Washington University (1997-99); Manager, Muscle Power (1994-96). **Associations & Accomplishments:** Tri-cities Guardsman Association; WWRNG. **Education:** Eastern Washington University. **Personal Information:** Married to Brandy in 1991. Two children: Eva and Catherine. Mr. Dossett enjoys outdoor activities.

Kevin E. Gehrt
Manager of Development and Communications
Information Services International
100 International Drive
Mount Olive, NJ 07828
(973) 691-3710
Fax: (973) 691-3548
kevin.gehrt@effem.com

7375

Business Information: Functioning in the capacity of Manager of Development and Communications for Information Services International, Mr. Gehrt oversees and coordinates all aspects of training and leadership development activities for the Company's network in North and South America. As a savvy, nine year professional, Mr. Gehrt maintains external client relations and promotes associate training programs to develop future managers. Before joining Information Services International, he served as a Human Resource Director for AlliedSignal Specialty Chemicals. In order to remain on top of changes in technical and human resources development, Mr. Gehrt reads publications such as Information World, as well as surfing the Internet. Looking toward the 21st century, he aspires to work abroad in the area of European development. His success reflects his ability to think outside the box, produce results, and aggressively take on new challenges. Information Services International is a full service information technology provider for the M&M/Mars Corporation. Established in 1979, the Company provides large corporations with the technical information necessary for research, development, and marketing of new and existing products. A staff of 1,500, works toward the common goal of client satisfaction. With headquarters in Mount Olive, New Jersey, the Company operates seven locations nationwide. **Career Highlights:** Manager of Development and Communications, Information Services International (1998-Present); Human Resource Director, Allied Signal Specialty Chemicals (1995-98); Corporate Recruiting Manager, Wiz Distributors, Ltd. (1993-95); Transportation Manager, LaSalle County Asphalt Company (1990-93). **Associations & Accomplishments:** Society for Human Resource Management; American Society for Training and Development. **Education:** Rutgers University, M.B.A. (1996); University of Illinois, B.S. in Industrial Psychology. **Personal Information:** Mr. Gehrt enjoys downhill skiing, scuba diving, golf and auto racing.

Rebecca E. Harte
Chief Information Officer
BRTRC
8260 Willow Oaks Corporate Drive, Suite 800
Fairfax, VA 22031
(703) 205-1528
Fax: (703) 204-9447
bharte@brtrc.com

7375

Business Information: Ms. Harte serves as Chief Information Officer of BRTRC, overseeing local area network support staff as well as participating in corporate planning and the development of the corporate vision. She also supervises the collaboration and development of system applications and addresses information technology related requests from clients. Ms. Harte plans to remain in her current position with the Consultancy, encouraging efforts for the expansion of the client base and available services. BRTRC offers a variety of technical services to clients, including information management, network design, and system administration. The Consultancy also provides web publishing, data base design, computer programming, and Internet related services. Established in 1985, BRTRC currently employs 200 people and has reached $15 million in annual revenue from the provision of technical engineering, support, and analysis. **Career Highlights:** Chief Information Officer, BRTRC (1989-Present); Mathematics Assistant, Hollins College (1987-89). **Associations & Accomplishments:** Association for Computing Machinery; Institute for Electrical and Electronics Engineers; Networking Professionals Association; Mathematical Association of America; American Mathematics Society; Phi Beta Kappa; Sigma Xi; Featured in Communications Week. **Education:** George Washington University, M.S. in Information Management (1994); Hollins College, B.A. in Mathematics (1989); Novell Inc., Certified

Netware Engineer (1996). **Personal Information:** Ms. Harte enjoys showing dogs and photography.

Fred A. Hopkins
LAN Administrator
Dun & Bradstreet Corporation
1 Diamond Hill Road
New Providence, NJ 07974
(908) 665-5833
Fax: (908) 665-5252
hopkinsf@dnb.com

7375

Business Information: As LAN Administrator of Dun & Bradstreet Corporation, Mr. Hopkins manages the communications network within the Corporation. His overall responsibilities include network security, installing new applications, distributing software upgrades, monitoring daily activity, and enforcing licensing agreements. Before joining Dun & Bradstreet, he assertively served as Communications Supervisor with eunetcom.ISD and as Senior Data Communications Technician with for Dunsnet. An expert, Mr. Hopkins developed a state-of-the-art storage management program and continuously provides routine backups. Additionally, he oversees and directs the Helps Desk, as well as configures machines. His career success reflects his ability to think out-of-the-box and take on new challenges and responsibilities. Strategic plans are focused on obtaining his MCSE. Dun & Bradstreet Corporation is a holding company for Dun and Bradstreet, one of the world's largest business to business credit, marketing, and purchasing information providers with a database of more than 50 million businesses worldwide. Established in 1841, the Corporation employs a work force of more than 10,000 people who help generate revenues in excess of $2.1 billion annually. **Career Highlights:** LAN Administrator, Dun & Bradstreet Corporation (1996-Present); Communications Supervisor, eunetcom, ISD (1994-96); Senior Data Communications Technician, Dunsnet c/o Dun & Bradstreet Corporation (1986-94). **Associations & Accomplishments:** American Management Association; USGA. **Education:** Brandywine College of Widener University. **Personal Information:** Married to Judith in 1995. Mr. Hopkins enjoys golf, motorcycling and bicycling.

Vishvesh Kanumilli
Director of Customer Implementation
Dun & Bradstreet
3 Sylvan Way
Parsippany, NJ 07054
(973) 605-6266
Fax: (973) 605-6938
kanumilliv@dnb.com

7375

Business Information: A prominent and respected professional, Mr. Kanumilli serves as Director of Customer Implementation for Dun & Bradstreet. Directly supervising 12 skilled professionals and the help desk staff, he works with clients and systems management to determine the type of information technology system that will provide them with optimum benefits. As a 10 year professional, Mr. Kanumilli designs and develops the system architecture, installing it at the client's location and training new users on its proper use. He remains on the cutting edge of technology by reading trade journals, networking on the Internet, and through hands on experiences. Establishing goals that are compatible with those of the Company, Mr. Kanumilli looks forward to a future promotion to Vice President. His success reflects his ability to think outside the box and aggressively take on new challenges. The largest information technology consulting agency in the United States, Dun & Bradstreet is the leading provider of business to business information and delivery systems. Currently, the Firm is headquartered in New Jersey. **Career Highlights:** Director of Customer Implementation, Dun & Bradstreet (1997-Present); Senior Consultant, Database Solutions (1994-97); Project Leader, Thai Carbon Black (1993-94). **Education:** Loyola College, B.A. in Economics (1984).

Ram Mohan
Vice President/Chief Technical Officer
Infonautics Corporation
590 North Gulph Road
King of Prussia, PA 19406
(610) 971-8840
Fax: (610) 971-8859

7375

Business Information: Serving with Infonautics Corporation since 1995, Mr. Mohan currently holds the position of Vice President and Chief Technical Officer. As such, he is responsible for the strategic business management and formulating and implementing marketing techniques and various campaigns. In addition, he monitors production rates and direction and authorizes decisions regarding distribution of the product. He oversees profit and loss records and presides over the recruitment and release of employees. A

recognized professional, Mr. Mohan has been published in the "Journal of Management Technology" and "National Computers Techxonics." In the future, he would like to remain with the Corporation and help it to expand into a $2 billion business. Infonautics Corporation is a fast growing 50 person Internet start-up company providing Internet software and information retrieval capabilities for businesses and individuals. Programs offered include the Sleuth line of consumer products, the award-winning Electric Library service and Encyclopedia.com, the Internet's first free online encyclopedia. Agents offer technical support for clients with questions regarding software and service. **Career Highlights:** Infonautics Corporation: Vice President/Chief Technical Officer (1999-Present), Director of Technology (1995-99); Software Project Lead, First Data Resources (1995-96); Software Engineer, UNISYS (1992-94). **Associations & Accomplishments:** Instiute of Electronics and Electrical Engineering; National Honor Society; Eastern Technology Council; Named to International WHO'S WHO of Information Technology; Philadelphia Area New Media Association; Association for Interactive Media; Mayor's E-Commerce Commission. **Education:** Drexel University, M.S. (In Progress); B.I.M., M.B.A.; Mangalore University, B.S. **Personal Information:** Mr. Mohan enjoys flying gliders, camping, hiking, writing, running and sports.

Jeff L. Reed
Manager, International Programs
UUNET Technologies
162 Brenda Court
Warrenton, VA 20186
(703) 208-3768
Fax: (703) 645-4166
jreed@uu.net

7375

Business Information: Mr. Reed has worked in the technology field since 1984. He arrived at UUNET Technologies in 1997, after 10 solid years as Senior Systems Engineer and Project Manager for GTE. Now, Mr. Reed fulfills the role of Manager of International Programs. He owns a significant record of delivering results by paying close attention to technical details and solving problems and challenges in a superb fashion. Currently, Mr. Reed is charged with management of UUNET's international backbone expansion in Asia, Latin America, and Canada. Relying on his strategic management skills and technology expertise, he is responsible for negotiating contracts and network designing and ordering. Developing schedules, time lines, and budgets; coordinating architectural specifications; facilitating resolution of utilities; maintaining design standards throughout all phases of project development; and synthesizing large quantities of data into monthly reports to keep project on track also fall within the realm of Mr. Reed's management responsibilities. His career accomplishments include developing a defense network for the government and building the first network allowing automated health care services. He attributes his success to his education and industry mentors. Keeping on top of emerging technologies and staying with the Company serves as Mr. Reed's future goals. His advice to others is "go to college." A global leader in Internet communications solutions, UUNET is a subsidiary of MCI WorldCom. International in scope, the Company is headquartered in Virginia. UUNET, founded in 1987, employs more than 9,600 people generating in excess of $5 billion in annual revenues. **Career Highlights:** Manager, International Programs, UUNET Technologies (1997-Present); GTE: Senior Systems Manager (1996-97), Project Manager (1989-96). **Associations & Accomplishments:** Institute of Electronics and Electrical Engineers; National Rifle Association; PSPES; Pennsylvania State University Alumni Association. **Education:** George Mason University, M.S. in Electrical Engineering (1998); Pennsylvania State University: Bachelor's degree (1984), Associate's degree (1982). **Personal Information:** Mr. Reed enjoys country western dancing.

Joy Remuzzi
Manager
UUNET
22001 Loudoun County Parkway
Ashburn, VA 20147
(703) 886-6669
jremuzzi@uu.net

7375

Business Information: Serving as the Manager of Global Web Site for UUNET, Ms. Remuzzi works hard to maintain the best site on the Web. Her main focus is on keeping the newest technology integrated in the Web page. Ms. Remuzzi also provides the marketing department updates, develops e-commerce strategies, and increases product information. She oversees three developers who work on the Web site in order to ensure its professional appearance and up-to-date reports. The most rewarding aspect of her career is building the Web site at GTS and coordinating all Web sites with UUNET. Ms. Remuzzi plans to continue working for UUNET in a position which gives her more work in formulating Web strategies and daily business processes. Her success is attributed to her innovativeness, problem solving skills, and not being afraid to ask questions. Established in 1987, UUNET is an Internet service provider and a division of MCI WorldCom. The Company works mostly for large companies with clients such as Disney and AOL. UUNET specializes in digital distribution, Internet communications, and Web hosting. The Company also designs and builds a wide variety of networks and Internet communications. Considered the most comprehensive server in the service provider industry, UUNET strives to maintain its excellent reputation by providing customers the highest quality service possible. Presently, UUNET employs a work force of over 7,000 people who helps generate in excess of $3.5 billion in annual revenues. **Career Highlights:** Manager of Global Web Site, UUNET (1999-Present); Communication Specialist, GTS (1995-99); Editor, Union Bank of Switzerland (1995). **Associations & Accomplishments:** New Media Society; Washington DC AIDS Ride; Phillips Gallery Contemporary; Friend of the Alexandria Art Legue; American Wine and Food Association. **Education:** Columbia University, M.A. 1986; School of Visual Arts; University of Rochester: B.A. in English, Russian Studies Certificate. **Personal Information:** Ms. Remuzzi enjoys travel, art, literature, running and biking.

Shashank Tripathi

Chief Executive Officer
Inaltus.com
9, 49 Onslow Garden, South Kensington
London, England, United Kingdom SW7 3QF
+44 2087997436
Fax: +44 2087997430
shashank@inaltus.com

7375

Business Information: Serving in the position of Chief Executive Officer of Inaltus.com, Mr. Tripathi is responsible for the development and implementation of policies and procedures that are incorporated into all courses of action. Throughout daily acitivities, he is charged with the obligation to performs such duties as departmental management, employee and client relations, and financial aspects such as profit and loss management. With more than five years of extensive experience in business management, Mr. Tripathi is currently utilizing his knowledge and talent to devise plans for assisting the Company in gaining more international recognition and exposure. His success reflects his ability to take on challenges and deliver results on behalf of the Company and its clientele. Inaltus.com is an Internet company engaged in the provision of all overhead services including accounting, human resources, and information technology. The Company targets small to medium sized companies throughout Europe, to include Germany, France, and England. Established in 2000, the Company is headquartered in London, England and functions under the direction of more than 20 professionals who facilitate smooth business operations on a daily basis. **Career Highlights:** Chief Executive Officer, Inalto.Com (1999-Present); Senior Manager, Andersen Consulting (1999); Manager, Schlumberger (1995). **Associations & Accomplishments:** Tripathi Memorial Trust. **Education:** Imd-Lousanne, M.B.A. in Finance with Honors (1995); Bachelor of Technology in Mechanical Engineering; Indian Institute of Technology (1986). **Personal Information:** Married to Gauri in 1991. One child: Tarini. Mr. Tripathi enjoys adventure activities.

Rhonda M. Vetere

Department Head
UUNET - A Division of MCI/WorldCom
5000 Britton Road
Hilliard, OH 43026
(614) 723-1426
Fax: (614) 723-1201
rvetere@wcom.net

7375

Business Information: Ms. Vetere is Department Head of UUNET's Network Operations Center. She is responsible for oversight and management of all day-to-day administration and operations, including the Center's work force. As the senior manager, she sets the strategic direction and vision, as well as ensures the functionality and fully operational status of the networking infrastructure. Ms. Vetere has assertively served with UUNET (formerly Compuserve) in a variety of roles since coming on board in 1993 as a Manager of Network Implementation and Integration. Overseeing personnel recruitment and management, implementing UUNET's policies and procedures, and supervising the research, evaluation, and deployment of advanced network technology also fall within the realm of her responsibilities. Ms. Vetere credits her career success to being goal oriented, decision making skills, focused with exuberant energy. Her success directly reflects her ability to build strong teams with synergy and technical strength and take on new challenges. Ms. Vetere has received numerous Quarterly Associate awards and yearly recognition from the officers. UUNET is the Internet services division of MCI/WorldCom. UUNET is a name that stands for excellence in Business Internet Communication Services. UUNET offers the world's highest capacity, most expandable and reliable IP Network. Providing Internet access, Web Hosting, Remote Access, VPN Solutions, and other "Value Added" services. Services are provided in 114 countries to more than 70,000 customers. **Career Highlights:** UUNET - A Division of MCI/WorldCom: Department Head (1998-Present), Service Level (1997-98), Manager of Network Implementation and Integration (1993-96). **Associations & Accomplishments:** National Association for Female Executives; Women in Telecommunications; American Management Association; Numerous Quarterly Awards and Yearly Recognitions from the Officers; Volunteer Trainer. **Education:** George Mason University, B.S. in Business Administration; Communications and Business degree. **Personal Information:** Ms. Vetere enjoys skiing, swimming, scuba diving and interior design.

Fred R. Anderson

Advanced Systems Engineer
EDS
13600 EDS Drive, Mail Stop A3S-D53
Herndon, VA 20171
(703) 742-2000
Fax: (703) 904-8919
fred.anderson.@eds.com

7376

Business Information: Serving in the position of Advanced Systems Engineer of EDS or Electronic Data Systems, Mr. Anderson fulfills a number of duties on behalf of the Company and its clientele. He oversees and directs LAN/WAN and related network operations. In his capacity, he serves as a network, server, and storage design engineer for United States naval ships, specializing in NT server and storage hardware design. Highly regarded, Mr. Anderson possesses superior talents and an excellent understanding of technology. He is a recipient of the Eagle Award for his role as a sales engineer. In the future, he looks forward to a chance to obtain a position as a Storage Engineer, designing and developing solutions for server networks. Founded in 1962, EDS is a professional services firm, specializing in management consulting, e-solutions, business process management, and information solutions. The Company utilizes technology to assist clients in staying current in the business world and remaining one step ahead of the competition. A global leader in the industry, the Company maintains a presence in 50 countries around the world. Employing a global work force of more than 120,000 professionals, EDS reports annual earnings of $12 billion. **Career Highlights:** Advanced Systems Engineer, EDS (1994-Present); Tempest Workstation Engineer, Zenith Inteq, Inc. (1989-94); RF Communications Engineer, Vega Precision Labs (1977-89). **Associations & Accomplishments:** Microsoft certified; Novell Certified; Cisco Certified. **Education:** EDS University: Microsoft Certified Professional (1998), Microsoft Certified Systems Engineer (1998). **Personal Information:** Married to Karin in 1992. Two children: Dylan and Logan. Mr. Anderson enjoys raquetball, kids ball and outdoor activities.

Wesley Dwayne Buhler

Manager
Electronic Data Systems
5400 Legacy Drive, B3-2A-40
Plano, TX 75024
(972) 604-4699
Fax: (972) 796-5561
dwayne.buhler@eds.com

7376

Business Information: Utilizing years of experience obtained thorough an extensive employment history, Mr. Buhler holds the title of Manager for Electronic Data Systems. Mr. Buhler leads an infrastructure management team that is responsible for service and support to internal employees and financial properties. As a savvy, 13 year professional, he leads a team of 11 employees in providing 3-Tier LAN and software tools development and support. Overseeing level II initiatives and directing change control, system migrations, and software packaging also fall within the realm of Mr. Buhler's responsibilities. His professional success and longevity reflects his ability to stay on top of emerging technology and aggressively taking on new challenges. Establishing goals that are compatible with the Company, Mr. Buhler would eventually like to attain the position of Division Manager. Electronic Data Systems is an international service provider for the information technology field that offers systems integration of computers for clients. Company headquarters are located in Plano, Texas. Established in 1963, the Company's operations employ the skilled services of 64 individuals to meet the demands of a growing clientele. **Career Highlights:** Electronic Data Systems: Manager (1993-Present), Manager/Supervisor of Database Administration (1991-93), Advanced Systems Engineer (1989-91). **Associations & Accomplishments:** NASPA; Microsoft Developers Network. **Education:** University of Tulsa, B.S. in Computer Information Systems (In Progress); University of Texas at Dallas, B.S. in Computer Information Systems (In Progress); Tulsa Junior College, A.A.S. in Computer Sciences (1986); Cohin County Community College. **Personal Information:** Married to Erin in 1982. Two children: Jennifer and Nicholas. Mr. Buhler enjoys car restoration and softball.

Kevin A. Burgess

Network Engineer
EDS System House
7001 Mumford Road, Suite 300, Tower 1
Halifax, Nova Scotia, Canada B3L 4N9
(902) 426-3538
Fax: (902) 426-9991
kburgess@cmhcschc.gc.ca

7376

Business Information: As a Network Engineer of EDS System House, Mr. Burgess designs and manages customer infrastructure, determing what the needs of the client are and developing a plan to meet those needs. A savvy, 10 year veteran of the information technology field, Mr. Burgess works closely with management and systems users to analyze, specify, and design cutting solutions to harness more of the computer's power. Participating in the analysis, design, evaluation, testing, and implementation of LAN, WAN, and Internet/Intranet related networking environments also fall within the technical realm of Mr. Burgess' responsibilities. He plans on keeping himself current on all aspects of client relations and emerging technology by reading trade journals and other forms of self study engagements. Success according to Mr. Burgess is due to his ability to think out-of-the-box, tackle new challenges, and deliver results on behalf of his clientele. EDS System House operates as an international company providing system integration and outsourcing network management services to big businesses. The Company currently employs a work force of more than 105,000 professional, technical, and support staff who help generate annual revenues in excess of $14 billion. **Career Highlights:** Network Engineer, EDS System House (1995-Present); Network Consultant, Downhome Computer Services (1994-95); Network Manager, Hub Meat Packers (1993-94); Support Manager, Atlantis Kobetek (1991-93). **Associations & Accomplishments:** Novell Certified; Cisco Certified; Netware Users International. **Education:** C.D.I. in Computer Maintenance (1990). **Personal Information:** Married to Nancy in 1986. Two children: Rachel and Joseph. Mr. Burgess enjoys golf and volleyball.

Charles E. DeLaPorte, Jr.

Information Analyst
EDS
600 Kellwood Parkway
St. Louis, MO 63017
(314) 576-3163
Fax: (314) 576-3310
chuck_delaporte@kellwood.com

7376

Business Information: Currently contracted by the Kellwood Company to help design a new information technology system and provide day-to-day information technology services, Mr. DeLaPorte serves as Information Analyst for EDS. He uses new GeneXus to maintain Kellwood's Enterprise Critical System, DOS400. This includes periodic maintenance and new development for DOS400, ensuring that it is functioning properly and at its optimum level. Continually striving to improve performance, Mr. DeLaPorte plans to learn more about the systems side of technology and the business practices of Kellwood. His career success reflects his ability to think out-of-the-box and take on new challenges and responsibilities. He is committed to the successful development of the Company and is searching for ways to make it more marketable. Since inception in 1962, EDS has been a leader in the information technology field. The Company offers services in three different areas: Management Consulting, Information Services, and E-business Solutions. More than 120,000 skilled employees serve clients in 49 countries around the globe. **Career Highlights:** Information Analyst, EDS (1996-Present); Programmer Analyst, Kellwood (1995-96); GeneXus Consultant, Software Application Professionals, Inc. (1993-95). **Education:** University of Missouri at St. Louis, B.S. in Business Administration with an emphasis in Management Information Systems (1993). **Personal Information:** Mr. DeLaPorte enjoys church, reading, movies, gardening and the theater.

B. F. Donohoe

Senior Consultant
EDS
1600 Smith Street
Houston, TX 77002
(713) 324-4450
Fax: (713) 324-8813
bdonoh@coair.com

7376

Business Information: Functioning in the capacity of Senior Consultant with EDS or Electronic Data Systems, Mr. Donohoe is the problem escalation point of contact for all systems and services and support. He has served with EDS in a variety of positions since joining the team as Senior Manager of Engineering and Project Management in 1992. Before joining EDS, Mr. Donohoe served as Vice President of System One. He also has over 25 years in various management capacities with several major airlines. In his role, he is responsible for all day-to-day operations to include hardware and software acquisition and installation. Coordinating resources, time lines, schedules, and budgets; working with users and management to analyze, specify, and design new solutions; and synthesizing large quantities of data into monthly reports also fall within the realm of Mr. Donohoe's responsibilities. Managing his staff of experts, he credits his success to luck and academics and his ability to think out-of-the-box and take on new challenges and responsibilities. Remaining on the bleeding edge of new technology is cited as his future goal. A public company, EDS offers consulting, hardware, software, and staffing services to an international clientele. EDS currently provides Continental Airlines with all of its daily communication needs, including data, voice, and fax. Headquartered in Plano, Texas, the Company presently employs a global workforce of more than 100,000 professional, technical, and support personnel. **Career Highlights:** EDS: Senior Consultant (1996-Present), Senior Manager of Engineering and Project Management (1992-95); Vice President, System One/Continental (1988-92); Over 25 years in various management capacity with several major airlines. **Associations & Accomplishments:** Auxiliary, United States Coast Guard; U.S. Power and Sail; T.A.S.S.; Museum Society. **Education:** College of San Mateo, B.A. (1990). **Personal Information:** Two children: Michael and Kathleen. Mr. Donohoe enjoys sailing, running (marathon runner) and Harley biking.

Ruth A. Garrels

Information Associate
EDS
902 East Hamilton Drive
Flint, MI 48550
(810) 236-9397
Fax: (810) 953-0685
lrgarrnet@ibm.net

7376

Business Information: Functioning in the role of Information Associate with EDS, Mrs. Garrels conducts system management, system analysis, and consulting services for clients in order to assess and meet their information technology needs. Drawing from an extensive education and previous occupational experience, Mrs. Garrels has developed the skills needed to maintain the highest standards of professional excellence. She attributes her success to her flexibility and her thorough understanding of the market. Mrs. Garrels hopes to expedite continued promotion and begin focusing on project management. Established in 1962, EDS is a publicly owned company providing management services for information systems. Serving an international client base, the Company employs a staff of 10,000 individuals dedicated to serving the diverse needs of the clientele. **Career Highlights:** Information Associate, EDS (1998-Present); Data Analyst, General Motors (1998-95); Financial Assistant, Central Garden & Pet (1992-95). **Associations & Accomplishments:** Order of Eastern Star. **Education:** Kennedy-Western University, degree in Management Information Systems (1999). **Personal Information:** Married to Lawrence B. in 1971. Three children: Erica, Elissa, and Matthew. Mrs. Garrels enjoys sewing, reading and computers.

Elbert W. Johnston

Technical Team Lead
EDS
401 South Valley Forge Road
Lansdale, PA 19446
(610) 669-1360
Fax: (610) 669-6870
jamkraine@compuserve.com

7376

Business Information: Dedicated to the success of EDS, Mr. Johnston applies his knowledge and expertise in the field of electrical engineering in serving as Technical Team Lead. He consults with clients regarding their individual business needs and goals to design and develop customized networks or system applications. Once a project is begun, he serves as the technical team leader and is in charge of six to twelve information technology professionals at a time. Mr. Johnston oversees each project from the design stage to its implementation. Consistently achieving quality performance, he looks forward to increasing his professional responsibilities in a higher management role. His success reflects his ability to build teams with synergy and technical strength, as well as deliver results and aggressively tackle new challenges. Nationally renowned, EDS is a leading consulting firm in the information technology industry. EDS employs a worldwide workforce of 130,000 knowledgeable individuals to provide clients with cutting edge technological solutions for software and hardware designed to enhance their business operations. Time management and business management services are also offered. **Career Highlights:** Technical Team Lead, EDS (1998-Present); Systems Administrator, Alternative Resources Corporation (1995-97); Henkels & Mckoy (1993-95); Corrosion Engineer, CorrPro Companies Inc. (1988-93). **Associations & Accomplishments:** Institute of Electrical and Electronics Engineers Computer Society; Institute of Electrical and Electronics Engineers; Institute of Electrical and Electronics Engineers Communication. **Education:** Temple University, B.S. in Electrical Engineering Technology (1990); RETS Electronics School (1978). **Personal Information:** Married to Mary Anne in 1983. Two children: Chloé and Nicholas. Mr. Johnston enjoys soccer, coaching and biking.

Joseph R. Lamberson

Senior Information Specialist
EDS
One Bell Center, MC 19-K-8
St. Louis, MO 63101
(314) 235-3742
Fax: (314) 331-3457

7376

Business Information: Serving as Senior Information Specialist of EDS, Mr. Lamberson is also the technical architect and project leader. Responsible for every aspect of applications, from the beginning to the end of projects, Mr. Lamberson is dedicated to accommodating the Company's clients needs in order to better enhance their business. Coordinating resources, time lines, schedules, assignments, and budgets also fall within the realm of his responsibilities. Beginning his association with EDS in 1991, Mr. Lamberson has received recognition for his diligence and management skills through several promotions to his current position. He continues to grow professionally and hopes to begin focusing on Java while also being involved in the advancement of operations. His success reflects his ability to think out-of-the-box, produce results, and aggressively take on new challenges. EDS is engaged in the development of information technology systems. Employing over 150,000 employees world-wide, the Company helps its clients in all aspects of the digital business such as consulting, outsourcing, and development projects. **Career Highlights:** EDS: Senior Information Specialist (1997-Present), Project Technical Consultant (1998-99), Y2K Project Leader (1996-98), Account Senior Technician (1995-96). **Associations & Accomplishments:** Trustee, Bethany Baptist Church. **Education:** Purdue University, B.S. in Industrial Management (1972). **Personal Information:** Married to April in 1980. Two children: Amy and Ashley. Mr. Lamberson enjoys tennis and other sports.

Himadri P. Mukherjee

Software Engineer
ABB Systems Control
451 Elcamino Real
Santa Clara, CA 95050
(408) 615-6326
Fax: (408) 615-6495
himadri.mukherjee@ustral.mail.abb.com

7376

Business Information: Functioning in the role of Software Engineer at ABB System Control, Mr. Mukherjee develops Oracle software used to properly feed real time database and control operations in electric utilities all over the world. Utilizing his extensive practical experience and academic background in computer science and electrical engineering, Mr. Mukherjee is charged with design and development of a variety of software such as systems information, programmed in Oracle; Spider, an in-house real time database software; and Oracle historical systems used for information storage. His success reflects his ability to think out-of-the-box and aggressively take on new challenges. Mr. Mukherjee's future goal is to become a mid level manager, working in both the technical side and management side. This will enable him effectively deal with major projects on a management level. ABB System Control is an electric utility vendor for control system software and business software for utilities and independent power operators. Global in scope, ABB Systems Control is a subsidiary of of Global ABB Company, a $50 billion company that maintains a presence in 100 countries around the world. ABB Systems Control is the transmission and distribution section manned by over 200 employees who help generate revenues in excess of $50 million annually. Additionally, ABB Systems Control specializes in cross continental involvement and collaboration in developing and implementing new software systems. **Career Highlights:** Software Engineer, ABB Systems Control (1996-Present); Software Engineer, Optimal Care Inc. (1995); Engineer, Jyoti, Ltd. (1993-94). **Associations & Accomplishments:** Institute of Electronics and Electrical Engineers; Oracle Users Group; Crusers Cricket Club; Secretary, Northern California Cricket Association; Association for Promotion Primary Education in the World. **Education:** Arizona State University, M.S. (1996); Regional Engineering College (1993). **Personal Information:** Married to Indrani in 1997. Mr. Mukherjee enjoys astrology, cooking and playing cricket in California league.

Herald Soohang Soon

Project Manager
EDS
200 1st Street SE
Cedar Rapids, IA 52401-1409
(319) 286-1336
Fax: (319) 398-8119
heraldsoon@yahoo.com

7376

Business Information: As a Project Manager for EDS, Mr. Soon provides strategic and operational information technology services for utilities, financial, and healthcare markets. He is responsibe for developing strategic plans, project management, and all training opportunities. Possessing superior talents and an excellent understanding of technology, Mr. Soon handles and is responsible for the operations of six departments. Coordinating resources, time lines, assignments, and budgets also fall within the realm of his responsibilities. He is also a certified Project Management Professional. In the future, Mr. Soon plans to continue in information technology in a more global industry. EDS provides state-of-the-art information technology systems to the utilities industry. The Company assists companies, which provide electricity and water to cities, implement information technology into their business processes. EDS's wide range of services also includes repair and maintenance of systems and upkeep of existing systems. **Career Highlights:** Project Manager, EDS (1997-Present); Systems Development and Quality Manager, EDS/Cars (1996-97); Technical Leader, EDS/GMAC (1991-93). **Associations & Accomplishments:** Project Management Professional; Project Management Institute. **Education:** Purdue University/ESC Rouwn, M.B.A./M.S. in Management (1996); National University of Singapore, Electrical Engineering degree (1986). **Personal Information:** Married to Felecia Tan in 1994. Mr. Soon enjoys white water rafting.

Karin Tuniewicz

Systems Supervisor
Electronic Data Systems
1471 Elmwood Avenue
Cranston, RI 02910
(401) 784-3893
Fax: (401) 467-9581
ktuniewicz@aol.com

7376

Business Information: Functioning in the capacity of Systems Supervisor at Electronic Data Systems or EDS, Mrs. Tuniewicz oversees and directs all aspects of project management, as well as supervises the technical staff, forecasts technology needs and resource requirements, and sets the technical priorities. Before joining EDS in 1998, Mrs. Tuniewicz served as Business Process Analyst with Matthew Thornton Healthcare and Senior Trainer and Technology Training Coordinator. As an eight year technology professional, she owns an established record of producing results in support of goals and objectives. Her present position primarily involves supervising and guiding 18 systems administrators and business analysts in the design and deployment of cutting edge solutions to enhance systems performance. Coordinating plans, resources, and schedules; analyzing client needs and developing solutions; and overseeing time lines and assignments are also an integral part of Mrs. Tuniewicz's responsibilities. She attributes her success to good mentors and her ingenuity. "Learn as much as you can and don't be stifled by people that say you can't do it," is cited as her advice. Continuing to fine tune her skills through education and certifications serves as her future endeavors. Electronic Data Systems is a large systems integration and consulting firm who provides consultants to work with local, state, and federal government agencies. Currently, EDS is working with 19 states providing data processing electronic solutions for the Medicaid program. Established in 1962, EDS is global in scope and is headquartered in Rhode Island. Presently, 100,000 professional, technical, and support personnel are employed by EDS. **Career Highlights:** Systems Supervisor, Electronic Data Systems (1998-Present); Business Process Analyst, Matthew Thornton Healthcare (1996-97); Senior Trainer/Technology Training Coordinator (1993-96). **Education:** Syracuse University, B.S. (1989). **Personal Information:** Married to Mark in 1997. Mrs. Tuniewicz enjoys vocal jazz, literature, hiking and cooking.

Kevin J. Vinson

Infrastructure Specialist
EDS
7013 Fox Drive
The Colony, TX 75056-4458
(972) 796-5335
Fax: (972) 796-5448
kevin.vinson@eds.com

7376

Business Information: Mr. Vinson has served in several different positions since beginning his career with EDS in 1985. At the present time, he fulfills the responsibilities of

Infrastructure Specialist. He consults with clients, designing platform engineering solutions based on their individual requirements. Solutions can be designed in a NetWare, Windows NT, or UNIX operating environment and is implemented at the client site by the solutions designer. In addition to his extensive experience in the field, Mr. Vinson has completed the telecommunication professional development program and is Novell NetWare Certified. He is currently pursuing his Microsoft Certification and credits his professional success to his parents, education, and hands on experience. His future endeavors include eventually getting involved in the consulting side of technology. EDS is an information technology services company, providing systems integration, e-commerce, data processing, and consulting services. Founded by Ross Perot in 1962, the Company employs a work force of approximately 104,000 skilled professionals in 10 locations. Headquartered in Plano, Texas, EDS boasts $17 billion in annual revenue. **Career Highlights:** EDS: Infrastructure Specialist (1999-Present), Advanced Systems Administrator (1991-99), Product Line Specialist (1989-91), Office Automation Analyst (1987-89). **Associations & Accomplishments:** Dallas Novell Users Group. **Education:** University of Illinois at Springfield, B.A. in Management (1985); Illinois Central College, Associate's degree (1981); Novell NetWare Certification: CNE - NetWare 4, CNE - IntranetWare, CNE - NetWare 5, MCNE - Internet/Intranet Solutions, MCNE - Integrating Windows NT, NCIP - Novell Certified Internet Professional; CIM - Certified Intranet Manager; Master Certified Novell Engineer. **Personal Information:** Married to Linda in 1985. Mr. Vinson enjoys running, biking, weight lifting and golf.

Paul C. Chambers

Chief Executive Officer/Co-Owner
Siteserv2000 LLC
6403 Tanglewood Drive
Troy, MI 48098-2281
(248) 879-8614
Fax: (248) 828-3712
paul@siteserv2000.com

7378

Business Information: Serving as Chief Executive Officer and Co-Owner of Siteserv2000 LLC, Mr. Chambers oversees and directs daily activities and is responsible for making executive decisions. Demonstrating an extensive knowledge of the industry, he recruits clients by offering informative explanations of technical services and capabilities, then negotiating contracts with a personable ease. Mr. Chambers handles all marketing campaigns, developing creative messages for the community to convey features such as customer support and impressive Web site formulation. Delving into the industry was an easy decision for Mr. Chambers, who simply combined his hobby with a strong work ethic to result in a superior technical company. Currently initiating expansion plans that include acquisition of smaller, related businesses and an increased international clientele, Mr. Chambers attributes his success to his mother, who offered much encouragement and his stepfather, who provided business related guidance. Siteserv2000 LLC was established in 1997, and currently employs two people to oversee daily operations. Providing Internet services, computer repair, and Web site development, the Company serves a local region of lower Michigan and is headquartered in Troy. **Career Highlights:** Chief Executive Officer/Owner, Siteserv2000 LLC (1997-Present). **Education:** Technology related courses; High School.

D'Wayne I. Da Costa

Network Installer/Service Technician
Vistec Electronic Services Inc.
3B-376 Kingston Road
Pickering, Ontario, Canada L1V 6K4
(905) 509-7399
Fax: (905) 509-7401
vistec@globalserve.net

7378

Business Information: As Network Installer and Service Technician at Vistec Electronic Services Inc., Mr. Da Costa oversees the implementation and maintenance of networks. Demonstrating extensive technical knowledge, he handles on-site client consulting, evaluating needs and designing innovative solutions. A systems expert, Mr. Da Costa creates custom networks to fulfill all aspects of client needs and oversees the purchasing and maintenance as well. Crediting his success to versatile problem solving techniques, Mr. Da Costa looks forward to continued advancement throughout the corporate structure. Established in 1989, Vistec Electronic Services Inc. provides computer sales and electronic services to local businesses and individuals. Employing five techncially knowledgeable people, the Corporation has developed a reputation of quality services and value priced products. **Career Highlights:** Network Installer/Service Technician, Vistec Electronic Services Inc. (1989-Present). **Associations & Accomplishments:** The Ontario Association of Certified Engineering Technician and Technologists; Canadian Electronic and Appliance Service Association. **Education:** R.C.C. **Personal Information:** Mr. Da Costa enjoys scuba diving, riding, hiking and rollerblading.

Frederick A. Heald

Senior Test Engineer
DecisionOne
4400 Longwood Lane
Columbus, OH 43228
(614) 883-0041
Fax: (614) 883-2100

7378

Business Information: Serving as Senior Test Engineer for DecisionOne, Mr. Heald is respsonsible for developing screen test applications and counteractive software that adjusts and repairs system errors. Mr. Heald also performs technician training, and monitors diagnostic projects, generating over 10 million screen analysis reports annually. Using the motivational skills aquired while serving in the United States Navy, Mr. Heald continually produces quality results among his training staff, and is regarded as a indelible asset to DecisionOne. He attributes his successful career to his father, who introduced him to the world of engineering. DecisionOne is an established and reputable computer consulting firm that provides screen testing and repair services to corporations nationwide, such as Dell Computers. Performing over 1,000 screen tests daily, the Firm is noted for its reliable counteractive software. Operating out of Columbus, Ohio, DecisionOne employs skilled technicians to facilitate every aspect of quality client service and software design; thus maintaining cutting edge technology. **Career Highlights:** Senior Test Engineer, DecisionOne (Present).

Joseph W. McNutt

Chief Technical Officer
The Computer & Network Fixer
28 Ambling Lane
Levittown, PA 19055-1253
(215) 629-5700
Fax: (215) 629-5714
jmcnutt@compfixer.com

7378

Business Information: Mr. McNutt holds the position of Chief Technical Officer with The Computer & Network Fixer. He is the Company's senior network field engineer as well as the senior systems analyst. Mr. McNutt holds current A+ certification, Compaq Netware ASE certification, Compaq Netware ASE certification, and multiple Netware OS CNE certifications. Mr. McNutt functions as his Company's principal technical liaison to their numerous client sites in the Philadelphia, Pennsylvania region. His daily responsibilities include maintaining and upgrading computer systems, making purchase recommendations for software, hardware, and serving as the senior decision-maker in the technology selection process. Mr. McNutt's affiliation with relevant industry organizations enables him to stay technologically up to date and allows for interaction with the many professionals in his field. In the future, Mr. McNutt anticipates significantly increased focus on Internet based e-commerce, and achieving CISCO and Microsoft MCSE certification. The Computer & Network Fixer, established in 1985, provides corrective and preventative computer and network maintenance services in WAN, LAN, and stand-alone environments. Employing 20 associates, the Company produces revenues in excess of $2 million and serves numerous clients in the Philadelphia, Pennsylvania metropolitan area. Surviving in such an evolving and competitive industry requires offering clients practical cost effective solutions combined with state-of-the-art troubleshooting techniques. Staying current with emerging technologies, The Computer & Network Fixer remains a leader in southeastern Pennsylvania. The Company takes pride in the fact that it successfully updates and modernizes computing infrastructures with minimal or no downtime. **Career Highlights:** Chief Technical Officer, The Computer & Network Fixer (1988-Present); Senior Field Engineering Specialist, Monroe System for Business (1972-88). **Associations & Accomplishments:** Institute of Electronics and Electrical Engineers; Association for Computing Machinery; Network Professional Association; Netware Users International. **Education:** Cleveland Institute of Electronics, Certificate in Electronics Technology with Laboratory (1981); Certified Novell Engineer (1995); Compaq Netware ASE (1998); A+ Certified (1995). **Personal Information:** Married to Suzanne in 1973. Two children: Jennifer L. and Barbara J. Mr. McNutt enjoys gardening.

Michael G. Simousek, A+, Net+

Owner/Repair and Installation Manager
Micro Technix
1841 Kropf Avenue
Madison, WI 53704-3415
(608) 235-0485
Fax: (608) 242-5662
mgsa@itis.com

7378

Business Information: As the Owner of Micro-Technix, Mr. Simousek serves as Repair and Installation Manager. He provides on site repair of personal computers and the installation of WAN equipment. Possessing an excellent understanding of technology, he is A+ and Network+ certified and is also certified by IBM in Desktop Systems and Warranty Basics. An independent contractor with 12 years of hands-on experience, Mr. Simousek is also an Authorized Network provider for Equant. Highly regarded by his clients, he provides warranty service on a range of network connectivity equipment. The highlights of his career are the experiences with customers and clients and the certifications he has obtained during his career. In the future, Mr. Simousek would like to become more involved in data communication, specifically switched packet data systems and computer networks. Customer service and being pleasant with people have contributed to his success. A local technology firm, Micro-Technix is a computer warranty service provider. Established in 1995, the Company is located in the Madison, Wisconsin area. Providing quality and expert services, the Company's motto is "Don't despair, we repair." **Career Highlights:** Owner/Repair and Installation Manager, Micro-Technix (1995-Present). **Associations & Accomplishments:** COMPTIA Certifications, IBM Personal Computer Certification; Techforce (Equant) Authorized Network Service Provider. **Education:** Madison Area Technical School, A.S. in Electronics (1988). **Personal Information:** Married to C. J. Johnson-Simousek in 1993. Mr. Simousek enjoys doing his work and travel with his wife.

Dave E. Yount

Lead Technician
MI Technologies
3310 East Peterson Road
Troy, OH 45373
(937) 335-4560
Fax: (937) 339-6344

7378

Business Information: As Lead Technician of MI Technologies, Mr. Yount is responsible for maintaining the integrity of technical support in his field. His primary responsibilities include such operations as providing leadership for his team in the areas of customer service, departmental management, employee relations, and client relations. Mr. Yount is noted for his contribution to a book written in 1998 and 1999, with his father, called the "Tech Tip Repair Book." Possessing an excellent understanding of his field, Mr. Yount grew up into the technology field. His father is a 35 year veteran of the field. Attributing his professional success to his father and his own persistence, he has aspirations to continue repairing more flat panels, while involving himself in more networking. MI Technologies engages in such endeavors as reverse engineering and technological repairs. The Company develops monitor schematics, while repairing data software and other electronic supplies within client companies. Established in 1994, the Company offers a host of other forms of support for their clients. Operating out of one local location, the Company enjoys annual revenues exceeding $180,000. Presently, MI Technologies is manned by a staff of three professional engineers. **Career Highlights:** Lead Technician, MI Technologies (Present). **Education:** Mobile Electronic Installers Certificate.

Mahmood Ahmed Abdulla

Manager of Internet Platform Development
Batelco
P.O. Box 14
Manama, Bahrain
+973 883507
Fax: +973 331351
mahmood@batelco.com.bh

7379

Business Information: Joining Batelco as Senior Technical Officer of Internet and Messaging Services in 1998, Mr. Abdulla fulfills a number of functions on behalf of the Company and his national clientele. His responsibility covers managing, administering, and maintaining the Company's Internet platforms. Possessing superior talents and an excellent understanding of technology, Mr. Abdull was promoted to the post of Manager of Internet Platform Development in June 2000. His focus is now on developing and deploying cutting-edge Internet and network technologies to help the Company remain at the forefront of industry as well as enhance and provide better services to clients. In the future,

Mr. Abdulla plans on continuing to help the Company to expand its operations. Situated in Muharraq, Bahrain, Batelco is a telecommunication and Internet service provider with a large customer base and a work force of more than 2,000 employees. The Company is committed to providing state-of-the-art, fast, efficient, and quality services to all of Bahrain. It is also has a regional presence through several joint ventures in the Middle East. **Career Highlights:** Batelco: Manager of Internet Platform Development (2000-Present), Senior Technical Officer of Internet Services (1998-00); Instructor of Computer Science, Univeristy of Bahrain (1991-98). **Associations & Accomplishments:** Internet Club; Bahrain Information Technology Society; Bahrain Al-Eslah Society. **Education:** Arizona State University, Master's degree in Computer Science (1996); King Fahd University of Petroleum and Minerals, B.Sc. in Computer Science (1991). **Personal Information:** Married to Samya Ali Juma in 1993. Two children: Ahmed and Nada. Mr. Abdulla enjoys reading, writing and do-it-yourself jobs.

Amin Adatia, Ph.D.

President
Knowtech Solutions, Inc.
66 Pineglen Crescent
Nepean, Ontario, Canada K2G 0G8
(613) 226-8378
Fax: (613) 226-7004
amin@knowtech.on.ca

7379

Business Information: As the President of Know Tech Solutions Inc., Dr. Adatia is responsible for the strategic and tactical direction for the Company. He formulates new business and marketing plans to keep the Corporation at the forefront within the industry sector of interest. Possessing superior talents and an excellent understanding of information technology, Dr. Adatia is in the process of creating a generic business model to better support data warehouse type of analysis. Established in 1986, Know Tech Solutions Inc. performs information technology related services to provide a competitive advantage. Located on the Internet at www.knowtech.on.ca, the Company designs and develops database models for business and research applications. In the past few years, the modeling has focused on the data warehouse implementations. Know Tech also provides Oracle database administration and Oracle Financials support. Working with other consultants having the same dedication and drive, Know Tech takes pride in providing clients with consulting services that make for better deployment of information technology. **Career Highlights:** President, Know Tech Solutions Inc. (1986-Present). **Associations & Accomplishments:** International Oracle Users Group; Oracle Development Tools Users Group; Oracle Applications Users Group. **Education:** University of London, Ph.D. (1980); University of British Columbia, M.B.A. (1983); University of London, B.S. in Engineering (1973). **Personal Information:** Two children: Sabrina and Moez. Dr. Adatia enjoys chess, cricket, current affairs, photography and ice hockey.

Braj Agarwal

Owner
Affordable PC Systems, Inc.
2309 Spruce Street
Seaford, NY 11783
(516) 783-7615
Fax: (516) 783-7615
cmagarwal@aol.com

7379

Business Information: Dedicated to providing technical and software training for his clients, Mr. Agarwal is the Owner of Affordable PC Systems, Inc. Offering customized hardware systems and cutting edge software applications, he remains at the forefront of all industry related technology, maintaining the most innovative products at compatible prices for his customers. Recipient of the Teaching Excellence Award, Mr. Agarwal is renowned for his communication skills, dedicating his professional career to not only PC development, but also the further education of his clientele. Presently focusing his entrepreneurial ability on the growth of Affordable PC Systems, the Company is expanding nationally, traveling more into Internet activity. Offering the most diverse technological services catering to all the needs of their clients, Affordable PC Systems, Inc. creates individually crafted hardware and software equipment, builds and maintains networks, and provides education and training on the use of computer systems. Established in 1988, the Corporation serves the regional Seaford, New York area, generating annual revenues in excess of $250,000. **Career Highlights:** Owner, Affordable PC Systems, Inc. (1988-Present); Senior Project Engineer, Shore Plastics (1983-87); Owner, Aloke Enterprises (1973-82). **Associations & Accomplishments:** Society of Mechanical Engineers; Adjunct Faculty at New York University. **Education:** Long Island University, M.B.A. (1988); State University of New York at Stony Brook, M.S.; Massachusetts Institute of Technology, B.S. **Personal Information:** Married to Puslipa in 1972. One child: Aloke. Mr. Agarwal enjoys soccer and reading.

Ismail Al-Jamal

Founder/Chief Executive Officer/Webmaster
Blue Dragon Network
965 Quarry Street
Petaluma, CA 94954-7477
(707) 486-5460
Fax: (707) 765-6478
webmaster@bluedragon.net

7379

Business Information: As Founder of Blue Dragon Network, Mr. Al-Jamal serves in his positions of Chief Executive Officer and Webmaster. Possessing superior talents and an excellent understanding of technology, he assumes responsibilities for all day to day operations. He maintains the Company's budget, facilitates promotional projects, and presides over the completion of all administrative tasks. Additionally, Mr. Al-Jamal supervises employee productivity, formulating a hands-on management style with and above average aptitude for problem solving. Through the development and implementation of policies and procedures, he encourages optimum performance among the staff, ensuring that all personnel work together to achieve a common goal. Mr. Al-Jamal has enjoyed substantial success in his present position and looks forward to Company expansion and growth. Blue Dragon Network is a consolidation company, which engages in Web page design, software repair and installation, and Internet selling and buying. Established in 1994, the Company employs the skilled services of seven individuals to facilitate all aspects of operation. Located in Petaluma, California, Blue Dragon Network provides its services to clients nationally. **Career Highlights:** Founder/Chief Executive Officer/Webmaster, Blue Dragon Network (1999-Present); Consultant, Sidi Mahammad Press (1993-99). **Education:** Santa Rosa Junior College. **Personal Information:** Mr. Al-Jamal enjoys surfing the Internet, power boating and cars.

Gerry Albright

President
Albright Ideas, Inc.
4031 Pumice Lane
Eagan, MN 55122
(612) 688-2726
Fax: (612) 688-9773
wvbh76a@prodigy.net

7379

Business Information: Mr. Albright founded Albright Ideas, Inc. in 1992 in order to provide clients with quality and much needed services. As President, he is responsible for all day-to-day activities, as well as coordinating administration, new business development, consulting, programming, and strategic planning. Future plans include targeting large corporations and airline industries. He would also like to attribute his success to perseverance. Albright Ideas, Inc. is a computer consulting firm, providing contracted maintenance services for Unisys computer systems. Services offered include programming, software enhancement, and network development. Established in 1992, Albright Ideas employs five people. **Career Highlights:** President, Albright Ideas, Inc. (1992-Present); Staff Consultant, ADIA Information Technology (1988-92); Staff Consultant, Datronics, Inc. (1984-88). **Associations & Accomplishments:** Microsoft Developer Network; Unisys Mapper Associates; Independent Business Alliance. **Education:** Gettysburg College, B.A. in Physics (1983). **Personal Information:** Married to Theresa.

Carol Elizabeth Allen

Network Specialist
Base Technologies, Inc.
P.O. Box 13097
Alexandria, VA 22312-9097
(202) 267-3157
Fax: (202) 267-5229
callen6216@aol.com

7379

Business Information: Serving as Network Specialist with Base Technologies, Inc. since 1997, Ms. Allen specializes in the building of complex network and database systems, the development of software and hardware, and the troubleshooting and maintenance of these specialized systems. Forming major client relations, she provides technical solutions to establish a more productive and efficient network structure for their various businesses. Utilizing four years of experience in this highly specialized field, Ms. Allen plans to further her education to facilitate promotional opportunities within Base Technologies. Her success is atttibuted to her ability to think out-of-the-box, take on challenges and new responsibilities, and deliver cutting-edge results on behalf of the Corporation and client base. Affiliated with the federal government, Base Technologies, Inc. was established in McLean, Virginia providing specialized consulting services for major corporations and businesses nationwide. Employing the skilled services of 5,000 individuals to acquire business, meet with clients, facilitate projects, and market services, the Corporation generates $100 billion in annual revenues. Incorporating the latest technological advancments into their products and services, the Corporation is dedicated to the meeting the diverse needs of a continually expanding clientele. **Career Highlights:** Network Specialist, Base Technologies, Inc. (1997-Present); Systems Analyst, AMA Technoliges (1996-97); Systems Analyst, I-Net, Inc. (1996). **Associations & Accomplishments:** Coriolis; Microsoft Certified Systems Engineer; Certified Novell Engineer; Master Certified Novell Engineer. **Education:** Computer Learning Center, Network Engineering Management (1996); PPI/Knowlogy, Microsoft Certified Systems Engineer. **Personal Information:** Three children: Tapresa Allen, John Calloway, and George Powell. Ms. Allen enjoys computers. Her favorite quote is "Change the things you control. Ignore the ones you can't."

Mark Allen

Systems Architect
Unisys Corporation
6410 Vicksburg Court NW
Acworth, GA 30101
(770) 368-6027
Fax: (770) 368-6121
mark.allen1@unisys.com

7379

Business Information: Serving as a Systems Architect for Unisys Corporation, Mr. Allen fulfills a number of technical functions on behalf of the Corporation. He oversees a team of professionals who analyze, design, implement, and manage cutting-edge technology and e-business solutions. Possessing an excellent understanding of technology, Mr. Allen researches potential client companies, negotiates contract agreements, and oversees the finances. He also ensures customer satisfaction and facilitates promotional activities on behalf of the Corporation to recruit new clients. Mr. Allen anticipates his promotion to practice lead as a result of his continuing efforts to increase his skills through training and professional development activities. He also aspires to increase his knowledge in order to expand the Corporation's international market share. Unisys is a provider of information solutions, technology, and software. Specializing in the development of critical business solutions, the Corporation creates a variety of software projects that facilitate the building of user applications, and the management of distribution systems. Established in the 1950s, the Corporation employs more than 35,000 individuals worldwide to meet the demands of a growing clientele. Unisys is headquartered in Pennsylvania and generates annual revenues in excess of $100 million. **Career Highlights:** Systems Architect, Unisys Corporation (2000-Present); DCS Consulting/Project Manager, Diversified Computer Solutions (1999-00); Systems and Network Administrator, National Distributing Company (1996-99); Systems and Network Administrator, Atlantic Video Corporation (1991-96). **Associations & Accomplishments:** Microsoft Solution Partner; Microsoft Developer Network. **Education:** Habersham Central High School (1988). **Personal Information:** Mr. Allen's credo is, "In today's business, you don't get what you deserve, you get what you negotiate."

Gwyn C. Anderson

Owner
Enhanced Ideas
P.O. Box 3602
La Crosse, WI 54602
(608) 788-6156
Fax: (608) 788-6156
gwyn96@earthlink.net

7379

Business Information: As Owner of Enhanced Ideas, Ms. Anderson is also the Chief Executive Officer. After working for a company that was sold out, she decided to take her chances on her own. She determines the overall strategic direction and business contribution of the information systems function. In her capacity, she is responsible for on site client support, training, public relations, and technician supervision. Ms. Anderson keeps employees aware of their importance to the Company and attains results through the proper direction of employees. Coordinating future resources, time lines, schedules, and assignments also fall within the purview of her responsibilities. She attributes her success to her parents and her local SCORE chapter, as well as her ability to take on new challenges. Her goal is to acquire additional employees to enable the Company to serve additional clients. Ms. Anderson's favorite quotable quote is, "Think about it really hard. You have to want it more than air." Enhanced Ideas is a computer consulting Firm specializing in hardware and software technical repair. The Company also offers software training for stand alone and network for both residential and commercial clients. Established in 1996, the Company has a total of three individuals to promote services, facilitate scheduling, address customer queries, repair, and client training. **Career Highlights:** Owner, Enhanced Ideas (1996-Present). **Personal Information:** Ms. Anderson enjoys rollerskating, camping, horseback riding and sci-fi.

Scott K. Anderson
President
Internet Ventures
602 Lewis Street
Pasadena, TX 77502-3707
(713) 648-0728
Fax: (713) 797-9326
scotta@intventure.com

7379

Business Information: Serving in the role of President of Internet Ventures, Mr. Anderson oversees day-to-day administration and operations. Concerned with all aspects of the Company, he focuses on employee development and customer relation improvement. Demonstrating extensive knowledge of the industry, he is directly involved in the creation of strategic business planning by lending his insight and guidance at departmental meetings. Recognized as an innovative and proactive leader, Mr. Anderson implements countless empowerment activities to foster a sense of teamwork among his staff. Citing strong networking abilities as the key to his success, Mr. Anderson intends to continue expanding his Company as he adds Web casting and automated billing to the corporate structure. Internet Ventures is a technical consulting firm that specializes in Internet and Intranet based solutions. Located in Pasadena, Texas, the Company employs seven people to assist in the completion of daily activities such as Web application development. The Company was established in 1997 and is experiencing considerable growth and expansion as reputation of quality services spreads throughout the professional community. **Career Highlights:** President, Internet Ventures (1997-Present); Owner, Internet Technology Services (1996-97); Internet Consultant, Berger & Company (1995-96); Electronic Marketing, IBM Corporation (1993-95). **Associations & Accomplishments:** Gulf Coast Conservation Association; Houston Livestock Show and Radeo. **Education:** Southwest Texas State, B.B.A. (1994). **Personal Information:** One child: Devyn.

Jonathan Andrews
President
Andrell Corporation
P.O. Box 5425
El Dorado Hills, CA 95762
(916) 803-1974
Fax: (530) 672-0637
jandrews@andrell.com

7379

Business Information: As President of Andrell Corporation, Mr. Andrews is responsible for all aspects of administration, consulting, public relations, and marketing. He attributes his success to the encouragement of his mentors. Mr. Andrews' plans for the future include expanding the size and visibility of the Corporation. Andrell Corporation provides custom software development and consulting services for local, state, and federal government agencies, as well as industries, insurance, and financial organizations. Established in 1994, the Corporation reports estimated annual revenue of $300,000. **Career Highlights:** President, Andrell Corporation (1994-Present); Senior Engineer Consultant, Tenera LP (1992-94); Director Special Projects, Environmental Products and Services (1988-92); Radiological Controls Engineer, Newport News Shipbuilding and Dry Dock (1985-88). **Associations & Accomplishments:** American Institute of Chemical Engineers; Jaycees. **Education:** Clarkson University (1985).

Christopher T. Ansell
Systems Consultant
Mesa Solutions
248 Eastview Drive
Madison, AL 35758
(256) 864-0400
Fax: (256) 864-0251
cansell@mesahq.com

7379

Business Information: As Systems Consultant of Mesa Solutions, Mr. Ansell contributes to the overall effectiveness of the Company by offering his insight and guidance on technical issues. Designing and developing applications to fulfill specific needs of clients, he demonstrates an extensive technical knowledge gained by education and practical work experience. Recognized for his superior abilities, he performs designing, coding, data modeling, and database expertise for the Company's new products. Attributing his success to an ongoing education, Mr. Ansell looks forward to integrating his knowledge into the Company's current operating procedures. Established in 1996, Mesa Solutions provides consulting expertise for AM/FM/GIS systems in the telecommunications and utilities arena. Headquartered in Alabama, the Company employs over 50 technically trained people to provide assistance to clients in all areas of business operations. **Career Highlights:** Systems Consultant, Mesa Solutions (1996-Present); Senior Systems Engineer, Intergraph (1993-96); Systems Engineer, Science Applications

International Corporation (1990-93). **Associations & Accomplishments:** Industry related. **Education:** University of Tennessee at Chattanooga, B.S. (1990). **Personal Information:** Married. Mr. Ansell enjoys reading and family time.

Ashraf M. Arafeh
Senior Account Manager
International Turnkey Systems
P.O. Box 23102
Jeddah, Saudi Arabia 21426
+966 26572669
Fax: +966 26572616
aarafeh@itsksa.com

7379

Business Information: As Senior Account Manager, Mr. Arafeh holds the responsibility of maintaining all corporate accounts with International Turnkey Systems. Utilizing two years of practical experience in his technical field of expertise, he introduces the client to the specific services offered by the Company in e-commerce and banking solutions, providing resolutions for the improvement of their financial status. Mr. Arafeh plans to expedite continued promotion through dedication and the perpetuation of additional clientele growth with International Turnkey Systems. His success reflects his ability to think outside the box, aggressively take on challenges, and deliver results on behalf of the Company and its clientele. Offering a variety of technological solutions to the financial sectors of major corporations, International Turnkey Systems was established in 1981. Headquartered in Jeddah, Saudi Arabia, the Company extends its highly specialized services globally operating out of offices in 12 countries throughout the Middle East. Employing the expertise of 600 professionals, the Company provides an expansive array of telecommunications and e-commerce solutions and services to their clients. Offering consulting services, the Company evaluates the client's business and implements specific systems in order to improve their financial status. **Career Highlights:** Senior Account Manager, International Turnkey Systems (1999-Present); Tantash Information Systems Group: Hardware Division Manager (1998-99), Sales Manager (1994-98). **Associations & Accomplishments:** Jordanian Engineers Association. **Education:** University fo North Carolina at Charlotte, B.Sc. in Engineering (1986). **Personal Information:** Married to Rimah in 1995. Two children: Anwar and Raneem. Mr. Arafeh enjoys chess.

Bryan N. Ard
Information Technology Manager
Maryville Technologies
540 Maryville Centre Drive
St. Louis, MO 63141
(314) 519-4100
Fax: (314) 519-4141
bryan.ard@maryville.com

7379

Business Information: Functioning in the capacity of Information Technology Manager of Maryville Technologies, Mr. Ard determines the overall strategic direction and vision, as well as business contribution of the information systems function. Before joining Maryville Technologies in 1994, Mr. Ard assertively served as a Technical Manager with Andersen Consulting. His history includes stints as Senior Application Development Specialist with Citicorp Mortgage and Programmer at HOK, Inc. In his present role, Mr. Ard works with users to analyze, specify, and design state-of-the-art systems solutions. Determining future resource requirements; overseeing time lines, schedules, and assignments; implementing and maintaining systems; and providing technical support also fall within the purview of his responsibilities. His success reflects his ability to build and lead teams with synergy and technical strength, think out-of-the-box, and take on new challenges and responsibilities. Eventually attaining the position of Director of Information Technology serves as one of Mr. Ard's future endeavors. A technology firm, Maryville Technologies engages in enterprise systems management consulting, systems integration, and applications management. Established in 1994, the Company employs a work force of more than 125 professional and technical experts who help generate revenues in excess of $45 million annually. **Career Highlights:** Information Technology Manager, Maryville Technologies (1994-Present); Technical Manager, Andersen Consulting (1990-94); Senior Application Development Specialist, Citicorp Mortgage (1989-90); Programmer, HOK, Inc. (1987-89). **Education:** University of Missouri at Rolla, B.S. in Electrical Engineering (1987). **Personal Information:** Married to Diana in 1998.

Julian Sol Ares
Software and Hardware Integrator
Chicago Microsystems
4117 North Oakley Avenue
Chicago, IL 60618
(773) 784-8164
Fax: (773) 784-8177
jsares@ix.netcom.com

7379

Business Information: As Software and Hardware Integrator of Chicago Microsystems, Mr. Ares utilizes his technical knowledge as he creates innovative solutions to assist in systems development. Specializing in the area of hardware and equipment, he regularly meets with clients to evaluate their computing and systems needs. He then formulates a business plan that fulfills the requirements set by the customers, amplifying quality and productivity. Mr. Ares is a dedicated employee, who credits his success in the industry to his superb timing skills; he also believes that you must know your customers and understand their needs before you can serve them. Keeping his goals consistent with corporate objective, Mr. Ares looks forward to continual advancement within the Company as he focuses on the implementation of WANs. Serving the greater metropolitan area, Chicago Microsystems is a local based company employing six people in the state of Illinois. Established in 1982, the Company is a networking reseller handling technical issues from clients who range from small businesses to schools. Offering hardware and software support, Chicago Microsystems has earned a reputation of well deserved respect throughout the community. **Career Highlights:** Software and Hardware Integrator, Chicago Microsystems (1995-Present); Instructor of Physical Sciences, Harold Washington College (1992-95); Research Assistant, University of Illinois (1979-91). **Associations & Accomplishments:** Society of Physics Students; Sigma Pi Sigma; American Association for the Advancement of Science; Smithsonian Institution; National Park Conservation Association; National Audobon Society; Nature Conservancy; World Wildlife Fund; National Wildlife Association; National Geographic Society; United States Figure Skating Association. **Education:** University of Illinois, M.S. (1981); Northwestern University, B.A. in Physics (1979). **Personal Information:** Mr. Ares enjoys figure skating competition and computer gaming.

Brett C. Arroyo
Systems Engineer
Jannon Group
3820 Freedom Drive
Charlotte, NC 28208
(708) 393-0485
Fax: (203) 461-9201
arroyob@jannon.com

7379

Business Information: Serving as Systems Engineer for Jannon Group, Mr. Arroyo supports and implements local area networks using Microsoft Back Office Suite. He also initiates routers, the use of Microsoft servers, and technical support programs. Mr. Arroyo plans to further his technical education, advancing to positions of greater responsibility. Established in 1991, Jannon Group operates as a consultancy, specializing in providing network solutions to Fortune 500 companies. The Firm operates offices in Stamford, Connecticut, Hartford, Connecticut, Chicago, Illinois, and Charlotte, North Carolina with the support of 125 representatives who perform local and wide area network integration, installation, and design as well as offering system training. **Career Highlights:** Systems Engineer, Jannon Group (1997-Present); Network Administrator, Conklin & Conklin, Inc.; Network Analyst, USCO Distribution, Inc.; Input/Output Specialist, Chesebrough-Ponds USA. **Education:** Computer Processing Institute, Diploma (1989); Microsoft Certified Systems Engineer. **Personal Information:** Mr. Arroyo enjoys computers and reading.

Senthil K. Arumugam
Software Consultant
Baton Rouge International Inc.
110 Winding Wood Drive, Apartment 5B
Sayreville, NJ 08872
(732) 949-1709
Fax: (732) 432-6583
indhian@hotmail.com

7379

Business Information: Demonstrating expertise in the real-time embedded systems firmware development field, Mr. Arumugam has served as Software Consultant for Baton Rouge International, Inc. since 1995. Currently performing contract duties for Lucent Technologies, he is responsible for infrastructural provisioning in the design and development of Lucent's famous Packetstar Voice Gateway products. Coordinating resources and schedules, overseeing time lines and assignments, and ensuring integrity and security of systems also fall within the realm of Mr. Arumugam's responsibilities. As a solid, 12 year professional, he credits his success to his knowledge of the industry and networking with colleges. His advice to others is to keep your eyes and ears open and browse the Internet to assimilate tech trends. Continually striving to improve performance, he plans to remain in the technology field. The Technology Division of Baton Rouge International Inc. originated in 1968 when the bank of the same name began developing software for a fully integrated banking system. In 1991, the Corporation was purchased by India based CMC Ltd. Since 1991, Baton Rouge International has served companies throughout the United States, offering a full range of software development services. Presently, the Corporation employs a workforce of more than 160 professional and technical experts. **Career Highlights:** Software Consultant, Baton Rouge International Inc. (1995-Present); Senior Development Consultant, CMC Ltd. (1990-98). **Education:** M.I.T., Anna Uty, India, Bachelor's degree in Technology (1990); Thiagarajar College of Engg, Madurai, India, B.Sc. (1987). **Personal Information:** Married to Sharmili S. Kumaran in 1993. One child: Roshan S. Kumaran. Mr. Arumugam enjoys Web hosting e-groups for professionals, friends and community.

Tarek Atia

Managing Director/Chief Executive Officer
Technologica Trading & Computer Systems
Nasr City, 2 Abas El Akkad Street
Cairo, Egypt
+20 22725330
Fax: +20 22725544
tarekati@technologica.com.eg

7379

Business Information: Displaying advanced technical skills and adept leadership abilities, Mr. Atia currently serves as Managing Director and Chief Executive Officer for Technologica Trading & Computer Systems. In his capacity since 1998, he is responsible for overseeing all daily operations and directing new business development. Concurrently Mr. Atia supervises all technical, administrative, and commercial aspects for the Company, and is tasked with reviewing corporate account actitvities and negotiating all contracts. Establishing goals that are compatible with those of the Company, Mr. Atia's current focus is to develop operations in Libiya. Enjoying tremendous success in his current position, he attributes his success to team work and his dedicated work ethic. Established in 1998, Technologica Trading & Computer Systems is a leading international information technology firm engaged in corporate consulting, e-commerce solutions, and Internet services. Located in Cairo, Egypt, the Company currently employs the talents and expertise of 20 highly skilled technicians who generate over $750 thousand in annual revenue. The Company specializes in providing comprehensive state of the art hardware, software, and netware as well as multi-media training. Serving a regional client base, Technologica Trading & Computer Systems is looking to expand operations towards the Libyan market. **Career Highlights:** Managing Director/Chief Executive Officer, Technologica Trading & Computer Systems (1998-Present); Engineering Construction Company: Management Auditor (1996-98), Chief Accountant (1994-96); English Teacher, Berlitz-Essen-Germany (1989-93). **Education:** College of Arts and Science, B.A. (1987). **Personal Information:** Married to Lula in 1987. Two children: Yosra and Amr. Mr. Atia enjoys playing the piano.

Igmar E. Avendano

Design Engineer II
SYMTX
4401 Fredrich Lane, Building 2, Suite 200
Austin, TX 78744
(512) 328-7799
Fax: (512) 328-7778
iavendano@syntx.com

7379

Business Information: Possessing superior talents in the engineering field, Mr. Avendano joined SYMTX in 1999 as a Design Engineer II. In his position, he is responsible for working closely with management and users to analyze, specify, and design systems including PCB boards, analog, and digital systems. A systems expert, Mr. Avendano also creates and resolves problems on all equipment and provides interface training to users. Proud of his many accomplishments, Mr. Avendano has received several Company awards for his exceptional work. Consistently achieving quality performance in his field, he plans to attain the position of senior engineer of a telecommunications company. SYMTX specializes in the custom creation of test equipment for the telecommunications, semiconductor, and satellite industries. The Company builds, manufactures, implements, and trains for the software, hardware, and equipment for different companies. Established in 1986, SYMTX is a global company that is located in Austin, Texas. Over 200 professional, technical, and support staff are employed to facilitate every aspect of day to day operations. Presently, the Company reports annual revenues in excess of $20 million. **Career Highlights:** Design Engineer II, SYMTX (1999-Present); Product Engineer, Motorola (1997-99); Design Engineer, Symmetrix, now SYMTX (1996-97). **Associations & Accomplishments:** Institute for Electronics and Electrical Engineers. **Education:** Texas Tech University, B.S. in Electrical Engineering (1996). **Personal Information:** Married to Jhenny Rasales in 1997. One child: Indira. Mr. Avendano enjoys soccer coaching.

Olusegun Babajide

Information Technology Consultant
Jano Multicom AS
Ensjovien 7, P.O. Box 0655
Oslo, Norway
+47 22626701
Fax: +47 22626614
obabajid@online.no

7379

Business Information: Functioning in the capacity of Information Technology Consultant at Jano Multicom AS, Mr. Babajide coordinates with users and management and provides technical and analytical assistance and advice in the realm of network operations. He arrived at Jano Multicom in 1999, after years of practical experience as Information Technology Consultant with Telenor Bedrift AS. An expert in his role, he owns a strong record in delivering results in support of the Company and major users and clients. Analyzing, supporting, and monitoring network operations; installing and maintaining hardware and software; troubleshooting network usage; and coordinating resources, schedules, and assignment also fall within the purview of Mr. Babajide's responsibilities. His future endeavors include increasing his knowledge base of network by interacting with his colleagues in the field, reading trade journals, and attending seminars and workshops. Jano Multicom AS operates as a cable network specializing in technology, Internet, and data communications technology. The Company has established itself as a full-service multimedia provider in competition with traditional telecommunications companies. It is also possible to subscribe to television, telephone, and Internet services, via the same cable. Jano Multicom is currently offering high speed cable modem access to the Internet over existing cable plant. **Career Highlights:** Information Technology Consultant, Jano Multicom AS (1999-Present); Information Technology Consultant, Telenor Bedrift AS (1996-98). **Education:** Naeringsakademet IT-Tech., C.N.E. (1996); Petroleum Engineer. **Personal Information:** Married to Mary Tnuli in 1992. Three children: Olaniyi, Olushina, and Akinsile. Mr. Babajide enjoys football, tennis and data.

James M. Babcock

Managing Principal
Unisys Corporation
110 Wall Street
New York, NY 10005
(212) 504-9617
Fax: (914) 988-5421

7379

Business Information: Possessing a strong background in information technology, Mr. Babcock fulfills the responsibilities of Managing Partner for Unisys Corporation. In this capacity, he provides management oversight of the consulting services' profit and loss statement for the eastern region of the United States and Canada. Utilizing 28 years of extensive experience and a strong academic history, Mr. Babcock oversees all aspects of sales and delivery of network and desktop services. Maintaining quality customer relations and personnel management also falls under the realm of Mr. Babcock's responsibilities. A recognized authority in the industry, he also provides new computer systems and cutting edge solutions to meet the needs of the organization and the clientele. Striving for maximum effectiveness, Mr. Babcock's long-term goal is to ultimately attain the position of Chief Information Officer. Unisys is an information management company. A provider of hardware and software solutions, the Corporation specializes in network integration and information technology consulting services. Located in New York, the Corporation's local operation in Warwick is part of a vast network of satellites situated throughout the world. **Career Highlights:** Managing Principal, Unisys Corporation (1993-Present); Vice President of Marketing, Timeplex (1990-93; Vice President of Coms Production, Unisys Corporation. **Associations & Accomplishments:** Central Valley United Methodist Church. **Education:** University of Phoenix, M.S. in Computer Science (In Progress); State University of New York at Albany: B.S. in Math (1970), M.S. in Computer Science course work; Crosby Quality College, Wharton Executive Development Program. **Personal Information:** Married to Beatrice in 1974. One child: Jason. Mr. Babcock enjoys golf and church activities.

Sandra A. Bacik

Network Consultant
Bacik Consulting Service
34402 14th Way SW
Federal Way, WA 98023
(253) 661-9327

7379

Business Information: Recurited by Advanced Communication Services (ACS) in 1999, Ms. Bacik fulfilled the responsibilities of Network Consultant, specializing in security. She has received the status of Certified Information Systems Security Professional. In her capacity, dealing with various operating system security, data center security, and general network security and disaster recovery fall into her realm of responsibility for clients. Drawing from over 15 years of experience in the data processing field, Ms. Bacik can perform network security audits and implement the required changes to be in compliance with Company policies. In addition, she can perform requirement findings, evaluate and analyze software, and implement the recommended security solutions. Ms. Bacik has spoken at various MIS conferences, teaches Internet and Your Child Safety classes, and is instructing at a local university for Computer Forensics. She has copyrighted a few documents on NT security, policy outlines, and a PERL class for security monitoring. Gaining more knowledge of new, cutting edge security features, spreading knowledge, and opening up her own consulting business serve as her long-term goals. After departing from ACS, Ms. Bacik ventured out on her own and opened a consulting firm called Bacik Consulting Service. **Career Highlights:** Network Consultant, Bacik Consulting Service (1999-Present); University Instructor, LightPoint Learning/City; Network Consultant, ACS (1999); Information Security Operating Systems Specialist, Weyerhaeuser (1997-99); Operating Systems Specialist, Bank of America (1995-99); LAN Specialist, HBO and Company (1993-95). **Associations & Accomplishments:** Agora; International Information Systems Security Certiication Consortium, Inc.; Certified Information Systems Security Professional; Computer Security Institute; Computer Techology Investigators Northwest; High Tech Computer Crime Consortium; Information Systems Security Association; Named to World's Who's Who of Women. **Education:** Villa Marie College, B.A. in Math minor in Management Information Systems (1984); University of North Carolina at Charlotte; Central Piedmont Community College. **Personal Information:** Ms. Bacik enjoys outdoors, hiking, camping, volleyball, music, cooking and working with Aromatherapy and herbs.

Dawn D. Badinger

Network Administrator
EMCO
8900 South Choctaw
Baton Rouge, LA 70815
(225) 925-8900
Fax: (225) 925-9334
ddbadinger@emcobr.com

7379

Business Information: As Network Administrator of EMCO, Mrs. Badinger supervises the direction of technical applications in the network department. Supervising the LAN and WAN, she lends her expertise to provide service and outstanding support for both internal employees and customers. Mrs. Badinger conducts regular evaluations of the Company, recommending specific equipment to be purchased for the maximization of customer support. A self-starter, she credits success to her initiative, understanding that she must accomplish tasks with skills she acquires through continued education. Enjoying the challenges of her position, Mrs. Badinger currently is working to put the Company in a more competitive position in the industry, focusing on e-commerce and an updated Web site. Specializing in computer network administration, EMCO is headquartered in Baton Rouge, Louisiana and employs over 170 people. Founded in 1962, the Company offers services for Motorola two-way radios and personal computers, including Internet access for individuals and businesses. **Career Highlights:** Network Administrator, EMCO (1990-Present). **Associations & Accomplishments:** National Association of Female Executives. **Education:** Southern Technical College, Associate's degree (1989). **Personal Information:** Married to Leo Badinger Jr. in 1995. One child: Caitlin. Mrs. Badinger enjoys dance and music.

Kathleen A. Bagley

Owner
Excel Consulting
P.O. Box 142
Winthrop, ME 04364-0142
(207) 377-5406
excl@ime.net

7379

Business Information: Mrs. Bagley is the Owner of Excel Consulting. Her business provides computer system consultation and business consultation, specializing in adaptive technology for the visually impaired and blind. Excel also provides in-service education for businesses and educational organizations, computer support for State of Maine Employees, and work-site evaluations for a variety of clientele including individuals, state agencies, and private businesses. Mrs. Bagley has also been instrumental in the set-up and maintenance of Adaptive Computer Sites in high schools and colleges around the state of Maine. The sole proprietor, Mrs. Bagley presently has a small staff, but hopes to see the Company increase in it's numbers and go national within the next five to seven years. An expert in her field, her advice to others is, "make sure your business has a firm foundation and find a good niche." Being able to deliver results and aggressively tackle new challenges has contributed to Mrs. Bagley's career success. Established in 1996, the Company has a total yearly revenue of $70,000. Presently, the Company is located in Winthrop, Maine. **Career Highlights:** Owner, Excel Consulting (1996-Present); Branch Manager, JobSmart (1995-96); Sales Manager/Head of Marketing, Combined Management (1994-95). **Associations & Accomplishments:** Citizens Advisory Council; Business Associate/Secretary, Pine Tree Guide Dog Users; Association for Education and Rehabilitation of the Blind and Visually Impaired; Initiate Advisor, Phi Sigma Pi Honor Fraternity; Psycho-social Rehabilitation Certification; Assistive Technology in the Workplace Certification. **Education:** University of Massachusetts at Boston, work towards Master's degree (1999); University of Maine at Farmington: B.A. in Business and Economics (1994), A.A. in Business Administration (1992). **Personal Information:** Married to Robert in 1998. Mrs. Bagley enjoys Alpine skiing, theatre, investing, travel and reading.

Gene Charles Baker, Jr.

Computer Systems Architect
Inventa
656 Tanglewood Drive
Eldersburg, MD 21784
gene.baker@inventa.com

7379

Business Information: Recruited to Inventa as Computer Systems Architect in 2000, Mr. Baker works closely with management and systems user to identify, analyze, specify, and design new solutions to harness more of the computer's power. Possessing an excellent understanding of his role, he is responsible for the functionality and operational status of the client's infrastructure. His focus is on designing, developing, and deploying new technology solutions to help keep client companies at the forefront as well as remain flexible, efficient, and profitable in the information technology age. Highly regarded, Mr. Baker is also responsible for identifying system problems and systems validation, programming, and installation. Drawing from 14 years of hands-on experience, he utilizes his talents and intellect to aggressively take on challenges and deliver results on behalf of the Firm and its clientele. Aspiring for a higher position, Mr. Baker is presently looking into management positions available to him. Established in 1984, Inventa is a professional services consulting firm. The Firm specializes in providing information technology solutions for businesses choosing to upgrade systems or customize a system for specific business needs. National in scope, Inventa is headquartered in Redwood Shores, California and operates a network of six satellite locations. **Career Highlights:** Computer Systems Architect, Inventa (2000-Present); Sybase, Inc.: Area Lead Architect (1998-00), Architect (1997-98), Principal Consultant (1997), Senior Consultant (1996-97), Consultant (1995-96); Technical Consultant, Autotote Lottery (1994-95); Senior Engineer, Ohmeda Critical Care (1992-94); Senior Program Analyst, Autotote Lottery (1990-92); Member of Technical Staff, Computer Sciences Corporation (1989-90); Engineer, Martin Marietta (1986-89). **Associations & Accomplishments:** President, Local Homeowner's Association; Vice President, Local Swim Club. **Education:** Loyola College, M.E.S. in Computer Science (1994); University of Maryland, B.S. in Computer Science (1988). **Personal Information:** Married to Lydia in 1988. Three children: Evan, Pierce, and Victoria. Mr. Baker enjoys stamp collecting and music.

Gerair D. Balian

Web Applications Developer
Digital Conversions
13922 Tustin East Drive, Apartment 39
Tustin, CA 92780-5925
(714) 327-2702
gbalian@earthlink.net

7379

Business Information: Serving as Web Applications Developer for Digital Conversions, Mr. Balian performs a number of technical duites on behalf of the Company. He is responsible for researching, designing, and developing cutting edge Web based applications. Possessing superior talents and an excellent understanding of technology, Mr. Balian is also responsible for implementing these applications for its clientele. Successfully staying on top of the ever changing information technology environment, his focus is helping is clients remain flexible, efficient, and profitable in the Information Technology Age. He attributes his success to his role model, Dr. Steven Franklin and his friend and mentor, Mr. Steven Yamanaka. Continue to research and develop new technology solutions serves as Mr. Balian's future endeavors. Digital Conversions is a public consulting company. Providing services to small and large sized companies, the Company writes and installs systems for clients getting ready to expand. Established in 1998, the Company employs 73 professional, technical, and support staff. Presently, Digital Conversions is national in scope and is located in Tustin, California. **Career Highlights:** Web Applications Developer, Digital Conversions (2000-Present); Developer, Mine Share Inc. (1998-00); Developer, Kofax Image Products (1997-98). **Education:** University of California at Irvine, B.S. in Computer Science (1998). **Personal Information:** Mr. Balian enjoys comedy, pool, singing and soccer.

Mark Barasch

Technical Director
Barasch Music & Sound
260 5th Avenue, Apartment 15S
New York, NY 10001-6417
(212) 986-6445
markb@bmands.com

7379

Business Information: A successful, 20 year veteran of the technology industry, Mr. Barasch ventured out to start up Barasch Music & Sound in 1990. As Owner and Operator, he oversees and directs all day-to-day administration and operations. He determines the overall strategic direction and formulates new business and marketing plans to keep the Company out-front of competitors in the music industry. Utilizing his business savvy and expertise, Mr. Barasch is in charge of all aspects of production. He also composes music and develops cutting edge concepts for advertising and Internet applications. A well known and respected professional, he owns and operates another business venture called "cy-fidelity.com" that was established in 1999. Future strategic plans are to focus more on business expansion and Web based applications. One of many career accomplishments, his greatest is producing a children's film "Magical Journey of Edgar and His Crayola Crayons" for Hallmark. He also wrote all the music for this film. Success according to Mr. Barasch is attributed to hard work, love of what he does, and luck. Barasch Music & Sound engages in music and sound production for the media indusrtries. The Company offers its clients advertising, Web site creation, audio, graphics, programming on computer platforms, and home market entertainment on CDRom. A small staff of eight professional and technical experts, the Company's major clients include American Express, IBM, Kleenex, Hallmark, and "I can't believe its not butter." Established in 1990, Barasch Music & Sound reports annual revenues in excess of $1.4 million. **Career Highlights:** Owner/Operator, Barasch Music & Sound (1990-Present). **Associations & Accomplishments:** American Society of Composers Authors, and Publishers; A.F.M.; S.A.G.; A.F.T.R.A. **Education:** Sarah Lawrence College, B.A. (1980). **Personal Information:** Married. Mr. Barasch enjoys spending time with his son, creating music, skiing, sailing, travel and sports.

Barbie Barta

Director of Operations
Comsys
4000 McEwen Road, Suite 200
Dallas, TX 75244-5014
(972) 455-3430
bbarta@comsys.com

7379

Business Information: Mrs. Barta has served with Comsys in various positions since joining the Company in 1997 as a Recruiter. Highly recruited to the Company, she currently serves as Director of Operations of the Dallas branch. She is responsible for all aspects of daily administration and operations, such as profitability and controlling expenses. In the position for a year, Mrs. Barta directs his staff of 15 people and manages a staff of 150 to 200 consultants. Handling corporate immigration and human resources also fall within the realm of her responsibilities. Before joining Comsys, she worked in the retail sales management field. One of her future endeavors include attaining the position of Account Executive and eventually working toward a Vice President capacity within the Company. Mrs. Barta's career success is attributed to attention to detail and perseverance, and her leadership ability to take on challenges and deliver results in support of corporate goals and objectives. A reputable, international recruiting company, Comsys places technical professionals for Fortune 500 clients. The Company specializes in placement of professionals in help desk, project management, and project consultant positions. Based in Houston, Texas, Comsys operates branches throughout the United States as well as one office in India. Established in 1989, the Company employs a staff of 165 people who help generate annual revenues in excess of $20 million. **Career Highlights:** Comsys: Director of Operations (1999-Present), Systems Trainer (1998-99), Recruiter (1997-98). **Associations & Accomplishments:** Board of Directors, United Way; Chairman of the Board, YMCA. **Personal Information:** Married to Mike in 1993. One child: Jordan.

Roy H. Bartlett

Vice President
GSI Consulting Services
55 University Avenue, Sutie 1601
Toronto, Ontario, Canada M5J 2H7
(416) 777-2525
Fax: (416) 777-2547
rbartlett@gsigroup.com

7379

Business Information: As Vice President of GSI Consulting Services, Mr. Bartlett is responsible for the delivery of quality services for all consulting practices. He works closely with users to analyze, specify, and design new solutions to help customers maintain the competitive edge in the market place. Overseeing and directing business development and daily operations, Mr. Bartlett focus is on growing and expanding the Company's clientele and bottom line. The most rewarding aspect of his career is being part of a team that designed and implemented a new process used in supermarkets. Committed to customer satisfaction, Mr. Bartlett plans to continue his work, becoming more involved in Internet business solutions, and assist the Company grow internationally. Established in 1980, GSI Consulting Services is involved in technology and management consulting. The Company also deals with intelligent building design, development, operation, and maintenance and is also involved in impementation of Web sites and e-commerce. Employing more than 500 people, the Company reports annual revenues in excess of $50 million. **Career Highlights:** Vice President, GSI Consulting Services (1998-Present); Chief Technology Officer, Ministry Defense and Aviation (1992-98); General Manager of Canada, Intellisys Inc. (1990-92); Director of Management Information Systems, J.D. Irving (1988-90). **Education:** University of New Brunswick (1973). **Personal Information:** Married to Naomi in 1980. Three children: Donna, Ross, and Patti-Bree. Mr. Bartlett enjoys physical fitness and jogging.

William Daniel Basinger

Senior Systems Analyst
M-Cubed Information Systems
3700 East-West Highway
Hyattsville, MD 20782-2015
(202) 874-7775
Fax: (202) 874-6878
basinger@wam.umd.edu

7379

Business Information: Mr. Basinger has worked in the information technology field since 1977. He has been with M-Cubed Information Systems since 1997, and now fulfills the role of Senior Systems Analyst. Mr. Basinger, demonstrating strategic systems and technology skills, is charged with assessing and updating IBM assemblers and COBOL codes for Y2K compliancy. In addition to supervising and guiding an eight member team, he handles numerous resource planning functions to include configuration and project management, systems design and coding, and testing and debugging. Determining future resource requirements, compiling statistical data, and providing technical support also fall within the realm of Mr. Basinger's responsibilities. One of his many career accomplishments include participating in a comprehensive software inventory and assessment of Department of Treasury Financial Systems Management COBOL and Assembly programs in preparation for rendering these programs Year 2000 compliant. He was able to effectively utilize IBM tools for expanding dates to include the century without modifying input or output file formats or procedural logic. Mr. Basinger is a recognized authority as he authored and published over seven technical publications including his Master's thesis "Set Theory and the Monoid." He attributes his success to the Christian values instilled in him by is parents. His future endeavors are to attain positions of Team Leader, Project Manager, and eventually an executive position. M-Cubed Information Systems operates as a government contracting firm. Established in 1983, the Company specializes in software development, engineering, consulting, Y2K remediation, out-sourcing services, and project management. International in scope, M-Cubed employs more than 90 professional and technical staff. **Career Highlights:** Senior Systems Analyst, M-Cubed Information Systems (1997-Present); Senior Computer Programmer/Analyst, PRC, Inc. (1996-97); Senior Computer Programmer/Analyst/Research Associate, George Washington University (1989-Present). **Associations & Accomplishments:** Association for Computing Machinery; American Geophysical Union; New York Academy of Sciences; Statue for Liberty-Ellis Island Foundation; Knight's of Columbus; Recipient, Technical Achievement Award, Vitro Corporation (1984); Marquis Who's Who in America; Marquis Who's Who in Science and Engineering. **Education:** Johns Hopkins University, M.S. in Computer Science (1989); Georgetown University, M.S. in Linguistics (1977); University of Maryland, B.S. in Linguistics, Anthropology, and Geology (1974). **Personal Information:** Married to Mary in 1988. Mr.

Basinger enjoys Bible study, violin, viola, poetry, science fiction and bridge.

Chris Batt-Ptaszek

Financial Analyst
GTE Internetworking, Powered by BBN
9810 Patuxent Wood Drive
Columbia, MD 21046
(410) 309-8362
Fax: (410) 794-4034
cbatt@bbn.com

7379

Business Information: Blending skills in technology and administration, Mrs. Batt-Ptaszek functions in the role of Financial Analyst. She bears responsibility for translating technical requirements into financial justifications. Before joining GTE Internetworking in 1995, Mrs. Batt-Ptaszek served as Program Administrator with BBN Communications. As an expert in her field, she oversees and handles the various purchasing processes, auditing procedures, and assists management in numerous capacities. Her success reflects her ability to aggressively take on new challenges and responsibilities. Seeking to provide the best in customer service, she frequently meets with vendors. Mrs. Batt-Ptaszek attributes her professional success to her tenacity. Her quotable quote to those considering the field is "be honest." GTE Internetworking, Powered by BBN functions as an Internet service provider. The Company provides a host of technology services, including electronic commerce and Web hosting. A core group of 20 people handle day-to-day administration and operational activities. **Career Highlights:** Financial Analyst, GTE Internetworking, Powered by BBN (1995-Present); Program Administrator, BBN Communications (1989-95). **Education:** Strayer University. **Personal Information:** Married. Mrs. Batt-Ptaszek enjoys her profession.

Richard P. Bayman

Instructor Development Manager
Chubb Computer Services
7 Entin Road
Parsippany, NJ 07054-5020
(973) 599-8013
Fax: (973) 599-8034
rbayman@chubb.com

7379

Business Information: Mr. Bayman has faithfully served with Chubb Computer Services for two years in the dual role of Instructor Development Manager. As part of the corporate training division, he is responsible for the training of each instructor and the monitoring of their classes. Possessing over 28 years of expertise, he coordinates with the 12 instructors under his direct supervision, to help develop courses and handle the ordering and scheduling of classes. Mr. Bayman ensures that all aspects of the classes are current and in accordance with the rigid standards of Chubb Computer Services. Before coming on board to the Chubb Computer Services team of professionals, he served as Director of Customer Service with the Institute of Electrical and Electronics Engineers. For the future, Mr. Bayman wants to continue his work internationally and to eventually become Director of the Company. His success reflects his ability to think outside the box and aggressively take on challenges. Chubb Computer Services is a wholly owned branch of the Chubb Corporation, which offers various types of technical services to the business industry. Chubb Computer Services was created to help the Corporation find experienced and compatible staffing. The Company now provides staffing to not only its parent company, but to many corporate clients in need of better staffing and IT training. Chubb Computer Services also offers programs through the Chubb Institue in programming, network engineering, and technical support so that all interested in furthering their technical career can earn their diploma. The institute then encourages all students to continue in their education to find the best technical positions available. **Career Highlights:** Instructor/Development Manager, Chubb Computer Services (1998-Present); Documentation & Configuration Control Manager, Ortho-Diagnostics (1996-98); Director of Customer Service, Institute of Electrical and Electronics Engineers (1994-95); Manager of Training and Documentation, Liz Claiborne, Inc. (1992-94). **Associations & Accomplishments:** Certified by the International Board of Trainers **Education:** Seton Hall University, M.A. (1992); Rutgers University, B.A.; International Board of Certified Trainers, CT; Chauney Group International, Ltd., CTT. **Personal Information:** Married to Cathy in 1966. Four children: Darren, David, Nicole, and Michelle. Mr. Bayman enjoys his daughter's soccer games, creative writing and science fiction.

Kishore Bayyapureddy

Senior Systems Architect
Equifax E-Banking Solutions, Inc.
100 West Main Street
Hahira, GA 31632
(770) 740-4010
Fax: (404) 847-7780
kishore.bayyapureddy@efx-ebanking.com

7379

Business Information: Possessing a superior background in the information technology field, Mr. Bayyapureddy functions as the Senior Systems Architect for Equifax E-Banking Solutions, Inc. In this capacity, he is in charge of designing software solutions using the double-up process based on Windows NT and Web features. Implementation of software also falls within the realm of his responsibilities. Utilizing years of extensive experience and a strong academic foundation, Mr. Bayyapureddy is the decision maker on technical tools and infrastructure resources used for software production. A respected expert in the field, he is responsible for regulating the growth of software products. One of many professional accomplishments, the greatest was design and development of a cutting edge software for on line banking. Becoming Microsoft certified and attaining other industry related certifications remain his future goals. Aggressively moving forward, Mr. Bayyapureddy's aspiration is to eventually attain the Position of Chief Information Officer or Chief Architect. Creating state-of-the-art software for commercial banks, Equifax E-Banking Solutions, Inc. was established in 1990. Software developed by the Company includes electronic transactions such as debits and direct deposits. Originally started as a back room software development business, the Company has expanded and now sells software packages to a clientele of more than 2,000 banks. Presently, the Company employs a staff of 70 people. **Career Highlights:** Senior Systems Architect, Equifax E-Banking Solutions, Inc. (1996-Present); Software Engineer, Lucent Bell Laboratories (1995-96). **Associations & Accomplishments:** Microsoft Certified Professional. **Education:** Louisiana State University, M.S.; Andhra University, B.S. **Personal Information:** Married to Priya in 1997. Mr. Bayyapureddy enjoys travel, reading and computers.

James F. Becker

Sales Manager
AOP Solutions
105 Brisbane Building
Buffalo, NY 14203
(716) 854-0872
Fax: (716) 854-0875
jbecker@aopsolutions.com

7379

Business Information: Mr. Becker has recently assumed the responsibilities of Sales Manager of AOP Solutions. He is responsible for assigning sales territories, formulating goals, establishing training programs, and managing and advising sales representatives. Duties include overseeing regional managers and their staffs, maintaining contact with dealers, distributors, and vendors as well as analyzing sales statistics and monitoring the preference of customers. Utilizing effective communication and interpersonal skills, Mr. Becker is able to network with other professionals and establish new business relationships in an effort to enter new markets. Achieving his sales quota by 120 percent for the last two years is cited as his career highlight to date. His goal is to advance to the position of vice president of sales or marketing, playing a vital role in the success of AOP Solutions. Professional success is attributed to his family values, mentors, and desire to achieve set goals. Mr. Becker also credits the Dale Carnegie training that he received as a vital reason for his advancement. AOP Solutions is a business specializing in document management and healthcare solutions. Providing services since 1990, this regional company employs a staff of approximately 90 people to lend their expertise and assist in meeting the demands of clients. **Career Highlights:** Sales Manager, AOP Solutions (1992-Present); Applications Support Manager, Barrister Information (1987-91). **Associations & Accomplishments:** Medical Group Management Association; W.N.Y.H.I.M.A. **Education:** Canisius College, B.S. (1987). **Personal Information:** Mr. Becker enjoys time with his family and golf.

John W. Beckner, M.C.P., C.N.A.

Senior Systems Analyst
Droege Computing Services
20 West Colony Place, Suite 120
Durham, NC 27705-5590
(919) 403-9459
Fax: (919) 403-8199
johnwmbeckner@hotmail.com

7379

Business Information: As Senior Systems Analyst of Droege Computing Services, Mr. Beckner performs applications development, utility programming, and systems analyzation. Additionally, he creates language applications and provides system design and integration. Mr. Beckner attributes his professional success to his consistent effort to keep up with technology. He currently plans to further his knowledge and experience regarding Internet developmental applications. Established in 1985, Droege Computing Services develops custom software solutions for small companies. The Company also offers consulting and on site training services. Headquartered in Durham, North Carolina, the Company markets services and products to an international clientele. **Career Highlights:** Senior Systems Analyst, Droege Computing Services (1994-Present); President, Beckner Vision Inc. (1977-94). **Associations & Accomplishments:** Developed: Relational Database Application Generator for Visual Database (1997), Windows 95 Startup Toolset (1997), Clipper to FoxPro language converter (1996), Beckner Library and Utilities for Clipper Language (1986-94), Insurance Premium Financing System available nationwide (1981-Present), Macro Assembler for 8086 architecture (1980), First Logical Disassembler for 280 and 8086 architecture (1979-80), First RPG language complier for microcomputers (1978). **Education:** Computer Learning Centers, Diploma in Computer Programming (1977). **Personal Information:** Two children: Elizabeth Anne and Joseph Alan. Mr. Beckner enjoys philately, programming, reading and activities with children.

Vickram A. Bedi

President/Owner
Datalink Computer Products Inc.
175 East Main Street
Mount Kisco, NY 10549-2950
(914) 666-2358
Fax: (914) 666-5528
datalink.cp.com

7379

Business Information: As President and Owner of Datalink Computer Products Inc., Mr. Bedi performs all administrative tasks, including assignment delegation and personnel acquisition. He also conducts performance evaluations and accounting reviews. Additionally, Mr. Bedi is engaged in designing, sourcing, and marketing desktops and laptops, as well as performs programming, coding, and testing on new software applications. In a customer relations capacity, Mr. Bedi confers with clients, recommending equipment purchases and conducts on site training on any Datalink products. Established in 1945, Datalink Computer Products Inc. manufactures and assembles personal computers. Additionally, the Company develops customized software for the vertical market, is a real estate management concern, and is in the process of developing an investment company. With customers in 40 countries, the Company generates annual sales near $35 million. **Career Highlights:** President/Owner, Datalink Computer Products Inc. (1945-Present). **Associations & Accomplishments:** Association of Better Computer Dealers; Ingram Alliance. **Education:** Manhattanville: M.S. in Strategic Management (1997), B.A. (1996). **Personal Information:** Mr. Bedi enjoys computers and coin collecting.

George I. Bekov, Ph.D.

President
Spectrum International, Inc.
6500 Fairmount Avenue, Suite 4
El Cerrito, CA 94530
(925) 798-8513
Fax: (925) 798-8913
laservizn@aol.com

7379

Business Information: Dr. Bekov is the President of Spectrum International, Inc. He oversees management, research and development, and marketing throughout his day and strives to motivate the staff to become fully effective and work together to create their designs. A savvy, 27 year veteran, Dr. Bekov determines the overall strategic direction and business contribution of the information systems function, as well as formulates business and marketing plans to keep the Corporation out-front of competitors. A consumer oriented worker, he devotes his attention to serving their needs. Recognizing a void of left by larger lazer corporations, Dr. Bekov quickly established his niche in the lazer market by creating Spectrum International. Looking to the next millennium, Dr. Bekov hopes to stay in the same business and remain at the cutting edge of technology by reading all pertinent information. Spectrum International, Inc. specializes in the service and custom development of lasers and laser based systems. Established in 1996, the Corporation has been dedicated to its clientele since creation and strives to ensure their satisfaction with every product. The Corporation turns over $250,000 annually and operates effectively through its staff of five personnel. **Career Highlights:** President, Spectrum International, Inc. (1996-Present); Director of Laboratory, Atom Science, Inc. (1992-96); Director of Laboratory, Institute of Spectroscopy, Russian Academy of Sciences (1980-92). **Associations & Accomplishments:** American Chemical Society; The International Society for Optical Engineering. **Education:** Institute of Spectroscopy, Ph.D. (1978); Moscow Institute of Physics and Technology,

M.S. (1972), B.S. (1972). **Personal Information:** Married to Galina in 1975. One child: Veronika. Dr. Bekov enjoys jazz, Alpine skiing and tennis.

Rodney S. Bellak

Account Manager
Chubb Computer Services
8 Sylvan Way
Parsippany, NJ 07054
(973) 971-3040
Fax: (973) 971-3080
rbellak@chubb.com

7379

Business Information: Utilizing over 15 years of experience, Mr. Bellak serves as Account Manager of Chubb Computer Services. He is responsible for corporate information technology staffing and training. Before joining Chubb Computer Services, Mr. Bellak assertively served as International Technology Coordinator, Programmer, and Computer Operator with Chubb & Son Inc. in a variety of positions. In his present role, he directly supervises over 100 consultants who works with each corporate client on a one on one basis, ultimately providing a customized solution based on specific individual needs. He presides over the consulting projects, ensuring that each client is provided with quality service. Identifying new clients, analyzing their needs, and proposing viable solutions also fall within the realm of his functions. Mr. Bellak has a true interest in his profession and credits much of his success to tenacity. Adapt and overcome is his personal key phrase. Committed to further development of the Company, he coordinates strategic planning to ensure a bright future as an Area Director. A subsidiary of Chubb Insurance, Chubb Computer Services specializes in corporate information technology. Maintaining corporate headquarters in Warren, New Jersey, a work force of 250 knowledgeable professionals provide computer consulting, training, and staffing to companies across the nation. Presently, the Company reports annual revenues in excess of $120 million. **Career Highlights:** Account Manager, Chubb Computer Services (1997-Present); Chubb & Son Inc.: International Technology Coordinator (1996-97), Programmer (1992-96), Computer Operator (1985-92). **Education:** Chubb Institute, degree in Programming (1992); County College of Morris. **Personal Information:** Mr. Bellak enjoys whitewater rafting, biking and photography.

Andre Benayoun

General Manager
IBSYS
47, Rue Raymond Poincaré
Nanterre, France 92000
+33 147259466
Fax: +33 147291109
abenayoum@ibsys.fr

7379

Business Information: Utilizing over a decade of skills and knowledge attained through an extensive employment and educational history, Mr. Benayoun founded IBSYS, a corporation that specializes in e-business consultation. Currently serving as General Manager of the Corporation, Mr. Benayoun is responsible for overseeing all operational and administrative aspects, to include development of detailed marketing strategies, network management, and consultation support. In his current capacity, he directs all marketing policies and market research to better approach the business market as well as plan for future business developments. Mr. Benayoun works closely with clients, analyzing current business procedures and corporate needs, to determine what technology would be most appropriate to enhance their current business ventures. Fluent in many foreign languages, Mr. Benayoun is able to conduct business in the French, English, Hebrew, Arabic and Spanish, thereby creating a broader range of clientele within Europe and allowing IBSYS to actualize their goals of attaining global expansion. Established in 1998, IBSYS is also known as Information Business Systems. Engaged in business-to-business e-commerce solutions and network services for the corporate environment, the Company is headquartered in Nanterre, France. The Company presently employs the talents and expertise of 12 highly skilled technicians who generate revenues in excess of $15 million annually. IBSYS specializes in providing clients with cutting edge global network design, application assistance, and consultation for window NT, UNIX and Lynox operating platforms. The Company is growing rapidly and has future plans for global operational development. **Career Highlights:** General Manager, IBSYS (1998-Present); Chief Information Officer, SAGA Transportation (1993-98); Engineer, ALSTON (1989-93). **Education:** ENSAM, Degree in Engineering (1988). **Personal Information:** Married to Joanna in 1998. Two children: Leah and Liam. Mr. Benayoun enjoys sports.

Abdul R. Berlas

Senior Systems Engineer
Technology Totems Inc.
3612 Marlborough Way
College Park, MD 20740
(703) 624-6301
Fax: (815) 425-9275
abe.berlas@techtotems.com

7379

Business Information: Educated in the field of computer and information sciences, Mr. Berlas serves as the Senior Systems Engineer for Technology Totems Inc. He plans, manages, and implements technological business solutions to help companies and corporations become better and more efficient in its own trade. Additionally, he provides training and technical support to clients on their new network systems and applications. Before joining Technology Totems, he served as a Network Engineer with both Advanced Communication Systems and Health Information Designs. Mr. Berlas attributes his professional success to a high level of ambition and stays abreast of technological advancements through continuing educational efforts. Committed to the further development of the Corporation, he looks forward to a future position as Director. Technology Totems Inc. is a Microsoft solutions provider and offers information technology consulting services such as systems integration to an international clientele. Over 20 skilled professionals are employed in operations based out of College Park, Maryland. Privately owned, the Corporation was established in 1997. **Career Highlights:** Senior Systems Engineer, Technology Totems Inc. (1997-Present); Network Engineer, Advanced Communication Systems (1996-97); Network Engineer, Health Information Designs (1995-96). **Education:** University of Maryland, degree in Computer and Information Science. **Personal Information:** Married in 1998. Mr. Berlas enjoys mountain biking, gardening and reading.

Marco Bertolucci

Vice President of Engineering
Le Groupe BRT
4608 Rue Hutchison
Montreal, Quebec, Canada H2V 3Z9
(450) 433-7113
Fax: (450) 433-8515
mbertolucci@groupebrt.com

7379

Business Information: Possessing superior talents in the information technology field, Mr. Bertolucci joined Le Groupe BRT in 1996 as the Vice President of Engineering. He is responsible for seven project teams, to include project managers and two to eight consultants on each team. Possessing an excellent understanding of his position, Mr. Bertolucci provides marketing assistance for new clients, creates the financial outlook, and provides the vision and direction for the Company. In addition, he creates specialist teams, performs as a technical advisor, coordinates project set up, documents data, and formulates short- and long-term planning strategies on behalf of his clients. Mr. Bertolucci attributes his success to his creativity and setting high goals of himself. An accomplished professional, he writes technical and business publications. His future plans include expanding the services of the Company into the United States, and later into Europe as well as becoming more involved in ERP and MRP consulting. Le Groupe BRT provides consulting in CAD and CAM design production with a goal of reducing market time for client companies. The Company's services include CAD/CAM software integration and automation, data management system integration, and outsourcing. Established in 1996, Le Groupe BRT employs a staff of 25 qualified personnel to serve the diverse needs of its clientele. **Career Highlights:** Vice President of Engineering, Le Groupe BRT (1996-Present); Senior Applications Engineer, Parametric Technology Corporation (1995-96); Applications Engineer, ICAM Technologies Corporation (1994-95). **Education:** University of New Brunswick, Bachelor's degree in Engineering and Mechanical Engineering (1994). **Personal Information:** Mr. Bertolucci enjoys automobile racing.

Zulfiqar Ahmed Bhatty

Manager of Logistics and Service Center
Digital Natcom Company
8th Floor, South Tower, Abraj Atta Awuneya, King Fahd Road, Ulaya District
Riyadh, Saudi Arabia 11414
+966 12180909
Fax: +966 12180900
zulfiqar.bhatty@digital-natcom.com

7379

Business Information: Serving in the role of Manager of Logistics and Service Center of Digital Natcom, Mr. Bhatty oversees and manages all aspects of day-to-day logistics and services provided to the Company's clientele. He is a 17 year veteran of the technology field. Possessing strong business savvy and academics, he determines the overall strategic direction of the logistical and customer services functions within the Company. Mr. Bhatty supervises the logistics department and strives to ensure each customer received timely advice and quality technical support. Coordinating time lines, schedules, and resources also fall within the purview of his responsibilities. For the future, he wants to continue growing with the Company and maintain his technical competence within the computer industry. His leadership ability to form teams with synergy and technical strength, think outside the box, and aggressively take on new challenges have contributed to his professional success. Digital Natcom is the Saudi Arabian subsidiary of the American-based Compaq Computer Corporation. The Company provides cutting edge technology services and products to commerical businesses and private citizens throughout the region. Working to increase the information technology available, the Company is dedicated to keeping pace with advancing technology. **Career Highlights:** Manager of Logistics and Service Center, Digital Natcom (1988-Present); Instrument Engineer, Schlumberger Overseas S.A. (1984-88); Research Engineer, National Institute of Electronics (1983). **Education:** B.S. in Electrical Engineering (1993). **Personal Information:** Married to Hummaira in 1987. Three children: Hareem, Aqsaa, and Laiba. Mr. Bhatty enjoys learning about the Internet.

Catherine B. Blake

National Account Executive
GTE Internetworking, Inc.
34 Brown Street
Marblehead, MA 01945-3739
(781) 262-2981
Fax: (781) 262-5124
cbblake@bbnplanet.com

7379

Business Information: Combining strategic management skills and consulting expertise, Ms. Blake serves as National Account Executive for GTE Internetworking, Inc. for the Corporation's highest revenue producing customers. In this capacity, Ms. Blake assumes responsibility for global account management for major companies such as John Hancock, Mutual Life Insurance, Reebok, TJX, Novell, Raytheon, and 3Com. In her previous marketing career, she was responsible for driving all marketing activities for the $350 million division which accounts for 85 percent of the Corporation's earnings. Ms. Blake possesses over 14 years of experience in the high technology industry. Owning a consistent record for delivering results in support of business objectives, she hopes in the near future to move into the business strategy area where she can work with corporate managers to demonstrate the value of GTE products and services. At some point, she would like to become Vice President of Marketing of a small company in the interactive media industry where she can orchestrate new, interactive Internet technologies. GTE Internetworking, formerly BBN was established in 1950, is a world leader in communications systems and Internet services. The GTE Internetworking provides e-commerce, videoconferencing, and interactive multimedia applications over the Internet. The Corporation employs approximately 150,000 professional, technical, and support staff, and posts annual revenues of $54 billion. **Career Highlights:** National Account Executive, GTE Internetworking, Inc. (1998-Present); Senior Marketing Manager, Picturetel Corporation (1995-98); Senior Account & Channel Manager, Novell, Inc. (1992-95); Systems Engineer & Consultant, IBM Corporation (1984-92). **Associations & Accomplishments:** United States Coast Guard Academy Course Work; Old North Church; Eastern Yacht Club; Recipient of various special awards from IBM Corporation: AS/400 New England User's Group Award, Consulting Contract Award, Northeast Region General Manager's Award, Branch Manager's Award; 100 Percent Club; Awarded Telecom XVI Print Advertising Award (1997). **Education:** Harvard University Extension School, Certificate in Information Technology & International Marketing (1995); Rensselaer Polytech Institute, M.B.A. Course work in International Marketing and Corporate Finance (1992); Pine Manor College, B.A. in Business Administration and French (1983); Novell Authorized Education Center: Certification Program Videoconferencing Engineer (1997), Certification Program NetWare Engineer (1995). **Personal Information:** Married to Robert S. in 1991.

Roger A. Blocchi

Director of Sales and Marketing
Network Engineering, Inc.
7155 Shadeland Station Way, Suite 190
Indianapolis, IN 46256-3922
(317) 595-6387
Fax: (317) 595-6370
rab@ne-inc.com

7379

Business Information: Demonstrating extensive business savvy and expertise in the technology field, Mr. Blocchi serves as the Director of Sales and Marketing of Network Engineering, Inc. Recruited to the Corporation in 1996, he is responsible for corporate account management and sales and the sales force. Utilizing more than nine years of experience, Mr. Blocchi develops and implements both strategic and tactical marketing plans to keep the Corporation out-front of industry competitors. Aggressive marketing of the

Corporation's services as well as determining and penetrating new markets and avenues for additional revenues also fall within the realm of his executive responsibilities. His accomplishments include directing the ATM development in Alaska and hooking up a major industrial company to the Internet. Attributing his success to positive, win win attitude, Mr. Blocchi's future endeavor is to become a Product Architect. His credo is "everything begins and ends in the mind." A subsidiary of David Spilkey, Network Engineering, Inc. operates as a network and information engineering company. Established in 1997, the Corporation specializes in data and Web consulting as well as integration services. International in scope, the Corporation is based in Indianapolis, Indiana. Presently, Network Engineering, Inc. employs a 25 professional, technical, and administrative support staff who assist in the generation of annual revenues in excess of $3.6 million. **Career Highlights:** Director of Sales and Marketing, Network Engineering, Inc. (1996-Present); Account Manager, Health Network Ventures, Inc. (1995-96); Senior Consultant, Administrator Information Technology (1991-95); Director of Systems, GTE EFT Services. **Associations & Accomplishments:** Columbia Club of Indianapolis.

Karl E. Bode

Branch Technical Manager
Sprint Paranet
1376D South Boulder Street
Gilbert, AZ 85296
(602) 266-9242
Fax: (602) 266-6086
kebode@sprintparanet.com

7379

Business Information: Possessing unique talent in information systems management, Mr. Bode joined Sprint Paranet in 1998 in his current position of Branch Technical Manager. He oversees efforts of technical solutions consultants assigned to Fortune 1000 accounts in Phoenix and Las Vegas. Before joining the Company, Mr. Bode served as Technical Operations Manager for Coactiv Systems, Inc. His background history includes a three and half year stint as Management Information Systems Manager at the Westin Maui as well as two and half years as the Assistant Information Systems Manager at the Grand Wailea Resort in Maui, Hawaii. Mr. Bode has direct profit and loss responsibilities for his business unit. Mr. Bode continues to grow professionally through the fulfillment of his responsibilities and his involvement in the advancement of operations. His success reflects his ability to think outside the box and aggressively tackle new challenges. Sprint Paranet specializes in the planning, implementation, and management of distributed computing environments. Founded in 1990, the Company currently has over 1,800 Technical Solutions Consultants throughout the United States. Forty two Consultants work on Mr. Bode's two major accounts, Motorola and American Express. Sprint Paranet boasts $200 million in annual sales. **Career Highlights:** Branch Technical Manager, Sprint Paranet (1998-Present); Technical Operations Manager, Coactiv Systems, Inc. (1997-98); Management Information Systems Manager, The Westin Maui Resort (1994-97). **Education:** Kennedy-Western University, M.S. in Management Information Systems (1999); University of Maryland, B.S. in Business Management. **Personal Information:** Married to Ann in 1999. Mr. Bode enjoys hiking, racquetball, shooting and archery.

Anand K. Bollineni

Senior Software Consultant
PSW Technologies
10926 Jollyville Road #308
Austin, TX 78759
(512) 342-3691
Fax: (512) 345-4976
bollinieni@psw.com

7379

Business Information: As the Senior Software Consultant of PSW Technologies, Mr. Bollineni is a key member of the information technology department engaged in maintenance and enhancement of back office tools. He is charged with the responsibility to oversee accounting matters including budgetary integrity and timesheet accuracy. Possessing an excellent understanding of his field, Mr. Bollineni also builds and develops Web pages, ensuring that all programs are user-firendly and proficient in providing useful information and enhanced efficiency. Very strong in computer expertise, he maintains software and goes on-site with clients to provide consulting to corporate engineers and programmers. A savvy, seven year veteran of technology, his highlights include writing the systems programs for hand held devices. Mr. Bollineni plans on remaining with the Corporation and continuing to design and develop cutting edge enterprise integrated systems. PSW Technologies, established in 1990, provides software solutions and technology for corporate clients. Services offered include program development, Web design, training programs, and consulting on useage. With emphasis on quality and efficieny, the Corporation operates out of five locations. Over 400 highly skilled and professional individuals are incorporated into the strategic operations of the Corporation. **Career Highlights:** Senior Software Consultant, PSW Technologies (1996-Present); Software Engineer, GTE-GSC (1996); Software Engineer, Ellsworth Associates Inc. (1995-96). **Associations & Accomplishments:** Association of Computing Machinery. **Education:** George Mason University, M.S. (1996); Nagarjuna University, B.S. **Personal Information:** Married to Sunitha in 1999. Mr. Bollineni enjoys music, travel and outdoor sports.

C. Scott Bonaparte

President/Chief Information Officer
Elite Systems Support Inc.
254 Long Beach Road
Hempstead, NY 11550
(212) 623-0853
scottb@csc-services.com

7379

Business Information: Having a love for computers, and a yearning for advancements in technology, Mr. Bonaparte did not hesitate to begin his own consulting firm in 1997. He is responsible for determining the overall strategic direction and business contribution of the information systems function. Using over ten years of experience in the information technology field, he is able to provide his customers with answers to all of their needs. He is the sole proprietor and therefore he completes everything from meeting with clients to keeping the accounting records in order to maintain a smooth operation for his Corporation. Mr. Bonaparte also installs the networking systems for his clients and has become an expert in troubleshooting and remaining on the cutting edge of technology. Coordinating resources and schedules, overseeing time lines and assignments, and managing the fiscal year budget also fall within the purview of Mr. Bonaparte's executive functions. For his next project, he is looking to move to the next level of success by allowing his business to expand and incorporate employees and a broadened client base. Established in 1997, Elite Systems Support Inc. is a network systems consulting firm. Offering computer support for banks and traders, the Corporation focuses on providing networking through the Windows NT system, as well as Novell OS2. The Corporation also installs the chosen networking systems for their clients, and helps with the regular maintenance as needed. **Career Highlights:** President/Chief Information Officer, Elite Systems Support Inc. (1997-Present); Infrastructure Engineer, Chase Manhattan Bank (1999-Present); Infrastructure Engineer, Bankers Trust (1997-98); Infrastructure Engineer, Formats/MediaForm (1990-97). **Associations & Accomplishments:** New York Network Engineering Group; Microsoft Technical Engineers Group; Compaq Systems Engineer. **Education:** State University of New York at Farmingdale, A.S. (1990); M.C.S.E.; A.S.E. **Personal Information:** Mr. Bonaparte enjoys motorcycle riding, weight lifting and roller blading.

Ron A. Boostrom

Senior Systems Engineer
Symbiont Inc.
8418 Timber Belt
San Antonio, TX 78250
(210) 637-2415
rboostrom@aol.com

7379

Business Information: Serving as Senior Systems Engineer of Symbiont, Inc., Mr. Boostrom is repsonsible for the recovery and design of enterprise systems for network management, four-tier support applications, helpdesk, infrastructure, and routers. He maintains a system of 144 enterprise servers, answers questions, and is integral in all aspects of network management, ensuring all new applications will integrate with the exisiting system. He also selects software to support network management and training in the UNIX environment. While serving in the United States Air Force, he was a personnel systems manager for five years and an instructor for five years, training over 4,000 students as well as network administrators. He has written four instructional manuals and had significant input into the production of three integration plans. Mr. Boostrom also assisted in the writing of a 90-page manual entitled "How to Install and Maintain Systems." His goal is to move up into higher levels of management. An AT&T certified instructor for network technicians, he attributes the success he has enjoyed to his technical expertise, social intelligence, and personality. An international company established in 1996, Symbiont Inc. provides government contracted health and medical support, systems architecture, and software development services to the United States Army, Navy, and Air Force globally. The Corporation currently employs 250 personnel and has estimated annual revenues in excess of $6 million. **Career Highlights:** Symbiont Inc.: Social Intelligence and Personality Engineer (1998-Present), Senior Systems Engineer (1995-Present), Network Training Instructor (1996-98), Development Techinician (1995-96), Network Training Instructor (1994-95), AT&T Instructor (1994-95); Systems Development Technician, Computer Data Systems (1994). **Associations & Accomplishments:** Openview Forum International. **Education:** University of Berkley, B.S. in Computer Information Systems (1998); University of Maryland; Community College of the Air Force. **Personal Information:** Married to June Katherine in 1991. Four children: Ronnie, Scott, Robin, and Jeannie. Two Stepchildren: Denver and David. Mr. Boostrom enjoys time with his family, tennis, ping pong and flying.

Michael Booth

Web Intelligence Consultant
IBM Global Services
MP193 Hursley Park
Winchester, England, United Kingdom S021 2JN
+44 1962817788
mike.booth@uk.ibm.com

7379

Business Information: Recruited to the e-business division of IBM Global Services in 1999, Mr. Booth serves as a Web Intelligence Consultant. In this capacity, he uses the information built into clients' web sites to assist them in improving their digital branding and web presence to cater more toward their target customers and to deliver business and marketing metrics. Mr. Booth has taken every opportunity to learn emerging technologies as they appear, including Java and e-commerce; as well as more traditional database and programming roles. He was responsible for implementing the entire computer infrastructure for Ezee-Fix Ltd., from network hardware and operating system installation to training and accounting systems migration. His development work led him to designing the publishing engine for paper catalogue publishing, writing a catalogue CD ROM and e-commerce website. Looking to the future, he plans to continue working in I-net technology and possible venture into consulting down the line. Mr. Booth advises other entering the field to "keep up to date with the latest technologies, but don't forget the fundamentals." IBM Global Services is a division of the giant IBM Corporation. The Division has offices worldwide and is dedicated to providing businesses with e-business development designed to enhance each one's current operations. One of the Division's e-business centers of excellence is Web Intelligence in Hursley, United Kingdom. Web Intellegence allows clients to leverage their groundbreaking web technology to their advantage by obtaining raw data and processing it into valuable customer and marketing information for real benefits. Data mining, database querying, and data capture allow businesses to better target customers through traditional media and improve their return on web investment. **Career Highlights:** Web Intelligence Consultant, IBM Global Services (1999-Present); Information Technology Manager, Ezee-Fix Ltd.; Customer Care Specialist, PC World; Body Engineer, Rover Group Ltd. **Education:** Leeds University (1998). **Personal Information:** Mr. Booth enjoys scuba diving. Mr. Booth is also currently training for BSAC Dive Leader Qualification.

Ambrose Carl Boudreaux

Systems Administrator/Site Manager
Ingenium Corporation
9200 Basil Court, Suite 400
Upper Marlboro, MD 20774
(619) 545-7486
Fax: (619) 545-8773
boudreauxc@sand.disa.mil

7379

Business Information: Mr. Boudreaux, serving as Systems Administrator and Site Manager for Ingenium Corporation, assumes the responsibilities for security access registrations of local and networked customers. Utilizing years of practical experience, he works closely with five other specialists whose duties involve regulating security systems and keeping track of existing and potential problems. A prominent leader in the business community, Mr. Boudreaux is in charge of programming, connecting and disconnecting access, and regulating local and network users located across the country. His goals are to get his contract extended, to continue to learn about information systems technologies, and grow along with the Agency. Striving to provide reliable and efficient service, Ingenium Corporation provides a wide range of application support operations for the Tandem and Himalaya Systems. Contracted by the Federal Government, the Corporation specializes in providing information technology services and support of operational systems. National in scope, the Corporation is part of a network of offices located across the United States. Located in Upper Marlbor, Maryland, the Corporation presently employs a staff of 103 people. **Career Highlights:** Systems Administrator/Site Manager, Ingenium Corporation (1998-Present); Data Processing Technician, DFCM (1997-98); Computer Programmer, Comprehensive Technologies Inc. (1996-97); Master Chief, United States Navy (1971-95). **Associations & Accomplishments:** The Association for Data Center Network and Enterprises Systems Management; Cursillo Movement of the Roman Catholic Church; Fleet Reserve Association; Organization of Sea Service Veterans; American Legion & Disable American Veterans. **Education:** La Verne University, A.A. (1977); Certificate of Apprenticeship - Certified Data Processing

Technician. **Personal Information:** Married to Perla in 1975. Mr. Boudreaux enjoys singing in the church choir, travel and gardening.

Matthew Bovell

Senior Business Analyst
IBM Global Services
150 Kettletown Road
Southbury, CT 06488
(203) 486-3678
Fax: (203) 486-5945
mcbovel@us.ibm.com

7379

Business Information: As a Senior Business Analyst of IBM Global Services, Mr. Bovell performs midrange business analysis, studying tools and techniques for cost modeling. He has served with IBM in a variety of roles since coming on board as a Programmer in 1983. Mr. Bovell assists in costing the Company's midrange services and determines methodologies by studying the various industry sources available to him. Coordinating resources and schedules and overseeing time lines and assignments also fall within the realm of Mr. Bovell's responsibilities. Applying his 16 years of experience in this field, he uses research and networking to determine what is best for his area. Attributing his success to good communication skills and logical thinking, he advises newcomers to learn the vocabulary of the industry. A division of IBM, IBM Global Services provides information technology services and began operations in 1991 as ISSC. The Division offers a wide variety of services such as data center outsourcing and technical consulting, and hosts Web sites for clients on a global scale. Presently, IBM Global Services employs a work force of more than 100,000 people worldwide. **Career Highlights:** IBM Global Services: Program Manager (1999-Present), Manager of WWW Services (1997-99), Manager of Infrastructure Technology (1995-97). **Associations & Accomplishments:** President, Southern New England Chapter, Project Management Institute. **Education:** Harvard University, B.A. (1983); Certified Project Management Professional. **Personal Information:** Mr. Bovell enjoys being a pop culture enthusiast.

Geri D. Bowden

President/Chief Operating Officer
Navant Corporation
112 East Hargett Street, Suite 203
Raleigh, NC 27601-1450
(919) 828-6044
Fax: (919) 828-9884
geri@navant.com

7379

Business Information: In her role as President and Chief Operating Officer of Navant Corporation, Ms. Bowden handles a myriad of responsibilities as she focuses on the development of the business market. Demonstrating innate ability combined with learned skills, she is directly involved in the development of extensive sales and marketing campaigns. Her impressive communicative skills are appreciated by clients and employees alike; civic organizations, public conventions, and seminars frequently request her presence as the guest of honor as she is a noted authority in her field. Ms. Bowden currently is planning growth and expansion plans that include cutting edge techonogy implementation as she prepares the Corporation for inital public offering in 2001. Navant Corporation is a consultancy firm located in Raleigh, North Carolina. Specializing in business-to-business infrastructure, the Corporation provides turnkey solutions for companies that are looking for comprehensive plans. Established in 1998, the Corporation focuses on technological advances in today's progressive society that includes networking solutions in their offerings. **Career Highlights:** President/Chief Operating Officer, Navant Corporation (Present); Technology Services Supervisor, The Vanguard Corporation; Business Development Manager, Main Line Bank; Marketing Analyst, Siemens Energy and Automation. **Associations & Accomplishments:** Society of Human Resource Management. **Education:** Rosemont College, M.S. in Management (1998); Temple University, B.A. in Political Science.

Jerrold A. Bowzer

Senior Consultant
IBM Global Services
14417 Remington Way
Oklahoma City, OK 73134-1800
(405) 748-3265
jbowzer@us.ibm.com

7379

Business Information: Mr. Bowzer is a Senior Consultant of IBM Global Services. Specializing in ERP packages, concentrating on PeopleSoft software, he assists in the implementation of new financial systems and the re-engineering of business processes. IBM Global Services hosts a staff of over 15,000 consultants worldwide which produces $25 billion in revenue each year. Mr. Bowzer has been recognized as a Golden Circle member for IBM which is an honor given to the top one percent of IBM employees. He plans to continue within IBM and the consulting group but is interested in getting more involved with e-Business. Mr. Bowzer attributes his professional success to his faith in God and keeping up-to-date with technology. **Career Highlights:** Senior Consultant, IBM Global Services (1996-Present); Project Manager, Integris Health (1995-96); Payroll Assistant Manager, The Hertz Corporation (1984-88). **Education:** University of Oklahoma, B.B.A. (1977). **Personal Information:** Married to Karen in 1989. One child: Joanna. Mr. Bowzer enjoys music, reading, the Internet and travel.

Richard A. Bradford

Owner
Never-Enuff Enterprises
2609 Bigler Avenue
Northern Cambria, PA 15714-0788
(814) 951-0226
dbradford@never-enuff.net

7379

Business Information: As the Owner of Never-Enuff Enterprises, Mr. Bradford monitors every aspect of Company operations, focusing on general administration, strategic planning, and service promotion. Utilizing his education, and capitalizing on more than eight years of solid experience, he is responsible for setting up new systems and evaluating new software. In addition, he provides on site technical support. Committed to further development, and always alert to new opportunities, techniques, and approaches, Mr. Bradford's future plans include expansion to ensure a bright future for the Company. His career highlights include fulfilling a mentor role and having a positive impact on the growth of the Company. Providing quality customer service laced with value and reliability is cited as his reasons for success. Established in 1998, and located in Northern Cambria, Pennsylvania, Never-Enuff Enterprises is an Internet service provider and computer repair company. To serve the diverse needs of its clientele, the Company employs a staff of four qualified personnel to provide services such as Web site development and e-mail to the general public. Additionally, the Company donates Internet service to Northern Cambria Catholic School and provides free house call support. **Career Highlights:** Owner, Never-Enuff Enterprises (1998-Present); NVR, Inc.: Network/Computer Specialist (1998-Present), Computer Operator (1995-97); Systems Operator, Joseph Horne Company (1992-94). **Education:** Computer Tech-Pittsburgh, diploma in Computer Science (1990). **Personal Information:** Married to Marilee. Two children: Brayo Lee and Britney Ann. Mr. Bradford enjoys building street rods and comptuer games.

Rupert R. Bradshaw

Owner/Operator
PC Net
13279 Andy Street
Gulfport, MS 39503
(288) 377-4036
Fax: (228) 377-3712
rupert.bradshaw@kessler.af.mil

7379

Business Information: The Owner of PC Net, Mr. Bradshaw also fulfills the role of Operator. He is responsible for all aspects of day-to-day administration and operational activities. Assisted by his wife, he determines the overall strategic direction and vision of the Company, as well as the business contribution of the information systems function. Mr. Bradshaw, drawing from his extensive academic ties and on the job experience as Webmaster, helps his clients set up an Internet access capability. For the last three years, PC Net has been experiencing position growth in all areas of operations. Concurrently, he works civil service for the United States Air Force Reserves as a Network Administrator. As a 13 year professional, Mr. Bradshaw's significant accomplishment is that of receiving his Microsoft Certified Systems Engineer certification. His future goals include moving up into a high level GS civil service position and continue to gain technical knowledge across the technology spectrum. His success reflects his ability to deliver results and aggressively tackle new challenges. A sole proprietorship, PC Net provides technology consultation and Web page design for small businesses and corporations. Currently, the Company was established in 1989 and is located in Gulfport, Mississippi. **Career Highlights:** Owner/Operator, PC Net (1986-Present); United State Air Force: Functional Systems Administrator/Information Manager (1996-Present), Computer Manager (1989-96). **Associations & Accomplishments:** AFCA Networking Work Shops; Interplanetary Society; Microsoft Site Developers; Ordained Deacon of Saucier Holiness Church. **Education:** Community College of the Air Force, A.S.; Microsoft Systems Certified Engineer; Certified Novell Administrator; Department of Defense Certification, A.S., B.A. (1998); Cabletron, Inc. Training; Government School's and In house Training. **Personal Information:** Married to Cynthia in 1980. Two children: Robert A. and Richard A. Mr. Bradshaw enjoys computers and salt water fishing.

Robert T. Bray, RCDD

Vice President
TSI, Inc.
953 Harmsted Court
St. Charles, MO 63301
(636) 949-8889
Fax: (636) 925-2111
rbray@tsi-inc.com

7379

Business Information: Mr. Bray has aggressively served with TSI, Inc. in a variety of capacities since first joining the team as Installation Supervisor in 1987. In 1998, he was elevated to the role of Vice President with oversight of all aspects of the design, bidding, and scheduling phases of project development. Mr. Bray, relying on his extensive business experience and technical skills, is charged with formulating new business and marketing strategies to increase the clientele base. Responsible for taking a lead role in driving growth, he uses his thorough knowledge of service and product offerings, markets, and competitors to determine and penetrate new markets and avenues for additional revenues. Concurrent to his executive duties, he performs project and operation managerial functions. Determining future resource requirements; overseeing time lines, schedules, assignments, and budgets; and managing multiple projects and project managers also fall within the realm of Mr. Bray's functions. He attributes his success to never backing away from challenges and taking pride in what he does. "Relationships are very important, don't burn bridges. Train people to do it right the first time and stay on top of the standards," is cited as Mr. Bray's advice to others. A telecommunications service provider, TSI, Inc. installs computer network cable infrastructure for government and commercial clients. Founded in 1987, TSI employs a work force of 60 persons who help generate in excess of $8 million annually. **Career Highlights:** TSI, Inc.: Vice President (1998-Present), Project Manager (1993-98), Installation Supervisor (1987-93). **Associations & Accomplishments:** Midwest Telecommunication Association; BICSI Telecommunication Associations; AFL-CIO Union Affiliation. **Education:** BICSI, Registered Communication Distribution Designer; Designing Telecommunications Distribution Systems Certificate; Local Area Networks and LAN Cabling Systems Certificate.

Sherry Lee Breitkreutz

Sioux Falls Client Care Source Coordinator
Gateway
700 East 54th Street North
Sioux Falls, SD 57104-0643
(605) 357-1000

7379

Business Information: Utilizing previous experience and education, Mrs. Breitkreutz is the Sioux Falls Client Care Source Coordinator for Gateway. She has faithfully served with the Company since coming on board as a Technical Support Representative in 1996. In her position, Mrs. Brietkreutz promotes morale, presides over client recognition to technicians, and keeps cleint care part of the Intranet Site. Mrs. Brietkreutz owns her own business called Brites Lites Design which develops Web sites for businesses and nonprofit organizations. Her goals include establishing her business into one which she can retire to, having more control of the Intranet, and staying on top of the technical industry. Mrs. Brietkreutz's success is attributed to her personality and leadership ability to deliver results and aggressively take on new challenges. Offering services in a variety of areas, Gateway is an established and reputable computer business. The Company is involved the building, selling, and supporting computers for individuals and business clients. Headquartered in North Sioux City, South Dakota, Gateway serves an international client base. Local operations in Sioux Falls, South Dakota employs a workstaff of 1,500 employees that devotes all concentrations on client care and technical support. **Career Highlights:** Gateway: Sioux Falls Client Care Source Coordinator (Present), Web Page Designer/Editor (1998-Present), Technical Support Representative (1996-98); Web Editor/Designer, Brite Lites Design (1995-Present). **Associations & Accomplishments:** Children Charities. **Education:** National College. **Personal Information:** Married to Timothy in 1991. Three children: Angela, Bud, and Joseph. Mrs. Breitkreutz enjoys computers, web designing, photography, art, writing, reading and hiking.

William B. Brenneman

Senior Network Engineer
AT&T Technical Services
2401 E Street NW, Room H438
Washington, DC 20037
(202) 663-3384
Fax: (202) 663-3411
w.brenneman@state.gov

7379

Business Information: As the Senior Network Engineer, Mr. Brenneman has been providing professional technical services with AT&T Technical Services since joining the Company in 1997. Focusing on the design of cutting-edge system routers, switches, and servers involved in telecommunication processes, he strives to implement the latest technological advances. Actively involved in day-to-day testing and research, Mr. Brenneman guarantees state-of-the-art products and services, with a firm emphasis on quality, value, and reliablity. Concurrently, he owns and operates Mountain Vista Communications, a company involved in consulting, PC work, networking, and minor repairs. Maintaining his current status with the Company, Mr. Brenneman's goals include becoming involved in systems management. Attributing his success to work ethic, his advice is, "always look for a way to improve existing processes and keep an open mind." Concentrating on governmental contracts, AT&T Technical Services is a wholly owned subsidiary of AT&T providing telecommunication services since the 1980s. Headquartered in Washington, D.C., the Company employs the skilled services of more than 500 professional technicians, engineers, and administrators to facilitate every aspect of design, manufacture, quality assurance, and distribution of products. Dedicated to providing excellent sales and services, the Company offers a variety of telecommunication services including the design and integration of data switching and networks. **Career Highlights:** Senior Network Engineer, AT&T Technical Services (1997-Present); Officer, United States Coast Guard Reserves (1997-Present); Officer, United States Coast Guard (1987-97). **Associations & Accomplishments:** Microsoft Certified Systems Engineer; Chief Executive Officer, Mountain Vista Communications. **Education:** University of Maryland, M.S. in Information Systems Management (1997); United States Coast Guard Academy, B.S. in Math and Computer Science. **Personal Information:** Married to Kim in 1999. Mr. Brenneman enjoys antique cars, golf and wood working.

Donald R. Bristow

Director of Worldwide Porting
Unify Corporation
3927 Lennane Drive
Sacramento, CA 95834-1922
(916) 928-6220
Fax: (916) 928-6403
don@unify.com

7379

Business Information: As Director of Worldwide Porting for Unify Corporation, Mr. Bristow is responsible for making Unify database and e-commerce application development products available for a worldwide marketplace on all major UNIX computer platforms. With 17 years of experience in the field and 15 years with Unify Corporation, he has acquired the skills necessary to effectively lead his Department. Mr. Bristow selects new computer platforms, procures computer hardware and software, schedules new ports, and allocates the engineering resources to accomplish ports from his team of engineers. In addition to overseeing all ports of new products, Mr. Bristow continues to utilize his expertise with older Unify software products by porting some of them himself. He plans to continue to be on the cutting edge of computer technology and to use this technology to enhance the porting process. Unify Corporation is a leading provider of software that helps companies create Internet and e-commerce applications. Software products include enterprise application development tools, database servers, Web-enablement tools, and a suite of e-commerce application products. Service products include training, consulting, and technical support. Founded in 1980, this $32 million company employs the expertise of approximately 140 dedicated and highly skilled employees. Headquartered in San Jose, California, there are six locations worldwide to provide sales and services. **Career Highlights:** Unify Corporation: Director of Worldwide Porting (1999-Present), Porting Manager (1990-99), Software Engineer (1984-90); Programmer, Jones Futura Foundation (1983-84); Oceanographic Systems Technician, United States Navy (1974-78). **Associations & Accomplishments:** Advisor, Key Friendships Ministry; Board Member, Air Time Ministries and Cornerstone Assembly. **Education:** California State University at Sacramento: B.A. (1983), B.A. (1982); American River College, A.A. (1974). **Personal Information:** Married to Sandra in 1978. One child: Elissa. Mr. Bristow enjoys digital

photography. He owns a home-based photography and photo restoration business, Lightray Photoimagery. Mr. Bristow and Sandra are involved with helping Russian immigrants in the Sacramento area.

Kirk Broadwater

Network Engineer
Techni-core
6539 Willow Springs Boulevard NW
Huntsville, AL 35806
(256) 658-1988
kirk@techni-core.com

7379

Business Information: As a Network Engineer for Techni-core, Mr. Broadwater is responsible for providing software and network engineering to government and local client companies. He is accountable for engineering all programs, including network setup and Web programming as well as ensuring the functionality and operational status of the early warning radar systems. Drawing from over 21 years of hands on experience, Mr. Broadwater continually strives to enhance systems performance, while also constructing plans to remain in his current position and becoming more involved in database management. His success reflects his ability to think outside the box, aggressively take on challenges, and deliver results. Techni-core is an information technology firm that provides technical and professional services to the government and local companies. Such services incude consulting, Web site design, strategic planning, and business development. Established in 1978, the Firm is located in Huntsville, Alabama and functions under the talents and full support of more than 100 professionals who facilitate smooth business operations. **Career Highlights:** Network Engineer, Techni-core (1999-Present); Software and Network Engineer, Waterjet Systems (1995-99); Software Engineer, Brannon And Tilly (1995); Software Consultant, Intergraph Corporation (1984-94). **Associations & Accomplishments:** Huntsville Network Users Group. **Education:** B.S. in Computer Science (1979); Microsoft Certified Systems Engineer (1999). **Personal Information:** Mr. Broadwater enjoys reading, research, running and dancing.

Jeffrey A. Brooks

Senior Systems Engineer
Planning Consultants, Inc.
P.O. Box 1676
Dahlgren, VA 22448
(540) 663-2739
Fax: (540) 663-2633
jbrooks@pci-dahl.com

7379

Business Information: As a Senior Systems Engineer for Planning Consultants, Inc., Mr. Brooks serves as the group leader for the test and evaluation group. Joining the Corporation's group of professionals in 1989, he is currently responsible for supervising the 25 employees in his department, providing technical oversight for the test and evaluation of Navy Combat Direction Systems, and overseeing the all aspects of the Corporation's daily engineering operations. The highlight of his career was participating in the development of innovative design changes to the Navy CDS computer programs allowing the system to be used more effectively and efficiently. Looking to the future, Mr. Brooks plans on continuing with the Corporation in his current position. Located in Dahlgren, Virginia, Planning Consultants, Inc. conducts test and evaluation services for United States Navy. Founded in 1985, the Corporation engages in services for a variety of topics and inquiries for confidential use by the Navy. A staff of 100 members are dedicated to performing test and evaluation and engineering for military purposes. **Career Highlights:** Senior Systems Engineer, Planning Consultants, Inc. (1989-Present); Systems Analyst, Comptek Research (1987-89); Systems Analyst, Vitro Corporation (1985-87); Operations Specialist, United States Navy (1980-85). **Associations & Accomplishments:** American Legion; Veterans of Foreign Wars. **Personal Information:** Married to Susan W. in 1982. Two children: Corey and Kyle. Mr. Brooks enjoys baseball and being a youth basketball coach.

Yvonne Brooks

Owner/President
Brooks Office Solutions
1 Hawthorne Court
Maple Shade, NJ 08052-1907
(856) 779-0077
Fax: (856) 779-0753
ybrooks@boss44.com

7379

Business Information: Serving as the President of Brooks Office Solutions, Ms. Brooks is also a Training Solutions Specialist, Consultant, and Owner of the Company. In her many capacities, she is a solutions provider focusing on user skills within the corporate market as well as individuals and

small offices. Also responsible for the training of the office support staff, Ms. Brooks customizes learning programs about software skills. She attributes her success to an ability to teach with understanding and an ability to break down the technology. Ms. Brooks hopes to become an authority in the user training field and facilitate continued growth for the Company. Established in 1989, Brooks Office Solutions provides result oriented counsulting and training services for proprietary or shrink wrapped software applications. Operating under the idea "Training does matter," the Company currently employs a staff of four individuals dedicated to serving the diverse needs of their growing clientele. **Career Highlights:** Owner/President, Brooks Office Solutions (1989-Present); Instructor, National Schools (1989-92). **Associations & Accomplishments:** Independent Computer Consultants Association; International Association of Administrative Professionals; Trainers and Educators of Metropolitan Philadelphia Organizations. **Education:** Thomas Edison University, B.S. (1999); Burlington County College A.S. (1994); National Schools, A.S.B. degree in Medical Secretarial Sciences (1991); Philadelphia Suburban Business School, degree in Legal Secretary. **Personal Information:** One child: Brenda. Ms. Brooks enjoys writing, poetry, reading, music and history.

Roy Brotman

Applications Development Manager
IBM Global Services
34 Maple Avenue #PB04
Pine Brook, NJ 07058-9769
(973) 276-3982
roycb@erols.com

7379

Business Information: Recruited to IBM Global Services in 1991, Mr. Brotman serves as Applications Development Manager for Actuarial Systems of the Prudential Insurance account. In this capacity, he is involved with project management, resource budgeting, technical support, implementing new systems, and training. Possessing an excellent understanding of his field, Mr. Brotman's focus is on changes that will allow IBM Global Services and its clients to take advantage of any newly developed technology to remain flexible, efficient, and profitable in the information technology age. Highly regarded by management and colleagues, Mr. Brotman's career highlight includes implementing a point of sale system for Disney World. Attributing his career success to his persistence, his goals are to remain in management, move into e-commerce, and conduct more training for the Company. IBM Global Services provides global outsourcing for large insurance companies and financial institutions. The Company also provides outsourcing application development and maintenance to industrial and commercial businesses. Established more than 100 years ago, the Company's headquarters is located in Armonk, New York and is involved in global applications development services. **Career Highlights:** Applications Development Manager, IBM Global Services (1991-Present); Senior Systems Analyst, Pathmark Supermarkets (1985-91). **Associations & Accomplishments:** Project Management Institute. **Education:** California Coast University: Postgraduate degree (In Progress), B.B.A. (1995); Briarcliff College/Grumman Data Systems Institute, Programming (1980). **Personal Information:** Married to Adrienne in 1977. Two children: Ian Matthew and Rachel Taylor. Mr. Brotman enjoys audiophile.

Jeff R. Broughton

Senior Consultant
Solution Bank
15202 Silverman Street
Webster, TX 77598
(713) 306-4975
Fax: (281) 286-8432
jeff@thebroughtous.com

7379

Business Information: Serving Solution Bank as a Senior Consultant, Mr. Broughton provides consulting services in the area of enterprise resource planning. He works closely with management and on-site clients to develop software that is designed to meet the customer's specific needs. Possessing an excellent understanding of technology, Mr. Broughton designs and develops software applications using Baan and MK7 technologies. He remains on the cutting edge of technology by keeping up on new technology and reading technical magazines and books. Attributing his career success to being in the right place at the right time, Mr. Broughton plans to remain with the Company and move into e-commerce or the technical area of day to day operations. Solution Bank is an information technology consulting firm. Serving an international clientele, the Company specializes in e-commerce and ERP solutions. Headquartered in Salt Lake City, Utah, the Company's local operations in Webster, Texas employs the skills and expertise of more than 200 professional, technical, and support staff. **Career Highlights:** Senior Consultant, Solution Bank (1999-Present); Systems Consultant, Wilson Solutions (1996-99); Database Analyst/Security Administrator, Haliburton Companies (1980-84). **Associations & Accomplishments:** Professional Association of Diving Instructors. **Education:**

University of Houston, B.S. (1978); San Sacinto College, A.S. in Business Data Processing. **Personal Information:** Married to Jane in 1990. One child: Mike. Mr. Broughton enjoys travel and scuba diving.

Charles Brown

Network Security Engineer
Trident Data Systems
21300 Alder Drive #101
Santa Clarita, CA 91321
(310) 338-3543
charlie_brown@tds.com

7379

Business Information: As a Network Security Engineer for Trident Data Systems, Mr. Brown has a vast number of responsibilities. He is the manager of the west coast information protection team and deals with network assessments and firewall installation. Possessing an excellent understanding of his field, he also trains employees, contacts customers who have problems, assists engineers, approves proposals, performs lab testing, and certifies new equipment. He plans to obtain his CCIE and keep up to date with certifications in order to stay ahead of the power curve with up and coming VPN technologies. Satisfied in his current job, Mr. Brown plans to stay with the Company, helping to facilitate growth and production. Established in 1974, Trident Data Systems is involved in information protection, threat analysis, penetration testing, and firewall installation. Serving an international clientele, the Company has 3,500 employees country-wide, 70 of which are employed in the commerical security division. The Company is a subsidiary of Veridian. **Career Highlights:** Network Security Engineer, Trident Data Systems (1999-Present); Senior Network Engineer, CPI Network Solutions (1998-99); Senior Network Engineer, Inca Computers (1997-98); Network Administrator, Mountain High Ski Resort (1996-97); United States Air Force (1988-93). **Education:** Montana State University, B.S. (1996); Microsoft Certified Systems Engineer; Microsoft Certified Trainer; Cisco Certified Network Professional; Checkpoint Certified Systems Engineer; Checkpoint Certified Security Instructor. **Personal Information:** Married to Tiffany in 1993. Mr. Brown enjoys being in a ski instructor in his off duty time.

Ed Brown

Director of Information Systems
Instruction Set, Inc.
16 Tech Drive
Natick, MA 01760
(808) 657-9085
Fax: (808) 651-9084
edb@instructionset.com

7379

Business Information: Serving as Director of Information Systems of Instruction Set, Inc., Mr. Brown is responsibile for taking the Company to the next level of technology. Credited with setting up the Company's extensive infrastructure, he maintains its functionality and operational status. Possessing an excellent understanding of technology, Mr. Brown remains focused and sets continuous goals, leading to his success in the industry. Maintaining a postion at the forefront of modern technology, he engages in constant research utilizing magazines and seminars. As a result of his academics and occupational experience, Mr. Brown is positioned himself for continued success in one of the most dynamic fields in the market. His strategic plans include completing his Master's degree and enter a chief information officer or chief technology Officer position. Advising others to stay focused and keep the frustration down, Mr. Brown's favorite quote is "a smart man learns from his mistakes, a wise man learns from others." Offering Web-based training and certification on a nationwide level, Instruction Set, Inc. provides a variety of on-line courses, in-house course development, and organized new hire programs. Utilizing office locations in New York, Massachusetts, Maryland, North Carolina, and Texas, the Corporation generates over $8 million in annual revenue, making it one of the most successful technological education companies in the world. In service since 1991, Instruction Set currently employs 100 personnel throughout the country, all focused on providing the most intensive and up-to-date education possible. **Career Highlights:** Instruction Set, Inc.: Director of Information Systems (2000-Present), Systems Manager (1998-00); Help Desk Specialist, Associate X-Ray (1996-97). **Education:** Wentworth Institute of Technology, B.S. in Computer Science (1998). **Personal Information:** Married to Helena Ramner-Brown in 1998. One child: Kevin.

Harold A. Brown II

Staff Software Engineer - Network Engineering Department
IBM Thomas J. Watson Research Center
P.O. Box 218
Yorktown Heights, NY 10598
(914) 945-3701
Fax: (212) 583-1802
habrown@watson.ibm.com

7379

Business Information: Serving IBM since 1995, Mr. Brown is currently a Staff Software Engineer with the Network Engineering Department at IBM Thomas J. Watson Research Center. He is responsible for research, design, and the development of innovative infrastructure technologies. Mr. Brown's research supports information utilized throughout the Corporation in new technology. He also performs fourth level customer support, personnel training, and presentations to Chief Information Officers and other high level executives. Additionally, he developed and coordinates the help desk support processes. Recently, Mr. Brown developed an I.D. tracking tool and created visual aids to introduce the program. He is currently conducting research and development on incorporating new technology into existing networking infrastructure to enable workstation mobility, greatly reduce human administrator intervention, and automate updates of information on workstations connected to networks. Founded in 1911, IBM has become one of the world's leading computer manufacturing, service, maintenance, retail, and financing companies. With over 200,000 employees around the globe, IBM yields annual revenues close to $80 billion. **Career Highlights:** IBM: Staff Software Engineer - Network Engineering Department (1996-Present), Senior Associate Programmer in OS/2 Development (1995-96), Supplement Programmer - IBM AdStar Division (1993); Research Assistant, Flight Controls Lab at California Polytechnic State University (1991-92); Manager of Information Systems, Brown's Enterprises (1985-88). **Associations & Accomplishments:** President, Cal Poly Robotic Society (1992); Key Member, Cal Poly Robotic Air Vehicle Team (1991); Alumni Association of Computer Engineering - California Poly Tech University at San Luis Obispo; Alumni Association of Computer Science, Purdue University Graduate School; Tau Beta Pi - National Engineering Honor Society; Recording and Corresponding Secretary of Epsilon Phi Chapter, Eta Kappa Nu - Electrical Engineering Honor Society; Upsilon Pi Epsilon - Computer Science Honor Society at Purdue University; Upsilon Pi Epsilon - Computer Science Honor Society at California Poly Tech; Golden Key National Honor Society; Purdue University Graduate School Alumni Association; Cal Poly University Alumni Association; Recipient, Bonus for new corporate standards - IBM Thomas J. Watson (1996); Andrews Doctoral Fellowship, Purdue University (1993-95); Certificate for Engineer-in-Training (1992); Certificate of Appreciation and Bonus, IBM AdStar Division (1993); Varian Academic Achievement Scholarship (1991); Chevron Academic Achievement Scholarship (1991); Second Place, First International Aerial Robotics Competition (1991); Letter of Commendation, State of California Department of Education (1984). **Education:** Purdue University at West Lafayette - Indiana, M.S. in Computer Science (1995); California Polytechnic State University, B.S. in Computer Engineering - Magna Cum Laude (1992). **Personal Information:** Mr. Brown enjoys weight lifting, swimming and horseback riding.

Francois Brunelle

President
Intelligence Architects LLC
2519 John Eppes Road, Unit 102
Herndon, VA 20171
(703) 930-1156
Fax: (703) 858-2593
francois.brunelle@mciworld.com

7379

Business Information: As President of Intelligence Architects LLC, Mr. Brunelle is an information management advisor and project leader. He is responsible for the execution of management consulting mandates, organizational structure, and sales planning. Utilizing 15 years of experience, he analyzes and manages conflicts in information technology projects together with the alignment of people, strategy, and technology. An accomplished professional, Mr. Brunelle negotiates the sale of information management solutions, analyzes cross-functional dependencies, and streamlines operations for total quality, customer satisfaction, and growth. His success is reflected within the company's successful relations with an extensive prominent clientele, including, Lunettaries New Look, Konkal & Associates, and the United States Department of Defense. Intelligence Architects LLC is a busi ness engineering practice that assists companies in designing highly adaptive business architectures through the alignment and redesign of their operational and system infrastructures. Using a side-by-side consultative approach, the Company follows a distinct methodology of modeling the systemic structure, aligning the system infrastructure, and supporting technologies. Offering audit and point services on a per-case basis, the Company maintains an eminent and growing client base. **Career Highlights:** President, Intelligence Architects LLC (1997-Present); Senior Account Manager, Oracle Canada, Inc. (1995-97); Senior Sales Representative, Data General (Canada) Inc. (1992-95); Sales Consultant/Sales Representative, Xerox Canada Ltd. (1984-92); Account Administrator, IBM Canada Ltd. (1981-84); International Banking Payment Officer, Bank of Montreal (1979-81). **Associations & Accomplishments:** American Production and Inventory Control Society (APICS); Project Management Institute (PMI); Society for Competitive Information Professionals (SCIP). **Education:** Hamilton University, B.Sc. in Management Information Systems.

Barbara J. Brunzell

Senior Director
Computer Network Technology
605 North Highway 169, Suite 1800
Minneapolis, MN 55441
(612) 797-6629
Fax: (612) 797-6800
barb_brunzell@cnt.com

7379

Business Information: Demonstrating more than 18 years of experience in the technology field, Mrs. Brunzell serves as the Senior Director of Education Services for Computer Network Technology. She serves as the leader of a group of instructors who provide technical curricula to internal and external presales and postsales audience. In charge of all of the technical and financial aspects of Computer Network Technology, she facilitates promotional activities to increase public awareness of the Company's products and services. Mrs. Brunzell oversees all of the sales activities and provides backup and support to business clients. Continually striving to improve performance, she looks forward to assisting in the completion of future corporate goals. Her success reflects her ability to produce results and aggressively tackle new challenges. Founded in 1980, Computer Network Technology offers cutting edge technology solutions to companies and corporations. The Company employs a knowledgeable staff of 600 professionals to provide high-performance, high-speed WAN/LAN networking hardware and software to its business clients. **Career Highlights:** Senior Director, Computer Network Technology (1996-Present); Cray Research, Inc.: Director of Education Services (1994-96), Manager of Technical Publications (1988-94). **Associations & Accomplishments:** President, Resources & Counseling for the Arts; Sunny Hollow Montessori; Mentor, St. Paul Minority Encouragement Program. **Education:** University of Minnesota, B.A. (1982). **Personal Information:** Married to Michael J. Looney in 1988. Three children: Meghan, Ian, and Erin. Mrs. Brunzell enjoys gardening, cooking, water sports and basketball with her kids.

John A. Bryant

Web Administrator
Orscheln Management Company
101 West Coates Street
Moberly, MO 65270
(660) 269-3461
Fax: (660) 269-3950
jbryant@mcmsys.com

7379

Business Information: As Web Administrator of Orscheln Management Company, Mr. Bryant designs, develops, and administers Orscheln Web sites. Over 15 years of experience in the technolgical field has enabled him to acquire the skills necessary to effectively complete his job duties. Dedicated to the success of Company, Mr. Bryant keeps abreast on new developments in the field and incorporates pertinent information into his job. He plans to develop his own Web site to provide customer support for information on technology products. Being flexible and the ability to quickly learn new concepts has attributed to Mr. Bryant's professional success. Orscheln Management Company is an information technology department for Orscheln Industries. Established in 1945, approximately 5,000 people lend their expertise in various aspects of the operation. **Career Highlights:** Orscheln Management Company: Web Administrator (1998-Present), Help Desk Manager (1995-98); Consultant/Developer, CTG (1994-95). **Associations & Accomplishments:** Technology Committee, Local Vocational School; Designer/Judge, Future Business Leader's of America Contest for Computer Repair; Microsoft Developers Network. **Education:** Columbia College (1997); Wisconsin University; Missouri University; Moberly Area Community College; Northeast Missouri State University. **Personal Information:** Two children: Michael S. and Daniel C. Mr. Bryant enjoys model building and camping.

William H. Buker

Master Database Administrator
Maxim Group
10900 Nuckols Road, Suite 210
Glen Allen, VA 23060
(804) 968-6000
Fax: (804) 968-5972
sealteam@hotmail.com
7379

Business Information: Mr. Buker holds the prestigious position of Master Database Administrator of the Maxim Group. He oversees and directs all projects and database administration and operations. His primary responsibility is to suggest and implement solutions to database administration problems. As an experienced, 13 year technology expert, Mr. Buker works closely with users and systems management, providing them detailed technical and analytical advice during the development of a major application. He is employed by outside companies and provides both analytical and programming services on a per project basis. Mr. Buker reports his findings to the client and makes recommendations for a solution. He credits his professional success to his quest for advanced knowledge and ability to think outside the box, deliver results, and aggressively tackle new challenges. The Maxim Group is a full service, team-oriented consulting firm with offices all across the United States. **Career Highlights:** Master Database Administrator, Maxim Group (1999-Present); Principal Consultant, Oracle Corporation (1997-99); Consultant, Signal Corporation (1996-97). **Education:** ECPI Computer Institute, Certificate (1991); George Washington University, B.S. (1986). **Personal Information:** Married to Jan in 1979. One child: Will. Mr. Buker enjoys golf, working out, water sports and surfing the Internet.

Kenneth B. Bumgarner

Principal/Chief Consultant
Bumgarner Global Enterprises
P.O. Box 872
Bloomington, IL 61702-0872
(309) 735-1930
kbumgarner@worldnet.att.net
7379

Business Information: Mr. Bumgarner is the Principal and Chief Consultant of Bumgarner Enterprises. Working within a mainframe environment, he is able to provide effective service to his clients and designs the neccessary equipment to facilitate their needs. He originally entered the business world as a truck driver and through the trucking company was given a data processing position. This sparked a yearning desire to further explore the world of computers and led to the creation and expansion of his current company. Mr. Bumgarner's highlight occurred in Saudi Arabia after a company closure. He and three other people successfully moved three major systems to another company and recoverted it back. In the future, he hopes to remain at the top of mainframe technology while experiencing a 15 percent growth rate every year. His success reflects his ability and willingness to accept other cultures and ways. Bumgarner Global Enterprises is an information technology consulting firm that also provides assistance in other technological areas outside of computer implementation. The Firm counsels its clients in establishing a home or business security system and is also involved in business recovery and business contingency planning. Established in 1983, the Firm has expanded to incorporate an international clientele with business in Moscow, Germany, France, Norway, England, Saudi Arabia, Hong Kong, and Singapore. **Career Highlights:** Principal/Chief Consultant, Bumgarner Enterprises (1983-Present). **Associations & Accomplishments:** Computer Security Institute; International Executive Guild. **Education:** Eastern Montana College, B.S. in Business Administration IRM (1985). **Personal Information:** Married to Martha in 1994. Mr. Bumgarner enjoys gospel music, scuba diving and golf.

Neal F. Burch, J.D.

Network Administrator
EFC Systems
5345 Atlanta Way
Montgomery, AL 36109-3323
(334) 386-7171
Fax: (334) 386-7164
sburch@faulkner.edu
7379

Business Information: As Network Administrator, Mr. Burch adminsters to the needs of student networks while developing the public relations with teachers and students. He constructs the networks with the specific qualities needed by the students and school administration. A savvy, five year veteran, he runs the needed cable to maintain efficient operations. Through the operation of a helpdesk, Mr. Burch ensures that each client of every project can gain the proper instruction and assistance with possible problem areas. Mr. Bruch has constructed over 700 servers and 400 systems with superior success and high quality. In the future, Mr. Burch will develop his skills and utilize his law education to assist EFC Systems. He also plans to acquire a higher administrative position within the Company. His success reflects his good Christian upbringing and his honesty and trustworthiness. Established in 1989, EFC Systems is a full service information technology company providing custom software, Web development, server support, cabling, and custom built hardware. The in-house Company employs 50 staff members to fulfill the individual needs of each client. EFC Systems currenly operates seven locations with the headquarters located in Nashville, Tennessee. **Career Highlights:** Network Administrator, EFC Systems (1996-Present); Helpdesk, Sirote & Permuit (1994-96). **Associations & Accomplishments:** President, Montgomery Chapter of Faulkner University Alumni Association; President, Zeta Eta Theta National Alumni Association. **Education:** Jones School of Law, J.D. (1998); Faulkner University, B.S. in History (1994). **Personal Information:** Married to Shannon in 1996. One child: Neal F. II. Mr. Burch enjoys soccer and family.

Scott A. Burch

Senior Network Engineer
Bulldog Information Services
120 Church Street, Suite A
San Francisco, CA 94114
(415) 397-2223
Fax: (415) 553-3661
scott@bulldoginfo.com
7379

Business Information: As Senior Network Engineer of Bulldog Information Services, Mr. Burch assists in the resolution of challenges other members of the department have on a daily basis. Demonstrating knowledge gained from practical work experience, he evaluates technical needs, then formulates innovative solutions. After successful implementation of these solutions, Mr. Burch maintains the programs with outstanding support services. He regularly meets with clients to discuss potential contract possibilities and serves as an upstanding representative of the Company. Recognized for his acheivements in the technical industry, Mr. Burch currently has plans to expand the department's involvement into varied aspects of the Company. Bulldog Information Services is a network communications firm that specializes in high end network design. Using sophisticated tools such as sniffers, the Company engages in consulting activities as well. Established in 1998, annual sales are estimated to be in excess of $250,000 proving that the fledging Company has built a solid reputation in the professional community. **Career Highlights:** Network Engineer, Bulldog Information Services (1999-Present); Network Engineer, Robert Half International (1998-99); Network Engineer, Network Associates (1999); Network Engineer, ICF (1998-99). **Associations & Accomplishments:** Network Professionals Association. **Education:** Western Oregon State University (1990). **Personal Information:** Mr. Burch enjoys cycling and sailing.

Jeanne Burtnett

Technical Services Manager/Webmaster
ITS Inc.
3355 Spring Mountain Road, Suite 270
Las Vegas, NV 89102-8639
(702) 596-7082
Fax: (503) 326-3957
jeanne@wizard.com
7379

Business Information: Starting as a Police Officer with the Department of Veterans Affairs, Ms. Burtnett made a decisive career move to technology after being laid off. Self taught in technology, she interviewed for a position with ITS Inc. in 1996 and was hired on as Technical Services Manager and Webmaster. A testimony to her commitment and dedicated work ethic, Ms. Burtnett oversees all aspects of design, implementation, and management of Internet Websites. As Webmaster, she is in charge of programming and deploying the strategic vision of her area of responsibility. One of her greatest accomplishments include coming into the Corporation and creating three state-of-the-art Websites from the ground up. Providing assistance and advice to the clientele, interpreting problems, and providing quality technical support for Website hardware and software difficulties also falls under the realm of her responsibilities. She attributes her professional success to good supervisors who gave her encouragement. Focusing more on the Internet and eventually attaining the position of Website Administrator serves as Ms. Burtnett's long-term goals. Established in 1995, ITS Inc. operates as a Website service provider. Based in Las Vegas, the Corporation special focus is on horse racing computer software. Operating three Websites on the Internet, ITS Inc. is manned by a staff of nine technology professionals. **Career Highlights:** Technical Services Manager/Webmaster, ITS Inc. (1996-Present); Police Officer, Department of Veterans Affairs (1991-95). **Associations & Accomplishments:** HTML Writers Guild; National Association for Female Executives. **Education:** Shippensburg University, B.S. (1990). **Personal Information:** Ms. Burtnett enjoys website design and camping.

Linda L. Butcher

President/Founder
Cyberlogic Business Services
2510-G Las Posas Road #232
Camarillo, CA 93010-2513
(805) 484-1710
linda@cyberlogic-interactive.com
7379

Business Information: Utilizing her vast experience in the field of information technology, Ms. Butcher founded Cyberlogic Business Services in 1996. Presently serving as President, Ms. Butcher oversees the general operation of the business in providing quality customer service for clients. She offers strategic analysis of Internet opportunities and is involved in the design and development of Web pages to meet individual client needs. Consulting directly with clients, Ms. Butcher provides Web site analysis to determine which design will best suit marketing and sales goals. Ms. Butcher enjoys assisting clients in the field of new media design and hopes to continue in this area by providing additional marketing opportunities for small businesses. Cyberlogic Business Services has one location in California and currently serves an international market in providing an array of Internet consulting services as well as new media design opportunities. With plans of expanding its services in the near future, the Company plans to continue providing individual customer service. **Career Highlights:** President/Founder, Cyberlogic Business Services (1996-Present); Chief Operations Officer, Computer Age Dentist, Inc. (1994-95); Administrator, Neer, McClellan and Neumeister Dental Corporation (1992-94). **Associations & Accomplishments:** National Association of Female Executives; International Webmaster's Association; The HTML Writer's Guild. **Education:** Moorpark College, A.S. in Business Administration (1989). **Personal Information:** One child: Justin M. Ms. Butcher enjoys rollerblading, weight training, fitness and computing technologies.

Khawar Butt

Owner/Managing Director
Trinet Networking & Training, Inc.
20957 Jade Court
Diamond Bar, CA 91765
(661) 284-3600
Fax: (661) 284-3086
khawarb@hotmail.com
7379

Business Information: As Owner and Managing Director of Trinet Networking & Training, Inc., Mr. Butt also teaches Cisco and Microsoft classes to a host of aspiring professionals and executive officers who look for more productive ways to utilize software capabilities. Throughout daily activities, he is charged with the responsibilities of managing all aspects of operations including administration, project development, and client relationships. Capitalizing on seven years of information technology management, combined with three years of extensive experience in all phases of corporate operations, Mr. Butt monitors tha productivity of the staff, formulating a hands-on management style with an above average aptitude for problem solving. His plans for the future include assisting the Corporation in expansion efforts to include the development of eight new business sites. Trinet Networking & Training, Inc. is a information technology training company that teaches Microsoft, Cisco, and Internet classes for a host of corporate clients. Also offering consulting, the Corporation provides services that assist clients in areas of business development, systems design, and employee training. Established in 1997, the Corporation is located in Diamond Bar, California and functions under the direction of more than 20 professionals who assist in generating $1.5 million in annual revenues. **Career Highlights:** Owner/Managing Director, Trinet Networking & Training, Inc. (1997-Present); Microsoft Contract Trainer (1996-97); Technical Manager, Mount Sierra College (1993-96). **Education:** Azusa Pacific University, Master's degree (2000); DeVry Institute of Technology (1992). **Personal Information:** Married to Shaziya in 1994. Mr. Butt enjoys tennis, basketball and reading.

Joe A. Cairns

Technical Leader
Database Consultants, Inc.
4835 LBJ Freeway, Suite 900
Dallas, TX 75244
(972) 392-0955
Fax: (972) 490-9439
jcairns@dci-ltd.com
7379

Business Information: An invaluable asset to the Corporation, Mr. Cairns functions in the role of Technical Leader for Database Consultants, Inc. He works with large and small businesses, but mainly assists medium range companies. Not only does Mr. Cairns manage multiple projects but he is a technical expert for 10 different sites. Consulting for five Web sites and conducting weekly training on the proper use of Oracle tools are his additional responsibilities. Mr. Cairns works with database management systems software and reorganizes and restructures data to better suit the needs of users. Also, he is responsible for maintaining the efficiency of the database, system security, and aids in design implementation. Recognized for his technology capabilities, Mr. Cairns was featured in an article in "International Oracle User Group Magazine" on the use of Oracle tools. He attributes his professional success to networking. As a long-term goal, Mr. Cairns desires to continue to learn more about technology. Operating as a consulting firm for Oracle database and software development, Database Consultants, Inc. has a strong work force of approximately 300 individuals. The Corporation focuses on consulting, but also has an education and product sales group. Headquartered in Texas, the Corporation has a network of 15 sites including 3 international sites in the United Kingdom. **Career Highlights:** Technical Leader, Database Consultants, Inc. (1996-Present); Michaels Stores, Inc.: Development Manager (1996-96), Technical Consultant (1994-96). **Personal Information:** Married to Marlo D. in 1990. Two children: Ashley and Caroline. Mr. Cairns enjoys remote control planes and working on 3D graphics design on his PC.

Gregory L. Campbell
Senior Principal
Technology Solutions Company
215 Foxworth Chase
Alpharetta, GA 30022
(770) 350-6400
Fax: (770) 350-6401
gregory_campbell@techsol.com

7379

Business Information: Mr. Campbell serves as the Senior Principal for Technology Solutions Company. He is responsible for day-to-day administration and operational activities, including maintaining client relationships, overseeing human resources development, and recruiting strategic partners and alliances. Before joining the Company, Mr. Campbell served as a Partner with Deloitte & Touche Consulting Group. His background history also includes stints as Member of Computer Sciences Corporation and Senior Industrial Engineer with General Dynamics, Inc. A systems expert, Mr. Campbell, in 1994, developed the first virtual management company that incorporated nine distributors and twenty-one manufacturers. He cites as his career highlight the implementation of a 140 person call center in only nine weeks. Looking to the next millennium, he is interested in helping to create supply chains and expand its virtual corporations. Technology Solutions Company is a consulting firm focusing on computers and technology. The Company creates computer networking systems for residential or business clients desiring access to the Internet and their business partners. The Company was established in 1987 at the start of the technology era and has continued to remain on the cutting edge of technology. **Career Highlights:** Senior Principal, Technology Solutions Company (Present); Partner, Deloitte & Touche Consulting Group; Member, Computer Sciences Corporation; Senior Industrial Engineer, General Dynamics, Inc. **Associations & Accomplishments:** Certified Production and Inventory Manager; American Production and Inventory Control Society; Certified Manager; Institute of Certified Professional Managers; Statistical Process Control; International Quality Institute; Delegate, Citizen Ambassador Program. **Education:** Bowling Green State University, M.B.A.; College of Idaho, B.A. in Recreation Management, Health, and Physical Education.

Robert W. Campbell, FLMI
President/Owner
Insursoft, Ltd.
2 Long Spur
Littleton, CO 80127-5728
(303) 933-2749
Fax: (303) 265-9474
rcampbell@insursoft.com

7379

Business Information: As Owner of Insursoft, Ltd., Mr. Campbell is responsible for all aspects of day-to-day administration and operational activities, to include determining the overall strategic direction and formulating business and marketing plans to keep the Company out-front in the industry. A savvy, 15-year professional, Mr. Campbell provides technical and analytical consulting services while concentrating his work in the software design analysis and development realm. A one person company, he is also involved in programming, focusing on VB, C, and C++. For the future, Mr. Campbell has aspirations to expand his new Company, incorporate a staff and larger clientele, and obtain the MCSD credential to balance the technical with the insurance side of the business. Attributing his success to networking, his advice is, "Absolutely do it!" He believes the future is owning your own business. Insursoft, Ltd. provides a consulting service for life insurance software development. Established in 1998, the Company counsels its clients on the implementation of the most effective software program that will meet the needs of their benefits monitoring needs. The Company turns over a revenue of $100,000 each year and has

doubled its profitability in just one year in the market. **Career Highlights:** President/Owner, Insursoft, Ltd. (1998-Present); Manager of Technical Development, Insurance Technologies (1996-98); Senior Programmer/Analyst, System Innovations (1991-96); Programmer/Analyst, First Capital Life (1984-91). **Associations & Accomplishments:** Fellow Life Management Institute. **Education:** San Diego State University, B.A. in Economics (1984). **Personal Information:** Married to Chiarme Leah in 1990. One child: Leah Marie.

Roderick G. Caraballo
Senior Systems Administrator
Avant Go
1700 South Amphlett Boulevard, Suite 300
San Mateo, CA 94402
(650) 235-3438
rcaraballo@avantgo.com

7379

Business Information: As Senior Systems Administrator, Mr. Caraballo provides connectivity for all locations concerning upgrades, maintenance, research, and development for all networks. As a five-year veteran, he troubleshoots any network problem areas and administers new applications to improve present systems for 250 users worldwide and all servers of Avant Go. An expert, Mr. Caraballo has standarized all systems for 140 users and all the servers of RMW Architecture & Design. In the future, Mr. Caraballo will become Cisco and MCSE certified. His success reflects his ability to think outside-the-box, deliver results, and aggressively take on new challenges. Established in 1996, Avant Go specializes in application software for personal digital assistants, PDAs. **Career Highlights:** Senior Systems Administrator, Avant Go (1999-Present); Information Systems Administrator, RMW Architecture & Design (1998-99); Software Engineer, TEC America (1997-98). **Associations & Accomplishments:** Institute of Electrical and Electronics Engineers Computer Society; Institute of Electrical and Electronics Engineers; Microsoft Certified Professional; Certified Novell Administrator; Speechcrafters. **Education:** Masters Institute, A.S. in Systems Administration (1999); Clemson University: Computer Science, Mathematics; University of Georgia at Athens, Software Engineer. **Personal Information:** Mr. Caraballo enjoys performing as a DJ, snowboarding and soccer.

Timothy S. Carl
President/Chief Executive Officer
The Carl Group
3 Highschool Court
Los Gatos, CA 95030
(408) 399-9740
Fax: (408) 399-9731
www.thecarlgroup.com

7379

Business Information: As President and Chief Executive Officer of The Carl Group, Mr. Carl is responsible for all aspects of company operations. He also supervises 50 employees, as well as acquires, terminates, and trains staff members. Mr. Carl also uses his expertise in negotiating business contracts. Concurrently, he is a part-owner of Invest in Yourself. The Company specializes in career transitions for professional athletes. Among the present clientele are members of the Green Bay Packers, Philadelphia Eagles, and Toronto Blue Jays. The Carl Group provides web page design and development, technical documentation, and training for technology companies. Hewlett-Packard and Sun are among its major accounts. Established in 1985, the Company also offers contract and staff placement. **Career Highlights:** President/Chief Executive Officer, The Carl Group (1985-Present); Principal, Business Writing Services (1983-84); Director of Training, Dialogic Systems (1984); Vice President/Board Member, Invest in Yourself, LLC; Owner/Board Member, IntraCom Corporation. **Associations & Accomplishments:** Society for Technical Communication: Senior Member, 2nd Vice President, First Vice President, President; President, Sumner Woods Homeowners Association Board of Directors. **Education:** University of California at Los Angeles, M.A. (1995); University of California at Santa Barbara: B.A. in History (1973), B.A. in Political Science (1969), Secondary Teaching Credential; Community College Teaching Credential. **Personal Information:** Married to Joan Bosworth in 1995. Two children: Matthew and Julia. Mr. Carl enjoys history.

Keith Carlascio
Principal Consultant
Application Consulting Group
121 Headquarters Plaza, 9th Floor, North Tower
Morristown, NJ 07960
(973) 898-0012
Fax: (973) 898-9054
kcarlascio@acgi.com

7379

Business Information: Serving as Principal Consultant of Application Consulting Group, Mr. Carlascio designs data warehouse and management systems from conception to implementation. He is responsible for providing services to his clientele in areas such as business management, managing full system life cycle projects, and overseeing critical management resources. Throughout his daily routine, Mr. Carlascio is also in charge of personnel management, interviewing, recruiting, and training. The most rewarding aspects of his career include being recruited to a large department store, working with MicroStrategy, and growing the managerial side of the business. A successful 11-year professional, Mr. Carlascio utilizes his superior knowledge and expertise in devising marketing and business plans to advance the Company's international operations and maintain its standing in the markets. The Application Consulting Group is a business intelligence consulting firm that offers a broad range of advisory services to various client companies. Specializing in relational technologies and business intelligence, the Company is listed among both Fortune 500 and Fortune 100 businesses. Headquartered in Morristown, New Jersey, the Company functions under the direction of more than 100 professionals who facilitate smooth business operations. Presently, the Company reports annual revenue in excess of $15 million. **Career Highlights:** Principal Consultant, Application Consulting Group (1999-Present); Technical Specialist, Liz Claiborne (1997-99); Associate Systems Consultant, Heublern, Inc. (1995-97); Senior Program Analyst, Goody's Family Clothing (1994-95). **Associations & Accomplishments:** Oracle Certified Professional; MicroStrategy Certified. **Education:** WTBY State Tech, A.S. in Data Processing (1989). **Personal Information:** Married to Michelle in 1995. One child: Giana. Mr. Carlascio enjoys home theater, car audio and golf.

Christopher M. Carrigan
Business Development and System Consultant
Enterprise Technology Group Inc.
327 Summer Street, 5th floor
Boston, MA 02210
(617) 262-8330
Fax: (617) 262-8303

7379

Business Information: Drawing on his extensive occupational experience and educational history, Mr. Carrigan serves as a Business Development and Systems Consultant for Enterprise Technology Group Inc. (ETG). He assumes accountability for several job functions. For starters, he works as an information technology consultant and provides clients in the SMB marketplace with systems and integration consulting services. Second, he heads the marketing effort and manages the strategy, plannings and implementation of ETG's partnerships with leading technology vendors, including Cisco, Compaq, HP, IBM, Novell, and Microsoft. Third, he handles business development and develops and proposes business plans based on market and business trends and competitive analysis. Lastly, he negotiates product and service agreements with channel vendors based upon business needs and market direction. Mr. Carrigan attributes his success to having a "never give up" attitude. He aspires to continue to provide management information systems support to the Corporation, keep abreast of new information technology and trends and practices, and eventually move into a management position in the field of information technology. Founded in 1997, ETG is a professional systems consulting firm, headquartered in Boston, Massachusetts. ETG specializes in providing clients in the SMB space with consulting services and turnkey solutions in the areas of LAN/WAN design and implementation, Internet security, and computer telephony. ETG's vertical focus covers several areas, such as venture capital, equity, insurance, legal, and high tech. At present, ETG employs a staff of 20 highly trained, certified and qualified personnel to serve the diverse needs of its clientele and has a projected $5 million in annual sales revenue for fiscal year 1999. **Career Highlights:** Business Development and System Consultant, Enterprise Technology Group Inc. (1998-Present); Associate Analyst/Account Manager, Summit Strategies, Inc. (1997-98); Network Integration Consultant, General Electric Capital Consulting (1995-97); Automation Technology Operations Local Area Network Administrator, Parsons Brinckerhoff, Central Artery/Tunnel Project (1993-95). **Associations & Accomplishments:** International WHO'S WHO of Information Technology (1998); Sales & Marketing Professionals of New England (1998); Enterprise Relationship Management Alumni Institute (ERMAI) (1998); Alumni, Radcliffe College, Harvard University (1998); Notary Public, Commonwealth of Massachusetts (1996); Alumni, University of Vermont (1992); American Marketing Association (1999-Present); Accomplishments: Certified Internet Business Strategist (1999); Compaq Advocate

(1999); IBM Computer Telephony Specialist (1999); "Power to Influence," Anthony Robbins & Associates (1999). **Education:** Suffolk University Frank Sawyer School of Management, M.B.A. (In Progress); Radcliffe Graduate College, Harvard University, Graduate Certificate in Management with Honors (1994-98); University of Vermont, B.A. in Liberal Arts with a minor in Chemistry (1992). **Personal Information:** Mr. Carrigan enjoys reading, history, antiques, classical piano, travel and visiting Vermont.

Bruce A. Carson
Director of Technology
Edgewater Technology
20 Harvard Mill Square
Wakefield, MA 01880
(781) 246-3343
bac@world.std.com

7379

Business Information: Serving as Director of Technology for Edgewater Technology, Mr. Carson researches new technology, incorporating that knowledge into the software solutions he designs for businesses. He presides over development efforts. Acting as mentor to his staff of programmers, he provides valuable input on technical staff reviews. Determining the overall strategic direction and business contribution of the information systems function, coordinating resources and schedules, and selecting technical solutions also fall within the realm of his functions. Mr. Carson credits his success of today to his ability to learn new information quickly and follows the adage of "If it ain't broke, don't fix it." Committed to providing continued optimum service to the Company, he anticipates becoming Vice President. Created in 1993, Edgewater Technology is owned by a publically held company offering custom consulting and systems integration. The Company has a staff of 130 qualified professionals and is a subsidiary of Staff Mark. A Microsoft business partner, Edgewater Technology is a Microsoft solutions provider. The Company boasted revenue of $21 million last year. **Career Highlights:** Director of Technology, Edgewater Technology (1995-Present); Senior Consultant, Charles River Development (1993-95); Programmer, Duracell, Inc. (1985-93). **Associations & Accomplishments:** Mass Go Association. **Education:** University of Wisconsin, B.A. (1984). **Personal Information:** Mr. Carson enjoys volleyball, rollerblading and playing war games.

Calvin L. Chan

Solutions Architect
Yellow Shirt
800 East Colorado Boulevard
Pasadena, CA 91101
(626) 817-6236

7379

Business Information: Leading a savvy team of systems engineers at Yellow Shirt, Mr. Chan serves in the positions of Solutions Architect. In his current capacity, he undertakes the challenges of designing company networks and troubleshooting for their diversified client portfolio of residents and corporations. Renowned as one of the most advanced, highly educated specialists in the field, Mr. Chan looks forward to several years of future success and further achievement in his industry. His strategic plans include becoming involved with systems integration projects and supply chain management systems as well as attaining the positions of Lead Engineer and Chief Information Officer. Serving the region of Pasadena, California, Yellow Shirt provides high quality, uninterrupted Internet service to an area of over 135,000 residents. In addition to their ISP activity, Yellow Shirt also provides business package integration for local companies, in situations where specialized software and services are required to accommodate the most efficient service. Concentrating on information management systems, design and implementation, and e-commerce, Yellow Shirt provides some of the most diverse and well rounded services available on the market. **Career Highlights:** Solutions Architect, Yellow Shirt (Present); Computer Technology Consultant, Delta Pacific International; Engineer, Kofax Image Products; Web Designer, Liquid Shadow Factory. **Associations & Accomplishments:** Association of Computing Machinery. **Education:** University of California at Irvine, degree in Information and Computer Science. **Personal Information:** Mr. Chan enjoys reading, writing, snowboarding and sports.

David R. Chapman

Training Manager
TenFold Corporaotin
180 West Election Road
Draper, UT 84020
(801) 619-8187
Fax: (801) 495-0353
dchapman@10fold.com

7379

Business Information: As a Training Manager for TenFold Corporation since 1999, Mr. Chapman manages and develops multimedia training software applications. Bringing an impressive knowledge of information technology to the Corporation, he has published more than 12 articles worldwide. Highly regarded, he possesses superior talents and an excellent understanding of the technology field. Continually achieving quality performance in his field, Mr. Chapman is presently involved in the development of simulated mission critical software, ensuring corporate longevity and success. His success reflects his ability to think outside-the-box, take on challenges, and deliver results on behalf of the Corporation and its clientele. Established in 1993 TenFold Corporation is a computer software company primarily engaged in providing large scale e-business applications for communications, energy, financial services, healthcare, insurance, and investment management industries. With 19 locations worldwide and an estimated annual revenue of $150 million, the Corporation presently employs 600 highly skilled computer technicians that develop custom corporate software. TenFold Corporation has grown rapidly since its conception and continues worldwide expansion as a leader in software development. **Career Highlights:** Training Manager, TenFold Corporation (1999-Present); Senior Instructional Designer, American Stores Company (1996-99). **Associations & Accomplishments:** International Society for Performance Improvement; American Society for Training and Development. **Education:** Utah State University, M.S. in Instructional Technology (1996); Brigham Young University, B.S. in Communications (1994). **Personal Information:** Married to Milette in 1991. Two children: Skye and Joshua. Mr. Chapman enjoys spending time with his family, creative writing and developing performance improvement models.

Nagaraju Chayapathi
Director, Systems Development
AMS Informatix Inc.
3150 Almeden Expressway, Suite 224
San Jose, CA 95118
(415) 352-6627
Fax: (408) 225-9100
CNAGARAJU@TRIU.COM

7379

Business Information: Utilizing 14 years of experience in the technology industry, Mr. Chayapathi serves as Director of Systems Development for AMS Informatix Inc. He is responsible for managing client projects related to Data Architecture, Data Migration, and Business intelligence solutions. Currently, he manages the development of products for Database Administration, Data Migration, and Decision Support System. Attributing his success to hard work, Mr. Chayapathi keeps abreast of advances in the technology field by attending seminars, reading industry publications, and visiting user groups online. Establishing goals that are compatible with the Corporation, he looks forward to one day managing the product development group. Established in 1993, AMS specializes in the development of Client/Server, Business intelligence, and e-commerce applications. AMS is an approved system integrator and business partner with leading technology firms including Powersoft, Oracle, Netscape, and GE. AMS has a proven track record of implementing several large scale projects for Fortune 500 companies. On a time and material basis, AMS can provide consultants with extensive project management experience who can be made available to the clients' premises, and work directly with the clients' IT staff. Having corporate headquarters in San Jose, AMS has a development and training center in India. AMS is manned by more than 80 professional, technical, and support personnel. **Career Highlights:** Director, Systems Development, AMS Informatix Inc. (1997-Present); Senior Consultant, Square D Software Ltd. (1995-97); EDP Manager, OMC Computers Ltd. (1992-95). **Associations & Accomplishments:** Computer Society of India; International Data Warehousing Association. **Education:** Sri Venkateswara University, Master's degree (1985). **Personal Information:** Married to Gayatri in 1992. One child: Preeti. Mr. Chayapathi enjoys reading, listening to music and playing with his daughter.

Deanford Chen
Software Specialist
Litton PRC
5312 Ayrshire Drive
San Jose, CA 95118
(408) 752-6373
dfchen@aol.com

7379

Business Information: As Software Specialist of Litton PRC, Mr. Chen handles a number of responsibilities within the Company. He is responsible for client server support and providing consulting and training services. A savvy, seven year professional, he also oversees database management systems as well as maintaining and upgrading the operating and database systems software. He supervises three employees who report directly to him on a daily basis. Career highlights include starting a Toastmaster's Club and earning numerous speaking awards. In the future, Mr. Chen looks forward to learning new technology and eventually moving up into a Chief Executive Officer's position. He attributes his success to his education, intelligence, and network and his ability to tackle new challenges and deliver results. Located in San Jose, California, the Company is a leading provider of information technology and systems based solutions. Litton PRC, a subsidiary of Litton Industries, Inc., has over 5,300 employees in 80 offices worldwide. The Company's core capabilities are in functional and information technology outsourcing, e-business and critical information and infrastructure integration. **Career Highlights:** Software Specialist, Litton PRC (1995-Present); Software Developer, Computer Science Corporation (1993-94). **Associations & Accomplishments:** Outstanding Young Men of America (1996); Jaycees; Association of Computing Machinery; Institute of Electronics and Electrical Engineers; Computer Society; Commonwealth Club. **Education:** San Jose State University, B.S. in Computer Science (1991). **Personal Information:** Mr. Chen enjoys swimming, chess, reading and theatres.

Jean Cheng
Senior Operations Specialist
Ajilon
100 Meridian Center, Suite 250
Rochester, NY 14623
(719) 423-8838
jcheng@flash.net

7379

Business Information: Displaying a thorough understanding of computer technology, Ms. Cheng functions in the role of Senior Operations Specialist for Ajilon. Her job entails working within the Company to implement software programs and portals which are used to search and find information. Ms. Cheng also services the Web browser and client server. She has been employed with the Ajilon since 1999. Effectively determining workable objectives, Ms. Cheng would like to go back to work in the developing industry. She credits her career success to her ability to learn and adapt to any situations, as well as deliver results and aggressively tackle new challenges. Serving an international client base, Ajilon is a computer consulting company. Services are provided to business and individuals in need of upgrading present computer systems or buying a new system altogether. Ajilon assumes responsibility for meeting with clients, determining their needs, finding the best product that will most suit the company, and then installing and offering education about the new system or software program. Contracting oversees and in the United States, a work staff of over 100 individuals is employed to provides clients with products and services laced with quality, value, and selection. **Career Highlights:** Senior Operations Specialist, Ajilon (1999-Present); Software Engineer, Lockheed Martin. **Education:** University of Houston at Clear Lake, M.S. in Computers (1998); Boston University, B.S. in Biomedical (1993).

Frank Cheung
Chief Technology Officer
Dynatek Infoworld, Inc.
13200 Crossroads Parkway North, Suite 360
City of Industry, CA 91746
(562) 699-6400
Fax: (562) 699-1891
frankc@dynatek.net

7379

Business Information: Mr. Cheung serves as Chief Technology Officer of Dynatek Infoworld, Inc. He is responsible for planning and delivering new advancements within the Corporation, including determining the strategic and technical direction of Dynatek and contributions of the information systems function. Before joining Dynatek Infoworld, Inc. in 1996, Mr. Cheung assertively served as Systems Administrator with the Kam Song Company, where he administered and controlled data resources and installed computer operating systems software. In 1998, Mr. Cheung was promoted to his current role of Dynatek's Chief Technology Officer. With an established track record of delivering results, his professional success reflects his ability to build strong teams with synergy and technical strength and take on new challenges and responsibilities. Determining future technical requirements, overseeing time lines, schedules, and budgets, and providing cohesive leadership also fall within the realm of his functions. He attributes his success to his technical background and interest in computers. Mr. Cheung is also a Microsoft Certified Systems Engineer. His goal is to eventually move up the hierarchy into a high level management position. "You must know how to manage effectively," is cited as his advice. An international technology company, Dynatek Infoworld, Inc. is an Internet and Web posting provider. The Corporation also specializes in database consulting. Established in 1996, Dynatek Infoworld presently employs a staff of more than 20 professional and technical experts. **Career Highlights:** Chief Technology Officer, Dynatek Infoworld, Inc. (Present); System Administrator, Kam Song Company. **Education:** University of Southern California: M.S. (1994), B.S. in Computer Science.

Mani A. Chinnaiah

President
AUM Technologies, Inc.
15 Richmond
Irvine, CA 92620
(714) 329-3635

7379

Business Information: Combining strategic management skills and information technology expertise, Mr. Chinnaiah serves in the role of President of AUM Technologies, Inc. He oversees and directs all aspects of day-to-day administration and operational activities, as well as performs market research to develop strategic plans for future business growth. Working closely with commercial clients, he is able to analyze their systems and propose up to date ERP, Y2K, and e-commerce technological solutions. Coordinating resources, schedules, time lines, and assignments; building teams with synergy and technical strength; and calculating and managing the fiscal year budget also fall within the purview of his executive responsibilities. Concurrent to his present position, Mr. Chinnaiah fulfills the capacity of Consultant for Solbourne. His future objectives for AUM Technologies is to expand the Company's national operations and add on an international department. AUM Technologies, Inc. was established in 1998 and offers computer consulting services to businesses across the country. Five skilled and knowledgeable professionals are employed. **Career Highlights:** President, AUM Technologies, Inc. (1998-Present); Consultant, Solbourne (1998-Present); Consultant, Utility Partner (1997-98); Consultant, Carter Burgess (1994-97). **Education:** University of Nevada at Reno, M.S. (1996); National University of Singapore, Master's degree in Engineering; University of Madras, Master's degree in Engineering; Annamalah University, Bachelor's degree in Engineering. **Personal Information:** Married to Uma in 1987. One child: Adithya. Mr. Chinnaiah enjoys tennis and golf.

Rajasekaran S. Chockalingam

Senior Database Support Specialist
CAM Systems LLC.
12980 Saratoga Avenue, Suite C
Saratoga, CA 95070
(408) 446-7094
Fax: (408) 446-7001
raja@camsystems.com

7379

Business Information: Drawing from 13 years of experience in the information technology field, Mr. Chockalingam serves as Senior Database Support Specialist for CAM Systems LLC. Recruited to the Company in 1999, he fulfills a number of operational duties on behalf of CAM Systems. He directly administers and controls the Company's data resources and ensures data integrity and security. Maintaining database functionality and operational status, eliminating data redundancy, and tuning tools to improve database performance also fall within the realm of Mr. Chockalingam's responsibilities. The most rewarding aspect of his career is staying on the cutting edge of Oracle technology. Attributing his success to his ability to communicate, think outside-the-box, take on challenges, and deliver innovative results, Mr. Chockalingam's strategic plans include strengthening focus on the Internet. CAM Systems LLC. provides cable application software and software consultation for the cable advertising industry. Established in 1996, the Company employs the skills of 20 employees, all of which have been specifically trained in the industry. Presently, the Company is located in Cupertino, California. **Career Highlights:** Senior Database Support Specialist, CAM Systems LLC. (1999-Present); Senior Database Administrator, Pacific Bell (1998-99); Regional Database Administrator, Quantum Asia-Pacific Singapore (1997-98). **Associations & Accomplishments:** International Oracle User Group. **Education:** Bharathidasan University, M.B.A. (1990); St. Joseph's College, B.Sc. (1982); Oracle Certified DBA. **Personal Information:** Married to A. Vijaya Lakshmi in 1995. One child: Prithvi. Mr. Chockalingam enjoys tennis, photography, books and surfing the Internet.

Terry L. Chrisman

Project Manager
Technology Solutions Company
1730 Edgewood Hill Circle, Apartment 103
Hagerstown, MD 21740-3364
(800) 759-2250
Fax: (410) 243-5001
terry_chrisman@techsol.com

7379

Business Information: Serving as Project Manager for Technology Solutions Company, Mr. Chrisman is charged with the overall productivity in daily operations. Possessing an excellent understanding of his field, he develops and guides information technology training strategies for major ERP implementations. He also assists in system testing and analysis. In addition, Mr. Chrisman assists and guides change management initiatives. He has established himself as a valuable company asset by demonstrating his superior communication skills and ability to manage multiple tasks simultaneously. His goals include learning new applications to standardize best practices, becoming involved in e-commerce, and obtaining his Master's degree in computer science. Technology Solutions Company provides information technology consulting services. Established in 1987, the Company has grown to employ over 1,200 people who generate multi million dollar annual revenues. Technology Solutions Company builds and manages e-business solutions. By providing quality services and components, the Company has become a leader in a lucrative, complex, and competitive industry. **Career Highlights:** Technology Solutions Company: Project Manager (1999-Present), Advisor/Assistant Project Manager (1999), Developer (1998-99). **Associations & Accomplishments:** International Society for Performance Improvement; American Society for Training & Development. **Education:** Frostburg State University, B.A. (1996).

Robert J. Chromy

President/Project Manager/Consultant
Information Technology Consulting, Inc.
12 Golf Course Road
Succasunna, NJ 07876
(973) 884-8511
rchromy@aol.com

7379

Business Information: Mr. Chromy ventured out on his own to start Information Technology Consulting, Inc. in 1997. At the present time, he serves as President, Project Manager, and Consultant. He leverages his experience and skills to help clients and staff successfully manage and implement IT solutions to business problems. Working on an individual basis, he answers questions consistently and researches solutions to any technical problems that clients may experience. His vast knowledge in the industry manifests itself in his expertise in the field. A member in several national organizations, Mr. Chromy is current with technological advancements and upgrades. He performs research on systems he feels will be especially successful and recommends them to his clients. In addition, he makes public presentations to all levels and audiences in corporations on various topics in information technology. In the future, Mr. Chromy intends to continue in his current position while working to develop strategies to help businesses with evolving technology. Attributing his considerable success to his experience, his contacts, and his education, Mr. Chromy's involvement in the consulting industry has proven to be an enlightening and worthwhile endeavor. Information Technology Consulting, Inc. was established in 1997. The Corporation specializes in software consulting in application development, systems analysis and design, data modeling, and network protocols in addition to systems quality assurance and metrics and project management. **Career Highlights:** President/Project Manager/Consultant, Information Technology Consulting, Inc. (1997-Present); Project Manager/Consultant, Telecommunications and Insurance Companies (1992-Present); Software Engineering Manager, Unisys Corporation (1984-91); Quality Assurance Manager, Dell Publishing Company (1981-84). **Associations & Accomplishments:** MIS Network Associates; Unisys Corporate Representative, International Function Point Users Group (1990-91); Unisys Corporation and Department Software Metrics Committees (1989-90); Data Processing Management Association (1980-91): International Director (1981-85), Chapter President (1986-87); Inducted into Delta Mu Delta, National Honor Society in Business Administration (1988); Awarded Certified Systems Professional (1985); Earned FLMI (1975); LOMA Pension Systems Committee (1978-81); BISAC Committee (1981-84). **Education:** Fairleigh Dickinson University, M.B.A. (1988); Marietta College, B.S. in Math and Physics (1964). **Personal Information:** Married to Patricia in 1968. Two children: Jennifer and Brett. Mr. Chromy enjoys writing.

Brian W. Cilley

Systems Engineer
RouterWare
6651 Walton Drive
Huntington Beach, CA 92647
(949) 442-0770
brian-cilley@routerware.com

7379

Business Information: Recruited to RouterWare in 1995, Mr. Cilley serves as a Systems Engineer. He assumes accountability for a variety of tasks, including product research and maintenance for the Information Technology Department. Mr. Cilley is also responsible for many of the Corporation's major accounts, providing customer support, technical assistance, and troubleshooting any problems which may arise. Looking forward to expanding his professional responsibilities by entering into upper management, he also entertains the entrepreneurial dream of owning his own consulting company in the future. His success reflects his ability to think outside the box, produce results, and aggressively take on new challenges. RouterWare is engaged in specialized software development within the information technology industry. The Corporation produces routers, a computer system that transfers data from one network to another. Protocol level routers are produced and the Corporation performs networking and embedded command and sytems functions as well. Founded in 1991, operations employ the skilled services of over 700 professionals in its two locations. **Career Highlights:** Systems Engineer, RouterWare (1995-Present). **Personal Information:** Mr. Cilley enjoys motorcross, snowboarding, river rafting, biking and surfing.

Ronald L. Clark

Lotus Notes Administrator
IBM Global Services
4111 Northside Parkway NW
Atlanta, GA 30327
(404) 238-5950
chclark@bellsouth.net

7379

Business Information: Serving as the Lotus Notes Administrator, Mr. Clark coordinates the code levels within the Lotus Notes and servers. He administrates and controls network security and deploys applications to individual servers, ensuring that the correct department and country information is in place. Before joining IBM Global Services, Mr. Clark served as a Systems Analyst with Drake Software. In his present role, he is responsible for the majority of aspects of the department as well as manages the employee security clearance for all employees. Mr. Clark feels that his most significant professional achievement is his complete certification in Lotus Notes Administration. Dedicated to the success of IBM Global Services, he plans to pursue additional technological certifications to capitalize on the promotional opportunities offered by the Company. His success reflects his ability to think outside the box and aggressively take on new challenges. IBM Global Services provides network administration and support for the World Wide Lotus Notes Network. This Department of IBM Global Services sets the technological standard globally for all IBM divisions. Approximately 50 knowledgeable professionals are employed in departmental operations. **Career Highlights:** Lotus Notes Administrator, IBM Global Services (1997-Present); Systems Analyst, Drake Software (1990-97). **Associations & Accomplishments:** Volunteer, Firefighter. **Education:** Western Carolina University, B.S. in Business Administration and Computer Information Systems (1997); Certified Novell Administrator; Certified Lotus Specialist. **Personal Information:** Married to Melissa in 1990. Mr. Clark enjoys golf, tennis, scuba diving and softball.

Perry R. Clawson

Director of Operations
Universal Systems and Technology Inc.
7005 University Boulevard
Winter Park, FL 32792
(407) 679-8700
Fax: (407) 679-0743
clawsonp@unitech-tsd.com

7379

Business Information: Educated in the field of systems management, Mr. Clawson serves as the Director of Operations for Universal Systems and Technology Inc. He assumes accountability for all daily activities, contractual requests, and new employee hires. Responsible for the simulation directorship, he provides training for each of the 60 staff members and ensures the training simulators built by his department are of the highest standards. Coordinating resources, time lines, schedules, and assignments also fall within the realm of his responsibilities. Mr. Clawson has received internal recognition for his work and at one point was chosen the "Manager of the Year for 1991." Attributing his success to his drive and attention to detail, he is maneuvering himself to gain a position as Vice President. An aerospace and information technology contract company, Universal Systems and Technology Inc. specializes in training simulators, computer based instructions, and technical assistance. The Corporation primarily works with the Federal Aviation Administration and the Department of Defense but does do some commercial contracts and international programs. Established in 1988, the Corporation employs 300 individuals generating in excess of $35 million annually. **Career Highlights:** Director of Operations, Universal Systems and Technology Inc. (1996-Present); Lieutenant Colonel, United States Army Reserve (Present); Program Manager, Lockheed Martin Corporation (1992-95); Business Manager, Martin Marietta Corporation (1989-91). **Associations & Accomplishments:** United States Army Reserve Officers Association; Association of Graduates, United States Military Academy. **Education:** Florida Institute of Technology, M.S. in Systems Management (1988); United States Military Academy at West Point, B.S. in General Engineering (1980). **Personal Information:** Married to Lisa in 1993. Mr. Clawson enjoys spending time with his family, reading, boating and golf.

Mark G. Clements

Owner
e-technicalsupport.com
P.O. Box 600009
Dallas, TX 75360
(214) 724-0392
Fax: (214) 853-4115
techmgr@e-technicalsupport.com

7379

Business Information: Utilizing over 10 years of extensive experience in the technology field, Mr. Clements is the Owner and Founder of e-technicalsupport.com. He performs tests on accounting software for Y2K compliancy and answers technical and bookkeeping and math questions for users. Performing statistical analysis of employee wages, he also ensures that he delivers quality customer services. Before venturing out on his own, he served as Technical Support Representative with M-USA Business Systems, Inc. and Administrative Accountant for Conlee Brothers Farm/Ranch. Concurrent to his role with e-technicalsupport.com, he assumes the responsibility of Senior Technical Support Engineer for Property Automation Software Corporation. An expert in his field, Mr. Clements attributes his career success to his ability to listen to his clients. His advice to new entrepreneurs is "do your homework before going into business for themselves." Becoming a dominant presence on the Internet serves as one of his future goals. e-technicalsupport.com is a Web based support, consulting, and tutoring firm. Created in 1999, the Company offers Y2K testing, preemployment screening, and tutoring statistics for clients through the Internet. **Career Highlights:** Owner, e-technicalsupport.com (1999-Present); Senior Tech Support Engineer, Property Automation Software Corporation (1995-Present); Technical Support Representative, M-USA Business Systems, Inc. (1994-95); Administrative Accountant, Conlee Brothers Farm/Ranch (1993-94). **Associations & Accomplishments:** American Institute of Professional Bookkeepers. **Education:** Sam Houston State University: B.B.A. in Accounting (1992), B.B.A. in International Business (1989). **Personal Information:** Married to Patricia in 1998. Mr. Clements enjoys collecting old foreign coins and bills, collecting artwork of Escher and golf.

Jon Cline

Chief Information Officer
Enthusiast, Inc.
PMB 194 3579 East Foothill Boulevard
Pasadena, CA 91107
(626) 523-9788
Fax: (626) 578-0717
jon@enthusiastonline.com

7379

Business Information: Possessing superior talents in the information technology field, Mr. Cline joined Enthusiast, Inc. in 2000 as the Chief Information Officer. He oversees and directs all technical elements within the Corporation's corporate structure. Ensuring the functionality and serviceability of the infrastructure, he utilizes strategic planning to increase business and establish new contacts. In addition, Mr. Cline manages business development and oversees newsite approval. He attributes his success to innovation and his ability to empower other people. Committed to further development of the Corporation, Mr. Cline coordinates strategic planning to ensure a bright future for Enthusiast, Inc. His goals include getting the Corporation's name out in the markets and continuing to grow the network. Striving to provide customers with reliable and efficient service, Enthusiast, Inc. offers community based Web sites with online content development for vertical portals and content specific online destinations. The Corporation also provides technical support for problems with connecting to the Internet. Established in 2000, Enthusiast is located in Pasadena, California and employs the expertise of four individuals to promote services and answer customer queries. **Career Highlights:** Chief Information Officer, Enthusiast, Inc. (2000-Present); System Engineer/Designer, American Film Institute (1998-00); Network Engineer/Instructor, Pasadena City College (1996-98); Software Supervisor, Lighthouse Partners (1996-98). **Education:** Pasadena City College (1997). **Personal Information:** Mr. Cline enjoys volleyball, guitar, Ultimate frisbee and teaching low income kids.

Marc G. Clouse

Manager of Business Systems Support
Systems Documentation Inc.
100 Metroplex Drive, Suite 100
Edison, NJ 08817
(732) 572-1111
Fax: (732) 572-9444
mclouse@sdicorp.com

7379

Business Information: Functioning in the role of Manager of Business Systems Support of Systems Documentation, Inc., Mr. Clouse oversees the entire internal systems infrastructure, including networks and business systems. Before joining Systems Documentation Inc. in 1996, Mr. Clouse served as DCS Coordinator with BMW of North America. Utilizing nine years of practical experience and a firm academic base, he oversees and directs the analysis, specification, and design of state-of-the-art business solutions and applications. Identifying new clients, analyzing their specific needs, developing proposals, and negotiating contracts also fall within the purview of Mr. Clouse's responsibilities. He attributes his success to being open-minded, being able to understand the needs of his clients, being a jack-of-all-trade, and an unquenchable thirst for knowledge. "Work hard. Get as much information as possible from the people you do business with, and don't burn any bridges," is cited as his advice. Becoming Vice President of Solutions and continuing his education serves as his future endeavors. Systems Documentation Inc. provides information systems consulting, product based solutions, Web applications, technical documentation, and contract labor for Fortune 500 clients. Established in 1979, the Corporation employs a work force of more than 160 people who help generate revenues in excess of $6.5 million annually. **Career Highlights:** Manager of Business Systems Support, Systems Documentation Inc. (1996-Present); DCS Coordinator, BMW of North America (1994-96). **Education:** Ramapro College, degree in Computer Science (1990); The Chubb Institute. **Personal Information:** Married to Stacy in 1994. One child: Marc Jr.

Cynthia A. Collins

President
Collins & Collins Consulting, Inc.
22365 El Toro Road, Suite 228
Lake Forest, CA 92630
(949) 588-9535
Fax: (949) 588-9530
collins_c3@earthlink.net

7379

Business Information: The Founder of Collins & Collins Consulting, Inc., Mrs. Collins also serves as its President. She established the Firm to provide her customers with quality information technology consulting services for their companies. A savvy professional since 1984, she determines the overall strategic direction and formulates business and marketing plans to keep the Corporation on the cutting edge in the technology industry. Keeping abreast of technological advancements through her vender contacts, seminars, and her membership in the Association of Information and Image Management, she attributes her success to a high level of quality service and the self-motivation which allows her to maintain it. She has performed several speaking engagements, including those at the Government Technology Conference, A.I.I.M. and A.R.M.A. Her success reflects her ability to think outside the box, produce results, tackle new challenges, and design viable solutions. Collins & Collins Consulting, Inc. specializes in the niche market of document technology but offers project management and process analysis as well. Created in 1997, current operations employ the talents of a single professional with an expectation to grow and expand. **Career Highlights:** President, Collins & Collins Consulting, Inc. (1997-Present); Area Manager, Eastman Kodak Company (1997); Director, Carrera Consulting Group (1995-96); Regional Practice Manager, Automated Concepts, Inc. (1992-95); Eastman Kodak Company (1984-91): Customer Support Manager, Systems Engineer, Design Engineer. **Associations & Accomplishments:** Past President/Vice President, Los Angeles Chapter, Association of Information and Image Management; Distinguished Service Award, AIIM. **Education:** University of Wisconsin, B.S. degree in Electrical Engineering (1983); A.I.I.M., Master of Information Technology; Certified Document Imaging Architect, Comptia. **Personal Information:** Married to Timothy W. in 1987. One child: Michael. Mrs. Collins enjoys golf, gardening and reading.

Louis H. Collins, Jr.

Systems Integration Specialist
Strategic Technologies
4975 Avalon Ridge Parkway
Norcross, GA 30071
(404) 841-4915
Fax: (404) 841-4049
collinll@imshealth.com

7379

Business Information: Specializing in the maintenance of complex network systems, Mr. Collins serves as Systems Integration Speicalist with Strategic Technologies. Utilizing an extensive knowledge in the field of information technology, he incorporates the latest technologies into the design and development of networks, ensuring an efficient and productive system. Overseeing small project management, Mr. Colllins provides the necessary funds and materials to the development of new network and software. Offering technical support and troubleshooting, he ensures complete client satisfaction of a quality product through tests and evaluations of the specific operations of the network. Consistently achieving quality performance in his field, Mr. Collins anticipates his promotion to Project Manager through hard work and dedication. Serving an international clientele, Strategic Technologies was established in 1985, and is dedicated to providing software solutions to large pharmaceutical companies. Located in Norcross, Georgia, the Company employs the technical expertise of 700 individuals to facilitate ever aspect of design, manufacture, quality assurance, and integration of complex systems. Generating $60 million in annual revenues, the Company remains dedicated to the expansion of their product line gauranteeing client satisfaction. **Career Highlights:** Systems Integration Specialist, Strategic Technologies (1996-Present); Field Engineer, Digital Equipment Corporation (1984-96); Administrative Manager, Lanier Worldwide (1979-84); Distribution Supervisor, Butterick Fashion Marketing (1972-78). **Education:** DeVry Technical College, B.S. in Electrical Engineering (1986). **Personal Information:** Married to Barbara in 1993. One child: Sheri. Mr. Collins enjoys travel, boating and fishing.

W. David Collins

Independent Consultant
David Collins
122 Vanderbilt Lane
Waxahachie, TX 75165-1744
(214) 914-0169
wdavidcollins@hotmail.com

7379

Business Information: In his role as an Independent Consultant for David Collins, Mr. Collins handles a variety of technical and administrative issues on a daily basis. Utilizing adept technical abilities, he implements and maintains 3.1H and 4.0 versions of the SAP operating systems for clients. He also provides valuable support services to his clientele as he demonstrates an extensive knowledge of the industry. Recognized for his impressive achievements and accomplishments, Mr. Collins is credited for the successful development of a mentoring program that is known throughout the community as "Pathways to Success." A dedicated professional with exceptional drive and motivation, he also maintains financial activities for a local family restaurant. In the future, Mr. Collins looks forward to handling more independent contracts as he increases his responsibilities. Attributing his success to a positive attitude and a supportive family, his advice is "take the risk." National in scope, David Collins operates as an independent specializing in information systems solutions, including corporate organization, reengineering, and technical support. Offering SAP 3.1 and 4.0 consulting services, David Collins provides training for clients on technical operating systems as they implement strategic business solutions. **Career Highlights:** Independent Consultant, David Collins (1999-Present); Management Consultant, Ernst & Young (1998-99); Consultant, ESoft Consulting (1998); Business Analyst, Amoco (1996-98). **Education:** University of Michigan Business School, B.B.A. (1996); University of Madrid (1997); London School of Economics (1995); University of Paris (1994). **Personal Information:** Mr. Collins enjoys flying, travel and researching on the Internet.

Ana Iris Colon

Administrator/Partner
Devnet Systems Corporation
P.O. Box 3667
Guaynabo, Puerto Rico 00970-3667
(787) 749-0463
Fax: (787) 783-0644
anaiscolon@usa.net

7379

Business Information: As Administrator and Partner of Devnet Systems Corporation, Mrs. Colon handles a multitude of responsibilities on a daily basis. Demonstrating an extensive knowledge of the industry, she focuses on business development and administrative operations to ensure that each department is operating at maximum efficiency. With a throughough understanding of policies in human resources and accounting, she designs strategic business plans that contribute to the overall effectiveness of the Corporation as a whole. Mrs. Colon enjoys dedicating time and attention to her business; she currently is initiating plans to further the business in the Latin American market as the Corporation becomes an Internet host. Mrs. Colon's success is attributed to her perseverance and ability to mark a target and shoot straight at it. Established in 1997, Devnet Systems Corporation is a technical consultancy firm located on the beautiful island of Puerto Rico. Offering services such as network integration, hardware installation, software implementation, and Web page design, the Corporation is involved in a partnership with Microsoft. Major clients include banks, pharmaceutical companies, and various corporations. The Corporation currently employs 15 professionals and generates revenues of $700,000 annually. **Career Highlights:** Administrator/Partner, Devnet Systems Corporation (1997-Present); Nuclear Medicine Technologist, TMR Diagnostic Imaging (1993-97). **Associations & Accomplishments:** Nuclear Medicine Association. **Education:** University of Puerto Rico, Nuclear Medicine (1993). **Personal Information:** Married to Rafael A. in 1993. Two children: Gabriel Antonio and Nicole Ariana. Mrs. Colon enjoys home improvement.

Philip J. Connolly
Director of Information Systems/Chief Technology Officer
Akropolis.net
1504 Brookhollow Drive, Suite 116
Santa Ana, CA 92075
(714) 751-1175
Fax: (714) 751-1185
pconnolly@akropolis.net

7379

Business Information: As Director of Information Systems and Chief Technical Officer, Mr. Connolly oversees all aspects of engineering, applications, and information technology. Possessing an excellent understanding of his field, he develops and implements new technology for future strategy aligned with business objectives. Working closely with the business and marketing teams, he uses his trained eye and keen analytical sense to work through problems that arise. Devoting time to the engineering and development divisions, he coordinates the business needs with technology. Highlights for Mr. Connolly include helping the Company grow and being in charge of developing the Intranet in 1994 while at the University of Southern California. His plans for the future are no less ambitious than his past. He would like to remain on the leading edge of implementing solutions and strategy to build an e-com and e-business and take over the "NET" market. Established in 1996, Akropolis.net provides business-to-business portals for the design and building industries. National in scope, the Company also offers commercial building tools. Presently, the Company located in Santa Ana, California employs the services of 12 professional, technical, and support staff. **Career Highlights:** Director of Information Systems/Chief Technical Officer, Akropolis.net (1999-Present); Network Engineer, Bernard Hodes Advertising (1998-99); Senior Analyst, Aegis Comminications Group (1997-98); Programmer/Analyst, University of Southern California (1991-97). **Education:** UCSB, B.S. (1991). **Personal Information:** Married in 1996. Mr. Connolly enjoys travel.

Charlie D. Cook
Systems Administrator
Edge Technologies, Inc.
3701 Pender Drive, Suite 150
Fairfax, VA 22030
(301) 435-5957
charlie.cook@edge-technologies.com

7379

Business Information: Drawing from an extensive educational and previous occupational experience, Mr. Cook joined Edge Technologies, Inc. in 1998 as Systems Administrator. Utilizing his vast technical knowledge, he is responsible for establishing and maintaining network systems, upgrading systems, evaluating new technologies, and working with NIH-NCBI. Possessing an excellent understanding of technology, he handles all Web, backups, and security services. Mr. Cook has received recognition for his diligence and skills through several internal awards from the Corporation. Continually striving for maximum effectiveness, he plans to pursue his Master's degree, enabling him to capitalize on the opportunities provided by the Company. Mr. Cook's favorite quote is "get involved and ask questions." Established in 1993, Edge Tehncologies, Inc. is an information technology solutions company. Located in Fairfax, Virginia, the Corporation employs the services of 100 individuals responsible for dealing with network, Internet, and security. **Career Highlights:** Systems Administrator, Edge Technologies, Inc. (1998-Present); Bridgewater College: Network Support Specialist (1995-98), Computing Center Assistant (1993-95). **Associations & Accomplishments:** USENIX; SAGE. **Education:** James Madison University, M.S. in Computer Science with a concentration in Information

Security (In Progress); Bridgewater College: B.S. in Political Science, B.S. in Mathematics and Computer Science. **Personal Information:** Mr. Cook enjoys snow skiing and reading science fiction.

John J. Creevy
Senior Customer Engineer
ENTEX Information Services, Inc.
6 International Drive
Rye Brook, NY 10573-1058
(847) 969-3420
Fax: (847) 969-8012
john.creevy@entex.com

7379

Business Information: Dedicated to the success of ENTEX Information Services, Inc., Mr. Creevy applies his knowledge and expertise in the technology industry in serving as Senior Customer Engineer. He provides help desk support, on-site desktop and LAN support, and site coordination functions for corporate clients, such as Avery Dennison's Schaumburg, Illinois and Edison New Jersey locations. Before joining ENTEX, Mr. Creevy served as an Account Manager for both Liuski International, Inc. and 3D-MICRO, Inc. As a 23 year technology professional, he coordinates resources, time lines, schedules, and assignments in providing pre- and post-sales technical support. Currently pursuing his Bachelor's degree in Technical Management, Mr. Creevy looks forward to advancing in network design and development. He keeps abreast of technological advances in his field through his college studies, trade magazines, and e-mail services. ENTEX Information Services, Inc., the nation's premier network integrator, is the industry's leading architect of advanced business computing solutions. The Corporation's philosophy is "Total PC management, because you've got a business to run." Created in 1993, operations employ over 5,500 people. Yearly revenue is reported to be over $500 million. **Career Highlights:** Senior Customer Engineer, ENTEX Information Services, Inc. (1997-Present); Account Manager, Liuski International, Inc. (1996-97); Account Manager, 3D-Micro, Inc. (1995-96). **Associations & Accomplishments:** Board of Education School District #87, Cook County, Illinois(1989-93); Director, Lombard Jaycees(1988); National Team Champion, 16-17 Year Old Division, AAU National Cross Country Championships(1975); All State Cross Country, Illinois (1975); National Association of Realtors. **Education:** DeVry Institute of Technology, B.S. in Technical Management (In Progress); Triton College, A.S. (1978). **Personal Information:** Married to Maria A. in 1997. One child: Alexander. Mr. Creevy enjoys bass fishing and riding his Harley-Davidson motorcycle.

Matthew J. Cross
System Administrator
SAIC
12479 Research Parkway
Orlando, FL 32826
(407) 207-2707
Fax: (407) 381-8436
crossm@odin.orl.saic.com

7379

Business Information: As System Administrator of SAIC, Mr. Cross is responsible for the maintenance of three NT servers, one Mac server, 130 personal computers, and 30 Macs. Additionally, he maintains network connections, troubleshoots malfunctions, installs upgrades, and recommends budget allocations for the purchase of technical equipment. Mr. Cross' plans for the future include completing his Bachelor's degree in Computer Science and his MCSE certification. Founded in 1969, SAIC currently operates as a computer engineering firm, contracted to develop new technical applications. With over 30,000 locations and 5,000 employees around the world, the Company primarily completes assignments for military, medical, and commercial organizations. Annual revenues of the California-based company are currently estimated at $1 billion. **Career Highlights:** System Administrator, SAIC (1995-Present); NT Administrator, University of Central Florida (1997-Present); System Administrator, SAIC (1990-94). **Associations & Accomplishments:** Alpha Phi Omega - National Coed Service Fraternity (1995-Present). **Education:** University of Central Florida; Gulf Coast Community College, A.A. in Engineering (1991); Microsoft Certified Professional Product Specialist (1996-Present). **Personal Information:** Mr. Cross enjoys service projects, sports and reading.

Brandon G. Curtis
Area Manager/International Dealer Director
TDSI, a Division of Randstad North America
4079 Ingot Street
Fremont, CA 94538
(800) 611-8374
Fax: (916) 315-1362
BCurtis@TDSI-HQ.com

7379

Business Information: Mr. Curtis serves in the dual role of Area Manager and International Dealer Director of TDSI, a Division of Randstad North America. He is responsible for four different areas of expertise that includes: outside and international dealer, public safety, sales management, and work force management of Blue Pumpkin Software. Mr. Curtis handles the management of the voice recording systems, LAN systems design and development, and the installation and technical support of the Althogen PC Systems. Playing such a large role for TDSI only fuels his desire to continue growing with the Company, expanding the international distribution channels and new emerging technologies. Success, according to Mr. Curtis, came when he sold his own company, Method Technology to TDSI in November of 1999. TDSI is a technical consulting firm. All clientele are provided with necessary tools to help keep their businesses up and running, such as computer telephony, staffing, communications; and network design, development, and management. TDSI is one of many subsidiaries branching from Rondstad North America, which was founded in 1985. TDSI has an experienced team of 80 plus consultants. **Career Highlights:** Area Manager/International Dealer Director, TDSI, a Division of Randstad North America (1999-Present); Owner, Method Technology (1999); Project Manager, Delta Wireless (1995-99); Project Manager/Lead Technician, Northwest Technology (1989-95). **Personal Information:** Married to Michelle in 1993. One child: Taylor. Mr. Curtis enjoys motorcycles, snowboarding and youth ministry. In addition, Mr. Brandon enjoys motivational speaking to high school students. He is also a high school pastor and counselor for teens.

Sujal Dalia
Quality Assurance Engineer
Systems Link
2711 Village Drive
Avenel, NJ 07001-1056
(609) 409-0909
sujaldalia@hotmail.com

7379

Business Information: As a Quality Assurance Engineer of Systems Link, Mr. Dalia is responsible for testing the software that converts wireless data and sends that information to the fraud detection software. In his current position for only one year, he has learned all of the facets involved in the job due to his ability to quickly grasp new concept methodologies. Additionally, Mr. Dalia regulates the testing of the software, composes the scripts used during testing, and also works on development of new tools. Possessing an excellent understanding of his field, he is currently working on two projects. Proud of the fact that he has been certified in New Jersey by the Quality Assurance Association, Mr. Dalia's future plans include developing more software. Founded in 1995, Systems Link is a computer software development company. Specializing in intrusion countermeasures, or software that that detects fraudulent use, the Company employs 90 individuals. Presently, the Company is located at 2540 Route 130, Suite 124, Cranberry, New Jersey 08512. **Career Highlights:** Quality Assurance Engineer, Systems Link (1999-Present); Quality Assurance Analyst, Westchester Medical Center (1998-99); Quality Assurance Engineer, FX Net (1998). **Education:** New Jersey Institute of Technology, B.S. (1998). **Personal Information:** Mr. Dalia enjoys reading computer books.

John L. Dashiell
Outbound Resource Manager
IMI Systems, Inc.
8133 Leesburg Pike, Suite 800
Vienna, VA 22182-2733
(703) 734-7057
Fax: (703) 821-7945
jdashiell@imisys.com

7379

Business Information: Providing his skilled services as Outbound Resource Manager of IMI Systems, Inc., Mr. Dashiell recruits new consultants to the Corporation and works closely with Fortune 400 companies to place consultants within their businesses. He researches new Internet tools and software programs, testing each one and programming them to serve each client's individual needs. Mr. Dashiell states that the key to success in technology is to obtain as much education as possible, and always keep abreast of new technology and when it is offered, take it. Planning to remain in the technology field, he enjoys the challenges of networking and Web design. Mr. Dashiell looks forward to building stronger relationships with his clients and performing more consulting. IMI Systems, Inc. is an information technology consulting company. Approximately 4,000 skilled consultants are employed in the United States, the United Kingdom, and Canada. The Corporation provides information technology consultants to clients, filling technical positions at client sites as needed. Targeting the telecommunications and financial industries, IMI Systems also specializes in Y2K remediation and writing new programs. However, each consultant remains an employee of the Corporation. Presently, IMI Systems reports annual revenues in excess of $500 million. **Career Highlights:** Outbound Resource Manager, IMI Systems, Inc. (1999-Present); Assistant Principal Plant Manager/Grounds Keeper, Equine Medical Center/VA Tec (1992-99); Environmental Site Engineer, MKM Engineers/Marmo Contracting (1997-98). **Associations & Accomplishments:** Virginia Thoroughbred Association; Virginia Horsemens Association; Church Softball. **Education:** Strayer University (Currently Attending). **Personal Information:** Mr. Dashiell enjoys outdoor sports, football, baseball, soccer, hunting, fishing, competitive shooting, hiking, biking and horseback riding.

Pravin W. Datar

Business Consultant
SE Technology
2355 Main Street
Irvine, CA 92614
(949) 250-7442
Fax: (949) 250-7443
pwdatar@yahoo.com

7379

Business Information: Displaying his skills in this highly specialized position, Mr. Datar serves SE Technology as a Business Consultant and has been with the Company since 1998. Forming and maintaining major client relations, he performs extensive evaluations in order to determine the necessary systems integration that will improve the efficiency and effectiveness of the Company's main networking system. Involved in enterprise resource planning, Mr. Datar organizes client reports and accounts in order to provide for the diverse needs of his clients. Looking for invovlement more in e-business, he continues to grow professionally through the fulfillment of his responsibilities with SE Technology and his involvement in the advancement of operations. Founded in 1985, SE Technology is an established and reputable enterprise resource planning consulting firm. Serving a national client base, the Company is headquartered in Connecticut and employs the expertise of 250 qualified personnel to direct all aspects of administration, integration, and customer service. **Career Highlights:** Business Consultant, SE Technology (1998-Present); Assistant Project Manager, Bluestar Ltd. (1997-98); Senior Industrial Engineer, Larsen & Toubro Ltd. (1995-97); Assistant Director, National Productivity Council (1989-95). **Associations & Accomplishments:** Indian Institute of Industrial Engineering; Institute of Cost and Works Accountants of India; Institution of Engineers. **Education:** National Product Council, P.L.D.I.E. (1991); Bachelor's degree in Engineering, Cost and Works Accountancy. **Personal Information:** Married to Padmini in 1996. Mr. Datar enjoys evolution and dramatics.

Maulik Avantikumar Dave, Ph.D.

Member of Technical Staff
Bhasha, Inc.
251, West Dekalb Pike, Apartment C411
King of Prussia, PA 19406
(610) 975-9325
mad@workmail.com

7379

Business Information: As a Member of the Technical Staff for Bhasha, Inc., Dr. Dave is responsible for writing software which will meet customer requirements. Consulting with his clients, he determines their needs, wants, and desires and strives to develop the software best suited to their system. Falling under the realm of his responsibilities are analyzing, designing, configuring, and implementing operating and database systems, compilers, utilities, and hardware and software. He also assumes accountability for necessary modifications, offering support and tracking the systems in order to prevent system crashes. Dr. Dave enjoys information technology, and looks forward to working with the machines the Corporation will soon be receiving. Attributing his success to his attitude, Dr. Dave believes that a person should constantly refer to publications, Web sites, and magazines in order to remain current within the industry. Bhasha, Inc. is involved in information extraction and classification. The Company's objective is to make information more accessible and easier to understand. Bhasha is applying techniques from a wide variety of advanced technology areas to solve some of the problems associated with high precision information retrieval. **Career Highlights:** Member of Technical Staff, Bhasha, Inc. (1999-Present); Software Technical Staff Member, Sun Microsystems, Inc. (1998-99); Senior Software Analyst, IBM Global Services (1998); Systems Analyst, Advanced Synergic Microsystems (1997-98). **Associations & Accomplishments:** Institute of Electrical and Electronic Engineers; Association for Computing Machinery. **Education:** Indian Institute of Science, Ph.D. in Computer Science (1998); M.S.

Derold L. Davis

President/Principal Consultant
Ddavis Software Consulting, Inc.
8763 Cottonwood Lane North
Maple Grove, MN 55369
(612) 425-0666
Fax: (612) 425-4599
ddavissci@aol.com

7379

Business Information: Mr. Davis serves in the dual role of President and Principal Consultant at Ddavis Software Consulting, Inc. He is responsible for consulting on all aspects of maintenance and software. He assists various institutions and companies in selecting the appropriate and most efficient software for their computers. An extensive background in the information technology and consulting field has enabled Mr. Davis to acquire the skills and knowledge necessary to keep clients on the cutting edge, as well as lead the Corporation in its growth and development. He is currently completing a system for the University of Minnesota that will be used to document and track maintenance procedures. Talent and dedication motivates Mr. Davis to continue his work. Ddavis Software Consulting, Inc. provides maintenance management and software consulting to clients. Established in 1997, the Corporation employs one individual who is solely responsible for all aspects of the day-to-day administration and operational activities. **Career Highlights:** President/Principal Consultant, Ddavis Software Consulting, Inc. (1997-Present); Senior Consultant, EMA Services, Inc. (1984-97); Data Processing Manager, Redline Medi-Mart (1982-84). **Associations & Accomplishments:** Minnesota Rural Water Association. **Personal Information:** Married to Charlotte in 1975.

James V. Davis

Project Manager
Perkin-Elmer Corporation
1505 Habbot Drive
Raleigh, NC 27603
(919) 779-4379
Fax: (919) 772-7398
davisjv@perkin_elmer.com

7379

Business Information: As Project Manager of Perkin-Elmer Corporation, Mr. Davis is responsible for determining and coordinating project resource requirements, schedules, assignments, and budgets. As a 17 year technology professional, Mr. Davis provides state-of-the-art information management consulting to the drug stability testing and pharmaceutical industries. Before joining Perkin-Elmer Corporation, he served as Systems Analyst for Bayer Corporation. His history includes Senior LIM's Coordinator with Merck & Company, Inc. and Captain in the United States Air Force. In addition to supervising his staff of three employees, Mr. Davis handles numerous resource planning functions to include personnel evaluations, determining future resource requirements, and synthesizing large quantities of data in monthly reports. An expert, he credits his professional success to his God given talents. Eventually attaining the position of Project Leader within three years serves as one of Mr. Davis' future goals. Perkin-Elmer Corporation is the leading supplier of laboratory information management systems. A public corporation, Perkin-Elmer is the parent to the PE Biosystems Group and Celera Genomics Group. National in scope, the Corporation is headquartered in Norwalk, Connecticut. **Career Highlights:** Project Manager, Perkin-Elmer Corporation (1998-Present); Quality Assurance Systems Analyst, Bayer Corporation (1993-98); Senior LIMs Coordinator, Merck & Company, Inc. (1989-93); Captain, United States Air Force (1983-88). **Associations & Accomplishments:** Garner Optimist Club; Optimist International. **Education:** East Carolina University, B.A. in Chemistry (1982). **Personal Information:** Married to Sabrina B. in 1983. One child: Lauren Amanda. Mr. Davis enjoys home improvement, working on his 1965 Mustang, gardening, softball, basketball, deep sea fishing and being a private pilot.

Steve Dean

Software Manager
Intermec
P.O. Box 4280
Everett, WA 98203-9280
(425) 356-1854
Fax: (425) 348-2721
sdean@intermec.com

7379

Business Information: Mr. Dean serves as Software Manager of Intermec. He oversees the enormous collection of software libraries and development tools to guarantee that all programs are made accessible by all clients. Utilizing 17 years of experience, he manages and guides a staff of 15 employees in all aspects of program management. The analysis, acquisition, installation, modification, configuration, and support of operating systems, utilities, and software and hardware also fall within the realm of his responsibilities. He focuses in the discovery, investigation, and initial deployment of advanced technologies within Intermace. A recognized expert, his software suite 250 was rated the best utilities in 1995 by PC Magazine. For the future, Mr. Dean hopes to advance into mid level management and become a software architect or director. Attributing his success to understanding changes in technology in a timely manner, his advice is "come in with your eyes open." Established in 1970, Intermec is a wholly owned subsidiary of the Unova Corporation of Beverly Hills, California. The Company specializes in the data collection of software such as bar code readers, access points, and warehouse management accessories. Each of the 2,000 employees within the Company are trained to provide expert consultation and advice to government, military, retail, and healthcare businesses. **Career Highlights:** Software Manager, Intermec (1998-Present); Software Development Manager, Airborne Express (1990-98); Software Engineer, Procomm Emeralds (1987-90); Software Engineer, Dillingham Construction (1985-87). **Education:** University of Calgary, B.Sc. (1981). **Personal Information:** Married to Kim in 1990.

Jim Demarest

Chief Instructor/Senior Managing Consultant
Power 2000 Inc.
940 East Diehl Road, Suite 100
Naperville, IL 60563-1482
(630) 536-0500
Fax: (630) 536-0599
jdemarest@power2000.com

7379

Business Information: Functioning in the dual role of Chief Instructor and Senior Managing Consultant for Power 2000 Inc., Mr. Demarest provides cutting edge training and consulting services to his clients. While spending 60 percent of his time training both publicly and on the Internet, Mr. Demarest also offers consulting services for projects based on mentoring. While working for the Powersoft Corporation, Mr. Demarest was ranked the number two instructor in North America in 1994 and Top Instructor in 1998. Drawing from more than 10 years of experience in the field, Mr. Demarest attributes his success to networking. He continues to grow professionally and hopes to build a training program. A Fortune 1000 company, Power 2000 Inc. is a computer software development company and consulting firm. Based out of Chicago, the Corporation was established in 1993 and currently employs a staff of 90 individuals to orchestrate every aspect of the operation. **Career Highlights:** Chief Instructor/Senior Managing Consultant, Power 2000 Inc. (1996-Present); Training and Consulting, Powersoft Corporation (1993-96); Training and Consulting, Computer Sciences Corporation (1988-93). **Associations & Accomplishments:** Harvest Bible Chapel; Chicagoland Java Users Group; Vice President, Chicagoland Silverstream Users Group. **Education:** Purdue University, B.S. (1988). **Personal Information:** Married to Deborah in 1995. One child: Hannah. Mr. Demarest enjoys biking, jogging, camping and racing.

Patrick P. Dempsey

Senior Systems Analyst
Affiliated Computer Services
2848 California Street, #3
San Francisco, CA 94115
(415) 267-0431
Fax: (415) 267-0333

7379

Business Information: Serving as a Senior Systems Analyst with Affiliated Computer Services, Mr. Dempsey maintains the credit card phone processing, pricing, and taxation portion of the business. He also conducts database analysis, handles customer correspondence, and oversees mainframe and PC technologies. Working with major companies such as AT&T, he has been involved in pay phone management throughout California and northern Nevada in the electronic transfer of funds. Established in 1988, Affiliated Computer Services, formerly OBS, is a time-sharing vendor to business clients, with some outsourcing as well. Originally, the Company was a start-up operation which obtained 50 percent of its revenue from outsourcing applications, 35 percent from professional services, and five percent from individual clients. Operating divisions internationally, Affiliated Computer Services is now a publicly traded firm on the New York Stock Exchange (AFA) and is headquartered in Dallas, Texas. **Career Highlights:** Senior Systems Analyst, Affiliated Computer Services (1980-Present); Help Desk Analyst, Cincom Systems Inc. (1979-80); Analyst/Programmer, Spreckels Sugar (1978-79). **Associations & Accomplishments:** Voting Member, Association for Computing Machinery (1977-Present); Affiliate Member, Institute of Electrical and Electronics Engineers - Computer Society (1977-Present); Active in alumni fund-raising for University of San Francisco; Contributes to Washington State Alumni Association; Chess buff - The USCF has scaled him as 1650 - been in chess tournaments, but has not joined as a member. **Education:** Washington State University, M.S. in Computer Science (1977); University of San Francisco, B.S. in Computer Science (1973). **Personal Information:** Married to Teresa M. in 1996. Mr. Dempsey enjoys chess, salt and fresh water fishing, golf and black jack.

William DesJarlais
Systems Engineer
Mercury Interactive
8201 Corporate Drive, Suite 750
Landover, MD 20785-2257
(301) 459-2163
billd@merc-int.com

7379

Business Information: Mr. DesJarlais was recruited to Mercury Interactive as tier 3, Product Expert in 1994. Currently, he fulfills the responsibility of Systems Engineer accountable for pre and post sales support. In this context, he supervises the demonstration and on-site testing of the Company's product line. Possessing an excellent understanding of his field, Mr. DesJarlais provides customer follow-up on products and supports three main product lines. He was the founding member of the customer support program for Mercury Interactive and is a product expert for load runner. Mr. DesJarlais plans for the future are to develop new technologies and eventually start a consulting firm. His success is attributed to his ability to keep on top of emerging technologies, tackle new challenges, and deliver results. Established in 1989, Mercury Interactive provides software testing tools. The Company sells automated tools for functional, regressional, and low testing to determine implementation strategy for any industry, corporation, and Fortune 100 companies. Headquartered in Sunnyvale, California Mercury Interactive is an International company with 40 offices worldwide. Presently, the Company employs more than 900 professional, technical, and support staff. **Career Highlights:** Mercury Interactive: Systems Engineer (1999-Present), Product Expert (1994-99); Developer, Lockheed (1985-94). **Education:** Georgia Tech University, B.S. in I.C.S. (1984). **Personal Information:** Married to Dava in 1981. Two children: Nathan and Brooke. Mr. DesJarlais enjoys sports and guitar.

Derrik Deyhimi
Founder/President/Chief Executive Officer
EnterpriseWorks, LLC
5301 Hollister Street, Suite 400
Houston, TX 77040
(713) 934-0200
Fax: (713) 934-7711
3d@ewllc.com

7379

Business Information: The Founder of EnterpriseWorks, LLC, Mr. Deyhimi serves as President and Chief Executive Officer. With the notable ability to understand complex problems and communicate solutions to both the client and the staff, he presides over the entire spectrum of the Company's operational, administrative, and consulting functions. Entrusted with the responsibility of business development, he utilizes strategic and tactical planning to ensure future growth. Mr. Deyhimi believes his success is due to simple human will power. He states that if you set your mind to something, then with effort, focus, and drive, your goal is achievable. EnterpriseWorks has already achieved remarkable growth in the first two years of operation. However, Mr. Deyhimi is looking forward to the Company's first initial offering by the year 2001. EnterpriseWorks, LLC first began operations in 1997 and offers systems integration and computer software consulting. The Company's infrastructure is based on the sales force automation but customer relations management, e-commerce, and front office and e-business integration are also offered. Presently, the Company employs 100 professional, technical, and support personnel. **Career Highlights:** Founder/President/Chief Executive Officer, EnterpriseWorks, LLC (1997-Present); Vice President/Owner, BSI Consulting (1995-97); Technical Manager, BSG Consulting (1992-94); Senior Systems Analyst, Compaq Computer Corporation (1991-92). **Associations & Accomplishments:** Board Member, Massachusetts Institute of Technology Enterprise Forum. **Education:** University of Houston, M.B.A. (1991); University

of Texas, B.A. (1989). **Personal Information:** Married to Jane Wolfe in 1994. Mr. Deyhimi enjoys golf, tennis, travel and skiing.

Armand Difilippo
Project Manager
Intershop Communication
30 Beacon Drive
South Beach, NY 11789-2017
(631) 673-6500
a.difilippo@intershop.com

7379

Business Information: As Project Manager of Intershop Communication, Mr. Difilippo handles the planning for the timing and budgeting of all projects and reviews existing projects. He is also a consultant, performing duties such as visiting clients, scoping analysis, writing proposals from both client teams and Intershop consulting teams, and developing the schedules for training of the sales force, providing them knowledge of products and services offered by the Company. Mr. Difilippo joined Intershop Communication in 1999, and has already had a positive impact on day-to-day operations. His goals include moving up the corporate structure into the role of Director of Business Models and developing a new E.R. package to better prepare people for change. "Listening and communicating skills are important in expanding and advancing your career goals," is cited as Mr. Difilippo's credo. Intershop Communication provides e-commece technology, specializing in the sale side of e-commerce products. The Company is first and foremost in the assessment of business needs. Intershop offers consulting, analysis, and on-site visitations to get a better perspective on customer needs. Over 600 experienced individuals, including consultants, auditors, and customer services representatives make up the wonderful staff of this international e-commerce company. **Career Highlights:** Project Manager, Intershop Communication (1999-Present); Consultant, Andersen Consulting (1998-99); Consultant, Brookhaven National Lab (1990-98). **Education:** Dowling College: M.B.A. in Management (1998), B.S. in Computer Information (1995). **Personal Information:** Married to Lynanne in 1994. One child: Marc. Mr. Difilippo enjoys racquetball, trap shooting, spending time with son and mountain biking.

Barry A. Dobyns
Director
The Windward Group
973 University
Los Gatos, CA 95032
(408) 395-9442
Fax: (408) 395-9642
barry@wwg.com

7379

Business Information: Functioning in the role of Director for the Windward Group, Mr. Dobyns manages the strategic technology practice, which focuses on early product definition and strategy. Before joining The Windward Group in 1997, he served as Vice President of Technology Development with Online Focus, Inc., Director of Multimedia and Online at SRA International, Inc., and Director of Software Development for Photonics Corporation. Providing Chief Technical Officer services, Mr. Dobyns participates in the early stages of consulting offered to clients. His focus is on product strategies and definitions and oversees six employees. Success has been attributed to careful listening, and reflects his ability to build teams with synergy and technical strength, think out-of-the-box, and take on new challenges. Strategic plans are focused on continued growth to 30 percent annually and making the Company three times larger with a strong international presence. The Windward Group operates as a software services company that focuses on developing revenue generating systems for clients based on emerging technology. Software consulting strategies are available to clients. National in scope, The Windward Group operates a network of six locations. Formed in 1989, a core group of 100 people is employed. **Career Highlights:** Director, The Windward Group (1997-Present); Vice President of Technology Development, Online Focus, Inc. (1996-97); Director of Multimedia and Online, SRA International, Inc. (1995-96); Director of Software Development, Photonics Corporation (1993-95). **Associations & Accomplishments:** Institute of Electronics and Electrical Engineers; Association of Computing Machinery; IRDA. **Personal Information:** Married to Lydia J. in 1985. Two children: Abigail and Rebecca. Mr. Dobyns enjoys family activities.

Jeremy Domingue
Systems Administrator
Cybersurfers
202 South Green Street
Tehachapi, CA 93561-1719
(661) 823-2200
Fax: (661) 823-2411
jer@cybersurfers.com

7379

Business Information: Utilizing several years of experience in the technology field, Mr. Domingue founded Cybersurfers in 1998 and currently serves as Systems Administrator. In this capacity, he offers technical support for local business clients and the local newspaper. Presiding over the daily operations of the Company, Mr. Domingue ensures that customers receive the very best in service and connectability to the Internet. Before venturing out into the entrepreneurial world, he served as Programmer for Selecta Switch and Systems Administrator with Tehachapi Mountain Internet. He developed an interest in technology through his job and the secret to his current success is "treat customers the way you would want to be treated." Continually formulating new goals and objectives, Mr. Domingue is looking into higher Internet access for his customers through wireless technology and the cable industry. His success reflects his ability to think out-of-the-box and aggressively tackle new challenges. Cybersurfers is a Internet service provider and offers additional services to businesses and individuals such as Web design, Web hosting, and ISDN accounts. Created in 1998, the Company employs the skilled services of two employees. **Career Highlights:** Systems Administrator, Cybersurfers (1999-Present); Programmer, Selecta Switch (1999); Systems Administrator, Tehachapi Mountain Internet (1996-98). **Personal Information:** Mr. Domingue enjoys computers and motorcycle riding.

Matthew T. Donoghue
Director of Technology
Digital Access Control
4433 East Brookfield Corporate Drive
Chantilly, VA 20151
(703) 631-9077
Fax: (703) 631-3175
matt@dacinc.com

7379

Business Information: As Director of Technology for Digital Access Control, Mr. Donoghue fulfills a number of duties on behalf of the Company and its clientele. He is responsible for providing professional oversight on all aspects of day to day technical services. Throughout his daily activities, Mr. Donoghue is charged with the obligation to perform such tasks as maintaining all network support systems, recruit new technology, and implement changes and upgrades to all systems. Highly regarded, he possesses an excellent understanding of his field. Utilizing four years of hands on experience and his communication skills, Mr. Donoghue negotiates for new business set ups that directly initiates expansion in the Company. His plans for his career include remaining in his current position in order to obtain more responsibility. Digital Access Control is a firm that was started as a debit card system, to later develop into a print management solutions business providing information technology consulting and contracting services for libraries and universities. Established in 1985, the Company offers networking initiatives and support for all facilities that invest in their services. Local operations in Chantilly, Virginia employ the expertise of 10 individuals to promote services, facilitate scheduling, and address customer queries. The Company currently generates annual revenues in excess of $3 million. **Career Highlights:** Director of Technology, Digital Access Control (2000-Present); Network Engineer, Advanced Digital Solutions (1998-00); Technician, PRC Litton (1996-98); Technician, DRI (1996). **Education:** American University, B.A. (1997). **Personal Information:** Mr. Donoghue enjoys tennis and reading.

Bryan A. Drexler
Software Developer
HSB Reliability Technology
3850 Tunlaw Road NW, Apartment 103
Washington, DC 20007-4852
bdrexler@hsbrt.com

7379

Business Information: Serving as Software Developer for HSB Reliability Technologies, Mr. Drexler is responsible for the creation of innovative software applications that will fulfill the specific needs of clients. Drawing on his vast technical knowledge gained from education and practical work experience, he handles projects from conception to implementation while effectively eliminating any problems that may occur. Mr. Drexler has been internally recognized for his numerous achievements within the Company, and is credited with the design of an innovative application that tracks inventory for customers. Enjoying the opportunities that accompany the challenges of his position, Mr. Drexler intends to continue in this capacity while aspiring to a management role within the corporate structure. HSB Reliaiblity Techonology is headquartered in Alexandria, Virginia, and maintains five other facilities throughout the United States. Presenting outsourced computerized maintenance management software solutions, the Company provides clients with access to the home server through the Internet or telephone lines. The Company specializes in preventative maintenance and factory consulting, offering resource, parts, and purchasing manager applications. These specific programs handle responsibilities such as the planning and scheduling of work orders, inventory control, and basic purchasing activities allowing staff to focus on daily activities instead of administrative tasks. **Career Highlights:** Sofware Developer, HSB Reliability Technology (1999-Present); Manager of Software Development, Penn, Schoen, & Berland Associates (1998-99); Software Engineering Intern, Xerox Corporation (1997-98). **Associations & Accomplishments:** Upsilon Pi Epsilon; Past President, American University College Democrats; Past President, American University College of Arts and Sciences. **Education:** The American University, B.S. in Computer Science (In Progress). **Personal Information:** Mr. Drexler enjoys travel and scuba diving.

Terry L. Drost

Network Administrator
Allgeier Martin & Associates
P.O. Box 2667
Joplin, MO 64803-2627
(417) 624-5703
Fax: (417) 624-7558
tdrost@clandjop.com

7379

Business Information: Utilizing the power of computers, Mr. Drost serves in the dual position of CAD Manager and Network Administrator of Allgeier, Martin & Associates. A successful, 16 year veteran in the technology field, he designs and develops the drafting and marketing for new projects, troubleshoots, and coordinates client education as well as customizes drafting software. Additionally, Mr. Drost oversees all drafting, computer, and networking administration duties for three microstations. At the same time, he oversees the final inspection of his design for the Pacific Railroad project and serves as a key member of the curriculum committee at Missouri Southern State College. Mr. Drost intends to continue his education, as well as expand networking and training of personnel for Allegeier, Martin & Associates. Established in 1954, Allegeier, Martin & Associates is a small engineering consulting firm. Headquartered in Joplin, Missouri, the Firm employs 130 individual to meet the demands of the local clientele. **Career Highlights:** Allgeier, Martin & Associates: Network Administrator (1992-Present), CAD Manager (1990-Present); CAD Manager, Benchmark Group (1984-90). **Associations & Accomplishments:** Beta Sigma Psi Fraternity; University of Nebraska Alumni Association. **Education:** Missouri Southern State College (1999); Creighton University; University of Nebraska. **Personal Information:** Married to Joann in 1992. Three children: Sarah, Kari, and Clay. Mr. Drost enjoys golf and hunting.

Sherry L. Dwyer, CPP

Software Support Manager
Optimum Solutions, Inc.
210 25th Avenue North, Suite 700
Nashville, TN 37203
(615) 329-2313
Fax: (615) 329-4448
sdwyer@optimum-solutions.com

7379

Business Information: Serving in her capacity as Software Support Manager for Optimum Solutions, Inc., Mrs. Dwyer draws upon her extensive background in computer based accounting and other similar areas. She provides timely and professional customer support services, does extensive research regarding proposed changes to the Corporation's software products, determines solutions to possible problem areas, and is also instrumental in customer training. Additionally, Mrs. Dwyer presides over all customer support personnel training and has oversight responsibilities for all facets of customer support. She is a Certified Payroll Professional and looks forward to further advancement in product development for NT based applications. Optimum Solutions, Inc. is a human resource software development and distribution company with a staff of 45 highly trained specialists. Established in 1994, the Corporation is based in Nashville, Tennessee and distributes IBM AS400 and Windows-based NT software applications throughout the United States, Canada, Puerto Rico, Africa, and Guam. **Career Highlights:** Software Support Manager, Optimum Solutions, Inc. (1994-Present); Office Manager, Management Service Group (1992-94); Account Executive, Automatic Data Processing (1991-92); Accountant, Corporate Child Care (1989-91). **Associations & Accomplishments:** Certified Payroll Professional; American Payroll Association. **Education:** M.T.S.U., B.B.A. (1982). **Personal Information:** Married to William M. in 1999. Mrs. Dwyer enjoys reading and swimming.

Dana Carl Ehlig

Consultant/Systems Engineer/Systems Administration/LAN Management
Dana Unlimited
872 Figueroa Drive
Altadena, CA 91001
(626) 292-0373
ehlig@ips.net

7379

Business Information: Possessing a wide variety of skills and talent in the fields of information technology and computer services, Mr. Ehlig has taken on and completed numerous consulting and contracting jobs. Serving in positions ranging from systems engineer to project coordinator, he has been instrumental in completing projects and contracts at or under budget while ensuring the work exceeds all specifications. With WANG/Getronics, he managed the roll-out and deployment of PC networks to three business centers. In 1999, at So Cal Edison, he coordinated the successful Y2K enterprise level server upgrade project. In his capacity as Desktop Network Support Case Manager with OAO Corporation, he managed the support for over 15 NASA flight teams and projects at the Jet Propulision Laboratory. With ALLTEL Information Services, he served for 5 years as the Operations Supervisor at a major national banking center. He enjoys making a difference and being of service. He looks forward to forging ahead into web administration and evolving with the new on-line technology. **Career Highlights:** Consultant/Systems Engineer/Administration/LAN Management, Dana Unlimited Consulting (1997-Present); Mobile Resource Representative, GETRONICS (1999-2000); DNS Case Manager, OAO Corp/JPL (1998-99); Operations Supervisor/Acting Operations Manager, ALLTEL Information Services (1992-97); Systems Sponsor/DBM Administration, Legal Personnel Inc. (So Cal Edison Litigation Support Contract) (1989-90); Section Group Supervisor, Information/Sterling Software, Viking Mars & Voyager Jupiter/Staturn Projects, JPL/NASA (1976-82). **Associations & Accomplishments:** American Red Cross, Health Services & Disaster Services Volunteer; California State Military Reserve, Installation Support Group, Los Alamitos AFRC, NCO Volunteer; ALLTEL Achievement Award for Service (1997), CalFed Center Manager's Award for centers first Superior Audit (1996), ALLTEL Employee of the Month (1995), CalFed Data Center Significant Contribution Award (1995), Alltel/Systematics Employee of the Month (1993), NASA Group Achievement Award, Voyger Flight Operations, General Science Data Team (1981). **Education:** Amer. Institute of Computer Sciences; New Horizons Computer Training Center; Certified Novell Administrator; Microsoft Certified Systems Engineer; Pasadena City College: Electro-Optics and Laser Technologist (1984), A.A. (1976). **Personal Information:** Married to Nina E. K. in 1981. One child: Elliott Justin. Mr. Ehlig enjoys geology, archeology, kayaking, minerology, hiking and backpacking, time with family and friends, photography, fishing, computers and the Internet and camping.

Charles E. Ellisor

Senior Project Manager/Systems Consultant
ENTEX Information Services
1205 Morningside Drive
Lufkin, TX 75904
(409) 634-9717
Fax: (409) 634-9718
cee001@lcc.net

7379

Business Information: As Senior Project Manager and Systems Consultant of ENTEX Information Systems, Mr. Ellisor presides over enterprise project design and implementation. Additionally, he fulfills a management capacity that includes full line consulting and outsourcing. As one of three people who handle the troubleshooting of information structure problems, Mr. Ellisor ensures all employees are aware of proper procedures and policies when carrying out repair tasks. He attributes his professional success to having integrity and commitment as well as being able to provide solutions. Always alert to new opportunities, techniques, and approaches, Mr. Ellisor looks forward to the progression of Web based technology within the Company. Established in 1982, ENTEX Information Services specializes in full line systems integration, network consulting, infrastructure design, and analysis for the PC environment. Employing over 5,000 people, annual sales currently exceeded $2 billion. At this time, ENTEX is the largest privately held systems intergration company in the United States. **Career Highlights:** Senior Project Manager/Systems Consultant, ENTEX Information Systems (1998-Present); District Services Operations Manager, Sears, Roebucks, & Company (1995-97); Engineer III, IBM (1991-95). **Associations & Accomplishments:** Rotary; Society of Broadcast Engineers; National Association of Broadcasters; Project Management Institute. **Education:** DeVry. **Personal Information:** Married to Pamela in 1991. Two children: Riley and Sean. Mr. Ellisor enjoys family time, being outdoors and photography.

Jeremy Elshire

Network Administrator
Ketel Thorsten Son, LLP
5140 Twilight Drive
Rapid City, SD 57709-6578
(605) 342-5630
Fax: (605) 342-2172
jeremy@ktllp.com

7379

Business Information: In his role as Network Administrator of Ketel Thorsten Son, LLP, Mr. Elshire oversees network access and systems integrity through the stellar maintenance of both hardware and software. Demonstrating extensive knowledge of the field, he handles troubleshooting for all systems and services including personal computers, fax machines, and telephones. Internally recognized for his valuable contributions to the operations of the Company, Mr. Elshire intends to continue in his current role as he furthers his education. His future endeavors include graduating with a Bachelor's degree in Computer Science, move into administration integration, and obtaining his certification in Novell and Cisco. Remaining on the cutting edge of technology and surrounding him with supportive professionals are reasons for Mr. Elshire's career success to date. Ketel Thorsten Son, LLC is a financial consulting firm, located in Rapid City, South Dakota's business center. The Firm offers certified financial accounting services to assist with the completion of taxes and auditing requests. K.T. Connecting, the parent company, offers information systems management services to local businesses. Operating together, these two progressive companies provide outstanding financial and technical support services to the professional community. **Career Highlights:** Network Administrator, Ketel Thorsten Son, LLP (1999-Present); Co-Manager, SDSM&T (1997-99); Cook, Royal Fork Buffet (1994-97). **Associations & Accomplishments:** Vice President, Association of Computing Machinery Local Chapter; Aircraft Owners and Pilot Association; I.V.C F. **Education:** South Dakota School of Mines and Technology, C.S.C. (In Progress).

Samuel G. Emory

Owner/Consultant
SGE Consulting
8534 Headford Road
Charlotte, NC 28277
(704) 904-1698
semory@carolins.rr.com

7379

Business Information: The Owner of SGE Consulting, Mr. Emory assumes the responsibilities of Consultant. In this capacity, he designs, codes, and implements system programs which increase the functionality of existing software utilized within client companies. One such program which was recently implemented by a customer added functions to the existing billing system. The system now serves a much larger client base than the old configuration allowed, and can provide a broader account history, as well as relational data links to other areas of the company's global database. Mr. Emory is very glad to have been interested in satellite technologies at the earliest stages of its development, as he now has a solid background on which to build toward state-of-the-art multimedia technologies now exploding into the world of communications. He anticipates similar advances in the demand for his services as clients venture into the leading technologies of that segment of the industry. Accumulating over 15 solid years of experience and with a firm educational background, Mr. Emory also formulates the Company's vision and develops innovative technology, business, and marketing strategies. His favorite advice to others is "Try to think outside of the nine dots." Established in 1996, SGE Consulting provides information technology consulting throughout the Charlotte, North Carolina region. SGE specializes in computer systems technologies, business applications, and data management issues. In addition, the Company offers business operational analysis and project management for a variety of industrial, corporate, and medium-sized businesses. One of the Company's principal clients at this time is DirectTV. SGE Consulting posts annual revenues of more than $100,000. **Career Highlights:** Owner/Consultant, SGE Consulting (1996-Present); Project Manager/Analyst, DBS Systems Corporation (1993-96); Application Manager, NCC Systems Inc. (1983-93). **Education:** University of North Carolina at Charlotte, B.S. (1980). **Personal Information:** Married to Meredith in 1978. Two children: Arwen and Philip. Mr. Emory enjoys electronics.

Richard L. English

President/Owner
Anglais Consulting Inc.
5224 West State Road 46, #413
Sanford, FL 32771
(407) 257-2400
richenglish@worldnet.att.net

7379

Business Information: Combining strategic management skills and consulting expertise, Mr. English ventured out on his own to start Anglais Consulting Inc. in 1998. As Owner, he assumes the responsibilities of President. In his capacity, he exercises oversight of all aspects of project planning and computer programming, design, testing, and documentation. Mr. English, relying on over 25 solid years of experience in the field, develops and designs powerful strategic and tactical marketing and business plans. Identifying new markets and service opportunities as well as maintaining personalized client relations also falls within the realm of his overall responsibilities. Starting with the United States Army Corps of Engineers, he has three years active military time, three years reserve time, and 19 years as a reserve officer. An accomplished professional with a consistent record of delivering results, he has taught technology courses at business colleges and in the United States Army Reserves. Heading into the 21st Century, he hopes to continue to work in the same line of business and become more involved in engineering activities. Anglais Consulting Inc. provides computer consulting for financial institutions. Primarily, the Company offers services to banks, savings and loan institutions, and credit unions. Located in Florida, the Company's international service offerings include maintenance, upgrades, and user modifications to mainframe software. **Career Highlights:** President/Owner, Anglais Consulting Inc. (1998-Present); Consultant, Hurst Companies (1996-98); Consultant, Citibank Singapore (1994-96); Programmer, National City Bank (1990-94); Alltel/Systematics Inc. (1984-90). **Associations & Accomplishments:** Reserve Officer Association; Veterans of Foreign Wars; Seminole County Chamber of Commerce; First Christian Church of Longwood. **Education:** Fort Hays Kansas State University, B.S. in Business (1976); Military Command and General Staff. **Personal Information:** Married to Jeanine in 1973. Mr. English enjoys water skiing, snow skiing , travel and visiting Hard Rock Cafés. In addition, he also enjoys collecting art by Wyland, America's leading environmental marine life artist.

Bjorn Enroth

Systems Engineer/Consultant
Dotcom Solutions AB
Box 4029
Solna, Sweden 17104
+46 708996363
Fax: +46 708996353
bjorn@enroth.nu

7379

Business Information: Focusing on network security, Mr. Enroth serves as Systems Engineer and Consultant of Dotcom Solutions AB. A successful, 16-year professional, he works closely with management and users to provide technical and analytical advice in the design of network infrastructures. In the role of technical consultant for the Company, Mr. Enroth contributes his experience and expertise in the industry to provide troubleshooting of network usage and developmental services including resolving LAN and WAN and Internet and Intranet communictions problems. Dedicating his career to the information technology field, he is continuing his education in Cisco, presently completing the highest level of training made available. Mr. Enroth attributes his success to the enjoyment of his work. "Don't do tomorrow what you can do today," is cited as his advice. Catering to the specific demands of medium and large size corporations, Dotcom Solutions provides the construction and maintenance of enterprise computer networks. Operating from 60 locations in Sweden, the Company employs over 800 information technology professionals to perform the extensive tasks of network management. Headquartered in Solna, Sweden, Dotcom Solutions draws on over a decade of customer service and satisfaction to provide the highest quality professional business available on the market. **Career Highlights:** Systems Engineer/Consultant, Dotcom Solutions AB (1995-Present); Systems Engineer, Vexa Svenska AB (1990-95); Engineer, Mobitmontage i Sverige AB (1984-90). **Education:** Cisco Certified Network Associate (2000); Checkpoint Certified Security Expert (1999). **Personal Information:** Married to Josefin in 1997. Four children: Erika, Dennis, Jesper, and Linus.

Regina M. Farage

Chief Executive Officer
Creative Computers & Networking, Inc.
77-72nd Street
Brooklyn, NY 11209
(718) 745-3963
Fax: (718) 745-3963
(718) 745-8186

7379

Business Information: As Chief Executive Officer for Creative Computers & Networking, Inc.; Ms. Farage exercises oversight of the day-to-day operations of the Corporation. She handles all financial matters including payroll, purchases, receivables, and investments. Ms. Farage directly supervises and assigns work to the eight employees of Creative Computers & Networking. She and her staff design and develop customized software and package the product for marketing on the Internet. One of the highlights of her career involved the design of an explosion-proof enclosure to house computers in a hazardous environment. The product was well received in the industry and a patent is pending. Ms. Farage focuses significant attention on new client development and hopes to continue expanding her customer base. Established in 1994, Creative Computers & Networking, Inc. is a computer consulting firm located in Brooklyn, New York. The Corporation markets hardware and software for custom configurations that serve the needs of clients from a wide range of business and individual interest areas. Additionally, the Corporation designs and markets training programs for standard and customized products, as well as providing help desk resources for clients. **Career Highlights:** Chief Executive Officer, Creative Computers & Networking, Inc. (1994-Present); Senior Consultant/Education Instructor, Oracle Corporation (1997); Project Manager, Merck & Company, Inc. (1990-97); Computer Programmer/Instructor, Pfizer Inc. (1989). **Associations & Accomplishments:** National Association of Female Executives. **Education:** Polytechnic University, B.S. in Electrical Engineering and Computer Science (1990); New York University. **Personal Information:** Ms. Farage is artistically inclined and has sold pictures at art shows.

Chuck Fender

Owner
Wazoo's Computers
P.O. Box 454
Alamogordo, NM 88311
(505) 434-5090
Fax: (505) 437-2265
chuck@wazoo.com

7379

Business Information: Mr. Fender is the Founder and Owner of Wazoo's Computers in Alamogordo, New Mexico. Overseeing the daily activites of the Company, he is responsible for all aspects of operations. Mr. Fender handles all procurement for the Company, including the negotiation of contracts with vendors. Serving a human resources role, he recruits and hires staff and trains them on technical issues. Completing all financial reports, he approves payroll and maintains accounts payable and receivable. Crediting his success to his grasp on the ever changing technology in today's progressive society, Mr. Fender intends to continue in his current capacity while initiating plans for growth and expansion. His advice is "do the research and preparation." Established in 1994, Wazoo's Computers provides Internet services to local residents, small to large businesses, and government agencies. Employing three dedicated people, the Company also offers Web hosting. **Career Highlights:** Owner, Wazoo's Computers (1994-Present). **Education:** Chapman College, Associate's degree (1984). **Personal Information:** Married to Janice in 1992. Two children: Stacie and Jessica.

Wendy Q. Feng, Ph.D.

Product Manager
Tom Sawyer Software
804 Hearst Avenue
Berkeley, CA 94710
(510) 665-3007
Fax: (510) 848-0854
wfeng@tomsawyer.com

7379

Business Information: Possessing an excellent understanding in technology, Dr. Feng joined Tom Sawyer Software as Product Manager in 1999. Her responsibilities include managing all phases of Microsoft product development including requirement analysis, architectural design, implementation, and quality assurance. Enjoying her prominence with Tom Sawyer Software, Dr. Feng continues to assist in the completion of corporate goals. Highly regarded, her career highlights include attaining her Ph.D. in Computer Science from the University of Newcastle in 1997 and receiving the "Best Computer Science Thesis of the Year" award from the Australian Computer Science Association. Caring deeply about the kind of work she produces, she aspires to develop useful products in the future. Established in 1991, Tom Sawyer Software is a software technology company that is the leading provider of relational information visualization solutions to areas of telecommunication, networking, data mining, process modeling, bioinformatics, and criminal analysis. Located in Berkeley, California, the Company employs 50 individuals to facilitate day-to-day operations. **Career Highlights:** Tom Sawyer Software: Product Manager (1999-Present), Research Staff Member (1997-99); Assistant Professor, East China Institute of Technology (1991-93). **Associations & Accomplishments:** Professional Member, Association for Computing Machinery; Institute of Electrical and Electronics Engineers; Institute of Electrical and Electronics Engineers Computer Society; New York Academy of Sciences; Silicon Valley Software Developer Forum; Best Computer Science Ph.D. Dissertation Award (1997), Australian Computer Science Association. **Education:** University of Newcastle, Ph.D. in Computer Science (1997); East China Institute of Technology, M.S. in Computer Science (1991); Nanjing University, B.S. in Computer Science (1988). **Personal Information:** Married to Huaizhong Li in 1991. Dr. Feng enjoys cooking, music and tennis.

Joseph R. Filippone

Consultant
Lead Trac
865 Pomeroy Avenue 313B
Santa Clara, CA 95051
(650) 655-4682
Fax: (209) 796-8450
joseph_filippone@usa.net

7379

Business Information: Serving as Consultant of Lead Track, Mr. Filippone works closely with management and systems users to analyze, specify, and design new solutions to harness more of the computer's power. In his capacity, he engages in various tasks including managing databases, overssing administrative duties, and directing installation and implementation of software. Possessing superior talents and an excellent understanding of technology, Mr. Filippone utilizes several years of hands on experience in technical positions to help the Company maintain a competitive edge in the markets. Currently, Mr. Filippone is working towards his Oracle DBA certification. His success reflect his ability to think outside the box, aggressively tackle new challenges, and deliver results on behalf of the Company and its clientele. Established in 1992, Lead Track currently employs a staff of 30. Recently the Company was been purchased by E-Partners and now reports annual revenues in excess of $1 million. The company operates as a consulting firm offering advice on sales logics and software implementation and customization. **Career Highlights:** Consultant, Lead Track (1999-Present); Manager, Micro Center Education (1999); Assistant Director, Hofstra University (1995-98). **Education:** Hofstra University, M.B.A. (1998); Oracle Database certified (In Progress). **Personal Information:** Mr. Filippone enjoys weightlifting, soccer and dancing.

Kenneth W. Finley, Jr.

Performance Measurement Analyst
Check Point Software Technology Ltd.
10822 Quest Drive
Frisco, TX 75035
(817) 606-6621
kwfinley@ts.checkpoint.com

7379

Business Information: As Performance Measurement Analyst at Check Point Software Technology Ltd., Mr. Finley designs and validates job performance models. He is directly responsible for Checkpoint's certified network security program and conducts intricate knowledge tests to judge the design of the models. Using his extensive technical knowledge and communication skills, he is recognized as a leader in the industry and offers training classes in teaming, instructional design, training skills, supervision, and software tools. A motivated, self-directed learner, Mr. Finley is continually revising his problem solving approach to include new information and current technology updates. Currently completing extensive research on internet based learning, Mr. Finley is working to complete his Ph.D. as he advances through the corporate structure. The number one provider of firewall hardware and software, Check Point Software Technology Ltd. secures server transmissions through technical solutions including Firewall-1, FloodGate, and Meta 1P. Established in 1993, the international company focuses time and resources on network management services and employs over 1,000 nationwide. **Career Highlights:** Performance Measurement Analyst, Check Point Software Technology Ltd. (Present); Associate Professor, Collin County Community College (1995-Present); Senior Analyst, Consulting Partners (1998-99); Senior Analyst, Texas

Instruments (1979-96). **Associations & Accomplishments:** International Society of Performance Improvement; American Society for Training and Development; SALT; Association for Educational Communications and Technology. **Education:** University of North Texas: Ph.D. in ATTD with Minor in Psychology (In Progress), M.S. in Computer Education & Cognitive Systems (1992); West Virginia University, B.A. in Speech Communication (1976). **Personal Information:** Married to Dorothy L. in 1975. Two children: Caitlin Michelle and Brian Cameron. Mr. Finley enjoys camping, hunting, water sports, reading and writing, scouting and church activities.

Kevin A. Fitzgerald

President/Chief Executive Officer
Cynrede Inc.
23161 Lake Center Drive, Suite 125
Lake Forest, CA 92630-6803
(949) 829-9028
Fax: (949) 829-9029
cynrede@aol.com

7379

Business Information: The founder of Cynrede Inc., Mr. Fitzgerald serves as President and Chief Executive Officer. Assuming responsibility for the corporate management, he also works personally with his clients. As a 12 year professional, he determines the overall strategic direction and business contribution of the information systems function. In his present capacity, he devotes attention to marketing the Corporation in an effort to increase the number of current projects and looks forward to future expansion of overall operations. Currently holding the rights to two patents, he has been published internationally and attributes his success thus far to his ability to focus on his goals. He advises others to be open minded, learn as much as possible, and talk with as many people as you can. Mr. Fitzgerald plans to expand his Corporation and take on a more administrative role. Cynrede Inc. provides document imaging, backfile conversions, and information management consulting to various types of businesses including title companies, the banking industry, and state and local governments. Founded in 1998, the Corporation performs the majority of its work from virtual locations through the program ILoc. Currently, Cynrede Inc. serves companies on a national level through seven locations. **Career Highlights:** President/Chief Executive Officer, Cynrede Inc (1998-Present); Vice President of Asia Pacific, Anacomp Inc. (1996-98); Vice President of Product Development, COM Products (1987-96). **Associations & Accomplishments:** Association of Information and Image Management. **Education:** University of Phoenix. **Personal Information:** Married to Anne in 1994. One child: Brian. Mr. Fitzgerald enjoys scuba diving and kayaking.

Michael G. Fitzgerald

Network Engineer
Road Runner
25-20 Brooklyn-Queens Expressway
Woodside, NY 11377
(718) 267-5251
Fax: (718) 721-2296
mfitzgerald@va.rr.com

7379

Business Information: Demonstrating his expertise in this highly specialized field, Mr. Fitzgerald serves Road Runner as a Network Engineer, providing complete monitoring of the network infrastructure, maintaining its functionality, scalability, and operational status. Operating out of a Regional Network Operations Center in Woodside, New York, the Network encompasses an area serving New York City, providing residential and commercial customers with a high-speed broadband Internet content solution using cable modem technology deployed over Time Warner Cable's vast hybrid fiber and coaxial cable infrastructure. IP management, network traffic analysis, affiliate support, and the design, development, and implementation of software solutions include some of the responsibilities Mr. Fitzgerald holds in maintaining the advanced network. Peering with major Internet service providers, Road Runner routes high-speed traffic to and from its almost one million subscribers nationally. Headquartered in Herndon, Virginia, the Company is a joint venture between a number of media and technology groups, including Microsoft Corporation, Compaq Computer Corporation, AT&T, and Time Warner Inc. Always alert to new opportunities, he concentrates on the further advancement of the Company and the products and services it provides. Continually striving for maximum effectiveness, Mr. Fitzgerald is currently pursuing his Master's degree in Electrical Engineering and his Cisco certification to enable him to capitalize on the opportunities afforded by Road Runner. His success is attributed to strong support from his wife and parents, and his strong personal drive. He graduated with Magna Cum Laude honors in 1996 with a Bachelor of Science degree in Electrical Engineering boasting a 4.0 GPA. **Career Highlights:** Network Engineer, Road Runner (2000-Present); Senior Headend Engineer, Time Warner Cable (1999-00). **Associations & Accomplishments:** Eta Kappa Nu Honor Society; Nu Ypsilon Tau Honor Society; Who's Who of American Students (1995); Louis Liss Presidential Award for Academic Achievement (1996). **Education:** New York Institute of Technology, B.S. in Electrical Engineering (1996); Limerick Regional Technical College, Ireland, Diploma in Electronic Engineering (1987). **Personal Information:** Married to Mary. Mr. Fitzgerald enjoys soccer, golf, snooker and working out at the gym.

Frank Flowers Jr.

Technician
Federated Systems Group
680 Austin Road
Ellenwood, GA 30294-3201
(678) 474-2282
fflowersjr@mindspring.com

7379

Business Information: Drawing on his love of computers, Mr. Flowers fulfills the daily acitivities of Management Information Systems Manager. In this capacity, he designs sophisticated client server applications and develops and maintains data programs using IBM's DB2 database package. Additionally, Mr. Flowers creates and pulls data for the inventory systems team as well as performs research into new technology products. Boasting a career highlight of completing the EET training, he plans on keeping the Group on the bleeding edge and out-front of competitors in the industry. In the future, Mr. Flowers plans on broadening his knowledge base, obtaining his Oracle certification, and exploring other advanced applications. His professional success reflects his ability to deliver results and take on new challenges. Established in 1989, Federated Systems Group is the information technology division of the Federated Department Stores, Inc. The Group provides technical support and design services for Federated Department Store such as Bloomingdales, Maces, and many more. Based in Georgia, Federated Systems Group employs 2,000 individuals. **Career Highlights:** Management Information Systems Manager, Federated Systems Group (1998-Present). **Associations & Accomplishments:** Association of Computing Machinery. **Education:** Mercer University, B.S. (1998). **Personal Information:** Mr. Flowers enjoys bowling, coin collecting, and movies, arts, and theater.

Janice Forrester

Director of Strategic and Analytical Services
Cytera Systems
4318 Northeast Glisan Street
Portland, OR 97213-1642
(503) 235-4481
janicef@hevanet.com

7379

Business Information: A respected professional, Mrs. Forrester serves as the Director of Strategic and Analytical Services for Cytera Systems. She presides over all aspects of project management for the software development team, providing training, troubleshooting, and assistance with implementation. Additionally, she supervises the project's design and marketing issues. She oversees the consultants and assists them with their work. Mrs. Forrester recently rebuilt the Budget Department and was largely responsible for the creation of Strategic and Analytical Services Department. Crediting her success to her education and listening skills, she is currently pursing her Doctorate. Continually formulating new goals and objectives, she looks forward to future professional challenges. A prominent information technology consulting company in the United States, Cytera Systems provides a variety of services for its high level executive clients. The Company offers strategic consulting and bench market analysis to assist its business clients become more competitive within each one's respective markets utilizing technology. Customized software development is provided according to individual needs and the 20-member staff in Portland, Oregon also offers technical support. Cytera Systems has three locations to better serve its clients. **Career Highlights:** Director of Strategic and Analytical Services, Cytera Systems (1996-Present); Director of Strategic Analysis, Best Buy Company Inc. (1994-96); Statistical Analyst, National Institute for Occupational Safety and Health (1993-94). **Associations & Accomplishments:** American Statistical Association; Society for Industrial and applied Mathematics; Mathematical Association of America; Institute for Operations Research and Management Sciences; Productivity Analysis Research Network; National Association of Female Engineers. **Education:** Portland State University, Ph.D. (In Progress); Pennsylvania State University, Master's degree in Engineering and Technology Management; Miami University, Master's degree in Mathematics and Statistics. **Personal Information:** Married to Roger Joys in 1998. Three children: Nicole, Erin, and Drew. Mrs. Forrester enjoys rock climbing, biking and racing crew boats.

Steven W. Fox

President
Onyx Solutions, Inc.
350 Windermere Circle
Newnan, GA 30625
(770) 304-5773
onyxsolutions@mindspring.com

7379

Business Information: A respected professional within the information technology field, Mr. Fox brings more than 20 years of experience to his position as President of Onyx Solution, Inc. Also the owner, Mr. Fox created the Corporation to be the realization of his dream to have the freedom to be his own boss. He makes all of the decisions affecting the Corporation's operations as well as performs consulting on SAP software and develops customized interfaces for clients. Mr. Fox is currently working with Coca Cola Enterprise. A certified SAP SDMM configurer, he has completed eight full cycle implementations of SAP to date. He advises other potential entreprenuers, "Get as much experiences as you can in your area of expertise if you want to start a business." Staying on the cutting edge of technology through continuous training and self study, Mr. Fox attributes his professional success to his persistence and perfectionism. Established in 1999, Onyx Solutions, Inc. offers its services to area businesses as a software consultancy. The Corporation provides local small to mid-size businesses in Atlanta, Georgia and the surrounding communities with expert advice regarding their SAP software. Some Fortune 500 companies also rely upon the Corporation's expertise. A knowledgable staff of two consultants is employed, generating an estimated $280,000 turnover for the Corporation's first year of business. **Career Highlights:** President, Onyx Solutions, Inc. (1999-Present); Senior Software Consultant, Whittman-Hart (1996-99); Systems Analyst, Georgia-Pacific (1978-96). **Education:** University of Arkansas, B.S. in Computer Science (1990). **Personal Information:** Married to Vickie L. in 1980. Two children: Jason W. and Miranda L. Mr. Fox enjoys hunting, fishing, travel and gardening.

Ben Allen Francis

Senior Director - Business Solution Methodology
CreMoS Partners
P.O. Box 294482
Lewisville, TX 75029-4482
(972) 221-2736
ben_francis@cremosp.com

7379

Business Information: As Senior Director of Business Solution Methodology, Mr. Francis is providing leadership in the arenas of business and technology consulting, client communications, technology implementation, systems delivery, and services in the telecommunications and non-profit arenas. He provides direction in the area of application platform design, exercising oversight of system integration and application testing. He serves, in addition, as a methodology implementation consultant, working closely with design teams to assess practical application on highly complex electronic transactions through system architectures. Mr. Francis relies on almost 20 years of experience in the telecommunications industry as well as his involvement with non-profit organizations for over 15 years in his decision-making processes; this experience is the key to his status as an industry change pioneer. One of the highlights of Mr. Francis' career was leading the multi-corporate team through the design and implementation of inter-company compensation systems for the local exchange carriers (LECs) and the Texas Public Utility Commission (PUC). Another highlight is his involvement in the design, implementation, and support of the systems environments that enabled an international telecommunications firm's entry and success in both the long-distance and Competitive Local Exchange Carrier (CLEC) markets while successfully implementing spiral, fusion, and pattern methodologies. Mr. Francis currently is pioneering his developed methodology in CreMoS Partners' consulting engagements with multiple clients. CreMoS Partners, the name for the firm created from the consolidation of several firms to form the single entity, is delivering world-class business solution methodologies that result in business process development, integration, and implementation, as well as system integration and solutions for multiple platforms. Concentrating in the telecommunications and banking industries, CreMoS is initiating its expansion to deliver strong methodology-based solutions to non-profit agencies. **Career Highlights:** Senior Director - Business Solution Methodology, CreMoS Partners (1999-Present); Domain Expert, GTE (1997-99); Project Lead, GTE Long Distance (1996-97); Business Process Expert, GTE Telephone Operations (1994-96). **Associations & Accomplishments:** Board of Directors (1996-98), Lewisville Lake Symphony; Board of Directors (1990-93), San Angelo Civic Ballet; Board of Directors (1981-93), San Angelo Symphony Society. **Education:** Austin College, B.A. in Business Administration (1977); University of Texas at Austin Graduate School of Business, Postgraduate study. **Personal Information:** Married to Beverly Lois in 1985. Two children: Matthew and Sarah. Mr. Francis is a classically trained violinist and composer as well as a writer of science fiction. He is currently organizing works for submission to be published.

Braden S. Franklin

Owner
Third Wave Services
1034 Riviera Street
Jacksonville, FL 32207
(904) 288-1504
Fax: (904) 288-2930
braden@3rdmail.com

7379

Business Information: Utilizing an extensive knowledge in the computer field, Mr. Franklin is the Owner of Third Wave Services. In his position, he determines the overall strategic direction and business contribution of the systems functions. He meets with the management staff of client companies to discuss the specific needs of the business. Then, Mr. Franklin analyzes the specifications and advises them on technology that best meets their requiremens. Moreover, he conducts the design, implmentation, and setup of the programs and provides all maintanance and upgrades as needed. Mr. Franklin displays a hard working and dedicated attitude towards his work and enjoys what he does. In the future, he looks forward to getting more involved with project management. Additionally, Mr. Franklin works for Bombardier Capital in network administration where he is responsible for maintaining backups and providing technical support. Founded in 1992, Third Wave Services is a computer consulting firm that works mainly with small to medium sized clients. Located in Jacksonville, Florida, the Company provides a variety of consulting services for all the needs and wants of their clients. Operating on a regional level, the Company has a staff of four professionals who are committed to supplying clients with the best possible advice and achieving complete client satisfaction. **Career Highlights:** Owner, Third Wave Services (1992-Present); Senior Technical Specialist, Bombardier Capital (1999-Present). **Associations & Accomplishments:** Volunteer, Provides Housing and Education for the Underprivelaged. **Education:** London University, B.S. (1982). **Personal Information:** Mr. Franklin enjoys being a nutritionalist and weight lifting.

Stephen J. Fredette

President
Electronic Systems Associates
11 West 42nd Street, 3rd Floor
New York, NY 10036
(212) 843-3601

7379

Business Information: Demonstrating more than 15 years of expertise in the information technology industry, Mr. Fredette serves as President for the Electronic Systems Associates. His primary responsibilities are sales and marketing to promote the Company and internal administration functions. A system consultant, he also spends time consulting with clients regarding their computer systems. Before being recruited to Electronic Systems Associates, he served as Chief Operating Officer for Donnelly Enterprise Solutions. His background history also includes stints as Vice President and General Manager and Executive Director of Sales for LANsystems, Inc. Mr. Fredette has a passionate love for his field and an appreciation for all facets of each individual company he has worked for. He states that you have to understand the technology and people in order to be successful. A turnaround specialist, he looks forward to expanding the Company either internationally or by going public. A subsidiary of Cyska & Hennesey, Electronic Systems Associates is an international provider of information technology consulting and engineering services. The Company focuses on computer and security networks and offers project management for its clientele. A single source provider of six low voltage services, Electronic Systems Associates proffered services include voice, data, and audio visual as well as intelligent building, fire, and life safety systems. Over 80 individuals are engaged in daily operations. The Company was established in 1986. **Career Highlights:** President, Electronic Systems Associates (1998-Present); Chief Operating Officer, Donnelly Enterprises Solutions (1997-98); LANsystems, Inc.: Vice President/General Manager (1993-97), Executive Director of Sales (1991-93). **Education:** Siena College, B.S. in Finance (1982). **Personal Information:** Married to Christine in 1991. Three children: Sean, Peter, and Catherine. Mr. Fredette enjoys golf and spending time with his family.

Richard Freedman

Chief Executive Officer
Consulting Strategies
8603 Redbud Lane
Shawnee Mission, KS 66220
(913) 422-8214

7379

Business Information: As Chief Executive Officer of Consulting Strategies, Mr. Freedman oversees all aspects of the business he founded. Coupling his business savvy with extensive technical knowledge, he is able to handle information technology consulting issues with ease. Consistently devleoping creative action plans, he meets with clients and acts as a model representation of the Company. A published author, Mr. Freedman is recognized throughout the industry as a capable, gifted leader in his field. Focusing time and attention on the geographical expansion of the Company to the East Coast, he looks forward to continual success and prosperity in his current role. Established in 1998 in Shawnee Mission, Kansas, Consulting Strategies currently employs three technically inclined people. The Company is engaged in information technology consulting and project management, offering innovative solutions to local businesses. Annual revenues exceed $650,000, proving that the growing company has upheld the mission statement of value, integrity, and quality products and services. **Career Highlights:** Chief Executive Officer, Consulting Strategies (1998-Present); Regional Consulting Manager, Entex Consulting Services (1995-99); Principal Consultant, Cap Gemini Consulting (1992-95); Network Manager, Dun and Bradstreet (1990-92). **Associations & Accomplishments:** Independent Computer Consultants Association; The Author's Guild. **Education:** Kingsborough College, A.A.S. (1985).

John C. Fremont

Senior Computer Specialist
Systems Support Alternatives, Inc.
14502 Greenview Drive #500
Laurel, MD 20703
(703) 607-7398
Fax: (703) 522-8316
fremontj@digizen.net

7379

Business Information: As Senior Computer Specialist of Systems Support Alternatives, Inc., Mr. Fremont is responsible for UNIX systems administration, Informix database administration and 4GL development, and hardware, software, and network configuration and management. As a 12 year computer science professional, Mr. Fremont provides on-site support to clients, including the National Guard Bureau located in Arlington, Virginia. Overseeing database applications development and screening telephone calls and resumes, he is in charge of all daily maintenance of the intricate interoffice network system. "Keeping a general overview of the industry and stay up to date with emerging technology," is cited as Mr. Fremont's advice to others. Receiving many informal internal recognition, he attributes his success to his curiosity and never accepting defeat. His goals are to stay in technology and move into a role that would accentuate his leadership talents. Systems Support Alternatives, Inc. is a privately owned business that offers services throughout the United States, but is concentrated in the East Coast and works primarily with Government agencies. Established in 1989, the Corporation contracts information technology support systems, primarily help desk functions. The Corporation also offers programming services and specializes in providing Microsoft solutions. National in scope, the Corporation operates branch offices across the United States. Presently, 100 personnel is employed at the Laurel, Maryland location. **Career Highlights:** Senior Computer Specialist, Systems Support Alternatives, Inc. (1996-Present); Contract Consultant, New Boston Systems, Inc. (1996); PC Specialist, Mid-Atlantic Medical Services, Inc. (1995-96). **Associations & Accomplishments:** Life Member, National Guard Bureau Alumni Association; Army National Guard Retiree. **Education:** Strayer University, degree in Information Systems Management (In Progress); Hawkeye Institute of Technology; Buena Vista College. **Personal Information:** Mr. Fremont enjoys reading, biking and gourmet cooking.

Paul Charles Fry

Senior Applications Consultant
Prime Systems, Inc.
13012 Terminal Avenue
Cleveland, OH 44135
paul_fry@email.msn.com

7379

Business Information: Serving as Senior Applications Consultant for Prime Systems, Mr. Fry is contracted by businesses to perform an analysis of its current system and its needs. Performing specification development and the allocation of resources, he determines how long the project will take and the necessary tools for completion. Mr. Fry works closely with each of his clients and customizes each system to the client's unique situations and needs, administering the new system's integration with the client's other existing systems. Coordinating resources, schedules, time lines, and assignments also fall within the realm of Mr. Fry's responsibilities. In 1994, he received recognition for integrating a customized program which resulted in the client saving a great deal of money. Attributing his success to hard work, faith in God, and continued involvement in the technology industry, Mr. Fry plans to continue to broaden and expand his knowledge of the everchanging technology field. Prime Systems, Inc. is a privately owned programming services consulting firm specializing in manufacturing Enterprise Database Systems such as MFG/PRO, Glovia, Progress, and Oracle on large and midrange systems. Established in 1992 and serving clients internationally from a single location in Cleveland, Ohio, operations consist of a 25 member staff. **Career Highlights:** Senior Applications Consultant, Prime Systems, Inc. (1998-Present); Software Consultant, Progressive Systems Consulting (1997-98); Programmer, Decision Resources, Inc. (1994-97). **Associations & Accomplishments:** APICS, Cleveland Chapter. **Education:** Grove City College; University of Pittsburgh. **Personal Information:** Mr. Fry enjoys marathon running.

Horst Fuhrmann

Chief Executive Officer/President
Skypro AG
Gewerbestrasse 7
Cham Zug, Switzerland 6330
+41 417414770
Fax: +41 417415071
horst@skypro.ch

7379

Business Information: As the Founder of Skypro AG, Mr. Fuhrmann functions in the dual role of Chief Executive Officer and President. He oversees and directs all aspects of day-to-day administration and operations of the Company, ensuring that activities function smoothly and without incident. A savvy, 13 year professional, he determines the overall strategic direction and formulates business and marketing plans to keep Skykpro on the leading edge within the technolgoy field. To maximize profits, Mr. Fuhrmann develops all the methodologies and concepts needed to keep the company on its projected path. In addition, he accounts for the fiscal budget, keeping the Company financially secure and not over-budget. As for the future, Mr. Fuhrmann plans to expand and develop the Company, watching it prosper into a leader within the industry. His success reflects his ability to build teams with synergy, technical strength, and a customer oriented attitude, as well as deliver results. Established in 1987, Skypro AG is involved in computer networking, Internet operations, Internet television and video technologies, boadcasting, and a variety of other functions. Building on years of experience, 30 employees have all contributed greatly to an estimated annual sales figure of $5 million. **Career Highlights:** Chief Executive Officer/President, Skypro AG (1987-Present). **Education:** Florida Tech, M.Sc. (1986). **Personal Information:** Married in 1991.

Allyson Fulmer

Director of Recruiting
SCB Computer Technology, Inc.
950 North Point Parkway, Suite 300
Alpharetta, GA 30005
(770) 346-7778
Fax: (770) 346-7746
afulmer@scb.com

7379

Business Information: Ms. Fulmer oversees and directs day-to-day operations of one of SCB's Computer Technology, Inc.'s eight regions. Fulfilling the accountability of Director of Recruiting, her area of responsibility includes all of North Carolina, South Carolina, Georgia, and ALabama. In her directorship role, Ms. Fulmer manages a staff of eight recruiters who are always searching for talented information technology professionals to staff projects. With some recruiting responsibilities, Ms. Fulmer also maintains and updates the Corporation's Web site. She has played a major role in transitioning the Corporation from the traditional recruiting methods to using the Internet in it's search for information technology professionals. As for the future, Ms. Fulmer future goals include assuming a larger role in the evolvement of virtual career fairs and video interviewing. She attributes her success to her organiztional skills and ability to remain complete multiple tasks. Established in 1976, SBC Computer Technology, Inc. offers consulting services, e-commerce solutions, and professional staffing services. Many of the Corporations clients include Fortune 500 companies and governmental agencies. The Coorporation's stock went public in 1976. Presently, SCB Computer Technology reports annual revenues in excess of $150 million. The Corporation employs 12,000 professional, technical, and support personnel in six regions across the United States. **Career Highlights:** Director of Recruiting, SCB Computer Technology, Inc. (1998-Present); Sales and Recruiting Manager, Executemp Training Resources (1997-98); Account Executive, MSI International (1996-97); Human Resources Manager, Pearson & Smithart (1989-96). **Associations & Accomplishments:** Society of Human Resources; Southeast Employment Network. **Education:** University of Alabama, M.A. (1996).

Shakil Sattar Gagan

Chief Information Officer
Texas Micro Computers
220 East Spring Valley Road
Richardson, TX 75081
(972) 699-3100
Fax: (972) 699-3103
tmcomp@flash.net

7379

Business Information: Dedicated to the success of Texas Micro Computers, Mr. Gagan applies his knowledge and expertise in the field of information technology and business management in serving as Chief Information Officer. He determines the policies and procedures which determine the Company's conduct of business and assumes responsibility for its strategic vision. Working closely with his staff of nine qualified professionals, he utilizes a management style that incorporates input and feedback from all personnel members. Mr. Gagan attributes his current success to his previous practical experience and his parents, wife, and children. He looks forward to publicly trading Texas Micro Computers. Texas Micro Computers specializes in Web development and hosting, providing Web maintenance, networking, interfacing, and connecting services. Also a manufacturer of computer hardware components, the Company installs cabling upgrades and implements automation equipment. The Company sells its products internationally, providing after sales technical support to clients. Texas Micro Computers was created in 1995 and now employs a staff of nine skilled professionals. **Career Highlights:** Chief Information Officer, Texas Micro Computers (1999-Present); Chief Financial Officer/Chief Information Officer, Intelligo Corporation (1996-99); General Manager, Micro Net System (199496). **Associations & Accomplishments:** United States Chamber of Commerce; Dallas Chamber of Commerce; Who's Who Executive and Business; Richardson Chamber of Commerce; Better Business Bureau; Small Business Network; Member of several local community and charity associations. **Education:** University of Illinois; College of Dupage. **Personal Information:** Married to Saniyah S. in 1994. One child: Shayan S. Mr. Gagan enjoys history reading and gardening.

Allan F. Gagnon

Owner/Administrator
Net Tryx Computer Services LLC
10625 North 25th Avenue, Suite 200
Phoenix, AZ 85029
(602) 944-3535

7379

Business Information: Serving as the Owner and Administrator of Net Tryx Computer Services LLC, Mr. Gagnon determines the overall strategic direction and business contribution of the information technology function. In this capacity, he is accountable for document imaging, including the design, development, and implementation of network systems, development of databases for hardware and software systems as well as the resale of products with the help of his staff of four individuals. Demonstrating tremendous troubleshooting skills, Mr. Gagnon designed and implemented the refurbishment of the Company's entire networking infrastructure. He has future plans to become information systems director for a Fortune 500 or 1000 company, and redesigning an entire information system. His aspirations also include doing more as a database administrator such as programming and involving himself with the Internet and Intranet and creation of cutting-edge Web pages. Based in Phoenix, Arizona, Net Tryx Computer Services LLC specializes in computer consulting. The Company also excels in networks, programs, databases, and office training. **Career Highlights:** Owner/Administrator, Net Tryx Computer Services LLC (2000-Present); Management Information Systems Director, Innovision Imaging, Inc. (1999-00); Network Engineer, Aztech Professional Services (1998-99); Management Information Systems Director, Kenney Aerial Mapping, Inc. (1997-98). **Education:** DeVry Institute of Technology, Bachelor's degree in Computer Information Systems (In Progress). **Personal Information:** Mr. Gagnon enjoys camping, hiking and hunting.

Prashant Gaitonde

System Architect
O.S.S. Inc.
11901 Hobby Horse Court, Apartment 325
Austin, TX 78758
(512) 699-6130
p_gaitonde@yahoo.com

7379

Business Information: Possessing a unique talent for the analysis and design of computer systems, Mr. Gaitonde is the Systems Architect for O.S.S. Inc. He determines the clients specifications and needs for their computer systems, and designs the most efficient and elaborate programs. Having six years experience in his field and starting out as a software programmer, Mr. Gaitonde came to the United States for the immense opportunities afforded to everyone in America. Intrigued by the freedom of choice in the United States, he plans to open his own firm and obtain an e-commerce certification. Mr. Gaitonde attributes his success to his joy of learning new and exciting things. His advice is "get involved in the Web." Established in 1993, with approximately 250 employees, O.S.S. Inc. is a consulting firm. The Firm provides professional manpower for the hardware, software, and network consulting project needs of a diverse clientele. O.S.S. Inc. specializes in computer systems consulting and architectural and programming designs. **Career Highlights:** Systems Architect, O.S.S. Inc. (1998-Present); Systems Analyst, Sunrise Logistics, Inc. (1997-98); Senior Programmer, Blue Star, Inc. (1995-97). **Education:** Mumbai University, B.S. in Computer (1992). **Personal Information:** Married. Mr. Gaitonde enjoys driving, travel, music, movies and vacations.

Prenston Gale, Sr.

Senior Computer Technician
MTISC
Unit 4962
APO, AA34037
(301) 985-9318
galep@cms.southcom.mil

7379

Business Information: Capitalizing on an extensive occupational and educational background, Mr. Gale began his career with MTISC in 1994. As the Senior Computer Technician he is charged with installing and maintaining software as well as providing personnel training. Responsible for designing and implementing new software into existing systems, he coordinates tests to ensure optimal performance, and he also maintains the functionality of existing systems. Mr. Gale corrects any errors found on the systems, ensuring fully operational status at all times. Constantly striving for maximum effectiveness, Mr. Gale is striving for his bachelor's degree to capitalize on the opportunities afforded by MTISC. Founded in 1980, MTISC is contracted by the United States government to provide technical support, installation upgrades, and systems maintenance to computer systems in United States embassies around the world. Employing over 100,000 technically trained individuals, the Company updates and modifies government computers and establishes networks between existing systems. **Career Highlights:** Senior Computer Technician, MTISC (1994-Present); Special Operations Officer, United States Army Special Forces (1974-94). **Associations & Accomplishments:** Special Forces Decade Association; Benevolent Protective Order of the Elks. **Education:** Grantham College of Engineering, B.S. (In Progress); Fayetteville Community College, A.A. in Business Administration. **Personal Information:** Married to Jenny in 1995. Two children: Saskia and Prenston, Jr.

Jagan Garimella

Architect
Sapient Corporation
10 Exchange Place, Suite 21
Jersey City, NJ 07302-3913
(201) 521-3957
jgarimella@sapient.com

7379

Business Information: In his role as Architect for Sapient Corporation, Mr. Garimella handles technical design activities for customers. Utilizing his practical work experience and related education, he conducts research to ensure proper design of systems and applications. With exceptional communicative skills, he meets with clients to evalute their needs and discuss their expectations. After gathering pertinent data, he is able to formulate technical products that consistently exceed all requirements. Credited for his impressive ability, he is recognized for his contributions to the formation of the Corporation. He attributes his success to internal motivation and currently is striving for advancement within the corporate structure. Sapient Corporation is an Internet consulting firm located in Jersey City, New Jersey. Established in 1992, the $150 million firm handles various e-commerce and e-business accounts for customers. The Corporation employs 1,500 people to assist in the completion of daily responsibilities. **Career Highlights:** Architect, Sapient Corporation (1996-Present). **Education:** University of Miami, M.S. (1995); Osmania University, B.S. in Civil Engineering.

Angie R. Garrett

Partner/Senior Consultant
Quantum Resources
819 Davis Hill Road
Center Conway, NH 03813
(708) 636-4007
Fax: (718) 636-4007
quantum@ncia.net

7379

Business Information: As Partner of Quantum Resources, Ms. Garrett also serves as Senior Consultant. She is responsible for quality assurance and process improvement. Her occupational background history includes engagements with various consulting companies. In her present role with Quantum, she oversees all aspects of daily operations, and has become a well-versed and talented sales and marketing representative as well. In this context, she is charged with negotiating contracts, managing the fiscal year budget, and developing new business endeavors. Project management also falls within the purview of her responsibilities. Ms. Garrett hopes to extend the services the Company is able to provide, increase her clientele base, and possibly spread internationally. She attributes her success to integrity and her personal commitment to do her best, as well as collaborating with other professionals. Established in 1994 as a first-time entrepreneurial adventure, Quantum Resources offers local businesses computer consulting services. The Corporation specializes in quality assurance in information systems. Clients are offered consultations on software support, testing, and quality assurance. The Corporation develops specific software programs for customers and then continues in its customer service excellence to provide extensive testing and reworking of the programs to make the finished product more adaptable for the client. **Career Highlights:** Partner/Senior Consultant, Quantum Resources (1994-Present); Project Manager, Sprint (1989-94); Computer Scientist, General Accounting Office (GAO) (1987-89); Programmer/Analyst, Sprint (1987-89). **Associations & Accomplishments:** National Association of Female Executives; American Society For Quality; Board of Directors, Chicago Quality Assurance Association; Participant, Chicago Software Process Improvement; Instructor, Quality Assurance Principles; Leader, Brownie Girl Scouts; Finance Secretary, Faith Lutheran Church; Recruiter, Pennsylvania State University. **Education:** Pennsylvania State University, B.S. (1986); George Washington University; Certified Quality Analyst; Certified Software Test Engineer. **Personal Information:** Married to Malachy in 1988. Four children: Caitlin, Padric, Morgan, and Briana. Ms. Garrett enjoys crafts, sewing, reading, travel and computers.

David A. Gatewood, MCP, MCSE

Consultant
CGI
402 BNA Drive, Suite 403
Nashville, TN 37217
(615) 366-4074
Fax: (615) 366-5582
dages@knuth.mtsu.edu

7379

Business Information: Functioning in the capacity of Consultant with CGI, Mr. Gatewood is involved in specialty systems management, setting up networks, software delivery, and providing the final level of support. Drawing from an extensive education and previous occupational experience, Mr. Gatewood provides continuous professional excellence in the fulfillment of his responsibilities. Before joining CGI, he served as a Consultant with Deloitte Consulting, DRT Systems. His background history also includes a stint as Information Technology Specialist for Systems Management for IBM Global Services. He attributes his substantial professional success to God and the encouragement he has received from his wife. Mr. Gatewood's goal is to continue to take classes and read in order to stay up to date in his field and to expedite continued promotion within the Company. CGI is a

Canadian based information service providing end to end information technology services. Established in 1976, the Company employs in excess of 10,000 individuals to orchestrate every aspect of the operations and reports an annual turnover of $1.5 billion. **Career Highlights:** Consultant, CGI (1999-Present); Consultant, Deloitte Consulting, DRT Systems (1999); Information Technology Specialist for Systems Management, IBM Global Services (1997-98). **Education:** Middle Tennessee State University, B.S. in Computer Science (1996); Electrical Engineering/ITT Technical Institute, A.S. **Personal Information:** Married to Lea Anne in 1993. One child: Connor Clay. Mr. Gatewood enjoys spending time with his family, 3D graphic art, scuba diving, woodworking and martial arts.

Ronald S. Gatlin

Webmaster
Nichols Research
4090 Memorial Parkway SW
Huntsville, AL 35802
(601) 634-3175
gatlinr@nichols.com

7379

Business Information: Serving as Webmaster of Nichols Research, Mr. Gatlin is responsible for internal and external Web design. Mr. Gatlin draws from an extensive education and previous occupational experience in maintaining internal Web sites, providing graphic support, and helping with servers and file structures. An eight year veteran, he has achieved substantial success in his career including having developed a program that is now a Congressional standard. Mr. Gatlin feels that teamwork is the reason for his success and he stays at the top of his field by reading trade magazines, attending conferences, and surfing the Internet. He continues to excel in his current position and looks forward to increasing the usability of Web sites. Nichols Research is engaged in providing information technologies for the Department of Defense as well as commercial and health care industries. Established in 1976, the Company employs a staff of 3,000 individuals dedicated to providing their clients with quality technical and computer support. **Career Highlights:** Webmaster, Nichols Research (1997-Present); Visual Designer/Technician, SESI (1993-97); Visual Designer, Boeing (1991-93). **Associations & Accomplishments:** Phone Crisis Counselor, Crisis Services of North Alabama; International Guild of Gay Webmasters; Chairman of the Board, Integrity Alabama. **Education:** Alabama A&M, B.A. in Graphics (1994). **Personal Information:** Mr. Gatlin enjoys singing, rollerblading and community service.

Charles W. Gautney

Director of Core Technologies Division
Noblestar Systems
12021 Sunset Hills Road, Suite 600
Reston, VA 20190-3296
(703) 464-4059
Fax: (703) 464-4220
cgautney@noblestar.com

7379

Business Information: As Director of Core Technologies Division for Noblestar Systems, Mr. Gautney is responsible for the direction and vision of a business unit that focuses on core systems architectures. He started the division based on his own expertise in UNIX, message oriented middleware, database administration, and networking. In a few short years, he has grown the division to 40 consultants working on projects all across the United States and Europe. Mr. Gautney is responsible for operations based in Reston, Virginia and Loenen a/d Vecht, Netherlands. He believes keeping up with ever changing technology and expanding knowledge at every opportunity is the key to succeeding in any field. His plans are to continue his success with the Company, expanding his offering in middleware and mobile computing. A systems integration consultancy, Noblestar Systems was established in 1987. The Company now employs over 500 individuals and conducts operations internationally. **Career Highlights:** Noblestar Systems: Director of Core Technologies Division (1996-Present), Manager (1994-96); Independent Consultant (1990-94). **Education:** Old Dominion University, B.S. in Computer Sciences (1987). **Personal Information:** Married to Rebecca in 1992. Two children: Tara Ashley and Heather Michelle. Mr. Gautney enjoys marine reef keeping and coin collecting.

Thomas E. Geist

Regional Vice President
Computer Horizons Corporation
1401 17th Street, Suite 900
Denver, CO 80202
(800) 409-2421
Fax: (303) 293-8402
tgeist@computerhorizons.com

7379

Business Information: Mr. Geist is the Regional Vice President of Computer Horizons Corporation. He has served with Computer Horizons since joining the Corporation as District Manager of Chicago in 1994. In his present role, he is responsible for the 19-state western region of the Corporation. As a 17 year professional Mr. Geist motivates 400 consultants in the region throughout the ten offices he is accountable for. He reports directly to the President of the Corporation regarding his progress and future goals. Utilizing his expertise in the training industry, he instructs employees on procedures and policies as well as personal development through their career. Mr. Geist hopes to continue to provide quality services to his clients and would like to see the West Coast businesses grow. His success reflects his leadership ability to build teams with synergy, technical strength, and a customer oriented attitude, as well as produce results in support of business objectives and aggressively tackle new challenges. Computer Horizons Corporation provides Information Technology consulting services to its clientele. Celebrating its 30th anniversary, the Corporation is publicly traded on NASDAQ and hosts 55 locations around the globe specializing in technological solutions. Over 5,000 employees strive to teach e-business to clients and open the doors to new staffing and outsourcing possibilities through the World Wide Web. Providing customer relations management and centralized vendor management to Fortune 500 companies, the Corporation turns over $615 million every year through its support assistance and tutorial instruction. **Career Highlights:** Computer Horizons Corporation: Regional Vice President (1997-Present), Area Vice President (1996-97), District Manager of Chicago (1994-96). **Education:** Central Michigan University, B.A. (1982). **Personal Information:** Married to Pamela K. in 1990. Two children: Jenna Kaye and Evan Andrew. Mr. Geist enjoys travel, playing sports, gardening and fishing.

William T. Georges

Project Manager
Science Applications International Corporation
10260 Campus Point Drive
San Diego, CA 92121
(858) 826-5388
Fax: (858) 826-3470
william.t.georges@saic.com

7379

Business Information: Mr. Georges functions in the role of Project Manager for Science Applications International Corporation or SAIC. He is responsible for ensuring systems reliability, availability, functionality, and fully operational status. Conducting in-depth maintainability studies, Mr. Georges is able to explore the business process and integration of technology into a variety of industries. Specializing in mission critical systems, he researches, investigates, and analyzes an array of areas within the information technology field. Several major highlights include overseeing a client management software project that increased the sales automation effort; and moving the investment department and trading desk from Manhattan to New Jersey and migrating the systems to a new technology platform. Looking to the next millennium, Mr. Georges hopes to become more developed in reliability studies and modeling of complex systems. His success is attributed to his flexibility, continuous learning, and persistence. SAIC provides systems integration and technology management. Established in 1969, the Corporation develops satelites, communication equipment, computer security systems, and Lotus Notes support programs. The Corporation also highlights a division dedicated to the development of software programs for hospital automation. Presently, SAIC employs a global staff of 38,000 people who help generate in excess of $4.7 billion annually. **Career Highlights:** Project Manager, Science Applications International Corporation (1997-Present); Metropolitan Live Insurance Company: Project Manager of Customer Contact Management (1996-97), Internal Management Consultant (1994-96), Senor Consultant of Strategic Consultancy (1993-94). **Education:** University of California at San Diego, Systems Engineering Certification Program (In Progress); Duke University, B.A. (1981). **Personal Information:** Married to Elizabeth in 1989. Two children: Alexander and Maxwell. Mr. Georges enjoys coaching little league soccer.

Dimitris A. Geragas

Engineer
Aera Inc.
2500 Clarendon Boulevard, Apartment 734
Arlington, VA 22201-3831
(703) 415-4667
Fax: (703) 415-1059
dgeragas@aol.com

7379

Business Information: Beginning his career with Aera Inc. as a Student Intern, Mr. Geragas has moved through the ranks to acheive the position of Engineer. This position allows him to assist the Corporation in the design, development, and implementation of software applications and other technical plans. Maintaining the decision support systems, he demonstrates his versatile abilities by formulating impressive data management and analysis strategies. Utilizing a variety of techniques to solve research and development challenges, Mr. Geragas is credited with the impressive creation of a software system that is now being used nationwide. Keeping his goals consistent with the objectives of the Corporation, he looks forward to advancement within the corporate structure. Aera Inc. is a nationwide technical company that focuses on Department of Defense contracts for the United States Navy. Offering commerical setups of LANs, WANs, and MANs, the Corporation also develops software applications to fit specific client needs. Established in 1988, the Corporation generates estimated annual revenues of over $22 million. **Career Highlights:** Engineer, Aera Inc. (1995-Present); Science Staff Writer, Maryland Media, Inc. (1992-95); Antenna Engineer, UMCP Radio Association (1993-94). **Education:** University of Maryland at College Park, Electrical Engineer (1996). **Personal Information:** Married to Eleni Valasiadou in 1998. Mr. Geragas enjoys swimming, skydiving, reading, anything dangerous and anything scientific.

Yuriy Gervagin

UNIX and Oracle Administrator
Websci Technologies
4214 Route 1 North
Monmooth Junction, NJ 08852
(303) 294-6727
Fax: (303) 391-7124
ggh1998@yahoo.com

7379

Business Information: As UNIX and Oracle Administrator of Websci Technologies, Mr. Gervagin consults with Company's clients regarding UNIX and Oracle administration and problems. He assists users to maintain their systems and databases and writes scripts for administering backups of these systems. Installing operating systems software, compilers, and utilities; administering and controlling data resources; and resolving systems difficulties also fall within the realm of Mr. Gervagin's responsibilities. With 30 years of experience in the industry, Mr. Gervagin is an expert in his field. He attributes his success simply to hard work. "Study, study, study." Always alert to new opportunities, techniques, and approaches, he wishes to expand his knowledge and obtain more industry certifications. Websci Technologies is a software development and consulting company. Employing approximately 150 individuals as programmers, systems administrators, and database administrators, the Company recruits most of its employees from India, China, and Russia. The Company was created in 1989 and performs consulting for private companies in the United States. **Career Highlights:** UNIX and Oracle Administrator, Websci Technologies (1998-Present); UNIX and Oracle Administrator, Sandy Info (1997-98); Technical Department Chief, ICT, Ltd. (1995-97); System Administrator, Transal Company (1992-95). **Associations & Accomplishments:** Assistant Professor, Caleulation Math and Cybernetics Department, Nizhny Nougorod State University **Education:** Transport University, B.S. (1978). **Personal Information:** Married to Elena in 1978. Two children: Katherine and Dmitriy. Mr. Gervagin enjoys jazz music and biking.

Amitava Ghosh

Consultant
Instasofte, Inc.
173 Essex Avenue
Metuchen, NJ 08840
(732) 271-2303
Fax: (508) 519-2683
aghosh@netscape.net

7379

Business Information: Functioning in the capacity of Consultant at Instasofte, Inc., Mr. Ghosh is responsible for the design and development of database model, as well as administering UNIX, database, and application server. As a six year technology professional, Mr.Ghosh oversees and controls database resources, database architecture, and Web server applications. Before arriving at Instasofte, he served as Database Developer and Administrator with AT&T and Programmer and Analyst at J&B Software. Mr. Ghosh concurrently fulfills the responsibility of Database Administrator for Lucent Technologies. Crediting his success to his academic background and work ethic, his professional success reflects his ability to think out-of-the-box and take on new challenges and responsibilities. He remains current with new technology by reading trade journals and taking classes. Eventually attaining the position of Chief Information Officer serves as one of Mr. Ghosh's future endeavors. A private software consulting company, Instasofte, Inc. specializes in business software solutions, as well as total solutions for database and e-commerce platforms. Established in 1996, Instasofte is headquartered in Delaware. Presently, the Corporation employs a work force of eight professional and technical experts. **Career Highlights:** Consultant, Instasofte, Inc. (Present); Database Administrator, Lucent Technologies (1998-Present); Database Developer and Administrator, AT&T (1996-98); Programmer/Analyst, J&B Software (1996). **Associations & Accomplishments:** Computer Society of India (1995). **Education:** Bangalore University, B.S. (1995). **Personal Information:** Married to Jayamadhuri Paladagu in 1996. Mr. Ghosh enjoys philately and writing computer games.

Stephen Gibson

President/Founder
SAP Professional Organization
305 Caldwell Avenue, Suite 2
Mooresville, NC 28115
(704) 660-1408
Fax: (704) 660-1400
(Alt) . P-h.: (800) 722-7614
stevegibson@sap-professional.org

7379

Business Information: After 15 years in Houston, Texas, and experience in various high level sales positions, Mr. Gibson returned to his native North Carolina to begin a new career in the high tech world. His Firm is an all-inclusive organization that provides services to the SAP community (see sap.com). SAP America works closely with Mr. Gibson as the sole advertiser at his sap-professional.org web site. There, he now offers a free forum to discuss software solutions. He also offers executive placement, executive search, training, and Internet recruiting tools from the Organization's sister companies. He is partnered with Mike Clark, founder of commercial-directory.com and supermail.com to offer innovative services and products. Recruiting contracts signed with Microsoft, SAP America, Georgia Pacific, Deloitte Touche ICS, and others keep his recruiting skills pushed to the limit providing SAP IT talent to those firms via permanent staffing and/or contract consulting via Principal Consulting in Tampa, Buffalo, and Charlotte. Mr. Gibson has held management positions with USX Corporation from 1975 to 1982, and served as Vice President for Gulf Coast Sources from 1984 to 1987, Lechman Brothers from 1987 to 1990, and Oppenheimer and Company from 1990 to 1997. Current staffing for SAP Professional Organization is 10 with expansion planned in 1999. Revenue from contracts and placement services should exceed $2.0 million in 1999. **Career Highlights:** President/Founder, SAP Professional Organization (1998-Present); Owner/President, Executive Recruiters LLC (1997-Present); Owner/President, flip-search.com (1998-Present); Vice President, Oppenheimer & Company, Houston (1990-95); Vice President, Lehman Brothers, Houston (1987-90); President, Gulf Coast Sources (1984-87); General Sales Manager, Nichimen America, Nitex Pipe Division (1983-84); General Sales Manager, Promo Steel Division, Tubos Reunidos SA (1982-84); Senior Sales Manager, USX (1976-82); Account Representative, Brant Snavely Agency, Northwestern Mutual Life Insurance Company (1974-76). **Associations & Accomplishments:** International Association of Human Resources (1998); Faith Partner (1997-Present), Coral Ridge Ministries; Chapter Founder (1996), Business Network International; Cove Christian Church (1998); Phi Delta Theta Alumni Representative, Duke University Alumni Association; Pepperdine University Alumni Association. **Education:** Clayton School of Natural Health, N.D. (1998); University of Houston School of Law (1982-83); Pepperdine University, M.B.A. in Finance (1978); Duke University, B.A. in Economics (1974). **Personal Information:** One child: Jacob Taylor age 15. Mr. Gibson enjoys water sports, poetry, music (guitar) and travel. He is a licensed Naturapathic Doctor in the state of North Carolina with a "virtual" practice maintained on the Internet throughout the United States. He resides in Mooresville, North Carolina (Race City USA) where he maintains close ties to several of NASCAR's drivers and owners. He attributes his modest success in life to his personal decision to accept Jesus Christ as his personal Savior.

Kimberly S. Gillette

Human Resources Administrator
Perspective Technology Corporation
1595 Spring Hill Road, Suite 310 West
Vienna, VA 22182
(703) 821-8800
Fax: (703) 821-8809
kgillett@perspect.com

7379

Business Information: Serving as Human Resources Administrator of Perspective Technology Corporation, Ms. Gillette orchestrates the compensation and benefits for all of the Corporation's employees. She maintains the employees' files, ensuring compliance with EEO and FMLA rules and regulations. Coordinating seminars and manual updates, Ms. Gillette conducts employee training for both of the Corporation's locations. In an effort to offer Perspective Technology the best and latest in training, she stays current with technology and new state and federal regulations by attending workshops, seminars, and training courses. Her success reflects her leadership ability to take on new challenges and follow through with responsibilities. Ms. Gillette's goals within the Corporation is to maintain and assist with its current growth, taking on more responsibility and expanding the employee benefits package. A subsidiary of MOTIS, Perspective Technology Corporation is a information technology consulting firm catering primarily to commercial clients. Established in 1989, the Corporation has experienced tremendous growth in the past year and recently opened a second office in Atlanta, Georgia. The Corporation now employs a total work force of 120 knowledgeable individuals and reports $25 million in annual revenue. **Career Highlights:** Human Resources Administrator, Perspective Technology Corporation (1998-Present); Human Resources Administrator, Government Micro Resources (1997-98); Office Administrator, National D.J. Connection (1997). **Associations & Accomplishments:** Society for Human Resource Management; Washington Technical Forum. **Education:** James Madison University, Business Management (1998). **Personal Information:** Ms. Gillette enjoys modeling, dancing and music.

Joyce Goldburgh

Operations Manager
Client Server Consulting
1151 Tower Lane
Bensenville, IL 60106-1027
(630) 766-2030
Fax: (630) 787-1312
joyce@ccscg.com

7379

Business Information: Ms. Goldburgh has recently assumed the title and responsibilities of Operations Manager of Client Service Consulting. Possessing 12 years of business savvy and technical expertise She retains overall accountability for sales, technical support, marketing, and help desk aspects of the Company. Additional duties include human resources, accounting, scheduling technicians, reviewing candidates for hire, and authorizing billing. Ms. Goldburgh's primary duties include ensuring all operations of Client Server Consulting run according to plan, meeting client expectations, and complying with set regulations and policies. Future plans include receiving a Master's degree in Communications and eventually moving into a smaller company where she can utiize her skills to assist in its growth, development, and expansion. Her advice to others in the field is "listen, be flexible, and learn as much as possible. Client Server Consulting, established in 1992, is a systems solutions provider based in Bensonville, Illinois. This technology firm offers a variety of services and is capable of meeting the demanding needs of clients with the assistance of a staff of 20 professionals. Top management of the Company keeps abreast on new developments in the field and incorporate pertinent information into daily activities. **Career Highlights:** Operations Manager, Client Server Consulting (1999-Present); Director of Development, Bear Necessities Pediatric Cancer Foundation (1998-99); Manager of Sales Operations, Inset Systems (1993-95). **Associations & Accomplishments:** Volunteer Counselor for Battered Women and Rape Victims. **Education:** Western Connecticut State University, B.S. (1988). **Personal Information:** Married to Mitchell in 1991. Two children: Christopher and Denise. Ms. Goldburgh enjoys running.

David Goldschmidt

Owner
Mobile MIS Consulting
8796 Carrousel Park Circle #136
Cincinnati, OH 45251
(513) 357-3096
Fax: (513) 641-2144
daveg7@aol.com

7379

Business Information: Possessing extensive knowledge and experience in the computer field, Mr. Goldschmidt decided to establish Mobile MIS Consulting in 1993. As the Owner and Consultant, he specializes in providing design services in the establishment of networks for corporate clients. After determining the best method of developing a network for businesses of varied sizes, Mr. Goldschmidt oversees the installation of computer systems to provide quality customer service to all clients. Attributing his success to his educational background and work ethics, Mr. Goldschmidt also serves as the Network Administrator for World Color Press. Mr. Goldschmidt enjoys his work in the field of information technology and hopes to continue to expand the services of Mobile MIS Consulting in the near future. The Company provides computer consulting, local area network design and installation services to clients in the Cincinnati area. Mobile MIS Consulting also conducts network administration and offers troubleshooting to assist clients with any computer systems problems. **Career Highlights:** Owner, Mobile MIS Consulting (1993-Present); Network Administrator, World Color Press (1997-Present); Certified Novell Engineer/Hardware Technician, Cincinnati Network Solutions (1995-97); Computer Sales, Scot Business Machines (1991-93). **Education:** Thomas More College, B.A. in Business Administration (1991). **Personal Information:** Mr. Goldschmidt enjoys cooking, the Internet and camping.

Deborah L. Goldsmith, Ph.D.

Lead Scientist Networking Systems Distributed Systems
Mitre Corporation
4106 Galt Street
San Diego, CA 92117-1125
(619) 758-7829
Fax: (619) 222-2260
dgoldsm1@ucsd.edu

7379

Business Information: A proven and tested technical expert, Dr. Goldsmith was recruited to MITRE Corporation as Lead Scientist of Networking Systems and Distributed Systems in 1992. A key team member of the systems engineering division, she is responsible for providing cutting edge communications networking capabilities to the United States Navy. Diligently working with the Department of Defense and primary systems users, Dr. Goldsmith provides naval vessels with state-of-the-art communications. She accomplishes her mission by participating in the analysis, design, evaluation, testing, and implementation of operating and networking related systems. Always looking for new challenges, Dr. Goldsmith plans on shifting gears in the future to Internet security. Established in the 1950s, the MITRE Corporation is an international, high tech electrical and communications firm primarily producing large scale command, control, and communication systems for the United States Air Force. Headquartered in Bedford, Massachusetts, the Corporation is in partnership with several government clients. As a non-profit organization, the Corporation works in the public interest issues. The Corporation is divided into three centers: systems engineering, systems research and development, and strategic technical management consulting. Presently, the Corporation is manned by over 4,000 professional, technical, and administrative support staff. **Career Highlights:** Lead Scientist of Networking Systems and Distributed Systems, MITRE Corporation (1992-Present); President/Chief Executive Officer, Goldsmith Computers (1988-Present); Member of Technical Staff, Compusec (1988-92). **Associations & Accomplishments:** Institute of Electronics and Electrical Engineers; American Academy of Actuaries; Association of Computing Machinery. **Education:** University of California at San Diego, Ph.D. (1988); Princeton University, Ph.D. (1972). **Personal Information:** Married to Reg E. Stanley in 1980. One child: Dena Goldsmith. Dr. Goldsmith enjoys piano, computers, jogging, hiking and French.

Debbie A. Golebiewski

Vice President/Corporate
Contract Computer Services
2213 West Jackson Street
Tupelo, MS 38801-3075
(662) 842-7800
Fax: (662) 842-3077
debbie@contractcomputer.com

7379

Business Information: Recruited to Contract Computer Services in 1997, Mrs. Golebiewski serves as the Vice President. She assumes responsibility for a variety of administrative and operational tasks including sales, business development, marketing, and purchasing. In addition, she also serves as the Corporate Secretary and is in charge of office management and computer system management. Mrs. Golebiewski is a Microsoft Certified System Engineer and is C++ certified. She maintains the internal database with a total of 800 clients nationally. Prior to her current position, Mrs. Golebiewski worked for Efficiency Billing Service in a variety of capacities. At the present time, she plans to expand the Company by creating new avenues of business and revenue. She also wants to continue to pursue her independent songwriting career. A full service computer company, Contract Computer Services offers all types of services to its clients including sales, repair service, network set-up, and monitoring. The Company also designs and implements hardware and software applications; performs upgrades and Web design; and installs desktops and printers. Best known for its software billing applications for utility companies, the Company has clients from across the country. A work force of 11 professionals is employed and works diligently to generate an annual income of $250,000. The Company was established in 1988. **Career Highlights:** Vice President, Contract Computer Services (1997-Present). **Associations & Accomplishments:** International Poetry Hall of Fame; International Society of Poets; National Author's Registry; 1998 Famous Poet Award; Homer Diamond Award; 1999 Editor Choice Award; Roberts Publishing Creative Writer's Award; 2000 Outstanding Intellectuals of 20th Century; 500 Leaders of Influence; Who's Who of Business & Professional Women; International WHO'S WHO of Professional Management; Mississippi Top 50 Leading Business Women; 2000 Notable American Women; american Business Women's Association; American Management Association; National Association of Female Executives. **Education:** Memphis State University, degree in Business Management and Journalism (1977); ICC, degree in Computers. **Personal Information:** Married to Mike in 1996. Three children: James Powell, Paden, and Logan. Mrs. Golebiewski enjoys creative writing, song writing and co-writing.

Carlos Gomes

Business Solutions Manager
IFS Portugal
Rua 5 Outubro, 615
Riba de Ave, Portugal 4765-219
+35 1939985498
carlos_gomes_pt@yahoo.com.br

7379

Business Information: Highly recruited to IFS in 2000, Mr. Gomes currently serves in the role of Business Solutions Manager responsible for coordinating resources, time lines, schedules, and communications for applications implementation and development projects. In his capacity, he helps management determine the overall strategic direction and business contribution of the Company. Possessing 10 years of business savvy and technical expertise, Mr. Gomes develops project schedules and assigns tasks as well as performs both analysis and implementation when required. Translating German, Spanish, and English to Portuguese, administering personnel appraisals and salaries, hiring, and budgets also fall within the preview of Mr. Gomes' responsibilities. Keeping up with the ever-changing technology and helping the Company remain out-front of competitors in the industry serves as his long-term goals. His success reflects his ability to think outside the box, deliver results, and take on new challenges. IFS develops and supplies IFS Applications, which is a complete ERP system that covers e-Business, CRM, SCM, manufacturing, distribution, financials, maintenance management, human resources, engineering, and front office. IFS Applications is entirely developed using a componet-based architecture and IFS is the world's fastest-growing company in the ERP and maintenance software market. The IFS business concept is to increase the freedom of action and competitiveness of companies by offering standardized business systems based on leading technologies. **Career Highlights:** Business Solutions Manager, IFS Portugal (2000-Present); Project Manager, BRAIN Portugal (1997-00); IT/IS Consultant, Freelancer (1994-97); IT/IS Director, F.T.O.F. SA (1989-94). **Associations & Accomplishments:** Clube Golf Braga; Regional Table Tennis Champion; University Table Tennis Champion. **Education:** Universidade do Minho, IT/IS Management (1997). **Personal Information:** Mr. Gomes enjoys squash, photograhpy, philately, golf and travel.

Ivan J. Gomes
Senior Consultant
Interactive Business Systems, Inc.
2625 Butterfield
Oak Brook, IL 60523
(847) 384-5439
Fax: (847) 384-5424
gomesivan@hotmail.com

7379

Business Information: Working in the industry for more than 11 years, Mr. Gomes currently fills the position of a Senior

Consultant for Interactive Business Systems, Inc. It is his responsibility to work with clients to design and implement solutions for business problems using Microsoft, Lotus, Novell, and OS/2 solutions. Possessing superior talents and an excellent understanding of technology, Mr. Gomes also installs LAN/WAN systems architectures for clients and ensures that systems are in proper running order at all times. The highlight of his career is inventing new solutions to help the Reserve Bank of Australia in migrating to an advanced systems environment. In the future, he plans to continue staying on the cutting edge of technology and enhance his knowledge of Internet and e-business technologies. Interactive Business Systems, Inc. provides information technology consulting services to Fortune 500 and 1000 companies. Founded in 1983, the Corporation engages in LAN and WAN design and implementation using Microsoft products and personal computer based technology. Employing more than 1,000 personnel, the Corporation reports estimated annual revenue exceeding $200 million. **Career Highlights:** Senior Consultant, Interactive Business Systems, Inc. (1998-Present); Senior LAN Specialist/Engineer, Reserve Bank of Australia (1995-98); Project Manager/Engineer, MicroHelp Computers Sydney, Australia (1993-95); Technical Manager/Field Engineer, Oasys Computer Center Sydeny, Australia (1988-93). **Associations & Accomplishments:** Eight year Member, Institute of Electrical and Electronics Engineers, Inc. and the Computer Society. **Education:** University of New South Wales, Bachelor's degree in Electrical Engineering (1987); Mount Eliza School of Management (1993). **Personal Information:** Married to Shelomi in 1995. Mr. Gomes enjoys computer operating systems, real estate and the stock market.

Timothy A. Goodwin
Programmer/Analyst
Commercial Data Corporation
3600 Regal Boulevard
Memphis, TN 38118
(901) 375-1000
Fax: (901) 375-9197
tgoodwin@cdc.1.com

7379

Business Information: As Programmer and Analyst for Commercial Data Corporation, Mr. Goodwin writes software in COBOL computer programming language. He also creates, designs, and installs custom configurations for clients, utilizing existing software as the operational basis. Analysis, acquisition, modification, support, and tracking of operating systems, databases, utilities, software, and hardware also fall within the scope of his functions. Mr. Goodwin attributes his success to his intelligence, and ability to translate knowledge into a profitable enterprise. Mr. Goodwin plans to obtain his CCP designation from the Institute for Certification of Computing Professionals, and hopes to keep abreast of current technologies. His favorite advice for others in the industry is "Educate yourself as much as possible." Established in 1967, Commercial Data Corporation provides computer system and software products and consultative services to clients across the United States. The focus audiences for Commercial Data's products and services are healthcare companies and MLM/Network Marketing Companies. CDC's products are primarily healthcare financial accounting systems and employee management software. CDC's services include healthcare financial consultative services, MLM/Network Marketing services, fulfillment services, call center operations, and data processing services. Around 42 professional, technical, and support staff are employed by the Corporation. **Career Highlights:** Programmer/Analyst, Commercial Data Corporation (1988-Present); Computer Analyst, Tyler Computers and Office Supplies (1986-88). **Associations & Accomplishments:** Institute of Electrical and Electronics Engineers Computer Society; Phi Theta Kappa International Honor Society; Delta Mu Delta National Honor Society in Business Administration; Delta State University Alumni Association; American Philatelic Society; Black Belt Club. **Education:** State Technical Institute, A.A.S. in Information Technology (1999); Delta State University, B.B.A. in Computer Information Systems (1985); University of Memphis; Northeast Mississippi Community College; Northwest Mississippi Community College. **Personal Information:** Mr. Goodwin enjoys karate, philosophy, stamp collecting and personal computing.

Eric M. Gool
Chief Executive Officer
SECI, Inc.
1307 South 14th Street
Lamar, CO 81052
(877) 876-6999
Fax: (719) 336-8245
e.gool@att.net

7379

Business Information: As Chief Executive Officer of SECI, Inc., Mr. Gool oversees daily operations and engineering of sites with coordination from AT&T, CISCO, Compaq, and Adcom. He bought the Company in 1997 and assisted in its

development into a profitable business. Mr. Gool formulates policies and procedures, develops goals, and implements strategies to achieve those goals. In collaboration with other top executives, he ensures that all aspects of the operation run according to the policies set by SECI, Inc. His career highlights include building a solid cable company from the ground up and selling it in 1997. Mr. Gool plans to be rated as one of the top national Internet providers. Setting trends and standards for others to emulate, he is actively involved in research and development of new products and Web pages. His success reflects his leadership ability to form teams with synergy, technical strength, and a customer oriented attitude, as well as deliver results and aggressively take on new challenges. Established in 1999, SECI, Inc. is a downstream Internet provider for rural clients living in the Midwest. Approximately nine highly skilled individuals, assist in fulfilling a variety of duties, such as ensuring all 30,000 customers are satisfied with their services. **Career Highlights:** Chief Executive Officer, SECI, Inc. (1998-Present); President, CFF, Inc. (1995-98); Nuclear/Biological Technology, United States Army (1985-90). **Associations & Accomplishments:** A.N.S.I.; Institute of Electronics and Electrical Engineers; Business Industries Consulting Service International; Local Jaycees; Fraternal Order of Eagles. **Personal Information:** Married to Robbie Sue in 1999. Mr. Gool enjoys fishing, clock repair and travel.

Rajan Gopalan
Principal Consultant
Cap Gemini America, Inc.
115 Perimeter Center Place, Suite 1100
Atlanta, GA 30346
(770) 481-6800
Fax: (770) 677-3521
rgopalan@usa.capgemini.com

7379

Business Information: As Principal Consultant of Cap Gemini America, Inc., Mr. Gopalan fulfills the responsibility of Project Manager. He supervises a team of 15 skilled professionals that provides client-server solutions to BellSouth. These applications are provided across state lines. Mr. Gopalan acts as a liaison between the client and the Corporation, planning client projects and monitoring its progress. Coordinating resources and schedules, overseeing time lines and assignments, and taking a lead role in driving products and services to market also fall within the realm of Mr. Gopalan's functions. He attributes his success to dedication, commitment, and his ability to learn and apply that knowledge. As an experienced, 10 year technology professional, his advice to others is "work smart, not hard." Mr. Gopalan surfs the Internet and reads industry magazines to keep current with new technology. Cap Gemini America, Inc. is one of the largest information technology and management consulting companies in the United States. Providing services such as Y2K solutions, project management, and management solutions, the Corporation has 45 locations in the United States. Cap Gemini America boasts more than $600 million in annual revenue and is a privately held, United States subsidiary of Paris-based Cap Gemini Group. Cap Gemini America is based out of New York and employs a workforce of 4,500 people. **Career Highlights:** Principal Consultant, Cap Gemini America, Inc. (1998-Present); Technical Manager, NIIT (USA) Inc. (1991-98). **Associations & Accomplishments:** A.A.C. **Education:** Indian Institute of Management, M.B.A. (1991); Indian Institute of Technology, Bachelor's degree in Technology (1989). **Personal Information:** Mr. Gopalan enjoys astronomy.

Ravichandran Gopalan
Programmer Analyst
Mascon
1515 East Woodfield Road
Schaumburg, IL 60173
(847) 240-2444
ravicha@worldmailer.com

7379

Business Information: Mr. Gopalan is the Programmer Analyst and works as a consultant for Mascon. He maintains the software that controls the operation of an entire computer infrastructure. A six year veteran, he is responsible for making changes in the sets of instructions that determine how the central processing unit of the system handles the various jobs it has been given. Because of his knowlege of the entire computer system, he often assists other programmers in determining the source of difficulties that may occur within programs. Before coming on board to Mascon, Mr. Gopalan served as Programmer Analyst with Synergysoft Solutions Inc. His background also includes a stint as Project Leader at Goldwire. Mr. Gopalan also meets with clients to determine any problems with the computer systems and finds adequate solutions. His plans for the next five years includes attaining the position of Senior Systems Analyst or obtaining a management role. Success is attributed to a firm faith in God, as well as reading articles on the Internet. Established in 1985, Mascon provides information technology and consulting services throughout the United States. Presently, the Company employs a work force of more than 120 professional, technical, and support personnel. **Career Highlights:** Programmer Analyst, Mascon (1999-Present);

Programmer Analyst, Synergysoft Solutions Inc. (1998-99); Project Leader, Goldwire (1996-98). **Education:** Loyola College, Madras University, B.Sc. (1993). **Personal Information:** Mr. Gopalan enjoys reading, music, gardening and Web surfing.

Frank J. Gordon, Jr.

Owner
Gordon Computer Services
9269 Campo Road, Suite One
Spring Valley, CA 91977
(619) 697-9148
Fax: (619) 466-3600
fgordon@gordoncs.com

7379

Business Information: As the Owner and sole employee of Gordon Computer Services, Mr. Gordon is responsible for all daily operations. He serves as a systems engineer and information technology consultant for clients, and develops all systems sold by the Company. Dedicated to the satisfaction of customers, he responds to all customer service calls and monitor clients' systems. Having faithfully served his country in the United States Navy for more than 20 years, Mr. Gordon retired in 1998 in the rank of Chief Petty Officer. In the future, he looks forward to the expansion of the Company, hiring employees and assisting small businesses in taking advantage of the Internet. His success reflects his self-discipline, determination, and customer service attitude. Gordon Computer Services provides information technology products and support services for small business. Founded in 1987, the Company develops software programs suited for small businesses, and then installs the systems and networks for the client. Utilizing the resources of one employee, the Company reports annual revenue exceeding $100,000. **Career Highlights:** Owner, Gordon Computer Services (1987-Present); Senior Information Technology Manager, Afldat Training Group Pacific (1994-98); United States Navy (1978-98). **Associations & Accomplishments:** Board Member, San Diego Netware Users Association; Small Business Specialist, Novell Cyannel Partner. **Education:** High School, G.E.D. (1977).

Randi-Lyn Gordon, Ph.D.

Training Coordinator
IBM-Knowledge Factory
4317 Village Oaks Lane
Dunwoody, GA 30338
(770) 835-7691
Fax: (770) 835-7579
vdrandi@us.ibm.com

7379

Business Information: Dr. Gordon has been the Training Coordinator for the IBM-Knowledge Factory since 1997. Established in 1994, the Knowledge Factory develops technology-based training for internal and external clients and is part of IBM's Global Learning Services. In her capacity as Training Coordinator, Dr. Gordon orchestrates internal training, develops, and implements skills-based workshops, and provides advanced skills training to various learning services courseware development teams. Dr. Gordon is also instrumental in helping to establish other Knowledge Factories worldwide, providing on-site team training and mentoring. Always alert to new techniques and opportunities, she plans to expand the training program for 2000 by providing a wider range of training opportunities and delivery methods. Dr. Gordon attributes her success to her extensive teaching background stretching from elementary grades through university graduate courses as well as her creativity, open-mindedness, and ability to view the potential curriculum "through the learner's eyes." She believes that everyone should follow their own dreams and desires, keep a wide focus, learn something new every day, and embrace change. **Career Highlights:** Training Coordinator, IBM-Knowledge Factory (1997-Present); Instructional Technologist, CD Group, Inc. (1995-97); Instructional Technology Instructor, Georgia State University (1984-95); Education Instructional Specialist, IBM Education Services (1981-93); Coordinator of Gifted Program, Mitchell County, Georgia (1978-80); Teacher of Elementary Grades (1972-78). **Associations & Accomplishments:** International Society for Technology in Education; American Society for Training and Development; Volunteer, City of Hope Fundraising; Most Outstanding Dissertation Award (1992), Georgia State University, Atlanta, Georgia. **Education:** Georgia State University, Ph.D. (1992); University of Miami, M.Ed.; University of Maine, B.S. in Education. **Personal Information:** Dr. Gordon enjoys needlework, theatre, skiing, photography, reading and surfing the net.

Charles F. Graul

Owner/President/Consultant
Centillion Computer Services, Inc.
521 Brookfield Drive
Largo, FL 33771-1401
(727) 535-7770
Fax: (727) 533-8440
chasgrual@centillion-largo.com

7379

Business Information: Mr. Graul is the Owner and President of Centillion Computer Systems, Inc. He also works as a computer consultant, technical writer, desktop publisher, and medical electronic claims processor. As a computer consultant, Mr. Graul aids client businesses in the selection of computer hardware and software, both for single systems and networks. He also project manages client businesses during the installation, upgrade and replacement, and systems checkouts. As a technical writer, Mr. Graul designs and writes business documents for client businesses. As a desktop publisher, he designs and publishes Web sites, flyers, brochures, and like documents for client businesses. As a medical electronic claims processor, he processes electronic claims for client medical practices. He is also published in several local, internal, and Internet papers. Mr. Graul's major accomplishments include, involvement with the Y2K major upgrade and replacement of the City of Dunedin's computer and network systems while employed as a microcomputer specialist; and employed as a field engineer for Harris Corporation CSD, he was responsible for the documenting, testing, and installation of the computer systems used in the first six F-15 flight simulators installed in the United States and Germany; and as a product engineer, he was responsible for the documenting, environmental testing, preproduction research and development, and production training for the Company's "ruggedized" computer system to be used on military aircraft carriers. **Career Highlights:** Owner/President/Consultant, Centillion Computer Services, Inc. (1999-Present); Microcomputer Specialist, City of Dunedin (1996-99); Network Administrator, Prudential Breliant Realty (1994-96); Membership/Computer Systems Manager, St. Pete Beach Chamber of Commerce (1993-94); Owner/President/Consultant, Ipsilon Corporation (1989-93). **Associations & Accomplishments:** Association of Information Technology Professionals, Pinellas County Chapter; City of Largo Public Works Advisory Board; Named to Who's Who Worldwide (1992-93); Named to International WHO'S WHO of Information Technology. **Education:** Fort Lauderdale Technical College, Diploma in Computer Programming (1969); Broward Community College; St. Petersburg Junior College. **Personal Information:** Married to Kay D. in 1993. Two children: Charles F. F. and Christina M. Two stepchildren: Lynn Scott and Lisa M. Three grandchildren: Joshua A., Jacob M., and Eugene F. Mr. Graul enjoys spending time with his family, music, photography and computers.

yoh SUPPORT SERVICES

E. G. Green

Operations Manager
Yoh Support Services
1010 Adams Avenue
Norristown, PA 19403
(610) 650-6246
Fax: (610) 650-6234
eg.green@yoh.com

7379

Business Information: Demonstrating considerable expertise in her field, Mrs. Green joined Yoh Support Services as Operations Manager in 1999. She oversees and directs a number of functions on behalf of the Company and its clientele. Possessing an excellent understanding of information technology, Mrs. Green supervises approximately 60 to 70 employees. She is responsible for overseeing sales, ensuring productive time management, evaluating staff performance, and maintaining client relationships. Displaying strong leadership skills, Mrs. Green builds on her previous experience as a consultant, territorial sales representative, and technical manager to deliverer consistent, reliable administration in his present position. Her career success reflects her ability to communicate, take on challenges and responsibilities, on deliver results on behalf of the Company and its clientele. Remaining with the Company and moving the corporate structure serves as her future endeavors. Yoh Support Services specializes in helpdesk outsourcing, providing valuable computer support to customers nationally. Since 1901, Yoh Support Services has provided the best in up-to-date scientific research and staffing. With innovation and vision, the Company has kept abreast of the latest science breakthroughs, thus, seamlessly moving to the forefront of the computer age. Presently, the Company employs a work force of more than 26,000 people. **Career Highlights:** Operations Manager, Yoh Support Services (1999-Present); Business Partner/Technical Manager, Soft-Switch/Lotus (1995-97); Wang: Territory Sales Representative (1992-95), Consultant (1978-92). **Associations & Accomplishments:** Eastern Technology Council; Help Desk Institute. **Personal Information:** Married to Michael Lucci in 1984.

N. Wayne Green

Engineering Associate
TRUTech, L.L.C.
2550 Duportail Street, Apartment E230
Richland, WA 99352
Fax: (209) 796-8958
wgreen@aol.com

7379

Business Information: Mr. Green was recruited to TRUTech, L.L.C. as an Engineering Associate in 1998. He is responsible for conducting technical surveys, providing consulting services, and performing evaluations. Possessing superior talents and an excellent understanding of his environmental role, he devises engineering plans, attends meetings, collects data, composes data reports, and deals with the technical writing and programming of the systems. Currently, Mr. Green is working on areas for nuclear waste, enabling the Company to help better the world. Highly regarded, he is credited with designing several pilot plans and being involved in chemistry to enhance the environment. Mr. Green's future plans include remaining with the Company and conducting more environmental work. Founded in 1996, TURTech, L.L.C. is a technology services firm that specializes in bettering the environment. Located in Richland, Washington, the Company conducts extensive research, enabling the employees to devise plans that will help in the quest to clean up the nation. A staff of 15 dedicated employees are dedicated to finding a solution to the environmental problems the nation is facing at present. **Career Highlights:** Engineering Associate, TRU Tech, L.L.C. (1998-Present); Manager, Fluor Daniel Hanford, Inc. (1996-98); Technical Director, Fluor Daniel, Inc. (1981-96). **Associations & Accomplishments:** American Institute of Chemical Engineers. **Education:** University of Kansas: Ph.D./Ch.E. (1969), M.S. in Nuclear Engineering, B.S. in Chemical Engineering. **Personal Information:** Four children: Wendy, Jason, Rebecca, and David. Mr. Green enjoys skiing, photography and music.

Daniel Gueguen

Operations Manager
Elantiel
8 Rue Raphaël
Asnieres, France 92600
+33 140864824
Fax: +33 147905655
daniel.gueguen@elantiel.net

7379

Business Information: Serving in the position of Operations Manager of Elantiel, Mr. Gueguen provides oversight and direction of all daily technical operations, fulfilling a number of duties on behalf of the Company and its clientele. Possessing superior talents and an excellent understanding of technology, he is responsible for information technology management, Web site design and development, and teaching his clients' employees on new, cutting-edge technology. With the notable ability to understand complex problems and communicate solutions to both customers and the Company's internal staff, Mr. Gueguen focuses his attention on client satisfaction. In the future, he plans to continue working in this capacity and looking forward to assisting in the completion of future corporate goals. His success reflects his leadership ability to form teams with synergy and technical strength, take on challenges, and deliver results. Established in 1996, Elantiel engages in the development of Internet sites. Employing 10 personnel, the Company also provides clients with courses in the use of computer science. Utilizing new and innovative technological advances, the Company provides services to a clientele throughout France. **Career Highlights:** Operations Manager, Elantiel (1999-Present); Product Manager, Credit du Nord (1994). **Education:** INSEEC (1986). **Personal Information:** Mr. Gueguen enjoys sailing.

Riccardo Guerrera

Systems Analyst/Programmer
Hi Nrg Webdesigns
2355 Rue de Troyes
Laval, Quebec, Canada H7K 3R2
(514) 781-7687
Fax: (450) 668-9719
hinrgweb@funcow.com

7379

Business Information: Utilizing his extensive expertise in Web design, Mr. Guerrera serves as Systems Analyst and

Programmer for Hi Nrg Webdesigns. He is in charge of managing the entire work flow of the Company in the conduct of daily programming of software programs and assisting with the creating Web sites and contents. Highly regarded, Mr. Guerrera is responsible for the analysis, design, evaluation, testing, and implementation of cutting edge Web technologies on behalf of the Company and its clientele. The most rewarding aspects of his career is his savvy customer relations and programming skills. In the nea future, he looks forward to continuing with the Company and possibly moving to the United States. Attributing his career success to dedication, his problem solving ability, and his willingness to learn new things, Mr. Guerrera stays on top of technology by reading and researching new products and companies. Located in Laval, Canada, Hi Nrg Webdesigns engages in the design of networks for small and medium sized companies. Founded in 1998, the Company builds programs and composes Web designs for their clients sites. Operating on a national level, the Company employs a small staff of professionals who help generate annual revenues in excess of $60,000. **Career Highlights:** Systems Analyst/Programmer, Hi Nrg Webdesigns (Present). **Associations & Accomplishments:** Association Pontelandofese of Montreal. **Education:** McGill University, Certificate (1999); Systems Analyst/Design Certificate. **Personal Information:** Mr. Guerrera enjoys down hill skiing and information technology.

Christopher Guido

President
Shore Systems, Inc.
37 Berry Place
Albertson, NY 11507
(212) 564-1818
cguido@shoresys.com

7379

Business Information: Mr. Guido serves as President of Shore Systems, Inc. He is currently partnering with other firms in direct sales, financing of jobs, and ensuring all clients' needs are met. A savvy, 11 year professional, he ensures customer satisfaction and oversees new technical solutions development and acquisition. Pushing the Corporation toward expansion and growth in the global markets, Mr. Guido is starting to provide additional cutting edge services to a growing clientele. His father, founder of "Computer Land" in 1982, got him interested in the technology field. Mr. Guido's future plans include moving Shore Systems into the area of supportive Internet, installing cameras on DOS line that will enable clients to view thier office "bus" from any location in the country as well as around the world. Securing a contract with New York City, servicing the infrastructure for 22 different offices is cited as Mr. Guido's greatest accomplishment to date. His success reflects his leadership ability to think out-of-the-box, deliver results, and take on new challenges. Since 1996, Shore Systems, Inc. has been providing quality computer networking to the community. The Corporation also provides office automation systems and integrations. Shore Systems is also a Microsoft provider. The Corporation provides services throughout New York and New Jersey. **Career Highlights:** President, Shore Systems, Inc. (1996-Present); Vice President, Electronic Filing Centers, Inc. (1992-96); Vice President, Top Notch Computer Service, Inc. (1988-92). **Associations & Accomplishments:** New Cassell Business Association; Long Island Help Desk Association. **Education:** Pace University, B.B.A. (1988). **Personal Information:** Married to Gina in 1994.

Peter Gulotta

Senior Systems Architect
North American Performance Group (NAPG, Inc.)
2597 Charlestown Road
Phoenixville, PA 19460
(610) 933-0922
Fax: (209) 671-9694
peteg@napg.com

7379

Business Information: With 20 years of extensive practical experience in the technology field, Mr. Gulotta joined North American Performance Group in 1998. Serving as Senior Systems Architect, he assumes responsibility for distributed systems consulting for Unix systems. Displaying his skills in this highly technical position, Mr. Gulotta provides consulting to firms with large Unix data centers and advises the clientele on performance analysis, high system availability, and overall distributed systems management. Security audits and general systems management also falls under the realm of his responsibilities. Additionally, Mr. Gulotta designs new computer systems and conducts research to improve their design, and develop and adapt principles for applying computers to new uses. One of many professional accomplishments, the greatest has been development of high level courses and teaching them to other consultants. An authority in the field, Mr. Gulotta attributes his success to working for Hewlett-Packard early in his career where he was able to grow academically, professional, and personally. Keeping pace with new Unix technology and attaining an Oracle DBA Certificate serves as his long-term goals. A group within the North American Performance Group, Unix System's Group operates as a consulting organization with a focus on performance and security analysis. National in scope, the Group was established in 1996 with local operations in Pennsylvania manned by three technology professionals. **Career Highlights:** Senior Systems Architect, North American Performance Group (NAPG, Inc.) (1998-Present); Senior Systems Architect, Livingston Consulting (1997-98); Systems Consultant, Hewlett-Packard (1983-97). **Associations & Accomplishments:** USENIX; SAGE; Smithsonian Institute; Computer Measurement Group. **Education:** Drexel University, B.S. in Computer Science (1980). **Personal Information:** Mr. Gulotta enjoys home remodeling and trips to Key West.

Rajesh Gupta

Project Manager
4C Solutions
P.O. Box 832
East Moline, IL 61244
(309) 751-6111
Fax: (309) 755-3099
rajesh_k_gupta@hotmail.com

7379

Business Information: As Project Manager of 4C Solutions, Mr. Gupta manages projects from conception to implementation, decides on new employees job descriptions, and interviews prospective employees. He oversees 18 highly skilled employees and ensures all aspects of the operation run according to the policies set by top executives. Years of education and experience has enabled Mr. Gupta to acquire the necessary skills to effectively complete his job duties. Keeping abreast on new developments in the field, he relays pertinent information to his staff. He plans to obtain the position of an executive level manager, gaining greater responsibilities and authority. Established in 1995, 4C Solutions specializes in E-solutions, providing Web solutions to fit the needs of individual clients. The consulting Firm prides itself on creativity, collaboration, committment, and computing excellence. This $18 million Firm presently employs the expertise of 200 people to assist in various aspects of the business. **Career Highlights:** Project Manager, 4C Solutions (1997-Present); Head Programmer, ITASCA Group (1996-97); Programmer Analyst, Eagle Point (1994-96). **Associations & Accomplishments:** Project Management Institute; Delta Sigma Pi Professional Fraternity. **Education:** Angelo State University, B.S. (1994). **Personal Information:** Married to Renu in 1996. One child: Rohan. Mr. Gupta enjoys driving, spending time with family and reading.

Thomas A. Gust

Senior Network Administrator/Supervisor
TeleCommunication Systems, Inc.
60 Second Street, Suite 201
Shalimar, FL 32579
(850) 651-6007
Fax: (850) 651-2650
gustt@hqafsoc.hurlhurt.af.mil

7379

Business Information: With an extensive background in computer software analysis and design, Mr. Gust serves as Senior Network Administrator and Supervisor of TeleCommunication Systems, Inc. He manages multiple Sun UNIX work stations and servers for the Global Command and Control System at Headquarters Air Force Special Operations Command. Mr. Gust assumes accountability for system, network, security, and Oracle database administration. Previousley during his career, he was responsible for the development of object-oriented computer models using the Joint Modeling and Simulation System architecture at Eglin Air Force Base. He designed the Weapons Delivery System calculation engine software now being used by the United States Air Force fighter pilots for mission planning, developed simulation software for the United States Navy, and developed Magnetic Resonance Imaging systems software. Demonstrating expertise in the information technology field, Mr. Gust plans to remain cognizant of technical innovations in the future. TeleCommunication Systems, Inc. specializes in providing commercial and government installations of telecommunications systems and computer contract support for the Department of Defense. Established in 1987, the Annapolis, Maryland based Corporation employs 500 professionals throughout three facilities. **Career Highlights:** Senior Network Administrator/Supervisor, TeleCommunication Systems, Inc. (1996-Present); Senior Software Engineer, Computer Science and Applications, Inc. (1995-96); Senior Senior Analyst, Suncoast Scientific, Inc. (1994-95); Lead Software Engineer, Keystone Computer Associates, Inc. (1987-89); Systems Analyst, Philips Medical Systems (1985-87). **Associations & Accomplishments:** Mathematical Association of America; Assistant Scoutmaster, Boy Scouts of America; American Tae Kwon Do Association; Institute of Electrical and Electronic Engineers; Association for Computing Machinery, Computer Science Conference Proceedings (1994); Computer Society Proceedings of the Conference on Software Maintenance (1992); Author of "An Illustration of Extending Structured Software Development to Include Object-Oriented Techniques"; Co-Author of "Locating User Functionality in Old Code". **Education:** University of West Florida, M.S. in Software Engineering (1994); Brigham Young University, B.S. in Civil Engineering (1977); Certified Solaris Network Administrator, Sun Microsystems, Inc. (1999). **Personal Information:** Married to Lorelei in 1978. Three children: Clint, Brent, and Tabitha. Mr. Gust enjoys Tae Kwon Do and scouting.

Assad Haddad

Managing Director
I.D.A.
Rue du Poncha 19
Nil-Staint Vincent, Belgium 1457
+32 10650860
Fax: +32 10657706
assad.haddad@village.uunet.ve

7379

Business Information: Mr. Haddad is the Managing Director for I.D.A. or International Data Access. In this highly profesional position, he concentrates his efforts on business operations in the Middle East and Africa. Mr. Haddad is also the Owner of I.D.A.'s international side of operations. He directs the day-to-day administration and operational activities, presides over meetings, and monitors financial transactions. Mr. Haddad also reports to the Board of Directors, prepares presentations, as well as implements Company policies and objectives. His goal is to develop specific areas that play an important part to security networks. His ability to speak English, French, and Dutch, as well as Spanish, German, and Arabic has enabled him to work unhindered in the global market place. Success is attributed to his ability to produce results and aggressively take on new challenges. I.D.A. is an established data networking consultancy and solutions provider. Founded in 1997, the Company is involved in the design, sales, and installation services to clients all over the world. Employing a qualified and skilled staff of 12 individauls, I.D.A. mainly serves the banking and corporate network industries. Headquartered in Maryland, operations in St. Vincent, Belgium are partners with several companies within the United States. I.D.A. reports an annual income of $600,000. **Career Highlights:** Managing Director, I.D.A. (1997-Present); Senior Area Director, Verifone/HP (1995); Area Director, Motorola (1981). **Associations & Accomplishments:** Past Member, Institute of Electronics and Electrical Engineers. **Education:** Boston University, M.B.A. (1985); University of Louvain, B.Sc. in Telecommunications. **Personal Information:** Married to Anne Puttemans in 1980. Two children: Pierre-Antoine and Thomas. Mr. Haddad enjoys sports.

Laurence A. Hall Jr.

President
Spacenet, Inc.
907 East Strawbridge Avenue, Suite D
Melbourne, FL 32901
(407) 951-1717
Fax: (407) 308-3225
hall@spacey.net

7379

Business Information: Mr. Hall serves as the President of Spacenet, Inc. He performs all administration, network, and software consulting for the Corporation. Working closely with clients, he discusses their situation and evaluates their problems hoping to discover and implement a feasible solution. A savvy, 17 year professional, Mr. Hall encourages newcomers to the industry to complete their education and stay current on all issues while getting the needed experience. Looking to the 21st Century, Mr. Hall hopes to remain up-to-date on all technologies and is coordinating plans to expand the Corporation's locations. His success reflects his ability to think outside the box, deliver results, and take on new challenges. Spacenet, Inc. is a full service Internet service provider offering dialup, ISDN, FR, e-commerce hosting, database hosting, virtual private networks, and dedicated lines to facilitate the needs of its clients. The Corporation is also a Compaq authorized reseller and Microsoft certified solutions provider. Established in 1996, the Corporation continues to remain on the cutting edge of technology and adapts to the constant changes in the industry by updating its services as frequently as possible. **Career Highlights:** President, Spacenet, Inc. (1996-Present); Senior Consultant, Northrop Grumman Corporation (1989-99); Senior Engineer, DBA Systems, Inc. (1982-89). **Associations & Accomplishments:** Who's Who Among Students in American Universities and Colleges (1979); Florida Internet Service Providers Association. **Education:** Florida Technical University: M.S. (1983), M.B.A. (1980), B.S. (1979). **Personal Information:** Mr. Hall enjoys scuba diving, boating, snow skiing and travel.

Raymond V. Hall

Chief Trainer
Raymond V. Hall Training & Consultant Services
900 South Wabash Avenue, #504
Chicago, IL 60605-2224
(312) 322-1061
Fax: (312) 322-1062
raymondvhall@usa.net

7379

Business Information: A prominent and respected professional, Mr. Hall founded Raymond V. Hall Training & Consultant Services in 1988. Serving as Chief Trainer of the Company, he identifies businesses that are in need of services then designs and delivers appropriate interventions or training courses for these clients. Highly regarded and possessing an excellent understanding of technology, Mr. Hall is also responsible for maintaining computer networks and formulating and deploying all marketing and sales strategies. Attributing his success to his ability to embrace change, he looks forward to continuing to promote corporate advancement. An established and reputable company, Raymond V. Hall Training & Consultant Services provides technical consulting assistance. Utilizing innovative training techniques, the Company works with clients to determine if businesses are in need of new technology or procedures. The Company implements procedures and installs new technology, and then trains employees on the use of these cutting-edge developments. **Career Highlights:** Chief Trainer, Raymond V. Hall Training & Consultant Services (1999-Present); Technical Support Specialist, Institute of Real Estate Management (1997-99); Program Director, Chicago Department of Public Health (1994-96); Instructor, Wang Laboratories (1981-88). **Associations & Accomplishments:** International Society for Performance Improvement; Chicago Land Chapter American Society for Training and Development. **Education:** Roosevelt University, B.B.A. (1974); University of Illinois at Chicago (1989); Northeastern Illinois University (1976); DePaul University (1977).

Rodney D. Hall

Division Director
Solutions By Design
2807 North Parham Road, Suite 360
Richmond, VA 24401
(804) 270-3636
Fax: (804) 270-4646
rhall@sbd.com

7379

Business Information: Utilizing more than 10 years of experience in the technology field, Mr. Hall joined Solutions By Design in 1998. In the capacity of Division Director, he is in charge of all aspects of client project management. He provides Lotus Certified Training for Notes for the Company's internal staff and corporate clients. Additionally, Mr. Hall visits client sites, offering consulting services in Lotus Notes and Domino. Coordinating resources and schedules, overseeing time lines and assignments, and determining the overall strategic direction also fall within the purview of Mr. Hall's responsibilities. Taking classes, reading trade journals, and obtaining additional certifications keep him on the cutting edge of technology. His success reflects his leadership ability to build strong teams with synergy, technical strength, and a customer oriented attitude, as well as take on new challenges. Looking to the future, Mr. Hall is utilizing strategic planning in order to position himself to launch his own company. Headquartered in Vienna, Virginia, Solutions By Design provides computer consulting services to businesses throughout the United States. The Company performs application development, systems administration, and offers technological consulting. Established in 1987, the Company consists of a staff of 75 qualified professionals. **Career Highlights:** Division Director, Solutions By Design (1998-Present); Executive Vice President, Solution 2000 Inc. (1995-98); Lead Trainer and Developer, Quality Systems, Inc. (1994-95); Service and Support Manager Connecting Point Computer Centers (1990-93). **Associations & Accomplishments:** North American Certified Lotus Instructor Advisory Council; Certified Lotus Professional: Principal Notes System Administrator (R4), Principal Notes Application Developer (R4), Certified Notes System Administrator (R5), Certified Notes Application Developer (R5), Certified Lotus Instructor (Level 3). **Education:** Eastern Mennonite University B.A. Computer Information Systems and Business Administration (1990). **Personal Information:** Married to Terry in 1988. One child: Evanna Christine. Mr. Hall enjoys keyboard and vocal music.

Brent M. Han, Ph.D.

President
HNA Consulting, Inc.
7078 Falls Reach Drive, Suite 301
Falls Church, VA 22043
(703) 241-9331
Fax: (703) 241-2120
bhan@hnac.com

7379

Business Information: Dr. Han functions in the capacity of President with HNA Consulting Inc. He is responsible for the overall management of the Company, as well as providing leading edge consulting services to a local clientele. A topnotch, eight year veteran of technology, Dr. Han determines the overall technical direction and formulates business and marketing plans to keep HNA outfront of industry competitors. His background history includes stints as Project Manager of Federal Data Corporation and Member of Technical Staff with MITRE Corporation. Drawing from this extensive occupational experience and academic ties, Dr. Han designs, specifies, and develops state-of-the-art database systems management software. Recognized as an expert and authority, he maintains customer relationships, sells and pushes products and services to market, and oversees general business administration and solutions. He started HNA Consulting because of the many challenges and wanting to be his own boss. Strategic plans include expanding the Company to the national level. Dr. Han's advice is "Expect to spend a lot of time at home and at work if you don't have dedication. Sacrifices have to be made." HNA Consulting, Inc., established in 1998, engages in computer consulting services and manufacturing activities, mainly on a local level. Located in Falls Church, Virginia, HNA Consulting specializes in database design, development, and implementation. Presently, two professional experts oversee all aspects of day-to-day operations of the Company. **Career Highlights:** President, HNA Consulting, Inc. (1998-Present); Project Manager, Federal Data Corporation (1994-98); Member of Technical Staff, MITRE Corporation (1991-94). **Associations & Accomplishments:** Institute of Electronics and Electrical Engineering; National Honor Society; National Artificial Intelligence Honor Society. **Education:** George Washington University, Ph.D. (1999). **Personal Information:** Dr. Han enjoys skiing, soccer, golf, reading and sky diving.

Wayne A. Haney

Chief Executive Officer/President
In-Net
116 Cedar Hill Church Road
Clinton, TN 37716
(865) 289-5125
wayneh@in-netcorp.com

7379

Business Information: As Chief Executive Officer of In-Net, Mr. Haney also fulfills the responsbility of President. He oversees and directs all daily adminstration and operations, to include financial and profit and loss statistics, business accounts, and contract negotiations. A savvy professional of technology, Mr. Haney successfully builds and implements essential programs so that clients may make full use of their software capabilities. With high aspirations for the future of his Firm, he plans to take the steps necessary for growth and expansion of products and services. His success reflects his ability to take on new challenges and deliver results on behalf of the Firm and its clientele. In-Net engages in the provision of computer related consulting services for client companies The Firm specializes in such areas as application and Web development and Internet programming. Established in 2000, the Firm is dedicated to producing user friendly programs and other comprehensive services to clients who need to upgrade their systems for future business development. The Company operates out of one convenient location, while functioning under the talents and expertise of four professional consultants and technology experts. **Career Highlights:** Chief Executive Officer/President, In-Net (2000-Present); Systems Engineer, Pomeroy Computers (1999); Technical Instructor, Roane State Community (1999); Support Analyst, Covenant Health (1998). **Education:** Roane State Community College.

Larry Harker

Director of e-Solution Services
Dewpoint, Inc.
90 Executive Drive
Carmel, IN 46032
(317) 814-8289
Fax: (317) 814-8264
larry@dewptinc.com

7379

Business Information: Possessing superior talents in the information technology field, Mr. Harker serves as Director of e-Solution Services for Dewpoint, Inc. In this capacity since 1997, he utilizes his advanced skills to manage all technical resources and maintain the network infrastructure, performing diagnostic tests, systems upgrades, and server configurations. Possessing an excellent understanding, Mr. Harker is also responsible for conducting all technical training, and assumes oversight of all technicians, providing them with guidance and comprehensive direction as they strive to meet client needs. He has enjoyed tremendous success in his current position with Dewpoint, Inc., and he aspires to be promoted to Chief Information Officer in the future. Established in 1995 Dewpoint, Inc. is engages in state-of-the-art Web development and e-commerce solutions for the corporate environment. Headquartered in Carmel, Indiana, the Corporation employs the talents and expertise of 30 highly skilled technicians who generate revenues in excess of $30 million annually. Dewpoint, Inc. specializes in providing clients with cutting edge global network designs, and also offers electronic commerce setup with round-the-clock systems assistance. **Career Highlights:** Director of e-Solution Services, Dewpoint, Inc. (1997-Present); Consultant, Whittman-Hart (1996-97); Network Administrator, Anthm (1991-96); Service Technician, Computerland, Carmel (1989-91). **Associations & Accomplishments:** Indiana Information Technology Association. **Education:** Southern Illiniois University: B.S. (1987), A.A.S. in Electronics (1986). **Personal Information:** Married to Teri in 1989. Three children: Kalyn, Isaac, and Tori. Mr. Harker enjoys water skiing and basketball.

Morgan Webb Harman

Manager of Production
Warner Brothers Online
2210 West Olive Avenue, 3rd Floor
Burbank, CA 91505
(818) 977-3438
Fax: (818) 841-6106
morgan@wb.com

7379

Business Information: Possessing unique talent in the Web design field, Mr. Harman joined Warner Brothers Online in 1999 as the Manager of Production. He presides over the management of around a dozen online productions for the Company's Web site and ensures that each service offered online is kept updated with the latest information. Assisting in the development of the Web site, he designs Web pages to be posted. Before joining Warner Brothers, he served as Webmaster with Pleasant Holidays, LLC. His background history also includes stints as Information Systems Manager for Illusion Inc. and Multimedia Engineer at AND Interactive. Mr. Harman stays abreast of new technological advances in his field by reading trade journals, networking online, and experimentation. His career success reflects his ability to think out-of-the-box and aggressively take on new challenges and responsibilities. Committed to the further development of Warner Brothers Online, he looks forward to assisting in the completion of future corporate goals. Warner Brothers Online, a division of Warner Brothers, provides the hosting, development, and production of online entertainment content for the Company. The Division was created in 1995 and operations employ approximately 100 skilled individuals. **Career Highlights:** Manager of Production, Warner Brothers Online (1999-Present); Webmaster, Pleasant Holidays, LLC (1998-99); Information System Manager, Illusion Inc. (1996-98); Multimedia Engineer, AND Interactive (1995-96). **Education:** California State University at Northridge, B.S. in Physics (1994). **Personal Information:** Married in 1991.

Wesley G. Harris

Senior Trainer/Consultant
Main Control, Inc.
7900 Westpark Drive, Suite T500
McLean, VA 22102
(703) 827-7056
Fax: (703) 748-7790
harriswg@maincontrol.com

7379

Business Information: As Senior Trainer and Consultant for Main Control, Inc., Mr. Harris is responsible for a great deal of training and consulting for the Corporation. In this capacity, he trains new employees and consults with clients in an attempt to improve information technology services. Possessing an excellent understanding of technology, he assists customers in redesigning systems to better utilize information technology within their organizaiton. The most rewarding aspect of his career his making a difference in troubled products. Attributing his success to being in the right place at the right time, Mr. Harris plans to follow technology, moving further up within the Corporation if the opportunity arises, and taking on new challenges. Main Control, Inc. engages in information technology infrastructure resource management. Established in 1994, the Corporation helps clients keep track of and save assets and attempts to show customers that information technology is more than just supplying support. Employing 200 personnel, the Corporation is dedicated to informing other companies of the advantages of utilizing informaiton technology within day to day business. **Career Highlights:** Senior Trainer/Consultant, Main Control, Inc. (1999-Present); Assistant Director of Education, Computer Learning Center (1997-99); Electrical Engineer, Universal Dynamics (1997-98). **Associations & Accomplishments:** Institute of

Electrical & Electronics Engineers; NHS; AMCE; American Institute of Electrical Engineers. **Education:** American Intercontinental University, Master's degree in Information Technology (Present); North Carolina A&T State University, B.S. in Electrical Engineering (1996): Advantec Institute, Windows NT diploma (1998). **Personal Information:** Mr. Harris enjoys roller blading, music, recording and modeling.

Eric A. Harrison

Program Manager
Unisys Corporation
10850 Via Frontera
San Diego, CA 92127-1788
(858) 451-4299
Fax: (858) 451-4153
eric.harrison@unisys.com

7379

Business Information: An invaluable asset of the Unisys Corporation team since it was founded, Mr. Harrison used his extensive computer training to work his way up through the ranks of Unisys. Starting as a Repair Operations Manager, Mr. Harrison has steadily advanced to his present position of Program Manager through hard work, diligence, and company loyalty. Possessing an excellent understanding of his field, Mr. Harrison currently supervises marketing, quality assurance, and network maintenance. Now an irreplaceable asset to Unisys, Mr. Harrison is working hard to ensure the Corporation's products are number one in a complex and competitive industry. One of the premiere manufacturers of information technology, Unisys is a key component in the computer industry. Established in 1986, Unisys employs over 30,000 people and has estimated annual revenuesof $8.5 billion. Headquartered in San Diego, California, Unisys builds servers and mainframes for computers as well as creates network software solutions. **Career Highlights:** Unisys Corporation: Program Manager (1997-Present), Director of Technical Services (1991-97), Manager of Repair, Test, and Engineering (1989-91), Repair Operations Manager (1987-89). **Education:** Weber State, B.A. in Business (1986); Utah Valley State College, A.A.S. in Electronic Technology. **Personal Information:** Married to Robin in 1980. One child: Alisha. Mr. Harrison enjoys reading, motorcycle riding, fishing and racquetball.

Judith A. Hartman

Database Administrator
Limited Technology Services
206 Merrimack Meadows Lane
Tewksbury, MA 01876
(978) 975-6137
Fax: (978) 975-6700
jhartman@mast.com

7379

Business Information: As the Database Administrator for Limited Technology Services, Ms. Hartman has been with the Company since 1999. In her position, she is responsible for overseeing the Oracle database management system, networking infrastructure, and tuning of systems. Moreover, she oversees the systems backups and installing, upgrading, and maintaining the system's functionality and operational status. Troubleshooting for any glitches that may occur, Ms. Hartman ensures data security, integrity, and reliability. Looking to the future in the 21st century, she plans on getting Oracle, Internet, and Web database experience. Highly regarded, she also attributes her success to staying on top of technology and striving to be the best. Located in Tewksbury, Massachusetts, Limited Technology Services is a leading manufacturer of clothing for national wear. The Company is a division of The Limited Stores, Inc. and produces quality, durable clothing for men and women for all types of weather. A staff of 700 employees works hard to produce up-to-date styles and comfortable garments for everyday use. **Career Highlights:** Database Administrator, Limited Technology Services (1999-Present); Director of Database, Colonial Gas Company (1976-99). **Associations & Accomplishments:** International Oracle Users Group. **Education:** University of Massachusetts, A.A. (1976). **Personal Information:** Two children: Leslie and Brittany. Ms. Hartman enjoys time with her children, dancing and crafts.

Kashif R. Hashmi

Director of Information Technologies Services
Base Technologies, Inc.
1749 Old Meadow Road #500
McLean, VA 22102
(703) 848-2400
Fax: (703) 848-0804
kashhashmi@yahoo.com

7379

Business Information: Proficient in all areas of technology, Mr. Hashmi was recruited to Base Technologies, Inc. more than two years ago. Serving as Director of Information Technologies Services, he utilizes over 10 years of practical experience in the field of technology in order to direct daily operations in the development of databases, network systems, and software. Overseeing the Corporation's IT infrastructure, he is proactively involved in multiple projects and implements the latest technologies in order to promote a more efficient and productive corporate structure. Always alert to new opportunities, techniques, and approaches, Mr. Hashmi's goal is to facilitate continued corporate growth and geographic expansion with Base Technologies, Inc. Established in 1987, Base Technologies, Inc. is dedicated to providing information technology services for federal and state government such as Department of Defense, Department of Commerce, Department of Justice, and Department of Transportation, in addition to commercial clients. Headquartered in McLean, Virginia, the Corporation employs a staff of over 200 qualified personnel to meet the demands of a growing clientele. BTI is the one-stop shop of IT consulting and IT solution provider, providing services ranging from software development, Intranet/e-commerce Internet development, database full life cycle development to LAN and WAN solutions. Presently, the Corporation generates in excess of $18.7 million in annual revenues. **Career Highlights:** Director of Information Technologies Services, Base Technologies, Inc. (1998-Present); Senior Systems Analyst, International Database Systems (1997). **Associations & Accomplishments:** Vice President, Association of Pakistan's Engineers and Scientists of North American; Board of Directors, Pakistan National League, Washington, D.C.; Board of Directors, Jagtech, USA; Project Management Institute; Vice President, Pakistan's Student Association GWU; Alpha Sigma Lamda Honors Society; George Washington University Alumni Association. **Education:** George Washington University, M.S. in Management Information Systems (1998); Strayer University, B.S. in Computer Information Systems with Honors (1996). **Personal Information:** Married to Iram in 2000.

Larry R. Haskell

Vice President/Owner
NeighborNet
P.O. Box 11608
Spring, TX 77391
(281) 251-6381
Fax: (281) 376-3125
neighbornet@neighbornet.com

7379

Business Information: Functioning in the role of Vice President and Owner of NeighborNet, Mr. Haskell is involved in the set up of services and marketing of the business. He determines the overall strategic direction and business contriubtion of the information systems function. In addition, he is responsible for overseeing the Company's operations on a day-to-day basis. Drawing from years of occupational experience, Mr. Haskell has developed the skills needed to maintain the highest standards of professional excellence. He attributes his success to a willingness to adapt or change and the willingness to stay in tune with the technical industry. Mr. Haskell's goal is to expand the operation throughout Houston and other cities. His advice is "make sure you've done all your homework and research." Established in 1994, NeighborNet provides Internet services for 64 communities in Houston, Texas with private Intranets, enabling them to talk amongst each other regarding serious topics. The Company is also dedicated to the development and design of Web sites for the advertisement of commercial companies online. Employing a staff of 13 individuals, the Company reports an estimated annual revenue of $250,000. **Career Highlights:** Vice President/Owner, NeighborNet (1997-Present); Compaq Computers: Quality Customer Services (1996-97), Electronic Services (1994-96); Data Management, IT (1991-94). **Associations & Accomplishments:** Memorial Northwest Homeowners Association; Chamber of Commerce; Joint Economic Development Committee, Houston Northwest Chamber; National Collegiate Handball Champion; Cypress Creek United Civic Association; Community Association Institute; Better Business Bureau. **Education:** Lake Forest College: Master's degree in Engineering (In Progress), Bachelor's degree in Chemistry (1990). **Personal Information:** Married to Patti in 1993. Two children: Avery and Monika. Mr. Haskell enjoys handball and snowskiing.

Nancy K. T. Hayata

Owner
South Bay Online
P.O. Box 11236
Torrance, CA 90510
(310) 517-9926
nancy@sbol.com

7379

Business Information: The Owner of South Bay Online, Ms. Hayata started this business with her husband in 1995 and currently serves as President. Thrilled to be doing her small part in helping the community, she is primarily responsible for overseeing the daily operations. Ms. Hayata stays involved in the Web programming aspect of her business, enjoying it the most because of her background in art. Determining the overall strategic direction and business contribution of the information systems function also fall within her realm of responsibilities. She believes that her current success is due to support from friends and the community, meeting new people, and the attitude that drives her to move forward. This success reflects her ability to aggressively take on new challenges. Looking to the new millennium, Ms. Hayata is expecting further Company growth. She eventually plans to put in new access lines and go public. An Internet service provider, South Bay Online offers Web design, Web hosting, and Internet access to small businesses and residential clients in the Greater Los Angeles area. The Company began operations in 1995 and employs a dedicated work force of 35 persons. **Career Highlights:** Owner, South Bay Online (1995-Present); Manager, Executive Pen & Pencil (1985-95). **Associations & Accomplishments:** Vice President, PTA Board. **Education:** University of California at Los Angeles, B.S. (1979); Fashion Institute Design and Merchandising, A.A. **Personal Information:** One child: Bradley.

John P. Heger, Ph.D.

Director
Pro-Tech
P.O. Box 169
Lucens, Switzerland 1522
+41 213839335
protec@altavista.net

7379

Business Information: As Director of Pro-Tech, Dr. Heger oversees all daily administration and operations of the Company. He determines the strategic direction and vision, and formulates business and marketing plans. His focus is on keeping the Company out-front of industry competitors. Possessing an excellent understanding of technology, Dr. Heger analyzes his clients' needs and creates state-of-the-art Webssites. He also consults with clients on production management, advising on necessary changes and implementation. Highly regarded by his customers and colleagues, he strives to change his clientele's approach in their production management including information technology and other area, such as management consulting. He attributes his success to confidence in himself and his ability to aggressively taking on all challenges and deliver results. Dr. Heger plans to stay with the business, continuing to expand operations internationally. Established in 1983, Pro-Tech provides Internet and management consultancy. Reporting annual sales of $75,000, the Company is located in Lucens, Switzerland. **Career Highlights:** Director, Pro-Tech (1995-Present); Director, Unics (1983-95); Branch Manager, Control Data Corporation (1978-83). **Associations & Accomplishments:** Swiss Association for Prevention of Violence within Families and Against Sexual Abuse of Children. **Education:** EPFL, Ph.D. (1975). **Personal Information:** Married to Andrea in 1996. Three children: J. Christopher, Sibylle, and Ghislaine. Dr. Heger enjoys reading books and walking his dog.

Melody J. Henderson

Telecommunications Manager
Computer Services
202 East 4th Street
Hughes Springs, TX 75656
(903) 572-4336
melody028@msn.com

7379

Business Information: Recruited to Computer Services as Telecommunications Manager in 1996, Ms. Henderson fulfills a number of duties on behalf of the Company. She is responsible for technical sales, network design, and systems administration. In this context, she explains technical aspects of a product to the sales force and clients, maintains and upgrades the network infrastructure, and administers and controls all daily operations of the systems functions. Possessing an excellent understanding of technology, Ms. Henderson is charged with management and oversight of the analysis, acqusistion, installation, and maintenance as well as support and tracking of operating systems, databases, compilers, utilities, software, and hardware. In the future, she plans on continuing to advance and make an impact in the computer industry Established in 1960, Computer Services is a banking service provider. The Company provides banking and financial services to corporations. Computer Services provides a software and Internet package to customers to provide them with their banking needs. The Company also employs consultants to help provide quality customer services to the clients. Headquartered in Texas, Computer Services employs 600 skilled professionals. **Career Highlights:** Telecommunications Manager, Computer Services (1996-Present); Software Engineer, ISYS (1995-96); Systems Engineer, Electronic Date Systems (1990-95). **Associations & Accomplishments:** IBM Advanced Technical Experts; Association of Computing Machinery.

Education: University of Texas, B.S. in Computer Science (1990). **Personal Information:** Married to Stephen I. in 1997. One child: Cheyenne Nicole. Ms. Henderson enjoys karate, tennis, golf and gardening.

Paul A. Henry

Manager of Business Development
Cyberguard
2000 West Commercial Boulevard, Suite 200
Fort Lauderdale, FL 33309-3061
(954) 958-3904
Fax: (954) 938-3901
controls@mediaone.net

7379

Business Information: Utilizing more than 20 years of practical experience in the technology industry, Mr. Henry serves as the Manager of Business Development for Cyberguard. He is responsible for the management of the Asian operations and assumes responsibility for the Company's worldwide business development and growth. Performing research on the latest software security applications, he is continually looking for new programs that can add to the Cyberguard armory against data theft. Mr. Henry holds no formal education degree. Instead, he holds several technical certifications and is completely self-educated. He cites setting priorities as the reason for his success and looks forward to working more in sales. Mr. Henry was the keynote speaker in the United States and Sweden on the subject of network security and has been published in numerous magazines. Created in 1995, Cyberguard is engaged in the specialty field of network security. The Company provides system security and firewalls utilizing the B-1 Orange Book Standard to businesses such as banks to prevent data loss and theft from unauthorized access by internal personnel or external individuals. Employing a staff of 145 personnel members, the Company reports an estimated $20 million in annual revenue. **Career Highlights:** Manager of Business Development, Cyberguard (1998-Present); Director, RTP Corporation (1996-98); Manager Control/International Group, Indeck (1980-98). **Education:** Community College; Microsoft Certified System Engineer; Microsoft Certified Professional & Internet; Certified Information System Security Professional. **Personal Information:** Married to Nancy in 1989. Mr. Henry enjoys boating.

Joseph Hershman

Consultant
IMI Systems, Inc.
300 Delaware Avenue
Wilmington, DE 19801
(302) 453-9930
joeh19012@aol.com

7379

Business Information: In his role as Consultant of IMI Systems, Inc., Mr. Hershman handles a variety of customer service related technical functions on a daily basis. Included in his responsibilities are activities such as data architecture, software creation and implementation, systems configuration, and strategic technical planning. Demonstrating extensive knowledge of his field gained through practical work experience and related education, Mr. Hershman lends his guidance and direction to the development and completion of database maintenance and programming functions, in addition to special interest projects such as Y2K compliance. Recognized for outstanding achievements in the industry, Mr. Hershman attributes success to his extensive education and a strong interest in learning. He realizes the importance of flexibility, and strives to include more technical project management into his role as he adapts to his ever changing working enviornment. IMI Systems, Inc. is a consulting firm that specializes in information technology consulting for industries ranging from financial institutions to manufacturing companies. Offering technical support for technical outsourcing solutions, the Corporation strives to implement cutting edge technology into standard operating procedures to ensure maximum satisfaction from customers. **Career Highlights:** Consultant, IMI Systems, Inc. (1998-Present); Senior Database Analyst, EDS-GMAC Mortgage Corporation (1992-98); Senior Programmer, Delaware Valley Regional Planning Commission (1987-92); Senior Consultant, Mellon Bank (1982-87). **Education:** University of Pennsylvannia, Post Graduate Studies; Temple University, M.A. in Computer Science and Information Science (1978); Muhlenberg College, B.S. in Natural Science (1976). **Personal Information:** Married. Four children.

Paul A. Hibbs

Information Systems Director
Coleman Research Corporation
9302 Lee Highway, Suite 800
Fairfax, VA 22031
(703) 934-7800
Fax: (703) 934-7810
paul_hibbs@mail.crc.com

7379

Business Information: Functioning as Information Systems Director for Coleman Research Corporation, Mr. Hibbs is accountable for plotting the overall strategic direction and determining the business contribution of the information systems function. In addition, he formulates cost effective solutions wile troubleshooting problems, as well as technical solutions. As for the next three to five years, he plans to advance from within the ranks of Coleman Research Corporation. Dedication and persistence have been major factors behind Mr. Hibbs' success. His advice is, "Be a good communicator." Coleman Research Corporation employs 1,200 people which are currently engaged in projects for the federal government. The Corporation oversees all information systems support for Fort Mead and the Medical University of South Carolina. Established in 1980, the Corporation's lucrative relationship with the American military has lead to a $150 million estimated revenue a year. **Career Highlights:** Information Systems Director, Coleman Research Corporation (1992-99); Senior Programmer, Best Programs (1991-92); Associate Programmer, Westat Inc. (1990-91). **Associations & Accomplishments:** Institute of Electronics and Electrical Engineers Computer Society; Associate Member, Fraternal Order of Police. **Education:** George Mason University, M.S. in Information Systems (1995); Illinois State University, B.S. in Computer Science (1990). **Personal Information:** Married to Sherri in 1991. One child: Michael.

Mark J. Hicks

Vice President
Hicks Technology Services
3640 Belvedere Street NW
Salem, OR 97304
(503) 588-9330
Fax: (503) 581-2794
mhicks@rocketmail.com

7379

Business Information: As Vice President of Hicks Technology Services, Mr. Hicks is responsible for maintaining the Company's competitive edge through ongoing technical training and skills enhancement. He seeks new opportunities to expand the relationship between HTS, its customers, and other industry partners. His knowledge of PC platforms and network environments provide customers and employees with informed consultation and solid solutions. He attributes much of his achievement to his family and his faith in Christ, and states that instinct and initiative are two keys to success. Hicks Technology Services is an Oregon based IT solutions firm founded in 1993. Specializing in the large scale rollout PC operating systems and software, the Company provides a fleet of services and ongoing technical support for their clientele. By continuing to research new ways to deploy both existing and emerging technologies, Hicks Technology is ensured a solid place in the IT industry. **Career Highlights:** **Education:** Microsoft Certified Systems Engineer (MCSE); IBM Router Bootcamp; ATM Concepts and Planning; Accelerated training on Windows 2000. **Personal Information:** Mr. Hicks enjoys camping and working with young adults in the Salem area. Mr. Hicks enjoys camping and working with young adults in the Salem area.

Charles Aaron Hite

Systems Engineer
Compunet Engineering
6901 Shawnee Mission Parkway, Suite 112
Overland Park, KS 66202
(913) 722-0007
Fax: (913) 651-5664
aaronh@cne-kc.com

7379

Business Information: As Systems Engineer of Compunet Engineering, Mr. Hite is involved in the design and development of WAN networking. Utilizing his technical background, he evaluates needs of clients to formulate strategic action plans to improve their networks or software applications. Overseeing training of employees, Mr. Hite demonstrates exceptional communcation skills as he conducts informative on-the-job training seminars. Credited with several impressive contributions to the overall effectiveness of the Company, he is recognized for his involvement in the design of the Gold Bank infastructure. Currently focusing time and attention on the implementation of video conferencing, Mr. Hite attributes his success to his

dedication to his personal savior, Jesus Christ. Headquartered in Overland Park, Kansas, Compunet Engineering employs 750 technically trained employees to assist in the completion of daily activities. Established in 1990, the subsidary of Gold Bank is engaged in LAN and WAN networking and consultancy. **Career Highlights:** Systems Engineer, Compunet Engineering (1999-Present); Systems Engineer, Computer Consultants (1996). **Education:** Johnson County Community College, Drafting Tech. (1995); Cisco Certified Network Professional; Microsoft Certified Systems Engineer; Citex Certified Administrator. **Personal Information:** Married to Amy R. in 1995. Two children: Aaron and Adin. Mr. Hite enjoys golf.

Matthew Stephen Hobbs

Technical Service Manager
Madge.web
One State Street Plaza, 12th Floor
New York, NY 10004
(212) 709-1150
matt.hobbs@madge.com

7379

Business Information: Serving as Technical Services Manager for the North American division of Madge.web, Mr. Hobbs is responsible for all technical services for the Company. He is charged with overseeing all research and development of virtual private networks and hosted web, application, servers, and services for a global market and maintaining a high level of productivity by his staff. Mr. Hobbs develops and implements new policies and procedures, negotiates contracts, and builds hardware and software capable of handling web hosted applications. Possessing an excellent understanding of technology, Mr. Hobbs' highlights include writing a code generator to migrate and port legacy mainframe applications to standard Unix systems and working as a team leader building the ANS/AOL European hosting infrastructure. A visionary, he plans to advance to a Director's position to better support Madge.web and achieve occupational success. Madge.web is an application service provider for international markets, focusing primarily on financial and media markets. Madge.web provides a European extention to the Real Networks broadcast network that will enable streaming media to be transferred seamlessly from the United States Real Broadcast Network (RBN) to the European Madge Broadcast Network (MBN). Established in 1986, the Madge groups of companies has grown to employ over 500 people worldwide generating large annual revenue. Becoming a global leader of automation system software and technology, Madge.web has established itself as a competent and reliable service provider for private and corporate businesses. **Career Highlights:** Technical Service Manager, Madge.web (1999-Present); Systems Engineer, MCI WorldCom (1998-99); Hosting Engineer, ANS Communications (1997-98); Lead Database Administrator, Agresso (1993-97). **Education:** Bournemouth University, B.S. in Engineering (1993); Oracle Certified Database Administrator, Cisco Certified, Microsoft Certified Systems Engineer. **Personal Information:** Married to Natasha in 1998. Two children: Naomi and Alexandra. Mr. Hobbs enjoys soccer, diving and karate.

Sami A. Hoda
Executive Manager
Digital Pyramid
7 Rising Hill Road
Pomona, CA 91766-4960
(909) 868-7418
Fax: (909) 868-0428
sami@digitalpyramid.com

7379

Business Information: Mr. Hoda functions in the capacity of Executive Manager for Digital Pyramid. He founded the Company several years ago and has dedicated his time to promoting the success of his entrepreneurial dream. Utilizing five years of experience, Mr. Hoda determines the overall strategic direction and business contribution of the information systems function. In this context, he oversees and directs Web design and Web hosting activities conducted within the Company. An expert troubleshooter, Mr. Hoda works with his staff and clients to locate the problem and uncover the solution. To better serve the Company, he has become a successful management by listening to his employees and taken their concerns into consideration. In the future, he prays for the success of Digital Pyramid and would like to move more into the administrative side of the Company. Mr. Hoda's success reflects his ability to think outside the box, deliver results, and aggressively take on new challenges. Digital Pyramid is a computer and network consulting firm. Established in 1998, the Company has acquired the skills of six information technology experts and is working to further its client base through extensive advertising and word of mouth referrals. The Company is available to customers in Pomona, California interested in upgrading or designing a computer network for their home or office. **Career Highlights:** Executive Manager, Digital Pyramid (1998-Present); Project Manager/Web Developer, Outwest Network Services

(1995-98); Student Technology Representative, Temple City Unified School District (1994-97). **Associations & Accomplishments:** Director of Web Development, Interactive Web Development Student Association; Site Builder Network-Level 12; California State Assembly Achievement Award, Outstanding Service to the Community. **Education:** California State Polytechnic University at Pomona, B.S. in Business Administration. **Personal Information:** Mr. Hoda enjoys volleyball and travel.

Tammy Lou Holden

Owner/Consultant
The Jesra Company
5710 East 7th Street #223
Long Beach, CA 90803
(310) 251-1595
wecc.tammyh@mailcity.com

7379

Business Information: As Owner and Consultant of The Jesra Company, Ms. Holden is in charge of the computer consulting for AS400 and Web development using Microsoft products. In this context, she engages in analysis, designing, programming, and consulting services. Utilizing 20 years of exceptional organizational skills and superior intellect, she has maintained an outstanding rapport with her customers and has yet to have unsatisfactory business dealings. Ms. Holden found herself in this profession purely by accident but it is obvious that some mistakes are worth making. Her career highlights include working as a team leader for many client companies, defining, analyzing, and organizing the projects for the programming teams. She is extremely proud of her accomplishments and has the compulsion to endeavor much more, if not all, in Web development. Ms. Holden's success reflects her leadership ability to form teams with synergy and technical strength, think outside the box, take on challenges, and deliver results. Established in 1993, The Jesra Company provides analysis, design, and programming services for client companies with AS/400 operating platforms as well as Internet and Intranet environments. Solely owned and operated, the Company specializes in computer and Web design consultation. **Career Highlights:** Owner/Consultant, The Jesra Company (1993-Present); Owner, Sysware, Inc. (1984-93); Consultant, Computer Systems & Applications (1981-84); Consultant, Independent Consulting Services (1982); Programmer/Analyst, Papa Gino's Restaurant (1981); Operations Supervisor, C.D. Burns of Boston (1980-81). **Associations & Accomplishments:** Aircraft Owners and Pilots Association; American Ostrich Association; Past Chairman, 99's The International Women's Pilots Association; Past Treasurer, Houston System 38 Users' Group; Past Vice President, Gulf Coast System 34/36 Users' Group; Recipient, Outstanding Service Award; Who's Who Among American Women. **Education:** California State University at Fullerton: Webmaster Certificate, Software Education of America, Principles of Infrastructure Deployment; California State University (1997); Learning Tree University; Boston College, Cobol Programming (1980). **Personal Information:** Ms. Holden enjoys photography, sailing, power boating, golf, skiing, crafts, bicycling, walking, hiking and backpacking.

John P. Holmertz

Independent Contractor
John Holmertz
3534 Highland Avenue
San Diego, CA 92105-3524
(619) 281-3310
jphnsd@aol.com

7379

Business Information: Demonstrating strategic systems and technical expertise, Mr. Holmertz serves as Independent Contractor. He is currently outsourced to the San Diego City Schools. Focusing his attention and effort on developing leading edge technologies, he is migrating a payroll system for the Schools from a main frame to a PC based system utilizing Cobal. He owns a consistent record of delivering results in support of objectives through communication and interpersonal skills, use of technology, and creative problem solving. Recently, Mr. Holmertz has recognized an increased need for Y2K consultants, and has efficiently responded to all his customers demands. An expert in Y2K conversions, Mr. Holmertz conducts systematic reviews of all internal hardware, software, and functions to verify that the systems is Year 2000 compliant. He has 20 years extensive experience in computer technology and prefers to work with operating systems such as UNIX. Mr. Holmertz's strategic plans include reeducating himself in HTML, Java, and Web-based programs. He anticipates future success with the continued delivery of quality services. San Diego City Schools is a network of public elementary, junior high, and senior high schools in the San Diego area. Specializing in general education, the Schools write their own curriculum, establish school times, offer extracurricular programs, and employ a quality staff of teachers, administrators, and support staff. **Career Highlights:** Independent Contractor, John Holmertz (1998-Present); Computer Programmer, Education Systems Exchange (1997-98); Computer Programmer, Otay Water District (1995-97). **Associations & Accomplishments:** UNIX General Interest Group. **Education:** Colemen College, A.S. in Computer Science (1976); California Polytechnic, B.S. in Business Administration (1973). **Personal Information:** Mr. Holmertz enjoys computers and programming.

Stuart B. Holoman

Consultant
Holocon, Inc.
2617 Countrywood Road
Raleigh, NC 27615-1222
(919) 847-8806
Fax: (919) 848-0572
holocon@compuserve.com

7379

Business Information: An experienced information technology Consultant with Holocon, Inc., Mr. Holoman performs a number of duties on behalf of the Corporation and its clients. He also fulfills the dual position of chief executive officer and president responsible for all daily administration and operational activities. In his capacity, Mr. Holoman provides consulting services, while conducting research, security analysis, and technical training. He determines the strategic direction and formulates all business and marketing plans, keeping the Corporation in the forefront of the industry. In the future, Mr. Holoman plans on facilitating new growth as well as developing innovative concepts. His professional success reflects his ability to tackle new challenges and deliver the appropriate results. Established in 1981, Holocon, Inc. is a computer and telecommunications consulting firm. Currently specializing in distributed systems operation, audio engineering, and general technology consulting services, the Corporation is focused on providing quality services to a growing clientele. Holocon is headquartered in Raleigh, North Carolina. **Career Highlights:** Consultant, Holocon, Inc (1981-Present); Senior Member of Technical Systems, Affiniti Group International (1999-00); Director of Computing Technology, Nortel (1978-81); Member of Technical Staff, Bell Laboratories (1970-78). **Associations & Accomplishments:** øKø; HKN; TBii; Volunteer, WCPE Radio. **Education:** Stevens Institute of Technology, ABD-MA (1976); North Carolina State University: M.S. in Electrical Engineering (1970), B.S. in Electrical Engineering (1965). **Personal Information:** Married to Elizabeth M. in 1993. Three children: Kristine Clements, Patricia, and Megan Smith. Mr. Holoman enjoys playing guitar, clarinet, radio announcing, music performance and music performance and astronomy.

Hassan Rezaei Homami

Senior System Engineer
Parson Brinkerhoff Farradyne
One Penn Plaza
New York, NY 10119
(212) 465-5492
Fax: (212) 465-5442
rezaei@pbworld.com

7379

Business Information: Utilizing 12 years of extensive academic and occupational experience in the technology field, Mr. Homami serves as Senior System Engineer of Parson Brinkerhoff Farradyne. In his role, he is responsible for all aspects of information technology systems and fiber optics network design, deployment, and upgrade as well as systems integration. Before joining the Parson Brinkerhoff Farradyne's professional team of experts, Mr. Homami served as Head of Research and Development for Tehran Traffic Control Company. His indepth background history also includes a stint as Teacher at Iran University of Science and Technology. Upgrading the employees' skill levels, and designing the Company's current network environment from a subsystem using cutting edge cabling technology is cited as Mr. Homami's career highlights to date. Staying abreast of new technology, he looks forward to providing continuing upgrades to hardware and software equipment within the Parson Brinkerhoff Farradyne infrastructure. Success is attributed to his involvement in research and associating with the right people. Established in 1980, Parson Brinkerhoff Farradyne engages in intelligent transportation systems design. Based out of Maryland, the Company provides optimal services and convenience for an international clientele. Presently, Parson Brinkerhoff Farradyne operates six facilities nationwide manned by a 300 professional, technical, and support staff. **Career Highlights:** Senior System Engineer, Parson Brinkerhoff Farradyne (1998-Present); Head of Research and Development, Tehran Traffic Control Company (1991-98); Technology Teacher, Iran University of Science and Technology (1994-96). **Associations & Accomplishments:** Institute of Electrical and Electronics Engineers; Signal Processing Society; Circuit and System Society; Vehicular Technology Society; Instrument and Measurement Society; Electron Device Society; Computer Society; World Scientific and Engineering Society; Iranian Mathematical Society. **Education:** Tehran University, M.S. in Electrical Engineering (1990); Isfahan University of Technology, B.S. in Electrical Engineering (1988); Sharif University of Technology, Certificate of Transportation Planning (1992). **Personal Information:** Married to Nadereh Moini in 1995. Two children: Nima and Sonya. Mr. Homami enjoys bike riding.

Jon K. House

President
House of Sedes
11717 West 99th Street
Overland Park, KS 66214
(913) 269-7562
Fax: (913) 381-8004
farmfile@mwis.net

7379

Business Information: The Owner of the House of Sedes, Mr. House assumes the responsibilities of President. He develops software, handles product marketing, and performs technical support. Coordinating resources and schedules, overseeing time lines and assignments, and taking a lead role in driving products to market also fall within the realm of Mr. House's functions. Concurrently, Mr. House serves as Systems Developer for Cdi Corp Allied Signal. In this capacity, he programs and administers Oracle 8.05 databases, develops and designs Oracle 2000 programs, and develops new Oracle products for Web applications. In addition, he fulfills the responsibility of Programmer with Farm Files, a computer software company. His role with Farm Files involves developing computer software. Mr. House believes the reason for success was his parents' investment in his future. Dedicated to his work, Mr. House lives the phrase "Commitment to Excellence." Looking to the future, he is maneuvering to establish his own consulting firm. Founded in 1996 by Mr. House, the House of Sedes is a computer software company. The Company develops software programs that are sold to selected businesses. Technical support is offered by the Company for its programs. **Career Highlights:** President, House of Sedes (1996-Present); System Developer, Cdi Corp Allied Signal (1998-Present); Programmer, Farm Files (1996-Present); Programmer Analyst, Sprint PCS (1997-98). **Education:** Kansas State University, Management Information System (1996). **Personal Information:** Mr. House enjoys playing semipro football.

Barry Arthur Howarth, Ph.D.

President
The Howbury Group Ltd.
1 Elmsley Crescent
Nepean, Ontario, Canada K2H 6T9
(613) 596-9635
Fax: (613) 596-6153
howbury@istar.ca

7379

Business Information: Dr. Howarth is President of The Howbury Group Ltd. He is responsible for writing policies for the Canadian government information technology departments. Before starting The Howbury Group, Dr. Howarth assertively served as Government Liaison with Motorola Inc. and Engineering Manager at Paramax Electronics. As a tested and proven, 27 year technology professional, he started The Howbury Group with his wife because of an unquenchable desire to be on his own and responsible for determining strategic direction and vision. Coordinating resources and schedules, overseeing time lines and assignments, managing the fiscal year budget, and taking a lead role in driving service offerings to market also fall within the purview of Dr. Howarth's executive functions. Crediting his professional success to his luck and taking calculated risks, Dr. Howarth's leadership reflects his ability to think out-of-the-box and aggressively take on new challenges. Looking forward to the next millennium, his primary objectives are to double sales and increase his staff. The Howbury Group is dedicated to providing quality consulting and networking services. Established in 1989, and located in Nepean, Canada, the Company has offered 10 years of providing software solutions on a wide range of technological areas. Systems security is a primary focus of the Company, insuring privacy of information from other networking systems. **Career Highlights:** President, The Howbury Group Ltd. (1992-Present); Government Liaison, Motorola (1990-92); Engineering Manager, Paramax Electronics (1985-90). **Associations & Accomplishments:** New York Academy of Sciences; National Association of Radio and Telecommunications Engineers; Professional Engineers of Ontario. **Education:** McGill University: Ph.D (1972), Master's degree in Engineering, Bachelor's degree in Engineering Physics. **Personal Information:** Dr. Howarth enjoys hiking and body building.

Franklyn L. Howell
Director, Technical Support and Network Operations
Intermedia Business Internet
12091 Beltsville Drive
Beltsville, MD 20705
(301) 847-6224
Fax: (301) 847-5082
franklyn@digex.net

7379

Business Information: Highly skilled in network management, Ms. Howell serves as the Director of Technical Support and Network Operations for Intermedia Business Internet and is responsible for technical support and network operations. In her capacity, she presides over the Technical Support Call Centers and the Network Operation Center. Serving as the escalation point for the backbone and customer issues, she was responsible for developing and implementing the current customer satisfaction policy. Her background history includes a three year stint at Digex, Inc. as Senior Manager of the NOC and Technical Support, Manager of Technical Support, and Leased Line Technician. Ms. Howell's success reflects her leadership ability to build teams with energy, pride, and a customer oriented attitude, as well as take on new challenges and responsibilities. She is continuously striving to improve her performance and looking forward to working with the challenges that the future of new technology in the new millennium holds. Intermedia Business Internet specializes in connectivity and applications, providing Internet services to large and medium sized businesses. The Company began operations in 1987 and now employs over 2,000 dedicated professionals. **Career Highlights:** Director, Technical Support and Network Operations, Intermedia Business Internet (1998-Present); Digex, Inc.: Senior Manager of NOC (1997-98), Technical Support Manager (1997), Leased Line Technician (1996-97). **Education:** Texas A&M University. **Personal Information:** Ms. Howell enjoys running her home network, learning new technology and spending time with her family and friends.

Tien-hao Hsiung
Consultant
Luminant Worldwide
520 Post Oak Boulevard, Suite 400
Houston, TX 77027
(713) 479-7203
Fax: (713) 479-7101
tien.hsiung@luminant.com

7379

Business Information: As Consultant for Luminant Worldwide, Mr. Hsiung is responsible for negotiating service terms to all clients while assisting them in the business development and maintenance. His daily activities include document management, overseeing the development of quality products and ensuring client satisfaction. With more than eight years of professional technology experience, Mr. Hsiung is fully capable of providing technical support of the highest quality. His future plans include development of international clients for the establishment of his own business. A strong family support systems is attributed to Mr. Hsiung's success. Luminant Worldwide is a computer, Internet, and e-commerce consulting firm that provides specialized services for a number of international client companies. Services include technology support, project development, and staffing. Established in 1999, the Company is headquartered in Houston, Texas and operates facilities in several international locations. The Company currently employs more than 850 professionals who assist in the annual generation of revenues exceeding $78 billion. **Career Highlights:** Consultant, Luminant Worldwide (1998-Present); Systems Enigneer, Future Computer (1998); Assistant Scientist, National Science Council (1995-98); Programmer, Furtune Consulting (1992-93). **Associations & Accomplishments:** Information System Audit Association; MIS Association in Taiwan. **Education:** University of Houston, M.B.A. (1998); National Sun Yat-sen University, B.B.A. (1995); National Tainei Institute of Technology, B.S. (1992). **Personal Information:** Married to Chu-Jung Shih in 1997. Mr. Hsiung enjoys golf, swimming, community involvement and singing in church choir.

James B. Hubbell
Senior Manager of Engineering
BBN Technologies
1300 North 17th Street, Suite 1200
Arlington, VA 22209
(703) 284-4795
Fax: (703) 284-2766
jhubbell@bbn.com

7379

Business Information: As the Senior Manager of Engineering, Mr. Hubbell oversees engineering and network architecture. He is responsible for directing conceptual design and management on a large scale. Before joining BBN, Mr.

Hubbell assertively served as Senior Manager of Internetworking for GTE Information System Division. His solid background history also includes a stint as Senior Consultant of Information Technology with Ernst & Young LLP. Assuring quality implementation of advanced technologies, he supervises his staff of 20 employees to achieve a common goal. Utilizing his years of education and occupational experience, he understands that departments must work as a team to produce at the optimum level. Coordinating resources, schedules, time lines, and assignments also fall within the purview of Mr. Hubbell's responsibilities. His success reflects his leadership ability to coordinate efforts to ensure that his department meets all objectives, think out-of-the-box, and take on new challenges and responsibilities. Looking toward the next millennium, Mr. Hubbell looks forward to continued success in his field. BBN Technologies is an internet service provider. Serving an international market, the Company offers Internet solutions and advanced technologies. Established in 1966, BBN Technologies provides quality service through trained individuals working tirelessly to assure customer satisfaction around the clock. **Career Highlights:** Senior Manager of Engineering, BBN Technologies (Present); Senior Manager of Internetworking, GTE Information System Division; Senior Consultant of Information Technology, Ernst & Young LLP. **Associations & Accomplishments:** Institute of Electronics and Electrical Engineers; American Society for Industrial Security Today; International Associatino for Counter Terrorism & Security Professionals. **Education:** University of Florida: M.S. in Decision and Information Sciences (1994), M.B.A., B.S. in Business Administration.

Kevin L. Hudson
UNIX System Administrator
RHI Consulting
9514 Lexham Drive
Houston, TX 77083
(281) 988-0029
klhudson@flash.net

7379

Business Information: After 15 successful years at AT&T in consulting, Mr. Hudson joined PGS Tensor as UNIX System Administrator in 1996. In 1999, he was highly recruited to RHI Consulting. In his current position of UNIX System Administrator for RHI, Mr. Hudson is a consultant specializing in Y2K program compliance and implmentation of backup servers for a 900 workstation information technology infrastructure. Always alert to new opportunities, techniques, and approaches, he intends to conform to industry standards and become more involved in Linux technologies. Mr. Hudson attributes his career success to his passion for technology and his ability to think outside the box, deliver results, and aggressively take on challenges. Founded in 1970, RHI Consulting employs the skilled services of 200 individuals to acquire business, meet with clients, faciltate projects, and market services. The Firm provides consultancy services on the UNIX platform and recruits information technology professionals for clients. Currently, RHI Consulting is performing outsource work for Slumberger Corporation. **Career Highlights:** UNIX System Administrator, RHI Consulting (1999-Present); Unix System Administrator, PGS Tensor (1996-99); Database Administration, AT&T (1993-96). **Education:** Oklahoma Christian (Currently Attending); Control Data Institute, Certified Computer Technician; AT&T UNIX Systems and PowerBuilder Certificate. **Personal Information:** Married to Leslie in 1983. Mr. Hudson enjoys Linux, computer networking, reading science fiction, surfing the Internet and spending time with his wife.

James E. Huffman
Chief Executive Officer
J&E Technology, Inc.
6362 Meeting House Way
Alexandria, VA 22312
(703) 927-7277
jim_huffman@yahoo.com

7379

Business Information: As Chief Executive Officer and founder, he assumes responsibility for overseeing the Corporation's daily operations, administering employee payroll and benefits. He determines the overall strategic direction and business contribution of the information systems function. Keeping track of the market, Mr. Huffman submits bids for potential contracts and is responsible for performing the Corporation's product research and development. Before starting J&E Technology, Mr. Huffman served as Director of Information Systems with e.spire Communications, Inc. and Manager of Information Systems and Information Systems Specialist at Bell Atlantic. An expert, he stays current in the industry by reading trade journals and attending seminars. Attributing his success to his smart work ethics, Mr. Huffman is working hard to ensure the future growth and success of J&E Technology. His years of success in the field reflects his ability to think out-of-the-box and take on new challenges. Created in 1999, J&E Technology, Inc. is an information technology

consulting Firm focusing on data warehousing, telecommunications, and customer facing systems. The Corporation employs three skilled and dedicated individuals and reports estimated revenue in excess of $150,000. **Career Highlights:** Chief Executive Officer, J&E Technology, Inc. (1999-Present); Director of Information Systems, e.spire Communications, Inc. (1998-99); Bell Atlantic: Manager of Information Systems (1997-98), Information Systems Specialist (1995-97). **Associations & Accomplishments:** Professional Management Institute; Peace Lutheran Church. **Education:** Virginia Tech: M.B.A. (1995), M.S. in Agricultural Economics. **Personal Information:** Married to E. Chuni Petros in 1993. Mr. Huffman enjoys computers, investing, basketball and tennis.

Barbara A. Hughes
Vice President of Product Development
WORLDSPAN
100 Galleria Parkway SE #705-1
Atlanta, GA 30339
(770) 563-6987
Fax: (770) 563-7003
barbara.hughes@worldspan.com

7379

Business Information: Serving in the role of Vice President of Product Development for WORLDSPAN, Ms. Hughes focuses her attention on the development of cutting edge computer products for her clientele. Accordingly, she heads up the team that creates and provides travel technology solutions that enhances clients' company growth and expansion. Working closely with her clients, she analyzes, specifies, and determines client needs in maintaining their systems infrastructure that ensures quality, value, and selection as well as keeping them ahead of industry competitors. A savvy, 22-year veteran, Ms. Hughes has worked with WORLDSPAN in a variety of positions since joining the team of prefessionals as Director of Applications Development in 1993. Ms. Hughes has enjoyed substantial success in her career and looks forward to a bright and properous future. She attributes her success to her ability to be flexible and embrace change and new systems technology. Founded in 1990, WORLDSPAN employs the skilled services of 3,000 individuals to serve the global business needs of the travel industry. As an enabler through the Internet, the Company proudly provides services to Trans World Airlines, Northwest, and Delta Airlines, 18,000 travel agencies, 500 airlines, rental car companies, hotels, and tour operators. To better accomodate clients, WORLDSPAN has two locations, one in Atlanta, Georgia, and an international location in London, England. **Career Highlights:** WORLDSPAN: Vice President of Product Development (1996-Present); Vice President of Airline Services (1995-96); Director of Applications Development (1993-96). **Associations & Accomplishments:** Women in Technology; Georgia 100 Mentoring Association; Presidential Circle, Habitat for Humanity; Three times named as One of the Most Powerful Women in Travel. **Education:** University of Missouri at Kansas City, M.B.A. (1977); University of Missouri at Columbia, B.A. in Math (1973). **Personal Information:** Ms. Hughes enjoys travel, poetry, collecting and sports.

Shane R. Hughes
President
Pyxis Consulting
60 State Street, Suite 700
Boston, MA 02109
(508) 277-6516
Fax: (508) 839-8578
shughes@pyxis-consulting.com

7379

Business Information: The Founder of Pyxis Consulting, Mr. Hughes serves as its President and assumes accountability for the day to day operations and administrative functions of the Firm. As a six year professional, he sets the overall strategic direction and formulates marketing and business plans. He is in charge of the Firm's sales, offering cutting edge technological solutions to corporate clients. Following up after the sale, Mr. Hughes offers technical support and ensures that good customer relations are maintained. Additionally, he performs the vendor management functions of the Firm. Mr. Hughes credits his willingness to take risks as the reason for his professional success with Pyxis Consulting and anticipates a growth rate of 75 to 100 percent through the use of e-commerce. Established in 1998, Pyxis Consulting specializes in information technology consulting, systems integration, and project management for large financial corporations. Approximately 60 percent of the Firm's business is obtained through the utilization of e-commerce. The Firm currently employs the services of four skilled professionals and boasts $750,000 in annual revenue. **Career Highlights:** President, Pyxis Consulting (1998-Present); Consultant, Andersen Consulting (1993-97). **Associations & Accomplishments:** F.L.M.I. **Education:** University of Massachusetts, B.B.A. (1993). **Personal Information:** Married in 1993. Two children: Connor and Keeghan.

Todd Hutchins
Senior Engineer
AV Associates
305 West Grand Avenue
Montvale, NJ 07645
(201) 476-1400
Fax: (201) 476-1307
todd.hutchins@aval.com

7379

Business Information: Serving as Senior Engineer for AV Associates, Mr. Hutchins fulfills a number of duties on behalf of the Company and its clientele. A successful, 11 year professional, he is responsible for providing professional oversight of a broad area of operations. His primary field of expertise includes systems integration, project management, and architectural design. Utilizing his engineering experience, Mr. Hutchins travels to regional locations overseeing project management and attending to technical calls. He has gained various training certificates and is CTS certified. Mr. Hutchins' plans for his career include remaining in his current position in order to assist the Company in developing plans and strategies to enhance growth and expansion. He aspires to grow the office and expand the Company by 100 percent. AV Associates is a production company that provides services in the design and building of audio, video, and network systems. Catering to the needs of a host of client companies, the Company also offers bandvision management design, consultation, and integration. Established in 1975, the Company is located in Montvale, New Jersey, and employs a total of 90 professionals including production staff, engineers, and administration. **Career Highlights:** Senior Engineer, AV Associates (1999-Present); Manufacturing/Consultant Interface, Crestron Electronics (1998-99); Manager/Senior Engineer, Crimson Tech (1989-98). **Associations & Accomplishments:** International Communications Industries Association. **Education:** Community College of the Air Force; Belleville Area College; Sony Training; Barco Training; NEC Training; Crestror Training. **Personal Information:** Mr. Hutchins enjoys the gym and reading.

Eric A. Hutchinson-Surette
Senior Software Quality Engineer
EarthLink
3100 New York Drive
Pasadena, CA 91107
(626) 296-5291
Fax: (626) 296-4168
erichs@corp.earthlink.net

7379

Business Information: Serving as the Senior Software Quality Engineer of EarthLink, Mr. Hutchinson-Surette is the supervisor of software quality engineering responsible for maintaining quality software for Internet connectivity. A visionary who had proven himself correct on many occasions, he is the team lead on a number of projects, including establishment of new baseline for software products and development of software for Windows operations. Highly regarded in the software industry, Mr. Hutchinson-Surette oversees the testing of new software for functionality and ease of use throughout its development. In the future, he plans to continue developing new software products, including new Microsoft operating systems. He believes his success is a result of his life experiences and his ability to aggressively tackle new challenges and deliver results. Headquartered in Atlanta, Georgia, EarthLink is an Internet service provider. Recently merged with Mindspring, EarthLink is now the second largest ISP in the U.S. The Corporation provides easy software for Internet connection as well as Web space, Web hosting services, and 24-hour technical support. Established in 1994, EarthLink operates a satellite of eight locations in the U.S. **Career Highlights:** EarthLink: Senior Sofware Quality Engineer (2000-Present), Lead Product Tester (1996-00); Senior Instructor, Prosoft I-Net Solutions (1996-97); Operations Assistant, United States Navy (1991-94). **Education:** Learning Tree University, C/C++ Certification (1999). **Personal Information:** Mr. Hutchinson-Surette enjoys photography and problem puzzle solving.

Ken Ishimoto
President
K's Room
2-16-1-409 Yamakubo, Urawa-shi
Saitama-ken, Japan 338-0821
+81 9017767274
Fax: +81 357763462
ishimoto@ksroom.com

7379

Business Information: Serving as President of K's Room, Mr. Ishimoto is charged with the overall success of the Company. He is responsible for day to day business activities including translation, sales, workload distribution, employee supervision, and customer service. Also performing administrative duties, Mr. Ishimoto conducts contract negotiations, policy and procedure development, strategic

business planning, marketing campaign design, and client consultation. Demonstrating his keen business sense and strong leadership skills, Mr. Ishimoto has become an esteemed member of his community. Continuing to deliver insightful guidance to K's Room, Mr. Ishimoto plans to remain with the Company promoting its best interests, thereby achieving personal satisfaction and occupational success. K's Room is a software and database development company providing essential services to a global market. Established in 1997, the Company has grown to employ four people who generate a substantial annual revenue. Specializing in the production of quality programs that maximize profit potential and streamline operating procedures, the Company has impacted client companies' efficiency and overall performance. Becoming an international leader in a complex and competitive industry by consistently delivering quality services and comprehensive client support, K's Room plans to expand to additional cities and countries throughout the world to gain consumer recognition and additional market shares. **Career Highlights:** President, K's Room (1997-Present); Technical Manager, ACI Japan (1998); System Engineer, BIOS (1990). **Education:** Police Akademie (1984); School for Computer and Technology. **Personal Information:** Married in 1991. Three children: Ato, Alice, and David. Mr. Ishimoto enjoys video, music and time with family.

Mohammed N. Islam
President
Websoft Technologies
101 Willoughby Street
Brooklyn, NY 11201
(718) 422-0696
Fax: (718) 422-0694
nazrul@aol.com

7379

Business Information: As President of Websoft Technologies, Mr. Islam is responsible for a number of responsibilities within the Company, such as designing, implementing, and supporting PC networks. In his capacity, he oversees all daily operations, handles management issues, and develops strong employee relations. Highly regarded in the industry, he coordinates, designs, and implements marketing for new investments, and oversees the setup of networks. Additionally, Mr. Islam maintains good client relations with both new and existing clients. For the near future, he looks forward to growing and expanding Company operations, providing optimum technical support, and advertising with a more personal touch. His success is attributed to his interpersonal and public relations skills. Established in 1995, Websoft Technologies provides technical support, enhances and updates networks, and provide consulting for new and existing clients. The mission of the Company is to provide cost effective Internat solutions for small and medium sized businesses. The main focus of the Company is the wide variety of Internet business applications. Presently, the Company has a work force of 250 employees and an annual revenue of $90 million. **Career Highlights:** President, Websoft Technologies (1999-Present); LAN Manager, Bell Atlantic (1998-99); Systems and Network Administrator, Credit Suisse First Boston (1996-98); Network Administrator, FDIC Headquarter (1991-96). **Education:** University of Arkansas, B.S. in Electrical Engineering (1991). **Personal Information:** Married to Saleha Khanam. Two children: Tahiya and Tahiya. Mr. Islam enjoys tennis and travel.

Michael Iwashita
Assistant Systems Administrator
Midwest Technology Management
1167 Meadows, Suite 700
Manhattan Beach, CA 90266
(909) 869-6771
Fax: (209) 671-5818
miwashita@usa.net

7379

Business Information: Serving as the Assistant Systems Administrator for Midwest Technology Management, Mr. Iwashita fulfills a number of technical duties on behalf of the Firm and its clientele. He administers and controls all systems resources and tools, ensures the functionality of the systems functions, and tunes systems tools, accessories, and peripherals. Possessing an excellent understanding of financial software development, Mr. Iwashita also works with outsource services, custom design software, and project proposals and development. Attributing his success to knowing the right people and luck, he plans to continuing working in this capacity, while looking forward to attaining his bachelor's degree. Established in 1995, Midwest Technology Management is a consulting firm. Providing services to a clientele located across the United States, the Firm offers business solutions for all types of industries on a contractual basis. Located in Manhattan Beach, California, the Firm employs the skills and expertise of a staff of two professionals. **Career Highlights:** Assistant Systems Administrator, Midwest Technology Management (2000-Present); Systems Engineer, State of California (1998-00); Junior System Engineer, Qualcom Inc. (1997-98). **Associations &**

Accomplishments: Delta Sigma Pi; Circle K International. **Education:** California Polytechnical at Pomona, B.A. (2000).

Nader S. Iznait
Information Technology and Systems Manager
Mohammed Bin Masaood & Sons
P.O. Box 322
Abu Dhabi, United Arab Emirates
+971 26967810
Fax: +971 2766523
nader-iznait@hotmail.com

7379

Business Information: Utilizing more than ten years of experience, Mr. Iznait serves as Information Technology and Systems Manager for Mohammed Bin Masaood & Sons. Expert in setting up and configuring secure LANs and WANs, he oversees and directs the information technology department in providing services to 30 remote locations connected to the Company's main systems infrastructure. Understanding networking concepts and setting up fully functional networks, Mr. Iznait ensures the functionality and operational status of a computer environment that encompasses over 600 PCs operating on UNIX and Windows NT platforms. Mr. Iznait is also involved in designing, implementing, and supporting an integrated financial system together with a number of associated workgroup business systems. Serving faithfully with the Company since 1989, he has been published in local newspapers. He is most proud of establishing the 30 remote locations. Very confident in his capabilities, he believes this has contributed to his success. Mr. Iznait's future endeavors include concentrating more on the major network protocol, worldwide web, and e-commerce. A leading retail and multi-trading company, Mohammed Bin Masaood & Sons operates out of Abu Dhabi, United Arab Emirates. Trading mostly air freight and jewelry, the Company represents United States and French companies including Tiffany and Company. Mohammed Bin Masaood & Sons has sole distribution of Nissan automobiles, Harley Davidson bikes, Bridgestone Tires, heavy vehicles, and trucks. The Company is also involved in the assembling and sale of engineering and marine products, prefabricated buildings, property and real estate management, hotel management, jewelry, and farms. Established in 1956, the Company employs a work force of more than 1,700 skilled workers and reports annual revenues in excess of $60 million. **Career Highlights:** Mohammed Bin Masaood & Sons: Information Technology and Systems Manager (1991-Present), Computer & Network Engineer (1989-91). **Associations & Accomplishments:** Jordanian Engineering Association; Siemon Cabling Company Certified Designer; Canadian Engineering Association. **Education:** University of Belgrade, Yugoslavia, College of Economics and Informatics, Degree in Engineering for Informatics. **Personal Information:** Married to Suha Nader in 1995. One child: Halla.

Qudsia A. Jaffery
Chief Executive Officer/President
Clecslov Inc.
1105 Heather Circle
Cedar Hill, TX 75104
(972) 291-0847
Fax: (972) 293-6303
qudsia@onraiup.net

7379

Business Information: As the Chief Executive Officer and President of Clecslov Inc., Ms. Jaffery fulfills a number of duties on behalf of the Corporation and its clientele. In her position, she oversees and directs all daily administration and operations, to include planning the fiscal budget and formulating new business and marketing ventures. Her focus is to keep Clecslov at the forefront of industry competitors as well as flexible, efficient, and profitable. Possessing an excellent understanding of technology, Ms. Jaffery's concentrates her efforts on providing clients' telecommunications software solutions. She also ensures complete customer satisfaction. In the future, she plans on remaining with Clecslov, staying in her current position, and expanding and growing daily operations. Located in Cedar Hill, Texas, Clecslov Inc. is a database consulting agency. Established in 1993, the Corporation provides consulting advice to clients in the Cedar Hill area. With a staff of dedicated employees who are committed to providing the best possible services, the Corporation reports annual revenues in excess of $200,000. **Career Highlights:** Chief Executive Officer/President, Clecslov Inc. (2000-Present); Consultant, GTECH (1996-00); Consultant, Ericsson (1995-96); Consultant, Sprint (1993-94). **Associations & Accomplishments:** Association of Computing Machinery; Institute of Electrical and Electronics Engineers; Assistant Troop Leader, Girl Scouts of America. **Education:** Cambridge Univeristy, Postgraduate diploma (1988); University of Engineering and Technology, B.S. in Engineering. **Personal Information:** Married to Tariq in 1991. Three children: Manall, Noor, and Hebah. Ms. Jaffery enjoys hiking, sewing and photography.

W. K. "Vitek" Janowski, P.Eng.

Principal Consultant
VP Systems Inc.
120 Thornbury Cresent
Nepean, Ontario, Canada K2G 6C2
(613) 762-0046
Fax: (613) 727-7494
vitek@vp-systems.com
7379

Business Information: As the Principal Consultant of VP Systems Inc., Mr. Janowski oversees and directs all daily operations and determines overall strategic direction and business contribution of information systems functions. In his capacity, he provides cutting-edge consultations on systems design and supervises his staff in field installation and dealing with clients. Dedicated to the future success of the Corporation, Mr. Janowski plans on leading VP Systems Inc. into the 21st century to play a larger role in today's world of wireless communications. VP Systems Inc. is involved in satellite telecommunication, network design and implementation, and consulting. Established in 1997, the Corporation employs three personnel within the consulting department. The Corporation's consulting department deals with consulting on information systems. **Career Highlights:** Principal Consultant, VP Systems Inc. (1997-Present); Sales Manager, Com Stream (1995-97); Project Manager, PTT Telecom (1991-95); Sales Engineer, Telesat Canada (1988-91). **Associations & Accomplishments:** Professional Engineers of Ontario; Institute for Electrical and Electronics Engineers. **Education:** Carleton University, Bachelor's degree in Engineering (1988). **Personal Information:** Married to Maeda in 1985. One child: Robert. Mr. Janowski enjoys windsurfing.

Wassim A. Jazi

eBusiness Consultant
Sprint Paranet
3010 Hollow Creek Drive
Houston, TX 77082
(713) 626-4800
Fax: (713) 622-4828
wajazi@sprintparanet.com
7379

Business Information: Mr. Jazi serves in the position of eBusiness Consultant with Sprint Paranet. Responsible for assisting the sales force in need analysis activities, he demonstrates his knowledge of the industry as he develops customized technical solutions for clients. Internally recognized for his impressive skills, Mr. Jazi has been in charge of such projects as Y2K compliance, and customer needs. Striving to bridge the gap between e-commerce and networking systems, he is continually reformulating solutions as technical processes are updated and refined. Attributing his success to adaptability and flexibility, Mr. Jazi intends to continue in his current role as he prepares to open his own consulting business. The planned focus will be Internet localization and globalization. Sprint Paranet is a division of Sprint, a leading telecommunications company. This Branch is concerned with technology consulting, management, and solutions for e-businesses. Originally established in 1993, the Company was acquired by Sprint in 1997. Currently, there are 3,000 employees and this number is expected to grow with the merger of Sprint and MCI. **Career Highlights:** eBusiness Consultant, Sprint Paranet (1997-Present); Information Technology Consultant, Gulf States (1995-97). **Associations & Accomplishments:** Houston Area Advisory Committee; University of Houston Alumni Association. **Education:** University of Houston: M.B.A. in International Business (1999), B.B.A. in Management Information Systems. **Personal Information:** Mr. Jazi enjoys skiing, soccer, camping and teaching.

Ritu Johorey

Project Manager
HCL America
13555 Breton Ridge Street, Apartment 1212
Houston, TX 77070-5828
(281) 514-6503
Fax: (281) 514-8192
ritu_johorey@hotmail.com
7379

Business Information: Possessing unique talents in the technology field, Mr. Johorey was recruited to HCL America in 1995. As Project Manager, he plans and oversees the development and support of all new software applications in a variety of functional areas. A savvy, 12 year veteran in technology, he is responsible for building his team with synergy and technical strength, and together, ensure projects are completed on time and within budgetary contraints. Mr. Johorey also ensures his clientele are completely satisfied with products and services they receive. Currently, his team is aggressively working on restructuring a distribution system for a client in the hardware industry. Coming to America about five years ago, his future strategic plans include getting into upper management and leading larger projects dealing with Internet and e-commerce. His success reflects his ability to think outside the box, take on challenges, and deliver results. HCL America, based in India, provides software development and consulting for a diverse clientele. Established in 1987, the Company employs over 600 individuals to facilitate every aspect of design and manufacture of customized software. The Company also serves as an information think tank and clearing house of technical services. **Career Highlights:** Project Manager, HCL America (1994-Present); Project Leader, Nucleus Software (1993-94); Software Engineer, Datamatics Ltd. (1990-93). **Education:** Lucknow University, B.Sc. (1988). **Personal Information:** Married to Vivek Kumar in 1992. Mr. Johorey enjoys trekking, water sports and home decorations.

Rabon S. Jones

Network Engineer
ISSI, Inc.
417 Muddy Branch Road, #101
Gaithersburg, MD 20878
(301) 755-0440
Fax: (815) 461-4589
rsjones@issilnc.com
7379

Business Information: Serving in the capacity of Network Engineer of ISSI, Inc., Mr. Jones is engaged in the implementation and maintenance of technical systems. Coupling practical work experience with an extensive education, he assists in the formulation of intricate processes. Specializing in all aspects of Web server operations, Mr. Jones also maintains LAN and WAN activities within the Corporation. Internally recognized for his creative problem solving approach, he is credited for his involvement in the design and development of the IRS's Teletax systems in which his ability and guidance led to increased production and lowered research expenditures. He attributes his success to strong family values and ongoing training of the industry. Enjoying the challenges of his position, Mr. Jones intends to continue in his current capacity as he initiates strategic technical solutions. Founded in 1988, ISSI, Inc. offers information technology consulting to clients in the United States and abroad. Employing 300 trained professionals, the Corporation specializes in network and database administration. **Career Highlights:** Network Engineer, ISSI, Inc. (1999-Present); Network Engineer, NCBPNP/N (1996-Present); Network Engineer, Landscape Gallery (1996-99). **Education:** Orange Technical Institute, Microsoft Certified Systems Engineer (1998). **Personal Information:** Married to Margaret F. in 1985. Two children: Ryan and Neisha. Mr. Jones enjoys golf and computers.

Tim H. Jones

President/Chief Executive Officer
Advanced Concepts Engineering and Technology
5804C Breckenridge Park
Tampa, FL 33610
(813) 630-2744
Fax: (813) 630-9823
jonest1ace@netzero.net
7379

Business Information: Serving in the dual capacity of President and Chief Executive Officer of Advanced Concepts Engineering and Technology, Mr. Jones oversees all activities within the Company, from engineering to human resources. He is responsible for formulating powerful strategic marketing and business plans, monitoring new business developments and growth opportunities, developing policies and procedures, and handling various budgeting and financial tasks. Mr. Jones' includes establishing the Department of Defense activities in Tampa, Florida. Through his effective leadership, this 42,000 square feet facility produced $40 million in annual revenues. Dedicated to the success of the Company, Mr. Jones, already on the cutting edge, hopes to remain on the top of the technology field. Good mentors have contributed to his success. Founded in 1999, Advanced Concepts Engineering and Technology is an up and coming business engaged in the design, integration, testing, installation, and training of individuals on voice, video, and data communications hardware and software for use in tactical and/or strategic applications. Employing a staff of 22 individuals, the Company is a start up network offering consulting, research, development, and verification of various information systems. **Career Highlights:** President/Chief Executive Officer, Advanced Concepts Engineering and Technology (1999-Present); Director of Joint Operations, Space and Naval Warfare Systems (1996-99); Meteorological/Oceanographer, Naval Command and Control (1994-96); Equipment Specialist, Naval Oceanographic Office (1991-94). **Associations & Accomplishments:** Armed Forces Communications Electronics Association; Florida Chamber of Commerce; Tampa Chamber of Commerce. **Education:** University of Phoenix, B.S. in Information Systems (1999). **Personal Information:** Mr. Jones enjoys golf.

David S. Jordan

Management Information Systems Manager
BBC, Inc.
230 Broadway, Suite 101
Lynnfield, MA 01905
(781) 593-6088
Fax: (781) 593-0050
djordache@hotmail.com
7379

Business Information: Serving as Management Information Systems Manager of BBC, Inc., Mr. Jordan demonstrates extensive technical knowledge as he maintains all computers and handles networking issues. Working closely with his staff, he performs systems back-ups, troubleshooting, accounts set-up, and programming activities. Administratively, he is responsible for departmental hiring, budgeting, procurement activities, and training programs. Recognized for his creative problem solving approach, he is credited with the development of several innovative tactics that contribute to the overall effectiveness and cost efficiency of the Corporation as a whole. Enjoying the prominence of his position, Mr. Jordan intends to continue in his current role, seeking advancement throughout the corporate structure. BBC, Inc. is an information technology consulting firm that assists local and international companies with technical and business issues. Additionally, the Corporation assists in the job placement process for those individuals who demonstrate exceptional talent and technical ability. Talented software engineers design innovative applications and tools to ensure clients are receiving maximum results and benefits. **Career Highlights:** Management Information Systems Manager, BBC, Inc. (1999-Present); Owner, Jordan Services (1994-99); PC Specialist, New England Computer Depot (1992-95); Systems Administrator, ICM (1984-92). **Associations & Accomplishments:** American Journal of Physics; Association of Black Engineers. **Education:** Massachusetts Institute of Technology, Ph.D. (In Progress); University of Wisconsin: Master's degree in Philosophy, B.S. **Personal Information:** Mr. Jordan enjoys golf, computer animation and pool.

Deepu Joseph

Senior Engineer/Development & Consulting Member/Technical Staff
Call Center Services, Inc.
13375 North Stemmons Freeway, Suite 200
Dallas, TX 75234
(972) 488-2333, Ext. 124
Fax: (972) 488-2340
Deepu@Joseph.MailHost.org
7379

Business Information: Functioning as Senior Engineer, Development, for Call Center Services, Inc. (CCS), Mr. Joseph designs and develops software solutions for computer telephony integration, as well as manages the Corporation's development staff. Before joining CCS, he served as a Consultant with Motorola, American Airlines/SABRE Group, and Keane, Inc. Directing day-to-day technical administration and operation of the Development Group, he provides field teams and sales associates with technical and analytical assistance to ensure successful solutions implementation. As an 11 year programming professional, Mr. Joseph is a mentor to junior engineers. His history includes stints as a Teaching Assistant in the United States and Lecturer in India. Wanting to be on the forefront of the Information Technology wave, Mr. Joseph moved to the United States in 1992 and attended Texas Tech University where he earned his Master's degree specializing in Management Information Systems. He attributes his success to God and the inspiration he received from his parents (his father was also an engineer). To find new horizons, stay on the leading edge of technology, synergize his technical and business skills, and attain the position of Vice President with a company dealing in emerging markets, serve as his near term goals. Wholly owned by Bell Atlantic, CCS is an international computer telephony integration company. Part of a large organization business and management channel, the Corporation is a technical solutions provider with a niche in call center implementation and training. Established in 1995, the Corporation employs more than 80 professional, technical, and support personnel. **Career Highlights:** Senior Engineer/Development & Consulting Member/Technical Staff,

Call Center Integration, Inc. (1997-Present); Consultant, Motorola (1997); Consultant, American Airlines/SABRE Group (1995-97); Consultant, Keane, Inc. (1994-95). **Associations & Accomplishments:** Institute of Electronics and Electrical Engineers; North Texas Linux User's Group; Java MUG; MEA of North Texas; DPMA Scholarship (1993); Outstanding Performance Award (1990). **Education:** Texas Tech University, M.S. in Business Administration (1997); Calicut University, B.Tech. in Production Engineering (1990). **Personal Information:** Married to Rebecca in 1996. One child: Ruth. Mr. Joseph enjoys music, tennis, apologetics, geometrical puzzles and teaching technology.

Anil B. Kale

President/Principal Technical Consultant
BAVS Corporation
3015 North Pointe Drive, #K
Jackson, MI 49202
(517) 788-0041
Fax: (517) 778-0502
bavs@aol.com

7379

Business Information: The President of BAVS Corporation, Mr. Kale also serves as the Principal Technical Consultant. He consults with clients, studying their systems and performing a series of tests in an effort to assist each client determine the best database system for their business. Providing a wide range of database services utilizing the IBM DB2 database, Mr. Kale performs database design and implementation. He is responsible for negotiating client contracts and provides training and technical support to the client after the sale. Crediting his success to his strong family values, Mr. Kale feels that his technical competency and excellent human relations are his greatest accomplishments. Looking to the future, he plans to expand his business operations into the field of e-commerce. BAVS Corporation is an information technology consulting firm specializing in DB2 database services. The majority of the Corporation's business, approximately 60 percent, is directly related to DB2 database consultations with commercial clients. Boasting $250,000 in annual revenue, operations employ a staff of five skilled professionals. The Corporation was founded in 1997. **Career Highlights:** President/Principal Technical Consultant, BAVS Corporation (1997-Present); DB2 Consultant, Volt Services Group (1996-97); Technical Consultant, Florida Power & Light (1994-96). **Associations & Accomplishments:** Vice President of Public Relations, Jackson Chamber of Commerce; Power Toastmasters. **Education:** Walchand College of Engineering, India, Bachelor's degree in Computer Technology (1991). **Personal Information:** Mr. Kale enjoys travel, music, movies and cultural psychology.

Kimberly Kalke

President/Chief Executive Officer
Kaltech International Corporation
2152 Tallapoosa Drive
Duluth, GA 30097
(678) 584-1940
Fax: (678) 584-1849
kimberly@kaltechintl.com

7379

Business Information: Overseeing the Company's operations, Mrs. Kalke currently serves as the President and Owner of Kaltech International Corporation. Within the boundaries of her position, she is responsible for developing new business for the Corporation, maintaining client relations, and overseeing both accounts receivable and accounts payable. She works directly with company recruiters in the development of market and placement objectives to help the organization meet its strategic goals in the information technology industry. Mrs. Kalke has opened a location in Texas, where the information technology business growth is second only to Silicon Valley. Seeking quick solutions that provide cost effective answers for the advancement of technology, Kaltech International Corporation serves its customers as a software consulting firm. Founded and incorporated in 1998, Kaltech International brings strength and resources to companies across the nation enabling them to progress in today's business environment. Kaltech's larger clients include IBM, CSC, iXL, and EDS. Services provided by Kaltech include customizing applications for business strategies, migration services to reduce cycle times and lower costs, offering alternatives to meeting requirements, training and certification programs, and e-service consultancy with sophisticated Internet-based solutions to established and startup businesses. **Career Highlights:** President/Chief Executive Officer, Kaltech International Corporation (1999-Present); Operations Manager, Datamatics (1995-99); Telecommunications Coordinator, Executive Business Center (1993-95); Clinique Manager, Macy's East (1986-93). **Associations & Accomplishments:** National Association of Women Business Owners (NAWBO); Company Representative to United States Consulates in Manila, Philippines; Madras, India; and Colombo, Sri Lanka; Member, Rebuilding Macy's Committee.

Dutt N. Kalluri

Director of Strategic Account Development
Kumaran Systems Inc.
12300 Twinbrook Parkway, Suite 660
Rockville, MD 20852-1606
(301) 984-4445
Fax: (301) 984-4446
duttk@kumaran.com

7379

Business Information: As Director of Strategic Account Development of Kumaran Systems Inc., Mr. Kalluri leads the department in the development of strategies, via the use of off-site development centers. Possessing an excellent understanding of his field, he creates and leads his teams in research and development of new technology. In this context, he ensures the quality, value, and reliability of the products delivered. With the Corporation since its conception in India, Mr. Kalluri has since moved to the Toronto, Canada facility in order to better serve his North American clientele. Highly regarded by his colleagues, he has authored over 20 papers on the role of industrial engineering. The highlights of his career include obtaining his Master's degree from a premier institute in India; developing new software concept methodologies; and being a founding member of SPIN worldwide. In the future, Mr. Kalluri hopes to assist in the improvement of software worldwide as well as starting his own company. His confidence, knowledge of technology, and strong determination have all contributed to his professional success. Established in 1990, Kumaran Systems Inc. is a software migration solutions provider. The Corporation deals with major Oracle applications. Through the ingenuity of its engineers, Kumaran Systems is the only Corporation that has developed an automated migration tool. Employing over 400 individuals, the Corporation is headquartered in Toronto, Canada. **Career Highlights:** Director of Strategic Account Development, Kumaran Systems Inc. (1997-Present); Division Head, Kumaran Software (1995-97); Process Engineer, Vetri Systems Inc. (1993-95); Information Systems Manager, Alcam Consulting (1989-93). **Associations & Accomplishments:** Indian Institute of Industrial Engineers; Software Process Improvement Network. **Education:** I.I.I.E., P.G.D.I.E. (1989); National Computing Center, diploma in Computer Programming and Applications. **Personal Information:** Married to Uma in 1994. Two children: Lakshmi and Gautam. Mr. Kalluri enjoys golf and reading.

Shawn Ivan Kammerdiener

Senior Consultant
Questra, Inc.
350 Linden Oaks
Rochester, NY 14625
(716) 381-0260
Fax: (716) 381-8098
sik@questra.com

7379

Business Information: As Senior Consultant for Questra, Inc., Mr. Kammerdiener does project studies for technology that can be used for client companies. Owning a proven record of delivering results by paying close attention to technical details and solving problems and challenges in a systematic manner, he designs and develops cutting edge software to enhance his clients' flexibility, efficiency, and profitability in the market place. In addition to his numerous planning functions, he also facilitates needs analysis, budgeting, design, coding, testing, and Web site development. His career highlights include designing and building software that controlled the train and switching system from Kowloon to Canton in Hong Kong. Continually striving for maximum effectiveness, Mr. Kammerdiener is learning more about personal electronics that connect to the Web. His future goals include moving up the Corporate ladder. Questra, Inc., established in 1991, provides consulting in e-services. Located in Rochester, New York, the Corporation employs a staff of 250 qualified individuals to help companies market their products by way of Internet service. The main goal of the Corporation is to provide analysis, design, installation, modification, configuration, support, and tracking of operating and networking infrastructures for the clients. **Career Highlights:** Senior Consultant, Questra, Inc. (1994-Present); Software Engineer, Northern Telecom (1989-94); Software Engineer, AIC (1987-89). **Associations & Accomplishments:** Reverend, Universal Life Church. **Education:** Empire State College, B.S. (2000); Monroe Community College, A.A.S.

Richard L. Kane

President/Senior Consultant
Coastal Technologies Group
5030 Champion Boulevard, Suite 6-183
Boca Raton, FL 33496
(800) 448-2835
Fax: (561) 988-0924
rkane@coastaltechnologies.com

7379

Business Information: Wearing many different hats, Mr. Kane serves as President and Senior Consultant for Coastal Technologies Group. In his role, he assumes responsibilities for all management aspects of daily administrative and operational activities. He is in charge of formulating the vision and creative and high powered business and marketing strategies. Drawing on years of experience and a firm academic background, he also serves as project manager and software developer who oversees all work on software aspects of systems design and development. Additionally, Mr. Kane uses his vast interpersonal skills as chief customer liaison to ensure customers' specific software needs are fulfilled and fully satisfied. An expert, he wrote a copy protection for Apple Computer while in high school, worked on very large engineering projects such as signaling for an Australia company, and owns a patent for artificial intelligence. Mr. Kane expects to grow and expand Group operations. A technology company, Coastal Technologies Group is dedicated to the development of software for telephone companies and is very specific about the types of projects the Group will accept. Local in scope and based in Florida, the Group was established in 1996 and employs eight consultants. **Career Highlights:** President/Senior Consultant, Coastal Technologies Group (1996-Present); Director of Network Product Development, EDS (1991-96). **Associations & Accomplishments:** Carrier Fraud Control Association; IBM Partners in Development; Microsoft ISV. **Education:** Florida Atlantic University, B.A. in Mathematics (1986). **Personal Information:** Married to Susan in 1998.

Suhas R. Kanitkar

Director
Complete Business Solutions
32605 West 12 Mile Road, Suite 250
Farmington Hills, MI 48334
(734) 254-5488
Fax: (734) 254-6473
skanitka@cbsinc.com

7379

Business Information: Mr. Kanitkar serves as Director for Complete Business Solutions. In this capacity, he utilizes extensive practical work experience to provide consulting services to businesses and individuals. Demonstrating his expertise, he also acts as Technical Architect for the Company, leading the technical support group. An advocate for open communication, Mr. Kanitkar utilitzes a direct, efficient style of management that incorporates employee feedback. Crediting his success to his unwavering perseverance, he currently is working to shift the Company's focus to business to business communications. Complete Business Solutions is a business consulting firm that also offers technical support. The international firm serves clients throughout the United States and Europe as well as India, Australia, and the Philippines. Keeping pace with today's technically progressive society, the Company is moving towards e-commerce as a main aspect of business. **Career Highlights:** Director, Complete Business Solutions (1994-Present); Assistant Consultant, Tata Consultancy (1987-94). **Education:** Kennedy Western, M.S. (1999); Institute of Technology, B.H.U. B-Tech (1984). **Personal Information:** Married to Pratibha in 1989. Two children: Chaitanya and Asawari. Mr. Kanitkar enjoys playing tennis, badmiton, and watching cricket.

Krishnakumar Kanthawar

President
Infinity Solutions Inc.
P.O. Box 3494, GCS
New York, NY 10163
(718) 631-0096
Fax: (718) 631-3534
kumark@infinity-solutions-inc.com

7379

Business Information: Mr. Kanthawar, serving as President for Infinity Solutions Inc, is engaged in the technology needs for a growing company. Infinity Solutions Inc is a complete technoloyg company that provides the technology needs for a growing client base. Infinity specializes in Web and network integraton and security, Web development, and medical transcription. A start-up company that has Fortune 500 clients under its belt, Infinity is making strong progress in the field of e-commerce. **Career Highlights:** President, Infinity Solutions Inc (1999-Present); Systems Manager, Manhattan Office Products (1995-99); Service Manager, Micro 2000 Computer Center of New York (1992-95); Service Technician, Mico Bosch, GmbH of India (1980-91). **Associations &**

Accomplishments: Association of Indian Engineers; Certified Engineers; Network Professional Engineers; Institute of Electronics and Electrical Engineers; Association of Computing Machinery; NPA. **Education:** NYIT, M.S. in Computer Science (1994); MCSE; CNE; CSA (Solaris); CNA (Solaris). **Personal Information:** Mr. Kanthawar enjoys bowling, golf, trivia and tennis.

Wayne Kao
Implementation Manager
eHNC
8148 Genesee Avenue, #32
San Diego, CA 92122
wkao@ehnc.com
7379

Business Information: Serving as Implementation Manager, Mr. Kao provides dual services in account management and implementation engineering for eHNC. He ensures quality customer services, supervises sales, and informs clients of all available services offered by the Corporation. Possessing an excellent understanding of technology, Mr. Kao also oversees systems implementation in order to provide flawless day to day operation for customers. His multi-tasking ability is vital to corporate success and in the future, Mr. Kao plans to expedite continued promotion through dedication and the perpetuation of additional growth through increased sales. eHNC is the leading applications service provider of e-commerce value added services that boost sales and minimize risks through customer interaction management. Through the utilization of simple interfaces, eHNC assists clients control transactions risk, build relationships, and enjoy the online experience. Established in 1991, the Corporation employs the skilled services of 45 individuals to facilitate all aspects of operation. The Corporation is located in San Diego, California and operates worldwide. **Career Highlights:** Implementation Manager, eHNC (1999-Present); Senior Software Engineer, Autometric, Inc. (1998-99); Software Engineer, Dynamic Instrument, Inc. (1994-96). **Education:** Babson College, M.B.A. (1998); University of California at Riverside. **Personal Information:** Mr. Kao enjoys reading and attending classes.

Hasan Karaburk
Director of Computer Services
Truestar, Inc.
9900 Main Street
Fairfax, VA 22031
(703) 591-7042
Fax: (703) 591-7046
hkaraburk@viu.edu
7379

Business Information: As Director of Computer Services of Truestar, Inc., Mr. Karaburk fulfills a number of duties on behalf of the Corporation and its clientele. He ensures the functionality and operational status of the systems infrastructure, accessories, and peripherals. Throughout daily duties, Mr. Karaburk is charged with the obligation to maintain all hardware, while also purchasing software, hosting Web sites, and implementing new systems. Attributing his success to time management, Mr. Karaburk cites as his career highlight his affiliation with the United States educational system. An accomplished professional, he has published five chemistry books. His future goals include teaching computers and chemistry at the collegiate level. Founded in 1993 Truestar, Inc. is an educational facility and consulting firm that offers a broad range of services to benefit the rising professionals. The Corporation provides professional consulting in various areas including management, financial aspects, and training. Headquartered in the United Kingdom, the U.S. headquarters was established in Fairfax, Virginia in 1997. Offering academic and scientific journals, the Corporation caters to an international client base. **Career Highlights:** Director of Computer Services, Truestar, Inc. (1997-Present); Educator/Writer, Surat/Truestar (1995-97); Toros Educational, Inc.: College Administrator/Director (1994-95), Faculty Member (1993-94). **Associations & Accomplishments:** World Academians Club; World Chemists' Club. **Education:** METU, B.S. (1993); Information Science/Computer Science Certificate. **Personal Information:** Married to Melek in 1994. One child: Enes. Mr. Karaburk enjoys travel, reading, sports and swimming.

R. S. Kashmirian
Partner/Director
IN3 Consulting, Canada
P.O. Box 976
Bragg Creek, Alberta, Canada T0L 0K0
(403) 519-0195
Fax: (403) 949-4164
ritchie.kashmirian@in3.net
7379

Business Information: Mr. Kashmirian serves as a Partner and Director of IN3 Consulting, Canada. Drawing from a strong background in information technology, he is responsible for conducting consulting services, assisting with planning strategies and attending to customers on a daily basis. Moreover, he helps to build companies, composes software development, acts as an information technology architect, and oversees all of the design and implementation of projects. Mr. Kashmirian looks forward to continuing with the Firm, moving more in business development, desiging more products and software, and becoming a leader in e-commerce. He attribute his success to being able to deal with change effectively and successfully. Founded in 1997, IN3 Consulting, Canada is an information techology consulting firm. Located in Bragg Creek, Alberta, Canada, the Firm provides software development, e-commerce and e-business solutions, and ERP implementation. Additionally, the Firm provides general consulting services such as planning, business relations, and public relations. With a staff of 12 employees, the Firm is rapidly becoming a successful entity among business owners. **Career Highlights:** Partner/Director, IN3 Consulting, Canada (1998-Present); Senior Consultant, IBM Canada, Ltd. (1997-98); Director/Senior consultant, Halbannah P/L, Australia (1984-97). **Associations & Accomplishments:** The Australian Computer Society. **Education:** Victoria University of Melbourne, Australia, Graduate diploma in Accounting (1986); Monash University of Melbourne, Australia, B.S. in Computer Science (1980). **Personal Information:** Married to Jennifer in 1994. Two children: Michael S. and Richard S. Mr. Kashmirian enjoys skiing, hiking, climbing, golf and chess.

Ralph J. Keiffer
Conference Director
Florida Government Technology Conference
University Center, Building C, Suite 2200
Tallahassee, FL 32306-3002
(850) 644-0157
Fax: (850) 644-7360
rkeiffer@garnet.acns.fsu.edu
7379

Business Information: Mr. Keiffer acts as Conference Director of Florida Government Technology Conference. He is responsible for the daily activities and planning for statewide government training conferences on information technology. The events include logistics, programs, and Web services planning and implementation. Mr. Keiffer relies on the personal edge of his profession, in that he excels in gaining knowledge through continuous study, due to requirements to stay up-to-date in training seminars. His future goals include a number of career oriented opportunities including the creating an online registration for vendors, staying with the Institute to streamline technology, getting involved with non-profit management, and attaining a position within the state government. The Florida Government Technology Conference is a division of Florida State University. Focused on consulting, training, and holding conferences for government entities of Florida and the United States, the Institute provides a forum to exchange ideas and merge buyers and sellers of corporations and industries nationwide. The Institute is the fifth leading technical conference in the nation, and is now in the process of holding its ninth session with the help of eight personnel. **Career Highlights:** Conference Director, Florida Government Technology Conference (1998-Present); Program Administrator, Florida Certified Public Manager Program (1994-98); Research Associate, Florida Center for Public Management (1991-94). **Associations & Accomplishments:** Board of Directors, Florida Society for Certified Public Manager (1994-98); Chair, Florida Government Technology Conference Vendor Advisory Committee. **Education:** Florida State University: Master's degree in Public Adminsitration (1992), B.A. in History/Political Science/International Affairs; St. John's River Community College, A.A. **Personal Information:** Mr. Keiffer enjoys NASCAR racing, antiques and collectibles, science fiction and sporting events.

Sadrudin B. Keshoojee
Senior Consultant
Condor Technologies
499 Thornall Street
Edison, NJ 08837
(732) 635-2557
Fax: (732) 635-0850
sadrudin.keshoojee@titantg.com
7379

Business Information: As Senior Consultant of Condor Technologies, Mr. Keshoojee handles a myriad of highly specialized tasks on a daily basis. He demonstrates an extensive knowledge of the industry as he engages in the implementation of ERP packages into client's current operating systems. Applying practical education and related work experience, he is able to conduct financial accounting and controlling activities as he utilizes the complex techniques of profitability analysis. Internally recognized for impressive acccomplishements while serving in his position, Mr. Keshoojee attributes his success to hard work and patience. He currently has plans to increase his effectiveness in the Company through effective goal planning and enhanced global reputation. Condor Technologies is a technical consulting firm located in Edison, New Jersey. Working closely with area businesses, the Firm implements SAP software to provide maximum solutions to technically challenging situations. **Career Highlights:** Senior Consultant, Condor Technologies (1997-Present); Financial Advisor, MetLife (1994-97); Account Manager, Walker International (1982-94). **Education:** Bombay University, M.B.A. (1981); SAP Partners Academy, Certified FI/CO and Profitability Analysis (1999). **Personal Information:** Married to Samira in 1987. Two children: Sasha and Alyzain. Mr. Keshoojee enjoys sports car and stamp collecting.

Tammy L. Keyes
Regional Coordinator
Fleet Technology Solutions
200 Exchange Street
Malden, MA 02148
(781) 397-5390
Fax: (781) 397-3279
7379

Business Information: Ms. Keyes has served in various positions with Fleet Bank since 1996. At the present time, she fulfills the responsibilities of Regional Coordinator for Fleet Technology Solutions, a department within Fleet Bank. In this capacity, she coordinates with vendors in an effort to resolve customer problems that have been referred to her office from the Corporate Help Desk. She also provides project management services for client server upgrades, LAN and WAN networks, and troubleshoots problems as necessary. Concurrently working as a Technical Analyst and Executive Onboarding Coordinator, Ms. Keyes duties include managing trouble tickets for Massachusetts, directing interaction with LAN and Network Engineering support groups, and monitoring service level agreements and vendor resources to optimize customer satisfaction. Identifying problematic trends and recommending corrective and preventative measures also fall within the scope of her functions. Instrumental in developing "scripts" for the Corporate Help Desk, Ms. Keyes is currently involved on a technical swat team and merger integration team. She enjoys her work and looks forward to increased involvement in project management, ultimately achieving the position of Project Manager and/or Business Analyst. Fleet Technology Solutions is an in-house telecommunications company providing vendor and project management and systems and infrastructure support. The Company consults with clients, determining the type of equipment needed for the business. In house technicians install the systems and provide technical support as needed. **Career Highlights:** Regional Coordinator, Fleet Technology Solutions (1998-Present); Corporate Program Administrator, Fleet Corporate Properties (1998); Administrative Assistant, Fleet Services Corporation (1996-98). **Associations & Accomplishments:** Humane Society of United States; Sierra Club. **Education:** New England College of Finance, certificates in Accounting, Finance, and Information Technology (In Progress); Castleton State College, Bachelor's degree in Sociology. **Personal Information:** Ms. Keyes enjoys golf, skiing, tennis and reading.

Nadeem M. Khalid
General Manager
Techno Serv
P.O. Box 2240
Manama, Bahrain
+973 712443
Fax: +973 713627
nmkhalid@batelco.com.bh
7379

Business Information: Serving as the General Manager for Techno Serv, Mr. Khalid joined the Company in 1997 and is currently responsible for overseeing all of the daily operations and management within the Manama facility. He is deeply involved with the strategic planning methods, provides direction for the Company and employees, as well as ensuring the commitment of quality service. Additionally, Mr. Khalid is in charge of making sure that all policies and procedures are being followed and that all of the clients are satisfied with their services. Highly regarded and possessing an excellent understanding of technology, he has received numerous awards and prizes for being the "top in sales" and exceeding quotas. In the future, Mr. Khalid looks forward to continuing with the Company and helping the Company become the leading information technology firm in the Persian Gulf region. His success reflects his ability to form teams with synergy, take on challenges, and deliver results on behalf of the Company and its clientele. Created in 1997, Techno Serv is an information systems firm that provides services to the Persian Gulf countries. Located in Manama, Bahrain, the Company focuses on assisting firms with services to better their business and also helping clients with the recruitment of new employees. At this location, the Company has a staff of seven hard working employees who are committed to providing the best possible service to their clientele. **Career Highlights:** General Manager, Techno Serv (1997-Present); Territory Manager, Oracle Corporation (1995-97); Sales Manager, Mantech Computers (1986-95). **Education:** Chartered Institute of Marketing, Diploma in Marketing Management (1992). **Personal Information:** Married to Huda Yusuf in 1988. Three children: Mohd, Ahmed, and Fatima. Mr. Khalid enjoys sports, adventure, travel, squash and running.

Ramzi Nabhan Khalil
Owner/Chief Executive Officer
MASSC
336 Dakota Street
Paterson, NJ 07503
(888) 656-2772
Fax: (973) 279-2898
rkhalil@massc.com

7379

Business Information: Drawing from an extensive education and previous occupational experience, Mr. Khalil leads MASSC as Owner and Chief Executive Officer. Primarily responsible for maintaining an efficient and effective corporate structure, he establishes high standards of excellence for employees of the Company. Heading all administrative and financial aspects of the Company, he directs the proper staffing, funds, and materials to the necessary areas of project development. Specifically involved in the executive decision making process, Mr. Khalil oversees negotiations and contracts established from the purchasing of client accounts. Extensively involved in formulating market strategies, Mr. Ramzi Khalil continues to promote the excellent sales and services offered by MASSC. Mr. Khalil's future goal is to build community development centers for the upcoming youth. These centers will provide the technology and cultural experiences the youth will need to mature and strive in our new technological society. MASSC is an established and reputable consulting firm providing clients with technological support in promoting the growth of their businesses. Located in Patterson, New Jersey, the Company was founded in 1995 employing 10 expert computer technicians, designers, and administrators who deal directly with setting up computer hardware and software systems according to their client's individual needs. Offering services in consulting for Web design, e-commerce, networking, graphics design, hosting services, and technical support the Company guarantees complete client satisfaction. **Career Highlights:** Owner/Chief Executive Officer, MASSC (1999-Present); Technology Information Specialist, Canning Gumm, Inc. (1997-99); Executive Manager, Three Stars Import & Export (1996). **Associations & Accomplishments:** American Society of Mechanical Engineers; Institute of Electronics and Electrical Engineers; Society of Automotive Engineers. **Education:** New Jersey Institute of Technology, degree in Computer Information Systems (In Progress); Passaic County Technical Institute, degree in Engine Mechanics with Honors. **Personal Information:** Mr. Khalil enjoys technology, art, martial arts and music.

Alamdar Hussain Khan
Senior Oracle Database Administrator
Sigma Projects Services
3383 North Millbrook Avenue, Apartment 35
Fresno, CA 93726
(559) 455-5042
ahussaiukhan@yahoo.com

7379

Business Information: As Senior Oracle Database Administrator of Sigma Projects Services, Mr. Khan fulfills a number of duties on behalf of the Company and its clientele. Managing the database mainframes, he oversees the proper installation and application of systems software. Actively involved in the development of new projects, he utilizes his vast knowledge of the computer field in order to implement new technologies. Committed to providing complete service, Mr. Khan maintains technical support for his clients. Continuing his training and focusing on the development of new projects, he is committed to furthering the success of Sigma Projects Services. Highly regarded, his goals include attaining the position of project manager or leader. Established in 1995, Sigma Projects Services is a reputable computer services company. With over 200 professional computer experts, Sigma Projects Services offers technical support and development of software and databases for their clients. Consulting with customers, the Company designs state-of-the-art systems according to their clients' specific requirements. **Career Highlights:** Senior Oracle Database Administrator, Sigma Projects Services (1998-Present); Senior Database Administrator/Consultant, Fresno County Computer Services Division (1998-Present); Senior Database Consultant, Oracle Corporation (1998); Oracle Database Administrator, L&T, India (1995-98). **Education:** California State University at Fresno, M.B.A. in Management Information Systems (In Progress); Madras University India, Master's in Computer Application, Bachelor's degree in Computer Science; National Institute of India, Advanced degree in Systems Management. **Personal Information:** Mr. Khan enjoys photography, reading, sports, fishing and travel.

Michael S. Kinnard
Consultant
Maxim Group (BioLab Inc.)
843 Riverstone Lane
Woodstock, GA 30188
(404) 378-1761
Fax: (770) 592-1361
mkinnard@mindspring.com

7379

Business Information: Functioning in the role of Consultant with Maxim Group, Mr. Kinnard is subcontracted out to BioLab Inc. BioLab engages in pool water treatment chemical research, manufacturing, and distribution. In his position, Mr. Kinnard is responsible for development and implementation of software and database solutions for internal corporate use. As a seven year professional, he is an experienced business solutions programmer and analyst who develops state-of-the-art accounting and financial software applications. In addition, Mr. Kinnard provides analytical and technical assistance in designing new solutions to enhance the overall performance of the information systems function. His success reflects his ability to think out-of-the-box and take on new challenges and responsibilities. He keeps on top of new technology by reading a variety of publications such as PC Magazine and Oracle. Remaining with Maxim Group and remaining at the cutting edge of technology serves as Mr. Kinnard's future goals. Maxim Group is an information technology contracting company. The Group's staff of information technology consultants are outsourced to various companies to enhance their information systems and technology infrastructure. Presently, Maxim Group reports estimated annual revenues in excess of $380 million. **Career Highlights:** Consultant, Maxim Group (BioLab Inc.) (1999-Present); Supply Officer, United States Navy (1992-98). **Education:** American Inter Continental University, M.I.T. (1999); University of Arizona, B.S. in Business Administration in Management Information Systems (1992). **Personal Information:** One child: Karl Duncan. Mr. Kinnard enjoys motorsports, photography and travel.

James H. Klempner
System Consultant
Newel Systems, Inc.
935-G North Plum Grove Road
Schaumburg, IL 60173
(847) 969-0600
Fax: (847) 969-0622
jimk@newelsys.com

7379

Business Information: Mr. Klempner is System Consultant of Newel System, Inc. He is a member of the board and is responsible for fulfilling the overall functions of Senior Consultant. Before coming on board to Newel Systems, he has assertively served as Project Manager with both Dun & Bradstreet Corporation and Caremark, Inc., and Senior Systems Consultant at Access Health Marketing. As a solid, 13 year technology professional with an established record of producing results, Mr. Klempner is responsible for network consulting, infrastructure design, software development and implementation of new, emerging technologies. Determining the strategic direction and guiding the business contributions of the information systems function also fall within the purview of Mr. Klempner's responsibilities. He credits his career success to his ability to successfully see the job through from conception to completion. Growing the Corporation to 25 employees and software development department serves as his future goals and objectives. A small privately owned consulting firm, Newel Systems, Inc. engages in network design, implementation, and support as well as custom software development. Local in scope, Newel Systems was established in 1987 and presently employs a staff of six professional and technical experts. **Career Highlights:** System Consultant, Newel System, Inc. (1996-Present); Project Manager, Dun & Bradstreet Corporation (1994-96); Project Manager, Caremark, Inc. (1992-94); Senior System Consultant, Access Health Marketing (1990-92); System Consultant, Baxter Healthcare Corporation (1986-90). **Education:** Keller Graduate School of Management (Currently Attending); Western Illinois University, B.S. in Computer Science. **Personal Information:** Married to Victoria in 1993. Two children: Nathan and Rebekah. Mr. Klempner enjoys tennis, bowling, winter camping and backpacking.

David S. Klinkefus
Internet Engineer/ATM Engineer
Iowa Communications Network
7700 Northwest Beaver Drive
Johnston, IA 50131-1902
(515) 323-4431
Fax: (515) 323-4425
dave.klinkefus@icn.state.ia.us

7379

Business Information: As an Internet Engineer of Iowa Communications Network, Mr. Klinkefus is responsible for ATM, WAN, and Internet engineering. Also, he serves as a DNS naming authority for the State of Iowa and is responsible for IP numbering. Providing service to over 300,000 users, Mr. Klinkefus also provides training, directs news feed access, and oversees web server operations. Iowa Communications Network provides Internet services to public and private schools at the elementary and secondary level. Libraries and community colleges are also served in the state of Iowa. The fibre optic network has been in operation since 1994 and has achieved annual Internet revenues of $2.5 million. **Career Highlights:** Internet Engineer, Iowa Communications Network (1985-Present); Field Technician, MWR - Telecom (1994-95); Field Technician, Iowa Network Services (1994). **Associations & Accomplishments:** Certified Network Administrator, Novell; Wide Area Network Technician, 3COM; Engineer, Hewlett-Packard; Bay Networks: Service Technician, Centillion Field Engineer; Technician, Toshiba; Field Technician, Windows 95; Field Technician, Windows NT; Bind DNS for Windows NT; NTMail for Windows NT; Service Engineer, GDC-APEX; ATM Switch Administration. **Education:** DMACC at Ankeny, Iowa, Electronics (1977). **Personal Information:** Married to Karen in 1985. Two children: Amy Lynn and Matthew Scott. Mr. Klinkefus enjoys Tae Kwon Do and has achieved his Black Belt.

Kathy Hawkins Knight
Business Analyst/Software Consultant
McKinley Group, Inc.
P.O. Box 53182
Atlanta, GA 30355-1182
(804) 385-4169
Kathy_Knight@hotmail.com

7379

Business Information: Serving with McKinley Group, Inc. since 1996, Ms. Knight assumes the responsibilities of Business Analyst and Software Consultant. In this capacity, she analyzes a variety of programs and computer systems and consults with clients regarding their software systems. She performs some COBOL programming as well as maintenance and development of various applications. Her career milestones include working on a critical project to get clients in Puerto Rico up and running after Hurricane Hugo. She attributes her success to persistence, perseverance, and taking advantage of opportunities afforded to her. Ms. Knight would like to continue to stay on the cutting edge of technology and stay abreast of new advancements. Her credo is "if you want to excel and realize your own potential, this is definitely the industry for you to begin." McKinley Group, Inc. based out of Virginia and with locations worldwide provides technical system consultation services. The Corporation also offers systems integration and technical support for clients with questions regarding their computer software and hardware applications. Agents of the Corporation provide individuals and businesses with information on various programs and applications that offer upgrade capabilities and faster, more in-depth processes. Internet access and Y2K technical support is also available. **Career Highlights:** Business Analyst/Software Consultant, McKinley Group, Inc. (1996-Present); Information Technology Consultant, Matrix, Inc. (1994-96); Senior Programmer Analyst, American Software (1992-94). **Associations & Accomplishments:** Black Data Processing Associates; National Association of Investors Corporation; Co-Founder, God is My Source Investors Corporation; Partner, Expert Consulting Services. **Education:** Seton Hall University, B.S. in Management Information Systems (1986). **Personal Information:** Married to Kenneth in 1993. One child: Kameron Joseph. Ms. Knight enjoys reading, investment club activities, surfing the Internet and family travel.

Claus Koppert
Data Center and Customer Service Manager
Euro-Log GmbH
Am Soeldnermoos 17
Hallbergmoos, Germany 85399
+49 8119595775
Fax: +49 8751843706
claus.koppert@t-online.de

7379

Business Information: Serving in the dual role of Data Center and Customer Service Manager for Euro-Log GmbH, Mr. Koppert fulfills a number of duties on behalf of the Company and its clientele. He is responsible for ensuring the functionality and operational status of the data infrastructure as well as running program systems, managing the help desk, and providing on site installation. In his current capacity, Mr. Koppert supervises a technical staff of 20 people. Having taken courses in software engineering, he possesses superior talents and an excellent understanding of of the industry. He is proud of his present job that gives him the opportunity to do a lot of things. A successful 14 year veteran of the field, Mr. Koppert plans to pursue his education and obtain a higher position as director. His professional success reflects his ability to think outside the box, aggressively take on challenges, and deliver results. Operating from Hallbergmoos, Germany, Euro-Log GmbH is a data service center. Established in 1995, the Center offers consultation and support on software development for transportation and logistics. Presently, the Company employs a work force of 50 professional, technical, a support staff who help generate in excess of $10 million in annual revenues. **Career Highlights:** Data Center and Customer Service Manager, Euro-Log GmbH (1997-Present); Quality Assurance Manager, Rolute & Sduven (1990-97); Quality Assurance Manager, Didel Company (1986-90). **Associations & Accomplishments:** Shareholder of the EuroLog GmbH. **Education:** Software Engineering (1986). **Personal Information:** Married in 1984. Two children: Florion and Fabian. Mr. Koppert enjoys walking and underwater rugby.

Ronald Kramer
Vice President, Application Services
UPAQ Ltd.
Mühlebachstrasse 6
Zürich, Switzerland 8008
+41 12542760
Fax: +41 12542701
ron.kramer@upaq.com

7379

Business Information: Combining management skills and technological expertise, Mr. Kramer began his career with UPAQ in 1999. As Vice President of Application Services, he fulfills a number of executive duties on behalf of the Company and its clientele. Possessing excellent technical and managerial skills, Mr. Kramer is responsible for the development and management of UPAQ's products and services portfolio as well as tending to outsourced system integrator relationships. He is proud of taking a lead role in driving growth and fostering excellence in his team. Always alert to new market opportunities, technologies, and approaches, Mr. Kramer is committed to assisting the Company in solving its challenges as it strives for its IPO. He attributes his success to his drive for continual personal growth, assuming responsibility, and sharing his humor. Founded in 1999, UPAQ is a Digital Asset Services Provider company specializing in the secure distribution and storage of important large data files and digital products via the Internet and satellite. The Zürich, Switzerland headquarters has a team of 30 experienced individuals to design, market, and provide digital asset services. UPAQ continues to provide the business-to-business market with essential technology solutions enabling reliable, convenient, and secure services in a fast-paced and mobile society. **Career Highlights:** Vice President, Applications Services, UPAQ Ltd. (1999-Present); Swisscom-The Blue Window: Head of Organizational Development (1998-99), Product Manager (1997-98); Dow Europe S.A.: Electronic Messaging Specialist (1994-97), Senior Information Systems Analyst (1991-94); Telecommunications Software Developer, Standard Telephon & Radio AG (1983-87). **Education:** Cornell University, Master's degree in Electrical Engineering (1983), B.S. in Electrical Engineering (1982); SAWI, Marketing/Advertising Diploma (1991); American School of Zürich (1978). **Personal Information:** Mr. Kramer enjoys travel, aikido, salsa dancing and reading.

Richard E. Kretz, Ph.D.
Consultant
Business Edge Solutions
773 Whitman Drive
Allen, TX 75002
(972) 359-0470
rkretz7761@aol.com

7379

Business Information: Serving as a Consultant with Business Edge Solutions, Dr. Kretz is directly involved in the development of cutting edge training and technical business solutions. Demonstrating his vast knowledge and commendable interpersonal skills, he regularly meets with executive client representatives, evaluating their needs and goals. Dr. Kretz has developed a model for a taxonomy that improves training and management development quality and performance. He formulates strategic plans to meet his client's requests, successfully implementing programs that maximize daily operations, training, and productivity. Keeping fully abreast of changes in the industry as the world gears up for the impending millennium, he networks, studies journals, attends seminars, and gathers information from the internet. Dr. Kretz looks forward to continual achievements with the Company as they lead the industry into the next millennium with repeatable best practice solutions. Business Edge Solutions is high value-add industry solution integration firm headquartered in Edison, New Jersey. Specializing in

delivering value through applying industry-specific solutions to solve industry specific-challenges. They work with clients to create, plan, and deploy solutions to achieve competitive differentiation through business process innovation and enabling technology solutions. Established in 1999, Business Edge Solutions has already developed a strong reputation of quality service and performance throughout the industry. **Career Highlights:** Consultant, Business Edge Solutions (1999-Present); Senior Technology Information Developer, Nortel Networks (1996-99); Developer, GTE (1985-96). **Associations & Accomplishments:** International Society for Performance Improvement. **Education:** American State University: Ph.D. (1997), M.S. in Education Administration; University of the State of New York: B.S. in Sociology and Business Management, A.A. in Liberal Studies. **Personal Information:** Married to Pamela Wilson in 1994. Dr. Kretz enjoys genealogy and genealogy.

Charles J. Krueger
Technical Manager
Image Computers Inc.
3149 Joshua Court
Holland, MI 49424
(616) 392-4455
Fax: (616) 392-1639
chuckk@image-computers.com

7379

Business Information: Following 21 years of distinguished service in the United States Navy, Mr. Krueger joined Image Computers Inc. as Technical Manager. He is responsible for providing technical support to the manufacturing and testing laboratories. A seven year veteran of Image Computers, Mr. Krueger is charged with providing sales and network support, as well as building, testing and repairing computers and setting up systems for internal users and clients. Recommending purchases and performing research and analysis also fall within the purview of his responsibilities. Designing and building state-of-the-art systems, providing quality, value, and selection and added value services to a loyal clientele, and putting the client first is cited as Mr. Krueger's career highlights. In addition, he worked on some history making electronic data communication projects while in the Navy. Formulating creative marketing plans and increasing the client base is cited as his future strategic objectives. Established in 1984, Image Computers Inc. engages in building and selling computers and offering services such as network and hardware consulting. With an international client base, Image Computers employs a staff of six dedicated professional experts who continuously provide services and products laced with quality, value, and selection. **Career Highlights:** Technical Manager, Image Computers Inc. (1992-Present); Aviation Electronics Technician, United States Navy (1971-92). **Associations & Accomplishments:** Fleet Reserve Association. **Education:** University of Laverne, degree in Business Administration (1985). **Personal Information:** Married to Sherry in 1977. One child: Ian.

Stefan Chi Ho Kung
Consultant
Stefan Chi Ho Kung, Freelance
18B, Yee King Building, 67 East Waterloo Road
Homantin, Hong Kong
+852 22966628
Fax: +852 27136381
stefan@hkmedia.net

7379

Business Information: Serving as an independent Internet technology Consultant, Mr. Kung utilizes his excellent capabilities in providing Internet solutions for an expanding clientele. Extensively involved in the creation and production of cutting edge Web sites, he consults with client companies and corporations to establish future goals and interests in order to create a site best suited to fill their specific needs. Utilizing his vast knowledge and expertise of computer technology, Mr. Kung holds the notable ability to understand complex problems and present possible solutions to his clients. Highly regarded and possessing superior talents and an excellent understanding of technology, Mr. Kung continues to grow professionally through the fulfillment of his responsibilities and his involvement in the advancement of operations. His success reflects his ability to think out-of-the-box, tackle new challenges, and deliver leading edge results on behalf of his clientele. Mr. Kung plans on spending time as a freelance consultant internationally and eventually plans to start up his own consulting firm **Career Highlights:** Consultant, Stefan Chi Ho Kung, Freelance (2000-Present); New Media Manager, South China Media (1999); Webmaster, Apple Daily Online (1999). **Associations & Accomplishments:** Co-Founder, Webmaster (HK) Association. **Education:** Ohio University, Degree in Communications and Business (2000); HKAL. **Personal Information:** Mr. Kung enjoys golf, football and tennis.

Frank C. LaBorde
General Manager
Magnetic Data Technologies
600 Pine Avenue
Goleta, CA 93117-2828
(805) 692-4723
Fax: (805) 967-2828
flaborde@magneticdata.com

7379

Business Information: Utilizing a strong managerial and technical background, Mr. LaBorde is currently the General Manager for Magnetic Data Technologies' Goleta Division. In his position, he is responsible for managing the manufacturing plant in Goleta, California. He oversees all finances and profit and loss statements as well as compiling and managing the fiscal budget. Moreover, he is charged with project management and implementation, conducting quality assurance, and ensuring client satisfaction. Highly regarded in the industry, Mr. LaBorde also supervises a staff of employees who report directly to him and provides support to the manufacturing staff. In the future, he looks forward to continuing with the Company and expanding within the industry. Headquartered in Goleta, California, the Company engages in the reverse logistics and repair operations of hi-tech equipment such as disk and optical drives, tape drives, telecommunication devices, and security equipment. Additionally, the Company performs and supports most customer service support activities such as inventory management, test screen, help desk, and return authorization management. Currently, the Company has a staff of 140 employees at the Goleta location and 1,650 employees worldwide. **Career Highlights:** General Manager, Magnetic Data Technologies, Goleta Division (1997-Present); Director of Materials, Pinacle Micro (1996-97); Director of Operations, ETA Technologies (1995-96); Senior Manufacturing Manager, Digital Equipment Corporation (1971-95). **Associations & Accomplishments:** Instructor, Universal Kempo Karate School Association; United Way Allocation Committee. **Education:** University of Phoenix, B.B.A. (1984); Springfield Technical College, A.S. in Electrical Technology. **Personal Information:** Married to Diane S. in 1972. Three children: Brett, Tammy, and Jason. Mr. LaBorde enjoys martial arts, golf, bowling and biking.

Evelyn Labbate
Owner/Operator
TechnoSphere Services
22 Kennedy Street
Howell, NJ 07731-2520
(732) 427-2888
Fax: (732) 942-1204
eve@learningchoices.com

7379

Business Information: Ms. Labbate is in the position of Owner and Operator of TechnoSphere Services. She ventured out on her own to start the Company in 1999. Ms. Labbate provides educational technical consulting services for her clients. Possessing an excellent understanding of technology, she oversees the online and telephone services for the Company. Her future plans include growing and expanding operations and increasing the clientele. She attributes her success to hands-on experience. The highlight of Ms. Labbate's 20 years of industry experience is starting her own business while simultaneously working towards her Ph.D. TechnoSphere Services is an educational technology consultancy. The Company consults and coaches educational technology online and by telephone for information technology and other businesses. Currently, TechnoSphere Services is headquartered in Howell, New Jersey. **Career Highlights:** Owner/Operator, TechnoSphere Services (1999-Present). **Associations & Accomplishments:** Association of Computing Machinery; Institute of Electrical and Electronics Engineers; A.A.C.E. **Education:** Nova Southeastern University, Ph.D. (In Progress); Monmouth University, Master's degree in Software Engineering. **Personal Information:** One child: Jamie (daughter).

David Thomas Lang, Ph.D. (abd)
Program Manager
Trident Data Systems
9413 Van Arsdale Drive
Vienna, VA 22181
(410) 981-0121
Fax: (703) 281-2661
dlang@mgfairfax.rr.com

7379

Business Information: Mr. Lang has served with Trident Data Systems in various positions since joining the team of professionals as computer forensic examiner in 1999. At the present time, serving in the role of Program Manager, he is responsible for program management of computer forensics at the Department of Defense computer forensics laboratory. Assigned to the government division of the Company, Mr.

Lang utilizes several years of technology experience to work on defense computer forensics, defense intrusion systems, and counter intelligence projects. His plans for the future include obtaining his Ph.D. and authoring a textbook on the computer forensics field with on-line delivery. Mr. Lang's success reflects his technical ability to think out-of-the-box, aggressively take on challenges, and deliver results on behalf of his clients. Offering a wide variety of quality services, Trident Data Services engages in the provision of data security services to both consumer and government clients. Trident is an information assurance company that maintains the inner office systems of all clients while providing consulting for software programs. Having been in business for several years, the Company operates out of several international locations, and functions under the talents and expertise of more than 1,100 professionals including consultants, legal advisors, and administrative staff. **Career Highlights:** Trident Data Systems: Program Manager (2000-Present), Computer Forensic Examiner (1999-2000); Senior Computer Forensic Examiner, Systems Integration (1998-99). **Associations & Accomplishments:** Former Wing Commander, Wyoming Wing, Civil Air Patrol (1991-93); Institute Electrical and Electronics Engineers; CSI. **Education:** Nova Southeastern University, Ph.D. (In Progress); Bowie State University, M.S. in Management Information Systems (1998). **Personal Information:** Married to Thresa in 1994. Two children: Danny Jolovich and Brandon Greathouse. Mr. Lang enjoys scuba diving.

Bjorn J. P. Larsen

Manager
Larsen Consulting
19 Royal Terrace
Southend-on-Sea, England, United Kingdom SS1 1DU
+44 1702332596
Cell Phone: 44 7931522058
bjorn@larsen-consulting.com

7379

Business Information: Striving toward achieving higher standards and goals, Mr. Larsen serves as a Manager of Larsen Consulting. A professional consultant in Lotus Notes application development, he utilizes his knowledge within information technology in forming reliable relationships with his clients in order to provide specifically designed Lotus Notes databases for their businesses. He attributes his professional success to being a well-organized perfectionist with computer skills dating as far back as 1983. Larsen Consulting is proud to be recognized as a specialized Lotus company, offering the full range of professional Lotus Notes services. Larsen Consulting primarily provides Lotus Professional Services and Alpharma IPD with professional advice and tailor made database software. Mr. Larsen also conducts seminars and courses related to Lotus Notes and application development. **Career Highlights:** Manager, Larsen Consulting (1999-Present); Senior Consultant, Lotus Professional Services (1998-99); Manager, Studio 97 (1995-98). **Associations & Accomplishments:** LPS (Lotus Professional Services). **Education:** Lotus Notes R5 Instructor enablement, IBM (1999); University Atheens, Lotus Notes, Lotus e-business (1999); MS-NT4.0 Core Technologies and Administration, Azlan (1997); Lotus Notes System Administrator, Leylock (1997); Lotus Notes Application Developer, Leylock (1997); Developing Interactive Internet Applications, Lotus Notes, Leylock (1997); Introduction to Lotus Script, Leylock (1997); Developing Clipper applications, STF Engineering (1993); Certified Lotus Notes Instructors; Certified Lotus Notes Specialist; Certified Lotus Notes Professional Application Developer. **Personal Information:** Mr. Larsen enjoys diving, kayaking and martial arts.

Fredrik Larsson

Chairperson
Mendosus
Tornstigen 3
Mendosus, Sweden 13244
+46 856202776
fln@mendosus.org

7379

Business Information: Ensuring quality services and customer satisfaction for clients of Mendosus as a whole, Mr. Larsson serves as the Company's Chairperson, overseeing the strategical development and strategy of their operations. Working in association with 25 additional freelance technical professionals in other locations, the Company communicates from satellite offices via email to coordinate activities and assignments. A published author and developer of a CD-Rom for use in the industry, Mr. Larsson works with Campusnet, a Web site established to help students from around the country develop new skills. Having achieved the honor of Employee of the Year for 1999 within Mendosus, Mr. Larsson has been widely recognized for his accomplishments in the field, which will lead to his promotion to Chief Technology Officer in the near future. Formed in 1995, and later established and operational in 1997, Mendosus is one of Sweden's leading technological software companies, encouraging the use of Linux and free software. Engaged in the purchase of domain names and creation and maintenance of Web sites for residents in the local area, the Company utilizes several networking contacts to create the most innovative and high quality sites on the Internet. **Career Highlights:** Chairperson, Mendosus (1997-Present); Developer/Development Manager, Campusnet (1999-Present); Instructor, Frontec (1999); Instructor, Korrnux (1998-99). **Associations & Accomplishments:** Ung-Invest. **Education:** Välkommaskolan, Electronic Technician (1996); Lulea University. **Personal Information:** Mr. Larsson enjoys scuba diving and sky diving.

Peter Laxström

Consultant
Locotech Oy
Kangasalantie 2
Helsinki, Finland 00550
+35 8505252988
Fax: +35 8977406720
peter@locotech.fi

7379

Business Information: Functioning in the capacity of Consultant for Locotech Oy, Mr. Laxström is responsible for computer consulting services. As a solid, four year information technology professional, Mr. Laxström assists in maintaining his clientele's information systems infrastructures' functionality and fully operational status. Working closely with users and systems management, he analyzes, specifies, and designs new solutions to improve the overall systems performance, as well as harness more of the computer's power. He also installs, repairs, plans, and creates cutting edge Web sites. Mr. Laxström chose the information technology field because of its very challenging and competitive environment. He believes the field is challenging because of the constant changes in information technology systems. Coordinating resources, time lines, schedules, assignments, and budgets also fall within the purview of his responsibilities. Mr. Laxström's strategic plans include networking and interacting with colleagues to help create new systems, maintain their efficiency, and expand and grow Company operations. His success reflects his ability to think outside the box and aggressively take on new challenges. Locotech Oy provides information technology consulting services as well as software packages. Established in 1995, Locotech is local in scope and employs a staff of five dedicated individuals. Presently, the Company reports estimated annual revenues in excess of $400,000. **Career Highlights:** Consultant, Locotech Oy (1996-Present); Teacher, A Upper Secondary School (1997-98). **Education:** Heslinge Upper Secretary School (1995). **Personal Information:** Mr. Laxström enjoys motor sports.

Kendall J. Leaman

Help Desk Manager
IntelliMark, Inc.
5020 Richard Lane
Mechanicsburg, PA 17055
(717) 790-0404
Fax: (717) 795-9153
kleaman@intellimark.pa.com

7379

Business Information: A savvy, 12 year veteran of the technology field, Mr. Leaman serves as Help Desk Manager of IntelliMark, Inc. responsible for the outsource and insource help desks. Supervising 50 employees, he handles all customer issues and technical support. Assisitng in the implementation of policies and procedures, monitoring productivity, and handling customer problems and queries are all duties fall within Mr. Leaman's responsibilities. One of Mr. Leaman's greatest advancememts within IntelliMark was the development of "Remed," a cutting edge call tracking system. Looking to the next millennium, he hopes to advance into other positons, accuring greater responsibility and authority. Keeping abreast on new developments in the field and taking technology courses have allowed Mr. Leaman to be successful in his position. Established in 1989, IntelliMark, Inc. provides information technology service, gaining an annual revenue of $8.3 million. Over 150 employees, working at the Mechanisburg location, assist in providing various services. Services include training, consulting, systems integration, and help desk. **Career Highlights:** Help Desk Manager, IntelliMark, Inc. (1998-Present); Help Desk Manager, The Wolf Organization, Inc. (1987-98). **Associations & Accomplishments:** Help Desk 2000; Help Desk Institute. **Education:** Pennsylvania State, Associates degree in Computer Science (1987). **Personal Information:** Married to Karen. One child: Zackary. Mr. Leaman enjoys church, youth group, computers and Internet.

Gregory L. Lear

Technical Consultant
Database Consultants, Inc.
613 Northwest Loop 410, Suite 520
San Antonio, TX 78216
(210) 733-4884

7379

Business Information: Displaying his expertise in this highly specialized position, Mr. Lear joined Database Consultants, Inc. in 1998. In the capacity of Technical Consultant, he works directly at the clients' sites to install, maintain, and troubleshoot databases. His responsibility is to rescue clients' critical data to prevent data loss or corruption. Mr. Lear has extensive experience in Oracle database administration, previously implementing an Oracle application for 100,00 users during his 20 year United States Air Force career. He credits his current success to his education and attention to detail. Continually striving to improve performance, he has plans to further his education and aspires to attain a position in the production or development of database administration. Database Consultants is a technical consultancy firm specializing in the Oracle software programs and system applications. The Corporation installs, manages, and administrates databases for large corporate clients. A work force of 357 skilled professionals are engaged to maintain the clients' various databases. **Career Highlights:** Technical Consultant, Database Consultants, Inc. (1998-Present); Database Administrator, Diversified Technical Services (1995-98); United States Air Force (1975-95). **Associations & Accomplishments:** San Antonio Oracle Users Group. **Education:** San Antonio College, B.S. (1998); Troy State University. **Personal Information:** Married to Elaine in 1998. Four children: Scott, Benjamin, Jeffrey, and Lisa. Mr. Lear enjoys hunting, woodworking, camping, boating and fishing.

Roger E. Lee

Research and Development Senior Software Support Specialist
Getronics/Wang
150 East 58th Street
New York, NY 10155
(212) 644-5717
Fax: (212) 644-8540

7379

Business Information: Servicing an area from Canada to Florida, Mr. Lee has faithfully served with Getronics/Wang in various positions since 1983. At the present time, he fulfills the responsibilities of Research and Development and Senior Software Support Specialist. In his role, he ensures all operating systems are fully operational at all times. As senior troubleshooter, Mr. Lee utilizes extensive technical expertise in resolving systems difficulties in the local area as well as upgrading systems when required. Additionally, he provides expert assistance and advice to users, interpreting problems, and providing technical support for hardware, software, and systems. As a member of Gentronics/Wang swat team, Mr. Lee uses his knowledge and technology skills in helping the organization analyze and implement state-of-the-art technology to realize the maximum benefit from investment in equipment, personnel, and business processes. An accomplished professional, he was recognized as Wang Laboratories' "Most Valuable Engineer" for 1995 and was presented the "Customer Service Pride and Service Award" for 1993, 1995, and 1996. Attaining Microsoft, NT, and A+ certification; becoming the number two man in Customer Engineering and Software Support; and earning a Master's degree serves as his long-term goals. Getronics/Wang is the world's largest engineering group specializing in INETs, PCs, LANs, networks, and mainframes. International in scope, more than half of Wang Laboratories' 13,500 staff works with the Pentagon, Internal Revenue Service, and United States Air Force. Presently, Getronics/Wang generates in excess of $3 billion in annual revenues. **Career Highlights:** Research & Development/Sernior Software Support Specialist,Getronics/ Wang (1983-Present); Senior Regional Software Support Specialist, Wang Laboratories (1981-99); Consulting, E.P. Dutton Inc. (1980-83); Senior Systems Analyst, International Paper (1974-80). **Associations & Accomplishments:** Co-Fund Raising Chairman, Seton Foundation for Children with Special Needs; St. Joseph/St. Thomas Holy Name Society; St. Joseph/St. Thomas Ushers Association; WHO'S WHO in Computer Industry. **Education:** Manhattan Community College, A.A.S. in Continuing Education; Brooklyn College; Pace University. **Personal Information:** Married to Maria in 1970. Two children: Roger John and Philip Joseph. Mr. Lee enjoys bowling and golf.

William Lee
Managing Principal
C-bridge Internet Solutions
12 Rosemary Court
Roseville, CA 95678-6010
(916) 920-6072
Fax: (707) 220-1974
wlee@c-bridge.com

7379

Business Information: Mr. Lee is a successful, five year professional of the technology field. He currently serves as Managing Principal for C-bridge Internet Solutions responsible for a number of duties on behalf of the Company and its clientele. Serving his position since 2000, Mr. Lee interacts with all divisions of program development and oversees employees and group contact. Possessing an excellent understanding of the industry, he also develops solutions and conducts field tests, and performs troubleshooting and indepth consulting work. Mr. Lee is highly regarded by his colleagues and plans on eventually attaining the role of Vice President of the iSolutions group, and becoming more involved in strategic initiatives. His success reflects his ability to take on challenges and deliver the appropriate solutions. C-bridge Internet Solutions provides consulting services for Internet companies on a business-to-business level. International in scope, the Company is headquartered in Cambridge, Massachusetts. The Company's San Francisco, California location employs the services and expertise of a work force of 150 professional, technical, and support staff. **Career Highlights:** Managing Principal, C-bridge Internet Solutions (2000-Present); Management Consultant for Retail and Distribution, IBM Global Services (1999-00); Management Consultant, KPMG Consulting (1997-99); Logistics Manager, Frito Lay, Inc. (1995-97). **Associations & Accomplishments:** Vice President, Alumni Association; CSUF ROTC Chapter; Golden Key National Honor Society; National Retail Federation; Scabbard & Blade. **Education:** California State University at Sacramento, M.B.A.; California State University at Fresno, B.S. in Finance. **Personal Information:** Married to Lillie Lai (nee Young) in 1986. Two children: Alexandria Lai and William Jonathan. Mr. Lee enjoys restoring vintage Porsches.

Hal Leeds

Chief Operating Officer/Managing Partner
Morrow Technical Services
201 Main Street, Suite 600
Fort Worth, TX 76123
(817) 339-1137
Fax: (817) 339-1138
hleeds@morrownet.com

7379

Business Information: As Chief Operating Officer of Morrow Technical Services, Mr. Leeds is also a Managing Partner with a position on the executive board. Utilizing over 18 years in the industry, he effectively supervises the administrative duties within the Company and oversees all aspects of financial, sales, and marketing activities. A recognized leader, he works as a mediator between customers and the staff to ensure the complete satisfaction of each customer with products and services provided. He also works with the accounting department to negotiate the payment on all products. Mr. Leeds is currently reviewing the opportunity to expand into 35 international markets and several information technology fields. His quote is "Don't expect to get rich overnight, be economical and look for long term growth. Do it right for the customer and expect to do a lot of hard work." Morrow Technical Services provides information technology consulting and installation services. Established in 1992, the Company hosts a team of 10 computer consultants working to offer clients auditing, planning, and upgrading services for their businesses. The Company is able to accommodate the needs of clients with ten computers all the way to a network of several thousand. Reviewing current systems and software programs for clients and determining the necessity of new software and hardware, Morrow Technical Services produces over $1 million in revenue each year through its reputable repairs and upgrades. In addition, Morrow Technical Services prides itself on pushing cost effective solutions, not the latest and greatest in new technologies. **Career Highlights:** Chief Operating Officer/Managing Partner, Morrow Technical Services (1998-Present); Director of Operations, Facility Works (1996-97); Senior Operations Manager, WorldCom (1984-96). **Associations & Accomplishments:** Cowtown Executives Association; Rotary; Fort Worth Workforce Development Committee; Economic Development Committee; Small Business Council; Big Brothers & Sisters; Boys & Girls Club; Casa Manama Theatre. **Education:** Ohio State University, B.S. (1976). **Personal Information:** Married to Harriet in 1992. Two children: Todd and Matthew. Mr. Leeds enjoys golf, tennis and snorkeling.

Robert P. Lehman

Consultant
New Horizon Management & Consulting
35735 Brushwood Drive
Solon, OH 44139-2403
(440) 542-0992
Fax: (440) 542-0537
rpl@nls.net

7379

Business Information: Mr. Lehman functions in the role of Consultant with New Horizon Management & Consulting. He evaluates the needs of every customer and aids them in determining their specific desires and establishing a comparable budget. Once the objectives of the customer are recognized, he works with the customer to design and write an effective program that accommodates their requests. He is also a partner of the Company and assisted in its establishment from the early planning stages. In the future, Mr. Lehman is hoping to move into a more managerial role that eliminates the excessive time spent in the consulting aspects of the Company but retain his involvement as a supervisor and motivator. A 20 year veteran of the United States Air Force, Mr. Lehman's success is attributed to his persistence and his leadership ability to build teams with synergy, technical strength, and a customer oriented attitude, as well as deliver results and tackle new challenges. New Horizon Management & Consulting engages in software consulting. Specializing in manufactured software programs, the Company has provided expert representation of its clients for three years. The Company works to assist clients in designing new software programs for their businesses and, because of the extensive training each employee undergoes, is able to make effective recommendations. The Company turns over $500,000 annually and employs a staff of 50 personnel. **Career Highlights:** Consultant, New Horizon Management & Consulting (1998-Present); Contract Manager, Phoenix Management (1994-98); Enlisted Member, United States Air Force (1974-94). **Associations & Accomplishments:** National Rifle Association. **Education:** United States Air Force Non-Commissioned Officer Academy (1984). **Personal Information:** Two children: Christopher and Wendy. Mr. Lehman enjoys the outdoors.

Sean Frederick Leinen

Senior Systems Specialist
Intergraph Corporation
47 Boyd Place
Bronxville, NY 10708-2107
(201) 460-7421
Fax: (914) 395-0495
sfleinen@ingr.com

7379

Business Information: Mr. Leinen serves in the role of Senior Systems Specialist for Intergraph Corporation, demonstrating adept ability as he completes technical tasks. Meeting with clients, he evaluates their operating systems and makes suggestions pertaining to upgrades and new purchases. Mr. Leinen is a 20 year veteran of the technical industry. He utilizes his extensive career experience to design customized, innovative technical solutions. A celebrated author, he is considered to be a leader in his field, recognized for his contributions to the industry. His book "Windows NT Server 4 Administrators Guide" is well known and used in the industry. Enjoying the challenges his position represents, Mr. Leinen intends to continue in his current capacity. Intergraph Corporation provides professional services to Fortune 1000 companies on a national and international level. Services are geared towards businesses in the computer graphic design and software development industries, and include digital medical, pre-press, publishing, and information technology enterprise marketing. Established in 1969, the Corporation currently employs 8,000 highly trained professionals to assist in the completion of daily activities. **Career Highlights:** Intergraph, Inc.: Senior Systems Specialist (1995-Present), Branch Support Analyst (1993-95), Senior Field Engineer (1990-93). **Associations & Accomplishments:** Microsoft Most Valued Professional; Microsoft Certified Systems Engineer. **Education:** Microsoft University, Windows 2000 Deployment Specialist. **Personal Information:** Mr. Leinen enjoys computer software development, six-string bassist, music and billiards.

Uwe Lemke
Senior Systems Architect
Asera, Inc.
300 Saginawa Drive
Rednvodaty, CA 94063
(650) 480-6073
Fax: (408) 248-1256

7379

Business Information: As Senior Systems Architect of Asera, Inc., Mr. Lemke oversees the design of systems customers currently own. He is responsible for hardware and software configurations, software applications, and ensuring systems have horsepower and speed. A systems expert, he has made great achievements in his position such as optimizing and streamlining computer systems as well as implementing cutting edge software production systems. Years of experience in the technological field has enabled Mr. Lemke to acquire the skills necessary to efectively fulfill his job obligations. Attributing his career success to being open-minded, he plans to stay in his position and continue to grow professionally throughout his career. Established in 1999, Asera, Inc. specializes in business to business e-commerce solutions. Over 135 dedicated and highly skilled individuals assists in various areas of the Company's business. The Company also provides quotes and catalogue information and implements systems within 60-90 days. **Career Highlights:** Senior Systems Architect, Asera, Inc. (1999-Present); Siemens: Manager (1999), Team Leader (1995-99), Software Configuration Manager (1990-95). **Education:** German University: M.S. (1984), M.S. (1979). **Personal Information:** Mr. Lemke enjoys flying and computer designing.

Jeremy R. Lemmon

Application Developer
SMS Data Products Group, Inc.
1501 Farm Credit Drive
McLean, VA 22102
(901) 874-4009
Fax: (901) 874-2668
jeremylemmon@hotmail.com

7379

Business Information: Educated in the technology field, Mr. Lemmon serves as Application Developer for SMS Data Products Group, Inc. He works with a team of three other developers to design, develop, and implement applications for the Corporation's Web enablement and Y2K upgrades with the United States Navy. Before joining SMS Data Products Group, Inc. in 1999, he served as an Intern at NCR Corporation and Honors Intern for the Federal Bureau of Investigation. Mr. Lemmon also works to upgrade and enhance existing applications. The analysis, configuration, installation, maintenance, support, and tracking of operating systems, databases, client server utility programs, software, and hardware also fall within the realm of Mr. Lemmon's functions. His career success reflects his ability to learn quickly, think out-of-the-box, and aggressively take on new challenges and responsibilities. Continually striving to improve performance, he looks forward to a future promotion to Information Technology Manager. SMS Data Products Group, Inc. is an information technology corporation offering advanced data storage solutions to such clients as the United States Navy. With two locations in the United States, the Corporation maintains corporate headquarters in McLean, Virginia. **Career Highlights:** Application Developer, SMS Data Products Group, Inc. (1999-Present); Intern, NCR Corporation (1997-99); Honors Intern, Federal Bureau of Investigations (1998). **Associations & Accomplishments:** Association for Computing Machinery. **Education:** University of South Carolina, B.S. in Customer Service (1999). **Personal Information:** Married to Julie Wilson in 1999. Mr. Lemmon enjoys making home improvements.

Terry M. Lentz, Jr.

Network Specialist/Technician
Systems Computer Technology
150 West University Boulevard
Melbourne, FL 32901
(321) 674-8107
admin@teejay.net

7379

Business Information: As Network Specialist and Technician of Systems Computer Technology, Mr. Lentz helps students and teachers with systems and oversees and installs network components. In his capacity, he attends to all aspects of programming software and database management systems, CGI scripting, supporting Web-based and e-mail services, and network administration. Possessing an excellent understanding of his field, he also maintains the automated setup system that allows people to register themselves. Mr. Lentz also works for BAF Satellite & Technology designing networks, creating automated software, providing support, and performing administration for all networked computer systems in the Company. He is proud of being able to provide networking and server services to his clients. Mr. Lentz loves to help others. He is currently starting a new business of his own providing Web services and colocation. Systems Computer Technology is affiliated with the Florida Institute of Technology. The Department provides network facilities including routing and dorm room connections at the Institute. The Department also maintains student registration databases, ensuring that all students' accounts are properly managed. **Career Highlights:** Network Specialist/Technician, Systems Computer Technology (1999-Present); Network Administrator/Technician, Artemis International (1999-Present); Network Administrator/Technician, Quest Capital Finance Management (1997-99). **Associations & Accomplishments:** Institute of Electrical and Electronics Engineers Computer Society; Microsoft Certified Systems Engineer+Internet. **Education:** International School of Bangkok, Diploma (1999). **Personal Information:** Mr. Lentz enjoys computer troubleshooting, network maintenance and loves to travel. He has lived in Thailand for more than four years and has traveled to many countries including Malaysia, Vietnam, Laos, Philippines, Taiwan, China, South Korea, India, South Africa, Germany, Luxembourg, and France.

Jeffrey A. Lester

Network Systems Engineer
International Network Services
2000 Aerial Center
Morrisville, NC 27560
(919) 319-0400
Fax: (919) 870-1107
jeff_lester@inx.com

7379

Business Information: Mr. Lester serves as a Network Systems Engineer for International Network Services, designing and implementing LAN and WAN systems and performing network consulting. As a 12 year technology professional and prior to joining International Network Services, Mr. Lester served as Information Technology Manager with IBM Corporation and Network Services Manager for Medic Computer Systems. Assigned to various International Network Services' projects throughout the United States, he advises client companies on the feasibility of its networks and ways to improve its internal processes. Mr. Lester designs new networks for the organizations, managing each project from start to finish. Ensuring network functionality and fully operational status, deploying advanced technology within the Company, and ensuring the security and reliability of networks also fall within the purview of Mr. Lester's functions. Beginning his career as a computer engineer, he has continued to move forward in the industry. Attributing his success to motivation and a desire to succeed, Mr. Lester keeps abreast of changes in the industry by additional training and reading. Founded in 1991, International Network Services is a global provider of network consulting and software solutions. The Company's 2,200 knowledgeable professionals provide expert technological advice to businesses around the world, responding to specific needs and resolving problems in an efficient manner. **Career Highlights:** Network Systems Engineer, International Network Services (1999-Present); Information Technology Manager, IBM Corporation (1998-99); Network Services Manager, Medic Computer Systems (1987-97). **Education:** North Carolina State University, B.S. in Computer Science (1991). **Personal Information:** Married to Kelly in 1994. Two children: Brittany and Bryant. Mr. Lester enjoys golf.

Dennis G. Levenhagen

Manager
MicroGo'L
228 Cherokee Road
Beaver Dam, WI 53916-1057
(920) 887-0642

7379

Business Information: The owner of MicroGo'L, Mr. Levenhagen serves as Manager. He determines the overall strategic direction and business contribution of the information systems function. A systems expert, he performs all of the troubleshooting, installation, and repair of client microcomputers. Additionally, Mr. Levenhagen outlays the system software, offers network support, and gives technical support and training to the users. He oversees and handles all of the bookkeeping and accounting details of the Company. Concurrently, he fulfills the role of Production Layout Inspector with John Deer Horicon Works. Attributing his entrepreneurial success to his persistence, Mr. Levenhagen stays on the cutting edge of new technological advances in the industry by attending seminars and classes. A+ certified, he is currently studying to obtain his Microsoft Professional Certification to enable him to offer his clients better quality service. A microcomputer consulting company, MicroGo'L first began operations in 1994. The Company installs, troubleshoots, and repairs microcomputers for companies. **Career Highlights:** Manager, MicroGo'L (1994-Present); Production Layout Inspector, John Deere Horicon Works (1972-Present). **Associations & Accomplishments:** Former Post Commander/Former County Commander, American Legion; Rental Manager, Church Parsonage. **Education:** Marion College, B.B.A. (1989); Moraine Technical College, Associate's degree in Supervisors Management. **Personal Information:** Married to Lois in 1981. Three children: Matthew, Jennifer, and Katherine. Mr. Levenhagen enjoys singing, aerobics, biking and computers.

John H. Lewis

Owner
Lewis Colorado
4570 Fenwood Drive
Littleton, CO 80126
(720) 331-2428
john@lewiscolorado.com

7379

Business Information: As Owner of Lewis Colorado, Mr. Lewis is responsible for the implementation of comprehensive programs and services for all prospective professionals. He determines the overall strategic direction and formulates new business ventures and marketing plans to keep the Company out-front of competitors in the industry. Mr. Lewis' primary functions with the Company include reinforcing policies and procedures, coordinating all classes, and providing one-on-one training for selective students. With more than six years of information technology experience, Mr. Lewis plans to utilize his professional talents in the training arena to provide his client companies with the best possible staffing. Lewis Colorado engages in the provision of customized systems training. The focus of the Company is to offer specialized courses to client businesses for the adaptivity of staff members. Established in 1999, the Company operates out of one convenient location in Littleton, Colorado, and functions under the direct expertise and talents of several professionals who assist the Company in generating annual revenues in excess of $120,000. **Career Highlights:** Owner, Lewis Colorado (1999-Present); Systems Trainer, Knowledge Alliance (1997-99); Systems Trainer, PCE (1994-97). **Associations & Accomplishments:** Denver Systems Management Users Group. **Education:** University of Western Ontario, B.A. (1994); Microsoft Certified Systems Engineer. **Personal Information:** Married to Suzette in 1999. Mr. Lewis enjoys golf.

Min Liao, Ph.D.

Internet Engineer
Advanced Network & Services, Inc.
200 Business Park Drive
Armonk, NY 11204
(914) 765-1126
Fax: (914) 273-1809
liao@advanced.org

7379

Business Information: Dr. Liao is an Internet Engineer for Advanced Network & Services, Inc. Operating from Armonk, New York, he is responsible for the core Internet performance. As a savvy software developer, he also assists in the development of state-of-the-art programs as well as maintenance of the database management system. Ten years of extensive experience as an electrical engineer enables Dr. Liao to be creative in the Internet industry. An accomplished professional, he currently owns two patents in China and five papers he published at Institute of Electronics and Electrical Engineers' international conferences. Attributing his success to his ability to track the direction of technology, Dr. Liao's future endeavors include continuing in this field and expanding his horizons via the Internet. Advanced Network & Services, Inc. is a nonprofit organization specializing in education and Internet technology. Founded in 1990, the Corporation works to enhance nationwide awareness of knowledge and new technologies. The Corporation's most reputable activity is its sponsorship of an annual competition in Web site design for children aged 10 to 18 years. Presently, the Corporation employs a staff of 30 professional and technical experts. **Career Highlights:** Internet Engineer, Advanced Network & Services, Inc. (1997-Present); Computer Consultant, Context Integration (1996-97); Adjunct Instructor, Polytechnic University of New York (1994-96). **Associations & Accomplishments:** Institute of Electrical and Electronics Engineers Computer Society. **Education:** Polytechnic University of New York, Ph.D. (1998), M.S.; Chong Qing University, M.S. **Personal Information:** Married to Yan in 1987. Two children: Ying and Linda. Dr. Liao enjoys reading and sports.

William "Keeko" Liddell

Support Manager
Sage Software, Inc.
17950 Preston Road, Suite 50
Dallas, TX 75252
(972) 732-7500
Fax: (972) 818-2337
keeko.liddell@sage.com

7379

Business Information: Mr. Liddell currently serves as Customer Support Services Manager for DacEasy software, a division of Sage Software Inc. He began his employment with Sage in 1995 as a frontline technical support analyst. In 1997, he was promoted to team supervisor, and in 1998 to his current position of department manager. In the capacity as Manager, he oversees and directs a 24 member staff in the daily operations of a high volume call and contact center. His background includes a six-year enlistment with the United States Marine Corps in the field of communication technology, serving as a communications consultant for a Washington D.C. based consulting firm, and participating for a period with EDS. Highly regarded by his colleagues, Mr. Liddell attributes his success to a strong dedication to family and profession, common sense, the ability to learn from other's mistakes or successes, a strong and honest work ethic, and opportunity. Sage Software is an industry leading developer of cutting edge software that assists business professionals with the ability to maintain a competitive edge in the business world. **Career Highlights:** Customer Support Services Manager, Sage Software, Inc. (1998-Present). **Associations & Accomplishments:** Software Support Professional Association (SSPA); Association of Support Professionals (ASP). **Education:** Brookhaven Community College and Richland Community College, Certificate, Business Systems and Software; Franklin Convey Seminar, 4 Roles of Leadership; MCRD San Diego, USMC Basic Training; USMC, Formal Communication Technology Training. **Personal Information:** Mr. Liddell enjoys music, playing guitar and technology.

Jin Lin

Web Developer
Savantnet Solutions
545 5th Avenue, Suite 1101
New York, NY 10017
(212) 370-1101
Fax: (212) 370-1145
jin@savantnet.com

7379

Business Information: Serveing as Web Developer of Savantnet Solutions, Ms. Lin oversees a number of duties on behalf of the Firm and its clientele. She is responsible for obtaining information necessary to develop a comprehensive, user-friendly Web site for her clients. Joining the Firm after being in involved in a technical support role with another company, Ms. Lin aggressively took on the challenge of creating, maintaining, and updating the Firm's Web site for the convenience of site visitors. With years of experience in the technolgy field, Ms. Lin anticipates her promotion as a result of her continuing efforts to increase her skills through training and professional development activities. Her success reflects her creative ability to think out-of-the-box and deliver results. A Web developer, Savantnet Solutions offers technical support in such forms as network set up, Web site design, and consulting. Established in 1985, the Firm is located in New York, New York and serves a regional clientele. Presently, the Firm functions under the direction of a number of professionals who facilitate smooth business operations. **Career Highlights:** Web Developer, Savantnet Solutions (2000-Present). **Education:** B.S. in Computer Science; CCNA Certification.

Patricia A. Link

Network Support Specialist/Webmaster
Area 2 Learning Tech Hub
119 West Madison Street, Suite 102
Ottawa, IL 61350-5014
(815) 434-0780
Fax: (815) 434-8699
plink@lth2.k12.il.us

7379

Business Information: Following 25 successful years of clerical experience, Ms. Link now serves as Network Support Specialist and Webmaster for Area 2 Learning Tech Hub. She coordinates and works closely with engineers in order to support the systems and networking infrastructure as well as assume accountability for the Web design and content. Dedicated to the computer literacy enhancement of area children, Ms. Link looks forward to working with schools and new technology. She plans on continuing her education and attending workshops while also expanding her opportunities as a Mary Kay Consultant. A self-motivator, Ms. Link attributes her success to her curiousity, desire and want for change, and ability to take on new challenges. Created in 1996 through the Illinois State Board of Education, Area 2 Learning Tech Hub coordinates with 17 counties and their school systems to facilitate Internet connectivity. The Organization employs the skilled services of six individuals. **Career Highlights:** Area 2 Learning Tech Hub: Network Support Specialist/Webmaster (1994-Present), Secretary; Independent Beauty Consultant, Mary Kay Cosmetics (2000-Present); Secretary, Noel-Smyser Engineering Company (1984-94). **Education:** IVCC (In Progress). **Personal Information:** Ms. Link enjoys camping, hiking, reading and gardening.

Ryan P. Litwin

Director
Information Systems Professionals
2323 North Mayfair Road, Suite 260
Milwaukee, WI 53226
(414) 443-2600
Fax: (414) 443-2619
rlitwin@mixcom.com
7379

Business Information: Functioning in the capacity of Director at Information Systems Professionals, Mr. Litwin assumes responsibility for the day-to-day administration and operational activities at the Milwaukee office, including all financial aspects such as profit and loss statements. He actively recruits information technology professionals and works with businesses to place each professional. Ensuring that each person has the proper skills and qualifications necessary for the business in which he is placed, Mr. Litwin resolves any problems arising from placements quickly and efficiently. He has gained much experience through his career by trial and error. In the process, he has learned what methods of business work and what do not. His advice to others, "Try not to take too much stress home with you, work towards a solution." Establishing goals that are compatible with those of the Company, Mr. Litwin wants to continue expanding his knowledge and skills in order to better serve his clients. Serving businesses in the state of Wisconsin, Information Systems Professionals specializes in the staffing and placement of information technology professionals. The Company maintains two main offices and a variety of satellite locations in the Southeast region of the state. A staff of 55 skilled individuals contract temporary and permanent placement of information technology professionals. The Company interviews, recruits, and maintains each of the professionals that are placed in the client businesses. **Career Highlights:** Director, Information Systems Professionals (1998-Present); Account Manager, Compuware (1996-98); Account Manager, Trusty Software Design (1995-96). **Education:** University of Wisconsin at Milwaukee, B.A. (1997). **Personal Information:** Married to Diane in 1993. Two children: Amanda and Morgan. Mr. Litwin enjoys gardening, reading, electronics, automobiles, swimming, water skiing and spending time with his family.

Manish Lodaya

Technical Manager
NextLinx Corporation
806 I Trotters Ridge Lane
Gaithersburg, MD 20879
(301) 977-4641
Fax: (301) 922-3892
manish_lodaya@nextlinx.com
7379

Business Information: As a technical member of the initial team that founded NextLinx Corporation Services Division, Mr. Lodaya serves as Technical Manager responsible for all aspects of day-to-day activities, such as projects and services. A brilliant person with an excellent understanding of his field, Mr. Lodaya manages the 12 staff technical consultants. Highly regarded as a hardware and software technical consultant, he works closely with management and users to analyze, specify, and design new solutions to harness the power of IT systems. In the future he hopes to be recognized as a hardware and software technical guru. Success, according to Mr. Lodaya, is attributed to his ability to think outside the box, take on challenges, and deliver results on time and within budget. NextLinx Corporation Services Division helps companies implement Oracle ERP, E-Commerce, and database software. Clients include: telecom, food production, publishing, hi-tech, and distribution companies. Established in 1997, NextLinx Services currently employs 60 professional technical and support staff. **Career Highlights:** Technical Manager, NextLinx Corporation (1997-Present); Technical Manager, Computer Science and Technology (1996-97); Technical Support Manger, ICL Singapore Pte. Ltd. (1995-96). **Associations & Accomplishments:** Institute of Electrical and Electronics Engineers Computer Society. **Education:** National Center for Software Technology: PGDST (1992); Bachelors in Engineering: B.E. (Electronics) (1990).

Vincent D. Lowe

Vice President of Business Development
Aqueduct Information Services
650 Castro Street #120-195
Mountain View, CA 94041
(248) 557-4848
Fax: (248) 557-8442
vincent@compclass.com
7379

Business Information: Mr. Lowe serves as Vice President of Business Development for Aqueduct Information Services. He facilitates new business opportunities, acts as the General Manager, conducts training workshops, and provides consulting services. Established in 1997, Aqueduct Information Services is an information technology engineering consultancy. The Firm offers clients Internet and intranet development, software and database design and implementation, and user training. Specialized training is conducted using an in-house developed curriculum combined with ongoing technical support. Aqueduct Information Services reports estimated annual revenue of $250,000. **Career Highlights:** Vice President of Business Development, Aqueduct Information Services (1997-Present); Technical Trainer, The Computer Classroom (1994-97); Cable and Wireless: Programmer/Analyst (1992-94), Data Analyst (1990-92). **Associations & Accomplishments:** Toastmasters International; Reading For The Future; Distinguished Instructor of the Year, Santa Cruz Operations (1996); Teacher, Sunmicro System Employees Program Language. **Personal Information:** Mr. Lowe enjoys science fiction and amateur film making.

Eric Q. Lunstead

Senior Account Manager
AMR Research
2 Oliver Street, Fifth Floor
Boston, MA 02109-4925
(617) 574-5213
Fax: (617) 542-5670
elunstead@amrresearch.com
7379

Business Information: As Senior Account Manager of AMR Research, Mr. Lunstead is responsible for maintaining relations with Chief Information Officers, Vice Presidents, and Directors of global companies in order understand their business strategies. By doing so, he can successfully evaluate their differing situations and advise them on technical solutions to make them more competitive. With a successful history of financial consulting to lean on, Mr. Lunstead is able to devlop innovative and creative approaches to improve client situations. Internally recognized for his ability to accurately assess financial and marketing profiles, he has closed several quarter to half million dollar deals for the Company. Always alert to new approaches, opportunities, and techniques, Mr. Lunstead currently is expanding his involvement in the e-business industry. AMR Research is an industry and marketing analysis firm providing independent advice on e-business strategy and e-commerce, using technologically advanced applications to make the business more cost and time effieicent. Established in 1986, the Company employs 200 people in the greater Boston area, with annual revenue exceeding $100 million. **Career Highlights:** Senior Account Manager, AMR Research (1998-Present); Account Manage, Interleaf Inc. (1995-98); Financial Consultant, Merrill Lynch (1993-95). **Education:** Harvard Extension School. **Personal Information:** Mr. Lunstead enjoys golf.

Robert Garon "Bob" Lynn

Independent Systems Consultant
6510-C Clavell Lane
Charlotte, NC 28210
(704) 552-2702
bob@boblynn.com
7379

Business Information: Portfolio Acquisition Application Data Base Conversion Manager is a job description title best describing Mr. Lynn's last nine years of tenure in the financial industries as a systems consultant in three predominate niches. They are: Bank and S & L client servicing and whole bank merger acquisition; Mortgage bank servicing portfolio and whole company acquisitions; and Project Management of systems regulatory compliance and feature functionality development. Mr. Lynn's engagement in First Union entailed development of a team and its infrastructure, processes and procedures for the Enterprise Information Management's Customer Data Warehouse, Extraction Development. The Extraction Development team develops extract applications from MVS production environments, which execute at cycled intervals extracting data files' from legacy systems. Via these modules, the extracted files' data is scrubbed, appended, and formatted for the Informix/Unix environments. These extracted files are further conditioned, transformed, and loaded to the Informix database for clients' appropriate data distribution or the business partner's date mart or hotel for their ultimate disposition. Mr. Lynn's charge and tenure with both Fleet Mortgage and Fiserve was to manage the development of, and production implementation for, corporate modus-operandi of staff and infrastructure on systems application and processes to meet large corporate growth objectives via portfolio acquisition and subsequent application data base and operational conversion and implementation. At Fleet during a 33-month period, 40 servicing acquisition conversion loads from 12 different seller servicing applications totaling over 578,000 loans and 35 servicing sale de-conversion service releases totaling over 250,000 loans were performed. During this time Mr. Lynn designed and directed the development, benchmark certification, implementation, and production use of XREF, a CICS/VSAM based conversion vendor cross referencing, field mapping, conversion field, and JCL run parameter application. Also during this time, Mr. Lynn oversaw the development and production use of a loosely coupled system for the sale of loan portfolios, FMSL, which was used from the due negligence to actual data base de-conversion. At Fiserve, Mr. Lynn developed the team and departmental infrastructure as well as was an integral part of the building through client acquisition conversion of a 65 bank all application NCR Bank service bureau in Miami, Florida. During the 1980 decade of bank re-regulation masked as de-regulation, Mr. Lynn's oversight entailed regulatory systems compliance for many regulations including Reg C, Reg Z, Reg CC, Reg D, FASB91, and FASB95. These and others were production implemented into all the appropriate applications used by those 65 client banks and supported by the service bureau staff. **Career Highlights:** Compuware Corporation, Systems Consultant, First Union National Bank's Enterprise Information Management Division - EIM (1998-99); Logical Computer Systems System Consultant, RR Donnelly & Sons Publishing (1998); Information Systems Development Project Manager, Fleet Mortgage Group (1994-98); Fiserv Systems Inc.: Assistant to the President (Technical Position), Manager of Customer Support Division, Manager of Product Applications, Senior Project Analyst, Manager of Programming and Analysis, Systems and Operations Analyst, Applications Analyst (1984-94); Manager, User Services, Citizens Federal S&L (1984-85); Manager, Loan Operations, Royal Trust Bank (1983-84); First Financial Management Corporation: Manager of Computer Services Department, Manager of Computer Operations Department, Senior Marketing Analyst of Marketing Department (1981-83); Federal Reserve Bank of Miami: Manager of Computer Services Department, Senior Operations Analyst/Supervisor of High Speed Operations/Supervisor of Computer and Sorter Operations/Supervisor of Dispatch Unit of Check Collection Department (1974-81); Staff Sergeant, United States Army (1972-74). **Associations & Accomplishments:** International WHO'S WHO of Information Technology (1999); International WHO'S WHO of Professional Management (1996); Phantom Post #10068, Veterans of Foreign Wars - Miami, Florida; American Legion - Florence, South Carolina. **Personal Information:** Two children: Jennifer Rae Lynn, born 1981, and Jessica Robin Lynn, born 1983. Mr. Lynn enjoys strength training, exotic travel to remote areas and being a PADI certified diver.

William W. Lynt III

President
Right Connection, Inc.
1649 Birch Road
Kenosha, WI 53140
(262) 597-5528
Fax: (262) 597-5529
will@rightconnection.com
7379

Business Information: As the President of the Right Connection, Inc., Mr. Lynt oversees all aspects of day-to-day administration and all technical operations, such as going on-site to analyze, specify, and design the client's needs. Possessing skills and the desire to use them freely, he has streamlined Corporation ideas and established procedures to help the Corporation remain flexible, efficient, and profitable in the Information Technology Age. With over 15 years of experience in technology, Mr. Lynt keeps the Corporation on the leading edge. He got his start in technology during his high school days. Never giving up, he now reaps the financial benefits of doing what he likes. Proud of his life's accomplishments, Mr. Lynt plans on building up his client base and expanding the Corporation's daily operation as well as increasing the number of employees. Attributing his professional success to honesty and integrity, his advice is "research the field you wan to go into." Established in 1999, the Right Connection Inc. provides computer consulting services including information systems solutions and custom hardware and software design. The Company is also the Information Systems Department for small to medium sized bsuinesses on a part time basis. Performing all technological duties including maintenance, upgrades, and troubleshooting are an integral part of the Company's functions. Local in scope, the Company employs a staff of three people who help generate in excess of $200,000 annually. **Career Highlights:** President, Right Connection, Inc. (1999-Present); Senior Engineer, Merge, Inc. (1998-99); Software Engineer, Cherry Corporation (1993-98). **Associations & Accomplishments:**

National Eagle Scout Association; Captain, Volunteer Response Squad, Scout Leaders Rescue; WEMSA; Institute of Electrical and Electronics Engineers. **Education:** University of Wisconsin at Platteville, B.S. in Electrical Engineering (1992). **Personal Information:** Married to Kris in 1994. One child: Jessica. Mr. Lynt enjoys rock climbing, rock climbing rescue, camping and backpacking.

Michelle MacIntosh
Technical Support Manager
Northern Computers
146 Terrace Avenue
Pawtucket, RI 02860
(401) 727-4870
Fax: (401) 727-4873
mkmac3@home.com

7379

Business Information: Involved with the highly demanding technical support industry, Mrs. MacIntosh maintains a leading positon as Technical Support Manager with Northern Computers. Offering specialized services in access control, time, and attendance, she focuses her technical skills to contact equipment dealers, and custom install computer programs for her clients. Conducting training courses and technical support services for her individual customers, Mrs. MacIntosh engages in a personal form of business conduct, one unique to the information technology industry. Before joining the Company, she served as technical support supervisor for both Associated Data, Inc. and Ames Department Stores. Mrs. MacIntosh's success is attributed to her ability to take on challenges and deliver the appropriate results. Blazing new pathways for other access control technology companies to follow, Northern Computers is a large installation and PC training specialist. Employing the diverse talent and knowledge of 300 trained professionals, Northern Computers has been in operation since the 1970s, making it one of the oldest and most established information technology consulting firms in the industry. **Career Highlights:** Technical Support Manager, Northern Computers (1997-Present); Technical Support Supervisor, Associated Data Inc. (1990-97); Technical Support Supervisor, Ames Department Stores (1973-89). **Education:** Somerville High, Diploma (1975). **Personal Information:** Married to Brian in 1993. Three children: Jessica, Katelyn and Michelle. Mrs. MacIntosh enjoys dart tournaments and sports.

John MacKrell
Senior Consultant
CIMdata, Inc.
3909 Research Park Drive
Ann Arbor, MI 48108-2299
(734) 668-9922
Fax: (734) 668-1957
j.mackrell@cimdata.com

7379

Business Information: As Senior Consultant of CIMdata, Inc., Mr. MacKrell provides leadership and direction on techincal marketing issues. Managing his staff with a proactive style, he demonstrates his extensive knowledge of the industry through innovative solution design. He conducts extensive research of the market to analyze trends, ensuring a competitive position within the industry for the Corporation. Recognized for impressive communicative skills, Mr. MacKrell's presence is frequently requested at conferences, seminars, and Company meetings so that he may lend his insight on complicated technical topics. Enjoying his position as a highly respected member of the professional community, Mr. MacKrell looks forward to continued prosperity in his role as he assists in future corporate growth. His advice is "understand and use technology to improve your own efficiency." CIMdata, Inc. specializes in technical consultancy for the engineering and manufacturing industries. Focusing time and attention of CAD, CAM, and PDM developments, the Corporation is able to maintain a competitive position in the computer solutions field. Established in 1983, the international corporation employs 25 people at the Ann Arbor, Michigan location. **Career Highlights:** Senior Consultant, CIMdata, Inc. (1990-Present); Director of Marketing, Holland Systems Corporation (1987-90); Director of CAD Products, Information Displays (1982-84); Director of Solid Modeling, Computer Vision (1981-82). **Associations & Accomplishments:** Member of Board of Directors, Barton Hills Village; Member of Board of Directors, Michigan Museum of Art Friends; Member of Board of Directors, Michigan Library Friends. **Education:** University of Michigan, B.S. in Naval Architecture (1970). **Personal Information:** Married to Cheryl in 1987. Mr. MacKrell enjoys music (choral singing), book collecting and map collecting.

Markian W. Maceluch
Senior Systems Analyst
General Physics Corporation
509 South Exeter Street
Baltimore, MD 21022
(410) 951-2850
Fax: (410) 951-2855
mmaceluch@yahoo.com

7379

Business Information: As Senior Systems Analyst of General Physics Corporation, Mr. Maceluch is in charge of Web systems integration, Web based training, distance learning, and e-commerce implementation. He determines what computer hardware and software will be needed to set up the system and implements chages to it. A six year veteran, he coordinates tests and observes the intital use of the system to ensure it performs as planned. In addition, Mr. Maceluch prepares specifications, work diagrams, and structure charts for computer programmers to follow and works with them to debug or eliminate errors from the system. He continues to grow professionally and hopes to continue to improve his products and assist Fortune 500 companies in the development of cutting edge Web based solutions. Mr. Maceluch attributes his success to his integrity and enjoying what he does. Established in 1965, General Physics Corporation is dedicated to evaluating companies and providing suggestions for performance improvement. Employing a staff of 2,500 individuals, the Company reports an estimated annual revenue of $250 million. **Career Highlights:** Senior Systems Analyst, General Physics Corporation (1995-Present); System Analyst/Lead Project Manager, Info JED (1994-95); Associate Software Engineering Technician, Paramax-Unisys (1993-94). **Associations & Accomplishments:** International Webmaster Association. **Education:** Herzing, DEC Computer Science (1993). **Personal Information:** Married to April in 1999. One child: Colby.

Neerruganti Madhusudan
Senior Software Consultant
Complete Business Solutions
301 West Preston Street
Baltimore, MD 21201
(410) 767-8776
Fax: (410) 333-7290
madhusudhan-n@hotmail.com

7379

Business Information: Utilizing several years of extensive experience as a systems analyst, Mr. Madhusudan serves as Senior Software Consultant for the Baltimore, Maryland location of Complete Business Solutions. In this capacity, he assumes accountability for project design and development as well as its implementation at the client site. As a 12 year professional, Mr. Madhusudan also provides technical and system maintenance for the network after its installation. Coordinating resources, time lines, schedules, and assignments; overseeing budgets; and providing cohesive leadership also fall within the realm of his responsibilities. A systems expert in his field, Mr. Madhusudan credits his career success to solid work ethics and a work smart philosophy, in addition to his ability to think outside the box and aggressively take on new challenges. Continually striving to improve performance, he looks forward to a future promotion of Project Manager. Complete Business Solutions is a software and information system management consulting firm. A full service provider, the Corporation assists customers to improve and enhance their operations through the use of technological systems, software, and business applications. **Career Highlights:** Senior Software Consultant, Complete Business Solutions (1998-Present); Senior Systems Analyst, Tata Consultancy Services (1991-98). **Education:** Junior Venkateswpra University, India, M.S. (1987). **Personal Information:** Married to Polu Padmavathi in 1999. Mr. Madhusudan enjoys travel.

Michael Magolnick
President
Solution Home.com
6424 Northwest 19th Court
Margate, FL 33063

7379

Business Information: Utilizing his philosophy of not being afraid to take risks, as well as advancing his hobby to a business level, Mr. Magolnick serves as President of Solution Home.com. In this context, he determines the overall strategic direction and formulates new business and marketing plans to keep the Company on the leading edge of the industry. A veteran of the field, he is responsible for overseeing all aspects of day-to-day administration and operational activities. Mr. Magolnick is in charge of employee and customer relations, and ensuring services offered by Solution

Home.com are laced with quality, value, and reliability. Looking to the future, he plans on launching a new division and taking the Company public. Demonstrating expertise in his field, Mr. Magolnick offers this piece of advice to up and coming business professionals, "Stay tuned with the latest technology and don't be afraid to take risks. This will allow you to capitalize on all opportunities afforded." Joining the Internet solutions market in 1999, Solutions Home.com is an Internet service provider for the Margate, Florida area. Supplying optimal services, the Company specializes in brokerage, appraisals,and development. Presently, the Company is headquartered in Miami, Florida. **Career Highlights:** President, Solution Home.com (1999-Present).

Quanteer D. Magwood
Associate Software Engineer
RWD Technologies
40480 Little Patuxent Parkway
Columbia, MD 21044
(410) 772-5147
Fax: (410) 772-5150
quanteer@hotmail.com

7379

Business Information: As Associate Software Engineer of RWD Technologies, Ms. Magwood assumes accountability for all aspects of software development. She is responsible for software and Web site design, graphics, testing, analysis, and implementation activities. In addition, she conducts on-site testing operations and works closely with a "knowledge management solutions" team to assist in the development of leading edge user oriented products. Excited about information technology, Ms. Magwood is a motivational speaker who addresses high school and college level students on the growth and opportunities in technology. A positive and tremendously productive spokesperson, she plans to continue in her current position taking on a variety of tasks in pursuit of following her destined career path in the technological industry. Ms. Magwood's advice is "be determined, let your dreams become reality, and set goals." RWD Technologies operates as an information technology company that provides professional services in e-commerce consulting and development. Specifically, the Corporation offers e-commerce and Internet solutions to clients throughout the United States. RWD Technologies provides connection services for user networks and implementation of new systems. Established in 1988, the Corporation aims to institute a user friendly atmosphere, promoting a greater acceptance of technological advancement by all users from novices to experts. A necessary enterprise, operations employ the skilled services of 1,500 qualified personnel to meet the demanding and rapidly changing needs of systems users. **Career Highlights:** Associate Software Engineer, RWD Technologies (1997-Present). **Associations & Accomplishments:** Board of Directors, Youth Enrichment Program of Howard County. **Education:** North Carolina A&T State University, B.S. in Computer Science (1997). **Personal Information:** Ms. Magwood enjoys Tae Kwon Do.

Anand Mahajani
Consultant
Diversified Computer Consultants
1928 Johnson Ferry Road NE, Apartment U
Atlanta, GA 30319
(404) 262-6606
anandmahajani@hotmail.com

7379

Business Information: Serving as a Consultant for Diversified Computer Consultants, Mr. Mahajani primarily performs Oracle database administration for the Company's various clients. In addition to his duties as an Oracle database administrator, he performs on-site consultancy for everything from installing upgrades to setting up computer systems. Before joining Diversified Computer Consultants, Mr. Mahajani served as System Manager for Nipro Ltd. and Supervisor with Indian Aluminium Company Ltd. As a 15 year technology professional, his scope of responsibilities also include analyzing, specifying, and designing new solutions to harness more of the computer's power. A systems expert, his career success reflects his sincerity and hard work ethic, as well as ability to think out-of-the-box and take on new challenges and responsibilities. Mr. Mahajani plans to become more heavily involved in project management for the Company. Diversified Computer Consultants is a consulting firm and offers a variety of services including Oracle database administration. Established in 1990, the Company employs a staff of 150 skilled professionals to deal one on one with each client, providing them with top of the line customized service. **Career Highlights:** Consultant, Diversified Computer Consultant (1998-Present); System Manager, Nipro Ltd. (1989-98); Supervisor, Indian Aluminium Company Ltd. (1985-89). **Education:** Government Polytechnic, Panaj, Croa, Diploma (1984). **Personal Information:** Married to Kamini in 1990. One child: Monika. Mr. Mahajani enjoys reading, movies and learning more about latest computer technology.

Jeff L. Majcher

Systems Engineer
Companion Tech
193 Business Park Drive, Suite A
Ridgeland, MS 39157
(601) 978-1983
Fax: (601) 978-3078
jmajcher@ctjms.com
7379

Business Information: As the Systems Administrator and Engineer of Companion Technologies, Mr. Majcher works closely with systems management and users to analzye, specify, and design solutions to harness more of the computer's power. Supervising a work force of 55 employees, his responsibilities include administering call tracking, e-mails, end user applications, and network development. Proficient in all aspects of Internet services and NT servers, Mr. Majcher has contributed much to the Company. Always alert to new opportunities, techniques, and approaches, his goal is to learn everything he can and stay on the cutting edge. Enthusiasm and energy is attributed to his professional success. Companion Technologies specializes in medical records and insurance computer systems. Working for Blue Cross Blue Shield, the Company provides software, new applications, and call tracking for hospitals, clinics, and private offices. The Company works from 40 different locations and employs over 500 individuals. Presently, the Company report revenues in excess of $100 million annually. **Career Highlights:** Systems Administrator and Engineer, Companion Technologies (1997-Present); Engineer, Westinghouse (1990-97). **Associations & Accomplishments:** Microsoft Certified Systems Engineer. **Education:** Pennsylvania State University, B.S. in Electrical Engineering (1989). **Personal Information:** Married to Ann in 1997. Mr. Majcher enjoys mountain biking and skiing.

Srinivas Mankala

Technical Consultant
Database Consultants, Inc.
11701 Metric Boulevard, Apartment 521
Austin, TX 78758
(512) 330-0066
Fax: (419) 831-8167
mankala@hotmail.com
7379

Business Information: Serving as a Technical Consultant of Database Consultants, Inc., Mr. Mankala assumes a number of responsibilities including hiring and training staff, overseeing the budget, and maintaining all administrative duties. Possessing an excellent understanding of technology, Mr. Mankala also consults as well as designs and develops software for use in business. Encouraging and facilitating optimum performance among the staff, he ensures all units work together to achieve a common goal. In the future, Mr. Mankala plans to become further involved in Web development and e-commerce. He attributes his professional success to his creative thinking. Database Consultants, Inc. is a consulting firm that provides expert information technology advice to businesses across the nation. Established in 1999, the Corporation employs a skilled staff to acquire business, meet with clients, facilitate projects, and market services. Headquartered in Austin, Texas, the Corporation provides services to clients across the nation. **Career Highlights:** Technical Consultant, Database Consultants, Inc. (1997-Present); Software Engineer, Information Technology Solutions, Inc. (1997); Senior Systems Officer, Tata Engineering & Locomotive Company, Ltd. (1994-97). **Education:** Osmania University, M.S. in Computer Science (1994); J.N.T. University, B.S. in Civil Engineering. **Personal Information:** Married to Sujani in 1996. One child: Pranavi. Mr. Mankala enjoys chess.

John Mao, Ph.D.

President
Rocsoar, Inc.
44 Spring House Court
Wilmington, DE 19810
(302) 529-7278
Fax: (302) 529-7439
mao@rocsoar.com
7379

Business Information: Dr. Mao is President of Rocsoar, Inc. He oversees and directs all day-to-day administration and operational activities. As a solid, 10 year software and programming professional, he develops and implements sales and marketing strategies, maintains supplier relationship, and drives software production. Dr. Mao, drawing from his extensive academic ties and business experience, determines the overall strategic direction and vision and business contribution of the information systems function. Maintaining fiscal responsibility, he monitors and tracks profit and loss statements and accounting ledgers, as well as calculates and manages the fiscal year budget. Determining future technical requirements, coordinating resources and schedules, and providing cohesive leadership also fall within the purview of Dr. Mao's responsibilities. His success reflects his ability to build teams with synergy and technical strength, think out-of-the-box, and take on new challenges head on. Growing and expanding business operations and becoming more involved with e-commerce technology serves as his strategic objectives. A software company, Rocsoar, Inc. provides Internet based procurement solutions. The Corporation offers clients the latest software technology and applications. Established in 1997, the Corporation presently employs a staff of eight professional and technical experts. **Career Highlights:** President, Rocsoar, Inc. (1997-Present); Project Leader, Spree.Com (1997); Programmer, Vision Tel (1996-97); Software Engineer, China Academy of Launch (1989-93); Group Manager, Vehicle Technologies. **Associations & Accomplishments:** American Association for Artificial Intelligence; Committee of Knowledge Management Consortium; Chairman, Philadelphia Association of Chinese Computer Professionals. **Education:** University of Delaware, Ph.D. (1999); Harbin Institute of Technology, M.S. (1989). **Personal Information:** Married to Yonggi in 1990. One child: Daniel. Dr. Mao enjoys fishing, photography and astronomy.

Lou Maraschiello

Owner
Smart Web Sales
975 East Avenue #118
Chico, CA 95926
(800) 996-0634
7379

Business Information: Mr. Maraschiello is the Owner of Smart Web Sales. He determines the overall strategic direction and formulates marketing and business plans to keep Smart Web Sales outfront of its competitors. A savvy, eight year veteran, he creates and designs Web sites to the specifications of his customers and helps some create audio and visually interactive CD-ROMs. These programs store information onto a disc which is then able to be linked through the Internet to a particular site. Inspired by attending a Forest Miller seminar, he conducted a skills inventory and recognized his talents and skills and began working towards his own business. In 1996, Mr. Maraschiello pioneered the first automation testimonial and he is currently looking to witness the tripling in size of his clientele. His advice is "work hard and believe in self and products." A balancing life style and enjoying what he does has contributed to Mr. Maraschiello's success. Smart Web Sales was established in 1997 and has assisted several of the local businesses in establishing new Web sites. The Company features a devoted staff of five individuals who are each talented in graphic design and Web page development. Expanding its role in the computer technology industry, the Company also builds interactive CD-ROM programs specifically designed to meet the specific needs of clients. **Career Highlights:** Owner, Smart Web Sales (1997-Present); Process Manager TES, Pacific Bell Directory (1996-98); Sales, CMC (1995-96); Collections Manager, Centennial Media Corporation (1991-95). **Associations & Accomplishments:** Le Tip International; Chico Chamber of Commerce; Association of Directory Publishers. **Education:** University of Arizona at Phoenix (1998). **Personal Information:** Mr. Maraschiello enjoys music.

Marc E. Marchioli

President/Owner
The Database Group Inc.
4011 Travis Street
Dallas, TX 75204-7512
(214) 528-3091
Fax: (214) 528-9459
marcm@databasegroup.com
7379

Business Information: Gathering years of extensive experience in various technology positions within corporate America, Mr. Marchioli decided that he was both knowledgeable and stable enough to venture out on his own and establish The Database Group Inc. Overseeing the daily operations, Mr. Marchioli's company specializes in Oracle software consulting. As the President and Owner, he provides strategic direction and planning, consults directly with clients to ascertain their needs, and recommends various software and hardware. Mr. Marchioli sets an example for his 15 employees as an advocate of customer relations and service. He provides insight into Web development, policy creation, and performance evaluations. In addition, Mr. Marchioli manages the budget and finances for the Corporation. He enjoys the rewards of owning his own business and anticipates the growth of The Database Group. Established in 1996, The Database Group Inc. is a software consulting company. Specializing in Oracle databases and applications, the Corporation assists clients in installation, set-up, and implementation of various programs that will increase profitability and productivity. Targeting medium to large companies, The Database Group also offers advice in Web development, e-commerce strategies, project management, search engines, and outsourcing services. With more than $3 million in annual revenue, the Corporation will double in size in the near future. **Career Highlights:** President/Owner, The Database Group Inc. (1995-Present); Principal, American Airlines Dec. Technician (1991-94); Senior Analyst, Pacific Enterprise Oil Company (1990-91); Senior Engineer, General Dynamics (1987-90). **Education:** University of Florida: Master's degree (1987), B.S. in Mechanical Engineering. **Personal Information:** Mr. Marchioli enjoys computers, volleyball, weightlifting, video and music.

Christopher W. Marini

Principal
C.W. Marini & Associates
1105 MacArthur Boulevard, Suite B
San Leandro, CA 94577
(510) 633-1784
chris@marinis.com
7379

Business Information: As founder and owner of C.W. Marini & Associates, Mr. Marini serves as Principal. He is responsible for all aspects of day-to-day administration and operational activities. Possessing an excellent understanding of technology, he determines the overall strategic direction and business contribution of the systems function. As the lead consultant, Mr. Marini maintains client relationships and assigns projects to his staff as well as coordinates resources, schedules, and budgets. He started C.W. Marini & Associates because he saw a need while working as a Manager of Technical Support at Santa Clara Unified School District. His career highlights include setting up the functional networks for metropolitan clients. Attributing his success to keeping pace with the technology world, Mr. Marini's goals are to become more involved in Internet and global networking and continue growing his Company. C.W. Marini & Associates is a computer network consulting agency. The Company is involved in systems integration. The Company specializes in LAN, WAN, NT Solaris, and Novel technologies. Consistenly acheiving high quality performance, the Company is also involved in troubleshooting and Web server configurations to the retail industry, educational arena, and small businesses. Established in 1998, the Company employs a staff of six technical experts to serve organizations throughout the state of California. **Career Highlights:** Principal, C.W. Marini & Associates (1998-Present); Manager of Technical Support, Santa Clara Unified School District (1995-97); Senior Consultant, Monolith Computer Services (1994-95). **Associations & Accomplishments:** Institute of Network Professionals; The Network Professional Association. **Education:** California State at Bakersfield, B.S. in Business Administration (1997); CNP certification; MCNE certification; CNX certification; Certified NetAnalyst Level 2.

Wendy C. Marker

Owner
Marker Consulting
7167 Princeton Avenue
St. Louis, MO 63130-2344
(314) 727-1163
Fax: (314) 727-3926
7379

Business Information: Serving as Owner of Marker Consulting, Ms. Marker utilizes her extensive expertise in engineering and system consulting to perform computer system implementation and organizational development for client organizations. Fluent in Spanish, she worked with Andersen Consulting on a previous project in Mexico to install a computerized banking system. All of the applications, analysis, and strategies were done in the Spanish language. Her other background history includes stints with McDonnell Douglas as Systems Consultant and Walt Disney as Industrial Engineer. Looking to the 21st Century, Ms. Marker is currently pursuing her Master's degree in Nonprofit Management and International Affairs. Her future goal is to enter into international development, merging Spanish and an international interest with nonprofit organizations and agencies into a successful avenue. She remains on the cutting edge by networking with her husband and colleagues in the same field. Newly established in 1999, Marker Consulting offers its services to nonprofit organizations on an independent contract basis. The Company assists organizations to establish new fundraising systems and event planning. **Career Highlights:** Owner, Marker Consulting (1999-Present); Systems Consultant, McDonnell Douglas (1995-96); Systems Consultant, Andersen Consulting (1990-95); Industrial Engineer, Walt Disney (1989). **Associations & Accomplishments:** Chair, Latin American Task Force; Board Member, First Presbyterian Church of St. Louis; Tutoring for Hispanic Youth; Sister Community in El Salvador. **Education:** Washington University, M.A. in Nonprofit Management and International Affairs (In Progress); Iowa State University, B.S. in Engineering (1990). **Personal Information:** Married to Jeffrey in 1995. Two children: Elise and Grace.

Harri Markkula

President/Chief Executive Officer
Tilator Oy
Sydanmaantie 178
Sakyla, Finland 27800
+35 8405746697
tilator@netti.fi

7379

Business Information: Mr. Markkula is the President and Chief Executive Officer of Tilator Oy and is responsible for overseeing the day-to-day operations of this successful company. A partner with his brother, he determines the overall strategic direction and formulates new business and marketing plans to keep the Company at the forefront of the industry. He directs all contract negotiations, personnel management, accounting, and marketing procedures. Mr. Markkula plans to use his keen business sense to effectively expand the business and its services to accommodate a larger clientele. Under Mr. Markkula's leadership, Tilator Oy has achieved a record of excellence by offering comprehensive customer support in addition to competent technical service solutions to its clients. Tilator Oy provides information technology to healthcare facilities and wellness providers of Finland. This Company was founded in 1993, and has grown to employ 3 people generating an annual revenue of over $100,000. By continuously expanding its services, Tilator Oy plans to promote its operations to an international level and gain recognition as a world class information technology provider. **Career Highlights:** President/Chief Executive Officer, Tilator Oy (1995-Present); Physician, Kuaerner Masa-Yards (Present); Physician, The Social Insurance Institution (1998-99). **Associations & Accomplishments:** Lions Club. **Education:** University of Turku, Physician (1989). **Personal Information:** Married to Minna in 1996. One child: Paula. Mr. Markkula enjoys information technology.

Gerald D. Marlow

Executive Vice President/Owner
Helios System Inc.
800 Roosevelt Road, Building E, Suite 320
Glen Ellyn, IL 60137
(630) 858-4708
Fax: (630) 858-4853
jmarlow@heliosystem.com

7379

Business Information: After working for other major companies for the last 17 years, Mr. Marlow decided to venture out on his own to start up Helios System Inc. in 1997. As Owner, he relies on his firm academics and extensive business experience and technical skills while performing in the role of Executive Vice President. He is charged with setting Helios System's technical direction and vision, as well as developing strategic and tactical marketing plans. Mr. Marlow's position principally involves providing clients with network and management consulting, creating cutting-edge network infrastructures, and providing technical support for the mortgage industry. He saw an entrepreneurship opportunity while working for a Fortune 18 bank and quickly took advantage of the situation. Analysis, design, evaluation, test, and implementation of security mechanism and advanced computer network environments also fall within the purview of Mr. Marlow's executive responsibilities. He attributes his success to development and maintenance of good customer relationships. Building up the Corporation and expanding operations, adding more employees and offices, and continuing to be a success in all future endeavors serves as Mr. Marlow's goals. Helios System Inc. operates as a reputable computer network design and implementation company. Targeting clients nationally and internationally, Helios System employs 10 persons helping to generate in excess of $1.5 million in annual revenues. **Career Highlights:** Executive Vice President/Owner, Helios System Inc. (1998-Present); Systems Design Engineer, ABN AMRO Banks (1995-97); Network Engineer, Entex (1989-95); Hardware Technician, Xerox (1985-89). **Associations & Accomplishments:** Chairman Technology Committee, Illinois Association of Mortgage Brokers. **Education:** DeVry Institute of Technology, Certified Novell Engineer (1995), Technical Diploma (1982). **Personal Information:** Married to Ann in 1989. Two children: Jennifer and Daniel. Mr. Marlow enjoys fishing and skiing.

Heiko Bernd Marschall

Chief Executive Officer
Marschall Electronics, Ltd.
Kreuzackerstrasse 2, Garmish-Parten Kirchen
Bavaria, Germany 82467
+49 88219439111
Fax: +49 882194391099
mec@armisch.net

7379

Business Information: As Chief Executive Officer of Marschall Electronics, Ltd., Mr. Marschall is dedictated to providing optimal services to the surrounding businesses. Utilizing his vast knowledge of the field of technologies, he continues to implement new concepts in the further development of software, programs, and databases. Overseeing the basic operations of his Company, Mr. Marschall presides over all financial, administrative, and marketing issues. Determining where funds should be placed, he ensures the necessary equipment and materials for certain projects. Providing the necessary staffing for jobs and projects, he also handles all personnel problems. Coordinating with various advertising companies, he further promotes his Company. Continuing his growth with Marshall Electronics, Mr. Marschall plans on concentrating his efforts towards the Company's further expansion throughout Europe. Specializing in information technologies, Marschall Electronics, Ltd. was established in 1991. Over 15 knowledgable technicians provide development and maintenance services for their clients. Specifically dealing with Internet applications, the Company focuses on providing excellent services in telecommunications. Coordinating with their various clients, Marschall Electronics concentrates their efforts towards implementing technologies necessary to the further expansion of their clients' businesses. Devoted to providing outstanding client satisfaction, the Company continues to offer a complete range of computer services. **Career Highlights:** Chief Executive Officer, Marschall Electronics, Ltd. (1991-Present). **Education:** Technical University of Munich, Physicist diploma (1998). **Personal Information:** Mr. Marschall enjoys ballroom dancing.

Lauren J. Massa-Lochridge

Chief Executive Officer/Chief Technology Strategist
exlr8, Inc.
1678 Shattuck Avenue #133
Berkeley, CA 94709
(510) 644-0644
Fax: (510) 644-0644
laurenml@acm.org

7379

Business Information: As co-founder of exlr8, Inc. Mrs. Massa-Lochridge serves as Chief Executive Officer and Chief Technology Strategist. She determines the technology strategy and formulates business and marketing plans, helping the Corporation to find and maintain its niche in the market place. A savvy business person, Mrs. Massa-Lochridge's responsibilities include hands-on technology architecture and mentoring of her team, leading them in the planning and execution of exlr8's product and service offerings. A recognized professional, she has had the prestigious honor of working with researchers at NASA and the University of California at Berkeley. Staying on the leading edge of technology, she takes an active role in numerous industry-related associations. Her future goals include continuing participation in exlr8's success and advisory board roles with other technology startups. Established in 1999, exlr8, Inc. is a startup in the Internet application software and e-commerce sector. exlr8's primary objective is to provide its customers with the most sophisticated tools for enhanced utilization of the Web and Internet. exlr8, Inc. is presently located in Berkeley, California. **Career Highlights:** Chief Executive Officer/Chief Technology Strategist, exlr8, Inc. (1999-Present); Principal Business Technologist, Sun Microsystems (1997-99); Core Engineer/Senior Software Architect, Applied Materials (1996); Senior Systems Analyst, NASA AMES Research Center, Information Sciences Division (1995); Research, Programmer/Analyst, University of California at Berkeley (1989-94). **Associations & Accomplishments:** Institute of Electronics and Electrical Engineers; Association of Computing Machinery. **Education:** Pratt Institute, BID (1984); University of California at Berkeley; SIGS: Artificial Intellegence, Knowledge Management; Engineering Database Management; Machine Learning, Information Sciences and Systems; Industrial Engineering and Operations Research, Computer Science. **Personal Information:** Married to Mark H. Lochridge in 1990.

Samir Matabudul

Information Technology and Management Consulting Manager
BTI Consulting
Reunion Road
Vacoas, Mauritius 01
+23 02128000
Fax: +23 02108989
sma@bti.intent.mu

7379

Business Information: A true innovator and problem solver by nature, Mr. Matabudul joined BTI Consulting in 1998 based upon his knowledge and experience in the information technology industry. Serving as Information Technology and Management Consulting Manager with a team of associated consultants, Mr. Matabudul works directly with the public, consulting in information technology planning and service promotions. Utilizing his education and capitalizing on more than five years of solid experience, he is responsible for project management based on emerging technologies. Always alert to new opportunities, Mr. Matabudul's goal for the future is to eventually attain the position of director of BTI Consulting. Established in 1998, BTI Consulting provides information technology and management consulting services. To serve the diverse needs of its clientele, the Company employs a staff of 20 highly qualified personnel to provide services such as Web site development and e-mail to the general public of Mauritius. **Career Highlights:** Information Technology and Management Consulting Manager, BTI Consulting (1999-Present); Senior Consultant, DCDM Consulting (1996-98); General Manager, Proliquest (Mauritius) (1995-96). **Associations & Accomplishments:** Executive Member, Mauritius Computer Society. **Education:** Imperial College at London, Bachelor's degree in English, with First Class Honors (1995). **Personal Information:** Married to Smita in 1999. Mr. Matabudul enjoys technical reading.

Nithyanandam "Mathi" Mathiyazhagan

Senior Consultant
IMR Global Corporation
100 South Missouri Avenue
Clearwater, FL 33756
(727) 467-8000
mathi@aol.com

7379

Business Information: Recruited to IMR Global in 1995, Mr. Mathiyazhagan currently serves as Senior Consultant. He assumes responsibility for providing support to the Company's sales staff, ensuring value selling to the client. An information systems professional with 17 years in the field, Mr. Mathiyazhagan is experienced in all aspects of analysis, design, development, implementation, and project management. During the course of his duties as Senior Consultant, he directly supervises seven regional and country managers. Coordinating resources, time lines, schedules, assignments, and budgets; working closely with users and systems management to analyze, specify, and design new solutions; and taking a lead role in driving products and services to a global market also fall within the realm of his responsibilities. Mr. Mathiyazhagan attributes the success he has achieved throughout his professional career to teamwork, a concerted effort of many individuals. Continually striving for maximum effectiveness, he looks forward to entering into business development. A publicly traded company, IMR Global Corporation offers consulting and software services to an international clientele. Approximately 3,000 skilled professionals strive to provide the most advanced technological solutions from strategically placed locations around the globe. Boasting $200 million in annual revenue, the Corporation was founded in 1988. **Career Highlights:** Senior Consultant, IMR Global Corporation (1995-Present); Consultant, Syntel Inc. (1993-95); Manager of Software, Verifone Inc. (1990-93); Senior Executive Software, Sudaram-Clayton Ltd. (1986-90). **Associations & Accomplishments:** Institute of Electrical & Electronics Engineers; Computer Society. **Education:** Capella University, M.S. (1998); Bharathidasan University, M.S. (1985); Madras University, B.S. (1982). **Personal Information:** Married to Anitha in 1989. Two children: Vidhya and Venkat. Mr. Mathiyazhagan enjoys photography.

Bill D. Matthews

Senior Manager
Union Pacific Technologies
1416 Dodge Street, Room 419
Omaha, NE 68179
(402) 271-6406
Fax: (402) 233-2996
bill_matthews@notes.up.com

7379

Business Information: As Senior Manager of Union Pacific Technologies, Mr. Matthews manages teams that support e-mail for all Union Pacific Corporation companies and teams supporting the Desktop Productivity suite for Union Pacific Railroad. Overseeing a total of 12 employees in his department, Mr. Matthews exemplifies the leadership abilities necessary to orchestrate the day-to-day administration and operational activities of his department. With 19 years of experience, he has acquired the skill, knowledge, and determination to assist Union Pacfic in its growth, development, and expansion. He is in charge of monitoring the time on servers, reacting to failures, and providing client account support. Mr. Matthews has made many great changes while in his position including consolidating the e-mail environment from 130 to 12 devices and also moved the environment from Omaha to St. Loius in two hours. He would like to become more involved in data security in the future. Mr. Matthews believes that the key to his success is the staff he presently works with. Union Pacific Technologies, an information technology development company, primarily supports railroad companies as well as commercial interests. Established in 1987, the Company is a subsidiary of Union Pacific which currently has a staff of 53,000 people. **Career Highlights:** Senior Manager, Union Pacific Technologies (1987-Present); Senior Systems Programmer, Union Pacific Railroad (1980-87). **Associations & Accomplishments:** Sigma Phi Epsilon Fraternity. **Education:** Southern Illinois University at Edwardsville, B.S. 1981. **Personal Information:**

Married to Rhonda in 1977. Two children: Brook and Brent. Mr. Matthews enjoys hunting.

David B. McCarson

Network Consulting Engineer
International Network Services
2000 Aerial Center Parkway
Morrisville, NC 27560
(919) 319-0400
Fax: (919) 467-3650
mccarsond@computer.org

7379

Business Information: After completion of a computer science degree while fulfulling an obligation to the United States Army, Mr. McCarson was sought out and recruited to International Network Services in 1998. Recently promoted to the position of Network Consulting Engineer, he handles the evaluation of need for clients who request a network consultation. Demonstrating his extensive knowledge of various aspects of information technology, Mr. McCarson maintains and repairs equipment, performs troubleshooting, and offers technical support to those in need of his services. Crediting peer support as a factor in his success, Mr. McCarson looks forward to assisting in the completion of future corporate goals. International Network Services is a global company that specialies in network consulting. Established in 1992, the Company is located in Morrisville, North Carolina. With the depth of resources to meet any need, the Company supports clients in an unsurpassed version of customer service based on the merit of 2,100 empoyees. **Career Highlights:** International Network Services: Network Consulting Engineer (1999-Present), Network Systems Engineer (1998-99); Senior Network Analysis, United States Army (1995-98). **Associations & Accomplishments:** Institute of Electronics and Electrical Engineers. **Education:** United State Military Academy at West Point, B.S. (1993). **Personal Information:** Married to Kristie in 1994. Two children: Brian and Taylor. Mr. McCarson enjoys auto racing.

Philip F. McCracken, III

Systems Analyst/Consultant
Actionet, Inc.
3214 Hewitt Avenue, Apartment 93
Silver Spring, MD 20906-4974
(202) 366-0354
burmajapan@aol.com

7379

Business Information: As Systems Analyst and Consultant of Actionet, Inc., Mr. McCracken advises the growing organization on all it's information technology needs. A devout lover of technology, he creates a variety of leading edge programs ranging from administrative to Web based. Exercising his skills in information management, his programs support existing software and hardware applications while controlling NT and SQL servers. Coupling his vast knowledge and skills in computers with his team player mentality, Mr. McCracken reports directly to the Vice President and President of the Corporation while cultivating a positive climate for maintaining mutually beneficial business relationships with clientele. An innovative professional, he plans to continue in his capacity perpetuating a shift in his duties to more Internet-based applications. Actionet, Inc. is a certified Microsoft provider. Serving a national and government clientele, the Corporation engages in software, programming, and hardware consulting for businesses and individuals. Presently, the Corporation is located in Vienna, Virginia. **Career Highlights:** Systems Analyst/Consultant, Actionet, Inc. (1999-Present); Systems Analyst, Dyn Corporation It ET (1997-99); Computer Consulting, Self-Employed (1995-Present). **Associations & Accomplishments:** Free Burma Coalition; Aided in Demonstrations for Free Tibet, Free Taiwan, and Free China Movements; Boholanos of Greater Washington. **Education:** DeVry Institute of Technology, B.S. in Electronics Engineering Technology (1990). **Personal Information:** Married to Emi K. in 1997. Mr. McCracken enjoys international activism and community activism.

Ted M. McElroy

President
Diversified Consulting International
471 McElroy Cove Road
Waynesville, NC 28786-7472
(828) 627-2173
Fax: (828) 627-1958
ted_mc@yahoo.com

7379

Business Information: Mr. McElroy serves as President and Consultant of Diversified Consulting International. He plans and oversees the research, evaluation, development and integration of new cutting-edge technologies. Diversified Consulting International engages in Oracle application consulting. The Company specializes in Oracle developing and programming of financial software applications as well as conducting integration services. As the company's senior systems analyst, Mr. McElroy works closely with clients to analyze, specify, design, and program financial software applications. Believing in quality customer service, he travels extensively to the client's site to perform programming and consulting services. The Company also engages in consulting for Laboratory Information Management Systems (LIMS). Mr. McElroy has over 15 years of experience with the design, programming, and development of Laboratory Information Management Systems. **Career Highlights:** President/Consultant, Diversified Consulting International (1997-Present); Computer Systems Manager, Quanterra Environmental Services (1996-97); Computer Systems Manager, International Technology (1978-96). **Education:** Western Carolina University: M.B.A. (1977), M.S. in Chemistry (1975), B.S. in Chemistry (1972). **Personal Information:** Mr. McElroy enjoys landscaping.

Thomas D. McElroy II

Member of Technical Staff
Unisource Network Services
10 North Dearborn, 2nd floor
Chicago, IL 60602
(312) 516-3800
tdmii@aol.com

7379

Business Information: Serving as Member of Technical Staff of Unisource Network Services, Mr. McElroy oversees voice and data network infrastructures. As the senior consultant, he is responsible for designing, specifying, developing, and constructing leading edge data centers for his clients. Utilizing more than seven years of experience in his field, Mr. McElroy is in charge of all aspects of project management functions, to include coordinating resources, schedules, communications, and budgets. One of his career highlights include building the data center for the Sears Tower in Chicago, Illinois. Mr. McElroy was also with a team that built state-of-the-art data ceters for Cellular One and Southwest. In the future he would like to assume a greater role in system projects for environmental back-ups and disasters. A savvy technical expert, Mr. McElroy's success reflects his leadership ability to think outside the box, tackle challenges, and deliver results. Unisource Network Services provides consulting for voice and data design systems. Established in 1986, the Company is based in Chicago, Illinois. National in scope, the Company currently employs a staff of 130 qualified personnel to serve the diverse needs of its clientele. **Career Highlights:** Member of Technical Staff, Unisource Network Services (1999-Present); Senior Consultant, Sullivan & Cagliano (1999); Senior Communications Consultant, Ernst & Young LLP (1995-99); Data Communications Consultant, Alternative Resource Corporation (1992-95). **Associations & Accomplishments:** Chicago Community Trust; Association of Technology Professionals; Art Institute of Chicago; Association of Impala SS Owners-the Herd of Chicago. **Education:** DePaul University: Master' degree (In Progress), B.S. (1989).

Thomas L. McGibbon

Department Manager
ITT Industries
210 West Pine Street
Rome, NY 13440-3457
(315) 334-4933
Fax: (315) 334-4964
tom.mcgibbon@itt.com

7379

Business Information: Mr. McGibbon serves as Department Manager of ITT Industries. He oversees and directs all day-to-day operations of the data and analysis center for software. Responsible for advanced engineering and sciences and research and development, Mr. McGibbon provides support information for technical radios for the United States Army. A trusted and tested, 27 year technology professional, he conducts special studies and research on classified and unclassified projects for the government. He is also responsible for compiling and synthesizing status reports and providing training to users when requested. His career highlights include serving as Director of DACS Center and receiving various internal awards. Attributing his success to technical awareness of the field, Mr. McGibbon looks foward to attaining his Master's degree and transitioning the Company into e-commerce. Located in Rome, New York, ITT Industries designs and engineers software for satellite communications under government contracts. The Company also provides connectors for personal computers and mobile phones in the telecommunications arena. The target market for the Company is the military and chemical processing plants. Founded in 1989, teh Company currently has a work force of 25 employees and an annual revenue of $5 million. **Career Highlights:** Department Manager, ITT Industries (1993-Present); Project Manager, PAR Technology (1993); Manager of Applications Software, PAR Microsystems (1990-93). **Associations & Accomplishments:** Institute of Electrical and Electronics Engineers; Association of Computing Machinery. **Education:** Southern Methodist University: M.S. (In Progress), B.S. in Math/Computer Science (1973). **Personal Information:** Married to Theresa in 1980. Two children: Jason and Tricia. Mr. McGibbon enjoys singing.

Tom McGuire

Network Consultant
Marc Mintz & Associates LLC
2 Lebeda Drive
Fairfield, NJ 07004
(473) 808-9040

7379

Business Information: As Network Consultant of Marc Mintz & Associates LLC, Mr. McGuire handles a variety of technical responsibilities within the corporate structure. Included in his daily schedule are activities such as network installation and maintenance and client support. Demonstrating adept abilities in the field, Mr. McGuire conducts evaluations of current systems to determine technical needs, then submits purchase requests for necessary equipment and software for upgrades. With exceptional communicative skills, he meets with clients to lend on-site support and consultancy services, explaining complex technical issues and offering training on software. Crediting his success to good mentors and role models, Mr. McGuire intends to continue in his current role as he furthers his education. Obtaining his MCSE and working on the new accounting software called "Time Switch" serves as his future endeavors. Aspiring to a position within a large corporation, his advice is "study hard and learn as much as you can." Marc Mintz & Associates LLC provides network consulting and accounting software to businesses in the Fairfield, New Jersey area. Established in 1984, the Company employs eight trained people to assist in the completion of daily activities. Focusing on networks and hardware, the Company strives to uphold high standards of quality as they work with clients. **Career Highlights:** Network Consultant, Marc Mintz & Associates LLC (1998-Present); Library Paige, Fairfield Public Library (1997-98); Maintenace, Mintz Rosenfield & Company (1996-97). **Education:** William Paterson University (In Progress). **Personal Information:** Mr. McGuire enjoys baseball.

Charles "Chuck" McKaskle

President
Mac Electronics
9770 East Mary Drive
Tucson, AZ 85730
(520) 886-7265
kitsune97@aol.com

7379

Business Information: As President of Mac Electronics, Mr. McKaskle oversees and directs day-to-day operational and administrative functions for the Company. He acts as a Consultant, providing the most up-to-date information to clients and working hard to maintain good client relations. Mr. McKaskle's background history includes 26 years of distinguished service with the United States Army as well as a stint with SOL Telecommunications as Engineering Assistant. In addition to his present duties of President, he serves as an Instructor at Pima Community College. Always alert to new opportunities, techniques, and approaches, Mr. McKaskle strives to make Mac Electronics as successful as possible. His personal and professional success reflects his leadership ability to build teams with synergy and technical strength and aggressively take on new challenges. Mac Electronics is a computer consulting firm offering clients technical advice and servicing for their businesses. Beginning operations in 1979, the Company employs a staff of three skilled professionals. **Career Highlights:** President, Mac Electronics (1987-Present); Instructor, Pima Community College (1980-Present); Engineering Assistant, SOL Telecommunications (1976-82); Sergeant Major, United States Army (1950-76). **Education:** Pima Community College, Associates of Science (1980); University of Maryland, CREI. **Personal Information:** Four children: Caroline Kyoko, Wayne Toshiyuki, Carl Akira, and Barbara Reiko. Mr. McKaskle enjoys photography, family history and keeping current in technology.

Michelle McKay, Ph.D.

Lead Instructional System Designer
C2 Multimedia
4350 Will Rogers Parkway, Suite 100
Oklahoma City, OK 73108-1836
(405) 948-7800
Fax: (405) 948-7887
michellemybelle@prodigy.net

7379

Business Information: As Lead Instructional System Designer of C2 Multimedia, Dr. McKay oversees three associates who assist in the completion of design and development of Web training curricula. A successful, 12 year veteran, she is involved in the development of departmental plans and setting of goals and maintenance of deadlines. Dr. McKay ensures quality control and training strategies are completed per Company guidelines. At the same time, she is currently completing her dissertation in Psychology. Consistently achieving quality performance in her field, Dr. McKay intends to expand her skills in the technical and Web training fields in an effort to attain her own training company. She attributes her career success to hands-on experience and persistence. Founded in 1989, C2 Multimedia is a privately owned company employing the skilled services of 100 individuals to acquire business, meet with clients, facilitate projects, and market services. The Company provides Web based training for the government and private sector. As the ninth fastest growing company in Washington D.C., C2 Multimedia's goal is to apply advanced technology solutions to workforce training. **Career Highlights:** Lead Instructional System Designer, C2 Multimedia (1999-Present); University of Oklahoma: Course Coordinator (1997-99), Software Skills Trainer (1995-97). **Associations & Accomplishments:** American Society for Training and Development; American Educational Research Association; Association for Educational Communications and Technology. **Education:** University of Oklahoma: Ph.D. (1999), M.S. in Experimental Psychology (1993); University of Tulsa, M.A. in Industrial and Organizational Psychology (1993); Oral Roberts University, B.S. in Biology (1987). **Personal Information:** Dr. McKay enjoys scuba diving.

D. Gregory McNeil

President/Chief Executive Officer
e-Business Express
23240 Chagrin Boulevard, Suite 600
Cleveland, OH 44122
(216) 514-6199
Fax: (330) 995-3246
gmcneil@e-businessexpress.com

7379

Business Information: As the founder of e-Business Express, Mr. McNeil serves as its President and Chief Executive Officer. He oversees and directs all day to day administration and operations, such as finances and profit and loss statistics as well as determining the direction and vision. Pushing products and services to the markets, he formulates both new business and marketing plans with a focus on maintaining a competitive edge in the industry. He also approves the budget, procures supplies, supervises all projects, and oversees the hiring of new employees. Mr. McNeil's possesses extensive managerial experience with companies, such as Ernst & Young and Unitech Systems. His innovative leadership style is instrumental to e-Business Express' continued success. In the future, he plans to keep the Company private and triple the bottom line. e-Business Express is an application service provider and e-business enabler. Dedicated to helping small and medium businesses, the Company develops individual e-business plans for its clientele that is perfectly suited to their business needs. The Company also hosts Web sites and helps promote e-businesses. Established in 1999, the Company is located in Cleveland, Ohio. **Career Highlights:** President/Chief Executive Officer, e-Business Express (1999-Present); Associate Director, Ernst & Young (1999); Unitech Systems: Managing Director (1995-98), Business Unit Leader (1993-94). **Education:** Kent State University, B.B.A. (1981). **Personal Information:** Married to Lori in 1999. Three children: Mathew, Amy Marie, and Samuel. Mr. McNeil enjoys travel, skiing and boating.

Craig R. McWilliams

Consultant
Senco-Argonne National Lab
1540 East Dundee Road, Suite 160
Palatine, IL 60067
(630) 252-0973
Fax: (630) 252-4607
craigm@anl.gov

7379

Business Information: Beginning his association with Senco-Argonne National Lab more than six years ago, Mr. McWilliams serves in the positions of a Consultant. Currently as a systems architect, he provides subject matter expertise and designs software systems. Focusing primarily nonproliferation, Mr. McWilliams is responsible for on weapons nonproliferation issues. Before joining the Lab, Mr. McWilliams served in the role of Director of Information Technology at Chicago Data Storage. His background also includes pharmacology and time in investment banking as a Programmer Analyst. Interested in researching and contributing to the evolution of information technology, Mr. McWilliams anticipates eventual ownership of his own information technology business. Senco-Argonne is a consulting and systems distribution company. Specializing in software consulting, Argonne caters to small and midsize businesses. Located in Palatine, Illinois, Senco-Argonne presently employs a staff of more than 40 professional, technical, and support staff. **Career Highlights:** Consultant, Senco-Argonne National Lab (1994-Present); Director of Information Technology, Chicago Data Storage (1993-94); Programmer Analyst, Harris Associates (1992-93). **Education:** Northwestern University, B.A. (1981). **Personal Information:** Married to Cindy in 1995.

Jatin Mehta, Ph.D.

Senior Consultant
MIC, Inc.
195 Bergen Avenue
Kearny, NJ 07032-3340
(800) 378-7890
mehtajatin@hotmail.com

7379

Business Information: Working with MIC, Inc. as a Senior Consultant for more than a year, Dr. Mehta is responsible for providing consulting services to clients. Working closely with management and systems users, he analyzes, specifies, designs, and implements cutting-edge solutions to enhance operating and networking systems operations. Serving mainly Fortune 500 and 1000 customers, Dr. Mehta is capable of working with clients in private industries and the federal government. Highly regarded, he also does a great deal of staff administration, with employees reporting to him. Attributing his success to staying informed, Dr. Mehta notes the highlight of his career as establishing an Internet portal for the health industry. In the future, he plans to continue working in the field of information technology, becoming a pioneer in the industry. Established in 1984, MIC, Inc. is a software consulting agency. Providing services in the areas of e-commerce, PeopleSoft, and Oracle software, the Corporation is the fastest growing of its kind in the Northeastern United States. Employing 200 personnel, the Corporation reports estimated annual revenue exceeding $25 million. **Career Highlights:** Senior Consultant, MIC, Inc. (1999-Present); Consultant, Software International (1997-99); Consultant, DJSCOE (1997). **Associations & Accomplishments:** NAFMFP; IPHE; ISTE. **Education:** IIT of Bombay, Ph.D. (1993); TKIET, Bachelor's degree in Engineering (1987). **Personal Information:** Married to Parul in 1994. One child: Sarth. Dr. Mehta enjoys surfing the Internet, basketball and e-business.

Steven D. Meisinger

President
Penguin Consulting Company, Inc.
1861 Brown Boulevard, Suite 743
Arlington, TX 76006-4697
(817) 467-7789
Fax: (817) 784-8030
penguin1@airmail.net

7379

Business Information: Very good at what he does and not needing a middle man as part of his business, Mr. Meisinger ventured out to start up Penguin Consulting Company, Inc. in 1993. As President, he is devoted to the success of the Corporation by concentrating his work within the custom programming arena. A highly savvy, systems expert, he meets and stays with clients from the conception of an idea to delivery of a finished program, ensuring the satisfaction of his clients throughout the entire process. Mr. Meisinger leads in the acquisition of new clients and their design ideas, focusing on the appropriate development of design coding within the programs. Looking to the year 2000 and beyond, Mr. Meisinger hopes to continue enhancing himself while maintaining his technical skills and advancing the systems of his customers. Penguin Consulting Company, Inc. specializes in computer consulting for the Arlington, Dallas, and Fort Worth, Texas areas. Since its establishment in 1993, the Corporation has updated the businesses of clients within the area through the implementation of new technologies and systems support equipment. The Corporation determines the exact needs of the clients and then works with them to develop an appropriate system of computer parts and networking tools to facilitate their needs. **Career Highlights:** President, Penguin Consulting Company, Inc. (1993-Present). **Associations & Accomplishments:** Independent Computer Consultants Association; Metro Midrange Systems Association; North Texas Personal Computer Users Group. **Personal Information:** Married to Kathleen J. in 1995. Two children: Eric and Mitchell. Mr. Meisinger enjoys computers and golf.

Martin Melconian

President/Founder
Globebyte
12/50 Kingsgate Road, Surrey
Kingston upon Thames, England, United Kingdom KT2 5AA
+44 1815413426
Fax: +44 1815467248
martin_melconian@globebyte.co.uk

7379

Business Information: Serving as President and Founder of Globebyte, Mr. Melconian superivses daily operations and functions within the Company. Fulfilling a variety of roles within the Company, he handles administrative tasks and serves a human resources capacity in the recruitment and training of staff. Demonstrating his impressive skills in the technical field, he develops and implements strategic business plans that incorporate market research, modern advances, and employee input. Mr. Melconian meets with clients to negotiate contracts for services and discuss business development. Striving for expansion, he is currently working to acheive public holding status for the Company. Globebyte is a world class provider of innovative Internet and Intranet services to international clients in 35 countries. Operating with a staff of 20 technically adept employees, the Company provides customers with a competitive edge in our modern society. **Career Highlights:** Founder/President, Globebyte (1993-Present); Associate Consultant, Microsoft Corporation (1992-93); Principal Developer, Pilot, Inc. (1991-92); Principle Developer, Thorn EMI Plc (1990-91). **Education:** London, Bachelor's degree in Engineering (with honors) (1989). **Personal Information:** Married to Gaye in 1995. Two children: Lia and Martin, Jr. Mr. Melconian enjoys assisting local IT start-ups, cryptography and data comprehension research.

Jalane M. Meloun

Chief Executive Officer
Meloun Consulting
2412 Cooledge Avenue
Akron, OH 44305
(330) 630-8210
Fax: (330) 630-8215
jmeloun@uakron.edu

7379

Business Information: An indendent contractor for hire as a computer instructor, Mrs. Meloun serves as Chief Executive Officer of Meloun Consulting. The founder and owner, she oversees and directs all day to day administration and operations. She determines the overall strategic direction and formulates powerful marketing and business plans to maintain the competitive edge in the market place. Highly regarded, Mrs. Meloun works closely with management and users to analyze, specify, and design new solutions to enhance program operations. In this capacity, she provides indepth training in technology and Microsoft office applications. Possessing an excellent understanding of technology, she also works at both JPC Computer Learning Center and the University of Akron as an Instructor. An accomplished professional, she has written course materials and serveral technical manuals. Mrs. Meloun's future aspirations include expanding her Company and gaining respect in the work place. A reputable technology company, Meloun Consulting provides state of the art information technology and industry consulting services. Founded in 1997, the Firm is regional in scope and is currently headquartered in Akron, Ohio. **Career Highlights:** Chief Executive Officer, Meloun Consulting (1997-Present); Instructor, JPC Computer Learning Center (1996-Present); Instructor, University of Akron (1996-Present). **Associations & Accomplishments:** Society of Industrial and Organizational Psychologists; Society for Human Resource Management; Volunteer, Akron Blind Center Technology Board. **Education:** University of Akron: Ph.D. in Industrial Organizational Psychology (In Progress), M.A. in Industrial Organizational Psychology (1998); Baldwin Wallace College, B.A. in Business Administration (1994); Microsoft Office User Specialist Expert Level Certification in Word, Excel, Access, and PowerPoint. **Personal Information:** Mrs. Meloun enjoys reading and dancing.

Greg Merkt

Senior Technical Services Consultant
PegaSystems Inc.
101 Main Street
Cambridge, MA 02142
(617) 374-9600
Fax: (617) 374-9620
merkg@pegasystems.com

7379

Business Information: As Senior Technical Services Consultant of PegaSystems Inc., Mr. Merkt is responsible for all aspects of technical project management. In this context, he oversees and directs systems installation and API development and performance tuning of operating systems, databases, and software. With an excellent understanding of his field, he also performs systems integration. Currently, Mr. Merkt is supervising two teams of 18 and 25 people on Blue Cross Blue Shield and Freed Credit Card projects. He is also working on obtaining his Sun and Oracle certifications. In the future, he plans on attaining his M.B.A. and eventually moving up into a Chief Operating Officer's position. Success, according to Mr. Merkt, is due to his persistence and honesty. PegaSystems Inc. is a systems software developer that contracts business for various clientele on a national level. The Corporation developes customized software and hardware for corporations and small business alike. Establishing itself as an information technology leader since its founding, PegaSystems Inc. has earned a reputation for superior customer service. Continuing to offer quality services, the Corporation is planning to expand to meet consumer demands and technological advances. **Career Highlights:** Senior Technical Services Consultant, PegaSystems Inc. (1998-Present); Operations Analyst, Continental Express Airlines (1995-98); Assistant Project Manager, Smit Americas- Offshore Salvage (1991-94) **Education:** Texas A&M University, degree in Management Information Systems (1996). **Personal Information:** Mr. Merkt enjoys moutain biking, golf, boating and fishing.

Dirk Meyer

Owner/General Manager
Dinoex
Im Grund 4, Habichtswald
Hessen, Germany 34317
+49 560655021
Fax: +49 560655023
dirk.meyer@dinoex.net

7379

Business Information: Serving as Owner and General Manager of Dinoex, Mr. Meyer is responsible for the provision of technical knowledge and diagnostics for customers, and management for various organizations. Possessing an excellent understanding of technology, he personally sets up e-mail servers and protocols. Mr. Meyer is very gifted in his computer knowledge and he dedicates his efforts to creating and enhancing user-friendly programs. His hope is that every client can incorporate these programs into their business operations. Mr. Meyer was inspired to start Dinoex because of the opportunity and a strong desire to be challenged. A solid telecommunications provider, his strategic plans include expanding the company's Internet presence and continuing to develop advanced communication protocols. Mr. Meyer is proud of his involvement with the complete restructure of an ISP program, providing his client an outcome three times greater than what was expected. Dinoex, established in 1993, provides communications and network services to both small and large businesses. The Company specializes in the design of LAN and WAN networks including application protocols. International in scope, the Company is recognized throughout the United States as a first class telecommunications provider. **Career Highlights:** Owner/General Manager, Dinoex (1993-Present); PMA: Information Technology Manager (1999), Developer (1995-99); Developer, Philips IA (1991-95). **Associations & Accomplishments:** German Unix User Group; Nederlanse Kubus Club; SETI@home; Linux User Group. **Education:** F.H. Darmstadt, B.S. in Computer Science (1990). **Personal Information:** Mr. Meyer enjoys playing with Rubik cubes, reading science fiction and watching whales.

Gregory S. Miles, Ph.D.

Program Manager
AverStar
6305 Ivy Lane, Suite 701
Greenbelt, MD 20770
(717) 267-9993

7379

Business Information: Following six years of service to the United States Air Force, Dr. Miles serves as a Program Manager at AverStar. Utilizing his knowledge of information systems, he provides technical information security support in an effort to ensure information systems and networks are secure, reliable, and available. Interfacing with customers and employees to analyze and specify workable solutions is one of Dr. Miles' primary responsibilites. Dr. Miles intends to gain additional hands-on experience that will enable him to capitalize on the vast opportunities offered by AverStar and the information technology field. His technical talents, being a team player, and his ability to take on challenges and deliver results are the reasons for his success. Established in 1996, AverStar's Information Security Group is engaged in information security and assurance for goverment and commerical customers. With the main office in Burlington, Massachusetts, the Company provides some the top information technology services to meet the demands of a growing clientele. The Greenbelt, Maryland office employs approximately 60 professional, technical, and support staff. **Career Highlights:** Program Manager, AverStar (1996-Present); Communication-Computer Systems Officer, United States Air Force (1990-96); Systems Engineer, Consolidated Aluminum (1987-89). **Education:** Kennedy-Western University, Ph.D. in Engineering Management (1999); Central Michigan University, M.S. in Administration (1993); University of Cincinnati, B.S. in Electrical Engineering (1990). **Personal Information:** Married to Brenda in 1989. Two children. Dr. Miles enjoys music, golf, reading, surfing the Internet for information on IT and physical fitness.

Stephen W. Miller

Solution Architect/Principal Consultant
Stonebridge Technologies
19617 Harness Court
Edmond, OK 73003
(405) 340-4357
Fax: (405) 340-3086
steve.miller@sbti.com

7379

Business Information: Mr. Miller functions in the dual capacity of Solution Architect and Principal Consultant with Stonebridge Technologies. He oversees the brainstorming behind the e-commerce and data warehousing solutions and serves as the Oklahoma area Consulting Manager. A savvy, 17 year expert, he plans, manages, and implements large scale solutions for client trouble spots. He coordinates several proposals to clients to solve business problems while expressing technical requirements. Responsible for all tasks performed within the department, Mr. Miller encourages the success of his staff. In the future, he hopes to enhance his role within the Company to become a multiple Project Manager. His success reflects his ability to deliver results and aggressively take on new challenges. Stonebridge Technologies is a leading provider of e-business solutions, computer network integration, and consulting services. Established in 1981, the Company specializes in database management, providing its clients with secure methods to save their files and create a back up system for the data. The Company turns over $150 million annually. **Career Highlights:** Solution Architect/Principal Consultant, Stonebridge Technologies (1997-Present); Technical Director, MicroAge/the Computer Professionals (1991-97); Computer Aided Engineering Systems Manager, The Benham Group (1984-91). **Associations & Accomplishments:** American Society of Manufacturing Engineers; Oracle Users Group. **Education:** Oklahoma State University, A.S. (1982). **Personal Information:** Married to Lori in 1980. Three children: Hallie Brooke, Stephen Easton, and Addison Paige. Mr. Miller enjoys scuba diving, digital graphic arts, research and reading.

Creflo R. Mims

President/Chief Executive Officer
Medical Knowledge Systems Inc.
4829 Woodward Avenue, Suite 200
Detroit, MI 48201-1330
(313) 832-1500
Fax: (313) 832-3423
mimsc@mksi.com

7379

Business Information: The President of Medical Knowledge Systems, Mr. Mims also serves as its Chief Executive Officer. He performs strategic planning in an effort to increase the Corporation's market share within the industry. In addition, he prepares business development presentations and supervises the efforts of a staff of 13 personnel members. A long time entreprenuer, Mr. Mims started this Company when he discovered an opportunity to make a difference in the medical industry. He has been published in the Crane business journal. Consistently achieving quality performance, he looks forward to venturing into software development for other areas of the medical field. Mr. Mims' success reflects his ability to think outside the box, deliver results, and take on new challenges. Serving a large regional clientele within the United States, Medical Knowledge Systems Inc. is an information technology service provider. The Corporation develops various types of medical software with a specialty in software design used in the radiation encology field. Medical Knowledge Systems was founded in 1986. A staff of 15 skilled professionals is dedicated to developing quality software programs. **Career Highlights:** President/Chief Executive Officer, Medical Knowledge Systems Inc. (1998-Present); Director Corporate Computer Services, Detroit Medical Center (1992-98); Manager Technical Development, EDS (1989-92). **Associations & Accomplishments:** Detroit Chamber of Commerce; Booker T. Washington Business Association; National Black MBA Association; 100 Blackmen of Gafater Detroit; Trustee, Hartford Memorial Baptist Church. **Education:** Wayne State University, M.B.A. (1972). **Personal Information:** Married to Voncile in 1983. Four children: Creflo III, Christina, Marcus, and Cesare. Mr. Mims enjoys golf.

Leo Mitchell Jr., P.E.

Vice President/Program Manager
DJG & Associates
11242 Brougham Drive
Sterling Heights, MI 48312
(248) 680-5570
Fax: (248) 680-5440
(248) 421-7358
lmitchellj@aol.com

7379

Business Information: Displaying his expertise in this highly specialized position, Mr. Mitchell currently is providing outsourcing technology services to the General Motors Metal Fabricating Division. Filling the dual role of Vice President and Program Manager, his primary responsibility was the implementation of the Y2K metal fabrications program to ensure that the Division would be effectively running during the transition to the new millennium. In his previous duties with Motorola, Mr. Mitchell received the Executive Award in 1988 for his role in the grand opening of its only state-of-the-art testing facility. He was elected the Key Architect and was the Chief Engineer on electrical instrumentation. Crediting his success to hard work, a positive attitude, and strategic planning, Mr. Mitchell is dedicated to the success of the General Motors Metal Fabricating Division and plans to gain Web access and get involved on the Internet. Serving the regional area around Troy, Michigan, DJG & Associates provides electronic engineering and computer information systems consulting outsourcing services. The Company was founded in 1994 and employs 25 knowledgeable professionals to provide the proffered services. **Career Highlights:** Vice President/Program Manager, General Motors Metal Fabricating Division (1998-Present); Information Technology Supervisor, United Technologies Auto (1992-97); Senior Automotive Engineer/Supervisor, Motorola Inc. (1985-92). **Associations & Accomplishments:** Engineering Society of Detroit; Airplane Owners and Pilots Association. **Education:** Syracuse University, B.S. in Business Administration (1994); Lawrence Technological University, B.S. in Electrical Engineering (1994). **Personal Information:** Two children: Kimberly and Leo. Mr. Mitchell enjoys flying and golf.

Michael J. Monaghan

Co-Founder/Internet Consultant
Cyberjava
7080 Hollywood Boulevard
Hollywood, CA 90028
(310) 466-6327
mj@mj.org

7379

Business Information: Mr. Monaghan is the Co-Founder of Cyberjava and Internet Consultant. He is also currently the Vice President of New Product Development for Matchcraft Inc. Performing detailed system analyses, he consults with clients to determine the type of Internet service that will allow them to experience the most benefits, increased productivity, and sales. He designs customized Extranets, Intranets, and e-commerce solutions for each individual client. Additionally, he also designs customer support sites. Mr. Monaghan is dedicated to the further development of his Company and looks forward to the day when the Company will attain public trading status. His success reflects his ability to think outside the box, produce results, and aggressively tackle new challenges. Since its inception in 1995, Cyberjava has been providing local companies and corporations in the Los Angeles area with internet access and services. Over 500 knowledgeable information technology professionals are employed in the development of applications tailored to the computer original equipment manufacturing industry. Cyberjava is the first premier Internet Coffee House in Los Angeles, California. **Career Highlights:** Co-Founder/Internet Consultant, Cyberjava (1995-Present); Founder, DragonFly Corporation (1994-Present); Vice President of New Product Development, Matchcraft Inc. (Present); Project Manager, Clecim-France (1990-94). **Associations & Accomplishments:** MENSA; Co-Founder, La First Internet Coffee House; Tech Team Developing Neccommercial Website. **Education:** American Graduate School of International Management, M.B.A. (1995); Case Western Reserve University, B.S. in Electrical Engineering and Applied Physics (1988). **Personal Information:** Mr. Monaghan enjoys flying helicopters.

Diana Moncoqut, Ph.D.

Member of Consulting Staff
Cadence Design Systems
482 Ridgewood Avenue
Glen Ridge, NJ 07028
(908) 898-2441
Fax: (908) 898-1435
moncoqut@cadence.com

7379

Business Information: Dr. Moncoqut serves as a Member of the Consulting Staff with Cadence Design Systems. She specializes her talents within the physical verification group where she analyzes reports and strives to guarantee current programs are operating effectively. Working with analog and RF circuit simulators, she educates her staff on new technologies and interprets problems to ensure future advancement of the Company. Before joining Cadence Design Systems, Dr. Moncoqut served as a member of the technical staff with both Lucent Technologies and Motorola. Her success reflects her ability to think out-of-the-box, tackle new challenges and responsibilities, and deliver results. Founded in 1988, the Company offers sophisticated software for electronic design combined with comprehensive, skilled methodology and design service expertise. Cadence's electronic design automation (EDA) software and services give customers a distinct competitive edge by improving time-to-market, quality, and productivity. The Company's technology is sold and supported throughout the world. **Career Highlights:** Member of Consulting Staff, Cadence Design Systems (1998-Present); Member of Technical Staff, Lucent Technologies (1998); Member of Technical Staff, Motorola (1997-98). **Associations & Accomplishments:** Association of Computing Machinery; Institute of Electrical and Electronics Engineers. **Education:** University of Toulouse: Ph.D. (1997), Master's degree in Electrical Engineering, B.S. **Personal Information:** Married to Jean-Michel in 1994. One child: Ines. Dr. Moncoqut enjoys ., hiking, sports, travel, swimming, and skiing.

Jeffery G. Morse

Senior Systems Engineer

AB Floyd, Inc.

1900 Beauregard Street
Alexandria, VA 22311
(703) 998-1882
morsej@erols.com

7379

Business Information: As the Senior Systems Engineer of AB Floyd Inc., Mr. Morse is responsible for computer systems analysis and programming. In this capacity, he designs and develops systems level software for Windows NT and UNIX platforms as well as Oracle database management and defense information systems. He is an expert in UMX and Informix/C. Possessing an excellent understanding of his field, Mr. Morse is also responsible for the analysis, acquisition, installation, modification, configuration, support, and tracking of operating systems, databases, utilities, software, and hardware. He enjoys his work and plans to further progress his knowledge of the industry by learning new programs and dealing more with Web based technology. Mr. Morse attributes his success to being goal oriented and having the ability to meet any challenges that might come his way. AB Floyd Inc. operates as a federal government contractor. Located in Alexandria, Virginia the Corporation employs 65 professional, technical, and support staff. **Career Highlights:** Senior Systems Engineer, AB Floyd Inc. (1999-Present); Consultant, Informix Software (1998-99); Senior Systems Analyst, Blue Cross Blue Shield NCA (1991-94). **Associations & Accomplishments:** Washington Area Informix User Group. **Education:** Delta Computer Engineering (1999); Computer Learning Center (1983-84); Montgomery College (1980); Virginia Tech (1977-79); Northern Virginia Community College (1980). **Personal Information:** Two children: Angel and Alexander. Mr. Morse enjoys sports and quality time with his sons.

Tarek M. Mourad

Engineering Manager

Telegyr Systems, Inc.

1730 Technology Drive
San Jose, CA 95110
(408) 452-5392
Fax: (408) 452-5260
tmmd@sj.znet.com

7379

Business Information: Mr. Mourad functions in the capacity of Engineering Manager for Telegyr Systems, Inc. He oversees and controls the day-to-day operational activities of the software integration team. A savvy, nine year veteran, he manages all aspects of project development, including coordinating resources, time lines, schedules, assignments, and budgets. An expert problem solver who is involved in testing pre-developed software, Mr. Mourad is able to quickly locate difficulties and resolve them in an effecient and successful manner. In the future, Mr. Mourad plans to contribute to the stream living project, bringing more technology into the software testing industry and determining new methods to fully utilize the technology. His success reflects his ability to think outside the box, deliver results, and take on new challenges. Telegyr Systems, Inc. is a value added reseller to electrical utilities and manufactures software solutions for controlling electrical grids and generation. Established in 1860, the Corporation recently converted from its previous role to incorporate the world of information technology and began assisting clients in creating software products to aid the manufacturing world. **Career Highlights:** Telegyr Systems, Inc.: Engineering Manager (1998-Present), Staff Engineer (1996-98); Senior System Analyst, Landis & Gyr (1990-96). **Associations & Accomplishments:** Board Member, Granada Islamic School. **Education:** Santa Clara University, Continuing Education (1997); Cornell University, B.S. in Civil Engineering (1975). **Personal Information:** Married to Nihad in 1982. Three children: Abdullah, Asmaa, and Mennatullah.

Kalyan Mukhopadhyay

Senior Systems Engineer

Cylogix

1305 Rivendell Way
Edison, NJ 08817
(609) 750-5250
kalyan.mukhopadhyay.msdw.com

7379

Business Information: Serving as the Senior Systems Engineer for Cylogix, Mr. Mukhopadhyay is responsible for implementing his knowledge and expertise into all aspects of software design and development. He works closely with management and systems users to analyz, specify, and design solutions to enhance operating and network architectures. Throughout daily duties, Mr. Mukhopadhyay manages all projects from start to finish, while also monitoring the actions of supporting staff for maximum quality control. Utilizing more than 23 years of extensive experience in the information technology field, Mr. Mukhopadhyay is currently devising plans to start up his consulting firm. His success reflects his ability to think outside the box, take on challenges, and deliver results on behalf of the Company and its clientele. An information technology firm, Cylogix offers information technology and applications consulting. The Company provides professional advisory in such areas as systems development and maintenance, staff training, and strategic planning. Established in 1996, the Company employs a work force of more than 200 professional, technical, and support staff who facilitate smooth day to day business operations. Presently, the Company reports annual revenue in excess of $20 million. **Career Highlights:** Senior Systems Analyst, Cylogix (1999-Present); Senior Systems Engineer, Electronic Data Systems (1998-99); Member of Technical Staff, Network Programs (1996-97); Systems Engineer, Nicco Corporation (1995-96). **Associations & Accomplishments:** Institute of Electrical and Electronics Engineers Computer Society; Association of Computing Machinery. **Education:** NITIE, M.S. (1987); Indian Institute of Technology, B.S. (1985). **Personal Information:** Married to Ranjawa in 1989. Two children: Abhigyan and Kaustan. Mr. Mukhopadhyay enjoys sports and reading.

Ramarao Mullapudi

President

Premier Consultancy

8024 Grand Canyon Drive
Plano, TX 75025
(972) 335-6539
Fax: (972) 335-6626
ramarad@pcs-us.com

7379

Business Information: Mr. Mullapudi functions in the capacity of President for Premier Consultancy. He strives to keep himself updated every day on the advancements within the information technology industry. An experienced consultant, he deals with the Company's corporate contracts and, after careful evaluation of their needs and concerns, coordinates a cost-effective plan to boost the client into the 21st Century. He plays a key role during contract negotiations and utilizes his charismatic character to alleviate the stress of the dealings. In the future, Mr. Mullapudi plans to open up the market, transfer into high quality technologies, and expand operations. Attributing his success to good contacts and networking, his quote is "hard work takes a lot of time." Premier Consultancy is a software consulting firm. Established in 1998, the Company has created a reputable name for its products and superior customer service. The Company primarily markets itself to the small to medium sized businesses in the surrounding areas of Plano, Texas. The Company assists its clients in the implementation of new programs and networking accessories. **Career Highlights:** President, Premier Consultancy (1998-Present); Consultant, DBS Systems (1993-98). **Associations & Accomplishments:** Independent Computer Consultant Association. **Education:** Andhra University: M.C.A. (1990), B.S. in Statistics. **Personal Information:** Married to Kalyani in 1991. Two children: Harika and Jitesh. Mr. Mullapudi enjoys politics and business.

Peter T. Mulé

Senior Account Executive

RCG Information Technology

55 Broad Street
New York, NY 10004-2501
(212) 547-2062
Fax: (212) 547-2027
pmule@rcgit

7379

Business Information: As the Senior Account Executive for RCG Information Technology, Mr. Mulé assumes a number of duties on behalf of the Company and its clientele. Possessing over 17 years of hands on experience, he maintains relations with existing client base and helps customers with information technology solutions. A savvy professional, Mr. Mulé's responsibilities also include generating new business and identifying and penetrating new avenues for additional revenues. His extensive experience is vital to the Company's enduring success. In the future, Mr. Mulé plans to continue in this field and looks forward to assisting the Company in the completion of Company goals and objectives. RCG Information Technology engages in information technology solutions and staff augmentation. Through expert research and analysis, the Company devises answers to solve business difficulties. Established in 1974, the Company employs the skilled services of 1,500 individuals to acquire business, meet with clients, facilitate projects, and market services. Located in New York, New York, the Company generates annual revenue of $250 million. **Career Highlights:** Senior Account Executive, RCG Information Technology (1995-Present); Owner/President, APG Associates (1990-95); Senior Marketer, Warren Enterprises (1984-90). **Education:** State University of New York at Farmingdale, B.S. (1983). **Personal Information:** Two children: Andrew and Elyza. Mr. Mulé enjoys water gardening, guitar and golf.

Brian E. Murphy

President

Cyberdeck Consultants

96 Linshaw Avenue
Pittsburgh, PA 15205
(412) 919-0848
Fax: (412) 291-1054
bmurphy@cyberdecks.com

7379

Business Information: Mr. Murphy has enjoyed substantial success while serving as President of Cyberdeck Consultants. Finding his work greatly rewarding, he is responsible for all aspects of day-to-day administration and operations include financial and profit and loss statements. In addition, he manages the fiscal budget and formulation of business and marketing strategies. Utilizing his vast experience and technical expertise, Mr. Murphy is involved in custom programming, that includes analysis, design, evaluation, testing, and implementation processes. Also, fulfilling the responsibilities of programmer and consultant, his focus is on the discovery, investigation, and initial deployment of advanced technologies to help his clients remain flexible, efficient, and profitable. Looking to the near future, Mr. Murphy's goals are to facilitate continued Company growth and geographic expansion, hoping to eventually have locations across the United States. Cyberdeck Consultants is a regional computer consulting and custom programming company headquartered in Pittsburgh, Pennsylvania, serving western Pennsylvania, Ohio, and West Virginia. Established in 1998, the Company targets small businesses. Cyberdeck specializes in building customized computers and software, developing customer training programs, and providing training for implementing software. The Company is also involved in the Internet. **Career Highlights:** President, Cyberdeck Consultants (1998-Present); Support Technician, ADAMMS Consulting Group (1990-99); Sales Representative, Sears, Roebuck & Company (1987-90). **Education:** Riverhead Training Inc. (1997-98); School of Computer Technology, Certificate in Applied Business Programming (1986). **Personal Information:** Mr. Murphy enjoys baseball and trains.

Jack Murphy

President

CyberPatriot.com

P.O. Box 8499
Myrtle Beach, SC 29578
(843) 222-4652
Fax: (801) 838-3262
jackmurphy@cyberpatriot.com

7379

Business Information: The Founder of CyberPatriot.com, Mr. Murphy serves as President. Utilizing more than 18 years of experience in the radio and television industry, he administrates the day-to-day maintenance of the Internet projects and is the writer, producer, and host of various other broadcast projects. Mr. Murphy has won Addy Awards for outstanding advertising copy and production. Dedicated to the success of this entrepreneurial venture, he also plans to expand his professional efforts into the field of Internet radio. Mr. Murphy compliments his duties at CyberPatriot.com with a position as Morning Radio Host at WKZQ. He also hosts the very popular TV show, "River Talk with Jack Murphy" which is seen daily on WFXB-Fox 43. CyberPatriot.com is an online resources provider, featuring a monthly politically oriented newsletter and a weekly Internet radio show. The Company also offers marketing and advertising services to small businesses. The Company utilizes radio and television production services as well as designing and reselling web sites. Established in 1998, broadcast consultancy services are also available. **Career Highlights:** President, CyberPatriot.com (1998-Present); Host, "River Talk with Jack Murphy," WFXB-Fox 43 (1997-Present); Morning Host/Production, WKZQ (1989-Present); Host/Writer/Producer, "Myrtle Beach Daze," a nationally syndicated television show (1994-96); Morning Host/Production, WEQR/WGBR (1987-89); Announcer/Production, WZZU (1985-86). **Associations & Accomplishments:** Sertoma; Board of Directors, Bethany Christian Services; Leadership Grand Strand; Coastal Carolina University Lifelong Learning Society. **Education:** Central Carolina Community College (1984). **Personal Information:** Married to Barbara Ann Krumm in 1997.

James M. Murray

Systems Administrator
CPU, Inc.
4200 South I-10 Service Road West, Suite 205
Metairie, LA 70001
(504) 889-2784
Fax: (504) 889-2799
jmm@cpu.com
7379

Business Information: Serving as Systems Administrator for CPU, Inc. since 1995, Mr. Murray designs, plans, and implements hardware and software for CPU and the Corporation's clientele. He provides user training for new hardware and software for clients and information system support staff. Installing operating systems software, compilers, and utilities; tuning software tools to enhance infrastructure performance; resolving systems difficulties; and coordinating resources and schedules also fall within the purview of his responsibilities. An expert in UNIX and NT integration and networking, Mr. Murray remains at the cutting edge of technology by reading industry publications, taking classes, and talking with other experts in the industry. He is currently Microsoft certified and is studying to become a Microsoft Engineer. His career success reflects his ability to think out-of-the-box and aggressively take on new challenges and responsibilities. Eventually, Mr. Murray anticipates becoming Chief Information Officer and being involved in project management on a larger scale. Created in 1985, CPU, Inc. is a system integration and consulting corporation. Businesses contract CPU, Inc. to evaluate their computer networks and design and implement a system that would best benefit their needs. Fifty knowledgeable and qualified professionals currently assist the Corporation in this endeavor. **Career Highlights:** CPU, Inc.: Systems Analyst (1999-Present), Programmer II (1997-99), Programmer I (1995-97). **Associations & Accomplishments:** USENIX/SAGE; Association for Computing Machinery. **Education:** Louisiana Tech University, B.S. in Computer Science (1995). **Personal Information:** Mr. Murray enjoys mountain biking and guitar.

John E. Myers

Consultant
Myers Consulting Inc.
1026 6th Street, Apartment B
Boonville, MO 65233
(660) 882-7163
Fax: (573) 445-9181
jmyers@sis-solutions.com
7379

Business Information: Mr. Myers serves as a Consultant of Myers Consulting Inc. He is responsible for providing technical and analytical assistance and advice in designing solutions to harness more of the computer's power. Mr. Myers has previously served as Management Information Systems Director with Alliance Water Resources, Inc., Technical Support Manager for Datastorm Technologies, Inc., and Programmer Analyst at Silvey Companies, Inc. As a solid, 12 year network and systems professional, Mr. Myers owns an established track record of producing results. In this context, he is responsible for technical support, network troubleshooting, on site training, and technical writing for the School Information System, a software system designed for the state Missouri. He has received numerous awards for customer satisfaction. Expanding operations, purchasing a building to house his business, and adding personnel to his staff serves as Mr. Myers' future endeavors. A private technology firm, Myers Consulting Inc. provides consulting services for public schools in the state of Missouri. Regional in scope, the Myers Consulting Corporation is located in Boonville, Missouri. Established in 1995, the Corporation presently employs a staff of four professional and technical experts. **Career Highlights:** Consultant, Myers Consulting Inc. (1996-Present); Management Information Systems Director, Alliance Water Resources, Inc. (1995-96); Technical Support Manager, Datastorm Technologies, Inc. (1989-91); Programmer Analyst, Silvey Companies, Inc. (1987-89). **Education:** University of Missouri at St. Louis, Certified Novell Administrator (1998); Central Methodist College at Fayette, B.A. (1987). **Personal Information:** Three children: Grant Daniel, Brooke Ashley, and Kara Renee. Mr. Myers enjoys trout fishing and coin collecting.

Dennis E. Nagel

Software Engineer
Onsale, Inc.
1350 Willow Road
Menlo Park, CA 94025
(650) 470-5223
dnagel@onsale.com
7379

Business Information: Serving as Software Engineer of Onsale, Inc., Mr. Nagel designs, encodes and administers the support of Company-wide forms packages using VB, C++, and Oracle backend databases. Before joining Onsale, Inc., Mr. Nagel served as Software Engineer with Co Development Technologies. In his present capacity, he acts as a consultant, developing and implementing customized programs for corporate clients using the latest in cutting edge technology. As a four year technology professional, he works with users and management to analyze, specify, and design technical solutions to harness more of the computer's power. Keeping abreast of changes and new ideas in the industry, Mr. Nagel attributes his career success to his continuing education. His success reflects his ability to think out-of-the-box and aggressively take on new challenges and responsibilities. Committed to further development of the Corporation, Mr. Nagel continues to grow professionally through the fulfillment of his responsibilities and his involvement in the advancement of operations. Utilizing a custom designed sales automation system, Onsale, Inc. is an e-commerce retailer of computers, printers, and other related equipment and offers online auctions in a straight sale format. Employing a staff of 150 personnel, the Corporation was established in 1995 and boasts annual sales of $400 million. **Career Highlights:** Software Engineer, Onsale, Inc. (1996-Present); Software Engineer, Co Development Technologies, Inc. (1995-96). **Associations & Accomplishments:** Elks Lodge; Honda Riders Association. **Education:** DeAnza College (Currently Attending); Down Business College, Certificate, honor graduate. **Personal Information:** Mr. Nagel enjoys sailing, skiing, camping and swimming.

DeVonna R. Naivar

Senior Programming Development Manager
IBM Server Development Group
1905 Meadow Ridge Drive
Taylor, TX 76574
(512) 838-1316
Fax: (512) 838-7939
navivar@ibm.net
7379

Business Information: Mrs. Naivar has served with IBM Server Development Group in various positions during her term of employment. At present, she fulfills the role of Senior Programming Development Manager. Acting as an area manager, she presides over the systems management and programs Intel personal computers. Coordinating resources and schedules, overseeing time lines and schedules, and ensuring the reliability and security of systems also fall within the scope of her responsibilities. Mrs. Naivar has 17 years of experience and has obtained the bulk of her education out of IBM. Her professional success reflects her ability to think out-of-the-box and aggressively take on new challenges and responsibilities. Committed to further development of the IBM, she coordinates strategic planning to ensure a bright future for a position as a Third Line Director. IBM Server Development Group specializes in AIX Operating System Development. Updating and upgrading AIX systems, the Company performs area systems development, ensuring that systems are of the latest and most advanced technology. **Career Highlights:** IBM Server Development Group: Senior Programming Development Manager (1997-Present), Architecture and Standards Manager (1995-97), Kermel Development and Bring Up Manager (1993-95). **Education:** University of Texas at Austin, B.B.A. (1982). **Personal Information:** Married to David L. in 1969. One child: Craig W. Mrs. Naivar enjoys college football, music, crafts and cooking.

Udaya Sankar Nallabathula, Ph.D.

Vice President
UCA Computer Systems, Inc.
114 Elizabeth Street
Dover, NJ 07801
(973) 887-2758
Fax: (973) 887-2762
7379

Business Information: Displaying his skills in this highly specialized position, Dr. Nallabathula serves as the Vice President of UCA Computer Systems, Inc. He offers computer consulting to clients on an individual basis, working with them to determine their specific needs and offering up-to-date technological solutions. Actively focusing on new employee recruitment, Dr. Nallabathula draws technology professionals from various countries, offering them employment opportunities in the United States. He also personally provides them with the training necessary to get them started in their new position. Continually striving for improved performance, he plans to maneuver the Corporation to take advantage of the business opportunities afforded companies by the Internet. Dr. Nallabathula credits his professional success to determination and the ability to aggressively take on new challenges. UCA Computer Systems, Inc. provides system integration, computer consulting, and e-commerce services to businesses across the state of New Jersey. The Corporation was founded in 1996 and has experienced tremendous growth since its inception. Employing the skilled services of 80 professionals, annual sales are boasted upwards of $20 million. **Career Highlights:** Vice President, UCA Computer Systems, Inc. (1998-Present); Engineer, Atlas Batteries, Inc. (1998); Director, Minerva Information Systems (1996-98); Managing Director, Power Packs, Pvt. Ltd. (1984-92). **Associations & Accomplishments:** Indian Institute of Metals. **Education:** Andhra University, Ph.D. (1997); Osmania University, M.B.A. (1983). **Personal Information:** Married to Gayatri in 1977. Two children: Harish and Suresh. Dr. Nallabathula enjoys reading, travel and computers.

Sheryl F. Namoglu

Executive Vice President
Arris Systems, Inc.
1160 West Swedesford Road, Suite 350
Berwyn, PA 19312
(610) 240-7203
Fax: (610) 407-9855
snamoglu@arrissys.com
7379

Business Information: Serving as the Executive Vice President of Arris Systems, Inc., Mrs. Namoglu is responsible for business development and managing day to day operations. Working in her position since 1995, she supervises a staff of 18 employees and he is accountable for marketing, hiring, firing, budget, strategic plans, customer relations, and organizational and employee issues. Attributing her career success to a strong engineering background, Mrs. Namoglu notes her most rewarding accomplishment as starting the Corporation. She plans on continuing to facilitate corporate growth and expansion locally and internationally. Arris Systems, Inc. is a software and consulting firm. Established in 1994, the Corporation provides products capable of delivering voice and data services over hybrid fiber coax networks. Focused on custom application development and systems integration, Arris Systems also specializes in e-business solutions. Presently, the Corporation's Berwyn, Pennsylvania location employs the skills and expertise of 35 personnel. **Career Highlights:** Executive Vice President, Arris Systems, Inc. (1995-Present). **Education:** Worcester Polytechnic Institute, B.S. (1984). **Personal Information:** Married to Gazanfer. Two children: Esin and Aydin. Mrs. Namoglu enjoys sailing, her kids and horseback riding.

Somnath Nandi

Senior Data Architect
Connectria
23 Hamilton Road
Maple Shade, NJ 08052
(610) 817-3117
Fax: (610) 831-1943
snandi@connectria.com
7379

Business Information: As the Senior Data Architect for Connectria, Mr. Nandi is responsible for number of duties on behalf of the Company and its clientele. He works closely with management and systems users to analyze, specify, design and implement new solutions to enhance overall operations. Possessing superior talents and an excellent understanding of technology, Mr. Nandi manages two data centers for his clients while simultaneously provides valuable insight into the latest storage technologies in network attached storage file systems, protocols, and internal operations. Building scalable storage networks, high availability subsystems, and managing several databases also fall within the realm of his responsibilities. A savvy, 14-year veteran, Mr. Nandi has earned various internal awards. His future plans include starting up his own company, similar in operations to Connectria. Headquartered in St. Louis, Missouri, Connectria is an e-scheduling firm that offers applications and consulting services and Web development packaging. In addition, the Company builds data centers for its clientele. Established in 1996, Connectria employs the skilled services of 71 people at the St. Louis, Missouri, and Philadelphia, Pennsylvania location. **Career Highlights:** Senior Data Architect, Connectria (1999-Present); Senior Database Consultant, Netera (1998-99); Senior Database Analyst, MFS Transtech Inc. (1996-98); Senior Systems Engineer, IBM India Ltd. (1996). **Education:** Foreman Training Institute, Degree in Production and Industrial Engineering (1986); S.J.P. at B'Lore, Diploma in Mechanical Engineering. **Personal Information:** Married to Sanhita in 1994. One child: Rohon. Mr. Nandi enjoys an active role in Indian classical music.

Matthew N. Nathan

Chief Executive Officer
Vison Education Inc.
250 West 57th Street, Suite 2632
New York, NY 10107
(212) 245-0444
Fax: (212) 245-4372
matthew@visioneducation.com

7379

Business Information: Mr. Nathan serves as Chief Executive Officer of Vision Education Inc. since 1998. He coordinates business development, manages the staff, oversees human resources, and implements projects. Possessing an excellent understanding of technology, he determines the overall strategic direction and business contribution of the information systems functions. In addition, he custom creates programs, performs future casting, and coordinates new projects. Mr. Nathan attributes his success to his forethought and having a focus on detail and imaging. His future plans are to expand Vision Education in more schools and deliver the technology on the Internet without losing quality teaching. Vision Education Inc. provides education technology training and consulting. The Corporation addresses schools nationwide to help teachers integrate technology into education. Established in 1998, the Corporation is headquartered in New York and employs 14 skilled consultants and administrative personnel. **Career Highlights:** Chief Executive Officer, Vison Education Inc. (1998-Present); Technology Systems Manager, Little Red School House, Institute for Learning Technologies (1997-98); Curriculum Designer, Teachers College (1997-98); Staff Developer, Teaching Matters (1997-98). **Education:** Bandoin College, B.A. (1997).

Raymond H. Naugle

Consultant
Xceed
5801 South Rita Lane
Tempe, AZ 85283-3021
(480) 383-5421
rww140@email.com

7379

Business Information: Mr. Naugle serves as a Consultant of Xceed. Behind the start-up of the Company, he specializes on design, development, and implementation of state-of-the-art semiconductor network environments onsite for his diverse clientele. A proven and tested leader in the Information Technology Age, Mr. Naugle's occupational background includes a 25-year stint with Motorola as a consultant and senior staff engineer. Presently, he is also involved in the analysis, design, evaluation, testing, and implementation of advanced LAN/WAN and Internet/Intranet-related computer networks. His highlight is cited as the reputation he established over the years in the design and maintenance of network technology. Attributing his success to being in the right place at the right time, Mr. Naugle future plans include designing new leading edge systems. Xceed is an in-house and remote destination consulting group. Working with clients throughout the state of Arizona, the Firm strives to carefully examine situations within the client's office and design appropriate reconstruction plans and solutions. The Firm had its start in 1999, and is presently located in Tempe, Arizona. **Career Highlights:** Consultant, Xceed (1998-Present); Senior Staff Engineer, Motorola (1973-98). **Education:** Arizona State University, M.S. (1978); Devry Institute, B.S. in Electrical Technology (1973). **Personal Information:** Married in 1982. Mr. Naugle enjoys family time and his grandchild.

Steve W. Nessel

Director of Learning and Development
Los Alamos Technical Associates
2400 Louisiana Boulevard NE, Suite 400
Albuquerque, NM 87110-4303
(505) 880-3428
Fax: (505) 880-3560
shessel@lata.com

7379

Business Information: As Director of Learning and Development of Los Alamos Technical Associates, Mr. Nessel is concerned with the development and management of a Company-wide training program that focuses on technical topics. Coupling his practical work experience with exceptional communicative skills, he is able to effectively interact with his students as he lends his knowledge and guidance. Internally recognized for his creative educational and instructional approaches, Mr. Nessel has successfully implemented several programs that have greatly contributed to overall effectiveness of the Company. Crediting his father for instilling a strong work ethic into him, he looks foward to continued prosperity within the corporate structure. Los Alamos Technical Associates provides information technology and environmental consulting for federal, city, and state governments as well as private industries. Established in 1976, the Company employs 600 people at the headquarters location in Albuquerque, New Mexico. **Career Highlights:** Director of Learning and Development, Los Alamos Technical Associates (1999-Present); Corporate Training Director, Montgomery Kone, Inc. (1998-99); Senior Instructor, Wackenhut Services, Inc. (1989-98). **Associations & Accomplishments:** American Society for Training and Development; Screen Actors Guild. **Education:** University of South Carolina, M.S. (1988); Ohio State University, B.A. **Personal Information:** Married to Sandra. Mr. Nessel enjoys acting, photography and travel.

Moses N. Newman

President
Point of Sale Technology Corporation
34 East 29th Street, 3rd Floor
New York, NY 10016
(212) 532-5383
Fax: (212) 252-1983
mosesn@mindspring.com

7379

Business Information: Serving as President of Point of Sale Technology Corporation, Mr. Newman is responsible for all aspects of daily operations. As the sole employee, he is in charge of programming and installation as well as support. Serving from an administrative capacity, he interviews and hires consultants for subcontracting. Overseeing accounting activities, he handles all bookkeeping, tax documents, and sales. Additionally, he uses his professional expertise to engage in marketing activities for the benefit of the Corporation. Crediting his open communication style as the main reason for his exemplary customer service skills, Mr. Newman has an adept ability to determine the needs of the customer and offer an efficient solution that often exceeds the expectations of the customer. Always alert to new opportunties and approaches, he currently has plans to begin national product sales from an Internet site, without the need for technicians. Point of Sale Technology Corporation is a multi-faceted business offering clients a variety of technologically advanced solutions. From the product support division they create, sell, and install computer based inventory control software and point of sale applications. The other division offers visual and network consulting as well as technical support. **Career Highlights:** President, Point of Sale Technology Corporation (1999-Present); Consultant, American International Group (1998-99); Consultant, Chase Manhattan Bank (1996); Consultant, GE Capital (1995-96). **Education:** New York University, B.A. in Computer Science (1988); Yale University; Southern Connecticut State University. **Personal Information:** Married to Jill M. Horn in 1999. Mr. Newman enjoys photography, gardening, skiing, driving and laser experimentation.

Bac Hai Nguyen

President
Jasmine Computers Technologies, Inc.
67 St. Catherine West #200
Montreal, Quebec, Canada H2X 1Z7
(514) 499-9996
Fax: (514) 499-9997
www.jasmine_tech.com

7379

Business Information: Mr. Nguyen is the President of Jasmine Computers Technologies, Inc., responsible for the general supervision of all daily operations. Under his direction, the Corporation has reached annual sales more than $5 million. Mr. Nguyen's plans for the future include pursuing an M.B.A. and deploying his business skills in further marketing and promotion of the Corporation. Jasmine Computers Technologies, Inc. offers computer consulting services to large corporations. Founded in 1985, the Canadian Firm currently operates from one office with the support of a six member professional staff. **Career Highlights:** President, Jasmine Computers Technologies, Inc. (1996-Present); President, CPC (1995); President, Netco (1993-95); Director, Alco Technology Inc. (1990-92). **Associations & Accomplishments:** Featured on a Canadian television broadcast throughout the Vietnamese Community regarding the Corporation (1995,1996).

Brittney T. Nguyen

Database Administrator
The Trizetto Group
6061 South Willow Drive
Englewood, CO 80111
(303) 495-7055
Fax: (303) 495-7001
brittney.nguyen@trizetto.com

7379

Business Information: As Database Administrator of The Trizetto Group, Ms. Nguyen fulfills a number of duties on behalf of the Group. A successful seven-year veteran of technology, she administers and controls data resources and ensures data security, integrity, and reliability. Primarily focusing her attention on managing projects and supporting Trizetto's intricate data warehouse environments, Ms. Nguyen designs and develops software specifically concerning physician reporting, patient transactions, and health claim processing. Presiding over all administrative responsibilities, she ensures the proper staffing and funding of each project. Continuing her growth with The Trizetto Group, Ms. Nguyen dedicates her efforts towards providing customer satisfaction. The most rewarding aspects of her career is being able to help customers and being appreciated. Her success reflects her ability to think outside-the-box, take on challenges, and deliver results. Specializing in providing application services to healthcare providers, The Trizetto Group was founded in 1997. Offering support and business enhancements, the Group offers customers a choice of best-of-class applications through its vendor-neutral position. Consulting with various physicians and practices, the Group establishes goals and interests in order to select application programs that will enhance productivity within the work environment. Committed to providing state-of-the-art equipment and services, The Trizetto Group focuses its attention to implementing new technologies. **Career Highlights:** Database Administrator, The Trizetto Group (1998-Present); Senior Analyst, Andersen Consulting (1997-98). **Associations & Accomplishments:** International Oracle Users Group; Rocky Mountain Cognos Users Group. **Education:** University of Colorado, M.B.A. (1998); Regis University, B.S. (1993). **Personal Information:** Ms. Nguyen enjoys reading, shopping and travel.

Anders Nilsson

Technical Lead
Absalon Group
Kalendegatan 26
Malmo, Sweden 21135
+46 406992070
Fax: +46 406117525
anders.nilsson@absalon.net

7379

Business Information: Serving as the Technical Lead for the Absalon Group, Mr. Nilsson oversees a number of functions on behalf of the Group and its global clients. He is responsible for deciding on the type of methodology and technique to be employed in each project. Possessing an excellent understanding of technology, Mr. Nilsson also is charged with managing the research department and supervising his staff of 15 employees. Using his skills and expertise, he effectively leads his staff during the testing phase of all new technical platforms. In the future, Mr. Nilsson looks forward to continuing with the Group, developing himself, and gaining more experience in his field. Located in Malmo, Sweden, the Absalon Group engages in providing services in the e-commerce industry. Founded in 1994, the Group offers knowledge management, customer relations management, and software development advice to a large clientele. Operating on an international level, the Malmo location has a staff of 38 employees who are dedicated to providing quality services. In 1999, the Group reported a substantial annual revenue and is constantly growing and developing. **Career Highlights:** Technical Lead, Absalon Group (1999-Present); System Developer, Nimrod Information Technology (1998-99). **Education:** Lund University, B.S. in System Design (1998). **Personal Information:** Mr. Nilsson enjoys sports and time with his friends.

Thomas J. Nolan, Jr.

Vice President/Director
Transaction Information Systems
115 Broadway, Floor 20
New York, NY 10006
(212) 962-1550
Fax: (212) 962-7175
tnolan@tisny.com

7379

Business Information: Possessing unique talent in the field of technology, Mr. Nolan serves in the dual role of Vice President and Director for Transaction Information Systems. He is responsible for the internal computing, networking, and telecommunication technological aspects of the Company. Before joining Transaction Information Systems, he served as Director of Distributed Architecture with Chase Mellon Shareholder Services. His solid background also includes stints as New York Region Senior Technical Manager for Automated Concepts Inc. and Advisory Process Manager at IBM Research. As an executive officer, he maintains the Information Technology Department's budget, approves vendors, and initiates technology purchases within budgetary guidelines. Additionally, Mr. Nolan acts as the personnel manager, interviewing and hiring qualified professionals. An accomplished professional, he holds a patent for one of his innovations in the information technology field. Always alert to new opportunities and approaches, he looks forward to assisting in the completion of future corporate goals. Boasting $125 million in yearly revenue, Transaction Information Systems specializes in the financial service industry, providing e-commerce solutions, development, and professional placement. Beginning operations in 1989, the Company consists of a staff of 550 skilled and knowledgeable professionals. **Career Highlights:** Vice President/Director, Transaction Information Systems (1997-Present); Director of Distributed Architecture, Chase Mellon Shareholder Services (1996-97); New York Region Senior Technical Manager, Automated Concepts Inc. (1994-96); Advisory Program Manager, IBM Research (1976-93). **Associations & Accomplishments:** President (1988-94), Mahepac Central Schools Board of Education. **Education:** Syracuse University, M.S. in Computer Engineering (1986); Fairleigh Dickinson University, B.S. in Electronic Technology. **Personal Information:** Married to Ellen in 1971. Four children: Kristen, Erin, Lauren, and Thomas. Mr. Nolan enjoys computer design and programming.

Barbara North

Owner
Great White North
280264 Grey Road #34, Rural Route 2
Proton Station, Ontario, Canada N0C 1L0
(416) 706-0846
Fax: (519) 923-6556
bnorth@bmts.com

7379

Business Information: As Owner and sole proprietor of Great White North, Mrs. North provides unequalled services as a consultant, analyst, and computer development specialist. She determines the direction and formulates new business development and marketing plans. Drawing on experiences as a programmer and analyst for three separate information technology companies since 1988, combined with her academic background, Mrs. North contributes her superior skills and knowledge to the industry. Currently, Mrs. North is specializing in the LANZA CASE Tool and AS/400 platforms. Presently expanding the horizons of her Company, she is planning the strategic direction of Great White North, introducing new company employees to the service in the near future. Her success reflects her ability to aggressively take on challenges and deliver results on behalf of her Company and its clientele. Serving the greater Toronto area, Ontario, Great White North provides computer development and business consulting services for a wide range of clients varying from small, family-run businesses to large corporations. Founded in 1996, Great White North offers specialized software maintenance and the highest quality corporate advice available on the market today, establishing customer contacts and referrals from across the nation. **Career Highlights:** Owner, Great White North (1996-Present); Programmer/Analyst, Insight Business Consultants (1993-96); Programmer/Analyst, National Sea Products (1988-93). **Associations & Accomplishments:** CIPS. **Education:** Dalhousie University, B.Sc. (1987). **Personal Information:** Married to Todd in 1993. One child: Alyson. Mrs. North enjoys scuba diving and horseback riding.

Kevin O'Brien

Owner/President
Island Services Network
129 Kent Street, Suite 303
Charlottetown, Prince Edward Island, Canada C1A 1N4
(902) 892-4476
Fax: (902) 894-6012
whoswho@isn.net

7379

Business Information: Utilizing a strong background and extensive knowledge, Mr. O'Brien is the Owner and President of Island Services Network. In his position, he is responsible for administering all management functions, such as the designing of systems and the development of new business opportunities. He oversees all of the daily operations within the Network, ensures complete customer satisfaction, and provides support for every employee. Moreover, Mr. O'Brien has daily communications with several clients and reviews all feedback from customers. He looks forward to continuing with the Network and expanding and growing. Located on Prince Edward Island, Canada, Island Services Network is an Internet service provider. Founded in 1994, the Network is the Island's oldest Internet company, providing a range of services such as wireless data services, systems integrations, custom solutions, and e-commerce. Operating on a regional basis, the Network has a staff of six employees who are committed to providing quality services to each customer. **Career Highlights:** Owner/President, Island Services Network (1994-Present); Systems Manager, PEI Federation of Agriculture (1992-93); Carpenter, Schurmans Building (1982-90); Speedskater, Team Canada (1978-81). **Associations & Accomplishments:** Rotary, Information Technology Association of PEI; Director, Metro Credit Union Board; Charlottetown Chamber of Commerce; Board Member, Health Information Resource. **Education:** Holland College, Business Applications Programmer (1992); University of Prince Edward Island, Political Science. **Personal Information:** Married to Ellie Reddin in 1991. Two children: Ryan Conway and Julia Conway. Mr. O'Brien enjoys model aircraft, quantum mechanics, nature and folk music.

Sean M. O'Brien

President/Chief Executive Officer
Modis Technologies
5756 South Semoran Boulevard
Orlando, FL 32822
(407) 380-7222
Fax: (407) 380-7569
sobrien@mgsd.com

7379

Business Information: Mr. O'Brien functions in the dual role of President and Chief Executive Officer with Modis Technologies. He concurrently sits on the Board of Directors of Modis UK, a joint venture of Modis Technologies. An 11-year veteran, he maintains the vision and focus of Modis Technologies' mission statement through all of the activities he involves the Company in. Mr. O'Brien works with the interactive expertise, synergy, and creativity of his staff to direct the future goals of the Company. For the future, he hopes to become more involved with merging into a larger group as an integrator for understanding how businesses operate on a more global angle. To fully uphold his position, he has confirmed his beliefs in his motto, "Always ask why at least five times." His success reflects his leadership ability to build teams with synergy, technical strength, and a customer oriented attitude, as well as produce cutting edge results, and aggressively tackle new challenges. Having excellent mentors and being a below the zone type of person has also contributed to his career success. Modis Technologies specializes in the virtual reality for the Internet supporting the market event, Business in Prothesis. Established in 1996, the Company trains customers on the possibilities available to them through the Internet and educates them on every product. With a staff of 52 employees, the Company also facilitates the training programs for IBM Corporation, Motorolla, and the Department of Defense computer users. Althogether, Modis Technologies produces $6 million annually through its international training programs. **Career Highlights:** Modis Technologies: President/Chief Executive Officer (1999-Present), Chief Operating Officer (1998-99), Executive Vice President (1997-98), Vice President (1996-97). **Associations & Accomplishments:** Association of the United State Army; International Society of Performance Improvements; Founder/Chairman, Total Knowledge Management Consortium. **Education:** University of Colorado, B.S. (1988); United States Army Ranger School; United States Paratrooper Training; Total Productive Manufacturing Certified Instructor. **Personal Information:** Married to Lynn in 1999. Mr. O'Brien enjoys surfing, running and weightlifting.

Brian K. O'Connor

Information Technology Manager
RESPEC
4775 Indian School Road NE, Suite 300
Albuquerque, NM 87110
(505) 260-8429
Fax: (505) 268-0040
bkoconn@respec.com

7379

Business Information: Mr. O'Connor is the Information Technology Manager for RESPEC. He is responsible for providing consulting and services to Sandia National Laboratories. Mr. O'Connor has served with RESPEC in a variety of roles since joining the Company as Systems Administrator in 1995. In his present position, he helps determine the overall strategic direction and business contribution of the information systems function. As a four-year professional, Mr. O'Connor supervises and guides the effort of his staff in providing computer support and maintaining the information systems infrastructure's functionality and fully operational status. As for his future, Mr. O'Connor would like to expand his professional reputation, move up the corporate hierarchy, grow the Company, and attain increased responsibilities. He attributes his success enjoying what he does and hard work. His advice is "Find out what you enjoy doing, find a niche, and read." RESPEC is a consulting firm that specializes in information technology, engineering, and environmental engineering. Averaging an estimated annual revenue of $10.5 million, the Company employs over 130 professional, technical, and support personnel. Founded in 1969 by a college professor and a group of students, RESPEC grew from a School of Mining project to a profitable, multimillion dollar industry. **Career Highlights:** RESPEC: Information Technology Manager (1997-Present), Operations Manager (1996-97), Systems Administrator (1995-96). **Associations & Accomplishments:** President's Quality Award; Turquoise Award. **Education:** University of New Mexico, B.B.A. in Business Computer Systems (1995). **Personal Information:** Married to Lisa in 1989. Two children: Sara and Darrin. Mr. O'Connor enjoys running, fly fishing, cycling and reading.

Timothy S. O'Malley

Director of Information Technology Strategy
IBM Global Services
62 Berkeley Place
Glen Rock, NJ 07452
(914) 766-2433

7379

Business Information: A prominent and respected professional, Mr. O'Malley serves as the Director of Information Technology Services for IBM Global Services. He assumes accountability for the Information Technology Strategy team responsible for defining the technology investments which produce a bottom line return. Before joining IBM Global Services as Director of Architecture and Standards in 1997, he served as both Managing Principal for the Northeast and Principal for Information Technology Strategy for IBM Consulting. Mr. O'Malley and his team locate the technology practitioners and business partners that are creating the technology of the future. Citing his networking skills as the reason for his success, he visits research laboratories and attends industry seminars to stay abreast of new advancements in his field. A new division of IBM established in 1997, IBM Global Services provides business information services to companies. Proffered services include information technology consulting, systems integration, managed operations, education, and systems maintenance. Over 120,000 qualified individuals are employed around the world. The Division reports an estimated $45 billion in annual revenue. **Career Highlights:** IBM Global Services: Director of Information Technology Strategy (1997-Present), Director of Architecture and Standards (1995-97); IBM Consulting: Managing Principal for the Northeast (1994-95), Principal for Information Technology Strategy (1994). **Associations & Accomplishments:** New Community Corporation, Newark New Jersey; Lead Council of IBM for Global Service. **Education:** Wharton School, University of Pennsylvania, M.B.A. (1999); Rider University, B.S. in Computers and Decision Sciences (1977). **Personal Information:** Married to Helen in 1982. Four children: Robert, Kaitlyn, Mary, and Peter. Mr. O'Malley enjoys sailing, coaching, community service and investing.

Manasse O. Obibi

Director
Zebra Systems Ltd.
526 Bath Road
Hounslow Middlesex, England, United Kingdom TW5 9UP
+44 0956247652
Fax: +44 1817549000
+44 1817594114
m.obibi@virgin.net

7379

Business Information: Mr. Obibi serves Zebra Systems Ltd. as Director, displaying his expertise in this highly skilled position. He is responsible for introducing prospective clients to the Corporation and negotiating any contracts which may be initiated. Overseeing accounting activities, he directs departmental personnel and fulfills a human resources role in the evaluation and promotion of management personnel. Providing input on the plans used when evaluating the needs of a particular client, Mr. Obibi is directly involved in the development of digital strategies. Enjoying his prominence, he intends to continue in his role, initiating impressive expansion plans to further increase the success of the Corporation in such countries as Nigeria, Ghana, and Zimbabwe. Established in 1997, the international computer consulting firm Zebra Systems Ltd. is headquartered in England. The Corporation is involved in computer development, project management, computer consultancy, computer training, and property investment. Top clients include corporations such as Hewlet-Packard, Cisco, and Britiania Airways. **Career Highlights:** Director, Zebra Systems Ltd. (1997-Present); Consultant, ICL-CFM (1997); Consultant, Glaxo Wellcome (1996); Consultant, Proctor & Gamble (1995); Director/Consultant, Corobal Ltd. **Associations & Accomplishments:** Institute of Information Systems; Institute of Computer Technology; Association of Computer Professionals. **Education:** London School of International Business, M.B.A. in International Marketing; Indiana University, Bachelor's degree in International Business Administration. **Personal Information:** Married to Augustina in 1986. Four children: Oghenekaro, Ekemera, Okemina, and Odiri. Mr. Obibi enjoys praying, reading the Bible, preaching and tennis.

Ruben J. Ochoa

Presidents
Computer Savers, Inc.
161 West 23rd Street, 2nd Floor
New York, NY 10011
(212) 807-1600
Fax: (212) 633-9957
ruben@pc-savers.com

7379

Business Information: Combining his technical skills and management expertise, Mr. Ochoa is the founder of Computer Savers, Inc. and serves in the role as President. In this capacity, he assumes the responsibility for all aspects of the Corporation's operational and administrative functions. He personally ensures that each client receives quality customer service. Presiding over the financial planning of the Corporation, he utilizes strategic planning to effect its continued growth and development. Mr. Ochoa is always alert to new opportunities, techniques, and approaches and plans to continue to provide quality products and services to his clientele. His success reflects his ability to build teams with synergy, technical strength, and a customer oriented attitude, produce results, and aggressively take on new challenges. Computer Savers, Inc. provides a wide range of hardware and software solutions for local businesses in the New York City area. The Corporation provides computer repair, software upgrades, system backup, and network support to its clients. Employing the skilled services of a six person work force, yearly revenue is estimated to be approximately $850,000. The Corporation was founded in 1993. **Career Highlights:** President, Computer Savers, Inc. (1993-Present); Manager, Rockwell Computers & Software (1995-96); Manager, Computer Services Group (1992-95); Manager, Merit Oil Corporation (1981-92). **Education:** Massachusetts Technical Institute Business School, Micro Computer Technology (1987). **Personal Information:** Married to 1991 in Maria. Two children: Daphnee and Yasmine. Mr. Ochoa enjoys boating and water sports.

Victor A. Ogunmodede

Senior Oracle Database Administrator
Teletech Holdings Inc.
1700 Lincoln Street, Suite 1400
Denver, CO 80203-4514
(303) 894-4168
Fax: (303) 365-0328
victor.ogunmodede@teletech.com

7379

Business Information: Mr. Ogunmodede functions in the role of Senior Oracle Database Administrator for Teletech Holdings Inc. Specializing in Oracle Financial database applications, he is responsible for development of advanced computer systems for the newly created call centers of his clients. A savvy, six-year database professional, Mr. Ogunmodede creates operable software programs and works to maintain the database throughout the duration of the contract with the clientele. Looking to the Year 2000 and beyond, his goals include eventually attaining the position of Director of Information Technology within the Corporation. Enthusiastically preparing for the completion of his Ph.D., his success reflects his ability to focus and work on one problem at a time to the best of his capability. Headquartered in Denver, Colorado, Teletech Holdings Inc. provides customer care management to its clients. Established in 1982, the Corporation has risen to become recognized as a Fortune 500 company. The Corporation supports a team of 12,400 employees who work to develop call centers for clients to enable them to better accommodate the needs of their customers. **Career Highlights:** Senior Oracle Database Administrator, Teletech Holdings Inc. (1998-Present); Oracle Database Administrator, Quark Corporated (1996-98); Oracle Database Administrator, Wamco Milk Industry (1993-96). **Associations & Accomplishments:** Institute of Electronics and Electrical Engineers; Oracle Development Tools User Group. **Education:** Rochester Institute of Technology, M.S. in Computer Science (1993); Al-mustansiyirah University, B.S. in Mathematics with Honors (1983). **Personal Information:** Married to Lola in 1991. Two children: Oluwaseun and Oluwatobi. Mr. Ogunmodede enjoys listening to music and photography.

Thada Olaric

Chief Executive Officer
Thaihosting
269/40 Sathupradit 17 Road
Yannawa, Thailand 10120
(909) 941-9620
Fax: +66 26741028
thada@thainet.org

7379

Business Information: As Chief Executive Officer of Thaihosting, Mr. Olaric also fulfills the responsibility of network systems administrator. He oversees and directs all daily administration and operations, such as financial and profit and loss statistics and managing the fiscal budget. A visionary who has proven himself correct on many occasions, Mr. Olaric established the Company at the age of 16 because he saw a need for the Company's services. Demonstrating leadership and managerial skills, he works closely with other members of the Company to ensure that all maneuvers are carried out according to strategic plans. His goals for the future include offering more data storage to his customers. Thaihosting serves as an Internet consultant and Web hosting provider. Located in Yannawa, Thailand, the Company engages in Web posting for 70 smalll and large customers in Thailand, providing such services as creating Web sites. Established in 1998, Thaihosting offers the expertise of eight professionals who work closely clients to analyze their specific needs and then specify and design solutions. Reporting an annual turnover of over $10,000, the Company is presently making arrangements to get more involved in Web posting and marketing as well as network systems administration. **Career Highlights:** Chief Executive Officer, Thaihosting (1998-Present); Systems Administrator, Thainet.org (1997-98). **Education:** LaSierra Academy (Currently Attending); St. Dominic School. **Personal Information:** Mr. Olaric enjoys ping pong and in-line skating.

Christopher M. Olexa

Senior Systems Engineer
Covad Communications
7918 Jones Branch Drive
McLean, VA 22033
(703) 394-1607
Fax: (703) 394-1601
chriso@covad.com

7379

Business Information: Mr. Olexa currently holds the position of Senior Systems Engineer with Covad Communications. He is responsible for technical advisement, hiring and training, market planning, and informational technology administration.

With an extensive educational and professional background in the field, Mr. Olexa has acquired the knowledge, dedication, and ambition to assist the Company in its overall advancement. His objective is to ensure Covad Communications has the ability to develop, grow, and expand its market. Technology is constantly changing, therefore Mr. Olexa keeps abreast in new developments by reading, speaking with coleagues, and attending professional seminars. Mr. Olexa plans to continue his work at Covad Communications and will continue to grow professionally. His success reflects his ability to think outside the box, produce results, and aggressively tackle new challenges. Covad Communications builds the world's largest DSL network utilizing IDSL, SDSL and ADSL in conjunction with ATM. Approximately 600 people are employed by the Company to assist in various services. **Career Highlights:** Senior Systems Engineer, Covad Communications (Present); Network Engineer, BBN/GTE Internetworking; UUNET Technologies: Internet Systems Engineer, Network Operations Engineer. **Associations & Accomplishments:** American Society of Mechanical Engineers. **Education:** Virginia Tech, B.S. Mechanical Engineering (1996). **Personal Information:** Mr. Olexa enjoys lacrosse, surfing, snowboarding, golf, church activities and reading.

Elizabeth K. Olson

Director, Project Management and Business System Analysis
Anexsys
525 West Monroe Street, Suite 925
Chicago,, IL 60661
(312) 441-4041
Fax: (312) 441-9340
eolson@anexsys.com

7379

Business Information: As Director of Project Management and Business System Analysis at Anexsys, Ms. Olson is concerned with a multitude of responsibilities on a daily basis. Managing project team leaders and staff members, she demonstrates a proactive leadership style as she incorporates their feedback and input into the creation of standard operating procedures. Focusing time and attention on project management, Ms. Olson is able to ensure all projects are running efficiently and accurately. She utilizes her education and practical work experience to prepare proposals that include details such as cost disclosure. Recognized for her impressive abilities, Ms. Olson frequently assists the Chief Information Officer with the development of strategic technical strategies. Attributing success to flexibility and adaptability within her role, Ms. Olson looks forward to expanding her role within the Company as she continues advancing through the corporate structure. Her advice is "understand true leadership." Providing e-commerce solutions to the government, Anexsys is recognized as an authority on business process development. Established in 1994 in Chicago, Illinois, the Company currently employs over 100 dedicated people to assist in the completion of corporate activities. **Career Highlights:** Director, Project Management and Business System Analysis, Anexsys (1998-Present); Vice President of Application Development, ABN AMRO (1996-98); Director of Application Development, Options Clearing Corporation (1994-96). **Associations & Accomplishments:** Project Management Institute; Board Member, Web SIG for Project Management Institute; Membership Chairperson, Winnetka Theatre. **Education:** Marquette University, B.S. (1981); Project Management Institute, Project Management Professional (1999). **Personal Information:** One child: Michelle. Ms. Olson enjoys theatre, dancing, needlework, and baking.

Herman Oosthuysen

Software Engineer/President
Aerospace Software Ltd.
217 Edgedale Gardens NW
Calgary, Alberta, Canada T3A 4M7
(403) 241-8773
Fax: (403) 241-8841
aerosoft@aerospacesoftware.com

7379

Business Information: As the Software Engineer and President of Aerospace Software Ltd., Mr. Oosthuysen oversees and directs all daily administration and operational functions. He determines overall strategic direction and formulates business and marketing plans to keep the Company competitive in the marketplace. A 16-year veteran of technology, Mr. Oosthuysen provides cutting-edge telephone equipment, Real Time, and DSP software for call centers and stockbrokers. He works closely with both management and users to analyze, specify, and design new solutions to harness more of the computer's power. An accomplished professional, he authored a book on CD form about the objective of Real Time software. Noting that others in the field should find a good mentor and make themselves known, Mr. Oosthuysen plans to become an independent consultant and find other professional contracts in the future. Established in 1995, Aerospace Software Ltd. is a software designer and developer. Located in Calgary, Alberta, the Company provides DSP software used in math-intensive signal processing applications, as well as Real Time software that is programmed to give an immediate response to any changes detected. Presently, a staff of two people man day-to-day operations. **Career Highlights:** Software Engineer/President, Aerospace Software Ltd. (1995-Present); Software Engineer, Computing Devices Canada (1995-98); Senior Engineer, Grinel (1995-97). **Associations & Accomplishments:** Institute of Electrical and Electronics Engineers; Captain, SA Army Core of Signals. **Education:** Stellenbosch University, Bachelor's degree in Electronic Engineering (1984). **Personal Information:** Married to Lona in 1984. One child: Gustav. Mr. Oosthuysen enjoys underwater diving and white water rafting.

Mehrdad Ordoobadi

Software Project Manager
Michael Baker Jr., Inc.
420 Rouser Road
Coraopolis, PA 15108
(412) 269-2975
Fax: (412) 269-7901
mordoobadi@mbakercorp.com

7379

Business Information: Drawing upon a broad experience in the software and construction field, Mr. Ordoobadi serves in the capacity of Software Project Manager for Michael Baker Jr., Inc. He works closely with management and systems users to analyze, specify, and design new software applications used to design and determine load rating for bridges. Rich in talents and possessing an excellent understanding of technology, Mr. Ordoobadi is well versed in Oracle Database and Sybase SQL Database and Server, and is able to used technology to solve engineering problems. In the future, Mr. Ordoobadi looks forward to remaining with Michael Baker Jr. and evenutally move up the corporate hierarchy. Located in Coraopolis, Pennsylvania, Michael Baker Jr., Inc. engages in consulting, construction, and engineering. For several years, the Corporation has provided bridge consultancy and bridge design for large construction companies nationwide. Furthermore, the Corporation has a staff of 3,600 professionals who are dedicated to providing quality services and durable structures. **Career Highlights:** Software Project Manager, Michael Baker Jr., Inc. (1997-Present); Structural Engineer, Sakhtemaan Sanaat (1993-96); Structural Engineer, Foundation for Construction of Public Schools (1992). **Education:** Carnegie Mellon University, M.S. in Computer Aided Engineering (1997); Shiraz University: M.S. in Structural Engineering (1991), B.S. in Civil Engineering (1988). **Personal Information:** Mr. Ordoobadi enjoys surfing the net, computer programming and picnics.

Rishikesh R. Pagnis

E-Commerce Architect
TexSYS RD Corporation
5333 North MacArthur Boulevard, Apartment 1105
Irving, TX 75038
(972) 582-3775
Fax: (972) 550-8454
rpagnis@texsysrd.com

7379

Business Information: Possessing unique talents in the information technology field, Mr. Pagnis joined TexSYS RD Corporation as E-Commerce Architect in 1999. He provides high level architecture of integrated systems and serves as a technical lead person overseeing all aspects of project management. Mr. Pagnis turns potential into action through preparation and skilled training. Concurrently, he serves asd Director of Information Technology at the University of Texas. Future plans for Mr. Pagnis include climbing the corporate ladder to achieve the Director's position at TexSYS RD through his involvement in the advancement of operations. His success reflects his ability to take on challenges and deliver results on behalf of the Corporation and its clientele. TexSYS RD Corporation is an e-business consulting firm. The Corporation provides integration of middle market ERP packages with e-business systems for mid-size companies. Established in 1983, the Corporation is located in Irving, Texas and employs 450 skilled individuals to acquire business, meet with clients, facilitate projects, and market services. TexSYS RD has estimated annual revenues of $65 million. **Career Highlights:** E-Commerce Architect, TexSYS RD Corporation (1999-Present); Director of Information Techology, TransAction Partners Inc. (1999); Assistant Director, Cait University of Dallas (1998-Present). **Associations & Accomplishments:** Center for Applied Information Technology at the University of Dallas; Microsoft Insiders Club; Microsoft Solution Developers Network; Sigma Iota Epsilon. **Education:** University of Dallas, Master's degree in Information Systems Management (1999); European University of Begium, International Management School, M.B.A; Mangalore University of India, Bachelor's degree in Engineering. **Personal Information:** Mr. Pagnis enjoys travel and reading.

Gregory S. Palatinus

Network Engineer
Pomeroy Computer Resources
3144 North Shadeland Avenue
Indianapolis, IN 46236
(317) 543-3660
Fax: (317) 543-3655

7379

Business Information: As a Network Engineer of Pomeroy Computer Resources, Mr. Palatinus is responsible for the design and implementation of technical solutions for wide area networks. He connects companies to the Internet on a large scale, visits sites, obtains customer needs, and designs and implements solutions in order to meet those needs. Mr. Palatinus has enjoyed substantial career success. One of his accomplishments include having been involved in various projects for large scale companies. He attributes his success to hard work ethic and personal motivation, as well as the ability to deliver results and aggressively take on new challenges. Mr. Palatinus plans on remaining with Pomeroy and become more involved common home users and cabling technologies. Headquartered in Hebron, Connecticut, Pomeroy Computer Resources is ranked as the fifth largest systems integration company in the United States. Also listed as the fastest growing in the United States by Fortune 500, the Company currently employs a staff of 10,000 individuals dedicated to serving clients in the Midwest. The Company reports an estimated annual revenue of $600 million. **Career Highlights:** Network Engineer, Pomeroy Computer Resources (1990-Present); Engineering Technician, MiL/600 (1981-90). **Associations & Accomplishments:** Nontel: NSP, ESP, TSP; Novell: Certified Network Engineer, Certified Network Engineer 3/4/5; Microsoft, MCPI; Cisco, CCIE. **Education:** IUPUI, B.A. (1981). **Personal Information:** Married to Janice in 1984. Two children: Brittany and Annah. Mr. Palatinus enjoys boating, snow and water skiing and fishing.

Dee A. Parker

Vice President of Education
HIE
15301 Dallas Parkway, Suite 950
Addison, TX 75001
(972) 361-3072
Fax: (972) 361-3094
dee.parker@hie.com

7379

Business Information: Getting started in technology while in college, Mrs. Parker currently serves as Vice President of Education for HIE. In her capacity, she provides software education to clients and employees that use the Company's software programs. She also trains employees in application, programming, and software use. An accomplished educator as well as a talented manager and organizer, Mrs. Parker ensures that all training programs are running smoothly, and that new classes are designed, developed, and implemented. She also oversees marketing projects and campaigns. Mrs. Parker intends to keep pace with emerging technology and share her knowledge with others, advance into higher management, and help the Company grow and expand. Her greatest accomplishment is growing the Department by 40 percent in 1998. Mrs. Parker attributes her success to ambition. Established in 1991, HIE is engaged in design and development of software applications and services for data integration. Based in Atlanta, Georgia, the Company develops data integration software for applications used in various industries, including health care and finance. The Company's strategic plan is to expand into other vertical markets. A staff of 200 people mans offices in the United States, Germany, and England. **Career Highlights:** Vice President of Education, HIE (1995-Present); Project Manager, R&D Systems (1990-95); Purchasing Manager, Hydraulic Supply Company (1988-90). **Associations & Accomplishments:** American Society For Training and Development; Society For Technical Communications; Health Level Seven; Texas A&M Century Club; DFW Unix Users Group. **Education:** Texas A&M University, B.S. degree (1988). **Personal Information:** Married to Chris in 1995. Two children: Mitchell and Bradley. Mrs. Parker enjoys playing the saxophone and being a Texas Aggies football fan.

Shawn Parkes

Consulting Manager
Lante Corporation
600 West Fulton
Chicago, IL 60661
(312) 696-5000
sparkes@lante.com

7379

Business Information: As the Consulting Manager for the Lante Corporation, Mr. Parkes is responsible for the implementation of policies and procedures in all areas of e-commerce consulting for client companies. Throughout his daily routine, he is charged with managing multiple consulting competencies, such as strategy, user experience, and technology in the building of products for the customers. With more than 18 years of professional business management experience, Mr. Parkes utilizes his talents and expertise to take the steps necessary to become an industry expert in the field of electronic marketplaces. Supervising up to 25 employees, he also provides a strong quality assurance and control presence. His future endeavors include becoming a chief information officer for software development or a dotcom start-up company. Mr. Parkes attributes his success to his passion for quality, efficiency, and the innovative management of people. Offering quality services, Lante Corporation is an e-commerce consulting firm. Specifically focused on the Internet, the Corporation's emphasis is on development of e-market and e-business solutions for dotcom and traditional corporate businesses. Established in 1985, the Corporation's services include e-commerce strategy, user research, branding, mutimedia interface design, and transactional system development. Headquartered in Chicago, Illinois, Lante operates internationally and functions under the direction of 475 people who facilitate day-to-day business operations and help generate annual revenues in excess of $30 million. **Career Highlights:** Consulting Manager, Lante Corporation (1997-Present); Systems Manager, CNA Insurance (1996-97); Project Manager, Baxter Healthcare Corporation (1984-96). **Associations & Accomplishments:** Recipient, Team Awards (1997), "CIO Magazine - Most Innovative Systems of the Decade"; Recipient, Team Awards (1998), Microsoft's "Best E-Commerce Application Developed Worldwide"; Recipient, Team Awards (2000), Comdex's "Best in Class Business to Business Application and Best Clix and Bricks Application". **Education:** Indiana University, B.S. in Business (1982). **Personal Information:** Married to Melia in 1982. Two children: Zachary and Harrison. Mr. Parkes enjoys Tai Chi instruction, scuba diving and physical health and fitness.

Kanti R. Patel

e-Commerce Practice Director
PCSI
60 Cohasset Court
Holmdel, NJ 07733-1081
(201) 488-7222
Fax: (201) 488-5040
kpatel@pcsiusa.com

7379

Business Information: Mr. Patel, PCSI's e-Commerce Practice Director, is responsible for overseeing daily business development and all e-commerce activities. This includes generation of new business, assisting the sales force, generating leads, directing technical services, managing a staff of five employees, overseeing the fiscal budget, and performing all aspects of personnel management including hiring and firing. Highly regarded and possessing an excellent understanding of technology, Mr. Patel specializes in e-commerce services, such as Web site design and development. Attributing his success to dedication and perseverance, he plans to continue working in this capacity, looking forward to a chance to move up within the corporate structure. Founded in 1985, PCSI is a consulting firm that provides information technology services. Headquartered in Holmdel, New Jersey, the Corporation works mainly with Fortune 500 companies. Employing 150 personnel, the Corporation reported estimated annual revenue exceeding $30 million in 1999. **Career Highlights:** e-Commerce Practice Director, PCSI (1997-Present); Director, DMR Consulting (1995-97). **Associations & Accomplishments:** Steering Commitee, New Jersey eCommerce User Group. **Education:** Brunel University of West London, B.S. (1984). **Personal Information:** Married.

Kiran K. Patel

Information Technology Specialist
IBM Global Services
717 Rutgers Lane
Parsippany, NJ 07054
(908) 931-4362
patelk@us.ibm.com

7379

Business Information: Drawing from an extensive educational history and occupational experience, Mr. Patel serves as the Information Technology Specialist for IBM Global Services. In his capacity, he is responsible for providing information technology solutions for the networking side. Accordingly, Mr. Patel facilitates the implementation and servicing support for LAN systems and infrastructure, and coordinates new products to service the clients' specific needs. Further, Mr. Patel monitors and tracks the upgrading of several networking envrionments, and is currently working with a government agency upgrading LAN, Windows NT, and Novell networks to Windows 2000 or NetWares. Consistently striving for optimal knowledge and expertise, Mr. Patel is MCSE and CNE certified. Looking to the future in the 21st Century, he plans on becoming a professional network architect, as well as designing and managing projects on a larger scale for IBM. A subsidiary of IBM Corporation, IBM Global Services provides global consulting of information technology solutions worldwide. With the assistance of 10,000 employees, the Company services Fortune 100 and small business companies. Serving an international clientele, the Company maintains offices throughout the world. **Career Highlights:** Information Technology Consultant, IBM Global Services (1996-Present); Assistant Manager, Fountain Technologies (1994-96). **Education:** Nova University at Florida, M.B.A. (1992); University of Baroda, B.S. in Engineering; Certified NetWare Engineer; Microsoft Certified Systems Engineer. **Personal Information:** Married. Two children. Mr. Patel enjoys reading and time with his family..

Lalit Patel

Consultant
Inforbit Inc.
89 Franklin Drive
Voorhees, NJ 08043
(609) 841-4888
(856) 772-0101
lpatel@erols.com

7379

Business Information: The President of Inforbit Inc., Mr. Patel also serves as a Consultant. He determines the overall strategic and tactical direction, as well as business contribution of the information systems function. Visiting the client sites, Mr. Patel works one on one with them to evaluate the individual needs of their businesses, and delivers cutting edge technological solutions that will enable them to improve their businesses and give them a competitive edge. Coordinating resources, schedules, time lines, and assignments also fall within the realm of his responsibilities. Mr. Patel plans to develop and expand his business by building good trusting client relationships. His success reflects his ability to think out-of-the-box and take on new challenges. He complements his duties at Inforbit with a position of Project Leader at Sancoa International. Created in 1997, Inforbit Inc. is a computer programming consulting firm. Operations employ the services of two skilled individuals and annual revenue has already reached $120,000. **Career Highlights:** Consultant, Inforbit Inc. (1997-Present); Project Leader, Sancoa International (1999-Present); Senior Consultant, Conti Mortgage (1998-99); Consultant, Rosenbluth International (1998). **Associations & Accomplishments:** DVCUG; AS/400; RPG; CLP; DB2/400. **Education:** Gujarat University, B.S. in Physics (1988), Computer Applications diploma; Atlantic Community College, AS/400. **Personal Information:** Married to Kinnari in 1995. One child: Rahie. Mr. Patel enjoys photography and camping.

Neelanjan Patri

Owner
NVT Consulting Services
2430 Columbine Trail
Chattanooga, TN 37421-1877
(423) 751-3233
Fax: (423) 751-4160
npatri@chattanooga.net

7379

Business Information: Serving as Owner of NVT Consulting Services, Mr. Patri oversees and directs all aspects of day-to-day administration and operational activities. Fulfilling the role of project leader, he is in charge of development of large projects in Web and e-commerce as well as assisting clients entering these areas. He provides technical service and support to customers and has developed offshore cost savings of 40 percent and more for international clients. In the future, Mr. Patri would like to establish one single point of control for e-commerce and Web pages, thus increasing their overall efficiency and flexbility. His advice is "read where you are going instead of where your are today so you can forecast projects and recruitment." Mr. Patri's success reflects his ability to think outside the box, aggressively take on new challenges, and deliver results on behalf of the Firm and its clientele. NVT Consulting Services is a consulting firm specializing in business solutions and work management concerns. The Firm also focuses on Oracle front end technology, development of Web pages, and e-commerce. Established in 1998, the Firm employs the talent of two qualified individuals to serve every aspect of customers' needs. **Career Highlights:** Owner, NVT Consulting Services (1998-Present); Project Leader, Professional Consulting Services (1993-98); Systems and Business Analyst, TELCO-India (1989-93). **Education:** KREC Suratkal, Bachelor's degree in Engineering (1989). **Personal Information:** Married to Vandana Lunawat in 1992. One child: Tanay. Mr. Patri enjoys writing poems, music, reading, badminton and tennis.

Robert T. Patton

Vice President of Data Systems and Operations
Bizrate Com
4053 Redwood Avenue
Los Angeles, CA 90066
(310) 305-3506
robpatton@earthlink.net

7379

Business Information: As Vice President of Data Systems and Operations of Bizrate Com, Mr. Patton oversees a multitude of duties. He assists in the formulation of policies and procedures, develops goals and objectives, and implements strategic plans. Dedicated to the success of Bizrate Com, Mr. Patton keeps abreast on new developments in the field and incorpoartes pertinent information into his daily duties. He has full knowlege of all aspects of the operation, excluding software development. A successful veteran, Mr. Patton is proud of being a part of the Pascal Project that developed part of the code at Apple. In the future, he plans to stay in the e-commerce field and apply data warehousing. His advice to others is to not only learn technolgy, but also business and people. Bizrate Com is a company providing e-commerce services. Established in 1996, approximately 140 people assist in various aspects of the business. The Company acts as an intermediary between consumers and merchants. Services include market research, consumer confidence, shop searches, rebate programs, and other services. With over 2,600 merchants online, the Company is ranked eigth in the world in their field. **Career Highlights:** Vice President of Data Systems/Operations, Bizrate Com (1999-Present); Senior Principal Consultant, Intelligent Solutions (1997-99); Senior Manager of Information Systems, AMGEN (1992-97). **Associations & Accomplishments:** Institute of Electronics and Electrical Engineers; Association of Computing Machinery. **Education:** La Salle University, Master's degree in Computer Engineering (In Progress); University of California at San Diego, Computer Engineering. **Personal Information:** Married to Kathryn in 1990. One child: Wes. Mr. Patton enjoys technology, books, travel and Boy Scouts.

Matthew R. Pavlovich

President
Media Driver, LLC
14902 Preston Road, Suite 404 #303
Dallas, TX 75240-1919
(214) 244-9607
mpav@debian.org

7379

Business Information: Mr. Pavlovich, the founder and President of Media Driver, LLC, is responsible for overseeing all aspects of operation. Experienced in all areas of technology, he oversees the technical direction of the Company's development and formulates new business and plans to keep the Company on the leading edge. A highly successful individual, Mr. Pavlovich is the founder of a number of media projects and groups. Demonstrating expertise in the field, he also deals with planning, hiring, and designing aspects for the Company. In the future, Mr. Pavlovich looks forward to the Company's growth and expansion, while hoping for a chance to further the advancement of other Linux projects. Founded in 2000, Media Driver, LLC provides advanced media
content delivery and monitoring technology. Dedicated to technological advancments in the area of media content drivers, the Company's applications include video streaming and systems monitoring. **Career Highlights:** President, Media Driver, LLC (1999-Present); Systems Administrator, Allegiance Telecom PC (1999); Network and Systems Administrator, Purdue University (1996-00). **Associations & Accomplishments:** Founder, Linux Video and DVD Project (www.linuxvideo.org); Founder, Open DVD Group (www.openvd.org); Lead Technician, Witness in New York DMCA MPAA vs 2600 (cryptome.org); Developer Debien NGU/Linux (www.debian.org); Institute of Electrical and Electronics Engineers. **Education:** Purdue University. **Personal Information:** Mr. Pavlovich enjoys ski diving, hiking, rock climbing, rafting, reading and running.

Kendrew Peacey

Development Manager
Informix
1099 18th Street, Suite 2500
Denver, CO 80202-1945
(303) 672-1254
Fax: (303) 672-1200
kendrew.peacey@cmpnetmail.com

7379

Business Information: Serving as a Development Manager for Informix, Mr. Peacey is responsible for all project development and implementation. He performs duties that include personnel management, workload distribution, and employee training. In addition to his management obligations, he actively develops tools for data model mapping and migration of applications on Legacy databases to ORDBMS and RDBMS. Mr. Peacey has become an esteemed company leader by demonstrating his effective management skills in conjunction with an expanded background in computer technology. Planning to obtain an executive management position, he is currently initiating projects to launch existing customer base into the competitive and profitable area of wireless communications. Based in Menlo Park, California, Informix is the technology leader in software infrastructure solutions for the Internet. Informix is the first and only company to integrate e-commerce and business intelligence on a true Internet infrastructure. Informix provides a fast, simple and complete way to bring businesses to the Web. The Company's solutions can personalize content management, and analyze information real-time. This, with Informix's highly scalable Web engines and media asset management capabilities, gives its customers a unique competitive advantage. **Career Highlights:** Development Manager, Informix (2000-Present); Development Manager, Ardent Software, Inc. (1998-2000); Development Team Lead/Architect, Unidata (1996-98); Support and Development Engineer, Systems Builder (1991-96). **Education:** Computer Learning Center (1986). **Personal Information:** Married to Angela in 1998. Mr. Peacey enjoys wine collecting.

Daniel Peake

Principal Consulting Manager
FutureNext Consulting, Inc.
16780 Lark Avenue
Los Gatos, CA 95032-7646
(408) 335-2507
Fax: (408) 395-0805
daniel@peake.org

7379

Business Information: As the Principal Consulting Manager of FutureNext Consulting, Inc., Mr. Peake oversees and directs daily operations of the Corporation's Technical Services Engineering Group. He is currently responsible for developing bes practices to be utilized for the technical implementations of leading edge systems solutions. Possessing an excellent understanding of emerging technology, Mr. Peake directs the recruiting, training, and mentoring of principal and senior level consultants including Oracle database administrators, Web and e-technology architects as well as network and systems engineers. Managing help desk, network, and telecommunications operations also fall within the realm of his functions. Mr. Peake has been involved with computers since he received his first computer at the age of 12. He also wrote his own software and ran his own BBS while in high school. Mr. Peake aspires to become a chief information officer and/or the chief technology officer of an Internet or hi-tech firm in the near future. Established in 1998, FutureNext Consulting, Inc. is a rapidly growing consulting firm dedicated to delivering "end to end" e-businesses and supply chain solutions. Focused on the mid-market and divisions of Fortune 500 companies, FutureNext Consulting currently employs a staff of 450 highly trained consultants. Located in Los Gatos, California, the Corporation reports annual revenues exceeding $100 million. **Career Highlights:** Principal Consulting Manager, FutureNext, Inc. (1998-Present); Owner/President, Peake Consulting (1994-Present); Principal Consultant, Core Technology Group, Inc. (1999); Manager, Information Technology, Metricom, Inc. (1995-99). **Associations & Accomplishments:** MENSA International; International Oracle Users Group; Oracle Applications Users Group; Silicon Valley Public Access Link. **Education:** San Diego State University (1988); Miracosta College. **Personal Information:** Married to Jennifer in 1994. Two children: Noelle and Alexis. Mr. Peake enjoys RC offroad car racing and water skiing.

Ehsan Peermamode

Executive Director
BTI Consulting
3rd Floor, Orchid Tower, Sir William Newton Street
Port Louis, Mauritius
+23 02128000
Fax: +23 02108989
ehsanp@bow.intnet.mu

7379

Business Information: Serving as Executive Director of BTI Consulting, Mr. Peermamode is also a partner of the Company. He determines the strategic direction as well as formulating and deploying market and business plans to keep the Company at the forefront of technology field. Possessing superior talents and an excellent understanding of his field, he is responsible for technical quality assurance, project management, and methodologies implementation. Utilizing his education and years of hands-on experience, Mr. Peermamode guides the Company, overseeing prospects marketing and identifying new projects. Committed to further development of the Company, he is focused on changes that will allow BTI Consulting and its clientele to take advantage of newly developed technology to remain flexible, efficient, and profitable in the Information Technology Age. Estabished in 1998, BTI Consulting engages in business and information technology consulting, utilizing software development geared toward the latest technologies. Located in Port Louis, Mauritius, the Company employs the expertise of 17 individuals highly skilled in the technological field to facilitate specialized consulting to travel, manufacturing, and finance companies. **Career Highlights:** Executive Director, BTI Consulting (1999-Present); Partner, DCDM Consulting (1998); Analyst Programmer, Currimjee, Ltd. (1990). **Education:** Lille University at France, M.S. in Computer Science (1988). **Personal Information:** Married to Jeannine in 1989. Two children: Adam and Joachim. Mr. Peermamode enjoys golf and photography.

Philip G. Pees

Computer Programmer
Mynd
1700 Wadsworth Drive
Cayce, SC 29033
(803) 333-7613
Fax: (803) 333-3860
philippees@mynd.com

7379

Business Information: As Computer Programmer for Mynd, Mr. Pees fulfills a number of duties on behalf of the Company and its clientele. He is charged with the responsibilities of providing technical support and administration of day to day operations of payroll systems, Oracle database, and daily applications of state of the art software. Utilizing more than four years of information technology experience, Mr. Pees takes advantage of every opportunity to benefit from his extensive education and hands on occupational experience. His long-term plans for his career include remaining in the field of Oracle administration, while gaining additional experience in database design and engineering. Mynd is an outside consulting firm that offers a host of programs and services for various insurance companies. Such services include custom creating software and implementing strategies and plans for future business development. Established in 1985, the Company is headquartered in Cayce, South Carolina and operates out of several international locations. The Company currently employs the skills and expertise of more than 6,500 professionals who facilitate smooth business operations. **Career Highlights:** Computer Programmer, Mynd (1998-Present); Emergency Medical Service Technician, Rural Metro Ambulance (1996-98); Salesman, Pullian Ford (1994-96). **Associations & Accomplishments:** Palmetto Mastersingers. **Education:** University of South Caroling, Bachelor's degree in Media Arts (1993); Midlands Technical College, Computer related classes. **Personal Information:** One child: Austin Philip.

Andrew M. Pegalis

President
Next Millennium Consulting, Inc.
7988-A Old Georgetown Road
Bethesda, MD 20814
(301) 565-4550
Fax: (301) 986-8504
pegalis@consult2000.com

7379

Business Information: Currently the President of Next Millennium Consulting, Inc., Mr. Pegalis develops and implements corporate strategies for business process improvement. A lawyer by training, he researches the best possible solutions to Y2K problems posed by internal IS systems, external business dependencies, vendor contracts, and other factors. Accomplished in the risk management field, Mr. Pegalis is credited with publishing the first article to deal with Y2K and Risk Management entitled, "For Risk Managers the Year 2000 is Now." A frequent public speaker, he looks to continue in his current career path with NMC. A member of the Society for Information Management's Working Group for the Year 2000, Next Millennium Consulting, Inc. is an independent risk management consulting firm. Dedicated exclusively to dealing with the year 2000 problem, NMC is involved in the conversion of client data. The Firm assists clients in assessing Y2K costs, including remediation, business interruption, and litigation expenses. Working directly under corporate executives, NMC utilizes multi-disciplined expertise and traditional risk management practices. The first business of its kind in the nation, NMC employs professional consultants, experienced in the fields of technology, law, finance, and insurance. **Career Highlights:** President, Next Millennium Consulting, Inc. (1997-Present); Contract Attorney, Akin, Gump, Strauss, Hauer & Feld (1997); Contract Attorney, MCI Metro (1997). **Associations & Accomplishments:** American Bar Association; Maryland State Bar Association; National Chapter of Friends of the Red Cross. **Education:** Washington College of Law, Juris Doctor (1995); Emory University, B.A. in Economics (1990). **Personal Information:** Mr. Pegalis enjoys sports and travel.

Kenneth M. Pepe

President
Pepe Enterprises
65 Florida Avenue
Island Park, NY 11558-1105
(631) 692-1752

7379

Business Information: Inspired to start his own business, Mr. Pepe is the owner and founder of Pepe Enterprises and currently serves as President. In his capacity, he oversees all aspects of technology consulting and systems and applications design, development, and implementation. Drawing from over 20 years of extensive occupational experience and wanting to maintain his independence, creativity, and hands on management style, Mr. Pepe started up Pepe Enterprises. Mr. Pepe attributes his success to keeping focused on quality, ability to learn quickly, and an attitude of "reliability and adaptability." Committed to further development and always alert to new opportunities, his professional goals are to grow the PC side of the Company and build onto his mainframe skills. Founded in 1994, Pepe Enterprises offers high quality computer consulting and design. An independent contractor reporting an annual revenue in excess of $100,000, Pepe Enterprises provides an affordable and reliable alternative. Computer related services include applications design and development, programming, coding, and testing for mainframe, client server, Internet and Intranet environments, and IBM DB2 products. Regional in scope, the Company located in Island Park, New York services the Greater New York area. **Career Highlights:** President, Pepe Enterprises (1994-Present); Senior Analyst, BACG, Inc. (1991-94); Project Manager, S-P Drug Company (1987-90); Project Leader, Charge-It, Inc. (1986-87). **Associations & Accomplishments:** National Small Business United; Independent Computer Consultants Association. **Education:** Lehigh University, B.S. (1977); Grumman Data Systems, Computer Programming. **Personal Information:** Mr. Pepe enjoys watching auto racing, aviation, reading and collectibles.

Nina L. Petrovich

Coastal Resources Social Scientist
NOAA Coastal Services Center
2234 South Hobson Avenue
Charleston, SC 29405
(843) 740-1203
Fax: (843) 740-1313
npetrovich@csc.noaa.gov

7379

Business Information: As Coastal Resources Social Scientist of NOAA Coastal Services Center, Ms. Petrovich facilitates the flow of information regarding coastal resource management, particularly as it relates to human uses and management decisions. Utilizing eight years of experience, she uses applied social sciences to evaluate the products and services program in an effort to discover what clients are doing and the information needed to help them connect. The ocean has served as a refuge for Ms. Petrovich since she was a little girl, leading to her current occupation. Attributing her success to enthusiasm, she is proud to have coordinated the project to promote Coastal Stewardship through volunteers and produced its Web site and a video for use as a recruitment tool. Ms. Petrovich's immediate professional plans are to engage in a study of the finer points of culture relating to coastal lines and eventually anticipates obtaining a leadership role in assisting the community. A part of the National Ocean Service, the NOAA Coastal Services Center provides spatial information and technology services for state level coastal resource managers. Employing a staff of 120 skilled individuals, the Center was established in 1994. **Career Highlights:** Coastal Resources Social Scientist, NOAA Coastal Services Center (1997-Present); Consultant, Coastal Vision (1997); Interim Manager, Wells National Estuarine Research Reserve (1996-97); Project Manager, National Association of Counties (1993-95). **Associations & Accomplishments:** The Coastal Society; Ultimate Players Association. **Education:** University of Delaware, Master's degree in Marine Policy (1993); University of Miami, B.S. in Marine Science and Biology. **Personal Information:** Ms. Petrovich enjoys photography, scuba diving, Ultimate Frisbee and jazzercise.

James L. Petrucelli

President/Chief Financial Officer
Tri Tech Systems, Inc.
251 North Dupont Highway, Suite 125
Dover, DE 19901
(302) 284-4582
Fax: (847) 589-8008
petrucelli@ttechsystems.com

7379

Business Information: Since joining Tri Tech Systems, Inc. in 1987, Mr. Petrucelli has achieved the position of President and Chief Financial Officer. In his dual role, he is responsible for the oversight of all financial aspects including accounts and tax certification. Moreover, he is charged with conducting certain legal issues, providing consulting services, and is involved with the marketing methods. Possessing an excellent understanding of technology, Mr. Petrucelli also performs the building of client servers and Oracle systems. In the future, he looks forward to moving more within the client server side and utilizing his degree and potential more. Located in Dover, Delaware, Tri Tech Systems, Inc. is a professional services firm that provides production and project management. Founded in 1987, the Corporation serves a national clientele offering main frame and client server development. With a staff of four employees, the Corporation reports an estimated annual revenue of $3 million. **Career Highlights:** Tri Tech Systems, Inc.: President/Chief Financial Officer (2000-Present), President/Chief Executive Officer (1987-00); Programmer/Analyst, Computer Aid, Inc. (1997-Present). **Associations & Accomplishments:** Chief Financial Officer, Class Act, Inc.; Knights of Columbus; Toastmasters. **Education:** Wilimington College, M.B.A. (1993); Shepherd College, B.S. (1986). **Personal Information:** Married to Chantal in 1994. Mr. Petrucelli enjoys yardwork, stocks, PC work and movies.

Ulf Pettersson

Chief Executive Officer
Tempogon AB
Scheelegatan 11
Stockholm, Sweden 112 28
+46 703213831
Fax: +46 706128448
ulf.pettersson@tempogon.se

7379

Business Information: Mr. Pettersson functions in the capacity of Chief Executive Officer for Tempogon AB. He determines the overall strategic direction and formulates powerful business and marketing plans to keep the Firm outfront of its competitors. A savvy, five year professional expert, Mr. Pettersson monitors all aspects of day-to-day activities of the office and provides a valuable resource for the Firm through his guidance and leadership skills. Maintaining client relationships and overseeing public relations, as well as coordinating resources, time lines, schedules, assignments, and fiscal year budgets also fall within the purview of Mr. Pettersson's responsibilities. Most proud of a completing project utilized by 25,000 users, his 21st Century goals are to multiply the annual turn over of the Firm and complete his MBA course. His professional success reflects his leadership ability to deliver results and aggressively take on new challenges. Tempogon AB is an information technology consulting firm. The Firm provides technical management for the computer networks in several businesses within Sweden. Established in 1997, the Firm hosts a staff of three technology experts to assists its clients in designing and implementing new systems or upgrading an old system within their home or office. Today, the Firm turns over skr 5 million every year in revenue. **Career Highlights:** Chief Executive Officer, Tempogon AB (1997-Present); Consultant, Enea Data AB (1995-97); Consultant, Memtek Development (1994-95). **Education:** Linkoping University, M.S. in Computer Science and Engineering (1994). **Personal Information:** Married to Eva in 1999. Two children: William and Noah. Mr. Pettersson enjoys mountain biking, rock climbing and sailing.

Scott P. Pfeiffer

Project Manager
V4 Consulting
501 Madison Avenue, Suite 205
Indianappolis, IA 46225
(317) 423-1809
spfeiffer@v4c.com

7379

Business Information: Mr. Pfeiffer serves as Project Manager of V4 Consulting. He is responsible for projects dealing with e-business solutions as well as computer graphics and multimedia technology. Utilizing over eight years of business experience and technical savvy, he plans, oversees, designs, and implements Web design and computer animation projects. He concurrently fulfills the role of lead designer. His career highlights include winning awards for photography. Additionally, Mr. Pfeiffer was recognized for his innovative interactive CD Rom resume. Coordinating project resouces, time lines, schedules, and communications and managing project and fiscal budgets also fall within the realm of his responsibilities. His future goals is to start his own company after V4 Consulting gets off the ground. Success, according to Mr. Pfeiffer, is attributed to his ability to think outside the box, take on challenges, and deliver results. Established in 1999, V4 Consulting operates as a medical and healthcare group providing e-business solutions. National in scope, the Company assists offers technology solutions for the financial industry, coporations, and small practices. Presently, V4 Consulting is staffed by a team of two professional and technical experts. The Company is headquartered in Indianapolis, Indiana. **Career Highlights:** Project Manager, V4 Consulting (1999-Present); Designer/Lead Author, Aeon Design Team (1999); Owner/Lead Designer, Digital Fx (1998); Graphics Editor, MIU (1992-99). **Associations & Accomplishments:** National Deans List; Who's Who Among Students in American Colleges and Universities. **Education:** Marycrest International University, B.A. in Computer Graphics (1999); Indiana University, degree in Mathematics and Computer Science. **Personal Information:** Mr. Pfeiffer enjoys sky diving, rafting, sports and travel.

Flemming Philipsen

Consultant/Owner
Kapa Consulting
Boegeraenget 2
Munkebo, Denmark 5330
+45 65975300
Fax: +45 65975315
mp@management_partners.com

7379

Business Information: Mr. Philipsen is the Owner and Consultant of Kapa Consulting. As the sole proprietor of the Firm, he is responsible for all aspects of administration and operational activities. Drawing from 25 years of business experience and academics, he provides the consulting services, produces the budget for the Firm, conducts the strategic planning, marketing, and advertising methods, and achieves new clients on a daily basis. Possessing an excellent understanding of technology, Mr. Phillipsen formulates innovative marketing and business plans to keep the Firm out-front of industry competitors. Moreover, he ensures that the clients are satisfied with his services and coordinates public relations to promote the services. In the future, Mr. Philipsen plans on remaining and taking the Firm to the next level with the addition of a few new clients. His success reflects his ability to take on challenges and deliver results on behalf of his clients. Created in 1988, Kapa Consulting is an information technology consulting and business development firm. Located in Munkebo, Denmark, the Firm works with all types of industries and several banks throughout the country providing consulting services on new business developments to ensure success. Working mainly on a national level, the Firm does have a select international clients. Presently, the Firm reports annual revenues in excess of $1 million. **Career Highlights:** Consultant/Owner, Kapa Consulting (1988-Present); Management Director, Philipsen Aps (1983-88); Sales Manager, Jacobs Kafee GmbH (1981-83). **Associations & Accomplishments:** Danish Management Council; DICMC; FDC. **Education:** University of Odense, M.BSc. (1980); Odense Technical High School, Production Engineer (1975). **Personal Information:** Married to Karin Pagh in 1974. Two children: Linda and Sandie. Mr. Philipsen enjoys reading and current technology issues.

Brian J. Pierron

Consultant/President/Treasurer
MJP Solutions Inc.
4694 Cemetary Road, PMB #305
Hilliard, OH 43026
(614) 534-4514
brianpierron@hotmail.com

7379

Business Information: Following his independent and entrepreneural spirit, Mr. Pierron started MJP Solutions, Inc. in 1999. He serves as Consultant, President, and Treasurer. In this context, he assumes all aspects of accountability for day-to-day business development and marketing. He also provides cutting edge solutions for his clients in the realm of software design and development. A savvy, sharp professional, Mr. Pierron controls and monitors financial and profit and loss statements as well as handles all human resource issues. He is Visual Basic 5 and 6 and will receive his M.C.S.E. certification within a year. Looking to the future, Mr. Pierron plans on building up his consulting business to eventually provide IT solutions and possibly develop a software product to be marketed through his Web site. Newly established in 1999, MJP Solutions, Inc. engages in software consulting. Offering services, such as software development, design, implementation and training, the Corporation specializes in visual basic, C++, Access, and Sequel. MJP Solutions is proudly operated by two individuals, whom founded the Corporation. **Career Highlights:** Consultant/President/Treasurer, MJP Solutions, Inc. (1999-Present); Computer Consultant, Quick Solutions, Inc. (1997-99); Programmer, EMRO Marketing (1995-96). **Education:** University of Dayton, B.S. (1997).

Ronald R. Plew

Vice President
Perpetual Technologies, Inc.
925 North 1050 East
Indianapolis, IN 46234
(317) 824-0393

7379

Business Information: As Partner and Owner of Perpetual Technologies, Inc., Mr. Plew fulfills the role of Database Administrator. He is responsible for all aspects of day-to-day administration and operational activities. In coordination with other partners, he determines the overall strategic direction and business contribution of the information systems function. A sharp professional, Mr. Plew is also accountable for establishing new business relations, providing user training, overseeing financial and profit and loss statements, and conducting research and development of new, cutting edge technologies. He utilizes his business and systems savvy in writing and implementing database manuals. Mr. Plew owes his involvement and success in the industry to his 16 plus years in the National Guard as a programming specialist. He has three publications to his credit and his working on a fourth. His strategic plans include expansion and more training. Hard work and dedication are cited as Mr. Plew's reasons for success. Perpetual Technologies, Inc., partnered with Oracle Corporation, is a company that provides database training and recruitment and placement of information technology professionals. The Company also offers consulting services to new and upcoming businesses. Perpetual Technologies is headquartered in Indianapolis, Indiana. **Career Highlights:** Database Administrator/Partner/Owner, Perpetual Technologies, Inc. (Present). **Associations & Accomplishments:** Oracle Certified Professional. **Personal Information:** Mr. Plew enjoys golf, chess and fishing.

Michael J. Podemski

Technical Consultant
Leapnet, Inc.
2015 Spring Road, Suite 600
Oak Brook, IL 60523
(630) 586-8795
(847) 910-5537
mpodemski@leapnet.com

7379

Business Information: Serving as a Technical Consultant for Leapnet, Inc., Mr. Podemski is responsible for working with clients within the insurance industry. He develops improvements for customers' existing systems, serving as a systems analyst and project leader responsible for testing and evaluating new technologies. Utilizing skills learned through an extensive educational background, Mr. Podemski performs all tasks in an efficient manner, ensuring that each client is satisfied with their services. The most rewarding aspect of his career is implementing Y2K solutions within the Corporation's infrastructure. Dedicated to the Corporation's success, he anticipates his promotion to lead solution architect as a result of his continuing efforts to increase his skills through training and professional development activities. Established in 1973, Leapnet, Inc. provides information technology consulting services. The Corporation specializes in e-business, data warehousing, broadvision, and software development. Local operations in Oak Brook, Illinois employs the expertise of 500 individuals to promote services, facilitate scheduling, and address customer queries. **Career Highlights:** Technical Consultant, Leapnet, Inc. (1997-Present). **Associations & Accomplishments:** Fenwick High School Alumni Association; University of Illinois Alumni Association; The Field Museum. **Education:** Keller Graduate School of Management, Graduate Certificate in Information Systems (1999); University of Illinois at Urbana, B.S. in Liberal Arts and Sciences (Psychology) (1996).

Srinivasa R. Ponakala, Ph.D.

Senior Systems Analyst
Cylogix, Inc.
1915 Hunters Glen Drive
Plainsboro, NJ 08536
(609) 750-5144
Fax: (609) 275-0305
s_ponakala@yahoo.com

7379

Business Information: As Senior Systems Analyst, Dr. Ponakala has been providing professional skills for Cylogix, Inc. since joining the Corporation in 1999. He focuses on research, design, and development of real-time systems using object oriented techniques and and design patterns and distributed concepts in order to promote and implement new technologies. Researching the development of new projects, he analyzes specific information in order to produce software products designed for the client's individual needs. Overseeing a staff of experienced technicians and designers, he arranges training courses and various assistance in order to expand the product line. Continuing his involvement with the development of Internet services and development, Dr. Ponakala remains committed to the furthering success of Cylogix, Inc. Specializing in software development and consulting services, Cylogix, Inc. was established in 1997. Consulting with clients on an individual basis, the Corporation establishes future goals and purposes in order to produce efficient software products. Located in Plainsboro, New Jersey, Cylogix performs a wide range of information technological services for the surrounding area including Internet development and creation of specific databases. Employing over 170 dedicated technicians and consulting agents, the Corporation gaurantees excellent end results in higher productivity levels and value added to sales. Committed to the furthering success of their client's businesses, Cylogix continues to provide quality services, ensuring complete client satisfaction. **Career Highlights:** Senior Systems Analyst, Cylogix, Inc. (1999-Present); Senior Programmer/Analyst, Tomorrow Technology, Inc. (1997-98); Associate Professor, University of Hydorabad (1986-97). **Associations & Accomplishments:** Institute of Electrical and Electronics Engineers; Association of Computing Machinery; American Association for the Advancement of Science. **Education:** Indian Institute of Technology, Ph.D. (1986); Regional Engineering College, M.S. (1981). **Personal Information:** Married to Madhavi in 1989. Two children: Puneet and Mounika. Dr. Ponakala enjoys yoga, reading and helping the underprivileged.

Mickey Poppitz

Chief Information Officer/Chief Executive Officer
DataSoft LLC.com
6979 Noble Court
Arvada, CO 80007-7053
(303) 431-8076
mickey@datasoftllc.com

7379

Business Information: Serving as DataSoft LLC.com's Chief Information Officer and Chief Executive Officer, Mr. Poppitz's responsiblilities involve various aspects of network engineering operations. On a daily basis, he works with the customers on a hands on basis, evaluating their needs, developing technical strategies, and implementing products and services to ensure the success of their network. A diverse member of the professional community, Mr. Poppitz is well versed in several areas of information technology such as UNIX administration and software development. Crediting much of his success to a combination of constant training and strong business alliances, he recommends a good business plan and a stable financial situation to those who would consider the same career path. Currently, Mr. Poppitz has plans underway for the development of a Web site that offers online features for customers interested in the Company's services. DataSoft LLC.com provides network and Internet solutions to businesses seeking a diversified approach to daily operations. Established in 1998, the Company employs three hardworking employees who offer assistance to customers that requires services such as dedicated line access and Web site development. **Career Highlights:** Chief Information Officer/Chief Executive Officer, DataSoft LLC.com (1998-Present); Senior Network Engineer, Eclipse Micro Systems (1997-98); Senior Network Engineer, Budget Computers, Inc. (1996). **Associations & Accomplishments:** Microsoft Developers Network; Internet Chamber of Commerce; Cisco Partner RISAC; Habitat for Humanity. **Education:** Morris County College, A.A.S. (1989).

Mark E. Porterfield

E-Commerce Practice Lead
ACS Professional Services
Northridge Office Plaza, 117 Vip Drive, Suite 210
Wexford, PA 15090
(724) 935-6655
Fax: (724) 935-7577
mporterf@mcsiweb.com

7379

Business Information: Mr. Porterfield is E-Commerce Practice Lead of ACS Professional Services. For the past two years, he has provided Web design, project management, system design, e-commerce management. As an eight year technology professional, Mr. Porterfield is charged with determining any problems within the Company including its nature and extent. Phases of his job require analyzing data and observing the operations of the Company. He develops solutions to problems, taking in account the general nature of the business and making recommendations. Experienced in the field, Mr. Porterfield has the capabilities to lead ASC Professional Services to the top. His plans for the Company is to triple in size, increase the client base, attain bigger projects, and achieve a wealth of success. Mr. Porterfield's success reflects his ability to build teams with synergy, technical strength, and a customer oriented attitude, as well as deliver results and aggressively take on new challenges. ACS Professional Services provides consulting, outsourcing, Web development, and enterprise solutions. Approximately 15,000 people are employed by the Company. It is the third largest Company of its kind that provides outsourcing. **Career Highlights:** Senior Consultant, ACS Professional Services (1997-Present); Senior Consultant, Deloitte & Touche (1995-97); Senior Systems Analyst, PPG Industries, Inc. (1994-95). **Education:** Carnegie Mellon University (1993); University of Pittsburgh, SLIS, B.S. in Information Systems (1991). **Personal Information:** Married to Jodi in 1997. Mr. Porterfield enjoys skiing and sailing.

Guy C. Prentice, Jr., MSIA (MBA), CDP

Owner
GCP Consulting
416 Dogwood Lane
Webster, NY 14580
(716) 785-0500
gcp@iname.com

7379

Business Information: As Owner of GCP Consulting, Mr. Prentice works closely with interfacing among Fortune 500 companies to determine needs, costs, methods, and project implementation. With more than 27 years of professional management experience, and 30 years of information technology expertise, he utilizes his superior talents to monitor the productivity of the staff, while formulating a hands-on management style with an above average aptitude for problem solving. He detemines the overall strategic direction and formulates business and marketing plans to maintain the Company's competitive edge. Highly regarded, Mr. Prentice continues to grow professionally through the fulfillment of his responsibilities and his involvement in the advancement of company operations. GCP Consulting specializes in the integration of new business technologies and methods with leading-edge computer technologies. The Company offers services that fill a variety of technological communication interface needs between Fortune 500 company professionals and their systems. Established in 1962, the Company is located in Webster, New York and provides services to a national clientele. Currently, the Company employs a staff of 25 qualified people to serve the demands of a growing clientele. **Career Highlights:** Owner, GCP Consulting (1962-Present); Program Manager, Xerox (1973-89). **Associations & Accomplishments:** DPMA; Association of Computing Machinery; President, Rochester T'ai Chi Ch'uan Center; Former President, Local Association of Computing Machinery; Former Explorer Scouting Advisor; Psychology Consultant, University of Rochester Medical Center; Certificate in Data Processing Lifetime Award. **Education:** Carnegie-Mellon University, MSIA (MBA) (1970); University of Rochester, B.A. in Business & Psychology (1969); Continued Education with Microsoft, IBM, and Hewlett-Packard.

Charles W. Primmer
Corporate Information Systems Director
IB Industries
P.O. Box 215
Brownsdale, MN 55918
(507) 567-2704
cprimmer@ibidata.com

7379

Business Information: Mr. Primmer is Corporate Information Systems Director of IB Industries. He is responsible for all day-to-day administration and operations of the systems infrastructure and management of data resources. Before joining IB Industries in 1991, Mr. Primmer served as Chief of Training Control Division and Post OIC of Weapons Safety while serving in the United States Air Force. His history includes membership in the Retired Officers Association. A professional, he plans and oversees systems maintenance, upgrades, and software design, development, and implementation of advanced software applications. In addition to supervising his staff of seven employees, Mr. Primmer is in charge of staff training, coordinating systems resources and schedules, and tuning systems software to enhance overall performance. His success reflects his ability to build strong teams with synergy and technical strength and take on new challenges and responsibilities. Mr. Primmer's future goals include continuing to provide services laced with quality, value, and selection. A privately held domestic company, IB Industries engages in database management. Established in 1986, IB Industries is located in Brownsdale, Minnesota. Presently, IB Industries employs a staff of more than 100 professional, technical, and administrative support personnel. **Career Highlights:** Corporate Information Systems Director, IB Industries (1991-Present); United States Air Force: Chief of Training Control Division (1985-87), Post Officer in Charge, Weapons Safety (1983-85). **Associations & Accomplishments:** Retired Officers Association. **Education:** University of Northern Colorado

(1980); LaVerne College, B.A. (1977); Allan Hancock Junior College, A.A. (1974). **Personal Information:** Married to Patricia A. in 1967. Two children: Michelle and Jeffrey. Mr. Primmer enjoys computers, cooking and gardening.

Steven Pulsipher
President
Net Designs and Creations, Inc.
3130 Reeves Avenue
Ogden, UT 84401
(801) 394-6755

7379

Business Information: As President of Net Designs and Creations, Inc., Mr. Pulsipher is responsible for overall operations on a day-to-day basis. Demonstrating impressive skill and ability, he designs and implements various Web based applications, incorporating employee feedback and input into his creations. A systems expert, Mr. Pulsipher handles installation and implementation of both hardware and software systems for clients, and conducts training courses for his employees to ensure they are well-versed on all aspects of operations. Overseeing marketing activities, Mr. Pulsipher formulates innovative campaigns that have successfully gained visibility for the growing corporation. He attributes his accomplishments to a strong family upbringing, as he was always taught to seek out his goals; Mr. Pulsipher looks forward to continued growth of the Corporation. Established in 1996, Net Designs and Creations, Inc. is a Web solution applications provider and development firm. Employing a technical staff of eight, the Corporation focuses on the creation and formulation of strategic business applications that will increase effectiveness and competitiveness of their clients when utilized. **Career Highlights:** President, Net Desings and Creations, Inc. (1996-Present); Senior Developer/Manager, Data Systems International (1994-96); Senior Developer, Design One (1992-94). **Associations & Accomplishments:** Life Member, Microsoft Developers Network; Life Member, Site Bulders Network; Life Member, National Rifle Association; Microsoft Certified Professional+Internet; MCSD+I. **Education:** C.C.I., Associate's degree in Programming (1999); O.W.A.T.C., Associate's degree in Business. **Personal Information:** Mr. Pulsipher enjoys Internet, hunting and water sports.

Ronald Punako, Jr.

Technician
American Precision Technology
1405 Moonlite Park Road
Hollsopple, PA 15935
rpunako@hotmail.com

7379

Business Information: Mr. Punako possesses an excellent understanding of the technology field. Previously employed as a Technician with American Precision Technology, he is currently enrolled as a full-time student at Mount Aloysius College. Working towards his Bachelor's degree in Computer Science, he is a certified free-lance Web Master and still conducts Web design and content on the side. Highly regarded, Mr. Punako has worked on databases and was responsible for systems installation, software programming and implementation, hardware upgrade and maintenance, customer service, training, and assisting other technicians. His background history also includes stints as Management Information Systems Specialist at Johnstown Corporation and Web Master with Lee Regional Hospital. Ambitious about sharing in the success of the information technology field, Mr. Punako plans to establish himself in the Internet field, specializing in client server work. Holding a 4.0 GPA at Mount Aloysius College and attributing his success to his overwhelming curiosity, he is constantly challenging himself of find out how much better he can become. **Career Highlights:** Technician, American Precision Technology (1998-2000); Management Information Systems Specialist, Johnstown Corporation (1997-98); Web Master/Intern, Lee Regional Hospital (1997). **Associations & Accomplishments:** A+ Certified Technician; Freelance Web Master. **Education:** Mount Aloysius College, Bachelor's degree in Computer Science (In Progress); CCACC, A.S. (1997). **Personal Information:** Mr. Punako enjoys weight lifting, reading and semi-pro football.

Fang Qian

Senior Software Engineer
OPTIMUS Corporation
8601 Gerogia Avenue, Suite 700
Silver Spring, MD 20910
(301) 585-7075
flora_qian@hotmail.com

7379

Business Information: A successful, 11 year veteran of the information technology field, Ms. Qian serves as the Senior Software Engineer of OPTIMUS Corporation. A technical lead and key member of the Corporation's Research and Development division, she provides oversight and management of high-tech projects. Possessing systems and software expertise, Ms. Qian coordinates and works closely with the U.S. govenment on all aspects of high-tech products, telecommunications, and information systems. An accomplished professional, she currently has two patents pending. Citing her strong interests and challenges in technology, she plans on continuing to work in the advanced research technology area. Her success reflects her ability to tackle these challenges and deliver results. The OPTIMUS Corporation provides its clientele with consulting services and research and development in telecommunications and information technology. With a reported annual sales of $30 million, the Corporation provides cutting edge services to its clients. Presently employing 100 professional and technical staff, OPTIMUS is headquartered in Silver Spring, Maryland. **Career Highlights:** Senior Software Engineer, OPTIMUS Corporation (1989-Present); Technical Staff Member, Telogy Networks (1996-97); Webmaster/System Engineer, Hamilton Securities Group (1996). **Associations & Accomplishments:** Institute of Electrical and Electronics Engineers; Association of Computing Machinery; Accoustical Society of America; Biomedical Engineering Society. **Education:** Drexel University, M.S. in Biomedical Engineering (1995).

Robert A. Quinn

Network Administrator
Vertek Corporation
330 Shore Drive, Apartment F18
Highlands, NJ 07732
(908) 464-8400
rob@vertekcorp.com

7379

Business Information: As Network Administrator of Vertek Corporation, Mr. Quinn oversees a variety of technical operations on a daily basis. Responsible for the network located at Vertek's executive office, he utilizes his education and practical work experience to conduct accurate appraisals of current systems. By gaining this insight, Mr. Quinn is able to purchase needed hardware and/or software that will fulfill the specific needs of clients' systems thereby maximizing all available resources. He is responsible for the design and construction of the company's intercom paging network. Mr. Quinn is shifting his career focus to network consulting, keeping pace with today's progressive society. He attributes his success to his foresight and continued education. His advice is, "Start at a small company, because you get a broad area of expertise." Headquartered in Murray Hill, New Jersey, the Vertek Corporation provides technical consultancy for business and networking issues. Employing 300 people throughout the Eastern region of the United States, the Company strives to formulate novel solutions and operating procedures for an array of Fortune 500 businesses. Established in 1988, the Company's annual revenues exceed $20 million and continue to grow as reputation of quality spread throughout the industry. **Career Highlights:** Network Administrator, Vertek Corporation (1997-Present). **Associations & Accomplishments:** Microsoft Certified Systems Engineer and Internet; Cisco Certified Network Associate. **Education:** Seton Hall University: M.B.A. in Management (In Progress), B.S. in Management Information Systems (1998). **Personal Information:** Mr. Quinn enjoys scuba diving.

Rajesh Suresh Raikar

Project Manager
Whalen & Company
3675 Mount Diablo Boulevard, #360
Lafayette, CA 94549
(925) 283-7700
rajeshraikar@unforgettable.com

7379

Business Information: Functioning in the role of Project Manager, Mr. Raikar utilizes years of education and experience to execute a multitude of tasks with ease. Performing market analysis and construction management, he distinguishes the most cost efficient methods for project completion. Mr. Raikar is also a software designer for the Company. Before joining the Company, he assertively served as Research Assistant with the Texas Transportation Institute. As an experienced, seven year technology professional, he coordinates resources and schedules, oversees time lines and assignments, and calculates and manages project budgets. Mr. Raikar attributes his professional success to his academics and his ability to quickly grasp new concepts and systems design methodologies. This success reflects his ability to build teams with synergy, think out-of-the-box, and take on new challenges and responsibilities. "You have to keep yourself open to all kinds of information and get a feel of how the end users use it," is cited as Mr. Raikar's advice. Founded in 1985, Whalen & Company is a consulting firm for computer software. With more than 210 employees, the Company is an international force in the market. With operations in three countries, the Company has 25 offices world wide. Whalen & Company designs and implements software systems for Fortune 500 companies. **Career Highlights:** Project Manager, Whalen & Company (1995-Present); Research Assistant, Texas Transportation Institute (1993-95). **Education:** Texas A&M University, M.S. (1995); G.I.T., Bachelor's degree in Civil Engineering (1990). **Personal Information:** Married to Radmika in 1997. Mr. Raikar enjoys soccer, cricket, drawing and computer animation.

Amie J. Ramczyk

Computer Programmer/Consultant
System Request Consultants
8626 Greenway Boulevard, Apartment 203
Middletown, WI 53562
(608) 836-7756
ramczyk@sysrg.com

7379

Business Information: As Computer Programmer and Consultant for System Request Consultants, Ms. Ramczyk executes technical consultation for clients via in-house network support. In her capacity, she meets with clients, determines their programming needs, and develops custom applications to suit their needs. Ms. Ramczyk also performs diagnostic testing, constructs coding applications, and performs program maintenance. Highly regarded, she possesses superior talents and an excellent understanding of technology. By continually staying alert to new techniques, opportunities, and technological advancements, Ms. Ramczyk is staying at the forefront in her field, thereby ensuring the Company's longevity as well as her personal occupational success. System Request Consultants is an independent computer consulting agency serving the local corporate community of Middleton, Wisconsin. Established in 1990, System Request Consultants currently employs seven highly skilled technicians who provides clients with premium online e-commerce support, programming, and on-site systems analysis for a multitude of applications. Specializing in new media, the Company also develops comprehensive state of the art software and is dedicated to providing new technology consultation around the clock. **Career Highlights:** Computer Programmer/Consultant, System Request Consultants (1998-Present). **Associations & Accomplishments:** Big Brothers/Big Sisters Program; University of Wixconsin Alumni Association of Oshkosh. **Education:** University of Wisconsin at Oshkosh, Bachelor's degree in Information Technology and Finance (1997). **Personal Information:** Ms. Ramczyk enjoys running, rollerblading, weight training, horses and swimming.

John Ranalli

President
Computer-Information Services Consulting
7100 Kinsella Court
Wilmington, NC 28409
(910) 343-4656
Fax: (910) 793-9460
ranallij@mindspring.com

7379

Business Information: Functioning in the role of President of Computer-Information Services Consulting, Mr. Ranalli works primarily with nonprofit organizations. He determines the overall strategic direction and formulates business and marketing plans. As a 29 year professional, Mr. Ranalli assists organizations in obtaining grant funding, offers workshops, and reaches out to help children who have poor access to technological resources. Prior to starting up Computer-Information Services Consulting, he served as Vocation Director and Executive Director with the Diocese of Raleigh. Mr. Ranalli also works with Communities That Care and applies 12 years of technical knowledge and expertise in an effort to help people. His future goals include offering services through the Internet, designing a Web page to offer tips, and to explore e-commerce to offer computer components and supplies. Mr. Ranalli's success reflects his ability to think out-of-the-box and take on new challenges and responsibilities. Established in 1999, Computer-Information Services Consulting offers a variety of services to companies and nonprofit organizations along the East Coast and mid United States. The Company builds and sells computers, offers software training, and performs group facilitation and strategic planning. **Career Highlights:** President, Computer-Information Services Consulting (1999-Present); Program Coordinator, Communities That Care (1998-Present); Diocese of Raleigh: Vocation Director(1989-99), Executive Director (1986-90). **Associations & Accomplishments:** Co-Chair, Teen Court Program Development; Steering Committee, Teen Leadership Experience; Committee Member, Parish Nurse Program; Committee Member, Collaborative Community Assistance Network. **Education:** University of Notre Dame, M.Div. (1982); Boston College, M.Ed. (1976); Manhattan College, Bachelor's degree in Mechanical Engineering (1970). **Personal Information:** Married to Marie Elena in 1998. Three children: Thomas, Patrick, and Laura. Mr. Ranalli enjoys gardening, music, exercise, sports and movies.

Shashank Rastogi

Senior Consultant
Open Systems
30 Newport Parkway, Apartment 905
Jersey City, NJ 07310
(201) 896-7445
srastogi@sbi.com

7379

Business Information: As Senior Consultant of Open Systems, Mr. Rastogi also serves as the Company's lead consultant for design and development of state-of-the-art information technology systems. Utilizing over eight years of business savvy and technical expertise, he develops leading edge, real-time systems for bond trading. Mr. Rastogi oversees all employees and ongoing projects and works with clients, while currently working to create an online real-time indexing system. He has been recognized by Wall Street Technology for a high yeild pricing engine he is proud to have developed. Attributing his success to academics, Mr. Rastogi's future aspirations include growing in the area of technology consulting. Established in 1990, Open Systems operates as a international consulting firm. Located in New York, the Company focuses primarily on developing cutting edge distributed global systems for the financial industry. Presently, Open Systems employs a 200 professional, technical, and administrative support staff who help generate revenues in excess of $35 million annually. **Career Highlights:** Senior Consultant, Open Systems (1997-Present); Assistant Vice President, Deutsche Bank (1996-97); Lead Architect, Office of the Future (1995-96). **Associations & Accomplishments:** Institute of Electrical and Electronics Engineers; Association of Computing Machinery. **Education:** BITS Pilani, India, M.S. in Microelectronics (1992). **Personal Information:** Married to Ritu Gupta in 1998.

Bud Ratliff, MCSE, MCP+I, MCT

Technology Consultant
Koinonia Computing
P.O. Box 4184
Midway, KY 40347
(502) 868-4039
Fax: (502) 808-2008
bratliff@gate.net

7379

Business Information: Mr. Ratliff is the Lexington, Kentucky manager for Koinonia Computing, a Microsoft Solution Provider based in Louisville, Kentucky. He provides project management, technology planning, support, and consulting services to enterprise customers. As a Microsoft Certified Trainer (MCT), he also trains students to become Microsoft Certified Systems Engineers (MCSE). Mr. Ratliff began his career as an English teacher who used technology to enhance learning; he then went on to provide computer-related support for over 1,700 employees. Having recently completed the Year 2000 remediation for Toyota Motor Manufacturing North America's 3,300 personal computer systems at four geographical dispersed sites, Mr. Ratliff is now implementing Office 2000 and Windows 2000 for those same sites. He plans to obtain his Project Management Professional certification from PMI this year, as well as complete the new Microsoft MCSE 2000 certification. Koinonia, known for its relationship-based consulting practices, and award-winning application design services recently merged with Cotton & Allen to provide a more comprehensive range of services to its clients, including business process planning and financial consulting. Having begun operations in 1986, Koinonia employs more than 40 consultants to provide quality service at reasonable rates. **Career Highlights:** Technology Consultant, Koinonia Computing (1998-Present); Procurement/Support Specialist (1996-98); Instructor of English, Asbury College (1995-96). **Associations & Accomplishments:** Vice President of Public Relations, Toastmaster of the Bluegrass; Project Management Institute; Phi Kappa Delta, International Speech Society. **Education:** Asbury College, B.S. in English Education (1991); University of Kentucky, Masters Program in English Literature. **Personal Information:** Married to Fran in 1994. Mr. Ratliff enjoys fencing, playing guitar in a local band and the history of frontier Kentucky.

Tony Ray

Owner
ARay Computer Services
P.O. Box 429405
Cincinnati, OH 45242
(513) 791-5155
Fax: (513) 791-5155
www.aray.com
aray@aray.com

7379

Business Information: With over 20 years of experience in his field, Mr. Ray is the Owner of ARay Computer Services, performing as Consultant and Business Administrator. He controls all daily activities from inventory purchases to consulting contract negotiation. Mr. Ray is planning to incorporate his Business and continue operations until his retirement. ARay Computer Services provides business, management, and computer consulting, as well as the sale, implementation, service, and system integration of software applications. Established in 1994, the Cincinnati, Ohio based Company reports estimated annual revenue of $1 million. **Career Highlights:** Owner, ARay Computer Services (1994-Present); Management Information Systems Manager, Johnson Electric (1993-94); Business Analyst, O&S (1991-93); Consultant/Business Analyst, Dataflow (1985-91). **Associations & Accomplishments:** Certified Professional Consultant - International Guild of Professional Consultants; National Consultants Network; Certified Management Consultant - International Society of Speakers, Authors, and Consultants. **Education:** West Valley Junior College, A.S. in Accounting (1976). **Personal Information:** Married to Margory in 1990. Five children: Kristen, Keith, Michael, Daniel, and Sean. Mr. Ray enjoys fishing and baseball.

Jagan M. Reddy

President
Proficient Software Expo Consulting Inc.
15 Hyacinth Drive, Apartment 1-L
Fords, NJ 08863
(908) 284-1224
reddyj@hotmail.com

7379

Business Information: Mr. Reddy holds the demanding position of President at Proficient Software Expo Consulting Inc. He oversees all operations ensuring all projects operate within the framework of the Corporation's overall plan. A successful professional, he also assists clients on various projects, creating software and overseeing the entire project from start to finish. Mr. Reddy formulates policies and procedures, develops goals and objectives, implements strategic goals, and directs the activities of individual departments. Dedicated to the success of the Corporation, he keep abreast on new developments in the field and reads current literature on changing technology. Mr. Reddy's fundamental objective is to assist Proficient Software Expo Consulting Inc. in its growth, development, and expansion into new markets. Proficient Software Expo Consulting Inc. is a consulting firm located in Fords, New Jersey. The Corporation, with the assistance of a highly qualified and trained staff, creates and designs software. **Career Highlights:** President, Proficient Software Expo Consulting Inc. (1999-Present); Cost Center Manager, Software Resources (1998-99); Managerial Lead Consultant, Mastech (1995); Software Engineer, INROSYS, India (1993). **Education:** University: M.A. (1993), Bachelor's degree in Technology. **Personal Information:** Married to Vasudha in 1997. One child: Abhinav. Mr. Reddy enjoys reading.

Julie A. Rediker

GIS Technical Trainer
Senior Geographic Information Systems Trainer
5 East Greenway Plaza, Suite 1700
Houston, TX 77046-0507
(713) 627-7878
Fax: (713) 627-7888
julile.rediker@idea.com

7379

Business Information: Serving as Senior Geographic Information Systems Trainer for Idea Integration, Ms. Rediker is responsible for providing technical training for geographic information systems. Utilizing past experience as a GIS specialist and GIS analyst, Ms. Rediker skillfully conducts research of new technology and develops up-to-date GIS curriculum for Idea Integration. Ms. Rediker also oversees the mobile technical support division for the Company, traveling to clients for on-site course instruction. Continually striving for maximum effectiveness, Ms. Rediker has current plans to obtain her Master's degree in geographic information systems, thereby, assisting Idea Integration's plans for e-business expansion and ensuring corporate longevity as well as her personal occupational success. Headquartered in Jacksonville, Florida, Idea Integration is a leader in providing end-to-end e-business solutions. Specializing in new media solutions, the Company provides comprehensive state-of-the-art software and new technology solutions. Idea Integration is comprised of 2,000 trained technicians who are instrumental in the Company's rapid growth and high net yields. With the growing demand for information technology consultation and round-the-clock network support, Idea Integration is one of the fastest growing firms in the industry, and is leading the globe to soaring heights in new media solutions. **Career Highlights:** Senior Geographic Information Systems Trainer, Idea Integration (1998-Present); Geographic Information Systems Specialist, Post, Buckley Schuh & Jernigan (1996-98); Geographic Information Systems Analyst, County of Volusia (1994-96); Digital Cartographer, American Automobile Association (1990-94). **Associations & Accomplishments:** International Cartographic Honor Society; Gamma Theta Upsilon, Cartographic Honor Society; American Society of Training and Development; Geospatial Information & Technology Association; Petroleum Users Group. **Education:** University of Idaho: B.S. in Geography (1990), B.S. in Cartography (1990); Idaho State University, A.A. in Graphic Arts. **Personal Information:** Ms. Rediker enjoys sports, WNBA, reading and collecting WNBA trading cards.

Donald W. Rice, Jr.

Owner/President
Next Generation Ideas
115 Forest Edge Drive
Raleigh, NC 27606
(919) 303-3693
Fax: (919) 303-3693
drice@nextgenideas.com

7379

Business Information: Leading Next Generation Ideas to establishing high standards of excellence for other individuals in the industry as President and Owner, Mr. Rice focuses on maintaining a high status within the field of information technology. Overseeing basic operations of the Company, he implements specific procedures and policies ensuring client and profit increase, and a continuing improvement of efficiency and productivity. Maintaining an organized annual budget, Mr. Rice initiates necessary purchases of materials and the direction of funds within budgetary guidelines. Turning potential into action through preparation and skilled training, he presides over all administrative aspects. Mr. Rice' goal is to facilitate continued Company growth and geographic expansion of Next Generation Ideas. Founded in 1996, Next Generation Ideas is an established and reputable software integration company with a focus on business e-commerce. Located in Raleigh, North Carolina, the Company employs the skilled services of 1,600 individuals to acquire business, meet with clients, market services, and develop complex software and networking systems. Striving to meet the demands of a growing clientele, the Company incorporates the latest technologies ensuring quality control and efficiency. **Career Highlights:** Owner/President, Next Generation Ideas (2000-Present); Senior Consultant, Answerthink Consulting (1999-00); Independent Contractor, Oxford (1997-99); Quality Analysis Lead, BSG (1995-97). **Associations & Accomplishments:** Phi Beta Sigma; March of Dimes. **Education:** University of North Carolina at Charlotte, B.A. in Computer Science (1995). **Personal Information:** Married to Aretha B. in 1999. Mr. Rice enjoys paintball and basketball.

Thomas P. Roberts

President
Saber Systems & Consulting, Inc.
PO Box 3916
Jackson, MS 39207
(601) 948-8183
Fax: (601) 948-8184
tomroberts@sabersci.com

7379

Business Information: Serving as President, Mr. Roberts is the co-owner and founder of Saber Systems & Consulting, Inc. He manages the daily operations of Saber Systems & Consulting as well as performing software development, management, and implementation for the Corporation's clients. As the Corporation's chief executive, Mr. Roberts determines the overall strategic direction and business contribution of the systems function. Coordinating resources and schedules, overseeing contract negotiations, and taking a lead role in driving products and services to market also fall within the realm of his responsibilities. Demonstrating a love of technology, he taught himself software engineering. His success reflects his ability to think out-of-the-box and take on new challenges. Mr. Roberts hopes to expand the Corporation in the future and be able to devote more time to his first love of software development. Established in 1997, Saber Systems & Consulting, Inc. performs software development and systems consulting for both governmental and commercial clients. The Corporation is already reporting an annual revenue of $700,000 and continues to grow. **Career Highlights:** President, Saber Systems & Consulting, Inc. (1997-Present); Data Resource Manager, AMS, Inc. (1995-97); Software Engineer, Litton Data Systems, Inc. (1991-94); Software Engineer, Syscon Services, Inc. (1989-91); Field Engineer, Raytheon Service Company (1986-89); Weapons Technician, United States Navy (1982-86). **Associations & Accomplishments:** Institute of Electronics and Electrical Engineers; First President, Gulf Coast Oracle User's Group. **Personal Information:** Married to Lori in 1982. Three children: Maslin, Logan, and Madelyn. Mr. Roberts enjoys scuba diving, shooting and writing.

Mark K. Robinson

Vice President
Computer Design & Integration
696 Route 46 West
Teterboro, NJ 07608
(201) 931-1420
Fax: (201) 931-0101
mark_robinson@cdillc.com

7379

Business Information: Mr. Robinson serves as Vice President of Computer Design & Integration or CDI. In his role, he manages the e-services and SUN services division of CDI. Highly regarded in the technology industry, he oversees the design and implementation of Internet/Intranet security and e-commerce solutions. He also delivers SUN and UNIX services solutions to an international clientele. Utilizing 16 years of experience in the information systems field, Mr. Robinson is responsible for advising clients, maintaining vendors relations, writing proposals, and performing security assessments as well as overseeing day-to-day business activities and conducting follow ups to ensure clients are completely satisfied. The highlight of his career is taking the lead role in a government contract dealing with the design and development of tactical security software. Bringing CDI to the forefront in the industry, Mr. Robinson's goals include delivering cutting edge security solutions to Fortune 1000 and 1500 companies. His success is attributed to doing a little more than the average and surrounding himself with successful people. CDI is a design and integration technology company. The Company engages in reselling Sun Microsystems and Hewlett-Packard equipment, and providing computer consulting services in the area of information security network infrastructures. Established in 19995, CDI presently employs a professional staff of 65 experts who help generate revenues in excess of $40 million annually. CDI nurtures an international presence from one corporate office located in Teterboro, New Jersey. **Career Highlights:** Vice President, Computer Design & Integration (1999-Present); Vice President, Citigroup, N.A., (1998-99); Senior Network and Information Security Engineer, Viacom International (1997-98); Consultant, SIAC (1996-97). **Personal Information:** Mr. Robinson enjoys bowling, reading, listening to jazz, dancing and time with his children.

Wesley D. Roe

President/Owner
Roetech Services
6325 Fairview Avenue
Downers Grove, IL 60516-3011
(630) 728-9685

7379

Business Information: As President and Owner of Roetech Services, Mr. Roe is involved in every aspect of operations. His duties are vast and include such tasks as recruitment, procurement approval, and payroll audit. Demonstrating extensive knowledge and exceptional skill of the industry, he works with staff members to develop innovative operational procuedures. Working closely with clients, Mr. Roe is able to effectively evaluate their needs, then offer custom designed solutions that incorporate available services and products. Enjoying the challenges of his position, Mr. Roe intends to continue in his current role as he initiates impressive growth plans that include expansion of services. Located in Downers Grove, Illinois, Roetech Services is recognized throughout the professional community as a leading provider of information technology recruiting services and consulting. Established in 1991, the Company employs three trained people to assist in various daily activities, such as staffing assessments for clients. **Career Highlights:** President/Owner, Roetech Services (1991-Present); Recruiting Consultant, Motorola (1999); Recruiting Consultant, Winstar Telecommunications (1999); Recruiting Consultant, Sybase, Inc. (1998). **Education:** Prairie State College, A.A.S. (1990); Dale Carnegie Certificate; Institute for Technical and Management Training, three Certificates. **Personal Information:** Married to Dawn in 1992. Mr. Roe enjoys computing, photography and electronics.

James R. Rogers

Infosec Analyst
Averstar
1 Overcash Avenue, Letterkenny Army Depot
Chambersburg, PA 17201-4122
(717) 267-8114
russr@planetcable.net

7379

Business Information: Mr. Rogers is Infosec Analyst for Averstar, formerly Intermetrics. He is responsible for performing penetration test and security vulnerability resolution on computer networks for the Department of Defense and its military departments. Before joining Averstar, Mr. Rogers served as a Systems Administrator for SAIC. His solid background history also includes a stint with the United States Air Force as Arabic Linguist and Systems Administrator. With firm academic ties and extensive occupational experience, he is able to focus on analyzing, making assessments, and designing cutting edge solutions to ensure the security and integrity of network environments. As a valuable member of a team of 10 skilled infosecurity analysts, Mr. Rogers enjoys working with computers. He credits his father, who gave him a computer while he was in the fifth grade, for his success. Eventually attaining the role of Director of Development serves as one of his future endeavors. A public company, Averstar engages in research and development of information technology security systems. International in scope, the Company's corporate headquarters is located in Burlington, Massachusetts. Presently, Averstar employs a highly qualified workforce of more than 2,000 professional, technical, and support personnel. **Career Highlights:** Infosec Analyst, Averstar (formerly Intermetrics) (1998-Present); Systems Administrator, SAIC (1997-98); Arabic Linguist/Systems Administrator, United States Air Force (1992-97). **Associations & Accomplishments:** Ducktank Computer Security; DefCon Planning Committee; The Planetary Society. **Education:** University of Maryland: M.S. in Information Resource Management (In Progress), B.S. in Computer Science (1995); Community College of the Air Force, A.S. in Applied Communications Technology (1995). **Personal Information:** Married to April in 1991. One child: Kynda. Mr. Rogers enjoys programming, reading and spending time with his family.

James Rogers

Manager of Global Technical Solutions
Teletech Services
2130 North Hollywood Way
Burbank, CA 91505-1522
(303) 894-4006
Fax: (818) 295-6246
jrogers@teleteck.com

7379

Business Information: As Manager of Global Technical Solutions for Teletech Services, Mr. Rogers oversees a number of duties on behalf of the Company. He provides technical services to personnel and customer service representatives. Possessing an excellent understanding of technology, he ensures employee productivity through the implementation of policies and procedures that encourage optimum performance. With a notable ability to understand complex problems and communicate solutions to clients and internal staff, Mr. Rogers is a vital part of the Company's global success. The most rewarding aspect of his career is participating in networking and migration as well as meeting project time lines. In the future, his goals are to facilitate continued Company growth and geographic expansion, and obtain a higher management position within the Company's corporate structure. Teletech Services is a leading provider of integrated, e-commerce enabled customer management solutions for global organizations predominatntly in the telecommunications, financial services, technology, and transportation industries. Teletech operates more than 11,900 state-of-the-art customer interaction center workstations and employs more than 16,300 people in nine countries. Presently, the Company reports annual income of more than $1 billion. **Career Highlights:** Teletech Services: Manager of Gloal Technical Solutions (1999-Present), Application Desktop Management Supervisor (1999-99), Network Engineer (1996-99). **Associations & Accomplishments:** Los Angeles Netware User Group. **Education:** University of Phoenix (Currently Attending); Barstow Community College, A.S.in Computer Science; The Learning Center, Certified Novell Engineer; Anet Education Center, CLP. **Personal Information:** Mr. Rogers enjoys bicycling, aquarist, travel and PC gaming.

Thomas G. Rogillio II

Senior Information Developer
Candle Corporation
366 West California Avenue, Apartment 7
Glendale, CA 91203
(310) 727-4849
Fax: (818) 500-7721
tgr2@pacbell.net

7379

Business Information: As Senior Information Developer of Candle Corporation, Mr. Rogillio is the lead technical writer and editor. In this position, he takes abstract data and numbers and spins it into coherent sentences for memos and manuals. As an editor, he supervises a team of eight writers who remains true to science and the clarity of good prose. Most of Mr. Rogillio's work has centered on middle wear systems and software controlling communications. As for the future, he plans to finish his current project and assume new duties. Success, he asserts, is the final product of his innate curiosity, as well as his leadership ability to enhance systems software by thinking outside the box and deliver results and aggressively take on new challenges. "Never stop asking questions, never assume," is cited as Mr. Rogillio's advice. Part of the booming technology industry, Candle Corporation engages in the development of systems management and automation software for a full line of computers. On the basic Windows-PC platform, the Corporation has endeavored to improve workstations, as well as the AS 400 mini-computer. With headquarters in California, Candle Corporation has become an transnational corporation. Utilizing the efforts of 1,900 people, the Corporation was founded in 1977. Since that year, the Corporation has grown to the point where it now grosses an estimated annual revenue of $360 million. **Career Highlights:** Senior Information Developer, Candle Corporation (1995-Present); Senior Technical Specialist, Dassault Systems (1984-95); Software Analyst, Louisiana State University (1977-84). **Education:** Louisiana State University: M.S. (1984), B.S. (1976). **Personal Information:** Mr. Rogillio enjoys theater, AIDS support and service.

Edward John Roman

Development Manager
Industri-Matematik North American Operations, Inc.
305 Fellowship Road
Mount Laurel, NJ 08054
(856) 793-3294
Fax: (856) 793-4401
edro@im.se

7379

Business Information: Drawing from years of extensive academic and occupational experience in the industry, Mr. Roman joined Industri-Matematik North American Operations Inc. as Advisory Consultant in 1995. Now serving as Development Manager, he manages and directs a team of business analysts and software engineers working on client projects to provide custom software solutions. In the future, he would like to help the Corporation to move into the e-commerce arena. Attributing his success to his persistence and patience, Mr. Roman's high career points have been providing expertise to customers to become more effective and bringing larger customers into the new Information Technology Age. Established in 1967, Industri-Matematik North American Operations Inc. provides high performance fulfillment and customer service software solutions for e-commerce. The Corporation is a sales and service organization providing software for wholesalers, retailers, manufacturers, and logistics. Employing 700 individuals and reporting annual sales of $90 million, the Corporation assists clients execute supply chains and manage customer relations and e-commerce fulfillments. **Career Highlights:** Industri-Matematik North American Operations, Inc.: Development Manager (1999-Present), Advisory Consultant (1995-99); Consultant, Unisys Corporation (1980-95). **Associations & Accomplishments:** American Production and Inventory Control Society; Certified Production Inventory Management. **Education:** Temple University: M.B.A. (1986), B.A. in Psychology (1979). **Personal Information:** Married to Kathy in 1987. One child: Tyler. Mr. Roman enjoys fishing, golf and family fun.

Antonio Romano

Research Director
IDC (International Data Corporation)
Via Gallarate 28
Milan, Italy 20151
+39 228457340
Fax: +39 228457333
aromano@idc.com

7379

Business Information: Mr. Romano assertively serves in the role of Research Director at IDC or International Data Corporation. He is responsible for oversight and management of IDC's research activities in Europe's southern region, including coordinating a multinational team of analysis. Before joining IDC as Information Technology Research Manager in 1996, Mr. Romano served as IT&TLC Research Manager for GFK Italy and Senior Consultant with Nomos Ricerca Italy. As a 13 year technology professional with an established record of delivering results, he plans and oversees the strategic direction and business contributions of the information systems functions. Overseeing and coordinating resources, schedules, and assignments and calculating and managing the fiscal year budget also fall within the purview of his functions. Mr. Romano's success as a leader reflects his ability to build and develop strong teams with synergy and technical strength, as well as take on new challenges and responsibilities. IDC, headquartered in Boston, Massachusetts, is the world's leading provider of market analysis and consulting to information technology and telecommunications vendors. The Italian subsidiary, established in Milan in 1986, presently employs a work force of more than 30 professional and technical experts who help generate revenues in excess of $8 million annually. **Career Highlights:** Research Director, IDC (1998-Present); Information Technology and TLC Research Manager, GFK Italy (1998); Information Technology Research Manager, IDC Italy (1996); Senior Consultant, Nomos Ricerca (1993). **Personal Information:** Married to Valeria Vicentini in 1999. Mr. Romano enjoys writing books on economy and philosophy.

Sasan Rostami

Vice President of Hardware Development
BITCOM Inc.
20010 Century Boulevard, Suite 101
Germantown, MD 20874-1118
(301) 916-9300
Fax: (301) 916-9325
rostami@bitcom.com

7379

Business Information: Serving in the role of Vice President of Hardware Development at BITCOM Inc., Ms. Rostami oversees all aspects of hardware engineering and development. She is responsible for staffing all projects, recruiting personnel, and supervising corporate administration. A savvy, 16 year professional in the technology field, Ms. Rostami's hands on management style ensures crucial technical details are not overlooked. Working closely with her clients, she is directly invovled in creating new technological solutions, affecting direct TV and PCs operations. Her future endeavors include developing an advanced telecommunications market voice IP/network and moving towards an optical communication network. Ms. Rostami's favorite credo is "experience and background success equals education." Her success reflects her ability to think outside the box, deliver results, and take on new challenges. A national technology company, BITCOM Inc. engages in engineering consulting within the communications area. Specializing in telecommunications and datacommunications, the Corporation provides cutting edge technology on wireless communication, Internet services and satellite systems. Established in 1997, BITCOM presently employs a staff of 15 professional and technical experts. **Career Highlights:** Vice President of Hardware Development, BITCOM Inc. (1998-Present); Principal Engineer, Hughes Network Systems (1994-98); Member of Technical Staff (I, II, III, Senior), HNS (1984-94). **Associations & Accomplishments:** Institute of Electrical and Electronics Engineers Communications Society; Etta Kappa Nu Engineering Society; Mu Epsilon Mathematics Society. **Education:** George Washington University: Ph.D. (In Progress), M.S. in Electrical Engineering (1991); University of Texas at Austin, B.S. in Electrical Engineering (1984). **Personal Information:** Married in 1995. Ms. Rostami enjoys reading books and sports.

Randall E. Rotz

Vice President/Chief Financial Officer
Innernet, Inc.
P.O. Box 21
Shady Grove, PA 17256-0021
(717) 593-5053
rerotz@innernet.net

7379

Business Information: Demonstrating extensive technical knowledge in his role as Vice President and Chief Executive Officer of Innernet, Inc., Mr. Rotz guides staff members through the completion of daily activities. Handling tasks that range from procurement approval to investment research, he oversees all financial aspects of the Corporation to ensure profitability and maximization of benefits of resources. Incorporating experience gained throughout his 31-year career in the industry into the operations of the Corporation, Mr. Rotz is able to develop innovative business strategies as he presents a clear model of customer satisfaction to his staff. An entrepreneur by nature, Mr. Rotz is also one of the founders of Sites-Unlimited.com, a Web site development company that offers services to businesses in the tri-state area. Keeping his personal goals consistent with the completion of corporate objectives, Mr. Rotz continues to provide superior customer service as he supports the growth and expansion of both Innernet, Inc. and Sites-Unlimited.com. Innernet, Inc. is an Internet service provider in Chambersburg, Pennsylvania. Serving more than 8,500 residents of nine different counties, the Corporation provides online training and assistance to every customer. **Career Highlights:** Vice President/Chief Financial Officer, Innernet, Inc. (2000-Present); Grove Worldwide: Director, Information Technology (1996-2000), Technical Support Manager (1992-96), Application Programs Manager (1989-92); Project Leader (1986-89). **Education:** Wilson College: B.A. in Business and Economics (1997), A.A. in Computer Information Systems (1968). **Personal Information:** Married to Nancy B. in 1970. Two children: Nathan A. and Angela N.

Richard Carl Rowe, Jr.

Consultant
Ajilon
4600 Mason Dale Court
Richmond, VA 23234
(804) 285-1751

7379

Business Information: As a Consultant for Ajilon, Mr. Rowe designs computerized business systems to coordinate work flows and facilitate operations. He analyzes codes and writes technical programs utilized in software development. Mr. Rowe also travels to client offices, performing need analyses, recommending and implementing upgrades, servicing equipment, and conducting user training classes. Mr. Rowe plans to become an independent consultant. Headquartered in Richmond, Virginia, Ajilon specializes in computer systems consulting, management, and service as well as the customization of software and hardware. The Firm also manufactures applications and offers auditing and processing. **Career Highlights:** Consultant, Ajilon (1996-Present); Registry Consultant, America's Registry (1991-Present); Independent Consultant, Regional Computer Resources (1977-91). **Associations & Accomplishments:** Association of Information and Technology Professionals; Promise Keepers; Omega Psi Phi Fraternity; St. John Baptist Church. **Education:** Purdue University, B.S. (1977). **Personal Information:** Married to Deborah in 1991. Four children: Richard III, Raoul, Deleyse, and Renard. Mr. Rowe enjoys fishing, working out, Bible study and gospel singing.

Albert E. Ruehli

Research Staff Member
IBM Thomas J. Watson Research Center
P.O. Box 218
Yorktown Heights, NY 10598-0218
(914) 945-1592
Fax: (914) 945-4244
ruehli@us.ibm.com

7379

Business Information: As Research Staff Member of IBM's Thomas J. Watson Research Center, Dr. Ruehli focuses on interconnectivity modeling issues. His research applies to chip and circuit packaging. Among the concerns addressed in Dr. Ruehli's work are the mathematical algorithms for scientific applications. He serves as a team leader within his department and facilitates group-based efforts on project goals. Dr. Ruehli has great appreciation for the nature of the work performed at the Research Center, and plans to remain with the organization to model complex chips, and to continue learning as that work progresses. It is his belief that in order to succeed and remain at the top in your field, you must have a real interest in the work you do and you must work hard. The IBM Thomas J. Watson Research Center in Yorktown Heights, New York is the corporate facility dedicated to developing new techniques. The focus of the TJW research team is to overcome the electromagnetic problems inherent to most computer hardware structures. More than 1,000 researchers and support staff are employed at the facility. The IBM Corporation, headquartered in Armonk, New York, is an international marketer of computers and other business machines with more than 270,000 employees worldwide. **Career Highlights:** Research Staff Member, IBM Thomas J. Watson Research Center (1963-Present). **Associations & Accomplishments:** Fellow, Institute of Electronics and Electrical Engineers; SIAM. **Education:** University of Vermont, Ph.D. (1972). **Personal Information:** Married to Robin in 1983. Dr. Ruehli enjoys skiing. He also reads numerous trade publications, and attends many conferences and seminars to learn as much about his industry as possible.

Frank Russello, Jr.

President/Owner
Habanero Software
86 Yates Street
West Haven, CT 06516
(203) 389-8066

7379

Business Information: As President of Habanero Software, Mr. Russello establishes the Firm's direction and serves as the lead technical architect. He participates in the physical development of technology products as well as provides administration for the Firm's daily operations. Mr. Russello enjoys his career and plans to continue creating innovative products for the world's businesses. Habanero Software performs computer software development and consulting. Headquartered in West Haven, Connecticut, the Firm has been providing solutions to large companies for three years and has recently begun processing software for retail applications. **Career Highlights:** President/Owner, Habanero Software (1994-Present); Manager, Coopers and Lybrand (1991-94); Programmer, Connecticut Department of Transportation (1988-91). **Education:** University of New Haven, A.S. (1989). **Personal Information:** Mr. Russello enjoys chess, photography, sailing, football and golf.

Eric Rutter

Internet Sales Consultant
Comcast Telecommunications
519 Columbia Boulevard
Cherry Hill, NJ 08002-1629
(610) 491-8844
ericrutter@aol.com

7379

Business Information: Mr. Rutter functions in the role of Internet Sales Consultant for Comcast Telecommunications. He works closely with clients and systems management to analyze, specify, and design cutting edge frame relay, WAN, and Internet solutions, as well as VPN Internet applications. In the future, Mr. Rutter hopes to take advantage of new technologies to capture a large portion of the technology market, and open a private consultancy where he can help small start up companies network their offices. His career highlights include developing a 9-system cable operation in Romania as a Partner with Rom Telecom; and helping take Poland Cablevision from being a back-end to a financial end operation. Mr. Rutter's success reflects his ability to think outside the box, produce results, and aggressively take on new challenges. Comcast Telecommunications is affiliated with Comcast International. The Company hosts a staff of 200 telecommunications experts that are able to provide information technology consulting to businesses in New Jersey. Taking advantage of the booming computer era, the Company provides Internet development, business hardware, and Internet solutions. **Career Highlights:** Internet Sales Consultant, Comcast Telecommunications (1998-Present); Eastern Division Start-up Manager, Communications Resources, Inc. (1996-98); Chief Accountant, 3R Associates, Inc. (1993-96). **Education:** University of Pennsylvania (Currently Attending); Bucknell University, B.A. (1993). **Personal Information:** Married to Rebecca in 1998. Mr. Rutter enjoys technology.

Robert Saerens

Managing Partner/Information Technology Consultant
Jovenko
Nieuwelaan 39A
Meise, Belgium 1860
+32 22704716
Fax: +32 22704722
robert.saernens@jovenko.com

7379

Business Information: Serving as Managing Partner and Information Technology Consultant of Jovenko, Mr. Saerens oversees and directs all day-to-day activities on behalf of the Company. A family owned business, he took the opportunity to start the Company because he knew he had capability and determination of making it on his own. Relying on his extensive training and business and technology expertise, he focuses on banks and insurance companies, suggesting solutions to information technology problems. Possessing rich talents and an excellent understanding of technology, Mr. Saerens first collects, reviews, and analyzes information, and then makes recommendations and often assists in the implementation of his proposal. Proud of the fact that he has been recognized for his contribution to Windows 2000 Architecture by being given an award by Microsoft, Mr. Saerens plans for the future include remaining in his highly respected position and continuing to facilitate expansion plans for the Company. Established in 1998, Jovenko engages in information technology consulting. An independent organization, the Company consists of two partners providing the latest in technology solutions. Located in Meise, Belgium, the Company serves not only regionally, but caters to international clients as well. **Career Highlights:** Managing Partner/Information Technology Consultant, Jovenko (1998-Present); Business Development Manager, Tandem (1994-97); Unisys: Marketing Manager (1993-94), Account Manager (1990-92). **Associations & Accomplishments:** K.V.I.V. Organization of Civil Engineers in Belgium. **Education:** University Gent, degree in Civil Engineering (1982). **Personal Information:** Married to Megskens Karlin in 1983. Three children: Steven, Koen, and Jolien. Mr. Saerens enjoys young soccer players. Mr. Saerens enjoys presiding over the local Young Soccer Players Association.

Vanilo Saint-Louis

President
Belimage Communications
783 Hempstead Turnpike
Franklin Square, NY 11010
(516) 355-0200
Fax: (516) 355-0673
vanilo@belimage.com

7379

Business Information: As President of Belimage Communications, Mr. Saint-Louis specializes in computer programming for HCML, Java, and database. He determines the overall strategic direction and vision, as well as business contribution of the information systems function. His current project is a network of television shows for the Internet to ensure quick implementation when the technology becomes readily available to the public. Mr. Saint-Louis also coordinates a portion of the graphic design in the Company. He is proud to be a part of a business remaining above the competition, on the cutting edge of Web casting technology. His goal is to see the growth of the Company in the near future and take the Company public in two to three years. Belimage Communications was established in 1997 to provide Internet technology to a diverse clientele. With a staff of six personnel, the Company specializes in Web and graphic design. Utilizing a multitude of skills, the staff also conducts video recording and editing and creates slogans and jingles for television advertising. With clients in the New England area, Florida, Haiti, France, Australia, and French Islands, the Company is a rapidly expanding service provider in the industry. **Career Highlights:** President, Belimage Communications (1997-Present); Webmaster, DSI Computer Services (1996-97). **Associations & Accomplishments:** Alpha Beta Gamma; International Business Honor Society; Alumni Association; New Jersey Press Association. **Education:** Queens College (1998); Queensborough Community College, A.S.; Essex County College, A.A.S. **Personal Information:** Mr. Saint-Louis enjoys thrilling rides, racquetball and working out.

Michael C. Samoska

Senior Systems Consultant
Micros-to-Mainframes
97 Mill Road
Woodbury, CT 06798
(860) 563-9099
Fax: (860) 563-8397
msamoska@ix.netcom.com

7379

Business Information: Serving as a Senior Systems Consultant for Micros-to-Mainframes, Mr. Samoska works closely with systems management and users, providing detailed technical and analytical advice for systems and process enhancements. In his capacity, he designs cutting-edge LAN and WAN architectures and focuses on emerging technologies and end-to-end solutions and integration. An expert, Mr. Samoska also contacts customers, determining their needs and creating customer programs to meet these needs. In the future, he would like to become a Chief Technology Officer. Established in 1986, Micros-to-Mainframes is a technology solutions provider. This includes design, implementation, and support of LAN/WAN, Windows NT, security solutions, messaging platforms, and Netware. Employing 250 personnel, the Company constructs customer systems for various companies and industries. **Career Highlights:** Senior Systems Consultant, Micros-to-Mainframes (1998-Present); Consultant, MicroAge (1996-98); Senior Systems Engineer, Compucom (1994-96). **Associations & Accomplishments:** United States Marine Corps (1985-89). **Education:** Waterbury State Technical College, A.S. Electrical Engineering (1992); Microsoft Certified Systems Engineer; Cisco Certified Internetworking Expert; CCDA; Certified Novell Engineer; Compaq ASE; IBM PSE; A+ Certification; Citrix Certificaiton. **Personal Information:** Married to Charmaigne in 1992. Two children: Michael Charles and Vania. Mr. Samoska enjoys skiing, mountain biking, golf and running.

Ravi Sathya

Director
Megasoft Consultants
8618 Westwood Center Drive, Suite 300
Vienna, VA 22182
(703) 734-9700
Fax: (703) 734-9799
rs@megasoftus.com

7379

Business Information: As Director, Mr. Sathya oversees the daily operations of the technical departments within Megasoft Consultants. Working closely with his team of 120 people, he utilizes a proactive style of management by incorporating employee feedback into operational procedures. On a regular basis, Mr. Sathya evaluates upcoming projects, then creates a business solution action plan that includes a team of employees specifically chosen for their individual abilities. Utilizing his extensive experience in the industry, Mr. Sathya formulates innovative marketing campaigns to emphasize product features and benefits. A published philosopher, he is recognized for his direct work style and credits success to his diligence and education. Aspiring to advancement within the corporate structure, Mr. Sathya looks forward to implementing procedures that will allow the Company to go public. Established in 1994, Megasoft Consultants offers consulting services for small scale e-commerce firms. Focusing on the lastest technical developments for the industry, the Company provides superior service for Internet based businesses as well. Megasoft Consultants employs over 200 people on an intenational scale with annual sales of over $20 million. **Career Highlights:** Director, Megasoft Consultants (1995-Present); Senior Engineer, MICO/Robert Bosch (1991-95). **Associations & Accomplishments:** Network of South Asian Professionals. **Education:** Bachelor's of Electrical and Electronics Engineering (1990). **Personal Information:** Married. Mr. Sathya enjoys travel, philosophy and classical music.

Steven Savage

Programming Consultant
Advanced Programming Resources
5282 Tamrarack Cirlce East, Apartment D
Columbus, OH 43229
(614) 761-9994
Fax: (614) 761-3397

7379

Business Information: As a Programming Consultant, Mr. Savage creates and implements systems and procedures allowing clients to utilizes technology in more profitable and effective methods. He works directly with clients and tailors programs and Internet capabilities of their systems to specific commercial needs. Advanced Programming Resources is a computer technology systems consulting firm. The Firm specializes in the placement of expert consultants at specific client sites to aid in systems development. Advanced Programming Resources aids its clients in achieving the most profitable use of the information technology and support systems. Advanced Programming currently employs 120 people. **Career Highlights:** Programming Consultant, Advanced Programming Resources (1996–Present); Technical Writer/Webmaster, Developer Systems Inc. (1995–96); Secretary/Developer, Exxcel Contract Management (1994–95); Administrator, Barthelmes-Stevens Inc. (1994). **Associations & Accomplishments:** Mr. Savage has done personal tutoring and individual job counselling. **Education:** The Ohio State University, B.S. (1990). **Personal Information:** Married to Michele in 1995. Mr. Savage enjoys being a Webmaster, history, technology and reading.

Jeffery H. Sawyer, Ph.D.

Chief Executive Officer
The Consultants
305 Winterlochen Road
Raleigh, NC 27603
(919) 819-0431
Fax: (919) 772-4577

7379

Business Information: Serving as the Chief Executive Officer, Dr. Sawyer is involved in all aspects of business operations in The Consultants. His primary responsibility is to fix technology red issues and provide marketing insights to corporate clients' Chief Information Officers. He demonstrates the technologies that are available for their use and helps them to design and implement a system customized for their business needs. Technology has always held a fascination for Dr. Sawyer. Continually striving to give a quality performance for his customers, he cites this and his faith in God as his reason for his success. "If you're not connected to what you are doing, then get connected, take action," he states. Dr. Sawyer is putting into effect strategic business plans to grow and expand The Consultants. He looks forward to tripling the Company's current revenue. The Consultants was first established in 1987 as a computer manufacturer underneath the name of Computer Wholesalers of Raliegh. Since that time, the Company has changed its business direction as well as its name. The Consultants now offers corporate clients executive level consulting services to Chief Information Officers. Current operations employ 12 dedicated individuals and boast $2.7 million in annual earnings. **Career Highlights:** Chief Executive Officer, The Consultants (1986–Present); Vice President, Branch Banking & Trust (1996–99); Consulting Guru, First USA Bank (1994–95); Senior Systems Analyst, MCI (1992–94); Lead Internet Consultant, IBM (1993–95). **Associations & Accomplishments:** IBM Best Team; Certified Systems Engineer; Certified Master of Industry Standard Architecture; Project Management Certified; Inventory Control Management; Apogee Betatester; Microsoft System Builder; US Robotics Excellence Award for System Design and Implementation; Round Table Manager **Education:** University of San Moritz, Ph.D. (1998); Columbia State University, M.S. in Computer Science (1996). **Personal Information:** Dr. Sawyer enjoys tennis and swimming.

Thomas Eric Sawyer

Owner/Consultant
dba Computer Consultant
8717 South 80th East Avenue
Tulsa, OK 74133-4824
(918) 459-8409
Fax: (918) 294-8266
74020.1265@compuserve.com

7379

Business Information: As Owner of dba Computer Consultant, Mr. Sawyer serves in the role of Consultant. He works closely with management and systems users to analyze, specify, and design new solutions to enhance the computer's power. Concurrently, he also serves as a Systems Administrator with the Oklahoma Air National Guard responsible for maintaining the systems infrastructure's functionality and operational status. Mr. Sawyer has been in business for himself since 1992. In this context, he provides leading edge technical consultations on turnkey solutions, including Internet and systems design, development, and deployment. The analysis, acquisition, installation, modification, configuration, and support of operating systems, utilities, and software and hardware also fall within the technical scope of his functions. Mr. Sawyer's objective is to discover, investigate, and implement advanced technologies in client companies' systems infrastructures. His future endeavors include retiring from the Air Force, expanding his Company, and providing Internet services. Key to success according to Mr. Sawyer is due to his diligence. dba Computer Consultant is an regional technology consulting firm. Located in Tulsa, Oklahoma, the Company engages in all aspects of turnkey solutions. **Career Highlights:** Owner/Consultant, dba Computer Consultant (1989–Present). **Associations & Accomplishments:** Institute of Internal Auditors; Associate Member, Association of Certified Fraud Examiners. **Education:** Oklahoma State University, B.S. in Accounting (1994); Tulsa Community College, A.S. in Accounting (1992); Community College of the Air Force, A.A. in Criminal Justice.

Personal Information: Married to Collette in 1995. One child: David. Mr. Sawyer enjoys travel.

Adam J. Schiavi

Partner/President
Advanced Technologies Consulting Group Inc.
12555 Biscayne Boulevard, PMB 901
North Miami, FL 33181
(305) 947-8981
Fax: (305) 447-8193
adschia@ibm.net

7379

Business Information: One of three Partners in the Advanced Technologies Consulting Group, Mr. Schiavi serves as President. He performs the executive management of the Corporation, overseeing the administration and management of the individual projects and the subcontractors used to deliver services. Responsible for the generation of new clients through the quality work by the Corporation, he works on business logistics such as timing and organization in order to accomplish this goal. Mr. Schiavi's best recommendations thus far for his work has been received from clients. His Corporation began operations by correcting system mistakes that previous companies had made. As demand for Advanced Technologies Consulting Group services increase, Mr. Schiavi intends to construct its own corporate infrastructure without the use of subcontractors and expand operations to meet the needs of its clients. Serving the South Florida area, Advanced Technologies Consulting Group Inc. provides the integration of new technologies into existing systems. The Corporation primarily services health care agencies, legal firms, and small businesses. Acting as a project management group, the Corporation utilizes subcontractors to deliver services and receives new business solely through recommendations. **Career Highlights:** Partner/President, Advanced Technologies Consulting Group Inc. (1998–Present); Principle Partner, Valu-Tech Computers (1994–97); Consultant, Research Atlantica (1994). **Education:** University of Miami, Ph.D. (In Progress); Barry University, M.S.; Florida State University, B.S. **Personal Information:** Married to Shari in 1996. One child: Anastasia Maria. Mr. Schiavi enjoys gardening and being a musician.

Mike Schifano

Principal Consultant
Applications Solutions
3800 Audley Street, # 7306
Houston, TX 77098
(281) 467-4830
mschifan@ix.netcom.com

7379

Business Information: Mr. Schifano is the Principal Consultant at Application Solutions. He is in charge of all Oracle accounts regarding financial and manufacturing software customizations. An expert, he completes the forms and paperwork and authors the reports necessary to ensure the satisfaction of his clients with their finished product. He is involved in Web page customization and development for corporate repository. Working in the industry for the last four years, Mr. Schifano has learned valuable techniques to organize his office operations. His time is devoted between designing Web pages and organizing the Oracle form reports. Looking to continue with the Firm for the next few years, Mr. Schifano is planning to move forward in his career and eventually open his own independent consulting firm. Attributing his success to his academics, perseverance, and hard work, his advice is "consulting is the quickest way to build career skills and marketing your skill sets." Application Solutions was established in 1996. Primarily composed of past Oracle employees, the consulting Firm offers clients application solutions through its help desk and available technicians. A boutique firm, Applications Solutions employs 25 professional and technical experts accommodating the expanding need for technology consulting. Each employee hosts a virtual location on the Internet which allows them to access clients across the nation although the majority of their concerns come from the Texan market. **Career Highlights:** Principal Consultant, Applications Solutions (1997–Present); Software Consultant, Oracle Corporation (1995–97). **Education:** Rice University, M.B.A. (1995); University of Rochester, B.A. in Mathematics.

Ryan Wm. Schlagheck

Integration Consultant
Unisys Corporation
10 Univac Lane
Windsor, CT 06095
(860) 298-1257
Fax: (860) 298-1300
ryan.schlagheck@unisys.com

7379

Business Information: Functioning in the role of Integration Consultant in the Commercial Practice of Unisys Corporation, Mr. Schlagheck is responsible for interface design and development, business process modeling, and program specification, as well as production support. Before joining Unisys Corporation in 1997, Mr. Schlagheck served as Consultant for Numetrix Ltd. As an expert, three year technology professional, he is involved in strategic planning, optimization studies, and implementation. Overseeing the full life cycle as Team Lead, he provides budget inputs, conducts cost analysis, provides technical support, and coordinates resources, schedules, and assignments. He credits his success to being highly selective and providing his clients with products laced with quality, value, and selection. Growing with the Corporation, moving up the corporate hierarchy, and becoming more involved in project management serve as Mr. Schlagheck's future goals. The Commercial Practice of the Unisys Corporation is involved in demand side management and integration, package based implementations, printing and publishing solutions, and consulting and sales. The Practice also engages in outsourcing services, Y2K remediation, and interface, Web development, and e-commerce solutions. Established in 1986, Unisys is based in Blue Bell, Pennsylvania and operates over 200 offices internationally. Presently, the Corporation employs a staff of 30 people at the Windsor, Connecticut location. **Career Highlights:** Integration Consultant, Unisys Corporation (1997–Present); Consultant, Numetrix Ltd. (1996). **Education:** Pennsylvania State University, B.S. in Management Science and Information Systems (1996). **Personal Information:** Married to Nicole C. in 1999. Mr. Schlagheck enjoys Internet emerging technologies, recreational motorsports and digital photography.

Jonatan Schmidt

Chief Technical Officer/Founder
1 Venture Inc.
540 Bryant Street
Palo Alto, CA 94301
(408) 246-4112
Fax: (408) 733-2130
jonatan@evision.com

7379

Business Information: Serving as the Chief Technical Officer and Founder of 1 Venture Inc., Mr. Schmidt guides all operations of the Corporation. A graduate of Tel-Aviv University, his vast experience and practical skills have culminated in leading 1 Venture Inc. to unlimited success. Mr. Schmidt also ensures total customer satisfaction and develops new business clientele. He is pleased with the success of the Corporation and plans to ensure the continued growth and vitality of 1 Venture Inc. Established in 1995, 1 Venture Inc. specializes in the distribution of network applications. With estimated annual revenues exceeding $18 million, the Corporation serves major multinational companies and corporations including AT&T, Microsoft, IBM, Intel, and Gateway. 1 Venture Inc. also provides system integration services, connecting data and other information technologies of large corporations with the Internet so as to provide a complex networking system. The Corporation has developed the 1LAW link, which connects four million attorneys through the Internet, and the MEDNET link, which connects sixteen million physicians. 1 Venture Inc. is the first to provide this networking systems to the public and has received overwhelming success. Currently, the Corporation employs 87 people. For the future, 1 Venture Inc. plans to post estimated annual revenues of $1 billion in the near future. **Career Highlights:** Chief Technical Officer/Founder, 1 Venture Inc. (1997–Present); Vice President of Development, Evision Group (1995–97); Vice President of Development, Advantec (1993–95). **Associations & Accomplishments:** European Communications Association; World Trading Association; Information Technology Association; Spectra. **Education:** Tel-Aviv University, Computer Science (1989); Sorbonne University of France, Business Psychology; Moscow University of C.I.S., M.B.A. **Personal Information:** Married to Karen in 1995. Two children: Katrina and Rachelle. Mr. Schmidt enjoys flying and graphic design.

Mads Rosendahl Schmidt

Software Engineer
Novo Nordisk IT A/S
Randersgade 27 4th
Copenhagen, Denmark 2100
+45 44422562
mads@twilight.dk

7379

Business Information: Drawing on extensive technical expertise, Mr. Schmidt is a Software Engineer for Novo

Nordisk IT A/S. He assumes the accountability for the custom design of cutting edge software programs for an international clientele. In this context, he constantly meets one on one with customers to discover their specific needs. From the information gathered, he analyzes the data and designs the software according to his client's program specifications. In addition, he programs applications for affiliates. A systems expert with an established track record of delivering results, Mr. Schmidt's success reflects his ability to think out-of-the-box and to aggressively take on new challenges. As Active in the technology field, he concurrently operates his own software company called Twilight Applications. Looking towards the next millennium, Mr. Schmidt plans to finish a current project, a utility program for Lotus Notes, for his Twilight Applications and eventually attain the position of Program Manager. Novo Nordisk IT A/S is a medical company that produces much needed scientific supplies. Growth hormones, insulin, and enzymes are a few of the products manufactured by Novo Nordisk. The Company aslo develops Web and software solutions. Established in 1950, the Company has devoted almost fifty years in the pursuit of science. With the strong and valid efforts of 15,000 people, Novo Nordisk has grown from its headquarters in Copenhagen to be an international business with over 40 different locations. **Career Highlights:** Software Engineer, Novo Nordisk IT A/S (Present); Owner, Twilight Applications (1997). **Education:** Technical University of Denmark, Master's degree in Civil Engineering (1996); Microsoft Certified Solutions Developer. **Personal Information:** Mr. Schmidt enjoys playing the guitar and boxing. He is also fluent in English, Danish, and French.

Debra Schneider

Owner
Techni Logic Consulting
6536 Deerfield Drive, Suite 211
Sagamore Hills, OH 44067-3107
(330) 592-3386
tlconsult1@aol.com

7379

Business Information: As the Owner of Techni Logic Consulting, Ms. Schneider serves as the sole proprietor of the Company. Utilizing over seven years of industry savvy and technical expertise, she fulfills the responsibilities of trainer, developer, and consultant. A Certified Microsoft User Specialist and an experienced programmer, Ms. Schneider provides cutting edge information technology assistance and support. Traveling throughout the United States to perform training presentations, she ensures classes are in plain English and easy to understand, taking the intimidation factor out of learning how to use computers. Desiring more freedom to operate in her own unique style, Ms. Schneider ventured out on her own to establish Techni Logic Consulting with nothing but vast knowledge and a strong will to succeed. In the future, she would like to have more direct clients, that are not acquired through sub-contracting. Success is attributed to Ms. Schneider's strong organizational skills and her ability to take on challenges and deliver results. She remains current by conducting beta testing for Microsoft and lots of reading. Established in 1997, Techni Logic Consulting offers software training in Microsoft Windows, Office, Project, and Lotus Notes as well as custom database development. With 80 percent of the Company deriving from sub-contracts, Techni Logic provides services to both large and small companies. **Career Highlights:** Owner, Techni Logic Consulting (1997-Present); Trainer/Software Specialist, TLG Corporation (1996-97); Associate Programmer Analyst, Ohio Edison (1993-96). **Associations & Accomplishments:** Delta Sigma Pi; American Cancer Society Relay for Life Participant; Volleyball Coach, CYO 8th Grade Girls. **Education:** University of Akron, B.S. in Information Management (1993); Certified Microsoft Office User Specialist. **Personal Information:** Ms. Schneider enjoys travel, softball, volleyball and the Cleveland Indians.

Doug J. Schneider

President
Appdepot Web Services
1911e Truesdale Drive
Regina, Saskatchewan, Canada S4V 2N1
(306) 569-8519
Fax: (306) 569-8518
doug.schneider@appdepot.com

7379

Business Information: Having specialized in the technical consultation industry for over a decade, Mr. Schneider serves in the position of President of Appdepot Web Services. Drawing from his extensive experience and knowledge, he oversees day to day administration and operational activities, to include sales, marketing, and human resources management. He also determines the overall strategic direction. Recognized for taking part in some of the most innovative advances in the technological field, Mr. Schneider played a crucial role in the development of the 1x Data Entry System, while serving as the National Project Officer. Attributing his success in the field to impeccable timing, human relations skills, and years of experience, Mr. Schneider plans on growing and expanding operations. Established in 1998, Appdepot Web Services provides specialized business and technical solutions related to Web application development projects. Serving the entire Canadian population, the Company utilizes the skills of seven technology software specialists who maintain the high quality service through continued education and networking. **Career Highlights:** President, Appdepot Web Services (1997-Present); Senior Technical Analyst, Agrevo Canada (1995-97); Informatics Project Officer, Agriculture Canada (1991-95). **Education:** University of Regina, B.Sc. (1989). **Personal Information:** Mr. Schneider enjoys hockey, golf, skiing, outdoor activities and music.

Keiko K. Schneider

Owner
Saboten Web Design
10704 Constitution Avenue NE
Albuquerque, NM 87112
(505) 271-5044
Fax: (505) 271-5044
kschnei@sabotenweb.com

7379

Business Information: As the Owner of Saboten Web Design, Ms. Schneider provides professional leadership services for the Company. Utilizing her knowledge gained from her certification in Online Teaching and Web Design and Internet, she concentrates her efforts towards the development of optimal products and services. Coordinating efforts with her numerous clients, she gains perspective on their future goals and interests in order to create a Web site suited for their individual purposes. Presiding over all financial and marketing aspects of the Company, Ms. Schneider directs funds to the necessary areas of development, managing within a yearly budget and stratigically planning market strategies in order to further promote her products and services. Committed to the furthering expansion of her clientele, Ms. Schneider continues the advancement of Saboten Web Design. Specializing in Web site designing, Saboten Web Design was established in 1999. Located in Albuquerque, New Mexico, the Company provides excellent bilingual Web applications in educational Web sites and offers consulting pertaining to educational technologies. Focusing on designing creative and effective Web sites, Saboten Web Design remains committed to the promotional services for their clients. **Career Highlights:** Owner, Saboten Web Design (1999-Present); Japanese Instructor, University of New Mexico (1995-99); Japanese Instructor, School for International Training (1992-95). **Associations & Accomplishments:** WAOE; ATJ; NCJLT; AAS; ACTFL; AATJ; IAJLT; HWG. **Education:** School for International Training, M.A.T. (1994); University of California, Online Teaching Certificate (2000); University of New Mexico: Programming for the Web Certificate (2000), Web Design and Internet Certificate (1999). **Personal Information:** Married.

Scott A. Schreffler

Network Engineer
Road Runner
1125 Chambers Road
Columbus, OH 43212
(614) 255-6622
Fax: (614) 255-5614
scott@twcol.com

7379

Business Information: As Network Engineer of Road Runner a division of Time Warner, Mr. Schreffler utilizes his expertise in the field to design, install, troubleshoot, and maintain a 30,000 user high speed cable modem network. A demanding job, he possesses the skills and knowledge neessary to effectively fulfill his job obligations. An integral and vital member of the operation, he assisst on numerous projects and offers advice that affects the future of Road Runner and Time Warner. Mr. Schreffler plans to continue to grow professionally and acquire the skills needed to achieve a Senior Network Engineer position for the Ohio Data Center or the Mid Atlantic Center. His advice is "hardwork and going the extra miles for details is essential for a successful career in the technical field." Road Runner, Time Warner is a high speed on line Internet business offering access ISP. Founded in 1998, this technologically advanced Company employs a staff of approximately 500 people to assist in various aspects of the operation. Quality and professional services are offered statewide. **Career Highlights:** Road Runner, Time Warner: Network Engineer (1999-Present), System Administrator (1996-99); Senior Sonet Technician, Time Warner Telephony (1995-96); Senior Field Engineer, MCI WorldCom (1989-95). **Associations & Accomplishments:** FCC License from United States Government; CISCO, CCNA. **Education:** United States Air Force & Trade School. **Personal Information:** Married to Barbara in 1981. Two children: Alyssa and Zack.

Todd J. Schuelka

Director of Operations
Ortho Computer Systems, Inc.
1107 Buckeye Avenue
Ames, IA 50010-8064
(515) 233-1026
Fax: (515) 233-1454
toddjs@orthoii.com

7379

Business Information: Serving as Director of Operations of Ortho Computer Systems, Inc., Mr. Schuelka exhibits proficiency and dedication within his field. In his capacity, he oversees the entirety of the Corporation's business, including computer production, user support, building systems, and installations. Possessing more than eight years with Ortho Computer Systems, he is one of three responsible for corporate management of the Corporation. Rich in talents and abilities, Mr. Schuelka orchastrates the Corporation's long-term planning by setting new salary schedules, and writing new employee and department policies. Additionally, he is responsible for the training of new employees and various Corporation management. Attributing his success to the ability to solve problems, and gradually working his way up the corporate ladder, he is looking forward to becoming more involved with the Internet. Ortho Computer Systems, Inc. is an established and reputable company offering solutions to orthodontis through advanced software and computer networks. Established in 1982, Ortho is devoted to providing practice management software and computer networks to Orthodonitists. As one of the largest independent software and computer networks company, Ortho utilizes the skilled services of 1,100 employees throughout several locations in both United States and Canada. **Career Highlights:** Ortho Computer Systems, Inc.: Director of Operations (1999-Present), Systems Support Manager (1996-99), Software Support Manager (1995-96), Software Support Representative (1992-95). **Education:** Iowa State University, B.S. in Physics (1992). **Personal Information:** Mr. Schuelka enjoys the great outdoors, camping and hiking.

Kathleen M. Schwendiger

Software Consultant
En-Data
380 South State Road, Suite 1004-272
Altamonte Springs, FL 32714
(407) 522-6868

7379

Business Information: A prominent and respected professional, Ms. Schwendiger serves as a Software Consultant for the En-Data. She works specifically with the GEAC financial and human resources software, customizing it to client's specifications and implementing the software at the client's site. Before joining En-Data, she served as a Software Consultant for both CSC and Republic Industries. Utilizing more than 20 years of extensive experience in the field of information technology, Ms. Schwendiger assists En Data in the completion of corporate goals. She remains current with the latest technological advancements through hands on practice, networking on the Internet, and reading trade journals. Ms. Schwendiger's professional success reflects her ability to deliver results, think outside the box, and aggressively tackle new challenges. Serving companies and corporations across the country, En-Data specializes in the placement of software consultants within the information technology industry. The Corporation is based out of the state of Florida. Created in the early 1990s, a work force of 25 dedicated professionals are employed in the recruitment and placement of information technology consultants. **Career Highlights:** Software Consultant, En-Data (1999-Present); Software Consultant, EDS (1999); Software Consultant, CSC (1998-99); Software Consultant, Republic Industries (1998). **Education:** Northwood Institute, B.A. (1989); Clarke College; Loras College. **Personal Information:** Four children: Michael, Lea, Kathy, and Barbara. Ms. Schwendiger enjoys needlework, in line skating and volleyball.

Gregory M. Sciullo

Director of Enterprise Technologies
Equitable Resources
One Oxford Centre, Suite 3300
Pittsburgh, PA 15219
(412) 553-5861
Fax: (412) 553-5757
gms@eqt.com

7379

Business Information: Utilizing more than 30 years of experience, Mr. Sciullo serves as the Director of Enterprise Technologies for Equitable Resources. He has received internal recognition for his outstanding performance through several promotions to his current position. Mr. Sciullo assumes accountability for the voice, data, and video technology for the entire corporate enterprise. It is his responsibility to ensure that the overall systems are updated to meet the demands of the technology industry's everchanging market. He ensures that the various networks function efficiently and addresses system security issues. Always alert to new opportunities, techniques, and approaches, Mr. Sciullo is planning to expand corporate operations into e-commerce. An energy provider and supplier of services primarily to government clientele, Equitable Resources offers a variety of computer services to companies across the United States. The Corporation is also an information technology consulting firm. Established over 100 years ago, national operations employ over 1,500 skilled professionals. Annual sales for the Corporation top $400 million. **Career Highlights:** Equitable Resources: Director of Enterprise Technologies (1996-Present), Manager of Enterprise Networks (1980-96). **Associations & Accomplishments:** Telecommunications Management Association; National Communication Advisory Board; Plum Borough School District; Franklin Regional School District. **Education:** University of Pittsburgh, B.S. in Chemistry (1969). **Personal Information:** Married to Linda in 1972. Two children: Michael and Joseph. Mr. Sciullo enjoys gardening, pottery and hiking.

Albert Sciurca
Database Administrator/Project Manager
Meta Group
208 Harbor Drive
Stamford, CT 06902
(203) 705-6535
Fax: (203) 359-8066
albert.sciurca@metagroup.com

7379

Business Information: Serving as the Database Administrator and Project Manager of Meta Group, Mr. Sciurca administers and controls all data resources and system tools, ensuring data security, integrity, and reliability. Possessing an excellent understanding of his position, he is responsible for performing database backups, maintaining the functionality and operational status of the database management system, and overseeing critical aspects of project development. Drawing from over six years of hands on experience and expertise in the field, Mr. Sciurca utilizes his superior talents to construct strategic plans for the continuation of quality services. His future endeavors include moving up in upper management, obtaining certification as an Oracle Certified Professional, and eventually becoming a consultant. He attributes his success to his perseverance and a "never give up" attitude. Meta Group is an information technology consulting firm that specializes in new technology, software, hardware issues, and systems engineering for international companies. Established in 1989, the Firm offers a variety of consulting services in such areas as business development, software development, and staffing. Currently, the Firm functions under the full support of more than 450 professionals who facilitate smooth business operations. **Career Highlights:** Database Administrator/Project Manager, Meta Group (1998-Present); Product Manager, Faconic Data Corporation (1996-98). **Education:** Pace University, B.B.A. (1994).

Glania Sebastian
Systems Engineer Advanced
Duererstr. 7
Balingen, Germany 72336
+49 7433276948
Fax: +49 7433276949
s.glania@seppl.com

7379

Business Information: Mr. Sebastian has provided EDS (Schweiz) AG with exceptional professional direction for over two years. Serving in the capacity of Systems Engineer Advanced, he is responsible for network security and Internet services and Sun Solaris operations. Possessing superior talents and an excellent understanding of his field and effective communication skills, he is currently working to develop more knowledge about Hewlett-Packard and Cisco security requirements in order to better comprehend the needs of customers and objectives of the Company. Mr. Sebastian is an invaluable asset in the computer industry, and looks forward to assisting in the completion of future EDS goals. Established in 1962, EDS is a technology consulting firm. Targeting Fortune 1000 companies, EDS utilizes global information technology to develop protective measures for clients who hire EDS consultants. The Company is the second-largest technology business in the world, and specializes in creating firewalls and network security. **Career Highlights:** Systems Engineer Advanced, EDS (Schweiz) AG (1998-Present); Working Student, Brameur Ltd. (1996); Computer Technician, SINUS GmbH (1995). **Education:** Fachhochschule, Dipl.Ing. (1998); Aufbaugymnasium, University Entrance Exam. **Personal Information:** Mr. Sebastian enjoys sports and playing ice hockey.

Palachandra Seetharam
Senior Consultant
Cap Gemini America
2542 Chain Bridge Road, Suite 204
Vienna, VA 22181
(703) 206-7597
Fax: (703) 206-8841
pseethar@usa.capgemini.com

7379

Business Information: Functioning as Senior Consultant with Cap Gemini America, Mr. Seetharam works with users and systems management to analyze, specify, and design new technological solutions to harness more of the computer's power. Before joining Cap Gemini America, Mr. Seetharam served as Systems Analyst for Leading Edge Systems, Inc. His broad background history also includes employment as Senior Systems Engineer with BFL Software of India and Programs Officer at Baharat Earth Movers of India. Utilizing is academic ties and experience in the technology field, Mr. Seetharam coordinates, schedules, and works directly with clients to better serve their technology needs. Mr. Seetharam's goal is to enhance services provided and ensure products and services are laced with quality, value, and selection. He plans on becoming more involved in Internet application development. Continuously producing results and aggressively taking on new challenges and responsibilities has contributed to his career success. Cap Gemini America is a management firm that offers information technology services and software consulting. Producing in excess of $600 million each year, the Company employs 4,000 personnel to meet the technology needs of each client. The Company is available to update software programs and build new networking systems. **Career Highlights:** Senior Consultant, Cap Gemini America (1996-Present); Systems Analyst, Leading Edge Systems, Inc. (1994-96); Senior Systems Engineer, BFL Software, India (1993-94); Programs Officer, Bharat Earth Movers, India (1991-93). **Associations & Accomplishments:** International Sybase and PowerBuilder User Groups; American Production and Inventory Control Society. **Education:** Mysor University at India, B.S. in Engineering (1990). **Personal Information:** Married to Suma in 1996. Mr. Seetharam enjoys Indian classical music, sports and spirituality.

Pedro J. Sepulveda
LAN Administrator
Debug Computers
44 Henna Street
Cabo Rojo, Puerto Rico 00623
(787) 851-2015
Fax: (787) 851-6872
debug@cogui.net

7379

Business Information: In order for clients to access information stored on a mainframe server from personal workstations in corporate offices, a link has to be created. To this end, Mr. Sepulveda created Debug Computers and currently serves as LAN Administrator. In his capacity, he develops and adapts network communication specifications to cater to the needs of each clients system. Distinguished by a higher level of theoretical expertise, Mr. Sepulveda is an innovative programmer and technician. With numerous certifications from various institutes, the practical application of education allows him to further develop his skills and help other people. Attributing much of his success to hard work, Mr. Sepulveda would like to continue advancing within the technology field. His success reflects his ability to think outside the box and deliver results. Debug Computers engages in network configuration and repair of hardward and software, such as printers, programs, and cables. Located in Cabo Rojo, Puerto Rico, the Company was established in 1994. Presently, local operations employ the services of three technical experts. **Career Highlights:** LAN Administrator, Debug Computers (1994-Present): Hanes Menswear, Inc.: LAN Administrator (1994-99), PC Administrator (1993-94). **Associations & Accomplishments:** Rotary International; Association for Computer Machinery; Phi Eta Mu Fraternity; Boqueron Power Squadron. **Education:** InterAmerican University, B.S. in Computer Programming (1992); Horizons, A Plus Certification. **Personal Information:** Married to Luz N. Torres Pagán in 1998. One child: Pedro A. Sepulveda Torres. Mr. Sepulveda enjoys shooting, diving and reading books.

Christopher J. Sersic
Consultant
Ambassador Consulting
838 Park Central South Drive, Apartment A
Indianapolis, IN 46260
(317) 277-0085
Fax: (317) 277-3382
cseric@yahoo.com

7379

Business Information: Functioning in the role of Consultant for Ambassador Consulting, Mr. Sersic is responsible for helping clients design, build, and implement both decision support systems and executive information systems. Before joining Ambassador Consulting, he served as Programmer and Analyst with Day Dream Publishing. His employment history also includes a stint as Software Engineer for Ventura Technologies International. An expert, Mr. Sersic closely coordinates and works with clients on development of Oracle data warehouse management software, and putting data in a usable format. He became involved in technology because he saw how he could utilize his creativity. Receiving internal recognition, Mr. Sersic plans to remain and grow with the Firm. "Learn from experience. It is important to listen and communicate," serves as his advice. His success reflects his ability to think out-of-the-box and take on new challenges and responsibilities. Ambassador Consulting operates as a firm specializing in Microsoft, Oracle, UNIX, and data warehousing consulting, and project development and maintenance. The targeted clientele include government agencies and pharmaceuticals, insurance, and banking industries. International in scope, the Firm was founded in 1989 and is located in Indianapolis, Indiana. **Career Highlights:** Consultant, Ambassador Consulting (1997-Present); Programmer/Analyst, Day Dream Publishing (1996-97); Software Engineer, Ventura Technologies International (1995-96). **Associations & Accomplishments:** Management Information Systems Association of Indiana State. **Education:** Indiana State University, B.S. (1995). **Personal Information:** Married to Priscilla in 1998. Mr. Sersic enjoys softball, bikes, travel and charity work.

Bellave S. Shashikumar
President
Techcircle.com inc.
28 Willow Way Drive
Enola, PA 17025
(717) 213-9292
Fax: (717) 772-1277
shashi@techcircle.com

7379

Business Information: As President of Techcircle.com inc., Mr. Shashikumar coordinates all day-to-day office administration and operational activities. He is responsible and vocal in all design and creation. Seeing the need for personalized service, Mr. Shashikumar works directly with clients and management to evaluate individual situations and determine the best solutions. In addition, Mr. Shashikumar is in charge of his staff and determines hiring, advertising, and marketing strategies. As a tested and proven, 15 year technology professional, his career success reflects his ability to solve problems in a systematic and efficient manner, think out-of-the-box, and take on new challenges. One of Mr. Shashikumar's future goals is to expand the Company in the international market. Techcircle.com inc. is an information technology services company. Established in 1999, the Corporation hires the best information technology professionals and offers information technology consulting services to large corporations and government agencies. The Corporation also designs and implements a variety of software programs for businesses nationally. The corporate Web site at <www.techcircle.com> will be developed into an Internet portal for Information Technology professionals and companies. **Career Highlights:** President, Techcircle.com inc. (1999-Present); Independent Software Consultant (1997-98); Senior Software Consultant, Infosys International Inc. (1992-97); Senior Software Consultant, Mastech Corporation (1989-92). **Education:** Bangalore University, B.S. (1982). **Personal Information:** Married to Usha L. Rao in 1993. Mr. Shashikumar enjoys painting and photography.

Mounir Shehata
Country Sales Manager
SBM-IBM
P.O. Box 5648
Jeddah, Saudi Arabia 21432
+966 26600007
shehata@sa.ibm.com

7379

Business Information: As the Country Sales Manager of SBM-IBM, Mr. Shehata takes on the challenges of marketing and selling Web servers as an intregal portion of SBM's activities. Affiliated with the Company for 17 years, he plays an active role in pre-sale organization of products before they are introduced to the general public. One of the most vital positions within the Company, Mr. Shehata's marketing factors often determine the overall success of a product and the accompanied sales. Seeking to expand upon his professional career within SBM, he is acquiring greater responsibility and further instruction in the field to maximize his intellectual potential. SBM, a division of the international IBM Corporation, is engaged in the global service of e-business solutions. Dedicated to providing the most innovative of technological advances to their customers, the Saudi Arabia division of IBM designs, develops, and manufactures components for the world's most state-of-the-art hardware and software systems. Employing 370 skilled technicians in the Jeddah location, SBM generates over $200 million in annual revenue. **Career Highlights:** SBM-IBM: Country Sales Manager (1997-Present), Country Channels Manager (1995-97), Regional Marketing Manager

(1993-95). **Education:** Ain Shahs University, B.S. in Commerce (1981). **Personal Information:** Married to Maria-Graziella in 1982. Two children: Alexandre and Philippe-Michel. Mr. Shehata enjoys squash and scuba diving.

Eduard Shprints
Senior Principal
ClearCommerce Corporation
11500 Metric Boulevard, Suite #300
Austin, TX 78758
(512) 977-5567
Fax: (512) 832-8901
edgsh@mailcity.com

7379

Business Information: Mr. Shprints functions in the role of Senior Principal for the Professional Services department of the ClearCommerce Corporation. He devotes the majority of his time to project management and assists his staff in designing and organizing the Corporation's development programs. A savvy, eight-year veteran, Mr. Shprints also is involved in systems architecture. Working closely with a team of engineers and consultants, he works to motivate them toward creativity and brainstorming and strives to encourage them to experiment with their talents. Very encouraged by his new position, Mr. Shprints plans to continue with ClearCommerce Corporation and enhance his education in the industry in order to advance to a higher position. His success reflects his ability to think outside the box, produce results, and aggressively take on new challenges. The Corporation engages in conducting e-commerce. ClearCommerce Corporation, an Internet software and services company, provides complete transaction processing solutions for large merchants and commerce service providers. Focused around the expanding world of the Internet, the Corporation is taking advantage of this newly established audience and has opened the world of Internet trade and financial planning. The ClearCommerce Engine improves profits and efficiencies by automating the back-end purchasing process. ClearCommerce brings you the best solutions in Internet Commerce transaction processing, fraud tracking, and reporting. The Corporation was founded in 1995 and has brought an increasing number of explorers and business executives to the future way of conducting business. **Career Highlights:** Senior Principal, ClearCommerce Corporation (1999-Present); Consultant, Decision Consultants Inc. (1998-99); Consultant, PSW Technologies Inc. (1997-98); President, E.D.I. & Company, Information Technology Consultants (1992-96). **Education:** BSUCSRE, M.S. in Computer Science (1996). **Personal Information:** Mr. Shprints enjoys sports, music and travel.

Suzanne Silliman
Group Director
Management Science Associates Inc.
6565 Penn Avenue
Pittsburgh, PA 15206
(412) 362-2000
Fax: (412) 363-5598
ssilliman@msa.com

7379

Business Information: Demonstrating expertise in the information technology field, Ms. Silliman serves as the Group Director of Syndicated Business Solutions within the Information Management Solution Division of Management Science Associates Inc. She is involved in every aspect of designing the syndicated business solutions for clients from the drawing board to the application implementation. Striving to keep the business solutions simple for increased ease of use, she also ensures that it is based on the latest in cutting edge technology. Ms. Silliman continues to grow professionally through the fulfillment of her responsibilities and her involvement in the advancement of operations. The Management Science Associates Inc. offers analytical software and information based services tailored to meet the needs of the CPG industry. Based in Pittsburgh, Pennsylvania, the Corporation provides data management services such as business analysis and media advertising. The Corporation was founded in 1963 and has grown to employ more than 650 knowledgeable individuals. **Career Highlights:** Group Director, Management Science Associates Inc. (1996-Present); Brand Management, H.J. Heinz (1993-96); Account Executive, Information Resources Inc. (1991-93). **Associations & Accomplishments:** Advertising Research Foundation; American Marketers Association; National Association Female Executives; National Advisory Group; NAMA; NAC. **Education:** St. Vincent College, B.A. in Math (1988).

Reginold T. Simmons
President
Resources Technical Services
5714 16th Avenue, Apartment 302
Hyattsville, MD 20782
(301) 853-8921
Fax: (301) 779-6417
simmrts@aol.com

7379

Business Information: Functioning in the role of President with Resources Technical Services, Mr. Simmons oversees all aspects of day-to-day internal operations of the Company. He conducts computer programming, main frame programming, technical work, subcontracting, and various consulting services. Having founded the Company after 30 years of practical experience in the field, Mr. Simmons is dedicated to providing clients with the highest quality of services. Determining the overall strategic direction and coordinating resources, time lines, schedules, assignments, and budgets are also an integral part of Mr. Simmons' responsibilities. He attributes his career success to reading literature and staying up to date in his field. Dedicated to the success of the Company, Mr. Simmons looks forward to handling state-of-the-art Legacy systems. Established in 1995, Resources Technical Services is an up and coming information technology service providing consulting services and automated data processing systems. Employing the expertise of two qualified individuals, the Company reports an estimated annual revenue in excess of $70,000. **Career Highlights:** President, Resources Technical Services (1998-Present); ADP Technical Specialist, Computer Technology Associates (1997-98); Senior Programmer Analyst, MITECH, Inc. (1996); Functional Analyst/Conversion Analyst/Programmer Analyst, Southside Hospital (1985-89). **Associations & Accomplishments:** Black Data Processing Associates; American Legion; Boy Scouts of America. **Education:** Molloy College, Certificate (1991); Burroughs Education Program, Certificate (1984). **Personal Information:** Married to Linda C. in 1972. Two children: Reginold T. Jr. and Richard W. Mr. Simmons enjoys fishing, camping, bowling and hiking.

Theodore L. Siska
Account Manager
Fujitsu
2 Carlson Parkway, Suite 225
Plymouth, MN 55447
(612) 249-6545
Fax: (612) 249-6549

7379

Business Information: Serving as Account Manager for Fujitsu, Mr. Siska is responsible for analyzing, designing, implementing, and managing intelligently-integrated voice, video, and data networks for multi-locations and call center customers. In addition, he develops and maintains account relationships with new and existing customers, designing and providing system solutions that solve customer's business problems. Mr. Siska attributes his success to having the ability to apply technology to meet specific business objectives. Established in 1968, Fujitsu is a developer of business communications systems, such as customer based data equipment, in-house telephone systems, ATM switches, and other video, voice and data communications products and equipment. Headquartered in Tokyo, Japan, Fujitsu employs 140,000 people and has an estimated annual revenue in excess of $43.3 billion. **Career Highlights:** Fujitsu: Account Manager (1997-Present), Senior Sales Engineer (1991, 1993, and 1995-97), Operations Manager (1993-94), Senior Sales Engineer (1991-93), Senior Application Engineer (1989-91). **Associations & Accomplishments:** Fujitsu's "Account Manager of the Year" (1998); Minnesota Telecommunications Association; Precinct Captain, Republican Party - City of Minnetonka; Association For Services Management International (Past). **Education:** University of Phoenix, M.B.A. (1991); University of Virginia, B.A. in History and Government (1982). **Personal Information:** Mr. Siska enjoys reading and golf.

Anca E. Slusanschi
Team Leader
Advantage Group
117 Realm Drive
Paraparaumu, New Zealand
+64 44715600
anca@acm.org

7379

Business Information: As the Team Leader for Advantage Group, Ms. Slusanschi fulfills the responsibility of a project manager within the e-commerce division of the Group. In her capacity, she plans, oversees, and directs the development and support of cutting-edge software applications. Possessing superior technical talents and an excellent understanding of technology, Ms. Slusanschi effectively utilizes her expertise in coordinating resources, schedules, and communications for applications development projects. A savvy, eight-year professional, she also performs systems analysis and programming, and serves as the chief liaison with user groups and systems management. The acquisition, installation, modification, configuration, support, and tracking of all operating systems, databases, utilities, software, and hardware also fall within the purview of Ms. Slusanschi's responsibilities. Continuing to grow professionally through fulfillment of her responsibilities and her involvement in the advancement of operations, she plans to remain and grow with the Company. Located in Wellington, New Zealand, Advantage Group is an information services provider. In this capacity, the Company is involved in the building and implementing of software in the government and private sectors. The Company is dedicated to providing the clientele with the highest quality of services possible. **Career Highlights:** Team Leader, Advantage Group (1997-Present); Analyst/Programmer, Anchor Trust, U.K. (1996-97). **Associations & Accomplishments:** Institute of Electronics and Electrical Engineers; Institute of Electronics and Electrical Engineers Computer Society; Association of Computing Machinery; American Association for the Advancement of Science (A.A.A.S.); New York Academy of Science; National Geographic Society. **Education:** University, M.Sc. (1992); Research Fellow, Surrey University, U.K. (1995-96). **Personal Information:** Married to Horia-Cristian in 1995.

Barry W. Smith
Information Systems Director
Warren County
165 County Road 519
Belvidere, NJ 07823-1927
(908) 475-6560
Fax: (908) 475-6582
bwsmith@bellatlantic.net

7379

Business Information: Mr. Smith is Information Systems Director for Warren County. In this capacity, he serves as manager of a countywide wide-area computer network which links various information resources. He represents the Information Services Office in meetings with county managers and boards, soliciting funding as appropriate for equipment and staff support. He also serves as liaison between Warren County and the state of New Jersey. Mr. Smith exercises oversight of computerized billing activities, information sharing protocols, and confidentiality issues. He directs the County's Y2K compliance and testing program to ensure coding adjustments and software replacements are in place. His efforts will circumvent the potential disruption of services anticipated upon the arrival of the new millennium. A highlight of Mr. Smith's career was implementation of an automated Welfare Board package which assists in the management of more than 15,000 child support and food stamp cases. He hopes to continue expanding his technological knowledge-base, and to rise through the management ranks within Warren County. Warren County's Information Services Office provides integrated information systems support for a wide variety of county government operations. Included in ISO services are voice, data, and video linkage for emergency, welfare, health, and medical providers. Agencies served include sheriff's department, 911 emergency switchboard, nursing homes, social services department, fire and EMT departments, and the office of the clerk of court. Warren County was established in 1825, and employs around 900 people to serve the governmental and community service needs of citizens. **Career Highlights:** Information Systems Director, Warren County (1997-Present); Data Processing Coordinator, Warren County Welfare Board (1976-96). **Associations & Accomplishments:** President, Harmony Township Volunteer Fire Department; Financial Chairman/Trustee, Bloomsbury United Methodist Church. **Education:** New Jersey Institute of Technology: M.S. in Mechanical Engineering (1989), B.S. in Electrical Engineering (1975).

Cheryl L. Smith
Assistant Project Manager
MIL Corporation
11148 Worchester Drive
New Market, MD 21774-6266
(301) 496-4591
Fax: (301) 480-3437
cheri_smith@nlm.nih.gov

7379

Business Information: Utilizing over 10 years of expertise in the information technology field, Ms. Smith fulfills the role of Assistant Project Manager at MIL Corporation. Coming on board to MIL's team of professionals in 1997, she currently is responsible for providing LAN support to the National Library of Medicine. Her background in the field includes stints as Software Engineer with First Data Corporation and Senior Systems Analyst at Orbital Sciences Corporation. In addition, Ms. Smith uses her years of experience in effectively managing day to day Help Desk operations. She is the chief customer liaison for government employees. Her realm of responsibilities also includes scheduling, work flow control, management of short and long term projects, space management, and systems troubleshooting. A recognized professional, Ms. Smith received an award for introducing knowledge base on the Web at the National Library of Medicine. Her future goal includes becoming a Project Manager and remaining on the leading edge of technology. MIL Corporation provides information technology consulting and support to an international clientele. One of the Corporation's clientele include the National Library of Medicine. Located in New Market, Maryland, MIL Corporation presently employs a highly trained staff of 20 technical experts and administrative and support personnel. **Career Highlights:** Assistant Project Manager, MIL Corporation (1997-Present); Software Engineer, First Data Corporation (1997); Senior Systems Analyst, Orbital Sciences Corporation (1990-97). **Associations & Accomplishments:** Association of Computing Machinery; Institute of Electrical and Electronics Engineers, Computer Society; Honor Society of Phi Kappa Phi, Hood Chapter. **Education:** Hood College, M.S. in Computer Science and Information Systems (1997); University of Maryland, B.S. in Education. **Personal Information:** Married to Jimmy R. in 1999. Three children: Kristen Yukov, Traci Sarni, and Amy Sarni. Ms. Smith enjoys golf and fishing.

Eric E. Smith, Ph.D.

Principal
Evan Design Group
2218 Sherman Street
Longmont, CO 80501-1332
(303) 776-6464
Fax: (303) 776-6464
esmith@evandesign.com

7379

Business Information: As Principal of Evan Design Group, Dr. Smith serves as the Lead Consultant and Project Manager. He coordinates experts to assist him in the design and implementation of network systems and related applications, primarily in the education industry. Dr. Smith also organizes and conducts training programs for newly installed equipment. As the Firm continues to prosper, Dr. Smith is hoping for the opportunity to engage in more conceptual consulting projects. Established in 1994, Evan Design Group provides consulting services regarding performance technology and training. Located in Longmont, Colorado, the Firm serves mostly a regional clientele, performing occasional national projects. **Career Highlights:** Principal, Evan Design Group (1994-Present); Faculty, International University (1995-Present); Assistant Professor, University of Northern Colorado (1988-94). **Associations & Accomplishments:** International Society for Performance Improvement; Association for Educational Communications and Technology; Federal Education and Training Association; HTML Writers Guild; Elder, Westview Presbyterian Church. **Education:** Purdue University: Ph.D. (1988), Master's degree; Wittenberg University, B.A. **Personal Information:** Married to Jennifer in 1991. One child: George Evan. Dr. Smith enjoys swimming, skiing, bicycling, reading and collecting comics.

Jeremy A. Smith

Owner/Consultant
Smith Consulting
1815 Cassel Road
Quakertown, PA 18951-3838
jasmith@easy-pages.com

7379

Business Information: The Owner of Smith Consulting, Mr. Smith serves as its Consultant. He handles all of the financial and administrative functions of the Company as well as its day-to-day operations. Making educated technological recommendations, he assists clients in deciding the best computer to purchase for their businesses. In this way, clients are able to create functional specifications to which hardware and software vendors can respond. Mr. Smith also performs repairs on computer equipment. When he was seven years old, his family bought him a computer and a future career was born. Attending a technical college, he attributes his success to the solid education he received there. He stays on the cutting edge of technology by continuing education and surfing the Internet for the latest technological developments. Looking to the future, Mr. Smith is eager to increase his responsibilities and work with expanding information systems. His success reflects his ability to produce results and aggressively take on new challenges. Established in 1998 by Jeremy Smith, Smith Consulting is a privately owned consulting firm. **Career Highlights:** Owner/Consultant, Smith Consulting (1998-Present); Computer Technician, TEKsystems (1999-Present); Technician, Lehigh Valley Wireless (1999); Help Desk, IT Career Connectors (1999). **Education:** Allentown Business School, Associate's degree (1999); Upper Bucks County Technical School, Diploma in Computer Service Technology.

Michele Smith

Senior Associate Software Consultant
1111 West 22nd Street
Oak Brook, IL 60523
(630) 574-3333
micsmith41@yahoo.com

7379

Business Information: Formerly Senior Associate Software Consultant of BMC Software, Inc., Miss Smith was responsible for pre and post sales of software products to the computer industry. During her time with the Corporation, she helped build the help desk and integrated numerous software products. In her work with Veteran's Affairs, she was responsible for implementing Windows95 at the Veteran's data center. In this endeavor, Miss Smith was involved in all phases of operation to include architecture, design, and systems integration. Recently in receipt of her Master's degree, Miss Smith has excelled in all areas of technology and consulting through continuous study on related subjects. She is looking for a project management position within three industries: e-commerce, cable media, or network engineering. Miss Smith is very confident in her abilities to take on challenges and deliver results. In possession of the knowledge to handle work of the most complex nature, Miss Smith has kept well informed of the marketing world and makes full use of leading edge software capabilities. She is highly skilled in the delivering of software solutions and developing requests for proposals and sales presentations. **Career Highlights:** Senior Associate Software Consultant, BMC Software, Inc. (1999-00); Sales Systems Engineer, Loyola University Medical (1998-99); Network Engineer, Salomon Smith Barney (1997-98); Network Administration, United States Department Veteran Affair (1995-97). **Associations & Accomplishments:** Institute of Electronics and Electrical Engineers Computer Society; National Council of Negro Women; National Association for the Advancement of Colored People; Association for Women in Computing; Women in Technology International. **Education:** Roosevelt University, M.S. (1999). **Personal Information:** Miss Smith enjoys galleries, theatre, arts and museums.

Walter E. Smith Jr.

Senior Consultant
Herman Miller
555 Lakehaven Circle
Orlando, FL 32828
(800) 250-8111
Fax: (407) 658-6183

7379

Business Information: Utilizing more than five years of experience in the industry, Mr. Smith serves as the Senior Consultant for Herman Miller. He administers to customers' inbound and outbound sales and service calls, providing pragmatic solutions to complex situations. These problems range from technical platform concerns to customer relationship management. Presented with the AT&T True Spirit Award for outstanding past performance, he credits his professional success to his surroundings and having great people as leaders. Mr. Smith's goal is to facilitate continued Company growth and geographic expansion, becoming a leader and teacher within the call center industry. His success reflects his ability to think outside the box, produce results, and take on new challenges. Herman Miller offers call center consulting support to Fortune 500 and Fortune 1000 companies within the United States. The Company's mission is to provide quality customer service at an unmatched affordable price. One staff member is used to conduct daily operations. The Company was recently founded in 1999. **Career Highlights:** Senior Consultant, Herman Miller (1999-Present); Call Center Director, Alignmark (1998-99); Call Center Director, Nextel (1997-98); Director of Outbound, Precision Response Company (1996-97). **Associations & Accomplishments:** Direct Marketing Association; American Television Association; Orlando Economic Development Commission and National Trust For Historic Preservation; DMA Teleservices Council. **Education:** Nova University, B.S. in Business Management (1994); Purdue University, Call Center Campus. **Personal Information:** Married to Sherri in 1990. Two children: Kourtney and Keith. Mr. Smith enjoys golf and swimming.

Brian D. Smoot

LAN Administrator
CSG Systems International
5970 South Greenwood Plaza Boulevard
Englewood, CO 80111
(303) 200-3143
Fax: (303) 200-3225
brian_smoot@csgsystems.com

7379

Business Information: Functioning in the role of LAN Administrator of CSG Systems International, Mr. Smoot oversees and directs daily LAN administration and operational activities. He installs and maintains hardware, software, and infrastructure resources, as well as troubleshoots network usage. Prior to joining CSG Systems, Mr. Smoot served as Systems Administrator with Management Technology and Associate Systems Analyst at Ford & Loral Aerospace. As a nine year technology professional, he is in charge of network design, technical support, and customer service issues. Coordinating and working with a team of experts, Mr. Smoot provides support for ongoing LAN problems, and gives recommendations on technological advances to improve or automate systems. Crediting his success to his supportive family, Mr. Smoot's overall success reflects is ability to think out-of-the-box and aggressively take on new challenges and responsibilities. CSG Systems International is one of the world's leading providers of customer care and billing solutions for the telecommunications industry. A publicly traded company, CSG Systems was established in 1994. Presently, the Company employs a work force of more than 1,600 professional, technical, and support personnel who help generate revenues in excess of $236 million annually. **Career Highlights:** LAN Administrator, CSG Systems International (1998-Present); Systems Administrator, Management Technology (1993-98); Associate Systems Analyst, Ford & Loral Aerospace (1990-93). **Associations & Accomplishments:** Minority Representative, Equal Employment Opportunity Board; Noncommissioned Officers Association. **Education:** University of Maryland (Currently Attending); Community College of the Air Force; United State Air Force Technical School. **Personal Information:** Married to Lanise D. in 1986. Three children: B. J., Brittani, and Brandi. Mr. Smoot enjoys sports.

Ed Sobieray

Consultant
eJiva
3801 Connecticut Avenue #428
Washington, DC 20008
(202) 258-9734
esobieray@ejiva.com

7379

Business Information: Recruited to eJiva in 1999, Mr. Sobieray serves as a Consultant. He works within the supply chain management division, which focuses on large core client companies in the manufacturing industry. Building collaborative relationships with the client companies, he devises technical strategies for their enterprise system environments, assessing their suitability to software functionality and helps implements new software products for cost savings. Mr. Sobieray also performs supply chain assessments, performance measurement, and internal business development in addition to his sales, marketing, and recruiting duties. Beginning his professional career in the Marine Corps, he worked as a logistics officer and moved into software implementation. He continuously strives to improve his performance, and looks forward to assisting eJiva go public. In the long-term, Mr. Sobieray plans to one day own his own consulting business. Recently founded in 1999, eJiva conducts its business activities in the field of enterprise technology consulting. The Company specifically focuses on supply chain management, customer relationship management, e-business, and technical architect and design. An approximate work force of 150 skilled professionals is employed to cater to clients' business needs. The Company reported its annual sales at $15 million for its first year in business. **Career Highlights:** Consultant, eJiva (1999-Present); Consultant, Avicon (1999); Supply Chain Consultant, Manugistics (1998); Captain, Logistics Office, United States Marine Corps (1993-97). **Associations & Accomplishments:** Association of Production and Inventory Control Systems; Marine Corps Association. **Education:** Virginia Military Institute, B.S. in Mechanical Engineering (1992); Naval Post Graduate School, Certificate in Logistics Planning. **Personal Information:** Mr. Sobieray enjoys running, basketball and volunteering.

Sanjay V. Sohoni

Software Development Manager
Informix Software, Inc.
4100 Bohannon Avenue
Menlo Park, CA 94025
(650) 923-1949
ssohoni@hotmail.com

7379

Business Information: After extensive study and work experience in the field of information technology, Mr. Sohoni was recruited to Informix Software Inc. as Software Development Manager. Included in his daily schedule are a variety of issues such as formulating technical strategies for state-of-the-art Web based and e-commerce solutions. Developing custom applications, Mr. Sohoni strives to incorporate specific features for each possible avenue. A highly respected and accomplished member of the professional community, Mr. Sohoni holds one U.S. and international patent for method and apparatus related to creation of prismatic letter sign making. His contribution to this patent was algorithm design and Microsoft Windows front-end development. In the future, Mr. Sohoni looks forward to expanding his knowledge on e-commerce while continually developing innovative products to meet customer demands. Informix Software, Inc. provides database software tools to power large company servers. Targeting the telecommunications, retail, and finance industries, the Corporation has been slowly evolving towards Internet based solutions. With 3,500 employees, the global Company sees annaul revenues in excess of $750 million. **Career Highlights:** Software Development Manager, Informix Software, Inc. (1995-Present); Senior Software Engineer, Gerber Scientific Products (1990-95); Senior Software Engineer, Innovative Systems/Summa Technologies (1985-90). **Education:** Louisiana State University, M.S. (1985); Indian Institute of Technology, Bachelor's degree in Technical Civil Engineering (1981). **Personal Information:** Married to Shyla in 1985. Two children: Utsav and Pooja.

Richard J. Speck

Lead Consultant
Relational Technologies
30000 Northwestern Highway
Farmington Hills, MI 48334
(248) 626-6800
rspeck@reltec.com

7379

Business Information: As Lead Consultant of Relational Technologies, Mr. Speck works with customers to analyze, specify, and design new, feasible applications to enhance their day-to-day operations. Overseeing a team of programmers performing site management, he designs and develops Web applications and software solutions. Possessing an excellent understanding of his field, Mr. Speck also fulfills the responsibility of database administrator. Coordinating and allocating resources, managing time lines and dead lines, and determining assignments, Mr. Speck is also an expert at troubleshooting and maintaining systems functionality and operational status. A visionary, his future plans include moving up the corporate structure and helping the Company implement and execute new technological strategies. As Lead Consultant of Relational Technologies, Mr. Speck works with customers to analyze, specify, and design new, feasible applications to enhance their day-to-day operations. Overseeing a team of programmers performing site management, he designs and develops Web applications and software solutions. Possessing an excellent understanding of his field, Mr. Speck also fulfills the responsibility of database administrator. Coordinating and allocating resources, managing time lines and dead lines, and determining assignments, Mr. Speck is also an expert at troubleshooting and maintaining systems functionality and operational status. A visionary, his future plans include moving up the corporate structure and helping the Company implement and execute new technological strategies. Founded in 1994, Relational Technologies provides software consulting services. Specializing in database applications, the Corporation assists businesses in improving the quality and efficiency of their work by providing them cutting edge software. Clients include middle markets, tier-1 suppliers, and the automotive industry. Presently, the Corporation is manned by 35 professional, technical, and support staff. Founded in 1994, Relational Technologies provides software consulting services. Specializing in database applications, the Corporation assists businesses in improving the quality and efficiency of their work by providing them cutting edge software. Clients include middle markets, tier-1 suppliers, and the automotive industry. Presently, the Corporation is manned by 35 professional, technical, and support staff. **Career Highlights:** Relational Technologies: Lead Consultant (1999-Present), Consultant (1996-99); Systems Engineer, Advance Data Research (1995-96). **Associations & Accomplishments:** Co-Founder, Christmas in April; Detroit Oracle Users Group; Michigan Oracle Application User Group. **Education:** University of Michigan, B.S. in General Studies (1994). **Personal Information:** Married to Tonya in 1997. Mr. Speck enjoys boating and hockey.

Russell F. Speed

Consultant
Rebel.com
151 Isabella
Ottawa, Ontario, Canada K1S 1V5
(613) 788-3600
rs@home-eh.com

7379

Business Information: Displaying his skills in this highly specialized position, Mr. Speed serves as Consultant for Rebel.com. His primary responsibilities include Web development, customer application assessment, and a wide range of consulting for a growing clientele. With more than six years of professional experience, Mr. Speed utilizes his superior talents and experience to establish comprehensive programs for all new and existing employees. His future plans include maintaining his present position while obtaining more knowledge and experience to enable him to provide better services for the Company and its customers. His success reflects his ability to think outside the box, take on new challenges, and deliver results. Serving a national client base, Rebel.com engages in the manufacturing and sales of netwinders for corporate and individual clients. The Company also offers professional consulting on the uses and operations of unique and beneficial products. Established in 1989, the Company caters to all business in need of systems upgrading and new implementations of software. Operating out of several locations throughout Canada, the Company functions under the talents and expertise of more than 150 professionals who facilitate strategic business operations. **Career Highlights:** Consultant, Rebel.com (Present); Internet Gateway Implementation and Developer, Nortel Networks; x.500/x.400 Implementation and Developer, Enterprise Solutions (1994-97). **Personal Information:** Married to Nathalie in 1995. One child: Christopher. Mr. Speed enjoys new technologies.

Bill E. Spell

Senior Account Manager
KForce.com
520 Post Oak Boulevard, Suite 700
Houston, TX 77027
(713) 479-3500
Fax: (713) 622-3778
bspell@romac.com

7379

Business Information: Displaying strengths in generating revenues for the Houston, Texas office, Mr. Spell serves as the Senior Account Manager of KForce.com. Working closely with the recruiting teams, he performs internal resume screening, facilitates relationships with new clients, and oversees human resource managers in the hiring process. In addition, Mr. Spell presides over current projects and monitors deficiencies as well as networks information technology functions. Possessing business savvy and expertise, he has been recognized for his diligence and hard work by being selected to cover the entire spectrum of the business. In the future, Mr. Spell plans to remain in his field, tripling the contact base through marketing, selling total solutions, as well as venturing into Web technologies and e-commerce business to business activities. Working smartly and having the ability to tackle new challenges and deliver results are reasons for his career successes. Established in 1963, KForce.com is an information technology solutions and placement company. The Company provides online job boards and solution through strategic resource planning and outsourcing. Employing over 3,000 people, KForce.com provides permanent placements as well. Annually, the Company reports annual revenues in excess of $1 billion. Headquartered in Tampa, Florida, the Company operates 110 locations nationally. **Career Highlights:** Senior Account Manager, KForce.com (2000-Present); Relationship Manager, Romac International (1999-00); Information Technology Recruiter, Magic (1996-99). **Associations & Accomplishments:** Texas A&M Century Club. **Education:** Texas A&M University, Bachelor's degree (1996). **Personal Information:** Mr. Spell enjoys racquetball and golf.

Matthias E. Stauch

Director/Owner
PRISMA Marketing
Rothenbuecherweg 23 B
Berlin, Germany 14089
+49 3026550792
Fax: +49 302629092
matthias@stauch.de

7379

Business Information: As the Director and Owner, Mr. Stauch is the visionary force behind the entire corporate structure. He meets with clients, assesses goals and needs, negotiates contracts, and works diligently with his staff to devise workable solutions to meet the diverse needs of his clients. A recognized professional, Mr. Stauch has written industry-related articles and has been interviewed in local newspapers. He is especially proud of his ability to provide quality solutions and services to large corporate clients. Future plans include the continued expansion of PRISMA Marketing and the opening of another business. Recognizing a market niche that he knew he could fill, Mr. Stauch established PRISMA Marketing in 1990 as an import and export trading company. Based on this experience, FIST (First International Sourcing Team), was invented to help German businesses establish long-term businesses worldwide. Located in Berlin, Germany, the Company specializes in the provision of business consultations, development, and realization of hardware and software solutions, as well as marketing, corporate design, Web presence, and call center solutions. Staffed by a five-member team, the Company also provides advisory services in regards to marketing and computer telecommunications. Services are provided primarily to the German market. **Career Highlights:** Director/Owner, PRISMA Marketing (1990-Present); Business Consultant: Krone AG, Plaut AG, SAP AG, SNI AG, UBW GmbH, TeraCom GmbH (1990-Present); Webmaster (1997-Present); Lecturer in Marketing Economics/Business, Deutsche Akademie fur Bank & Immobilien Wirtschaft (1996). **Associations & Accomplishments:** Chartered Senior Consultant, (UBW the German Chamber of Commerce); Partner, HTDC; IWA; IPPA; HWG; Net ProCon; ACSA; SAP Professional Organization; AKC; i-Consulting. **Education:** Volkswirt (FU-Berlin), Diploma; Wirtschafbingenieur cand. (Tu-Berlin), Diploma; Senior Business Consultant, Anlange-und Wirtschaftsberater, diploma. **Personal Information:** Mr. Stauch enjoys skiing and art.

Frederic Stemmelin

President/Chief Executive Officer
IDB Consulting
351 Monroe Drive
Palo Alto, CA 94306-4418
(650) 559-9353
Fax: (650) 559-9353
stemmelin@idbconsulting.com

7379

Business Information: Combining management skills and software expertise, Mr. Stemmelin joined the IDB Consulting team in 1995 as President and Chief Executive Officer of United States operations based in Palo Alto. In this capacity, he develops and implements both strategic and tactical marketing and sales plans. He is charged with orchestrating aggressive expansion into new markets, developing new service offering, and engaging in strategic alliances, joint ventures, and acquisitions. Mr. Stemmelin, accountable for taking a lead role in driving growth, manages client-specific marketing programs, maintains personalized contacts with the clientele, and conducts service presentations for potential clients. With overall responsibilities for administrative activities, he identifies new service and marketing opportunities to support the Company's annual growth target. An accomplished professional, e was interviewed by television networks in France on upcoming client server architecture and methodology. Mr. Stemmelin, owning a consistent record of delivering results in support of business objectives, plans on opening offices on the East Coast of the United States. He also is pushing for an increase in the market shares and enhancing the United States professional network. Mr. Stemmelin's favorite advice for others in the industry is "make the money before you look for too much growth." IDB Consulting is a consulting and software development company. Headquartered in Paris, France, the Companys' United States headquarters is located in Palo Alto, California. The Company specializes in databases using Oracle and Sybase platforms. Currently, the producs include editing and managing PL/SQL codes, and business document management. Targeting banking and pharmaceutical industries, IDB Consulting employs a global staff of 35 people with five assigned to the Palo Alto office. Established in 1995, the Company reports annual revenue of excess of $2 million. **Career Highlights:** President/Chief Executive Officer, IDB Consulting (1995-Present); General Manager, James Martin & Company (1995-96); Sales Manager, Powersoft (formerly SDP) (1993-94). **Education:** Institute of Technology, Associate's degree (1989). **Personal Information:** Mr. Stemmelin enjoys snowboarding, windsurfing and golf. He is also fluent in German, French, and English.

Daniel Stence

Consulting Partner
Silicon Plains Technologies
227 Zwart Road
Des Moines, IA 50312-5401
(515) 243-1300
Fax: (515) 225-8787
dstence@worldnet.att.net

7379

Business Information: Mr. Stence, displaying his skills in this highly specialized position, serves as Consulting Partner for Silicon Plains Technologies. In his current capacity, he is responsible for designing and implementing a wide array of high technology electronic document management systems. Drawing on 20 years of occupational experience, Mr. Stence is in charge of conducting analysis and identifying new data services and methods. An expert professional and rich in skills and knowledge, he is a Certified Document Imaging Architech and has received the Master of Information Technologies from AIIM. Mr. Stence, always alert to opportunities and techniques, continues to set high goals and objective. His goals are to become a Certified Records manager, organize industry educational events, enhance leadership skills, and be more involved in Junior Achievement. Founded in 1994, Silicon Plains Technologies provides custom application development, network and infrastructure design, and electronic document management solutions. Reporting an estimated annual revenue in excess of $2 million, the Company, an IBM and Microsoft business partner, helps its clients leverage information technology to solve business challenges. National and diverse in scope, Silicon Plains is centrally located in Des Moines, Iowa. Presently, the Company employs a staff of nearly 25 technical professionals. **Career Highlights:** Consulting Partner, Silicon Plains Technologies (1999-Present); Document Imaging Specialist, Hughes Image Systems (1998-1999); Strategic Application Manager, Crest Information Technologies (1996-98); Vice President of Sales, Digital Data Resources (1994-96); District Sales Manager, First Image Management Company (1979-94). **Associations & Accomplishments:** Association for Information and Image Management; Association for Record Managers and Administrators; Junior Achievement. **Education:** University of Iowa, Bachelor's degree in Business Administration (1976). **Personal Information:** Married to Beth in 1977. Mr. Stence enjoys golf and politics.

Ryan K. Stephens
President, Oracle DBA
Perpetual Technologies, Inc.
3500 DePauw Boulevard, Suite 2008
Indianapolis, IN 46217
(317) 824-0393
Fax: (317) 824-0394
ryan@perptech.com

7379

Business Information: Mr. Stephens is President of Oracle DBA for Perpetual Technologies, Inc. He is responsible for day-to-day administration and operational activities. Identifying a need in the industry, Mr. Stephens found his niche and started up Perpetual Technologies. As founder and owner, he determines the overall strategic direction and vision and business contribution of the information systems function. Before starting the Corporation, he served as Oracle Database Administrator for both Unisys Corporation and EDS. His success as a leader reflects his ability to build and lead teams with synergy and technical strength, think out-of-the-box, and take on new challenges. Administering and controlling Oracle database resources, Mr. Stephens is in charge of development and implementation of new software, as well as providing technical support and training. Maintaining public relations and coordinating resources, schedules, and communications for applications development projects also fall within the purview of his responsibilities. He keeps on top of emerging technologies and systems development methodologies by training and reading. Expand and grow business operations and clientele to a national and international level serves as Mr. Stephens' strategic objectives. Mr. Stephens is also a six-time published author for MacMillan Computer Publishing USA. Some of his works include: "Teach Yourself SQL in 21 Days, 2E," "Teach Yourself SQL in 21 Days, 3E," "Teach Yourself SQL in 24 Hours," "Oracle Unleashed, 2E," "Oracle 8 Server Unleashed," and "Oracle Development Unleashed." Mr. Stephens is an Instructor for Indiana University-Purdue University at Indianapolis, Division of Continuing Studies, where he has developed an Oracle and UNIX training program from the ground up. Perpetual Technologies, Inc. is a computer consulting and training provider specializing in Oracle and UNIX operating systems. Local in scope, the Corporation is located in Indianapolis, Indiana. Established in 1997, Perpetual Technologies presently employs a staff of 11 professional and technical experts. **Career Highlights:** President, Oracle DBA, Perpetual Technologies, Inc. (1997-Present); Instructor, Indiana University (1997-Present); Database Administrator, Unisys Corporation (1996-97); Database Administrator, EDS (1995-96). **Associations & Accomplishments:** Independent Computer Consultant Association; Indiana Oracle Users Group. **Education:** Indiana University (Currently Attending); United States Army Computer Science School. **Personal Information:** Married to Tina in 1992. One child: Daniel. Mr. Stephens enjoys outdoor sports, chess and writing.

Winston M. Stewart
Information Systems Consultant
ComDyn Group, LLC
651 East 4th Street, Suite 100
Chattanooga, TN 37403
(423) 763-3585
stewartw@edge.net

7379

Business Information: Mr. Stewart is an Information Systems Consultant for the ComDyn Group, LLC. Working for Blue Cross Blue Shield of Tennessee, he is responsible for consulting services in the realm of operating and database management and data warehouse systems software. Project management, including coordinating resources and schedules and determining future resource requirements also fall within the scope of Mr. Stewart's functions. Before joining ComDyn Group, he served as both Consultant and Manager of Database Administration with OAO, Inc. His active affiliation with industry related associations enables him to remain current, and allows him to network and interact with the many professionals in the field. As a solid, 36 year professional, Mr. Stewart owns an established track record of producing results in support of the Company's technical and business objectives. Eventually attaining the position of Project Manager working with decision support software in the

Data Warehouse Department serves as one of his future endeavors. A fully integrated provider of networking solutions, ComDyn Group, LLC specializes in software consulting and business systems design, development, and implementation. National in scope, the Company operates a network of several nationwide locations. **Career Highlights:** Information Systems Consultant, ComDyn Group, LLC (1997-Present); OAO, Inc.: Consultant (1996-97), Manager of Database Administration (1985-96). **Associations & Accomplishments:** International Data Warehouse; Federal Government Information Processing Council; National Management Association. **Education:** University of Kansas (1963). **Personal Information:** Married to Rachel in 1961. One child: Kevin. Mr. Stewart enjoys hunting and tae-kwon-do.

Keith Stokes
West Region Projects Manager
Entex Information Technology Services, A Siemens Company
1200 Northwest Naito Parkway
Portland, OR 91209-2830
(503) 243-5416
Fax: (503) 241-8414
keithstokes@entex.com

7379

Business Information: Responsible for all technological projects within Entex Informations Technology Services, A Siemen's Company, Mr. Stokes serves as West Region Projects Manager. He is accountable for all projects in a 17 state region located West of the Mississippi. A successful, 14 year veteran of the field, Mr. Stokes is engaged in contract negotiation and pricing as well as management and oversight of project managers and delivery teams in his region. Coordinating resources, time lines, and assignments and monitoring both profit and loss statistics also fall within the realm of his responsibility. Presently seeking ways to expand upon his intellectual territory, Mr. Stokes is introducing new policies and innovative technologies into his operations. Established in 1996, Entex Information Technology Services, A Siemens Company, is one of the country's leading information technology services firm. Providing a full range of services to build, maintain, and manage entire company infrastructures, Entex Information Technology Services is a unique combination of several service companies, making them a first choice among major corporations nationwide. **Career Highlights:** West Region Projects Manager, Entex Information Technology Services, A Siemens Company (1997-Present); Project Manager, Columbia College (1996-97); Consultant, Self Employed (1993-96); Department Head, Winco Foods (1986-93). **Education:** University of Phoenix, Master's degree (In Progress); Portland State University, B.S. **Personal Information:** Four children: Genavee, Benjamin, Jared, and Justin. Mr. Stokes enjoys seminars, reading and writing.

Keith Stolle
President
Internet Gateway, Inc.
1915 South Austin Avenue #108
Georgetown, TX 78626
(512) 930-1022
Fax: (512) 868-9080
keith@thegateway.net

7379

Business Information: Possessing natural ability, Mr. Stolle got into technology at the young age of 17 and became fascinated with computer technology. Pursuing his goal, he worked for State Farm Insurance as a Network Administrator till 1997 when he ventured out on his own and established Internet Gateway, Inc. One of three partners, Mr. Stolle presently serves as President and is responsible for all aspects of technical support and systems administration. He also oversees Internet services to include dial-up access and Web page hosting. Drawing from over 16 years of practical experience, Mr. Stolle is in charge of reorganizing and restructuring data to better suit the specific needs of the Corporation and clientele. Helping clients realize the maximum benefit from the monies invested in technology equipment and processes also fall under the realm of his responsibilities. He attributes his professional success to excellent work ethic by his parents. Continuing to grow the Corporation, becoming more involved with hands-on operations, hiring additional people, and doing more for his community serves as Mr. Stolle's long-term goals. One of only three Internet service providers in the Georgetown, Texas area, Internet Gateway, Inc. was established in 1996 and operates as a state-of-the-art Internet service provider. Local in scope, the Corporation is manned by a staff of four technology professionals generating in excess of $300,000 in annual revenues. **Career Highlights:** President, Internet Gateway, Inc. (1997-Present); Network Administrator, State Farm Insurance (1982-97). **Associations & Accomplishments:** Texas Internet Service Providers Association. **Education:** St. Edwards University. **Personal Information:** Married to Donna in 1982. Two children: Ryan

and Gene. Mr. Stolle enjoys handcrafts, bowling, canoeing and kite flying.

Bev Stowell
Chief Executive Officer/Owner
Stowell Data Solutions
P.O. Box 864
Stanton, MI 48888-9702
(517) 831-5237
(517) 831-9233
bstowell@rocketmail.com

7379

Business Information: Stowell Data Solutions provides consulting services to physicians, local government officials, and health care companies. Offering insight on data systems and medical billing, the Company strives to offer the most accurate information possible to the public. Ms. Stowell serves as Chief Executive Officer and Owner of the Company, overseeing the daily operations and making all executive decisions. She regularly meets with local officials and health care industry representatives to discuss and evaluate current data systems. Working closely with her staff, she directs the information systems department to acheive maximum results by utilizing procedures derived from employee input and feedback. Ms. Stowell attributes her success to her love of the industry and her ability to teach herself vital technical concepts. Striving to expand her Company, she looks forward to becoming a major provider of information services to public and private health care companies. Additionally, she serves as Manager of Information Systems Coordinator for Mid Michigan District Health Department. Lending her technical expertise, she oversees the telecommunications, networking, and computer systems for the entire three county region. **Career Highlights:** Chief Executive Officer/Owner, Stowell Data Solutions (1999-Present); Management Information Systems Coordinator, Mid Michigan District Health Department (1999-Present); Office Manager/Information Systems Manager, United Memorial Hospital (1973-90). **Associations & Accomplishments:** National Association of Female Executives; National CMHC User Group. **Education:** Various college courses. **Personal Information:** Married to Lester in 1975. Two children: Carrie and Brandon. Ms. Stowell enjoys reading, music, the wilderness, family time and her work. She also researches and studies the changes in health care data systems and data collection.

Robert J. Strechay Jr.
Consultant
On Source Consulting
15603 Kuykendahl Road, Suite 114
Houston, TX 77090
(281) 880-1100
Fax: (281) 880-1150
strechayr@onsource.com

7379

Business Information: Functioning in the role of Consultant with On Source Consulting, Mr. Strechay specializes in performance management, technical consulting, capacity planning, and providing sales and business developments with technical regiment. In addition, Mr. Strechay also offers internal marketing services. An expert, he attributes his substantial success to having a foundation laid for him by a former boss at his first information technology job. He continues to grow professionally and hopes to continue to help the Company plan and implement e-commerce and Web technologies. Mr. Strechay attributes his success to his ability to think outside the box, deliver results, and aggressively tackle on new challenges. Established in 1994, On Source Consulting is a network consultancy to Fortune 2000 companies. Operating from two locations, the Company focuses on information technology organizations and specializes in business processes, technical engineering, e-commerce, and mergers. The Company currently employs a staff of 100 individuals dedicated to serving the needs of their clientele. **Career Highlights:** Consultant, On Source Consulting (1999-Present); Consultant, Predictive Systems, Inc. (1998-99); Consultant, Strategic Networks (1996-98). **Associations & Accomplishments:** American Management Association; Eagle Scout. **Education:** Boston University: M.S. in Telecommunications (In Progress), B.S. in Business Administration (1997).

Thomas K. Strickland, Jr.
President
Source Net Inc
5881 Leesburg Pike #503
Falls Church, VA 22041-2312
(703) 931-5800
Fax: (703) 820-4990

7379

Business Information: Drawing from a rock solid occupational experience and a firm educational foundation, Mr. Strickland serves as President. In his capacity, he oversees all aspects of day-to-day management and administration activities. In addition, Mr. Strickland orchestrates the formulation of innovative and high impact marketing, business, and new technology strategies. A prominent and respected professional, he is able to effectively and efficiently do more with less resources. An accomplished technical writer, Mr. Strickland has authored internal technical manuals that are used to conduct system training. Mr. Strickland is very proud of his Company and where it is today and has set goals of getting more involved in using Internet and Intranet Protocol. Established in 1990, Source Net, Inc. is an established and reputable management consulting firm. Located in Falls Church, Virginia, the focused attention of Source Net, Inc. is on providing a wide spectrum of Internet consulting services for clients on the East coast. Presently, Source Net, Inc. employs a highly skilled and dedicated work staff of 21 management consultants and administrators. **Career Highlights:** President, Source Net, Inc. (1990–Present); Instructor of Information Systems Technology, North Virginia Community College (1990–Present); Data Manager, Strickland Company (1988–90). **Associations & Accomplishments:** Agricultural Communicator in Education. **Education:** University of Georgia, B.S. in Computer Sciences (1990). **Personal Information:** Mr. Strickland enjoys flying.

Greg D. Strutt
Technician/Programmer
Software Creations
9529 Chaton Road
Laurel, MD 20723
(301) 483-0710
Fax: (301) 483-0748
gstrutt@home.com

7379

Business Information: Dedicated to the success of the Software Creations, Mr. Strutt serves in a dual role of Technician and Programmer. A savvy, 14 year technology professional, he assumes responsibility for all of the computer hardware functions and the majority of the help desk services of the Company. Performing state-of-the-art clipper programs, he also develops customized software for his clients. As the Principal of Software Creations, Mr. Strutt oversees and directs all daily administration and operational activities. In this context, he performs both market research and business development. His success reflects his ability to think out-of-the-box and aggressively take on new challenges. Mr. Strutt's solid background history includes stints as Programmer and Field Engineer with CDSI and Singer Company LSSD. Looking to the new millennium, his strategic focus is on taking Software Creations international. Created in 1992, Software Creations offers computer consulting and a wide variety of other information technology services to its clients. The Company provides hardware upgrades, network installations, and help desk services as well as clipper and access programming. **Career Highlights:** Technician/Programmer, Software Creations (1992–Present); Programmer, CDSI (1990–92); Field Engineer, Singer Company LSSD (1985-90). **Associations & Accomplishments:** Institute of Electrical and Electronics Engineers. **Education:** George Washington University, M.S. in Engineering Management (1990); Capitol College, B.S. in Electrical Engineering Technology (1985). **Personal Information:** Married to Nancy in 1990. Mr. Strutt enjoys computers.

Michelle Yu Su
Application Engineer
Asera, Inc.
600 Clipper Drive, Suite 100
Belmont, CA 94002
(650) 745-2176
michell_su@yahoo.com

7379

Business Information: In her position as Application Engineer for Asera, Inc, Ms. Su designs and activates leading edge e-commerce infrastructures for clients and utilizes various API to integrate with different components. She researches client needs in order to ensure accurate designs and solutions. Excellent at critical and analytical thinking, and creativity and resourcefulness in problem solving, Ms. Su is an invaluable asset to the Corporation's overall success and demonstrates her abilities through excellent task planning and project scheduling. Highly regarded, she encourages and motivates others, and is able to provide suggestions and unique opinions. Appreciated for her intelligence, resourcefulness, and competency, Ms. Su has enjoyed tremendous success in her position and looks forward to assisting in the completion of future corporate goals. Asera provides high value Internet solutions for the business-to-business demand chain. Asera is dedicated to delivering the most comprehensive, flexible, and highest quality e-business application services to encourage client growth, innovation, and the ability to compete at Web speed. The Corporation is headquartered in California and employs a staff of industrious personnel to orchestrate all facets of operations. **Career Highlights:** Application Engineer, Asera, Inc. (2000-Present); Informative Inc.: Architect (2000), Senior Software Engineer (1999-00); Software Developer,

Medical Simulation Corporation (1999); System Administrator, University of Houston (1998); Data Analyst, University of Missouri (1995-97). **Associations & Accomplishments:** Association of Computer Machinery; International WHO'S WHO in Information Technology; Paper "Server-side session management techniques for World Wide Web" presented to Proceedings of ETCE/OMAE2000 Joint Conference. **Education:** University of Houston, M.S. in Computer Science (1998); Sun Certified Java Architect.

Suhendra Sutan
Software Developer
Netforce, Inc.
42 Plymouth Drive
Daly City, CA 94015
(510) 541-3825
ssutan@hotmail.com

7379

Business Information: Serving as a Software Developer of Netforce, Inc., Mr. Sutan develops software systems utilizing actuate reporting tools and Oracle databases. Possessing an excellent understanding of technology, he works with management and systems users to analyze, specify, and design state-of-the-art software solutions and user base compilers for FDA programs. Enjoying what he does, Mr. Sutan hopes to become a software engineer lead in the realm of Internet technology. The highlight of his career is the development of a credit interface software for credit reporting agencies while employed with Loadsoft, Inc. Attributing his success to his faith in God, Mr. Sutan looks forward to assisting in the completion of future corporate goals. Established in 1996, Netforce, Inc. is dedicated to providing clients with consulting services. The Corporation provides software solutions and consulting services to the pharmaceutical and biotechnology industries. Located in Daly City, California, the Corporation employs 25 personnel who works with a number of different clients, such as Pizers. **Career Highlights:** Software Developer, Netforce, Inc. (2000–Present); Software Developer, Loansoft, Inc. (1999); Intern, General Electric (1999). **Associations & Accomplishments:** UPE Computer Honors Society; Institute of Electrical and Electronics Engineers Computer Society; Association of Computing Machinery; ASO Programming Team; Arkansas State University International Student Association. **Education:** Arkansas State University, B.S. (1999). **Personal Information:** Mr. Sutan enjoys basketball, chatting and surfing internet.

Paula Emery Sutton
Technical Team Leader
Pegasus Consulting Group
P.O. Box 670
Londonderry, NH 03053
(603) 661-0817

7379

Business Information: Combining her strategic technical expertise and management skills, Ms. Sutton serves as the Technical Team Leader for the Pegasus Consulting Group. She consults with clients in an effort to accommodate their individual needs and provide them with cutting edge technological solutions. Converting cable into modules, she designs, develops, and implements cutting edge SAP solutions. Ms. Sutton has been working diligently on this project for companies within the chemical industry for over a year. Before joining Pegasus Consulting, she served as a Consultant with PricewaterhouseCoopers. Her background history also includes a stint as Team Lead for IBM Global Services. Establishing goals that are compatible with those of the Pegasus Consulting Group, Ms. Sutton is committed to providing continued optimum service and looks forward to increasing her professional responsibilities as Project Manager. Her success reflects her ability to think outside the box, deliver results, and aggressively take on new challenges and responsibilities. Beginning operations in 1992, Pegasus Consulting Group provides SAP consulting services to an international clientele. The Group employs an approximate work force of 500 knowledgeable personnel. **Career Highlights:** Technical Team Leader, Pegasus Consulting Group (1998-Present); Consultant, PricewaterhouseCoopers (1998); Team Leader, IBM Global Services (1996-98). **Education:** California State University at Chico, B.S. in Management Information Systems and Accounting (1995). **Personal Information:** Married to Scott in 1997. Ms. Sutton enjoys kayaking, hiking, skiing and snow boarding.

Hilary W. Swanson
Director of Information Systems
Ontempo
655 North Central Avenue
Glendale, CA 91203-1400
(818) 649-7785
Fax: (818) 649-8315
hswanson@ontempo.com

7379

Business Information: Utilizing an extensive knowledge of information technology, Mrs. Swanson is the Director of Information Systems for Ontempo. She fulfills a number of technical duties on behalf of the Company and its clientele. Demonstrating strong leadership, Mrs. Swanson determines the technical direction and vision as well as formulates new business and marketing plans, keeping the Company on the cutting edge. In addition, she is active in the architecture design functions, providing solutions and maintaining the Company's system functionality and services. Moreover, she supervises the production, staging, testing, and development of data center teams. Located in Glendale, California, Ontempo engages in providing online services to the media. Founded in 1998, the Company focuses mainly on newspapers but does, however, cater to other media sources. Operating internationally, the Company has a staff of over 50 employees dedicated to providing quality products and services. **Career Highlights:** Director of Information Services, Ontempo (2000-Present); Manager of System Technology, California Power Exchange (1998-00); UNIX System Specialist, Delta Technology (1997-98); UNIX System Specialist, IBM (1996-97); Hewlett Packard (1995-96). **Associations & Accomplishments:** Network and Systems Professional Organization. **Education:** California State University at Long Beach (1998); University of Southern California, B.S. (1996). **Personal Information:** Married to Jeremy in 1999.

Orest Roman Swystun
President
BDC 4 You
8014 Old Georgetown Road
Bethesda, MD 20814
(301) 538-7876
Fax: (603) 308-3090
oswystun@bdc4you.com

7379

Business Information: Mr. Swystun is President of BDC 4 You. Identifying a need in the industry, he decided to go at it alone and establish BDC 4 You in 1999. He is responsible for setting the strategic direction and vision, and overseeing business development, including investments and strategic alliances. Before starting BDC, Mr. Swystun served as Technical Practice Lead with Appix, Inc., where he was responsible for developing cutting edge methodology for the design and development of new technologies. An expert, his history includes Senior Consulting Manager at Noblestar, Independent Consultant working with the United States Navy, and Systems Analyst and Programmer for Unisys. As the chief executive, Mr. Swystun is charged with meeting clients' needs, maintaining public relations, recruiting consultants, and overseeing the staff. Determining future resource requirements and overseeing time lines and schedules also fall within the realm of Mr. Swystun's responsibilities. His active affiliation with industry user groups enables him to remain current, and allows him to network and interact with the many professionals in different fields. He credits his faith in God for his success. Expanding operations internationally serves as one of his future goals. BDC 4 You is a computer consulting company. National in scope, BDC 4 You operates a network of three locations. **Career Highlights:** President, BDC 4 You (1999-Present); Technical Practice Lead, Appix, Inc. (1997-99); Senior Consulting Manager, Noblestar (1995-97); Independent Consultant, Independent Oracle, United States Navy (1991-95); Systems Analyst/Programmer, Unisys (1986-91). **Associations & Accomplishments:** International Oracle Users Group; Middle Atlantic Oracle Professionals; The Washington Group; Oracle Developers Tool User Group; PLASAT, Ukrainian Scouting Organization. **Education:** Edinboro University, B.S. in Computer Science (1986). **Personal Information:** Married to Teresa Stasiuk in 1998. Mr. Swystun enjoys camping.

Aamir Mazhar Syed
Senior Consultant/Owner
A&S Solutions, Inc.
196 Dock Road
Matawan, NJ 07747
asyed@erols.com

7379

Business Information: The Owner of A&S Solutions, Inc. Mr. Syed functions as Senior Consultant responsible for all day-to-day administration and operational activities. An information systems professional with 15 years in the field, Mr. Syed provides state-of-the-art consulting services to his international clientele. Before starting A&S, he served as a Consultant at RIS Information Systems and as a Systems

Analyst with Bellcore. Concurrently, Mr. Syed also serves as Project Leader with AT&T Corporation. He owns an established track record of producing results. His track record includes: development of an integrated financial software system to automate changes in the account technical field; design and development of an Internet payable and purchasing system using bar codes; and increased cost efficiency by eliminating 12 manpower positions in the Management Information Systems Department. Mr. Syed's future strategic objective is to increase the client base. An expert, his career success reflects his ability to think outside the box and aggressively take on new challenges. A&S Solutions, Inc. engages in computer software consulting. Providing services on a contract basis to large companies, A&S Solutions specializes in financial and accounts payable and receivable software development for clients internationally. Established in 1997, the Corporation is manned by three dedicated professional experts. **Career Highlights:** Senior Consultant/Owner, A&S Solutions, Inc. (1997-Present); Project Leader, AT&T Corporation (1996-Present); Consultant, RIS Information Systems (1995-96); Systems Analyst, Bellcore (1990-95). **Associations & Accomplishments:** Oracle Applications User Group. **Education:** Stevens Institute of Technology, M.S. (1990); Jersey City State College, B.S. (1987). **Personal Information:** Married in 1994. One child: Faiz. Mr. Syed enjoys swimming and biking.

Leela Shankar Tamma
Software Developer
Rapidigm
1470 West 116th Avenue, Apartment 30
Denver, CO 80234
(303) 926-8518
ltamma@yahoo.com

7379

Business Information: As Software Developer for Rapidigm, Mr. Tamma is responsible for implementing and developing new software. He focuses his attention on such areas as design, project development, learning systems performance, and the development of algorithms. With more than three years of experience with the Company, Mr. Tamma is considered a powerful asset in that he demonstrates his abilities to conduct work of the most complex nature. His future aspirations for his career include staying well informed of changing technologies in order to provide only quality in his chosen profession. Mr. Tamma attributes his success to his supportive parents as well as his ability to take on challenges and deliver results. Rapidigm engages in the provision of information technology services for the management and development of software and corresponding processes. Primary projects are implemented for the production of electical appliances and other electronic devices used in businesses all over the world. Established in 1995, the Company is headquartered in Pittsburgh, Pennsylvania, and operates out of 12 other convenient locations. The Company functions under the guidance and dedication of more than 750 highly skilled professionals at the Denver, Colorado facility. **Career Highlights:** Software Developer, Rapidigm (1997-Present); Systems Analyst, Remote Servicing Instruments (1995-97). **Associations & Accomplishments:** Institute of Electrical and Electronics Engineers. **Education:** IPGSR JNTU India, Master's in Technical (1997)

Kenny T. H. Tan
President/Chief Executive Officer
Berjaya USA Group, Inc.
83-26 Broadway
Elmhurst, NY 11373
(718) 458-1600
Fax: (718) 639-6389
ktan5377@aol.com

7379

Business Information: Looking for new challenges and taking calculated risks, Mr. Tan ventured out into the corporate world with a partner to establish Berjaya USA Group, Inc. At the present time, he assumes the responsibilities of President and Chief Executive Officer. In these roles, Mr. Tan oversees all management aspects of day-to-day administrative and consulting activities. He facilitates formulation of the Corporation's creative vision and development of powerful technology, sales, marketing, and business strategies. Utilizing his strong academic background and Microsoft and Novell certifications, Mr. Tan is responsible for all training activities at the Corporation's computer training school. Providing consultation and advice to users, Mr. Tan implements the means for computer technology to meet the specific needs of individual clients. Directing and participating in the analysis, acquisition, modification, and configuration to harness more of the computer's power also falls within the realm of his responsibilities. An independent business operation, Mr. Tan's goal is to change along with technology and learn more and more everyday. The strategic plan is to expand operations in the market place and become more successful. Berjaya USA Group, Inc. is a computer training, retail, and consulting firm. Based in New York, the Corporation operates a network of four offices along with the largest training school in Queens. Established in 1992 and local in

scope, the local operation in Elmhurst presently employs a work force of more than 20 technology professionals. **Career Highlights:** President/Chief Executive Officer, Berjaya USA Group, Inc. (1997-Present); Chief Executive Officer, ANK. **Associations & Accomplishments:** Microsoft Certified Solution Provider; Computing Technology Industry Association; Network Professional Association. **Education:** New York Institute of Technology, M.S. (1992); University of Toledo; Certified Novell Engineer; Microsoft Certified System Engineer; Microsoft Certified Trainer. **Personal Information:** Married to Mallory in 1992. Two children: Samuel and Elaine. Mr. Tan enjoys to travel.

Andrew L. Tang
Vice President of Global Customer Relationship Management Practice
TEQ International
234 St. Francis Street, #2H
San Gabriel, CA 91776
(949) 433-3258
andrewtang@home.com

7379

Business Information: Displaying his skills in this highly specialized position, Mr. Tang serves as Vice President of Global Customer Relationship Management Practice for TEQ International. He oversees and directs CRM projects in Europe, North America, Latin America, and Asia. Offering global vision with local strategies, Mr. Tang handles new business development and designs the project team infrastructure. Assisting the managing directors for the various companies, he ensures that the companies reach its target revenue. Mr. Tang achieved his current position after only four years in the profession through his exceptional job performance and his ability to understand and solve complex problems on a global scale. His goal is to expand the Company from the present 250 employees up to 2,000, ensuring a solid company base before going public. Mr. Tang's career success reflects his ability to deliver results as promised and aggressively take on new challenges. TEQ International is a rapidly growing global consulting firm, offering technology consulting and implementation services. Headquartered in Amsterdam, Netherlands, the Company provides consulting on application systems, customer relations management, business improvements, and e-commerce solutions. Additional services in the European Recovery Program and SAP are offered. Presently, TEQ International employs a staff of more than 250 individuals. **Career Highlights:** Vice President of Global Customer Relationship Management Practice, TEQ International (1999-Present); Director of Technology Solutions, Keane (CRM Solutions Practice) (1998-99); Technology Consultant, Andersen Consulting (1996-98). **Education:** California State University at Long Beach, Bachelor's degree in Management Information Systems (1996). **Personal Information:** Married to Holly Qian in 1994.

Dan Tansanu
Owner
Datainterdev, Ltd.
24-5975 Av De L'authion
Montreal, Quebec, Canada H1M 2W3
(514) 493-6187
dan@tansa.nu

7379

Business Information: As Owner of Datainterdev, Ltd., Mr. Tansanu drew upon his proven business skills and technical expertise to found the Company two years ago. The Company's sole employee, he specializes in Web development and database integration services. He is accustomed to working with large projects and was responsible for the development of the shell for a European database prototype and the development of the largest freelance network on the Web for the Opus 360 Company based in New York. A believer in continuous learning, Mr. Tansanu advises newcomers to the field of information technology to get a varied amount of experience. He is the author of several books which were published in the Romanian and Sans script languages. Attributing his professional success to self-knowledge and his spirituality, he looks forward to being completely independent as well as developing and owning several of his own Web sites. Datainterdev, Ltd. is a consulting service, focusing its efforts on providing Web and database architecture. Founded in 1997, the Company offers its services to an international clientele primarily based in the United States and Canada. **Career Highlights:** Owner, Datainterdev, Ltd. (1997-Present); Web Developer, U.S. WEB/CKS (1999); Consultant, Videotron (1995-99). **Associations & Accomplishments:** A.R.T.; Microsoft Network. **Education:** Master's degree (1984).

Ron A. Tanuwidjaja
Principal Consultant
FutureNext Consulting, Inc.
10720 Ridgefield Terrace
Moreno Valley, CA 92557
(909) 536-8307
rtanuwidjaja@futurenext.com

7379

Business Information: Serving as the Principal Consultant for FutureNext Consulting, Inc., Mr. Tanurwidjaja oversees and directs all day to day database administration. He is responsible for working with clients to assist in the administration of systems within the organizations including systems assessment and upgrade. As a systems architect, he works closely with systems management and users to analyze, specify, and design and implement new solutions into exiting architectures, thereby enhancing overall systems operations. Attributing his success to his ability to seamlesssly implement new system without any glitches, Mr. Tanuwidjaja remains on the cutting edge of technology by training, reading, and participating in user groups. In the future, he plans on obtaining an executive management position, in addition to continuing working hands on. Located in Moreno Valley, California, FutureNext is a consulting firm. Providing services mainly in the areas of enterprise resource planning and e-commerce, the Firm employs 400 talented professionals. The Firm offers clients new and innovative technological solutions used by clients in the process of daily operations. **Career Highlights:** Principal Consultant, FutureNext Consulting, Inc. (1999-Present); Senior Principal Consultant, Oracle (1996-99); Senior Programmer/Analyst, Health Net (1993-96). **Education:** California State University at Santa Barbara, B.S. in Computer Systems (1989).

Thomas A. Tay
Vice President/Founder
Hawaii Multimedia Corporation
1019 University Avenue, Suite 2A
Honolulu, HI 96826-1509
(808) 946-6123
Fax: (808) 946-2750
tom@rainbows.net

7379

Business Information: A savvy, four year veteran of technology, Mr. Tay ventured into the multimedia industry to start up Hawaii Multimedia Corporation. As the Founder, he serves as Vice President responsible for daily administration and operational activities. He determines the overall strategic direction and formulates new business and marketing plans to maintain the Corporation's competitiveness and position in the markets. Drawing from his academics and business experience, Mr. Tay takes a hands on approach on technical related issues, such as field work adn solutions implementation. He believes that e-business is the driving force behind successful companies. One of many strategic objectives, he plans on establishing additional locations to promote the Corporation and provide clients with solutions on demand. Success according to Mr. Tay is attributed to his knowledge base, curiosity, and desire as well as his ability to think out-of-the-box and deliver cutting edge results. An international technology company, Hawaii Multimedia Corporation operates as a Microsoft certified solutions provider. Established in 1998, the Corporations provides on-line computer and telecommunications support, consulting and integration services, and Web and e-business solutions. Headquartered in Honolulu, Hawaii, the Corporation operates two locations, providing customers with services laced with quality, value, and reliability. **Career Highlights:** Vice President/Founder, Hawaii Multimedia Corporation (1997-Present); Sales Associate/Financial Representative, Prudential Financial Services (1996). **Associations & Accomplishments:** Microsoft Certified Systems Engineer. **Education:** University of Hawaii, B.B.A. (1996). **Personal Information:** Married. Mr. Tay enjoys reading and sports, primarily basketball.

George V. Tereshko
Database Administrator
Genesys Labs
1155 Market Street
San Francisco, CA 94103-1522
(415) 437-1065
Fax: (415) 432-1260
george@genesyslab.com

7379

Business Information: In his current position as a Database Administrator for Genesys Labs, Mr. Tereshko is responsable for data base administration, UNIX/NT, and overseeing development support. Utilizing his information technological skils, he is able to assist numerous departments in computer and telephone integration, management solutions, and the Internet. Years of education and experience in the field have enabled Mr. Tereshko to acquire the skills necessary to effectively complete his job duties. Dedicated to the success of Genesys Labs, he keeps abreast on new developments in the field, reads current literature, and attends professional seminars. Enjoying the satifaction he receives from helping others, Mr. Tereshko attributes his success to determination. Genesys Labs produces enterprise interactive management software such as computers, telephony, and integration. Established in1990, the Company employs the expertise of 7,500 dedicated and highly skilled individuals. Headquartered in San Francisco, California, the Company strives to provide the most current, technological products in the field. **Career Highlights:** Database Administrator, Genesys Labs (1996-Present); Senior Software Engineer, Chicago Financial Tech. (1997); Unix Admininstrator, Transnet Company, Moscow (1995-96). **Education:** Moscow Institute of Physics and Technology, M.S. (1989). **Personal Information:** Married to Tanya in 1978. Two children: Valentine and Eugene. Mr. Tereshko enjoys computers.

Malcolm W. Tester II

Manager of Information Systems
Cambric Corporation
110 West Business Park Drive
Draper, UT 84020
(801) 816-8900
Fax: (801) 816-8908
mtester@cambric.com

7379

Business Information: Recruited to Cambric Corporation in 1998, Mr. Tester serves as Manager of Information Systems. He presides over the Information Technology Department and serves as the chief liaison and technical consultant for two local and six off site locations. Responsible for the administration, maintenance, and software installation and updates, he ensures that any revised programs are made available to the off site locations and are functioning properly. Keeping abreast of industry changes through his personal drive and thirst for knowledge, Mr. Tester states that there is no catching up within the technology field. He is continually learning by reading, networking on the Internet, and attending seminars. His goal is to achieve a Senior Management or Director's position within the Information Technology Department. Established in 1989, Cambric Corporation provides data conversion and collaborative engineering outsourcing to commercial companies, large corporations, and the government. The Corporation's essential function is to convert a paper drawing into a 3D model, making it easier to understand. International operations employ over 400 skilled professionals. **Career Highlights:** Manager of Information Systems, Cambric Corporation (1998-Present); Networking Consultant, TEKsystems (1997-98); Manager of Information Systems, Universal Gym Equipment (1995-97). **Education:** Davidson County Community College (1997); Purdue University, B.S. in Computer Technology. **Personal Information:** Married to Joanie in 1977. Two children: Brianne and Jasmine. Mr. Tester enjoys taking family vacations.

Ajit Tharaken

Software Developer
Data Downlink Corporation
322 West 104 Street, #1R
New York, NY 10025
(212) 218-6843
Fax: (212) 218-6841
ajit.tharaken@ibm.net

7379

Business Information: Mr. Tharaken is a Software Developer at Data Downlink Corporation. Data Downlink, established in 1996, provides online data on various subjects via their flagship service .xls. In this capacity, he develops and creates Internet based tools and data warehousing applications. .xls is a Web-based information service providing knowledge professionals with access to a broad array of quantitative business information. Data Downlink Corporation gathers data from multiple sources, then provides cross-indexes and cross-links before making the data available to information consumers in spreadsheet format over the World Wide Web. .xls contains company financials, economic, demographic, industry, country, and market-specific data, all in one easy-to-search Web site at http://www.xls.com. He also created a product called privatesuite(TM). Privatesuite(TM) is the fastest, easiest, and most cost-effective way to identify and retrieve profiles on privately-held companies around the world. A new .xls application, privatesuite(TM), simultaneously searches across multiple private company databases for companies that meet user-defined criteria. He has more recently been working on a search protal called PortalB. PortalB is a search engine which "breaks the search barrier." Not only does it search the Web but also searches premium data from .xls and provides results to the users in an easy format. This new approach in search technology is the first of its kind. He also has helped raise over a million dollars in venture funding from investors for PortalB. Prior to working at Data Downlink, he served as the Director of Technology for the Arista Group. In this capacity, he developed and created investor an tool for analysis and reporting. He is the co-founder and creator of www.altvest.com, which grew rapidly and became an independent "spin-off" operation. This product directly impacted the hedge fund industry by providing timely and accurate information on hedge funds in real time. Arista Group provides financial advisory services to high net worth clients worldwide. **Career Highlights:** Software Developer, Data Downlink Corporation (Present); Director of Technology, Arista Group (1996-99); Systems Administrator, Columbia Law School (1995-96); Software Programmer, Lawrence Berkeley Labs (1995). **Associations & Accomplishments:** Institute of Electronics and Electrical Engineers; American Association for the Advancement of Science. **Education:** Columbia University, Master's degree (1996); R.V. College of Engineering, Bachelor's degree in Computer Science and Engineering (1994). **Personal Information:** Mr. Tharaken enjoys tennis and bicycling.

Gary A. Therens

Director of Channel Development
Control Data Systems, Inc.
4201 North Lexington Avenue
Arden Hills, MN 55126
(651) 415-4208
Fax: (651) 415-4344
gary.therens@cdc.com

7379

Business Information: Mr. Therens functions in the capacity of Director of Channel Development with Control Data Systems, Inc. He is responsible for all aspects of electronic commerce marketing and channel development for Control Data Systems' United States and European operations. A 10 year expert, Mr. Therens orchestrates the development of the strategic direction and formulates powerful marketing and business plans to keep the Company at the forefront in the industry. He has faithfully served with Control Data Systems in a variety of positions since coming on board as Messaging Marketing Manager in 1996. In addition to supervising and mentoring his staff of six employees, Mr. Therens is responsible for channel security, reliable, and efficiency. His future plans include eventually attaining the position of Vice President. Control Data Systems, Inc., a subsidiary of Syntegra, offers a variety of quality services to customers. Founded in 1992, the Corporation is a provider of systems integration services, e-commerrce solutions, and outsourcing in which they plan, implement, and manage all aspects for Fortune 1000 companies' information systems infrastructure. Control Data Systems employs a work force of 1,100 individuals who help generate annual sales in excess of $280 million. Headquarters are located in Arden Hills, Michigan. **Career Highlights:** Control Data Systems, Inc: Director of Channel Development (1999-Present), Manager, EIS Marketing (1998-99), Messaging Marketing Manager (1996-98). **Associations & Accomplishments:** Electronic Messaging Association. **Education:** University of Minnesota, B.S. in Marketing (1989) **Personal Information:** Married to Patricia in 1995. Four children: Rich, Julie, Brian, and Scott.

K. Michael Thomas

Consultant
Insys Inc.
8141 Greentree Drive
Elkridge, MD 21075-6226
(410) 799-4450
kmthomas@home.com

7379

Business Information: A savvy, 13 year veteran of technology, Mr. Thomas serves as Consultant of Insys Inc. He works closely with management and users to analyze, specify, and design financial solutions to keep clients on the leading edge in their industries. In this context, he performs gap analysis, creates functional and technical designs, and configures financial aspects of products which enables him to implement cutting edge strategies. Utilizing his personal quality of astute attention to detail, Mr. Thomas is currently working on a project for the American Red Cross for which he finds quite fulfilling. Looking into the future, he intends to stay abreast of up and comming Web based applications which will enable him to capitalize on opportunities offered by the Corporation. His success reflects his ability to think outside the box, take on challenges and new responsibilities, and deliver results. One of the largest in the industry, Insys Inc. is a management systems integrator, aiding in the development and implementation of Oracle financial systems. Providing LAN/WAN connectivity designs, the Corporation also provides Internet solutions, products, and services as well as design and configurations for file and CD-ROM servers, custom programming solutions, and other related products. Utilizing the expertise of 20 skilled professionals, Insys Inc. is able to match the organizational needs of their clientele. **Career Highlights:** Consultant, Insys Inc. (1997-Present); Senior Applications Analyst, Squires Group (1996-97); Senior Applications Analyst, Kenda Systems (1995-96). **Education:** University of Maryland College Park, B.S. (1987). **Personal Information:** Mr. Thomas enjoys travel, tennis and going to the beach.

Norman Thompson

Director/Principal Consultant
International Data Solutions
1721 Blanding Boulevard, Suite 106
Jacksonville, FL 32210
(904) 388-3966
Fax: (904) 388-5069
nthompson@idsonline.net

7379

Business Information: Serving as Director and Principal Consultant for International Data Solutions, Mr. Thompson oversees and directs all daily administration and operational activities, such as monitoring financial and profit and loss statistics as well as approving the fiscal budget. Overseeing all operations, Mr. Thompson supervises his staff of 20 employees, to include the Jacksonville, Florida office of 5 people. Possessing an excellent understanding of technology, he has been Oracle certified for over 13 years and he is designated as the Company's technical troubleshooter. Among his many professional accomplishments, he created the first cluster database in Dallas in 1992. In the future, Mr. Thompson plans on designing and developing more e-commerce applications. Established in 1997, International Data Solutions is a software consulting firm. Headquartered in Atlanta, Georgia, the Firm specificalizes in developing, consulting, placement, and training of the client's employees. Employing 15 individuals of varying professional specializations, the Firm provides these services internationally. **Career Highlights:** Director/Principal Consultant, International Data Solutions (1997-Present); Senior Oracle Database Administrator, CSX Technologies (1996-97). **Associations & Accomplishments:** Jacksonville Chamber of Commerce. **Education:** University of Southern Mississippi, B.A. in Science (1986). **Personal Information:** Married to Olive in 1981. Three children: Mevannie, Mark, and Melissa.

Wesley Thompson

Network Administrator
Application Partners, Inc.
235 Camelback Raod, Apartment 239
Pleasant Hill, CA 94523-1473
(925) 552-8230
Fax: (925) 552-8243
wthompson@goapi.com

7379

Business Information: Following a distinguished career in the United States Navy, Mr. Thompson now serves in the capacity of Network Administrator for Application Partners, Inc. Radiating excellence in the computer science field, he oversees all aspects of daily administration and operations. He also helps determines the overall technical direction and business contribution of the systems function. In this context, Mr. Thompson is responsible for administering the network infrastructure, maintaining LAN/WAN connectivity, purchasing hardware and software, and ensuring the reliability and security of systems. Looking to the future in the 21st century, Mr. Thompson plans on attending college and obtaining a role as Information Systems Manager. Completing his MCSE and administering the largest network while stationed aboard a U.S. Navy aircraft carrier serves as his career highlights. His success is attributed to discipline and consistency and the ability to deliver results and take on challenges. Application Partners, Inc. is a software development company. Catering to insurance imaging and workflow, the Corporation staffs 30 individuals to meet the demands of a growing clientele. Application Partners is headquatered in Pleasant Hill, California. **Career Highlights:** Network Administrator, Application Partners, Inc. (1999-Present); Systems Administrator/Support, United States Navy (1996-99). **Associations & Accomplishments:** Microsoft Certified Systems Engineers; Veteran, United States Navy. **Personal Information:** Mr. Thompson enjoys sports and cooking.

Michael Anthony Tiemann

Director of Division of Architecture and Standards
Office of the Chief Information Officer, United States Department of Energy
1000 Independence Avenue SW, Room 8H-068 (50-321)
Washington, DC 20585
(202) 586-5461
michael.tiemann@hq.doe.gov

7379

Business Information: Mr. Tiemann serves as Director of the Division of Architecture and Standards within the Office of the Chief Information Officer, United States Department of Energy. He is responsible for establishing a technology framework and roadmap to ensure alignment of information systems and resources for business needs. A savvy, 23-year veteran, he is an information architect responsible for supervising 12 federal and 25 contracted support staff members and ensuring the highest professional excellence and innovation. Managing approximately a $4 million annual budget and affecting $1.4 billion in information technology decisions, he represents the Department at forums, conferences, and seminars. Development of Department wide information architect procedures also falls within Mr. Tiemann's responsibilities. A recognized professional, he was a recipient of the 1998 Federal Computer Week/Federal 100 Award. Mr. Tiemann aspires to become the first federal Chief of Information Achitect or an agency Chief Information Officer. The U.S. Department of Energy is a diverse and large agency in the Federal government. It addresses issues involving energy supply, environmental cleanup, national and world security, and scientific research. The Office of the Chief Information Officer is responsible for advising senior Departmental officials on the deployment of information technology and for establishing policy. The Architecture and Standards Division is responsible for establishing and managing the Department wide Information Architecture and IT standards to guide the overall deployment of IT to align to DOE business needs and to meet the requirements of law. The Department's leadership in Information Architecture has affected and influenced OMB policy and the Federal Enterprise Architecture Framework. **Career Highlights:** United States Department of Energy: Director of Divsion of Architecture and Standards, Office of the Chief Information Officer (1998-Present), Information Architecture Program Manager, CIO (1994-98), Information Resource Management Planner, IM (1990-94), IM Project Manager, IRM (1988-90). **Associations & Accomplishments:** Armed Forces Communication and Electronics Association; Association for Federal International Resources Managers; Federal CIO Council's Emerging; Information Technology and Enterprise Interoperability Committee; Former Chair, Federal Agencies Information Architecture Working Group; Former Member, Energy Federal Credit Union Technology Advisory Committee. **Education:** University of Southern California, M.S.S.M. (1977); Texas A&M University, Bachelor's degree in Environmental Design (1972); Chemical Officers Basic School (1972). **Personal Information:** Married to Cynthia in 1981. Two children: Michelle and Matthew. Mr. Tiemann enjoys drawing, painting, writing fictional stories, collecting toys and family activities.

Ronald L. Tiongco

Network Analyst
Unisource Network Services
10 North Dearborn Street, Suite 200
Chicago, IL 60602
(312) 516-3800
Fax: (312) 516-3810
tiongcor@bigfoot.com

7379

Business Information: Possessing advanced technical abilities, Mr. Tiongco serves with Unisource Network Services as a Network Analyst. Utilizing seven solid years of strong practical experience, he manages the information technology infrastructure for the whole enterprise, which currently consists of three offices. He possesses an excellent understanding of his field. Mr. Tiongco's responsibilities include network and telecommunications management, researching new technologies and methods, and planning the budget and overall strategy of the Company's information technology infrastructure. His plan for the future is to become more integrated in his knowledge of network and telecommunication technologies. Highly regarded by his colleagues, Mr. Tiongco's motto is "improvise, adapt, and overcome." Established in 1986, Unisource Network Services is a professional services firm that focuses on the strategic application of telecommunications and network technologies. Headquartered in Chicago, Illinois, the Firm operates from three locations. Reporting annual revenue of $15 million, the Firm employs 100 individuals to ensure that clients derive the highest quality integration of voice, data, and video technologies. **Career Highlights:** Network Analyst, Unisource Network Services (1997-Present); Network Technician, Altheimer & Gray (1996-97); Computer Technician, CompUSA, Inc. (1995-96); Computer Technician, Best Buy Company, Inc. (1993-95). **Education:** DeVry Institute of Technology at Chicago, B.S. in Computer Information Systems (1998).

Christophe Tissier

Web Designer
Graphtis
3C Rue Des Iris
Antony, France 92160
+33146749750
Fax: +33146749750
manager@graphtis.com

7379

Business Information: As Web Designer of Graphtis, Mr. Tissier is also the manager responsible for all day-to-day activities. Drawing from his superior talents and excellent understanding of technology, he posts an amazing 6,500 advertisements monthly. Working in the comfort of his own home, he is also responsible for the strategic and tactical marketing techniques for individualized projects. He takes pride in helping his clientele find opportunities that they never before knew existed. Highlights of his career includes publishing a book in French that has been published in the New York Times and a number of French magazines. Attributing his success to enjoying what he does, Mr. Tissier plans to continue developing and selling Web sites and increasing his clientele. Through his technological vision, combined with his entreprenuerial spirit, Mr. Tissier founded Graphtis in 1998. An information technology business, the Company is involved in designing Web sites. Specifically, the Company recieves the information to be designed and creates an original piece that gets the consumer's attention. Reporting an annual sales mark at an estimated $80,000, the Company also performs printing of old postcards, that is marketed through the Internet. **Career Highlights:** Web Designer, Graphtis (1998-Present). **Associations & Accomplishments:** Who's Who in International Art; Greci Marino Italian University of Art; Published arthur. **Education:** Cambridge University, Proficiency (1992); International Business; Graphic Arts; HTML and Internet related courses. **Personal Information:** Married to Isabelle in 1992. One child: Morgane. Mr. Tissier enjoys reading, surfing the Internet and writing.

John K. Tobison

Vice President/Chief Information Officer
Mapinfo Corporation
1 Global View
Troy, NY 12180
(518) 285-7144
Fax: (518) 285-7420
john.tobison@mapinfo.com

7379

Business Information: Beginning his employment with Mapinfo Corporation more than six years ago, Mr. Tobison has received recognition for his diligence and management skills through several promotions to his current position of Vice President and Chief Information Officer. He assumes overall responsibility for managing the global information technology functions and the corporate network infrastructure. Performing competitor assessments in order to respond quickly to market changes, he presides over the remote mobile field service sales force and the finance department. Mr. Tobison devotes a considerable amount of his time to strategic planning and intends to continue to bring new technology into the Corporation to increase its competitiveness. He attributes his professional success to his ability to communicate on both the business side and the technical side of the Corporation. Serving an international clientele, Mapinfo Corporation is a independent software vendor, providing decision support and mapping solutions for a broad range of applications. The Corporation was created in 1984. Boasting $61 million in annual sales, over 400 knowledgeable employees offer their skills to businesses from various locations. **Career Highlights:** Vice President/Chief Information Officer, Mapinfo Corporation (1994-Present); Managing Associate, Coopers & Lybrand (1984-94); Manager, Arthur Young & Company (1980-84); Software Engineer, Royal Insurance (1977-80). **Education:** State University of New York at Albany: M.B.A. (1990), B.S. (1977). **Personal Information:** Mr. Tobison enjoys backpacking, running, scuba diving, cycling and kayaking.

Barbara J. Todisco

Information Technology Customer Services Manager
GTE Internetworking, Inc.
50 Moulton Street, 2/1B
Cambridge, MA 02138-1119
(617) 873-2896
Fax: (617) 873-2024
btodisco@bbn.com

7379

Business Information: Ms. Todisco serves as the Information Technology Customer Services Manager for GTE Internetworking, Inc. In her position, she is responsible for a wide array of day-to-day customer support functions. An intelligent, sharp, 22-year veteran, she directs internal customer support and service level agreement management. She presides over Help Desk operations, Knowledge Resource Management, and the IT Education and Training Center. Her organization supports the IT needs of more than 6,000 employees. Goals for Ms. Todisco include expanding support operations globally. She credits her success to surrounding herself with knowledgeable and successful people. Headquartered in Cambridge, Massachusetts, GTE Internetworking, a unit of the GTE Corporation (NYSE: GTE) offers customers, from consumers to Fortune 500 companies, a full-spectrum of integrated Internet services using IP networking technologies. GTE Internetworking delivers complete network solutions, including dial-up and dedicated Internet access, high-performance Web hosting, virtual private networks (VPNs), managed Internet security, network management, systems integration, and Web-based application development for integrating the Internet into business operations. Additional information about GTE Internetworking can be found on the Internet at http://www.bbn.com, and about GTE Corporation at http://www.gte.com. GTE Internetworking establishes high standards of professional excellence for all companies within the industry. **Career Highlights:** Information Technology Customer Services Manager, GTE Internetworking, Inc. (1996-Present); Information Technology Business Applications Manager, BBN Corporation (1994-96); Business Applications Manager, Magix Software, Inc. (1987-94). **Associations & Accomplishments:** Women in Technology Information; Help Desk Institute; Gartner Group Research Associate; GTE Chairman Leadership Awards (1998): Bronze Level, Team Leadership, Gold Level Channel Award for Outstanding Team Performance. **Education:** Suffolk University, B.S. in Business Administration (1977). **Personal Information:** Two children: Elena and Daniel. Ms. Todisco enjoys exercising, walking along the ocean, boating and reading. She is an accomplished classical pianist.

Robert N. Toro

Systems Specialist
Fleet Technology Solutions
500 Center Street
Wallingford, CT 06492-3806
(860) 756-5383
robt@snet.net

7379

Business Information: As Systems Specialist of Fleet Technology Solutions, Mr. Toro works with a team of client and server programmers to develop financial information systems using PC, midrange and mainframe technologies. Recruited to manage and redefine the infrastructure, he worked diligently to bring the facilities into compliance and continues to do so with no customer impact. A savvy, nine-year professional, Mr. Toro spearheaded a successful effort to replace and reinstall all production equiptment, including 12 production servers. Mr. Toro's strategic plans include remaining focused on his responsibilities and executing a considerable business investment with Smart Card Technology. His continued success is the result of creating opportunities and establishing solid contacts. Fleet Technology Solutions specializes in technical solutions to business problems and for professional development opportunities. A subsidiary of Fleet National Bank, the Company possesses an international client base. The Company is comprised of a 30,000 member strong workforce supplying quality products and services to a diverse group of clients. Generating $10 million in annual sales, the Company conducts research and makes recommendations for inclusions at offices in New York, Rhode Island, Massachusetts, and Conneticut. **Career Highlights:** Systems Specialist, Fleet Technology Solutions (1997-Present); Senior Network Engineer, ENTEX Information Services (1995-97); Lead Field Technician, TSSI (1993-94); Customer Engineer, Vanstar (1993). **Education:** South Central Connecticut Community College (1991); Connecticut State Certificate in Electronics Theory, Hardware Technician Certified. **Personal Information:** Mr. Toro enjoys writing, playing music and desiging Intranet web sites.

Joe Torrez

Project Success Manager
Vantive Corporation
J. Kumps Str. 28
Overijse, Belgium 3090
+32 26577509
Fax: +32 26577511
joe_torrez@vantive.com

7379

Business Information: Mr. Torrez functions in the capacity of Project Success Manager for the Vantive Corporation. Having been working with the Corporation for years, he has just recently received promotion to this current position. At the present time, Mr. Torrez oversees all aspects of customer loyalty and success in implementing their products. Before joining Vantive as Customer Success Manager, he assertively served with SWIFT in a variety of roles that includes Support Team Lead, Senior Suppjort Specialist, and Tools Coordinator. A 13 year veteran in his field, Mr. Torrez designs customer appreciation campaigns to attract new clients and retain the old. Looking to the next millennium, he plans on remaining with Vantive and help the Company grow and expand operations. His career highlight occurred while working for SWIFT, where he implemented a highly successful call service. Mr. Torrez's success reflects his ability to deliver results and aggressively take on new challenges. Vantive Corporation was established in 1990 and is involved in the enhancement of information technology usage around the world. The Corporation promotes five different software applications through its experienced sales force. Dedicated to customer resource management, the Corporation conducts e-commerce to survey the needs and concerns of the customer. **Career Highlights:** Vantive Corporation: Project Success Manager (1999-Present), Customer Success Manager (1997-99); SWIFT: Support Team Lead (1996-97), Senior Support Specialist (1994-96), Tools Coordinator (1992-94). **Education:** H.I.R.T.O. Deurne, Graduate Level (1986). **Personal Information:** Married to Greet Van Torre in 1992. Three children: Lisa, Enya, and Robin. Mr. Torrez enjoys jogging, biking, reading and films.

Stefan Toth

Business Consultant
DATESSA
Box 81
Sodertalje, Sweden 15121
+46 706271569
Fax: +46 706271569
toth@wartech.com

7379

Business Information: Serving in the capacity of Business Consultant for DATESSA, Mr. Toth fulfills a number of functions on behalf of the Firm and its clientele. He is responsible for sales in corporate portals and business intelligence and consulting in corporate portals and business intelligence as well as identifying new prospects and avenues for additional revenues. Possessing an excellent understanding of business and technology, Mr. Toth provides technical consultations for IBM portal and the business intelligence knowledge center in the Nordic region. In the future, he plans to start up a new company and move to the United States. His success reflects his ability to grasp new concept methodologies, take on challenges, and deliver the appropriate results. Established in 1986, DATESSA operates as a consulting firm. Providing services in database progress, business intelligence, and corporate portals, the Company works closely with large corporations such as Brio Technology, IBM, and DB2. Employing a staff of 24 personnel, the Company develops and updates databases for client use. **Career Highlights:** Business Consultant, DATESSA (1998-Present); Owner, WarpTech (1997-99); Systems Administrator, Dresser Wayne (1997-98). **Associations & Accomplishments:** Rotary Youth Leadership Award. **Education:** Royal Institute of Technology, Bachelor's degree in Computers (2000); High School Electrical Engineer (1996). **Personal Information:** Mr. Toth enjoys travel, diving and jet kundo.

Allan T. Towl

Owner
Information Systems Services
3, 4th Street
Attleboro, MA 2703
(508) 226-8704
atowl44@naisp.net

7379

Business Information: Mr. Towl is Owner of Information Systems Services, and also serves as Senior Consultant. Maintaining both of these roles, he is able to demonstrate impressive technical abilities and business savvy. With seemingly innate communicative ease, he meets with customers who are largely involved in the publishing industry to evalutate their current business situations. After developing action plans, Mr. Towl makes necessary purchases to streamline and upgrade networks as he personally installs and maintains the systems. Credited with the creation of a cost-cutting, time-saving e-business application to fully automate a publishing company, Mr. Towl feels a great deal of his success stems from his flexibility and open mindedness. A celebrated author, he looks forward to continued success in the consulting industry. Information Systems Services is located in the bustling city center of Attleboro, Massachusetts. The sole proprietorship of information technology consulting services in the area, the Company was established in 1998. Recognized throughout the professional community as a quality provider of technical services, the Company looks forward to continued success and prosperity. **Career Highlights:** Owner, Information Systems Services (1998-Present); Chief Systems Architect, Mostby Consumer Health (1996-97); Director of Information Systemes, Madison Publishing (1994-96); Prinicpal Consultant, Information Systems Services (1992-94). **Associations & Accomplishments:** Microsoft Developers Network. **Education:** University of Connecticut, B.S. (1974). **Personal Information:** Married to Janina in 1969. One child: Brandon N.

Daniel J. R. Tripaldi

Client Manager
Catapult Software Training
36 Hillside Drive
New FairField, CT 06812
(860) 947-4040

7379

Business Information: Possessing unique talent in the information technology field, Mr. Tripaldi joined Catapult Software Training in 1999 as its Client Manager. He assumes responsibility for maintaining existing customer relationships as well as developing new ones through the sale of software training products and services. Focusing his efforts primarily on the sales end of customer service, Mr. Tripaldi performs software demonstrations and coordinates software training for clients in addition to his other duties. A savvy professional, he was responsible for generating and putting together a team to close a half million dollar deal with Cola-Cola in his previous position with CDI Information Services. He is a team player and feels he owes his current success to being dedicated, staying focused, and his association with good people. Continually formulating new goals and objectives, Mr. Tripaldi looks forward to moving up the corporate ladder into a managerial position within a larger district with the Company. Headquartered in the state of Washington, Catapult Software Training is an IBM Company and provides end-user, advanced technical, and proprietary software training. A skilled workforce of 500 individuals is employed to offer company services which include Microsoft product training. Established in 1989, the Company has steadily grown and now reports an estimated annual revenue of $55 million. **Career Highlights:** Client Manager, Catapult Software Training (1999-Present); Account Manager, CDI Information Services (1997-99); Project Manager, Nemeth Martin Consulting (1996-97); Registered Representative, Corporate Securities Group (1993-96). **Associations & Accomplishments:** Hartford Area Trainers. **Education:** Western Connecticut State University, B.A. (1993). **Personal Information:** Married to Caterina in 1999. Mr. Tripaldi enjoys mountain biking, water skiing and cooking.

Yudhi S. Trisno, Ph.D.

President
Acucomm Inc.
4699 Old Ironside Drive, Suite 150
Santa Clara, CA 95054-1846
(408) 567-9968
Fax: (408) 567-9969
yudhi.trisno@acucomm.com

7379

Business Information: Possessing a solid family background in the technology industry, Dr. Trisno ventured out into the corporate world with three other partners to establish Acucomm Inc. At the present time, he assumes the accountability of President. In this capacity, Dr. Trisno oversees all aspects of technology implementation, product development, marketing study, and day-to-day operational activities. He facilitates the formulation of creative visions and development of powerful technology and business strategies. Drawing from several years of extensive engineering experience and a strong academic background, Dr. Trisno is involved in the discovery, investigation, and global deployment of new, leading edge technologies. Directing and participating in the acquisition, installation, modification, configuration, and support and tracking of operating systems, databases, utilities, and software and hardware also falls within the realm of his executive responsibilities. He attributes his professional success to a combination of hard work and his technical skills. One of his career accomplishments is the introduction of fiber optics technology to the television cable industry. Grow the Corporation, bring in more employees, and help make the Internet more than it is serves as Dr. Trisno's long-range strategies. Acucomm Inc. is engaged in the design and development of telecommunication and Internet infrastructures based on IP transport access networks. Based in California and international in scope, the Corporation was established in 1997 and presently employs a staff of 15 technology professionals. **Career Highlights:** President, Acucomm Inc. (1997-Present); North American Marketing Manager, OKI Semiconductor (1994-97); Lead Development Engineer, Fujitsu (1991-94); Senior Scientist, General Instruments (1988-91). **Associations & Accomplishments:** Institute of Electrical and Electronic Engineers; Instruments and Measurements Transaction Review Committee. **Education:** State University of New York, Ph.D. (1988). **Personal Information:** Married to Lany in 1985. Two children: Stephen and Daniel. Dr. Trisno enjoys biking, sightseeing, reading and experimenting.

Albert P. Tse

Managing Partner
Duke Technology, Inc.
131-58 Maple Avenue
Flushing, NY 11355
(718) 784-8815
atse@duketech.com

7379

Business Information: Displaying his expertise in the field of information technology, Mr. Tse serves Duke Technology, Inc. as Managing Partner. Utilizing eight years of practical experience in his highly specialized field, he strives to incorporate the latest technologies into the development of diverse programs, and integrate systems into client's businesses that help improve efficiency and productivity. Providing troubleshooting, Mr. Tse offers systems support and customer services guaranteeing complete customer satisfaction. Planning out market strategies, he focuses on the promotional aspects of the Corporation in order to widen the clientele. Committed to his career with Duke Technology, Inc., Mr. Tse's goal is to facilitate continued corporate growth and geographic expansion. Established in 1997, Duke Technology, Inc. specializes as an Internet service provider offering consulting services. Devoted to servicing the diverse needs of a growing clientele, the Corporation provides Cisco, Adtran, APC, Flowpoint, Paradyne, Tut, and Sonic Wall resales, video streaming, Web Design, E-commerce, and B2B solutions. Located in Flushing, New York, the Corporation employs the expertise of four highly qualified individuals to acquire business, meet with clients, facilitate projects, and market services. **Career Highlights:** Managing Partner, Duke Technology, Inc. (2000-Present); Internet Engineer, Rockefeller Group Telecommunications (1998-00); Systesm Analyst, Ziff Brothers, LLC (1997-98); Network Manager, Damon G. Douglas Company (1996-97); Sotheby's Inc. (1994-96); City University of New York Graduate Center (1992-94). **Education:** Pace University, B.S. (1996); Microsoft Certified Systems Engineer; Microsoft Certified Professional+Internet; Cisco Certified Network Administrator. **Personal Information:** Married to Anna in 1999. Mr. Tse enjoys travel, music and outdoor activities.

Simon Lai Yan Tse

Senior Software Consultant
VSI
5604 Southwest Parkway, Suite 3918
Austin, TX 78735
(512) 936-2176
tse_simon@hotmail.com

7379

Business Information: Serving as Senior Software Consultant of VSI, Mr. Tse has a variety of tasks he performs throughout the work day. As a consultant, he integrates and implements systems primarily focused on database and secured Internet applications. A savvy, six-year veteran of technology, he is able to work on six or seven different projects at a time. As chief network architect, he is responsible for the Company's networking infrastructure and consults on the Company's high level projects. Additionally, Mr. Tse teaches and trains how to use and apply HTML, Java, DTML, SQL, C++, and LISP languages. Looking forward to becoming known and recognized globally as a technical expert, he plans on starting up his own consulting company in the near future. His success reflects his ability to tackle new challenges and deliver results on behalf of his the Company's clientele. Established in 1990, VSI is an international computer consulting firm. The Company provides information technology solutions to federal and state governments as well as local businesses. Providing outsource services, the Company places information technology professionals with clients. VSI currently operates three locations in Taiwan, Hong Kong, and Washington, D.C. With headquarters in Austin, Texas, VSI employs a work force of 100 employees helping to generate annual revenues in excess of $20 million. **Career Highlights:** VSI: Senior Software Consultant (1997-Present), Design Engineer (1996-97); Systems Administrator, Southwest Texas University (1993-96). **Associations & Accomplishments:** Association of Computing Machinery. **Education:** Southwest Texas University, B.S. in Computer Science (1995). **Personal Information:** Married to Sarah in 1998. Mr. Tse enjoys scuba diving and marathon running.

Frank P. Tutone

Novell Netware Instructor
Lanop Corporation
1880 Hartog Drive
San Jose, CA 95131
(408) 297-2234
Fax: (408) 297-2234
delphysfl@aol.com

7379

Business Information: Demonstrating strategic expertise in the technology field, Mr. Tutone has served as the Novell Netware Instructor for the Lanop Corporation since 1995. He currently teaches one class but has plans to begin instruction in additional classes. Before joining Lanop, he served as Senior Network Engineer with Mathesongas Products. His background history also includes a stint as Senior Programmer Analyst for Business Records Corporation. Mr. Tutone feels that the most significant achievement of his professional career came when he assumed the responsibility of building a network system that interfaced county, state, and federal operations to one another. He cabled the LAN and WAN systems to link to headquarters and each individual location. Establishing goals that are compatible with those of the Lanop Corporation, Mr. Tutone plans to continue teaching and looks forward to the addition of new classes in his location. His success reflects his ability to think outside the box, deliver results, and aggressively tackle new challenges. The Lanop Corporation is a test preparatory center, offering training in Novell and Microsoft based programs. Headquartered in New York, network computer consulting and training is offered through the Corporation's 14 test centers across the country. Current operations in San Jose, California employ the dedicated services of one skilled individual. **Career Highlights:** Novell Netware Instructor, Lanop Corporation (1995-Present); Senior Network Engineer, Mathesongas Products (1996-98); Senior Programmer Analyst, Business Records Corporation (1992-96). **Associations & Accomplishments:** Silicon Valley Netware Users International. **Education:** Lanop Corporation, Certified Novell Engineer 3 (1997); Adelphi University, Psychology and Religion. **Personal Information:** Two children: Alexander

Paul and Samantha Jane. Mr. Tutone enjoys modeling, camping and biking.

Peter G. Tuttle
Senior Procurement Analyst
CEXEC, Inc.
13921 Park Center Road, Suite 400
Dulles, VA 20171
(202) 268-7010
ptuttle@erols.com

7379

Business Information: As the Senior Procurement Analyst with CEXEC, Inc., Mr. Tuttle provides contract and program management support to the United States Postal Service headquarters as well as technology support to offices on major information technology acquisitions. Drawing on several years of military experience during his service in the United States Army, Mr. Tuttle displays superior leadership and organizational skills, the two most vital qualities of a senior procurement analyst position. Presently seeking ways to expand upon his intellectual and professional territory, Mr. Tuttle is building his experiences in information technology contracting. His success reflects his ability to think out-of-the-box, take on challenges, an deliver results on behalf of the Corporation and its clientele. Founded in 1976, CEXEC, Inc. is a national provider of network services, engineering and information technology services, acquisition, contracting, and program management to the federal government. Specifically serving the diverse needs of the United States Postal Service, CEXEC, Inc. maintains one of the largest nationwide networks in the world. **Career Highlights:** CEXEC, Inc.: Senior Procurement Analyst (1998-Present), Contracting Officers Administrative Representative (1994-98); United States Army: Competition Advocate, TRADOC (1991-94), Production Officer , PEO ASM (1990-91). **Associations & Accomplishments:** National Contract Management Association; Company of Military Historians. **Education:** Webster University, M.A. (1985); Certified Professional Contracts Manager; NCMA (1995). **Personal Information:** Married to Janell in 1975. One child: Erin. Mr. Tuttle enjoys United States military history.

Ayoub B. Ukani
Chief Executive Officer
PC Troubleshooter, Inc.
1977 South Oak Haven Circle
Miami, FL 33179
(305) 970-7778
Fax: (305) 933-1964
wehave@solution4u.com

7379

Business Information: Maintaining an incredible standing and reputation as the Chief Executive Officer of three information technology companies, Mr. Ukani manages all the personnel and contracted staff of PC Troubleshooter, Inc., a $60 million company located in Miami, Florida. An expert in the technology consulting industry, Mr. Ukani personally provides consultation, integration, and project management services as well as Web design and hosting for major clients from across the globe. Integrated with the services of PC Troubleshooter, the two companies also operated under his ownership, Global Enterprise Telecommunication, and World Web are dedicated to providing Internet access, Web hosting, Internet organization and design for major companies as well as disaster recovery site services. Striving to conquer the challenges of the Internet market, Mr. Ukani is currently focusing his business expertise on creating technological solutions for the global market. Serving Fortune 500 companies from 40 countries around the world, PC Troubleshooter, Inc. specializes in consulting, integration, and project management. Currently in their sixth year of service, the Corporation employs a staff of eleven who dedicate their skills and expertise to a service desk in operation twenty-four hours a day, seven days a week. **Career Highlights:** Chief Executive Officer, PC Troubleshooter, Inc. (1995-Present); Senior Project Leader, Interval International (1997-Present); Senior Systems Engineer, AeroTek (1997-98); Senior Systems Engineer, MagicBox (1994-97). **Associations & Accomplishments:** Better Business Bureau; Chamber of Commerce. **Education:** ShipOwner, B.S. (1979). **Personal Information:** Married to Ramona in 1984. Three children: Azim, Minhas, and Salima. Mr. Ukani enjoys volleyball, swimming, basketball and time with his children.

Annette van der Laan
• • • ━━━◖◉◗━━━ • • •
Chief Executive Officer
CS Computer Services Holdings Ltd.
P.O. Box 786691, Sandton
Johannesburg, South Africa 2146
+27 118022182
Fax: +27 118047501
avdlaan@cs.co.za

7379

Business Information: Ms. van der Laan functions in the capacity of Chief Executive Officer for CS Computer Services Holdings Ltd. She has provided strong leadership that has enhance the Company's overall reputation in the global market place. A savvy, three year veteran, Ms. van der Laan monitors communications and oversees the acquisition of new contracts and accounts. In addition, she ensures that day-to-day operations function smoothly and do not hinder business. Ms. van der Laan has formulated powerful strategic plans in order to expand the Company's profit margins and scope of business. In this regard, she spearheads all marketing initiatives. On many occasions, Ms. van der Laan has traveled extensively on behalf of the CS Computer Services Holdings speaking on issues of importance. By doing this, Ms. van der Laan has increased the Company's visibility in the international marketplace. In addition, she has met with other heads of industry. Her diplomacy has resulted in new strategic alliances, partnerships, and joint ventures. As for the future, Ms. van der Laan plans to watch CS Computer Services Holdings become a leader in systems integration. Her success reflects her leadership ability to form teams with synergy, deliver results, and aggressively take on challenges and responsibilities. CS Computer Services Holdings Ltd. is an information technology company that specializes in ERP implementations. Specifically, the Company specialize in SAP, BAAN, Oracle, and so much more. Throughout South Africa, the Company has been central in expanding computer literacy and information technology training. In turn, these services assists further developing networking services for corporate and public sectors of business. Established in 1990, the CS Computer Services Holdings has seen substantial growth in the Internet. Currently, the Company employs more than 400 professional, technical, and suppport personnel. **Career Highlights:** Chief Executive Officer, CS Computer Services Holdings Ltd. (1996-Present); Partner, PricewaterhouseCoopers (1991-96). **Associations & Accomplishments:** South African Institute of Chartered Accountants; Public Accountants and Auditors Board. **Education:** University of Pretoria, BCom (Acc), Hons; C.T.A. (1996); C.A. (S.A.). **Personal Information:** Two children: Wiebe and Jeandre. Ms. van der Laan enjoys golf and jogging.

Michael Van Houten
Lead Consultant
Cannaissance Consulting
25 Independence Boulevard
Warren, NJ 07054
(973) 257-2121
Fax: (973) 257-2006
mvanhout@oracle.com

7379

Business Information: Employing his extensive technical expertise, Mr. Van Houten serves as Cannaissance Consulting's Lead Consultant. He is responsible for software application and database design, development, and implementation. Before moving to Cannaissance, Mr. Van Houten filled the capacity of Senior Consultant at Oracle Corporation. His background history also includes a stint as Systems Engineer with Anheuser-Busch Inc. As a six year technology professional, he works closely with users and systems management to analyze, specify, and design cutting edge technical solutions to harness more of the computer's power, as well as resolve system difficulties. Drawing upon years of solid academic ties and occupational experiences, Mr. Van Houten provides individualized consulting services to meet the needs of clients. His career success reflects his ability to solve difficult problems and deliver end solutions to satisfy customers. Creating sound, workable solutions, he ensures database security, reliability, and integrity. Mr. Van Houten's future goals include remaining in a technical role and enhancing his level of expertise through reading and attending seminars and training classes. A technology consulting firm, Cannaissance Consulting specializes in ERP solutions. **Career Highlights:** Lead Consultant, Cannaissance Consulting (1999-Present); Senior Consultant, Oracle Corporation (1997-99); Systems Engineer, Anheuser Busch, Inc. (1993-97). **Education:** New Jersey Institute of Technology, B.S. in Computer Science (1994). **Personal Information:** Married to Lori in 1997. Mr. Van Houten enjoys building plastic models, programming and quiet time with his wife.

Enid T. Vargas
• • • ━━━◖◉◗━━━ • • •
Senior Vice President
Advanced Computer Technologies
P.O. Box 361697
San Juan, Puerto Rico 00936-1697
(787) 756-5620
Fax: (787) 756-5150

7379

Business Information: Providing her skilled services as Senior Vice President of Consulting Services, Ms. Vargas was recruited to Advanced Computer Technologies in 1996. She assumes responsibility for Company projects for clients in the banking industry and the government. Additionally, she directly oversees 12 project managers and their staff to ensure the quality of offered services. Ms. Vargas has defined clear goals for her professional career and has worked diligently to obtain her current success. She states that success is not easy, be prepared to work hard and learn from your failures. Her success reflects her leadership ability to build teams with synergy, technical strength, and a customer oriented attitude, as well as aggressively tackle new challenges. Continually striving for maximum effectiveness, Ms. Vargas intends to obtain her Master's degree and looks forward to assisting in the completion of future corporate goals. Advanced Computer Technologies provides local businesses with information systems and project management on mainframe computer systems. Additional services in the client server environment are also offered. The Company was established in 1994 and has grown to employ the professional services of 125 qualified individuals. Advanced Computer Technologies boasts $26 million in revenue a year. **Career Highlights:** Senior Vice President, Advanced Computer Technologies (1996-Present); Senior Project Manager, ProData Services (1994-96); Manager, GM Group (1987-94). **Associations & Accomplishments:** Founder/President, Puerto Rico Chapter of the Project Management Institute; City of San Juan Distinguished Women's Award (1998). **Education:** University of Puerto Rico, B.B.A. (1985). **Personal Information:** Ms. Vargas enjoys reading.

Sudharshan S. Vazhkudai
Senior Consultant
SAIR, Inc.
125 Heritage Drive
Oxford, MS 38655
(662) 236-2484
Fax: (662) 236-2428
ssvahku@olemiss.edu

7379

Business Information: Serving SAIR Inc. as the Senior Consultant, Mr. Vazhkudai serves with the core team and is involved in Linux exam development. A successful professional, he writes chapters for publication in industry leading publications. Well versed in Linux technology, he also administers the testing of people of all levels of Linux experience, from novice to experienced professionals. Drawing from his extensive technological education, he executes his position to his utmost ability. Proud of his published papers on the principles of DBIA, Mr. Vazhkudai's future aspirations are to attain his Ph.D. and become involved in a wider area of computing. His success reflects his ability to think outside the box, aggressively tackle new challenges and responsibilities, and deliver results. Established in 1997, SAIR Inc. is a world leader and premier organization in Linux certification. Dealing mainly with large corporations, the Corporation also administers certification exams worldwide, validates Linux professionals, and trains those who are not. Globally experienced and oriented, the Corporation employs a total of 50 individuals. **Career Highlights:** Senior Consultant, SAIR Inc. (Present); Instructor, Department of Computer Science-University of Mississippi (1998-Present); Summer Researcher, ESRI, Inc. (1998-98); Design Engineer/Research and Development, Wipro Infotech (1996-97). **Associations & Accomplishments:** Referee, Association of Computing Machinery; Institute of Electrical and Electronics Engineers; Upsilon Pi Epsilon Acaemic Honor Society. **Education:** University Mississippi: Ph.D. in Computer Sciences (In Progress), M.S. in Computer Sciences; GIT, Bachelor's degree in Engineering in Computer Sciences. **Personal Information:** Mr. Vazhkudai enjoys research on distributed systems and reading.

Vignesh Velappan
Technical Support Engineer
Wavetek Wandel Goltermann
102, Jalan Chenderai Dua, Bangsar
Kuala Lumpur, Malaysia 59100
+60 37032518
Fax: +60 32524102
vignesh76@hotmail.com

7379

Business Information: Serving as a Technical Support Engineer for Wavetek Wandel Goltermann, Mr. Velappan oversees all aspects of daily support on test solutions for the telecommunications, enterprise networks, and wireless industries. Possessing superior talents and an excellent understanding of technology, he also provides software testing and systems upgrades for the information systems infrastructure. Demonstrating his unique expertise, Mr. Velappan provides training and offers network analysis services for various clients. In the next three to five years, Mr. Velappan plans to transition into a telecommunications consultant position, attributing his success to hard work. Wavetek Wandel Goltermann is quickly becoming a leader in providing test solutions for technologies in the communications industry. The Company partners with its customers to develop and implement solutions that meet individual testing requirements. Customers then use these test solutions to develop, manufacture, install, and maintain their communications systems. The Company operates dual headquarters in Research Triangle Park, North Carolina and in Eningen, Germany. Currently, Wavetek Wandel Goltermann employs 2,600 people worldwide and reports annual sales of over $469 million. **Career Highlights:** Technical Support Engineer, Wavetek Wandel Goltermann (1999-Present). **Associations & Accomplishments:** Institute of Electrical Engineers, United Kingdom. **Education:** University of Hertfordshire, Bachelor's degree in Engineering with Honors (1997), Degree in Electrical and Electronic Engineering (1998); The Nottingham Trent University. **Personal Information:** Mr. Velappan enjoys weight training and the Internet.

Ravindra V. Vellanki

Director of Systems Integration
C A Consultants Int. Ltd.
4204 Eureka Street, #D
Metairie, LA 70001-6558
(504) 889-2225
Fax: (504) 779-6828
rvellanki@cacil.com

7379

Business Information: Highly skilled in the field of technology, Mr. Vellanki was recruited to C A Consultants Int. Ltd. in 1999. Currently serving as the Director of Systems Integration, he fulfills a number of technical tasks on behalf of the Company and its clientele. Possessing superior talents and an excellent understanding of his field, Mr. Vellanki oversees all systems integration operations. He is also responsible for designing systems architecture and implementing GIS projects for a national corporate clientele. The most rewarding aspect of his career is obtaining two Master's degrees in his field. In the future, Mr. Vellanki plans to continue designing software and upgrading existing systems, and consistently achieving quality performance in his field. Established in 1997, C A Consultants Int. Ltd. is an established and reputable consulting firm specializing in software development and systems integration. The Company currently employs a team of skilled individuals to meet the demands of a growing clientele. Presently, C A Consultants is located in Metairie, Louisiana. **Career Highlights:** Director of Systems Integration, C A Consultants Int. Ltd. (Present); Plangraphics, Inc.: Director of Systems Integration (1998), Executive Consultant (1997). **Associations & Accomplishments:** GITA. **Education:** North Dakota State University: M.S. in Computer Science (1995), M.S. in Engineering. **Personal Information:** Married to Charulata in 1997. Mr. Vellanki enjoys photography.

Jean-Pierre Venancio

Director/Manager
Activeweb
130 Avenue Joseph Kessel
Voisins Le Bretonneux, France 78960
+33 139441636
Fax: +33 139441721
jpv@activeweb.fr

7379

Business Information: Leading Activeweb to higher standards of computer networking, Mr. Venancio actively holds the positions of Director and Manager. Utilizing over 10 years of expertise attained through an extensive employment and educational history, he strives to incorporate the latest technology into the development of new projects. Demonstrating leadership, Mr. Venancio determines the overall strategic direction and formulates new business and marketing plans to keep Activeweb out-front of competitors in the industry. Forming major client accounts, he is proactively involved in the negotiation and establishment of contracts. The most rewarding aspects of his career include starting up the Company, expanding its services, and working for Lotus. Committed to the increase of clients and the expansion of services, Mr. Venancio's goal is to facilitate continued Company growth and geographic expansion. Established in 1997, Activeweb is an Internet services provider through ASP based on Lotus Notes and Domino. Located in France, the Company extends its specialized services to an international client base. Employing the skilled services of five expert computer technicians, and designers who orchestrate all activities in design, development, and integration, the Company remains dedicated towards providing for the specific needs of their expanding clientele, and the development of programs, and services utilizing the latest technologies. **Career Highlights:** Director/Manager, Activeweb (1997-Present); Technical Sales Representative, Lotus Development (1990-98). **Education:** Control Data School, Computer Technician. **Personal Information:** Married to Adelia. Two children: Sonia and Lauriane. Mr. Venancio enjoys windsurfing, tennis, skiing and time with family.

Michel Villetorte

Technical Manager/Owner
GVL
3535 Avenue Papineau, Apartment 508
Montreal, Quebec, Canada H2K 4J9
(514) 990-3865
Fax: (514) 521-7876
mivide@videotron.ca

7379

Business Information: An expert veteran in the field of technology, Mr. Villetorte is the current Technical Manager and Owner of GVL. He determines the overall strategic direction and formulates marketing and business plans to keep the Company out-front of competitors in the industry. Drawing from his extensive knowledge and 16 solid years of hands on experience, Mr. Villetorte supervises and performs programming and is responsible for recruiting and all administrative aspects of the Company. Optimistic about the future of his Company, Mr. Villetorte expects to see GVL expand throughout the entire North American continent. His success is attributed to his ability to take on challenges and deliver results on behalf of the Company and its clientele. Located in Montreal, Canada, GVL is a company builds custom databases and provide data processing services. The current client base includes small and medium sized corporations in the surrounding area. Presently, the Company is manned by two professionals who generates in excess of $70,000 annually. **Career Highlights:** Technical Manager/Owner, GVL (1994-Present); Vice President, 7 Generation (1991-94); Vice President, SAO (1988-94): Vice President (1984-88). **Education:** ENSBA, Ana (1968). **Personal Information:** Married to Marie Francoise Lascaray in 1971. Three children: Laetitia, Malthias, and Melanie. Mr. Villetorte enjoys racquetball.

Martin von Pfaler

Art Director/Designer
Pollenpolen
Alvdalen
Vallentuna, Sweden 18660
+46 851235500
Fax: +46 851235500
pollenpo@pollenpolen.com

7379

Business Information: Serving with Pollenpolen as Art Director and Designer, Mr. von Pfaler manages and designs projects and oversees all aspects of daily Web development activities. Possesssing superior talents and an excellent understanding of technology, he decided to start Pollenpolen with a focus on providing quality services to his clients. An accomplished professional, Mr. von Pfaler co-wrote an article in a magazine about pollen related topics. He attributes his professional success to his interest in the field of computers as well as his ability to think outside the box, take on challenges, and deliver results on behalf of the Company and its clientele. In the future, Mr. von Pfaler would like to see his Company expand and grow nationally and internationally. Established in 1996, Pollenpolen specializes in Web design and provides Internet solutions. The Company provides consultancy in Pollenpolen, Sweden and network access to Scandanavia, Germany, and the Nordic Countries. Headquartered in Vallentuna, Sweden, Pollenpolen is manned by one skilled professional. **Career Highlights:** Art Director/Designer, Pollenpolen (1996-Present); First Assistant, Swedish Museum of Natural History (1996-Present); Assistant, National Institute of Occupational Health (1995-96); Assistant, Swedish Museum of Natural History (1994-96) **Associations & Accomplishments:** Treasurer, Nordic Aerobiology Association. **Education:** University of Stolkholm, B.S. (1994). **Personal Information:** Married to Lena Von Pfaler in 1997. Two children: Saga and Edvard. Mr. von Pfaler enjoys gardening and botanical excursions.

John T. Vu

Senior Consultant/President
Distributed Network Administration
6 Marc Court
Parlin, NJ 08859
(732) 602-1893
john@cyberdna.com

7379

Business Information: As Senior Consultant and President of Distributed Network Administration, Mr. Vu monitors every aspect of Company operations focusing on general administration, strategic planning, and service promotions. Utilizing his education and capitalizing on more than 10 years of solid experience, he is responsible for setting up new systems and evaluating software. In addition, he provides on site technical support and consulting to financial industries such as Goldman Sachs & Company, Merrill Lynch & Company, and Chase Manhattan Bank. Demonstrating his technical skills, he advises clients utilizing information technology resources. Mr. Vu is proud of his new business and attributes his success to "God giving him the opportunity to work with good people." Distributed Network Administrtion is a computer hardware and software consulting business. Established in 1999, the Company is located in Parlin, New Jersey. To serve the diverse needs of its clientele, the Company employs a staff of two personnel to provide services such as Web site development, e-mail, phone service, databases, hardware, and software. **Career Highlights:** Senior Consultant/President, Distributed Network Administration (1999-Present); Senior Systems Engineer, Goldman Sachs & Company (Present); Systems Administrator, Merrill Lynch & Company (1997-99); Chase Manhattan Bank N.A. (1996-97). **Associations & Accomplishments:** Microsoft Certified Professional; Novell Certified Engineer. **Education:** Queens College, B.A. (1990). **Personal Information:** Married to Ha Le in 1996. Mr. Vu enjoys making money.

John S. Wallmark

Owner
Millstone River Systems, Inc.
20 Robin Drive
Skillman, NJ 08558
(609) 921-7484
Fax: (609) 921-9504
john_wallmark@compuserve.com

7379

Business Information: Fueled by an entrepreneurial spirit and a unquenchable desire for independence, Mr. Wallmark started Millstone Rive Systems, Inc. in 1992. As the Owner, he oversees all day-to-day administration and operational activities, including determining the overall strategic direction. His present scope encompasses design and programming Oracle database and DBMS software, as well as implementation and maintenance functions. The senior consultant, Mr. Wallmark's strategic plans include taking on larger projects and hiring independent contractors to accomplish specific objectives. With 27 years of experience, he ensures data integrity and security, eliminates data redundancy, and fine tunes software tools to enhance overall database performance. Coordinating resources and schedules, overseeing time lines and assignments, calculating and managing the the fiscal year budget, and resolving technical issues also fall within the realm of Mr. Wallmark's responsibilities. He attributes his success to his willingness to go out and do something different. Mr. Wallmark believes in order to be successful you have to get out of the employee mold, be prepared to take risk, and think like a business person. His advice is "deliver a solution rather than put in time." Millstone River Systems, Inc. is a self sufficient Oracle consultant. Founded in 1992, Millstone River Systems operates with a modest staff to meet the needs of clients. The Corporation requires nothing from the client except the assignment itself, while designing and implementing new software. **Career Highlights:** Owner, Millstone River Systems, Inc. (1992-Present). **Associations & Accomplishments:** International Oracle Users Group. **Education:** The College of William and Mary in Virginia, B.S. (1972). **Personal Information:** Married.

Daniel Q. Wan

Senior Network Engineer
Strategic Alliance International Corporation
1 World Trade Center, Suite 4627
New York, NY 10048
(212) 432-0684
Fax: (201) 242-0175
wan@sprintmail.com

7379

Business Information: Utilizing more than 10 years of experience in the technology field, Mr. Wan serves as Senior Network Engineer for Strategic Alliance International Corporation. In this capacity, he works at the client sites, providing network design, configuration, and implementation. Mr. Wan maintains client system servers and workstations by providing network security, administering upgrades, and troubleshooting problems as necessary. As a technology professional, he owns an established track record of producing results in support of business and technical objectives. His active affiliation with industry associations enables him to remain current, and allows him to network and interact with colleagues and other professionals in different fields. Attributing his career success to strong family support, he advises others to set goals, gain hands-on experience, and always strive to improve your career. Privately held, Strategic Alliance International Corporation is a software and network consulting firm providing a wide range of services for Fortune 500 financial companies. The Corporation offers software development and integration, Internet services, systems integration, information technology professional staffing, and legal services. Created in 1996, approximately 20 knowledgeable individuals are employed. **Career Highlights:** Senior Network Engineer, Strategic Alliance International Corporation (1998-Present); Network Engineer, Omnitech Corporate Solutions, Inc (1997-98); Software Engineer, Dictaphone Corporation (1995-96); Software Engineer, China Tongda Network System Corporation (1990-95). **Associations & Accomplishments:** Retired, Association of Computing Machinery; Microsoft Certified System Engineer; Sun Microsystem Certified System Administrator; Citrix Certified Win Frame Administrator; Microsoft Certified Trainer. **Education:** University of Bridgeport, M.S. (1996); Xidian University, B.Sc. (1990). **Personal Information:** Married to Lizzie Y. Ling in 1996. One child: Matthew. Mr. Wan enjoys tour swimming.

Jonathan Wanagel

Senior Technologist
Lante Corporation
3180 139th Avenue SE, Suite 100
Bellevue, WA 98005
(425) 564-8971
Fax: (425) 564-8801
jjw@lante.com

7379

Business Information: As the Senior Technologist of Lante Corporation, Mr. Wanagel is responsible for the development of Microsoft related topics. Guiding his staff of developers, he also organizes and manages the effort of the team in analyzing, specifying, and designing technical solutions. He is responsible for recruiting and interviewing as well as training employees on emerging technologies. Possessing an excellent understanding of technology, Mr. Wanagel conducts presentations, oversees all project management and research activities and works closely with clients and systems architects to plan, estimate, design, and implement new systems. He is most proud of starting at an entry-level position and working his way up to his current capacity. His highlights include helping Microsoft create a technical information CD. Getting more involved with Java and UNIX and continue to better himself serves as Mr. Wanagel's future endeavors. Established in 1984, the Lante Corporation is a consulting firm. Specializing in Internet and e-commerce consulting, the Corporation also develops digital marketing places, accessible to all. Employing approximately 400 professionals of varying degrees, the Corporation has reported an estimated $33 million in annual sales. **Career Highlights:** Senior Technologist, Lante Corporation (1996-Present); Programmer/Analyst, Diamond Management Systems (1995-96); PC Specialist, Specialty Testing and Equipment (1991-95).

Byron Nigel Warmsley

Senior Test Specialist
McDonald Bradley
8200 Greensboro Drive
McLean, VA 22102
(202) 401-2381
b_warmsley@yahoo.com

7379

Business Information: Mr. Warmsley is the Senior Test Specialist for McDonald Bradley. A Y2K specialist for the Company, he regularly performs IV, V, & Y2K technical support for the Department of Housing and Urban Development's property tracking system. He is the Technical Project Manager and attends several meetings to coordinate the efforts of his team within the Company. Some of his larger projects include his involvement with the Department of Energy DBA project and his work on a portion of the Hubble Space Telescope. In the future, Mr. Warmsley is planning to obtain his Oracle certification to better his career position. His parents taught him outstanding work ethics very early in life, and he believes that is the reason behind his current success. McDonald Bradley provides computer consulting services to businesses in McLean, Virginia. Established in 1983, the Company is dedicated to the technological advancement of every corporation and private residence in the area. The Company offers software development and design services to facilitate the specific needs of each client. A staff of 15 employees meet with clients and advise them throughout the adaptations of new technology and updating of older systems. **Career Highlights:** Senior Test Specialist, McDonald Bradley (1994-Present); TRW: Senior Database Administrator (1992-94), System Programmer (1984-92). **Associations & Accomplishments:** Digital Equipment Computer User's Society; Giga Information Group; North American Ingres User's Association; Society Institute of Electrical and Electronics Engineers. **Education:** Morgan State University, B.S. in Computer Science (1991). **Personal Information:** Two children: Amber and Marcus. Mr. Warmsley enjoys reading, billiards, computers and history events.

Paul L. Washington Jr.

Security Systems Engineer
Litton/TASC
131 National Business Parkway, Suite 110
Annapolis Junction, MD 20701-1027
(301) 483-6000
Fax: (301) 604-0500
plwashington@tasc.com

7379

Business Information: Possessing unique talent in the information technology field, Mr. Washington serves as Security Systems Engineer for Litton/TASC. He assumes accountability for orchestrating project security issues. Concurrent to his position, Mr. Washington is pursuing a Doctoral degree in Computer & Communications Security. Previously during his career, he served as a Military Intelligence Officer in the United States Army. In the future, Mr. Washington would like to continue advancing with Litton/TASC and become a college instructor. Employing more than 2,800 professionals, Litton/TASC provides systems engineering and technical solutions to government agencies and business establishments throughout the world. The Massachusetts based Company operates over 25 offices throughout the United States and the United Kingdom, generating estimated annual revenue of $480 million. **Career Highlights:** Security Systems Engineer, Litton/TASC (1996-Present); Systems Engineer, DIA (1996); Company Commander, United States Army (1995-96). **Associations & Accomplishments:** Information System Security Associations, Vice President National Capital Chapter; Prince Hall Free and Accepted Masons; Kappa Alpha Psi Fraternity Inc.; Boy Scouts of America; Armed Forces Communications and Electronics Association; Military Intelligence Corps Associations; Armed Forces Communications; Electronics Associations; Committee for Computing Machinery. **Education:** George Washington University, D.Sc. (In Progress); Golden Gate University, M.S.; United States Military Academy, B.S. **Personal Information:** Married to Cyndie in 1989. One child: Chloe. Mr. Washington enjoys golf and scuba diving.

Richard Wasilewski

President
AAC Inc.
830 East Higgins Road, Suite 111-I
Schaumburg, IL 60173
(815) 758-9430
Fax: (847) 969-1908
marketing@aac-consulting.com

7379

Business Information: Mr. Wasilewski is the President of AAC, Inc. He oversees all departments including marketing, sales and promotion, purchasing, finance, personnel, trining, and quality control. He is also responsible for formulating policies and procedures, developing goals and objectives, and implementing strategic plans. In collaboration with other top executives, Mr. Wasilewski ensures all aspects of the operation run within the framework of the Firms' overall plan. Future plans include increasing the staff and customer base and doubling the size of the Firm. Wanting to fulfill the needs of his customers, Mr. Wasilewski attributes his success to the people he works with. Established in1984, AAC Inc. is a consulting firm assisting businesses with their computer needs. Presently three people work at the Firm, lending their expertise in various aspects of the operation. **Career Highlights:** President, AAC Inc. (Present); Consultant Analyst, Monsanto (1996-Present); Consultant Analyst, Quaker Oats (1995-96); Consultant Anaalyst, Griffith Laboratories (1990-95). **Associations & Accomplishments:** National Association of the Self-Employed; NACCB. **Education:** College of Lake County; Write College. **Personal Information:** Married.

Sascha Watermann

Online Producer
LN-Online GmbH, Luebeck
Staunsfeld 3
Hernberg, DE 23923
+49 4571442208
sw@sasche-watermann.de

7379

Business Information: A prominent and highly respected professional, Mr. Watermann performs a host of duties as Online Producer for LN-Online GmbH, Luebeck. He fulfills the responsibility of Web master accountable for building sites, technical project management, and creation and implementation of content and templates. With more than 13 years of strong academics and technical experience, Mr. Watermann administers and controls the Company's data resources and ensures data integrity, security, and reliability. He is also responsible for directing and participating in the analysis, design, evaluation, and deployment of LAN/WAN and Internet related computer programs. Highly regarded, Mr. Watermann never perceives his profession as a job, because he enjoys it and utilizes it as a way of life. His plans for his career include getting more involved on the technical side of business operations, including real programming. A reputable subsidiary of the Hernberg, German local newspaper, LN-Online GmbH, Luebeck engages in the provision of Internet services to local and regional citizens. Services includes news and local information, Web access, and other multimedia services. Established in 1998, the Company functions out of the one convenient location in Hernberg, Germany under the direct guidance and talents of nine professionals. **Career Highlights:** Online Producer, LN-Online GmbH, Luebeck (1998-Present). **Education:** Fachhoch Koelin, Diploma (1997).

Demian K. Weaver

Supervisor of LAN Engineers
PSINet
510 Huntmar Park Drive
Herndon, VA 20170
(703) 375-1113
weaverd@psi.com

7379

Business Information: Mr. Weaver serves as Supervisor of LAN Engineers for SAGA SOFTWARE, Inc. In this capacity, he exercises oversight of two teams of three engineers charged with the installation and maintenance of over 120 servers in 15 locations for the Corporation's North American operations. He provides troubleshooting advice as needed and prioritizes work assignments for the engineering team members. It is within the scope of his position to develop and implement quality control procedures which ensure seamless integration among systems both within the Corporation and for client users of the Corporation's products. Mr. Weaver currently has around 30 projects in process which involve all stages of engineering from analysis through completion. He manages all new product evaluations and makes recommendations to corporate executives regarding purchases and upgrades. In addition, he assumes accountability for adherence to budgetary constraints as mandated by the Board of Directors. Mr. Weaver hopes to assume greater levels of responsibility as he rises through the management ranks within SAGA SOFTWARE, Inc. and to further develop his Web site and electronic commerce skills. SAGA SOFTWARE, Inc., established in 1972, develops, markets, installs, and services enterprise-class software which allows customers to leverage their IT investment by linking valuable information from enterprise class systems to the desktop, helping them free their information. Approximately 1,000 professional, technical, and support staff are employed by the Corporation which is headquartered in Reston, Virginia. **Career Highlights:** Supervisor of LAN Engineers, PSINet (1999-Present); SAGA SOFTWARE, Inc.: Supervisor of LAN Engineers (1998-99), LAN Engineer (1998), Desktop Specialist (1997-98). **Associations & Accomplishments:** Member (1994-Present), United States Army Reserve; Commanding General's Award for Excellence; Top of Commandant's List, Basic and Advanced Training; Dean's List Scholar. **Education:** University of Colorado, B.S. in Information Systems (1997). **Personal Information:** Mr. Weaver enjoys travel, snow skiing, water skiing, scuba diving and playing golf.

Gregory Weber

Program Manager/Courseware Presenter
Volt Computer Services/Entirenet
14151 Brightmore Drive
Sterling Heights, MI 48312
(810) 274-0531
Fax: (810) 979-8356
a-gregwe@microsoft.com

7379

Business Information: As Program Manager for Microsoft, Mr. Weber acts as subject matter expert for Microsoft Official Curriculum courseware. As Courseware Presenter for Entirenet, he travels throughout the world delivering technical subject matter to clients and customers of Microsoft. Mr. Weber received a patent for his contributions to a fuel system control algorithm with his work at Cummins. He also aided in the development of the M1A2 tank for General Dynamics. Attributing his success to "working smart," he aspires to a position with Microsoft that will allow him to further develop his technical abilities. Contracted to Microsoft through Volt Computer Services, Mr. Weber serves as Program Manager and a subject matter expert for developing courses. He also works with Entirenet, a Microsoft preferred vendor, delivering technical content to clients. **Career Highlights:** Program Manager, Volt Computer Services/Entirenet (1999-Present); Courseware Presenter, Entirenet (1999-Present); Lead Curriculum Coordinator, Electronic Data Systems (1995-99); Software Engineer, Cummins (1993-95); Systems Engineer, General Dynamics (1992-93). **Education:** Oakland University, Bachelor's degree (1992).

John B. Weeks

Senior Systems Administrator
Quintus Corporation
47212 Mission Falls Court
Fremont, CA 94539
(510) 624-2845
Fax: (510) 770-1377
john@weeksweb.com

7379

Business Information: As Senior Systems Administrator of Quintus Corporation, Mr. Weeks handles the Solaris network system support and Web server administration. He is responsible for the infrastructure design and maintenance of NT and UNIX systems. Working closely with his team of seven associates, Mr. Weeks excels in the areas of web tool development. Before joining Quintus, he assertively served as Senior Systems Administrator with Sun Microsystems. Capitalizing on more than 10 years of extensive experience in all phases of operation, Mr. Weeks plans to further his education with a Master's degree to broaden his technical skills in leading edge technologies. Quintus Corporation is a software engineering company. The Corporation is a privately held software provider of customer call tracking software. Founded in 1995, operations employ the skilled services of 200 individuals to acquire business, meet with clients, facilitate projects, and market services. **Career Highlights:** Senior Systems Administrator, Quintus Corporation (1997-Present); Senior Systems Administrator, Sun Microsystems (1990-97). **Education:** University of California, Santa Cruz, B.S. in Computer Science (1990). **Personal Information:** Mr. Weeks enjoys spending time with family and friends, high technology, stock trading, skiing, camping, hiking and biking.

Jeffrey Haoran Wei, Ph.D.

President
UHERE Corporation
2 North Second Street, Suite 1225
San Jose, CA 95113
(408) 817-9000
Fax: (408) 297-4277
jwei@uhere.com

7379

Business Information: Dr. Wei serves as President of the UHERE Corporation. Having founded the Corporation a year ago, his business savvy and technical expertise has led to the successful launch of the Corporation as well as the advancement of its own operations for the betterment of business. He is responsible for determining the overall strategic direction and business contribution of the information systems function. Utilizing a strong academic background, Dr. Wei oversees all day-to-day administration and operations, such as financial and profit and loss statement and fiscal year budgeting. The highlights of his career include publishing a physics paper on biological questions at the age of 18, as well as having the ability to start from scratch and build a successful business. In the future, Dr. Wei plans on establishing the Corporation as dominent force in the e-commerce arena. UHERE Corporation is an Internet start-up business providing consulting services to all clients in the San Jose, California region. Founded in 1999, the Corporation is dedicated to the successful launch of several Web-based businesses. Employing 15 individuals, the Corporation works to advance the computer abilities of each client through the implementation of cutting edge comptuer technologies and Web sites. **Career Highlights:** President, UHERE Corporation (1999-Present); Product Manager, Infoseek (1998-99); Business Development Manager, Applied Materials (1997-98); Marketing Research Manager, Emerson Electric (1996). **Education:** University of Minnesota at Twin Cities, Ph.D.; Massachusetts Institute of Technology, Sloan School of Management, M.B.A. (1997); University of Science and Technology of China, B.S. **Personal Information:** Married to Sarah in 1983. Three children: Richard, William, and Henry. Dr. Wei enjoys hiking, movies, socializing and going out to dinner.

Ted P. Weis

Principal Owner
PROTOCOL Technology Partners, LLC
PMB 154, 23623 North Scottsdale Road, D3
Scottsdale, AZ 85255
(480) 563-5405
Fax: (480) 473-3226
tedweis@protocoltechnology.com

7379

Business Information: As Principal and co-founder for PROTOCOL Technology Partners, LLC, Mr. Weis is primarily responsible for the overall account strategy and development, including the direction and implementation of sales and marketing throughout the organization. Mr. Weis is responsible for developing and maintaining client relationships at the highest level and developing professional partner relationships that enhance PROTOCOL in the marketplace. Prior to co-founding PROTOCOL, Mr. Weis served as an Account Executive and Recruiting Associate for Alliance Consulting Group, an IT Consulting Services company and Source Services Corporation, an IT Recruitment and Consulting Services company. Mr. Weis played an early role in the development of Alliance and Source Services and, in addition, spent time as an internal recruiter for a prominent staffing initiative at AlliedSignal, Inc. for its Information Technology Group. Prior to that, Mr. Weis was a top performing Senior Associate at Harris, Kovacs, Alderman, one of the premier medical recruitment and consulting companies in the industry. PROTOCOL Technology Partners, LLC is an Information Technology Recruiting and Consulting firm, specializing in Internet and ERP advances. The Company employs highly trained people with solid industry track records to asisst clients in filling their IT staffing needs. Established in 1999, the Company is headquartered in Scottsdale, Arizona where reputation of quality and value services is rapidly spreading throughout the professional community. **Career Highlights:** Principal Owner, PROTOCOL Technology Partners, LLC (1999-Present); Associate, Alliance Consulting Group (1998-99); Independent Consultant, Allied Signal (1997-98); Partner, Source EDP (1995-97). **Associations & Accomplishments:** Arizona Technical Recruiters Association; Sigma Alpha Epsilon. **Education:** Kansas State University, B.S. in Business Administration (1992). **Personal Information:** Mr. Weis enjoys golf, community activities and outdoor recreation.

Ross Weisberg

Computer Support Hardware Technician
Edmunds & Associates
333 Tilton Road
Northfield, NJ 08225
(609) 645-7333
Fax: (609) 646-6041
rolen3@msn.com

7379

Business Information: As Computer Support Hardware Technician for Edmunds & Associates, Mr. Weisberg offers his knowledge and skill in the field of information technology for customers and local government agencies. His daily responsibilities include monitoring help desk lines, offering hardware support, and backing up software as well as providing assistance with Microsoft Office solutions, troubleshooting, and overseeing on-site reimbursements. Possessing an excellent understanding of technology, Mr. Weisberg also is accountable for maintaing vendor relationships and Web site programming using HCML and Java. Looking to the future, Mr. Weisberg's goals include gaining employment with a brokerage firm to utilize all of his expertise. His success reflects his ability to think outside the box, take on challenges, and deliver state-of-the-art results on behalf of the Firm and its clientele. A software developer, Edmunds & Associates produces computer solutions to local governments in the state of New Jersey. Regional in scope, the Firm specializes in writing tax and financial software solutions. Presently, Edmunds & Associates is located in Northfield, New Jersey. **Career Highlights:** Computer Support Hardware Technician, Edmunds & Associates (1997-Present). **Education:** Mommouth University, B.S. in Business Administration (1996). **Personal Information:** Mr. Weisberg enjoys travel.

Abbott D. Weiss

Vice President
Digital Equipment Corporation
200 Forest Street
Marlborough, MA 01752
(508) 467-5718
Fax: (508) 467-1640

7379

Business Information: As Vice President, Mr. Weiss is responsible for all aspects of operations, including industry marketing for systems business in the Americas. There are five business areas: retail, wholesale, consumer packaging, travel/hospitality, and transportation. Digital Equipment Corporation specializes in the manufacture, distribution, and service of computer systems worldwide (100 countries). Established in 1957, Digital Equipment Corporation employs 60,000 people with annual sales of $13 billion. **Career Highlights:** Digital Equipment Corporation: Vice President (1994-Present), Vice President - Retail/Wholesale Industries (1991-94), Secretary - Executive Committee (1988-90), United States Area Manufacturing Manager (1983-88). **Associations & Accomplishments:** Former Director, Digital Credit Union; Digital Corporation Contributions Committee; Partner, Logistics Systems, Inc. (1968-74). **Education:** Harvard Business School, D.B.A. (1970); Massachusetts Institute of Technology, M.S. in Management (1965); Webb Institute, B.S. in Naval Architecture and Marine Engineering (1963). **Personal Information:** Married to Barbara in 1965. Two children: Sarah and Aaron. Mr. Weiss enjoys travel, food, wine, fishing and photography.

Richard A. Weiss

President/Chief Executive Officer
ComTech Labs
443 Dell Place
Stanhope, NJ 07874-2743
(973) 347-1088
Fax: (801) 505-8564

7379

Business Information: Possessing unique talent in the information technology field, Mr. Weiss serves as the President and Chief Executive Officer of ComTech Labs. Mr. Weiss founded the Company after working with other consulting firms for several years. While he enjoyed his work, he wanted to be able to satisfy the client's needs the way he felt was best. He advises others following his entrepreneurial path to ensure that they deliver on their promises to their clients and states that his honesty and integrity with his clients is the key to his success. Utilizing strategic planning, Mr. Weiss is looking to expand to other states along the East Coast. His goal is to diversify his Company and to offer additional "Innovative Technology Solutions" such as e-commerce and other Internet-based services. ComTech Labs offers a variety of computer consulting services, including server administration, client support, and LAN/WAN management to the private and public sector as well as local and state government agencies throughout New Jersey. Established in 1999 by Mr. Weiss, the Company already boasts sales upwards of $250, 000. **Career Highlights:** President/Chief Executive Officer, ComTech Labs (1999-Present); Systems Support and Migration Coordinator, Worldwide Headquarters Warner Lambert Company (1996-98); Off Hours Emergency Support Team Member, Exxon Company International Headquarters (1996-98); Help Desk Coordinator, Data Tech Associates (1995-96). **Associations & Accomplishments:** Microsoft Certified Systems Engineer; Microsoft Certified Professional Internet Specialist; Member, HTML Writers Guild; Member, Microsoft Developers Network; NAUI Open Water SCUBA Diver; PADI Advanced SCUBA Diver. **Education:** Suxxex County Vocational Technical School, Degree in Data Processing (1982); Word of Life Bible Institute, Diploma (1984); CEF Leadership Training Institute, Diploma (1986); Computer Science/Information Technology Courses, Seminars, and Self-Directed Learning Programs (1979-Present). **Personal Information:** Married to Melissa, R.N., M.S., C.D.E., C.S Mr. Weiss enjoys travel and scuba diving.

Michael J. Welker, Jr.

Technology Consulting/Project Manager
IBM Global Services
319 Prospect Street
Warren, PA 16365
(216) 664-7345
Fax: (216) 664-7345
michaelk.welker@us.ibm.com

7379

Business Information: As Technology Consultant with IBM Global Services, Mr. Welker is responsible for all concepts related to Microsoft technology integration. Working on various projects such as data center migration and government network implementation, he demonstrates exceptional skill in his field. With versatility and adaptability, Mr. Welker shifts his expertise to various aspects of the field as he handles Netware, UNIX, Solaris, and HP-UX issues. Also recognized for a forte in SNA connections and e-mail solutions, his daily schedule includes network achitecture and systems design, maintenance, and upgrades as well as troubleshooting of all systems. Recognized for a creative problem solving approach, Mr. Welker is credited with the successful implementation of several innovative time saving techniques. One of his career highlights occurred at ASAP Computer, where he set up an MCSE boot camp to train the staff to teach MCSE courses. Mr. Welker aspires to the position of Chief Technology Officer, a role which would allow him to fully utilize his education, experience, and adept ability. IBM Global Services is the support and service branch of the IBM Corporation. Lending services to technology research, engineering, and manufacturing, the Company is recognized as a leading provider of technical solutions. Over 250,000 trained individuals work for the Company, striving to assist fellow team members and clients with daily tasks related to operations. **Career Highlights:** Technology Consultant, IBM Global Services (1998-Present); Chief Enterprise Engineer, ASAP Computer (1998); Project Manager, TEKsystems (1997-98); Information Technology Support Engineer, RHI Consulting (1997). **Associations & Accomplishments:** Past Member, Red Cross Disaster Action Team; Past CPR, First Aid, and Professional Instructor, Red Cross. **Education:** Industry Certifications. **Personal Information:** Married to Kimberly in 1993. Two children: David Morris and Steven

Michael. Mr. Welker enjoys scuba diving, skiing and volunteering.

Kevin Wheatland

••• ◗━━◉━━◖ •••

Managing Partner
CCG Consulting Associates
Nybrogatan #24
Stockholm, Sweden 11439
+46 87571732
kevin.wheatland@telia.com

7379

Business Information: After a distinguished 10 year career with Ericsson Telecommunications, Mr. Wheatland jumped at the opportunity to explore other aspects of the technology market and willingly joined forces with several other business executives to form CCG Consulting Associates. As Managing Partner with the Company, he concentrates his service to the consulting field, where he is able to fully utilize his talents acquired from previous positions. For the future, Mr. Wheatland hopes to continue with this new Company and help it strengthen and grow internationally. An expert, his success reflects his ability to think outside the box, deliver results, and aggressively take on new challenges. Established in 1999, CCG Consulting Associates provides general management, education, business development, and training within the information technology industry. Operating on an international level, the Company facilitates the educational needs of its clients throughout the various markets. The Company specializes its services to those businesses functioning within the high technology industries, however, it also works with clients in Sweden to establish their businesses and create their first computer network for the office. **Career Highlights:** Managing Partner, CCG Consulting Associates (1999-Present); Director of Strategic Marketing and Professional Services, Ericcson Radio Systems (1998-99); Ericcson Telecom: Director of Service Innovation (1992-98), Executive Consultant (1991-92); Director of Customer Service, Ericcson Business Communications (1988-91). **Associations & Accomplishments:** Board of Directors, Association for Services Management International; Visiting Fellow in Hi Technology Services Management, Faculty of Liverpool John Moores University; Board of Directors, Aro, Ltd.; Institute of Directors. **Education:** Liverpool University, M.S. (1999). **Personal Information:** Married to Inger in 1980. One child: Karolina. Mr. Wheatland enjoys travel, food and wine.

Michael Henry White
UNIX System Administrator
Envision
12977 North Outer 40 Drive, Suite 310
St. Louis, MO 63141
(314) 737-6776
michael.h.white@monsanto.com

7379

Business Information: With more than 20 solid years in the information systems field, Mr. White fulfills the responsibility of UNIX System Administrator for Envision. Continually striving to improve performance and maintain quality, he is responsible for design, development, and implementation of cutting edge systems programs for a variety of clients. Utilizing the credibility he has fostered by working closely with a team of 20 personnel, Mr. White also coordinates space management, backup programming, and network transfer. In keeping with high standards set by Envision, he plans to remain with the Firm and continue his success in the field. His success reflects his ability to think out-of-the-box, solve system difficulties, design new solutions, and aggressively take on new challenges. Eventually attaining the position of Database Administrator serves as one of Mr. White's future endeavors. A consulting Firm, Envision specializes in information technology. Established in 1963, the Firm employs 200 qualified individuals at the St. Louis office to conduct operations and meet the needs of a diverse clientele. The Firm is an international force in the consultancy field. **Career Highlights:** UNIX System Administrator, Envision (1999-Present); UNIX Administrator, Mars (1998-99); UNIX Administrator, Manpower Technical (1997-98). **Associations & Accomplishments:** Square Deal Lodge #159; Eureka Consistory #29; AASA. **Education:** Tarkio College, degree in Management Information System (1985); St. Louis Community College at Forest Part, A.A. (1978); University of Missouri at St. Louis. **Personal Information:** Married to Patricia K. in 1976. Five children: Michael Jr., Michelle, Malinda, Erica, and Felicia. Mr. White enjoys football, baseball, basketball, track and music.

Susan L. Whitney
Senior Technical Specialist
AverStar, Inc., Geospacial Services Group
4099 Southeast International Way, Suite 206
Portland, OR 97222
(503) 794-1344
Fax: (503) 794-1350

7379

Business Information: Functioning in the role of Senior Technical Specialist of AverStar, Inc., Ms. Whitney is responsible for the development of in house GIS software, sales, and customer support. A smart, 16-year professional, she serves as the Geospacial Services Group's Technical Production Advisor. In addition, Ms. Whitney monitors the testing of newly developed software applications. Her career highlights include working with the U.S. Forest Service, mapping data on Cedar River Watershed landswap that was eventually submitted to Congress. Attributing her success to her very supportive husband, Ms. Whitney continues to grow professionally and hopes to successfully complete the current software development project. Established in 1964, AverStar, Inc. is engaged in information technology assurance, development, operations, and consulting. Also involved in principle GIS application development, the Company currently employs a staff of 2,000 individuals nationwide. **Career Highlights:** Senior Technical Specialist/Human Relations Liaison, AverStar, Inc., Geospacial Services Group (1995-Present); GIS Technical Services/Trainer/Human Resources, Infotec Development/AverStar, Inc. (1993-95); Cartographer, U.S. Department of Agriculture/USPS (1990-93). **Associations & Accomplishments:** Master Gardener Volunteeer, Oregon State Extension Service; Oregon Army National Guard, Retired. **Education:** Bowling Green State University, B.S. in Geology (1983). **Personal Information:** Ms. Whitney enjoys bowhunting, hiking, cross country skiing and riding the Harley.

David D. Wilkinson
Chief Executive Officer
Wilkinson Consulting Group, Inc.
200 Douglas Lane
Pleasant Hill, CA 94523
(925) 944-7062
Fax: (925) 944-7062
davidwil@msn.com

7379

Business Information: Mr. Wilkinson is Chief Executive Officer of Wilkinson Consulting Group, Inc. He is responsible for all day-to-day administration and operational activities. After working for some of the giants in the information technology field such as Gateway Group, Summit Integration Group, and CG Computer Services, Inc., Mr. Wilkinson ventured out into the entrepreneurial world in 1997 to start Wilkinson Consulting Group, Inc. His wife Sindy presently serves as its Vice President. A 24 year information systems professional, he owns a wealth of experience across the technology spectrum to include analysis, design, development, implementation, and project management. During his long career, Mr. Wilkinson has worked with financial applications and is familiar with operations and production control; operational, application, and systems EDP auditing. His accomplishments include a Y2K assessment engagement at Longs Drug Stores, as well as a technical audit of the network infrastructure and Human Resources system at American President Lines. Currently, Mr. Wilkinson is implementing an NT server conversion for over 4,000 users at Clorox Company. He credits his success to his ability to remain calm in a fiery situation and help others understand technology. Attaining the position of Chief Technology Officer with an Internet start up company and continue go grow his own Company serves as his future endeavors. Established in 1997, Wilkinson Consulting Group, Inc. provides computer consulting and information technology services. Located in Pleasant Hills, California, Wilkinson Consulting Group engages in a wide range of services, including project management, database development, messaging, Microsoft Backoffice technology, and Web design and development. **Career Highlights:** Chief Executive Officer, Wilkinson Consulting Group, Inc. (1997-Present); Senior Back Office Engineer, Gateway Group (1996-97); Manager, Summit Integration Group (1994-96); Senior Consultant, CG Computer Services, Inc. (1992-94). **Education:** California State University at Los Angeles, 105 units completed (1982); Long Beach City College, Structured Cobol and Assembler with Keyes and Cashman (1973-74). **Personal Information:** Married to Sindy in 1986. Two children: Danielle and Brianna. Mr. Wilkinson enjoys chess, music, playing the flute, tennis, astronomy and spending time with his family.

Edward A. Winter
President
Computer Consultant
535 Park Avenue
Revere, MA 02151
(781) 317-2326
eawinter@mediaone.net

7379

Business Information: As President of Computer Consultant, Mr. Winter oversees and directs all aspects of operation including monitoring financial and profit and loss statements and managing the budget. He determines the strategic direction and develops marketing and business plans to keep the Company on the competitive edge. Possessing an excellent understanding of technology, Mr. Winter fulfills the responsibility of project lead. In this context, he is in charge of tracking customer accounts, coordinating on-site work, developing Web sites. In the future, he plans on offering Internet hosting and e-commerce business, expanding operations, and increasing the clientele. He is also a professor at Salem State College. Attributing his success to a strong commitment to excellence and being at the right place at the right now, Mr. Winter looks forward to continued success and prosperity. Located in Revere, Massachusetts, Computer Consultant provides computer consultancy for small to medium sized companies. The Company specializes in assessing and computerizing their clients' needs using both hardware and software, building networks, and training users, as well as creating Web sites. Established in 1980, the Company employs five experts to facilitate every aspect of daily operations. **Career Highlights:** President, Computer Consultant (1980-Present); Professor, Salem State College (1990-Present). **Associations & Accomplishments:** Knights of Columbus. **Education:** Salem State University, M.S. (1978); Boston State University, B.S. (1973). **Personal Information:** Married to Denise in 1980. Two children: Daniel and Kimberly. Mr. Winter enjoys computers and vacations in Disney World.

W. Scott Winter
SAP Consultant
Clarkston Potomac
2605 Meridian Parkway
Durham, NC 27713-2294
(919) 484-4695
swinter@clarkstonpotomac.com

7379

Business Information: As a SAP Consultant for Clarkston Potomac, Mr. Winter fulfills a number of technical functions on behalf of the Company and its clientele. He is responsible for the design and implementation of management and technical infrastructures. Possessing an excellent understanding of SAP software, Mr. Winter works closely with management and users to analyze, specify, and design creative database software as well as ensure data security, integrity, and reliability. The most rewarding aspects of his career include identifying a need for integrated systems. Highly regarded, Mr. Winter's success is attributed to his decision-making ability and his intuitiveness. In the future, he aspires to be an independent consultant and his own boss. Clarkston Potomac provides consultation services for security and control to mid-sized businesses. Established in 1991, the Company provides technical support, Enterprise Resource Planning, and SAP implementation as well as information technology strategies to its customers. The Company employs an enterprising staff of 200 and is headquartered in Durham, North Carolina. **Career Highlights:** SAP Consultant, Clarkston Potomac (1998-Present); SAP Consultant, IBM (1997-98); Staff Sergeant, Crew Chief for KC-135R, United States Air Force (1989-98). **Education:** San Diego State University, B.S. in Computer Science (1997). **Personal Information:** Mr. Winter enjoys travel, computers, sports and music.

R. David Woodburn, ISP
Director
Canam Software Labs, Inc.
199 Glenway Circle
Newmarket, Ontario, Canada L3Y 7S6
(905) 898-3279
Fax: (905) 898-7808
woodburn@canamsoftware.com

7379

Business Information: Serving as Director of Canam Software Labs, Inc., Mr. Woodburn is charged with the overall success of the Corporation. He is responsible for day to day business activities including employee supervision, client consultation, workload distribution, and programming guidance. A member of the board of directors, he oversees and monitors financial and profit and loss statistics as well as managing the fiscal budget. Also performing administrative duties, Mr. Woodburn conducts contract negotiations, policy and procedure developement, strategic business planning, and personnel management. Continuing to lead the Corporation to new levels of prosperity, Mr. Woodburn plans to promote the best interests of Canam Software Labs from his current position; thereby gaining personal satisfaction and occupational success. Canam Software Labs, Inc. engages in software development. Established in 1994, the Corporation has grown to employ over 30 people who generate a substantial annual revenue. Specializing in the custom development of business programs, Canam Software Labs has become an international leader in the software engineering industry. Maintaining an impeccable product record, the Corporation is expanding operations to additional cities and countries throughout the world, gaining profit potential and consumer recognition. **Career Highlights:** Director, Canam Software Labs. Inc. (1994-Present); Director, Castek Software Factory (1993); Manager of Information Engineering, Imperial Oil (1990-92). **Associations & Accomplishments:** CIPS; Former President, CIPS Toronto Section. **Education:** University of Waterloo, B.A. in Math (1977). **Personal Information:** Married to Barbara in 1976. Two children: Shanna Lea and Tracy Elizabeth. Mr. Woodburn enjoys golf, squash and tennis.

Marguerite E. Woods

Senior Software Engineer
eMerge Interactive
10315 102nd Terrace
Sebastian, FL 32958
(561) 581-7175
Fax: (561) 589-3779
mwoods@emergeinteractive.com

7379

Business Information: As Senior Software Architect for eMerge Interactive, Ms. Woods is responsible for data warehousing and collection. Utilizing her education and many years of extensive experience, Ms. Woods has just recently joined the Company. Possessing advanced technical abilities, she is responsible for building models for all data; e-commerce, engineering, Oracle DBA, and enterprise applications integration programs in several languages. Continually striving for maximum effectivess, Ms. Woods plans to pursue her Ph.D. to enable her to capitalize on the opportunities provided by the Company as well as build undiscovered data mining and neural networks. Attributing her career success to the example exhibited by her parents, Ms. Wood's highlights include being the technical lead on various projects and resourcing all equipment and software. Established in 1996, eMerge Interactive provides e-commerce for the cattle industry. Located in Sebastian, Florida, the Company employs 100 highly skilled individuals responsible for supplying track data and vertical data from business to business to certify cattle in the United States. **Career Highlights:** Senior Software Engineer, eMerge Interactive (1999-Present); Engineering Specialist, Northrop Grumman (1983-99). **Associations & Accomplishments:** Institution of Electric and Electronics Engineers. **Education:** Webster University, M.S. in Computer Science (1998); Rollins College, B.S. **Personal Information:** Ms. Woods enjoys reading, billiards and technology.

Jason Worley

CDOE Manager
Auto Desk Inc.
24 Morrison Road
Windham, NH 03087
(415) 507-5508

7379

Business Information: Mr. Worley fulfills the responsibility of CDOE Manager with Auto Desk Inc. Working with the hardware and software aspects of systems design and development, Mr. Worley guides his team in creating new devices and computer-related equipment. He is responsible for developing both packaged and systems software. A systems exper, Mr. Worley sets global standards for software licensing and keeps abreast on technological advancements and forecasts. Because of the implemetation of new programs designed by Mr. Worley, Auto Desk, Inc. has saved a large amount of money and is therefore able to expand their profitability. He plans to continue his work in the field and expand his knowledge of computer science and Web development. Passion for the job and watching the market keeps Mr. Worley on the cutting edge. His success reflects his ability to aggressively tackle new challenges and deliver results. Part of the Informational Technology field, Auto Desk Inc. is a software development company located in Windham, New Hampshire. The fourth largest software company in the world, the Corporation specializes in CAD engineering software packages. Headquartered in California, Auto Desk operates a network of 58 glabol locations. Presently, the Corporation is manned by more than 2,600 professional, technical, and support personnel who help generate in excess of $500 million annually. **Career Highlights:** CDOE Manager, Auto Desk Inc. (Present).

Rik Wright

Project Manager
ZoneNetwork.com
1415 Western Avenue #300
Seattle, WA 98101
(206) 621-8630
Fax: (206) 621-0651
rikw@zonenetwork.com

7379

Business Information: Mr. Wright serves as the senior Project Manager of ZoneNetwork.com directing and managing ongoing e-commerce initiatives and keeping them in line with the Corporation's business plan across multiple Internet-based properties. Crediting his success to quick wit and fast perception, he is recognized for using his creative skills to solve unique problems within the aggressive timelines of an Internet business model. Enjoying the challenge of his position, Mr. Wright intends to continue in his current capacity. Established in 1996, ZoneNetwork.com is a leading online media company. Its targeted websites provide high-quality, comprehensive information, news, and online shopping to passionate outdoor communities. The Corporation's best-known property is MountainZone.com, the premier mountain sports website offering community, commerce, and content. A trusted and well-known brand among mountain sport enthusiasts, the site is a complete resource for skiing, snowboarding, mountain biking, climbing, hiking, photography, and other outdoor sports. **Career Highlights:** Project Manager, ZoneNetwork.com (1998-Present); Director, Systems, Knowware LLC; Director, Systems, Numinous Technologies; Systems Analyst, Bennington Capital Management. **Associations & Accomplishments:** Washington State Software Association; Washington State Technology Alliance; HTML Writers Guild. **Education:** Virginia Commonwealth University. **Personal Information:** Mr. Wright enjoys music. He majored in jazz guitar performance in college and performs regularly in several jazz ensembles.

Scott D. Yelich

Owner
Computer System Consulting
P.O. Box 5178
Santa Fe, NM 87502
(505) 992-8359
scott@spy.org

7379

Business Information: Utilizing his extensive experience and skills in the technology industry, Mr. Yelich ventured out on his own to start Computer System Consulting. With the assistance of his two employees, he performs consulting services and network administration for client companies but specializes in providing Internet services. Mr. Yelich is very knowledgeable in computer security issues and in 1994, assisted in the apprehension of the perpetrator of a computer fraud. A systems expert, he currently has an e-commerce application in the patent process. He hopes to be the first person with a patent on e-commerce. Computer System Consulting serves the regional area around Santa Fe, New Mexico at the present time however, Mr. Yelich is planning to expand operations into California and New York. His entrepreneurial and professional success reflects his leadership ability to build a team with synergy, technical strength, and a customer oriented attitude, as well as think out-of-the-box and aggressively take on new challenges. Computer System Consulting first began operations as a side business. In 1996, Mr. Yelich devoted his attention to the Company full time and offers computer consulting, Internet services, network administration and security features, and e-commerce to small businesses. **Career Highlights:** Owner, Computer System Consulting (1993-Present). **Associations & Accomplishments:** Gave Seminar, University of Science and Technology in Hong Kong (1992).

Frances L. Yoakley

President
Independent Truckers Group, Inc.
3172 North Rainbow Boulevard, Suite 68
Las Vegas, NV 89108
(702) 395-5726
Fax: (702) 395-5728
fyoakley@itruckers.com

7379

Business Information: Ms. Yoakley functions in the role of President of the Independent Truckers Group, Inc. Concentrating on the weather reporting needs of the Web site, she assists in locating new information that is the most accurate prediction of upcoming weather situations. Other information provided includes truck stops and parts availability in the event of breakdowns. As the owner of the Independent Truckers Group, Ms. Yoakley determines the overall strategic direction and formulates new business and marketing plans to keep the Corporation out-front of industry competitors. For the future, she hopes to see the Corporation advance into the public market and she is currently organizing a discount group that provides new services at a lower cost to truck drivers around the world. Ms. Yoakley's strategic goals include taking the Corporation public and organizing a discount group for truckers. Her advice is "research everything you plan to do." Independent Truckers Group, Inc. provides transportation information to truck drivers and dispatch centers through the use of the World Wide Web. Founded in 1998, the Corporation was created after the need for up-to-the-minute information within this market was recognized. A team of six employees work to locate information and continuously update the information available to the client, turning over $500,000 each year. **Career Highlights:** President, Independent Truckers Group, Inc. (1998-Present); Senior Programmer, Movipartners, Inc. (1998); Internet Consultant, Computerama, Inc. (1997-98); Internet Consultant, BlitzNet Online Communications (1995-97). **Education:** East Tennessee State University (1996).

Carol Young

Assistant Manager - Programming
AT&T Solutions/McDermott Inc. Account
2600 East Main Street
Lancaster, OH 43130
(740) 687-4216
Fax: (740) 687-4347
cyoung02@aol.com

7379

Business Information: Possessing advanced technical abilities, Ms. Young serves as a Programmer for AT&T Solutions on the McDermott account. She assumes accountability for performing electronic data interchange, programming in Synergy DBL, Powerhouse, and Microsoft Access. Ms. Young incorporates customer orders into the network, designs Access databases, and assists with the help desk. Ms. Young plans to continue in her current capacity and acquire more system networking responsibilities. With headquarters in Florham Park, New Jersey, AT&T Solutions was founded in February 1995 and provides networking services worldwide. The Company services over 1,000 clients and employs more than 7,000 personnel. **Career Highlights:** Assistant Manager - Programming, AT&T Solutions (1999-Present); Diamond Power: Programmer (1997-99), Payroll Technician (1988-97), Clerk A (1982-88). **Associations & Accomplishments:** Golden Key National Honor Society; Gamma Pi Delta. **Education:** Ohio University at Lancaster: A.A. in Computer Science (1995), Outstanding Graduate in Computer Science Technology. **Personal Information:** Ms. Young enjoys walking, reading, 3-D puzzles and outdoor activities.

Gary Zaika, Ph.D.

Owner
Integral Software Corporation
1688 Saint Marks Avenue
Merrick, NY 11566
(212) 217-9214
Fax: (212) 217-9205
gzaika@dlj.com

7379

Business Information: As the Owner of the Integral Software Corporation, Dr. Zaika oversees and directs all day-to-day administration and operations. He determines the strategic and tactical direction of the Corporation and formulates new business and marketing plans to keep the Corporation in the forefront of the industry. Possessing superior talents and an excellent understanding of the field, Dr. Zaika is involved with programming and design of system architecture for small to medium-sized companies in New York. He is proud of his invention of state-of-the-art search engines. Concurrently, Dr. Zaika is the Managing Associate of Plural, Inc., a consulting company. Support and maintenance of search engines, Web applications, and worldwide applications also fall within the realm of his responsibilities. A supportive family, previous scientific experience, and MCSE and CNE certifications have contributed to Dr. Zaika's success. His goals for the future include becoming more involved in the Internet, e-commerce, and e-business as well as increasing his clientele and expanding his Corporation. Founded in 1994, Integral Software Corporation is a computer consulting firm. Services include support and development of Internet, Intranet, and client-server applications. Presently, the Corporation is located in Merrick, New York. **Career Highlights:** Owner, Integral Software Corporation (1994-Present); Managing Associate, Plural, Inc. (2000-Present); Technical Director, Blackberry Technology (1997); Project Leader, Muze, Inc. (1995). **Education:** Saratov University of Russia, Ph.D. (1989); Donetsk University of Ukraine, M.S. (1982); Microsoft Certified Solution Developer (1999); Certified Novell Engineer (1994). **Personal Information:** Married to Olga in 1982. Two children: Anna and Natalya. Dr. Zaika enjoys ice hockey, movies, reading, soccer and theatre.

Hong Zhang, Ph.D.
Senior Technical Architect
Emerald Solutions Inc.
20 Independence Boulevard, Suite 2
Warren, NJ 07059
(908) 542-4500
hong_zhang@emeraldsolutions.com

7379

Business Information: Dr. Zhang is a Senior Technical Architect at the Warren, New Jersey location of Emeral Solutions, Inc. On a daily basis, he demonstrates impressive technical ability as he designs and develops intricate coding programs. Configurating testing projects for customers, Dr. Zhang conducts extensive research to ensure all needs will be met by his creation. He stays current on progressive methods by attending seminars and reading pertinent material; success in this industry stems from being a team player. Focusing on the future, Dr. Zhang intends to incorporate systems integration into his career by becoming more involved in the design of technology. Emerald Solutions, Inc. provides consulting services to e-commerce businesses. Established in 1996, the Corporation is headquartered in Oregon and employs over 350 people at various locations throughout the United States. The Corporation has been recognized for the creation of impressive technical plans and outstanding customer support. **Career Highlights:** Senior Technical Architect, Emerald Solutions Inc. (1997-Present); Systems Engineer, EDS (1994-97); Visiting Scientist, Brookheaven National Lab (1993-94). **Associations & Accomplishments:** American Physics Society. **Education:** Ohio University, Ph.D. in Physics (1993); Tsinghua University at Beijing, Bachelor's degree in Engineering. **Personal Information:** Dr. Zhang enjoys golf and bridge.

Wei Zhao, Ph.D.
Senior Software Engineer
Netpliance, Inc.
515 Palm Valley Boulevard, #831
Round Rock, TX 78664
(512) 493-8322
zw@cs.umd.edu

7379

Business Information: Drawing from an extensive academic background and years of occupational experience, Dr. Zhao joined Nepliance, Inc. in 1999 as Senior Software Developer. He works closely with top management and users to analyze, specify, design, and implement the distributed personalization architecture. Possessing an excellent understanding of technology, Dr. Zhao focus is on the discovery, investigation, and initial deployment of state-of-the-art technologies to keep the Corporation and its clients flexible, efficient, and profitable in the Information Technology Age. Enjoying his prominence and success with the Corporation, Dr. Zhao intends to remain in his current position while researching new technology. Highlights include his research work at the University of Maryland and his recruitment to his present role. His success is attributed to taking advantage of the opportunities afforded to him throughout his school years and career. Established in 1999 and located in Round Rock, Texas, Netpliance, Inc. is an Internet service provider and manufacturer of Internet personal access devices. The Corporation employs the services of 125 individuals responsible for administration, overseeing the development and design processes, manufacturing, marketing, and sales of equipment smaller than PC. With a United States market expanding into Canada and Europe, Netpliance, Inc. is one of the first to deliver the consumer information appliance, the I-opener. **Career Highlights:** Senior Software Engineer, Netpliance, Inc. (1999-Present); Research Assistant, University of Maryland (1996-99); Software Engineer, Hewlett-Packard (1992-94). **Associations & Accomplishments:** Institute of Electrical and Electronics Engineers; Association of Computing Machinery. **Education:** University of Maryland at College Park: Ph.D. (1999), M.S. (1996); FuDan University, B.S. (1989). **Personal Information:** Married to Yi Qiu in 1993. One child: Elliot. Dr. Zhao enjoys travel and sports.

Jonathan R. Ziehl
Consultant
Schafer-CIT
575 Willow Brook Office Park
Fairport, NY 14450
(716) 218-4170
Fax: (716) 218-9192
jonathan@ziehl.net

7379

Business Information: As Consultant for Schafer-CIT, Mr. Ziehl works closely with management and systems users to analyze, specify, and design new systems solutions and applications. Possessing an excellent understanding of technology, he focuses on Web development, project management, and sales. A savvy consultant, Mr. Ziehl is highly regarded by both technologists and the customers he serves. He would like to further the Company's growth in project management. His career highlights include the development of an Extranet business to business solution for a utility company, a fully automated system that was profiled in the local computer magazine, Computer Link. Mr. Ziehl enjoys working in this industry and attributes his success to gaining experience while still in school. A subsidiary of Schafer Corporation, Schafer-CIT engages in computer consulting, e-business, Web applications, and visual basic. Schafer Corporation services government contracts, from military to research. Schafer-CIT deals with commercial contracts, providing clients with custom applications development. The Company was established in 1972, employs 380 individuals, and reports annual sales of $55 million. **Career Highlights:** Consultant, Schafer-CIT (2000-Present); Senior Consultant, Actium (1997-00); Analyst, Andersen Consulting (1996-97). **Associations & Accomplishments:** Microsoft Certified Professional; Microsoft Certified Trainer. **Education:** Rochester Institute of Technology, B.S. in Information Technology (1996).

Frank Sanchez
Director of Information Systems
Veridicom
276 Gold Mine Drive
San Francisco, CA 94131
(408) 565-6111
Fax: (415) 550-8911
fks@veridicom.com

7381

Business Information: A savvy, 11 year professional gaining hands on experience from several information systems positions with previous employers, Mr. Sanchez is renowned as one of the leading experts in the technological industry. Serving as Director of Information Systems, he currently maintains the operations within the information systems department for Veridicom. Possessing an excellent understanding of technology, Mr. Sanchez is responsible for the systems infrastructure, database management system, software implementation, and all applications. Certified as a computer engineer, Mr. Sanchez comes to the business with extensive qualifications, placing him in a position to advance through all levels of management. His future goal is to attain the position of Chief Information Officer with Veridicom or another company. Established in 1997 as an innovative technology firm, Veridicom is a major manufacturer of fingerprint security system devices. Meeting the demand of the technology industry in the year 2000, Veridicom has expanded, to include a staff of 70 manufacturers, designers, marketers, and other professionals, while their sales have grown to reach $9.3 million dollars. **Career Highlights:** Director of Information Systems, Veridicom (1998-Present); Manager of Information Systems, Teggera (1997-98); Manager of Information Systems, Cypress Semiconductor (1989-97). **Education:** UUP, CDI Certificate in Computer Engineering (1999) **Personal Information:** Mr. Sanchez enjoys working out at the gym and outdoor sports.

Louis T. De Stefano
Owner
Louis T. De Stefano, Inc.
P.O. Box 177
Stanardsville, VA 22973
(804) 990-4237
Fax: (804) 990-4239

7382

Business Information: As Owner of Louis T. De Stefano, Inc., Mr. De Stefano oversees and directs all aspects of day-to-day operations. He is responsible for the development and implementation of policies and procedures incorporated into all areas of the Corporation's business. Throughout daily functions, Mr. De Stefano is accountable for specifying and designing electronics security systems, performing security audits, and preparing security testing programs. Highly regarded, Mr. De Stefano continues to grow professionally through the fulfillment of his responsibilities and his involvement in the advancement of operations. His plans for Louis T. De Stefano, Inc. includes expansion and increasing clients and employees. Hard work and study is cited as his reasons for success. Louis T. De Stefano, Inc. is engaged in the provision of security systems consulting for government facilities, public utilities, and corporate offices. The Corporation offers a host of services including security design, surveys, testing, and installation. Established in 1981, the Corporation caters to national clients. Headquartered in Stanardsville, Virginia, the Corporation operates out of several other locations that function under the direction and full support of several professionals who facilitate smooth business operations. **Career Highlights:** Owner, Louis T. De Stefano, Inc. (1981-Present); Security System Engineer, NUSAC (1980-81); Staff Security Specialist, Bechtel Power Corporation (1976-80). **Associations & Accomplishments:** American Society of Industrial Security; Institute of Electrical and Electronics Engineers; National Society of Professional Engineers; Tau Beta Pi. **Education:** Polytechnic Institute of Brooklyn: M.S. in Electrical Engineering (1972), B.S. in Electrical Engineering (1970). **Personal Information:** Married to Deborah Anne in 1999. Five children: Noah, Abraham, Samuel, Anna, and Simeon. Mr. De Stefano enjoys stamp collecting.

Peter C. Garenani
Y2K Coordinator
Ademco Group
165 Eileen Way
Syosset, NY 11791
(516) 921-6704
peter_garenani@ademco.com

7382

Business Information: Demonstrating expertise in the technology field, Mr. Garenani has served with Ademco Group in various positions since 1993. At the present time, he assumes the responsibilities of Y2K Coordinator. In this role, he is responsible for the creation and implemention of global Y2K aremediation plans for all desktop and network systems across the domestic and worldwide enterprises of the Ademco Group. Combining management and supervisory skills, he coaches and guides a team of five employees who delivers support, research and development, and remediation services to offices in every Ademco location worldwide. Mr. Garenani takes charge of hiring, firing, training, and performance evaluations for the members of his technology team. He also exercises oversight of budgetary compliance within his area. Mr. Garenani hopes to continue his rise through the management ranks of Ademco and to eventually become the Chief Information Officer. A positive mental attitude and a good family has attributing to his success. Ademco Group is the world's largest manufacturer of business and personal security products including motion detectors, alarms, card access systems, and glass breakage sensor devices. Ademco has been in business for more than 30 years and supports over 50 operational centers internationally. At least 2,500 professional, technical, and support staff is employed by the Company which posts annual revenues greater than $1.5 billion. **Career Highlights:** Ademco Group: Y2K Coordinator (1998-Present), Help Desk Manager (1997-98), Manager of Support Services (1993-97). **Associations & Accomplishments:** Sovereign Military Order of Malta; American Association Auxiliary; Board of Directors, Christmas in April, Jersey City Branch; Founder/Director, Long Island Writers and Storytellers Guild. **Education:** The University of Albany, B.A., cum laude (1988). **Personal Information:** Mr. Garenani enjoys biking, sailing, community service, jazz music, world travel, cultures and languages.

Marty P. Johnston
Manager of Information Services
Kalatel Engineer Inc.
728 Southwest Wake Robin Avenue
Corvallis, OR 97333-1612
(541) 752-9194

7382

Business Information: Mr. Johnston functions in the capacity of Manager of Information Services for Kalatel Engineer Inc. He is responsible for networking of local and wide area networks and the configuration of all neccessary systems to ensure their functionality and operability. A savvy, 18 year professional, Mr. Johnston also monitors the Internet and LAN/WAN networking environment, as well as assists in designing and programming the Web site. In the future, Mr. Johnston hopes to complete his MCSE certification and eventually move into a Director's role. His success is attributed to his ambition and going the extra mile. Kalatel Engineer Inc. engages in the design and technology advancement of closed circuit television. The Corporation creates cameras and video surveillance equipment for use in stores and automobiles to protect the merchandise and customers in a variety of circumstances. Established in 1989, the Corporation employs 120 personnel and turns over $20 million annually. **Career Highlights:** Manager of Information Services, Kalatel Engineer Inc. (1997-Present); Business Owner, LynxTech (1988-97). **Education:** ITT Technical Institute, Associate's degree (1981); MCP+I. **Personal Information:** Married to Marci in 1991. Two children: Marissa and Amanda. Mr. Johnston enjoys water skiing and yard work.

Ryan J. Lee
Corporate Programmer/Analyst
ADT Security Services, Inc.
18383 Pleasant View Drive
Weston, MO 64098
(816) 801-4697
Fax: (816) 801-4550
rlee@adt.com

7382

Business Information: Serving as Corporate Programmer and Analyst of ADT Security Services, Inc., Mr. Lee oversees a number of technical duties on behalf of the Corporation and its clientele. Since joining ADT Security Services in 1998, he has focused his attention to programming and developing database solutions for productivity, and payroll and service delivery Company wide. Mr. Lee is responsible for maintaining the functionality and operational status of the Legacy systems. His concentration is on the discovery, investigation, and initial deployment of advanced technologies within ADT Security Services. Attributing his professional success to his determination and ambition, Mr. Lee continues to strive towards excellence in product evaluation and development with ADT Security Services. He aspires to attain an e-commerce or database developer position. Serving a global client base, ADT Security Services, Inc. has been providing specialized fire and security devises and services for residential and commercial establishments since 1874. The largest security service provider in the world, ADT Security Services also serves government clients and educational institutions. Headquartered in Florida, the Corporation employs over 30,000 expert technicians and installers worldwide. Striving towards meeting the demands of their clients, ADT Security Services remains committed to providing excellent sales and services. **Career Highlights:** Corporate Programmer/Analyst, ADT Security Services, Inc. (1998-Present); Lead Service Agent, Avis Rent-A-Car (1996-98); Crew Trainer, McDonalds (1994-96). **Associations & Accomplishments:** Microsoft Certified Professional. **Education:** National American University. **Personal Information:** Mr. Lee enjoys philosophical ideologies. Mr. Lee's fiancée is Amada Keogh.

Russell Rumley
General Manager
Infipro Inc.
P.O. Box 5609
Greenville, MS 28704-5609
(601) 335-5300
Fax: (601) 332-5072
rir@techinfo.com

7382

Business Information: Functioning in the role of General Manager for Infipro Inc., Mr. Rumley oversees the day-to-day operations within the Corporation. He schedules the project assignments for the six employees that report directly to him throughout the day. He understands the importance of technology in his career field and Mr. Rumley devotes a large portion of his time to remaining on the cutting edge of information technology through researching literary sources, such as trade journals and networking himself in the industry through his clients and business relations. A newcomer to Infipro Inc., Mr. Rumley is planning on an extensive stay with the Corporation and would like to use his time with them to excel in his field and become the Director of his department within the next few years. Infipro Inc. was established in 1976 to provide security to the residents of Greenville, Missouri. The Corporation features residential and business security systems for its clients. The systems offer everything from a simple upgraded door lock to the most state-of-the-art, technologically enhanced motion sensory systems to prevent break-ins and theft. **Career Highlights:** General Manager, Infipro Inc. (1998-Present); Technical Support, Sentrynet (1992-98); Electronic Technician, VSDA AMS Cotton Division (1990-92); Security Police, United States Air Force. **Associations & Accomplishments:** Home Builders Association; Chamber of Commerce; Boy Scouts of America. **Education:** Mississippi Delta Junior College (1990). **Personal Information:** Married to Nancy in 1989. One child: Patrick. Mr. Rumley enjoys hunting, camping, fishing, whitewater canoeing and riding his motorcycle.

Gene Turner
Owner
Industrial Data and Magic
612 East 7th Street
El Dorado, AR 71730
(870) 863-5115
Fax: (870) 863-8823
genet@ipa.net

7382

Business Information: As Owner of Industrial Data and Magic, Mr. Turner strives to bring technology into the rural community utilizing information systems to increase productivity with less physical effort. He determines the overall strategic direction and vision, as well as contribution of the information systems function. With more than 20 years of extensive experience in the technology field, he coordinates and directs all services offered by the Company. Services and products offered by Mr. Turner includes application programming, network administration, interfacing of new technology, and video over Web at home. Possessing high customer orientation and focus, he trains clients to effectively apply systems technology to their particular needs. His professional success reflects his ability to think out-of-the-box and aggressively take on new challenges. Mr. Turner's goal is to learn and implement new technology for himself and for clients while building a larger customer base. Established in 1987, Industrial Data and Magic offers many services in the technology field. Providing networking implementation, cabling projects, and database work, the Company employs a staff of two to conduct office operations on a daily basis. **Career Highlights:** Owner, Industrial Data

and Magic (1998-Present); President, Protective Systems, Inc.; Project Manager/Business Systems Manager, Con Agra Poultry Company. **Associations & Accomplishments:** Den Leader, Boy Scouts of America. **Education:** Louisiana Technical University, B.S. (1995); A.S. in Business (1993); A.S. in Electronics (1978). **Personal Information:** Two children: E. Campbell IV and E. Carson. Mr. Turner enjoys camping, travel, scuba diving and computers.

Lu Ann Born
NT Systems Engineer
Associated Press
15 Kildare Lane
Jackson, NJ 08527-3925
(609) 860-6956
Fax: (609) 860-6992
luanne_born@ap.org

7383

Business Information: Drawing on numerous technological certifications and years of success and experience in the industry, Ms. Born serves as NT Systems Engineer for the Associated Press. Specializing in managing and engineering of the Adsend System, Ms. Born oversees advertisements, projects, and new systems utilizing the latest innovations in publication technology. Adsend delivers over a million advertisements per year to newspapers in North America. Looking to extend the boundaries of her professional career, Ms. Born is upgrading her present certifications, and emphasizing her education on networking skills. Her professional success is attributed to her genuine interest in technology. Renowned around the world for its services and journalism, the Associated Press is a cooperative newspaper organization that supports all phases of radio, television, and newspaper communications. Employing more than 3,000 associates internationally, the Organization has been in operation since 1848, ranking it as one of the longest standing and most highly established news companies of all time. **Career Highlights:** Associated Press: NT Systems Engineer (2000-Present), Systems Manager (1998-2000), Production Supervisor (1996-98). **Education:** Brookdale Community College; Certified NetWare Administrator-3; Certified NetWare Administrator-4; Certified NetWare Engineer-5; Microsoft Certified Professional+Internet; Microsoft Certified Systems Engineer; University of Rhode Island; New York University; William Paterson College; Ramapo College. **Personal Information:** Ms. Born enjoys antiques, biking and music.

Danielle M. Villegas
Project Manager
Associated Press
19 Commerce Court West
Cranbury, NJ 08512
(609) 860-7252
Fax: (609) 860-6994
dvillegas@home.com

7383

Business Information: Serving as Project Manager of Business Development for the Associated Press, Mrs. Villegas is responsible for managing AdRES, the AP's dynamic and Internet based reservations service. AdRES is an electronic system used for reserving advertisement space in publications. A seasoned professional, with over 10 years of hands-on experience, she maintains vendor relationships by serving as the business development liaison between advertiser and newspaper clients, Research and Development, and Sales and Technical Support in regards to AdRES. Highly regarded by her colleagues in the field, Mrs. Villegas' current strategic plans center around the promotion and development of this AP AdSEND service, and making it the electronic standard for advertisement reservations. The Associated Press provides state, national, and international news through such methods as broadcasting, online services, graphics, and photography to the publishing industry. Established in 1848, the Associated Press is headquartered in New York City, with its main technical center based in Cranbury, New Jersey. The Associated Press operates out of a number of locations worldwide under the direct support of more than 3,500 professionals. **Career Highlights:** Project Manager, Associated Press (1999-Present); Princeton Learning Systems: Senior Project Manager, Content Management (1999), Project Manager/Senior Account Manager/Client Services (1998-99); Client Services Account Representative (outsourced), Blackwell's Information Services (1995-98). **Associations & Accomplishments:** National Association of Female Executives. **Education:** Mary Washington College, B.A. in History (1990); Mercer County Community College, Certification in Web Design (1999). **Personal Information:** Married to Juan C. in 1999. Mrs. Villegas enjoys travel, cooking, reading and dancing.

Lori Acheson
Operations Director
Marketlink, Inc.
21 North 6th Street
Esterville, IA 51334-2227
(712) 362-8556
Fax: (712) 362-5560
mlink@ncn.net

7389

Business Information: Ms. Acheson functions in the role of Operations Director of Marketlink, Inc. He is responsible for all day-to-day administration and operational activities of a satellite call-center located in Esterville, Iowa. She supervises and monitors her staff of 50 employees ensuring proper etiquette and procedures are adhered to. A professional in her field for over two years, Ms. Acheson faithfully served with Marketlink in a variety of positions since coming on board to the Corporation in 1998. In addition to overseeing part of the Corporation, she is in charge of hiring, firing, evaluations, as well as coordinating resources, time lines, schedules, assignments, and operational and maintenance budgets. Her greatest accomplishment with Marketlink is appointment to the Operations Director capacity. She is the youngest person to ever be placed in this position. Ms. Acheson's next career goal is to follow her established trend and become the youngest Vice President at Marketlink. Her success is attributed to her persistence, determination, consistency, and her integrity. Marketlink, Inc. provides telemarketing services for the cable television industry. Established in 1992, the Corporation works to promote its clients through telemarketing campaigns. The staff of 50 employees also conduct consumer research to determine the most profitable markets certain products should be recommended to. The Corporation has a total of three centers to manage the steady flow of customers that need to be contacted on a daily basis. **Career Highlights:** Marketlink, Inc.: Operations Director (1999-Present), Operation Manager (1999), Client Service Representative (1998-99). **Associations & Accomplishments:** Estherville Chamber of Commerce. **Education:** Central College at Pella, B.A. (1998). **Personal Information:** Ms. Acheson enjoys volunteering in the community.

Tommy L. Allen
Project Manager
e-Marketworld.com
252 James River Drive
Newport News, VA 23601
(804) 643-8875
Fax: (804) 643-2198
tallen@e-marketworld.com

7389

Business Information: Serving as e-Marketworld.com's Project Manager, Mr. Allen oversees and directs new vertical research and development. He owns an extensive background and expertise in information technology. Responsible for transitioning the Company to hosting services, he also attends to cutting edge Web design and development. Possessing superior talents and an excellent understanding of technology, Mr. Allen is also accountable for servers, applications, ensuring Web content is accurate, tracking sales information, and hiring new employees. Dedicated to the Company's success, Mr. Allen hopes to continue to provide his superior services, possibly obtaining a position as the chief technical officer in the future. Established in 1997 e-Marketworld.com deals in the production of Internet conferences and tradeshows. A premier organization, the Company brings buyers and sellers together through Internet conferences and tradeshows to produce business opportunities. Employing 100 personnel, the Company reports annual revenues in excess of $40 million. **Career Highlights:** Project Manager, e-Marketworld.com (1999-Present); e-Commerce Project Manager, Dataline Inc. (1995-99); Project Manager, LEM Solutions-Africa (1995-98); Linguist/Analyst, Central Intelligence Agency (1984-95). **Associations & Accomplishments:** African Explorers Association; Association of e-Commerce Developers; International Association for the Preservation of Afro/Tropical Rainforest. **Education:** University of Virginia. **Personal Information:** Married to Deborah in 1982. Three children: Monique, Stuart, and Dannielle. Mr. Allen enjoys African art collecting, big game hunting and photography.

James H. Barnard
Senior Integration Analyst
First Consulting Group
1038 Chaphan Pine Circle, Apartment 206
Winter Springs, FL 32708-5209
(877) 332-8763
Fax: (877) 332-8763

7389

Business Information: Having joined First Consulting Group in 1999 as Integration Analyst, Mr. Barnard has been recognized for his diligence and skills through a promotion to Senior Integration Analyst. Responsible for management of the overall systems architecture, he utilizes his engineering knowledge to design, develop, and implement software solutions. His success reflects his persistence and ability to tackle new challenges and deliver results as well as identify new avenues for technology. Mr. Barnard shares his wisdom with the public forum through articles and presentations. Enjoying the challenges his position presents, he intends to continue in his current role as he gains increased recognition for his efforts. First Consulting Group, a national organization located in Winter Springs, Florida, was established to provide the latest cutting edge information technology to the health care sector. The Group has grown to employ over 1,400 highly skilled individuals to facilitate day to day operations and provide solutions and engineering programs. Combining their technological expertise with their knowledge of the healthcare industry's specialized needs, the employees of the Group strive to determine particular requirements and objectives. They then analyze all this information and develop a technical plan tailored to the clients' needs. **Career Highlights:** Senior Integration Analyst, First Consulting Group (1999-Present); Systems Analyst, Florida Hospital (1998-99). **Associations & Accomplishments:** Association of International Advertising Agencies; INFORMS; St. Andrews Society of Central Florida. **Education:** University of Central Florida: M.S. in Engineering Management (1998), B.S. in Aerospace Engineering. **Personal Information:** Married to Haven Taylor in 1994. Mr. Barnard enjoys water skiing, reading and information technology.

Tina Bartolotta

Manager of Development & Operations
National Data Corporation
4 Corporate Square Northeast Expressway
Atlanta, GA 30329
(404) 728-2873
Fax: (404) 728-3871
tina.bartolotta@globalpay.com

7389

Business Information: Ascending rapidly up the corporate ladder at National Data Corporation, Ms. Bartolotta now serves as the Manager of Development and Operations. Her division develops and tests new software and operational services. In charge of the quality assurance testers and the technical support group, she administers performance reviews, gives project quotations, and personally checks the new and existing services. Since beginning her career in the credit card industry with NDC, Ms. Bartolotta has kept abreast of new technological developments by reading magazines, surfing the Internet, and attending in/out training resources. As a solid, 12 year technology professional, her success reflects her ability to solve problems in a systematic and efficient manner and take on new challenges. Committed to providing continued optimum service, she is looking forward to a promotion to the position of Director of Development and Operations. Headquartered in Atlanta, Georgia, National Data Corporation is one of the top four credit card processors in the United States. Serving clients on a global scale, the Corporation offers all types of transactions including credit card, debit cards, checks, and health claims. **Career Highlights:** National Data Corporation: Manager of Development & Operations (1997-Present), Supervisor II of Development & Operations (1997), Supervisor of Customer Service (1993-97). **Associations & Accomplishments:** Service Awards, National Data Corporation: Employee of the Month (July 1990, May 1992, December 1992, February 1993); Go For The Goals Finalist (1996); Circle of Excellence Winner (1996); Committment and Achievement Awards (1993, 1998, 1999). **Personal Information:** Ms. Bartolotta enjoys bowling and dancing.

Carlene Beall

Certified Trainer
dba computer moms®
1301 Lipan Trail
Austin, TX 78733
(512) 263-4084
sweetp42@aol.com

7389

Business Information: Utilizing an extensive knowledge in the computer field, Ms. Beall ventured out to establish her own company called dba computer moms®. Currently serving as a Certified Trainer, she possesses superior talents and an excellent understanding of technology. She teaches computer classes on programs, such as Windows95/98, AOL, Internet Explorer and Netscape, Microsoft Office, and Quicken to adults and high school students. Highly regarded in her field, Ms. Beall also provides technical support for all areas of daily technical operations. Determining the overall strategic direction and vision for her business as well as formulating new business and marketing plans fall within the purview of her responsibilities. In the future, Ms. Beall looks forward to continuing building up her client base and staying on top of emerging technology. Founded in 1998, dba computer moms® is located in Austin, Texas. The Company provides computer classes and technical support at the customer's home or office, providing one-on-one professional services at the client's convenience. Furthermore, the Company offers additional training in other areas of computers, enabling the students to acquire the necessary skills for jobs and careers. The Company is constantly growing and expanding, quickly becoming a success. **Career Highlights:** Certified Trainer, dba computer moms® (1998-Present); Teacher, Rockdale High School (1996); Vice President/Manager, Zilker Park R.R. Austin (1985-89); Sales Representative, Philip Morris USA (1978-81). **Associations & Accomplishments:** Past Member, Ballet Austin Guild; Austin National Science Association; Lawyers Wives Club. **Education:** Southwest Texas State University, Master's degree in Career and and Technical Education (In Progress); St. Edwards, B.L.S. (1991). **Personal Information:** Two children: Jennifer and Ashley. Ms. Beall enjoys reading, ranching, boating, hunting, football, cooking, gardening and fine dining.

Kevin Blumenthal

Information Systems Director
Budd Van Lines
24 School House Road
Somerset, NJ 08873
(732) 627-0600
Fax: (732) 627-0678
kblumenthal@buddvanlines.com

7389

Business Information: Mr. Blumenthal serves as Information Systems Director for Budd Van Lines. Because Budd Van Lines have been one of the fastest growing companies in America today, the Company is opening new locations across the country. These new locations will help to maintain the high quality of service customers have come to expect from Budd Van Lines. Working with a staff of four employees, he helps to maintain the entire computer and telecommunications infrastructure, develops new industry applications, and promotes new technology throughout the Company. Mr. Blumenthal hopes to become the Chief Information Officer of the Company by keeping up with technology and increasing the networking of its offices and marketing costs. His advice to others is to "keep up with technology" as much as possible. Budd Van Lines relocates executives around the world. Focused on Fortune 500 companies, the Company prides itself on its high level of professionalism and high level of quality. Established in 1975, the Company has built a reputation for product superiority and customer service satisfaction from over two decades in the field. **Career Highlights:** Information Systems Director, Budd Van Lines (1998-Present); Consultant, Bell Atlantic Mobile (1996-98); Systems Analyst, Kenworth Truck Company (1993-96); Systems Analyst, Port of Seattle (1994-96). **Education:** DeVry Institute of Technology, B.S. in Information Technology Systems (1989). **Personal Information:** Married to Melody in 1990. Mr. Blumenthal enjoys being with his family, racquetball, bicycling and travel.

Anne B. Campbell

Manager of Information Technology
Blackwell's Information Services
901 Route 168, Suite 204
Blackwood, NJ 08012-3203
(609) 227-1100
Fax: (609) 232-5397
campbell@blackper.com

7389

Business Information: Serving as Information Technology Manager of Blackwell's Information Services, Mrs. Campbell is responsible for LAN/WAN network administration, technical support and training, and customer support for EDI transactions. Before joining Blackwell's Information Services, she served as Network Administrator at Blackwell North American. Her background history also includes a stint as Project Manager with Sunbelt Business Computer. In her present role, Mrs. Campbell ensures that all technological aspects of the Company are in a running order, and that customers are satisfied and can call for assistance if needed. In addition to supervising a staff of two employees, she oversees the information infrastructure as well as coordinates resources, time lines, schedules, and assignments. Mrs. Campbell entered the information technology field after earning a degree in English. She decided to try her hand at technology because of the challenge and opportunities. Mrs. Campbell's quote is "Have you rebooted?" Her aspirations are to eventually attain the position of Chief Information Officer and increase her staff. Blackwell's Information Services resells subscriptions to academic libraries and universities all over the world. Established over 100 years ago, this international company has a total of six network locations located around the globe. Presently, the Company is staffed by a work force of more than 85 professional, technical, and support personnel. **Career Highlights:** Manager of Information Technology, Blackwell's Information Services (1996-Present); Network Administrator, Blackwell North America (1991-96); Project Manager, Sunbelt Business Computer (1989-91). **Education:** West Virginia Wesleyan University, B.A. in English (1990); New York University; Public Relations Institute; Microsoft NT and Exchange Technical Training. **Personal Information:** Married to Jack in 1990. Two children: Joseph and John. Mrs. Campbell enjoys modern dance and jazz dancing.

Cary Donovan Conover

Senior Corporate Systems Consultant
Conseco Services LLC
3021 Gateway, Suite 200
Irving, TX 75063
(972) 550-5416
Fax: (972) 550-5410
caryd@usa.net

7389

Business Information: As a Senior Corporate Systems Consultant, Irving office for Conseco Services, Mr. Conover plans, implements, and maintains NT, Novell, and Windows 95 systems. Mr. Conover advises on issues in the UNIX arena. With the support of one staff member, he performs daily management of systems, conducts user training, and develops and enforces policies regarding systems operations and security. Mr. Conover plans to maintain his personal standards of excellence through his strident efforts to stay abreast of the latest technology, guiding the facility in technological changes and upgrades. Conseco Companies is a Fortune 500 company striving to use technology to improve customer service. **Career Highlights:** Senior Corporate Systems Consultant, Conseco Services LLC (1997-Present); Senior Systems Programmer - UNIX, Parkland Health and Hospital System (1996-97); Systems Analyst, All Saints Health and Hospital System (1995-96); UNIX Systems Administrator, Hogan Systems (1995). **Associations & Accomplishments:** Institute of Electrical and Electronics Engineers, Computer Society; Association for Computing Machinery; Power Engineers Society, Dallas; Team OS/2. **Education:** Colorado Technical College (1995); Angelo State Unviersity; University of Maryland; Central Texas College - East Asian Division; Monterey Peninsula College, Graduate; Koren language course; Presidio of Monterey Defense Language Institute. **Personal Information:** Married to Kirsten Mele in 1993. Mr. Conover enjoys golf, bowling, computers and the Internet.

Andrew M. Denis

Director of Management Information Systems
Hotel Interactive
160 East Main Street
Huntington, NY 11743
(631) 424-7755
andy@hotelinteractive.com

7389

Business Information: Functioning in the capacity of Director of Management Information Systems for Hotel Interactive, Mr. Denis oversees and directs all aspects of day-to-day administration and design and development of emerging technology. Considering his work a labor of love, Mr. Denis began his interest in computer science during his years in high school. Success for him comes from keeping abreast of changes through both education and hands on experience. In addition to his duties as Webmaster, Mr. Denis' goal for the future is the to stay in communications technology and utilize digital resources, as well as reduce the manual effort of technology. Concurrently, he serves as an Adjunct Professor and Lecturer of Advanced Multimedia Design and Development at the State University of New York at Stony Brook. His success reflects his ability to think outside the box and aggressively tackle new challenges. Established in 1999, Hotel Interactive offers news, information, and other related tools for individuals searching for hospitality information through mediums such as online and interactive design. A staff of six coordinates office operations on a daily basis. Serving a national market, the Company responds to the need for custom form information. **Career Highlights:** Director of Management Information Systems, Hotel Interactive (1997-Present); Vice President/Director of Technology Development, Quantum Research and Technologies (1998-Present); Scientist, io Wave, Inc. (1995-Present). **Associations & Accomplishments:** Apple Fellowship; Software Affiliations/Accreditations from Microsoft; Adobe; MacroMedia; Borland; Sun Microsystems; Stratos. **Education:** University of Illinois, B.S. (1986); University of Virginia, Computer Science; Ohio State University, Physics and Advanced Mathematics. **Personal Information:** Mr. Denis enjoys travel, biking, reading, surfing the Internet and computer graphics and animation.

Jackie Lea Dobrovolny

Principal
Triple Play
12281 East Villanova Drive
Aurora, CO 80014-1903
3033687290
jdoffice@home.com

7389

Business Information: As the sole owner and operator of Triple Play, Ms. Dobrovolny accepts calls from her clients to discuss any problems and solutions. As Principal of Triple Play, she implements her outstanding technical intellect and experience to make technology the main ingredient in her recipe for success. Possessing over 23 years of expertise, she provides updates on information technology, guaranteeing her clients' acheivement in their future business goals. Ms. Dobrovolny is very proud of her present station in life and is hoping for a merger to expand her Company. Her incentive to maintain a solid grasp on her future is her belief that there are a lot of things that will catch one's eye, but only a few things will catch one's heart. She advises that we all follow our hearts. Attributing her professional success to networking with her colleagues, Ms. Dobrovolny's future endeavors include completing her dissertation and attaining her Ph.D. Triple Play is an independent consulting company, which engages in instructional design and evaluation of technology-based instruction. The Company utilizes the advantages of technology to counsel and audit various business to ensure impending success. Presently, the Company is located in Aurora, Colorado. **Career Highlights:** Principal, Triple Play (1993-Present); Instructor, University of Colorado at Denver (1997-Present); Manager of Commercial Products, McDonnell Douglas (1977-92). **Associations & Accomplishments:** International Society for Performance Improvement; American Educational Research Association: Association for the Advancement of Computing in Education; Association for Educational Computing and Technology. **Education:** University fo Colorado-Denver: Doctoral Candidate (1999), Master's degree in Education (1975), Bachelor's degree in Psychology (1971). **Personal Information:** Married to Kenneth in 1970. Ms. Dobrovolny enjoys home improvement activities and physical fitness.

Dennis A. Drown

Senior Programmer/Analyst
American Frozen Foods Inc.
355 Benton Street
Stratford, CT 06615
(203) 378-7900
ddrown@sprintmail.com

7389

Business Information: As Senior Programmer and Analyst of American Frozen Foods Inc., Mr. Drown is responsible for overall programming computer operations. To this end, he installs new software, designs and maintains systems, and sets up company-wide networks of personal computers. Also, Mr. Drown monitors newly released software, noting if they can benefit the Corporation in new ways, and he keeps American Frozen Foods abreast of all technological developments to keep the Corporation modern. As for the future, Mr. Drown wishes to stay in programming. Success, he maintains, is the end product of challenges and persistence. American Frozen Foods Inc. delivers frozen foods that last from four to six months. Established in 1960, the Corporation has profited from those who need large stockpiles of foods that can remain in storage. With a headquarters located in Connecticut, American Frozen Foods operates 14 sales offices across the Untied States. The Corporation's dedication to quality has lead to an estimated annual sales figure of $60 million. To earn such a high figure, the American Frozen Foods has relied on the skilled efforts of a work force of 1,500 people. **Career Highlights:** Senior Programmer/Analyst, American Frozen Foods Inc. (1983-Present); Programmer, Hartford Provision (1979-93); Programmer, Bob Broadway Computer Services (1973-79). **Education:** Vannuys College of Business (1973). **Personal Information:** Married to Cheryl in 1993. Mr. Drown enjoys motorcycles and camping.

Kenneth L. Guthrie, Jr.

Senior Systems Engineer
Spherion Corporation
2929 Jasmine Brook Court
Dacula, GA 30019
(404) 240-3763
Fax: (770) 339-4116
klgjr@mindspring.com

7389

Business Information: As the Senior Systems Engineer, Mr. Guthrie extends his expertise to Spherion Corporation in maintaining the systems infrastructure of the business sports center's 300 branches. Managing all operations, he implements necessary procedures and policies, ensuring efficiency and effectiveness of the Corporation's WindowsNT and WAN environments. Leading day to day administrative tasks, he turns potential into action through preparation and skilled training. Microsoft certified, Mr. Guthrie utilizes his knowledge and skills to integrate state-of-the-art systems into each facility, thereby enhancing the overall productivity. Committed to the furhter expansion of Spherion Corporation, he continues to strive towards improving his professional performance. Offering a variety of quality services, Spherion Corporation specializes in consulting services for capital management and human resources. Established in 1951, the Corporation employs the skilled services of over 20,000 professional administrators to acquire business, meet with clients, facilitate projects, and market services. Striving towards implementing the latest technologies, the Corporation establishes high standards of excellence for others in the industry. Presently, the Corporation reports annual revenues in excess of $4 billion. **Career Highlights:** Senior Systems Engineer, Spherion Corporation (1998-Present); Senior LAN/WAN Support Administrator, Prudential Insurance (1998); PC and LAN Administrator, C&P/Sovran Corporation (1978-91). **Associations & Accomplishments:** Microsoft Certified Systems Engineer (1997); Atlanta Back Office User Group. **Education:** Tidewater Community College, A.S. (1985). **Personal Information:** Married to Denise in 1980. Three children: Patricia, Kenneth, and Jonnie Ranae. Mr. Guthrie enjoys networking, time with his family, walking and travel.

Michael F. Hemsey

Director
Consumer Financial Network
705 Norfleet Road
Atlanta, GA 30305
(770) 291-7120
mhemsey@cfn.com

7389

Business Information: Demonstrating high standards of professional excellence, Mr. Hemsey functions in the role of Director for the Consumer Financial Network. He has been employed with the Company since 1997. In his capacity, Mr. Hemsey presides over the marketing of products and services to existing and potential clients. He works to develop brand strategies, collects informations for the database, in addtion to user- interface. Mr. Hemsey also supervises the work activity of the design teams, creates the Web design, and works with the print and electronic media. His goal is to eventually become the Chief Information Officer for Consumer Financial Network. "Set-up partnerships," is cited as Mr. Hemsey's advice. Serving an international client base, Consumer Financial Network was establishsed in 1993. The Company offers financial services and benefits through the Internet in addition to consumer advice through teleweb. Service to clients, consumers, and providers are free. A workstaff of 200 individuals are employed within the 20 locations of the Company. **Career Highlights:** Director, Consumer Financial Network (1997-Present); Director, Mutual of New York (1993-97). **Associations & Accomplishments:** Board Member, New Jersey Notre Dame Alumni Association; Co-Founder, St. Peter's St. Foundation. **Education:** University of Notre Dame, B.A. (1993); School of Writing Arts, Series 7 Licensed; Princeton Consulting, Business Plan Development. **Personal Information:** Married to Shaheen in 1998. Mr. Hemsey enjoys travel, sports and writing.

Richard V. Hennessy

Programmer
Harte-Hanks
2080 Cabot Boulevard
Longhorne, PA 19047
(215) 970-3515
richard_hennessy@harte-hanks.com

7389

Business Information: Functioning in the role of Programmer with Harte-Hanks, Mr. Hennessy is in charge of the customization, design, and development of Foxpro applications. He writes and maintains the detailed instructions that list in a logical order the steps that computers must execute to perform their functions. Mr. Hennessy is responsible for both systems analysis and programming. Working directly with experts from various fields, Mr. Hennessy creates software for general use. He is involved in updating, repairing, and modifying code for existing programs. He also assists in training users. Success can be attributed to Mr. Hennessy's honesty and ability to understand the Company's information technology needs. Established in 1995, Harte-Hanks, a Fortune 500 company, provides telemarketing response management. Global in scope, the Company is located in Longhorne, Pennsylvania. Presently, Harte-Hanks employs more than 150 professional, technical, and support personnel. **Career Highlights:** Programmer, Harte-Hanks (1999-Present); Programmer/Analyst, Abilitech (1998-99); Independent Consultant (1994-98); Programmer, Handisoft (1990-94). **Associations & Accomplishments:** Planetary Society. **Education:** CIR, Computer Training, Certificate (1989); Temple University. **Personal Information:** Mr. Hennessy enjoys physics and learning more about exact sciences.

Delwin R. Hinkle

Founder/President
24/7 University, Inc.
4201 Wingren Drive Suite 202
Irving, TX 75062
(972) 717-9170
Fax: (972) 717-1481
dhinkle@247university.com

7389

Business Information: A 17 year veteran of the technology field, Mr. Hinkle founded 24/7 University, Inc. in March 2000. Recognizing the convergence of streaming multimedia technology and the availability of affordable broadband Internet access, Mr. Hinkle identified a business opportunity to deliver continuing professional education, product education, and internal employee training using streaming multimedia. As the Founder of the Corporation, developer of the business plan that obtained first round private investment capital, and the designer of the database system underlying the Corporation's web site, Mr. Hinkle is involved in all of the daily activities of 24/7 University. The Corporation currently employs a staff of five personnel. **Career Highlights:** Founder/President, 24/7 University, Inc. (2000-Present); Director of Information Services, SEI Incentives, Ltd. (1995-00); Founder/President, ProSys, Inc. (1988-95); Vice President/Controller/Chief Financial Officer, Pepper Industries, Inc. (1986-87). **Associations & Accomplishments:** International WHO'S WHO of Information Technology (1998); Outstanding Young Men in America (1989, 1990); Who's Who in the Computer Industry (1989); Past President, Dallas Clipper User Group; Who's Who in Leading American Executives (1993); Technology Advisory Committee, Dallas Chapter of Arthritis Foundation (1988-95); Preschool Advisory Committee, VRBC Weekday Preschool. **Education:** Baylor University, B.B.A. in Accounting Cum Laude (1977); Texas Certified Public Accountant. **Personal Information:** Married to Anne in 1978. Two children: Lindsay and Stacey. Mr. Hinkle enjoys reading and surfing the Internet.

Connie C. Inman

Senior Technical Director of Software Development
Nova Information Systems
7300 Chapman Highway
Knoxville, TN 37920
(800) 725-1243
Fax: (423) 609-2711
connie.inman@novainfo.com

7389

Business Information: As Senior Technical Director for Nova Information Systems, Mrs. Inman supervises the activities of the software development staff. In charge of team building, she implements innovative processes developed through employee input and feeback to improve quality and maximize productivity. Also serving as a Project Manager, Mrs. Inman has the responsibility of overseeing specific jobs within the Company, ensuring proper processing techniques are being carried out. Recognized for acheivements in the field, she is credited with the development of an automated in-house system that greatly improved the operational efficiency and allows for easy gathering of client data. Crediting her success to the tremendous support she receives from her family, Mrs. Inman is looking forward to attaining a technology related executive position and aspires to be named Chief Information Officer. Nova Information Systems provides credit card transaction processing for Visa, Master Card, Discover, and American Express. Approximately 500 people are employed at the Knoxville, Tennessee location, where various vendors have business contracts to transact the payments. **Career Highlights:** Senior Technical Director of Software Development, Nova Information Systems (1997-Present); Project Data Manager, CDM Federal Programs (1993-96); Senior Information Specialist, IT Corporation (1991-93). **Associations & Accomplishments:** Director, Homeowners' Association. **Education:** Pellissippi Technical; University of Tennessee, Computer Science. **Personal Information:** Married to Kent in 1987. One child: Marylyn Elle. Mrs. Inman enjoys scuba, photography and family.

John S. Kot, Jr.

Database Administrator
Total Response Inc.
4405 Blue Ribbon Road
Indianapolis, IN 46203
(317) 781-4600
Fax: (317) 781-4612
jkot@totalresponse.com

7389

Business Information: Functioning in the role of Database Administrator at Total Response Inc., Mr. Kot manages and controls the day-to-day operations and data resources. He provides invaluable inputs in establishing the technical direction and vision of Total Response and developing the strategic business and marketing plans. In his present position, Mr. Kot oversees an Oracle database infrastructure. He became involved with computer science after taking a programming course in high school. Studying, reading manuals and technical magazines, taking classes and on the job training are ways Mr. Kot is able to stay on the cutting edge of technology. An expert in the field, he coordinates with clients to analyze, design, and implement a state-of-the-art marketing database that meets all their specific needs. Diversified and multifunctional, Mr. Kot concurrently serves as the Corporation's Systems Administrator for the AS400 operating platform. Installing operating systems software, ensuring data security and integrity, tuning software tools to enhance overall performance, and resolving systems problems are also an integral part of his responsibilities. Mr. Kot attributes his professional success to the learning opportunities afforded to him by Total Response. Eventually attaining the corporate position of Information Systems Director serves as one of his future endeavors. A subsidiary of The Jackson Group, Total Response Inc. is an integrated and database marketing communications company. Established in 1992, Total Response Inc.'s sister companies include

Jackson Press and Communico. Presently, the Corporation employs more than 250 professional, technical, and administrative personnel who help generate annual revenues in excess of $8 million. Currently, Total Response is headquartered in Indianapolis, Indiana. **Career Highlights:** Database Administrator, Total Response Inc. (1994-Present); Computer Operator, Woods Wire (1993-94). **Education:** Professional Career Institute (1992). **Personal Information:** Married to Vickie.

Flavio De Araujo Leao

Information Systems and Technology Director
BMG
Av. Das Americas, 500-Bl.12
Rio de Janiero, Brazil 22640-100
+55 214384584
Fax: +55 214833232
flavio.leao@bmge.com

7389

Business Information: As Information Systems and Technology Director of BMG, Mr. Leao is responsible for the technical activities of over 10 countries and United States Latin business units. On a daily basis, he evaluates the operating status of hardware and software to ensure that production potentials are being maximized. Working closely with his staff, Mr. Leao develops strategic cost cutting techniques that will contribute to the competition of the Company by lowering overhead costs without compromising quality. Recgonized for his creative problem solving approach to challenges, the Company requires him to travel extensively to utilize his skills at several locations of global operations. Keeping his goals consistent with the completion of corporate objectives, Mr. Leao looks forward to continued success in his current role. Established in 1980, BMG is an entertainment company that offers music compact discs, cassette tapes, video tapes, and digital video discs to the general public. Additionally, the Company records music for various artists, a factor that has helped to achieve a strong presence in the international branch of the music and entertainment industry. Employing several thousand people worldwide, the Company has estimated revenues of $4 billion annually. **Career Highlights:** Information Systems and Technology Director, BMG (1993-Present); Management Information Systems Manager, Bausch & Lomb and Waicon (1986-93); Systems Engineer, Electrobras (1978-86). **Education:** PUC at Rio De Janiero: Engineering degree (1978), Systems Engineering, Telecommunications Engineer. **Personal Information:** Married to Monica Avellar. Three children: André, João Marcelo, and Mirela. Mr. Leao enjoys tennis and gardening.

Marc S. McCray

Manager of Engineering Services
Compath Inc.
3007 Williams Drive
Fairfax, VA 22031
(703) 207-0500
Fax: (703) 206-9616
marc@compath.com

7389

Business Information: Mr. McCray has served with Compath Inc. in various roles since his arrival in 1997. At present, he fulfills the position of Manager of Engineering Services. A savvy expert, Mr. McCray owns a record of delivering results in support of business objectives by paying close attention to technical details and solving problems and challenges with a positive, can-do attitude. In addition to managing and guiding his team, he is responsible for maintaining existing networks, and numerous resource planning functions to include hiring, firing, employee evaluations, and project scheduling and assignments. Mr. McCray, an innovative and focused information technology leader, is also responsible for troubleshooting, upgrading, and designing new, state-of-the-art computer networking environments. Additionally, he is charged with recommending purchases, coordinating training, and formulating powerful strategic and tactical plans. Mr. McCray's long-term goals include becoming the Manager of Engineering, earning Cisco certification, attaining a Chief Executive Officer position, and starting his own systems integration company. He attributes his success to seeing and acting upon opportunities when they arise. Compath Inc. provides network support and solutions to cable companies and the United States government. The Corporation offers systems integration for the government and cable companies. Hardware is sold, designed, installed, and supported. Outsourcing projects are conducted, networks are maintained, and consulting is offered. Founded in 1985, the Corporation presently employs a team of 180 professional and technical personnel. **Career Highlights:** Compath Inc.: Manager of Engineering Services (1998-Present), Project Manager (1997-98); Systems Administrator, Henderson & Phillips Inc. (1995-97). **Education:** Old Dominion University, B.S. in Business Administration (1995). **Personal Information:** Mr. McCray enjoys the outdoors, tennis and hiking.

Webb R. McDowell

Account Manager
Xpedite Systems
2221 Rosecrans Avenue, #126
El Segundo, CA 90245
(310) 727-1807
Fax: (310) 377-9898
xsiweb@primenet.com

7389

Business Information: Serving as Account Manager for Xpedite Systems, Mr. McDowell fulfills a number of duties on behalf of the Company and its clients. He is responsible for daily business activities including shipping itineraries, production schedules, order fulfillment, customer service, employee supervision, and workload distribution. Also performing administrative duties, Mr. McDowell conducts contract negotiations, strategic business planning, policy, and procedure development, personnel management, and client consulation. Bringing the Company to new financial milestones, Mr. McDowell plans to remain with Xpedite Systems promoting its best interests, thereby achieving personal satisfaction and occupational success. "Have preseverance and always stick to it," is cited as his advice. Xpedite Systems provides telecommunications services to international clients. Established in 1988, the Company has grown to employ over 250 peolple who generate annual revenues topping $200 million. Specializing in fax services, e-mail provision, and teleconferencing, Xpedite Systems has become a global leader in a complex and competitive industry. Maintaining an impeccable service record, Xpedite Systems plans to expand operations to additional cities and countries around the world to gain consumer recognition and growth potential. **Career Highlights:** Account Manager, Xpedite Systems (1996-Present); Technical Sales, Components Plus (1992-96); Technical Sales, Touchstone Technical Sales (1988-92). **Education:** B.S. in Information Systems (2000). **Personal Information:** Married. Mr. McDowell enjoys art, fishing, golf and reading.

Mazda T. Miles

Director of Systems Support
Pennrose Properties, Inc.
1650 Market Street, Suite 3810
Philadelphia, PA 19103-7301
(215) 979-1682
Fax: (215) 979-1101
mazda_miles@pennrose.com

7389

Business Information: Working as a liaison between the three divisions of Pennrose Properties, Inc., Mrs. Miles has been providing professional technical services with the Corporation for two years as Director of Systems Support. Overseeing the basic maintenance of the network system, she incorporates the latest technologies into upgrading the systems, providing a more efficient and effective network. Utilizing skills and knowledge attained from her certification in Microsoft, Mrs. Miles also provides technical support and troubleshooting, ensuring a quality networking system. Committed to her career with Pennrose Properties, Inc., Mrs. Miles' goal is to facilitate continued Corporation growth and geographic expansion. Founded in the 1980s, Pennrose Properties, Inc. is an established and reputable real estate agency providing affordable housing development, management, and service. Serving a national client base, the Corporation is located in Philadelphia, Pennsylvania and employs the skilled services of 500 individuals to promote services, facilitate scheduling, and address client queries. **Career Highlights:** Director of Systems Support, Pennrose Properties, Inc. (1998-Present); Human Resources Manager, Compass International (1997-98); Writing Specialist, Eastern College (1996-97). **Education:** Microsoft Certified Professional (1999); IBM Right Source Certificate. **Personal Information:** Mrs. Miles enjoys family time and surfing the Internet.

Richard G. Pinkall-Pollei

Security Analyst/Systems Engineer
Cooperative Resources International
135 Enterprise Drive - P.O. Box 930230
Verona, WI 53593
(608) 845-1900
Fax: (608) 845-1999
whraven@msn.fullfeed.com

7389

Business Information: Serving as the Security Analyst and Systems Engineer for Cooperative Resources International, Mr. Pinkall-Pollei fulfills a variety of responsibilities. A graduate of Carthage College, he ensures the efficiency and total security of all computer system operations. With over 15 years of experience with Cooperative Resources International, Mr. Pinkall-Pollei engineers and monitors all network and software operations and functions for the Company. Regarded as an expert in his field, he conducts several training sessions in computer systems operation and security. In the future, Mr. Pinkall-Pollei plans to continue in computer system security while expanding his technical knowledge. Cooperative Resources International is a holding company for dairy and agricultural cooperatives. With estimated annual revenues exceeding $70 million, the Company owns and operates four subsidiary companies. Currently, Cooperative Resources International employs 1,300 people. **Career Highlights:** Cooperative Resources International: Security Analyst/Systems Engineer (1990-Present), Systems Analyst (1985-90), Assistant Manager, Data Entry (1982-85). **Associations & Accomplishments:** Association for Computing Machinery; American Association for the Advancement of Science; Aircraft Owners and Pilots Association; Experimental Aircraft Association. **Education:** Carthage College: B.A. (1976); University of Georgia at Athens. **Personal Information:** Married to Patricia in 1986. One child: Richard E.

Michael J. Powers

Director of Information Systems
The Charlton Group
644 Science Drive
Madison, WI 53711-1073
(608) 232-9444
Fax: (608) 232-9411
mpowers@thecharltongroup.com

7389

Business Information: As Director of Information Systems of The Charlton Group, Mr. Powers provides direction for the activites of the technical departments. Concerned with software and hardware, he works closely with his staff to develop innovative strategies for the improvement of operations. He utilizes his practical work experience and related education to handle programming issues for the Company, offering his insight and guidance to create exceptional results. Maintaining the corporate Web sites, he is involved in the design and upkeep, ensuring customers and potential clients receive a good impression when visiting. Mr. Powers relies on his dediction to assist him in the completion of personal and business goals; he currently is striving to expand the regional Company to a national level. The Charlton Group was founded in 1987, and employs over 300 people. Engaged in telemarketing, the main focus of the Company is outbound cable. Headquartered in Madison, Wisconsin, the Company operates three locations to serve an extensive clientele, with annual revenues exceeding $12 million. **Career Highlights:** Director of Information Systems, The Charlton Group (1998-Present); Advanced Data Comm, Inc.: Senior System Administrator (1996-98), Director of Systems & Programming (1990-96). **Education:** Indian Hills Community College, Associate's degree (1989). **Personal Information:** Mr. Powers enjoys NASCAR.

Jeffrey D. Reese

Geographic Information Systems Specialist
Delaware County Information Services
100 West Main Street, Room 204
Muncie, IN 47305
(765) 213-1269
Fax: (765) 747-7744
marine@iquest.net

7389

Business Information: Mr. Reese serves in the role of Geographic Information Systems Specialist of Delaware County Information Services. He is in charge of project management and systems implementation of the Agency's mapping operations. Utilizing business and technical savvy, he uses computers in the mapping of land features and political boundaries. Currently, Mr. Reese is working on a parcel project measuring property boundaries for 55,000 parcels, garthering data on building layers to compute municiple's tree inventory, side walks, ditches, and legal drains. In addition, he is heading a data sharing project that will combine Muncie City, Delaware County, Department of Muncie Sanitary Division, and Ball State University on one database. Recognized for his accomplishments, Mr. Reese was nominated for the "Muncie and Delarware Clean and Beautiful Environment" award. His long-range plans include remaining in his current position and eventually starting up his own company. Delaware County Information Services is currently involved in mapping property boundaries in Delaware county. The Agency is also involved in processing the data to determine zoning and equitable distribution of County resources. Operating since 1998, the Agency employs a skilled technical staff of four people. Delaware County Information Services is located in Muncie, Indiana. **Career Highlights:** Geographic Information Systems Specialist, Delaware County (1998-Present); Geographic Information Systems Technician, Ball State University (1996-98); Landscape Architect Assistant, Paws Incorporated (1991-96); United States Marine Corps Reserve (1991-99). **Associations & Accomplishments:** Eagle Scout, Boy Scouts of America; Optimist International; Big Brothers, Big Sisters. **Education:** Ball State University, Bachelor's degree (1998). **Personal Information:** Married to

Lisa J. in 1994. Mr. Reese enjoys sculpting, camping, image processing and staining glass.

Matthew R. Rossi

Business Manager
Internet World Media, Inc.
16 Thorndale Circle
Darlen, CT 06820
(203) 341-2918
Fax: (203) 226-8284
mrossi@iw.com

7389

Business Information: Mr. Rossi serves as Business Manager for Internet World of Internet World Media, Inc. He is responsible for maintaining the financial success of the Corporation. By using his superior communication skills, he maintains an open door policy condusive to employee feedback, ensuring positive working conditions and a productive team. Possessing an impressive educational background as well as hands on experience, Mr. Rossi has established a reputation for results and a keen business sense. His career highlight is the launch of a joint venture that brought in approximately $20 million in one year for the Gartner Group. Attributing his success to common sense, Mr. Rossi plans to remain with the Internet World Media, gaining experience and climbing the ladder to the position of Chief Financial Officer. Internet World Media, Inc. provides Internet trade shows and international and domestic publications. This international company employs over 100 people generating an annual income of over $200,000. Targeting large corporations and smaller businesses, the Corporation provides Internet exposure and increased community recognition of client services and capabilities. By increasing public awareness and technology upgrades to private homes and expanding businesses, Internet World Media has secured a successful future in an aggressive and complex industry. **Career Highlights:** Business Manager for Internet World, Internet World Media, Inc. (1999-Present). **Education:** University of Connecticut, M.B.A. in Finance (1994). **Personal Information:** Married to Barbara in 1995. One child: Samantha.

Eukarlgen A. Rothe

Product Manager
First Data Corporation
10825 Farnam Drive C-31
Omaha, NE 68154-3277
(402) 222-7148
Fax: (402) 222-7045
geno.rothe@firstdatacorp.com

7389

Business Information: As the Product Manager of First Data Corporation, Mr. Rothe engages in product development and proper management of the Buiness Unit. An expert, he has done a lot of work to improve the business relationships and the work of the Corporation. He works to motivate employees to be customer service oriented and to effectively respond to the needs of each client. A recognized professional, Mr. Rothe has been published in newspapers and magazines relating to the products and services he provides. His success reflects his ability to think outside the box, deliver results, and aggressively tackle new challenges. First Data Corporation is a Fortune 500 company established in 1970 in Omaha, Nebraska. The Corporation is involved in credit card processing and collection. **Career Highlights:** First Data Corporation: Project Manager (1998-Present), Implementation Manager (1997-98), Team Leader of Client Services (1994-97). **Associations & Accomplishments:** American Management Association-International; Lambda Chi Alpha; Special Olympics. **Education:** University of Nebraska at Kearney, B.S. in Business Administration (1993). **Personal Information:** Married to Darcee in 1994. Mr. Rothe enjoys bike riding and golf.

Mike M. Salem

Technology Specialist
UOP
25 East Algonquin
Des Plaines, IL 60017
(847) 391-2270
Fax: (847) 391-2758
mmsalem@uop.com

7389

Business Information: As Technology Specialist for UOP, Mr. Salem is responsible for the development of various software and network programs to ensure the functionality and operational status of the systems infrastructure. Fulfilling the accountability of project manager, he is charged with the obligation to conduct extensive research and strategic planning to maximize the utilization of advanced technology throughout the Company. With more than 13 years of professional experience, Mr. Salem continues to grow professionally through the fulfillment of his responsibilities, and his involvement in the advancement of day to day operations. Attributing his success to his upbringing, Mr. Salem's plans for his career include becoming highly recognized in the field of technology. UOP specializes in the provision of liscensing for engineering design and technolgy operations. The Company issues liscensing for international oil companies that engage in activities as drilling, refining, and distribution. Established in 1914, the Company is headquartered in Des Plaines, Illinois, and operates out of several international locations. The Company currently employs the highly skilled services of more than 5,000 professionals who assist in the annual generation of revenues exceeding $1.5 billion. **Career Highlights:** Technology Specialist, UOP (1995-Present); Project Engineer, Ferro Corporation (1993-95); Project Engineer, ARI Technologies (1991-93). **Associations & Accomplishments:** American Institute of Chemcial Engineering. **Education:** Illinois Institute of Technology (1987-89); University of Alabama, B.S. Chemical Engineering (1983). **Personal Information:** Married to Manal in 1990. Mr. Salem enjoys travel, reading, golf, theatre, tennis, bicycling, music and physical fitness.

Kerry M. Wiemokly

Chief Executive Officer
Graphic Consultants
5 Nanuk Road
Hopewell Junction, NY 12533
(914) 882-0345
kwiemokly@frontiernet.net

7389

Business Information: Functioning in the capacity of Chief Executive Officer for Graphic Consultants, Mr. Wiemokly determines the overall strategic direction and business contribution of the information systems function, as well as formulates business and marketing plans to keep the Company out-front of competitors. A savvy, 15 year professional, Mr. Wiemokly is responsible for setting up in house imaging equipment, software programs, networking, and Web page development. In addition, he is involved with the development and implementation of policies and procedures throughout the Company and handles various legal and public relations issues. Mr. Wiemokly continues to grow professionally and looks forward to being involved in the continued success of his Company. Founded in 1999, Graphic Consultants is an up and coming electronic consulting firm. The Company specializes in electronic pre-press, creative design, and digital work flows, and equipment. The Company currently employs a staff of eight individuals dedicated to serving the diverse needs of their clientele. **Career Highlights:** Chief Executive Officer, Graphic Consultants (1999-Present); Director of Imaging, AGA Inc. (1998-99); Director of Technology, Ro-Ark Printing Inc. (1991-98); Pre-Press Manager, Allied Printing (1988-91). **Education:** Sand Diego State, B.A. (1984). **Personal Information:** Married to Karla J. in 1991. Two children: Tanner Michael and Maya Michell. Mr. Wiemokly enjoys baseball, golf and water skiing.

Michael C. Wright

Director of Information Services and Information Technology
MCB Collection Services Inc.
2066 14th Avenue
Vero Beach, FL 32960
(800) 749-8811

7389

Business Information: Serving as Director of Information Services and Information Technology, Mr. Wright is the key developer of custom programs for customers of MCB Collection Services Inc. Supervising the design of networking systems, he demonstrates an extensive knowledge of the industry as he implements technical solutions. Mr. Wright utilizes information he has gained throughout his 25 year career in the field to guide his staff as they face challenges while working with customers. Recognized for his outstanding achievements in the industry, he is credited with the design of nearly 80 percent of the Kennedy Space Center's computer systems infrastructure. Mr. Wright attributes success to his ability to remain fully abreast of technological changes by reading journals, attending courses, and participating in Internet groups. Enjoying the variance associated with his position, Mr. Wright looks forward to assisting the Corporation in the completion of future goals as he continues in his position. Specializing in data collection, MCB Collection Services Inc. works closely with the utilities and medical industry. Headquartered in Vero Beach, Florida, the Corporation strives to formulate innovative business solutions for the industry. **Career Highlights:** Director of Information Services and Information Technology, MCB Collection Services Inc. (1999-Present). **Personal Information:** Mr. Wright enjoys boating, scuba diving, Ham radio and working on hot rods.

C. "Bud" Wychulis

Owner
The Rhythm Section Lab
101 West Ruddle Street
Coaldale, PA 18218
(570) 645-9835
trsl@losch.net

7389

Business Information: As the Owner of The Rhythm Section Lab, Mr. Wychulis provides services as a recording engineer and Web site designer. In this capacity, he performs all booking for the studio, orders digital equipment, maintains equipment functionality and operational status, and designs Web sites. A savvy professional, he determines the strategic direction and vision, and formulates new marketing and business plans on keep the Lab on the leading edge. Possessing an excellent understanding of his field, Mr. Wychulis is dedicated to providing all clients with a high quality of service and ensuring that each customer is properly cared for. Attributing his success to his dedication to learning new technology, Mr. Wychulis hopes to soon provide Web weddings to his customers. Established in 1997, The Rhythm Section Lab is involved in two different types of business. The Lab offers services as a recording studio as well as designs and hosts Web sites. Employing a technical staff of three personnel, the Lab also provides Internet server access throughout the United States. **Career Highlights:** Owner, The Rhythm Section Lab (1977-Present); Musician, The Mudflas (1991-Present); Musician, Bill Haleys Comets (1980-91). **Associations & Accomplishments:** American Cancer Society; Volunteer Fireman; Sons of the American Legion. **Education:** C.C.A.V.T.S. (1999). **Personal Information:** Married to Sandra in 1989. Two children: Cheryl and Andrea. Mr. Wychulis enjoys music.

7500 Auto Repair, Services, and Parking

- 7513 Truck rental and leasing, no drivers
- 7514 Passenger car rental
- 7515 Passenger car leasing
- 7519 Utility trailer rental
- 7521 Automobile parking
- 7532 Top and body repair and paint shops
- 7533 Auto exhaust system repair shops
- 7534 Tire retreading and repair shops
- 7536 Automotive glass replacement shops
- 7537 Automotive transmission repair shops
- 7538 General automotive repair shops
- 7539 Automotive repair shops, nec
- 7542 Carwashes
- 7549 Automotive services, nec

E. Joel Camunias

Inside Sales Supervisor
Bonfiglioli
7941 Jane Street, Unit 2
Concorde, Ontario, Canada L4K 4L6
(905) 738-4466
Fax: (905) 738-9833
joel.camunias@sympatico.ca

7539

Business Information: Recruited to Bonfiglioli as Inside Sales Supervisor in 1998, Mr. Camunias also fulfills the responsibility of quality manager as well as information technology support and training. In his position, he establishes and maintains customer relations, ensures the functionalilty and operational status of the A/S400 platform, and provides support to the customer service representatives. Possessing an excellent understanding of his capacity, Mr. Camunias oversees client relations, resolving any problems that might occur. The most rewarding aspect of his career is being employed by a nationally recognized company, such as Bonfiglioli and having the opportunity to manage individuals. He attributes his success to his intuition and looks forward to continuing with the Company, integrating the way business is conducted and maintaining good customer relations. Founded in 1986, Bonfiglioli provides services and engages in the sales of gear motors and gear reducers. The Concorde, Canada location serves as the sales department for the main office headquartered in Italy. With a staff of 17 employees in Canada, the Company as a whole has reports annual revenues in excess of $12 million. **Career Highlights:** Inside Sales Supervisor, Bonfiglioli (1998-Present); Product Specialist, Rexnord Canada (1995-98); Senior Inside Sales and Applications Supervisor, Maple Leaf Drives (1990-95); Inside Sales and Technical Support Supervisor, Sm. Cyclo Canada (Sumitomo Ind.) (1987-89). **Education:** DeVry Institute of Technology, Technologist diploma (1985). **Personal Information:** Married to Laura in 1985. Mr. Camunias enjoys music and reading.

Hosam Mahmoud Ismail

Information Technology Manager

Toyota Egypt

43 Mohamed Kamel Al Harone, Naser City

Cairo, Egypt

+20 123252534

Fax: +20 24858286

hosam@link.com.eg

7539

Business Information: As Information Technology Manager of Toyota Egypt, Mr. Ismail is responsible managing all information technology functions for the Company. Highly regarded, he is responsible for maintaining the functionality and operational status of the information systems infrastructure, as well as determining the strategic direction and business contribution of the information systems functions. Compiling the technology budget, designing and implementing new software applications, managing all technology projects, and overseeing all training opportunities also fall within the realm of his responsibilities. Possessing an excellent understanding of technology, Mr. Ismail demonstrated a broad range of knowledge that assisted him in his promotional climb to his present position. With more than eight years of information technology experience, Mr. Ismail utilizes his superior professional talents in his field to implement better programs that will improve the information technology field. Toyota Egypt engages in the provision of automobile and components for vehicular maintenance. One of four in a family of businesses, the Company also maintains a service center for such functions as tune-ups, oil changes, and tire maintenance. Established in 1981, the Company is headquartered in Cairo, Egypt while operating out of a number of subsidiaries for more convenient services. The Company presently functions under the direct guidance and expertise of more than 300 professionals who facilitate smooth business operations. **Career Highlights:** Information Technology Manager, Toyota Egypt (2000-Present); Project Systems Manager, Al Futtaim Group NTE (1996-00); Senior Analyst Programmer, Al Naboo DAH Group (1990-96). **Associations & Accomplishments:** IBM Technical Courses. **Education:** IDPM UK: Higher Diploma (1992), Diploma (1990); Aim Shams University Faculty of Commerce, Degree (1979). **Personal Information:** Married in 1981. Two children: Dina and Tariq. Mr. Ismail enjoys fishing.

Shyam Keshavmurthy, Ph.D

Systems Engineer

Perceptron

47827 Halyard Drive

Plymouth, MI 48170-2461

(734) 214-5466

Fax: (734) 214-2604

spkeshav@perceptron.com

7549

Business Information: Drawing from an extensive academic history and occupational background, Dr. Keshavmurthy fulfills the accountability of Systems Engineer with Perceptron. He is responsible all aspects of product design and development. Before joining Perceptron, Dr. Keshavmurthy served as Research Fellow with the University of Michigan. His background also includes a stint as Senior Engineer at Nuclear Power Corporation of India Ltd. A 12 year veteran, Dr. Keshavmurthy specializes his services to the inspection of paint jobs on automobiles. Together with his staff, he scans newly painted cars for flaws in paint and in the application process. Dr. Keshavmuthy currently owns two patents in the United States, one for a landmine detection machine and another one for a piece of machinery that detects errors on a variety of painted surfaces. His success reflects his technical ability to think outside the box, deliver results, and aggressively take on new challenges. Perceptron engages in automated inspection and gauging. Established in 1987, the Company assists in promotion of consumer awareness and fair treatment during the purchase of automobiles and car repair services. The Company employs a staff of 300 personnel who are trained in the meticulous inspection techniques to ensure the proper completion of all automobile jobs. **Career Highlights:** Systems Engineer, Perceptron (1998-Present); Research Fellow, University of Michigan (1996-98); Senior Engineer, Nuclear Power Corporation of India Ltd. (1987-92). **Associations & Accomplishments:** Society of Photo Optical Engineers; Association of Physicists in Medicine. **Education:** University of Florida, Ph.D. (1996); University of Mysore, B.S in Mechanical Engineering. **Personal Information:** Married to Shashi Kowole in 1997. One child: Deepthi. Dr. Keshavmurthy enjoys tennis and painting.

7800 Motion Pictures

7812 Motion picture and video production
7819 Services allied to motion pictures
7822 Motion picture and tape distribution
7829 Motion picture distribution services
7832 Motion picture theaters, ex drive-in
7833 Drive-in motion picture theaters
7841 Video tape rental

George Bliss

Senior Manager of Information Technology

Walt Disney Company BVHE

350 South Buena Vista Street

Burbank, CA 91521

(818) 295-3681

7812

Business Information: Displaying his skills in this highly specialized position, Mr. Bliss serves as Senior Manager of Information Technology for Walt Disney Company BVHE. Before joining Walt Disney Company, he served as Manager of Finance Systems for Carolco Pictures. As a topnotch, 11 year veteran of the technology field, Mr. Bliss stimulates management efficiency and effectiveness. He is responsible for strategic and tactical planning and upkeep of all aspects of technology within the division. A systems expert, he installs and repairs hardware and software, researches and develops new technology, and serves as chief vendor liaison. Coordinating resources, schedules, time lines, and assignments also fall within the realm of his responsibilities. Setting realistic goals, Mr. Bliss' objective is to eventually attain the position of Chief Information Officer. Serving an international client base, Walt Disney Company is an established media, production, entertainment, and publication company. The Company has several locations inside and outside of the United States. Walt Disney BVHE is located in Burbank, California. Local operations employ 600 qualified personnel to distribute Walt Disney products and produce motion pictures for television. Annual sales of the Company are reported at $3.5 billion. **Career Highlights:** Senior Manager of Information Technology, Walt Disney Company BVHE (1993-Present); Manager of Finance Systems, Carolco Pictures (1989-93). **Associations & Accomplishments:** Microsoft Certified Professional; THX Certified, George Lucas Company, Ltd. **Education:** American State University, B.S. (1988). **Personal Information:** Mr. Bliss enjoys surfing the Internet, skiing and reading.

John Neal Crossman

President/Partner

Crossman Post Production

35 Lone Hollow

Sandy, UT 84092

(801) 553-1958

Fax: (801) 553-0953

xmanpost@hotmail.com

7812

Business Information: Mr. Crossman serves as President and Partner of Crossman Post Production and utilizes nearly 20 years experience in the industry. His professional background includes graphics animation, video editing, and audio sweeting or sound effects. Mr. Crossman recently acquired non-linear as well as linear editing systems. Crossman Post Production operates as a corporate broadcast studio, producing training films, educational films, and commercials for public broadcast. Established in 1992, the Company has completed assignments contracted by Wilsons Sports, Yamaha, Icon Health and Fitness, Inc., the Utah Jazz, Kued, KJZZ, The Oddessy Channel, and Yonex. Located in Utah, the Company also edits an ongoing monthly series of educational videos, distributed to 22 counties. **Career Highlights:** President/Partner, Crossman Post Production (1992-Present); Partner, Beta Bay, Inc. (1986-92); Chief Editor, KSLTV News (1978-86); Staff Member/Band Director (1974-76). **Education:** University of Utah, B.A. (1981). **Personal Information:** Married to Wendy Wood in 1983. Two children: J.J. and Luke. Mr. Crossman enjoys music.

Lee Goldstein

Disaster Recovery Specialist

20th Century Fox

P.O. Box 900

Beverly Hills, CA 90213-0900

(310) 369-3134

Fax: (310) 369-5797

leego@fox.com

7812

Business Information: Serving as the Disaster Recovery Specialist for 20th Century Fox, Mr. Goldstein provides disaster recovery planning, documentation, and testing for the information technology group as well as studio operations and various business units on the lot. Before joining 20th Century Fox, Mr. Goldstein served as systems security administrator with Underwriters Reinsurance Company where he was in charge of disaster recovery planning and IT systems security. His history also includes a stint as senior network engineer at Litton Computer Services. In his present role, he is responsible for disaster prevention, response, and recovery for both emergency management and business contingencies. Continuing to grow professionally through the fulfillment of his responsibilities and active participation in the disaster recovery industry, Mr. Goldstein sees disaster recovery planning becoming increasingly more important. His success reflects his ability to aggressively tackle new challenges. Established in 1904, 20th Century Fox is a large entertainment provider of feature films, television programs, and home entertainment programming throughout the world. Operations at the Century City lot employ the talented services of approximately 3,000 individuals. **Career Highlights:** Disaster Recovery Specialist, 20th Century Fox (1998-Present); Systems Security Administrator, Underwriters Reinsurance Company (1997-98); Senior Network Engineer, Litton Computer Services (1996-97); Network Administrator, Whittaker Corporation (1994-96). **Associations & Accomplishments:** Survive-The Business Continuity Group International; Member of the Board of Directors, Business and Industry Council for Emergency Planning and Preparedness; Project Management Institute. **Education:** California State University at Northridge, B.S. (1989); Certified Business Continuity Professional; Certified Novell Engineer in Netware & Groupwise. **Personal Information:** Mr. Goldstein enjoys travel and playing and watching hockey.

Timothy G. Teramoto

Lead FX Animator

Tippett Studios

239 Glen Park Avenue

San Rafael, CA 94901-1308

(510) 649-9711

quaker@tippett.com

7812

Business Information: Mr. Teramoto is a Lead FX Animator for Tippett Studios. Overseeing effects animation sequences, he creatively designs techniques to most efficiently generate the desired effects. He meets with production, discussing alternatives and obtaining a more definitive idea of the production plans. One of Mr. Teramoto's proudest moments was a presentation he made at an industry conference regarding a computer-generated creature for video games. Some of his most successful film work has been seen in "Star Wars" and "The Haunting." In the future, Mr. Teramoto plans on becoming more involved in Web media and online graphics. His success has been attributed to his ability to think out-of-the-box, tackle new challenges, and deliver the desired results. Mr. Teramoto is a lead FX Animator for Tippett Studios. Overseeing effects animation sequences, he creatively designs techniques to most efficiently generate the desired effects. He meets with production discussing alternatives and obtaining a more definitive idea of the production plans. One of Mr. Teramoto's proudest moments was a presentation he made at an industry conference regarding a computer-generated creature for video games. Some of his most successful film work has been seen in "Star Wars" and "The Haunting." In the future, Mr. Teramoto plans on becoming more involved in Web media and online graphics. Success has been attributed to his ability to think out-of-the-box, tackle new challenges and deliver the desired results. Tippett Studios provides the entertainment industry with computer generated visual effects. Located in the heart of motion picture development, the Studios operate out of Berkeley, California. Presently, the Studios employ a staff of 100 professional and technical experts that provide graphic animation for major motion pictures. **Career Highlights:** Lead FX Animator, Tippett Studios (1999-Present); Technical Director, Industrial Light & Magic (1998-99); Senior Technical Director, Square USA (1996-98); Technical Director, Sony Imageworks (1994-96). **Associations & Accomplishments:** Tau Beta Pi. **Education:** University of Pennsylvania, B.S. in Engineering (1993). **Personal Information:** Mr. Teramoto enjoys art, photography and Ultimate Frisbee.

Ruth Caspary

Digital Texture Artist

Cinesite

8464 Kittyhawk Avenue

Los Angeles, CA 90045-4270

(323) 468-2166

ruth@cinesite.com

7819

Business Information: Serving as Cinesite' Digital Texture Artist, Ms. Caspary engages in digital texture and matte painting. In this role, she is involved in the visual effects in the 3D department, computer paints for animation, organizing pipline, working with modelers and lighting departments, maintaining the 3D paint program, and gathering reference and managing files. She is interested in staying in this industry, learning more about lighting, and becoming more involved in sound and Internet video. Ms. Caspary attributes her succes to her people and communication skills. The highlight of Ms. Caspary's career was managing a group that worked on the film "Air Force One" and various other 3D Imax films. As a subsidiary of Kodak, Cinesite provides digital effects for films. The Company is involved in image processing, film restoration for film production, and retail marketing. Local operations in Los Angeles, California employ 300 individuals to facilitate every aspect of an international clientele's needs, and strives to provide customers with a way to preserve priceless occasions on quality film. **Career Highlights:** Digital Testure Artist, Cinesite (1999-Present); Digital Painter, Rhythm & Hues (1999); Digital Painter, VIFX (1998-99); Digital Painter, Boss Film Studios (1996-97). **Associations & Accomplishments:** Siggraph Member/Volunteer, Art Gallery; Technoasis; Volunteer, W.L.A. Animal Shelter. **Education:** Fashion Institute, A.A. (1990); Kent State University; University of California at Los Angeles. **Personal Information:** Ms. Caspary enjoys ballroom dancing, salsa dancing and being a halloween freak.

Thom Sanford

Application Developer
Warner Bros.
4000 Warner Boulevard, Suite 2707
Burbank, CA 91522
(818) 954-3653
thomas.sanford@warnerbros.com

7829

Business Information: In 1994, Mr. Sanford was contacted by Warner Bros.'s Human Resources Department with an offer to become a valuable member of the Warner Bros.'s team as an Application Developer. Before joining Warner Bros.'s, Mr. Sanford served as Senior Programmer and Analyst with Miller's Outpost and as an independent. He designs, develops, and implements state-of-the-art systems for the tracking of film. Mr. Sanford is continually upgrading his systems and spent two years writing a program for tracking prints. This program is his own theatre and collection piece. In addition to his work at Warner Bros., Mr. Sanford is an Instructor at California State University and teaches advanced Web design. His career success reflects his ability to think out-of-the-box and aggressively take on new challenges and responsibilities. For his future, he intends to open his own business focusing on Web development, specifically for e-commerce. Warner Bros. is an entertainment corporation with its own television station and programs. Additionally, the Corporation makes and distributes films to a wide audience. The corporate IT Department deals with film distribution, specifically the 4 Star project. The project tracks all theatre film bookings and tickets purchased. Upon return of the film, the project tracks where the film was used and its quality. Information gathered from this system is used for ticket sales and submitted to appropriate agencies. Presently, Warner Bros. employs a work force of more than 20,000 people. **Career Highlights:** Application Developer, Warner Bros. (1994-Present); Senior Programer/Analyst, Miller's Outpost (1991-94); Senior Programer/Analyst, Self-Employed (1989-91). **Associations & Accomplishments:** Institute of Electronics and Electrical Engineers. **Personal Information:** Three children: Thomas, Gwendolyn, and Tiffany. Mr. Sanford enjoys digital sound design and electronic music.

7900 Amusement and Recreation Services

- 7911 Dance studios, schools, and halls
- 7922 Theatrical producers and services
- 7929 Entertainers and entertainment groups
- 7933 Bowling centers
- 7941 Sports clubs, managers, and promoters
- 7948 Racing, including track operation
- 7991 Physical fitness facilities
- 7992 Public golf courses
- 7993 Coin-operated amusement devices
- 7996 Amusement parks
- 7997 Membership sports and recreation clubs
- 7999 Amusement and recreation, nec

Deborah Elizabeth Bukis

Strategic Advisor
Seattle Center
4638 First Northeast Street
Seattle, WA 98109
(206) 615-0388
Fax: (206) 386-1978
liz.bukis@ci.seattle.wa.us

7941

Business Information: As Strategic Advisor of the Seattle Center, Ms. Bukis has a myriad of technology duties and responsibilities. Among these are network installation, fiberoptics infrastructure maintenance, and program implementations. A successful, nine year veteran, Ms. Bukis began his association with the Center as Technical Services Manager in 1991. She utilizes her strong business experience and technical expertise in helping determine the overall strategic direction and formulate technical plans to keep the Seattle Center at the forefront. In addition to her operational management of the development, set-up, and repair of the Center's mainframe, Ms. Bukis is also accountable for the Center's security and fire systems. Her highlights include putting in a new, in-house digital system. Eventually working in the private sector designing and deploying advanced technologies is cited as Ms. Bukis' future endeavors. "Knowing what you want to do and going for it as well as setting goals," serves as her keys to success. The Seattle Center is a sports/cultural complex that was established in 1962. Hosting trade shows, conferences, sporting events, and concerts, the Center also hosts five major outdoor festivals in its 20 plus acre area. This area is beatifully landscaped with gardens, plazas, fountains, and sculptures. The home of three major performing arts companies, the Center is also home to three professional sports franchises. With 9 million visitors a year, the Center is at the hub of the bustling metropolis of Seattle. Presently, a 350 professional, technical, and support staff man day-to-day operations. **Career Highlights:** Seattle Center: Strategic Advisor (1999-Present), Physical Assets Manager (1995-99), Technical Services Manager (1991-95). **Associations & Accomplishments:** Association of Energy Engineers. **Education:** City University (1999); University of Washington; Seattle Central University; Wayne State University, degree in Marine Engineering. **Personal Information:** One child: Nicholas. Ms. Bukis enjoys dog training and rock climbing.

Yury A. Izrailevsky

Artificial Intelligence Software Engineer
GetFit.com
460 East 19th Avenue #3
San Mateo, CA 94403
(650) 551-6719
yury@getfit.com

7991

Business Information: Serving as GetFit.com's Artificial Intelligence Software Engineer, Mr. Izrailevsky is responsible for providing artificial intelligence support for custom workout generation based on personal data and goals. He works with fitness experts and users to create programs and develops artificial intelligence engines. Highly regarded, he possesses superior talents and an excellent understanding of artificial intelligence technology. The high light of his career is working as an Artificial Intelligence Consultant for the Department of Defense at NASA. At NASA, he is credit with writing a leading edge simulation program. Attributing his success to a diversified background, Mr. Izrailevsky plans to bring more functionality and features to the Company in the future. The premier online fitness training service, GetFit.com is a personalized online fitness trainer. The first of its kind to tailor a personalized fitness program to each individual's goals and needs, the Company employs 45 personnel to meet customers needs. GetFit's customers include corporations, athletic teams, and organizations that want to provide their employees, athletes or members a new service that will help them reach their goals. **Career Highlights:** Artificial Intelligence Software Engineer, GetFit.com (1999-Present); Artificial Intelligence Software Engineer, Stottler Menke Association, Inc. (1997-99); Research Assistant, FLUX Group University of Utah (1998-99); Research Assistant, GRECC VA Administration (1995-97). **Associations & Accomplishments:** Association of Computing Machinery; U.S.E.N.I.X. **Education:** University of Utah: M.S. in Computer Science (In Progress), B.S. in Computer Science (1997).

Mark A. Greene

Management Information Systems Director
Linkscorp
245 Waukegan Road, Suite 204
Northfield, IL 60093-2761
(847) 441-1010
Fax: (847) 441-0602
markgreene@linkscorp

7992

Business Information: Serving as Management Information Systems Director for Linkscorp, Mr. Greene supervises all technical operations and activities. Demonstrating an extensive knowledge of the industry, he utilizes a proactive style of management as he incorporates staff feedback and input into standard operating procedures. He evaluates technical needs, then implements and maintains necessary equipment. Supervising the LAN and WAN, Mr. Greene handles Intranet sites for the Company. Concerned with telecommunications, he operates the phone systems to ensure accurate and efficient services. Recognized for his outstanding achievements in the industry, Mr. Greene is credited with automating the entire Company. Striving to gain the position of Project Manager, he looks forward to offering exceptional customer service to clients. Established in 1993, Linkscorp is a property management firm that owns and operates 25 golf courses. Headquartered in Chicago, Illinois, the Company is recognized as a leading provider of consulting services. The Company maintains several facilities throughout the state and employs a total of 1,000 people. **Career Highlights:** Management Information Systems Director, Linkscorp (1995-Present); Account Manager, Digital Technologies (1995); Police Officer, Glenville, Illinois Police Department (1986). **Associations & Accomplishments:** National Golf Course Owners Association.

Jeffrey J. Witkowski

Manager of Information Systems
American Junior Golf
2415 Steeplechase Lane
Roswell, GA 30076-3592
(770) 998-4653
Fax: (770) 992-9763
jwitkowski@ajga.org

7992

Business Information: Beginning his association with the American Junior Golf in 1999, Mr. Witkowski presently serves as the Manager of Information Systems. Utilizing his business savvy and experience in the technological field, he is responsible for all day-to-day operations, to include computer networking, Web site design and content, and ensuring the reliability and accuracy of the database. Maintaining client relations, Mr. Witkowski relays pertinent information from the golfers onto their Web sites such as member information, tournament dates, and scholarship results for potential colleges. Future aspirations include continuing in his career with American Junior Golf, keeping abreast on new developments in the field, and helping the Association grow and expand and eventually become a premier program in the country. Academics, knowledge, and resources availability are reasons for Mr. Witkowski's success. A golf association, American Junior Golf is headquartered in Roswell, Georgia. The Association's main objective is to offer exposure for young golfers, ages 13 to 18, who are expected to acquire college sport scholarships. Manned by a staff of 32 individuals, the Association's 61 event schedule are made available on the Web. **Career Highlights:** Manager of Information Systems, American Junior Golf (1999-Present); Help Desk, Westminster College (1998-99); Intern, Western Pennsylvania Golf Association (1998-99). **Education:** Wesminster College, B.A. in Science (1999). **Personal Information:** Mr. Witkowski enjoys sports.

James A. Raymondo

Senior System Analyst
The Walt Disney Company
345 Bayshore Boulevard, Apartment 905
Tampa, FL 33606-2350
(813) 631-7545
james.raymondo@disney.com

7996

Business Information: Mr. Raymondo is Senior System Analyst at The Walt Disney Company's reservation center in Tampa, Florida. He is responsible for a Novell NT-based environment and oversees an infrastructure consisting of more than 500 computers and 700 users. Providing support for the LAN network also is an integral part of Mr. Raymondo's functions. He fell in love with the first computer he was ever given when he was just a child, and continued to enhance his knowledge throughout all of his educational ventures. After working with the State Attorney's office and converting them to a PC environment, Mr. Raymondo was ready for more challenges. He applied with the Disney Company, and has enjoyed the challenges and opportunities he has been fortunate enough to receive. In the future, Mr. Raymondo hopes to continue to be challenged with the Company and would like to prove himself through a new position as a Technical Specialist in the next year. The Walt Disney Company was created to provide entertainment to the youngsters in the world. The Company has four major theme parks to offer thrill rides and imagination journeys for children and adults, but Disney is primarily known throughout the world for their animated cartoons. With features such as "Cinderella" and "Mary Poppins," they have been recognized as world-renouned leaders in the cartoon animation and motion picture industries for decades. At the Company's animation studios in Tampa, Florida, the Walt Disney Company sponsors over 45,000 employees creating weekly cartoons and animated films for the Company. **Career Highlights:** Senior System Analyst, The Walt Disney Company (Present); Network Engineer, State Attorney Office; Network Engineer, Applied Benefits Research. **Education:** Hillsborough Community College: A.S, A.A. **Personal Information:** Married to Cynthia in 1998. Mr. Raymondo enjoys studying and reading technical publications.

Gus Dandas
Network Specialist
Arizona Lottery
4740 East University Drive
Phoenix, AZ 85034
(480) 921-4529
Fax: (480) 921-4501
gdandas@home.com

7999

Business Information: Mr. Dandas functions in the role of Network Specialist with the Arizona Lottery. He is responsible for support of the entire LAN/WAN Lottery infrastructure. Before joining Arizona Lottery as Technical Support Specialist in 1992, he served as a Technical Support Specialist with Coastal Corporation. The Lottery has become very popular throughout the state and with online accessability, it is able to advertise the possibilities and attract a larger audience. In his current position, Mr. Dandas oversees and monitors the file servers carefully to ensure the equality and protection during the selection of the winning numbers. For the future, Mr. Dandas hopes to move into a position of Network Manager within the Arizona Lottery. A systems expert, his success reflects his ability to think outside the box, deliver results, and aggressively tackle new challenges and responsibilities. Established in 1983, Arizona Lottery was created to provide the state of Arizona with additional funds for its governmental programs. The Lottery produces millions of dollars through its sale of lottery tickets. Avid residents wanting to test their luck are able to purchase a combination of numbers in hopes of acquiring the winning combination and celebrate their multi-million dollar earnings. **Career Highlights:** Arizona Lottery: Network Specialist (1994-Present), Technical Support Specialist (1992-94); Technical Support Specialist, Coastal Corporation (1969-92). **Associations & Accomplishments:** Phoenix Netware Users Group. **Education:** Wayne State University, B.A. (1969). **Personal Information:** Married to Erine in 1986.

Mark K. Mavis
Information Technology Manager
Ticketmaster
3100 Broadway Street
Kansas City, MO 64111-2406
(816) 753-6286
Fax: (816) 753-3612
markm@kc.ticketmaster.com

7999

Business Information: As Information Technology Manager of Ticketmaster, Mr. Mavis is responsible for overseeing all the technology involved in the Kansas and western Missouri locations. Working closely with a team of two individuals, Mr. Mavis is invovled in the maintenance of equipment and printing reports. He has enjoyed substantial success in his career and attributes it to being in the right place at the right time, as well as his ability to think outside the box, deliver results, and take on new challenges. Mr. Mavis hopes to begin working in an administrative role and begin focusing on the network end of technology such as in the Internet and e-mail. Established in 1979, Ticketmaster is engaged in the sale of tickets to sporting events, concerts, the circus, and any other event other than movies. Headquartered in Los Angeles, California, the Company currently employs more than 5,000 individuals dedicated to serving an international client base. **Career Highlights:** Information Technology Manager, Ticketmaster (1990-Present); Technology Manager, Image Electronics (1987-89); Carrier, Orange County Register (1982-87). **Education:** Video Technical Institute, A.A.S. (1987). **Personal Information:** Married to Shellie in 1989. Four children: Christopher, Auston, Shelby, and Marissa. Mr. Mavis enjoys sports, martial arts and automobiles.

Atique R. Shah
Director of DBM/CRM
Uproar.com
240 West 35th Street, 9th Floor
New York, NY 10591
(917) 351-2874
Fax: (212) 279-8892
ashah@uproar.com

7999

Business Information: Currently serving as Director of DBM/CRM for Uproar.com, Mr. Shah evaluates raw data and transforms it into business intelligence. In his current capacity, he orchestrates marketing, designs products, creates tables, fields and marketing backgrounds, and targets advertisements and products for clients. Mr. Shah has been credited for helping to implement the database at Uproar.com. Thanks to much perseverance on Mr. Shah's part, the database greatly increased business for the Company. Highly regarded in his field, he possesses superior talents and an excellent understanding of technology. Attributing his success to his wife's support, continued learning, and solid relationships he has developed with other professionals, he aspires to become Executive Vice President of the Company, seeing them through future expansion and success.

Established in 1995, Uproar.com is an online entertainment company currently staffing 150 employees. Serving an international clientele of Internet surfers, Uproar.com provides new humor, games, and uplifting material daily for its clients. Presently, the Company is located in New York City, New York. **Career Highlights:** Director of DBM/CRM, Uproar.com (2000-Present); Database Marketing Manager, Cross World Network Inc (1998-00); Interactive Graphic Artis, Tascor/IBM Somers (1997-98); Department Manager, Bloomingdale's (1995-96). **Associations & Accomplishments:** President, Alpha Kappa Psi Professional Business Fraternity; Phi Kappa Psi; President, American International Association; Web Designer, W.A.M.A. **Education:** New York University, Professional Certificate (1999-Present). **Personal Information:** Married to Bayberry L. in 1997. Mr. Shah enjoys animation, datamining, programming, reading and skiing.

8000 Health Services

8011 Offices and clinics of medical doctors
8021 Offices and clinics of dentists
8031 Offices of osteopathic physicians
8041 Offices and clinics of chiropractors
8042 Offices and clinics of optometrists
8043 Offices and clinics of podiatrists
8049 Offices of health practitioners, nec
8051 Skilled nursing care facilities
8052 Intermediate care facilities
8059 Nursing and personal care, nec
8062 General medical and surgical hospitals
8063 Psychiatric hospitals
8069 Specialty hospitals exc. psychiatric
8071 Medical laboratories
8072 Dental laboratories
8082 Home health care services
8092 Kidney dialysis centers
8093 Specialty outpatient clinics, nec
8099 Health and allied services, nec

Barbara H. Obeirne, MMIS, RN
Clinical System Supervisor
Renal Care Group, Inc.
155 North Market, Suite 305
Wichita, KS 67202
(316) 261-9990
Fax: (316) 261-9966
bobeirn@renalcaregroup.com

8011

Business Information: Serving as a Clinical System Supervisor of Renal Care Group, Ms. Obeirne is responsible for systems administration. She oversees help desk activities, installs equipment, performs software troubleshooting, and conducts training and development activities. Possessing adept technical abilities, Ms. Obeirne is credited for the design of the Group's current network. Her plans for the future include remaining in her current position and acquiring more software responsibilities. Renal Care Group, Inc. is a healthcare establishment specializing in the treatment of kidney related disorders. Offering high quality nephrology dialysis services, the Clinics treat approximately 26,000 patients. Established in 1996, Renal Care Group is headquartered in Nashville, Tennessee and employs 7,500 professionals. **Career Highlights:** Renal Care Group, Inc.: Clinical System Supervisor (1999-Present), Computer Specialist (1996-99); Clinical Manager, Kansas Nephrology Association (1986-96); St. Francis Regional Medical Center: Assistant Director (1980-86), Patient Care Supervisor (1977-80). **Associations & Accomplishments:** American Nephrology Nurse Association. **Education:** Friends University, Master's degree in Management Information Systems (1996); Alfred University, B.S. in Nursing (1975). **Personal Information:** Married to Stephen in 1974. Three children: Kevin, Sean, and Bridget. Ms. Obeirne enjoys computers and painting.

Joe Rodriguez
Network Engineer
The Sports Club
11100 Santa Monica Boulevard, Suite 300
Los Angeles, CA 90025
(310) 479-5200
Fax: (310) 479-5740
joecoolr@pacbell.net

8011

Business Information: Dedicated to the success of The Sports Club, Mr. Rodriguez applies his knowledge and expertise in the information technology field in serving as the Network Engineer. In this capacity, he designed the enterprise management environment for the Institute's numerous systems, enabling the systems to function seemlessly as one network. Mr. Rodriguez assumed responsibility for building

the entire network from the beginning cable to the finished product. He currently oversees its management and administration. Continually formulating new goals and objectives, he is planning to increase the Institute's business through the use of e-commerce. His success reflects his ability to think outside the box and aggressively take on new challenges and responsibilities. The Sports Club is a healthcare facility, specializing in sports injuries and medicine. Created in 1980, the Institute caters to the sports industry, assisting its athletic members to heal as quickly as possible from their job-related injuries. Over 3,000 administrative, medical, and support personnel are employed. **Career Highlights:** Network Engineer, The Sports Club (1987-Present). **Education:** WVOC, Microprocessor Design (1997). **Personal Information:** Married to Veronica in 1991. Mr. Rodriguez enjoys dancing, skiing and fitness.

John Tang, Ph.D.
Manager of Information Technology
BAART/CDP
1111 Market Street
San Francisco, CA 94103
(415) 552-7914
Fax: (415) 552-3455
john_tang@boart.cdp.com

8011

Business Information: Supervising the network support department for BAART/CDP, Dr. Tang actively holds the position of Manager of Information Technology. Concentrating his efforts towards integrating software and network systems to improve efficiency and productivity, he is extensively involved in the development of specific software, hardware, links, and other applications designed specifically for use in medical practices. Utilizing his expansive knowledge in the field of computer technology, Dr. Tang also teaches part time at the local computer learning center. Consistently achieving quality performance in his field, he is committed to providing optimum performance to BAART/CDP. Attributing his success to his ability to remain calm under pressure, his most rewarding aspect of his career is implementing a cutting edge enterprise system and training 24 people for Microsoft Certified Systems Engineer certification. "Don't attribute fault to people who came before you," is cited as Dr. Tang's advice. Specializing in free healthcare services for the community of San Francisco, California, BAART/CDP is a chain of primary care clinics established in 1977. Employing the expertise of 350 healthcare personnel, the Clinics offers a wide variety of medical services for patients on a walk in and scheduled appointment basis meeting the diverse needs of its growing patient base. **Career Highlights:** Manager of Information Technology, BAART/CDP (1997-Present); Technical Support Manager, County of Almeda (1996-97); Management Information Systems Manager, Oakland Private Industry Council (1991-95); Human Resources Manager, Cogide Recycling Company (1990-91). **Associations & Accomplishments:** President, Board of Directors, Dance for Power; Board of Advisors, American Vict League. **Education:** University of Virginia: Ph.D. (1991), M.A. (1987); San Francisco State University: M.A. (1983), B.A. (1981). **Personal Information:** Married to Juana Enriquez in 1990. One child: Jonathan Alexander.

Charles W. Coyle

Senior Systems Engineer
Olsten Health Services
18002 Regency Park Drive, Apartment 1116
Tampa, FL 33647
(813) 264-3159
Fax: (913) 814-4357
chuck.coyle@olstenhs.com

8059

Business Information: Dedicated to the success of Olsten Health Services, Mr. Coyle applies his extensive knowledge and expertise in the engineering field in serving as Senior Systems Engineer. He is responsible for designing network and computer solutions, performing business analysis, and managing and coordinating the systems infrastructure in the Southeast region of the United States. As a savvy, senior registered technician, Mr. Coyle maintains hardware and software, ensures the functionality and fully operational status of the BUS, and provides technical and help desk support to over 100 users. He has been a key team member of Olsten Health Services for five years. Continually formulating new goals and objectives, Mr. Coyle owns a business and is currently pioneering with a partner to start up a data recovery business. He hopes to establish both and open a location in Singapore. His advice is, "keep your head down and listen to your users so that you can give them the best possible answer." He attributes his career success to having good people mentoring and supporting him. Offering a variety of services, Olsten Health Services is a healthcare solutions company. The Company provides home health care services and staffing for the health industry, as well as works with flying nurses and hospices. Company headquarters are located in Melville, New York. The Company has 250 home health offices, between 70 to 100 managed offices, and 6 resource centers located in the United States, Canada, and Europe. An estimated 613,000 qualified personnel are employed by Olsten Health Services who help generate revenues in excess of $4.7 million annually. **Career Highlights:** Senior Systems Engineer, Olsten Health Services (1997-Present); Account Executive, United Health Care (1997); Senior Coordinator, Olsten Health Services (1995-97).

Jason M. Mokros

Information Systems Manager
Wexner Heritage Village
1151 College Avenue
Colombus, OH 43209
(614) 231-4900
Fax: (614) 237-1175
jmokros@netexp.net

8059

Business Information: Utilizing a strong knowledge in information systems, Mr. Mokros serves as Information Systems Manager for Wexner Heritage Village. He oversees all daily administration and operations of the informations systems infrastructure as well as maintain its functionality. Possessesing an excellent understanding of technology, Mr. Mokros provides support of all in-house telecommunications and personal computers, which consists of 217 telephones and 150 computer nodes. Moreover, he conducts the server maintanance, repairs, and attends to all technical advance within the network. In the future, Mr. Mokros looks forward to continuing with the Village in his current position. His professional success reflects his ability to take on challenges and deliver results on behalf of the Village and its clientele. Founded in 1951, Wexner Heritage Village is a long term health care center. Located in Colombus, Ohio, the Center is equipped with approximately 300 beds throughout five buildings and provides patients with exceptional care and attention for all of their needs. With a staff of over 500 employees, the Center has become a full success and reports a substantial annual revenue each year. **Career Highlights:** Information Systems Manager, Wexner Heritage Village (1999-Present); Service Engineer, ADS System, Inc. (1997-99). **Associations & Accomplishments:** Netware Users International; CNA Certified; A+ Certified. **Education:** DeVry Institute of Technology, Associate's degree (1998-99).

Carla V. Bender

Management Information Systems Manager
Pikes Peak Mental Health
220 Ruskin Drive
Colorado Springs, CO 80910
(719) 572-6110

8062

Business Information: With over 14 years of experience and a Master's degree in Software Engineering, Ms. Bender joined the Institution as Management Information Systems Manager. In this capacity, she manages the maintenance of all databases and programs which track patients and treatments. Commended for effieciency and accuracy, she facilitates the filing of reports to the state of Colorado on behalf of the Institution. With her practical experience, she offers technical support to employess and also handles systems integration. Frequently recongized for her professionalism in a often trying working enviornment, Ms. Bender is considered an asset to her colleagues, who value her work ethics and business strategies. She is continually striving to ensure all employees of the Institution are knowledgeable about the technology they work with every day. In the future, Ms. Bender hopes to help the Institution develop more independence in information access. Pikes Peak Mental Health is a non-profit organization that provides full service counseling and support to the residents of the Colorado Springs, Colorado community. Working closely with other health specialists, they emphasize the development of coping skills to help individiuals work out their mental and emotional health issues. Within the Institution, the Management Information Systems Department provides all maintenance and support of database, technical, and information systems including telecommunications and network services. **Career Highlights:** Management Information Systems Manager, Pikes Peak Mental Health (1998-Present). **Personal Information:** One child. Ms. Bender enjoys collecting Pok-E-Mon cards, hiking, rollerblading and composing music.

Briget R. Bishop

Project Coordinator
Fauquier Hospital
500 Hospital Drive
Warrenton, VA 20186
(540) 347-2550

8062

Business Information: Displaying a unique talent in the medical field, Ms. Bishop serves as Project Coordinator for Fauquier Hospital. As a healthcare professional, she presides over the JCAHO survey for the Hospital, Nursing Home, and Home Health services which is utilized to verify the quality of health care received by patients. Ms. Bishop also assumes responsibility for the clinical information systems in the Hospital and serves as a resource person for its daily operational issues. She was recently recognized as one of 99 most outstanding nurses in the state of Virginia for 1999. Ms. Bishop's plans to remain with the Hospital and grow professionally. Fauquier Hospital provides medical and acute care services to the residents of Warrenton, Virginia and surrounding communities. Established in 1959, the Hospital maintains 86 beds for its patients. Over 600 dedicated administrative, medical, and support personnel work to ensure that patients receive the best in modern medical care. **Career Highlights:** Fauquier Hospital: Project Coordinator (1998-Present), QI/RM Assistant Director (1995-96); QI Director, Culpeper Hospital (1989-94). **Associations & Accomplishments:** National Association for Healthcare Quality; Certified Professional in Healthcare Quality; Virginia Association for Healthcare Risk Managers; Capital Area Roundtable for Informatics in Nursing Group; Virginia Organizations for Nursing Executives. **Education:** Averett College, M.B.A. (1997); Western Connecticut State University, R.N., B.S.N. (1989). **Personal Information:** Married to Fred A. in 1985. Ms. Bishop enjoys refinishing furniture.

Darnell Busch

Management Information Systems Director
Samuel Rodgers Community Health Center
825 Euclid Avenue
Kansas City, MO 64124-2323
(816) 889-4620
Fax: (816) 474-6475
dbusch@samuel-rodgers.org

8062

Business Information: Educated in the field of Computer Science, Mr. Busch joined Samuel Rodgers Community Health Center as Management Information Systems Director in 1995. In this capacity, he coordinates and manages the Management Information Systems Department and staff to ensure that the Center's vital computer systems are performing at its optimum level at all times. Mr. Busch provides technical leadership to senior management, assisting them in technological decision-making for the Center's benefit. Determining and coordinating resources and schedules, overseeing time lines and assignments, and ensuring the security, reliability, and security of the infrastructure also fall within the realm of his responsibilities. Crediting his success to perseverance, he advises other to stay in the same field but gain more experience. Mr. Busch's career success reflects his ability to think out-of-the-box and take on new challenges and responsibilities. He continues to grow professionally through the fulfillment of his responsibilities and his involvement in the advancement of operations. Established in 1968, Samuel Rodgers Community Health Center was the first community healthcare center in Kansas City. The Center employs 213 healthcare professionals and support personnel to provide valued local services. **Career Highlights:** Management Information Systems Director, Samuel Rodgers Community Health Center (1998-Present); Systems Analyst, Lockheed-Martin (1995-98); Teacher, Kansas City Missouri School District (1993-95); Technical Analyst, Ellerbe Becket (1992-93). **Associations & Accomplishments:** Black Data Processors Association; Officer, Kappa Alpha Psi. **Education:** Park College, Teacher Certificate (1991), B.S. in Mathematics & Computer Science.

Peter J. Cox

Network Manager of Information Technical Services
New York Methodist Hospital
506 6th Street
Brooklyn, NY 11215
(718) 780-5993

8062

Business Information: Recruited to the New York Methodist Hospital in 1989, Mr. Cox currently serves as Network Manager of Information Technical Services. A systems expert, he oversees all day-to-day administration and management of the network infrastructure and offers desktop support to individual users. Performing new server and desktop installations, he configures the specifications for the equipment and applications. Coordinating time lines, resources, schedules, and assignments; tuning software tools to improve overall performance; and providing cohesive leadership is also an integral part of his functions. In addition, Mr. Cox travels extensively to eight other locations affiliated with the Hospital and provides network support. Committed to providing continued optimum service, his success reflects his ability to aggressively take on new challenges. The New York Methodist Hospital is a 500 bed facility, offering a full range of medical services to the residents of Brooklyn, New York. The Information Technical Services Department within the Hospital provides technical services to over 600 users. Established in 1881, the Hospital presently employs a work force of more than 1,750 professional, medical, technical, and administrative personnel. **Career Highlights:** New York Methodist Hospital, Network Manager of Information Technical Services (1989-Present).

Mike Dauplaise

Desktop Publisher
St. Mary Hospital Medical Center
1726 Shawano Avenue
Green Bay, WI 54303
(920) 498-4236
Fax: (920) 497-3745
mdauplai@stmgb.org

8062

Business Information: Serving as a Desktop Publisher for St. Mary Hospital Medical Center, Mr. Dauplaise fulfills a number of duties on behalf of the Center and its clients. He is responsible for maintaining accurate medical transcripts. Possessing an excellent understanding of the medical field, he communicates directly with Center doctors to thoroughly determine a patient's condition so that it may be entered correctly into patient files. A successful 16 year professional, he is the noted state winner of the WHPRM Award. Illustrating his attention to detail and superior communication skills, Mr. Dauplaise has established himself as a key part of the Center's faculty, thereby ensuring a bright future in healthcare administration. St. Mary Hospital Medical Center is a facility that provides superior healthcare to the citizens of Greenbay, Wisconsin. Established in 1900, the Center has grown to employ over 650 people who provide quality services to patients. Recognized as a leader in the healthcare industry, the center incorporates cutting edge technology and a soft touch to deliver comprehensive care to patients and their families. Maintaining a wide variety of care options, the Center's motivated team of professionals capable of treating trauma, cardiac, and chronic ailment emergencies on a moments notice. Continuing to provide top qualtiy healthcare utilizing innovative medical procedures, the Center is expanding its services to accomodate increased patient referrals and technological advancements. **Career Highlights:** Desktop Publisher, St. Mary Hospital Medical Center (1996-Present); Special Agent, Northwestern Mutual Life (1993-96); Writer, Green Bay Press Gazette (1990-93); Editor, Green Bay News Chronicle (1989-90). **Associations & Accomplishments:** Wisconsin Healthcare Public Relations and Marketing Society; Greater Green Bay Optimists; Friends of the Brown County Library. **Education:** St. Norbart College, B.A. (1984). **Personal Information:** Married to Bonnie Groessl in 1999. Two children: Nickolas Groessl and Benjamin Groessl. Mr. Dauplaise enjoys running and golf.

C. Lewis Dingman, Ph.D.

Computer and Telecommunications Operations Manager
Medical Center Hospital
P.O. Box 7329
Odessa, TX 79760-7239
(915) 640-2323
Fax: (915) 640-1378
ldingman@echd.org

8062

Business Information: As Computer and Telecommunications Operations Manager for the Medical Center Hospital, Dr. Dingman is responsible for the direction of various technical activities. Throughout daily activities, he is charged with the obligation to design, develop, and implement courseware for PC specialists in computer support and telecommunications areas. With more than 21 years of information technology experience, Dr. Dingman utilizes his superior professional talents to devise plans for continuing his efforts to build and develop technology education in a health care environment. His credo is "your college degree means absolutely nothing." The Medical Center Hospital of Odessa, Texas is a non-profit health care facility that provides thorough, comprehensive care to patients needing treatment for a host of medical problems. The Hospital consists of 398 beds and various medical programs for regional citizens of 27 surrounding counties. Established in 1949, services include emergency, inpatient-outpatient surgery, and pediatrics. The Hospital functions under the direction of more than 1,700 individuals including certified medical technicians, physicians, administrators, and counseling staff. **Career Highlights:** Computer and Telecommunications Operations Manager, Medical Center Hospital (1993-Present); Technology Instructor/Classroom Teacher, Public and Private Schools in Texas and Louisiana (1979-93). **Associations & Accomplishments:** Help Desk Institute; Microsoft HUG Charter; HIM. **Education:** Kennedy Western, Ph.D. (2000); Texas Christian University: M.Ed., B.S. **Personal**

Information: Married to Barbara in 1990. Four children: Rhonda, Sharon, Travis, and Danielle. Dr. Dingman enjoys stainglass design and riding touring motorcycles.

Richard D. Groves

User Support Analyst
Covenant Health
1410 Centerpoint Boulevard, Suite 400
Knoxville, TN 37932-1960
(423) 374-4534
Fax: (423) 374-4860
rgroves@netgrp.net

8062

Business Information: Utilizing more than 10 years of experience in the field of technology, Mr. Groves serves as the User Support Analyst for Covenant Health. He provides computer support services to the many end users, training them in the use of system applications and software programs used by the Company. Troubleshooting problems as they arise, he is responsible for hardware repair. Before joining Covenant Health, he served as Lead Engineer and Owner of Consulting Associates. His background history also includes stints as Sales and Technical Associate for American Speedy Printing and Wideband Communications Equipment Maintenance Specialist with the United States Air Force. In his present role, Mr. Groves also installs new softwares upgrades as needed. Attributing his professional success to his ability to access information quickly, he stays current with technology through research, the Internet and industry vendors. He credits his success to his electronics background gained through service in the U.S. Air Force and his continuing education effort. Covenant Health is a healthcare management organization. The Company provides services to seven hospitals and several physicians clinics in the state of Tennessee. Approximately 9,000 qualified individuals handle the administration, employee payroll and benefits, and medical billing and claims for the Company's various clients. **Career Highlights:** User Support Analyst, Covenant Health (1996-Present); Lead Engineer/Owner, Consulting Associates (1994-96); Sales and Technical Associate, American Speedy Printing (1991-96); Wideband Communications Equipment Maintenance Specialist, United States Air Force (1989-91). **Associations & Accomplishments:** International Society of Certified Electronics Technicians. **Education:** ITT Technical Institute, A.S. in Applied Science (1996). **Personal Information:** Mr. Groves enjoys antique cars and computers.

Jeremy E. Houghton

Network Administrator
Pikes Peak Mental Health
220 Ruskin Drive
Colorado Springs, CO 80910
(719) 572-6114
Fax: (719) 597-6199
jhoughton@rmi.net

8062

Business Information: Following a distinguished military intelligence career in the United States Army, Mr. Houghton now serves as a Network Administrator for Pikes Peak Mental Health. He handles the administration of the NT, Novell, and UNIX networks of the Center. In this capacity, he purchases the software and hardware equipment, sets up the on-site users, and troubleshoots the account problems for the accounting department. Additionally, he trains users and managerial personnel, offering internal technical support. Mr. Houghton states that his work philosophy is "Work honestly and stick with it." Continually formulating new goals and objectives, he plans to own his own network consulting business in the future. His success reflects his ability to think outside the box, produce results, and tackle new challenges. Pikes Peak Mental Health is a not-for-profit mental health center dedicated to improving the emotional and psychological stability of its patients. The largest mental health facility of its kind, the Center features a hospital and family counseling center. An approximate work force of 4,000 is involved in all aspects of operation. The Center was founded in 1875. **Career Highlights:** Network Administrator, Pikes Peak Mental Health (1999-Present); Owner, Whitefire Technology (1999); Network Administration, Compaq (1999); Military Intelligence, United States Army (1993-97). **Associations & Accomplishments:** Speak Out Survivors. **Education:** Knowledge Alliance, Micrososft Certified Systems Engineer+I, A+ Certification (1999). **Personal Information:** Married to Anjeanette in 1998. Mr. Houghton enjoys speak out survivors, writing and computers.

Arnold M. Jenkins, III

Local Area Network Administrator
Johns Hopkins Hospital
1830 East Monument Street
Baltimore, MD 21287
(410) 614-4329
Fax: (410) 614-3750
ajenkin@jhmi.edu

8062

Business Information: Possessing excellent organizational skills and the ability to quickly grasp technical concepts, Mr. Jenkins was recruited to Johns Hopkins Hospital in 1996. At the present time, he assumes the responsibilities of Local Area Network Administrator. In his role, he exercises management oversight of six Windows NT servers and more than 600 Windows NT desktops. Drawing from nearly eight years of experience and a firm academic background, he is responsible for directing and participating in the analysis, design, evaluation, testing, and implementation of LAN, WAN, and Internet and Intranet related computer systems. Analysis, acquisition, installation, modification, configuration, support and tracking of operating systems, databases, utilities, and software and hardware also falls within the realm of Mr. Jenkins' responsibilities. Completing his Ph.D. in Computer Science and getting into teaching and technology research serves as his long-range strategic plans. His favorite advice is "Don't ever stop reading, even after you get your degree." The flagship of Johns Hopkins Medicine, Johns Hopkins Hospital is an acute care hospital. Housing 1,025 beds, the Hospital is staffed primarily by full-time faculty physicians of the Johns Hopkins University School of Medicine. Founded in 1887 and based in Baltimore, the Hospital is presently manned by more 5,000 individuals. **Career Highlights:** Local Area Network Administrator, Johns Hopkins Hospital (1996-Present); Network Technician, O/E Mid-Atlantic (1993-96); Lab Assistant/Tutor, Towson State University (1990-93). **Education:** Johns Hopkins University, Master's degree (In Progress); Towson State University, B.S. **Personal Information:** Mr. Jenkins enjoys snow skiing, mountain biking and rollerblading.

Catherine Lee Litten

Senior Programmer/Analyst
Valley Presbyterian Hospital
15107 Vanowen Street
Van Nuys, CA 91405-4597
(818) 782-6600
Fax: (818) 902-5202
cat@littenfamily.com

8062

Business Information: Serving in the dual role of Senior Programmer and Analyst for Valley Presbyterian Hospital, Ms. Litten is responsible for applications development and software integration. She directs and participates in the analysis, design, evaluation, testing, and implementation of inhouse specific software as well as installing and troubleshooting completed projects. Ms. Litten plans to climb the corporate ladder to achieve the position of Chief Financial Officer or Systems Manager position for a supply company. She has demonstrated her leadership qualities by effectively communicating Hospital goals and implementing techniques of reaching those goals. Success, according to Ms. Litten, is attributed to being in the right place at the right time and her ability to take on challenges and deliver results. Valley Presbyterian Hospital provides healthcare to the community of Van Nuys, California. The Hospital was established in 1954 and employs over 1,000 people contributing to the wellness of the community. Proceeding with plans for structural expansion, the Hospital plans to provide increasingly superior care in numerous fields of medicine. Valley Presbyterian Hospital has earned the reputation for curing illness and being sensitive to the patient's needs. **Career Highlights:** Senior Programmer/Analyst, Valley Presbyterian Hospital (1996-Present); Systems Administrator, Monk Office Supply (1993-95); Controller, Modern Service Office Supply (1989-93). **Associations & Accomplishments:** Parent Leader, Boy Scouts; United States Figure Skating Association; Assistant Den Leader, Cub Scouts. **Education:** DeVry Institute; College of the Canyons, A.A. **Personal Information:** One child: William Thomas. Ms. Litten enjoys being assistant den leader.

Sue Lopardo

Director of Enterprise Systems
Northwestern Memorial Hospital
259 East Erie Street
Chicago, IL 60611
(312) 926-3978
Fax: (312) 926-0086
slopardo@nmh.org

8062

Business Information: Mrs. Lopardo serves as the Director of Enterprise Systems at Northwestern Memorial Hospital. She is responsible for all aspects of the information systems functions related to the help desk, systems administration, network accessability, and technology standards. Her most recent project has been the Hospital-wide upgrade of all computer systems for year 2000 readiness. For the future, Mrs. Lopardo hopes to become more involved in strategic planning, and she plans to expand her career into teaching at possibly Lake Forest Graduate School of Management or Northwestern University. Her success reflects her ability to think outside the box, deliver results, and tackle challenges. Northwestern Memorial Hospital provides medical services to the Chicago, Illinois area. Founded in 1974, the Hospital has expanded to accommodate a 500 bed facility and employs a staff of 4,500 personnel. Associated with Northwestern University, the Hospital is recognized as the most technologically advanced facility of its kind in Chicago. **Career Highlights:** Director of Enterprise Systems, Northwestern Memorial Hospital (1995-Present); Vice President, Bank of America/Continental Bank (1972-95). **Associations & Accomplishments:** Help Desk Institute. **Education:** Lake Forest Graduate School of Management, M.B.A. (1996); DePaul University, B.S. in Operations Management (1991). **Personal Information:** Married to Patrick in 1983. Two children: Angela and Patrick. Mrs. Lopardo enjoys exercise, ski, travel and shopping.

Steven C. Peterson

Director of Information Systems and Telecommunications
Magee Rehabilitation Hospital
6 Franklin Plaza
Philadelphia, PA 19102
(215) 587-3336
Fax: (215) 977-9740
speterson@mageerehab.org

8062

Business Information: As Director of Information Systems and Telecommunications at Magee Rehabilitation Hospital, Mr. Peterson oversees the entire telecommunications and information technology systems infrastructure within the Hospital. He manages the staff, troubleshoots all system problems, is responsible for the maintenance and upgrade of the systems, and ensures that the Hospital is Y2K compliant. A savvy, 18 year professional, he attributes his substantial success to hardwork, dedication, and staying up-to-date by attending seminars and reading trade magazines. Mr. Peterson continues to grow professionally and hopes to expedite continued promotion in the technology field. Established in 1958, Magee Rehabilitation Hospital is a 96 bed medical facility specializing in providing physical therapy to individuals with spinal cord and brain injuries. Also offering an outpatient facility, the Hospital currently employs a staff of 350 individuals dedicated to serving the diverse medical needs of their patients. **Career Highlights:** Director of Information Systems and Telecommunications, Magee Rehabilitation Hospital (1986-Present); Systems Leader, HBOC (1984-86); Systems Programmer, Data-Tek (1981-84). **Education:** Computer Learning Center, Philadelphia, Certified Netware Engineer. **Personal Information:** Married to Linda in 1984. Two children: Kristin and Steven Jr. Mr. Peterson enjoys sports, restoring old cars, fishing and family time.

Stephen L. Pladna

Senior Analyst Programmer
Duke University Medical Center
P.O. Box 3900
Durham, NC 27710
(919) 286-6315
Fax: (919) 286-6369
pladn001@mc.duke.edu

8062

Business Information: Mr. Pladna serves as Senior Analyst Programmer with Duke University Medical Center. He is responsible for day-to-day administration and mainframe programming for patient care. As a 25 year technology professional, Mr. Pladna has served with Duke University's Medical Center in a variety of roles since joining the University in 1982. Working closely with users and systems management, he analyzes, specifies, and designs new technology solutions to harness more of the computer's power and improve the overall performance of the systems infrastructure. A recognized leader, Mr. Pladna will soon become Chairman of the Centers' ADS Technical Symposium Planning Committee in which he presently serves as Treasurer. His success reflects his ability to find and document answers to difficulties for use at a later date. Attaining a higher level technical advisory role and PC experience serves as his future goals. "It is a lucrative and exciting market, become proficient in the basics," is cited as Mr. Pladna's advice. Duke University's Medical Center is one of the top medical schools in the Southeast. A separate entity of Duke University, the Medical Center was established in the 1930s. Local and regional in scope, the Duke University employs a staff of more than 10,000 professional, medical, technical, and administrative support personnel. **Career Highlights:** Senior Analyst Programmer, Duke University Medical Center (1982-Present). **Associations & Accomplishments:** Treasurer, ADS Technical Symposium Planning Committee. **Education:** University of Notre Dame, B.B.A. in Management (1974). **Personal Information:** Married to Rosemarie in 1974. Three children: Todd, Brett, and Matthew. Mr. Pladna enjoys gardening.

John Edward Robbins

Director of Information Services
Community Medical Center
1822 Mulberry Street
Scranton, PA 18510-2375
(570) 969-8274
Fax: (570) 969-8796
john.robbins@cmchealthsvs.org

8062

Business Information: Since beginning his career with the Community Medical Center, Mr. Robbins has served in a variety of roles. At the present time, he fulfills the responsibilities of Director of Information Services. Reporting directly to the Vice President, he oversees the daily operation and maintenance of the LAN and WAN networks for the Center and its satellite locations. Mr. Smith presides over hardware and software acquisitions for the server and individual workstations and supervises its implementation through the 10 departmental employees. Continually striving to improve performance, he anticipates a promotion to Chief Information Officer. His success reflects his ability to produce results in support of medical objectives and aggressively take on new challenges. The Community Medical Center is a nonprofit primary health care facility. Established in 1960, the Scranton, Pennsylvania location is licensed for 325 beds. There are two satellite facilities underneath the Center's jurisdiction with an approximate work force of 1,600 staff members between the three facilities. **Career Highlights:** Community Medical Center: Director of Information Services (1997-Present), Network Administrator, Senior Analyst. **Education:** Marywood University, M.B.A. (1999); King's College, B.S. (1990). **Personal Information:** Married to Jeanann in 1989. One child: Lauren. Mr. Robbins enjoys golf and tennis.

Sarah E. Robertson, R.N.

RegisteredNurse/NetworkInformationSystemsCoordinator
Seton Healthcare Network
408 Wood Bine Drive
Austin, TX 78745-2252
(512) 324-1027
srobertson@seton.org

8062

Business Information: Serving dual roles of Registered Nurse and Network Information Systems Coordinator at Seton Healthcare Network, Ms. Robertson's daily schedule is full of varied tasks. Utilizing her medical knowledge, she assists the Perinatal Division, ensuring equipment and services meet the specific needs of her patients. As Systems Administrator for the Watchchild IS, Ms. Robertson manages the systems database and handles troubleshooting, maintenance, and upgrades of hardware and software. A leader for the National Focus Group for WatchChild IS, she is also responsible for charting and report writing. With exceptional communicative skills, Ms. Robertson conducts training courses for employees on technical equipment used within the Network. Attributing her success to a life long desire to learn, Ms. Robertson intends to continue in her current role as she furthers her education and builds the networking capabilities of Seton Healthcare Network. Seton Healthcare Network is recognized as a major health care management network in the greater Austin area that provides level four trauma services. Comprised of eight hospitals and numerous clinics totaling over 700 beds, the Network employs nearly 2,000 people to assist in the administration of operating policies. Established in 1930, the Network is continually striving to implement the best procedures possible for the benefit of total patient care. **Career Highlights:** Seton Healthcare Network: Registered Nurse/Network Information Systems Coordinator (1999-Present), Registered Nurse/Educator (1994-99); Registered Nurse/Educator, Baptist Medical Center (1991-94); Registered Nurse/Charge Nurse, Brackenridge Hospital (1988-91). **Associations & Accomplishments:** AWHONN; Texas Nurses Association; Executive Secretary, American Red Cross; Secretary, Nurse Advisory Board. **Education:** Angelo State University, Associate's degree in Nursing; Austin Community College (1999). **Personal Information:** Married to James Trimmier in 1997. One child: Elizabeth. Ms. Robertson enjoys computer design, art and gardening.

Andrew F. Shever

Network and Communications Manager
Lourdes Hospital
1530 Lone Oak Road
Paducah, KY 42003-7900
(502) 444-2899
Fax: (502) 444-2868
ashever@lourdes-pad.org

8062

Business Information: As Network and Communications Manager for Lourdes Hospital, Mr. Shever manages the network and telecommunications infrastructure. He is responsible for the day-to-day operations of the telephony system, LAN and WAN network, and all computer hardware and peripherals. A systems expert, he oversees all acquisitions and acts as chief vendor liaison. Working closely with his team of three employees, Mr. Shever utilizes a management style that incorporates input and feedback from all staff members. His success reflects his ability to build teams with synergy and take on new challenges and responsibilities. Mr. Shever plans to expedite continued promotion through the fulfillment of his responsibilities and his involvement in the advancement of operations. Lourdes Hospital is a 325 bed medical facility located in Wester, Kentucky. The Hospital is a not for profit organization and a subsidiary of Mercy Health Partners, headquartered in Cincinnati, Ohio. Established in 1970, the Hospital employs a staff of 1,500 individuals dedicated to providing quality health care and improving the quality of life for their patients. **Career Highlights:** Lourdes Hospital: Network and Communications Manager (1996-Present), Communications Manager (1995-96). **Associations & Accomplishments:** Microsoft Certified Professional+Internet; Microsoft Certified Engineer; Certified Novell Administration. **Education:** Wheeling Jesuit. **Personal Information:** Married to Nickie in 1993. Three children: Kristen, Ashley, and Drew. Mr. Shever enjoys the upkeep of rental properties.

Sue E. Terrell

Manager of Information Systems
Floyd Memorial Hospital
1850 State Street
New Albany, IN 47150-4997
(812) 981-6665
Fax: (812) 949-5795
sterrell@fmhhs.com

8062

Business Information: Drawing upon many years of directorial and managerial experience, Ms. Terrell serves in the position of Manager of Information Systems for Floyd Memorial Hospital. Drawing upon an extensive knowledge in the information systems field, she is responsible for overseeing all of the day to day operations including program setup and upgrades. Moreover, she is charged with supervising the data center, conducting systems backup, and coordinating help desk activities. An expert, Ms. Terrell provides programming and technical support to her staff members. She is dedicated to her work and has become a invaluable asset to the Hospital. In the future, Ms. Terrell looks forward to continuing with the Hospital in her current position and staying abreast of emerging technologies. Founded in 1953, Floyd Memorial Hospital is a 215 bed acute care hospital. Located in New Albany, Indiana, the Hospital provides a wide range of home health and acute care services to patients and is currently county owned. The Hospital is staffed with over 1,100 professionals and volunteers who are dedicated to providing the best medical services available. **Career Highlights:** Manager Information Systems, Floyd Memorial Hospital (1999-Present); Caritas Health Services: Interface Specialist (1995-96), Interim Information Systems Director (1995-96), Manager of Systems and Programming (1985-97). **Associations & Accomplishments:** HIMMS. **Education:** Oakland City University, B.S. in Organizational Management (1999); Indiana University: A.S. in Business, A.S. in Computer Science. **Personal Information:** Married to Jess Jr. in 1979. Two children: Micah and Allison. Ms. Terrell enjoys coaching sports and cabinet design and building.

Pierre Vassallo, M.D., Ph.D., FACA, ARZT for Radiology

Consultant Radiologist
Department of Radiology, St. Luke's Hospital
Gwardamangia, Malta
+356 25951673
Fax: +356 382695
pvassallo@mail.link.net.mt

8062

Business Information: Dr. Vassallo serves as a Consultant Radiologist at St. Luke's Hospital. Using radiologic equipment, he diagnoses patients and consults with them regarding their illnesses. Before joining St. Luke's Hospital, he served as Research Associate with Memorial Sloan Kettering Cancer Center in New York, and Staff Radiologist at the University of Muenster. In addition to his work at the Hospital, Dr. Vassallo teaches Radiology. He lectures classes and works with students in the field, allowing them to gain experience. He feels that he has been successful in his field due to internal motivation and family support. For his future, Dr. Vassallo sees himself spending more time at the Hospital with his patients and performing more lectures. Founded in 1850, St. Luke's Hospital serves the people of Malta. The Department of Radiology uses sophisticated diagnostic equipment to diagnose patients for different types of illnesses such as cancer. **Career Highlights:** Consultant Radiologist, Department of Radiology, St. Luke's Hospital (1995-Present); Research Associate, Memorial Sloan Kettering Cancer Center (1992-95); Staff Radiologist, University of Muenster, Germany (1987-92). **Associations & Accomplishments:** Radiological Society of North America; Society of Magnetic Resonance; European Association of Radiology; European Society of Magnetic Resonance; Fellow, American College of Angiologists. **Education:** University of Muenster, Ph.D. (1991); University of Malta, M.D. (1984); German Medical Association, Board Certified in Radiology. **Personal Information:** Married to Josanne in 1987. One child: Rachel Anne. Dr. Vassallo enjoys music, travel and literature.

Bradley T. Wells

Director of Information Systems Planning
Iroquois Memorial Hospital
200 East Fairman Avenue
Watseka, IL 60970
(815) 432-4444
Fax: (815) 432-4421

8062

Business Information: Combining his 20 years of extensive experience in the healthcare industry with technical expertise, Mr. Wells serves as the Director of Information Systems Planning for the Iroquois Memorial Hospital. He plans the information systems infrastructure for the Hospital's various units and ensures that they function efficiently according to strict healthcare industry standards for the deliverance of quality care. Directly supervising 18 staff members, he assumes responsibility of 50 nodes and 40 independent Internet and Intranet connections. Coordinating resources, time lines, schedules, and assignments; compiling and synthesizing large quantities of data for management reports; and calculating and managing the technology fiscal year budget also fall within the purview of his responsibilities. Continually formulating new goals and objectives, Mr. Wells looks forward to utilizing his skills in a consulting capacity. Founded in 1916, the Iroquois Memorial Hospital provides a variety of services to the residents of Watseka, Illinois and its surrounding areas. A healthcare hospital with 98 beds, the Hospital maintains a residential home and several physicians' clinics. Approximately 380 administrative, healthcare, and support personnel are employed. A $30 million budget is given annually to the Hospital. **Career Highlights:** Iroquois Memorial Hospital: Director of Information Systems Planning (1997-Present), Director of Cardiopuluanary (1990-97); Director of Respiratory Care, Hoopeston Hospital (1982-90); Owner, Respiratory Health Services, Inc. (1980-90). **Associations & Accomplishments:** Toast Masters International; American Association for Respiratory Care; Advisory Board, Kanhabe Community College Respiratory Program (1987-95). **Education:** University of Illinois, B.S. (1979); Parkland College, A.A.S. **Personal Information:** Married to Meredith in 1979. Two children: Nathan Bradley and Rachel Marie. Mr. Wells enjoys golf, walking and Bible studies.

Robert M. Wells

Hospital Director of Information Systems
Summit Medical Center
5655 Frist Boulevard
Hermitage, TN 37076-2053
(615) 316-3531
Fax: (615) 316-3565
robb.wells@columbia.net

8062

Business Information: Providing his skilled services as Hospital Director of Information Systems for Summit Medical

Center, Mr. Wells presides over the administration of the LAN and WAN systems and coordinating end user acquisitions and Y2K remediation. He is responsible for hardware and software purchases and implementation, network security, and technical and strategic direction of the Center. Before joining Summit Medical Center, Mr. Wells served as Network Analyst with Columbia Healthcare Corporation, Owner of Computer Solutions, and International Trade and Customer Service Representative with Kempf Machinery Company. Coordinating resources and schedules and overseeing time lines and assignments also fall within the purview of Mr. Well's functions. His success reflects his leadership ability to build strong teams with synergy, technical strength, and a customer oriented attitude, as well as aggressively taking on new challenges. Keeping abreast of the latest technological advances by attending classes and seminars, Mr. Wells is looking forward to expanding his professional horizons and offering his services to other countries. A part of the Columbia Healthcare Corporation, Summit Medical Center is a 205 bed facility providing healthcare services to Hermitage, Tennessee and its surrounding communities. Presently, operations are handled by more than 900 healthcare and administrative support personnel. **Career Highlights:** Hospital Director of Information Systems, Summit Medical Center (1997-Present); Network Analyst, Columbia Healthcare Corporation (1996-97); Owner, Computer Solutions (1994-96); International Trade and Customer Service Representative, Kempf Machinery Company (1990-94). **Associations & Accomplishments:** World Missions Committee, Christ Community Church; Deacon, International Chapel. **Education:** Belmont University, M.B.A. (1994); University of Tennessee at Knoxville, B.A.; German Certification Upper Levels. **Personal Information:** Married to Jennifer in 1991. Three children: Connor, Reid, and Marissa. Mr. Wells enjoys golf, water skiing and snow skiing.

Joe M. Wilson

Director
Sunnyside Community Hospital
3030 Northeast 10th Street, Suite 209
Renton, WA 98056
(425) 255-9232
jmwilson82@hotmail.com

8062

Business Information: Displaying his expertise in the technology field, Mr. Wilson serves as Director for the Sunnyside Community Hospital. He assumes responsibility for the management of the Hospital's entire information systems function and personnel. Supervising daily network and system administration and maintenance, he oversees application product and services development for various departments within the Hospital. Mr. Wilson is assisted in his duties by a staff of eight dedicated individuals. Attributing his professional success to his faith and belief in God, he believes his most significant achievement in his career was the implementation of an advanced communication system integrating voice, graphic, and data systems with one another. Mr. Wilson's future goal is to become actively involved in broad band communication services for the market industry. Providing exceptional healthcare services to valley residents of Sunnyside, Washington, the Sunnyside Community Hospital is rated one of the top 100 rural hospitals in the nation. A Level Three trauma center available for the community's emergency use, the Hospital was founded in 1962. **Career Highlights:** Director, Sunnyside Community Hospital (1999-Present); Telecommunication Manager, Boeing Employee Credit Union (1998-99); Engineering Standards Specialist, Boeing (1987-98). **Associations & Accomplishments:** Association of Testing & Materials; Ordained Baptist Minister. **Education:** City University, Master's degree (1998); Pierce Community College: B.S. in Computer Systems and Telecommunications, Associate's degree in Technology. **Personal Information:** One child: Shailee Jenay. Mr. Wilson enjoys cycling.

Reid McCoppen

Telecommunications Services Manager
Baycrest Centre for Geriatric Care
3560 Bathurst Street
Toronto, Ontario, Canada M6A 2E1
(416) 785-2500
Fax: (416) 785-2864
mccopen@baycrest.org

8069

Business Information: Mr. McCoppen has provided his exceptional skills and experience to the Baycrest Centre for Geriatric Care since February of 1990, and he is presently fulfills the position of Telecommunications Services Manager. In his daily capacity, Mr. McCoppen oversees and directs all telecommunication aspects of the Center, supervising paging and cellular phone technology installation and maintenance. Currently undergoing a technical upgrade, he is responsible for all project management aspects of Baycrest Centre for Geriatric Care's voice and data network expansion project. Drawing on his previous management and supervisory positions, he conducts contract negotiations, regulates infostructure upgrades, and oversees telephone activities. Committing his extensive expertise to the Center, Mr. McCoppen plans to continue implementing further advances in technology into the Center, maintaining their leading position in the industry. Located in Toronto, Ontario, Baycrest Centre for Geriatric Care is a full service geriatric hospital integrated with a retirement residence in the combined facility. Employing a large staff of 1,300 professionals in the medical and nursing industry, the Center is renowned for the quality of their services and caring support of their staff. **Career Highlights:** Telecommunications Services Manager, Baycrest Centre for Geriatric Care (1990-Present); Field Manager, Installex Telecom (1988-90); Project Supervisor, Riser Teleconnect Inc. (1983-88). **Associations & Accomplishments:** Committee Member, Peel Childrens Aid Society. **Education:** Mohawk College, Industrial Management Technology degree (1980). **Personal Information:** Married to Julia in 1985. One child: Jennifer. Mr. McCoppen enjoys home repair, camping and family time.

Hugo Jimenez

Lead Support Analyst
Lifechem Lab
8 King Road
Rockleigh, NJ 07647-2502
(201) 767-7070
hugo.jimenez@fmc-na.com

8071

Business Information: Displaying his expertise in the demanding field of information technology, Mr. Jimenez serves as the Lead Support Analyst for Lifechem Lab. In this capacity, he assumes responsibility for applications development and support for the Company's network and systems. He works diligently to ensure that every aspect of the local area network is functioning perfectly so that the staff is able to perform their work and the sensitive medical data is safely saved and easily accessible. Mr. Jimenez began his career as a medical technologist and uses his knowledge of the field to better able to serve the Company in the performance of his duties. The highlight of his career came when he served as the program manager for a software upgrade to a main application. He is currently pursuing new technological avenues for the Company, including upgrading its operating system to a UNIX-based environment. Mr. Jimenez attributes his success to a willingness to learn new things and deliver results. Serving a local and regional clientele, Lifchem Lab is a reference medical laboratory, providing dialysis and laboratory services to clinics in the area. The Company receives various types of samples such as blood, urine, and tissue, and is able to perform numerous tests in accordance with the requests received from medical clinics. Beginning operation in 1980, the Laboratory has built a reputation for quality work in the past 20 years. A staff of 300 technicians, administrative, and support personnel are employed. **Career Highlights:** Lead Support Analyst, Lifechem Lab (1997-Present); Lab Information Systems Coordinator, Bergen Pines (1996-97); Lab Information Systems Coordinator, Meadowlands Hospital (1991-96). **Education:** University of Phoenix Online Campus, M.S. (In Progress); Fairleigh Dickinson University, B.S. in Chemistry. **Personal Information:** Married to Nancy in 1983. Two children: Barbara and Daisy. Mr. Jimenez enjoys fishing and reading.

Walter J. Symczyk Jr.

Systems Manager
Beth Israel Medical Center
1st Avenue at 16th Street
New York, NY 10003
(212) 420-4413
w.symczyk@worldnet.att.net

8071

Business Information: Serving as Systems Manager for Beth Israel Medical Center's Pathology Department, Mr. Symczyk is responsible for maintaining the Center's robotic and laboratory computer systems. Supervising his staff of five people, Mr. Symczyk maintains the systems infrastructure, in addition to integrating new systems and assisting the Department remain on the cutting edge of technology. A 29 year professional, he served as Systems Manager for Nyack Hospital prior to being recruited to Beth Israel Medical Center. His background history also includes a stint as Principal Specialist for Business Applications at American Express Health Systems Group. Coordinating resources, time lines, schedules, assignments, and budgets also fall within the purview of Mr. Symczyk's responsibilities. He attributes his success to his family upbringing and their support, as well as his ability to think out-of-the-box and aggressively take on new challenges. Continuing to grow professionally, Mr. Symczyk looks forward to any advancement opportunities that may arise. Beth Israel Medical Center is a 1,000 bed, non profit medical center. Established in 1890, the Center is a reputable facility employing a staff of 2,500 individuals dedicated to provide superior health care. The Pathology Department is the core lab for Continuum Health Care Partners. Specimens are processed for 6 hospitals and 300 clients by a robotics line. **Career Highlights:** Systems Manager, Beth Israel Medical Center (1996-Present); Systems Manager, Nyack Hospital (1992-96); Principal Specialist for Business Applications, American Express Health Systems Group (1989-92). **Education:** Seton Hall University, B.A. (1970). **Personal Information:** Married to Marian in 1974. Mr. Symczyk enjoys amateur radio (KB2BQK) and remote controlled aircraft.

Roger D. Theriault

Information Technology Manager
Fresenius Medical Care
95 Hayden Avenue Ledgmnt
Lexington, MA 02421-7942
(781) 402-9000
Fax: (781) 402-9730
roger.theriault@fmc-na.com

8092

Business Information: Performing as in the role of Information Technology Manager for Fresenius Medical Care of North America, Mr. Theriault is responsible for all aspects of data warehouse operations. Accordingly, he maintains the largest patient statistical profile database system, develops support questions and answers for the Internet, and oversees development and project management of new applications. Before joining Fresenius, he served as both Programmer and Senior Systems Analyst for NEC Technologies developing large systems. He originally started his career managing restaurants and later switched after seeing the enormous growth opportunities available in the technology field. Demonstrating expertise in the computer field, Mr. Theriault anticipates promotion to the position of Chief Informations Officer or Chief Technological Officer of a technology related-company. His success reflects his ability to think "out-of-the-box" and deliver results. Originating in Germany, Fresenius Medical Care of North America manufactures dialysis equipment and supplies. The Company provides services through medical clinics, hospitals, and home care. Established in 1970, Fresenius Medical Care of North America currently employs 20,000 individuals who help generate in excess of $3.6 billion in annual revenues. **Career Highlights:** Information Technology Manager, Fresenius Medical Care of North America (1995-Present); Senior Systems Analyst, NEC Technologies (1985-95); Manager, Carrol's Corporation (1981-85). **Associations & Accomplishments:** Data Warehouse Institute; Northeast Oracle Users Group; New Hampshire Mensa. **Education:** University of Maine at Orono, B.A. (1976); Computer Processing Institute; Bentley College. **Personal Information:** Two children: Jennifer Lynn and Roger David. Mr. Theriault enjoys music, reading and playing the trumpet.

OMD OFFICE OF THE MEDICAL DIRECTOR
Pinellas County Emergency Medical Services

Jeffery R. Barnard, NEMTP, BHRM

President/Executive Director
Emergency Medical Services Group, Inc., d.b.a. EMSG
12490 Ulmerton Road
Largo, FL 33774-2700
(727) 582-2036
Fax: (727) 582-2076
cyberOMD@AOL.com
jbarnard@medcontrol.com

8099

Business Information: Mr. Barnard serves as the President and Executive Director of EMSG. He is a Board Certified Healthcare Risk Manager and has been a certified paramedic for 22 years. The Company he manages is the full-time contract provider for Medical Direction and Clinical Quality Control for the Pinellas County Emergency Medical Services system, the third largest provider in the nation of EMS service. Utilizing over 24 years of experience, he oversees all of the business operations including 37 full and part-time staff. Mr. Barnard also serves on the elite medical staff that provides online medical direction to the 1,400 personnel operating in the EMS system. A firm believer in the benefits of information technology in healthcare, he plans to become an information technology consultant for the EMS field. Mr. Barnard states,

"Information is the catalyst in understanding the type and quality of service we deliver to our customers. Without information, we wander aimlessly without due regard for human life." His success reflects his ability to deliver results and aggressively tackle new challenges. He has been directly involved in the conceptual design and the invention of many software systems currently used in the EMS system today. These systems include the Strategic Placement Initiative (SPI) for the placement of the community's Automated External Defibrillator (AED) program, and BestCare, an out-of-hospital medical information system directing the appropriate managed care pathway. Mr. Barnard's Company continues to be an industry leader influencing others in using data for healthcare success stories. **Career Highlights:** President/Executive Director, EMSG (1995-Present); Executive Director, JLR, Inc. (1989-95); Assistant Fire Chief, City of St. Petersburg Beach, Florida (1975-89). **Associations & Accomplishments:** Associate Member, National Association of Emergency Medical Services Physicians; Tampa Bay Healthcare Risk Management Association; National Association of EMS Quality Professionals; Associate Member, Florida Association of EMS Medical Directors; Associate Member, American Health Lawyers Association; Staff Member (1990-Present), EMS Online Medical Control; EMS Medical Communications Officer (1996-Present); Executive Editor, Scene 911, "The Voice of Florida Emergency Service Providers; Executive Editor, "Today's EMS," Office of the Medical Director; Numerous State and Local Committees; Local/National Speaker. **Education:** Columbia Southern University, B.S./M.S. with a major in Health Administration (In Progress); St. Petersburg Junior College; Licensed Paramedic, Florida; Licensed Healthcare Risk Manager, Florida; Board Certified in Healthcare Risk Management by the American Board of Risk Managers. **Personal Information:** Married to Debra in 1976. One child: Noelle. Mr. Barnard enjoys church, family time, residential construction and a variety of hobbies. Mr. Barnard is a Christian.

Michael J. Botnan

Systems and Database Administrator
Courage Center - Department of MIS
2522 Pioneer Trail
Hamel, MN 55340
(612) 520-0269
Fax: (612) 520-0299
michaelb@courage.org

8099

Business Information: As Systems and Database Administrator for Courage Center's Department of MIS, Mr. Botnan exercises oversight of all UNIX computers that comprise the Center's network. He keeps track of donation data and the functions of various programs operated by the Center such as the Courage Card promotion which markets a line of Christmas Cards. Mr. Botnan hopes to obtain another base system for the Center with which he can replace the primary control functions and to complete his certification on NT networking. Courage Center has been assisting people with disabilities since 1928. Their mission is to empower people with disabilities to reach for their full potential in every aspect of life. The Courage Center provides rehabilitation, environment, and independent living services for people with physical disabilities and sensory or neurological impairments. More than 70 services are provided to 20,000 children and adults each year. Headquartered in Golden Valley, Courage Center operates four satellite locations nationally and employs more than 1,035 professional, technical, and support personnel. **Career Highlights:** Systems and Database Administrator, Courage Center - Department of MIS (1991-Present); In-Site Systems, Project Leader - Medical (1990-91); Assistant Administrator/MIS Manager, Minneapolis Clinic of Neurology (1965-90). **Associations & Accomplishments:** Medical Group Management Association. **Education:** Brown Institute, Diploma (1981); University of Minnesota; Mankato State. **Personal Information:** One child: Julie. Mr. Botnan enjoys motorcycling riding, gun collecting, dog training and photography.

Bart L. Hubbs

Information Systems Audit Supervisor
Columbia HCA
1 Park Plaza Building 2 2-E
Nashville, TN 37203-1548
(615) 344-8107
bart.hubbs@home.com

8099

Business Information: Mr. Hubbs has been a hard-charging team member of Columbia/HCA since 1997, and presently holds the position of Information Systems Audit Supervisor. As such, he coordinates and manages Information Systems audits to ensure that Columbia/HCA maintains a high level of systems integrity, confidentiality, and availability. Years of education and extensive experience in the field have enabled Mr. Hubbs to acquire the vast skills necessary to superbly complete his job responsibilities. A successful systems expert, he has received numerous awards for his dedication and knowledge including the "Best Technical Skills Award." Mr. Hubbs' future plans include the continued development of professionals who can understand technical problems and explain the solutions to business executives. Columbia/HCA, formed after a 1994 merger, provides healthcare and hospital administration. More than 180,000 people are employed by Columbia/HCA to assist in various aspects of the business. Ranked the largest healthcare organization in the United States, Columbia/HCA has recently spun-off two new companies and operates over 200 hospitals. **Career Highlights:** Information Systems Audit Supervisor, Columbia HCA (1997-Present); Supervisor, CNA Insurance (1995-97). **Associations & Accomplishments:** ISACA; ISC□; Certified Information Systems Auditor; Certified Information System Security Professional. **Education:** Murray State University, B.S. in Business (1995). **Personal Information:** Mr. Hubbs enjoys mountain biking, scuba diving, water skiing and travel.

Justin A. Salandra

Technical Support Specialist
Mount Kisco Medical Group
110 South Bedford Road
Mount Kisco, NY 10549
(914) 242-1544
Fax: (914) 242-1590
jsalandra@mkmg.com

8099

Business Information: Serving as Technical Support Specialist for Mount Kisco Medical Group, Mr. Salandra is responsible for all technical support for the network, as well as local machines and telephony infrastructure. An expert, he devotes a substantial amount of time to designing customized programs such as computerized child birth term calculations for the OB/GYN Department. His career success reflects his ability to aggressively take on new challenges and responsibilities. In the future, Mr. Salandra looks to specialize in the network administration realm. Coordinating resources, time lines, schedules, and assignments also fall within the scope of his functions. Looking toward advancing up the corporate hierarchy, he plans to obtain more certifications to facilitate promotional opportunities within Mount Kisco Medical Group, and specialize in the network administration realm. Created in 1947, Mount Kisco Medical Group provides medical services to individuals within New York state through its three locations. Sixty-seven doctors and approximately 400 administrative and support personnel are employed to fulfill Mount Kisco Medical Group's creed of providing quality health care. **Career Highlights:** Technical Support Specialist, Mount Kisco Medical Group (1999-Present). **Associations & Accomplishments:** Alpha Beta Kappa Honor Society; Hawthorne Fire Department; Emergency Medical Technician; Who's Who in American Junior Colleges. **Education:** Westchester Business Institute, A.O.S. (1999).

Wendy M. Towner

Network Development Manager
HFN, Inc./Kinetra IMIN
1315 West 22nd Street, Suite 300
Oak Brook, IL 60523
(630) 472-6543
Fax: (630) 954-1308
townerw@hfninc.com

8099

Business Information: Ms. Towner is Network Development Manager of HFN, Inc. She oversees development of software applications for internal and external clients, including project management. Before joining HFN, Inc.'s team as Sponsor Services Manager in 1997, Ms. Towner served as LAN Administrator with Capital Cities/ABC Inc. As a 20 year technology professional, she owns an established record of producing results. In her role, she is responsible for directing a team of 12 programmers and analyst in designing and maintaining the Web. Ms. Towner's focus is on enhancing systems functions and decision-critical information flow within the healthcare field. Her career success reflects her flexibility and ability to think out-of-the-box and take on new challenges and responsibilities. A hard charger, Ms. Towner currently has her name on two patents. Eventually attaining the role of Chief Information Officer serves as one of her future goals. A for profit company, HFN, Inc. is a preferred provider organization (PPO) in a joint venture with Kinetra IMIN, a leader in providing health information networks and e-commerce services. Established in 1985, HFN, Inc. focuses on medical and disability healthcare management services. Products encompass workers compensation, group health, health management, and long-term care. Presently, HFN, Inc.'s office in Oak Brook, Illinois employs a staff of over 65 professional, healthcare, and administrative support personnel. **Career Highlights:** HFN, Inc./Kinetra IMIN: Network Development Manager (1997-Present), Sponsor Services Manager (1997-97); LAN Administrator, Capital Cities/ABC Inc. (1993-95). **Associations & Accomplishments:** Director of Events, Bolingbrook Community Basketball League; Webmaster, Community of Bolingbrook. **Personal Information:** Three children: Jesse David, Sean Erik, and Christopher George. Ms. Towner enjoys basketball, biking, reading and puzzles. Also, Ms. Towner serves as Director of events for a youth basketball league of 1,200 children.

8100 Legal Services

8111 Legal services

Robert D. Baker

Information Systems Director
Schreck Morris
300 South 4th Street, Suite 1200
Las Vegas, NV 89101
(702) 464-7072
Fax: (702) 382-8135
rbaker@schreckmorris.com

8111

Business Information: Possessing unique talents and savvy in the information technology field, Mr. Baker joined Schreck Morris in 1997. He serves as Information Systems Director. In this highly specialized management position, he oversees and directs daily administration and operations of the information and telecommunications infrastructure. He maintains software, hardware, and associated peripherals; researches and develops new technology; supervises employees within his Department; and troubleshoots and repairs systems difficulties. Coordinating resources, schedules, time lines, and assignments also fall within the purview of Mr. Baker's responsibilities. One of many highlights include being awarded the Bronze Star Medal while serving with the United States Army during the Persian Gulf War. Effectively blending personal goals with the Firm's objectives, Mr. Baker's goals are to eventually attain the position of Chief Information Officer. An AV rated Law Firm, Schreck Morris is a group of lawyers specializing in all areas of law. The Firm represents clients throughout the state of Nevada. Founded in 1997, the Firm presently employs a staff of 120 qualified lawyers, paralegals, administrators, and information specialists to orchestrate operations within the Firm. **Career Highlights:** Information System Director, Schreck Morris (Present); Adjunct Professor, Webster University (1996-Present); Implementation Planner, GES (1998); Logistics Manager, United States Army (1993-95). **Associations & Accomplishments:** Veterans of Foreign Wars; American Legion. **Education:** Webster University, M.A. in Computer Resource and Information Management (1994); Hawaii Pacific College, B.S. in Business Administration. **Personal Information:** Married to Vicky in 1983. Mr. Baker enjoys flyball and golf.

Whitney L. Bolyard

Help Desk Supervisor
Reinhart, Boerner, et al
1000 North Water Street, P.O. Box 514000
Milwaukee, WI 53203
(414) 298-8526
Fax: (414) 298-8097
wbolyard@reinhartlaw.com

8111

Business Information: Mrs. Bolyard functions in the role of Help Desk Supervisor with Reinhart, Boerner, et al. She is responsible for all aspects of day-to-day administration and operations of the Help Desk. Before joining Reinhart, Boerner, et al as Help Desk Analyst in 1999, Mrs. Bolyard served as a Help Desk Specialist with Waukesha Engine. In her present capacity, she ensures that all calls are answered properly, as well as providing quality user training on software utilized by the Firm. Supervising her staff of three employees, Mrs. Bolyard is responsible for personnel evaluations, determining the overall strategic direction and goals, overseeing all resources and schedules, and establishing systems and help desk policies and procedures. She stays up to date with emerging technology by taking courses and reading technical magazines. Her professional success reflects her strong customer service attitude and her ability to build teams with synergy and technical strength. The highlights of her career include obtaining her MCSE and becoming an integral part of the Firm's Information Technology Department. With a positive look to the new millennium, Mrs. Bolyard's future goals include becoming the Firm's Network Administrator and eventually attaining the position of Information Systems Director. Reinhart, Boerner, et al is a corporate law firm. Privately owned, the Firm was founded in 1894. International in scale, the Firm located in Milwaukee, Wisconsin, presently employs a staff of more than 400 professional and technical personnel as well as legal administrators. **Career Highlights:** Reinhart, Boerner, et al: Help Desk Supervisor (1999-Present), Help Desk Analyst (1998-99); Help Desk

Specialist, Waukesha Engine (1998). **Associations & Accomplishments:** Professional Help Desk Association; Leader and Service Unit Manager, Girl Scouts of America. **Personal Information:** Married to Rick A.

Brian R. Clayton

Information Systems Manager
Coolidge Wall Womsley Lombard
33 West 1st Street
Dayton, OH 45402-1298
(937) 223-8177
Fax: (937) 223-8711
clayton@coollaw.com

8111

Business Information: Possessing unique talent in the field of technology, Mr. Clayton serves as the Information Systems Manager for Coolidge Wall Womsley Lombard. He manages LAN and WAN network services, internet services, application development, photocopiers and fax units, and telecommunications for the Firm. Mr. Clayton assumes the responsibility of the LAN and WAN networks, performing its maintenance and presiding over the development and implementation of new system applications and software upgrade purchases. Keeping abreast of advancements within the technology field by attending seminars, reading books, and consulting with industry vendors, he credits his success to determination and a willingness to learn. Mr. Clayton is committed to providing continued optimum performance. A prominent and respected law firm, Coolidge Wall Womsley Lombard specializes in providing corporate and business law; labor and employment law; litigation; real estate; tax; estate planning and probate; and environmental legal services. The Firm employs a professional staff of 120 personnel members, 50 of which are highly qualified attorneys. Coolidge Wall Womsley Lombard was founded in 1853. **Career Highlights:** Information Systems Manager, Coolidge Wall Womsley Lombard (1996-Present); Network Services Manager, Intrepid Technology (1995-96); Technical Consultant, Rippe & Kingston (1995-96); General Manager, Compu-Net City (1993-95). **Associations & Accomplishments:** Dayton Bar Association Technology; Commissioner, City of Vandalia Youth Soccer. **Personal Information:** Married to Dana in 1994. Two children: Whitney and Elizabeth. Mr. Clayton enjoys soccer, baseball, computers, gardening and spending time with his family.

Roseland M. Davis

Technology Trainer
Jones Day Reavis & Pogue
599 Lexington Avenue
New York, NY 10022
(212) 326-3687
Fax: (212) 755-7306
rosdavis@jonesday.com

8111

Business Information: Demonstrating exceptional skill and communication abilities, Ms. Davis serves in the position of Technology Trainer for Jones Day Reavis & Pogue. An advocate for life-long education, she prepares courses for employees that highlight the focal points of software and related applications. The training is offered for beginners to advanced users of technology systems, touching on topics such as Microsoft Word and network faxing. Attributing success to her organizational skills and patience, Ms. Davis enjoys the challenges of her position and intends to continue in her current capacity. Her strategic plans include learning as much as possible and eventually starting her own business. Established in Cleveland in 1893, the legal practice of Jones Day Reavis & Pouge has a professional staff that consists of over 1,200 lawyers worldwide. One of the largest and most geographically diverse law fims in existance, more than half of the Fortune 500 companies and a wide array of other entities seek representation and cousel for issues such as mergers and acquisitions, joint ventures, regulatory matters, and finance matters. **Career Highlights:** Technology Trainer, Jones Day Reavis & Pogue (1999-Present); Trainer, Tiger Information Systems (1999-Present); Training Coordinator, Proskavor Rose (1998-99). **Associations & Accomplishments:** Professional Legal Trainers Group; Corel Legal User's Group. **Education:** Fordham University, B.A. (1996); Trainee, New Horizons, HTML Certificates. **Personal Information:** Ms. Davis enjoys exercising, reading, tutoring and dancing.

Jerome A. Farquharson

Technology Development Senior Analyst
Bryan Cave
211 North Broadway, Suite 3600
St. Louis, MO 63102
(314) 259-2657
Fax: (314) 259-2020
jfarquharson@bryancave.com

8111

Business Information: As Technology Development Senior Analyst of Bryan Cave, Mr. Farquharson is responsible for all WAN and LAN implementation, contract negotiations, and equipment purchases. Before joining Bryan Cave, he served as Software Engineer with the Spencer Reed Group. His history also includes stints as Systems Engineer for NBC Olympics and Project Manager at GTE Telephone Operations. As a seven year professional, he concurrently fulfills the role of Senior Project Manager responsible for technology deployment, cabling, work flow processes, and providing inputs to the Firm's fiscal year budget. Throughout his career, Mr. Farquharson has accomplished many goals, but his greatest achievement came in 1996 at the Olympic Games in Atlanta, Georgia. He is credited with creating the Games' network infrastructure and was responsible for all aspects of communications and cabling. His success is solely attributed to God. Publishing articles, obtaining his Ph.D., getting more involved in project management and consulting, earning his project management certification, and eventually becoming Chief Executive Officer of his own company serves as Mr. Farquharson's future endeavors. Established in 1847, Bryan Cave provides legal representation to an international clientele. Ranked as the top law firm in St. Louis, Missouri, the Firm is also recognized as the fourth best in the United States. Headquartered in St. Louis, Bryan Cave operates a network of eight offices in the United States and six throughout Europe and Asia. Presently, the Firm employs a work force of more than 1,500 personnel who help generate revenues in excess of $115 million annually. **Career Highlights:** Technology Development Senior Analyst, Bryan Cave (1999-Present); Software Engineer, Spencer Reed Group (1997-99); Systems Engineer, NBC Olympics (1994-96); Project Engineer, GTE Telephone Operations (1994-95). **Associations & Accomplishments:** Certified Systems Engineer; Certified NetWare Engineer; Microsoft Certified Systems Engineer; Elder Ministers Guild; National Association for the Advancement of Colored People; Toastmasters Club; Kiwanis Club; Red Cross Volunteer; Boy's & Girls Club of America; Institute of Electrical and Electronics Engineers Computer Society. **Education:** Clark Atlanta University: M.S. in Computer Science (1997), B.S. in Computer Science (1995); College of the Bahamas, A.A. in Business Administration (1992). **Personal Information:** Married to Desiree in 1999. Mr. Farquharson enjoys reading, public debating and studying poetry.

Britt L. Jackson

Systems Administrator
Frith Anderson & Peake, PC
3140 Chaparral Drive
Roanoke, VA 24018
(540) 725-3374
Fax: (540) 772-9167
britt.jackson@prodigy.net

8111

Business Information: Ms. Jackson is the Systems Administrator at Frith Anderson & Peake, PC. She has the continual task of training the staff on all hardware and software adaptations put into the Firm's computer databases. She installs all new product and routinely tests the operational effectiveness of the Firm's current technology. With computers becoming a integral part of the legal industry, Ms. Jackson has undertaken the difficult task of maintaining and updating the databases. She also designs upgrade programs to bring the older systems in the office up-to-date with the current technology. Conducting seminars on the technology has proven to be the most effective method to teach the staff, and she designs courses that will speak to her students in a language they will be able to interpret. On the legal side of the Firm, Ms. Jackson assists in general case management of personal injury clients by interviewing them, processing subpoenas, and analyzing medical records. In the future, she hopes to be appointed as Chief Information Officer at the Firm. She credits her success to her rich legal and technical expertise. Frith Anderson & Peake, PC is a law firm. With a clientele expanding across the state, the Firm has employed a staff of 23 lawyers, paralegals, and legal secretaries. Established in 1997, Frith Anderson & Peake has continued to expand its practice and currently focuses on corporate law. **Career Highlights:** Systems Administrator, Frith Anderson & Peake, PC (1997-Present); Paralegal, Gentry Locke Rakes & Moore (1995-97); Legal Assistant, Johnson Ayers & Matthews (1993-95); Relocation Director, Waldrop Realty (1992-93). **Associations & Accomplishments:** Roanoke Valley Paralegal Association: Vice President, Committee Chairman; Volunteer, Court Appointed Special Advocate for Abused and Neglected Children; Roanoke Bar Association Foundation. **Education:** University of Tampa, B.Sc. (1992); American Institute of Paralegal Studies, Certificate (1993).

Personal Information: Married to Kevin in 1996. Ms. Jackson enjoys travel.

Lowell J. Lysinger Jr.

Technical Specialist
BSA & I, LLP
856 Callowhill Road
Perkasie, PA 18944
(215) 864-8449
Fax: (215) 864-8244
lowelllysinger@hotmail.com

8111

Business Information: As the BSA&I, LLP's Technical Specialist, Mr. Lysinger oversees project management and supports the computer and network infrastructure. In this capacity, he works on computers, monitors systems warranty, and ensures the functionality of software, printing, network, and cabling. Possessing an excellent understanding of technology, Mr. Lysinger supports users to resolve complex level 2 problems, provides machine upkeep, maintains address billing systems, negotiates with vendors, and works with software and legal applications and configurations. Highly regarded, he leads his team in replicating systems, editing base filing systems, and giving multimedia presentations. Constantly getting new products at work, Mr. Lysinger plans staying on top of emerging technologies and keeping his options open for anything that might come his way. Established in 1880, BSA&I, LLP is a law firm concentrating on corporate law. With 1,000 employees and 7 branch offices, the Firm deals with business from corporate to start up companies. The Firm has locations throughout the United States, with headquarters located in Philadelphia, Pennsylvania. **Career Highlights:** Technical Specialist, BSA&I, LLP (1997-Present); Help Desk Technician, Freedom Systems Corporation (1996-97); Lab Technician, Bucks County Community College (1995-96). **Education:** Bucks County Community College, Associate's degree (1996). **Personal Information:** One child: Jacob. Mr. Lysinger enjoys automobiles, choral music, do it yourself computers and reading.

Ruddy Marchena

Management Information Systems Assistant Manager
Pellerano & Herrera
P.O. Box 524121
Miami, FL 33152-4121
(809) 541-5200
Fax: (809) 567-0773
r_marchena@hotmail.com

8111

Business Information: As Management Information Systems Assistant Manager of Pellerano & Herrera, Mr. Marchena administers LANs with Novell NetWare 4.1 and WindowsNT 4.0. He supervises two technical support and users assistant personnel. An eight year veteran, Mr. Marchena maintains the software that controls the operation of the entire computer system. He makes changes in the sets of instructions and determines how the central processing unit of the system handles the various jobs it has ben given and communicates with peripheral equipment, such as terminals, printers, and disk drives. Because of his knowledge of the entire computer system, Mr. Marchena often helps determine the source of problems that may occur with the Firm's computer programs. He would like to move to a larger company and possibly obtain a Consultant position. Both reading and networking with his peers keep Mr. Marchena abreast on new technology, better enabling him to provide services with quality and value. Established in 1952, Pellerano & Herrera is a full service law firm located in Miami, Florida. Over 160 people are currently employed by the Firm to assist in various duties. Attorneys at the Firm act as both advocates and advisors in our society. They perform in-depth research into the purposes behind the applicable laws and into judicial decisions that have been applied to those laws under circumstances similar to those currently faced by their clients. Other service include consulting businesses on legal matters. **Career Highlights:** Management Information Systems Assistant Manager, Pellerano & Herrera (1998-Present); Profamilia, Inc.: Systems Analyst (1995-98), Computer Department Assistant (1991-95). **Education:** Universidad Nacional Pedro Henriquez Urena, Computer Systems Engineer (1991). **Personal Information:** Mr. Marchena enjoys tennis and guitar.

William H. Mongon

Manager of Information Systems
Cook Yancey King and Galloway
333 Texas Street, Suite 1700
Shreveport, LA 71101
(318) 227-7746
Fax: (318) 227-7746
mongonw@cykg.com

8111

Business Information: As the Manager of Information Systems for Cook Yancy King and Galloway, Mr. Mongon is responsible for managing the information operating systems and network infrastructures. He serves as the Firm's Web master and ensures that all employees are properly trained in the usage of the network. Following 20 years of distinguished service in the U.S. Air Force, Mr. Mongon joined the Firm in 1997. Highly regarded, he possesses superior talents and an excellent understanding of the technology field. Attributing his success to a love for what he does, Mr. Mongon plans to continue his work with the Firm and eventually moving to Dallas, Texas and become involved with systems test and evaluation. Cook Yancey King and Galloway is a professional law corporation. More than 40 attorneys and 130 staff members are employed to provide a variety of services to residents of the Shreveport, Louisiana area. The Firm is dedicated to ensuring that the law is properly upheld and citizens are represented in any capacity needed in a court of law. **Career Highlights:** Manager of Information Systems, Cook Yancey King and Galloway (1997-Present); Intergration Manager, United States Air Force (1977-97). **Associations & Accomplishments:** Association of Information Technology Professionals. **Education:** University of Maryland. **Personal Information:** Two children: Allison and William S. Mr. Mongon enjoys sports.

Yolanda Muhammad

Training Manager
Legal Aid Society
90 Church Street, 14th Floor
New York, NY 10007-2919
(212) 577-3945
Fax: (212) 587-7999
ymuhamma@legalaid.org

8111

Business Information: Possessing over 10 years of occupational and educational experience, Ms. Muhammad was recruited to Legal Aid Society in 1995. As the Firm's Training Manager, she fulfills a number of duties on behalf of the Legal Aid Society and its clientele. Possessing superior talents and an excellent understanding of technology, Ms. Muhammad is responsible for training staff members on computer software applications, such as Windows, Word Perfect, Group Wise, and Microsoft Word and Excel. Overseeing support services, to include help desk and writing the training curriculum, also fall within the realm of her responsibilities. The most rewarding aspects of her career include winning an award for her Master's thesis which was also published. Ms. Muhammad is an advocate of open communication, fostering a strong sense of teamwork and purpose among others in the office. Becoming more involved in consulting and project management serves as her future endeavors. Her credo is "treat people how you want to be treated." Created by 12 immigrants in 1876, the Legal Aid Society is now the largest legal service provider in the world. Specializing in family law practices, the Firm employs the skilled services of 1,800 individuals to meet with clients, negotiate cases, and attend legal litigations. With 22 locations, Legal Aid Society continues to provide skilled legal expertise to lower wealth clientele at fees within their means of support. **Career Highlights:** Training Manager, Legal Aid Society (1999-Present); Trainer, Kaye Insurance (1993-95); User Support, Union Bank of Switzerland (1990-93). **Associations & Accomplishments:** Professional Legal Trainers Group; Literacy Volunteers (1986-92); American Cancer Society (1998-99). **Education:** Andrey Cohen College, M.S. (1999); City College of New York, B.A. in History and Education. **Personal Information:** Married to Fareed. Three children: Unique, Nadir, and Waheed. Ms. Muhammad enjoys jewelry design, writing and walking.

Sharon E. L. Munajj

Senior Trainer
Long Aldridge & Norman
303 Peachtree Street, Suite 5300
Atlanta, GA 30308
(404) 527-8498
Fax: (404) 527-4198
smunajj@lanlaw.com

8111

Business Information: Employed with Long Aldridge & Norman since 1997, Mrs. Munajj is the Senior Trainer of Information Systems. In this position, she coordinates all day-to-day aspects of technology training programs for employees within the Firm. Training is provided in computer applications with concentrations in Word Perfect and Microsoft Suite. Before joining the Firm, she served as Systems Administrator and Trainer for Hurt Richardson Gainer et al. Her background also includes a stint as Senior Trainer with Chabourner & Parke. Currently, Mrs. Munajj serves as a consultant to lawyers where she recommends appropriate applications that should be used on certain projects. She also handles all public relations within the Information Systems Department. Her goal is to beome more involved in training in Web base and global teleconferencing. Mr.s Munajj credits her success to her interest in the industry, as well as her ability to think outside the box, produce results, and aggressively take on new challenges. Offering effective legal service to all clients, Long Aldridge & Norman was established in 1974. The Firm concentrates services in the area of corporate, real estate, and taxes. The Firm has 180 trained and qualified lawyers and a total work force of 425 individual who serves as paralegals, legal secretaries, office receptionists, legal assistants, and investigators. Offices are located in Atlanta, Georgia and Washington, D.C and is presently expanding. **Career Highlights:** Senior Trainer, Long Aldridge & Norman (1997-Present); Systems Administrator/Trainer, Hurt Richardson Garner et al (1990-92); Senior Trainer, Chadbourne & Parke (1988-90). **Associations & Accomplishments:** American Society of Training & Development; American Management Association; Secretary for Information Technology Ministry, 1st African Presbyterian Church. **Education:** C.W. Post College. **Personal Information:** Married to Gerard in 1989. Two children: Amir and Illyasah.

Linda L. Powell

Information Systems Manager
McDermott, Will & Emery
600 13th Street NW
Washington, DC 20005-3005
(202) 756-8085
Fax: (202) 756-8087
lpowell@mwe.com

8111

Business Information: Working out of the Washington D.C. office, Mrs. Powell serves as the Information Systems Manager for McDermott, Will & Emery. She is responsible for providing technological support for other employees of the Practice and assisting them in fully understanding the applications available through their personal computers. A systems expert, Mrs. Powell assists the Firm in implementation of all software and hardware accessories and evaluates the network for management to advise them on difficulties and future improvements. Looking to the Year 2000 and beyong, she hopes to continue applying new technologies to the Firm, and she would like to increase her understanding of the business operations in order to design a specialized program that more fully accommodates the needs of the staff. McDermott, Will & Emery is a law firm providing services to a nationally based clientele. Headquartered in Chicago, Illinois, the Firm supports 13 sites across the United States and is recognized as the ninth largest legal practice in the country. A staff of 1,800 employees operate the Firm's offices and strive to uphold the reputation that was built through 40 years of successful representation of its clients. **Career Highlights:** Information Systems Manager, McDermott, Will & Emery (1998-Present); Project Manager, United States Army Legal Automation (1994-98); Legal Administrator, United States Army Legal Services Agency (1992-94); Legal Administrator, United States Army Litigation Center (1991-92). **Education:** University of Maryland European Division, Paralegal Certificate (1981). **Personal Information:** Married to Gregory in 1977. Two children: Lisa and Keith. Mrs. Powell enjoys family time.

Eric D. Reichert

Information Technology Officer
Mbh Settlement Group
6862 Elm Street, Suite 200
McLean, VA 22101
(703) 734-8900
Fax: (703) 714-8655
ereiche@mbh.com

8111

Business Information: As the Information Technology Manager for Mbh Settlement Group, Mr. Reichert is responsible for the management of all technology aspects for the maintenance and continuing operation of the computer's infrastructure, to include networks, copiers, and printers. Highly regarded, he is also responsible for purchasing Web projects. Possessing over four years of professional technology experience, Mr. Reichert utilizes his superior knowledge and expertise to devise strategic plans to help the Group remain on the leading edge in support of its clientele. Concurrently, he owns and operates a consulting business with plans for future expansion. Mr. Reichert's success is attributed to his ability to think outside the box, aggressively take on challenges and new responsibilities, and deliver results on behalf of the Group and its clientele. Mbh Settlement Group provides a variety of settlements and legal services in the real estate industry. The Group offers comprehensive assessments of claims, relative information, and quality settlement options for each client according to severity of claims. Established in 1996, the Group is located in McLean, Virginia and employs the talents of more than 150 individuals including executive officers, legal professionals, and administrative staff. **Career Highlights:** Information Technology Officer, Mbh Settlement Group (1998-Present); Technology Project Manager, Images, Inc. (1997-98); Owner, Any Key Computer Specialists (1996-97); Computer Technician, Seminole County Sheriff's Office (1996). **Education:** Seminole Community College, A.S. (1997). **Personal Information:** Mr. Reichert enjoys reading and researching on the Web.

Lee Schwing

Director of Information Services
Ziffren, Brittenham, Branca & Fischer LLP
1801 Century Park West
Los Angeles, CA 90067
(310) 552-3388
Fax: (310) 553-7068
lees@zbbf.com

8111

Business Information: Serving as Director of Information Services for the law firm of Ziffren, Brittrnham, Branca & Fischer LLP, Ms. Schwing is responsible for both technical direction and implementation of all the Firm's technology. With the expansive variety of clients handled by ZBBF, Ms. Schwing is involved in the review, analysis, and evaluation of technical issues for many of the Firm's new and current clients. Her involvement with these clients has let her play a crucial role in the development of some of the largest entertainment related Internet companies in the world. In addition to her direct role with the ZBBF clients, Ms. Schwing has also made sure that the Firm maintains its place on the technological cutting-edge. Whether it has been successful deployments of Windows 2.1 through Windows 2000 with Word .9 through Office 2000 or building a network infrastructure to handle the next generation of broadband technology, Ms. Schwing always makes sure the Firm is able to take advantage of the new technologies. Located in Los Angeles, California, Ziffren, Brittenham, Branca & Fischer LLP is an entertainment law firm. With over 80 employees and a client roster that includes Harrison Ford, Eddie Murphy, the Backstreet Boys, and Carlos Santana, the Firm is recognized as the premier entertainment law firm in the world. **Career Highlights:** Director of Information Services, Ziffren, Brittenham, Branca & Fischer LLP (Present). **Education:** Antioch College, B.A. (1974). **Personal Information:** Married to Mark Griffin in 1989.

Mark A. Teague

PC Training and Support Specialist
Winthrop/Stimson
1 Battery Park Plaza, Floor 30
New York, NY 10004-1405
(212) 858-1415
Fax: (212) 858-1500
teaguem@winstim.com

8111

Business Information: In his role as PC Training and Support Specialist at the legal practice of Winthrop/Stimson, Mr. Teague handles a variety of technical responsibilities at the New York and Palm Beach, Florida offices. Utilizing extensive knowledge of the industry, he evaluates current operating procedures, implementing changes such as upgrades as he sees fit. Demonstrating exceptional communication skills, Mr. Teague conducts training courses to ensure staff members are fully up-to-date on equipment and corporate procedures. He acts as a liaison between technical employees and users, smoothing the bridge between laypersons and complex issues. Lending his ability to the development of technology on an international level for the Practice, he is recognized as an authority within his field. Mr. Teague enjoys the challenges his position represents and intends to continue in his current capacity as he prepares to open his own consulting firm. Winthrop/Stimson is an international law firm that handles diverse areas of legal matters. Global offices are located in London, Hong Kong, Singapore, and Tokyo, and additional American offices are in Washington D.C. and Stanford, Connecticut. The New York branch was established as the international headquarters. **Career Highlights:** PC Training and Support Specialist, Winthrop/Stimson (1999-Present); Senior Trainer, CTEC (1997-99). **Education:** University of Ulster, Magee College, B.A. with honors (1994). **Personal Information:** Mr. Teague enjoys travel, theater and reading.

Cynthia Buchan Thiele

Project Coordinator
Pillsbury Madison & Sutro
4 Windsor Place
San Francisco, CA 94133
(415) 983-1149
Fax: (415) 983-1080
thiele-cb@pillsburylaw.com

8111

Business Information: Ms. Thiele functions in the role of Project Coordinator for Pillsbury Madison & Sutro. She is responsible for purchasing equipment, overseeing Y2K compatability and compliance, managing and maintaining the budget for the Information Technology department, and playing an important role within the majority of the large task projects. Ms. Thiele assists in forcasting the fiscal year budget and acts as a liaison between her department and the accounting department. Coordinating resources, time lines, schedules, and assignments are also an integral part of her responsibilities. Looking to the next millennium, Ms. Thiele is working toward a project management position. Pillsbury

Madison & Sutro is a commercial law firm. Founded in 1874, the Firm is one of the largest legal representation in California and is recognized worldwide as a reputable firm. The Firm has expanded its subsidiaries over the years to include two branches in Virginia, seven in California, one in New York, and one in Tokyo. Utilizing its reputation and the talents of its staff, the Firm has continued to be successful in the court room. **Career Highlights:** Project Coordinator, Pillsbury Madison & Sutro (1998-Present); Technology Buyer, Andersen Consulting (1997-98); Customer Service Representative/Agent, Village Insurance Agency (1995-97). **Education:** Sweet Briar College, B.A. (1992). **Personal Information:** Married in 1998.

8200 Educational Services

8211 Elementary and secondary schools
8221 Colleges and universities
8222 Junior colleges
8231 Libraries
8243 Data processing schools
8244 Business and secretarial schools
8249 Vocational schools, nec
8299 Schools and educational services, nec

Chuck Bayne
Technology Director
Laramie High School
1275 North 11th Street
Laramie, WY 82072
(307) 721-4420
Fax: (307) 721-4419
cbaynesr@aol.com

8211

Business Information: Serving as Technology Director for Laramie High School, Mr. Bayne oversees and manages all multimedia equipment, while instructing teachers in the area of computer systems and technology implementation in the classroom. With the School for more than 28 years, he has recieved many internal recognitions for his efforts in the advancement of technology throughout the School. He was a key player in receiving funding from the state legislature to get all Schools in the state connected to the Internet. In the future, Mr. Bayne is looking forward to getting all Schools connected through video connection in order to provide a distance learning capability. He attributes his success to his desire to make a difference. Laramie High School offers learning opportunities for students in grades 10 through 12. The School employs a staff and faculty of 103 to provide instruction in many subjects. Approximately 1,000 students attend the School each year. **Career Highlights:** Laramie High School: Technology Director (1985-Present), Teacher (1971-85). **Associations & Accomplishments:** National Education Association; Life Member, American Vocational Association; Past Vice President, Wyoming Education Association; Phi Delta Kappa, Professional Education Fraternity; National Rifle Association; Benevolent and Protective Order of Elks; Loyal Order of Moose; State Technology Educational Leaders (1999). **Education:** University of Wyoming, B.S. (1991); Certification in Multimedia. **Personal Information:** Married to Mina in 1960. Three children: Charles, Jeff, and Michael. Mr. Bayne enjoys hunting, fishing, crafts and computers.

Sandra L. Becker, Ed.D.
Director of Technology
Governor Mifflin School District
101 South Waverly Street
Shillington, PA 19607-2644
(610) 775-5089
Fax: 6107967471
sbecker@gmsd.k12.pa.us

8211

Business Information: An 29-year veteran in education, Dr. Becker joined the Governor Mifflin School District team of professionals in 1994. At present, she fulfills the role of Director of Technology responsible for all aspects of day-to-day administrative and operational activities. Dr. Becker, an innovative and impact information technology leader, is charged with oversight of the Web site, Intranet Virtual Private Net Administration, and technology integration into curriculum assessment. Relying on strong academics and strategic management skills, she concurrently serves as Chairman of the Technology Committee composed of 11 teachers who love and are dedicated to technology and students. Dr. Becker guides the committee in evaluating current systems and networks, and making upgrade or purchase recommendations. She also keeps the School Board current on status of new technologies implemented within the School District. Determining future resources; developing schedules, budgets, and policies; and providing

cohesive leadership also fall within the realm of her responsibilities. Recognized for her high impact leadership, Dr. Becker has won the Computer World Smithsonian Site and Apple Distinguished Educator Award for two years. Getting the School District more involved with the Internet, building an Intranet that would improve the efficiency of business planning, and developing an Extranet that will provide parents access to their children's records and grades serves as Dr. Becker's innovative goals. Microsoft and Apple Computer created case studies on the technology implementation in this district. Governor Mifflin School District, founded in 1955, operates as a K-12 educational system with a $37 million annual budget. Located in Reading, the District also offers advanced college courses for students willing to participate. Presently, 550 faculty staff and administrators is employed by the School District. **Career Highlights:** Governor Mifflin School District: Director of Technology (1994-Present), Mathematics Teacher (1971-94); Management Information Systems Internship, Hofmann LaRoche Pharmaceuticals (1993). **Associations & Accomplishments:** Apple Distinguished Educator; Association For Educational Communications and Technologies; Board of Directors, Tech Corp PA; Conference Faculty, Classroom Connect & E School News; Phi Delta Kappa; Computer Society; AACE; ISTE; Institute of Electronics and Electrical Engineers; Advisory Board, International Conference on Learning with Technology. **Education:** Lehigh University, Ed.D. (1994); Kutztown University: M.S. in Education (1973), B.S. in Secondary Education (1971). **Personal Information:** Married to Robert H. in 1972. Dr. Becker enjoys Web sites, computer graphics, music and hiking.

Peter M. Cline
Consultant
Manhattan Village Academy
43 West 22nd Street
New York, NY 10010-5101
(212) 242-8752
Fax: (212) 242-7630
petercline@earthlink.net

8211

Business Information: A savvy, three veteran of the technology field, Mr. Cline currently serves as Computer Coordinator of Manhattan Village Academy. He oversees all student interns and day-to-day technology functions, including network administration. In this context, he maintains software and hardware infrastructure and user accounts, as well as creates database and installs and upgrades operating and networking systems. Drawing from his wealth of technical knowledge, Mr. Cline also teaches HTML, JavaScript, and C++; serves as a technical advisor; maintains an Appletalk network with roughly 160 nodes; develops Web sites; and provides technical support to systems users. A respected professional in technology, he is charged with writing grants, assessing new technologies, making purchasing decisions, and helping teachers integrate leading edge technology into their curriculums. Starting his master's program and getting more involved in developing teachers through training is cited as Mr. Cline's future endeavors. His success is attributed to his motivation, desire to make a difference, and belief in what he's doing. public high school in Manhattan, part of the NYCBOE's Superintendency for Alternative Education **Career Highlights:** Computer Coordinator, Manhattan Village Academy (1997-Present); Consultant, Freedom House (1998-Present); Technician, Hunter College Elementary School (1998); Member/Volunteer, AmerCorps/Corporation for National Service (1994-97). **Associations & Accomplishments:** Trail Organization; Hiking Societies; Human Rights Organizations; Eagle Scout; Amateur Musician. **Education:** New York University, B.A. (1997). **Personal Information:** Mr. Cline enjoys hiking, birding, music, reading, writing, travel, sports and French and Slavic languages.

Scott Colbert
Personal Computer Support Technician
Capital Area Intermediate Unit
P.O. Box 489
Summerdale, PA 17093
(717) 732-8404
Fax: (717) 732-8414
scolbert@caiu.k12.pa.us

8211

Business Information: Demonstrating expertise in his field, Mr. Colbert serves as the Personal Computer Support Technician for Capital Area Intermediate Unit. He provides technical support for the School's desktops, ensuring that the hardware, software, and operating systems operate at optimum levels. In charge of in house account management, he handles all of the network accounts, access, and e-mail configurations. Before joining Capital Area Intermediate Unit in 1997, Mr. Colbert assertively served with Richfood of Pennsylvania as Computer Support Technician and Senior Computer Operator. Coordinating resources, time lines, and schedules, as well as ensuring the entire systems functionality also fall within the scope of his functions. Mr. Colbert performs research to stay up to date and attributes his professional success to this fact. Continually striving to improve

performance, he anticipates a promotion to Network Administrator. Founded in 1972, Capital Area Intermediate Unit is a private school located in Summerdale, Pennsylvania. The School provides courses on technology for special needs children in an effort to give them the same technological advantage as other children. Presently, the School employs a staff of more than 490 individuals. **Career Highlights:** Computer Support Technician, Capital Area Intermediate Unit (1997-Present); Richfood of Pennsylvania: Computer Support Technician (1996-97), Senior Computer Operator (1991-96). **Education:** Coastal Carolina Community College (1984-85). **Personal Information:** Married to Maryanne in 1992. One child: Jessica. Mr. Colbert enjoys music, piano, guitar, writing and hiking.

Daniel J. Cornwall
Computer Aided Drafting and Design Instructor
Grundy Area Vocational Center
1002 Union Street
Morris, IL 60450
(815) 942-4390
Fax: (815) 942-6650
uicaregion3@yahoo.com

8211

Business Information: Serving as Computer Aided Drafting and Design Instructor of Grundy Area Vocational Center, Mr. Cornwall educates students on the basic and advanced principals of Auto CAD 2000. Demonstrating exceptional technical knowledge, he is able to guide students through the basic operation of equipment as he offers insight to the program's techniques. With superior communication skills, he is able to explain complex technical terms in a manner easily comprehendible to inexperienced students. Citing the discipline and motivation gained through his military career as the key to his success in the civilian world, Mr. Cornwall intends to continue in his current role as he continually implements technical updates and changes into the cirriculum. High school students in grades 11 and 12 living in the community of Morris, Illinois, can sharpen their technical skills at the Grundy Area Vocational Center. The Center is comprised of various departments that offer training and graduation certificates in areas such as woodworking and industrial technology. Established in 1972, the Center is recognized as a cornerstone of the educational community as generation after generation of students successfully complete valuable training courses. **Career Highlights:** Computer Aided Drafting and Design Instructor, Grundy Area Vocational Center (1993-Present); Corporate Draftsman, Duplex Producers (1991-93); Construction Equipment Supervisor, United States Army (1976-90). **Associations & Accomplishments:** Life Member, 82nd Airborne Division Association; 4th Infantry Division Association; 1st Armored Division Association; DeKalb County VietNOW; Life Member, Veterans of Foreign Wars. **Education:** Lewis University (Currently Attending); Kishwaukee College: Associate's degree in Mechanical Computer Aided Design, Architectural Computer Aided Design. **Personal Information:** Married to Diane in 1980. Three children: Travis, Cassandra, and Jacob. Mr. Cornwall enjoys archery, designing homes, hunting and woodworking.

Phyllis C. David
Director for Operational Technology
Kershaw County School District
1301 DuBose Court
Camden, SC 29020
(803) 432-8416
Fax: (803) 425-8918
davidp@do.kershaw.k12.sc.us

8211

Business Information: Functioning in the capacity of Director for Operational Technology at Kershaw County School District, Mrs. David is responsible for determining the overall strategic direction and academic contribution of the information systems function. She has worked in the training and development and education arenas since 1987. Joining Kershaw County School District faculty in 1996, Mrs. David directly oversees and manages the life cycle of the IT/IS infrastructure for the entire School District. She is charged with recommending and acquiring advanced technologies such as hardware, software, LAN and WAN, Internet, and e-mail. Her focus is to deploy the most up-to-date technologies within the School District, and help the Kershaw County remain on the leading edge of education. In addition to supervising a staff of six persons to include high school and college interns, Mrs. David also plans and oversees the evaluation and integration of new technology; coordinates resources, schedules, and budgets; and provides technical support and problem resolution. She credits her success to her extensive academic ties, and remaining on the bleeding edge of technology by attending seminars and trades shows and interacting with her colleagues in the field. Kershaw County School District provides pre-kindergarten to grade 12 education to more than 9,500 students. Local in scope, Kershaw County is located in central South Carolina. The School District encompasses 20 school locations manned by over 1,200 educators, administrators, and support staff. **Career Highlights:** Kershaw County School District: Director for Operational Technology (1999-Present), Coordinator for

Technology (1996-99); District Technology Trainer, District 5 of Richland County (1996); Training and Development, PMSC, Inc. (1994-95); Teacher, Kershaw County School District (1987-94). **Associations & Accomplishments:** AAIM; Who's Who in American Junior Colleges; SCADPD; AECT. **Education:** Webster University, M.A. in Computer Resource Management (1990); Limestone College, B.S. in Management; Midlands Technical College, Business degree. **Personal Information:** Married to Robert in 1985. Two children: Trey and Jessica. Mrs. David enjoys fishing, singing, handbells and guitar.

Dirk A. DeLo, Ph.D.
Director of Technology
Westminster School
995 Hopmeadow Street
Simsbury, CT 06070
(860) 408-3056
Fax: (860) 408-3001
dadelo@westminister-school.org

8211

Business Information: Serving as Director of Technology for Westminster School, Dr. DeLo manages the Technology Department, directly supervising a staff of five. He is responsible for keeping the School up-to-date and on the cutting edge of today's technological advances. To that effect, he performs long-term planning for the Department to predict what will be needed for Westminster's future. Additionally, Dr. DeLo trains the faculty members in the use of the computer system. As a technology professional, he determines the overall strategic direction and educational contribution of the information systems function. Coordinating resources and schedules; overseeing time lines and assignments; and ensuring the reliability, integrity, and security of the infrastructure also fall within the purview of Dr. DeLo's executive responsibilities. Establishing goals that are compatible with the mission of the School, he plans to keep the School on the cutting edge of technology. Westminster School is a private boarding school providing a quality education for ninth through 12th grade students. Employing a staff of 150 teaching, administrative, and support personnel, the School was founded in 1888. **Career Highlights:** Director of Technology, Westminster School (Present). **Associations & Accomplishments:** Published, "Using Multimedia Technologies for Teaching High School Mathematics" (1997); Awarded "Presidential Award for Excellence in Science and Mathematics Teaching (1996); Awarded "GTE Gift Fellowship for Technology and Mathematics" (1995); Awarded "Woodrow Wilson National Foundation Fellowship for Mathematics" (1993). **Education:** Columbia University: Ph.D. (1997), M.S. (1993), M.A. (1990); Amherst College, B.A. (1989). **Personal Information:** Married to Sarah in 1991. Two children: Piper Elizabeth and Cameron Alexander. Dr. DeLo enjoys sailing, sculling, squash and scuba diving.

Carol A. Derrick
Technology Facilitator
A.C. New Middle School
3700 South Belt Line Road
Mesquite, TX 75181
(972) 882-5600
cderrick@mesquiteisd.org

8211

Business Information: Utilizing more than 20 years of experience in education, Ms. Derrick currently serves as the Technology Facilitator for A.C. New Middle School. Meeting with student representatives each summer to discuss troubleshooting and basic database spreadsheet system, she also coordinates with a five member teacher's team to write and plan the computer related curriculum. In addition, Ms. Derrick manages and schedules classes in the School's two computer labs, providing technical assistance to students and teachers alike as well as supervising between 14 and 21 student assistants. As a 27 year technology professional, Ms. Derrick's success reflects her ability to take on new challenges and responsibilities. Her goal is to educate the teachers more about computers and help them feel more at ease in the use of today's technology. Part of the Mesquite Independent School District, A.C. New Middle School is a public school providing a middle school education to 6th, 7th, and 8th grade students. Over 900 students are enrolled and 70 administrative, teaching, and support personnel work diligently to enhance and perfect educational opportunities for the District's youth. **Career Highlights:** Technology Facilitator, A.C. New Middle School (1996-Present); Mesquite Independent School District: Computer Literacy Teacher (1995-96), Reading Teacher (1989-95), Special Education Teacher (1972-89). **Associations & Accomplishments:** State Officer, Alpha Delta Kappa; Association for Supervision and Curriculum Development; Mesquite Education Association; Association of Texas Professional Educators. **Education:** University of Texas at Tyler, M.Ed. (1977).

David Elliott
Technology Coordinator
Hong Kong International School
1 Red Hill Road
Tai Tam, Hong Kong
+852 28139211
Fax: +852 28137300
delliott@hs.hkis.edu.hk

8211

Business Information: Mr. Elliott has been with the School for over 16 years and currently serves as Technology Coordinator. In this capacity, he is responsible for the development of curriculum for computer related courses, monitoring advances in computer software applications, and adapting updated applications to current curriculums. In addition, Mr. Elliott develops workshops on a variety of technology related subjects and conducts training programs for teachers at the School. Established in 1966, the Hong Kong International School is an independent, private school providing educational opportunities to approximately 2,500 students in grades pre-kindergarten through 12. Operating two campuses, the School prepares graduating students for admittance into colleges and universities in Hong Kong, the United States, and other international locations. **Career Highlights:** Hong Kong International School: Technology Coordinator (1987-Present), Technology Coordinator (1982-97); Management of Projects, Institute of Cultural Affairs (1974-82). **Associations & Accomplishments:** International Society for Technology in Education; Association for Supervision and Curriculum Development. **Education:** University of Oregon, M.S. (1990); Chicago Theological Seminary, Master in Divinity; Purdue University, B.S. **Personal Information:** Married to Mary Jane in 1968. Three children: Sarah, Michael, and Diane. Mr. Elliott enjoys music, singing, socializing and coaching golf.

Judith M. Green
Technology Coordinator
Waukegan Public Schools
1201 North Sheridan Road
Waukegan, IL 60085-2081
(847) 263-4729
Fax: (847) 360-5355
jgreen@mail.wps.lake.k12.il.us

8211

Business Information: Mrs. Green has served with Waukegan Public Schools in various positions since 1990. At the present moment, she fulfills the responsibilities of Technology Coordinator. In this capacity, she is the K-12 technology and learning coordinator for Unified District 60. Accumulating over eight years of experience and with a strong academic background, Mrs. Green coordinates professional development and oversees grant and district funds earmarked for integration of technology across the curriculum. As the coordinator for the entire District, she serves as decision maker for technology integration and purchases as well as for all aspects of the day-to-day operations of the Technology Department. Respected in her field, Mrs. Green is also responsible for formulating the technology budget and training teachers on engaged learning models and applications. One of her greatest accomplishments include designing an amazing picture machine educational software using NCR technology. Published on the web, this software provided wetland issue based problems for classroom learning. Mrs. Green's future plan is to implement cutting edge distance and video learning technology into the Distrct's classrooms. Waukegan Public Schols is an urban school district with over 14,500 students. The District encompasses twenty-two sites to include fourteen elementary schools, one combined preschool and kindergarten, five middle schools, and one high school. Regional in scope, the District presently employs a staff of more than 1,200 professional, technical, and support personnel. **Career Highlights:** Waukegan Public Schools: Technology Coordinator (1997-Present), K-8 Technology Consultant (1996-97), Science Teacher (1990-96). **Associations & Accomplishments:** International Society for Technology in Education; Illinois Computing Educators; Illinois Science Teacher Association. **Education:** St. Xavier University, M.A. (1997); Carthoge College, B.A.; College of Lake County, Associate's degree. **Personal Information:** Married to Martin in 1972. Five children: Kristopher, Katherine, Andrew, Sarah, and Matthew. Mrs. Green enjoys reading, walking, hiking and childrens activities.

Leland G. Hall
Chairman of Academic Computer Department
The Hotchkiss School
Box 800
Lakeville, CT 06039-0800
(860) 435-2591
Fax: (860) 435-1355
lhall@hotchkiss-school.org

8211

Business Information: Mr. Hall serves in the role of Chairman of Academic Computer Department for The Hotchkiss School. He is responsible for all aspects of day-to-day administration and operations of the Academic Computer Department. Mr. Hall, utilizing over 36 years of academic ties and occupational experience, determines the overall strategic direction of the Department and educational contributions of the information systems function. He teaches faculty members and students about the proper use of computer applications within their daily routine. Mr. Hall promotes the newest technologies throughout the School and is always looking for opportunities to enhance the performance of the School's information technology infrastructure. He works closely with the Director of Photography on developing the digital technology course, and Head of the Music Department overseeing projects and developing the technology curriculum. His career highlights include integrating process writing and word processing in the early 1980s. Mr. Hall's goal is to set up a Teacher Development Center to help develop curriculum material for courses on line through the Intranet. He is also coordinating plans for a sabbatical vacation to Florida where he is planning to explore the world of computer graphics. The Hotchkiss School is an independent boarding school. Concentrating its educational talents to the secondary level of education for students in the ninth through twelfth grades. Founded in 1891, the School blossomed into a facility that supports 540 students. The School has a staff of 100 educators and offers a complete curriculum that features over 200 courses. **Career Highlights:** Chairman of Academic Computer Department, The Hotchkiss School (1990-Present); Director Technology, Region I School District (1988-90); Director Technology, Winchester School District (1985-88). **Associations & Accomplishments:** International Society for Technology in Education; Former Trustee, Salisbury Family Services; Habitate for Humanity. **Education:** Lesley College, M.Ed. (1984); Ricker Coller, B.A. (1963). **Personal Information:** Married to Pamela in 1971. Mr. Hall enjoys photography, carpentry and computer graphics.

Michael Hall
Network Manager
Century High School
2000 Southwest 234th Avenue
Hillsboro, OR 97123
(503) 848-1850
Fax: (503) 848-1825
hallm@hsd.k12.or.us

8211

Business Information: Possessing advanced technical skills, Mr. Hall serves as Network Manager for Century High School. In this capacity, he manages the network's infrastructure, performs diagnostic testing, and constructs custom program applications. Mr. Hall is also responsible for upgrading the system network and conducts detailed network training for all staff members. Continually staying alert to new techniques and progressive technology, Mr. Hall is currently involved in a large-scale network deployment in effort to keep Century High School up-to-date with today's technological advancements. His future goal is to continue studies in information technology and branch out into the private sector of Network Management. Century High School is an educational institution that provides higher learning to students from grades nine through twelve. Located in Hillsboro, Oregon, the Institution employs the expertise of 110 skilled professionals who are dedicated to ensuring the highest quality of education available. Providing character education and technology developments to students for decades, the Institution also offers college preparatory educational programs, and career development courses to aid students in exploring future endeavors. **Career Highlights:** Network Manager, Centruy High School (1999-Present); Patch Database Technician, Symantec Corporation (1999); Support Services Representation, Stream Internation, Inc. (1997-99). **Associations & Accomplishments:** Stage manager for several local theater productions; Active participant of local church. **Education:** Portland Community College, (Currently Attending). **Personal Information:** Mr. Hall enjoys motorcycles and photography.

Scott A. Heinssen
Information Systems Manager
St. Joseph's Indian School
North Main
Chamberlain, SD 57326
(605) 734-3322
Fax: (605) 734-3480
sheinssen@stjo.org

8211

Business Information: Drawing from extensive occupational experience, Mr. Heinssen performs as Informations Systems Manager for St. Joseph's Indian School overseeing all aspects of computer relates tasks. In so doing, he designs and develops programs for the computer systems infrastructure, reorganizes and restructures data to better suit the needs of the user as well as maintaining the efficiency and security of the database. Further, Mr. Heinssen provides assistance and advice to users, interpreting problems and providing technical support for hardware, software, and systems. Presiding over a staff of 10 employees, he demonstrates productive managerial techniques which successfully builds and reinforces essential staff and management relations. Mr. Heinssen was instrumental in keeping the Y2K bug in check, in over 3,000 programs he only had to correct 7. Enjoying substantial success in his field, he intends to continue with his current career path with the possibility of working with another company. Mr. Heinssen attributes his success to patience, never assuming, and being able to socialize with a wide variety of people. Since 1927, St. Joseph's Indian School has provided full service care and education for children. As a non-profit organization, the School coordinates education with the everyday care of students through feeding and providing a home. Employing 200 staff, and adminstration personnel, St. Joseph's Indian School works within the constraints of a $25 million a year budget. **Career Highlights:** Information Systems Manager, St. Joseph's Indian School (1997-Present); Technical Support Specialist, Midcontinent Media, Inc. (1992-97); Technical Support Specialist, PAM Oil, Inc. (1989-92); Computer Operator, Citibank of South Dakota (1981-88). **Associations & Accomplishments:** Common Users Group. **Education:** Southeast Area Vocational and Technical (1980). **Personal Information:** One child: Matthew. Mr. Heinssen enjoys being a beer connoisseur, darts, bowling and boating.

Arnold Dale Kimble
Coordinator of Data Processing and Systems Management
Garrett County Board of Education
40 South Fourth Street
Oakland, MD 21550
(301) 334-8911
Fax: (301) 334-8916
dkimble@ga.k12.md.us

8211

Business Information: Getting his start in technology through the United States Army as a electronic warfare specialist, Mr. Kimble was recruited to the Garrett County Board of Education in 1997. At the present time, he fulfills the responsibilities of Coordinator of Data Processing and Systems Management. With extensive electronics and computer expertise, he is responsible for installation, upgrade, and maintenance of the WAN and LAN networks. Additionally, Mr. Kimble oversees data processing systems and all systems administrator's functions. Management of administration and student software and maintaining the efficiency of the database and system security also falls under the realm of his responsibilities. A new project, Mr. Kimble designed and installed the wide area network (WAN) that connects the 15 schools and one specialized training facility to the central office data processing facilities. A prominent expert in the field, he attributes his success to persistence and sticking firmly to his goals. Concurrently, Mr. Kimble works part-time as an Adjunct Professor for Allegany College of Maryland and Garrett Community College teaching computer repair and computer networking classes. Becoming more involved in the industry, continuing to expand and improve services on his WAN project and continuing his education serves as Mr. Kimble's long-term goals. The public school system for Garrett County, Garrett County Board of Education encompasses 15 schools in the County. Local in scope, Garrett County Board of Education is manned by 1,000 educators providing educational services to over 5,000 students. **Career Highlights:** Coordinator of Data Processing and Systems Management, Garrett County Board of Education (1997-Present); Network Administrator, Allegany College of Maryland (1995-97); Platoon Sergeant, United States Army (1980-94). **Associations & Accomplishments:** Retired United States Army Non-Commissioned Officer. **Education:** Frostburg State University, M.B.A. (1998); University of the State of New York Board of Regents, B.S. **Personal Information:** Married to Ellen in 1971. Two children: Christopher and Andrea. Mr. Kimble enjoys travel and gardening.

John J. Kopaczewski
Department Chairman
Kennedy Kenrick Catholic High School
250 East Johnson Highway
Norristown, PA 19401
(610) 275-2846
coachkop@aol.com

8211

Business Information: Challenging students to gain their potential mentally, physically, and socially, Mr. Kopaczewski has held the position as Department Chairman for four years with Kennedy Kenrick Catholic High School. Working specifically with the technology department, he strives to incorporate the latest technology in the education process. Mr. Kopaczewski has enjoyed substantial success as an educator and finds his work greatly rewarding. Serving as moderator for the student council, overseeing the Technology Club, and teaching five computer classes, he is dedicated to providing his students with the most practical and comprehensive education, sharing ideas and techniques in an enthusiastic and persuasive manner. Continually striving for maximum effectiveness, Mr. Kopaczewski goals include obtaining his Ph.D. to enable him to teach at a college level after his career with Kennedy Kenrick Catholic High School. Establishing higher standards in education since the early 1950s, Kennedy Kenrick Catholic High School provides quality education to students grades 9 through 12. The School staffs over 50 administrative, teaching, and support personnel who work diligently to enhance and perfect educational opportunities for its 700 students. **Career Highlights:** Department Chairman, Kennedy Kenrick Catholic High School (1996-Present); Assistant Vice President, Meritor Savings Bank (1986-95); Manager, Wells Fargo Alarm (1980-86). **Associations & Accomplishments:** National Association of Teachers; Pennsylvania Association of Student Council Advisors; Pennsylvania Football Association of High School Athletes. **Education:** Rosemont College, M.Ed. in Technology (In Progress); St. Joseph's University, B.S. (1985). **Personal Information:** Married to Joanne in 1982. Two children: Dana and Allison. Mr. Kopaczewski enjoys fishing and coaching.

Erika P. Lapham
Technology Technician
West Noble School Corporation
5050 North U.S. 33
Ligonier, IN 46767-9606
(219) 894-3191
Fax: (219) 894-7394
elpham@ligtel.com

8211

Business Information: Ms. Lapham has served with West Noble School Corporation in various positions since 1993. At the present time, she fulfills the responsibilities of Technology Technician. In that capacity, Ms. Lapham oversees all aspects of installation and maintenance of the Corporation's LAN and WAN networks that includes 13 Windows NT and 3 NetWare servers and 1,000 workstations. Utilizing five years of experience and a firm academic foundation, she is responsible for providing support to over 3,000 users. Additional responsibilities recently have included Internet access at every desktop through a TI connection and fully automating corporation food service. Troubleshooting difficulties, setting up servers, and implementing hardware and software also falls under the Ms. Lapham's diverse responsibilities. A respected expert in the field, she designs new computer systems and solutions to meet the specific needs of the organization. Solving Y2K problems is an additional function of Ms. Lapham's role. She attributes her success to possessing excellent problem solving skills, natural abilities, and her love of learning new technology. Supporting growth within the Corporation, keeping up with evolving technology, and keeping costs down for users serves as Ms. Lapham's long-term goals. West Noble School Corporation provides K-12 education services to over 2,500 students. Encompassing two elementary schools, one middle school, and one high school, the Corporation's services are regional in scope. Located in Indiana, 300 dedicated educators and administrators man the Corporation. **Career Highlights:** West Noble School Corporation: Technology Technician (1994-Present), Elementary Building Technician (1993-94). **Associations & Accomplishments:** Indiana Computer Educators; Northeast Indiana Computer Coordinators; Hoosier Educational Computer Coordinators; Deacon in Ligonier Presbyterian Church. **Education:** Kennedy-Western University, B.S. in Management Information Systems (1998). **Personal Information:** Married to William in 1969. One child: Heather. Ms. Lapham enjoys swimming, reading, crossstitching and gardening.

Karstyn McCoy
Management Information Systems Administration Officer
Horizon Instructional Systems
4213 Alan Drive
North Highlands, CA 95660
(916) 645-5167
Fax: (916) 434-3708
mccoy@hiscs.org

8211

Business Information: As Management Information Systems Administration Officer for Horizon Instructional Systems, Mr. McCoy oversees computer purchasing and leasing and distribution tracking. He determines the strategic direction and the academic contribution of the information systems functions as well as administrates ISP and multiple POP sites. Possessing an excellent understanding of technology and academics, Mr. McCoy is in charge of recommending services and hardware, providing backup, and overseeing routine maintenance on the network and computer infrastructure. In the future, he hopes to remain with Horizon Instructional Systems and continue to transform the School's database and network environments. Horizon Instructional Systems is a California charter school providing alternative education for grades K-12. The School provides its own ISP and offers computers and Internet connections to further education. Enrolling approximately 6,000 individuals, the School employs 130 professionals of varying degrees. Presently, the School reports an estimated $15 million in annual revenue. **Career Highlights:** Management Information Systems Administration Officer, Horizon Instructional Systems (Present). **Education:** University of California at Davis Extension (1998). **Personal Information:** Married to Catherine in 1980. One child: Ryan. Mr. McCoy enjoys arts.

Joel W. Mengerink
Teacher
Paulding High School
622 North Jefferson
Van Wert, OH 45891
(419) 399-4656
jmenger452@aol.com

8211

Business Information: A dedicated and determined individual, Mr. Mengerink serves as a Teacher for Paulding High School. Educating students in the areas of accounting, clerical records, business law, keyboarding, and computer applications, he also serves as a coach for the School's basketball and cross track teams. Mr. Mengerink is dedicated to providing his students with the most practical and comprehensive education, sharing ideas and techniques in an enthusiastic and persuasive manner. Continually striving for maximum effectiveness, he is currently pursing his Master's degree in order to enable him to capitalize on the opportunities afforded by the School. His success reflects his ability to take on challenges and new responsibilities and deliver results. Paulding High School provides academic opportunities for students in ninth through twelfth grades. Located in Van Wert, Ohio, the School provides a full range of educational services to several hundred students each year. More than 150 professionals are employed to fulfill all aspects of administrative, teaching and support duties. **Career Highlights:** Teacher, Paulding High School (1998-Present); Financial Aid Administrator, ITT Technical Institute (1997-98); Sports Announcer, Wert/WKSD Radio (1995-Present). **Associations & Accomplishments:** School Technology Committee; Ohio High School Basketball Coaches Assocaition; United Methodist Church. **Education:** Bowling Green State University, B.S. (1997). **Personal Information:** Married to Erin in 1997. Mr. Mengerink enjoys cross country running, basketball and announcing football on radio.

Anne Moy
Teacher
Rosses Community School
Sandfield Ardara
Donegal, Ireland
+35 37521122
annemoy@eircom.net

8211

Business Information: As a Teacher at Rosses Community School, Mrs. Moy facilitates business and technology classes for junior and senior students. Specifically, she teaches business development and information technology courses. A pioneer in the regional area, Mrs. Moy introduces information technology to the students via Rosses Community School and implemented a video conferencing system between area schools and international sites. She encourages young people to take advantage of every learning opportunity, including participation in national competitions in the business area, in which her students have clearly established themselves. In the future, she plans to continue facilitating business development and information technology programs in pursuit of increased personal and professional development for herself and her students. Mrs. Moy is currently pursuing a Master's degree in Information Communication Technology. Her success reflects her ability to think outside-the-box and deliver results. The Rosses Community School provides general education for young adults ages 12 to 18 years old. Established in 1978, the School provides developmental and educational instruction to its students. In this capacity, the School intends to educate, train, and prepare students for the diverse roles they will assume in future business and life situations. **Career Highlights:** Teacher, Rosses Community School (1991-Present); Lecturer, Catering College (1988-91); Teacher of Business, Donegal V.E.C. (1979-87). **Associations & Accomplishments:** Business Teachers Association of Ireland. **Education:** University College Galaway, Bachelor's degree in Commerce (1977); Diploma: Typewriting, Shorthand, Wordprocessing. **Personal Information:** Married to Hugh in 1980. Two children: Maria and Daniel. Mrs. Moy enjoys information technology, politics and industrial relations.

Buddy Pride

Director of Technology
McHenry School District #15
1011 North Green Street
McHenry, IL 60050-5720
(815) 385-7210
Fax: (815) 344-7121
bpride@d15.org

8211

Business Information: Serving as Director of Technology, Mr. Pride is responsible for the maintenance of all personal computers, software, and hardware in McHenry School District #15. Responsible for the supervision of one assistant and two teachers per building, he also conducts purchases and performs upgrades. Mr. Pride is responsible for three full-time staff and one teacher per building. He also conducts all purchases and performs upgrades. McHenry School District #15 is comprised of elementary schools serving 4,500 students in grades kindergarten through eighth. Employing 500 people, the district operates two middle schools and five elementary buildings equipped with local area networks, wide area networks, and 500 personal computers and over 700 desktop and laptop computers. **Career Highlights:** McHenry School District #15: Director of Technology (1994-Present), Music Teacher (1993-94). **Associations & Accomplishments:** IDEA Fellows Program; ASCD; MENC/IMEA; Speaker for Reforming Education Through Technology, Illinois Education and Technical Conference - October (1996); Attends the National Technical Conference, hosted by the National School Board Association. **Education:** Saint Xavier University, Master's degree; Northern Illinois University, B.M. Ed. (1993). **Personal Information:** Married to Heidi in 1992. Mr. Pride enjoys musical theatre and singing.

Mark C. Robinson

Technology Coordinator
Archmere Academy
3600 Philadelphia Pike
Claymont, DE 19703
(302) 798-6632
Fax: (302) 798-7290
robinson@archmereacademy.com

8211

Business Information: Functioning in the role of Technology Coordinator for Archmere Academy, Mr. Robinson manages campus wide network and supports users including both faculty and students. He is responsible for troubleshooting and providing back up support. Before joining Archmere Academy as Assistant Computer Coordinator in 1998, he served as a Computer Lab Assistant for Neumann College. An expert, Mr. Robinson demonstrates a strong ability to solve computer malfunctions and ensures that they are used to generate meaningful information and increase efficiency. Coordinating resources, time lines, schedules, assignments, and budgets also fall within the purview of his functions. Continually striving for maximum effectiveness, Mr. Robinson is currently pursuing his Master's degree to enable him to capitalize on the opportunities provided by the Academy. Founded in 1932, Archmere Academy is a private, Catholic, co-educational high school serving as a college preparatory educational facility. An established and prestigious school, Archmere staffs over 60 administrative, teaching, and support personnel who work diligently to enhance and perfect educational opportunities for its students. **Career Highlights:** Archmere Academy: Technology Coordinator (1999-Present), Assistant Computer Coordinator (1998-99); Computer Lab Assistant, Neumann College (1993-98). **Education:** Neumann College: Candidate for M.S. (In Progress), B.A. (1996). **Personal Information:** Mr. Robinson enjoys coaching. Mr. Robinson coaches both women's varsity basketball and co-ed varsity track at Archmere Academy.

John A. Roina

Information Systems Operations Supervisor
Eaglecrest High School
5100 South Picadilly Street
Aurora, CO 80015
(303) 699-0408
Fax: (303) 400-7395
jroina@earthlink.net

8211

Business Information: Serving as the Information Systems Operations Supervisor of Eaglecrest High School, Mr. Roina coordinates the technical support and integration of technology into instruction. Utilizing 31 years of technical expertise, he ensures that all computers are used to provide meaningful information and increase efficiency. Mr. Roina is also heavily involved in the development of the Sci-Tech Certificate Program, a career focused, advanced learning opportunity with corporate, higher education, and international partnerships. This innovative program offers unique opportunities for his students to get ahead in the world of information technology, thereby providing them a better, brighter outlook on the future. Mr. Roina's long-term objectives are to continue with the Sci-Tech Certificate Program and expand learning opportunities. His advice to others is, "Keep a sense of humor and stay flexible." Eaglecrest High School is an educational facility focused on teaching teenagers. Established in 1990, the School's curriculum carries a strong technical emphasis, specializing in future careers. All teachers are provided training to integrate technology into their teaching. Eaglecrest students, studying general or advanced diploma programs, are given appropriate computer skills to make learning more interesting and challenging. **Career Highlights:** Information Systems Operations Supervisor, Eaglecrest High School (1990-Present); Communications/Technical Specialist, Cherry Creek Schools (1986-89); Instructor, California State University at San Francisco (1975-77); Production Coordinator, KSFO Radio (1969-74). **Associations & Accomplishments:** Colorado Technology in Education Conference. **Education:** University of Colorado at Denver, M.A. (1995). **Personal Information:** Married to Laurie Roina in 1979. Three children: Chris, Luke, and Marybeth. Mr. Roina enjoys music composition and fossil collecting.

Janice M. Sankot

Information Technology Assistant
Parkview Center School
701 West County Road B
Roseville, MN 55113
(651) 487-4360
Fax: (651) 487-4379
jsankot@pcs.roseville.k.12.mn.us

8211

Business Information: As Information Technology Assistant at Parkview Center School, Ms. Sankot handles various aspects of technical operations. Demonstrating impressive technical ability within her role, she oversees all 230 computers within the School. Conducting extensive evaluations, she troubleshoots computers including software applications and related hardware. With excellent communicative skills, Ms. Sankot is able to effectively and accurately instruct the staff and faculty on software used by the School. She is personally responsible for the preparation of manuals and handouts as she prepares the curriculum, translating complex technical terms and concepts into easily understandable material. Attributing success to the guidance and assistance of the people she works with, Ms. Sankot intends to continue in her current role as she assists in the completion of future corporate goals. Established in 1989 in Roseville, Minnesota, Parkview Center School provides instruction for students in kindergarden through grade eight. Over 750 students are led through daily activities by a dedicated, professional staff of 150. The School is part of a district that is responsible for the education of over 6,500 students, and is the only school that houses nine different grades in one building. **Career Highlights:** Information Technology Assistant, Parkview Center School (1995-Present); Roseville Area Schools: Program Assistant (1992-95), Office Clerical (1990-92); Reference Librarian, University of Cincinnati/Raymond Walters College (1987-89). **Associations & Accomplishments:** American Library Association; Michael Servetus Unitarian Society; Mindy Greiling Volunteer Committee (Nuts & Bolts); Virtuous Womens Book Club; Minnesota Public Radio. **Education:** St. Cloud State University (1997); University of Kentucky, M.S. in Library Science (1986); Iowa State University, B.S. in History (1973). **Personal Information:** Married to Jerry J. in 1970. One child: Jennifer A. Ms. Sankot enjoys computers, reading, travel and volunteering.

Dale F. Schaidle

Technology Coordinator
Tremont High School
400 West Pearl Street
Tremont, IL 61568
(309) 925-2051
Fax: (309) 925-3236
dschaidl@roe53.k12.il.us

8211

Business Information: Mr. Schaidle serves as the Technology Coordinator for the Tremont High School. He is responsible for coordinating the local and wide area networks as well as the software for students and faculty. In charge of six computer laboratories, he supervises the administration of 150 computers and the people using them. Mr. Schaidle is currently expanding the School's Internet services and is updating the business functions for the administrative personnel. The respected author of several software books, he strives to remain abreast of changes in the information technology field and has written several software reviews for industry publications. Establishing goals that are compatible with those of the School, Mr. Schaidle strives to provide students with as much technical knowledge as possible. Tremont High School is one of the public schools within the Tremont School District. Providing a quality education to students in grades nine through twelve, the School strives to prepare its students to attain a job after graduation or for studies in a higher educational institution. A staff of 80 administrative, faculty, and support personnel are employed. **Career Highlights:** Tremont High School: Technology Coordinator (1996-Present), Technology Instructor (1978-96). **Associations & Accomplishments:** Illinois Computing Educators; Association for Supervision and Curriculum Development; Kappa Delta Pi. **Education:** St. Xavier University, M.A. (1999). **Personal Information:** Married to Susan in 1977. Three children: Justin, Corrine, and Stacie.

Keith N. Schlarb

Director of Management Information Systems
Worthington City Schools
406 East Wilson Bridge Road
Worthington, OH 43085-2370
(614) 883-3130
Fax: (614) 883-3125
csdirec@worthington.k12.oh.us

8211

Business Information: Functioning in public education for 26 years, Mr. Schlarb presently serves as Director of Management Information Systems for the Worthington City Schools. In this capacity, he provides management oversight of all technical aspects of computer technology and management software applications for Worthington City Schools. Mr. Schlarb has strong leadership skills in supervising a 16-person staff. The network systems which he coordinates include 23 Novell LANs, WAN connectivity, UNIX systems with approximately 3.000 nodes comprised of Pcs and Macs. The networks are used by over 11,000 students and staff. A widely respected professional, Mr. Schlarb directs district level technology plans while identifying and outlining program development needs for management software. This includes development, training, and support of in-house software used to maintain student and human resource information. Always alert to opportunities, his long-term goal is to advance professionally in the realm of management information systems. A city school system, the Worthington City Schools, provides educational services for approximately 10,500 students. Facilities available for education include twelve elementary schools, four middle schools, two high schools, one special education center, and an alternative school which serves 150 students. **Career Highlights:** Worthington City Schools: Director of Management Information Systems (1980-Present), Teacher (1974-80). **Education:** Ohio State: M.A. (1979), B.S. (1973). **Personal Information:** Married to Cindy in 1974. Two children: Evan and Jonathan. Mr. Schlarb enjoys spending time with his family and doing web database design.

Martha F. Schlosser

Library Media Specialist
Truman High School
3301 South Noland Road
Independence, MO 64055
(816) 521-2710
Fax: (816) 521-2924
mscholosser@indep.k12.mo.us

8211

Business Information: Displaying her superior technical talents in this specialized position, Mrs. Schlosser serves as a Library Media Specialist for Truman High School. She provides training in information technology, problem solving, and research skills. In addition, she fulfills the responsibility of a technical librarian who works with computers, machines, systems software, and videos. Working with students and teachers on finding and analyzing information also fall within the purview of her responsibilities. Proud of her many accomplishments, Mrs. Schlosser was instrumental in securing a $300,000 grant for the School. Her plans for the future include continuing in her position and accessing more on-line information for the use of the students. Truman High School is an educational institution teaching grades nine through twelve and enrolls 1,700 students yearly. Designated a blue ribbon school, it received the 1995 Technology Award. Special courses are taught in computer troubleshooting and electronic research. Established in 1964, Truman High School is located in Independence, Missouri and staffs 120 administrative, teaching, and support personnel who work diligently to enhance and perfect educational opportunities for the youth. **Career Highlights:** Library Media Specialist, Truman High School (1979-Present); Library Assistant, University of Missouri Libraries (1976-79). **Associations & Accomplishments:** American Association of School Librarians; American Library Association; Missouri Association of School Libraries; Greater Kansas City Association of School Libraries. **Education:** Lesley College, M.A. (1982); University of Missouri at Kansas City, B.A. **Personal Information:** Married to Doug in 1982. Two children: Holly Elfanbaum and Cindy Owens. Mrs. Schlosser enjoys travel, duplicate bridge and hiking.

Bruce R. Schwartz

Director of Computing and Information Systems
The Principia
13201 Clayton Road
St. Louis, MO 63131
(314) 275-3500
Fax: (314) 275-3534
brs@prin.edu

8211

Business Information: As Director of Computing and Information Systems, Mr. Schwartz provides direction to the technical departments within The Principia. To do so, he must effectively ascertain the needs of each individual department, then purchase the necessary software or hardware for the required improvement. After installation, he then provides support and maintenance for whatever issues may arise. Additionally, he upgrades all computer systems and maintains the satellite campus' WAN connection. An innovative thinker, who always finds creative, technical solutions to challenges, Mr. Schwartz is involved in a four year plan to replace all computers, with the current equipment being donated to area schools. Enjoying the prominence of his position, he intends to continue in his current capacity, focusing on the technical education of the faculty to further quality education. The Principia is a private school for sons and daughters of Christian Scientists, comprised of a college prep high school, a small liberal arts college, and housing units for all students. Adhering strictly to the mission statement, which states the main priority of the School is to serve the cause of Christian Science through the education of the whole man, the School provides countless opportunities for social, mental, and physical growth. **Career Highlights:** The Principia: Director of Computing and Information Systems (1981-Present), Dean of Boys (1972-81); Army Security Agency, United States Army (1966-71). **Associations & Accomplishments:** Dads' Club Representative; Named to Who's Who in the Midwest; Governing Board, Local Church; Sunday School Teacher; Commissioner, Local Wildlife Commission. **Education:** University of Maryland, Business degree (1971); University of Missouri, Managerial Communications; Washington University, graduate courses; New York Institute, Modern Photography degree. **Personal Information:** Married to Diane in 1968. Two children: Christine and Brie Anne. Mr. Schwartz enjoys photography.

Donna E. Slusher

Network Administrator
Floyd Public Schools
140 Harris Hart Road
Floyd, VA 24091
(540) 745-9400
Fax: (540) 745-9496
slusherd@floyd.k12.va.us

8211

Business Information: Functioning in the role of Network Administrator for the Floyd Public Schools, Ms. Slusher assumes responsibility for the administration for all of the Schools' network and individual computers. She oversees all day-to-day administration and operational activities of the systems infrastructure. A systems expert, Ms. Slusher is in charge of setting up the information systems and network environment in the Schools, providing both students and teachers with the required training and education to use and work networks and computers. Coordinating resources, time lines, schedules, and assignments; overseeing the systems budget; and tuning software tools to enhance the overall systems performance is also an integral part of her responsibilities. Ms. Slusher performs the network maintenance, installing software upgrades as necessary and monitoring systems activity. Enjoying her work in the educational system, she plans to continue in her current position. Providing a quality education for students in grades kindergarten through 12th grade, Floyd Public Schools serves the residents of Floyd, Virginia. Approximately 200 administrative, teaching, and support personnel are employed to provide the youthful students with the best in educational opportunities for their future in tomorrow's world. **Career Highlights:** Network Administrator, Floyd Public Schools (1991-Present); Partner, Hubbell Lighting (1978-81). **Associations & Accomplishments:** Guard Instructor, Floyd County High School Band; Floyd Baptist Church. **Education:** New River Community College, B.S. (1995). **Personal Information:** Married to F. M. Jr. in 1980. Two children: Joseph and Logan.

Lisa A. Snare

Technology Technician
ACCS @ St. Mary Site
1400 4th Avenue
Altoona, PA 11602
(814) 944-1250
Fax: (814) 942-0894
stmarys@aasdcat.com

8211

Business Information: As Technology Technician of ACCS @ St. Mary Site, Ms. Snare oversees the computer laboratory and classroom computers. She also works closely with the students with AR and CCC programs. Years of academic ties and 11 years of experience in the field has enabled Ms. Snare to acquire her extensive skills and knowledge necessary to fulfill her technical responsibilities. Her fundamental objectives are to help students become computer literate at a young age and be available to answer any questions and resolve current computer application issues. Ms. Snare hopes that her positon will allow her to acquire a position in the corporate arena, gaining greater authority and responsibility. She strives for professional success to set a positive example for her children as well as to achieve her personal goals. Established in 1889, ACCS @ St. Mary Site is an elementary school offering an educational atmosphere to students grades pre-kindergarten through fifth. A variety of courses and programs are offered to students. The School provides a specifically designed curriculum to meet the individual needs of students. A staff of 15 people are readily available to assist students in their scholastic activities. **Career Highlights:** Technology Technician, ACCS @ St. Mary Site (1994-Present); Grant Eagle: Assistant Office Manager (1992-94), Cheese Shoppe Manager (1989-92). **Associations & Accomplishments:** American Legion; Fraternal Order of Eagles. **Education:** AAVTS, Certificate in Computer Programming (1980). **Personal Information:** Two children: Justin Michael and Justine Elisabeth. Ms. Snare enjoys crafts, swimming, hunting, boating and skiing.

Juan H. Sustaita

Teacher
Keys Academy
2809 North 7th Street
Harlingen, TX 78550
(956) 427-3220
Fax: (956) 427-3223
drsus12@hotmail.com

8211

Business Information: Serving as a Teacher with Keys Academy, Mr. Sustaita demonstrates his expertise in the computer field in his taught courses in keyboarding and business computer information systems. Maintaining the hardware and software of computers provided by the Academy, he also provides troubleshooting services and trains the faculty in how to use these systems. The most rewarding aspect of his career is publishing articles in business magazines on computer education. Highly regarded, he was also named "Teacher of the Year," while employed at a military school. Continuing in his career with Keys Academy, Mr. Sustaita has goals to expand the distance learning program, attain his Ph.D. in computers, and then teach at a collegiate level. His success is attributed to his insatiable curiosity and being very analytical. Established in 1991, Keys Academy is an educational institution providing general and specialized course instruction for individuals at risk of not graduating. The Academy staffs 30 administrative, teaching, and support personnel who work diligently to enhance and perfect educational opportunities for its youth. Concentrating on meeting the needs of its students, the Academy provides a four year program, enrolling 300 and offering internet access and distance learning capabilities. **Career Highlights:** Teacher, Keys Academy (1993-Present); Chairman, OST Department, Austin Community College (1990-92); Computer Teacher, Austin School District (1989-90). **Associations & Accomplishments:** Texas Computer Education Association; Texas Business Education Association. **Education:** University of Texas at Austin, Post Graduate (1985-90); University of North Texas at Denton, Master's degree in Business Education; Texas A&I University at Kingsville, B.S. in English and Business Education. **Personal Information:** Mr. Sustaita enjoys raising Shih-tzu puppies, gardening and reading.

Carl Thomas

Network Administrator/Webmaster
St. Labre Indian School
1000 Tongue River Road
Ashland, MT 59003
(406) 784-4500
Fax: (406) 784-6161
cthomas@stlabre.org

8211

Business Information: Functioning in the dual capacity of Network Administrator and Webmaster of St. Labre Indian School, Mr. Thomas is responsible for installation and maintenance of local area network hardware and software, including troubleshooting network usage and computer peripherals. Before joining St. Labre in 1998, Mr. Thomas served as an independent VB Consultant. His professional success reflects his ability to think out-of-the-box and take on new challenges. An expert, he oversees and directs repairs and assembly of computers and peripherals, as well as maintains the networking environment for all three campus locations. Providing technical and analytical support to more than 300 users, Mr. Thomas' prime focus is on maintaining the functionality and fully operational status of the systems infrastructure. Designing Web sites, performing system backups and data recovery, acquiring hardware and software, and resolving communications problems also fall within the realm of Mr. Thomas' responsibilities. Obtaining his CNE certification serves as one of his future goals. St. Labre Indian School is an nonprofit educational ministry affiliated with the Roman Catholic Church. Regional in scope, the Ministry is headquartered in Ashland, Montana. Established in 1884, St. Labre operates a network of three locations manned by more than 300 people. **Career Highlights:** Network Administrator/Webmaster, St. Labre Indian (1998-Present); VB Consultant (1997-98). **Education:** Northern Michigan State University, B.A. (1997); Miles Community College, A.A.S. in Small Computer Systems. **Personal Information:** Married to Judy in 1966. Three children: Tina, Thomas, and Brian. Mr. Thomas enjoys spending time with his family and grandchildren.

Michael J. Thompson

Agri-Technology Teacher
Glades Central High School
1001 Southwest Avenue M
Belle Glade, FL 33430
(561) 993-4445
Fax: (561) 993-4414
thompson_m@firn.edu

8211

Business Information: Serving as Agri-Technology Teacher at Glades Central High School, Mr. Thompson handles the instruction of students in both agricultural science and technology. Demonstrating an extensive knowledge of the industry, he serves as network administrator of over 745 computers and 6 servers. Lending his knowledge to students, he directs satellite distance learning programs to assist in the education of non-traditional students. Recognized for his valuable contributions to the field, Mr. Thompson is the receipient of prestigious awards such as the William T. Dyer certificate. Attributing his success to his ability to focus and a strong commitment to achieve, Mr. Thompson looks forward to continued advancement in his field as he furthers his education. Glades Central High School offers educational instruction to over 1,500 students in grades nine through twelve. Recognized throughout the community as an excellent insititution, the School boasts consecutive football champion titles, Black History Brain Bowl Champions, and dozens of other academia awards. **Career Highlights:** Agri-Technology Teacher, Glades Central High School (1983-Present); Agricultural Teacher, Fort Pierce Central High School (1981-83); Assistant Director of Agricultural and Weather Center, University of Kentucky (1979-81). **Associations & Accomplishments:** National Association of Agriculture Educators; Florida Association of Agriculture Educators; Palm Beach County School District Technology Standards Task Force; Technology In-Service Steering Committee. **Education:** University of Kentucky: M.S. (1979), B.S. (1976). **Personal Information:** One child: Nancy. Mr. Thompson enjoys hydroponic gardening, scuba diving and horse training. Mr. Thompson is the proud grandfather of three children: David, Rachel, and Jordon.

Allan S. Timmins

Technology Coordinator
Westside Elementary School
5400 Applegate Drive
Spring Hill, FL 34606
(352) 797-7080
Fax: (352) 797-7180

8211

Business Information: Mr. Timmins functions in the role of Technology Coordinator for Westside Elementary School. With the blossoming opportunities presented through the world of computers, he recognized the importance of increasing the School's technology. A 30 year veteran in elementary education, Mr. Timmins developed the overall technical direction and strategy, and today, the School operates a state-of-the-art 200-computer infrastructure. In addition to managing the information systems function, he oversees the in-house television studio. Establishing Internet access, Mr. Timmins' efforts has allowed students to advance their exploration capabilities in all areas of study. Utilizing his extensive skills, he monitors the system and ensures its functionality and operable condition everyday. Looking to the next millennium, Mr. Timmins is encouraged by the positive response the computers have brought to the School and hopes to increase the new opportunities available through technology in the School District. Westside Elementary School is dedicated to the successful education adventure of the young minds of Spring Hill, Florida. The School features a top quality pre-kindergarten class where the youngest students are able to sharpen their skills and prepare for intense classroom studies. Students remain with the School through the fifth grade where, upon completion of the course requirements, they continue their education at the next level. The School also devotes its time to the exploration of extra curricular talents outside of the classroom. **Career Highlights:** Technology Coordinator, Westside Elementary School (1995-Present). **Education:** Massachusetts State College at Lowell, M.Ed. in Administration (1974); Lowell State College, B.S. in Elementary Education (1967).

Stephen Waldeck
Information Systems Instructor
Warsaw Area Career Center
1 Tiger Lane
Warsaw, IN 46580-4807
(219) 267-5174
Fax: (219) 267-5174
basiasplace@kconline.com

8211

Business Information: Utilizing more than 15 years as an educator, Mr. Waldeck serves as Information Systems Instructor for the Warsaw Area Career Center. He teaches students at both the high school and college levels. At the high school level, he teaches C++ and Visual Basic programming. To students enrolled in the local college, Mr. Waldeck provides instruction in systems analysis and design, C++, Visual Basic, and data communications. Complementing his duties at the Warsaw Area Career Center, he also teaches technical courses at the Ivy Tech College. Mr. Waldeck enjoys working with people and teaching them about technology. He plans to continue his work as an educator. His success reflects his ability to deliver results in support of educational objectives and aggressively tackle new challenges and responsibilities. Warsaw Area Career Center provides educational opportunities for high school students in grades 9 through 12, as well as local college students. The Center assists the students in determining a career path and teaches them the basic job skills of their chosen field of study. **Career Highlights:** Information Systems Instructor, Warsaw Area Career Center (1984-Present); Information Systems Instructor, Ivy Technical College (1985-Present); Systems Analysis Consultant/Web Designer, Agogic Vision, Inc. (1998-Present). **Associations & Accomplishments:** President Elect, Indiana Business Education Association; National Business Education Association; Vice President, Warsaw Community Education Association; District Coordinator, Business Professionals of America. **Education:** Ball State University: M.A.E. (1987), Vocational Endorsement (1987), Data/Info Processing Endorsement (1987), two Bachelor's degrees in Business Education (1984). **Personal Information:** Mr. Waldeck enjoys gardening, computers and his pets.

Norma E. Welsh
Project Coordination Manager
GV-WFL EduTech
131 Drumlin Court
Newark, NY 14513
(315) 332-7250
Fax: (315) 331-7045
nwelsh@edutech.org.

8211

Business Information: Acting as the chief liaison between 47 school districts and GV-WFL EduTech, Ms. Welsh fulfills the responsibility of Project Coordination Manager. She works directly with the technical coordinators from each school to evaluate and determine needs and construct long-term arrangements. She believes the key to success is to remain active by attending seminars and gaining knowledge from a variety of sources. As a topnotch 20-year technology professional, she is also responsible for determining and coordinating future resource requirements; overseeing time lines, schedules, assignments; and calculating and managing the technology fiscal year budget. In addition to her duties with EduTech, Ms. Welsh serves as a Lieutenant Colonel in the field of intelligence for the New York Air National Guard. Her goal is to expand her role in the technology departments of the schools and increase development. Ms. Welsh's success reflects her adaptability and excellent people skills. Working for the education of students, GV-WFL EduTech provides 47 suburban school districts with technical solutions, counseling, and support. Employing a staff of 100, EduTech plans, orders, installs, services, and supports the necessary computer equipment for the schools. The Service continues to provide opportunities for the staff to become knowledgeable in the information systems field. **Career Highlights:** Project Coordination Manager, GV-WFL EduTech (1997-Present); Lieutenant Colonel/Chief of Intel, 107 Air Refuel Wing, New York Air National Guard (Present); Technology Trainer, GV-WFL EduTech (1993-97); Technology Specialist, WFL

Teacher Resource Center (1986-91). **Education:** State University of New York at Potsdam, B.A. in Mathematics (1978); Texas A&M, degree in Meteorology; State University of New York at Genesco, degree in Education. **Personal Information:** Married to Timothy. Ms. Welsh enjoys golf, bowling and reading.

Rachel A. West
Systems Engineer
Carlsbad Municipal School District
408 North Canyon Street
Carlsbad, NM 88220
(505) 234-3300
westr@carlsbad.k12.nm.us

8211

Business Information: Mrs. West demonstrates strategic systems and technology expertise while serving as Systems Engineer for the Carlsbad Municipal School District. In this capacity, she is accountable for the design and implementation of state-of-the-art networks. In addition, Mrs. West draws on over nine solid years of practical experience and a firm academic background in assuming the responsibilities of Systems Administrator. In this context, she is responsible for the analysis, acquisition, installation, modification, configuration, support, and tracking of operating systems, e-mail and Web servers, databases, server utilities, software, and hardware. Mrs. West's goals include becoming a Cisco Certified Internet Engineer. She attributes her success to her mentors, Cecil Thomas, Bill Behner, and Praveen Talum. Carlsbad Municipal School District provides a full-range of educational services in grades K-12. Professional development programs and staff support is provided for teachers and administrators. Presently, the District employs 730 people to serve the educational needs of the Carlsbad Municipal School District. **Career Highlights:** Systems Engineer, Carlsbad Municipal School District (1995-Present); Systems Analyst, Westinghouse Electric Corporation (1991-95); Technician I, Peak Technical (1990-91). **Associations & Accomplishments:** 4-H Leader; Organizational Leader for Canyon Kids 4-H Club. **Education:** Thomas Edison State College, B.A. (1995); New Mexico State University, Associate's degree in Business; Microsoft Certified Professional; Microsoft Certified Systems Engineer. **Personal Information:** Married to Richard G. in 1979. Three children: Thomas, Michael, and Christopher. Mrs. West enjoys rancing, 4-H, studying space, stars and constellations.

Thomas A. Wiewiora
SAP Systems Manager
Holland Hitch Company
467 Ottawa Avenue
Holland, MI 49423
(616) 396-6501
Fax: (616) 396-1511
tom.wierwiora@hollandhitch.com

8211

Business Information: Mr. Wiewiora is SAP Systems Manager for the Holland Hitch Company. Responsible for the technical programming and professional staff, he coordinates the activities of eight personnel to effectively control the information technology systems throughout the offices in Holland, Michigan. His duties include writing several reports and attending a wide variety of meetings to demonstrate the current technology needs of the Company. He and his staff conducts regular analysis of the many computer systems and strives to maintain an operable database with the most up-to-date technology. Having a strong mentor throughout his career, Mr. Wiewiora has been a valuable addition to the team at the Holland Hitch Company. He implemented the SAP program at the Company and is presently working to move all facilities into the SAP systems. Mr. Wierwiora attributes his success to his peers, reading, and keeping on top of new technology. Holland Hitch Company is a manufacturer for the heavy truck transportation industry. Operating within the industry for 85 years, the Company has become the leading manufacturer of coupling fifth wheel landing gear components. The Company supports a staff of 3,500 personnel throughout its 23 manufacturing and distribution centers. Through its production of suspension parts and axles, the Company produces $534 million annually. **Career Highlights:** Holland Hitch Company: SAP Systems Manager (1999-Present), Management Information Systems Manager (1993-99), Database Administrator (1988-93). **Education:** Grand Valley State University, M.S. in Computer Information Systems (1991); Western Michigan University, B.S. in Computer Science (1985); Grand Rapids Community College, A.S. (1981). **Personal Information:** Married to Mary Ann in 1986. One child: Haley Elizabeth. Mr. Wiewiora enjoys water sports and running.

Teresa Wilkins
Technology Coordinator/Assistant Principal
Our Lady of Mount Carmel School
1706 Old Eastern Avenue
Baltimore, MD 21221-2203
(410) 686-1023

8211

Business Information: Mrs. Wilkins fulfills a variety of responsiblities within the educational structure of Our Lady of Mount Carmel School as she serves the roles of Technology Coordinator and Assistant Principal. Demonstrating adept technical ability, she handles technical troubleshooting with ease as she maintains hardware and software resources. Utilizing superior communicative skills, Mrs. Wilkins leads upperclass students through technology courses as she offers insight and guidance to solve their questions. Working closely with staff members, she ensures each instructor is adequately familiar with operating systems and software. Recognized as an authority within her field, Mrs. Wilkins recently spoke at the White House during a press briefing as she represented the 21st Century Teachers Organization. Citing a supportive staff and strong dedication as the keys to her success, Mrs. Wilkins intends to continue in her current role as she furthers the use of technology in the classroom. Baltimore, Maryland is home to Our Lady of Mount Carmel School, a co-educational Catholic school that provides educational instruction for 700 students from grades pre-kindergarten to 12. The Parish was established in the early 1900s with an elementary school following closely in 1920; the more modern version of the current School was developed in 1959. **Career Highlights:** Our Lady of Mount Carmel School: Technology Coordinator (1994-Present), Assistant Principal (1998-Present), Faculty Member (1983-Present). **Associations & Accomplishments:** Maryland Chapter Leader, 21st Century Teachers Organization; Maryland Instructional Computer Coordinators Association; National Catholic Educators Association; Tandy Technology Teacher. **Education:** Loyola College: M.M.S. (1990), B.A. (1982). **Personal Information:** Married to Harry in 1982. Three children: Stephanie, Charlotte, and Trey. Mrs. Wilkins enjoys travel, reading and politics.

John R. Yarrow
Executive Director, Applications and Operations
Richardson Independent School District
400 South Greenville Avenue
Richardson, TX 75081
(972) 705-2121
Fax: (972) 301-3443
jyarrow@tenet.edu

8211

Business Information: As Executive Director of Applications and Operations of Richardson Independent School District, Mr. Yarrow retains responsibility for the completion of daily objectives. Demonstrating adept technical abilities, he maintains smooth operation of the network by carefully conducting observation of systems. He monitors the computers, help desk, and telecommunication activities, contributing to the overall effectiveness of the District. Directing his staff with a proactive management style, Mr. Yarrow is able to incorporate employee feedback and input into the creation of standard operating proceudres as he fosters a sense of teamwork and empowerment. Recognized for impressive accomplishments in the field, he attributes professional success to his skills and luck of timing in the industry. Attending countless seminars and conferences, he is able to keep abreast of current technological changes and updates. Mr. Yarrow aspires to become the Chief Information Officer of the District or a large business. His advice is "learn project management." Richardson Independent School District provides educational instruction for nearly 35,000 students in grades kindergarden through 12. Encompassing several suburbs in the Dallas area, the District offers traditional education with progressive twists such as computers in the classroom and applied technology classes. The District employs 4,500 highly trained people to assist in the completion of District objectives. **Career Highlights:** Executive Director of Applications and Operations, Richardson Independent School District (1997-Present); Director of Technology, Grand Independent School District (1995-97); Technology Coordinator, White Settlement Independent School District (1994-95). **Associations & Accomplishments:** Texas Computer Education Association. **Education:** University of North Texas, Master's degree (1994). **Personal Information:** Married to Leanne in 1987. Three children: Hope, Olivia, and Myles. Mr. Yarrow enjoys sports, reading and writing.

Dennis A. Yoshimura

Director of Technology
Johnston Community School District
6600 Northwest 62nd Avenue
Johnston, IA 50131
(515) 278-0470
Fax: (515) 278-0470
dyosh@johnston.k12.ia.us

8211

Business Information: Mr. Yoshimura has been Director of Technology for the Johnston Community School District since 1991. When he began in this position, there was merely one computer laboratory of Apple 2E and Mac Plus computers available to the students. Since that time, Mr. Yoshimura has incorporated many new programs and began the transition to Windows and NT servers. He is in the process of bringing in a digital analog line and a dual satellite dish. He is very proud to have established the Iowa Communications Network or ICN to every school building in the entire school district. Mr. Yoshimura is looking forward to increasing the number of computers in the School District and wants to see a minimum of six in each classroom. He will continually update the systems and implement new programs in an effort to familiarize and prepare students for the technology of today. Johnston Community School District provides a quality public education for students in Kindergarten through 12th grade. The School District offers interactive learning for students across the state via telemetric cameras, ICN sites, and laser disc players. Advanced placement programs are available for foreign language teachers. The only one of its kind in Iowa, these programs are provided through an ATM backbone with a fiberoptic line. Students in the school use Macintosh and IBM compatible computers. **Career Highlights:** Johnston Community School District: Director of Technology (1996-Present), Technology Coordinator (1993-96), Technology Consultant (1991-93), Teacher (1974-93); Captain, United States Air Force (1968-72). **Associations & Accomplishments:** Co-chairman of Evaluations, Iowa Technology and Education Connection; International Society for Technology in Education; Association for Supervision and Curriculum Development; Iowa Association for Supervision and Curriculum Development; Iowa Distant Learning Association; Deacon/Board Member, Local Church. **Education:** Drake University, M.M.E. (1974). **Personal Information:** Married to Margaret Ann in 1974. Three children: David, Scott, and Michelle. Mr. Yoshimura enjoys playing the trumpet.

Samer S. Abusoud

Information Systems Director
Washington University
4444 Forest Park, Campus Box 8505
St. Louis, MO 63108
(314) 286-1600
Fax: (314) 286-1601
samer@ot-link.wustl.edu

8221

Business Information: Providing his skilled services as Information Systems Director of Washington University, Mr. Abusoud oversees the operations of all of the information systems used by the University in its various departments. As a five year technology professional, he sets the overall technical direction and educational contribution of the information systems function. He ensures that the servers are running at optimum level, monitoring its activity and that of the system users. Searching the Internet, he finds and downloads the latest program updates, installing those and other software upgrades to improve efficiency. Mr. Abusoud administers the helpdesk and departmental databases. Coordinating resources, schedules, time lines, and assignments, as well as the fiscal year budget for the Information Systems Department also fall within the purview of his responsibilities. He anticipates further managerial promotions as a result of his continuing efforts to increase his skills through training and professional development activities. Washington University is a higher educational facility dedicated to fulfilling its core mission of path breaking medical research in such areas as Occupational Therapy. A private, four-year, coed, liberal arts and specialized university, Washington University was established in 1853, and is located on a 169 acre, suburban campus in St. Louis, Missouri. **Career Highlights:** Washington University: Information Systems Director (1998-Present), Manager of Information Technology (1994-97). **Associations & Accomplishments:** Certified Novell Engineer. **Education:** SIUC Carbondale, B.S. in Finance (1993). **Personal Information:** Mr. Abusoud enjoys being a Triathlete.

Leah Dawn Baker-Cross

Senior Systems Analyst
University of Nebraska
6001 Dodge Street, Epply, Room 110
Omaha, NE 68182-0051
(402) 554-3751
Fax: (402) 554-3475
lcorss@mail.unomaha.edu

8221

Business Information: Displaying her expertise in the demanding field of information technology, Mrs. Baker-Cross serves as Senior Systems Analyst for the University of Nebraska at Omaha. She assumes all responsibility for design and support of the student's information system, communications support, and hands-on financial aid on campus. Coordinating the monthly focus user group, she is also a part-time instructor for information technology systems and teaches mainframe spreadsheets, C++, word processing, and the Internet. Keeping abreast of new developments in the industry through reading and self-study, she attributes her success to support from family and friends, the community, and church organizations. Mrs. Baker-Cross served proudly in the United States Army for eight years and was among the first women to receive instruction in the communications security field. Continuing to further her education, she is learning Web programming tools and looks forward to advancing to the next level of management within the University's structure. The University of Nebraska at Omaha is a higher educational institution dedicated to providing students with a quality education that will assist them in all areas of their lives. Established in 1909, the University has grown in size as well as student body in its 90 years of operation. Consisting of three seperate campuses, the University of Nebraska offers a wide variety of degrees, disciplines, certifications, and course studies. **Career Highlights:** Senior Systems Analyst, University of Nebraska at Omaha (1993-Present); Senior Systems Analyst, Mutual of Omaha (1978-92); Staff Sergeant, United States Army (1964-72). **Associations & Accomplishments:** Association of Computing Machinery; State Officer, Disabled Veterans Auxiliary. **Education:** University of Nebraska at Omaha: M.S. (In Progress), Bachelor's degree in General Studies. **Personal Information:** Married to Howard in 1966. One child: Jon Carter. Mrs. Baker-Cross enjoys reading, sewing and crochet.

Sudip Bhattacharjee, Ph.D.

Assistant Professor
University of Connecticut
School of Business Administration, 2100 Hillside Road, U41 IM
Storrs, CT 06269
(860) 486-1274
Fax: (860) 486-4839
sudip@sba.uconn.edu

8221

Business Information: An Assistant Professor at the University of Connecticut, Dr. Bhattacharjee influences the lives of over 200 students annually through his graduate and undergraduate programs. He is responsible for day to day operations and information management at the University's School of Business Administration. Respected and highly regarded, Dr. Bhattacharjee specializes in basic and applied research regarding the information systems and technology, as well as electronic commerce. He is also involved in research, analysis of information and new methodologies, teaching, and serving on several committees. Dr. Bhattacharjee is honored to be associated with this prestigious University, and is currently working towards status as a tenured professor. The University of Connecticut, centrally located in Storrs, Connecticut, is home to well over 28,000 students, and is prided as being regarded as the only public research facility in the state. Offering several degree programs, the University of Connecticut draws students from around the globe to experience the educational services offered within. Established in 1850, the University is a prominent institution of higher education, employing the skill and honor of more than 5,000 professors, administrators, and educational professionals. **Career Highlights:** Assistant Professor, University of Connecticut (1998-Present); Research Assistant/Instructor, State University of New York at Buffalo (1992-98); Projects Executive, Shaw Wallace & Company, India (1990-92). **Associations & Accomplishments:** Association of Information Systems; Beta Gamma Sigma; Omega Rho; Certified Novell Netware Administrator; President, School of Management Ph.D. Association; Chairman, Student Teaching Review Committee; House Captain, High School; Who's Who Among Students in American Universities and Colleges (1996). **Education:** State University of New York at Buffalo, Ph.D. (1999); Indian Institute of Technology, Bachelor's degree in Mechanical Engineering with Honors. **Personal Information:** Married to Sarbari in 1996. One child: Aditya. Dr. Bhattacharjee enjoys building computer systems, travel, soccer and cooking.

Matthew C Burden

Director
Northwestern University
357 East Chicago Avenue, MCB71
Chicago, IL 60611
(312) 503-0193
m-burden@northwestern.edu

8221

Business Information: Mr. Burden serves as the Director for Northwestern University. He is responsible for all computer applications, such as LAN/WAN, database, client server, and Web development for the University's Law School. In addition, he provides support and administration for information technology functions and ensures the functionality and operational status of the systems infrastructure. Before joining the University, Mr. Burden served with Boise Cascade Office Products as ITSS Supervisor and Operations Supervisor. His background also includes eight years of military service with the U.S. Army. Mr. Burden attributes his success to having very good mentors. In the future, he looks forward to a promotion to vice president or assistant to the chief information officer as well as continuing to learn more about network security. Northwestern University is an institution of higher learning providing general and specialized course instruction for individuals wishing to advance their educational studies. The University is a major college enrolling over 15,000 students yearly. Established in 1854, the University is located in Chicago and staffs more than 1,500 administrative, teaching, and support personnel who work diligently to enhance and perfect educational opportunities for its students. **Career Highlights:** Director, Northwestern University (1999-Present); Boise Cascade Office Products: ITSS Supervisor (1998-99), Operations Supervisor (1996-98); Captain, United States Army (1989-96). **Associations & Accomplishments:** Veterans Foreign Wars; American Legion; Special Forces Association; Reserve Officer Association. **Education:** DePaul University, Information Technology (1998); University of Illinois; University of South Carolina. **Personal Information:** Married to Jennifer in 1997.

Amy L. R. Buse

Computer Resource Manager
Ferris State University
119 South Street
Big Rapids, MI 49307
(231) 591-2415
Fax: (231) 591-2407
busea@ferris.edu

8221

Business Information: Joining Ferris State University as Computer Resource Manager in 1995, Mrs. Buse is responsible for managing computing resources for the University's colleges of business and technology. With more than 18 years of teaching experience, she utilizes her extensive knowledge in the areas of information technology to demonstrate the importance of maintaining comprehensive programs and helpful information. Supervising nine full time computer technicians and seventy students, Mrs. Buse is accountable for controlling and administering the University's computer resources, ensuring computer availability for use by students and the faculty. Her future plans include remaining with the University in order to continue providing excellence and quality in her technical capacity. Ferris State University engages in the provision of higher education for aspiring professionals. The University offers more of a hands-on approach to technology and other majors for a wide selection of degrees and certifications. Established in 1884, the University enrolls a student body of 10,000, while operating out of a location that is the base for several satellite campuses. The University presently functions under the direct guidance and talents of more than 1,500 professional educators who facilitate smooth academic administration on a daily basis. **Career Highlights:** Computer Resource Manager, Ferris State University (1995-Present); Teacher, Augres-Sims Schools (1986-95); Teacher, Jefferson Parish Schools (1982-86). **Associations & Accomplishments:** Leader, Cub Scouts; Leader, Boy Scouts; Leader, Girl Scouts; School Volunteer. **Education:** Central Michigan University: M.S. in Computer Science (1995), B.S. Math with minor in Computer Science (1982). **Personal Information:** Married to Robert C. in 1982. Two children: Jacob and Bridgette.

Mary M. Cagney

Quality Assurance/Editor
Northern Illinois University
926 East Indiana Street
Wheaton, IL 60187
(815) 75306795
mcagney766@aol.com

8221

Business Information: Displaying her extensive skills in this highly specialized position, Ms. Cagney serves as Quality Assurance and Editor for E-Learning Services at Northern Illinois University. She oversees the Web pages and has the final say on Web contents. In addition, she manages educational eligibility, graphics, and audio and video quality as well as creates the Web guide. Ms. Cagney attributes her success to the ability to make the most out of every opportunity and being at the right place at the right time. Her future plans include achieving a position working with an Internet service provider. E-Learning Services at Northern Illinois University provides Internet services. The University is a four-year college and offers graduate and doctorate degrees. The University is located in Dekalb, Illinois and employs skilled teachers, counselors, and administrative personnel who utilize their professional abilities to provide an excellent education for students. **Career Highlights:** Quality Assurance/Editor, Northern Illinois University (2000-Present); E-Web Developer/Editor, E-Learning Services (1999-2000); Correspondent, Religion New Service (1998); Editor/Writer, Christianity Today (1997-98). **Associations & Accomplishments:** Chicago Council on Foreign Relations. **Education:** Northern Illinois University, M.Ed. (2000); Wheaton College, M.A. in Communications; University College Dublin, B.Sc. in Physics and Math. **Personal Information:** Ms. Cagney enjoys reading the "New York Times" newspaper. His quote is "the truth is always the strongest argument."

Clay B. Carley III

Assistant Professor
East Central University
Rural Road 7, Box 193D
Ada, OK 74820
(580) 310-5659
cbc@cs3.ecok.edu

8221

Business Information: Starting his diverse computer background in the United States Navy, Mr. Carley moved into the private sector in 1988. Manuvering throughout the private work force, he now serves as Assistant Professor of East Central University. Here, Mr. Carley teaches software engineering and design, computer literacy, and programming one as well as object oriented programming. However, in the fall of 2000, he will be adding another course of study to include computer architecture. Having received numerous awards throughout his career, Mr. Carley is currently pursuing a Doctorate in Computer Science, which will enable him to advance in the fields of research and computer publishing. His professional success reflects is ability to think out-side-the-box and tackle challenges and deliver results. A branch of the Okalahome University system, East Central University is a midwestern educational institution. Established in the late 1800s, the Institution offers Bachelor's and Master's degrees. Employing approximately 500 staff members, East Central University is well known for the foreign exchange students program. **Career Highlights:** Assistant Professor, East Central University (1998-Present); Programmer/Analyst, Jack Henry & Associates (1996-98); Business Systems Delivery Specialist, Aetna Life and Casualty (1990-96); Consultant/Programmer, The Systems Group (1988-90). **Associations & Accomplishments:** Association of Computing Machinery; SIG for Computer Science Education; Head of Competitions Committee, Marlborough Fife & Drum Corps; Committee Member, Colonel John Chester Fife & Drum 50th Anniversary. **Education:** Rensselaer Polytechnic Institute, M.S. in Computer Science (1997); Sonoma State University, B.A. in Mathematics (1970). **Personal Information:** Married to Leslie M. in 1977. Two children: Clay (Scott) B. IV and Colin B. Mr. Carley enjoys programming, coin collecting and raising quail.

James Anthony Castaldi

Instructor
The Chubb Institute
8 Sylvan Way
Parsippany, NJ 07054
(973) 971-3027
Fax: (973) 656-2761
Jcataldi@chubb.com

8221

Business Information: As an Instructor at The Chubb Institute, Mr. Castaldi fulfills a number of duties on behalf of the Institute and the student body. He is responsible for teaching his students computer science and applications as well as programming. Possessing an excellent understanding of technology, Mr. Castaldi ensures each student receives the required training to be able to effectively deploy their technology skills in the corporate world to the benefit management and users. Highly regarded, he provides support for logic structure using C++, DB2, Oracle, HTML, and Java as well as Novell and Windows 98 platforms. The most rewarding aspect of his career is the development of a telemarketing software to tract number of calls and sales. Dedicated to the success of the Institute and its students, Mr. Castaldi plans to continue to provide his services in the years to come. He aspires to eventually attain the position of director. Located in Parsippany, New Jersey, The Chubb Institute is a school for computer programming. Established in 1970, the Institute employs the skill and expertise of more than 500 personnel. The Institute is dedicated to providing students with an education which will be of use in today's constantly advancing technological world. **Career Highlights:** Instructor, The Chubb Institute (1996-Present); Project Leader, Reed Reference Publishing (1994-96); Senior System, GAF Corporation (1995-96). **Education:** Fairleigh Dickinson University, M.B.A. (1981); University of Miami at Coral Gables, B.A.; The Chubb Institute (1977). **Personal Information:** Married to Eilleen in 1972. Two children: Nathan and Leah. Mr. Castaldi enjoys theater and ballet.

Ferdinand T. Chew

Program Coordinator
Texas A&M University, Texas Engineering Extension Services
1525 East 29th Street, Apartment 404
Bryan, TX 77802-1415
(409) 845-8605
fchew@computer.org

8221

Business Information: Mr. Chew joined the Texas A&M University System's Texas Engineering Extension Service in 1992, and over the last six years, has provided extensive consulting work on information technology. In the capacity of a Program Coordinator, his duties include reviewing and analyzing technological equipment and processes for commercial use, identifying and evaluating software, and analyzing business processes for improvement through use of information technology services. Mr. Chew is always alert to new opportunities and will be transferring to the largest information technology and management consulting company, Andersen Consulting. Established in 1919, the Texas Engineering Extension Service provides training and consulting on state-of-the-art space and information technology for the National Aeronautics and Space Agency, Department of Defense, National Institute of Standards and Technology, and the Department of Energy. Texas Engineering Extension Service employs a staff of 500 individuals capable of providing educational and technical services to 75,800 students. Headquartered in College Station, the Institute generates over $55 million in revenues. **Career Highlights:** Texas A&M University, Texas Engineering Extension Services: Program Coordinator (1995-Present), Senior Manager (1994-95), Manager (1992-94). **Associations & Accomplishments:** Associate Member, Institute of Electrical and Electronics Engineers; Reservist Officer, Singapore Armed Forces. **Education:** Texas A&M University: M.S. in Electrical Engineering in Computers (1997), M.B.A. in Management Information Systems (1991); Wayne State University, B.Sc. in Electrical Engineering, cum laude; Singapore Polytechnic, Diploma in Electrical Engineering. **Personal Information:** Mr. Chew enjoys travel, movies and classical music.

Kristine U. Chua

Assistant Director of Academic Services
Columbia University Law School
435 West 116th Street
New York, NY 10027-7297
(212) 854-2669
Fax: (212) 854-1135
kchua@law.columbia.edu

8221

Business Information: Serving in the role of Assistant Director of Academic Services of Columbia University Law School, Ms. Chua oversees coordination of all student records on multiple computer systems, develops and maintains integrity and reliability of the Department's database, and designs and develops advanced software applications. Before coming on board to the University in 1994, she served as Research Assistant of Phil Institute for Development Studies. Ms. Chua's intense curiosity influenced her interest in her particular field, and after six years of sharpening her skills and enhancing her abilities, she is endeavoring to create a special, more high-tech and digitized, database for the Department. Success is attributed to Ms. Chua's ability to take on challenges and positive deliver results. Founded in 1754, Columbia University is an institute of higher learning, which is located in New York. The University's enrollment stands at approximately 3,800 students per year who engage in either a three-year general study program or a one-year master's program. Columbia University has, regionally, over 10,000 employees who work in various branches, such as The Foundation of Engineering and Applied Science and the Columbia University Law School. **Career Highlights:** Columbia University Law School: Assitant Director of Academic Services (1999-Present), Administrator (1994-99); Research Assistant, Phi Institute for Development Studies. **Associations & Accomplishments:** Philippine Economics Society; International Honor Society of Pi Kappa Phi; Pi Gamma Mu Honor Society. **Education:** Columbia University Teachers College, M.A. (In Progress); Columbia University Graduate School of Arts and Sciences, Economics Department: Ph.D. Candidate (1991-96), Master's degree in Philosophy (1991), M.A. (1998); University of the Philippines, B.A. (1996).

Galen R. Collins

Associate Professor/Associate Dean
Northern Arizona University
2631 North Elk Run Street
Flagstaff, AZ 86004-7607
(520) 523-7333
Fax: (520) 523-1711
galen.collins@ndu.edu

8221

Business Information: Mr. Collins serves in the dual role of Associate Professor and Associate Dean at Northern Arizona University's School of Hotel and Restaurant Management. Since the inception of the School, he has been responsible for maintaining the fluid operation of the academic unit and distance learning initiatives. He is responsible for managing the information technology curriculum and planning and deploying technology resources. Possessing an excellent understanding of his field, Mr. Collins successfully developed the first Web course in the United States on hospitality information technology. Highly regarded, he consistently displays his extensive experience in the development, implementation, evaluation, and selection of industry and educational systems. He is an advisory board member for several hospitality-related companies, has published a text on hospitality information technology, and has been recognized in several journals. Mr. Collins is an approved information technology expert for Giga Information Systems. He attributes his success to his academic ties and ability to take on challenges and deliver results. Northern Arizona University is an institution of higher learning. This facility provides quality education and degrees in various areas of study. Establishing itself as a leader in the educational community, Northern Arizona University offers its students a variety of extra curricular activities including fraternities, sororities, clubs, and athletics. Continuing to provide superior learning opportunities to more than 20,000 students, Northern Arizona University plans to further expand its research and development areas to accommodate a growing student body and technological advances. **Career Highlights:** Northern Arizona University: Associate Professor/Associate Dean (1999-Present), Associate Professor/Assistant Dean (1992-96); Assistant Professor (1987-92); Chairperson, Abacus Internet Services, Inc. Phoenix, Arizona (1996-Present). **Associations & Accomplishments:** Association of Computing Machinery; Founding President (1992-97), Hospitality Information Technology Association; President (1996-97)/Charter Member, Flagstaff Sunrise Lions Club; Hospitals Financial Technology Professional; Publisher, International Journal of Hospitality Information Technology. **Education:** Florida International University, M.S. in Hotel & Food Service Management (1980), B.B.A. (1978). **Personal Information:** Married to Melissa in 1991. One child: Robbie. Mr. Collins enjoys raquetball, painting and golf.

Len Cooley

Director of Computing Services
University of Oregon Athletics
2727 Leo Harris Parkway
Eugene, OR 97401
(541) 346-5474
Fax: (541) 346-0907
lcooley@oregon.uoregon.edu

8221

Business Information: As Director of Computing Services of the University of Oregon Athletics, Mr. Cooley takes charge of specific technology related projects. In addition, he handles the Department's purchasing, upgrading, and telecommunications. One of the Athletic Department's goals is to have football games casted live on the Internet and with the new existing scoreboard, to offer video feed such as plays of the game. Mr. Cooley is currently coordinating efforts to allow the distance learner to access the University via video conferencing. Establishing goals that are compatible with his Department, he wishes to implement the Windows CE Machine and each new project as efficiently and quickly as possible to enhance University Athletics. He is also taking the lead role in testing a new fax server. Under his leadership, the University has been chosen as the first beta site for software testing of report writing applications. Mr. Cooley stays on the cutting edge of technology by reading magazines such as PC Week and Windows, attending conferences, and networking. The University of Oregon is state-supported and is a nationally and internationally recognized research university. The Athletics Department offers almost every sport imaginable and is a member of the NCAA. Presently, the Athletics Department employs 150 individuals. **Career Highlights:** Computing Services Director, University of Oregon Athletics (1998-Present); College of Business: Director of Technology (1997-98), Network Administrator (1994-98); Manager of Computing Services, Cabot Oil & Gas Corporation (1991-94). **Education:** University of Houston, Accounting degree (1983). **Personal Information:** Married in 1978. Mr. Cooley enjoys reading.

Jean Frances Coppola
Manager of Client Support
Pace University at Pleasantville
235 Elm Road, Suite 100
Briarcliff, NY 10510-2256
(914) 923-2682
Fax: (914) 923-2754
coppola@pace.edu

8221

Business Information: Ms. Coppola has faithfully served with Pace University in various positions since joining the University as University Manager of Microcomputer Systems in 1994. Currently, she fulfills the responsibility of Manager of Client Support responsible for information technology procurements and establishing standards. Utilizing extensive her academics and experience in the technology field, Ms. Coppola is also manager of the Help Desk, e-classroom designer and coordinator, and professor. Demonstrating strong organizational skills, she leads a staff of 21 technicians in managing seven sites and providing 2nd and 3rd level support to over 4,000 users. Strategic planning of information technology capital, ensuring compliance with virus control procedures, and providing consultations also fall within the purview of Ms. Coppola's functions. Finishing her Ph.D., she authored a cover story for www.thejournal.com in January 2000. Attributing her success to having a sense of humor, her career goals include attaining a position of Chief Information Officer at a small college. A private, four year, coed university, Pace University was established in 1906. Situated on a 200-acre, suburban campus in Briarcliff, the University provide both undergraduate and graduate programs. The University's Information Technology Department administers, designs, develops, and implements all technology strategies. **Career Highlights:** Pace University: Manager of Client Support (1998-Present), Chief of Computer Information Office (1997-98), University Manager of Microcomputer Systems (1994-97). **Associations & Accomplishments:** Board of Directors, EMG Health Communications; Board of Directors, Association of Computing Machinery, New York City, SIGGRAPH; Alumni Board Member, St. Francis Preparatory School; Choir Member/Flutist, Our Lady of Lourdes; Choir Member/Flutist, Our Lady & Blessed Sacrament; Choir Member/Flutist, St. Andrew's Andream Musical Theatre Players. **Education:** Nova Southeastern University, Ph.D. in Computer Science (2000); Pace University: M.S. in Telecommunications (1992), M.S. in Computer Science (1990); Hofstra University, B.S. in Computer Science (1986). **Personal Information:** Ms. Coppola enjoys music and playing the flute.

Deborah Creech
Manager of University Infrastructure
Embry-Riddle Aeronautical University
4515 Saxon Drive
New Smyrna, FL 32619
(904) 226-6415
Fax: (904) 226-6008
creechd@db.erau.edu

8221

Business Information: Proficient in all areas of technology, Ms. Creech serves Embry-Riddle Aeronautical University as Manager of University Infrastructure. Maintaining the University's complex computer network, she concentrates her efforts towards incorporating the latest technologies in order to provide a more efficient and effective system. Coordinating the efforts of her team of associates, Ms.Creech focuses on the continuing development of telecommunications services and the upgrading of server functions. Always alert to new opportunities, approaches, and techniques, Ms. Creech remains committed to providing optimum services to Emby-Riddle Aeronautical University. Her success is attributed top her diligence and a desire to learn more. Providing specialized training programs for worldwide pilots as well as course instruction as a business school for the computer sciences, the University focuses on providing quality educational development to an international student body. Established in 1925, the University staffs expert administrative, teaching, and support personnel who work diligently to enhance and perfect educational opportunities for its expanding student body of 60,000. **Career Highlights:** Embry-Riddle Aeronautical University: Manager of University Infrastructure (2000-Present), Senior Systems Administrator (1998-00); Desktop Analyst, Eclipsys Corporation (1996-98). **Associations & Accomplishments:** Vice President, NetWare Users International. **Education:** Daytona Beach Community College, Associate's degree (2000); Novell Certifiedf NetWare Engineer; Microsoft Certified Professional. **Personal Information:** Married to Howard in 1986. One child: Courtney. Ms. Creech enjoys reading, golf and computers.

Peggy Dalious
Manager of Operations & Applications
University of Colorado Hospital
13001 East 17th Place
Aurora, CO 80045
(303) 724-5107
peggy.dalious@uncolorado.edu

8221

Business Information: Ms. Dalious is the Manager of Operations and Applications at the University of Colorado Hospital. In this position, Ms. Dalious must oversee the functionality of the data center, maintain all equipment, and upgrade all software applications. She brings with her a nursing background to this technical job, using it to ensure that all equipment has a valid therapeutic usage. During her tenure at the hospital, Ms. Dalious has contributed strongly to the drive towards Y2K compliance, and she has been instrumental in shaping the strategic direction of information technology at the Hospital. As for the future, Ms. Dalious plans to provide network infrastructure and applications for all new facilities. Current success, she asserts, has been the final product of her openess to new concepts and people. In 1921, the University of Colorado Hospital was founded. It included a tertiary care and a truama center working in conjunction with the Univeristy of Colorado. As a result, the Schools of Medicine, Nursing, and Pharmacy have all benefited from this strong relationship. Currently, the Hospital employs 2,000 people. **Career Highlights:** Manager of Operations & Applications, University of Colorado Hospital (1992-Present); Senior Consultant, Andersen Consulting (1989-92); Registered Nurse, University of Chicago Hospital (1983-87). **Associations & Accomplishments:** Colorado Healthcare Information and Management Systems Society; Healthcare Information and Management Systems Society. **Education:** University of Texas, Austin, M.B.A. (1989); Duke University, B.S. in Nursing (1983). **Personal Information:** Ms. Dalious enjoys being a triathlete and half marathon runner.

Jeanne DeVore
Director of Information Technology
Dr. William M. Scholl College of Podiatric Medicine
1001 North Dearborn
Chicago, IL 60610
(312) 280-2936
Fax: (312) 280-2997
jdevore@scholl.edu

8221

Business Information: Serving as Dr. William M. Scholl College of Podiatric Medicine's Director of Information Technology, Ms. DeVore retains sole responsiblity for the technical operations within the College. Utilizing her recently acquired Microsoft Certified Systems Engineer certification, she deals with the challenges of the information systems on a daily basis, implementing creative solutions to solve technical problems. Maintaining networking systems, Ms. DeVore performs troubleshooting tasks to ensure hardware, software, and equipment are all functioning properly. Internally recognized for her superior abilities, she looks forward to advancing Web based developments within the College. Enjoying the activities of her current position, Ms. DeVore intends to continue in this capacity. Dr. William M. Scholl College of Podiatric Medicine is located in Chicago, Illinois. The independent school offers bachelor's, doctoral, and first professional degrees with one major offered: biology. Founded in 1912, the College employs 75 people to assist with administrative functions. **Career Highlights:** Director of Information Technology, Dr. William M. Scholl College of Podiatric Medicine (Present). **Education:** Northern Illinois University, B.A. (1982). **Personal Information:** Ms. DeVore enjoys writing and textile arts.

Brian D. Downs
Technical Support Administrator
University of St. Thomas
2115 Summit Avenue, #5020
St. Paul, MN 55105
(651) 962-6773
Fax: (651) 962-6775
bddowns@stthomas.edu

8221

Business Information: Serving as Technical Support Administrator of the University of St. Thomas, Mr. Downs assumes responsibility for the administration of the Novell Intranetware 4.11 network. Consisting of 25 users, the network is used by the Career and Personal Counseling Departments. Mr. Downs presides over every aspect of the Novell network except for the software development. He has received recognition for his role in implementing the first NT system used within the Computing Department and for the TSS program currently being utilized by the University. Attributing his success to perseverance and his willingness to ask questions, he states that there is no such thing as a dumb question. Mr. Downs plans to get involved in Web development for the University and continue to diversify his interests within the technology industry. The largest private college in the state of Minnesota, the University of St. Thomas is well known for its School of Business and Registered Social Work studies. At the present time, approximately 10,000 students are enrolled in the University, half of which are undergraduates. Voted number 8 on Minnesota's "Best Places to Work" list, 1,500 administrative, faculty, and support personnel are employed. The University was founded in 1885 and maintains four campuses across the state. **Career Highlights:** University of St. Thomas: Technical Support Administrator (1997-Present), Hardware Technician (1996-97); Hardware Technician, Datasource/Hagan (1994-96). **Associations & Accomplishments:** Strictly Business Advisory Council. **Education:** CDI Computer Academy, Associate's degree (1994); St. Cloud State University. **Personal Information:** Married to Leah in 1989. Two children: Mackenzie and Jackson. Mr. Downs enjoys hunting, fishing, old cars and spending time with his family.

Barbara Drago
Director/Founder
New York Institute of Entrepreneurship
41 State Street, Suite 110M
Albany, NY 12207
(518) 443-5606
Fax: (518) 443-5610
dragoba@nyssbdc.com

8221

Business Information: Ms. Drago is Director and one of the Founders of the New York Institute of Entrepreneurship. She presides over day-to-day administration and operations, providing on-line business education for middle schools, high schools, and the adult population. Before joining the New York Institute of Entrepreneurship, Ms. Drago served as Director of the Technical Development Organizations within the New York State Science and Technology Foundation. Prior to this position, Ms. Drago served as the statewide Director of the New York State Small Business Advocacy Service and Acting Director for the New York State Work and Family Resource Center for Empire State Development. In her present capacity, she maintains and upgrades the current system and also devotes her time towards designing more effective online systems processing "any time, any place" business education. Determining the overall strategic direction and formulating marketing and educational plans also fall within the realm of Ms. Drago's responsibilities. Utilizing her experience in observing the Institute's growth from the start, she compiled the budget reports and is a key member of the planning committee for the Institute. Always looking for an adventure, Ms. Drago hopes to witness the Institute's expansion that will maximize its student base. New York Institute of Entrepreneurship acts as a Web based business educational institution affiliated with the State University of New York system and private universities and colleges. Through the programs at the Institute, individuals are able to earn their certification in various programs from associate's, bachelor's, or master's degrees in business studies. Established in 1998, the Institute prides itself on the adapted programs for students of all ages to accomplish their goals. **Career Highlights:** Director/Founder, New York Institute of Entrepreneurship (1998-Present); NYS TDO/MEP, New York State Science & Technology Foundation (1997-98); Empire State Development: Director, New York State Small Business Advocate (1994-97), Acting Director, New York State Work & Family Resource Center (1991-94); Teacher, High School. **Associations & Accomplishments:** United States International Year of the Older Person Executive Committee, United Nations; Board Member, New York State Small Business Development Center; New York State Women's Advisory Committee; United States Science & Technology Association; Chairperson, Governor's Women's Economic Conference; Governor's Commission Honoring the Achievements of Women. **Education:** State University of New York at Albany, B.A. (1977). **Personal Information:** One child: Alexandra Velella. Ms. Drago enjoys travel, reading, music and work.

Dennis LeRoy Duncan
Information Systems Office Manager
Emmanuel College
P.O. Box 129
Franklin Springs, GA 30639-0129
(706) 245-7226
Fax: (706) 245-4424
dduncan@emmanuel-college.edu

8221

Business Information: Following 20 years of distinguished services in the United States Air Force, Mr. Duncan joined Emmanuel College as Information Systems Office Manager. He assumes accountability for all administration on the servers and management of over 350 peices of computer and telephone hardware. In addition, he oversees all product coordination and customer satisfaction. Also, Mr. Duncan is responsible for maintaining all equipment, as he is the College's hardware technician. An expert, his career highlight includes turning an ex-biology lab at the College into two computer laboratories. As for the future, he hopes to complete his studies in higher education and obtain A+ certification. Currently, Mr. Duncan attributes his success to hard work, God-given organizational skills, and a determined attitude. Emmanuel College is a Christian educational facility that is part of a ministry. With a student body of 850 people, the College offers up to 13 majors. Each student has the possibility to learn Pastoral Studies, Pre-Medical, and Pre-Pharmacy studies, among other possibilities. To assist all students, the College has retained a faculty and staff of 150 people. **Career Highlights:** Information Systems Office Manage, Emmanuel College (1995-Present); Vehicle Maintenance Supervisor, United States Air Force (1975-95). **Associations & Accomplishments:** Coalition of Retired Military Veterans; Toastmasters; Angel Award, United States Air Force. **Education:** Emmanuel College, Bachelor's degree with minor in Information Systems (In Progress); Community College of the Air Force, Associate's degree in Production Management. **Personal Information:** Married to Connie Marie in 1975. One child: Erika Faith. Mr. Duncan enjoys sound systems and church activities.

Peter K. Dunn

Telecommunication Operations Manager
Auraria Higher Education Center
P.O. Box 173361
Denver, CO 80217-3361
(303) 556-2207
Fax: (303) 556-2207
peterdunn@pobox.com

8221

Business Information: Mr. Dunn is the Telecommunication Operations Manager for Auraria Higher Education Center. He plans new and retrofits voice and data network services for the Center, and together with his staff, he educates users on the new adaptations involved in new systems while ensuring the effectiveness of each product. Involved in the purchasing for his division, Mr. Dunn produces several financial reports and discusses larger purchases with the Board of Directors. In the future, he would like to move into the private sector of the Center while promoting e-commerce. His success reflects his hard work ethic and ability to adapt to changes, as well as produce results and take on new challenges. Auraria Higher Education Center provides voice and data network services to 3,500 users throughout a higher education campus featuring three institutions. Established in 1974, the Center is the only one of its kind, providing a governing authority to the information technology applications and systems utilized by the campus. Hosting a staff of 350 personnel, the Center implements new software and provides new technology opportunities to its students and the surrounding community. **Career Highlights:** Telecommunication Operations Manager, Auraria Higher Education Center (1988-Present); Manager of Financial Systems, U S West Financial Corporation (1987-88); Financial Planning Director, Sears Communications Network. **Associations & Accomplishments:** American Institute of Certified Public Accountants; Leukemia Foundation; A.C.U.T.A.; A.A.N.R.; S.S.U.G.; A.U.G.; R.M.B.; R.M.N. **Education:** DePaul University, M.B.A. (1977); Roosevelt University, B.A. (1973). **Personal Information:** Two children: Chase and Greta. Mr. Dunn enjoys gourmet cooking, travel, photography and gardening.

Alan N. Fels

Senior Information Technology Support Specialist
University of Pennsylvania Graduate School of Education
3700 Walnut Street
Philadelphia, PA 19104-6216
(215) 573-3299
Fax: (215) 573-2119
alanf@gse.upenn.edu

8221

Business Information: As Senior Information Technology Support Specialist at the University of Pennsylvania Graduate School of Education, Mr. Fels manages all support services including desktop and research centers as well as end user support. A savvy, nine year veteran of technology, he is responsible for network design, introduction of policies, implementation of new technology, and the video conferencing room. Utilizing his expertise, Mr. Fels conducts cutting edge technology research, and supervises seven individuals, whom he trains in systems repair. Possessing invaluable hands on, technical consulting experience, his resume includes work for a number of international corporations located in Israel, Canada, Australia, Austria and Germany. Future plans include getting the new video conferencing research laboratory he designed up and running. He also desires to keep bringing the University closer to 21st century technology. Mr. Fels' success is attributed to his love for technology and what he does. The University of Pennsylvania is one of the oldest schools in the United States. Founded in the 1740s by Benjamin Franklin, the University has 12 separate schools. With an annual budget of $1.3 billion, the School has about 10,000 students enrolled. Affiliated with a hospital, the University employs about 3,600 faculty members. Offering a variety of courses and majors, the University also offers associate's, bachelor's, master's, doctoral, and first professional degrees. With its campus set in an urban environment, the University allows the student a myriad of cultural experiences. **Career Highlights:** Senior Information Technology Support Specialist, University of Pennsylvania Graduate School of Education (1995-Present); Consultant, Canadian Embassy, Tel Aviv (1991-95); Consultant, United Technologies, Tel Aviv (1991-95); Consultant, Boring, Tel Aviv (1991-95). **Associations & Accomplishments:** New York Academy of Science. **Personal Information:** Married to Elyse in 1978. One child: Adam.

Lawrence Forman, Ph.D.

Professor of Computer and Information Systems
City College
1313 12th Avenue
San Diego, CA 92101-4787
(619) 230-2666
Fax: (619) 230-2063
lforman@sdccd.net

8221

Business Information: As a Professor of Computer and Information Systems at City College, San Diego, California, Dr. Forman is responsible for curriculum development, lesson preparation, and class instruction. Utilizing his vast education and over 24 years of solid experience, Dr. Forman specializes in teaching students how to create, design, and implement interactive multimedia systems. Proud of the fact that he has been instrumental in obtaining grants for the College for underprivileged students, his reward is seeing students transfer to high quality institutions and graduate with honors. With a passion for teaching, Dr. Forman's goal is to continue to instill and inspire students to embrace technology in their futures. Established in 1914, City College located in San Diego, California is an institution of higher learning dedicated to helping young men and women continue their education, enabling them to enjoy richer, more meaningful lives. The College prepares people for higher institutions of learing and employs 500 qualified staff members, including post graduates to Ph.D. educators to facilitate daily functions. **Career Highlights:** Professor of Computer and Information Systems, City College (1984-Present); Information Scientist/Consultant (1978-Present); Research Associate, Scripps Institution of Oceanography (1976-78). **Associations & Accomplishments:** Association of Computing Machinery; Institute of Electronics and Electrical Engineers; SIGGRAPH; Founder, Walkabout International. **Education:** University of California at Berkeley: Ph.D. (1999), M.A.; Brown University, B.S. **Personal Information:** Married to Diane Bradley in 1989. One child: Jenay. Dr. Forman enjoys camping, marathon walking, travel and reading.

Larry B. Frazier, II

Education Manager
Oracle University
1015 Hiawatha Lane
Morengo, IL 60601
(972) 401-5821
Fax: (603) 452-7613
larry.frazier@oracle.com

8221

Business Information: Serving as Education Manager with Oracle University, Mr. Frazier fulfills a number of duties on behalf of the University. In his capacity, he is responsible for teaching a wide range of subjects, such as programming languages, Web sites, and application servers. Possessing an excellent understanding of technology, Mr. Frazier oversees nine classrooms, providing on-site education and lecturing on such topics as custom front-end applications. With more than two years of experience in education and nine years of programming experience, Mr. Frazier plans on remaining in his current capacity, writing computerized training curriculum, and generating CBTs. The most rewarding aspects of his career include programming an interactive flight simulator for Bell Helicopter, as well as teaching 12 classes and becoming OCP and CTTcertified within his first year of employment at Oracle. Success, according to Mr. Frazier, is due to support from his peers and mentors. Oracle University is an educational establishment that offers programs and courses in database software administration. The University develops databases and powers 90 percent of Web sites for Fortune 500 and Web companies. Founded in the mid 1970s, the University also designs and develops cutting-edge application servers and systems tools. Headquartered in Redwood Shores, California, the University operates internationally. **Career Highlights:** Education Manager, Oracle University (1998-Present); Senior Programmer, Bell Helicopter (1996-98); Programmer, United States Air Force (1987-96). **Associations & Accomplishments:** High School Umpire; High School Coach. **Education:** Chapman University, B.S. (1996); Community College of the Air Force, A.S.; Oracle Certified Professionals; Certified Technical Trainer. **Personal Information:** Mr. Frazier enjoys baseball.

Sharon L. Gander

Instructional Designer/Senior Learning Analyst
Cerner Corporation, Cerner Virtual University
2800 Rockcreek Parkway, MD W0721
Kansas City, MO 64117-2519
(816) 201-2623
sgander@cerner.com

8221

Business Information: As the Senior Learning Analyst of Cerner Corporation's Cerner Virtual University, Ms. Gander fulfills the responsibility of instructional designer. Utilizing 18 years of extensive experience and technical expertise, she is dedicated to providing the most practical and comprehensive educational ideas and techniques. As a specialist in her field, she designs intelligent educational-based games. Ms. Gander is an entrepreneur by nature and her goal is to continue to develop the Corporation and move into a position of leadership. She attributes her success to unique thinking, making leaps, and risk taking. The Cerner Corporation develops software for the health care industry. Located in Kansas City, Missouri, the Cerner Corporation employs 2,500 individuals to oversee development and manufacturing processes, manage sales, and market products. Cerner Virtual University is the educational arm of Cerner Corporation serving Cerner's 2,500 associates and clients world-wide. The Cerner Corporation was established in 1984. **Career Highlights:** Senior Learning Analyst, Cerner Corporation, Cerner Virtual University (1997-Present); Independent Consultant (1993-97); Employee Development Specialist, State of Minnesota (1982-93). **Associations & Accomplishments:** National Association of Female Executives; International Society for Performance Improvement, Twin Cities (1992-97); President, SIG (1996); Camp Fire Boys and Girls, Inc: Chapter Board President (1990-91), Board Vice President (1989-90); Club Leader (1989-93). **Education:** Montana State University, M.Ed. (1981); University of Northern Colorado, B.A. in Education. **Personal Information:** Ms. Gander enjoys amateur photography, painting, dogs and reading.

Victor E. Garcia-Barreras

Assistant Director of Technology and Operations
Nova Southeastern University
3601 College Avenue, #142
Davie, FL 33314
(954) 262-4925
Fax: (954) 262-3917
barreras@scis.nova.edu

8221

Business Information: Mr. Garcia-Barreras serves in the position of Assistant Director of Technology and Operations for Nova Southeastern University. He has been with the University since 1999. Posssessing an excellent understanding of technology, he determines the strategic direction and academic contribution of the informations systems function. In his present role, Mr. Garcia-Barreras is responsible for maintenance of all the ISDN networks and video conference Web for distance education. He provides support for the entire computer networking environment at the University. Plans for the future for Mr. Garcia-Barreras are to start teaching courses in computers, and obtain his doctorate in technology. Established in 1965, Nova Southeastern University is a private higher educational institution. The University enrolls 27,000 students a year, 11,000 students on campus and the rest of the students are through the Internet Conference. Nova Southeastern University is one of the largest private universities in the United States. Located in Florida, Nova Southeastern University employs 2,000 educators and administrators. The University has an estimated annual revenue of $242 million. **Career Highlights:** Assistant Director of Technology and Operations, Nova Southeastern University (1999-Present); Systems Programmer II, Puerto Riceo Department of Agriculture (1987-90); Computer Programming Professor, Catholic University of Puerto Rico (1989-90). **Associations & Accomplishments:** Association of Computing Machinery; Institute for Electrical and Electronics Engineers; Alpha Phi Omega Service Fraternity. **Education:** Nova Southeastern University, M.S. in Computer Science (1998); BMIS Catholic University of Puerto Rico; Institute of Multiple Technology, A.A. in Computer Programming. **Personal Information:** Married to Norma I. Padilla-Casiano in 1987. Two children: Victor Andres Garcia Padilla and Paola del Mar Garcia Padilla. Mr. Garcia-Barreras enjoys photography and scuba diving.

Daniel J. Garrison

Professor
Rochester Institute of Technology
P.O. Box 384
Pittsford, NY 14534-0384
(716) 475-6929
Fax: (716) 248-0890
djgarrison@hotmail.com

8221

Business Information: As Professor of the Rochester Institute of Technology, Mr. Garrison conducts research and teaches three classes a quarter on technology, such as Web design and programming. He is responsible for project management, coordinating resources, time lines, schedules, and assignments. Concurrently, he is the owner and president of Digital Audio Notebook, a print Christian music publication. Multi-faceted, Mr. Garrision also oversees daily operations of christianmusicindustry.com, an online Christian music information source and e-commerce Web site. Mr. Garrison plans to stay with the Institute, where he can continue his research into information technology; and further the growth of his company and have more partnerships with other companies. His success reflects his leadership ability to form teams with synergy and technical strength, take on challenges, and deliver results. Rochester Institute of Technology provides higher education in the field of electronics and technology. Over 2,000 students attend the information technology courses; therefore, making up a combined total of 10,000 students for the entire school. The Institute offers various degrees in the fields of imaging arts printing, engineering, information technology, and liberal arts. **Career Highlights:** Professor, Rochester Institute of Technology (1999-Present); President, Digital Audio Notebook (1990-Present); Store Manager, Alpha & Omega Books and Gifts (1996-97). **Associations & Accomplishments:** Phi Kappa Phi National Honor Society; Phi Theta Kappa National Honor Society; Lexington Publishing Who's Who. **Education:** Rochester Institute of Technology, Master's degree in Fine Arts (1999); Liberty University, B.S.; Word of Life Bible Institute, A.A.S.; Rochester Institute of Technology, A.G.C.

Binto George, Ph.D.

Faculty Member
Western Illinois University
558 South Dudley Street
Macomb, IL 61455
(309) 298-1073
Fax: (309) 298-2302
b-george@wiu.edu

8221

Business Information: Dr. George is a Faculty Member of Western Illinois University's Computer Science Department. He instructs his students in artificial intelligence and telecommunications networks. An expert in his field, he also conducts leading edge research on electronic auctions, business operations systems, security of real-time database systems, and concurrency control and buffer management. Recognized, Dr. George's joint work with Professor J. Haritsa in buffer management was selected as one of the best papers in the VLDB, a premier international conference in database technology. An accomplished author, he owns many journals, conference publications, and a book on Multilevel Transaction Processing. He was asked to be a reviewer of international conferences and journals and was selected as one of the chairs of the international conference on information technology to be held in Cochin in 2000. Dr. George encourages future members of the profession to "be early and set the pace for those coming behind you." His success is attributed to academics and hard work. Western Illinois University is an institution of higher learning. Established in 1899, the University is a state-owned facility providing graduate and undergraduate degrees. Boasting a student body of 13,000 eager minds, the University is most proud of its 15 to 1 student to faculty ratio. The University's two campuses are operated through a staff of 1,000 faculty, administrative, and support personnel. **Career Highlights:** Faculty Member, Western Illinois University (1999-Present); Assistant Research Professor, Rutgers State University, New Jersey (1999). **Associations & Accomplishments:** Association for Computing Machinery; Chair International conference on Software Technology, Cochin (2000); Nominee, Best Alumni Research Award, Indian Institute of Science, Bangalore; Graduate Aptitude Test Examination, National Level Aptitude Test, Score 95.52; National Merit Scholarship for SSLC. **Education:** Indian Institute of Science, Ph.D. in Computer Science (1998); Cochin University of Science and Technology, Master of Technology (1994); Mahatma Gandhi University, Bachelor of Technology (1992). **Personal Information:** Dr. George enjoys reading, cycling, photography and travel.

John P. Guevara

Program Manager
USUHS
4301 Jones Bridge Road, Room A2066
Bethesda, MD 20814
(301) 295-9778
Fax: (301) 295-0752
jguevara@ushhs.mil

8221

Business Information: Achieving great strides in the computer field, Mr. Guevara is the Program Manager for the Uniformed Service University of Health Sciences. He manages the traditional course and development of the online distance learning course. In this context, Mr. Guevara designed, developed, and maintained the Internet based curriculum which provides audio, video, automation, and text courses. His goal is to have this technology innovation up and running by the Spring of 2000. A systems expert, Mr. Guevara also created a software template format to help students take the courses and enable them to receive their certificates immediately upon completion. Concurrently, he serves in the role of Executive Officer for the Army Reserve Pilot Project Information Center. Looking to the future, Mr. Guevara plans to attend Princeton Law School and pursue a career in the area of licensing of software and Internet services. Bethesda, Maryland is home of the Uniformed Service University of Health Sciences. Established in 1972, the University is a military school with one campus. The University helps commanders of medical treatment facilities develop their executive skills through traditional and on online courses. Presently, the University employs a staff of four professional and technical experts to oversee day-to-day operations. **Career Highlights:** Program Manager, Uniformed Service University of Health Sciences (Present); Program Manager, Henry Jackson Foundation (1998-Present); Web Developer, Jewish Institute for National Security Affairs (1997-98); Systems Administrator, Casais & Associate (1996-97). **Associations & Accomplishments:** Reserve Officer's Association; Executive Office, United States Army Reserve 344th Information Operations Center. **Education:** George Washington University, B.A. (1998). **Personal Information:** Married to Marilyn in 1994. Mr. Guevara enjoys reading.

Gary J. Habermann

Director of Technical Resources
Widener University
One University Place
Chester, PA 19013
(610) 499-1030
Fax: (610) 499-1201
gary.j.habermann@widener.edu

8221

Business Information: Serving as Director of Technical Resources of the Information Services Department of Widener University since 1996, Mr. Habermann is responsible for implementing technology and managing the University's ATM infrastructure. He has served with Widener University in a variety of positions since coming on board in 1985. As an 18 year professional with an established track record of producing results, Mr. Habermann's primary responsibility is to research new technology and introduce it into the teaching curriculum. Possessing a love for technology, Mr. Habermann seeks to improve the educational environment of the students through the use of technology. In addition to supervising a technical staff of 14 employees, he coordinates resources and schedules, oversees time lines and assignments, and maintains the functionality and fully operations status of the University's UNIX/Novell/NT based systems. Mr. Habermann looks forward to one day owning his own consulting firm and making a difference in the technology industry. Widener University is a four year liberal arts college. Founded in 1821, the University has 7,500 students enrolled in its three educational facilities. **Career Highlights:** Widener University: Director of Technical Resources (1996-Present), Various Positions (1985-96); Technical Specialist, SCT Corporation (1981-85). **Associations & Accomplishments:** 3Com Technical Advisory Board; 3Com Users Group. **Education:** Widener University, B.S. (1998). **Personal Information:** Married to Deborah in 1985. Mr. Habermann enjoys golf and computers.

Karen Hanford

Dean/Program Director
Western University of Health Sciences
1395 Ridgewood Drive, Suite 300
Chico, GA 95973
(530) 898-7026
Fax: (530) 898-7038
khanford@western.eud

8221

Business Information: As Dean and Program Director of Western University of Health Sciences, Mrs. Hanford is also the founding Dean for the College of Nursing. She is responsible for recruitment and technical administration and oversees the graduate programs such as Nursing and Family Practitioners, MSN, and post Masters. Before joining Western University, she served with California State University at Chico as Family Nurse Practitioner and Assistant Professor. Her background history also includes a stint as Clinical Nurse Specialist Respiratory at Enhoe Hospital. Highly qualified, Mrs. Hanford also presides over the completion of all administrative tasks. She has been requested to speak at conferences in 1997 and 1998 and the University was the first Web based university in the nation. She attributes her success to being prepared for a job of responsibility before it comes. Mrs. Hanford's goal is to assist the Institution become more diversified. Western University of Health Sciences is a private, non profit university specializing in health provisions. Established in 1975, the Institution includes programs for allied health, physical therapy, and physicians assistants. Headquartered in Pomona, California, the Institution currently has over 1,400 students enrolled. **Career Highlights:** Dean/Program Director, Western University of Health Sciences (Present); California State University at Chico: Family Nurse Practitioner (1992-97), Assistant Professor (1987-92); Clinical Nurse Specialist Respiratory, Enhoe Hospital (1987-91). **Education:** University of North Dakota, F.N.P. P.A. (1993); San Francisco State University, B.S. in Nursing; California State University at Chico, M.S. in Nursing. **Personal Information:** Married to Robert in 1969. Two children: Sarah and Emily. Mrs. Hanford enjoys gardening and speed walking.

Wayne C. Harvester

Computer Service Specialist III
Fort Valley State University
P. O. Box 4061
Fort Valley, GA 31030-0400
(912) 825-6345
Fax: (912) 825-6988
harvesterw@mail.fvsu.edu

8221

Business Information: Mr. Harvester serves as Computer Service Specialist III for Fort Valley State University. In this capacity, he operates a mobile computerized classroom and maintains system operations across the campus. He also designs and implements hardware and software applications, primarily used in research. Mr. Harvester plans to earn his Windows NT certification and become Network Administrator. Founded in 1896, Fort Valley State University has become the largest research facility in the Western United States. The University is comprised of one main campus and two remote campuses, all offering a wide range of undergraduate and graduate programs. **Career Highlights:** Computer Service Specialist III, Fort Valley State University (1992-Present); IBM Educational Sales, CBM (1991-92). **Associations & Accomplishments:** Agricultural Communicator in Education. **Education:** University of Georgia, B.S. in Computer Sciences (1990). **Personal Information:** Mr. Harvester enjoys watersports.

Paul Henry Hickey

Information Technology Coordinator
Loyola University
7214 St. Charles Avenue, Campus Box 901
New Orleans, LA 70118-3538
(504) 861-5732
Fax: (504) 861-5786
paulhickey@mindspring.com

8221

Business Information: A Certified Network Engineer, Mr. Hickey serves as the Information Technology Coordinator for the Law School within the Loyola University. He manages all of the technical resources for the School from software purchase to hardware repair. Presiding over the administration of the Novell and Windows NT network file servers, he monitors its daily activity and provides a routine backup system to prevent data loss. He is in charge of the audio and video resources, ensuring that the systems are in optimum working order. Establishing goals that are compatible with those of the University, Mr. Hickey anticipates an eventual promotion to Vice President of the Information Technology Department. Loyola University provides higher educational instruction to students from across the country and some international students as well. Founded in 1914, this private Catholic university has over 5,500 students enrolled, including 3,400 undergraduates, 1,300 graduates, and 700 prospective law professionals. A work force of 150 instructional, administrative, and support personnel are employed by the University's Law School. **Career Highlights:** Information Technology Coordinator, Loyola University (1998-Present); Senior Network Analyst, Bank One (1997-98); Network Analyst, First Commerce Corporation (1994-97). **Education:** Tulane University: Certified Networking Engineer Four (1997), Certified Networking Engineer Three (1997); Loyola University, Bachelor's degree in Applied Science (1989); Delgado Community College, A.S. (1984). **Personal Information:** Mr. Hickey enjoys boating, camping and tennis.

Lawrence W. Hill

Assistant Professor of Information Technology
Rochester Institute of Technology
119 Glen Iris Drive
Rochester, NY 14623
(716) 475-7064
lwh@it.rit.edu

8221

Business Information: In his capacity as Asistant Professor of Information Technology of Rochester Institute of Technology, Mr. Hill is integral in development of new courses for the Institute. He prepares and delivers lectures on existing courses, and is activly involved in software development and management. An expert, he also provides additional consulting services to a variety of clients. A savvy, 23 year veteran of technology, he was nominated for the Eisenhower Teaching Award. Establishing goals compatible with the Institute's objectives, Mr. Hill plans on continuing in his technical role, advancing within the Institute hierarchy, and researching in other areas of interest. He attributes his success to staying current in his chosen field and setting his mind to finsh whatever he starts. "Do the job right the first time," is cited as Mr. Hills' credo. Rochester Institute of Technology, founded in 1829, is a four year university currently staffed by approximately 1,500 educators and administrators. An independent, comprehensive, and coed institute, Rochester Institute of Technology is situated on a 1,300 acre campus with easy access to Buffalo. Presently, over 11,500 graduate and undergraduate students attend the Institute seeking associate, bachelor's, master's, and doctoral degrees and post-master's certificates. **Career Highlights:** Assistant Professor of Information Technology, Rochester Institute of Technology (1998-Present); Senior Engineer, Harris Corporation (1980-98); Graphics Manager, Giltspur Exhibits International (1977-80). **Associations & Accomplishments:** Institute of Electronics and Electrical Engineers; Association of Computing Machinery, National and Local Chapters; Genesee Repeater Association; National Rifle Association; Past President, St. Patrick Neighborhood Association. **Education:** Rochester Institute of Technology: M.S. (1997), B.S. (1976). **Personal Information:** Married to Theresa in 1977. One child: Jennifer. Mr. Hill enjoys computers, electronics, Ham radio, photography, robotics and sailing.

Rosana Holliday

Customer Support Manager, Information and Technology Services
American College of Cardiology
6726 Selkirk Court
Bethesda, MD 20817
(301) 493-2319
Fax: (301) 897-5400
rhollida@acc.org

8221

Business Information: Displaying her expertise in the technology field, Mrs. Holliday serves as Customer Support Manager of Information and Technology Services at the American College of Cardiology. She presides over the Institute's entire computer infrastructure, primary systems, and general operations. Before joining the Institute, she served as a self employed Computer Consultant. Her background history includes a stint as Electrical Engineer for Escelsa. In her present role, Mrs. Holliday performs routine maintenance, providing a backup system for the Institute to prevent accidental data loss and ensuring that network security is updated regularly to guard against computer viruses and unauthorized access. Continually striving for maximum effectiveness, Mrs. Holliday is currently pursuing her Ph.D. in Information Technology to enable her to capitalize on the opportunities presented to her by the Institute. Her success reflects her ability to aggressively take on new challenges. The American College of Cardiology provides continuing educational opportunities to doctors and other professionals within the medical field. Founded in 1949, the Institute is a leader in Cardiology research, incorporating its discoveries into its classroom curriculum. An approximate staff of 200 administrative, faculty, and support personnel are dedicated to providing premium instruction in this specialized field. **Career Highlights:** Customer Support Manager, Information and Technology Services, American College of Cardiology (1994-Present); Computer Consultant, Self Employed (1992-94); Electrical Engineer, Escelsa (1986-92). **Associations & Accomplishments:** Institute of Electronics and Electrical Engineers; Aircraft Owners and Pilots Association; National Society of Professional Engineers; Society of Executive Women. **Education:** George Mason, Ph.D. in Information Technology (In Progress); M.S. in Computer Information Systems; B.S. in Electrical Engineering. **Personal Information:** Married to George in 1989. Mrs. Holliday enjoys flying as a private pilot, skydiving, scuba diving and riding motorcycles.

P. Kent Hooker

Senior Systems Programmer
University of Wisconsin at Madison
1210 West Dayton Street
Madison, WI 53706
(608) 263-1990
Fax: (608) 265-4945
khooker@doit.wisc.edu

8221

Business Information: With extensive experience in systems administration, Mr. Hooker serves as the Senior Systems Programmer for the University of Wisconsin at Madison. Before taking on his present role at the the University, he served as the University's Project Manager. Mr. Hooker's background history also includes a stint as Senior Systems Analyst for the State of Wisconsin. Currently, he oversees the administration of the UNIX vases computers used by campus students, buying and selling UNIX related equipment and software. Additionally, he debugs, repairs, and upgrades the computers for continued use. As a 21 year professional, Mr. Hooker's success reflects his ability to think out-of-the-box and aggressively take on new challenges. Establishing goals that are compatible with those of the University, Mr. Hooker is committed to providing continued optimum service. The University of Wisconsin at Madison is a higher learning institution and was founded in 1849. Offering advanced computing and super computing support as well as many other academic subjects, they provide students with an education in today's technology. Presently, the University employs a staff of more than 12,500 individuals generating in excess of $4.75 million in annual revenues. **Career Highlights:** University of Wisconsin at Madison: Senior Systems Programmer (1995-Present), Project Manager (1990-95); Senior Systems Analyst, State of Wisconsin (1989-90). **Associations & Accomplishments:** USENIX; SAGE; SHARE; Security Working Group; CIC; FIRST. **Education:** University of Wisconsin at Madison, B.A. (1978). **Personal Information:** Married to Gayle in 1978. Mr. Hooker enjoys pipe organs and the harpsichord.

Ernest W. Howell

Network Systems Administrator
Colgate University
107 Ray Street North
Ilion, NY 13357
(315) 228-7478
bhowell@mail.colgate.edu

8221

Business Information: Mr. Howell serves in the capacity of Network Systems Administrator for Colgate University. In this role, he handles a multitude of highly specialized technical tasks such as Microsoft Exchange Administration. Demonstrating adept abilities, he oversees networking and systems design to ensure smooth operations within the organizational structure of the Institution. He is credited with the successful implementation of an Internet background that supports campus-wide email, in addition to several other innovative developments that have contributed to the overall effectiveness of the educational process. Mr. Howell attributes his professional accomplishments to helpful mentors who spent time teaching him industry practices. Enjoying the challenges of his position, Mr. Howell intends to continue in his current role as he prepares to implement Windows 2000 and Exchange 2000. His advice is, "Get involved with as many resources as possible and have fun." Colgate University is an independent, co-ed university located in Hamilton, New York. The educational institution awards Bachelor's and Master's degrees for the successful completion of programs in fields such as anthropology, biochemistry, peace and conflict studies, and theater arts. Over 2,500 undergraduate students attend the University, and participate in programs such as NCAA Division I athletic clubs and student government associations. **Career Highlights:** Network Systems Administrator, Colgate University (1998-Present); Computer Instructor, Air Force Research Laboratory (1996-98); Active Duty, United States Navy (1975-96). **Associations & Accomplishments:** Fleet Reserve Association; American Legion. **Education:** St. Leo College, A.A. (1997). **Personal Information:** Married to Sharon Gleasman-Howell in 1986. Three children: Matthew, Amanda, and Sharon E.

Xiaohong Hu, Ph.D.

Computer Specialist
USUHS
4301 Jones Bridge Road, Room 006
Bethesda, MD 20814-4799
(301) 295-1130
Fax: (301) 295-3935
xhu@usuhs.mil

8221

Business Information: Serving as a full time programmer and database administrator, Dr. Hu fulfills the responsibility of Computer Specialist with the USUHS or United States University of Health and Sciences. In his capacity, he works with the University's Department of Information Systems and is responsible for maintaining the functionality and serviceability of the operating and networking environments. Drawing on years of experience in the industry and possessing natural computer talents, Dr. Hu analyzes, specifies, and develops new software as well as offers computer consultation and advice. Receiving recognition for his accomplishments within the University, he is credited with the development of a pharmaceutical program which is now fully utilized by the University, and as a result of its success, he has gained a larger client portfolio. Fully certified in Microsoft, Dr. Hu plans to continue on his current career path with the University, dedicating his time to the future of the students. Located in Bethesda, Maryland, the USUHS operates in coordination with the Department of the Navy. Dedicated to providing medical instruction for military students, the University utilizes the most innovative equipment and teaching methods in their educational programs. **Career Highlights:** Computer Specialist, USUHUS (1998-Present); Computer Specialist, Hubei Textile Design Institute (1989-92). **Education:** Darmouth College, Ph.D. (1998); HUST: M.S., Bachelor's degree in Engineering. **Personal Information:** Married to Xinzhang Li in 1988. One child: Kun Li. Dr. Hu enjoys travel.

Jian Huang, Ph.D.

Research Assistant
University of Minnesota
11013 Quebec Circle
Bloomington, MN 55438-2804
(612) 624-8545
Fax: (612) 625-0572
huangj@cs.umn.edu

8221

Business Information: Serving as Research Assistant at the University of Minnesota, Dr. Huang performs related research on computer architechture. His affinity for computers has led him in his vocational decisions. Utilizing his technical expertise, Dr. Huang's research is focused on improving the micro-proccessors or the computer's brain. His background history includes a stint as Intern with Cray Research. Recently, he started working for Sun Microsystems as the Senior Engineer. In this capacity, Dr. Huang will be involved in the discovery, investigation, and initial deployment of advanced technologies within Sun Microsystems. His focus will be on changes that will allow Sun Microsystems' clients to take advantage of any newly developed advanced technologies to remain flexible, efficient, and profitable in the Information Technology Age. Proud of his achievements in micro-proccessing, Dr. Huang attributes his success to the feedback from his many colleagues; preparation, and intervention. In the future, he would like to study the Web-community. Founded in the 1850s, the University of Minnesota enjoys a reputation as an institution for technological medical schooling. Enrolling 10,000 students, the University is set in a large community enivronmment. Providing a variety of majors, the University is a state funded institution. A four year public university, many degrees are also offered at the University of Minnesota. **Career Highlights:** Research Assistant, University of Minnesota (1995-Present); Senior Engineer, Sun Microsystems (2000-Present); Intern, Cray Research (1996). **Associations & Accomplishments:** Computer Architecture, Association of Computing Machinery; Institute of Electrical and Electronics Engineers Computer Society. **Education:** University of Minnesota: Ph.D. (2000), M.S. in Computer Science, B.A. in Computer Science.

David Jeff Jackson, Ph.D.

Associate Professor
University of Alabama
P.O. Box 870286
Tuscaloosa, AL 35487-0286
(205) 348-2919
Fax: (205) 348-6959
jjackson@eng.ua.edu

8221

Business Information: As an Associate Professor with the University of Alabama, Dr. Jackson teaches both graduate and undergraduate levels of computer engineering, electrical, and mechanical systems as well as conducting research projects. His skills and knowledge are demonstrated through his formulation of a computer program that is now utilized by the University. Highly regarded by his colleagues and students, he possesses superior talents and an excellent understanding of technology. Attributing his success to motivation provided by peers and students, Dr. Jackson plans to continue in his present position, aspiring to the level of full professor. The University of Alabama is an institute of higher learning that offers general and specialized course curricula for individuals desiring more formal educational opportunities. Established in 1831, the University is home to approximately 18,000 students from across the United States as well as from 83 different countries. The University of Alabama located in Tuscaloosa is one of the institutions that make up the University system. **Career Highlights:** Associate Professor, University of Alabama (Present). **Associations & Accomplishments:** Institute of Electrical and Electronics Engineers; Institute of Electrical and Electronics Engineers

Computer Society; International Society for Computers and their Applications; American Society Engineering Education; Association of Computing Machinery. **Education:** University of Alabama, Ph.D. (1990); Auburn University: M.S. in Electrical Engineering (1986), B.S. (1984). **Personal Information:** Married to Laura in 1995. One child: Julie.

Vicki S. Jacobs

Systems Analyst
Wharton County Junior College
911 East Boling Highway
Wharton, TX 77488-3298
(409) 532-6563
Fax: (409) 532-6545
vickij@wcjc.cc.tx.us

8221

Business Information: Utilizing 20 solid years of experience in the information technology field, Ms. Jacobs joined Wharton County Junior College in 1990. In the capacity of Systems Analyst, she oversees all the computer systems in the College, giving reports on its status. Additionally, she is responsible for programming and maintaining the accounting payroll and student financial aid systems. Directing and participating in the analysis, design, configuration, installation, maintenance, supporting, and tracking operating and networking systems, databases, client server utility programs, software, and hardware also fall within the purview of her responsibilities. Ms. Jacobs credits her success to an ability to work well with others and having an open mind. Her success also reflects her ability to think out-of-the-box and aggressively take on new challenges and responsibilities. Always alert to new opportunities, techniques, and approaches, she anticipates her promotion to Chief Information Officer. Wharton County Junior College was founded in the 1940s with the goal of providing students with a quality education after high school. The College consists of two campuses and has approximately 4,000 students enrolled. **Career Highlights:** Systems Analyst, Wharton County Junior College (1990-Present); Data Processing Manager, Matagorda County (1989-90); Programmer Analyst, Duke Energy (formerly Texas Eastern) (1980-84). **Associations & Accomplishments:** Vice President, Van Vleck Little League; East Matagorda County Youth Boosters; Van Vleck Athletics Booster, Van Vleck Band Boosters. **Education:** Sam Houston State University, B.S. (1980). **Personal Information:** Married to Michael in 1981. Two children: Christina L. and Kyle S. Ms. Jacobs enjoys gardening, waterskiing and horseback riding.

Sallie J. Johnson

Associate Director for Distance Learning
Troy State University Dothan
500 University Drive, P.O. Box 8368, #174
Dothan, AL 36304
(334) 983-6556
Fax: (334) 983-6322
Sjohnson@tsud.edu

8221

Business Information: Recently attaining her position, Ms. Johnson serves as the Associate Director for Distance Learning at the Troy State University Dothan. Advancing the distance learning program into the 21st century, she is responsible for the development and implementation of online and telecommunication courses. Through her dedication to community service, Ms. Johnson offers continuing education classes as well as implementation of satellite systems. Enjoying her current position, she plans to build up the online program which will enable her to develop a total online degree program, but at the same time, she looks forward to the pursuit of a Ph.D. in Computing Technology of Education. A savvy professional, Ms. Johnson was a presenter at the 1st Annual Alabama Distance Learning Symposium in March 2000. She received a commendation for her work in helping quadruple the enrollment at Embry-Riddle Aeronautical University. Attributing her success to a positive attitude, faith, and team work, Ms. Johnson's advice is "keep an open mind and be flexible." Founded in the 1950s, Troy State University Dothan is a separately accredited school, however still a part of the Troy State University Group. A four year institution, the University offers graduate studies in education, arts and science, and business. Located on 255 acres of land, Troy State University Dothan provides traditional classes as well as online courses. **Career Highlights:** Associate Director for Distance Learning, Troy State University Dothan (1999-Present); Computer Science Director, University of Maryland (1991-Present); Computer Science Director, Embry-Riddle Aeronautical University (1991-Present); Computer Science Director, Troy State University Dothan (1991-Present); Center Director/Administrator, Embry-Riddle Aeronautical University (1996-99); Multi Media Labs Director, University of Maryland, Asian Division (1991-93). **Associations & Accomplishments:** Association of Computing Machinery; Association of Computing Machinery Special Interest Groups: Computer-Human Interaction, Data Communication, Computer Science Education, Computer Uses in Education, Multimedia, Hypetext, Hypermedia and Web. **Education:** Nova Southeastern Univesity, Ph.D. in Computing Technology in Education (In Progress); Webster University, M.A.; University of the State of New York, B.S., A.S. **Personal Information:** Married to Charlie Johnson in 1988. Four children: Daniel, Chad, Grant, and Luke. Ms. Johnson enjoys spending time with family, reading and praise/worship team singing.

Sunil Joseph

Senior Database Consultant
Harvard Medical School
1 Kendall Sq. Bldg 600 Ste 260
Cambridge, MA 02139
(617) 867-3145
tylerbacalkorn@earthlink.net

8221

Business Information: Mr. Joseph serves Harvard Medical School as the Senior Database Consultant. Maintaining the extensive Oracle based systems, Mr. Joseph ensures quality control while producing customized reports and summary sheets for medical professionals from around the world. Operating with a team of trained database professionals, he preserves the activity and function of all networks that are relied upon by research facilities, hospitals, and institutions on a large scale. Author of 67 publications in the fields of disease research and development, Mr. Joseph has earned a position among the most highly dignified and respected medical professionals in the world. Currently, he is dedicating his time to upholding his several technical certifications, and is anticipating playing a leading role in project management. Providing international service from the Cambridge, Massachusetts location, Harvard Medical School was designed to produce a global database on researchable types of cancer, in the benefit of cancer patients and victims who may otherwise have gone with inadequate treatment. **Career Highlights:** Harvard Medical School: Senior Database Consultant (1999-Present), Research Coordinator, Senior Research Data Analyst, Administrative Coordinator; Database Administrator, Wyeth-Ayerst Pharmaceuticals (1999). **Associations & Accomplishments:** Society of Clinical Data Management; Drug Information Association; Oracle Clinical User Group; World Alzheimer 2000 Congress; Brandeis University Alumni Association; Contributor, Health Data Management Magazine. **Education:** Brandeis University, B.S. in Biochemistry cum laude (1997); Oracle Education Corporation: Database Administration (2000), SQL Plus (1997).

Jai W. Kang, Ph.D.

Assistant Professor
Medaille College
18 Agassiz Circle
Buffalo, NY 14214
(716) 884-3281
Fax: (716) 884-0291
jwkang@jkang.com

8221

Business Information: Dr. Kang is a unique individual, completely dedicated to the teaching field. He currently serves as an Assistant Professor in the computer information systems department at Medaille College. He instructs four courses per semester, which vary from programming, C++, system analysis, and data communications. He is also a member of the College Technology Committee and helps to shape the College's strategic technical direction. In addition to his work with the College, Dr. Kang is a Computer Applications Consultant presently contracted by the Department of Energy. Crediting his success to motivation and support from his family, Dr. Kang looks forward to increasing his participation in information technology research. His advice to others is, "Keep up-to-date with technology." Located in Buffalo, New York, Medaille College is a four-year, accredited higher education institution. The College was founded in 1937 and offers students various types of degrees including Associate's, Bachelor's, and Master's in different professional disciplines. A staff of 150 administrative, faculty, and support personnel work diligently to ensure that students not only excel in their career concentrations but receive a well-rounded education that helps them grow as individuals and later as members of society in general. **Career Highlights:** Assistant Professor, Medaille College (Present); Computer Consultant, URS Greiner Woodward Clyde (1999-Present); Computer Applications Manager, Ecology and Environment, Inc. (1981-97). **Associations & Accomplishments:** Certified Computing Professional; Institute for Certification of Computing Professionals; Association for Computing Machinery; Association for Information Systems; Institute for Operations Research and the Management Sciences. **Education:** State University of New York at Buffalo, Ph.D. (1984); Georgia Institute of Technology: M.S. in Operations Research (1978), M.S. in Computer and Information Science (1976); Kent State University, M.A. in Mathematics (1974); Seoul National Univeristy, B.S. in Pharmacy (1969). **Personal Information:** Married to Kyung S. in 1981. Two children: James Minsuk and Jennifer Hagyoung. Dr. Kang enjoys tennis and trap shooting.

Heather Alicia Katz

Instructional Technologist
University of Texas at Austin, Charles A. Dana Center
2315 Town Lake Circle, Apartment 306
Austin, TX 78741-3063
(512) 447-8415
Fax: (512) 475-9445
hakatz@mail.utexas.edu

8221

Business Information: As Instructional Technologist of the University of Texas at Austin's Charles A. Dana Center since 1997, Ms. Katz is responsible for effectively integrating technology into the educational curriculum. She consults with the University regarding multimedia development and is a member of the technology team under the Star Center. As Webmaster, she develops, maintains, and updates Web sites at the Star Center and Charles A. Dana Center. Her responsibilities include interface design, graphical design, HTML coding, PDF documentation, JavaScript, and staff training. Before accepting this position, Ms. Katz was looking for something to marry her two fields of training. Developing technology integration training materials for the K-12 education community and facilitating respective workshops also fall within the purview of her functions. She attributes her success to strong motivation, perseverance and setting definite goals. Looking to the future, she intends to work in a research and development capacity, writing grants, multimedia development, and setting up technological centers in urban areas. An accomplished professional, Ms. Katz credits include eleven presentations and four publications. Founded in 1992, the Charles A. Dana Center is located at the University of Texas at Austin. Dedicated to the equity and excellence of students at all levels of public education, the Center is engaged in research and program development. Presently, the Dana Center is manned by more than 119 people. **Career Highlights:** Instructional Technologist, University of Texas at Austin, Charles A. Dana Center (1997-Present); Web Developer/Instructional Technologist, University of Texas, Texas Education Network (1996-97); Special Educator, Prince George's County Public Schools (1993-94). **Associations & Accomplishments:** Who's Who Among Women in America; Pi Lambda Theta; Who's Who Among Students in American Universities and Colleges; Phi Delta Kappa; Association for Advancement of Computing in Education; Kappa Delta Pi; International Society for Technology in Education. **Education:** University of Texas at Austin, Ph.D. in Instructional Technology (In Progress); Howard University: M.Ed. in Special Education (1993), B.S. in Environmental Science with minors in Civil Engineering and Allied Science (1992). **Personal Information:** Ms. Katz enjoys cycling, swimming, gardening, jazz, foreign films, sewing, weight lifting, meditating and reading.

Christian Jon Keck

Computer Systems Coordinator
University of Dayton
300 College Park, MH3
Dayton, OH 45469-2201
(937) 229-2278
Fax: (937) 229-3528
keck@udayton.edu

8221

Business Information: Mr. Keck serves as Computer Systems Coordinator for the University of Dayton. In this capacity, he is charged with the maintenance and support of all computer systems within the College of Arts and Sciences which involves 65 percent of the University facilities. This responsibility includes upkeep of the University's principal 43 computer labs, networks, hardware, software, and system architecture. Other responsibilities include the upkeep of all faculty and staff machines, over 350 machines network hardware and software. He ensures the stability of operating systems throughout his domain and conducts regular backups of all mainframe activities. In addition, Mr. Keck serves as System Administrator with authority over security issues and access assignments. He monitors upgrade and new installation implementation to provide optimum functionality and support for all users both in the administrative and student areas. He attributes his success to persistence and strong problem-solving skills. Mr. Keck is also charged with the supervision of five technical support staff members and a student lab staff of around 45 part-time assistants who help operate the various campus computer labs. His future objective is to complete his bachelor's degree in Management Information Systems and Communications with a minor in Criminal Justice. Once completed, he plans to utilize his background in the Criminal Justice area to seek a position involved in computer investigative work. The University of Dayton is a private, four-year, coed, liberal arts university with graduate programs. Affiliated with the Roman Catholic Church, the University was established in 1850 and provides post-secondary educational opportunities to more than 12,000 students. More than 70 major areas of study are offered at the University of Dayton which employs approximately 900 professional, technical, and support staff. **Career Highlights:** Computer Systems Coordinator, University of Dayton (1996-Present); Assistant Computer Facilitator, Northmont City Schools (1990-96). **Associations & Accomplishments:** Englewood Police Department; Boy

Scouts of America; Clayton United Methodist Church. **Education:** University of Dayton, Bachelor's degree in Management Information Systems and Communications with minor in Criminal Justice (In Progress). **Personal Information:** Mr. Keck enjoys a wide variety of music and outdoor activities such as hiking and fishing. He works part-time as a police officer with a local department.

Anthony R. Korwin

Director of Technology Support Services
Oregon State University
3140 Pine Drive
Prescott, AZ 86301
(541) 737-3685
Fax: (541) 737-3453
tony.korwin@orst.edu

8221

Business Information: As Director of Technology Support Services, Mr. Korwin is credited for the superior management of several aspects within the department's operation at Oregon State University. In his position, he focuses his superior ability and skill in the supervision of centralized computer applications, desktop support systems, and the support of the University's self-sufficient technological departments. Analyzing and supporting computer operations, monitoring system resources and response times, and providing first line support for operational problems also fall within the realm of his responsibilities. Striving to maintain the most innovative and cutting-edge facilities, Mr. Korwin is working to direct Oregon State University to the leading position as the most highly technologically integrated school in the world. One of the most prestigious public education facilities in the country, Oregon State University is a Carnegie 1 Research Institution and is a land, sea, and space grant university. Currently enrolling over 16,000 students each year, the University is located in Corvallis, Oregon. Mr. Korwin telecommutes to OSU from his home in Prescott, Arizona. The University's information technology services, a vital division of the main campus, employs a staff of 25 technical professionals who maintains and upgrades the modern technology utilized within the University. **Career Highlights:** Director of Technology Support Services, Oregon State University (1997-Present); Technology Coordinator, Nestucca Valley School District, Cloverdale, Oregon (1991-97). **Associations & Accomplishments:** NCCE; ACTE; ITEA; Project Management Institute. **Education:** Bowling Green State University, M.Ed. (1986); Eastern Illinois University, B.S. **Personal Information:** Married to Kathleen Aviña in 1994.

Miroslav Kubat, Ph.D.

Associate Professor
University of Louisiana at Lafayette, Center for Advanced Computer Studies
2 Rex Street Conference Center
Lafayette, LA 70504-4330
(337) 482-6606
Fax: (337) 482-5791
mkubat@cacs.usl.edu

8221

Business Information: Specializing in computer science, Dr. Kubat serves as an Associate Professor at University of Louisiana at the Lafayette's Center for Advanced Computer Studies. Dedicated to providing his students with the most practical and comprehensive education, he shares ideas and techniques in an enthusiastic and persuasive manner. His focus at the Center is on research, discovery, investigation, development, and deployment of leading edge technologies. He hopes to one day be able to focus more on his own research. Success, according to Dr. Kubat, takes talent, being in the right place, and time. The University of Louisiana at Lafayette is an institution of higher learning providing general and specialized course instruction for individuals wishing to advance their educational studies. With a wide range of majors, the University offers degrees, such as associate's, bachelor's, master's, and doctoral degrees and post-master's certificates. The University was established in 1900 and now serves over 16,000 students. The University's Center for Advanced Computer Studies strives to incoporate the latest technology in the education process. **Career Highlights:** Associate Professor, University of Louisiana at Lafayette, Center for Advanced Computer Studies (1998-Present); Senior Researcher, University of Ottawa (1995-97); Senior Researcher, University of Linz (1994-95). **Associations & Accomplishments:** Institute of Electrical and Electronics Engineers Computer Society; Association of Computing Machinery; American Association of Artificial Intelligence. **Education:** Brno Technical University: Ph.D. (1990), M.S. (1982). **Personal Information:** Married to Vera in 1990. One child: Jaroslav.

Damon L. Landis

Software Developer/Network Specialist
DeVry Institute of Technology
4800 Regent Boulevard
Irving, TX 75063
(972) 929-6777
Fax: (972) 929-6778
dlandis@dal.devry.edu

8221

Business Information: Serving as Software Developer and Network Specialist for DeVry Institute of Technology since 1998, Mr. Landis assumes responsibility for the design, development, and implementation of new software for the administration side of the University. Before joining the DeVry Institute of Technology, he served as Software Developer with Integrated Concepts Inc. and Software Engineer at Plexsys Wireless. Maintaining the computer network upon which the students depend, Mr. Landis provides network security, installs new applications, distributes software upgrades, and performs routine system backup. In his spare time, he enjoys teaching C++, C, and Java. His career success reflects his ability to think out-of-the-box and take on new challenges and responsibilities. Mr. Landis is currently pursuing his Master's degree to enable him to capitalize on the opportunities provided by the University. DeVry Institute of Technology is a fully accredited private university providing a quality education to people seeking expertise in the business world. The University located in Irving, Texas was founded in 1969 and offers 9 different degrees to prospective students. **Career Highlights:** Software Developer/Network Specialist, DeVry Institute of Technology (1998-Present); Software Developer, Integrated Concepts Inc. (1998); Software Engineer, Plexsys Wireless (1997-98). **Education:** DeVry Institute of Technology, B.S. (1997). **Personal Information:** Mr. Landis enjoys canoeing, kayaking, marksmanship and body building.

Yvonne M. Ledford

Systems Administrator
University of Oklahoma Health Sciences Center
1100 North Lindsay Avenue, SCB-101
Oklahoma City, OK 73104
(405) 271-2101
Fax: (405) 691-1696

8221

Business Information: Utilizing more than 15 years of experience, Ms. Ledford serves as the Systems Administrator for the University of Oklahoma Health Sciences Center. She administrates and maintains the UNIX and VMS systems as well as the NT server. Presiding over the backup support of the databases, she manages the academic application, PeopleSoft application, and the library automation system. In addition, she is in charge of the efficient functioning of the mail exchange server. Ms. Ledford cites quality colleagues and mentors as the reason for her success. Consistently achieving quality performance, she continues to grow professionally through the fulfillment of her responsibilities and her involvement in the advancement of operations. University of Oklahoma Health Sciences Center provides specialized higher educational opportunities for students across the country. Approximately 4,000 students enroll in classes on an annual basis. The University was established in 1890. **Career Highlights:** University of Oklahoma Health Sciences Center: Systems Administrator (1995-Present), Programmer (1991-94), Programmer/Operator (1986-91). **Associations & Accomplishments:** DECUS LUG, Compaq Users Group. **Education:** Rose State College, Associate's degree in Business Technology, Major in Management Information Systems. **Personal Information:** Two children: Corey Ray and Taylor Renee.

Xuhong "Linda" Li, Ph.D.

Assistant Professor
City College of New York
Computer Science Department, Convent Avenue, 138th Street
New York, NY 10031
(212) 650-6175
Fax: (212) 650-6184
linda@csfaculty.engr.ccny.cuny.edu

8221

Business Information: Serving as Assistant Professor of City College of New York since 1999, Dr. Li is a faculty member in the Department of Computer Science. Possessing an excellent understanding of computer science, she teaches software engineering courses and performs computer science research. Highly regarded, Dr. Li also promotes funding for her research and serves as a mentor to her students. She is the co-chair for the document processing program IDPT2000. An acccomplished technical authority, Dr. Li has published over 10 conference papers. A visionary, she is planning partnership programs with IBM. She also aspires to publish more papers and a book. City College of New York is a four-year college. The College offers graduate, undergraduate, and doctorate programs. City College of New York has approximately 1,000 students enrolled in the Computer Science Department. Located in New York, New York, the College employs 26 educators and administrators in the Computer Science Department. **Career Highlights:** Assistant Professor, City College of New York (1999-Present); Software Engineer, Beijing Brilliance Industrial Corporation (1995-96); Software Engineer, Jade Bird System Software, Inc. (1994-95). **Associations & Accomplishments:** Association of Computing Machinery. **Education:** New Jersey Institute of Technology, Ph.D. (1999); Beijing University, Master's degree in Computer Science (1994); Tianjin University, Bachelor's degree in Computer Engineering (1991). **Personal Information:** Married to Zhenfu Cheng in 1993. Dr. Li enjoys playing cards and tennis.

Weidong Liao

Research Analyst
Kent State University
1340 Allerton Street
Kent, OH 44240
(330) 672-4004
Fax: (330) 672-7825
wliao@kent.edu

8221

Business Information: As Research Analyst of Kent State University, Mr. Liao performs a number of functions on behalf of the University and its students. Joining Kent State in 1997, he focuses his attention to conducting research on networking technology. Possessing an excellent understanding of his field, Mr. Liao provides instruction on programming and building systems and software. He also writes specifications for architecture and communications networks as well as develops protocols. Highly regarded, he authored an article on Java programming that was published in a Chinese publication. Acheiving two Master's degrees from his studies in China and the United States, Mr. Liao is currently working on his Ph.D. Continuing his career at Kent State, Mr. Liao remains focused on his research for new technologies. His keys to success include his intuition and his ability to establish good relations with his co-workers. Concentrating on raising the standards for higher education, Kent State University was established in 1919. Considered to be one of the top 100 public universities in the United States, the University enrolls 20,700 students. Offering a wide range of programs including undergraduate, graduate, and nocredit programs, the University provides more than 170 fields of study. Focusing their attention towards the student body, the University also provides facilities and organizations suited for the students' individual desires including 230 student organizations and over 100 academic, residential, and administrative facilities. Dedicated to the provision of quality education, Kent Sate University employs an 850 faculty staff. **Career Highlights:** Research Analyst, Kent State University (1997-Present); Software Engineer, Software Institute, Chinese Academy of Sciences; System Analyst, Microsoft Corporation; Graduate Assistant, Northeastern University. **Associations & Accomplishments:** Institute of Electrical and Electronics Engineers; Association of Computing Machinery. **Education:** Kent State University, M.S. in Engineering Science (1998); Northeastern University at China, Bachelor's degree. **Personal Information:** Married to Mei Chen in 1996. One child: Frank. Mr. Liao enjoys chess, table tennis and time with family.

Sue Linder-Linsley

Director of Collections Management
Department of Anthropology
Southern Methodist University
Dallas, TX 75275-0336
(214) 768-2938
Fax: (214) 768-2906
slinder@mail.smu.edu

8221

Business Information: As Director of Collections Management with the Department of Anthropology, Ms. Linder-Linsley oversees information technology support and management information systems functions. Applying 25 years of extensive experience, she manages 650 Web page files and is responsible for Web content development and publishing. She draws upon her considerable professional expertise as she handles systems maintenance, upgrades, and troubleshooting. Ms Linder-Linsley would like to expand her archeological consulting activities to include on-line cultural resource development services. Looking to the 21st Century, she plans to establish a complete highly reputable anthropology multimedia Web site. Her success reflects her ability to think outside the box, deliver results, and aggressively tackle new challenges. The Department of Anthropology at Southern Methodist University specializes in anthropology and archeology. The Department employs over 30 educators providing quality instruction to students. The University offers individuals a wide selection of academic studies to challenge the mind. Possessing an international client base, the Institution encourages participation in extracurricular activities, which enhance academic scholarship. **Career Highlights:** Director of Collections Management, Department of Anthropology (1990-Present);

Director of Special Programs, Dallas Museum of Natural History Association (1988-90); Assistant Director/Director of Information Systems and Field Operations, Archaeology Research Program, Institute for the Study of Earth Hand Man (1987-88). **Associations & Accomplishments:** Certified Professional Archeologist by the Society of Professional Archeologists (1995); Professional Member, The Association of Internet Professionals (1995); Register of Professional Archaeologists; Web Page Committee (1997-Present)/Chair, Council of Texas Archaeologists; Society of American Archaeology; Omicron Delta Kappa Honor Society. **Education:** Southern Methodist University, M.A. (1995); Certified Field Reviewer, Accreditation Review Council (1999); Beloit College, B.A. in Anthropology and Museum Studies (1984). **Personal Information:** Married to Mike in 1982. Ms. Linder-Linsley enjoys geneaology, swimming and NASCAR.

Gregory T. Litchfield

Computer Systems Manager
Grace University
1311 South 9th Street
Omaha, NE 68108
(402) 449-2914
Fax: (402) 341-9587
glitchfield@mail.graceu.edu

8221

Business Information: Following 30 years of distinguished service in the United States Air Force, Mr. Litchfield joined the Grace University staff as Computer Systems Manager in 1995. Utilizing four years of experience and technical expertise, Mr. Litchfield delivers consistent results in support of the educational objectives of Grace University through effective use of emerging technologies, and solving both problems and challenges in a systematic and efficient manner. His focus is on deploying and maintaining advanced technologies within Grace University, and helping the Institution remain in the forefront of education. In addition to fulfilling his diverse duties, Mr. Litchfield handles numerous resource planning functions to include determining future resource requirements, as well as keeping the operating and networking infrastructures fully operational and functional. Analysis, modification, configuration, upgrade, implementation, support, and tracking operating systems, databases, server utilities, software, and hardware also fall within the scope of Mr. Litchfield's responsibilities. Seeing a major expansion of systems within the network, Mr. Litchfield's future goals include remaining with Grace University, and taking the Institution to the next level of technology. Grace University, founded in 1943, is an institution of higher education. Affiliated with the Mennonite faith, the Institution provides a curricula that is fundamental in doctrine, spiritual in emphasis, and interdenominational in scope. Presently, a staff of 120 persons provide for the educational needs of the student body. **Career Highlights:** Computer Systems Manager, Grace University (1995-Present); United States Air Force: Quality Facilitator/Tracker (1994-95), Superintendent of Maintenance (1992-94), Communications Maintenance Manager (1981-92), Communications Maintenance Supervisor (1972-81), Communications Maintenance Technician (1965-72). **Associations & Accomplishments:** Air Force Association; POISE Users Group. **Education:** University of Maryland, B.Sc. (1996). **Personal Information:** Two children: Christopher and Andrew.

Xiaoqing "Frank" Liu, Ph.D.

Assistant Professor
University of Missouri - Rolla
1870 Miner Circle
Rolla, MO 65409
(573) 341-4848
Fax: (573) 341-4501
fliu@cs.umr.edu

8221

Business Information: Providing his skilled services as Assistant Professor for the University of Missouri - Rolla's Computer Science Department, Dr. Liu conducts research and instruction on software engineering. In this capacity, he teaches undergraduate and graduate students. Concurrently, Dr. Liu serves as the Director of Software Engineering Laboratory at the University. Utilizing 15 solid years of occupational experience and a firm academic history, he performs a wide range of cutting edge research on software systems with a primary focus on software improvement and quality. An active member of two industry related associations, he has published over 30 journal and conference articles on software. Getting into the field because of his fascination with technology, Dr. Liu's long-range goals are to continue with software engineering research and strengthen the University's software engineering program. Established in 1870, the University of Missouri - Rolla operates as a technical university serving over 4,500 students. The University generates in excess of $78 million in annual revenues. Offering a fine educational program covering all aspects of engineering technology, the Computer Science Department currently serves 350 undergraduate and 50 graduate students. **Career Highlights:** University of Missouri - Rolla: Assistant Professor (1995-Present), Director of Software Engineering Laboratory (1996-Present). **Associations & Accomplishments:** Institute of Electronic and Electrical Engineers, Inc.; Association of Computing Machinery; Who's Who in Science and Engineering; International WHO'S WHO of Professionals. **Education:** Texas A&M University, Ph.D. (1995); Southeast University - Peoples Republic of China, M.S. (1985); Changsha Institute of Technology - Peoples Republic of China, B.S. (1982). **Personal Information:** Married to Xiaoxia in 1988. One child: Jesse. Dr. Liu enjoys travel, fishing and sports.

Kevin J. Loeffler

Systems Administrator
Purdue University
1149 South Campus Courts E10
West Lafayette, IN 47907
(765) 496-2856
loeffler@purdue.edu

8221

Business Information: Dedicated to the educational success of Purdue University, Mr. Loeffler applies his knowledge and expertise in the field of technology in serving as Systems Administrator. He assumes accountability for the computer and local area network administration for a division of the Office of the Dean of Students. Performing software and hardware installation and maintenance, he ensures that the network and its systems are performing at optimum levels. Mr. Loeffler also offers his technical expertise to the systems users, assisting them with any questions or problems. Citing enthusiasm for his work and an appreciation for the technology industry as the reason for his success, he is continually striving to improve his performance by keeping abreast of new developments in his field. He looks forward to gaining his technical certifications in the near future. Purdue University is a higher education academic institution offering majors in accounting, communications, and mathematics as well as numerous others. Undergraduate and graduate degrees are offered in the University's course studies. Purdue University was established in 1869 and employs more than 14,800 administrative, instructional, and support personnel. **Career Highlights:** Systems Administrator, Purdue University (1997-Present). **Associations & Accomplishments:** Association for Computing Machinery; The Institute of Electronics and Electrical Engineers; Theta Tau Fraternity, Phi Chapter. **Education:** Purdue University, B.S. (1997). **Personal Information:** Mr. Loeffler enjoys racquetball and playing the guitar.

Judith M. Marged, Ed.D.

Information Technology Faculty
American Intercontinental University
8151 West Peter's Road, Crossroad Two, Suite 1000
Plantation, FL 33324
(954) 835-0939
margedj@prodigy.net

8221

Business Information: Providing her superior talents as Information Technology Faculty, Dr. Marged joined American Intercontinental University in 1999. In her position, she teaches computer networking using a variety of leading edge programs that includes Windows NTand Server, AT, Net Essentials, and Windows 2000. Highly regarded, Dr. Marged attributes her professional success to her quest for knowledge. Dedicated to providing her students with the most practical and comprehensive education, Dr. Marged shares ideas and techniques in an enthusiastic and persuasive manner. The most rewarding aspect of her career is developing a nine week health course at Ramblewood Middle School. Consistently achieving quality performance in her field, Dr. Marged plans to continue learning and changing with emerging technology to capitalize on opportunites at American Intercontinental University. American Intercontinental University, a private institution, provides specialized course instruction in information technology and business for individuals wishing to advance their educational studies. The University offers bachelor's and master's degrees. Established in 1970, the University is located in Plantation, Florida and maintains six campuses. Presently, the Plantation location staffs 50 administrative, teaching, and support personnel who work diligently to enhance and perfect educational opportunities for students. **Career Highlights:** Infomation Technology Faculty, American Intercontinental University (1999-Present); Teacher of Special Education and Substance Abuse Prevention, Ramblewood Middle School (1984-96); Teacher of Learning for Disabled Students, American Academy (1980-83). **Associations & Accomplishments:** Association for Career and Technical Education; Phi Delta Kappa. **Education:** Nova University, Ed.D. (1991); Florida Atlantic University: M.Ed. in Guidance and Counseling (1984), B.A. in Exceptional Education (1980), B.A. in Biology (1984). **Personal Information:** Dr. Marged enjoys travel, sports, reading, music and computers.

Warren D. Mayer

Programmer/Analyst
Rutgers University
190 University Avenue
Newark, NJ 07102-1818
(973) 353-5764
Fax: (973) 353-1246
jmcintire@nugget.nqc.peachnet.edu

8221

Business Information: Possessing advanced technical abilities, Mr. Mayer serves as Programmer and Analyst for the Newark campus of Rutgers University. He assumes accountability for developing, maintaining, and upgrading the Web site. In addition, Mr. Mayer oversees client server applications and assists in the development of the curriculum utilizing the Internet. He also teaches a course on building Web sites and serves on the Web Advisory Committee for the Rutgers system. Proficient in Windows 95, Sun operations, Unix, and Mac, Mr. Mayer aspires to continue advancing in his career and hopes to become more involved in Internet application development in the future. Rutgers University is an institute of higher learning offering undergraduate and graduate degrees in various fields of study. The University currently employs 600 faculty members to serve 27,000 students. **Career Highlights:** Programmer/Analyst, Rutgers University Computing Services Department (1988-Present). **Associations & Accomplishments:** Association of Online Professionals; Society of Applied Learning Technology; National Trust for Historic Preservation. **Education:** Rutgers University: M.S. (In Progress), B.A. (1979). **Personal Information:** Mr. Mayer enjoys travel, computers, hiking, museums, historical preservation and restoration and 18th and 19th Century antiques.

Virgil L. McDonald

Computer Science Instructor
Mesa Technical College
911 South 10th Street
Tucumcari, NM 88401-3352
(505) 461-4413
Fax: (505) 461-1901
virgilm@mesatc.cc.nm.us

8221

Business Information: As a Computer Science Instructor at Mesa Technical College, Mr. McDonald teaches students how to complete all aspects of computer operations. Beginning with programming and applications, he demonstrates his extensive knowledge by providing hands on examples of proper procedures. Utilizing several years of experience, he directs students on the repair and maintenance of operating systems and hardware. An advocate of open communication, he encourages feedback and input from his students, fostering an environment that is conducive to learning. Currently, he is working to develop Web-based applications and computer support programs for the improvement of the circiculum. Mesa Technical College offers technical degrees of higher education. Established in 1981, the state legislature granted the power to issue degrees to the college in 1994. Employing over 50 people to direct students, the Institution provides quality education and modern facilities. **Career Highlights:** Mesa Technical College: Computer Science Faculty (1983-Present), Computer Support (1983-99); Programmer, Ben Rose, C.P.A. (1982-83). **Associations & Accomplishments:** Council for Higher Education Computing Services. **Education:** University of Phoenix, M.S. in C.I.S. (1999); Eastern New Mexico University, B.S. in Computer Science. **Personal Information:** Married to Brenda in 1978. Two children: Chris and Nathan. Mr. McDonald enjoys being outdoors, hunting, fishing, camping and sports.

Armando Ibarra Medina

Computer Manager
ITESM Campus Laguna
Paseo Del Technologico S/N Col., Coahuila
Torreon, Mexico 27250
+52 17296381
aibarra@campus.lag.itesm.mx

8221

Business Information: A successful veteran of the technology industry for the last 10 years, Mr. Medina serves as the Computer Manager for ITESM Campus Laguna. In his capacity, he fulfills a number of technical duties on behalf of the Institution. Possessing an excellent understanding of his field, Mr. Medina oversees and directs all aspects of day to day operations of the systems and networking infrastructure and ensures its functionality and operational status. In addition, he provides management oversight of computer technology on all campus extensions, overseeing installation of computers in computer labs. In the future, Mr. Median's goals include moving to another university and continuing to move up the corporate ladder. His success reflects his ability to take on challenges and deliver results. ITESM Campus Laguna is an educational institution providing higher learning in the area of technology. With seven campuses located throughout Mexico, the Institution educates more than 11,000 students every year. Presently, the Institution is situated in Torreon,

Mexico. **Career Highlights:** Computer Manager, ITESM Campus Laguna (Present). **Education:** ITESM, Master's degree in Computer Science (1994); Bachelor's degree in Computer Science (1990). **Personal Information:** Married to Rosa Eluira Mora in 1994. One child: Jessica Ibarra Mora. Mr. Medina enjoys swimming, sleeping and travel.

Janie E. Montgomery

Internet Manager
Ottawa University
1001 South Cedar Street
Ottawa, KS 66067
(785) 229-1094
Fax: (785) 242-0182
janiem@ottawa.edu

8221

Business Information: As Internet Manager of Ottawa University, Ms. Montgomery is responsible for Internet hardware and software design and content. She is in charge of all hardware including servers, routers, switches, and software. Additional responsibilties include designing previous Web sites and is involved in creating interactive sites. Ms. Montgomery handles e-mail usage on campus and is invovled in project management for recent equipment changes. She is also in charge of UNIX box and administrative contact for online courses. Current projects include working with Lucent to design new interactive Web sites. She hopes to move into a project management position outside the university setting. Ms. Montgomery believes that the key to success is to be dedicated to work and always be up for a challenge. Ottawa University is an Independent American Baptist, higher education facility with six locations. Set on a 60-acre campus with easy access to Kansas City, approximately 500 undergraduate students presently take advantage of the educational opportunities available at the University. Established in 1865, a staff of 150 individuals are available to assist students in all aspects of their college career. **Career Highlights:** Internet Manager, Ottawa University (1995-Present); Partner, Hydrapac, L.L.C. (1998-Present); Network Administrator, Flatland Gun & Supply, Inc. (1993-96). **Education:** Ottawa University, B.A. in Computer Information Systems (1995). **Personal Information:** Married to John Pollock in 1995. Two children: Brenton and Justin. Ms. Montgomery enjoys horseback riding, boating and working out.

Pedro Morales

Management Information Systems Director
University of Southern California School of Medicine
2025 Zonal Avenue, Room 6602
Los Angeles, CA 90033-1034
(323) 226-4634
Fax: (323) 226-2796
pmorales@hsc.usc.edu

8221

Business Information: Mr. Morales directs computing operations and services for the clinical research center at the University of Southern California's School of Medicine. In his current role as Management Information Systems Director, he exercises oversight of computer system operations from his office near the School's research center, where the mainframe is housed. Mr. Morales monitors technical services operations and the system's help desk service log to keep an eye on operational integrity across systems and platforms within the facility and across campus. He also consults with technicians when problems arise, and provides his troubleshooting expertise as needed. Mr. Morales monitors data processing and storage activities to analyze local and wide area network utilization and resource margins to ensure seamless access and operation of the systems and software for critical research requirements. He plans to continue expanding his technological knowledge-base, and hopes to advance through the management hierarchy. The University of Southern California is a highly-selective, private, four-year, coed, liberal arts university with graduate programs. Established in 1880, USC is located in Los Angeles, and serves a student population of around 28,000. The USC School of Medicine facilities are operated separately from the central USC campus. **Career Highlights:** Management Information Systems Director, University of Southern California School of Medicine (1995-Present); Systems Manager, Harbor UCLA Research and Educational Institute (1988-95); Systems Operator, Whittier College (1985-88). **Associations & Accomplishments:** National Association of General Clinical Research Center Systems Manager. **Education:** Whittier College, B.B.A. in Computer Networks (1988). **Personal Information:** Married to Evelyn in 1997. Mr. Morales enjoys cross-country skiing and sailing.

Padmavathi Muvvala

Database Administrator
University of Bahrain
Flat 24, Building 189, Road 2608
Area 326, Bahrain
+973-9634716
Fax: +973-714891
mpadmavathi@hotmail.com

8221

Business Information: Proficient in all areas of technology, Mrs. Padmavathi was recruited to the University of Bahrain in 1998. Serving as Database Administrator, she manages the University's Oracle based database, performing routine maintenance, monitoring daily activity, providing network security, and a backup system to prevent data loss. An expert, Mrs. Padmavathi also assists staff programmers in the design and programing of the database. Currently researching new trends in the field of technology, she is studying the effect of technology on geographical systems and the output of data in an analysis environment. As a 12 year technology professional, Mrs. Muvvala' career success reflects her ability to think outside the box and aggressively take on new challenges. The University of Bahrain is a higher learning institute. Approximately 1,000 administrative, faculty, and support personnel work diligently to provide students with quality educational opportunities. **Career Highlights:** Database Administrator, University of Bahrain (1998-Present); Computer Specialist, Environmental Affairs (1994-98); Scientist and Engineer C, National Remote Sensing A (1991-94). **Associations & Accomplishments:** Indian Society of Remote Sensing; Indian Cartographic Association; Land Use Management Society. **Education:** Anna University, India, Master's degree in Technology (1988). **Personal Information:** Married to M R in 1992. One child: Nil. Mrs. Muvvala enjoys reading technical reviews and books.

Leonard J. Nester

Director of Information Services
St. Joseph's University
5600 City Avenue
Philadelphia, PA 19131
(610) 660-1287
Fax: (610) 660-1536
nester@sju.edu

8221

Business Information: Mr. Nester has been with St. Joseph's University since 1998, and has spent that time keeping students and staff current with the latest in multimedia. As the Director of Information Services, he works in the information technology department where he oversees and directs call center and help desk operations. He recruited, hired, and trained a coop staff of 30 to provide students online assistance. Possessing an excellent understanding of technology, Mr. Nester developed and documented computing standards, procedures, and policies. He also prepares weekly operations for his group, adjusting staff and schedules in response to planned and unplanned absences and operational contingencies. Overseeing the computing lab, running workshops and seminars, and deploying new software and hardware also fall within the realm of Mr. Nester's functions. In the future, he plans on completely rebuilding his Department, have the Company fully wired, and have the call center and help desk at an 80 percent call resolution on the first call. St. Joseph's University is a Catholic Jesuit university located in Philadelphia, Pennsylvania. A member of NCAA Division I, more than 3,200 undergraduates attend the University. St. Joseph's student body is vastly diverse, educating people from more than fifty foreign countries. More than 90 percent of the faculty at St. Joseph's hold doctoral or terminal degrees, and they strive to extend office hours so as to give students the opportunity for private assistance. **Career Highlights:** Director of Information Services, St. Joseph's University (1998-Present); Senior Systems Engineer, InfoSystems Inc. (1997-98); Senior Systems Engineer, Digital Equipment Corporation (1996-97). **Education:** St. Joseph's University, Bachelor's degree. **Personal Information:** Married to Doreen Cassady-Nester in 1982. Five children: Carly, Ashley, Ben, Len, and Nicole.

Marjana Newman

Technical Support Specialist 2
Louisiana State University at Eunice
P.O. Box 1129- Information Tech
Eunice, LA 70535-1129
(337) 550-1307
Fax: (337) 550-1306
mnewman@lsue.edu

8221

Business Information: Ms. Newman has faithfully served with Louisiana State University at Eunice in a variety of roles since joining the University as Equipment Operator in 1983. In her current position of Technical Support Specialist 2, she analyzes and supports computer operations, monitors system resources, and provides operational support. Utilizing her extensive skills in technology, she is responsible for programming, PC repair, help desk support, and network administration. Ms. Newman, with an excellent understanding of her field, is involved in troubleshooting of hardware, software, and PCs; and is responsible for adding users to the system and ensuring the system is functional and operational. Attributing success to her supportive family, she enjoys her current position and takes pride in the system that she implemented from a manual card to an on-line system. Louisiana State University at Eunice is a higher education facility providing degrees in office management, secretarial work, criminal justice, paralegal, nursing, and general studies. As a part of the Louisiana State University system, the Eunice location employs 160 administrative, teaching, and support personnel. Educating more than 3,000 individuals, the University works diligently to enhance and perfect educational opportunities for students. **Career Highlights:** Lousiana State University at Eunice: Technical Support Specialist 2 (1999-present), Applications Programmer (1992-99), Equipment Operator (1983-92). **Associations & Accomplishments:** FUPC Youth Group. **Education:** Louisiana State University, Associate's degree in CIT (1992). **Personal Information:** One child: Brock. Ms. Newman enjoys needlework and reading.

Quan Nguyen

Manager
McGill University
805 Sherbrooke Street, Room 200
West Montreal, Quebec, Canada H3A 2K6
(514) 398-3709
Fax: (514) 398-6876
quan@cc.mcgill.ca

8221

Business Information: As Manager of McGill University, Mr. Nguyen oversees and maintains the functionality and operational status of the University's netwoking infrastructure, providing excellent services in information technologies. Specifically heading all design and implementation of new systems and programs, Mr. Nguyen ensures an efficient database suited for the University's particular needs. Utilizing his vast knowledge of information technologies, he concentrates his efforts towards working closely with networking vendors in order to gain more knowledge and assume more responsibilities within his Department. Dedicated to the further advancement of higher education, McGill University was established in 1821. Located in West Montreal, Canada, the University is positioned on a beautiful campus attracting students from all over the country. Over 10,000 professional and adminsitrative staff devote their time towards providing quality education and support. Programs are offered in variety in order to assist the student in reaching their career goals. Special assistance such as financial aid and counseling are available to direct students in making their decisions as to course load and academic activities. **Career Highlights:** Manager, McGill University (1993-Present); Senior Telecommunications Analyst, Pratt & Whitney Canada (1982-93); Communications Specialist, Bell Canada (1980-82). **Associations & Accomplishments:** Institute of Electrical and Electronics Engineers. **Education:** Ecole Polytechnique de Montreal, Bachelor's in Engineering (1978). **Personal Information:** Married to Thi Ngoc in 1995. One child: Hoang.

Gary B/ Nickerson

Director of Computer and Information Technology
Oklahoma Baptist University
500 West University Street
Shawnee, OK 74801-2589
(405) 878-2056
Fax: (405) 878-2047
gary_nickerson@mail.okbu.edu

8221

Business Information: As Director of Computer and Information Technology for Oklahoma Baptist University, Mr. Nickerson is responsible for computer systems throughout 14 buildings. The systems are comprised of 525 network computers with Web servers and on-line library catalog access. Mr. Nickerson also controls an MIT program for the University's satellite campuses in seven states. He plans to remain on the cutting edge of technology, entering a new and diverse range of technical fields. Oklahoma Baptist University was established in 1910 as a private liberal arts educational facility. In the past eight years, the University has been recognized by U.S. News for excellence in the academic field. Oklahoma Baptist University reports estimated annual revenue of $25 million. **Career Highlights:** Oklahoma Baptist University: Director of Computer and Information Technology (1997-Present), Assistant Director of Information Systems (1993-97), Microcomputer Services Manager (1990-93), Computer Lab Supervisor (1989-90). **Associations & Accomplishments:** Minister. **Education:** Oklahoma Baptist University, B.A. (1989). **Personal Information:** Married to Tina Mannon in 1978. Three children: Shawna, Brad, and Adam. Mr. Nickerson enjoys trout fishing.

James Novitzki, Ph.D.
Director of IT Credit Programs
Johns Hopkins University
201 North Charles Street, Suite 20-D
Baltimore, MD 21201-3933
(301) 294-7103
Fax: (301) 294-7010
j.novitzki@jhu.edu

8221

Business Information: As Director of Information Technology Credit Programs for John Hopkins University, Dr. Novitzki is responsible for implementing guidance and integrity in all projects. His primary functions include gathering information for educational development, classroom instruction, designing and modifying programs, and coordinating annual conferences. Dr. Novitzki regularly attends meetings and seminars to keep abreast of structural changes to curriculum, which will help him in his endeavors to develop classes on line. John Hopkins University engages in the provision of higher education for students aspiring to careers in today's competitive professional world. A school of complex study programs, the University offers two information technology courses for degrees for educating technically inclined students on computer related issues. The information technology department was established in 1992, and has programs for concentration on telecommunicatiohns, e-business, and e-commerce. With the assistance of more than 800 trained professional educators, the University presently provides knowledge for over 1,100 students in the information technology credit program. **Career Highlights:** Director of IT Credit Programs, Johns Hopkins University (1995-Present); MIS Coordinator, North Central College (1989-95); Associate Professor, Naval Post Graduate School and University of Montana (1978-85). **Associations & Accomplishments:** Board of Directors, International Academy of Information Management; Society of Information Management; Institute of Electrical and Electronic Engineers; Association of Information Technology Professionals. **Education:** United States International University, Ph.D. (1978); LaVern University, M.A. (1974); University of Southern California, B.A. (1964); University of Minnesota, Post Doctorate Study (1987); Indiana University (1985). **Personal Information:** Married to Linda in 1964. Five children: Kathleen, Brenda, James, Lisa, and Mary. Dr. Novitzki enjoys being a member of the Knights of Columbus and model trains.

Jonas Öberg
Systems Administrator
Mälardalens Mögskola
Kaserngatan 6
Vasteras, Sweden 72347
+46 21144831
Cell Phone: +46 733423962
jonas@gnu.org

8221

Business Information: A savvy Systems Administrator of Mälardalens Mögskola, Mr. Öberg is responsible for managing all aspects of the computer systems and network infrastructure. His responsibilities include ensuring that e-mail, networks, and free software are running properly at all times. Possessing an excellent understanding of his field, Mr. Öberg has published numerous articles on working with free software in various Swedish newspapers. In the future, he plans to continue working in this capacity, possibly moving more into applications service provisioning. Mälardalens Mögskola is an institution of higher learning providing specialized course instruction for individuals wishing to advance their educational studies. The University staffs 900 administrative, teaching, and support personnel who work diligently to enhance and perfect educational opportunities for its students. Founded in 1975, the University educates more than 14,000 students each year. **Career Highlights:** Systems Administrator, Mälardalens Mögskola (1999-Present); Owner, CIXIT, A.B. (1998-99); Systems Administrator, Aros Internet, A.B. (1997-98); Systems Administrator, Ericsson Telecom, A.B. **Associations & Accomplishments:** Volunteer, Free Software Foundation. **Education:** Mälardalens Mögskola (1999). **Personal Information:** Mr. Öberg enjoys writing, reading, cooking, biking and travel. Mr. Öberg actively participates in the free software community as a programmer, speaker, and writer.

Vazi P. Okhandiar
Department Head of Computer Science
National University
10 Gettysburg
Irvine, CA 92620-3266
(714) 429-5131
vpok@aol.com

8221

Business Information: Possessing broad technical expertise in software technology, Ms. Okhandiar was recruited to National University in 1998. At the present time, she fulfills the diverse responsibilities of Department Head of Computer

Science. In that capacity, she provides management oversight of the entire operation of the department. Teaching objective database and information technology courses also falls in the realm of her role. Utilizing 12 years of extensive experience and strong knowledge in technology, Ms. Okhandiar develops course curriculum, advises students, and formulates innovative marketing strategies. Concurrent to her teaching role, she conducts part-time consulting on the side. She attributes her success to a strong professional background, excellent leadership skills, and solid family background. Always alert to new opportunities, Ms. Okhandiar's long-term goal is to simultaneously continue in consulting, information technology, and education. National University is an institution of higher learning. A private, upper-division, coed, liberal arts university with graduate programs, the Institution was founded in 1971. Located on 15-acres of land in San Diego, the Institution operates 20 branch campuses in California, Las Vegas, and Costa Rica. Majors with largest enrollment are computer science and behavioral science. **Career Highlights:** Department Head of Computer Science, National University (1998-Present); Project Manager, NetVision (1997-98); Senior Software Engineer, Computer Science Corporation (1996-97); Senior System Engineer, EDS/General Motors (1991-96). **Associations & Accomplishments:** Institute of Electronics and Electrical Engineers; Association of Computing Machinery; President, Syban User Group Orange County; Received Award for Outstanding Job on EDS Project Management Software Development. **Education:** University of California at Irvine: Executive MBA (2000), B.S. in Electrical Engineering (1986); Illinois Institute of Technology at Chicago, M.S. in Computer Science (1988). **Personal Information:** Married to Amitabh in 1989. Two children: Neil and Rohit. Ms. Okhandiar enjoys travel, swimming, reading and biking.

Patrick C. Olson, Ph.D.
Director of Information Technology
Menlo College
1000 El Camino Real
Atherton, CA 94027-4301
(650) 688-3830
Fax: (650) 322-0407
olsonp@menlo.edu

8221

Business Information: As Director of Information Technology of Menlo College, Dr. Olson oversees the computer and networking environment at the College. In this context, he oversees and directs the day-to-day administration and operations of technology laboratories as well as servers and business systems. He determines the overall technical direction of the College and formulates new technical plans to keep the College at forefront of academic excellence. Dr. Olson approves computer purchases, assists in the decision making of policies and procedures, helps with admissions and financial registration. Because of Dr. Olson's innovativeness, Menlo College is the first school with a gigabyte backbone infrastructure for library computing. Building USI, a new mainframe at Hughes Aircraft Corporation; implementing Cal Poly's first LAN, and designing a Master's Program at the University of Redland are a few of Dr. Olson's career accomplishments to date. Enjoying substantial success in the information technology field, he plans to continue in his role at Menlo College for the next five years before returning to the faculty as a professor. Established in 1927, Menlo College is a reputable, four-year institution of higher learning. Offering undergraduates studies, the College employs more than 180 professional and administrative faculty. Providing educational services to a regional population, Menlo College boasts an enrollment of 600 to 700 students. Presently, the College reports annual revenues in excess of $1 million. **Career Highlights:** Director of Information Technology, Menlo College (1999-Present); Visiting Assistant Professor, University of Nevada (1998-99); Adjunct Professor, University of Redlands (1995-98); Assistant Professor, California State Polytechnic University (1987-95); Computing Staff, Hughes Aircraft Company (1981-87). **Associations & Accomplishments:** International Society for Technology in Education; Association of Computing Machinery; Educause. **Education:** Claremont Graduate School, Ph.D. (1999); University of Southern California, M.S. in Systems Management (1985); University of Montana, B.A. (1979). **Personal Information:** Dr. Olson enjoys books, music, television, trains, pens and computer games.

John Paden, M.B.A.
Director of Information Management
St. Mary College
4100 South 4th Street
Leavenworth, KS 66048-5082
(913) 758-6230
Fax: (913) 758-6140
padenj@swbell.net

8221

Business Information: Concentrating efforts on providing innovative technology for St. Mary College, Mr. Paden serves as the Director of Information Management. He oversees the

local area networks, telecommunications, and distance learning applications for three campuses. In addition, Mr. Paden negotiates contracts, purchases hardware and software according to the specific needs of the departments, and aids local schools in the procurement of updated systems and applications. Providing staffing solutions for his division, Mr. Paden coordinates training activities to ensure employees maintain a high understanding of technology to provide assistance to both students and faculty. Mr. Paden aspires to advance into a Chief Information Officer position in the near future. Serving the world of academia since 1921, St. Mary College is a private liberal arts institution offering four-year degrees. The College is located in Leavenworth, Kansas and has an enrollment of approximately 300 students annually. **Career Highlights:** Director of Information Management, St. Mary College (1996-Present); President/Owner, Cyber Design Group (Present); Interim Executive Director, Heartland Technology Consortium (1996-Present); Owner, First Capital Source (1988-96). **Associations & Accomplishments:** Heartland Technology Consortium; Advisory Board, Information Technology Program, Johnson County Community College. **Education:** Johnson County Community College, Telecommunications and Networks Specialist Certificate (1994); University of Missouri at Columbia: M.B.A. (1973), B.S. in Business Administration (1971). **Personal Information:** Married to Kristin in 1983. One child: Rebecca. Mr. Paden enjoys being a pilot, woodworking, reading business and technical journals and skiing.

Randy J. Pagulayan
Web Designer
University of Cincinnati
P.O. Box 210376, Department of Psychology
Cincinnati, OH 45221-0376
(513) 556-5583
Fax: (513) 556-1904
pagular@email.uc.edu

8221

Business Information: As a Web Designer at the University of Cincinnati, Mr. Pagulayan is responsible for the Department web page. Utilizing his vast technical skills, he focuses on general administration of the Web site and strategic planning for the information technology systems. Responsible for setting up new systems and evaluating software, he provides on-site technical support. His career highlights include being part of Motorola's design group and receiving a scholarship from Motorola as well as writing publication records, book chapters, book reviews, and technical journals. Committed to further development and always alert to new opportunities, techniques, and approaches, his future plans include using his education and social skills to move into a position in industry and better himself even further. Mr. Pagulayan says, "No matter how smart a person may be, he has to have social skills." University of Cincinnati is a state supported institution of higher learning located in Cincinnati, Ohio. The 19,451 undergraduate students and 7,506 gaduate students at the University receive an outstanding education where they can choose from 325 academic programs, exceptional co-op opportunities, and 275 student organizations. Rich with opportunity and fascinatingly diverse, the University prepares students for their future job, graduate school, and life. **Career Highlights:** University of Cincinnati: Web Designer, Department of Psychology (1999-Present), Statistical Consultant, Institute for Nursing Research (1999-Present); Human Factors Specialist, Motorola (1999). **Associations & Accomplishments:** Human Factors & Economics Society; Association of Computing Machinery; Special Interest Group Computer-Human Interaction; International Society for Ecological Psychology. **Education:** University of Cincinnati, M.A. (1998); University of Maryland at College Park, B.A. (1995). **Personal Information:** Mr. Pagulayan enjoys Macintosh computers, rollerblading, skiing and soccer.

Scott M. Parrill
Senior Systems Programmer
University of Wyoming, Department of Space and Data & Visualization Center
16th & Gibbon Street
Laramie, WY 82071
(307) 766-2524
Fax: (307) 766-2744
sparrill@uwyo.edu

8221

Business Information: Serving as the Senior Systems Programmer for the University of Wyoming's Department of Spatial Data & Visualization Center, Mr. Parrill is responsible for systems administration, programming for Geographic Information System projects, and Web programming. Drawing from his previous occupational experience, he also manages all of the computers, peripherals, and networking for the Department. He works closely with management and users to analyze, specify, and design new solutions to harness more of the computer's power. Maintaining an edge in the advancement of technology, Mr. Parrill also advises on the current affairs in the information technology industry. Highly regarded, he plans to continue excelling in the industry. Founded in 1886, the University of Wyoming is a state supported, co-ed institution of higher learning. Providing the student population of over 11,250 with a high quality education, the University offers a variety of major areas of study. Within the University, the Department of Spatial Data and Visualization Center provides aspects of support for the University's GIS computer systems. Specifically providing geographic information systems, the Department employs the skills of 20 specially trained individuals. **Career Highlights:** Senior Systems Programmer, University of Wyoming, Department of Spatial Data & Visualization Center (1997-Present); Senior Systems Analyst, Sykes Enterprises (1994-97). **Education:** University of Wyoming, B.S. in Electrical Engineering (1991). **Personal Information:** Mr. Parrill enjoys reading, hunting, photography and computers.

Stephen M. Patti

Information Technology Manager
Yale University
ITS/Telecommunications
221 Whitney Avenue, 3rd Floor
New Haven, CT 06520
(203) 432-2022
Fax: (203) 436-4376
stephen.patti@yale.edu

8221

Business Information: Mr. Patti assists in the intergration of all programs and services offered by the Yale University telecommunications department through his role as Desktop Support Manager. Through his extensive knowledge of the industry, he supports the University's users by lending technical support services to solve challenges. Demonstrating his educational ties and technical expertise, he maintains hardware and software, including servers, as he handles upgrades and troubleshooting. Enjoying the challenges of his position, Mr. Patti aspires to a role that will allow him to further develop his skills, such as that of director of information technology of a small business or university department. One of the most distinguished institutions of higher learning in the world, Yale University was established in 1701 in New Haven, Connecticut. Offering Bachelor's, Master's, Doctoral, and first professional Degress in majors ranging from American studies to South Asian languages, the University also provides a wide array of extracurricular clubs and athletic programs. **Career Highlights:** Desktop Support Manager, Yale University (1999-Present); Consultant, PricewaterhouseCoopers (1999); Computer Support Professional, Simsburg Public Schools (1999); Business Analyst, Industrial Risk Insurer's (1986-97). **Associations & Accomplishments:** Microsoft Certified Systems Engineer. **Education:** Trinity College, B.A. in Economics (1986). **Personal Information:** Married to Lisa Patrice in 1996. Mr. Patti enjoys massage therapy, golf and martial arts.

Michael Pietrowski

Director of Videography
Stonehill College
320 Washington Street
Easton, MA 02356-1202
(508) 565-1082
Fax: (508) 565-1446

8221

Business Information: Mr. Pietrowski functions in the role of Director of Videography at Stonehill College. He was appointed by the President of the College to redesign and restructure the technology program involving videography. Since his appointment, he has integrated computer and video technologies into the program and has correlated credit programs for students involved in special events at the College. His primary motivation is to successfully promote all types of technology within the College. Highlights include design and implementation of spearhead technology for Mastree High School and establishment of the first SMPTE high school student section in the world. Attributing his success to the students and being very committed, Mr. Pietrowski hopes to continue being the first of many events in the future. Stonehill College is a four-year liberal arts facility challenging the students of Easton, Maine. The College encourages its student body to achieve higher educational goals than they had ever imagined and expand their curiousity into new topics. Students attending the College have been provided with top quality educational opportunities for over fifty years. Today, the students have the opportunity to participate is a wide assortment of extra curricular activities. **Career Highlights:** Director of Videography, Stonehill College (1998-Present); Director of Video, Mass Marine Theater (1980); Director of Audio and Visual Technology, Mastree Public (1977). **Associations & Accomplishments:** Society of Motion Picture & Television Enanrean. **Education:** Cape Cod Regular Technical High School. **Personal Information:** Mr. Pietrowski enjoys racquetball, basketball, travel and golf.

Katharine Purnell

Career Services Manager
American Intercontinental University
American Intercontinental University
Plantation, FL 33324
(954) 835-0951
Fax: (954) 835-1020
kpurnell@aiuniv.edu

8221

Business Information: As the Career Services Manager with American Intercontinental University, Ms. Purnell is responsible for working with community employers in order to match students and graduates to various employment opportunities. Highly regarded, she maintains a 96 percent placement rate for graduates. Throughout her duties, she is charged with the obligation to perform such activities as hosting career fairs and conducting campus visits for student evaluations. With more than seven years of hands-on experience, Ms. Purnell plans on using her superior knowledge and expertise to devise innovative plans with an emphasis on maintaining excellence and maximizing the career potential of all American Intercontinental University students. American Intercontinental University is an academic institute that provides higher education to aspiring professionals and those who wish to expand current knowledge. The University offers a wide variety of courses and programs primarily for obtaining Bachelor's and Master's degrees in such fields as information technology and international business. Established in 1970, the University is headquartered in Florida. **Career Highlights:** Career Servics Manager, American Intercontinental University (1999-Present); University of Phoenix: Director of Student Services (1996-99), Operations Supervisor (1995-96), Lead Counselor (1993-95). **Associations & Accomplishments:** International Association of Career Management Professionals; Education and Workforce Development Council at Fort Lauderdale; Volunteer, Red Cross of America. **Education:** University of Phoenix: M.A. in Organizational Management (1998), B.S. in Business Administration; Chaparrel Career College, A.A. in Business Computer Science. **Personal Information:** Ms. Purnell enjoys playing brain teaser-type games and caring for children.

Todd M. Quasny

Research Technician
Texas Tech University
3315 35th Street
Lubbock, TX 79413-2316
(806) 438-8633
todd@quasny.com

8221

Business Information: A savvy professional, Mr. Quasny serves as a Reasearch Technician of Texas Tech University's Computer Science Department in AI and Robotics. Along with his duties inside the laboratory, he plans programs, orders epuipment for the use of fellow technicians, and handles all computer set up and installations. A key technical member of the team for one year and a half, Mr. Quasny is still working on his education. He is endeavoring to complete his Master's degree, then eventually his Ph.D. His career highlight is the implementation of a leading edge system for the computer laboratory, providing students with an up-to-date operating platform to enhance their academic process. His success is attributed to networking and knowing the right people. Established in 1923, Texas Tech University is an institution of higher education that caters to over 25,000 students from around the United States and 99 other countries. Students have more than 300 graduate and undergraduate degree programs to chose from. Texas tech University is the second largest continuing education campus in the United States. **Career Highlights:** Texas Tech University: Research Technician (Present), System Administrator, Math Department (1998-99), Systems Programmer, ACS (1997-98), Student Assistant (1996-97). **Associations & Accomplishments:** Association of Computing Machinery; Coach, Computer Programming Team, Texas Tech University; Judge, UIL State Programming Contest; Lubbock Linx Users Group. **Education:** Texas Tech University, B.S. in Computer Science (In Progress). **Personal Information:** Mr. Quasny enjoys movies, music and travel.

Daniel D. Reneau, Ph.D.

President
Louisiana Tech University
Railroad Avenue, Wyly Tower, Room 1620
Ruston, LA 71272
(318) 257-3785
Fax: (318) 257-2928

8221

Business Information: As President, Dr. Reneau is the chief executive administrator responsible for all aspects of academic operations, particularly serving as the University's representative in all outreach and community relations. A full-tenured Professor of Biomedical Engineering, Dr. Reneau continues to conduct research in the field. He was also responsible for the implementation, in 1973, of the Biomedical Engineering Department. Louisiana Tech University is a public, four-year, coed, specialized university with diversified graduate programs. Established in 1894, the University has 407 full-time faculty, 75 part-time faculty and over 1,100 administrative and support staff. Special programs of study include: Preprofessional Programs in Law; Medicine; Veterinary Science; Pharmacy; Dentistry and Optometry. Six colleges within the University are Engineering; Administration and Business; Education; Life Sciences; Human Ecology, and Graduate School. **Career Highlights:** Louisiana Tech University: President (1988-Present), Vice President of Academic Affairs (1980-87), Professor and Head of the Biomedical Engineering Department (1973-80), Associate Professor and Head of the Biomedical Engineering Department (1972-73). **Associations & Accomplishments:** American Chemical Society; American Institute of Chemical Engineers; American Society of Engineering Education; Biomedical Engineering Society; European Society for Micro circulation; International Association for Oxygen Transport Tissue; Louisiana Engineering Society; Louisiana Teachers Association. **Education:** Clemson University, M.S. in Chemical Engineering (1964); Louisiana Tech University, B.S. (1963). **Personal Information:** Married to Linda in 1961. Two children: Dana Reneau Bernhard and John Reneau. Dr. Reneau enjoys reading, fishing, scuba diving and collecting North Louisiana Indian artifacts.

Robert Randall Robbins

Systems Technician
Sam Houston State University
12129 Andwood Street
Willis, TX 77318-7213
(409) 294-3955
Fax: (409) 294-1231

8221

Business Information: Utilizing more than 12 years of experience in the telecommunications field, Mr. Robbins serves as Systems Technician for the Computer Services Department of the Sam Houston State University. He assumes accountability for the 5,000 number telephone system on campus, administering the system, and troubleshooting any problems that arise. Additionally, he assists other staff members with the maintenance and troubleshooting of the computer network systems for the University. Mr. Robbins assumed the responsibility for coordinating the voice and data communications wiring for the largest dormitory on campus, configuring the specifications, and bringing the systems up to par with the rest of the campus. Crediting his education, work ethics, and military background as the key to his success, Mr. Robbins is currently pursuing his certifications in CISCO and MCSC. The Computer Services Department of the Sam Houston State University provides data and telecommunication support for 500 faculty members and over 14,000 students. Employing a staff of 25 dedicated individuals, the Department has 20 to 30 servers working at any one time and supplies Internet access to all dormitories and video to the classrooms in addition to its normal data and telecommunication functions. **Career Highlights:** Sam Houston State University: Computer Systems Technician (1999-Present), Student Network Technician (1998-99); Communications Maintenance Technician, United States Army (1987-93). **Associations & Accomplishments:** Golden Key Honor Society; National Dean's List (3 Years); Who's Who of Computers (1987). **Education:** Sam Houston State University. **Personal Information:** Married to Diana in 1998. One child: Jeremy Hoskins. Mr. Robbins enjoys martial arts, boating and skiing.

Brian M. Rothschild

Internet Strategist
Fordham University
113 West 60th Street, #1321
New York, NY 10023
(212) 636-6094
Fax: (212) 636-7222
rothschild@fordham.edu

8221

Business Information: Serving as an Internet Strategist for Fordham University, Mr. Rothschild is responsible for maintaining the University's Web site. In his capacity, he evaluates strategies and technologies for future implementation and integration for Fordham's Internet and Intranet sites. Demonstrating strong technical skills, Mr. Rothschild also ensures the upkeep of the existing sites and posts new information concentrating on University activities and operations. Attributing his success to networking and education, he notes the highlight of his career as organizing international conferences in England. In the future, Mr. Rothschild plans to continue working in this capacity, looking forward to the chance to continue to learn. Fordham University is an institution of higher learning providing general and specialized course instruction for individuals wishing to advance their educational studies. Established in 1841, the University is a private Catholic institution, which educates more than 14,000 undergraduate and graduate students annually. **Career Highlights:** Fordham University: Internet Strategist (1999-Present), Project Manager (1998-99); Adjunct Faculty, Dowling College (1996-98). **Associations & Accomplishments:** New York State Higher Educational Web Professionals; International WHO'S WHO of Professionals. **Education:** Fordham University, Ph.D. Candidate (In Progress); Iona College: M.B.A. (1992), B.A. (1990).

Damon E. Russell

Assistant Director of Computer Sciences
The Catholic University of America Columbus School of Law
3600 John McCormack Road
Washington, DC 20064
(202) 319-6087
Fax: (202) 319-6792
russelld@law.edu
8221

Business Information: As Assistant Director of Computer Services of The Catholic University of America Columbus School of Law, Mr. Russell supports and maintains daily computer operations by controlling systems level software. A solid, 10 year veteran of technology, he oversees network operations, e-mail systems, hubs, routers, and client server utility programs. He sets the technical direction, as well as formulates research and development strategies to help the University law school stay on top of emerging technologies. In addition to supervising his staff of five persons, Mr. Russell handles numerous other functions to include providing hardware and software and monitoring system resources. Ensuring electronic components meets IEEE standards before it hits the market also fall within the scope of his responsibilities. He is the recipient of a sizeable cash bonus and Letter of Appreciation from the Department of Defense for his phenomenal efforts. Mr. Russell attributes his success to a strong faith in God and guidance of the Holy Spirit. "To everyone who has, more will be given, but as for the one who has nothing, even what he has will be taken away," is cited as his quote from Luke 19:26. Opening his own computer store and gathering more technology knowledge serves as his future goals. A private, four-year, coed, liberal arts university, The Catholic University of America is home to the Columbus School of Law. The University provides international law programs and a Catholic based education. Founded in 1887, the University located on a 155-acre suburban campus in Washington, D.C., employs a faculty of more than 500 educators and administrators. **Career Highlights:** Assistant Director of Computer Services, The Catholic University of America Columbus School of Law (1997-Present); Information Systems Manager, Preston, Gates, Ellis Atly (1996-97); Production Supervisor, CDA Investment Technology (1994-96). **Education:** George Washington University, Associate's degree (1989). **Personal Information:** Married to Osvena A. in 1990. Two children: Picasso and Mikasa. Mr. Russell enjoys reading, chess and basketball.

Marvin G. Ryder

Assistant Vice President
McMaster University
1280 Main Street West
Hamilton, Ontario, Canada L8S 4L8
(905) 525-9140
Fax: (905) 524-5288
ryderm@mcmaster.ca
8221

Business Information: As Assistant Vice President of McMaster University, Mr. Ryder has been providing excellent educational services for over 16 years. Overseeing the basic operations of the University's administration, Mr. Ryder is responsible for the necessary staffing and meetings and conferences regarding University policies. Along with his duties as Vice President, he is in charge of the information services and technology portfolio containing telecommunications, audiovisual services, computing services, and printing services. Highly regarded by his colleagues, he possesses superior talents and an excellent understanding of technology. Involved in the preservation of academic quality, Mr. Ryder plans on staying at the University. "One must have excellent communication skills," is cited as his advice to others. Established in 1887, McMaster University, through its innovative education and groundbreaking research, has become one of the leading post-secondary institutions in Canada. Supported by more than $74 million in grants, the University is able to provide programs through six facilities and offers first class libraries and other sophisticated amenities. Included in these facilities are modern language labs, music rehearsal rooms, art studios, an art gallery, and seminar rooms for the programs in humanities. Resources in the science and engineering include a nuclear reactor and Van de Graaf accelerator. Computing facilities include mainframes, terminal clusters, and microcomputers. Enrolling over 13,000 full-time students, a staff of over 1,000 teaches both graduate and undergraduate courses. Among the 1,000 faculty, most hold doctorate degrees in their specific area of studies. **Career Highlights:** McMaster University: Assistant Vice President (1997-Present), Lecturer of Marketing and Entereprenuership (1984-Present), Assistant to the Dean (1987-97). **Associations & Accomplishments:** North American Case Research Association; Chair, Transition Board for the New City of Hamilton; Director, Hamilton Entertainment and Convention Facilities, Inc. **Education:** McMaster University, M.B.A. (1984); Carleton University: B.A. in Mathematical Sciences, B.Sc. with Honors in Chemistry. **Personal Information:** Mr. Ryder enjoys antiques, National Geographic magazines and golf.

Farhad Saba, Ph.D.

Founder
F. Saba & Associates
6863 Cominito Montanoso, Apartment 9
San Diego, CA 92119-2349
(619) 461-0625
Fax: (619) 303-6779
saba1@home.com
8221

Business Information: Dr. Saba is Founder of F. Saba & Associates. He also fulfills the role of Professor of Technology at San Diego State University. Dr. Saba's research and development interests focus is on design, implementation, and evaluation of leading edge distance learning systems. With 22 years of extensive experience in distance education, Dr. Saba has been involved in all aspects of the field, from policy analysis and design to implementation and evaluation. In this context, he works with the Internet to conduct experimentation and evaluation projects regarding the effectiveness of conducting e-courses via online lectures, demonstrations, and examinations. Concurrently, Dr. Saba serves as the Executive Editor of The Distance Educator and Media Review Editor of the American Journal of Distance Education. In addition to the US, he has presented professional seminars and conferences in countries including Afghanistan, France, Great Britain, The People's Republic of China, and Turkey. Looking to the next millennium, Dr. Saba hopes to stay on the cutting edge of the information technology industry. Established in 1995, F. Saba & Associates is a consulting firm that operates within the information technology industry. The Firm engages in the design, implementation, and evaluation of distance education systems, with its virtual offices located on the World Wide Web. The Firm assists its clients in the production and successful promotion of a more efficient computer network to effectively communicate the needs of online lectures and examinations. **Career Highlights:** Founder, F. Saba & Associates (1995-Present); Professor of Educational Technology, San Diego State University (1984-Present); The University of Connecticut: Director of Telecommunications Division (1981-84), Radio/Television Producer (1980-81); Lecturer, Syracuse University (1979); Managing Director of Educational Radio and Television of Iran, National Iranian Radio and Television (1973-78). **Associations & Accomplishments:** National Society for Performance and Instruction; President of International Division, Association for Educational Communications and Technology; Association for the Advancement of Computing in Education; Vice President (1983-84), Institute of International Media Communication; Association for Development of Computer-Based Instructional Systems; Advisory Council Member, Institute of International Media Communication; Phi Beta Delta Honor Society for International Scholars; Alliance for Distance Education in California. **Education:** Syracuse University, Ph.D. in Instructional Technology (1976); San Francisco State University: M.A. in Broadcast Communication Arts, B.A. in Radio, Television, and Film. **Personal Information:** Dr. Saba enjoys distance education.

Lawrence V. Saxton, Ph.D.

Professor of Computer Science
University of Regina Computer Science Department
3737 Wascana Parkway
Regina, Saskatchewan, Canada S4S 0A2
(306) 585-4745
Fax: (306) 585-4745
saxton@cs.uregina.ca
8221

Business Information: Dr. Saxton officially started his tenure at the Institution in 1973 as a professor and researcher, then in 1994 moved into the position of Head of Computer Science Department. He has since returned to teaching and research which is his first love. Concurrently, Dr. Saxton is on the Information Technology committee and is conducting research in Theoretical Databases with a focus on understanding database languages. A respected professional, he is very proud of his students and attributes his success to being the best he can be, being free of stress, and loving his work. University of Regina is a full service institution of higher learning offering undergraduate and graduate programs. A public, four-year, and coed institution, the University of Regina is comprised of one main campus. Originally founded as Regina College in 1906, the name was changed to University of Saskatchewan, then in 1974 was changed to University of Regina. Local in scope, the Institution is located in Regina, Canada. **Career Highlights:** University of Regina: Professor of Computer Science (1999-Present), Professor/Department Head of Computer Science (1994-99), Professor/Researcher, (1973-94); Visiting Professor, University of Waterloo (1999-00); Visiting Researcher, Indiana University (1991-92); Visiting Associate Professor, Vanderbilt University (1982-83). **Associations & Accomplishments:** Association for Computing Machinery; Institute of Electrical and Electronics Engineers Computer Society; Canadian Information Processing Society; Society for Industrial and Applied Mathematics; Lakeshore Tennis Club; University Club; Published articles in peer review journals and major science journals; Presentations at major international conferences; Recognized by Institute of Electrical and Electronics Engineers for award winning papers. **Education:** University of Waterloo: Ph.D. (1973), Master's degree in Mathematics (1970), Bachelor's degree in Mathematics (1969). **Personal Information:** Dr. Saxton enjoys tennis, slow pitch softball, reading novels and playing pool.

Shane Schlosser

PC LAN Administrator
University College of the Fraser Valley
33844 King Road
Abbotsford, British Columbia, Canada V2S 7M8
(604) 853-7441
Fax: (604) 853-4502
shane@uniserve.com
8221

Business Information: Mr. Schlosser functions under the title of PC LAN Administrator of University College of the Fraser Valley. He is charged of operating the department of computer technology. Possessing an excellent understanding of technology, Mr. Schlosser realm of responsibility includes compute systems administration as well as server and workstation setup, troubleshooting, repair, upgrade. He ensures computer laboratories are functional, properly configured, and operational. Highly regarded, Mr. Schlosser does some consulting and teaches the Microsoft Certified Systems Engineer course. Attributing his success to a knack for troubleshooting systems difficulties, Mr. Schlosser plans to stay on top of emerging technology. University College of the Fraser Valley is an institute of higher education. Established in 1975, the College offers courses in various fields including international trade, computer science, and medical. The College provides courses for over 6,000 full-time students and more than 10,000 part-time students. On-line courses are also available for those students who prefer or require a more convenient form of study. Presently, the College is staffed by 750 educators and administrators. **Career Highlights:** PC LAN Administrator, University College of the Fraser Valley (1998-Present); Supervisor, Uniserve Online (1995-98); Computer Technician, Panther Computers (1993-95). **Associations & Accomplishments:** Netware Users International; Microsoft Technet. **Education:** Capilano College, Network Specialist Program (1998); Microsoft Certified Systems Engineer; Certified Netware Administrator. **Personal Information:** Mr. Schlosser enjoys chess, computers, reading and skiing.

Conrad Shayo, Ph.D.

Management Information Systems Professor
California State at San Bernardino
2674 South Pleasand Avenue
Ontario, CA 91761
(909) 880-5798
Fax: (909) 880-5994
cshayo@cactus.csusb.edu
8221

Business Information: As Management Information Systems Professor at California State University at San Bernardino, Dr. Shayo is responsible for providing comprehensive instructions on management information systems. Primarily, his realm of expertise includes systems analysis, electronics, ERP technology, and strategic information systems. With more than 15 years of professional education and lecturer background, Dr. Shayo utilizes his superior talents in managing three classes per quarter, while providing consulting services and devising new plans to develop and enhance programs for critical thinking. His future endeavors also include publishing more written works. Dr. Shayo's success reflects his ability to communicate, take on challenges, and deliver results. California State University at San Bernardino is an educational facility that engages in the provision of advanced academics to individuals seeking to further their knowledge or prepare for professional careers. The University, one of twenty-three state colleges in

California, offers a wide variety of programs for both graduate and undegraduate degrees in majors ranging from science to computer technology. Located in Ontario, California, the University employs more than 500 individuals including professional educators and administrative personnel. **Career Highlights:** California State at San Bernardino: Management Information Systems Professor (1998-Present), Assistant Professor (1994-97); Lecturer, University of Dar-es-Salaam (1985-93). **Associations & Accomplishments:** Association of Computing Machinery; A.I.S.; International Information Management Association. **Education:** Claremont Graduate University: Ph.D. (1995), M.S. in Information Sciences (1992); University of Nairobi, M.B.A. (1985); University of Dar-es-Salaam, Bachelor's degree in Communications (1981).

V. Janene Sikkink

Manager
University of Alaska
P.O. Box 755320
Fairbanks, AK 99775-5320
(907) 474-5310
Fax: (907) 474-7127
sxvjs@alaska.edu

8221

Business Information: Mrs. Sikkink is Manager of the Helpdesk and Training at the University of Alaska's Information Technology Services department. Managing a staff of four people within the Helpdesk, she is able to answer the questions of all students and faculty members visiting the department. To ensure the effectiveness of the Helpdesk, she devotes countless hours to the training and education of each staff member working at the desk. Her team works with all computer users at the University to expand their knowledge on the use and opportunities available to them through the computer network. To expand her personal effectiveness in her position, Mrs. Sikkink is aggressively working towards obtaining her Ph.D. in Computer Security. Her professional success reflects her ability to think outside the box and take on new challenges. University of Alaska is an institution for higher learning focused on the students aspiring to become business leaders within Alaska. To utilize the natural environment surrounding its campus, the University features specialized programs in fishery, science, and research. The University supports three major campuses throughout the state and hosts 23 sites in its entirety. One of these sites is the Information Technology Services department which provides information technology resources and support for all faculty, staff, and students at the campus' various locations. **Career Highlights:** Manager, University of Alaska (1999-Present); Project Coordinator, Arctic Region Super Computing Center (1997-98); Direct/Marketing Statewide, Internet Alaska, Inc. (1995-97). **Associations & Accomplishments:** Toastmaster's International. **Education:** University of Alaska at Fairbanks, M.B.A. **Personal Information:** Married to Jeffrey Alan in 1996. Mrs. Sikkink enjoys crocheting, cross-stitching and web design.

Judith S. Sotir

Information Technology Design Director
Waubonsee College
5 East Galena Boulevard
Aurora, IL 60506-4178
(630) 801-7900
Fax: (630) 892-5063
jsotir@mail.wcc.cc.il.us

8221

Business Information: Ms. Sotir functions in the role of Information Technology Design Director for Waubonsee College. She determines the overall strategic direction and designs and develops new educational technology uses. A savvy, 25 year veteran of the field, Ms. Sotir governs the activities of all students within her classrooms and instructs several courses each semester. Her greatest enjoyment stems from the hands-on laboratory facility where she assists students in conducting research and designing new, cutting edge software programs. Looking to the new millennium, Ms. Sotir plans to continue in the field and stay abreast of new technology to better serve her students. Success is attributed to her ability to analyze and apply data. Waubonsee College is a higher learning institution dedicated to the successful training of tomorrow's business leaders. The College highlights an adult education program where returning students can recieve their education while working. The Program accentuates the knowledge they will have already gained in life and teaches them the background needed to make them increasingly successful in their careers. **Career Highlights:** Information Technology Design Director, Waubonsee College (1992-Present). **Associations & Accomplishments:** Trustee, Fox Metro Water Reclamation District; Board Member, Indian Prairie School District 204. **Education:** Elmhurst College, B.A. (1974). **Personal Information:** Ms. Sotir enjoys tennis and travel.

Tami Spurlin

Computer Support Specialist
University of Florida, Horticultural Science Department
Box 110690, 1301 Fifield Hall
Gainesville, FL 32611
(352) 392-1928
Fax: (352) 392-8649
tamis@ufl.edu

8221

Business Information: In her position as Computer Support Specialist for the University of Florida, Ms. Spurlin maintains the computers for the Horticultural Science Department. She performs troubleshooting operations, maintains the local area network, and installs systems upgrades. Additionally, she provides equipment for faculty presentations and serves as a liaison between the Department and the University. Beginning her career more than 13 years ago, Ms. Spurlin has received recognition for her diligence and skills in Web page design and she has utilized her knowledge to implement policies that enhance her Department's effectiveness. Ms. Spurlin has enjoyed substantial success in her present position and in the future plans to attain a position in the private sector as well as become involved in the Web environment and JavaScripting. The University of Florida is an institution of higher learning providing general and specialized course instruction for individuals wishing to advance their educational studies. Established in 1853, the University staffs administrative, teaching, and support personnel who work diligently to enhance and perfect educational opportunities for its students. Home to more than 28,000 students, the University is located in Gainesville, Florida and offers graduate and undergraduate degrees in such areas as accounting, engineering, and phsychology. **Career Highlights:** University Florida, Horticulture Science Department: Computer Support Specialist (1999-Present), Senior Word Processor (1993-99), Secretary (1990-93), Clerk/Typist (1987-90). **Education:** University of Florida. **Personal Information:** Married to Keith in 1988. Ms. Spurlin enjoys going to the beach and gardening.

Moawiya A. Taj

Web Master/Computer Programmer
King Fahd University of Petroleum and Minerals
P.O. Box 626
Dharan, Saudi Arabia 31261
+966 38604290
Fax: +966 38603927

8221

Business Information: Loyal and dedicated, Mr. Taj has served with King Fahd University of Petroleum and Minerals since 1981. At the present time, he fulfills the responsibilities of Computer Programmer and assumes the prestigious title of Web Master. In this context, he is responsible for the development of cutting edge web sites for the University. Furthermore, he utilizes extensive technical career experiences in training three co-workers in the development of Web sites. He is also the Internet Section Supervisor of King Fahd University of Petroleum and Minerals. Capitalizing on his expertise in the field and his longevity with the Organization, within three to five years, Mr. Taj would like to work in the management department. Established in 1963, the King Fahd University of Petroleum and Minerals first opened its doors to a college class of 67 students. Thirty-five years later, that enrollment number has gone up to 7,000 students. The University is best known for its science department and is comprised of eight college divisions to include Graduate Studies, Applied Engineering, Engineering Sciences, Sciences, Industrial Management, Environmental Design, Computer Science and Engineering, and the Preparatory Year Program. All eight of the divisions share a facility and utilize similar disciplines. University programs that are offered include Chemistry, Mathematics, Chemical Engineering, Mechanical Engineering, Electrical Engineering, Civil Engineering and Petroleum Engineering. **Career Highlights:** Web Master/Computer Programmer, King Fahd University of Petroleum and Minerals (1981-Present). **Associations & Accomplishments:** Chairman of the Technical Committee of GulfNet (Arabian Gulf Countries Computer Network 1989-92); Association of Computing Machinery International; Saudi-Arabia Chapter of the ACM; Saudi Computer Society; Egypt Computer Society. **Education:** Boeing Computer Services, Diploma (1983). **Personal Information:** Married to Mona in 1991. Mr. Taj enjoys swimming and reading newspapers and computer books.

Cecilia T. Taylor

Academic Computing Specialist
Mercer University
3001 Mercer University Drive
Atlanta, GA 30341
(770) 986-3314

8221

Business Information: Serving as an Academic Computing Specialist at Mercer University, Ms. Taylor trains faculty, staff, and students on various software programs. She works and interacts with students, teaches software classes, and has previously developed and maintained a database which is still in use. Beginning her career more than seven years ago, Ms. Taylor has developed the skills needed to maintain the highest standards of professional excellence and builds relationships built on trust and respect. She attributes her substantial success to persistance. A savvy systems expert, she continues to grow professionally and hopes to establish her own sewing business in the future. Mercer University is a church related institution founded by Georgia Baptists in 1833. Composed of the College of Liberal Arts, the Stetson School of Business and Economics, the School of Engineering, the Walter F. George School of Law, the School of Medicine, the School of Education, the Southern School of Pharmacy, and the McAfee School of Theology, the University is dedicated to providing a comprehensive and practical education to all its students. **Career Highlights:** Academic Computing Specialist, Mercer University (1998-Present); Lab Coordinator/Clinician, Morris Brown College (1992-98). **Associations & Accomplishments:** American Society for Training and Development. **Education:** Keller Graduate School of Management: M.B.A. (1997), Master's degree in Human Resources Management (1998); Olivet Nazarene University, B.A. in Mathematics. **Personal Information:** Ms. Taylor enjoys sewing, cross-stitching, knitting and roller skating.

Frank P. Tedesco

Director of Network Services
William Paterson University
300 Pompton Road
Wayne, NJ 07470-2152
(973) 720-2304
Fax: (973) 720-3598
tedesco@gw.wilpaterson.edu

8221

Business Information: Mr. Tedesco is the Director of Network Services for William Paterson University. He develops, implements, and supports the University network system providing access to faculty, staff, and students to technology resources. Having dedicated nearly a decade of service to the University, he has focused his projects on the networking services and the automated teller machines. He feels his success is the result of constantly trying to look at the future of his field and exploring the technologies people find useful in today's society. With 18 employees reporting directily to him, Mr. Tedesco has been repsonsible for developing and implementing a fiber-backbone system for the University. The system was designed to run approximately 25 years and has been installed in 33 buildings throughout the Campus. Within the next three to five years, Mr. Tedesco would like to add courses inthe areas of training and manufacturing. William Paterson University is an educational facility preparing the minds of future business leaders for all areas of the world. Founded in 1855, the University provides a historical heritage for its students that has demonstrated its dedication and commitment to appropriate educational training for over 150 years. A body of 10,000 eager minds compose the force of students within each classroom, laboratory, and organization at the University. **Career Highlights:** Director of Network Services, William Paterson University (1991-Present); Software Quality Assurance Engineer, Kearfott Guidance & Navigation (1989-90). **Education:** William Paterson University, B.S. in Computer Sciences (1990). **Personal Information:** Mr. Tedesco enjoys his work.

Rebecca Ann Tyler

Director of Information Systems
Eastern Mennonite University
1200 Park Road
Harrisonburg, VA 22802
(540) 432-4478
Fax: (540) 432-4444
tylerr@emu.edu

8221

Business Information: Providing her skilled services as Director of Information Systems for the Eastern Mennonite University, Mrs. Tyler presides over the administration of all aspects of the administrative, academic, and technical systems. She directly supervises a staff of 25 skilled personnel members who assist her in the coordination, planning, and implementation of software and network upgrades and maintenance. Acting as vendor liaison for the University, Mrs. Tyler purchases the necessary hardware and software for the 465 computers and LAN system. She continues to grow professionally through the fulfillment of her responsibilities and anticipates her promotion to vice president as a result of her continuing efforts to increase her skills through training and developmental activities. Mrs. Tyler's success reflects her ability to produce results and aggressively tackle new challenges. Founded in 1917, the Eastern Mennonite University is a private university affiliated with the Mennonite Church. The University is considered to be in the nation's Top 10 in liberal arts studies and has the largest cross cultural program in the country. Approximately 1,400 students are enrolled in undergraduate and graduate seminary programs. **Career Highlights:** Director of Information Systems, Eastern Mennonite University (1999-Present); Assistant Director of Computer Information Systems, Mary Baldwin College (1994-99); Systems Analyst, CMDS (1988-94). **Associations & Accomplishments:** Valley Voice Toastmasters International; President, CTM (1996-97); Steering Committee Member, Virginia Regional Users Group (1995-Present); Mrs. Harrisonburg, Mrs. International Pageant (1998); United States Army Commendation Medal (1979); Service Award of the Year (1992), CMDS. **Education:** James Madison University, B.B.A. (1995); Tidewater Community College, A.S. in Data Processing (1987); Signal School at Fort Gordon, Georgia (1977). **Personal Information:** Married to Thomas Harrison in 1993. Two children: Melissa and David. Mrs. Tyler enjoys downhill snow skiing, running, gardening and restoration of furniture.

Marla J. Van Baren

Publications Editor
National Technological University
700 Centre Avenue
Fort Collins, CO 80526
(970) 495-6449
Fax: (970) 484-0668
marla@mail.ntu.edu

8221

Business Information: Ms. Van Baren functions in the capacity of Publications Editor for National Technological University. She is responsible for editing non-credit course information for continuity and ensuring the correctness of all information provided to students through the Internet. A seven year veteran in the technical field, Ms. Van Baren maintains all publications and Web sites to assist the University in its marketing strategies. Looking to the 21st Century, Ms. Van Baren plans on obtaining her Master's degree in Technology Communications. The highlight of her career is being able to network and interact with industry leaders. Her success reflects her extensive academic background and her ability to produce results and take on new challenges. National Technological University is a distance education facility which offers Master degree programs and non-credit training courses to people working in technological organizations. All of the courses are taught via the satellite and the Internet, providing students the opportunity to study and attend lectures within the comforts of their own homes. The University was created in 1984 and has increased its role in the market through its expansion into the Internet world. **Career Highlights:** Publications Editor, National Technological University (1998-Present); Graphics Designer, North American Directory Services (1995-98); Office Manager, American West Realty, Inc. (1992-95). **Associations & Accomplishments:** Completed Leadership Loveland Program (1993-95). **Education:** Colorado State University, M.S. (In Progress); Hope College: B.A. in Sociology, B.A. in English and Communications. **Personal Information:** Ms. Van Baren enjoys reading, photography and hiking.

Brian C. Wechsler

Technology Mentor
Wolf Creek Elementary
P.O. Box 1937, Wolf Creek School Housing
Pine Ridge, SD 57770
(605) 867-5174
Fax: (605) 867-5067
wech@scpschls.k12.sd.us

8221

Business Information: Highly recruited to Wolf Creek Elementary as Technology Mentor in 1999, Mr. Wechsler teaches children and teachers technology skills. Possessing an excellent understanding of technology, he is also responsible for the School's computer infrastructure. In this context, Mr. Wechsler maintains and upgrades computers and peripherals as well as provides database and network services and Internet connectivity. Selected as a TTL Instructor, he teaches computer skills during the summer to teachers from all across the state of South Dakota. Continually training to hone his technology skills, Mr. Wechsler hopes to continue in the technical field. In the future, he would like to become responsible for the entire systems function and teach classes on the Internet to students and teachers. The Shannon County School District is located in South Dakota. Employing 110 professionals, the Wolf Creek School is an elementary school, which maintains pre-kindergarten through eighth grades. **Career Highlights:** Technology Mentor, Wolf Creek Elementary (1999-Present); Technology for Teaching and Learning Instructor, State of South Dakota (1999-00); Kindergarten Teacher, Shannon County School District (1994-99). **Associations & Accomplishments:** South Dakota National Education Association; National Education Association; Volunteer, National Association of American Indian Children and Elders. **Education:** University of South Dakota, B.S. (1994); Oglala Lakota College, degree in Early Childhood Special Education. **Personal Information:** Mr. Wechsler enjoys volunteer work, bicycling, canoeing, fishing and hunting.

Paul Wermager

Head of Science and Technology Department
University of Hawaii
Hamilton Library, Room 304B, 2550 The Mall
Honolulu, HI 96822
(808) 956-2541
Fax: (808) 956-2547
wermager@hawaii.edu

8221

Business Information: Dedicated to the success of the students and faculty of the University of Hawaii, Mr. Wermager applies his knowledge and expertise in the field of information technology in serving as the Head of Science and Technology Department at Hamiliton Library. Included in his daily schedule are such duties as supervision of professional staff, maintainance of department budget, and upgrade of networking systems. Continually formulating new goals and objectives, he plans to expand total Internet accessibility to better serve students, faculty, and researchers. Using his knowledge of computers and technology, Mr. Wermager is continuously improving the Department's Web page. He is proud of being a published author in several journals, and attributes his success to being an informed decision maker. Founded in 1910, the University of Hawaii is a land grant institution composed of 10 campuses throughout the 50th state. The main campus is located in Honolulu, where Mr. Wermanger is employed. The Science and Technology Department supports all the science degree programs of the University and is a valubale resource to students, faculty, researchers, and the general public. **Career Highlights:** Head of Science and Technology Department, University of Hawaii (1992-Present); Registered Nurse, Kapiolani Medical Center (1982-92). **Associations & Accomplishments:** Special Libraries Association; Medical Library Association; Hawaii Library Association. **Education:** University of Hawaii: M.P.H. (1999), Master's degree in Library Information Studies, B.S.N.; North Dakota State University, Bachelor's degree in Pharmacy. **Personal Information:** Mr. Wermager enjoys reading, writing and computers.

David M. Wessels, Ph.D.

Assistant Professor
University of Arkansas
3090 West Wildflower Street
Fayetteville, AR 72704-6745
(501) 575-2635
wessels@engr.var6.edu

8221

Business Information: Serving as a Professor at the University of Arkansas, Dr. Wessels is responsible for teaching graduates and undergraduates, and conducting research in software engineering and systems testing. A sharp, 11 year veteran of the field, he is actively involved in cutting edge analysis and development of research projects that attracts grant monies to the University. Maintaining computer labs and teaching two courses a semester is also an integral part of Dr. Wessels' academic responsibilities. An accomplished expert, he has been published in professional journals. His success is attributed to his hardwork ethic, flexibility, and innovativeness. Located in the Northwestern section of the state of Arkansas, the Unversity of Arkansas is a state supported 420-acre campus providing a large variety of courses leading to bachelor's, master's or even doctoral and first professional degrees. The University offers various majors to include accounting, computer engineering, French, mathematics, and zoology. Approximately 17,000 students attend the University which is staffed by 1,000 educators and administrators. **Career Highlights:** Professor, University of Arkansas (1998-Present); Lecturer, James Cook University (195-98); Lecturer, University of Victoria (1992-95). **Associations & Accomplishments:** Institute of Electrical and Electronics Engineers; Association of Computing Machinery. **Education:** University of Victoria: Ph.D. (1995), M.Sc. (1990), B.Sc. (1989). **Personal Information:** Dr. Wessels enjoys scuba diving and snorkeling.

Brad Whitecotton

Systems Administrator
University of Evansville
1800 Lincoln Avenue
Evansville, IN 47722
(812) 488-1171
Fax: (812) 479-2088
bw9@evansville.edu

8221

Business Information: Possessing unique skills in systems administration, Mr. Whitecotton joined the University of Evansville in 1997 as a Systems Administrator. A systems expert, he oversees the administration of the UNIX system and server as well as the NT server and network. Designing the computer workstations for the University staff members and students, Mr. Whitecotton is responsible for purchasing the necessary hardware and software. Additionally, he provides technical support to the 700 University employees and the entire student body. Monitoring and tuning systems software; installing new users; and resolving systems problems; and coordinating resources, time lines, and schedules also fall within the realm of his responsibilities. Consistently achieving quality performance in his field, Mr. Whitecotton anticipates a future promotion to Director. His career success reflects his ability to think out-of-the-box and aggressively take on new challenges and responsibilities. A private university with approximately 2,500 students enrolled, the University of Evansville was founded in 1854. The University is an institution of higher learning providing general and specialized course instruction for individuals wishing to advance their educational studies. **Career Highlights:** Systems Administrator, University of Evansville (1997-Present). **Education:** University of Evansville (Currently Attending). **Personal Information:** Mr. Whitecotton enjoys sports, reading and going out.

Guoliang Xue, Ph.D.

Professor of Computer Science
University of Vermont
325 Votey Building, Department of Computer Science
Burlington, VT 05405
(802) 656-8688
Fax: (802) 656-0696
xue@cs.uvm.edu

8221

Business Information: Recruited to the University of Vermont as Assistant Professor in 1993, Dr. Xue now serves as Professor of Computer Science. He is responsible for modern media communications, writing and translating computer languages, and teaching courses on parallel and data programming, database management systems, and computer languages. Daily, his duties include giving lectures, leading small seminars, supervising students, and advising and working with students individually. Keeping abreast of new develoments in the field, Dr. Xue reads current literature, talks with colleagues in the field, and participates in professional conferences. Students at the University rely on his expertise to effectively prepare them for further schooling or a career in the field. Dr. Xue has authored and published numerous books and plans to continue to learn and grow academically and professionally. Located in Burlington, Vermont, the University of Vermont is a state supported, co-educational institution of higher learning. Set a a suburban 425-acre campus, the University offers a variety of courses and programs specifically designed to meet the individual needs to students. A dedicated and skilled staff assists students in their college careers. About 7,500 undergraduate students annually take advantage of the opportunities available at the University. **Career Highlights:** University of Vermont: Professor of Computer Science (2000-Present), Associate Professor (1999-00), Assistant Professor (1993-99); Postdoctoral Fellow, University of Minnesota (1991-93). **Associations & Accomplishments:** Senior Member, Institute of Electrical and Electronics Engineer; Association of Computing Machinery; Institute of Electrical and Electronics Engineers Circuits and Systems Society; Institute of Electrical and Electronics Engineers Communications Society; Institute of Electrical and Electronics Engineers Computer Society. **Education:** University of Minnesota, Ph.D. (1987-91). **Personal Information:** Married to Shangyun Sun in 1983. Two children: Tongke and Alfred. Dr. Xue enjoys running and watching NBA games.

Akmal A. Younis, Ph.D.

Research Assistant Professor
University of Miami
P.O. Box 24-8421
Coral Gables, FL 33124
(305) 284-3454
Fax: (305) 284-4044
ayounis@miami.edu

8221

Business Information: Utilizing a vast education and many years of solid experience, Dr. Younis joined the University of Miami as a Research Associate in l995, and has received recognition for his diligence and skills through promotion to his current position of Research Assistant Professor. Responsible for research, development, and teaching of graduate and undergraduate classes in the university's computer engineering and information technology program, he establishes high standards of excellence for his students. Dr. Younis leads and supervises graduate students' research in information management, multimedia databases, and medical imaging. Striving to incorporate the latest technology in the education process, he oversees the development of information technology labs with state-of-the-art equipment and software tools. Dr. Younis' goals for the future include developing the foundation for the information technology program. Located in Miami, Florida, the University of Miami is a private higher education institute established in 1925. The 8,000 qualified individuals employed by the University, including postgraduates to Ph.D. educators, are dedicated to giving students a better appreciation of such fields as art, literature, history, human relations, and science. The University prepares people for professional careers as doctors, lawyers, teachers, and engineers. **Career Highlights:** University of Miami: Research Assistant Professor (1998-Present), Research Associate (1995-97), Research Assistant (1989-94); Assistant Scientist, IBM World Trade Corporation (1988). **Associations & Accomplishments:** Institute of Electrical and Electronics Engineers; Tau Beta Pi; Eta Kappa Nu. **Education:** University of Miami: Ph.D. (1998), M.S. in Electrical and Computer Engineering (1991); Ain Shams University, B.S. in Electrical and Computer Engineering (1986). **Personal Information:** Married to Amal M. Ali in 1996. One child: Muhammad. Dr. Younis enjoys swimming and jogging.

Luis M. Zornosa Cabrera

Associate Professor
Inter American University of Puerto Rico
P.O. Box 5100, San German Campus
San German, Puerto Rico 00623
(787) 264-1912
Fax: (787) 892-6350
lzornosa@sg.inter.edu

8221

Business Information: Staying loyal to the education of the youth of Puerto Rico, Mr. Zornosa Cabrera is an Associate Professor of Inter American University of Puerto Rico San German campus. Teaching the subject of management information systems for graduate and undergraduate students, all courses are taught in computer languages. Other courses he teaches include database design, system analogy and design, marketing, and information technology. In addition to his teaching role, Mr. Zornosa Cabrera also does private consulting in the areas that he teaches. Dealing with computers has always come naturally, since his first job was in information technology. In the future, he would like to integrate new technologies into the University's curriculum, and finish his doctoral degree. Founded in 1912, the Inter American University of Puerto Rico at San German is a co-educational institute of higher learning. With over 4,800 students enrolled, the University is part of the Inter American University of Puerto Rico. The most popularly chosen majors are business administration, secretarial science, and accounting. Providing a small town environment for its students, the University offers associate's, bachelor's, and master's degrees. **Career Highlights:** Associate Professor, Inter American University of Puerto Rico (1985-Present); Management Information Systems Consultant, Bank of Bogota (1984-85); Management Information Systems Consultant, Codi-Mobil (1982-84). **Associations & Accomplishments:** Lion International; Masonic Lodge; American Society of Mechanical Engineers; Phi Delta Kappa; Data Processing Managers Association; AIIE. **Education:** Boston University, Master's degree in Manufacturing Engineering; Universidad de los Andes, B.S. in Indutrial Engineering; Nova University. **Personal Information:** Married to Cisly de Jesus in 1974. Two children: Luis A. and Erick. Mr. Zornosa Cabrera enjoys photography and tennis.

Brian Sterling Ackley

Technical Specialist
Tompkins Cortland Community College
Box 139, 170 North Street
Dryden, NY 13053
(607) 844-8211
Fax: (607) 844-9665
ackleyb@sunytccc.edu

8222

Business Information: As a Technical Specialist for Tompkins Cortland Community College, Mr. Ackley is responsible for the support and governing of computer equipment for use by students, while also overseeing a staff that provides assistance to students using software. His other obligations include assisting with the installation and maintenance of the network infrastructure and maintaining the department's Web site. With more than 13 years of professional education experience with the College, Mr. Ackley is committed to further development of the College and is currently involved in the formation of a new technology plan to help ensure a bright future. His credo is "timing is everything." Tompkins Cortland Community College is an institution of higher learning that provides general and specialized course instruction for individuals wishing to advance their educational studies. Established in 1968, the College offers degrees and certifications in a variety of programs. Presently more than 250 professional educators, administrators, and support personnel staff the College. **Career Highlights:** Tompkins Cortland Community College: Technical Specialist (1987-Present), Lab Assistant (1985-87); Aircraft Mechanic, United States Air Force (1981-85). **Associations & Accomplishments:** National Education Association; Microsoft Advisory Panel; State University of New York Officers Association. **Education:** Tompkins Cortland Community College, A.S. in Liberal Arts, Math/Science (1991). **Personal Information:** Married to Jeannie in 1991. Five children: Stephen, Rebekah, Jennifer, Benjamin, and Brianna. Mr. Ackley enjoys travel, history and baseball.

Janet B. Ayers

President
Carroll Technical Institute
997 South Highway 16
Carrollton, GA 30116
(770) 836-6820
Fax: (770) 836-4742
jayers@falcon.carroll.tec.ga.us

8222

Business Information: In her role as President of Carroll Technical Institute, Ms. Ayers oversees daily activities and is responsible for economic direction and progress. Demonstrating business savvy with financial know-how, she is able to effectively manage portfolios and other business obligations. Concerned with capital improvements and accreditation, she is continually revamping curriculum requirements to ensure each student receives a superior education. By lending her insight and guidance at departmental meetings, Ms. Ayers is directly involved in the creation of strategic operational policies. A pillar in the educational community, her presence is frequently requested at civic and corporate assemblies. Recognized for impressive leadership skills and clearly stated goals, Ms. Ayers attributes her success to hard work and focus. She intends to continue in her current capacity as she assists in the development of a new campus and the implementation of new instructional programs. Carroll Technical Institute provides educational instruction programs that, upon successful completion, may lead to certificates, diplomas or terminal associate degrees. Popular majors include fields such as accounting, dental hygiene, and electronic engineering technology. Most students are able to complete requirements for graduation in two years or less. The Institute maintains four campuses throughout western Georgia, with a total enrollment of over 2,000 students. **Career Highlights:** Carroll Technical Institute: President (1995-Present), Vice President of Instructional and Student Services (1993-95), Vice President of Student Services (1988-93). **Associations & Accomplishments:** West Georgia League of Women Voters; Georgia Education Advisement Council; Chamber of Commerce; Who's Who of Business Leaders; Who's Who of Global Leaders; American Association of University Women. **Education:** State University of West Georgia: M.Ed., B.S. in Education, Specialist in Education. **Personal Information:** Two children: Jesset and Cole. Ms. Ayers enjoys church activities and reading.

James G. Beachner

Network Engineer
The Metropolitan Community College
500 Southwest Longview Road
Lee's Summit, MO 64081
(816) 672-2363
Fax: (816) 672-2439
beachj@longview.cc.mo.us

8222

Business Information: Mr. Beachner's reputation of adept technical ability and innovative problem solving techniques preceeds his work as The Metropolitan Community Colleges' Network Engineer. Demonstrating impressive skill, he oversees technical project management to ensure smooth operations and accurate completion of tasks. Concerned with maintenance, troubleshooting, and installation of hardware and software, he utilizes his education and training to devise ingenous strategies that maximize available resources. To remain current on technology changes and updates, Mr. Beachner attends seminars, researches on the Internet, and reads trade journals. With plans to further his education already in motion, he is initiating another network conversion that will involve all seven campuses. His advice is "get the certifications, do it one step at a time." The Metropolitan Community Colleges operates an educational system comprised of seven campuses spanning across Missouri and Kansas. A total of 20,000 students attend the higher learning Institution; Lee's Summit, Missouri is home to Longview Community College, a member of the educational system. The College was established in 1968 and employs 1,300 people to assist students seeking their certificate or two year degree in areas such as accounting, criminal justice, or postal management. **Career Highlights:** The Metropolitan Community Colleges: Network Engineer (1997-Present), Campus Network Coordinator (1995-97), Computer Support Specialist (1993-95). **Associations & Accomplishments:** Boy Scout Leader. **Education:** University of Missouri at Kansas City, B.S./CSTP (1995); Longview Community College, A.S. in Computer Science (1993). **Personal Information:** Married to Tiffany in 1988. Two children: Dalton and Baili. Mr. Beachner enjoys coaching sports for children and being a Boy Scout den leader.

Jake Beaver

Assistant Director of Network Services
Texas State Technical College
3801 Campus Drive
Waco, TX 76705
(254) 867-4830
Fax: (254) 867-3403
jake@tstc.edu

8222

Business Information: Since joining Texas State Technical College as Technician I in 1993, Mr. Beaver has rapidly ascended to his current position as Assistant Director of Network Services. In his current position, he is responsible for installing Cat 5 twisted pair cable, fiber optic cable, Cisco switches, and Cabletron routes as well as terminating all ends. Moreover, Mr. Beaver supervises 12 to 14 employees in the design and implementation of the campus' network as well as the installation and repair of the systems infrastructure. Possessing superior talents and an excellent understanding of technology, Mr. Beaver looks forward to remaining with the College in his current position. His success attributes his ability to take on challenges and deliver results on behalf of the College and its student body. Located in Waco, Texas, Texas State Technical College is an institute of higher learning. Founded in 1970, the College is a two year institution that provides students with a core technical and vocational curriculum of approximately 216 courses. With a diverses student population of 831 full time students, the College enrolls students come from three different states and territories and three countries. Currently, the College has a staff of hard working employees who committed to providing the students with the best possible education. **Career Highlights:** Texas State Technical College: Assistant Director of Network Services (1997-Present), Technician II (1996-97), Technician I (1993-96). **Associations & Accomplishments:** Texas State Technical College Alumni Association; Texas State Technical College Native American Student Association. **Education:** Texas State Technical College, A.A.S. (1991). **Personal Information:** Married to Sharon in 1991. One child: Shantell. Mr. Beaver enjoys fishing, hunting, camping and outdoors.

Anthony R. Bichel, Ph.D.

Director of Technology Center
Juniata College
1700 Moore Street
Huntingdon, PA 16652
(814) 641-3665
Fax: (814) 641-3706
bichela@juniata.edu

8222

Business Information: As Director of Technology Center at Juniata College, Dr. Bichel determines the strategic direction and academic function of the Technology Center. He is responsible for administering and controlling aspects of the multimedia, digital, audiovisual technologies. A savvy, 11 year professional, Dr. Bichel is also the webmaster accountable for 75 students who handle daily activities at the Technology Center. Purchasing equipment and creating smartboards and computer simulations used in the classrooms also is an integral part of Dr. Bichel's responsibilities. He is also an instructor of political science and international relations. A respected expert, he hopes to build a program at the College that will redefine excellence. After that, he hopes to take his skills to a larger university. Dr. Bichel's highlights include building the Technology Center from the ground up. His success is attributed to his ability to aggressively tackle new challenges and deliver results. Juniata College is a private liberal arts college. Located in Huntington, Pennsylvania, the College is a four year institute. The College has a different education philosophy and they try to create a fun atmosphere with lots of opportunities for the students. Established in 1998, the College presently employs a staff of 65 people. **Career Highlights:** Director of Technology Center, Juniata College (1999-Present); Director of Center for Innovative Learning, Sam Houston State University (1998-99). **Associations & Accomplishments:** Certified Distance Education Instructor; VTEL Certified Trainer. **Education:** University of Hawaii at Manoa, Ph.D. (1997); Valdosta State University: M.A. in History (1991), B.A. in Philosophy (1990), B.A. in Political

Science (1989). **Personal Information:** Married to Rebecca M. in 1987. Dr. Bichel enjoys collecting shells.

Dale Blackburn
Academic Department Head
ECPI College of Technology
7015G Albert Pick Road
Greensboro, NC 27409
(336) 665-1400
Fax: (336) 664-0801
dblackburn@ecpi.edu

8222

Business Information: Holding the position as Academic Department Head, Mr. Blackburn has been a major part of ECPI College of Technology since 1989. Responsible for curriculum develpment, he maintains student success rates and is an instructor of classroom observations. Presiding over administrative issues, he presents his input into faculty reviews, manages the scheduling of instructors and classes, and oversees the academic advising, tutoring, and the performance assessment of PBTE/CBSD modules. Focusing on the current upsizing of ECPI College of Technology, Mr. Blackburn remains committed towards providing excellent student services. Very passionate about the educational field, his success is attributed to his patience and surrounding himself with positive people. Serving North Carolina, South Carolina, and Virginia from nine campuses, ECPI College of Technology is an independent, private college offering associate of applied science degrees, diplomas, and certificate programs. Established in 1966, the College is located in Greensboro, North Carolina. Providing state accredited course curriculum to its expansive student body, the College employs an experienced and knowledgable staff of 100. Dedicated towards raising its standards, ECPI College of Technology continues to provide quality educational services. **Career Highlights:** Academic Department Head, ECPI College of Technology (1989-Present); Electronics Technician, United States Navy (1965-89). **Associations & Accomplishments:** Electronics Technician Association; Carolina NT Users Group; GTCC Advisory Board. **Education:** Regents College, B.S. (1989). **Personal Information:** Married to Anita in 1998. Two children: Julie and Michael. Mr. Blackburn enjoys bass fishing.

Antonio Cesar Corradi
Technical Coordinator
Senai
Muniz de Souza #3R
Sao Paulo, Brazil 01534-000
+55 112782455
Fax: +55 112782925
corradi@sp.senai.br

8222

Business Information: A highly successful, 21 year veteran of technology, Mr. Corradi serves as the Technical Coordinator at Senai. Focusing on the technical programs at the School, he doubles in his role as Principal of the School. In charge of approximately 65 students, Mr. Corradi's leadership talents assist in the successful mentorship of the School. Before joining Senai in 1985, he served as a Quality Assurance Analyst with Fiação Camp Belo. His background also includes a stint as Quality Assurance Analyst for S.G.S. do Brasil. For the near future, Mr. Corradi hopes to finish his Master's degree and continue to enhance the overall performance of the School. Senai is a specialized learning institution focusing its services on the education of students aspiring for future careers within the textile industry. With approximately 65 students, the School centers its classroom programs around spinning and weaving techniques that will provide the students with the skills necessary to create wonderful patterns and exquisite textiles. **Career Highlights:** Technical Coordinator, Senai (1985-Present); Quality Assurance Analyst, Fiação Campo Belo (1981-85); Quality Assurance Analyst, S.G.S. do Brasil (1979-81). **Associations & Accomplishments:** Brasilien Association for Textile Technical; Consil of Engineers Association. **Education:** UNICAMP, Master's degree (1999); Business Administration Pedagogy. **Personal Information:** Three children: Daniel, Samantha, and Tabatha. Mr. Corradi enjoys volleyball.

Shahid M. Dardai
Computer Science Professor
Richard J. Daley College
7500 South Pulaski Road
Chicago, IL 60652-1242
(773) 838-7750
Fax: (773) 838-7524

8222

Business Information: Mr. Shahid Dardai currently serves as a Computer Science Professor for Richard J. Daley College. As such, he is responsible for instructing students in the field of information technology. Richard J. Daley College is a junior community college, one of the City Colleges of Chicago engaged in offering higher education programs. **Career Highlights:** Chairperson of Computer Information System Department, Richard J. Daley College (August 1991-May 1995); Teacher of Math and Computer Science, Chicago State University (1993-Present); Associate Professor, Richard J. Daley College (1983); Instructor, Harry Truman College (1982). **Associations & Accomplishments:** Data Processing Management Association - Chicago (1990); Honorary Member, Phi Theta Kappa (1990); Member, Data Process Management Association (1990). **Education:** Northeastern Illinois University - Chicago, B.S. in Computer Science (1981); Other Technical Degrees or Certifications include an M.S. in Statistics and a B.S. in Math. **Personal Information:** Married to Husn B. Shahid in 1965. Five children: Akram, Ahsan, Fauzia, Aslam, and Asghar.

Donald A. Davidson, Ph.D.
Professor
Laguardia Community College
3110 Thomson Avenue
Long Island City, NY 11101-3083
(718) 349-4052
Fax: (718) 349-4061
dadlg@aol.com

8222

Business Information: A leader in the educational field, Dr. Davidson is a Professor of Computer Informations Systems for Laguardia Community College. Employed with College since the beginning in 1971, he performs many activities within the course of a day. Dr. Davidson, also a Founder of the College, makes administrative decisions, presides over the choosing of new curriculum, and serves as a Chairperson for the Laguardia Community College Computer Policy Committee. Dr. Davidson also instructs classes, assists students with academics, and works with research and development. His goal is to continue as a consultant for his son's business as well as his position in academic studies. Dr. Davidson credits his success to his keen interest in business and technology in addtion to his ability to interact. Laguardia Community College was established in 1971. The College is an institution of higher education that provides students with many degree programs and classes to choose from. Laguardia Community College is the second largest commuity college within New York. In addtion to various degree programs, the College has paid internship programs, co-operative education, and interest organizations for students to partake in. A dedicated and skilled workstaff of 450 personnel members are employed by the College to meet the demands of a growing student body. **Career Highlights:** Professor, Laguardia Community College (1971-Present); Consultant, Cornell Design (1966-71); Programmer, IBM Corporation (1961-66). **Associations & Accomplishments:** D.P.M.A.; Vice President, Hewlett-Woodmere Public Library. **Education:** City University of New York, Ph.D. (1973); Blackstone Law School, J.D.; Columbia College, B.S. **Personal Information:** Married to 1962 in Esther. Two children: Phyllis and Jacob. Dr. Davidson enjoys bowling and chess.

Ann L. Degner
Director of Learning Technologies
San Juan College
4601 College Boulevard
Farmington, NM 87402-4699
(505) 599-0310
Fax: (505) 599-0555
degner@sjc.cc.nm.us

8222

Business Information: Serving as Director of Learning Technologies of San Juan College, Ms. Degner leads the formulation of institutional policy for instructional and new learning methodologies. Her additional responsibilities include faculty education and distance learning. Before assuming her supervisory duties, she was an Assistant Professor at the College for 10 years. Due to her efforts, the College now has 17 computer labs and 1,000 computers on campus. Ms. Degner is able to perform consulting work through MultiMedia Solutions, a service provided by the College. In the future, she hopes to delve further into distance education. Her keys to success have been her sense of humor and her ability to think outside-the-box and deliver results. Founded in 1956, San Juan College is a two-year, county-supported college. With an undergraduate population of 4,500 students, the College offers certificates, transfer associate, and terminal associate degrees. Set in a picturesque 698-acre, small town campus, the College offers its students an environment believing a tranquil setting is condusive to the learning process. San Juan College employs over 800 individuals. **Career Highlights:** San Juan College: Director of Learning Technologies (1998-Present), Director of Instructional Computing (1992-98), Associate Professor of Computer Science (1982-92). **Associations &**

Accomplishments: National Council of Instructional Administrators; Association for Educational Communications and Technology; New Mexico Council of Higher Education Computing/Communications; Chairperson (1999), New Mexico Council on Technology in Education; Farmington Museum Foundation; PEO. **Education:** New Mexico State University: M.A. (1988), B.S. (1974). **Personal Information:** Married to Robert in 1979. Ms. Degner enjoys fishing and boating.

Cheryl L. Evans
Network Technician
Rockingham Community College
P.O. Box 38
Wentworth, NC 27375
(336) 342-4261

8222

Business Information: Serving as Network Technician, Ms. Evans oversees the installation of software and hardware on each of the 600 computers, and hiring of part time, qualified staff to assist in the administration of the department. She maintains the network system, ensuring a smooth operation and providing back up systems for the College's various departments. Additionally, Ms. Evans handles faculty staff development, coordinating and conducting classes for their continuing education. Coordinating resources, time lines, schedules, and assignments also fall within the purview of Ms Evans' functions. Owing her success to perseverance, she advises others to remember the three D's: dedication, determination, and desire. Looking toward the next millennium, Ms. Evans plans include assisting in the College's growth and recruitment of more students and employees. Founded in 1967, Rockingham Community College is a higher learning institute. Well known for great instructors, the College's size allows much one on one student-teacher interaction. An advisory committee struggles to bring in teachers from different industries in an effort to offer a broader curriculum. Presently, the College employs a staff of more than 415 people. **Career Highlights:** Rockingham Community College: Network Technician (1998-Present), Instructor (1996-Present); Dog Breeder, Self-Employed (1988-93). **Associations & Accomplishments:** American Association of Women in Community Colleges; Rockingham Amateur to Talk Society; Amateur Radio Club. **Education:** Rockingham Community College, A.A.S. (1996). **Personal Information:** Ms. Evans enjoys amateur radio, electronics and computers.

Ronald Gibson
Head of Industrial Technology
Walters State Community College
500 South Davy Crocket Parkway
Morristown, TN 37813-6899
(423) 318-2758
Fax: (923) 585-6895
ronald.gibson@wscc.cc.tn.us

8222

Business Information: Dr. Gibson serves as Head of Industrial Technology for Walters State Community College. He is responsible for teaching manufacturing and CIM technology curriculums. Before joining Walters State Community College in 1995, Dr. Gibson served as a Ph.D. Intern at the University of Tennessee's Oakridge National Laboratory. His solid technology background includes employment as Senior Project Engineer with Schegel Tennessee Inc. and Senior Electrical Engineer for Becton Dickinson. In his capacity, he also fulfills the responsibilities of Associate Professor responsible for designing and promoting advanced technology courses. Dr. Gibson, in addition to supervising and mentoring his staff of three employees, is charged with personnel evaluations; overseeing academic time lines, schedules, and assignments; and providing students with cutting edge technologies. His success reflects his ability to communicate, think out-of-the-box, and aggressively take on new challenges as well as his drive for perfection. Walters State Community College is a state supported, two year, coed institution which is an integral part of State University and Community College System of Tennessee. Established in 1970, the Institution is located on a 100 acre campus in Morristown, Tennessee. Specializing in industrial and manufacturing technologies, Walters State Community College employs a staff of four people in the Industrial Technology Department. **Career Highlights:** Head of Industrial Technology, Walters State Community College (1995-Present); Senior Project Engineer, Schlege Tennessee Inc. (1991-93); Senior Electrical Engineer, Becton Dickinson (1983-91). **Associations & Accomplishments:** Friends Disaster Relief; Alenwick Community Center. **Education:** University of Tennessee, Ph.D (1999); Clemson University: M.S. (1976), B.S. (1975). **Personal Information:** Married to Gwynn L. in 1973. Two children: Forrest N. and Heather N. Dr. Gibson enjoys camping, hiking and hunting.

Brandon Hamilton

Instructor
Ivy Tech State College
12801 South Justice Street
Calumet Park, IL 60827
(219) 464-8514
Fax: (219) 464-9751
blhamilt@ny.tec.in.us

8222

Business Information: With over 22 years of experience in operations management, systems engineering, telecommunications, and computer science, Mr. Hamilton joined the Ivy Tech State College faculty team in 1997, and presently fulfills the role of Instructor. His position principally involves teaching computer information systems in the College's Business Division. Mr. Hamilton, a multi-functional professional, specializes in office automation, records management, and training. Other major fields of expertise include policy and procedural writing, computer programming, database and spreadsheet design, and managerial accounting. As a computer systems developer, Mr. Hamilton has designed software applications in relationship marketing, marketing analysis, and financial planning. He has served on the boards of many profit and non-profit organizations in Los Angeles. Owning a consistent record of delivering results, Mr. Hamilton is well versed in VAX, MVS, DOS, Windows95 and NT as well as COBOL, Fortran, ADA, Visual Basic, Pascal, C++ and RBG. Having studied Nuclear Power Technology while serving in the United States Navy, he has authored a number of professional publications to include "Specifications for North Anna Nuclear Power Plant," and "Operating Procedures for a Power Plant Computer." His future plan is to move into educational consulting. Mr. Hamilton's credo is "find a niche if you like what your doing, success will follow." Ivy Tech State College is the third largest state-supported college in Indiana. Founded in 1963, it has grown to be a network of 24 community-based campuses offering quality career and transfer programs. **Career Highlights:** Instructor, Ivy Tech State College (1997-Present); Adjunct Professor, DeVry Institute of Technology (1996); Chief Executive Officer, World Marketing Services (1995); Strategic Planner, Milburn, Maiello, and Church (1995); Instructor, Los Angeles Valley College (1995); Instructor, Glendale Career College (1995); Instructor, Premiere Career College (1995); Adjunct Professor, University of Phoenix (1994-95). **Associations & Accomplishments:** Association of Computing Machinery; University of Illinois Alumni Association; Indiana Coalition of Blacks in Higher Education; Fellow, Coro Foundation. **Education:** Indiana State University, Ph.D. in Educational Leadership, Administration, and Foundations (In Progress); University of Southern California, M.B.A. (1991); University of Illinois, B.S. (1979); Kennedy King College, A.A (1975). **Personal Information:** Mr. Hamilton enjoys jogging, cycling, swimming, scuba diving, skiing, tennis, dancing, writing and reading.

William R. Harding III

Instructor
ECPI Technical College
201 Tapestry Terrace
Cary, NC 27511
(919) 571-0057
Fax: (919) 571-0780
bhardling@ecpi.edu

8222

Business Information: Drawing from over 23 years of extensive experience in the field, Mr. Harding serves in the capacity of Instructor at ECPI Technical College. He provides students with an education in the areas of Linnux, Sisco, Microsoft NT, and Novell. With 20 students in each of his classes, Mr. Harding also serves as the head of the ECPI Technical College's information technology department. Looking to the future, he plans to complete his MCSE and CCNA certifications and continue to teach. His success reflects his ability to think out-of-the-box, communicate effectively, take on challenges, and deliver results on behalf of the College and its student body. ECPI Technical College is an institution of higher learning that provides education in technical areas. Located in Cary, North Carolina, the College provides a full range of educational services dealing with Microsoft NT and Novell to 300 students each year. A great number of professionals are employed to fulfill all aspects of administrative, teaching, and support duties. **Career Highlights:** ECPI Technical College: Instructor (1994-Present), Director of Education (1998-99). **Education:** Southwestern Baptist, M.Div. (1977); Old Dominion Univeristy: B.S., Associates degree. **Personal Information:** Married to Margaret in 1994. One child: Scott Edward. Mr. Harding enjoys family time, reading and the Internet.

Jim Hemgen

Director of Information Technology Training
Frederick Community College
7932 Opossumtown Pike
Frederick, MD 21702
(301) 846-2681
Fax: (301) 846-2689
jhemgen@fcc.cc.md.us

8222

Business Information: As Director of Information Technology Training of Frederick Community College, Mr. Hemgen assumes accountability for all computer related training classes. He is responsible for developing the curriculum, organizing class schedules, and administering information technology training in continuing education and contracting. Determining which courses are to be taught, he hires qualified instructors, markets special projects, and performs information technology assessments. An expert, Mr. Hemgen custom creates some courses and administers Cisco and Prosoft training to the students. Recently, he formed a partnership with ITech which assisted in obtaining an additional 200 training programs for the College. Always alert to new opportunities, techniques, and approaches, Mr. Hemgen is looking forward to developing and running information technology training programs on a larger scale. Founded in 1958, Frederick Community College is a public community college with approximately 5,000 students enrolled. Providing information technology training through continuing education programs, the College staffs 200 administrative, teaching, and support personnel who work diligently to enhance and perfect educational opportunities for students. **Career Highlights:** Director of Information Technology Training, Frederick Community College (1997-Present); Computer Business Teacher, Giathersburg High School (1991-97); Information Technology Analyst, World Bank (1990-92); Cellular Sales Representative, Cellular One (1989-91). **Associations & Accomplishments:** American Society for Training and Development. **Education:** University of Maryland, B.S. (1990); University of California at Los Angeles, Online Teaching Certificate. **Personal Information:** Married to Tami in 1994. One child: Calie. Mr. Hemgen enjoys coaching high school lacrosse.

Thomas A. Hennigan, Ph.D

Instructor
Lewis-Clark State College
500 8th Avenue
Lewiston, ID 83501
(208) 799-2452
Fax: (208) 799-2175
thennigan@lesc.edu

8222

Business Information: In his position as an Instructor for Lewis-Clark State College, Dr. Hennigan provides training sessions on technology based courses to instruct employees in the use of multimedia tools for education enhancement. Additionally, he manages and operates laboratory maintenance systems, oversees network infrastructure, and installs and upgrades hardware and software for College computers. Building on more than 20 years of extensive employment and educational experience, Dr. Henningan ensures the College utilizes the best in cutting edge technology. Enjoying substantial success in his present position and finding his work greatly rewarding, Dr. Henningan plans on expanding laboratory services, reaching more students, and providing recognition for all. Lewis-Clark State College is an institution of higher learning providing general and specialized course instruction for individuals wishing to advance their educational studies. Established in 1913 as a two year teaching college, Lewis-Clark now offers four year degrees and is well known for its nursing and teaching instruction. The College is located in Lewiston, Idaho and is home to more than 1,000 students from around the world. **Career Highlights:** Instructor, Lewis-Clark State College (1997-Present); U.S. West Grant Manager, University of Idaho (1995-97). **Associations & Accomplishments:** American Society of Curriculum Developers; Delta Psi Omega. **Education:** University of Idaho, ABD (2000); Washington State University, M.A. (1984); LCSC, B.S. (1976). **Personal Information:** Four children: Issac Wilson, Megan Orine, Samson, and Beth Newstrom. Mr. Hennigan enjoys church activities.

Timothy A. Hollabaugh

Dean of Technology
College of the Sequoias
4466 East Huntsman Avenue
Fresno, CA 93725
(559) 730-3843
timh@giantsequoias.cc.ca.us

8222

Business Information: Serving as Dean of Technology, Mr. Hollabaugh has been providing excellent educational services with the College of the Sequoias since 1987. Managing a group of four programmers, two technicians, and four laboratory aides, he focuses on the maintaining and upgrading of the College's complex computer network. Organizing transcript and administrative data, Mr. Hollabaugh concentrates his efforts towards implementing new technologies in order to run a more effective and efficient networking system. Involved in the designing and installation of the College's Web site, he assists in technical promotional services in order to extend the College of the Sequoias' services to a more expansive area. Specializing in higher education, the College of the Sequoias was established in 1930. Located in Fresno, California, the College offers an expansive variety of degrees, courses, and programs to its enrolled 10,000 students. Employing 800 knowledgable faculty members, and staff, the College remains dedicated to the furthering advancement in quality educational development. **Career Highlights:** Dean of Technology, College of the Sequoias (1987-Present); Team Leader, Army National Guard (1984-87); Shift Sergeant, Pinkterton Inc. (1980-84). **Associations & Accomplishments:** Board Member, Chief Information Systems Officer Association; Past Trustee, Immanuel Lutheran Church. **Education:** California State University at Fresno, B.S. in Computer Science (1999); Regents University of New York, A.S. in Computer Science. **Personal Information:** Married to Tammy in 1999. Three children: Chris, David, and Michael. Mr. Hollabaugh enjoys gardening.

Christopher L. Kennedy

Manager of Network Services
Frederick Community College
7932 Opossumtown Pike
Frederick, MD 21702
(301) 846-2591
Fax: (301) 846-2498
ckennedy@fcc.cc.md.us

8222

Business Information: Functioning in the role of Manager of Network Services with Frederick Community College, Mr. Kennedy oversees and directs all administration and operational activities of the systems infrastructure. He is responsible for program installation and upgrade. Before joining Frederick Community College as Computer Systems Specialist in 1993, Mr. Kennedy served as a Computer Technician with Frederick County. In his present position, he performs backups and data recovery, resolves communications problems, and troubleshoots network usage and computer peripherals. Having received several internal awards, Mr. Kennedy works with a team of individuals to insure the successful operation of all information systems. His future endeavors include becoming more of a technical expert in PeopleSoft and obtaining his M.B.A. degree. Mr. Kennedy's success reflects his ability to produce results and aggressively tackle new challenges. Frederick Community College is an institute of learning serving a local population. Established in 1958, the College is a two year, accredited institution offering a diverse educational format and a multitude of student activities. A staff and faculty of 300 oversee the daily instruction of students on campus. **Career Highlights:** Frederick Community College: Manager of Network Services (1998-Present), Computer System Specialist (1993-98); Computer Technician, Frederick County, Maryland Government (1990-91). **Associations & Accomplishments:** Maryland Community College Information Technology Managers. **Education:** Frostburg State University, M.B.A. (In Progress); University of Maryland, B.S. in Information System Management; Frederick Community College, A.A. in Business Administration. **Personal Information:** Mr. Kennedy enjoys dancing and collecting coins, baseball cards and miniature die cast metal cars.

Gail D. Klatkiewicz

Enrollment Coordinator
Lake Land College
P.O. Box 359
Sheboygan, WI 53082
(920) 565-1218
Fax: (920) 565-1206
klatkiewiczg@lakeland.edu

8222

Business Information: As Enrollment Coordinator of Lake Land College, Ms. Klatkiewicz oversees all aspects of the Instructor Department. Her responsibilities as Enrollment Coordinator include assisting students at the beginning of their time at the Institution, planning all activities, and monitoring students and instruction. Ms. Klatkiewicz has been a member of the Lakeland staff for 10 years and has plans to further her education to obtain her Doctorate. She credits her success to the support of her family and her friends and considers being the Head of the Computer Committee to be a major highlight of her career. Lakeland College is an educational facility located just 55 miles north of Milwaukee. Originally founded, in 1875, within a liberal arts tradition, the Institution places a large emphasis on preparation for sound careers. Lakeland College has a student body of approximately 3,800. The Institution also operates a campus in Tokyo, Japan and provides other foreign study programs in Asia and Europe. **Career Highlights:** Lake Land College:

Enrollment Coordinator (1989-Present), Instructor (1999). **Associations & Accomplishments:** Parent to Parent Facilitator. **Education:** Lakeland College, M.B.A. (1998); Marian College, B.A. **Personal Information:** Married to Michael in 1970. Four children: Mathew, Sara, Diane, and Rebecca. Ms. Klatkiewicz enjoys white water rafting, wood carving and stained glass.

Edward Maloney

Education Supervisor
ITT Technical Institute
17901 1/2 Bullock Avenue
Encino, CA 91316
(818) 364-5151
Fax: (818) 364-5150
ed_maloney@usa.net

8222

Business Information: Functioning in the role of Education Supervisor for ITT Technical Insititute, Mr. Maloney has fulfilled a long list of duties. He has coordinated computer visualization technology and networking, modeling, and software design for libraries. A three year veteran, Mr. Maloney has offered his technical expertise to many students via tutoring in the realm of CAD and computer visualization. In addition, he has advised students in regards to educational and professional oppurtunities. As for the future and looking to the 21st Century, Mr. Maloney plans to advance in both technical and educational fields. His quote is "teaching is awesome." His ability to deliver results and take on new challenges has been contributing factors to his professional success. ITT Technical Institute provides an education in electrical engineering and information technology. As a chain of schools across the United States, ITT Technical Institute has facilitated the professional growth of many Americans. As a result, many of the the Intstitute's graduates have gone on to prosperous careers in technical fields. **Career Highlights:** Education Supervisor, ITT Technical Institute (Present); Automated Test Engineer, Sentex Systems; Senior Programming Technician, Telecommunications Consulting Group. **Associations & Accomplishments:** Alpha Beta Kappa; Institute of Electronics for Electrical Engineers. **Education:** ITT Technical Institute, B.S. (1996).

Randy C. Marchany

Senior Computer Systems Engineer
Virginia Tech Computing Center
1700 Pratt Drive
Blacksburg, VA 24060
(540) 231-9523
randy.marchany@vt.edu

8222

Business Information: As Senior Computer Systems Engineer with Virginia Tech Computing Center since 1975, Mr. Marchany is responsible for management of systems administration. Within the Electrical and Computer Engineering Department, he also manages the technology infostructure and workstation laboratories. Accumulating 23 years of technology experience working at the University and with a strong academic background, he teaches Internet and UNIX security courses including World Wide Web security, network attack analysis, and the formulation of effective site security policies. Mr. Marchany is a member of the SANS Institute, which is one of the foremost computer security organizations. Additionally, he teaches UNIX system management training courses for internal and external administrators. He also guides his staff of four experts in planning yearly budgets, approving equipment and software acquisition, preparing grant requests for funds, and conducting training and orientation seminars for laboratory users. An expert in the field, Mr. Marchany has authored nine publications, conducted over 100 presentations at various conferences, and has orchestrated over 50 professional seminars. His future goals include increasing security awareness and eventually attaining the position of Information Security Officer. Virginia Tech Computing Center is the information systems department within the Virginia Polytechnic Institute and State University. Serving over 30,000 students, the University is known for infostructure research to include both Internet and networking. The Center presently employs a faculty staff of more than 500 professional, technical, and support personnel. **Career Highlights:** Senior Computer Systems Engineer, Virginia Tech Computing Center (1989-Present); Assistant Director, Virginia Tech Department of Electrical and Computer Engineering Workstation Labs (1995-Present); Associate, Ernst & Young - New York (1993-Present); Lecturer, Information, Security, Audit, and Control Association (1992-Present). **Associations & Accomplishments:** Association of Computing Machinery; Institute of Electrical and Electronics Engineers; Digital Equipment Computer User's Society; Sun Microsystems Users Group; International Computer Music Association; Broadcast Music Inc.; Usenix/SAGE. **Education:** Virginia Polytechnic Institute and State University: M.S. in Electrical Engineering (1992), B.S. in Computer Science (1981). **Personal Information:** Married in 1996. Mr. Marchany enjoys being a member of the award winning band. The award winning band is "No Strings Attached."

Margaret R. Morrell, M.A.

Director of Internet Development Center
Valencia Community College
1800 South Kirkman Road
Orlando, FL 32811
(407) 299-5000
mmorrell@virtualgateways.com

8222

Business Information: Holding the position of Director of Internet Development Center at Valencia Community College since 1997, Mrs. Morrell presides over a range of duties. She is responsible for managing all aspects of Internet development collegewide with a full time staff and numerous interns. Mrs. Morrell administers and controls all data resources. She recovers corrupted data and eliminates redundancy to improve Internet services. Some of her greatest accomplishments at the College includes leading a team on a Y2K project, making numerous presentations at national conventions for healthcare, and designing and implementing a program for a student portfolio. Mrs. Morrell plans to specialize in instructional technology in the future and obtain certification for Microsoft. Perseverance is the main characterstic that has allowed Mrs. Morrell to succeed in her professional career. Founded in 1967, Valencia Community College is a state-supported, two-year, co-educational educational facility. Part of the Florida Community College System, the College offers awards certificates, transfer associate, and terminal associate degrees. Approximately 19,500 undergraduates are currently taking advantage of the educucation opportunities at Valencia Community College. **Career Highlights:** Director of Internet Development Center, Valencia Community College (1997-Present); Business Systems Analyst, Orlando Regional Healthcare System (1992-97); Programmer Analyst, St. Anthony's Hospital (1987-92); President/Owner, Gateway Designs (1997-present). **Associations & Accomplishments:** Editor, Briefme Magazine & Computer Web & Internet; Chief Editor, First Internet Bird Club. **Education:** Webster University, Master's degee in Computer Resources and Information Systems (1997); B.S. in Chemistry (1974); St. Petersburg Community College, A.S. (1969). **Personal Information:** Married to M. L. Morrell, Jr. in 1977. One child: Mari Patrice.

Joyce E. Nelson

315 1/2 Main Street
Ashland, WI 54806

8222

Business Information: A savvy, 15 year professional in the field of technology, Ms. Nelson served as Network Administrator and Technician for WITC-Ashland. She was responsible for facilitating the computer network functionality for 4,300 students and more than 75 employees. Ms. Nelson was an invaluable member of the WITC-Ashland team of professionals, providing excellent educational course direction. Responsible for the test and evaluation of day to day operations, she created cutting edge problematic solutions and implemented new procedures and policies in order to provide a more effective and efficient operation. Highly regarded, Ms. Nelson believes satisfaction of a good job comes only from personal satisfaction. Her occupational background history includes stint as Network Technician with Pierce County in Wisconsin; Computer Support Specialist for The Barbers; and Computer Operator at Gourmet Award Foods. Attributing her success to hard work ethic and her ability to take on challenges and deliver results, she plans on developing, growing, adapting, and making changes in her personal growth. Ms. Nelson's advice to others is "believe in growing and be honest to yourself." **Career Highlights:** Network Administrator/Technician, WITC-Ashland (1999-00); Network Technician, Pierce County, Wisconsin (1998-99); Computer Support Specialist, Regis Corporation, formerly The Barbers (1997-98); Computer Operator, Gourmet Award Foods (1997). **Education:** National American University, B.S. in Computer Information Systems (1998); Hibbing Vocational Technical College, A.S. in Electronics (1985). **Personal Information:** Ms. Nelson enjoys network integration and computer network design.

Horia Pop, Ph.D.

Professor
Mount San Antonio College
1000 North Grand Avenue, #26A, Room 212B
Walnut, CA 91789
(909) 594-5611
hpop@mtsac.edu

8222

Business Information: Serving as a Professor at Mount San Antonio College, Dr. Pop teaches computer science and mathematic courses. A visionary who has proven himself correct on many occasions, he is involved in building the computer science and network programs. Possessing an excellent understanding of his field, Dr. Pop is responsible for developing new courses and facilitating grant writing, gaining funding for the computer science and mathematics departments. Highly regarded, he has published more than 10 papers in several trade journals. Dr. Pop attributes his success to his determination and ability to communicate effectively and deliver results. Looking to the future, his future aspirations are to grow the programs already in place, and develop more toward networking. Founded in 1946, Mount San Antonio College is a district-supported two year, co-ed college. A part of the California Community College System, the College awards transfer associates degrees. With a student population of 32,000 individuals, the campus is located in a small town environment. Over 450 faculty members are employed here, and the College offers day and night classes. **Career Highlights:** Professor, Mount San Antonio College (1998-Present); Professor, Occidental College (1997-98); Professor, University of Iowa (1995-97). **Associations & Accomplishments:** Institute of Electrical and Electronics Engineer; Association of Computing Machinery; American Mathematical Society. **Education:** University of Southern California, Ph.D. (1995); Institute of Mathematics, Ph.D. in Mathematics; University of Iowa, M.S. in Computer Science. **Personal Information:** Married to Vanda in 1977. Two children: Andrei and Irina. Dr. Pop enjoys math, math/computer systems programming competitions, classical music and skiing.

Timothy E. Reese

Division Manager
Eastern Idaho Technical College
1600 South 25th East
Idaho Falls, ID 83404
(208) 524-3000
Fax: (208) 524-3007
tim@eitc.edu

8222

Business Information: Mr. Reese has faithfully served with Eastern Idaho Technical College since coming board to the College's faculty as Division Manager in 1976. He oversees daily administration and operations of the Business Technology Center. In this context, Mr. Reese determines the overall technical direction and academic contribution of the information systems functions. Highly regarded, he supervises and guides a staff of 18 full time and 40 part time employees in coordinating computer usage and availability, conducting business and information scheduling, and developing new program software to enhance the learning process. Maintaining the functionality and operational status of the systems infrastructure is also a very integral part of Mr. Reese's responsibilities. In the future, he looks forward to remaining with the College in his current position. Founded in 1969, Eastern Idaho Technical College is a two-year technical college that is owned and operated by the state. Located in Idaho Falls, Idaho, the College offers students a variety of courses to choose from while working to obtain a diploma. The College was the first college in Idaho to form a partnership with the Microsoft Corporation concerning the bettering of student education. Currently, the College has a staff of approximately 106 employees who are committed to the students. **Career Highlights:** Division Manager, Eastern Idaho Technical College (1976-Present). **Associations & Accomplishments:** Greater Idaho Falls Chamber of Commerce; American Vocational Association; Idaho Marketing Education Association; Better Business Bureau Education Foundation; Idaho Vocational Education Association; Northwest Academic Forum. **Education:** California State University at Northridge; Idaho State University, M.A.; Boise State University; University of Idaho. **Personal Information:** Mr. Reese enjoys show dogs.

Andre Schonken

Information Technology Director
PE Technikon
Private Bag X 6011
Port Elizabeth, South Africa 6000
+27 415043237
Fax: +27 415043189
andre@ml.petech.ac.za

8222

Business Information: Mr. Schonken has been employed with the PE Technikon since 1980. At the beginning of his employment with PE, he was hired as the Project Manager. Years later and with a wealth of practical experience under his belt, Mr. Schonken now assumes responsibility of Information Technology Director. He oversees the systems and network infrastructures, as well as determines the overall strategic direction and educational contribution of the information systems function. A systems expert, he does research and development of new technology on the market, manages computer technicians, serves as chief liasion between the Technology Department and other departments, and troubleshoots problems. Establishing realistic goals that are compatible with PE Technikon, Mr. Schonken would like to transition PE into using effective knowledge management system. His success reflects his ability to produce results and aggressively tackle new challenges. The PE Technikon is an established institute of higer education located in Port Elizabeth, South Africa. The University, offers many degree programs that incorporates the latest technology which provides each student with an edge on opportunity. Nationally based, the University employs over 700 professional educators who are dedicated to the success of each student. **Career Highlights:** PE Technikon: Information Technology Director (1986-Present), Project Manager (1980-86). **Associations & Accomplishments:** Computer Society of South Africa. **Education:** B.Sc. with Honors in Computer Science. **Personal Information:** Married to Alta in 1980. Two children: Elandré and Renaldo. Mr. Schonken enjoys Austrian Philately.

Lynn A. Usack

Instructional Technologist
Corning Community College
1 Academic Drive
Corning, NY 14830
(607) 962-9417
Fax: (607) 962-9466
usack@corning-cc.edu

8222

Business Information: As Instructional Technologist at Corning Community College, Mrs. Usack assists the faculty in the integration of technology into their curriculum. Throughout daily activities, she is responsible for such aspects as Web design, work shops, and systems maintenance. With more than two years of extensive experience in technology, Mrs. Usack capitalizes on her knowledge and talents as she continues the pursuit of her doctorate in small business management. A multi-faceted professional, she also plans on conducting some consulting, desk top publishing, and film production work. Her success is attributed to her ability to think outside the box, take on challenges, and deliver results on behalf of the College. Corning Community College of Corning New York is a is a two-year educational facility that provides higher learning to include both corporate and distance educational programs. Supplying two-year degrees and certificates, the College offers various courses in host subjects including business administration, nursing, and information technology. Established in 1957, the College utilizes the highly skilled services of more than 300 employees including professionals, executive staff, and administrative personnel. **Career Highlights:** Instructional Technologist, Corning Community College (1999-Present); Business Development Representative, Cornell Fingerlakes Credit Union (1998-99); Graduate Fellow, Ithaca College (1997-98); Research Assistant III, Boyce Thompson Institute (1992-96). **Associations & Accomplishments:** Middle States Association of Colleges and Schools; Evaluator Association for Computing Machinery; SIGGRAPH; Educause Jane Ryland Fellow. **Education:** Ithace College, M.S. in Communications (1998); Cornell University, B.S. in Microbiology (1986). **Personal Information:** Married to Ryszard in 1984. One child: Krystopher Stephan. Mrs. Usack enjoys freelance art, playing the fife and film production.

Mike Walinder

Senior Computer Technician
McCook Community College
1205 East 3rd Street
McCook, NE 69001-2631
(308) 345-6303
Fax: (308) 345-3305
mwalindr@mcc.mccook.cc.ne.us

8222

Business Information: Holding the position of Senior Computer Technician since 1994, Mr. Walinder maintains the functionality and operational status of the network environment of McCook Community College. Utilizing his expansive knowledge in computer software and hardware development, he concentrates his efforts towards the organization of satellite classes, and troubleshooting for the College's database. Assembling bids and designing video classrooms, Mr. Walinder focuses on Novell networking and database with McCook Community College. Looking to the future, he plans on becoming more involved in Novell networking and database development. Serving the region of McCook, Nebraska, McCook Community College provides higher education in specialized information technology courses. Established in 1926, this two year college staffs 75 teachers and administration dedicated to the provision of quality education. Extensively involved in the information techological sciences, the College focuses on fiber district learning, the development of online course curriculum, and technical resource for grant writing. **Career Highlights:** Senior Computer Technician, McCook Community College (1994- Present); Owner, A&M Aviation & Computers (1992-94); Chief Mechanic, Obeilin Flying Service (1984-92). **Education:** McCook Community College, A.A.S. in Computer Science (1995); Certified Novell Administrator; Federal Aviation Administration Private Pilot; Federal Aviation Administration Airframe & Powerplant Mechanic. **Personal Information:** Married to Glenda in 1973. Two

children: Melissa and Angie. Mr. Walinder enjoys walking and reading.

Jim Wallace

Technology Coordinator
Great Rivers Tech Institute
P.O. Box 747
McGehee, AR 71654
(870) 222-5360
Fax: (870) 222-4709
jwallace@grvts.tec.ar.us

8222

Business Information: Beginning his association with Great Rivers Technical Institute as a business teacher, Mr. Wallace was promoted to Technology Coordinator in 1998. With no previous computer experience, but strongly motivated to achieve optimal results, he has excelled in his current position. Mr. Wallace assumes accountability for the development of the Web page for the College and a local high school. In addition, he maintains the network, coordinates the implementation of new technology, provides assistance to the help desk, and maintains IP connections. Displaying a strong sense of purpose, Mr. Wallace anticipates growth within his department and wishes to attain some assistants to help with his growing responsibilities. His success reflects his ability to deliver results and take on new challenges. Established in 1974, Green Rivers Technical Institute is a state funded two-year college resulting in degrees, certifications, and licensing. With a faculty and staff of 40 people, the College is able to offer education in computers, industrial technology, graphic arts and other related technical fields. The College estimates an annual revenue of $350,000. **Career Highlights:** Great Rivers Technical Institute: Information Technology Coordinator (1998-Present), Business Education Instructor (1984-98); Data Processing Manager, United Dollar Stores Inc. (1967-84). **Associations & Accomplishments:** American Vocational Association; Arkansas Business Teachers; Data Processing Management Association. **Education:** UAF (1998-99). **Personal Information:** Married to Patricia in 1968. Two children: Andrew and Bethanie. Mr. Wallace enjoys wood burning, small crafts and woodworking.

Alan L. Wise

Microcomputer Technician
Pima Community College
2202 West Anklam Road
Tucson, AZ 85709-0170
(520) 206-6053
Fax: (520) 206-6972
awise@pimacc.pima.edu

8222

Business Information: Following 21 years of distinguished service in the United States Air Force, Mr. Wise was recruited to Pima Community College as Microcomputer Technician in 1981. His present role principally involves providing technical support to a small-scale user interface and database-oriented application infrastructure. Mr. Wise, utilizing his firm academic ties and technical strength gained while in the U.S. Air Force, is charged with analyzing and supporting computer operations by controlling production applications, monitoring system resources, and providing first-line support for operational problems. A tested and proven, 17 year veteran of Pima Community College, he loves learning new, emerging technology. Troubleshooting and repairing personal computers, installing and setting up computer systems and networks, and operating system software also fall within the purview of Mr. Wise's responsibilities. His prime focus is on helping the College leverage and maximize the investments in technology, personnel, and processes to achieve educational objectives and goals. Taking the College to the next level of technology and success serves as Mr. Wise's future endeavors. A state-supported, two year, coed college, Pima Community College is part of the Arizona State Community College System. Founded in 1966, the College is located on a 350-acre urban campus in Tucson. Presently, the College is manned by a staffed of 1,567 serving the educational needs of more than 27,900 students annually. **Career Highlights:** Microcomputer Technician, Pima Community College (1981-Present); Master Sergeant, United States Air Force (1961-81). **Associations & Accomplishments:** American Legion; Lifetime Member, Retired Enlisted Association; American Association for Retired Persons; Lifetime Member, Handyman Club of America; Tucson Computer Society. **Education:** Pima Community College, A.A.S. (1991); A+ Certified Technician; Compaq Certified Technician; Apple Certified Technician. **Personal Information:** Married to Antonia "Toni" in 1992. Two children: Patricia Lynne Campbell and Diana Jean Miller. Mr. Wise enjoys bowling, hiking and biking.

Tess Wymore

Systems Analyst/Oracle Database Administrator
Coconino Community College
3000 North Fourth Street
Flagstaff, AZ 86003-8000
(520) 527-1222
Fax: (520) 527-8998

8222

Business Information: Serving as Systems Analyst and Oracle Database Administrator for the Coconino Community College, Ms. Wymore utilizes Oracle's BANNER application to run programs for the finance, accounts receivable, and human resources departments as well as for students and various Web products. She administrates the Oracle relational database management system on the DG/UX host, providing technical software and application support and system implementation. Ms. Wymore states that her current professional success came as a result of taking advantage of the opportunities presented to her during her career. She is proud to have presented a 1.5 hour session at the SCT Summit '99 Banner Conference and has been accepted to present at the Summit 2000 in March. Continually striving to improve her performance, she plans to attain her certification as a Database Administrator to facilitate promotional opportunities within the College. Coconino Community College is a higher educational institution offering a variety of occupational and academical courses and two year degrees to residents in Flagstaff, Arizona and the surrounding communities. Founded in 1991, the College enrolls 3,300 students each semester. Approximately 300 administrative, instructional, and support personnel are dedicated to providing quality educational opportunities to students. **Career Highlights:** System Analyst/Oracle Database Administrator, Coconino Community College (1994-Present); Programmer/Analyst, Chevron Corporation (1991-93). **Associations & Accomplishments:** Girl Scouts; National Organization of Women. **Education:** San Diego State University, B.S. (1989). **Personal Information:** Ms. Wymore enjoys hiking, kayaking, camping and volleyball.

Thomas P. Gray

Assistant Manager of Networking and Computing
Toledo Lucas County Public Library
325 North Michigan Street
Toledo, OH 43624-1614
(419) 259-5261

8231

Business Information: As Assistant Manager of Networking and Computing of Toledo Lucas County Public Library, Mr. Gray is concerned with network and computing management. Demonstrating an exceptional technical knowledge gained through practical work experience, Mr. Gray maintains the WAN network for all branches of the Library. Utilizing his impressive abilities, he efficiently and accurately maintains Internet-based functions as he monitors 12 WindowsNT servers. With superior communicative and speaking abilities, he is able to conduct intensive application training programs for staff as he translates technical jargon into easily comprehensible terms. Attributing success to good networking skills, Mr. Gray realizes the importance of learning by example and strives to study the images of his mentors. He intends to continue in his current capacity as he updates the technology used throughout the Library. Located in Toledo, Ohio, the Toledo Lucas County Public Library ranks seventh among the ninety libraries serving populations of between 250,000 and 499,000. Offering a wide range of reading material, reference books, and study aids, the Library also provides lending services to members. Over 19 branches are located throughout the region. The goal of the Library is to make educational materials and informative data readily available while teaching generations that reading is an important form of entertainment. **Career Highlights:** Assistant Manager of Networking and Computing, Toledo Lucas County Public Library (1996-Present); Part Time Instructor, Owens Community College (1985-Present); Programmer/Analyst, Unisys Corporation (1986-96). **Associations & Accomplishments:** Epsilon Pi Tau International Honor Society for Technology Professionals; Tau Alpha Pi National Honor Society for Engineering Technology. **Education:** Bowling Green State University (Currently Attending); Owens Technical College, A.A.S. in Electronic Engineering Technology. **Personal Information:** Married to Wendy in 1984. Three children: Courtney, Brittany, and Kaleigh. Mr. Gray enjoys basketball and model rocketry.

Ricardo S. Vilchez

Evening Supervisor
Fordham University Library
13 Van Pelt Avenue
Staten Island, NY 10303
(212) 636-6062
Fax: (212) 636-6766
ul-vilchez@rhoda.fordham.edu

8231

Business Information: Serving as an Evening Supervisor with the Fordham University Library, Mr. Vilchez is responsible for instructing students on information, literacy skills, and managing book circulation. Additionally, he educates and trains students on computer systems. Currently, he is in the process of preparing himself to write sources on computer technology. Fordham University is a private, four-year, coed, liberal arts university with graduate programs. Affiliated with the Roman Catholic Church, the University was established in 1841 and is situated on an 85-acre campus at Rose Hill in the Bronx and a seven-acre Lincoln Center campus in midtown Manhattan. The Fordham University Library is engaged in circulating books and other materials for reading, study, and reference. **Career Highlights:** Evening Supervisor, Fordham University Library (1989-Present); Counselor, Pratt Institute (1984-89); Administrative Assistant, Central Bank of Nicaragua (1974-84). **Associations & Accomplishments:** American Library Association; American Society for Information Science; Pratt Institute Computer and Technology Club; Nicaragua Philanthropic Club; Reforma National Library; President, Commission Hispana Pro Obra Ruben Dario; Vice President, Nicaragua Children Foundation of New York. **Education:** Pratt Institute: M.L.S. (1995), M.S.; Fordham University, B.A. in Politcal Science; Private University - Managua, Nicaragua, B.Bus.Admin. **Personal Information:** Two children: Ricardo E. and Nidia E.

Victoria M. Castillo

Software Applications Instructor
Alphatrain
219 Burnett Avenue
Maplewood, NJ 07040
(908) 686-1990
lizva@hotmail.com

8243

Business Information: As a savvy, Computer Software Instructor at Alphatrain, Ms. Castillo teaches out of the Newark, New Jersey facility. Educating her students on personal computer fundamentals, Windows98, Microsoft 97 Office Suite, Microsoft 2000 Office Suite and the Internet, she also provides corporate training. Seeing that her skills were lacking in a constantly changing industry, she took the initiative and acquired the necessary skills through education. Expecting her computer A+ certifications soon, Ms. Castillo looks to the future to improve herself both spiritually and physically. Her professional success is due to her patience and faith and belief in God, as well as her ability to take on challenges and deliver results. Established in 1992, Alphatrain is a minority business school that offers training in computer technology. With four locations, the School serves the New Jersey region and offers courses of instruction that include MCSE, MOUS, PC help and support specialist, multimedia, photoshops, and Web design. Headquartered in New Providence, New Jersey, Alphatrain provides its courses in a classroom setting at three locations. **Career Highlights:** Software Applications Instructor, Alphatrain (1999-Present); Manager of Contract & Lease, Battery Park City Authority (1990-96); Apprenticeship Specialist, Non-Traditional Employment for Women (1985-90). **Associations & Accomplishments:** Ordained Deacon (1999), Liberation in Truth Unity Fellowship Church; Microsoft Office User Specialist Certifications: MS Word, MS Excel. **Education:** Alphatrain, PC Support Specialist (1999); Cornell University, degree in Labor Relations. **Personal Information:** Three children: John L., Jeffrey A., and Michael A. Ms. Castillo enjoys music, writing, reading and mentoring. Aspiring to fulfill a dream of starting her own school, Ms. Castillo is currently in the process of accomplishing her vision with the establishment of Apprentice Options for Women, which is scheduled to open for business in the near future.

Michael D. Finch

PC Repair/Network Administration Supervising Instructor
BMR Training Centers
14156 Amargosa Road, Suite G
Victorville, CA 92392
(760) 243-1105
Fax: (760) 243-6216
mfvvca@usa.net

8243

Business Information: Demonstrating an extensive knowledge in the technical industry, Mr. Finch serves as PC Repair and Network Administration Supervising Instructor for BMR Training Centers. Every day he trains students with an innovative, hands-on approach to computer repairs to ensure they grasp multiple concepts. Supervising the repair of Novell and Microsoft networks, he guides his class to search for less obvious solutions to seemingly complicated problems. An advocate for open communication and teamwork, he also maintains the systems and network used by the Center, including the LAN and WAN. Recognized for his technical expertise, he is credited with the development and implementation of the current cirriculum of his courses. Keeping his goals consistent with the objectives of the Center, he currently is working to gain additional certifications while allowing his personal drive to continue pushing him towards success. BMR Training Centers is a higher education vocational school, specializing in technology training such as software training and computer repair. Professional staff members instruct pupils on various techniques to enforce modern concepts taught in class. The Center strives to offer practical applications of the training such as networking skills and theory to provide students with an advantage in today's technically progessive society. **Career Highlights:** PC Repair Network Administration Supervising Instructor, BMR Training Centers (1995-Present); Business Manager/Instructor, El Dorado Colleges, Inc. (1991-95). **Education:** Center for Degree Studies, Associate's degree in Business; El Dorado College, Certificate of Completion in Information Computer Systems; Victor Valley College, Certificate of Completion in Information Computer Systems. **Personal Information:** Mr. Finch enjoys horseback riding and writing.

Lily H. Yang

Information Technology Specialist
WFSATC
3031 South 200 East
Salt Lake City, UT 84115
(801) 481-7272
Fax: (801) 481-7167
lyang@wfsatc.org

8243

Business Information: Demonstrating her expertise in the field of information technology, Ms. Yang serves as Information Technology Specialist with WFSAT concentrating her efforts on developing programs and curriculum in the instruction of computer and certification courses. Utilizing 15 years of extensive practical experience in her particular field, Ms. Yang implements specific procedures and technologies dedicated to providing her students with the most practical and comprehensive educational development. Always alert to new opportunities, techniques, and approaches, Ms. Yang is committed to providing optimum service to WFSATC. Established in 1992, WFSATC specializes in information technology education programs for professionals who wish to advance their educational studies in the field of technology. The Institution staffs 45 administrative, teaching, and support personnel who work diligently to enhance and perfect educational opportunities for its students. Incorporating the latest technologies into educational development, the Institution establishes high standards of excellence for others in the industry. **Career Highlights:** Information Technology Specialist, WFSATC (1998-Present); Programmer and Project Manager, Paragon Technologies (1998); Programmer Leader, Allen Communications (1985). **Associations & Accomplishments:** Vice Chairman of Chinese Scholar and Students Associations, Brigham Young University (1982-83). **Education:** Brigham Young University, M.A. (1984); IKON Technical, Microsoft Certified Systems Engineer (1998). **Personal Information:** Married to George Battle in 1995. Ms. Yang enjoys stamp collecting and reading.

Pamela J. Knight

Technical Director
The Wharton School
3733 Spruce Street, Vance 344
Philadelphia, PA 19104
(215) 898-0400
Fax: (215) 898-2695
knightp@wharton.upenn.edu

8244

Business Information: Utilizing more than 15 years of experience in the technology field, Mrs. Knight joined The Wharton School in 1997. In the capacity of Technical Director for the External Affairs Department, she performs systems planning and evaluation, systems design and implementation, and oversees data warehousing and distributed systems. Mrs. Knight directly supervises a staff of five and is responsible for the Public Affairs and Funding Department. She provides technical support, manages projects, and serves as a liaison to other universities. Attributing her success to a good basic education and technical background, Mrs. Knight also received valuable support from family and colleagues within the field. She advises others to obtain the most affordable education possible and consider volunteering to gain more experience and knowledge. Mrs. Knight stays current in her field with conferences, magazines, staff training, and networking with colleagues on the Internet. For the future, she hopes to perform more technical and project management. Mrs. Knight plans to continue her studies and anticipates obtaining a Directorship. Rated number one in Business Schools in Newsweek, The Wharton School is one of the top three business schools in the country. The School offers undergraduate, postgraduate, and executive MBA courses. Many of the nation's top business leaders are graduates of Wharton. Officially founded in 1850, the School can trace its roots back to the 1700s and Benjamin Franklin. **Career Highlights:** The Wharton School: Technical Director (1997-Present), Information System Specialist (1994-97); Programmer/Analyst, Drexel University (1989-94); Information System Specialist, Abbott Northwestern Hospital (1986-89). **Education:** Drexel University, M.S. in Information System (1994); Loughborough University of Technology, B.S. in Civil Engineering. **Personal Information:** Married to Richard in 1985.

Patrick Belpaire

General Manager/Owner
U&I Learning
Hogeweg 12
Steenhuize, Belgium 9550
+32 54502294
Fax: +32 54502294
pat@uni.be

8299

Business Information: Serving as General Manager of U&I Learning, Mr. Belpaire is also the Owner of the Company. He is responsible for the overall management of the Company and guides employees in the development of the educational programs. Coordinating resources, time lines, schedules, and assignments; taking a lead role in driving services to market; and providing cohesive leadership also fall within the realm of Mr. Belpaire's responsibilities. The Company was founded when Mr. Belpaire decided he wanted to combine his computer knowledge with his psychology degree. He feels the proudest moment in his career was the moment he became successful with his own Company. Dedicated to the success of U&I Learning, Mr. Belpaire formulates strategic planning to facilitate continued Company growth and to enable U&I Learning to operate on an international level. Established in 1997, U&I Learning is an up and coming company specializing in online learning environments. Employing a staff of five individuals, the Company currently serves a local client base with education online dealing from business to business. **Career Highlights:** General Manager/Owner, U&I Learning (1994-Present); Dolmen: Sales Manager (1990-94), Training Officer (1986-90). **Associations & Accomplishments:** Belgian Network for Open and Distant Learning; VOV; ASTD. **Education:** University Antwerp, Master's degree (1994); University Gent: Master's degree in Education and Psychology, Post Graduate in Artificial Intelligence and Business Economics. **Personal Information:** Married in 1999. One child: Tibo. Mr. Belpaire enjoys his work.

Barbara L. Frisvold

Lead Instructor
Computer Learning Centers, Inc.
312 Marshall Avenue, Suite 100
Laurel, MD 20707
(301) 317-3617
brisvold@hotmail.com

8299

Business Information: Mrs. Frisvold is the Lead Instructor at Computer Learning Centers, Inc. in Laurel, Maryland. In this role, she is responsible for the direction of course material when presented to students who desire to gain a technical education. Demonstrating exceptional communicative skills, she translates sophisticated technical jargon into laymans terms to ensure all students are able to grasp the complicated concepts presented in class. Additionally, Mrs. Frisvold provides end-user support by assisting at the Help Desk; she also fulfills the needs of both Database and Systems Administrator. She credits her success to being flexible within the ever-changing industry and is internally recognized for her impressive accomplishments. In the future, Mrs. Frisvold intends to continue in her current role as she implements more database technology into students' cirriculum. With 27 locations throughout the United States, Computer Learning Centers, Inc. is recognized as one of the leading information technology technical schools. Providing training on all operational systems, the Center offers courses in customer service, call center software, network engineering, and programming. Originally established in 1947, the Laurel, Maryland location opened in 1996; nationwide employees total 1,200. **Career Highlights:** Lead Instructor, Computer Learning Centers, Inc. (1998-Present); Technical Writer, Excalibur Technologies (1997-98); Director of Client Services, Dakota Imaging, Inc. (1993-96). **Associations & Accomplishments:** Institute of Electronics and Electrical Engineers Computer Society; Association for Supervision and Curriculum Development; Outstanding Faculty Member of the Quarter (1999). **Education:** Washington State University: B.A. (1973), Teaching Credential (1973); Loyola College, Graduate courses in Educational Technology. **Personal Information:** Married to Gary A. in 1972. Three children: David, Brian, and Andrew.

Hugh Haggerty

Publishing Systems Manager
Kaplan
888 Seventh Avenue
New York, NY 10106
(212) 492-5874

8299

Business Information: Possessing superior talents in the information technology field, Mr. Haggerty joined Kaplan in 1999 as a Publishing Systems Manager. He manages the technical aspects of the desktop publishing department and provides MacIntosh support and networking. In addition, he oversees the operation of the computer infrastructure and implements new technology. Utilizing three years of experience in his field, Mr. Haggerty continues to assist the Company in the completion of corporate goals. He anticipates his promotion to Network Manager with Kaplan as a result of his continuing efforts to increase his skills through training and professional development activities. He also plans to obtain Cisco and MCSE certifications. Mr. Haggerty's success is attributed to his ability to take on challenges and deliver results on behalf of the Company. Kaplan operates as an educational firm that conducts training for standardized tests located at most major colleges. National in scope, the Company is located in New York. Currently, Kaplan employs the skilled services of 3,000 individuals to acquire business, meet with clients, facilitate projects, and market services. **Career Highlights:** Publishing Systems Manager, Kaplan (1998-Present); Technical Manager, Pubworks (1997-98). **Associations & Accomplishments:** New York Mac Users Group.

Donna L. Harris

Systems Director
Christian Educational Ministries
1820 Shilo Drive
Tyler, TX 75703
(903) 509-2999
Fax: (903) 509-1139
cem@ballistic.com

8299

Business Information: Committed to the success of the Christian Educational Ministries, Ms. Harris serves as the Systems Director. She presides over the administration of the Organization's network, system applications, and individual PCs. Additionally, she oversees the database administration, handles the Web site, and troubleshoots any problems. Ms. Harris also assumes the responsibilities of Webmaster and coordinating the scheduling and distribution of the taped sermons to the radio stations and updates the audio online which enables users to listen to the sermons over the Internet. After her recent divorce, Ms. Harris put herself through college, juggling work and three children to go from a full-time mother to Systems Director in a short four year period. Currently pursuing her certifications in Novell and NT, Ms. Harris looks forward to assisting the Organization in the completion of future goals. Established in 1995, the Christian Educational Ministries focuses on a child's educational level, providing nondenominational study materials such as video, tapes, and books for use in Sunday School or home study with parents. Each week, the Organization gives Christian sermons through over 100 radio stations. **Career Highlights:** Systems Director, Christian Educational Ministry (1997-Present); Marketing, Griffin Communications (1997); Local Area Network Administrator, NWCCD (1995-97). **Associations & Accomplishments:** Phi Theta Kappa; Girl Scouts Leader; Odessy of the Mind Coach. **Education:** Tyler Junior College; NWCCD, A.A.S. **Personal Information:** Three children: Hope, Heather, and Heidi. Ms. Harris enjoys outdoors, bowling and children's sporting events.

Jeanne Huddle, Ed.D.

Educational Programmer
ARESC
420 Sierra Madren Drive
North Little Rock, AR 72118
(870) 534-6129
huddlej@USA.net

8299

Business Information: Dr. Huddle serves as Educational Programmer of Arkansas Educational Service Corporation. She is responsible for program and service design for professional and educational growth. A successful, 34 year professional, she designs and evaluates software and technology that will assist students in learning increasingly complex concepts in today's classroom. Dr. Huddle identifies ideas and methods to improve educational programs for community youth and adult outreach facilities. She also has influence over school districts and local government agencies concerning SOLs and technologies utilized in the classrooms. Dr. Huddle plans to remain with the Corporation, expand her involvement to the sales of classroom technology, and further increase the scholastic capabilities of school systems to relate to students on various levels. Her educational background as well as her superb communication skills allow Dr. Huddle to effectively direct the future of scholastic achievement in the state of Arkansas, giving her the satisfaction of making a difference in the community. The Arkansas Educational Service Corporation is an educational service provider that coverer 12 school districts as well as the Department of Corrections. Serving as a link to the Department of Education, the Corporation provides information on new legislation regarding education, technical training, lesson planning, and educational equipment. Establsished in 1984, and employing over 100 people, the Corporation has greatly improved educational standards for primary and secondary schools as well as provided powerful lobbying for educational needs. **Career Highlights:** Educational Programmer, Arkansas Educational Service Corporation (1992-Present); Educational Consultant, Micro Computer Center (1988-92); Director of Leadership Development, Arkansas Department of Education (1986-88); Director of Professional Growth/Library Media Director, Pulaski County Schools (1968-86). **Associations & Accomplishments:** Co-Founder, Annual Hot Springs Technology Institute ofr Education; Arkansas Association of Educational Administrators; March of Dimes; American Heart Association; American Cancer Society; National Staff Development Council; American Society for Curriculum and Supervision. **Education:** University of Arkansas: Ed.D. (1993), Education Specialist (1981); University of Oklahoma, MLS (1972); Arkansas State University, B.S. in Education (1966). **Personal Information:** One child: Jeffrey. Dr. Huddle enjoys outdoor sports and reading.

Karen Landry

Information Technology/Information Systems Instructor
Computer Learning Centers, Inc.
436 Broadway
Methuen, MA 01844
(978) 794-0233
Fax: (978) 685-6011
karen.landry@clcx.com

8299

Business Information: With extensive experience as an educator, Ms. Landry serves as Information Technology and Information Systems Instructor for the Computer Learning Centers, Inc.. She specializes in database and sequel oriented management, instructing several introductory and support management classes. Before coming on board to Computer Learning Centers, Ms. Landry faithfully served as Manager for Automated Medical Systems. Her background history also includes a stint as Teacher with the Boston Public Schools. An accomplished professional, her most significant achievement during her career came when she developed and maintained the computer laboratory in the Boston Public Schools. Consistently achieving quality performance in the educational field, Ms. Landry is committed to providing continued optimum service to the Computer Learning Centers. She states that seeing her students graduate is a great highlight for her. Founded in 1957, the Computer Learning Centers, Inc. is a technological training and education facility. The Centers instructs individuals from around the world who are interested in beginning a technical career or who are obtaining continuing education in an effort to progress further in their established fields. Several certifications are offered including CNA, CNE, MCSE, and MOUS. Established in 1957, there are 28 separate locations throughout the United States. **Career Highlights:** Information Technology/Information Systems Instructor, Computer Learning Centers, Inc. (1992-Present); Manager, Automated Medical Systems (1986-92); Teacher, Boston Public Schools (1980-86). **Associations & Accomplishments:** Nu Gamma Chapter; Phi Betta Kappa. **Education:** University of Massachusetts, B.S. (1982). **Personal Information:** Ms. Landry enjoys photography, computers and fishing.

Christopher S. Leblanc

Supervisor/Instructor
Porter & Chester Institute
132 Hubbard Street
Ludlow, MA 01056
(413) 593-1508
Fax: (413) 583-6019
csl@aol.com

8299

Business Information: Providing his skilled services as Supervisor and Instructor for the Porter & Chester Institute, Mr. Leblanc oversees and directs the Computer and Architectural Drafting and Engineering Division. He directly supervises a staff of three qualified individuals. An expert, Mr. Leblanc sets the curriculum for the Department and teaches students in the discipline of architecture and CAD practices. Before joining the Institute in 1993, Mr. Leblanc assertively served as CAD Manager and Designer for The O'Leary Company, Inc. His solid, 16 year history in the technology field also includes a stint as Drafter and CAD Operator with Friendly Restaurants. Crediting his professional success to a sincere love of his work, he keeps up with the latest developments in his field by attending seminars, continuing education, and the Internet. Committed to providing continued optimum service to Porter & Chester Institute, Mr. Leblanc looks forward to deeper involvement in educative project architecture. Headquartered in Standford, Connecticut, Porter & Chester Institute maintains a total of six campuses. The Institute offers post-secondary education in architectural and civil CADD technology and was founded in 1954. **Career Highlights:** Supervisor/Instructor, Porter & Chester Institute (1993-Present); CAD Manager/Designer, The O'Leary Company, Inc. (1987-93); Drafter/CAD Operator, Friendly Restaurants (1985-87). **Education:** Porter & Chester Institute, Certificate (1983); Wentworth Institute of Technology, Certificate. **Personal Information:** Married to Kathleen in 1983. Mr. Leblanc enjoys sports and general aviation.

Lynn A. Makar

Director of Management Information Systems
Luzerne Intermediate Unit
368 Tioga Avenue
Kingston, PA 18704-5153
(570) 287-9681
Fax: (570) 287-5721
lamakar@liu.18.k12.pa.us

8299

Business Information: Ms. Makar is the Director of Managment of Information Systems for the Luzerne Intermediate Unit. Having served the Unit for almost 25 years, she specializes her talents within the network administration responsibilities. She compiles department data for the special education students and she assists them in generating funds with the results she provides. A systems expert, she also runs the computer lab, training other staff members on the proper use of computer technology. In the future, Ms. Makar hopes to become an Adjunct faculty member at the university level of education while she continues to upgrade her own education by completing her Master's degree. Luzerne Intermediate Unit is an educational agency concentrating its services to those students requiring specialized education structures. Since 1971, the Unit has provided occupational therapy and physical therapy programs within the regular classrooms of Kingston, Pennsylvania. The Unit also offers unique educational opportunities for homeless children, adults, and other students requiring alternatives to obtain their educational goals. **Career Highlights:** Director of Management Information Systems, Luzerne Intermediate Unit (1990-Present). **Associations & Accomplishments:** Technology Education Association of Pennsylvania; Attendance/Child Accounting Professional Association. **Education:** Marywood University, M.S. (1993); Wilkes College, B.S. in Elementary Education and Early Childhood Education (1987). **Personal Information:** Ms. Makar enjoys computers and mystery novels.

Angela D. Roberts

Marketing Administrator
AMBC-CCTC/ICTS
6660 Security Boulevard, Suite 13
Baltimore, MD 21207
(919) 384-9032
Fax: (410) 298-6641
aroberts@icts.com

8299

Business Information: As the Marketing Administrator within AMBC-CCTC/ICTS, Ms. Roberts is engaged in several aspects of the Company's operations. Focusing her extensive experience in the field, she provides the marketing services for AMBC-CCTC/ICTS, promoting the career development of professionals and students throughout the Baltimore, Maryland region. In addition to her promotional activity, Ms. Roberts also takes on a leading role in registering students, entering their vital information into the campus-wide database, taking course payments, setting up classroom arrangements, and maintaining the campus database. Looking to expand upon her current ability in the field, Ms. Roberts is currently attaining her Windows 2000 certification, and is seeking further advancement in her career. Providing career development to professionals from all industries, AMBC-CCTC/ICTS offers specific certification training, instruction on the development of resumes, and assistance in job placement. Dedicated to promoting success among professionals in today's dynamic careers, AMBC-CCTC/ICTS offers development and instruction in nearly every available field offered on the East Coast. **Career Highlights:** Marketing Administrator, AMBC-CCTC/ICTS (Present). **Associations & Accomplishments:** Who's Who Among High School Students.

Nancy A. Rudins

Systems Programmer
National Center for Supercomputing Applications
1011 West Springfield Avenue
Urbana, IL 61801-3072
(217) 244-6180
Fax: (217) 244-7396
nrudin@ncsa.vive.edu

8299

Business Information: As Systems Programmer of National Center for Supercomputing Applications, Ms. Rudins collects and analyzes systems performance metrics and prepares disaster recovery contingencies. She has assertively served with the Center since coming on board to the team as Computer Analyst in 1987. An expert, she provides software and systems support for high performance computers. In addition, Ms. Rudins maintains statistics and ensures their availability to other technology professionals as well as systems management. She has enjoyed substantial success in her career by having put together a disaster recovery plan from scratch for a center with 25 systems and having written a software package that automatically keeps track of both up and down times, availability, and reliability and markets it on her personal Web site. Ms. Rudins attributes her success to being in the right place at the right time. Her goal is to continue growing in her field and to become more involved in UNIX and Windows. National Center for Supercomputing Applications is an educational institution providing supercomputing facilities to researchers throughout the country. Established in 1985, the Center employs a staff of 300 individuals to help meet the diverse needs of its clientele. **Career Highlights:** National Center for Supercomputing Applications: Systems Programmer (1995-Present), Computer Analyst (1987-95). **Associations & Accomplishments:** Disaster Recovery Institute. **Education:** Parkland College, A.A.S. (1991). **Personal Information:** Ms. Rudins enjoys her work.

Paula Kaur Singh

Founder/President/Chief Executive Officer
The International Academy of Information Sciences, Systems and Technologies
160 West Portola Avenue
Los Altos, CA 94022-1251
(650) 941-8761

8299

Business Information: As Founder, President, and Chief Executive Officer of the International Academy of Information Sciences, Systems and Technologies, Paula Singh is in charge of all day-to-day activities. She also serves as Chairman of the Board of Directors. A respected professional in her field, she is a member of International WHO'S WHO of Professionals, International WHO'S WHO of Professional Management, International WHO'S WHO of Entrepreneurs, International WHO'S WHO of Information Technology, and International WHO'S WHO of Intellectuals. Ms. Singh is a leader with great vision, integrity, and a strong sense of social commitment. Her extraordinary contribution to molding international societies is recognized by several leading research institutions and important biographers. She is honored with numerous awards and is recognized as one of 2,000 Outstanding People of the 20th Century for her contribution to International Peace and Technological Advancement, one of 2,000 Outstanding Community Leaders of the 20th Century for her contribution to Education and Public Health, and one of 2,000 Outstanding Scientists of the 20th Century for her contribution to Medical and Information Sciences. Ms. Singh also holds the coveted International 20th Century Achievement Award with the distinct selectivity as one of Five Hundred Leaders of Influence. She has been inducted into the Millennium Hall of Fame in honor of her extraordinary leadership and contributions including positive and humane changes molding international societies, scientific insights and works giving current and future generations examples to follow, and enlightenment in regard to what has been and what can be through education. Established in 1994, the International Academy of Information Sciences, Systems and Technologies is an international educational institution for information sciences, systems, and technologies. The International Academy of Information Sciences, Systems, and Technologies strengthens the link between industry and education, promotes breakthroughs by facilitating the transfer of knowledge and technologies, and promotes business and public awareness of technologies and their impacts. **Career Highlights:** Founder/President/Chief Executive Officer, The International Academy of Information Sciences, Systems and Technologies (1994-Present); Director of Seminars and Information Services, Mind Matter Seminars, Stanford, California (1993); Founder, President, and Chief Executive Officer, Medical Information Management Research and Development (1984-Present). **Associations & Accomplishments:** International Association of Women in Technology; American Association for the Advancement of Science; Scientist/Mentor, Boston Museum of Science; Member, Smithsonian Institute; Founding Member, The Library of Congress; Association of Women in Science; American Public Health Association - Forum on Bioethics, Health Education, and Legislative Action Committee; National Association of Female Executives; American Association of University Women; International Federation of University Women; Citizen Ambassador, People to People International; World Affairs Council. **Education:** Oxford University, The Oxford Strategic Leadership Programme (1998); Stanford University, Stanford Leadership Academy (1998); Harvard University and Massachusetts Institute of Technology, Senior Executive Education Programs (1997); Stanford University, Executive Education Programs (1996); University of California - Davis, B.S. (1988); Numerous national and international forums,

congresses, symposiums, and conferences. **Personal Information:** Ms. Singh enjoys triathlons, white water river guiding, playing the saxophone, singing, photography and yacht racing.

Edward Tippins
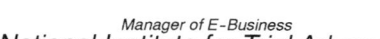

Senior Database Administrator
Sylvan Prometric
1429 R Street NW, Unit A
Washington, DC 20009
(410) 843-6217
Fax: (410) 843-8050
edward.tippins@educate.com

8299

Business Information: Mr. Tippins is the Senior Database Administrator for Sylvan Prometric. He is responsible for maintaining the computer systems functionality and fully operational status. Before joining Sylvan Prometric, he served as a Database Administrator at both Sprint and Office Comptroller of Currency. Remaining on the cutting edge of technology, Mr. Tippins educates himself on the current events and future expectations for the industry through reading field-related magazines and attending seminars. He updates the Company's database regularly to assure it is not overloaded with unnecessary information and operating at its peak capacity. Mr. Tippins is working to become a top level consultant in the Information Technology industry and data warehousing. His success reflects his ability to think outside the box, produce results, and aggressively take on new challenges. Sylvan Prometric provides educational services in a diverse realm of studies. Originally founded in 1994, today's students are able to study and be examined for certification tests and driver licensing. Primarily focused on serving the private industry, the Company's largest population of students arrive for Microsoft certification, Novell certification, and general education certification. Eight employees coordinate the schedules of courses and the specific instructors needed to accredit a particular program. The employees also oversee testing and exam days at the Company. **Career Highlights:** Senior Database Administrator, Sylvan Prometric (1999-Present); Senior Database Administrator, Sprint (1998-99); Senior Database Administrator, Office Comptroller of Currency (1994-98). **Associations & Accomplishments:** Data Warehousing Institute; Institute of Electrical and Electronics Engineers; National Association of System Programmers. **Education:** Northwestern University, Bachelor's degree (1976). **Personal Information:** Mr. Tippins enjoys playing chess and is recognized localy as a chess master.

Susan Toth
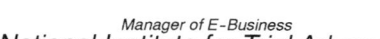

Manager of E-Business
National Institute for Trial Advocacy
1602 North Ironwood Drive
South Bend, IN 46635
(800) 225-6482
Fax: (219) 282-1263
suetoth@hotmail.com

8299

Business Information: Serving as Manager of E-Business for the National Institute for Trial Advocacy, Mrs. Toth is responsible for managing the strategic business units. Her responsibilities include electronic publishing, e-commerce, technical programs, parnerships, and distance learning programs. Mrs. Toth is an extremely determined individual, demonstrated by five years of active duty in the United States Navy and current duty with the United States Naval Reserves. She is a veteran of the Gulf War and the recent Kosovo conflict. In the future she plans to continue to train lawyers in using technology in the courtroom. Mrs. Toth's success reflects her ability to take on challenges and deliver results on behalf of the Institute and its clientele. Established in 1972, the National Institute for Trial Advocacy is the premier provider of continuing legal education courses. Providing trial skills to lawyers internationally, the Institute ensures that new techniques are presented to clients. Employing 50 personnel, the Institute reports estimated annual revenue of $8 million. **Career Highlights:** Manager of E-Business, National Institute for Trial Advocacy (1997-Present); Assistant General Cousel, NIBCO, Inc. (1994-97); Officer, United States Navy (1986-91). **Associations & Accomplishments:** Naval Reserve Association; New York Bar Association; Texas Distance Learning Association; Texas-Exes; Vice-Chair, St. Joseph County Republican Partry; Notre Dame Law School Alumni Association. **Education:** Notre Dame Law School, Juris Doctorate with Honors (1994); University of Texas at Austin, B.A. (1986). **Personal Information:** Married to

Christopher in 1990. One child: Kit. Mrs. Toth enjoys reading, cooking, running, swimming, cycling and playing with her son and pets.

Michael Louis Turchiaro
Information Technology Specialist
Atlantic Technical Center
4700 Coconut Creek Parkway
Coconut Creek, FL 33063-3999
(954) 977-2053
turchiaro@directnet1.net

8299

Business Information: As Information Technology Specialist of Atlantic Technical Center, Mr. Turchiaro performs technical support and network administration duties. With impressive technical abilities, he regularly evaluates needs throughout the Center, then formulates solutions that include purchasing, systems set up, and implementations of both hardware and software. He handles troubleshooting of internal systems with exceptional ease, utilizing a creative problem solving approach that consistently allows him to acheive positive results. Recognized for his accomplishments throughout the industry, he credits his persistance and dedication as the main factors of his success. Mr. Turchiaro currently has plans to further his involvment in community-related technical activities as he assists in the completion of the center's educational objectives. His advice is, "Get good technical training." Atlantic Technical Center is the second largest adult education facility in the state of Florida. Employing over 200 staff members, the Center provides technical training for fields such as electrical maintenance, plumbing, and nursing. The county school was established in 1970 in Coconut Creek, Florida. **Career Highlights:** Information Technology Specialist, Atlantic Technical Center (1990-Present); Associate Professor, College of Aeronautics (1987-89); Technology Teacher/Media Specialist/Trainer, New York City School Board (1977-86). **Education:** Lehman College, M.S. (1980); Fordham University, B.A. (1977). **Personal Information:** Married to Marie in 1981. Two children: Michael Jr. and Matthew. Mr. Turchiaro enjoys both playing and coaching basketball, is an avid reader, and loves working with computer and the internet and technology.

8300 Social Services

8322 Individual and family services
8331 Job training and related services
8351 Child day care services
8361 Residential care
8399 Social services, nec

Steven G. Ebrahimi
Architect
Ga Childcare Online
P.O. Box 77701
Atlanta, GA 30357
(404) 272-5220
gachildcare@gachildcare.com

8322

Business Information: Providing his skilled services as Architect of Ga Childcare Online, Mr. Ebrahimi is responsible for the design and development of the Company's Web site. He maintains the Web site and works with licensing bureaus to ensure the accuracy of the information posted. Working closely with users and management, he analyzes, specifies, and designs new, cutting Web technology and to harness more of the computer's power. His focus is to help the Company become firmly established and ensure information provided online is accurate and reliable. Crediting his success to perseverance and hands on experience, he also occupies a full time position with BellSouth as a Systems Analyst. Mr. Ebrahimi is committed to the success of Ga Childcare Online and coordinates strategic planning to ensure a bright future for further development and growth. Offering services to parents and teachers in Atlanta, Georgia and the surrounding communities, Ga Childcare Online was established in 1999. The Company provides Internet information and referral sources for childcare regionally. **Career Highlights:** Architect, Ga Childcare Online (1999-Present); Systems Analyst, BellSouth (Present). **Education:** Emory University, B.S. (1997); Georgia Institute of Technology. **Personal Information:** Mr. Ebrahimi enjoys white water rafting and hiking.

Juanita E. Hagemeier
Executive Director
Disabled Citizen Alliance for Independence
369 Crabtree Road
Steelville, MO 65565
(573) 244-3315
Fax: (523) 244-5609
dcitizen@misn.com

8322

Business Information: Displaying her expertise in this highly specialized position, Ms. Hagemeier serves as the Executive Director for the Disabled Citizen Alliance for Independence. She is responsible for the coordination of the planning and program expansion for the Company and writes grant proposals to obtain government and private funding. Working directly with the community to increase public awareness, she is a frequent public speaker and an advocate for personnel management. Ms. Hagemeier is dedicated to the Company and patients and looks forward to serving as a mentor to the local community on its behalf. Disabled Citizen Alliance for Independence is an independent living center dedicated to teaching disabled individuals the necessary living skills that will enable them to attain and maintain their independence. Founded in in 1980, the Center empowers its patients with the courage to get back on their feet to reenter the work force and accomplish their individual goals. **Career Highlights:** Disabled Citizen Alliance for Independence: Executive Director (1987-Present), Assistant Director/Independent Living Specialist (1985-87), Independent Living Specialist (1980-85). **Associations & Accomplishments:** Missouri Organization Centers for Independent Living; Association Programs of Rural Independent Living Center; National Council Independent Living; National Rehabilitation Association; Missouri Rehabilitation Association. **Personal Information:** Four children: Dora Grgurich, Delores, Shane, and Susan Markland. Ms. Hagemeier enjoys crafts, doll collecting, gardening, her family and grandchildren.

Susan K. Stone
Information Technology Operations Manager
Texas Department of Protective & Regulatory Services
826 Riveroak Drive
Austin, TX 78753
(512) 834-4471
Fax: (512) 719-6144
stonesk@tdprs.state.tx.us

8322

Business Information: Educated in the field of systems engineering, Ms. Stone serves as the Information Technology Operations Manager for the Texas Department of Protective & Regulatory Services. Responsible for supervising the technical staff in the field, she oversees the network's operations, administering upgrades, performing routine maintenance, and providing a backup system for emergencies. As a 10 year technology veteran with an established track record of producing results, her success reflects her leadership ability to build teams with synergy, technical strength, and a client focused attitude; and take on new challenges and responsibilities. Ms. Stone anticipates her promotion to Director as a result of her continuing efforts to increase her skills through training and professional development activities. Texas Department of Protective & Regulatory Services is a state agency assigned the responsibility of protecting abused children and aged and disabled adults and licensing child care facilities. Split from the Texas Department of Human Services in 1991, the Agency now employs 7,000 counseling, administrative, and support personnel who work diligently to ensure that each individual gets the quality care and protection he or she deserves. **Career Highlights:** Texas Department of Protective & Regulatory Services: Information Technology Operations Manager (1997-Present), Regional Manager of Information Technology (1994-97), System Analyst IV (1989-94). **Associations & Accomplishments:** Volunteer, Lone Star Hospice; Crestview Baptist Church. **Education:** Lamar University, Bachelor of Medical Technology (1994); Tarrant County Junior College; Microsoft Certified Training; Novell Certified Training. **Personal Information:** Two children: Jennifer Hayes and Jeremy Merren. Ms. Stone enjoys swimming, camping and volunteer work.

Salena Wilson
Database Developer
SASI
2101 South Indiana
Chicago, IL 60616
(312) 808-3210
Fax: (312) 824-9550

8322

Business Information: Possessing unique talents in the technology field, Ms. Wilson joined SASI in 1999 as Database Developer. Displaying her skills in this highly specialized position, she is charged with the tremendous task of converting, distributing, and maintaining the Agency's database from Access to SQL. Ms. Wilson enjoys the challenges her position presents, and utilizing considerable experience, she downloads, maintains, and upgrades the database and provides technical support. Committed to further development and always alert to new opportunities, techniques, and approaches, Ms. Wilson's future plans include obtaining her Master's degree, enabling her to capitalize on the promotional opportunities provided by the Agency. SASI, established in 1976, is an agency dedicated to helping individuals with addictions caused by the misuse of alcohol, narcotics, and other drugs. Located in Chicago, Illinois, the Agency employs 80 highly qualified people devoted to helping addicts live a clean and productive life. **Career Highlights:** Database Developer, SASI (1999-Present). **Education:** Chicago State University, B.S. (1998). **Personal Information:** One child: Derrick Giovanni. Ms. Wilson enjoys writing poetry and painting.

Ethel G. Harris
Instructor
OICW/Sequoia Adult School
1200 O'Brien Drive
Menlo Park, CA 94025
(650) 322-8431
Fax: (650) 324-3419
(650) 462-6331
harris@oicw.org

8331

Business Information: Ms. Harris has faithfully served with OICW/Sequoia Adult School in a variety of positions since joining the Agency as a Receptionist in 1977. In 1983, she was promoted to her current position of Instructor. Her duties include training and instructing students in the realm of computer technology and teaching student's skills, such as keyboarding and composing business letters. Possessing an excellent understanding of her field, Ms. Harris also teaches students how to take memos, use a 10 key calculator, follow simple DOS commands on the computer, and deciphering medical terminology. In the future, Ms. Harris looks forward to continuing with the Agency in her current position, being a financial success, and starting up her own business with a goal of helping people. Located in Menlo Park, California, OICW/Sequoia Adult School is a job-training agency. Founded in 1962, the Agency provides training courses for individuals who are seeking enhancement of their job skills to better themselves within the career desired. Moreover, the Agency offers job placement for unemployed individuals who are looking for jobs whether in specific fields or in general. With a staff of over 100 employees, the Agency is a non-profit organization. **Career Highlights:** OICW/Sequoia Adult School: Instructor (1983-Present), Counseling Clerk (1980-83), Receptionist (1977-80). **Associations & Accomplishments:** Past Member, National Association for the Advancement of Colored People. **Education:** University of Phoenix, B.A. in Business Management (1995); DeAnza College; San Jose State; College of San Mateo; Utica Junior College; University of California at Santa Cruz. **Personal Information:** Three children: Pamela, Anthony, and Ashley. Ms. Harris enjoys walking, reading, movies, parks and theater.

Fernando A.Callo
Technical Operations Manager
Sunrise Assisted Living
9401 Lee Highway, Suite 300
Fairfax, VA 22031-1824
(703) 352-6648

8361

Business Information: Mr. Callo serves in the role of Technical Operations Manager at Sunrise Assisted Living, a position that entails the completion of a multitude of specialized tasks. Demonstrating adept technical ability, he maintains high-end computers and oversees the administration of the databases and systems. Recognized for communicative skills that allow him to explain complex technical concepts in easily comprehendible terms, Mr. Callo is credited with the development of successful training programs. A savvy, 10 year expert in the field, he currently has plans to continue in his role, implementing continual changes of the information technology industry. Recognizing the needs of independent senior adults, Sunrise Assisted Living strives to maintain an atmosphere of unregimented and self-reliant living conditions. A highly trained staff is employed to assist the residents who live in various areas of the facility, including the retirement apartments. **Career Highlights:** Technical Operations Manager, Sunrise Assisted Living (1997-Present); Senior Consultant, Manugistics (1994-97); Senior Project Manager, Cedar Cliff Systems (1992-94); Senior Consultant, ASI (1990-92). **Education:** George Washington University, M.S. (1996). **Personal Information:** Mr. Callo enjoys tennis, soccer and camping.

Teri Czarnik
Information Systems Manager
Friendship Village
350 West Shaumburg Road
Schaumburg, IL 60194
(847) 884-5407
Fax: (847) 884-5828
tczarnik@friendshipvillage.net

8361

Business Information: Demonstrating her considerable expertise in the field of information technology, Mrs. Czarnik serves as the Information Systems Manager for Friendship Village. In charge of the LAN network and computer systems, she also presides over the administration of the security systems within the Center, the telecommunications equipment and system, and photocopiers. Additionally, she assumes responsibility for the in-house training facility, training the internal staff on the Center's computer systems. Citing family support as the basis of her success, she advises newcomers to the field to get a lot of experience quickly to ensure their future success. Mrs. Czarnik is dedicated to the further development of the Center, and looks forward to becoming the Information Systems Director for multiple locations. Her success reflects her ability to deliver results and take on new challenges. Established in 1977, Friendship Village is a continuing care retirement community serving the local area of Schaumburg, Illinois and the surrounding communities. Currently, approximately 900 residents live and receive medical care at the facility. The only community care and retirement community under one roof in the state, the Center employs the dedicated services of over 400 personnel members including three doctors and a nursing staff. **Career Highlights:** Information Systems Manager, Friendship Village (1999-Present); Systems Analyst, Zurich Kemper; Supervisor/Information Technology, G.E. Capitol; Systems Administrator, OCE-USA. **Education:** Roosevelt College. **Personal Information:** Married to Gary in 1995. One child: Anthony.

Scott F. Fenwick
Director of Performance Improvement and Utilization Review
Edgemeade
13400 Edgemeade Road
Upper Marlboro, MD 20772-8088
(301) 888-1330
Fax: (301) 579-2342
late40s@aol.com

8361

Business Information: As Director of Performance Improvement and Utilization Review, Mr. Fenwick is responsible for improving organizational performance by continuously improving the outcomes of care and services provided to agency clients and for updating standards in control of budget, manpower and utilization review. Mr. Fenwick supervises the information systems manager, clinical records, data base, and computer systems specialist functions. He attributes his success to the support of his wife and children. Edgemeade is a residential treatment center for severely emotionally disturbed adolescents. A private, non-profit organization, Edgemeade operates three Residential Treatment Programs, three Therapeutic Group Homes, and three Outpatient Community Mental Health Centers. **Career Highlights:** Director of Performance Improvement and Utilization Review, Edgemeade (1990-Present); NCOIC - Quality Assurance and Medical Inspections, United States Air Force (1986-90); Team Executive Officer, United States Medical Inspector General's Staff - United States Air Force (1984-86). **Associations & Accomplishments:** National Association of Quality Assurance Professionals; Vice President of the Board of Directors, Charles County Mental Health Authority - Charles County, Maryland; Charles County Foster Care Review Board; Volunteer in Mall Annex, Charles County Sheriff's Department; Recipient of numerous Air Force and Air National Guard awards and decorations, including two meritorious service medals and the New Jersey Medal of Honor. **Education:** LaSalle University, M.S. (1995). **Personal Information:** Mr. Fenwick enjoys computers, reading, family activities, sports and cooking.

Robin C. Metzler
Senior Systems Analyst
KidsPeace
3438 Route 309
Orefield, PA 18069
(610) 799-8585
Fax: (610) 391-8280
rmetzler@kidspeace.org

8361

Business Information: Mr. Metzler serves as Senior Systems Analyst of KidsPeace. He is responsible for working with users and management to analyze, design, and develop new business applications. Before joining KidsPeace as Senior Systems Administrator in 1995, Mr. Metzler served as Systems Analyst and Programmer with Weiler Brush

Company, Inc. Mr. Metzler is also an adjunct faculty member for the Center for Business and Industry at Northampton Community College in Bethlehem, Pennsylvania. As an instructor, he teaches Introduction to UNIX and UNIX Systems Administration classes part-time to other IT professionals. Combining his extensive technical expertise and academic ties, he is involved with program installation, user support, and program development. Providing technical and analytical assistance to programmers to harness more of the computer's power, and overseeing deployment and integration of new technologies within KidsPeace are an integral part of Mr. Metzler's responsibilities. He credits his career success to his perseverance. His success as a technology professional reflects his ability to think out-of-the-box and take on new challenges and responsibilities. Eventually attaining the position Information Technology Manager serves as one of his future goals. KidsPeace provides a full range of healthcare services to children in crisis and foster care homes. Both outpatient and inpatient medical care are provided. Established in 1886, KidsPeace is national in scope and operates a healthcare network of nine locations. Presently, KidsPeace employs a staff of more than 1,900 people who regularly serve more than 2,000 children with a comprehensive continuum of kids' mental health treatment programs. **Career Highlights:** Senior Systems Analyst, KidsPeace (1996-Present); Senior Systems Administrator (1995-96); System Analyst/Programmer, Weiler Brush Company, Inc. (1990-95). **Associations & Accomplishments:** Metro Regional Lawson Users Group; Morning Star Rotary Club; Advisory Board, Bethlehem Salvation Army. **Education:** Marshall University, M.S. in Physical Education; Georgetown College, B.S. in Physical Education; ICSI, Data Processing Diploma (1990). **Personal Information:** Three children: Todd, Allyson, and Meredith. Mr. Metzler enjoys walking and tennis.

William D. Bailey

Management Information Systems Manager
Catholic Charities
2625 Zanker Road, Suite 200
San Jose, CA 95134
(408) 325-5142
Fax: (408) 744-0275
wbailey@ccsj.org

8399

Business Information: Serving as Management Information Systems Manager of Catholic Charities, Mr. Bailey is responsible for management and oversight of the systems infrastructure. Throughout daily activities, he is held accountable for multiple personal computer support, while implementing policies and procedures for software maintenance, purchasing, engineering, and technical administration. The most rewarding aspect of his career is participating in the installation of a virtual private network. With over six years of hands on and technical experience, Mr. Bailey utilizes his superior talents in order to devise plans for pursuing network technology and identifying ways to streamline the systems functions. The Catholic Charities of San Jose, California is a non-profit organization that engages in helping needy citizens. Providing various services for helping people, the Organization offers advocates for youth, adult, and senior citizens, while also provides programs for behavioral health, foster care, immigration and refugee, property management, and community education and awareness. Established in 1955, Catholic Charities functions under the direction of more than 200 professionals and volunteers. **Career Highlights:** Management Information Systems Manager, Catholic Charities (1998-Present); Network Administrator, Valley Credit Union (1996-98); Computer Instructor, Sunnyvale School District (1994-96); Tennis Professional, Almaden Swim & Racquet Club (1990-96). **Associations & Accomplishments:** Advisory Board, Computer Technological Care. **Education:** sollege, A.A. (1989); San Diego State; San Jose State; Microsoft Certified Professional: NT Server 4.0, Networking. **Personal Information:** Married to Maribel in 2000. Mr. Bailey enjoys tennis and information technology.

Thomas P. Farney

Manager of CSC
Illinois Primary Health Care
3430 Constitution Drive, Suite 118
Springfield, IL 62707-9402
(217) 547-6070
Fax: (217) 547-6071
tfarney@earthlink.net

8399

Business Information: As Manager of CSC of Illinois Primary Health Care, Mr. Farney manages the computer solutions center (repair facility) that provides technical support for a statewide dial on demand computer network. He also manages 26 people, handles all technical warehouse data, installs networks, provides maintanence, and upgrades records. Years of education and experience in the field has enabled Mr. Farney to acquire the skills necessary to effectively complete his job duties. He plans to obtain a higher postion, gaining greater authority and responsibility as well as becoming a people manager. Mr. Farney attributes his professional success to being blessed by God with the ability to identify and resolve problems. Illinois Primary Health Care is a nonprofit organization that provides educational and communication services to member clinics which in turn offer medical services to patients with no means to pay for medical services. Established in 1982, approximately 1,000 people provide assistance in various areas of the business. Headquartered in Springfield, Ilinois, there are presently 115 clinics. **Career Highlights:** Manager of CSC, Illinois Primary Health Care (1999-Present); Network Analyst, CTG Inc. (1999); Network Consultant, Manpower Technical (1997-98); ATC Coordinator, Illinois State University (1994-97). **Associations & Accomplishments:** Golden Key National Honor Society; National Rifle Association; Volunteer, Illinois Special Olympics. **Education:** Illinois State University, B.S. in Mathematics (1998); Lincoln Land Community College, A.S. **Personal Information:** Mr. Farney enjoys weight lifting and walking.

Keith R. Hamm

Management Information Systems Director
Catholic Charities of Buffalo
525 Washington Street
Buffalo, NY 14203
(716) 856-4494
Fax: (716) 856-2005
keith1@pcom.net

8399

Business Information: Possessing more than 20 years of extensive experience in the technology field, Mr. Hamm was recruited to the Catholic Charities of Buffalo in 1998. At the present time, he serves as the Management Information Systems Director. He is accountable for the administration, maintenance, and design of all of the Organization's computer systems. Before joining Catholic Charities of Buffalo, Mr. Hamm served as Systems Engineer with Frontier Network Systems. His broad background history also includes stints as Systems Engineer for RG Data Inc. and Senior Systems Technician at Intelogic Trace Inc. In his current capacity, he configures workstations for each of the Organization's 120 users as well as the Internet access. Coordinating resources, time lines, schedules, and assignments; calculating and managing the fiscal year budget; and fine tuning system software tools to improve systems performance also fall within the purview of his functions. Continually striving to improve performance, Mr. Hamm is dedicated to providing continued optimum service. Catholic Charities of Buffalo is a nonprofit organization dedicated to helping those in need of consoling, education, drug abuse, resettlement, adoptions, and many other services. Approximately 400 dedicated individuals work to provide these services at little or no charge. **Career Highlights:** Management Information Systems Director, Catholic Charities of Buffalo (1998-Present); Systems Engineer, Frontier Network Systems (1997-98); Systems Engineer, RG Data Inc. (1994-97); Senior Systems Technician, Intelogic Trace Inc. (1987-94). **Education:** Buffalo State College, B.S. (1977). **Personal Information:** Mr. Hamm enjoys car restoration.

Jonathan Schneider

PC Network Technician
SCL Health Services
1602 5th Avenue, Apartment #A
Leavenworth, KS 66048
(913) 682-1338
Fax: (580) 481-1241
antolycus@operamail.com

8399

Business Information: Serving as a PC Network Technician for SCL Health Services, Mr. Schneider fulfills a number of duties on behalf of the Company and its clientele. He is responsible for maintaining the functionality and operational status of the Company's WAN/LAN and Internet related network environment. Possessing an excellent understanding of technology, Mr. Schneider provides technical support to other locations and purchases new software for the Company's use. He also reviews new software, deciding which would be the most effective, efficient, and economical for Company. In the future, Mr. Schneider plans to further his education to facilitate greater promotional opportunities in the information technology field. Headquartered in Leavenworth, Kansas, SCL Health Services operates as a health system. Owning multiple hospitals, the Company owns a reputation for excellence. Rapidly expanding operations, the Company is presently manned by more than 35 professional, technical, and administrative support staff. **Career Highlights:** PC Network Technician, SCL Health Services (1999-Present); Technician, Andy Graham Computers (1997-99); Candy Striper, St. John's Hospital (1994-98) **Associations & Accomplishments:** LHS Alumni. **Education:** Lansing High School, Diploma (1994). **Personal Information:** Mr. Schneider enjoys surfing the internet, especially Ebay, reading, research, the stock market and accounting.

Eric H. Scott

Information Services Director
D/FW Hospital Council
250 Decker Court
Irving, TX 75062-2706
(972) 719-4900
Fax: (972) 719-4009
escott1@compuserve.com

8399

Business Information: As Information Services Director of D/FW Hospital Council, Mr. Scott presides over the Organization's communications, including telephones, the local area network, hardware, software, and the Internet. He performs installations, upgrades, troubleshooting, and hardware repairs, as well as web page development, vendor relations, and equipment purchasing. As the organization continues to thrive, Mr. Scott is hoping to hire additional staff members in his department. D/FW Hospital Council was founded in 1968 as a nonprofit organization dedicated to providing administrative support to area hospitals. The Organization presently employs 60 people who perform human resources functions and coordinate meetings. **Career Highlights:** Information Services Director, D/FW Hospital Council (1995-Present); Network Manager, Metrica, Inc. (1994-Present); Field Service Engineer, Compucel Service Corporation (1992-94); Repair Center Supervisor, Microdyne Corporation (1990-92). **Associations & Accomplishments:** Received letters of appreciation from the United States Air Force. **Personal Information:** Mr. Scott enjoys watching movies, coaching little league and attending basebase games.

James White

Computer Specialist
YAI
460 West 34th Street
New York, NY 10001-2382
(212) 273-6511
Fax: (212) 695-5838
TDD: (212) 290-2787
jwhite@yai.org

8399

Business Information: As Computer Specialist for the YAI or Young Adult Institute, Mr. White is responsible for technical support and services, as well as overseeing all aspects of communications, networks, and infrastructure hardware. He manages the LAN systems and is involved in the implementation of new programs to the system. An expert, he advises the help desk team on proper procedures to follow when repairing hardware or advising clients over the telephone about the condition of their systems. Mr. White's success comes from his enduring persistence and continuous goal setting, and his ability to deliver results and aggressively tackle new challenges. Believing firmly in "seizing the day," Mr. White has been in the right place at the right time on several occasions. He aspires to eventually attain the position of Chief Information Officer. YAI is a health organization providing education and residential services to people with disabilities. Established in 1957, the Institute has dedicated itself to the promotion of independence within the society of disabled persons. The Institute employs over 5,000 personnel to meet with clients and determine their personalized needs. A non-profit organization, the Institute has office locations across the country, all reporting to its headquarters in New York. **Career Highlights:** Computer Specialist, YAI (1996-Present); Sales Engineer, NCS, Inc. (1996); Environmental Engineer, EPA (1993-96); Electronics Helper, Ponce Marine Farm (1991-93). **Associations & Accomplishments:** Institute of Electronics and Electrical Engineers; Association of Computing Machinery; Boy Scouts of America. **Personal Information:** Mr.White enjoys music, computers running, biking, and Shakespeare.

8600 Membership Organizations

8611 Business associations
8621 Professional organizations
8631 Labor organizations
8641 Civic and social associations
8651 Political organizations
8661 Religious organizations
8699 Membership organizations, nec

Jon B. Lorange

Manager of Computer Department
The Farmers Association of Iceland
Baendahollin v/Hagatorg
Reykjavik, Iceland IS-107
+35 45630300
Fax: +35 45625177
jbl@bi.bondi.is

8611

Business Information: Recruited to The Farmers Association of Iceland in 1991, Mr. Lorange serves as the Manager of Computer Department for the Association. He is responsible for maintaining the functionality and operational status of the Association's systems infrastructure. A successful, nine-year veteran of technology, Mr. Lorange is striving to build up the Association's 110-year reputation through the implementation of operable computer technology. In addition, he works closely with his staff to keep all advisories and online databases current and connected to international business partners. Keeping on top of the latest in technology and maintaining the internal computers online serve as Mr. Lorange's future endeavors. His career success is attributed to his ability to aggressively tackle challenges and deliver positive results. The Farmers Association of Iceland was developed to help farmers keep up-to-date with the latest statistics in the agricultural industry. The Association also acts as an advisor to farmers in all agricultural aspects. **Career Highlights:** Manager of Computer Department, The Farmers Association of Iceland (1991-Present); Manager, The Social Democratic Party (1986-87). **Associations & Accomplishments:** The Farmers Association of Iceland. **Education:** RSP Computer Science, Systems Analyst (1991). **Personal Information:** Married to Steinunn Georgsdottir in 1989. Three children: Asta, Hjordis, and Jon Jr. Mr. Lorange enjoys chess.

Daniel J. Autry

Knowledge Management Technical Support Coordinator
American Institute of Certified Public Accountants
Harborside Financial Center 201 Plaza 3
Jersey City, NJ 07311
(201) 938-3247
Fax: (201) 938-3546
dautry@aicpa.org

8621

Business Information: As Knowledge Management Technical Support Coordinator for the American Institute of Certified Public Accountants, Mr. Autry manages and handles the technical aspects of knowledge management projects. He performs the evaluation and implementation of each of the systems to assure maximum performance. Coordinating resources and schedules, overseeing time lines and assignments, and managing project budgets also fall within the realm of his responsibilities. Before joining the Institute, Mr. Autry served as Network Engineer with SDS Computers. The American Institute of Certified Public Accountants is a non profit organization for aspiring certified public accountants. Established in 1887, the Institute designs courses and tests to become certified as a public accountant with three facilities located throughout the United States. The Institute has various committees established to perform examples of the best practices, and instructs the proper adherence to certified public accounting guidelines and rules. Headquartered in Jersey City, New Jersey, the Institute employs over 600 employees. **Career Highlights:** Knowledge Management Technical Support Coordinator, American Institute of Certified Public Accountants (1999-Present); PC Systems Specialist, American Institute of Certified Public Accountants (1996-99); Network Engineer, SDS Computers (1992-96). **Associations & Accomplishments:** Boy Scouts National Organization; Eagle Scouts National Organization. **Education:** Kean University, B.A. in Political Sciences (1993). **Personal Information:** Mr. Autry enjoys motorcycling, cycling and computers.

Robin L. Bader

Assistant Network Administrator
ARDC
130 East Randolph, Suite 1100
Chicago, IL 60601
(312) 540-5206
bird143 @aol.com

8621

Business Information: As the Assistant Network Administrator of ARDC or Attorney Registration and Disciplinary Commission, Miss Bader is concerned with the completion of daily technical activities. Utilizing her knowledge and expertise of technology, she effectively maintains over 100 workstations, handling troubleshooting and upgrades as needed. By lending her insight at technical departmental meetings, Miss Bader is directly involved in the development of technology procedures and guidelines. Recognized throughout the technology field as a motivated team player, Miss Bader intends to continue in her current role as she familiarizes herself with Internet functions and cutting-edge wireless technology. Attributing her success to being in the right place at the right time, her quote is "you have to work toward your goal and stay current." ARDC registers attorneys and lawyers within the state of Illinois. Acting as a regulatory committee, the Commission investigates complaints and generates data to support evidence of findings. If needed, the questionable parties are disciplined as deemed wholly necessary by the Commission. **Career Highlights:** Assistant Network Administrator, ARDC (1999-Present); Systems Analyst, Carvill America (1987-99). **Associations & Accomplishments:** Treasurer of Library District. **Education:** Governers State University, B.A. (1992); Morainne Valley Community College, A+ Class; Prairie State College, A.A.S. in Programming; Suburban Heights College, Visual Basic and other Miscellaneous Classes.

Phillip L. Duncan, Jr.

Online Communications Manager
American Society for Quality
611 East Wisconsin Avenue
Milwaukee, WI 53202
(800) 248-1946
Fax: (414) 272-1734
pduncan@asq.org

8621

Business Information: Mr. Duncan is the Online Communications Manager for the American Society for Quality. Responsible for the team of site administrators, he manages the work flow of his department, guiding upcoming technologies into the operations of the Society. His most recent project involves the revamping of sites by creating and building a Web site that features an on-line registration for Sector Specific Spin-off of ISO-9000. In the future, Mr. Duncan is working towards establishing himself in the publications end of the Society and he would like to conduct more research projects. He attributes his success to collaborative skills. American Society for Quality is a professional society that supports an extensive network of quality business clients desiring the opportunity to better educate its staff. Established in 1946, the Society offers certification and training courses for business professionals looking to accentuate their talents within specific areas of their career. The Society features 135,000 international members that stay linked to the new programs and ideas through several periodicals published by the Society and its Web site. **Career Highlights:** Online Communications Manager, American Society for Quality (Present). **Associations & Accomplishments:** Sacred Military Order of the Temple of Jerusalem. **Education:** University of Wisconsin at Milwaukee, M.F.A. (1997); University of Tennessee, B.F.A. (1993). **Personal Information:** Married to George Anne Boyle in 1995. Mr. Duncan enjoys playing classical guitar and British/Antique motorcycles.

Michael J. Gilbert

Technology Director
Massachusetts Association of School Committees
1 McKinley Square
Boston, MA 02109
(617) 523-8454
mgilbert@masc.mee.edu

8621

Business Information: Utilizing more than 20 years of experience in the technology field, Mr. Gilbert serves as the Technology Director for the Massachusetts Association of School Committees. He offers his technical expertise to the school districts, providing each one with voice and data technological education and training. In this manner, he assists the districts form their technology goals and direction, enabling them to provide quality equipment and training programs for students. Mr. Gilbert strives to incorporate the latest technology in the education process and is committed to providing continued optimum service. His success reflects his leadership ability to build teams with synergy and technical strength, as well as deliver results and aggressively tackle new challenges. The Massachusetts Association of School Committees was established in 1947 and is a membership based, educational organization for school districts within the state of Massachusetts. A staff of 12 personnel members run the Association and are dedicated to providing quality educational opportunities for students in grades kindergarten through 12th. **Career Highlights:** Technology Director, Massachusetts Association of School Committees (1996-Present); Project Manager, Flexxparts LP (1993-96); Various Positions, Digital Equipment (1977-93). **Associations & Accomplishments:** Massachusetts Local Government Advisory Council; Massachusetts School Pensowell Advisory Council; Massachusetts Education Technology Advisory Council; Advisor, NSBA/ITTE. **Education:** Bryant College. **Personal Information:** Married to Pamela in 1974. Three children: Scott, Ruth, and Meghan.

Baoping Guo, Ph.D.

Senior Program Analyst
American Chemical Society
1155 Sixteenth Street NW
Washington, DC 20036
(202) 872-6309
Fax: (202) 776-8289
b_guo@acs.org

8621

Business Information: As the Senior Perogram Analyst for the American Chemical Society, Dr. Guo provides leadership and organization to the information technology department. Possessing an excellent understanding of his field, he is responsible for developing and maintaining the Oracle database for the processing of new and existing memberships and subscriptions to the Society's publication. With more than two years of on the job experience, Dr. Guo utilizes other resources of knowledge, such as education and expertise, to apply excellence to his support of the Society's systems infrastructure. Looking to the future, his aspirations include becoming an authority in his profession. Dr. Guo's success reflects his ability to think outside the box, aggressively take on challenges, and deliver results on behalf of the Society and and its members. The American Chemical Society is a non-profit organization that engages in providing accommodations for professional chemists. The Society allows members to congregate and discuss current topics, while demonstrating new discoveries and hypothesis. Established in 1876, the Society currently has more than 200,000 members who attend on a regular basis, utilizing it as a learning tool to be applied to daily activities on the job. The Society maintains operational status through over 550 professionals including coordinators, senior chemists, and administrators. **Career Highlights:** Senior Program Analyst, American Chemical Society (1998-Present); Professor, College of West Virginia (1995-98). **Associations & Accomplishments:** International Oracle User Group. **Education:** Xian Jiautong University, Ph.D.; Nanjing University, Master's degree; Taiyuan Engineering Institute, Bachelor's degree. **Personal Information:** Married to Ying Wu One child: Alyssa Yao. Dr. Guo enjoys travel, swimming, reading and sports.

Evelyn N. Heitman

Assistant Director
CCNE
1 Dupont Circle NW, Suite 530
Washington, DC 20036
(202) 887-6791
Fax: (202) 887-8476
eheitman@aacn.riche.edu

8621

Business Information: Displaying her skills in this highly specialized position, Ms. Heitman functions in the role of Assistant Director for CCNE. Beginning her stay with the Association in 1998, she assists in providing direction, leadership, and day-to-day management to operational activities. She presides over writing, editing, and Webmaster projects. Ms. Heitman also handles billings, directs the nominating committee for the board of directors, and supervises employees. Effectively developing objectives, Ms. Heitman wants to increase her computer skills and learn more about the World Wide Web. She credits her success to desire, flexibility, understanding, drive, and educational ties, as well as her ability to think outside the box, deliver results, and aggressively take on new challenges. CCNE is a non-profit association located in Washington, DC. Founded in 1997, the Association provides accreditation to colleges and universities that offers a nursing degree program of study. CCNE performs comprehensive evaluations on the schools and ensures compliance of each school with all organizational policies and goals before accreditation is met. Local operations employ the skilled services of five individuals to supervise evaluations, facilitate scheduling, manage the database, and answer client queries. **Career Highlights:** Assistant Director, CCNE (1997-Present); President, Pocket Full of Posies (1994-99); Marketing Analyst, The Washington Post (1989-93); Account Executive, Govatos, Dunn & Boroz (1988-89). **Education:** George Mason University, M.B.A. (1989); Stanford University, B.A. **Personal Information:** Married to Thomas Haile in 1984. One child: Evan Thomas. Ms. Heitman enjoys travel, weight lifting, cooking, reading and the outdoors.

Otis Lee Jones

Senior Oracle Database Administrator
National Nephrology Association
511 Union Street, Suite 1800
Nashville, TN 37219
(615) 777-8221
Fax: (615) 259-0693

8621

Business Information: As the Senior Oracle Database Administrator of the National Nephrology Associates, Mr. Jones administers and controls all data resources. In his position, he designs and developments cutting-edge database applications and information systems to position National Nephrology Associates as a leader in the Renal Disease Management arena. Keeping pase with electronic commerce, Mr. Jones designs databases level code and constructs for electronic clains and purchase orders submission and processing. Established in 1998, the National Nephrology Associates is located in Nashville, Tennessee. Currently, National Nephrology Associates own and manage over 90 renal clinics. Mr. Jones' previous career highlights include designing and implementing information systems for NASA and Mission Critical Software Systems for the Department of Defense. A savvy, 16-year veteran of the field, he attributes his success to attention to detail and continuing education. Future plans for Mr. Jones include staying on the cutting edge of information system technology and continuing his education and training. **Career Highlights:** Senior Oracle Database Administrator, National Nephrology Association (1999-Present); Senior Oracle Developer, Envoy Corporation (1997-99); Computer Scientist, Computer Science Corporation (1995-97). **Education:** Alabama A&M, M.S. in Industrial Engineering (1990); University of Mississippi School of Engineering, B.S. in Computer Science. **Personal Information:** Mr. Jones enjoys golf, racquetball and outdoor activities.

Allan V. Kotmel, Ph.D., CDP

Manager of Information Services
New York State Teachers Retirement System
10 Corporate Woods Drive
Albany, NY 12211-2395
(518) 447-2932
Fax: (518) 447-2764
akotmel@nystrs.state.ny.us

8621

Business Information: Beginning his association with the New York State Teachers' Retirement System over 27 years ago, Dr. Kotmel is now the Manager of Information Services. In this capacity, he is responsible for a staff of 65 covering three departments. Accordingly, he monitors business applications, provides technical services for the database system, and oversees all employee relations. Accomplishing much within his field, Dr. Kotmel is responsible for the conversion of GRS to a client server based system. Looking into the future, he intends to become involved with e-commerce and Web processing within the district which will enable him to provide field services to clients, therefore expanding into video conferencing. Dr. Kotmel attributes his success to his integrity and self-confidence. Based in Albany, New York, New York State Teachers' Retirement System is a member of the Public Teachers' Retirement Association. The Association collects funds and invests money for the readiment of the retirement for teachers. In 1976, legislation was passed whiich requires all members to contribute three percent to the retirement fund. Established in 1921, the Association employs a staff of 330 people. **Career Highlights:** New York State Teachers' Retirement System: Manager of Information Services (1995-Present), Manager of Systems and Programs (1983-95), Supervisor of EDP (1977-83), Programmer (1972-77). **Associations & Accomplishments:** Association of Information Technology Professionals; Public Retirement of Information Systems Management; New York State Forum for Information Resource Management; Guilderland Board of Education. **Education:** Southern University of New York-Albany, Ph.D. (1973); Dartmouth College, M.A. (1966); Harturich College, B.A. (1964). **Personal Information:** Married to Marjorie in 1969. Two children: Allan V. Jr. and David W. Dr. Kotmel enjoys baseball, math games and crossword puzzles.

Jeffrey Lynn Plunkett

Information Service Operator
ARDC
221 West 1st Street
Duluth, MN 55802
(218) 722-5545
Fax: (218) 529-7592
jplunkett@mall-ardc.com

8621

Business Information: Mr. Plunkett functions in the role of Information Service Operator of ARDC. He provides computer and network technical support to all employees and monitors the productivity and efficiency of 145 computer servers. A savvy, five year veteran of the information technology field, Mr. Plunkett is responsible for training his staff and instructing the remaining employees on proper computer usage and safety precautions they can use throughout the year to secure the documents and information they work with. Looking to the 21st Century, Mr. Plunkett hopes to remain with the Firm and would like to graduate from his position to acquire his own business. His success is attributed to his expertise and people skills. ARDC was established by the United States Government to develop rural communities in several areas of basic needs. The Firm enhances the transportation capabilities within the communities while increasing the recycling and reorganization of the areas natural resources. The human resources division of ARDC examines the effective use of every business' staff and encourages the use of children and the elderly within applicable positions. **Career Highlights:** Information Service Operator, ARDC (1998-Present); Manager, Funco Land (1998); Technician, Computer Renaissance (1995-98). **Education:** W.I.T.C. (1996). **Personal Information:** Mr. Plunkett enjoys golf, travel and computer games.

Timothy Reed

Systems Engineering Coordinator
American Urological Association
2425 West Loop, Suite 333
Houston, TX 77027
(713) 622-2700
treed@houston.avanet.org

8621

Business Information: Providing the American Urological Association with maintenance and operational support of their computer network systems, Mr. Reed serves in the position Systems Engineering Coordinator. Demonstrating a strong understanding of technology, he is responsible for all day to day systems operations and ensuring the functionality of the entire infrastructure. Highly regarded and certified in all Microsoft programs, Mr. Reed dedicates his education and skills in the field to maintain all servers throughout the Association as well as the purchase of cutting edge hardware and software upgrades available through further advancements in modern technology. Attributing his past career successes and future performance to his determination to succeed, Mr. Reed ensures the continuing efforts of the American Urological Association to become the most advanced medical association in the world. Providing continued education to urologists and medical students from across the country, the American Urological Association is a non-profit organization. Offering the support of a nationwide network to professional doctors and specialists, the Association facilitates future advancements in the field. In addition to their networking ability, educational material and testing authorities are available including videos, study sheets, home study material, and exam creation. One of the most extensive and diverse medical associations in the world, the American Urological Association is experiencing great member growth and geographic expansion. **Career Highlights:** Systems Engineering Coordinator, American Urological Association (1998-Present); Assistant Systems Administrator, J.E. Stone & Associates (1997-98); LAN Support Specialist, Health Administration Services (1995-97); Computer Lab Specialist, Prairie View A&M (1990-94). **Education:** TPrairie View A&M University, degree in Technology (1994); Microsoft Certified Professional. **Personal Information:** Married to Reyna in 1994. Two children: Alisa N. and Timothy L. Mr. Reed enjoys reading and computers.

Regina V. Barton

Instructional Technology Coordinator
United Federation of Teachers, Teacher Centers Professional Development Program
48 East 21st Street, 10th Floor
New York, NY 10010
(212) 475-3737
Fax: (212) 475-9049
rbarton@ufttc.org

8631

Business Information: As Instructional Technology Coordinator of the United Federation of Teachers, Teacher Centers Professional Development Program, Ms. Barton assists educators in integrating technology, the New York City Performance Standards and curriculum. Before joining the Teacher Center, Ms. Barton served as an English Teacher in Newtown High School where she taught English (grades 9-12), taught desktop publishing, and advised the school newspaper. As a 15-year professional, she now collaborates with the New York City Board of Educator's Division of Instructional Support on a Professional Development program called Project Smart Schools. Ms. Barton also teaches educators emerging technologies such as interactive distance learning, as well as how to effectively and efficiently use new technologies. Her objectives include designing and implementing new programs to support instructional technology in the classroom, assisting in the adaptation of technology standards for New York City and helping to shape the vision for professional development in instructional technology. The United Federation of Teachers is the teacher's union in New York City. The UFT negotiates for better benefits and opportunities for teachers. The Teacher Centers Professional Development Program is the educational program of the UFT, which offers professional development services across all content areas for pre-kindergarten through 12th grade. Established in New York state in 1987, the UFT Teacher Center is one of approximately 118 statewide Teacher centers. In New York City, the UFT Teacher Center has 250 school-based sites and five instructional technology laboratories. Teacher Centers are funded through a state grant and other funding sources. **Career Highlights:** Instructional Technology Coordinator, United Federation of Teachers, Teacher Centers Professional Development Program (1993-Present); Teacher of English, Newtown High School, Elmhurst New York (1984-93). **Associations & Accomplishments:** International Society of Technology in Education. **Education:** Queens College, M.S. in Education, Secondary Education in English (1984). **Personal Information:** Married to Anthony in 1990. Ms. Barton enjoys gardening and singing in a four part church choir.

James Hurtak, Ph.D., Ph.D.

President
AFFS Corporation
Box FE
Los Gatos, CA 95031
(408) 741-0964
Fax: (408) 741-0964

8641

Business Information: A prominent and respected scientist, Dr. Hurtak serves as President of the AFFS Corporation or the Academy for Future Science Corporation. Facilitating conferences and symposiums to gather associate members for scientific discussion, he is a frequent lecturer worldwide. From his work through the years, Dr. Hurtak realized that the future's problems had to be faced on an international scale. He states that a person must recognize the paradigm of science is changing for the 21st Century; the synthesizing of science and knowledge provides a whole new image in the science market. Attributing his success as a scientist to the inspiration of work with young people throughout the world and their interests, he continues to work internationally through the media of electronic textbooks. Dr. Hurtak also looks forward to expanding his scientific research Web site, www.affs.org, using CDS and broadband while making it more interactive. Founded in 1973, the AFFS Corporation is a scientific association for new energy futures and the application of new technologies in international applications. There are 12,000 members of the Corporation throughout the world with 500 of those members within the United States. **Career Highlights:** President, AFFS Corporation (1977-Present); International Director, Lasertech Corporation (1988-97); Senior Scientific Consult, Advanced Scientific Applications (1993-96); International Director, Technology Marketing Analysis Corp. (1982-87). **Associations & Accomplishments:** Director, Institute for New Energy, Palo Alto, California; New York Academy of Sciences; Society of Professional Industrial Engineers; Latin American Remote Sensing Society; Developer,

Award-Winning Computer Animation Films and Interactive CDs; Important publications: "Marketing and Legislation in Outer Space," "Remote Sensing and the Ryukyu Submerged Landforms in the Pacific Ocean," "Innovate Technique for In Situ Treatment of Contaminated Surface Waters and Submerged Sediments by Enhanced Aerobic Bioremediation," "Cold Fusion Research: Models and Potential Benefits," "Survey and Critical Review of Recent Innovative Energy Conversion Technologies," "RQM/Swiss Technologies: Summary and Status," "High Temperature Superconductivity," and "Liquid Hydrogen: Fuel for Future Space Transportation." **Education:** University of California at Irvine, Ph.D. (1976); University of Minnesota: Ph.D., M.A.; University of Chicago. **Personal Information:** Married to Desiree. Dr. Hurtak enjoys producing films. His latest project is a collection of international films on information technology.

Marc L. Stiehr

Director of Information Technology
Young Men's Christian Association of Metropolitan Chicago
801 North Dearborn Street
Chicago, IL 60610-3316
(312) 932-1260
Fax: (312) 932-1332
mstiehr@ymcachgo.org

8641

Business Information: As Director of Information Technology for the Young Men's Christian Association of Metropolitan Chicago, Mr. Stiehr directs all technology related initiatives association-wide. He oversees the implementation of software and systems that will enhance and improve the overall functions of the YMCA. Mr. Stiehr began his career 27 years ago as an urban planner. Realizing his fascination with technology, he began studying the practical uses it offers. Now, he is a leader in his industry and he offers sound advice to other professionals in his field. In addition and in conjunction with YMCA, he has worked with a disabilities provider to design technical solutions for graphical workstations for the blind and voice-activated workstations for the disabled. He accepts his responsibilities dutifully and attributes his success to asking appropriate questions and listening to mentors. He completed the three-year plan he developed to prepare the YMCA for Y2K compliance and position technology for the future. Young Men's Christian Association of Metropolitan Chicago provides health, fitness, and social service programs to build strong kids, strong families, and strong communities. Established in 1858, the YMCA is renowned for improving the neighborhoods it serves and society overall through its efforts to strengthen families, build individual self-sufficiency, and develop young leaders. The Association employs 3,500 employees throughout the Chicago metropolitan area in its 36 centers, camps, and corporate offices, providing services to nearly one million people. In addition, the YMCA is recognized as the largest childcare and residence provider in Chicago. **Career Highlights:** Director of Information Technology, Young Men's Christian Association of Metropolitan Chicago (1997-Present); Sears, Roebuck & Company: Financial Planning Project Manager (1995-97), Technical Consultant (1995), Systems Planning Consultant (1987-95). **Associations & Accomplishments:** Former President, Data Processing Management Association of Sheboygan, Wisconsin. **Education:** University of Wisconsin at Oshkosh, B.S. (1971). **Personal Information:** Married to Bari in 1971. Two children: Matthew and Kristin.

Ken R. Klassy

Network Administrator
First Baptist Church Raytown
10500 East 350 Highway
Raytown, MO 64138
(816) 353-1994
Fax: (816) 778-1134
kklassy@fbc-raytown.org

8661

Business Information: Maintaining the challenging position of Network Administrator for the First Baptist Church in Raytown, Mr. Klassy ensures the efficient operation of all equipment involved with this widely broadcasted church. He administers and controls all network tools and resources, ensuring functionality and operational status. Possessing an excellent understanding of technology, Mr. Klassy is in charge of running the NT server and makes sure that the most innovative of technological advances are utilized in his service. Presently engaged in extending the boundaries of his intellectual and professional career, Mr. Klassy is continuing his education with further Microsoft Certified Systems Engineering training. Located in Raytown, Missouri, outside of Kansas City, the First Baptist Church of Raytown offers a

unique type of service. Established in 1840, this 6,000 member Church broadcasts its service live on the Internet to those unable to attend in person. Specializing in bridge events, the First Baptist Church provides direction and strength to residents and communities from around the country. **Career Highlights:** Network Administrator, First Baptist Church Raytown (1999-Present); Student Network Administrator, Hannable La Grange College (1998-99). **Associations & Accomplishments:** Phi Beta Delta; Student Government Association. **Education:** Hannibal La Grange, Degree in Computer Science (1999). **Personal Information:** Mr. Klassy enjoys saltwater aquariums.

Donald Durand

Information System Manager
American Radio Relay League
225 Main Street
Newington, CT 06111
(860) 594-0317
Fax: (860) 594-0298
ddurand@arrl.org

8699

Business Information: Volunteering his expertise in the information technology field, Mr. Durand serves in the role of Information Systems Manager for the American Radio Relay League. Orchestrating a wide range of technology projects, he overees and directs day-to-day operations, maintains the security of the membership database, and keeps members aware of FCC regulations through e-mail and networking. Mr. Durand chaired the committee that designed and built a frame relay network statewide for health care organizations which was used as a model for other states. This innovation was presented at a national information technology forum. His future plans include moving the League's current systems to a SQL platform as well as providing a full e-commerce solution to members by the years end. Attributing his success to flexibility, Mr. Durand's advice is, "Learn people skills." A nonprofit organization since 1914, American Radio Relay League is the national association of amatuer radio operators. A membership run organization, the League serves as an advocate to government as well as publishes magazines, books, and multimedia videos for members. The League proudly holds a membership of 162,000 individuals, who are located throughout the United States. **Career Highlights:** Information Systems Manager, American Radio Relay League (1997-Present); Chief Information Technology Consultant, Phillips National Inc. (1995-Present); Director of Distributive Information Systems, Lawrence & Memorial Hospital (1991-94). **Associations & Accomplishments:** American Registry of Radiologic Technologists; Committee Chair, Troop 11, New London, Connecticut Boy Scouts of America; Appeared as a guest on Dee Snider radio, WMRQ, Hartford, to discuss Y2K issues. **Education:** Providence College: M.Ed. (1985), B.A. in Education; Rhode Island Community College, A.A.S. **Personal Information:** Married to Kathryn in 1992. Three children: Zachary, Emily, and Hayley. Mr. Durand enjoys motorcycling, camping, and historical research.

Mark H. Gamble

Technical Director
South Carolina Arts Commission
1506 Friars Court
West Columbia, SC 29169
(803) 734-8684
Fax: (803) 734-8562
mgamble@arts.state.sc.us

8699

Business Information: As Technical Director of the South Carolina Arts Commission, Mr. Gamble offers technical support and expertise to film and videomakers in the Southeast United States. Among his many responsibilities, he researches funding for projects in the film and video industry, manages the equipment access program, provides equipment training, and meets with film and videomakers for consultations. Mr. Gamble's achievements include publishing a "Boxing Simulation" computer game for which he was nominated an award, and other video productions. Planning to stay in the film production industry, Mr. Gamble anticipates creating documentaries and feature films in the future. His success is attributed to his ability to think outside the box and deliver results. Established in 1967, the South Carolina Arts Commission operates as a state arts agency and regional media center. The 40 employees work diligently to assist South Carolina artists in funding projects and grants, as well as offering educational information. Presently, the Commission is located in Columbia, South Carolina. **Career Highlights:** Technical Director, South Carolina Arts Commission (1999-Present); Cameraman, Image Productions (1998-99); Video Production Coordinator, Palmetto Richland Memorial Hospital (1997-98); Freelance Cameraman (1994-97). **Education:** University of South Carolina, M.A. (1995); Wofford College, B.A. (1988). **Personal Information:** Mr. Gamble enjoys writing, travel and model building.

Jim Shamlin

Webmaster
Boy Scouts of America
P.O. Box 152079
Irving, TX 75015
(972) 580-2415
jshamlin@netbsa.org

8699

Business Information: Proficient in the information architecture, Mr. Shamlin was recruited to the Boy Scouts of America in 1998. Serving in the position of Webmaster, he developed and implemented the Organization's Web sites used to raise Scouting awareness on a national level. In addition, he is responsible for all aspects of the Internet activities aimed towards the general public. Coordinating resources, schedules, and time lines; analyzing, specifying, and designing new solutions; and enhancing the overall performance of the networking environment also fall within the purview of his responsibilities. Attributing his success to personal innovation and an ability to take on new challenges, Mr. Shamlin keeps current with the changing technology field by reading trade journals and networking with colleagues on the Internet. Consistently achieving quality performance, he anticipates a promotion to Chief Information Officer. Boy Scouts of America is a nonprofit youth organization designed to teach boys ages 11 to 18 to become good citizens and leaders of our society. The Organization was established in 1907 in Great Britain and brought to the United States in 1909 by William D. Boyce. Approximately 10,000 individuals dedicated to the nation's youth are employed nationwide by the Boy Scouts of America. **Career Highlights:** Webmaster, Boy Scouts of America (1998-Present); Senior Analyst, Web Development, GTE Internet Solutions (1996-98); Consultant, Ajilon (1995-96); Graphic Designer, R.R. Donnelley (1993-95). **Education:** East Carolina University: M.A. (1993), B.A. (1989).

8700 Engineering and Management Services

8711 Engineering services
8712 Architectural services
8713 Surveying services
8721 Accounting, auditing, and bookkeeping
8731 Commercial physical research
8732 Commercial nonphysical research
8733 Noncommercial research organizations
8734 Testing laboratories
8741 Management services
8742 Management consulting services
8743 Public relations services
8744 Facilities support services
8748 Business consulting, nec

Walt Burton

Principal Systems Engineer
Rand Technologies
2030 East Algonquin Road
Schaumburg, IL 60173
(847) 303-6460
Fax: (847) 303-6471
wburton@rand.com

8711

Business Information: Demonstrating technical expertise in the technological field since 1985, Mr. Burton was recruited to Rand Technologies in 1991. At the present time, he distinguishably serves as Principal Systems Engineer and is responsible for all aspects of information systems integration planning. Drawing from years of practical occupational experience and a firm academic background, Mr. Burton oversees implementation and installation of customer's hardware on-site as well as conducting vendor and product evaluations. The world's largest seller of mechanical design automation tools, Rand Technologies specializes in mechanical engineering computer systems integration and related services. Also providing installation, training, and consulting services, the Company's products are found in cars, computers, planes, recreational vehicles, television, and stereo equipment. Headquartered in Canada, Rand Technologies operates 75 international office locations employing 800 people and generating in excess of $300 million in annual revenues. **Career Highlights:** Principal Systems Engineer, Rand Technologies (1991-Present); Applications Engineer, Calay Systems (1990-91); Senior Technical Associate, Technetics (1985-90). **Education:** Indiana State University, B.S. in Engineering Technology (1984); Sun Microsystems Enterprise Certified. **Personal Information:** Married to Maggie in 1982. Three children: Elizabeth, Kimberly, and Lillian.

Shawn Edward Caldwell
Computer Aided Design and Drafting Manager
Anderson and Associate's, Inc.
100 Ardmore Street
Blacksburg, VA 24060
(540) 552-5592
Fax: (540) 552-5729
caldwell@andassoc.com

8711

Business Information: Highly skilled in the computer technology field, Mr. Caldwell serves as Computer-Aided Design and Drafting Manager of Anderson and Associates, Inc. Staying on the leading edge, he is responsible for maintaining the Corporation's design software up-to-date. A successful, five year veteran, he also provides software support and is involved in all aspects of software analysis, design, development, and installation. Currently the designer technician for a water/waste water treatment plant, Mr. Caldwell does the design, drafting, and inspection as well as field work. Continually striving for maximum effectiveness, his goal is to take software design and develpment to the next level; and better himself. His professional career highlight is his appointment to his present position after only two years with the Corporation. Success according to Mr. Caldwell is due to his values instilled by his parents and industry mentors. Anderson and Associates, Inc. is a hi-tech, leading edge, employee owned company. Located in Blackburg, Virginia, the Corporation specializes in civil engineering. Established in 1968, the Corporation employs over 170 individuals to facilitate surveying, land development, transportation, and water and sewer utilities design. **Career Highlights:** Computer-Aided Design and Drafting Manager, Anderson and Associates, Inc. (1998-Present). **Associations & Accomplishments:** AutoCAD Users Group International; Chairman, Virginia Tech AutoCAD User Group. **Education:** Virginia Western Community Colleg, A.S. in Engineering (1995). **Personal Information:** Mr. Caldwell enjoys computers, the outdoors, and games.

Mark A. Chamberlain
CADD Systems Manager
Landtech Consultants, Inc.
484 Groton Road, Unit 1
Westford, MA 01886-1152
(978) 672-6100
Fax: (978) 692-6668
mchmbrln@landtechinc.com

8711

Business Information: Joining Landtech Consultants, Inc. in 1993, Mr. Chamberlain serves as CADD Systems Manager. In his present capacity, he is responsible for production, planning, designing, and systems upgrade as well as GPS translation and training new employees on the CADD program. Highly regarde, he possesses superior talents and an excellent understanding of technology. With a degree from New Hamshire Technical Institute and 15 years of hands on experience in the engineering and surveying fields, Mr. Chamberlain is a self taught Auto CADD expert. Attributing his success to his flexibility, he stresses that in order to expand yourself as a person, one must not be afraid to try something new. Establishing goals compatible to the Corporation's objectives, he plans on becoming involved in geographic information systems. Established in 1990, Landtech Consultants, Inc. is a civil engineering and land surveying business. Catering to the needs of commercial businesses, Landtech Consultants, Inc. perform various surveys including subdivision, boundary, the ALTA Survey, title search surveys, and the GPS Survey. Presently, the Corporation is manned by a 14 professional, technical, and support staff. **Career Highlights:** CADD Systems Manager, Landtech Consultants, Inc. (1993-Present); Drafting Supervisor/Systems Manager, Storch Associates (1991-93); CADD Operator/Applications Programmer, Holden Engineering & Surveying (1985-90). **Education:** New Hampshire Technical Institute, Associate's in Architecture Technology (1983). **Personal Information:** Mr. Chamberlain enjoys military history.

Paul DeVincentis
Network Systems Administrator
Burns & Roe Enterprises
2237 Trinity Drive, Building 2
Los Alamos, NM 87544
(505) 661-4423
Fax: (505) 661-2525
pdevincentis@brapt.com

8711

Business Information: Mr. DeVincentis has worked in the computer science field since 1990, the same year he joined the Burns & Roe Enterprises team. An proactive team member, he has served in a variety of capacities since his arrival at Burns & Roe. He now serves as Network Systems Administrator responsible for managing and maintaining the entire network infrastructure. Owning a proven record of delivering high impact results, Mr. DeVincentis oversees all day-to-day operations of the LAN, file servers, and the mail server. He leverages his extensive management skills and technical expertise in providing network security and desk top and CADD support. In addition, Mr. DeVincentis handles numerous resource planning functions to include personnel management, resource requirements in an ever changing business environment, and mentoring other associates. Analysis, design, evaluation, test, and implementation of advanced computer based networking environments also fall within the purview of his responsibilities. He attributes his success to persistence and drive to be the best. Remaining in the computer field and becoming more involved in Web pages design serves as Mr. DeVincentis' future goals. An engineering and design firm, Burns & Roe Enterprises is heavily engaged in the power industry that involves nuclear, fossil, and cogen energy. A reputable company founded in 1932, Burns & Roe Enterprises also works for the Department of Energy on a contract basis. Presently, the Company employs a work force of more than 550 people who help generate annual revenues in excess of $300 million. **Career Highlights:** Burns & Roe Enterprises: Network Systems Administrator (1996-Present), Mechanical Engineer II (1990-96); Autocad Designer, EI Associates (1996). **Associations & Accomplishments:** Associate Member, American Society of Mechanical Engineers; MCSE (2000), Microsoft Certified Systems Engineer; Lexington's Who's Who of Information Technology; Institute of Electrical and Electronics Engineers, Inc. Computer Society (IEEE). **Education:** Western New England College, B.S. in Mechanical Engineering (1989). **Personal Information:** Mr. DeVincentis enjoys ice hockey, inline hockey, golf, comedy, classic rock and coaching youth hockey.

Robert T. Fink
Group Leader
MPR Associates, Inc.
6712 Fisher Avenue
Falls Church, VA 22046
(703) 519-0561
Fax: (703) 519-0224
rfink@mpr.com

8711

Business Information: A Group Leader of MPR Associates Inc., Mr. Fink serves as senior manager in charge of the MPR business sector, that includes all aspects of information technology products and services. Possessing an excellent understanding of technology, Mr. Fink manages a savvy group of engineers and supervisors accountable for engineering research and development in computer systems. An active member of various industry related organizations, he is able to remain on top of advancing technology by networking with the many professionals in different fields. His accomplishments include the development of methods for safe and reliable use of computers and software in critical, real-time applications. Mr. Fink's future endeavors include becoming more involved with product development using new technology. His success reflects his ability to take on challenges and deliver results to help clients remain at the forefront in the Information Technology Age. Founded in 1964, MPR Associates, Inc. is an engineering consulting firm. Providing high-tech engineering consultation, the Firm is presently headquartered in Alexandria, Virginia. Employing 130 individuals, the Firm offers its services internationally. **Career Highlights:** Group Leader, MPR Associates, Inc. (1974-Present). **Associations & Accomplishments:** Association of Computing Machinery; Institute of Electrical and Electronics Engineers. **Education:** Rice University: Master's degree in Electronic Engineering (1974), B.S. in Engineering summa cum laude (1973). **Personal Information:** Married to Cathy in 1984. Three children: Nathan, Alex, and Christopher.

Timothy G. Granger
Vice President
American Engineering
P.O. Box 650
North East, MD 21901
(410) 398-5000
Fax: (410) 287-3661
timothygranger@juno.com

8711

Business Information: Drawing upon 15 years of experience, Mr. Granger is the Vice President for American Engineering. In his position, he is responsible for overseeing all of the office operations including all field work and client calls. Moreover, he is charged with developing networks and implementing changes and upgrades to the networks. Mr. Granger also terminates, tests, and installs custom programs on each network as well as troubleshoots network difficulties. During his illustrious career in the technical field, he has received many awards and looks forward to expanding the Company, succeeding, and moving into fiber optics. Founded in 1985, American Engineering engages in civil engineering and network design. Located in North East, Maryland, the Company also conducts network activities and provides consulting services to a local clientele. The Company offers installation and support including cabling, terminations, and testing. Presently, American Engineering employs a work force of 7 employees, and reports annual revenues of $400,000. **Career Highlights:** Vice President, American Engineering (1985-Present). **Associations & Accomplishments:** Maryland Society of Surveyors. **Education:** Cecil Community College; Delaware Technical and Community College. **Personal Information:** Married to Carrie Lynn in 1988. Six children: Brooke, Levi, Lane, Brielle, Lief, and Jace. Mr. Granger enjoys weight lifting, fishing and water skiing.

Andrew T. Harris
CAD Supervisor
Hicks & Ragland Engineering Company
P.O. Box 65800
Lubbock, TX 79464-5800
(806) 722-7600
Fax: (806) 722-7802
aharris@hreng.com

8711

Business Information: As CAD Supervisor of Hicks & Ragland Engineering Company, Mr. Harris oversees all computer aided design aspects of the operation. He began his career with the Company five years ago and has held trhe supervisory title for six months. Mr. Harris was promoted to his present role due to demonstrating his skill, knowledge, and determination in the field. With a passion for the work, he is acapable and ready to take on new projects and developing new ways to accomplish goals. He also hopes to continue to learn and improve his skills to possibly teach others. Mr. Harris's best advice is "stay in school." Established in 1937, Hicks & Ragland Engineering Company specializes in telecommunication engineering for the majority of independent telephone companies. Approxiamtley 130 highly skilled and trained individuals are employed by the Company. **Career Highlights:** Hicks & Ragland Engineering Company: CAD Supervisor (1999-Present), Graphics Technician (1994-99). **Education:** Barton County Community College, A.A.S. (1994). **Personal Information:** Mr. Harris enjoys shooting, fishing, listening to music and watching classic movies.

Erasmus W. McEady, Ph.D.
Project Leader/Senior Communications Engineer
Vector Data Systems
P.O. Box 71557
Fort Bragg, NC 28307
(910) 396-1686
Fax: (910) 396-4249
mceadye@bragg.army.mil

8711

Business Information: Proficient in all areas of technology, Dr. McEady has served with Vector Data Systems in various positions since 1993. At the present time, he fulfills the responsibilities of Project Leader and Senior Communications Engineer. In his capacity, he provides centralized information systems support for the 18th Airborne Corps stationed at Fort Bragg. Along with three technology professionals, Dr. McEady provides project management, systems integration, application performance testing, telecommunications support, and Web site management. On the hardware side, he draws from over 17 years of experience and a strong academic background to maintain 39 end-user desktops and 16 notebooks. A recognized authority, Dr. McEady's military awards include the Defense Meritorious Service Award; Meritorious Service Award (1OLC); Legion of Merit; and Bronze Star. And in 1972, he was recipient of the "Distinguished Instructor Award." His goals include increasing the manpower in his department to 10 technology experts and looking for opportunities to start his own business. A global engineering and information technology company, Vector Data Systems provides systems technology and networking expertise. Primarily serving a government and military clientele, the Company's focus is on engineering, communications, networks, and logistics automation. With a worldwide presence, the Company operates offices in the United Kingdom, Germany, and Australia. Purchased in 1998, Vector Data Systems is now a subsidiary of Anteon Corporation. Over 100 people staff operations at headquarters in Alexandria, Virginia. **Career Highlights:** Project Leader/Senior Communications Engineer, Vector Data Systems (1997-Present), Systems Engineer (1995-97), Engineer (1993-95); Adjunct Professor, Webster University & Campbell University, Pope Air Force Base (1999-Present). **Associations & Accomplishments:** Omega Psi Phi Fraternity Inc.; Tau Gamma Gamma Chapter; Prince Hall Mason. **Education:** La Salle University, Ph.D. in Education (1996); Webster University, Dual M.A. in Computer Resources and Information Management, Security Management (1994); Chapman University, B.A. in Economics and Business Administration (1981). **Personal Information:**

Married to Loverette in 1967. Two children: Erasmus Jr. and Eric. Dr. McEady enjoys computers, yard work and golf.

Roya Noorbakhsh

Engineering Department Manager
Fluor Global Services
One Fluor Daniel Drive
Aliso Viejo, CA 92698-0001
(949) 349-4202
Fax: (949) 349-3081
roya.noorbakhsh@fluor.com

8711

Business Information: As Engineering Department Manager of Fluor Global Services, Ms. Noorbakhsh fulfills a number of duties on behalf of the Company and its clientele. Concentrating her efforts towards project management, she oversees and provides direction to 100 engineers. Maintaining an efficient staff, she ensures the needed support for the development of various products. Providing training courses for new workers, Ms. Noorbakhsh strives towards excellence in service. Managing the fiscal budget, personnel and resources management, and quality assurance is also an integral part of her responsibilities. Furthering her growth with Fluor Global Services, she devotes her time and attention to the successful completion of projects. Her success reflects her ability to think outside the box, aggressively take on new challenges, and deliver results. Providing quality equipment and consulting in telecommunications, Fluor Global Services was established in 1984. Located in Aliso Viejo, California, the Company employs a knowledgable staff of over 550. Specifically dealing with clients, Fluor Global Services offers a variety of telecommunications in order to promote business growth. Consulting with the clients, the Company is able to evaluate and research problematic areas, then implement the specific product needed for the solution. Dedicated to providing state-of-the-art equipment and excellent client services, Fluor Global Services remains committed to the success of their projects. **Career Highlights:** Engineering Department Manager, Fluor Global Services (1996-Present); Project Engineer/Project Manager, CALTRANS (1992-96); Electrical Engineer, Satellite Technology Management (1990-92). **Associations & Accomplishments:** Association of Public Safety Communications; Item Writer, California Board for Professional Engineers and Land Surveyors; CSULB Alumni. **Education:** University of Southern California, M.B.A. (1998); California State University, B.S. in Electrical Engineering (1991); Registered Electrical Engineer in State of California (PE). **Personal Information:** Ms. Noorbakhsh enjoys music, reading and rollerblading.

Ike D. Penney

Projects Director
Lockard & White
14511 Falling Creek, Suite 507
Houston, TX 77014
(281) 586-0574
Fax: (281) 586-0044
ipenney@lawtelecom.com

8711

Business Information: Mr. Penney was recruited to Lockard & White as Projects Engineer in 1992. In his current capacity as Projects Director, he is responsible for applying project management principles in the performance of his job to ensure quality services is being provided to the Company's clients. He also oversees and directs specific projects or a number of projects on behalf of the Company and its' clientele. Possessing strong leadership skills, Mr. Penney supervises the workflow that includes providing project scope compliance, project scheduling, and project budgetingl. Delivery of services and identifying new avenues for additional revenues also fall within the realm of his responsibilities. His background history includes employment with Motorola as Systems Engineer, Project Engineer, and Project Manager. His career highlights include a three-year project on a nationwide system implementation of the first portable data terminal network that benefited hundreds of cities and resulted in the establishment of new companies. In another three0year period, Mr. Penney was the lead engineer and project manager for the design and deployment of an extensive offshore two-way radio system for a major oil company. Mr. Penney attributes his success to the people he has had the pleasure of working with. He gives credit to the engineers, sales people, and project managers he has associated with in the past who have given him a positive direction. His goals include becoming PMI certified and focusing more on project management tasks. Ambitious about the future, Mr. Penney plans to see Lockard & White become an international company as he takes on greater roles in management. Lockard & White, founded in 1984 by Marcus Lockard and Charles White, is a telecommunications system engineering, consulting, and project management firm which currently employs in excess of 50 persons and reports annual sales of $4.5 million. **Career Highlights:** Projects Director, Lockard & White (1992-Present); Motorola C&E: Project Manager (1988-92), Project Engineer (1982-87), Systems Engineer (1979-81). **Associations & Accomplishments:** Project Management International. **Education:** University of Houston, B.S. (1979). **Personal Information:** Mr. Penney enjoys gardening, reading and naturism.

Dana W. Rippon

Senior Project Manager/Prinicpal Technologist
CHZM Hill
2525 Airpark Drive
Redding, CA 96001-2443
(530) 229-3311
Fax: (530) 243-1654
drippon@ch2m.com

8711

Business Information: Beginning his career with CH2M Hill more than 30 years ago, Mr. Rippon has received recognition for his diligence and management skills through several promotions to his current position of Senior Project Manager and Principal Technologist. Utilizing a vast education and solid experience, his responsibilities include design of water treatment plants; planning specifications; quality control; and education of technology, teaching others to know "the latest technology." Having piloted a state of the art water treatment plan by designing a system to replace five million gallons of water a day with treated water, he is very proud of his accomplishments. Possessing an excellent understanding of his field, Mr. Rippon attributes his success to "empathizing with clients." Established in 1946, CH2M Hill is an engineering consultant. Located in Redding, California, the Firm employs over 7,000 highly qualified individuals to facilitate international consulting focusing on water and hazard waste engineering and transportation. **Career Highlights:** CH2M Hill: Senior Project Manager/Principal Technologist (1999-Present), Senior Project Manager (1990-99), Sanitary Engineer (1971-90). **Associations & Accomplishments:** Water Environment Association of Texas; California Water Environment Association; American Water Works Association. **Education:** Stanford University, M.S. (1972); Humboldt State University, B.S. (1971). **Personal Information:** Married to Anne in 1990. Two children: Rebecca and Tyler. Ms. Rippon enjoys weight lifting.

Daniel Serfaty

Founder/Chief Scientist
Aptima, Inc.
600 West Cummings Park, Suite 3050
Woburn, MA 01801-6369
(781) 935-3966
Fax: (781) 935-4385
serfaty@aptima.com

8711

Business Information: Serving as Founder and Chief Scientist since 1996, Mr. Serfaty is the owner of Aptima, Inc. In this capacity, he is responsible for the management and organization of the Corporation as well as coordinating various aspects of research. Formulating the vision and fresh strategic direction, Mr. Serfaty establishes technology teams and provides solutions to a variety of technical problems. An authority in the field, he has written well over 100 articles and has written complete chapters for books involved with Psychology, Human Engineering, and Team Work. The spark which spurred Mr. Serfaty into starting his own business was born out of curiosity. Among his goals are to continue to be a scientist and do research especially involving the Internet. He wants to continue to write articles and do lectures. A human-centered engineering business, Aptima, Inc. was founded in 1996. The Corporation performs research in human factors and supports the design of complex human-machine systems. Aptima, Inc. contracts services through the United States government with a majority of the business involving the Department of Defense, NASA, and the Education Department. Employees have backgrounds in engineering, behavioral science, and computer science. With a core group of 30 employees, the Corporation generates over $3 million in annual sales and is fast becoming a market leader in the field of human engineering. **Career Highlights:** Founder/Chief Scientist, Aptima, Inc. (1996-Present); Alpha Tech, Inc.: Group Leader (1989-95), Program Manager (1987-89); Lecturer, University of Connecticut (1986-87). **Associations & Accomplishments:** Institute of Electronics and Electrical Engineers; Systems, Man, & Cybernetics Society; Human Factors Society; Elta Kappa Nu; Sigma Xi Honors Society. **Education:** University of Connecticut, M.B.A. (1985); Technion; Israel Institute of Technology, Master's degree in Aeronautical Engineering. **Personal Information:** Married to Irene in 1980.

Laura Barrett Silsbee

Project Coordinator
Earth Tech
1452 Corporate Pointe
Warner Robins, GA 31088-3431
(912) 329-8870
Fax: (912) 329-1062
laurasilsbee@earthtech.com

8711

Business Information: As Project Coordinator for Earth Tech, Mrs. Silsbee oversees all aspects of project management and coordination. Demonstrating exceptional knowledge of her field gained through practical work experience and related education, she lends guidance and support as she directs her staff through the completion of daily tasks. Offering technical support, Mrs. Silsbee works closely with customers and employees to develop applicable solutions and business plans. She handles marketing related activities for available services with an innovative, creative approach. Crediting success to the flexibility she demonstrates throughout her career, Mrs. Silsbee intends to continue with the Company as she assists in the development of advanced GIS systems and Web based applications. Earth Tech is an enviornmental waste service center located in Warner Robins, Georgia. Specializing in waste water management services, the Company offers geographic information systems assistance. The Company employs 7,000 throughout the entire Corporation to assist in the completion of corporate goals. **Career Highlights:** Project Coordinator, Earth Tech (1999-Present); CSC, Inc.: GIS Analyst (1997-99); Environmental Analyst (1996-97); Technical Lead Cultutal Resources (1994-96). **Associations & Accomplishments:** Urban and Regional Information Systems Associations; Society for Georgia Archaeology; Society for American Archaeology; Warner Robins Little Theatre. **Education:** University of California Los Angeles, M.A. in Archaeology (1993); University of California Riverside Extension; GIS Certificate (1997); University of California Davis, B.A. in Anthrolpology (1988); University of Phoenix Online, M.S. in Computer Information Systems (In Progress). **Personal Information:** Married to David in 1993. Mrs. Silsbee enjoys theatre, biking, camping, reading, writing, handcrafts and music.

Daniel S. Wagner

Design Supervisor
Foster Wheel Environment Corporation
67 Wilson Road
Monroe, NY 10950
(914) 783-4229
Fax: (973) 597-7433
dwagner@fwenc.com

8711

Business Information: Serving as Foster Wheel Environmental Corporation's Design Supervisor since 1977, Mr. Wagner is a 32-year veteran of technology responsible for every aspect of the day-to-day technical operations. He is accountable for maintaining CAD systems, developing CAD software and files, and archiving. A faithful and assertive employee, Mr. Wagner has seen the Corporation go through several changes throughout his tenure with the Corporation. He is the person responsible for setting up and maintaining LAN/WAN connectivities. Maintaining open communications with staff members on a daily basis, he is the person responsible for settting up and keeping LAN/WAN networks functional and operational. The most rewarding aspect of his career was getting involved in computers with no degree and still making it to his current position. Mr. Wagner plans on obtaining certification in Microsoft and networking in the near future. Attributing his success to determination and work ethics, his advice is, "Start early and get as much training as you can." Headquartered in Morris Plains, New Jersey, Foster Wheeler Environmental Corporation is an environmental engineering service that specializes in site development, remediation, reporting, and conducting investigations for the Environmental Protection Agency (EPA). The Corporation started out as a contractor to the EPA, and gradually grew to its current state. As a national corporation, Foster Wheeler Environmental employs a staff of 2,000 members located throughout the United States. Presently, the Corporation reports annual revenues in excess of $350 million. **Career Highlights:** Design Supervisor, Foster Wheeler Environmental Corporation (1977-Present); Squad Leader, Chomico Construction Company (1973-77); Application Engineer, Johnson Service Company (1970-72). **Associations & Accomplishments:** Senior Member, Instrument Society of America. **Personal Information:** Married to Genevieve in 1967. Four children: Barbara, Elizabeth, Christine, and Daniel. Mr. Wagner enjoys gardening and computers.

Jerry L. Wallenborn

Geographic Information Systems and CAD Manager
Earth Tech
9365 Carmichael Drive
La Mesa, CA 91941
(858) 536-5610
Fax: (858) 536-5620
wallenborn@earthtech.com

8711

Business Information: Contributing 22 years of hard work to the field, Mr. Wallenborn serves as Geographic Information Systems and CAD Manager for Earth Tech. Gaining incredible amounts of valuable experience and industry knowledge during his career, he is responsible for all aspects of daily network administration, CAD and GIS mapping, and graphics for marketing. Before joining Earth Tech in 1990, Mr. Wallenborn served as CAD Instruction Director for the Computer Graphics Institute. His background history also include stints as CAD and Construction Director with Muir Institute and Head CAD Instructor at Grossmont Community College. Administering and controlling systems tools, tuning systems software, peripherals, and networks, and resolving systems problems also fall within the realm of Mr. Wallenborn's responsibilities. In the future, he plans on taking on bigger projects and becoming more involved on the design aspects of technology. Supporting the architectural design and graphics of major companies around the country, Earth Tech employs a staff of 33 highly trained and industry educated professionals. Specializing in environmental and civil engineering, Earth Tech generates annual sales in excess of $5.7 million. Presently, Earth Tech is operating in their 25th year. **Career Highlights:** Geographic Information Systems and CAD Manager, Earth Tech (1990-Present); CAD Instruction Director, Computer Graphics Institute (1987-90); CAD and Construction Director, Muir Institute (1983-87); Head CAD Instructor, Grossmont Community College (1978-83). **Associations & Accomplishments:** California Association of Computer Users; Autocad Users of America; Bently Select. **Education:** National University, Master's degree in Digital Technology (1994); San Diego State Univeristy, Master's degree in Computer Science; Grossmont Community College, Bachelor's degree in Music. **Personal Information:** Three children: Heide, Jason, and Heather. Mr. Wallenborn enjoys model building and computer programming.

Richard L. Bland

Director of Computer Services
Giffels Associates, Inc.
25200 Telegraph Road
Southfield, MI 48034
(248) 936-8036
Fax: (248) 936-8037
rbland@giffels-usa.com

8712

Business Information: Mr. Bland serves as Director of Computer Services for Giffels Associates, Inc. He is responsible for all computer applications, telecommunications, LAN and WAN networks, bar code systems, records management, and Y2K compliance. Before joining Giffels Associates, Mr. Bland served as Data Center Services Manager and Systems and Procedures Manager for Black & Veatch, Consulting Engineers. As a 30-year professional in the field, he has developed several engineering systems for noise and vibration, fluid distribution analysis, and software development procedures for nuclear safety related systems. He has presented or published more than 40 technical papers on four continents. In addition to supervising and leading his staff, he handles special assignments, such as replacing traditional analog blueprints with direct digital plotting, and implementing video conferencing to facilitate fast track projects, thus setting the overall strategic direction of the technology environment. He is most proud of his appointment to teams that traveled to China and South Africa to present technology based applications to government agencies, universities, and private engineering and architectural firms. Mr. Bland attributes his success to good genes and work ethics provided by his parents and the grace of God. Giffels Associates, Inc. is a privately owned architectural engineering company. Established in 1925, the Corporation employs over 500 personnel who provide strategic planning, design, and systems integration services to a broad range of markets. Presently, the Corporation produces $70 million in annual revenues. **Career Highlights:** Director of Computer Services, Giffels Associates, Inc. (1978-Present); Black & Veatch: Manager of Data Center Services (1976-78), Manager of Systems and Procedures (1974-76), Applications Engineer (1968-74). **Associations & Accomplishments:** Past Chairman, Technical Council on Computer Practices; American Society of Civil Engineers; Silver Beaver and Eagle Scout, Boy Scouts of America; Delegation Leader, People to People, South Africa; Delegation Representative, Computer Applications Delegation to the People's Republic of China. **Education:** University of Missouri, M.S. (1972); University of Kansas, B.S. (1966); Illinois Institute of Technology (1962); Short Courses at the University of Wisconsin; Colorado State University. **Personal Information:** Married to Sharon in 1966. Two children: Richard and Joseph. Mr. Bland enjoys metal and wood working, studying ancient architecture and being involved with the Boy Scouts of America.

Jeffrey Allen Block

Systems Administrator/Leader
Kahler Slater Architects
611 East Wisconsin Avenue
Milwaukee, WI 53202
(414) 272-2000
Fax: (414) 272-2000
jblock@kahlerslater.com

8712

Business Information: Mr. Block serves as the Systems Administrator and Leader in charge of technological development for Kahler Slater Architects. Possessing an excellent understanding of his field, he is responsible for maintaining the network infrastructure as well as designing and administering the data base. He is also accountable for the development of Web applications and evaluation of new technology that may benefit the Firm. Highly regarded by his colleagues, Mr. Block is working to achieve an executive role within Kahler Slater Architects and evenutally start his own consulting company. His success is a result of having good colleagues and good mentors. Established in 1918 and located in Milwaukee, Wisconsin, Kahler Slater Architects provides architectural services to non-residential clients. Involved mostly with large corporations, the Firm starts from scratch and uses the most state of the art design technology to generate a custom design for interior or exterior structures. The Firm then generates a technical blueprint to be used during construction. Generating annual sales in excess of $10 million, Kahler Slater Architects employs 130 people. **Career Highlights:** Systems Administrator/Leader, Kahler Slater Architects (1998-Present); Network Administrator, CNR Health (1997-98); Systems Administrator, Wisconsin Color Press (1995-97). **Associations & Accomplishments:** Association of Information Technology Professionals; Non Profit Work for Association that need Computer Assistance. **Personal Information:** Married to Melisa M. in 1999. Mr. Block enjoys dogs, woodworking and computers.

John R. Brown III

CAD Supervisor
Tarquini Organization
1812 Federal Street
Camden, NJ 08105-1899
(856) 365-7270
jbrown3@snip.net

8712

Business Information: As Tarquini Organization's CAD Supervisor, Mr. Brown serves the Organization in a number of different aspects. Possessing an excellent understanding of CAD technology, he is involved in drafting, designing, and project management. A savvy, CAD operator with over five years of hands on experiece, Mr. Brown utilizes high speed workstations and PCs to design graphic illustrations in the performance of his duties. Highly regarded, he also mentors his staff. Continually striving for maximum effectiveness, Mr. Brown is planning on pursuing a degree in architecture to enable him to capitalize on the opportunities provided by Tarquini Organization. He continues to grow professionally through the fulfillment of his responsibilities and his involvement in the advancement of operations. Success, according to Mr. Brown, is attributed to his ability to think out-of-the-box, aggressively take on challenges, and deliver results. Established in 1947, Tarquini Organization specializes in architecture and planning. Employing 20 personnel, the Organization provides architectural services, schematic design, and construction administration. The Organization is dedicated to ensuring that clients are given the best services available. **Career Highlights:** CAD Supervisor, Tarquini Organization (1997-Present); Digital Editor, Aerial Data Reduction (1996-97). **Education:** Lincoln Technical Institute, diploma (1995). **Personal Information:** Mr. Brown enjoys reading, computers and stock car racing.

Sparkle N. Fleming

IST Coordinator
BSW International
One West Third Street, Suite 100
Tulsa, OK 74103
(918) 582-8771
Fax: (918) 587-3594
sparkle_fleming@bswintl.com

8712

Business Information: Serving in the position of IST Coordinator for BSW International, Ms. Fleming is responsible for troubleshooting, maintenance, and software and hardware upgrades. Demonstrating strategic management skills, she coordinates and develops projects, time lines, schedules, and serves as chief liaison between clients and project managers. Utilizing extensive academic and occupational experience in her field, Ms. Fleming proactively deals with utility companies and civil engineers, and is responsible for working closely with city government officials to design and develop city projects. Attributing her success to her determination and good parental support, Ms. Fleming would like to become a fashion designer or technical consultant in the future. Established in 1983, BSW International operates as an architectural engineering firm. Employing 180 personnel, the Company constructs buildings for clients and is involved in the process from beginning to end. The Company designs inside and outside of buildings, inspects proposed sites, and monitors the building project. **Career Highlights:** BSW International: IST Coordinator (1998-Present), IST Administrator (1998), Team Associate (1998). **Education:** McLain Career Academy, Diploma (1997); Tulsa Vo-Tech, 2000 Computer Introduction Certification. **Personal Information:** Ms. Fleming enjoys being a Mary Kay consultant.

Jim Harmon

Information Technology Administrator
MKC Associates, Inc.
380 North Main Street, Suite 500
Mansfield, OH 44902
(419) 525-1102
Fax: (419) 525-1428
jharmon@mkcinc.com

8712

Business Information: Serving as the Information Technology Administrator of MKC Associates, Inc., Mr. Harmon fulfills a number of duties on behalf of the Corporation. He administers and controls all aspects of network tools and ensures the functionality and operational status of LAN/WAN and Internet related network environment. Possessing superior talents and an excellent understanding of technology, Mr. Harmon is actively involved in troubleshooting systems difficutlties, performing computer maintenance, and providing technical assistance for all three corporate offices, to include Mansfield, New Philadelphia, and Coshooton. He is also involved network installation, ensuring that users have proper network access. In the future, Mr. Harmon plans to obtain his Microsoft Certified Systems Engineer certification to facilitate promotional opportunities within the industry. Established in 1925, MKC Associates, Inc. is an architectural and engineering firm. Headquartered in Mansfield, Ohio, the Corporation employs 86 personnel to fulfill all aspects of operation. Estimated annual revenues were reported exceeding $125 million in 1999. **Career Highlights:** MKC Associates, Inc: Information Technology Administrator (1998-Present), Draftsman/Roofing (1989-98); Draftsman/Designer, Architectural Metal & Glass (1989). **Education:** North Carolina State University, Associate's Degree (1989); Microsoft Certified Systems Engineer Training. **Personal Information:** Two children: Matt and Jennifer. Mr. Harmon enjoys motorcycling and fishing.

Nabil H. Kafrouni

Technical Director
Mancini Duffy
2 World Trade Center, Suite 2110
New York, NY 10048
(212) 393-0389
Fax: (212) 393-0352

8712

Business Information: Serving as a Technical Director for Mancini Duffy, Mr. Kafrouni is responsible for firm wide staffing and policy mangement. Overseeing a group of 30 personnel, he deals with technical standards and management and technical supervision. He is also in charge of staffing and budgeting for the group and must ensure that all employees follow the proper technical regulations for the Company. Dedicated to the Company's successful operations, Mr. Kafrouni plans to continue working in his capacity, looking forward to the chance to expedite his promotion. Highly regarded and possessing an excellent understanding of technology, his success reflects his ability to take on challenges and deliver results. Established in 1920, Mancini Duffy specializes in providing architectural services. Working with commercial, retail, financial institutions, publishing, and facilities management corporations, the Company provides clients with interior architecture design services. Headquartered in New York, New York, the Company employs the skills and expertise of 200 personnel and reports estimated annual revenue exceeding $26 million. **Career Highlights:** Technical Director, Mancini Duffy (1998-Present); Project Manager, SNS Architects & Engineers (1986-98). **Associations & Accomplishments:** American Institute of Architects. **Education:** New Jersey Institute of Technology, M.S. in Construction Management (1985); New York Institute of Technology, Bachelor's degree in Architecture (1983). **Personal Information:** Married to Alina Perez in 1992. Mr. Kafrouni enjoys technical and design and reading trading magazines. His credo is, "Diligence is the mother of good luck."

Michael D. Medsker
Systems and Technology Development Manager
Archer Engineers
21309 South Bronson Acres Road
Peculiar, MO 64078
(913) 362-9753
Fax: (913) 362-6847

8712

Business Information: Serving as Systems and Technology Development Manager, Mr. Medsker oversees all technical operations. Utilizing advanced technical skills, he develops new technology applications, while keeping abreast of innovations in technology, to assist Archer Engineers in maintaining a competitive edge. Mr. Medsker's plans for the future include remaining with the Firm and assisting in expanding the clientele base. Founded in 1907, Archer Engineers is a firm specializing in providing civil and architectural engineering services. The Kansas based Company operates eight offices in Missouri and Kansas and employs 130 professionals. **Career Highlights:** Systems and Technology Development Manager, Archer Engineers (1994-Present); Computer Aided Engineering Development Programmer, Black & Veatch (1989-94); Air/Mixed Gas Deep Sea Diver, United States Air Force. **Associations & Accomplishments:** Institute of Electrical and Electronics Engineers - Computer Society; Historical Diving Society. **Education:** Longview College; Missouri Western State College; St. Phillips College; Platte College; College of Oceaneering. **Personal Information:** Married to Marla Two children: Michael Jr. and Micayla. Mr. Medsker enjoys aviation, computer animation and programming.

Stephen M. Palasciano
Director of Management Information Systems
Cannon
2170 Whitehaven Road
Grand Island, NY 14072-2091
(716) 774-3291
Fax: (716) 773-5909
spalasciano@cannondesign.com

8712

Business Information: Serving as Director of Management Information Systems for Cannon, Mr. Palasciano oversees and directs systems administration and operations for all offices nationwide. Before joining Cannon, Mr. Palasciano served in the role of Senior Systems Consultant with Western New York Computing Systems, and as Senior Systems Analyst for State University of New York at Buffalo's School of Medicine. He supervises and mentors a staff of four employees at each branch office. As a six year computer science expert, Mr. Palasciano determines the strategic and tactical direction, including hardware and software acquisition. Providing consultation to high level design clients also fall within the realm of his functions. He remains abreast of changes through attending seminars and extensive research. Looking toward the next millennium, Mr. Palasciano's goals include revamping the Company's ERP system, and eventually attaining the position of Chief Information Officer for Cannon. Established in 1946, Cannon is an architectural and engineering firm. Also offering project management, the Company employs a trained staff of 450 personnel to provide efficiency and quality. Headquartered in Grand Island, New York, Cannon operates nine other locations across the United States. Cannon reports estimated annual revenues in excess of $40 million. **Career Highlights:** Director of Management Information Systems, Cannon (1997-Present); Senior Systems Consultant, Western New York Computing Systems (1995-97); Senior Systems Analyst, State University of New York at Buffalo School of Medicine (1995-95). **Associations & Accomplishments:** State University of New York at Buffalo Alumni Association; State University of New York at Buffalo Engineering Alumni Association; State University of New York at Buffalo School of Management Alumni Association. **Education:** State University of New York at Buffalo: M.B.A. (1998), B.S. in Electrical and Computer Engineering (1993). **Personal Information:** Married to Maureen in 1992. One child: Allison. Mr. Palasciano enjoys playing the guitar and wine tasting.

Steven D. Papke
Architect/3D Design Specialist
PQH Architects, Inc.
4141 Southpoint Drive East, Suite 200
Jacksonville, FL 32216
(904) 296-0041

8712

Business Information: As Architect and 3D Design Specialist of PQH Architects, Inc., Mr. Papke is responsible for design of structures as well as technical aspects of network administration. Demonstrating his versatility and impressive organizational skills, Mr. Papke handles 3D design of various buildings as he strives to create a product that exceeds both customer expectations and corporate standards. A technically inclined employee, he excels in computerized photo manipulation and Web design as he continually finds inventive ways in which to carry out daily tasks. As he maintains the network, Mr. Papke oversees the data test of all software and he ensures the corporate Web site is user friendly and informative. Attributing success to a strong personal motivation to achieve, he has been recognized within his field as a leader. Enjoying the challenges of his current position, Mr. Papke intends to continue in his role as he designs quality spaces. Employing 30 professionals, PQH Architects, Inc. is the fifth largest architectural firm in Jacksonville, Florida. Desiging commercial, medical, industrial, and educational buildings, the Corporation has also created several multifamily dwellings. Annual revenues are estimated to exceed $15 million; among the critically acclaimed structures the Corporation is responsible for, they have also created a solid reputation of quality, creativity, and integrity throughout the professional industry. **Career Highlights:** PQH Architects, Inc.: Architect/3D Design Specialist (1997-Present), Intern (1993-97); Intern, The Stellar Group (1988-89). **Associations & Accomplishments:** Associate, American Institute of Architects. **Education:** University of Florida, Master's degree in Architecture (1997). **Personal Information:** Mr. Papke enjoys surfing.

J. Schumacher
Information Systems Administrator
Abbot & Abbot Architects, PLL
130 East Chestnut Street, Suite 302
Columbus, OH 43215
(614) 461-0101
Fax: (614) 461-1107
webmaster@abbot-abbot.com

8712

Business Information: Serving as Information Systems Administrator for Abbot & Abbot Architects, PLL, Mr. Schumacher combines his knowledge of architecture and technology to bring the Company to the forefront of retail architectural design. He administers the Company's information database and drafting programs, working to bring the Drafting Department to a quicker, more efficient level through the use of new technology. Mr. Schumacher designed the Company's Web page, performs and implements marketing strategies, and interacts with existing and potential clients. He is proud to have built an advanced system, even building machines from scratch, on limited funds to make the Company the leader in the industry. His success reflects his ability to think out-of-the-box and aggressively take on new challenges and responsibilities. Planning a Web development project for the purpose of coordination and sharing in the architectural industry, Mr. Schumacher intends to continue advancing professionally within Abbot & Abbot Architects. Abbot & Abbot Architects, PLL is an architectural firm specializing in retail design and roll out. The Company was founded in 1958 and employs a staff of 25 skilled personnel that design retail outlets for companies across the country. **Career Highlights:** Information Systems Administrator, Abbot & Abbot Architects, PLL (Present). **Education:** Ohio State University, B.S. in Architecture (1997). **Personal Information:** Married to Michelle in 1997. Mr. Schumacher enjoys astronomy, Habitat for Humanity and relaxation.

Gim Hong Tan
Senior Systems Engineer
SembCorp Construction
60 Admiralty Road West
Singapore, Singapore 759947
+65 8497829
gimhong@stanfordalumni.org

8712

Business Information: Entering the challenging field of technology in 1995, Mr. Tan has always remained on the cutting edge of new technology. After a year as a programmer with the Oracle Corporation, Mr. Tan joined the team of professionals at SembCorp Construction in 1995. In his current capacity of Senior Systems Engineer with SembCorp, Mr. Tan is responsible for the maintenance, functionality, and upgrade of the information technology and management information systems infrastructure. Utilizing his expertise, he is responsible for the development of e-commerce and set up of the Internet environment for his company. A recognized leader, Mr. Tan is credited with the development of Web-based employee self-service system and online procurement system. His success reflects his ability to think outside the box, deliver results, and take on challenges. Originally established in 1979 and merged in 1999, SembCorp Construction serves an international client base. An architectural and construction company, SembCorp Construction engages in all types of construction for commercial and private clients. **Career Highlights:** Senior Systems Engineer, SembCorp Construction (1996-Present); Programmer, Oracle Corporation (1995-96). **Education:** Stanford University, M.Sc. (1995); University of California at Berkeley, B.Sc. in Electrical Engineering and Computer Science. **Personal Information:** Married to Low Wei Joo in 1997. Mr. Tan enjoys jogging and badminton.

Clark F. Tucker
Director of Technology
The Haskell Company
111 Riverside Avenue, Floor 1
Jacksonville, FL 32202
(904) 791-4777
Fax: (904) 791-4693

8712

Business Information: Recruited to The Haskell Company in 1995, Mr. Tucker provides his skilled services in serving as the Director of Technology. He determines the overall technical direction and business contribution of the information systems function. A systems expert in his field, he assumes the accountability for all technological related issues from remote access, the Internet, and phones to reprographic computer graphics. Before joining The Haskell Company, Mr. Tucker assertively served as Senior Project Manager with CCG Chesapeake Consulting Group. His background history also includes a stint as Director of Information Systems for EA Engineering and Manager of Distributed Information Systems with General Instrument Corporation. Establishing goals that are compatible with those of the Company, Mr. Tucker looks forward to a future position as Vice President. He credits his current professional success to his extensive knowledge of project management and his leadership ability to build teams with synergy and technical strength, as well as aggressively take on new challenges. Boasting more than $500 million in annual earnings, The Haskell Company is engaged in the architect, engineering, and construction industry. The Company provides project and construction management, designing and building commercial structures and corresponding property landscape. **Career Highlights:** Director of Technology, The Haskell Company (1996-Present); Senior Project Manager, Chesapeake Consulting Group (1995-96); Director of Information Systems, EA Engineering (1987-95); Manager of Distributed Information Systems, General Instrument Corporation. **Associations & Accomplishments:** Association of Computing Machinery; Institute of Electronics and Electrical Engineers; SMPTE; AISM. **Education:** University of Phoenix, M.B.A. (1995); Nashville State Technical Institute, A.A. in Electrical Engineering (1974); MTSU: B.S. in Mass Communication and Technology Theatre & Broadcasting, B.S. (1972); University of Tennessee, Architectural Major (1970). **Personal Information:** Married to Mary in 1976. Two children: Robert and John. Mr. Tucker enjoys running, rollerblading, bicycling and reading.

Smith Young
Contract Professional
Superior Technology Resources
1190 East Long Place
Littleton, CO 80122
(919) 541-3805
smithyoung@ntr.net

8712

Business Information: Mr. Young is a Contract Professional of Superior Technology Resources. He is responsible software design and implementation. In his present role, he offers his technical services as an Architect and Software Engineer. Mr. Young travels from company to company primarily dealing with original equipment manufacturing companies specializing in Oracle and digital equipment. Currently, he is outsourced to Andersen Consulting developing a United States Physicians network. Mr. Young's history includes working with EPA and assisting them on a Lockheed Martin contract. This contract focused on helping Lockheed Martin analyze and design solutions to be able to operate as an enterprise entity in the private sector. Exhibiting perseverance, his strategic focus is on helping clients find solutions from simple to long-term problems. Mr. Young is in the process of establishing a start up, "think tank" company with several colleagues and create a forum exclusive to technology networking. A solid, 26 year professional, his success reflects his ability to think out-of-the-box and aggressively take on new challenges and responsibilities. Superior Technology Resources provides contract professional support for companies. **Career Highlights:** Contract Professional, Superior Technology Resources (Present); Oracle Functional Expert, Lockheed Martin (1999-Present); Chief Architect, Citicorp (1998-99); Senior Software Engineer, Migration Software System (1995-98). **Education:** University of Florida, B.S. in Business Administration (1973). **Personal Information:** Married to Rita in 1972. Two children: Joshua and Laura. Mr. Young enjoys research and simulation.

Dean E. Daffron

S.I.T. (Surveyor in Training)
Tuttle Maddux Surveying
16582 Eastchase
Montgomery, TX 77316-6704
(281) 367-2052
Fax: (281) 292-9220
daff@lcc.net

8713

Business Information: As a land and construction surveyor, Mr. Daffron began his employment with Tuttle Maddux Surveying in 1989. With 15 employees, the Company is based in the county of Montgomery and provides quality services for a large portion of southeast Texas. With years of combined service, the Company is contracted by real estate companines, home owners, and business owners. As a Surveyor in Training at Tuttle Maddux Surveying, Mr. Daffron analyzes boundary surveys. He also coordinates most of the drawings and calculations in the office. With more than 17 years of experience in the business, he utilizes his knowledge and practical experience to complete tasks with accuracy and efficiency. Mr. Daffron's goal is to continue his education and become a Licensed Land Surveyor in the future. **Career Highlights:** S.I.T. (Surveyor in Training), Tuttle Maddux Surveying (1989-Present); S.I.T. (Surveyor in Training), LandTech Consultants (1996-97); Senior Party Chief, Precision Survey Services (1983-89). **Associations & Accomplishments:** Texas Society of Professional Surveyors, State Chapter, Gulf Coast Chapter. **Education:** Southern Ohio College; Houston Community College; Montgomery College. **Personal Information:** Married. One child: Leah. Mr. Daffron enjoys land surveying, playing the guitar, listening to music, math, travel and spending time with family.

Brandon A. Schoettle

Project and Information Technology Manager
Information Transfer System
1250 North Main Street
Ann Arbor, MI 48104
(734) 994-0003
Fax: (734) 994-1228
brandon7@provide.net

8713

Business Information: Educated in the field of engineering, Mr. Schoettle currently serves as Project and Information Technology Manager. Presiding over survey research projects, he works with the Company to determine the system design, supervises the engineers during system development, and oversees its final integration in the client's network. Before joining Information Transfer System in 1995, Mr. Schoettle served as Data Processing Manager's Assistant with Market Strategies Inc. In his current capacity as Information Technology Manager, he manages the internal network of the Company, ensuring that the system is functioning properly and efficiently as well as providing technical support as needed. Establishing goals that are compatible with the Company, Mr. Schoettle plans to continue to grow with the Company and take it to the next level of information technology. Information Transfer System performs survey research, primarily for public health. A full service research facility, the Company also performs value added system development for Microsoft and Novell environments. The majority of the research is done for the military, universities, and federal, state, and county governments. Established in 1987, Information Transfer System employs a staff of more than 60 people. **Career Highlights:** Project and Information Technology Manager, Information Transfer System (1995-Present); Data Processing Managers Assistant, Market Strategies Inc, (1994-95). **Education:** University of Michigan, degree in Engineering.

Roland S. N. Wiseman

Land Surveyor/Geographic Information Systems Specialist
Lands & Surveys Division
Maitagual Street
Tunapune, Trinidad & Tobago
(868) 625-0427
rolwise@yahoo.com

8713

Business Information: A successful Land Surveyor, Mr. Wiseman also serves as a Geographic Information Systems Specialist for the Land & Surveys Division located in the West Indies. He is responsible for overseeing the digital mapping system, ensuring its functionality in order to conduct operations, such as exploration, demographics, and tracking of Trinidad and Tobago and its surrounding areas. As officer in charge of LIS langauge development that is used in conjunction with the GIS system, Mr. Wiseman promotes the technological advancement and strategic development of the Company. To remain at the forefront of the industry, he takes an active role in MCIS courses, industry specific conferences, and reading trade journals. Attributing his success to his strong faith and belief in God, Mr. Wiseman's plans to focus more on GIS aspects of the mapping industry, providing a more highly specialized product. Lands & Surveys Division provides specific production and mapping for Trinidad and Tobago. Headquartered in Trinidad, West Indies, the Company employs a work force of over 750 highly trained and skilled surveyors, professionals, and administrators who ensure the success of Lands & Surveys Division. Specializing in the creation, maintenance, and management of LIS development, the Company has established itself among the leaders in the field. **Career Highlights:** Land Surveyor/Geographic Information Systems Specialist, Lands & Surveys Division, Trinidad & Tobago (1990-Present). **Associations & Accomplishments:** Community Services Department, Tunapuna Seventh-day Adventist Church; Geographic Information System Society of Trinidad and Tobago; Institute of Surveyors of Trinidad and Tobago. **Education:** University of West Indies: M.S. in Geographic Information Systems (In Progress), B.S. (1990). **Personal Information:** Married to Marcia Castillo-Wiseman in 1991. One child: Brittany Cassandra Danielle. Mr. Wiseman enjoys tennis, badminton, soccer and community work.

Suraj Babal

Senior Associate
PricewaterhouseCoopers LLP
399 Thornall Street
Edison, NJ 08837
(732) 632-3934
Fax: (732) 906-6012
suraj.babal@us.pwcglobal.com

8721

Business Information: As Senior Associate of PricewaterhouseCoopers LLP, Mr. Babal performs information technology management consulting. Mr. Babal presides over the client projects, currently managing three teams consisting of eight skilled professionals. Coordinating between the individual teams, he oversees the project roll outs and performs systems integration. Before joining PricewaterhouseCoopers in 1997, he served as Software Consultant with Hewlett-Packard and Software Engineer for HCL Consulting. As a seven year technology professional with an established track record of delivering results, Mr. Babal attributes his success to family support and states, "Apart from education and hard work, you must be at the right place at the right time. Take calculated risks and maintain confidence in your client and yourself." He plans to expedite continued promotion through dedication and his involvement in the advancement of operations. Headquatered in Switzerland, PricewaterhouseCoopers LLP provides management consulting services to businesses in more than 155 countries world wide. The Company consults with clients, developing programs and working with the businesses from the time of conception to completion. Boasting $15 billion in annual revenue, more than 150,000 individuals are employed around the world. **Career Highlights:** Senior Associate, PricewaterhouseCoopers LLP (1997-Present); Software Consultant, Hewlett-Packard Singapore (1997); Software Engineer, HCL Consulting (1995-97). **Education:** BITS Pilani, M.S. (1994); Nagpur University, B.S. **Personal Information:** Married to Anuja in 1996. One child: Roshni. Mr. Babal enjoys golf and travel.

Daniel M. Cassat

Information Technology Consultant
RSM McGladrey, Inc.
1011 Ashford Drive
Cheyenne, WY 82007
(307) 637-2680
Fax: (307) 634-4939
dcassat@mail.com

8721

Business Information: As Information Technology Consultant of RSM McGladrey, Inc., Mr. Cassat conducts evaluations of computer network systems, noting their needs. After completing the analysis, he designs a technical plan to fulfill the requests made. Demonstrating a broad knowledge of the information technology industry, Mr. Cassat is able to fully implement the solutions he formulates, from physical installation to systems integration and maintenance. He remains current on technical issues by reading journals, surfing the Internet for pertinent information, and attending training courses. His success stems from a drive to understand technology and a desire to manipulate it to benefit society. Looking towards the future, Mr. Cassat looks foward to assisting in the geographical expansion of the Corporation. RSM McGladrey, Inc. is an international firm that offers accountancy consulting. Specializing in projects that involve small to medium-sized businesses, the Corporation is one of the 40 largest consulting firms serving American businesses. Focusing on geographical expansion and clientele growth in the next century, the Corporation looks forward to continued success within the professional community. **Career Highlights:** Information Technology Consultant, RSM McGladrey, Inc. (1993-Present); Network Administrator, Unicover Corporation (1987-93); Computer Technician, LSCD #1 (1987); Service Manager, Computer Land (1983-87). **Associations & Accomplishments:** Microsoft Certified Engineer; Citrix Administrator. **Education:** Denver Institute of Technology, Associate's degree in Electronics (1982). **Personal Information:** Two children: Vanessa and Samantha. Mr. Cassat enjoys biking, music writing and performance, sports and tennis.

Kevin W. Cornwell

Information Technology Consultant
Cotton and Allen
200 South 5th Street, Suite 201S
Louisville, KY 40202
(502) 566-1011
Fax: (502) 568-4311
kevinc@cottonandallen.com

8721

Business Information: Dedicated to the success of Cotton and Allen, Mr. Cornwell serves as an Information Technology Consultant. He visits the clients' sites, performs a needs analysis of their current systems, and provides them with cutting edge technological solutions. "Listen to the client and identify the problem," is the method he uses in his work as a consultant. Inside the accounting Firm, Mr. Cornwell performs internal MIS planning and technical support. Working with users and management to analyze, specify, and design new solutions to harness more of the computer's power also fall within the purview of Mr. Cornwell's responsibilities. Continually formulating new goals and objectives, he is looking forward to becoming more involved in the needs analysis portion of his responsibilities. Serving medium to small sized businesses, Cotton and Allen is a public accounting firm providing tax and audit services. Founded in 1920, the Company consists of 55 qualified professionals and boasts $4.5 million in yearly revenue. **Career Highlights:** Information Technology Consultant, Cotton and Allen (1997-Present); Senior Consultant/Accountant, McCaulgy, Nicolas, & Company (1990-97). **Associations & Accomplishments:** American Institute of Certified Public Accountants; Indiana Society of Certified Public Accountants; Kentucky Society of Certified Public Accountants. **Education:** Indiana University Southeast, B.A. in Business (1990). **Personal Information:** Married to Amy in 1989. Two children: Caleb and Ethan. Mr. Cornwell enjoys teaching Sunday School, home improvements and reading.

Marcus J. D'Andrea

Network Administrator
PricewaterhouseCoopers
200 East Randolph
Chicago, IL 60601
(312) 540-2714
Fax: (312) 503-0903
bsmtd@wans.net

8721

Business Information: Educated in the field of computer science, Mr. D'Andrea functions in the role of Network Administrator for PricewaterhouseCoopers. He travels extensively to client company sites, troubleshooting their networks and servers for connectivity, performance, and configuration issues. Additionally, he performs software upgrades and works on an environment team of 35 consultants. Concurrent to his present position, Mr. D'Andrea serves as an Instructor at Moraine Valley Community College. His background history also includes employment at Equity Office Properties (EOP) as a Network Administrator and as a Lucent Technical Associate with Lucent Technologies, as well as service in the United States Air Force. An expert, Mr. D'Andrea remains on the cutting edge of technology by networking on the Internet, reading trade journals, and hands-on experience. Crediting his success thus far to his education and focusing on his goals, his long-term plan for the future is to own his own consulting business. One of the top consulting Companies in the United States, PricewaterhouseCoopers offers high end information technology and network consulting services. Publicly held, the Company reports $15 billion in annual revenue. Approximately 60,000 professional consultants are employed nationwide. **Career Highlights:** Network Administrator, PricewaterhouseCoopers (1999-Present); Instructor, Moraine Valley Community College (1999-Present); Equity Network Administrator, Equity Office Properties (EOP) (1999); Lucent Technical Associate, Lucent Technologies (1998). **Associations & Accomplishments:** Microsoft Certified Systems Engineer+Internet; Microsoft Certified Systems Engineer; Certified Systems Engineer; Microsoft Certified Professional+Internet; Microsoft Certified Professional; Certified NetWare Administrator 5; CCA WF1-8; A+ Certification; Network Plus; Hewlett-Packard Certified. **Education:** Chicago State University, B.S. in Computer Science (1998); Moraine Valley Community College. **Personal Information:** Mr. D'Andrea enjoys taking certification exams.

Thomas J. Decker, III

Management Consultant
Ernst & Young LLP
326 Edgewood Avenue
Horsham, PA 19044
(215) 448-4035
decketh@aol.com

8721

Business Information: As a Management Consultant at Ernst & Young LLP, Mr. Decker efficiently fullfills the responsibilities of his position. With the Firm since 1997, he is a valuable resource to the Firm. His primary responsibility is the quality assurance of computer programs offered by the Firm. Essentially, he breaks down various programs and rebuilds them piece by piece to ensure quality for the consumer. Aside from this task, he has lent his knowledge on numerous projects including lectures on issues of the industry, creation of the fee structure and ad hoc models, and the implementation of the redesign of the Firm's knowledgable management database. With a vast knowledge of several systems, Mr. Decker is an invaluable asset to Ernst & Young. His goal is to obtain his Ph.D. in Business Administration with concentration in International Management. Ernst & Young LLP serves a national market in the field of information services and e-commerce. Established in 1894, the Firm has become a leader in the industry. Employing a growing staff of 30,000 nationally, Ernst & Young is well known for offering flexible service programs. Representatives are knowledgeable and readily available to answer all questions and offer solutions to various problems. **Career Highlights:** Management Consultant, Ernst & Young LLP (1997-Present); Independent Contractor, Longshore & Simmons (1994-97); Healthcare Consultant, The Health Care Group (1993-94). **Associations & Accomplishments:** Academy of Management; International Society of Logistics; Healthcare Financial Management Association; Nova Southeastern University Doctoral Student Association; La Salle University Alumni Healthcare Association; The Fraternity of Phi Gamma Delta. **Education:** Nova Southeastern University, School of Business and Entrepreneurship, Ph.D. in Business Administration with a concentration in International Management (In Progress); Eastern College, M.B.A. (1997); La Salle University, B.S. in Business Administration (1993).

Michael S. Evanco

Manager of eSecurity Solutions
Ernst & Young LLP
1400 Key Tower, 50 Fountain Plaza
Buffalo, NY 14202
(716) 843-5047
Fax: (716) 843-5175
michael.evanco@ey.com

8721

Business Information: As a Manager of eSecurity Solutions for Ernst & Young LLP, Mr. Evanco is responsible for e-commerce and information security consulting. He assists clients with using information technology for competitive business advantage and utilizes that opportunity to demonstrate the opportunities available on the World Wide Web. Recognized for his research projects and extensive knowledge in several areas, Mr. Evanco has been invited to speak at several local and national conventions and seminars. He hopes to expand the Firm's use of e-commerce in the future and also open the door to e-procurement with extended goals of lowering the price of purchasing M.R.O. supplies. Mr. Evanco's success reflects his ability to design innovations by thinking outside the box, produce leading edge results, and tackle new challenges. Ernst & Young LLP provides professional services in consulting, tax, and audit. Ernst & Young is a connected consulting firm that transforms mature companies and start-up .coms into companies, creating strategies, systems, and product and service bundles that integrate the Internet and advanced technologies. Hosting over 85,000 employees, the Firm turns over $10.3 billion annually through its assistance on the national and international arenas. **Career Highlights:** Manager of eSecurity Solutions, Ernst & Young LLP (1996-Present); Director of Technology, WNY Technology Development Center (1993-96); Enterprise Consultant, CTG (1991-93); Team Manager, Marine Midland Bank (1986-91). **Associations & Accomplishments:** American Production and Inventory Control Society; Christ the King Technology Committee. **Education:** State University of New York at Buffalo: M.B.A. (1986), B.A. in Statistics (1979). **Personal Information:** Married to Noreen in 1985. Two children: Maura and Karalyn.

Peter C. H. Guo

Manager, Global Risk Management Solutions
PricewaterhouseCoopers LLP
Suite 1700, 601 West Hastings Street
Vancouver, British Columbia, Canada V6B 5A5
(604) 806-7649
Fax: (604) 806-7667
peter.guo@ca.pwcglobal.com

8721

Business Information: As an experienced professional, Mr. Guo provides exceptional services in information systems risk management, security, and controls, including integrating risk-mitigating solutions into each enterprise's strategy and operations. He consults on numerous platforms and applications, including UNIX, NT, AS/400, SAP, JD Edwards, Oracle, and numerous industry-specific systems. Mr. Guo also has expertise in business process controls (particularly order fulfillment, logistics, and inventory management) project management, systems development, quality assurance over programming changes and information technology due diligence. Mr. Guo has led and implemented several projects in the above areas for numerous clients, including multinationals operating in the high technology, pharmaceutical, biotechnology, financial services, and forestry industries. Leveraging his undergraduate background in life sciences and his extensive professional experience, Mr. Guo maintains a focus on the high technology and pharmaceutical industries, particularly in the application and control of e-commerce solutions. Drawing on the expertise, knowledge and technology of the globe's largest professional services firm, PricewaterhouseCoopers LLP, Mr. Guo is able to focus world-class resources to assist clients in achieving critical results and turn risks into opportunities. **Career Highlights:** Manager, Global Risk Management Solutions, PricewaterhouseCoopers LLP (1997-Present); Senior Staff Accountant, Ernst & Young (1994-97); President & CEO, Students' Administrative Council (1991-92). **Associations & Accomplishments:** Canadian Institute of Chartered Accountants; Institute of Chartered Accountants of Ontario; Institute of Chartered Accountants of British Columbia; Information Security, Audit and Control Association; Canadian Information Processing Society; Federation of Chinese Canadian Professionals. **Education:** University of Toronto, M.B.A. (1995), B.Sc. (1992); Chartered Accountant; Certified Information Systems Auditor. **Personal Information:** Married One child. Mr. Guo enjoys variety of sports, reading, music and fine dining. Mr. Guo is involved in professional and personal education and development.

Ivan B. Hardaway

Manager of Technology Operations
Ernst & Young Technologies, Inc.
14100 Park Meadow Drive
Chantilly, VA 20151
(703) 814-8178
Fax: (703) 814-7690
ivan.hardaway@ey.com

8721

Business Information: As Manager of Technology Operations with Ernst & Young Technologies, Inc., Mr. Hardaway manages all technical operations including voice and data technology allocated for internal and external support. With over 20 years of experience in the technology field, Mr. Hardaway is capable of managing the operations of his department. He provides professional support for Fortune 500 companies and networks with executives and other top management. Attention to detail, building relationships, and teamwork are all characterisitic attributed to his professional success. Mr. Hardway believes that strong work ethics are necessary in the technological field. Established in 1994, Ernst & Young Technologies, Inc. presently reports annual revenues in excess of $200 million. **Career Highlights:** Manager of Technology Operations, Ernst & Young Technologies, Inc. (1997-Present); Technology Manager, Price Waterhouse (1995-97); Computer Programmer/Analyst, United States Navy (1976-89). **Education:** Strayer University, B.S. in Computer Information Systems (1998). **Personal Information:** Married to Carolyn.

Byron T. Hawkins

Information Security Consultant
Ernst & Young
701 Market Street, Suite 1400
St. Louis, MO 63101
(314) 259-1097
Fax: (314) 259-1613
hawkinsby@ey.com

8721

Business Information: As a Information Security Consultant of Ernst & Young, Mr. Hawkins is responsible for many technical duties on behalf of the Firm. Recruited to the Firm's team of professionals as staff consultant in 1997, he is in charge of technical architectural design and implementation of cutting edge firewall technology to support emerging e-commerce initiatives. Overseeing information system audits and Internet security, Mr. Hawkins provides superior technical support to the Firm's clients. His focus is on implementation of internal solutions that will allow the clients to stay ahead of competitors and remain flexible, efficient, and profitable. Mr. Hawkins continues his growth with Ernst & Young and looks to extend security initiatives to online and public applications. For over 70 years, Ernst & Young has been providing tax and auditing consulting services worldwide. Professional services specialize in providing business solutions. One of the "Big 5," Ernst & Young provides information systems assurance and security, along with e-commerce assurance and security, and information systems. The Firm also provide solutions to a variety of complex issues, helping clients become more flexible, productive, efficient, and profitabl e. **Career Highlights:** Ernst & Young: Information Security Consultant (1998-Present), Staff Consultant (1997-98). **Associations & Accomplishments:** Microsoft Certified Professionals; Microsoft Certified Systems Engineer. **Education:** St. Louis University, B.S. in Business Administration (1997).

Cathryn A. Hennes

Programmer Analyst
Intellinex, an Learning Venture of E&Y
1300 Huntington Building, 925 Euclid Avenue
Cleveland, OH 44115
(216) 737-1144
Fax: (216) 583-1122
cathryn.valliere@ey.com

8721

Business Information: Serving as Programmer Analyst, Mrs. Hennes develops Lotus Notes/Domino applications and assists other with Lotus Notes for Intellinex, an eLearning Venture of E&Y. She sets up and maintains database programming, system administration, and specialized training in Lotus Notes. Mrs. Hennes designs, develops, builds, and completes Lotus Notes projects, and works closely with E&Y clients with consulting issues. Becoming more involved in database development and Domino web programming serves as her long-range plans. Mrs. Hennes' favorite quote is, "Don't let anyone tell you there is only one way to do things, as there is always a different way you can do it." **Career Highlights:** Programmer Analyst, Intellinex, an Learning Venture of E&Y (Present). **Associations & Accomplishments:** Lifetime Member, International Society of Poets. **Education:** Burlington County College, A.A. (1993); Certified Lotus Specialist (CLS) Lotus Notes Release 4 in Application Developmet; Certified Lotus End-User Instructor (CLEI) Lotus Notes Release 4 and 5. **Personal Information:** Married to Robert in 1997. One child: Cassiopeia. Mrs. Hennes enjoys poetry, music and crafts. She also enjoys spending time and playing with her new daughter. Mrs. Hennes enjoys computers, and her home computer, scanner, and digital camera.

Nicholas A. Horton

Systems Engineer/Software Engineer
Hertzbach & Company
10 Music Fair Road
Owings Mills, MD 21117
(410) 363-3200
Fax: (410) 363-9295
ny_mail@zdnetonebox.com

8721

Business Information: As Systems Engineer and Software Engineer of Hertzbach & Company, Mr. Horton orchestrates Web site design and applications conversions. Exhibiting an exceptional command of computer technology, he researches programs and monitors networking activities. He provides instruction in Office 2000 and teaches classes in Windows operation for clients as well as personnel. Mr. Horton explores opportunities for new business development and consistently maintains the internal network. In the future, he would like to further enhance his professional credentials and eventually join the FBI as a Tax Fraud Investigator. Success, according to Mr. Horton, is attributed to his mentor and his ability to taking time step to away and think about the best decision. Hertzbach & Company is a management consulting and accounting firm. The Company assists business owners and their management teams in enhancing efficiency, profitability, cash flow, and overall financial stability. Drawing upon the professional talents of 75 representatives, Hertzbach & Company enables clients to better understand the critical tax issues which effect business operations. The Company provides customized services for several industries including construction, law, automobile, and information technology. **Career Highlights:** Hertzback & Company: Systems Engineer/Software Engineer (1998-Present), Accountant (1998-Present); Surf Rescue Technician, Ocean City Beach Patrol (1996). **Associations & Accomplishments:** Martial Arts Instructor; Camp Counselor, Cerebral Palsy Children and Adults; Towson University Alumni Association. **Education:** Towson University, B.S. in Accounting (1998); Microsoft Certified Professional; Microsoft Certified Systems Engineer+Internet; Windows 2000; Web Development;

CompuMaster. **Personal Information:** Mr. Horton enjoys computers, martial arts and movies.

Wong Mee Hunt

• • • ◀━━◉━━▶ • • •

Information Technology Consultant
PricewaterhouseCoopers
448, Taman Asean
Melaka, Malaysia 75250
+60 193173248
wmhunt@pc-jaring.my

8721

Business Information: As Information Technology Consultant for PricewaterhouseCoopers, Mrs. Hunt works on project management and implementation, primarily in the utilities, manufacturing, and human resources industries. Throughout her daily routine, she coordinates with management, users, and software engineers, providing detailed technical and analytical advice for design and development of major applications. Beginning her association with the Firm three years ago, Mrs. Hunt has worked diligently to develop her skills and acquire expertise in her field. Always alert to new opportunities, techniques, and approaches, she plans to become more involved in project management for multinational companies. Her success reflects her ability to think out-of-the-box, take on challenges, and deliver results on behalf of the Firm and its clientele. A global firm, PricewaterhouseCoopers specializes in a professional advisory services. One of the largest financial and information technology advisory companies, the Firm offers six major lines of services, to include auditing, assurance, business and financial advisory services, and management consulting. Established in 1850, the Firm is headquartered in Rosemont, Illinois. Presently, the Firm employs a staff of more than 150,000 professionals in 150 countries. **Career Highlights:** Information Technology Consultant, PricewaterhouseCoopers (1997-Present); Consultant, Magnus Consulting Sdn. Bhd. (1997); Systems Analyst, Malaysia Airlines (1990). **Associations & Accomplishments:** Yayasan Salam; Crest-Crisis Relief Services and Training; International Christian Ministries; SAP Certified Consultant; Former Volunteer (1998), Common Wealth Games Malaysia. **Education:** University of Malaya, B.A. in Economics (1989); Diploma of Computer Science (1990). **Personal Information:** Married. Mrs. Hunt enjoys outdoor activities, arts and crafts and cooking.

James Lam
Senior Manager
Ernst & Young LLP
P.O. Box 118
Mendham, NJ 07945
(212) 773-2037
lamj@acm.org

8721

Business Information: Mr. Lam functions as the Senior Manager of Ernst & Young LLP's office in Mendham, New Jersey. He is responsible for maintaining and implementing emerging technology for the New York Advanced Development Center. Before coming on board to Ernst & Young in 1995, Mr. Lam served as Manager for Coopers & Lybrand. His solid consultant background history also includes a stint as Associate with J.P. Morgan. An 18 year professional in his field, he plays a major role as senior manager and field consultant. He travels extensively to client sites to help in the software design, development, and deployment process. Working with a team of three to twelve people, Mr. Lam assists in determining the overall technical direction and vision. He credits his career success to his ability to work well with other people. An accomplished expert, he received recognition for developing a middleware solution for IBM. Moving up the corporate hierarchy within the Firm, remaining in the middleware and financial side of technology, and eventually attaining Partner status with the Firm serves as Mr. Lam's future endeavors. Ernst & Young LLP engages as a global management consulting firm. As the second largest consultant in the world, the Firm specialties include financial, accounting, and information technology. Established in the 1940s, the Firm operates a network of over 250 offices around the globe. Manned by more than 10,000 individuals, Ernst & Young reports estimated revenues in excess of $2 billion annually. **Career Highlights:** Senior Manager, Ernst & Young LLP (1996-Present); Manager, Coopers & Lybrand (1994-95); Associate, J.P. Morgan (1984-94). **Associations & Accomplishments:** Association for Computing Machinery; USENIX; Object Developers Group. **Education:** Rider University, B.S. (1981). **Personal Information:** Married to Elise.

Stephen T. Lyle
Consultant
PricewaterhouseCoopers
12902 Federal Systems Park Drive
Fairfax, VA 22033
(703) 322-5552
Fax: (703) 322-7552
stephen.lyle@uspwcglobal.com

8721

Business Information: Serving as a Consultant for PricewaterhouseCoopers, Mr. Lyle focuses on developing information systems in educational realm. In his capacity, he conducts reviews of existing technology and education practices and recommends improvements to these systems. Highly regarded, he possesses an excellent understanding of technology and the ability to communcated effectively. Mr. Lyle notes his greatest accomplishment as working with schools and providing them with a chance to work with a professional in the area who deeply cares about the education of their youth. Keeping on the cutting edge of technology through the use of journals and conferences, Mr. Lyle attributes his success to his networking ability. PricewaterhouseCoopers provides consulting services in a variety of areas. Consulting services include technology, business practices, and strategic change, focusing on the public education industry. Established in 1988, the Firm employs more than 150,000 employees globally. **Career Highlights:** Consultant, PricewaterhouseCoopers (1998-Present); Systems Administrator/Office Manager, United States Senate (1997-98); Technology Specialist, Falls Church Public Schools (1996-97). **Education:** University of Virginia: M.Ed., B.A. (1994); Carnegie Mellon University, Undergraduate Studies in Engineering (1988-90). **Personal Information:** Mr. Lyle enjoys mountain biking, piano, trumpet, skiing and camping.

José R. Marín
Manager
PricewaterhouseCoopers LLP
254 Munoz Rivera Avenue, BBV Tower, Suite 900
San Juan, Puerto Rico 00918
(787) 772-7942
Fax: (787) 766-1094
jose.r.marin@us.pwcglobal.com

8721

Business Information: Serving as a Manager for PricewaterhouseCoopers LLP, Mr. Marín fulfills a number of consulting duties on behalf of the Firm and its clientele. Demonstrating strong technology skills, he is responsible for operational systems and risk management on a day to day basis. In this capacity, he provides leading edge consulting services in information systems security, ensuring that clients are offered the best available systems in order to guarantee smooth operations. In the future, Mr. Marín would like to obtain a position as a Partner with one of the "Big 5" accounting firms. His success reflects his ability to think out-of-the-box, take on challenges and new responsibilities, and deliver the desired results. Established in 1925, PricewaterhouseCoopers LLP is an international accounting firm. One of the largest accounting firms in the world, the Firm is a part of the "Big 5." Headquartered in New York, New York, the Firm also provides consulting services and reports estimated annual revenue exceeding $28 million. Local operations in San Juan, Puerto Rico employ the skills and expertise of 175 personnel. **Career Highlights:** Manager, PricewaterhouseCoopers LLP (1999-Present); Experienced Senior, Arthur Andersen, LLP (1998-99); Senior Associate, Coopers & Lybrand, LLP (1996-98); Financial Analyst, Bristol-Myers - S Qui BB (1994). **Associations & Accomplishments:** Puerto Rico Industrial Development Company; Information Systems Audit and Control Association; Technology Consultant, State Society of CPAs; National Society of Hispanic MBAs. **Education:** University of Wisconsin, Master's degree in Accounting (1996); University of Puerto Rico, B.B.A. in Accounting. **Personal Information:** One child: Genesis A. Mr. Marín enjoys sports and reading.

Shyamkumar Narayana
Senior Associate II
Ernst & Young Application Services LLC.
22700 Lake Forest Drive, Apartment 535
Lake Forest, CA 92630
(949) 260-7353
nshyamk@gte.net

8721

Business Information: Possessing superior talents in the information technology field, Mr. Narayana serves as Senior Associate II with Ernst & Young Application Services LLC. Fulfilling the position of team lead, he works closely with systems management and users to analyze, specify, design, and deploy advanced technology to keep the Firm and its client base flexible, efficient, and profitable in the global market place. A successful 14-year veteran, Mr. Narayana determines the strategic direction and business contribution of the information system functions. He is also responsible for aspects of systems analysis, design, evaluation, testing, and implementation of software and computer related systems as well as generating status reports. Recognized for his professionalism, Mr. Narayana received the "Excellence Award". He anticipates his promotion to project manager as a result of his continuing efforts to increase his skills through training and professional development activities. Ernst & Young Application Services LLC. specializes in consulting and software services. The Firm was established in 1999 and has offices in Chicago, Illinois and Irvine, California as well as other cities in the United States. Employing a skilled staff of professionals to acquire business, meet with clients, facilitate projects, and market services, the Firm continues to provide cutting-edge technical services on behalf of its clientele. **Career Highlights:** Senior Associate II, Ernst & Young Application Services LLC (1999-Present); Project Lead/Senior Software Consultant, HCL Technologies India Pvt. Ltd./HCL Technologies America, Inc. (1996-99); Systems Manager, WIPRO Systems (1995-96); Systems Analyst, Sonata Software Limited (1992-95). **Associations & Accomplishments:** Project Management Institute, membership #146764; International Executive Guild, membership #1253166; United States Tennis Association, Inc., membership # 919505828. **Education:** California State University, U.S.A., M.B.A. (In Progress); Kerala University, India, B.Sc. in Physics (1985); DTE Maharashtra, India, Advanced Diploma in Computer Software, Systems Analysis, and Application. **Personal Information:** Married to Krishna Shyamkumar in 1999. Mr. Narayana enjoys sports, tennis, reading and listening to music.

Floyd Parks

• • • ◀━━◉━━▶ • • •

Partner
PricewaterhouseCoopers
333 Market Street, Suite 1700
San Francisco, CA 94105-2118
(415) 281-5197

8721

Business Information: Mr. Parks functions in the capacity of Partner with PricewaterhouseCoopers. Working out of the Firm's office in San Francisco, California, he manages the information technology strategy practice for the West region. Before joining PricewaterhouseCoopers in 1999, Mr. Parks served as Manager of Information Technology Systems for Coopers & CT Brand. His extensive background also includes a stint as Manager for Deloitte Haskins & Sells. Currently, he assists clients in designing and implementing cutting edge computer networks within their offices and provides them with the accessibility to the Internet and cross-continent networking. In the future, Mr. Parks hopes to work in technology strategizing work in its "real-time" phases instead of its planning stages. PricewaterhouseCoopers specializes in professional services such as management consulting, systems integration, process management, audit and tax services, and human resources consulting. With multiple subsidiaries around the world, the Firm is regarded as the largest professional service in the world. The Firm features an integrated staff of 155,000 employees carefully networked to provide the most optimum level of service to its clients. Altogether, the Firm turns over $15 billion annually. **Career Highlights:** Partner, PricewaterhouseCoopers (1999-Present); Manager of Information Technology Systems, Coopers & CT Brand (1988-99); Manager, Deloitte Haskins & Sells (1987-88). **Associations & Accomplishments:** Association of M.B.A. Executives; American MENSA Ltd. **Education:** University of Utah, M.B.A. (1982); University of Southern Colorado: B.S. in Business Administration (1978), A.A.S. (1976). **Personal Information:** Married to Melanie in 1979. Two children: William and Molly. Mr. Parks enjoys Cub Scouts and the local swim club.

Abhijit B. Patil

• • • ◀━━◉━━▶ • • •

Senior Associate
PricewaterhouseCoopers
144 Middlesex Turnpike
Burlington, MA 01854
(781) 359-5446
p_abhijit@hotmail.com

8721

Business Information: Demonstrating expertise in the technology field, Mr. Patil currently serves as Senior Associate with PricewaterhouseCoopers. In this capacity, he acts as a consultant to various companies, performing needs analysis and developing system solutions. Mr. Patil presides over project management and directly supervises 5 to 6 employees at a time. He develops and configures network systems, administering its programming and specification development. Before joining PricewaterhouseCoopers, he served as a Programmer for both Teleon and Anz Bank. Mr. Patil owes his success to his family who worked hard and sacrificed everything to give him a solid education. A tribute goes to his father, Mr. Bahaskar Patil. Consistently achieving quality performance in his field, Mr. Patil looks forward to moving into higher management and anticipates an eventual position as a Partner. His career success reflects his ability to think out-of-the-box and take on new challenges. Serving an international clientele, PricewaterhouseCoopers is the largest consulting firm in the world. The Data Warehousing Division offers consulting services, outsourcing services, project management, and Web development and hosting. Additionally, the Division builds databases and performs system integration and analysis. Presently, more than 250 professional and technical experts man the Data Warehousing Division. **Career Highlights:** PricewaterhouseCoopers: Senior Associate (1996-Present), Associate (1996); Programmer, Teleon (1994-96); Programmer, Anz Bank. **Associations & Accomplishments:** Institute of Electrical and Electronics Engineers. **Education:** University of New Hampshire: Ph.D. (In Progress), M.B.A. (1995), M.S. (1995), B.S. in Engineering. **Personal Information:** Mr. Patil enjoys shopping, travel, squash and racquetball.

Kyle B. Plummer

Network Administrator
Norman Jones Enlow Company
1418 Brice Road
Reynoldsburg, OH 43068
(614) 864-3134
Fax: (614) 864-8117
kplummer@nje.com

8721

Business Information: Dedicated to the success of Norman Jones Enlow Company, Mr. Plummer applies his knowledge and expertise in the field of information technology in serving as Network Administrator. He assumes responsibility for all of the Company's computer equipment including the PCs, servers, routers, and software, as well as the LAN/WAN, Web site, and other Internet issues. Additionally, Mr. Plummer performs industry research in an effort to provide the Company with the latest accounting programs and provides technical support and training to users. He is continually striving for maximum effectiveness and is currently pursuing his M.C.S.E., C.P.A., and Master's degree in Business Administration to enable him to capitalize on the opportunities presented by the Company. Norman Jones Enlow Company is a Certified Public Accountant firm providing a wide range of accounting services to companies and individuals in the state of Ohio. Founded in 1954, the Company has four locations statewide. Over 50 administrative, accounting, and support personnel are employed. Annual earnings are estimated to be upwards of $4 million. **Career Highlights:** Network Administrator, Norman Jones Enlow Company (1996-Present). **Associations & Accomplishments:** Golden Key National Honor Society. **Education:** Ohio University, B.B.A. (1996); Palomar College at San Marcos, A.A. **Personal Information:** Married to Paula in 1996. Mr. Plummer enjoys family activities, scale models and computer training.

Stephanie A. Pritchett

Director of Business Alliances
Ernst & Young LLP
14100 Park Meadow Drive, Suite 100
Chantilly, VA 20151
(703) 841-8475
stephanie.pritchett@ey.com

8721

Business Information: Functioning in the role of Director of Business Alliances for Ernst & Young LLP, Ms. Pritchett is responsible for developing joint ventures and strategic alliances to keep the Firm on the cutting edge of the technology industry. Before coming on board to Ernst & Young, Ms. Pritchett served as Regional Account Manager for PricewaterhouseCoopers. Her background history also includes a stint as Federal Business Development Manager at Epach. In her position with Ernst & Young, she guides and conducts all alliance contracts to ensure the interests of the Corporation are met. Utilizing 11 years of experience, Ms. Pritchett conducts conferences with top executives of each department to guarantee a profitable margin. Her long term goals include continuing to move up the corporate ladder at Ernest & Young LLP. Key to success has been attributed to her determination and ability to deliver results and aggressively take on new challenges. Ernst & Young provides information technology consulting for global Fortune 500 companies, as well as small to medium-sized businesses. The Firm is ranked 12th in Forbes' Fortune 500 and 173rd in Hoover's 500. It is the fourth-largest of the Big Five accounting firms. As a division of Ernst & Young, Ernst & Young LLP focuses on accounting services including tax and consultations. The Firm has published several guides for running business in different markets and industries, offering tips for planning strategies and tax savings. **Career Highlights:** Director of Business Alliances, Ernst & Young (1998-Present); Regional Account Manager, PricewaterhouseCoopers (1995-98); Federal Business Development Manager, Epach.

Steven E. Robichaud

National Government Information Technology Consulting Coordinator
RSM McGladrey, Inc.
303 East Vanderbuilt Way, #200
San Bernardino, CA 92408
(909) 386-1720
Fax: (909) 386-7009

8721

Business Information: Mr. Robichaud functions in the role of National Government Information Technology Consulting Coordinator for RSM McGladrey, Inc responsible for sales and project delivery. He coordinates national consulting services for the technologically related needs of area government offices. A savvy, 19 year professional, Mr. Robichaud ensures the effective operation of every individually designed system, working with the client to understand their needs and utilize them in designing the new network. In the future, he plans to expand his involvement in e-business and increase his information technology planning clientele. Attributing his career success to a position attitude and a thirst to learn, Mr. Robichaud's advice is "get into something that you want to do and you will be successful." RSM McGladrey, Inc. provides information technology consulting, specializing in serving the needs of government offices within the United States. The Corporation also offers some tax consulting advice for other businesses in the area. Hosting a staff of 400 employees, the Corporation turns over $50 million annually. **Career Highlights:** National Government Information Technology Consulting Coordinator, RSM McGladrey, Inc. (1990-Present); Executive Sales Manager, Unisys Corporation (1980-90); Account Manager, Sun Gard Recovery Services, Inc. (1990-95). **Associations & Accomplishments:** Associate Member, National League of Cities; Associate Member, National Association of Counties; Associate Member, National Government Finance Officer's Association. **Education:** Moorhead State University, B.A. (1980); Certified Business Continuity Planner. **Personal Information:** Married to Sara. Two children: Paul and Alison. Mr. Robichaud enjoys adult hockey and long distance running.

Nancy L. Scott, M.B.A.

Manager
Ernst & Young LLP
233 South Wacker Drive
Chicago, IL 60606-6306
(312) 879-2135
Fax: (312) 879-6864
niscott@aol.com

8721

Business Information: Displaying extensive expertise in technology and consulting, Ms. Scott serves as a Manager for Ernst & Young LLP. In her role, she leads or co-leads project development teams. It is her responsibility to introduce new systems and procedures to clients in her contact with them. Ms. Scott, owning a consistent record of delivering results, serves as a vital representative of the Firm and usually works only on top, high visibility projects and important accounts. She provides suggestions for system selection and implementation and offers step-by-step assistance in the deployment of advanced technologies. Ms. Scott bases her success on the concern she has for each individual client and enjoys the challenge that technology offers. In the future, Ms. Scott plans to stay with Ernst & Young LLP and would like to continue working on top projects and with leading edge software packages. Established in the early 1900s, Ernst & Young LLP is set apart as a pioneer in the consulting field. Based in New York, the Firm has over 60,000 professionals in its various practices. Ernst & Young LLP's health practice serves the healthcare technology industry with over 1,500 professionals employed nation wide. The Firm specializes in the training and instruction of healthcare employees in systems designed to enhance and improve record-keeping procedures. The Firm conducts evaluations of information systems and makes recommendations on new systems that will benefit clients. **Career Highlights:** Ernst & Young LLP: Manager (1999-Present), Senior Consultant (1996-99); Enterprise Systems, Inc. (ESi): Financial Products Manager (1995-96), Implementation Project Manager (1994-95), Implementation Specialist (1993-94). **Associations & Accomplishments:** Director At Large, University of Chicago Women's Business Group; Associate, American College of Healthcare Executives; HIMSS; Chicago Health Executives Forum. **Education:** University of Chicago, M.B.A. with Honors (1991); University of Illinois, B.S. (1983). **Personal Information:** Ms. Scott enjoys opportunities technology presents her.

Paul Sehmbey

Manager
Ernst & Young
1959 Upper Water Street, Suite 1301
Halifax, Nova Scotia, Canada B3J 2Z1
(902) 421-6251
Fax: (902) 420-1080
ab255@chebucto.ns.ca

8721

Business Information: Utilizing over 13 years experience in the information technology field, Mr. Sehmbey currently serves as Manager of Ernst & Young. He plans and oversees the development and support of e-businesss technologies. Recruited to Ernst & Young in 1998, Mr. Sehmbey is responsible for determining e-business and data warehousing strategies, evaluating cutting edge software, and designing data and technical architecture. A methodology expert, he is the lead in providing knowledge management consulting as well as conducting cutting edge research, design, and delivery of turnkey projects for the Firm's clientele. Coordinating resources, time lines, schedules, assignments, and budgets also fall within the purview of Mr. Sehmbey's functions. Showcasing his ability to think out-of-the-box, take on challenges, and deliver results, he received an information technology systems professional designation. Leading larger teams, 10 to 20 people, in larger e-commerce projects is cited as Mr. Sehmbey's future endeavors. Ernst & Young is a "Big Five" public accounting firm specializing in providing accounting services, tax preparation and planning, and management e-business consulting services to clients throughout the world. Established in 1864, the Firm employs an international staff of 45,000 professional, technical, and support personnel. The Halifax, Nova Scotia site is currently manned by a 35-member staff. **Career Highlights:** Manager, Ernst & Young (1998-Present); Senior Consultant, Keane Canada Inc. (1997-98); Senior Consultant, Andersen Consulting (1992-98). **Associations & Accomplishments:** Canadian Information Processing Society; Canadian Association of Management Consultants. **Education:** Dalhousie University: B.Sc. in Computer Science (1991), Diploma in Engineering (1987). **Personal Information:** Married to Wendy in 1993. Two children: Dhillon and Wendy. Mr. Sehmbey enjoys playing with his two children.

Andrew V. Shields

Knowledge Transfer Manager
PricewaterhouseCoopers
30 South 17th Street, 18th floor
Philadelphia, PA 19103
(215) 523-6551
Fax: (610) 429-5992
andrewvshields@netscape.net

8721

Business Information: As Knowledge Transfer Manager of the Philedelphia, Pennsylvannia location of PricewaterhouseCoopers, Mr. Shields develops and implements internal technical training. Demonstrating decisive leadership abilities as he works closely with his team of technical writers, he incorporates feedback and input to foster a sense of empowerment among the staff. Mr. Shields has an extensive knowledge of the technical industry, gained through practical work experience and education and coupled with innate abilities. Continually formulating applicable instruction programs for computer and Web based training, he is credited with smooth implementation of educational procedures used by the Firm to ensure the entire staff is techncially inclined. Realizing his success stems from his ability to be a versatile employee, Mr. Shields believes self-motivation is essential for achievements in any career. Enjoying the challenges of his current position, he looks forward to helping the Firm become more involved in distance learning courses for the busy professional. PricewaterhouseCoopers is recognized as one of the top five consulting firms in the world, with more than 150,000 global employees. Offering services ranging from accounting to tax consulting, the Firm provides technical training for employees and clients. **Career Highlights:** Knowledge Transfer Manager, PricewaterhouseCoopers (1997-Present); Creative Director, Spree.com (1997); Instructional Designer, Provident Mutual (1995-97). **Associations & Accomplishments:** American Society for Training and Development. **Education:** Pennsylvania State University, Advertising and Business degree (1991); Master Trainer Institute, Master Trainer Certificate. **Personal Information:** Mr. Shields enjoys creative writing and painting.

Gary M. Stine

Information Technology Director
Payroll Systems.com
39 Argonaut Street, Suite 200B
Aliso Viejo, CA 92656
(949) 206-0411
Fax: (949) 206-9175
gstine@payrollsystems.com

8721

Business Information: Serving as Information Technology Director for Payroll Systems.com, Mr. Stine oversees and manages all daily management of the systems infrastructure. He determines the overall strategic direction and business contributions of the information systems functions. Possessing an excellent understanding of technolgy, Mr. Stine's primary duties include software alterations, searching and identifying new software applications new enhance the overall operations, recruiting new staff members, and negotiating contracts. Drawing from three years of experience, Mr. Stine manages the LAN/WAN and Internet related computer networks as well as ensures that all computers are used to generate meaningful information. His plans for his career include becoming more involved in programming, while also focusing of Web sites and software consulting. Payroll Sytems.com engages in the coordination and regulation of employee payrolls for an array of client companies. The Company offers a broad spectrum of services for their clients including tax preparation and tax auditing for companies who do not need payroll services. Established in 1997, the Company utilizes two divisions for operations, while functioning under the direction and talents of more than 75 highly skilled professionals. **Career Highlights:** Information Technology Director, Payroll Systems.com (1999-Present); Management Information Systems Manager, Southland Payroll Services (1998-99); Associate Systems Engineer, Electronic Data Systems (1997-98); Partner, The Inquisitor (1994-97). **Associations & Accomplishments:** Epsilon Delta Pi; Honor Society for the Computer Sciences. **Education:** DeVry University, Bachelor's degree (1997). **Personal Information:** One child: Gavin.

Dimitri Trikoz

Senior Auditor
Ernst & Young Audit
13 Rue Dulong
Paris, France 75017
+33 146936578
Fax: +33 149015420
dimitri_trikoz@ernst-young.fr

8721

Business Information: Mr. Trikoz functions in the capacity of Senior Auditor for Ernst & Young Audit. He is responsible for analyzing the systems function to determine adequate security and controls, mostly for the banking sector. Before joining Ernst & Young Audit in 1998, Mr. Trikoz faithfully served as Head of Information Technology Department with Credit Lyonnais Ukraine. Drawing from his extensive academic background and occupational experience, he travels around Europe to evaluate the security for his clients' systems infrastructures to ensure the continual security, reliability, and efficiency of systems. Evaluating systems and operational procedures and reporting findings to senior management also falls within the purview of his responsibilities. Looking to the next millennium, Mr. Trikoz plans on directing his efforts in learning more about e-Commerce. His success reflects his ability to deliver results and aggressively take on new challenges. The Department of Information Systems Assurance and Advisory Services of Ernst & Young Audit, in which Mr. Trikoz works, specializing in the auditing of information systems. This activity includes reviews of the information technology systems and the supporting procedures of different businesses in order to ensure their availability as well as the confidentiality and integrity of the information stored and processed. **Career Highlights:** Senior Auditor, Ernst & Young Audit (1998-Present); Head of the Information Technology Department, Credit Lyonnais Ukraine (1993-97). **Education:** Ecole Nationale des Ponts et Chaussees, M.B.A. (1999); Kiev Polytechnic Institute, System Engineer (1993). **Personal Information:** Mr. Trikoz enjoys horseback riding, travel and reading.

Scott D. Williams

Director of Technology
Dixon Odom PLLC
1829 Eastchester Drive
High Point, NC 27265
(336) 889-5156
Fax: (336) 889-2812
swilliams@disonodom.com

8721

Business Information: Functioning in the capacity of Director of Technology at Dixon Odom PLLC, Mr. Williams works with users to determine the overall strategic direction and business contribution of the information systems function. He manages the Technology Group and guides his seven member staff in supporting 300 plus users and managing the technology budget. As a solid, five year technology professional, Mr. Williams has served with Dixon Odom in a variety of positions since joining the Firm as Network Administrator in 1995. In his present role, he maintains all computer systems and LAN and WAN networks fully functional and operational at all times. Hardware and software acquisition, coordinating resources and schedules, and overseeing time lines and assignments also fall within the realm of his responsibilities. An expert with an established track record of producing results, Mr. Williams is a member of the the Firm's Technical Advisory Committee. Eventually attaining the position of Chief Information Officer and becoming a Partner in the Firm serves as his future goals. A member of Moores Rowland International, Dixon Odom PLLC is ranked as the second largest accounting and consulting firm and among the nation's top 35. Services offered include: accounting, auditing, tax, and consulting. Headquartered in High Point, North Carolina, the Firm operates a network of 11 offices to serve clients nationally and internationally. Established in 1959, Dixon Odom employs a staff of more than 300 professionals. **Career Highlights:** Dixon Odom PLLC: Director of Technology (1999-Present), Network Systems Supervisor (1998-99), Network Administrator (1995-98); R&D Technician, MCS Dracon Division (1994-95). **Associations & Accomplishments:** CPA/Manager of Information Systems; Information Technology Alliance. **Education:** High Point University, B.S. in Accounting (1995); Guillford Technical Community College, A.S. in Electrical Engineering. **Personal Information:** Married to Annette in 1991. Three children: Chase, Tyler, and Alaina. Mr. Williams enjoys spending time with family, mountain biking and cars.

Todd A. Zabel

Manager
HLB Tautges Redpath, Ltd.
4810 White Bean Parkway
White Bear Lake, MN 55110
(651) 426-7000
Fax: (651) 426-5004
tzabel@hlbtr.com

8721

Business Information: As Manager for HLB Tautges Redpath, Ltd., Mr. Zabel is responsible for the implementation of accounting software. He manages an advisory group, meets with prospects, and oversees sales and marketing for the Company. Highly regarded, he possesses superior talents and an excellent understanding of technology. Noting the highlight of his career as assisting small businesses in becoming more successful, Mr. Zabel attributes his success to striving to always do the best and his ability to take on challenges and deliver results. In the future, he plans to continue working in this capacity, looking forward to assisting in the completion of future corporate goals. Founded in 1970, HLB Tautges Redpath, Ltd. is one of the world's largest tax and accounting consulting firms, providing international clients with current, accurate, and in-depth audits and tax advisories. HLB Tautges Redpath provides services to commercial and government clients in the areas of individual taxes, total solutions, investment services, and financial planning. **Career Highlights:** Manager, HLB Tautges Redpath, Ltd. (1987-Present). **Associations & Accomplishments:** Information Technology Alliance; American Institute of Certified Public Accountants; Minnesota Society of Certified Public Accountants; White Bear Chamber of Commerce, 1996 Chairs Choice Award Winner; National Soccer Coaches Association; White Bear Soccer Club. **Education:** Gustavus Adolphus College, B.A. (1987); Certified Public Accountant (1990). **Personal Information:** Married to Michelle in 1990. Three children: Amanda, Megan, and Brenna. Mr. Zabel enjoys soccer, hockey, biking and coaching.

Randy Anderson

Technical Support Manager
Eaton Corporation
4201 North 27th Street
Milwaukee, WI 53216-1807
(414) 449-6686
Fax: (414) 449-7084
randyanderson@eaton.com

8731

Business Information: Functioning in the role of Technical Support Manager with Eaton Corporation, Mr. Anderson is responsible for providing technical support to the Corporation's Research and Development Innovation Center. Before joining Eaton in 1998, Mr. Anderson served as Technical Support Manager for FMLH and Help Desk Manager at Harley-Davidson Motor Company. His background history also includes a stint as Field Coordinator for Manpower Inc. In his present capacity, Mr. Anderson oversees and directs PC support for two buildings in Milwaukee, Wisconsin and one in Detroit, Michigan. A 17 year technology professional, he helps answer user questions and maintain the functionality and operational status of the systems infrastructure. His success is attributed to his networking and his ability to think outside the box, as well as deliver results and aggressively tackle new challenges. "Keep in contact with everyone you meet throughout your career," is cited as Mr. Anderson's advice. Eventually attaining the position of Information Systems Director serves as one of his future endeavors. Eaton Corporation is a research and development company. A Fortune 500 manufacturer of technical controls, Eaton Corporation's international market is focused on three primary areas: automotive, commercial, and appliance. Currently, the Corporation is headquartered on Cleveland, Ohio. **Career Highlights:** Technical Support Manager, Eaton Corporation (1998-Present); Help Desk Manager, Harley-Davidson Motor Company (1996-98); Technical Support FMLH (1998); Field Coordinator, Manpower Inc. (1987-96). **Education:** North Park College, B.S. in Computer Science (1982); Certified Novell Administrator. **Personal Information:** Married to Dawn in 1993. Two children: Benjamin and Katherine.

Joseph A. Aprile

Systems Administrator
Fred Hutchinson Cancer Research Center
1100 Fairview Avenue North
Seattle, WA 98109-4417
(206) 667-6116
Fax: (206) 667-5530
japrile@fhcrc.org

8731

Business Information: Mr. Aprile has served with the Fred Hutchinson Cancer Research Center in a variety of capacities since joining the Center in 1980. He spend the first 10 years involved in research investigations. Drawing from his 10 years of information technology experience, he currently administers network servers and printers and manages the desktops for users in the programs he supports. Additional duties include managing the web site for his division and maintaining SQL-based system data. Mr. Aprile is currently involved in Intranet development. The Fred Hutchinson Cancer Research Center was established in 1975, and is renowned for performing the first human bone marrow transplant. It has been a pioneer in helping to develop bone marrow transplant centers throughout the world. The Public Health Sciences division, of which Mr. Aprile is a member, employs many scientific experts and is part of numerous collaborative efforts with other institutions with a focus on preventive medicine. The best known example of such efforts is the Women's Health Initiative which encompasses over 40 centers throughout the country. **Career Highlights:** Fred Hutchinson Cancer Research Center: Systems Administrator (1995-Present), Systems Analyst/Programmer (1991-95), Research Investigator (1980-90). **Education:** North Carolina State University, M.S. in Biochemistry (1970); Manhattan College, B.S. in Biology (1966). **Personal Information:** Two children: Lia and Julian. Mr. Aprile enjoys poetry, photography and being an artist.

Ruth Ann Barkin

SEG Information Systems Project Manager
DynCorp
6101 Stevenson Avenue
Alexandria, VA 22304
(703) 461-2203
barkinr@dycorp.com

8731

Business Information: Serving as SEG Information Systems Project Manager for DynCorp, Mrs. Barkin is responsible for the management of information modeling and systems. Supervising the direction of specially designated projects, she ensures her staff follows corporate policy and they conduct research and implement design techniques for data tracking and analysis. She demonstrates an extensive knowledge of the industry as she pens proposals on behalf of the Corporation, stating facts in a clear and concise manner. Proud of her accomplishments, Mrs. Barkin is recognized for her creative approaches to challenges and is credited with the acquisition of serveral contract through well designed bids. Keeping her goals consistent with corporate objectives, she looks forward to continual advancement within the hierarchy as she provides outstanding customer support. DynCorp specializes in science and engineering consulting and provides services primarilly to the enviornmental sector. Handling serveral contracts for the United States government, they assist the administrative staff of many military bases as well as the Environmental Protection Agency. Established in 1950, the Corporation has estimated annual revenues of over $1.6 billion, and employs 200 people at the Alexandria, Virginia location. **Career Highlights:** DynCorp: SEG Information Systems Project Manager (1996-Present), Task Manager (1991-96); Systems and Applications Developer, Viar & Company (1987-91). **Associations & Accomplishments:** National Association for Female Executives. **Education:** Memphis State University, M.S. in Industrial Psychology (1982); University of Maryland: B.S. in Psychology (1980), B.A. in Economics (1980). **Personal Information:** Married to Craig Bond in 1986. Two children: Kelcey and Kyle Bond. Mrs. Barkin enjoys skiing, music, theater and dancing.

Peter J. Bartoli
Lead Network Security Specialist

SAIC
10260 Campus Point Drive
San Diego, CA 92121
(858) 826-5495
Fax: (858) 826-5112
peter.j.bartoli@saic.com

8731

Business Information: As the active head hacker in charge of ethical network penetration services for SAIC, Mr. Bartoli has been offering his excellent skills to clients and personel. Serving as Lead Network Security Specialis, he designs special training for hackers as well as leads the training courses and brings in eligible recruits to the Corporation. Mr. Bartoli, along with his team of experts, specialize in networking and breaking codes to get into computer systems for their customer contacts. Responsible for new hiring and sales training and marketing, he determines who and what will better the promotion of the Corporation. Utilizing his excellent skills and knowledge, Mr. Bartoli focuses on the expansion and success of SAIC. Since 1969, SAIC has been providing security consultants and large scale integrators for the area of San Diego, California. With over 40,000 employees, the Corporation offers security assessments and locates security holes. Concentrating on the technological safety of their clients, SAIC offers quality control and service. Presently, the Corporation reports annual earnings in excess of $6 billion. **Career Highlights:** Lead Network Security Specialist, SAIC (1997-Present); Lead Systems Administrator, MillenniaNet (1995-97); Network Administrator, University of Texas (1994-95). **Associations & Accomplishments:** Association of Computing Machinery; CCNA. **Education:** San Diego State University, B.S. in Computer Science (1997).

Carlton L. Bjerkaas
Division Manager

SAIC
619 West U.S. Highway 50
O'Fallon, IL 62269-1942
(618) 624-9005
Fax: (618) 624-9008
carlb@aristotle.saic.com

8731

Business Information: Mr. Bjerkaas serves as the Division Manager of Applied Telecommunications for SAIC. In his current capacity, he supervises 100 staff members and is responsible for maintaining telecommunications equipment and applications. Mr. Bjerkaas plans to continue his career with the Company, encouraging expansion of his Division and the services it offers. Established in 1969, SAIC is a diversified, international company offering a variety of technical services. System programming, integration, and training are among the Company's primary services. Consulting and telecommunications options are also offered. **Career Highlights:** Division Manager, SAIC Science Applications (1996-Present); Senior Scientist, SAIC International Corporation (1995-96); Director of Technology and Requirements, United States Air Force (1995). **Associations & Accomplishments:** Armed Forces Communications and Electronics Association; American Society of Public Administration; American Association for the Advancement of Science; Fellow, American Meteorological Society; Rotary International. **Education:** Auburn University, M.P.A. (1983); Massachusetts Institute of Technology, S.M. (1977); University of North Dakota, B.S. (1970). **Personal Information:** Three children: Kristopher, Eric, and Todd. Mr. Bjerkaas enjoys participating in youth activities, Boy Scouts and coaching soccer.

Gideon Paul Caplovitz
Systems Programmer

Abratech Corporation
475 Gate 5 Road, Suite 275
Sausalito, CA 94965
(415) 289-7453
gcap@abratech.com

8731

Business Information: Serving as Systems Programmer of Abratech Corporation, Mr. Caplovitz applies his extensive education and scientific knowledge to maintain all technical operations. His duties include administraton of the LAN, including troubleshooting and maintenance. Developing scientific programming, he writes applications for digital signal and fourier processes with the goal of improving current industry standards. Also serving as Webmaster and Mathematical Analyst, Mr. Caplovitz is credited with the creation and implementation of the corporate network. Attributing his success to the values and ethics instilled in him by his parents, he credits his career advancement to his problem solving ability. Mr. Caplovitz currently is working to shift his responsibilities to a private company, keeping the same career path in mind. Abratech Corporation is a

biomedical research firm specializing in the study of auditory brain stem response. Employing four trained professionals who conduct hearing and sleep experiments, the 14 year old Corporation is recognized for contributions to the health research industry. **Career Highlights:** Systems Programmer, Abratech Corporation (1998-Present); Independent Contractor, Lucent Technologies (1997-98); Scientific Programmer, AT&T Bell Laboratories (1995-97); Intern UNIX Programmer, Nava Undersea Warfare Center (1994-95). **Associations & Accomplishments:** American Mathematical Society. **Education:** Couvant Institute/New York University, M.S. in Math (1998); University of California at Santa Cruz, B.A. in Computational Math (1996). **Personal Information:** Mr. Caplovitz enjoys Ultimate Frisbee, cars, guitar and sports.

Cameron K. Coursey
Director

SBC Technology Resources
9505 Arboreturm Boulevard
Austin, TX 78759
(512) 372-5816
Fax: (512) 372-5891
coursey@tri.sbc.com

8731

Business Information: As Director of SBC Technology Resources, Mr. Coursey is responsible for research and development of wireless services. Combining 12 years of strategic management and occupational experience, he effectively leads his team in creating new technology in support of personal communication services and digital wireless capabilities, and evaluates and develops the requirements for products and mobile phone vendors. A recognized expert, Mr. Coursey recently published a book entitled, "Understanding Digital PCS, the TDMA Standard," which explores the expanding world behind digital networking. Always focused on his goals and objectives, he has made plans to continue in his leadership role with SBC Technology Resources, as well as expand SBC's responsibilities and broaden the Company's scope. He attends several conferences correlating to his field to increase his knowledge so he may better assist in new innovations. In reaching towards another goal, Mr. Coursey, is currently in the process of obtaining a patent for one of his creations. Keeping focused on the ultimate goal has contributed to his career success. SBC Technology Resources operates as the telecommunications research and development arm of the parent, SBC Communications. Today, the Company is an expanding branch of the cellular and digital communications industry. International in scope, SBC is headquartered in Austin, Texas and operates a network of two locations. Presently, there are over 300 professional, technical, and administrative support employees at the Company's office in Austin, Texas involved in applied research and technical work. **Career Highlights:** Director, SBC Technology Resources (1992-Present); Electronics Engineer, McDonnell Douglas Aircraft Company (1989-91). **Associations & Accomplishments:** Institute of Electronics and Electrical Engineers. **Education:** University of Missouri at Rolla: M.S. in Electrical Engineering (1988), B.S. in Electrical Engineering (1987). **Personal Information:** Married to Karen in 1987. Two children: Nathanael and Joshua. Mr. Coursey enjoys water sports, jogging, reading, writing and spending time with his family.

Reynaldo J. Fadri
Management Information Systems Supervisor

Vivorx Inc.
2825 Santa Monica Boulevard, Suite 200
Santa Monica, CA 90404
(310) 264-7768
rey@vivorx.com

8731

Business Information: As the Management Information Systems Supervisor of Vivorx, Inc., Mr. Fadri plans and oversees multiple projects and works with senior management to determine systems development strategy and standards. He is responsible for the maintenance of the network infrastructure as well as installation of new software, roll out of technology, backing up systems, and training employees on network procedures. Possessing superior talents and an excellent understanding of his field, Mr. Fadri ensures network security by installing firewalls and assigning and tracking user passwords. Attributing his success to academics, he is self taught on the intricacies of software and database system. Obtaining his MCSE certification and starting up his own consulting business serves as his future endeavors. Established in 1990 and headquartered in Santa Monica, California, Vivorx Inc. is a biotechnology company involved in scientific and medical research. A knowledgeable team of doctors and scientist conduct research with the disease diabetes. Conducting worldwide research, the Corporation investigates the disease itself, its effect on human cells, and possible treatments. Working for the pharmaceutical companies, the Corporation investigates chemicals that may be used for a treatment or cure. **Career**

Highlights: Management Information Systems Supervisor, Vivorx Inc. (1999-Present); Management Information Systems Manager, Frankel, Lodgen, Lacher, Golditch, Sardi & Howard (1998-99); Management Information Systems Manager, Nat Sherman Inc. (1996-97); Design Engineer, Signal Transformer Inc. (1994-96). **Associations & Accomplishments:** Certified Novell Engineer, 3.xx. **Education:** Polytechnic University (1996); Manhattan College, Bachelor's degree in Electrical Engineering. **Personal Information:** Mr. Fadri enjoys playing the guitar.

Barbie V. Hackney
Software Applications Engineer

SAIC
14609 Runfeldt Street
Austin, TX 78725-1837
(512) 326-6642
bvhack@excite.com

8731

Business Information: Having spent 18 years in the field troubleshooting, Ms. Hackney joined SAIC in 1999 as Software Applications Engineer. She creates and designs cutting-edge Oracle relational databases and warehouse and data marketing software. Her responsibilities include performing data modeling, data analysis, and mapping. Possessing superior talents and an excellent understanding of technology, Ms. Hackney works closely with systems management and users to analyze, specify, and design new technical solutions, presenting a logical model and drafting system requirements. She is currently working with the Veterans Affair Administration to design an advanced database for their UNIX Server. Her plans for the future include specializing in one area of data model and design. Ms. Hackney attributes her success to being a fast learner and taking the initiative to handle problems and solve them. Established in 1969, SAIC is an international corporation involved in research and engineering for the health sector. Located in Austin, Texas, the Corporation contracts out to the military and other government agencies. Employing 36,000 individuals responsible for daily operations, the Corporation reports annual revenues in excess of $4.7 billion. **Career Highlights:** Software Applications Engineer, SAIC (1999-Present); Technical Consultant, SAP (1998-99); Database Administrator, Texas Workforce Commission (1997-98). **Education:** St. Edwards University, Bacherlor's degree in Liberal Studies and Computer Information Science (1997); Tyler Junior College, degree in Computer Science; Austin Community College, degree in Computer Science. **Personal Information:** One child: Erik Coleman. Ms. Hackney enjoys inspirational messages, church ministries, going to the beach and travel.

Jeff L. Holliday
Systems Engineer

Honda Research and Development
21001 State Route 739
Raymond, OH 43067-9705
(937) 645-6319
jholliday@columbus.rr.com

8731

Business Information: As a Systems Engineer for Honda Research and Development, Mr. Holliday is responsible for the procurement of information systems equipment and providing NT and systems support. Before joining Honda Research and Development, he served as Owner and Contractor for Holliday Wiring. His background history also includes a stint as Field Technician for Ameritech Company. An expert with 12 years experience, he also works to ensure the effective work performance of the Company's computer network database and trains fellow co-workers on any new software or hardware that may be new to the system. In the future, Mr. Holliday hopes to advance into a position on the administrative side of business operations that will more fully utilize his organizational and supervisory skills. He attributes his success to his honesty and his ability to think outside the box, produce results, and tackle new challenges. Honda Research and Development specializes in the exploration of new designs and technologies within the automotive industry. Established in 1994, the division in Raymond, Ohio hosts a staff of 1,300 dedicated innovators. These innovators work to test and refine the newest technologies for the next line of Honda automobiles and motorcycles. The Honda Corporation produces $30 million annually from its world wide sale of mobile transportation. **Career Highlights:** Systems Engineer, Honda Research and Development (1996-Present); Owner/Contractor, Holliday Wiring (1990-96); Field Technician, Ameritech Company (1987-90). **Associations & Accomplishments:** Jehovah's Witness; Theocratic studies and speaking. **Education:** Bell and Howell Database Certification; NT Core Systems Certification; HVAC-Advanced Refrigeration Certification; Windows 95 Registry Certification; TCP/IP Certification; T.Q.M. Certification; I.S.O. Certification. **Personal Information:** Married to Tina in 1983. Mr. Holliday enjoys automation and remote control technologies.

Istella Chui-Mei Ko
Database Programmer
Ouintiles Pacific, Inc.
331a East Evelyn Avenue
Mountain View, CA 94041
(650) 567-2000
Fax: (650) 567-4000
iko@omtn.quintiles.com

8731

Business Information: Functioning in the role of Database Programmer for Quintiles Pacific, Inc., Ms. Ko is responsible for the design and implementation of new programs within the Corporation. Establishing her presence in the computer science field, Ms. Ko utilizes eight years of on the job experience and academic ties in instructing users of new applications and systems. A systems expert, she works closely with users and systems management to analyze, specify, and design new solutions. Developing and supporting user interface and database oriented applications, ensuring data integrity and security, and tuning software tools to enhance overall performance also fall within the purview of Ms. Ko's responsibilities. Her goal is to remain with the Corporation in the database programming realm. Ms. Ko's career success reflects her ability to think outside the box, produce results, and aggressively take on new challenges. Established in 1987, Quintiles Pacific, Inc. is a leading full service contract research organization serving clients in key drug development. Offering expertise in both therapeutic drugs and regulatory drugs, the Corporation services include strategic product development, health economics, data management, product evaluation, and clinical trials. With more than 1,700 employees world wide, the Corporation operates 29 offices through out the United States, Europe, and Asia. Annual revenue often exceeds $60,000. **Career Highlights:** Database Programmer, Quintiles Pacific, Inc. (1991-Present). **Education:** San Jose State University, B.S. (1989); Tien Medical Nursing School, R.N. **Personal Information:** Married to Share Wing in 1984. One child: Brittany. Ms. Ko enjoys travel and reading.

Helmuth E. Kristen, Ph.D.

Doctor
Harvard-Smithsonian Center for Astrophysics
60 Garden Street, MS 42
Cambridge, MA 02138
(617) 495-7294
hkr.sten@cfa.harvard.edu

8731

Business Information: Dr. Kristen serves as a post doctoral research affiliate at the Harvard-Smithsonian Center for Astrophysics. In his role, he conducts astrophysical research and develops Web sites and database management systems. A member of the center's star formation department, Dr. Kristen works closely with 35 other professionals in performing research and development of information systems, and making presentations on research findings. In the future, Dr. Kristen's objective is to push and deliver his findings out into the information technology community. His success is attributed to his in-depth networking and his ability to prioritize his career plans, as well as his ability to think outside the box, take on challenges, and deliver results in support of systems users. The Harvard-Smithsonian Center for Astrophysics houses the Astrophysical Research Center. The Center was established in 1974 and is located in Cambridge, Massachusetts. The World's largest astrophysics research center, the Center presently employs a staff of more than 900 professional, technical, and administrative support staff. **Career Highlights:** Doctor, Harvard-Smithsonian Center for Astrophysics (1998-Present); Partner/Board Member, Vindobona A.B. (1995-Present); System Administrator, Stockholm University (1993-98). **Associations & Accomplishments:** Swedish Space and Aeronautics Society. **Education:** Stockholm University, Ph.D. (1998); Royal Institute of Tehnology, M.Sc. (1993). **Personal Information:** Dr. Kristen enjoys keeping up on financial markets and cognitive computing.

Lisa Anne Markel
Director, Clinical Data Management Operations for North America
Covance
First Union Tower, 150 Fourth Avenue North, Suite 1400
Nashville, TN 37219
(615) 313-6877
Fax: (615) 313-6701
lisa-anne.markel@covance.com

8731

Business Information: Ms. Markel serves as Director of Clinical Data Management Operations for North America for the Clinical Development Group of Covance. She assumes accountability for all data handling, database design, data collection, diagnostic programming, data review, query generation and resolution, data coding, and quality control. As a member of the data management team, Ms. Markel participates in client development, striving to expand the existing client base and enhance customer relations. She liaises with North American, European, and Asia-Pacific representatives to identify and implement solutions to global data management issues and concerns. Ms. Markel assists with the formulation of strategies to improve data management efficiencies through collaboration with clients and multi-discipline representatives. Her plans for the future include remaining with Covance and assisting in expansion operations. Covance offers pharmaceutical research and development services to compliment the in-house departments of companies in the industry. At present, Covance is one of the largest international contract research organization in the world. Additionally, the Company offers central laboratory; commercialization and marketing; and product packing and labeling prior to distribution services. **Career Highlights:** Covance: Director, Clinical Data Management Operations for North America (1998-Present), Director of Data Management (1996-98); Clinical Research Scientist, Cato Research, Ltd. (1991-96); Principal Biomedical Engineer, ABB Environmental (1978-91); Research Assistant, Duke University Medical Center (1974-78). **Associations & Accomplishments:** Sigma Xi, Research Triangle Park Chapter; DIA; Covance Key Contributor (1997); Cato Research President's Award (1991, 1994-96). **Education:** Duke University: M.S. in Biomedical Engineering (1981), B.S.E. in Biomedical Engineering (1976). **Personal Information:** Two children: Erick J. and Heather L. Collins. Ms. Markel enjoys travel and participating in her children's soccer, track and basketball activities.

Allen K. Moore

Senior Systems Engineer
SAIC
9480 Pease Avenue, Suite B8
Elmendorf Air Force Base, AK 99506
(907) 552-5704
Fax: (907) 352-9260
nicotine@gci.net

8731

Business Information: As Senior Systems Engineer of SAIC's location at Elmendorf Air Force Base, Alaska, Mr. Moore handles all of the different aspects of systems engineering, technical support, and redesigning networks. Possessing an excellent understanding of his field, he is responsible for six employees who work on a five year contract basis to provide all of the services the Corporation offers to the United States Air Force. His highlight includes being the site lead after only being with the Corporation six months. Attributing his success to being in the right place at the right time and networking, Mr. Moore hopes to improve performance, work more efficiently, help promote growth, and become a program manager for the Corporation. Established in 1969, SAIC operates as a systems engineering and technical assistance contracting services company. In this capacity, the Corporation's 45,000 professional, technical, and support staff provides systems engineering and technical support of UNIX and NT systems, user accounts, and redesign of networks for classified projects. **Career Highlights:** Senior Systems Engineer, SAIC (1998-Present); Senior Systems Analyst, Lockheed Martin (1997). **Education:** Hawaii Pacific University, M.S. in Information Systems (1997); Wayland Baptist University, B.S. **Personal Information:** Married to Jackie in 1988. Three children: Alexis, Jesseca, and Julia. Mr. Moore enjoys camping, computers, fishing and rock climbing.

William E. Nova

Analyst
Caro Research
3401 Stearns Hill Road
Waltham, MA 02451
(978) 371-1660
wnova@caroresearch.com

8731

Business Information: As an Analyst with Caro Research, Mr. Nova is responsible for integrating pharmacoeconomics models and technology, producing computer-assisted solutions, and optimizing and displaying model results. Drawing from an extensive education, Mr. Nova also provides slides and presentations for other companies. Beginning his association with the Company in 1998, Mr. Nova has quickly established himself as an important and vital contributor to the success of the Company. He continues to grow professionally and hopes to begin offering independent services while also becoming more computer oriented. Mr. Nova's success reflects his ability to think outside the box, deliver results, and take on new challenges. Founded in 1992, Caro Research is involved in technology assessments, epidemiology studies, and pharmacoeconomics. A young growing company, Caro Research conducts studies on the evalution of drugs and reveals their results to drug manufacturers. Employing a staff of 40 individuals, the Company also offers seminars displaying how their studies are conducted. **Career Highlights:** Analyst, Caro Research (1998-Present); Analyst, Andersen Consulting (1997-98); Programmer, University of Los Andes (1995-96). **Associations & Accomplishments:** Colombia Volunteer (1991-92), ICYE. **Education:** University of Los Andes, Computer Science and Systems Engineer (1997). **Personal Information:** Mr. Nova enjoys travel, reading, languages, playing cards, movies, swimming, biking, hiking and camping.

Gillian Ralph

Information Manager
Industrial Research Ltd.
P.O. Box 2225
Auckland, New Zealand
+64 93034116
Fax: +64 93028117
g.ralph@irl.cri.nz

8731

Business Information: Recruited to Industrial Research Ltd. in 1992, Mrs. Ralph serves in the position of Information Manager responsible for oversight and management of the information services area of the Company. Possessing a superior talent and an excellent understanding of technology, she is part of a professional staff of experts who provide valuable information and systems to enhance day-to-day operations. Her focus is on keeping the Company out-front of the competition in the markets as well as helping the Company remain flexible, efficient, and profitable. Before joining the Company's team of professionals, Mrs. Ralph was employed as a Library Manager and Librarian for AIDD, DSIR. Striving to attain her goals, she plans on delivering information electronically online to further the Company's success and prosperity. Established in 1947, Industrial Research Ltd. specializes in industrial and technological research and development. The Company is a Crown Research Institute and is government funded. Industrial Research Ltd. produces scientific engineering material, mechanical engineering advanced technology, and robotic applications in industrial areas. Headquartered in Auckland, the Company presently employs 400 professional, technical, and support staff. **Career Highlights:** Information Manager, Industrial Research Ltd. (1992-Present); AIDD, DSIR: Library Manager (1983-92), Librarian (1972-83). **Associations & Accomplishments:** American Libraries Association; Australian Libraries and Information Association; Library and Information Association of New Zealand. **Education:** M.B.A. (1998); B.A. (1979). **Personal Information:** Married in 1973. Mrs. Ralph enjoys reading, horticulture and gardening.

Jimmy Ruffin

Systems Administrator
Promega
5445 East Cheryl Parkway
Madison, WI 53711-5373
(608) 277-2486
Fax: (608) 233-5379
jruffin@home.com

8731

Business Information: Serving as Promega's Systems Administrator since 1997, Mr. Ruffin is concerned with various aspects of the Company's highly technical daily operations. Working closely with his team of 19 associates, he strives to develop technical solutions to improve current procedures and solve operational challenges. Implementing software specifically created to fill corporate needs, Mr. Ruffin is able to formulate business strategies that allow the Company to remain competitive. He additionally handles all areas of hardware and phone line set up including upgrades; he is in charge of equipment relocation when a departmental move is necessary. Mr. Ruffin attributes the majority of his success to his interactions with others who had a clear vision of the information technology field and what role he could play in it. He looks forward to assisting the Company in the completion of corporate goals as he aspire to the position of Information Systems Manager. Established in 1979, Promega engages in the research and development of biotechnology and biopharmaceuticals. Employing nearly 500 people, the global Company focuses a great deal of their efforts on criminology and DNA studies. The Company also operates a Web site, complete with mail boxes and an international helpdesk. **Career Highlights:** Systems Administrator, Promega (1997-Present); WAN Administrator, Sitel Tech (1997); Computer Lab Technician, University of Wisconsin at Madison (1996). **Associations & Accomplishments:** MS Direct Access; MSDN; TechNet; IntelliQuest; Harris Pall Individual Readiness Reserve; Army National Guard Officers Club. **Education:** Edgewood, B.S. (1999); Milwaukee Area Technical College, A.A.S. **Personal Information:** Two children: Xavier and Jared.

Anthony A. Salazar

Systems Engineer
Los Alamos National Laboratory
P.O. Box 1663, MS: D440, Bikini Atoll Road
Los Alamos, NM 87545
(505) 667-2508
Fax: (505) 665-4197
aasalazar@lanl.gov

8731

Business Information: A 12 year veteran of Los Alamos National Laboratory, Mr. Salazar currently serves as Systems Engineer. In this position, he is the software development lead exercising oversight of integrating hardware and software systems for the Adaptive Deployable Processing Systems Project. Analysis, installation, modification, configuration, support, and tracking of prototype systems, utilities, software, and hardware also fall within the realm of Mr. Salazar's responsibilities. One of many accomplishments during his fine career was his software integration work on the DAPS on the Laser Ranger Program that was launched during the late 1990s. He attributes his success to his supportive management, his willingness to learn, and a supportive wife. Mr. Salazar plans to continue integrating new, prototype software for the benefit of the Laboratory Projects. Los Alamos National Laboratory is a Department of Energy contractor that conducts government research and experiments. Responsible for the creation of the "Bomb" and many other weapons, the Laboratory was originally founded in 1945. Located in Los Alamos, New Mexico, the primary responsibility of the Laboratory is research of weapons and new technologies. Presently, more than 7,000 professional, technical, and support staff are employed by the Laboratory. **Career Highlights:** Los Alamos National Laboratory: Systems Engineer (1992-Present), Systems Manager and Administrator (1988-92), Junior Computer Programmer (1985-88). **Associations & Accomplishments:** Institute of Electronics and Electrical Engineers Computer Society; Mexican American Engineers and Scientists (MAES). **Education:** New Mexico State University, B.S. in Computer Science (1986); Northern New Mexico Community College. **Personal Information:** Married to Helen C. in 1987. Two children: Valerie and Daniel. Mr. Salazar enjoys coaching soccer, motorcycling, racquetball and playing musical instruments.

Karen R. Staples

Division Administrator
SAIC
16541 Commerce Drive
King George, VA 22485-5806
(540) 663-3215
Fax: (540) 663-0640
karen.r.staples@cpmx.saic.com

8731

Business Information: Functioning in the capacity of Division Administrator for SAIC, Ms. Staples oversees all daily administrative functions, including tracking and monitoring the financial activities of each contract, fiscal year budget, and bottom line profits. Before joining SAIC, Ms. Staples served as Legal Secretary with Mason & Mason. Her employment history also include stints as Administrative Assistant for Turf & Tree Equipment Center, as well as Data Entry Operator with the Potomac River Fisheries Commission. Well versed in the realm of accounting, she is in charge of employee travel and time expenditures and expense accounts. Attributing her success to her educational history, family support, and industry mentors, Ms. Staples success reflects her ability to aggressively take on new challenges and responsibilities. Eventually attaining the position of Administrative Supervisor within SAIC serves as one of her future goals. A research and engineering firm, SAIC was established in 1969 and engages in systems and software development. With corporate headquarters in San Diego, California, the Corporation specializes in technology analysis, design, development, and integration as well as technical support services. Targeting Fortune 500 companies, SAIC presently employs a workforce of more than 35,000 personnel to meet the needs of clients around the globe. **Career Highlights:** Division Administrator, SAIC (1998-Present); Legal Secretary, Mason & Mason (1995-97); Administrative Assistant, Turf & Tree Equipment Center (1993-95); Data Entry Operator, Potomac River Fisheries Commission (1991-93). **Education:** Mary Washington College, B.S. in Business Administration (1993). **Personal Information:** Ms. Staples enjoys reading, bowling, board games, animals, crossword puzzles and going to the beach.

John A. Wick, Ph.D.

Senior Scientist
SAIC
1710 Saic Drive, MS 1-12-2
McLean, VA 22102
(703) 676-2738
Fax: (703) 676-2746
john.a.wick@saic.com

8731

Business Information: As Senior Scientist for SAIC, Dr. Wick is a 34 year veteran of the technology field. Demonstrating strong strategic systems and technical expertise, he fills the role of technical director with oversight of EC and IC research and development activities. He also performs systems engineer functions in conducting day-to-day business development for telecommunication companies. Dr. Wick, an innovative and high-impact information technology leader, invents leading edge solutions and e-commerce enhancements. An authority in the field who owns a record of delivering results, he guides and mentors more than 1,000 employees in the performance of high-tech innovations. Dr. Wick's favorite credo is "knowledge is your key to success." His success is attributed to being well positioned - in the right place at the right time and knowing the market and competitors. Becoming involved with more exotic areas of technology and putting together more solutions serves as Dr. Wick's goals. One of the largest information technology providers in the world, SAIC generates over $4 billion in annual revenues. Systems integrations consulting is offered to government agencies and commercial businesses. Established in 1969, the Company employs a global work force of 35,000 people. **Career Highlights:** Senior Scientist, SAIC (1989-Present); Technical Partner, Bell Technical Operations (1986-89); Associate Department Head, The MITRE Corporation (1974-86). **Associations & Accomplishments:** Potomac Valley Radio Club; American Radio Relay League. **Education:** University of Wisconsin, Ph.D. in Electrical Engineering (1972); University of Nebraska: M.S. in Electrical Engineering (1966), B.S. in Electrical Engineering (1965). **Personal Information:** Married to Gail in 1968. Two children: Chris and Matt. Dr. Wick enjoys amateur radio, hiking, swimming and video production.

Carla Zaragoza

Information Manager
Saguaro Clinical Research
4892 North Stone Avenue, Suite 180
Tucson, AZ 85704-5749
(520) 887-5212
Fax: (520) 887-5226
cjzaragoza@aol.com

8731

Business Information: Ms. Zaragoza demonstrates adept technical ability in her role as Information Manager of Saguaro Clinical Research. On a regular basis, she must evaluate current operating systems to ensure proper functioning, implementing upgrades or changes as she sees fit. Utilizing exceptional communication skills, she trains staff members on equipment and machinery, ensuring they fully benefit from all available resources. Paying close attention to detail, she handles the administration of patent records and prepares documentation to be submitted for approval to the Food and Drug Administration. Ms. Zaragoza attributes her success to dedication and motivation she developed during her prosperous military career. Currently, she aspires to the position of Operations Officer of the Company. Saguaro Clinical Research is engaged in the investigation of the effects of specific drugs on the human body. Highly trained professionals who strive for total efficiency and accuracy while carrying out their daily tasks are conducting various studies at any given time. Much of the data gathered from the research is managed through an extensive network of databases, capable of generating tables, graphs, and reports in preparation of Food and Drug Administration trials. **Career Highlights:** Information Manager, Saguaro Clinical Research (1997-Present); Superintendent/School Registrar, 355th Training Squadron, U.S. Air Force (1987-97); Military Training Instructor, 3743rd Basic Military Training Squadron, U.S. Air Force (1980-84). **Associations & Accomplishments:** American Legion; National Notary Association. **Education:** Pima Community College. **Personal Information:** Ms. Zaragoza enjoys exercise, travel, sports, reading and movies.

Nikhil Chitre

Software Consultant
Information Resources, Inc.
525 Monroe Street West
Chicago, IL 60661-3629
(312) 627-4858
Fax: (312) 474-8553
nikhil.chitre@infores.com

8732

Business Information: As Software Consultant for Information Resources, Inc. Mr. Chitre is responsible for the development of software, project management, and database design. Possessing superior talents and an excellent understanding of technology, he work with management and users to analyze, specify, and design new solutions new harness more of the computer's power. Utilizing his experience as an information technology consultant since 1996, Mr. Chitre also participates in the acquisition, installation, modification, configuration, support, and tracking of operating systems, databases, utilities, software, and hardware. Highly regarded, Mr. Chitre attributes his success to being able to work well with others and his ability to think outside the box, tackle new challenges, and deliver results on behalf of the Corporation and its clients. Established in 1979, Information Resources, Inc. is a market research company offering a wide variety of services to their clients. Headquartered in Chicago, Illinois, Information Resources currently employs 5,000 and reports annual revenues of $500 million. The Corporation offers services such as software consulting and design of custom software. **Career Highlights:** Software Consultant, Information Resources, Inc. (1998-Present); Consultant, WorldCom, Inc. (1998); Programming Consultant, Loyola University at Chicago (1996-98). **Education:** Loyola University at Chicago, M.S. in Computer Science (1998); Nagpur University, Bachelor's in Mechanical Engineering (1993). **Personal Information:** Married to Reshma in 1999. Mr. Chitre enjoys reading, technical publications and travel.

Richard W. Phillips

Senior Member of the Technical Staff
Software Engineering Institute
2260 Cremora Drive
Pittsburgh, PA 15241
(412) 835-0949
Fax: (412) 835-8914
dwp@sei.cmu.edu

8732

Business Information: As Senior Member of the Technical Staff, Mr. Phillips assists client organizations in the software development community to assess their current software development practices and then adopt the necessary new technologies, processes, and organizational changes to ensure an ongoing program of software engineering improvement. The Software Engineering Institute is a federally funded research and development center for the purpose of developing and transitioning new software technologies and management practices into the software development community. Established in 1984 and serving government, military, and industrial customers, the Software Engineering Institute has become a leading source of technical and management practices for cost-effective design and development of complex software systems. The Institute consists of about 200 scientists and engineers, and is part of the Carnegie Mellon University in Pittsburgh, Pennsylvania, with offices also in Washington, D.C. **Career Highlights:** Senior Member of the Technical Staff, Software Engineering Institute, Carnegie Mellon University (1992-Present); Senior Programmer and Development Manager, International Business Machines Corporation, assigned to software development laboratories in Poughkeepsie, New York, Amsterdam, Netherlands, and Vienna, Austria (1964-92); Prior to joining IBM's software development operations, Mr. Phillips held a number of technical and management positions in IBM HQ and customer support locations at St. Paul, Minnesota, Endicott, New York, White Plains, New York, and Detroit, Michigan (1954-64); Adjunct Associate Professor at Rensselaer Polytechnic Institute where he taught Software Engineering courses in the graduate study program (1984-91). **Associations & Accomplishments:** Mr. Phillips can be counted among the early pioneers in defining and managing the development process for complex systems of the 1960s and 1970s. In the current era of the 1980s and 90s, he co-authored numerous technical journal articles in the field of software engineering. Co-author of the book "Software Engineering: An Industrial Approach" (Prentice Hall, 1988); Association for Computing Machinery; International Council on Systems Engineering; Senior Member, Institute of Electricl and Electronics Engineers; Holder of two patents; United States Naval Reserve (1946-54). **Education:** Systems Research Institute, Certification (1984); University of Wisconsin (1951). **Personal Information:** Married to Leona

J. in 1950. Three children: Gregory, Gwen, and Nancy. Mr. Phillips enjoys playing jazz music.

Jeffrey A. Pillers

Director
Information Resources, Inc.
150 North Clinton Street
Chicago, IL 60661
(312) 726-1221
Fax: (312) 474-3417
8732

Business Information: Mr. Pillers, a 10-year veteran of the Information Resources, Inc. team of professionals, operates under the title of Director responsible for all aspects of PC technology, including all desktop software and hardware. Utilizing his business savvy and technical expertise, he maintains the functionality and serviceability of the computer infrastructure. He also performs all upgrades as well as installation of desk tops and laboratory computers. Creating cutting edge databases and overseeing project management, Mr. Pillers focuses on changes that will allow Information Resources to take advantage of new developed technology to remain flexible, efficient, and profitable in the Information Technology Age. He is self-taught in the technology field. Success is attributed to his persistence and his ability to take on challenges and deliver results. Mr. Pillers' aspirations include attaining a role of vice president in charge of end user computer support to include voice, message, and email technologies. Information Resources, Inc. is a market research company engaged in the development and distribution of software for various businesses. An international company, Information Resources is based in Chicago, Illinois and operates with the help of 3,500 highly skilled and intelligent individuals. The Corporation reports an annual revenue of $600 million. **Career Highlights:** Information Resources, Inc.: Director (1998-Present), Project Manager (1994-98), Supervisor (1992-94), Specialist (1990-92). **Associations & Accomplishments:** International Who's Who Among College Students. **Personal Information:** Married to Christina in 1992. One child: Zachary. Mr. Pillers enjoys coin collecting, golf and family time.

Matthew Sonnentag

Director of Operations and Technology
Gantz Wiley Research
901 Marquette Avenue
Minneapolis, MN 55402
(612) 217-5027
Fax: (612) 342-2922
msonnentag@gantzwiley.com
8732

Business Information: As Director of Operations and Technology with Gantz Wiley Research, Mr. Sonnentag divides his responsibilities into two categories: operations and technology. Serving in the operational capacity, he supervises the employees who perform client and research related tasks such as analysts and surveyors. Mr. Sonnetag works closely with his staff to develop strategies that will allow for increased internal effectiveness. Relying on the strong sense of teamwork in the various departments, he demonstrates an efficient management style as he delegates tasks to carefully chosen, capable groups for completion. Additionally, Mr. Sonnentag handles several technological responsibilities which he must tend to on a daily basis. Demonstrating technical expertise gained from practical work experience and education, he maintains the networking systems of the Company, handling installation and upgrades. Familiar with progressive techniques, Mr. Sonnentag implements Internet survey applications that have been developed as a result of careful research. Attributing success to his good luck and great interpersonal skills, he looks forward to continued advancement within the Company, as he encourages the client base to become more reliant on the Internet. Gantz Wiley Research is a consulting company that specializes in employee and customer relations in the areas of satisfaction research. Established in 1987, the Company currently only works with focus groups of business to business services. With over 45 emplyees at the headquarters location of Minneapolis, Minnesota, the international firm is recognized as a leader in the survey reseach field. **Career Highlights:** Director of Operations and Technology, Gantz Wiley Research (1999-Present); Network Architect, Deluxe Corporation (1998-99); Network Operations Manager, Piper Jaffray Company (1996-98); Network Systems Manager, Compucane/Health Systems Integration (1992-96). **Associations & Accomplishments:** Institute of Electrical and Electronics Engineers (1997). **Education:** University of Wisconsin, Bachelor's degree in Business Science (1987). **Personal Information:** Married to Jeannette in 1999. Seven children: Cori, Aaron, Jamie, Jimmy, Jessica, Jackie, and Jenna. Mr. Sonnentag enjoys horseback riding, skiing and outdoor activities.

Hong Heather Yu, Ph.D.

Scientist
Panasonic Technology Inc.
2 Research Way
Princeton, NJ 08540
(609) 734-7325
Fax: (609) 987-8827
heathery@acm.org
8732

Business Information: Functioning in the role of Scientist at Panasonic Technology Inc., Dr. Yu is responsible for all day-to-day administration and research and development functions of the Corporation's Information Technology Department. Recruited to Panasonic Technology in 1998, Dr. Yu extensive academic history includes a Ph.D. and Master's from the University of Princeton. This, along with his nine year experience in the technology field, enables her to effectively and efficiently lead her staff in performing leading edge research and development of new methodologies, techniques, and products to enhance Panasonic Technology's operations in the national and international arenas. Dr. Yu's professional success reflects her leadership ability to build teams with synergy, technical strength, and a customer oriented attitude; think out-of-the-box, and take on new challenges and responsibilities. Her future goals include remaining and growing with Panasonic. Panasonic Technology Inc. operates as a research laboratory specializing in state-of-the-art information technology development. The Corporation maintains a firm presence in over 150 countries around the globe, and is presently manned by a worldwide work force of more than 80,000 professional, technical, and support personnel. **Career Highlights:** Scientist, Panasonic Technology Inc. (1998-Present). **Associations & Accomplishments:** Institute of Electronics and Electrical Engineers; Association for Computing Machinery; International Society for Optical Engineering. **Education:** Princeton University: Ph.D. (1998), Master's degree (1996); Peking University.

Winifreda Floro Alvarado

Information Technology Manager
Brookings Institution
1775 Massachusetts Avenue NW
Washington, DC 20036-2188
(202) 797-6175
Fax: (202) 797-6264
walvarado@brook.edu
8733

Business Information: Mrs. Alvarado got her start with Brookings Institution in 1991 as Senior Programmer. At the present time, she assumes the accountability of Information Technology Manager. In this role, Mrs. Alvarado oversees all aspects of network administration and also serves as a consultant to the Institution's research staff. With over 20 years of rich practical experience and education, she coaches and guides a staff of two people in managing the network infrastructure, and Web site as well as support of all on-going research projects. A respected expert in the field, Mrs. Alvarado manages the Institution's Y2K inventory, assessment, and testing program. Directing the analysis, acquisition, and installation as well as modification, configuration, and support of operating systems, databases, and utilities also falls within the realm of her responsibilities. She has been quoted in National Journal, Colleges and Universities Compensation Survey and Charter School Survey Research publications. Attributing her success to her technical skills and educational background, Mrs. Alvarado's favorite advice is, "Keep learning is the key, stay up with both technology and work experience." Brookings Institution is a research and education organization. A "Think Tank," the Institution conducts government, foreign, and economic research studies. Employing a global staff of more than 350 people, the Institution is located in Washington, D.C. **Career Highlights:** Brookings Institution: Information Technology Manager (1993-Present), Senior Programmer of Research Program (1991-93); Senior Programmer of Computer Services, International Food Policy Research Institute (1987-91); Technical Staff of EDP Management Consulting Services, Sycip, Gorres, Velayo and Company (1978-81). **Associations & Accomplishments:** Treasurer, V.P. Math Major Circle. **Education:** University of Pennsylvania, M.S. in Computer Science (1983); University of Philippines, B.S. in Mathematics cum laude (1978). **Personal Information:** Married to Domingo in 1984. Mrs. Alvarado enjoys swimming, gardening and collecting stamps and coins.

Kelly Marie Dilks

Principal Investigator
ERDC-CNC
P.O. Box 9005
Champaign, IL 61826-9005
(217) 352-6511
Fax: (217) 352-6511
k-dilks@cecer.army.mil
8733

Business Information: Ms. Dilks is the Principal Investigator of ERDC-CNC in Champaign, Illinois. It is her responsibility to set the direction for research projects and to lead teams of researchers working to integrate models and geospatial data to support military training. Managing 12 to 16 projects a year, she is responsible for team management and integration. Possessing an excellent understanding of her field, Ms. Dilks also teaches computer science to Third World countries. Currently working with intelligence agencies to teach applications, she believes success is a result of being fair and engaging in lots of teamwork. Established in 1992, ERDC-CNC is a U.S. Army research center involved in studying conservation as it pertains to environmental issues reguarding land management for all the branches of the military. The Center uses computer based modeling to provide an analyst tool for their engineers. Located in Champaign, Illinois, the Center employs a 2,000 professional, technical, and support staff. **Career Highlights:** Principal Investigator, ERDC-CNC (1992-Present). **Associations & Accomplishments:** American Association of Geographers. **Education:** Illinois State University, Doctorate (In Progress); University of Illinois: M.S. (1994), B.S. (1990). **Personal Information:** Married to Chris in 1989. One child: Clay. Ms. Dilks enjoys outdoors, reading and sports.

Ronald J. Fehd

Programmer/Analyst
Centers for Disease Control
4770 Buford Highway
Atlanta, GA 30341
(770) 488-8102
Fax: (770) 488-8282
rjf2@cdc.gov
8733

Business Information: Possessing unique talent in the technology field, Mr. Fehd serves in a dual role of Programmer and Analyst for the Centers for Disease Control. Before joining the Agency in 1988, he served as a Research Coordinator at Georgia State University. In his present capacity, he writes programs in the SAS and S-Plus languages for use by the medical staff in their research. Presiding over the data management of the Agency, Mr. Fehd performs software and program upgrades and devotes considerable effort to network security and data loss prevention. Establishing goals that are compatible with those of the Agency, he looks forward to increasing his professional responsibilities and obtaining a managerial position. As a 13 year professional, Mr. Fehd's success reflects his ability to think outside the box and aggressively take on new challenges. The Centers for Disease Control is an independent agency of the federal government, established to provide Health and Human Services to the citizens of the United States. Founded in 1945, the Agency's primary function is to perform research on existing and possibly emerging diseases in an effort to prevent its spread or effect its elimination. The Agency is often called upon by other countries to assist in crisis and employs over 8,000 dedicated medical professionals and support personnel. **Career Highlights:** Programmer/Analyst, Centers for Disease Control (1988-Present); Research Coordinator, Georgia State University (1986-88). **Associations & Accomplishments:** Association of Computing Machinery; Institute of Electrical and Electronics Engineers. **Education:** University of Hawaii at Manoa, B.S. in Computer Science (1986). **Personal Information:** Mr. Fehd enjoys origami and motorcycles.

Darren L. Lowe

Computer/Network Specialist
NIST
100 Bureau Drive, Stop 8601
Gaithersburg, MD 20899-8601
(301) 975-6667
Fax: (301) 975-4737
dlowe@nist.gov
8733

Business Information: Maintaining the vital role of Computer/Network Specialist within NIST, Mr. Lowe supplies web development, network administration, hardware, software, and system administration support to the Building and Fire Research Laboratory (BFRL). As a certified UNIX System Administrator and TCP/IP Network Professional, Mr. Lowe comes to the Agency among the highest qualified technical specialists in the world. He is working toward his

MCSE and continues to stay current on the latest WWW technologies. Mr. Lowe attributes his success to effective time management and the ability to quickly diagnose and solve a myriad of technical challenges. As a laboratory within NIST, BFRL's mission is to enhance the competitiveness of U.S. industry and public safety through performance prediction and measurement technologies and technical advances that improve the life cycle quality of constructed facilities. NIST is a federal government organization, operating under the U.S. Department of Commerce. Employing the skills of over 3,000 scientific professionals, the Institute is responsible for working with the industry to develop and apply technology, measurements, and standards. **Career Highlights:** Computer Network Specialist, NIST (1989–Present). **Education:** Capitol College, B.S. in Electrical Engineering in Technology (1991); SGI Administrator Cerificate; TCP/IP and Webmaster Certification. **Personal Information:** Married to Melanie in 1989. Three children: Jeffrey, Paige, and Taylor. Mr. Lowe enjoys fishing, ice hockey and coaching little league.

Barbara L. Peterson
Project Manager
Department of Energy at Idaho National Engineering and Environmental Laboratory
135 West 4th North
Rigby, ID 83442-1212
(208) 526-3518
blp@ida.net

8733

Business Information: Serving as Advisory Engineer for the Department of Energy at Idaho National Engineering and Environmental Laboratory, M&O Contractor, Ms. Peterson oversees the accurate and timely completion of specific projects. Lending her technical knowledge and expertise, she develops systems and strategies that facilitate the coordination of information movement between the various agency locations. By preparing reports, she demonstrates her ability to conduct thorough analysis of complex operating systems. She is credited with the successful implementation of several innovative business strategies, and looks forward to continued prosperity as she advances throughout the corporate structure. The Department of Energy at Idaho National Engineering and Environmental Laboratory is concerned with the maintenance and support of research facilities. Many of the facilities conduct analysis of nuclear energy and waste management, striving to devise techniques and tactics that will contribute to the overall effectiveness of the conservation process of the state. **Career Highlights:** Advisory Engineer, Department of Energy at Idaho National Engineering and Environmental Laboratory (2000-Present); Project Manager, Limitco/EG&G (1990-00); EG&G: Unit Manager (1987-90), Engineering Specialist (1985-87). **Associations & Accomplishments:** Institute of Electrical and Electronics Engineers; American Computing Machinery; I.N.C.O.S.E. **Education:** Eastern Michigan University, B.S. (1978). **Personal Information:** Married to David in 1990. Three children: Joshua Privett, Daniel Privett, and Eric Peterson.

Li-Sheng Shen, Ph.D.
Director
CCL
Building 51, 195-11 Section 4, Chung Hsing Road, Chutung
Hsinchu, Taiwan
+886 35917302
Fax: +886 35829732
shen@ccl.itri.org.tw

8733

Business Information: Serving in the position of Director of CCL, Dr. Shen fulfills a number of duties on behalf of the Company and its clientele. He is responsible for developing core technologies in virtual reality with an emphasis in fostering the creation of new industry. Utilizing over 20 years of academic ties and hands-on experience, Dr. Shen supervises 60 personnel within the Company's information technology department and ensure the functionality and operational status of the systems infrastructure. Proud of developing numerous virtual reality projects, Dr. Shen attributes his success to the infrastructure and environment. In the future, he looks forward to developing leading-edge human computer interaction and human interface technologies. Founded in 1990, CCL is a computer laboratory. Providing services in the areas of computers, communications, and consumer electronics, the Company performs research and development to help local industry in techniques for operations in these areas. **Career Highlights:** Director, CCL (1998-Present); Deputy Director, Advanced Technology Center/CCL (1996-98); Manager, Computer Communication Division/CCL (1993-96). **Associations & Accomplishments:** Association of Computing Machinery; Institute of Electrical and Electronics Engineers. **Education:** Delft University of Technology, Ph.D. (1993); National Chiao Tung University: M.S. in Electronics, B.S. in Electronic

Engineering. **Personal Information:** Married to Li-Wen Wang. Three children. Dr. Shen enjoys golf and basketball.

Gregory Dickinson
Systems Manager
Paradigm Analytical Laboratories
2627 Northchase Parkway SE
Wilmington, NC 28405-7419
(910) 350-2839
paradigm-labs@compuserve.com

8734

Business Information: Possessing unique talent in the information technology field, Mr. Dickinson joined Paradigm Analytical Laboratories in 1994 as the Systems Manager. With the Laboratory since its inception, he is responsible for all computer information systems. Included in his duties is the management of all data systems and local area and wide area network connectivity. Attributing his success to clear thinking and an enjoyment of his work, Mr. Dickinson's plans for the future include improving the way the Lab does business with networking upgrades and the Internet. Paradigm Analytical Laboratories is a regional environmental laboratory based in Wilmington, North Carolina. Created with the ideal that new approaches were needed in the field of environmental research, the Lab creates innovative testing methods to be applied to wastewater, sewage systems, and related areas of refuse. These results are then applied by the Lab to statistical analysis, and improvements and necessary changes. Established in 1994, the Paradigm Analytical Laboratory employs a professional staff of 15 technicians and administrators. **Career Highlights:** Systems Manager, Paradigm Analytical Laboratories (1994-Present); Director of Automation, IEA, Inc. (1991-93); Senior Technical Specialist, Envirofacts (1990-91). **Associations & Accomplishments:** Institute of Electrical and Electronics Engineers Computer Society. **Education:** Montgomery College, A.A. in Electronics Technology (1985); Virginia Polytechnic Institute and State University, B.S. in Biology (1974). **Personal Information:** Married to Diana in 1978. One child: Alia. Mr. Dickinson enjoys reading science fiction and involvement with his daughter's activities.

Dwayne L. Knirk, Ph.D.
Software Quality Engineer
Sandia National Laboratories
9208 Mabry Avenue NE
Albuquerque, NM 87109-6400
(505) 844-7183
Fax: (505) 844-3920
dlknirk@sandia.gov

8734

Business Information: Possessing an excellent understanding of technology, Dr. Knirk serves as Software Quality Engineer at Sandia National Laboratories. Being with the Lab for seven years, he is responsible for software engineering methods, software process assessments, improvements, methods adoption, and training. He is the principal member of the information technology group. Dr. Knirk is the only software testing expert working on an $18 million modernization project, remodeling operations for all support questions in the software department. His accomplishments include developing a cutting edge software testing product that is now used by both IBM and AT&T. He has published many articles in chemical journals. Dr. Knirk's success is attributed to good memory skills, his ability to organize information, and his parents encouraging him and providing him with a good education. Established in 1949, Sandia National Laboratories provides nuclear weaponry, microelectronic mechanical machines, information security, robotics, teraflops simulations, and global test ban treaty monitoring. Sandia is a national lab service for the United States government run by the Department of Energy with a focus on disassembling nuclear weapons. Sandia National Laboratories provides safe transport of nuclear weapons internationally. The Lab is the leader in micro electromachines. Located in Albuquerque, New Mexico, the Lab employs 7,600 professional, technical, and support staff. **Career Highlights:** Software Quality Engineer, Sandia National Laboratories (1993-Present); Chief Software Engineer, Programming Environments, Inc. (1984-93); Advanced Methods Research/Development, Electronic Associates, Inc. (1977-84). **Associations & Accomplishments:** Institute of Electrical and Electronics Engineers; Institute of Electrical and Electronics Engineers Computer Society; American Society of Quality. **Education:** Rice University, Ph.D. in Theoretical Chemistry (1972); Michigan State University: M.A. in Chemistry (1967), B.S. (1967). **Personal Information:** Dr. Knirk enjoys classical pianist.

Linda Ciabatoni
Founder
Catalyst 2020
5742 North 4th Street
Arlington, VA 22205
(703) 522-6191
Fax: (703) 522-6147
sonolinda@msn.com

8741

Business Information: Ms. Ciabatoni founded Catalyst 2020 in 1997 and assumed the post of Founder, performing all strategic planning services for clients. Utilizing a technical background and strong business development and marketing skills, she has successfully increased the revenues of several clients by 50 percent or more. She is dedicated to leaders producing extraordinary results. Catalyst 2020 provides services to high technology companies who are interested in expansion or increasing profitability. The Company develops customized business strategies to assist businesses with progression and taking market share. **Career Highlights:** Founder, Catalyst 2020 (1997-Present); Vice President for Marketing, ENTEVO (1997-99); Office of President, Suite Software (1996-97); Executive Vice President, New Dimension Software (1994-95); Division Marketing Group Manager, Sun Microsystems (1989-94). **Associations & Accomplishments:** Recipient of 1999 Marketing Computers ICON Award; Russian Teen Mentor; Licensed Transformational Leader, PATH; Child and Youth Advocate. **Education:** University of Maryland, B.S. (1970); Massachusetts Institution of Technology, International Relations Executive Program. **Personal Information:** Ms. Ciabatoni enjoys ballroom dancing, athletics, writing and international cultures.

Michael A. Marino
President
Carolina Manufacturer's Service, Inc.
2650 Pilgrim Court
Winston-Salem, NC 27104
(910) 631-2867
Fax: (910) 631-2906
mike.marino@cms.inmar-inc.com

8741

Business Information: Incorporating 28 successful years of experience with NYNEX Corporation, a world leading telecommunications conglomerate, Michael Marino's expertise in communications and information technology led him to serve in many key positions. His extensive communications background includes serving as Group Vice President for NYNEX Corporation; Executive Vice President and Chief Operating Officer for NYNEX Mobile Communications Company; Vice President of Strategy and Planning for NYNEX Worldwide Services Group; Executive Vice President and Chief Operating Officer with NYNEX Business Centers; and Vice President of Finance and Administration for NYNEX Business Information Systems Company. Utilizing his vast skills acquired in the telecommunications field, Mr. Marino joined Carolina Manufacturer's Service, Inc. as President in 1996. Carolina Manufacturer's Service, Inc. leads the North American market as the longest-standing provider of promotion planning and management services to major consumer product manufacturers and their distribution partners. Currently the largest of three operating subsidiaries of Inmar Enterprises, Inc., Carolina Manufacturer's Service, Inc. is headquartered along with them in Winston-Salem, North Carolina. Formed in 1983, the Company employs 2,500 people in North Carolina and in various locations throughout Mexico and Texas. **Career Highlights:** President, Carolina Manufacturer's Service, Inc. (1996-Present); Group Vice President, NYNEX Corporation (1995-96); Executive Vice President/Chief Operating Officer, NYNEX Mobile Communications Company (1992-94); Vice President of Strategy and Planning, NYNEX Worldwide Services Group (1991-92); Executive Vice President/Chief Operating Officer, NYNEX Business Centers (1988-91); Vice President of Finance and Administration, NYNEX Business Information Systems Company (1987-88). **Associations & Accomplishments:** Alumni Board, Pace University, Lubin Graduate School of Business; Alumni Association, Tufts University; Board of Directors, Wireless Telecom, Inc.; Alumni Association, Beelzebubs of Tufts University; Delta Mu Delta Honorary Society for M.B.A. Graduates; Fund-raiser: United Way, Junior Achievement, March of Dimes, Juvenile Diabetes Foundation; Board of Advisors, International WHO'S WHO of Information Technology. **Education:** Pace University, Lubin Graduate School of Business, M.B.A. (1979); Tufts University, B.A. (1969). **Personal Information:** Married to Diane in 1988. Two children: Christie and Loryn. Mr. Marino enjoys playing golf, reading and travel.

Michael R. Passe, M.C.S.E.

Senior Systems Engineer
Care Group
1135 Tremont Street
Boston, MA 02120
(617) 754-8051
Fax: (617) 754-8060
mpasse@caregroup.harvard.edu

8741

Business Information: In his role as Senior Systems Engineer, Mr. Passe is concerned with the strategic development of technology for Care Group. Utilizing education and related work experience, he completes activities such as development and implementation of hardware and software. Overseeing network systems, he gathers data to generate applications and tools for messaging and Intel service support groups. Keeping his personal goals in line with corporate objectives, Mr. Passes intends to continue in his current role as he assist in the completion of corporate goals such as the administration of an NT Windows 2000 platform. His success reflects his ability to think outside the box, deliver results, and take on new challenges. Headquartered in Boston, Massachusetts Care Group is comprised of a collaboration of five hospitals and a community physician. Additionally, the Group maintains several clinics, rehabilitation centers, and outpatient facilities, resulting in the formation of the largest healthcare organization granted by NIH in the country. **Career Highlights:** Senior Systems Engineer, Care Group (1998-Present); Systems Consultant, Michael R. Passe Consulting (1992-Pesent); Systems Engineer III, Boston University (1994-98); Systems Engineer, Xerotex (1993-94). **Associations & Accomplishments:** National Eagle Scout Association. **Education:** Worcester Polytechnic Institute, B.S. in Electrical Engineering (1993); Microsoft Certified Systems Engineer. **Personal Information:** Mr. Passe enjoys travel.

Brian W. Alger

Principal
KPMG Consulting
Suite 100, Waterpark Place, 20 Bay Street
Toronto, Ontario, Canada M5J 2X9
(416) 228-7205
Fax: (416) 363-6150
brian.alger@sympatico.ca

8742

Business Information: As the Principal for KPMG Consulting, Mr. Alger designs, produces, and implements educational systems including system changes and updates for distribution to an international clientele. Possessing an excellent understanding of technology, he works closely with management and systems users to analyze, specify, and design new solutions to enhance the overall operations of the technical infrastructure. Mr. Alger's skills and knowledge were instrumental in the development of the first multi-media school in the United States, and his extensive experience continues to inspire new, quality educational software. Mr. Alger plans to continue in his present position, fostering growth and expansion in e-learning projects and education via the computer. KPMG Consulting specializes in computer consulting for various markets. The Firm maintains headquarters in Toronto, Ontario that specializes in educational systems consulting. Established in 1999, local operations employ the services of 20 individuals to facilitate all aspects of design, research, marketing, and systems implementation. **Career Highlights:** Principal, KPMG Consulting (1998-Present); Director, Mind Wave, Inc.; Educator, Halton District School Board. **Education:** York University, Master's degree in Fine Arts (1985). **Personal Information:** Mr. Alger enjoys computers and music.

Joel P. Attri

Manager of CRM Infrastructure Team
KPMG Consulting, Inc.
500 East Middlefield Road
Mountain View, CA 94043
(408) 307-9511
Fax: (954) 827-0452
jattri@pacbell.net

8742

Business Information: Highly skilled in the technical consulting industry, Mr. Attri serves as the Manager of the CRM Infrastructure Team for KPMG Consulting, Inc. In his capacity, he fulfills a number of technical functions on behalf of the Firm and its international clientele. Leading the global task force in systems design, Mr. Attri oversees and directs the deployment of infrastructure layouts that are capable of supporting all information technology concepts and methodologies, from mail to file storage to applications. Remaining with KPMG, Mr. Attri is well on his way to becoming Senior Manager, thereby achieving personal satisfaction and occupational success. Established in 1887, KPMG Consulting is one of the "Big 5" consulting firms specializing in stock values, corporate tax, and investment consultation. Internationally recognized, KPMG Consulting employs the expertise of over 30,000 professionals who generate annual revenues of over $2 billion. Providing state of the art information technology solutions to private and commercial clients, KPMG is achieving great notoriety all over the world. **Career Highlights:** Manager of CRM Infrastructure Team, KPMG Consulting, Inc. (1999-Present); Technology Manager, Centerbeam (1999); Implementation Manager, CBT Systems (1998-99). **Associations & Accomplishments:** Lifetime Alumni of De La Salle High School; Volunteer Member of Contra Costa County. **Education:** St. Marys College of California, B.A. in Sports Management (1995); Certifications: Microsoft, Citrix, and Sichel. **Personal Information:** Mr. Attri enjoys volunteer work and aerobic dancing.

Carol M. Benner

Database Manager
Templin Management Associates
265 Locust Grove Road
Greenfield Center, NY 12833-1501
(518) 893-7760
Fax: (518) 893-2215
cbenner@templin.com

8742

Business Information: As Database Manager of Templin Management Associates, Ms. Benner is responsible for information management. She collects data and statistics for consultant evaluations and processes the data into an accessible database to facilitate its assimilation into presentations. Ms. Benner has held her present position since 1994 and is confident in her ability to take on further responsibilities in the future. Templin Management Associates provides consulting services to organizations in the health care industry. Established in 1986, the Consultancy focuses on productivity and staffing studies designed to assist health care facilities to become more efficient, and to improve the quality of patient care and customer service. Templin Management Associates currently operates offices in New York and California, generating annual revenues near $300,000. **Career Highlights:** Database Manager, Templin Management Associates (1994-Present); Adjunct Faculty Member, Adirondack Community College (Present); Investment Assistant, Evergreen Bancorp (1987-94); Teacher, Lake George Central School (1972-75). **Associations & Accomplishments:** Executive Secretary of the Consulting Alliance; Former Board Member, Lower Adirondack Regional Arts Council; National Association of Female Executives. **Education:** Kennedy Western University, Master's Candidate; State University of New York at Fredonia, B.S. in Education (1966). **Personal Information:** Married to Timothy in 1965. Two children: Glen S. and Wayne B. Ms. Benner enjoys playing classical guitar, fiber arts and painting.

Moninder S. Birdi

Project Manager
Parsons Engineering Science
10521 Rosehaven Street
Fairfax, MD 22030
(703) 934-2338
Fax: (703) 591-1305
moninder.birdi@parsons.com

8742

Business Information: Mr. Birdi is Project Manager of Parsons Engineering Science. He is responsible for leading project teams in analyzing, designing, and implementing software applications, including identifying client requirements and developing cutting edge systems specifications. Mr. Birdi first came on board to Parsons Engineering Science as an Associate Engineer in 1996. Prior to that, he served as a Project Manager with the Urban Development Institute. As a seven year technology veteran, he owns an established track record for producing results in support of objectives and goals. Mr. Birdi, in his current position, leads and manages projects, fulfills the role of Oracle database administrator, designs and implements software applications, and performs ERP development for the aviation industry. In addition to supervising his staff of 11 employees, he handle numerous resource planning functions, to include determining future resource requirements; overseeing time lines, schedules, assignments, and budgets; and providing cohesive leadership during all phases of operation. He credits his success to his aptitude and ability to build strong teams and think out-of-the-box. Eventually moving up the corporate hierarchy and managing a team of 25 people serve as his future aspirations. A large international consulting firm, Parsons Engineering Science specializes in design, construction, and program management in civil and environmental engineering. Established in 1958, Parsons Engineering Science is manned by workforce of more than 12,100 professional, technical, and support people. **Career Highlights:** Parsons Engineering Science: Project Manager (1998-Present), Associate Engineer (1996-98); Project Manager, Urban Development Institute (1992-93). **Associations & Accomplishments:** Water Environment Federation. **Education:** University of Maryland, M.S. in Environmental Engineering (1996), B.S. in Civil Engineering. **Personal Information:** Mr. Birdi enjoys cricket.

Linda G. Blockus

Manager
KPMG Consulting
10 Hamilton Road
Basking Ridge, NJ 07920
(973) 912-4638
lblockus@kpmg.com

8742

Business Information: Demonstrating adept technical abilities, Mrs. Blockus serves as Manager for the KPMG Consulting. In her capacity, she is responsible for conducting OSS tests on performance metrics, and providing clients with strategic planning methods based on reviewed technical information. Posssessing an excellent understanding of her field, Mrs. Blockus also supervises administrative aspects, conducts systems training, and oversees operational developments. She continues to grow professionally through the fulfillment of her responsibilities and her involvement in the advancement of operations. Staying technical, but moving and learning more about the e-business arena serves as Mrs. Blockus' future plans. Headquartered in Basking Ridge, New Jersey, KPMG Consulting is a "Big 5" management consulting firm providing specialized consultation for the telecommunications industry. The Firm operates offices across the nation that provides clients with corporate restructuring programs designed to improve operational management and enhance performance measures. Dedicated to ensuring quality services, KPMG Consulting handles each corporate account with special attention by researching client needs, expenditures, and analyzing revenues, whereupon, a custom plan is formulated to directly suit client needs. **Career Highlights:** Manager, KPMG Consulting (1998-Present); Division Manager, AT&T (1971-97); Disrtict Manager, Lucent Technologies (1985-89). **Education:** Fordham University, M.B.A. (1974); Russell Page College, B.A. in Economics and Retailing; George Washington University, Project Management Certificate. **Personal Information:** Married to Bruce. Mrs. Blockus enjoys reading, wine and ballroom dancing.

Michael G. Burkhart

Software Engineer
Watson Wyatt Worldwide
1717 H Street NW
Washington, DC 20006-3900
(202) 715-7740
Fax: (707) 221-2156
mike_burkhart@watsonwyatt.com

8742

Business Information: Serving as a Software Engineer with Watson Wyatt Worldwide, Mr. Burkhart develops software for the compensation practice, as well as supports the software technically and develops and teaches training curricula. He attributes his success in designing easy-to-read and easy-to-use applications to his background in photography and drafting. Watson Wyatt brings together two disciplines - people and financial management - to help clients improve business performance. Through cost-effective compensation and benefits programs that help companies attract, retain, and motivate a talented workforce, Watson Wyatt helps clients achieve competitive advantage through their people. Watson Wyatt has more than 5,000 associates in 35 countries and has corporate offices in Reigate, England and Bethesda, Maryland. **Career Highlights:** Software Engineer, Watson Wyatt Worldwide (1994-Present); Senior Programmer/Analyst, Weston Brothers Software (1991-94); Programmer/Analyst, Software Synergistics (1989-91); Integrated Circuit Board Designer, Texas Instruments (1979-89). **Associations & Accomplishments:** American Compensation Association; Boy Scouts of America: Assistant Cub Master Pack 846, Troop Committee Member Troop 847; Former member of the Dallas Professional Photographers Association. **Education:** Eastfield Community College, Associate's degree (1986). **Personal Information:** Married to Roxane W. in 1983. Two children: Paul Michael and Matthew Jacob. Mr. Burkhart enjoys photography, scouting and woodworking.

John Cary

President
ComCore
Two Ravinia Drive, Suite 860
Atlanta, GA 30346
(770) 390-1770
Fax: (770) 390-1771
jcary@comcore.com

8742

Business Information: Mr. Cary serves as President of ComCore. Utilizing an extensive background knowledge of recruitment consulting, he is responsible for leading the Company's daily administration and operational functions. He determines strategic direction and business contribution of the information systems function. Mr. Cary attends to client development and relationships, ensuring all services provided are laced with quality and value. Keeping the customer his number one priority, Mr. Cary maintains daily communications, enabling him to receive feedback on the services provided. In the future, he looks forward to growing the Company to a position where he is able to delegate and lead. "The world is a small place, never burn bridges," is cited as his advice. His success reflects his ability to communicate effectively, take on challenges, and deliver results on behalf of his clientele. Founded in 1999, ComCore provides state-of-the-art outsourcing and management consulting, specifically in the recruitment area. Located in Atlanta, Georgia, the Company targets the placement of technology professionals from computer programmers to chief information officers. The Company's main focus is the fast-growing technology based companies around the United States. With a staff of approximately 20 employees, the Company reports annual revenues in excess of $3 million. **Career Highlights:** President, ComCore (1999-Present); Director of Recruiting, Diversified Computer Consultants (1999-Present); Managing Director, Cornerstone Resources (1996-99). **Associations & Accomplishments:** TAG Georgia; TRN Chicago; AIRS; BNI Atlanta; SEN Atlanta; Orlando Chamber of Commerce. **Education:** Texas A&M University, B.S. in Accounting (1995). **Personal Information:** Married to Meredith in 1997. Mr. Cary enjoys golf, flying and water sports.

Jane Caudullo

Director
Arthur Andersen
100 Arthur Andersen Parkway
Sarasota, FL 34232
(941) 341-5952
Fax: (941) 341-5893
jane.caudullo@us.arthurandersen.com

8742

Business Information: A topnotch, 13 year veteran of the consulting and technology field, Mrs. Caudullo joined the Arthur Andersen team as Director in 1998, after 12 solid years as Associate Director with Ernst & Young LLP. She owns a consistent record of delivering results through communication and interpersonal skills, use of emerging technology, and solving system problems and challenges in a systematic and efficient manner. Her present position involves oversight of all internal systems development. Mrs. Caudullo leverages her extensive management skills and technical expertise in maintaining all client servers and systems infrastructure, as well as ensuring technical products and services are laced with quality, value, and selection. An expert in the field, she is able to take ideas and turn them into cutting edge software designs. Installing operating systems software, database management systems software, and servers; monitoring and tuning systems software, peripherals, and networks; and resolving system problems and challenges also fall within the purview of Mrs. Caudullo's responsibilities. Creating more up to date Web sites for consumers and giving them the highest quality is cited as Mrs. Caudullo's future endeavors. A global Big 5 accounting firm, Arthur Andersen provides up-to-date technical services to clients. Presently, the Firm employs a global staff of more than 55,000 professional, technical, and support personnel who help generate annual revenues in excess of $7 billion. **Career Highlights:** Director, Arthur Andersen (1998-Present); Associate Director, Ernst & Young LLP (1987-98). **Associations & Accomplishments:** Sun Coast Technology Organization. **Education:** Montclair State University, B.A. (1985). **Personal Information:** Married to Sal in 1971. Three children: Debbie, Jennifer, and Al.

Kishore Chakraborty, Ed.D.

Chief Executive Officer
Kishore Chakraborty Consulting
104 Coolidge Hill Road, Unit 15
Watertown, MA 02472-5025
(617) 926-8785
chak@gis.net

8742

Business Information: As founder and owner of Kishore Chakraborty Consulting, Dr. Chakraborty consults with businesses on strategy to best help their company. As the Company's Chief Executive Officer, he determines the strategic direction and vision. Possessing an excellent understanding of his field, he demonstrates consulting expertise as he collects, reviews, and analyzes information prior to making recommendations to his clients on technical solutions. Dr. Chakraborty also advises companies about the Internet. Sharing his knowledge in the public forum, he has written various books on impact technology and strategy planning and also teaches. Having been voted "Professor of the Year," he is constantly asked to be keynote speaker by major corporations. Dr. Chakraborty's advice to others is "get involved with the Internet." Attributing his success to education and intelligence, his future goals include teaching, consulting, and publishing research. Established in 1997, Kishore Chakraborty Consulting provides corporations and small businesses solutions to management and organizational problems. Presently, the Company is located in Watertown, Massachusetts and serves a regional clientele. **Career Highlights:** Chief Executive Officer, Kishore Chakraborty Consulting (1997-Present); Professor of Strategy, Arthur D. Little School of Management (1998-Present); Assistant Professor of Management, Babson College (1989-97). **Education:** Harvard Graduate School of Education, Ed.D. (1982); Harvard University, M.Ed.; Brandeis University, B.A.

Larry J. Conway

Manager
Arthur Andersen
225 Franklin Street
Boston, MA 02110-2804
(617) 330-5514
Fax: (617) 439-9731
laurence.j.conway@us.arthurandersen.com

8742

Business Information: For the past year, Mr. Conway has adhered to the responsibilities of Manager of Arthur Andersen. He provides senior project management for consulting engagements, establishes new business, distributes work load, and sells technical assignments. Overlapping duties require Mr. Conway to be a strategic planner and dedicated leader. One demonstration of Mr. Conway's achievements is the movement of the entire data center in one day. The Data Center took over a month to plan, however he had the knowledge and abilities to complete the task correctly and efficiently. Mr. Conway also stripped 20 percent off the informational technology budget, leaving additional funds to be available for other projects. He believes in recruiting a great team to get jobs done and assist the Firm in its advancement. Reading, training, and keeping current on new technology are all attributed to Mr. Conway's great success. Arthur Andersen is a consulting firm for e-commerce, customer relationship management, data warehousing, and one to one marketing. Providing services since 1913, the Firm has a total of 70,000 employees to assist in a variety of duties. Arthur Andersen prides itself on the reputation of providing the best in advanced technology and assisting clients in defining their strategies. **Career Highlights:** Manager, Arthur Andersen (1998-Present); Infrastructure Service Manager, Sybase, Inc. (1996-98); Infrastructure Services Director, Epsilon Data Management (1994-96); Development Manager, Wang Laboratories (1980-94). **Associations & Accomplishments:** Deputy Chief of Staff for Information Management; Massachusetts Army National Guard; Information Systems Advisory Council; School Superintendent's Advisory Committee; National Guard Associations; Second Corps Cadets Veterans Association; Yankee Division Veterans Association. **Education:** Anna Maria College, M.B.A. (1998); Northeastern University, B.A. in Mathematics, Certificate in Computer Programing; United States Army Command and General Staff School Certificate. **Personal Information:** Married to Linda in 1977. Two children: Larry and Mike. Mr. Conway enjoys canoe racing and coaching youth sports.

Jerry D. Croswell

Senior Technical Writer
Cendant Corporation
40 Oakview Drive
Trumbull, CT 06611
(203) 416-2670
Fax: (203) 416-2088
jcroswell@cms.cendant.com

8742

Business Information: As the Senior Technical Writer for Cendant Corporation, Mr. Croswell develops, writes, and edits program and system documentation, user manuals, training courses, and procedures. Coming on board to Cendant in 1992, he uses his extensive technical skills and hands on experience to develop state of the art Microsoft Access databases for the Corporation's management and system users. Highly regarded, he continues to grow as he fulfills the many responsibilities of his position. Attributing his success to knowledge and his ability to take on challenges and deliver results, Mr. Croswell plans on remaining with Cendant Corporation in his present position and assisting in the completion of corporate goals. Cendant Corporation is a direct marketing firm providing local companies with a chance to concentrate on providing services, while another company performs the marketing. The Company provides discounts on a variety of products and services, primarily for hotels and the transportation industry. National in scope, Cendant Corporation is headquartered in Long Island, New York. **Career Highlights:** Senior Technical Writer, Cendant Corporation (1992-Present); Supervisor of 2nd Shift, Duracell (1989-90); Senior Production Control Analyst, GE Capital (1979-89). **Associations & Accomplishments:** United States Marine Corps (1966-74). **Education:** Sacred Heart Universtiy, A.S. in Paralegal (1979). **Personal Information:** Married to Jane in 1975. One child: Patricia. Mr. Croswell enjoys reading and history.

Linda A. Fousek

Information Architect
Intend Change
1080 Sherman Court
Lindsay, CA 93247
(650) 207-6660
jerilaf@leland.standford.edu

8742

Business Information: As an Information Architect of Intend Change, Ms. Fousek is responsible for developing user interface design for e-commerce Web sites. Other obligations include discussing advantages and disadvantages of new and existing programs, user testing, market research, and the creation of prototypes. With more than two years of technical experience, Ms. Fousek utilizes her professional talents to implement excellence and precision into every design. Highly regarded, her plans for the future include remaining with the Company, with the possibility of returning to Stanford for a year to earn a Master's degree in Media Studies. Success, according to Ms. Fousek, is attributed to her ability to take on challenges and deliver results on behalf of the Company and its clients. Intend Change engages in the provision of professional consulting services for client companies. The Company offers such services as building marketing strategies and creating interfaces. Established in 1999, the Company operates out of Palo Alto, California. The Company currently has 30 professionals including consultants, administrative staff, and executive officers. **Career Highlights:** Information Architect, Intend Change (2000-Present); User Interface Designer, U.S. Web/CKS (1999-00); Computer Technician, Stanford Residential Computing (1998-00); Therapist, Independent (1996-98). **Education:** Stanford University, B.S. (2000). **Personal Information:** Ms. Fousek enjoys being an interpreter for the deaf, triathalons, backpacking, rowing and sailing.

John R. Holderread

Consultant
Quality Solutions
1011 South 5th
Springfield, IL 62703
(217) 523-8922

8742

Business Information: The sole proprietor and serving as a Consultant for Quality Solutions, Mr. Holderread provides consulting services for his clients in an effort to enhance the start-up of new businesses, the initiation of new programs, and the provision of workable solutions to common problems throughout the corporate world. But Mr. Holderread's activities far surpass the boundaries established by his consulting and management services. He continues to focus efforts on research and development and continually strives to develop and promote his own inventions in the area of information technology. Also a poet, he has a poem published (Days of Futures Past) in a book titled "Dance on The Horizon," a collection from beginning writers, and entertains aspirations of publishing more poetry in the future. In an effort to provide more comprehensive services through his Business, Mr. Holderread is a Y2K expert, he recently developed a proposed ISO standard for quality and productivity, and at this time is initiating a national and global program to give benefits to the Y2K problems. The standard is in the form of a business integration system that allows for the delivery of the Malcomb Baldrige Award. Quality Solutions is actively seeking new clients and referrals are appreciated. An entrepreneur in the truest sense of the word, Mr. Holderread had an idea for a product that he hoped to develop and market. In his attempt to take it from the conceptualization stage to the finished product, he encountered many obstacles and realized that the only way to showcase his invention was through an entrepreneurial endeavor. Thus, Quality Solutions was founded in 1986. Located in Houston, Texas, the Company focuses efforts on consultation and research activities, as well as total quality management, information technology, and software applications for state and federal government organizations and area businesses. **Career Highlights:** Consultant, Quality Solutions (1986-Present). Clients include the Illinois Department of Public Aid, Union Pacific, and GND. **Associations & Accomplishments:** Co-Founder, Houston Inventors Association. **Personal Information:** Three children: Jon, Carrie, and Allison. John R. Holderread is a Vietnam era veteran.

Karen Hurst

Experience Manager
Arthur Andersen
631 Preston Woods Treal
Dunwoody, GA 30338
(404) 221-4687
Fax: (404) 681-8400
karen.g.hurst@us.arthurandersen.com

8742

Business Information: Ms. Hurst functions in the capacity of an Experience Manager with Arthur Andersen. She is responsible for guiding and leading both database administrators and technical architects in assessing, designing, and implementing technical infrastructures that meet the clients short and long term strategic goals. Before joining the Arthur Andersen team, Ms. Hurst served as Senior Database Administrator and Architect for Matrix Consulting as well as Senior Systems Analyst with Science & Technology. As an 11 year professional, she assists in establishing and implementing the client's technology environments, identifies new avenues for increased revenues, and develops powerful data architect and data warehouse marketing plans. Ms. Hurst also is responsible for outsourcing consultants and other professionals to staff clients' staff. She supervises a staff of five employees providing regional and international solutions. Her milestones include her ability to introduce and teach new technology to clients. Creating cutting edge ideas and practicing them, conducting hands on research and implementation, reading, and surfing the Internet helps Ms. Hurst remain on the leading edge. Becoming a Partner or Senior Principal in a large firm and taking the lead in designing an innovation and development center serves as her future endeavors. Arthur Andersen is a global business, management, finance, and information technology consulting firm. A respected Fortune 500 company, Arthur Andersen is the number one financial services company in the United States. In addition, the Firm offers technology services ranging from networking to data warehousing, ERP, and Y2K. Established in 1920, Arthur Andersen employs a global staff of over 100,000 professionals, technical, and administrative support personnel. Presently, the Firm reports estimated revenues in excess of $1 billion annually. **Career Highlights:** Experience Manager, Arthur Andersen (1998-Present); Senior Database Administrator/Architect, Architect Matrix Consulting (1996-97); Senior System Analyst, Science & Technology (1991-95); **Associations & Accomplishments:** Institute of Electronics and Electrical Engineers; IOUG; DECUS. **Education:** Tennessee Technical University, B.S. in Business Administration (1988). **Personal Information:** Ms. Hurst enjoys hiking, flying and sky diving.

Carrie D. Ingersoll

Manager
Deloitte Consulting
19167 110th Place SE
Renton, WA 98055-8112
(425) 635-9400
Fax: (425) 646-9009
cingersoll@dttus.com

8742

Business Information: Serving as Manager for Deloitte Consulting, Ms. Ingersoll supervises a client service team of 10 people. She specializes in SAP implementation software, as well as business process design. In addition, Ms. Ingersoll engages in specifications testing. She, in turn, reports all results to her superiors. Also, to maintain a talented staff, Ms. Ingersoll interviews, recruits, and hires new employees. As for the future, she plans to become actively engaged in e-commerce, and attain new knowledge of that ever-changing facet of business and administration. Current success, Ms. Ingersoll asserts, is the final product of good mentors and peers who have pushed her to reach her goals. Deloitte Consulting is a "Big 5" firm. Providing services for different areas of consulting, representatives of the Firm has fostered awareness in every subject from information control to assurance, tax, and law. The Firm's client service teams combine insight, business knowledge, and industry expertise to assist clients achieve success. **Career Highlights:** Manager, Deloitte Consulting (1996-Present); Consultant, Andersen Consulting (1995-96); Quality Engineer, Carver Corporation (1994-95). **Education:** University of Washington, B.S. in Industrial Engineering (1994). **Personal Information:** Ms. Ingersoll enjoys horseback riding, hiking, biking and snow skiing.

Francesca F. Keating

Manager
KPMG Consulting
1676 International Drive
McLean, VA 22102
(703) 347-4338
Fax: (703) 747-3947
fkeating@kpmg.com

8742

Business Information: As a Manager within KPMG Consulting, Mrs. Keating is responsible for ERP/XRP sales, implementations, and package solution integrations. A ten year veteran, and two with KPMG, her primary focus is on improving business through software implementation. Possessing business savvy and technical expertise, Mrs. Keating is involved in the discovery, assessment, and deployment of advanced technologies to help her clients remain flexible, efficient and profitable in the Information Technology Age. Her primary clientele are universities and research institutes. Staying on the crest of the wave, Mrs. Keating's strategic plans are deployment of new technologies and bringing e-business and portal usage to the forefront. Her highlights include bringing a number of multi-package implementation programs to completion on time and within budgetary constraints. Aggressively taking on challenges and delivering results is key to Mrs. Keating's success. Established in 1897, KMPG LLP is one of the "Big 5" accounting firms that provides Audit, Tax, and Consulting services. The Firm has recently spun off its consulting arm by creating KPMG Consulting. This new Company provides a wealth of consulting services within the following lines of business: High Tech, Consumer and Industrial Markets, Communications and Content, Public Sector, Finance, and Health Care. Over 25,000 consultants work together to assist a large international clientele. **Career Highlights:** Manager, KPMG Consulting (1998-Present); Principal, Oracle Corporation (1995-98). **Education:** Southern Methodist University, M.B.A. (1991); Pace University, B.A. (1990). **Personal Information:** Married.

Michael Kennedy

Partner/Recruiter
The Kennedy Connection
314 Stamford Drive
Powell, OH 43065
(614) 523-9975
kconnect@ibocity.com

8742

Business Information: Serving in the dual role of Partner and Recruiter at The Kennedy Connection, Mr. Kennedy is responsible for the recruiting and training of other professionals to develop their own Internet based business. His fundamental objective is to network to promote the Company and its services in order to establish new business and client relationships. Utilizing his extensive knowledge in the technological field, Mr. Kennedy is able to fulfill his job obligations unhindered. He hopes to assist the Company in its growth, development, and expansion in the future. His success is attributed to his strong belief in God. The Kennedy Connection is a multilevel Internet marketer involved with the Internet shopping business. Established in 1999, two people assist in various areas of the business. **Career Highlights:** Partner/Recruiter, The Kennedy Connection (1999-Present); Finance Manager, Jack Maxton Chevrolet (1981-99). **Personal Information:** Married to Constance Elaine in 1996. Two children: Brandon and Troy. Mr. Kennedy enjoys music and golf.

Rajesh Kumawat

Consultant
KPMG LLP
757 3rd Avenue
New York, IL 10017
(212) 758-9700
Fax: (212) 872-7951
rkumawat@netscape.net

8742

Business Information: Providing his skilled services as an information technology Consultant for KPMG LLP, Mr. Kumawat primarily focuses on outsourcing, needs assessment, and administering professional advice. He develops strategic plans for companies to enable each one to effectively utilize information technology to enhance business growth. Mr. Kumawat has received much recognition from satisfied clients for a job well done. He credits his success to a topnotch university education, ability, and the good fortune to have met the right people in his career. Looking forward to the next millennium, Mr. Kumawat plans to obtain a position as an Integrator where he can utilize his combined technical and managerial skills to assist in the development of new technology. With a global presence in 157 countries, KPMG LLP provides information technology consulting with a strong focus on the media and entertainment industry. Corporate headquarters are located in Amsterdam, Holland. Founded in 1872, the Firm bases its business on firm core values such as no boundaries between industries, leadership, and partnership. Presently, the Firm employs a work force of more than 95,000 individuals. **Career Highlights:** Consultant, KPMG LLP (1999-Present); On-Site Consultant, University of Illinois (1998-99); Assistant Manager, Eicher Ltd. (1996-97). **Associations & Accomplishments:** Vice President, Technology Management Association. **Education:** University of Illinois at Urbana/Champaign, M.B.A. (1999); Mangalore University, Bachelor's degree in Engineering (1996). **Personal Information:** Mr. Kumawat enjoys singing, tennis and jogging.

Bonnie L. Lawrence

President
Lawrence Associates
P.O. Box 9645
New Haven, CT 06536
(203) 624-9995
Fax: (203) 624-6488
www.bllawrenceassoc/ne@msn.com

8742

Business Information: The owner and founder of Lawrence Associates, Ms. Lawrence serves in the role of President. She is responsible for determining the overall strategic direction and vision the Company, as well as formulating marketing and business plans. Her solid background history includes stints as General Manager with Productivity Point International and National Account Manager for Frontier Communications. As topnotch professional in her field, Ms. Lawrence utilizes strategic client development techniques to gain business and establish a trusting relationship with clients. Primarily dealing with the larger accounts, she consults with clients to determine their needs, and offer cutting edge solutions to better enhance their business. Ms. Lawrence is committed to the further development of the Company and plans to facilitate continued growth and geographic expansion by utilizing strategic planning to grab a larger portion of the current market share. Created in 1996, Lawrence Associates provides consulting for telecommunications and business management. In addition to consulting service offerings, the staff of 10 qualified professionals also give technical training and sell related telecommunications equipment. **Career Highlights:** President, Lawrence Associates (1996-Present); General Manager, Productivity Point International; National Account Manager, Frontier Communications. **Associations & Accomplishments:** Fairfield Network of Executive Women; Institute of Management Consultants; American Marketing Association; Women in Communication; Sales & Marketing Executives International; Ambassador at Yale; Volunteer, New Haven Hospital. **Education:** Quinnipiae College; Ricker College; Fairfield University. **Personal Information:** Ms. Lawrence enjoys adventure travel, skiing, backpacking, painting, inline skating and sailing.

Brenda Lewis

Founder/President
Transactions Marketing Inc.
2 Greenwich Plaza, Suite 100
Greenwich, CT 06830-6353
(203) 622-3933
b.lewis@transactionsmarketing.com

8742

Business Information: Drawing on her extensive background in wireless data communications, beginning with satellite services in the late 1960s, Brenda Lewis founded Transactions Marketing Inc. in 1982. Serving as President of the Company, she works directly for investors and CEOs on a turn-key basis, managing project employees, negotiating customer and supplier contracts and developing strategic marketing partnerships. Transactions Marketing Inc. provides project management for business-to-business, mission critical digital commerce services. TMI has in-depth expertise in wireless media and specializes in turn-key and high risk projects, including pilots, product launch, IPOs, company start-up operations, early growth stage marketing, and restructuring for electronic commerce. Primary vertical markets served include financial services, telecommunications, and logistics. **Career Highlights:** Founder/President, Transactions Marketing Inc. (1982-Present); Director of Marketing, Howmet Aluminum Corporation (1976-81); Senior Analyst, Marine Management Systems (1974-75); Analyst, Exxon International (1967-73). **Associations & Accomplishments:** Software & Information Industry Association, Wireless Data Forum; New York New Media Association; City of Stamford, Connecticut Planning Board; Co-Chair Cove Task Force; Founder, Cove East Side Neighborhood Coalition. **Education:** University of Connecticut, M.B.A. (1981); Smith College, B.A., cum laude (1967); Harvard Business School, P.M.D. 41; New York University, Certificate in Telecommunications Management. **Personal Information:** Ms. Lewis is an active racing sailor and skier.

Humbert Low

Manager
KPMG LLP
Suite 3300, Commerce Court West, P.O. Box 31
Toronto, Ontario, Canada M5L 1B2
(416) 777-8862
Fax: (416) 777-8818
hlow@kpmg.ca

8742

Business Information: As Manager of KPMG LLP, Mr. Low is responsible for providing leadership and support in a practice related to information technology risk. His specific duties include such activities as Internet and e-commerce security services, information technology assurance services, and security related consulting services. Mr. Low is deeply involved in practice and service development, consulting clients on information risk mitigation. With years of experience in the technology field, he engages in research and conference attendance and speaking, all of which contribute to his reputation of excellence. His strategic plans for the future include keeping abreast of new technology and continuing to better himself. "Got to have determination," is cited as Mr. Low's advice. KPMG LLP engages in the provision of services in the areas of accounting and consulting. The Firm offers such services as information technology consulting and financial auditing for client companies. Established in 1870, the Firm operates many locations in 159 countries, and functions under the talent and expertise of more than 100,000 dedicated professionals. **Career Highlights:** Manager, KPMG LLP (1999-Present); Senior Consultant, Deloitte & Touche LLP (1998-99); Specialist, Andersen

Consulting (1996-98). **Associations & Accomplishments:** Institute of Management Accountants; Information Systems Audit & Controls Association; American Institute of Certified Public Accountants; Colorado Society of Certified Public Accountants; Shaw College Representative, Federation of Alumni Association of Chinese University. **Education:** University of Toronto, M.B.A. (1996); Chinese University of Hong Kong, B.B.A. (1994); Certified Information Systems Auditor (2000); State of Colorado, Certified Public Accountant (1997).

Robert A. Martin

Webmaster/Manager/Enterprise Engineer
PTI
2872 Woodcock Boulevard, Suite 150
Atlanta, GA 30341-4012
(770) 936-3181
Fax: (770) 936-3180

8742

Business Information: Utilizing over 15 years of experience in the field of information technology, Mr. Martin serves as Webmaster for PTI or Planning Technologies Inc. He designs and develops Web pages and Web sites used by the Corporation's various clients on its Intranet and on the Internet. As a 16 year veteran, Mr. Martin also serves as Manager and Enterprise Engineer. He uses his considerable engineering skills to integrate clients' myriad computer systems with one another, as well as into a seemlessly functioning network. Crediting his success to his strong Microsoft background and his continuous education efforts, he complements his duties at the Corporation with his own business of creating Web sites. Mr. Martin is committed to providing continued optimum performance and aspires to the position of Head Developer or Manager of the Application Division. Established in 1981, PTI provides enterprise network business management consulting services to large companies and corporations. In addition, the Corporation offers telecommunication and Internet services as well. Over 100 talented professionals are employed in this professional service organization. PTI reports $77 million in annual revenue each year. **Career Highlights:** Webmaster/Manager/Enterprise Engineer, PTI (1997-Present); Owner, Net Expressions Web Design (1985-Present); Management Information Systems Manager, Micro Equipment Corporation (1983-85). **Education:** Stockton State College, B.A. 91983); Microsoft Certified Professional; Windows NT 4.0; Internet Information Server 4.0; Microsoft Certified Systems Engineer. **Personal Information:** Married to Tammy in 1991. Mr. Martin enjoys the guitar, surfing, writing and performing.

Michael J. McDonnell

Oracle Database Administrator
Andersen Consulting
1601 Market Street
Philadelphia, PA 19103
(610) 695-1653
mcdonnelm@voicenet.com

8742

Business Information: Displaying his skills in this highly specialized position, Mr. McDonnell serves as Oracle Database Administrator for Andersen Consulting. He is responsible for installation, configuration, and upgrading Oracle Software, IT integration, Systems support, and UNIX administration. Mr. McDonnell coordinates with other teams to schedule and implement all system upgrades and enhancements. Administering and controlling data resources, fine tuning applications and databases to enhance database performance, and ensuring data integrity and security also fall within the purview of Mr. McDonnell's responsibilities. Prior to joining Andersen Consulting in 1994, he served as Programmer and Analyst with PRC Inc. He continues to grow professionally and gain experience through the fulfillment of his responsibilities and his involvement in the advancement of operations. Mr. McDonnell's success reflects his ability to think out-of-the-box and take on new challenges and responsibilities. Serving an international clientele, Andersen Consulting offers consulting services on various types of database administration. The Firm administers Oracle Relational Database Management Systems software, OnLine Analytical Processing databases, ROLAP, MOLAP, and Data Warehousing. Established in 1989, a staff of 65,000 qualified professionals are employed worldwide. **Career Highlights:** Oracle Database Administrator, Andersen Consulting (1994-Present); Programmer/Analyst, PRC Inc. (1990-94). **Associations & Accomplishments:** Association of Computing Machinery. **Education:** University of Scranton, B.S. (1990). **Personal Information:** Married to Angela in 1992. Two children: Michael Jarrett and Shane Vincent. Mr. McDonnell enjoys bicycle riding.

Dale T. McGuff

Director of Distance Learning Development
Arthur Andersen
1405 North 5th Avenue
St. Charles, IL 60174
(630) 444-6469
Fax: (630) 584-5581
dale.t.mcguff@us.arthurandersen.com

8742

Business Information: Mr. McGuff is the Director of Distance Learning Development for Arthur Andersen Performance and Learning. He is responsible for the successful deployment of interactive distance learning applications and associated technologies for internal use as well as consulting with external clients who want to identify alternative performance and learning strategies. Utilizing fifteen years of experience including five years with the Firm, Mr. McGuff has become an Expert at identifying strategic process methodologies for the implementation of successful interactive distance learning programs. For the future, Mr. McGuff plans to remain with Arthur Andersen and hopes to oversee the development of a Firm-wide global distance learning strategy. His success reflects his leadership and his ability to think outside the box, deliver results, and aggressively tackle new challenges. Arthur Andersen is one of the Big 5 accounting firms providing professional services to customers around the world. Throughout all of its offices, the Firm employs over 130,000 personnel who assist clients with a wide range of services that include tax, auditing, risk management, technology systems, and performance and learning. This year, the Firm will surpass $16 billion in revenues. **Career Highlights:** Arthur Andersen: Director of Distance Learning Development (1998-Present), Satellite Television Manager (1995-98); Producer/Director, WTSP-TV, Tampa (1979-89). **Associations & Accomplishments:** American Society of Training and Development; International Council for Open and Distance Education; United States Distance Learning Association. **Education:** University of South Florida, M.A. (1992); University of Northern Arizona, B.S. **Personal Information:** Married to Deborah in 1985. Mr. McGuff enjoys boating, fishing and golf.

Kevin J. Miller

Consultant
Andersen Consulting
19216 Munger Farm Road
Pollesville, MD 20837-2174
(703) 947-2246
Fax: (978) 246-0518
kevin.j.miller@ac.com

8742

Business Information: In his role as Consultant of Andersen Consulting, Mr. Miller handles various aspects of technical consultancy. Coupling excellent communicative skills with practical work experience, he regularly works with clients off-site to evaluate their needs and determine solutions. Gathering data through observations and client reports, Mr. Miller is able to generate technical action plans that most often involve the implementation of software. Specializing in PeopleSoft Human Resources, he works with analysis and design and oversees business process design and the conversion of Legacy systems. Attributing his success to the courage to try new things and take educated risks, Mr. Miller intends to continue with the Company as he progresses through the Firm's structure to the position of partner. Andersen Consulting is a leading global management and technology consulting firm whose mission is to help its clients create their future. The Firm works with clients from a wide range of industries to bring far-reaching change by aligning their people, processes, and technology with their strategy. Mr. Miller is part of the Firm's enterprise business solutions group, working with clients to implement package applications such as Oracle, SAP, or PeopleSoft. Over 65,000 men and women worldwide are employed by the global management company, that is continually improving and revising policies and procedures to ensure clients receive maximum results from their efforts. **Career Highlights:** Andersen Consulting: Consultant (1999-Present), Conversion/Software Fix Team (1999), Reporting Team Lead (1998-99), Business Process Design Team (1997-98). **Education:** James Madison University, B.B.A. in Finance and Economics (1997). **Personal Information:** Mr. Miller enjoys skiing, scuba, hiking and golf.

Bobby S. Mukundan

Domain Expert
Sapient Corporation
14131 Midway Road, Suite 900
Addison, TX 75001
(972) 982-0301
Fax: (972) 934-9206
bmukundan@sapient.com

8742

Business Information: Functioning as a Domain Expert in the Core Technology Group within Sapient's Technology Discipline, Mr. Mukundan works actively with multiple project teams, clients, and vendors to support the creation of e-Business solutions. He is the driver of key design tradeoff decisions about product offerings of various product suites and it's intergration in the overall solution. He educates project teams and clients about the feasibility of technical implementations. A savvy, seven-year professional, he communicates points of view on the applicability of database and application server product offerings based upon the requirements of the client that the solution is being built for. He has a strong background in Enterprise e-commerce and ERP systems architecture and is a certified Oracle product specialist. Mr. Mukundan has worked on implementations for several large clients like Harvard University, Siemans, Symbios Logic, First USA/Paymentech Merchant Services and Ares-Sereno International SA, to name a few. His success is attributed to his ability to think ahead and see the big picture as well as deliver results and take on new challenges. Sapient Corporation is a leading e-services consultancy providing Internet strategy consulting and sophisticated Internet-based solutions to Global 1000 companies and start-up businesses. Sapient helps clients define their Internet strategies and design, architect, develop, and implement solutions to execute those strategies. Founded in 1991, Sapient has been providing Internet solutions for over five years and employs approximately 1,900 people in offices in Cambridge, Massachusetts, the Corporation's headquarters, as well as London, Sydney, Milan, New York, San Francisco, Chicago, Atlanta, Dallas, Washington D.C., and Los Angeles. Sapient has been listed in Forbes' 200 Best Small Companies for the past three years. **Career Highlights:** Domain Expert, Sapient Corporation (1996-Present); Contract Database Administrator, Sabre Decision Tech (1995-96); Contract Systems Analyst, Deutsche Bank (1994-95); Contract Software Engineer, Siemens Nixdorf (1994); Application Developer, COMPIN, UAE (1993). **Associations & Accomplishments:** I.E.E.E. Computer Society; Oracle Database Administrator. **Education:** University of Madras, Bachelor of Engineering, Computer Science, and Engineering (1992); Oracle Certified Professional

Frank S. Nestore

Consultant
Arthur Andersen LLP
1869 Charter Lane, Suite 301
Lancaster, PA 17601
(717) 390-2533
Fax: (717) 397-8688
frank.s.nestore@us.arthurandersen.com

8742

Business Information: As Consultant of Arthur Andesen LLP, Mr. Nestore is responsible for low-level, on-site project management. Demonstrating remarkable talent in his field, he continually evaluates current projects to ensure events are occuring on schedule and proper procedures are being carried out. Mr. Nestore oversees software implementation and troubleshooting of equipment, offering maintenance and excellent customer support. Internally recognized for the development of several innovative technical solutions, he credits his professional success to a strong willingness to learn. Constantly updating his education through trade journals, the Internet, and current events, Mr. Nestore looks forward to future advancement within the corporate structure. His advice is "don't be afraid to step back and get experience." Arthur Andersen LLP is an international firm that was established in the 1800s. Offering services such as professional information technology and business process counsultancy, the Firm operates facilities around the globe, employing a total of 80,000 professionals. **Career Highlights:** Consultant, Arthur Andersen LLP (1998-Present); Commissioning Engineer, Fuller Company (1995-98). **Associations & Accomplishments:** American Chemical Society; American Institute of Chemical Engineers; American Production and Inventory Control Society. **Education:** Lehigh University, B.S. in Chemistry (1995). **Personal Information:** Mr. Nestore enjoys scuba diving and is a PADI certified diver.

Chris D. Paladino

Project Manager
Andersen Consulting
5374 Chieftain Circle
Alexandria, VA 22312-2324
(703) 947-2394
Fax: (703) 354-8564
chris.d.paladino@ac.com

8742

Business Information: Leading operations as Project Manager for Andersen Consulting, Mr. Paladino heads the high technology and business integration teams, delivering knowledge management services and human performance applications. Taking on the multi-faceted challenges of planning, designing, and developing the strategic plans within Andersen Consulting, he leads a team of 25 professional advisors. Credited as being an integral part of the team that assisted South Africa through their new constitution, Mr. Paladino will lead his team of associates through the future success of the Firm. Attributing his professional success to the concern he has for those who work for him, his future endeavors include moving up the corporate ladder. Offering respected and devoted services in this dynamic field, Andersen Consulting provides technological and management consulting for an international clientele. Utilizing the expertise of over 40,000 specialists around the world, the Firm was established in 1930. Earning a status as one of the oldest and most prestigious in their field, Andersen Consulting reports annual revenues of $9 billion. **Career Highlights:** Project Manager, Andersen Consulting (1997-Present); Executive Consultant, Automation Research Systems (1994-97); Civilian Technical Manager, United States Department of Navy (1989-94). **Associations & Accomplishments:** United States Tennis Association. **Education:** University of Southern California, M.S. in Systems Management (1993); California Polytechnic State University, B.S. in Electronic Engineering Technology. **Personal Information:** Married to Bonnie J. in 1995. One child: Michael V. Mr. Paladino enjoys tennis, family, church, technology and public speaking.

Gary A. Randles
Senior Consultant
Arthur Andersen
33 West Monroe
Chicago, IL 60603
(312) 507-4689
Fax: (312) 507-8380
grandles@prodigy.net

8742

Business Information: Offering his knowledge, skills, and dedicated service to Arthur Andersen since 1998, Mr. Randles currently serves as the Senior Consultant engaged in the multifaceted tasks of technological research and development of new methodologies. Highly regarded, he possesses superior talents and an excellent understanding of existing and emerging technologies. Mr. Randles views and evaluates new vendor products, assessing their potential for use within various client corporations. Looking to extend his ability in PC based operations, Mr. Randles is currently improving his skills through continued education and service in the field. Providing evaluation and implementation of processes and technologies to reduce risk in major companies and corporations, Arthur Andersen is one of the most innovative and advanced technology risk consulting firms in the country. Generating $130 million in annual revenue, Arthur Andersen provides the services of over 50,000 professionals who specialize in the effects of major technical implementations on all aspects of company operations. **Career Highlights:** Senior Consultant, Arthur Andersen (1998-Present); Systems Analyst, Northwest Community Hospital (1994-98). **Associations & Accomplishments:** International Computer Security Association; Digital Equipment User Society; Finish Line Director; Humanitarian Service Project's Galloping Ghost 5K Run. **Education:** Northern Illinois University, B.S. (1995); Microsoft Certified Systems Engineer; Certified Netware Administrator; Cisco Certified Network Associate; Citrix Certified Administrator; BreezeCom Certified Implementer. **Personal Information:** Married to Sandra in 1999. One child: Michael. Mr. Randles enjoys running, kayaking and flying.

Jack G. Rex

Proprietor
JGR Consulting, LLP
3130 Shoreland Avenue
Toledo, OH 43611
(419) 727-9679
Fax: (419) 727-9683
jrex@toast.net

8742

Business Information: Utilizing more than 20 years of experience in the information technology field, Mr. Rex is Proprietor of JGR Consulting, LLP and serves as Senior Consultant. He oversees and directs all aspects of day-to-day operations of the Company and presides over the completion of all administrative tasks. Offering his state-of-the-art services as Senior Consultant, he performs many types of computer systems consulting. He performs feasibility studies to determine the best system for each client and once decided, provides project management to oversee the implementation. The most significant achievement in Mr. Rex's professional career came when he coordinated a $56 million SAP implementation in just 15 months. His success reflects his ability to deliver results and aggressively tackle new challenges. JGR Consulting, LLP offers innovative information technology consulting services. The Company specializes in systems consulting, project management, feasibility studies, and business process reengineering. JGR Consulting, LLP was established in 1997. **Career Highlights:** Senior Consultant, JGR Consulting, LLP (1997-Present); Manager of Applications Development, Holnam (1995-97); Manager of Distribution Systems, Revco Drugs (1994-95); Manager of Special Projects, Owens Corning (1981-94). **Associations & Accomplishments:** Toledo Chamber of Commerce; Better Business Bureau of Northwest Ohio; International Order of Blue Gavel. **Education:** University of

Toledo, M.B.A. (1982); Bowling Green State University, B.S. (1979); Certified Data Processor (1984). **Personal Information:** Married to Denise in 1985. Two children: Sarah and Elizabeth. Mr. Rex enjoys boating, fishing and golf.

John Seelander

Vice President of Information Technology
The Plus Group
555 East Butterfield Road
Lombard, IL 60148-5680
(630) 515-0500
Fax: (630) 515-0510
theplusjns@aol.com

8742

Business Information: Mr. Seelander is the Vice President of Information Technology for The Plus Group. Leading all information technology services, he has full charge of related departments and staff members, including LAN, WAN, systems integration, and full support. Mr. Seelander is also involved in shaping the direction of the Company's future. The Plus Group is a human resources consulting firm. Services include consulting in personnel, acquisitions and mergers, and financial planning issues. Operating nine offices nationally, The Plus Group employs 1,000 people and was established in 1992. **Career Highlights:** Vice President of Information Technology, The Plus Group (1992-Present); Systems Integrator, Expert Business Systems (1990-92); EDP Coordinator, SEC Companies of The United States of America (1987-90). **Education:** Valparaiso University, B.S. in General Business (1987). **Personal Information:** Married to Suzanne in 1987. Four children: Christen, Sean, Kevin, and Eric. Mr. Seelander enjoys activities with family and friends, boating and skiing.

Jason E. Sherlock

Analyst
Andersen Consulting LLP
11951 Freedom Drive
Reston, VA 20190
(703) 947-2959
jason.e.sherlock@ac.com

8742

Business Information: Mr. Sherlock functions as Analyst at Andersen Consulting LLP, overseeing software design and programming for clients. He uses his knowledge and skills in a problem solving capacity, implementing the means for computer technology to meet the individuals needs of the Firm. He studies business data processing problems and designs new solutions using computers. Mr. Sherlock plans and develops new computer systems and devises ways to apply exisiting systems to operations still completed manually. Quickly establishing his presence in the field, Mr. Sherlock considers himself to be methodical and committed which has helped him to achieve professional success. His advice is "know what your interests are." Established in 1989, Andersen Consulting LLP offers technology and management consulting to clients. With the assistance of approximately 58,000 highly skilled employees, the Firm averages $6.8 billion per year. Andersen Consulting is ranked one of the world largest firms of its kind, operating in 49 countries. **Career Highlights:** Analyst, Andersen Consulting LLP (1998-Present). **Associations & Accomplishments:** American Guild of Organists; Organist at Unitarrian University Church of Arlington; Volunteer, SMYAL. **Education:** University of Rochester, B.A. in Music (1998), B.S. in Chemical Engineering (1998); University College Cork. **Personal Information:** Mr. Sherlock enjoys music.

Bryan E. Skiles
Program/Project Manager of Software
KPMG LLP
1630 Tahoe Circle
Tracy, CA 95376
(650) 404-4917
Fax: (650) 960-1176
bskiles@kpmg.com

8742

Business Information: As Program and Project Manager of Software for KPMG LLP, Mr. Skiles supervises a team of employees who strive to develop innovative applications to ensure that their clients stay ahead of the competition. On a daily basis, he handles administrative tasks for the teams he manages such as scheduling and budgeting. He must also maintain accurate records of each project currently in operation, to ensure proper company procedures are followed. Offering his insight and guidance at departmental meetings to formulate strategic business planning, he is utilizing 12 years of extensive experience within the financial

industry. Mr. Skiles demonstrates an effective, productive style of management that incorporates employee input and feedback to create a sense of teamwork among his staff. Attributing his success to his ability to communicate well with both clients and staff, Mr. Skiles is currently preparing literary works for publication. KPMG LLP is one of the top five consulting firms in the United States. Specializing in customer management software, the Tracy, California location offers services to enhance automated sales and marketing. With over 20,000 employees worldwide, the Firm has annual revenues in excess of $4 billion. **Career Highlights:** Program/Project Manager of Software, KPMG LLP (1998-Present); Senior System Analyst, SBC Corporation (1997-98); Owner/Consultant, BES Consulting (1990-97); Experienced Senior, Andersen Consulting (1987-90). **Education:** Brigham Young University: Master's degree in Accounting (1987), B.Sc.; Ricks College, A.S. **Personal Information:** Married to Tammy in 1995. Five children: Carlene, David, Marc, Janai, and Caleb. Mr. Skiles enjoys music and reading.

Greg W. Sluka
Information Systems Manager
Watson Wyatt Worldwide
28411 Northwestern Highway, Suite 500
Southfield, MI 48034
(248) 358-7742
Fax: (248) 358-7971
greg_sluka@watsonwyatt.com

8742

Business Information: Mr. Sluka functions in the role of Information Systems Manager for Watson Wyatt Worldwide. He is responsible for all aspects of day-to-day administration and operational activities of the systems infrastructure. Before joining the Watson Wyatt Worldwide team in 1995, Mr. Sluka served as Network Administrator with Compass Bank. His background history also includes a stint as Systems Analyst at the University of Texas' Health Science Center. As a solid, 11 year veteran of information technology, Mr. Sluka provides internal systems support for all of the Company's consultants. In addition to supervising 10 employees, he is charged with recommending and approving purchases, maintaining the budget, studying projects, and sourcing outside consultants to ensure clients technological needs are being met. An expert, Mr. Sluka had to overcome many obstacles and personal trials. Now a success, he stays on leading edge of technology through reading, researching, asking questions, and using resources to the utmost. Attaining a higher management role, obtaining is academic degree, and enhance his ability to communicate with others serves as his future endeavors. Watson Wyatt Worldwide operates as an international consulting firm with a focus on people and financial management. Employing more than 5,000 associates around the globe, Watson Wyatt Worldwide is headquartered in both Reigate, United Kingdom and Bethesda, Maryland. **Career Highlights:** Information Systems Manager, Watson Wyatt Worldwide (1995-Present); Network Administration, Compass Bank (1992-95); Systems Analyst, University of Texas Health Science Center (1988-92). **Associations & Accomplishments:** HAL-PC. **Education:** Certified NetWare Administrator. **Personal Information:** Mr. Sluka enjoys martial arts, bridge, soccer, flying, camping and bonsai trees.

Bill Stough
Director/Owner
Professional Consulting Services
508 Central Boulevard
Tallassee, AL 36078
(334) 283-2533
Fax: (334) 283-3302

8742

Business Information: The Owner of Professional Consulting Services, Mr. Stough created the Company in 1990 after his retirement from the business sector. Serving as Director, he designs custom machinery, assisting his partner in the building of the actual machine. As a topnotch, 44 year professional, he installs the necessary operating systems and application programs, setting up the computers up for individual clients. In charge of the Human Resources Department as well, Mr. Stough actively recruits professionals in the engineering and technology fields from large plants and from abroad in Europe and Asia. He states that in order to be a successful entrepreneur, you must build your knowledge and academic base, measuring in calculated risks. "Sometimes you have to go out on the limb where the fruit is," is cited as his quote. In the future, Mr. Stough plans to expand his humanitarian aid to the construction of hospital facilities and domestic fish farming. Created in 1990, Professional Consulting Services is a management and technical consulting firm. The Company offers free state-of-the-art construction to various humanitarian causes. Operations employ the services of 24 dedicated individuals. **Career Highlights:** Director/Owner, Professional Consulting Services (1990-Present); Engineering/Industrial Relations Manager, Mount Vernon Mills (1975-90); Engineering Manager, Diversified Products (1970-75); Operations

Manager, Orrox Corporation (1973-75). **Associations & Accomplishments:** Trustee Director, Community Hospital; Alabama Council on Economic Education; Tallassee City School Foundation; Advisory Council, Alabama Christian College. **Education:** Auburn University, B.S. in Mechanical Engineering (1955); William & Mary; Georgia Tech (1960). **Personal Information:** Married to Betty Joyce Richburg in 1953. Mr. Stough enjoys water skiing, snow skiing, wind surfing and wood working.

Gerald "Gerry" Tetrault

General Manager
TetraTech Consulting Service
209 Joseph Street
Chatham, Ontario, Canada N7L 3H2
(519) 352-8573
Fax: (519) 352-9881
gerry@tetratechsrvs.com

8742

Business Information: Utilizing the extensive skills he acquired during 29 years working at a natural gas utility, Mr. Tetrault established TetraTech Consulting Service and serves as its General Manager. His journey into the entrepreneurial world of self-employed consulting has been a very gratifying experience and a situation that he thrives on. Working in numerous positions from computer operator to the senior IT manager, he has the capability to create and implement strategic, marketing, and business plans. By virtue of his personable nature, Mr. Tetrault is able to develop strong and trusting bonds with his clients, resulting in word-of-mouth advertising. He is well-versed in numerous computer applications and technology platforms. His responsibilities with the Company are to provide project leadership and structure to IT departments that are struggling. His ability to explain the most complex of computer problems is just one facet of his incredible curriculum Vitae. TetraTech Consulting Services, a consulting company, provides senior level project and strategic management services. The Company has the experience and knowledge to complete any consulting service. Reporting an estimated $200,000 in annual profits, the Company's list of specializations include Microsoft Certified Systems Engineers, Certified CISCO Engineers, UNIX, NT, PeopleSoft, and SAP. **Career Highlights:** General Manager, TetraTech Consulting Services (1998-Present); Union Gas Ltd.: Manager of Information Technology Solutions (1969-98), Manager of Information Delivery (1995-97), Manager of Systems Development (1994-95), Manager of Data Resources (1987-93). **Education:** University of Windsor, B.A. in Economics (1992). **Personal Information:** Married to Sharon in 1997. Four children: Jaclyn and Lisa Tetrault and Jennifer and Joshua Robinson. Mr. Tetrault enjoys sports.

Michael Thompson

Principal Technology Consultant
DMR Consulting Group
252 Adelaide Street East
Toronto, Ontario, Canada M5A 1N1
(416) 594-2021
michael_thompson@dmr.ca

8742

Business Information: Renowned for his architecture, data warehouse architecture, data applications architecture, and technical expertise, Mr. Thompson was recruited to DMR Consulting Group as Principal Technology Consultant in 1999. A savvy, 17-year professional, he is responsible for coordinating strategic and business plans for data and applications management. Highly regarded and possessing superior talents, he works closely with systems management and users to analyze, specify, design, and implement advanced technical solutions into the client's systems functions. The most rewarding aspect of his career is publishing an article in the "Data Management Review" on "Andyne GQL" now known as "Hummingbird BI Query." Formulating goals compatible with the Company, Mr. Thompson plans to expand and formulate a complete architectural composite, functioning within DMR Consulting Group as a leader in a highly competitive industry. Established in 1972, DMR Consulting Group is a management consulting firm that is a leading global provider of consulting services and solutions to Fortune 1000 companies and business clientele all over the world. Headquartered in Montreal, Canada, the Corporation employs the skilled services of over 9,000 individuals to expedite the diverse requirements of a growing patronage. Reporting $920 million gross revenue per year, DMR Consulting Group continues to pilot professional consumers with prevailing technological advances. **Career Highlights:** Principal Technology Consultant, DMR

Consulting Group (1999-Present); Data Architect, Sprint Canada (1997-99); Applications Architect, Canadian Pacific Railway (1991-97). **Education:** London Graduate School of Business Studies, M.S. in Business Studies (1980); London School of Economics and Political Science, B.S. in Economics (1978); Microsoft Certified Professional+Internet (1999); Microsoft Certified Systems Engineer (1999); Microsoft Certified Database Administrator (1999); Certified Oracle Database Administrator Learning Tree International (1995). **Personal Information:** Mr. Thompson enjoys walking, gardening and tennis. His favorite quotation is, "Far away there in the sunshine are my highest aspirations. I may not reach them, but I can look up and see their beauty, believe in them, and try to follow where they lead," by Louisa May Alcott.

Jeremy Toback

Information Technology Director/Senior Consultant
Strategy Partners Group
4620 Saint Croix Lane, Unit 936
Naples, FL 34109
(888) 886-5013
Fax: (561) 673-5809
toback1@aol.com

8742

Business Information: Mr. Toback is the Information Technology Director and Senior Consultant of Strategy Partners Group. Drawing on several years of experience in the consulting industry, combined with skills in all aspects of technology, Mr. Toback oversees the operation of two computer networks, an e-mail system, and supplies the technological support for 200 users. Having received Microsoft certification and training in various software programs, Mr. Toback is highly certified for the management of several projects in his undertaking. Anticipating further development in the e-commerce industry, he intends to further his education, remaining at the forefront of the technology. His success reflects his ability to think outside the box, take on new challenges, and deliver results. Established in 1997, Strategy Partners Group is a management consulting firm dedicated to supplying clients with the most accurate and professional advice in technological and corporate fields. Offering service internationally, the Firm now operates with a staff of 12 professional consultants and worldwide marketing experts. **Career Highlights:** Information Technology Director/Senior Consultant, Strategy Partners Group (1998-Present); Technical Trainer, AOL (1997-98). **Associations & Accomplishments:** Phi Gamma Delta. **Education:** Jacksonville University, B.S. (1995); Microsoft Certified Systems Engineer.

Tracey Townsend
Senior Consultant
Arthur Andersen Technology Solutions
1 North State Street
Chicago, IL 60607
(312) 507-2664
Fax: (312) 507-0440
tracey.townsend@us.arthurandersen.com

8742

Business Information: Possessing more than three years of experience and educated in the field of computer science, Ms. Townsend serves as the Senior Consultant for Arthur Andersen Technology Solutions. She assumes the responsibility of integrating cutting edge technology into the local office infrastructures. Presiding over the information technology solutions for the desktops, LANs, WANs, Intranet, and Extranet, she designs, develops, and implements the various networks and system applications. Ms. Townsend credits her professional success to her mother, brother, and mentors. Committed to providing continued optimum service, she looks forward to obtaining a managerial position and increasing her professional responsibilities. Her success reflects her ability to think outside the box, produce results, and aggressively tackle new challenges and responsibilities. Headquartered in Chicago, Illinois, the Arthur Andersen Technology Solutions is an internal department within Arthur Andersen. The Department oversees the technological aspects of the Company, designing the internal data infrastructures for individual offices around the world as well as connecting networks on a global scale. **Career Highlights:** Arthur Andersen Technology Solutions: Senior Consultant (1997-Present), Consultant (1996-97). **Associations & Accomplishments:** National Association of Female Executives; Lexington Who's Who Among Business Leaders and Professionals; In Roads National Alumni Association; United Way of Chicago. **Education:** Loyola University of Chicago, B.S. in Computer Sciences (1996). **Personal Information:** Ms. Townsend enjoys reading and running.

D. Brian Hoffman

Maintenance Planner
Maryland Stadium Authority
Maintenance at Camden Yards
555 Russell Street, Suite A
Baltimore, MD 21230
(410) 576-0300
Fax: (410) 539-7640
brian@mdstad.com

8744

Business Information: Mr. Hoffman functions in the capacity of Maintenence Planner at Maryland Stadium Authority Maintenance at Camden Yards. In this capacity, he researches and develops cutting edge software programs. He determines recommendations, and supports all day-to-day database operations. In addition, he has also overseen server and systems administration. As for the future, Mr. Hoffman plans to countinue working on computer maintenence prgrams, as well as manage technical services. Current success, he asserts, was made possible by his ability to organize and reason. The Maryland Stadium Authority Maintenance at Camden Yards is a public sports facility. Built in 1990, the Stadium has been home to many baseball teams, including the Baltimore Orioles. In addition, the Authority completes bidding and negotiates contracts for maintenence and upkeep. Currently, the Authority employs 70 people. **Career Highlights:** Maintenance Planner, Maryland Stadium Authority Maintenance at Camden Yards (1998-Present); Master Security Guard, The Johns Hopkins Hospital (1996-98); Technical/Industrial Sales, L.A. Benson and Sons, Inc. (1995-96); Educator, Anne Arundel County Public Schools (1991-95). **Associations & Accomplishments:** National Spinal Cord Injury Network; University of Maryland University Hospital Volunteer Services. **Education:** University of Maryland, B.S. (1990); Johns Hopkins University, Computer Programming. **Personal Information:** Married to Sharon in 1998. One child: W. Tristan. Mr. Hoffman enjoys antique British sports cars.

Anupam D. S. Bal, Eng.

Technical Specialist-Software Engineer
ICOM Solutions Pty. Ltd.
Level 7, 114-120 Castlereagh Street
Sydney, New South Wales, Australia 2000
+61 292612499
Fax: +61 292612599
Mobile: +61 417419176
anupam_bal@sunbeam.com.au

8748

Business Information: As Technical Specialist, Mr. Bal is responsible for engineering support systems and software application developments. Mr. Bal also spends a great deal of his time training his clients in the use of Notes, assisting them with re-engineering their business processes, and working with them to document their policies, procedures, and systems. With several years of computer experience, Mr. Bal is currently pursuing a Master's degree in the field of Engineering Management from the University of Technology in Sydney. His future plans include achieving software engineering excellence and advancement in the computer engineering industry in order to assume an executive position. Mr. Bal also plans to study business administration at Stanford University or Harvard Business School and aspires to work at the White House. Established in 1992, ICOM Solutions Pty. Ltd. is an Information Technology (IT) consulting and Technical Services company based in Sydney, Parramatta in New South Wales, and Melbourne in Victoria. The Company provides IT Training and Education, software development and engineering, as well as application design and Help Desk services for major international clients including Nestle, American Express, Westpac Banking Corporation, AGL, AMPOL, IBM Global Services and the Defense Department. ICOM Solutions also offers second and third line support, as well as performance management and software application training. In the future, the Company plans to continue global expansion into the Asia Pacific region. **Career Highlights:** Technical Specialist-Software Engineer, ICOM Solutions Pty. Ltd. (1997-Present). **Associations & Accomplishments:** Association for Computing Machinery; Australian Computer Society; IEEE and IEEE Computer Society; Institution of Engineers, Australia; Association of Professional Engineers, Scientists and Managers, Australia; Institution of Industrial Engineers, United States. **Education:** University of Technology, Sydney (In progress); Newcastle University, Graduate Diploma in Computer Science (1996); Amravati University, Bachelor of Engineering in Computer Engineering. **Personal Information:** Mr. Bal enjoys reading American literature, running, weight training and golf.

Robert T. Barr

Director of Information Systems
HSI Geotrans, Inc.
46050 Manekin Plaza, Suite 100
Sterling, VA 20166-6519
(703) 444-7000
Fax: (703) 444-1685
rbarr@hsigeotrans.com

8748

Business Information: Mr. Barr has served with HSI Geo Trans, Inc. in several positions since 1995. At the present time, he fulfills the responsibilities of Director of Information Systems. In this capacity, Mr. Barr is responsible for development of personal computer and networking strategies as well as implementation of new, state-of-the-art information systems. He provides management of networks at all satellite locations and personal computer support activities Corporation-wide. Utilizing extensive occupational experience and a firm academic foundation, Mr. Barr is in charge of integrating new technologies and working Y2K computer issues. He attributes his professional success to a hard work ethic. One of many professional accomplishments, the greatest was assisting with the 1997 merger between Geo Trans and HSI. To this end, he contributed to the smooth transfer of technology and completed the systems integration between the two companies. Working for a consulting firm in the area of computer integration serves as Mr. Barr's long-range goal. Incorporated in 1997, HIS Geo Trans, Inc. operates as an environmental consulting firm. National and international in scope, the Corporation specializes in ground water modeling, clean up activities, and environmental assessments. Headquartered in Virginia, the Corporation operates a network of 12 satellites offices worldwide and employs a staff of 180 professional consultants. **Career Highlights:** Director of Information Systems, HSI Geo Trans, Inc. (1996-Present); Systems Administrator, Geo Trans (1995-96); Trades Utility Worker, James Madison University (1995-Present). **Education:** James Madison University, B.B.A. (1994). **Personal Information:** Married to Tabitha in 1995. Mr. Barr enjoys outdoor activities, home repair and improvement and woodworking.

David Brand

Information Technology Manager
Fers Business Services Inc.
401 North Michigan Avenue
Chicago, IL 60611-4255
(312) 245-1730
Fax: (312) 644-4423
dbrand@fers.com

8748

Business Information: Serving in the capacity of Information Technology Manager at Fers Business Services Inc., Mr. Brand is responsible for implementing cutting edge technologies, managing help desk operations, and maintaining the existing systems infrastructure. He determines the overall strategic direction and business contribution of the information systems function. Clients rely on his extensive technolgical expertise in the field to meet their individual needs. Mr. Brand is MCSE certified. He possesses the skills and knowledge necessary to facilitate and harness the computer's power to the benefit of his clients. Because the industry is constantly changing, Mr. Brand keeps abreast of new developments in the field by reading current literature, networking and interacting with colleagues, and attending professional seminars. His success reflects his ability to deliver results and take on challenges and new responsibilities. Fers Business Services Inc. offers accounting, systems, pension, personal financing, and human resources consulting. Established in 1971, the consulting firm strives to provide quality services to clients with the assistance of 300 employees. **Career Highlights:** Fers Business Services Inc.: Information Technology Manager (1997-Present), Network and Systems Engineer (1995-97); Benefits System Programmer, Aon Consulting (1994-95). **Education:** Northern Illinois University, B.S. (1994). **Personal Information:** Mr. Brand enjoys skiing, camping, golf, fishing and reading.

LeAnnette Carvajal

Independent Representative of I Link World Wide, LLC
I Link Worldwide, LLC (Independent Representative)
2320 Ragland Street
Las Vegas, NV 89108
(702) 499-5699
Fax: (888) 237-4291
leonet@wordnet.att.net

8748

Business Information: Ms. Carvajal functions as an Independent Representative of I Link Worldwide, LLC. She is responsible for maximizing the client's communications infrastructure, including saving them money on long distance services. As both owner and operator, Ms. Carvajal determines the overall strategic direction and business contribution of the communications function. Before starting up I Link Worldwide, LLC (Independent Representative), she assertively served as a Cellular Sales Specialist with AT&T Wireless Division. She has also held part time positions with the University of Nevada at Las Vegas. A nine year professional, Ms. Carvajal is able to gain her client's trust by offering products that genuinely meets their specific needs. Sixty-six percent of her customers were referred. Her success reflects her ability to maintain excellent client relations by knowing her customers' needs and accommodating them. Involved in her community, Ms. Carvajal works with adult and children literacy programs. She tutors children in math and reading and holds classes for the elderly and Y2K preparation. Her continuing long term goal is to be as successful as possible. I Link Worldwide, LLC (Independent Representative) operates as an intelligent, fully integrated communications provider of tools used to increase the value and flexibility of telephones, cellulars, pagers, and faxes and integrating them into a single environment. Presently, I Link Worldwide, LLC (Independent Representative) employs a skilled work force of more than 36 individuals in down line operations. **Career Highlights:** Independent Representative of I Link World Wide, LLC, I Link Worldwide, LLC (Independent Representative) (1999-Present); Cellular Sales Specialist, AT&T Wireless Division (1997-99). **Associations & Accomplishments:** The American Marketing Association; Alumni of University of Nevada; Board of Directors, Planned Parenthood. **Education:** University of Nevada, B.S. in Business Administration (1995). **Personal Information:** Ms. Carvajal enjoys water skiing, fishing and rock climbing.

Gayle Coffman

Senior Database Administrator
Adecco at Boeing
14528 Northeast 1st Street
Bellevue, WA 98007-4902
(425) 603-0208
wccomp@nwlink.com

8748

Business Information: Demonstrating expertise in the technology field, Mrs. Coffman is a Senior Database Administrator. Mrs. Coffman and her husband are the sole proprietors of World Class Computing business established in 1993. In her role with World Class Computing, she provides her customers with architecture and technology consulting services. As a former Microsoft Corporation employee, Mrs. Coffman possesses intimate knowledge of the Microsoft computer architectures. She provides advice and troubleshooting services as well as custom configuration for systems and software as requested by her customers. An accomplished professional, she is an author of information technology books. Her most notable work to date is "The Complete Reference: SQL Server 7," that was published by Osborne/McGraw-Hill in 1998. She plans in the near future to begin another such project focusing on the changing world of computer technologies toward a digital universe. Mrs. Coffman's goals are to continue learning about current computer technologies and to move into Internet programming and Web site development technology. Mrs. Coffman's advice to others in the industry is to "keep on the leading edge of technology." **Career Highlights:** Senior Database Administrator, Boeing Corporation (1999-Present); Senior Database Administrator, Corbis Corporation (1998-99); Senior Database Administrator/Senior Operations Analyst, Microsoft Corporation (1997-98); Author, Osborne/McGraw-Hill (1997-98); Owner/Data Architect, World Class Computing (1993-98). **Education:** University of Northern Colorado, B.S. in Administration and Management Information Systems (1983); Microsoft Certified Professional. **Personal Information:** Married to Christopher J. in 1989. Two children: Kelly Collins and Christopher S. Mrs. Coffman enjoys sewing and time with her family.

Tamara L. Davis

Information Technology Professional
International Management Communication Corporation, Inc.
1201 Brickle Avenue, Suite 200
Miami, FL 33231
(305) 371-2776
Fax: (305) 371-2193
tdavis@imcc.com

8748

Business Information: Educated in the field of information technology, Ms. Davis serves as an Information Technology Professional for International Management Communication, Inc. She is responsible for visiting individual clients, working with them in an effort to determine their unique business needs, and providing them with up-to-date technological solutions. Before joining International Management Communication, she served as Media Director with Deal Direct Inc. Her background history also includes a stint as Project Manager at DavoCom One. In her current role, Ms. Davis is also charge with preparing all financial proposals and portfolios for the Corporation's clients. Additionally, she performs the network administration and the implementation of new business products. Looking to the future, Ms. Davis plans to begin working more with database management. Her success reflects her ability to think outside the box and aggressively take on new challenges. Founded in 1984, International Communication Corporation, Inc. provides business clients with financial, internal management communications, project management, and economic development pensions. The Corporation reports $6 million in yearly sales and employs a work force of 60 staff members. **Career Highlights:** Information Technology Professional, International Management Communication Corporation, Inc. (1997-Present); Media Director, Deal Direct Inc. (1995-97); Project Manager, DavoCom One (1993-95). **Associations & Accomplishments:** Institute of Electronics and Electrical Engineers; NetWare Users International. **Education:** Kennedy Western, degree in Management Information Systems (1999); Microsoft Systems Certified Engineer. **Personal Information:** Married to David Sanchez in 1999. Two children: Alex and Blaire. Ms. Davis enjoys being a scuba diving instructor.

Wanda S. Dembeck

Vice President
Triad Performance Technologies
30101 Northwestern Highway, Suite 330
Farmington Hills, MI 48334
(616) 956-6850
Fax: (248) 737-0333
wandad@triadperform.com

8748

Business Information: Ms. Dembeck, in her current position of Vice President, assumes accountability for the overall sales of the Company, supervising the sales associates and setting sales goals and objectives. Performing client consultations, she advises companies in the types of training and computer systems that will best benefit them and achieve maximum results. Ms. Dembeck credits her professional success to a relentless focus on the customer. She was able to build a previous business from $100,000 to $2 million in yearly sales by following that philosophy. Her goal for the immediate future is to create a Web based training program for use by the Company. She looks forward to incorporating more technology into Triad Performance Technologies' solutions. A recognized professional in her field, Ms. Dembeck is the recipient of an International ISPI Award. A performance improvement consulting firm, Triad Performance Technologies specializes in improving company organizations through its employees utilizing process improvement, training, and technology. The Company improves human performance by teaching employees the skills and knowledge needed to improve a company's business results, ensuring that they have good systems to work with, and making sure that all standard methods are processed. Triad Performance Technologies was founded in 1988 and employs a staff of 50 skilled individuals. **Career Highlights:** Triad Performance Technologies: Vice President (1998-Present), Consulting Director (1997-98), Senior Performance Consultant (1995-97). **Associations & Accomplishments:** International Society for Performance Improvement; American Society of Training and Development; Institute of Management Consultants; Product

Management Association. **Education:** Wright State University, B.S. (1984). **Personal Information:** Married to Craig in 1988. Two children: Carsten and Collin. Ms. Dembeck enjoys golf.

Mary Dinota

Consultant
MWD Consultants
5645 Arbor Circle
St. Leonard, MD 20685
(410) 586-3683
Fax: (301) 494-0595
mdinota@aol.com

8748

Business Information: A tested and proven professional, Mrs. Dinota is a 39 year veteran in the communications field. She ventured into the corporate world in 1983 to start MWD Consultants. As Owner, she serves as Consultant responsible for planning and designing communications systems. Before becoming an entrepreneur and business owner, Mrs. Dinota was employed as Telecommunications Specialist with the Department of Commerce, NTIA/PTFP. Her solid background history also includes a stint as Program Officer for HEW/Education Office/EBFP in Washington D.C. Experienced in a number of facets of her field, she also writes grant proposals for non-profit organizations to attain federal funding for their distance learning and public broadcasting projects. Bidding on communication contracts is an integral part of her functions. Reflecting on her distinguished career, Mrs. Dinota believes that success came from hiring the right staff for the job. Her success reflects her leadership ability to build teams with synergy, technical strength, and a customer oriented attitude, and aggressively take on new challenges. MWD Consultants is a privately owned telecommunications consulting firm. Established in 1983, the Firm works with non-profit organizations and other businesses to ascertain the educational and informational needs of the area which can be served by a state-of-the-art telecommunications system or systems. Once determined, the Firm recommends and/or develops comprehensive plans for one or more systems to meet identified needs. **Career Highlights:** Consultant, MWD Consultants (1983-Present); Telecommunications Specialist, Department of Commerce, NTIA/PTFP (1970-83); Program Officer, HEW/Education Office/EBFP (1962-70). **Associations & Accomplishments:** SALT; Beta Sigma Phi. **Education:** Platt-Gard University (1939-40); Various communications courses, workshops, conferences, and on-the-job-training. **Personal Information:** Married to Edward F. Three children: Patricia, Diane, and Edward J.

Arthur M. Griffin

Senior Technical Writer
Independent Contractor and Consultant
119 Roycroft Avenue
Long Beach, CA 90803
(310) 813-8894
art.griffin@trw.com

8748

Business Information: Looking for a way to broaden his educational horizons within his field of expertise, Mr. Griffin found it through the establishment of his own business, Independent Contractor and Consultant. His solid background history includes stints as Systems Engineer for TRW, Inc. and Communications Staff Officer with the United States Air Force. In his present capacity as Senior Technical Writer, Mr. Griffin is responsible for developing, writing, and updating software user guides, operations and management procedures, and proposal documents. Documents are written in order to explain to customers or employees, the various software developed by a company. Coordinating resources, schedules, time lines, and assignments; determining the overall strategic and tactical direction; and driving product and service offerings to market also fall within the realm of Mr. Griffin's functions. To better understand software applications and procedures, he works with a team of programming professionals. Mr. Griffin is wishing to continue working independently on various projects and in conjunction with businesses in the area. His advice his "Network, network, network." The Company works with written and technical documents for the law enforcement, manufacturing, petrochemical, and pharmaceutical warehousing industries as well as the accounting and financing industries. **Career Highlights:** Senior Technical Writer, Independent Contractor and Consultant (1995-Present); Systems Engineer, TRW, Inc. (1982-95); Communications Staff Officer, United States Air Force (1962-82). **Associations & Accomplishments:** Armed Forces Communications and Electronics Association (1975-Present); Society of Technical Communications (1997-Present); Long Beach Grand Prix (1988-Present). **Education:** University of Southern California, M.S. in Systems Management (1972); University of New Hampshire, B.A. in Chemistry (1962). **Personal Information:** Two children: Laura and Amy. Mr. Griffin enjoys snow skiing, attending the Long Beach Grand Prix and participating in cart races.

Thomas W. Nielsen

Technology Manager
BMC Consultants, Inc.
5105 DTC Parkway, Suite 219
Englewood, CO 80111-2600
(303) 770-6613

8748

Business Information: Mr. Nielsen has worked in the computer science field since 1990. He joined the BMC Consultants, Inc. team as Retirement Plan Consultant in 1994. In 1996, Mr. Nielsen was elevated to the role of Technology Manager with oversight of development and implementation of new technologies. Leveraging his extensive academic ties, business experience, and technical expertise, he is charged with management of Y2K compliance and testing, office automation, Internet and network communications and integration with business partners, electronic trading, and disaster recovery after systems crash. He is known to deliver results in support of technical objectives through effective decision-making, use of emerging technologies, and solving problems and challenges in a highly efficient manner. Planning and directing all computer and peripheral machines operations, data entry, data control scheduling, and quality control also fall within the purview of Mr. Nielsen's responsibilities. He attributes his success to perseverance. "Don't give up," is cited as Mr. Nielsen's advice to others in the field. Established in the 1970s, BMC Consultants, Inc. provides full service retirement plan consulting and administration services. With a solid reputation for timely and professional service, the BMC's team of consultants provide expertise for pension, profit sharing, and 401(k) plans as well as plan administration, reporting, and compliance testing. National in scope, the Corporation targets clients in the professional service and financial industries. Presently, the Englewood office employs 32 persons. **Career Highlights:** BMC Consultants, Inc.: Technology Manager (1997-Present), Retirement Plan Consultant (1994-97); Retirement Plan Administrator, Milliman & Roberston, Inc. (1992-94); Program Manager, Martin Luther Homes (1990-92). **Education:** University of Denver, M.S. (1992); University of Mary, B.S.; Microsoft Certified Professional.

Donald R. Pigeon

President of Technology and Product Services
The Human Factor, Inc.
1840 Hilton, Suite 1
Ferndale, MI 48220
(248) 399-2211
Fax: (248) 399-2213
dpigeon@h-factor.com

8748

Business Information: Mr. Pigeon serves as President with The Human Factor, Inc. One of the founding members, he first became interested in the database consultation industry when he and a partner saw an opportunity to provide more efficient services than were currently available. In his position of President of technology and product services, Mr. Pigeon orchestrates all technical services provided by the Corporation. Besides developing leading-edge services and products, he is also the Corporation's lead technical consultant. Developing both strategic and tactical marketing plans, orchestrating aggressive expansion into new geographic markets, and developing new service offerings also falls with the realm of his responsibilities. A respected expert in his field, Mr. Pigeon conducts presentations at conferences and seminars with major vendors such as "PeopleSoft". His greatest accomplishment is building a reputation for excellence. Mr. Pigeon attributes his success to his ability to get along and communicate with others. The Human Factor, Inc. is an employee-owned corporation that specializes in Oracle and database activities. Founded in 1998, The Human Factor offers consultations in database administration, performance, and remote database administration services. The Corporation is headquartered in Ferndale, Michigan and employs a staff of six highly skilled and trained persons. The Corporation is currently thriving in a competitive national market and has already initialized plans to expand their operations. **Career Highlights:** President of Technology and Product Services, The Human Factor, Inc. (1998-Present); Project Manager/Consultant, Dimension Systems Inc. (1994-98). Oracle DBA/Developer, Business News Publishing (1994). Analyst, Hughes Aircraft Company (1984-93). **Associations & Accomplishments:** Oracle Developers Program. **Education:** California State University, B.A. in Business Administration and Computer Information Management (1991); University of New York at Albany, A.A. (1982). **Personal Information:** Mr. Pigeon enjoys golf and fishing.

Francena Purchase-Owens

President
Purchase Business Institute
1486 44th Street SE, Suite 201
Kentwood, MI 49508
(616) 534-6811

8748

Business Information: As the President, Ms. Purchase-Owens, working alongside her associate, focuses attention on the facilitation of all projects and activities. Utilizing her ability to communicate via the public platform, she personally conducts seminars, expunding on numerous topics and providing her students with workable solutions to meet specific needs. Further, she concentrates efforts on marketing research and provides services as an advertising campaign specialist. Ms. Purchase-Owens enjoys the many challenges and rewards of business ownership and attributes her success to her desire to learn and her ability to help others achieve their goals. Future plans includes completion of her Ph.D. program and being the recipient of an Associate's degree from the American Workshop. Drawing from a desire to extend more than 20 years of experience working in the community, Ms. Purchase-Owens established Purchase Business Institute in 1998. Located in Kentwood, Michigan, the Institute specializes in the provision of comprehensive instruction in project marketing. Students are taught how to achieve success, work as a team, and bring about a successfuly resolution to the completion of projects. Instruction is also provided to customer service representatives in the areas of dealing with difficult customers, proper telephone etiquette, and the timely provision of service. The human resources field is also addressed. All instruction is provided through motivational workshops and seminars to such clients as churches, community centers, and corporations. **Career Highlights:** President, Purchase Business Institute (1998-Present); President, Creative Works (1990-98); Marketing Coordinator, Michigan National Bank (1980-81). **Associations & Accomplishments:** American Management Association; Marketing Research Association; Jaycees International; American Society for Training and Development; SEENA Neighborhood Association; Professional Secretaries of America; Secretary, Phi Beta Lamda Honors Society; Manpower Sales and Service Certificate; Advisory Board of Transitions, Touchtone Innovare Division. **Education:** Western Michigan University, B.S. in Applied Liberal Studies (1997); Milwaukee Stratton College, A.A.; Dale Carnegie, Human Relations and Public Speaking; Michigan Professional School of Modeling, diploma. **Personal Information:** Ms. Purchase-Owens enjoys travel.

Eric S. Ransden

Manager, Network Services
Ceridian Performance Partners
930 Commonwealth Avenue
Boston, MA 02215
(617) 582-0357
Fax: (617) 566-2806
eric.ransden@ceridian.com

8748

Business Information: As the Manager of Network Services and a member of the senior management team for Ceridian Performance Partners, Mr. Ransden leads several teams including network infrastructure systems, database services, procurement, and the help desk. Throughout his career, he has exceeded in several technical roles, managed technical teams, and created and grown new technical departments. As for the future, Mr. Ransden looks to lead the information technology division of a small growth company. Ceridian Performance Parnters, a business unit of Ceridian Corporation, is the leading provider of fully-integrated workplace effectiveness solutions including work-life, employee assistance, and organizational development programs. **Career Highlights:** Manager, Network Services, Ceridian Performance Partners (1998-Present); Network Services Manager, Work/Family Directions (1996-98); Sun Life of Canada: Senior Technical Analyst (1992-96), Network Analyst (1991-92). **Education:** Bentley College, M.S. in Computer Information Systems (1999); State University of New York at Albany, B.S. in Management Information Systems. **Personal Information:** Married. Two children. Mr. Ransden enjoys golf and family time.

Carl W. Seidel

Owner
Carl Seidel Consulting
208 Royal Oaks Place
Denton, TX 76205
(940) 381-3036
Fax: (940) 381-3036
carl.w.seidel@mindspring.com

8748

Business Information: In January 2000, Mr. Seidel founded Carl Seidel Consulting. As Owner, he presently serves as the Firm's consultant. With an excellent understanding of his field, he advises people and client companies on technology transfer, product development, manufactuing, and marketing of radio pharmaceuticals. Working to push client's products into the market as quickly as possible, he attends many different meetings and seminars learning new skills and strategies. Highly regarded, Mr. Seidel also determines the overall strategic direction and formulates busienss and marketing plans to keep the Firm out–front of competitors. Mr. Seidel plans to enlarge Carl Seidel Consulting so that companies throughout Europe and Asia are aware of the Firm's reputable for quality services. Carl Seidel Consulting is a consulting agency, providing service primarily to pharmaceutical areas. The Firm assists these type of companies in making decisions with the company's best interest in mind, conducting market analysis, supporting in manufacturing and distribution decisions, and helping to find new facilities. Working with regulatory agencies such as FDAWRC, the Firm aids in design and implementation of new business plans. **Career Highlights:** Owner, Carl Seidel Consulting (2000–Present); President/Chief Executive Officer, International Isotopes, Inc. (1997–99); DuPont Merck: Associate Director (1991–97), Manufacturing Manager (1981–91). **Associations & Accomplishments:** Society of Nuclear Medicine; European Association of Nuclear Medicine; American Chemical Society; American National Standards Institute; International Isotope Society; United States Pharmacoeia. **Education:** University of Notre Dame, M.S. (1963); University of Wisconsin, B.S. in Chemistry (1959). **Personal Information:** Married to Suzanne Winslow in 1963. Four children: Lisa Marie, Michael Dana, Rebecca Suzanne, and Elaine Marie. Mr. Seidel enjoys tennis.

Alfred E. Walker, IV, AICP
Lead Planner
GAI Consulting Southeast Inc.
10199 Southside Boulevard, Suite 103
Jacksonville, FL 32256
(904) 363-1110
Fax: (904) 363-1115
walkeral@bellsouth.net

8748

Business Information: Mr. Walker serves as Senior Planner and Management Information Systems Director for Parsons Harland Bartholomew and Associates, Inc. He performs in a managerial capacity for system operations, projects, and the computer aided drafting department. In addition, Mr. Walker serves as a client liaison, visiting client job sites and coordinating project implementations. Supervising six employees, he also conducts performance evaluations and recommends alterations in personnel. Parsons Harland Bartholomew and Associates, Inc. provides civil consulting for the military and government organizations. The Consultancy offers planning, economic analysis, environmental impact forecasting, data analysis, and computer systems operation services. Headquartered in St. Louis, Missouri, Parsons Harland Bartholomew and Associates, Inc. operates five facilities which offer service to 20 countries. **Career Highlights:** Lead Planner, GAI Consulting Southeast In. (Present); Senior Planner/Management Information Systems Director, Parsons Harland Bartholomew and Associates, Inc. (1992–99); Regional Planner/Management Information Systems Director, Northeast Florida Regional Planning Council (1986–92); Office Manager, Florida Department of Environmental Regulation (1979–86). **Associations & Accomplishments:** Director, Society of American Military Engineers; Director, Florida Planning and Zoning Association, Northeast Florida Section. **Education:** University of Tennessee, B.A. (1975). **Personal Information:** Mr. Walker enjoys fishing, family time and outdoor activities.

Patricia A. Watkins
Manager of Information Resources
Morpace International
31700 Middlebelt Road
Farmington Hills, MI 48334
(248) 737-5300
Fax: (248) 737-5325
pwatkins@morpace.com

8748

Business Information: As Manager of Information Resources for Morpace International, Ms. Watkins supervises the corporate library as she conducts research. Utilizing her education, she develops innovative means to gather data that will benefit the Company by serving as examples of competitors, thereby making the Company aware of necessary steps to take to become cutting edge. A motivated and self-directed employee, Ms. Watkins is recognized for her abilities to accomplish tasks efficiently and accurately. Attributing her success to a strong ambition and a desire to make knowledge easily accessible to all employees, she looks forward to continuing in her current capacity as she shifts the focus of the department to the Internet to create international contacts. Providing market research on an global scale, Morpace International employs over 150 people at the Farmington Hills, Michigan location. Offering full services, the Company handles all aspects of the operations, from telephone services to focus groups. Established in 1975, the Company has estimated revenues of $940 million annually. **Career Highlights:** Manager of Information Resources,

Morpace International (1999-Present); Senior Project Director, Creative Marketing Consultant (1986–97); Project Director, Campbell Ewald Advertising (1984–86). **Associations & Accomplishments:** President (1999–00), Women in Communication of Detroit; President (1983–84), International Association of Personnel Women. **Education:** Wayne State University, Master's degree in Library Information Science (In Progress); University of Michigan, B.A. **Personal Information:** Ms. Watkins enjoys literature, film, music and photography.

8900 Services, Nec

8999 Services, nec

Harold G. Hedelund
President/Chief Executive Officer
HH Technologies, Inc./Hedelund Engineering
7505 Barkentine Street
Las Vegas, NV 89128-5279
(702) 340-3706
Fax: (702) 870-1070
hhtech@hhtechnology.com

8999

Business Information: Utilizing his vast experience gained from previous career positions, Harold Hedelund founded HH Technologies, Inc./Hedelund Engineering in 1987 (formerly HV Technologies, Inc. & Hedelund Engineering starting in 1971). Handling all aspects of operations, he serves as Author and Publisher of technical books, manuals, software, and publications. Facilitating continuous improvement, he keeps abreast of the rapid changes in the technology field to improve his own Company. During his career, Mr. Hedelund authored and published several correspondence courses, books, manuals, and publications including books on Alternator/Generator and Detailed Starter Rebuilding, as well as an Author/Publisher Training Manual, real estate publications and publications on microwave cooking techniques, starting and setting up a home business, and gaming. His real estate publications appeared in a National Board of Realtors magazine. A description of all these publications appears on the World Wide Web. He would like to attribute his success to rapid growth of technology, and his ability to advertise. **Career Highlights:** President/Chief Executive Officer, HH Technologies, Inc./Hedelund Engineering (1972–Present); Senior Member Technical Staff, Teledyne Microelectronics (1968); Staff Engineer, TRW Systems Microelectronics Center; Various Electronic Companies (1948–68). **Associations & Accomplishments:** Former Co-Owner/C.O.B. of a Nevada real estate corporation; Former Property Manager/Broker, Veterans Administration; Nevada Real Estate License; Who's Who; BBB. **Education:** College of Electrical/Electronics Engineering; Microelectronic Processing courses; Advanced Real Estate courses. **Personal Information:** Mr. Hedelund enjoys reading and computers.

Mark J. Nightingale
Area Manager
Pro Staff Personnel
1300 Post Oak Boulevard
Houston, TX 77056
(713) 626-8822
Fax: (713) 626-8827
mark_nightingale@prostaff.com

8999

Business Information: Mr. Nightingale functions in the role of Area Manager for Pro Staff Personnel. He is responsible for all administration and operational activities at the Houston office, to include accounting, profit and loss statements, information technology and engineering, business strategies, hiring and firing, and creative services. An esteemed representative of the Agency, he concurrently fulfills the position of Regional Director of Accounting for the Southeast Texas locations. Recognized as the top producer within the Agency, Mr. Nightingale's future endeavors include becoming the Manager of all offices within the Houston area and increasing his involvement in the technical aspects of the Agency. His quote is "a year in information technology is three months in real-time." Pro Staff Personnel operates as a staffing and recruiting agency. Established in 1985, the Agency serves the surrounding businesses to assist in finding appropriate employees to fill a particular position. The Agency offers a temporary assistance program where clients are able to "test" an employee in a certain position before hiring them into the actual position. Facilitating the needs of businesses across the United States, the Agency supports a staff of 1,000 traveling representatives and a network of 250 office locations

across the country. **Career Highlights:** Area Manager, Pro Staff Personnel (1999–Present); Robert Half International: Area Manager (1997–99), Branch Manager (1997), Division Director (1993–96). **Associations & Accomplishments:** Institute of Management Accountants. **Education:** Lanchester Polytechnic, Accounting (1980). **Personal Information:** Married to Barbara in 1993. Two children: Jessica and Tony. Mr. Nightingale enjoys golf and swimming.

Arli Quesada
Freelance Writer
14 Steven Way
San Rafael, CA 94903
Fax: (415) 479-7227
aq99@aol.com

8999

Business Information: As a Freelance Writer, Mrs. Quesada has become established in the media education field, recognized for her publications of online articles and stories. Utilizing a Bachelor's degree in Journalism, and experience as a Freelance Writer for the Autodesk Foundation, she contributes intensive research, writing, and editing to the media industry. An active member of various writing associations and councils, Mrs. Quesada has established a role as one of the most highly respected authors in the country. Recognized for coordinating the United States's first multimedia contest for American students, Mrs. Quesada enjoys working with young students from around the country, and she is currently working towards a position as a writer for the media education field. Co-Author of "Changing the World Through Media Education," Mrs. Quesada works with specialty publications focusing on technology and media literacy. Her articles are utilized in international magazines who emphasize project based, educational technology and Internet services, all of which are founded around extensive research. **Career Highlights:** Freelance Writer (1996–Present); Freelance Web Writer, Antodesk Foundation (1998–00); Marketing Director, Academic Therapy Publications/High Nook Books (1987–95). **Associations & Accomplishments:** Education Writers Association; Founder, North Bay Multimedia Association; Co-Chairman, San Francisco Bay Area Book Festival Multimedia Committee (1994–95); Coordinator, Student Multimedia Contest for Merin County Fair and Exposition (1996). **Education:** University of California at Berkeley: Course in Integrating Technology Into the Cirriculum (1989), Certificate in Book Publishing (1987); San Francisco State University, B.A. in Journalism (1980). **Personal Information:** Married to Allen in 1986. One child: April.

9100 - 9799
PUBLIC
ADMINISTRATION

9100 Executive, Legislative, and General

9111 Executive offices
9121 Legislative bodies
9131 Executive and legislative combined
9199 General government, nec

Saud A. Almogbel
Computer Consultant
Royal Cabinet of Saudi Arabia
45813 Colonnade Terrace
Sterling, VA 20166
(703) 863-1790
Fax: (703) 433-0566
almogbel@aol.com

9121

Business Information: Displaying his professional expertise, Mr. Almogbel is a Computer Consultant for the Royal Cabinet of Saudi Arabia. He handles technical problems associated with the computer infrastructure, ensuring the complete functionality and operational status of the information systems function. A 13-year veteran, Mr. Almogbel presides over programming, researches new and upcoming technological products that could be of benefit, implements and coodinates training programs for employees on all new systems, and oversees and directs network administration. Attributing his success to his parents and prayers, his career highlight includes working for the Chief of the Royal Cabinet. Displaying innovation, Mr. Almogbel would like to complete his Ph.D. and introduce automatic ideas to ease work flow. **Career Highlights:** Computer Consultant, Royal Cabinet of Saudi Arabia (1986-Present). **Associations & Accomplishments:** Institute of Electrical and Electronics Engineers; Association of Computing Machinery. **Education:** George Washington University, Ph.D. (In Progress); University of Southern California School of Engineering, M.S. in Computer Science. **Personal Information:** Married to Areej Aldahash in 1990. Two children: Aljohara and Sara. Mr. Almogbel enjoys reading, swimming and travel.

Nehme George Chakhtoura
Information Technology Officer
Prince George's Accounting Government/Department of Environmental Resources
9400 Peppercorn Place, Suite 600
Upper Marlboro, MD 20774-5359
(301) 883-5926
Fax: (301) 883-7298
sealion@cais.com

9121

Business Information: Mr. Chakhtoura serves as Information Technology Officer for Prince George's Accounting Government's Department of Environmental Resources. The information technology department provides strategic information technology planning and services to a 500 user community. Mr. Chakhtoura oversees the coordination of new applications, development of new hardware, and procurement of new hardware and software. Mr. Chakhtoura utilized his superior project management skills on the Agency's Y2K project, and was able to meet the demand of developing new applications within very strict budget and time requiremens. He stresses that in order to stay ahead in technology, you must research the stock market and remain current with trends. Attributing his success to having well rounded education and knowledge in a variety of disciplines, Mr. Chakhtoura anticipates moving forward to a higher position in the county service within the near future. Prince George's Accounting Government's Department of Environmental Resources is a local organization providing a variety of regulatory and service programs to area residents in the Upper Marlboro, Maryland area. Established in the 1970s, the Agency specializes in environmental planning, construction regulations, solid waste management, animal control, and recycling. Empoying 500 individuals, the Agency reports annual revenues in excess of $180 million. **Career Highlights:** ASCPrince George's County Government/Department of Environmental Resources: Information Technology Officer (1999-Present); Project Manager/Section Head/Associate Director (1988-99); Plant Engineer/Production Supervisor, Gold Bond Building Products (1985-88). **Associations & Accomplishments:** Past Member, American Society of Civil Engineers; Past Member, American Society of Professional Engineers. **Education:** University of Maryland, M.S. (1998); University of North Carolina, B.S. in Engineering (1983). **Personal Information:** Married to Candice in 1985. Three children: George N., James A., and Danielle D. Mr. Chakhtoura enjoys sports and travel.

Michael D. Deltano
Information Systems Manager
Town of Easton
136 Elm Street
North Easton, MA 02356
(508) 230-3411
Fax: (508) 230-3421
mdeltano@easton.ma.us

9121

Business Information: Serving the Town of Easton as Information Systems Manager, Mr. Deltano oversees network administration and management of the systems functions within the governmental institution. Utilizing 23 years of expertise and knowledge attained through an extensive employment history, Mr. Deltano concentrates his attention on the maintenance of server back up systems, Internet capabilities, and system upgrades. Striving to incorporate the latest technologies, he focuses on providing a more efficient and effective network system for the Municipality. Always alert to new opportunities, techniques, and approaches, Mr. Deltano remains committed to providing optimum services with the Town of Easton. The ability to learn quickly is cited as one of his reasons for success. Serving as a commonwealth government to the community of North Easton, Massachusetts, the historic Town of Easton municipality was established in 1725. Employing a government administration of 300, the Municipality provides specialized services of city leadership in diversified areas of legal aspects to its surrounding community. Dedicated toward providing for the diverse needs of the people, the Municipality offers services in marriage licensing, divorce court, traffic court, individual representation, and other legal issues. **Career Highlights:** Information Systems Manager, Town of Easton (1998-Present); Senior Application Engineer, Foxboro Company (1977-98). **Associations & Accomplishments:**

Massachusetts Government Information Systems Association. **Education:** Northeastern University, B.S. in Electrical Engineering (1981); Microsoft Cetrified Systems Engineer. **Personal Information:** Married to Cynthia in 1992. One child: Kristin. Mr. Deltano enjoys history, computers and golf.

George M. Dykes, IV
Systems Administrator
Senator Craig Thomas
United States Senate
Washington, DC 20510-0001
(202) 224-6441
Fax: (202) 224-6441
george_dykes@thomas.senate.gov

9121

Business Information: Mr. Dykes brings 10 years of leadership, political, and technology experience to his position as Systems Administrator for the office of Senator Craig Thomas. In that role, he manages all aspects of technology and information systems for the Senator's office and five field offices in Wyoming. He provides and performs analysis, procurement, installation, and configuration of technology for an office of 40 legislative and administrative professionals. He also provides training, maintenance, and technical support, and has implemented and maintained the Senator's first Intranet and external web site. As long-terms goals, he would like to finish requirements for a Bachelor's degree in Business Administration. Concurrently, Mr. Dykes owns and runs a small business, GMD Technologies, that provides technology and Internet solutions to small businesses. His future goals include continuing to work for Senator Craig Thomas while expanding GMD Technologies' operations. Senator Craig Thomas has represented Wyoming in the United States Congress since 1989. **Career Highlights:** Systems Administrator, Senator Craig Thomas, United States Senate (1995-Present); Owner/President, GMD Technologies (1998-Present); Systems Administrator, Congressman Christopher Cox (1993-95); Reconnaissance Communications and Team Leader, United States Marine Corps with combat duty in Operation DESERT STORM (1988-92). **Associations & Accomplishments:** Senate Systems Administrator Association, Vice President and Chairman of New Products Review Committee (1997); Quality Assurance Council, Senate Sergeant-at-Arms (1997). **Education:** Northern Virginia Community College, B.B.A. (Candidate). **Personal Information:** Mr. Dykes enjoys golf, skiing, camping and off road 4x4 trips. He also enjoys volunteering as a consultant for inexperienced computer users.

Michael R. Flowers
Senior Systems Analyst
Contra Costa County
40 Douglas Drive
Martinez, CA 94520-2205
(952) 313-1673
Fax: (925) 313-1757
mikflowr@pacbell.net

9121

Business Information: As Senior System Analyst of Contra Costa County, Mr. Flowers provides county level management for State and Local Systems, including the California Medi-Cal Eligibility Data System, SAWS Information System, and Automated Finger Image Reporting and Match System. Responsibilities include: coordination of systems usage, creation of User Documentation for systems under his responsibility (he is proud of his ability to create "user friendly user documentation"), development and coordination of large scale systems training projects, and troubleshooting. Mr. Flowers represents his systems to county staff, medical providers, clients, and the public. Currently, Mr. Flowers is heavily involved in implementing changes resulting from Federal and State Welfare Reform. Mr. Flowers enjoys his career in public service, and attributes his success to his dedication to the people that his systems serve, not to the systems themselves. Contra Costa County, employing approximately 7,000 public servants, is the local government responsible for the health, welfare, and education of its residents through the facilitation of various social and economic programs. **Career Highlights:** Contra Costa County: Senior Systems Analyst (1982-Present), Program Analyst (1978-82), Worker/Supervisor (1970-78). **Associations & Accomplishments:** International MENSA Society; Association of Delightfully Alive Humans. **Education:** Diablo Valley Junior College, A.A. (1967). **Personal Information:** Mr. Flowers enjoys home remodeling, cooking and reading.

Anthony M. Jones
Office Systems Analyst
San Joaquin County Public Works
1810 East Hazelton Avenue
Stockton, CA 95205-6232
(209) 468-8474
Fax: (209) 468-2999
amjones@co.san.joaquin.ca.us

9121

Business Information: Possessing rich talents in the information technology field, Mr. Jones fulfills a number of duties on behalf of San Joaquin County Public Works as Office Systems Analyst. Operating in collaboration with the local county government, he owns several years of experience as a laboratory technician and office systems technician in his professional portfolio. Demonstrating his management and technical expertise, Mr. Jones administers and controls the LAN/WAN network architecture, manages client server rights and software, and oversees all troubleshooting activities. In the future, he plans on becoming certified in more area of the information technology field and receive his master's degree. San Joaquin County Public Works' information systems division engages in maintaining the County's network infrastructure. Employing over 500 professionals in the county government, the Public Works department is able to run efficiently supporting the community of more than 250,000 residents. **Career Highlights:** San Joaquin County Public Works: Office Systems Analyst (1996-Present), Office Systems Technician (1995-96); Lab Technician, Jeff's Computers (1989-90). **Education:** San Joaquin Delta College. **Personal Information:** Four children: Ashanti, Aliah, Michael, and Miyanna.

Charles C. Nixon
Hydraulic Engineer
Bureau of Indian Affairs - Navajo Area Office
P.O. Box 619
Fort Defiance, AZ 86504-0619
(520) 729-7357
Fax: (520) 729-7356
73243.llll@compuserve.com

9121

Business Information: With 16 solid years experience working for the Bureau of Indian Affairs, Mr. Nixon fulfills the responsibilities of Hydraulic Engineer. He has held various positions with the Bureau including Civil Engineer and Hydrologist. At the present time, Mr. Nixon is in charge of the water dam safety program for the Navajo Indian Reservation. Supervising a variety of engineering programs is one of his major functions. Additionally, he utilizes years of extensive experience and a strong academic history in performing dam inspections to ensure that local and federal regulations are being met. Handling project management and the repairs and maintenance for 13 dams falls under his realm of responsibility. Mr. Nixon focuses on the safety of those living in close proximity to the dams. As a long-term professional goal, he would like to develop a state-of-the-art early warning system for dam failures. Functioning as a government agency, the Bureau of Indian Affairs - Navajo Area Office was established in 1776 during the colonial era in the United States. The Agency's major function is the supervision of reservation resources and assets and is located in Washington, DC. **Career Highlights:** Bureau of Indian Affairs - Navajo Area Office: Hydraulic Engineer (1990-Present), Civil Engineer (1992-98); Hydrologist, Bureau of Indian Affairs - Flathend Agency (1989-90). **Education:** Kansas State University: M.S. (1976), B.S. (1974). **Personal Information:** Married to Susan E. in 1977. Two children: Amanda S. and Patricia A. Mr. Nixon enjoys AWANA youth ministry, being a church elder and computer consulting.

Kevin Ian Nonweiler
Manager of Information Technology Services
Mosman Municipal Council
5 Simeon Place
Liberty Grove, New South Wales, Australia 2138
+61 299784015
Fax: +61 299784132
k.nonweiler@computer.org

9121

Business Information: With over 18 years of experience in the technological field, Mr. Kevin Nonweiler was recruited to Mosman Municipal Council in 1996. At the present time, he fulfills the responsibilities of Manager of Information Technology Services. In his capacity, he oversees all aspects of information technology services as well as recommendation and implementation of technology products and services. Drawing on his technical expertise, he also works on software and hardware. Additionally, Mr. Kevin Nonweiler is in charge of the local area network ensuring it is maintained in a fully operational status. Continuing to provide quality services serves as his long-term goal. A local government organization founded in 1798, Mosman Municipal Council is responsible for rates and property management of land and facilities owned by the government. With approximately 12,000 parcels of land, the Council employs a staff of more than 150 people manning two locations. **Career Highlights:** Manager of Information Technology Services, Mosman Municipal Council (1996-Present); Lumley Technology: Data Center Manager (1989-96); Technical Support Manager (1988-89). **Associations & Accomplishments:** Association of Computing Machinery; Institute of Electrical and Electronic Engineers; Australian Computer Society; Australian Institute of Management; Competent Toastmaster. **Education:** Southern Cross University of Australia, M.B.A. (In Progress); Victoria University of Wellington, B.A. (1980). **Personal Information:** Married to Pek Fun in 1980. Two children: Jason and Alana. Mr. Nonweiler enjoys reading and playing chess.

Emmanuel E. A. Alexis

Computer Operator
Quebec Government
8827 9th Avenue
Montreal, Quebec, Canada H1Z 3A3
(514) 864-1161
Fax: (514) 873-6130
emmanuel.alexis@mfe.gouv.qc.ca

9131

Business Information: Drawing upon a strong background in computers, Mr. Alexis is the Computer Operator for the Quebec Government's information technology department. In his position, he is responsible for administering the Norton Antivirus program on the governmental computers as well as supplying workstations with the necessary programs to disable viruses. Moreover, he is charged with creating solutions for virus problems and works with a team of five other employees within the antivirus department. During his career, Mr. Alexis has performed numerous upgrades in several companies and his ability to fluently speak several languages has made him an asset to the Department and government. In the future, he looks forward to continuing with the Department, becoming a HTML Programmer, and advancing in networking. Located in Montreal, Canada, the Quebec Government information technology department maintains the upkeep of the information systems infrastructure and implements antivirus programs. Established in 1996, the Department provides a variety of programs to government agencies and other businesses to safeguard computer systems from threatening viruses. Currently, the Department supports a user base of 450 and operates on a local level. **Career Highlights:** Computer Operator, Quebec Government (2000-Present); Computer Operator, Microcell (1998-99). **Education:** Montreal University (2000). **Personal Information:** Mr. Alexis enjoys jogging and gospel music.

Stephen D. Armstrong

Chief of Information Systems Support
State of Kansas
2800 Southwest Topeka
Topeka, KS 66611
(785) 274-1432
Fax: (785) 274-1426
sdarmstrong@agtop.state.ks.us

9131

Business Information: Displaying his expertise in the technology field, Mr. Armstrong serves as Chief of Information Systems Support responsible for providing technical support for all statewide systems under the Adjutant General. An information systems professional with 20 years experience in the industry, Mr. Armstrong is experienced in all aspects of analysis, design, development, implementation, and project management. He supervises a staff of five employees. Before joining the Adjutant General's staff in 1999, he served as Director of Information Resources at the Topeka Juvenile Correctional Facility. His background history also includes that of Owner of Innovative Computer Systems. An expert, Mr. Armstrong keeps abreast of the latest technological advancements by reading trade journals and continuous education. Committed to continued optimum performance, he anticipates a promotion to Chief Information Officer. Founded in 1862, the Adjutant General office is a state government agency, coordinating with the Kansas National Guard and State Department of Emergency Management to provide emergency services to the citizens of the state of Kansas. Approximately 2,000 dedicated individuals are employed throughout the state. **Career Highlights:** Chief of Information Systems Support, State of Kansas (1999-Present); Director of Information Resources, Topeka Juvenile Correctional Facility (1992-99); Owner, Innovative Computer Systems (1991-92). **Associations & Accomplishments:** International WHO'S WHO of Professionals (1996). **Education:** Washburn University, B.A. (1979). **Personal Information:** Married to Laura in 1995. One child: Benjamin. Mr. Armstrong enjoys travel and sailing.

Amanda M. Cooper

AS/400 Manager
RF Wolters Company, Inc.
426 Campbell Hill Street
Marietta, GA 30060

9131

Business Information: Beginning her career more than 13 years ago, Ms. Cooper has worked diligently to develop skills and knowledge in all areas of information technology field. She is dedicated to ensuring that the needs of her clients are met and that all projects are completed efficiently and effectively. As of September 27, 1999, Ms. Cooper joined RF Wolters Company, Inc as its AS/400 Manager. An expert, Ms. Cooper has previously served with the City of Aiken in South Carolina as a Systems Analyst. Her background history also include stints as Software Engineer with Logistic Systems Architects and Programmer at Raytheon Support Services. She has developed the skills needed to maintain the highest standards of professional excellence and attributes her substantial success to her faith. A highly active member in her community, Ms. Cooper hopes to continue learning about networking and integrating systems. She attributes her success to her faith and ability to produce results and aggressively take on new challenges. Ms. Cooper continues to provide quality consultations and is also engaged in the installation of networks and fiber optics. **Career Highlights:** AS/400 Manager, RF Wolters Company, Inc. (1999-Present); Self Employed Systems Analyst (1999); Systems Analyst, City of Aiken (1990-99); Software Engineer, Logistic Systems Architects (1988-90); Programmer, Raytheon Support Services (1986-88). **Associations & Accomplishments:** Volunteer, United Way of Aiken County; Ambassador, City of Aiken Chamber of Commerce. **Education:** Spelman College, B.S. (1986). **Personal Information:** Married to Freddie in 1999. Ms. Cooper enjoys wedding floral design.

Sheryl A. Duggan

Civil Engineering Technician
City of Owasso
P.O. Box 180
Owasso, OK 74055
(918) 272-4959
Fax: (918) 272-4996
duggans47@aol.com

9131

Business Information: Since 1998, Mrs. Duggan has served in the position of Civil Engineer Technician for the City of Owasso. In her role, she is responsible for creating computer generated drawings of maps using state-of -the-art computed aided design programs. She manages the City projects from building, remodeling, to street repair that the City contracts out to different companies. Furthermore, Mrs. Duggan conducts inspections of the finished projects, supervises her staff, and ensures that the projects stay within budgetary constraints. She looks forward to continuing with the City, growing in her position, and taking on more responsibilities. Highly regarded, Mrs. Duggan attributes her success to family support and perseverance. Located in Owasso, Oklahoma, the City of Owasso is a municipal government. Since its establishment, the City has engaged in providing streets, buildings, and funds as well as overseeing the public and government agencies, such as the police and fire departments. With a staff of over 100 employees, the City is dedicated providing a safe place to live. **Career Highlights:** Civil Engineering Technician, City of Owasso (1988-Present), Document Controller, AMI (1986-88); Site Office Coordinator, ENSCO (1985-86). **Associations & Accomplishments:** Representative, Red Ribbon Campaign (anti-drug); Erosion and Sedimentation Control Training; Involved in helping formulate city regulations and enforcements of erosion control. **Education:** S.E.K. Technical University, degree in Drafting and Design (1992); Northwestern Oklahoma State University; Tulsa Vocational Tech, Auto CAD; CadTech, Maximizing Auto CAD; Drug Prevention Training, Training the Trainer. **Personal Information:** Married to Michael in 1967. Four children: Danny, Terry, Kimberly Young, and Mendy Baty. Mrs. Duggan enjoys writing poetry, painting, quilting, crafts and reading murder mysteries.

Ahmed Azzam Elmasri, Ph.D.

Head of Computer Department
Ministry of Cabinet Affairs & Information
P.O. Box 15851
Manama, Bahrain
+973 686091
Fax: +973 686653
Mobile: +973 9613932
mndl@bateleco.com.bh

9131

Business Information: Serving as the Head of the Computer Department for Bahrain's Ministry of Cabinet Affairs and Information, Dr. Elmasri determines and develops the overall technical strategic plan for the Ministry. Possessing an excellent understanding of technology, he is responsible for proposing new software applications and hardware. Dr. Elmasri ensures the functionality and operational status of the operating systems and network infrastructures, troubleshoots difficulties, and programs new solutions. With a staff of seven people in this Department, all departments within the Ministry come to him for every information technology need. A successful, 18-year professional, Dr. Elmasri's plans for the future include the development of the Bahrain electronic government project. The Ministry of Cabinet Affairs & Information coordinates the activities of the various ministries of the government of Bahrain, while providing advice and expertise to the country's executive administration. Established in 1963, the Ministry employs a 1,000 professional, technical, and support staff. **Career Highlights:** Head of the Computer Department, Ministry of Cabinet Affairs & Information (1997-Present); Information Technology Advisor, Ministry of Education (1993-97); Director of Computer Center, Ajman University (1988-93); Lecturer, University of Bahrain Computer Science Department (1985-88). **Associations & Accomplishments:** Oxford Club; Bahrain Information Technology Society; Seven papers in various magazines, journals, and conferences. **Education:** Bradford University, Ph.D. (1993); Montreal University, B.S. in Electronics/Communications (1980). **Personal Information:** Married to Maha Al-Mandeel in 1982. Five children: Fatima, Mohammed, Ebrahim, Maryam, and Noor. Dr. Elmasri enjoys reading, surfing the Internet and swimming.

Nicholas R. Hardgrove

Information Systems Analyst
City of Laramie
406 East Ivinson Avenue
Laramie, WY 82070
(307) 721-5219
Fax: (307) 721-5211
nhardgrave@ci.laramie.wy.us

9131

Business Information: Serving as Information Systems Analyst with the City of Laramie, Mr. Hardgrove presides over the Information Services Division. He supervises the administration of all of the hardware and software operations of the NT server, the work stations, and remote access user support applications. Additionally, he acts as the Company's liaison to industry vendors and provides technical support to the system's 175 users. In addition to supervising two employees, he handles numerous resource planning functions such as personnel evaluations, oversees time lines and schedules, and coordinates resources and assignments. Mr. Hardgrove has written some articles relating to the computer field and was published in The Laramie Boomerang. Continually striving to improve performance, he looks forward to a future promotion to Chief Information Officer. In 1868, a group of pioneers banded together to form a settlement in the wilderness of Wyoming. That settlement is known today as the City of Laramie. Approximately 28,000 people now reside within the City's limits and the municipal government of Laramie focuses on improving the quality of life for each of its great citizens. Presently, the City employs a work force of more than 360 public servants. **Career Highlights:** Information Systems Analyst, City of Laramie (1998-Present); Network Administrator, Wind River Visual Communication (1997-98); Web Programmer, Geology Department (1996-97). **Associations & Accomplishments:** National Soccer Coaching Association of America; Palm Developers. **Education:** University of Wyoming, B.S. in Computer Science (1994). **Personal Information:** Mr. Hardgrove enjoys mountain biking and soccer.

Alvin A. Hunter

Technology Consulting Branch Manager
Commonwealth of Virginia - Department of Information Technology
110 South 7th Street, Floor 3
Richmond, VA 23219-3931
(804) 371-5958
Fax: (804) 320-8797

9131

Business Information: Mr. Hunter serves as the Technology Consulting Branch Manager for the Department of Information Technology within the Commonwealth of Virginia. He manages a team of consultants that assist state agencies and local governments in network development and design. Mr. Hunter specializes in Network design, LAN, WAN communications, WAN, LAN to mainframe communications, and Windows NT Server and Windows NT BackOffice Applications. His greatest accomplishment to date is designing the Governor's network. The Commonwealth of Virginia performs all legislation and congressional acts within the state. The government body is divided into a number of departments, each with a specific purpose. The Department of Information Technology administers, develops, upgrades, and maintains computer information systems of all the state's agencies. The department was formed in 1984 and staffs 480 professionals. **Career Highlights:** Commonwealth of Virginia - Department of Information Technology: Technology

Consulting Branch Manager (2000-Present), Computer Systems Lead Engineer (1996-99), Computer Systems Senior Engineer (1985-96), Computer Systems Engineer (1984-85); Programmer Analyst (1981-84). **Education:** Virginia State University, B.A. (1976). **Personal Information:** Married to Laura in 1986. Two children: Alvin Jr. and Tarnesha. Mr. Hunter enjoys weightlifting and bicycling.

Kim A. Kleppe

Manager of Information Systems
City of Mount Vernon
1401 Britt Road
Mount Vernon, WA 98273-6511
(360) 336-0624
Fax: (360) 336-0623
kimk@ci.mount-vernon.wa.us

9131

Business Information: As Manager of Information Systems for the City of Mount Vernon, Mr. Kleppe administers and controls all database resources as well as the systems and network infrastructure. Possessing an excellent understanding of technology, he is responsible for maintaining computer and telephone systems throughout the City. A savvy, technical professional, Mr. Kleppe is also involved in database programming and oversees set up, servers, routers, wiring, installation of software, and budgeting. Ensuring systems and database reliability, security, and integrity; and coordinating resources, time lines, and assignments also fall within the realm of Mr. Kleppe's functions. Striving to reach his highest potential, Mr. Kleppe plans on remaining in his field and becoming an expert in the information technology arena. Currently staffing 274 employees, the City of Mount Vernon is a local government that provides a range of services to include computer and phone systems, emergency, police protection, water, sewage, road repair, and recreation to City residents. **Career Highlights:** Manager of Information Systems, City of Mount Vernon (Present). **Education:** Skagit Valley College. **Personal Information:** One child: Corey. Mr. Kleppe enjoys hiking, rafting, skiing, softball, golf and travel.

Long Minh Le

Database Administrator
County of Ingham, Management Information Services
121 East Mapple
Mason, MI 48854
(517) 676-7382
Fax: (517) 676-7396
dp_long@ingham.org

9131

Business Information: Mr. Le serves as Database Administrator for Ingham County's Management Information Services. He controls and administers all data systems and tools and ensures data security, integrity, and reliability. Possessing an excellent understanding of his field, he also fulfills the responsibilities of client server developer and systems analyst. Highly regarded, Mr. Le is accountable for the analysis, acquisition, installation, modification, configuration, support, and tracking of operating systems, databases, utilities, software, and hardware. Recognized for his incredible efforts, he single-handedly took small database systems and implemented and integrated them into a large Oracle database. Driven to provide faster and more accurate results in the medical industry, Mr. Le plans on working towards the creation of a medical research database. Given the opportunity to locate a limitless supply of medical information including the diagnosis of diseases, recommended medications, treatment, and available cures, the medical industry would reflect a profound change. His success reflects his ability to think outside the box, take on challenges, and deliver results. Continuing his research and training through Ingham County's Management Information Services, Mr. Le is one of the 1,211 county employees involved with the operation of local government, enforcement of laws and regulations, and development of the community. Ingham County was founded in 1838. **Career Highlights:** Ingham County, Management Information Services: Database Administrator (1998-Present), Systems Analyst (1995-98); Programmer/Analyst, Continental Systems (1987). **Education:** Northwood University, B.B.A. (1995); Dalat University, B.A. (1974). **Personal Information:** Married to Hien Thanh Trinh in 1976. Five children: Lam, Nguyen, Johnny, Thomas, and Julia. Mr. Le enjoys classical guitarist and a tropical fish hobbyist.

Scott J. Liske

Director of Information Services
City of Appleton
100 North Appleton Street
Appleton, WI 54911-4702
(920) 832-6008
Fax: (920) 832-5885
scott.liske@appleton.org

9131

Business Information: As Director of Information Services for the City of Appleton, Mr. Liske is responsible for the management and support of computer hardware, software, connectivity, and telephones. Also involved in overseeing a staff of 12 individuals, Mr. Liske ensures all project quality, presides over the budget, and handles all procurement. He has enjoyed substantial success in his career including having established a computer network from the ground up and having written articles for several technical publications. He hopes to keep up with technology and continue his standardization. City of Appleton is a local government municipality engaged in handling all matters for the local community. Engaged in the organization of community programs and festivals, the City reports an estimated annual turnover of $1.2 million. **Career Highlights:** City of Appleton: Director of Information Services (1999-Present), Police LAN Administrator (1994-99), Police Officer (1992-94). **Associations & Accomplishments:** Past Chairman, Local County Red Cross Agency; Past President, Local United Way Agency; Retired Major, United States Army Reserve. **Education:** Mount Senario College, B.S. (1990). **Personal Information:** Married to Nancy in 1989. Two children: Nicholas and Adam. Mr. Liske enjoys woodworking, fishing and cooking.

Raymond Long

Network Administrator
City of El Paso
P.O. Box 23098
El Paso, TX 79923
(915) 541-4393

9131

Business Information: As the Senior Network Administrator for the City of El Paso, Mr. Long is currently responsible for all computer networks within the City. He began by creating a local area network at all 10 library branches of the City and is also working on building its wide area network. Drawing from over 12 years of experience in networking, Mr. Long was also in charge of ensuring the City was Y2K compliant. He has enjoyed substantial success in his career including having received several grants, and in 1993 building the largest network in the history of the University of Texas at El Paso. Mr. Long attributes his success to his family values and support. He hopes to continue building the network and expedite continued promotion within the City. The City of El Paso is a government municipality in far west Texas. The site of Fort Bliss military base and the annual Sun Bowl, the City is growing economically with major assembly plants such as Chevron and Ford and a growing population of 615,000 residents. **Career Highlights:** Senior Network Administrator, City of El Paso (1996-Present); Management Information Systems Associate, Security Capitol (1995-96); Network Manager, University of Texas at El Paso (1991-95). **Associations & Accomplishments:** Microsoft Certified Professional; Certified Novell Administrator. **Education:** University of Texas at El Paso, B.S. (1990). **Personal Information:** One child: Priscilla Rose. Mr. Long enjoys basketball and comic book collecting.

John W. Mayer

Software Services Manager
City of Irving
825 West Irving Boulevard
Irving, TX 75060
(972) 721-3690
Fax: (972) 721-2560
jmayer@ci.irving.tx.us

9131

Business Information: Mr. Mayer is a resident and employee of the City of Irving, serving as Software Services Manager for the city government. In his role, he supervises a 12 person staff comprising of programmer analysts, database administrators, systems programmers, and computer operators. A systems expert, he oversees and directs mainframe and midrange systems operations, as well as designs his own programming projects using Oracle and Mircrosoft. Mr. Mayer is well recognized within the City for his ability to transform dead-end projects into highly functional programs. He plans to become more involved with industry related associations and civic organizations within the community. Attributing his success to consistency, Mr. Mayer is working to gain more responsibilities within the City government. City of Irving is a municipal government hosting a current city with a population of 180,000 residents. Irving, Texas is located between Dallas and Fort Worth and is the home of several industrial leaders headquarters. The City also houses Valley Ranch, the training facility for the Dallas Cowboys football team and Dallas Stars hockey team. **Career Highlights:** Software Services Manager, City of Irving (1998-Present); Conversion Programmer, Agency Management Services (1998); Programmer Analyst, City of College Station (1997-98); Programmer Analyst, Brookshire Grocery Company (1994-96). **Education:** Texas A&M University, Bachelor's degree (1994). **Personal Information:** Married to Kimberly Ann in 1990. One child: Kenneth Allen. Mr. Mayer enjoys reading, scuba diving, playing racquetball and spending time with his family.

Michael Noble

Director of Telecommunications
City of Greenfield
P.O. Box 456
Greenfield, IN 46140
(317) 462-8507
Fax: (317) 462-8610

9131

Business Information: Serving as Director of Telecommunications, Mr. Noble oversees daily technical activites for the City of Greenfield, Indiana. Maintaining the City's telephone network, he demonstrates a superior technical ability as he works closely with mulitmedia aspects of telecommunications such as the Internet. He regularly performs evaluations of hardware, software, and other equipment to ensure the Department is operating at maximum efficiency; recently he orchestrated the television station's equipment upgrade. Keeping his goals consistent with the objectives of the Department and of the City, he currently is working to implement technology that will allow the station to operate faster and more efficiently. Located less than 20 miles east of Indianapolis, Indiana, the City of Greenfield is home to approximately 20,000 people. The City of Greenfield's Telecommunications Department provides telephone services to City agencies and provides programming for the government access television station. **Career Highlights:** Director of Telecommunications, City of Greenfield (1998-Present); Design Engineer, Bennett Innovations (1997-98); Gaffer/Grip/Videographer, Freelance (1996); Production Assistant, Innovative Edit (1995-96). **Education:** Indiana University, B.A. (1995).

Stephen L. Pastorik

Planner II/Geographic Information System Specialist
West Valley City
3600 Constitution Boulevard
Salt Lake City, UT 84119
(801) 963-3545
Fax: (801) 963-3559
spastorik@ci.west-valley.ut.us

9131

Business Information: In his position as Planner II and Geographic Information Systems Specialist, Mr. Pastorik oversees all global information services, digital mapping, and zoning administration. Utilizing skills and knowledge acquired from an extensive academic background, he authors and requests federal grants, creates city grants for local residents, and reviews construction plans to ensure compliance with local, state, and federal regulations. Continually striving for maximum effectiveness, Mr. Pastorik is currently pursuing his M.B.A. degree to enable him to capitalize on opportunites afforded by the City. West Valley City is a community of 100,000 citizens located in scenic Utah. The local government contributes many services designed to protect residents and improve the quality of life available. City Planning is an integral part of city life, providing mapping services and zoning ordinances for area residents. Established in 1980, the Department employs the skilled services of 600 individuals to facilitate all aspects of operation. **Career Highlights:** Planner II/Geographic Information System Specialist, West Valley City (1995-Present). **Associations & Accomplishments:** American Planning Association. **Education:** University of Utah: M.B.A. (In Progress), B.S. in Planning (1997). **Personal Information:** Married to Jennifer Pastorick in 1995. One child: Jacob. Mr. Pastorik enjoys hiking, camping and church activities.

Craig A. Phillips

Systems Analyst
City of Las Vegas
4354 Silver Bay Street
Las Vegas, NV 89147
(702) 229-6842
numb1fan@aol.com

9131

Business Information: Functioning in the role of Systems Analyst, Mr. Phillips is responsible for maintaining and updating the computer system and networking infrastructure for the City of Las Vegas. He primarily oversees the financial system, written to calculate procurement and payroll, and manage the cash flow. His current project is preparing all systems for the Y2K adjustment for transition to the new millennium. Before joining the City of Las Vegas, Mr. Phillips served as a Technician for Hi-Tech Services and as Programmer and Analyst with Sports Form. As an experienced, 12 year computer professional, he is charged with oversight responsibility for purchasing new technology equipment and applications. Participating in the analysis, design, implementation, configuration, test, support, and tracking of operating systems, database software, client server utility programs, software, and hardware also fall within the realm of Mr. Phillips' functions. His success reflects his ability to take on new challenges and responsibilities. Working and eventually attaining the position of Senior Analyst serves as one of his future goals. The City of Las Vegas is located in southern Nevada. Incorporated in 1905, the City is known for the casinos and clubs that line the main street and beyond. Gambling, however, did not become the City's primary industry until the 1940s, when a military institution was built just outside of the City. The local government consists of 2,500 elected and hired officials who strive for the progress of the City. **Career Highlights:** Systems Analyst, City of Las Vegas (1988-Present); Technician, Hi-Tech Services (1985-88); Programmer, Sports Form (1982-85). **Associations & Accomplishments:** Chairman, Advisory Council, Las Vegas Chapter, De Molay International. **Education:** University of Nevada at Las Vegas, B.S. in Computer Science with a minor in Mathematics (1987). **Personal Information:** Married to Linda in 1987. Mr. Phillips enjoys golf, bowling and softball.

John M. Raby

Director of Management Information Systems
City of Pensacola
180 West Government Street
Pensacola, FL 32501
(850) 435-1825
Fax: (850) 435-1838
jraby@ci.pensacola.fl.us

9131

Business Information: Mr. Raby serves in the role of Director of Management Information Systems for the City of Pensacola. He is responsible for supervising 20 people and ensuring all aspects of the operation run within the framework of the City's overall strategic plan and vision. In collaboration with other top executives, Mr. Raby resolves any current problems or issues which may otherwise prohibit the daily duties of the office. A smart systems expert, he determines the overall strategic direction and business contributions of the information systems function. He is also responsible for overseeing personnel management and advising city officials on more effective and efficient means of operation. Mr. Raby attributes his professional success to the ability to get along with others and networking to establish new business contacts and relationships. City of Pensacola provides administration and city services to residents of Pensacola. Pensacola, an urban region, is located on the Northwestern coast of Florida with a population of more than 60,000 people. Florida is ranked one of the leading tourist sites in the United States. **Career Highlights:** Director of Management Information Systems, City of Pensacola (1997-Present); Principal Engineer, Svendrup Technology (1991-97); Colonel, United States Air Force (1965-91). **Associations & Accomplishments:** Past President, Pensacola Heritage Foundation; 33rd Mason. **Education:** New York University, M.S. (1970); United States Air Force Academy, B.S. (1965). **Personal Information:** Married to Janine in 1985. Mr. Raby enjoys golf and investing.

Michael A. Ritcher

Director of Management Information Systems
City of Oxford
101 East High Street
Oxford, OH 45056-1887
(513) 524-5278
Fax: (513) 523-7298
mritcher@cityofoxford.org

9131

Business Information: Drawing from 17 years of experience in the technology field, Mr. Ritcher is the Director of Management Information Systems for the City of Oxford. In his capacity, he oversees and directs a number of technical duties, to include the installation and maintenance of software and hardware accessories and peripherals. Demonstrating strong leadership, Mr. Ritcher determines the strategic direction and business contribution of the information systems functions on behalf of the City. Administering and controlling database software and software applications, he ensures the integrity and security of all data resources. Moreover, he provides field technical support, conducts long term planning, and works with legal counselors on various issues. In the future, Mr. Ritcher looks forward to continuing with the City, while upgrading and creating an environment that allows easy electronic exchange. The City of Oxford, Ohio serves a population of approximately 22,000 residents. The City government comprises of various departments that manages a variety of duties on behalf of the City's residents. The City's information systems function is responsible for maintaining the technical infrastructure and providing computer training to City employees. **Career Highlights:** Director of Management Information Systems, City of Oxford (1999-Present); City of Sarasota: Computer Systems Administrator (1989-94), Systems Analyst (1989-94). **Education:** Manatec Community College: A.A. (1984), A.S. (1983). **Personal Information:** Married to Denise in 1983. Mr. Ritcher enjoys classic car restoration.

Brent R. Robson

Information Analyst
Halifax Regional Municipality
P.O. Box 1749 Station Central
Halifax, Nova Scotia, Canada B3J 3A5
(902) 490-7068
Fax: (902) 490-6389
robsonb@region.halifax.ns.ca

9131

Business Information: Serving as an Information Analyst for Halifax Regional Municipality, Mr. Robson is a key part of a team that attends to the Municipality's information needs. Services provided by Mr. Robson includes records management, library services, indexing, and database development. Possessing superior talents and an excellent understanding of technology, he is also responsible for indexing, cataloging, reference inquiries, budgeting, ordering, and a number of administrative duties on behalf of the Municipality. Very dedicated and having a strong passion for his job, Mr. Robson plans on developing and implementing an electronic virtual library that will greatly assist the Municipality's staff in conducting day-to-day business operations. Halifax Regional Municipality is a municipal government for a population of 354,000 citizens. Located in Halifax, Nova Scotia, the Municipality was established in 1841, and employs more than 5,000 personnel. Within the Municipality is a library which serves the staff, offering online and indexing services and an Intranet site for staff. **Career Highlights:** Information Analyst, Halifax Regional Municipality (1998-Present); Database Specialist, Nova Scotia Department of Justice (1997-98); Information Specialist, Nova Scotia Records Management (1993-96). **Associations & Accomplishments:** Canadian Library Association; Special Libraries Association. **Education:** Dalhousie University, Bachelor's in Education (1985); University of Kings College, B.A. (1984). **Personal Information:** Married to Kelly in 1996. Mr. Robson enjoys camping.

Donald A. Saunders

Design Engineer
County of Cuyahoga
1370 Ontario Street, Suite 1910
Cleveland, OH 44113-1701
(440) 439-6364
Fax: (216) 348-3896
saundersward6@sprintmail.com

9131

Business Information: A 23 year veteran of the technology field, Mr Saunders fulfills the responsibilities of Design Engineer for the County of Cuyahoga. Focused and innovative, he works in the Engineering Department and is accountable for the design and building of highways in addition to overseeing the Department's computer systems. He supervises the operation and maintenance of the hardware and software components of the Department's computers in the performance of his duties that he assumed in 1977. Concurrently, Mr. Saunders serves as a City Councilman in Bedford, Ohio, a small Cuyahoga County city of 15,000 people about 15 miles southeast of Cleveland. Attributing his career success to his communication ability, he is currently pursuing a goal to complete a G.I.S. database for the City of Bedford. Mr. Saunders owns a consistent record of delivering results through leadership, effective decision-making, and interpersonal skills. The County of Cuyahoga is a regional government agency in the United States that concerns itself with providing the range of engineering and public works services to county government projects throughout a region of the country's tenth largest state. Providing services in the most populous region of Ohio, the Department is located in Cleveland, the seat of Cuyahoga County, which is home to more than 1.5 million people. The Engineering Department activities of County of Cuyahoga involves the building of roads, highways, utility facilities, water and waste treatment plants and systems, and other infrastructures to support the county and local citizens. The County of Cuyahoga employs 250 professional, technical, and administrative staff. **Career Highlights:** Design Engineer, County of Cuyahoga (1977-Present); Ward 6 Councilman, City of Bedford (1998-Present). **Associations & Accomplishments:** University of Akron, B.S. in Civil Engineering (1979); University of Dayton.National Society of Professional Engineers; American Society of Highway Engineers; Bedford Historical Society; Suburban Community Council Association. **Education:** University of Akron, B.S. in Civil Engineering (1979); University of Dayton. **Personal Information:** Married to Judy in 1995. Two children: Matthew and Andrew.

Mark A. Silhavy

Systems Analyst
City of College Station
P.O. Box 9960
College Station, TX 77842-7960
(409) 764-3498
Fax: (409) 764-3664
msilhavy@tca.net

9131

Business Information: Mr. Silhavy functions in the role of Systems Analyst at the City of College Station. He is responsible for program implementation, requirements analysis, database and systems administration, and integregating new ideas. As a project team leader, he coordinates the activities of his department during system implementations that involve working with other departments. One of his greatest accomplishments while at the Municipality has been his leadership behind a joint project with Texas A&M University where students from the University enroll in a course aimed at developing, designing, and maintaining the city's Intranet site. In the future, Mr. Silhavy would like to move into a position of Project Manager and in the mean time he plans to continue implementing and updating the current systems. His success reflects his ability to adapt to changes, think outside the box, produce cutting edge results, and tackle new challenges. The City of College Station is the local governing body for College Station, Texas. Established in 1938, the Municipality controls the legislative activities for over 60,000 residents. Aside from establishing laws, enforcing regulations, and other legal activities, the Municipality also creates community events to promote the friendly environment of the City. College Station has a staff of nearly 800 sworn and civilian personnel all working to ensure a safe and habitable city is provided for its residents. **Career Highlights:** Systems Analyst, City of College Station (1997-Present); Finance and Accounting Intern, City of Rosenberg (1993-97). **Associations & Accomplishments:** Texas A&M University: Association of Former Students, Hospitality Committee, Fish Camp Counselor, New Student Orientation Leader; Past President, Church Youth Organization; Executive Committee, High School Council. **Education:** Texas A&M University at College Station, B.B.A. in Accounting and Business Analysis (1998). **Personal Information:** Mr. Silhavy enjoys golf.

Douglas Thompson

Systems Security Officer
City of Orlando
400 South Orange Avenue, 5th Floor
Orlando, FL 32801-2589
(407) 246-3020
Fax: (407) 246-2878
doug.thompson@ci.orlando.fl.us

9131

Business Information: As the Systems Security Officer for the City of Orlando, Mr. Thompson oversees and directs all systems security functions. He is responsible for the provision of new data entry, investigative reports, and general security and integrity of all systems. Possessing an excellent understanding of technology, he creates backup systems, he is also accountable for physical and platform security. A savvy 21 year civil servant of the City of Orlando, Mr. Thompson's primary focus is on maintaining the functionality, operational status, and reliability of the City's systems infrastructure. With a background of government service, he has previously served with the United States Navy. He joined the City as Police Dispatcher in 1979, and has since faithfully served in a variety of capacities with the City government. Attributing his success to networking with others in the field as well as support of family and friends, Mr. Thompson's future goals include getting more involved in risk management and utilizing new technical assessment methodologies to enhance overall systems security. The City of Orlando's information technology department oversees and manages the City's technology infrastructure. The Department is charged with protecting all City government computer systems through the provision of security systems that prevent unlawful entry into confidential files, programs, and Web sites. Established in the 1800s, the City of Orlando is local in scope and it employs more than 3,000 civil servants. **Career Highlights:** City of Orlando: Systems Security Officer (1999-current), Senior Computer Operator (1991-99), Police Dispatcher (1979-91). **Associations & Accomplishments:** XPLOR International, Teaching in Elementary Schools with Junior Acheviements Program. **Education:** Florida Technical College, PC Repair. **Personal Information:** Married to Carol in 1988. One child: Shayna. Mr. Thompson enjoys woodworking and sports.

Dane Van Pelt
Network Information Systems Manager
City of Albuquerque
P.O. Box 1293
Albuquerque, NM 87103
(505) 768-2797
Fax: (505) 768-4615

9131

Business Information: As Network Information Systems Manager of the City of Albuquerque DFA/ISD, Mr. Van Pelt oversees the operation of all local, midrange, and wide area networks utilized by the Municipality. He coordinates infrastructure development, help desk operations, and file sharing server programs, while providing technical support for desktop applications and platforms. The City of Albuquerque DFA/ISD operates as a local government office, responsible for the administration of public works and public safety, taxation, zoning, and transportation. **Career Highlights:** Network Information Systems Manager, City of Albuquerque DFA/ISD (1995-Present); Defense Information System Agency of Europe - United States Army: Division Chief of Implementation (1994-95), Branch Chief (1991-94). **Education:** Missouri Western State College, B.S. (1978). **Personal Information:** Married to Maria Three children: Loretta, Dane, and Chad. Mr. Van Pelt enjoys woodworking, auto mechanics and family time.

Charles Barber
LAN Coordinator
Social Security Administration
110 Frederick Street, Suite A
Greenville, SC 29607
(864) 233-8110
Fax: (864) 233-9377
charles.barber@ssa.gov

9199

Business Information: Displaying skills in this highly specialized position, Mr. Barber joined the Social Security Administration in 1968 as a Claims Representative. In 1992, Mr. Barber was elevated to the role of LAN Coordinator responsible for maintaining the functionality and fully operational status of the regional and national LAN infrastructure, including 53 intelligent work stations in the Greenville, South Carolina Social Security Office. As a 25 year technology professional, he is responsible for making sure that all software and software bridges work in Greenville, South Carolina. He also travels to Birmingham and Baltimore to access story devices. Formulating realistic objectives, Mr. Barber plans to retire from the Agency within three years and open a high speed communications architecture company with a direct focus on hardware and software. Crediting his success to his father, Mr. Barber's career highlight includes designing a cutting edge database used to control folders. Providing outstanding service to all residents, the Social Security Administration is a federal government owned organization. The Agency provides economic security to individuals facing retirement, disability, death, and unemployment. Medical care is also available through the Agency. Established in 1936, regional headquarters are located in Atlanta, Georgia. The Agency is the largest user of the Windows NT system. **Career Highlights:** Social Security Administration: LAN Coordinator (1992-Present), Assistant Manager (1986-91), Area Administration Assistant (1981-86). **Associations & Accomplishments:** Social Security Administration Managers Association; Optimist International Club; Who's Who Among Students in Colleges and Universities (1968). **Education:** Benedict College, B.S. (1968); Compumaster Certificate (1999); Georgetown University (1970); United States Army, Computer Training. **Personal Information:** Married to Mabel C. in 1975. Two children: Charles Kelvin and Jessica Charlene. Mr. Barber enjoys golf, riding ATVs, and repairing old computers and making them Y2K ready through the use of software.

Jeffrey L. Caffey
Computer Specialist
Department of Justice, Immigration Naturalization Service
United States Government
Washington, DC 20536
(202) 307-0134
jc1159@aol.com

9199

Business Information: Functioning in the capacity of a Computer Specialist with the Department of Justice, Immigration Naturalization Service, Mr. Caffey administers and controls all aspects of the Agency's data resources. Before joining the Immigration Naturalization Service in 1998, he served as Senior Systems Programmer with Computer Resource Management. His background history includes a stint as Systems Programmer at GEICO Insurance. Offering technical support and overseeing all computer systems within the Agency, Mr. Caffey ensures data integrity, security, and reliability, as well as recover corrupted data and eliminate redundancy. A systems expert, he also fine tunes software tools to improve database performance and resolves systems problems. Mr. Caffey stays abreast of changes in his field by reading and surfing the Internet. He attributes his substantial success to his upbringing and his ability to deliver results and tackle new challenges and responsibilities. His future aspirations include moving into an upper level management role. Immigration Naturalization Service is a division of the Department of Justice. A government agency, the Department specializes in ensuring that illegal aliens are apprehended and returned to their home or that immigrants are able to find asylum in the United States. **Career Highlights:** Computer Specialist, Department of Justice, Immigration Naturalization Service (1998-Present); Senior Systems Programmer, Computer Resource Management (1997-98); Systems Programmer, GEICO Insurance (1996-97). **Associations & Accomplishments:** Alpha Phi Alpha Fraternity, Inc. **Education:** Alabama State University, B.S. (1982); Certified Novell Engineer; Certified Novell Administrator. **Personal Information:** Married to Tina in 1994. Mr. Caffey enjoys computers, listening to music, bowling and fishing.

Joyce E. Endres, CFSP
Strategic Information Technology Consultant
State of Wisconsin, Department of Administration
P.O. Box 7844
Madison, WI 53707
(608) 264-8506
Fax: (608) 266-2164
joyce.endres@doa.state.wi.us

9199

Business Information: As Strategic Information Technology Consultant for the Department of Administration, Mrs. Endres provides information and state data to other departments within the State of Wisconsin government. Serving as a strategic consultant, she coordinates activities with data forms that have been standardized statewide to provide applicable solutions to challenges. From an administrative standpoint, Mrs. Endres maintains vital records and supervises the direction of training programs to ensure that governmental policies are adhered to. The recipient of several internal performance awards, Mrs. Endres attributes success to her strong feelings of self-value, realizing her attitude is reflected in her work. Striving to gain a more broad perspective of the technical fields related to her position, Mrs. Endres currently has plans to increase her involvement in state policy as she continually learns new aspects of progressive technology. A central service agency for the State of Wisconsin, the Department of Administration employs over 1,200 of the total 25,000 state employees. Fulfilling needs for several aspects of state government, the Department provides documents, organizes campaigns, and assists with the planning of committees and events. **Career Highlights:** State of Wisconsin, Department of Administration: Strategic Information Technology Consultant (1995-Present); State of Wisconsin, Industry, Labor, and Human Relations: Business Systems Analyst (1970-95), Data Entry Manager (1964-70). **Associations & Accomplishments:** President (Present), Business Forms Management Association; B.F.M.A. **Education:** C.E.U.; Management Systems; Professional Organization and Training Companies. **Personal Information:** Married to Leo A. in 1966. Three children: Lucinda Fritchen, Leo S., and Leane Rielly. Mrs. Endres enjoys collecting clowns, antiques and collectables, reading and cards.

Cindy L. Hamilton
Systems Support Coordinator
Kentucky Department for Libraries & Archives
300 Coffee Tree Road
Frankfort, KY 40601-9267
(502) 564-8300
Fax: (502) 564-5773
cindy.hamilton@kdla.net

9199

Business Information: Serving in several positions throughout her career with the Kentucky State Government, Ms. Hamilton currently serves as the Systems Support Coordinator with the Kentucky Department for Libraries & Archives. A systems expert, she supervises the information technology systems infrastructure for the Department and other smaller related agencies. Presiding over the network administration, she assumes accountability for the efficient operation of six servers and the workstations for 200 users. Ms. Hamilton works hard and is continually striving to stay abreast of the latest technological advancements in her field. Consistently achieving quality performance, she looks forward to a future promotion to Information Systems Manager. Her success reflects her ability to deliver results and aggressively tackle new challenges. Founded during the 1960s, the Kentucky Department for Libraries & Archives is the state government agency and records center responsible for the collection and storage of state and government documents and records. The Agency is also performs genealogy research. Several regional offices are located throughout the state and agency headquarters is maintained in Frankfort, Kentucky. An approximate work force of 160 qualified staff members is employed statewide. **Career Highlights:** Kentucky Department for Libraries & Archives: Systems Support Coordinator (1999-Present), Computer Operator/Senior Analyst (1991-99); Kentucky Department for Military Affairs, Computer Operations Analyst (1989-91). **Education:** Morehead State University, B.B.A. (1986); Prestonsburg Community College, A.A. **Personal Information:** Ms. Hamilton enjoys the gym, walking and reading.

Stephen A. Keppler
Director, Vehicle Systems Department
ITS America
400 Virginia Avenue SW, Suite 800
Washington, DC 20024
(202) 484-4662
Fax: (202) 484-3483
skeppler@itsa.org

9199

Business Information: Mr. Keppler functions in the role of Director, Vehicle Systems Department for the Intelligent Transportation Society of America (ITS America). He oversees activities regarding technology applications for vehicle and vehicle-infrastructure based information systems, products and services in transportation. Projects involving the automotive, commercial vehicle, and intermodal sectors are within Mr. Keppler's purview as the department director. Before joining the Society as a Senior Engineer in 1998, Mr. Keppler faithfully served as an Engineer for the Federal Highway Administration. Currently, he assists both the public and private sectors in developing and implementing various technologies in transportation that saves lives, time, money, and improve the quality of life. Fulfilling his role as the Project Manager for a large scale vehicle-based technology demonstration event in Ohio during the summer of 1999, showcasing the latest international technology developments in cars, trucks, buses, and transit vehicles is cited as his career highlight. Attributing his success to a strong upbringing, always wanting to learn, and surrounding himself with knowledgeable and socially conscious people, Mr. Keppler plans to become more prominent in the industry and continue his service to the Society as he enters the 21st Century. ITS America is a public-private, not-for-profit organization chartered by the U.S. Congress to promote technology in transportation and to enhance the safety and productivity of our nation's transportation system. Founded in 1991, the Society is an organization of organizations numbering over 1,000 member companies worldwide including State Departments of Transportation and Federal Agencies on the public side, and private companies such as Microsoft, Intel, Motorola, Ford, General Motors, DaimlerChrysler, Nissan, and others - all combining forces in hopes of enhancing the performance and reliability of our transportation network through advanced technology applications. **Career Highlights:** ITS America: Director, Vehicle Systems Department (1998-Present), Senior Engineer (1998); Engineer, Federal Highway Administration (1992-97). **Associations & Accomplishments:** Society for Automotive Engineers; Institute for Transportation Engineers; Chi Epsilon, Honorary Civil Engineering Fraternity; Named to International WHO'S WHO of Information Technology. **Education:** Drexel University: B.S. in Civil Engineering (1992), B.S. in Architectural Engineering (1992). **Personal Information:** Married to Dana in 1997. Mr. Keppler enjoys soccer, playing sports, golf and outdoor activities.

Allison W. Latmore
Senior Fixed Income Research Analyst
Florida State Board of Administration
P.O. Box 13300
Tallahassee, FL 32317-3300
(850) 413-1438
Fax: (850) 413-1419
latmore_allison@fsba.state.fl.us

9199

Business Information: Beginning her career with the Florida State Board of Administration several years ago, Ms. Latmore has received recognition for her diligence and expert technical skills through several promotions to her current position of Senior Fixed Income Research Analyst. In this capacity, she manages internal and external porfolios while tracking and reporting her findings. She also assists in risk budgeting analysis, and credit research on technology for REIT sectors. Ms. Latmore has achieved significant occupational success and was recently involved in developing and designing a program for the governor of Florida and his board of directors on asset management. "We make a living by what we get, but we make a life by what we give," from the legendary Winston Churchill, is her favorite quote. The Florida State Board of Administration is an agency that operates as a fixed income research analysis center. Located in Tallahasse, Florida, current operations utilize a collective work force of over 250 highly trained professionals who help expedite all daily activities. The Agency specializes in quantitive performance work and credit analysis of the technology and REIT sectors. **Career Highlights:** Florida State Board of Administration: Senior Fixed Income Research Analyst (Present), Fixed Income Research Analyst III (1998), Fixed Income Research Analyst II (1996), Quantitative Analyst/Investment Analytics (1994). **Associations & Accomplishments:** Tallahassee Woman's Club; Tallahassee 25. **Education:** Valdosta State University, B.B.A. (1986). **Personal Information:** Married to Bobby in 1987. Two children: Peyton and Grant. Ms. Latmore enjoys snow skiing and rollerblading.

9200 Justice, Public Order, and Safety

9211 Courts
9221 Police protection
9222 Legal counsel and prosecution
9223 Correctional institutions
9224 Fire protection
9229 Public order and safety, nec

Dawn L. Diestelkamp

Information Systems Manager
Superior Court of California, County of Fresno
1255 Fulton Mall
Fresno, CA 93775
(559) 488-2598
ddiestelkamp@fresno.ca.gov

9211

Business Information: Serving as Information Systems Manager for the Superior Court of California of the County of Fresno, Ms. Diestelkamp manages all daily operations of the technology department. She detemines the strategic direction and business contributions of the information systems functions. Supervising a staff of six employees, Ms. Diestelkamp fulfills the responsibility of a project manager for large case management. She is also accountable for planning meetings, overseeing billing reviews, and analyzing new systems and new technology. Highly regarded, she possesses an excellent understanding of technology and her role with the Court. Conducting research in her field, Ms. Kiestelkamp plans to stay with the Court and continue to teach the M.B.A. program at the local university. The Superior Court of California for the County of Fresno is a trial court. Dealing with both civil and criminal cases, the Court's primary main objective is to facilitate adherence to legal precedents and procedures and the determination of criminal and civil responsibilities as well as verdicts. The Court employing 460 people in the conduct of its day-to-day activities. **Career Highlights:** Information Systems Manager, Superior Court of California, County of Fresno (1991-Present); Valley Medical Center of Fresno: Systems and Procedures Analyst (1990-91), Clinical Laboratory Technologist (1977-89). **Associations & Accomplishments:** Fresno Womens Network: First Vice President/President (2001); Co-Chair, Training and Certificate Committee, California Court Clerks Association; National Association for Female Executives. **Education:** California State University at Fresno: M.B.A. (1995), Master's degree in Public Administration (1983), B.S. in Microbiology (1976). **Personal Information:** Ms. Diestelkamp enjoys women's athletics and reading.

William A. Gast

Computer Systems Manager
U.S. Bankruptcy Court
110 East Court Avenue, Suite 300
Des Moines, IA 50306
(515) 284-6234
Fax: (515) 284-6404
wag@iasb.uscourts.gov

9211

Business Information: Mr. Gast serves as Computer Systems Manager with the U.S. Bankruptcy Court located in Des Moines, Iowa. He is responsible for design and development of cutting edge software to maintain the efficiency and improve the overall performance of the Court's systems and data infrastructure. Concurrent to his role with the U.S. Bankruptcy Court, Mr. Gast is Owner of Gast Electric Service which he started in 1976. Responsible for the Court's operational architecture, he plans the installation of new data storage innovations and provides the necessary training to bring new systems on line without interruption of case services. Mr. Gast is an accomplished professional. His career highlights include development of a new operational software methodology that has been universally accepted by the Court system. In addition, he was hand-picked to travel to Romonia to design a network system specifically for their court system. Mr. Gast's strategic goal is to integrate his case management software into the World Wide Web. An agency of the federal government, the U.S. Bankruptcy Court was established in 1776. National in scale, the federal government currently operates a network of three Bankruptcy Courts located across the United States. In addition to its primary functions, the Courts manages and exchanges data between other Bankruptcy Courts. **Career Highlights:** Computer Systems Manager, U.S. Bankruptcy Court (Present); Owner, Gast Electric Service (1976-Present). **Associations & Accomplishments:** National Conference of Bankruptcy Clerks; Technical Advisory Group, Judicial Conference of the United States (1995-98); Technical Advisory Group, Judicial Conference of the 8th Circuit (1998-Present). **Education:** Buena Vista College, B.S. (1967). **Personal Information:** Married to Carolyn in 1967. Two children: Bob and Michelle. Mr. Gast enjoys building and piloting airplanes and golf.

Robert R. Hayhurst

Information Security Specialist
United States Department of Justice
3625 FCI Road
Marianna, FL 32446
(850) 526-6376
Fax: (850) 482-6837
compspec@technologist.com

9211

Business Information: Functioning in the role of Information Security Specialist with United States Department of Justice, Mr. Hayhurst administers and oversees all security aspects of network and operating systems infrastructures. He maintains networks and acts as the service manager for 400 computers, 270 of which are part of the Department's intricate network system. A 28 year law enforcement professional, Mr. Hayhurst keeps up with applicable laws and ensures compliance with software copyrights. Looking to the next millennium, Mr. Hayhurst's goals include attaining the position of Information Technology Manager and eventually retiring and transitionging to the consulting field. Remaining on the cutting edge by attending classes and surfing the Internet, his success is attributed to his easy comprehensiion of technology. United States Department of Justice engages in law enforcement. Established in 1935, the Department is involved corrrectional facilities' operation and has made strong efforts to rehabilitate criminals. Through the use of educational, social, and psychological programs, many hardened criminals have undergone a metamorphisis. The efforts of 350 employees have helped facilitate these transformations. **Career Highlights:** United States Department of Justice: Information Security Specialist (1995-Present), Computer Service Manager (1991), Legal Technician (1988-91). **Associations & Accomplishments:** Faternal Order of Police. National Law Enforcement State President for West Virginia. **Personal Information:** Married to Deborah Sue in 1979. Two children: John Keith and Victoria Lee. Mr. Hayhurst enjoys photography.

Steven R. Lauer

Software Specialist
Maricopa County Superior Courts
201 West Jefferson Street
Phoenix, AZ 85003
(602) 390-2286
slauer@cosc.maricopa.gov

9211

Business Information: Serving as a Software Specialist for Maricopa County Superior Courts, Mr. Lauer is responsible for the design and development of software applications for the Superior Courts' computer systems. Providing excellent technical and software support, he maintains the functionality of the information systems infrastructure, troubleshooting and offering problematic solutions concerning the 700 user database. His focus is maintaining the integrity, reliability, and security of the Courts' database management functions. Implementing new technologies, he strives to develop a more efficient and cost worthy software product. Continuing his career with Maricopa County Superior Courts, Mr. Lauer remains committed to the furthering advancement in computer technologies. His success reflect his ability to think outside the box, aggressively take on challenges, and deliver results on behalf of the Courts. Maricopa County Superior Courts is a governmental agency engaged in providing protection under the law for those individuals residing within the juisdiction of the Maricopa County in Phoenix, Arizona. **Career Highlights:** Maricopa County Superior Courts: Software Specialist (1998-Present), Supervisor (1995-98), Data Entry (1991-95). **Education:** Arizona State University, B.A. (1992).

Katherine Wieland

Regional Computer Specialist
US Trustee
P.O. Box 1064
Wichita, KS 67201
(316) 269-6213
wielandk@aol.com

9211

Business Information: Serving as Regional Computer Specialist, Ms. Wieland fulfills a variety of tasks within the corporate structure of the US Trustee. Overseeing the technical operations of separate agencies within three states, she handles technical evaluations of operating systems. After conducting research, Ms. Wieland implements applicable software and hardware to ensure each agency is running with optimal efficiency. Demonstrating extensive knowledge in her field, she directs troubleshooting, maintenance, and upgrades for all systems. Crediting her success to good mentors and role models, she continually updates her education through courses and trade journals. Ms. Wieland aspires to a position that will give her increased responsibilities within a large corporation in the private sector. The US Trustee is a division of the Department of Justice. A federal agency, the Department administers bankruptcy claims on a governmental level. With over 1,100 employees, the Department has maintained efficient operations since establishing in 1979. **Career Highlights:** Regional Computer Specialist, US Trustee (Present). **Associations & Accomplishments:** Association of Information Technology Professionals. **Education:** Friends University, B.S. in Computer Information Systems (1994); Kearney State College, B.A. in Education; Microsoft Certified Systems Engineer (1999).

Robert W. Erdely

Trooper
Pennsylvania State Police
4221 Route 286 Highway West
Indiana, PA 15701
(724) 357-2000
Fax: (724) 357-2001
rerdely@psp.state.pa.us

9221

Business Information: As a Trooper for the Pennsylvania State Police, Mr. Erdely has a unique job description. He searches for and investigates cases of Internet fraud. Through his diligent work, he finds fraudulent companies, then seizes computer harddrives for use as evidence in court cases. He is one of three police officers in the state who perform this valuable service and attributes his success to his belief in God, and his experience and discipline gained while serving in the United States Air Force. In the future, Mr. Erdely plans to continue in his present position thereby guaranteeing safety for all citizens, and eventually move up the hierarchy. The Pennsylvania State Police is dedicated to protecting the citizens of Pennsylvania. Because of the Department's determined efforts, crime is steadily declining throughout the state, thus ensuring safety and prosperity for all. Established in 1905, the Department supplies patrols for highway safety and investigates crime on a statewide level. Presently, the Department employs a staff of more than 4,000 professionals. **Career Highlights:** Pennsylvania State Police: Trooper (1998-00), Trooper Vice (1994-98), Trooper Patrol (1991-94). **Associations & Accomplishments:** International Association of Computer Investigative Specialists. **Education:** FBI Academy, Basic Unix; IACIS, Forensics Computer. **Personal Information:** Married to Lynda in 1999. Three children: Shane, Brandon, and Hannah.

Gary Edward Glick

Computer Systems Administrator
Riley County Police Department
610 Colorado
Manhattan, KS 66502
(785) 537-2112
Fax: (785) 537-4930
glick@pd.co.riley.ks.us

9221

Business Information: Proficient in systems administration, Mr. Glick serves as the Computer Systems Administrator for the Riley County Police Department. He assumes the responsibility for administrating and controlling the Department's LAN and WAN networks in a 24 hour/7 day a week environment. Additionally, he coordinates projects, plans software and network application upgrades, and performs network security. Before joining Riley County Police Department, he served as Imaging System Administrator for Shawnee County, Kansas. His background history also includes stints as Programmer with SystemWorks and Computer Specialist at Nelson's Electronics. In his present role, Mr. Glick is also responsible for writing grants for the Department and coordinated all Y2K compliance issues. Consistently achieving quality performance in his field, he continues to grow professionally through the fulfillment of his responsibilities and involvement in the advancement of operations. Mr. Glick's success reflects his ability to think out-of-the-box and aggressively take on new challenges. The Riley County Police Department was established in 1974 to protect residents' lives and property, preserve the peace, and prevent crime. The Department is dedicated to serving the county's residents and utilizes various methods of law enforcement to accomplish its edicts. Approximately 170 administrative, law enforcement officers, and support personnel are employed. **Career Highlights:** Computer Systems Administrator, Riley County Police Department (1998-Present); Imaging System Administrator, Shawnee County, KS (1996-98); Programmer, SystemWorks (1994-96); Computer Specialist, Nelson's Electronics (1992-96). **Education:** Washburn University, B.S. (1992). **Personal Information:** Mr. Glick enjoys camping and golf.

Michael P. Jacobs

Systems Administrator
City of Asbury Park Police
One Municipal Plaza
Asbury Park, NJ 07712
(732) 502-5784
Fax: (732) 774-8352
mpjacobs@monmouth.com

9221

Business Information: Serving as Systems Administrator of City of Asbury Park's Police Department, Mr. Jacobs has served with the City since 1984. In this capacity, he exercises oversight and control of all management aspects of day-to-day system operations. Accumulating extensive experience, he manages the Police's Data Processing Department in addition to coordinating the purchase, installation, and maintenance of all computer hardware. Combining management skills and technical expertise, Mr. Jacobs coaches and guides his staff in storing, indexing, filing, and retrieving crime related data. Additionally, he is responsible for three UNIX and NT servers as well as providing technical support for 85 users. Directing and participating the analysis, modification, configuration, support, and tracking of operating systems, databases, utilities, software, and hardware also falls within the scope of Mr. Jacobs' functions. His career highlights include convincing the Department to move into the Information Technology Age, and earning MCPS certification. Additionally, he has added mobile computing to the Agency, allowing individuals the ability to gather state and local information directly from a laptop computer. Within the year, they will also show the creation of the agencies Web page. Obtaining more Microsoft certifications and implementing new technologies serves as his long-term goals. City of Asbury Park's Police Department is responsible for enforcing city, state, and federal statutes, laws, and regulations designed to protect life and property. Also, the Police Department spends time patrolling designated areas to preserve the peace and to prevent crimes; resolve problems within the community; and enforce laws governing motor vehicle operations. **Career Highlights:** Systems Administrator, City of Asbury Park Police (1984-Present); Director of Loss Prevention, Hahnes Department Store (1979-84). **Associations & Accomplishments:** Microsoft Certified Product Specialist; Life Member, Republican National Committee; Sterling Registry Who's Who Executive Edition. **Education:** Brookdale College (1985). **Personal Information:** Married to Cynthia in 1986. Mr. Jacobs enjoys collecting stamps and coins.

L. J. Johnson, Jr.

Supervisory Special Agent
South Carolina Law Enforcement Division
4400 Broad River Road
Columbia, SC 29210
(803) 896-7031
Fax: (803) 896-7192
cjohnson@mak.sled.state.sc.us

9221

Business Information: Serving as Supervisory Special Agent for South Carolina Law Enforcement Division, Lt. Johnson fulfills a number of law enforcement duties on behalf of the state of South Carolina. Possessing an excellent understanding of technology, he is responsible for investigating a wide range of computer, telecommunications, and high technology crimes. Working closely with seven special agents, Lt. Johnson provides the technical training required and guides his team in employing special techniques in solving crimes in the technology realm. With more than 13 years of hands on law enforcement experience and technical expertise, Lt. Johnson utilizes his skills to devise strategic plans to remain on top of emerging technology and develop his unit. "Develop patience! You will always be behind technology. Be flexible. You have to be able to change with the industry. You must have a desire to be challenged," is cited as Lt. Johnson's advice to others following the same career path. A government agency, the South Carolina Law Enforcement Division provides law enforcement. Under the direction of more than 600 officers, the Division is responsible for the investigation of crimes, forensic laboratory management, and strategic tactic planning. Established in 1947, the Division is located in Columbia, South Carolina. **Career Highlights:** South Carolina Law Enforcement Division: Supervisory Special Agent (1997-Present), Special Agent (1992-97), Assistant Chief (1987-92). **Associations & Accomplishments:** South Carolina Law Enforcement Officers Association; International Association of Chiefs of Police; National Tactical Officers Association; National Association of Technical Investigators. **Personal Information:** Married to Laura Whelchel in 1999. Lt. Johnson enjoys running, golf and reading.

Michael B. Stoopman

Branch Manager, ISB
Queensland Police
100 Roma Street
Brisbane, Queensland, Australia 4001
+61 733643900
Fax: +61 733643858
stoopman.mike@mailbox.police.old.gov.au

9221

Business Information: Beginning his career nine years ago with Queensland Police, Mr. Stoopman has received recognition for his diligence and skills through several promotions to Branch Manager, ISB. Utilizing his education and years of hands on experience, he manages a branch of information technicians who support information technology used by police. His responsibilities include maintaining computers, file servers, and all related infrastructure and software. Overseeing the daily network systems, Mr. Stoopman also coordinates repair services, purchasing of equipment, Web development, and information technology strategies. Proud of the fact that he was the first information technology professional to receive the National Achievement Award from the Australian Post, Mr. Stoopman attributes his success a supportive family and a strong desire to excel. Queensland Police is the law enforcement and public safety agency for Queensland, Australia. The Department's mission is to preserve and protect life, property, peace and order, and maintain a quality of life by oriented policing. The Department employs a staff of 10,000 highly qualified officers and administration workers to carry out daily operations. **Career Highlights:** Queensland Police: Branch Manager, ISB (1998-Present), Manager of Technical Information (1997-98), Manager of Communications and Network Service (1991-96); Facilities Manager, Australia Post (1987-91). **Associations & Accomplishments:** Australia Postel Institution; Built Enviroment Engineering and Surveying Alumni; Royal Queensland Yacht. **Education:** Queensland University of Technology, B.S. in Electrial Engineering (1979). **Personal Information:** Married to Bernadine M. in 1983. Mr. Stoopman enjoys sailing, travel and wood working.

Michael Sean Tuomey

Senior Administrator
Chicago Police Department
1830 West Monterey Avenue
Chicago, IL 60643
(312) 747-4881
Fax: (312) 747-6455
stuomey@aol.com

9221

Business Information: Mr. Toumey is a Senior Administrator for the Chicago Police Department. He is the Chief of Staff for a precinct commander and is in charge of 12 internal personnel and has staff authority over more than 350 officers. He provides back up support for all employees and is responsible for the organization and completion of all administrative duties. Paperwork is a large part of the police officer's day, and Mr. Tuomey and his staff are responsible for maintaining searchable and undertstandable files and records on each case worked on in the office. Prior to his service as a Senior Administrator, Mr. Toumey served in the United States Army. Today, he is also a Major in the Army Reserves and has recieved his qualifications in Combat Arms and Combat Service Support. In this context, he commands a transportation battalion with more than 600 personnel in five states. Having recently returned from service in Bosnia, Mr. Toumey has been selected for the rank of Lieutenant Colonel. The Chicago Police Department provides law enforcement for the residents of Chicago, Illinios. Established in 1843, the Department hosts over 18,000 personnel dedicated to assisting and benefitting the citizens they serve. The Department is involved in community activities and charity events throughout the city. The officers in the Department are also involved in the nationwide drug and alcohol abuse awareness program. **Career Highlights:** Senior Administrator, Chicago Police Department (1994-Present); United States Army Officer, United States Army (1982-94). **Associations & Accomplishments:** American Association of Public Administrators; Reserve Officers' Association. **Education:** Illinois Institute of Technology, M.P.A. (1998); The Citadel, B.Sc. in Business Administration (1982).

Jerry Vickers

Technical Specialist
Manchester Police Department
200 West Fort Street
Manchester, TN 37355-1521
(931) 728-2099
Fax: (931) 723-1591
jerryv@edge.net

9221

Business Information: Faithfully serving with the Manchester Police Department for over 25 years, Mr. Vickers fulfills the accountability of Technical Specialist. Performing many computer duties, he is responsible for providing all technical support. Accordingly, Mr. Vickers has designed and developed a LAN/WAN networking system. Further, he is responsible for purchasing new technology and administering, installing, and maintaining the networking infrastructure to ensure its functionality and fully operational status. Looking forward to the new millennium, Mr. Vickers wishes to become a networking installer for a software company. He attrubutes his success to the creation and maintenance of goals, as well as his ability to deliver results and aggressively take on challenges and new responsibilities. Manchester is located in the middle Northeastern portion of Tennessee. The Manchester Police Department, with 30 employees, serves as protectors of life and property for over 7,000 people. The Department ensures the enforcement of statutes, laws, and regulations set by state and federal governments. **Career Highlights:** Technical Specialist, Manchester Police Department (1989-Present); Criminal Investigator, Coffee County Sheriff's Department (1983-89); Investigator, Tullahoma Police Department (1975-83). **Education:** State University of New York, B.S. (1994); Microsoft Certified Systems Engineer (In Progress).

Serge Al Pavlovsky

Information Technology Unit Manager
Office Of The Corporation Counsel
441 Fourth Street NW, Suite 1060-North
Washington, DC 20001
(202) 724-4082

9222

Business Information: A prominent and respected professional, Mr. Pavlovsky serves as Information Technology Unit Manager for the Office Of The Corporation Counsel. He presides over the Information Technology Department and oversees the administration for 600 workstations within the local area network. In addition, Mr. Pavlovsky is in charge of the connection exchange for the wide area network connecting the Counsel to other government agencies within the District of Columbia. Before joining Office Of The Corporation Counsel, Mr. Pavlovsky served as Senior Network Engineer and Team Chief for Artel, Inc. His extensive background history also includes stints as Senior Network Engineer with Xenia, Inc. and Owner and President of Globus Company. An expert, he continues to grow professionally through the fulfillment of his responsibilities and his involvement in the advancement of operations. His success reflects his ability to think outside the box and aggressively take on new challenges. The Office of The Corporation Counsel is the organization within the government of the District of Columbia which serves as the legal counsel on behalf of the federal government in all legal matters. Founded in 1971, the Counsel employs the dedicated services of 600 administrative, legal, and support personnel in the District of Columbia. **Career Highlights:** Information Technology Unit Manager, Office of The Corporation Counsel (1998-Present); Senior Network Engineer/Team Chief, Artel, Inc. (1997-98); Senior Network Engineer, Xenia, Inc. (1994-97); Owner/President, Globus Company (1989-94). **Education:** M.S. in Business Management (1983); M.S. in Computer Science (1976).

Brian A. Bailey

Management Information Systems Manager
Rappahannock Regional Jail
P.O. Box 8390
Fredericksburg, VA 22404
(540) 371-3838
Fax: (540) 371-6184

9223

Business Information: As Management Information Systems Manager of Rappahannock Regional Jail, Mr. Bailey presides over a wide range of responsibilities. He administers the Facility's network, performs computer repair, authorizes purchasing, trains new users, and oversees telecommunications. When Mr. Bailey became Management Information Systems Manager in 1996, the Facility only had five computers. Mr. Bailey helped design and implement the current WAN system used by the four counties, enabling them to share vital information. Thanks to him, the counties now are linked to Virginia's criminal information network and can access data across the United States. Each county can obtain any information used for identification purposes offered through the Sheriff's Department and mobile units within five minutes. Mr. Bailey has recently begun implementing video imaging and is looking forward to becoming a part of a regional to national criminal network, linking all law enforcements agencies to one WAN system. Built in 1940, Rappahannock Regional Jail houses inmates for four counties in the area surrounding Fredericksburg. The Facility employs a workforce of 150 administrative, guard, and support personnel to maintain the Facility and is supported by the counties served, receiving state funds to complement its income. Set to open in the year 2000, a new Facility is being constructed that will increase the Facility's housing capacity. **Career Highlights:** Management Information Systems Manager, Rappahannock Regional Jail (1995-Present); Computer Systems Analyst, Department of Defense (1983-95); Electronics Technician, United States Navy (1977-83). **Education:** American Institute, M.S. (1999); American Institute for Computer Sciences: M.S., B.S. **Personal Information:** Married to Pamela in 1998. Four children: Andrew, Bobby, Alison, and Charity.

Stephen P. Frazier

Manager of Technical Services
Oklahoma Department of Corrections
3400 North Martin Luther King Avenue
Oklahoma City, OK 73111
(405) 425-2549
Fax: (405) 425-2554
stevef@doc.state.ok.us

9223

Business Information: Functioning in the capacity of Manager of Technical Services of Oklahoma Department of Corrections, Mr. Frazier plans and oversees research and development, evaluation and test, and integration of new technology within the Department's infrastructure. As an expert VM and VSE systems programmer, he installs and maintains IBM operating systems and utility programs. In addition to supervising his staff of three employees, Mr. Frazier handles numerous resource planning functions such as personnel evaluations, determining future resource requirements, and overseeing time lines, schedules, and assignments. His success reflects his ability to build teams with synergy and technical strength and take on new challenges. Overseeing projects on a management level, as well as hands on implementation also fall within the realm of Mr. Fazier's responsibilities. His short term objectives include a smooth transition into the new millennium, continue deploying advanced technologies, and keep the Department on the cutting edge of technology. A state agency, Oklahoma Department of Corrections operates as a state government law enforcement system responsible for prisons, parole, tracking crime, and criminal records. Established in 1907, the Department is regional in scope and manned by more than 5,000 employees. **Career Highlights:** Manager of Technical Services, Oklahoma Department of Corrections (Present). **Associations & Accomplishments:** American Corrections Association; National Association of Systems Programmers; Lions Club; Boy Scouts. **Education:** University of Oklahoma (1975).

John D. Guy

Management Information Systems Field Service Manager
Tennessee Department of Correction
Route 1 Box 660
Tiptonville, TN 38079
(615) 350-3326
Fax: (901) 253-0136
jguy@mail.state.tn.us

9223

Business Information: Mr. Guy functions in the capacity of Management Information System Field Service Manager for the Tennessee Department of Correction. Responsible for 18 networks across the state, he determines the overall strategic direction and contribution of the information systems function. An eight year professional, Mr. Guy has served with Tennessee Department of Corrections in a variety of role since joining the Department as Information Systems Support Specialist 2 in 1991. In addition to supervising and mentoring his staff of 16 personnel, he is engaged in traveling throughout the state to install Novell networks between 19 Department facilities. Working within the networking system, Mr. Guy facilitates the communication needs of the Department through his services. Looking toward the next millennium, he plans to eventually attain the position of Director or Assistant Director within the Department. Tennessee Department of Correction is a state government agency designed to rehabilitate criminals from the state while also punishing them for the crimes they were a part of. The Department has 19 facilities across the state which, together, house 17,000 inmates. A team of 5,000 employees are working to ensure the safety of inmates and protection of the communities they reside in. **Career Highlights:** Tennessee Department of Correction: Management Information System Field Service Manager (1998-Present), Information System Support Specialist 5 (1996-98), Information System Support Specialist 2 (1991-96). **Education:** University of Tennessee at Martin (1992). **Personal Information:** Married to Cathi in 1990. Three children: Jacob, John, and Sarah. Mr. Guy enjoys fishing.

William W. Minion

Computer Services Manager
Federal Bureau of Prisons
501 Capital Circle NE
Tallahassee, FL 32304-9225
(850) 878-2173
Fax: (850) 671-6119

9223

Business Information: Mr. Minion has served with the Federal Bureau of Prisons in various positions since 1979. At the present time, he fulfills the responsibilities of Computer Services Manager. Presiding over the local area network administration for 300 users, he devotes considerable attention to computer security to prevent unauthorized access in any form. He performs detailed system training for new users and oversees the hardware maintenance as well as the software upgrades and the implementation of new system applications. Mr. Minion was personally responsible for creating and implementing the LAN currently used by the administration. Crediting his work ethics as the reason for his success, he stays up-to-date through the Internet, technical books, and self training. He has enjoyed substantial success in the information technology field, but is now considering a move into law enforcement. Many of his subordinates have been trained and promoted to IS Managers, and some have gone into private computer consulting from the exposure and experience gained from Mr. Minion. The Federal Bureau of Prisons is the federal government's system of correctional institutions. First established in 1930, there is a federal prison for each region of the United States. Over 31,000 administrative, correctional, and support personnel are employed in the nation's prison system network. The Federal Prison located in Tallahassee, Florida houses approximately 900 inmates. **Career Highlights:** Federal Bureau of Prisons: Computer Services Manager (1990-Present), Computer Analyst (1983-90), Computer Programmer (1979-83). **Associations & Accomplishments:** Tau Kappa Delta Fraternity; Boy Scouts. **Education:** Cleary College, B.B.A. (1971). **Personal Information:** Married to Marsha K. in 1970. Two children: Michael George, an Independent Distributor for Starlight International, and Lindsey Elaine. Mr. Minion enjoys golf, swimming, boating, snow skiing and remodeling houses.

Carlina Duggan

Systems Administrator
Lake Dillon Fire Protection District
P.O. Box 4428
Dillon, CO 80435-4428
(970) 262-1337
Fax: (970) 262-6434
carlina@bewellnet.com

9224

Business Information: Providing her skilled services as Systems Administrator to the Lake Dillon Fire Protection District, Ms. Duggan is responsible for the development of the wide area network that is currently used to service volunteers and personnel. Prior to serving the Lake Dillon Fire Protection District, she served as Administrative Assistant at Frisco Fire District/Lake Dillon Fire Authority and as Public Finance Associate with George K. Brown & Company in Denver, Colorado. In her present role, she continues any engineering work needed on the wide area network, programs the District's databases, performs routine maintenance for the network and databases, and provides all PC technician services. Providing office systems support and training, Ms. Duggan serves as the help desk for end users. She also produces all graphic design/desktop publishing work for the District. Complementing her duties at the Department, she owns and operates three thriving "home-run" businesses with her husband. These businesses are American Fire Stop Shop, Lifespace, Inc., and CJ's Desktop Designs. Ms. Duggan enjoys her work and plans to remain in the information technology field. Lake Dillon Fire Protection District provides fire and rescue services serving four different towns with three main stations. Additionally, the District provides fire and rescue services in mutual aid agreements with other fire districts in the county, responding 20 miles north, 10 miles south, and 10 miles each to the east and west of the main station in Silverthorne. Eighteen full-time employees and more than 70 volunteers work for the District to provide these services. **Career Highlights:** Systems Administrator, Lake Dillon Fire Protection District (1995-Present); Administrative Assistant, Frisco Fire District/Lake Dillon Fire Authority (1992-95); Public Finance Associate, George K. Baum & Company (1990-92). **Associations & Accomplishments:** President (1991), Women's Securities Association of Denver; Planning & Zoning Commissioner (1995-97), Town of Dillon. **Personal Information:** Married to Gip in 1992. Two children: Catherine Lockwood and James Lockwood.

Mark A. Whitt

Information Systems Administrator
Houston Fire Department
1205 Dart Street
Houston, TX 77077
(713) 247-5053
Fax: (713) 247-5980

9224

Business Information: Serving as the Information Systems Administrator for the Houston Fire Department, Mr. Whitt orchestrates all technical operations. Included in his schedule are varied tasks that include budgeting, planning, and scheduling for the Department. Utilizing his technical abilities, Mr. Whitt evaluates the needs of the current systems and hardware, then develops and implements improvements. Recgonized for his superior results in challenging situations, he has been named project leader for four different programs: emergency, lifesaving, CAD dispatch locator, and pilot mobile data computing. Attributing his success to his persistent dedication, Mr. Whitt currently is planning to shift his career focus back into the research area of technology. The fourth largest fire department in the United States is the Houston Fire Department, located in the southeastern section of Texas. Serving 660 square miles of the metropolitan area, the Department strives to provide efficient service under incredible time constraints. **Career Highlights:** Information Systems Administrator, Houston Fire Department (Present); Systems Engineer, BSM (1992); Engineer, Procter & Gamble (1985); Engineer, Rockwell International CCSD (1983). **Associations & Accomplishments:** National Society of Black Engineers; Institute of Electronics and Electrical Engineers; Eagle Scout, Boy Scouts of America; Most Worshipful Prince Hall Grand Lodge of Texas and Jurisdiction; F.A.M. **Education:** Texas State University, M.B.A. (In Progress); University of Houston, B.S. (1987). **Personal Information:** Married to Carla in 1993. One child: Marcus. Mr. Whitt enjoys camping, fishing and golf.

Shelby Ross Fox

Computer Specialist
FEMA
2432-211 Berryville Pike
Winchester, VA 22603
(540) 542-2630
Fax: (540) 542-2489
shelby.fox@fema.gov

9229

Business Information: Dedicated to the success of FEMA or Federal Emergency Management Agency, Mrs. Fox is a Computer Specialist who fulfills the responsibility of team leader of a service desk consisting of six people. Employed with the Agency since 1984, she works within the Information Technology Services Directorate Operations Division of the Agency. A property officer, Mrs. Fox presides over a large equipment account and troubleshoots equipment malfunctions as well as assists employees who use the equipment. She also supervises all service desk employees and is a certified Help Desk Manager, maintains an equipment database and personnel records of the branch, and attends department meetings. Mrs. Fox would like to move back to her home state of North Carolina and still work for the government. FEMA was establised in 1979. A part of the United States government, the Agency offers assistance to counties, states, and their islands in the event of a disaster, such as hurricanes, earthquakes, flooding, tornadoes, and human made disasters. FEMA operates many temporary disaster field offices throughout the United States that houses employees ready to assist as well as a variety of equipment to aid in the recovery process. Local operations in Bluemont, Virginia employ a workstaff of hundreds to respond to individual disasters when needed and serves as one of the centers for disaster victims aid. They serve as a liaison between local, state, and the federal governments. **Career Highlights:** FEMA: Computer Specialist (1997-Present), Telecommunications Technician (1984-96); Secretary, U.S. Department of Commerce (1978-84); Internal Revenue (1976-78); United States Air Force (1974-76). **Education:** Lord Fairfax College, Network Engineer Certificate (1998); Asheboro Commercial College, Diploma (1973). **Personal Information:** Married to Thomas in 1987. Mrs. Fox enjoys decorating and antiques. Mrs. Fox has four children and eight grandchildren.

Malcolm M. Pullen

Information Systems Manager
BOEC/City of Portland
9911 SE Bush Street
Portland, OR 97266
(503) 823-4670
Fax: (503) 823-4630
malcolm@ci.portland.or.us

9229

Business Information: As Information Systems Manager of BOEC or Bureau Of Emergency Communications for the City of Portland, Mr. Pullen oversees all day-to-day computer operations. He is accountable for the maintenance of the systems infrastructure as well as updating with ever changing technology. He must have the ability and knowledge to locate new systems that are cost effective, easily integrated, and have the potential for long term use before becoming obsolete. Mr. Pullen's latest project is the implementation and integration of a digital voice recording device. In addition to supervising his staff of 12 employees, he handles numerous resource planning functions, to include coordinating resources and schedules, overseeing time lines and schedules, and evaluating personnel. As an experienced, 22 year professional, his goal is to develop a staff qualified to operate a system based on the latest technology. His success reflects his ability to build teams with synergy and technical strength and take on new challenges. Mr. Pullen also plans to become a part-time consultant after his retirement. BOEC is the office fielding 911 emergency calls for the city of Portland, Oregon. All calls received by the Office are time critical and rely on the presence of efficient computer operations. A staff of 155 personnel utilizes BOEC's systems on a daily basis to insure the safety of the citizens of the city. Presently, the Bureau operates on a budget of over $12 million annually. **Career Highlights:** BOEC/City of Portland: Information Systems Manager (1995-Present), Information Systems Supervisor (1989-95), Management Information Systems Analyst (1983-89), Public Safety Analyst (1977-83). **Education:** Portland State University, B.A. in Mathematics (1977). **Personal Information:** Four children: Johnchai, Tyree, Leif, and Destini. Mr. Pullen enjoys Qi Gong.

9300 Finance, Taxation, and Monetary Policy

9311 Finance, taxation and monetary policy

Omogbemiboluwa I. Acholonu

Computer Specialist
Internal Revenue Service, Financial and Administrative Systems
11330 Booth Bay Way
Bowie, MD 20720-3429
(202) 283-5023
Fax: (202) 283-3429
gbacholonu@yahoo.com

9311

Business Information: A successful professional, with extensive academic and occupational experience in the technology field, Mrs. Acholonu serves as a Computer Specialist for the Internal Revenue Service's Financial and Administrative Systems division. Throughout daily activities, she is responsible for a host of duties, such as programming, performing software engineering, project development, and database configuration management. Mrs. Acholonu is highly regarded and possesses an excellent understanding of her field. Capitalizing on nine years of information technology experience, Mrs. Acholonu is currently devising plans for taking advantage of all opportunities afforded by the Internal Revenue Service. Attributing her success to God and strong family support system, she aspires to become branch chief and eventually start up her own business. The Internal Revenue Service, Financial and Administrative Systems is an agency of the U.S. government. The Agency provides taxpayers' services by applying tax laws and responsibilities to all, equally and fairly. Developed in the early 1900s, the Financial and Administrative Systems division is responsible for personnel systems and the maintenance of personnel information within internal systems. **Career Highlights:** Computer Specialist, Internal Revenue Service, Financial and Administrative Systems (1999-Present); Computer Specialist, Internal Revenue Service, Electronic Graphics and Archives Systems (1991-99). **Associations & Accomplishments:** Association for the Improvement of Minorities; Deacon for Young Adults II, Clifton Park Baptist Church. **Education:** Bowie State University, M.S. (1999); University of Maryland, B.Sc. in Computer Science. **Personal Information:** Married to Anderson in 1992. One child: Uzoamaka. Mrs. Acholonu enjoys reading mystery novels and playing the piano.

Janie Benfield

Appraiser/Programmer Analyst
San Juan County Assessor
100 South Oliver Drive, Suite 400
Aztec, NM 87410-2435
(505) 334-4223
Fax: (505) 334-1669
jbenfield@co.san-juan.nm.us

9311

Business Information: Ms. Benfield serves in the dual role of Appraiser and Programmer Analyst for San Juan County Assessor. Aside from her responsibilities as a property appraiser, she is also responsible for the network system of the Agency. Supervising 35 workstations, Ms. Benfield installs and undates hardware and software within the system and is involved in the maintenance of each station. She also advises on purchasing, programming, and user education for the information technology department. Looking to the next millennium, Ms. Benfield hopes to implement a cutting edge relational database for the Agency. She attributes her success to being open-minded and flexible. San Juan County Assessor is a property tax service that conducts tax assessments for the county. The Agency determines the property values for use in processing property taxes on mobile homes, personal property, and real property, such as homes, businesses, farms, and churches. The Agency strives to ensure the equitable evaluation of a property using state regulations and the industry standards. **Career Highlights:** San Juan County Assessor: Appraiser/Programmer Analyst (1993-Present), CAMA Appraiser (1991-93), Appraisal Clerk (1985-91). **Associations & Accomplishments:** Secretary/Treasurer, GIS/Rural Addressing Affiliate of New Mexico Association of Counties; Piano/Organ, Aztec Presbyterian Church Accompanist. **Education:** San Juan College; I.A.A.O., New Mexico Certified Appraiser; Long Ridge Writers Group; USDA Graduate School. **Personal Information:** Married to Keith in 1969. Three children: Russell, David, and Brian. Ms. Benfield enjoys sewing, crochet, knitting and house plants.

Martin O. Bridges, Sr.

Senior Computer Systems Analyst
Internal Revenue Service
P.O. Box 24551
Kansas City, MO 64131
(816) 926-1651
Fax: (816) 823-1948
marty.o.bridges@irs.gov

9311

Business Information: Demonstrating expertise in the information technology field, Mr. Bridges currently serves as Senior Computer Systems Analyst for the Internal Revenue Service. Working closely with management and systems users, he is responsible for operations performance evaluations, Web site design and programming, and applications designing. In addition, Mr. Bridges acts as a consultant to the branch chief and conducts on-the-job training for new systems analysts. Beginning his association with the Agency in 1971 as a Computer Operator, Mr. Bridges has worked diligently to develop his skills to acquire expertise in his field. Proud of his many accomplishments, he is credited with the design of an AI Expert System for workload setup, scheduling, and balancing, which is still used by the Agency. He designed and developed the first Web-based application in IRS to integrate a Web browser and an Oracle database. Mr. Bridges attributes his success to having a strong base of logic. His future plans are to achieve his Novell and Windows 2000 certifications, and to start up his own computer consulting firm. The Internal Revenue Service is an agency of the U.S. Department of Treasury that collects income taxes. The Agency enforces tax laws, offers advice to taxpayers, and collects estate, excise, gift, and other taxes. Established in 1913, the Internal Revenue Service is headquartered in Washington, D.C. and employs the expertise of 86,000 individuals in collections, processing, data entry, and administration. **Career Highlights:** Internal Revenue Service: Senior Computer Systems Analyst (1998-Present), Senior Knowledge Systems Analyst (1990-98), Computer Performance Analyst (1985-90), Computer Systems Analyst (1979-85), Computer Programmer (1971-79), Computer Operator (1971-77). **Associations & Accomplishments:** Our Lady of the Presentation Catholic Church. **Education:** University of Missouri at Rolla. **Personal Information:** Married to Vicki in 1985. Four children: Dana Marie Colville, Angela Lynn Pope, Martin Jr., and Kathy Jo Barnett. Mr. Bridges enjoys Web design.

Kenneth L. Green Jr.

Systems Administrator
United States Department of Treasury
15th & Pennsylvania Avenue NW
Washington, DC 20220
(202) 622-1812
Fax: (202) 622-1822
kennethgreen@erols.com

9311

Business Information: Mr. Green serves in the role of Systems Adminstrator for the United States Department of Treasury responsible for maintaining the functionality and operational status of the information systems infrastructure in the Office of the Fiscal Assistant Secretary. A savvy, 23-year professional, Mr. Green works in the Office of Cash and Debt Management, where he is involved with budget and government finances. Employed with the Government since 1977, he attends FRB conferences and makes financial decisions concerning a $5 billion account. Mr. Green also tracks the progress of Treasury Tax and Loan (TT&L) within the United States. His highlight includes ensuring OFAS's Y2K readiness in 1998. Mr. Green believes that fate brought him to his job. The United States Department of Treasury is a division of the executive branch of the government. This Department provides a variety of quality service to residents of the United States which includes collecting federal taxes, presiding over customs, holding all payments received to the government, as well as paying all government expenses. Headquartered in Washington, D.C., the Department was establised in 1789 and employs 5,000 workers. **Career Highlights:** Systems Administrator, United States Department of Treasury (1991-Present); Manager of Banking Systems, Financial Management Services (1982-91); Manager of Equipment Maintenance Depots, United States Army Medical Material Agency (1979-82). **Associations & Accomplishments:** Lions Club International; American Legion; A.I.I.M. **Education:** Hood College, B.A. in Management (1981). **Personal Information:** Married to Magaly in 1974. Three children: James-Michael, Jon-Paul, and Kenneth III. Mr. Green enjoys golf and coaching youth sports.

Jason F. Haught

Computer Security Analyst
United States Treasury, Bureau of Public Debt
P.O. Box 1328
Parkersburg, WV 26106-1328
(304) 480-7498
jhaught@bpd.treas.gove

9311

Business Information: Mr. Haught functions in the capacity of Computer Security Analyst for the United States Treasury, Bureau of Public Debt. He maintains and monitors incident response capability, reviews security controls of applications, identifies potential risks, and trains end users on security and security responses. Focused on virus protection, he is involved in managing the anti-virus campaign within the several computer databases and repairing systems during a virus scare. In the future, Mr. Haught hopes to increase his involvement in computer security, particularly within the boundary between wide area and local area networks. His success reflects his ability to deliver results and aggressively take on new challenges. United States Treasury, Bureau of Public Debt is the financial accountant for the United States Government. The Agency is involved in publishing monthly financial summaries for the legislators and processing payments and claims throughout the year. Employing 1,800 personnel, the Agency has successfully monitored the financial activity of the government for several decades. **Career Highlights:** United States Treasury, Bureau of Public Debt: Computer Security Analyst (1998-Present), Computer Specialist (1997-98); Software Engineer, Science Application International Corporation (1994-97). **Associations & Accomplishments:** Association for Computing Machinery. **Education:** Marshall University, B.S. in Computer Science (1994). **Personal Information:** Mr. Haught enjoys boating, computer research and gaming.

Larry L. Hoffman

Computer Specialist
Federal Government
1704 Ramblewood Avenue
Columbus, OH 43235
(614) 692-9523

9311

Business Information: Mr. Hoffman has served in various positions with the Federal Government for the past 26 years. At the present time, he fulfills the responsibilities of Computer Specialist in the Defense Financial Accounting Systems Department. He maintains, updates, and installs new systems, hardware, and software for the accounting department. His job takes him to all of the states throughout the country. Interested in the technology field since childhood,

Mr. Hoffman stays on the cutting edge by attending classes, computer based training, and the exchange of information with colleagues. He is currently taking training on the client server networks that the Federal Government is planning to install. Mr. Hoffman will be deeply involved in its implementation. The United States Federal Government's Defense Financial Accounting Systems Department assumes responsibility for the accurate accounting of the government's budget for the nation's defense. Presently, the Financial Accounting Systems Department employs a staff of more than 55 people. **Career Highlights:** Computer Specialist, Federal Government (1974-Present). **Associations & Accomplishments:** Sierra Club, Environmental Organization; Space Studies Institute. **Education:** Institute of Computer Management, Associate's degree (1974). **Personal Information:** Married to Mary M. in 1992. Two children: Pamela Marie and Mary Beth. Mr. Hoffman enjoys golf, soccer and leisurely vacations.

Joan Serocki McGrory

Manager of Information Systems
Shelby County Trustee
P.O. Box 2751
Memphis, TN 38101
(901) 545-4826
Fax: (901) 545-4421
jmcgrory@memphisonline.com

9311

Business Information: Thoroughly educated in the field of information technology, Mrs. McGrory serves as the Manager of Information Systems for Shelby County Trustee. She assumes accountability for the entire spectrum of the Agency's data communication infrastructure from the individual workstations to the network server's operating environment. Purchasing software programs and applications as well as the necessary hardware equipment, she troubleshoots any problems that arise and ensures that the systems are operating at optimum levels. A team of four skilled professionals assist her in her duties. Continually striving for maximum effectiveness, Mrs. McGrory is currently pursuing her Ph.D. in Information Systems and attributes her professional success to her determination. A local governmental agency, Shelby County Trustee is responsible for the property tax collection of over 300,000 tax payers. The Agency operates with a yearly budget of over $500 million and also serves as the County's bank. Established in 1800, a staff of 100 personnel members work diligently to collect and distribute the County's tax dollars for the benefit of all. **Career Highlights:** Manager of Information Systems, Shelby County Trustee (1991-Present). **Education:** Nova Southeastern, Ph.D. in Information Systems (In Progress); Christian Brothers University: M.B.A .(1996), B.S. in Electrical Engineering (1988). **Personal Information:** Married to John in 1997. Mrs. McGrory enjoys water skiing.

Timothy N. Oakeley

Network Administrator
State of New Mexico Taxation and Revenue Department
1100 South St. Francis Drive
Santa Fe, NM 87505-4147
(505) 827-2309
Fax: (505) 827-0469
toakeley@state.nm.us

9311

Business Information: Mr. Oakeley has served with the State of New Mexico Taxation and Revenue Department in a variety of positions since 1995. At the present time, he fulfills the responsibilities of Network Administrator. His specific duties include overseeing facility maintenance and providing technical support solutions for over 1,000 users statewide. Mr. Oakeley is highly recognized for his ability to understand complex problems and is always alert to new opportunities, techniques, and approaches. Encouraging and facilitating optimum performance among the staff, he is an advocate for open communication, fostering a strong sense of teamwork and purpose among others in the office. Remaining with the Department, Mr. Oakeley is well on his way to becoming information systems manager, thereby achieving personal satisfaction and occupational success. The State of New Mexico Taxation and Revenue Department is a state government agency. With local operations in Santa Fe, New Mexico, the Department employs a small team of qualified personnel to serve the diverse needs of state residents. **Career Highlights:** State of New Mexico Taxation and Revenue Department: Network Administrator (1998-Present), Information Systems Analyst I (1995-98); Programmer, Los Alamos National Laboratory (1994-95). **Associations & Accomplishments:** Who's Who of High School. **Education:** Benedictine College, B.A. in Computer Science (1994); New Horizons Computer Learning Center, Microsoft Certified Systems Engineer (1999). **Personal Information:** Married to Louise M. in 2000. One child: Joshua R. Vigil. Mr. Oakeley enjoys hunting, fishing and biking.

James D. Strutton

Staff Information System Analyst
Department of Finance for State of California
915 L Street
Sacramento, CA 95814-3700
(916) 323-3104
jdstrutton@aol.com

9311

Business Information: As an Information Systems Analyst for Department of Finance for State of California, Mr. Strutton designs and implements information systems. Utilizing 35 years of extensive experience in the computer and information management field, he is responsible for systems analysis, determining current and projected requirements, developing new systems, and modifying existing systems. Mr. Strutton hopes to retire in six years and then teach at a local junior college. His career highlight is being part of a team that implemented the U.S. Army's worldwide payroll system and the development of the Statewide Waste Water Information System in California. Attributing his success to his supportive wife and his intelligence, Mr. Strutton's advice is, "Stay in school and get a good grounding in your chosen field." The Department of Finance for the State of California provides budgetary organization and monitoring for the State. Under the direction of the Governor, the Finance assembles the Governor's Budget and implements it based on legislation passed by the California Legislature. The Department also advises the Governor on revenues and expenditures. With a work force of approximately 350 individuals, the Department is dedicated to assuring that the taxpayer's money is spent fairly. **Career Highlights:** Staff Information Systems Analyst, Department of Finance for State of California (1986-Present); Associate Information Systems Analyst, State EDP Education Program (1978-84); Information Systems Analyst/Programmer, State of California (1970-77); Staff Sergeant, United States Army (1966-69). **Associations & Accomplishments:** MENSA; Data Management Association; Association for the Advancement of Human Computer Interaction; The Highlander Association; The World Futurist Society. **Education:** Sierra College in Rockland, California, Post Graduate Studies (In Progress); California State University of Sacramento, California, B.S. (1975); San Bernardino Valley College, A.A. (1970). **Personal Information:** Married to Charlotte E. in 1966. Mr. Strutton enjoys Internet surfing, computer programming, fuzzy logic and Chaos Theory, scuba diving, sheep farming and stock trading.

9400 Administration of Human Resources

9411 Admin. of educational programs
9431 Admin. of public health programs
9441 Admin. of social and manpower programs
9451 Administration of veterans' affairs

Darlene A. Andre

Elementary Technology Coordinator
Northbrook Community School District 28
1475 Maple Avenue
Northbrook, IL 60062
(847) 498-7950
Fax: (847) 498-7970

9411

Business Information: Displaying her skills in this specialized position, Mrs. Andre serves as the Elementary Technology Coordinator for the Northbrook Community School District 28. Her primary responsibility is to teach the staff and students how to use today's technology and its tools in an academic setting. She assumes responsibility for the local area network and the wide area network, performing routine maintenance, monitoring daily activity, and troubleshooting problems as needed. Acting as the software and hardware purchasing agent, three aides assist her in the completion of her responsibilities. Mrs. Andre cites her solid education and a strong belief in what she does as the secret to her success. She quotes Eleanor Roosevelt, "The future belongs to those who believe in the beauty of their dreams." The Northbrook Community School District 28 is a public school system providing quality educational opportunities for students in the local community of Northbrook, Illinois. More than 1,700 students in kindergarten through eighth grade attend the District's four schools. A staff of over 250 faculty, administrative, and support personnel are dedicated to providing the best education possible for the city's youth. **Career Highlights:** Elementary Technology Coordinator, Northbrook Community School District 28 (1993-Present); Training Director, Educational Resources (1992-93); Instructional Technologist, Lake Forest District 67 (1989-92). **Associations & Accomplishments:** International Society for Technology in Education; Illinois Computing Educators; Illinois Technology Leadership Academy; Technology and Learning Illinois Teacher of the Year (1995). **Education:** National-Louis University, M.Ed. (1991); University of Wisconsin at Whitewater, B.S. in Education (1982). **Personal Information:** Married to William in 1987. Two children: Nicolette and W. Alexander. Mrs. Andre enjoys coaching soccer, being a scout leader, cooking, bicycling and crafts.

David Thomas Ansley

Technology Specialist
Warren County Schools
107 Academy Street
Warrenton, GA 30828
(706) 465-3383
Fax: (706) 465-9141

9411

Business Information: Recruited to Warren County Schools in 1980 as a Teacher, Mr. Ansley currently serves as its Technology Specialist. He oversees the installation and maintenance of personal computers in the schools for the 80 teachers and 1,000 students as well as the administration of the local area network. Acting as a vendor liaison, he purchases software programs and hardware equipment. Mr. Ansley's primary responsibility is to train teachers how to incorporate technology into their normal curriculum. He also offers help desk support to the system's numerous users. Crediting his success to his stubbornness, he continues to grow professionally through the fulfillment of his responsibilities. Warren County Schools is a public school system located in the east central portion of Georgia. The County has two schools and offers quality educational opportunities to students in grades kindergarten through 12th grade. A staff of 104 administrative, faculty, and support personnel are dedicated to providing the very best education possible for its young students. **Career Highlights:** Warren County Schools: Technology Specialist (1993-Present), Assistant Principal (1988-93), Teacher (1980-88). **Associations & Accomplishments:** Professional Association of Georgia Educators; Georgia Association of Educational Technology Professionals. **Education:** Augusta State University: Specialist in Education (1985), M.Ed. (1982); University of Georgia, B.A. (1978). **Personal Information:** Mr. Ansley enjoys reading and sports.

Jamey Fern Baiter

Principal Technology Consultant
Illinois State Board of Education
100 North 1st Street
Springfield, IL 62777-0002
(217) 782-5439
Fax: (217) 785-7650
jbaiter@smtp.isbe.state.il.us

9411

Business Information: Demonstrating expertise in the information technology field, Ms. Baiter currently serves as Principal Technology Consultant with the Illinois State Board of Education. Working in the technical outreach division she manages grants, implements technology with the schools and teachers, hosts workshops, and performs consulting. Attributing her success to creative thinking, Ms. Baiter has the ability to turn potential into action through preparation and skilled training. Highly regarded by her colleagues and posssessing an excellent understanding of technology, she plans to expedite continued promotion through dedication to her responsibilities at the Illinois State Board of Education. Her success reflects her ability to communicate effectively, take on challenges, and deliver results on behalf of the Board of Education. The Illinois State Board of Education manages the public schools and oversees the hiring and testing of the teachers for educational positions. Established decades ago, the Illinois State Board of Education staffs 800 administrative, teaching, and support personnel who work diligently to enhance and perfect educational opportunities for its youth. **Career Highlights:** Principal Technology Consultant, Illinois State Board of Education (1999-Present); Teacher, Southwestern School District (1998-99); Teacher/Technical Director, Gibualt High School (1993-98); Teacher Aide, Columbia High School (1991-93). **Associations & Accomplishments:** Association for Supervision and Curriculum Development. **Education:** Southern Illinois University at Edwardsville: M.S. (1993), B.S. (1989).

Thomas M. Bradley

Network Infrastructure Manager
Val Verde Unified School District
975 Morgan Street
Perris, CA 92571-3157
(909) 940-6100
Fax: (909) 940-6146
tbradley@valverde.edu

9411

Business Information: Since beginning his employment with Val Verde Unified School District as Consultant in 1991, Mr. Bradley has served in several different technological positions since. Utilizing his extensive knowledge in the technological field, he currently fulfills the responsibilities of Network Infrastructure Manager. As a solid, 26-year professional, he assumes accountability for the entire School District's LAN/WAN wiring, design, and installation. Additionally, he troubleshoots problems, repairing the network infrastructure and acts as a purchasing agent for hardware and software acquisitions. Mr. Bradley currently supervises one skilled professional in the course of his duties as well as four additional staff members indirectly. He looks forward to increasing the departmental staff in the near future. His success reflects his ability to think outside the box and aggressively take on new challenges. The Val Verde Unified School District provides quality educational opportunities for the youth of Perris, California. Serving students from kindergarten on up to the 12th grade, the District has a total of 12 schools. Approximately 7,500 qualified administrative, faculty, and support personnel are dedicated to offering the best education to the city's youthful residents. **Career Highlights:** Val Verde Unified School District: Network Infrastructure Manager (1997-Present), Technology Technician (1995-97), Consultant (1991-95). **Personal Information:** Mr. Bradley enjoys off road vehicles and camping.

Barbara Smith Camp

Associate Director of Student Services
Klein Independent School District
14307 Pheasant Hill
Houston, TX 77104
(281) 655-6231
Fax: (281) 349-5439
bscamp@mail.esc4.com

9411

Business Information: As an Associate Director of Student Services with the Klein Independent School District in Houston, Texas and as a professional in the publishing and oil and gas industry, Ms. Camp has held a variety of information technology positions. She has served as an instructional administrator for 10 content areas including Technology Applications, K-12. She administered the development and implementation of a K-5 technology applications curriculum series and the computer literacy and computer science courses. Ms. Camp has purchased and managed the installation of 14 instructional labs and is currently the project manager for automating 30 libraries. She also managed the installation of security software and serves as the system administrator for the library automation project. She has published over 62 curriculum guides, plans staff development training, and develops and administers bids for library media services. In the future, Ms. Camp looks forward to continuing to implement library projects, providing Internet access, and facilitating advanced technology into classroom development. She enjoys her work and serving students and her community. Located in Houston, Texas, the Klein Independent School District provides students an exceptional education. Fully accredited by the Texas Education Agency, the District was founded in 1928 and covers an area of 87.5 square miles. Currently, the District is equipped with 19 elementary schools, which have 763 classrooms, 6 intermediate schools with 469 classrooms, and 3 high schools with 446 classrooms. At present, the District houses a student population of over 31,500 students. **Career Highlights:** Klein Independent School District: Associate Director of Student Services (Present), Student Services Officer (1988-2000), Department Chairperson (1984-88); Editorial Specialist, Coastal Corporation (1979-81); Records Analyst, Tenneco, Inc. (1975-78); Editor, Non-Profit Organization (1972-73). **Education:** Stephen F. Austin University, M.Ed. (1985); Texas Tech University, B.A.; Kilgore College, A.A. **Personal Information:** Married to Walter in 1980. Ms. Camp enjoys photography.

Ronnie D. Chandler

District Technology Specialist
Muskogee Public Schools
202 West Broadway Street
Muskogee, OK 74401
(918) 684-3700
Fax: (918) 684-3701
rdc@muskogee.org

9411

Business Information: Following an intense interest in technology, Mr. Chandler serves as District Technology Specialist for the Muskogee Public Schools. In this context, he is responsible for the infrastructure upgrade, integration, development, and implementation of software and hardware. He is also charged with oversight of the LAN system and supervision of the Schools two TV stations. Additionally, Mr. Chandler orchestrates the development and implementation of the Schools' Internet strategies, ensuring the Schools remain and the cutting edge of technology. Originally in heavy equipment field, Mr. Chandler is now an IBM Certified Technical with experience in network design and implementation and software development. Looking forward to completing his CNE certification, his long-term plans include pursuing his MCSE. Muskagee Public Schools provides the educational needs of students from kindergarten to twelvth grade. Employing 800 administrative, teaching, and support staff, the Schools provides educational opportunities to over 6,500 students. With a large focus on technology, Muskagee Public Schools operates over 4,800 PCs, a LAN system with all schools connected as well as 2 stations with live broadcasts. **Career Highlights:** District Technology Specialist, Muskogee Public Schools (1997-Present); Field Engineer, Viacom Inc. (1997); Project Coordinator, TCI Cablevision (1996-97). **Education:** Novell Certification. **Personal Information:** Married to Debra in 1978. Two children: Michael Z. and David M. Mr. Chandler enjoys woodworking, hunting and fishing.

David Clemis

Director of School Net Operations
Industry Canada
155 Queen Street
Ottawa, Ontario, Canada K1A 0H5
(613) 952-0598
Fax: (613) 834-2021
davidclemis@home.com

9411

Business Information: With extensive knowledge and experience in the field of technology, Mr. Clemis serves as Director of School Net Operations for Industry Canada. His specific area of expertise lies in the area of connecting local and regional schools to the Internet, for more comprehensive programs and better learning potential for the children. In doing so, Mr. Clemis is obligated to carry out such functions as developing plans for connections, facilitating a national registry, and providing Web support. Possessing an excellent understand in of technology, Mr. Clemis' plans for his future include remaining with the Agency in order to maintain the technical state of the local establishments. His success reflects his ability to take on challenges and deliver results. Industry Canada engages in the provision of a wide array of professional services as a federal government initiative for connecting Canadians through the Internet and providing them a modern learning environment. Founded in 1996, the Agency incorporates such technology into such establishments as schools, postal services, and shopping centers. Presently, Industry Canada is located in Ottawa, Canada. **Career Highlights:** Industry Canada: Director of School Net Operations (1999-Present), Senior Technical Analyst (1997-99); Telecommunications Standards, Advisory Council of Canada (1991-99). **Associations & Accomplishments:** Armed Forces Communication and Electronics Association; Association of Computing Machinery. **Education:** University of Ottawa, M.B.A. (1995); Brock University, B.A. with Distinction. **Personal Information:** Married to Elizabeth in 1973. Two children: Christina and Jonathan. Mr. Clemis enjoys sailing, badminton and competitive swimming.

Tammy L. Evans

Business Leader of Technology Services
Oakland Schools
2100 Pontiac Lake Road
Waterford, MI 48328-2735
(248) 209-2187
Fax: (248) 209-2207
tammy.evans@oakland.k12.mi.us

9411

Business Information: Serving as Business Leader of Technology Services of Oakland Schools, Ms. Evans is responsible for all mainframe and microcomputing services. Working with her staff to develop the systems infastructure and WAN strategies, she coordinates the strategic direction of the department. She maintains all client servers which handle internal and external activity. Overseeing the technical aspects of the finance, payroll, and human resources departments, Ms. Evans utilizes her education to implement upgrades and changes that benefit the District. Crediting success to her ongoing education and her up-to-date skills, she intends to continue in her current capacity, seeking advancements within the corporate structure. The Oakland Schools provides education for approximately 250,000 students in grades kindergarten through twelve. Comprised of over 500 different school and administration buildings, the District also employs 3,500 staff members in capacities ranging from teachers and principals to coaches and custodians. **Career Highlights:** Oakland Schools: Business Leader of Technology Services (1998-Present), Manager of Network Services (1996-98); Manager of User Services, Oakland Community College (1992-96). **Associations & Accomplishments:** Michigan School Business Officials; Michigan Area Computer Users; Oakland Schools Business Officials; State Director, Michigan Department of Education. **Education:** Baker College, M.B.A. (1995), B.B.A. in Computer Information (1992).

Bonnie L. Harris

Director of Technology
Harris County Department of Education
6300 Irvington Boulevard
Houston, TX 77022
(713) 696-8230
Fax: (713) 696-0736
bharris@hcde-texas.org

9411

Business Information: Serving as the Director of Technology for the Harris County Department of Education, Ms. Harris is responsible for establishing leadership and integrity throughout the information technology division. Her primary functions include network management, Web page design, and upgrade of enterprise software for business components. With more than 20 years of educational experience, Ms. Harris is also involved in a number of public programs and community organizations, which are coordinated to further the educational potential of all students. Attributing her success to a varying educational background, she plans to remain with the Department to further her education and then move on to the legal community. The Harris County Department of Education provides services, personnel, and alternative education for all schools public and private within the County. A resource for 24 school districts, the Department engages in the provision of adult educational programs, reading programs, peer counseling, occupational therapy, and physical therapy. Established in 1986, the Department operates out of five convenient locations for a growing attendance, and more advanced curriculum. The Department functions under the guidance and expertise of 1,500 professionals. **Career Highlights:** Director of Technology, Harris County Department of Education (1987-Present); Supervisor of General Rehabilitation, Medical Center Del Oro (1983-87); Supervisor of Alcohol, Drug, Pain, Hermann Hospital, (1982-83). **Associations & Accomplishments:** Houston Historical Society, Texas Educators Computer Association; Texas Center for Education Technology; Texas Prevention of Cruelty to Animals. **Education:** University Wisconsin at Madison, B.S. in Occupational Therapy (1981). **Personal Information:** Ms. Harris enjoys reading, music, choir, theater and animals.

Sharon M. Hennessy

Information Systems Manager
Parkway School District
455 Northwoods Mill Road
Chesterfield, MO 63017
(314) 415-8031
Fax: (314) 415-8035

9411

Business Information: Combining her knowledge of education with her technical skills, Mrs. Hennessy serves as the Information Systems Manager for the Parkway School District. A systems expert, she presides over the management of the AS/400 computer system and administrative software, performing routine maintenance, monitoring daily activity, and providing backup for the system. Mrs. Hennessy reads industry publications, attends seminars, and networks on the Internet in an effort to stay up to date on the latest in educational technology. Incorporating this knowledge into her job, she ensures that the School District is able to offer its students quality education in today's technology. As a 21 year technology professional, her success reflects her ability to think out-of-the-box and aggressively take on new challenges. Remaining with the School District and taking the District to the next level of technology serves as one of Mrs. Hennessy's future goals. Parkway School District works to provide quality education for students in grades kindergarten through 12th grade. A public school district, there are a total of 28 schools altogether. Over 3,000 administrative, teaching, and support personnel strive to enhance and perfect educational opportunities for its youth.

Career Highlights: Information Systems Manager, Parkway School District (1998-Present); Lead Programmer/Analyst, H.B.E. Corporation (1982-98); Data Processing Manager, Mehlville School District (1978-82). **Education:** Southeast Missouri State University, B.S. in Secondary Education (1976). **Personal Information:** Three children: Sean, Patrick, and Andrew. Mrs. Hennessy enjoys fishing, camping, photography and bicycling.

Patricia Iuele, Ed.D.

Director of Technology
Tenafly Public Schools
19 Columbus Drive
Tenafly, NJ 07670
(201) 816-6677
Fax: (201) 871-9577
patricia@tenafly.k12.nj.us

9411

Business Information: Dr. Ivele has served in several different positions since beginning her career with Tenafly Public Schools more than 25 years ago. At the present time, she serves as the Director of Technology, responsible for all technological aspects of the District's computer systems. Directly supervising a staff of four qualified staff members, she oversees the administrative and student networks. Additionally, Dr. Ivele is in charge of the LAN and WAN maintenance as well as the Internet and satellite access. She cites her willingness to learn and explore new things as the reason for her success. Establishing goals that are compatible with those of the District, Dr. Ivele is committed to providing continued optimum service. Tenafly Public Schools provides students in grades kindergarten through 12th grade with quality educational opportunities to enable them to become productive members of society. Composed of six schools with approximate enrollment of 2,600 students, the District employs 350 administrative, faculty, and support personnel. **Career Highlights:** Tenafly Public Schools: Director of Technology (1994-Present), Vice Principal (1989-94), Science Teacher (1975-89). **Associations & Accomplishments:** American Chemical Society; American Educational Research Association; Association for Supervision and Curriculum Development; NECC; Association for Supervision and Curriculum Development. **Education:** Rutgers University, Ed.D. (1991). **Personal Information:** Dr. Ivele enjoys gardening.

Frank J. Klein, M.B.A./T.M.

Director of Technology
Brighton School District -Technology Department
630 South 8th Avenue
Brighton, CO 80601
(303) 655-2912
Fax: (303) 655-2870
fklein6501@aol.com

9411

Business Information: Demonstrating expertise in the information technology field, Mr. Klein serves as Director of Technology for the Technology Department of Brighton School District. He oversees the maintenance of telecommunications and video systems and orchestrates technical training classes. In addition, Mr. Klein programs and maintains switches and networks. With over 12 years of experience in his field, Mr. Klein attributes his success to effective interpersonal and communications skills. His plans for the future include remaining on the cutting edge of technology, assisting students in developing technical skills, and establishing an independent consultancy. Brighton School District administers the educational services provided by public schools in Brighton, Colorado. The District employs 523 faculty and staff members to serve 4,400 students enrolled at nine elementary, middle, and high schools. **Career Highlights:** Brighton School District, Technology Department: Director of Technology (Present), Management Information Systems Coordinator (1995-2000); Testing and Assessment Lab Administrator, Delta School District (1990-95); Store Manager, Delta Computer Store (1985-90). **Associations & Accomplishments:** United States Navy Reserves; Teacher of the Year (1974, 1991, 1992). **Education:** University of Phoenix, M.B.A./T.M. (1998); N.I.U.: B.S. in Civil Engineering, B.S. in Education. **Personal Information:** Married. Two children: Robert and Brandon. Mr. Klein enjoys camping, fishing, rafting and golf.

Adele G. Morris

Technology Director
Craig County Public Schools
2670 Turnberry Road
Salem, VA 24153
(540) 864-5185
Fax: (540) 989-6174

9411

Business Information: Functioning in the role of Technology Director for Craig County Public Schools, Mrs. Morris is responsible for procurement of hardware and software, maintenance of the technology infrastructure, and training the professional staff and student classes in emerging technology. Before joining Craig County Public Schools, Mrs. Morris served as a Claims Representative II for Kemper Insurance Company. Her background history also includes stints as Computer Coordinator for Trinity Episcopal School and Instructor at Mediaah Middle School. A solid professional with over 25 years of extensive academic and occupational experience, she owns an established track record of producing results in support of educational, technical, and business objectives. Possessing a Master's degree in Biology, Mrs. Morris is credited with computerizing the Science Department. Under her technology leadership, the School has gone from Apple IIE computers to an environment with Internet and multimedia access. An accomplished professional, she was recipient of the Illinois Governor's Master Teacher Award. Attributing her success to a desire to learn and a good foundation provided by her parents, Mrs. Morris enjoys what she does when students light up and say, "I got it!" Craig County Public Schools operates as a one-site school campus with elementary and secondary schools for kindergarten through 12th grade students. Presently, the School employs a staff of 90 educators, administrators, and support personnel. **Career Highlights:** Technology Director, Craig County Public Schools (Present); Claims Representative II, Kemper Insurance Company; Computer Coordinator, Trinity Episcopal School; Instructor, Mediaah Middle School (1974). **Associations & Accomplishments:** Daughters of the American Revolution; Mayflower Society; Senior Sponsor for Mill Mount Valley of Virginia N.S.C.A.R. Society. **Education:** Northeastern Illinois University, Master's degree in Biology; Frostburg State University, Bachelor's degree; Elmhurst College; National College of Education; Virginia Western Community College. **Personal Information:** Married to Charles in 1974. Two children: Nora and Emmalee. Mrs. Morris enjoys genealogy.

Richard L. Ralstin

Director of Technology
Sacaton Public School District #18
P.O. Box 98
Sacaton, AZ 85247-0098
(520) 562-3339
Fax: (480) 735-9343

9411

Business Information: Serving as Director of Technology of the Sacaton Public School District #18, Mr. Ralstin is responsible for all of the media and systems infrastructure in the District. He proposes and writes grants, constructs the curriculum and is involved with the student database system. A savvy, technical expert, he currently has the District on a five year technology plan, and is working to get all of the campuses connected online to the Internet. Future strategic plans for Mr. Ralstin include upgrading the District's infrastructure to wireless technology. His manufacturing manual for curriculum development called "Building Linkages" is cited as his career highlight. Mr. Ralstin's success reflects his leadership ability to take on challenges and deliver results. Founded in 1960, the District is located on the Gila River Indian Reservation in Sacaton, Arizona. The Districts' main focus is to prepare students from kindengarten to eighth grade for a higher education. There are currently two districts on the reservation and both include public schools. **Career Highlights:** Director of Technology, Sacaton Public School District #18 (1999-Present); State Supervisor, Arizona Department of Education (1996-99); Teacher, Gila Bend (1993-96); Teacher, Deer Valley V-Tec. **Associations & Accomplishments:** American Vocational Association; International Technology Education Association; National Association of Trade and Industrial Education; Arizona Coaches Association. **Education:** Northern Arizona University, M.A. (1998). **Personal Information:** Married to Linda in 1986. One child: Brian. Mr. Ralstin enjoys collecting coins and John Wayne videos.

Ramon J. Ray

Program Manager
Savannah-Chatham County Board of Education
106 Greenbriar Drive
Savannah, GA 31419-2916
(912) 651-0910
rrayjar@aol.com

9411

Business Information: Displaying unique talent in this specialized field, Mr. Ray serves as Instructional Technology Program Manager for the Savannah - Chatham County Board of Education. He is in charge of all instructional computer and technology issues as well as software programs for the entire school system. Maintaining responsibility for all classrooms wired to the Internet, he performs hands-on and textbook training for the faculty, administrative personnel, and students on software use. Mr. Ray also serves as a liaison to vendors on behalf of the Board of Education. He has equipped 1,500 classes, grades kindergarten through 12th, with new technology. Planning to continue to move forward with the development and implementation of technology, he would like to contribue more to the Department and take on more administrative duties. Mr. Ray credits his success thus far to his parents and upbringing. The Savannah - Chatham County Board of Education was founded in 1870 with the purpose of providing educational opportunities to the citizens youth in an effort to improve their quality of life. Today, that tradition continues and the school system has grown along with the counties' populations. A total of 55 schools are utilized for the 36,000 students in grades kindergarten through 12th. The Board of Education also offers adult education programs for citizens' continuing education after high school. Approximately 5,000 administrative, faculty, and support personnel are employed to ensure students receive a quality education. **Career Highlights:** Savannah - Chatham County Board of Education: Instructional Technology Program Manager (1999-Present), Network Administrator (1997-99), Technology Specialist (1995-97), Computer Facilitator (1993-95). **Associations & Accomplishments:** Alpha Phi Alpha Fraternity, Inc. **Education:** Savannah State University: Master's degree in Public Administration (1998), B.S. in Computer Science Technology (1990), A.S. in Computer Engineering Technology (1990). **Personal Information:** Married to Sheryl in 1999. One child: Ariel.

Mark Wesley Robinson

Manager of Systems Development Group
United States Department of Education
7th & D Streets SW
Washington, DC 20202-0001
(202) 205-9500
Fax: (202) 401-2455
mark.robinson@ed.gov

9411

Business Information: Serving as Manager of Systems Development Group of the United States Department of Education, Mr. Robinson oversees all day-to-day activities of systems development group. A key member of the Office of the Chief Financial Office, he is responsible for developing advanced financial management software. Possessing 19 years of technical expertise, Mr. Robinson manages his staff of 10 technical professionals as well as oversees a contractor staff of 90 employees. He was recruited to the Department as the Deputy Program Manager for the implementation of the EDCAPS program. His background history also includes working on an auto system tracking railcar activities for the Washington Metro Transit Authority. Mr. Robinson became involved in the technology field while attending the University of Pennsylvania where he worked in the University's data center. Advancing into the future, Mr. Robinson goal is to move to a senior executive level position within the federal government. His advice is "read industry periodicals, take training courses, and stay abreast of what is happening in the technical field." Faith and prayer are reasons for Mr. Robinson's success. Since 1978, the United States Department of Education has served the educational needs of the nation. The Department is responsible for managing the federal education policy and administering student financial aid programs. The United States Department of Education currently employs 4,000 individuals to meet the educational demands of Americans. **Career Highlights:** United States Department of Education: Manager of Financial Systems Development Group (1998-Present), Computer Specialist (1997-98); United States Office of Personnel Management: Special Assistant (1995-97), Staff Director (1992-95). **Associations & Accomplishments:** Affiliated Member, Institute of Electrical and Electronics Engineers Computer Committee; Associate Member, Project Management Institute; Chairman, Asbury United Methodist Church Computer Committee. **Education:** University of

Pennsylvania, B.A. (1981); George Washington School of Business and Public Administration, Graduate Certificate in Information Technology Project Management. **Personal Information:** Married to Susan F. in 1988. One child: Daryn Susan. Mr. Robinson enjoys church and family time.

Kitty Sanchez-Pfeiffer

Coordinator of Technology and Information Systems
San Marcos United School District
1 Civic Center Drive, Suite 300
San Marcos, CA 92069
(760) 752-1204
Fax: (760) 591-0426
kitty@sdcoe.k12.ca.us

9411

Business Information: Ms. Sanchez-Pfeiffer serves as Coordinator of Technology and Information Systems for San Marcos United School District. She manages the Educational Technology Department and coordinates the design and implementation of WAN and LAN networks. Each school has its own local area network and is connected by the district wide area network to the central office. At least one computer lab is available for use in each school with half of all classrooms having one computer available to students. All schools have Internet access but the elementary schools' access is restricted. Ms. Sanchez-Pfeiffer allows students in the middle and high schools Internet access on an acceptable use policy after they receive a network education class. The Technology Department offers additional training to teachers and holds evening classes to faculty, students, general staff, and the community. Responsible for the implementation of all of the District's educational programs and training, Ms. Sanchez-Pfeiffer coordinates the reviewing and testing of new educational software for future use in the classrooms. Her goal is to put a computer in every classroom and permit students to access library reference material without leaving the room and make media retrieval available to teachers online. She is in the process of improving the WAN by adding additional components that will enhance and expand its functions. San Marcos United School District provides educational opportunities for children in grades kindergarten through 12th grade. The District is composed of 17 elementary, middle, and high schools with an overall total of 12,000 students. Approximately 1,200 administrative, teaching, and support personnel are employed in the District during the school year. **Career Highlights:** Coordinator of Technology and Information Systems, San Marcos United School District (1995-Present); System Integrity Analyst, Jostens Learning Corporation (1988-94); Coordinator of Developmental Education, Central Arizona College (1982-88). **Associations & Accomplishments:** Designer/Implementor, Developmental Education Learning Lab for local Community College. **Education:** Northern Deye University, B.S. (1969); Northern Arizona University, Special Certification in Remedial Reading. **Personal Information:** Married to Jim in 1993. Two children: Jason David Payne and Jennifer Diane Payne. Ms. Sanchez-Pfeiffer enjoys gardening and home remodeling.

John W. Schroth

Technology Coordinator
Strongsville City Schools
13200 Pearl Road
Strongsville, OH 44136-3494
(440) 572-7017
Fax: (440) 238-7242
schroth@strongnet.org

9411

Business Information: Providing his skilled services as Technology Coordinator for the Strongsville City Schools, Mr. Schroth assumes responsibility for all of the information technology functions for the entire School District. He is in charge of the faculty's academic file servers and provides students with computers on which to learn and practice future skills. Reviewing new software programs and hardware equipment on the market, he makes informed purchasing decisions. Mr. Schroth installs new programs and equipment, training faculty and students alike in its use. Additionally, he oversees the adult college classes offered at night. His most memorable accomplishment with the District was the development and implementation of a desktop security system. Dedicated to the educational success of the District, Mr. Schroth plans to bring on more technological support staff and looks forward to attaining a promotion to a Trainer User Support position. The Strongsville City Schools offer quality educational instruction to students from the kindergarten level through graduation. Founded in 1914, the Public School System is composed of eight elementary schools, two middle schools, and one high school. Over 800 administrative, educational, and support personnel work diligently to provide students with a solid educational base for their future. **Career Highlights:** Technology Coordinator, Strongsville City Schools (1996-Present); Chagrin Falls Schools: Technology Director (1995-96), Teacher (1985-95). **Education:** Kent State University: M.A. (1993), B.A. (1984). **Personal Information:** Married to Rebecca in 1984. Four children: Spencer, Hanna, Christopher, and Cameron. Mr. Schroth enjoys British car restoration.

Arthur R. Scott

Director of Operational Technology & Telecommunications Department
Atlanta Public Schools
2352 Bagwell Drive SW
Atlanta, GA 30315-6418
(404) 635-2845
Fax: (404) 635-2859
ascott@atlanta.k12.ga.us

9411

Business Information: Mr. Scott serves as Director of Operational Technology & Telecommunications Department of the Atlanta Public Schools. His responsibilities include overseeing a 40-person team responsible for media systems incorporating satellite, broadcast and digital video, computer systems, and Internet communication data to further the education and understanding of the students in his District. Mr. Scott directed the construction of a brilliant computer network system connecting all 112 schools in his District, and decreasing extraneous expenditures by 30 percent. His accomplishments have lead to networking and communications with other school districts, further expanding the resources from which the educational system has to draw from. Mr. Scott has greatly improved the School's ability to teach and the student's desire to learn. He plans to finish current projects and to someday be employed as Chief Information Officer of a large corporation. This Atlanta, Georgia school district is responsible for the education and life skills development for over 6,000 students. The District operates 112 academc sites offering a diverse student population educational opportunities. School board administrators emphasize the feeling of security and comfort by maintaining "Zero Tolerance" and "Open Door" policies for both parents and students alike. The current administration is responsible for a drop in overall campus misbehavior, and a rise in standardized test scores. **Career Highlights:** Atlanta Public Schools: Director of Operational Technology & Telecommunications Department (1995-Present), Systems Analyst/Network Administrator (1992-95); Computer Operations Coordinator, Kaiser Foundaiton Health Plan of Georgia (1990-91). **Associations & Accomplishments:** Computerworld/Smithsonian Institute Award Winner for Technology in Education (1999); Mayor's Task Force for Technology, City of Atlanta. **Education:** Clark Atlanta University, B.A. in Business Education/Management (1990); Southern Polytechnic University, Graduate Studies; Georgia Institute of Technology: Information Technology Project Management, Middle Management Program, Microsoft NT/Exchange and Cisco Network Administration. **Personal Information:** Four children. Mr. Scott enjoys reading, computers, listening to music and physical fitness.

Rick K. Smith, Ed.D.

Director of Technology
Ignacio School District
P.O. Box 460
Ignaciao, CO 81137
(970) 563-4522
Fax: (970) 563-4524
rsmith@ignacio.k12.co.us

9411

Business Information: Displaying exceptionally advanced technilogicall skills, Dr. Smith serves as Director of Technology for Ignaciao School District. In this capacity, he manages the network's infrastructure, performs diagnostic testing, and operates as the LAN network administrator. Dr. Smith is also responsible for server upkeep and upgrading the system network as well as purchasing software, hardware, and technology. In addition, he conducts detailed network training for all staff members and leads technology research utilizing acquired grant monies. Dr. Smith has written numerous articles regarding Internet access that has been published in curriculum periodicals and instructional computer magazines nationwide. He has enjoyed tremendous success in his current position with the School District and aspires to attain a network administration position in the corporate world. Software skills and his supportive wife, Becky, are cited as reasons for his success. Ignaciao School District is a regional public school system that provides higher learning to students from pre-kindergarten through grade twelve. Located on the Southern Ute American Indian Reservation in Ignaciao, Colorado, the District is comprised of four schools and employs a collective work force of over 120 certified teachers that are dedicated to ensuring the highest quality of education available. **Career Highlights:** Ignacio School District: Director of Technology (1999-Present), Computer Instructor (1993-99); Technology Consultant, Office of Rick Smith (1997-98). **Education:** Nova Southeastern University, Ed.D. (1999); Adams State College, Master's degree; Fort Lewis College, B.A. **Personal Information:** Married to Becky in 1980. Two children: Eileen Marie and Timothy Michael. Dr. Smith enjoys volunteer coaching, hunting, fishing and camping.

Sheldon K. Smith, Ed.D.

Director of Technology and Information Services
Paso Robles Public School District
2990 Union Road
Paso Robles, CA 93447
(805) 237-3362
Fax: (805) 460-0740
sheldonsmith@email.com

9411

Business Information: As Director of Technology and Information Services at Paso Robles Public School district, Dr. Smith is responsible for all aspects of business and instructional computer uses. As a former English teacher and assistant principal, Dr. Smith brings a wealth of classroom insights and experiences in utilizing computers to improve instruction and student learning. Currently, Dr. Smith oversees a growing wide area network comprising over 25 servers and 1,500 clients, all connected via T-1 lines. Demonstrating his extensive knowledge of the information technology field, he regularly evaluates technical needs within the District and implements any necessary upgrades or changes. Working closely with his staff, he oversees all network communication and desktop computing uses. Additionally, Dr.Smith develops training programs to help ensure that his district staff are able to utilize computers efficiently, and that students utilize computers to improve their knowledge. Dr. Smith handles the purchasing of hardware, software, computer services, and equipment, in addition to making approvals on purchasing requests. Enjoying the challenge of the information technology department, he intends to continue in his current role to help bring the District's schools into the information age, while finding creative methods for additional technology funding. Paso Robles Public School District is concerned with the education of youths in the schools of the Paso Robles, California area. Serving over 6,000 students, the District seeks to promote the most modern and innovative forms of education possible to offer students the best educational opportunities. **Career Highlights:** Director of Technology and Information Services, Paso Robles Public School District (1999-Present); Technology Program Coordinator, San Luis Obispo County Office of Education (1997-99); Assistant Principal, Atascadero Unified (1995-97). **Associations & Accomplishments:** Advisory Panel, California Commission on Teacher Credentialing Computer Education; Category One Cyclist, United States Cycling Federation; Collegiate National Cycling: Champion of Team Pursuit, Two-Time State Champion of Time Trial; California Polytechnic State University Wheelmen Cycling Team; Phi Delta Kappa; California School Leadership Academy; Very Special Person Honorary Service Award, Parent Teacher Student Association; Published Articles: "Safe Internet Use in Schools" (1999), "Why You Need a Pager: Now There is No Excuse for Being Out of Touch with Your Office" (1998), "Never Out of Touch" (1997), "Administrative Paging" (1996), "Pagers Provide the Link" (1996), "Classroom-Based Telecommunication" (1994). **Education:** University of Southern California, Ed.D. (1998); California Polytechnic State University - San Luis Obispo: M.A with Distinction, B.A. **Personal Information:** Married to Patricia in 1991. One child: Riley.

Samuel "Sam" Thomas Wallace

Data Processing Manager
Education Service Center-2
209 North Water Street
Corpus Christi, TX 78401-2599
(361) 561-8669
Fax: (361) 883-3442
swallace@esc2.net

9411

Business Information: Mr. Wallace functions as the Data Processing Manager for Education Service Center-2. He is responsible for managing of the Data Processing Department. As an information systems professional with 13 years in the field, Mr. Wallace has served with the Center in a variety of roles since joining the Center as Media Manager in 1994. He also serves in the capacity of Telecommunications Coordinator for Education Service Center-2. To this end, he provides technical support and coordinates all activities, as well as works with network design and development and implementation. His highlights includes connecting the infrastructure of 22 school districts into a single AT network environment. Having 37 school districts connected and providing Interact access and video conferencing serves as Mr. Wallace's future goal. His advice to others is "never say no." Mr. Wallace's success reflects his determination and is attributed to reading, talking with vendors, and attending trade shows. Education Service Center-2 engages the search and discovery of resources for School District 42 in Corpus Christi, Texas. Coordinating and working with two universities and two community colleges, the Center serves eleven counties and seven charter schools. Established in 1968, Education Service Center-2 presently employs a staff of more than 118 professional, technical, and support personnel. **Career Highlights:** Education Service Center-2: Data Processing Manager (1998-Present), Management Information System Project Manager (1997-98), Instructional Technology

Consultant (1995-97), Media Manager (1994-95). **Associations & Accomplishments:** Texas Computer Educators Association. **Education:** Texas A&M University at Kingsville: M.S. (1993), B.S. **Personal Information:** Married to Julie Ann in 1986. Two children: Katherine "Katie", Lanaughn, and Alyssa Marie. Mr. Wallace enjoys hunting, fishing and golf.

E. Hayet Woods
Instructional Technology Resource Teacher
Independence School District
537 Clyde Street
Liberty, MO 64068
(816) 796-4885
hayetw@aol.com

9411

Business Information: Presently, Ms. Woods serves as the Instructional Technology Resource Teacher for the Independence School District. Utilizing 10 years of hands on experience, she is a renowned instructor on new advances in the technological world. Ms. Woods devotes her professional career to educating the country's teachers who are engaged in technological instruction. Striving to keep America's teachers in the forefront of this very dynamic field, Ms. Woods offers assistance in lesson creation and technology integration into the classroom. A member of the Who's Who Among American Teachers, she is continuing to expand upon her intellectual territory, working towards a career educating teachers at a college level. One of the most prestigious not-for-profit educational facilities in the nation, Independence School District utilizes a three building campus in the education of students specifically in grades 6 to 8. Employing over 1,600 professional teachers, administrators, and additional staff, the District is renowned for providing the most state-of-the-art education to their expanding student base. **Career Highlights:** Instructional Technology Resource Teacher, Independence School District (2000-Present); Computer Teacher, Kearney Junior High School (1996-00); Sixth Grade Teacher, Holt Elementary School (1990-96). **Associations & Accomplishments:** National Education Association; Kearney Education Association; National Middle School Association; Drug Education Curriculum Committee; Founder/Student Council, Holt Elementary School; Principals Advisory Committee; Grant Writing Committee. **Education:** Lesley College, M.A. in Education, Technology in Education (1996); Central Missouri State University, B.S. in Elementary Education with a minor in Mathematics. **Personal Information:** Married to Kenneth Patrick in 1992. Ms. Woods enjoys walking in charity events, reading and spending time with his nephew.

Gordon J. Asbach
Web Administrator
State of Washington, Department of Social and Health Services
P.O. Box 45842
Olympia, WA 98504-5842
(360) 664-5817
Fax: (360) 664-5630
asbacgj@dshs.wa.gov

9431

Business Information: Mr. Asbach serves as Web Administrator for the State of Washington, Department of Social and Health Services. He designs, implements, and maintains Web sites for the Department's finance division. Utilizing his creative talents, Mr. Asbach strives to successfully display all areas of the State government facilities through a user-friendly, navigable Web site. His career highlight includes being named the United States Navy Reserve Sailor of the Year and earning a Navy and Marine Achievement Award while serving in the United States Navy. Looking to the next millennium, Mr. Asbach hopes to remain on the cutting edge of technology and advance his position in the industry. His success is attributed to his unyielding devotion and deep commitment. State of Washington, Department of Social and Health Services monitors the safety and welfare concerns of the state of Washington. The Department is responsible for the distribution of all government assistance throughout the area and also hosts the abuse management division. This division reponds to reports of violence or neglect within the area in hopes of saving a family and maybe a life. **Career Highlights:** Web Administrator, State of Washington, Department of Social and Health Services (1997-Present); Webmaster, Asbach Web Creations (1996-Present); Network Administrator/Office Manager, Hanemann, Bateman & Jones (1988-97). **Associations & Accomplishments:** International Webmasters Association; The HTML Writers Guild. **Education:** National Academy for Paralegal Studies (1990). **Personal Information:** Married to Linda Lee in 1999. Three children: Noah, Skye, and Hope.

Linda M. Baxter
Management Information Systems Manager
Neuse Center
P.O. Box 1636
New Bern, NC 28563
(919) 636-1510
Fax: (919) 633-1237

9431

Business Information: With several years of experience in her field, Ms. Baxter is the Management Information Systems Manager of Neuse Center, presiding over mini computer, personal computer, and network operations. She performs system maintenance, training, and troubleshooting, as well as giving help desk support and in house consulting for management personnel. Ms. Baxter also monitors data input and retrieval, ensuring system integrity and security for electronic medical records. She plans to continue her career with Neuse Center, hoping for further advancement as the Company grows through the implementation of innovative technology. Neuse Center provides treatment and assistance to individuals with mental health disorders, substance abuse issues, and developmental disabilities. The Center operates 38 sites under the authority of county and local governments in Jones, Pamlico, Carteret, and Craven counties of North Carolina. In order to provide adequate service, Neuse Center currently employs 350 full time people and 400 part time contract staff members. **Career Highlights:** Management Information Systems Manager, Neuse Center (1988-Present); Management Information Systems Manager, Robinson Insurance Inc. (1985-88); Management Information Systems Manager, Stallings-Woodruff Insurance (1982-85). **Associations & Accomplishments:** BCP Advisory Committee, Craven Community College; Secretary, North Carolina Finance and Reimbursement Officers; President, Lady Elks of New Bern - Lodge #764. **Education:** North Carolina Wesleyan University, B.S. in Computer Information Systems (1993). **Personal Information:** Married to John R. in 1965. Two children: James R. and Kathryn E. Ms. Baxter enjoys family activities, crafts and cooking.

Misty M. Beelman
LAN Administrator
Consultech, Inc.
7755 Office Plaza Drive, Suite 145
West Des Moines, IA 50266
(515) 327-0950
misticb@netins.net

9431

Business Information: Serving as the LAN Administrator for Consultech, Inc., Ms. Beelman assumes the responsibility for the management and documentation of the Corporation's network security and resources, AVARS, PBX, and other LAN/WAN related issues for the state of Iowa. She trains and supervises the technical department's support staff, coordinating multiple projects with multiple vendors and sites. Responsible for the administration of the Cold and Winframe servers, she is the primary contact for vendors and handles the product purchasing for the LAN/WAN and other Corporation equipment. Ms. Beelman analyzes various departmental data needs, creating databases or system applications in response to growing data needs and concerns. Her advice to industry newcomers is "strive to reach your goals and don't quit." She is committed to the further development of the Corporation, coordinating strategic planning to ensure a bright future for Vice President. Headquartered in Atlanta, Georgia, Consultech, Inc. is an information technical consulting services firm. The Corporation was established in 1997 in Iowa as the fiscal agent for that state's Medicaid program. An approximate work force of 200 staff members work diligently to provide medical services to the state's indigent population. **Career Highlights:** LAN Administrator, Consultech, Inc. (1997-Present); System Administrator, ICIS (1996-97). **Education:** Buena Vista University, B.A. (1996). **Personal Information:** Ms. Beelman enjoys sports, swimming, reading, writing poetry and socializing.

Glen A. Coleman
MDS/OASIS Technical Coordinator
Ohio Department of Health, DQA
246 North High Street, 3rd Floor
Columbus, OH 43215
(614) 752-4795
Fax: (614) 466-8692
gcoleman@gw.odh.state.oh.us

9431

Business Information: Serving as MDS/OASIS Technical Coordinator of Ohio Department of Health, DQA, Mr. Coleman is responsible for administration of Ohio's MDS/OASIS systems and also for maintaining the division's NT and Oracle network. He assures the accuracy and consistency of the Department's data set system which is the program used to intake information required by the government from nursing homes, called the minimum data set, and processes it to ensure the submitted data is in an acceptable form. On the OASIS side, the program applies the same specifications to home health care management and establishes maximized data security. Mr. Coleman provides system support for the offices and reports to the federal government on a consistent basis as to the security levels in place and the opportunities for improvement or enhancement on the system. A certified Novell and Microsoft product tester, Mr. Coleman gains much of his experience through hands-on instruction and is able to offer the Department with cutting edge information regarding new products, programs, and opportunities. Success was achieved, for Mr. Coleman, through his enduring faith in God. Ohio Department of Health, DQA is a state run government agency who's primary goals are to validate and discipline nursing home facilities and home health agencies. The Department employs approximately 1,500 personnel throughout their offices in the state of Ohio. **Career Highlights:** Ohio Department of Health, DQA: MDS/OASIS Technical Coordinator (1998-Present), Network Administrator (1994-98), Programmer (1992-94). **Associations & Accomplishments:** Security Panel, National MDS/OASIS System; Youth Pastor, Living Word Assemblies of God. **Education:** N.A.E.C., CNA (1998). **Personal Information:** Married to Theresa R. in 1985. One child: Angela S. Mr. Coleman enjoys playing golf and tennis and participating with his church.

Charles "Chuck" F. Cornwall, II
Director of Information Technology for the Bureau of WIC
Mississippi State Department of Health, WIC Program
2423 North State Street
Jackson, MS 39216
(601) 987-6757
Fax: (601) 825-7026
craigiz@bellsouth.net

9431

Business Information: Functioning in the capacity of Director of Information Technology for the Bureau of WIC, Mr. Cornwall is responsible for determining the overall strategic direction and contribution of the information systems function to the WIC Program. Mr. Cornwall has assertively served with the Mississippi State Department of Health's WIC Program since joining the Mississippi State Department of Health as Branch Director in 1981. In his position, he oversees all day-to-day administration and operation of the information systems infrastructure, to include designing, implementing, and maintaining systems. Conducting Year 2000 remediation and systematic reviews, formulating strategic and tactical plans, and supervising a staff of 25 professional and technical experts also fall within the realm of Mr. Cornwall's responsibilities. He credits his success to his ability to work as a team and his motivation. "Failure is not an option," is cited as his credo. Mississippi State Department of Health's WIC Program offers nutritional foods to women, infants, and children. Established in 1974, the WIC Program operates a network of 104 locations across the state. Presently, the WIC Program office in Jackson, Mississippi is manned by 25 people who help manage a budget of $56 million annually. **Career Highlights:** Mississippi State Department of Health, WIC Program: Director of Information Technology for the Bureau of WIC (1997-Present), Technical Specialist (1994-97), Branch Director (1981-94); Administrative Officer, City of Jackson (1971-81). **Associations & Accomplishments:** American Society of Public Administrators; Mississippi Society of Public Administrators; Junior Achievement Advisor; National Geriatric Society; Mississippi Computer Society. **Education:** M.C., B.S. (1970); Mississippi State University; University of Georgia; University of Missouri; University of Wisconsin School of Engineering. **Personal Information:** Married to Connie S. in 1971. Two children: Chris and Craig. Mr. Cornwall enjoys gardening, walking, soccer and baseball.

Patricia C. Ellis
Bureau Chief
South Carolina Department of Health and Human Services
1801 Main Street
Columbia, SC 29202
(803) 898-2787
Fax: (803) 898-4510
ellis@dhhs.state.sc.us

9431

Business Information: Serving as Bureau Chief of South Carolina Department of Health and Human Services, Ms. Ellis assumes responsibility for the administration of the Department's PC workstations, laptops, telephones, modems, and fax lines. An experienced professional, she oversees the server and PC-based applications as well as the WAN and LAN administration for the Department's 20 offices. Ms. Ellis negotiates technology related contracts with private companies and developed the long term technology plan currently in use by the Department. Reporting directly to the Executive Director and the Deputy Director for Fiscal Management, Ms. Ellis owns an established track record of producing results. Her career success reflects her leadership ability to form teams with synergy and a customer oriented attitude, and aggressively take on new challenges and responsibilities. Always alert to new opportunities, techniques, and approaches, Ms. Ellis looks forward to one day opening a private consulting business. The South Carolina Department of Health and Human Services is the state level government agency that administers Medicaid. Established in 1984, the Department receives a $2.3 billion annual budget and employs 650 staff members. **Career Highlights:** South Carolina Department of Health and Human Services: Bureau Chief (1997-Present), Information Technology Manager/Special Projects Manager (1996-97), Director of Child Support Enforcement System Automation Project (1993-96); Systems Manager for Administrative Support, South Carolina Security Commission (1983-93). **Associations & Accomplishments:** Greater Columbia Community Relations Council Luncheon Club; Lexington Network of Executive Women; Association for Women on Boards and Commissions; Automation Advisory Board, Lexington County Arts Association; National Child Support Enforcement Association; International Association of Personnel in Employment Security; National Data Processing Advisory Board for the Department of Labor. **Education:** University of South Carolina, B.A. in Applied Professional Sciences with emphasis on Management (1987); National Dean's List; University of South Carolina's Dean's List; Midlands Technical College, A.S. in Computer Science (1971). **Personal Information:** One child: Michael Scott. Ms. Ellis enjoys travel, reading and kick boxing.

Sylvie Grimes

Distributed Computer Systems Analyst
Leon County Health Department
2065 Municipal Way
Tallahassee, FL 32304
8504873162
Fax: 8504877954

9431

Business Information: A savvy professional, Ms. Grimes serves as the Distributed Computer Systems Analyst of the Leon County Health Department's management information systems department. She fulfills a number of technical functions on behalf of the Department while serving as network and systems administrator and Webmaster. Possessing an excellent understanding of technology, Ms. Grimes is also a supervisor responsible for recommending and approving purchases as well as providing employee evaluations. Providing support for programming, software applications, and installation of hardware and software, and tracking statistics also fall within the realm of Ms. Grimes' responsibilities. In the future, she looks forward to continuing in her line of work, taking joy in helping the Department to help others. A part of Florida state government, the Leon County Health Department provides public health services to residents of Leon County. Working with an annual budget of $7 million, the Department employs four personnel in the management information systems department. Presently, the Department is located in Tallahassee, Florida. **Career Highlights:** Distributed Computer Systems Analyst, Leon County Health Department (1998-Present); Network Administrator, Florida Department of Labor/Division of Blind Services (1995-98); Project Coordinator, IBM/Leon County Conversion Project (1991-93). **Associations & Accomplishments:** Phi Theta Kappa; Davis Productivity Award, Florida Taxwatch (1994); Florida Department of Education Excellence through Teamwork Award (1994); Lambda Delta Sigma Sorority. **Education:** Florida State University, B.S. in Computer Science (In Progress); Tallahassee Community College, A.S. in Networking Technologies (In Progress), A.S. (1995); AT&T/Lucent Technologies Cabling Specialist Certification (1998). **Personal Information:** Married to Robert D. in 1999. Ms. Grimes enjoys speleology, canoeing and gardening. She is currently pursuing Microsoft's MCSE Certification and Cisco's CCNA Certification.

Patty Hubbert

Network Administrator
Spalding County Health Department
1007 Memorial Drive
Griffin, GA 30223
(770) 467-4736
Fax: (770) 229-3169
phub2361@aol.com

9431

Business Information: Serving as Network Administrator for the Spalding County Health Department, Ms. Hubbert presides over the daily operations of Information Systems. She has faithfully served with Spalding County Health Department since joining the Department in 1989. In this capacity, she assumes responsibility for the Department's system implementation as well as the implementation of software. Ms. Hubbert is in charge of hardware and software purchases and provides technical support and training for the systems users. Coordinating resources, time lines, schedules, and assignments also fall within the purview of Ms. Hubbert's responsibilities. Continually striving to improve her performance, she looks forward to a future position as Director. Her success reflects her ability to aggressively tackle new challenges. The Spalding County Health Department provides public health services to the general public of Spalding County, Georgia. Services such as physical examinations, children's immunizations, and the Women, Infant, and Children Program are offered. **Career Highlights:** Network Administrator, Spalding County Health Department (1989-Present). **Associations & Accomplishments:** Business & Professional Women's Association; Georgia Public Health Association; Georgia Government Finance Officers Association; Griffin/Spalding Leadership. **Personal Information:** Married to Michael in 1985. Two children: Andrew and Stephen White. Ms. Hubbert enjoys gardening, latch hook, reading, working and playing with her dogs.

Walter James Hull

Chief of Management Information Services
Ohio Department of Alcohol and Drug Addiction Services
280 North High Street, Floor 12
Columbus, OH 43215-2537
(614) 644-8434
Fax: (614) 752-8645
hull@ada.state.oh.us

9431

Business Information: As Chief of Management Information Services of the Ohio Department of Alcohol and Drug Addiction Services, Mr. Hull provides internal and external support services for hardware, software, and networks used by the Agency. Utilizing a direct, productive style of management, he acheives maximum results from his staff by creating an atmosphere conducive to teamwork. Demonstrating an adept ability, Mr. Hull is noted for the design, installation, and maintenance of LANs and WANs used by the Agency. Additionally, he has created customized sofware applications to improve the overall performance of the Agency, including a touch screen technical program and an automatic reimbursement database system. Mr. Hull also supervises and approves the purchase of software and hardware and often negotiates procurement agreements with vendors. Always alert to new approaches and techniques, he has initiated several in-depth, expansive renovation programs for the Agency's network to increase effectiveness. Attributing his prominence to the firm belief that success is the only option, Mr. Hull intends to continue his career by seeking advancement opportunities within the corporate structure. The Ohio Department of Alcohol and Drug Addiction Services provides planning and funding for alcohol and drug addiction providers in Ohio. Employing 100 people, the Agency strives to create applicable treatments for ease of transition into society for those afflicted. **Career Highlights:** Chief of Management Information Services, Ohio Department of Alcohol and Drug Addiction Services (1989-Present); Management Information Services Coordinator, Ohio Department of Health (1973-89). **Associations & Accomplishments:** National Association of State Information Resource Executives; Ancient Accepted Scottish Rite; Shrine; United Methodist Church; Gamma Beta Phi. **Education:** Temple University, M.A. (1972); Union College, B.A. (1969); Ohio State University; Rutgers University; Western Michigan University. **Personal Information:** Married to Sylvia in 1991. Three children: Christopher, Seth, and Mandy Pfannenschmidt. Mr. Hull enjoys woodworking and collecting German nutcrackers.

Richard P. Milligan

Computer Technician/Analyst
Peterborough County-City Health Unit
Apartment 203, 467 Chamberlain Street
Peterborough, Ontario, Canada K9J 4L3
(705) 743-1000
Fax: (705) 743-7914
rmilliga@peterboro.net

9431

Business Information: With several years of experience in the information technology field, Mr. Milligan serves as Computer Technician and Analyst of Peterborough County-City Health Unit. Overseeing the information systems, he assumes accountability for installing and maintaining five Novell network units, two Unix servers, and a Web server. In the future, he would like to create Web pages for customers over the Internet. Peterborough County-City Health Unit is a non-profit organization engaged in providing community health promotion and protection services to citizens in the Peterborough community. Operating since 1964, the Organization employs 100 professionals. **Career Highlights:** Computer Technician/Analyst, Peterborough County-City Health Unit (1991-Present); Computer Technician/Analyst, Bowes & Cocks Ltd. (1988-91). **Education:** Fleming College, Computer Programming (1987). **Personal Information:** Married to Geesien in 1982. Mr. Milligan enjoys computers, computer graphics, landscape oil painting and cross-country skiing.

Susan E. Watson

Director of Information Technology
Alberta Health and Wellness
10025 Jasper Avenue, 21st Floor
Edmonton, Alberta, Canada T5J 2N3
(780) 415-1503
Fax: (780) 427-2411

9431

Business Information: Ms. Watson has served with Alberta Health and Wellness in various positions since 1989. At the present time, she fulfills the responsibilities of Director of Information Technology. Possessing superior talents in the field, she oversees and directs all day to day adminstration and operational activities. Utilizing her strong management skills, Ms. Watson manages a staff of 25 skilled employees, balances the budget, performs human resources functions, plans marketing and business strategies, and oversees customer relations. In addition, Ms. Watson is responsible for the installation and set up of the computer systems, management and maintenance of hardware and software, and delivery of new systems to the users. Highly regarded, she attributes her success to using a good common sense approach and having excellent communication skills. Proud of her accomplishments, Ms. Watson is currently working on developing and implementing a big project. In the future, she anticipates her promotion to Chief Information Officer with Alberta Health and Wellness as a result of her continuing efforts to increase her skills through training and professional development activities. Alberta Health and Wellness is a government agency responsible for evaluating and monitoring the health care system in the Alberta, Canada. Established in the 1900s, the Agency is located in Edmonton and employs a work force of 20 people to oversee administrative duties and to perform evaluations on the health care system. The Agency is working to improve the health care system and to provide superior medical care for the citizens of Alberta. **Career Highlights:** Alberta Health and Wellness: Director of Information Technology (1998-Present), Head of Information Technology New Development (1989-98); Director of Motor Vehicle Systems, Alberta Socicitos General (1982-89). **Education:** NAIT, Diploma of Applied Arts (1973). **Personal Information:** Married to Robert Lederer in 1986. One child: Steven Lederer.

Michael P. Broward

Information Systems Manager III
New Mexico Department of Labor, Information Systems Bureau
401 Broadway NE
Albuquerque, NM 87103
(505) 841-9002
Fax: (505) 841-8993
mbroward@state.nm.us

9441

Business Information: As Information Systems Manager III of New Mexico Department of Labor, Mr. Broward directs computer activities of two divisions and three departments. Managing Information Systems Bureau's systems function, he is responsible for supervising employment services, overseeing job training, and acting as a labor relations specialist. Dealing with peolpe is an essential part of the job, therefore Mr. Broward strives to establish excellent communication between employers and employees. He is available to answer any questions or concerns on labor issues such as payroll, benefits, compensation, human rights, and other related issues. A savvy, 15 year professional, Mr. Broward oversees three managers who are responsible for directing the activities of their departments and implementing Company policies on a daily basis. Mr. Broward has been recognized numerous times for his skill, dedciation, and achievemnts made in the New Mexico Department of Labor. He hopes to eventually attain the position of Bureau Chief, assuming greater responsibilties and authority. Keeping abreast on new developments and issues in the field, Mr. Broward attends national and regional seminars where he is also able to network, promoting the Department and establishing new business and relationships. New Mexico Department of Labor is the state employment services agency, which also services an Information Systems Bureau. Approxiamtely 10 employees assist in fulfilling various job positions. **Career Highlights:** Information Systems Manager III, New Mexico Department of Labor, Information Systems Bureau (1998-Present); Information Systems Manager, Laguna Industries (1994-98); Senior Systems Analyst, Honeywell DASD (1986-94); Computer Solutions Analyst, Sperry Flight Systems (1984-86). **Associations & Accomplishments:** Toastmaster's International. **Education:** University of Phoenix, B.S. in Business Administration (1988); Aba Technical Vocational Institute, A.A. in Data Processing

Technology (1984). **Personal Information:** Married to Bernadette in 1994. Two children: Philip and Jacky. Mr. Broward enjoys motorcycling, skiing and weightlifting.

James A. Konicki

UI Tax Auditor 2
New York State Department of Labor
State Campus Bloc 12, Room 238A
Albany, NY 12240-0001
(518) 485-5781
Fax: (518) 485-5787
jkonick1@nycap.rr.com

9441

Business Information: As UI Tax Auditor II, Mr. Konicki performs audits and investigations for the New York State Department of Labor. Here, he provides support for the staff conducting audits and investigations. Possessing business savvy and expertise in the technology field, Mr. Konicki is the lead programmer responsible for all aspects of database management systems, coding client servers, and ensuring integrity and reliability of programs as well as making sure systems are in compliance with regulations. Furthermore, Mr. Konicki researches and reports on studies of industry compliances. A proven performer, he designed the entire tax program for the Department. Always alert to new and upcoming technology techniques, Mr. Konicki intends to remain in the technology field, further automation, and redesign and reengineer the infrastructure of the Department to a paperless system. His ability to influence people is cited as his reasons for success. A state agency, the New York State Department of Labor engages in administering and enforcing laws promoting the welfare of wage earners, thereby improving their working conditions as well as advancing their opportunities for employment. Currently, the Department employs the skilled services of 300 individuals. **Career Highlights:** New York State Department of Labor: UI Tax Auditor II (1994-Present), UI Tax Auditor 1 (1991-94); Accounts Receivable Supervisor, New York State Association for Retarded Children. **Associations & Accomplishments:** Association of Government Accountants; Albany Polish American Citizens Club; Pomost International. **Education:** Canisius College: B.S. (1991), A.A. (1988). **Personal Information:** Married to Renee in 1996. Two children: Adam and Stephanie. Mr. Konicki enjoys Polish history, language culture, cooking and surfing the Internet.

Brian V. Rhodes
Systems Analyst
Illinois Department of Children and Family Services
2916 Rend Drive
Springfield, IL 62707-6903
(217) 524-3556
bvrhodes@fgi.net

9441

Business Information: As a Systems Analyst for the Illinois Department of Children and Family Services, Mr. Rhodes writes new and maintains existing programs to maintain the functionality and oerational status of the systems infrastructure. Possessing superior talents and an excellent understanding of technology, he also analyzes data used to specify and design new solutions in which to harness more of the computer's power. Mr. Rhodes utilizes his extensive educational and work experiences to tailor programs and systems to meet the special needs of the Department. He maintains his competitive edge through networking and reading industry related literature. In the future, Mr. Rhodes plans on attaining the position of Senior Analyst and also a management role. He aspires to keep on advancing and staying on top of technology. The Illinois Department of Children and Family Services is a department of the state government. The Department tracks information concerning foster children's medical treatments, foster parents, and child abuse and adoption records. Located in Springfield, Illinois, the Department presently employs a work force of more than 1,000 professional, counseling, and administrative staff. **Career Highlights:** Systems Analyst, Illinois Department of Children and Family Services (1997-Present); Programmer Analyst III, Illinois Department of Public Aid (1993-97); Systems Program Analyst, Systems Evaluation and Analysis Group (1991-92). **Associations & Accomplishments:** Knights of Columbus; Fraternal Order of Eagles. **Education:** Southern Illinois University at Carbondale, Bachelor's degree (1991); Associate's degree in Computer Information Processing. **Personal Information:** Married to Dorothy in 1992. One child: Megan. Mr. Rhodes enjoys coin collecting, computers and playing darts.

Robert P. Bubniak
Associate Deputy Assistant Secretary for Telecommunications
Department of Veterans Affairs
810 Vermont Avenue NW
Washington, DC 20420-0001
(202) 273-8069
Fax: (202) 273-5401
robert.bubniak@mail.va.gov

9451

Business Information: A successful, 39 year veteran of the communications field, Mr. Bubniak currently fulfills the responsibility of Associate Deputy Assistant Secretary for Telecommunications of the Department of Veterans Affairs. He determines the overall strategic direction and formulates new technology plans to keep the Department in the forefront of emerging technology. In this context, Mr. Bubniak is accountable for planning, organizing, and implementing a full range of information technology services, such as voice, data, radio, and imaging services. Maintaining the WAN interconnectivity of three central databases functional and operational, Mr. Bubniak ensures real time data availability for 172 medical centers, 58 benefit offices, over 600 out-patient centers, and 200 counseling centers. Possessing a strong academic background, he graduated from the National Defense University's Information Resource Management College. Also, Mr. Bubniak attended the Signal Officer Basic and Advance Course while serving in the United States Army. His future plans include attaining the position of vice president of a telecommunications firm. The Department of Veterans Affairs operates as a federal agency responsible for administering health care and benefits for veterans of the armed forces. Headquartered in Washington, D.C., the Department presently serves more than 26 million veterans and their dependents. A staff of over 230,000 assists in daily operations of the Department and satellite offices located across the country. **Career Highlights:** Associate Deputy Assistant Secretary for Telecommunications, Department of Veterans Affairs (1998-Present); Chief of Telecommunications, Department of the State (1987-98). **Associations & Accomplishments:** Past President, National Capitol Chapter, Independent Telecommunications Pioneer Association; Past President, Returned and Services League of Australia, Washington, DC Chapter; Founder/Past President, Dike Club of Washington, DC; Co-founder/Executive Vece-President, Armed Forces Broadcasters Association; Chairman, Federal Technology Service Interagency Management Council; Federal Technology Service. **Education:** The American University, M.A. (1974); Syracuse University, A.B. **Personal Information:** Married to Joan in 1961. Two children: Alison and Erica. Mr. Bubniak enjoys tennis and reading.

Robert N. Huffman
Systems Manager
Veterans Administration Medical Center
Rural Route 9
Martinsburg, WV 25401-9809
(304) 263-0811
Fax: (304) 264-3988

9451

Business Information: Mr. Huffman functions in the role of Systems Manager for the Veterans Administration Medical Center in Martinsburg, West Virginia. He is responsible for overseeing the entire systems and network infrastructure at the Center, as well as monitoring the activities of the computer databases. Eliminating data redundancy and tuning software tools to improve database performance also fall within the realm of Mr. Huffman's responsibilities. Looking to the 21st Century, Mr. Huffman plans on continuing with technology and remaining on track within the industry. Attributing his success to always doing his best, one of his career highlights include being a 10 year veteran of the United States Navy. Veterans Administration Medical Center is a branch of the Department of Veterans Affairs that accommodates the medical needs of veterans. At its location in Martinsburg, West Virginia, the Martinsburg Veterans Administration Medical Center is a 99-bed primary and secondary care facility, providing medical, surgical, and psychiatric services. Long-term care is provided in a 148-bed nursing home care unit and 312-bed domiciliary. A full range of medical, surgical, and psychiatric outpatient services are offered. **Career Highlights:** Systems Manager, Veterans Administration Medical Center (1974-Present); Yeoman, United States Navy (1965-74). **Associations & Accomplishments:** Air National Guard, Retired; Boy Scouts of America; Knights of Columbus; United States Navy. **Education:** United States Navy, Technical Schools. **Personal Information:** Married to Mary in 1969.

Two children: Rachel Stack and Ann. Mr. Huffman enjoys scouting, camping, hiking and fishing.

9500 Environmental Quality and Housing

9511 Air, water, and solid waste management
9512 Land, mineral, and wildlife conservation
9531 Housing programs
9532 Urban and community development

Daniel J. Clark
Local Area Network Administrator
Michigan Department of Environmental Quality
333 South Capitol
Lansing, MI 48933
(517) 335-6808
Fax: (603) 917-2660
clarkdj@state.mi.us

9511

Business Information: Mr. Clark functions in the role of Local Area Network Administrator for the Michigan Department of Environmental Quality. He oversees and controls database administration and is involved in setting up and installing new computer and database systems within the surrounding offices. A savvy, 14 year professional, Mr. Clark puts offices online, programs database user-interfaces, and troubleshoots network usage and computer peripherals. Performing system backups and data recovery and resolving communications problems also fall within the realm of his responsibilities. In the future, Mr. Clark hopes to expand the Department, complete his NT networking certification while staying abreast of certification. His success is attributed to a strong desire to learn and his ability to produce results and aggressively take on new challenges. Michigan Department of Environmental Quality is a state government agency specializing in guaranteeing the superior quality of the environmental habitat of the state of Michigan. Established by local legislators originally to monitor the effect of harmful chemicals on the surrounding habitat, the Department is now involved with tracking and distrubuting low interest loans to needy communities. The Department is striving to upgrade their waste and drinking water systems to improve their environmental quality for the protection of public health and natural resources. **Career Highlights:** Local Area Network Administrator, Michigan Department of Environmental Quality (1994-Present); Microcomputer Support Technician, Michigan Department of Social Services (1990-94); Microcomputer Support Technician, Michigan Department Treasury (1985-90). **Associations & Accomplishments:** Certified Novell Engineer; Microsoft Professional; ISCET; Author, SRF and DWRF Databases. **Education:** University of Michigan, B.S. (1990); Certified Electronics Technician; Certified Computer Technician; Advanced Computer Technician; Computer Programming; Microsoft Certified Professional. **Personal Information:** Mr. Clark enjoys contributing columnist and designing database.

Mark Day
Deputy Chief Information Officer
United States Environmental Protection Agency
401 M Street SW
Washington, DC 20460
(202) 260-4465
Fax: (202) 260-4542
day.mark@epa.gov

9511

Business Information: Serving as Deputy Chief Information Officer of United States Environmental Protection Agency or US EPA, Mr. Day directs the daily operations of the information technnology department. To ensure maximum effectiveness of the Agency, it is essential that locations from across the country can communicate quickly with each other. Mr. Day fulfills this need by installing and maintaining headquarters Intranets. Supervising a staff of 184 employees and 1,000 contractors, he utilizes his 13 years of industrial experience to formulate and implement innovative strategic planning and technical solutions. Internally recognized for his achievments within the Agency, he was named the "Top Innovator" of 1999 for his creative, applicable contributions to society. Crediting his success to his ability to communicate technical statistics into accessable information, Mr. Day plans to seek business opportunities within the private sector aspiring to the position of Chief Information Officer. The US EPA sets regulations for protection of the resources of the country. Operating with a $7 billion budget, the Agency is staffed by 18,000 employees in Washington, D.C., in addition to the 18,000 nationwide employees. These dedicated employees strive to maintain and improve the United States by organizing studies to monitor the effects of particular situations, inspecting potential hazards, and enforcing complicance of the policies set. **Career Highlights:** United States Environmental Protection Agency: Deputy Chief Information Officer (1997-Present), Director of Information Resource Planning (1995-97); Missouri Department of Natural Resources: Chief Information Officer/Environmental Quality (1987-92), Director Residental Energy (1983-86). **Associations & Accomplishments:** Adjunct Professor, George Mason University at Virginia. **Education:** Southwest Baptist University, B.A. magna cum laude (1997). **Personal Information:** One child: Rachel. Mr. Day enjoys reading, history, roses and NASCAR.

Thang Diep

Computer Programmer
State Water Resource Control Board; SWRCB
3929 48th Avenue, Apartment 14
Sacramento, CA 95823
(916) 657-0903
Fax: (916) 391-3427
q_diep@hotmail.com

9511

Business Information: Serving as Computer Programmer for the State Water Resource Control Board of California or SWRCB, Mr. Diep oversees a number of duties on behalf of the Board and its customers. He is responsible for the maintenance and upgrade of all systems programs utilized within the Department. His day to day functions include working with the stenewater unit, managing database information, processing customer information, and offering technical support to all system users. With more than four years of professional engineering experience, Mr. Diep is utilizing his superior knowledge and expertise to devise plans for continuing in his current capacity. His success is attributed to his ability to think outside-the-box, take on challenges, and deliver results. SWRCB is a state government office that engages in the prevention of water polution. The Department contracts various professionals to test water resources for contaminants, while also incorporating the expertise of water works employees for comprehensive water treatment. Local operations in Sacramento, California employs more than 500 professinals to orchestrate all activities of testing and research. **Career Highlights:** Computer Programmer, State Water Resource Control Board; SWRCB (1997-Present); Paper Boy, Sacto Bee (1995). **Education:** Computer and Mechanical Engineering degree (In Progress). **Personal Information:** Mr. Diep enjoys learning and evaluating the newest software.

Toni Trinette Frazier-Rousey

Program Analyst
United States Environmental Protection Agency
1200 Pennsylvania Avenue NW
Washington, DC 20004
(202) 564-5979
Fax: (202) 501-0656
rousey.toni@epa.gov

9511

Business Information: Mrs. Frazier-Rousey has faithfully served with the United States Environmental Protection Agency in a variety of positions since joining the Agency's team of professionals as Executive Office Manager in 1999. She is responsible for developing, executing, and evaluating systems and processes related to strategic planning, communications and outreach, and decision-making in support of the director's priority programs and activities. Highly regarded by her supervisor and her colleagues, Mrs. Frazier-Rousey possesses an excellent understanding of environmental management and matters and concerns of corporate businesses and the public. Mrs. Frazier-Rousey's future plans include remaining with the Agency in order to continue contributing to the successful management of the environment. Her success reflects her ability to take on challenges and new responsibilities and deliver results on behalf of the Agency. The United States Environmental Protection Agency engages in the safeguarging of the natural environment, air, water, and land, upon which life depends. Protecting human health, the Agency was established in 1970, and now operates out of 14 offices to provide various services to public establishments, such as natural parks, landfills, water systems, wildlife, and other organizations which protect natural resources. **Career Highlights:** United States Environmental Protection Agency: Program Analyst (1998-Present), Staff Assistant to Director (1997-98), Executive Office Manager (1991-97). **Associations & Accomplishments:** National United Church Ushers Association of America, Inc. **Education:** Central Senior High. **Personal Information:** Married to Harry G., II Two children: Tesha Frazier and Seth. Mrs. Frazier-Rousey enjoys reading the Bible, singing and listening to music.

Matthew J. Heringer

Computer Systems Specialist
Ministry of the Environment
331-435 James Street South
Thunder Bay, Ontario, Canada P7E 6S7
(807) 475-1721
Fax: (807) 475-1754
heringma@ene.gov.on.ca

9511

Business Information: Joining the Ministry of the Environment in 1980, Mr. Heringer serves as Computer Systems Specialist. In his role, he manages the Northern region computer systems infrastructure, ensuring the functionality and operational status of the systems function at six different offices located throughout Ontario, Canada. Possessing an excellent understanding of technology, Mr. Heringer is responsible for all aspects of WAN, Internet, and Intranet networks, including security and support functions. Planning the technology budget is also an integral part of his responsibilities. Attributing his career success to effective listening skills and patience, Mr. Heringer's goals include helping the Ministry change with technology and introducing new innovations. The Ministry of the Environment is a government agency that closely monitors air, water, and sewage for Ontario, Canada. The Agency conducts remote monitoring of the environment using telementry systems and also monitors industries, ensuring compliance of government environmental regulations. Currently, the Ministry of the Environment is manned by 1,500 dedicated individuals. **Career Highlights:** Computer Systems Specialist, Ministry of the Environment (1980-Present); Systems Coordinator, Ministry of Natural Resources (1979-80). **Education:** Lakehead University (1976); Confederated College (1980). **Personal Information:** Married to Lena in 1980. Five children: Jeff, Sean, Christopher, David, and Brian. Mr. Heringer enjoys hockey, scuba diving, baseball, softball, water skiing, downhill skiing and coaching. Mr. Heringer also coaches and covers hockey and baseball and promotes and lives by the philosophy that "an active mind is a productive mind; steer children in the right direction and they will prosper."

Gary A. McDanel

Team Leader of Engineering Support
United States Bureau of Reclamation
P.O. Box 36900
Billings, MT 59107
(406) 247-7659
Fax: (406) 247-7898
gmcdanel@gp.usbr.gov

9511

Business Information: As Team Leader of Enginnering Support for the United States Bureau of Reclamation, Mr. McDanel is responsible for accurate and timely engineering information relevant to the current projects. Providing computer-aided design and drafting is also an integral part of his team leader functions. Working closely with his team of associates, Mr. McDanel utilizes a management style that incorporates input and feedback from staff members in the drawing of records and showing of designs. It is Mr. McDanel's responsibility to ensure software is up and working, including digital photography. A leader in establishing electronic data systems, Mr. McDanel's goal is to improve the current systems and move forward. His success reflects his ability to build teams with synergy and technical strength, take on challenges, and deliver results. United States Bureau of Reclamation, established in the 1920s, is a department of the United States Government dedicated to reclaiming and maintaining deserts, dams, and reservoirs. The Great Plains regional office located in Billings, Montana employees 10 highly skilled individuals to investigate and oversee hydroelectric power and water levels of current projects. **Career Highlights:** Team Leader of Engineering Support, United States Bureau of Reclamation (1992-Present). **Associations & Accomplishments:** City Council, City of Billings. **Personal Information:** Married to Adelita in 1978. Three children.

Mohammad Pakuwibowo

Information Technology Manager
Skafab
Box 92172, Hammarbyvägen 71
Stockholm, Sweden 12008
+46 87729331
Fax: +46 86401940
mohammad.pakuwibowo@skafab.stockholm.se

9511

Business Information: Following 16 solid years of working with SL, Mr. Pakuwibowo was recruited to the Skafab team in 1991. At the present time, he assumes the responsibilities of Information Technology Manager. In his capacity, he exercises oversight of all aspects of the Company's day-to-day information technology operations. Mr. Pakuwibowo, with over seven years of experience in the field and with a firm academic base, is responsible for his staff, acting as liaison with operations, program support, training program, and coordinating new technologies objectives. Directing and participating in the analysis, acquisition, installation, modification, configuration, support, and tracking of operating systems, databases, utilities, software, and hardware also fall within the realm of Mr. Pakuwibowo's responsibilities. His focus is on providing assistance and advice to users, interpreting problems, and designing new solutions to help the Company realize the maximum benefit from the investment in equipment, personnel, and waste cycle processes. Skafab operates as a waste recycling company. Targeting Stockholm households and restaurants who respectively produce approximately 200,000 and 25,000 tons of waste annually, Skafab ensures clients comply with sorting requirements prior to pickup. Once processed, the Company then markets reusable waste to industries. Established in 1976, the Company is headquartered in Stockholm, Sweden. Presently, Skafab employs 110 professional, technical, and support staff generating in excess of 250 million SEK. **Career Highlights:** Information Technology Manager, Skafab (1991-Present); SL: Traffic Production Planner (1988-91), Bus Driver (1975-88). **Associations & Accomplishments:** JUSEK; Dataföeringen; During his student years, Mr. Pakuwibowo was Chairman of the Coordinating Body of Indonesian Students Associations in Europe (1963-70). **Education:** The Prague School of Economics, M.S. (1970); Educational, Computer, and Network Courses. **Personal Information:** Married to Adeline in 1968. One child: Yanto. Mr. Pakuwibowo enjoys reading books, badminton, travel and jogging.

Jeanette E. Paul

Database Administrator
TNRCC
P.O. Box 13087-Industrail Emissions MC-164
Austin, TX 78711
(512) 239-1929
Fax: (512) 239-1515
jpaul@tnrcc.state.tx.us

9511

Business Information: As Database Administrator of TNRCC or Texas Natural Resource Conversation Commission, Ms. Paul assumes the responsibility for ensuring that the Commission's data information is in order and enables the employees to access that information easily and efficiently. She has assertively served with TNRCC in a variety of roles since joining the Commission as Administrative Technician. She performs application development with Sterling design, Window implementation testing, and data model development. Administering and controlling data resources, ensuring data integrity and security, and tuning software tools to enhance the overall performance also fall within the purview of Ms. Paul's responsibilities. Attributing her success to perseverance and strategic planning, Ms. Paul plans to become Microsoft Systems Engineer certified. Employing a work force of approximately 3,000 individuals, TNRCC is the state of Texas' leading environmental agency. The Commission is involved in administering the rules and regulations relating to most areas of the Texas environment such as water, air, and solid waste. The Commission works with a yearly appropriated budget of $369 million. **Career Highlights:** TNRCC: Database Administrator (Present), System Support Specialist, Administrative Technician. **Education:** Shenandoah Conservatory: Bachelor's degree in Music in Piano Performance (1986), Bachelor's degree in Music in Piano Composition (1986); Juilliard School of Music. **Personal Information:** Married to Mark. One child: Melissa. Ms. Paul enjoys playing the piano.

Albert W. Stockell

Information Systems Analyst 4
State of Tennessee Department of Environment and Conservation
401 Church Street, 15th Floor LNC Tower
Nashville, TN 37219
(615) 532-0253
Fax: (615) 532-1199
astockell@mail.state.tn.us

9511

Business Information: As Information Systems Analyst 4 of State of Tennessee Department of Environment and Conservation, Mr. Stockell works directly with management and users to analyze, specify, and design new applications. An experience, 15-year veteran of information systems technology, he has served with the State of Tennessee in a variety of capacities since joining the Department of Environment and Conservation team of professionals. He is an expert who delivers results by effectively using technology and solving problems and challenges in a highly efficient manner. Mr. Stockell's present role involves systems programming using PowerBuilder; working on technical projects and being part of a team built with synergy, technical strength, and customer oriented focus; and building state-of-the-art environmental and conservation applications on site. Troubleshooting difficulties, conducting inventories and determining resource requirements, and deploying advanced technologies within the Department of Environment and Conservation also fall within the purview of Mr. Stockell's responsibilities. His focus is helping the Department maintain flexibility and efficiency in the conduct of day-to-day administration and operational activities. An ex-Marine and retired Naval Reservist, he attributes his success to being in the right place at the right time, and taking advantage of opportunities. Continue with what he is doing and eventually retire and get into the consulting business serves as a few of his future goals. State of Tennessee Department of Environment and Conservation is responsible for monitoring state streams, pollution, treatment plans and forestry. Founded in 1796, the state of Tennessee employs a work force of more than 40,000 civil servants. **Career Highlights:** State of Tennessee Department of Environment and Conservation: Information Systems Analyst 4 (1996-Present), Information Systems Analyst 3 (1989-96), Information Systems Analyst 2 (1984-89). **Associations & Accomplishments:** Sons of the American Revolution; American Legion; Veterans of Foreign Wars; Who's Who of the South and Southwest. **Education:** Nashville State Technical Institute, A.S. (1984).

James C. Berry

Computer Specialist
USDA Forest Service, HMR
1621 North Kent Street, Room 900
Arlington, VA 22209
(703) 605-5200
Fax: (703) 605-5105
cberry/wo@fs.fed.us

9512

Business Information: Functioning in the role of Computer Specialist for the USDA Forest Service, HMR, Mr. Berry is a program leader for implementation of human resource management. He is responsible for supporting users, analysis of needs, and manages projects. Mr. Berry joined the USDA Forest Service, HMR in 1981. An expert, he establishes high standards of excellence for other individuals in the industry. As an 18 year technology professional, he owns an established record of producing results in support of USDA objectives and goals. His success reflects his leadership ability to effectively coordinate resources, schedules, time lines, and assignments. Mr. Berry plans to expedite continued promotion through the fulfillment of his responsibilities and his involvement in the advancement of operations. He aspires to eventually attain the position of Manager of Human Resources for the Department. The USDA Forest Service, HMR manages vast amounts of road, lands in the national forest, and recreational areas. Established in 1905, the Department employs a domestic staff of 30,000 employees to orchestrate every aspect of managing the large amounts of land under their supervision. **Career Highlights:** Computer Specialist, USDA Forest Service, HMR (1981-Present); **Associations & Accomplishments:** The Ballyshaners, Inc.

Kelly A. Griggs

Computer Specialist
Minerals Management Services
1201 Elmwood Park Boulevard
New Orleans, LA 70123-2394
(504) 731-3009
Fax: (504) 731-3004
kelly.griggs@mms.gov

9512

Business Information: As Computer Specialist of Minerals Management Services, Mr. Griggs oversees all systems integragation, facility design, computer room design, and new technology acquisitions. The Agency relies on his expertise in the technological area to ensure all aspects of the operation run according to the overall plan. His skill, knowledge, and determination were all acquired through extensive educational ties and hands on experience. Understanding the ever changing field of technology, Mr. Griggs keeps abreast by reading current literature, networking and interacting with colleagues, and attending professional seminars. His professional accomplishments include redesigning the offshore corporate database and designing all computer rooms. Minerals Management Services, established in 1982, is part of the U.S. Department of Interior. The regulatory agency's purpose is to manage the mineral resources of the outer continental shelf in an environmentally safe manner. The Agency collects, verifies, and distributes mineral revenues from Federal and Indian lands. A team consisting of 1,000 people lend their expertise in various areas of the operation. **Career Highlights:** Minerals Management Services: Computer Specialist (1996-Present), Computer Specialist/Database Administrator (1992-96), Computer Specialist/Applications Development Analyst (1990-92), Supervisory Computer Specialist (1987-90). **Education:** University of New Orleans, B.S. in Computer Science (1984). **Personal Information:** Married to Deborah in 1991. Three children: Charles Andrew and Step Children: Brandi N. and Joshua S. Ward. Mr. Griggs enjoys hiking.

Jeanette M. Gum

Technical Support Supervisor
Oregon Department of Forestry
2600 State Street
Salem, OR 97310
(503) 945-7271
Fax: (503) 945-7314
jgum@odf.state.or.us

9512

Business Information: Serving as the Technical Support Supervisor of Oregon Department of Forestry, Mrs. Gum maintains the Department's information technology infrastructure. Utilizing skills she has gained throughout the past 12 years, she manages the Department's network, evaluates software and hardware, conducts research and development, and ensures all systems are running properly to support over 1,100 users. In the future, Mrs. Gum plans to continue in her current role, and is looking forward to implementing new, more advanced systems. Her professional success reflects her ability to take on challenges and deliver results on behalf of the Department of Forestry. Established in 1911, the Oregon Department of Forestry is responsible for planting trees and caring for the state's forests. A division of Oregon's state government, the Department maintains 40 offices located throughout the state. **Career Highlights:** Oregon Department Forestry: Technical Support Manager (1998-Present), Senior Network Administrator (1988-98); Supervisor Computer Specialist, U.S. Forest Service (1980-88). **Associations & Accomplishments:** State Management Association; Agency Leadership (1999); Oregon Leadership (1999). **Education:** Linn Benton Community College, degreee in Business (1999); Microsoft University, Microsoft Certified; GTE University; Portland State University. **Personal Information:** Married to Harold in 1994. Two children: Yvonne Snider and Launa Periman. Mrs. Gum enjoys travel, day trading, quilting and camping.

William Lyle Lobato

Computer Specialist
Minerals Management Services
770 Paseo Camarillo
Camarillo, CA 93010
(805) 389-7636
Fax: (805) 389-7637
william.lobato@mms.com

9512

Business Information: Mr. Lobato functions as a Computer Specialist of Minerals Management Services, responsible for working and maintaining the Company's computer infrastructure. Overseeing all day-to-day operations, he installs various equipment including software, printers, and internal components, as well as retrieves files. Utilizing his knowledge and skills in a problem solving capacity, Mr. Lobato implements the means for computer technology to meet the needs of individuals or businesses. His plans include attaining the position of Chief of Automated Data Processing, assuming greater responsibilities and authority. Srategic plans include converting old mainframes to NT platforms and migrating over 110 PCs from CC Mail to Microsoft Exchange. Professional success can be attributed to Mr. Lobato' knowledge, perseverence, dedication, and a "middle of the road" personality. Minerals Management Services is a business involved with the federal government. Currently employing approximately 140 dedicated workers and headquartered in Herndan, Virginia, the Copmany operates a network of 10 office locations. Presently, the Company offers leasing and selling of mineral rights and offshore gas and oil rights. **Career Highlights:** Computer Specialist, Minerals Management Services (1984-Present); Clerk, Department of Motor Vehicles (1983-84); Assistant Manager, Chief Auto Parts (1982-83). **Associations & Accomplishments:** Knights of Columbus; Camarillo Pony Baseball Association. **Education:** California Polytechnic at Pomona, B.S. (1982).

Robin L. Perez

System Administrator
Bureau of Land Management
300 South Richmond Road
Ridgecrest, CA 93555
(760) 384-5412

9512

Business Information: Demonstrating extensive skills in the technology field, Ms. Perez serves as System Administrator for the Bureau of Land Management. She has served with the Bureau of Land Management in a variety of roles since joining the Bureau as a Computer Assistant and Student Trainee in 1993. In her present position, Mrs. Perez performs system administration, maintenance of the local area network, and handles all software and hardware aspects for the Ridgecrest Field Office. Additionally, she administrates all e-mail functions, training users on the Lotus e-mail packages as well as the Windows 95, NT, and UNIX operating systems. An expert, Ms. Perez continues to grow professionally through the fulfillment of her responsibilities and involvement in the advancement of operations. Her career success reflects her ability to think outside-the-box and aggressively take on new challenges. A government agency, the Bureau of Land Management is a division of the Department of the Interior. The Bureau is responsible for the conservation and land management of the state of California. The Ridgecrest Field Office is located in the California Desert District and employs 55 dedicated individuals to perform its services. **Career Highlights:** Bureau of Land Management: System Administrator (1995-Present), Computer Assistant/Student Trainee (1993-95); Configuration and Documentation Assistant, Comarco (1990-93). **Associations & Accomplishments:** Alpha Kappa Psi-Professional Business Fraternity, Mu Upsilon Chapter. **Education:** California State University at Bakersfield, Bachelor's degree (1998); BLM Nation Training Center: UNIX training courses, PC based training courses. **Personal Information:** Ms. Perez enjoys working on computers for friends and family.

Waheed H. Ansari

Assistant Director of Systems of Network
Illinois Housing Development Authority
401 North Michigan Avenue
Chicago, IL 60611
(312) 836-5255
Fax: (312) 832-2180
wansari@ihda.org

9531

Business Information: As the Assistant Director of Systems and Network for the Illinois Housing Development Authority, Mr. Ansari supervises a group of five technical people who work to manage Novell, Network, NT, and Sun and UNIX systems. Utilizing 15 years of experience in the field, Mr. Ansari is responsible for designing the network and the infrastructure. Mr. Ansari's advice is that a person get as much knowledge as possible and decide what area is desirable for employment. He attributes his success to a great amount of reading he has done, which has helped to increase his knowledge in the field. Illinois Housing Development Authority is a quasi government agency that serves as a mortgage management organization. Employing 200 individuals, the Agency reports annual revenue of $8 million. The Agency also manages a number of retirement homes. The Agency helps families to buy homes by providing money to lend to these families. **Career Highlights:** Assistant Director of Systems and Network, Illinois Housing Development Authority (1997-Present); Systems Manager, University of Illnois (1994-97); Systems Manager, Digital Equipment Corporation (1985-94). **Education:** Northeastern Illinois University, B.S. in Computer Science (1985). **Personal Information:** Married to Mona in 1988. Two children: Farrah and Shaan. Mr. Ansari enjoys computers, reading and travel.

Wesley A. Dumeer

Data Center Manager
Virginia Housing Development Authority
601 South Belvidere
Richmond, VA 23234-6504
(804) 343-5806
Fax: (804) 343-8640
wes.dumeer@vhda.com

9531

Business Information: As the Data Center Manager, Mr. Dumeer manages a staff of systems administrators responsible for maintaining all VHDA computer systems. He ensures that all business applications personnel have access to the appropriate systems and data to support the daily operation of the most successful housing authority in the United States. He ensures that VHDA production systems and data are safe and secure from outside sources. Founded in 1972, VHDA employs the skilled services of more than 300 associates that work together in support of a common mission "To help fellow Virginians obtain safe, sound, and decent housing otherwise unaffordable to them." VHDA assists low to moderate income families to achieve their goal to own a home of their own. **Career Highlights:** Data Center Manager, Virginia Housing Development Authority (1999-Present); Data Center Manager, Fruit of the Loom (1996-99); Data Center Manager, Richfood, Inc. (1994-96); Director of Technical Services and Computer Operations, First Dominion Mutual Life Insurance Company (1990-94); Manager, Financial Systems, Aetna Life Insurance Company (1981-89). **Education:** Computer Processing Institute, Advanced Computer Programming degree (1971). **Personal Information:** Married to Linda in 1970. Two children:

Matthew and David. Mr. Dumeer enjoys golf and family oriented activities.

Vincent S. Tong
Management Information Systems Technician
Chester Housing Authority
1010 Madison Street
Chester, PA 19013
(610) 876-5561
chamis@bellatlantic.net

9531

Business Information: Providing his skilled services as Management Information Systems Technician for the Chester Housing Authority, Mr. Tong stands as the Agency's only technical employee. As such, he assumes responsibility for every aspect of technical operations from networking systems to user technical support. He oversees the Agency's software and application implementation, system maintenance, and PC repair, as well as troubleshooting problems as they arise. Crediting his success to an exceptional ability to learn and network, he has received internal recognition for his outstanding performance. Mr. Tong plans to continue in his current position, keeping the Agency up to date as technology changes. Founded in the 1800s, Chester Housing Authority is a local government agency designed to deal with housing and real estate issues for the local community. The Agency works with Section A housing and other programs, employing 100 dedicated personnel members throughout its five office locations. **Career Highlights:** Management Information Systems Technician, Chester Housing Authority (1997-Present); Management Information Systems Manager, Luen Tat Electrical Engineering Ltd. (1995-97); Systems Administrator, Nancy Electronics Industrial Company Ltd. (1993-95). **Associations & Accomplishments:** Novell Association; The Chartered Association of Certified Accountants; Information Systems Audit and Control Association. **Education:** Pennsylvania State University, B.S. (1991). **Personal Information:** Mr. Tong enjoys golf and computers.

Michael L. Walker
Senior Information Systems Auditor
HUD Office of Inspector General
451 Seventh Street SW, Room 8172
Washington, DC 20410
(202) 708-3444
Fax: (202) 401-4920
michael_l._walkek@hud.gov

9531

Business Information: Recruited to the HUD Office of Inspector General in 1992, Mr. Walker currently serves as a Senior Information Systems Auditor for the OIG's Information System Audit Division. In this capacity, he manages the audits dealing with telecommunications, mainframes, the Internet, and client server utility programs. After each audit, he issues reports to HUD on the results. Mr. Walker has been recognized for his extraordinary performance in past audits and credits his success to perseverance and hard work. He is always working to improve himself by gaining knowledge and experience, taking success one step at a time. Striving to improve performance, Mr. Walker is continually formulating new goals and objectives. His future aspirations include eventually retiring and going into the private sector. Established in 1965, the Housing and Urban Development agency provides funding for those members of the population who are having difficulty in paying for adequate housing. HUD's vision is to provide a decent, safe, and sanitary home and suitable living environment for every American. Presently, the Office of Inspector General employs a staff of 16 individuals. The HUD Office of Inspector General is an independent department within the agency and is responsible for performing audits and investigating potential fraud. **Career Highlights:** Senior Information Systems Auditor, HUD Office of Inspector General (1992-Present); Supervisory Auditor, Department of Transportation Office of Inspector General (1982-92); Auditor, United States General Accounting Office (1976-79). **Associations & Accomplishments:** Information Systems Audit & Control Association; Association of Certified Fraud Examiners; Association of Governmental Financial Managers. **Education:** Delaware State University, degree in Business Administration (1974); United States Army, Command and General Staff College. **Personal Information:** Married to Patricia in 1972. Two children: Michael and Andrew. Mr. Walker enjoys blacksmithing and gardening.

Thomas A. Ruddiman
Project Manager
Portland Development Commission
1900 Southwest Fourth Avenue, Suite 7000
Portland, OR 97201
(503) 823-3289
Fax: (503) 279-1883
truddiman@portlanddev.org

9532

Business Information: In 1997, Mr. Ruddiman began his career with Portland Development Commission as a Senior Budget Analyst. Today he serves as Project Manager, a position that entails a multitude of responsibilities on a daily basis. He is concerned with the progress of various programs and projects that pertain to rental housing statistics and scheduling processes. Recognized for his accuracy and efficiency, he is also in charge of auditing and accounting requirements. With impressive technical abilities, he oversees software implementation, handling troubleshooting or maintenance issues as the need arises. Enjoying the challenges his position presents, Mr. Ruddiman intends to continue in his current capacity as he keeps abreast of technological updates and advances. His success reflects his association with quality people and his ability to aggressively take on new challenges. The state of Oregon established the Portland Development Commission in 1958 to assist the city of Portland with economic development issues. Focusing on job creation, the Commission promotes the city as a progressive, cosmopolitan area when lobbying to potential employers. By creating an environment that is conducive to economic advancement, the Commission entices current companies to remain in the area. Overall, the Commission plays an instrumental role in the lives of Portland residents, planning housing and bringing in new business opportunities. **Career Highlights:** Portland Development Commission: Project Manager (1999-Present), Accounting Manager (1999), Senior Budget Analyst (1997-99). **Associations & Accomplishments:** Vice President/Treasurer/President Elect, Rotary Club of Newport; Newport Lions Club; Board of Trustees, Special Districts Association of Oregon. **Education:** Oregon State University, B.S. in Accounting (1984); Novell Network Training; Microsoft Applications Training. **Personal Information:** One child: Kirsten Marie. Mr. Ruddiman enjoys fishing and skiing.

9600 Administration of Economic Programs

9611 Admin. of general economic programs
9621 Regulation, admin. of transportation
9631 Regulation, admin. of utilities
9641 Regulation of agricultural marketing
9651 Regulation misc. commercial sectors
9661 Space research and technology

Douglas M. Anderson
Software Engineer
Los Angeles County Mass Transit Agency
One Gateway Plaza
Los Angeles, CA 90012
(213) 922-7042
Fax: (213) 922-3961
anderson@mta.net

9621

Business Information: Serving in the capacity of Software Engineer for the Los Angeles County Mass Transit Agency, Mr. Anderson oversees the design and development of telecommunications and computer systems for the customer relations division. Demonstrating an adept ability and extensive technical knowledge, Mr. Anderson formulates both voice processing and geoprocessing capabilities. The end result of his work is a division that accurately provides information such as transportation routes and schedules to customers. Recognized throughout the industry as a gifted leader, Mr. Anderson currently is preparing to retire and establish his own telephony business firm. Attributing his success to enthusiasm, his advice is "learn how things work, both software and hardware. Resulting from a corporate merger over 5 years ago, Los Angeles County Mass Transit Agency employs over 8,000 people throughout the state of California. Operating with a $2.5 billion budget, the Agency oversees all bus, rail, heavy, and light transportation in Los Angeles County. Each day, 1.3 million citizens utilize the services offered as they strive to regulate polution within the City. **Career Highlights:** Software Engineer, Los Angeles County Mass Transit Agency (1994-Present); SCRTD: Senior Systems Analyst (1990-94), Systems Coordinator (1985-90). **Associations & Accomplishments:** Culver

Palms YMCA Annual Campaign Leader. **Education:** West Los Angeles College (1992-93); Price College, (1973-74). **Personal Information:** Married to Paula E. in 1989. Two children: Kelly and Shelby. Mr. Anderson enjoys aerodynamic research, thermodynamic research, backpacking and playing the guitar.

George Anthochy

Computer Specialist
Federal Aviation Administration
4215 Glen Hollow Circle
Arlington, TX 76016
(817) 222-5117
Fax: (817) 222-5952
george.antochy@faa.gov

9621

Business Information: As a Computer Specialist of the Federal Adviation Administration or FAA, Mr. Antochy is responsible for all aspects of day-to-day LAN administration and end-user support and training. Fulfilling the dual role of software mentor and PC support specialist in the rotocraft division, he analyzes and supports computer operations, monitors systems resources, and provides first-line support for operational problems. Possessing technical savvy and expertise, Mr. Anthochy certifies the manufacturers' helicopter production processes, ensuring compliance with industry standards and regulations. A key member of the information technology department within the rotorcraft division, his diverse responsibilities also include administering Lotus Notes and working with microcomputer applications as well as evaluating and intalling both PCs and associated peripherals. Looking to the future, Mr. Anthochy goals include becoming an owner of a successful home networking PC company, or possibly attaining the position of Chief Information Officer for a Fortune 1000 company. Strong work ethic, desire to provide the best products and services to clients, adapting to change, and practicing common sense have contributed to Mr. Anthochy's career success in the field. Founded in 1958, the FAA is an agency of the U.S. government. With a work force of 38,000 professional, technical, and administrative support staff, the Agency's two major priorties are to regulate the air traffic control and navigation systems to ensure the safety of U.S. airways; and provide regulatory compliance of the aircraft manufacturing process and pilot and aircrew training. **Career Highlights:** Computer Specialist, Federal Aviation Administration (1990-Present); Computer Systems Analyst, FKW, Inc. (1988-90); Regional Sales Manager, GTSI (1986-88). **Associations & Accomplishments:** Past Member, Microcomputer Managers Association. **Education:** Bloomsburg University, B.A. in History (1979). **Personal Information:** Married to Laura A. in 1979. Three children: Diana E., Carolyn J., and Eric G. Mr. Anthochy enjoys youth soccer, Cub Scouts, softball, biking and running.

Nicholaos Antoniou

Network and Information Systems Administrator
Transcom
111 Pavonia Avenue, Suite 605
Jersey City, NJ 07310-1955
(201) 963-4033
Fax: (201) 963-4113
antoniou@xcm.org

9621

Business Information: Recruited to Transcom in 1999, Mr. Antoniou serves in the capacity of Network and Information Systems Administrator. He is responsible for the information, communications, network, and system infrastructure. Utilizing his business savvy and technical expertise, he ensures the functionality, operational status, reliability, and security of the agency's networking and operating environment. Before joining Transcom, Mr. Antoniou served as a systems administrator with the New Jersey Institute of Technology. He supervises and manages technical and support people working in the field as well as internal offices. The Agency relies upon Mr. Antoniou to develop and maintain transportation systems used to transmit service allocations and monitor and track accidents, travel speeds, telephony, and private networks. Compiling and analyzing data, he ensures the Agency customers with safe and timely transportation modes. His future plans include remaining with Transcom and completing ongoing projects. Mr. Antoniou attributes his success to his ability to provide software, hardware, and communications networks with the least amount of capital expenditure. An agency of several state governments, Transcom is a coalition of agencies in the New York, New Jersey, and Connecticut metro areas, providing a cooperative, coordinated approach to regional transportation management. Established in 1986, the Agency is located in Jersey City, New Jersey. **Career Highlights:** Network and Information Systems Administrator, Transcom (1999-Present); Systems Administrator, New Jersey Institute of Technology (1992-98). **Associations & Accomplishments:** Institute of Electrical and Electronics Engineers; Association of Computing Machinery. **Education:** New Jersey Institute of Technology: Ph.D. (In Progress), M.S. in Electrical Engineering (1994), B.S. in Computer Engineering (1992). **Personal Information:** Mr. Antoniou enjoys racquetball, motorcycle riding and water activities.

Furat C. Babilla

Information Technology Department Manager
Alameda County, Public Works Agency
399 Elmhurst Street, Room 234
Hayward, CA 94544
(510) 670-6544
Fax: (510) 782-1939
furat@acpwa.mail.co.alameda.ca.us

9621

Business Information: As Information Technology Department Manager of Public Works Agency of Alameda County, Mr. Babilla is responsible for a multitude of duties. He oversees a team of 17 systems engineers, authorizes purchases, conducts research and studies on new devices, and analyzes relevant information. Years of experience in the technology field has enabled Mr. Babilla to acquire the skills and knowledge necessary to effectively fulfill his job obligations with the Public Works Agency. Dedicated to the success of the Alameda County, he keeps abreast on new developments in the field and fields pertinent information into daily activities. Mr. Barilla has made great contributions in support of the Agency and plans to continue to learn and grow professionally. Future aspirations include becoming Information Technology Department Director and recieving his M.B.A. in Information Technology. He also hopes to become a leader in establishing fundamental footnotes in technical advancements throughout the state of California. The Public Works Agency provides all civil, traffic, environmental, and architectural engineering services within Almeda County. Founded in 1968, the Agency employs a staff of 315 individuals to assist in meeting the needs of the local community. **Career Highlights:** Information Technology Department Manager, Public Works Agency, Alameda County (1998-Present); Systems Engineering Consultant, Galoob Toys, Inc. (1998); Systems Engineering Consultant, Entex Information Services (1995-97). **Associations & Accomplishments:** Institute of Electrical and Electronics Engineers; Microsoft Systems Development; Technical Professional Society; BARMA Society. **Education:** University of the Pacific, M.B.A. in Information Technology (In Progress); San Francisco State University, B.S. in Electrical Engineering (1988); High Tech Academy, Certified Novel Engineer; IBM Certified Technician; Microsoft Certified Systems Engineer. **Personal Information:** Mr. Babilla enjoys carpentry, coin collecting, hiking, tennis and soccer.

Connie H. Klass

Information Technology Manager
Virginia Department of Transportation
1700 North Main Street
Suffolk, VA 23434
(757) 925-3665
Fax: (757) 925-3638
klass_ch@vdot.state.va.us

9621

Business Information: Ms. Klass serves as Information Technology Manager for Virginia Department of Transportation. She is responsible for determining the overall strategic direction and business contribution of the systems function. In her capacity, she oversees 12 employees who work in three different divisions: help desk, networking group, and software applications. As coordinater of these three groups, Ms. Klass ensures that all files are updated and flowing smoothly. She prides herself on being a "people person," and her favorite credo is "computers don't talk back." Her future endeavors include transitioning the Department to Microsoft 2000 and eliminating the existing networking platform. Established in 1925, Virginia Department of Transportation is an agency of the state of Virginia organized to deal with primary maintenance and construction of roads. One of the divisions of the Agency is the Information Technology Department. This division supports all technical programs used for desk to users laptop. The Agency employs over 130 inspectors working in remote areas in a 12-county radius who use lap top computers. **Career Highlights:** Information Technolgy Manager, Virginia Department of Transportation (1985-Present). **Education:** Averett College, B.B.A. (1999).

Raymond F. Levesque

Project Analyst
Federal Aviation Administration
800 Independence Avenue SW
Washington, DC 20591
(202) 267-9544
Fax: (202) 267-5580
ray.levesque@faa.gov

9621

Business Information: Serving as Project Analyst for the Federal Aviation Administration, Mr. Levesque is charged with the overall success of the aircraft inspection process. He is responsible for daily compliancy testing including equipment inventories, systems checks, mechanical function, structural stability, and maintenance logs. Also performing systems analyst duties, Mr. Levesque conducts systems evaluations, program accents, and systems diagnosis. Leading the Federal Aviation Administration to achieve an impeccable safety record, Mr. Levesque plans to remain with the Agency to promote public safety and corporate accountability. His success reflects his ability to tackle new challenges and deliver results on behalf of the Agency and the public. The Federal Aviation Administration is a government agency that regulates the aviation industry. Established decades ago, the Agency has grown to employ thousands of people ensure public safety and corporate compliance of aviation laws. Specializing in the regulation of the aircraft industry, the Federal Aviation Administration conducts aircraft inspections, logbook audits, aviation professional testing, policy and procedure development, and accident investigations. Continuing to lead the world in aircraft safety, the Federal Aviation Administration plans to expand operations to more effectively supervise airport activities. **Career Highlights:** Project Analyst, Federal Aviation Administration (1996-Present); Hamilton Standard: Business Manager (1993-96), Senior Proposal/Marketing Manager (1989-93). **Associations & Accomplishments:** Information System Auditing & Control Association. **Education:** Western New England Colle, B.S. in Business Administration and Computer Information Systems (1993). **Personal Information:** Married.

Nancy L. Michaelsen

GIS Programmer/Analyst
Virginia Department of Transportation
9211 Lambs Creek Chruch Road
King George, VA 22485-6901
(703) 383-2262
michaelsen_nl@dot.state.va.us

9621

Business Information: Serving in the dual role of GIS Programmer and Analyst for the Virginia Department of Transportation or VDOT, Ms. Michaelsen is the senior technical resource and project leader for the VDOT user community. She works on multiple projects with tight deadlines. Possessing an excellent understanding of her field, she develops and disseminates customized GIS interfaces adn templates to VDOT users, providing specialized trainining as needed. Highly regarded, Ms. Michaelsen establishes effective business relationships with VDOT GIS users adn GIS experts in other local agencies. Her goals are to maintain and improve the capabilities of the District GIS, incorporating new technology after technical review. Providing GIS quality control and assurance, Ms. Michaelsen uses her technical expertise to incorporate existing and proposed VDOT systems, such as ICAS, PPMS, and HTRIS. Attributing her success to her drive and determination, she would like to develop and implement a natural resource based application and become more GIS literate. Virginia Department of Transportation is responsible for the design, construction, and maintenance of highways and bridges throughout the state. The GIS Department of the Agency is involved in providing geographic information to the Agency about the state of Virginia. **Career Highlights:** GIS Programmer/Analyst, Virginia Department of Transportation (1999-Present); GIS Program Manager, NVPDC (1998-99); GIS Planner, RADCO (1997-98). **Associations & Accomplishments:** MENSA; Urban and Regional Information Systems Association; Conservation Consultant, Northern Virginia Soil and Water Conservation District; Vounteer Judge, Fairfax County High School Science Fair. **Education:** George Mason University, M.S. in Cartographic and Geographic Information Systems (1997); State University of New York College of Environmental Science and Forestry, B.S. in Natural Resources Management with minor in Forestry (1977); City University of New York at Queensboro, A.A.S. (1973). **Personal Information:** Married to Larry in 1984. Ms. Michaelsen enjoys creating habitats for butterflies.

Gregory D. Zimmerman

Network Engineer
Minnesota Department of Transportation
1400 Gervais Avenue
Maplewood, MN 55109-2044
(651) 779-5934
gdzim@attglobal.net

9621

Business Information: Serving as a Network Engineer for the Minnesota Department of Transportation, Mr. Zimmerman fulfills a number of duties on behalf of the Department and state. He manages and supervises a wide area network, ensuring its functionality and operational status. Demonstrating strong technological skills, he is responsible for planning projects, coordinating and purchasing materials, and managing a host of other day-to-day activities. With over four years of information technology experience, Mr. Zimmerman plans to continue his education in order to take advantage of opportunities for advancement. His key to success is persistence and his "I can" attitude as well as his ability to take on challenges and deliver results. The Minnesota Department of Transportation is an agency of the state government of Minnesota established to administer and regulate transportation activities throughout the state. Specializing in road research and development for the state, the Department concentrates on road and highway construction and maintenance. Presently, the Department employs a work force of over 2,250 people who facilitate smooth day-to-day operations. **Career Highlights:** Minnesota Department of Transportation: Network Engineer (1998-Present), Systems Administrator (1997-98); LAN Administrator, Northwest Airlines (1996-97); Training, Green Tree Financial (1996). **Education:** University of Wisconsin at Lacrosse, B.S. (1996). **Personal Information:** Married to Nichol in 1996.

Robert J. Barton Jr.

Systems Analyst II
City of Virginia Beach Department of Public Utilities
3500 Dam Neck Road
Virginia Beach, VA 23546
(757) 563-1409
Fax: (757) 427-3507
rbarton@city.virginia-beach.va.us

9631

Business Information: Mr. Barton has been serving the City of Virginia Beach Department of Public Utilities since 1984. As Systems Analyst II, he oversees the operation and maintenance of the workgroup and equipment used to monitor and control the City's water and sewer services. He manages nine employees, performs equipment upgrades, installations, and develops system architecture and specifications for equipment replacements under Capital Improvement Projects. Possessing an excellent understanding of his field, Mr. Barton designs and implements distributed process control systems, called SCADA. Maintaining an organized annual budget, he initiates the direction of funds within budget guidelines. Striving to incorporate the latest technologies, Mr. Barton concentrates his efforts toward improving the quality, reliability, and usability of the systems used by the Department. Affiliated with the local government, City of Virginia Beach Department of Public Utilities was established in 1952. Employing the skilled services of over 200 individuals to facilitate every aspect of distribution, collection, control, testing, and maintenance, the Department services the water needs for over 123,000 customers. The Department provides pumping and distribution of purified water and collection of wastewater throughout the City, generating $60 million in annual revenues. **Career Highlights:** City of Virginia Beach Department of Public Utilities: Systems Analyst II (1987-Present), Operations Supervisor (1984-87); Computer Technician, Mega Byte Computer Associates (1978-80). **Education:** Old Dominion University, B.S. in Electrical Engineering Technology (1982); Norfolk Vocational Technical School (1974). **Personal Information:** Mr. Barton enjoys music, computers and movies.

Olga Lizcano

Systems Support Specialist
Public Utility Commission
P.O. Box 13326
Austin, TX 78711-3326
(512) 936-7103
Fax: (512) 936-7098
olga.lizcano@puc.state.tx.us

9631

Business Information: Recruited in 1997, Ms. Lizcano serves in the capacity of Systems Support Specialist for the Public Utility Commission. A successful, 10 year professional, she currently works in the information technology division of the Commission and provides computer support for the entire agency as well as the general public using the Commission's interchange system. Possessing an excellent understanding of her field, Ms. Lizcano assists help desk personnel by providing e-mail support and answering the phones. She also helps maintain the systems infrastructrure, improving existing systems and upgrading to new technologies as needed. Highly regarded in the technology industry, she looks forward to remaining with the Commission and eventually moving up the corporate structure. Ms. Lizcano's success reflects her ability to take on challenges and new responsibilities and deliver results. Established in 1975, the Public Utility Commission is a state agency that provides consumer protection. Located in Austin, Texas, the Commission provides regulation in the telephone and electric industries in the state of Texas. Serving the communities in and around Austin, the Commission has a staff of 250 dedicated employees who work hard to provide these services to the communities. **Career Highlights:** Systems Support Specialist, Public Utility Commission (1997-Present); Computer Support Specialist/Librarian, Office of Public Utility Counsel (1992-97); Quality Assurance Supervisor, United States Bureau of the Census (1990-91). **Education:** Austin Community College (1994); Pan American University of Edinburg, Texas. **Personal Information:** Married to George Samuelson in 1998. Ms. Lizcano enjoys outdoor activitites, crafts, technological activities and reading.

Cecil L. Pearce, Jr.
Information Technology Director
PSC
2705 Johnson Road
Loganville, GA 30052
(404) 651-8397
Fax: (404) 463-6185
lamarp@psc.state.ga.us

9631

Business Information: In his position as Information Technology Director of PCS or Public Service Commission for the state of Georgia, Mr. Pearce is responsible for all aspects of design, implementation, and maintenance of computers for the Agency. He oversees network operations and analyzes hardware and software to ensure flawless performance. Additionally, he maintains the department budget, supervises employees, and presides over administrative tasks. Highly regarded, Mr. Pearce's innovative management style encourages optimum staff performance and ensures that all employees work together to achieve a common goal. Mr. Pearce has enjoyed substantial success and aspires to the position of Chief Information Officer for the Agency. The PSC is the Georgia state government utility regulatory agency. Established in 1879, the Agency employs a skilled staff to facilitate all aspects of day to day operations. Located in Loganville, Georgia, PSC is a vital part of the state community. **Career Highlights:** Information Technology Director, PSC (1999-Present); Tollway Operations Division Manager, Tollway Operations Division Manager, Georgia 400 Tollway Authority (1997-98); Adminstrative Specialist, Georgia Department of Transportation (1993-97). **Education:** Georgia State University (1999); Microsoft Professional+Internet; Cisco Certified Network Administrator; Microsoft Certified Systems Engineer. **Personal Information:** Married to Cindy in 1995. Two children: Sandy and Victoria. Mr. Pearce enjoys martial arts and Bonsai Trees.

John M. Nassif
Information Technology Division Chief of the Farm Service Agency
United States Department of Agriculture
1520 Market Street (Mail Code 54)
St. Louis, MO 63103
(314) 539-6875
Fax: (314) 539-2762
jmnassif@kcc.fsa.usda.gov

9641

Business Information: Utilizing more than 20 years of experience garnered in a large part within the United States Department of Agriculture, Mr. Nassif currently serves as the Information Technology Division Chief of the Farm Service Agency. He oversees the effective use of the various resources which are assigned to him. Mr. Nassif assumes responsibility for the management of people and projects in terms of dollars, equipment, techical services, decision making, and problem solving. Additionally, Mr. Nassif is in charge of network support, databases, Web base conversions, and business data. Recognized for his outstanding performance by the Department of Agriculture, he received the Honor Award in 1992 for his superb evaluation and reconstruction of the Department's database, leading to its increased efficiency and ease of use. Mr. Nassif credits his current success to several factors: understanding people, being a motivator, possessing a strong sense of loyalty, having a good staff, and maintaining political contacts. Continually striving to improve his performance, he is strengthening his management skills and plans to stay on top of changes in the evolving technological field. Established in the 1940s, the United States Department of Agriculture is dedicated to the

development of the country's rural areas, providing a variety of services. The Farm Service Agency is an agency within the Department offering loans to farmers for equipment and commodities funded by the United States Congress. The Agency's office in St. Louis, Missouri employs a skilled workforce of 51 individuals. **Career Highlights:** United States Department of Agriculture: Information Technology Division Chief of the Farm Service Agency (1995-Present), Information Technology Division Director of the Rural Development Agency (1995), Information Technology Branch Chief of the Farmers Home Administration Agency (1983-95). **Associations & Accomplishments:** Chairperson (1996-Present), St. Louis Region, Missouri DECA State Business Partnership; Chairperson (1999-Present), St. Louis Federal Executive Board; Board Member (1990-Present), St. Louis Arthritis Foundation. **Education:** Missouri Valley College, B.S. in Accounting (1966); St. Louis Community College, Meramec, Associate's degree in Data Processing (1976); degree in Information Technology. **Personal Information:** Married to Judith in 1996. Five children: Aimee, Pete, Dan, Tom, and Matt. Mr. Nassif enjoys golf and volunteer work.

Kathy M. Tankersley
Computer Specialist
United States Department of Agriculture Food and Nutrition Service
10 Causeway Street, Room 501
Boston, MA 02222-1069
(617) 565-6467
Fax: (617) 565-6472
ziggyll@att.world.att.net

9641

Business Information: Highly skilled in the information technology field, Ms. Tankersley serves as a Computer Specialist for the United States Department of Agriculture Food and Nutrition Service. Providing technical assistance and project oversight of information systems, she administers programs on the national, state, and local levels. Presently Ms. Tankersley is supervising multiple projects for FNS program administration including electronic benefit transfer. She plans to keep abreast of technical advancements and develop chip card technology for food stamps, WIC, school lunch, and breakfast programs in the future. The United States Department of Agriculture Food and Nutrition Service is a federal government agency dedicated to providing citizens with food assistance and nutritional education. Employing more than 1,000 personnel, the Agency administers various food and nutrition service programs. Programs include food stamps, WIC, school lunch, food distribution, and child nutrition. **Career Highlights:** Computer Specialist, United States Department of Agriculture Food and Nutrition Service (1987-Present); Navy Regional Data Automation Command (1975-87): Database Administrator, Systems Analyst, Computer Specialist. **Associations & Accomplishments:** American Public Human Services Association; Data Processing Management Association; NPCA; NARDAC Women of the Year (1980); Received National Accommodation for consolidating FNS Handbooks into a single system advance planning document guidance, FNS Handbook 901 (1992, update - 1997); Published in "CIO Magazine" and government technology periodical. **Education:** Edison College, B.A. in Computer Science and Technology (1994); Louisiana State University; Pennsylvania State University; Microsoft Certification (In Progress). **Personal Information:** Ms. Tankersley enjoys travel, playing the piano, music, reading and writiing.

Brenda C. Taylor
Computer Specialist
National Information Technology Center - Department of Agriculture
2827 North 55th Street
Kansas City, KS 66104-2304
(816) 926-2321
Fax: (913) 287-8986
tenda@kcnet.com

9641

Business Information: Serving as a Computer Specialist with National Information Technology Center - Department of Agriculture, Ms. Taylor implements and executes information security, system security, and data access restriction. She also resolves technical problems, performs general systems service, and provides technical assistance regarding software and hardware. Ms. Taylor was inspired to enter the technical field by a Weekly Reader article she read while in the sixth grade, and continues to excel in her chosen profession. National Information Technology Center - Department of Agriculture is the service bureau and data processing center for the United States Department of Agriculture. Headquartered in Washington, D.C., the Department employs 126,000 people nationwide, with three main service centers. **Career Highlights:** Computer Specialist, National Information Technology Center - Department of Agriculture (1988-Present); Programmer Analyst, USDA ASCS

(1984-88). **Associations & Accomplishments:** American Business Women's Association; National Association of Female Executives; Youth Friends. **Education:** Kansas State University, B.S. (1978); Kansas City, Kansas Community College. **Personal Information:** Ms. Taylor enjoys needlepoint, reading, embroidery, working with children and computers.

Edwin Y. Lee
Data Processing Manager II
Contractors State Licensing Board
9821 Business Park Drive
Sacramento, CA 95827-1703
(916) 255-4324
Fax: (916) 361-3783
elee@dca.ca.gov

9651

Business Information: As the Data Processing Manager for the Contractors State Licensing Board, Mr. Lee manages information technology and telecommunications usage along with its staff. Demonstrating his strong technology leadership, he oversees all aspects of data entries. He is also responsible for Internet protocol, voice and data communications, local dial-in, wireless infrastructures, work flow, digital imaging, interactive voice response equipment, and Web design and content. Possessing an excellent understanding of his field, Mr. Lee maintains the Board's Legacy database, ensuring data integrity, reliability, and security. He is also responsible for staff development. In the future, he hopes to attain a higher level of management. His success reflects his ability to take on challenges and deliver results. Established in 1929, the Contractors State Licensing Board is the state of California's governing body that establishes policy and procedures, and issues contract licenses. Functioning under the state's Department of Consumer Affairs, there are 15 offices state-wide manned by a staff of more than 500 people. **Career Highlights:** Data Processing Manager II, Contractors State License Board (1999-Present); Senior Information Systems Analyst, Department of Consumer Affairs (1994-99); Associate Analyst, State Teachers Retirement System (1985-94). **Education:** California State University at Sacramento, B.S. (1984).

Ziad Kamil Muhammad Ali
Spacecraft System Engineer
Canadian Space Agency
6767 Rue De L'Aeroport
Saint-Hubert, Quebec, Canada J3Y 8Y9
(450) 926-4496
Fax: (450) 926-6620
ziad.ali@space.gc.ca

9661

Business Information: A savvy, 15 year professional, Mr. Ali currently serves as a Spacecraft System Engineer for the Canadian Space Agency. He is responsible for an number of duties on behalf of the Agency, to include monitoring satellite manufacturing processes to ensure optimal levels of operations. Possessing superior talents and an excellent understanding of technology, Mr. Ali demonstrates high level of dedication by ensuring that all procedures are performed correctly, thus maintaining smooth running operations. He also ensures that all government specifications, safety regulations, and guidelines are strictly enforced. Attributing his success to patience and his ability to take on challenges and deliver results, Mr. Ali's future plans include implementing procedures that reduce space program costs. The Canadian Space Agency is a government agency that monitors all space activity, such as satellites and spacecraft as well as developing and implementing a national space program. The Agency also hires contractors to build and maintain satellites and micro-satellites for use in telecommunications, weather monitoring, and navigational purposes. Established in 1989, the Agency presently employs a work force of more than 700 professional, technical, and support staff. **Career Highlights:** Canadian Space Agency: Spacecraft System Engineer (1999-Present), Spacecraft Operations Engineer (1996), P/L Engineer (1990). **Education:** Concordia University, M.Sc. (1985). **Personal Information:** Married to Janine in 1994. One child: Basil.

Jeffrey S. Corn
Director of Systems and Compliance
United Space Alliance
8550 Astronaut Boulevard
Cape Canaveral, FL 32920
(407) 861-5252
Fax: (407) 861-6221
cornjs@usano.ksc.nasa.gov

9661

Business Information: Functioning in the role of Director of Systems and Compliance for United Space Alliance or USA, Mr. Corn conducts and develops policies, procedures, audits, and reviews of all subcontracting and purchasing activities. He maintains the operation of the automated, enterprise acquisition systems. To ensure the proper completion of projects, Mr. Corn reviews the legality of contracts and obtains software from various companies to install, utilize, and train employees. An accomplished professional, his many career highlights include obtaining his present position and seeing Shuttle launches. Looking to the 21st Century, next millennium, Mr. Corn plans on becoming more involved with the information technology venue of USA. He attributes his success to a strong set of values instilled in him by his parents. Headquartered in Houston, Texas, United Space Alliance was established in 1996 as a joint venture of the Boeing Company and Lockhead Martin Corporation. Currently, USA employs people in Texas, Florida, Alabame, California, and Washington, DC. NASA Space and Shuttle program contracts the services of United Space Alliance to manage and oversee space systems including mulit-service systems and NASA's human space flight program. USA manages one-third of NASA's space shuttle budget. **Career Highlights:** United Space Alliance: Director of Systems and Compliance (1999-Present), Manager of Material Administration (1997-99), Manager of Purchasing (1996-97); Manager of Purchasing, Lockheed Space Operations (1989-96). **Associations & Accomplishments:** National Association of Purchasing Management; National Contract Management Association; National Management Association. **Education:** California Polytechnical State University, B.A. (1977). **Personal Information:** Married to Kimberly in 1997.

Cynthia Irene Hintz

Project Manager
United Space Alliance
5464 Flint Road
Cocoa, FL 32927-2213
(321) 861-5063
Fax: (407) 861-0785
cinhintz@aol.com

9661

Business Information: Ms. Hintz serves as Project Manager with United Space Alliance. She oversees and directs information technology projects. Ms. Hintz served as Supervisor with Lockheed Martin prior to joining United Space Alliance as Project Engineer in 1996. In her current position, she is tasked with complete oversight and management of design, development, test, production, and maintenance of existing and new software and hardware. Coordinating resources, time lines, schedules, and assignments; compiling and synthesizing large quantities of information into management reports; and calculating and managing project budgets also fall within the realm of Ms. Hintz's responsibilities. Her professional highlights include migrating the system from an old IBM mainframe to client server environment, and developing the largest interface ever integrated at Kennedy Space Center. Ms. Hintz's success reflects the old fashioned values instilled in her by her mom and dad. Obtaining her Master's in Information Technology with a focus on being a Webmaster and automating the grade card reporting system in the state of Florida serves as her future endeavors. A joint venture created by The Boeing Company and Lockheed Martin, United Space Alliance is the prime contractor for NASA's Space Shuttle Program. Responsible for all aspects of day-to-day operation and management of the Shuttle fleet, United Space Alliance is manned by a skilled work force in Texas, Florida, Alabama, California, and Washington, D.C. **Career Highlights:** United Space Alliance: Project Manager (1998-Present), Project Engineer (1996-97); Supervisor, Lockheed Martin (1991-95). **Associations & Accomplishments:** National Management Association; Children's Miracle Networks; PSJ Football and Cheerleading Association; PSJ Baseball Association; Women's International Bowling Congress. **Education:** Barry University, M.S. in Information Technology (In Progress), B.S. in Information Technology (1996); Brevard Community College, A.A. (1996). **Personal Information:** Married to Todd in 1982. Two children: Todd and Stacey. Ms. Hintz enjoys bowling and children's sports.

9700 National Security and International Affairs

9711 National security
9721 International affairs

William D. Akridge

Information Management Officer
90th Regional Support Command
8000 Camp Robinson Road
North Little Rock, AR 72118
(501) 771-8778
Fax: (501) 771-8745
william.akridge@usarc-emh2.army.mil

9711

Business Information: Following 20 years of distinguished services in the United States Army, Mr. Akridge retired in 1998 as a full Colonel. At the present time, he serves as the Information Management Officer for the United States Army Reserve's 90th Regional Support Command, and assumes accountability for a five state region encompassing more than 25,000 soldiers. He maintains all communications, records, automation, and mail for the Command's troops. Self-educated in the field of information technology, Mr. Akridge has enjoyed substantial professional success in his new field. He is currently in the process of switching the local area network to a regional level automation system to better enhance his operations. Mr. Akridge was a combat leader in Vietnam and was a successful personnel affairs manager throughout his military career. A division of the United States Army Reserve, the 90th Regional Support Command stands ready to assist our active duty troops in the event of a large scale war. The troops attend monthly and yearly training sessions to maintain their state of readiness and sharpen their skills. Currently, the Command employs 48 administrative and support personnel. **Career Highlights:** Information Management Officer, 90th Regional Support Command (1998-Present); 120th ARCOM: Military Personnel Officer (1990-95), Public Affairs Officer (1986-90). **Associations & Accomplishments:** United States Army Officer candidate, School Hall of Fame. **Education:** St. Leo College, B.A. (1982). **Personal Information:** Married to Heidi. Three children: Kevin, Heather, and Juanita.

Joseph F. Bertrand

Staff Sergeant/Computer Technology Supervisor
United States Marine Corps
2045A Brown Drive
Kailua, HI 96734-4801
(808) 257-5929
bertrandjf@mcbh.usmc.mil

9711

Business Information: As Computer Technology Supervisor of United States Marine Corps, 1st Radio Battallion at Kaneohe Bay, Staff Sergeant Bertrand is concerned with technical aspects of daily operations. Included in his schedule are activities such as maintenance, troubleshooting, upgrade, and repair of all computer equipment and Intel systems infrastructures. Demonstrating his extensive knowledge of the field, he supports essential data communications and telecommunication functions. SSgt. Bertrand has traveled extensively to serve his country, lending technical support services to troops at Camp Pendleton and in Somalia. An entreprenuer by nature, he also runs a computer solutions business from his home that serves area companies. Looking forward to a long awaited retirement after enjoying his military career, SSgt. Bertrand looks forward to continued success in military, professional, and personal aspects of his life. The United States Marine Corp is an intergal department of the United States Navy. Established in 1775, the purpose of the U.S. Marine Corps is to provide support for land, air, and amphibious combat missions. Presently, the U.S. Marine Corps is manned by 170,000 marines. **Career Highlights:** United States Marine Corps: Staff Sergeant/Computer Technology Supervisor, 1st Radio Battalion (1998-Present), Data Communications Technician, 8th Communications Battalion Service Company (1995-98), Data Communications Technician, H&S Batallion Communications Company (1992-93), Computer Technician, 1st Batallion 3rd Marines Communications Platoon (1991-92). **Education:** Hawaii Pacific University, Associate's degree in Computer Science (1999). **Personal Information:** Married to Emily in 1994. Two children: Kyle and Kiana. SSgt. Bertrand enjoys martial arts and surfing the Web.

Myrna Boone-Shuford

Communication Engineer
Westinghouse - Savannah River Site
P.O. Box 1144
Aiken, SC 29808
(803) 952-7757
Fax: (803) 952-8765
myrna.shuford@srs.gov

9711

Business Information: Functioning as Communication Engineer at Westinghouse Savannah River Site's DOE Complex, Ms. Boone-Shuford is responsible for the education of 16,000 current site employees to ensure that all needs are met for changes in site license software, voice, and data communications. WSRC's Information Technology Organizational Consolidation and Business Alignment recent consolidation of computing resources and functions in the new business and technical computing organization reflects its sustained pursuit of improved cost effectiveness and standardization through consolidation. The Company's organizational strategy remains focused on three primary objectives: consolidation of computing load on large-scale, centrally managed technology; elimination of duplicate effort in the field organizations; and training efforts to keep 16,000 site employees up-to-date on information technology services and products. She has also been involved in design development of network infrastructure. Before joining Westinghouse, Ms. Boone-Shuford was Manager of Williston Telephone Company and Home Cable, Inc., and System Analyst with Allied - General Nuclear Services. Ms. Boone-Shuford keeps abreast of changes in the computer industry by attending seminars, various workshops, and training courses. Her career began approximately 30 years ago, and has developed the skills needed to maintain the highest standards of professional excellence. She is now looking forward to retirement and hopes to use her experience and education to do volunteer work for schools, hospitals, and nursing homes. She will also work with the Miss North Carolina as an advisor and with the Parkway Playhouse in Burnsville. **Career Highlights:** Communication Engineer, Westinghouse - Savannah River Site (1988-Present); Manager, Williston Telephone Company (1984-88); System Analyst, Allied - General Nuclear Services (1971-84). **Education:** University of South Carolina, degree in Computer Science (1973). **Personal Information:** Married to Jerry in 1959. Two children: Kimberly (USC Graduate) and Timothy (Georgia State Graduate). Ms. Boone-Shuford enjoys shopping, shopping, and more shopping, motorcycles, antiques and travel.

Dave Eizember

Director of Information Management
Army National Guard
2823 West Main Street
Rapid City, SD 57702
(605) 737-6676
Fax: (605) 737-6245
dave.eizember@sd.ngb.army.mil

9711

Business Information: As Director of Information Management for the Army National Guard of South Dakota, Mr. Eizember is responsible for management and oversight of all aspects of the wide and local area network and computer and telephony infrastructure. He determines the overall strategic direction and formulates plans for contingency taskings. In addition, he presides over the completion of all administrative and operational tasks. Mr. Eizember has enjoyed substantial success in his career and attributes it all to the people he has around him. He hopes to remain in the information technology field, begin pursuing his Master's degree in Information Services, and become involved in consulting in systems integration. The Army National Guard of South Dakota is a reserve component of the United States Army. An outgrowth of the volunteer militia that was first authorized in 1792, South Dakota's Army National Guard is under the control of the Governor of South Dakota, and may be called into federal service at the direction of the President of the United States. Employing a full time staff of 500 individuals, the Guard is dedicated to preserving the national security of the United States. **Career Highlights:** Director of Information Management, Army National Guard (1988-Present). **Associations & Accomplishments:** Elks Club; Life Member, Veterans of Foreign Wars; Life Member, National Guard Association of the United States; Life Member, National Guard Association of South Dakota. **Education:** South Dakota School of Mines, B.S. in Mechanical Engineering (1981); Microsoft Certified Systems Engineer. **Personal Information:** Married to Ceclila in 1983. Two children: Jordan and Jiliane.

Dimas Espinoza

Senior Information Assurance Policy Analyst
DEISSC2
2379 Northeast Loop 410, Suite 15
San Antonio, TX 78217
(210) 946-2221
Fax: (210) 946-5559
eapinoza_d@msn.com

9711

Business Information: Since 1993, Mr. Espinoza has performed duties of Senior Information Assurance Policy Analyst for the United States Army. He possesses over 20 years of experience in technology security systems. Providing management of information systems security programs, Enterprise networks, security firewalls, policies and procedures, and training programs also falls under the realm of Mr. Espinoza's responsibilities. In addition, he assumes accountability for budgetary functions and implementation of blocks to protect information from unauthorized individuals. Additionally, he monitors the network, intrusion detection system, and plant design security. His long-term goal is to perform a complete review of policies and regulations to facilitate and enhance overall systems security. **Career**

Highlights: Senior Information Assurance Policy Analyst, DEISSC2 (1993-Present); DDN Network Manager, USAHCSSA (1987-92); Computer Specialist, U.S. Army Academy of Health Sciences (1983-86). **Associations & Accomplishments:** Computer Security Institute; Chair of HQDA Committee to Rewrite Army Policy for Information Systems Security. **Education:** Webster University, M.A. (1985); Trinity University, B.S. in Computer Science (1975). **Personal Information:** Married to Gina in 1987. Five children: Nicholas Edware, John Thomas, Lynda Ann, Randall, and Elizabeth Ann. Mr. Espinoza enjoys playing computer chess and doing home improvement.

Kathryn A. Evans
Project Manager
United States Army Corps of Engineers
3909 Halls Ferry Road
Vicksburg, MS 39180-6133
(601) 634-2674
evansk@mail.wes.army.mil

9711

Business Information: Ms. Evans has served with the United States Army Corps of Engineers since 1985 and presently holds the position of Project Manager. In charge of the Agency's software electronic meeting facility, she presides over the project management development of software systems designed specifically for the federal government. Ms. Evans and her team have the added responsibility of training government employees in the use of their specific programs. Coordinating resources and schedules, overseeing time lines and assignments, and managing project budgets also fall within the purview of her responsibilities. Keeping abreast of the latest in technology by reading industry publications, attending classes, and hands on experience, she credits her success to education and networking with colleagues. Her success reflects her ability to think out-of-the-box and take on new challenges and responsibilities. Always alert to new opportunities, techniques, and approaches, Ms. Evans sees herself working with the Agency on larger and more innovative projects. The United States Army Corps of Engineers is a federal government agency underneath the United States Army. The Corps of Engineers maintains eight laboratories nationwide, employing more than three hundred research scientists and administrative personnel at each location. **Career Highlights:** Project Manager, United States Army Corps of Engineer (1985-Present). **Associations & Accomplishments:** Leadership Vicksburg through Chamber of Commerce. **Education:** Mississippi College, B.S. (1992). **Personal Information:** One child: Carmen E. Parmegiani. Ms. Evans enjoys interior decorating, painting and remodeling.

Norma Wheatley Favaro
Logistics Management Specialist
HQ CPSG/LGLP
230 Hall Boulevard
San Antonio, TX 78243
(210) 977-2596
Fax: (210) 622-5448
nfavaro@aol.com

9711

Business Information: As Chief of Logistics Management and Systems Branch of for HQ CPSG/LGLP, Mrs. Favaro is responsible for identifying and managing process flow, procedures, regulatory guidance, and public law. A specialist who possesses an excellent understanding of her field, she is involved in managing standard and non-standard systems and usage of support items. Effectively deploying her staff, Mrs. Favaro ensures the capability to support the Group's mission and that all reporting actions are completed and sent to senior management. Dedicated to the success of the Group, she continues to develop internal programs as she continues to better herself by interacting with developers, contractors, and designers. In the future, Mrs. Favaro hopes to obtain a higher position within the Group and keeping the business moving higher and faster and getting everything upgraded. "Learn from others and always be award," is cited as her advice to others. Located in San Antonio, Texas, HQ CPSG/LGLP engages in logistics management and data systems support for cryptologic systems group. Employing 10 personnel, the Group provides a number of services to the United States Air Force. **Career Highlights:** Chief of Logistics Management and Systems Branch, HQ CPSG/LGLP (1998-Present); C-17 System Manager, United States Air Force (1997-98); San Antonio Air Logistic Center: International Program Manager (1991-97), NATO Program Manager (1985-90). **Associations & Accomplishments:** Past Chapter Chairman, Society of Logistics Engineers; Air Force Association; Board of Directors, Nogalitos Gear, Inc. **Education:** University of Texas at San Antonio: Master's in Public Administration (1997), B.A. in Psychology (1979). **Personal Information:** Married to Joseph D. in 1984. Two children: Constance and Colleen. Mrs. Favaro enjoys gardening.

Mark E. Fileger
Chief of Finance Automation
United States Air Force
216 Sweeney Boulevard
Langley Air Force Base, VA 23665-2714
(757) 764-5743
Fax: (757) 764-4047
mark.fileger@langley.af.mil

9711

Business Information: As Chief of Finance Automation of United States Air Force's Financial Management Division at Langley Air Force Base, Mr. Fileger directs the activities of the Air Combat Command's financial automation team. Demonstrating exceptional technical knowledge, he maintains the system by overseeing troubleshooting, maintenance, and upgrades of hardware and software. A sharp professional, Mr. Fileger oversees several types of financial management systems and provides outstanding user support. Recognized by the White House, Department of Defense, and U.S. Air Force as a leader in his field, he looks forward to continued developments in his field such as automated financial management systems and processes. He received a DoD award for an Automated Battle System his team developed, as well as the ACC/FM Outstanding Contributor Award in 1999. Mr. Fileger attributes his success to his willingness to learn new things and apply them in his life. His plans include retirement in 2002, obtaining his certifications and Bachelor's degree in Computer Science, and finding employment in the information technology corporate sector. The U.S. Air Force is a military department within the Department of Defense responsible for the aerospace defense posture of the United States around the world. Langley Air Force Base serves as headquarters for the Air Combat Command and home for the 1st Fighter Wing and other related DoD organizations. The Financial Management Division was established in 1996 as the automated center responsible for accurate record keeping and timely report preparation. Over 80 people are employed at this Division that supports twenty-one other U.S. Air Force facilities located throughout the continental United States and two overseas. **Career Highlights:** United States Air Force: Chief of Finance Automation, Headquarters, Air Combat Command/FM (1997-Present), Superintendent, 32nd Regional Accounting and Finance Office (1996-97), Superintendent, Management Branch Headquarters, Air Combat Command/FM (1992-96). **Associations & Accomplishments:** Air Force Sergeants Association; American Society of Military Comptrollers. **Education:** St. Leo College: B.A. (1999), A.A. in Liberal Arts; Community College of the Air Force, A.A. in Financial Management. **Personal Information:** Two children: Bonnie and Eric. Mr. Fileger enjoys computer maintenance, golf and computer gaming.

Andrew L. Forte, M.B.A., C.P.A., C.G.F.M.
Senior Technical Support Auditor
Department of Defense Inspector General
400 Army Navy Drive #858
Arlington, VA 22202
(703) 604-8932
Fax: (703) 604-8932
aforte@dodig.osd.mil

9711

Business Information: Since joining the Department of Defense as project leader and auditor in 1991, Mr. Forte has achieved promotion to the position of Senior Technical Support Auditor. In his current capacity, he meticulously evaluates internal operations and coordinates all performance and auditing results when compiling reports to be turned over to the United States Congress. Possessing an excellent understanding of his position and his field, Mr. Forte also is responsible for working with service audit agencies' coordinators to ensure solutions to findings that impact the Department of Defense's military readiness, effectiveness, and efficiency are implemented. Providing support to internal audit agencies with programming also fall within the realm of his responsibilities. The most rewarding aspects of his career include auditing the White House Communications Agency, as well as auditing the retired pay system of the Philippines. Attributing his success to self-motivation, Mr. Forte's future plans include conducting more electronic audits and completing his Master's degree in Information Technology. The Department of Defense Inspector General has auditing oversight of the Department of Defense, to include all of its operations and agencies. Chartered by the United States Congress, the Inspector General was established in 1978. Located in Arlington, Virginia, the DoD Inspector General is manned by a staff of 620 civilian and military professionals. **Career Highlights:** Department of Defense Inspector General: Senior Technical Support Auditor (1998-Present), Project Leader/Auditor (1991-98); Corporate Income Tax Auditor, Missouri Department of Revenue (1989-91); Comptroller, Forte Buick, Inc (1986-89). **Associations & Accomplishments:** Association of Government Accountants; American Institute of Certified Accountants; Scout Master, Boy Scout Troop #1866, Arlington, Virginia. **Education:** Savannah State University, M.B.A. in

Management (1985); Tuskagee University, B.S. in Accounting (1977); Certified Defense Financial Auditor (1999); Certified Defense Logistics Auditor (1998); Certified Government Financial Manager (1996); Certified Public Accountant (1994). **Personal Information:** Married to Violeta in 1999. One child: Ke'Andra. Mr. Forte enjoys softball and jogging.

Arthur W. Garrett, II
Accounting Supervisor
Naval Support Activity
2300 General Myers Avenue, Building 2, 2nd Floor
New Orleans, LA 70142
(504) 678-2256
Fax: (504) 678-2323

9711

Business Information: As Accounting Supervisor of Naval Support Activity in New Orleans, Mr. Garrett is accountable for the supervision of four department technicians and the maintenance of the Fastdata computer system. He also monitors departmental project completion and budget compliance. The Naval Support Activity is responsible for maintaining fiscal concerns of the Naval base. Established in 1954, each base utilizes the Department, employing reservist, active duty, tenant commanders, and civilian staff members. The Department also provides assistance with housing and recreation for military personnel. **Career Highlights:** Accounting Supervisor, Naval Support Activity (1973-Present); Boatswain Mate - 3rd Class, United State Coast Guard (1969-73). **Associations & Accomplishments:** American Society of Military Comptrollers. **Education:** Southern University, B.S. in Accounting (1981). **Personal Information:** Married to Emelda T. in 1992. Four children: Arthur, Leslie, Nathan, and Dainette. Mr. Garrett enjoys swimming, reading and swimming.

Kenneth O. Glenn
Network Engineer
Metamore
2600 North Woodlawn
Wichita, KS 67220
(316) 681-1759
glennk@89rsc.net

9711

Business Information: Mr. Glenn is the Network Engineer for Metamore. Concentrating on the system administration responsibilities, he maintains seven exchange servers and troubleshoots all problems that may arise in addition to maintaining the e-mail systems. Configuring systems and providing assistance to users are also tasks included in the course of Mr. Glenn's day. For the future of his career, he hopes to advance his role within the Company and obtain aditional responsibilities. Metamore is a technical support business that specializes in the information technology industry. The Company's largest contract is with the United States Government and the team of 1,000 employees travel around the country to enhance the computer networks and the software programs of government offices. The Company hosts a total of nine branch offices throughout the United States and tackles every project from system design to program upgrades. **Career Highlights:** Network Engineer, Metamore (1996-Present); Exchange/Network Administrator, 89th Regional Support Command-RAM, United States Army Reserve (1996-Present); Technical Specialist, Honewell (1989-96). **Associations & Accomplishments:** Alexander Graham Bell Association for the Deaf. **Education:** Friends University, B.S. in Computer Science Information Systems (1995); Butler County Community College, A.A.S. in Engineering Electronic Technology. **Personal Information:** Two children: Kristine and James. Mr. Glenn enjoys racquetball, snow and water skiing and cooking.

Marcia K. Hanson-Gorby
Plans and Programs Manager
New Jersey Air National Guard
3324 Charles Boulevard
McGuire Air Force Base, NJ 08641
(609) 724-5806
Fax: (609) 724-6158
57tigress@adelphia.net

9711

Business Information: Functioning in the capacity of Plans and Programs Manager for the New Jersey Air National Guard, Ms. Hanson-Gorby is responsible for program management and database development. She processes requirements for users including giving access to systems and determining their specific service needs. A systems expert, Ms. Hanson-Gorby also develops and implements specific systems and also monitors the progress of these systems. The highlight of her career is ensuring Y2K program compliance for New Jersey Air National Guard's system and network infrastructures. Looking to the new millennium and beyond, Ms. Hanson-Gorby will pursue a new position as the Manager of Technical Systems as well as Webmaster. She attributes her professional success to her people skills and her ability to think outside the box, deliver results, and aggressively take on challenges and new responsibilities. The New Jersey Air National Guard is a reserved component of the United States Air Force and falls under the control of the Governor of New Jersey. The National Guards of the Army and Air Force have an authorized strength of over 560,000 men and women, with about 114,000 in the Air National Guard. Members are enlisted voluntarily into this reserved-based unit. State funds provide armories and storage facilities while the federal funding provides clothing, weapons, and equipment. During peacetime, the members attend 48 weekly drill and training periods per year. Founded in 1792, the National Guard has established departments in all states to provide protection to the civilians of the United States. **Career Highlights:** Plans and Programs Manager, New Jersey Air National Guard (1997-Present). **Associations & Accomplishments:** Institute of Electrical and Electronics Engineers Computer Society; Enlisted Association of the National Guard; Past President, Parent Teacher Association. **Education:** Ocean County College: B.S. in Computer Science (In Progress); Community College of the Air Force, A.A.S. in Avionic Systems Technology (1993). **Personal Information:** Three children: Joshua, Sean, and Leigh. Ms. Hanson-Gorby enjoys computers.

Peter V. Huynh
Chief of Network Operations
United States Army
6825 16th Street NW, Building T-2
Washington, DC 20307
(202) 782-5511
Fax: (760) 281-7679
pvh@writemail.com

9711

Business Information: As Chief of Network Operations at the United States Army's Walter Reed Army Medical Center, Mr. Huynh handles the automation of the network. Demonstrating his extensive knowledge of information technology, he maintains the infastructure and installs hardware and software upgrades. Working closely with his staff, Mr. Huynh strives to develop innovative technical solutions to continually improve the effectiveness of the department. Mr. Huynh has received internal recognition for the implementation of a 21 state regional network and email system. Keeping his goals consistent with those of the Center, he aspires to a higher position within the corporate structure while initiating plans for the opening of his own business. The United States Army's Walter Reed Army Medical Center provides healthcare to military personnel and their dependents. The 1,200 bed hosptial employs 6,000 trained people, 70 percent of which are civilians. Established in 1917, the Center conducts reasearch in the medical technology field. **Career Highlights:** Chief of Network Operations, United States Army (1999-Present); Senior Information Technology Manager, North Atlantic Regional Medical Command (1996-99). **Associations & Accomplishments:** Institute of Electrical and Electronics Engineers; H.I.M.S.S.; V.A.S. **Education:** Nova Southeastern University, Ph.D. (In Progress); Central Michigan University, M.S. in Administration; University of Washington, B.A. **Personal Information:** Mr. Huynh enjoys skiing, camping, tennis and outdoors.

Cheryl D. Jewel
Information Systems Management Officer
United States Army Visual Information Center
Room 5B266, The Pentagon
Washington, DC 20310
(703) 697-6335
Fax: (703) 695-3370
donna.jewel@hqda.army.mil

9711

Business Information: As Information Systems Management Officer of the United States Army Visual Information Center, Mrs. Jewel is charged with the responsibility of managing the entire networking infrastructure. Possessing an excellent understanding of technology, she is responsible for all software and hardware, troubleshooting, and U.S. Army wide network systems. Mrs. Jewel is also in charge of overseeing integral security issues, to include equipment security. She is proud of her every accomplishments within the Center, as she has acquired several awards due to her outstanding professional performance including implementing the LAN and automating the entire Center. Attributing her success to being in the right place at the right, Mrs. Jewel plans on remaining at the Center and introduce new technology. The United States Army Visual Information Center engages in electronic imaging and graphics. Established in 1917, the Center also handles photographic and television services support to the Headquarters, United States Army. A staff of 186 carefully selected individuals work hard to maintain worldwide presence and precise historical documentation. Maintaining a worldwide presence, the Center provides state of the art

graphics and support services. **Career Highlights:** Information Systems Management Officer, United States Army Visual Information Center (1991-Present); Computer Specialist, Office Deputy Chief of Staff (1986-91); Administrative Secretary, Office for Personnel, Deputy Chief of Staff (1979-86); Secretarial Assistant, United States Senate (1967-78). **Associations & Accomplishments:** Pentagon Personal Computer Users Group. **Education:** Learning Tree International, Access Programming (1999); Gadsden Business College, A.A.; Northern Virginia Community College, A.A. in Computer Science. **Personal Information:** Married to James in 1998. Two children: Michael Reid Barrett and Cherylyn Michelle Merwine. Mrs. Jewel enjoys her home computer, reading and her grandchildren.

D. Timothy Jones
Network Engineer and Administrator
United States Navy
PSC 1008, Box 3022
FPO, AA 34051
(787) 865-3463
standingfire@altavista.com

9711

Business Information: Faithfully serving as a member of the United States Navy since 1984, Mr. Jones has been recognized for his professionalism and technical expertise by several promotions, and currently serves as an Assistant Planning and Projects Officer. Presently stationed at NCTS Puerto Rico, he is charged with coordinating network and telecommunication upgrades and additions, in addition to facilitating communication with other naval units. Drawing from his continuing education and hands on experience, Mr. Jones assists with the design of new network circuits, the contracting and installation of new equipment, and maintains the functionality of an operational status of NCTS's netowkring architectures. Administering and controlling system resources, providing technical expertise to assigned technicians, analyzing security, and resolving systems difficulties also fall within the scope of his functions. Continually striving for maximum effectiveness, Mr. Jones is pursing a college education to enable him to build a large scale network and capitalize on the opportunities provided by the U.S. Navy. The United States Navy is a branch of the armed forces designated to protecting U.S. waters and territories. The U.S. Navy maintains a strong presence nationally and internationally in ports and seas around the world. Over one million men and women serve in the U.S. Navy around the globe to protect U.S. interests from hostile actions. **Career Highlights:** United States Navy: Network Engineer and Administrator (1998-Present), Network Installer/Analyst (1993-97), Operations Supervisor (1991-93), Network Administrator/Operator (1988-91), Systems Analyst/Operator (1984-88). **Education:** Military Technical Schools: Network Security Vulnerability Technician, LAN Administration, Programming, Network Switch Management. **Personal Information:** Mr. Jones lives with his small house pet near the beach.

Steve F. LaFata
Technical Director
480 Intelligence Group
34 Elm Street
Langley Air Force Base, VA 23665-2092
(757) 764-4444
Fax: (757) 764-4507
steve.lafata@langley.af.mil

9711

Business Information: As the Technical Director for the 480 Intelligence Group at Langley Air Force Base, Virginia, Mr. LaFata fulfills the duties of a GS-15. Working closely with the commander's staff, he is responsible for advising the commander and senior officers in the technology fields on automated and weapons systems technologies. Moreover, he is charged with conducting innovations and providing future planning and requirements for the Group. The chief liaison on critical issues, Mr. LaFata also manages manpower as well as oversees the annual budgeting process and future planning of strategic resources. During his career, he has won several awards for his dedication and loyalty to the Group. He is also a 20 year, distinguished veteran of the United States Marine Corps. In the future, Mr. LaFata looks forward to continuing with the Group, becoming a major part of its growth, achieving the position of a senior advisor, and creating a diversified staff. His quote is "data is data." Located at Langley Air Force Base, Virginia, the 480 Intelligence Group is an intel unit consisting of six squadrons. The Group provides imagery and logic support to defense combat units with threat and mission duties. Furthermore, the Group employees a mixed group of 1,020 civilians, contractors, and military personnel who oversee and manage a fiscal budget of $14 million. **Career Highlights:** 480 Intelligence Group: Technical Director (1994-Present), Technical Advisor (1991-94), Chief of Systems (1989-91), Systems Manager (1986-89); Imagery Analysis and Collection Management, United States Marine Corps

(1965-85). **Associations & Accomplishments:** ARCIA; National Military Intelligence Association. **Personal Information:** Married to Angela in 1991. Two children: Donna and Steven. Mr. LaFata enjoys golf and gardening.

John A. Leonelli
Information Management Officer
Defense Information Systems Agency, Department of Defense
701 South Court House Road, #D43
Arlington, VA 22204-2164
(703) 607-4448

9711

Business Information: Beginning his association with the Defense Information Systems Agency in 1992 as the Space Management Officer, Mr. Leonelli has received recognition for his diligence and management skills through the promotion to his current role of Information Management Officer. In his capacity, he works in the Acquisitions and Logistics Department coordinating corporate planning, budgeting, and strategic direction. He reports to the Chief Information Officer. Dedicated to the betterment of the Department of Defense, Mr. Leonelli developed the cutting edge computer aided Facilities Management Program that helped program directors better manage the utilization and maintenance of real-estate and facilities. Enjoying substantial success, he wishes to continue in his current position as well as attain more knowledge and experience. Mr. Leonelli attributes his success to his foresight and his ability to deliver results and aggressively take on new challenges. The Defense Information Systems Agency is an internal agency within the United States Department of Defense. The Agency provides information technology support, enforces standards of information technology, and consolidates information technology projects. This Agency currently employs the skilled services of 130 competent individuals. **Career Highlights:** Defense Information Systems Agency: Information Management Officer (1997-Present), Management Analyst (1995-97), Space Management Officer (1992-95); Budget Analyst, 5th Signal Command, Germany (1989-92). **Education:** University of Southern California, M.S. (1986); National Defense University, CIO Certificate; United States Army Comptroller School (1988). **Personal Information:** Mr. Leonelli enjoys sailing, photography and travel.

Lashika L. Mikel
Oracle Application Developer
Westinghouse
804 Cross Court Drive
Augusta, GA 30909
(803) 952-8769
lashika_mikel@yahoo.com

9711

Business Information: As the Oracle Application Developer for Westinghouse, Ms. Mikel is responsible for developing in-house forms from scratch. In her position, she is charged with planning budgets and implementing the application software for the entire Company. Moreover, she supervises a staff of employees who report directly to her on a daily basis and conducts meeting with the other managers. The most rewarding aspects of her career include receiving two Vice President Awards for budgeting. In the future, Ms. Mikel looks forward to continuing with the Company in her current position, as well as becoming a project manager and receiving her certification in Oracle in August of 2000. Founded in 1950, Westinghouse is a government nuclear contractor. Located in Augusta, Georgia, the Company is also a subcontractor for the Department of Energy. Presently, the Company is international in scope, and employs a work force of more than 13,500 professional, technical, and support staff. **Career Highlights:** Oracle Application Developer, Westinghouse (1998-Present); Programmer Analyst, Union Camp Corporation (1996-98). **Associations & Accomplishments:** International Oracle Users Group - Americas; Black Data Processing Associates - CSRA Chapter. **Education:** Georgia Southern University, B.B.A. in Informations Systems (1996). **Personal Information:** Ms. Mikel enjoys volunteer work, travel, meeting people and shopping.

Robin M. Mosby
Chief CSS/Work Group Manager
United States Air Force
2221 Grissom Road, 6 AS/CCA
Trenton, NJ 08641-5209
(609) 724-4732
Fax: (609) 724-4708

9711

Business Information: Functioning in the dual role of Chief CSS and Work Group Manager of the United States Air Force, Ms. Mosby supervises the entire computer office and personnel section under the Squadron Commander. Also serving as Chief Support Personalist, Ms. Mosby trains crews in the use of the computers as opposed to leaving a paper trail. Beginning her career in the U.S. Air Force more than one year ago, Ms. Mosby has enjoyed substantial success in her career. She attributes her professional success to the values instilled in her by her parents, as well as her ability to deliver results and aggressively take on new challenges. Ms. Mosby continues to grow professionally and looks forward to continuing in her current position. The United States Air Force is a military department within the Department of Defense responsible for air operations. The U.S. Air Force was officially established in 1947. The Base in Trenton, New Jersey currently consists of 265 individuals dedicated to protecting the national security of the United States. **Career Highlights:** United States Air Force: CSS Chief/Work Group Manager (1998-Present), Resource Advisor (1998-98); Bank of America (1998-Present). **Associations & Accomplishments:** McGuire Top 3 Association; African American Committee. **Education:** Burlington County College, A.A. (1998); Community College of the Air Force, Information Resources Management. **Personal Information:** One child: Michael W. Ms. Mosby enjoys computers, bowling and golf.

James M. Naff, C.G.F.M.

Systems Administrator
Department of Defense
4716 Andover Square
Indianapolis, IN 46226
(317) 510-3432
Fax: (317) 510-3406
jim.naff@dfas.mil

9711

Business Information: A distinguished, 26-year veteran of the United States Army, Mr. Naff currently serves in the role of Systems Administrator for the Department of Defense. Coming on board to the DoD in 1989, he administers and controls systems resources and tools. Possessing an excellent understanding of technology, he maintains the functionality and operational status of the DoD's information systems infrastructure located at the Department's Indianapolis, Indiana facility. Highly regarded, Mr. Naff determines the systems strategic direction as well as contribution of the systems functions on behalf of his customers' mission. Currently, he is working closely with systems management and users to create and implement new software applications to turn the Department into a paperless environment. In the future, Mr. Naff plans to remain in his present position and continue providing quality products and services in a timely manner. The U.S. Department of Defense is a cabinet level agency of the Executive Branch of the federal government tasked with the mission of ensuing the defense of the national interest at home and abroad. The Department of Defense is headquartered in Washington, D.C. and its operations include all branches of the U.S. armed forces and other national security agencies. **Career Highlights:** Systems Adminstrator, Department of Defense (1989-Present); Sergeant Major, United States Army (1962-88). **Associations & Accomplishments:** Association of Government Accountants; American Society of Military Comptrollers. **Education:** Texas Tech University, B.B.A. in Accounting (1974); Orange Coast College: A.A. in Accounting and History, A.A. in Liberal Arts. **Personal Information:** Married to Judith in 1961. Two children. Mr. Naff enjoys numismatics and philately.

Steven S. Orndoff

Computer Specialist
United States Army Corps of Engineers
Box 2250
Winchester, VA 22604
(540) 665-3707
Fax: (540) 665-4043

9711

Business Information: In his current position as Computer Specialist for the United States Army Corps of Engineers, Mr. Orndoff is responsible for providing a great deal of information technology services. This includes offering recommendations to enhance technology, overseeing benefit analysis and hardware and software configurations, updating and upgrading systems, serving as an information security officer, and investigating security breeches. He also supports and maintains satellite receiving and broadcasting systems and designs WAN and LAN networks for the Corps. A dedicated and determined individual, Mr. Orndoff trains personnel once every six months in the area of current viruses and security awareness. Attributing his success to mentoring received from his college math professor, he plans to obtain a management position in information systems security and attain Windows 2000 certification. United States Army Corps of Engineers was established in order to provide military construction, engineering, flood control, and waterway navigation. During peacetime, the Corps plans and directs the construction of navigation and flood control works such as harbors, dams, and levees for the federal government. In times of military action, the Corps builds bridges, roads, airfields, and military camps, in addition to carrying out mapping for use by the Armed Forces. The United States Army Corps of Engineers was orginally founded in 1780 and today employs more than 30,000 personnel. **Career Highlights:** United States Army Corps of Engineers: Computer Specialist (1990-Present), LAN Administrator (1987-90). **Education:** Shenandoah University, B.S. in Mathematics (1984). **Personal Information:** Mr. Orndoff enjoys swimming and gardening.

Charles R. Pedersen, Ph.D.

Visiting Scientist
Air Force Research Laboratory
IFTC 26 Electronic Parkway
Rome, NY 13441
(315) 330-4846
Fax: (315) 330-2953
pedersencr@worldnet.att.net

9711

Business Information: Dr. Pedersen functions in the capacity of Visiting Scientist for the Air Force Research Laboratory in Rome, New York. Focused within modern high performance computing technology, he participates in a nation wide community for exploration and software development for advanced parallel computers. A savvy, 38 year research professional, Dr. Pedersen also mentors a team of researchers within the Laboratory and provides them with technical leadership as well as business and career development strategies. Involved in many day-to-day technical activities of the Laboratory, he spearheads the preparation of proposals that generate funding for a number of research programs. In the future, Dr. Pedersen plans to remain in his profession and enhance his services through another position. His success is attributed to his management and people skills as well as his leadership ability to think outside the box, deliver results, and aggressively take on new challenges and responsibilities. "Learn as much as you can and stay at the forefront," is cited as Dr. Pedersen's advice. Air Force Research Laboratory is one of a collection of laboratory facilities established by the United States Air Force in 1945. The Laboratory is involved in the continued exploration of the information technology industry and every one of the 1,000 staff members work towards the discovery and testing of the next generation of avionics computer technology. Presently, the Laboratory operates on an annual budget in excess of $100 million. **Career Highlights:** Visiting Scientist, Air Force Research Laboratory; Senior Research Scientist, Research Association for Defense Conversion (1997-Present); Riverside Research Institute: Consultant (1993), Research Director (1995-97, 1961-93). **Associations & Accomplishments:** Institute of Electronics and Electrical Engineers Computer Society; Phi Beta Kappa; Tau Beta Pi; Eta Kappa Nu; Sigma Xi. **Education:** Columbia University: Ph.D. in Electrical Engineering (1966), M.S., B.S., A.B. with highest honors. **Personal Information:** Married to Althea. Four children: Jean, Sharon, Robert, and John. Dr. Pedersen enjoys cryptography and market statistics.

William F. Severin

Systems Integrator
United States Air Force, Headquarters Air Combat Command
1238 Springwell Place
Newport News, VA 23608
(757) 764-3723
severomw@erols.com

9711

Business Information: Serving as Systems Integrator of United States Air Force, Headquarters Air Combat Command, Major Severin assumes accountability for Command-wide systems integration as well as maintaining systems functionality and operational status. In this context, he evaluates old and present systems in order to divulge their worth and decide whether a new system is necessary to keep operations on the cutting edge. Keeping out-front of emergin technology, he participates in a variety of research and development activities promoting fluency in the latest technology. A savvy, 20 year veteran, Major Severin's career highlights include participating in with the United Nations' forces in Somalia and his role as Deputy J6 for joint task force operations in the Southwest Asia theater. An innovative communications and information professional, Major Severin plans to retire from the United States Air Force in order to pursue a career as a freelance consultant on defense contracting operations. His success is attributed to his academics and a desire to "just do it." Established in 1947, the United States Air Force is the branch of the armed forces responsible for carrying out the majority of the nation's aerial military operations. The United States Air Force, Headquarters Air Combat Command's mission is to project tactical air power worldwide to meet national objectives. Presently, the United States Air Force is manned by 645,000 airmen capable of initiating and sustaining combat operations. **Career Highlights:** Systems Integrator, United States Air Force, Headquarters Air Combat Command (1994-Present); Senior ADP Staff Officer, United Nations Operations Somalia (1993-94); Operations Inspector, United States Air Force, Headquarters Tactical Air Command (1989-93). **Associations & Accomplishments:** Armed Forces Communications Electronic Association; Outstanding Young Men of America. **Education:** Air Force Institute of Technology, M.S. (1987); University of South Carolina, B.S. (1980). **Personal Information:** Married to Helga in 1981. Two children: Ashley and Andrew.

Glenn A. Smith

Computer Scientist
United States Army Research Laboratory
ATTN: AMSRL-WM-IM
Aberdeen Proving Ground, MD 21005-5066
(410) 278-3485
Fax: (410) 278-9969
glenns@arl.mil

9711

Business Information: Mr. Smith serves in the capacity of Computer Scientist of the United States Army Research Laboratory at Aberdeen Proving Ground (APG) in Maryland. Fulfilling the role of systems, network, and teleconferencing administrator, his duties include monitoring and tuning systems software, peripherals, and networks as well as administering and controlling operating systems, compilers, and utilities. Mr. Smith, possessing extensive expertise, is also involved in systems analysis and integration, providing installation and help desk support for new systems, and installing and configuring new and upgrade systems. He plans to attain certifications in new technology and gain more experience with networking. Mr. Smith attributes his success to his willingness to take on new jobs with enthusiasm, training, keeping an open mind, and his problem solving skills. Mr. Smith serves in the capacity of Computer Scientist of the United States Army Research Laboratory at Aberdeen Proving Ground (APG) in Maryland. Fulfilling the role of systems, network, and teleconferencing administrator, his duties include monitoring and tuning systems software, peripherals, and networks as well as administering and controlling operating systems, compilers, and utilities. Mr. Smith, possessing extensive expertise, is also involved in systems analysis and integration, providing installation and help desk support for new systems, and installing and configuring new and upgrade systems. He plans to attain certifications in new technology and gain more experience with networking. Mr. Smith attributes his success to his willingness to take on new jobs with enthusiasm, training, keeping an open mind, and his problem solving skills. The United States Army Research Laboratory has not always existed in its present form. Battlefields constantly change and victory usually depends upon superior technology and general know-how. As the battlefield has changed, so has the direction of research into weapons, materials, and surveillence systems. From missile systems to close-combat techniques and thermographic imaging, the Army Research Laboratory is on the cutting edge of battlefield technology. Established in 1992, the Laboratory presently employs a staff of 400. The United States Army Research Laboratory has not always existed in its present form. Battlefields constantly change and victory usually depends upon superior technology and general know-how. As the battlefield has changed, so has the direction of research into weapons, materials, and surveillence systems. From missile systems to close-combat techniques and thermographic imaging, the Army Research Laboratory is on the cutting edge of battlefield technology. Established in 1992, the Laboratory presently employs a staff of 400. **Career Highlights:** Computer Scientist, United States Army Research Laboratory (1992-Present); Computer Scientist, Ballistic Research Laboratory (1986-92). **Education:** The Johns Hopkin's University, Master's degree in Computer Science (1992); University of Maryland, B.S. in Computer Science. **Personal Information:** Mr. Smith enjoys snow skiing.

Richard K. Smith

Telecommunications Manager
United States Air Force
Hanscom Air Force Base
Boston, MA 01731-5000
(781) 377-7500
Fax: (781) 377-7276
rksmith@webtv.net

9711

Business Information: Drawing from more than 30 years of military services, Mr. Smith is the Telecommunications Manager for the United States Air Force at Hanscom Air Force Base. In his position, he is responsible for overseeing and maintaining the functionality and operational status of the Base's communications and information systems infrastructure, to include computers, pagers, and cell phones. Possessing superior talents and an excellent understanding of technology, Mr. Smith's focus is on maintaining the Base's readiness to support U.S. Air Force contingency taskings assigned. His active participation with industry-related associations enables him to remain on the cutting edge and provides him avenues to network and interact with other communications and information systems professionals. In the future, Mr. Smith looks forward to working possibly with the United Nations or an international networking company. Established in 1948, the United States Air Force is a military department within the Department of Defense. Hanscom Air Force Base, located 17 miles northwest of Boston, Massachusetts is part of the Air Force Materiel Command. Currently, Hanscom Air Force Base's telecommunications, computer network, and information systems services/control center is manned by 250 military and civilian personnel. **Career Highlights:** Telecommunications Manager, United States Air Force, Hanscom Air Force Base (Present); Program Element Monitor, Secretary of the Air Force, ACQN (1996-98); Engineering Supervisor, Joint STARS E8-C, Ground Systems (1992-96); Software IV & V Program Manager, Joint STARS E-8A, Software Development (1987-91). **Associations & Accomplishments:** American Institute of Aeronautics and Astronautics; Armed Forces Communication and Electronics Association; Air Force Association; Association of Old Crows; Institute of Electronics and Electrical Engineers; National Association of Retired Federal Employees; Armaga Springs Homeowners Association; Chief Information Officer Certification. **Education:** Golden Gate University, Master's degree of Public Administration; Antioch University, B.A. in Engineering and Management; Allan Hancock College, Associate's degree in Quality Technology; Information Resources Management College, Advance Management (1998); Defense Systems Management College, Program Management; Air University, Air War College Seminar Program. **Personal Information:** Married to Carol A. in 1963. Two children: Susan and Richard. Mr. Smith enjoys research on technology effects on socialization.

Timothy R. Smith

Network Control Center Manager
Washington Army National Guard
Building 106, Camp Murray
Tacoma, WA 98430
(253) 512-7777
Fax: (253) 512-8679
smithtr@wa-army.ngb.army.mil

9711

Business Information: Mr. Smith functions in the capacity of Network Control Center Manager for the Washington Army National Guard. He manages the local area network and wide area network connectivity and domain servers. An expert troubleshooter, he advises the Internet accessibility of the Guard within the state of Washington. He is also involved in fire watch security control for the dense forest areas of the state. Awarded as the Army Chief of Staff Award, Mr. Smith hopes to become involved in implementing Windows 2000 and gain his Cisco certification. His success is attributed to his constant study and remaining on the cutting edge of technology. Washington Army National Guard operates as a reserve component of the United States Army. Under the control of the state governor, the Army National Guard was established in 1835 to protect and defend citizens of the United States. Today, the Guard is the first response team for any nationwide emergencies and the reserve team for the United States Army during times of war. Presently, the Washington Army National Guard is manned by more than 8,000 national guardsmen. **Career Highlights:** Network Control Center Manager, Washington Army National Guard (1999-Present); Master Engineer, POA (1990-98). **Associations & Accomplishments:** Back Office Professional Association. **Education:** Cornell University, B.A. (1985); Microsoft Certified Professional; Microsoft Certified Professional+Internet; Microsoft Certified System Engineer. **Personal Information:** Married to Chan in 1990.

Stephen E. Stoner

Chief of ET&S
USAED Sacramento
1325 J Street, Room 1055
Sacramento, CA 95814
(916) 557-7676
Fax: (916) 557-7026
sstoner@spk.usace.army.mil

9711

Business Information: Serving as the Chief of ET&S for USAED Sacramento, Mr. Stoner supervises seven units that support automation within his Department. Possessing an excellent understanding of his field, he also guides his staff in performing quality control reviews, applications development, specification writing, and data architecture. Ensuring compliance with ISO Standards and criteria also fall under the purview of his responsibilities. Mr. Stoner compiles the budgets, oversees project management, and provides strategic planning methods for the Department. He oversees the systems functions, directs replacement and upgrade of hardware and software, and troubleshoots. His plans for the future include attaining his Ph.D. "Do everything in moderation," is cited as Mr. Stoner's advice. Established in 1774, USAED Sacramento is part of the United States Army Engineer district, employing 1,100 private and public engineers around the world. Department, located in Sacramento, California, engages in project design of navigational streams, locks, dams, civil work missions, and infrastructures in and around Sacramento. Regionally, the Department reports an annual revenue of $400 million. **Career Highlights:** USAED Sacramento: Chief fo ET&S (1993-Present), Chief Arms TCX (1990-93), Assistant Chief of Technical Support Branch (1987-90), Design Quality Assurance (1982-87). **Education:** University of California at Davis: M.B.A. (1986), B.S. in Electrical Engineering (1977). **Personal Information:** Married to Alice in 1973. Two children: Armineh and Amelia. Mr. Stoner enjoys complexity in organizational behavior.

Per Svensson, Ph.D.

Director of Research
Defense Research Establishment
FOA
Stockholm, Sweden 17290
+46 87063696
Fax: +46 87063686
pers@sto.foa.se

9711

Business Information: Holding the position of Director of Research, Dr. Svensson provides his technical expertise with Defense Research Establishment for 26 years. Concentrating his efforts towards research and development, he oversees a knowledgable and experienced team of researchers supplying them with necessary equipment, and materials. Authoring in C[] systems technology, he performs lectures in regards to established research in newly developed products. Continuing his specialized research with the Defense Research Establishment, Dr. Svensson remains committed to providing excellent information technology development. Possessing the tenacity to pursue what he believes in, Dr. Svensson attributes his success to the availability of quality education and his desire to absorb knowledge to develop new ideas and concepts. Serving a national client base, the Defense Research Establishment is a government institution founded in 1945. Located in Stockholm, Sweden, the Establishment employs 1,100 technical experts who are extensively involved in performing defense research in C[] oriented information fusion and information systems architecture. **Career Highlights:** Defense Research Establishment: Director of Research (1987-Present), Senior Scientist (1982-87); Adjunct Professor, Royal Institute of Technology (1996). **Associations & Accomplishments:** Association of Computing Machinery; Institute of Electrical and Electronics Engineers; Institute of Electrical and Electronics Engineers Computer Society; American Association for the Advancement of Science. **Education:** Royal Instiute of Technology: Associate Professor of Docent (1983), Ph.D. in Computing Science (1979), Licentiate of Technology (1970), M.S. in Engineering Physics (1965). **Personal Information:** Three children: Orjan, Sigrid, and Ragni. Dr. Svensson enjoys travel, diving, classical music and reading.

Charlene C. Trachtenberg

Technical Specialist
Space & Naval Warfare Systems Command
1949 South George Mason Drive
Arlington, VA 22204
(703) 697-9876
Fax: (703) 931-3437
charlene_trachtenberg@yahoo.com

9711

Business Information: A successful, 25 year veteran of information technology, Ms. Trachtenberg serve as a Technical Specialist with the Space & Naval Warfare Systems Command. She is responsible for all aspects of computer programming, budget excecution, and contract acquisition. Fulfilling a number of technical duties since joining the Command in 1996, Ms. Trachtenberg directs and participates in the analysis, installation, configuration, modification, support, and tracking of operating systems, database management systems, utilities, software, and hardware. Her focus is on the discovery, investigation, and initial deployment of new technologies within the Space & Naval Warfare Systems Command. The most rewarding aspects of her career is creating applications laced with quality, value, and reliability. In the future, Ms. Trachtenberg anticipates her promotion to systems analyst as a result of her continuing efforts to increase her skills through training and professional development activities, as well as her ability to work with Web applications. Space & Naval Warfare Systems Command provides technical support to naval and space warfare systems. The Command specializes in computer programming and problem solving. Established in the 1900s, the Command is located in Arlington, Virginia and employs many skilled technicians and administrative personnel. **Career Highlights:** Technical Specialist, Space & Naval Warfare Systems Command (1996-Present); Computer Specialist, Naval Telecommunication & Computer Organization (1991-95); Computer Programmer/Analyst, United States Army Military Transportation Management Command (1981-91). **Associations & Accomplishments:** National Association of Retired Federal Employees; Wilde Oak Home Association. **Education:** Northern Virginia Community College, Computer Science degree; China Medical College, B.S. (1975). **Personal Information:** Married to Jack in 1975. Ms. Trachtenberg enjoys travel, movies, reading and computer browsing.

Emily H. Vandiver

Director/Technology Program Manager
United States Aviation and Missile Command
Amsam-Rd-At
Redstone Arsenal, AL 35898
(256) 876-4857
Fax: (256) 876-4033
evandiver@redstone.army.mil

9711

Business Information: Ms. Vandiver is Director and Technology Program Manager with the United States Aviation and Missile Command. She is responsible for all aspects of applied and advanced technology initiatives for Army weapon systems for soldiers. Together with her co-workers, she designs new programs and creates new techniques to more fully utilize the current aircraft and missile launching devices. For her outstanding efforts while in the Army, Ms. Vandiver has been recognized as one of the "Outstanding Women" within the Department of the Army and has received the "Civilian Service Award." To advance within her field, she continuously attends seminars and workshops that keep her abreast of the newest advancements. Ms. Vandiver believes that tenacity is the reason for success and she looks forward to the future of Army technology and the upcoming implementation projects within her division. United States Aviation and Missile Command is a division of the Department of Defense. Operating within the Army, the Missile Command researches and develops new armory and battle plans to enhance the performance of the troops during times of war. The Command works to link the efforts of the Air Force, Army, Navy, and Marine Corps together with the latest technology to implement new tracking devices, radar techniques, missiles, and protective gear. **Career Highlights:** United States Aviation and Missile Command: Director/Technology Program Manager (1997-Present), Technology Program Manager (1994-97), Rapid Force Projection Initiative Manager (1992-94). **Associations & Accomplishments:** Association of United States Army; American Helicopter Society; American Institute of Aeronautics and Astronautics; Senior Member, Institute of Electrical and Electronics Engineers; National Defense Industrial Association; National Space Club; Society of Women Engineers; Rotary Club. **Education:** University of Alabama at Huntsville: B.S. in Business Administration Management (In Progress), B.S. in Electrical Engineering Magna Cum Laude. **Personal Information:** Two children: Melissa and David. Ms. Vandiver enjoys water sports, golf and arts and crafts.

Clarence E. Weaver

LAN Manager
Headquarters, Air Force Audit Agency
1125 Air Force Pentagon
Washington, DC 20330-1125
(703) 696-8029
Fax: (703) 696-8034

9711

Business Information: Getting started in technology through high school, Mr. Weaver's success is due to is hard work ethic and ambition. Joining Headquarters, Air Force Audit Agency in 1997, he fulfills the responsibilities of LAN Manager. In his role, he oversees all management aspects of day-to-day network operations. Drawing from over 20 years of practical experience and a firm academic foundation, Mr. Weaver also presides over customer services. A testament to his technical and management skills, the network has not been down except for intermittent power outages. Remaining on the leading edge of technology, he continually reads various trade magazines, surfs the Internet, and attends trade shows. Becoming head of another government agency and getting more into design and procurement serves as Mr. Weaver's long-term goals. Headquarters, Air Force Audit Agency is part of the Department of Defense. The Agency performs Air Force directed audits on Air Force units with a focus on inventory and audit policies, procedures, documentation, and corrective actions. Based in Washington, DC, the Agency's local operation is staffed by more than 500 auditors and administrators. **Career Highlights:** LAN Manager, Headquarters, Air Force Audit Agency (1997-Present); LAN Support Manager, Department of the Navy (1989-97); Computer Analyst, Vitro Corporation (1978-89). **Education:** Virginia State University, B.S. in Information Services (1978); Lear Siegler Institute, Associate degree in Computer Programming. **Personal Information:** Mr. Weaver enjoys art, photography and individual sports.

Barry H. Young

Mathematician
White Sands Missile Range
Department of the Army
Las Cruces, NM 88002
(505) 678-4480
youngbl@wsmr.army.mil

9711

Business Information: Serving as a Mathematcian for White Sands Missile Range, Mr. Young is responsible for the development of cutting edge software for data reduction. Possessing superior talents and an excellent understanding of his field, he is accountable for reducing the amount of paperwork the Range deals with by providing a system, which will allow all employees and military personnel access to required data in the performance of their duties. Highly regarded and attributing his success to good fortune and intelligence, Mr. Young notes the highlight of his career as developing a state of the art data reading software as well as a network for monitoring realtime. In the future, he looks forward to completing his assignment with with White Sands Missile Range and retiring. The White Sands Missile Range supports missle development for Department of Defense, Department of the Army, Department of the Air Force, and National Aeronautics and Space Administration. Operated by the United States Army Test and Evaluation Command, the Range covers more than 3,200 square miles and is the largest military installation in the country. **Career Highlights:** White Sands Missile Range: Mathematician (1986-Present), General Engineer (1982-86), Mechanical Engineer. **Associations & Accomplishments:** American Mathematical Society; Institute Electrical and Electronics Engineers Computer Society. **Education:** New Mexico State University, M.S. in Mathematics (1982); Southern Methodist University, M.S. in Mechanical Engineering (1971).

Richard W. Peppe Jr.
Senior Project Manager
United States Department of State
2401 East Street NW
Washington, DC 20522
(202) 261-8242
Fax: (703) 242-0891
pepperwjr@aol.com

9721

Business Information: Serving as Senior Project Manager of the United States Department of State, Mr. Peppe is responsible for sourcing and selecting equipment for the information technology department. He is accountable for developing software applications and redesigning existing systems. A successful, 26 year veteran of the technology field, Mr. Peppe establishes policy and rules, as well as manages all aspects of hiring and educating project managers. Recognized for his contributions, he is credited with implementing a Prisoner of War Information System use to document information on enemy prisoners of war, such as citizenship and next of kin. His is also recognized for his involvement in the OASYS project from 1992-95. This project provided a new search engine of a much quicker speed using technologies that includes RISC processing, Raid, and HAMCP. In the future, Mr. Peppe plans to attain an administrative role, continue his education, retire, and become a college professor. Established in 1775, the Department of State is responsible for establishing diplomatic relationships with foreign countries throughout the world. Together with the agencies of these countries, the Department develops and enforces policies concerned with health, welfare, education, environment, human rights, and other worldwide issues. **Career Highlights:** Senior Project Manager, United States Department of State (1988-Present); Systems Development Division Manager, Continental Insurance Company (1988-95); Senior Accountant/Systems Developer, MCI Corporation (1994-95). **Associations & Accomplishments:** USARWA; Data Processing Managers Association; Masons; Moose; American Legion; Veterans of Foreign Wars; BPOE. **Education:** University of South Florida, B.S. (1981); A.A. in Business Administration; Basic Law Enforcement; Advanced Law Enforcement; Economics; Mathematics. **Personal Information:** Married to Margaret in 1989. One child: Thomas Anthony. Mr. Peppe enjoys skiing, oil painting, hiking, camping, snowmobiling and travel.

John R. Rogers

Counselor for Telematics
South African Embassy
3051 Massachusetts Avenue NW
Washington, DC 20008-3693
(202) 274-7999
Fax: (202) 364-6008
golfmad@erols.com

9721

Business Information: Mr. Rogers is the Counselor for Telematics and Information Services for the Embassy of the Republic of South Africa in Washington D.C. He is responsible for managing all the computer, telecommunications, and Internet networks and facilities for all the accredited South African Missions in Canada as well as North, South, and Central America. The South African Embassy's role in the United States is to promote South Africa's national interests by encouraging and fostering the flow of resources between the two countries in order to further the quality of life of the people of South Africa. In the age of technological and information revolution, it is Mr. Rogers' responsibility to assure the Embassy of the technological means with which to accomplish its goals. The South African Embassy is staffed by several dipomats and their assistants under the leadership and guidance of the Ambassador. **Career Highlights:** Counselor for Telematics, South African Embassy (1998-Present); Deputy Director of Telematics, Department of Foreign Affairs (Present); Technology/Communications Official to the President Mandela's office during numerous state visits around the world; Attaché, Communications Systems, South African Embassy, United States (1991-95); Counsel, Communications Systems, South African Embassy, London, United Kingdom (1983-89); Senior Electronics Laboratory Technician, South African Bureau of Standards (1975-77); Air Traffic Control Radar Technician, South African Air Force (1968-72). **Associations & Accomplishments:** Past Associate Member, South African Institute of Electrical and Radio Engineers; Invited to the opening of South Africa's New Antartica Research Base: Sanae (IU) in Antarctic in January 1997. **Education:** Pretoria College for Advanced Technical Education (1968-72). **Personal Information:** Married to Anna in 1972. Four children: John Jr., Phillip, Gareth, and Christopher. Mr. Rogers enjoys taking part in sports with his sons, sailing and golf.

Iris D. Williams

Project Manager
United States Department of State
7374 Boston Boulevard
Springfield, VA 22153-3149
(703) 912-8483
Fax: (703) 912-8668
williamsid@state.gov

9721

Business Information: As a Project Manager for the United States Department of State, Ms. Williams is responsible for overseeing the division which handles cables, telegrams, and e-mails. She maintains the budget and initiates departmental purchases within budgetary guidelines. Demonstrating strong leadership, she supervises the technical staff in order to ensure accurate and dependable communications. Her superior managerial skills are vital to the Department's seamless day to day operation. In the future, Ms. Williams plans to obtain certification for project management, obtain a branch chief position, and gain additional responsibilities. Her success reflects her ability to take on tough challenges and deliver results. The United States Department of State is an executive department of the U.S. government that facilitates relationships with other governments. The Department advises the President of the United States on foreign policy and is responsible for carrying out policies, negotiating treaties, and attending to official business with foreign embassies in Washington, D.C. **Career Highlights:** United States Department of State: Project Manager (1999-Present), Legislative Affairs Special Assistant (1998-99), Acting Branch Chief (1998), Help Desk Supervisor (1996-98). **Education:** University of Maryland, B.A. (1990); Syracuse University. **Personal Information:** Married to Kevin F. in 1987. Two children: Jennifer Jewel and Victor F. Ms. Williams enjoys tai chi, fencing and sewing.

Members Indexed Alphabetically
by
Last Name

Section 2

A

Abbott, Lisa, Office Depot, Delray Beach, FL *Page 1-128*

Abdulla, Mahmood Ahmed, Batelco, Manama, Bahrain *Page 1-216*

Abercrombie, Richard D., Datapoint Corporation, San Antonio, TX *Page 1-170*

Abramczyk, Edward S., Concert, Reston, VA *Page 1-95*

Abu-Zahra, Bill, MICROS Systems, Inc. - Southern California Region, Aliso Viejo, CA *Page 1-49*

Abusoud, Samer S., Washington University, St. Louis, MO *Page 1-320*

Acheson, Lori, Marketlink, Inc., Esterville, IA *Page 1-299*

Acholonu, Omogbemiboluwa I., Internal Revenue Service, Financial and Administrative Systems, Bowie, MD *Page 1-379*

Ackermann, Anthony, LA Dye & Printworks, Inc., Pico Rivera, CA *Page 1-11*

Ackley, Brian Sterling, Tompkins Cortland Community College, Dryden, NY *Page 1-335*

Adams
   Rick, IHS Engineering, Colorado Springs, CO *Page 1-18*
   Sharon K., Process Software Corporation, Chelmsford, MA *Page 1-170*

Adatia, Amin, Knowtech Solutions, Inc., Nepean, Ontario, Canada *Page 1-217*

Ademidun, Olumide A., Spar Aerospace, Ikey Lagos, Nigeria *Page 1-56*

Aden, Steve E., ITS Communications, Grand Rapids, MI *Page 1-95*

Adesh, Vivek S., Starternet, Douglasville, GA *Page 1-170*

Adkins
   Jeffrey M., Coldwater Creek, Mineral Wells, WV *Page 1-130*
   Kaye W., K & R Splicing, Pekin, IL *Page 1-6*

Agarwal, Braj, Affordable PC Systems, Inc., Seaford, NY *Page 1-217*

Aguero Blanco, Marjorie, DaimlerChrysler Aerospace Orbital Systems Inc., Houston, TX *Page 1-170*

Ahmed, Shakir, ETISALAT, Fujairah, United Arab Emirates *Page 1-95*

Akhtar, Hasan, Innovex, Litchfield, MN *Page 1-48*

Akridge, William D., 90th Regional Support Command, North Little Rock, AR *Page 1-392*

Al Hadad, Shariff, Golden Enterprises, Melbourne, FL *Page 1-70*

Al-Jamal, Ismail, Blue Dragon Network, Petaluma, CA *Page 1-217*

Al-Nimri, Nabil Isa, JTC, Amman, Jordan *Page 1-91*

Albright, Gerry, Albright Ideas, Inc., Eagan, MN *Page 1-217*

Aldridge, Brad W., Radio Advertising Bureau, Dallas, TX *Page 1-165*

Alexis, Emmanuel E. A., Quebec Government, Montreal, Quebec, Canada *Page 1-372*

Alger, Brian W., KPMG Consulting, Toronto, Ontario, Canada *Page 1-362*

Ali
   Murtaza, Texas Instruments, Dallas, TX *Page 1-63*
   Ziad Kamil Muhammad, Canadian Space Agency, Saint-Hubert, Quebec, Canada *Page 1-391*

Allain, Jean-Marc, New Bridge Technology, Houston, TX *Page 1-54*

Allen
   Almon, Bowater Inc., Catawba, SC *Page 1-14*
   Carol Elizabeth, Base Technologies, Inc., Alexandria, VA *Page 1-217*
   Mark, Unisys Corporation, Acworth, GA *Page 1-217*
   Pamela T., ABN AMRO Bank, Chicago, IL *Page 1-137*
   Tommy L., e-Marketworld.com, Newport News, VA *Page 1-299*

Almeda, Gilbert S., Grubb & Ellis Company, Northbrook, IL *Page 1-158*

Almeida-Coffron, Katty, Hewlett-Packard Company, Palo Alto, CA *Page 1-39*

Almogbel, Saud A., Royal Cabinet of Saudi Arabia, Sterling, VA *Page 1-370*

Alsedek, Steven M., Coastal Securities LP, Dallas, TX *Page 1-147*

Altan, Ergin, Turkish Aerospace Industries, Ankara, Turkey *Page 1-75*

Alvarado, Winifreda Floro, Brookings Institution, Washington, DC *Page 1-360*

Alvarez, Isidro, Motorola, Fort Lauderdale, FL *Page 1-64*

Anandan, Israel D., IMS HEALTH Strategic Technologies, Norcross, GA *Page 1-171*

Ananya, Brigit, Ananya Systems, Inc., Los Gatos, CA *Page 1-194*

Anderson
   Bruce N., Duke Energy Corporation, Charlotte, NC *Page 1-113*
   Douglas M., Los Angeles County Mass Transit Agency, Los Angeles, CA *Page 1-389*
   Fred R., EDS, Herndon, VA *Page 1-214*
   Gwyn C., Enhanced Ideas, La Crosse, WI *Page 1-217*
   Maribeth, First Chicago/Mercantile Services, Chicago, IL *Page 1-171*
   Michael E., Integrated Chipware, Reston, VA *Page 1-171*
   Randy, Eaton Corporation, Milwaukee, WI *Page 1-356*
   Scott K., Internet Ventures, Pasadena, TX *Page 1-218*
   Terri W., Breed Technologies, Lakeland, FL *Page 1-72*

Andre, Darlene A., Northbrook Community School District 28, Northbrook, IL *Page 1-380*

Andrews, Jonathan, Andrell Corporation, El Dorado Hills, CA *Page 1-218*

Angle, Brenda K., A. Louis Supply Company, Ashtabula, OH *Page 1-122*

Anniko, P. Peter, Fidelity & Deposit Company of Maryland, Baltimore, MD *Page 1-153*

Ansari, Waheed H., Illinois Housing Development Authority, Chicago, IL *Page 1-388*

Ansell, Christopher T., Mesa Solutions, Madison, AL *Page 1-218*

Ansley, David Thomas, Warren County Schools, Warrenton, GA *Page 1-380*

Anthochy, George, Federal Aviation Administration, Arlington, TX *Page 1-389*

Antle, M. D. Paka, DRS Optronics, Viera, FL *Page 1-84*

Anton, Patrice, Novacel, deville Les Rouen, France *Page 1-26*

Antoniou, Nicholaos, Transcom, Jersey City, NJ *Page 1-389*

Aprile, Joseph A., Fred Hutchinson Cancer Research Center, Seattle, WA *Page 1-356*

Arafeh, Ashraf M., International Turnkey Systems, Jeddah, Saudi Arabia *Page 1-218*

Archer, Kelley P., FSI International, Chaska, MN *Page 1-64*

Ard, Bryan N., Maryville Technologies, St. Louis, MO *Page 1-218*

Ares, Julian Sol, Chicago Microsystems, Chicago, IL *Page 1-218*

Arias, Jorge M., Hules Tecnicos S.A., San Jose, Costa Rica *Page 1-29*

Aris, Harold A., Vibe Magazine, New York, NY *Page 1-16*

Armstrong
   Jay, Tivoli Systems, Austin, TX *Page 1-194*
   Stephen D., State of Kansas, Topeka, KS *Page 1-372*

Arpide, Jose I., Osram Sylvania, Beverly, MA *Page 1-53*

Arroyo, Brett C., Jannon Group, Charlotte, NC *Page 1-218*

Arumugam, Senthil K., Baton Rouge International Inc., Sayreville, NJ *Page 1-218*

Asbach, Gordon J., State of Washington, Department of Social and Health Services, Olympia, WA *Page 1-384*

Ashford
   Anne, NEC Technologies, Inc., Littleton, MA *Page 1-48*
   Paul L., Software Consulting Services, Nazareth, PA *Page 1-194*

Athey, Harry C., Philips P.C. Peripherals, Colorado Springs, CO *Page 1-128*

Atia, Tarek, Technologica Trading & Computer Systems, Cairo, Egypt *Page 1-219*

Attri, Joel P., KPMG Consulting, Inc., Mountain View, CA *Page 1-362*

Austin, Richard, Nortel Networks, Brampton, Ontario, Canada *Page 1-54*

Autry, Daniel J., American Institute of Certified Public Accountants, Jersey City, NJ *Page 1-345*

Avendano, Igmar E., SYMTX, Austin, TX *Page 1-219*

Awan, Tajammul H., Command Web Offset, Secaucus, NJ *Page 1-17*

Ayers, Janet B., Carroll Technical Institute, Carrollton, GA *Page 1-335*

Azar, Lawrence, ppb, Inc., Portola Valley, CA *Page 1-64*

Azizi, Peyman, Loral Cyberstar, Rocksville, MD *Page 1-108*

B

Babajide, Olusegun, Jano Multicom AS, Oslo, Norway *Page 1-219*

Babal, Suraj, PricewaterhouseCoopers LLP, Edison, NJ *Page 1-352*

Babcock, James M., Unisys Corporation, New York, NY *Page 1-219*

Babilla, Furat C., Alameda County, Public Works Agency, Hayward, CA *Page 1-390*

Babu, Venkatesha, Innosoft Inc., Edison, NJ *Page 1-31*

Bachrach, Daniel A., BEST! Software, Inc., St. Petersburg, FL *Page 1-171*

Bacik, Sandra A., Bacik Consulting Service, Federal Way, WA *Page 1-219*

Badar, Ijaz Ul Haq, Emirates Telecom Corporation, Abu Dhabi, United Arab Emirates
Page 1-95

Bader, Robin L., ARDC, Chicago, IL Page 1-345

Badinger, Dawn D., EMCO, Baton Rouge, LA Page 1-219

Baez, Ramon F., Northrop Grumman, Dallas, TX Page 1-75

Bagley, Kathleen A., Excel Consulting, Winthrop, ME Page 1-219

Bahrami, Ali, The Boeing Company, Seattle, WA Page 1-75

Bailey
    Brian A., Rappahannock Regional Jail, Fredericksburg, VA Page 1-377
    Larry J., Southern California Edison, Rosemead, CA Page 1-113
    William D., Catholic Charities, San Jose, CA Page 1-344

Baiter, Jamey Fern, Illinois State Board of Education, Springfield, IL Page 1-380

Baker
    Gene Charles, Inventa, Eldersburg, MD Page 1-220
    Melvin, PROSOFT, Hampton, VA Page 1-201
    Robert D., Schreck Morris, Las Vegas, NV Page 1-311

Baker-Cross, Leah Dawn, University of Nebraska, Omaha, NE Page 1-320

Bal, Anupam D. S., ICOM Solutions Pty. Ltd., Sydney, New South Wales, Australia Page 1-367

Baliakhov, Dmitri, EMC Corporation, Hopkinton, MA Page 1-212

Balian, Gerair D., Digital Conversions, Tustin, CA Page 1-220

Balkema, Allan, Regional Transportation District, Denver, CO Page 1-87

Ball, Sharron L., Jon Barry & Associates, Inc., Conord, NC Page 1-165

Bandong, Lydia M., Arris Interactive, Suwanee, GA Page 1-58

Bandyopadhyay, Abhijit, Cypress Semiconductor Corporation, Cupertine, CA Page 1-63

Banerjee, Ayananshu, SBC Communications Inc., St. Louis, MO Page 1-95

Bansal, Kapil, Sapient Corporation, Union City, NJ Page 1-201

Barasch, Mark, Barasch Music & Sound, New York, NY Page 1-220

Barber
    Charles, Social Security Administration, Greenville, SC Page 1-375
    Clifton J., Oki Network Technologies, Suwanee, GA Page 1-57

Barkin, Ruth Ann, DynCorp, Alexandria, VA Page 1-356

Barnard
    James H., First Consulting Group, Winter Springs, FL Page 1-299
    Jeffery R., Emergency Medical Services Group, Inc., d.b.a. EMSG, Largo, FL Page 1-310

Barr
    Angela Lynn, ALCOA Engineered Products, Cressona, PA Page 1-32
    Robert T., HSI Geotrans, Inc., Sterling, VA Page 1-368

Barrow, Rudy, DMB&B Advertising, Los Angeles, CA Page 1-163

Barrows, Donald A., Lassen Municipal Utility, Susanville, CA Page 1-113

Barta, Barbie, Comsys, Dallas, TX Page 1-220

Bartlett, Roy H., GSI Consulting Services, Toronto, Ontario, Canada Page 1-220

Barto, Bill L., RWJ & Associates, Oklahoma City, OK Page 1-167

Bartoli, Peter J., SAIC, San Diego, CA Page 1-357

Bartolotta, Tina, National Data Corporation, Atlanta, GA Page 1-300

Barton
    Regina V., United Federation of Teachers, Teacher Centers Professional Development Program, New York, NY Page 1-346
    Robert J., City of Virginia Beach Department of Public Utilities, Virginia Beach, VA Page 1-390

Basinger, William Daniel, M-Cubed Information Systems, Hyattsville, MD Page 1-220

Bass, Barbara A., Pagemart Wireless, Dallas, TX Page 1-92

Bates
    Charles P., Northeast Utilities, Berlin, CT Page 1-116
    Christopher A., Catalina Marketing, Tampa, FL Page 1-165

Batiste, Joshua, Reliant Energy HL&P, Houston, TX Page 1-115

Batmazian, Krikor, Cisco Systems, Inc., Santa Clara, CA Page 1-58

Batt-Ptaszek, Chris, GTE Internetworking, Powered by BBN, Columbia, MD Page 1-221

Baukman, Robert, Mynd, Eastover, SC Page 1-171

Baxter, Linda M., Neuse Center, New Bern, NC Page 1-384

Bayman, Richard P., Chubb Computer Services, Parsippany, NJ Page 1-221

Bayne, Chuck, Laramie High School, Laramie, WY Page 1-314

Bayyapureddy, Kishore, Equifax E-Banking Solutions, Inc., Hahira, GA Page 1-221

Beachner, James G., The Metropolitan Community College, Lee's Summit, MO Page 1-335

Beall, Carlene, dba computer moms[], Austin, TX Page 1-300

Bearce, James E., Copeland Associates, Inc., East Brunswick, NJ Page 1-156

Beard, Gunilla, Tetra Pak Americas, Inc., Atlanta, GA Page 1-37

Beasley, Mark S., U.S. Tobacco Manufacturing LP, Nashville, TN Page 1-10

Beaumont, Patrick A., Housing Fiscal Services, New York, NY Page 1-158

Beaver, Jake, Texas State Technical College, Waco, TX Page 1-335

Bechard, Richard, Siemens Canada, Ontario, Ontario, Canada Page 1-72

Bechtel, Lawrence J., Blue Cross & Blue Shield of Louisiana, Baton Rouge, LA Page 1-149

Becker
    Andrew D., DNA Systems Inc., Somerville, NJ Page 1-171
    James F., AOP Solutions, Buffalo, NY Page 1-221
    Sandra L., Governor Mifflin School District, Shillington, PA Page 1-314

Beckner, John W., Droege Computing Services, Durham, NC Page 1-221

Bedi, Vickram A., Datalink Computer Products Inc., Mount Kisco, NY Page 1-221

Beebe, David H., Automation Research Systems, Limited, Alexandria, VA Page 1-171

Beelman, Misty M., Consultech, Inc., West Des Moines, IA Page 1-384

Bekov, George I., Spectrum International, Inc., El Cerrito, CA Page 1-221

Bellak, Rodney S., Chubb Computer Services, Parsippany, NJ Page 1-222

Belousov, Katrina, CSC Consulting Firm, Cincinnati, OH Page 1-201

Belpaire, Patrick, U&I Learning, Steenhuize, Belgium Page 1-340

Benavides, Rafael, Fisher-Rosemount, El Paso, TX Page 1-81

Benavidez, Eduardo D., The Wornick Company - Right Away Division, McAllen, TX Page 1-10

Benayoun, Andre, IBSYS, Nanterre, France Page 1-222

Bender
    Carla V., Pikes Peak Mental Health, Colorado Springs, CO Page 1-307
    Kendra, Tipper Tie, Apex, NC Page 1-34

Benedict, Michael, Telxon Corporation, Akron, OH Page 1-39

Benfield, Janie, San Juan County Assessor, Aztec, NM Page 1-379

Benner, Carol M., Templin Management Associates, Greenfield Center, NY Page 1-362

Bennett, John C., Ravenna Aluminum, Ravenna, OH Page 1-32

Benson, Stephen T., GMAC Commercial Mortgage, Horsham, PA Page 1-140

Berg, Linda M., West Wisconsin Telecom Cooperative, Inc., Menomonie, WI Page 1-95

Berlas, Abdul R., Technology Totems Inc., College Park, MD Page 1-222

Berner, Georg, Siemens AG, Munich, Germany Page 1-72

Berry, James C., USDA Forest Service, HMR, Arlington, VA Page 1-388

Bertolucci, Marco, Le Groupe BRT, Montreal, Quebec, Canada Page 1-222

Bertrand, Joseph F., United States Marine Corps, Kailua, HI Page 1-392

Besiso, Marwan Y., Al Zamil Group of Companies, Riyadh, Saudi Arabia Page 1-161

Betty, Joseph M., The Vanguard Group, Valley Forge, PA Page 1-145

Beukhof, Martin, Fingerhut, Plymouth, MN Page 1-130

Bhandary, Manoj S., Annuncio, San Jose, CA Page 1-163

Bhattacharjee, Sudip, University of Connecticut, Storrs, CT Page 1-320

Bhatty, Zuliqar Ahmed, Digital Natcom Company, Riyadh, Saudi Arabia Page 1-222

Bichel, Anthony R., Juniata College, Huntingdon, PA Page 1-335

Billings, Claire, Lockheed Martin, Gaithersburg, MD Page 1-79

Birdi, Moninder S., Parsons Engineering Science, Fairfax, MD Page 1-362

Bishop, Briget R., Fauquier Hospital, Warrenton, VA Page 1-307

Bjerkaas, Carlton L., SAIC, O'Fallon, IL Page 1-357

Black, Randy M., Simplot Livestock Company, Grand View, ID Page 1-1

Blackburn, Dale, ECPI College of Technology, Greensboro, NC Page 1-336

Blake
    Brian C., VERITAS Software, Buffalo, NY Page 1-194
    Catherine B., GTE Internetworking, Inc., Marblehead, MA Page 1-222

Bland, Richard L., Giffels Associates, Inc., Southfield, MI Page 1-350

Blankers, Galen C., Dethmers Manufacturing Company, Boyden, IA *Page 1-35*

Blaylock, William A., Checkfast, Salt Lake City, UT *Page 1-138*

Bliss, George, Walt Disney Company BVHE, Burbank, CA *Page 1-304*

Blocchi, Roger, Network Engineering, Inc., Indianapolis, IN *Page 1-222*

Block, Jeffrey Allen, Kahler Slater Architects, Milwaukee, WI *Page 1-350*

Blockus, Linda G., KPMG Consulting, Basking Ridge, NJ *Page 1-362*

Blumenthal, Kevin, Budd Van Lines, Somerset, NJ *Page 1-300*

Bode, Karl E., Sprint Paranet, Gilbert, AZ *Page 1-223*

Boegeman, Steven M., Ashten Racks, Inc., Irvine, CA *Page 1-123*

Boettger, Hans-Bernd, Battenfeld Extlenrusionstechnik GmbH, Bad-Muender, Germany *Page 1-36*

Boffardi, Marc G., Factset Research Systems, Greenwich, CT *Page 1-201*

Bogner, Wilhelm, Frequentis, Vienna, Austria *Page 1-55*

Boland, Dennis G., American Family Insurance Company, Madison, WI *Page 1-149*

Bollineni, Anand K., PSW Technologies, Austin, TX *Page 1-223*

Bolyard, Whitney L., Reinhart, Boerner, et al, Milwaukee, WI *Page 1-311*

Bonaparte, C. Scott, Elite Systems Support Inc., Hempstead, NY *Page 1-223*

Bonner, Barbara D., AT&T, Bridgewater, NJ *Page 1-95*

Boone-Shuford, Myrna, Westinghouse - Savannah River Site, Aiken, SC *Page 1-392*

Boostrom, Ron A., Symbiont Inc., San Antonio, TX *Page 1-223*

Booth
  Mark M., Southern Wine & Spirits, Miami, FL *Page 1-125*
  Michael, IBM Global Services, Winchester, England, United Kingdom *Page 1-223*

Bordonaro, Robert, Sulzer Metco, Westbury, NY *Page 1-34*

Borgmann, Philip M., Aurora Foods, St. Louis, MO *Page 1-8*

Borisov, Gennadiy, MTVi Group, New York, NY *Page 1-107*

Born, Lu Ann, Associated Press, Jackson, NJ *Page 1-299*

Bosworth, Kimberly A., Minibar Systems, Rockville, MD *Page 1-120*

Botnan, Michael J., Courage Center - Department of MIS, Hamel, MN *Page 1-311*

Boudreaux, Ambrose Carl, Ingenium Corporation, Upper Marlboro, MD *Page 1-223*

Bourdon, Philippe M., IKON Office Solutions, Glastonbury, CT *Page 1-50*

Bouwma, Michael, Alliant Energy, Madison, WI *Page 1-113*

Bovell, Matthew, IBM Global Services, Southbury, CT *Page 1-224*

Bowden, Geri D., Navant Corporation, Raleigh, NC *Page 1-224*

Bowen, Lynn A., Talbot's, Tampa, FL *Page 1-127*

Bowens, Dewitt, AlliedSignal Technical Services, La Plata, MD *Page 1-26*

Bowzer, Jerrold A., IBM Global Services, Oklahoma City, OK *Page 1-224*

Boyd, Ashley Aubrey, Rheem Manufacturing Company, Montgomery, AL *Page 1-53*

Boyles
  Alan L., AAA Business Machines, Fayetteville, AR *Page 1-128*
  Dana A., SRP, Tempe, AZ *Page 1-116*

Bradford
  Kirby R., Lucent Technologies, Alameda, CA *Page 1-58*
  Richard A., Never-Enuff Enterprises, Northern Cambria, PA *Page 1-224*

Bradish, Edward, Channel Communications, Wyano, PA *Page 1-108*

Bradley
  Dennis R., IBM Corporation, New York, NY *Page 1-39*
  Thomas M., Val Verde Unified School District, Perris, CA *Page 1-381*

Bradshaw, Rupert R., PC Net, Gulfport, MS *Page 1-224*

Brady, Brian J., Crown American Hotels Company, Johnstown, PA *Page 1-162*

Braggs, Genelle R., IBM Corporation, Atlanta, GA *Page 1-39*

Braithwaite, Wayne N., Bonneville International Corporation, Salt Lake City, UT *Page 1-107*

Brammer, Douglas E., Bell Atlantic, Silver Spring, MD *Page 1-96*

Brand, David, Fers Business Services Inc., Chicago, IL *Page 1-368*

Brauner, Darrell R., Ericsson, Inc., Research Triangle Park, NC *Page 1-58*

Bray, Robert T., TSI, Inc., St. Charles, MO *Page 1-224*

Breitkreutz, Sherry Lee, Gateway, Sioux Falls, SD *Page 1-224*

Brenneman, William B., AT&T Technical Services, Washington, DC *Page 1-225*

Brickerd, D. Dean, Orbcomm, Sterling, VA *Page 1-96*

Brickley, Douglas J., De Bellas & Co., Houston, TX *Page 1-142*

Brickman, Eric R., Prudential, Newark, NJ *Page 1-148*

Bridges, Martin O., Internal Revenue Service, Kansas City, MO *Page 1-379*

Bristow, Donald R., Unify Corporation, Sacramento, CA *Page 1-225*

Broadwater, Kirk, Techni-core, Huntsville, AL *Page 1-225*

Brocious, Mary Anne, Valassis Communications, Livonia, MI *Page 1-20*

Brooks
  Jeffrey A., Planning Consultants, Inc., Dahlgren, VA *Page 1-225*
  Yvonne, Brooks Office Solutions, Maple Shade, NJ *Page 1-225*

Brotman, Roy, IBM Global Services, Pine Brook, NJ *Page 1-225*

Broughton, Jeff R., Solution Bank, Webster, TX *Page 1-225*

Broward, Michael P., New Mexico Department of Labor, Information Systems Bureau, Albuquerque, NM *Page 1-385*

Brown
  Charles, Trident Data Systems, Santa Clarita, CA *Page 1-226*
  Chris N., Sybase, Inc., Greenwood Village, CO *Page 1-194*
  Dennis J., Grubb & Ellis Company, Northbrook, IL *Page 1-158*
  Ed, Instruction Set, Inc., Natick, MA *Page 1-226*
  Harold A., IBM Thomas J. Watson Research Center, Yorktown Heights, NY *Page 1-226*
  John R., Tarquini Organization, Camden, NJ *Page 1-350*
  John S., Optical Coating Laboratory, Santa Rosa, CA *Page 1-82*
  Kent, Donovan Data Systems, New York, NY *Page 1-165*
  Michael W., RIA - Research Institute of America, Carrollton, TX *Page 1-172*
  Robert W., Employers Unity, Arvada, CO *Page 1-155*
  Sharon M., GMAC Commercial Mortgage, Horsham, PA *Page 1-140*
  Thomas K., Resource Systems, Inc., New York, NY *Page 1-194*
  Thomas S., Square D Company, Nashville, TN *Page 1-52*

Brumley, Isaac, Attachmate Corporation, Bremerton, WA *Page 1-195*

Brunelle, Francois, Intelligence Architects LLC, Herndon, VA *Page 1-226*

Bruno, Rae Ann, Siemens Energy and Automation, Cumming, GA *Page 1-55*

Brunzell, Barbara J., Computer Network Technology, Minneapolis, MN *Page 1-226*

Bryant
  John A., Orscheln Management Company, Moberly, MO *Page 1-226*
  Tom, RCN Corporation, Arlington, MA *Page 1-96*

Bubniak, Robert P., Department of Veterans Affairs, Washington, DC *Page 1-386*

Bucchino, Nicolas A., VERITAS Software, Mountain View, CA *Page 1-195*

Buchner, Pamela J., Alaska Airlines, Seattle, WA *Page 1-89*

Budd, Daniel L., Control Systems International, Merriam, KS *Page 1-51*

Bufford, Peter, Solectron Corporation, Foster City, CA *Page 1-39*

Buhler, Wesley Dwayne, Electronic Data Systems, Plano, TX *Page 1-214*

Buker, William H., Maxim Group, Glen Allen, VA *Page 1-227*

Bukis, Deborah Elizabeth, Seattle Center, Seattle, WA *Page 1-305*

Bullied, Perry Leon, Information Retrieval, Cary, NC *Page 1-172*

Bullock, Steven H., Computer Sciences Corporation, Rockville, MD *Page 1-201*

Bumgarner, Kenneth B., Bumgarner Global Enterprises, Bloomington, IL *Page 1-227*

Bunt, Christopher Allen, Nortel Networks, Richardson, TX *Page 1-55*

Burch
  Neal F., EFC Systems, Montgomery, AL *Page 1-227*
  Scott A., Bulldog Information Services, San Francisco, CA *Page 1-227*

Burchfield, Bill, Police and Firemen's Disability, Columbus, OH *Page 1-155*

Burden, Matthew C., Northwestern University, Chicago, IL *Page 1-320*

Burg, Hans, ALPS Electric Europa GmbH, Duesseldorf NRW, Germany *Page 1-68*

Burgess
  Kevin A., EDS System House, Halifax, Nova Scotia, Canada *Page 1-214*
  Ronald A., IER Industries, Inc., Macedonia, OH *Page 1-28*

Burgoyne, Ann C., Berwanger Overmyer Associates, Columbus, OH *Page 1-155*

Burkhart, Michael G., Watson Wyatt Worldwide, Washington, DC *Page 1-362*

Burns, Elizabeth J., ProcureNet, Inc., New Hartford, CT *Page 1-172*

Burroughs, Vonda M., Hunter Douglas, Tupelo, MS *Page 1-13*

Burtnett, Jeanne, ITS Inc., Las Vegas, NV *Page 1-227*

Burton, Walt, Rand Technologies, Schaumburg, IL *Page 1-347*

Busch, Darnell, Samuel Rodgers Community Health Center, Kansas City, MO *Page* 1-307

Buse, Amy L. R., Ferris State University, Big Rapids, MI *Page* 1-320

Butcher, Linda L., Cyberlogic Business Services, Camarillo, CA *Page* 1-227

Butt, Khawar, Trinet Networking & Training, Inc., Diamond Bar, CA *Page* 1-227

Buzby, Carrie D., IBM Corporation, Denver, CO *Page* 1-39

Byrd, Melody D., IDX, Lombard, IL *Page* 1-201

C

Caffey, Jeffrey L., Department of Justice, Immigration Naturalization Service, Washington, DC *Page* 1-375

Cagney, Mary M., Northern Illinois University, Wheaton, IL *Page* 1-320

Cairns, Joe A., Database Consultants, Inc., Dallas, TX *Page* 1-227

Calderbank, Kevin, Southern Internet, Palm Beach Gardens, FL *Page* 1-108

Caldwell, Shawn Edward, Anderson and Associate's, Inc., Blacksburg, VA *Page* 1-348

Callahan, Gerard W., I Connection Inc., Waukegan, IL *Page* 1-172

Callaway, Lawrence A., United States Postal Service, Merrifield, VA *Page* 1-88

Callo, Fernando A., Sunrise Assisted Living, Fairfax, VA *Page* 1-343

Caloza, Racquel D., Merck & Co., Inc, Bridgeport, PA *Page* 1-22

Camp, Barbara Smith, Klein Independent School District, Houston, TX *Page* 1-381

Campbell
 Anne B., Blackwell's Information Services, Blackwood, NJ *Page* 1-300
 Chris A., BsG Inc., Dallas, PA *Page* 1-172
 Eileen Rose, Merallis Company, Rocky Hill, CT *Page* 1-147
 Gregory L., Technology Solutions Company, Alpharetta, GA *Page* 1-228
 Robert W., Insursoft, Ltd., Littleton, CO *Page* 1-228

Camunias, Joel, Bonfiglioli, Concorde, Ontario, Canada *Page* 1-303

Caplovitz, Gideon Paul, Abratech Corporation, Sausalito, CA *Page* 1-357

Caraballo, Roderick G., Avant Go, San Mateo, CA *Page* 1-228

Carl, Timothy S., The Carl Group, Los Gatos, CA *Page* 1-228

Carlascio, Keith, Application Consulting Group, Morristown, NJ *Page* 1-228

Carley, Clay B., East Central University, Ada, OK *Page* 1-321

Carlton, Rodney A., Cooper Tire Company, Texarkana, AR *Page* 1-28

Carrigan, Christopher M., Enterprise Technology Group Inc., Boston, MA *Page* 1-228

Carson, Bruce A., Edgewater Technology, Wakefield, MA *Page* 1-229

Carter, Jeffrey W., Consolidated Natural Gas, Pittsburgh, PA *Page* 1-115

Carvajal, LeAnnette, I Link Worldwide, LLC (Independent Representative), Las Vegas, NV *Page* 1-368

Cary, John, ComCore, Atlanta, GA *Page* 1-362

Casabon, Sylvain, Groupe Cantrex, Inc., Saint-Laurent, Quebec, Canada *Page* 1-132

Caspary, Ruth, Cinesite, Los Angeles, CA *Page* 1-304

Cassat, Daniel M., RSM McGladrey, Inc., Cheyenne, WY *Page* 1-352

Castaldi, James Anthony, The Chubb Institute, Parsippany, NJ *Page* 1-321

Castelino, Flavian M., National Telephone Services, Muscat, Oman *Page* 1-96

Caster, Charles, Gulfstream Aerospace, Savannah, GA *Page* 1-75

Castillo, Victoria M., Alphatrain, Maplewood, NJ *Page* 1-340

Catalone, Gregory S., Sprint, Reston, VA *Page* 1-96

Caudullo, Jane, Arthur Andersen, Sarasota, FL *Page* 1-363

Causey, Gary D., Comforce Info Tech, Dike, TX *Page* 1-167

Cauzzo, Luiz Henrique, Filtros Mann, Ltda., Indaiatuba, Brazil *Page* 1-72

Cerda, Ken H., Verizon Wireless, Carrollton, TX *Page* 1-92

Cerqueira, Joao Roberto Monteiro, Hewlett-Packard Company, Sao Paulo, Brazil *Page* 1-39

Chabrier, Donna R., Reactor, Mountain View, CA *Page* 1-166

Chaikin, Jamie A., Telcordia Technologies, Piscataway, NJ *Page* 1-172

Chakhtoura, Nehme G, Prince George's Accounting Government/Department of Environmental Resources, Upper Marlboro, MD *Page* 1-371

Chakraborty, Kishore, Kishore Chakraborty Consulting, Watertown, MA *Page* 1-363

Chamberlain, Mark A., Landtech Consultants, Inc., Westford, MA *Page* 1-348

Chambers
 Paul C., Siteserv2000 LLC, Troy, MI *Page* 1-216
 Teressa S., United Parcel Service, Louisville, KY *Page* 1-90

Chami, Ahmed R., Microsoft Corporation - North West Africa, Casablanca, Morocco *Page* 1-195

Chan
 Calvin L., Yellow Shirt, Pasadena, CA *Page* 1-229
 Joe, Orient Overseas Container Line, Ltd., Wanchai, Hong Kong *Page* 1-89
 Monte Tak Ho, MVP Health Plan, Schenectady, NY *Page* 1-152
 Rodney W., American Megatrends Inc., Norcross, GA *Page* 1-195

Chandler, Ronnie D., Muskogee Public Schools, Muskogee, OK *Page* 1-381

Chang, David W., Cisco Systems, Inc., San Jose, CA *Page* 1-58

Channell, John L., Resource Technologies Corporation, Troy, MI *Page* 1-167

Chapman
 David R., TenFold Corporaotin, Draper, UT *Page* 1-229
 Gregory P., EFTC, Olathag, KS *Page* 1-76

Charpentier, Elizabeth, Wasco Products Inc., Sanford, ME *Page* 1-53

Chawla, Inder, Schlumberger, Houston, TX *Page* 1-2

Chayapathi, Nagaraju, AMS Informatix Inc., San Jose, CA *Page* 1-229

Chbeir, Ziad E., If and Then, Croton On Hudson, NY *Page* 1-113

Chee, Adrian U., International Savings, Honolulu, HI *Page* 1-136

Chen
 Deanford, Litton PRC, San Jose, CA *Page* 1-229
 Yuan-Yuan "Chrissie", Genentech, South San Francisco, CA *Page* 1-22

Cheng
 David Hui-Wen, TrustMed.com, Taipei, Taiwan *Page* 1-212
 Jack Y., Infoloan, San Jose, CA *Page* 1-140
 Jean, Ajilon, Rochester, NY *Page* 1-229
 Kin Wing Horace, Atek Electronics Company Ltd., Kowloon, Hong Kong *Page* 1-121
 Michael P. K., Independent, Alhambra, CA *Page* 1-202

Cherry, Donald Thomas, Computer Sciences Corporation, Meriden, CT *Page* 1-202

Cheung, Frank, Dynatek Infoworld, Inc., City of Industry, CA *Page* 1-229

Chew, Ferdinand T., Texas A&M University, Texas Engineering Extension Services, Bryan, TX *Page* 1-321

Chia, Teck-Hng, Colour Scan Company Private Limited, Singapore, Singapore *Page* 1-20

Chien, David, Atima Technology Inc., Fremont, CA *Page* 1-119

Childs
 Keith F., Inmet Corporation, Ann Arbor, MI *Page* 1-57
 Robert L., Sapient Corporation, Cambridge, MA *Page* 1-202

Chinnaiah, Mani A., AUM Technologies, Inc., Irvine, CA *Page* 1-230

Chitre, Nikhil, Information Resources, Inc., Chicago, IL *Page* 1-359

Chizmarik, Joseph J., The Knowledge Sculptors, Chatham, NJ *Page* 1-202

Chockalingam, Rajasekaran S., CAM Systems LLC., Saratoga, CA *Page* 1-230

Chohrach, Michael J., Reliant Energy, Houston, TX *Page* 1-116

Chow, Thomas, Computer Curriculum Corporation, Sunnyvale, CA *Page* 1-202

Chrisman, Terry L., Technology Solutions Company, Hagerstown, MD *Page* 1-230

Christly, John A., The Golf Network, Inc., Pompano Beach, FL *Page* 1-172

Chromy, Robert J., Information Technology Consulting, Inc., Succasunna, NJ *Page* 1-230

Chu, Tung S., Ever Glitter International Ltd., New York, NY *Page* 1-123

Chua
 Chephren, Digital Scanning Corporation, Singapore, Singapore *Page* 1-48
 Kristine U., Columbia University Law School, New York, NY *Page* 1-321

Chugg, Ginger M., Inland Northwest Health Services, Spokane, WA *Page* 1-152

Chui, Carol Y., Sprint, Burlingame, CA *Page* 1-96

Churetta, Scott, Accu Sort Systems Inc., Telford, PA *Page* 1-173

Ciabatoni, Linda, Catalyst 2020, Arlington, VA *Page* 1-361

Ciarlette, Karen L., Computer Associates, Oakbrook Terrace, IL *Page* 1-173

Cilley, Brian W., RouterWare, Huntington Beach, CA *Page* 1-230

Clan, Jean, AT&T, La Grange, KY *Page 1-96*

Clark
Brian E., The Zenith, Sarasota, FL *Page 1-153*
Bruce A., Cal-Pak Systems, Modesto, CA *Page 1-119*
Daniel J., Michigan Department of Environmental Quality, Lansing, MI *Page 1-386*
Maynard S., Vegetarian Resource Center, Cambridge, MA *Page 1-163*
Ronald L., IBM Global Services, Atlanta, GA *Page 1-230*

Clarke, Tracy J., Symantec Corporation, Hackensack, NJ *Page 1-195*

Clawson, Perry R., Universal Systems and Technology Inc., Winter Park, FL *Page 1-230*

Clayton, Brian R., Coolidge Wall Womsley Lombard, Dayton, OH *Page 1-312*

Clements
Gregory Alexander, W.W. Grainger, Vernon Hills, IL *Page 1-123*
Kerry Keith, U S WEST, Denver, CO *Page 1-97*
Larry, Viquity, Sunnyvale, CA *Page 1-195*
Mark G., e-technicalsupport.com, Dallas, TX *Page 1-231*

Clemis, David, Industry Canada, Ottawa, Ontario, Canada *Page 1-381*

Cline
Jon, Enthusiast, Inc., Pasadena, CA *Page 1-231*
Peter M., Manhattan Village Academy, New York, NY *Page 1-314*

Clouse, Marc G., Systems Documentation Inc., Edison, NJ *Page 1-231*

Cobb, Gary A., Corning Inc., Wilmington, NC *Page 1-69*

Cochran, John A., DuPont Photomasks, Inc., Round Rock, TX *Page 1-64*

Cofer, Eric C., CN Bioscience, San Diego, CA *Page 1-22*

Coffman, Gayle, Adecco at Boeing, Bellevue, WA *Page 1-368*

Colaianne, John J., Crown Communications Inc., Canonsburg, PA *Page 1-97*

Colbert, Scott, Capital Area Intermediate Unit, Summerdale, PA *Page 1-314*

Colclough Bennett, Judith, North Carolina State Education Assistance Authority, Research Triangle Park, NC *Page 1-138*

Cole, Michael A., Analysts International, Fort Worth, TX *Page 1-173*

Coleman
Glen A., Ohio Department of Health, DQA, Columbus, OH *Page 1-384*
Marquis R., Advanced Web Design, Detroit, MI *Page 1-202*

Collier, H. James, Advanta Corporation, Spring House, PA *Page 1-140*

Collins
Cynthia A., Collins & Collins Consulting, Inc., Lake Forest, CA *Page 1-231*
Galen R., Northern Arizona University, Flagstaff, AZ *Page 1-321*
Louis H., Strategic Technologies, Norcross, GA *Page 1-231*
W. David, David Collins, Waxahachie, TX *Page 1-231*

Colon, Ana Iris, Devnet Systems Corporation, Guaynabo, Puerto Rico *Page 1-231*

Condon, J. Emmett, Hercules Inc., Tervose, PA *Page 1-26*

Coniglio, Allen P., Unilever, Trumbull, CT *Page 1-25*

Connell, Donna M., Comforce Company, Cumming, GA *Page 1-167*

Connolly, Phil J., Akropolis.net, Santa Ana, CA *Page 1-232*

Conover, Cary Donovan, Conseco Services LLC, Irving, TX *Page 1-300*

Conway, Larry J., Arthur Andersen, Boston, MA *Page 1-363*

Cook, Charlie D., Edge Technologies, Inc., Fairfax, VA *Page 1-232*

Cooley, Len, University of Oregon Athletics, Eugene, OR *Page 1-321*

Cooper, Amanda M., RF Wolters Company, Inc., Marietta, GA *Page 1-372*

Coplu, Ali, Goldman Sachs & Company, Lyndhurst, NJ *Page 1-142*

Coppola, Jean Frances, Pace University at Pleasantville, Briarcliff, NY *Page 1-322*

Cordle, Ruth, Anteon Corporation, Montgomery, AL *Page 1-173*

Corn, Jeffrey S., United Space Alliance, Cape Canaveral, FL *Page 1-391*

Cornwall
Charles "Chuck" F., Mississippi State Department of Health, WIC Program, Jackson, MS *Page 1-384*
Daniel J., Grundy Area Vocational Center, Morris, IL *Page 1-314*

Cornwell, Kevin W., Cotton and Allen, Louisville, KY *Page 1-352*

Corradi, Antonio Cesar, Senai, Sao Paulo, Brazil *Page 1-336*

Corsello, Michael Phillip, The Upper Deck Company, LLC, Carlsbad, CA *Page 1-85*

Corson, Charlton E., Lockheed Martin Enterprise Information Systems, Denver, CO *Page 1-79*

Costa, Anthony P., Sher Distributing, Leonardo, NJ *Page 1-125*

Costis, Nickolaos C., Eurisko S.A., Attica, Greece *Page 1-173*

Cothern, Rick, Cothern Computer Systems, Inc., Jackson, MS *Page 1-173*

Coullard, Jeremy B., Barco, Inc., South Windsor, CT *Page 1-69*

Coursey, Cameron K., SBC Technology Resources, Austin, TX *Page 1-357*

Cowan, Patrick Neal, Qwest Communications, Denver, CO *Page 1-97*

Cox
Benjamin Bryan, Micro Technology Unlimited, Raleigh, NC *Page 1-173*
Dale, Integrated Systems Engineering, Logan, UT *Page 1-85*
David W., Dana Corporation, Fort Wayne, IN *Page 1-73*
Joel A., Hollister Inc., Libertyville, IL *Page 1-83*
Peter J., New York Methodist Hospital, Brooklyn, NY *Page 1-307*

Coyle
Charles W., Olsten Health Services, Tampa, FL *Page 1-306*
Stephen F., Gilbane, Providence, RI *Page 1-4*

Craft, Michael K., Sprint PCS, Kansas City, MO *Page 1-92*

Crane, Douglas G., Kent Datacomm, Austin, TX *Page 1-203*

Craven, Brett, Ciber Custom Solutions Group, Overland Park, KS *Page 1-173*

Crawford
James A., Schneider Electric, Westford, MA *Page 1-64*
Jen, Royal Oak Boring, Lake Orion, MI *Page 1-73*
Michael W., United Titanium Inc., Wooster, OH *Page 1-85*

Creech, Deborah, Embry-Riddle Aeronautical University, New Smyrna, FL *Page 1-322*

Creevy, John J., ENTEX Information Services, Inc., Rye Brook, NY *Page 1-232*

Cremerius, Guillermo, Best Foods Brazil, Sao Paulo, Brazil *Page 1-10*

Crincoli, Diane J., Bank of New York Trust Company, Jacksonville, FL *Page 1-161*

Crockett, Kimberly L., NASA's Sounding Rocket Operations Contract, Chincoteague Island, VA *Page 1-78*

Cross, Matthew J., SAIC, Orlando, FL *Page 1-232*

Crossman, John Neal, Crossman Post Production, Sandy, UT *Page 1-304*

Croswell
David C., Majestic Systems Integration, Castaic, CA *Page 1-203*
Jerry D., Cendant Corporation, Trumbull, CT *Page 1-363*

Crowl, Jerry L., Michigan Production Machining, Inc., Macomb, MI *Page 1-73*

Cunningham, Linda S., Michelin, Duncan, SC *Page 1-28*

Curcio, Barry M., Lydall, Inc., Manchester, CT *Page 1-15*

Curry, Gary, Irwin Research and Development, Yakima, WA *Page 1-29*

Curtis
Brandon G., TDSI, a Division of Randstad North America, Fremont, CA *Page 1-232*
Steve D., The Coffee Beanery Ltd., Flushing, MI *Page 1-9*

Curto, Philip A., KBC Bank New York N.V., New York, NY *Page 1-134*

Czarnik, Teri, Friendship Village, Schaumburg, IL *Page 1-343*

D

D'Amico, Stephen, Aegon Equity Group, Palm Harbor, FL *Page 1-148*

D'Andrea, Marcus J., PricewaterhouseCoopers, Chicago, IL *Page 1-352*

D'Sylva, Leon J., Hughes Christensen, Dubai, United Arab Emirates *Page 1-3*

Da Costa, D'Wayne I., Vistec Electronic Services Inc., Pickering, Ontario, Canada *Page 1-216*

Daffron, Dean E., Tuttle Maddux Surveying, Montgomery, TX *Page 1-352*

Dalal, Alex F., The Vanguard Group, Honey Brook, PA *Page 1-145*

Dalia, Sujal, Systems Link, Avenel, NJ *Page 1-232*

Dalious, Peggy, University of Colorado Hospital, Aurora, CO *Page 1-322*

Dalton, Robin S., The Boeing Company, Seattle, WA *Page 1-75*

Dandas, Gus, Arizona Lottery, Phoenix, AZ *Page 1-306*

Danguillecourt, Sergio, Bacardi Ltd., Miami, FL *Page 1-9*

Dar, Arif A., General Electric Company, Atlanta, GA *Page 1-76*

Darby, Philip D., Siemens Energy and Automation, Atlanta, GA *Page 1-55*

Dardai, Shahid M., Richard J. Daley College, Chicago, IL *Page 1-336*

Darichuk, Glenn J., TAF-TECH Cable Systems, Calgary, Alberta, Canada *Page 1-6*

Darmenio, Greg, Chain Store Guide, Tampa, FL *Page 1-128*

Dashiell, John L., IMI Systems, Inc., Vienna, VA *Page 1-232*

DaSilva, Elsie, Schein Pharmaceuticals, Florham Park, NJ *Page 1-22*

Datar, Pravin W., SE Technology, Irvine, CA *Page 1-233*

Daugherty, J. Max, PharMerica, Pearland, TX *Page 1-130*

Dauplaise, Mike, St. Mary Hospital Medical Center, Green Bay, WI *Page 1-307*

Dave, Maulik Avantikumar, Bhasha, Inc., King of Prussia, PA *Page 1-233*

David, Phyllis C., Kershaw County School District, Camden, SC *Page 1-314*

Davidson, Donald A., Laguardia Community College, Long Island City, NY *Page 1-336*

Davis
    Cindy, Maidenform, Inc., Bayonne, NJ *Page 1-12*
    Derold L., Ddavis Software Consulting, Inc., Maple Grove, MN *Page 1-233*
    Donald N., MicroAge, Gilbert, AZ *Page 1-119*
    James V., Perkin-Elmer Corporation, Raleigh, NC *Page 1-233*
    Roseland M., Jones Day Reavis & Pogue, New York, NY *Page 1-312*
    Tamara L., International Management Communication Corporation, Inc., Miami, FL *Page 1-368*

Davison, Glenn L., Maxson Young Associates, Inc., San Francisco, CA *Page 1-157*

Day, Mark, United States Environmental Protection Agency, Washington, DC *Page 1-386*

De Cesare, Vito, Solectron Technology Company, Charlotte, NC *Page 1-40*

de Freitas, André A., Vital Network Services, New York, NY *Page 1-109*

De Shazer, Ronelle, Code Hennessy & Simmons, Chicago, IL *Page 1-142*

De Stefano, Louis T., Louis T. De Stefano, Inc., Stanardsville, VA *Page 1-298*

Dean, Steve, Intermec, Everett, WA *Page 1-233*

DeCarlo, Fred H., Bozell Group, New York, NY *Page 1-163*

Decker, Thomas J., Ernst & Young LLP, Horsham, PA *Page 1-353*

Defiesta, Clarence B., Microsoft Corporation, Redmond, WA *Page 1-195*

Degner, Ann L., San Juan College, Farmington, NM *Page 1-336*

DeLaPorte, Charles E., EDS, St. Louis, MO *Page 1-214*

Delgado-Lopez, Lupe, Computer Sciences Corporation, Austin, TX *Page 1-203*

DeLo, Dirk A., Westminster School, Simsbury, CT *Page 1-315*

Deltano, Michael D., Town of Easton, North Easton, MA *Page 1-371*

Demarest, Jim, Power 2000 Inc., Naperville, IL *Page 1-233*

Dembeck, Wanda S., Triad Performance Technologies, Farmington Hills, MI *Page 1-368*

DeMent, Ryan A., Tyco Packaging Systems, Hayward, CA *Page 1-121*

DeModna, Christina K., Purdue Pharma L.P., Ardsley, NY *Page 1-23*

Dempsey, Patrick P., Affiliated Computer Services, San Francisco, CA *Page 1-233*

DeNigris, Ernest G., Actel, Mendham, NJ *Page 1-64*

Denis, Andrew M., Hotel Interactive, Huntington, NY *Page 1-300*

Dernoga, Kathleen A., American Society for Testing and Materials, West Conshohocken, PA *Page 1-16*

Derrick
    Carol A., A.C. New Middle School, Mesquite, TX *Page 1-315*
    Charles E., Revacomp Inc., Ellicott City, MD *Page 1-128*

DeSantis, Lori Ann, ASAP II, Oakland Park, FL *Page 1-174*

DesJarlais, William, Mercury Interactive, Landover, MD *Page 1-234*

Desroches, Dennis, Radian International Software, Houston, TX *Page 1-174*

DeVincentis, Paul, Burns & Roe Enterprises, Los Alamos, NM *Page 1-348*

DeVore, Jeanne, Dr. William M. Scholl College of Podiatric Medicine, Chicago, IL *Page 1-322*

Deyhimi, Derrik, EnterpriseWorks, LLC, Houston, TX *Page 1-234*

Di Luna, Leasa M., S1 Corporation, Littleton, MA *Page 1-196*

Dickinson, Gregory, Paradigm Analytical Laboratories, Wilmington, NC *Page 1-361*

Dickman, Lowell V., ITC Delta Com, Bronson, FL *Page 1-97*

Diep, Thang, State Water Resource Control Board; SWRCB, Sacramento, CA *Page 1-387*

Diestelkamp, Dawn L., Superior Court of California, County of Fresno, Fresno, CA *Page 1-376*

Difilippo, Armand, Intershop Communication, South Beach, NY *Page 1-234*

Dilks, Kelly Marie, ERDC-CNC, Champaign, IL *Page 1-360*

Dima-Ala Villanueva, Lorli, Sequel Communications, New York, NY *Page 1-109*

Dingman, C. Lewis, Medical Center Hospital, Odessa, TX *Page 1-307*

Dinota, Mary, MWD Consultants, St. Leonard, MD *Page 1-369*

Dinsmore, David L., Linear Technology Corporation, Dallas, TX *Page 1-64*

Dinsmore, David L., Linear Technology Corporation, Dallas, TX *Page 1-64*

Dix, Brian Douglas, NCR Corporation, Peachtree City, GA *Page 1-50*

Dixon, Richard T., LTV Steel, East Chicago, IN *Page 1-31*

Do
    Hai Thanh, Electronics Arts, San Jose, CA *Page 1-196*
    Minh-Kha, Nortel Networks, Saint-Laurent, Quebec, Canada *Page 1-55*

Doan
    Cody, S 304, Minneapolis, MN *Page 1-83*
    Phillip K., Marvell, Sunnyvale, CA *Page 1-65*

Dobrovolny, Jackie Lea, Triple Play, Aurora, CO *Page 1-300*

Dobyns, Barry A., The Windward Group, Los Gatos, CA *Page 1-234*

Doddapaneni, Srinivas P., Lucent Technologies, Emmaus, PA *Page 1-58*

Dodge, Jon, Lotus Development Corporation, Alexandria, VA *Page 1-174*

Domingue, Jeremy, Cybersurfers, Tehachapi, CA *Page 1-234*

Donato, Anthony M., ASCOT Communications, Greenwood Lake, NY *Page 1-109*

Donoghue, Matthew T., Digital Access Control, Chantilly, VA *Page 1-234*

Donohoe, B. F., EDS, Houston, TX *Page 1-214*

Dorman, Gregory J., Information Builders Inc., New York, NY *Page 1-196*

Dossett, Robert W., TerraComm, Inc., Spokane, WA *Page 1-212*

Dover, Pamala V., Mountaire Farms, Lumberbridge, NC *Page 1-1*

Downs, Brian D., University of St. Thomas, St. Paul, MN *Page 1-322*

Drago, Barbara, New York Institute of Entrepreneurship, Albany, NY *Page 1-322*

Drexler, Bryan A., HSB Reliability Technology, Washington, DC *Page 1-234*

Dritsas, George E., Wells Fargo Bank, Whiting, IN *Page 1-133*

Drost, Terry L., Allgeier Martin & Associates, Joplin, MO *Page 1-235*

Drown, Dennis A., American Frozen Foods Inc., Stratford, CT *Page 1-301*

Duay, Cheryl L., GE Supply, Shelton, CT *Page 1-121*

Dubnicka, Leigh C., Philips Medical Systems, Shelton, CT *Page 1-69*

Duda, Andrew, AM Search Consulting, Inc., Rockville, MD *Page 1-168*

Duggan
    Carlina, Lake Dillon Fire Protection District, Dillon, CO *Page 1-378*
    Sheryl A., City of Owasso, Owasso, OK *Page 1-372*

Duggins, Ginger B., Prudential Carolinas Realty, Greensboro, NC *Page 1-159*

Dumeer, Wesley A., Virginia Housing Development Authority, Richmond, VA *Page 1-388*

Duncan
    Dennis LeRoy, Emmanuel College, Franklin Springs, GA *Page 1-322*
    Phillip L., American Society for Quality, Milwaukee, WI *Page 1-345*

Dunlap, Thomas S., Themis, Inc., Westerville, OH *Page 1-196*

Dunn, Peter K., Auraria Higher Education Center, Denver, CO *Page 1-323*

Dunston, Corlis Yvette, Fleet & Industrial Supply Center, Norfolk, VA *Page 1-91*

Duong, Huy M., General Chemical Corporation, Parsippany, NJ *Page 1-26*

Durand, Donald, American Radio Relay League, Newington, CT *Page 1-347*

Dwyer, Sherry L., Optimum Solutions, Inc., Nashville, TN *Page 1-235*

Dykes, George M., Senator Craig Thomas, Washington, DC *Page 1-371*

Dzhidzhora, Karen Ann Estelle, Mortgage Guaranty Insurance Corporation, Milwaukee, WI *Page 1-156*

E

Eblowitz, Michael, MacroSoft, Highland, CA *Page 1-174*

Ebrahimi, Steven G., Ga Childcare Online, Atlanta, GA *Page 1-342*

Eckert, John F., Insulgard Corporation, Hyattsville, MD *Page 1-85*

Edwards
    Albert L., Computer Sciences Corporation, San Diego, CA *Page 1-203*
    Ginger F., McInturff Miligan & Brooks, Greeneville, TN *Page 1-156*
    Tony J., Telxon Corporation, Dallas, TX *Page 1-40*

Eggleston, Kevin B., Bank of America, Jacksonville, FL *Page 1-133*

Ehlig, Dana Carl, Dana Unlimited, Altadena, CA *Page* 1-235

Eisman, Ariane M., Fala Direct Marketing, Inc., Melville, NY *Page* 1-165

Eizember, Dave, Army National Guard, Rapid City, SD *Page* 1-392

Elaprolu, Srikanth, USI, Chantilly, VA *Page* 1-174

Elfadel, Abe, IBM Corporation, Yorktown, NY *Page* 1-40

Elkin, L. Daniel, Macrophage International, Brentwood, TN *Page* 1-174

Elliott, David, Hong Kong International School, Tai Tam, Hong Kong *Page* 1-315

Ellis
Allan D., Telxon Corporation, Seattle, WA *Page* 1-40
Patricia C., South Carolina Department of Health and Human Services, Columbia, SC *Page* 1-384

Ellisor, Charles E., ENTEX Information Services, Lufkin, TX *Page* 1-235

Elmasri, Ahmed Azzam, Ministry of Cabinet Affairs & Information, Manama, Bahrain *Page* 1-372

Elshire, Jeremy, Ketel Thorsten Son, LLP, Rapid City, SD *Page* 1-235

Ely, Mark, Dreher & Associates, Inc., Oakbrook Terrace, IL *Page* 1-142

Embry, Dale L., Phillips Petroleum Company, Bartlesville, OK *Page* 1-27

Emory, Samuel G., SGE Consulting, Charlotte, NC *Page* 1-235

Endres, Joyce E., State of Wisconsin, Department of Administration, Madison, WI *Page* 1-375

English, Richard L., Anglais Consulting Inc., Sanford, FL *Page* 1-236

Engvall, Thomas J., RLI Corporation, Peoria, IL *Page* 1-174

Enlow, Jeffrey Dale, Sunbeam Outdoor Products, Neosho, MO *Page* 1-53

Enos, Dennis, AT&T Wireless Services, Orlando, FL *Page* 1-92

Enroth, Bjorn, Dotcom Solutions AB, Solna, Sweden *Page* 1-236

Ensor, Bettina Rice, Applied Materials, Richardson, TX *Page* 1-65

Ercolani, Gianantonio, Intel Corporation, Ottobrunn, Germany *Page* 1-65

Erdely, Robert W., Pennsylvania State Police, Indiana, PA *Page* 1-376

Erickson, Scott W., CBS, New York, NY *Page* 1-107

Ernst, Kelli A., Computer Curriculum Corporation, Alexandria, VA *Page* 1-203

Eshelman, Scott Walter, 1-800-VIDEO-ON, Boulder, CO *Page* 1-109

Espinoza, Dimas, DEISSC2, San Antonio, TX *Page* 1-392

Evanco, Michael S., Ernst & Young LLP, Buffalo, NY *Page* 1-353

Evans
Cheryl L., Rockingham Community College, Wentworth, NC *Page* 1-336
Kathryn A., United States Army Corps of Engineers, Vicksburg, MS *Page* 1-393
Tammy L., Oakland Schools, Waterford, MI *Page* 1-381

F

Fadely, Gary, Thomson Consumer Electronics, Indianapolis, IN *Page* 1-54

Fadri, Reynaldo J., Vivorx Inc., Santa Monica, CA *Page* 1-357

Fallacara, Flo, MetLife, Bridgewater, NJ *Page* 1-148

Fällberg, Christian, Telia AB, Stocksund, Sweden *Page* 1-97

Fang, Jesse, Intel Corporation, Santa Clara, CA *Page* 1-65

Fanshteyn, Timur, CDS Inc., New York, NY *Page* 1-175

Farage, Regina M., Creative Computers & Networking, Inc., Brooklyn, NY *Page* 1-236

Farmer, Ira Anthony, Hubbard Company, Bremen, GA *Page* 1-12

Farney
Kerry G., I/N Tek, New Carlisle, IN *Page* 1-31
Thomas P., Illinois Primary Health Care, Springfield, IL *Page* 1-344

Farquharson, Jerome A., Bryan Cave, St. Louis, MO *Page* 1-312

Farral, Travis M., Nokia, Inc., Irving, TX *Page* 1-55

Farris, Terrance J., OSF Healthcare Systems, Peoria, IL *Page* 1-152

Favaro, Norma Wheatley, HQ CPSG/LGLP, San Antonio, TX *Page* 1-393

Fedele, Alan R., Zagar Inc., Euclid, OH *Page* 1-36

Fee, John A., MCI Corporation, Richardson, TX *Page* 1-70

Fehd, Ronald J., Centers for Disease Control, Atlanta, GA *Page* 1-360

Felix, Donald F., CBM Business Machines Inc., Johnstown, PA *Page* 1-48

Feliz, Luis R., KRM Risk Management and Insurance Services, Inc., Fresno, CA *Page* 1-157

Fels, Alan N., University of Pennsylvania Graduate School of Education, Philadelphia, PA *Page* 1-323

Fender, Chuck, Wazoo's Computers, Alamogordo, NM *Page* 1-236

Feng
Wendy Q., Tom Sawyer Software, Berkeley, CA *Page* 1-236
Wu-Chang, Puma Technology, Emeryville, CA *Page* 1-92

Fenwick, Scott F., Edgemeade, Upper Marlboro, MD *Page* 1-343

Ference, William F., Golden Eagle Credit Corporation, Ridgefield, CT *Page* 1-167

Fernandez
Marino A., Cisco Systems, Inc., Chelmsford, MA *Page* 1-58
Rafael Manuel, Infosinergia, S.A., Miami, FL *Page* 1-109

Ferrao, Helder Flavio, Netstream Telecom, Sao Caetano Du Sol, Brazil *Page* 1-97

Ferraro, Brian D., C&C Ford Sales Inc., Horsham, PA *Page* 1-126

Ferrier, William Wayne, Dresser-Rand Company, Tulsa, OK *Page* 1-37

Fey, Eugenia, Crystallize, West Bloomfield, MI *Page* 1-175

Fiacco, Philip, Diamond Packaging, Rochester, NY *Page* 1-14

Fidelman, Jennifer Faith, Playa Vista, Los Angeles, CA *Page* 1-160

Fielden, Jeanette, U S WEST Interprise Networking Services, Denver, CO *Page* 1-97

Fig, Susan B., HNC Software, Inc., San Diego, CA *Page* 1-175

Fileger, Mark E., United States Air Force, Langley Air Force Base, VA *Page* 1-393

Filippone, Joseph R., Lead Trac, Santa Clara, CA *Page* 1-236

Finch, Michael D., BMR Training Centers, Victorville, CA *Page* 1-340

Fincke, Greg, Pasco Inc., Dade City, FL *Page* 1-7

Fink
Dean R., ATL Ultrasound, Bothell, WA *Page* 1-84
Robert T., MPR Associates, Inc., Falls Church, VA *Page* 1-348

Finklestein, Ronald, OMNOVA Solutions Inc., Mogadore, OH *Page* 1-27

Finley, Kenneth W., Check Point Software Technology Ltd., Frisco, TX *Page* 1-236

Finney, M. Parker, Outokumpu American Brass, Buffalo, NY *Page* 1-32

Fiore, Stephanie A., PAREXEL International, Lowell, MA *Page* 1-23

Fiorito, Juliann M., May Department Stores, Lorain, OH *Page* 1-126

Fischer, Jennifer L., UPS Information Services, Jersey City, NJ *Page* 1-90

Fisher
Angela M., Lear Corporation, Port Huron, MI *Page* 1-73
Terrance, Horizon Healthware, Inc., Raleigh, NC *Page* 1-175

Fitzgerald
Kevin A., Cynrede Inc., Lake Forest, CA *Page* 1-237
Michael G., Road Runner, Woodside, NY *Page* 1-237
Patricia J., Bank Boston, Boston, MA *Page* 1-134

Fleming
James C., T&T Pump Company, Inc., Fairmont, WV *Page* 1-37
Sparkle N., BSW International, Tulsa, OK *Page* 1-350

Flowers
Frank, Federated Systems Group, Ellenwood, GA *Page* 1-237
Michael R., Contra Costa County, Martinez, CA *Page* 1-371

Folk, Gene E., Harcourt, Inc., Orlando, FL *Page* 1-17

Forman, Lawrence, City College, San Diego, CA *Page* 1-323

Forquer, Christy S., US Telecom - PhoneMaster Division, Joplin, MO *Page* 1-98

Forrester, Janice, Cytera Systems, Portland, OR *Page* 1-237

Forte, Andrew L., Department of Defense Inspector General, Arlington, VA *Page* 1-393

Foster Carter, Linda Marie, Ford Motor Company, Lathrup, MI *Page* 1-71

Fousek, Linda A., Intend Change, Lindsay, CA *Page* 1-363

Fowler
Darren L., Raytheon Travel Air, Wichita, KS *Page* 1-75
Susan E., Nosco Inc., Waukegan, IL *Page* 1-20

Fox
Jeffrey W., Pacific Investment Management Company, Newport Beach, CA *Page* 1-161
Kathleen, Michigan Spring and Stamping, Muskegon, MI *Page* 1-34
Roberta J., Roberta Fox Group Inc., Toronto, Ontario, Canada *Page* 1-203
Shelby Ross, FEMA, Winchester, VA *Page* 1-378
Steven W., Onyx Solutions, Inc., Newnan, GA *Page* 1-237

Frackman, David A., Madscience, New York, NY *Page 1-175*

Fraedrich, D. David, Home Mortgage Inc., Phoenix, AZ *Page 1-140*

Frager, Yehuda Stuart, T. Rowe Price Associates, Baltimore, MD *Page 1-161*

Francis
Ben Allen, CreMoS Partners, Lewisville, TX *Page 1-237*
Philip H., Mascon Information Technologies, Schaumburg, IL *Page 1-203*
Pinkley, Cable & Wireless, Castries Bwi, St. Lucia *Page 1-98*

Franco, Vicente, Nutreco Spain, Madrid, Spain *Page 1-10*

Frangieh, Robert T., elcom.com, Inc., Framingham, MA *Page 1-175*

Franklin
Braden S., Third Wave Services, Jacksonville, FL *Page 1-238*
Douglas N., McKesson HBOC, Alpharetta, GA *Page 1-175*

Franz, John F., V.I.P.S., Plantation, FL *Page 1-156*

Fraser, Neal D., South Bay Bank, Torrance, CA *Page 1-134*

Fraze, John T., Verio, Inc., Englewood, CO *Page 1-109*

Frazier
Larry B., Oracle University, Morengo, IL *Page 1-323*
Stephen P., Oklahoma Department of Corrections, Oklahoma City, OK *Page 1-378*

Frazier-Rousey, Toni Trinette, United States Environmental Protection Agency, Washington, DC *Page 1-387*

Fredette, Stephen J., Electronic Systems Associates, New York, NY *Page 1-238*

Freedman, Richard, Consulting Strategies, Shawnee Mission, KS *Page 1-238*

Fremont, John C., Systems Support Alternatives, Inc., Laurel, MD *Page 1-238*

French, Cynthia, Ahlers & Associates, Waco, TX *Page 1-176*

Friend, Richard E., Computer Sciences Corporation, Millersville, MD *Page 1-204*

Fries, Michel, Dexia Bank International in Luxembourg, Athus, Belgium *Page 1-137*

Frisvold, Barbara L., Computer Learning Centers, Inc., Laurel, MD *Page 1-340*

Fritz, Laura, Hastings Entertainment, Inc., Amarillo, TX *Page 1-130*

Fry
Paul Charles, Prime Systems, Inc., Cleveland, OH *Page 1-238*
Susan F., Weatherford International Inc., The Woodlands, TX *Page 1-3*

Frye, Randy E., Country Oven, Inc., Harrisburg, PA *Page 1-129*

Fuhrmann, Horst, Skypro AG, Cham Zug, Switzerland *Page 1-238*

Fujisaku, Kiminori, Fujitsu Microelectronics, Inc., San Jose, CA *Page 1-65*

Fulmer, Allyson, SCB Computer Technology, Inc., Alpharetta, GA *Page 1-238*

G

Gabardi, Felice R., MFS Investment Management, Raynham, MA *Page 1-145*

Gabriel, Darren K., ERDAS, Inc., Atlanta, GA *Page 1-176*

Gaddam, Ravi, Analysts International, Littleton, CO *Page 1-176*

Gagan, Shakil Sattar, Texas Micro Computers, Richardson, TX *Page 1-239*

Gagnon, Allan F., Net Tryx Computer Services LLC, Phoenix, AZ *Page 1-239*

Gaither, Mark A., Cisco Systems, Inc., San Jose, CA *Page 1-59*

Gaitonde, Prashant V., O.S.S. Inc., Austin, TX *Page 1-239*

Gajic, Dragan, E-Greetings, Santa Cruz, CA *Page 1-21*

Gale, Prenston, MTISC, APO AA *Page 1-239*

Gallegos, Joanne C., Charles Schwab, Danville, CA *Page 1-142*

Gamble, Mark H., South Carolina Arts Commission, West Columbia, SC *Page 1-347*

Gander, Sharon L., Cerner Corporation, Cerner Virtual University, Kansas City, MO *Page 1-323*

Gao, Hui, General Electric Company, Schenectady, NY *Page 1-77*

Garcia-Barreras, Victor E., Nova Southeastern University, Davie, FL *Page 1-323*

Gardner
Chris D., Micron Technology, Boise, ID *Page 1-65*
Jeffrey L., Ericsson, Plano, TX *Page 1-59*
Mac, Bell Atlantic, Wilmington, DE *Page 1-98*

Garenani, Peter C., Ademco Group, Syosset, NY *Page 1-298*

Garg
Arun, Cisco Systems, Inc., San Jose, CA *Page 1-59*
Rajiv, U S WEST/Global Crossing, Minneapolis, MN *Page 1-98*

Garimella, Jagan, Sapient Corporation, Jersey City, NJ *Page 1-239*

Garinger, Phillip D., Microman, Inc., Washington Central Heights, OH *Page 1-204*

Garner, Michael W., IBM Corporation, Cary, NC *Page 1-40*

Garrels, Ruth A., EDS, Flint, MI *Page 1-215*

Garrett
Angie R., Quantum Resources, Center Conway, NH *Page 1-239*
Arthur W., Naval Support Activity, New Orleans, LA *Page 1-393*

Garrison, Daniel J., Rochester Institute of Technology, Pittsford, NY *Page 1-324*

Gartin, Edward, The Pezrow Companies Inc., Ramsey, NJ *Page 1-144*

Garverick, Arthur E., Labor Ready, Inc., Auburn, WA *Page 1-48*

Garza, Johnny Kim, DACOR, Pasadena, CA *Page 1-52*

Gaspar, Victor, DIS-Process S.L., Bilbao, Spain *Page 1-204*

Gaspardino, Amy L., Public Opinion, Chambersburg, PA *Page 1-15*

Gast, William A., U.S. Bankruptcy Court, Des Moines, IA *Page 1-376*

Gates
Dramise D., Sonic Foundry, Inc., Madison, WI *Page 1-176*
Maurice R., Dow Agrosciences, EDC/LL, Indianapolis, IN *Page 1-26*

Gatewood, David A., CGI, Nashville, TN *Page 1-239*

Gatlin, Ronald S., Nichols Research, Huntsville, AL *Page 1-240*

Gaul, Donna F., Regional Network Communications, Inc., Bethlehem, PA *Page 1-176*

Gautney, Charles W., Noblestar Systems, Reston, VA *Page 1-240*

Gautreaux, Wayne J., El Paso Energy, Houston, TX *Page 1-115*

Gauvin, Lorraine Leandra, Havas Interactive, Inc., Bellevue, WA *Page 1-176*

Geary, Matthew, Sprint PCS, Lenexa, KS *Page 1-92*

Gee, Nicholas L., TYCO Valves & Control, Sparks, NV *Page 1-34*

Geer, David W., NCR Corporation, Severna Park, MD *Page 1-50*

Gehrt, Kevin E., Information Services International, Mount Olive, NJ *Page 1-213*

Geist, Thomas E., Computer Horizons Corporation, Denver, CO *Page 1-240*

Gelfenbain, Alexander, Sun Microsystems, Inc., Palo Alto, CA *Page 1-40*

Gellineau, Antonio C., Raytheon, Madison, AL *Page 1-80*

Genser, Mira E., InfoRay, Inc., Cambridge, MA *Page 1-176*

George
Binto, Western Illinois University, Macomb, IL *Page 1-324*
Dorina, PSEG Services Corporation, West New York, NJ *Page 1-87*
Michael, Lockheed Martin Federal Systems, Owego, NY *Page 1-80*
Sunil, Merrill Lynch, Princeton, NJ *Page 1-142*

Georges, William T., Science Applications International Corporation, San Diego, CA *Page 1-240*

Geragas, Dimitris A., Aera Inc., Arlington, VA *Page 1-240*

Gerlick, Joshua A., Obsidian Corporation, Oswego, IL *Page 1-177*

German, James, Wartsila NSD Corporation, Annapolis, MD *Page 1-35*

Gerstner, Kyle, IBEX Capital Markets, Boston, MA *Page 1-145*

Gervagin, Yuriy, Websci Technologies, Monmooth Junction, NJ *Page 1-240*

Ghosh
Amitava, Instasofte, Inc., Metuchen, NJ *Page 1-240*
Sukumar, MCI WorldCom, Inc., Tulsa, OK *Page 1-98*

Giannotta, Cel, Liberty Health, Markham, Ontario, Canada *Page 1-150*

Gibbons, Jim, National Rural Telecommunications Cooperative, Herndon, VA *Page 1-98*

Gibson
Ronald, Walters State Community College, Morristown, TN *Page 1-336*
Stephen, SAP Professional Organization, Mooresville, NC *Page 1-241*

Gilbeaux, Jeffrey J., Trane, Timonium, MD *Page 1-122*

Gilbert, Michael J., Massachusetts Association of School Committees, Boston, MA *Page 1-345*

Gililland, Michael E., Burlington Northern Santa Fe Railway, Fort Worth, TX *Page 1-86*

Gillette, Kimberly S., Perspective Technology Corporation, Vienna, VA *Page 1-241*

Gilley, Darryl W., Marconi Services Corporation, Fort Walton Beach, FL *Page 1-71*

Gilliam, Ken W., State Farm Insurance, Bloomington, IL *Page 1-154*

Gilmore, Cary W., Black & Veatch, Overland Park, KS *Page 1-204*

Glaeser, Paul H., CSI Maximus, Inc., Wayne, PA *Page 1-177*

Glenn
John D., Van Kampen Funds, Houston, TX *Page 1-145*
Kenneth O., Metamore, Wichita, KS *Page 1-393*
Terry M., Eddie Bauer, Inc., Redmond, WA *Page 1-131*
Tyrone L., Genentech, South San Francisco, CA *Page 1-23*

Glick, Gary Edward, Riley County Police Department, Manhattan, KS *Page 1-376*

Glover, John D., Reynolds & Reynolds, Dayton, OH *Page 1-21*

Godsey
Chene W., Standard Federal Bank, Troy, MI *Page 1-135*
Vicki Lynn, Royal Ordnance North America, Bloomingdale, TN *Page 1-34*

Goggins, Dennis R., National Semiconductor, Arlington, TX *Page 1-65*

Goins, Raphael D., Flexon, Pittsburgh, PA *Page 1-177*

Goldburgh, Joyce, Client Server Consulting, Bensenville, IL *Page 1-241*

Goldman, Sergey, ADP, Portland, OR *Page 1-211*

Goldschmidt, David, Mobile MIS Consulting, Cincinnati, OH *Page 1-241*

Goldsmith, Deborah L., Mitre Corporation, San Diego, CA *Page 1-241*

Goldstein, Lee, 20th Century Fox, Beverly Hills, CA *Page 1-304*

Golebiewski, Debbie A., Contract Computer Services, Tupelo, MS *Page 1-241*

Gomes
Carlos, IFS Portugal, Riba de Ave, Portugal *Page 1-242*
Ivan J., Interactive Business Systems, Inc., Oak Brook, IL *Page 1-242*

Gong, Youhong Wade, Cisco Systems, Inc., Burlington, MA *Page 1-59*

Gonzalez, Danny E., Fairfield Communities, Inc., Fort Lauderdale, FL *Page 1-160*

Goodhart, Daniel L., Procter & Gamble, Cincinnati, OH *Page 1-25*

Goodwin, Timothy A., Commercial Data Corporation, Memphis, TN *Page 1-242*

Gool, Eric M., SECI, Inc., Lamar, CO *Page 1-242*

Gopalan
Rajan, Cap Gemini America, Inc., Atlanta, GA *Page 1-242*
Ravichandran, Mascon, Schaumburg, IL *Page 1-242*

Gorby, Bryan, Equant, Dunedin, FL *Page 1-204*

Gordon
Frank E., Quad Systems Corporation, Willow Grove, PA *Page 1-59*
Frank J., Gordon Computer Services, Spring Valley, CA *Page 1-243*
Randi-Lyn, IBM-Knowledge Factory, Dunwoody, GA *Page 1-243*

Gorgen, Nancy A., Soft Ad, Dearborn, MI *Page 1-177*

Gorman, Daniel W., Nypro, Inc., Clinton, MA *Page 1-29*

Gorney, John P., Teaco Inc., Tulsa, OK *Page 1-98*

Gosnell, Phillip K., Regions Financial Corporation, Mobile, AL *Page 1-140*

Graf, Sebastian, PROMATIS Corporation, San Ramon, CA *Page 1-177*

Graham
Charles K., W.H. Linder & Associates, Metairie, LA *Page 1-5*
Deborah L., Astra Zeneca, Woodland Hills, CA *Page 1-23*
Douglas M., Commonwealth Credit Union, Frankfort, KY *Page 1-136*

Granato, Orazio, Hewlett-Packard Company, Bergamo, Italy *Page 1-40*

Granger, Timothy G., American Engineering, North East, MD *Page 1-348*

Graul, Charles F., Centillion Computer Services, Inc., Largo, FL *Page 1-243*

Gray, Thomas P., Toledo Lucas County Public Library, Toledo, OH *Page 1-339*

Green
E. G., Yoh Support Services, Norristown, PA *Page 1-243*
Joseph E., American Express One, Mount Laurel, NJ *Page 1-91*
Judith M., Waukegan Public Schools, Waukegan, IL *Page 1-315*
Kenneth L., United States Department of Treasury, Washington, DC *Page 1-379*
N. Wayne, TRUTech, L.L.C., Richland, WA *Page 1-243*

Greenbank, Martin P., Garden Burger, Clearfield, UT *Page 1-8*

Greene
John E., Stonehenge Telecom Americas, Maitland, FL *Page 1-5*
Mark A., Linkscorp, Northfield, IL *Page 1-305*
Michael, 3Com, Santa Clara, CA *Page 1-48*
William F., Sprint, Overland Park, KS *Page 1-99*

Greenlaw, Valdonna, edu.com, Boston, MA *Page 1-132*

Gregory, Peter H., AT&T Wireless Services, Redmond, WA *Page 1-92*

Griffin
Arthur M., Independent Contractor and Consultant, Long Beach, CA *Page 1-369*
Lianne H., BellSouth, Atlanta, GA *Page 1-99*

Griffiths, Andrea M., Analytical Graphics, Phoenixville, PA *Page 1-177*

Griggs, Kelly A., Minerals Management Services, New Orleans, LA *Page 1-388*

Grigoryev, Alex, ATS, Ellicott City, MD *Page 1-52*

Grilk, Andrew H., Thomson Financial Securities Data, Newark, NJ *Page 1-145*

Grimes, Sylvie, Leon County Health Department, Tallahassee, FL *Page 1-385*

Grindle, Mark J., General Electric, Schenectady, NY *Page 1-77*

Griskell, Ivory J., Lucent Technologies, Orlando, FL *Page 1-59*

Groves, Richard D., Covenant Health, Knoxville, TN *Page 1-308*

Grunstad, Chandler R., Pentacon Industry Group, Inc., Fort Wayne, IN *Page 1-86*

Gu, Sheena, Lucent Technologies, Westford, MA *Page 1-59*

Guald, Andrew G., AT&T, Lincroft, NJ *Page 1-99*

Gueguen, Daniel, Elantiel, Asnieres, France *Page 1-243*

Guerrera, Riccardo, Hi Nrg Webdesigns, Laval, Quebec, Canada *Page 1-243*

Guevara, John P., USUHS, Bethesda, MD *Page 1-324*

Guido, Christopher, Shore Systems, Inc., Albertson, NY *Page 1-244*

Guild, Brian K., Bridgewater Associates, Greenwich, CT *Page 1-145*

Gulling, Mark, Eastman Kodak Company, Rochester, NY *Page 1-84*

Gulotta, Peter, North American Performance Group (NAPG, Inc.), Phoenixville, PA *Page 1-244*

Gum, Jeanette M., Oregon Department of Forestry, Salem, OR *Page 1-388*

Gunawan, Kingson, Excite@Home, San Jose, CA *Page 1-109*

Guo
Baoping, American Chemical Society, Washington, DC *Page 1-345*
Ju, MediaFair, San Gabriel, CA *Page 1-177*
Peter C. H., PricewaterhouseCoopers LLP, Vancouver, British Columbia, Canada *Page 1-353*

Gupta, Rajesh, 4C Solutions, East Moline, IL *Page 1-244*

Gust, Thomas A., TeleCommunication Systems, Inc., Shalimar, FL *Page 1-244*

Guthrie, Kenneth L., Spherion Corporation, Dacula, GA *Page 1-301*

Guy, John D., Tennessee Department of Correction, Tiptonville, TN *Page 1-378*

Guyton, Thomas C., Carlyle, Inc., Seattle, WA *Page 1-178*

Guzzetta, Jacqueline R., Macklowe Properties, New York, NY *Page 1-160*

H

Habermann, Gary J., Widener University, Chester, PA *Page 1-324*

Hackney, Barbie V., SAIC, Austin, TX *Page 1-357*

Haddad, Assad, I.D.A., Nil-Staint Vincent, Belgium *Page 1-244*

Hafen, Lynn R., MarkeStar, Odgen, UT *Page 1-163*

Hagemeier, Juanita E., Disabled Citizen Alliance for Independence, Steelville, MO *Page 1-343*

Haggerty, Hugh, Kaplan, New York, NY *Page 1-340*

Halaut, Jeffrey D., Radian Inc., Alexandria, VA *Page 1-178*

Hale
Chris L., Russellville Realty, Russellville, AR *Page 1-159*
Christie Callahan, Randol International, Ltd., Denver, CO *Page 1-18*
Pamela D., AdminaStar Federal, Louisville, KY *Page 1-157*

Hall
Laurence A., Spacenet, Inc., Melbourne, FL *Page 1-244*
Leland G., The Hotchkiss School, Lakeville, CT *Page 1-315*
Michael, Century High School, Hillsboro, OR *Page 1-315*
Michael R., State Government of Illinois Telecommunications, Springfield, IL *Page 1-99*
Raymond V., Raymond V. Hall Training & Consultant Services, Chicago, IL *Page 1-245*
Rodney D., Solutions By Design, Richmond, VA *Page 1-245*

Hamilton
Brandon, Ivy Tech State College, Calumet Park, IL *Page 1-337*
Cindy L., Kentucky Department for Libraries & Archives, Frankfort, KY *Page 1-375*

Hamm, Keith R., Catholic Charities of Buffalo, Buffalo, NY *Page 1-344*

Hammons, Lois G., Rubber Products Distributors, Indianapolis, IN *Page 1-123*

Hamner, Clinton W., Charter One Bank, Middleburg Heights, OH *Page 1-135*

Hamzei, Nader, Internet Solution Group, West Lake Village, CA *Page 1-178*

Han, Brent M., HNA Consulting, Inc., Falls Church, VA *Page 1-245*

Haney, Wayne A., In-Net, Clinton, TN *Page 1-245*

Hanford, Karen, Western University of Health Sciences, Chico, GA *Page 1-324*

Hanson-Gorby, Marcia K., New Jersey Air National Guard, McGuire Air Force Base, NJ *Page 1-393*

Hardaway, Ivan B., Ernst & Young Technologies, Inc., Chantilly, VA *Page 1-353*

Hardgrove, Nicholas R., City of Laramie, Laramie, WY *Page 1-372*

Hardin, Rohdonda R., American Electric Power Company, Columbus, OH *Page 1-113*

Harding, William R., ECPI Technical College, Cary, NC *Page 1-337*

Hardjowirogo, Jono, Association for Computing, New York, NY *Page 1-16*

Hare, Angela D., Central Electric, Sanford, NC *Page 1-114*

Hargreave, Andrew G., Geneer, Inc., Des Plaines, IL *Page 1-178*

Harker, Larry, Dewpoint, Inc., Carmel, IN *Page 1-245*

Harlap, Jonathan, Reel Film Festival, Inc., Montreal, Quebec, Canada *Page 1-166*

Harman, Morgan Webb, Warner Brothers Online, Burbank, CA *Page 1-245*

Harmon
Jim, MKC Associates, Inc., Mansfield, OH *Page 1-350*
Margaret, America Online Inc., Sterling, VA *Page 1-110*

Harper, deAnna A., Capital Thinking, Inc., New York, NY *Page 1-140*

Harris
Andrew T., Hicks & Ragland Engineering Company, Lubbock, TX *Page 1-348*
Bonnie L., Harris County Department of Education, Houston, TX *Page 1-381*
Dana B., Systems Made Simple, Inc., Syracuse, NY *Page 1-178*
Donna L., Christian Educational Ministries, Tyler, TX *Page 1-341*
Ethel G., OICW/Sequoia Adult School, Menlo Park, CA *Page 1-343*
Mark W., Standard Register, Dayton, OH *Page 1-21*
Wesley G., Main Control, Inc., McLean, VA *Page 1-245*

Harrison, Eric A., Unisys Corporation, San Diego, CA *Page 1-246*

Hart
Byron Dean, Excel Communications, Howe, TX *Page 1-99*
Ryan L., Vanalco, Inc., Vancouver, WA *Page 1-32*

Harte, Rebecca E., BRTRC, Fairfax, VA *Page 1-213*

Hartman, Judith A, Limited Technology Services, Tewksbury, MA *Page 1-246*

Harty, Dave F., Acsis, Inc., Marlton, NJ *Page 1-178*

Harvell, J. Larry, AlliedSignal, Chester, VA *Page 1-27*

Harvester, Wayne C., Fort Valley State University, Fort Valley, GA *Page 1-324*

Hasan, Anis S., Sun Microsystems, Inc., Khobar, Saudi Arabia *Page 1-41*

Hashmi, Kashif R., Base Technologies, Inc., McLean, VA *Page 1-246*

Haskell, Larry R., NeighborNet, Spring, TX *Page 1-246*

Hassan, Abdulla K. E., Bahrain Telecommunications Company, Manama, Bahrain *Page 1-99*

Hatch, Robert Duane, Iomega Corporation, Kaysville, UT *Page 1-48*

Hattenhauer, Wallace L., SBC Communications Inc., Bryant, AR *Page 1-99*

Haught, Jason F., United States Treasury, Bureau of Public Debt, Parkersburg, WV *Page 1-379*

Hawkins
Byron T., Ernst & Young, St. Louis, MO *Page 1-353*
Joyce L., DuPont Pharmaceuticals Company, Wilmington, DE *Page 1-23*

Hayata, Nancy K. T., South Bay Online, Torrance, CA *Page 1-246*

Hayhurst, Robert R., United States Department of Justice, Marianna, FL *Page 1-376*

Haynes
Dawn M., Rational Software, Lexington, MA *Page 1-178*
Lettie K., Burlington Northern Santa Fe Railway, Fort Worth, TX *Page 1-86*

He, Yingbin "Ian", Spur Ventures Inc., Vancouver, British Columbia, Canada *Page 1-2*

Heald, Frederick A., DecisionOne, Columbus, OH *Page 1-216*

Hedelund, Harold G., HH Technologies, Inc./Hedelund Engineering, Las Vegas, NV *Page 1-370*

Hedenberg, Judy A., Medical Manager West, Van Nuys, CA *Page 1-179*

Hedges, Bradley, Entegris, Chaska, MN *Page 1-29*

Hedgley, David, NASA-DFRC, Edwards, CA *Page 1-78*

Hedtke, David J., Birch Telecom, Inc., Kansas City, MO *Page 1-179*

Heger, John P., Pro-Tech, Lucens, Switzerland *Page 1-246*

Heinssen, Scott A., St. Joseph's Indian School, Chamberlain, SD *Page 1-315*

Heitman, Evelyn N., CCNE, Washington, DC *Page 1-345*

Helfenstein, Dirk, Independent, Stuttgart, Germany *Page 1-5*

Hemgen, Jim, Frederick Community College, Frederick, MD *Page 1-337*

Hemsey, Michael F., Consumer Financial Network, Atlanta, GA *Page 1-301*

Henderson
George W., Unifirst Corporation, Owensboro, KY *Page 1-12*
Melody J., Computer Services, Hughes Springs, TX *Page 1-246*

Hennes, Cathryn A., Intellinex, an Learning Venture of E&Y, Cleveland, OH *Page 1-353*

Hennessy
Richard V., Harte-Hanks, Longhorne, PA *Page 1-301*
Sharon M., Parkway School District, Chesterfield, MO *Page 1-381*

Hennigan, Thomas A., Lewis-Clark State College, Lewiston, ID *Page 1-337*

Henry
Karen E., Eastern Health System, Inc., Birmingham, AL *Page 1-152*
Paul A., Cyberguard, Fort Lauderdale, FL *Page 1-247*

Hepp, Jean-Paul, Pharmacia & Upjohn, Peapack, NJ *Page 1-23*

Hering, Rich, ADP Marshall, a Fluor Daniel Company, Mesa, AZ *Page 1-66*

Heringer, Matthew J., Ministry of the Environment, Thunder Bay, Ontario, Canada *Page 1-387*

Hermann, Edwin C., CitiFinancial, Owings Mills, MD *Page 1-138*

Hernández González, Luis Marcial, General Motors, Mesa, AZ *Page 1-71*

Herrmann, Scott M., Edelbrock Corporation, Torrance, CA *Page 1-71*

Herron, Kristine M., Chain Link Technologies Inc., Sunnyvale, CA *Page 1-179*

Hersey, Phil A., Dentsply International, York, PA *Page 1-83*

Hershfield, David M., Lucent Technologies, Alameda, CA *Page 1-60*

Hershman, Joseph, IMI Systems, Inc., Wilmington, DE *Page 1-247*

Hibbs, Paul A., Coleman Research Corporation, Fairfax, VA *Page 1-247*

Hickey, Paul Henry, Loyola University, New Orleans, LA *Page 1-324*

Hickman, Michael J., GTE, Thousand Oaks, CA *Page 1-100*

Hicks, Mark J., Hicks Technology Services, Salem, OR *Page 1-247*

Hidary, Jack D., EarthWeb, Inc., New York, NY *Page 1-179*

Highland, Franklin J., L.T.G. Technologies, Inc., Greenfield, WI *Page 1-38*

Hill
David J., Power FCU, Syracuse, NY *Page 1-136*
Derek P., Hewlett-Packard Company, Santa Clara, CA *Page 1-41*
Geoffrey D., Lucent Technologies LTCP, Chester, NJ *Page 1-60*
Lawrence W., Rochester Institute of Technology, Rochester, NY *Page 1-325*

Hilliard, Marion, Federal Express, Irving, TX *Page 1-90*

Hillman, Jack Dyer, Amica, Lincoln, RI *Page 1-148*

Hilton
Jon M., Vishay-Sprague, Sanford, ME *Page 1-69*
Mark R., NCR Corporation, Duluth, GA *Page 1-50*

Hines, Daniel J., Baxter Healthcare Corporation, Rolling Meadows, IL *Page 1-83*

Hinkle, Delwin R., 24/7 University, Inc., Irving, TX *Page 1-301*

Hinkston, Kevin L., Hewlett-Packard Company, Palo Alto, CA *Page 1-41*

Hinson, Kevin, Quebecor World Hawkins, Church Hill, TN *Page 1-20*

Hintz, Cynthia Irene, United Space Alliance, Cocoa, FL *Page 1-392*

Hite, Charles Aaron, Compunet Engineering, Overland Park, KS *Page 1-247*

Hix, Darrell R., Electronic Systems, Inc., Virginia Beach, VA *Page 1-204*

Ho, Kelvin K., YKE International Inc., Corona, NY *Page 1-70*

Hobbs
Dan J., Mylex, San Jose, CA *Page 1-179*
Matthew Stephen, Madge.web, New York, NY *Page 1-247*
Steve, Cable & Wireless Global Mobile, London, England, United Kingdom *Page 1-100*

Hockman, James E., Merck & Co., Inc., Elkton, VA *Page 1-23*

Hoda, Sami A., Digital Pyramid, Pomona, CA *Page 1-247*

Hodgin, Charles L., Crowder Construction, Charlotte, NC *Page 1-5*

Hoey, Brent M., IBM Corporation, Orange, VA *Page 1-41*

Hoffman
D. Brian, Maryland Stadium Authority Maintenance at Camden Yards, Baltimore, MD *Page 1-367*
Larry L., Federal Government, Columbus, OH *Page 1-379*

Hoggard
Kevin, City Mortgage Corporation, Anchorage, AK *Page 1-140*
Robin L., Beasley Enterprises, Ahoskie, NC *Page 1-126*

Holden, Tammy Lou, The Jesra Company, Long Beach, CA *Page 1-248*

Holder, Michele, Madison International Sales, Stamford, CT *Page 1-124*

Holderread, John R., Quality Solutions, Springfield, IL *Page 1-363*

Hollabaugh, Timothy A., College of the Sequoias, Fresno, CA *Page 1-337*

Holland
Adam, Verizon Wireless, Dublin, OH *Page 1-92*
Paul R., Logicon, Inc., Herndon, VA *Page 1-77*

Hollands, Brian P., ADP Hayes Ligon, Riverview, FL *Page 1-212*

Holliday
Jeff L., Honda Research and Development, Raymond, OH *Page 1-357*
Rosana, American College of Cardiology, Bethesda, MD *Page 1-325*

Holmertz, John P., John Holmertz, San Diego, CA *Page 1-248*

Holoman, Stuart B., Holocon, Inc., Raleigh, NC *Page 1-248*

Holzeisen, Thomas, Musipl@y GmbH, Bad Wiessee, Germany *Page 1-107*

Homami, Hassan Rezaei, Parson Brinkerhoff Farradyne, New York, NY *Page 1-248*

Hooke, Edward C., Southern New England Telephone, Meriden, CT *Page 1-100*

Hooker, P. Kent, University of Wisconsin at Madison, Madison, WI *Page 1-325*

Hope, Teresa M., Lemo USA, Inc., Santa Rosa, CA *Page 1-68*

Hopkins, Fred A., Dun & Bradstreet Corporation, New Providence, NJ *Page 1-213*

Horn, David J., Entergy Services, Gretna, LA *Page 1-116*

Horton, Nicholas A., Hertzbach & Company, Owings Mills, MD *Page 1-353*

Houghton, Jeremy E., Pikes Peak Mental Health, Colorado Springs, CO *Page 1-308*

House
Jeffrey A., Campbell Soup Company, Camden, NJ *Page 1-7*
Jon K., House of Sedes, Overland Park, KS *Page 1-248*

Howard
Charles L., Pulau Electronics Corporation, Colorado Springs, CO *Page 1-71*
Donald R. B. "Donn", American General Finance, Evansville, IN *Page 1-138*
Jason, Blue Cross & Blue Shield of Alabama, Birmingham, AL *Page 1-150*
Pat E., Commonwealth Energy, Tustin, CA *Page 1-114*

Howarth, Barry Arthur, The Howbury Group Ltd., Nepean, Ontario, Canada *Page 1-248*

Howell
Ernest W., Colgate University, Ilion, NY *Page 1-325*
Franklyn L., Intermedia Business Internet, Beltsville, MD *Page 1-249*

Hsiung, Tien-hao, Luminant Worldwide, Houston, TX *Page 1-249*

Hu, Xiaohong, USUHS, Bethesda, MD *Page 1-325*

Huang, Jian, University of Minnesota, Bloomington, MN *Page 1-325*

Hubbard, Keith J., Seagate Technology, Minneapolis, MN *Page 1-46*

Hubbell, James B., BBN Technologies, Arlington, VA *Page 1-249*

Hubbert, Patty, Spalding County Health Department, Griffin, GA *Page 1-385*

Hubbs, Bart L., Columbia HCA, Nashville, TN *Page 1-311*

Huddle, Jeanne, ARESC, North Little Rock, AR *Page 1-341*

Hudson
Kevin L., RHI Consulting, Houston, TX *Page 1-249*
Melanie, Lexmark, Lexington, KY *Page 1-49*

Huffman
James E., J&E Technology, Inc., Alexandria, VA *Page 1-249*
Robert N., Veterans Administration Medical Center, Martinsburg, WV *Page 1-386*

Hughes
Adrienne, Sea Ray Boats, Inc., Knoxville, TN *Page 1-78*
Barbara A., WORLDSPAN, Atlanta, GA *Page 1-249*
Chris, Micrografx, Allen, TX *Page 1-196*
Mary Ann, Arizona Central Credit Union, Phoenix, AZ *Page 1-136*
Shane R., Pyxis Consulting, Boston, MA *Page 1-249*

Hull, Walter James, Ohio Department of Alcohol and Drug Addiction Services, Columbus, OH *Page 1-385*

Hume, Stephen G., Maxim Integrated Products, Inc., Beaverton, OR *Page 1-66*

Humphreys, Timothy J., USI Prescription Benefits, East Haven, CT *Page 1-157*

Hunt
Desmond, Habberstad Nissan, Jamaica, NY *Page 1-71*
Jeff L., Fruit of the Loom, Bowling Green, KY *Page 1-11*
Kelly K., Time Warner Communications, Columbus, OH *Page 1-107*
Wong Mee, PricewaterhouseCoopers, Melaka, Malaysia *Page 1-354*

Hunter
Alvin A., Commonwealth of Virginia - Department of Information Technology, Richmond, VA *Page 1-372*
Craig M., Vancouver/Richmond Health Port, Vancouver, British Columbia, Canada *Page 1-152*

Hurst, Karen, Arthur Andersen, Dunwoody, GA *Page 1-363*

Hurtak, James, AFFS Corporation, Los Gatos, CA *Page 1-346*

Hussain, Masood, Saudi Lighting Company, Riyadh, Saudi Arabia *Page 1-54*

Hussey, Michael P., Wells Fargo, San Francisco, CA *Page 1-133*

Hutchins, Todd, AV Associates, Montvale, NJ *Page 1-250*

Hutchinson-Surette, Eric A., EarthLink, Pasadena, CA *Page 1-250*

Hutson, Tom, United Defense, San Jose, CA *Page 1-60*

Huynh, Peter V., United States Army, Washington, DC *Page 1-394*

Hwang, Kyunam, oCen Communications, Irwindale, CA *Page 1-100*

I

Ikeda-Hayes, Rieko, Omaha Public Power District, Papillion, NE *Page 1-114*

Im, Sang H., Kurgan & Cheviot, Los Angeles, CA *Page 1-85*

Ingersoll, Carrie D., Deloitte Consulting, Renton, WA *Page 1-364*

Inman, Connie C., Nova Information Systems, Knoxville, TN *Page 1-301*

Irve, Morten, BRF Kredit a/s, Lyngby, Denmark *Page 1-141*

Ishimoto, Ken, K's Room, Saitama-ken, Japan *Page 1-250*

Islam, Mohammed N., Websoft Technologies, Brooklyn, NY *Page 1-250*

Ismail, Hosam Mahmoud, Toyota Egypt, Cairo, Egypt *Page 1-304*

Israel, Burt, National Search Associates, Carlsbad, CA *Page 1-168*

Ivele, Patricia, Tenafly Public Schools, Tenafly, NJ *Page 1-382*

Ivey, Gabrielle, Lexmark International, Inc., Lexington, KY *Page 1-119*

Iwashita, Michael, Midwest Technology Management, Manhattan Beach, CA *Page 1-250*

Iznait, Nader S., Mohammed Bin Masaood & Sons, Abu Dhabi, United Arab Emirates *Page 1-250*

Izrailevsky, Yury A., GetFit.com, San Mateo, CA *Page 1-305*

J

Jablonske, Patricia J., Blue Cross & Blue Shield of Minnesota, St. Paul, MN *Page 1-150*

Jackson
Alan W., Nortel Networks, Stoughton, MA *Page 1-55*
Anna L., BP Amoco, Sante Fe, TX *Page 1-2*
Britt L., Frith Anderson & Peake, PC, Roanoke, VA *Page 1-312*
David Jeff, University of Alabama, Tuscaloosa, AL *Page 1-325*

Jacobs
Michael P., City of Asbury Park Police, Asbury Park, NJ *Page 1-377*
Vicki S., Wharton County Junior College, Wharton, TX *Page 1-326*

Jaffer, Akbar G., Snapfish.com, San Francisco, CA *Page 1-179*

Jaffery, Qudsia A., Clecslov Inc., Cedar Hill, TX *Page 1-250*

Jain, Kunwar, Express Computer Supply, San Diego, CA *Page 1-119*

Jamieson, John M., Chesapeake Sciences, Millersville, MD *Page 1-205*

Janowski, W. K. "Vitek", VP Systems Inc., Nepean, Ontario, Canada *Page 1-251*

Jathanna, Kenneth S., Carrier Saudi Arabia, Riyadh, Saudi Arabia *Page 1-122*

Jaworski, Zdzislaw "Jess", B.R.M., West Sussex, England, United Kingdom *Page 1-46*

Jay, Henry D., Siebel Systems, Inc., San Mateo, CA *Page 1-196*

Jazi, Wassim A., Sprint Paranet, Houston, TX *Page 1-251*

Jenkins, Arnold M., Johns Hopkins Hospital, Baltimore, MD *Page 1-308*

Jennings, Travis Wayne, NCH Corporation, Irving, TX *Page 1-8*

Jensen, Kristen A., Intel Corporation, Portland, OR *Page 1-66*

Jeunesse, Braden P., ADP, Minneapolis, IN *Page 1-212*

Jewel, Cheryl D., United States Army Visual Information Center, Washington, DC *Page 1-394*

Jha, Ashok S., Goldman Sachs & Company, New York, NY *Page 1-143*

Jimenez, Hugo, Lifechem Lab, Rockleigh, NJ *Page 1-310*

Jimeno, Andy, Lincoln County Technology Group, Libby, MT *Page 1-110*

Jimmo, Steven M., Genesys Computing Technologies, Chicopee, MA *Page 1-205*

Joeckel, Tamie, Catalyst Software Evaluation Centers Inc., Dallas, TX *Page 1-179*

Joerg, Werner B., Netessence, Salt Lake City, UT *Page 1-180*

Johnsen, Melissa C., Netstock Direct Corporation, Bellevue, WA *Page 1-110*

Johnson
Deke Andrew, Oracle Corporation, Redwood Shores, CA *Page 1-196*
Gary, Petro-Canada, Calgary, Alberta, Canada *Page 1-27*
Ginger Sears, Dean Oliver International, Savannah, GA *Page 1-205*
Janet Lee, SCT, Lexington, KY *Page 1-180*
L. J., South Carolina Law Enforcement Division, Columbia, SC *Page 1-377*
Lucy J., Alcon Laboratories, Fort Worth, TX *Page 1-84*
Patricio, Cyberweb Telecommunications, Quito, Ecuador *Page 1-180*
Ron D., SciQuest.com, Morrisville, NC *Page 1-132*
Sallie J., Troy State University Dothan, Dothan, AL *Page 1-326*

Johnston
Barry David, Scudder Investments, London, England, United Kingdom *Page 1-146*
Elbert W., EDS, Lansdale, PA *Page 1-215*
James W., Shoe Carnival, Evansville, IN *Page 1-127*
Marty P., Kalatel Engineer Inc., Corvallis, OR *Page 1-298*

Johorey, Ritu, HCL America, Houston, TX *Page 1-251*

Jones
Anthony M., San Joaquin County Public Works, Stockton, CA *Page 1-371*
Benedict, R R Donnelley & Sons, Torrance, CA *Page 1-18*
Beth E., Scott Hull Associates, Dayton, OH *Page 1-166*
Billy R., Siemens Energy and Automation, Bristol, TN *Page 1-56*
D. Timothy, United States Navy, FPO AA *Page 1-394*
Jeffrey M., Pacific Bell, San Ramon, CA *Page 1-100*
Jennifer L., Hewlett-Packard Company, San Jose, CA *Page 1-41*
Otis Lee, National Nephrology Association, Nashville, TN *Page 1-346*
Rabon S., ISSI, Inc., Gaithersburg, MD *Page 1-251*
Russell W., Healthcare Management, Philadelphia, PA *Page 1-150*
Stephen, Als Cartage Ltd., Kitchener, Ontario, Canada *Page 1-88*
Tim H., Advanced Concepts Engineering and Technology, Tampa, FL *Page 1-251*

Joplin, Toby L., TaascFORCE, Tulsa, OK *Page 1-180*

Jordan
David S., BBC, Inc., Lynnfield, MA *Page 1-251*
Roxanne M., Rockwell, Melbourne, FL *Page 1-75*

Joseph
Deepu, Call Center Services, Inc., Dallas, TX *Page 1-251*
Sunil, Harvard Medical School, Cambridge, MA *Page 1-326*

Juettner, Michael J., AEG/Electrolux, Rothenburg Bay, Germany *Page 1-53*

Justicia, José A., Justice Communications, San Diego, CA *Page 1-60*

Jutras, Cindy M., InterBiz of Computer Associates, Andover, MA *Page 1-180*

K

Kafrouni, Nabil H., Mancini Duffy, New York, NY *Page 1-350*

Kale, Anil B., BAVS Corporation, Jackson, MI *Page 1-252*

Kalkar, Sanjiv, National Standard Mortgage, Tarrytown, NY *Page 1-141*

Kalke, Kimberly, Kaltech International Corporation, Duluth, GA *Page 1-252*

Kalluri, Dutt N., Kumaran Systems Inc., Rockville, MD *Page 1-252*

Kalmar, Steve, Southdown, Inc., Brea, CA *Page 1-30*

Kaltenbach, Shirley J., Compaq Computer Corporation, Nashua, NH *Page 1-41*

Kammerdiener, Shawn Ivan, Questra, Inc., Rochester, NY *Page 1-252*

Kamssu, Honore, The Wornick Company, McAllen, TX *Page 1-10*

Kane, Richard L., Coastal Technologies Group, Boca Raton, FL *Page 1-252*

Kang, Jai W., Medaille College, Buffalo, NY *Page 1-326*

Kanitkar, Suhas R., Complete Business Solutions, Farmington Hills, MI *Page 1-252*

Kantaria, Jay K., Nextlink, Plano, TX *Page 1-100*

Kanthawar, Krishnakumar, Infinity Solutions Inc., New York, NY *Page 1-252*

Kanumilli, Vishvesh, Dun & Bradstreet, Parsippany, NJ *Page 1-213*

Kao
Kevin J., General Electric (GE) Corporate Research and Development, Niskayuna, NY *Page 1-77*
Wayne, eHNC, San Diego, CA *Page 1-253*

Karaburk, Hasan, Truestar, Inc., Fairfax, VA *Page 1-253*

Karlsen, Rolf, Gulius Maske, Trondheim, Norway *Page 1-124*

Kashmirian, R. S., IN3 Consulting, Canada, Bragg Creek, Alberta, Canada *Page 1-253*

Kaskoun, Anthony Joseph, Proconex, Hatboro, PA *Page 1-205*

Katz, Heather Alicia, University of Texas at Austin, Charles A. Dana Center, Austin, TX *Page 1-326*

Kaufman, Jeremy, Cranel Inc., Columbus, OH *Page 1-119*

Kavanaugh, Keith J., StorageTek, Silver Spring, MD *Page 1-46*

Kawasaki, Gregory, CSC Consulting, Waltham, MA *Page 1-205*

Keane, James B., Northstar Steel & Aluminum, Inc., Manchester, NH *Page 1-121*

Keating, Francesca F., KPMG Consulting, McLean, VA *Page 1-364*

Keaton-Culp, Carolyn R., Lucent Technologies, Naperville, IL *Page 1-60*

Keck, Christian Jon, University of Dayton, Dayton, OH *Page 1-326*

Keenan, Marvin P., Air Touch, Pleasant Hill, CA *Page 1-93*

Keiffer, Ralph J., Florida Government Technology Conference, Tallahassee, FL *Page 1-253*

Kemp, Karen L., GAF, Wayne, NJ *Page 1-28*

Kennedy
Christopher L., Frederick Community College, Frederick, MD *Page 1-337*
Michael, The Kennedy Connection, Powell, OH *Page 1-364*

Kenney, Sean R., Commerce One, Dublin, CA *Page 1-196*

Keoghan, Leo E., Nabisco, East Hanover, NJ *Page 1-8*

Keppler, Stephen A., ITS America, Washington, DC *Page 1-375*

Kerry, Marianne L., SSB-City, New York, NY *Page 1-135*

Keshavmurthy, Shyam, Perceptron, Plymouth, MI *Page 1-304*

Keshoojee, Sadrudin B., Condor Technologies, Edison, NJ *Page 1-253*

Keyes, Tammy L., Fleet Technology Solutions, Malden, MA *Page 1-253*

Khalid, Nadeem M., Techno Serv, Manama, Bahrain *Page 1-253*

Khalifa, Kathy L., IBM Corporation, Apex, NC *Page 1-42*

Khalil, Ramzi Nabhan, MASSC, Paterson, NJ *Page 1-254*

Khan
Alamdar Hussain, Sigma Projects Services, Fresno, CA *Page 1-254*
Tameen, Siemens Electrocom LP, Arlington, TX *Page 1-50*

Khong, Huy T., HMT Technology, Fremont, CA *Page 1-49*

Kilbashian, Rick, Fishman Transducers, Wilmington, MA *Page 1-69*

Kim
Alice, Gast Manufacturing, Benton Harbor, MI *Page 1-37*
Kyle "Ki Jong", SDS America, Boston, MA *Page 1-205*

Kimble, Arnold Dale, Garrett County Board of Education, Oakland, MD *Page 1-316*

Kindermans, Marc, Hewlett-Packard Belgium, Oud Haverlee, Belgium *Page 1-42*

King, Keith A., Puget Sound Naval Shipyard, Bremerton, WA *Page 1-78*

Kinnard, Michael S., Maxim Group (BioLab Inc.), Woodstock, GA *Page 1-254*

Kirkland, William Michael, BellSouth Business Systems, Jacksonville, FL *Page 1-101*

Kirkpatrick, Mindy L., Visa International, San Francisco, CA *Page 1-138*

Kislow, Christopher K., DI, Egg Harbor City, NJ *Page 1-60*

Kitajima, Hiroyuki, Hitachi, Ltd., Kanagawa, Japan *Page 1-121*

Kittredge, Gregory J., Gamesville, Watertown, MA *Page 1-197*

Kitts Malik, Kathleen, SAS Institute, Cary, NC *Page 1-180*

Kjelvik, Vickey A., Transamerica Tax Service, Dallas, TX *Page 1-162*

Klass, Connie H., Virginia Department of Transportation, Suffolk, VA *Page 1-390*

Klassy, Ken R., First Baptist Church Raytown, Raytown, MO *Page 1-347*

Klatkiewicz, Gail D., Lake Land College, Sheboygan, WI *Page 1-337*

Klatt, Bruce K., Corporate Air, Billings, MT *Page 1-90*

Klein
> David E., Bertch Cabinet Manufacturing Inc, Waterloo, IA *Page 1-12*
> Frank J., Brighton School District - Technology Department, Brighton, CO *Page 1-382*

Kleinman, John V., SCT Corporation, Fort Wayne, IN *Page 1-180*

Kleinschmidt, James E., Gulf Telephone, Foley, AL *Page 1-101*

Klemba, Keith S., Hewlett-Packard Company, Mountain View, CA *Page 1-42*

Klempner, James H., Newel Systems, Inc., Schaumburg, IL *Page 1-254*

Kleppe, Kim A., City of Mount Vernon, Mount Vernon, WA *Page 1-373*

Klinkefus, David S., Iowa Communications Network, Johnston, IA *Page 1-254*

Knight, Kathy Hawkins, McKinley Group, Inc., Atlanta, GA *Page 1-254*

Knight
> Lophney H., Marsh USA, Inc., New York, NY *Page 1-157*
> Pamela J., The Wharton School, Philadelphia, PA *Page 1-340*

Knirk, Dwayne L., Sandia National Laboratories, Albuquerque, NM *Page 1-361*

Knorr, Patrick, Sunflower Cablevision, Lawrence, KS *Page 1-108*

Knotts
> James Brian, SCT, Malvern, PA *Page 1-180*
> Martha J., Continental Airlines, Houston, TX *Page 1-89*

Ko, Istella Chui-Mei, Ouintiles Pacific, Inc., Mountain View, CA *Page 1-358*

Kochanowski, Mark, McWhorter Technologies, Carpentersville, IL *Page 1-22*

Koehn, Kathy Lynn, Midwest Cooperative, Quinter, KS *Page 1-122*

Köhler, Andreas, LKW Walter AG, Vienna, Austria *Page 1-88*

Kolber, Jeffrey A., Computer Sciences Corporation, West Orange, NJ *Page 1-205*

Koluch, Andrew R., Federal-Mogul, St. Louis, MO *Page 1-73*

Konicki, James A., New York State Department of Labor, Albany, NY *Page 1-386*

Kopaczewski, John J., Kennedy Kenrick Catholic High School, Norristown, PA *Page 1-316*

Koppert, Claus, Euro-Log GmbH, Hallbergmoos, Germany *Page 1-254*

Korber, Lorraine M., Henry Schein, Inc., Stevens, PA *Page 1-124*

Korwin, Anthony R., Oregon State University, Prescott, AZ *Page 1-327*

Kosco, Thomas John, American Reinsurance, Princeton, NJ *Page 1-154*

Kot, John S., Total Response Inc., Indianapolis, IN *Page 1-301*

Kotmel, Allan V., New York State Teachers Retirement System, Albany, NY *Page 1-346*

Koubek, Cindy, Fairmont Hotel, New Orleans, LA *Page 1-162*

Kozlov, Christopher M., Arlington Industries, Libertyville, IL *Page 1-120*

Kraft, Debra, ABB Alston Power, Kings Mountain, NC *Page 1-33*

Kramer
> Daune C., Clarus Software, Marietta, GA *Page 1-181*
> Ronald, UPAQ Ltd., Zürich, Switzerland *Page 1-255*

Kraut, Jeffrey B., Associated Textile Converters, New York, NY *Page 1-11*

Kreft, Bryan M., Silicon Graphics, Santa Clara, CA *Page 1-181*

Krell, Lori A., Pixel Magic Imaging, Austin, TX *Page 1-181*

Kretz, Richard E., Business Edge Solutions, Allen, TX *Page 1-255*

Kristen, Helmuth E., Harvard-Smithsonian Center for Astrophysics, Cambridge, MA *Page 1-358*

Kropp, Monica B., EER Systems, Inc., Fort Gordon, GA *Page 1-181*

Krueger, Charles J., Image Computers Inc., Holland, MI *Page 1-255*

Kubat, Miroslav, University of Louisiana at Lafayette, Center for Advanced Computer Studies, Lafayette, LA *Page 1-327*

Kuczerepa, Paul R., Baxter Healthcare Corporation, Round Lake, IL *Page 1-83*

Kueffel, Claudia, Leoni Kabel GmbH & Company KG, Roth, Germany *Page 1-35*

Kumawat, Rajesh, KPMG LLP, New York, IL *Page 1-364*

Kung, Stefan Chi Ho, Stefan Chi Ho Kung, Freelance, Homantin, Hong Kong *Page 1-255*

Kupfer, Mendy, Destia, Brooklyn, NY *Page 1-101*

Kwan, Vincent W., Marconi Data Systems, Inc., Deerfield, IL *Page 1-36*

L

L'Heureux, Colette M., Standard Insurance, Portland, OR *Page 1-150*

Labbate, Evelyn, TechnoSphere Services, Howell, NJ *Page 1-255*

LaBorde, Frank C., Magnetic Data Technologies, Goleta, CA *Page 1-255*

LaBounty, Rachael, Sprint, New Century, KS *Page 1-101*

LaFata, Steve F., 480 Intelligence Group, Langley Air Force Base, VA *Page 1-394*

Laforet, Christopher, Netpath, Inc., Burlington, NC *Page 1-110*

LaGrange, Palmer V., CBSI - Computer Based Systems, Inc., An AverStar Company, Fairfax, VA *Page 1-181*

Lalone, David J., Vengroff, Williams & Associates, Sarasota, FL *Page 1-165*

Lam
> James, Ernst & Young LLP, Mendham, NJ *Page 1-354*
> Kuet Leong, Kyoei Electronics (S) Pte. Ltd., Singapore, Singapore *Page 1-121*
> Wing, HK Net Company, Ltd., Kowloon, Hong Kong *Page 1-101*

Lamberson, Joseph R., EDS, St. Louis, MO *Page 1-215*

Lambert, Paul R., PFF Bank & Trust, Pomona, CA *Page 1-134*

Lambrache, Emil, Atmel Corporation, San Jose, CA *Page 1-66*

Landes, J. Christopher, Lucent Technologies, Basking Ridge, NJ *Page 1-60*

Landis, Damon L., DeVry Institute of Technology, Irving, TX *Page 1-327*

Landrigan, Shawn B., Novell, Inc., Herndon, VA *Page 1-197*

Landry, Karen, Computer Learning Centers, Inc., Methuen, MA *Page 1-341*

Lane, Michael J., Toyota Motor Manufacturing of Kentucky, Georgetown, KY *Page 1-73*

Lang
> David Thomas, Trident Data Systems, Vienna, VA *Page 1-255*
> Robert R., GE Harris Railway, Orlando, FL *Page 1-181*

Langford, Mark G., Southeastern Metals Manufacturing Company, Jacksonville, FL *Page 1-33*

Langley, William, Medscribe Information Systems, Inc., Jacksonville, FL *Page 1-167*

Lapham, Erika P., West Noble School Corporation, Ligonier, IN *Page 1-316*

Lapp, Jon E., Plantrol Systems, Ltd., Westfield, NY *Page 1-182*

Larkin, CorDell R., David Gomez & Associates, Inc., Chicago, IL *Page 1-168*

Larsen, Bjorn J. P., Larsen Consulting, Southend-on-Sea, England, United Kingdom *Page 1-256*

Larson
> Kenneth O., Compaq Computer Corporation, Schaumburg, IL *Page 1-42*
> Sheldon C., Canadian Pacific Railway, Minneapolis, MN *Page 1-86*

Larsson, Fredrik, Mendosus, Mendosus, Sweden *Page 1-256*

Lasky, Tami M., Stratum New Media, Chesapeake, VA *Page 1-182*

Latmore, Allison W., Florida State Board of Administration, Tallahassee, FL *Page 1-375*

Lauchlan, E. Anne, United Distillers & Vintners, Clackmannanshire, Scotland, United Kingdom *Page 1-9*

Lauda, Irene, Speed Link Inc., Pontiac, MI *Page 1-110*

Lauer, Steven R., Maricopa County Superior Courts, Phoenix, AZ *Page 1-376*

Lauffher, Wolfgang, T-Online International AG, Darmstadt, Germany *Page 1-110*

Lavardera, Danny, SITA, Bohemia, NY *Page 1-101*

Lawlor, James E., TASC, Inc., Reading, MA *Page 1-206*

Lawrence, Bonnie L., Lawrence Associates, New Haven, CT *Page 1-364*

Lawson
> Barbara D., Baltimore Gas & Electric, Lusby, MD *Page 1-117*
> John A., Houghton Mifflin, Attleboro, MA *Page 1-17*

Laxström, Peter, Locotech Oy, Helsinki, Finland *Page 1-256*

Layne, Theodore J., FT Mortgage Companies, Irving, TX *Page 1-160*

Le, Long Minh, County of Ingham, Management Information Services, Mason, MI *Page 1-373*

Le Melinaire, Pascal, Landmark Graphics, Austin, TX *Page 1-182*

Leach, David B., Air Products & Chemicals, Inc., GEGE Process Controls A32H2, Allentown, PA *Page 1-125*

Leaman, Kendall J., IntelliMark, Inc., Mechanicsburg, PA *Page 1-256*

Leao, Flavio De Araujo, BMG, Rio de Janeiro, Brazil *Page 1-302*

Lear, Gregory L., Database Consultants, Inc., San Antonio, TX *Page 1-256*

Leary, Mike W., The Montana Power Company, Butte, MT *Page 1-116*

LeBeauf, Shelia M., Equistar Chemicals, LP, Houston, TX *Page 1-26*

Leblanc, Christopher S., Porter & Chester Institute, Ludlow, MA *Page 1-341*

Lechner, Suzanne L., CCW, Fond du Lac, WI *Page 1-182*

Ledford, Yvonne M., University of Oklahoma Health Sciences Center, Oklahoma City, OK *Page 1-327*

Lee
    Edwin Y., Contractors State Licensing Board, Sacramento, CA *Page 1-391*
    Myungho, Sun Microsystems, Inc., Palo Alto, CA *Page 1-42*
    Roger E., Getronics/Wang, New York, NY *Page 1-256*
    Ryan J., ADT Security Services, Inc., Weston, MO *Page 1-298*
    William, C-bridge Internet Solutions, Roseville, CA *Page 1-257*

Leeds, Hal, Morrow Technical Services, Fort Worth, TX *Page 1-257*

LeFaive, Donna M., Trinary Systems Inc., Fennville, MI *Page 1-182*

Lefebvre, Guy, Graphic Resources, Scarborough, Ontario, Canada *Page 1-124*

Legault, Stephane, Wyeth-Ayerst Canada, Inc., Saint-Laurent, Quebec, Canada *Page 1-24*

Legutki, Gregory W., CTAP, San Bernardino, CA *Page 1-206*

Lehman
    Mary Jane Cottingham, Thomson Corporation, Cincinnati, OH *Page 1-18*
    Robert P., New Horizon Management & Consulting, Solon, OH *Page 1-257*

Leinen, Sean Frederick, Intergraph Corporation, Bronxville, NY *Page 1-257*

Leitzel, David R., Unisphere Solutions, Englewood, CO *Page 1-56*

Lembke, David R., Investors Fiduciary Trust, Kansas City, MO *Page 1-147*

Lemke, Uwe, Asera, Inc., Rednvodaty, CA *Page 1-257*

Lemmon, Jeremy R., SMS Data Products Group, Inc., McLean, VA *Page 1-257*

Lentz, Terry M., Systems Computer Technology, Melbourne, FL *Page 1-257*

Leonelli, John A., Defense Information Systems Agency, Department of Defense, Arlington, VA *Page 1-394*

Leskody, James J., Systems-Ensync, Las Vegas, NV *Page 1-6*

Lester, Jeffrey A., International Network Services, Morrisville, NC *Page 1-258*

Leung, Gregory D., EC Cubed, Nesconset, NY *Page 1-110*

Levenhagen, Dennis G., MicroGo'L, Beaver Dam, WI *Page 1-258*

Leveque, Gilles, Hewlett-Packard Company, Grenoble Cedex 9, France *Page 1-42*

Levesque, Raymond F., Federal Aviation Administration, Washington, DC *Page 1-390*

Levin, Maria, Compaq Computer Corporation, Methuen, MA *Page 1-42*

Levine
    William A., First Continental Trading, Chicago, IL *Page 1-143*
    Jerilee "Jeri" Goodman, Andrx, Weston, FL *Page 1-24*

Lewis
    Brenda, Transactions Marketing Inc., Greenwich, CT *Page 1-364*
    John H., Lewis Colorado, Littleton, CO *Page 1-258*
    R. Scott, Ericsson Messaging Systems, Woodbury, NY *Page 1-61*
    Winston E., Lockheed Martin, Los Banos, CA *Page 1-79*

Lewis A., Francisco, Plural, New York, NY *Page 1-182*

Li, Xuhong "Linda", City College of New York, New York, NY *Page 1-327*

Liao
    Min, Advanced Network & Services, Inc., Armonk, NY *Page 1-258*
    Weidong, Kent State University, Kent, OH *Page 1-327*

Liddell, William "Keeko", Sage Software, Inc., Dallas, TX *Page 1-258*

Liguori, Stephen D., Northrop Grumman, Bethpage, NY *Page 1-76*

Lim, Daniel K., Guittard Chocolate Company, Burlingame, CA *Page 1-8*

Liming, Ray D., Merck-Medco Rx, Columbus, OH *Page 1-131*

Limon, Jeffrey Jessey, J.L. Communications, Irving, TX *Page 1-111*

Lin, Jin, Savantnet Solutions, New York, NY *Page 1-258*

Lindberg, Reiulf, Scandinavian Airlines, Oslo, Norway *Page 1-89*

Linder-Linsley, Sue, Department of Anthropology, Dallas, TX *Page 1-327*

Lindner, Dale R., Texas Instruments, Dallas, TX *Page 1-66*

Linfante, Thomas P., Jerry's Precision Company, Dover, NJ *Page 1-52*

Link, Patty A., Area 2 Learning Tech Hub, Ottawa, IL *Page 1-258*

Lipson, Derek N., SCS, Inc., Fremont, NE *Page 1-13*

Lis, Ellen R., Wyeth-Ayerst Research, Radnor, PA *Page 1-24*

Liske, Scott J., City of Appleton, Appleton, WI *Page 1-373*

Litchev, Lubomir, Symantec Corporation, Cupertino, CA *Page 1-197*

Litchfield, Gregory T., Grace University, Omaha, NE *Page 1-328*

Litten, Catherine Lee, Valley Presbyterian Hospital, Van Nuys, CA *Page 1-308*

Little
    Dinah B., Computer Curriculum Corporation, Annapolis, MD *Page 1-206*
    Frank, Design Fabricators, Lafayette, CO *Page 1-54*

Littman, Karen G., Morphonix, San Rafael, CA *Page 1-182*

Litwin, Ryan P., Information Systems Professionals, Milwaukee, WI *Page 1-259*

Liu
    Chen, Motorola, Naperville, IL *Page 1-66*
    Kevin H., Bellcore, Red Bank, NJ *Page 1-101*
    Ningsheng, Experian, Englewood, CO *Page 1-182*
    Xiaoqing "Frank", University of Missouri - Rolla, Rolla, MO *Page 1-328*

Livingston, Mark A., Hewlett-Packard Labs, Palo Alto, CA *Page 1-43*

Lizcano, Olga, Public Utility Commission, Austin, TX *Page 1-390*

Llagostera, Domingo, El Paso Energy Corporation, Sugar Land, TX *Page 1-115*

Lo, Alen, HSBC, Heng Fa Chuen, Hong Kong *Page 1-143*

Lobato, William Lyle, Minerals Management Services, Camarillo, CA *Page 1-388*

Lodaya, Manish, NextLinx Corporation, Gaithersburg, MD *Page 1-259*

Loechner, Erich Karl, Computer Land, San Diego, CA *Page 1-206*

Loeffler, Kevin J., Purdue University, West Lafayette, IN *Page 1-328*

Lomax, Anissa M., Seaboard Credit Union, Jacksonville, FL *Page 1-137*

Lombardi, James, Robertson Stephens, Bronxville, NY *Page 1-143*

Lombardini, John T., Public Service/Electric & Gas, Newark, NJ *Page 1-116*

Londeree, Vicki Neal, Lexis Publishing, Charlottesville, VA *Page 1-18*

Long
    Barbara Anne, Computer Sciences Corporation, Crystal City, VA *Page 1-206*
    Cheryl C., Ross Systems, Atlanta, GA *Page 1-183*
    Raymond, City of El Paso, El Paso, TX *Page 1-373*

Longgood, Donna R., Cox Target Media, Largo, FL *Page 1-20*

Longstrom, Edward, Lockheed Martin, Owego, NY *Page 1-79*

Loo, Ringo, NetMedia International Ltd., Hong Kong, Hong Kong *Page 1-18*

Lopardo, Sue, Northwestern Memorial Hospital, Chicago, IL *Page 1-308*

Lopes, Duane A., Formglas, Inc., Toronto, Ontario, Canada *Page 1-7*

Lorange, Jon B., The Farmers Association of Iceland, Reykjavik, Iceland *Page 1-345*

Lord, John D., CAS Inc., Pelham, NY *Page 1-4*

Lorenzi, David L., Comcast, Oaks, PA *Page 1-108*

Losson, M. Melissa, Raytheon Company, Fullerton, CA *Page 1-80*

Louie, Victor C., IKOS Systems, Arlington Heights, IL *Page 1-206*

Loustaudaudine, Christophe, CAC Systèmes, Areines, France *Page 1-76*

Love, Darlene, Motorola, Schaumburg, IL *Page 1-57*

Low, Humbert, KPMG LLP, Toronto, Ontario, Canada *Page 1-364*

Lowe
    Darren L., NIST, Gaithersburg, MD *Page 1-360*
    Vincent D., Aqueduct Information Services, Mountain View, CA *Page 1-259*

Loy-Tate, Deanne, Reynolds & Reynolds, Oklahoma City, OK *Page 1-21*

Lozano, Hector Jose, Independent, San Jeronimo, Mexico *Page 1-73*

Luderer, Bob, Sloan & Company, Inc., West Caldwell, NJ *Page 1-7*

Ludwig, Mark A., AW Chesterton Company, Canton, MA *Page 1-37*

Lufkin, Keith S., Southern Trust Mortgage, Richmond, VA *Page 1-141*

Luiz, Dave P., Health & Welfare Agency, Sacramento, CA *Page 1-155*

Luman, Charles J., MCI Systemhouse, Minneapolis, MN *Page 1-206*

Lunstead, Eric Q., AMR Research, Boston, MA *Page 1-259*

Luther, Carolyn W., Independence Blue Cross, Philadelphia, PA *Page 1-150*

LuVisi, Michael A., IBM Corporation, Long Beach, CA *Page 1-43*

Lyle
Richard, StorageTek, Austin, TX *Page 1-46*
Stephen T., PricewaterhouseCoopers, Fairfax, VA *Page 1-354*

Lynch, Ron A., Tekmark Global Solutions, Wayne, PA *Page 1-170*

Lyng, Gary, VERITAS Software, Mountain View, CA *Page 1-197*

Lynk, Dennis R., Benedict Corporation, Norwich, NY *Page 1-126*

Lynn, Robert Garon "Bob", Independent, Charlotte, NC *Page 1-259*

Lynt, William W., Right Connection, Inc., Kenosha, WI *Page 1-259*

Lysinger, Lowell J., BSA & I, LLP, Perkasie, PA *Page 1-312*

M

Maceluch, Markian W., General Physics Corporation, Baltimore, MD *Page 1-260*

MacIntosh, Michelle, Northern Computers, Pawtucket, RI *Page 1-260*

MacKrell, John, CIMdata, Inc., Ann Arbor, MI *Page 1-260*

Madhusudan, Neeruganti, Complete Business Solutions, Baltimore, MD *Page 1-260*

Magnotta, Salvatore D., Union Switch and Signal, Washington, PA *Page 1-78*

Magolnick, Michael, Solution Home.com, Margate, FL *Page 1-260*

Magwood, Quanteer D., RWD Technologies, Columbia, MD *Page 1-260*

Mahajani, Anand, Diversified Computer Consultants, Atlanta, GA *Page 1-260*

Maher, Michael A., Weber Chevrolet, St. Louis, MO *Page 1-127*

Mahmud, Shamun, Amdahl Corporation, Washington, DC *Page 1-43*

Maholm, Timothy R., McDonald Investments, Cleveland, OH *Page 1-146*

Maimbourg, Michael A., Solectron Corporation, Gatesville, TX *Page 1-43*

Maio, Joseph A., Hilton Hotels Corporation, Elizabeth, NJ *Page 1-162*

Majcher, Jeff L., Companion Tech, Ridgeland, MS *Page 1-261*

Makar, Lynn A., Luzerne Intermediate Unit, Kingston, PA *Page 1-341*

Maley, Scott, TASC, Inc., Midwest City, OK *Page 1-206*

Mallouk, Ramez H., Nokia, Helsinki, Finland *Page 1-61*

Maloney, Edward, ITT Technical Institute, Encino, CA *Page 1-338*

Maltais, John R., CBSI, Springfield, MA *Page 1-183*

Mancini, James M., IKON Technology Services, Irvine, CA *Page 1-50*

Manges, John P., Primerica Financial Services, Duluth, GA *Page 1-139*

Manino, Brooke, American Express - TRS, Berkeley Heights, NJ *Page 1-138*

Mankala, Srinivas, Database Consultants, Inc., Austin, TX *Page 1-261*

Manning, Kevin W., MediaOne Group, Englewood, CO *Page 1-108*

Mao, John, Rocsoar, Inc., Wilmington, DE *Page 1-261*

Maraschiello, Lou, Smart Web Sales, Chico, CA *Page 1-261*

Marchany, Randy C., Virginia Tech Computing Center, Blacksburg, VA *Page 1-338*

Marchena, Ruddy, Pellerano & Herrera, Miami, FL *Page 1-312*

Marchioli, Marc E., The Database Group Inc., Dallas, TX *Page 1-261*

Marcus, Judith L., Oracle Corporation, New York, NY *Page 1-197*

Marged, Judith M., American Intercontinental University, Plantation, FL *Page 1-328*

Margison-Evans, Charel, Triplex Director Marketing Corporation, Novato, CA *Page 1-166*

Marín, José R., PricewaterhouseCoopers LLP, San Juan, Puerto Rico *Page 1-354*

Marini, Christopher W., C.W. Marini & Associates, San Leandro, CA *Page 1-261*

Marino, Michael A., Carolina Manufacturer's Service, Inc., Winston-Salem, NC *Page 1-361*

Marinoff, Ryan H., DynaLink, Cleveland, OH *Page 1-183*

Markel, Lisa Anne, Covance, Nashville, TN *Page 1-358*

Marker, Wendy C., Marker Consulting, St. Louis, MO *Page 1-261*

Markkula, Harri, Tilator Oy, Sakyla, Finland *Page 1-262*

Markowski, Violet E., IBM Corporation, Arlington, MA *Page 1-43*

Marlow, Gerald D., Helios System Inc., Glen Ellyn, IL *Page 1-262*

Marques, Ronaldo Pereiras, American Express, Phoenix, AZ *Page 1-139*

Marschall, Heiko Bernd, Marschall Electronics, Ltd., Bavaria, Germany *Page 1-262*

Marshall, Don H., Attachmate Corporation, Bellevue, WA *Page 1-197*

Martin
Eric M., Green Bay Packaging, Inc., Conway, AR *Page 1-15*
Robert A., PTI, Atlanta, GA *Page 1-365*

Martinsson, Lars E., Oracle Corporation, Redwood City, CA *Page 1-197*

Marton, Candace C., ProxyMed, Inc., Boca Raton, FL *Page 1-183*

Mason, Jeffrey W., Sundance Travel International, Irvine, CA *Page 1-91*

Massa-Lochridge, Lauren J., exlr8, Inc., Berkeley, CA *Page 1-262*

Massey, Thomas E., PageNet, Dallas, TX *Page 1-102*

Mastroianni, Dan A., MBI Inc., Norwalk, CT *Page 1-163*

Masuda, Yukie, IBM Japan, Kanagawa, Japan *Page 1-43*

Matabudul, Samir, BTI Consulting, Vacoas, Mauritius *Page 1-262*

Mathes, Jonathan R., U.S. Bank, Minneapolis, MN *Page 1-133*

Mathis, Belinda J., Mercedes Benz U.S. International, Tuscaloosa, AL *Page 1-127*

Mathiyazhagan, Nithyanandam "Mathi", IMR Global Corporation, Clearwater, FL *Page 1-262*

Mathur, Sameer, Phoenix Technologies Ltd., San Jose, CA *Page 1-183*

Matos, Ricardo R., Parkson Corporation, Fort Lauderdale, FL *Page 1-38*

Matsumoto, T. Steve, Computer Sciences Corporation, Sterling, VA *Page 1-207*

Matthews
Bill D., Union Pacific Technologies, Omaha, NE *Page 1-262*
John V., Lucent Technologies, Columbus, OH *Page 1-61*
Neil A., CIBC Offshore Banking Services Corporation, St. Michael, Barbados *Page 1-143*

Mavis, Mark K., Ticketmaster, Kansas City, MO *Page 1-306*

Mayer
John W., City of Irving, Irving, TX *Page 1-373*
Warren D., Rutgers University, Newark, NJ *Page 1-328*

McAndrew, Jeffrey M., Stuart Dean Company, New York, NY *Page 1-7*

McCalla, Izett M. E., Island Life Insurance Company, Kingston, Jamaica *Page 1-148*

McCandless, Doug, International Comfort Products, Hampshire, TN *Page 1-51*

McCarson, David B., International Network Services, Morrisville, NC *Page 1-263*

McCauley, Barney, SMUD, Sacramento, CA *Page 1-114*

McCoppen, Reid, Baycrest Centre for Geriatric Care, Toronto, Ontario, Canada *Page 1-310*

McCown, Renee, Polo Ralph Lauren, Lyndhurst, NJ *Page 1-132*

McCoy, Karstyn, Horizon Instructional Systems, North Highlands, CA *Page 1-316*

McCracken, Philip F., Actionet, Inc., Silver Spring, MD *Page 1-263*

McCraw, Shirley B., SYSCO Corporation, Houston, TX *Page 1-129*

McCray, Marc S., Compath Inc., Fairfax, VA *Page 1-302*

McCrea, Ianthe Helen, Reliant Energy, Inc., Houston, TX *Page 1-116*

McCusker, Clinton F., Lightbridge Inc., Burlington, MA *Page 1-93*

McDanel, Gary A., United States Bureau of Reclamation, Billings, MT *Page 1-387*

McDonald, Virgil L., Mesa Technical College, Tucumcari, NM *Page 1-328*

McDonnell, Michael J., Andersen Consulting, Philadelphia, PA *Page 1-365*

McDowell
Haywood, The Stock Market Reference Desk, Reston, VA *Page 1-183*
Webb R., Xpedite Systems, El Segundo, CA *Page 1-302*

McEady, Erasmus W., Vector Data Systems, Fort Bragg, NC *Page 1-348*

McElroy
Ted M., Diversified Consulting International, Waynesville, NC *Page 1-263*
Thomas D., Unisource Network Services, Chicago, IL *Page 1-263*

McElvy, Pam, InterVoice-Brite, Inc., Dallas, TX *Page 1-56*

McEntyre, Susan K., McKesson HBOC, Alpharetta, GA *Page 1-24*

McFarlane, Daniel C., Michelin North America, Greenville, SC *Page 1-28*

McFarlin, David J., Barco, Inc., South Windsor, CT *Page 1-69*

McGary, Steven M., Corning Inc. Science Division Products, Acton, MA *Page 1-69*

McGibbon, Thomas L., ITT Industries, Rome, NY *Page 1-263*

McGourty, Felicity F., Tivoli Systems, Austin, TX *Page 1-198*

McGrory, Joan Serocki, Shelby County Trustee, Memphis, TN *Page 1-380*

McGuff, Dale T., Arthur Andersen, St. Charles, IL *Page 1-365*

McGuire
    Michael R., Kaiser Health Plan, Walnut Creek, CA *Page 1-152*
    Tom, Marc Mintz & Associates LLC, Fairfield, NJ *Page 1-263*

McIntosh, Clarissa R., Alcatel USA, Plano, TX *Page 1-102*

McIntyre, David M., The Shoe Show of Rocky Mount, Concord, NC *Page 1-127*

McKaskle, Charles "Chuck", Mac Electronics, Tucson, AZ *Page 1-263*

McKay, Michelle, C2 Multimedia, Oklahoma City, OK *Page 1-263*

McKillip, West, AFI, Amarillo, TX *Page 1-125*

McKinney, Debi C., Nationwide Insurance, Columbus, OH *Page 1-148*

McLaughlin-Nelson, Lori K., Advanced Elastomer Systems, L.P., Akron, OH *Page 1-22*

McLemore, Shannon, Continuous Forms & Checks, Inc., Peachtree City, GA *Page 1-138*

McLennan, Gerald J., OC Transpo, Orleans, Ontario, Canada *Page 1-87*

McNeil, D. Gregory, e-Business Express, Cleveland, OH *Page 1-264*

McNutt, Joseph W., The Computer & Network Fixer, Levittown, PA *Page 1-216*

McQuillister, George A., Pacific Gas & Electric, Oakland, CA *Page 1-117*

McWilliams, Craig R., Senco-Argonne National Lab, Palatine, IL *Page 1-264*

Meckley, Hope Eyre, SAP, Atlanta, GA *Page 1-184*

Medina, Armando Ibarra, ITESM Campus Laguna, Torreon, Mexico *Page 1-328*

Medsker, Michael D., Archer Engineers, Peculiar, MO *Page 1-351*

Mehta, Jatin, MIC, Inc., Kearny, NJ *Page 1-264*

Meier, Debora L., Family Health Systems, Madison, WI *Page 1-153*

Meisinger, Steven D., Penguin Consulting Company, Inc., Arlington, TX *Page 1-264*

Melconian, Martin, Globebyte, Kingston upon Thames, England, United Kingdom *Page 1-264*

Mellin, Jorma, Telia Finland Ltd., Vantaa, Finland *Page 1-102*

Meloun, Jalane M., Meloun Consulting, Akron, OH *Page 1-264*

Mendoza, Julio Cesar, Lear Seating Inespo Comercial, Diadema Sp, Brazil *Page 1-74*

Menezes, Conrad O., American Express Company, New York, NY *Page 1-139*

Mengerink, Joel W., Paulding High School, Van Wert, OH *Page 1-316*

Merkt, Greg, PegaSystems Inc., Cambridge, MA *Page 1-264*

Merritt, Gary S., Greeley Gas Company, Denver, CO *Page 1-115*

Messes, Alexander P., The Allied Group Inc., Glastonbury, CT *Page 1-184*

Meszaros, Jason P., Retek Information System, Minneapolis, MN *Page 1-184*

Metzler, Robin C., KidsPeace, Orefield, PA *Page 1-343*

Meyer
    Dirk, Dinoex, Hessen, Germany *Page 1-265*
    Leo H., Humana Inc., Louisville, KY *Page 1-153*
    Patrick J., Information Graphics Systems Inc., Boulder, CO *Page 1-184*

Meyerson, James L., Hewlett-Packard Company, Cupertino, CA *Page 1-43*

Michael, Laura Anne, Attachmate Corporation, Bellevue, WA *Page 1-198*

Michaelides, Phyllis J., Textron, Inc., Providence, RI *Page 1-76*

Michaelsen, Nancy L., Virginia Department of Transportation, King George, VA *Page 1-390*

Michales, Thomas C., Af Associates, Northvale, NJ *Page 1-207*

Mikel, Lashika L., Westinghouse, Augusta, GA *Page 1-394*

Mikkelsen, Dean C., Schlumberger/GeoQuest, Houston, TX *Page 1-3*

Miler, Wyatt H., George Miler, Inc., Melbourne, FL *Page 1-90*

Miles
    Greg S., AverStar, Greenbelt, MD *Page 1-265*
    Mazda T., Pennrose Properties, Inc., Philadelphia, PA *Page 1-302*

Miller
    Jeffrey T., Simpson Housing Ltd. Partnership, Denver, CO *Page 1-160*
    Kevin J., Andersen Consulting, Pollesville, MD *Page 1-365*
    Stephen W., Stonebridge Technologies, Edmond, OK *Page 1-265*

Milligan, Richard P., Peterborough County-City Health Unit, Peterborough, Ontario, Canada *Page 1-385*

Mills, Dennis Joseph, Comsearch, Reston, VA *Page 1-61*

Milner, Dana, Home Depot, Atlanta, GA *Page 1-126*

Mims, Creflo R., Medical Knowledge Systems Inc., Detroit, MI *Page 1-265*

Minasyan, Georgiy R., Astro-Med, Inc., Lafayette Hill, PA *Page 1-83*

Mingin, Philip M., Olsten Corporation, Melville, NY *Page 1-168*

Minion, William W., Federal Bureau of Prisons, Tallahassee, FL *Page 1-378*

Mirau, Michael Glen, eLogo.com Encorporation, Dallas, TX *Page 1-118*

Misirian, Nathan J., Case Corporation, Racine, WI *Page 1-35*

Mitchell, Leo, DJG & Associates, Sterling Heights, MI *Page 1-265*

Mixon, Daniel A., AT&T, Fort Smith, AR *Page 1-102*

Mohamed
    Mohamed Ahmed, Cairo Barclay's Bank, Cairo, Egypt *Page 1-137*
    Noohu, 2GoTrade.com, Wanchai, Hong Kong *Page 1-184*

Mohammed, David S., Connection Staffing, Inc., Tampa, FL *Page 1-170*

Mohan, Ram, Infonautics Corporation, King of Prussia, PA *Page 1-213*

Moiseyev, Aleksey, Parametric Technology Corporation, Waltham, MA *Page 1-198*

Mokros, Jason M., Wexner Heritage Village, Colombus, OH *Page 1-307*

Moler, Dino D., The National Transportation Exchange, Inc., Downers Grove, IL *Page 1-147*

Moles, Patrick H., Integrated Solutions Group, Foothill Ranch, CA *Page 1-184*

Molnar, Andie, Lucent Technologies, Metuchen, NJ *Page 1-61*

Monaghan, Michael J., Cyberjava, Hollywood, CA *Page 1-265*

Moncoqut, Diana, Cadence Design Systems, Glen Ridge, NJ *Page 1-265*

Mongon, William H., Cook Yancey King and Galloway, Shreveport, LA *Page 1-312*

Monson, Barbara E., Carlson Hospitality Worldwide, Oceanside, CA *Page 1-111*

Monteiro, Walkiria, Compaq Computer Corporation, Sao Paulo, Brazil *Page 1-44*

Montgomery, Janie E., Ottawa University, Ottawa, KS *Page 1-329*

Montreuil, Benoit, SET Technologies, Inc., Sainte-Foy, Quebec, Canada *Page 1-184*

Moore, Allen K., SAIC, Elmendorf Air Force Base, AK *Page 1-358*

Moore-Fore, Iris Lynn, Lockheed Martin, Washington, DC *Page 1-80*

Moorehouse, Nina M., Novell, Inc., Bel Air, MD *Page 1-198*

Moosman, Elizabeth D., Equitable Tax Service, Logan, UT *Page 1-163*

Morales, Pedro, University of Southern California School of Medicine, Los Angeles, CA *Page 1-329*

Morrell, Margaret R., Valencia Community College, Orlando, FL *Page 1-338*

Morrill, Jane E., Duke Communications Windows 2000 Magazine, Loveland, CO *Page 1-16*

Morris
    Adele G., Craig County Public Schools, Salem, VA *Page 1-382*
    Michael P., Vitamin Shoppe Industries, Inc., North Bergen, NJ *Page 1-132*

Morrison, K. C., Principal Financial Group, Des Moines, IA *Page 1-148*

Morrow, Larry J., Newnan Technologies, Inc., Newnan, GA *Page 1-207*

Morse, Jeffery G., AB Floyd, Inc., Alexandria, VA *Page 1-266*

Mosby, Robin M., United States Air Force, Trenton, NJ *Page 1-394*

Moser, Ellen M., IBM Corporation, Redwood City, CA *Page 1-44*

Mourad, Tarek M., Telegyr Systems, Inc., San Jose, CA *Page 1-266*

Moxley, Greg D., Computer Sciences Corporation, Hampton, VA *Page 1-207*

Moy, Anne, Rosses Community School, Donegal, Ireland *Page 1-316*

Muehlius, David A., E.C. Styberg Engineering Company, Racine, WI *Page 1-74*

Muhammad, Yolanda, Legal Aid Society, New York, NY *Page 1-313*

Muhlstadt, Maryanne T., K-mart Distribution Center, Manteno, IL *Page 1-88*

Mui, Henry M., Chase Manhattan Bank, New York, NY *Page 1-135*

Mukherjee, Himadri P., ABB Systems Control, Santa Clara, CA *Page 1-215*

Mukhopadhyay, Kalyan, Cylogix, Edison, NJ *Page 1-266*

Mukundan, Bobby S., Sapient Corporation, Addison, TX *Page 1-365*

Mulé, Peter T., RCG Information Technology, New York, NY *Page 1-266*

Mullapudi, Ramarao, Premier Consultancy, Plano, TX *Page 1-266*

Mulleady, Michael F., Kay Elemetrics Corporation, Lincoln, NJ *Page 1-185*

Mullen, Frank L., SMA Inc., Humble, TX *Page 1-185*

Muller, Gary D., Eskom, Bellville, South Africa *Page 1-114*

Mulligan, John, Bureau of Translation Services Inc., Haddonfield, NJ *Page 1-185*

Mullinax, Cindy Tarte, Bobbin Group Publishing, Columbia, SC *Page 1-16*

Munajj, Sharon E. L., Long Aldridge & Norman, Atlanta, GA *Page 1-313*

Mundle, Sheldon, IBM Corporation, Marietta, GA *Page 1-44*

Munshi, Darius J., Houston Associates, Arlington, VA *Page 1-111*

Munukutla, Srinivasa S., AT&T, Edison, NJ *Page 1-102*

Murawaski, Michael R., Computer Sciences Corporation, Warren, MI *Page 1-207*

Murphy
  Brian E., Cyberdeck Consultants, Pittsburgh, PA *Page 1-266*
  George E., Premiere Conferencing, Colorado Springs, CO *Page 1-102*
  Jack, CyberPatriot.com, Myrtle Beach, SC *Page 1-266*

Murray
  James M., CPU, Inc., Metairie, LA *Page 1-267*
  Lee, Weyerhaeuser Company, Federal Way, WA *Page 1-12*

Muvvala, Padmavathi, University of Bahrain, Area 326, Bahrain *Page 1-329*

Mychalczuk, Michael G., Mission Critical Software, Houston, TX *Page 1-185*

Myers, John E., Myers Consulting Inc., Boonville, MO *Page 1-267*

N

Nachlis, Mark Neal, Cisco Systems, Inc., Belmont, CA *Page 1-61*

Naff, James M., Department of Defense, Indianapolis, IN *Page 1-395*

Nagarajan, Senthil Kumar, Cisco Systems, Inc., Union City, CA *Page 1-61*

Nagel, Dennis E., Onsale, Inc., Menlo Park, CA *Page 1-267*

Naivar, DeVonna R., IBM Server Development Group, Taylor, TX *Page 1-267*

Nallabathula, Udaya Sankar, UCA Computer Systems, Inc., Dover, NJ *Page 1-267*

Namoglu, Sheryl F., Arris Systems, Inc., Berwyn, PA *Page 1-267*

Nana, Rajesh C., Flexx Magazine, Lithia Springs, GA *Page 1-17*

Nandi, Somnath, Connectria, Maple Shade, NJ *Page 1-267*

Narayana, Shyamkumar, Ernst & Young Application Services LLC., Lake Forest, CA *Page 1-354*

Nassani, Joseph, ITT Avionics, Clifton, NJ *Page 1-77*

Nasser, Zaina, Oman Development Bank, Muscat, Oman *Page 1-139*

Nassif, John M., United States Department of Agriculture, St. Louis, MO *Page 1-391*

Nathan, Matthew N., Vison Education Inc., New York, NY *Page 1-268*

Naugle, Raymond H., Xceed, Tempe, AZ *Page 1-268*

Neal, Scott C., Nortel Networks, Overland Park, KS *Page 1-56*

Nebel, John K., Schenck Turner Inc., Orion, MI *Page 1-83*

Nelson, Joyce E., Independent, Ashland, WI *Page 1-338*

Nemchick, David C., Eastman Kodak Company, Rochester, NY *Page 1-84*

Nessel, Steve W., Los Alamos Technical Associates, Albuquerque, NM *Page 1-268*

Nester, Leonard J., St. Joseph's University, Philadelphia, PA *Page 1-329*

Nestore, Frank S., Arthur Andersen LLP, Lancaster, PA *Page 1-365*

Newberry, Del R., First Horizon Home Loans, Garland, TX *Page 1-141*

Newman
  Marjana, Louisiana State University at Eunice, Eunice, LA *Page 1-329*
  Moses N., Point of Sale Technology Corporation, New York, NY *Page 1-268*

Newsome, Teresa M., TASC, Inc., Chantilly, VA *Page 1-207*

Newton, Clifford R., Delphi Saginaw Steering Systems, Saginaw, MI *Page 1-74*

Nguyen
  Bac Hai, Jasmine Computers Technologies, Inc., Montreal, Quebec, Canada *Page 1-268*
  Brittney T., The Trizetto Group, Englewood, CO *Page 1-268*
  Duc V., Moore Business Forms, Nacogdoches, TX *Page 1-20*
  Khanh, Nova Bancorp Group, Ltd., Montreal, Quebec, Canada *Page 1-143*
  Peter N., Furon FHP, Anaheim, CA *Page 1-81*
  Quan, McGill University, West Montreal, Quebec, Canada *Page 1-329*
  Tony H., Chicago Title & Trust, Chatsworth, CA *Page 1-185*

Nial, Marjorie, SCIT, Mount Pleasant, MI *Page 1-162*

Nicholson
  Bill, Catellus Development Corporation, San Francisco, CA *Page 1-160*
  Peter D., CCL Label, Ontario, CA *Page 1-37*

Nickele, Margaret M., S&C Electric Company, Chicago, IL *Page 1-52*

Nickerson, Gary B., Oklahoma Baptist University, Shawnee, OK *Page 1-329*

Niel, Anthony L., Kaiser Permanente, Honolulu, HI *Page 1-150*

Nielsen, Thomas W., BMC Consultants, Inc., Englewood, CO *Page 1-369*

Nightingale, Mark J., Pro Staff Personnel, Houston, TX *Page 1-370*

Nilsson
  Anders, Absalon Group, Malmo, Sweden *Page 1-268*
  Sigward, CS Cybernetic Systems AB, Vallentuna, Sweden *Page 1-207*

Nixon, Charles C., Bureau of Indian Affairs - Navajo Area Office, Fort Defiance, AZ *Page 1-371*

Noble
  Amanda, CSC, Richmond, VA *Page 1-208*
  Michael, City of Greenfield, Greenfield, IN *Page 1-373*

Nofal, Mohamed El-Sayed, High Technology Systems Ltd. (Hitechnofal), Cairo, Egypt *Page 1-208*

Nolan, Thomas J., Transaction Information Systems, New York, NY *Page 1-269*

Nonweiler, Kevin Ian, Mosman Municipal Council, Liberty Grove, New South Wales, Australia *Page 1-371*

Noon, Patrick H., Saudi Arabian Bechtel Company, Al Khobar, Saudi Arabia *Page 1-5*

Noor, Nicholas N., International Online Relations, New Windsor, NY *Page 1-208*

Noorbakhsh, Roya, Fluor Global Services, Aliso Viejo, CA *Page 1-349*

Noortheen, Mohammed, Net Tours & Travel, Dubai, United Arab Emirates *Page 1-91*

North, Barbara, Great White North, Proton Station, Ontario, Canada *Page 1-269*

Norwood, Kevin W., Premier Systems Integrators, Richardson, TX *Page 1-208*

Nourse, Sharon, Packaging Technologies, Davenport, IA *Page 1-38*

Nova, William E., Caro Research, Waltham, MA *Page 1-358*

Novitzki, James, Johns Hopkins University, Baltimore, MD *Page 1-330*

Nutter, John J., Quantum Corporation, Shrewsbury, MA *Page 1-47*

Nuwer, Kevin, Xerox, Webster, NY *Page 1-50*

Nyeu, Maung, Odetics, Inc., Irvine, CA *Page 1-57*

Nylese, Tara Lyn, EDAX Inc., Fort Myers, FL *Page 1-81*

Nzabanita, Hakiza, United Bible Societies, Lome, Togo *Page 1-17*

O

O'Brien, Greg, G&L Enterprises, Pearisburg, VA *Page 1-164*

O'Brien
  Kevin, Island Services Network, Charlottetown, Prince Edward Island, Canada *Page 1-269*
  Sean M., Modis Technologies, Orlando, FL *Page 1-269*

O'Bryant, George H., Professional Duplicating, Media, PA *Page 1-20*

O'Connor, Brian K., RESPEC, Albuquerque, NM *Page 1-269*

O'Donnell
  Charlie, Pepsi Cola International, Somers, NY *Page 1-9*
  Shaun I., Anheuser-Busch, Inc., Lanexa, VA *Page 1-9*

O'Keefe, Curtis W., Winstar, Falls Church, VA *Page 1-93*

O'Malley, Timothy S., IBM Global Services, Glen Rock, NJ *Page 1-269*

Oakeley
  Agnes C., Inter-tel Technologies, Inc., Albuquerque, NM *Page 1-93*
  Timothy N., State of New Mexico Taxation and Revenue Department, Santa Fe, NM *Page 1-380*

Obeirne, Barbara H., Renal Care Group, Inc., Wichita, KS *Page 1-306*

Öberg, Jonas, Mälardalens Mögskola, Vasteras, Sweden *Page 1-330*

Obibi, Manasse O., Zebra Systems Ltd., Hounslow Middlesex, England, United Kingdom *Page 1-270*

Ochoa, Ruben J., Computer Savers, Inc., New York, NY *Page 1-270*

Odok, Erhan, Oracle Corporation, Orlando, FL *Page 1-198*

Oglensky, David S., Data Management Services, Cedar Knolls, NJ *Page 1-185*

Ogunmodede, Victor A., Teletech Holdings Inc., Denver, CO *Page 1-270*

Ohaeri, Kenneth O., Blue Cross & Blue Shield, St. Paul, MN *Page 1-151*

Okhandiar, Vazi P., National University, Irvine, CA *Page 1-330*

Olaric, Thada, Thaihosting, Yannawa, Thailand *Page 1-270*

Olexa, Christopher M., Covad Communications, McLean, VA *Page 1-270*

Oliva, Stephen A., Sprint, Overland Park, KS *Page 1-102*

Oliver, Thomas W., Furniture City Color, High Point, NC *Page 1-22*

Olney, Tiffany, American Microsystems Inc, Pocatello, ID *Page 1-67*

Olsen, William W., Madison River Communications, Manito, IL *Page 1-103*

Olson
Elizabeth K., Anexsys, Chicago, IL *Page 1-270*
Patrick C., Menlo College, Atherton, CA *Page 1-330*
Rob A., Freedom Plastics, Sun Prairie, WI *Page 1-29*

Omran, Abraham, Cyras Systems, Inc., Fremont, CA *Page 1-56*

Oo, Zaw W., Cookson Fibers, Inc., Ansonville, NC *Page 1-11*

Oosthuysen, Herman, Aerospace Software Ltd., Calgary, Alberta, Canada *Page 1-270*

Ordoobadi, Mehrdad, Michael Baker Jr., Inc., Coraopolis, PA *Page 1-271*

Orhon, Ahmet V., Siskon Electronic Company, Izmir, Turkey *Page 1-208*

Orndoff, Steven S., United States Army Corps of Engineers, Winchester, VA *Page 1-395*

Osmer, Corey, Native Textiles, Glens Falls, NY *Page 1-11*

Ostermann, Gerhard H., Panalpina Inc., Morristown, NJ *Page 1-88*

Ouellette, Beth, Prudential Insurance, Roseland, NJ *Page 1-149*

Oulundsen, George E., Millipore Corporation, Bedford, MA *Page 1-82*

Ownby, James O., IKON Education Services, Greenville, SC *Page 1-51*

Owrey, Richard, Ellwood Group Inc., Ellwood City, PA *Page 1-34*

P

Paddock, Janet, Alaska Power & Telephone Company, Port Townsend, WA *Page 1-103*

Paden, John, St. Mary College, Leavenworth, KS *Page 1-330*

Padilla, Reynaldo D., The Bank of Nova Scotia, Scarborough, Ontario, Canada *Page 1-135*

Page, William Walter, E-Citi, Los Angeles, CA *Page 1-186*

Pagliei, Jeffrey M., ESPS, Inc., Fort Washington, PA *Page 1-186*

Pagnis, Rishikesh R., TexSYS RD Corporation, Irving, TX *Page 1-271*

Pagulayan, Randy J., University of Cincinnati, Cincinnati, OH *Page 1-330*

Pakuwibowo, Mohammad, Skafab, Stockholm, Sweden *Page 1-387*

Paladino, Chris D., Andersen Consulting, Alexandria, VA *Page 1-365*

Palasciano, Stephen M., Cannon, Grand Island, NY *Page 1-351*

Palatinus, Gregory S., Pomeroy Computer Resources, Indianapolis, IN *Page 1-271*

Pang, Elmer S. B., Kazuo Totoki Ltd., Honolulu, HI *Page 1-159*

Papke, Steven D., PQH Architects, Inc., Jacksonville, FL *Page 1-351*

Pardy, Brian J., Oxford Health Plans, Branford, CT *Page 1-151*

Park, Hyun, Starmedia Network, Inc., New York, NY *Page 1-111*

Parker
Barry A., AT&T, Basking Ridge, NJ *Page 1-103*
Dee A., HIE, Addison, TX *Page 1-271*
Jeffrey T., Phillips Petroleum Company, Borger, TX *Page 1-27*
Keith A., Inca Metal Products, Lewisville, TX *Page 1-35*
Kerry, SalesSupport.com, Dallas, TX *Page 1-186*
Kevin M., McKinney & Silver, Raleigh, NC *Page 1-164*

Parkes, Shawn, Lante Corporation, Chicago, IL *Page 1-271*

Parks, Floyd, PricewaterhouseCoopers, San Francisco, CA *Page 1-354*

Parot, Philippe, Sarl Cyberjet, Etampes, France *Page 1-198*

Parrill, Scott M., University of Wyoming, Department of Space and Data & Visualization Center, Laramie, WY *Page 1-330*

Parrish
Brian P., J.C. Solutions, LLC, Fairmont, WV *Page 1-186*
Richard R., Randy's Professional Web Site Design, Winnsboro, TX *Page 1-186*

Passantino, George A., Manchester Equipment, Hauppauge, NY *Page 1-120*

Passe, Michael R., Care Group, Boston, MA *Page 1-362*

Pastorik, Stephen L., West Valley City, Salt Lake City, UT *Page 1-373*

Pate, Lonnie J., Southern Linc, Savannah, GA *Page 1-93*

Patel
Kanti R., PCSI, Holmdel, NJ *Page 1-271*
Kiran K., IBM Global Services, Parsippany, NJ *Page 1-271*
Lalit, Inforbit Inc., Voorhees, NJ *Page 1-272*
Mitool M., Z-Tel, Atlanta, GA *Page 1-103*

Patil
Abhijit B., PricewaterhouseCoopers, Burlington, MA *Page 1-354*
Ashutosh, Oracle Corporation, Redwood Shores, CA *Page 1-198*

Patri, Neelanjan, NVT Consulting Services, Chattanooga, TN *Page 1-272*

Patterson, Ollie C., MCI WorldCom, Inc., Atlanta, GA *Page 1-103*

Patti, Stephen, Yale University ITS/Telecommunications, New Haven, CT *Page 1-331*

Pattock, Suzanne Sacek, CIBER Enterprise Application Services, Carnegie, PA *Page 1-186*

Patton, Robert T., Bizrate Com, Los Angeles, CA *Page 1-272*

Paul
Charles, Rise Communications, Inc., Jacksonville, TX *Page 1-111*
Jeanette E., TNRCC, Austin, TX *Page 1-387*

Pavlovich, Matthew R., Media Driver, LLC, Dallas, TX *Page 1-272*

Pavlovsky, Serge Al, Office Of The Corporation Counsel, Washington, DC *Page 1-377*

Payne, Shirley S., Tri-Cities Regional Airport, Blountville, TN *Page 1-90*

Peacey, Kendrew, Informix, Denver, CO *Page 1-272*

Peake, Daniel, FutureNext Consulting, Inc., Los Gatos, CA *Page 1-272*

Pearce, Cecil L., PSC, Loganville, GA *Page 1-391*

Pearson, Kenneth W., Zilog, Cedar Park, TX *Page 1-67*

Pease, Michael A., Equinix, Ashburn, VA *Page 1-111*

Pedersen, Charles R., Air Force Research Laboratory, Rome, NY *Page 1-395*

Peermamode, Ehsan, BTI Consulting, Port Louis, Mauritius *Page 1-272*

Pees, Philip G., Mynd, Cayce, SC *Page 1-273*

Pegalis, Andrew M., Next Millennium Consulting, Inc., Bethesda, MD *Page 1-273*

Peltz, Raymond, TransCanada Energy, Omaha, NE *Page 1-2*

Peng, Vincent Cheng-Kun, Taiwan Cellular Corporation, Taipei, Taiwan *Page 1-93*

Penney, Ike D., Lockard & White, Houston, TX *Page 1-349*

Pepe, Kenneth M., Pepe Enterprises, Island Park, NY *Page 1-273*

Peppe, Richard W., United States Department of State, Washington, DC *Page 1-397*

Peram, Suresh, JobsMadeEasy.com, Marietta, GA *Page 1-168*

Percifield, George A., Raymond Building Supply, North Fort Myers, FL *Page 1-118*

Perez
Pedro P., Cross Country Home Service, Parkland, FL *Page 1-155*
Robin L., Bureau of Land Management, Ridgecrest, CA *Page 1-388*

Perez Munguia, Carlos Manuel, NCR de Mexico S.A. de C.V., Mexico City, Mexico *Page 1-51*

Perkins, Brian J., Sumitomo Machinery Corporation of America, Chesapeake, VA *Page 1-38*

Perras, Kathleen A., Dynamics Research Corporation, Andover, MA *Page 1-186*

Peters, Ryan M., Windsor Group, Atlanta, GA *Page 1-157*

Peterson
Barbara L., Department of Energy at Idaho National Engineering and Environmental Laboratory, Rigby, ID *Page 1-361*
Billie, Pervasive Software Inc., Austin, TX *Page 1-187*
Cynthia Sue, E&K Companies, Inc., Omaha, NE *Page 1-6*
Gregory, AT&T Labs, Lincroft, NJ *Page 1-103*
Randy, Citicorp International Communications Inc., Sioux Falls, SD *Page 1-135*
Richard, Illinois Power Company, Decatur, IL *Page 1-117*
Steven C., Magee Rehabilitation Hospital, Philadelphia, PA *Page 1-308*

Petroski, Thomas L., Motorola, De Soto, IL *Page 1-67*

Petrov, Alex, DirectNet Telecommunications, Newport Beach, CA *Page 1-111*

Petrovich, Nina L., NOAA Coastal Services Center, Charleston, SC *Page 1-273*

Petrucelli, James L., Tri Tech Systems, Inc., Dover, DE *Page 1-273*

Petsche, Christopher M., Cooperative Resource Services, Cleveland, OH *Page 1-168*

Pettersson, Ulf, Tempogon AB, Stockholm, Sweden *Page 1-273*

Pfeiffer, Scott P., V4 Consulting, Indianappolis, IA *Page 1-273*

Phatak, Shreyas, Micronpc.com, Boise, ID *Page 1-47*

Phenicie, Robert L., Independent, Herndon, VA *Page 1-208*

Philipsen, Flemming, Kapa Consulting, Munkebo, Denmark *Page 1-274*

Phillips
    Craig A., City of Las Vegas, Las Vegas, NV *Page 1-373*
    Howard C., Lexmark International, Inc., Lexington, KY *Page 1-120*
    Richard W., Software Engineering Institute, Pittsburgh, PA *Page 1-359*

Piazza, Sonya B., Blue Cross & Blue Shield of Alabama, Helena, AL *Page 1-151*

Picariello, Angela E., Rockwell Collins, Melbourne, FL *Page 1-77*

Picherot, Laurence, Honeywell, Sophia Antipolis, France *Page 1-81*

Pierron, Brian J., MJP Solutions Inc., Hilliard, OH *Page 1-274*

Pierson, Gina L., Prudential Insurance Company of America, Lafayette, NJ *Page 1-149*

Pietrowski, Michael, Stonehill College, Easton, MA *Page 1-331*

Pigeon, Donald R., The Human Factor, Inc., Ferndale, MI *Page 1-369*

Pillers, Jeff A., Information Resources, Inc., Chicago, IL *Page 1-360*

Pinkall-Pollei, Richard G., Cooperative Resources International, Verona, WI *Page 1-302*

Pittas, Douglas, Alltech Data Systems, Bensenville, IL *Page 1-93*

Pladna, Stephen L., Duke University Medical Center, Durham, NC *Page 1-308*

Plambeck, Pamela, Hall Kinion, Denver, CO *Page 1-168*

Plew, Ronald R., Perpetual Technologies, Inc., Indianapolis, IN *Page 1-274*

Plumb, Sean F., Schwab Institutional, Denver, CO *Page 1-146*

Plummer, Kyle B., Norman Jones Enlow Company, Reynoldsburg, OH *Page 1-355*

Plunkett, Jeffrey Lynn, ARDC, Duluth, MN *Page 1-346*

Poag, Bowie J., Propaganda, Tucson, AZ *Page 1-199*

Podemski, Michael J., Leapnet, Inc., Oak Brook, IL *Page 1-274*

Pollock, Francisco, Alcon Laboratories, Burleson, TX *Page 1-84*

Ponakala, Srinivasa R., Cylogix, Inc., Plainsboro, NJ *Page 1-274*

Pop, Horia, Mount San Antonio College, Walnut, CA *Page 1-338*

Poppitz, Mickey, DataSoft LLC.com, Arvada, CO *Page 1-274*

Porterfield, Mark E., ACS Professional Services, Wexford, PA *Page 1-274*

Post, John S., U.S. Steel-Clairton Works, Clairton, PA *Page 1-31*

Potowski, Christopher J., SBPA Systems, Inc., Houston, TX *Page 1-187*

Poupart, Christian, Buscom MKS, Montreal, Quebec, Canada *Page 1-128*

Powell, Linda L., McDermott, Will & Emery, Washington, DC *Page 1-313*

Powers, Michael J., The Charlton Group, Madison, WI *Page 1-302*

Prentice, Guy C., GCP Consulting, Webster, NY *Page 1-275*

Pribich, Jeff, BP Amoco, Naperville, IL *Page 1-2*

Pride, Buddy, McHenry School District #15, McHenry, IL *Page 1-317*

Primmer, Charles W., IB Industries, Brownsdale, MN *Page 1-275*

Pringle, James W., Compaq Computer Corporation, Redding, CA *Page 1-44*

Pritchett, Stephanie A., Ernst & Young LLP, Chantilly, VA *Page 1-355*

Private, John A., Zebra Technologies Corporation, Vernon Hills, IL *Page 1-51*

Pryor, Jason A., Greenlee Textron, Rockford, IL *Page 1-36*

Pulcine, Brian, Parkway Insurance, Franklin Park, NJ *Page 1-154*

Pullen, Malcolm M., BOEC/City of Portland, Portland, OR *Page 1-378*

Pulsipher, Steven, Net Designs and Creations, Inc., Ogden, UT *Page 1-275*

Punako, Ronald, American Precision Technology, Hollsopple, PA *Page 1-275*

Puranachoti, Sornkawee, KGI Securities One Public Company, Ltd., Bangkok, Thailand *Page 1-146*

Purchase-Owens, Francena, Purchase Business Institute, Kentwood, MI *Page 1-369*

Purnell, Katharine, American Intercontinental University, Plantation, FL *Page 1-331*

Q

Qian, Fang, OPTIMUS Corporation, Silver Spring, MD *Page 1-275*

Quasny, Todd, Texas Tech University, Lubbock, TX *Page 1-331*

Quesada, Arli, Independent, San Rafael, CA *Page 1-370*

Quinn
    James J., Newbridge Networks, Chantilly, VA *Page 1-49*
    Robert A., Vertek Corporation, Highlands, NJ *Page 1-275*

Quint, Al, Cal PERS, Sacramento, CA *Page 1-146*

Quintanilla, Chris A., Intellisource, Philadelphia, PA *Page 1-169*

Quist, Stephen C., John Deere Company, Lenexa, KS *Page 1-36*

R

Raby, John M., City of Pensacola, Pensacola, FL *Page 1-374*

Raikar, Rajesh Suresh, Whalen & Company, Lafayette, CA *Page 1-275*

Ralph, Gillian, Industrial Research Ltd., Auckland, New Zealand *Page 1-358*

Ralstin, Richard, Sacaton Public School District #18, Sacaton, AZ *Page 1-382*

Ramachandran, Shyam, Viking Range Corporation, Greenwood, MS *Page 1-53*

Ramczyk, Amie J., System Request Consultants, Middletown, WI *Page 1-276*

Ramey, Corey D., Tennessee Valley Authority, Knoxville, TN *Page 1-114*

Rampley, Douglas R., Sprint, Irving, TX *Page 1-103*

Ramsey, Kathryn L., Eclipse Inc., Boulder, CO *Page 1-187*

Ranalli, John, Computer-Information Services Consulting, Wilmington, NC *Page 1-276*

Randazzo, Leonard, Dwarf Holdings, LLC., South Hackensack, NJ *Page 1-139*

Randles, Gary A., Arthur Andersen, Chicago, IL *Page 1-366*

Ransden, Eric S., Ceridian Performance Partners, Boston, MA *Page 1-369*

Rao, Sonali, Arris Interactive, Suwanee, GA *Page 1-62*

Rash, Jeanne, Bayer Corporation, Tarrytown, NY *Page 1-24*

Rastogi, Shashank, Open Systems, Jersey City, NJ *Page 1-276*

Ratliff, Bud, Koinonia Computing, Midway, KY *Page 1-276*

Ravishankar, Channasandra, Hughes Network Systems, Germantown, MD *Page 1-94*

Rawsthorne, Daniel A., Access, Seattle, WA *Page 1-187*

Ray
    Ramon Jarrod, Savannah-Chatham County Board of Education, Savannah, GA *Page 1-382*
    Tony E., ARay Computer Services, Cincinnati, OH *Page 1-276*

Raymondo, James A., The Walt Disney Company, Tampa, FL *Page 1-305*

Recchioni, Mario J., Citigroup, Inc., Las Vegas, NV *Page 1-135*

Reddy
    Jagan M., Proficient Software Expo Consulting Inc., Fords, NJ *Page 1-276*
    K. B., Digiquest, Riverside, CA *Page 1-112*

Rediker, Julie A., Senior Geographic Information Systems Trainer, Houston, TX *Page 1-277*

Reed
    Dana E., Sprint, Kansas City, MO *Page 1-104*
    Jeff L., UUNET Technologies, Warrenton, VA *Page 1-213*
    Timothy, American Urological Association, Houston, TX *Page 1-346*

Reedy, Matthew K., J.E. Reedy, Inc., Seymour, IN *Page 1-5*

Reese
    Jeffrey D., Delaware County Information Services, Muncie, IN *Page 1-302*
    Timothy E., Eastern Idaho Technical College, Idaho Falls, ID *Page 1-338*

Regalado, Johnson, Mabuhay Philippine Satellite Corporation, New Manila, Philippines *Page 1-112*

Registe, Martin P., Cellstar, Carrollton, TX *Page 1-122*

Rehman, Razi Ur, Poly Products, LLC, Sultanate, Oman *Page 1-12*

Reicher
    Joshua S., Advance Business Graphics, Mira Loma, CA *Page 1-21*
    Stuart, Sure Air Ltd., Stamford, NY *Page 1-159*

Reichert, Eric D., Mbh Settlement Group, McLean, VA *Page 1-313*

Reid, Nathan D., Pepper Construction, Hainesville, IL *Page 1-4*

Reinert, Johannes, kohlpharma GmbH, Perl Saarland, Germany *Page 1-124*

Remuzzi, Joy, UUNET, Ashburn, VA *Page 1-213*

Renard, James A., JWR Systems, Edmonds, WA *Page 1-187*

Reneau, Daniel D., Louisiana Tech University, Ruston, LA *Page 1-331*

Renner, Amy, Clinical Pharmacologic Research Communications, Morgantown, WV *Page 1-49*

Rex, Jack G., JGR Consulting, LLP, Toledo, OH *Page 1-366*

Rexford, Victoria, ASAP Software Express, Atlanta, GA *Page 1-120*

Reyes, Sherry, American Express, Phoenix, AZ *Page 1-139*

Reynolds
Carl W., Hyperbole Software, Unlimited, Madison, IN *Page 1-187*
Teresa G., Alcatel USA, Plano, TX *Page 1-104*

Reyntjens, Bruno R. F., In Controls Inc., Hurricane, WV *Page 1-52*

Rhine, Chad D., Hughes Network Systems, Germantown, MD *Page 1-94*

Rhodes, Brian V., Illinois Department of Children and Family Services, Springfield, IL *Page 1-386*

Ricciardelli, Nicholas J., ICC International, Scottsdale, AZ *Page 1-187*

Rice, Donald W., Next Generation Ideas, Raleigh, NC *Page 1-277*

Richards, Sharon L., Safeco Life Insurance, Redmond, WA *Page 1-149*

Richardson, Susan E., Wang Healthcare, Hudson, NH *Page 1-188*

Richmond, Leon L., Applied Industrial Technologies, Cleveland, OH *Page 1-123*

Rightmer, Charles K., Entech Sales & Service Inc., Austin, TX *Page 1-123*

Riley, Cathy N., SPX Corporation, Portage, MI *Page 1-36*

Rinker, Ricky Lee, Legacy Bank of Texas, Plano, TX *Page 1-141*

Riopelle, Joanna M., ABN AMRO, Chicago, IL *Page 1-137*

Rios
Anthony A., Accelerated Imaging, Inc., Tustin, CA *Page 1-208*
Joe Gaudalupe, Peerless Manufacturing Company, Dallas, TX *Page 1-38*

Rippon, Dana W., CHZM Hill, Redding, CA *Page 1-349*

Ritcher, Michael A., City of Oxford, Oxford, OH *Page 1-374*

Rizzuto, Alan, Colorado Springs Utilities, Colorado Springs, CO *Page 1-116*

Robbins
John Edward, Community Medical Center, Scranton, PA *Page 1-309*
Robert Randall, Sam Houston State University, Willis, TX *Page 1-331*

Roberts
Angela D., AMBC-CCTC/ICTS, Baltimore, MD *Page 1-341*
Thomas P., Saber Systems & Consulting, Inc., Jackson, MS *Page 1-277*

Robertson, Sarah E., Seton Healthcare Network, Austin, TX *Page 1-309*

Robichaud, Steven E., RSM McGladrey, Inc., San Bernardino, CA *Page 1-355*

Robinson
Marck R., Power Data Corporation, Bellevue, WA *Page 1-188*
Mark C., Archmere Academy, Claymont, DE *Page 1-317*
Mark K., Computer Design & Integration, Teterboro, NJ *Page 1-277*
Mark Wesley, United States Department of Education, Washington, DC *Page 1-382*

Robson
Brent R., Halifax Regional Municipality, Halifax, Nova Scotia, Canada *Page 1-374*
Peter J., Oracle Corporation, Belmont, CA *Page 1-199*

Roden, Mark Philip, Delphi Automotive, Fenton, MI *Page 1-118*

Rodriguez
Joe, The Sports Club, Los Angeles, CA *Page 1-306*
Louis F., Techware Solutions, Inc., West Paterson, NJ *Page 1-209*

Roe, Wesley D., Roetech Services, Downers Grove, IL *Page 1-277*

Roebke, Laurence R., Barrick Goldstrike Mines, Inc., Elko, NV *Page 1-2*

Rofe, Michael Stuart, e-GM, Omiya City, Japan *Page 1-71*

Rogers
Alvina C., American Agrisurance, Council Bluffs, IA *Page 1-154*
David D., San Gabriel Valley Credit Union, El Monte, CA *Page 1-137*
James, Teletech Services, Burbank, CA *Page 1-277*
James R., Averstar, Chambersburg, PA *Page 1-277*
John H., Total Technology Services, South Portland, ME *Page 1-209*
John R., South African Embassy, Washington, DC *Page 1-397*

Rogillio, Thomas G., Candle Corporation, Glendale, CA *Page 1-278*

Roina, John A., Eaglecrest High School, Aurora, CO *Page 1-317*

Rolenz, Michael A., The Aerospace Corporation, Harbor City, CA *Page 1-78*

Rolfsmeyer, Kenneth T., American Family Insurance, Madison, WI *Page 1-151*

Roll, Gary V., ADP Dealer Services, Hoffman Estates, IL *Page 1-212*

Roman, Edward John, Industri-Matematik North American Operations, Inc., Mount Laurel, NJ *Page 1-278*

Romano
Angelo, Tritec Communications Inc., East Hanover, NJ *Page 1-104*
Antonio, IDC (International Data Corporation), Milan, Italy *Page 1-278*
Robert "Rob", BarPoint.com, Fort Lauderdale, FL *Page 1-188*

Romel, Jeffrey Lawrence, The Hartford, Hartford, CT *Page 1-154*

Romish, Lisa S., Sprint PCS, Kansas City, MO *Page 1-94*

Rook, Cynthia L., BellSouth Communications Systems, Orlando, FL *Page 1-104*

Rosado, Luis E., Sun Microsystems, Inc., Southlake, TX *Page 1-44*

Rosano, John L., barnesandnoble.com, New York, NY *Page 1-130*

Rose
David E., Physicians Health Plan, Fort Wayne, IN *Page 1-153*
Linda L., Hewlett-Packard Company, Vancouver, WA *Page 1-44*

Rosenbaum, Lisa Lenchner, General Motors, Bloomfield, MI *Page 1-72*

Rosenquist, Eric C., Internet of Lawton, Lawton, OK *Page 1-209*

Rosivach, Chris, Davis Standard/HES, Paucatuck, CT *Page 1-36*

Ross, Russell H., E Trade, Menlo Park, CA *Page 1-143*

Rossi, Matthew R., Internet World Media, Inc., Darlen, CT *Page 1-303*

Rostami, Sasan, BITCOM Inc., Germantown, MD *Page 1-278*

Rothe, Eukarlgen A., First Data Corporation, Omaha, NE *Page 1-303*

Rothschild, Brian M., Fordham University, New York, NY *Page 1-331*

Rotondo, Eugene M., MIB Inc., Westwood, MA *Page 1-157*

Rotz, Randy E., Innernet, Inc., Shady Grove, PA *Page 1-278*

Rowe, Richard Carl, Ajilon, Richmond, VA *Page 1-278*

Rubin, Nancy, Camp Cuisine, Parkland, NY *Page 1-129*

Rucker, Mark C., Service Merchandise, Brentwood, TN *Page 1-131*

Ruddiman, Thomas A., Portland Development Commission, Portland, OR *Page 1-389*

Rudins, Nancy A., National Center for Supercomputing Applications, Urbana, IL *Page 1-341*

Rudstrom, Lennart, Disney Consumer Products, Cannes, France *Page 1-130*

Rueger, Maria J., Bank of America, Jacksonville, FL *Page 1-134*

Ruehli, Albert E., IBM Thomas J. Watson Research Center, Yorktown Heights, NY *Page 1-279*

Ruffin, Jimmy, Promega, Madison, WI *Page 1-358*

Ruiz, Raul, Honeywell-Thermal Systems, Imperial, CA *Page 1-33*

Rumley, Russell, Infipro Inc., Greenville, MS *Page 1-299*

Russ, Jerry D., Walls Computers Etc., Hot Springs, AR *Page 1-188*

Russell
Christopher P., Engelberth Construction, Colchester, VT *Page 1-4*
Damon E., The Catholic University of America Columbus School of Law, Washington, DC *Page 1-332*
Lisa S., Key Staff, Seattle, WA *Page 1-169*

Russello, Frank V., Habanero Software, West Haven, CT *Page 1-279*

Rutter, Eric, Comcast Telecommunications, Cherry Hill, NJ *Page 1-279*

Rybiski-Joseph, Elizabeth, Kaiser Aluminum, Gramercy, LA *Page 1-3*

Ryder, Marvin G., McMaster University, Hamilton, Ontario, Canada *Page 1-332*

S

Saba, Farhad, F. Saba & Associates, San Diego, CA *Page 1-332*

Sabin, Matthew S., Radio Frequency Systems, Meriden, CT *Page 1-57*

Sachen, Richard J., KLA-Tencor, San Jose, CA *Page 1-67*

Sachs, Steven W., Telxon Corporation, The Woodlands, TX *Page 1-44*

Saerens, Robert, Jovenko, Meise, Belgium *Page 1-279*

Safford, Michael, Autodesk, Inc., Windham, NH *Page 1-188*

Sailer, Chrystiana, RoseTel Systems, Los Angeles, CA *Page 1-112*

Saint-Louis, Vanilo, Belimage Communications, Franklin Square, NY *Page 1-279*

Saladis, Frank P., Cisco Systems, Inc., Staten Island, NY *Page 1-62*

Salandra, Justin A., Mount Kisco Medical Group, Mount Kisco, NY *Page 1-311*

Salaver, Timothy R., Cornerstone Systems Solutions, Inc., Las Vegas, NV *Page 1-188*

Salazar, Anthony A., Los Alamos National Laboratory, Los Alamos, NM *Page 1-359*

Saldana, Carlos P., Los Angeles Department of Water and Power, Los Angeles, CA *Page 1-117*

Salem, Mike M., UOP, Des Plaines, IL *Page 1-303*

Salileh, Isam, Lucky Baby Company, Riyadh, Saudi Arabia *Page 1-15*

Salinas, Alexander, Perclose, Inc., Redwood City, CA *Page 1-83*

Salisbury, Andrew J., SCA Hygiene Products, Eddystone, PA *Page 1-15*

Salter, Jim, Patton General Contracting, Summerville, SC *Page 1-4*

Samadi, Marwan, National Bank of Kuwait, Beirut, Lebanon *Page 1-136*

Samoska, Michael C., Micros-to-Mainframes, Woodbury, CT *Page 1-279*

Sanchez, Frank, Veridicom, San Francisco, CA *Page 1-298*

Sanchez-Pfeiffer, Kitty, San Marcos United School District, San Marcos, CA *Page 1-383*

Sander, Tim A., Applied Systems, Inc, University Park, IL *Page 1-188*

Sandiego, Angelito H., Perot Systems, McKinney, TX *Page 1-169*

Sandoval, Fernando, Rich Products, Buffalo, NY *Page 1-8*

Sanford, Thom, Warner Bros., Burbank, CA *Page 1-305*

Sankot, Janice M., Parkview Center School, Roseville, MN *Page 1-317*

Santhumayor, Ivan NJ, Goldman Sachs & Company, New York, NY *Page 1-144*

Santoli, Nicolas, Campania Management Company Inc., Vienna, VA *Page 1-156*

Santos, Raul Jose, Informatica Asociada, Tecamachalco, Mexico *Page 1-189*

Santucci, Peter, G.O. Carlson Inc., Thorndale, PA *Page 1-31*

Sarkes, Robert A., Epronet, San Mateo, CA *Page 1-169*

Sathya, Ravi, Megasoft Consultants, Vienna, VA *Page 1-279*

Saunders, Donald A., County of Cuyahoga, Cleveland, OH *Page 1-374*

Savage
    Charles L., Atkinson-Baker, Inc., Glendale, CA *Page 1-167*
    Steven, Advanced Programming Resources, Columbus, OH *Page 1-279*

Sawyer
    Jeffery H., The Consultants, Raleigh, NC *Page 1-280*
    Thomas Eric, dba Computer Consultant, Tulsa, OK *Page 1-280*

Saxton, Lawrence V., University of Regina Computer Science Department, Regina, Saskatchewan, Canada *Page 1-332*

Sayian, Stephen, Teradyne Inc., Boston, MA *Page 1-82*

Schaefer, James F., Eat 'N Park Restaurants, Pittsburgh, PA *Page 1-129*

Schaeffer, Russell A., Seagate Technology, Longmont, CO *Page 1-47*

Schaetzlein, Eric R., Schlund + Partner AG, Karlsruhe, Germany *Page 1-112*

Schafft, Soren, Telenor, Inc., Reston, VA *Page 1-104*

Schaidle, Dale F., Tremont High School, Tremont, IL *Page 1-317*

Schall, Ronald G., Professional Communications Systems, Tampa, FL *Page 1-209*

Schartel, David M., Thomas Hardware, Reading, PA *Page 1-122*

Schettino, Antonio Ernesto, Kb/TEL, Mexico City, Mexico *Page 1-45*

Schiavi, Adam J., Advanced Technologies Consulting Group Inc., North Miami, FL *Page 1-280*

Schifano, Mike, Applications Solutions, Houston, TX *Page 1-280*

Schilero, Frank, New York Daily News, Jersey City, NJ *Page 1-15*

Schlabs, Heidi, Marketing Specialists, Irving, TX *Page 1-146*

Schlagheck, Ryan Wm., Unisys Corporation, Windsor, CT *Page 1-280*

Schlarb, Keith N., Worthington City Schools, Worthington, OH *Page 1-317*

Schlosser
    Martha F., Truman High School, Independence, MO *Page 1-317*

Shane, University College of the Fraser Valley, Abbotsford, British Columbia, Canada *Page 1-332*

Schmidt
    Christian A., Mead Corporation, Dayton, OH *Page 1-15*
    Donald, Karl Williams Inc., Springfield, IL *Page 1-119*
    Jonatan, 1 Venture Inc., Palo Alto, CA *Page 1-280*
    Mads Rosendahl, Novo Nordisk IT A/S, Copenhagen, Denmark *Page 1-280*

Schmitt, Warren L., Newport, Minneapolis, MN *Page 1-86*

Schneider
    Debra, Techni Logic Consulting, Sagamore Hills, OH *Page 1-281*
    Doug J., Appdepot Web Services, Regina, Saskatchewan, Canada *Page 1-281*
    Jonathan, SCL Health Services, Leavenworth, KS *Page 1-344*
    Keiko K., Saboten Web Design, Albuquerque, NM *Page 1-281*

Schoenung, Karen, Duni Corporation, Menomonee Falls, WI *Page 1-70*

Schoettle, Brandon A., Information Transfer System, Ann Arbor, MI *Page 1-352*

Schomaker, Paul A., Database Technologies, Boca Raton, FL *Page 1-209*

Schonken, Andre, PE Technikon, Port Elizabeth, South Africa *Page 1-338*

Schreffler, Scott A., Road Runner, Columbus, OH *Page 1-281*

Schroth, John W., Strongsville City Schools, Strongsville, OH *Page 1-383*

Schubert, William Anthony, Unlimited Solutions Inc., Columbus, OH *Page 1-189*

Schuelka, Todd, Ortho Computer Systems, Inc., Ames, IA *Page 1-281*

Schuetz, Jeffrey M., Sonoco, Hartsville, SC *Page 1-14*

Schultes, Stan J., Sun Hydraulic Corporation, Sarasota, FL *Page 1-35*

Schultz
    Cynthia L., Bosch Automation Technology, Racine, WI *Page 1-74*
    David A., Bank of New York Clearing Services, Milwaukee, WI *Page 1-147*

Schumacher, J., Abbot & Abbot Architects, PLL, Columbus, OH *Page 1-351*

Schupp, Felix A., MMT Corporation, San Jose, CA *Page 1-189*

Schwartz, Bruce R., The Principia, St. Louis, MO *Page 1-318*

Schweitzer
    Loren M., Bank of America, Dallas, TX *Page 1-134*
    Richard, Savvy Data, Pompano Beach, FL *Page 1-189*

Schwendiger, Kathleen M., En-Data, Altamonte Springs, FL *Page 1-281*

Schwing, Lee, Ziffren, Brittenham, Branca & Fischer LLP, Los Angeles, CA *Page 1-313*

Sciullo, Gregory M., Equitable Resources, Pittsburgh, PA *Page 1-281*

Sciurca, Albert, Meta Group, Stamford, CT *Page 1-282*

Scott
    Arthur R., Atlanta Public Schools, Atlanta, GA *Page 1-383*
    Barry Price, Sun Microsystems, Inc., San Jose, CA *Page 1-45*
    Dane C., Emcore, Somerset, NJ *Page 1-67*
    David L., Public Financial Management, Philadelphia, PA *Page 1-147*
    Eric H., D/FW Hospital Council, Irving, TX *Page 1-344*
    Nancy L., Ernst & Young LLP, Chicago, IL *Page 1-355*

Sebastian, Glania, Independent, Balingen, Germany *Page 1-282*

Seebo, Terry, May Logistics Services, Inc., Buena Park, CA *Page 1-88*

Seelander, John M., The Plus Group, Lombard, IL *Page 1-366*

Sees, Chris V., Micro Technology Groupe, Pennsburg, PA *Page 1-209*

Seetharam, Palachandra, Cap Gemini America, Vienna, VA *Page 1-282*

Sehmbey, Paul, Ernst & Young, Halifax, Nova Scotia, Canada *Page 1-355*

Seidel, Carl W., Carl Seidel Consulting, Denton, TX *Page 1-369*

Seney, Thomas R., RTC Technologies, Inc., Racine, WI *Page 1-189*

Sepulveda, Pedro J., Debug Computers, Cabo Rojo, Puerto Rico *Page 1-282*

Serfaty, Daniel, Aptima, Inc., Woburn, MA *Page 1-349*

Sersic, Christopher J., Ambassador Consulting, Indianapolis, IN *Page 1-282*

Sesay, Sahid, Baffin Inc., Alameda, CA *Page 1-27*

Severin, William F., United States Air Force, Headquarters Air Combat Command, Newport News, VA *Page 1-395*

Shackelford, Reba, Lucent Technologies, Garland, TX *Page 1-62*

Shah, Atique R., Uproar.com, New York, NY *Page 1-306*

Shami, Azmat Bilal, Cressoft Inc., Englewood, CO *Page 1-189*

Shamlin, Jim, Boy Scouts of America, Irving, TX *Page 1-347*

Shannon, Patricia A., Alcan Aluminum Corporation, Warren, OH *Page 1-32*

Sharp, Jeffrey A., Indy Residential Services, Indianapolis, IN *Page 1-159*

Shashikumar, Bellave S., Techcircle.com inc., Enola, PA *Page 1-282*

Shaw, M. Lea, Carleton Corporation, Billerica, MA *Page 1-189*

Shayo, Conrad, California State at San Bernardino, Ontario, CA *Page 1-332*

Shehata, Mounir, SBM-IBM, Jeddah, Saudi Arabia *Page 1-282*

Shen, Li-Sheng, CCL, Hsinchu, Taiwan *Page 1-361*

Shepard, Peter J., Charles J. Miller, Inc., Hampstead, MD *Page 1-4*

Sherlock, Jason E., Andersen Consulting LLP, Reston, VA *Page 1-366*

Sherman, David M., J Crew Group, Inc., New York, NY *Page 1-131*

Sherwood, John Anthony, Synermark, Austin, TX *Page 1-159*

Shever, Andrew F., Lourdes Hospital, Paducah, KY *Page 1-309*

Shields
    Andrew V., PricewaterhouseCoopers, Philadelphia, PA *Page 1-355*
    Daniel, Seagate Technology, Paris, France *Page 1-47*

Shih, William, Raytheon Systems, Covina, CA *Page 1-80*

Shin, Dong-Keun, Hwa Shin Building, Seoul, South Korea *Page 1-158*

Shindnes, Sergey, Information Builders Inc., Farmington, CT *Page 1-199*

Shoemaker, Linda L., Frontier Hotel Gambling, Las Vegas, NV *Page 1-162*

Shprints, Eduard, ClearCommerce Corporation, Austin, TX *Page 1-283*

Shreffler, Sue L., Federal Home Loan Bank, Topeka, KS *Page 1-136*

Shukla, Sandeep, Lucent Technologies, Altamonte Springs, FL *Page 1-62*

Shumway, Kathleen K., Niagara Mohawk Power Corporation, Lycoming, NY *Page 1-114*

Siddiqui, Khayyam, Goldman Sachs & Company, Bloomfield, NJ *Page 1-144*

Sikkink, V. Janene, University of Alaska, Fairbanks, AK *Page 1-333*

Silhavy, Mark A., City of College Station, College Station, TX *Page 1-374*

Sill, Gary L., Peirone Produce, Spokane, WA *Page 1-125*

Silliman, Suzanne, Management Science Associates Inc., Pittsburgh, PA *Page 1-283*

Silsbee, Laura Barrett, Earth Tech, Warner Robins, GA *Page 1-349*

Simkins, Steven R., MTA Solutions, Anchorage, AK *Page 1-112*

Simko, Edward J., Prudentual Reality and Relocation Services, Ossining, NY *Page 1-117*

Simmons
    John E., InAir, Chesterfield, MO *Page 1-190*
    Reginold T., Resources Technical Services, Hyattsville, MD *Page 1-283*

Simonsen, Peter, Amazon.com, Seattle, WA *Page 1-131*

Simousek, Michael G., Micro Technix, Madison, WI *Page 1-216*

Singh
    Jagdeep, Envision Financial System, Inc., Irvine, CA *Page 1-190*
    Paula Kaur, The International Academy of Information Sciences, Systems and Technologies, Los Altos, CA *Page 1-342*

Sink, Christi L., Latent Technology, Dallas, TX *Page 1-190*

Siska, Theodore L., Fujitsu, Plymouth, MN *Page 1-283*

Sitterberg, Wolfgang, Citrix System, Inc., Fort Lauderdale, FL *Page 1-190*

Skiles
    Bryan E., KPMG LLP, Tracy, CA *Page 1-366*
    Michael John, Eli Lilly and Company, Indianapolis, IN *Page 1-24*

Skomra, Stewart A., Telxon Corporation, The Woodlands, TX *Page 1-45*

Slater, Keith R., Medic Computer Systems, Raleigh, NC *Page 1-199*

Sluka, Greg W., Watson Wyatt Worldwide, Southfield, MI *Page 1-366*

Slusanschi, Anca E., Advantage Group, Paraparaumu, New Zealand *Page 1-283*

Slusher, Donna E., Floyd Public Schools, Floyd, VA *Page 1-318*

Smith
    Barry W., Warren County, Belvidere, NJ *Page 1-283*
    Bruce A., Metropolitan Life, Dunwoody, GA *Page 1-149*
    Cheryl L., MIL Corporation, New Market, MD *Page 1-283*
    Daniel J., BMC, Austin, TX *Page 1-199*
    Eric E., Evan Design Group, Longmont, CO *Page 1-284*
    Glenn A., United States Army Research Laboratory, Aberdeen Proving Ground, MD *Page 1-395*
    Jake, Zydeco.com, Seattle, WA *Page 1-133*
    Jeffrey W., Reebok International, Holden, MA *Page 1-30*
    Jennifer M., SS&C Technologies, Chicago, IL *Page 1-190*
    Jeremy A., Smith Consulting, Quakertown, PA *Page 1-284*
    Joshua D., Acxiom RTC, Inc., La Grange, IL *Page 1-209*
    Rebecca L., Nokia Networks, Irving, TX *Page 1-62*
    Richard D., TRW, Baldwin, MD *Page 1-210*
    Richard K., United States Air Force, Boston, MA *Page 1-395*
    Rick K., Ignacio School District, Ignaciao, CO *Page 1-383*
    Sheldon K., Paso Robles Public School District, Paso Robles, CA *Page 1-383*
    Steven E., Corepoint Technologies, Indianapolis, IN *Page 1-199*
    Timothy R., Washington Army National Guard, Tacoma, WA *Page 1-396*
    Walter E., Herman Miller, Orlando, FL *Page 1-284*
    Michele, Independent, Oak Brook, IL *Page 1-284*

Smoot, Brian D., CSG Systems International, Englewood, CO *Page 1-284*

Snare, Lisa A., ACCS @ St. Mary Site, Altoona, PA *Page 1-318*

Snetsinger, Leo V., ROI Systems, Minneapolis, MN *Page 1-190*

Snouffer, Bret Daniel, GTE, Marion, OH *Page 1-104*

Snyder
    Andrew H., Time Warner, New York, NY *Page 1-108*
    Larry, Control Contractors, Inc., Seattle, WA *Page 1-86*

Sobieray, Ed, eJiva, Washington, DC *Page 1-284*

Sobolewski, Michael W., GE, Schenectady, NY *Page 1-70*

Sohoni, Sanjay V., Informix Software, Inc., Menlo Park, CA *Page 1-284*

Solomon, Maria Luisa A., Financial Information, Inc., Jersey City, NJ *Page 1-19*

Songy, Michael P., Creative Labs, Inc., Milpitas, CA *Page 1-190*

Sonnentag, Matthew, Gantz Wiley Research, Minneapolis, MN *Page 1-360*

Soon, Herald Soohong, EDS, Cedar Rapids, IA *Page 1-215*

Sorstedt, Berthil, Lindex AB, Alingsas, Sweden *Page 1-127*

Sotir, Judith S., Waubonsee College, Aurora, IL *Page 1-333*

Spangler, Kerry, Raytheon, Marlborough, MA *Page 1-81*

Spaulding, Omar Young, NASA, Washington, DC *Page 1-78*

Speck, Richard J., Relational Technologies, Farmington Hills, MI *Page 1-285*

Speed, Russell F., Rebel.com, Ottawa, Ontario, Canada *Page 1-285*

Spell, Bill E., KForce.com, Houston, TX *Page 1-285*

Spence, Mike, Texas Instruments, Dallas, TX *Page 1-67*

Spencer
    Karen E., Aisin USA, Seymour, IN *Page 1-74*
    Terri J., Providian Financial, Fremont, CA *Page 1-94*

Spiegel, Steven M., Babcock & Wilcox, Dallas, TX *Page 1-33*

Spoon, John, A&L Lithography, Escondido, CA *Page 1-19*

Sporre, Matts, Telia Mobile, Nacka Strand, Sweden *Page 1-104*

Springer
    Michael, Tecmark LLC, Woodbury, MN *Page 1-164*
    Sarah Lee, AEMP Corporation, Jackson, TN *Page 1-74*

Sprouse, Matthew C., Bell Atlantic, Silver Spring, MD *Page 1-105*

Spurlin, Tami, University of Florida, Horticultural Science Department, Gainesville, FL *Page 1-333*

Spurlock, Samuel, FedEx, ITD/Finance in Legal Systems, Collierville, TN *Page 1-90*

Srinivasan, Savitha, IBM Corporation, San Jose, CA *Page 1-45*

St. Aubin, Roger, Atlantisус Promotions, Longueuil, Quebec, Canada *Page 1-74*

Stalker, Daniel E., Augmentix, Inc., Tucson, AZ *Page 1-190*

Standford, Don R., Target, Oakland, CA *Page 1-126*

Standley, David L., Biomophic VLSI, Thousand Oaks, CA *Page 1-67*

Stanley, Kenneth L., American Century Investments, Kansas City, MO *Page 1-144*

Staples, Karen R., SAIC, King George, VA *Page 1-359*

Starr, Laura A., Independent Health, Williamsville, NY *Page 1-151*

Stathopoulos, Dimitrios, Phillips Broad Band Network, Syracuse, NY *Page 1-32*

Stauch, Matthias E., PRISMA Marketing, Berlin, Germany *Page 1-285*

Stebenne, Andrew M., Pike Tool & Grinding, Colorado Springs, CO *Page 1-33*

Stein, Emmanuel, Elsevier Science, New York, NY *Page 1-19*

Stemmelin, Frederic, IDB Consulting, Palo Alto, CA *Page 1-285*

Stence, Daniel, Silicon Plains Technologies, Des Moines, IA *Page 1-285*

Stephens
    Amy E., Fascor, Cincinnati, OH *Page 1-191*
    C. Millard, Fidelity Investments, Dallas, TX *Page 1-161*
    Ryan K., Perpetual Technologies, Inc., Indianapolis, IN *Page 1-286*

Stetson, Audrey J., Newport Strategic Search LLC, Carlsbad, CA *Page 1-169*

Steven, Brad J., Print Tech, Inc., Ann Arbor, MI *Page 1-166*

Stewart, Winston M., ComDyn Group, LLC, Chattanooga, TN *Page 1-286*

Stewen, Robert, Mercedes-Benz USA, Inc., Bethesda, MD *Page 1-72*

Stiehr, Marc L., Young Men's Christian Association of Metropolitan Chicago, Chicago, IL *Page 1-347*

Stine, Gary M., Payroll Systems.com, Aliso Viejo, CA *Page 1-355*

Stockell, Albert W., State of Tennessee Department of Environment and Conservation, Nashville, TN *Page 1-387*

Stocker, Laura Baker, Pipeline Interactive, Lebanon, PA *Page 1-191*

Stokes, Keith, Entex Information Technology Services, A Siemens Company, Portland, OR *Page 1-286*

Stolle, Keith, Internet Gateway, Inc., Georgetown, TX *Page 1-286*

Stone, Susan K., Texas Department of Protective & Regulatory Services, Austin, TX *Page 1-343*

Stoner, Stephen E., USAED Sacramento, Sacramento, CA *Page 1-396*

Stoopman, Michael B., Queensland Police, Brisbane, Queensland, Australia *Page 1-377*

Stough, Bill, Professional Consulting Services, Tallassee, AL *Page 1-366*

Stowell, Bev, Stowell Data Solutions, Stanton, MI *Page 1-286*

Strechay, Robert J., On Source Consulting, Houston, TX *Page 1-286*

Strickland, Thomas K., Source Net Inc, Falls Church, VA *Page 1-286*

Stroud, Richard, BAE Systems, Rockville, MD *Page 1-76*

Strutt, Greg D., Software Creations, Laurel, MD *Page 1-287*

Strutton, James D., Department of Finance for State of California, Sacramento, CA *Page 1-380*

Stucki, Walter, NCI, La Tour De Peilz, Switzerland *Page 1-191*

Studer, Michael W., Sun Microsystems, Inc., Newark, CA *Page 1-45*

Su
    Alan P., Agilent Technologies, Inc., Westlake Village, CA *Page 1-82*
    Michelle Yu, Asera, Inc., Belmont, CA *Page 1-287*

Suárez del Real, Claudio, Valvu las Keystone de Mexico, Zatopan, Mexico *Page 1-74*

Sudula, Nagesh B., Merrill Lynch, Plainsboro, NJ *Page 1-144*

Suhaimi, Sunyo L., Integrated Device Technology, Inc., Santa Clara, CA *Page 1-68*

Sundell, Richard A., Tone Software Corporation, Anaheim, CA *Page 1-191*

Sustaita, Juan H., Keys Academy, Harlingen, TX *Page 1-318*

Sutan, Suhendra, Netforce, Inc., Daly City, CA *Page 1-287*

Sutherland, Stephanie K., Dan River, Inc., Danville, VA *Page 1-11*

Sutter, Rick, SutterTel.Com, Kennewick, WA *Page 1-128*

Sutton
    Curtis, Sierra Pine Adel Division, Hahira, GA *Page 1-13*
    Paula Emery, Pegasus Consulting Group, Londonderry, NH *Page 1-287*
    Ron R., Lifemark Corporation, Indianapolis, IN *Page 1-153*

Svendsen, Cary A., BellSouth, Atlanta, GA *Page 1-105*

Svensson, Per, Defense Research Establishment, Stockholm, Sweden *Page 1-396*

Swafford, Martin H., Compuware Corporation, Addison, TX *Page 1-191*

Swallow, Brett A., Archer Daniels Midland Company, Decatur, IL *Page 1-1*

Swanson
    Hilary W., Ontempo, Glendale, CA *Page 1-287*
    N. Diana, Aceomatic Recon, Pittsburgh, PA *Page 1-118*

Swetzig, DeAnnaKay, Hewlett-Packard Company, Greeley, CO *Page 1-45*

Swystun, Orest Roman, BDC 4 You, Bethesda, MD *Page 1-287*

Syed, Aamir Mazhar, A&S Solutions, Inc., Matawan, NJ *Page 1-287*

Symczyk, Walter J., Beth Israel Medical Center, New York, NY *Page 1-310*

T

Taj, Moawiya A., King Fahd University of Petroleum and Minerals, Dharan, Saudi Arabia *Page 1-333*

Tamas, Peter V., Barclays Global Investors, San Francisco, CA *Page 1-155*

Tamma, Leela Shankar, Rapidigm, Denver, CO *Page 1-288*

Tan
    Aik W., Colorscope, Inc., Monterey Park, CA *Page 1-166*
    Gim Hong, SembCorp Construction, Singapore, Singapore *Page 1-351*
    Kenny T. H., Berjaya USA Group, Inc., Elmhurst, NY *Page 1-288*

Tang
    Andrew L., TEQ International, San Gabriel, CA *Page 1-288*
    Carolyn B., PointStar.com, Schaumburg, IL *Page 1-166*
    John, BAART/CDP, San Francisco, CA *Page 1-306*

Tanigawa, David S., Thomson Financial, Boston, MA *Page 1-147*

Tankersley, Kathy M., United States Department of Agriculture Food and Nutrition Service, Boston, MA *Page 1-391*

Tansanu, Dan, Datainterdev, Ltd., Montreal, Quebec, Canada *Page 1-288*

Tanuwidjaja, Ron A., FutureNext Consulting, Inc., Moreno Valley, CA *Page 1-288*

Tash, Preston K., Dexter Shoe Company, Dexter, ME *Page 1-30*

Tauche, Julie, Knetico Inc., Newbury, OH *Page 1-51*

Tay, Thomas A., Hawaii Multimedia Corporation, Honolulu, HI *Page 1-288*

Taylor
    Brenda C., National Information Technology Center - Department of Agriculture, Kansas City, KS *Page 1-391*
    Brian J., Skymall Inc., Glendale, AZ *Page 1-191*
    Cecilia T., Mercer University, Atlanta, GA *Page 1-333*
    Isiah, New York City Transit Authority, Brooklyn, NY *Page 1-87*
    J. West, DIMON International, Inc., Farmville, NC *Page 1-10*
    Wendy E., Fullarton Computer Industries Inc., Winterville, NC *Page 1-45*

Teague, Mark A., Winthrop/Stimson, New York, NY *Page 1-313*

Tedesco, Frank P., William Paterson University, Wayne, NJ *Page 1-333*

Teller, Joel S., Thomas Consumer Electronics, Indianapolis, IN *Page 1-54*

Temple, TheresaMarie, Entology, Inc., Bedminister, NJ *Page 1-191*

Teramoto, Tim G., Tippett Studios, San Rafael, CA *Page 1-304*

Terault, Normand A., Simplex Time Recorder, West Minster, MA *Page 1-62*

Tereshko, George V., Genesys Labs, San Francisco, CA *Page 1-288*

Terrell
    Joseph A., Clinton Electronics Corporation, Loves Park, IL *Page 1-63*
    Sue E., Floyd Memorial Hospital, New Albany, IN *Page 1-309*

Terway, Jennifer D., MICROS Systems, Inc., Chicago, IL *Page 1-49*

Tester, Malcolm W., Cambric Corporation, Draper, UT *Page 1-289*

Tetrault, Gerald "Gerry", TetraTech Consulting Service, Chatham, Ontario, Canada *Page 1-367*

Thakkar, Vrajesh, AMS Inc., New York, NY *Page 1-121*

Thalanany, Sebastian, Motorola, Buffalo Grove, IL *Page 1-68*

Tharaken, Ajit, Data Downlink Corporation, New York, NY *Page 1-289*

Thelemaque, Tony, fp Label, Napa, CA *Page 1-21*

Thelin, Bradford, Connect South, Austin, TX *Page 1-192*

Therens, Gary A., Control Data Systems, Inc., Arden Hills, MN *Page 1-289*

Theriault, Roger D., Fresenius Medical Care, Lexington, MA *Page 1-310*

Thiele, Cynthia Buchan, Pillsbury Madison & Sutro, San Francisco, CA *Page 1-313*

Thomas
    Alexander, Alta Mesa Resources, Houston, TX *Page 1-3*
    Carl, St. Labre Indian School, Ashland, MT *Page 1-318*
    George A., Retro Studios, Austin, TX *Page 1-85*
    Inigo, Diamond State Port Corporation, Wilmington, DE *Page 1-89*
    Ivory L., Avantel, Garland, TX *Page 1-105*
    K. Michael, Insys Inc., Elkridge, MD *Page 1-289*
    Russell, Review Technology Group, Brookville, OH *Page 1-210*
    Taft H., Mansfiled Plumbing Products, Kilgore, TX *Page 1-30*

Thompson
    A. J., The Gazette, Penrose, CO *Page 1-16*
    Douglas, City of Orlando, Orlando, FL *Page 1-374*
    Michael, DMR Consulting Group, Toronto, Ontario, Canada *Page 1-367*
    Michael J., Glades Central High School, Belle Glade, FL *Page 1-318*
    Norman, International Data Solutions, Jacksonville, FL *Page 1-289*
    Wesley, Application Partners, Inc., Pleasant Hill, CA *Page 1-289*

Thornhill, C. Allen, US Filter Distribution, Thomasville, GA *Page 1-123*

Thorpe, James L., Rail Inc., Cary, NC *Page 1-87*

Thurogood, Brian A, William Reed, South Gostoden, England, United Kingdom *Page 1-19*

Tiemann, Michael Anthony, Office of the Chief Information Officer, United States Department of Energy, Washington, DC *Page 1-289*

Tignor, Doug J., Swiss Bank Corporation, Lisle, IL *Page 1-137*

Timberlake, Frank "Rusty", Orbital Sciences Corporation, Sterling, VA *Page 1-79*

Timmins, Allan S., Westside Elementary School, Spring Hill, FL *Page 1-318*

Tinelli, Felice, Lucent Technologies, Sun Rise, FL *Page 1-62*

Tiongco, Ronald L., Unisource Network Services, Chicago, IL *Page 1-290*

Tippins, Edward, Sylvan Prometric, Washington, DC *Page 1-342*

Tipton, Duane E., Aeroglide Corporation, Cary, NC *Page 1-38*

Tiseo, Roseann M., Arrow Electronics, Melville, NY *Page 1-122*

Tissier, Christophe, Graphtis, Antony, France *Page 1-290*

Toback, Jeremy, Strategy Partners Group, Naples, FL *Page 1-367*

Tober, Theresa J., Job Service North Dakota, Bismarck, ND *Page 1-169*

Tobison, John K., Mapinfo Corporation, Troy, NY *Page 1-290*

Tocco, Anthony J., Compsat Technology, St. Clair, MI *Page 1-210*

Todd, James A., Mcgraw-Hill Higher Education, Burr Ridge, IL *Page 1-17*

Todisco, Barbara J., GTE Internetworking, Inc., Cambridge, MA *Page 1-290*

Tollenaere, Caroline, Astrazeneca Belgium, Destelbergen, Belgium *Page 1-24*

Tolman, R. Brent, Premera Blue Cross, Nine Mile Falls, WA *Page 1-151*

Tomlin, Doyce E., Micro Revisions Inc., Houston, TX *Page 1-192*

Tomlinson, William W., Willis North America, Inc., Nashville, TN *Page 1-158*

Tong, Vincent S., Chester Housing Authority, Chester, PA *Page 1-389*

Toro, Robert N., Fleet Technology Solutions, Wallingford, CT *Page 1-290*

Torrez, Joe, Vantive Corporation, Overijse, Belgium *Page 1-290*

Torry, Billy D., Plaspro (Plastic Provisions Inc.), Sears, MI *Page 1-29*

Toth
    Stefan, DATESSA, Sodertalje, Sweden *Page 1-291*
    Susan, National Institute for Trial Advocacy, South Bend, IN *Page 1-342*

Towl, Allan T., Information Systems Services, Attleboro, MA *Page 1-291*

Towner, Wendy M., HFN, Inc./Kinetra IMIN, Oak Brook, IL *Page 1-311*

Townsend, Tracey, Arthur Andersen Technology Solutions, Chicago, IL *Page 1-367*

Trache, Jamal Eddine, Gasco, Abu Dhabi, United Arab Emirates *Page 1-27*

Trachtenberg, Charlene C., Space & Naval Warfare Systems Command, Arlington, VA *Page 1-396*

Trainor, John C., Epson Electronics America Inc., El Segundo, CA *Page 1-49*

Tramontana, Richard M., Chase Manhattan Mortgage Corporation, Edison, NJ *Page 1-141*

Tran, Ngoc-Diem T., Allergan, Inc., Irvine, CA *Page 1-25*

Tresidder, Garfield W., Tri State Hospital Supply Corporation, Salisbury, NC *Page 1-120*

Trice, David M., Bank of America, College Park, GA *Page 1-134*

Trikoz, Dimitri, Ernst & Young Audit, Paris, France *Page 1-356*

Tringali, Michael A., Dolby Laboratories, San Francisco, CA *Page 1-57*

Tripaldi, Daniel J. R., Catapult Software Training, New FairField, CT *Page 1-291*

Tripathi, Shashank, Inaltus.com, London, England, United Kingdom *Page 1-214*

Trisno, Yudhi S., Acucomm Inc., Santa Clara, CA *Page 1-291*

Tritt, Ralph, AT&T, Morristown, NJ *Page 1-105*

Trivedy, P., Multicom Business Systems Ltd., Wembley, England, United Kingdom *Page 1-210*

Tsai, Sunnie, Seagate Technology Inc., San Jose, CA *Page 1-47*

Tse
    Albert P., Duke Technology, Inc., Flushing, NY *Page 1-291*
    Simon Lai Yan, VSI, Austin, TX *Page 1-291*

Tsengouras, Michael D., Navigation Technology, Schaumburg, IL *Page 1-81*

Tsung, Theodore T., Digitrade Inc., New York, NY *Page 1-192*

Tucker, Clark F., The Haskell Company, Jacksonville, FL *Page 1-351*

Tuniewicz, Karin, Electronic Data Systems, Cranston, RI *Page 1-215*

Tuomey, Michael Sean, Chicago Police Department, Chicago, IL *Page 1-377*

Turchiaro, Michael Louis, Atlantic Technical Center, Coconut Creek, FL *Page 1-342*

Turner, Gene, Industrial Data and Magic, El Dorado, AR *Page 1-299*

Tutone, Frank P., Lanop Corporation, San Jose, CA *Page 1-291*

Tuttle
    Michael, Intermedia Communications, Tampa, FL *Page 1-105*
    Peter G., CEXEC, Inc., Dulles, VA *Page 1-292*
    Robert A., Kaiser Permanente, Oakland, CA *Page 1-151*

Tuzzo, Dominick, BetzDearborn division of Hercules, Inc., Croton On Hudson, NY *Page 1-5*

Tyeklar, Zoltan, EPIX Medical, Inc., Cambridge, MA *Page 1-25*

Tyler
    James E., Premier Systems Integrators, Charlotte, NC *Page 1-210*
    Mary F., The New England, Boston, MA *Page 1-156*
    Rebecca Ann, Eastern Mennonite University, Harrisonburg, VA *Page 1-333*

U

Udayamurthy, Sekar, Texas Instruments, Dallas, TX *Page 1-68*

Ujanen, Kari R., Ujanen, San Francisco, CA *Page 1-210*

Ukani, Ayoub B., PC Troubleshooter, Inc., Miami, FL *Page 1-292*

Ullah, Shamya M., Goldman Sachs, New York, NY *Page 1-144*

Urban, James J. "Jack", U S WEST, Omaha, NE *Page 1-105*

Urbanowicz, Robert Stanley, Parkway Insurance, Bridgewater, NJ *Page 1-154*

Usack, Lynn A., Corning Community College, Corning, NY *Page 1-339*

Usiak, Robert F., Home Shopping Network, St. Petersburg, FL *Page 1-131*

V

Valente, Jean-Luc, Homebid.com, Scottsdale, AZ *Page 1-159*

Vallon, Ronald Martin, CSC Consulting & Systems Integration, Waltham, MA *Page 1-211*

Valonzo, Avelino Mark A., Atlantic Express, Staten Island, NY *Page 1-87*

Van, My Tien, Livingston International, Etobicoke, Ontario, Canada *Page 1-91*

Van Baren, Marla J., National Technological University, Fort Collins, CO *Page 1-334*

Van Den Brink, Joost, Moore Clark, Vancouver, British Columbia, Canada *Page 1-1*

van der Laan, Annette, CS Computer Services Holdings Ltd., Johannesburg, South Africa *Page 1-292*

van der Linden, Nicoledean J., Engineering Information, Inc., Hoboken, NJ *Page 1-19*

Van Houten, Michael, Cannaissance Consulting, Warren, NJ *Page 1-292*

Van Huynh, Khoa, First Union National Bank, Charlotte, NC *Page 1-134*

Van Kallen, Ramon G. W., Continental Forge Company, Compton, CA *Page 1-34*

Van Pelt, Dane, City of Albuquerque, Albuquerque, NM *Page 1-375*

Vandenbos, Rod, Digital Internet Services Corporation, Indian Wells, CA *Page 1-112*

Vandiver, Emily H., United States Aviation and Missile Command, Redstone Arsenal, AL *Page 1-396*

VanDoorne, Vincent A., Ford Power Products, Southfield, MI *Page 1-118*

VanMeter, Jim, The Little Tikes Company, Hudson, OH *Page 1-85*

Vanover, Andrew, Amerada Hess Corporation, Tarrytown, NY *Page 1-28*

Vargas
    Enid T., Advanced Computer Technologies, San Juan, Puerto Rico *Page 1-292*
    Usha, Palm Beach County Health Care District, West Palm Beach, FL *Page 1-152*

Varghese, Sajini Sara, Instinet, New York, NY *Page 1-144*

Vassallo, Pierre, Department of Radiology, St. Luke's Hospital, Gwardamangia, Malta *Page 1-309*

Vassidiki, Soumahoro, Cote D'Ivoire Telecom, Abidjan, Ivory Coast (Cote d'Ivoire) *Page 1-105*

Vazhkudai, Sudharshan S., SAIR, Inc., Oxford, MS *Page 1-292*

Veach, Dale L., Dispatch Printing Company, Columbus, OH *Page 1-16*

Vedda, Michael S., S1 Corporation, Santa Clara, CA *Page 1-200*

Veguilla, John Anthony, Winstar Telecommunication, San Francisco, CA *Page 1-94*

Velappan, Vignesh, Wavetek Wandel Goltermann, Kuala Lumpur, Malaysia *Page 1-292*

Velez, George W., CSC, Jackson, NJ *Page 1-211*

Vellanki, Ravindra V., C A Consultants Int. Ltd., Metairie, LA *Page 1-293*

Venancio, Jean-Pierre, Activeweb, Voisins Le Bretonneux, France *Page 1-293*

Venz, Barbara E., MCI Telecommunications, McCormick, SC *Page 1-106*

Vermont, Lee M., American Megatrends Inc., Norcross, GA *Page 1-200*

Verna, Michael A., Inacom, Iselin, NJ *Page 1-211*

Verstraete, Edmond J., Janssen Pharmaceuticals, Washington Crossing, PA *Page 1-25*

Vertetis, Virginia A., AT&T, Somerset, NJ *Page 1-106*

Vetere, Rhonda M., UUNET - A Division of MCI/WorldCom, Hilliard, OH *Page 1-214*

Vickers, Jerry, Manchester Police Department, Manchester, TN *Page 1-377*

Vilchez, Ricardo S., Fordham University Library, Staten Island, NY *Page 1-339*

Villamil, Camilo E., Motorola, Fort Lauderdale, FL *Page 1-68*

Villegas, Danielle M., Associated Press, Cranbury, NJ *Page 1-299*

Villetorte, Michel, GVL, Montreal, Quebec, Canada *Page 1-293*

Vincent, Debbie A., GeoQuest, Houston, TX *Page 1-3*

Vincken, Wim, Coovi.com, Bat Yam, Israel *Page 1-164*

Vinson, Kevin J., EDS, The Colony, TX *Page 1-215*

Viswanathan, Narayanan, i2 Technologies, Irving, TX *Page 1-200*

Vitelli, Joseph D., Howmet Corporation, Hampton, VA *Page 1-32*

von Pfaler, Martin, Pollenpolen, Vallentuna, Sweden *Page 1-293*

Vu, John T., Distributed Network Administration, Parlin, NJ *Page 1-293*

Vurdela, Greg J., BCMEA, Vancouver, British Columbia, Canada *Page 1-89*

W

Wacker, Trent S., Missourian Publishing, Washington, MO *Page 1-21*

Wagner
Daniel S., Foster Wheel Environment Corporation, Monroe, NY *Page 1-349*
Paul W., Squeal Media Arts, Bloomington, IN *Page 1-192*

Wahn, Norman A., Chr. Hansen, Inc., Milwaukee, WI *Page 1-10*

Wai-Hung, Kwok, Nexcel Limited, Kowloon, Hong Kong *Page 1-192*

Waits, Julian W., BMC Software, Houston, TX *Page 1-200*

Walczak, Bryan T., Arian Lowe & Travis, Chicago, IL *Page 1-164*

Waldeck, Stephen, Warsaw Area Career Center, Warsaw, IN *Page 1-319*

Walden, Steven J., Pace/Butler Corporation, Edmond, OK *Page 1-129*

Walinder, Mike, McCook Community College, McCook, NE *Page 1-339*

Walker
Alfred E., GAI Consulting Southeast Inc., Jacksonville, FL *Page 1-370*
James A., WAHLCO Engineered Products, Inc., Lewiston, ME *Page 1-33*
Julie-Anne, Agilent Technologies, Inc., Westford, MA *Page 1-82*
Loren Mark, Lockheed Martin, Severna Park, MD *Page 1-80*
Michael L., HUD Office of Inspector General, Washington, DC *Page 1-389*

Wallace
James Ashford, FedEx, Collierville, TN *Page 1-90*
Jim, Great Rivers Tech Institute, McGehee, AR *Page 1-339*
Samuel "Sam" Thomas, Education Service Center-2, Corpus Christi, TX *Page 1-383*

Wallenborn, Jerry L., Earth Tech, La Mesa, CA *Page 1-350*

Wallmark, John S., Millstone River Systems, Inc., Skillman, NJ *Page 1-293*

Walls, Georgette F., CSC Consulting, West Orange, NJ *Page 1-211*

Walsh, Christopher W., RCN Corporation, Princeton, NJ *Page 1-106*

Walter, Dick, Laser Wireless Inc., Lancaster, PA *Page 1-63*

Wamara, Ian Kamese, Cargill Uganda, Ltd., Kampala, Uganda *Page 1-9*

Wamsley, Alan Maurice, Chiron America, Inc., Charlotte, NC *Page 1-38*

Wan, Daniel Q., Strategic Alliance International Corporation, New York, NY *Page 1-293*

Wanagel, Jonathan, Lante Corporation, Bellevue, WA *Page 1-294*

Wancio, Charlie, Alcatel USA, Plano, TX *Page 1-106*

Wang
Bruce, Draft Worldwide, New York, NY *Page 1-164*
Hong, Siliconix, Inc., Santa Clara, CA *Page 1-68*

Ward, Michael F., Genentech, South San Francisco, CA *Page 1-25*

Warmelink, Michael R., Thomson Consumer Electronics, Indianapolis, IN *Page 1-54*

Warmsley, Byron Nigel, McDonald Bradley, McLean, VA *Page 1-294*

Warrington, William "Sandy" E., EG&G Defense Materials, Toole, UT *Page 1-117*

Washington
Jacqulin R., PPG Industries, Inc., Huntsville, AL *Page 1-30*
Paul L., Litton/TASC, Annapolis Junction, MD *Page 1-294*

Wasilewski, Richard, AAC Inc., Schaumburg, IL *Page 1-294*

Watermann, Sascha, LN-Online GmbH, Luebeck, Hernberg, DE *Page 1-294*

Watkins
Patricia A., Morpace International, Farmington Hills, MI *Page 1-370*
Steve, Summit National Bank, Atlanta, GA *Page 1-136*

Watson, Susan E., Alberta Health and Wellness, Edmonton, Alberta, Canada *Page 1-385*

Watts, Dennis H., Weblink Wireless, Dallas, TX *Page 1-94*

Weaver
Clarence E., Headquarters, Air Force Audit Agency, Washington, DC *Page 1-396*
Demian K., PSINet, Herndon, VA *Page 1-294*
Sandra K., Roundy's Ohio Division, Lima, OH *Page 1-124*

Weber, Gregory, Volt Computer Services/Entirenet, Sterling Heights, MI *Page 1-294*

Wechsler, Brian C., Wolf Creek Elementary, Pine Ridge, SD *Page 1-334*

Weeks, John B., Quintus Corporation, Fremont, CA *Page 1-295*

Wei, Jeffrey Haoran, UHERE Corporation, San Jose, CA *Page 1-295*

Weigand, Michael R., Master Automation, Inc., Kirtland, OH *Page 1-211*

Weinberg, Laurie J., Management Recruiters International, Springfield, NJ *Page 1-169*

Weis, Ted P., PROTOCOL Technology Partners, LLC, Scottsdale, AZ *Page 1-295*

Weisberg, Ross, Edmunds & Associates, Northfield, NJ *Page 1-295*

Weiss
Abbott D., Digital Equipment Corporation, Marlborough, MA *Page 1-295*
Richard A., ComTech Labs, Stanhope, NJ *Page 1-295*

Welker, Michael J., IBM Global Services, Warren, PA *Page 1-295*

Wellnitz, Judi K., Tenneco Packaging, Deerfield, IL *Page 1-29*

Wells
Bradley T., Iroquois Memorial Hospital, Watseka, IL *Page 1-309*
Dwayne, Long Fence & Home, Riverdale, MD *Page 1-118*
Robert M., Summit Medical Center, Hermitage, TN *Page 1-309*

Welsh, Norma E., GV-WFL EduTech, Newark, NY *Page 1-319*

Wentzler, Tracy, United Distillers, Omaha, NE *Page 1-9*

Werkowitz, Derek, O'Neil Associates, Dayton, OH *Page 1-19*

Wermager, Paul, University of Hawaii, Honolulu, HI *Page 1-334*

Wessels, David M., University of Arkansas, Fayetteville, AR *Page 1-334*

West
Chris, Northrop Grumman-Canada Ltd., Burlington, Ontario, Canada *Page 1-76*
Rachel A., Carlsbad Municipal School District, Carlsbad, NM *Page 1-319*

Wheatland, Kevin, CCG Consulting Associates, Stockholm, Sweden *Page 1-296*

Wheeler
Barbara, ECCS, Tinton Falls, NJ *Page 1-47*
Revell, ACT Teleconferencing, Inc., Richardson, TX *Page 1-63*

White, James, YAI, New York, NY *Page 1-344*

White
Allen, Levi Strauss & Co., Westlake, TX *Page 1-12*
Kevin D., EURO RSCG DSW Partners, Salt Lake City, UT *Page 1-165*
Kimberly A., Commerce One, Orinda, CA *Page 1-200*
Michael Henry, Envision, St. Louis, MO *Page 1-296*

White Rayner, Nicole M., Ziff-Davis, Garden City, NY *Page 1-17*

Whitecotton, Brad, University of Evansville, Evansville, IN *Page 1-334*

Whitney, Susan L., AverStar, Inc., Geospacial Services Group, Portland, OR *Page 1-296*

Whitt
Mark A., Houston Fire Department, Houston, TX *Page 1-378*
Richard S., MCI WorldCom, Inc., Washington, DC *Page 1-106*

Whittington, Cathy D., Novell, Inc., East Norriton, PA *Page 1-200*

Wick, John A., SAIC, McLean, VA *Page 1-359*

Wieland, Katherine, US Trustee, Wichita, KS *Page 1-376*

Wiemokly, Kerry M., Graphic Consultants, Hopewell Junction, NY *Page 1-303*

Wiewiora, Thomas A., Holland Hitch Company, Holland, MI *Page 1-319*

Wilcox, Michael J., Hyperacuity Systems, Colorado Springs, CO *Page 1-82*

Wilkie, Timothy J., Republic Mortgage Insurance Company, Winston-Salem, NC *Page 1-156*

Wilkins
  Jackie D., Raytheon/TI Systems Company, Van Alstyne, TX *Page 1-81*
  Teresa, Our Lady of Mount Carmel School, Baltimore, MD *Page 1-319*

Wilkinson, David D., Wilkinson Consulting Group, Inc., Pleasant Hill, CA *Page 1-296*

Willerton, Shane L., Williams Refining, LLC, Memphis, TN *Page 1-28*

Williams
  Allen D., Ward Manufacturing Inc., Elmira, NY *Page 1-31*
  Alvis A., Merck & Co., Inc., Somerset, NJ *Page 1-25*
  Anthony, KSLA TV, Shreveport, LA *Page 1-108*
  Iris D., United States Department of State, Springfield, VA *Page 1-397*
  Laura H., Resource Information Management Systems, Inc., Naperville, IL *Page 1-192*
  Scott D., Dixon Odom PLLC, High Point, NC *Page 1-356*
  Terry, Palisades Safety & Insurance Management, Hoboken, NJ *Page 1-154*

Willis, Crissy M., Commonwealth Health Corporation, Bowling Green, KY *Page 1-153*

Wilsdon, Alex L., Leopard Communications, Boulder, CO *Page 1-192*

Wilson
  Edward Alton, State of Connecticut Workers Compensation, Hartford, CT *Page 1-155*
  Joe M., Sunnyside Community Hospital, Renton, WA *Page 1-310*
  Jonathan G., Hickory Springs Manufacturing, Hickory, NC *Page 1-13*
  Ralph Thomas, Compaq Computer Corporation, Newtown, CT *Page 1-46*
  Raymond E., Viewsonic, Walnut, CA *Page 1-49*
  Salena, SASI, Chicago, IL *Page 1-343*
  Sheryl A., Desert De Oro Foods Inc., Kingman, AZ *Page 1-129*

Wineteer, Stephen A., 1st National Bank of Omaha, Bellevue, NE *Page 1-161*

Wingenroth, Rebecca M., GPU Energy, Reading, PA *Page 1-115*

Winkler, Piotr, Uproar, Inc., Ridgewood, NY *Page 1-200*

Winklesky, James B., O'Brien Interactive, Acworth, GA *Page 1-193*

Winquist, John A., ADP Dealer Services, Portland, OR *Page 1-212*

Winship, Matthew, Washburn & Associates, Inc., Overland Park, KS *Page 1-200*

Winter
  Edward A., Computer Consultant, Revere, MA *Page 1-296*
  W. Scott, Clarkston Potomac, Durham, NC *Page 1-296*

Wise
  Alan L., Pima Community College, Tucson, AZ *Page 1-339*
  Michael, Mitsubishi Wireless Communications Inc., Duluth, GA *Page 1-57*

Wiseman, Roland S. N., Lands & Surveys Division, Tunapune, Trinidad & Tobago *Page 1-352*

Wisloff, Tomm, Kinetic Concepts, Inc., San Antonio, TX *Page 1-13*

Wismer, James D., Institute for Scientific Information (ISI), Philadelphia, PA *Page 1-19*

Witkowski, Jeffrey J., American Junior Golf, Roswell, GA *Page 1-305*

Wolf
  Gerald L., Kalas Manufacturing Inc., Denver, PA *Page 1-53*
  Randy L., IBM Corporation, Essex Junction, VT *Page 1-46*

Wong, Stephen, Philips Medical Systems, Mountain View, CA *Page 1-70*

Wonsang, Willmer B., CommVault System, Frisco, TX *Page 1-193*

Wood, Robert S., Auto Gas Systems Inc., New Braunfels, TX *Page 1-211*

Woodburn, R. David, Canam Software Labs, Inc., Newmarket, Ontario, Canada *Page 1-296*

Woodlee, Jason, CTech, West Orange, NJ *Page 1-193*

Woods
  E. Hayet, Independence School District, Liberty, MO *Page 1-384*
  Marguerite E., eMerge Interactive, Sebastian, FL *Page 1-297*

Woodworth, Juanita D., CVIS, Coarsegold, CA *Page 1-129*

Woolverton, Thomas, IXC Communications, Livonia, MI *Page 1-106*

Word, Glenn E., Kellogg Brown & Root, Houston, TX *Page 1-6*

Worley, Jason, Auto Desk Inc., Windham, NH *Page 1-297*

Wright
  Joel S., DigitalXpress, St. Paul, MN *Page 1-113*
  Michael C., MCB Collection Services Inc., Vero Beach, FL *Page 1-303*
  Richard A., Hazelwood Farms Inc., Hazelwood, MO *Page 1-8*
  Richard K., Siemens Microelectronics, OptoElectronics Division, Cupertino, CA *Page 1-56*
  Rik, ZoneNetwork.com, Seattle, WA *Page 1-297*

Wuosmaa, Shelby M., Cambar Software, Charleston, SC *Page 1-201*

Wychulis, C. "Bud", The Rhythm Section Lab, Coaldale, PA *Page 1-303*

Wymore, Tess, Coconino Community College, Flagstaff, AZ *Page 1-339*

Wynn, Sherri Peterson, Chesapeake Display & Packaging, Winston-Salem, NC *Page 1-14*

Wysocki, Thomas A., Select Comfort, Plymouth, MN *Page 1-13*

Wyss, Mark W., Bentley Management Corporation, Denver, CO *Page 1-141*

X

Xie, Ian Y., Medio Systems, Inc., San Jose, CA *Page 1-193*

Xue, Guoliang, University of Vermont, Burlington, VT *Page 1-334*

Y

Yan, David K. C., AmTelecom Group, Inc., Mississauga, Ontario, Canada *Page 1-106*

Yang
  Binglin "Bing", Cargill, Inc., Minnetonka, MN *Page 1-125*
  Charles X., USHarbor.com, Inc., Mountain View, CA *Page 1-131*
  Lily H., WFSATC, Salt Lake City, UT *Page 1-340*
  Ning, GTE Laboratories, Inc., Waltham, MA *Page 1-107*

Yarrow, John R., Richardson Independent School District, Richardson, TX *Page 1-319*

Yarussi, Richard A., Nanometrics, Inc., Sunnyvale, CA *Page 1-37*

Yates, Travis, Remington Agency, Gainesville, FL *Page 1-193*

Yearwood, Michael, Coretec, Inc., Toronto, Ontario, Canada *Page 1-63*

Yelich, Scott D., Computer System Consulting, Santa Fe, NM *Page 1-297*

Yilmaz, Haluk, 3M Turkey, Istanbul, Turkey *Page 1-14*

Yim, Aaron P., General Electric, Jonesboro, AR *Page 1-77*

Yoakley, Frances L., Independent Truckers Group, Inc., Las Vegas, NV *Page 1-297*

Yoneyama, Tsutomu, Livedoor, Inc., Tokyo, Japan *Page 1-107*

Yoshimura, Dennis A., Johnston Community School District, Johnston, IA *Page 1-320*

Young
  Aaron C., AppliedTheory, Syracuse, NY *Page 1-211*
  Barry H., White Sands Missile Range, Las Cruces, NM *Page 1-397*
  Carol, AT&T Solutions/McDermott Inc. Account, Lancaster, OH *Page 1-297*
  Leigh Irish, Cooper Communities, Inc., Bella Vista, AR *Page 1-160*
  Sandra Kay, Microcosm, Torrance, CA *Page 1-79*
  Smith, Superior Technology Resources, Littleton, CO *Page 1-351*

Younis, Akmal A., University of Miami, Coral Gables, FL *Page 1-334*

Yount, David E., MI Technologies, Troy, OH *Page 1-216*

Yrizarry, Lisa Marie, Federal Reserve Bank, Portland, OR *Page 1-133*

Yu
  Hong Heather, Panasonic Technology Inc., Princeton, NJ *Page 1-360*
  Simon P., M-Plus, Fremont, CA *Page 1-120*

Z

Zabel, Todd A., HLB Tautges Redpath, Ltd., White Bear Lake, MN *Page 1-356*

Zaika, Gary, Integral Software Corporation, Merrick, NY *Page 1-297*

Zaragoza, Carla, Saguaro Clinical Research, Tucson, AZ *Page 1-359*

Zepeda, Jesse H., IKON, Whittier, CA *Page 1-51*

Zepp, Gregg L., Infinite Wisdom Web Designs, Reisterstown, MD *Page 1-193*

Zhang
  Guogen, IBM Santa Teresa Lab, San Jose, CA *Page 1-46*

Hong, Emerald Solutions Inc., Warren, NJ *Page* 1-298

Zhao
Eric Yanguang, Solution Soft Systems, Inc., Cupertino, CA *Page* 1-193
Wei, Netpliance, Inc., Round Rock, TX *Page* 1-298

Zhu, Jack J., Avery Dennison, FRNA, Fort Wayne, IN *Page* 1-14

Ziegler, Jody Nyquist, Honeywell Home & Building Control, Minneapolis, MN *Page* 1-6

Ziehl, Jonathan R., Schafer-CIT, Fairport, NY *Page* 1-298

Zimmerman, Gregory D., Minnesota Department of Transportation, Maplewood, MN *Page* 1-390

Zornosa Cabrera, Luis M., Inter American University of Puerto Rico, San German, Puerto Rico *Page* 1-335

Zwickel, M. Susan, Snelling Personnel Services, Fairfield, NJ *Page* 1-170

Members Indexed Alphabetically by Company Name

Section 3

Numbers

1 Venture Inc., Chief Technical Officer/Founder, Schmidt, Jonatan, Palo Alto, CA *Page 1-280*

1-800-VIDEO-ON, Engineering Manager, Eshelman, Scott Walter, Boulder, CO *Page 1-109*

1st National Bank of Omaha, Systems Architect, Wineteer, Stephen A., Bellevue, NE *Page 1-161*

20th Century Fox, Disaster Recovery Specialist, Goldstein, Lee, Beverly Hills, CA *Page 1-304*

24/7 University, Inc., Founder/President, Hinkle, Delwin R., Irving, TX *Page 1-301*

2GoTrade.com, Software Engineer, Mohamed, Noohu, Wanchai, Hong Kong *Page 1-184*

3Com, e-Business Development Manager, Greene, Michael, Santa Clara, CA *Page 1-48*

3M Turkey, Information Technology Supervisor, Yilmaz, Haluk, Istanbul, Turkey *Page 1-14*

480 Intelligence Group, Technical Director, LaFata, Steve F., Langley Air Force Base, VA *Page 1-394*

4C Solutions, Project Manager, Gupta, Rajesh, East Moline, IL *Page 1-244*

90th Regional Support Command, Information Management Officer, Akridge, William D., North Little Rock, AR *Page 1-392*

A

A. Louis Supply Company, Systems Engineer, Angle, Brenda K., Ashtabula, OH *Page 1-122*

A.C. New Middle School, Technology Facilitator, Derrick, Carol A., Mesquite, TX *Page 1-315*

A&L Lithography, Lithography Specialist, Spoon, John, Escondido, CA *Page 1-19*

A&S Solutions, Inc., Senior Consultant/Owner, Syed, Aamir Mazhar, Matawan, NJ *Page 1-287*

AAA Business Machines, Network Engineer, Boyles, Alan L., Fayetteville, AR *Page 1-128*

AAC Inc., President, Wasilewski, Richard, Schaumburg, IL *Page 1-294*

AB Floyd, Inc., Senior Systems Engineer, Morse, Jeffery G., Alexandria, VA *Page 1-266*

ABB Alston Power, Systems Administrator, Kraft, Debra, Kings Mountain, NC *Page 1-33*

ABB Systems Control, Software Engineer, Mukherjee, Himadri P., Santa Clara, CA *Page 1-215*

Abbot & Abbot Architects, PLL, Information Systems Administrator, Schumacher, J., Columbus, OH *Page 1-351*

ABN AMRO, Senior Vice President, Riopelle, Joanna M., Chicago, IL *Page 1-137*

ABN AMRO Bank, Project Manager, Allen, Pamela T., Chicago, IL *Page 1-137*

Abratech Corporation, Systems Programmer, Caplovitz, Gideon Paul, Sausalito, CA *Page 1-357*

Absalon Group, Technical Lead, Nilsson, Anders, Malmo, Sweden *Page 1-268*

Accelerated Imaging, Inc., Chief Information Officer, Rios, Anthony A., Tustin, CA *Page 1-208*

Access, Director of Program Management/Development Practices/Chief Architect, Rawsthorne, Daniel A., Seattle, WA *Page 1-187*

ACCS @ St. Mary Site, Technology Technician, Snare, Lisa A., Altoona, PA *Page 1-318*

Accu Sort Systems Inc., Software Design Engineer, Churetta, Scott, Telford, PA *Page 1-173*

Aceomatic Recon, Systems Administrator, Swanson, N. Diana, Pittsburgh, PA *Page 1-118*

ACS Professional Services, E-Commerce Practice Lead, Porterfield, Mark E., Wexford, PA *Page 1-274*

Acsis, Inc., Director Research and Development, Harty, Dave F., Marlton, NJ *Page 1-178*

ACT Teleconferencing, Inc., National Technical Network Manager, Wheeler, Revell, Richardson, TX *Page 1-63*

Actel, President/Chief Executive Officer, DeNigris, Ernest G., Mendham, NJ *Page 1-64*

Actionet, Inc., Systems Analyst/Consultant, McCracken, Philip F., Silver Spring, MD *Page 1-263*

Activeweb, Director/Manager, Venancio, Jean-Pierre, Voisins Le Bretonneux, France *Page 1-293*

Acucomm Inc., President, Trisno, Yudhi S., Santa Clara, CA *Page 1-291*

Acxiom RTC, Inc., Industry Solutions Architect, Smith, Joshua D., La Grange, IL *Page 1-209*

Adecco at Boeing, Senior Database Administrator, Coffman, Gayle, Bellevue, WA *Page 1-368*

Ademco Group, Y2K Coordinator, Garenani, Peter C., Syosset, NY *Page 1-298*

AdminaStar Federal, Manager of Client Server Development, Hale, Pamela D., Louisville, KY *Page 1-157*

ADP
  PC Coordinator, Jeunesse, Braden P., Minneapolis, IN *Page 1-212*
  Software Developer, Goldman, Sergey, Portland, OR *Page 1-211*

ADP Dealer Services
  Repair Supervisor, Winquist, John A., Portland, OR *Page 1-212*
  Supervisor, Roll, Gary V., Hoffman Estates, IL *Page 1-212*

ADP Hayes Ligon, Client Operations Analyst, Hollands, Brian P., Riverview, FL *Page 1-212*

ADP Marshall, a Fluor Daniel Company, Manager of Telecommunications, Hering, Rich, Mesa, AZ *Page 1-66*

ADT Security Services, Inc., Corporate Programmer/Analyst, Lee, Ryan J., Weston, MO *Page 1-298*

Advance Business Graphics, Manager of Internet Systems Service, Reicher, Joshua S., Mira Loma, CA *Page 1-21*

Advanced Computer Technologies, Senior Vice President, Vargas, Enid T., San Juan, Puerto Rico *Page 1-292*

Advanced Concepts Engineering and Technology, President/Chief Executive Officer, Jones, Tim H., Tampa, FL *Page 1-251*

Advanced Elastomer Systems, L.P., Manager of Information Systems Operations, McLaughlin-Nelson, Lori K., Akron, OH *Page 1-22*

Advanced Network & Services, Inc., Internet Engineer, Liao, Min, Armonk, NY *Page 1-258*

Advanced Programming Resources, Programming Consultant, Savage, Steven, Columbus, OH *Page 1-279*

Advanced Technologies Consulting Group Inc., Partner/President, Schiavi, Adam J., North Miami, FL *Page 1-280*

Advanced Web Design, President, Coleman, Marquis R., Detroit, MI *Page 1-202*

Advanta Corporation, Director, Collier, H. James, Spring House, PA *Page 1-140*

Advantage Group, Team Leader, Slusanschi, Anca E., Paraparaumu, New Zealand *Page 1-283*

AEG/Electrolux, Information Technology Manager, Juettner, Michael J., Rothenburg Bay, Germany *Page 1-53*

Aegon Equity Group, Senior Database Administrator, D'Amico, Stephen, Palm Harbor, FL *Page 1-148*

AEMP Corporation, Business Systems Analyst, Springer, Sarah Lee, Jackson, TN *Page 1-74*

Aera Inc., Engineer, Geragas, Dimitris A., Arlington, VA *Page 1-240*

Aeroglide Corporation, Technical Manual Coordinator, Tipton, Duane E., Cary, NC *Page 1-38*

Aerospace Software Ltd., Software Engineer/President, Oosthuysen, Herman, Calgary, Alberta, Canada *Page 1-270*

Af Associates, Senior Project Manager, Michales, Thomas C., Northvale, NJ *Page 1-207*

Affiliated Computer Services, Senior Systems Analyst, Dempsey, Patrick P., San Francisco, CA *Page 1-233*

Affordable PC Systems, Inc., Owner, Agarwal, Braj, Seaford, NY *Page 1-217*

AFFS Corporation, President, Hurtak, James, Los Gatos, CA *Page 1-346*

AFI, RORC Support Specialist, McKillip, West, Amarillo, TX *Page 1-125*

Agilent Technologies, Inc.
  E-Business Manager, Walker, Julie-Anne, Westford, MA *Page 1-82*
  Software Design Engineer, Su, Alan P., Westlake Village, CA *Page 1-82*

Ahlers & Associates, Assistant Management Information Systems Director, French, Cynthia, Waco, TX *Page 1-176*

Air Force Research Laboratory, Visiting Scientist, Pedersen, Charles R., Rome, NY *Page 1-395*

Air Products & Chemicals, Inc., GEGE Process Controls A32H2, Technology Manager of Control Strategies, Leach, David B., Allentown, PA *Page 1-125*

Air Touch, Senior Project Manager, Keenan, Marvin P., Pleasant Hill, CA *Page 1-93*

Aisin USA, Network Specialist, Spencer, Karen E., Seymour, IN *Page 1-74*

Ajilon
Consultant, Rowe, Richard Carl, Richmond, VA *Page 1-278*
Senior Operations Specialist, Cheng, Jean, Rochester, NY *Page 1-229*

Akropolis.net, Director of Information Systems/Chief Technology Officer, Connolly, Phil J., Santa Ana, CA *Page 1-232*

Al Zamil Group of Companies, Consultant, Besiso, Marwan Y., Riyadh, Saudi Arabia *Page 1-161*

Alameda County, Public Works Agency, Information Technology Department Manager, Babilla, Furat C., Hayward, CA *Page 1-390*

Alaska Airlines, Management Information Systems Analyst/Instructor, Buchner, Pamela J., Seattle, WA *Page 1-89*

Alaska Power & Telephone Company, Management Information Systems Director, Paddock, Janet, Port Townsend, WA *Page 1-103*

Alberta Health and Wellness, Director of Information Technology, Watson, Susan E., Edmonton, Alberta, Canada *Page 1-385*

Albright Ideas, Inc., President, Albright, Gerry, Eagan, MN *Page 1-217*

Alcan Aluminum Corporation, System Analyst, Shannon, Patricia A., Warren, OH *Page 1-32*

Alcatel USA
EDI Manager for Order Management, Reynolds, Teresa G., Plano, TX *Page 1-104*
Software Development Engineer, McIntosh, Clarissa R., Plano, TX *Page 1-102*
Software Engineer, Wancio, Charlie, Plano, TX *Page 1-106*

ALCOA Engineered Products, Engineering Information Systems Manager, Barr, Angela Lynn, Cressona, PA *Page 1-32*

Alcon Laboratories
Senior Information Specialist, Pollock, Francisco, Burleson, TX *Page 1-84*
Technical Consultant, Johnson, Lucy J., Fort Worth, TX *Page 1-84*

Allergan, Inc., SAP Basic Consultant, Tran, Ngoc-Diem T., Irvine, CA *Page 1-25*

Allgeier Martin & Associates, Network Administrator, Drost, Terry L., Joplin, MO *Page 1-235*

Alliant Energy, UNIX Team Leader, Bouwma, Michael, Madison, WI *Page 1-113*

AlliedSignal, Systems Analyst, Harvell, J. Larry, Chester, VA *Page 1-27*

AlliedSignal Technical Services, Software Engineer, Bowens, Dewitt, La Plata, MD *Page 1-26*

Alltech Data Systems, Information Systems Director, Pittas, Douglas, Bensenville, IL *Page 1-93*

Alphatrain, Software Applications Instructor, Castillo, Victoria M., Maplewood, NJ *Page 1-340*

ALPS Electric Europa GmbH, Electronic Data Processing and Information Technology Manager, Burg, Hans, Duesseldorf NRW, Germany *Page 1-68*

Als Cartage Ltd., Information Systems Manager, Jones, Stephen, Kitchener, Ontario, Canada *Page 1-88*

Alta Mesa Resources, Engineering Technologist, Thomas, Alexander, Houston, TX *Page 1-3*

AM Search Consulting, Inc., Principal Consultant, Duda, Andrew, Rockville, MD *Page 1-168*

Amazon.com, Manager of System Services, Simonsen, Peter, Seattle, WA *Page 1-131*

Ambassador Consulting, Consultant, Sersic, Christopher J., Indianapolis, IN *Page 1-282*

AMBC-CCTC/ICTS, Marketing Administrator, Roberts, Angela D., Baltimore, MD *Page 1-341*

Amdahl Corporation, Staff Consultant, Mahmud, Shamun, Washington, DC *Page 1-43*

Amerada Hess Corporation, Senior Information Technology Specialist, Vanover, Andrew, Tarrytown, NY *Page 1-28*

America Online Inc., Traffic Manager, Harmon, Margaret, Sterling, VA *Page 1-110*

American Agrisurance, Network Administrator, Rogers, Alvina C., Council Bluffs, IA *Page 1-154*

American Century Investments, Manager of Electronic Development and Technology, Stanley, Kenneth L., Kansas City, MO *Page 1-144*

American Chemical Society, Senior Program Analyst, Guo, Baoping, Washington, DC *Page 1-345*

American College of Cardiology, Customer Support Manager, Information and Technology Services, Holliday, Rosana, Bethesda, MD *Page 1-325*

American Electric Power Company, Information Technology Training Specialist, Hardin, Rohdonda R., Columbus, OH *Page 1-113*

American Engineering, Vice President, Granger, Timothy G., North East, MD *Page 1-348*

American Express
Head of Production Control, Marques, Ronaldo Pereiras, Phoenix, AZ *Page 1-139*
Programmer Analyst II, Reyes, Sherry, Phoenix, AZ *Page 1-139*

American Express - TRS, Vice President of Information Technology, Manino, Brooke, Berkeley Heights, NJ *Page 1-138*

American Express Company, Lead Network Engineer, Menezes, Conrad O., New York, NY *Page 1-139*

American Express One, Senior Network Administrator, Green, Joseph E., Mount Laurel, NJ *Page 1-91*

American Family Insurance, Network Technology Analyst, Rolfsmeyer, Kenneth T., Madison, WI *Page 1-151*

American Family Insurance Company, Technology Consultant, Boland, Dennis G., Madison, WI *Page 1-149*

American Frozen Foods Inc., Senior Programmer/Analyst, Drown, Dennis A., Stratford, CT *Page 1-301*

American General Finance, Manager of Technology Asset Management, Howard, Donald R. B. "Donn", Evansville, IN *Page 1-138*

American Institute of Certified Public Accountants, Knowledge Management Technical Support Coordinator, Autry, Daniel J., Jersey City, NJ *Page 1-345*

American Intercontinental University
Career Services Manager, Purnell, Katharine, Plantation, FL *Page 1-331*
Information Technology Faculty, Marged, Judith M., Plantation, FL *Page 1-328*

American Junior Golf, Manager of Information Systems, Witkowski, Jeffrey J., Roswell, GA *Page 1-305*

American Megatrends Inc.
BIOS Engineer, Chan, Rodney W., Norcross, GA *Page 1-195*
Raid Test Engineer, Vermont, Lee M., Norcross, GA *Page 1-200*

American Microsystems Inc, Application Analyst, Olney, Tiffany, Pocatello, ID *Page 1-67*

American Precision Technology, Technician, Punako, Ronald, Hollsopple, PA *Page 1-275*

American Radio Relay League, Information System Manager, Durand, Donald, Newington, CT *Page 1-347*

American Reinsurance, Director, Kosco, Thomas John, Princeton, NJ *Page 1-154*

American Society for Quality, Online Communications Manager, Duncan, Phillip L., Milwaukee, WI *Page 1-345*

American Society for Testing and Materials, Manager of Acquisitions and Review, Dernoga, Kathleen A., West Conshohocken, PA *Page 1-16*

American Urological Association, Systems Engineering Coordinator, Reed, Timothy, Houston, TX *Page 1-346*

Amica, Information Technology Process Manager, Hillman, Jack Dyer, Lincoln, RI *Page 1-148*

AMR Research, Senior Account Manager, Lunstead, Eric Q., Boston, MA *Page 1-259*

AMS Inc., Account Executive for Sales, Thakkar, Vrajesh, New York, NY *Page 1-121*

AMS Informatix Inc., Director, Systems Development, Chayapathi, Nagaraju, San Jose, CA *Page 1-229*

AmTelecom Group, Inc., Director of Information Systems/Information Technology, Yan, David K. C., Mississauga, Ontario, Canada *Page 1-106*

Analysts International
Consultant, Cole, Michael A., Fort Worth, TX *Page 1-173*
Senior Database Administrator, Gaddam, Ravi, Littleton, CO *Page 1-176*

Analytical Graphics, Technical Trainer, Griffiths, Andrea M., Phoenixville, PA *Page 1-177*

Ananya Systems, Inc., President, Ananya, Brigit, Los Gatos, CA *Page 1-194*

Andersen Consulting
Consultant, Miller, Kevin J., Pollesville, MD *Page 1-365*
Oracle Database Administrator, McDonnell, Michael J., Philadelphia, PA *Page 1-365*
Project Manager, Paladino, Chris D., Alexandria, VA *Page 1-365*

Andersen Consulting LLP, Analyst, Sherlock, Jason E., Reston, VA *Page 1-366*

Anderson and Associate's, Inc., Computer Aided Design and Drafting Manager, Caldwell, Shawn Edward, Blacksburg, VA *Page 1-348*

Andrell Corporation, President, Andrews, Jonathan, El Dorado Hills, CA *Page 1-218*

Andrx, Information Systems Director, Levine, Jerilee "Jeri" Goodman, Weston, FL *Page 1-24*

Anexsys, Director, Project Management and Business System Analysis, Olson, Elizabeth K., Chicago, IL *Page 1-270*

Anglais Consulting Inc., President/Owner, English, Richard L., Sanford, FL *Page 1-236*

Anheuser-Busch, Inc., Systems Engineer, O'Donnell, Shaun I., Lanexa, VA *Page 1-9*

Annuncio, Software Development Manager, Bhandary, Manoj S., San Jose, CA *Page 1-163*

Anteon Corporation, Technical Advisor, Cordle, Ruth, Montgomery, AL *Page 1-173*

AOP Solutions, Sales Manager, Becker, James F., Buffalo, NY *Page 1-221*

Appdepot Web Services, President, Schneider, Doug J., Regina, Saskatchewan, Canada *Page 1-281*

Application Consulting Group, Principal Consultant, Carlascio, Keith, Morristown, NJ *Page 1-228*

Application Partners, Inc., Network Administrator, Thompson, Wesley, Pleasant Hill, CA *Page 1-289*

Applications Solutions, Principal Consultant, Schifano, Mike, Houston, TX *Page 1-280*

Applied Industrial Technologies, Manager of Logistics Information Systems, Richmond, Leon L., Cleveland, OH *Page 1-123*

Applied Materials, Management Information Systems Manager of North American Region, Ensor, Bettina Rice, Richardson, TX *Page 1-65*

Applied Systems, Inc, Senior Technical Advisor, Sander, Tim A., University Park, IL *Page 1-188*

AppliedTheory, Internal Technology Manager, Young, Aaron C., Syracuse, NY *Page 1-211*

Aptima, Inc., Founder/Chief Scientist, Serfaty, Daniel, Woburn, MA *Page 1-349*

Aqueduct Information Services, Vice President of Business Development, Lowe, Vincent D., Mountain View, CA *Page 1-259*

ARay Computer Services, Owner, Ray, Tony E., Cincinnati, OH *Page 1-276*

Archer Daniels Midland Company, Senior Information Systems Audit Manager, Swallow, Brett A., Decatur, IL *Page 1-1*

Archer Engineers, Systems and Technology Development Manager, Medsker, Michael D., Peculiar, MO *Page 1-351*

Archmere Academy, Technology Coordinator, Robinson, Mark C., Claymont, DE *Page 1-317*

ARDC
    Assistant Network Administrator, Bader, Robin L., Chicago, IL *Page 1-345*
    Information Service Operator, Plunkett, Jeffrey Lynn, Duluth, MN *Page 1-346*

Area 2 Learning Tech Hub, Network Support Specialist/Webmaster, Link, Patty A., Ottawa, IL *Page 1-258*

ARESC, Educational Programmer, Huddle, Jeanne, North Little Rock, AR *Page 1-341*

Arian Lowe & Travis, Director of Management Information Systems, Walczak, Bryan T., Chicago, IL *Page 1-164*

Arizona Central Credit Union, Director of Computer Operations, Hughes, Mary Ann, Phoenix, AZ *Page 1-136*

Arizona Lottery, Network Specialist, Dandas, Gus, Phoenix, AZ *Page 1-306*

Arlington Industries, Network Administrator, Kozlov, Christopher M., Libertyville, IL *Page 1-120*

Army National Guard, Director of Information Management, Eizember, Dave, Rapid City, SD *Page 1-392*

Arris Interactive
    Customer Operations Specialist, Bandong, Lydia M., Suwanee, GA *Page 1-58*
    Senior Marketing, Rao, Sonali, Suwanee, GA *Page 1-62*

Arris Systems, Inc., Executive Vice President, Namoglu, Sheryl F., Berwyn, PA *Page 1-267*

Arrow Electronics, Human Resource Information Systems Computer Programmer 2, Tiseo, Roseann M., Melville, NY *Page 1-122*

Arthur Andersen
    Director of Distance Learning Development, McGuff, Dale T., St. Charles, IL *Page 1-365*
    Director, Caudullo, Jane, Sarasota, FL *Page 1-363*
    Experience Manager, Hurst, Karen, Dunwoody, GA *Page 1-363*
    Manager, Conway, Larry J., Boston, MA *Page 1-363*
    Senior Consultant, Randles, Gary A., Chicago, IL *Page 1-366*

Arthur Andersen LLP, Consultant, Nestore, Frank S., Lancaster, PA *Page 1-365*

Arthur Andersen Technology Solutions, Senior Consultant, Townsend, Tracey, Chicago, IL *Page 1-367*

ASAP II, President, DeSantis, Lori Ann, Oakland Park, FL *Page 1-174*

ASAP Software Express, Reginal Sales Manager, Rexford, Victoria, Atlanta, GA *Page 1-120*

ASCOT Communications, Webmaster, Donato, Anthony M., Greenwood Lake, NY *Page 1-109*

Asera, Inc.
    Application Engineer, Su, Michelle Yu, Belmont, CA *Page 1-287*
    Senior Systems Architect, Lemke, Uwe, Rednvodaty, CA *Page 1-257*

Ashten Racks, Inc., Systems Administrator, Boegeman, Steven M., Irvine, CA *Page 1-123*

Associated Press
    NT Systems Engineer, Born, Lu Ann, Jackson, NJ *Page 1-299*
    Project Manager, Villegas, Danielle M., Cranbury, NJ *Page 1-299*

Associated Textile Converters, Controller, Kraut, Jeffrey B., New York, NY *Page 1-11*

Association for Computing, Publisher, Hardjowirogo, Jono, New York, NY *Page 1-16*

Astra Zeneca, Promotions Designer, Graham, Deborah L., Woodland Hills, CA *Page 1-23*

Astrazeneca Belgium, Information Systems and Information Technology Manager, Tollenaere, Caroline, Destelbergen, Belgium *Page 1-24*

Astro-Med, Inc., Senior Scientist, Minasyan, Georgiy R., Lafayette Hill, PA *Page 1-83*

AT&T
    District Manager, Bonner, Barbara D., Bridgewater, NJ *Page 1-95*
    Large Account Manager, Mixon, Daniel A., Fort Smith, AR *Page 1-102*
    Manager of Product Strategy & Development, Parker, Barry A., Basking Ridge, NJ *Page 1-103*
    Project Manager, Clan, Jean, La Grange, KY *Page 1-96*
    Senior Project Manager, Vertetis, Virginia A., Somerset, NJ *Page 1-106*
    Senior Systems Administrator, Munukutla, Srinivasa S., Edison, NJ *Page 1-102*
    Senior Systems Programmer/Administrator, Tritt, Ralph, Morristown, NJ *Page 1-105*
    Technical Consultant, Guald, Andrew G., Lincroft, NJ *Page 1-99*

AT&T Labs, Principal Technical Staff Member, Peterson, Gregory, Lincroft, NJ *Page 1-103*

AT&T Solutions/McDermott Inc. Account, Assistant Manager - Programming, Young, Carol, Lancaster, OH *Page 1-297*

AT&T Technical Services, Senior Network Engineer, Brenneman, William B., Washington, DC *Page 1-225*

AT&T Wireless Services
    Account Manager for the Information Technology National Support Services Team, Enos, Dennis, Orlando, FL *Page 1-92*
    Information Technology Manager, Gregory, Peter H., Redmond, WA *Page 1-92*

Atek Electronics Company Ltd., Field Application Engineer, Cheng, Kin Wing Horace, Kowloon, Hong Kong *Page 1-121*

Atima Technology Inc., President, Chien, David, Fremont, CA *Page 1-119*

Atkinson-Baker, Inc., Management Information Systems Director, Savage, Charles L., Glendale, CA *Page 1-167*

ATL Ultrasound, Lead Technical Writer, Fink, Dean R., Bothell, WA *Page 1-84*

Atlanta Public Schools, Director of Operational Technology & Telecommunications Department, Scott, Arthur R., Atlanta, GA *Page 1-383*

Atlantic Express, Management Information Systems Manager, Valonzo, Avelino Mark A., Staten Island, NY *Page 1-87*

Atlantic Technical Center, Information Technology Specialist, Turchiaro, Michael Louis, Coconut Creek, FL *Page 1-342*

Atlantiques Promotions, Space Management Specialist/Webmaster, St. Aubin, Roger, Longueuil, Quebec, Canada *Page 1-74*

Atmel Corporation, Senior Staff Design Engineer, Lambrache, Emil, San Jose, CA *Page 1-66*

ATS, Programmer, Grigoryev, Alex, Ellicott City, MD *Page 1-52*

Attachmate Corporation
    Senior Consultant, Brumley, Isaac, Bremerton, WA *Page 1-195*
    Senior Manager of Publications, Localization and Usability, Michael, Laura Anne, Bellevue, WA *Page 1-198*
    Technical Advisor, Marshall, Don H., Bellevue, WA *Page 1-197*

Augmentix, Inc., Systems Administrator, Stalker, Daniel E., Tucson, AZ *Page 1-190*

AUM Technologies, Inc., President, Chinnaiah, Mani A., Irvine, CA *Page 1-230*

Auraria Higher Education Center, Telecommunication Operations Manager, Dunn, Peter K., Denver, CO *Page 1-323*

Aurora Foods, Manager of Systems Development, Borgmann, Philip M., St. Louis, MO *Page 1-8*

Auto Desk Inc., CDOE Manager, Worley, Jason, Windham, NH *Page 1-297*

Auto Gas Systems Inc., Senior Software Engineer, Wood, Robert S., New Braunfels, TX *Page 1-211*

Autodesk, Inc., Manager of Desktop Technologies, Safford, Michael, Windham, NH *Page 1-188*

Automation Research Systems, Limited, Principal Information Engineer, Beebe, David H., Alexandria, VA *Page 1-171*

AV Associates, Senior Engineer, Hutchins, Todd, Montvale, NJ *Page 1-250*

Avant Go, Senior Systems Administrator, Caraballo, Roderick G., San Mateo, CA *Page 1-228*

Avantel, Project Manager, Thomas, Ivory L., Garland, TX *Page 1-105*

AverStar, Program Manager, Miles, Greg S., Greenbelt, MD *Page 1-265*

Averstar, Infosec Analyst, Rogers, James R., Chambersburg, PA *Page 1-277*

AverStar, Inc., Geospacial Services Group, Senior Technical Specialist, Whitney, Susan L., Portland, OR *Page 1-296*

Avery Dennison, FRNA, Senior Control System Engineer, Zhu, Jack J., Fort Wayne, IN *Page 1-14*

AW Chesterton Company, NT Server and Microsoft Exchange Administrator, Ludwig, Mark A., Canton, MA *Page 1-37*

B

B.R.M., Chairman, Jaworski, Zdzislaw "Jess", West Sussex, England, United Kingdom *Page 1-46*

BAART/CDP, Manager of Information Technology, Tang, John, San Francisco, CA *Page 1-306*

Babcock & Wilcox, Field Service Engineer, Spiegel, Steven M., Dallas, TX *Page 1-33*

Bacardi Ltd., Director of the Board, Danguillecourt, Sergio, Miami, FL *Page 1-9*

Bacik Consulting Service, Network Consultant, Bacik, Sandra A., Federal Way, WA *Page 1-219*

BAE Systems, Systems Administrator, Stroud, Richard, Rockville, MD *Page 1-76*

Baffin Inc., Chief Technical Officer, Sesay, Sahid, Alameda, CA *Page 1-27*

Bahrain Telecommunications Company, Senior Technical Officer, Hassan, Abdulla K. E., Manama, Bahrain *Page 1-99*

Baltimore Gas & Electric, Information Technology Technician, Lawson, Barbara D., Lusby, MD *Page 1-117*

Bank Boston, Project Manager, Fitzgerald, Patricia J., Boston, MA *Page 1-134*

Bank of America
Assistant Vice President, Rueger, Maria J., Jacksonville, FL *Page 1-134*
Associate Vice President, Schweitzer, Loren M., Dallas, TX *Page 1-134*
Senior Vice President, Eggleston, Kevin B., Jacksonville, FL *Page 1-133*
Vice President of Receivables Services, Trice, David M., College Park, GA *Page 1-134*

Bank of New York Clearing Services, Senior Network Administrator, Schultz, David A., Milwaukee, WI *Page 1-147*

Bank of New York Trust Company, Vice President of LAN Administration, Crincoli, Diane J., Jacksonville, FL *Page 1-161*

Barasch Music & Sound, Technical Director, Barasch, Mark, New York, NY *Page 1-220*

Barclays Global Investors, Trade Floor System Engineer, Tamas, Peter V., San Francisco, CA *Page 1-155*

Barco, Inc.
Director of Operations, McFarlin, David J., South Windsor, CT *Page 1-69*
Information Technology Manager, Coullard, Jeremy B., South Windsor, CT *Page 1-69*

barnesandnoble.com, Application Developer, Rosano, John L., New York, NY *Page 1-130*

BarPoint.com, Director, Romano, Robert "Rob", Fort Lauderdale, FL *Page 1-188*

Barrick Goldstrike Mines, Inc., Systems Analyst II, Roebke, Laurence R., Elko, NV *Page 1-2*

Base Technologies, Inc.
Director of Information Technologies Services, Hashmi, Kashif R., McLean, VA *Page 1-246*
Network Specialist, Allen, Carol Elizabeth, Alexandria, VA *Page 1-217*

Batelco, Manager of Internet Platform Development, Abdulla, Mahmood Ahmed, Manama, Bahrain *Page 1-216*

Baton Rouge International Inc., Software Consultant, Arumugam, Senthil K., Sayreville, NJ *Page 1-218*

Battenfeld Extlenrusionstechnik GmbH, Manager, Boettger, Hans-Bernd, Bad-Muender, Germany *Page 1-36*

BAVS Corporation, President/Principal Technical Consultant, Kale, Anil B., Jackson, MI *Page 1-252*

Baxter Healthcare Corporation
Senior Technical Analyst, Hines, Daniel J., Rolling Meadows, IL *Page 1-83*
Senior Technical Consultant, Kuczerepa, Paul R., Round Lake, IL *Page 1-83*

Baycrest Centre for Geriatric Care, Telecommunications Services Manager, McCoppen, Reid, Toronto, Ontario, Canada *Page 1-310*

Bayer Corporation, Manager of Customer & Technical Training, Rash, Jeanne, Tarrytown, NY *Page 1-24*

BBC, Inc., Management Information Systems Manager, Jordan, David S., Lynnfield, MA *Page 1-251*

BBN Technologies, Senior Manager of Engineering, Hubbell, James B., Arlington, VA *Page 1-249*

BCMEA, Information Technology Director, Vurdela, Greg J., Vancouver, British Columbia, Canada *Page 1-89*

BDC 4 You, President, Swystun, Orest Roman, Bethesda, MD *Page 1-287*

Beasley Enterprises, Management Information Systems Director, Hoggard, Robin L., Ahoskie, NC *Page 1-126*

Belimage Communications, President, Saint-Louis, Vanilo, Franklin Square, NY *Page 1-279*

Bell Atlantic
Senior Specialist for Strategic Planning, Brammer, Douglas E., Silver Spring, MD *Page 1-96*
Software Engineer, Sprouse, Matthew C., Silver Spring, MD *Page 1-105*
Systems Engineer, Gardner, Mac, Wilmington, DE *Page 1-98*

Bellcore, Research Scientist, Liu, Kevin H., Red Bank, NJ *Page 1-101*

BellSouth
Manager, Svendsen, Cary A., Atlanta, GA *Page 1-105*
Program Manager, Griffin, Lianne H., Atlanta, GA *Page 1-99*

BellSouth Business Systems, Systems Designer II, Kirkland, William Michael, Jacksonville, FL *Page 1-101*

BellSouth Communications Systems, Systems Technologist, Rook, Cynthia L., Orlando, FL *Page 1-104*

Benedict Corporation, Director of Programs, Lynk, Dennis R., Norwich, NY *Page 1-126*

Bentley Management Corporation, Manger of Networking Technologies, Wyss, Mark W., Denver, CO *Page 1-141*

Berjaya USA Group, Inc., President/Chief Executive Officer, Tan, Kenny T. H., Elmhurst, NY *Page 1-288*

Bertch Cabinet Manufacturing Inc, Management Information Systems Manager, Klein, David E., Waterloo, IA *Page 1-12*

Berwanger Overmyer Associates, Operations Manager of Financial Services, Burgoyne, Ann C., Columbus, OH *Page 1-155*

Best Foods Brazil, Information Technology Manager, Cremerius, Guillermo, Sao Paulo, Brazil *Page 1-10*

BEST! Software, Inc., Senior Network Administrator, Bachrach, Daniel A., St. Petersburg, FL *Page 1-171*

Beth Israel Medical Center, Systems Manager, Symczyk, Walter J., New York, NY *Page 1-310*

BetzDearborn division of Hercules, Inc., Technical Specialist, Tuzzo, Dominick, Croton On Hudson, NY *Page 1-5*

Bhasha, Inc., Member of Technical Staff, Dave, Maulik Avantikumar, King of Prussia, PA *Page 1-233*

Biomophic VLSI, Technical Lead Designer, Standley, David L., Thousand Oaks, CA *Page 1-67*

Birch Telecom, Inc., Manager of Information Systems Development, Hedtke, David J., Kansas City, MO *Page 1-179*

BITCOM Inc., Vice President of Hardware Development, Rostami, Sasan, Germantown, MD *Page 1-278*

Bizrate Com, Vice President of Data Systems and Operations, Patton, Robert T., Los Angeles, CA *Page 1-272*

Black & Veatch, Systems Support Specialist, Gilmore, Cary W., Overland Park, KS *Page 1-204*

Blackwell's Information Services, Manager of Information Technology, Campbell, Anne B., Blackwood, NJ *Page 1-300*

Blue Cross & Blue Shield, Senior Information Systems Manager, Ohaeri, Kenneth O., St. Paul, MN *Page 1-151*

Blue Cross & Blue Shield of Alabama
Manager of Corporate Quality Assurance, Piazza, Sonya B., Helena, AL *Page 1-151*
Systems Consultant, Howard, Jason, Birmingham, AL *Page 1-150*

Blue Cross & Blue Shield of Louisiana, Technical Trainer, Bechtel, Lawrence J., Baton Rouge, LA *Page 1-149*

Blue Cross & Blue Shield of Minnesota, Manager of Information Systems, Jablonske, Patricia J., St. Paul, MN *Page 1-150*

Blue Dragon Network, Founder/Chief Executive Officer/Webmaster, Al-Jamal, Ismail, Petaluma, CA *Page 1-217*

BMC, Quality Assurance Database Administrator, Smith, Daniel J., Austin, TX *Page 1-199*

BMC Consultants, Inc., Technology Manager, Nielsen, Thomas W., Englewood, CO *Page 1-369*

BMC Software, Director of Emerging Technologies, Waits, Julian W., Houston, TX *Page 1-200*

BMG, Information Systems and Technology Director, Leao, Flavio De Araujo, Rio de Janiero, Brazil *Page 1-302*

BMR Training Centers, PC Repair/Network Administration Supervising Instructor, Finch, Michael D., Victorville, CA *Page 1-340*

Bobbin Group Publishing, Information Technology Manager, Mullinax, Cindy Tarte, Columbia, SC *Page 1-16*

BOEC/City of Portland, Information Systems Manager, Pullen, Malcolm M., Portland, OR *Page 1-378*

Bonfiglioli, Inside Sales Supervisor, Camunias, Joel, Concorde, Ontario, Canada *Page 1-303*

Bonneville International Corporation, Information Systems Engineer, Braithwaite, Wayne N., Salt Lake City, UT *Page 1-107*

Bosch Automation Technology, Information Systems Supervisor, Schultz, Cynthia L., Racine, WI *Page 1-74*

Bowater Inc., Senior Database Administrator, Allen, Almon, Catawba, SC *Page 1-14*

Boy Scouts of America, Webmaster, Shamlin, Jim, Irving, TX *Page 1-347*

Bozell Group, Director, DeCarlo, Fred H., New York, NY *Page 1-163*

BP Amoco
    Project Manager, Jackson, Anna L., Sante Fe, TX *Page 1-2*
    Project Manager, Pribich, Jeff, Naperville, IL *Page 1-2*

Breed Technologies, Database Administrator, Anderson, Terri W., Lakeland, FL *Page 1-72*

BRF Kredit a/s, Systems Engineer, Irve, Morten, Lyngby, Denmark *Page 1-141*

Bridgewater Associates, Systems Administrator, Guild, Brian K., Greenwich, CT *Page 1-145*

Brighton School District –Technology Department, Director of Technology, Klein, Frank J., Brighton, CO *Page 1-382*

Brookings Institution, Information Technology Manager, Alvarado, Winifreda Floro, Washington, DC *Page 1-360*

Brooks Office Solutions, Owner/President, Brooks, Yvonne, Maple Shade, NJ *Page 1-225*

BRTRC, Chief Information Officer, Harte, Rebecca E., Fairfax, VA *Page 1-213*

Bryan Cave, Technology Development Senior Analyst, Farquharson, Jerome A., St. Louis, MO *Page 1-312*

BSA & I, LLP, Technical Specialist, Lysinger, Lowell J., Perkasie, PA *Page 1-312*

BsG Inc., Art Director, Campbell, Chris A., Dallas, PA *Page 1-172*

BSW International, IST Coordinator, Fleming, Sparkle N., Tulsa, OK *Page 1-350*

BTI Consulting
    Executive Director, Peermamode, Ehsan, Port Louis, Mauritius *Page 1-272*
    Information Technology and Management Consulting Manager, Matabudul, Samir, Vacoas, Mauritius *Page 1-262*

Budd Van Lines, Information Systems Director, Blumenthal, Kevin, Somerset, NJ *Page 1-300*

Bulldog Information Services, Senior Network Engineer, Burch, Scott A., San Francisco, CA *Page 1-227*

Bumgarner Global Enterprises, Principal/Chief Consultant, Bumgarner, Kenneth B., Bloomington, IL *Page 1-227*

Bureau of Indian Affairs – Navajo Area Office, Hydraulic Engineer, Nixon, Charles C., Fort Defiance, AZ *Page 1-371*

Bureau of Land Management, System Administrator, Perez, Robin L., Ridgecrest, CA *Page 1-388*

Bureau of Translation Services Inc., Senior Account Manager, Mulligan, John, Haddonfield, NJ *Page 1-185*

Burlington Northern Santa Fe Railway
    Information Systems Services Director, Haynes, Lettie K., Fort Worth, TX *Page 1-86*
    Senior Systems Developer I, Gililland, Michael E., Fort Worth, TX *Page 1-86*

Burns & Roe Enterprises, Network Systems Administrator, DeVincentis, Paul, Los Alamos, NM *Page 1-348*

Buscom MKS, Systems Integrator, Poupart, Christian, Montreal, Quebec, Canada *Page 1-128*

Business Edge Solutions, Consultant, Kretz, Richard E., Allen, TX *Page 1-255*

C

C A Consultants Int. Ltd., Director of Systems Integration, Vellanki, Ravindra V., Metairie, LA *Page 1-293*

C.W. Marini & Associates, Principal, Marini, Christopher W., San Leandro, CA *Page 1-261*

C&C Ford Sales Inc., Internet Manager, Ferraro, Brian D., Horsham, PA *Page 1-126*

C-bridge Internet Solutions, Managing Principal, Lee, William, Roseville, CA *Page 1-257*

C2 Multimedia, Lead Instructional System Designer, McKay, Michelle, Oklahoma City, OK *Page 1-254*

Cable & Wireless, ISP Manager/Head of Information Technology and Data Services, Francis, Pinkley, Castries Bwi, St. Lucia *Page 1-98*

Cable & Wireless Global Mobile, Technical Director, Hobbs, Steve, London, England, United Kingdom *Page 1-100*

CAC Systèmes, Project Manager, Loustaudaudine, Christophe, Areines, France *Page 1-76*

Cadence Design Systems, Member of Consulting Staff, Moncoqut, Diana, Glen Ridge, NJ *Page 1-265*

Cairo Barclay's Bank, Information Technology Director, Mohamed, Mohamed Ahmed, Cairo, Egypt *Page 1-137*

Cal PERS, Systems Analyst, Quint, Al, Sacramento, CA *Page 1-146*

Cal-Pak Systems, Director of Customer Service, Clark, Bruce A., Modesto, CA *Page 1-119*

California State at San Bernardino, Management Information Systems Professor, Shayo, Conrad, Ontario, CA *Page 1-332*

Call Center Services, Inc., Senior Engineer/Development & Consulting Member/Technical Staff, Joseph, Deepu, Dallas, TX *Page 1-251*

CAM Systems LLC., Senior Database Support Specialist, Chockalingam, Rajasekaran S., Saratoga, CA *Page 1-230*

Cambar Software, Project Manager, Wuosmaa, Shelby M., Charleston, SC *Page 1-201*

Cambric Corporation, Manager of Information Systems, Tester, Malcolm W., Draper, UT *Page 1-289*

Camp Cuisine, Vice President, Rubin, Nancy, Parkland, NY *Page 1-129*

Campania Management Company Inc., Management Information Systems Director, Santoli, Nicolas, Vienna, VA *Page 1-156*

Campbell Soup Company, Senior Project Manager, House, Jeffrey A., Camden, NJ *Page 1-7*

Canadian Pacific Railway, Senior Audit Specialist of Information Technology, Larson, Sheldon C., Minneapolis, MN *Page 1-86*

Canadian Space Agency, Spacecraft System Engineer, Ali, Ziad Kamil Muhammad, Saint-Hubert, Quebec, Canada *Page 1-391*

Canam Software Labs, Inc., Director, Woodburn, R. David, Newmarket, Ontario, Canada *Page 1-296*

Candle Corporation, Senior Information Developer, Rogillio, Thomas G., Glendale, CA *Page 1-278*

Cannaissance Consulting, Lead Consultant, Van Houten, Michael, Warren, NJ *Page 1-292*

Cannon, Director of Management Information Systems, Palasciano, Stephen M., Grand Island, NY *Page 1-351*

Cap Gemini America, Senior Consultant, Seetharam, Palachandra, Vienna, VA *Page 1-282*

Cap Gemini America, Inc., Principal Consultant, Gopalan, Rajan, Atlanta, GA *Page 1-242*

Capital Area Intermediate Unit, Personal Computer Support Technician, Colbert, Scott, Summerdale, PA *Page 1-314*

Capital Thinking, Inc., Systems Producer, Harper, deAnna A., New York, NY *Page 1-140*

Care Group, Senior Systems Engineer, Passe, Michael R., Boston, MA *Page 1-362*

Cargill Uganda, Ltd., Auditor/Manager of Information Technology, Wamara, Ian Kamese, Kampala, Uganda *Page 1-9*

Cargill, Inc., Corporate I/T Customer Relationship Manager, Yang, Binglin "Bing", Minnetonka, MN *Page 1-125*

Carl Seidel Consulting, Owner, Seidel, Carl W., Denton, TX *Page 1-369*

Carleton Corporation, Manager of Customer Educational Services, Shaw, M. Lea, Billerica, MA *Page 1-189*

Carlsbad Municipal School District, Systems Engineer, West, Rachel A., Carlsbad, NM *Page 1-319*

Carlson Hospitality Worldwide, Manager of Information Technology, Monson, Barbara E., Oceanside, CA *Page 1-111*

Carlyle, Inc., Data and Voice Account Manager, Guyton, Thomas C., Seattle, WA *Page 1-178*

Caro Research, Analyst, Nova, William E., Waltham, MA *Page 1-358*

Carolina Manufacturer's Service, Inc., President, Marino, Michael A., Winston-Salem, NC *Page 1-361*

Carrier Saudi Arabia, Information Technology Manager, Jathanna, Kenneth S., Riyadh, Saudi Arabia *Page 1-122*

Carroll Technical Institute, President, Ayers, Janet B., Carrollton, GA *Page 1-335*

CAS Inc., Vice President, Lord, John D., Pelham, NY *Page 1-4*

Case Corporation, Manager of Information System Training, Misirian, Nathan J., Racine, WI *Page 1-35*

Catalina Marketing, Manager of Store Systems, Bates, Christopher A., Tampa, FL *Page 1-165*

Catalyst 2020, Founder, Ciabatoni, Linda, Arlington, VA *Page 1-361*

Catalyst Software Evaluation Centers Inc., Partner, Joeckel, Tamie, Dallas, TX *Page 1-179*

Catapult Software Training, Client Manager, Tripaldi, Daniel J. R., New FairField, CT *Page 1-291*

Catellus Development Corporation, Director of Information Services, Nicholson, Bill, San Francisco, CA *Page 1-160*

Catholic Charities, Management Information Systems Manager, Bailey, William D., San Jose, CA *Page 1-344*

Catholic Charities of Buffalo, Management Information Systems Director, Hamm, Keith R., Buffalo, NY *Page 1-344*

CBM Business Machines Inc., General Manager/Vice President of Sales and Marketing, Felix, Donald F., Johnstown, PA *Page 1-48*

CBS, Senior Network Engineer, Erickson, Scott W., New York, NY *Page 1-107*

CBSI, Senior Consultant, Maltais, John R., Springfield, MA *Page 1-183*

CBSI - Computer Based Systems, Inc., An AverStar Company, Principal Programmer Analyst, LaGrange, Palmer V., Fairfax, VA *Page 1-181*

CCG Consulting Associates, Managing Partner, Wheatland, Kevin, Stockholm, Sweden *Page 1-296*

CCL, Director, Shen, Li-Sheng, Hsinchu, Taiwan *Page 1-361*

CCL Label, Technical Development Manager, Nicholson, Peter D., Ontario, CA *Page 1-37*

CCNE, Assistant Director, Heitman, Evelyn N., Washington, DC *Page 1-345*

CCW, Vice President/Consultant, Lechner, Suzanne L., Fond du Lac, WI *Page 1-182*

CDS Inc., Senior Developer, Fanshteyn, Timur, New York, NY *Page 1-175*

Cellstar, Network Specialist, Registe, Martin P., Carrollton, TX *Page 1-122*

Cendant Corporation, Senior Technical Writer, Croswell, Jerry D., Trumbull, CT *Page 1-363*

Centers for Disease Control, Programmer/Analyst, Fehd, Ronald J., Atlanta, GA *Page 1-360*

Centillion Computer Services, Inc., Owner/President/Consultant, Graul, Charles F., Largo, FL *Page 1-243*

Central Electric, Information Technology Specialist, Hare, Angela D., Sanford, NC *Page 1-114*

Century High School, Network Manager, Hall, Michael, Hillsboro, OR *Page 1-315*

Ceridian Performance Partners, Manager, Network Services, Ransden, Eric S., Boston, MA *Page 1-369*

Cerner Corporation, Cerner Virtual University, Instructional Designer/Senior Learning Analyst, Gander, Sharon L., Kansas City, MO *Page 1-323*

CEXEC, Inc., Senior Procurement Analyst, Tuttle, Peter G., Dulles, VA *Page 1-292*

CGI, Consultant, Gatewood, David A., Nashville, TN *Page 1-239*

Chain Link Technologies Inc., Software Developer, Herron, Kristine M., Sunnyvale, CA *Page 1-179*

Chain Store Guide, Director of Systems Development and Production, Darmenio, Greg, Tampa, FL *Page 1-128*

Channel Communications, Field Engineer, Bradish, Edward, Wyano, PA *Page 1-108*

Charles J. Miller, Inc., Management Information Systems Director, Shepard, Peter J., Hampstead, MD *Page 1-4*

Charles Schwab, Senior Project Coordinator, Gallegos, Joanne C., Danville, CA *Page 1-142*

Charter One Bank, Project Administrator, Hamner, Clinton W., Middleburg Heights, OH *Page 1-135*

Chase Manhattan Bank, Database Designer/Information System Developer, Mui, Henry M., New York, NY *Page 1-135*

Chase Manhattan Mortgage Corporation, Senior Technical Officer, Tramontana, Richard M., Edison, NJ *Page 1-141*

Check Point Software Technology Ltd., Performance Measurement Analyst, Finley, Kenneth W., Frisco, TX *Page 1-236*

Checkfast, Director of Management Information Systems, Blaylock, William A., Salt Lake City, UT *Page 1-138*

Chesapeake Display & Packaging, Applications Project Manager, Wynn, Sherri Peterson, Winston-Salem, NC *Page 1-14*

Chesapeake Sciences, Staff Engineer, Jamieson, John M., Millersville, MD *Page 1-205*

Chester Housing Authority, Management Information Systems Technician, Tong, Vincent S., Chester, PA *Page 1-389*

Chicago Microsystems, Software and Hardware Integrator, Ares, Julian Sol, Chicago, IL *Page 1-218*

Chicago Police Department, Senior Administrator, Tuomey, Michael Sean, Chicago, IL *Page 1-377*

Chicago Title & Trust, Network Administrator, Nguyen, Tony H., Chatsworth, CA *Page 1-185*

Chiron America, Inc., Show Manager/Applications Engineer, Wamsley, Alan Maurice, Charlotte, NC *Page 1-38*

Chr. Hansen, Inc., Telecommunications Manager, Wahn, Norman A., Milwaukee, WI *Page 1-10*

Christian Educational Ministries, Systems Director, Harris, Donna L., Tyler, TX *Page 1-341*

Chubb Computer Services
    Account Manager, Bellak, Rodney S., Parsippany, NJ *Page 1-222*
    Instructor Development Manager, Bayman, Richard P., Parsippany, NJ *Page 1-221*

CHZM Hill, Senior Project Manager/Prinicpal Technologist, Rippon, Dana W., Redding, CA *Page 1-349*

CIBC Offshore Banking Services Corporation, Information Technology Specialist, Matthews, Neil A., St. Michael, Barbados *Page 1-143*

Ciber Custom Solutions Group, Consultant, Craven, Brett, Overland Park, KS *Page 1-173*

CIBER Enterprise Application Services, Senior Oracle Database Administrator, Pattock, Suzanne Sacek, Carnegie, PA *Page 1-186*

CIMdata, Inc., Senior Consultant, MacKrell, John, Ann Arbor, MI *Page 1-260*

Cinesite, Digital Texture Artist, Caspary, Ruth, Los Angeles, CA *Page 1-304*

Cisco Systems, Inc.
    Business Development Manager, Gaither, Mark A., San Jose, CA *Page 1-59*
    CAD Applications Engineer, Batmazian, Krikor, Santa Clara, CA *Page 1-58*
    Global Project Management Advocate, Saladis, Frank P., Staten Island, NY *Page 1-62*
    Hardware Design Engineer, Fernandez, Marino A., Chelmsford, MA *Page 1-58*
    Senior Engineer, Gong, Youhong Wade, Burlington, MA *Page 1-59*
    Senior Manager of Support Services Market, Nachlis, Mark Neal, Belmont, CA *Page 1-61*
    Solutions Project Manager, Garg, Arun, San Jose, CA *Page 1-59*
    Technical Leader, Chang, David W., San Jose, CA *Page 1-58*
    Web Architect, Nagarajan, Senthil Kumar, Union City, CA *Page 1-61*

Citicorp International Communications Inc., Technical Engineer, Peterson, Randy, Sioux Falls, SD *Page 1-135*

CitiFinancial, Systems/Operations Analyst of the Investment Recovery Division, Hermann, Edwin C., Owings Mills, MD *Page 1-138*

Citigroup, Inc., Vice President of Data Center, Recchioni, Mario J., Las Vegas, NV *Page 1-135*

Citrix System, Inc., Group Manager, Sitterberg, Wolfgang, Fort Lauderdale, FL *Page 1-190*

City College, Professor of Computer and Information Systems, Forman, Lawrence, San Diego, CA *Page 1-323*

City College of New York, Assistant Professor, Li, Xuhong "Linda", New York, NY *Page 1-327*

City Mortgage Corporation, Computer Department Manager, Hoggard, Kevin, Anchorage, AK *Page 1-140*

City of Albuquerque, Network Information Systems Manager, Van Pelt, Dane, Albuquerque, NM *Page 1-375*

City of Appleton, Director of Information Services, Liske, Scott J., Appleton, WI *Page 1-373*

City of Asbury Park Police, Systems Administrator, Jacobs, Michael P., Asbury Park, NJ *Page 1-377*

City of College Station, Systems Analyst, Silhavy, Mark A., College Station, TX *Page 1-374*

City of El Paso, Network Administrator, Long, Raymond, El Paso, TX *Page 1-373*

City of Greenfield, Director of Telecommunications, Noble, Michael, Greenfield, IN *Page 1-373*

City of Irving, Software Services Manager, Mayer, John W., Irving, TX *Page 1-373*

City of Laramie, Information Systems Analyst, Hardgrove, Nicholas R., Laramie, WY *Page 1-372*

City of Las Vegas, Systems Analyst, Phillips, Craig A., Las Vegas, NV *Page 1-373*

City of Mount Vernon, Manager of Information Systems, Kleppe, Kim A., Mount Vernon, WA *Page 1-373*

City of Orlando, Systems Security Officer, Thompson, Douglas, Orlando, FL *Page 1-374*

City of Owasso, Civil Engineering Technician, Duggan, Sheryl A., Owasso, OK *Page 1-372*

City of Oxford, Director of Management Information Systems, Ritcher, Michael A., Oxford, OH *Page 1-374*

City of Pensacola, Director of Management Information Systems, Raby, John M., Pensacola, FL *Page 1-374*

City of Virginia Beach Department of Public Utilities, Systems Analyst II, Barton, Robert J., Virginia Beach, VA *Page 1-390*

Clarkston Potomac, SAP Consultant, Winter, W. Scott, Durham, NC *Page 1-296*

Clarus Software, Product/Consulting Competency Manager, Kramer, Daune C., Marietta, GA *Page 1-181*

ClearCommerce Corporation, Senior Principal, Shprints, Eduard, Austin, TX *Page 1-283*

Clecslov Inc., Chief Executive Officer/President, Jaffery, Qudsia A., Cedar Hill, TX *Page 1-250*

Client Server Consulting, Operations Manager, Goldburgh, Joyce, Bensenville, IL *Page 1-241*

Clinical Pharmacologic Research Communications, Product Information Coordinator, Renner, Amy, Morgantown, WV *Page 1-49*

Clinton Electronics Corporation, Systems Administrator, Terrell, Joseph A., Loves Park, IL *Page 1-63*

CN Bioscience, Senior Applications Analyst, Cofer, Eric C., San Diego, CA *Page 1-22*

Coastal Securities LP, Systems Administrator/OTC Trader, Alsedek, Steven M., Dallas, TX *Page 1-147*

Coastal Technologies Group, President/Senior Consultant, Kane, Richard L., Boca Raton, FL *Page 1-252*

Coconino Community College, Systems Analyst/Oracle Database Administrator, Wymore, Tess, Flagstaff, AZ *Page 1-339*

Code Hennessy & Simmons, Manager of Information Systems, De Shazer, Ronelle, Chicago, IL *Page 1-142*

Coldwater Creek, Data Center Manager, Adkins, Jeffrey M., Mineral Wells, WV *Page 1-130*

Coleman Research Corporation, Information Systems Director, Hibbs, Paul A., Fairfax, VA *Page 1-247*

Colgate University, Network Systems Administrator, Howell, Ernest W., Ilion, NY *Page 1-325*

College of the Sequoias, Dean of Technology, Hollabaugh, Timothy A., Fresno, CA *Page 1-337*

Collins & Collins Consulting, Inc., President, Collins, Cynthia A., Lake Forest, CA *Page 1-231*

Colorado Springs Utilities, Applications Lead/Y2K Project Manager, Rizzuto, Alan, Colorado Springs, CO *Page 1-116*

Colorscope, Inc., Systems Manager, Tan, Aik W., Monterey Park, CA *Page 1-166*

Colour Scan Company Private Limited, Production Manager, Chia, Teck-Hng, Singapore, Singapore *Page 1-20*

Columbia HCA, Information Systems Audit Supervisor, Hubbs, Bart L., Nashville, TN *Page 1-311*

Columbia University Law School, Assistant Director of Academic Services, Chua, Kristine U., New York, NY *Page 1-321*

Comcast, Director of Network Engineering, Lorenzi, David L., Oaks, PA *Page 1-108*

Comcast Telecommunications, Internet Sales Consultant, Rutter, Eric, Cherry Hill, NJ *Page 1-279*

ComCore, President, Cary, John, Atlanta, GA *Page 1-362*

ComDyn Group, LLC, Information Systems Consultant, Stewart, Winston M., Chattanooga, TN *Page 1-286*

Comforce Company, Consultant, Connell, Donna M., Cumming, GA *Page 1-167*

Comforce Info Tech, Consultant, Causey, Gary D., Dike, TX *Page 1-167*

Command Web Offset, Systems Analyst/Management Information Systems Manager, Awan, Tajammul H., Secaucus, NJ *Page 1-17*

Commerce One
Client Engagement Manager, Kenney, Sean R., Dublin, CA *Page 1-196*
Technical Manager, White, Kimberly A., Orinda, CA *Page 1-200*

Commercial Data Corporation, Programmer/Analyst, Goodwin, Timothy A., Memphis, TN *Page 1-242*

Commonwealth Credit Union, Manager of Information Systems, Graham, Douglas M., Frankfort, KY *Page 1-136*

Commonwealth Energy, Director of Information Services, Howard, Pat E., Tustin, CA *Page 1-114*

Commonwealth Health Corporation, Systems Analyst, Willis, Crissy M., Bowling Green, KY *Page 1-153*

Commonwealth of Virginia - Department of Information Technology, Technology Consulting Branch Manager, Hunter, Alvin A., Richmond, VA *Page 1-372*

Community Medical Center, Director of Information Services, Robbins, John Edward, Scranton, PA *Page 1-309*

CommVault System, Systems Engineer, Wonsang, Willmer B., Frisco, TX *Page 1-193*

Companion Tech, Systems Engineer, Majcher, Jeff L., Ridgeland, MS *Page 1-261*

Compaq Computer Corporation
Mail and Messaging Consultant, Levin, Maria, Methuen, MA *Page 1-42*
Project Manager, Kaltenbach, Shirley J., Nashua, NH *Page 1-41*
Senior Consultant, Larson, Kenneth O., Schaumburg, IL *Page 1-42*
Senior Enterprise Consultant, Wilson, Ralph Thomas, Newtown, CT *Page 1-46*
Senior Solution Architect, Pringle, James W., Redding, CA *Page 1-44*
Systems Manager, Monteiro, Walkiria, Sao Paulo, Brazil *Page 1-44*

Compath Inc., Manager of Engineering Services, McCray, Marc S., Fairfax, VA *Page 1-302*

Complete Business Solutions
Director, Kanitkar, Suhas R., Farmington Hills, MI *Page 1-252*
Senior Software Consultant, Madhusudan, Neeruganti, Baltimore, MD *Page 1-260*

Compsat Technology, Consultant, Tocco, Anthony J., St. Clair, MI *Page 1-210*

Compunet Engineering, Systems Engineer, Hite, Charles Aaron, Overland Park, KS *Page 1-247*

Computer Associates, Project Manager, Ciarlette, Karen L., Oakbrook Terrace, IL *Page 1-173*

Computer Consultant, President, Winter, Edward A., Revere, MA *Page 1-296*

Computer Curriculum Corporation
Curriculum Specialist, Ernst, Kelli A., Alexandria, VA *Page 1-203*
Data Center Manager, Chow, Thomas, Sunnyvale, CA *Page 1-202*
Manager of Professional Services, Little, Dinah B., Annapolis, MD *Page 1-206*

Computer Design & Integration, Vice President, Robinson, Mark K., Teterboro, NJ *Page 1-277*

Computer Horizons Corporation, Regional Vice President, Geist, Thomas E., Denver, CO *Page 1-240*

Computer Land, Senior Systems Engineer, Loechner, Erich Karl, San Diego, CA *Page 1-206*

Computer Learning Centers, Inc.
Information Technology/Information Systems Instructor, Landry, Karen, Methuen, MA *Page 1-341*
Lead Instructor, Frisvold, Barbara L., Laurel, MD *Page 1-340*

Computer Network Technology, Senior Director, Brunzell, Barbara J., Minneapolis, MN *Page 1-226*

Computer Savers, Inc., Presidents, Ochoa, Ruben J., New York, NY *Page 1-270*

Computer Sciences Corporation
Computer Programmer/Analyst, Long, Barbara Anne, Crystal City, VA *Page 1-206*
Computer Scientist, Cherry, Donald Thomas, Meriden, CT *Page 1-202*
Director of Desktop and Distributed Systems, Murawaski, Michael R., Warren, MI *Page 1-207*
Director, Bullock, Steven H., Rockville, MD *Page 1-201*
Program Manager, Edwards, Albert L., San Diego, CA *Page 1-203*
Senior Business Analyst, Delgado-Lopez, Lupe, Austin, TX *Page 1-203*
Senior Infosec Engineer, Friend, Richard E., Millersville, MD *Page 1-204*
Senior Manager, Moxley, Greg D., Hampton, VA *Page 1-207*
System Architect, Kolber, Jeffrey A., West Orange, NJ *Page 1-205*
Systems Administrator, Matsumoto, T. Steve, Sterling, VA *Page 1-207*

Computer Services, Telecommunications Manager, Henderson, Melody J., Hughes Springs, TX *Page 1-246*

Computer System Consulting, Owner, Yelich, Scott D., Santa Fe, NM *Page 1-297*

Computer-Information Services Consulting, President, Ranalli, John, Wilmington, NC *Page 1-276*

Compuware Corporation, ASQ Certified Software Quality Engineer and Quality Auditor, Swafford, Martin H., Addison, TX *Page 1-191*

Comsearch, Programmer Analyst, Mills, Dennis Joseph, Reston, VA *Page 1-61*

Comsys, Director of Operations, Barta, Barbie, Dallas, TX *Page 1-220*

ComTech Labs, President/Chief Executive Officer, Weiss, Richard A., Stanhope, NJ *Page 1-295*

Concert, Manager Network Management Systems, Abramczyk, Edward S., Reston, VA *Page 1-95*

Condor Technologies, Senior Consultant, Keshoojee, Sadrudin B., Edison, NJ *Page 1-253*

Connect South, Network Operations Center Specialist, Thelin, Bradford, Austin, TX *Page 1-192*

Connection Staffing, Inc., Information Technology Division Manager, Mohammed, David S., Tampa, FL *Page 1-170*

Connectria, Senior Data Architect, Nandi, Somnath, Maple Shade, NJ *Page 1-267*

Conseco Services LLC, Senior Corporate Systems Consultant, Conover, Cary Donovan, Irving, TX *Page 1-300*

Consolidated Natural Gas, Manager of Systems, Carter, Jeffrey W., Pittsburgh, PA *Page 1-115*

Consultech, Inc., LAN Administrator, Beelman, Misty M., West Des Moines, IA *Page 1-384*

Consulting Strategies, Chief Executive Officer, Freedman, Richard, Shawnee Mission, KS *Page 1-238*

Consumer Financial Network, Director, Hemsey, Michael F., Atlanta, GA *Page 1-301*

Continental Airlines, Senior Analyst of Electronic Product Development, Knotts, Martha J., Houston, TX *Page 1-89*

Continental Forge Company, Managing Director, Van Kallen, Ramon G. W., Compton, CA *Page 1-34*

Continuous Forms & Checks, Inc., Management Information Systems Manager, McLemore, Shannon, Peachtree City, GA *Page 1-138*

Contra Costa County, Senior Systems Analyst, Flowers, Michael R., Martinez, CA *Page 1-371*

Contract Computer Services, Vice President/Corporate, Golebiewski, Debbie A., Tupelo, MS *Page 1-241*

Contractors State Licensing Board, Data Processing Manager II, Lee, Edwin Y., Sacramento, CA *Page 1-391*

Control Contractors, Inc., Software Engineer, Snyder, Larry, Seattle, WA *Page 1-86*

Control Data Systems, Inc., Director of Channel Development, Therens, Gary A., Arden Hills, MN *Page 1-289*

Control Systems International, Software Engineer, Budd, Daniel L., Merriam, KS *Page 1-51*

Cook Yancey King and Galloway, Manager of Information Systems, Mongon, William H., Shreveport, LA *Page 1-312*

Cookson Fibers, Inc., IT Manager, Oo, Zaw W., Ansonville, NC *Page 1-11*

Coolidge Wall Womsley Lombard, Information Systems Manager, Clayton, Brian R., Dayton, OH *Page 1-312*

Cooper Communities, Inc., Assistant Database Administrator, Young, Leigh Irish, Bella Vista, AR *Page 1-160*

Cooper Tire Company, Network Specialist, Carlton, Rodney A., Texarkana, AR *Page 1-28*

Cooperative Resource Services, Vice President of Management Information Systems, Petsche, Christopher M., Cleveland, OH *Page 1-168*

Cooperative Resources International, Security Analyst/Systems Engineer, Pinkall-Pollei, Richard G., Verona, WI *Page 1-302*

Coovi.com, Research and Development Manager, Vincken, Wim, Bat Yam, Israel *Page 1-164*

Copeland Associates, Inc., Network Engineer, Bearce, James E., East Brunswick, NJ *Page 1-156*

Corepoint Technologies, Director of Information Technology, Smith, Steven E., Indianapolis, IN *Page 1-199*

Coretec, Inc., Information Technology Manager, Yearwood, Michael, Toronto, Ontario, Canada *Page 1-63*

Cornerstone Systems Solutions, Inc., President/Chief Executive Officer, Salaver, Timothy R., Las Vegas, NV *Page 1-188*

Corning Community College, Instructional Technologist, Usack, Lynn A., Corning, NY *Page 1-339*

Corning Inc., Program Office Manager, Cobb, Gary A., Wilmington, NC *Page 1-69*

Corning Inc. Science Division Products, Information Technology Manager, McGary, Steven M., Acton, MA *Page 1-69*

Corporate Air, Management Information Systems Director, Klatt, Bruce K., Billings, MT *Page 1-90*

Cote D'Ivoire Telecom, Consultant, Vassidiki, Soumahoro, Abidjan, Ivory Coast (Cote d'Ivoire) *Page 1-105*

Cothern Computer Systems, Inc., Co-Owner, Cothern, Rick, Jackson, MS *Page 1-173*

Cotton and Allen, Information Technology Consultant, Cornwell, Kevin W., Louisville, KY *Page 1-352*

Country Oven, Inc., Systems Coordinator, Frye, Randy E., Harrisburg, PA *Page 1-129*

County of Cuyahoga, Design Engineer, Saunders, Donald A., Cleveland, OH *Page 1-374*

County of Ingham, Management Information Services, Database Administrator, Le, Long Minh, Mason, MI *Page 1-373*

Courage Center - Department of MIS, Systems and Database Administrator, Botnan, Michael J., Hamel, MN *Page 1-311*

Covad Communications, Senior Systems Engineer, Olexa, Christopher M., McLean, VA *Page 1-270*

Covance, Director, Clinical Data Management Operations for North America, Markel, Lisa Anne, Nashville, TN *Page 1-358*

Covenant Health, User Support Analyst, Groves, Richard D., Knoxville, TN *Page 1-308*

Cox Target Media, Project Lead, Longgood, Donna R., Largo, FL *Page 1-20*

CPU, Inc., Systems Administrator, Murray, James M., Metairie, LA *Page 1-267*

Craig County Public Schools, Technology Director, Morris, Adele G., Salem, VA *Page 1-382*

Cranel Inc., Integration Service Manager, Kaufman, Jeremy, Columbus, OH *Page 1-119*

Creative Computers & Networking, Inc., Chief Executive Officer, Farage, Regina M., Brooklyn, NY *Page 1-236*

Creative Labs, Inc., Software Engineering Manager, Songy, Michael P., Milpitas, CA *Page 1-190*

CreMoS Partners, Senior Director - Business Solution Methodology, Francis, Ben Allen, Lewisville, TX *Page 1-237*

Cressoft Inc., Account Manager, Shami, Azmat Bilal, Englewood, CO *Page 1-189*

Cross Country Home Service, Project Manager, Perez, Pedro P., Parkland, FL *Page 1-155*

Crossman Post Production, President/Partner, Crossman, John Neal, Sandy, UT *Page 1-304*

Crowder Construction, Management Information Systems Director, Hodgin, Charles L., Charlotte, NC *Page 1-5*

Crown American Hotels Company, Information Systems Director, Brady, Brian J., Johnstown, PA *Page 1-162*

Crown Communications Inc., Project Manager, Colaianne, John J., Canonsburg, PA *Page 1-97*

Crystallize, Senior Software Architect, Fey, Eugenia, West Bloomfield, MI *Page 1-175*

CS Computer Services Holdings Ltd., Chief Executive Officer, van der Laan, Annette, Johannesburg, South Africa *Page 1-292*

CS Cybernetic Systems AB, Owner, Nilsson, Sigward, Vallentuna, Sweden *Page 1-207*

CSC
Senior Network Engineer, Velez, George W., Jackson, NJ *Page 1-211*
Technical Project Manager, Noble, Amanda, Richmond, VA *Page 1-208*

CSC Consulting
Principal Consultant, Kawasaki, Gregory, Waltham, MA *Page 1-205*
Senior Consultant, Walls, Georgette F., West Orange, NJ *Page 1-211*

CSC Consulting & Systems Integration, Senior Consultant, Vallon, Ronald Martin, Waltham, MA *Page 1-211*

CSC Consulting Firm, LAN Administrator, Belousov, Katrina, Cincinnati, OH *Page 1-201*

CSG Systems International, LAN Administrator, Smoot, Brian D., Englewood, CO *Page 1-284*

CSI Maximus, Inc., Software Engineer, Glaeser, Paul H., Wayne, PA *Page 1-177*

CTAP, Technology Mentor, Legutki, Gregory W., San Bernardino, CA *Page 1-206*

CTech, Chief Executive Officer, Woodlee, Jason, West Orange, NJ *Page 1-193*

CVIS, Applications Engineer, Woodworth, Juanita D., Coarsegold, CA *Page 1-129*

Cyberdeck Consultants, President, Murphy, Brian E., Pittsburgh, PA *Page 1-266*

Cyberguard, Manager of Business Development, Henry, Paul A., Fort Lauderdale, FL *Page 1-247*

Cyberjava, Co-Founder/Internet Consultant, Monaghan, Michael J., Hollywood, CA *Page 1-265*

Cyberlogic Business Services, President/Founder, Butcher, Linda L., Camarillo, CA *Page 1-227*

CyberPatriot.com, President, Murphy, Jack, Myrtle Beach, SC *Page 1-266*

Cybersurfers, Systems Administrator, Domingue, Jeremy, Tehachapi, CA *Page 1-234*

Cyberweb Telecommunications, Executive Director, Johnson, Patricio, Quito, Ecuador *Page 1-180*

Cylogix, Senior Systems Engineer, Mukhopadhyay, Kalyan, Edison, NJ *Page 1-266*

Cylogix, Inc., Senior Systems Analyst, Ponakala, Srinivasa R., Plainsboro, NJ *Page 1-274*

Cynrede Inc., President/Chief Executive Officer, Fitzgerald, Kevin A., Lake Forest, CA *Page 1-237*

Cypress Semiconductor Corporation, Staff Engineer, Bandyopadhyay, Abhijit, Cupertine, CA *Page 1-63*

Cyras Systems, Inc., Design Engineer, Omran, Abraham, Fremont, CA *Page 1-56*

Cytera Systems, Director of Strategic and Analytical Services, Forrester, Janice, Portland, OR *Page 1-237*

D

D/FW Hospital Council, Information Services Director, Scott, Eric H., Irving, TX *Page 1-344*

DACOR, Network Manager, Garza, Johnny Kim, Pasadena, CA *Page 1-52*

DaimlerChrysler Aerospace Orbital Systems Inc., Computer Programmer, Aguero Blanco, Marjorie, Houston, TX *Page 1-170*

Dan River, Inc., Data Translation Specialist, Sutherland, Stephanie K., Danville, VA *Page 1-11*

Dana Corporation, Information Systems Manager, Cox, David W., Fort Wayne, IN *Page 1-73*

Dana Unlimited, Consultant/Systems Engineer/Systems Administration/LAN Management, Ehlig, Dana Carl, Altadena, CA *Page 1-235*

Data Downlink Corporation, Software Developer, Tharaken, Ajit, New York, NY *Page 1-289*

Data Management Services, Sales Consultant/Sales Engineer, Oglensky, David S., Cedar Knolls, NJ *Page 1-185*

Database Consultants, Inc.
Technical Consultant, Lear, Gregory L., San Antonio, TX *Page 1-256*
Technical Consultant, Mankala, Srinivas, Austin, TX *Page 1-261*
Technical Leader, Cairns, Joe A., Dallas, TX *Page 1-227*

Database Technologies, Program Manager, Schomaker, Paul A., Boca Raton, FL *Page 1-209*

Datainterdev, Ltd., Owner, Tansanu, Dan, Montreal, Quebec, Canada *Page 1-288*

Datalink Computer Products Inc., President/Owner, Bedi, Vickram A., Mount Kisco, NY *Page 1-221*

Datapoint Corporation, Staff Systems Programmer, Abercrombie, Richard D., San Antonio, TX *Page 1-170*

DataSoft LLC.com, Chief Information Officer/Chief Executive Officer, Poppitz, Mickey, Arvada, CO *Page 1-274*

DATESSA, Business Consultant, Toth, Stefan, Sodertalje, Sweden *Page 1-291*

David Collins, Independent Consultant, Collins, W. David, Waxahachie, TX *Page 1-231*

David Gomez & Associates, Inc., Senior Consultant, Larkin, CorDell R., Chicago, IL *Page 1-168*

Davis Standard/HES, Senior Designer, Rosivach, Chris, Paucatuck, CT *Page 1-36*

dba Computer Consultant, Owner/Consultant, Sawyer, Thomas Eric, Tulsa, OK *Page 1-280*

dba computer moms☐, Certified Trainer, Beall, Carlene, Austin, TX *Page 1-300*

Ddavis Software Consulting, Inc., President/Principal Consultant, Davis, Derold L., Maple Grove, MN *Page 1-233*

De Bellas & Co., Vice President, Brickley, Douglas J., Houston, TX *Page 1-142*

Dean Oliver International, Chemicals Control Engineer, Johnson, Ginger Sears, Savannah, GA *Page 1-205*

Debug Computers, LAN Administrator, Sepulveda, Pedro J., Cabo Rojo, Puerto Rico *Page 1-282*

DecisionOne, Senior Test Engineer, Heald, Frederick A., Columbus, OH *Page 1-216*

Defense Information Systems Agency, Department of Defense, Information Management Officer, Leonelli, John A., Arlington, VA *Page 1-394*

Defense Research Establishment, Director of Research, Svensson, Per, Stockholm, Sweden *Page 1-396*

DEISSC2, Senior Information Assurance Policy Analyst, Espinoza, Dimas, San Antonio, TX *Page 1-392*

Delaware County Information Services, Geographic Information Systems Specialist, Reese, Jeffrey D., Muncie, IN *Page 1-302*

Deloitte Consulting, Manager, Ingersoll, Carrie D., Renton, WA *Page 1-364*

Delphi Automotive, Algorithm Engineer, Roden, Mark Philip, Fenton, MI *Page 1-118*

Delphi Saginaw Steering Systems, Consultant, Newton, Clifford R., Saginaw, MI *Page 1-74*

Dentsply International, Engineer, Hersey, Phil A., York, PA *Page 1-83*

Department of Anthropology, Director of Collections Management, Linder-Linsley, Sue, Dallas, TX *Page 1-327*

Department of Defense, Systems Administrator, Naff, James M., Indianapolis, IN *Page 1-395*

Department of Defense Inspector General, Senior Technical Support Auditor, Forte, Andrew L., Arlington, VA *Page 1-393*

Department of Energy at Idaho National Engineering and Environmental Laboratory, Project Manager, Peterson, Barbara L., Rigby, ID *Page 1-361*

Department of Finance for State of California, Staff Information System Analyst, Strutton, James D., Sacramento, CA *Page 1-380*

Department of Justice, Immigration Naturalization Service, Computer Specialist, Caffey, Jeffrey L., Washington, DC *Page 1-375*

Department of Radiology, St. Luke's Hospital, Consultant Radiologist, Vassallo, Pierre, Gwardamangia, Malta *Page 1-309*

Department of Veterans Affairs, Associate Deputy Assistant Secretary for Telecommunications, Bubniak, Robert P., Washington, DC *Page 1-386*

Desert De Oro Foods Inc., Systems Administrator, Wilson, Sheryl A., Kingman, AZ *Page 1-129*

Design Fabricators, Safety and Environmental Manager, Little, Frank, Lafayette, CO *Page 1-54*

Destia, Voice Engineer, Kupfer, Mendy, Brooklyn, NY *Page 1-101*

Dethmers Manufacturing Company, Engineer, Blankers, Galen C., Boyden, IA *Page 1-35*

Devnet Systems Corporation, Administrator/Partner, Colon, Ana Iris, Guaynabo, Puerto Rico *Page 1-231*

DeVry Institute of Technology, Software Developer/Network Specialist, Landis, Damon L., Irving, TX *Page 1-327*

Dewpoint, Inc., Director of e-Solution Services, Harker, Larry, Carmel, IN *Page 1-245*

Dexia Bank International in Luxembourg, Information Technology Manager, Fries, Michel, Athus, Belgium *Page 1-137*

Dexter Shoe Company, Manager of Desktop and Data Communication Services, Tash, Preston K., Dexter, ME *Page 1-30*

DI, Senior Programmer/Analyst, Kislow, Christopher K., Egg Harbor City, NJ *Page 1-60*

Diamond Packaging, Information Systems Director, Fiacco, Philip, Rochester, NY *Page 1-14*

Diamond State Port Corporation, Director of Management Information Systems, Thomas, Inigo, Wilmington, DE *Page 1-89*

Digiquest, President/Chief Executive Officer, Reddy, K. B., Riverside, CA *Page 1-112*

Digital Access Control, Director of Technology, Donoghue, Matthew T., Chantilly, VA *Page 1-234*

Digital Conversions, Web Applications Developer, Balian, Gerair D., Tustin, CA *Page 1-220*

Digital Equipment Corporation, Vice President, Weiss, Abbott D., Marlborough, MA *Page 1-295*

Digital Internet Services Corporation, Executive Vice President, Vandenbos, Rod, Indian Wells, CA *Page 1-112*

Digital Natcom Company, Manager of Logistics and Service Center, Bhatty, Zuliqar Ahmed, Riyadh, Saudi Arabia *Page 1-222*

Digital Pyramid, Executive Manager, Hoda, Sami A., Pomona, CA *Page 1-247*

Digital Scanning Corporation, Information Technology Manager, Chua, Chephren, Singapore, Singapore *Page 1-48*

DigitalXpress, President/Vice President Marketing and Business Development, Wright, Joel S., St. Paul, MN *Page 1-113*

Digitrade Inc., Chief Technology Officer, Tsung, Theodore T., New York, NY *Page 1-192*

DIMON International, Inc., End User Services Manager, Taylor, J. West, Farmville, NC *Page 1-10*

Dinoex, Owner/General Manager, Meyer, Dirk, Hessen, Germany *Page 1-265*

DirectNet Telecommunications, Project Manager, Petrov, Alex, Newport Beach, CA *Page 1-111*

DIS-Process S.L., Managing Director, Gaspar, Victor, Bilbao, Spain *Page 1-204*

Disabled Citizen Alliance for Independence, Executive Director, Hagemeier, Juanita E., Steelville, MO *Page 1-343*

Disney Consumer Products, Information Technology Manager, Rudstrom, Lennart, Cannes, France *Page 1-130*

Dispatch Printing Company, Corporate Telecommunications Manager, Veach, Dale L., Columbus, OH *Page 1-16*

Distributed Network Administration, Senior Consultant/President, Vu, John T., Parlin, NJ *Page 1-293*

Diversified Computer Consultants, Consultant, Mahajani, Anand, Atlanta, GA *Page 1-260*

Diversified Consulting International, President, McElroy, Ted M., Waynesville, NC *Page 1-263*

Dixon Odom PLLC, Director of Technology, Williams, Scott D., High Point, NC *Page 1-356*

DJG & Associates, Vice President/Program Manager, Mitchell, Leo, Sterling Heights, MI *Page 1-265*

DMB&B Advertising, Director of Information Technologies, Barrow, Rudy, Los Angeles, CA *Page 1-163*

DMR Consulting Group, Principal Technology Consultant, Thompson, Michael, Toronto, Ontario, Canada *Page 1-367*

DNA Systems Inc., Chief Financial Officer, Becker, Andrew D., Somerville, NJ *Page 1-171*

Dolby Laboratories, Technical Supervisor, Tringali, Michael A., San Francisco, CA *Page 1-57*

Donovan Data Systems, WAN Engineer, Brown, Kent, New York, NY *Page 1-165*

Dotcom Solutions AB, Systems Engineer/Consultant, Enroth, Bjorn, Solna, Sweden *Page 1-236*

Dow Agrosciences, EDC/LL, Senior Telecommunications Engineer, Gates, Maurice R., Indianapolis, IN *Page 1-26*

Dr. William M. Scholl College of Podiatric Medicine, Director of Information Technology, DeVore, Jeanne, Chicago, IL *Page 1-322*

Draft Worldwide, Help Desk Supervisor, Wang, Bruce, New York, NY *Page 1-164*

Dreher & Associates, Inc., Manager of Information Systems and Information Technology, Ely, Mark, Oakbrook Terrace, IL *Page 1-142*

Dresser-Rand Company, Associate, Ferrier, William Wayne, Tulsa, OK *Page 1-37*

Droege Computing Services, Senior Systems Analyst, Beckner, John W., Durham, NC *Page 1-221*

DRS Optronics, Director of Information Technology, Antle, M. D. Paka, Viera, FL *Page 1-84*

Duke Communications Windows 2000 Magazine, Editor at Large, Morrill, Jane E., Loveland, CO *Page 1-16*

Duke Energy Corporation, Manager of Technology Planning and Application Services, Anderson, Bruce N., Charlotte, NC *Page 1-113*

Duke Technology, Inc., Managing Partner, Tse, Albert P., Flushing, NY *Page 1-291*

Duke University Medical Center, Senior Analyst Programmer, Pladna, Stephen L., Durham, NC *Page 1-308*

Dun & Bradstreet, Director of Customer Implementation, Kanumilli, Vishvesh, Parsippany, NJ *Page 1-213*

Dun & Bradstreet Corporation, LAN Administrator, Hopkins, Fred A., New Providence, NJ *Page 1-213*

Duni Corporation, Information Technology Manager, Schoenung, Karen, Menomonee Falls, WI *Page 1-70*

DuPont Pharmaceuticals Company, Associate Director, Human Resources Information Services Group, Hawkins, Joyce L., Wilmington, DE *Page 1-23*

DuPont Photomasks, Inc., Solutions Architect, Cochran, John A., Round Rock, TX *Page 1-64*

Dwarf Holdings, LLC, Senior Partner, Randazzo, Leonard, South Hackensack, NJ *Page 1-139*

DynaLink, Field Technician, Marinoff, Ryan H., Cleveland, OH *Page 1-183*

Dynamics Research Corporation, Health and Human Services Director, Perras, Kathleen A., Andover, MA *Page 1-186*

Dynatek Infoworld, Inc., Chief Technology Officer, Cheung, Frank, City of Industry, CA *Page 1-229*

DynCorp, SEG Information Systems Project Manager, Barkin, Ruth Ann, Alexandria, VA *Page 1-356*

E

E Trade, Manager, System Security, Ross, Russell H., Menlo Park, CA *Page 1-143*

E.C. Styberg Engineering Company, Information Systems Manager, Muehlius, David A., Racine, WI *Page 1-74*

E&K Companies, Inc., Applications Analyst/Trainer, Peterson, Cynthia Sue, Omaha, NE *Page 1-6*

e-Business Express, President/Chief Executive Officer, McNeil, D. Gregory, Cleveland, OH *Page 1-264*

E-Citi, Manager, Page, William Walter, Los Angeles, CA *Page 1-186*

e-GM, Senior Project Manager, Rofe, Michael Stuart, Omiya City, Japan *Page 1-71*

E-Greetings, Director of Technical Operations and Information Systems, Gajic, Dragan, Santa Cruz, CA *Page 1-21*

e-Marketworld.com, Project Manager, Allen, Tommy L., Newport News, VA *Page 1-299*

e-technicalsupport.com, Owner, Clements, Mark G., Dallas, TX *Page 1-231*

Eaglecrest High School, Information Systems Operations Supervisor, Roina, John A., Aurora, CO *Page 1-317*

Earth Tech
Geographic Information Systems and CAD Manager, Wallenborn, Jerry L., La Mesa, CA *Page 1-350*
Project Coordinator, Silsbee, Laura Barrett, Warner Robins, GA *Page 1-349*

EarthLink, Senior Software Quality Engineer, Hutchinson-Surette, Eric A., Pasadena, CA *Page 1-250*

EarthWeb, Inc., President/Chief Executive Officer, Hidary, Jack D., New York, NY *Page 1-179*

East Central University, Assistant Professor, Carley, Clay B., Ada, OK *Page 1-321*

Eastern Health System, Inc., UNIX Administrator, Henry, Karen E., Birmingham, AL *Page 1-152*

Eastern Idaho Technical College, Division Manager, Reese, Timothy E., Idaho Falls, ID *Page 1-338*

Eastern Mennonite University, Director of Information Systems, Tyler, Rebecca Ann, Harrisonburg, VA *Page 1-333*

Eastman Kodak Company
Assistant Chief Information Officer, Gulling, Mark, Rochester, NY *Page 1-84*
Senior Systems Analyst, Nemchick, David C., Rochester, NY *Page 1-84*

Eat 'N Park Restaurants, Director of Information Systems Technology, Schaefer, James F., Pittsburgh, PA *Page 1-129*

Eaton Corporation, Technical Support Manager, Anderson, Randy, Milwaukee, WI *Page 1-356*

EC Cubed, Director of Global Systems Integration Alliances, Leung, Gregory D., Nesconset, NY *Page 1-110*

ECCS, Lead Developer/Manager of Software Tools, Wheeler, Barbara, Tinton Falls, NJ *Page 1-47*

Eclipse Inc., Manager of Technical Publications/Webmaster, Ramsey, Kathryn L., Boulder, CO *Page 1-187*

ECPI College of Technology, Academic Department Head, Blackburn, Dale, Greensboro, NC *Page 1-336*

ECPI Technical College, Instructor, Harding, William R., Cary, NC *Page 1-337*

EDAX Inc., Technical Sales Manager, Nylese, Tara Lyn, Fort Myers, FL *Page 1-81*

Eddie Bauer, Inc., Manager of Applications Development, Glenn, Terry M., Redmond, WA *Page 1-131*

Edelbrock Corporation, Chief Manufacturing Engineer, Herrmann, Scott M., Torrance, CA *Page 1-71*

Edge Technologies, Inc., Systems Administrator, Cook, Charlie D., Fairfax, VA *Page 1-232*

Edgemeade, Director of Performance Improvement and Utilization Review, Fenwick, Scott F., Upper Marlboro, MD *Page 1-343*

Edgewater Technology, Director of Technology, Carson, Bruce A., Wakefield, MA *Page 1-229*

Edmunds & Associates, Computer Support Hardware Technician, Weisberg, Ross, Northfield, NJ *Page 1-295*

EDS
    Advanced Systems Engineer, Anderson, Fred R., Herndon, VA Page 1-214
    Information Analyst, DeLaPorte, Charles E., St. Louis, MO Page 1-214
    Information Associate, Garrels, Ruth A., Flint, MI Page 1-215
    Infrastructure Specialist, Vinson, Kevin J., The Colony, TX Page 1-215
    Project Manager, Soon, Herald Soohong, Cedar Rapids, IA Page 1-215
    Senior Consultant, Donohoe, B. F., Houston, TX Page 1-214
    Senior Information Specialist, Lamberson, Joseph R., St. Louis, MO Page 1-215
    Technical Team Lead, Johnston, Elbert W., Lansdale, PA Page 1-215

EDS System House, Network Engineer, Burgess, Kevin A., Halifax, Nova Scotia, Canada Page 1-214

edu.com, Senior Director, Greenlaw, Valdonna, Boston, MA Page 1-132

Education Service Center-2, Data Processing Manager, Wallace, Samuel "Sam" Thomas, Corpus Christi, TX Page 1-383

EER Systems, Inc., Software Engineer, Kropp, Monica B., Fort Gordon, GA Page 1-181

EFC Systems, Network Administrator, Burch, Neal F., Montgomery, AL Page 1-227

EFTC, Systems Analyst, Chapman, Gregory P., Olathag, KS Page 1-76

EG&G Defense Materials, Instructor/Database Administrator, Warrington, William "Sandy" E., Toole, UT Page 1-117

eHNC, Implementation Manager, Kao, Wayne, San Diego, CA Page 1-253

eJiva, Consultant, Sobieray, Ed, Washington, DC Page 1-284

El Paso Energy, UNIX Systems Administrator, Gautreaux, Wayne J., Houston, TX Page 1-115

El Paso Energy Corporation, Senior Engineering Systems Analyst, Llagostera, Domingo, Sugar Land, TX Page 1-115

Elantiel, Operations Manager, Gueguen, Daniel, Asnieres, France Page 1-243

elcom.com, Inc., Customer Support Manager, Frangieh, Robert T., Framingham, MA Page 1-175

Electronic Data Systems
    Manager, Buhler, Wesley Dwayne, Plano, TX Page 1-214
    Systems Supervisor, Tuniewicz, Karin, Cranston, RI Page 1-215

Electronic Systems Associates, President, Fredette, Stephen J., New York, NY Page 1-238

Electronic Systems, Inc., Senior Network Consultant/Project Manager, Hix, Darrell R., Virginia Beach, VA Page 1-204

Electronics Arts, Software Release Engineer, Do, Hai Thanh, San Jose, CA Page 1-196

Eli Lilly and Company, Associate Information Consultant, Skiles, Michael John, Indianapolis, IN Page 1-24

Elite Systems Support Inc., President/Chief Information Officer, Bonaparte, C. Scott, Hempstead, NY Page 1-223

Ellwood Group Inc., Director of Information Systems, Owrey, Richard, Ellwood City, PA Page 1-34

eLogo.com Encorporation, Chief Information Officer, Mirau, Michael Glen, Dallas, TX Page 1-118

Elsevier Science, Information Technology Consultant, Stein, Emmanuel, New York, NY Page 1-19

Embry-Riddle Aeronautical University, Manager of University Infrastructure, Creech, Deborah, New Smyrna, FL Page 1-322

EMC Corporation, Software Systems Architect, Baliakhov, Dmitri, Hopkinton, MA Page 1-212

EMCO, Network Administrator, Badinger, Dawn D., Baton Rouge, LA Page 1-219

Emcore, Chief Engineer, Scott, Dane C., Somerset, NJ Page 1-67

Emerald Solutions Inc., Senior Technical Architect, Zhang, Hong, Warren, NJ Page 1-298

eMerge Interactive, Senior Software Engineer, Woods, Marguerite E., Sebastian, FL Page 1-297

Emergency Medical Services Group, Inc., d.b.a. EMSG, President/Executive Director, Barnard, Jeffery R., Largo, FL Page 1-310

Emirates Telecom Corporation, Engineer, Badar, Ijaz Ul Haq, Abu Dhabi, United Arab Emirates Page 1-95

Emmanuel College, Information Systems Office Manager, Duncan, Dennis LeRoy, Franklin Springs, GA Page 1-322

Employers Unity, Manager of Data Services, Brown, Robert W., Arvada, CO Page 1-155

En-Data, Software Consultant, Schwendiger, Kathleen M., Altamonte Springs, FL Page 1-281

Engelberth Construction, Application Specialist, Russell, Christopher P., Colchester, VT Page 1-4

Engineering Information, Inc., Publisher, van der Linden, Nicoledean J., Hoboken, NJ Page 1-19

Enhanced Ideas, Owner, Anderson, Gwyn C., La Crosse, WI Page 1-217

Entech Sales & Service Inc., Project Manager, Rightmer, Charles K., Austin, TX Page 1-123

Entegris, Network Engineer, Hedges, Bradley, Chaska, MN Page 1-29

Entergy Services, Video Services Product Line Manager, Horn, David J., Gretna, LA Page 1-116

Enterprise Technology Group Inc., Business Development and System Consultant, Carrigan, Christopher M., Boston, MA Page 1-228

EnterpriseWorks, LLC, Founder/President/Chief Executive Officer, Deyhimi, Derrik, Houston, TX Page 1-234

ENTEX Information Services, Senior Project Manager/Systems Consultant, Ellisor, Charles E., Lufkin, TX Page 1-235

ENTEX Information Services, Inc., Senior Customer Engineer, Creevy, John J., Rye Brook, NY Page 1-232

Entex Information Technology Services, A Siemens Company, West Region Projects Manager, Stokes, Keith, Portland, OR Page 1-286

Enthusiast, Inc., Chief Information Officer, Cline, Jon, Pasadena, CA Page 1-231

Entology, Inc., Senior Consultant, Temple, TheresaMarie, Bedminister, NJ Page 1-191

Envision, UNIX System Administrator, White, Michael Henry, St. Louis, MO Page 1-296

Envision Financial System, Inc., Senior Analyst, Singh, Jagdeep, Irvine, CA Page 1-190

EPIX Medical, Inc., Director of Management Information Systems, Tyeklar, Zoltan, Cambridge, MA Page 1-25

Epronet, Director of Information Technology, Sarkes, Robert A., San Mateo, CA Page 1-169

Epson Electronics America Inc., Manager of Information Technology, Trainor, John C., El Segundo, CA Page 1-49

Equant, Information Technology Manager, Gorby, Bryan, Dunedin, FL Page 1-204

Equifax E-Banking Solutions, Inc., Senior Systems Architect, Bayyapureddy, Kishore, Hahira, GA Page 1-221

Equinix, Network Specialist, Pease, Michael A., Ashburn, VA Page 1-111

Equistar Chemicals, LP, Information Technology Training Coordinator, LeBeauf, Shelia M., Houston, TX Page 1-26

Equitable Resources, Director of Enterprise Technologies, Sciullo, Gregory M., Pittsburgh, PA Page 1-281

Equitable Tax Service, Executive Assistant, Moosman, Elizabeth D., Logan, UT Page 1-163

ERDAS, Inc., Senior Applications Analyst, Gabriel, Darren K., Atlanta, GA Page 1-176

ERDC-CNC, Principal Investigator, Dilks, Kelly Marie, Champaign, IL Page 1-360

Ericsson, Senior Product Manager, Gardner, Jeffrey L., Plano, TX Page 1-59

Ericsson Messaging Systems, Systems Manager, Lewis, R. Scott, Woodbury, NY Page 1-61

Ericsson, Inc., Information Systems and Information Technology Controller, Brauner, Darrell R., Research Triangle Park, NC Page 1-58

Ernst & Young
    Information Security Consultant, Hawkins, Byron T., St. Louis, MO Page 1-353
    Manager, Sehmbey, Paul, Halifax, Nova Scotia, Canada Page 1-355

Ernst & Young Application Services LLC., Senior Associate II, Narayana, Shyamkumar, Lake Forest, CA Page 1-354

Ernst & Young Audit, Senior Auditor, Trikoz, Dimitri, Paris, France Page 1-356

Ernst & Young LLP
    Director of Business Alliances, Pritchett, Stephanie A., Chantilly, VA Page 1-355
    Management Consultant, Decker, Thomas J., Horsham, PA Page 1-353
    Manager of eSecurity Solutions, Evanco, Michael S., Buffalo, NY Page 1-353
    Manager, Scott, Nancy L., Chicago, IL Page 1-355
    Senior Manager, Lam, James, Mendham, NJ Page 1-354

Ernst & Young Technologies, Inc., Manager of Technology Operations, Hardaway, Ivan B., Chantilly, VA Page 1-353

Eskom, Senior Customer Support Officer, Muller, Gary D., Bellville, South Africa Page 1-114

ESPS, Inc., Technical Support Analyst, Pagliei, Jeffrey M., Fort Washington, PA Page 1-186

ETISALAT, Building Management Systems and Security Operations Specialist, Ahmed, Shakir, Fujairah, United Arab Emirates Page 1-95

Eurisko S.A., Information Technology Manager, Costis, Nickolaos C., Attica, Greece Page 1-173

EURO RSCG DSW Partners, Senior Technologist, White, Kevin D., Salt Lake City, UT *Page 1-165*

Euro-Log GmbH, Data Center and Customer Service Manager, Koppert, Claus, Hallbergmoos, Germany *Page 1-254*

Evan Design Group, Principal, Smith, Eric E., Longmont, CO *Page 1-284*

Ever Glitter International Ltd., Vice President of Operations, Chu, Tung S., New York, NY *Page 1-123*

Excel Communications, Information Technology Engineer III, Hart, Byron Dean, Howe, TX *Page 1-99*

Excel Consulting, Owner, Bagley, Kathleen A., Winthrop, ME *Page 1-219*

Excite@Home, Software Engineer, Gunawan, Kingson, San Jose, CA *Page 1-109*

exlr8, Inc., Chief Executive Officer/Chief Technology Strategist, Massa-Lochridge, Lauren J., Berkeley, CA *Page 1-262*

Experian, Senior Software Engineer, Liu, Ningsheng, Englewood, CO *Page 1-182*

Express Computer Supply, Vice President, Jain, Kunwar, San Diego, CA *Page 1-119*

F

F. Saba & Associates, Founder, Saba, Farhad, San Diego, CA *Page 1-332*

Factset Research Systems, Real-Time Systems Engineer, Boffardi, Marc G., Greenwich, CT *Page 1-201*

Fairfield Communities, Inc., Director of Data Administration, Gonzalez, Danny E., Fort Lauderdale, FL *Page 1-160*

Fairmont Hotel, Management Information Systems Manager, Koubek, Cindy, New Orleans, LA *Page 1-162*

Fala Direct Marketing, Inc., Management Information Systems Director, Eisman, Ariane M., Melville, NY *Page 1-165*

Family Health Systems, Senior Programmer/Analyst, Meier, Debora L., Madison, WI *Page 1-153*

Fascor, Director of Customer Service, Stephens, Amy E., Cincinnati, OH *Page 1-191*

Fauquier Hospital, Project Coordinator, Bishop, Briget R., Warrenton, VA *Page 1-307*

Federal Aviation Administration
Computer Specialist, Anthochy, George, Arlington, TX *Page 1-389*
Project Analyst, Levesque, Raymond F., Washington, DC *Page 1-390*

Federal Bureau of Prisons, Computer Services Manager, Minion, William W., Tallahassee, FL *Page 1-378*

Federal Express, Technical Recruiter, Hilliard, Marion, Irving, TX *Page 1-90*

Federal Government, Computer Specialist, Hoffman, Larry L., Columbus, OH *Page 1-379*

Federal Home Loan Bank, Computer Programmer Analyst, Shreffler, Sue L., Topeka, KS *Page 1-136*

Federal Reserve Bank, Technical Specialist, Yrizarry, Lisa Marie, Portland, OR *Page 1-133*

Federal-Mogul, User Support Analyst, Koluch, Andrew R., St. Louis, MO *Page 1-73*

Federated Systems Group, Technician, Flowers, Frank, Ellenwood, GA *Page 1-237*

FedEx, Recruiter, Wallace, James Ashford, Collierville, TN *Page 1-90*

FedEx, ITD/Finance in Legal Systems, Senior Programmer Analyst, Spurlock, Samuel, Collierville, TN *Page 1-90*

FEMA, Computer Specialist, Fox, Shelby Ross, Winchester, VA *Page 1-378*

Ferris State University, Computer Resource Manager, Buse, Amy L. R., Big Rapids, MI *Page 1-320*

Fers Business Services Inc., Information Technology Manager, Brand, David, Chicago, IL *Page 1-368*

Fidelity & Deposit Company of Maryland, Programmer/Analyst, Anniko, P. Peter, Baltimore, MD *Page 1-153*

Fidelity Investments, Consultant/Systems Analyst, Stephens, C. Millard, Dallas, TX *Page 1-161*

Filtros Mann, Ltda., Information Technology and Purchasing Manager, Cauzzo, Luiz Henrique, Indaiatuba, Brazil *Page 1-72*

Financial Information, Inc., Technical Support Specialist, Solomon, Maria Luisa A., Jersey City, NJ *Page 1-19*

Fingerhut, Director of Systems Management Group, Beukhof, Martin, Plymouth, MN *Page 1-130*

First Baptist Church Raytown, Network Administrator, Klassy, Ken R., Raytown, MO *Page 1-347*

First Chicago/Mercantile Services, Chief Information Officer, Anderson, Maribeth, Chicago, IL *Page 1-171*

First Consulting Group, Senior Integration Analyst, Barnard, James H., Winter Springs, FL *Page 1-299*

First Continental Trading, Information Technology Director, Levine, William A., Chicago, IL *Page 1-143*

First Data Corporation, Product Manager, Rothe, Eukarlgen A., Omaha, NE *Page 1-303*

First Horizon Home Loans, Systems Analyst, Newberry, Del R., Garland, TX *Page 1-141*

First Union National Bank, Lead Developer, Van Huynh, Khoa, Charlotte, NC *Page 1-134*

Fisher-Rosemount, Information Technology Manager, Benavides, Rafael, El Paso, TX *Page 1-81*

Fishman Transducers, Director of Management Information Systems, Kilbashian, Rick, Wilmington, MA *Page 1-69*

Fleet & Industrial Supply Center, Information Systems Security Officer, Dunston, Corlis Yvette, Norfolk, VA *Page 1-91*

Fleet Technology Solutions
Regional Coordinator, Keyes, Tammy L., Malden, MA *Page 1-253*
Systems Specialist, Toro, Robert N., Wallingford, CT *Page 1-290*

Flexon, Systems/Network Administrator, Goins, Raphael D., Pittsburgh, PA *Page 1-177*

Flexx Magazine, Graphic and Web Designer, Nana, Rajesh C., Lithia Springs, GA *Page 1-17*

Florida Government Technology Conference, Conference Director, Keiffer, Ralph J., Tallahassee, FL *Page 1-253*

Florida State Board of Administration, Senior Fixed Income Research Analyst, Latmore, Allison W., Tallahassee, FL *Page 1-375*

Floyd Memorial Hospital, Manager of Information Systems, Terrell, Sue E., New Albany, IN *Page 1-309*

Floyd Public Schools, Network Administrator, Slusher, Donna E., Floyd, VA *Page 1-318*

Fluor Global Services, Engineering Department Manager, Noorbakhsh, Roya, Aliso Viejo, CA *Page 1-349*

Ford Motor Company, System Analyst/Process Consultant, Foster Carter, Linda Marie, Lathrup, MI *Page 1-71*

Ford Power Products, Systems Director/Chief Information Officer, VanDoorne, Vincent A., Southfield, MI *Page 1-118*

Fordham University, Internet Strategist, Rothschild, Brian M., New York, NY *Page 1-331*

Fordham University Library, Evening Supervisor, Vilchez, Ricardo S., Staten Island, NY *Page 1-339*

Formglas, Inc., Network Administrator, Lopes, Duane A., Toronto, Ontario, Canada *Page 1-7*

Fort Valley State University, Computer Service Specialist III, Harvester, Wayne C., Fort Valley, GA *Page 1-324*

Foster Wheel Environment Corporation, Design Supervisor, Wagner, Daniel S., Monroe, NY *Page 1-349*

fp Label, Director of Information Technology, Thelemaque, Tony, Napa, CA *Page 1-21*

Fred Hutchinson Cancer Research Center, Systems Administrator, Aprile, Joseph A., Seattle, WA *Page 1-356*

Frederick Community College
Director of Information Technology Training, Hemgen, Jim, Frederick, MD *Page 1-337*
Manager of Network Services, Kennedy, Christopher L., Frederick, MD *Page 1-337*

Freedom Plastics, Management Information Systems Manager, Olson, Rob A., Sun Prairie, WI *Page 1-29*

Frequentis, Information Technology Security Administrator, Bogner, Wilhelm, Vienna, Austria *Page 1-55*

Fresenius Medical Care, Information Technology Manager, Theriault, Roger D., Lexington, MA *Page 1-310*

Friendship Village, Information Systems Manager, Czarnik, Teri, Schaumburg, IL *Page 1-343*

Frith Anderson & Peake, PC, Systems Administrator, Jackson, Britt L., Roanoke, VA *Page 1-312*

Frontier Hotel Gambling, Management Informations Systems Director, Shoemaker, Linda L., Las Vegas, NV *Page 1-162*

Fruit of the Loom, Data Center Manager, Hunt, Jeff L., Bowling Green, KY *Page 1-11*

FSI International, Information Technology Security Manager, Archer, Kelley P., Chaska, MN *Page 1-64*

FT Mortgage Companies, Vice President for Information Technology Services, Layne, Theodore J., Irving, TX *Page 1-160*

Fujitsu, Account Manager, Siska, Theodore L., Plymouth, MN *Page 1-283*

Fujitsu Microelectronics, Inc., General Manager, Fujisaku, Kiminori, San Jose, CA *Page 1-65*

Fullarton Computer Industries Inc., Management Information Systems Manager, Taylor, Wendy E., Winterville, NC *Page 1-45*

Furniture City Color, Web Manager, Oliver, Thomas W., High Point, NC *Page 1-22*

Furon FHP, Principal Engineer, Nguyen, Peter N., Anaheim, CA *Page 1-81*

FutureNext Consulting, Inc.
Principal Consultant, Tanuwidjaja, Ron A., Moreno Valley, CA *Page 1-288*
Principal Consulting Manager, Peake, Daniel, Los Gatos, CA *Page 1-272*

G

G.O. Carlson Inc., Information Systems Manager, Santucci, Peter, Thorndale, PA *Page 1-31*

G&L Enterprises, President, O'Brien, Greg, Pearisburg, VA *Page 1-164*

Ga Childcare Online, Architect, Ebrahimi, Steven G., Atlanta, GA *Page 1-342*

GAF, Manager of Quality Control, Kemp, Karen L., Wayne, NJ *Page 1-28*

GAI Consulting Southeast Inc., Lead Planner, Walker, Alfred E., Jacksonville, FL *Page 1-370*

Gamesville, NT Systems Administrator, Kittredge, Gregory J., Watertown, MA *Page 1-197*

Gantz Wiley Research, Director of Operations and Technology, Sonnentag, Matthew, Minneapolis, MN *Page 1-360*

Garden Burger, Technical Support Manager, Greenbank, Martin P., Clearfield, UT *Page 1-8*

Garrett County Board of Education, Coordinator of Data Processing and Systems Management, Kimble, Arnold Dale, Oakland, MD *Page 1-316*

Gasco, Senior Contract Engineer, Trache, Jamal Eddine, Abu Dhabi, United Arab Emirates *Page 1-27*

Gast Manufacturing, Web Site Administrator, Kim, Alice, Benton Harbor, MI *Page 1-37*

Gateway, Sioux Falls Client Care Source Coordinator, Breitkreutz, Sherry Lee, Sioux Falls, SD *Page 1-224*

GCP Consulting, Owner, Prentice, Guy C., Webster, NY *Page 1-275*

GE, Senior Computer Scientist, Sobolewski, Michael W., Schenectady, NY *Page 1-70*

GE Harris Railway, Manager, Lang, Robert R., Orlando, FL *Page 1-181*

GE Supply, e-Commerce Project Leader, Duay, Cheryl L., Shelton, CT *Page 1-121*

Geneer, Inc., Enterprise Technology Architect, Hargreave, Andrew G., Des Plaines, IL *Page 1-178*

Genentech
Managing Principal Database Administrator, Glenn, Tyrone L., South San Francisco, CA *Page 1-23*
Scientific Programmer/Data Analyst, Ward, Michael F., South San Francisco, CA *Page 1-25*
Human Resources Information Technology Manager, Chen, Yuan-Yuan "Chrissie", South San Francisco, CA *Page 1-22*

General Chemical Corporation, Senior Programmer Analyst, Duong, Huy M., Parsippany, NJ *Page 1-26*

General Electric
Information Technology Manager, Grindle, Mark J., Schenectady, NY *Page 1-77*
Information Technology Manager, Yim, Aaron P., Jonesboro, AR *Page 1-77*

General Electric (GE) Corporate Research and Development, Staff Engineer, Kao, Kevin J., Niskayuna, NY *Page 1-77*

General Electric Company
Computer Scientist, Gao, Hui, Schenectady, NY *Page 1-77*
Manager of Affiliates Y2K Program, Dar, Arif A., Atlanta, GA *Page 1-76*

General Motors
GMPT, Rosenbaum, Lisa Lenchner, Bloomfield, MI *Page 1-72*
Project Engineer, Hernández González, Luis Marcial, Mesa, AZ *Page 1-71*

General Physics Corporation, Senior Systems Analyst, Maceluch, Markian W., Baltimore, MD *Page 1-260*

Genesys Computing Technologies, President, Jimmo, Steven M., Chicopee, MA *Page 1-205*

Genesys Labs, Database Administrator, Tereshko, George V., San Francisco, CA *Page 1-288*

GeoQuest, Oracle Database Administrator, Vincent, Debbie A., Houston, TX *Page 1-3*

George Miler, Inc., Vice President, Miler, Wyatt H., Melbourne, FL *Page 1-90*

GetFit.com, Artificial Intelligence Software Engineer, Izrailevsky, Yury A., San Mateo, CA *Page 1-305*

Getronics/Wang, Research and Development Senior Software Support Specialist, Lee, Roger E., New York, NY *Page 1-256*

Giffels Associates, Inc., Director of Computer Services, Bland, Richard L., Southfield, MI *Page 1-350*

Gilbane, Senior Programmer/Analyst, Coyle, Stephen F., Providence, RI *Page 1-4*

Glades Central High School, Agri-Technology Teacher, Thompson, Michael J., Belle Glade, FL *Page 1-318*

Globebyte, President/Founder, Melconian, Martin, Kingston upon Thames, England, United Kingdom *Page 1-264*

GMAC Commercial Mortgage
Director of Network Operations, Benson, Stephen T., Horsham, PA *Page 1-140*
Team Leader, Brown, Sharon M., Horsham, PA *Page 1-140*

Golden Eagle Credit Corporation, Project Manager, Ference, William F., Ridgefield, CT *Page 1-167*

Golden Enterprises, Engineer, Al Hadad, Shariff, Melbourne, FL *Page 1-70*

Goldman Sachs, Associate, Ullah, Shamya M., New York, NY *Page 1-144*

Goldman Sachs & Company
Analyst/Developer, Coplu, Ali, Lyndhurst, NJ *Page 1-142*
Database Administrator, Santhumayor, Ivan NJ, New York, NY *Page 1-144*
Information Technology Specialist, Siddiqui, Khayyam, Bloomfield, NJ *Page 1-144*
Senior Programmer Analyst, Jha, Ashok S., New York, NY *Page 1-143*

Gordon Computer Services, Owner, Gordon, Frank J., Spring Valley, CA *Page 1-243*

Governor Mifflin School District, Director of Technology, Becker, Sandra L., Shillington, PA *Page 1-314*

GPU Energy, Director of Business Development, Wingenroth, Rebecca M., Reading, PA *Page 1-115*

Grace University, Computer Systems Manager, Litchfield, Gregory T., Omaha, NE *Page 1-328*

Graphic Consultants, Chief Executive Officer, Wiemokly, Kerry M., Hopewell Junction, NY *Page 1-303*

Graphic Resources, Network Administrator, Lefebvre, Guy, Scarborough, Ontario, Canada *Page 1-124*

Graphtis, Web Designer, Tissier, Christophe, Antony, France *Page 1-290*

Great Rivers Tech Institute, Technology Coordinator, Wallace, Jim, McGehee, AR *Page 1-339*

Great White North, Owner, North, Barbara, Proton Station, Ontario, Canada *Page 1-269*

Greeley Gas Company, Information Technology Manager, Merritt, Gary S., Denver, CO *Page 1-115*

Green Bay Packaging, Inc., Information Systems Coordinator, Martin, Eric M., Conway, AR *Page 1-15*

Greenlee Textron, Webmaster, Pryor, Jason A., Rockford, IL *Page 1-36*

Groupe Cantrex, Inc., Director of Information Systems, Casabon, Sylvain, Saint-Laurent, Quebec, Canada *Page 1-132*

Grubb & Ellis Company
Regional Supervisor of Central Region, Almeda, Gilbert S., Northbrook, IL *Page 1-158*
Technical Services Manager, Brown, Dennis J., Northbrook, IL *Page 1-158*

Grundy Area Vocational Center, Computer Aided Drafting and Design Instructor, Cornwall, Daniel J., Morris, IL *Page 1-314*

GSI Consulting Services, Vice President, Bartlett, Roy H., Toronto, Ontario, Canada *Page 1-220*

GTE
Instructor of Retail Markets, Snouffer, Bret Daniel, Marion, OH *Page 1-104*
Project Engineer, Hickman, Michael J., Thousand Oaks, CA *Page 1-100*

GTE Internetworking, Inc.
Information Technology Customer Services Manager, Todisco, Barbara J., Cambridge, MA *Page 1-290*
National Account Executive, Blake, Catherine B., Marblehead, MA *Page 1-222*

GTE Internetworking, Powered by BBN, Financial Analyst, Batt-Ptaszek, Chris, Columbia, MD *Page 1-221*

GTE Laboratories, Inc., Senior Member of Technical Staff, Yang, Ning, Waltham, MA *Page 1-107*

Guittard Chocolate Company, Chief Information Officer, Lim, Daniel K., Burlingame, CA *Page 1-8*

Gulf Telephone, Communications Engineer, Kleinschmidt, James E., Foley, AL *Page* 1-101

Gulfstream Aerospace, Senior Database Analyst, Caster, Charles, Savannah, GA *Page* 1-75

Gulius Maske, Information Technology Manager, Karlsen, Rolf, Trondheim, Norway *Page* 1-124

GV-WFL EduTech, Project Coordination Manager, Welsh, Norma E., Newark, NY *Page* 1-319

GVL, Technical Manager/Owner, Villetorte, Michel, Montreal, Quebec, Canada *Page* 1-293

H

Habanero Software, President/Owner, Russello, Frank V., West Haven, CT *Page* 1-279

Habberstad Nissan, Warranty Operations Manager, Hunt, Desmond, Jamaica, NY *Page* 1-71

Halifax Regional Municipality, Information Analyst, Robson, Brent R., Halifax, Nova Scotia, Canada *Page* 1-374

Hall Kinion, Account Manager, Plambeck, Pamela, Denver, CO *Page* 1-168

Harcourt, Inc., Acting Director of Business Systems, Folk, Gene E., Orlando, FL *Page* 1-17

Harris County Department of Education, Director of Technology, Harris, Bonnie L., Houston, TX *Page* 1-381

Harte-Hanks, Programmer, Hennessy, Richard V., Longhorne, PA *Page* 1-301

Harvard Medical School, Senior Database Consultant, Joseph, Sunil, Cambridge, MA *Page* 1-326

Harvard-Smithsonian Center for Astrophysics, Doctor, Kristen, Helmuth E., Cambridge, MA *Page* 1-358

Hastings Entertainment, Inc., Director of Product Systems, Fritz, Laura, Amarillo, TX *Page* 1-130

Havas Interactive, Inc., Corporate Recruitment Manager, Gauvin, Lorraine Leandra, Bellevue, WA *Page* 1-176

Hawaii Multimedia Corporation, Vice President/Founder, Tay, Thomas A., Honolulu, HI *Page* 1-288

Hazelwood Farms Inc., Director of Information Systems, Wright, Richard A., Hazelwood, MO *Page* 1-8

HCL America, Project Manager, Johorey, Ritu, Houston, TX *Page* 1-251

Headquarters, Air Force Audit Agency, LAN Manager, Weaver, Clarence E., Washington, DC *Page* 1-396

Health & Welfare Agency, System Software Specialist 1, Luiz, Dave P., Sacramento, CA *Page* 1-155

Healthcare Management, Project Manager, Jones, Russell W., Philadelphia, PA *Page* 1-150

Helios System Inc., Executive Vice President/Owner, Marlow, Gerald D., Glen Ellyn, IL *Page* 1-262

Henry Schein, Inc., ISO 9000 Coordinator/Quality Analyst, Korber, Lorraine M., Stevens, PA *Page* 1-124

Hercules Inc., Senior Systems Analyst, Condon, J. Emmett, Tervose, PA *Page* 1-26

Herman Miller, Senior Consultant, Smith, Walter E., Orlando, FL *Page* 1-284

Hertzbach & Company, Systems Engineer/Software Engineer, Horton, Nicholas A., Owings Mills, MD *Page* 1-353

Hewlett-Packard Belgium, Business Development Manager, Kindermans, Marc, Oud Haverlee, Belgium *Page* 1-42

Hewlett-Packard Company
Business Consultant/Project Manager, Hinkston, Kevin L., Palo Alto, CA *Page* 1-41
Chief Technology Advisor, Klemba, Keith S., Mountain View, CA *Page* 1-42
Consulting Manager, Cerqueira, Joao Roberto Monteiro, Sao Paulo, Brazil *Page* 1-39
Development Environment Manager, Hill, Derek P., Santa Clara, CA *Page* 1-41
Environmental Health and Safety Specialist, Rose, Linda L., Vancouver, WA *Page* 1-44
European Services Delivery Program Manager, Granato, Orazio, Bergamo, Italy *Page* 1-40
Functional Manager, Almeida-Coffron, Katty, Palo Alto, CA *Page* 1-39
Information Systems Manager, Leveque, Gilles, Grenoble Cedex 9, France *Page* 1-42
Information Technology Transition Manager, Jones, Jennifer L., San Jose, CA *Page* 1-41
Product Manager, Swetzig, DeAnnaKay, Greeley, CO *Page* 1-45
Senior Technical Consultant, Meyerson, James L., Cupertino, CA *Page* 1-43

Hewlett-Packard Labs, Research Programmer, Livingston, Mark A., Palo Alto, CA *Page* 1-43

HFN, Inc./Kinetra IMIN, Network Development Manager, Towner, Wendy M., Oak Brook, IL *Page* 1-311

HH Technologies, Inc./Hedelund Engineering, President/Chief Executive Officer, Hedelund, Harold G., Las Vegas, NV *Page* 1-370

Hi Nrg Webdesigns, Systems Analyst/Programmer, Guerrera, Riccardo, Laval, Quebec, Canada *Page* 1-243

Hickory Springs Manufacturing, Personal Computer Specialist, Wilson, Jonathan G., Hickory, NC *Page* 1-13

Hicks & Ragland Engineering Company, CAD Supervisor, Harris, Andrew T., Lubbock, TX *Page* 1-348

Hicks Technology Services, Vice President, Hicks, Mark J., Salem, OR *Page* 1-247

HIE, Vice President of Education, Parker, Dee A., Addison, TX *Page* 1-271

High Technology Systems Ltd. (Hitechnofal), Managing Director, Nofal, Mohamed El-Sayed, Cairo, Egypt *Page* 1-208

Hilton Hotels Corporation, Senior Manager, Maio, Joseph A., Elizabeth, NJ *Page* 1-162

Hitachi, Ltd., Technology Director, Kitajima, Hiroyuki, Kanagawa, Japan *Page* 1-121

HK Net Company, Ltd., Senior Business Development Manager, Lam, Wing, Kowloon, Hong Kong *Page* 1-101

HLB Tautges Redpath, Ltd., Manager, Zabel, Todd A., White Bear Lake, MN *Page* 1-356

HMT Technology, Automation Specialist, Khong, Huy T., Fremont, CA *Page* 1-49

HNA Consulting, Inc., President, Han, Brent M., Falls Church, VA *Page* 1-245

HNC Software, Inc., Director, Fig, Susan B., San Diego, CA *Page* 1-175

Holland Hitch Company, SAP Systems Manager, Wiewiora, Thomas A., Holland, MI *Page* 1-319

Hollister Inc., Manager of ERP Technical Services, Cox, Joel A., Libertyville, IL *Page* 1-83

Holocon, Inc., Consultant, Holoman, Stuart B., Raleigh, NC *Page* 1-248

Home Depot, Director of Information Services, Milner, Dana, Atlanta, GA *Page* 1-126

Home Mortgage Inc., Director of Information Technology, Fraedrich, D. David, Phoenix, AZ *Page* 1-140

Home Shopping Network, Associate Telecom Engineer - Data, Usiak, Robert F., St. Petersburg, FL *Page* 1-131

Homebid.com, Chief of Marketing and Operations, Valente, Jean-Luc, Scottsdale, AZ *Page* 1-159

Honda Research and Development, Systems Engineer, Holliday, Jeff L., Raymond, OH *Page* 1-357

Honeywell, Manager Data Services Europe, Picherot, Laurence, Sophia Antipolis, France *Page* 1-81

Honeywell Home & Building Control, Learning Solutions Development Leader, Ziegler, Jody Nyquist, Minneapolis, MN *Page* 1-6

Honeywell-Thermal Systems, Lead Manufacturing Engineer, Ruiz, Raul, Imperial, CA *Page* 1-33

Hong Kong International School, Technology Coordinator, Elliott, David, Tai Tam, Hong Kong *Page* 1-315

Horizon Healthware, Inc., Development Support Analyst, Fisher, Terrance, Raleigh, NC *Page* 1-175

Horizon Instructional Systems, Management Information Systems Administration Officer, McCoy, Karstyn, North Highlands, CA *Page* 1-316

Hotel Interactive, Director of Management Information Systems, Denis, Andrew M., Huntington, NY *Page* 1-300

Houghton Mifflin, Systems Specialist, Lawson, John A., Alttleboro, MA *Page* 1-17

House of Sedes, President, House, Jon K., Overland Park, KS *Page* 1-248

Housing Fiscal Services, Systems Administrator, Beaumont, Patrick A., New York, NY *Page* 1-158

Houston Associates, Software Engineer, Munshi, Darius J., Arlington, VA *Page* 1-111

Houston Fire Department, Information Systems Administrator, Whitt, Mark A., Houston, TX *Page* 1-378

Howmet Corporation, Information Systems Manager, Vitelli, Joseph D., Hampton, VA *Page* 1-32

HQ CPSG/LGLP, Logistics Management Specialist, Favaro, Norma Wheatley, San Antonio, TX *Page* 1-393

HSB Reliability Technology, Software Developer, Drexler, Bryan A., Washington, DC *Page* 1-234

HSBC, Information Technology Audit Manager, Lo, Alen, Heng Fa Chuen, Hong Kong *Page* 1-143

HSI Geotrans, Inc., Director of Information Systems, Barr, Robert T., Sterling, VA *Page* 1-368

Hubbard Company, Systems Operator, Farmer, Ira Anthony, Bremen, GA *Page* 1-12

HUD Office of Inspector General, Senior Information Systems Auditor, Walker, Michael L., Washington, DC *Page* 1-389

Hughes Christensen, Consultant, D'Sylva, Leon J., Dubai, United Arab Emirates *Page* 1-3

Hughes Network Systems
    Member of Technical Staff, Rhine, Chad D., Germantown, MD *Page* 1-94
    Senior Principal Engineer, Ravishankar, Channasandra, Germantown, MD *Page* 1-94

Hules Tecnicos S.A., Technical Service Manager, Arias, Jorge M., San Jose, Costa Rica *Page* 1-29

Humana Inc., Senior Consulting Systems Programmer, Meyer, Leo H., Louisville, KY *Page* 1-153

Hunter Douglas, Quality System Coordinator, Burroughs, Vonda M., Tupelo, MS *Page* 1-13

Hwa Shin Building, Independent Researcher, Shin, Dong-Keun, Seoul, South Korea *Page* 1-158

Hyperacuity Systems, Chief Executive Officer, Wilcox, Michael J., Colorado Springs, CO *Page* 1-82

Hyperbole Software, Unlimited, Owner/Operator, Reynolds, Carl W., Madison, IN *Page* 1-187

I

I Connection Inc., Chief Executive Officer, Callahan, Gerard W., Waukegan, IL *Page* 1-172

I Link Worldwide, LLC (Independent Representative), Independent Representative of I Link World Wide, LLC, Carvajal, LeAnnette, Las Vegas, NV *Page* 1-368

I.D.A., Managing Director, Haddad, Assad, Nil-Staint Vincent, Belgium *Page* 1-244

I/N Tek, Systems Analyst, Farney, Kerry G., New Carlisle, IN *Page* 1-31

i2 Technologies, Solutions Architect, Viswanathan, Narayanan, Irving, TX *Page* 1-200

IB Industries, Corporate Information Systems Director, Primmer, Charles W., Brownsdale, MN *Page* 1-275

IBEX Capital Markets, Senior Systems Analyst, Gerstner, Kyle, Boston, MA *Page* 1-145

IBM Corporation
    Advisory Programmer, Srinivasan, Savitha, San Jose, CA *Page* 1-45
    Advisory Software Engineer, Khalifa, Kathy L., Apex, NC *Page* 1-42
    Computer Security Specialist/Project Manager, Buzby, Carrie D., Denver, CO *Page* 1-39
    Data Management & Business Intelligence Sales Associate, Markowski, Violet E., Arlington, MA *Page* 1-43
    Information Technology Architect, LuVisi, Michael A., Long Beach, CA *Page* 1-43
    Open Systems Manager, Braggs, Genelle R., Atlanta, GA *Page* 1-39
    Principal, Hoey, Brent M., Orange, VA *Page* 1-41
    Project Executive, Moser, Ellen M., Redwood City, CA *Page* 1-44
    Research Staff Member, Elfadel, Abe, Yorktown, NY *Page* 1-40
    RF Engineer, Wolf, Randy L., Essex Junction, VT *Page* 1-46
    Senior Consultant, Mundle, Sheldon, Marietta, GA *Page* 1-44
    Senior Information Technology Specialist, Bradley, Dennis R., New York, NY *Page* 1-39
    Senior Software Developer, Garner, Michael W., Cary, NC *Page* 1-40

IBM Global Services
    Applications Development Manager, Brotman, Roy, Pine Brook, NJ *Page* 1-225
    Director of Information Technology Strategy, O'Malley, Timothy S., Glen Rock, NJ *Page* 1-269
    Information Technology Specialist, Patel, Kiran K., Parsippany, NJ *Page* 1-271
    Lotus Notes Administrator, Clark, Ronald L., Atlanta, GA *Page* 1-230
    Senior Business Analyst, Bovell, Matthew, Southbury, CT *Page* 1-224
    Senior Consultant, Bowzer, Jerrold A., Oklahoma City, OK *Page* 1-224
    Technology Consulting/Project Manager, Welker, Michael J., Warren, PA *Page* 1-295
    Web Intelligence Consultant, Booth, Michael, Winchester, England, United Kingdom *Page* 1-223

IBM Japan, Advisory Education Specialist, Masuda, Yukie, Kanagawa, Japan *Page* 1-43

IBM Santa Teresa Lab, Advisory Software Engineer, Zhang, Guogen, San Jose, CA *Page* 1-46

IBM Server Development Group, Senior Programming Development Manager, Naivar, DeVonna R., Taylor, TX *Page* 1-267

IBM Thomas J. Watson Research Center
    Research Staff Member, Ruehli, Albert E., Yorktown Heights, NY *Page* 1-279

    Staff Software Engineer - Network Engineering Department, Brown, Harold A., Yorktown Heights, NY *Page* 1-226

IBM-Knowledge Factory, Training Coordinator, Gordon, Randi-Lyn, Dunwoody, GA *Page* 1-243

IBSYS, General Manager, Benayoun, Andre, Nanterre, France *Page* 1-222

ICC International, President/Chief Executive Officer, Ricciardelli, Nicholas J., Scottsdale, AZ *Page* 1-187

ICOM Solutions Pty. Ltd., Technical Specialist-Software Engineer, Bal, Anupam D. S., Sydney, New South Wales, Australia *Page* 1-367

IDB Consulting, President/Chief Executive Officer, Stemmelin, Frederic, Palo Alto, CA *Page* 1-285

IDC (International Data Corporation), Research Director, Romano, Antonio, Milan, Italy *Page* 1-278

IDX, Consultant, Byrd, Melody D., Lombard, IL *Page* 1-201

IER Industries, Inc., Manager of Information Systems, Burgess, Ronald A., Macedonia, OH *Page* 1-28

If and Then, General Manager, Chbeir, Ziad E., Croton On Hudson, NY *Page* 1-113

IFS Portugal, Business Solutions Manager, Gomes, Carlos, Riba de Ave, Portugal *Page* 1-242

Ignacio School District, Director of Technology, Smith, Rick K., Ignaciao, CO *Page* 1-383

IHS Engineering, VAX/VMS Systems Administrator, Adams, Rick, Colorado Springs, CO *Page* 1-18

IKON, Director of Engineering, Zepeda, Jesse H., Whittier, CA *Page* 1-51

IKON Education Services, Southeast District Network Manager, Ownby, James O., Greenville, SC *Page* 1-51

IKON Office Solutions, UNIX System Administrator, Bourdon, Philippe M., Glastonbury, CT *Page* 1-50

IKON Technology Services, Executive Vice President of Service & Support, Mancini, James M., Irvine, CA *Page* 1-50

IKOS Systems, Technical Sales and Support Representative, Louie, Victor C., Arlington Heights, IL *Page* 1-206

Illinois Department of Children and Family Services, Systems Analyst, Rhodes, Brian V., Springfield, IL *Page* 1-386

Illinois Housing Development Authority, Assistant Director of Systems of Network, Ansari, Waheed H., Chicago, IL *Page* 1-388

Illinois Power Company, Supervisor of Technical Support Services, Peterson, Richard, Decatur, IL *Page* 1-117

Illinois Primary Health Care, Manager of CSC, Farney, Thomas P., Springfield, IL *Page* 1-344

Illinois State Board of Education, Principal Technology Consultant, Baiter, Jamey Fern, Springfield, IL *Page* 1-380

Image Computers Inc., Technical Manager, Krueger, Charles J., Holland, MI *Page* 1-255

IMI Systems, Inc.
    Consultant, Hershman, Joseph, Wilmington, DE *Page* 1-247
    Outbound Resource Manager, Dashiell, John L., Vienna, VA *Page* 1-232

IMR Global Corporation, Senior Consultant, Mathiyazhagan, Nithyanandam "Mathi", Clearwater, FL *Page* 1-262

IMS HEALTH Strategic Technologies, Manager of Database Team, Anandan, Israel D., Norcross, GA *Page* 1-171

In Controls Inc., Senior Control Systems Engineer, Reyntjens, Bruno R. F., Hurricane, WV *Page* 1-52

In-Net, Chief Executive Officer/President, Haney, Wayne A., Clinton, TN *Page* 1-245

IN3 Consulting, Canada, Partner/Director, Kashmirian, R. S., Bragg Creek, Alberta, Canada *Page* 1-253

Inacom, Professional Services Manager, Verna, Michael A., Iselin, NJ *Page* 1-211

InAir, Vice President of Product Design, Simmons, John E., Chesterfield, MO *Page* 1-190

Inaltus.com, Chief Executive Officer, Tripathi, Shashank, London, England, United Kingdom *Page* 1-214

Inca Metal Products, Manager of Information Systems, Parker, Keith A., Lewisville, TX *Page* 1-35

Independence Blue Cross, Senior Director of Managed Care Systems, Luther, Carolyn W., Philadelphia, PA *Page* 1-150

Independence School District, Instructional Technology Resource Teacher, Woods, E. Hayet, Liberty, MO *Page* 1-384

Independent
    Consultant, Lozano, Hector Jose, San Jeronimo, Mexico *Page* 1-73
    Freelance Writer, Quesada, Arli, San Rafael, CA *Page* 1-370

Independent Systems Consultant, Lynn, Robert Garon "Bob", Charlotte, NC *Page* 1-259

Nelson, Joyce E., Ashland, WI *Page* 1-338

Owner/Technical Consultant, Cheng, Michael P. K., Alhambra, CA *Page* 1-202

Phenicie, Robert L. Jr., Herndon, VA *Page* 1-208

Project Lead, Helfenstein, Dirk, Stuttgart, Germany *Page* 1-5

Senior Associate Software Consultant, Smith, Michele, Oak Brook, IL *Page* 1-284

Systems Engineer Advanced, Sebastian, Glania, Balingen, Germany *Page* 1-282

Independent Contractor and Consultant, Senior Technical Writer, Griffin, Arthur M., Long Beach, CA *Page* 1-369

Independent Health, Systems Manager, Starr, Laura A., Williamsville, NY *Page* 1-151

Independent Truckers Group, Inc., President, Yoakley, Frances L., Las Vegas, NV *Page* 1-297

Industri-Matematik North American Operations, Inc., Development Manager, Roman, Edward John, Mount Laurel, NJ *Page* 1-278

Industrial Data and Magic, Owner, Turner, Gene, El Dorado, AR *Page* 1-299

Industrial Research Ltd., Information Manager, Ralph, Gillian, Auckland, New Zealand *Page* 1-358

Industry Canada, Director of School Net Operations, Clemis, David, Ottawa, Ontario, Canada *Page* 1-381

Indy Residential Services, Sales and Marketing Representative, Sharp, Jeffrey A., Indianapolis, IN *Page* 1-159

Infinite Wisdom Web Designs, Account Executive, Zepp, Gregg L., Reisterstown, MD *Page* 1-193

Infinity Solutions Inc., President, Kanthawar, Krishnakumar, New York, NY *Page* 1-252

Infipro Inc., General Manager, Rumley, Russell, Greenville, MS *Page* 1-299

Infoloan, Information Technology Administrator, Cheng, Jack Y., San Jose, CA *Page* 1-140

Infonautics Corporation, Vice President/Chief Technical Officer, Mohan, Ram, King of Prussia, PA *Page* 1-213

InfoRay, Inc., Worldwide Marketing Manager, Genser, Mira E., Cambridge, MA *Page* 1-176

Inforbit Inc., Consultant, Patel, Lalit, Voorhees, NJ *Page* 1-272

Informatica Asociada, General Manager, Santos, Raul Jose, Tecamachalco, Mexico *Page* 1-189

Information Builders Inc.
Senior Programmer, Shindnes, Sergey, Farmington, CT *Page* 1-199
Vice President of Research and Development, Dorman, Gregory J., New York, NY *Page* 1-196

Information Graphics Systems Inc., Information Systems Manager, Meyer, Patrick J., Boulder, CO *Page* 1-184

Information Resources, Inc.
Director, Pillers, Jeff A., Chicago, IL *Page* 1-360
Software Consultant, Chitre, Nikhil, Chicago, IL *Page* 1-359

Information Retrieval, Systems Analyst, Bullied, Perry Leon, Cary, NC *Page* 1-172

Information Services International, Manager of Development and Communications, Gehrt, Kevin E., Mount Olive, NJ *Page* 1-213

Information Systems Professionals, Director, Litwin, Ryan P., Milwaukee, WI *Page* 1-259

Information Systems Services, Owner, Towl, Allan T., Attleboro, MA *Page* 1-291

Information Technology Consulting, Inc., President/Project Manager/Consultant, Chromy, Robert J., Succasunna, NJ *Page* 1-230

Information Transfer System, Project and Information Technology Manager, Schoettle, Brandon A., Ann Arbor, MI *Page* 1-352

Informix, Development Manager, Peacey, Kendrew, Denver, CO *Page* 1-272

Informix Software, Inc., Software Development Manager, Sohoni, Sanjay V., Menlo Park, CA *Page* 1-284

Infosinergia, S.A., President, Fernandez, Rafael Manuel, Miami, FL *Page* 1-109

Ingenium Corporation, Systems Administrator/Site Manager, Boudreaux, Ambrose Carl, Upper Marlboro, MD *Page* 1-223

Inland Northwest Health Services, Assistant Director information Services, Chugg, Ginger M., Spokane, WA *Page* 1-152

Inmet Corporation, RF/Microwave Engineer, Childs, Keith F., Ann Arbor, MI *Page* 1-57

Innernet, Inc., Vice President/Chief Financial Officer, Rotz, Randy E., Shady Grove, PA *Page* 1-278

Innosoft Inc., President, Babu, Venkatesha, Edison, NJ *Page* 1-31

Innovex, Customer Quality Engineer, Akhtar, Hasan, Litchfield, MN *Page* 1-48

Instasofte, Inc., Consultant, Ghosh, Amitava, Metuchen, NJ *Page* 1-240

Instinet, Director of Research Development, Varghese, Sajini Sara, New York, NY *Page* 1-144

Institute for Scientific Information (ISI), Manager of Current Awareness Products, Wismer, James D., Philadelphia, PA *Page* 1-19

Instruction Set, Inc., Director of Information Systems, Brown, Ed, Natick, MA *Page* 1-226

Insulgard Corporation, Network Administrator/Computer Specialist, Eckert, John F., Hyattsville, MD *Page* 1-85

Insursoft, Ltd., President/Owner, Campbell, Robert W., Littleton, CO *Page* 1-228

Insys Inc., Consultant, Thomas, K. Michael, Elkridge, MD *Page* 1-289

Integral Software Corporation, Owner, Zaika, Gary, Merrick, NY *Page* 1-297

Integrated Chipware, Chief Scientist, Anderson, Michael E., Reston, VA *Page* 1-171

Integrated Device Technology, Inc., Director, IT Infrastructure, Suhaimi, Sunyo L., Santa Clara, CA *Page* 1-68

Integrated Solutions Group, Owner/Operator, Moles, Patrick H., Foothill Ranch, CA *Page* 1-184

Integrated Systems Engineering, Systems Manager, Cox, Dale, Logan, UT *Page* 1-85

Intel Corporation
Engineer Manager, Fang, Jesse, Santa Clara, CA *Page* 1-65
Instructional Designer, Jensen, Kristen A., Portland, OR *Page* 1-66
Manager, Ercolani, Gianantonio, Ottobrunn, Germany *Page* 1-65

Intelligence Architects LLC, President, Brunelle, Francois, Herndon, VA *Page* 1-226

IntelliMark, Inc., Help Desk Manager, Leaman, Kendall J., Mechanicsburg, PA *Page* 1-256

Intellinex, an Learning Venture of E&Y, Programmer Analyst, Hennes, Cathryn A., Cleveland, OH *Page* 1-353

Intellisource, General Manager, Quintanilla, Chris A., Philadelphia, PA *Page* 1-169

Intend Change, Information Architect, Fousek, Linda A., Lindsay, CA *Page* 1-363

Inter American University of Puerto Rico, Associate Professor, Zornosa Cabrera, Luis M., San German, Puerto Rico *Page* 1-335

Inter-tel Technologies, Inc., Systems Engineer, Oakeley, Agnes C., Albuquerque, NM *Page* 1-93

Interactive Business Systems, Inc., Senior Consultant, Gomes, Ivan J., Oak Brook, IL *Page* 1-242

InterBiz of Computer Associates, Vice President of Production Strategy, Jutras, Cindy M., Andover, MA *Page* 1-180

Intergraph Corporation, Senior Systems Specialist, Leinen, Sean Frederick, Bronxville, NY *Page* 1-257

Intermec, Software Manager, Dean, Steve, Everett, WA *Page* 1-233

Intermedia Business Internet, Director, Technical Support and Network Operations, Howell, Franklyn L., Beltsville, MD *Page* 1-249

Intermedia Communications, Lead Technician, Tuttle, Michael, Tampa, FL *Page* 1-105

Internal Revenue Service, Senior Computer Systems Analyst, Bridges, Martin O., Kansas City, MO *Page* 1-379

Internal Revenue Service, Financial and Administrative Systems, Computer Specialist, Acholonu, Omogbemiboluwa I., Bowie, MD *Page* 1-379

International Comfort Products, Network Analyst, McCandless, Doug, Hampshire, TN *Page* 1-51

International Data Solutions, Director/Principal Consultant, Thompson, Norman, Jacksonville, FL *Page* 1-289

International Management Communication Corporation, Inc., Information Technology Professional, Davis, Tamara L., Miami, FL *Page* 1-368

International Network Services
Network Consulting Engineer, McCarson, David B., Morrisville, NC *Page* 1-263
Network Systems Engineer, Lester, Jeffrey A., Morrisville, NC *Page* 1-258

International Online Relations, President/Owner, Noor, Nicholas N., New Windsor, NY *Page* 1-208

International Savings, Management Information Systems Manager, Chee, Adrian U., Honolulu, HI *Page* 1-136

International Turnkey Systems, Senior Account Manager, Arafeh, Ashraf M., Jeddah, Saudi Arabia *Page* 1-218

Internet Gateway, Inc., President, Stolle, Keith, Georgetown, TX *Page* 1-286

Internet of Lawton, LAN Administrator, Rosenquist, Eric C., Lawton, OK *Page* 1-209

Internet Solution Group, Director of Software Development, Hamzei, Nader, West Lake Village, CA *Page* 1-178

Internet Ventures, President, Anderson, Scott K., Pasadena, TX *Page* 1-218

Internet World Media, Inc., Business Manager, Rossi, Matthew R., Darlen, CT *Page* 1-303

Intershop Communication, Project Manager, Difilippo, Armand, South Beach, NY *Page 1-234*

InterVoice-Brite, Inc., A/R Supervisor/Commissions Administrator, McElvy, Pam, Dallas, TX *Page 1-56*

Inventa, Computer Systems Architect, Baker, Gene Charles, Eldersburg, MD *Page 1-220*

Investors Fiduciary Trust, Network Services Manager, Lembke, David R., Kansas City, MO *Page 1-147*

Iomega Corporation, Senior Technical Training Manager, Hatch, Robert Duane, Kaysville, UT *Page 1-48*

Iowa Communications Network, Internet Engineer/ATM Engineer, Klinkefus, David S., Johnston, IA *Page 1-254*

Iroquois Memorial Hospital, Director of Information Systems Planning, Wells, Bradley T., Watseka, IL *Page 1-309*

Irwin Research and Development, Software Engineer, Curry, Gary, Yakima, WA *Page 1-29*

Island Life Insurance Company, Director of Computer Environment, McCalla, Izett M. E., Kingston, Jamaica *Page 1-148*

Island Services Network, Owner/President, O'Brien, Kevin, Charlottetown, Prince Edward Island, Canada *Page 1-269*

ISSI, Inc., Network Engineer, Jones, Rabon S., Gaithersburg, MD *Page 1-251*

ITC Delta Com, AEII, Dickman, Lowell V., Bronson, FL *Page 1-97*

ITESM Campus Laguna, Computer Manager, Medina, Armando Ibarra, Torreon, Mexico *Page 1-328*

ITS America, Director, Vehicle Systems Department, Keppler, Stephen A., Washington, DC *Page 1-375*

ITS Communications, Information Systems Manager, Aden, Steve E., Grand Rapids, MI *Page 1-95*

ITS Inc., Technical Services Manager/Webmaster, Burtnett, Jeanne, Las Vegas, NV *Page 1-227*

ITT Avionics, Systems Administrator, Nassani, Joseph, Clifton, NJ *Page 1-77*

ITT Industries, Department Manager, McGibbon, Thomas L., Rome, NY *Page 1-263*

ITT Technical Institute, Education Supervisor, Maloney, Edward, Encino, CA *Page 1-338*

Ivy Tech State College, Instructor, Hamilton, Brandon, Calumet Park, IL *Page 1-337*

IXC Communications, Area Technical Coordinator, Woolverton, Thomas, Livonia, MI *Page 1-106*

J

J Crew Group, Inc., Director of Telecommunications and Cell Center Technology, Sherman, David M., New York, NY *Page 1-131*

J.C. Solutions, LLC, Software Engineer, Parrish, Brian P., Fairmont, WV *Page 1-186*

J.E. Reedy, Inc., Vice President, Reedy, Matthew K., Seymour, IN *Page 1-5*

J.L. Communications, General Manager, Limon, Jeffrey Jessey, Irving, TX *Page 1-111*

J&E Technology, Inc., Chief Executive Officer, Huffman, James E., Alexandria, VA *Page 1-249*

Jannon Group, Systems Engineer, Arroyo, Brett C., Charlotte, NC *Page 1-218*

Jano Multicom AS, Information Technology Consultant, Babajide, Olusegun, Oslo, Norway *Page 1-219*

Janssen Pharmaceuticals, Director of Information Management, Verstraete, Edmond J., Washington Crossing, PA *Page 1-25*

Jasmine Computers Technologies, Inc., President, Nguyen, Bac Hai, Montreal, Quebec, Canada *Page 1-268*

Jerry's Precision Company, Programmer, Linfante, Thomas P., Dover, NJ *Page 1-52*

JGR Consulting, LLP, Proprietor, Rex, Jack G., Toledo, OH *Page 1-366*

Job Service North Dakota, Data Processing Coordinator, Tober, Theresa J., Bismarck, ND *Page 1-169*

JobsMadeEasy.com, Chief Executive Officer, Peram, Suresh, Marietta, GA *Page 1-168*

John Deere Company, Information Technology Analyst, Quist, Stephen C., Lenexa, KS *Page 1-36*

John Holmertz, Independent Contractor, Holmertz, John P., San Diego, CA *Page 1-248*

Johns Hopkins Hospital, Local Area Network Administrator, Jenkins, Arnold M., Baltimore, MD *Page 1-308*

Johns Hopkins University, Director of IT Credit Programs, Novitzki, James, Baltimore, MD *Page 1-330*

Johnston Community School District, Director of Technology, Yoshimura, Dennis A., Johnston, IA *Page 1-320*

Jon Barry & Associates, Inc., Information Systems Manager, Ball, Sharron L., Conord, NC *Page 1-165*

Jones Day Reavis & Pogue, Technology Trainer, Davis, Roseland M., New York, NY *Page 1-312*

Jovenko, Managing Partner/Information Technology Consultant, Saerens, Robert, Meise, Belgium *Page 1-279*

JTC, Telex Exchange Engineer, Al-Nimri, Nabil Isa, Amman, Jordan *Page 1-91*

Juniata College, Director of Technology Center, Bichel, Anthony R., Huntingdon, PA *Page 1-335*

Justice Communications, President/Chief Executive Officer, Justicia, José A., San Diego, CA *Page 1-60*

JWR Systems, Founder/Engineer, Renard, James A., Edmonds, WA *Page 1-187*

K

K & R Splicing, Owner, Adkins, Kaye W., Pekin, IL *Page 1-6*

K's Room, President, Ishimoto, Ken, Saitama-ken, Japan *Page 1-250*

K-mart Distribution Center, Manager of Special Projects, Muhlstadt, Maryanne T., Manteno, IL *Page 1-88*

Kahler Slater Architects, Systems Administrator/Leader, Block, Jeffrey Allen, Milwaukee, WI *Page 1-350*

Kaiser Aluminum, Senior Systems Engineer, Rybiski-Joseph, Elizabeth, Gramercy, LA *Page 1-3*

Kaiser Health Plan, Senior Software Developer, McGuire, Michael R., Walnut Creek, CA *Page 1-152*

Kaiser Permanente
Manager of Network Engineering, Niel, Anthony L., Honolulu, HI *Page 1-150*
Senior National Manager for National Web Services, Tuttle, Robert A., Oakland, CA *Page 1-151*

Kalas Manufacturing Inc., Director of Management Information Systems, Wolf, Gerald L., Denver, PA *Page 1-53*

Kalatel Engineer Inc., Manager of Information Services, Johnston, Marty P., Corvallis, OR *Page 1-298*

Kaltech International Corporation, President/Chief Executive Officer, Kalke, Kimberly, Duluth, GA *Page 1-252*

Kapa Consulting, Consultant/Owner, Philipsen, Flemming, Munkebo, Denmark *Page 1-274*

Kaplan, Publishing Systems Manager, Haggerty, Hugh, New York, NY *Page 1-340*

Karl Williams Inc., Service Manager, Schmidt, Donald, Springfield, IL *Page 1-119*

Kay Elemetrics Corporation, Software Project Manager, Mulleady, Michael F., Lincoln, NJ *Page 1-185*

Kazuo Totoki Ltd., Rental Agent/Programmer, Pang, Elmer S. B., Honolulu, HI *Page 1-159*

Kb/TEL, Hardware Design Manager, Schettino, Antonio Ernesto, Mexico City, Mexico *Page 1-45*

KBC Bank New York N.V., Technical Support Manager/Assistant Vice President, Curto, Philip A., New York, NY *Page 1-134*

Kellogg Brown & Root, Manager of Engineering Project Support, Word, Glenn E., Houston, TX *Page 1-6*

Kennedy Kenrick Catholic High School, Department Chairman, Kopaczewski, John J., Norristown, PA *Page 1-316*

Kent Datacomm, Technical Services and Project Manager, Crane, Douglas G., Austin, TX *Page 1-203*

Kent State University, Research Analyst, Liao, Weidong, Kent, OH *Page 1-327*

Kentucky Department for Libraries & Archives, Systems Support Coordinator, Hamilton, Cindy L., Frankfort, KY *Page 1-375*

Kershaw County School District, Director for Operational Technology, David, Phyllis C., Camden, SC *Page 1-314*

Ketel Thorsten Son, LLP, Network Administrator, Elshire, Jeremy, Rapid City, SD *Page 1-235*

Key Staff, Chief Operating Officer, Russell, Lisa S., Seattle, WA *Page 1-169*

Keys Academy, Teacher, Sustaita, Juan H., Harlingen, TX *Page 1-318*

KForce.com, Senior Account Manager, Spell, Bill E., Houston, TX *Page 1-285*

KGI Securities One Public Company, Ltd., Executive Director of Information Technology, Puranachoti, Sornkawee, Bangkok, Thailand *Page 1-146*

KidsPeace, Senior Systems Analyst, Metzler, Robin C., Orefield, PA *Page 1-343*

Kinetic Concepts, Inc., Manager of Application Development, Wisloff, Tomm, San Antonio, TX *Page 1-13*

King Fahd University of Petroleum and Minerals, Web Master/Computer Programmer, Taj, Moawiya A., Dharan, Saudi Arabia *Page 1-333*

Kishore Chakraborty Consulting, Chief Executive Officer, Chakraborty, Kishore, Watertown, MA *Page 1-363*

KLA-Tencor, Senior Production Supervisor, Sachen, Richard J., San Jose, CA *Page 1-67*

Klein Independent School District, Associate Director of Student Services, Camp, Barbara Smith, Houston, TX *Page 1-381*

Knetico Inc., Technology Services Manager, Tauche, Julie, Newbury, OH *Page 1-51*

Knowtech Solutions, Inc., President, Adatia, Amin, Nepean, Ontario, Canada *Page 1-217*

kohlpharma GmbH, Head of Information Technology, Reinert, Johannes, Perl Saarland, Germany *Page 1-124*

Koinonia Computing, Technology Consultant, Ratliff, Bud, Midway, KY *Page 1-276*

KPMG Consulting
  Manager, Blockus, Linda G., Basking Ridge, NJ *Page 1-362*
  Manager, Keating, Francesca F., McLean, VA *Page 1-364*
  Principal, Alger, Brian W., Toronto, Ontario, Canada *Page 1-362*

KPMG Consulting, Inc., Manager of CRM Infrastructure Team, Attri, Joel P., Mountain View, CA *Page 1-362*

KPMG LLP
  Consultant, Kumawat, Rajesh, New York, IL *Page 1-364*
  Manager, Low, Humbert, Toronto, Ontario, Canada *Page 1-364*
  Program/Project Manager of Software, Skiles, Bryan E., Tracy, CA *Page 1-366*

KRM Risk Management and Insurance Services, Inc., Information Systems Manager, Feliz, Luis R., Fresno, CA *Page 1-157*

KSLA TV, Management Information Systems Manager, Williams, Anthony, Shreveport, LA *Page 1-108*

Kumaran Systems Inc., Director of Strategic Account Development, Kalluri, Dutt N., Rockville, MD *Page 1-252*

Kurgan & Cheviot, Director of Information Systems, Im, Sang H., Los Angeles, CA *Page 1-85*

Kyoei Electronics (S) Pte. Ltd., Chief Application Engineer, Lam, Kuet Leong, Singapore, Singapore *Page 1-121*

L

L.T.G. Technologies, Inc., Mechanical Design Engineer, Highland, Franklin J., Greenfield, WI *Page 1-38*

LA Dye & Printworks, Inc., Information Systems Director, Ackermann, Anthony, Pico Rivera, CA *Page 1-11*

Labor Ready, Inc., Management Information Systems Director, Garverick, Arthur E., Auburn, WA *Page 1-48*

Laguardia Community College, Professor, Davidson, Donald A., Long Island City, NY *Page 1-336*

Lake Dillon Fire Protection District, Systems Administrator, Duggan, Carlina, Dillon, CO *Page 1-378*

Lake Land College, Enrollment Coordinator, Klatkiewicz, Gail D., Sheboygan, WI *Page 1-337*

Landmark Graphics, Project Leader, Le Melinaire, Pascal, Austin, TX *Page 1-182*

Lands & Surveys Division, Land Surveyor/Geographic Information Systems Specialist, Wiseman, Roland S. N., Tunapune, Trinidad & Tobago *Page 1-352*

Landtech Consultants, Inc., CADD Systems Manager, Chamberlain, Mark A., Westford, MA *Page 1-348*

Lanop Corporation, Novell Netware Instructor, Tutone, Frank P., San Jose, CA *Page 1-291*

Lante Corporation
  Consulting Manager, Parkes, Shawn, Chicago, IL *Page 1-271*
  Senior Technologist, Wanagel, Jonathan, Bellevue, WA *Page 1-294*

Laramie High School, Technology Director, Bayne, Chuck, Laramie, WY *Page 1-314*

Larsen Consulting, Manager, Larsen, Bjorn J. P., Southend-on-Sea, England, United Kingdom *Page 1-256*

Laser Wireless Inc., President/Founder, Walter, Dick, Lancaster, PA *Page 1-63*

Lassen Municipal Utility, IS/GIS Coordinator, Barrows, Donald A., Susanville, CA *Page 1-113*

Latent Technology, Marketer, Sink, Christi L., Dallas, TX *Page 1-190*

Lawrence Associates, President, Lawrence, Bonnie L., New Haven, CT *Page 1-364*

Le Groupe BRT, Vice President of Engineering, Bertolucci, Marco, Montreal, Quebec, Canada *Page 1-222*

Lead Trac, Consultant, Filippone, Joseph R., Santa Clara, CA *Page 1-236*

Leapnet, Inc., Technical Consultant, Podemski, Michael J., Oak Brook, IL *Page 1-274*

Lear Corporation, Management Information Systems Manager, Fisher, Angela M., Port Huron, MI *Page 1-73*

Lear Seating Inespo Comercial, Information Technology Director, Mendoza, Julio Cesar, Diadema Sp, Brazil *Page 1-74*

Legacy Bank of Texas, Banking Officer, Rinker, Ricky Lee, Plano, TX *Page 1-141*

Legal Aid Society, Training Manager, Muhammad, Yolanda, New York, NY *Page 1-313*

Lemo USA, Inc., Product Specialist, Hope, Teresa M., Santa Rosa, CA *Page 1-68*

Leon County Health Department, Distributed Computer Systems Analyst, Grimes, Sylvie, Tallahassee, FL *Page 1-385*

Leoni Kabel GmbH & Company KG, Technical Sales Manager, Kueffel, Claudia, Roth, Germany *Page 1-35*

Leopard Communications, Internet Strategist, Wilsdon, Alex L., Boulder, CO *Page 1-192*

Levi Strauss & Co., Supervisor of Information Technology Operations, White, Allen, Westlake, TX *Page 1-12*

Lewis Colorado, Owner, Lewis, John H., Littleton, CO *Page 1-258*

Lewis-Clark State College, Instructor, Hennigan, Thomas A., Lewiston, ID *Page 1-337*

Lexis Publishing, Financial Systems Analyst, Londeree, Vicki Neal, Charlottesville, VA *Page 1-18*

Lexmark, Account Manager/Marketing Analyst, Hudson, Melanie, Lexington, KY *Page 1-49*

Lexmark International, Inc.
  Application Architect, Phillips, Howard C., Lexington, KY *Page 1-120*
  Manager Business Systems Support, Ivey, Gabrielle, Lexington, KY *Page 1-119*

Liberty Health, Vice President of Information Technology, Giannotta, Cel, Markham, Ontario, Canada *Page 1-150*

Lifechem Lab, Lead Support Analyst, Jimenez, Hugo, Rockleigh, NJ *Page 1-310*

Lifemark Corporation, Information Technology Manager, Sutton, Ron R., Indianapolis, IN *Page 1-153*

Lightbridge Inc., Systems Integration Architect, McCusker, Clinton F., Burlington, MA *Page 1-93*

Limited Technology Services, Database Administrator, Hartman, Judith A, Tewksbury, MA *Page 1-246*

Lincoln County Technology Group, Systems Administrator, Jimeno, Andy, Libby, MT *Page 1-110*

Lindex AB, Information Technology Manager, Sorstedt, Berthil, Alingsas, Sweden *Page 1-127*

Linear Technology Corporation, Field Applications Engineer, Dinsmore, David L., Dallas, TX *Page 1-64*

Linkscorp, Management Information Systems Director, Greene, Mark A., Northfield, IL *Page 1-305*

Litton PRC, Software Specialist, Chen, Deanford, San Jose, CA *Page 1-229*

Litton/TASC, Security Systems Engineer, Washington, Paul L., Annapolis Junction, MD *Page 1-294*

Livedoor, Inc., Senior Engineer, Yoneyama, Tsutomu, Tokyo, Japan *Page 1-107*

Livingston International, Chief Information Officer, Van, My Tien, Etobicoke, Ontario, Canada *Page 1-91*

LKW Walter AG, Information Technology Manager, Köhler, Andreas, Vienna, Austria *Page 1-88*

LN-Online GmbH, Luebeck, Online Producer, Watermann, Sascha, Hernberg, DE *Page 1-294*

Lockard & White, Projects Director, Penney, Ike D., Houston, TX *Page 1-349*

Lockheed Martin
  Computer-Based Training (CBT) Team Lead, Billings, Claire, Gaithersburg, MD *Page 1-79*
  Enterprise Network Engineer, Longstrom, Edward, Owego, NY *Page 1-79*
  Information Security Engineer, Moore-Fore, Iris Lynn, Washington, DC *Page 1-80*
  Senior Systems Engineer, Walker, Loren Mark, Severna Park, MD *Page 1-80*

Systems Engineer, Lewis, Winston E., Los Banos, CA *Page 1-79*

Lockheed Martin Enterprise Information Systems, Systems Administrator and Integrator, Corson, Charlton E., Denver, CO *Page 1-79*

Lockheed Martin Federal Systems, Software Engineer, George, Michael, Owego, NY *Page 1-80*

Locotech Oy, Consultant, Laxström, Peter, Helsinki, Finland *Page 1-256*

Logicon, Inc., Deputy Director, Holland, Paul R., Herndon, VA *Page 1-77*

Long Aldridge & Norman, Senior Trainer, Munajj, Sharon E. L., Atlanta, GA *Page 1-313*

Long Fence & Home, Director of Information Technology, Wells, Dwayne, Riverdale, MD *Page 1-118*

Loral Cyberstar, Senior Internet Engineer, Azizi, Peyman, Rocksville, MD *Page 1-108*

Los Alamos National Laboratory, Systems Engineer, Salazar, Anthony A., Los Alamos, NM *Page 1-359*

Los Alamos Technical Associates, Director of Learning and Development, Nessel, Steve W., Albuquerque, NM *Page 1-268*

Los Angeles County Mass Transit Agency, Software Engineer, Anderson, Douglas M., Los Angeles, CA *Page 1-389*

Los Angeles Department of Water and Power, Senior Communications Electrician, Saldana, Carlos P., Los Angeles, CA *Page 1-117*

Lotus Development Corporation, Senior Systems Architect, Dodge, Jon, Alexandria, VA *Page 1-174*

Louis T. De Stefano, Inc., Owner, De Stefano, Louis T., Stanardsville, VA *Page 1-298*

Louisiana State University at Eunice, Technical Support Specialist 2, Newman, Marjana, Eunice, LA *Page 1-329*

Louisiana Tech University, President, Reneau, Daniel D., Ruston, LA *Page 1-331*

Lourdes Hospital, Network and Communications Manager, Shever, Andrew F., Paducah, KY *Page 1-309*

Loyola University, Information Technology Coordinator, Hickey, Paul Henry, New Orleans, LA *Page 1-324*

LTV Steel, Manager of Process Control, Dixon, Richard T., East Chicago, IN *Page 1-31*

Lucent Technologies
  Director of Information Systems Operations, Bradford, Kirby R., Alameda, CA *Page 1-58*
  Director of Technical Communications, Hershfield, David M., Alameda, CA *Page 1-60*
  Global Operations Manager, Shukla, Sandeep, Altamonte Springs, FL *Page 1-62*
  Market Development Manager, Landes, J. Christopher, Basking Ridge, NJ *Page 1-60*
  Member of Technical Staff, Matthews, John V., Columbus, OH *Page 1-61*
  Member of the Technical Staff, Keaton-Culp, Carolyn R., Naperville, IL *Page 1-60*
  Principal Software Engineer, Gu, Sheena, Westford, MA *Page 1-59*
  Product Manager, Molnar, Andie, Metuchen, NJ *Page 1-61*
  Regional Director, Tinelli, Felice, Sun Rise, FL *Page 1-62*
  Senior Manager of Information Technology, Griskell, Ivory J., Orlando, FL *Page 1-59*
  Technical Staff, Doddapaneni, Srinivas P., Emmaus, PA *Page 1-58*
  Training Consultant, Shackelford, Reba, Garland, TX *Page 1-62*

Lucent Technologies LTCP, Business Analyst, Hill, Geoffrey D., Chester, NJ *Page 1-60*

Lucky Baby Company, Information Technology Administrator, Salileh, Isam, Riyadh, Saudi Arabia *Page 1-15*

Luminant Worldwide, Consultant, Hsiung, Tien-hao, Houston, TX *Page 1-249*

Luzerne Intermediate Unit, Director of Management Information Systems, Makar, Lynn A., Kingston, PA *Page 1-341*

Lydall, Inc., Oracle Database Administrator, Curcio, Barry M., Manchester, CT *Page 1-15*

M

M-Cubed Information Systems, Senior Systems Analyst, Basinger, William Daniel, Hyattsville, MD *Page 1-220*

M-Plus, President, Yu, Simon P., Fremont, CA *Page 1-120*

Mabuhay Philippine Satellite Corporation, Head of Sales and Marketing, Regalado, Johnson, New Manila, Philippines *Page 1-112*

Mac Electronics, President, McKaskle, Charles "Chuck", Tucson, AZ *Page 1-263*

Macklowe Properties, Information Systems Manager, Guzzetta, Jacqueline R., New York, NY *Page 1-160*

Macrophage International, Senior Consultant, Elkin, L. Daniel, Brentwood, TN *Page 1-174*

MacroSoft, Chief Executive Officer, Eblowitz, Michael, Highland, CA *Page 1-174*

Madge.web, Technical Service Manager, Hobbs, Matthew Stephen, New York, NY *Page 1-247*

Madison International Sales, Information Systems Manager, Holder, Michele, Stamford, CT *Page 1-124*

Madison River Communications, Network Analyst, Olsen, William W., Manito, IL *Page 1-103*

Madscience, Chief Technical Officer/President, Frackman, David A., New York, NY *Page 1-175*

Magee Rehabilitation Hospital, Director of Information Systems and Telecommunications, Peterson, Steven C., Philadelphia, PA *Page 1-308*

Magnetic Data Technologies, General Manager, LaBorde, Frank C., Goleta, CA *Page 1-255*

Maidenform, Inc., Senior Vice President of Retail, Davis, Cindy, Bayonne, NJ *Page 1-12*

Main Control, Inc., Senior Trainer/Consultant, Harris, Wesley G., McLean, VA *Page 1-245*

Majestic Systems Integration, PeopleSoft Consultant, Croswell, David C., Castaic, CA *Page 1-203*

Mälardalens Mögskola, Systems Administrator, Öberg, Jonas, Vasteras, Sweden *Page 1-330*

Management Recruiters International, Account Manager, Weinberg, Laurie J., Springfield, NJ *Page 1-169*

Management Science Associates Inc., Group Director, Silliman, Suzanne, Pittsburgh, PA *Page 1-283*

Manchester Equipment, Systems Administrator, Passantino, George A., Hauppauge, NY *Page 1-120*

Manchester Police Department, Technical Specialist, Vickers, Jerry, Manchester, TN *Page 1-377*

Mancini Duffy, Technical Director, Kafrouni, Nabil H., New York, NY *Page 1-350*

Manhattan Village Academy, Consultant, Cline, Peter M., New York, NY *Page 1-314*

Mansfiled Plumbing Products, Information Systems Technician, Thomas, Taft H., Kilgore, TX *Page 1-30*

Mapinfo Corporation, Vice President/Chief Information Officer, Tobison, John K., Troy, NY *Page 1-290*

Marc Mintz & Associates LLC, Network Consultant, McGuire, Tom, Fairfield, NJ *Page 1-263*

Marconi Data Systems, Inc., Staff Chemist, Kwan, Vincent W., Deerfield, IL *Page 1-36*

Marconi Services Corporation, Manager of Business Development, Gilley, Darryl W., Fort Walton Beach, FL *Page 1-71*

Maricopa County Superior Courts, Software Specialist, Lauer, Steven R., Phoenix, AZ *Page 1-376*

Marker Consulting, Owner, Marker, Wendy C., St. Louis, MO *Page 1-261*

MarkeStar, IBM AS400 Systems Administrator, Hafen, Lynn R., Odgen, UT *Page 1-163*

Marketing Specialists, Director of Business Services, Schlabs, Heidi, Irving, TX *Page 1-146*

Marketlink, Inc., Operations Director, Acheson, Lori, Esterville, IA *Page 1-299*

Marschall Electronics, Ltd., Chief Executive Officer, Marschall, Heiko Bernd, Bavaria, Germany *Page 1-262*

Marsh USA, Inc., Assistant Vice President, Knight, Lophney H., New York, NY *Page 1-157*

Marvell, Senior Systems Administrator, Doan, Phillip K., Sunnyvale, CA *Page 1-65*

Maryland Stadium Authority Maintenance at Camden Yards, Maintenance Planner, Hofman, D. Brian, Baltimore, MD *Page 1-367*

Maryville Technologies, Information Technology Manager, Ard, Bryan N., St. Louis, MO *Page 1-218*

Mascon, Programmer Analyst, Gopalan, Ravichandran, Schaumburg, IL *Page 1-242*

Mascon Information Technologies, Managing Partner, Francis, Philip H., Schaumburg, IL *Page 1-203*

Massachusetts Association of School Committees, Technology Director, Gilbert, Michael J., Boston, MA *Page 1-345*

MASSC, Owner/Chief Executive Officer, Khalil, Ramzi Nabhan, Paterson, NJ *Page 1-254*

Master Automation, Inc., Vice President, Weigand, Michael R., Kirtland, OH *Page 1-211*

Maxim Group, Master Database Administrator, Buker, William H., Glen Allen, VA *Page 1-227*

Maxim Group (BioLab Inc.), Consultant, Kinnard, Michael S., Woodstock, GA *Page 1-254*

Maxim Integrated Products, Inc., Senior Member Technical Staff, Test Systems Development, Hume, Stephen G., Beaverton, OR *Page 1-66*

Maxson Young Associates, Inc., Information Technology Manager, Davison, Glenn L., San Francisco, CA *Page* 1-157

May Department Stores, Lead Programmer/Analyst, Fiorito, Juliann M., Lorain, OH *Page* 1-126

May Logistics Services, Inc., Network Systems Administrator, Seebo, Terry, Buena Park, CA *Page* 1-88

Mbh Settlement Group, Information Technology Officer, Reichert, Eric D., McLean, VA *Page* 1-313

MBI Inc., Manager of Systems and Programming, Mastroianni, Dan A., Norwalk, CT *Page* 1-163

MCB Collection Services Inc., Director of Information Services and Information Technology, Wright, Michael C., Vero Beach, FL *Page* 1-303

McCook Community College, Senior Computer Technician, Walinder, Mike, McCook, NE *Page* 1-339

McDermott, Will & Emery, Information Systems Manager, Powell, Linda L., Washington, DC *Page* 1-313

McDonald Bradley, Senior Test Specialist, Warmsley, Byron Nigel, McLean, VA *Page* 1-294

McDonald Investments, Manager of Technology Training, Maholm, Timothy R., Cleveland, OH *Page* 1-146

McGill University, Manager, Nguyen, Quan, West Montreal, Quebec, Canada *Page* 1-329

Mcgraw-Hill Higher Education, Webmaster/Business Development Mentor, Todd, James A., Burr Ridge, IL *Page* 1-17

McHenry School District #15, Director of Technology, Pride, Buddy, McHenry, IL *Page* 1-317

MCI Corporation, Fellow, Fee, John A., Richardson, TX *Page* 1-70

MCI Systemhouse, Managing Consultant, Luman, Charles J., Minneapolis, MN *Page* 1-206

MCI Telecommunications, Senior Manager, Venz, Barbara E., McCormick, SC *Page* 1-106

MCI WorldCom, Inc.
Senior Manager, Patterson, Ollie C., Atlanta, GA *Page* 1-103
Senior Policy Counsel, Whitt, Richard S., Washington, DC *Page* 1-106
Software Systems Engineer, Ghosh, Sukumar, Tulsa, OK *Page* 1-98

McInturff Miligan & Brooks, Accountant/Systems Administrator, Edwards, Ginger F., Greeneville, TN *Page* 1-156

McKesson HBOC
Manager, McEntyre, Susan K., Alpharetta, GA *Page* 1-24
Team Leader, Franklin, Douglas N., Alpharetta, GA *Page* 1-175

McKinley Group, Inc., Business Analyst/Software Consultant, Knight, Kathy Hawkins, Atlanta, GA *Page* 1-254

McKinney & Silver, Information Technology Support Engineer, Parker, Kevin M., Raleigh, NC *Page* 1-164

McMaster University, Assistant Vice President, Ryder, Marvin G., Hamilton, Ontario, Canada *Page* 1-332

McWhorter Technologies, Technical Analyst, Kochanowski, Mark, Carpentersville, IL *Page* 1-22

Mead Corporation, SAP Data Analyst, Schmidt, Christian A., Dayton, OH *Page* 1-15

Medaille College, Assistant Professor, Kang, Jai W., Buffalo, NY *Page* 1-326

Media Driver, LLC, President, Pavlovich, Matthew R., Dallas, TX *Page* 1-272

MediaFair, Principal Engineer, Guo, Ju, San Gabriel, CA *Page* 1-177

MediaOne Group, Manager of Web Services, Manning, Kevin W., Englewood, CO *Page* 1-108

Medic Computer Systems, Director of Clinical Implementations, Slater, Keith R., Raleigh, NC *Page* 1-199

Medical Center Hospital, Computer and Telecommunications Operations Manager, Dingman, C. Lewis, Odessa, TX *Page* 1-307

Medical Knowledge Systems Inc., President/Chief Executive Officer, Mims, Creflo R., Detroit, MI *Page* 1-265

Medical Manager West, Software Support Specialist, Hedenberg, Judy A., Van Nuys, CA *Page* 1-179

Medio Systems, Inc., President/Chief Executive Officer, Xie, Ian Y., San Jose, CA *Page* 1-193

Medscribe Information Systems, Inc., Operations and Information Systems Director, Langley, William, Jacksonville, FL *Page* 1-167

Megasoft Consultants, Director, Sathya, Ravi, Vienna, VA *Page* 1-279

Meloun Consulting, Chief Executive Officer, Meloun, Jalane M., Akron, OH *Page* 1-264

Mendosus, Chairperson, Larsson, Fredrik, Mendosus, Sweden *Page* 1-256

Menlo College, Director of Information Technology, Olson, Patrick C., Atherton, CA *Page* 1-330

Merallis Company, Business Writer, Campbell, Eileen Rose, Rocky Hill, CT *Page* 1-147

Mercedes Benz U.S. International, Human Resource Information Systems Specialist, Mathis, Belinda J., Tuscaloosa, AL *Page* 1-127

Mercedes-Benz USA, Inc., Information Technology Coordinator, Stewen, Robert, Bethesda, MD *Page* 1-72

Mercer University, Academic Computing Specialist, Taylor, Cecilia T., Atlanta, GA *Page* 1-333

Merck & Co., Inc, Systems Analyst/Programmer, Caloza, Racquel D., Bridgeport, PA *Page* 1-22

Merck & Co., Inc.
Information Services Manager, Williams, Alvis A., Somerset, NJ *Page* 1-25
Senior Systems Engineer, Hockman, James E., Elkton, VA *Page* 1-23

Merck-Medco Rx, Systems Analyst, Liming, Ray D., Columbus, OH *Page* 1-131

Mercury Interactive, Systems Engineer, DesJarlais, William, Landover, MD *Page* 1-234

Merrill Lynch
Vice President, Sudula, Nagesh B., Plainsboro, NJ *Page* 1-144
Webmaster, George, Sunil, Princeton, NJ *Page* 1-142

Mesa Solutions, Systems Consultant, Ansell, Christopher T., Madison, AL *Page* 1-218

Mesa Technical College, Computer Science Instructor, McDonald, Virgil L., Tucumcari, NM *Page* 1-328

Meta Group, Database Administrator/Project Manager, Sciurca, Albert, Stamford, CT *Page* 1-282

Metamore, Network Engineer, Glenn, Kenneth O., Wichita, KS *Page* 1-393

MetLife, Associate Business Systems Analyst, Fallacara, Flo, Bridgewater, NJ *Page* 1-148

Metropolitan Life, Project Consultant, Smith, Bruce A., Dunwoody, GA *Page* 1-149

MFS Investment Management, Assistant Vice President of Infrastructure, Gabardi, Felice R., Raynham, MA *Page* 1-145

MI Technologies, Lead Technician, Yount, David E., Troy, OH *Page* 1-216

MIB Inc., Software Quality Assurance Manager, Rotondo, Eugene M., Westwood, MA *Page* 1-157

MIC, Inc., Senior Consultant, Mehta, Jatin, Kearny, NJ *Page* 1-264

Michael Baker Jr., Inc., Software Project Manager, Ordoobadi, Mehrdad, Coraopolis, PA *Page* 1-271

Michelin, Business Systems Manager, Cunningham, Linda S., Duncan, SC *Page* 1-28

Michelin North America, Manager of Business Analysis, McFarlane, Daniel C., Greenville, SC *Page* 1-28

Michigan Department of Environmental Quality, Local Area Network Administrator, Clark, Daniel J., Lansing, MI *Page* 1-386

Michigan Production Machining, Inc., Network Administrator, Crowl, Jerry L., Macomb, MI *Page* 1-73

Michigan Spring and Stamping, Information Systems Manager, Fox, Kathleen, Muskegon, MI *Page* 1-34

Micro Revisions Inc., President, Tomlin, Doyce E., Houston, TX *Page* 1-192

Micro Technix, Owner/Repair and Installation Manager, Simousek, Michael G., Madison, WI *Page* 1-216

Micro Technology Groupe, Systems Engineer, Sees, Chris V., Pennsburg, PA *Page* 1-209

Micro Technology Unlimited, Customer Support Manager, Cox, Benjamin Bryan, Raleigh, NC *Page* 1-173

MicroAge, Advanced Systems Analyst 3, Davis, Donald N., Gilbert, AZ *Page* 1-119

Microcosm, Senior Software Engineer, Young, Sandra Kay, Torrance, CA *Page* 1-79

MicroGo'L, Manager, Levenhagen, Dennis G., Beaver Dam, WI *Page* 1-258

Micrografx, Senior Director of Development, Hughes, Chris, Allen, TX *Page* 1-196

Microman, Inc., Project Manager, Garinger, Phillip D., Washington Central Heights, OH *Page* 1-204

Micron Technology, Systems Manager, Gardner, Chris D., Boise, ID *Page* 1-65

Micronpc.com, Programmer/Analyst, Phatak, Shreyas, Boise, ID *Page* 1-47

MICROS Systems, Inc., Implementation Consultant, Terway, Jennifer D., Chicago, IL *Page* 1-49

MICROS Systems, Inc. - Southern California Region, Business Manager, Abu-Zahra, Bill, Aliso Viejo, CA *Page 1-49*

Micros-to-Mainframes, Senior Systems Consultant, Samoska, Michael C., Woodbury, CT *Page 1-279*

Microsoft Corporation, Application Developer Consultant, Defiesta, Clarence B., Redmond, WA *Page 1-195*

Microsoft Corporation - North West Africa, General Manager, Chami, Ahmed R., Casablanca, Morocco *Page 1-195*

Midwest Cooperative, Communications Manager, Koehn, Kathy Lynn, Quinter, KS *Page 1-122*

Midwest Technology Management, Assistant Systems Administrator, Iwashita, Michael, Manhattan Beach, CA *Page 1-250*

MIL Corporation, Assistant Project Manager, Smith, Cheryl L., New Market, MD *Page 1-283*

Millipore Corporation, Sales Engineer, Oulundsen, George E., Bedford, MA *Page 1-82*

Millstone River Systems, Inc., Owner, Wallmark, John S., Skillman, NJ *Page 1-293*

Minerals Management Services
Computer Specialist, Griggs, Kelly A., New Orleans, LA *Page 1-388*
Computer Specialist, Lobato, William Lyle, Camarillo, CA *Page 1-388*

Minibar Systems, Technical Services Manager, Bosworth, Kimberly A., Rockville, MD *Page 1-120*

Ministry of Cabinet Affairs & Information, Head of Computer Department, Elmasri, Ahmed Azzam, Manama, Bahrain *Page 1-372*

Ministry of the Environment, Computer Systems Specialist, Heringer, Matthew J., Thunder Bay, Ontario, Canada *Page 1-387*

Minnesota Department of Transportation, Network Engineer, Zimmerman, Gregory D., Maplewood, MN *Page 1-390*

Mission Critical Software, Product Manager, Knowledge Products, Mychalczuk, Michael G., Houston, TX *Page 1-185*

Mississippi State Department of Health, WIC Program, Director of Information Technology for the Bureau of WIC, Cornwall, Charles "Chuck" F., Jackson, MS *Page 1-384*

Missourian Publishing, Pre Press Manager, Wacker, Trent S., Washington, MO *Page 1-21*

Mitre Corporation, Lead Scientist Networking Systems Distributed Systems, Goldsmith, Deborah L., San Diego, CA *Page 1-241*

Mitsubishi Wireless Communications Inc., Technology Manager, Wise, Michael, Duluth, GA *Page 1-57*

MJP Solutions Inc., Consultant/President/Treasurer, Pierron, Brian J., Hilliard, OH *Page 1-274*

MKC Associates, Inc., Information Technology Administrator, Harmon, Jim, Mansfield, OH *Page 1-350*

MMT Corporation, Vice President of Software Engineering, Schupp, Felix A., San Jose, CA *Page 1-189*

Mobile MIS Consulting, Owner, Goldschmidt, David, Cincinnati, OH *Page 1-241*

Modis Technologies, President/Chief Executive Officer, O'Brien, Sean M., Orlando, FL *Page 1-269*

Mohammed Bin Masaood & Sons, Information Technology and Systems Manager, Iznait, Nader S., Abu Dhabi, United Arab Emirates *Page 1-250*

Moore Business Forms, Systems Analyst, Nguyen, Duc V., Nacogdoches, TX *Page 1-20*

Moore Clark, Business Unit Controller, Van Den Brink, Joost, Vancouver, British Columbia, Canada *Page 1-1*

Morpace International, Manager of Information Resources, Watkins, Patricia A., Farmington Hills, MI *Page 1-370*

Morphonix, President/Owner, Littman, Karen G., San Rafael, CA *Page 1-182*

Morrow Technical Services, Chief Operating Officer/Managing Partner, Leeds, Hal, Fort Worth, TX *Page 1-257*

Mortgage Guaranty Insurance Corporation, Tele-Education Systems Administrator, Dzhidzhora, Karen Ann Estelle, Milwaukee, WI *Page 1-156*

Mosman Municipal Council, Manager of Information Technology Services, Nonweiler, Kevin Ian, Liberty Grove, New South Wales, Australia *Page 1-371*

Motorola
Business Development Manager, Villamil, Camilo E., Fort Lauderdale, FL *Page 1-68*
Industrial Engineer, Love, Darlene, Schaumburg, IL *Page 1-57*
Lead Software Engineer/Wireless Network Architect, Thalanany, Sebastian, Buffalo Grove, IL *Page 1-68*
Software Engineer, Alvarez, Isidro, Fort Lauderdale, FL *Page 1-64*
Software Engineer, Petroski, Thomas L., De Soto, IL *Page 1-67*
Speech Technologist, Liu, Chen, Naperville, IL *Page 1-66*

Mount Kisco Medical Group, Technical Support Specialist, Salandra, Justin A., Mount Kisco, NY *Page 1-311*

Mount San Antonio College, Professor, Pop, Horia, Walnut, CA *Page 1-338*

Mountaire Farms, Manager, Dover, Pamala V., Lumberbridge, NC *Page 1-1*

MPR Associates, Inc., Group Leader, Fink, Robert T., Falls Church, VA *Page 1-348*

MTA Solutions, Chief Technology Officer, Simkins, Steven R., Anchorage, AK *Page 1-112*

MTISC, Senior Computer Technician, Gale, Prenston, APO AA *Page 1-239*

MTVi Group, Director, Digital Media Platform, Borisov, Gennadiy, New York, NY *Page 1-107*

Multicom Business Systems Ltd., Managing Director, Trivedy, P., Wembley, England, United Kingdom *Page 1-210*

Musipl@y GmbH, Webmaster/Application Programmer, Holzeisen, Thomas, Bad Wiessee, Germany *Page 1-107*

Muskogee Public Schools, District Technology Specialist, Chandler, Ronnie D., Muskogee, OK *Page 1-381*

MVP Health Plan, Programmer/Analyst, Chan, Monte Tak Ho, Schenectady, NY *Page 1-152*

MWD Consultants, Consultant, Dinota, Mary, St. Leonard, MD *Page 1-369*

Myers Consulting Inc., Consultant, Myers, John E., Boonville, MO *Page 1-267*

Mylex, Manager, Hobbs, Dan J., San Jose, CA *Page 1-179*

Mynd
Computer Programmer I, Baukman, Robert, Eastover, SC *Page 1-171*
Computer Programmer, Pees, Philip G., Cayce, SC *Page 1-273*

N

Nabisco, Senior Manager for Information Technology Manufacturing Systems, Keoghan, Leo E., East Hanover, NJ *Page 1-8*

Nanometrics, Inc., Senior Optical Engineer, Yarussi, Richard A., Sunnyvale, CA *Page 1-37*

NASA, Management Information Systems Consultant, Spaulding, Omar Young, Washington, DC *Page 1-78*

NASA's Sounding Rocket Operations Contract, Y2K Specialist, Crockett, Kimberly L., Chincoteague Island, VA *Page 1-78*

NASA-DFRC, Mathematician, Hedgley, David, Edwards, CA *Page 1-78*

National Bank of Kuwait, Information Technology Manager, Samadi, Marwan, Beirut, Lebanon *Page 1-136*

National Center for Supercomputing Applications, Systems Programmer, Rudins, Nancy A., Urbana, IL *Page 1-341*

National Data Corporation, Manager of Development & Operations, Bartolotta, Tina, Atlanta, GA *Page 1-300*

National Information Technology Center - Department of Agriculture, Computer Specialist, Taylor, Brenda C., Kansas City, KS *Page 1-391*

National Institute for Trial Advocacy, Manager of E-Business, Toth, Susan, South Bend, IN *Page 1-342*

National Nephrology Association, Senior Oracle Database Administrator, Jones, Otis Lee, Nashville, TN *Page 1-346*

National Rural Telecommunications Cooperative, Chief Information Officer, Gibbons, Jim, Herndon, VA *Page 1-98*

National Search Associates, Executive Director, Israel, Burt, Carlsbad, CA *Page 1-168*

National Semiconductor, Manager of Information Systems, Goggins, Dennis R., Arlington, TX *Page 1-65*

National Standard Mortgage, Systems Administration, Kalkar, Sanjiv, Tarrytown, NY *Page 1-141*

National Technological University, Publications Editor, Van Baren, Marla J., Fort Collins, CO *Page 1-334*

National Telephone Services, Manager of Data Communications, Castelino, Flavian M., Muscat, Oman *Page 1-96*

National University, Department Head of Computer Science, Okhandiar, Vazi P., Irvine, CA *Page 1-330*

Nationwide Insurance, Team Lead, McKinney, Debi C., Columbus, OH *Page 1-148*

Native Textiles, Manager of Research and Development, Osmer, Corey, Glens Falls, NY *Page 1-11*

Naval Support Activity, Accounting Supervisor, Garrett, Arthur W., New Orleans, LA *Page 1-393*

Navant Corporation, President/Chief Operating Officer, Bowden, Geri D., Raleigh, NC *Page 1-224*

Navigation Technology, Project Manager, Tsengouras, Michael D., Schaumburg, IL *Page 1-81*

NCH Corporation, Technical Systems Administrator, Jennings, Travis Wayne, Irving, TX *Page 1-8*

NCI, Development Manager, Stucki, Walter, La Tour De Peilz, Switzerland *Page 1-191*

NCR Corporation
Executive Vice President of European Operations and Worldwide Quality Assurance, Hilton, Mark R., Duluth, GA *Page 1-50*
Program Manager, Geer, David W., Severna Park, MD *Page 1-50*
Project Manager V, Dix, Brian Douglas, Peachtree City, GA *Page 1-50*

NCR de Mexico S.A. de C.V., Operations Manager, Perez Munguia, Carlos Manuel, Mexico City, Mexico *Page 1-51*

NEC Technologies, Inc., Senior Web Business Analyst/Webmaster, Ashford, Anne, Littleton, MA *Page 1-48*

NeighborNet, Vice President/Owner, Haskell, Larry R., Spring, TX *Page 1-246*

Net Designs and Creations, Inc., President, Pulsipher, Steven, Ogden, UT *Page 1-275*

Net Tours & Travel, Systems Analyst, Noortheen, Mohammed, Dubai, United Arab Emirates *Page 1-91*

Net Tryx Computer Services LLC, Owner/Administrator, Gagnon, Allan F., Phoenix, AZ *Page 1-239*

Netessence, President/Chief Technical Officer, Joerg, Werner B., Salt Lake City, UT *Page 1-180*

Netforce, Inc., Software Developer, Sutan, Suhendra, Daly City, CA *Page 1-287*

NetMedia International Ltd., Project Director, Loo, Ringo, Hong Kong, Hong Kong *Page 1-18*

Netpath, Inc., President, Laforet, Christopher, Burlington, NC *Page 1-110*

Netpliance, Inc., Senior Software Engineer, Zhao, Wei, Round Rock, TX *Page 1-298*

Netstock Direct Corporation, Chief Technology Officer, Johnsen, Melissa C., Bellevue, WA *Page 1-110*

Netstream Telecom, Operations Manager, Ferrao, Helder Flavio, Sao Caetano Du Sol, Brazil *Page 1-97*

Network Engineering, Inc., Director of Sales and Marketing, Blocchi, Roger, Indianapolis, IN *Page 1-222*

Neuse Center, Management Information Systems Manager, Baxter, Linda M., New Bern, NC *Page 1-384*

Never-Enuff Enterprises, Owner, Bradford, Richard A., Northern Cambria, PA *Page 1-224*

New Bridge Technology, Systems Engineer, Allain, Jean-Marc, Houston, TX *Page 1-54*

New Horizon Management & Consulting, Consultant, Lehman, Robert P., Solon, OH *Page 1-257*

New Jersey Air National Guard, Plans and Programs Manager, Hanson-Gorby, Marcia K., McGuire Air Force Base, NJ *Page 1-393*

New Mexico Department of Labor, Information Systems Bureau, Information Systems Manager III, Broward, Michael P., Albuquerque, NM *Page 1-385*

New York City Transit Authority, Computer Administrator, Taylor, Isiah, Brooklyn, NY *Page 1-87*

New York Daily News, Vice President of Technology, Schilero, Frank, Jersey City, NJ *Page 1-15*

New York Institute of Entrepreneurship, Director/Founder, Drago, Barbara, Albany, NY *Page 1-322*

New York Methodist Hospital, Network Manager of Information Technical Services, Cox, Peter J., Brooklyn, NY *Page 1-307*

New York State Department of Labor, UI Tax Auditor 2, Konicki, James A., Albany, NY *Page 1-386*

New York State Teachers Retirement System, Manager of Information Services, Kotmel, Allan V., Albany, NY *Page 1-346*

Newbridge Networks, Director, Research & Development, Quinn, James J., Chantilly, VA *Page 1-49*

Newel Systems, Inc., System Consultant, Klempner, James H., Schaumburg, IL *Page 1-254*

Newnan Technologies, Inc., Chief Technical Officer, Morrow, Larry J., Newnan, GA *Page 1-207*

Newport, Systems Network Manager, Schmitt, Warren L., Minneapolis, MN *Page 1-86*

Newport Strategic Search LLC, Office Manager/Systems Administrator, Stetson, Audrey J., Carlsbad, CA *Page 1-169*

Nexcel Limited, Project Manager, Wai-Hung, Kwok, Kowloon, Hong Kong *Page 1-192*

Next Generation Ideas, Owner/President, Rice, Donald W., Raleigh, NC *Page 1-277*

Next Millennium Consulting, Inc., President, Pegalis, Andrew M., Bethesda, MD *Page 1-273*

Nextlink, Technical Lead Engineer, Kantaria, Jay K., Plano, TX *Page 1-100*

NextLinx Corporation, Technical Manager, Lodaya, Manish, Gaithersburg, MD *Page 1-259*

Niagara Mohawk Power Corporation, Supervisor of Software Development, Shumway, Kathleen K., Lycoming, NY *Page 1-114*

Nichols Research, Webmaster, Gatlin, Ronald S., Huntsville, AL *Page 1-240*

NIST, Computer/Network Specialist, Lowe, Darren L., Gaithersburg, MD *Page 1-360*

NOAA Coastal Services Center, Coastal Resources Social Scientist, Petrovich, Nina L., Charleston, SC *Page 1-273*

Noblestar Systems, Director of Core Technologies Division, Gautney, Charles W., Reston, VA *Page 1-240*

Nokia, Project Manager, Mallouk, Ramez H., Helsinki, Finland *Page 1-61*

Nokia Networks, Documentation Services Manager, Smith, Rebecca L., Irving, TX *Page 1-62*

Nokia, Inc., Senior Project Manager, Farral, Travis M., Irving, TX *Page 1-55*

Norman Jones Enlow Company, Network Administrator, Plummer, Kyle B., Reynoldsburg, OH *Page 1-355*

Nortel Networks
Director of Information Services and Real Estate Systems, Austin, Richard, Brampton, Ontario, Canada *Page 1-54*
Internal Business Manager for Dallas, Bunt, Christopher Allen, Richardson, TX *Page 1-55*
Network Engineer, Neal, Scott C., Overland Park, KS *Page 1-56*
Verification Engineer, Do, Minh-Kha, Saint-Laurent, Quebec, Canada *Page 1-55*
WAN/LAN Manager, Jackson, Alan W., Stoughton, MA *Page 1-55*

North American Performance Group (NAPG, Inc.), Senior Systems Architect, Gulotta, Peter, Phoenixville, PA *Page 1-244*

North Carolina State Education Assistance Authority, Manager of Computer Services, Colclough Bennett, Judith, Research Triangle Park, NC *Page 1-138*

Northbrook Community School District 28, Elementary Technology Coordinator, Andre, Darlene A., Northbrook, IL *Page 1-380*

Northeast Utilities, Information Technology Account Manager, Bates, Charles P., Berlin, CT *Page 1-116*

Northern Arizona University, Associate Professor/Associate Dean, Collins, Galen R., Flagstaff, AZ *Page 1-321*

Northern Computers, Technical Support Manager, MacIntosh, Michelle, Pawtucket, RI *Page 1-260*

Northern Illinois University, Quality Assurance/Editor, Cagney, Mary M., Wheaton, IL *Page 1-320*

Northrop Grumman
Director of Software Engineering, Baez, Ramon F., Dallas, TX *Page 1-75*
Software Engineer, Liguori, Stephen D., Bethpage, NY *Page 1-76*

Northrop Grumman-Canada Ltd., Mechanical Designer, West, Chris, Burlington, Ontario, Canada *Page 1-76*

Northstar Steel & Aluminum, Inc., Information Technology Administrator, Keane, James B., Manchester, NH *Page 1-121*

Northwestern Memorial Hospital, Director of Enterprise Systems, Lopardo, Sue, Chicago, IL *Page 1-308*

Northwestern University, Director, Burden, Matthew C., Chicago, IL *Page 1-320*

Nosco Inc., Director of Information Systems, Fowler, Susan E., Waukegan, IL *Page 1-20*

Nova Bancorp Group, Ltd., Managing Director of Information Technology, Nguyen, Khanh, Montreal, Quebec, Canada *Page 1-143*

Nova Information Systems, Senior Technical Director of Software Development, Inman, Connie C., Knoxville, TN *Page 1-301*

Nova Southeastern University, Assistant Director of Technology and Operations, Garcia-Barreras, Victor E., Davie, FL *Page 1-323*

Novacel, Director of Innovative Technologies, Anton, Patrice, deville Les Rouen, France *Page 1-26*

Novell, Inc.
Consultant, Moorehouse, Nina M., Bel Air, MD *Page 1-198*
Consultant, Whittington, Cathy D., East Norriton, PA *Page 1-200*
Senior Account Executive, Landrigan, Shawn B., Herndon, VA *Page 1-197*

Novo Nordisk IT A/S, Software Engineer, Schmidt, Mads Rosendahl, Copenhagen, Denmark *Page 1-280*

Nutreco Spain, Information Technology Manager, Franco, Vicente, Madrid, Spain *Page 1-10*

NVT Consulting Services, Owner, Patri, Neelanjan, Chattanooga, TN *Page 1-272*

Nypro, Inc., Technical Director, Distance Learning Systems, Gorman, Daniel W., Clinton, MA *Page 1-29*

O

O.S.S. Inc., System Architect, Gaitonde, Prashant V., Austin, TX *Page 1-239*

O'Brien Interactive, Website Developer/Database Administrator/Server Administrator, Winklesky, James B., Acworth, GA *Page 1-193*

O'Neil Associates, Systems Support Manager, Werkowitz, Derek, Dayton, OH *Page 1-19*

Oakland Schools, Business Leader of Technology Services, Evans, Tammy L., Waterford, MI *Page 1-381*

Obsidian Corporation, President, Gerlick, Joshua A., Oswego, IL *Page 1-177*

OC Transpo, Director of Information Technology, McLennan, Gerald J., Orleans, Ontario, Canada *Page 1-87*

oCen Communications, Senior Network Engineer, Hwang, Kyunam, Irwindale, CA *Page 1-100*

Odetics, Inc., Computer Scientist, Nyeu, Maung, Irvine, CA *Page 1-57*

Office Depot, Senior Manager of Distributed Logistics Systems, Abbott, Lisa, Delray Beach, FL *Page 1-128*

Office of the Chief Information Officer, United States Department of Energy, Director of Division of Architecture and Standards, Tiemann, Michael Anthony, Washington, DC *Page 1-289*

Office Of The Corporation Counsel, Information Technology Unit Manager, Pavlovsky, Serge Al, Washington, DC *Page 1-377*

Ohio Department of Alcohol and Drug Addiction Services, Chief of Management Information Services, Hull, Walter James, Columbus, OH *Page 1-385*

Ohio Department of Health, DQA, MDS/OASIS Technical Coordinator, Coleman, Glen A., Columbus, OH *Page 1-384*

OICW/Sequoia Adult School, Instructor, Harris, Ethel G., Menlo Park, CA *Page 1-343*

Oki Network Technologies, Director, Barber, Clifton J., Suwanee, GA *Page 1-57*

Oklahoma Baptist University, Director of Computer and Information Technology, Nickerson, Gary B., Shawnee, OK *Page 1-329*

Oklahoma Department of Corrections, Manager of Technical Services, Frazier, Stephen P., Oklahoma City, OK *Page 1-378*

Olsten Corporation, Assistant Vice President, Procurement, Mingin, Philip M., Melville, NY *Page 1-168*

Olsten Health Services, Senior Systems Engineer, Coyle, Charles W., Tampa, FL *Page 1-306*

Omaha Public Power District, Programmer Analyst, Ikeda-Hayes, Rieko, Papillion, NE *Page 1-114*

Oman Development Bank, Computer Manager, Nasser, Zaina, Muscat, Oman *Page 1-139*

OMNOVA Solutions Inc., Divisional Information Systems Manager, Finklestein, Ronald, Mogadore, OH *Page 1-27*

On Source Consulting, Consultant, Strechay, Robert J., Houston, TX *Page 1-286*

Onsale, Inc., Software Engineer, Nagel, Dennis E., Menlo Park, CA *Page 1-267*

Ontempo, Director of Information Systems, Swanson, Hilary W., Glendale, CA *Page 1-287*

Onyx Solutions, Inc., President, Fox, Steven W., Newnan, GA *Page 1-237*

Open Systems, Senior Consultant, Rastogi, Shashank, Jersey City, NJ *Page 1-276*

Optical Coating Laboratory, Network Engineer, Brown, John S., Santa Rosa, CA *Page 1-82*

Optimum Solutions, Inc., Software Support Manager, Dwyer, Sherry L., Nashville, TN *Page 1-235*

OPTIMUS Corporation, Senior Software Engineer, Qian, Fang, Silver Spring, MD *Page 1-275*

Oracle Corporation
Electronic Sales Manager, Johnson, Deke Andrew, Redwood Shores, CA *Page 1-196*
Product Manager, Robson, Peter J., Belmont, CA *Page 1-199*
Project Lead, Patil, Ashutosh, Redwood Shores, CA *Page 1-198*
Senior Applications Architect, Martinsson, Lars E., Redwood City, CA *Page 1-197*
Senior Consultant, Marcus, Judith L., New York, NY *Page 1-197*
Senior Consulting Specialist, Odok, Erhan, Orlando, FL *Page 1-198*

Oracle University, Education Manager, Frazier, Larry B., Morengo, IL *Page 1-323*

Orbcomm, Director, Brickerd, D. Dean, Sterling, VA *Page 1-96*

Orbital Sciences Corporation, Senior Network Administrator, Timberlake, Frank "Rusty", Sterling, VA *Page 1-79*

Oregon Department of Forestry, Technical Support Supervisor, Gum, Jeanette M., Salem, OR *Page 1-388*

Oregon State University, Director of Technology Support Services, Korwin, Anthony R., Prescott, AZ *Page 1-327*

Orient Overseas Container Line, Ltd., Technical Analyst, Chan, Joe, Wanchai, Hong Kong *Page 1-89*

Orscheln Management Company, Web Administrator, Bryant, John A., Moberly, MO *Page 1-226*

Ortho Computer Systems, Inc., Director of Operations, Schuelka, Todd, Ames, IA *Page 1-281*

OSF Healthcare Systems, Project Manager, Farris, Terrance J., Peoria, IL *Page 1-152*

Osram Sylvania, Assistant Analyst, Arpide, Jose I., Beverly, MA *Page 1-53*

Ottawa University, Internet Manager, Montgomery, Janie E., Ottawa, KS *Page 1-329*

Ouintiles Pacific, Inc., Database Programmer, Ko, Istella Chui-Mei, Mountain View, CA *Page 1-358*

Our Lady of Mount Carmel School, Technology Coordinator/Assistant Principal, Wilkins, Teresa, Baltimore, MD *Page 1-319*

Outokumpu American Brass, Technical Director, Finney, M. Parker, Buffalo, NY *Page 1-32*

Oxford Health Plans, Programmer, Pardy, Brian J., Branford, CT *Page 1-151*

P

Pace University at Pleasantville, Manager of Client Support, Coppola, Jean Frances, Briarcliff, NY *Page 1-322*

Pace/Butler Corporation, Vice President, Walden, Steven J., Edmond, OK *Page 1-129*

Pacific Bell, Lead Project Manager, Jones, Jeffrey M., San Ramon, CA *Page 1-100*

Pacific Gas & Electric, Mobile Computing Product Manager, McQuillister, George A., Oakland, CA *Page 1-117*

Pacific Investment Management Company, Systems and Network Manager, Fox, Jeffrey W., Newport Beach, CA *Page 1-161*

Packaging Technologies, Systems Administrator, Nourse, Sharon, Davenport, IA *Page 1-38*

Pagemart Wireless, Senior Manager, Bass, Barbara A., Dallas, TX *Page 1-92*

PageNet, Senior Software Engineer, Massey, Thomas E., Dallas, TX *Page 1-102*

Palisades Safety & Insurance Management, Data Processing Specialist, Williams, Terry, Hoboken, NJ *Page 1-154*

Palm Beach County Health Care District, Operations and Database Manager, Vargas, Usha, West Palm Beach, FL *Page 1-152*

Panalpina Inc., Project Manager, Ostermann, Gerhard H., Morristown, NJ *Page 1-88*

Panasonic Technology Inc., Scientist, Yu, Hong Heather, Princeton, NJ *Page 1-360*

Paradigm Analytical Laboratories, Systems Manager, Dickinson, Gregory, Wilmington, NC *Page 1-361*

Parametric Technology Corporation, Software Engineer, Moiseyev, Aleksey, Waltham, MA *Page 1-198*

PAREXEL International, WW IS Security Manager, Fiore, Stephanie A., Lowell, MA *Page 1-23*

Parkson Corporation, Mechanical Engineer, Matos, Ricardo R., Fort Lauderdale, FL *Page 1-38*

Parkview Center School, Information Technology Assistant, Sankot, Janice M., Roseville, MN *Page 1-317*

Parkway Insurance
Help Desk/Assistant to Network Administrator, Urbanowicz, Robert Stanley, Bridgewater, NJ *Page 1-154*
Oracle Database Administrator, Pulcine, Brian, Franklin Park, NJ *Page 1-154*

Parkway School District, Information Systems Manager, Hennessy, Sharon M., Chesterfield, MO *Page 1-381*

Parson Brinkerhoff Farradyne, Senior System Engineer, Homami, Hassan Rezaei, New York, NY *Page 1-248*

Parsons Engineering Science, Project Manager, Birdi, Moninder S., Fairfax, MD *Page 1-362*

Pasco Inc., Support Manager, Fincke, Greg, Dade City, FL *Page 1-7*

Paso Robles Public School District, Director of Technology and Information Services, Smith, Sheldon K., Paso Robles, CA *Page 1-383*

Patton General Contracting, Information Systems Manager, Salter, Jim, Summerville, SC *Page 1-4*

Paulding High School, Teacher, Mengerink, Joel W., Van Wert, OH *Page 1-316*

Payroll Systems.com, Information Technology Director, Stine, Gary M., Aliso Viejo, CA *Page 1-355*

PC Net, Owner/Operator, Bradshaw, Rupert R., Gulfport, MS *Page 1-224*

PC Troubleshooter, Inc., Chief Executive Officer, Ukani, Ayoub B., Miami, FL *Page 1-292*

PCSI, e-Commerce Practice Director, Patel, Kanti R., Holmdel, NJ *Page 1-271*

PE Technikon, Information Technology Director, Schonken, Andre, Port Elizabeth, South Africa *Page 1-338*

Peerless Manufacturing Company, Project Engineer, Rios, Joe Gaudalupe, Dallas, TX *Page 1-38*

Pegasus Consulting Group, Technical Team Leader, Sutton, Paula Emery, Londonderry, NH *Page 1-287*

PegaSystems Inc., Senior Technical Services Consultant, Merkt, Greg, Cambridge, MA *Page 1-264*

Peirone Produce, Information Systems Manager, Sill, Gary L., Spokane, WA *Page 1-125*

Pellerano & Herrera, Management Information Systems Assistant Manager, Marchena, Ruddy, Miami, FL *Page 1-312*

Penguin Consulting Company, Inc., President, Meisinger, Steven D., Arlington, TX *Page 1-264*

Pennrose Properties, Inc., Director of Systems Support, Miles, Mazda T., Philadelphia, PA *Page 1-302*

Pennsylvania State Police, Trooper, Erdely, Robert W., Indiana, PA *Page 1-376*

Pentacon Industry Group, Inc., Business Support Specialist, Grunstad, Chandler R., Fort Wayne, IN *Page 1-86*

Pepe Enterprises, President, Pepe, Kenneth M., Island Park, NY *Page 1-273*

Pepper Construction, Systems Engineer, Reid, Nathan D., Hainesville, IL *Page 1-4*

Pepsi Cola International, Project Leader, O'Donnell, Charlie, Somers, NY *Page 1-9*

Perceptron, Systems Engineer, Keshavmurthy, Shyam, Plymouth, MI *Page 1-304*

Perclose, Inc., Information Technology Manager, Salinas, Alexander, Redwood City, CA *Page 1-83*

Perkin-Elmer Corporation, Project Manager, Davis, James V., Raleigh, NC *Page 1-233*

Perot Systems, Systems Integration Specialist, Sandiego, Angelito H., McKinney, TX *Page 1-169*

Perpetual Technologies, Inc.
President, Oracle DBA, Stephens, Ryan K., Indianapolis, IN *Page 1-286*
Vice President, Plew, Ronald R., Indianapolis, IN *Page 1-274*

Perspective Technology Corporation, Human Resources Administrator, Gillette, Kimberly S., Vienna, VA *Page 1-241*

Pervasive Software Inc., Human Resources Information Systems Specialist, Peterson, Billie, Austin, TX *Page 1-187*

Peterborough County-City Health Unit, Computer Technician/Analyst, Milligan, Richard P., Peterborough, Ontario, Canada *Page 1-385*

Petro-Canada, Senior Security Advisor, Johnson, Gary, Calgary, Alberta, Canada *Page 1-27*

PFF Bank & Trust, Database Administrator, Lambert, Paul R., Pomona, CA *Page 1-134*

Pharmacia & Upjohn, Director of Internet Communications, Hepp, Jean-Paul, Peapack, NJ *Page 1-23*

PharMerica, Director of Strategic Clinical Services Information Systems, Daugherty, J. Max, Pearland, TX *Page 1-130*

Philips Medical Systems
Change Analyst, Dubnicka, Leigh C., Shelton, CT *Page 1-69*
Chief Architect/Development Director, ICS, Wong, Stephen, Mountain View, CA *Page 1-70*

Philips P.C. Peripherals, Information Technology Manager, Athey, Harry C., Colorado Springs, CO *Page 1-128*

Phillips Broad Band Network, RF Design Engineer, Stathopoulos, Dimitrios, Syracuse, NY *Page 1-32*

Phillips Petroleum Company
Engineering Principal, Embry, Dale L., Bartlesville, OK *Page 1-27*
Systems Analyst Buyer, Parker, Jeffrey T., Borger, TX *Page 1-27*

Phoenix Technologies Ltd., Engineering Team Leader, Mathur, Sameer, San Jose, CA *Page 1-183*

Physicians Health Plan, Manager of Network Services, Rose, David E., Fort Wayne, IN *Page 1-153*

Pike Tool & Grinding, Process Engineering/CNC Programmer, Stebenne, Andrew M., Colorado Springs, CO *Page 1-33*

Pikes Peak Mental Health
Management Information Systems Manager, Bender, Carla V., Colorado Springs, CO *Page 1-307*
Network Administrator, Houghton, Jeremy E., Colorado Springs, CO *Page 1-308*

Pillsbury Madison & Sutro, Project Coordinator, Thiele, Cynthia Buchan, San Francisco, CA *Page 1-313*

Pima Community College, Microcomputer Technician, Wise, Alan L., Tucson, AZ *Page 1-339*

Pipeline Interactive, Director of Account Services, Stocker, Laura Baker, Lebanon, PA *Page 1-191*

Pixel Magic Imaging, Design Coordinator, Krell, Lori A., Austin, TX *Page 1-181*

Planning Consultants, Inc., Senior Systems Engineer, Brooks, Jeffrey A., Dahlgren, VA *Page 1-225*

Plantrol Systems, Ltd., Programmer, Lapp, Jon E., Westfield, NY *Page 1-182*

Plaspro (Plastic Provisions Inc.), Sales Engineer, Torry, Billy D., Sears, MI *Page 1-29*

Playa Vista, Marketing Manager, Fidelman, Jennifer Faith, Los Angeles, CA *Page 1-160*

Plural, Creative Lead, Lewis A., Francisco, New York, NY *Page 1-182*

Point of Sale Technology Corporation, President, Newman, Moses N., New York, NY *Page 1-268*

PointStar.com, Web Coordinator, Tang, Carolyn B., Schaumburg, IL *Page 1-166*

Police and Firemen's Disability, Development Manager, Burchfield, Bill, Columbus, OH *Page 1-155*

Pollenpolen, Art Director/Designer, von Pfaler, Martin, Vallentuna, Sweden *Page 1-293*

Polo Ralph Lauren, Systems Manager, McCown, Renee, Lyndhurst, NJ *Page 1-132*

Poly Products, LLC, Systems Manager, Rehman, Razi Ur, Sultanate, Oman *Page 1-12*

Pomeroy Computer Resources, Network Engineer, Palatinus, Gregory S., Indianapolis, IN *Page 1-271*

Porter & Chester Institute, Supervisor/Instructor, Leblanc, Christopher S., Ludlow, MA *Page 1-341*

Portland Development Commission, Project Manager, Ruddiman, Thomas A., Portland, OR *Page 1-389*

Power 2000 Inc., Chief Instructor/Senior Managing Consultant, Demarest, Jim, Naperville, IL *Page 1-233*

Power Data Corporation, President, Robinson, Marck R., Bellevue, WA *Page 1-188*

Power FCU, Assistant Director of Marketing/Webmaster, Hill, David J., Syracuse, NY *Page 1-136*

ppb, Inc., President, Azar, Lawrence, Portola Valley, CA *Page 1-64*

PPG Industries, Inc., Information Technology Manager, Washington, Jacqulin R., Huntsville, AL *Page 1-30*

PQH Architects, Inc., Architect/3D Design Specialist, Papke, Steven D., Jacksonville, FL *Page 1-351*

Premera Blue Cross, Information Technology Team Leader, Tolman, R. Brent, Nine Mile Falls, WA *Page 1-151*

Premier Consultancy, President, Mullapudi, Ramarao, Plano, TX *Page 1-266*

Premier Systems Integrators
Internet and Data Management Technology Practice Leader, Norwood, Kevin W., Richardson, TX *Page 1-208*
Systems Administrator, Tyler, James E., Charlotte, NC *Page 1-210*

Premiere Conferencing, Director of Network Operations, Murphy, George E., Colorado Springs, CO *Page 1-102*

PricewaterhouseCoopers
Consultant, Lyle, Stephen T., Fairfax, VA *Page 1-354*
Information Technology Consultant, Hunt, Wong Mee, Melaka, Malaysia *Page 1-354*
Knowledge Transfer Manager, Shields, Andrew V., Philadelphia, PA *Page 1-355*
Network Administrator, D'Andrea, Marcus J., Chicago, IL *Page 1-352*
Partner, Parks, Floyd, San Francisco, CA *Page 1-354*
Senior Associate, Patil, Abhijit B., Burlington, MA *Page 1-354*

PricewaterhouseCoopers LLP
Manager, Global Risk Management Solutions, Guo, Peter C. H., Vancouver, British Columbia, Canada *Page 1-353*
Manager, Marín, José R., San Juan, Puerto Rico *Page 1-354*
Senior Associate, Babal, Suraj, Edison, NJ *Page 1-352*

Prime Systems, Inc., Senior Applications Consultant, Fry, Paul Charles, Cleveland, OH *Page 1-238*

Primerica Financial Services, Technical Specialist, Manges, John P., Duluth, GA *Page* 1-139

Prince George's Accounting Government/Department of Environmental Resources, Information Technology Officer, Chakhtoura, Nehme G, Upper Marlboro, MD *Page* 1-371

Principal Financial Group, Systems Programmer, Morrison, K. C., Des Moines, IA *Page* 1-148

Print Tech, Inc., Information Technology Manager, Steven, Brad J., Ann Arbor, MI *Page* 1-166

PRISMA Marketing, Director/Owner, Stauch, Matthias E., Berlin, Germany *Page* 1-285

Pro Staff Personnel, Area Manager, Nightingale, Mark J., Houston, TX *Page* 1-370

Pro-Tech, Director, Heger, John P., Lucens, Switzerland *Page* 1-246

Process Software Corporation, Technical Support Coordinator, Adams, Sharon K., Chelmsford, MA *Page* 1-170

Proconex, Lead Engineer, Kaskoun, Anthony Joseph, Hatboro, PA *Page* 1-205

Procter & Gamble, Senior Accounting Manager, Goodhart, Daniel L., Cincinnati, OH *Page* 1-25

ProcureNet, Inc., Senior Database Administrator/Architect, Burns, Elizabeth J., New Hartford, CT *Page* 1-172

Professional Communications Systems, Director of Corporate Sales, Schall, Ronald G., Tampa, FL *Page* 1-209

Professional Consulting Services, Director/Owner, Stough, Bill, Tallassee, AL *Page* 1-366

Professional Duplicating, Systems Administrator/Digital Imaging Specialist, O'Bryant, George H., Media, PA *Page* 1-20

Proficient Software Expo Consulting Inc., President, Reddy, Jagan M., Fords, NJ *Page* 1-276

PROMATIS Corporation, Chief Operating Officer, Graf, Sebastian, San Ramon, CA *Page* 1-177

Promega, Systems Administrator, Ruffin, Jimmy, Madison, WI *Page* 1-358

Propaganda, Founder/Project Manager, Poag, Bowie J., Tucson, AZ *Page* 1-199

PROSOFT, Senior Training Analyst, Baker, Melvin, Hampton, VA *Page* 1-201

PROTOCOL Technology Partners, LLC, Principal Owner, Weis, Ted P., Scottsdale, AZ *Page* 1-295

Providian Financial, Technical Manager, Data Warehousing, Spencer, Terri J., Fremont, CA *Page* 1-94

ProxyMed, Inc., Y2K Project Manager, Marton, Candace C., Boca Raton, FL *Page* 1-183

Prudential, Director, Brickman, Eric R., Newark, NJ *Page* 1-148

Prudential Carolinas Realty, Manager of Information Systems, Duggins, Ginger B., Greensboro, NC *Page* 1-159

Prudential Insurance, Systems Director, Ouellette, Beth, Roseland, NJ *Page* 1-149

Prudential Insurance Company of America, PC/LAN Specialist, Pierson, Gina L., Lafayette, NJ *Page* 1-149

Prudentual Reality and Relocation Services, Network Engineer, Simko, Edward J., Ossining, NY *Page* 1-117

PSC, Information Technology Director, Pearce, Cecil L., Loganville, GA *Page* 1-391

PSEG Services Corporation, Information Technology Project Manager, George, Dorina, West New York, NJ *Page* 1-87

PSINet, Supervisor of LAN Engineers, Weaver, Demian K., Herndon, VA *Page* 1-294

PSW Technologies, Senior Software Consultant, Bollineni, Anand K., Austin, TX *Page* 1-223

PTI, Webmaster/Manager/Enterprise Engineer, Martin, Robert A., Atlanta, GA *Page* 1-365

Public Financial Management, Director of Information Technology, Scott, David L., Philadelphia, PA *Page* 1-147

Public Opinion, Management Information Systems Director, Gaspardino, Amy L., Chambersburg, PA *Page* 1-15

Public Service/Electric & Gas, Public Affairs Manager, Lombardini, John T., Newark, NJ *Page* 1-116

Public Utility Commission, Systems Support Specialist, Lizcano, Olga, Austin, TX *Page* 1-390

Puget Sound Naval Shipyard, Architect, King, Keith A., Bremerton, WA *Page* 1-78

Pulau Electronics Corporation, Site Manager, Howard, Charles L., Colorado Springs, CO *Page* 1-71

Puma Technology, Senior Architect, Feng, Wu-Chang, Emeryville, CA *Page* 1-92

Purchase Business Institute, President, Purchase-Owens, Francena, Kentwood, MI *Page* 1-369

Purdue Pharma L.P., Manager, PKDM Submissions Support Coordinator, DeModna, Christina K., Ardsley, NY *Page* 1-23

Purdue University, Systems Administrator, Loeffler, Kevin J., West Lafayette, IN *Page* 1-328

Pyxis Consulting, President, Hughes, Shane R., Boston, MA *Page* 1-249

Q

Quad Systems Corporation, Customer Support Manager, Gordon, Frank E., Willow Grove, PA *Page* 1-59

Quality Solutions, Consultant, Holderread, John R., Springfield, IL *Page* 1-363

Quantum Corporation, Senior Firmware Engineer, Nutter, John J., Shrewsbury, MA *Page* 1-47

Quantum Resources, Partner/Senior Consultant, Garrett, Angie R., Center Conway, NH *Page* 1-239

Quebec Government, Computer Operator, Alexis, Emmanuel E. A., Montreal, Quebec, Canada *Page* 1-372

Quebecor World Hawkins, Group Leader of Electronics Shop, Hinson, Kevin, Church Hill, TN *Page* 1-20

Queensland Police, Branch Manager, ISB, Stoopman, Michael B., Brisbane, Queensland, Australia *Page* 1-377

Questra, Inc., Senior Consultant, Kammerdiener, Shawn Ivan, Rochester, NY *Page* 1-252

Quintus Corporation, Senior Systems Administrator, Weeks, John B., Fremont, CA *Page* 1-295

Qwest Communications, Manager of Corporate Disaster Recovery, Cowan, Patrick Neal, Denver, CO *Page* 1-97

R

R R Donnelley & Sons, West Coast Information Technology Manager, Jones, Benedict, Torrance, CA *Page* 1-18

Radian Inc., Senior Systems Engineer, Halaut, Jeffrey D., Alexandria, VA *Page* 1-178

Radian International Software, Support Analyst, Desroches, Dennis, Houston, TX *Page* 1-174

Radio Advertising Bureau, SQL Server Administrator, Aldridge, Brad W., Dallas, TX *Page* 1-165

Radio Frequency Systems, Telecommunications Supervisor, Sabin, Matthew S., Meriden, CT *Page* 1-57

Rail Inc., Information Technology Project Manager, Thorpe, James L., Cary, NC *Page* 1-87

Rand Technologies, Principal Systems Engineer, Burton, Walt, Schaumburg, IL *Page* 1-347

Randol International, Ltd., Production Manager/Art Director/Web Designer, Hale, Christie Callahan, Denver, CO *Page* 1-18

Randy's Professional Web Site Design, Owner/Operator, Parrish, Richard R., Winnsboro, TX *Page* 1-186

Rapidigm, Software Developer, Tamma, Leela Shankar, Denver, CO *Page* 1-288

Rappahannock Regional Jail, Management Information Systems Manager, Bailey, Brian A., Fredericksburg, VA *Page* 1-377

Rational Software, Product Manager, Haynes, Dawn M., Lexington, MA *Page* 1-178

Ravenna Aluminum, Network Administrator, Bennett, John C., Ravenna, OH *Page* 1-32

Raymond Building Supply, Director of Management Information Systems, Percifield, George A., North Fort Myers, FL *Page* 1-118

Raymond V. Hall Training & Consultant Services, Chief Trainer, Hall, Raymond V., Chicago, IL *Page* 1-245

Raytheon
Principal Technical Support and Training Development Specialist, Spangler, Kerry, Marlborough, MA *Page* 1-81
Senior Software Engineer II, Gellineau, Antonio C., Madison, AL *Page* 1-80

Raytheon Company, Senior Principal Software Engineer, Losson, M. Melissa, Fullerton, CA *Page* 1-80

Raytheon Systems, Engineer, Shih, William, Covina, CA *Page* 1-80

Raytheon Travel Air, Senior Systems Developer, Fowler, Darren L., Wichita, KS *Page* 1-75

Raytheon/TI Systems Company, Senior Electrical Design Engineer, Wilkins, Jackie D., Van Alstyne, TX *Page* 1-81

RCG Information Technology, Senior Account Executive, Mulé, Peter T., New York, NY *Page* 1-266

RCN Corporation
   Director of Y2K Program, Walsh, Christopher W., Princeton, NJ *Page* 1-106
   Senior Manager of Operations, Bryant, Tom, Arlington, MA *Page* 1-96

Reactor, Principal/Account Manager, Chabrier, Donna R., Mountain View, CA *Page* 1-166

Rebel.com, Consultant, Speed, Russell F., Ottawa, Ontario, Canada *Page* 1-285

Reebok International, Principal SAP R/3, Smith, Jeffrey W., Holden, MA *Page* 1-30

Reel Film Festival, Inc., Director of Multimedia Design, Harlap, Jonathan, Montreal, Quebec, Canada *Page* 1-166

Regional Network Communications, Inc., Director of Information Technology, Gaul, Donna F., Bethlehem, PA *Page* 1-176

Regional Transportation District, Network Systems Administrator, Balkema, Allan, Denver, CO *Page* 1-87

Regions Financial Corporation, Microcomputer Systems Administrator, Gosnell, Phillip K., Mobile, AL *Page* 1-140

Reinhart, Boerner, et al, Help Desk Supervisor, Bolyard, Whitney L., Milwaukee, WI *Page* 1-311

Relational Technologies, Lead Consultant, Speck, Richard J., Farmington Hills, MI *Page* 1-285

Reliant Energy, Manager, SAP Applications Production Support, Chohrach, Michael J., Houston, TX *Page* 1-116

Reliant Energy HL&P, Applications Manager, Batiste, Joshua, Houston, TX *Page* 1-115

Reliant Energy, Inc., Senior Vice President of Information Technology/Chief Information Officer, McCrea, Ianthe Helen, Houston, TX *Page* 1-116

Remington Agency, Chief Executive Officer, Yates, Travis, Gainesville, FL *Page* 1-193

Renal Care Group, Inc., Clinical System Supervisor, Obeirne, Barbara H., Wichita, KS *Page* 1-306

Republic Mortgage Insurance Company, Senior Network Administrator, Wilkie, Timothy J., Winston-Salem, NC *Page* 1-156

Resource Information Management Systems, Inc., Director of Product Architecture, Williams, Laura H., Naperville, IL *Page* 1-192

Resource Systems, Inc., Technical Consultant, Brown, Thomas K., New York, NY *Page* 1-194

Resource Technologies Corporation, Information Technology Manager, Channell, John L., Troy, MI *Page* 1-167

Resources Technical Services, President, Simmons, Reginold T., Hyattsville, MD *Page* 1-283

RESPEC, Information Technology Manager, O'Connor, Brian K., Albuquerque, NM *Page* 1-269

Retek Information System, Information Technology Manager, Meszaros, Jason P., Minneapolis, MN *Page* 1-184

Retro Studios, Director of Information Technology, Thomas, George A., Austin, TX *Page* 1-85

Revacomp Inc., Area Manager, Derrick, Charles E., Ellicott City, MD *Page* 1-128

Review Technology Group, President/Chief Executive Officer, Thomas, Russell, Brookville, OH *Page* 1-210

Reynolds & Reynolds
   Database Administrator, Glover, John D., Dayton, OH *Page* 1-21
   Systems Administrator, Loy-Tate, Deanne, Oklahoma City, OK *Page* 1-21

RF Wolters Company, Inc., AS/400 Manager, Cooper, Amanda M., Marietta, GA *Page* 1-372

Rheem Manufacturing Company, Network Administrator, Boyd, Ashley Aubrey, Montgomery, AL *Page* 1-53

RHI Consulting, UNIX System Administrator, Hudson, Kevin L., Houston, TX *Page* 1-249

RIA - Research Institute of America, Developer, Brown, Michael W., Carrollton, TX *Page* 1-172

Rich Products, Senior Network Analyst, Sandoval, Fernando, Buffalo, NY *Page* 1-8

Richard J. Daley College, Computer Science Professor, Dardai, Shahid M., Chicago, IL *Page* 1-336

Richardson Independent School District, Executive Director, Applications and Operations, Yarrow, John R., Richardson, TX *Page* 1-319

Right Connection, Inc., President, Lynt, William W., Kenosha, WI *Page* 1-259

Riley County Police Department, Computer Systems Administrator, Glick, Gary Edward, Manhattan, KS *Page* 1-376

Rise Communications, Inc., President, Paul, Charles, Jacksonville, TX *Page* 1-111

RLI Corporation, Web Developer, Engvall, Thomas J., Peoria, IL *Page* 1-174

Road Runner
   Network Engineer, Fitzgerald, Michael G., Woodside, NY *Page* 1-237
   Network Engineer, Schreffler, Scott A., Columbus, OH *Page* 1-281

Roberta Fox Group Inc., President/Chief Executive Officer, Fox, Roberta J., Toronto, Ontario, Canada *Page* 1-203

Robertson Stephens, Information Technology Manager, Lombardi, James, Bronxville, NY *Page* 1-143

Rochester Institute of Technology
   Assistant Professor of Information Technology, Hill, Lawrence W., Rochester, NY *Page* 1-325
   Professor, Garrison, Daniel J., Pittsford, NY *Page* 1-324

Rockingham Community College, Network Technician, Evans, Cheryl L., Wentworth, NC *Page* 1-336

Rockwell, Systems Administrator, Jordan, Roxanne M., Melbourne, FL *Page* 1-75

Rockwell Collins, Information Technology Staff, Picariello, Angela E., Melbourne, FL *Page* 1-77

Rocsoar, Inc., President, Mao, John, Wilmington, DE *Page* 1-261

Roetech Services, President/Owner, Roe, Wesley D., Downers Grove, IL *Page* 1-277

ROI Systems, Information Technology Manager, Snetsinger, Leo V., Minneapolis, MN *Page* 1-190

RoseTel Systems, Director of Technology, Sailer, Chrystiana, Los Angeles, CA *Page* 1-112

Ross Systems, Manager of Information Development, Long, Cheryl C., Atlanta, GA *Page* 1-183

Rosses Community School, Teacher, Moy, Anne, Donegal, Ireland *Page* 1-316

Roundy's Ohio Division, Order Support for Management Information Systems, Weaver, Sandra K., Lima, OH *Page* 1-124

RouterWare, Systems Engineer, Cilley, Brian W., Huntington Beach, CA *Page* 1-230

Royal Cabinet of Saudi Arabia, Computer Consultant, Almogbel, Saud A., Sterling, VA *Page* 1-370

Royal Oak Boring, Systems Administrator, Crawford, Jen, Lake Orion, MI *Page* 1-73

Royal Ordnance North America, PC Support Technician, Godsey, Vicki Lynn, Bloomingdale, TN *Page* 1-34

RSM McGladrey, Inc.
   Information Technology Consultant, Cassat, Daniel M., Cheyenne, WY *Page* 1-352
   National Government Information Technology Consulting Coordinator, Robichaud, Steven E., San Bernardino, CA *Page* 1-355

RTC Technologies, Inc., Manager of Software Development, Seney, Thomas R., Racine, WI *Page* 1-189

Rubber Products Distributors, Computer Coordinator, Hammons, Lois G., Indianapolis, IN *Page* 1-123

Russellville Realty, Operations Director, Hale, Chris L., Russellville, AR *Page* 1-159

Rutgers University, Programmer/Analyst, Mayer, Warren D., Newark, NJ *Page* 1-328

RWD Technologies, Associate Software Engineer, Magwood, Quanteer D., Columbia, MD *Page* 1-260

RWJ & Associates, Information Technologies Division Head, Barto, Bill L., Oklahoma City, OK *Page* 1-167

S

S 304, Product Review Board Coordinator, Doan, Cody, Minneapolis, MN *Page* 1-83

S&C Electric Company, Computer Graphic Specialist, Nickele, Margaret M., Chicago, IL *Page* 1-52

S1 Corporation
   Information Technology Director, Vedda, Michael S., Santa Clara, CA *Page* 1-200
   Senior Data Architect, Di Luna, Leasa M., Littleton, MA *Page* 1-196

Saber Systems & Consulting, Inc., President, Roberts, Thomas P., Jackson, MS *Page* 1-277

Saboten Web Design, Owner, Schneider, Keiko K., Albuquerque, NM *Page* 1-281

Sacaton Public School District #18, Director of Technology, Ralstin, Richard, Sacaton, AZ *Page* 1-382

Saddle Creek Corporation, Network Analyst, Kessler, Peter W., Macon, GA *Page* 1-88

Safeco Life Insurance, Database Administrator, Richards, Sharon L., Redmond, WA *Page 1-149*

Sage Software, Inc., Support Manager, Liddell, William "Keeko", Dallas, TX *Page 1-258*

Saguaro Clinical Research, Information Manager, Zaragoza, Carla, Tucson, AZ *Page 1-359*

SAIC
    Division Administrator, Staples, Karen R., King George, VA *Page 1-359*
    Division Manager, Bjerkaas, Carlton L., O'Fallon, IL *Page 1-357*
    Lead Network Security Specialist, Bartoli, Peter J., San Diego, CA *Page 1-357*
    Senior Scientist, Wick, John A., McLean, VA *Page 1-359*
    Senior Systems Engineer, Moore, Allen K., Elmendorf Air Force Base, AK *Page 1-358*
    Software Applications Engineer, Hackney, Barbie V., Austin, TX *Page 1-357*
    System Administrator, Cross, Matthew J., Orlando, FL *Page 1-232*

SAIR, Inc., Senior Consultant, Vazhkudai, Sudharshan S., Oxford, MS *Page 1-292*

SalesSupport.com, Web Design Developer, Parker, Kerry, Dallas, TX *Page 1-186*

Sam Houston State University, Systems Technician, Robbins, Robert Randall, Willis, TX *Page 1-331*

Samuel Rodgers Community Health Center, Management Information Systems Director, Busch, Darnell, Kansas City, MO *Page 1-307*

San Gabriel Valley Credit Union, Information Systems Manager, Rogers, David D., El Monte, CA *Page 1-137*

San Joaquin County Public Works, Office Systems Analyst, Jones, Anthony M., Stockton, CA *Page 1-371*

San Juan College, Director of Learning Technologies, Degner, Ann L., Farmington, NM *Page 1-336*

San Juan County Assessor, Appraiser/Programmer Analyst, Benfield, Janie, Aztec, NM *Page 1-379*

San Marcos United School District, Coordinator of Technology and Information Systems, Sanchez-Pfeiffer, Kitty, San Marcos, CA *Page 1-383*

Sandia National Laboratories, Software Quality Engineer, Knirk, Dwayne L., Albuquerque, NM *Page 1-361*

SAP, E-Business Strategy Manager, Meckley, Hope Eyre, Atlanta, GA *Page 1-184*

SAP Professional Organization, President/Founder, Gibson, Stephen, Mooresville, NC *Page 1-241*

Sapient Corporation
    Architect, Garimella, Jagan, Jersey City, NJ *Page 1-239*
    Domain Expert, Mukundan, Bobby S., Addison, TX *Page 1-365*
    Software Engineer, Bansal, Kapil, Union City, NJ *Page 1-201*
    Training Manager, Childs, Robert L., Cambridge, MA *Page 1-202*

Sarl Cyberjet, President, Parot, Philippe, Etampes, France *Page 1-198*

SAS Institute, Ergonomics Coordinator, Kitts Malik, Kathleen, Cary, NC *Page 1-180*

SASI, Database Developer, Wilson, Salena, Chicago, IL *Page 1-343*

Saudi Arabian Bechtel Company, Information Technology Consultant, Noon, Patrick H., Al Khobar, Saudi Arabia *Page 1-5*

Saudi Lighting Company, Management Information Systems Manager, Hussain, Masood, Riyadh, Saudi Arabia *Page 1-54*

Savannah-Chatham County Board of Education, Program Manager, Ray, Ramon Jarrod, Savannah, GA *Page 1-382*

Savantnet Solutions, Web Developer, Lin, Jin, New York, NY *Page 1-258*

Savvy Data, President, Schweitzer, Richard, Pompano Beach, FL *Page 1-189*

SBC Communications Inc.
    Data Systems Engineer, Hattenhauer, Wallace L., Bryant, AR *Page 1-99*
    Senior Analyst, Banerjee, Ayananshu, St. Louis, MO *Page 1-95*

SBC Technology Resources, Director, Coursey, Cameron K., Austin, TX *Page 1-357*

SBM-IBM, Country Sales Manager, Shehata, Mounir, Jeddah, Saudi Arabia *Page 1-282*

SBPA Systems, Inc., Product Developer, Potowski, Christopher J., Houston, TX *Page 1-187*

SCA Hygiene Products, Network Specialist, Salisbury, Andrew J., Eddystone, PA *Page 1-15*

Scandinavian Airlines, Administration Manager, Lindberg, Reiulf, Oslo, Norway *Page 1-89*

SCB Computer Technology, Inc., Director of Recruiting, Fulmer, Allyson, Alpharetta, GA *Page 1-238*

Schafer-CIT, Consultant, Ziehl, Jonathan R., Fairport, NY *Page 1-298*

Schein Pharmaceuticals, Director of Application Software, DaSilva, Elsie, Florham Park, NJ *Page 1-22*

Schenck Turner Inc., Software Engineer, Nebel, John K., Orion, MI *Page 1-83*

Schlumberger, Program Manager, Chawla, Inder, Houston, TX *Page 1-2*

Schlumberger/GeoQuest, Consultant, Mikkelsen, Dean C., Houston, TX *Page 1-3*

Schlund + Partner AG, Partner/Manager of Domain Services, Schaetzlein, Eric R., Karlsruhe, Germany *Page 1-112*

Schneider Electric, Manager of Manufacturing Engineering, Crawford, James A., Westford, MA *Page 1-64*

Schreck Morris, Information Systems Director, Baker, Robert D., Las Vegas, NV *Page 1-311*

Schwab Institutional, Project Manager III, Plumb, Sean F., Denver, CO *Page 1-146*

Science Applications International Corporation, Project Manager, Georges, William T., San Diego, CA *Page 1-240*

SciQuest.com, Enterprise Architect, Johnson, Ron D., Morrisville, NC *Page 1-132*

SCIT, Information Technology Technical and Administrative Assistant, Nial, Marjorie, Mount Pleasant, MI *Page 1-162*

SCL Health Services, PC Network Technician, Schneider, Jonathan, Leavenworth, KS *Page 1-344*

Scott Hull Associates, Marketing Strategist, Jones, Beth E., Dayton, OH *Page 1-166*

SCS, Inc., Information Systems Manager, Lipson, Derek N., Fremont, NE *Page 1-13*

SCT
    Lead Programmer Analyst, Johnson, Janet Lee, Lexington, KY *Page 1-180*
    Senior Architect, Knotts, James Brian, Malvern, PA *Page 1-180*

SCT Corporation, LAN Administrator, Kleinman, John V., Fort Wayne, IN *Page 1-180*

Scudder Investments, Director of Information Technology Systems, Johnston, Barry David, London, England, United Kingdom *Page 1-146*

SDS America, Director, Kim, Kyle "Ki Jong", Boston, MA *Page 1-205*

SE Technology, Business Consultant, Datar, Pravin W., Irvine, CA *Page 1-233*

Sea Ray Boats, Inc., Senior Systems Analyst, Hughes, Adrienne, Knoxville, TN *Page 1-78*

Seaboard Credit Union, Data Processing Manager, Lomax, Anissa M., Jacksonville, FL *Page 1-137*

Seagate Technology
    Equipment Support Technician, Hubbard, Keith J., Minneapolis, MN *Page 1-46*
    Senior Director, Information Technology EMEA, Shields, Daniel, Paris, France *Page 1-47*
    Senior Director, Schaeffer, Russell A., Longmont, CO *Page 1-47*

Seagate Technology Inc., Consultant, Tsai, Sunnie, San Jose, CA *Page 1-47*

Seattle Center, Strategic Advisor, Bukis, Deborah Elizabeth, Seattle, WA *Page 1-305*

SECI, Inc., Chief Executive Officer, Gool, Eric M., Lamar, CO *Page 1-242*

Select Comfort, Director, Wysocki, Thomas A., Plymouth, MN *Page 1-13*

SembCorp Construction, Senior Systems Engineer, Tan, Gim Hong, Singapore, Singapore *Page 1-351*

Senai, Technical Coordinator, Corradi, Antonio Cesar, Sao Paulo, Brazil *Page 1-336*

Senator Craig Thomas, Systems Administrator, Dykes, George M., Washington, DC *Page 1-371*

Senco-Argonne National Lab, Consultant, McWilliams, Craig R., Palatine, IL *Page 1-264*

Senior Geographic Information Systems Trainer, GIS Technical Trainer, Rediker, Julie A., Houston, TX *Page 1-277*

Sequel Communications, Marketing Manager, Dima-Ala Villanueva, Lorli, New York, NY *Page 1-109*

Service Merchandise, Database Administrator, Rucker, Mark C., Brentwood, TN *Page 1-131*

SET Technologies, Inc., Chief Technology Officer, Montreuil, Benoit, Sainte-Foy, Quebec, Canada *Page 1-184*

Seton Healthcare Network, Registered Nurse/Network Information Systems Coordinator, Robertson, Sarah E., Austin, TX *Page 1-309*

SGE Consulting, Owner/Consultant, Emory, Samuel G., Charlotte, NC *Page 1-235*

Shelby County Trustee, Manager of Information Systems, McGrory, Joan Serocki, Memphis, TN *Page 1-380*

Sher Distributing, Information Technology Manager, Costa, Anthony P., Leonardo, NJ *Page 1-125*

Shoe Carnival, Computer Operations Manager, Johnston, James W., Evansville, IN *Page 1-127*

Shore Systems, Inc., President, Guido, Christopher, Albertson, NY *Page 1-244*

Siebel Systems, Inc., Product Manager, Siebel Call Center, Jay, Henry D., San Mateo, CA *Page 1-196*

Siemens AG, Head of Information & Communications Innovation Field, Berner, Georg, Munich, Germany *Page 1-72*

Siemens Canada, Reliability Technologist, Bechard, Richard, Ontario, Ontario, Canada *Page 1-72*

Siemens Electrocom LP, Software Engineer, Khan, Tameen, Arlington, TX *Page 1-50*

Siemens Energy and Automation
  Director of Information Systems Customer Service, Bruno, Rae Ann, Cumming, GA *Page 1-55*
  Quality Assurance Technician, Jones, Billy R., Bristol, TN *Page 1-56*
  Senior Information Security Analyst, Darby, Philip D., Atlanta, GA *Page 1-55*

Siemens Microelectronics, OptoElectronics Division, Senior Member of Technical Staff, Wright, Richard K., Cupertino, CA *Page 1-56*

Sierra Pine Adel Division, Management Information Systems Manager/Mill Analyst, Sutton, Curtis, Hahira, GA *Page 1-13*

Sigma Projects Services, Senior Oracle Database Administrator, Khan, Alamdar Hussain, Fresno, CA *Page 1-254*

Silicon Graphics, Intern of Strategy and Strategic Alliances Marketing Team, Kreft, Bryan M., Santa Clara, CA *Page 1-181*

Silicon Plains Technologies, Consulting Partner, Stence, Daniel, Des Moines, IA *Page 1-285*

Siliconix, Inc., Section Manager, Wang, Hong, Santa Clara, CA *Page 1-68*

Simplex Time Recorder, Principal Database Administrator, Terault, Normand A., West Minster, MA *Page 1-62*

Simplot Livestock Company, Network Engineer, Black, Randy M., Grand View, ID *Page 1-1*

Simpson Housing Ltd. Partnership, Vice President of Information Systems, Miller, Jeffrey T., Denver, CO *Page 1-160*

Siskon Electronic Company, Manager/Owner, Orhon, Ahmet V., Izmir, Turkey *Page 1-208*

SITA, Implementation Engineer, Lavardera, Danny, Bohemia, NY *Page 1-101*

Siteserv2000 LLC, Chief Executive Officer/Co-Owner, Chambers, Paul C., Troy, MI *Page 1-216*

Skafab, Information Technology Manager, Pakuwibowo, Mohammad, Stockholm, Sweden *Page 1-387*

Skymall Inc., Director of Technical Operations, Taylor, Brian J., Glendale, AZ *Page 1-191*

Skypro AG, Chief Executive Officer/President, Fuhrmann, Horst, Cham Zug, Switzerland *Page 1-238*

Sloan & Company, Inc., Manager of Accounting and Information Technology, Luderer, Bob, West Caldwell, NJ *Page 1-7*

SMA Inc., Consultant, Mullen, Frank L., Humble, TX *Page 1-185*

Smart Web Sales, Owner, Maraschiello, Lou, Chico, CA *Page 1-261*

Smith Consulting, Owner/Consultant, Smith, Jeremy A., Quakertown, PA *Page 1-284*

SMS Data Products Group, Inc., Application Developer, Lemmon, Jeremy R., McLean, VA *Page 1-257*

SMUD, Principal Information Technology Specialist, McCauley, Barney, Sacramento, CA *Page 1-114*

Snapfish.com, Manager, Sustaining and Performance Engineering, Jaffer, Akbar G., San Francisco, CA *Page 1-179*

Snelling Personnel Services, Owner/President, Zwickel, M. Susan, Fairfield, NJ *Page 1-170*

Social Security Administration, LAN Coordinator, Barber, Charles, Greenville, SC *Page 1-375*

Soft Ad, Operations Director, Gorgen, Nancy A., Dearborn, MI *Page 1-177*

Software Consulting Services, Senior Applications Developer, Ashford, Paul L., Nazareth, PA *Page 1-194*

Software Creations, Technician/Programmer, Strutt, Greg D., Laurel, MD *Page 1-287*

Software Engineering Institute, Senior Member of the Technical Staff, Phillips, Richard W., Pittsburgh, PA *Page 1-359*

Solectron Corporation
  Production Engineer, Maimbourg, Michael A., Gatesville, TX *Page 1-43*
  Project Manager, Bufford, Peter, Foster City, CA *Page 1-39*

Solectron Technology Company, Product Manager, De Cesare, Vito, Charlotte, NC *Page 1-40*

Solution Bank, Senior Consultant, Broughton, Jeff R., Webster, TX *Page 1-225*

Solution Home.com, President, Magolnick, Michael, Margate, FL *Page 1-260*

Solution Soft Systems, Inc., Software Architect, Zhao, Eric Yanguang, Cupertino, CA *Page 1-193*

Solutions By Design, Division Director, Hall, Rodney D., Richmond, VA *Page 1-245*

Sonic Foundry, Inc., Software Quality Assurance Manager, Gates, Dramise D., Madison, WI *Page 1-176*

Sonoco, Director of Technology, Schuetz, Jeffrey M., Hartsville, SC *Page 1-14*

Source Net Inc, President, Strickland, Thomas K., Falls Church, VA *Page 1-286*

South African Embassy, Counselor for Telematics, Rogers, John R., Washington, DC *Page 1-397*

South Bay Bank, Network Systems Administrator, Fraser, Neal D., Torrance, CA *Page 1-134*

South Bay Online, Owner, Hayata, Nancy K. T., Torrance, CA *Page 1-246*

South Carolina Arts Commission, Technical Director, Gamble, Mark H., West Columbia, SC *Page 1-347*

South Carolina Department of Health and Human Services, Bureau Chief, Ellis, Patricia C., Columbia, SC *Page 1-384*

South Carolina Law Enforcement Division, Supervisory Special Agent, Johnson, L. J., Columbia, SC *Page 1-377*

Southdown, Inc., Data Processing Supervisor, Kalmar, Steve, Brea, CA *Page 1-30*

Southeastern Metals Manufacturing Company, Management Information Systems Technician, Langford, Mark G., Jacksonville, FL *Page 1-33*

Southern California Edison, Technical Specialist/Scientist, Bailey, Larry J., Rosemead, CA *Page 1-113*

Southern Internet, President/Chief Executive Officer, Calderbank, Kevin, Palm Beach Gardens, FL *Page 1-108*

Southern Linc, Direct Sales Manager, Pate, Lonnie J., Savannah, GA *Page 1-93*

Southern New England Telephone, Manager of Switching Control, Hooke, Edward C., Meriden, CT *Page 1-100*

Southern Trust Mortgage, Systems Administrator, Lufkin, Keith S., Richmond, VA *Page 1-141*

Southern Wine & Spirits, Manager of Systems and Integration, Booth, Mark M., Miami, FL *Page 1-125*

Space & Naval Warfare Systems Command, Technical Specialist, Trachtenberg, Charlene C., Arlington, VA *Page 1-396*

Spacenet, Inc., President, Hall, Laurence A., Melbourne, FL *Page 1-244*

Spalding County Health Department, Network Administrator, Hubbert, Patty, Griffin, GA *Page 1-385*

Spar Aerospace, Information Technology Manager, Ademidun, Olumide A., Ikey Lagos, Nigeria *Page 1-56*

Spectrum International, Inc., President, Bekov, George I., El Cerrito, CA *Page 1-221*

Speed Link Inc., Technical Support Technician, Lauda, Irene, Pontiac, MI *Page 1-110*

Spherion Corporation, Senior Systems Engineer, Guthrie, Kenneth L., Dacula, GA *Page 1-301*

Sprint
  Director of Information Technical Services, LaBounty, Rachael, New Century, KS *Page 1-101*
  Manager of Systems Deployment, Reed, Dana E., Kansas City, MO *Page 1-104*
  Manager of Transport Planning, Oliva, Stephen A., Overland Park, KS *Page 1-102*
  Network Engineer I, Greene, William F., Overland Park, KS *Page 1-99*
  Network Engineer, Catalone, Gregory S., Reston, VA *Page 1-96*
  Systems Integrator, Rampley, Douglas R., Irving, TX *Page 1-103*
  Test Engineer, Chui, Carol Y., Burlingame, CA *Page 1-96*

Sprint Paranet
  Branch Technical Manager, Bode, Karl E., Gilbert, AZ *Page 1-223*
  eBusiness Consultant, Jazi, Wassim A., Houston, TX *Page 1-251*

Sprint PCS
  Professional Skills Curriculum Developer, Craft, Michael K., Kansas City, MO *Page 1-92*
  Senior Product Manager, Romish, Lisa S., Kansas City, MO *Page 1-94*
  Software Engineer II/Application Administrator, Geary, Matthew, Lenexa, KS *Page 1-92*

Spur Ventures Inc., President, He, Yingbin "Ian", Vancouver, British Columbia, Canada *Page 1-2*

SPX Corporation, Management Information Systems Manager, Riley, Cathy N., Portage, MI *Page 1-36*

Square D Company, Analytics Manager, Brown, Thomas S., Nashville, TN *Page 1-52*

Squeal Media Arts, President/Chief Executive Officer/3D Artist, Wagner, Paul W., Bloomington, IN *Page 1-192*

SRP, Senior Computer Analyst, Boyles, Dana A., Tempe, AZ *Page 1-116*

SS&C Technologies, Consultant, Smith, Jennifer M., Chicago, IL *Page 1-190*

SSB-City, Vice President, Strategic Marketing, Kerry, Marianne L., New York, NY *Page 1-135*

St. Joseph's Indian School, Information Systems Manager, Heinssen, Scott A., Chamberlain, SD *Page 1-315*

St. Joseph's University, Director of Information Services, Nester, Leonard J., Philadelphia, PA *Page 1-329*

St. Labre Indian School, Network Administrator/Webmaster, Thomas, Carl, Ashland, MT *Page 1-318*

St. Mary College, Director of Information Management, Paden, John, Leavenworth, KS *Page 1-330*

St. Mary Hospital Medical Center, Desktop Publisher, Dauplaise, Mike, Green Bay, WI *Page 1-307*

Standard Federal Bank, Lead Systems Administrator, Godsey, Chene W., Troy, MI *Page 1-135*

Standard Insurance, Senior Systems Integrator, L'Heureux, Colette M., Portland, OR *Page 1-150*

Standard Register, Senior Staff Engineer, Harris, Mark W., Dayton, OH *Page 1-21*

Starmedia Network, Inc., Associate, Park, Hyun, New York, NY *Page 1-111*

Starternet, Chief Executive Officer, Adesh, Vivek S., Douglasville, GA *Page 1-170*

State Farm Insurance, Technical Analyst, Gilliam, Ken W., Bloomington, IL *Page 1-154*

State Government of Illinois Telecommunications, Design Engineer, Hall, Michael R., Springfield, IL *Page 1-99*

State of Connecticut Workers Compensation, Technical Analyst 3, Wilson, Edward Alton, Hartford, CT *Page 1-155*

State of Kansas, Chief of Information Systems Support, Armstrong, Stephen D., Topeka, KS *Page 1-372*

State of New Mexico Taxation and Revenue Department, Network Administrator, Oakeley, Timothy N., Santa Fe, NM *Page 1-380*

State of Tennessee Department of Environment and Conservation, Information Systems Analyst 4, Stockell, Albert W., Nashville, TN *Page 1-387*

State of Washington, Department of Social and Health Services, Web Administrator, Asbach, Gordon J., Olympia, WA *Page 1-384*

State of Wisconsin, Department of Administration, Strategic Information Technology Consultant, Endres, Joyce E., Madison, WI *Page 1-375*

State Water Resource Control Board; SWRCB, Computer Programmer, Diep, Thang, Sacramento, CA *Page 1-387*

Stefan Chi Ho Kung, Freelance, Consultant, Kung, Stefan Chi Ho, Homantin, Hong Kong *Page 1-255*

Stonebridge Technologies, Solution Architect/Principal Consultant, Miller, Stephen W., Edmond, OK *Page 1-265*

Stonehenge Telecom Americas, Director of Network Operations and Management, Greene, John E., Maitland, FL *Page 1-5*

Stonehill College, Director of Videography, Pietrowski, Michael, Easton, MA *Page 1-331*

StorageTek
    Support Engineer, Lyle, Richard, Austin, TX *Page 1-46*
    Systems Engineer, Kavanaugh, Keith J., Silver Spring, MD *Page 1-46*

Stowell Data Solutions, Chief Executive Officer/Owner, Stowell, Bev, Stanton, MI *Page 1-286*

Strategic Alliance International Corporation, Senior Network Engineer, Wan, Daniel Q., New York, NY *Page 1-293*

Strategic Technologies, Systems Integration Specialist, Collins, Louis H., Norcross, GA *Page 1-231*

Strategy Partners Group, Information Technology Director/Senior Consultant, Toback, Jeremy, Naples, FL *Page 1-367*

Stratum New Media, Senior Project Manager, Lasky, Tami M., Chesapeake, VA *Page 1-182*

Strongsville City Schools, Technology Coordinator, Schroth, John W., Strongsville, OH *Page 1-383*

Stuart Dean Company, Systems Administrator, McAndrew, Jeffrey M., New York, NY *Page 1-7*

Sulzer Metco, Technical Engineer, Bordonaro, Robert, Westbury, NY *Page 1-34*

Sumitomo Machinery Corporation of America, Manager of Computer Systems, Perkins, Brian J., Chesapeake, VA *Page 1-38*

Summit Medical Center, Hospital Director of Information Systems, Wells, Robert M., Hermitage, TN *Page 1-309*

Summit National Bank, Assistant Vice President/Director of Information Technology, Watkins, Steve, Atlanta, GA *Page 1-136*

Sun Hydraulic Corporation, Information Technology Manager, Schultes, Stan J., Sarasota, FL *Page 1-35*

Sun Microsystems, Inc.
    Architect, Gelfenbain, Alexander, Palo Alto, CA *Page 1-40*
    Senior Consultant, Rosado, Luis E., Southlake, TX *Page 1-44*
    Senior Performance Technologist, Lee, Myungho, Palo Alto, CA *Page 1-42*
    Software Engineer, Studer, Michael W., Newark, CA *Page 1-45*
    Support Manager, Scott, Barry Price, San Jose, CA *Page 1-45*
    Systems Administrator, Hasan, Anis S., Khobar, Saudi Arabia *Page 1-41*

Sunbeam Outdoor Products, PC Technician/Network Administrator, Enlow, Jeffrey Dale, Neosho, MO *Page 1-53*

Sundance Travel International, Director of Information Services, Mason, Jeffrey W., Irvine, CA *Page 1-91*

Sunflower Cablevision, Datavision Manager, Knorr, Patrick, Lawrence, KS *Page 1-108*

Sunnyside Community Hospital, Director, Wilson, Joe M., Renton, WA *Page 1-310*

Sunrise Assisted Living, Technical Operations Manager, Callo, Fernando A., Fairfax, VA *Page 1-343*

Superior Court of California, County of Fresno, Information Systems Manager, Diestelkamp, Dawn L., Fresno, CA *Page 1-376*

Superior Technology Resources, Contract Professional, Young, Smith, Littleton, CO *Page 1-351*

Sure Air Ltd., Management Information Systems Manager, Reicher, Stuart, Stamford, NY *Page 1-159*

SutterTel.Com, President, Sutter, Rick, Kennewick, WA *Page 1-128*

Swiss Bank Corporation, Network Specialist, Tignor, Doug J., Lisle, IL *Page 1-137*

Sybase, Inc., Technology Specialist/Manager, Brown, Chris N., Greenwood Village, CO *Page 1-194*

Sylvan Prometric, Senior Database Administrator, Tippins, Edward, Washington, DC *Page 1-342*

Symantec Corporation
    Senior Software Engineer, Litchev, Lubomir, Cupertino, CA *Page 1-197*
    Senior Systems Engineer, Clarke, Tracy J., Hackensack, NJ *Page 1-195*

Symbiont Inc., Senior Systems Engineer, Boostrom, Ron A., San Antonio, TX *Page 1-223*

SYMTX, Design Engineer II, Avendano, Igmar E., Austin, TX *Page 1-219*

Synermark, Information Technology Director, Sherwood, John Anthony, Austin, TX *Page 1-159*

SYSCO Corporation, Senior Systems Programmer, McCraw, Shirley B., Houston, TX *Page 1-129*

System Request Consultants, Computer Programmer/Consultant, Ramczyk, Amie J., Middletown, WI *Page 1-276*

Systems Computer Technology, Network Specialist/Technician, Lentz, Terry M., Melbourne, FL *Page 1-257*

Systems Documentation Inc., Manager of Business Systems Support, Clouse, Marc G., Edison, NJ *Page 1-231*

Systems Link, Quality Assurance Engineer, Dalia, Sujal, Avenel, NJ *Page 1-232*

Systems Made Simple, Inc., Chairman of the Board/Chief Information Officer, Harris, Dana B., Syracuse, NY *Page 1-178*

Systems Support Alternatives, Inc., Senior Computer Specialist, Fremont, John C., Laurel, MD *Page 1-238*

Systems-Ensync, Owner, Leskody, James J., Las Vegas, NV *Page 1-6*

T

T. Rowe Price Associates, Senior Staff Associate, Frager, Yehuda Stuart, Baltimore, MD *Page 1-161*

T&T Pump Company, Inc., Director of Design and Development, Fleming, James C., Fairmont, WV *Page 1-37*

T-Online International AG, Network Designer, Lauffher, Wolfgang, Darmstadt, Germany *Page 1-110*

TaascFORCE, Accounting Division Manager, Joplin, Toby L., Tulsa, OK *Page 1-180*

TAF-TECH Cable Systems, Project Leader, Darichuk, Glenn J., Calgary, Alberta, Canada *Page 1-6*

Taiwan Cellular Corporation, Senior Engineer, Peng, Vincent Cheng-Kun, Taipei, Taiwan *Page 1-93*

Talbot's, Manager of Database Administration, Bowen, Lynn A., Tampa, FL *Page 1-127*

Target, DIS Supervisor, Standford, Don R., Oakland, CA *Page 1-126*

Tarquini Organization, CAD Supervisor, Brown, John R., Camden, NJ *Page 1-350*

TASC, Inc.
Manager of Information Systems Development, Lawlor, James E., Reading, MA *Page 1-206*
Senior Software Engineer, Maley, Scott, Midwest City, OK *Page 1-206*
Website Administrator, Newsome, Teresa M., Chantilly, VA *Page 1-207*

TDSI, a Division of Randstad North America, Area Manager/International Dealer Director, Curtis, Brandon G., Fremont, CA *Page 1-232*

Teaco Inc., Vice President/General Manager, Gorney, John P., Tulsa, OK *Page 1-98*

Techcircle.com inc., President, Shashikumar, Bellave S., Enola, PA *Page 1-282*

Techni Logic Consulting, Owner, Schneider, Debra, Sagamore Hills, OH *Page 1-281*

Techni-core, Network Engineer, Broadwater, Kirk, Huntsville, AL *Page 1-225*

Techno Serv, General Manager, Khalid, Nadeem M., Manama, Bahrain *Page 1-253*

Technologica Trading & Computer Systems, Managing Director/Chief Executive Officer, Atia, Tarek, Cairo, Egypt *Page 1-219*

Technology Solutions Company
Project Manager, Chrisman, Terry L., Hagerstown, MD *Page 1-230*
Senior Principal, Campbell, Gregory L., Alpharetta, GA *Page 1-228*

Technology Totems Inc., Senior Systems Engineer, Berlas, Abdul R., College Park, MD *Page 1-222*

TechnoSphere Services, Owner/Operator, Labbate, Evelyn, Howell, NJ *Page 1-255*

Techware Solutions, Inc., President/Senior Consultant, Rodriguez, Louis F., West Paterson, NJ *Page 1-209*

Tecmark LLC, Director Information Systems and Operations, Springer, Michael, Woodbury, MN *Page 1-164*

Tekmark Global Solutions, Branch Manager, Lynch, Ron A., Wayne, PA *Page 1-170*

Telcordia Technologies, Principal Performance Engineer, Chaikin, Jamie A., Piscataway, NJ *Page 1-172*

TeleCommunication Systems, Inc., Senior Network Administrator/Supervisor, Gust, Thomas A., Shalimar, FL *Page 1-244*

Telegyr Systems, Inc., Engineering Manager, Mourad, Tarek M., San Jose, CA *Page 1-266*

Telenor, Inc., Director of Business Development, Schafft, Soren, Reston, VA *Page 1-104*

Teletech Holdings Inc., Senior Oracle Database Administrator, Ogunmodede, Victor A., Denver, CO *Page 1-270*

Teletech Services, Manager of Global Technical Solutions, Rogers, James, Burbank, CA *Page 1-277*

Telia AB, Technical Coordinator, Fällberg, Christian, Stocksund, Sweden *Page 1-97*

Telia Finland Ltd., Development Manager, Mellin, Jorma, Vantaa, Finland *Page 1-102*

Telia Mobile, Senior Advisor and Strategist, Sporre, Matts, Nacka Strand, Sweden *Page 1-104*

Telxon Corporation
Director of Retail Systems Integration, Sachs, Steven W., The Woodlands, TX *Page 1-44*
Manager of Technical Services, Edwards, Tony J., Dallas, TX *Page 1-40*
Manager of Technical Services, Ellis, Allan D., Seattle, WA *Page 1-40*
Senior Director of Product Marketing, Skomra, Stewart A., The Woodlands, TX *Page 1-45*
Webmaster, Benedict, Michael, Akron, OH *Page 1-39*

Templin Management Associates, Database Manager, Benner, Carol M., Greenfield Center, NY *Page 1-362*

Tempogon AB, Chief Executive Officer, Pettersson, Ulf, Stockholm, Sweden *Page 1-273*

Tenafly Public Schools, Director of Technology, Ivele, Patricia, Tenafly, NJ *Page 1-382*

TenFold Corporaotin, Training Manager, Chapman, David R., Draper, UT *Page 1-229*

Tenneco Packaging, Senior Systems Analyst, Wellnitz, Judi K., Deerfield, IL *Page 1-29*

Tennessee Department of Correction, Management Information Systems Field Service Manager, Guy, John D., Tiptonville, TN *Page 1-378*

Tennessee Valley Authority, Information Systems Engineer, Ramey, Corey D., Knoxville, TN *Page 1-114*

TEQ International, Vice President of Global Customer Relationship Management Practice, Tang, Andrew L., San Gabriel, CA *Page 1-288*

Teradyne Inc., Training Group Manager, Sayian, Stephen, Boston, MA *Page 1-82*

TerraComm, Inc., Director, Dossett, Robert W., Spokane, WA *Page 1-212*

Tetra Pak Americas, Inc., Regional Support Center Manager, Beard, Gunilla, Atlanta, GA *Page 1-37*

TetraTech Consulting Service, General Manager, Tetrault, Gerald "Gerry", Chatham, Ontario, Canada *Page 1-367*

Texas A&M University, Texas Engineering Extension Services, Program Coordinator, Chew, Ferdinand T., Bryan, TX *Page 1-321*

Texas Department of Protective & Regulatory Services, Information Technology Operations Manager, Stone, Susan K., Austin, TX *Page 1-343*

Texas Instruments
Program Manager, Spence, Mike, Dallas, TX *Page 1-67*
Project Manager of Corporate Development, Lindner, Dale R., Dallas, TX *Page 1-66*
Senior Member of Technical Staff, Ali, Murtaza, Dallas, TX *Page 1-63*
Senior Technical Analyst, Udayamurthy, Sekar, Dallas, TX *Page 1-68*

Texas Micro Computers, Chief Information Officer, Gagan, Shakil Sattar, Richardson, TX *Page 1-239*

Texas State Technical College, Assistant Director of Network Services, Beaver, Jake, Waco, TX *Page 1-335*

Texas Tech University, Research Technician, Quasny, Todd, Lubbock, TX *Page 1-331*

TexSYS RD Corporation, E-Commerce Architect, Pagnis, Rishikesh R., Irving, TX *Page 1-271*

Textron, Inc., Director/Chief Technologist, Michaelides, Phyllis J., Providence, RI *Page 1-76*

Thaihosting, Chief Executive Officer, Olaric, Thada, Yannawa, Thailand *Page 1-270*

The Aerospace Corporation, Systems Engineer, Rolenz, Michael A., Harbor City, CA *Page 1-78*

The Allied Group Inc., Interactive Developer, Messes, Alexander P., Glastonbury, CT *Page 1-184*

The Bank of Nova Scotia, Senior Technical Analyst, Padilla, Reynaldo D., Scarborough, Ontario, Canada *Page 1-135*

The Boeing Company
Chief Architect, Bahrami, Ali, Seattle, WA *Page 1-75*
Computer Security Specialist, Dalton, Robin S., Seattle, WA *Page 1-75*

The Carl Group, President/Chief Executive Officer, Carl, Timothy S., Los Gatos, CA *Page 1-228*

The Catholic University of America Columbus School of Law, Assistant Director of Computer Sciences, Russell, Damon E., Washington, DC *Page 1-332*

The Charlton Group, Director of Information Systems, Powers, Michael J., Madison, WI *Page 1-302*

The Chubb Institute, Instructor, Castaldi, James Anthony, Parsippany, NJ *Page 1-321*

The Coffee Beanery Ltd., Information Systems Specialist, Curtis, Steve D., Flushing, MI *Page 1-9*

The Computer & Network Fixer, Chief Technical Officer, McNutt, Joseph W., Levittown, PA *Page 1-216*

The Consultants, Chief Executive Officer, Sawyer, Jeffery H., Raleigh, NC *Page 1-280*

The Database Group Inc., President/Owner, Marchioli, Marc E., Dallas, TX *Page 1-261*

The Farmers Association of Iceland, Manager of Computer Department, Lorange, Jon B., Reykjavik, Iceland *Page 1-345*

The Gazette, Microcomputer Specialist, Thompson, A. J., Penrose, CO *Page 1-16*

The Golf Network, Inc., Chief Technology Officer, Christly, John A., Pompano Beach, FL *Page 1-172*

The Hartford, Consultant, Romel, Jeffrey Lawrence, Hartford, CT *Page 1-154*

The Haskell Company, Director of Technology, Tucker, Clark F., Jacksonville, FL *Page 1-351*

The Hotchkiss School, Chairman of Academic Computer Department, Hall, Leland G., Lakeville, CT *Page 1-315*

The Howbury Group Ltd., President, Howarth, Barry Arthur, Nepean, Ontario, Canada *Page 1-248*

The Human Factor, Inc., President of Technology and Product Services, Pigeon, Donald R., Ferndale, MI *Page 1-369*

The International Academy of Information Sciences, Systems and Technologies, Founder/President/Chief Executive Officer, Singh, Paula Kaur, Los Altos, CA *Page 1-342*

The Jesra Company, Owner/Consultant, Holden, Tammy Lou, Long Beach, CA *Page 1-248*

The Kennedy Connection, Partner/Recruiter, Kennedy, Michael, Powell, OH *Page 1-364*

The Knowledge Sculptors, Founder, Chizmarik, Joseph J., Chatham, NJ *Page 1-202*

The Little Tikes Company, CAD Administrator, VanMeter, Jim, Hudson, OH *Page 1-85*

The Metropolitan Community College, Network Engineer, Beachner, James G., Lee's Summit, MO *Page 1-335*

The Montana Power Company, Supervisor of Gas Drafting, Leary, Mike W., Butte, MT *Page 1-116*

The National Transportation Exchange, Inc., Director of Business Development, Moler, Dino D., Downers Grove, IL *Page 1-147*

The New England, Senior Systems Manager, Tyler, Mary F., Boston, MA *Page 1-156*

The Pezrow Companies Inc., Systems Manager, Gartin, Edward, Ramsey, NJ *Page 1-144*

The Plus Group, Vice President of Information Technology, Seelander, John M., Lombard, IL *Page 1-366*

The Principia, Director of Computing and Information Systems, Schwartz, Bruce R., St. Louis, MO *Page 1-318*

The Rhythm Section Lab, Owner, Wychulis, C. "Bud", Coaldale, PA *Page 1-303*

The Shoe Show of Rocky Mount, Senior Analyst, McIntyre, David M., Concord, NC *Page 1-127*

The Sports Club, Network Engineer, Rodriguez, Joe, Los Angeles, CA *Page 1-306*

The Stock Market Reference Desk, Owner/Chief Executive Officer, McDowell, Haywood, Reston, VA *Page 1-183*

The Trizetto Group, Database Administrator, Nguyen, Brittney T., Englewood, CO *Page 1-268*

The Upper Deck Company, LLC, Information Systems Operations Manager, Corsello, Michael Phillip, Carlsbad, CA *Page 1-85*

The Vanguard Group
    Project Manager, Dalal, Alex F., Honey Brook, PA *Page 1-145*
    Technical Support Supervisor, Betty, Joseph M., Valley Forge, PA *Page 1-145*

The Walt Disney Company, Senior System Analyst, Raymondo, James A., Tampa, FL *Page 1-305*

The Wharton School, Technical Director, Knight, Pamela J., Philadelphia, PA *Page 1-340*

The Windward Group, Director, Dobyns, Barry A., Los Gatos, CA *Page 1-234*

The Wornick Company, Software Engineer, Kamssu, Honore, McAllen, TX *Page 1-10*

The Wornick Company - Right Away Division, Network Administrator/Systems Analyst, Benavidez, Eduardo D., McAllen, TX *Page 1-10*

The Zenith, Director of Enterprise Network Services, Clark, Brian E., Sarasota, FL *Page 1-153*

Themis, Inc., Co-Founder/Senior Systems Advisor, Dunlap, Thomas S., Westerville, OH *Page 1-196*

Third Wave Services, Owner, Franklin, Braden S., Jacksonville, FL *Page 1-238*

Thomas Consumer Electronics, Director of Quality Audio Products, Teller, Joel S., Indianapolis, IN *Page 1-54*

Thomas Hardware, Managed Information Systems Director, Schartel, David M., Reading, PA *Page 1-122*

Thomson Consumer Electronics
    Senior Systems Analyst, Warmelink, Michael R., Indianapolis, IN *Page 1-54*
    Technical Trainer, Fadely, Gary, Indianapolis, IN *Page 1-54*

Thomson Corporation, Business Systems Manager, Lehman, Mary Jane Cottingham, Cincinnati, OH *Page 1-18*

Thomson Financial, Senior Systems Administrator, Tanigawa, David S., Boston, MA *Page 1-147*

Thomson Financial Securities Data, Senior Software Engineer, Grilk, Andrew H., Newark, NJ *Page 1-145*

Ticketmaster, Information Technology Manager, Mavis, Mark K., Kansas City, MO *Page 1-306*

Tilator Oy, President/Chief Executive Officer, Markkula, Harri, Sakyla, Finland *Page 1-262*

Time Warner, Technical Manager, Snyder, Andrew H., New York, NY *Page 1-108*

Time Warner Communications, Operations Manager, Hunt, Kelly K., Columbus, OH *Page 1-107*

Tipper Tie, Information Technology Project Manager, Bender, Kendra, Apex, NC *Page 1-34*

Tippett Studios, Lead FX Animator, Teramoto, Tim G., San Rafael, CA *Page 1-304*

Tivoli Systems
    Director of Product Management Strategy, McGourty, Felicity F., Austin, TX *Page 1-198*
    Project Manager, Armstrong, Jay, Austin, TX *Page 1-194*

TNRCC, Database Administrator, Paul, Jeanette E., Austin, TX *Page 1-387*

Toledo Lucas County Public Library, Assistant Manager of Networking and Computing, Gray, Thomas P., Toledo, OH *Page 1-339*

Tom Sawyer Software, Product Manager, Feng, Wendy Q., Berkeley, CA *Page 1-236*

Tompkins Cortland Community College, Technical Specialist, Ackley, Brian Sterling, Dryden, NY *Page 1-335*

Tone Software Corporation, Software Developer, Sundell, Richard A., Anaheim, CA *Page 1-191*

Total Response Inc., Database Administrator, Kot, John S., Indianapolis, IN *Page 1-301*

Total Technology Services, Vice President of Operations/Partner, Rogers, John H., South Portland, ME *Page 1-209*

Town of Easton, Information Systems Manager, Deltano, Michael D., North Easton, MA *Page 1-371*

Toyota Egypt, Information Technology Manager, Ismail, Hosam Mahmoud, Cairo, Egypt *Page 1-304*

Toyota Motor Manufacturing of Kentucky, Skill Trade Technician, Lane, Michael J., Georgetown, KY *Page 1-73*

Trane, Systems Manager, Gilbeaux, Jeffrey J., Timonium, MD *Page 1-122*

Transaction Information Systems, Vice President/Director, Nolan, Thomas J., New York, NY *Page 1-269*

Transactions Marketing Inc., Founder/President, Lewis, Brenda, Greenwich, CT *Page 1-364*

Transamerica Tax Service, Help Desk Analyst/Department Web Editor, Kjelvik, Vickey A., Dallas, TX *Page 1-162*

TransCanada Energy, Software Engineer, Peltz, Raymond, Omaha, NE *Page 1-2*

Transcom, Network and Information Systems Administrator, Antoniou, Nicholaos, Jersey City, NJ *Page 1-389*

Tremont High School, Technology Coordinator, Schaidle, Dale F., Tremont, IL *Page 1-317*

Tri State Hospital Supply Corporation, Management Information Systems Officer, Tressidder, Garfield W., Salisbury, NC *Page 1-120*

Tri Tech Systems, Inc., President/Chief Financial Officer, Petrucelli, James L., Dover, DE *Page 1-273*

Tri-Cities Regional Airport, Communication Center Supervisor/Computer Specialist, Payne, Shirley S., Blountville, TN *Page 1-90*

Triad Performance Technologies, Vice President, Dembeck, Wanda S., Farmington Hills, MI *Page 1-368*

Trident Data Systems
    Network Security Engineer, Brown, Charles, Santa Clarita, CA *Page 1-226*
    Program Manager, Lang, David Thomas, Vienna, VA *Page 1-255*

Trinary Systems Inc., Product Manager, LeFaive, Donna M., Fennville, MI *Page 1-182*

Trinet Networking & Training, Inc., Owner/Managing Director, Butt, Khawar, Diamond Bar, CA *Page 1-227*

Triple Play, Principal, Dobrovolny, Jackie Lea, Aurora, CO *Page 1-300*

Triplex Director Marketing Corporation, Technical Department Manager, Margison-Evans, Charel, Novato, CA *Page 1-166*

Tritec Communications Inc., Vice President of Operations, Romano, Angelo, East Hanover, NJ *Page 1-104*

Troy State University Dothan, Associate Director for Distance Learning, Johnson, Sallie J., Dothan, AL *Page 1-326*

Truestar, Inc., Director of Computer Services, Karaburk, Hasan, Fairfax, VA *Page 1-253*

Truman High School, Library Media Specialist, Schlosser, Martha F., Independence, MO *Page 1-317*

TrustMed.com, Editor in Chief, Cheng, David Hui-Wen, Taipei, Taiwan *Page 1-212*

TRUTech, L.L.C., Engineering Associate, Green, N. Wayne, Richland, WA *Page 1-243*

TRW, Technical Writer, Smith, Richard D., Baldwin, MD *Page 1-210*

TSI, Inc., Vice President, Bray, Robert T., St. Charles, MO *Page 1-224*

Turkish Aerospace Industries, Senior Programmer, Altan, Ergin, Ankara, Turkey *Page 1-75*

Tuttle Maddux Surveying, S.I.T. (Surveyor in Training), Daffron, Dean E., Montgomery, TX *Page 1-352*

Tyco Packaging Systems, PC Technician, DeMent, Ryan A., Hayward, CA *Page 1-121*

TYCO Valves & Control, LAN Support Manager, Gee, Nicholas L., Sparks, NV *Page 1-34*

U

U S WEST
    Operations Manager, Clements, Kerry Keith, Denver, CO *Page 1-97*
    Senior Engineer, Urban, James J. "Jack", Omaha, NE *Page 1-105*

U S WEST Interprise Networking Services, Manager of Internet Services, Fielden, Jeanette, Denver, CO *Page 1-97*

U S WEST/Global Crossing, Data Consultant, Garg, Rajiv, Minneapolis, MN *Page 1-98*

U.S. Bank, Help Desk Manager, Mathes, Jonathan R., Minneapolis, MN *Page 1-133*

U.S. Bankruptcy Court, Computer Systems Manager, Gast, William A., Des Moines, IA *Page 1-376*

U.S. Steel-Clairton Works, LAN Administrator, Post, John S., Clairton, PA *Page 1-31*

U.S. Tobacco Manufacturing LP, Administrator, Beasley, Mark S., Nashville, TN *Page 1-10*

U&I Learning, General Manager/Owner, Belpaire, Patrick, Steenhuize, Belgium *Page 1-340*

UCA Computer Systems, Inc., Vice President, Nallabathula, Udaya Sankar, Dover, NJ *Page 1-267*

UHERE Corporation, President, Wei, Jeffrey Haoran, San Jose, CA *Page 1-295*

Ujanen, Chief Executive Officer/Principal Consultant, Ujanen, Kari R., San Francisco, CA *Page 1-210*

Unifirst Corporation, Systems Analyst, Henderson, George W., Owensboro, KY *Page 1-12*

Unify Corporation, Director of Worldwide Porting, Bristow, Donald R., Sacramento, CA *Page 1-225*

Unilever, Senior Systems Administrator, Coniglio, Allen P., Trumbull, CT *Page 1-25*

Union Pacific Technologies, Senior Manager, Matthews, Bill D., Omaha, NE *Page 1-262*

Union Switch and Signal, Computer Programmer, Magnotta, Salvatore D., Washington, PA *Page 1-78*

Unisource Network Services
    Member of Technical Staff, McElroy, Thomas D., Chicago, IL *Page 1-263*
    Network Analyst, Tiongco, Ronald L., Chicago, IL *Page 1-290*

Unisphere Solutions, Senior Systems Engineer, Leitzel, David R., Englewood, CO *Page 1-56*

Unisys Corporation
    Integration Consultant, Schlagheck, Ryan Wm., Windsor, CT *Page 1-280*
    Managing Principal, Babcock, James M., New York, NY *Page 1-219*
    Program Manager, Harrison, Eric A., San Diego, CA *Page 1-246*
    Systems Architect, Allen, Mark, Acworth, GA *Page 1-217*

United Bible Societies, Information Technology Consultant, Nzabanita, Hakiza, Lome, Togo *Page 1-17*

United Defense, Program Manager, Hutson, Tom, San Jose, CA *Page 1-60*

United Distillers, Information Systems Manager, Wentzler, Tracy, Omaha, NE *Page 1-9*

United Distillers & Vintners, Technical Information Manager, Lauchlan, E. Anne, Clackmannanshire, Scotland, United Kingdom *Page 1-9*

United Federation of Teachers, Teacher Centers Professional Development Program, Instructional Technology Coordinator, Barton, Regina V., New York, NY *Page 1-346*

United Parcel Service, Lead Technical Specialist, Chambers, Teressa S., Louisville, KY *Page 1-90*

United Space Alliance
    Director of Systems and Compliance, Corn, Jeffrey S., Cape Canaveral, FL *Page 1-391*
    Project Manager, Hintz, Cynthia Irene, Cocoa, FL *Page 1-392*

United States Air Force
    Chief CSS/Work Group Manager, Mosby, Robin M., Trenton, NJ *Page 1-394*
    Chief of Finance Automation, Fileger, Mark E., Langley Air Force Base, VA *Page 1-393*
    Telecommunications Manager, Smith, Richard K., Boston, MA *Page 1-395*

United States Air Force, Headquarters Air Combat Command, Systems Integrator, Severin, William F., Newport News, VA *Page 1-395*

United States Army, Chief of Network Operations, Huynh, Peter V., Washington, DC *Page 1-394*

United States Army Corps of Engineers
    Computer Specialist, Orndoff, Steven S., Winchester, VA *Page 1-395*
    Project Manager, Evans, Kathryn A., Vicksburg, MS *Page 1-393*

United States Army Research Laboratory, Computer Scientist, Smith, Glenn A., Aberdeen Proving Ground, MD *Page 1-395*

United States Army Visual Information Center, Information Systems Management Officer, Jewel, Cheryl D., Washington, DC *Page 1-394*

United States Aviation and Missile Command, Director/Technology Program Manager, Vandiver, Emily H., Redstone Arsenal, AL *Page 1-396*

United States Bureau of Reclamation, Team Leader of Engineering Support, McDanel, Gary A., Billings, MT *Page 1-387*

United States Department of Agriculture, Information Technology Division Chief of the Farm Service Agency, Nassif, John M., St. Louis, MO *Page 1-391*

United States Department of Agriculture Food and Nutrition Service, Computer Specialist, Tankersley, Kathy M., Boston, MA *Page 1-391*

United States Department of Education, Manager of Systems Development Group, Robinson, Mark Wesley, Washington, DC *Page 1-382*

United States Department of Justice, Information Security Specialist, Hayhurst, Robert R., Marianna, FL *Page 1-376*

United States Department of State
    Project Manager, Williams, Iris D., Springfield, VA *Page 1-397*
    Senior Project Manager, Peppe, Richard W., Washington, DC *Page 1-397*

United States Department of Treasury, Systems Administrator, Green, Kenneth L., Washington, DC *Page 1-379*

United States Environmental Protection Agency
    Deputy Chief Information Officer, Day, Mark, Washington, DC *Page 1-386*
    Program Analyst, Frazier-Rousey, Toni Trinette, Washington, DC *Page 1-387*

United States Marine Corps, Staff Sergeant/Computer Technology Supervisor, Bertrand, Joseph F., Kailua, HI *Page 1-392*

United States Navy, Network Engineer and Administrator, Jones, D. Timothy, FPO AA *Page 1-394*

United States Postal Service, Information Technology Specialist, Callaway, Lawrence A., Merrifield, VA *Page 1-88*

United States Treasury, Bureau of Public Debt, Computer Security Analyst, Haught, Jason F., Parkersburg, WV *Page 1-379*

United Titanium Inc., Director of Information Systems, Crawford, Michael W., Wooster, OH *Page 1-85*

Universal Systems and Technology Inc., Director of Operations, Clawson, Perry R., Winter Park, FL *Page 1-230*

University College of the Fraser Valley, PC LAN Administrator, Schlosser, Shane, Abbotsford, British Columbia, Canada *Page 1-332*

University of Alabama, Associate Professor, Jackson, David Jeff, Tuscaloosa, AL *Page 1-325*

University of Alaska, Manager, Sikkink, V. Janene, Fairbanks, AK *Page 1-333*

University of Arkansas, Assistant Professor, Wessels, David M., Fayetteville, AR *Page 1-334*

University of Bahrain, Database Administrator, Muvvala, Padmavathi, Area 326, Bahrain *Page 1-329*

University of Cincinnati, Web Designer, Pagulayan, Randy J., Cincinnati, OH *Page 1-330*

University of Colorado Hospital, Manager of Operations & Applications, Dalious, Peggy, Aurora, CO *Page 1-322*

University of Connecticut, Assistant Professor, Bhattacharjee, Sudip, Storrs, CT *Page 1-320*

University of Dayton, Computer Systems Coordinator, Keck, Christian Jon, Dayton, OH *Page 1-326*

University of Evansville, Systems Administrator, Whitecotton, Brad, Evansville, IN *Page 1-334*

University of Florida, Horticultural Science Department, Computer Support Specialist, Spurlin, Tami, Gainesville, FL *Page 1-333*

University of Hawaii, Head of Science and Technology Department, Wermager, Paul, Honolulu, HI *Page 1-334*

University of Louisiana at Lafayette, Center for Advanced Computer Studies, Associate Professor, Kubat, Miroslav, Lafayette, LA *Page 1-327*

University of Miami, Research Assistant Professor, Younis, Akmal A., Coral Gables, FL *Page 1-334*

University of Minnesota, Research Assistant, Huang, Jian, Bloomington, MN *Page 1-325*

University of Missouri - Rolla, Assistant Professor, Liu, Xiaoqing "Frank", Rolla, MO *Page 1-328*

University of Nebraska, Senior Systems Analyst, Baker-Cross, Leah Dawn, Omaha, NE *Page 1-320*

University of Oklahoma Health Sciences Center, Systems Administrator, Ledford, Yvonne M., Oklahoma City, OK *Page 1-327*

University of Oregon Athletics, Director of Computing Services, Cooley, Len, Eugene, OR *Page 1-321*

University of Pennsylvania Graduate School of Education, Senior Information Technology Support Specialist, Fels, Alan N., Philadelphia, PA *Page 1-323*

University of Regina Computer Science Department, Professor of Computer Science, Saxton, Lawrence V., Regina, Saskatchewan, Canada *Page 1-332*

University of Southern California School of Medicine, Management Information Systems Director, Morales, Pedro, Los Angeles, CA *Page 1-329*

University of St. Thomas, Technical Support Administrator, Downs, Brian D., St. Paul, MN *Page 1-322*

University of Texas at Austin, Charles A. Dana Center, Instructional Technologist, Katz, Heather Alicia, Austin, TX *Page 1-326*

University of Vermont, Professor of Computer Science, Xue, Guoliang, Burlington, VT *Page 1-334*

University of Wisconsin at Madison, Senior Systems Programmer, Hooker, P. Kent, Madison, WI *Page 1-325*

University of Wyoming, Department of Space and Data & Visualization Center, Senior Systems Programmer, Parrill, Scott M., Laramie, WY *Page 1-330*

Unlimited Solutions Inc., Software Architect, Schubert, William Anthony, Columbus, OH *Page 1-189*

UOP, Technology Specialist, Salem, Mike M., Des Plaines, IL *Page 1-303*

UPAQ Ltd., Vice President, Application Services, Kramer, Ronald, Zürich, Switzerland *Page 1-255*

Uproar.com, Director of DBM/CRM, Shah, Atique R., New York, NY *Page 1-306*

Uproar, Inc., System Network Engineer, Winkler, Piotr, Ridgewood, NY *Page 1-200*

UPS Information Services, Business Analyst, Fischer, Jennifer L., Jersey City, NJ *Page 1-90*

US Filter Distribution, Manager, Thornhill, C. Allen, Thomasville, GA *Page 1-123*

US Telecom – PhoneMaster Division, Communications Director/Alliance Liaison, Forquer, Christy S., Joplin, MO *Page 1-98*

US Trustee, Regional Computer Specialist, Wieland, Katherine, Wichita, KS *Page 1-376*

USAED Sacramento, Chief of ET&S, Stoner, Stephen E., Sacramento, CA *Page 1-396*

USDA Forest Service, HMR, Computer Specialist, Berry, James C., Arlington, VA *Page 1-388*

USHarbor.com, Inc., Chief Executive Officer/President, Yang, Charles X., Mountain View, CA *Page 1-131*

USI, Developer, Elaprolu, Srikanth, Chantilly, VA *Page 1-174*

USI Prescription Benefits, Senior Director of Business Information Systems, Humphreys, Timothy J., East Haven, CT *Page 1-157*

USUHS
    Computer Specialist, Hu, Xiaohong, Bethesda, MD *Page 1-325*
    Program Manager, Guevara, John P., Bethesda, MD *Page 1-324*

UUNET, Manager, Remuzzi, Joy, Ashburn, VA *Page 1-213*

UUNET – A Division of MCI/WorldCom, Department Head, Vetere, Rhonda M., Hilliard, OH *Page 1-214*

UUNET Technologies, Manager, International Programs, Reed, Jeff L., Warrenton, VA *Page 1-213*

V

V.I.P.S., President, Franz, John F., Plantation, FL *Page 1-156*

V4 Consulting, Project Manager, Pfeiffer, Scott P., Indianapolis, IA *Page 1-273*

Val Verde Unified School District, Network Infrastructure Manager, Bradley, Thomas M., Perris, CA *Page 1-381*

Valassis Communications, Telecommunications Manager, Brocious, Mary Anne, Livonia, MI *Page 1-20*

Valencia Community College, Director of Internet Development Center, Morrell, Margaret R., Orlando, FL *Page 1-338*

Valley Presbyterian Hospital, Senior Programmer/Analyst, Litten, Catherine Lee, Van Nuys, CA *Page 1-308*

Valvu las Keystone de Mexico, Information Systems Manager, Suárez del Real, Claudio, Zatopan, Mexico *Page 1-74*

Van Kampen Funds, Programming Analyst I, Glenn, John D., Houston, TX *Page 1-145*

Vanalco, Inc., Training and Communications Coordinator, Hart, Ryan L., Vancouver, WA *Page 1-32*

Vancouver/Richmond Health Port, Manager of Information Systems, Hunter, Craig M., Vancouver, British Columbia, Canada *Page 1-152*

Vantive Corporation, Project Success Manager, Torrez, Joe, Overijse, Belgium *Page 1-290*

Vector Data Systems, Project Leader/Senior Communications Engineer, McEady, Erasmus W., Fort Bragg, NC *Page 1-348*

Vegetarian Resource Center, Executive Director, Clark, Maynard S., Cambridge, MA *Page 1-163*

Vengroff, Williams & Associates, Management Information Systems Manager, Lalone, David J., Sarasota, FL *Page 1-165*

Veridicom, Director of Information Systems, Sanchez, Frank, San Francisco, CA *Page 1-298*

Verio, Inc., Sales Manager, Fraze, John T., Englewood, CO *Page 1-109*

VERITAS Software
    General Manager of Consumer Products, Lyng, Gary, Mountain View, CA *Page 1-197*
    Senior Consultant, Blake, Brian C., Buffalo, NY *Page 1-194*
    Senior Direct Response Manager, Bucchino, Nicolas A., Mountain View, CA *Page 1-195*

Verizon Wireless
    Information Security Manager, Holland, Adam, Dublin, OH *Page 1-92*
    Senior Systems Analyst, Cerda, Ken H., Carrollton, TX *Page 1-92*

Vertek Corporation, Network Administrator, Quinn, Robert A., Highlands, NJ *Page 1-275*

Veterans Administration Medical Center, Systems Manager, Huffman, Robert N., Martinsburg, WV *Page 1-386*

Vibe Magazine, Director of Information Technology, Aris, Harold A., New York, NY *Page 1-16*

Viewsonic, WAN Manager, Wilson, Raymond E., Walnut, CA *Page 1-49*

Viking Range Corporation, Systems Administrator/Management Information Systems Supervisor, Ramachandran, Shyam, Greenwood, MS *Page 1-53*

Viquity, Vice President of Operations, Clements, Larry, Sunnyvale, CA *Page 1-195*

Virginia Department of Transportation
    GIS Programmer/Analyst, Michaelsen, Nancy L., King George, VA *Page 1-390*
    Information Technology Manager, Klass, Connie H., Suffolk, VA *Page 1-390*

Virginia Housing Development Authority, Data Center Manager, Dumeer, Wesley A., Richmond, VA *Page 1-388*

Virginia Tech Computing Center, Senior Computer Systems Engineer, Marchany, Randy C., Blacksburg, VA *Page 1-338*

Visa International, Vice President of Global Intranet, Kirkpatrick, Mindy L., San Francisco, CA *Page 1-138*

Vishay-Sprague, Manager of Information Technology, Hilton, Jon M., Sanford, ME *Page 1-69*

Vison Education Inc., Chief Executive Officer, Nathan, Matthew N., New York, NY *Page 1-268*

Vistec Electronic Services Inc., Network Installer/Service Technician, Da Costa, D'Wayne I., Pickering, Ontario, Canada *Page 1-216*

Vital Network Services, Senior Engineer, de Freitas, André A., New York, NY *Page 1-109*

Vitamin Shoppe Industries, Inc., Chief Information Officer, Morris, Michael P., North Bergen, NJ *Page 1-132*

Vivorx Inc., Management Information Systems Supervisor, Fadri, Reynaldo J., Santa Monica, CA *Page 1-357*

Volt Computer Services/Entirenet, Program Manager/Courseware Presenter, Weber, Gregory, Sterling Heights, MI *Page 1-294*

VP Systems Inc., Principal Consultant, Janowski, W. K. "Vitek", Nepean, Ontario, Canada *Page 1-251*

VSI, Senior Software Consultant, Tse, Simon Lai Yan, Austin, TX *Page 1-291*

W

W.H. Linder & Associates, Senior Programmer, Graham, Charles K., Metairie, LA *Page 1-5*

W.W. Grainger, Electronic Data Interchange Manager, Clements, Gregory Alexander, Vernon Hills, IL *Page 1-123*

WAHLCO Engineered Products, Inc., Systems Manager, Walker, James A., Lewiston, ME *Page 1-33*

Walls Computers Etc., Senior Computer Technician, Russ, Jerry D., Hot Springs, AR *Page 1-188*

Walt Disney Company BVHE, Senior Manager of Information Technology, Bliss, George, Burbank, CA *Page 1-304*

Walters State Community College, Head of Industrial Technology, Gibson, Ronald, Morristown, TN *Page 1-336*

Wang Healthcare, Systems Administrator, Richardson, Susan E., Hudson, NH *Page 1-188*

Ward Manufacturing Inc., Maintenance Engineer, Williams, Allen D., Elmira, NY *Page* 1-31

Warner Bros., Application Developer, Sanford, Thom, Burbank, CA *Page* 1-305

Warner Brothers Online, Manager of Production, Harman, Morgan Webb, Burbank, CA *Page* 1-245

Warren County, Information Systems Director, Smith, Barry W., Belvidere, NJ *Page* 1-283

Warren County Schools, Technology Specialist, Ansley, David Thomas, Warrenton, GA *Page* 1-380

Warsaw Area Career Center, Information Systems Instructor, Waldeck, Stephen, Warsaw, IN *Page* 1-319

Wartsila NSD Corporation, WAN Administrator, German, James, Annapolis, MD *Page* 1-35

Wasco Products Inc., Acting Manager of Management Information Systems, Charpentier, Elizabeth, Sanford, ME *Page* 1-53

Washburn & Associates, Inc., Consultant, Winship, Matthew, Overland Park, KS *Page* 1-200

Washington Army National Guard, Network Control Center Manager, Smith, Timothy R., Tacoma, WA *Page* 1-396

Washington University, Information Systems Director, Abusoud, Samer S., St. Louis, MO *Page* 1-320

Watson Wyatt Worldwide
    Information Systems Manager, Sluka, Greg W., Southfield, MI *Page* 1-366
    Software Engineer, Burkhart, Michael G., Washington, DC *Page* 1-362

Waubonsee College, Information Technology Design Director, Sotir, Judith S., Aurora, IL *Page* 1-333

Waukegan Public Schools, Technology Coordinator, Green, Judith M., Waukegan, IL *Page* 1-315

Wavetek Wandel Goltermann, Technical Support Engineer, Velappan, Vignesh, Kuala Lumpur, Malaysia *Page* 1-292

Wazoo's Computers, Owner, Fender, Chuck, Alamogordo, NM *Page* 1-236

Weatherford International Inc., Systems and Programming Manager, Fry, Susan F., The Woodlands, TX *Page* 1-3

Weber Chevrolet, Management Information Systems Manager, Maher, Michael A., St. Louis, MO *Page* 1-127

Weblink Wireless, Manager of Information Technology Web Development, Watts, Dennis H., Dallas, TX *Page* 1-94

Websci Technologies, UNIX and Oracle Administrator, Gervagin, Yuriy, Monmooth Junction, NJ *Page* 1-240

Websoft Technologies, President, Islam, Mohammed N., Brooklyn, NY *Page* 1-250

Wells Fargo, Information Technology Manager, Hussey, Michael P., San Francisco, CA *Page* 1-133

Wells Fargo Bank, Senior Systems Engineer, Dritsas, George E., Whiting, IN *Page* 1-133

West Noble School Corporation, Technology Technician, Lapham, Erika P., Ligonier, IN *Page* 1-316

West Valley City, Planner II/Geographic Information System Specialist, Pastorik, Stephen L., Salt Lake City, UT *Page* 1-373

West Wisconsin Telecom Cooperative, Inc., Internet and Technical Support Administrator, Berg, Linda M., Menomonie, WI *Page* 1-95

Western Illinois University, Faculty Member, George, Binto, Macomb, IL *Page* 1-324

Western University of Health Sciences, Dean/Program Director, Hanford, Karen, Chico, GA *Page* 1-324

Westinghouse, Oracle Application Developer, Mikel, Lashika L., Augusta, GA *Page* 1-394

Westinghouse - Savannah River Site, Communication Engineer, Boone-Shuford, Myrna, Aiken, SC *Page* 1-392

Westminster School, Director of Technology, DeLo, Dirk A., Simsbury, CT *Page* 1-315

Westside Elementary School, Technology Coordinator, Timmins, Allan S., Spring Hill, FL *Page* 1-318

Wexner Heritage Village, Information Systems Manager, Mokros, Jason M., Colombus, OH *Page* 1-307

Weyerhaeuser Company, Senior Database Administrator, Murray, Lee, Federal Way, WA *Page* 1-12

WFSATC, Information Technology Specialist, Yang, Lily H., Salt Lake City, UT *Page* 1-340

Whalen & Company, Project Manager, Raikar, Rajesh Suresh, Lafayette, CA *Page* 1-275

Wharton County Junior College, Systems Analyst, Jacobs, Vicki S., Wharton, TX *Page* 1-326

White Sands Missile Range, Mathematician, Young, Barry H., Las Cruces, NM *Page* 1-397

Widener University, Director of Technical Resources, Habermann, Gary J., Chester, PA *Page* 1-324

Wilkinson Consulting Group, Inc., Chief Executive Officer, Wilkinson, David D., Pleasant Hill, CA *Page* 1-296

William Paterson University, Director of Network Services, Tedesco, Frank P., Wayne, NJ *Page* 1-333

William Reed, e-Business and Information Systems Manager, Thurogood, Brian A, South Gostoden, England, United Kingdom *Page* 1-19

Williams Refining, LLC, Database Analyst, Willerton, Shane L., Memphis, TN *Page* 1-28

Willis North America, Inc., Director of Technology, Tomlinson, William W., Nashville, TN *Page* 1-158

Windsor Group, Desktop Support Manager, Peters, Ryan M., Atlanta, GA *Page* 1-157

Winstar, Director of Product Marketing, O'Keefe, Curtis W., Falls Church, VA *Page* 1-93

Winstar Telecommunication, Senior Technical Consultant, Veguilla, John Anthony, San Francisco, CA *Page* 1-94

Winthrop/Stimson, PC Training and Support Specialist, Teague, Mark A., New York, NY *Page* 1-313

Wolf Creek Elementary, Technology Mentor, Wechsler, Brian C., Pine Ridge, SD *Page* 1-334

WORLDSPAN, Vice President of Product Development, Hughes, Barbara A., Atlanta, GA *Page* 1-249

Worthington City Schools, Director of Management Information Systems, Schlarb, Keith N., Worthington, OH *Page* 1-317

Wyeth-Ayerst Canada, Inc., Project Leader, Legault, Stephane, Saint-Laurent, Quebec, Canada *Page* 1-24

Wyeth-Ayerst Research, Principal Database Administrator, Lis, Ellen R., Radnor, PA *Page* 1-24

X

Xceed, Consultant, Naugle, Raymond H., Tempe, AZ *Page* 1-268

Xerox, UNIX Core Developer, Nuwer, Kevin, Webster, NY *Page* 1-50

Xpedite Systems, Account Manager, McDowell, Webb R., El Segundo, CA *Page* 1-302

Y

YAI, Computer Specialist, White, James, New York, NY *Page* 1-344

Yale University ITS/Telecommunications, Information Technology Manager, Patti, Stephen, New Haven, CT *Page* 1-331

Yellow Shirt, Solutions Architect, Chan, Calvin L., Pasadena, CA *Page* 1-229

YKE International Inc., Sales Manager, Ho, Kelvin K., Corona, NY *Page* 1-70

Yoh Support Services, Operations Manager, Green, E. G., Norristown, PA *Page* 1-243

Young Men's Christian Association of Metropolitan Chicago, Director of Information Technology, Stiehr, Marc L., Chicago, IL *Page* 1-347

Z

Z-Tel, Director of Database and Information Services, Patel, Mitool M., Atlanta, GA *Page* 1-103

Zagar Inc., Management Information Systems Manager, Fedele, Alan R., Euclid, OH *Page* 1-36

Zebra Systems Ltd., Director, Obibi, Manasse O., Hounslow Middlesex, England, United Kingdom *Page* 1-270

Zebra Technologies Corporation, Documentation Specialist, Private, John A., Vernon Hills, IL *Page* 1-51

Ziff-Davis, Design Director, White Rayner, Nicole M., Garden City, NY *Page* 1-17

Ziffren, Brittenham, Branca & Fischer LLP, Director of Information Services, Schwing, Lee, Los Angeles, CA *Page* 1-313

Zilog, Firmware Architect and Developer, Pearson, Kenneth W., Cedar Park, TX *Page* 1-67

ZoneNetwork.com, Project Manager, Wright, Rik, Seattle, WA *Page* 1-297

Zydeco.com, Vice President of Information Technology Strategy, Smith, Jake, Seattle, WA
   Page 1-133

Members Indexed
by
Geographic Location

Section 4

ARMY POST OFFICE

APO AA, MTISC, Gale, Prenston *Page* 1-239

FPO AA, United States Navy, Jones, D. Timothy *Page* 1-394

AUSTRALIA

New South Wales

Liberty Grove, Mosman Municipal Council, Nonweiler, Kevin Ian *Page* 1-371

Sydney, ICOM Solutions Pty. Ltd., Bal, Anupam D. S. *Page* 1-367

Queensland

Brisbane, Queensland Police, Stoopman, Michael B. *Page* 1-377

AUSTRIA

Vienna

Frequentis, Bogner, Wilhelm *Page* 1-55

LKW Walter AG, Köhler, Andreas *Page* 1-88

BAHRAIN

Area 326, University of Bahrain, Muvvala, Padmavathi *Page* 1-329

Manama

Bahrain Telecommunications Company, Hassan, Abdulla K. E. *Page* 1-99

Batelco, Abdulla, Mahmood Ahmed *Page* 1-216

Ministry of Cabinet Affairs & Information, Elmasri, Ahmed Azzam *Page* 1-372

Techno Serv, Khalid, Nadeem M. *Page* 1-253

BARBADOS

St. Michael, CIBC Offshore Banking Services   Corporation, Matthews, Neil A. *Page* 1-143

BELGIUM

Athus, Dexia Bank International in Luxembourg, Fries, Michel *Page* 1-137

Destelbergen, Astrazeneca Belgium, Tollenaere, Caroline *Page* 1-24

Meise, Jovenko, Saerens, Robert *Page* 1-279

Nil-Staint Vincent, I.D.A., Haddad, Assad *Page* 1-244

Oud Haverlee, Hewlett-Packard Belgium, Kindermans, Marc *Page* 1-42

Overijse, Vantive Corporation, Torrez, Joe *Page* 1-290

Steenhuize, U&I Learning, Belpaire, Patrick *Page* 1-340

BRAZIL

Diadema Sp, Lear Seating Inespo Comercial, Mendoza, Julio Cesar *Page* 1-74

Indaiatuba, Filtros Mann, Ltda., Cauzzo, Luiz Henrique *Page* 1-72

Rio de Janiero, BMG, Leao, Flavio De Araujo *Page* 1-302

Sao Caetano Du Sol, Netstream Telecom, Ferrao, Helder Flavio *Page* 1-97

Sao Paulo

Best Foods Brazil, Cremerius, Guillermo *Page* 1-10

Compaq Computer Corporation, Monteiro, Walkiria *Page* 1-44

Hewlett-Packard Company, Cerqueira, Joao Roberto Monteiro *Page* 1-39

Senai, Corradi, Antonio Cesar *Page* 1-336

CANADA

Alberta

Bragg Creek, IN3 Consulting, Canada, Kashmirian, R. S. *Page* 1-253

Calgary

Aerospace Software Ltd., Oosthuysen, Herman *Page* 1-270

Petro-Canada, Johnson, Gary *Page* 1-27

TAF-TECH Cable Systems, Darichuk, Glenn J. *Page* 1-6

Edmonton, Alberta Health and Wellness, Watson, Susan E. *Page* 1-385

British Columbia

Abbotsford, University College of the Fraser Valley, Schlosser, Shane *Page* 1-332

Vancouver

BCMEA, Vurdela, Greg J. *Page* 1-89

Moore Clark, Van Den Brink, Joost *Page* 1-1

PricewaterhouseCoopers LLP, Guo, Peter C. H. *Page* 1-353

Spur Ventures Inc., He, Yingbin "Ian" *Page* 1-2

Vancouver/Richmond Health Port, Hunter, Craig M. *Page* 1-152

Nova Scotia

Halifax

EDS System House, Burgess, Kevin A. *Page* 1-214

Ernst & Young, Sehmbey, Paul *Page* 1-355

Halifax Regional Municipality, Robson, Brent R. *Page* 1-374

Ontario

Brampton, Nortel Networks, Austin, Richard *Page* 1-54

Burlington, Northrop Grumman-Canada Ltd., West, Chris *Page* 1-76

Chatham, TetraTech Consulting Service, Tetrault, Gerald "Gerry" *Page* 1-367

Concorde, Bonfiglioli, Camunias, Joel *Page* 1-303

Etobicoke, Livingston International, Van, My Tien *Page* 1-91

Hamilton, McMaster University, Ryder, Marvin G. *Page* 1-332

Kitchener, Als Cartage Ltd., Jones, Stephen *Page* 1-88

Markham, Liberty Health, Giannotta, Cel *Page* 1-150

Mississauga, AmTelecom Group, Inc., Yan, David K. C. *Page* 1-106

Nepean

Knowtech Solutions, Inc., Adatia, Amin *Page* 1-217

The Howbury Group Ltd., Howarth, Barry Arthur *Page* 1-248

VP Systems Inc., Janowski, W. K. "Vitek" *Page* 1-251

Newmarket, Canam Software Labs, Inc., Woodburn, R. David *Page* 1-296

Ontario, Siemens Canada, Bechard, Richard *Page* 1-72

Orleans, OC Transpo, McLennan, Gerald J. *Page* 1-87

Ottawa

Industry Canada, Clemis, David *Page* 1-381

Rebel.com, Speed, Russell F. *Page* 1-285

Peterborough, Peterborough County-City Health Unit, Milligan, Richard P. *Page* 1-385

Pickering, Vistec Electronic Services Inc., Da Costa, D'Wayne I. *Page* 1-216

Proton Station, Great White North, North, Barbara *Page* 1-269

Scarborough

Graphic Resources, Lefebvre, Guy *Page* 1-124

The Bank of Nova Scotia, Padilla, Reynaldo D. *Page* 1-135

Thunder Bay, Ministry of the Environment, Heringer, Matthew J. *Page* 1-387

Toronto

Baycrest Centre for Geriatric Care, McCoppen, Reid *Page* 1-310

Coretec, Inc., Yearwood, Michael *Page* 1-63

DMR Consulting Group, Thompson, Michael *Page* 1-367

Formglas, Inc., Lopes, Duane A. *Page* 1-7

GSI Consulting Services, Bartlett, Roy H. *Page* 1-220

KPMG Consulting, Alger, Brian W. *Page* 1-362

KPMG LLP, Low, Humbert *Page* 1-364

Roberta Fox Group Inc., Fox, Roberta J. *Page 1-203*

Prince Edward Island

Charlottetown, Island Services Network, O'Brien, Kevin *Page 1-269*

Quebec

Laval, Hi Nrg Webdesigns, Guerrera, Riccardo *Page 1-243*

Longueuil, Atlantiques Promotions, St. Aubin, Roger *Page 1-74*

Montreal

Buscom MKS, Poupart, Christian *Page 1-128*

Datainterdev, Ltd., Tansanu, Dan *Page 1-288*

GVL, Villetorte, Michel *Page 1-293*

Jasmine Computers Technologies, Inc., Nguyen, Bac Hai *Page 1-268*

Le Groupe BRT, Bertolucci, Marco *Page 1-222*

Nova Bancorp Group, Ltd., Nguyen, Khanh *Page 1-143*

Quebec Government, Alexis, Emmanuel E. A. *Page 1-372*

Reel Film Festival, Inc., Harlap, Jonathan *Page 1-166*

Saint-Hubert, Canadian Space Agency, Ali, Ziad Kamil Muhammad *Page 1-391*

Saint-Laurent

Groupe Cantrex, Inc., Casabon, Sylvain *Page 1-132*

Nortel Networks, Do, Minh-Kha *Page 1-55*

Wyeth-Ayerst Canada, Inc., Legault, Stephane *Page 1-24*

Sainte-Foy, SET Technologies, Inc., Montreuil, Benoit *Page 1-184*

West Montreal, McGill University, Nguyen, Quan *Page 1-329*

Saskatchewan

Regina

Appdepot Web Services, Schneider, Doug J. *Page 1-281*

University of Regina Computer Science Department, Saxton, Lawrence V. *Page 1-332*

COSTA RICA

San Jose, Hules Tecnicos S.A., Arias, Jorge M. *Page 1-29*

DENMARK

Copenhagen, Novo Nordisk IT A/S, Schmidt, Mads Rosendahl *Page 1-280*

Lyngby, BRF Kredit a/s, Irve, Morten *Page 1-141*

Munkebo, Kapa Consulting, Philipsen, Flemming *Page 1-274*

ECUADOR

Quito, Cyberweb Telecommunications, Johnson, Patricio *Page 1-180*

EGYPT

Cairo

Cairo Barclay's Bank, Mohamed, Mohamed Ahmed *Page 1-137*

High Technology Systems Ltd. (Hitechnofal), Nofal, Mohamed El-Sayed *Page 1-208*

Technologica Trading & Computer Systems, Atia, Tarek *Page 1-219*

Toyota Egypt, Ismail, Hosam Mahmoud *Page 1-304*

FINLAND

Helsinki

Locotech Oy, Laxström, Peter *Page 1-256*

Nokia, Mallouk, Ramez H. *Page 1-61*

Sakyla, Tilator Oy, Markkula, Harri *Page 1-262*

Vantaa, Telia Finland Ltd., Mellin, Jorma *Page 1-102*

FRANCE

Antony, Graphtis, Tissier, Christophe *Page 1-290*

Areines, CAC Systèmes, Loustaudaudine, Christophe *Page 1-76*

Asnieres, Elantiel, Gueguen, Daniel *Page 1-243*

Cannes, Disney Consumer Products, Rudstrom, Lennart *Page 1-130*

deville Les Rouen, Novacel, Anton, Patrice *Page 1-26*

Etampes, Sarl Cyberjet, Parot, Philippe *Page 1-198*

Grenoble Cedex 9, Hewlett-Packard Company, Leveque, Gilles *Page 1-42*

Nanterre, IBSYS, Benayoun, Andre *Page 1-222*

Paris

Ernst & Young Audit, Trikoz, Dimitri *Page 1-356*

Seagate Technology, Shields, Daniel *Page 1-47*

Sophia Antipolis, Honeywell, Picherot, Laurence *Page 1-81*

Voisins Le Bretonneux, Activeweb, Venancio, Jean-Pierre *Page 1-293*

GERMANY

Bad Wiessee, Musipl@y GmbH, Holzeisen, Thomas *Page 1-107*

Bad-Muender, Battenfeld Extlenrusionstechnik GmbH, Boettger, Hans-Bernd *Page 1-36*

Balingen, Independent, Sebastian, Glania *Page 1-282*

Bavaria, Marschall Electronics, Ltd., Marschall, Heiko Bernd *Page 1-262*

Berlin, PRISMA Marketing, Stauch, Matthias E. *Page 1-285*

Darmstadt, T-Online International AG, Lauffher, Wolfgang *Page 1-110*

Duesseldorf NRW, ALPS Electric Europa GmbH, Burg, Hans *Page 1-68*

Hallbergmoos, Euro-Log GmbH, Koppert, Claus *Page 1-254*

Hessen, Dinoex, Meyer, Dirk *Page 1-265*

Karlsruhe, Schlund + Partner AG, Schaetzlein, Eric R. *Page 1-112*

Munich, Siemens AG, Berner, Georg *Page 1-72*

Ottobrunn, Intel Corporation, Ercolani, Gianantonio *Page 1-65*

Perl Saarland, kohlpharma GmbH, Reinert, Johannes *Page 1-124*

Roth, Leoni Kabel GmbH & Company KG, Kueffel, Claudia *Page 1-35*

Rothenburg Bay, AEG/Electrolux, Juettner, Michael J. *Page 1-53*

Stuttgart, Independent, Helfenstein, Dirk *Page 1-5*

GREECE

Attica, Eurisko S.A., Costis, Nickolaos C. *Page 1-173*

HONG KONG

Heng Fa Chuen, HSBC, Lo, Alen *Page 1-143*

Homantin, Stefan Chi Ho Kung, Freelance, Kung, Stefan Chi Ho *Page 1-255*

Hong Kong, NetMedia International Ltd., Loo, Ringo *Page 1-18*

Kowloon

Atek Electronics Company Ltd., Cheng, Kin Wing Horace *Page 1-121*

HK Net Company, Ltd., Lam, Wing *Page 1-101*

Nexcel Limited, Wai-Hung, Kwok *Page 1-192*

Tai Tam, Hong Kong International School, Elliott, David *Page 1-315*

Wanchai

2GoTrade.com, Mohamed, Noohu *Page 1-184*

Orient Overseas Container Line, Ltd., Chan, Joe *Page 1-89*

ICELAND

Reykjavik, The Farmers Association of Iceland, Lorange, Jon B. *Page 1-345*

IRELAND

Donegal, Rosses Community School, Moy, Anne *Page 1-316*

ISRAEL

Bat Yam, Coovi.com, Vincken, Wim *Page 1-164*

ITALY

Bergamo, Hewlett-Packard Company, Granato, Orazio *Page 1-40*

Milan, IDC (International Data Corporation), Romano, Antonio *Page 1-278*

IVORY COAST (COTE D'IVOIRE)

Abidjan, Cote D'Ivoire Telecom, Vassidiki, Soumahoro *Page 1-105*

JAMAICA

Kingston, Island Life Insurance Company, McCalla, Izett M. E. *Page 1-148*

JAPAN

Kanagawa

    Hitachi, Ltd., Kitajima, Hiroyuki *Page 1-121*

    IBM Japan, Masuda, Yukie *Page 1-43*

Omiya City, e-GM, Rofe, Michael Stuart *Page 1-71*

Saitama-ken, K's Room, Ishimoto, Ken *Page 1-250*

Tokyo, Livedoor, Inc., Yoneyama, Tsutomu *Page 1-107*

JORDAN

Amman, JTC, Al-Nimri, Nabil Isa *Page 1-91*

LEBANON

Beirut, National Bank of Kuwait, Samadi, Marwan *Page 1-136*

MALAYSIA

Kuala Lumpur, Wavetek Wandel Goltermann, Velappan, Vignesh *Page 1-292*

Melaka, PricewaterhouseCoopers, Hunt, Wong Mee *Page 1-354*

MALTA

Gwardamangia, Department of Radiology, St. Luke's Hospital, Vassallo, Pierre *Page 1-309*

MAURITIUS

Port Louis, BTI Consulting, Peermamode, Ehsan *Page 1-272*

Vacoas, BTI Consulting, Matabudul, Samir *Page 1-262*

MEXICO

Mexico City

    Kb/TEL, Schettino, Antonio Ernesto *Page 1-45*

    NCR de Mexico S.A. de C.V., Perez Munguia, Carlos Manuel *Page 1-51*

San Jeronimo, Independent, Lozano, Hector Jose *Page 1-73*

Tecamachalco, Informatica Asociada, Santos, Raul Jose *Page 1-189*

Torreon, ITESM Campus Laguna, Medina, Armando Ibarra *Page 1-328*

Zatopan, Valvu las Keystone de Mexico, Suárez del Real, Claudio *Page 1-74*

MOROCCO

Casablanca, Microsoft Corporation - North West Africa, Chami, Ahmed R. *Page 1-195*

NEW ZEALAND

Auckland, Industrial Research Ltd., Ralph, Gillian *Page 1-358*

Paraparaumu, Advantage Group, Slusanschi, Anca E. *Page 1-283*

NIGERIA

Ikey Lagos, Spar Aerospace, Ademidun, Olumide A. *Page 1-56*

NORWAY

Oslo

    Jano Multicom AS, Babajide, Olusegun *Page 1-219*

    Scandinavian Airlines, Lindberg, Reiulf *Page 1-89*

Trondheim, Gulius Maske, Karlsen, Rolf *Page 1-124*

OMAN

Muscat

    National Telephone Services, Castelino, Flavian M. *Page 1-96*

    Oman Development Bank, Nasser, Zaina *Page 1-139*

Sultanate, Poly Products, LLC, Rehman, Razi Ur *Page 1-12*

PHILIPPINES

New Manila, Mabuhay Philippine Satellite Corporation, Regalado, Johnson *Page 1-112*

PORTUGAL

Riba de Ave, IFS Portugal, Gomes, Carlos *Page 1-242*

PUERTO RICO

Cabo Rojo, Debug Computers, Sepulveda, Pedro J. *Page 1-282*

Guaynabo, Devnet Systems Corporation, Colon, Ana Iris *Page 1-231*

San German, Inter American University of Puerto Rico, Zornosa Cabrera, Luis M. *Page 1-335*

San Juan

    Advanced Computer Technologies, Vargas, Enid T. *Page 1-292*

    PricewaterhouseCoopers LLP, Marín, José R. *Page 1-354*

SAUDI ARABIA

Al Khobar, Saudi Arabian Bechtel Company, Noon, Patrick H. *Page 1-5*

Dharan, King Fahd University of Petroleum and Minerals, Taj, Moawiya A. *Page 1-333*

Jeddah

    International Turnkey Systems, Arafeh, Ashraf M. *Page 1-218*

    SBM-IBM, Shehata, Mounir *Page 1-282*

Khobar, Sun Microsystems, Inc., Hasan, Anis S. *Page 1-41*

Riyadh

    Al Zamil Group of Companies, Besiso, Marwan Y. *Page 1-161*

    Carrier Saudi Arabia, Jathanna, Kenneth S. *Page 1-122*

Digital Natcom Company, Bhatty, Zuliqar Ahmed *Page 1-222*

Lucky Baby Company, Salileh, Isam *Page 1-15*

Saudi Lighting Company, Hussain, Masood *Page 1-54*

SINGAPORE

Singapore

　　Colour Scan Company Private Limited, Chia, Teck-Hng *Page 1-20*

　　Digital Scanning Corporation, Chua, Chephren *Page 1-48*

　　Kyoei Electronics (S) Pte. Ltd., Lam, Kuet Leong *Page 1-121*

　　SembCorp Construction, Tan, Gim Hong *Page 1-351*

SOUTH AFRICA

Bellville, Eskom, Muller, Gary D. *Page 1-114*

Johannesburg, CS Computer Services Holdings Ltd., van der Laan, Annette *Page 1-292*

Port Elizabeth, PE Technikon, Schonken, Andre *Page 1-338*

SOUTH KOREA

Seoul, Hwa Shin Building, Shin, Dong-Keun *Page 1-158*

SPAIN

Bilbao, DIS-Process S.L., Gaspar, Victor *Page 1-204*

Madrid, Nutreco Spain, Franco, Vicente *Page 1-10*

ST. LUCIA

Castries Bwi, Cable & Wireless, Francis, Pinkley *Page 1-98*

SWEDEN

Alingsas, Lindex AB, Sorstedt, Berthil *Page 1-127*

Malmo, Absalon Group, Nilsson, Anders *Page 1-268*

Mendosus, Mendosus, Larsson, Fredrik *Page 1-256*

Nacka Strand, Telia Mobile, Sporre, Matts *Page 1-104*

Sodertalje, DATESSA, Toth, Stefan *Page 1-291*

Solna, Dotcom Solutions AB, Enroth, Bjorn *Page 1-236*

Stockholm

　　CCG Consulting Associates, Wheatland, Kevin *Page 1-296*

　　Defense Research Establishment, Svensson, Per *Page 1-396*

　　Skafab, Pakuwibowo, Mohammad *Page 1-387*

　　Tempogon AB, Pettersson, Ulf *Page 1-273*

Stocksund, Telia AB, Fällberg, Christian *Page 1-97*

Vallentuna

　　CS Cybernetic Systems AB, Nilsson, Sigward *Page 1-207*

　　Pollenpolen, von Pfaler, Martin *Page 1-293*

Vasteras, Mälardalens Mögskola, Öberg, Jonas *Page 1-330*

SWITZERLAND

Cham Zug, Skypro AG, Fuhrmann, Horst *Page 1-238*

La Tour De Peilz, NCI, Stucki, Walter *Page 1-191*

Lucens, Pro-Tech, Heger, John P. *Page 1-246*

Zürich, UPAQ Ltd., Kramer, Ronald *Page 1-255*

TAIWAN

Hsinchu, CCL, Shen, Li-Sheng *Page 1-361*

Taipei

　　Taiwan Cellular Corporation, Peng, Vincent Cheng-Kun *Page 1-93*

　　TrustMed.com, Cheng, David Hui-Wen *Page 1-212*

THAILAND

Bangkok, KGI Securities One Public Company, Ltd., Puranachoti, Sornkawee *Page 1-146*

Yannawa, Thaihosting, Olaric, Thada *Page 1-270*

TOGO

Lome, United Bible Societies, Nzabanita, Hakiza *Page 1-17*

TRINIDAD & TOBAGO

Tunapune, Lands & Surveys Division, Wiseman, Roland S. N. *Page 1-352*

TURKEY

Ankara, Turkish Aerospace Industries, Altan, Ergin *Page 1-75*

Istanbul, 3M Turkey, Yilmaz, Haluk *Page 1-14*

Izmir, Siskon Electronic Company, Orhon, Ahmet V. *Page 1-208*

UGANDA

Kampala, Cargill Uganda, Ltd., Wamara, Ian Kamese *Page 1-9*

UNITED ARAB EMIRATES

Abu Dhabi

　　Emirates Telecom Corporation, Badar, Ijaz Ul Haq *Page 1-95*

　　Gasco, Trache, Jamal Eddine *Page 1-27*

　　Mohammed Bin Masaood & Sons, Iznait, Nader S. *Page 1-250*

Dubai

　　Hughes Christensen, D'Sylva, Leon J. *Page 1-3*

　　Net Tours & Travel, Noortheen, Mohammed *Page 1-91*

Fujairah, ETISALAT, Ahmed, Shakir *Page 1-95*

UNITED KINGDOM
England

　　Hounslow Middlesex, Zebra Systems Ltd., Obibi, Manasse O. *Page 1-270*

　　Kingston upon Thames, Globebyte, Melconian, Martin *Page 1-264*

　　London

　　　　Cable & Wireless Global Mobile, Hobbs, Steve *Page 1-100*

　　　　Inaltus.com, Tripathi, Shashank *Page 1-214*

　　　　Scudder Investments, Johnston, Barry David *Page 1-146*

　　South Gostoden, William Reed, Thurogood, Brian A *Page 1-19*

　　Southend-on-Sea, Larsen Consulting, Larsen, Bjorn J. P. *Page 1-256*

　　Wembley, Multicom Business Systems Ltd., Trivedy, P. *Page 1-210*

　　West Sussex, B.R.M., Jaworski, Zdzislaw "Jess" *Page 1-46*

　　Winchester, IBM Global Services, Booth, Michael *Page 1-223*

Scotland

　　Clackmannanshire, United Distillers & Vintners, Lauchlan, E. Anne *Page 1-9*

UNITED STATES OF AMERICA

Alabama

Birmingham

Blue Cross & Blue Shield of Alabama, Howard, Jason *Page 1-150*

Eastern Health System, Inc., Henry, Karen E. *Page 1-152*

Dothan, Troy State University Dothan, Johnson, Sallie J. *Page 1-326*

Foley, Gulf Telephone, Kleinschmidt, James E. *Page 1-101*

Helena, Blue Cross & Blue Shield of Alabama, Piazza, Sonya B. *Page 1-151*

Huntsville

Nichols Research, Gatlin, Ronald S. *Page 1-240*

PPG Industries, Inc., Washington, Jacqulin R. *Page 1-30*

Techni-core, Broadwater, Kirk *Page 1-225*

Madison

Mesa Solutions, Ansell, Christopher T. *Page 1-218*

Raytheon, Gellineau, Antonio C. *Page 1-80*

Mobile, Regions Financial Corporation, Gosnell, Phillip K. *Page 1-140*

Montgomery

Anteon Corporation, Cordle, Ruth *Page 1-173*

EFC Systems, Burch, Neal F. *Page 1-227*

Rheem Manufacturing Company, Boyd, Ashley Aubrey *Page 1-53*

Redstone Arsenal, United States Aviation and Missile Command, Vandiver, Emily H. *Page 1-396*

Tallassee, Professional Consulting Services, Stough, Bill *Page 1-366*

Tuscaloosa

Mercedes Benz U.S. International, Mathis, Belinda J. *Page 1-127*

University of Alabama, Jackson, David Jeff *Page 1-325*

Alaska

Anchorage

City Mortgage Corporation, Hoggard, Kevin *Page 1-140*

MTA Solutions, Simkins, Steven R. *Page 1-112*

Elmendorf Air Force Base, SAIC, Moore, Allen K. *Page 1-358*

Fairbanks, University of Alaska, Sikkink, V. Janene *Page 1-333*

Arizona

Flagstaff

Coconino Community College, Wymore, Tess *Page 1-339*

Northern Arizona University, Collins, Galen R. *Page 1-321*

Fort Defiance, Bureau of Indian Affairs - Navajo Area Office, Nixon, Charles C. *Page 1-371*

Gilbert

MicroAge, Davis, Donald N. *Page 1-119*

Sprint Paranet, Bode, Karl E. *Page 1-223*

Glendale, Skymall Inc., Taylor, Brian J. *Page 1-191*

Kingman, Desert De Oro Foods Inc., Wilson, Sheryl A. *Page 1-129*

Mesa

ADP Marshall, a Fluor Daniel Company, Hering, Rich *Page 1-66*

General Motors, Hernández González, Luis Marcial *Page 1-71*

Phoenix

American Express, Marques, Ronaldo Pereiras *Page 1-139*

American Express, Reyes, Sherry *Page 1-139*

Arizona Central Credit Union, Hughes, Mary Ann *Page 1-136*

Arizona Lottery, Dandas, Gus *Page 1-306*

Home Mortgage Inc., Fraedrich, D. David *Page 1-140*

Maricopa County Superior Courts, Lauer, Steven R. *Page 1-376*

Net Tryx Computer Services LLC, Gagnon, Allan F. *Page 1-239*

Prescott, Oregon State University, Korwin, Anthony R. *Page 1-327*

Sacaton, Sacaton Public School District #18, Ralstin, Richard *Page 1-382*

Scottsdale

Homebid.com, Valente, Jean-Luc *Page 1-159*

ICC International, Ricciardelli, Nicholas J. *Page 1-187*

PROTOCOL Technology Partners, LLC, Weis, Ted P. *Page 1-295*

Tempe

SRP, Boyles, Dana A. *Page 1-116*

Xceed, Naugle, Raymond H. *Page 1-268*

Tucson

Augmentix, Inc., Stalker, Daniel E. *Page 1-190*

Mac Electronics, McKaskle, Charles "Chuck" *Page 1-263*

Pima Community College, Wise, Alan L. *Page 1-339*

Propaganda, Poag, Bowie J. *Page 1-199*

Saguaro Clinical Research, Zaragoza, Carla *Page 1-359*

Arkansas

Bella Vista, Cooper Communities, Inc., Young, Leigh Irish *Page 1-160*

Bryant, SBC Communications Inc., Hattenhauer, Wallace L. *Page 1-99*

Conway, Green Bay Packaging, Inc., Martin, Eric M. *Page 1-15*

El Dorado, Industrial Data and Magic, Turner, Gene *Page 1-299*

Fayetteville

AAA Business Machines, Boyles, Alan L. *Page 1-128*

University of Arkansas, Wessels, David M. *Page 1-334*

Fort Smith, AT&T, Mixon, Daniel A. *Page 1-102*

Hot Springs, Walls Computers Etc., Russ, Jerry D. *Page 1-188*

Jonesboro, General Electric, Yim, Aaron P. *Page 1-77*

McGehee, Great Rivers Tech Institute, Wallace, Jim *Page 1-339*

North Little Rock

90th Regional Support Command, Akridge, William D. *Page 1-392*

ARESC, Huddle, Jeanne *Page 1-341*

Russellville, Russellville Realty, Hale, Chris L. *Page 1-159*

Texarkana, Cooper Tire Company, Carlton, Rodney A. *Page 1-28*

California

Alameda

Baffin Inc., Sesay, Sahid *Page 1-27*

Lucent Technologies, Bradford, Kirby R. *Page 1-58*

Lucent Technologies, Hershfield, David M. *Page 1-60*

Alhambra, Independent, Cheng, Michael P. K. *Page 1-202*

Aliso Viejo

Fluor Global Services, Noorbakhsh, Roya *Page 1-349*

MICROS Systems, Inc. - Southern California Region, Abu-Zahra, Bill *Page 1-49*

Payroll Systems.com, Stine, Gary M. *Page 1-355*

Altadena, Dana Unlimited, Ehlig, Dana Carl *Page 1-235*

Anaheim

Furon FHP, Nguyen, Peter N. *Page 1-81*

Tone Software Corporation, Sundell, Richard A. *Page 1-191*

Atherton, Menlo College, Olson, Patrick C. *Page 1-330*

Belmont

Asera, Inc., Su, Michelle Yu *Page 1-287*

Cisco Systems, Inc., Nachlis, Mark Neal *Page 1-61*

Oracle Corporation, Robson, Peter J. *Page 1-199*

Berkeley

exlr8, Inc., Massa-Lochridge, Lauren J. *Page 1-262*

Tom Sawyer Software, Feng, Wendy Q. *Page 1-236*

Beverly Hills, 20th Century Fox, Goldstein, Lee *Page 1-304*

Brea, Southdown, Inc., Kalmar, Steve *Page 1-30*

Buena Park, May Logistics Services, Inc., Seebo, Terry *Page 1-88*

Burbank

Teletech Services, Rogers, James *Page 1-277*

Walt Disney Company BVHE, Bliss, George *Page 1-304*

Warner Bros., Sanford, Thom *Page 1-305*

Warner Brothers Online, Harman, Morgan Webb *Page 1-245*

Burlingame

Guittard Chocolate Company, Lim, Daniel K. *Page 1-8*

Sprint, Chui, Carol Y. *Page 1-96*

Camarillo

Cyberlogic Business Services, Butcher, Linda L. *Page 1-227*

Minerals Management Services, Lobato, William Lyle *Page 1-388*

Carlsbad

National Search Associates, Israel, Burt *Page 1-168*

Newport Strategic Search LLC, Stetson, Audrey J. *Page 1-169*

The Upper Deck Company, LLC, Corsello, Michael Phillip *Page 1-85*

Castaic, Majestic Systems Integration, Croswell, David C. *Page 1-203*

Chatsworth, Chicago Title & Trust, Nguyen, Tony H. *Page 1-185*

Chico, Smart Web Sales, Maraschiello, Lou *Page 1-261*

City of Industry, Dynatek Infoworld, Inc., Cheung, Frank *Page 1-229*

Coarsegold, CVIS, Woodworth, Juanita D. *Page 1-129*

Compton, Continental Forge Company, Van Kallen, Ramon G. W. *Page 1-34*

Covina, Raytheon Systems, Shih, William *Page 1-80*

Cupertine, Cypress Semiconductor Corporation, Bandyopadhyay, Abhijit *Page 1-63*

Cupertino

Hewlett-Packard Company, Meyerson, James L. *Page 1-43*

Siemens Microelectronics, OptoElectronics Division, Wright, Richard K. *Page 1-56*

Solution Soft Systems, Inc., Zhao, Eric Yanguang *Page 1-193*

Symantec Corporation, Litchev, Lubomir *Page 1-197*

Daly City, Netforce, Inc., Sutan, Suhendra *Page 1-287*

Danville, Charles Schwab, Gallegos, Joanne C. *Page 1-142*

Diamond Bar, Trinet Networking & Training, Inc., Butt, Khawar *Page 1-227*

Dublin, Commerce One, Kenney, Sean R. *Page 1-196*

Edwards, NASA-DFRC, Hedgley, David *Page 1-78*

El Cerrito, Spectrum International, Inc., Bekov, George I. *Page 1-221*

El Dorado Hills, Andrell Corporation, Andrews, Jonathan *Page 1-218*

El Monte, San Gabriel Valley Credit Union, Rogers, David D. *Page 1-137*

El Segundo

Epson Electronics America Inc., Trainor, John C. *Page 1-49*

Xpedite Systems, McDowell, Webb R. *Page 1-302*

Emeryville, Puma Technology, Feng, Wu-Chang *Page 1-92*

Encino, ITT Technical Institute, Maloney, Edward *Page 1-338*

Escondido, A&L Lithography, Spoon, John *Page 1-19*

Foothill Ranch, Integrated Solutions Group, Moles, Patrick H. *Page 1-184*

Foster City, Solectron Corporation, Bufford, Peter *Page 1-39*

Fremont

Atima Technology Inc., Chien, David *Page 1-119*

Cyras Systems, Inc., Omran, Abraham *Page 1-56*

HMT Technology, Khong, Huy T. *Page 1-49*

M-Plus, Yu, Simon P. *Page 1-120*

Providian Financial, Spencer, Terri J. *Page 1-94*

Quintus Corporation, Weeks, John B. *Page 1-295*

TDSI, a Division of Randstad North America, Curtis, Brandon G. *Page 1-232*

Fresno

College of the Sequoias, Hollabaugh, Timothy A. *Page 1-337*

KRM Risk Management and Insurance Services, Inc., Feliz, Luis R. *Page 1-157*

Sigma Projects Services, Khan, Alamdar Hussain *Page 1-254*

Superior Court of California, County of Fresno, Diestelkamp, Dawn L. *Page 1-376*

Fullerton, Raytheon Company, Losson, M. Melissa *Page 1-80*

Glendale

Atkinson-Baker, Inc., Savage, Charles L. *Page 1-167*

Candle Corporation, Rogillio, Thomas G. *Page 1-278*

Ontempo, Swanson, Hilary W. *Page 1-287*

Goleta, Magnetic Data Technologies, LaBorde, Frank C. *Page 1-255*

Harbor City, The Aerospace Corporation, Rolenz, Michael A. *Page 1-78*

Hayward

Alameda County, Public Works Agency, Babilla, Furat C. *Page 1-390*

Tyco Packaging Systems, DeMent, Ryan A. *Page 1-121*

Highland, MacroSoft, Eblowitz, Michael *Page 1-174*

Hollywood, Cyberjava, Monaghan, Michael J. *Page 1-265*

Huntington Beach, RouterWare, Cilley, Brian W. *Page 1-230*

Imperial, Honeywell-Thermal Systems, Ruiz, Raul *Page 1-33*

Indian Wells, Digital Internet Services Corporation, Vandenbos, Rod *Page 1-112*

Irvine

Allergan, Inc., Tran, Ngoc-Diem T. *Page 1-25*

Ashten Racks, Inc., Boegeman, Steven M. *Page 1-123*

AUM Technologies, Inc., Chinnaiah, Mani A. *Page 1-230*

Envision Financial System, Inc., Singh, Jagdeep *Page 1-190*

IKON Technology Services, Mancini, James M. *Page 1-50*

National University, Okhandiar, Vazi P. *Page 1-330*

Odetics, Inc., Nyeu, Maung *Page 1-57*

SE Technology, Datar, Pravin W. *Page 1-233*

Sundance Travel International, Mason, Jeffrey W. *Page 1-91*

Irwindale, oCen Communications, Hwang, Kyunam *Page 1-100*

La Mesa, Earth Tech, Wallenborn, Jerry L. *Page 1-350*

Lafayette, Whalen & Company, Raikar, Rajesh Suresh *Page 1-275*

Lake Forest

Collins & Collins Consulting, Inc., Collins, Cynthia A. *Page 1-231*

Cynrede Inc., Fitzgerald, Kevin A. *Page 1-237*

Ernst & Young Application Services LLC., Narayana, Shyamkumar *Page 1-354*

Lindsay, Intend Change, Fousek, Linda A. *Page 1-363*

Long Beach

IBM Corporation, LuVisi, Michael A. *Page 1-43*

Independent Contractor and Consultant, Griffin, Arthur M. *Page 1-369*

The Jesra Company, Holden, Tammy Lou *Page 1-248*

Los Altos, The International Academy of Information Sciences, Systems and Technologies, Singh, Paula Kaur *Page 1-342*

Los Angeles

Bizrate Com, Patton, Robert T. *Page 1-272*

Cinesite, Caspary, Ruth *Page* 1-304

DMB&B Advertising, Barrow, Rudy *Page* 1-163

E-Citi, Page, William Walter *Page* 1-186

Kurgan & Cheviot, Im, Sang H. *Page* 1-85

Los Angeles County Mass Transit Agency, Anderson, Douglas M. *Page* 1-389

Los Angeles Department of Water and Power, Saldana, Carlos P. *Page* 1-117

Playa Vista, Fidelman, Jennifer Faith *Page* 1-160

RoseTel Systems, Sailer, Chrystiana *Page* 1-112

The Sports Club, Rodriguez, Joe *Page* 1-306

University of Southern California School of Medicine, Morales, Pedro *Page* 1-329

Ziffren, Brittenham, Branca & Fischer LLP, Schwing, Lee *Page* 1-313

Los Banos, Lockheed Martin, Lewis, Winston E. *Page* 1-79

Los Gatos

    AFFS Corporation, Hurtak, James *Page* 1-346

    Ananya Systems, Inc., Ananya, Brigit *Page* 1-194

    FutureNext Consulting, Inc., Peake, Daniel *Page* 1-272

    The Carl Group, Carl, Timothy S. *Page* 1-228

    The Windward Group, Dobyns, Barry A. *Page* 1-234

Manhattan Beach, Midwest Technology Management, Iwashita, Michael *Page* 1-250

Martinez, Contra Costa County, Flowers, Michael R. *Page* 1-371

Menlo Park

    E Trade, Ross, Russell H. *Page* 1-143

    Informix Software, Inc., Sohoni, Sanjay V. *Page* 1-284

    OICW/Sequoia Adult School, Harris, Ethel G. *Page* 1-343

    Onsale, Inc., Nagel, Dennis E. *Page* 1-267

Milpitas, Creative Labs, Inc., Songy, Michael P. *Page* 1-190

Mira Loma, Advance Business Graphics, Reicher, Joshua S. *Page* 1-21

Modesto, Cal-Pak Systems, Clark, Bruce A. *Page* 1-119

Monterey Park, Colorscope, Inc., Tan, Aik W. *Page* 1-166

Moreno Valley, FutureNext Consulting, Inc., Tanuwidjaja, Ron A. *Page* 1-288

Mountain View

    Aqueduct Information Services, Lowe, Vincent D. *Page* 1-259

    Hewlett-Packard Company, Klemba, Keith S. *Page* 1-42

    KPMG Consulting, Inc., Attri, Joel P. *Page* 1-362

    Ouintiles Pacific, Inc., Ko, Istella Chui-Mei *Page* 1-358

    Philips Medical Systems, Wong, Stephen *Page* 1-70

    Reactor, Chabrier, Donna R. *Page* 1-166

    USHarbor.com, Inc., Yang, Charles X. *Page* 1-131

    VERITAS Software, Bucchino, Nicolas A. *Page* 1-195

    VERITAS Software, Lyng, Gary *Page* 1-197

Napa, fp Label, Thelemaque, Tony *Page* 1-21

Newark, Sun Microsystems, Inc., Studer, Michael W. *Page* 1-45

Newport Beach

    DirectNet Telecommunications, Petrov, Alex *Page* 1-111

    Pacific Investment Management Company, Fox, Jeffrey W. *Page* 1-161

North Highlands, Horizon Instructional Systems, McCoy, Karstyn *Page* 1-316

Novato, Triplex Director Marketing Corporation, Margison-Evans, Charel *Page* 1-166

Oakland

    Kaiser Permanente, Tuttle, Robert A. *Page* 1-151

    Pacific Gas & Electric, McQuillister, George A. *Page* 1-117

    Target, Standford, Don R. *Page* 1-126

Oceanside, Carlson Hospitality Worldwide, Monson, Barbara E. *Page* 1-111

Ontario

    California State at San Bernardino, Shayo, Conrad *Page* 1-332

    CCL Label, Nicholson, Peter D. *Page* 1-37

Orinda, Commerce One, White, Kimberly A. *Page* 1-200

Palo Alto

    1 Venture Inc., Schmidt, Jonatan *Page* 1-280

    Hewlett-Packard Company, Almeida-Coffron, Katty *Page* 1-39

    Hewlett-Packard Company, Hinkston, Kevin L. *Page* 1-41

    Hewlett-Packard Labs, Livingston, Mark A. *Page* 1-43

    IDB Consulting, Stemmelin, Frederic *Page* 1-285

    Sun Microsystems, Inc., Gelfenbain, Alexander *Page* 1-40

    Sun Microsystems, Inc., Lee, Myungho *Page* 1-42

Pasadena

    DACOR, Garza, Johnny Kim *Page* 1-52

    EarthLink, Hutchinson-Surette, Eric A. *Page* 1-250

    Enthusiast, Inc., Cline, Jon *Page* 1-231

    Yellow Shirt, Chan, Calvin L. *Page* 1-229

Paso Robles, Paso Robles Public School District, Smith, Sheldon K. *Page* 1-383

Perris, Val Verde Unified School District, Bradley, Thomas M. *Page* 1-381

Petaluma, Blue Dragon Network, Al-Jamal, Ismail *Page* 1-217

Pico Rivera, LA Dye & Printworks, Inc., Ackermann, Anthony *Page* 1-11

Pleasant Hill

    Air Touch, Keenan, Marvin P. *Page* 1-93

    Application Partners, Inc., Thompson, Wesley *Page* 1-289

    Wilkinson Consulting Group, Inc., Wilkinson, David D. *Page* 1-296

Pomona

    Digital Pyramid, Hoda, Sami A. *Page* 1-247

    PFF Bank & Trust, Lambert, Paul R. *Page* 1-134

Portola Valley, ppb, Inc., Azar, Lawrence *Page* 1-64

Redding

    CHZM Hill, Rippon, Dana W. *Page* 1-349

    Compaq Computer Corporation, Pringle, James W. *Page* 1-44

Rednvodaty, Asera, Inc., Lemke, Uwe *Page* 1-257

Redwood City

    IBM Corporation, Moser, Ellen M. *Page* 1-44

    Oracle Corporation, Martinsson, Lars E. *Page* 1-197

    Perclose, Inc., Salinas, Alexander *Page* 1-83

Redwood Shores

    Oracle Corporation, Johnson, Deke Andrew *Page* 1-196

    Oracle Corporation, Patil, Ashutosh *Page* 1-198

Ridgecrest, Bureau of Land Management, Perez, Robin L. *Page* 1-388

Riverside, Digiquest, Reddy, K. B. *Page* 1-112

Rosemead, Southern California Edison, Bailey, Larry J. *Page* 1-113

Roseville, C-bridge Internet Solutions, Lee, William *Page* 1-257

Sacramento

    Cal PERS, Quint, Al *Page* 1-146

    Contractors State Licensing Board, Lee, Edwin Y. *Page* 1-391

    Department of Finance for State of California, Strutton, James D. *Page* 1-380

    Health & Welfare Agency, Luiz, Dave P. *Page* 1-155

    SMUD, McCauley, Barney *Page* 1-114

    State Water Resource Control Board; SWRCB, Diep, Thang *Page* 1-387

    Unify Corporation, Bristow, Donald R. *Page* 1-225

    USAED Sacramento, Stoner, Stephen E. *Page* 1-396

San Bernardino

    CTAP, Legutki, Gregory W. *Page* 1-206

    RSM McGladrey, Inc., Robichaud, Steven E. *Page* 1-355

San Diego

City College, Forman, Lawrence *Page 1-323*

CN Bioscience, Cofer, Eric C. *Page 1-22*

Computer Land, Loechner, Erich Karl *Page 1-206*

Computer Sciences Corporation, Edwards, Albert L. *Page 1-203*

eHNC, Kao, Wayne *Page 1-253*

Express Computer Supply, Jain, Kunwar *Page 1-119*

F. Saba & Associates, Saba, Farhad *Page 1-332*

HNC Software, Inc., Fig, Susan B. *Page 1-175*

John Holmertz, Holmertz, John P. *Page 1-248*

Justice Communications, Justicia, José A. *Page 1-60*

Mitre Corporation, Goldsmith, Deborah L. *Page 1-241*

SAIC, Bartoli, Peter J. *Page 1-357*

Science Applications International Corporation, Georges, William T. *Page 1-240*

Unisys Corporation, Harrison, Eric A. *Page 1-246*

San Francisco

Affiliated Computer Services, Dempsey, Patrick P. *Page 1-233*

BAART/CDP, Tang, John *Page 1-306*

Barclays Global Investors, Tamas, Peter V. *Page 1-155*

Bulldog Information Services, Burch, Scott A. *Page 1-227*

Catellus Development Corporation, Nicholson, Bill *Page 1-160*

Dolby Laboratories, Tringali, Michael A. *Page 1-57*

Genesys Labs, Tereshko, George V. *Page 1-288*

Maxson Young Associates, Inc., Davison, Glenn L. *Page 1-157*

Pillsbury Madison & Sutro, Thiele, Cynthia Buchan *Page 1-313*

PricewaterhouseCoopers, Parks, Floyd *Page 1-354*

Snapfish.com, Jaffer, Akbar G. *Page 1-179*

Ujanen, Ujanen, Kari R. *Page 1-210*

Veridicom, Sanchez, Frank *Page 1-298*

Visa International, Kirkpatrick, Mindy L. *Page 1-138*

Wells Fargo, Hussey, Michael P. *Page 1-133*

Winstar Telecommunication, Veguilla, John Anthony *Page 1-94*

San Gabriel

MediaFair, Guo, Ju *Page 1-177*

TEQ International, Tang, Andrew L. *Page 1-288*

San Jose

AMS Informatix Inc., Chayapathi, Nagaraju *Page 1-229*

Annuncio, Bhandary, Manoj S. *Page 1-163*

Atmel Corporation, Lambrache, Emil *Page 1-66*

Catholic Charities, Bailey, William D. *Page 1-344*

Cisco Systems, Inc., Chang, David W. *Page 1-58*

Cisco Systems, Inc., Gaither, Mark A. *Page 1-59*

Cisco Systems, Inc., Garg, Arun *Page 1-59*

Electronics Arts, Do, Hai Thanh *Page 1-196*

Excite@Home, Gunawan, Kingson *Page 1-109*

Fujitsu Microelectronics, Inc., Fujisaku, Kiminori *Page 1-65*

Hewlett-Packard Company, Jones, Jennifer L. *Page 1-41*

IBM Corporation, Srinivasan, Savitha *Page 1-45*

IBM Santa Teresa Lab, Zhang, Guogen *Page 1-46*

Infoloan, Cheng, Jack Y. *Page 1-140*

KLA-Tencor, Sachen, Richard J. *Page 1-67*

Lanop Corporation, Tutone, Frank P. *Page 1-291*

Litton PRC, Chen, Deanford *Page 1-229*

Medio Systems, Inc., Xie, Ian Y. *Page 1-193*

MMT Corporation, Schupp, Felix A. *Page 1-189*

Mylex, Hobbs, Dan J. *Page 1-179*

Phoenix Technologies Ltd., Mathur, Sameer *Page 1-183*

Seagate Technology Inc., Tsai, Sunnie *Page 1-47*

Sun Microsystems, Inc., Scott, Barry Price *Page 1-45*

Telegyr Systems, Inc., Mourad, Tarek M. *Page 1-266*

UHERE Corporation, Wei, Jeffrey Haoran *Page 1-295*

United Defense, Hutson, Tom *Page 1-60*

San Leandro, C.W. Marini & Associates, Marini, Christopher W. *Page 1-261*

San Marcos, San Marcos United School District, Sanchez-Pfeiffer, Kitty *Page 1-383*

San Mateo

Avant Go, Caraballo, Roderick G. *Page 1-228*

Epronet, Sarkes, Robert A. *Page 1-169*

GetFit.com, Izrailevsky, Yury A. *Page 1-305*

Siebel Systems, Inc., Jay, Henry D. *Page 1-196*

San Rafael

Independent, Quesada, Arli *Page 1-370*

Morphonix, Littman, Karen G. *Page 1-182*

Tippett Studios, Teramoto, Tim G. *Page 1-304*

San Ramon

Pacific Bell, Jones, Jeffrey M. *Page 1-100*

PROMATIS Corporation, Graf, Sebastian *Page 1-177*

Santa Ana, Akropolis.net, Connolly, Phil J. *Page 1-232*

Santa Clara

3Com, Greene, Michael *Page 1-48*

ABB Systems Control, Mukherjee, Himadri P. *Page 1-215*

Acucomm Inc., Trisno, Yudhi S. *Page 1-291*

Cisco Systems, Inc., Batmazian, Krikor *Page 1-58*

Hewlett-Packard Company, Hill, Derek P. *Page 1-41*

Integrated Device Technology, Inc., Suhaimi, Sunyo L. *Page 1-68*

Intel Corporation, Fang, Jesse *Page 1-65*

Lead Trac, Filippone, Joseph R. *Page 1-236*

S1 Corporation, Vedda, Michael S. *Page 1-200*

Silicon Graphics, Kreft, Bryan M. *Page 1-181*

Siliconix, Inc., Wang, Hong *Page 1-68*

Santa Clarita, Trident Data Systems, Brown, Charles *Page 1-226*

Santa Cruz, E-Greetings, Gajic, Dragan *Page 1-21*

Santa Monica, Vivorx Inc., Fadri, Reynaldo J. *Page 1-357*

Santa Rosa

Lemo USA, Inc., Hope, Teresa M. *Page 1-68*

Optical Coating Laboratory, Brown, John S. *Page 1-82*

Saratoga, CAM Systems LLC., Chockalingam, Rajasekaran S. *Page 1-230*

Sausalito, Abratech Corporation, Caplovitz, Gideon Paul *Page 1-357*

South San Francisco

Genentech, Chen, Yuan-Yuan "Chrissie" *Page 1-22*

Genentech, Glenn, Tyrone L. *Page 1-23*

Genentech, Ward, Michael F. *Page 1-25*

Spring Valley, Gordon Computer Services, Gordon, Frank J. *Page 1-243*

Stockton, San Joaquin County Public Works, Jones, Anthony M. *Page 1-371*

Sunnyvale

Chain Link Technologies Inc., Herron, Kristine M. *Page 1-179*

Computer Curriculum Corporation, Chow, Thomas *Page 1-202*

Marvell, Doan, Phillip K. *Page 1-65*

Nanometrics, Inc., Yarussi, Richard A. *Page 1-37*

Viquity, Clements, Larry *Page 1-195*

Susanville, Lassen Municipal Utility, Barrows, Donald A. *Page 1-113*

Tehachapi, Cybersurfers, Domingue, Jeremy *Page 1-234*

Thousand Oaks

    Biomophic VLSI, Standley, David L. *Page 1-67*

    GTE, Hickman, Michael J. *Page 1-100*

Torrance

    Edelbrock Corporation, Herrmann, Scott M. *Page 1-71*

    Microcosm, Young, Sandra Kay *Page 1-79*

    R R Donnelley & Sons, Jones, Benedict *Page 1-18*

    South Bay Bank, Fraser, Neal D. *Page 1-134*

    South Bay Online, Hayata, Nancy K. T. *Page 1-246*

Tracy, KPMG LLP, Skiles, Bryan E. *Page 1-366*

Tustin

    Accelerated Imaging, Inc., Rios, Anthony A. *Page 1-208*

    Commonwealth Energy, Howard, Pat E. *Page 1-114*

    Digital Conversions, Balian, Gerair D. *Page 1-220*

Union City, Cisco Systems, Inc., Nagarajan, Senthil Kumar *Page 1-61*

Van Nuys

    Medical Manager West, Hedenberg, Judy A. *Page 1-179*

    Valley Presbyterian Hospital, Litten, Catherine Lee *Page 1-308*

Victorville, BMR Training Centers, Finch, Michael D. *Page 1-340*

Walnut

    Mount San Antonio College, Pop, Horia *Page 1-338*

    Viewsonic, Wilson, Raymond E. *Page 1-49*

Walnut Creek, Kaiser Health Plan, McGuire, Michael R. *Page 1-152*

West Lake Village, Internet Solution Group, Hamzei, Nader *Page 1-178*

Westlake Village, Agilent Technologies, Inc., Su, Alan P. *Page 1-82*

Whittier, IKON, Zepeda, Jesse H. *Page 1-51*

Woodland Hills, Astra Zeneca, Graham, Deborah L. *Page 1-23*

Colorado

Arvada

    DataSoft LLC.com, Poppitz, Mickey *Page 1-274*

    Employers Unity, Brown, Robert W. *Page 1-155*

Aurora

    Eaglecrest High School, Roina, John A. *Page 1-317*

    Triple Play, Dobrovolny, Jackie Lea *Page 1-300*

    University of Colorado Hospital, Dalious, Peggy *Page 1-322*

Boulder

    1-800-VIDEO-ON, Eshelman, Scott Walter *Page 1-109*

    Eclipse Inc., Ramsey, Kathryn L. *Page 1-187*

    Information Graphics Systems Inc., Meyer, Patrick J. *Page 1-184*

    Leopard Communications, Wilsdon, Alex L. *Page 1-192*

Brighton, Brighton School District - Technology Department, Klein, Frank J. *Page 1-382*

Colorado Springs

    Colorado Springs Utilities, Rizzuto, Alan *Page 1-116*

    Hyperacuity Systems, Wilcox, Michael J. *Page 1-82*

    IHS Engineering, Adams, Rick *Page 1-18*

    Philips P.C. Peripherals, Athey, Harry C. *Page 1-128*

    Pike Tool & Grinding, Stebenne, Andrew M. *Page 1-33*

    Pikes Peak Mental Health, Bender, Carla V. *Page 1-307*

    Pikes Peak Mental Health, Houghton, Jeremy E. *Page 1-308*

    Premiere Conferencing, Murphy, George E. *Page 1-102*

    Pulau Electronics Corporation, Howard, Charles L. *Page 1-71*

Denver

    Auraria Higher Education Center, Dunn, Peter K. *Page 1-323*

    Bentley Management Corporation, Wyss, Mark W. *Page 1-141*

    Computer Horizons Corporation, Geist, Thomas E. *Page 1-240*

    Greeley Gas Company, Merritt, Gary S. *Page 1-115*

    Hall Kinion, Plambeck, Pamela *Page 1-168*

    IBM Corporation, Buzby, Carrie D. *Page 1-39*

    Informix, Peacey, Kendrew *Page 1-272*

    Lockheed Martin Enterprise Information Systems, Corson, Charlton E. *Page 1-79*

    Qwest Communications, Cowan, Patrick Neal *Page 1-97*

    Randol International, Ltd., Hale, Christie Callahan *Page 1-18*

    Rapidigm, Tamma, Leela Shankar *Page 1-288*

    Regional Transportation District, Balkema, Allan *Page 1-87*

    Schwab Institutional, Plumb, Sean F. *Page 1-146*

    Simpson Housing Ltd. Partnership, Miller, Jeffrey T. *Page 1-160*

    Teletech Holdings Inc., Ogunmodede, Victor A. *Page 1-270*

    U S WEST Interprise Networking Services, Fielden, Jeanette *Page 1-97*

    U S WEST, Clements, Kerry Keith *Page 1-97*

Dillon, Lake Dillon Fire Protection District, Duggan, Carlina *Page 1-378*

Englewood

    BMC Consultants, Inc., Nielsen, Thomas W. *Page 1-369*

    Cressoft Inc., Shami, Azmat Bilal *Page 1-189*

    CSG Systems International, Smoot, Brian D. *Page 1-284*

    Experian, Liu, Ningsheng *Page 1-182*

    MediaOne Group, Manning, Kevin W. *Page 1-108*

    The Trizetto Group, Nguyen, Brittney T. *Page 1-268*

    Unisphere Solutions, Leitzel, David R. *Page 1-56*

    Verio, Inc., Fraze, John T. *Page 1-109*

Fort Collins, National Technological University, Van Baren, Marla J. *Page 1-334*

Greeley, Hewlett-Packard Company, Swetzig, DeAnnaKay *Page 1-45*

Greenwood Village, Sybase, Inc., Brown, Chris N. *Page 1-194*

Ignaciao, Ignacio School District, Smith, Rick K. *Page 1-383*

Lafayette, Design Fabricators, Little, Frank *Page 1-54*

Lamar, SECI, Inc., Gool, Eric M. *Page 1-242*

Littleton

    Analysts International, Gaddam, Ravi *Page 1-176*

    Insursoft, Ltd., Campbell, Robert W. *Page 1-228*

    Lewis Colorado, Lewis, John H. *Page 1-258*

    Superior Technology Resources, Young, Smith *Page 1-351*

Longmont

    Evan Design Group, Smith, Eric E. *Page 1-284*

    Seagate Technology, Schaeffer, Russell A. *Page 1-47*

Loveland, Duke Communications Windows 2000 Magazine, Morrill, Jane E. *Page 1-16*

Penrose, The Gazette, Thompson, A. J. *Page 1-16*

Connecticut

Berlin, Northeast Utilities, Bates, Charles P. *Page 1-116*

Branford, Oxford Health Plans, Pardy, Brian J. *Page 1-151*

Darlen, Internet World Media, Inc., Rossi, Matthew R. *Page 1-303*

East Haven, USI Prescription Benefits, Humphreys, Timothy J. *Page 1-157*

Farmington, Information Builders Inc., Shindnes, Sergey *Page 1-199*

Glastonbury

    IKON Office Solutions, Bourdon, Philippe M. *Page 1-50*

    The Allied Group Inc., Messes, Alexander P. *Page 1-184*

Greenwich

Bridgewater Associates, Guild, Brian K. *Page 1-145*

Factset Research Systems, Boffardi, Marc G. *Page 1-201*

Transactions Marketing Inc., Lewis, Brenda *Page 1-364*

Hartford

State of Connecticut Workers Compensation, Wilson, Edward Alton *Page 1-155*

The Hartford, Romel, Jeffrey Lawrence *Page 1-154*

Lakeville, The Hotchkiss School, Hall, Leland G. *Page 1-315*

Manchester, Lydall, Inc., Curcio, Barry M. *Page 1-15*

Meriden

Computer Sciences Corporation, Cherry, Donald Thomas *Page 1-202*

Radio Frequency Systems, Sabin, Matthew S. *Page 1-57*

Southern New England Telephone, Hooke, Edward C. *Page 1-100*

New FairField, Catapult Software Training, Tripaldi, Daniel J. R. *Page 1-291*

New Hartford, ProcureNet, Inc., Burns, Elizabeth J. *Page 1-172*

New Haven

Lawrence Associates, Lawrence, Bonnie L. *Page 1-364*

Yale University ITS/Telecommunications, Patti, Stephen *Page 1-331*

Newington, American Radio Relay League, Durand, Donald *Page 1-347*

Newtown, Compaq Computer Corporation, Wilson, Ralph Thomas *Page 1-46*

Norwalk, MBI Inc., Mastroianni, Dan A. *Page 1-163*

Paucatuck, Davis Standard/HES, Rosivach, Chris *Page 1-36*

Ridgefield, Golden Eagle Credit Corporation, Ference, William F. *Page 1-167*

Rocky Hill, Merallis Company, Campbell, Eileen Rose *Page 1-147*

Shelton

GE Supply, Duay, Cheryl L. *Page 1-121*

Philips Medical Systems, Dubnicka, Leigh C. *Page 1-69*

Simsbury, Westminster School, DeLo, Dirk A. *Page 1-315*

South Windsor

Barco, Inc., Coullard, Jeremy B. *Page 1-69*

Barco, Inc., McFarlin, David J. *Page 1-69*

Southbury, IBM Global Services, Bovell, Matthew *Page 1-224*

Stamford

Madison International Sales, Holder, Michele *Page 1-124*

Meta Group, Sciurca, Albert *Page 1-282*

Storrs, University of Connecticut, Bhattacharjee, Sudip *Page 1-320*

Stratford, American Frozen Foods Inc., Drown, Dennis A. *Page 1-301*

Trumbull

Cendant Corporation, Croswell, Jerry D. *Page 1-363*

Unilever, Coniglio, Allen P. *Page 1-25*

Wallingford, Fleet Technology Solutions, Toro, Robert N. *Page 1-290*

West Haven, Habanero Software, Russello, Frank V. *Page 1-279*

Windsor, Unisys Corporation, Schlagheck, Ryan Wm. *Page 1-280*

Woodbury, Micros-to-Mainframes, Samoska, Michael C. *Page 1-279*

Delaware

Claymont, Archmere Academy, Robinson, Mark C. *Page 1-317*

Dover, Tri Tech Systems, Inc., Petrucelli, James L. *Page 1-273*

Hernberg, LN-Online GmbH, Luebeck, Watermann, Sascha *Page 1-294*

Wilmington

Bell Atlantic, Gardner, Mac *Page 1-98*

Diamond State Port Corporation, Thomas, Inigo *Page 1-89*

DuPont Pharmaceuticals Company, Hawkins, Joyce L. *Page 1-23*

IMI Systems, Inc., Hershman, Joseph *Page 1-247*

Rocsoar, Inc., Mao, John *Page 1-261*

District of Columbia

Amdahl Corporation, Mahmud, Shamun *Page 1-43*

American Chemical Society, Guo, Baoping *Page 1-345*

AT&T Technical Services, Brenneman, William B. *Page 1-225*

Brookings Institution, Alvarado, Winifreda Floro *Page 1-360*

CCNE, Heitman, Evelyn N. *Page 1-345*

Department of Justice, Immigration Naturalization Service, Caffey, Jeffrey L. *Page 1-375*

Department of Veterans Affairs, Bubniak, Robert P. *Page 1-386*

eJiva, Sobieray, Ed *Page 1-284*

Federal Aviation Administration, Levesque, Raymond F. *Page 1-390*

Headquarters, Air Force Audit Agency, Weaver, Clarence E. *Page 1-396*

HSB Reliability Technology, Drexler, Bryan A. *Page 1-234*

HUD Office of Inspector General, Walker, Michael L. *Page 1-389*

ITS America, Keppler, Stephen A. *Page 1-375*

Lockheed Martin, Moore-Fore, Iris Lynn *Page 1-80*

McDermott, Will & Emery, Powell, Linda L. *Page 1-313*

MCI WorldCom, Inc., Whitt, Richard S. *Page 1-106*

NASA, Spaulding, Omar Young *Page 1-78*

Office of the Chief Information Officer, United States Department of Energy, Tiemann, Michael Anthony *Page 1-289*

Office Of The Corporation Counsel, Pavlovsky, Serge Al *Page 1-377*

Senator Craig Thomas, Dykes, George M. *Page 1-371*

South African Embassy, Rogers, John R. *Page 1-397*

Sylvan Prometric, Tippins, Edward *Page 1-342*

The Catholic University of America Columbus School of Law, Russell, Damon E. *Page 1-332*

United States Army Visual Information Center, Jewel, Cheryl D. *Page 1-394*

United States Army, Huynh, Peter V. *Page 1-394*

United States Department of Education, Robinson, Mark Wesley *Page 1-382*

United States Department of State, Peppe, Richard W. *Page 1-397*

United States Department of Treasury, Green, Kenneth L. *Page 1-379*

United States Environmental Protection Agency, Day, Mark *Page 1-386*

United States Environmental Protection Agency, Frazier-Rousey, Toni Trinette *Page 1-387*

Watson Wyatt Worldwide, Burkhart, Michael G. *Page 1-362*

Florida

Altamonte Springs

En-Data, Schwendiger, Kathleen M. *Page 1-281*

Lucent Technologies, Shukla, Sandeep *Page 1-62*

Belle Glade, Glades Central High School, Thompson, Michael J. *Page 1-318*

Boca Raton

Coastal Technologies Group, Kane, Richard L. *Page 1-252*

Database Technologies, Schomaker, Paul A. *Page 1-209*

ProxyMed, Inc., Marton, Candace C. *Page 1-183*

Bronson, ITC Delta Com, Dickman, Lowell V. *Page 1-97*

Cape Canaveral, United Space Alliance, Corn, Jeffrey S. *Page 1-391*

Clearwater, IMR Global Corporation, Mathiyazhagan, Nithyanandam "Mathi" *Page 1-262*

Cocoa, United Space Alliance, Hintz, Cynthia Irene *Page 1-392*

Coconut Creek, Atlantic Technical Center, Turchiaro, Michael Louis *Page 1-342*

Coral Gables, University of Miami, Younis, Akmal A. *Page 1-334*

Dade City, Pasco Inc., Fincke, Greg *Page 1-7*

Davie, Nova Southeastern University, Garcia-Barreras, Victor E. *Page 1-323*

Delray Beach, Office Depot, Abbott, Lisa *Page* 1-128

Dunedin, Equant, Gorby, Bryan *Page* 1-204

Fort Lauderdale

    BarPoint.com, Romano, Robert "Rob" *Page* 1-188

    Citrix System, Inc., Sitterberg, Wolfgang *Page* 1-190

    Cyberguard, Henry, Paul A. *Page* 1-247

    Fairfield Communities, Inc., Gonzalez, Danny E. *Page* 1-160

    Motorola, Alvarez, Isidro *Page* 1-64

    Motorola, Villamil, Camilo E. *Page* 1-68

    Parkson Corporation, Matos, Ricardo R. *Page* 1-38

Fort Myers, EDAX Inc., Nylese, Tara Lyn *Page* 1-81

Fort Walton Beach, Marconi Services Corporation, Gilley, Darryl W. *Page* 1-71

Gainesville

    Remington Agency, Yates, Travis *Page* 1-193

    University of Florida, Horticultural Science Department, Spurlin, Tami *Page* 1-333

Jacksonville

    Bank of America, Eggleston, Kevin B. *Page* 1-133

    Bank of America, Rueger, Maria J. *Page* 1-134

    Bank of New York Trust Company, Crincoli, Diane J. *Page* 1-161

    BellSouth Business Systems, Kirkland, William Michael *Page* 1-101

    GAI Consulting Southeast Inc., Walker, Alfred E. *Page* 1-370

    International Data Solutions, Thompson, Norman *Page* 1-289

    Medscribe Information Systems, Inc., Langley, William *Page* 1-167

    PQH Architects, Inc., Papke, Steven D. *Page* 1-351

    Seaboard Credit Union, Lomax, Anissa M. *Page* 1-137

    Southeastern Metals Manufacturing Company, Langford, Mark G. *Page* 1-33

    The Haskell Company, Tucker, Clark F. *Page* 1-351

    Third Wave Services, Franklin, Braden S. *Page* 1-238

Lakeland, Breed Technologies, Anderson, Terri W. *Page* 1-72

Largo

    Centillion Computer Services, Inc., Graul, Charles F. *Page* 1-243

    Cox Target Media, Longgood, Donna R. *Page* 1-20

    Emergency Medical Services Group, Inc., d.b.a. EMSG, Barnard, Jeffery R. *Page* 1-310

Maitland, Stonehenge Telecom Americas, Greene, John E. *Page* 1-5

Margate, Solution Home.com, Magolnick, Michael *Page* 1-260

Marianna, United States Department of Justice, Hayhurst, Robert R. *Page* 1-376

Melbourne

    George Miler, Inc., Miler, Wyatt H. *Page* 1-90

    Golden Enterprises, Al Hadad, Shariff *Page* 1-70

    Rockwell Collins, Picariello, Angela E. *Page* 1-77

    Rockwell, Jordan, Roxanne M. *Page* 1-75

    Spacenet, Inc., Hall, Laurence A. *Page* 1-244

    Systems Computer Technology, Lentz, Terry M. *Page* 1-257

Miami

    Bacardi Ltd., Danguillecourt, Sergio *Page* 1-9

    Infosinergia, S.A., Fernandez, Rafael Manuel *Page* 1-109

    International Management Communication Corporation, Inc., Davis, Tamara L. *Page* 1-368

    PC Troubleshooter, Inc., Ukani, Ayoub B. *Page* 1-292

    Pellerano & Herrera, Marchena, Ruddy *Page* 1-312

    Southern Wine & Spirits, Booth, Mark M. *Page* 1-125

Naples, Strategy Partners Group, Toback, Jeremy *Page* 1-367

New Smyrna, Embry-Riddle Aeronautical University, Creech, Deborah *Page* 1-322

North Fort Myers, Raymond Building Supply, Percifield, George A. *Page* 1-118

North Miami, Advanced Technologies Consulting Group Inc., Schiavi, Adam J. *Page* 1-280

Oakland Park, ASAP II, DeSantis, Lori Ann *Page* 1-174

Orlando

    AT&T Wireless Services, Enos, Dennis *Page* 1-92

    BellSouth Communications Systems, Rook, Cynthia L. *Page* 1-104

    City of Orlando, Thompson, Douglas *Page* 1-374

    GE Harris Railway, Lang, Robert R. *Page* 1-181

    Harcourt, Inc., Folk, Gene E. *Page* 1-17

    Herman Miller, Smith, Walter E. *Page* 1-284

    Lucent Technologies, Griskell, Ivory J. *Page* 1-59

    Modis Technologies, O'Brien, Sean M. *Page* 1-269

    Oracle Corporation, Odok, Erhan *Page* 1-198

    SAIC, Cross, Matthew J. *Page* 1-232

    Valencia Community College, Morrell, Margaret R. *Page* 1-338

Palm Beach Gardens, Southern Internet, Calderbank, Kevin *Page* 1-108

Palm Harbor, Aegon Equity Group, D'Amico, Stephen *Page* 1-148

Parkland, Cross Country Home Service, Perez, Pedro P. *Page* 1-155

Pensacola, City of Pensacola, Raby, John M. *Page* 1-374

Plantation

    American Intercontinental University, Marged, Judith M. *Page* 1-328

    American Intercontinental University, Purnell, Katharine *Page* 1-331

    V.I.P.S., Franz, John F. *Page* 1-156

Pompano Beach

    Savvy Data, Schweitzer, Richard *Page* 1-189

    The Golf Network, Inc., Christly, John A. *Page* 1-172

Riverview, ADP Hayes Ligon, Hollands, Brian P. *Page* 1-212

Sanford, Anglais Consulting Inc., English, Richard L. *Page* 1-236

Sarasota

    Arthur Andersen, Caudullo, Jane *Page* 1-363

    Sun Hydraulic Corporation, Schultes, Stan J. *Page* 1-35

    The Zenith, Clark, Brian E. *Page* 1-153

    Vengroff, Williams & Associates, Lalone, David J. *Page* 1-165

Sebastian, eMerge Interactive, Woods, Marguerite E. *Page* 1-297

Shalimar, TeleCommunication Systems, Inc., Gust, Thomas A. *Page* 1-244

Spring Hill, Westside Elementary School, Timmins, Allan S. *Page* 1-318

St. Petersburg

    BEST! Software, Inc., Bachrach, Daniel A. *Page* 1-171

    Home Shopping Network, Usiak, Robert F. *Page* 1-131

Sun Rise, Lucent Technologies, Tinelli, Felice *Page* 1-62

Tallahassee

    Federal Bureau of Prisons, Minion, William W. *Page* 1-378

    Florida Government Technology Conference, Keiffer, Ralph J. *Page* 1-253

    Florida State Board of Administration, Latmore, Allison W. *Page* 1-375

    Leon County Health Department, Grimes, Sylvie *Page* 1-385

Tampa

    Advanced Concepts Engineering and Technology, Jones, Tim H. *Page* 1-251

    Catalina Marketing, Bates, Christopher A. *Page* 1-165

    Chain Store Guide, Darmenio, Greg *Page* 1-128

    Connection Staffing, Inc., Mohammed, David S. *Page* 1-170

    Intermedia Communications, Tuttle, Michael *Page* 1-105

    Olsten Health Services, Coyle, Charles W. *Page* 1-306

    Professional Communications Systems, Schall, Ronald G. *Page* 1-209

Talbot's, Bowen, Lynn A. *Page 1-127*

The Walt Disney Company, Raymondo, James A. *Page 1-305*

Vero Beach, MCB Collection Services Inc., Wright, Michael C. *Page 1-303*

Viera, DRS Optronics, Antle, M. D. Paka *Page 1-84*

West Palm Beach, Palm Beach County Health Care District, Vargas, Usha *Page 1-152*

Weston, Andrx, Levine, Jerilee "Jeri" Goodman *Page 1-24*

Winter Park, Universal Systems and Technology Inc., Clawson, Perry R. *Page 1-230*

Winter Springs, First Consulting Group, Barnard, James H. *Page 1-299*

Georgia

Acworth

    O'Brien Interactive, Winklesky, James B. *Page 1-193*

    Unisys Corporation, Allen, Mark *Page 1-217*

Alpharetta

    McKesson HBOC, Franklin, Douglas N. *Page 1-175*

    McKesson HBOC, McEntyre, Susan K. *Page 1-24*

    SCB Computer Technology, Inc., Fulmer, Allyson *Page 1-238*

    Technology Solutions Company, Campbell, Gregory L. *Page 1-228*

Atlanta

    ASAP Software Express, Rexford, Victoria *Page 1-120*

    Atlanta Public Schools, Scott, Arthur R. *Page 1-383*

    BellSouth, Griffin, Lianne H. *Page 1-99*

    BellSouth, Svendsen, Cary A. *Page 1-105*

    Cap Gemini America, Inc., Gopalan, Rajan *Page 1-242*

    Centers for Disease Control, Fehd, Ronald J. *Page 1-360*

    ComCore, Cary, John *Page 1-362*

    Consumer Financial Network, Hemsey, Michael F. *Page 1-301*

    Diversified Computer Consultants, Mahajani, Anand *Page 1-260*

    ERDAS, Inc., Gabriel, Darren K. *Page 1-176*

    Ga Childcare Online, Ebrahimi, Steven G. *Page 1-342*

    General Electric Company, Dar, Arif A. *Page 1-76*

    Home Depot, Milner, Dana *Page 1-126*

    IBM Corporation, Braggs, Genelle R. *Page 1-39*

    IBM Global Services, Clark, Ronald L. *Page 1-230*

    Long Aldridge & Norman, Munajj, Sharon E. L. *Page 1-313*

    MCI WorldCom, Inc., Patterson, Ollie C. *Page 1-103*

    McKinley Group, Inc., Knight, Kathy Hawkins *Page 1-254*

    Mercer University, Taylor, Cecilia T. *Page 1-333*

    National Data Corporation, Bartolotta, Tina *Page 1-300*

    PTI, Martin, Robert A. *Page 1-365*

    Ross Systems, Long, Cheryl C. *Page 1-183*

    SAP, Meckley, Hope Eyre *Page 1-184*

    Siemens Energy and Automation, Darby, Philip D. *Page 1-55*

    Summit National Bank, Watkins, Steve *Page 1-136*

    Tetra Pak Americas, Inc., Beard, Gunilla *Page 1-37*

    Windsor Group, Peters, Ryan M. *Page 1-157*

    WORLDSPAN, Hughes, Barbara A. *Page 1-249*

    Z-Tel, Patel, Mitool M. *Page 1-103*

Augusta, Westinghouse, Mikel, Lashika L. *Page 1-394*

Bremen, Hubbard Company, Farmer, Ira Anthony *Page 1-12*

Carrollton, Carroll Technical Institute, Ayers, Janet B. *Page 1-335*

Chico, Western University of Health Sciences, Hanford, Karen *Page 1-324*

College Park, Bank of America, Trice, David M. *Page 1-134*

Cumming

    Comforce Company, Connell, Donna M. *Page 1-167*

    Siemens Energy and Automation, Bruno, Rae Ann *Page 1-55*

Dacula, Spherion Corporation, Guthrie, Kenneth L. *Page 1-301*

Douglasville, Starternet, Adesh, Vivek S. *Page 1-170*

Duluth

    Kaltech International Corporation, Kalke, Kimberly *Page 1-252*

    Mitsubishi Wireless Communications Inc., Wise, Michael *Page 1-57*

    NCR Corporation, Hilton, Mark R. *Page 1-50*

    Primerica Financial Services, Manges, John P. *Page 1-139*

Dunwoody

    Arthur Andersen, Hurst, Karen *Page 1-363*

    IBM-Knowledge Factory, Gordon, Randi-Lyn *Page 1-243*

    Metropolitan Life, Smith, Bruce A. *Page 1-149*

Ellenwood, Federated Systems Group, Flowers, Frank *Page 1-237*

Fort Gordon, EER Systems, Inc., Kropp, Monica B. *Page 1-181*

Fort Valley, Fort Valley State University, Harvester, Wayne C. *Page 1-324*

Franklin Springs, Emmanuel College, Duncan, Dennis LeRoy *Page 1-322*

Griffin, Spalding County Health Department, Hubbert, Patty *Page 1-385*

Hahira

    Equifax E-Banking Solutions, Inc., Bayyapureddy, Kishore *Page 1-221*

    Sierra Pine Adel Division, Sutton, Curtis *Page 1-13*

Lithia Springs, Flexx Magazine, Nana, Rajesh C. *Page 1-17*

Loganville, PSC, Pearce, Cecil L. *Page 1-391*

Macon, Saddle Creek Corporation, Kessler, Peter W. *Page 1-88*

Marietta

    Clarus Software, Kramer, Daune C. *Page 1-181*

    IBM Corporation, Mundle, Sheldon *Page 1-44*

    JobsMadeEasy.com, Peram, Suresh *Page 1-168*

    RF Wolters Company, Inc., Cooper, Amanda M. *Page 1-372*

Newnan

    Newnan Technologies, Inc., Morrow, Larry J. *Page 1-207*

    Onyx Solutions, Inc., Fox, Steven W. *Page 1-237*

Norcross

    American Megatrends Inc., Chan, Rodney W. *Page 1-195*

    American Megatrends Inc., Vermont, Lee M. *Page 1-200*

    IMS HEALTH Strategic Technologies, Anandan, Israel D. *Page 1-171*

    Strategic Technologies, Collins, Louis H. *Page 1-231*

Peachtree City

    Continuous Forms & Checks, Inc., McLemore, Shannon *Page 1-138*

    NCR Corporation, Dix, Brian Douglas *Page 1-50*

Roswell, American Junior Golf, Witkowski, Jeffrey J. *Page 1-305*

Savannah

    Dean Oliver International, Johnson, Ginger Sears *Page 1-205*

    Gulfstream Aerospace, Caster, Charles *Page 1-75*

    Savannah-Chatham County Board of Education, Ray, Ramon Jarrod *Page 1-382*

    Southern Linc, Pate, Lonnie J. *Page 1-93*

Suwanee

    Arris Interactive, Bandong, Lydia M. *Page 1-58*

    Arris Interactive, Rao, Sonali *Page 1-62*

    Oki Network Technologies, Barber, Clifton J. *Page 1-57*

Thomasville, US Filter Distribution, Thornhill, C. Allen *Page 1-123*

Warner Robins, Earth Tech, Silsbee, Laura Barrett *Page 1-349*

Warrenton, Warren County Schools, Ansley, David Thomas *Page 1-380*

Woodstock, Maxim Group (BioLab Inc.), Kinnard, Michael S. *Page 1-254*

Hawaii

Honolulu

Hawaii Multimedia Corporation, Tay, Thomas A. *Page* 1-288

International Savings, Chee, Adrian U. *Page* 1-136

Kaiser Permanente, Niel, Anthony L. *Page* 1-150

Kazuo Totoki Ltd., Pang, Elmer S. B. *Page* 1-159

University of Hawaii, Wermager, Paul *Page* 1-334

Kailua, United States Marine Corps, Bertrand, Joseph F. *Page* 1-392

Idaho

Boise

Micron Technology, Gardner, Chris D. *Page* 1-65

Micronpc.com, Phatak, Shreyas *Page* 1-47

Grand View, Simplot Livestock Company, Black, Randy M. *Page* 1-1

Idaho Falls, Eastern Idaho Technical College, Reese, Timothy E. *Page* 1-338

Lewiston, Lewis-Clark State College, Hennigan, Thomas A. *Page* 1-337

Pocatello, American Microsystems Inc, Olney, Tiffany *Page* 1-67

Rigby, Department of Energy at Idaho National Engineering and Environmental Laboratory, Peterson, Barbara L. *Page* 1-361

Illinois

Arlington Heights, IKOS Systems, Louie, Victor C. *Page* 1-206

Aurora, Waubonsee College, Sotir, Judith S. *Page* 1-333

Bensenville

Alltech Data Systems, Pittas, Douglas *Page* 1-93

Client Server Consulting, Goldburgh, Joyce *Page* 1-241

Bloomington

Bumgarner Global Enterprises, Bumgarner, Kenneth B. *Page* 1-227

State Farm Insurance, Gilliam, Ken W. *Page* 1-154

Buffalo Grove, Motorola, Thalanany, Sebastian *Page* 1-68

Burr Ridge, Mcgraw-Hill Higher Education, Todd, James A. *Page* 1-17

Calumet Park, Ivy Tech State College, Hamilton, Brandon *Page* 1-337

Carpentersville, McWhorter Technologies, Kochanowski, Mark *Page* 1-22

Champaign, ERDC-CNC, Dilks, Kelly Marie *Page* 1-360

Chicago

ABN AMRO Bank, Allen, Pamela T. *Page* 1-137

ABN AMRO, Riopelle, Joanna M. *Page* 1-137

ARDC, Bader, Robin L. *Page* 1-345

Arian Lowe & Travis, Walczak, Bryan T. *Page* 1-164

Arthur Andersen Technology Solutions, Townsend, Tracey *Page* 1-367

Arthur Andersen, Randles, Gary A. *Page* 1-366

Chicago Microsystems, Ares, Julian Sol *Page* 1-218

Chicago Police Department, Tuomey, Michael Sean *Page* 1-377

Code Hennessy & Simmons, De Shazer, Ronelle *Page* 1-142

David Gomez & Associates, Inc., Larkin, CorDell R. *Page* 1-168

Dr. William M. Scholl College of Podiatric Medicine, DeVore, Jeanne *Page* 1-322

Ernst & Young LLP, Scott, Nancy L. *Page* 1-355

Fers Business Services Inc., Brand, David *Page* 1-368

First Chicago/Mercantile Services, Anderson, Maribeth *Page* 1-171

First Continental Trading, Levine, William A. *Page* 1-143

Illinois Housing Development Authority, Ansari, Waheed H. *Page* 1-388

Information Resources, Inc., Chitre, Nikhil *Page* 1-359

Information Resources, Inc., Pillers, Jeff A. *Page* 1-360

Lante Corporation, Parkes, Shawn *Page* 1-271

MICROS Systems, Inc., Terway, Jennifer D. *Page* 1-49

Northwestern Memorial Hospital, Lopardo, Sue *Page* 1-308

Northwestern University, Burden, Matthew C. *Page* 1-320

PricewaterhouseCoopers, D'Andrea, Marcus J. *Page* 1-352

Raymond V. Hall Training & Consultant Services, Hall, Raymond V. *Page* 1-245

Richard J. Daley College, Dardai, Shahid M. *Page* 1-336

S&C Electric Company, Nickele, Margaret M. *Page* 1-52

SASI, Wilson, Salena *Page* 1-343

SS&C Technologies, Smith, Jennifer M. *Page* 1-190

Unisource Network Services, McElroy, Thomas D. *Page* 1-263

Unisource Network Services, Tiongco, Ronald L. *Page* 1-290

Young Men's Christian Association of Metropolitan Chicago, Stiehr, Marc L. *Page* 1-347

Chicago,, Anexsys, Olson, Elizabeth K. *Page* 1-270

De Soto, Motorola, Petroski, Thomas L. *Page* 1-67

Decatur

Archer Daniels Midland Company, Swallow, Brett A. *Page* 1-1

Illinois Power Company, Peterson, Richard *Page* 1-117

Deerfield

Marconi Data Systems, Inc., Kwan, Vincent W. *Page* 1-36

Tenneco Packaging, Wellnitz, Judi K. *Page* 1-29

Des Plaines

Geneer, Inc., Hargreave, Andrew G. *Page* 1-178

UOP, Salem, Mike M. *Page* 1-303

Downers Grove

Roetech Services, Roe, Wesley D. *Page* 1-277

The National Transportation Exchange, Inc., Moler, Dino D. *Page* 1-147

East Moline, 4C Solutions, Gupta, Rajesh *Page* 1-244

Glen Ellyn, Helios System Inc., Marlow, Gerald D. *Page* 1-262

Hainesville, Pepper Construction, Reid, Nathan D. *Page* 1-4

Hoffman Estates, ADP Dealer Services, Roll, Gary V. *Page* 1-212

La Grange, Acxiom RTC, Inc., Smith, Joshua D. *Page* 1-209

Libertyville

Arlington Industries, Kozlov, Christopher M. *Page* 1-120

Hollister Inc., Cox, Joel A. *Page* 1-83

Lisle, Swiss Bank Corporation, Tignor, Doug J. *Page* 1-137

Lombard

IDX, Byrd, Melody D. *Page* 1-201

The Plus Group, Seelander, John M. *Page* 1-366

Loves Park, Clinton Electronics Corporation, Terrell, Joseph A. *Page* 1-63

Macomb, Western Illinois University, George, Binto *Page* 1-324

Manito, Madison River Communications, Olsen, William W. *Page* 1-103

Manteno, K-mart Distribution Center, Muhlstadt, Maryanne T. *Page* 1-88

McHenry, McHenry School District #15, Pride, Buddy *Page* 1-317

Morengo, Oracle University, Frazier, Larry B. *Page* 1-323

Morris, Grundy Area Vocational Center, Cornwall, Daniel J. *Page* 1-314

Naperville

BP Amoco, Pribich, Jeff *Page* 1-2

Lucent Technologies, Keaton-Culp, Carolyn R. *Page* 1-60

Motorola, Liu, Chen *Page* 1-66

Power 2000 Inc., Demarest, Jim *Page* 1-233

Resource Information Management Systems, Inc., Williams, Laura H. *Page* 1-192

New York, KPMG LLP, Kumawat, Rajesh *Page* 1-364

Northbrook

Grubb & Ellis Company, Almeda, Gilbert S. *Page* 1-158

Grubb & Ellis Company, Brown, Dennis J. *Page 1-158*

Northbrook Community School District 28, Andre, Darlene A. *Page 1-380*

Northfield, Linkscorp, Greene, Mark A. *Page 1-305*

O'Fallon, SAIC, Bjerkaas, Carlton L. *Page 1-357*

Oak Brook

   HFN, Inc./Kinetra IMIN, Towner, Wendy M. *Page 1-311*

   Independent, Smith, Michele *Page 1-284*

   Interactive Business Systems, Inc., Gomes, Ivan J. *Page 1-242*

   Leapnet, Inc., Podemski, Michael J. *Page 1-274*

Oakbrook Terrace

   Computer Associates, Ciarlette, Karen L. *Page 1-173*

   Dreher & Associates, Inc., Ely, Mark *Page 1-142*

Oswego, Obsidian Corporation, Gerlick, Joshua A. *Page 1-177*

Ottawa, Area 2 Learning Tech Hub, Link, Patty A. *Page 1-258*

Palatine, Senco-Argonne National Lab, McWilliams, Craig R. *Page 1-264*

Pekin, K & R Splicing, Adkins, Kaye W. *Page 1-6*

Peoria

   OSF Healthcare Systems, Farris, Terrance J. *Page 1-152*

   RLI Corporation, Engvall, Thomas J. *Page 1-174*

Rockford, Greenlee Textron, Pryor, Jason A. *Page 1-36*

Rolling Meadows, Baxter Healthcare Corporation, Hines, Daniel J. *Page 1-83*

Round Lake, Baxter Healthcare Corporation, Kuczerepa, Paul R. *Page 1-83*

Schaumburg

   AAC Inc., Wasilewski, Richard *Page 1-294*

   Compaq Computer Corporation, Larson, Kenneth O. *Page 1-42*

   Friendship Village, Czarnik, Teri *Page 1-343*

   Mascon Information Technologies, Francis, Philip H. *Page 1-203*

   Mascon, Gopalan, Ravichandran *Page 1-242*

   Motorola, Love, Darlene *Page 1-57*

   Navigation Technology, Tsengouras, Michael D. *Page 1-81*

   Newel Systems, Inc., Klempner, James H. *Page 1-254*

   PointStar.com, Tang, Carolyn B. *Page 1-166*

   Rand Technologies, Burton, Walt *Page 1-347*

Springfield

   Illinois Department of Children and Family Services, Rhodes, Brian V. *Page 1-386*

   Illinois Primary Health Care, Farney, Thomas P. *Page 1-344*

   Illinois State Board of Education, Baiter, Jamey Fern *Page 1-380*

   Karl Williams Inc., Schmidt, Donald *Page 1-119*

   Quality Solutions, Holderread, John R. *Page 1-363*

   State Government of Illinois Telecommunications, Hall, Michael R. *Page 1-99*

St. Charles, Arthur Andersen, McGuff, Dale T. *Page 1-365*

Tremont, Tremont High School, Schaidle, Dale F. *Page 1-317*

University Park, Applied Systems, Inc, Sander, Tim A. *Page 1-188*

Urbana, National Center for Supercomputing Applications, Rudins, Nancy A. *Page 1-341*

Vernon Hills

   W.W. Grainger, Clements, Gregory Alexander *Page 1-123*

   Zebra Technologies Corporation, Private, John A. *Page 1-51*

Watseka, Iroquois Memorial Hospital, Wells, Bradley T. *Page 1-309*

Waukegan

   I Connection Inc., Callahan, Gerard W. *Page 1-172*

   Nosco Inc., Fowler, Susan E. *Page 1-20*

   Waukegan Public Schools, Green, Judith M. *Page 1-315*

Wheaton, Northern Illinois University, Cagney, Mary M. *Page 1-320*

Indiana

Bloomington, Squeal Media Arts, Wagner, Paul W. *Page 1-192*

Carmel, Dewpoint, Inc., Harker, Larry *Page 1-245*

East Chicago, LTV Steel, Dixon, Richard T. *Page 1-31*

Evansville

   American General Finance, Howard, Donald R. B. "Donn" *Page 1-138*

   Shoe Carnival, Johnston, James W. *Page 1-127*

   University of Evansville, Whitecotton, Brad *Page 1-334*

Fort Wayne

   Avery Dennison, FRNA, Zhu, Jack J. *Page 1-14*

   Dana Corporation, Cox, David W. *Page 1-73*

   Pentacon Industry Group, Inc., Grunstad, Chandler R. *Page 1-86*

   Physicians Health Plan, Rose, David E. *Page 1-153*

   SCT Corporation, Kleinman, John V. *Page 1-180*

Greenfield, City of Greenfield, Noble, Michael *Page 1-373*

Indianapolis

   Ambassador Consulting, Sersic, Christopher J. *Page 1-282*

   Corepoint Technologies, Smith, Steven E. *Page 1-199*

   Department of Defense, Naff, James M. *Page 1-395*

   Dow Agrosciences, EDC/LL, Gates, Maurice R. *Page 1-26*

   Eli Lilly and Company, Skiles, Michael John *Page 1-24*

   Indy Residential Services, Sharp, Jeffrey A. *Page 1-159*

   Lifemark Corporation, Sutton, Ron R. *Page 1-153*

   Network Engineering, Inc., Blocchi, Roger *Page 1-222*

   Perpetual Technologies, Inc., Plew, Ronald R. *Page 1-274*

   Perpetual Technologies, Inc., Stephens, Ryan K. *Page 1-286*

   Pomeroy Computer Resources, Palatinus, Gregory S. *Page 1-271*

   Rubber Products Distributors, Hammons, Lois G. *Page 1-123*

   Thomas Consumer Electronics, Teller, Joel S. *Page 1-54*

   Thomson Consumer Electronics, Fadely, Gary *Page 1-54*

   Thomson Consumer Electronics, Warmelink, Michael R. *Page 1-54*

   Total Response Inc., Kot, John S. *Page 1-301*

Ligonier, West Noble School Corporation, Lapham, Erika P. *Page 1-316*

Madison, Hyperbole Software, Unlimited, Reynolds, Carl W. *Page 1-187*

Minneapolis, ADP, Jeunesse, Braden P. *Page 1-212*

Muncie, Delaware County Information Services, Reese, Jeffrey D. *Page 1-302*

New Albany, Floyd Memorial Hospital, Terrell, Sue E. *Page 1-309*

New Carlisle, I/N Tek, Farney, Kerry G. *Page 1-31*

Seymour

   Aisin USA, Spencer, Karen E. *Page 1-74*

   J.E. Reedy, Inc., Reedy, Matthew K. *Page 1-5*

South Bend, National Institute for Trial Advocacy, Toth, Susan *Page 1-342*

Warsaw, Warsaw Area Career Center, Waldeck, Stephen *Page 1-319*

West Lafayette, Purdue University, Loeffler, Kevin J. *Page 1-328*

Whiting, Wells Fargo Bank, Dritsas, George E. *Page 1-133*

Iowa

Ames, Ortho Computer Systems, Inc., Schuelka, Todd *Page 1-281*

Boyden, Dethmers Manufacturing Company, Blankers, Galen C. *Page 1-35*

Cedar Rapids, EDS, Soon, Herald Soohong *Page 1-215*

Council Bluffs, American Agrisurance, Rogers, Alvina C. *Page 1-154*

Davenport, Packaging Technologies, Nourse, Sharon *Page 1-38*

Des Moines

   Principal Financial Group, Morrison, K. C. *Page 1-148*

   Silicon Plains Technologies, Stence, Daniel *Page 1-285*

   U.S. Bankruptcy Court, Gast, William A. *Page 1-376*

Esterville, Marketlink, Inc., Acheson, Lori *Page* 1-299

Indianappolis, V4 Consulting, Pfeiffer, Scott P. *Page* 1-273

Johnston

    Iowa Communications Network, Klinkefus, David S. *Page* 1-254

    Johnston Community School District, Yoshimura, Dennis A. *Page* 1-320

Waterloo, Bertch Cabinet Manufacturing Inc, Klein, David E. *Page* 1-12

West Des Moines, Consultech, Inc., Beelman, Misty M. *Page* 1-384

Kansas

Kansas City, National Information Technology Center - Department of Agriculture, Taylor, Brenda C. *Page* 1-391

Lawrence, Sunflower Cablevision, Knorr, Patrick *Page* 1-108

Leavenworth

    SCL Health Services, Schneider, Jonathan *Page* 1-344

    St. Mary College, Paden, John *Page* 1-330

Lenexa

    John Deere Company, Quist, Stephen C. *Page* 1-36

    Sprint PCS, Geary, Matthew *Page* 1-92

Manhattan, Riley County Police Department, Glick, Gary Edward *Page* 1-376

Merriam, Control Systems International, Budd, Daniel L. *Page* 1-51

New Century, Sprint, LaBounty, Rachael *Page* 1-101

Olathag, EFTC, Chapman, Gregory P. *Page* 1-76

Ottawa, Ottawa University, Montgomery, Janie E. *Page* 1-329

Overland Park

    Black & Veatch, Gilmore, Cary W. *Page* 1-204

    Ciber Custom Solutions Group, Craven, Brett *Page* 1-173

    Compunet Engineering, Hite, Charles Aaron *Page* 1-247

    House of Sedes, House, Jon K. *Page* 1-248

    Nortel Networks, Neal, Scott C. *Page* 1-56

    Sprint, Greene, William F. *Page* 1-99

    Sprint, Oliva, Stephen A. *Page* 1-102

    Washburn & Associates, Inc., Winship, Matthew *Page* 1-200

Quinter, Midwest Cooperative, Koehn, Kathy Lynn *Page* 1-122

Shawnee Mission, Consulting Strategies, Freedman, Richard *Page* 1-238

Topeka

    Federal Home Loan Bank, Shreffler, Sue L. *Page* 1-136

    State of Kansas, Armstrong, Stephen D. *Page* 1-372

Wichita

    Metamore, Glenn, Kenneth O. *Page* 1-393

    Raytheon Travel Air, Fowler, Darren L. *Page* 1-75

    Renal Care Group, Inc., Obeirne, Barbara H. *Page* 1-306

    US Trustee, Wieland, Katherine *Page* 1-376

Kentucky

Bowling Green

    Commonwealth Health Corporation, Willis, Crissy M. *Page* 1-153

    Fruit of the Loom, Hunt, Jeff L. *Page* 1-11

Frankfort

    Commonwealth Credit Union, Graham, Douglas M. *Page* 1-136

    Kentucky Department for Libraries & Archives, Hamilton, Cindy L. *Page* 1-375

Georgetown, Toyota Motor Manufacturing of Kentucky, Lane, Michael J. *Page* 1-73

La Grange, AT&T, Clan, Jean *Page* 1-96

Lexington

    Lexmark International, Inc., Ivey, Gabrielle *Page* 1-119

    Lexmark International, Inc., Phillips, Howard C. *Page* 1-120

Lexmark, Hudson, Melanie *Page* 1-49

SCT, Johnson, Janet Lee *Page* 1-180

Louisville

    AdminaStar Federal, Hale, Pamela D. *Page* 1-157

    Cotton and Allen, Cornwell, Kevin W. *Page* 1-352

    Humana Inc., Meyer, Leo H. *Page* 1-153

    United Parcel Service, Chambers, Teressa S. *Page* 1-90

Midway, Koinonia Computing, Ratliff, Bud *Page* 1-276

Owensboro, Unifirst Corporation, Henderson, George W. *Page* 1-12

Paducah, Lourdes Hospital, Shever, Andrew F. *Page* 1-309

Louisiana

Baton Rouge

    Blue Cross & Blue Shield of Louisiana, Bechtel, Lawrence J. *Page* 1-149

    EMCO, Badinger, Dawn D. *Page* 1-219

Eunice, Louisiana State University at Eunice, Newman, Marjana *Page* 1-329

Gramercy, Kaiser Aluminum, Rybiski-Joseph, Elizabeth *Page* 1-3

Gretna, Entergy Services, Horn, David J. *Page* 1-116

Lafayette, University of Louisiana at Lafayette, Center for Advanced Computer Studies, Kubat, Miroslav *Page* 1-327

Metairie

    C A Consultants Int. Ltd., Vellanki, Ravindra V. *Page* 1-293

    CPU, Inc., Murray, James M. *Page* 1-267

    W.H. Linder & Associates, Graham, Charles K. *Page* 1-5

New Orleans

    Fairmont Hotel, Koubek, Cindy *Page* 1-162

    Loyola University, Hickey, Paul Henry *Page* 1-324

    Minerals Management Services, Griggs, Kelly A. *Page* 1-388

    Naval Support Activity, Garrett, Arthur W. *Page* 1-393

Ruston, Louisiana Tech University, Reneau, Daniel D. *Page* 1-331

Shreveport

    Cook Yancey King and Galloway, Mongon, William H. *Page* 1-312

    KSLA TV, Williams, Anthony *Page* 1-108

Maine

Dexter, Dexter Shoe Company, Tash, Preston K. *Page* 1-30

Lewiston, WAHLCO Engineered Products, Inc., Walker, James A. *Page* 1-33

Sanford

    Vishay-Sprague, Hilton, Jon M. *Page* 1-69

    Wasco Products Inc., Charpentier, Elizabeth *Page* 1-53

South Portland, Total Technology Services, Rogers, John H. *Page* 1-209

Winthrop, Excel Consulting, Bagley, Kathleen A. *Page* 1-219

Maryland

Aberdeen Proving Ground, United States Army Research Laboratory, Smith, Glenn A. *Page* 1-395

Annapolis

    Computer Curriculum Corporation, Little, Dinah B. *Page* 1-206

    Wartsila NSD Corporation, German, James *Page* 1-35

Annapolis Junction, Litton/TASC, Washington, Paul L. *Page* 1-294

Baldwin, TRW, Smith, Richard D. *Page* 1-210

Baltimore

    AMBC-CCTC/ICTS, Roberts, Angela D. *Page* 1-341

    Complete Business Solutions, Madhusudan, Neeruganti *Page* 1-260

    Fidelity & Deposit Company of Maryland, Anniko, P. Peter *Page* 1-153

    General Physics Corporation, Maceluch, Markian W. *Page* 1-260

Johns Hopkins Hospital, Jenkins, Arnold M. *Page 1-308*

Johns Hopkins University, Novitzki, James *Page 1-330*

Maryland Stadium Authority Maintenance at Camden Yards, Hoffman, D. Brian
Page 1-367

Our Lady of Mount Carmel School, Wilkins, Teresa *Page 1-319*

T. Rowe Price Associates, Frager, Yehuda Stuart *Page 1-161*

Bel Air, Novell, Inc., Moorehouse, Nina M. *Page 1-198*

Beltsville, Intermedia Business Internet, Howell, Franklyn L. *Page 1-249*

Bethesda

American College of Cardiology, Holliday, Rosana *Page 1-325*

BDC 4 You, Swystun, Orest Roman *Page 1-287*

Mercedes-Benz USA, Inc., Stewen, Robert *Page 1-72*

Next Millennium Consulting, Inc., Pegalis, Andrew M. *Page 1-273*

USUHS, Guevara, John P. *Page 1-324*

USUHS, Hu, Xiaohong *Page 1-325*

Bowie, Internal Revenue Service, Financial and Administrative Systems, Acholonu, Omogbemiboluwa I. *Page 1-379*

College Park, Technology Totems Inc., Berlas, Abdul R. *Page 1-222*

Columbia

GTE Internetworking, Powered by BBN, Batt-Ptaszek, Chris *Page 1-221*

RWD Technologies, Magwood, Quanteer D. *Page 1-260*

Eldersburg, Inventa, Baker, Gene Charles *Page 1-220*

Elkridge, Insys Inc., Thomas, K. Michael *Page 1-289*

Ellicott City

ATS, Grigoryev, Alex *Page 1-52*

Revacomp Inc., Derrick, Charles E. *Page 1-128*

Fairfax, Parsons Engineering Science, Birdi, Moninder S. *Page 1-362*

Frederick

Frederick Community College, Hemgen, Jim *Page 1-337*

Frederick Community College, Kennedy, Christopher L. *Page 1-337*

Gaithersburg

ISSI, Inc., Jones, Rabon S. *Page 1-251*

Lockheed Martin, Billings, Claire *Page 1-79*

NextLinx Corporation, Lodaya, Manish *Page 1-259*

NIST, Lowe, Darren L. *Page 1-360*

Germantown

BITCOM Inc., Rostami, Sasan *Page 1-278*

Hughes Network Systems, Ravishankar, Channasandra *Page 1-94*

Hughes Network Systems, Rhine, Chad D. *Page 1-94*

Greenbelt, AverStar, Miles, Greg S. *Page 1-265*

Hagerstown, Technology Solutions Company, Chrisman, Terry L. *Page 1-230*

Hampstead, Charles J. Miller, Inc., Shepard, Peter J. *Page 1-4*

Hyattsville

Insulgard Corporation, Eckert, John F. *Page 1-85*

M-Cubed Information Systems, Basinger, William Daniel *Page 1-220*

Resources Technical Services, Simmons, Reginold T. *Page 1-283*

La Plata, AlliedSignal Technical Services, Bowens, Dewitt *Page 1-26*

Landover, Mercury Interactive, DesJarlais, William *Page 1-234*

Laurel

Computer Learning Centers, Inc., Frisvold, Barbara L. *Page 1-340*

Software Creations, Strutt, Greg D. *Page 1-287*

Systems Support Alternatives, Inc., Fremont, John C. *Page 1-238*

Lusby, Baltimore Gas & Electric, Lawson, Barbara D. *Page 1-117*

Millersville

Chesapeake Sciences, Jamieson, John M. *Page 1-205*

Computer Sciences Corporation, Friend, Richard E. *Page 1-204*

New Market, MIL Corporation, Smith, Cheryl L. *Page 1-283*

North East, American Engineering, Granger, Timothy G. *Page 1-348*

Oakland, Garrett County Board of Education, Kimble, Arnold Dale *Page 1-316*

Owings Mills

CitiFinancial, Hermann, Edwin C. *Page 1-138*

Hertzbach & Company, Horton, Nicholas A. *Page 1-353*

Pollesville, Andersen Consulting, Miller, Kevin J. *Page 1-365*

Reisterstown, Infinite Wisdom Web Designs, Zepp, Gregg L. *Page 1-193*

Riverdale, Long Fence & Home, Wells, Dwayne *Page 1-118*

Rocksville, Loral Cyberstar, Azizi, Peyman *Page 1-108*

Rockville

AM Search Consulting, Inc., Duda, Andrew *Page 1-168*

BAE Systems, Stroud, Richard *Page 1-76*

Computer Sciences Corporation, Bullock, Steven H. *Page 1-201*

Kumaran Systems Inc., Kalluri, Dutt N. *Page 1-252*

Minibar Systems, Bosworth, Kimberly A. *Page 1-120*

Severna Park

Lockheed Martin, Walker, Loren Mark *Page 1-80*

NCR Corporation, Geer, David W. *Page 1-50*

Silver Spring

Actionet, Inc., McCracken, Philip F. *Page 1-263*

Bell Atlantic, Brammer, Douglas E. *Page 1-96*

Bell Atlantic, Sprouse, Matthew C. *Page 1-105*

OPTIMUS Corporation, Qian, Fang *Page 1-275*

StorageTek, Kavanaugh, Keith J. *Page 1-46*

St. Leonard, MWD Consultants, Dinota, Mary *Page 1-369*

Timonium, Trane, Gilbeaux, Jeffrey J. *Page 1-122*

Upper Marlboro

Edgemeade, Fenwick, Scott F. *Page 1-343*

Ingenium Corporation, Boudreaux, Ambrose Carl *Page 1-223*

Prince George's Accounting Government/Department of Environmental Resources, Chakhtoura, Nehme G *Page 1-371*

Massachusetts

Acton, Corning Inc. Science Division Products, McGary, Steven M. *Page 1-69*

Alttleboro, Houghton Mifflin, Lawson, John A. *Page 1-17*

Andover

Dynamics Research Corporation, Perras, Kathleen A. *Page 1-186*

InterBiz of Computer Associates, Jutras, Cindy M. *Page 1-180*

Arlington

IBM Corporation, Markowski, Violet E. *Page 1-43*

RCN Corporation, Bryant, Tom *Page 1-96*

Attleboro, Information Systems Services, Towl, Allan T. *Page 1-291*

Bedford, Millipore Corporation, Oulundsen, George E. *Page 1-82*

Beverly, Osram Sylvania, Arpide, Jose I. *Page 1-53*

Billerica, Carleton Corporation, Shaw, M. Lea *Page 1-189*

Boston

AMR Research, Lunstead, Eric Q. *Page 1-259*

Arthur Andersen, Conway, Larry J. *Page 1-363*

Bank Boston, Fitzgerald, Patricia J. *Page 1-134*

Care Group, Passe, Michael R. *Page 1-362*

Ceridian Performance Partners, Ransden, Eric S. *Page 1-369*

edu.com, Greenlaw, Valdonna *Page 1-132*

Enterprise Technology Group Inc., Carrigan, Christopher M. *Page 1-228*

IBEX Capital Markets, Gerstner, Kyle *Page 1-145*

Massachusetts Association of School Committees, Gilbert, Michael J. *Page* 1-345

Pyxis Consulting, Hughes, Shane R. *Page* 1-249

SDS America, Kim, Kyle "Ki Jong" *Page* 1-205

Teradyne Inc., Sayian, Stephen *Page* 1-82

The New England, Tyler, Mary F. *Page* 1-156

Thomson Financial, Tanigawa, David S. *Page* 1-147

United States Air Force, Smith, Richard K. *Page* 1-395

United States Department of Agriculture Food and Nutrition Service, Tankersley, Kathy M. *Page* 1-391

Burlington

Cisco Systems, Inc., Gong, Youhong Wade *Page* 1-59

Lightbridge Inc., McCusker, Clinton F. *Page* 1-93

PricewaterhouseCoopers, Patil, Abhijit B. *Page* 1-354

Cambridge

EPIX Medical, Inc., Tyeklar, Zoltan *Page* 1-25

GTE Internetworking, Inc., Todisco, Barbara J. *Page* 1-290

Harvard Medical School, Joseph, Sunil *Page* 1-326

Harvard-Smithsonian Center for Astrophysics, Kristen, Helmuth E. *Page* 1-358

InfoRay, Inc., Genser, Mira E. *Page* 1-176

PegaSystems Inc., Merkt, Greg *Page* 1-264

Sapient Corporation, Childs, Robert L. *Page* 1-202

Vegetarian Resource Center, Clark, Maynard S. *Page* 1-163

Canton, AW Chesterton Company, Ludwig, Mark A. *Page* 1-37

Chelmsford

Cisco Systems, Inc., Fernandez, Marino A. *Page* 1-58

Process Software Corporation, Adams, Sharon K. *Page* 1-170

Chicopee, Genesys Computing Technologies, Jimmo, Steven M. *Page* 1-205

Clinton, Nypro, Inc., Gorman, Daniel W. *Page* 1-29

Easton, Stonehill College, Pietrowski, Michael *Page* 1-331

Framingham, elcom.com, Inc., Frangieh, Robert T. *Page* 1-175

Holden, Reebok International, Smith, Jeffrey W. *Page* 1-30

Hopkinton, EMC Corporation, Baliakhov, Dmitri *Page* 1-212

Lexington

Fresenius Medical Care, Theriault, Roger D. *Page* 1-310

Rational Software, Haynes, Dawn M. *Page* 1-178

Littleton

NEC Technologies, Inc., Ashford, Anne *Page* 1-48

S1 Corporation, Di Luna, Leasa M. *Page* 1-196

Lowell, PAREXEL International, Fiore, Stephanie A. *Page* 1-23

Ludlow, Porter & Chester Institute, Leblanc, Christopher S. *Page* 1-341

Lynnfield, BBC, Inc., Jordan, David S. *Page* 1-251

Malden, Fleet Technology Solutions, Keyes, Tammy L. *Page* 1-253

Marblehead, GTE Internetworking, Inc., Blake, Catherine B. *Page* 1-222

Marlborough

Digital Equipment Corporation, Weiss, Abbott D. *Page* 1-295

Raytheon, Spangler, Kerry *Page* 1-81

Methuen

Compaq Computer Corporation, Levin, Maria *Page* 1-42

Computer Learning Centers, Inc., Landry, Karen *Page* 1-341

Natick, Instruction Set, Inc., Brown, Ed *Page* 1-226

North Easton, Town of Easton, Deltano, Michael D. *Page* 1-371

Raynham, MFS Investment Management, Gabardi, Felice R. *Page* 1-145

Reading, TASC, Inc., Lawlor, James E. *Page* 1-206

Revere, Computer Consultant, Winter, Edward A. *Page* 1-296

Shrewsbury, Quantum Corporation, Nutter, John J. *Page* 1-47

Springfield, CBSI, Maltais, John R. *Page* 1-183

Stoughton, Nortel Networks, Jackson, Alan W. *Page* 1-55

Tewksbury, Limited Technology Services, Hartman, Judith A *Page* 1-246

Wakefield, Edgewater Technology, Carson, Bruce A. *Page* 1-229

Waltham

Caro Research, Nova, William E. *Page* 1-358

CSC Consulting & Systems Integration, Vallon, Ronald Martin *Page* 1-211

CSC Consulting, Kawasaki, Gregory *Page* 1-205

GTE Laboratories, Inc., Yang, Ning *Page* 1-107

Parametric Technology Corporation, Moiseyev, Aleksey *Page* 1-198

Watertown

Gamesville, Kittredge, Gregory J. *Page* 1-197

Kishore Chakraborty Consulting, Chakraborty, Kishore *Page* 1-363

West Minster, Simplex Time Recorder, Terault, Normand A. *Page* 1-62

Westford

Agilent Technologies, Inc., Walker, Julie-Anne *Page* 1-82

Landtech Consultants, Inc., Chamberlain, Mark A. *Page* 1-348

Lucent Technologies, Gu, Sheena *Page* 1-59

Schneider Electric, Crawford, James A. *Page* 1-64

Westwood, MIB Inc., Rotondo, Eugene M. *Page* 1-157

Wilmington, Fishman Transducers, Kilbashian, Rick *Page* 1-69

Woburn, Aptima, Inc., Serfaty, Daniel *Page* 1-349

Michigan

Ann Arbor

CIMdata, Inc., MacKrell, John *Page* 1-260

Information Transfer System, Schoettle, Brandon A. *Page* 1-352

Inmet Corporation, Childs, Keith F. *Page* 1-57

Print Tech, Inc., Steven, Brad J. *Page* 1-166

Benton Harbor, Gast Manufacturing, Kim, Alice *Page* 1-37

Big Rapids, Ferris State University, Buse, Amy L. R. *Page* 1-320

Bloomfield, General Motors, Rosenbaum, Lisa Lenchner *Page* 1-72

Dearborn, Soft Ad, Gorgen, Nancy A. *Page* 1-177

Detroit

Advanced Web Design, Coleman, Marquis R. *Page* 1-202

Medical Knowledge Systems Inc., Mims, Creflo R. *Page* 1-265

Farmington Hills

Complete Business Solutions, Kanitkar, Suhas R. *Page* 1-252

Morpace International, Watkins, Patricia A. *Page* 1-370

Relational Technologies, Speck, Richard J. *Page* 1-285

Triad Performance Technologies, Dembeck, Wanda S. *Page* 1-368

Fennville, Trinary Systems Inc., LeFaive, Donna M. *Page* 1-182

Fenton, Delphi Automotive, Roden, Mark Philip *Page* 1-118

Ferndale, The Human Factor, Inc., Pigeon, Donald R. *Page* 1-369

Flint, EDS, Garrels, Ruth A. *Page* 1-215

Flushing, The Coffee Beanery Ltd., Curtis, Steve D. *Page* 1-9

Grand Rapids, ITS Communications, Aden, Steve E. *Page* 1-95

Holland

Holland Hitch Company, Wiewiora, Thomas A. *Page* 1-319

Image Computers Inc., Krueger, Charles J. *Page* 1-255

Jackson, BAVS Corporation, Kale, Anil B. *Page* 1-252

Kentwood, Purchase Business Institute, Purchase-Owens, Francena *Page* 1-369

Lake Orion, Royal Oak Boring, Crawford, Jen *Page* 1-73

Lansing, Michigan Department of Environmental Quality, Clark, Daniel J. *Page* 1-386

Lathrup, Ford Motor Company, Foster Carter, Linda Marie *Page 1-71*

Livonia

    IXC Communications, Woolverton, Thomas *Page 1-106*

    Valassis Communications, Brocious, Mary Anne *Page 1-20*

Macomb, Michigan Production Machining, Inc., Crowl, Jerry L. *Page 1-73*

Mason, County of Ingham, Management Information Services, Le, Long Minh *Page 1-373*

Mount Pleasant, SCIT, Nial, Marjorie *Page 1-162*

Muskegon, Michigan Spring and Stamping, Fox, Kathleen *Page 1-34*

Orion, Schenck Turner Inc., Nebel, John K. *Page 1-83*

Plymouth, Perceptron, Keshavmurthy, Shyam *Page 1-304*

Pontiac, Speed Link Inc., Lauda, Irene *Page 1-110*

Port Huron, Lear Corporation, Fisher, Angela M. *Page 1-73*

Portage, SPX Corporation, Riley, Cathy N. *Page 1-36*

Saginaw, Delphi Saginaw Steering Systems, Newton, Clifford R. *Page 1-74*

Sears, Plaspro (Plastic Provisions Inc.), Torry, Billy D. *Page 1-29*

Southfield

    Ford Power Products, VanDoorne, Vincent A. *Page 1-118*

    Giffels Associates, Inc., Bland, Richard L. *Page 1-350*

    Watson Wyatt Worldwide, Sluka, Greg W. *Page 1-366*

St. Clair, Compsat Technology, Tocco, Anthony J. *Page 1-210*

Stanton, Stowell Data Solutions, Stowell, Bev *Page 1-286*

Sterling Heights

    DJG & Associates, Mitchell, Leo *Page 1-265*

    Volt Computer Services/Entirenet, Weber, Gregory *Page 1-294*

Troy

    Resource Technologies Corporation, Channell, John L. *Page 1-167*

    Siteserv2000 LLC, Chambers, Paul C. *Page 1-216*

    Standard Federal Bank, Godsey, Chene W. *Page 1-135*

Warren, Computer Sciences Corporation, Murawaski, Michael R. *Page 1-207*

Waterford, Oakland Schools, Evans, Tammy L. *Page 1-381*

West Bloomfield, Crystallize, Fey, Eugenia *Page 1-175*

Minnesota

Arden Hills, Control Data Systems, Inc., Therens, Gary A. *Page 1-289*

Bloomington, University of Minnesota, Huang, Jian *Page 1-325*

Brownsdale, IB Industries, Primmer, Charles W. *Page 1-275*

Chaska

    Entegris, Hedges, Bradley *Page 1-29*

    FSI International, Archer, Kelley P. *Page 1-64*

Duluth, ARDC, Plunkett, Jeffrey Lynn *Page 1-346*

Eagan, Albright Ideas, Inc., Albright, Gerry *Page 1-217*

Hamel, Courage Center - Department of MIS, Botnan, Michael J. *Page 1-311*

Litchfield, Innovex, Akhtar, Hasan *Page 1-48*

Maple Grove, Ddavis Software Consulting, Inc., Davis, Derold L. *Page 1-233*

Maplewood, Minnesota Department of Transportation, Zimmerman, Gregory D. *Page 1-390*

Minneapolis

    Canadian Pacific Railway, Larson, Sheldon C. *Page 1-86*

    Computer Network Technology, Brunzell, Barbara J. *Page 1-226*

    Gantz Wiley Research, Sonnentag, Matthew *Page 1-360*

    Honeywell Home & Building Control, Ziegler, Jody Nyquist *Page 1-6*

    MCI Systemhouse, Luman, Charles J. *Page 1-206*

    Newport, Schmitt, Warren L. *Page 1-86*

    Retek Information System, Meszaros, Jason P. *Page 1-184*

    ROI Systems, Snetsinger, Leo V. *Page 1-190*

    S 304, Doan, Cody *Page 1-83*

    Seagate Technology, Hubbard, Keith J. *Page 1-46*

    U S WEST/Global Crossing, Garg, Rajiv *Page 1-98*

    U.S. Bank, Mathes, Jonathan R. *Page 1-133*

Minnetonka, Cargill, Inc., Yang, Binglin "Bing" *Page 1-125*

Plymouth

    Fingerhut, Beukhof, Martin *Page 1-130*

    Fujitsu, Siska, Theodore L. *Page 1-283*

    Select Comfort, Wysocki, Thomas A. *Page 1-13*

Roseville, Parkview Center School, Sankot, Janice M. *Page 1-317*

St. Paul

    Blue Cross & Blue Shield of Minnesota, Jablonske, Patricia J. *Page 1-150*

    Blue Cross & Blue Shield, Ohaeri, Kenneth O. *Page 1-151*

    DigitalXpress, Wright, Joel S. *Page 1-113*

    University of St. Thomas, Downs, Brian D. *Page 1-322*

White Bear Lake, HLB Tautges Redpath, Ltd., Zabel, Todd A. *Page 1-356*

Woodbury, Tecmark LLC, Springer, Michael *Page 1-164*

Mississippi

Greenville, Infipro Inc., Rumley, Russell *Page 1-299*

Greenwood, Viking Range Corporation, Ramachandran, Shyam *Page 1-53*

Gulfport, PC Net, Bradshaw, Rupert R. *Page 1-224*

Jackson

    Cothern Computer Systems, Inc., Cothern, Rick *Page 1-173*

    Mississippi State Department of Health, WIC Program, Cornwall, Charles "Chuck" F. *Page 1-384*

    Saber Systems & Consulting, Inc., Roberts, Thomas P. *Page 1-277*

Oxford, SAIR, Inc., Vazhkudai, Sudharshan S. *Page 1-292*

Ridgeland, Companion Tech, Majcher, Jeff L. *Page 1-261*

Tupelo

    Contract Computer Services, Golebiewski, Debbie A. *Page 1-241*

    Hunter Douglas, Burroughs, Vonda M. *Page 1-13*

Vicksburg, United States Army Corps of Engineers, Evans, Kathryn A. *Page 1-393*

Missouri

Boonville, Myers Consulting Inc., Myers, John E. *Page 1-267*

Chesterfield

    InAir, Simmons, John E. *Page 1-190*

    Parkway School District, Hennessy, Sharon M. *Page 1-381*

Hazelwood, Hazelwood Farms Inc., Wright, Richard A. *Page 1-8*

Independence, Truman High School, Schlosser, Martha F. *Page 1-317*

Joplin

    Allgeier Martin & Associates, Drost, Terry L. *Page 1-235*

    US Telecom - PhoneMaster Division, Forquer, Christy S. *Page 1-98*

Kansas City

    American Century Investments, Stanley, Kenneth L. *Page 1-144*

    Birch Telecom, Inc., Hedtke, David J. *Page 1-179*

    Cerner Corporation, Cerner Virtual University, Gander, Sharon L. *Page 1-323*

    Internal Revenue Service, Bridges, Martin O. *Page 1-379*

    Investors Fiduciary Trust, Lembke, David R. *Page 1-147*

    Samuel Rodgers Community Health Center, Busch, Darnell *Page 1-307*

    Sprint PCS, Craft, Michael K. *Page 1-92*

    Sprint PCS, Romish, Lisa S. *Page 1-94*

    Sprint, Reed, Dana E. *Page 1-104*

Ticketmaster, Mavis, Mark K. *Page 1-306*

Lee's Summit, The Metropolitan Community College, Beachner, James G. *Page 1-335*

Liberty, Independence School District, Woods, E. Hayet *Page 1-384*

Moberly, Orscheln Management Company, Bryant, John A. *Page 1-226*

Neosho, Sunbeam Outdoor Products, Enlow, Jeffrey Dale *Page 1-53*

Peculiar, Archer Engineers, Medsker, Michael D. *Page 1-351*

Raytown, First Baptist Church Raytown, Klassy, Ken R. *Page 1-347*

Rolla, University of Missouri - Rolla, Liu, Xiaoqing "Frank" *Page 1-328*

St. Charles, TSI, Inc., Bray, Robert T. *Page 1-224*

St. Louis

Aurora Foods, Borgmann, Philip M. *Page 1-8*

Bryan Cave, Farquharson, Jerome A. *Page 1-312*

EDS, DeLaPorte, Charles E. *Page 1-214*

EDS, Lamberson, Joseph R. *Page 1-215*

Envision, White, Michael Henry *Page 1-296*

Ernst & Young, Hawkins, Byron T. *Page 1-353*

Federal-Mogul, Koluch, Andrew R. *Page 1-73*

Marker Consulting, Marker, Wendy C. *Page 1-261*

Maryville Technologies, Ard, Bryan N. *Page 1-218*

SBC Communications Inc., Banerjee, Ayananshu *Page 1-95*

The Principia, Schwartz, Bruce R. *Page 1-318*

United States Department of Agriculture, Nassif, John M. *Page 1-391*

Washington University, Abusoud, Samer S. *Page 1-320*

Weber Chevrolet, Maher, Michael A. *Page 1-127*

Steelville, Disabled Citizen Alliance for Independence, Hagemeier, Juanita E. *Page 1-343*

Washington, Missourian Publishing, Wacker, Trent S. *Page 1-21*

Weston, ADT Security Services, Inc., Lee, Ryan J. *Page 1-298*

Montana

Ashland, St. Labre Indian School, Thomas, Carl *Page 1-318*

Billings

Corporate Air, Klatt, Bruce K. *Page 1-90*

United States Bureau of Reclamation, McDanel, Gary A. *Page 1-387*

Butte, The Montana Power Company, Leary, Mike W. *Page 1-116*

Libby, Lincoln County Technology Group, Jimeno, Andy *Page 1-110*

Nebraska

Bellevue, 1st National Bank of Omaha, Wineteer, Stephen A. *Page 1-161*

Fremont, SCS, Inc., Lipson, Derek N. *Page 1-13*

McCook, McCook Community College, Walinder, Mike *Page 1-339*

Omaha

E&K Companies, Inc., Peterson, Cynthia Sue *Page 1-6*

First Data Corporation, Rothe, Eukarlgen A. *Page 1-303*

Grace University, Litchfield, Gregory T. *Page 1-328*

TransCanada Energy, Peltz, Raymond *Page 1-2*

U S WEST, Urban, James J. "Jack" *Page 1-105*

Union Pacific Technologies, Matthews, Bill D. *Page 1-262*

United Distillers, Wentzler, Tracy *Page 1-9*

University of Nebraska, Baker-Cross, Leah Dawn *Page 1-320*

Papillion, Omaha Public Power District, Ikeda-Hayes, Rieko *Page 1-114*

Nevada

Elko, Barrick Goldstrike Mines, Inc., Roebke, Laurence R. *Page 1-2*

Las Vegas

Citigroup, Inc., Recchioni, Mario J. *Page 1-135*

City of Las Vegas, Phillips, Craig A. *Page 1-373*

Cornerstone Systems Solutions, Inc., Salaver, Timothy R. *Page 1-188*

Frontier Hotel Gambling, Shoemaker, Linda L. *Page 1-162*

HH Technologies, Inc./Hedelund Engineering, Hedelund, Harold G. *Page 1-370*

I Link Worldwide, LLC (Independent Representative), Carvajal, LeAnnette *Page 1-368*

Independent Truckers Group, Inc., Yoakley, Frances L. *Page 1-297*

ITS Inc., Burtnett, Jeanne *Page 1-227*

Schreck Morris, Baker, Robert D. *Page 1-311*

Systems-Ensync, Leskody, James J. *Page 1-6*

Sparks, TYCO Valves & Control, Gee, Nicholas L. *Page 1-34*

New Hampshire

Center Conway, Quantum Resources, Garrett, Angie R. *Page 1-239*

Hudson, Wang Healthcare, Richardson, Susan E. *Page 1-188*

Londonderry, Pegasus Consulting Group, Sutton, Paula Emery *Page 1-287*

Manchester, Northstar Steel & Aluminum, Inc., Keane, James B. *Page 1-121*

Nashua, Compaq Computer Corporation, Kaltenbach, Shirley J. *Page 1-41*

Windham

Auto Desk Inc., Worley, Jason *Page 1-297*

Autodesk, Inc., Safford, Michael *Page 1-188*

New Jersey

Asbury Park, City of Asbury Park Police, Jacobs, Michael P. *Page 1-377*

Avenel, Systems Link, Dalia, Sujal *Page 1-232*

Basking Ridge

AT&T, Parker, Barry A. *Page 1-103*

KPMG Consulting, Blockus, Linda G. *Page 1-362*

Lucent Technologies, Landes, J. Christopher *Page 1-60*

Bayonne, Maidenform, Inc., Davis, Cindy *Page 1-12*

Bedminster, Entology, Inc., Temple, TheresaMarie *Page 1-191*

Belvidere, Warren County, Smith, Barry W. *Page 1-283*

Berkeley Heights, American Express - TRS, Manino, Brooke *Page 1-138*

Blackwood, Blackwell's Information Services, Campbell, Anne B. *Page 1-300*

Bloomfield, Goldman Sachs & Company, Siddiqui, Khayyam *Page 1-144*

Bridgewater

AT&T, Bonner, Barbara D. *Page 1-95*

MetLife, Fallacara, Flo *Page 1-148*

Parkway Insurance, Urbanowicz, Robert Stanley *Page 1-154*

Camden

Campbell Soup Company, House, Jeffrey A. *Page 1-7*

Tarquini Organization, Brown, John R. *Page 1-350*

Cedar Knolls, Data Management Services, Oglensky, David S. *Page 1-185*

Chatham, The Knowledge Sculptors, Chizmark, Joseph J. *Page 1-202*

Cherry Hill, Comcast Telecommunications, Rutter, Eric *Page 1-279*

Chester, Lucent Technologies LTCP, Hill, Geoffrey D. *Page 1-60*

Clifton, ITT Avionics, Nassani, Joseph *Page 1-77*

Cranbury, Associated Press, Villegas, Danielle M. *Page 1-299*

Dover

Jerry's Precision Company, Linfante, Thomas P. *Page 1-52*

UCA Computer Systems, Inc., Nallabathula, Udaya Sankar *Page 1-267*

East Brunswick, Copeland Associates, Inc., Bearce, James E. *Page 1-156*

East Hanover

Nabisco, Keoghan, Leo E. *Page 1-8*

Tritec Communications Inc., Romano, Angelo *Page 1-104*

Edison

AT&T, Munukutla, Srinivasa S. *Page 1-102*

Chase Manhattan Mortgage Corporation, Tramontana, Richard M. *Page 1-141*

Condor Technologies, Keshoojee, Sadrudin B. *Page 1-253*

Cylogix, Mukhopadhyay, Kalyan *Page 1-266*

Innosoft Inc., Babu, Venkatesha *Page 1-31*

PricewaterhouseCoopers LLP, Babal, Suraj *Page 1-352*

Systems Documentation Inc., Clouse, Marc G. *Page 1-231*

Egg Harbor City, DI, Kislow, Christopher K. *Page 1-60*

Elizabeth, Hilton Hotels Corporation, Maio, Joseph A. *Page 1-162*

Fairfield

Marc Mintz & Associates LLC, McGuire, Tom *Page 1-263*

Snelling Personnel Services, Zwickel, M. Susan *Page 1-170*

Florham Park, Schein Pharmaceuticals, DaSilva, Elsie *Page 1-22*

Fords, Proficient Software Expo Consulting Inc., Reddy, Jagan M. *Page 1-276*

Franklin Park, Parkway Insurance, Pulcine, Brian *Page 1-154*

Glen Ridge, Cadence Design Systems, Moncoqut, Diana *Page 1-265*

Glen Rock, IBM Global Services, O'Malley, Timothy S. *Page 1-269*

Hackensack, Symantec Corporation, Clarke, Tracy J. *Page 1-195*

Haddonfield, Bureau of Translation Services Inc., Mulligan, John *Page 1-185*

Highlands, Vertek Corporation, Quinn, Robert A. *Page 1-275*

Hoboken

Engineering Information, Inc., van der Linden, Nicoledean J. *Page 1-19*

Palisades Safety & Insurance Management, Williams, Terry *Page 1-154*

Holmdel, PCSI, Patel, Kanti R. *Page 1-271*

Howell, TechnoSphere Services, Labbate, Evelyn *Page 1-255*

Iselin, Inacom, Verna, Michael A. *Page 1-211*

Jackson

Associated Press, Born, Lu Ann *Page 1-299*

CSC, Velez, George W. *Page 1-211*

Jersey City

American Institute of Certified Public Accountants, Autry, Daniel J. *Page 1-345*

Financial Information, Inc., Solomon, Maria Luisa A. *Page 1-19*

New York Daily News, Schilero, Frank *Page 1-15*

Open Systems, Rastogi, Shashank *Page 1-276*

Sapient Corporation, Garimella, Jagan *Page 1-239*

Transcom, Antoniou, Nicholaos *Page 1-389*

UPS Information Services, Fischer, Jennifer L. *Page 1-90*

Kearny, MIC, Inc., Mehta, Jatin *Page 1-264*

Lafayette, Prudential Insurance Company of America, Pierson, Gina L. *Page 1-149*

Leonardo, Sher Distributing, Costa, Anthony P. *Page 1-125*

Lincoln, Kay Elemetrics Corporation, Mulleady, Michael F. *Page 1-185*

Lincroft

AT&T Labs, Peterson, Gregory *Page 1-103*

AT&T, Guald, Andrew G. *Page 1-99*

Lyndhurst

Goldman Sachs & Company, Coplu, Ali *Page 1-142*

Polo Ralph Lauren, McCown, Renee *Page 1-132*

Maple Shade

Brooks Office Solutions, Brooks, Yvonne *Page 1-225*

Connectria, Nandi, Somnath *Page 1-267*

Maplewood, Alphatrain, Castillo, Victoria M. *Page 1-340*

Marlton, Acsis, Inc., Harty, Dave F. *Page 1-178*

Matawan, A&S Solutions, Inc., Syed, Aamir Mazhar *Page 1-287*

McGuire Air Force Base, New Jersey Air National Guard, Hanson-Gorby, Marcia K. *Page 1-393*

Mendham

Actel, DeNigris, Ernest G. *Page 1-64*

Ernst & Young LLP, Lam, James *Page 1-354*

Metuchen

Instasofte, Inc., Ghosh, Amitava *Page 1-240*

Lucent Technologies, Molnar, Andie *Page 1-61*

Monmooth Junction, Websci Technologies, Gervagin, Yuriy *Page 1-240*

Montvale, AV Associates, Hutchins, Todd *Page 1-250*

Morristown

Application Consulting Group, Carlascio, Keith *Page 1-228*

AT&T, Tritt, Ralph *Page 1-105*

Panalpina Inc., Ostermann, Gerhard H. *Page 1-88*

Mount Laurel

American Express One, Green, Joseph E. *Page 1-91*

Industri-Matematik North American Operations, Inc., Roman, Edward John *Page 1-278*

Mount Olive, Information Services International, Gehrt, Kevin E. *Page 1-213*

New Providence, Dun & Bradstreet Corporation, Hopkins, Fred A. *Page 1-213*

Newark

Prudential, Brickman, Eric R. *Page 1-148*

Public Service/Electric & Gas, Lombardini, John T. *Page 1-116*

Rutgers University, Mayer, Warren D. *Page 1-328*

Thomson Financial Securities Data, Grilk, Andrew H. *Page 1-145*

North Bergen, Vitamin Shoppe Industries, Inc., Morris, Michael P. *Page 1-132*

Northfield, Edmunds & Associates, Weisberg, Ross *Page 1-295*

Northvale, Af Associates, Michales, Thomas C. *Page 1-207*

Parlin, Distributed Network Administration, Vu, John T. *Page 1-293*

Parsippany

Chubb Computer Services, Bayman, Richard P. *Page 1-221*

Chubb Computer Services, Bellak, Rodney S. *Page 1-222*

Dun & Bradstreet, Kanumilli, Vishvesh *Page 1-213*

General Chemical Corporation, Duong, Huy M. *Page 1-26*

IBM Global Services, Patel, Kiran K. *Page 1-271*

The Chubb Institute, Castaldi, James Anthony *Page 1-321*

Paterson, MASSC, Khalil, Ramzi Nabhan *Page 1-254*

Peapack, Pharmacia & Upjohn, Hepp, Jean-Paul *Page 1-23*

Pine Brook, IBM Global Services, Brotman, Roy *Page 1-225*

Piscataway, Telcordia Technologies, Chaikin, Jamie A. *Page 1-172*

Plainsboro

Cylogix, Inc., Ponakala, Srinivasa R. *Page 1-274*

Merrill Lynch, Sudula, Nagesh B. *Page 1-144*

Princeton

American Reinsurance, Kosco, Thomas John *Page 1-154*

Merrill Lynch, George, Sunil *Page 1-142*

Panasonic Technology Inc., Yu, Hong Heather *Page 1-360*

RCN Corporation, Walsh, Christopher W. *Page 1-106*

Ramsey, The Pezrow Companies Inc., Gartin, Edward *Page 1-144*

Red Bank, Bellcore, Liu, Kevin H. *Page 1-101*

Rockleigh, Lifechem Lab, Jimenez, Hugo *Page 1-310*

Roseland, Prudential Insurance, Ouellette, Beth *Page 1-149*

Sayreville, Baton Rouge International Inc., Arumugam, Senthil K. *Page 1-218*

Secaucus, Command Web Offset, Awan, Tajammul H. *Page 1-17*

Skillman, Millstone River Systems, Inc., Wallmark, John S. *Page* 1-293

Somerset

    AT&T, Vertetis, Virginia A. *Page* 1-106

    Budd Van Lines, Blumenthal, Kevin *Page* 1-300

    Emcore, Scott, Dane C. *Page* 1-67

    Merck & Co., Inc., Williams, Alvis A. *Page* 1-25

Somerville, DNA Systems Inc., Becker, Andrew D. *Page* 1-171

South Hackensack, Dwarf Holdings, LLC, Randazzo, Leonard *Page* 1-139

Springfield, Management Recruiters International, Weinberg, Laurie J. *Page* 1-169

Stanhope, ComTech Labs, Weiss, Richard A. *Page* 1-295

Succasunna, Information Technology Consulting, Inc., Chromy, Robert J. *Page* 1-230

Tenafly, Tenafly Public Schools, Ivele, Patricia *Page* 1-382

Teterboro, Computer Design & Integration, Robinson, Mark K. *Page* 1-277

Tinton Falls, ECCS, Wheeler, Barbara *Page* 1-47

Trenton, United States Air Force, Mosby, Robin M. *Page* 1-394

Union City, Sapient Corporation, Bansal, Kapil *Page* 1-201

Voorhees, Inforbit Inc., Patel, Lalit *Page* 1-272

Warren

    Cannaissance Consulting, Van Houten, Michael *Page* 1-292

    Emerald Solutions Inc., Zhang, Hong *Page* 1-298

Wayne

    GAF, Kemp, Karen L. *Page* 1-28

    William Paterson University, Tedesco, Frank P. *Page* 1-333

West Caldwell, Sloan & Company, Inc., Luderer, Bob *Page* 1-7

West New York, PSEG Services Corporation, George, Dorina *Page* 1-87

West Orange

    Computer Sciences Corporation, Kolber, Jeffrey A. *Page* 1-205

    CSC Consulting, Walls, Georgette F. *Page* 1-211

    CTech, Woodlee, Jason *Page* 1-193

West Paterson, Techware Solutions, Inc., Rodriguez, Louis F. *Page* 1-209

New Mexico

Alamogordo, Wazoo's Computers, Fender, Chuck *Page* 1-236

Albuquerque

    City of Albuquerque, Van Pelt, Dane *Page* 1-375

    Inter-tel Technologies, Inc., Oakeley, Agnes C. *Page* 1-93

    Los Alamos Technical Associates, Nessel, Steve W. *Page* 1-268

    New Mexico Department of Labor, Information Systems Bureau, Broward, Michael P. *Page* 1-385

    RESPEC, O'Connor, Brian K. *Page* 1-269

    Saboten Web Design, Schneider, Keiko K. *Page* 1-281

    Sandia National Laboratories, Knirk, Dwayne L. *Page* 1-361

Aztec, San Juan County Assessor, Benfield, Janie *Page* 1-379

Carlsbad, Carlsbad Municipal School District, West, Rachel A. *Page* 1-319

Farmington, San Juan College, Degner, Ann L. *Page* 1-336

Las Cruces, White Sands Missile Range, Young, Barry H. *Page* 1-397

Los Alamos

    Burns & Roe Enterprises, DeVincentis, Paul *Page* 1-348

    Los Alamos National Laboratory, Salazar, Anthony A. *Page* 1-359

Santa Fe

    Computer System Consulting, Yelich, Scott D. *Page* 1-297

    State of New Mexico Taxation and Revenue Department, Oakeley, Timothy N. *Page* 1-380

Tucumcari, Mesa Technical College, McDonald, Virgil L. *Page* 1-328

New York

Albany

    New York Institute of Entrepreneurship, Drago, Barbara *Page* 1-322

    New York State Department of Labor, Konicki, James A. *Page* 1-386

    New York State Teachers Retirement System, Kotmel, Allan V. *Page* 1-346

Albertson, Shore Systems, Inc., Guido, Christopher *Page* 1-244

Ardsley, Purdue Pharma L.P., DeModna, Christina K. *Page* 1-23

Armonk, Advanced Network & Services, Inc., Liao, Min *Page* 1-258

Bethpage, Northrop Grumman, Liguori, Stephen D. *Page* 1-76

Bohemia, SITA, Lavardera, Danny *Page* 1-101

Briarcliff, Pace University at Pleasantville, Coppola, Jean Frances *Page* 1-322

Bronxville

    Intergraph Corporation, Leinen, Sean Frederick *Page* 1-257

    Robertson Stephens, Lombardi, James *Page* 1-143

Brooklyn

    Creative Computers & Networking, Inc., Farage, Regina M. *Page* 1-236

    Destia, Kupfer, Mendy *Page* 1-101

    New York City Transit Authority, Taylor, Isiah *Page* 1-87

    New York Methodist Hospital, Cox, Peter J. *Page* 1-307

    Websoft Technologies, Islam, Mohammed N. *Page* 1-250

Buffalo

    AOP Solutions, Becker, James F. *Page* 1-221

    Catholic Charities of Buffalo, Hamm, Keith R. *Page* 1-344

    Ernst & Young LLP, Evanco, Michael S. *Page* 1-353

    Medaille College, Kang, Jai W. *Page* 1-326

    Outokumpu American Brass, Finney, M. Parker *Page* 1-32

    Rich Products, Sandoval, Fernando *Page* 1-8

    VERITAS Software, Blake, Brian C. *Page* 1-194

Corning, Corning Community College, Usack, Lynn A. *Page* 1-339

Corona, YKE International Inc., Ho, Kelvin K. *Page* 1-70

Croton On Hudson

    BetzDearborn division of Hercules, Inc., Tuzzo, Dominick *Page* 1-5

    If and Then, Chbeir, Ziad E. *Page* 1-113

Dryden, Tompkins Cortland Community College, Ackley, Brian Sterling *Page* 1-335

Elmhurst, Berjaya USA Group, Inc., Tan, Kenny T. H. *Page* 1-288

Elmira, Ward Manufacturing Inc., Williams, Allen D. *Page* 1-31

Fairport, Schafer-CIT, Ziehl, Jonathan R. *Page* 1-298

Flushing, Duke Technology, Inc., Tse, Albert P. *Page* 1-291

Franklin Square, Belimage Communications, Saint-Louis, Vanilo *Page* 1-279

Garden City, Ziff-Davis, White Rayner, Nicole M. *Page* 1-17

Glens Falls, Native Textiles, Osmer, Corey *Page* 1-11

Grand Island, Cannon, Palasciano, Stephen M. *Page* 1-351

Greenfield Center, Templin Management Associates, Benner, Carol M. *Page* 1-362

Greenwood Lake, ASCOT Communications, Donato, Anthony M. *Page* 1-109

Hauppauge, Manchester Equipment, Passantino, George A. *Page* 1-120

Hempstead, Elite Systems Support Inc., Bonaparte, C. Scott *Page* 1-223

Hopewell Junction, Graphic Consultants, Wiemokly, Kerry M. *Page* 1-303

Huntington, Hotel Interactive, Denis, Andrew M. *Page* 1-300

Ilion, Colgate University, Howell, Ernest W. *Page* 1-325

Island Park, Pepe Enterprises, Pepe, Kenneth M. *Page* 1-273

Jamaica, Habberstad Nissan, Hunt, Desmond *Page* 1-71

Long Island City, Laguardia Community College, Davidson, Donald A. *Page* 1-336

Lycoming, Niagara Mohawk Power Corporation, Shumway, Kathleen K. *Page* 1-114

Melville

    Arrow Electronics, Tiseo, Roseann M. *Page* 1-122

    Fala Direct Marketing, Inc., Eisman, Ariane M. *Page* 1-165

    Olsten Corporation, Mingin, Philip M. *Page* 1-168

Merrick, Integral Software Corporation, Zaika, Gary *Page* 1-297

Monroe, Foster Wheel Environment Corporation, Wagner, Daniel S. *Page* 1-349

Mount Kisco

    Datalink Computer Products Inc., Bedi, Vickram A. *Page* 1-221

    Mount Kisco Medical Group, Salandra, Justin A. *Page* 1-311

Nesconset, EC Cubed, Leung, Gregory D. *Page* 1-110

New Windsor, International Online Relations, Noor, Nicholas N. *Page* 1-208

New York

    American Express Company, Menezes, Conrad O. *Page* 1-139

    AMS Inc., Thakkar, Vrajesh *Page* 1-121

    Associated Textile Converters, Kraut, Jeffrey B. *Page* 1-11

    Association for Computing, Hardjowirogo, Jono *Page* 1-16

    Barasch Music & Sound, Barasch, Mark *Page* 1-220

    barnesandnoble.com, Rosano, John L. *Page* 1-130

    Beth Israel Medical Center, Symczyk, Walter J. *Page* 1-310

    Bozell Group, DeCarlo, Fred H. *Page* 1-163

    Capital Thinking, Inc., Harper, deAnna A. *Page* 1-140

    CBS, Erickson, Scott W. *Page* 1-107

    CDS Inc., Fanshteyn, Timur *Page* 1-175

    Chase Manhattan Bank, Mui, Henry M. *Page* 1-135

    City College of New York, Li, Xuhong "Linda" *Page* 1-327

    Columbia University Law School, Chua, Kristine U. *Page* 1-321

    Computer Savers, Inc., Ochoa, Ruben J. *Page* 1-270

    Data Downlink Corporation, Tharaken, Ajit *Page* 1-289

    Digitrade Inc., Tsung, Theodore T. *Page* 1-192

    Donovan Data Systems, Brown, Kent *Page* 1-165

    Draft Worldwide, Wang, Bruce *Page* 1-164

    EarthWeb, Inc., Hidary, Jack D. *Page* 1-179

    Electronic Systems Associates, Fredette, Stephen J. *Page* 1-238

    Elsevier Science, Stein, Emmanuel *Page* 1-19

    Ever Glitter International Ltd., Chu, Tung S. *Page* 1-123

    Fordham University, Rothschild, Brian M. *Page* 1-331

    Getronics/Wang, Lee, Roger E. *Page* 1-256

    Goldman Sachs & Company, Jha, Ashok S. *Page* 1-143

    Goldman Sachs & Company, Santhumayor, Ivan NJ *Page* 1-144

    Goldman Sachs, Ullah, Shamya M. *Page* 1-144

    Housing Fiscal Services, Beaumont, Patrick A. *Page* 1-158

    IBM Corporation, Bradley, Dennis R. *Page* 1-39

    Infinity Solutions Inc., Kanthawar, Krishnakumar *Page* 1-252

    Information Builders Inc., Dorman, Gregory J. *Page* 1-196

    Instinet, Varghese, Sajini Sara *Page* 1-144

    J Crew Group, Inc., Sherman, David M. *Page* 1-131

    Jones Day Reavis & Pogue, Davis, Roseland M. *Page* 1-312

    Kaplan, Haggerty, Hugh *Page* 1-340

    KBC Bank New York N.V., Curto, Philip A. *Page* 1-134

    Legal Aid Society, Muhammad, Yolanda *Page* 1-313

    Macklowe Properties, Guzzetta, Jacqueline R. *Page* 1-160

    Madge.web, Hobbs, Matthew Stephen *Page* 1-247

    Madscience, Frackman, David A. *Page* 1-175

    Mancini Duffy, Kafrouni, Nabil H. *Page* 1-350

    Manhattan Village Academy, Cline, Peter M. *Page* 1-314

    Marsh USA, Inc., Knight, Lophney H. *Page* 1-157

    MTVi Group, Borisov, Gennadiy *Page* 1-107

    Oracle Corporation, Marcus, Judith L. *Page* 1-197

    Parson Brinkerhoff Farradyne, Homami, Hassan Rezaei *Page* 1-248

    Plural, Lewis A., Francisco *Page* 1-182

    Point of Sale Technology Corporation, Newman, Moses N. *Page* 1-268

    RCG Information Technology, Mulé, Peter T. *Page* 1-266

    Resource Systems, Inc., Brown, Thomas K. *Page* 1-194

    Savantnet Solutions, Lin, Jin *Page* 1-258

    Sequel Communications, Dima-Ala Villanueva, Lorli *Page* 1-109

    SSB-City, Kerry, Marianne L. *Page* 1-135

    Starmedia Network, Inc., Park, Hyun *Page* 1-111

    Strategic Alliance International Corporation, Wan, Daniel Q. *Page* 1-293

    Stuart Dean Company, McAndrew, Jeffrey M. *Page* 1-7

    Time Warner, Snyder, Andrew H. *Page* 1-108

    Transaction Information Systems, Nolan, Thomas J. *Page* 1-269

    Unisys Corporation, Babcock, James M. *Page* 1-219

    United Federation of Teachers, Teacher Centers Professional Development Program, Barton, Regina V. *Page* 1-346

    Uproar.com, Shah, Atique R. *Page* 1-306

    Vibe Magazine, Aris, Harold A. *Page* 1-16

    Vison Education Inc., Nathan, Matthew N. *Page* 1-268

    Vital Network Services, de Freitas, André A. *Page* 1-109

    Winthrop/Stimson, Teague, Mark A. *Page* 1-313

    YAI, White, James *Page* 1-344

Newark, GV-WFL EduTech, Welsh, Norma E. *Page* 1-319

Niskayuna, General Electric (GE) Corporate Research and Development, Kao, Kevin J. *Page* 1-77

Norwich, Benedict Corporation, Lynk, Dennis R. *Page* 1-126

Ossining, Prudential Reality and Relocation Services, Simko, Edward J. *Page* 1-117

Owego

    Lockheed Martin Federal Systems, George, Michael *Page* 1-80

    Lockheed Martin, Longstrom, Edward *Page* 1-79

Parkland, Camp Cuisine, Rubin, Nancy *Page* 1-129

Pelham, CAS Inc., Lord, John D. *Page* 1-4

Pittsford, Rochester Institute of Technology, Garrison, Daniel J. *Page* 1-324

Ridgewood, Uproar, Inc., Winkler, Piotr *Page* 1-200

Rochester

    Ajilon, Cheng, Jean *Page* 1-229

    Diamond Packaging, Fiacco, Philip *Page* 1-14

    Eastman Kodak Company, Gulling, Mark *Page* 1-84

    Eastman Kodak Company, Nemchick, David C. *Page* 1-84

    Questra, Inc., Kammerdiener, Shawn Ivan *Page* 1-252

    Rochester Institute of Technology, Hill, Lawrence W. *Page* 1-325

Rome

    Air Force Research Laboratory, Pedersen, Charles R. *Page* 1-395

    ITT Industries, McGibbon, Thomas L. *Page* 1-263

Rye Brook, ENTEX Information Services, Inc., Creevy, John J. *Page* 1-232

Schenectady

    GE, Sobolewski, Michael W. *Page* 1-70

    General Electric Company, Gao, Hui *Page* 1-77

    General Electric, Grindle, Mark J. *Page* 1-77

    MVP Health Plan, Chan, Monte Tak Ho *Page* 1-152

Seaford, Affordable PC Systems, Inc., Agarwal, Braj *Page* 1-217

Somers, Pepsi Cola International, O'Donnell, Charlie *Page* 1-9

South Beach, Intershop Communication, Difilippo, Armand *Page* 1-234

Stamford, Sure Air Ltd., Reicher, Stuart *Page* 1-159

Staten Island

    Atlantic Express, Valonzo, Avelino Mark A. *Page* 1-87

    Cisco Systems, Inc., Saladis, Frank P. *Page* 1-62

    Fordham University Library, Vilchez, Ricardo S. *Page* 1-339

Syosset, Ademco Group, Garenani, Peter C. *Page* 1-298

Syracuse

    AppliedTheory, Young, Aaron C. *Page* 1-211

    Phillips Broad Band Network, Stathopoulos, Dimitrios *Page* 1-32

    Power FCU, Hill, David J. *Page* 1-136

    Systems Made Simple, Inc., Harris, Dana B. *Page* 1-178

Tarrytown

    Amerada Hess Corporation, Vanover, Andrew *Page* 1-28

    Bayer Corporation, Rash, Jeanne *Page* 1-24

    National Standard Mortgage, Kalkar, Sanjiv *Page* 1-141

Troy, Mapinfo Corporation, Tobison, John K. *Page* 1-290

Webster

    GCP Consulting, Prentice, Guy C. *Page* 1-275

    Xerox, Nuwer, Kevin *Page* 1-50

Westbury, Sulzer Metco, Bordonaro, Robert *Page* 1-34

Westfield, Plantrol Systems, Ltd., Lapp, Jon E. *Page* 1-182

Williamsville, Independent Health, Starr, Laura A. *Page* 1-151

Woodbury, Ericsson Messaging Systems, Lewis, R. Scott *Page* 1-61

Woodside, Road Runner, Fitzgerald, Michael G. *Page* 1-237

Yorktown, IBM Corporation, Elfadel, Abe *Page* 1-40

Yorktown Heights

    IBM Thomas J. Watson Research Center, Brown, Harold A. *Page* 1-226

    IBM Thomas J. Watson Research Center, Ruehli, Albert E. *Page* 1-279

North Carolina

Ahoskie, Beasley Enterprises, Hoggard, Robin L. *Page* 1-126

Ansonville, Cookson Fibers, Inc., Oo, Zaw W. *Page* 1-11

Apex

    IBM Corporation, Khalifa, Kathy L. *Page* 1-42

    Tipper Tie, Bender, Kendra *Page* 1-34

Burlington, Netpath, Inc., Laforet, Christopher *Page* 1-110

Cary

    Aeroglide Corporation, Tipton, Duane E. *Page* 1-38

    ECPI Technical College, Harding, William R. *Page* 1-337

    IBM Corporation, Garner, Michael W. *Page* 1-40

    Information Retrieval, Bullied, Perry Leon *Page* 1-172

    Rail Inc., Thorpe, James L. *Page* 1-87

    SAS Institute, Kitts Malik, Kathleen *Page* 1-180

Charlotte

    Chiron America, Inc., Wamsley, Alan Maurice *Page* 1-38

    Crowder Construction, Hodgin, Charles L. *Page* 1-5

    Duke Energy Corporation, Anderson, Bruce N. *Page* 1-113

    First Union National Bank, Van Huynh, Khoa *Page* 1-134

    Independent, Lynn, Robert Garon "Bob" *Page* 1-259

    Jannon Group, Arroyo, Brett C. *Page* 1-218

Premier Systems Integrators, Tyler, James E. *Page* 1-210

    SGE Consulting, Emory, Samuel G. *Page* 1-235

    Solectron Technology Company, De Cesare, Vito *Page* 1-40

Concord, The Shoe Show of Rocky Mount, McIntyre, David M. *Page* 1-127

Conord, Jon Barry & Associates, Inc., Ball, Sharron L. *Page* 1-165

Durham

    Clarkston Potomac, Winter, W. Scott *Page* 1-296

    Droege Computing Services, Beckner, John W. *Page* 1-221

    Duke University Medical Center, Pladna, Stephen L. *Page* 1-308

Farmville, DIMON International, Inc., Taylor, J. West *Page* 1-10

Fort Bragg, Vector Data Systems, McEady, Erasmus W. *Page* 1-348

Greensboro

    ECPI College of Technology, Blackburn, Dale *Page* 1-336

    Prudential Carolinas Realty, Duggins, Ginger B. *Page* 1-159

Hickory, Hickory Springs Manufacturing, Wilson, Jonathan G. *Page* 1-13

High Point

    Dixon Odom PLLC, Williams, Scott D. *Page* 1-356

    Furniture City Color, Oliver, Thomas W. *Page* 1-22

Kings Mountain, ABB Alston Power, Kraft, Debra *Page* 1-33

Lumberbridge, Mountaire Farms, Dover, Pamala V. *Page* 1-1

Mooresville, SAP Professional Organization, Gibson, Stephen *Page* 1-241

Morrisville

    International Network Services, Lester, Jeffrey A. *Page* 1-258

    International Network Services, McCarson, David B. *Page* 1-263

    SciQuest.com, Johnson, Ron D. *Page* 1-132

New Bern, Neuse Center, Baxter, Linda M. *Page* 1-384

Raleigh

    Holocon, Inc., Holoman, Stuart B. *Page* 1-248

    Horizon Healthware, Inc., Fisher, Terrance *Page* 1-175

    McKinney & Silver, Parker, Kevin M. *Page* 1-164

    Medic Computer Systems, Slater, Keith R. *Page* 1-199

    Micro Technology Unlimited, Cox, Benjamin Bryan *Page* 1-173

    Navant Corporation, Bowden, Geri D. *Page* 1-224

    Next Generation Ideas, Rice, Donald W. *Page* 1-277

    Perkin-Elmer Corporation, Davis, James V. *Page* 1-233

    The Consultants, Sawyer, Jeffery H. *Page* 1-280

Research Triangle Park

    Ericsson, Inc., Brauner, Darrell R. *Page* 1-58

    North Carolina State Education Assistance Authority, Colclough Bennett, Judith *Page* 1-138

Salisbury, Tri State Hospital Supply Corporation, Tresidder, Garfield W. *Page* 1-120

Sanford, Central Electric, Hare, Angela D. *Page* 1-114

Waynesville, Diversified Consulting International, McElroy, Ted M. *Page* 1-263

Wentworth, Rockingham Community College, Evans, Cheryl L. *Page* 1-336

Wilmington

    Computer-Information Services Consulting, Ranalli, John *Page* 1-276

    Corning Inc., Cobb, Gary A. *Page* 1-69

    Paradigm Analytical Laboratories, Dickinson, Gregory *Page* 1-361

Winston-Salem

    Carolina Manufacturer's Service, Inc., Marino, Michael A. *Page* 1-361

    Chesapeake Display & Packaging, Wynn, Sherri Peterson *Page* 1-14

    Republic Mortgage Insurance Company, Wilkie, Timothy J. *Page* 1-156

Winterville, Fullarton Computer Industries Inc., Taylor, Wendy E. *Page* 1-45

North Dakota

Bismarck , Job Service North Dakota, Tober, Theresa J. *Page 1-169*

Ohio

Akron

    Advanced Elastomer Systems, L.P., McLaughlin-Nelson, Lori K. *Page 1-22*

    Meloun Consulting, Meloun, Jalane M. *Page 1-264*

    Telxon Corporation, Benedict, Michael *Page 1-39*

Ashtabula, A. Louis Supply Company, Angle, Brenda K. *Page 1-122*

Brookville, Review Technology Group, Thomas, Russell *Page 1-210*

Cincinnati

    ARay Computer Services, Ray, Tony E. *Page 1-276*

    CSC Consulting Firm, Belousov, Katrina *Page 1-201*

    Fascor, Stephens, Amy E. *Page 1-191*

    Mobile MIS Consulting, Goldschmidt, David *Page 1-241*

    Procter & Gamble, Goodhart, Daniel L. *Page 1-25*

    Thomson Corporation, Lehman, Mary Jane Cottingham *Page 1-18*

    University of Cincinnati, Pagulayan, Randy J. *Page 1-330*

Cleveland

    Applied Industrial Technologies, Richmond, Leon L. *Page 1-123*

    Cooperative Resource Services, Petsche, Christopher M. *Page 1-168*

    County of Cuyahoga, Saunders, Donald A. *Page 1-374*

    DynaLink, Marinoff, Ryan H. *Page 1-183*

    e-Business Express, McNeil, D. Gregory *Page 1-264*

    Intellinex, an Learning Venture of E&Y, Hennes, Cathryn A. *Page 1-353*

    McDonald Investments, Maholm, Timothy R. *Page 1-146*

    Prime Systems, Inc., Fry, Paul Charles *Page 1-238*

Colombus, Wexner Heritage Village, Mokros, Jason M. *Page 1-307*

Columbus

    Abbot & Abbot Architects, PLL, Schumacher, J. *Page 1-351*

    Advanced Programming Resources, Savage, Steven *Page 1-279*

    American Electric Power Company, Hardin, Rohdonda R. *Page 1-113*

    Berwanger Overmyer Associates, Burgoyne, Ann C. *Page 1-155*

    Cranel Inc., Kaufman, Jeremy *Page 1-119*

    DecisionOne, Heald, Frederick A. *Page 1-216*

    Dispatch Printing Company, Veach, Dale L. *Page 1-16*

    Federal Government, Hoffman, Larry L. *Page 1-379*

    Lucent Technologies, Matthews, John V. *Page 1-61*

    Merck-Medco Rx, Liming, Ray D. *Page 1-131*

    Nationwide Insurance, McKinney, Debi C. *Page 1-148*

    Ohio Department of Alcohol and Drug Addiction Services, Hull, Walter James *Page 1-385*

    Ohio Department of Health, DQA, Coleman, Glen A. *Page 1-384*

    Police and Firemen's Disability, Burchfield, Bill *Page 1-155*

    Road Runner, Schreffler, Scott A. *Page 1-281*

    Time Warner Communications, Hunt, Kelly K. *Page 1-107*

    Unlimited Solutions Inc., Schubert, William Anthony *Page 1-189*

Dayton

    Coolidge Wall Womsley Lombard, Clayton, Brian R. *Page 1-312*

    Mead Corporation, Schmidt, Christian A. *Page 1-15*

    O'Neil Associates, Werkowitz, Derek *Page 1-19*

    Reynolds & Reynolds, Glover, John D. *Page 1-21*

    Scott Hull Associates, Jones, Beth E. *Page 1-166*

    Standard Register, Harris, Mark W. *Page 1-21*

    University of Dayton, Keck, Christian Jon *Page 1-326*

Dublin, Verizon Wireless, Holland, Adam *Page 1-92*

Euclid, Zagar Inc., Fedele, Alan R. *Page 1-36*

Hilliard

    MJP Solutions Inc., Pierron, Brian J. *Page 1-274*

    UUNET - A Division of MCI/WorldCom, Vetere, Rhonda M. *Page 1-214*

Hudson, The Little Tikes Company, VanMeter, Jim *Page 1-85*

Kent, Kent State University, Liao, Weidong *Page 1-327*

Kirtland, Master Automation, Inc., Weigand, Michael R. *Page 1-211*

Lancaster, AT&T Solutions/McDermott Inc. Account, Young, Carol *Page 1-297*

Lima, Roundy's Ohio Division, Weaver, Sandra K. *Page 1-124*

Lorain, May Department Stores, Fiorito, Juliann M. *Page 1-126*

Macedonia, IER Industries, Inc., Burgess, Ronald A. *Page 1-28*

Mansfield, MKC Associates, Inc., Harmon, Jim *Page 1-350*

Marion, GTE, Snouffer, Bret Daniel *Page 1-104*

Middleburg Heights, Charter One Bank, Hamner, Clinton W. *Page 1-135*

Mogadore, OMNOVA Solutions Inc., Finklestein, Ronald *Page 1-27*

Newbury, Knetico Inc., Tauche, Julie *Page 1-51*

Oxford, City of Oxford, Ritcher, Michael A. *Page 1-374*

Powell, The Kennedy Connection, Kennedy, Michael *Page 1-364*

Ravenna, Ravenna Aluminum, Bennett, John C. *Page 1-32*

Raymond, Honda Research and Development, Holliday, Jeff L. *Page 1-357*

Reynoldsburg, Norman Jones Enlow Company, Plummer, Kyle B. *Page 1-355*

Sagamore Hills, Techni Logic Consulting, Schneider, Debra *Page 1-281*

Solon, New Horizon Management & Consulting, Lehman, Robert P. *Page 1-257*

Strongsville, Strongsville City Schools, Schroth, John W. *Page 1-383*

Toledo

    JGR Consulting, LLP, Rex, Jack G. *Page 1-366*

    Toledo Lucas County Public Library, Gray, Thomas P. *Page 1-339*

Troy, MI Technologies, Yount, David E. *Page 1-216*

Van Wert, Paulding High School, Mengerink, Joel W. *Page 1-316*

Warren, Alcan Aluminum Corporation, Shannon, Patricia A. *Page 1-32*

Washington Central Heights, Microman, Inc., Garinger, Phillip D. *Page 1-204*

Westerville, Themis, Inc., Dunlap, Thomas S. *Page 1-196*

Wooster, United Titanium Inc., Crawford, Michael W. *Page 1-85*

Worthington, Worthington City Schools, Schlarb, Keith N. *Page 1-317*

Oklahoma

Ada, East Central University, Carley, Clay B. *Page 1-321*

Bartlesville, Phillips Petroleum Company, Embry, Dale L. *Page 1-27*

Edmond

    Pace/Butler Corporation, Walden, Steven J. *Page 1-129*

    Stonebridge Technologies, Miller, Stephen W. *Page 1-265*

Lawton, Internet of Lawton, Rosenquist, Eric C. *Page 1-209*

Midwest City, TASC, Inc., Maley, Scott *Page 1-206*

Muskogee, Muskogee Public Schools, Chandler, Ronnie D. *Page 1-381*

Oklahoma City

    C2 Multimedia, McKay, Michelle *Page 1-263*

    IBM Global Services, Bowzer, Jerrold A. *Page 1-224*

    Oklahoma Department of Corrections, Frazier, Stephen P. *Page 1-378*

    Reynolds & Reynolds, Loy-Tate, Deanne *Page 1-21*

    RWJ & Associates, Barto, Bill L. *Page 1-167*

    University of Oklahoma Health Sciences Center, Ledford, Yvonne M. *Page 1-327*

Owasso, City of Owasso, Duggan, Sheryl A. *Page 1-372*

Shawnee, Oklahoma Baptist University, Nickerson, Gary B. *Page 1-329*

Tulsa

    BSW International, Fleming, Sparkle N. *Page 1-350*

dba Computer Consultant, Sawyer, Thomas Eric *Page 1-280*

Dresser-Rand Company, Ferrier, William Wayne *Page 1-37*

MCI WorldCom, Inc., Ghosh, Sukumar *Page 1-98*

TaascFORCE, Joplin, Toby L. *Page 1-180*

Teaco Inc., Gorney, John P. *Page 1-98*

Oregon

Beaverton, Maxim Integrated Products, Inc., Hume, Stephen G. *Page 1-66*

Corvallis, Kalatel Engineer Inc., Johnston, Marty P. *Page 1-298*

Eugene, University of Oregon Athletics, Cooley, Len *Page 1-321*

Hillsboro, Century High School, Hall, Michael *Page 1-315*

Portland

ADP Dealer Services, Winquist, John A. *Page 1-212*

ADP, Goldman, Sergey *Page 1-211*

AverStar, Inc., Geospacial Services Group, Whitney, Susan L. *Page 1-296*

BOEC/City of Portland, Pullen, Malcolm M. *Page 1-378*

Cytera Systems, Forrester, Janice *Page 1-237*

Entex Information Technology Services, A Siemens Company, Stokes, Keith *Page 1-286*

Federal Reserve Bank, Yrizarry, Lisa Marie *Page 1-133*

Intel Corporation, Jensen, Kristen A. *Page 1-66*

Portland Development Commission, Ruddiman, Thomas A. *Page 1-389*

Standard Insurance, L'Heureux, Colette M. *Page 1-150*

Salem

Hicks Technology Services, Hicks, Mark J. *Page 1-247*

Oregon Department of Forestry, Gum, Jeanette M. *Page 1-388*

Pennsylvania

Allentown, Air Products & Chemicals, Inc., GEGE Process Controls A32H2, Leach, David B. *Page 1-125*

Altoona, ACCS @ St. Mary Site, Snare, Lisa A. *Page 1-318*

Berwyn, Arris Systems, Inc., Namoglu, Sheryl F. *Page 1-267*

Bethlehem, Regional Network Communications, Inc., Gaul, Donna F. *Page 1-176*

Bridgeport, Merck & Co., Inc, Caloza, Racquel D. *Page 1-22*

Canonsburg, Crown Communications Inc., Colaianne, John J. *Page 1-97*

Carnegie, CIBER Enterprise Application Services, Pattock, Suzanne Sacek *Page 1-186*

Chambersburg

Averstar, Rogers, James R. *Page 1-277*

Public Opinion, Gaspardino, Amy L. *Page 1-15*

Chester

Chester Housing Authority, Tong, Vincent S. *Page 1-389*

Widener University, Habermann, Gary J. *Page 1-324*

Clairton, U.S. Steel-Clairton Works, Post, John S. *Page 1-31*

Coaldale, The Rhythm Section Lab, Wychulis, C. "Bud" *Page 1-303*

Coraopolis, Michael Baker Jr., Inc., Ordoobadi, Mehrdad *Page 1-271*

Cressona, ALCOA Engineered Products, Barr, Angela Lynn *Page 1-32*

Dallas, BsG Inc., Campbell, Chris A. *Page 1-172*

Denver, Kalas Manufacturing Inc., Wolf, Gerald L. *Page 1-53*

East Norriton, Novell, Inc., Whittington, Cathy D. *Page 1-200*

Eddystone, SCA Hygiene Products, Salisbury, Andrew J. *Page 1-15*

Ellwood City, Ellwood Group Inc., Owrey, Richard *Page 1-34*

Emmaus, Lucent Technologies, Doddapaneni, Srinivas P. *Page 1-58*

Enola, Techcircle.com inc., Shashikumar, Bellave S. *Page 1-282*

Fort Washington, ESPS, Inc., Pagliei, Jeffrey M. *Page 1-186*

Harrisburg, Country Oven, Inc., Frye, Randy E. *Page 1-129*

Hatboro, Proconex, Kaskoun, Anthony Joseph *Page 1-205*

Hollsopple, American Precision Technology, Punako, Ronald *Page 1-275*

Honey Brook, The Vanguard Group, Dalal, Alex F. *Page 1-145*

Horsham

C&C Ford Sales Inc., Ferraro, Brian D. *Page 1-126*

Ernst & Young LLP, Decker, Thomas J. *Page 1-353*

GMAC Commercial Mortgage, Benson, Stephen T. *Page 1-140*

GMAC Commercial Mortgage, Brown, Sharon M. *Page 1-140*

Huntingdon, Juniata College, Bichel, Anthony R. *Page 1-335*

Indiana, Pennsylvania State Police, Erdely, Robert W. *Page 1-376*

Johnstown

CBM Business Machines Inc., Felix, Donald F. *Page 1-48*

Crown American Hotels Company, Brady, Brian J. *Page 1-162*

King of Prussia

Bhasha, Inc., Dave, Maulik Avantikumar *Page 1-233*

Infonautics Corporation, Mohan, Ram *Page 1-213*

Kingston, Luzerne Intermediate Unit, Makar, Lynn A. *Page 1-341*

Lafayette Hill, Astro-Med, Inc., Minasyan, Georgiy R. *Page 1-83*

Lancaster

Arthur Andersen LLP, Nestore, Frank S. *Page 1-365*

Laser Wireless Inc., Walter, Dick *Page 1-63*

Lansdale, EDS, Johnston, Elbert W. *Page 1-215*

Lebanon, Pipeline Interactive, Stocker, Laura Baker *Page 1-191*

Levittown, The Computer & Network Fixer, McNutt, Joseph W. *Page 1-216*

Longhorne, Harte-Hanks, Hennessy, Richard V. *Page 1-301*

Malvern, SCT, Knotts, James Brian *Page 1-180*

Mechanicsburg, IntelliMark, Inc., Leaman, Kendall J. *Page 1-256*

Media, Professional Duplicating, O'Bryant, George H. *Page 1-20*

Nazareth, Software Consulting Services, Ashford, Paul L. *Page 1-194*

Norristown

Kennedy Kenrick Catholic High School, Kopaczewski, John J. *Page 1-316*

Yoh Support Services, Green, E. G. *Page 1-243*

Northern Cambria, Never-Enuff Enterprises, Bradford, Richard A. *Page 1-224*

Oaks, Comcast, Lorenzi, David L. *Page 1-108*

Orefield, KidsPeace, Metzler, Robin C. *Page 1-343*

Pennsburg, Micro Technology Groupe, Sees, Chris V. *Page 1-209*

Perkasie, BSA & I, LLP, Lysinger, Lowell J. *Page 1-312*

Philadelphia

Andersen Consulting, McDonnell, Michael J. *Page 1-365*

Healthcare Management, Jones, Russell W. *Page 1-150*

Independence Blue Cross, Luther, Carolyn W. *Page 1-150*

Institute for Scientific Information (ISI), Wismer, James D. *Page 1-19*

Intellisource, Quintanilla, Chris A. *Page 1-169*

Magee Rehabilitation Hospital, Peterson, Steven C. *Page 1-308*

Pennrose Properties, Inc., Miles, Mazda T. *Page 1-302*

PricewaterhouseCoopers, Shields, Andrew V. *Page 1-355*

Public Financial Management, Scott, David L. *Page 1-147*

St. Joseph's University, Nester, Leonard J. *Page 1-329*

The Wharton School, Knight, Pamela J. *Page 1-340*

University of Pennsylvania Graduate School of Education, Fels, Alan N. *Page 1-323*

Phoenixville

Analytical Graphics, Griffiths, Andrea M. *Page 1-177*

North American Performance Group (NAPG, Inc.), Gulotta, Peter *Page 1-244*

Pittsburgh

Aceomatic Recon, Swanson, N. Diana *Page* 1-118

Consolidated Natural Gas, Carter, Jeffrey W. *Page* 1-115

Cyberdeck Consultants, Murphy, Brian E. *Page* 1-266

Eat 'N Park Restaurants, Schaefer, James F. *Page* 1-129

Equitable Resources, Sciullo, Gregory M. *Page* 1-281

Flexon, Goins, Raphael D. *Page* 1-177

Management Science Associates Inc., Silliman, Suzanne *Page* 1-283

Software Engineering Institute, Phillips, Richard W. *Page* 1-359

Quakertown, Smith Consulting, Smith, Jeremy A. *Page* 1-284

Radnor, Wyeth-Ayerst Research, Lis, Ellen R. *Page* 1-24

Reading

GPU Energy, Wingenroth, Rebecca M. *Page* 1-115

Thomas Hardware, Schartel, David M. *Page* 1-122

Scranton, Community Medical Center, Robbins, John Edward *Page* 1-309

Shady Grove, Innernet, Inc., Rotz, Randy E. *Page* 1-278

Shillington, Governor Mifflin School District, Becker, Sandra L. *Page* 1-314

Spring House, Advanta Corporation, Collier, H. James *Page* 1-140

Stevens, Henry Schein, Inc., Korber, Lorraine M. *Page* 1-124

Summerdale, Capital Area Intermediate Unit, Colbert, Scott *Page* 1-314

Telford, Accu Sort Systems Inc., Churetta, Scott *Page* 1-173

Tervose, Hercules Inc., Condon, J. Emmett *Page* 1-26

Thorndale, G.O. Carlson Inc., Santucci, Peter *Page* 1-31

Valley Forge, The Vanguard Group, Betty, Joseph M. *Page* 1-145

Warren, IBM Global Services, Welker, Michael J. *Page* 1-295

Washington, Union Switch and Signal, Magnotta, Salvatore D. *Page* 1-78

Washington Crossing, Janssen Pharmaceuticals, Verstraete, Edmond J. *Page* 1-25

Wayne

CSI Maximus, Inc., Glaeser, Paul H. *Page* 1-177

Tekmark Global Solutions, Lynch, Ron A. *Page* 1-170

West Conshohocken, American Society for Testing and Materials, Dernoga, Kathleen A. *Page* 1-16

Wexford, ACS Professional Services, Porterfield, Mark E. *Page* 1-274

Willow Grove, Quad Systems Corporation, Gordon, Frank E. *Page* 1-59

Wyano, Channel Communications, Bradish, Edward *Page* 1-108

York, Dentsply International, Hersey, Phil A. *Page* 1-83

Rhode Island

Cranston, Electronic Data Systems, Tuniewicz, Karin *Page* 1-215

Lincoln, Amica, Hillman, Jack Dyer *Page* 1-148

Pawtucket, Northern Computers, MacIntosh, Michelle *Page* 1-260

Providence

Gilbane, Coyle, Stephen F. *Page* 1-4

Textron, Inc., Michaelides, Phyllis J. *Page* 1-76

South Carolina

Aiken, Westinghouse - Savannah River Site, Boone-Shuford, Myrna *Page* 1-392

Camden, Kershaw County School District, David, Phyllis C. *Page* 1-314

Catawba, Bowater Inc., Allen, Almon *Page* 1-14

Cayce, Mynd, Pees, Philip G. *Page* 1-273

Charleston

Cambar Software, Wuosmaa, Shelby M. *Page* 1-201

NOAA Coastal Services Center, Petrovich, Nina L. *Page* 1-273

Columbia

Bobbin Group Publishing, Mullinax, Cindy Tarte *Page* 1-16

South Carolina Department of Health and Human Services, Ellis, Patricia C. *Page* 1-384

South Carolina Law Enforcement Division, Johnson, L. J. *Page* 1-377

Duncan, Michelin, Cunningham, Linda S. *Page* 1-28

Eastover, Mynd, Baukman, Robert *Page* 1-171

Greenville

IKON Education Services, Ownby, James O. *Page* 1-51

Michelin North America, McFarlane, Daniel C. *Page* 1-28

Social Security Administration, Barber, Charles *Page* 1-375

Hartsville, Sonoco, Schuetz, Jeffrey M. *Page* 1-14

McCormick, MCI Telecommunications, Venz, Barbara E. *Page* 1-106

Myrtle Beach, CyberPatriot.com, Murphy, Jack *Page* 1-266

Summerville, Patton General Contracting, Salter, Jim *Page* 1-4

West Columbia, South Carolina Arts Commission, Gamble, Mark H. *Page* 1-347

South Dakota

Chamberlain, St. Joseph's Indian School, Heinssen, Scott A. *Page* 1-315

Pine Ridge, Wolf Creek Elementary, Wechsler, Brian C. *Page* 1-334

Rapid City

Army National Guard, Eizember, Dave *Page* 1-392

Ketel Thorsten Son, LLP, Elshire, Jeremy *Page* 1-235

Sioux Falls

Citicorp International Communications Inc., Peterson, Randy *Page* 1-135

Gateway, Breitkreutz, Sherry Lee *Page* 1-224

Tennessee

Bloomingdale, Royal Ordnance North America, Godsey, Vicki Lynn *Page* 1-34

Blountville, Tri-Cities Regional Airport, Payne, Shirley S. *Page* 1-90

Brentwood

Macrophage International, Elkin, L. Daniel *Page* 1-174

Service Merchandise, Rucker, Mark C. *Page* 1-131

Bristol, Siemens Energy and Automation, Jones, Billy R. *Page* 1-56

Chattanooga

ComDyn Group, LLC, Stewart, Winston M. *Page* 1-286

NVT Consulting Services, Patri, Neelanjan *Page* 1-272

Church Hill, Quebecor World Hawkins, Hinson, Kevin *Page* 1-20

Clinton, In-Net, Haney, Wayne A. *Page* 1-245

Collierville

FedEx, ITD/Finance in Legal Systems, Spurlock, Samuel *Page* 1-90

FedEx, Wallace, James Ashford *Page* 1-90

Greeneville, McInturff Miligan & Brooks, Edwards, Ginger F. *Page* 1-156

Hampshire, International Comfort Products, McCandless, Doug *Page* 1-51

Hermitage, Summit Medical Center, Wells, Robert M. *Page* 1-309

Jackson, AEMP Corporation, Springer, Sarah Lee *Page* 1-74

Knoxville

Covenant Health, Groves, Richard D. *Page* 1-308

Nova Information Systems, Inman, Connie C. *Page* 1-301

Sea Ray Boats, Inc., Hughes, Adrienne *Page* 1-78

Tennessee Valley Authority, Ramey, Corey D. *Page* 1-114

Manchester, Manchester Police Department, Vickers, Jerry *Page* 1-377

Memphis

Commercial Data Corporation, Goodwin, Timothy A. *Page* 1-242

Shelby County Trustee, McGrory, Joan Serocki *Page* 1-380

Williams Refining, LLC, Willerton, Shane L. *Page* 1-28

Morristown, Walters State Community College, Gibson, Ronald *Page* 1-336

Nashville

CGI, Gatewood, David A. *Page* 1-239

Columbia HCA, Hubbs, Bart L. *Page 1-311*

Covance, Markel, Lisa Anne *Page 1-358*

National Nephrology Association, Jones, Otis Lee *Page 1-346*

Optimum Solutions, Inc., Dwyer, Sherry L. *Page 1-235*

Square D Company, Brown, Thomas S. *Page 1-52*

State of Tennessee Department of Environment and Conservation, Stockell, Albert W. *Page 1-387*

U.S. Tobacco Manufacturing LP, Beasley, Mark S. *Page 1-10*

Willis North America, Inc., Tomlinson, William W. *Page 1-158*

Tiptonville, Tennessee Department of Correction, Guy, John D. *Page 1-378*

Texas

Addison

Compuware Corporation, Swafford, Martin H. *Page 1-191*

HIE, Parker, Dee A. *Page 1-271*

Sapient Corporation, Mukundan, Bobby S. *Page 1-365*

Allen

Business Edge Solutions, Kretz, Richard E. *Page 1-255*

Micrografx, Hughes, Chris *Page 1-196*

Amarillo

AFI, McKillip, West *Page 1-125*

Hastings Entertainment, Inc., Fritz, Laura *Page 1-130*

Arlington

Federal Aviation Administration, Anthochy, George *Page 1-389*

National Semiconductor, Goggins, Dennis R. *Page 1-65*

Penguin Consulting Company, Inc., Meisinger, Steven D. *Page 1-264*

Siemens Electrocom LP, Khan, Tameen *Page 1-50*

Austin

BMC, Smith, Daniel J. *Page 1-199*

ClearCommerce Corporation, Shprints, Eduard *Page 1-283*

Computer Sciences Corporation, Delgado-Lopez, Lupe *Page 1-203*

Connect South, Thelin, Bradford *Page 1-192*

Database Consultants, Inc., Mankala, Srinivas *Page 1-261*

dba computer moms[], Beall, Carlene *Page 1-300*

Entech Sales & Service Inc., Rightmer, Charles K. *Page 1-123*

Kent Datacomm, Crane, Douglas G. *Page 1-203*

Landmark Graphics, Le Melinaire, Pascal *Page 1-182*

O.S.S. Inc., Gaitonde, Prashant V. *Page 1-239*

Pervasive Software Inc., Peterson, Billie *Page 1-187*

Pixel Magic Imaging, Krell, Lori A. *Page 1-181*

PSW Technologies, Bollineni, Anand K. *Page 1-223*

Public Utility Commission, Lizcano, Olga *Page 1-390*

Retro Studios, Thomas, George A. *Page 1-85*

SAIC, Hackney, Barbie V. *Page 1-357*

SBC Technology Resources, Coursey, Cameron K. *Page 1-357*

Seton Healthcare Network, Robertson, Sarah E. *Page 1-309*

StorageTek, Lyle, Richard *Page 1-46*

SYMTX, Avendano, Igmar E. *Page 1-219*

Synermark, Sherwood, John Anthony *Page 1-159*

Texas Department of Protective & Regulatory Services, Stone, Susan K. *Page 1-343*

Tivoli Systems, Armstrong, Jay *Page 1-194*

Tivoli Systems, McGourty, Felicity F. *Page 1-198*

TNRCC, Paul, Jeanette E. *Page 1-387*

University of Texas at Austin, Charles A. Dana Center, Katz, Heather Alicia *Page 1-326*

VSI, Tse, Simon Lai Yan *Page 1-291*

Borger, Phillips Petroleum Company, Parker, Jeffrey T. *Page 1-27*

Bryan, Texas A&M University, Texas Engineering Extension Services, Chew, Ferdinand T. *Page 1-321*

Burleson, Alcon Laboratories, Pollock, Francisco *Page 1-84*

Carrollton

Cellstar, Registe, Martin P. *Page 1-122*

RIA - Research Institute of America, Brown, Michael W. *Page 1-172*

Verizon Wireless, Cerda, Ken H. *Page 1-92*

Cedar Hill, Clecslov Inc., Jaffery, Qudsia A. *Page 1-250*

Cedar Park, Zilog, Pearson, Kenneth W. *Page 1-67*

College Station, City of College Station, Silhavy, Mark A. *Page 1-374*

Corpus Christi, Education Service Center-2, Wallace, Samuel "Sam" Thomas *Page 1-383*

Dallas

Babcock & Wilcox, Spiegel, Steven M. *Page 1-33*

Bank of America, Schweitzer, Loren M. *Page 1-134*

Call Center Services, Inc., Joseph, Deepu *Page 1-251*

Catalyst Software Evaluation Centers Inc., Joeckel, Tamie *Page 1-179*

Coastal Securities LP, Alsedek, Steven M. *Page 1-147*

Comsys, Barta, Barbie *Page 1-220*

Database Consultants, Inc., Cairns, Joe A. *Page 1-227*

Department of Anthropology, Linder-Linsley, Sue *Page 1-327*

e-technicalsupport.com, Clements, Mark G. *Page 1-231*

eLogo.com Encorporation, Mirau, Michael Glen *Page 1-118*

Fidelity Investments, Stephens, C. Millard *Page 1-161*

InterVoice-Brite, Inc., McElvy, Pam *Page 1-56*

Latent Technology, Sink, Christi L. *Page 1-190*

Linear Technology Corporation, Dinsmore, David L. *Page 1-64*

Media Driver, LLC, Pavlovich, Matthew R. *Page 1-272*

Northrop Grumman, Baez, Ramon F. *Page 1-75*

Pagemart Wireless, Bass, Barbara A. *Page 1-92*

PageNet, Massey, Thomas E. *Page 1-102*

Peerless Manufacturing Company, Rios, Joe Gaudalupe *Page 1-38*

Radio Advertising Bureau, Aldridge, Brad W. *Page 1-165*

Sage Software, Inc., Liddell, William "Keeko" *Page 1-258*

SalesSupport.com, Parker, Kerry *Page 1-186*

Telxon Corporation, Edwards, Tony J. *Page 1-40*

Texas Instruments, Ali, Murtaza *Page 1-63*

Texas Instruments, Lindner, Dale R. *Page 1-66*

Texas Instruments, Spence, Mike *Page 1-67*

Texas Instruments, Udayamurthy, Sekar *Page 1-68*

The Database Group Inc., Marchioli, Marc E. *Page 1-261*

Transamerica Tax Service, Kjelvik, Vickey A. *Page 1-162*

Weblink Wireless, Watts, Dennis H. *Page 1-94*

Denton, Carl Seidel Consulting, Seidel, Carl W. *Page 1-369*

Dike, Comforce Info Tech, Causey, Gary D. *Page 1-167*

El Paso

City of El Paso, Long, Raymond *Page 1-373*

Fisher-Rosemount, Benavides, Rafael *Page 1-81*

Fort Worth

Alcon Laboratories, Johnson, Lucy J. *Page 1-84*

Analysts International, Cole, Michael A. *Page 1-173*

Burlington Northern Santa Fe Railway, Gililland, Michael E. *Page 1-86*

Burlington Northern Santa Fe Railway, Haynes, Lettie K. *Page 1-86*

Morrow Technical Services, Leeds, Hal *Page 1-257*

Frisco

Check Point Software Technology Ltd., Finley, Kenneth W. *Page 1-236*

CommVault System, Wonsang, Willmer B. *Page 1-193*

Garland

Avantel, Thomas, Ivory L. *Page 1-105*

First Horizon Home Loans, Newberry, Del R. *Page 1-141*

Lucent Technologies, Shackelford, Reba *Page 1-62*

Gatesville, Solectron Corporation, Maimbourg, Michael A. *Page 1-43*

Georgetown, Internet Gateway, Inc., Stolle, Keith *Page 1-286*

Harlingen, Keys Academy, Sustaita, Juan H. *Page 1-318*

Houston

Alta Mesa Resources, Thomas, Alexander *Page 1-3*

American Urological Association, Reed, Timothy *Page 1-346*

Applications Solutions, Schifano, Mike *Page 1-280*

BMC Software, Waits, Julian W. *Page 1-200*

Continental Airlines, Knotts, Martha J. *Page 1-89*

DaimlerChrysler Aerospace Orbital Systems Inc., Aguero Blanco, Marjorie *Page 1-170*

De Bellas & Co., Brickley, Douglas J. *Page 1-142*

EDS, Donohoe, B. F. *Page 1-214*

El Paso Energy, Gautreaux, Wayne J. *Page 1-115*

EnterpriseWorks, LLC, Deyhimi, Derrik *Page 1-234*

Equistar Chemicals, LP, LeBeauf, Shelia M. *Page 1-26*

GeoQuest, Vincent, Debbie A. *Page 1-3*

Harris County Department of Education, Harris, Bonnie L. *Page 1-381*

HCL America, Johorey, Ritu *Page 1-251*

Houston Fire Department, Whitt, Mark A. *Page 1-378*

Kellogg Brown & Root, Word, Glenn E. *Page 1-6*

KForce.com, Spell, Bill E. *Page 1-285*

Klein Independent School District, Camp, Barbara Smith *Page 1-381*

Lockard & White, Penney, Ike D. *Page 1-349*

Luminant Worldwide, Hsiung, Tien-hao *Page 1-249*

Micro Revisions Inc., Tomlin, Doyce E. *Page 1-192*

Mission Critical Software, Mychalczuk, Michael G. *Page 1-185*

New Bridge Technology, Allain, Jean-Marc *Page 1-54*

On Source Consulting, Strechay, Robert J. *Page 1-286*

Pro Staff Personnel, Nightingale, Mark J. *Page 1-370*

Radian International Software, Desroches, Dennis *Page 1-174*

Reliant Energy HL&P, Batiste, Joshua *Page 1-115*

Reliant Energy, Chohrach, Michael J. *Page 1-116*

Reliant Energy, Inc., McCrea, Ianthe Helen *Page 1-116*

RHI Consulting, Hudson, Kevin L. *Page 1-249*

SBPA Systems, Inc., Potowski, Christopher J. *Page 1-187*

Schlumberger, Chawla, Inder *Page 1-2*

Schlumberger/GeoQuest, Mikkelsen, Dean C. *Page 1-3*

Senior Geographic Information Systems Trainer, Rediker, Julie A. *Page 1-277*

Sprint Paranet, Jazi, Wassim A. *Page 1-251*

SYSCO Corporation, McCraw, Shirley B. *Page 1-129*

Van Kampen Funds, Glenn, John D. *Page 1-145*

Howe, Excel Communications, Hart, Byron Dean *Page 1-99*

Hughes Springs, Computer Services, Henderson, Melody J. *Page 1-246*

Humble, SMA Inc., Mullen, Frank L. *Page 1-185*

Irving

24/7 University, Inc., Hinkle, Delwin R. *Page 1-301*

Boy Scouts of America, Shamlin, Jim *Page 1-347*

City of Irving, Mayer, John W. *Page 1-373*

Conseco Services LLC, Conover, Cary Donovan *Page 1-300*

D/FW Hospital Council, Scott, Eric H. *Page 1-344*

DeVry Institute of Technology, Landis, Damon L. *Page 1-327*

Federal Express, Hilliard, Marion *Page 1-90*

FT Mortgage Companies, Layne, Theodore J. *Page 1-160*

i2 Technologies, Viswanathan, Narayanan *Page 1-200*

J.L. Communications, Limon, Jeffrey Jessey *Page 1-111*

Marketing Specialists, Schlabs, Heidi *Page 1-146*

NCH Corporation, Jennings, Travis Wayne *Page 1-8*

Nokia Networks, Smith, Rebecca L. *Page 1-62*

Nokia, Inc., Farral, Travis M. *Page 1-55*

Sprint, Rampley, Douglas R. *Page 1-103*

TexSYS RD Corporation, Pagnis, Rishikesh R. *Page 1-271*

Jacksonville, Rise Communications, Inc., Paul, Charles *Page 1-111*

Kilgore, Mansfiled Plumbing Products, Thomas, Taft H. *Page 1-30*

Lewisville

CreMoS Partners, Francis, Ben Allen *Page 1-237*

Inca Metal Products, Parker, Keith A. *Page 1-35*

Lubbock

Hicks & Ragland Engineering Company, Harris, Andrew T. *Page 1-348*

Texas Tech University, Quasny, Todd *Page 1-331*

Lufkin, ENTEX Information Services, Ellisor, Charles E. *Page 1-235*

McAllen

The Wornick Company - Right Away Division, Benavidez, Eduardo D. *Page 1-10*

The Wornick Company, Kamssu, Honore *Page 1-10*

McKinney, Perot Systems, Sandiego, Angelito H. *Page 1-169*

Mesquite, A.C. New Middle School, Derrick, Carol A. *Page 1-315*

Montgomery, Tuttle Maddux Surveying, Daffron, Dean E. *Page 1-352*

Nacogdoches, Moore Business Forms, Nguyen, Duc V. *Page 1-20*

New Braunfels, Auto Gas Systems Inc., Wood, Robert S. *Page 1-211*

Odessa, Medical Center Hospital, Dingman, C. Lewis *Page 1-307*

Pasadena, Internet Ventures, Anderson, Scott K. *Page 1-218*

Pearland, PharMerica, Daugherty, J. Max *Page 1-130*

Plano

Alcatel USA, McIntosh, Clarissa R. *Page 1-102*

Alcatel USA, Reynolds, Teresa G. *Page 1-104*

Alcatel USA, Wancio, Charlie *Page 1-106*

Electronic Data Systems, Buhler, Wesley Dwayne *Page 1-214*

Ericsson, Gardner, Jeffrey L. *Page 1-59*

Legacy Bank of Texas, Rinker, Ricky Lee *Page 1-141*

Nextlink, Kantaria, Jay K. *Page 1-100*

Premier Consultancy, Mullapudi, Ramarao *Page 1-266*

Richardson

ACT Teleconferencing, Inc., Wheeler, Revell *Page 1-63*

Applied Materials, Ensor, Bettina Rice *Page 1-65*

MCI Corporation, Fee, John A. *Page 1-70*

Nortel Networks, Bunt, Christopher Allen *Page 1-55*

Premier Systems Integrators, Norwood, Kevin W. *Page 1-208*

Richardson Independent School District, Yarrow, John R. *Page 1-319*

Texas Micro Computers, Gagan, Shakil Sattar *Page 1-239*

Round Rock

DuPont Photomasks, Inc., Cochran, John A. *Page 1-64*

Netpliance, Inc., Zhao, Wei *Page 1-298*

San Antonio

    Database Consultants, Inc., Lear, Gregory L. *Page 1-256*

    Datapoint Corporation, Abercrombie, Richard D. *Page 1-170*

    DEISSC2, Espinoza, Dimas *Page 1-392*

    HQ CPSG/LGLP, Favaro, Norma Wheatley *Page 1-393*

    Kinetic Concepts, Inc., Wisloff, Tomm *Page 1-13*

    Symbiont Inc., Boostrom, Ron A. *Page 1-223*

Sante Fe, BP Amoco, Jackson, Anna L. *Page 1-2*

Southlake, Sun Microsystems, Inc., Rosado, Luis E. *Page 1-44*

Spring, NeighborNet, Haskell, Larry R. *Page 1-246*

Sugar Land, El Paso Energy Corporation, Llagostera, Domingo *Page 1-115*

Taylor, IBM Server Development Group, Naivar, DeVonna R. *Page 1-267*

The Colony, EDS, Vinson, Kevin J. *Page 1-215*

The Woodlands

    Telxon Corporation, Sachs, Steven W. *Page 1-44*

    Telxon Corporation, Skomra, Stewart A. *Page 1-45*

    Weatherford International Inc., Fry, Susan F. *Page 1-3*

Tyler, Christian Educational Ministries, Harris, Donna L. *Page 1-341*

Van Alstyne, Raytheon/TI Systems Company, Wilkins, Jackie D. *Page 1-81*

Waco

    Ahlers & Associates, French, Cynthia *Page 1-176*

    Texas State Technical College, Beaver, Jake *Page 1-335*

Waxahachie, David Collins, Collins, W. David *Page 1-231*

Webster, Solution Bank, Broughton, Jeff R. *Page 1-225*

Westlake, Levi Strauss & Co., White, Allen *Page 1-12*

Wharton, Wharton County Junior College, Jacobs, Vicki S. *Page 1-326*

Willis, Sam Houston State University, Robbins, Robert Randall *Page 1-331*

Winnsboro, Randy's Professional Web Site Design, Parrish, Richard R. *Page 1 – 186*

Utah

Clearfield, Garden Burger, Greenbank, Martin P. *Page 1-8*

Draper

    Cambric Corporation, Tester, Malcolm W. *Page 1-289*

    TenFold Corporaotin, Chapman, David R. *Page 1-229*

Kaysville, Iomega Corporation, Hatch, Robert Duane *Page 1-48*

Logan

    Equitable Tax Service, Moosman, Elizabeth D. *Page 1-163*

    Integrated Systems Engineering, Cox, Dale *Page 1-85*

Odgen, MarkeStar, Hafen, Lynn R. *Page 1-163*

Ogden, Net Designs and Creations, Inc., Pulsipher, Steven *Page 1-275*

Salt Lake City

    Bonneville International Corporation, Braithwaite, Wayne N. *Page 1-107*

    Checkfast, Blaylock, William A. *Page 1-138*

    EURO RSCG DSW Partners, White, Kevin D. *Page 1-165*

    Netessence, Joerg, Werner B. *Page 1-180*

    West Valley City, Pastorik, Stephen L. *Page 1-373*

    WFSATC, Yang, Lily H. *Page 1-340*

Sandy, Crossman Post Production, Crossman, John Neal *Page 1-304*

Toole, EG&G Defense Materials, Warrington, William "Sandy" E. *Page 1-117*

Vermont

Burlington, University of Vermont, Xue, Guoliang *Page 1-334*

Colchester, Engelberth Construction, Russell, Christopher P. *Page 1-4*

Essex Junction, IBM Corporation, Wolf, Randy L. *Page 1-46*

Virginia

Alexandria

    AB Floyd, Inc., Morse, Jeffery G. *Page 1-266*

    Andersen Consulting, Paladino, Chris D. *Page 1-365*

    Automation Research Systems, Limited, Beebe, David H. *Page 1-171*

    Base Technologies, Inc., Allen, Carol Elizabeth *Page 1-217*

    Computer Curriculum Corporation, Ernst, Kelli A. *Page 1-203*

    DynCorp, Barkin, Ruth Ann *Page 1-356*

    J&E Technology, Inc., Huffman, James E. *Page 1-249*

    Lotus Development Corporation, Dodge, Jon *Page 1-174*

    Radian Inc., Halaut, Jeffrey D. *Page 1-178*

Arlington

    Aera Inc., Geragas, Dimitris A. *Page 1-240*

    BBN Technologies, Hubbell, James B. *Page 1-249*

    Catalyst 2020, Ciabatoni, Linda *Page 1-361*

    Defense Information Systems Agency, Department of Defense, Leonelli, John A. *Page 1-394*

    Department of Defense Inspector General, Forte, Andrew L. *Page 1-393*

    Houston Associates, Munshi, Darius J. *Page 1-111*

    Space & Naval Warfare Systems Command, Trachtenberg, Charlene C. *Page 1-396*

    USDA Forest Service, HMR, Berry, James C. *Page 1-388*

Ashburn

    Equinix, Pease, Michael A. *Page 1-111*

    UUNET, Remuzzi, Joy *Page 1-213*

Blacksburg

    Anderson and Associate's, Inc., Caldwell, Shawn Edward *Page 1-348*

    Virginia Tech Computing Center, Marchany, Randy C. *Page 1-338*

Chantilly

    Digital Access Control, Donoghue, Matthew T. *Page 1-234*

    Ernst & Young LLP, Pritchett, Stephanie A. *Page 1-355*

    Ernst & Young Technologies, Inc., Hardaway, Ivan B. *Page 1-353*

    Newbridge Networks, Quinn, James J. *Page 1-49*

    TASC, Inc., Newsome, Teresa M. *Page 1-207*

    USI, Elaprolu, Srikanth *Page 1-174*

Charlottesville, Lexis Publishing, Londeree, Vicki Neal *Page 1-18*

Chesapeake

    Stratum New Media, Lasky, Tami M. *Page 1-182*

    Sumitomo Machinery Corporation of America, Perkins, Brian J. *Page 1-38*

Chester, AlliedSignal, Harvell, J. Larry *Page 1-27*

Chincoteague Island, NASA's Sounding Rocket Operations Contract, Crockett, Kimberly L. *Page 1-78*

Crystal City, Computer Sciences Corporation, Long, Barbara Anne *Page 1-206*

Dahlgren, Planning Consultants, Inc., Brooks, Jeffrey A. *Page 1-225*

Danville, Dan River, Inc., Sutherland, Stephanie K. *Page 1-11*

Dulles, CEXEC, Inc., Tuttle, Peter G. *Page 1-292*

Elkton, Merck & Co., Inc., Hockman, James E. *Page 1-23*

Fairfax

    BRTRC, Harte, Rebecca E. *Page 1-213*

    CBSI - Computer Based Systems, Inc., An AverStar Company, LaGrange, Palmer V. *Page 1-181*

    Coleman Research Corporation, Hibbs, Paul A. *Page 1-247*

    Compath Inc., McCray, Marc S. *Page 1-302*

    Edge Technologies, Inc., Cook, Charlie D. *Page 1-232*

    PricewaterhouseCoopers, Lyle, Stephen T. *Page 1-354*

    Sunrise Assisted Living, Callo, Fernando A. *Page 1-343*

Truestar, Inc., Karaburk, Hasan *Page 1-253*

Falls Church

HNA Consulting, Inc., Han, Brent M. *Page 1-245*

MPR Associates, Inc., Fink, Robert T. *Page 1-348*

Source Net Inc, Strickland, Thomas K. *Page 1-286*

Winstar, O'Keefe, Curtis W. *Page 1-93*

Floyd, Floyd Public Schools, Slusher, Donna E. *Page 1-318*

Fredericksburg, Rappahannock Regional Jail, Bailey, Brian A. *Page 1-377*

Glen Allen, Maxim Group, Buker, William H. *Page 1-227*

Hampton

Computer Sciences Corporation, Moxley, Greg D. *Page 1-207*

Howmet Corporation, Vitelli, Joseph D. *Page 1-32*

PROSOFT, Baker, Melvin *Page 1-201*

Harrisonburg, Eastern Mennonite University, Tyler, Rebecca Ann *Page 1-333*

Herndon

EDS, Anderson, Fred R. *Page 1-214*

Independent, Phenicie, Robert L. Jr. *Page 1-208*

Intelligence Architects LLC, Brunelle, Francois *Page 1-226*

Logicon, Inc., Holland, Paul R. *Page 1-77*

National Rural Telecommunications Cooperative, Gibbons, Jim *Page 1-98*

Novell, Inc., Landrigan, Shawn B. *Page 1-197*

PSINet, Weaver, Demian K. *Page 1-294*

King George

SAIC, Staples, Karen R. *Page 1-359*

Virginia Department of Transportation, Michaelsen, Nancy L. *Page 1-390*

Lanexa, Anheuser-Busch, Inc., O'Donnell, Shaun I. *Page 1-9*

Langley Air Force Base

480 Intelligence Group, LaFata, Steve F. *Page 1-394*

United States Air Force, Fileger, Mark E. *Page 1-393*

McLean

Base Technologies, Inc., Hashmi, Kashif R. *Page 1-246*

Covad Communications, Olexa, Christopher M. *Page 1-270*

KPMG Consulting, Keating, Francesca F. *Page 1-364*

Main Control, Inc., Harris, Wesley G. *Page 1-245*

Mbh Settlement Group, Reichert, Eric D. *Page 1-313*

McDonald Bradley, Warmsley, Byron Nigel *Page 1-294*

SAIC, Wick, John A. *Page 1-359*

SMS Data Products Group, Inc., Lemmon, Jeremy R. *Page 1-257*

Merrifield, United States Postal Service, Callaway, Lawrence A. *Page 1-88*

Newport News

e-Marketworld.com, Allen, Tommy L. *Page 1-299*

United States Air Force, Headquarters Air Combat Command, Severin, William F. *Page 1-395*

Norfolk, Fleet & Industrial Supply Center, Dunston, Corlis Yvette *Page 1-91*

Orange, IBM Corporation, Hoey, Brent M. *Page 1-41*

Pearisburg, G&L Enterprises, O'Brien, Greg *Page 1-164*

Reston

Andersen Consulting LLP, Sherlock, Jason E. *Page 1-366*

Comsearch, Mills, Dennis Joseph *Page 1-61*

Concert, Abramczyk, Edward S. *Page 1-95*

Integrated Chipware, Anderson, Michael E. *Page 1-171*

Noblestar Systems, Gautney, Charles W. *Page 1-240*

Sprint, Catalone, Gregory S. *Page 1-96*

Telenor, Inc., Schafft, Soren *Page 1-104*

The Stock Market Reference Desk, McDowell, Haywood *Page 1-183*

Richmond

Ajilon, Rowe, Richard Carl *Page 1-278*

Commonwealth of Virginia - Department of Information Technology, Hunter, Alvin A. *Page 1-372*

CSC, Noble, Amanda *Page 1-208*

Solutions By Design, Hall, Rodney D. *Page 1-245*

Southern Trust Mortgage, Lufkin, Keith S. *Page 1-141*

Virginia Housing Development Authority, Dumeer, Wesley A. *Page 1-388*

Roanoke, Frith Anderson & Peake, PC, Jackson, Britt L. *Page 1-312*

Salem, Craig County Public Schools, Morris, Adele G. *Page 1-382*

Springfield, United States Department of State, Williams, Iris D. *Page 1-397*

Stanardsville, Louis T. De Stefano, Inc., De Stefano, Louis T. *Page 1-298*

Sterling

America Online Inc., Harmon, Margaret *Page 1-110*

Computer Sciences Corporation, Matsumoto, T. Steve *Page 1-207*

HSI Geotrans, Inc., Barr, Robert T. *Page 1-368*

Orbcomm, Brickerd, D. Dean *Page 1-96*

Orbital Sciences Corporation, Timberlake, Frank "Rusty" *Page 1-79*

Royal Cabinet of Saudi Arabia, Almogbel, Saud A. *Page 1-370*

Suffolk, Virginia Department of Transportation, Klass, Connie H. *Page 1-390*

Vienna

Campania Management Company Inc., Santoli, Nicolas *Page 1-156*

Cap Gemini America, Seetharam, Palachandra *Page 1-282*

IMI Systems, Inc., Dashiell, John L. *Page 1-232*

Megasoft Consultants, Sathya, Ravi *Page 1-279*

Perspective Technology Corporation, Gillette, Kimberly S. *Page 1-241*

Trident Data Systems, Lang, David Thomas *Page 1-255*

Virginia Beach

City of Virginia Beach Department of Public Utilities, Barton, Robert J. *Page 1-390*

Electronic Systems, Inc., Hix, Darrell R. *Page 1-204*

Warrenton

Fauquier Hospital, Bishop, Briget R. *Page 1-307*

UUNET Technologies, Reed, Jeff L. *Page 1-213*

Winchester

FEMA, Fox, Shelby Ross *Page 1-378*

United States Army Corps of Engineers, Orndoff, Steven S. *Page 1-395*

Washington

Auburn, Labor Ready, Inc., Garverick, Arthur E. *Page 1-48*

Bellevue

Adecco at Boeing, Coffman, Gayle *Page 1-368*

Attachmate Corporation, Marshall, Don H. *Page 1-197*

Attachmate Corporation, Michael, Laura Anne *Page 1-198*

Havas Interactive, Inc., Gauvin, Lorraine Leandra *Page 1-176*

Lante Corporation, Wanagel, Jonathan *Page 1-294*

Netstock Direct Corporation, Johnsen, Melissa C. *Page 1-110*

Power Data Corporation, Robinson, Marck R. *Page 1-188*

Bothell, ATL Ultrasound, Fink, Dean R. *Page 1-84*

Bremerton

Attachmate Corporation, Brumley, Isaac *Page 1-195*

Puget Sound Naval Shipyard, King, Keith A. *Page 1-78*

Edmonds, JWR Systems, Renard, James A. *Page 1-187*

Everett, Intermec, Dean, Steve *Page 1-233*

Federal Way

Bacik Consulting Service, Bacik, Sandra A. *Page 1-219*

Weyerhaeuser Company, Murray, Lee *Page 1-12*

Kennewick, SutterTel.Com, Sutter, Rick *Page 1-128*

Mount Vernon, City of Mount Vernon, Kleppe, Kim A. *Page 1-373*

Nine Mile Falls, Premera Blue Cross, Tolman, R. Brent *Page 1-151*

Olympia, State of Washington, Department of Social and Health Services, Asbach, Gordon J. *Page 1-384*

Port Townsend, Alaska Power & Telephone Company, Paddock, Janet *Page 1-103*

Redmond

AT&T Wireless Services, Gregory, Peter H. *Page 1-92*

Eddie Bauer, Inc., Glenn, Terry M. *Page 1-131*

Microsoft Corporation, Defiesta, Clarence B. *Page 1-195*

Safeco Life Insurance, Richards, Sharon L. *Page 1-149*

Renton

Deloitte Consulting, Ingersoll, Carrie D. *Page 1-364*

Sunnyside Community Hospital, Wilson, Joe M. *Page 1-310*

Richland, TRUTech, L.L.C., Green, N. Wayne *Page 1-243*

Seattle

Access, Rawsthorne, Daniel A. *Page 1-187*

Alaska Airlines, Buchner, Pamela J. *Page 1-89*

Amazon.com, Simonsen, Peter *Page 1-131*

Carlyle, Inc., Guyton, Thomas C. *Page 1-178*

Control Contractors, Inc., Snyder, Larry *Page 1-86*

Fred Hutchinson Cancer Research Center, Aprile, Joseph A. *Page 1-356*

Key Staff, Russell, Lisa S. *Page 1-169*

Seattle Center, Bukis, Deborah Elizabeth *Page 1-305*

Telxon Corporation, Ellis, Allan D. *Page 1-40*

The Boeing Company, Bahrami, Ali *Page 1-75*

The Boeing Company, Dalton, Robin S. *Page 1-75*

ZoneNetwork.com, Wright, Rik *Page 1-297*

Zydeco.com, Smith, Jake *Page 1-133*

Spokane

Inland Northwest Health Services, Chugg, Ginger M. *Page 1-152*

Peirone Produce, Sill, Gary L. *Page 1-125*

TerraComm, Inc., Dossett, Robert W. *Page 1-212*

Tacoma, Washington Army National Guard, Smith, Timothy R. *Page 1-396*

Vancouver

Hewlett-Packard Company, Rose, Linda L. *Page 1-44*

Vanalco, Inc., Hart, Ryan L. *Page 1-32*

Yakima, Irwin Research and Development, Curry, Gary *Page 1-29*

West Virginia

Fairmont

J.C. Solutions, LLC, Parrish, Brian P. *Page 1-186*

T&T Pump Company, Inc., Fleming, James C. *Page 1-37*

Hurricane, In Controls Inc., Reyntjens, Bruno R. F. *Page 1-52*

Martinsburg, Veterans Administration Medical Center, Huffman, Robert N. *Page 1-386*

Mineral Wells, Coldwater Creek, Adkins, Jeffrey M. *Page 1-130*

Morgantown, Clinical Pharmacologic Research Communications, Renner, Amy *Page 1-49*

Parkersburg, United States Treasury, Bureau of Public Debt, Haught, Jason F. *Page 1-379*

Wisconsin

Appleton, City of Appleton, Liske, Scott J. *Page 1-373*

Ashland, Independent, Nelson, Joyce E. *Page 1-338*

Beaver Dam, MicroGo'L, Levenhagen, Dennis G. *Page 1-258*

Fond du Lac, CCW, Lechner, Suzanne L. *Page 1-182*

Green Bay, St. Mary Hospital Medical Center, Dauplaise, Mike *Page 1-307*

Greenfield, L.T.G. Technologies, Inc., Highland, Franklin J. *Page 1-38*

Kenosha, Right Connection, Inc., Lynt, William W. *Page 1-259*

La Crosse, Enhanced Ideas, Anderson, Gwyn C. *Page 1-217*

Madison

Alliant Energy, Bouwma, Michael *Page 1-113*

American Family Insurance Company, Boland, Dennis G. *Page 1-149*

American Family Insurance, Rolfsmeyer, Kenneth T. *Page 1-151*

Family Health Systems, Meier, Debora L. *Page 1-153*

Micro Technix, Simousek, Michael G. *Page 1-216*

Promega, Ruffin, Jimmy *Page 1-358*

Sonic Foundry, Inc., Gates, Dramise D. *Page 1-176*

State of Wisconsin, Department of Administration, Endres, Joyce E. *Page 1-375*

The Charlton Group, Powers, Michael J. *Page 1-302*

University of Wisconsin at Madison, Hooker, P. Kent *Page 1-325*

Menomonee Falls, Duni Corporation, Schoenung, Karen *Page 1-70*

Menomonie, West Wisconsin Telecom Cooperative, Inc., Berg, Linda M. *Page 1-95*

Middletown, System Request Consultants, Ramczyk, Amie J. *Page 1-276*

Milwaukee

American Society for Quality, Duncan, Phillip L. *Page 1-345*

Bank of New York Clearing Services, Schultz, David A. *Page 1-147*

Chr. Hansen, Inc., Wahn, Norman A. *Page 1-10*

Eaton Corporation, Anderson, Randy *Page 1-356*

Information Systems Professionals, Litwin, Ryan P. *Page 1-259*

Kahler Slater Architects, Block, Jeffrey Allen *Page 1-350*

Mortgage Guaranty Insurance Corporation, Dzhidzhora, Karen Ann Estelle *Page 1-156*

Reinhart, Boerner, et al, Bolyard, Whitney L. *Page 1-311*

Racine

Bosch Automation Technology, Schultz, Cynthia L. *Page 1-74*

Case Corporation, Misirian, Nathan J. *Page 1-35*

E.C. Styberg Engineering Company, Muehlius, David A. *Page 1-74*

RTC Technologies, Inc., Seney, Thomas R. *Page 1-189*

Sheboygan, Lake Land College, Klatkiewicz, Gail D. *Page 1-337*

Sun Prairie, Freedom Plastics, Olson, Rob A. *Page 1-29*

Verona, Cooperative Resources International, Pinkall-Pollei, Richard G. *Page 1-302*

Wyoming

Cheyenne, RSM McGladrey, Inc., Cassat, Daniel M. *Page 1-352*

Laramie

City of Laramie, Hardgrove, Nicholas R. *Page 1-372*

Laramie High School, Bayne, Chuck *Page 1-314*

University of Wyoming, Department of Space and Data & Visualization Center, Parrill, Scott M. *Page 1-330*

Non-Members Arranged
Alphabetically
by
Last Name

Section 5

Mr. Hend Abbed: FMC; 3022 Golf Terrace; Danville, IL 61832

Mr. Julian R. Abbott Jr.: Anderson School District 5; 1020 Jody Drive; Seneca, SC 29678-1004

Ms. Kristi Abbott: American United Life; P.O. Box 368; Indianapolis, IN 46206-0368

Mr. Raghunath Abburi: JD Edwards & Co.; 32427 Glen Cove; Farmington Hills, MI 48334-3612

Mr. Aiman A. Abdel-Malek: General Electric; 2901 East Lake Road, 9-315; Erie, PA 16531

Mr. Bryan Abel: Cinergy; 603 South East Street; Plainfield, IN 46168-1413

Mr. Alfred Aboulsaad: Warner Music Group; 414 East Cedar Avenue, Apartment 22; Burbank, CA 91501-2799

Mr. Jose Abraham: Computer Associate, Inc.; 6650 West Snowville Road; Brecksville, OH 44141

Ms. Doretha H. Abrams: AT&T Alascom; 210 East Bluff Drive, TC 230; Anchorage, AK 99501

Mr. John Abrams: McDonald's Corporation; 1 McDonalds Drive, 2nd Floor; Hinsdale, IL 60523-1900

Mr. Luis Abrego: Yucaipa Valley Water District; 12770 2nd Street, #730; Yucaipa, CA 92399-5670

Mr. Preeti Acharya: PTC International; 401 East Pratt Street; Baltimore, MD 21202-3117

Ms. Dawn Ackerman: Infoseek; 1399 Moffett Park Drive; Sunnyvale, CA 94089-1134

Ms. Debora M. Ackerman: Main Resource, Inc.; 74 Evergreen Drive; Portland, ME 04103-1066

Mr. Emmanuel Ackerman: Depository Trust & Clearance Company; 55 Water Street, Floor 23; New York, NY 10041-0098

Mr. Erik N. Ackerman: Lexmark International Inc.; 740 West New Circle Road; Lexington, KY 40550-0001

Mr. Mike Ackerman: Lextron Micro Tech; P.O. Box 1057; Greeley, CO 80632-1057

Ms. Elena Adames: Lockheed Martin; 12506 Lake Underhill Road; Orlando, FL 32825-5011

Mr. Allan Adams: Norwest Card Services; 2135 2100th Street; Manilla, IA 51454

Ms. Elsa Adams: AlliedSignal; 13819 South 33rd Street; Phoenix, AZ 85044-3649

Mr. Michael Adams: Louisville Science Center; 727 West Main Street; Louisville, KY 40202-2681

Ms. Sherry L. Adams: Texas Department of Public Safety; P.O. Box 4087; Austin, TX 78773

Mr. David Aden: Webworld Studies, Inc.; 898 North Lexington Street; Arlington, VA 22205

Mr. Timothy Adkins: Roadrunner Communications, Inc.; 12530 Iron Bridge Road, Suite G; Chester, VA 23831-1599

Dr. Marty Aduckes Ph.D.: Symbol Technologies, Inc.; 401 Hackensack Avenue; Hackensack, NJ 07601

Dr. Payman Afshari Ph.D.: Key Plastics, LLC; 21333 Haggerty Road; Novi, MI 48104

Mr. Nitin Agarwal: ABR Products, Inc.; 2 Tamarack Circle; Fishkill, NY 12524-2642

Mrs. Smita Agarwal: Ace Computers; 2707 Livingstone Lane; Vienna, VA 22180-7258

Mr. Joseph P. Agius: Sybase, Inc.; 561 Virginia Road; Concord, MA 01742-2732

Mr. Frank Agnello: Abacon Telecommunications; 4388 Federal Drive; Greensboro, NC 27410-8115

Mr. J. Robert Agno: APPNET; 650 Avis Drive, Suite 100; Ann Arbor, MI 48108-9649

Mr. Mark A. Aguilera: Genisys Consulting; 5209 South Kenneth; Chicago, IL 60632

Mr. Jerry Aguren: Compaq; 16115 Castlegrove Court; Tomball, TX 77375-8521

Mr. Charlie Agwumezie: Ubix Systems Technologies; 5402 Queens Chapel Road; Hyattsville, MD 20782-3901

Mr. Jalil U. Ahmad: Joher Consulting; 999 Via Colinas; Westlake Village, CA 91362-5051

Mr. Syed Suhail Ahmad: Oracle Corporation; 3242 Players Club Circle; Memphis, TN 38125

Mr. Syed Ahmad: NAVIS L.L.C.; 3954 Northumberland Terrace; Fremont, CA 94555-2264

Mr. Anis Ahmed: Aces; 4444 Memorial Dive, Apartment 2; Houston, TX 77007-7375

Mr. Farrukh Ahmed: GE Corporate; 3135 Easton Turnpike, #W21; Fairfield, CT 06431-0002

Mr. Watanabe Akira: Japan Aircraft Manufacturing Company, Ltd.; Showa-Cho 3175; Kanazawa-Ku, Japan 236-0001

Mr. Oktay Aksoy: Turkish Embassy; Dag Hammarskjolds Vag 20; Stockholm, Sweden 115 27

Mr. Abdullah M. Al-Harbi: Saudi Arabian Airlines; CC 990 P.O. Box 167; Jeddah, Saudi Arabia 21231

Dr. Muhammad Ali Al-Tayyeb: Saudi Aramco; P.O. Box 12240; Dhahran, Saudi Arabia 31311

Mr. Nazmin Alani: Rendall and Associates; 5000 Falls of Neuse Road, Suite 304; Raleigh, NC 27609-5480

Mr. Mohamad Albadawi: Harlan Corporation; P.O. Box 15159; Kansas City, KS 66115-0159

Dr. Alan Albarran Ph.D.: Southern Methodist University; P.O. Box 750113; Dallas, TX 75275-0113

Ms. Maria Albers: Industria Venoco; P.O. Box 025632, Vallendox #CV003; Miami, FL 33102-5632

Mr. David Albert: FSI International; 600 Millennium Drive; Allen, TX 75013

Mr. Fritz Albrecht: ARA Kunst Dr. Fritz Albrecht; Altrandsbert; Miltach, Germany 93468

Mr. Gerry S. Albright: Albright Ideas, Inc.; 4031 Pumice Lane; Eagan, MN 55122

Ms. Connie Alcala: Stanislaus County; P.O. Box 3322; Modesto, CA 95353-3322

Mr. Hector Aldaz: Saic; 45061 Fellowship Square; Ashburn, VA 20147-2737

Mr. Michael Alden: MCI World Com; 6312 South Fiddlers Green Circle, Suite 6; Englewood, CO 80111-4943

Mr. D. Alderdice: Lafayette High School; 370 Lafayette Avenue; Buffalo, NY 14213-1494

Ms. Ann Aldinger: WPI, Inc.; 1001 G Street NW, Suite 300; Washington, DC 20001-4545

Mr. Jason Aldrich: Iocologo.com, inc.; 3312 Piedmont Road NE, Suite 405; Atlanta, GA 30305-1714

Ms. Karen Aldridge: Mississippi State Department of Health; 2423 North State Street, #1700; Jackson, MS 39216-4504

Mr. Richard Alercia: Eds; 2 Crystal Hill; Fairport, NY 14450-4111

Mr. Carlos Alexandre: Oliff and Berridge, P.L.C.; 277 South Washington Street, Suite 500; Alexandria, VA 22314-3646

Mr. Mohammed Ali: Oracle Corporation; 9801 Meadowglen Lane, Apartment 190; Houston, TX 77042-4432

Dr. Walid Y. Ali-Ahmad Ph.D.: Maxim Integrated Products; 120 San Gabriel Drive; Sunnyvale, CA 94086-5150

Mr. Bala Alla: Metabasis Thermputics, Inc.; 9390 Towne Centre Drive; San Diego, CA 92121-3015

Ms. Sharon Allan: ABB; 1412 Shadowview Court; Raleigh, NC 27614

Mr. Brian R. Allen Jr.: Marshall & Williams Company; 46 Baker Street; Providence, RI 02905-4417

Ms. Donna Allen: Womens Care; 1450 West Granada Boulevard; Ormond Beach, FL 32174-9141

Mr. Grant R. Allen: Ernst & Young LLP; 9009 Norwick Road; Richmond, VA 23229-7758

Mr. Jack Allen: California ISO; P.O. Box 639014; Folsom, CA 95763-9014

Ms. Jacqueline J. Allen: Alltel Information Services; One Alltel Center, 13560 Morris Road; Alpharetta, GA 30091622

Ms. Leslie Frank Allen: Westinghouse Anniston; 1415 Laydens Mill Road; Jacksonville, AL 36201

Mr. Michael D. Allen: Burns & McDonnell; P.O. Box 419173; Kansas City, MO 64141-6173

Mr. Mitchell Allen: Warren Electric Group; 2929 McKinney Street; Houston, TX 77003-3823

Ms. Vicki C. Allen: Food Lion, Inc.; P.O. Box 1330; Salisbury, NC 28145-1330

Mr. Sergio Almada: Data General; 1650 Sioux Drive, Suite 44305; El Paso, TX 79925

Ms. Annie Almasi: Fortis Health; 501 West Michigan Street; Milwaukee, WI 53203-2706

Mr. Malik M. Altaf: Siemens; 2202 Silver Spur; Round Rock, TX 78681-7438

Ms. Lucille Altidor: Miami Dade Aviation Department; P.O. Box 592075; Miami, FL 33159-2075

Mr. Oscar Alvarado: Southwest Independent School District; 11914 Dragon Lane; San Antonio, TX 78252-2647

Mr. Oscar E. Alvarez Jr.: Earthlink; 3100 New York Drive; Pasadena, CA 91016

Mr. Greg Alvey: Unified Food Service Purchasing Corporation; 950 Breckenridge Lane; Louisville, KY 40207

Mr. Lubna N. Alvi: United States Committee for Refugees; 1717 Massachusetts Avenue NW, Suite 200; Washington, DC 20036

Mr. Wilker Ambooken: Computer Enterprises, Inc.; 216 Chatham Park Drive, Apartment TB; Pittsburgh, PA 15220-2107

Ms. Dani Ambrose: Acton Burnell, Inc.; 1500 North Beauregard, Suite 210; Alexandria, VA 22311

Mr. Jason Amick: Eakes Office Plus; 2401 Avenue A; Kearney, NE 68847-5498

Mr. Michael Amoroso: US WEB, Corp.; 733 3rd Avenue; New York, NY 10017

Mr. Roberto Amoroso: Southern Florida Water Management District; 3301 Gun Club Road; West Palm Beach, FL 33406-3089

Mr. G. Scott Amos: Grinnell Fire Protection System; 835 Sharon Drive; Westlake, OH 44145

Mr. Med Amr: CSC; 2000 East Imperial Highway; El Segundo, CA 90245-3571

Mr. Joe Amsdill: County of Niagara; 59 Park Avenue; Lockport, NY 14094-2758

Mr. Russell Ji Amundsen: MML Software; 45 Research Way, Suite 207; East Setauket, NY 11733-6401

Mr. Senthil Subbanan Anand: Krijal Softek, Inc.; 3644 White Eagle Drive; Naperville, IL 60564

Mr. Shivprasad Anantram: Edison; 2456 Corte Merlango; San Clemente, CA 92673-3618

Mr. Joseph Anastasio: Depository Trust Company; 55 Water Street, 20th Floor; New York, NY 10041-0098

Ms. Jeanette Anders: Cyracom International, Inc.; 7332 North Oracle Road; Tucson, AZ 85704-6305

Mr. Craig Anderson: Grant Thornton; 2 East Gilman Street; Madison, WI 53703-1497

Mr. David Anderson: M Corp; 10 Parsonage Road; Edison, NJ 08837-2429

Mr. Harry Anderson: Andex Executive Search; 101 River Street; Milford, CT 06460

Mr. Jeff Anderson: University of Alabama, Academic Computing & Technology; 901 13th Street South, EB 149; Birmingham, AL 35294-1250

Ms. Pamela Anderson: Polk Community College; 200 Avenue K SE; Winter Haven, FL 33880-7002

Mr. R. C. Anderson: Department of Information Technology; 110 South 7th Street; Richmond, VA 23219

Mr. Richard Anderson: Fleet Financial Group; P.O. Box 5080; Hartford, CT 06102-5080

Mr. Ross Anderson: U.S. District Court; 601 West Broadway; Louisville, KY 40202

Ms. Sherrie Anderson: Cache Mortgage Corporation; 167 East 6100 South, Suite 100; Murray, UT 84107-7260

Mr. Steve Anderson: Jones Financial Company, Ltd.; 201 Progress Parkway; Maryland Heights, MO 63043-3003

Ms. Saundra Andre: Inter-Tel Technologies; 3641 Ridge Mill Drive; Hilliard, OH 43026

Mr. Dave Andrews: University of Central Florida; Physical Plant, 4000 Central Florida Boulevard; Orlando, FL 32816-3600

Mr. Ed Andrews: Crosswinds Communities; 41050 Vincenti Court; Novi, MI 48375-1921

Mr. Jacob Andrews: Mobius Group; One Sansome, Suite 2100; San Francisco, CA 94104-4448

Mr. John Andrews: Elementis Pigments; 2001 Lynch Avenue; East St. Louis, IL 62204-1717

Mr. Paul Andrews: BG Transco; 31 Homer Road; Solihull, England, United Kingdom B91 3LT

Mr. Richard Andrews: Software Technologies Corporation; 404 East Huntington Drive; Monrovia, CA 91016-3633

Ms. Sherry Andrews: Medical College of Ohio; 3000 Arlington Avenue; Toledo, OH 4361402595

Mr. Wilburn E. Andrews Jr.: U.S. OPM; 4685 Log Cabin Drive; Macon, GA 31204-6317

Mr. Arnold Angel: Renaissance Worldwide Inc.; 4001 Weston Parkway; Cary, NC 27513

Mr. Luke Angelis: Microsoft; 14205 Ash Way; Lynwood, WA 98037

Mr. Joe Angerson : 1101 North Washington Street; Wilkes Barre, PA 18705-1817

Mr. Alfred F. Anzalone: Bank Boston; 81 West Main Street; Waterbury, CT 06702-2000

Mr. Vincent Anzelone: Integrated Partnerships; 8725 West Higgins Road; Chicago, IL 60631

Ms. Rosemary Appleton: United Interactive Technology; 11336 Wiles Road; Coral Springs, FL 33076-2114

Mr. Bill A. Aquino: California State 9 Credit Union; 2300 Clayton Road, Suite 220; Concord, CA 94520

Ms. Marie E. Aragon: General Services Department, Client Services Support Bureau; 715 Alta Vista Street, P.O. Box 26110; Santa Fe, NM 87502

Mr. Haji R. Aref: PPC; 2006 West Genesee Street; Syracuse, NY 13219-1683

Mr. Kev R. Arends: Lee Enterprises, Inc.; 63349 Saddleback Drive; Bend, OR 97701

Dr. Nabil Arman Ph.D.: XPAND Corporation; 2251 Pimmit Drive, No. 526; Falls Church, VA 22043

Mr. James M. Armitage: ZTECH Associates, Inc.; 22 Chester Road; Boxboro, MA 01719

Mr. Marvin W. Armstrong: Future Media Productions, Inc.; 25136 Anza Drive; Valencia, CA 91355

Mr. Tracy R. Armstrong: Sprint Corporation; 1604 Springhill Road; Vienna, VA 22182

Ms. Kelly Arndt: New Horizons Computer Learning; 14115 Farmington Road; Livonia, MI 48154-5457

Mr. Brian Arneson: US West; 600 Stinson Boulevard NE, Suite 3N; Minneapolis, MN 55413-2620

Mr. Dan Arnold: Absolute Quality; 10720 Gilroy Road; Hunt Valley, MD 21031-8207

Ms. Terry Lynn Arnold: T-n-J Computer Services; 107 Sharon Circle; Columbia, TN 38401

Mr. William L. Arnold: Diebold Inc.; 2283 South Von Braun Court; Harvey, LA 70058-3018

Ms. Jasmin Aronce: Decision Consultants Inc.; 3453 Northwest 44th Street, #6; Fort Lauderdale, FL 33309-4267

Mr. Nitu Arora: Sprint PCS; 4900 Main Street; Kansas City, MO 64112

Ms. Sheri Arrants: Novus Services; 2402 West Beardsley Road; Phoenix, AZ 85027-3301

Mr. Philip J. Arruda: Seattle Transportation; 600 4th Avenue, Room 410; Seattle, WA 98104-1826

Ms. Cindy Ashcraft: Naval Medical Center; 620 John Paul Jones Circle; Portsmouth, VA 23708-2111

Ms. Melissa Asher: Executrain of Sacramento; 1510 Arden Way; Sacramento, CA 95815-4025

Mr. Alex Ashford: Epiphany Marketing; 11424 Hatteras Street, Apartment 3; North Hollywood, CA 91601-1181

Mr. Yehia E. Ashi: Sinai Industrial and Marine Supplies; P.O. Box 112, Shubra Gardens; Cairo, Egypt

Mr. Adnan Ashraf: Earthweb, Inc.; 3 Park Avenue; New York, NY 10016

Ms. Sarah A. Ashworth: Purvis Systems; 1272 West Main Road; Middletown, RI 02842

Mr. Yuksel Aslandogan: Navigation Technologies, Inc.; 2206 South Goebbert Road, Apartment 303; Arlington Heights, IL 60005-4208

Mr. Munir H. Atalla: Near East Engineering Company; P.O. Box 1838; Amman, Jordan 11118

Mr. Ahmet Atan: Ideas, Inc.; 3500 Yankee Drive, Suite 350; St. Paul, MN 55121-1632

Mr. Philip Atarodian: Hollywood Touch Studio; P.O. Box 794; Annandale, VA 22003-0794

Mr. Peter Atkinson: Warman International Inc.; 2701 South Stoughton Road; Madison, WI 53716-3332

Mr. Sreedhar Atluri: Cambridge Technology Partners; 7650 Corporate Center Drive, #500; Miami, FL 33126

Ms. Valerie B. Attell: Cooper Lighting; 1121 Highway 74 South; Peachtree City, GA 30269

Mr. C. Atwood: Bedford Fair Apparel; 3131 Randall Parkway; Wilmington, NC 28403-2560

Mr. Thomas Aukett: GTE Enterprise Solutions; 100 North Tampa Street, Suite 3800; Tampa, FL 33602-5835

Mr. Troy Ault: Nationwide Insurance; 1 Nationwide Plaza; Columbus, OH 43215-2239

Mr. Rick Avvampato: Computer Sciences, Naytheon; 2295 Plantation Drive; Melbourne, FL 32935-7233

Ms. Maggie Hosni Awadalla: The American University in Cairo; 29 Shahid A. Moneim Hafez Street #6 Heliopolis; Cairo, Egypt

Mr. Reha Ayalp: Connect Point International, Inc.; 5020 Nicholson Court, Suite 204B; Kensington, MD 20895

Ms. Marcie Aylor: Reynolds Metals Company; 6605 West Broad Street; Richmond, VA 23230-1723

Mr. Morys Azcarte: Mutual Service Corporation; 250

Australian Avenue South, Suite 1800; West Palm Beach, FL 33401-5012
Ms. Caitlin Babb Martindale: Whittman-Hart; 394 Pacific Avenue, 5th Floor; San Francisco, CA 94111
Mr. Larry Babbio: Bell Atlantic; 180 Washington Valley Road; Bedminster, NJ 07921-2123
Mr. Jerry Babcock: Genco Distribution System; 100 Papercraft Park; Pittsburgh, PA 15238-3274
Mrs. Jude A. Baca: Teledyne Water Pik; 1730 East Prospect Road; Fort Collins, CO 80525-1310
Mr. Ben Baccarella: Dakotah Direct, Inc.; 9317 East Sinto Avenue; Spokane, WA 99206-4034
Mr. Robert T. Bach Jr.: V Span; 1100 1st Avenue, Suite 400; King of Prussia, PA 19406-1312
Mr. Sam Bacharach: Intergraph; 2051 Mercator Drive; Reston, VA 20191-3450
Mr. Jonathan Backus: Ab & C Group; 1 Executive Way; Ranson, WV 25438-1069
Ms. Patty Backus: Telergy; 5784 Widewaters Parkway; Syracuse, NY 13214-1878
Ms. Deborah Bacon: Environmental Data Resources; 3530 Post Road; Southport, CT 06490-1169
Ms. Penny Ellamar Bacon: Bergen Brunswig Medical; P.O. Box 53749; Fayetteville, NC 28305-3749
Mr. David C. Baden: Van Buren/Cass District Health Department; 57418 CR 681, Suite A; Hartford, MI 49057
Mr. Alan Badia: Internet Junction; P.O. Box 2218; Dunedin, FL 34697
Mr. Souheil Badran: Digital Insight; 26025 Mureau Road; Calabasas, CA 91302-3180
Mr. Tracy Baetzel: Honigman Miller Schwartz & Cohn; 2290 First National Building, 660 Woodward Avenue; Detroit, MI 48226-3583
Mrs. Sharmila Bagchi: Harrahs Casino Hotel; 219 North Center Street; Reno, NV 89501-1413
Mr. Van Baggett: Ingram; 1 Ingram Boulevard; La Vergne, TN 37086-3629
Mr. Habib Bagheri: EG&G Vactec, Inc.; 10900 Page Avenue; St. Louis, MO 63132-1097
Mr. Ali Abdallah Bahakim: Alfassel Shipping Company; P.O. Box 13175; Jeddah, Saudi Arabia 21493
Mr. Sam Bahour: Arab Palestinian Investment Company; P.O. Box 2323; Ramallah, Israel
Ms. Kathleen Bahr: PRC, Inc.; 5182 Potomac Drive; King George, VA 22485-5824
Mr. Benjamin Bahrenburg: Independent Consultant; P.O. Box 22063; Albany, NY 12222-0001
Mr. Kevin Bailey: Pro-Care Home Health; 1203 Ashley Circle; Bowling Green, KY 42104-1061
Mr. Roger Bailey: Computer Technology Association Inc.; 129 Rue Royal; Slidell, LA 70461
Mr. Shawn Bailey: WDS Telecommunications Services Group; 9220 Rumsey Road; Columbia, MD 21045-1956
Mr. Mark Baillie: Maurices; 105 West Superior Street; Duluth, MN 55802-2031
Mr. James Baird: City of Bellingham; 210 Lottie Street; Bellingham, WA 98225-4009
Dr. Waheed I. Bajwa: Oregon State University; 2040 Cordley Hall; Corvallis, OR 97331-8530
Ms. Angela Baker: Fisher Scientific; 822 Ohio River Boulevard, Apartment 10; Sewickley, PA 15143-1930
Ms. Colette Baker: Bureau of Prisons; 320 1st Street NW, Room 365; Washington, DC 20534-0002
Mr. Mike Baker: Excel Communications; 8036 Deer Trail Drive; Dallas, TX 75238-3353
Ms. D. Baker-Hussar: Graphic Enterprises, Inc.; 3874 Highland Park NW; North Canton, OH 44720-4538
Mr. Bruce Bakken: Badger Meter; 4545 West Brown Deer Road; Milwaukee, WI 53223
Mr. Venkateshwara S. Balaga: VSI, Inc.; 2018 Springfield Loop West; Birmingham, AL 35242
Mr. Krishnan Balasubramanian: Oracle Corporation; 110 Abernathy Road, Building 500, Suite 1120; Atlanta, GA 30328
Ms. Nancy Balcer: Transamerica Distributed Finance; 5595 Trillium Boulevard; Hoffman Estates, IL 60192-3405
Mr. David Balch: Rockland Trust Company; 288 Union Street; Rockland, MA 02370-1896
Mr. Paul J. Baldauf: KLRS; 5231 Elmwood Drive; Pittsburgh, PA 12557
Mr. Darrel A. Ballard: Wetzel County Schools; 333 Foundry Street; North Martinsville, WV 26155-1142
Ms. Desiree Ballard: Hewlett Packard; 3000 Waterview Parkway; Richardson, TX 75080-1400
Mr. Jacob Ballard: City of Rochester Hills; 1000 Rochester Hills Drive; Rochester, MI 48309-3033
Ms. Rosa M. Baltazar: State Government; P.O. Box 3869; Calexico, CA 92232-3869
Mr. Omoluabi Olu Bamisaiye: DSP; P.O. Box 4953; Brockton, MA 02303-4953
Ms. Angela Bandlow: Calico Commerce; 1809 California Street; San Francisco, CA 94109-4566
Mr. Kevin Bandy: Market Source; 2 Commerce Drive; Cranbury, NJ 08512-3501
Mr. Wayne Y. Bangsil: JCB Credit Card Company; 626 Wilshire Boulevard, Suite 200; Los Angeles, CA 90017-2915
Ms. Candida Banister: Micro Diagnostics, Inc.; 1133 Warrior Drive; Franklin, TN 37064-5031
Mr. Atal Bansal: APS Technologies; 630 West 84th Street; Hialeah, FL 33014-3617
Mr. Michael Banyas: Household International; 100 Mittel Drive; Wood Dale, IL 60191
Mr. Andy Barber: GTE TSI; 11400 4th Street North, Apartment 807; St. Petersburg, FL 33716
Mr. Billy Barber: BP Amoco; 260 The Bluffs; Austell, GA 30168
Ms. Mary Barber : 2505 Transportation Road P.O. Box 768; Willmar, MN 56201-0768
Ms. Angela Bargbieri: Novartis Consumer Health; 560 Morris Avenue; Summit, NJ 07901-1312
Mr. John J. Barlas : 8204 Southeast 62nd Street; Mercer Island, WA 98040-4919
Ms. Sherilynn Barlay: Nextlink Ohio; 2 Easton Oval; Columbus, OH 43219-6036
Mr. Eric Barnard: W.S. Erectors, Inc.; Rural Route 5 Box 45C; Bastrop, TX 78602-7603
Mr. Scot Barnard: Securities America; 130 East Kiowa Street, Suite 500; Colorado Springs, CO 80903-1733
Mr. N. H. Barnaschone: Claude Reid, Inc.; P.O. Box 277; Blumenfontein, South Africa 9300
Mr. Austen Barnes: Barnes Advanced Technology, Inc.; 1051 Clinton Street; Buffalo, NY 14206-2823
Mr. Harris H. Barnes: Barnes, Broom, Dallas & McLeod; P.O. Box 13956; Jackson, MS 39236-3956
Ms. Ramona G. Barnes: United States Air Force; 75th Communications Squadron, 7879 Wardleigh Road; Hill Air Force Base, UT 84056-5997
Mr. Jerry Barnett: Jackson Madison County General Hospital; 708 West Forest Avenue; Jackson, TN 38301-3900
Mr. John Barnovsky: Maximation, LLC; 376 Piedmont Road; Columbus, OH 43214-3816
Ms. Jennifer L. Baro: Desert Research Institute; 2215 Raggio Parkway; Reno, NV 89512-1095
Mr. Daniel Baron: Smurfit Newsprint Corporation; 2205 West Mount Vernon Avenue, P.O. Box 2364; Pomona, CA 91769
Mr. Robert Barone: St. John's University; 8000 Utopia Parkway; Jamaica, NY 11432-1343
Mr. William Barr: CBSI (Patent Office)/Averstar; 7116 Beulah Street; Alexandria, VA 22315-3502
Dr. E. A. Barrett: South Florida Water Management District; 233 Oleander Avenue; Palm Beach, FL 33480-3806
Mr. Ronald J. Barrett: Dixon Industries, Inc.; P.O. Box 1569; Coffeyville, KS 67337-0945
Mr. Michael C. Barrows: Cape & Islands District Attorneys Office; P.O. Box 455; Barnstable, MA 02630
Ms. Terttu Barsch: ITT Technical Institute; 2600 Lake Lucien Drive, Suite 140; Maitland, FL 32751-7288
Mr. Arthur F. Bartle: Paramount Industries, Inc.; P.O. Box 259; Croswell, MI 48422-0259
Mr. William L. Bartlett: Cox-Little & Company; 6201 Fairview Road, Suite 201; Charlotte, NC 28210
Ms. Heather Bartley: Physicians Primary Care; 12995 South Cleveland Avenue, Suite 206; Fort Myers, FL 33907-3890
Mr. John H. Bartol: National Geographic; 1145 17th Street NW; Washington, DC 20036
Ms. Kimberly Baskett: SBC Operations, Inc.; 4801 Northwest Loop 410; San Antonio, TX 78229
Mr. William P. Bass: CAMAC Corporation; 14401 Industrial Park Road; Bristol, VA 24203
Mr. Jamie Basswerner: Dima Ltda.; 4460 Northwest 74th Avenue; Miami, FL 33166
Mr. Kalyan K. Basu: Norfel Networks; 3605 Sage Brush Trail; Plano, TX 75023-5836
Mr. Sanjay Basu: Hewlett Packard; 14427 Wellesley Street #1; Dearborn, MI 48126
Mr. James P. Bates: Sitel Technology Services; 1117 Deming Way; Madison, WI 53717-1953
Mr. Richard Bates: Telehouse International; 7 Teleport Drive; Staten Island, NY 10311-1001
Ms. Lalitha Devi Battina: Applied Automation Techniques Inc.; 5753 Miami Lakes Drive; Miami Lakes, FL 33014-2417
Ms. Nona Battistella: Accessor Capital Management; 1420 Fifth Avenue, Suite 3600; Seattle, WA 98101
Mr. Kevin D. Battles: Dragons Realm Enterprises; 16450 South Tamiami Trail; Fort Myers, FL 33908
Mr. Gabrielle M. Baudendistel: Horton Medical Center; 60 Prospect Avenue; Middletown, NY 10940-4133
Mr. Eric Bauer: La Crosse Management System; 200 Main Street; La Crosse, WI 54601-9301
Mr. Damian J. Baumann: OSF Healthcare; 800 Northeast Glen Oak Avenue; Peoria, IL 61603-3255
Mr. Joe Baumgartner: Bogen Communications; 50 Spring Street; Ramsey, NJ 07446-1131
Mr. Josef Baumgartner: GALILEO Laboratories; 5301 Patrick Henry Drive; Santa Clara, CA 95054
Mr. Paul Baumgartner: Origin Technology in Business; 8044 Montgomery Road, Suite 200 West; Cincinnati, OH 45236-2929
Ms. Alireza Bavafa SSE: MCI System House; 12750 Center Court Drive; Cerritos, CA 90703
Mr. Thomas A. Bavuso: Highmark Blue Cross Blue Shield; 810 Parish Street; Pittsburgh, PA 15220
Mr. Barry Baxley: AT&T Solutions; 4825 Creekstone Drive 4E119; Durham, NC 27703-8051
Mrs. Kristie Baxter: United Information Technologies; 1051 Perimeter Drive, Suite 550; Schaumburg, IL 60173-5807
Mr. Geneane M. Bazan: North American Vaccine; 10150 Old Columbia Road; Columbia, MD
Ms. Kathryn Beard: Princeton Financial Systems; 600 College Road East; Princeton, NJ 08540-6636
Mr. Dan Bearwood: Key Tech Corporation; 12420 Evergreen Drive; Mukilteo, WA 98275
Mr. Jim Beasley: Province Healthcare; 4904 Manchester Pike; Murfreesboro, TN 37127-7714
Mr. Kelvin Beaton: Steck Medical Group; 147 Oak Point Drive; Chehalis, WA 98532-9668
Ms. Tammy Beatty: Advertex-Macy's; 420 Fulton Street; Brooklyn, NY 11201-5214
Mr. Jeffrey A. Beauchamp: Agency Computer Systems, Inc.; 36880 Woodward Avenue, Suite 100; Bloomfield, MI 48304-0921
Mr. Eugene S. Beaumont II: Orecomm; 44931 Falcon Place; Sterling, VA 20166-9500
Ms. Carol S. Bebb: UOP; 25 East Algonquin Road; Des Plaines, IL 60016-6100
Mr. Paul Bechta: Rand Worldwide; 321 Commonwealth Road, Suite 302; Wayland, MA 01778-5039
Ms. Judith Ann Becker: Protege Systems, Inc.; 300 North Martingale Road, Suite 750; Schaumburg, IL 60173-2097
Ms. Dianna P. Beckham: Ascent Management; 110 West 7th Street; Fort Worth, TX 76102
Mr. Alan Beckwith: Idx; 116 Huntington Avenue; Boston, MA 02116-5749
Ms. Margaret A. Bedell: New York State Department of Labor; Bulding 12 State Campus, Room 374; Albany, NY 12240-0001
Dr. Allan H. Beeber MBA: Campus Crusade For Christ; 100 Lake Hart Drive; Orlando, FL 32809-7875
Ms. Virginia Behnke: I/N Kote; 30755 Edison Road; New Carlisle, IN 46552-9695
Mr. John Beimler: Radiomind Studios; 213 Schuring Road; Portage, MI 49024
Mr. Mario Belbis: Industrial Adhesives Co.; 130 North Campbell Avenue; Chicago, IL 60612-2120
Mr. Steve Belcher: Citizens Insurance Company; 645 West Grand River Avenue; Howell, MI 48843-2184
Mr. Michael T. Belcourt Jr.: Heberly & Associates; 521 Fourth Street; Havre, MT 59501
Mr. Fred Belga: Ameritch Corporation; 225 West Randolph Street, Floor 22B; Chicago, IL 60606-1824
Ms. Ellen Belitzky: Unilever; 55 Meritt Boulevard; Trumbull, CT 06611-5435
Ms. Carol Bell: Compucare, Inc.; 1469 Southwest Covered Bridge Road; Palm City, FL 34990-1908
Mr. Fred Bell: Comcast Online; 8031 Corporate Drive; Baltimore, MD 21236-4986
Ms. Wendy Bell: Hiwaay Information Services; P.O. Box 551; Huntsville, AL 35804
Ms. Jackie Belles: Daniel & Yeager; 1200 South Pine Island Road, Suite 600; Plantation, FL 33324-4465
Mr. Tom Bellmer: Overland Data Center; 4550 West 109th Street; Overland Park, KS 66211-1317
Dr. Barbara J. Belon: Norwalk Community College; 188 Richards Avenue; Norwalk, CT 06854-1655
Mr. D. Lynnwood Belvin: Berry College; 102 Martha Drive SW; Rome, GA 30165-4138
Mr. Jon Bemis: Alltel Corporation; 1 Allied Drive; Little Rock, AR 72202-2099
Mr. Bob Bemmer: 5 Day Business Forms; 2910 East La Cresta Avenue; Anaheim, CA 92806-1818
Ms. Wendy Benaquista: Freemarkets; 1 Oliver Plaza; Pittsburgh, PA 15222-2600
Mr. Jeff Benfield: Media Comm; 9700 Southern Pines Boulevard; Charlotte, NC 28273-5559
Dr. Jacques Benkoski Ph.D.: Monterey Design Systems, Inc.; 894 Ross Drive, Suite 200; Sunnyvale, CA 94089-1443
Mr. Dale Bennett: Square D Company; 3700 6th Street SW; Cedar Rapids, IA 52404-5403
Mr. Gary R. Bennett: Forum Health Trumbull Memorial Hospital; 1350 East Market Street; Warren, OH 44483-6608
Mr. Randel J. Bennett: Sheriff's Office of the City of Jacksonville; 501 East Bay Street; Jacksonville, FL 32202
Mr. Jeffrey L. Benson: Syntek, Inc.; 4301 North Fairfax Drive; Arlington, VA 22203
Mr. Andresen Bent: Odense Windsor, A.G.; Oehningerstr 2; Stein Am Rhein, Switzerland 8260
Mr. Bob Benta: County Wide Communication; 78 River Street; Dover Foxcroft, ME 04426
Ms. Terri Bentley: Applied Systems; 15125 Royal Georgian Road; Orland Park, IL 60462-3890
Mrs. Marlene Bentzen: Watlow Controls; 1241 Bundy Boulevard; Winona, MN 55987-4873
Mr. Dennis Benzer: Healthcare Compare; 4141 North Scottsdale Road, Suite 220; Scottsdale, AZ 85251-3938
Mr. Michael A. Berardi Jr.: Hughes Supply, Inc.; 20 North Orange Avenue, Suite 1928; Orlando, FL 32801
Mr. Charles Berberich: American Water Works Association; 6666 West Quincy Avenue; Denver, CO 80235-3098
Mr. Bill Berg: Lake Superior College; 2101 Trinity Road; Duluth, MN 55811-3399
Mr. Jim Bergman: Hennigan Mercer & Bennett; 601 South Figueroa Street, Suite 3300; Los Angeles, CA 90017-5708
Mr. Mike Berkeland: Facciola Meat Company; P.O. Box 50548; Palo Alto, CA 94303-0548
Mrs. Daniele Berker: Conseco; 5405 Whittier Court; Indianapolis, IN 46250
Ms. Kathy L. Bernacki: P.T.B.O.E.; P.O. Box 98; Browns Mills, NJ 08015-0098
Mr. Frank Bernal: Citizens Communications; 8800 North Central Expressway; Dallas, TX 75231-6433
Mr. Mark A. Bernstein: Windsong West; P.O. Box 327; Lecompton, KS 66050-0327
Mr. Omer Berry: Orgill, Inc.; 2100 Latham Street; Memphis, TN 38109-7796
Mr. William G. Bertocchini: Nextlink California; 1924 East Deere Avenue; Santa Ana, CA 92705-5737
Ms. Joanne P. Bertone: Columbia, HCA; 2555 Park Place; Nashville, TN 37203-1512
Mr. Vincent Bertone: Anne Arundel County Schools; 427 Manor Road; Arnold, MD 21012
Mr. George A. Beshears: John Wood Community College; 150 South 48th Street; Quincy, MO 62301-0406
Mr. Mark Bess: Union Pacific Railroad; 1723 North 160th Street; Omaha, NE 68118-2408
Mr. Richard J. Bestany Jr.: Alterra Group, Inc.; 1330 Webster Street; Baltimore, MD 21230-4740
Ms. Jeani Bestys: Maryland Plastics, Inc.; P.O. Box 472; Federalsburg, MD 21632

Ms. Belinda M. Bethea: RenaLab; 197 Interstate Drive, Suite G; Richland, MS 39218

Mr. Craig S. Betzold: Affiliated Computer Services; 2901 3rd Street South; Waite Park, MN 56387

Ms. Pamela Q. Bevan: Williams Communication Solutions; 1290 Silas Deane Highway; Wethersfield, CT 06109

Mr. Scott Bevis: SIC@IYC Harrisburg; 1201 West Poplar Street; Harrisburg, IL 62946-3711

Mr. Nitesh Bharadia: Systems Group International, Ltd.; Systems House, Goldsworth Road; Surrey, England, United Kingdom GU21 1JT

Mr. Chetan Bhargave: University of Akron; 430 Sumner Street, Apartment 301; Akron, OH 44304-1793

Mr. Ronak Bhatt: Netscape Communications; 1248 Sunnyvale Saratoga Road, Apartment 28; Sunnyvale, CA 94087-2544

Mr. Debashis Bhattacharya: Castwell Products, Inc.; 7800 Austin Avenue; Skokie, IL 60077-2641

Mr. Yasser Biaz: Providian Financial; 180 Brannan Street, Apt. 109; San Francisco, CA 94107-2051

Mr. Fernand Bibeau: Computel; 520 Dartmouth Place Southeast; Albuquerque, NM 87106-2323

Ms. Shelley Bickel: Interactive Search (iSearch); 5959 West Century Boulevard, Suite 200; Los Angeles, CA 90045-6502

Mr. Jim Bicking: Stohlman Oldsmobile; 200 South Pickett Street; Alexandria, VA 22304-4784

Ms. Tiffany Biederman: Idexx Informatics; 2536 Alpine Road; Eau Claire, WI 54703-9560

Mr. Mike Biek: Robert Half International; 402 BNA Drive, Suite 410; Nashville, TN

Mr. Adam Bielawski: United Buying Service, Inc.; 39 South Milwaukee Avenue; Wheeling, IL 60090-3107

Mr. Paul J. Bierbower: Pacific Bell; 2600 Camino Ramon; San Ramon, CA 94583-5099

Ms. Renee Biles: Romac; 4965 U.S. Highway 42; Louisville, KY 40222

Mr. David T. Bill: Towers Perrin; 1500 Market Street, Floor 22E; Philadelphia, PA 19102-2103

Mr. Ernie Billingsley: Dale Rogers Training Center, Inc.; 2501 North Utah Avenue; Oklahoma City, OK 73107-1229

Mr. Joel Bingham: Aalfs Manufacturing; 1005 4th Street; Sioux City, IA 51101-1806

Mr. Paul N. Bingle: CMS Communications, Inc.; 715 Goddard; Chesterfield, MO 63005

Mr. Martin J. Binns: MEMC Electronic Materials, Inc.; 501 Pearl Drive; St. Peters, MO 63376-1071

Mr. Joe Birge: Department Of Veterans Affairs; 155 Van Gordon Street; Lakewood, CO 80228-1709

Mrs. Yondi Bitsko: Boeing Company; P.O. Box 582808; Tulsa, OK 74158-2808

Ms. Myra Bitzer: Villages of Lake Sumter; 1100 Main Street; The Villages, FL 32159-7719

Mr. Garth Black: Comcotec; 610 Rembrandt Circle; Irwin, PA 15642-9505

Mr. Thomas Scott Blackard: Lago Vista Independent School District; 8039 Bar-K Ranch Road; Lago Vista, TX 78645

Mr. Eugene Blackburn: Air Force Research Laboratory; 525 Brooks Road; Rome, NY 13441-4505

Mr. B. K. Blacker: The Edistona Partnership; West Winds, Inkford Brook; Wythall, England, United Kingdom

Mr. Max Blacknik: GFG Foodservice, Inc.; P.O. Box 14489; Grand Forks, ND 58208-4489

Mr. Anthony L. Blackson: Family Self Funding; P.O. Box 113; Lyndora, PA 16045-0113

Mrs. Cammie Blake: U.S. Cellular Corporation; 800 Cornerstone Drive; Knoxville, TN 37932-3231

Ms. Denise Blake: Round Lake Area School; 316 South Rosedale Court; Round Lake, IL 60073-2944

Mr. Kesten C. Blake: La Habra High School; 801 Highlander Avenue; La Habra, CA 90631-3720

Mr. Rob Blakely: Benedictine School; 14299 Benedictine Lane; Ridgely, MD 21660

Mr. Irving C. Blaney: PSC, Inc.; 12330 Pinecrest Road; Reston, VA 20121

Ms. Ann Blankinship: Tower Automotive; P.O. Box 29; Milan, TN 38358-0529

Mr. Kenneth J. Blansette: Life Search, Inc.; 2403 Baur Drive; Indianapolis, IN 46220-2828

Dr. Stephen Blatt Ph.D.: Sanders A Lockheed Martin Company; 88 Blanford Place; Bedford, NH 03110-4611

Ms. Lori Blaylock: First Interstate Data; 2825 3rd Avenue North; Billings, MT 59101-1949

Mr. William B. Blaylock: Rockwood School District; 1955a Shepard Road; Glencoe, MO 63038-1431

Mr. Serge Blinder: Bank Boston; 1 Bank Boston Place; Waltham, MA 02154

Ms. Leslie Ann Bliss: Regents College; 7 Columbia Circle; Albany, NY 12203-5156

Ms. Cynthia Blodgett: AlliedSignal Aerospace; P.O. Box 1404; Greer, SC 29652-1404

Mr. John B. Bloniarz: Ernst & Young; 1776 Old Mill Road; Wantagh, NY 11793-3243

Mr. James B. Bloom: ADAC; 540 Alder Drive; Milpitas, CA 95035-7443

Mr. Aaron S. Bloomfield: SOHO Consulting; P.O. Box 472; La Center, WA 98629-0472

Mr. Don Blosser: AT&T; 783 Colts Neck Road; Freehold, NJ 07728-8106

Mr. Ronald R. Bloyer: University of Utah; 4341 Mulholland Street; Salt Lake City, UT 84124-3840

Ms. Debora Bluestone: GSD/ISD Training Center; 715 Alta Vista, Simms Building; Santa Fe, NM 87502

Mr. Steven Bo: New World Consulting Corp.; 42-35 Bell Boulevard, Suite 148; Bayside, NY 11361

Mr. Keith Boatner: Vysis, Inc.; 3100 Woodcreek Drive; Downers Grove, IL 60515-5427

Mr. Robert Boeri: Factory Mutual; 15 Eli Whitney Street; Westborough, MA 01581-3517

Mr. Thomas Boesch: Mulay Plastics; 10 West Laura Drive; Addison, IL 60101-5100

Ms. Tania Bogner: DirecTV; 2230 East Imperial Highway; El Segundo, CA 90245-3531

Dr. Suzi Bogom Ph.D.: Capitol Region Education Council; 111 Charter Oak Avenue; Hartford, CT 06106-1912

Ms. Debbie Bohannan: Nevada Auto Auction; 8801 Las Vegas Boulevard South; Las Vegas, NV 89123-1641

Mr. Patrick Bohlinger : 1373 Lincoln Avenue; Holland, MI 49423-9389

Ms. Deborah Bohn: Geek Garb; 914 St. Clair Street, Suite 116; Melbourne, FL 32935-5963

Mr. Jeff Bohrer: Mahtomedi Public Schools; 8000 75th Street North; Mahtomedi, MN 55115-1795

Ms. Sherri L. Bolen: Day, Edwards, Et Al; 210 Park Avenue, Suite 2900; Oklahoma City, OK 73102-5605

Mr. Michael W. Boler: Vanausdall & Farrar Inc.; 1214 North Meridian Street; Indianapolis, IN 46204-1094

Mr. Jim Bolinder: First Health Group Corporation; 2610 Decker Lake Lane; Salt Lake City, UT 84119-2053

Ms. Kim Bolinger: Computer Science Corporation; 3811 Turtle Creek Boulevard; Dallas, TX 75219

Ms. Julie Bollman: Star-Telegram; 400 West 7th Street; Fort Worth, TX 76102-4701

Mr. Lucien C. Bomar: Remote Access Solutions, Inc.; 2331 Northwoods Lake Court; Duluth, GA 30096

Mr. John Bondon: Focus on Technology; 1170 Redfern Court; Concord, CA 94521-4739

Mr. Darren Z. Bondwif: Transcend PC Inc.; 1108 Laramie Street; Manhattan, KS 66502-5312

Ms. C. Elizabeth Bone: Insource Technology Corporation; 363 North Sam Houston Parkway East, Suite 1800; Houston, TX 77060-2413

Mr. Chris Bongartz: BMC Industries; 30 Kellogg Road; Cortland, NY 13045-3150

Mr. Francis J. Bonk: DBS Systems Corporation; 10925 Valley Spring Drive; Charlotte, NC 28277-3732

Mr. AJ Bonnell: Woodhaven Association; 509 La Moille Road; Sublette, IL 61637-9753

Mr. B. H. Bonner: Bonner Environmental; 400 FM 2547; Fairfield, TX 75840-5226

Ms. Patti Bonnette: Sonoco; 1 North 2nd Street; Hartsville, SC 29550-3305

Mr. Eric Booker: AT&T; 118 Milnor Avenue; Syracuse, NY 13224-1629

Mrs. Virginie Boone: Lonely Planet; 150 Linden Street; Oakland, CA 94607-2538

Mr. Adam Boornazian: Smithkline Beecham; 1 Franklin Plaza; Philadelphia, PA 19102-1225

Mr. Jon Borel: MCI Worldcom; 2424 Garden of the Gods Road; Colorado Springs, CO 80919-3190

Mr. Gunnar Borge: Advanced Manufacturing Center; 1205 Backus; El Paso, TX 79925

Mr. Daniel Borges: Franklin Insurance Company; 214 East Church Street; Lock Haven, PA 17745-2010

Mr. Tom Borneman: SGI; 1050 Lowater Road; Chippewa Falls, WI 54729

Mr. Jake Bosmeijer: Amway Corporation; 7575 Fulton Street East, Mailcode MB-1D; Ada, MI 49355-0001

Mr. Chris J. Bossong: Arthur Andersen, LLP; 2249 Elm Avenue, Appartment 320; Cleveland, OH 44113-2338

Mr. Romal Bostic: Independent Consultants, Inc.; 210 Lanier Drive, #1303; Statesboro, GA 30458

Mr. Larry Botsford: Ampco; 11400 Northwest 36th Avenue; Miami, FL 33167-2907

Ms. Maria Bottone : 460 West 34th Street, Floor 15; New York, NY 10001-2320

Mr. William D. Boudreaux: Wyeth Lederle; 211 Bailey Road; West Henrietta, NY 14586

Mr. Allen Bouknight: Systems Development; MSC 6202; Harrisonburg, VA 22807-0001

Mr. John C. Boulden: Praxair, Inc.; 175 East Park Drive; Tonawanda, NY 14150-7844

Dr. Jihad Boura Ph.D.: ASIC Alliance; 78 Dragon Court; Woburn, MA 01801

Ms. Stephanie Bourdage: Seagate Technology; 7801 Computer Avenue; Minneapolis, MN 55435-5489

Mr. Ernest Bourne: Ixl; 1010 Battery Street; San Francisco, CA 94111-1202

Ms. Deborah M. Bowen CPIM: GEC North America Corporation; 6100 Fairview Road, Suite 1100; Charlotte, NC 28210-3291

Ms. Susan Bowen: Business Tech Group; 14044 West Petronella Drive, Suite 2; Libertyville, IL 60048-9656

Ms. Rhonda Bowling: ICG Communications, Inc.; 161 Inverness Drive West; Englewood, CO 80112-5003

Ms. Carol Bowman: BMC Software; 6901 Rockledge Drive; Bethesda, MD 20817

Ms. Debra Bowman: Menominee Indian Tribe; P.O. Box 910; Keshena, WI 54135-0910

Ms. Julie Bowman: Business Communications, Inc.; 7903 Thorndike Road; Greensboro, NC 27409-9425

Ms. Rita A. Bowman: LIMRA International; 300 Day Hill Road; Windsor, CT 06095-4761

Mr. Zygmont J. Boxer: Com Ed; 227 West Monroe; Chicago, IL 60606

Mr. Leah Boyd: Houston Cellular Company; 3773 Southwest Freeway; Houston, TX 77027-7513

Mr. Eric Boyer: Boston Apartment Magazine; 14 Beechcroft Street; Brighton, MA 02135-2502

Mr. Rod Boyer: HPI Racing; 15321 Barranca Parkway; Irvine, CA 92618-2216

Mr. John V. Boyle: 100 C; 942 Congress Street; Portland, ME 04102-3033

Mr. Mark Boyles: Sybase Inc.; 322 1/2 East 50th Street; New York, NY 10022

Mr. Pat Boyles: LS3P Associates, Ltd.; 112 South Tryon Street, Suite 200; Charlotte, NC 28284-2192

Mr. James Alan Bozeman: City of Murfreesboro Tennessee; 111 West Vine Street; Murfreesboro, TN 37130-3573

Mr. Enrico Bozzetti: Mil Data Informatica; 900 Post Road, Apartment 104; Warwick, RI 02888

Mr. John T. Brack: Southeast Georgia Regional Medical Center; 2415 Parkwood Drive; Brunswick, GA 31520

Mr. Mark Brackenbury: Health Management Systems; 401 Park Avenue South; New York, NY 10016-8808

Ms. Donna Brackett: Mead Corporation; 35 Hartford Street; Rumford, ME 04276-2045

Mr. Rickard Braddock: Lockheed Martin/PMSC; Interstate 77 & U.S. 21; Blythewood, SC 29016

Mr. Ed Bradford: Hanover Pen Corporation; 501 Fame Avenue; Hanover, PA 17331-9539

Mr. Robert Bradford: Bangor Hydro Electric Company; 33 State Street; Bangor, ME 04401-5039

Ms. Fran Bradley: Ames Safety Envelope Package; 21 Rev Nazareno Properzi Way; Somerville, NH 02143-3255

Mr. Ivan Bradley: 49er R.O.P.; 360 Nevada Street; Auburn, CA 95603-3720

Mr. Claudio H. Braga: Brazilian Aeronautical Commission; 1701 22nd Street NW; Washington, DC 20008

Mr. James Eric Brahney: Systems Modeling Corporation; 504 Beaver Street; Sewickley, PA 15143-1755

Mr. Hank Brain: Tupperware Corporation; 14418 Flo Road; Orlando, FL 328326566

Mr. Leonard M. Bram: Ameritech; 7510 Whigham Court; Dublin, OH 43016-8796

Mr. Michael J. Brams: D.E. Shaw & Company; 401 West 47th Street, Apartment 8; New York, NY 10036-2339

Mr. Richard Brandel: PricewaterhouseCoopers; 9 Secora Road, Apartment K7; Monsey, NY 10952-3770

Mr. John Brandenburg: Damark International, Inc.; 7101 Winnetka Avenue North; Minneapolis, MN 55428-1619

Ms. Heather Brandli: Teligent; 12001 Sunrise Valley Drive, Suite 400; Reston, VA 20191-3404

Mr. Lars F. Brandt: Lunt Manufacturing Co. Inc.; 601-605 Lunt Avenue; Schaumburg, IL 60193-4410

Ms. Delorious Branic: District Child & Family Services; 609 H Street NE; Washington, DC 20002-4347

Mr. George Peter Branigan: Omnipoint Comm; 360 Newark Pompton Turnpike; Wayne, NJ 07470-6641

Ms. Toni L. Branscum: City of Torrance; One Civic Plaza Drive #500; Carson, CA 90745

Ms. Michelle Brantley: Hopkins Crawley Bagwell Upshaw; 2701 24th Avenue; Gulfport, MS 39501-4941

Ms. Patricia Brantley: Presbyterian New Covenant; 1110 Lovett Boulevard; Houston, TX 77006-3824

Mrs. Sondra D. Brasseur: Stupp Corporation; 12555 Ronaldson Road; Baton Rouge, LA 70570

Mr. Doug Braunschweig: Vucom New Media, Inc.; 1256 Kirts Boulevard, Suite 300; Troy, MI 48084-4838

Mr. Don Brayton: VLSI Standards, Inc.; 8534 Fenwick Street; Sunland, CA 91040-1920

Mr. Vinvent Brejtfus: General Employment; 2803 Butterfield Road, Suite 260; Oak Brook, IL 60523-1156

Mr. Lee Brennan: Intermedia Communications; 12007 Los Nietos Road; Santa Fe Springs, CA 90670-2539

Ms. Stephanie Brenner: Metamor Industry Solutions; 9030 Stony Point Parkway; Richmond, VA 23235-1936

Mr. Erik Brennom: Crystal Communications; 2611 Luther Drive, #116; Ames, IA 50010-4780

Mr. Michael P. Brescia: Instrument & Equipment Co.; 2 Wilson Drive, Unit #1; Emerson, NJ 07838

Mr. David Brethauer: Brethauer Consulting Group; 10019 North Miller Court; Mequon, WI 53092-6180

Mr. Eric Brewer: Microbilt; 1640 Airport Road NW; Kennesaw, GA 30144-7038

Mr. Kevin Brewer: Wake Forest University, School of Medicine; Medical Center Boulevard; Winston-Salem, NC 27157-0001

Ms. Lori Brewer: Safelite Glass Corporation; 2400 Farmers Drive, Floor 4; Columbus, OH 43235-2762

Mr. Russell Brewer: Dana Corporation Plumley; 100 Plumley Drive; Paris, TN 38242-8022

Mr. Donald Bricker: Fort Worth Star Telegram; 400 West 7th Street; Fort Worth, TX 76102-4701

Mr. John E. Brietz Jr.: Collegis; 807 Glen Arden Way; Altamonte Springs, FL 32701-6817

Ms. Linda Brigance: Federal Express; 31 Kaki Bukit Road, #3; Singapore, Singapore 417818

Mr. David T. Brill: Peak Technologies; 2915 Commers Drive, Suite 1300; Eagen, MN 55121-2362

Mr. Rob Brinberg: Baines Gwinner; 70 East 55th Street, Floor 22; New York, NY 10022-3222

Mr. Matthew Brink: Positive Communications, Inc.; 5753 West Las Positas Boulevard; Pleasanton, CA 94588-4084

Mr. Steve Britton: Andersen Corporation; 8236 113th Street South; Cottage Grove, MN 55016-4523

Ms. Kelly S. Brockman: Kutak Rock; 14109 Pierce Plaza, #42; Omaha, NE 68144

Mr. Michael Brockway: Bell Atlantic; 2 Blue Hill Plaza, Floor 1; Pearl River, NY 10965-3101

Mr. David Brodosi: University of Florida; 140 7th Avenue South, Suite 207; St. Petersburg, FL 33701-5016

Mr. Bob Brodsky: Celanese Acetate; P.O. Box 32414; Charlotte, NC 28232-2414

Mr. Howard L. Brokaw: Sherwood; 120 Church Street; Lockport, NY 14094

Mr. Dan Bromberg: Bell Atlantic; 13101 Columbia Pike, Room 102H; Silver Spring, MD 20904-5248

Ms. Lisa Brook: Jacobson Stores; 3333 Sargent Road; Jackson, MI 49201-8800

Mr. Chris A. Brooks: MTL Systems, Inc.; 3481 Dayton-Xenia Road; Beavercreek, OH 45432-2796

Ms. Heather Brooks: Raymond James & Associates; 880 Carillon Parkway; St. Petersburg, FL 33716-1100

Mr. Richard Brooks: TRW; 6522 Clagett Avenue; Tracy Landing, MD 20779-2536

Mr. Steve Brooks: Hardin Construction Group; 1380 West Paces Ferry Road NW; Atlanta, GA 30327-2465

Mr. Tim Brooks: Ico Global Communication; P.O. Box 66572; Washington, DC 20035-6572

Mr. William Brooks: Bancrott School; 110 Shore Drive; Worcester, MA 01605-3198

Ms. Farah Broom: Nextel Communications; 3212 Arrowhead Circle, Apartment A; Fairfax, VA 22030

Ms. Holly Brosam: Travel Technologies Group; 7557 Rambler Road, Suite 1300; Dallas, TX 75231-2392

Mr. John A. Broskey: The Penn Mutual Life Insurance Company; 600 Dresher Road; Horsham, PA 19044

Mr. Bill Brown: Aquent Partners; 6300 South Syracuse Way, Suite 470; Englewood, CO 8011-6792

Mr. Danny Brown: Universal Tax Systems; 6 Mathis Drive NW; Rome, GA 30165-1242

Mr. Ed Brown: Bunn-O-Matic Corporation; 1400 Stevenson Drive; Springfield, IL 62703-4291

Mr. James A. Brown: Bearing Services and Supply Inc.; P.O. Box 7497; Shreveport, LA 71137-7497

Mr. James Brown: Office of Cable Television & Telecommunications; 2217 14th Street NW; Washington, DC 20009-4401

Mr. Johnny Brown: City of Colorado Springs Utilities; P.O. Box 1103; Colorado Springs, CO 80901-1103

Mr. Joseph Brown: Wacom Technology Corporation; 1311 Southeast Cardinal Court; Vancouver, WA 98683-9589

Mr. Richard Brown: University of Louisville; 2126 South Floyd Street; Louisville, KY 40208-2751

Mr. Robert A. Brown: Docucorp International; 5910 North Central Expressway; Dallas, TX 75206-5125

Mr. Steven K. Brown: Hewlett-Packard; 1115 Southeast 164th Avenue; Vancouver, WA 98683-9625

Ms. Terri Brown: DOJ/JMD/IRM/CSS; United States Department of Justice 1151 Seven Locks Road; Rockville, MD 20854-2905

Mr. Gary Browning: Tube Forgings of America, Inc.; 5200 Northwest Front Avenue; Portland, OR 97210-1110

Ms. Patti J. Bruce: Duke Power Company; 526 South Church Street, Suite EC05M; Charlotte, NC 28202-1802

Mr. Stein Bruch: Northwest Airlines, Inc.; 15142 Cimarron Avenue; Rosemount, MN 55068-2754

Mr. Jason R. Bruecker: Carroll College; 100 North East Avenue; Waukesha, WI 53186

Mr. Michael W. Bruens: Southern Illinois University; 1275 Point Drive, Room 107; Carbondale, IL 62901-6633

Mr. Edward W. Bruette Jr.: Silverlink Corporation; P.O. Box 73; Silverdale, WA 98383-0073

Ms. Kimberly Brugier: KRB Productions; 4913 St. Thomas Place; Fort Worth, TX 76135-1544

Mr. Stephen Brumm: Olmsted County; 151 4th Street SE, ISC Department; Rochester, MN 55904-3710

Mr. Mike Bruner: State Personnel Department; 64 North Union Street; Montgomery, AL 36130-3020

Mr. Chris Brunn: DD Studios, Inc.; 1743 West 33rd Street; Chicago, IL 60608-6249

Mr. Frank Bruno: American Express; 1185 Avenue of Americas; New York, NY 10036

Mr. Rusty Bruns: Charleston Southern University; 9200 University Boulevard, P.O. Box 118087; Charleston, SC 29423-8087

Mr. Michael Bryars: Ford Motor Company; 48380 Red Run Drive; Canton, MI 48187-5434

Mr. Ze'ev Bubis: Globaloop; 5 Hanagar Street; Hod Hasharon, Israel 45800

Mr. Michael J. Buchetto: Citizens Utilities Company; 3 High Ridge Park; Stamford, CT 06905

Mr. Robert Budd: Honeywell, Inc.; 2701 4th Avenue South; Minneapolis, MN 55408-1771

Mr. Tim Budd: Cybertek; Rural Road 1 Box 11; Darlington, IN 47940-9703

Mr. Zoran Budzakoski: API Systems, Inc.; 264 Orient Way; Rutherford, NJ 07070-2843

Mr. Kris Bueltmann: AG Edwards; One North Jefferson; St. Louis, MO 63103

Mr. Jovy Buenaventura: Evergreen Supply Company; 11375 Sunrise Park Drive, Suite 500; Rancho Cordova, CA 95742

Mr. Jose G. Bueno: Americatel Corporation; 4045 Northwest 97th Avenue; Miami, FL 33178-2300

Ms. Noelle Bufton: Northern Trust; 50 South La Salle Street # MB-12; Chicago, IL 60675

Ms. Kathy Bugbee: Family Service Centers; 2960 Rossvelt Boulevard; Clearwater, FL 33760

Mr. Tom Buller: Lombard Elementary School District; 150 West Madison Street; Lombard, IL 60148-3317

Mr. Cecil Bunn: Raytheon E&C; P.O. Box 101; Birmingham, AL 35201-0101

Mr. Gary Bunzel: OK Industries, Inc.; 4601 North 6th Street; Fort Smith, AR 72904-2208

Mr. Bobby L. Burch Jr.: Allstate Insurance Company; 100 Galleria Officentre, Suite 300; Southfield, MI 48034-8429

Mr. Davis Burchette: Cellular South; 9471 Three Rivers Road; Gulfport, MS 39503

Mr. Alvin J. Burge: Midland Brake; 10707 Northwest Airworld Drive; Kansas City, MO 64153-1215

Ms. Suzanne Burgei: The Health Alliance, Information Systems Division; 3200 Burnet Avenue, Floor 5; Cincinnati, OH 45229-3099

Mr. Kirt Burgtorf: Dealer Computer Services; 1000 Town Center, Suite 350; Southfield, MI 48075-1258

Mr. Jim Burke: Fenton Press; 1544 West Wrightwood Court; Addison, IL 60101

Mr. John M. Burke: Bethany College; 636 Market Street; Santa Cruz, CA 95060

Mr. Robert M. Burkhead: Synet Service Corporation; 10 Park Crest Court, Apartment B; Novato, CA 94947-4761

Mr. Thomas Burleson: Calm Water Software; 4650 Oakwood Lane; West Des Moines, IA 50265-5413

Mr. Scott Burmann: Lear Corporation; 5200 Auto Club Drive; Dearborn, MI 48126

Ms. Alyson Burnett: Informix Software; 16011 College Boulevard; Shawnee, KS 66219-1366

Ms. Delphia Mynhier Burnett: IDX Information Systems, Inc.; 10400 Linn Station Road; Louisville, KY 40223-3839

Ms. Melanie Burns: Florida Citrus Mutual; 302 South Massachusetts Avenue; Lakeland, FL 33801-5091

Mr. Sean Burns: Horizon Health; 3308 North Shepard; Milwaukee, WI 53211

Mr. Steve Burns: University of Tennessee; P.O. Box 1071; Knoxville, TN 37901-1071

Ms. Kathleen E. Burr: Agency.com; 1701 North Market Street; Dallas, TX 75202-2013

Mr. Les Burrows: St. Petersburg High School; 2501 5th Avenue North; St. Petersburg, FL 33713

Mr. Spike Burrows: Colorado Department of Corrections; 2862 South Circle Drive, Suite 400; Colorado Springs, CO 80906-4106

Ms. Deborah C. Burton: University of Kentucky Medical Center/Kentucky Telecare; K-117 Kentucky Clinic, 740 South Limestone; Lexington, KY 40536

Mr. Alan Bush: Ahold Information Services; 650 Executive Center Drive; Greenville, SC 29615-4520

Mr. David Bush: Telecommunications Resources, Inc.; 8 Victory Lane, Suite 200; Liberty, MO 64068-1903

Mr. John C. Butkus: AT&T; 4 State Park Road; Chester, NJ 07930

Ms. Elisa Butler: Mastech Corporation; 1000 Commerce Drive, Parkridge 1; Pittsburgh, PA 15275

Mr. Marion B. Butler: University Health Care System; 1350 Walton Way; Augusta, GA 30901-2629

Mr. Wayne Buzby: Bull Information Systems; 13001 North 1st Street; Phoenix, AZ 85022-5201

Mr. William J. Byerly: FAA; 10 Aviation Avenue; Hilliard, FL 32046

Ms. Vivian Byers: TRW; 108 East 7th Street; Little Rock, AR 72201-4509

Mr. Dennis Byford Jr.: Esker U.S., Inc.; 100 East 7th Avenue; Stillwater, OK 74074

Mr. Johan Bygge: A.B. Electrolux; St. Goraiusgatan 143; Stockholm, Sweden 105 45

Ms. Louise Byrd : 5672 Lynnhurst Lane; Montgomery, AL 36117-2912

Ms. Roanette Byrd: Kentucky State University; 400 East Main Street, Suite 261; Frankfort, KY 40601-2334

Mr. Eric K. Byrtus: Computer Network Solutions; 2023 Bravado Street; Vista, CA 92083

Ms. Diane Cabral: Brooktrout Software; 333 Turnpike Road; Southborough, MA 01772-1755

Mr. Shawn Cadmes: Adt Security; 6260 Harvest Run Cove; Memphis, TN 38141-8360

Ms. Tanisha Caglin: Prudential Insurance; 1045 Grove Avenue, #3D; Edison, NJ 08820

Ms. Michele Cairns: Emerson College; 100 Beacon Street; Boston, MA 02116-1596

Mr. Edward Calabrese: IBM; 13 Catalpa Court; Avon, CT 06001-4511

Mr. Neal Calanni: Osicom Technologies, Inc.; 9020 Junction Drive; Annapolis Junction, MD 20701-1146

Mr. Frank Calderon: Zebra Books; 850 3rd Avenue, Floor 16; New York, NY 10022-6222

Mr. J. E. Caldwell: Lockheed Martin Tactical Aircraft Systems; 5308 Garrick Avenue; Fort Worth, TX 76133-2141

Mr. Rodney Calinisan: Norsat International, Inc.; 100-4401 Still Creek Drive; Burnaby, British Columbia, Canada V5C 6G9

Mr. Thomas S. Call: TACAN Corporation; 2330 Faraday Avenue; Carlsbad, CA 92008-7216

Mr. Steve Calvert: New Breed Transfer Corporation; 4239 Piedmont Parkway; Greensboro, NC 27410-8112

Mr. Paul Calvino: Shell Services International; 9715 Slate Field Drive; Houston, TX 77064-7632

Mr. Mark Campagnolo: Rittenhouse Paper Company; 250 South Northwest Highway; Park Ridge, IL 60068-4252

Ms. Cynthia A. Campbell: Entegris; 102 North Jonathan Boulevard; Chaska, MN 55318-2350

Ms. Joeann Campbell: APTECH Engineering Services; 1282 Reamwood Avenue; Sunnyvale, CA 94089-2233

Mr. Michael Campbell: Therma-Wave, Inc.; 1250 Reliance Way; Fremont, CA 94539-6100

Mr. Michael Campbell: Aldmyr Systems Inc.; 2002 Ruatan Street; Adelphi, MD 20783-2141

Mr. Robert Campbell: Medic Computer Systems; 647 Willamsburg Court; Sanford, NC 27330-3544

Mr. Scott D. Campbell: General Dynamics; 1450 Academy Park Loop; Colorado Springs, CO 80910-3725

Ms. Seham Campbell: Oneida Nation of New York; 336 Genesee Street; Oneida, NY 13421-2612

Mr. Walter Campbell: Ascent Consulting; 1613 Lake Salvador Drive; Harvey, LA 70058-5151

Ms. Jennifer Canik: Tech Fuel; 6540 Lusk Boulevard, Suite C261; San Diego, CA 92121

Mr. Edgar A. Cann: Jacobs Applied Technician; 121 Sandtrap Road; Summerville, SC 29483-2934

Mr. Tim Canney: CoCreate Software, Inc.; 3801 Automation Way, Suite 110; Fort Collins, CO 80525

Ms. Kelly Cannon: Ucs; 200 Quality Circle; Bryan, TX 77040-5331

Mr. Robert Terry Canup: Westvaco Corporation; P.O. Box 118005; Charleston, SC 29423-8005

Mr. Mike Cap: Inacom; 301 Cayuga Road, Suite 100; Buffalo, NY 14225

Mr. David Capeci: Harleysville Insurance; 355 Maple Avenue; Harleysville, PA 19438-2297

Mr. Mirkeya Capellan: CAP GEMINI America; 3333 Barker Avenue, Floor 1; Bronx, NY 10467-6303

Ms. Suzanne Capener: Project Control Solutions; 3024 North 425 East; Ogden, UT 84414-1960

Ms. Linda Capetillo Cunliffe: University of California at Los Angeles Laboratory of Neurological Imaging; 11997 Laurelwood Drive, #2; Studio City, CA 91604

Mr. Clint H. Carbaugh: Figis, Inc.; 3200 South Maple Avenue; Marshfield, WI 54404-0002

Mr. D. D. Carbonara: Bethel Park School District; 301 Church Road; Bethel Park, PA 15102-1696

Mr. Robert Card: Liebert Corporation; 1050 Dearborn Drive; Columbus, OH 43085-1544

Mr. Diego Cardenas : P.O. Box 40286; Downey, CA 90239-1286

Ms. Jean Cardeno: Micron Electronics Inc.; 460 West Orchard Avenue, Apartment 203; Nampa, ID 83651-1974

Ms. Dona Cardone: Medina County Career Center; 1101 West Liberty Street; Medina, OH 44256-1346

Mr. Tad Cardwell: Technical Management Group, Inc.; 15163 Dahlgren Road, Suite 101; King George, VA 22485

Mr. Don Carey: Darwin Networks; 101 South 5th Street, Suite 3650; Louisville, KY 40202-3126

Mr. M. Chad Carlile: PricewaterhouseCoopers; 6002 Wyndham Woods Drive; Powder Springs, GA 30127

Mr. Eric D. Carlson: ATX Telecommunications; 50 Monument Road; Bala Cynwyd, PA 19004-1723

Ms. Karleen Carlson: Van Diest Supply Company; P.O. Box 610; Webster City, IA 50595-0610

Mr. Kent A. Carlson: Massachusetts Water Resources Authority; 100 1st Avenue; Charlestontown, MA 02129-2043

Mr. Robert Carlson: Kane County; 719 South Batavia Avenue; Geneva, IL 60134-3077

Mr. Thomas Carlson: Stanford University; 562 Salvatierra Street; Stanford, CA 94305-8603

Dr. Tim Carlson Ph.D.: Santa Fe Institute; 1399 Hyde Park Road; Santa Fe, NM 87501-8943

Ms. Wendy Carlson: Harding Manufacturer; 6247 State Route 233; Rome, NY 13440-1037

Mr. Ron Carmanico: IOS Integrated Solutions; 8100 Three Chopt Road, Suite 119; Richmond, VA 23229-4833

Mr. Robert P. Carmichael: Sita; 3100 Cumberland Boulevard SE, Suite 2; Atlanta, GA 30339-5930

Mr. John Carocci: Noah's Ark; 712 C.G. Giffin Road; Locust Grove, GA 30248

Mr. David William Carolla: Auto Diesel Electric; 410 East Sixth Street; Reno, NY 89512

Ms. Barbara Carpenter: Temple College; 2600 South 1st Street; Temple, TX 765047435

Mr. Durant Carpenter: Gemisys Corporation; 7103 South Revere Parkway; Englewood, CO 80112-3992

Mr. John Carpenter: Georgetown University School of Business; 3600 North Street NW; Washington, DC 20007-2670

Mr. Mike Carpenter: Computer Guidance Corporation; 4742 North 24th Street; Phoenix, AZ 85016-4858

Ms. Pamela L. Carpenter-Summers: Port of San Diego; P.O. Box 120488; San Diego, CA 92112-0488

Mr. Michael Carpentier: Browning Auto Group; 18803 Studebaker Road; Cerritos, CA 90703-5386

Ms. Aliza D. Carpio: Kimberly Clark Printing Technology; 529 West 4th Avenue; Escondido, CA 92025-4037

Mr. Gary Carr: Interior Environment Inc.; 251 South 24th Street; Philadelphia, PA 19103-5529

Ms. Leigh Carr: Citrix Systems; 6400 Northwest 6th Way; Fort Lauderdale, FL 33309-6123

Mr. Randy Carr: Consumer Concepts; 5458 Highway 70 West; Morehead City, NC 28557-4516

Mr. Steven Carr: Department of Military Affairs; P.O. Box 988; St. Augustine, FL 32085-0988

Mr. Chris Carrara: Sartorius Corporation; 131 Heartland Boulevard; Edgewood, NY 11717-8358

Mr. Dan Carrera: Intermodal Transportation Services; 9 Campus Drive; Parsippany, NJ 07054-4408

Mr. Jay Carrier: Creative Software Technologies; 160 Turnpike Road, Suite One; Chelmsford, MA 01824

Mr. Ted Carrier: NBS Contract Group; 2139 Austin; Rochester Hills, MI 48309

Mr. Jeff Carrington: The Acacia Group; 7315 Wisconsin Avenue, Lobby 5; Bethesda, MD 20814-3207

Ms. Janet Carroll R.D., L.D.: Department of Veterans Affairs; 4314 Stagecoach Trail; Temple, TX 76502

Mr. Mark E. Carroll: Computer Mastery; 2609 Old Greenbrier Pike; Greenbrier, TN 37073-4507

Ms. Peggy Carroll: Advocate Healthcare; 2100 York Road; Oak Brook, IL 60523-1916

Mr. Terry Carroll: Hollins Consulting; Hollins House, Bishop Thornton; Harrogate, England, United Kingdom HG3 3JZ

Mr. John Carson: Digital Galaxy Net Works; 2226 Eastlake Avenue, #159; Seattle, WA 98102-3489

Mr. Scott Carstens: Metamor ITS; 15608 Marathon Circle, Apartment 404; North Potomac, MD 20878-5365

Ms. Maria Cartagena: Liberty Science Center; 251 Phillip Street; Jersey City, NJ 07305-4600

Mr. Steven Cartell: Southeastern Ohio Regional Medical Center; 1341 Clark Street; Cambridge, OH 43725-9614

Mr. Augustus Carter Jr.: McGraw-Hill; 148 Princeton Highstown Road #S2; Highstown, NJ 08520-1412

Mr. Dan Carter: Bruker; 19 Fortune Drive; Billerica, MA 01821-3957

Mr. John Carter: ARCO; 1545 Greenwich Road; San Dimas, CA 91773-3707

Mr. Paul S. Carter: IBM; 6813 Breezewood Road; Raleigh, NC 27607-4704

Ms. Tiffany Carter: Sarcom Inc.; 3020 South Tech Boulevard; Miamisburg, OH 45342-4860

Mr. Anthony Cartolaro: Torch Communications; 2 Peartree Lane; Levittown, PA 19054-3604

Mr. Terry Caruthers: Litton PRC; 1500 PRC Drive; McLean, VA 22102-5002

Mr. Ron Carver: Federal Express; 2828 Business Park Drive; Memphis, TN 38118-1555

Mr. Joe Casagranda: PP&L; 45 Basin Creek Road; Butte, MT 59701

Mr. Patrick A. Casale: Patrick A. Casale; 2785 East Desert Inn Road, # S-134; Las Vegas, NV 89121-3626

Mr. Jeffrey T. Case: Capital Blue Cross Information Technology; 2500 Elmerton Avenue, MD 7422; Harrisburg, PA 17110

Mr. Kenneth R. Casey Jr.: Traffic Management Services, Inc.; 612 East Superior Street; Alma, MI 48801-1936

Mr. Joseph Caskey: Ingram Micro; 1600 East Saint Andrew Place; Santa Ana, CA 92705-4926

Mr. Arthur Cason: Reliv International Inc.; 136 Chesterfield Industrial Boulevard; Chesterfield, MO 63005-1220

Mr. David D. Cason: United States Air Force Civil Service; 404 North 7th Street; Eglin Air Force Base, FL 32542-5642

Mr. Chester Cass: Cross Creek Apparel, Inc.; 510 Holly Springs Church Road; Mount Airy, NC 27030

Mr. Benjamin Cassan de Valry: Defi Start Up; 4 Place de Valaris; Paris, France 75001

Ms. Rachel M. Cassidy: Main Control Inc.; 3487 Evans Ridge Drive; Atlanta, GA 30341-5848

Mr. Michael Castelluccio: Strategic Finance; 10 Paragon Drive; Montvale, NJ 07645-1718

Mr. Adrian Castro: Rhythms; 708 Charcot Avenue; San Jose, CA 95131

Mr. Darren Castro: Viron Energy Services; 216 Northwest Platte Valley Drive; Kansas City, MO 64150-9793

Mr. Lundy Castro: Upper Peninsula Power Co.; 600 East Lakeshore Drive; Houghton, MI 49931-1868

Mr. Pete B. Catalena: Bettis Corporation; P.O. Box 508; Waller, TX 77484-0508

Mr. Henry P. Catoire III: Tanisys-USA, Inc.; 12201 Technology Boulevard; Austin, TX 78727

Ms. Cathie Cawthon : P.O. Box 440; Raymore, MO 64083-0440

Mr. Vidal Cazarez: Hewlett Packard; 1266 Kifer Road, #101F; Sunnyvale, CA 94086-5304

Mr. John R. Cease: Central & Southwest Services; 2 West 2nd Street; Tulsa, OK 74103

Mr. H. Frank Cervone: DePaul University; 2350 North Kenmore Avenue; Chicago, IL 60614

Ms. Teba Cespon: Miller Freeman PSN; 460 Park Avenue South, Floor 9; New York, NY 10016-7315

Ms. Ginger Chabot: City of Chandler; P.O. Box 4008; Chandler, AZ 85244-4008

Mr. Kent E. Chadrick: PACAF/SFMC; 25 East Street, Suite C-301; Honolulu, HI 96853

Mr. Keith Chadwick: Pittsburgh State University; 1701 South Broadway Street; Pittsburgh, KS 66762-7500

Mr. Rick Chainey: House of the Good Shepherd; 1750 Genesee Street; Utica, NY 13502

Mr. Nitant Chakranarayan: Compaq Computer Corporation; 12818 Justin Trail; Houston, TX 77070-4662

Mr. James Chambers: Ram Technologies; 2025 13th Street; Ashland, KY 41101-3517

Mr. Tam Chan: Shure, Inc.; 222 Hartrey Avenue; Evanston, IL 60202-3696

Mr. Wai Chan: Hawaii Pacific University; 11669 Fort Street, Suite 102; Honolulu, HI 96813

Mr. Mohit Chanana: Ultra International; 2968 Gessner Drive; Houston, TX 77080-2506

Mr. Byron Chancellor: J.F. Day & Company, Incorporated; 2820 6th Ave South; Birmingham, AL 35233-2899

Mr. Khem Chander: Wal-Mart Stores; 2900 North 22nd Street, Apartment P-6; Rogers, AR 72756-2174

Mr. Billy Ray Chandler: Sci Systems, Inc.; P.O. Box 1000; Huntsville, AL 35807-4001

Mr. Trevor Chandler: Drayton Drayton and Lamar; 4141 Columbia Road; Augusta, GA 30907

Mr. Sekhar Chandra: Lucent Technologies, Inc.; 432 Conover Drive; Neshanic Station, NJ 08853-1136

Dr. Joseph J. Chang Ph.D.: The Aerospace Corporation; 2350 East El Segundo Boulevard, M8-695; El Segundo, CA 90245

Mr. Steve Z. Chang: Citicorp; 2203 St. Francis Street; Wilmington, DE 19808

Mr. David Chaplin: Litho Krome Company; P.O. Box 988; Columbus, GA 31902-0988

Mr. Bill Chapman: Marshallnet, L.L.C.; 204 East State Street; Marshalltown, IA 50158-1737

Mr. T. L. Chapman: United Technologies Corporation; 300 Cold Spring Road, Apartment 302; Rocky Hill, CT 06067-3126

Mr. Maruan Charafeddine: Panamerican Chemical D.B.A.; 9449 Briar Forest Drive, Appartment 511; Houston, TX 77063-1040

Ms. Danielle E. Chard: Collier County Government; 2800 Horseshoe Drive North; Naples, FL 34104-6998

Mr. Geoffrey B. Charest: EDS; 137 Elm Lane; Shrewsbury, NJ 07702-4503

Mr. Matt Chase: Digital Think; 1098 Harrison; San Francisco, CA 94103

Mr. Michael L. Chase: Staples Business Advantage; 125 Mushroom Boulevard; Rochester, NY 14623

Ms. Desiree Chastine: Access Graphics; 1426 Pearl Street; Boulder, CO 80302-5340

Mr. Jitendra Chaturvedi: QCom Inc.; 9 Winding Wood Drive, #48; Sayreville, NJ 08872

Mr. Meng Chau: Boston Health Care for the Homeless; 461 Walnut Avenue Floor 3; Jamaica Plain, MA 02130-2331

Mr. Asma Chaudhri: Tran Systems Corporation; 4600 Madison Avenue, Suite 500; Kansas City, MO 64112-3017

Mr. Mario Chavarria: South Western Bell Mobile; 3501 South Padre Island Drive; Corpus Christi, TX 78415-2908

Mr. Manoj Chawla: Metier; 3150 Bristol Street, Suite 230; Costa Mesa, CA 92626-3052

Mr. Jim Cheatle: Motorola, Inc.; 1320 North Plum Grove Road, # I140; Schaumburg, IL 60173-4546

Mr. Kevin J. Check: University of Wisconsin-Madison; 610 Walnut Street, Room 1285; Madison, WI 53705-2336

Mrs. Cindy Cheek: Corporate Systems; 3030 Warrenville Road; Lisle, IL 60532-1000

Mr. Charles L. Chen: Phoenix Technologies Ltd.; 411 East Plumeria Drive; San Jose, CA 95134

Mr. David Chen: Qualitech System; 8882 Chambore Drive; Jacksonville, FL 32256-8485

Mr. David Chen: Advantis; 4440 Winding River Drive; Valrico, FL 33594-7830

Mr. Jian Hua Chen: George Mason University; 4400 University Drive, 5C4; Fairfax, VA 22030

Mr. Paul Chen: Ernst & Young LLP; 515 South Flower Street, #2500; Los Angeles, CA 90071

Mr. Ruxin Chen Ph.D.: Sony Research Lab; 3300 Zanker Road, SJ1B5; San Jose, CA 95134

Mr. Rathinavelu Chengalvarayan: Lucent Technologies; 339 Millcreek Lane; Naperville, IL 60540-8292

Mr. Robert L. Cheripko: American Electric Power; 4500 South Hamilton Road; Groveport, OH 43125-9563

Mr. Seth D. Chernoff: Streamline Internet; 1137 Pearl Street, Suite 205; Boulder, CO 80302

Mr. Peter Cherrick: Computer Land; 764 Long Hill Road; Groton, CT 06340-4273

Mr. Ivan K. Chestnutt: The Mitre Corporation; 7323 West US Highway 90, Suite 402; San Antonio, TX 78227-3562

Mr. Wilson Cheung: DuPont IS; 1515 Garnet Mine Road; Marcus Hook, PA 19061-2099

Mr. Felicia K. Chevis: Telecheck; 5251 Westheimer; Houston, TX 77071-3036

Ms. Donna Cheyne: Interwood Forest Products; 1500 Brooks Industrial Road; Shelbyville, KY 40065-8109

Mr. Prakash Chhatwani: UPP Business Systems; 984 Sweetflower Drive; Hoffman Estates, IL 60194-2394

Mr. M. Chimhanda: National Merchant Bank of Zimbabwe; First Street Union Avenue, Box 2564; Harare, Zimbabwe

Mr. Yuah-Yuan Chin: Lucent Technologies; 184 Liberty Corner Road, Suite 3; Warren, NJ 07059

Mr. Paul Chinnery: Memorial Medical Center West Michigan; P.O. Box 54; Ludington, MI 49431-1906

Mr. Paul Chinski: Motorola; 1301 East Algonquin Road; Schaumburg, IL 60196-1078

Mr. William D. Chipman: Tandy Information Services Corporation; 200 Taylor Street, Suite 500; Fort Worth, TX 76102-7308

Ms. Minda Chipurnoi: Caribiner International; 16 West 61st Street; New York, NY 10023-7606

Mr. Brian Chisholm: Newspaper Printing; 5210 South Lois Avenue; Tampa, FL 33611-3445

Mr. Robert Chisick: Medifor, Inc.; 647 Washington Street; Port Townsend, WA 98368-5743

Mr. Dean A. Choate: Systems Change Networks of Wisconsin; 100 Forest Street North; Stevens Point, WI 54481-1027

Mr. Yoon H. Choi: Ecco Design Inc.; 16 West 19th Street; New York, NY 10011-4205

Mr. Kevin Chopp: Fujitsu-Icl Systems, Inc.; 11085 North Torrey Pines Road; La Jolla, CA 92037-1007

Mr. James Chow: Metamor Software Solutions; 2851 Clover Street; Pittsford, NY 14534-1711

Mr. Sammy Chow: CNA Insurance; CNA Plaza; Chicago, IL 60685

Mr. S. Chowdavaram: Convoy/Neon; 8082 North Maroa Avenue, #102; Fresno, CA 93711

Mr. Rana T. Chowdhury: Whittman-Hart, Inc.; Rural Road 2 Box 220; Le Center, MN 56057-9646

Mr. Dwight Christensen: Philips Semiconductor; 811 East Arques Avenue, #79; Sunnyvale, CA 94086-4523

Mr. Todd Christensen: Mini-Cassia Development Commission; P.O. Box 640; Heyburn, ID 83336-0640

Ms. Lynette Christian: Picture Rocks Intermediate; 5875 North Sanders Road; Tucson, AZ 85743-8402

Ms. Karen N. Christiansen: Chicago Board of Trade; 2015 Glenview Road; Glenview, IL 60025-2849

Mr. Scott Christianson: Micrografx; 1303 East Arapaho Road; Richardson, TX 75081-2494

Ms. Karen Christmyer: Marconi Communications; 1122 F Street; Lorain, OH 44052-2200

Mr. Adam Christopher: University of Denver; 2020 South Race Street #BA367; Denver, CO 80210-4308

Mr. Dale A. Christopherson: Lawson Software; 380 St. Peter Street; St. Paul, MN 55102-1302

Ms. Cindi Lynn Chrzan-Lanigan: Across Frontiers International, Inc.; 211 East 43rd Street, Room 1400; New York, NY 10017-4707

Mr. William Chu: V D O, North America; 188 Brooke Road; Winchester, VA 22603-5762

Mr. F. Chun: Chun & Associates; P.O. Box 12093; San Francisco, CA 94112-0093

Mr. Patrick Chun: Greenwood Multimedia Company; 8200 Jones Road, #318; Richmond, British Columbia, Canada V6Y 3Z2

Mr. Bruno M. Chung: Brigham Young University, Hawaii; 55-220 Kulanai Street, Box 1891 ITG; Laie, HI 96762

Mr. Michael B. Chung: Andersen Consulting; 2101 Rosecrans Avenue, Suite 3300; El Segundo, CA 90245-4750

Ms. Knikkolette Church: Tri Net Corporate Realty Trust; 3480 Preston Ridge Road, Suite 575; Alpharetta, GA 30005-2054

Mr. Jonathan D. Churins: DCWWA; 27 High Street; Poughkeepsie, NY 12601-1962

Mr. Gregg Ciabattoni: Long Island University; 70 Route 340; Orangeburg, NY 10962-2219

Ms. Susan Cicirelli: American Land Title Association; 1828 L Street NW, Suite 705; Washington, DC 20036

Mr. Joe Ciconte: Tug; 1717 22nd Avenue; Melrose Park, IL 60160-1927

Dr. A. Cigada Ph.D.: Politecnico di Milano; Piazza Leonardo Da Vinci 32; Milan, Italy 20133

Mr. Jeffrey Cilcus: Health & Education Services, Incorporated; 131 Rantoul Street; Beverly, MA 01915

Mr. Michael Ciulla: Chase; 43 Pitt Avenue; Staten Island, NY 10314-5633

Mr. Mark Clabaugh: Advanced Computer Telephony Solutions; 336 Fort Pickens Road, Apartment E207; Gulf Breeze, FL 32561-2046

Mr. Taylor Clapp: Genetics & Ivf Institute; 3020 Javier Road; Fairfax, VA 22031-4609

Mr. James A. Clark: Hazlett Lewis & Bieter; 701 Broad Street, Suite 300; Chattanooga, TN 37402-1800

Mr. Jamie Clark: Bellsouth Mobility; 4540 O'Hara Drive; Evansville, IN 47711

Mr. Jason L. Clark: First South Bank; 10611 Deerwood Park Boulevard; Jacksonville, FL 32256-0509

Mr. Kenneth Clark: Adelphia Cable Company; 1 Adelphia Drive; Blairsville, PA 15717-1158

Ms. Lynn Clark: Maxager Technology; 2173 Francisco Boulevard E, Suite C; San Rafael, CA 94901-5523

Mr. Mike Clark: Idaho State University, School of Applied Technology; P.O. Box 8380; Pocatello, ID 83209-0001

Ms. Susan Clark: Alma College; 614 West Superior Street; Alma, MI 48801

Mr. Tom Clark: Arthur Andersen LLP; 424 Church Street, Suite 1000; Nashville, TN 37219-2304

Mr. Brian D. Clarke: Automatic Data Processing; 40 West Gude Drive, Suite 200; Rockville, MD 20850-1166

Mr. Glenn Clarke: Corbel & Company; 1660 Prudential Drive; Jacksonville, FL 32207-8197

Mr. Matthew Clarke: Clorox Services Company; 7208 Johnson Drive; Pleasanton, CA 94588-8005

Ms. Christine Clarson: Sprint; 850 East Altamonte Drive; Altamonte Spring, FL 32701-5002

Mr. Richard Clausen: Teradyne, Inc.; 880 Fox Lane; San Jose, CA 95131-1616

Ms. Robin Clausen: First Data Resources; 7305 Pacific Street #33; Omaha, NE 68114-5447

Mr. Adam W. Clawson C.E.T.: General Dynamics/GTE; 330 Twolick Drive; Indiana, PA 15701

Alan Clay: Peebles, Inc.; 1 Peebles Street; South Hill, VA 23970-3315

Dr. Connie Clayton Ph.D.: SAIC; 414 Henry Street; Alton, IL 60220-2609

Ms. Pillaure Cleary: Fidelity National Title; 810 Charleston Highway; West Columbia, SC 29169

Mr. Samuel Clem: Electronic Data System; P.O. Box 2247; Staunton, VA 24402-2247

Mr. Jim Cleppe: Global Crossing Conferencing; 12110 Pecos Street; Denver, CO 80234-2081

Mr. Kevin Clifford: ABM; 500 Howard Street, #300; San Francisco, CA 94133

Mr. Vivi Clift: GE-Industrial Systems; 7000 West Bert Kouns Industrial; Shreveport, LA 71129-3000

Mr. Steve Clinton: Picus LLC; 2877 Guardian Lane , Suite 301; Virginia Beach, VA 23452-7328

Mr. Christopher M. Clore Esq.: Acme Die Casting; 5626, 21st Street; Racine, WI 53406

Ms. Gilly Clough: Sun Microsystems Inc.; 6800 Paragon Place, Suite 226; Richmond, VA 23230-1652

Mr. David Clow : 853 North Edinburgh Avenue; Los Angeles, CA 90046-6903

Ms. Melissa Coan: Plc PC Control Systems; 1386 Sunset Road; Cleveland, OH 44124-1657

Ms. Melissa Coates: Bachow/Coastel Operations, Inc.; 4549 Johnston Street; Lafayette, LA 70503

Mr. Craig E. Cobb: Bell Atlantic; P.O. Box 6360; Syracuse, NY 13206-6360

Mr. Ed Coburn: Quantum Corporation; 10125 Federal Drive; Colorado Springs, CO 80908-4508

Mr. William C. Coburn III: The University of Texas Health Center at Tyler; 11937 US Highway 271; Tyler, TX 75708

Mr. Larry Cochran: Oce-USA; 5450 North Cumberland Avenue; Chicago, IL 60656-1484

Ms. Sandy Coffey: Cambridge Technology Partners; 841 Apollo Streeet; El Segundo, CA 90245

Mr. Joseph Cohen: Phoenix Web Services; 6001 Lakeside Avenue, Suite 33; Richmond, VA 23228-5735

Mr. Tom Coker: Communication Corporation; 1001 Lockwood Avenue; Columbus, GA 31906-2414

Mr. Michael E. Colbaugh: Union Switch & Signal; 1000 Technology Drive; Pittsburgh, PA 15219-3104

Ms. Bonnie Cole: Smarte Carte, Inc.; 4455 White Bear Parkway; St. Paul, MN 55110-7641

Mr. Curtis E. Cole: Carrier Transicold; 700 Olympic Drive; Athens, GA 30601-1652

Mr. Mark Cole: McCarter; P.O. Box 868; Laurinburg, NC 28353-0868

Mr. Robert Cole: IBM Global Services; 3200 Lake Emma Road; Lake Mary, FL 32746-3334

Dr. Roland Cole Ph.D.: Software Patent Institute; 9225 Indian Creek Parkway, Suite 1100; Overland Park, KS 66210-2029

Mr. Dale Colemere: Planthink Concepts, Inc.; P.O. Box 16177; Panama City, FL 32406-6177

Mr. David Coles: Decision Consultants, Inc.; 1654 Briar Ridge Drive; Ann Arbor, MI 48108-9400
Mr. Scott Collard: G.T.E. Internet Working; 10 Fawcett Street; Cambridge, MA 02138-1171
Mr. Ray Collazo: Loran, Inc.; 1705 East Colton Avenue; Redlands, CA 92374-4971
Ms. Joann Collins: Lincoln County High School; 345 Ward Avenue; Lincolnton, GA 30817-0579
Mr. Kevin Collins: Canon USA; 2110 Washington Boulevard, Suite 150; Arlington, VA 22204-5799
Mr. Lawton Collins: Bell and Howell; 6205 Summit Triangle; Norcross, GA 30092-2734
Ms. Shirley Collins: Software Applications and Computer; 10972 Northwest 41st Drive; Pompano Beach, FL 33065-7762
Mr. Jose Colom: CR Industries; 57 South Commerce Way, Suite 140; Bethlehem, PA 18017-8964
Ms. Cathy Colston: Prosoft, Inc.; 2300 Claredon Boulevard, #1111; Arlington, VA 22201
Mr. Derek Comeaux: Lafayette Parish Clerk; P.O. Box 2009; Lafayette, LA 70502-2009
Ms. Tammi Comer: Fruth, Inc.; Route 1, Box 332; Point Pleasant, WV 25550-9726
Mr. Thomas G. Comfort: US West; 1600 7th Avenue, #2000; Seattle, WA 98191-0002
Mr. Jim Conaway: Ameritech; 1100 East Waterloo Road; Akron, OH 44306-3861
Mr. Chris Condo: Adobe Air Inc.; 500 South 15th Street; Phoenix, AZ 85034-3399
Mr. Jon Conine: Department of Social and Health Services; P.O. Box 9162; Olympia, WA 98507-9162
Mr. Bruce A. Conklin: Edfund; 3300 Zinfandel Drive; Rancho Cordova, CA 95670-6043
Mr. Terry W. Conley: Hazard Technical College; 101 Vo Tech Drive; Hazard, KY 41701-1122
Ms. Teri Connally: Synovus Technnologies, Inc.; 500 11th Street; Columbus, GA 31901
Mr. Dang Conner: ANTEC; 4215 Willow Grass Court; Cumming, GA 30041-1247
Mr. George W. Conquest: Southeastern Community College; 1015 South Gear Avenue; West Burlington, IA 52655-1614
Mr. Jason Conrad: Consolidated Natural Gas; 445 West Main Street, #2450; Clarksburg, WV 26301
Mr. Jerome Charles Conrad: CWT; 193 Courtland Street; Rockford, MI 49341-1064
Mr. C. E. Conway: B-1B Training System Support Center (TSSC); 465 Second Avenue; Dyess Air Force Base, TX 79607-1745
Mr. Dwight Cook: Americold Logistics; 10 Glenlake Parkway, Suite 800; Atlanta, GA 30328
Mr. Edmund J. Cook: Test Technology Inc.; 1825 Underwood Drive; Delran, NJ 08075
Ms. Kathleen Cook: INTELSAT; 3400 International Drive, Box 24; Washington, DC 20008-3006
Mr. Robert J. Cook: Oracle Corporation; 400 Linden Oaks; Rochester, NY 14625
Mr. John Patrick Cooke Jr.: ESS Electronic Sales Systems; 55 Broad Street; New York, NY 10004
Mr. Guy Cooley: United States Air Force; 865 Misty Valley Road; O Fallon, IL 62269-1874
Ms. Anne R. Coolidge: W.P. Carey & Company, Inc.; 50 Rockfeller Plaza #2nd; New York, NY 10020-1605
Mrs. Inez Coon: Mercy Information Systems; 200 Jefferson Avenue; Grand Rapids, MI 49503-4502
Mr. Gary Cooper: Cannondale Corporation; 172 Friendship Village Road; Bedford, PA 15522-6600
Ms. Karen Cooper: Rhode Island Department of Education; 255 Westminster Street; Providence, RI 02903-3414
Ms. Kim Cope: Kiawah Island Community; 23 Beachwalker Drive; Johns Island, SC 29455-5652
Mr. Patrick Copland: Lockheed Martin IMS; 515 North Sycamore Street; Santa Ana, CA 92701-4637
Mrs. Kathy Coppes: University of Findlay; 349 Trenton Avenue; Findlay, OH 45840-3745
Ms. Deirdre Corio: MetLife Human Resources Spectrum; 1 Madison Avenue, Area 3F; New York, NY 10010-3603
Ms. Pamela Cornell: Chubb Computer Services; 8 Sylvan Way; Parsippany, NJ 07054-3801
Mr. Keith Corpier: United States Department of Agriculture Farm Service Agency; 700 West Capitol Avenue, Suite 3416; Little Rock, AR 72201-3215
Ms. Yvonne Corppetts: Corppetts & Associates; 6225 Honeysuckle Lane; Walls, MS 38680-9505
Mr. Conrad Corral: Medsep Corporation; 1630 West Industrial Park Street; Covina, CA 91722-3419
Ms. Pat Correa: Music Service of South Dakota, Inc.; 900 North Western Avenue; Sioux Falls, SD 57104-2001
Mr. Jose Francisco Correa Navas: Servicios Pulicitarios Computarizados; Farm Cuaria 200, 50 North, 75 0; Moravia, Costa Rica
Mr. Ted Corsaro: Hill-Rom; 1695 West Sandcroft Drive; Charleston, SC 29407-3068
Mr. Conrado Cortez: Kamehameha Schools Bishop estate KSBE; 567 South King Street, Suite 618; Honolulu, HI 96813-3036
Mr. Dave Corun: Shelter Systems, Ltd.; 633 Stone Chapel Road; Westminster, MD 21157
Mr. Corey Coscioni: Peapod; 1264 West Ardmore Avenue; Chicago, IL 60660-3410
Mr. Len Cossette: Averstar, Inc.; 21487A Great Mills Road; Lexington Park, MD 20653
Mr. Ben Costa: E-Plus, Inc.; 130 Futura Drive; Pottstown, PA 19464-3480
Ms. Mary Shelby Costello: Productivity Point International; 7160 Skillman Street, Apartment 2513; Dallas, TX 75231-5633
Mr. Jeffrey Cote: The Summit Group; 4215 Edison Lakes Parkway; Mishawaka, IN 46545-1424
Mr. Michael Coules: Wells Appel Land Strategies; 1516 Locust Street; Philadelphia, PA 19102-4401
Mr. Kevin Coulter: Brown Company; 15 Broken Tree Road; Medway, MA 02053-2447
Ms. Libbie Counselman: Rider University; 109 Delmere Drive, Apartment 10; Princeton, NJ 08540-7011
Ms. Donica Courter: REALTECH Systems Corporation; Empire State Building, 250 5th Avenue, 77th Floor; New York, NY 10118
Mr. Carl Cover: Speechlaw, Inc.; 27758 Santo Margarita, #282; Mission Viejo, CA 92691
Mr. Richard Cowan: Verifone-Hp Subsidiary; 100 Kahelu Avenue; Miliani, HI 96789391
Mr. Kevin A. Cowie: Tyco Healthcare/U.S. Surgical Corporation; 195 McDermott Road; North Haven, CT 06473
Mrs. Tanya Cox: Itawamba Community College; 2176 South Eason Boulevard; Tupelo, MS 38801-5981
Mr. Jason Coyan: Nationwide Insurance; 3 Nationwide Plaza 3-12-06; Columbus, OH 43215-2462
Mr. David R. Cozzi: SPSS Inc.; 1415 West Partridge Lane, Unit 5; Arlington Heights, IL 60004-7439
Mr. Rich Cozzi: Kutol Products; 7650 Camargo Road; Cincinnati, OH 45253-3108
Mr. Curtis M. Cragg: The Audible Difference; 5981 Skylinks Way; Livermore, CA 94550-1163
Mr. Benjamin Cramer: Keane, Inc.; 6031 Rutherglenn Drive; Houston, TX 77096-3828
Mr. Tim Crane: American States Insurance; P.O. Box 1636; Indianapolis, IN 46206-1636
Mr. Jeremy M. Crawf: Safe-Co Corporation; 12179 Sycamore Terrace Drive, Apartment E; Cincinnati, OH 45249-8132
Ms. Carrie L. Crawford: Group III Communications, Inc.; 204 West Kansas Avenue, Suite 103; Independence, MO 64050-3714
Mr. Leslie Crawford: Ameritech; 2001 Gulseth; Madison, WI 53703
Mr. Ted Crawford: Harris Corporation, GCSD; 150 South Wickham Road, MS W3/7755; Melbourne, FL 32904-1190
Mr. Jean M. Craye: Fleury Michon; BP 1; Pouzauges, France 85700
Ms. Elizabeth Creager: CMR; 1385 Enterprise Drive; West Chester, PA 19380-5959
Mr. James C. Crenner: Conmed Aspen Labs.; 14603 East Fremont Avenue; Englewood, CO 80112-4253
Mr. Michael Crews: Tri States Automotive Warehouse; 3966 Old Cottondale Road; Marianna, FL 32448-3612
Mr. Christopher S. Cripe: Gibson Insurance; 300 South St. Louis Boulevard; South Bend, IN 46617
Officer Bill Crippen: Western Correctional Institution; 13800 McMullen Highway SW; Cumberland, MD 21502-5622
Mr. Charles T. Crisler: Personal Computer Services; 10865 Indeco Drive; Cincinnati, OH 45241
Mr. Tedd Crist: Tacoma Public Utilities; 3628 South 35th Street; Tacoma, WA 98409-3115
Mr. Mark Cristiano: Malden Mills; P.O. Box 809; Lawrence, MA 01842-1609
Mr. Robert Crocker: Fort Wayne Wire Die, Inc.; 10004 Wheatfield Lane; Fort Wayne, IN 46825-1739
Mr. Jim Cromeenes: Metamor ITS; 3435 Marsh Creek Way; Elk Grove, CA 95758-4664
Mr. John Crooks: Delfin Systems; 8739 Cold Plain Court; Springfield, VA 22153-2423
Mr. Jim Cross: Montana Power; 40 East Broadway Street; Butte, MT 59701-9394
Mr. Brendan Crowe: Computer Sciences Corporation; 700 Washington Street; Bath, ME 04530
Ms. Cheryl Crowsey: Nextel; 201 State Route 17; Rutherford, NJ 07070-2574
Mr. Benjamin Cruz Jr.: TRW, Inc.; 1908 Faymont Drive; Manhattan Beach, CA 90266
Mr. Kenny J. Cruz: Warner Bros.; 4000 Warner Boulevard; Burbank, CA 91522
Mr. Jack Cuddy: Alabama Department of Industrial Relations; Room 521; Montgomery, AL 36131-0001
Mr. Robert F. Cudworth Jr.: Alltel Information Services; 3669 Wylam Avenue; Scranton, PA 18507-1540
Mrs. Patsy Lee Culbert: Solomon Software; 200 East Hardin Street; Findlay, OH 45840-4925
Mr. Jeff Culpepper: Cabot Corporation; 1095 Windward Ridge Parkway; Alpharetta, GA 30005-2257
Mr. Ross J. Culpepper: Protel Inc.; 4150 Kidron Road; Lakeland, FL 33811-1274
Mr. David A. Culver: Fisher Scientific; 2000 Park Lane; Pittsburgh, PA 15275
Mr. Henry Culver: Braun Consulting; 30 West Monroe; Chicago, IL 60603
Mr. Michael Culver: Mount Graham Alternative High School; 734 11th Street; Safford, AZ 85546
Mr. Donald A. Cumfer: Vapacon, Inc.; 464 Freeze Street; Cookeville, TN 38501
Mr. Deverett Cummings: University of Virginia; P.O. Box 234, Health Sciences; Charlottesville, VA 22902-0234
Mr. Mark Cummings: College of the Redwoods; 7351 Tompkins Hill Road; Eureka, CA 95501-9300
Mr. Michael Cummings: Honeywell Inc. Micro Switch Division; 6006 Sedgefield Terrace; Midlothian, VA 23112-6398
Mr. John Cummins: MedStar Health; 1009 Adcock Road; Lutherville Timonium, MD 21093-4802
Mr. Rob Cummons: Sears Credit; 6 Neshaminy Interplex, Suite 500; Feasterville Trevose, PA 19053-6999
Mr. Andrew Cunningham: Air New Zealand; 6001 Avion Drive; Los Angeles, CA 90045-5691
Ms. Christine Cunningham: American International Group; 1700 Market Street, Floor 18; Philadelphia, PA 19103-3913
Mr. John A. Cunningham: Gibson Greetings Inc.; P.O. Box 371804, Gibson Card Division; Cincinnati, OH 45222-1804
Ms. Karin Cunningham: Federal Home Loan Bank of Pittsburgh; 323 Caperton Street; Pittsburgh, PA 15210
Ms. Lori A. Cunningham: Nestle USA, Inc.; 800 North Brand Boulevard; Glendale, CA 91203-3213
Mr. Owen Cunningham: Fidelity Investments; 268 Hartford Turnpike, Apartment D6; Tolland, CT 06084-2831
Mr. Paul Cunningham: Vexcel Imaging Corporation; 3131 Indian Road; Boulder, CO 80301-2976
Ms. Susanne Currivan: Modis Consulting; 1290 East Main Street; Stamford, CT 06902-3555
Ms. Margaret Elizabeth Curtis: Mid State RV Center; P.O. Box 1330; Byron, GA 31008
Mr. Mark Curtis: Ciber, Inc.; 3327 Brockport Spencerport Road; Spencerport, NY 14559-2169
Mr. Matt Curtis: Yaskawa Electric; 2121 Norman Drive South; Waukegan, IL 60085
Ms. Denise Cyrus: Productivity Point International; 106 Association Drive; Charleston, WV 25311-1217
Ms. Rebecca Czupryna: Saratoga Systems, Inc.; 2s748 Grove Lane; Warrenville, IL 60555-2714
Ms. Lisa D'Alessio: Microage; 187 East Union Avenue; East Rutherford, NJ 07073-2123
Mr. Bill D'Alonzo Jr.: RCI; 298 New Churchmans Road; New Castle, DE 19720
Ms. Miriah G. D'Aponte: Baruch College; 17 Lexington Avenue; New York, NY 10010
Mr. Echo J. D'Uva: Benjamin Rush Center; 650 South Salina Street; Syracuse, NY 13202
Mr. Verlyn C. Dabell: FMC Corporation; P.O. Box 4111; Pocatello, ID 83205-4111
Mr. Stephen F. Dabney: Inverness Counsel, Inc.; 545 Madison Avenue, Floor 9; New York, NY 10022-4296
Dr. Vladimir Dadeshidze Ph.D.: Siemens Medical Systems; 2501 North Barrington Road; Hoffman Estates, IL 60195
Dr. Serhan Dagtas Ph.D: Phillip's Research; 345 Scarborough Road; Briarcliff Manor, NY 10510-2027
Ms. Kim Dahl: Mathison Company; 1213 North Avenue; Fargo, ND 58102-4627
Mr. Paul J. Daigle: GES Exposition Services; 3807 Toulouse; New Orleans, LA 70119
Mr. Jacques Dailey: Peregrine Systems; 9270 Amys Street, Apartment 29; Spring Valley, CA 91977-6606
Mr. Mike Dailey: Michigan I&C; 46200 Port Street, Lot 4; Plymouth, MI 48170-6048
Ms. Tisa Dais: NASDAQ; 4615 Captain Covington Place; Upper Marlboro, MD 20772
Mr. Kevin Dalgleish: Nortel Networks; 2924 11th Street Ne; Calgary, Alberta, Canada T2E 7L7
Mr. Mark Dalic: Alltel; 2000 Highland Road; Twinsburg, OH 44087-2248
Mr. Bill Dalton: LeMars Community Schools; 921, 3rd Avenue SW; LeMars, IA 51031
Mr. Gordon B. Daly: U.S. West; 1999 Broadway; Denver, CO 80111
Ms. Susan Daly: Broward Community College; 225 East Las Olas Boulevard, Room 330; Fort Lauderdale, FL 33301-2298
Mr. Bill Dana: Troy Systems; 3701 Pender Drive, Suite 500; Fairfax, VA 22030-6045
Mr. Behnam Danai: Abb Systems Control; 451 El Camino Real; Santa Clara, CA 95050-4300
Mr. Jon Dandrea: Charles E. Smith; 2345 Crystal Drive; Arlington, VA 22202-4801
Ms. Maily Dang: Mariner Post Acute Network; 15415 Katy Freeway, Suite 800; Houston, TX 77094
Ms. Jennifer Danielson: Diamond Technology Partners, Inc.; 10 Harries Street, Apartment 3; Boston, MA 02109-1133
Mr. Larry Dao: Toshiba America; 13741 Bewley Street; Garden Grove, CA 92843-4003
Ms. Mary Lynn Darcy: Micromedex Inc.; 6200 South Syracuse Way; Englewood, CO 80111-4737
Mr. David Darise: Sherwood Promotions; 1335 South Chillicothe Road; Aurora, OH 44202-8066
Ms. Melissa Darnell: Santa Clara Coastland; 3421 Monroe Street; Santa Clara, CA 95051-1417
Mr. Dan Dart: Computers Unlimited; 2407 Montana Avenue; Billings, MT 59101-2336
Mr. Ravindra Das: Alltel Information Services; 1853 Beacon Hill Circle, H24; Cuyahoga Falls, OH 44221
Dr. Subhasish Dasgupta Ph.D.: Farleigh Dickinson University; 1000 River Road, H323E; Teaneck, NJ 07666
Ms. Shannon M. Daugard: TRW; 823 Brookside Drive; Lansing, MI 48917-9295
Mr. Heath Daugherty: Precoat Metals; 4301 South Spring Avenue; St. Louis, MO 63116
Mr. Joe Daugirdas: Applied Industrial Technology; 3301 Euclid Avenue; Cleveland, OH 44115
Ms. Mirna Dault: Bremen Bearings; 1342 West Plymouth Street; Bremen, IN 46506-1954
Ms. Gina Davalos: Ameritech; 2000 West Ameritech Center Drive; Hoffman Estates, IL 60606
Ms. Tania Davey: Pacific Bell; 500 East Main Street; Alhambra, CA 91801-3961
Mr. Michael A. Davidson: Methodist Hospital; 6565 Fannin Street, Suite B 2-22; Houston, TX 77030-2707
Mr. E. Davies: The Magic Camera Company; Shepperton Studios; Shepperton, England, United Kingdom TW17 0QD
Mr. Tudor Davies: Spectrum Signal Processing; 200-2700 Produciton Way; Burnaby, British Columbia, Canada V3E 3J8
Mr. Gilberto Davila: Abbott Labs; P.O. Box 1345; Quebradillas, Puerto Rico 00678-1345
Ms. Anne Davis: Nationwide Insurance; 1 Nationwide Plaza 1-29; Columbus, OH 43215-2239
Ms. Kandy Davis: A&A

Services; 2136 West Park Place Boulevard; Stone Mountain, GA 30087-3538

Mr. Ken Davis: Bell & Howell Information and Learning; 300 North Zeeb Road; Ann Arbor, MI 48103-1553

Ms. Kim Davis: KD Technologies; 8600 Boulevard East, #4B; North Bergen, NJ 07047

Mr. Les Davis: Palm Beach County Court Administration; 205 North Dixie Highway, Suite 5.2500; West Palm Beach, FL 33401

Ms. Linda R. Davis: Hughes Network Systems; 100 Lake Forest Boulevard; Gaithersburg, MD 20877-2616

Mr. Michael Davis: Texas Technical University Health Sciences Center; Health Science Library; Lubbock, TX 79430-0001

Mr. Russ Davis: Diskriter Inc.; 3257 West Liberty Avenue; Pittsburgh, PA 15216-2390

Mr. Ted E. Davis: St. Petersburg Police; 1300 1st Avenue North; St. Petersburg, FL 33705-1588

Mr. Terry Davis: Division Professional Registration; 3505 Missouri Boulevard; Jefferson City, MO 65106-7111

Mr. Stratos Davlos: Inference; 100 Rowland Way; Novato, CA 94945

Mr. Brian Dawson: Midwest Hidta; 10220 North Ambassador Drive, Suite 620; Kansas City, MO 64153-2374

Mr. Dale Dawson: MSX International; 1765 Star Batt Drive; Rochester Hills, MI 48309-3708

Mr. Scott Day: Baylor University; P.O. Box 97268; Waco, TX 79798-7268

Ms. Shary Day: Sprint PCS; 7900 College Boulevard; Overland Park, KS 66210-1867

Ms. Susan Day: A Drive Computers Inc.; 630 Skylark Drive, Suite A; Charleston, SC 29407-1718

Mr. Don De Cristofaro: Kimberly-Clark; 401 North Lake Street; Neenah, WI 54956-2072

Mr. Peter A. de la Mora: Westlake Group; 4714 Lakeside Meadow Drive; Missouri, TX 77459-1644

Mr. Randy De Lorenzo: CommNet Cellular, Inc.; 8350 East Crescent Parkway; Englewood, CO 80111

Mr. Gerard De Man: New Jersey Transit; 1 Penn Plaza East; Newark, NJ 07105-2245

Mr. Sam De Marco: Black & Veatch; 11401 Lamar; Overland Park, KS 66211

Mr. Carl De Pasquale: Business Edge; 399 Thornall Street; Edison, NJ 08837

Ms. Catherine M. Deal: 136 Willow Street; Wollaston, MA 02170-2922

Mr. Lon R. Dean: ITT Industries Corporation, Systems Division; 775 Daedlian Drive; Rome, NY 13441

Mr. Paul Dean: C.C.I. Triad; 2 Wilshire Boulevard; Saratoga Springs, NY 12866-9062

Ms. Theresa Lea Dean: Vectra Bank Colorado; 616 East Speer Boulevard; Denver, CO 80203

Mr. Frank Deardurff III: Hane Training, Inc.; 120 South 7th Street; Terre Haute, IN 47807-3607

Mr. Dennis Deas: Andersen Consulting; 2612 East 11th Avenue; Denver, CO 80206-3206

Mr. Bert Debusschere: Engine Research Center; 1500 Engineering Drive; Madison, WI 53706-1609

Mr. Tom Decillis: Boeing; 14771 La Capelle Road; La Mirada, CA 90638-4608

Mr. Michael Decker: Litton PRC; 301 West Dominick Street; Rome, NY 13440

Mr. Vo Vann Decker: Allegany Arc; 240 Connor Street; Wellsville, NY 14895-1055

Mr. Tawfiq Deek: Winonics Brea; 660 North Puente Street; Brea, CA 92821-2880

Ms. Tina Deel: PCCA Head Start Program, Inc.; P.O. Box 1119; Chatham, VA 24531-1119

Mr. Eddie Deeney: Aiesec International; 135 West 50th Street, Floor 17; New York, NY 10020

Mr. Daniel P. Defonte: G.B.M.; 201 Basin Street Plaza; Williamsport, PA 17701

Mr. Albert A. Dekin Ph.D.: Binghamton University; P.O. Box 6000; Binghamton, NY 13902

Mr. Edward Del Gaudio: TTSI; 18 Worlds Fair Drive; Somerset, NJ 08873

Mr. Paul Del Giudice: Cablevision; 2045 State Route 27; Edison, NJ 08817-3334

Mr. Jimmy Dela Cruz: Sun America; 21650 Oxnard Street; Woodland Hills, CA 91367-4901

Ms. Karen Delaney: CVPH Medical Center; 75 Beekman Street; Plattsburgh, NY 12901-1437

Ms. Dina Delgiudice: Lewco Securities; 34 Exchange Place; Jersey City, NJ 07302-3885

Mr. Roger S. Delight: Cellnet Data Services; 2523 Sea Biscuit Court; Santa Rosa, CA 95401-5695

Mr. Emerson Deline: CDSC; 352 Classon Avenue, #358; Brooklyn, NY 11238-1306

Mr. Edward Dellget: Community Mental Health; 68353 Bannock Road; Saint Clairsville, OH 43950

Mr. Daryl Dellinger: Continental Teves; 1103 Jamestown Road; Morganton, NC 28655-9285

Ms. Lori Deloof: Venture Services; P.O. Box 229; Gurnee, IL 60031-0229

Ms. Darlene Delroy: Health First, Inc.; 1350 Hickory Street; Melbourne, FL 32901-3276

Mr. Joseph Deluise: Howard Systems International; 695 East Main Street; Stanford, CT 06901

Mr. Eric Demby: Applied Legal Technologies; 401 2nd Avenue South, Suite 822; Minneapolis, MN 55401-2306

Mr. Matthew Demetros: Network Catalyst; 1370 Reynolds Avenue, Suite 101; Irvine, CA 92614-5545

Ms. Tanya Demjanec: International Safety Instruments, Inc.; 922 Hurricane Shoals Road NE; Lawrenceville, GA 30043-4822

Mr. Stephen Demme: Zcom2; 1821 Miccosukee Commons Drive; Tallahassee, FL 32308-5433

Mr. Don Denman: Continuum Tech; 220 Continuum Drive; Fletcher, NC 28732-7444

Mr. Joseph Dennis: Speer & Associates; 8215 Roswell Road; Atlanta, GA 30350-6451

Mr. Robert Dennis: Maher & Maher; 530 Prospect Avenue; Little Silver, NJ 07739-1444

Mr. William David Denson: EDS; 10800 River Road; Westwego, LA 70094-2040

Mr. Gary Dentremont: Towers Perrin; 1500 Market Street; Philadelphia, PA 19102-2100

Mr. Timothy Desalvo: Newport News; 513 Oyster Point Road; Newport News, VA 23602-6919

Ms. Kathleen Desantis: Amalgamated Life; 730 Broadway; New York, NY 10003-9511

Mr. Franck H. Desbrandes: ATM Network Design; 10 Rue Jeanne D'Arc; Sevres, France 92704

Ms. Linda Desmond: Cycloid-Vision; 84 7th Street; Providence, RI 02906-2840

Ms. Mary Desmond: SPIN Design; 19 Pond Road; Gloucester, MA 01930-1834

Mr. Shyam Devadas: Peirce-Phelps, Inc.; 10000 Virginia Manor Road, Suite 350; Beltsville, MD 20705-4205

Mr. Venkatachalam Devanarayanan: Capital One; 11013 West Broad Street; Glen Allen, VA 23060

Mr. Murty Devata: MSD Engineering; 42 Tealham Drive; Etobicoke, Ontario, Canada M9V 3T6

Mr. Jim Devincentis: Thoughtware Inc.; P.O. Box 771; Helen, GA 30545-0771

Ms. Patricia Griffis DeWalt: The Carle Foundation; 611 West Park Street; Urbana, IL 61801-2529

Mr. Aaron Dewell: Akcess, Inc.; MB 2937, 3705 Arctic Boulevard; Anchorage, AK 99503-5774

Mr. Nazmin Dhanani: Bandai America; 21661 Brookhurst Street, Apartment 402; Huntington Beach, CA 92646-8165

Mr. Kartik Dhekne: Ciber Inc.; 20 Valley Avenue, Apartment B5; Westwood, NJ 07675-3605

Mr. J. Dia: Quarry Technologies; 8 New England Executive Park; Burlington, MA 01803-5007

Mr. Chris Diamond: Federated Group; 3025 West Salt Creek Lane; Arlington Heights, IL 60005-1083

Mr. Mark Diana: Virginia Commonwealth University; P.O. Box 980203; Richmond, VA 23298-0203

Mr. Hebert J. Diaz-Flores: University of California at Davis; 1811 Rushmore Lane; Davis, CA 95616-6654

Ms. Kathy Dicaltado: National Penn Bank; P.O. Box 547; Boyertown, PA 19512-0547

Mr. David Dicarlo: Marconi Medical Systems; 5471 State Route 322; Windsor, OH 44099-9754

Ms. Denise Dicataldo: TWJ Consulting; 5319 University, #310; Irvine, CA 92626

Mr. Paul Dichiara: City Wholesale Grocery; 300 Industrial Drive; Birmingham, AL 35211-4456

Mr. James Dick MD: 80 Cove Road; Oyster Bay, NY 11771

Dr. Kenneth L. Dick Ph.D.: University of Nebraska at Omaha; 1720 South 155 Circle; Omaha, NE 68144

Mr. Don Dickerson: Bozell Kamstra; 100 North 6th Street; Minneapolis, MN 55403-1505

Mr. Dallas Difrancesco: Utah State Tax Commission; 210 North 1950 West; Salt Lake City, UT 84134-0002

Mr. Rhagan Dillingham: Powertel; 10172 Linn Station Road; Louisville, KY 40223-3887

Mr. Michael Dimeo: Eastman Gelatine; 227 Washington Street; Peabody, MA 01960-6998

Mr. Patrick Dine: Edge Technologies Inc.; 3701 Pender Drive, Suite 150; Fairfax, VA 22030

Ms. L. K. Dingelstedt: Stautzenberger College; 5355 Southwyck Boulevard; Toledo, OH 43614

Mr. Michael F. Diruscio: Albany International; P.O. Box 5837; Greenville, SC 29606-5837

Ms. Marilyn Disbrow: Apl Limited; 1111 Broadway; Oakland, CA 94607-4036

Mr. Joseph DiStefano : 1159 Astor Avenue; Bronx, NY 10469-5434

Mr. Sean Dittmore: Microsoft Corporation; 19429 Normandy Park Drive SW; Normandy Park, WA 98166-4131

Mr. Mark Dixon: Pioneer-Standard Electronic; 4800 East 131st Street; Cleveland, OH 44105-7132

Mr. Rason Dobbs: Sweetheart Cup Company; P.O. Box 380, 1355 Highway 138; Conyers, GA 30012-0380

Mr. Igor Dobruskin: Hunter College; 695 Park Avenue, Suite E1323; New York, NY 10021-5085

Mr. Robert R. Dockery: Western Piedmont Community College; 1001 Burkemont Avenue; Morganton, NC 28655-4511

Ms. Karen Doescher: Saratogian; 20 Lave Avenue; Saratoga Springs, NY 12866-2356

Mr. Joseph A. Dohle: Love Lace Health Systems; 5400 Gibson Boulevard SE; Albuquerque, NM 87108-4729

Mr. Francis R. Dohrau Jr.: New York State Department of Family Assistance; 41 Wertman Lane; Loudonville, NY 12211-2142

Mr. Ram Dokka: Suntory Water Group; 2141 Powers Ferry Road SE; Marietta, GA 30067

Mr. Brian A. Doll: Quality Computer Products; 2709 South Queen Street; York, PA 17403-9718

Ms. Yasha Domanski: MSC Industrial Supply; 75 Maxess Road; Melville, NY 11747-3151

Mr. Martin Dombrowski: EG&G, Inc.; 3610 Collins Ferry Road, #K7; Morgantown, WV 26505-2353

Ms. Mayda Domenech: Children's Home Society; 800 Northwest 15th Street; Miami, FL 33136-1412

Mr. Paul Donaghy: Aquent Partners; 4835 Lyndon B. Johnson Freeway; Dallas, TX 75244-6005

Mr. Richard S. Donald: Lutheran Immigrant Refugee Service; 700 Light Street; Baltimore, MD 21230

Mrs. Debbie Donaldson-Tate: Navistar International; 2521 West Grunewald; Blue Island, IL 60406

Mr. Jim Donati: Nextel Communications; 851 Trafalgar Court; Orlando, FL 32810-5941

Mr. Luiz Felipe Donato: Sga - Systems & Service; Av. Ga. Felicissimo Gardozo 835/ 605 - Blockz; Rio de Janeiro, Brazil 22631360

Ms. Jin Jing Jennifer Dong: Country Wide Home Loan; 6400 Legacy Drive PTX 478; Plano, TX 75024

Mr. Ray Donnelly: New Venture Technologies Corporation; 176 South Road; Enfield, CT 06082-4414

Mr. Thomas M. Donnelly: Cargo System, Inc.; 88 Pine Street; New York, NY 10005-1801

Mr. Kevin Donoghue: Matrix Integrated Systems; 4050 Lakeside Drive; Richmond, CA 94806-1936

Mr. Terry Dooley: Shazam Network; 6700 Pioneer Parkway; Johnston, IA 50131-1605

Mr. Henk J. Doorenspleet: Rabofacet BV; P.O. Box 17100; Utrecht, Netherlands 3500 HG

Ms. Cheryl A. Dopp: Access Graphics; 1426 Pearl Street; Boulder, CO 80302-5340

Ms. Suresh Doraiswamy: Yazaki North America; 6801 North Haggerty Road; Canton, MI 48187-3538

Mr. Nick Dordea: BMC Software, Inc.; 10926 Jollyville Road, Apartment 1209; Austin, TX 78759-4863

Ms. Julie Dorey: Xerox Corporation; 54 Cranberry Circle; Sudbury, MA 01776-1063

Mr. Juzer Doriwala: The Internet Dnystive, Inc.; 4806 West 129th Street; Alsip, IL 60803

Mr. Daniel D. Dorsey: Siemens ICN, Inc.; 515 Madison Avenue; Cape Canaveral, FL 32920-5101

Mr. Oliver Dossman: Kirkland's; 805 North Parkway; Jackson, TN 38305-3039

Mr. Vered Dotan: Datatex, Ltd.; Haudem 3; Petah Tikva, Israel

Mr. Alan Doucet: Polaroid Corporation; 920 Winter Street; Waltham, MA 02451

Mr. Art D. Douglas: Arvin Industries, Inc.; 950 East 450 South; Columbus, IN 47201-9383

Mr. James A. Douglas: Modem Media; 230 East Avenue; Norwalk, CT 06855

Mr. Jason Douglas: Elizabeth School District; P.O. Box 660; Elizabeth, CO 80107-0660

Ms. Linda S. Douglas: Parking Management, Inc.; 1725 DeSales Street NW, Suite 300; Washington, DC 20036-4406

Ms. Susan Douglas: SAIC; 5107 Leesburg Pike, Suite 2200; Falls Church, VA 22041-3262

Mr. Gary Douglass: Boys Ranch School; P.O. Box 219; Boys Ranch, TX 79010

Mr. Mehran Doustan: Muze; P.O. Box 234108; Great Neck, NY 11023-4108

Ms. Peggy Dowell: Nortel Network; 640 Massman Drive; Nashville, TN 37210-3722

Mr. Stephen B. Downard: Install Shield Corporation; 1310 Cambia Drive; Schaumburg, IL 60193

Mr. Matt Downer: WWW Hotlinks Com; 1931 Old Middlefield Way; Mountain View, CA 94043-2557

Mr. John M. Downey: Beneficial Savings Bank; 106 South 16th Street; Philadelphia, PA 19102-2896

Mr. John Downey: Union County Vo-Tech Schools; 1776 Raritan Road; Scotch Plains, NJ 07076-2997

Mr. Richard T. Downey: United States Army Recruiting Command; 1307 3rd Avenue; Fort Knox, KY 40121

Mr. Jay Downing: Highmark Blue Cross Blue Shield; 120 5th Avenue; Pittsburgh, PA 15222-3000

Mr. George A. Downsbrough: Raytheon Systems Company; 300 Sciences Park Road; State College, PA 16803-2214

Ms. Joanna Doyle: The Limited, Inc.; Three Limited Parkway; Columbus, OH 43230

Mr. Federico Drada: Bellsouth Mobility; 7180 Lee Street; Hollywood, FL 33024

Mr. Bruce Drake: Valspar Corporation; P.O. Box 1461; Minneapolis, MN 55440-1461

Mr. Cheikh Drame: Enron; 2100 Tanglewilde Street, #699; Houston, TX 77063

Mr. Joseph E. Dregier: Bell Atlantic; 1 East Pratt Street; Baltimore, MD 21202-1002

Mr. Mike Drennan: The Tech Museum of Innovation; 145 West San Carlos Street; San Jose, CA 95113-2014

Mr. Chris A. Driggers: Pine State Knitwear Company, Inc.; P.O. Box 631; Mount Airy, NC 27030

Mr. Daniel S. Driscoll: University of Wisconsin Hospital; 610 North Whitney Way; Madison, WI 53705-2750

Ms. Theresa Drossos: East Islip High School; 47 Division Avenue; East Islip, NY 11730-1923

Ms. Lauren Drummond: Gensler; 2020 K Street NW, Suite 200; Washington, DC 20006

Mr. Shuyong Du: Alcatel USA; 8828 Christian Court; Plano, TX 75025-3872

Mr. Luiz G. Duarte: Galaxy Latin America; 9175 Ramblewood Drive, Apartment 516; Coral Springs, FL 33071-7065

Mr. Jared Dubey: Vitesse; 741 Calle Plano; Camarillo, CA 93012

Mr. Dion Dubois: Baron & Bud, P.C.; 3102 Oak Lawn Avenue, Suite 1100; Dallas, TX 75219-4281

Ms. Sandy DuBose: Duncanville High School; 900 West Camp Wisdom Road; Duncanville, TX 75116-3021

Mr. Scott P. Ducharme: Circuit City Service; 9270 Trade Place; San Diego, CA 92126-6317

Mr. Michael Dudley: Pinney Associates; 4800 Montgomery Lane; Bethesda, MD 20814-3249

Mr. Joe Duea: Minnesota Technology, Inc.; 111 Third Avenue South; Minneapolis, MN 55401

Mr. John A. Duffus: San Diego Data Processing; 5975 Santa Fe Street; San Diego, CA 92109

Mr. Ed Duffy: Kutak Rock; 225 Peachtree Street NE, Suite 2100; Atlanta, GA 30303-1701

Mr. Thomas Dufresne: Southbridge Savings Bank; 253 Main Street; Southbridge, MA 01550-2503

Ms. Kathy Dugas: SAS Institute, Inc.; 2901 North Central Avenue, Suite 1750; Phoenix, AZ 85012-2763

Ms. Pamela F. Dumas: Bell South; 6767 Bundy Road;

New Orleans, LA 70127-2563
Ms. Chauny Dunbar: Airline Tariff Publishing Company; P.O. Box 17415; Washington, DC 20041-0415
Ms. Elizabeth S. Dunbar: Baltimore City College; 3220 The Alameda; Baltimore, MD 21218-3641
Mr. Gregory D. Duncan: Mercantile Bank; 2513 Hunters Pointe Boulevard; Edwardsville, IL 62025-3066
Ms. Gwendolyn Duncan: Catalytica Pharmaceutical Inc.; P.O. Box 1887; Greenville, NC 27835-1887
Mr. John W. Duncan: Saic; 2114 Aluka Loop; Pearl City, HI 96782-1317
Mr. Charles Louis Dunham: Gary Fire Department; 200 East 5th Avenue; Gary, IN 46402
Mr. Blaine Dunlap: Adsell; 5001 Southwest Avenue; St. Louis, MO 63110
Ms. Amy Dunn: Columbia/HCA; 1 Park Plaza, #9; Nashville, TN 37203-1548
Ms. Doris Rugg Dunn: Whidbey Campus, Skagit Valley College; 1900 Souteast Pioneer Way; Oak Harbor, WA 98277
Mr. Jeffrey Dunning: Mobex Communications, Inc.; 400 Inverness Drive South, Suite 200; Englewood, CO 80112-5817
Ms. Lisa Dupree: Huntsville Madison County Mental Health; 660 Gallatin Street Southwest; Huntsville, AL 35801-4996
Mr. Donald M. Duran: Coors; 177850 West 32nd Avenue #CC276; Golden, CO 80401
Mr. Orlando Duran: U.S. Holdings, Inc.; 3200 West 84 Street; Hialeah, FL 33018
Ms. Cathy Durand: Sequent Computer Systems; 7701 France Avenue South; Edina, MN 55435-5288
Mr. Jonthan C. Durrence: Southeast Health Unit; 3015 Bentwood Drive; Waycross, GA 31503-4117
Mr. Mike Dutch: Hitachi Data Systems; 750 Central Expressway, MS 32-07; Santa Clara, CA 95050
Ms. Barbara Dutile: Lakes Region General Hospital; 80 Highland Street; Laconia, NH 03246-3298
Mr. Devon Duval: CPS Systems, Inc.; 3400 Carlisle Street; Dallas, TX 75204-1285
Ms. Kathleen Dwyer: Office Products Analyst; 1275 Bloomfield Avenue; Fairfield, NJ 07004-2708
Mr. Eric Dycus: Mayflower Vehicle Systems; P.O. Box 789; Kings Mountain, NC 28086-0789
Mrs. Paige Dyer: Aurora Enterprise Solutions; 12310 Pinecrest Road, Suite 200; Reston, VA 20191-1636
Mr. Brad Dyke: U.S.A.F./G.A.I., Inc.; 2479 Thornhill Drive; Troy, OH 45373-1022
Ms. Marily Dykstra: Haworth, Inc.; 1 Haworth Court; Holland, MI 49423
Mr. Gerard A. Dzierzanowski: Graphic Controls; 189 Van Rensselaer Street; Buffalo, NY 14210-1345
Mr. Greg Dzurisin: Illinois Staff Water Survey; 2204 Griffith Drive; Champaign, IL 61820-7463
Mr. David C. Eakin: NAVICP Code 0426; 5450 Carlisle Pike; Mechnicsburg, PA 17055-2411
Ms. Brenda Earley: Lucent Technologies; P.O. Box 20046; Greensboro, NC 27420-0046
Mr. Mark H. Easter: Election Systems & Software, Inc.; P.O. Box 321; Urbanna, VA 23175
Dr. Abe Eastwood Ph.D.: National MS Society; 733 Third Avenue; New York, NY 10017-3288
Mr. Raymond C. Eaton: Computer Curriculum Corporation; 53 Perimeter Center East, Suite 120; Atlanta, SC 30346
Ms. Margarita Echeverri: Interamerican Development Bank; 5901 Montrose Road, Apartment S405; Rockville, MD 20852-4747
Mr. Leonardo Echeverria: Jaboneria Nacional; Francisco De Marcos 102; Guayaquil, Ecuador
Mr. Steve Eckerman: Irwin Research Services; 4112 Northwest 22nd Drive; Gainesville, FL 32605-1769
Mr. Matthew Bryant Eckstine: Citibank/Citigroup; 14700 Citicorp Drive; Hagerstown, PA 21472
Mr. Will Eddy: Wam! Net; 492 Highland Avenue; Montclair, NJ 07043-1202
Mr. Jason Edgmon: TTC; 20400 Observation Drive; Germantown, MD 20876-4023
Mr. Dan J. Edwards: RHI; 5938 Scenic Place; Shoreview, MN 55126-9123
Mr. Dee Edwards: Strategic Weather Service; 610 South Belardo, #1000; Palm Springs, CA 92264
Mr. Rich Edwards: Norwest Mortgage; 1 Home Campus; Des Moines, IA 50328-0001
Mr. Robert F. Edwards: Alliance for Manufacturing & Technology; 61 Court Street, Floor 6; Binghamton, NY 13901-3270
Mr. Scott Edwards: Hewlett Packard; 20 Perimeter Summit Boulevard NE; Atlanta, GA 30319-1417
Ms. Sharon Edwards: Sara Lee Underwear; 1000 East Hanes Mill Road; Winston-Salem, NC 27105-1384
Mr. Wesley F. Edwards: Jetstream Internet Services Inc.; Box 142; Salmon Arm, British Columbia, Canada V1E 4N2
Mr. Harrison Egbiremolen: RMS Information Systems; 1304 Putty Hill Avenue; Towson, MD 21286-8043
Mr. Julius Eggert: Sault Tribe MIS; 531 Ashmun Street; Sault Ste. Marie, MI 49783-1907
Mr. Nick Eggleston: Data Communications Cons; 6320 Rucker Road, Suite E; Indianapolis, IN 46220-4879
Mr. Robert Ehly: National Aeronautic and Space Administration; Warehouse #6, Building 4876; Edwards, CA 93524-0001
Ms. Linda Ehret: Arthur Andersen; 101 Arthur Andersen Parkway; Sarasota, FL 34232-6323
Ms. Diana K. Eide: Champlain College; 163 South Willard Street; Burlington, VT 05401-3950
Mr. Shawn Ivin Einzinger: Geac Computers, Inc.; 1193 West 2400 South, Suite C; Salt Lake City, UT 84119-1547
Mr. Thomas S. Eisenhart: Lucent Technologies; 222 Mount Airy Road; Basking Ridge, NJ 07920-2329
Ms. Rachelle Ekstrom: Intertech; 400 Chesterfield Center, Suite 200; Chesterfield, MO 63017-4800
Mr. Shoreh Elhami: Delaware County Auditor; 94 North Sandusky Street; Delaware, OH 43015
Mr. Chris Elliott: Private Business; 9010 Overlook Boulevard; Brentwood, TN 37027-5242
Ms. Melissa Elliott: Odessa College; 201 West University Boulevard; Odessa, TX 79764-7127
Ms. Victoria Elliott: Quest Diagnostics; 821 Salem Road; Burlington, NJ 08016
Mr. Dave Ellis: Aurora Electric/DataTel; 1118 East 70th Avenue; Anchorage, AR 99518-2352
Mr. Marcella Ellis: Residence; 1037 West Colfax Avenue; South Bend, IN 46616-1030
Mr. Mike Ellis: Lund Cadillac; 1311 East Bell Road; Phoenix, AZ 85022-2797
Mr. Randall Ellis: Sawtek Inc.; 2565 Millwood Avenue; Deltona, FL 32725-2302
Mr. Kevin Ells: Magellan Software Corp.; 23201 Mill Creek Drive; Laguna Hills, CA 92653-1641
Mr. Ed Ellsworth: MCI Worldcom; 2424 Garden of the Gods Road; Colorado Springs, CO 80919-3172
Mr. Amir Elmasri: IT Solutions; 120 University Park Drive; Winter Park, FL 32792-4440
Mr. Gregory Elorette: Morris County Sheriff; P.O. Box 900; Morristown, NJ 07963-0900
Mr. Dennis C. Elrod: Hnedak Bobo Group, Inc.; 104 South Front Street; Memphis, TN 38103-2906
Mr. Tom Elsberry: Lodgenet Entertainment; 3900 West Innovation Street; Sioux Falls, SD 57107-7002
Dr. Rob Elsner: University of Georgia; Department of Psychology; Athens, GA 30602
Mr. Gordon Embry: Gerrard & Co.; 410 Gerrard Drive; Florence, AL 35630-6326
Ms. Krista Embry: Trevecca Nazarene University; 333 Murfreesboro Road; Nashville, TN 37210-2834
Ms. Amy H. Emery: Ticona; 8040 Dixie Highway; Florence, KY 41042-2904
Mr. R. J. Emmett: Chrome Data Corporation; 524 Main Street; Oregon City, OR 97045-1824
Mr. Fidel V. Encarnacion: California Department of Real Estate; 2201 Broadway; Sacramento, CA 95818-7000
Ms. Dorothy Enderle: Mid West Spring & Stamping; P.O. Box 337; Mentone, IN 46539-0337
Mr. Allen Enebo: HBS International Inc.; 411 108th Avenue NE; Bellevue, WA 98004-8404
Mr. Donald Enfinger: Inacom Corporation; 3937 Pointe North; Gainesville, GA 30506-5386
Mr. Nader Engheta: Moore School of Electrical Engineering Ms6314; 200 South 33rd Street; Philadelphia, PA 19104
Mr. Burzin Engineer : 22982 Mill Creek Drive; Laguna Hills, CA 92653-1214
Mr. Mark England: North Dakota State University Library; P.O. Box 5599; Fargo, ND 58105-5599
Mr. Patterson A. England: Motorola Internet Solutions Division; 55 Shuman Boulevard, Suite 600; Naperville, IL 60563
Ms. Judy Englert: Interim Technology Consulting; 1170 Pittsford-Victor Road; Pittsford, NY 14534
Mr. Tim English: Hart Information Services; P.O. Box 80649; Austin, TX 78708-0649
Mr. Mike Ennis: BMC Software; 2101 Citywest Boulevard; Houston, TX 77042-2827
Ms. Valerie E. Eno: Gorman Richardson Architects, Inc.; 1 Ash Street; Hopkinton, MA 01748-1822
Mr. Allan Enyart: Farm Bureau Financial Services; 403 Hall Street; West Union, IA 52175-1009
Ms. Pam Eppinette: Eppinette International; 1012 Pleasantview Road; Ephrata, PA 17522-1408
Mr. Jerry Erbesfield: Prudential Georgia Realty; 863 Holcomb Bridge Road; Roswell, GA 30076
Mr. Glenn Ericson: Pheonix Consulting LLC; P3141 76th Street; Flushing, NY 11370
Mr. Holger Ericson : 20 Wiltshire Place; Durham, NC 27713-6515
Ms. Robbie Ericson: SCT Utility Systems; 9 Science Court; Columbia, SC 29203-9344
Mr. Alan Ericsson: Norco International AB; P.O. Box 7146; Helsingborg, Sweden 250 07
Mr. Anyangwe Ericsyrol: Fannie Mae; 3900 Wisconsin Avenue NW; Washington, DC 20016-2892
Mr. Louis Ernest III: Ohio Savings Bank; P.O. Box 91003; Cleveland, OH 44101
Mr. Stanley C. Ernst: Ohio State University; 2120 Fyffe Road; Columbus, OH 43210-1067
Mrs. Linda Erskine: Instructional Technology-Museum Informatics; University of California at Berkeley, 2241 College; Berkeley, CA 94720-1094
Mr. Robert Ersoni: KPMG LLP; 1900-2000 Avenue McGill College; Montreal, Quebec, Canada H3A 3H8
Ms. Alana Erstad: Tharaldson Enterprises; P.O. Box 9118; Fargo, ND 58106-9118
Mr. Todd A. Ervin: One Communications; 183 West Market Street; Warren, OH 44481-1022
Mr. Jose Escudero: Blue Cross Blue Shield; 2379 Foxhaven Drive East; Jacksonville, FL 32224-2001
Mr. Raul Esguerra: Pacific Cold Storage; 19840 South Rancho Way; Dominguez Hills, CA 90221
Mr. Scott Eshelman: 1 800 Video On; University of Colorado, At Building 4001 Discovery Drive, Suite 270; Boulder, CO 80303
Mr. David Espos: Pilot Network Services, Inc.; 1080 Marina Village Parkway; Alameda, CA 94501-6427
Mr. Richard Esposito: Rapid Search; 88 Alexander Street, Apartment 2; Rochester, NY 14620-1129
Mr. Vincent Esposito: New York City Law Department; 100 Church Street, Suite 4-162; New York, NY 10007-2601
Mr. Scott Esry: TDS Computing Services; 8401 Greenway Boulevard; Middleton, WI 53562-4629
Mr. James Essinger: Student Loan Fund of Idaho; P.O. Box 730, DP Department; Fruitland, ID 83619-0730
Mr. Hans-Christian Essl: Infineon Technology; Wernerwerkstrasse 2; Regensburg, Germany 93049
Mrs. Zanetta D. Estelle: Andersen Consulting; 1876 Data Drive; Birmingham, AL 35244
Mr. Jeremy Estle: Logix Communications; 3555 Northwest 58th Street; Oklahoma City, OK 73112-4707
Mr. Ramasamy Eswaran: International Consultants, Inc.; 2414 North Vinegate; Wichita, TX 67226
Ms. Pat Eswein: Qwest Communications; 4650 Lakehurst Center; Dublin, OH 43016-3252
Mr. David B. Evans: East Carolina University; 600 Moye Road #1510, Room 15-10; Greenville, NC 27858-4301
Mr. Donald Evans: Zygo, Advanced Imaging System; 4136 Lemoyne Way; Campbell, CA 95008-3748
Mr. Gary Evans: Kamphaus Henning & Hood; 1000 Ohio Pike; Cincinnati, OH 45245-2346
Mr. Paul Evans: Avnet; 2211 South 47th Street; Phoenix, AZ 85034-6403
Mr. Sean R. Evans: Epitonic, Inc.; 123 Townsend Street, Suite 365; San Francisco, CA 94107-1979
Ms. Sharon Evans: MCI World Com; 7130 Glen Forest Drive; Richmond, VA 23226-3754
Mrs. Susan D. Evans: Amarillo Independent School District, Food Service Department; 7200 West Interstate 40; Amarillo, TX 79106-2598
Mr. Terry Evans: Union University; 1050 Union University Drive; Jackson, TN 38305-3697
Mr. Trenton Evenson: Lutheran Health Systems; 4310 17th Avenue South; Fargo, ND 58103-3339
Mr. Gerry Evenwel: Paw Print Direct Marketing; 2451 Lively Boulevard; Elk Grove Village, IL 60007-6726
Mr. Erich Everett: Sycamore School District; 5751 Cooper Road; Cincinnati, OH 45242-7015
Mr. Ricky Everly: Illinois Department of Children & Family Services; 2309 West Main Street; Marion, IL 62959-1187
Mr. Bob Everson: Oracle Corporation; 2101 Silent Rain Drive; Colorado Springs, CO 80919-3002
Mr. Mike Ewing: Greenwood School District; 444 East Gary Street; Greenwood, AR 72936-7016
Mr. Kurt V. Eychaner: Falcon Cable Television; P.O. Box 1027; Dalton, GA 30722-1027
Mr. Kyril Faenov: Microsoft Corporation; One Microsoft Way; Redman, WA 98052
Mr. Michael W. Fahnert: KeyLabs, Inc.; 385 South 520 West; Lindon, UT 84042-1770
Mr. John Fahs: Cytec Industries; P.O. Box 425; Wallingford, CT 06492-7050
Mr. Jeffrey J. Faison: United States Treasury-FMS; 3700 East West Highway; Hyattsville, MD 20782-2015
Mr. Rey Fajardo: 82 MDG/SGSI; 149 Hart Street, Suite 6; Sheppard Air Force Base, TX 76311
Ms. Jackie Falch: Omni Resources, Inc.; 131 West Madison Street, Suite 505; Madison, WI 53703-3233
Ms. Donna Falkenberg: Utah State University; 500 Old Main Highway; Logan, UT 84322-0500
Mr. Don Falter: Systems Management, Inc.; 10946 Golden West Drive; Hunt Valley, MD 21031-8218
Ms. Stacy Falwell: Eagle Ridge Institute; 124 North Main Street; Wagoner, OK 74467-4426
Dr. Thomas R. Fanning Ph.D.: New York State Department of Health; Corning Tower, Room 2038; Albany, NY 12237
Mr. Renato Flavio Fantoni: Ericsson Telecomunications SA; R. Maria Prestes Maia, 300-Cp 371; Sao Paulo, Brazil 02047-901
Mr. William C. Farabow: North State Telephone; 111 Hayden Place; High Point, NC 27260-4913
Dr. Abbas Farazdel Ph.D.: IBM Corporation; 522 South Road; Poughkeepsie, NY 12601
Mr. Khaled Farhang: Micro-Sery Corporation; 1531 31st Street NW, Apartment 4; Washington, DC 20007-3041
Mr. Mehrdad Farjadian: Nortel; 19111 Dallas Parkway, Suite 200; Dallas, TX 75287-6912
Mr. Jerone Farley: Valvoline Instant Oil Change; 3499 Blazer Parkway; Lexington, KY 40509-1830
Mr. Jerry Farley: Sioux City Foundry Company; 801 Division Street; Sioux City, IA 51105-2644
Mr. Roy Farmer: Stone Manufacturing; 3452 Main Street; Columbia, SC 29203-6435
Mr. Timothy Farnham: AT&T; 1350 Treat Boulevard, Suite 500; Walnut Creek, CA 94596-2153
Mr. Michael J. Farris: Van Ausdall & Farrar; 1214 North Meridian Street; Indianapolis, IN 46204-1094
Ms. Maria Fatouros: Textron Systems; 52 Sherburne Road South; Lexington, MA 02421-5552
Ms. Karen M. Faust-Longmire: Nicolet Instrument Corporation; 5225 Verona Road; Madison, WI 53711-4495
Dr. John Faverman Ph.D.: Commonwealth Financial Network; 29 Sawyer Road; Waltham, MA 02453
Mr. Muhammad Favid: Anderson Corporation; P.O. Box 2123; Stillwater, MN 55082
Mr. Derek Fawcett: Vartek Telecom; 3200 West Pleasant Run Road; Lancaster, TX 75146-1052
Mr. Daniel Fealko: Intelligent Query Engines, Inc.; 221 Walton Street, Suite 3B; Syracuse, NY 13202
Mr. Gregory E. Federline: Litton Advanced Systems Division; 9318 Gaither Road; Gaithersburg, MD 20877-1441
Mr. Arthur Fedich: Mailers Software; 22382 Avenida Empresa; Rancho Santa Maria, CA 92688-2112
Mr. David Feeney: Entex Information Services; 148 South Street Exit; Bristol, CT 06010-6419
Mr. Joshua Feldman:

Compaq Computer Corp.; 2 Penn Plaza; New York, NY 10121-3099

Mr. Elio J. Feliu: Nortel Networks; 1500 Concord Terrace; Sunrise, FL 33323-2808

Mr. Jeremy Fennessy: MacNeal Health Network; 3249 Oak Park Avenue; Berwyn, IL 60402-0715

Mr. Gary Fenstamaker: Census Bureau; 4700 Silver Hill Road; Washington, DC 20233-0002

Mr. James Ferguson: Oklahoma County; 320 Robert S. Kerr, Suite 321; Oklahoma City, OK 73102

Mr. Tony Ferguson: Emj America; 1434 Farrington Road; Apex, NC 27502-7358

Mr. William G. Ferguson: CITGO Petroleum; 6130 South Yale Avenue, 819 OWP; Tulsa, OK 74136-1930

Mr. Vincent Fernicola: Snyder Healthcare Sales; 200 Cottontail Lane, Eastwing; Somerset, NJ 08873-1231

Mr. Michael Ferranti: American Management System, Inc.; 75 Livingston Avenue; Roseland, NY 07068

Mr. Alejandro Ferrell: Bell South; 2300 Northlake Center Drive; Tucker, GA 30084-4007

Mr. Charlie Fessenden: AT&T; 55 Corporate Drive, #31A01; Bridgewater, NJ 08807-1206

Mr. Raoul Fiedler: BPS, Inc.; 1715 Wyatt Drive; Santa Clara, CA 95054-1524

Mr. Michael Fielden: Internet Technology Group; 645 East Arques Avenue; Sunnyvale, CA 94086

Mr. Matthew Fielder: Dove Tail Systems; 130 Clinton Road; Fairfield, NJ 07004

Mr. Greg C. Fields: Compaq Computers Corporation; 1604 Dickens Place; Upper Marlboro, MD 20774-6020

Mr. Julian Fields: Alopatek; 555 Utica Drive; Sunnyvale, CA 94087

Mr. Victor Fields: County of Kane; On445 Sulley Drive; Geneva, IL 60134

Mr. M. Figueiras: Goldman Sachs; 85 Broad Street; New York, NY 10004-2456

Mr. Ken Filete: Advo Inc.; 1 Univac Lane, Suite 3; Windsor, CT 06095-2614

Ms. Colleen E. Filtz: TDS Telecom; 946 Red Tail Ridge; Oregon, WI 53575-3233

Mr. Eric Finkelstein: PJM Interconnections L.L.C.; 955 Jefferson Avenue; Morristown, PA 19403

Ms. Kristin L. Finley: Swiss Colony Data Center; 1112 7th Avenue; Monroe, WI 53566

Mr. John Campbell Finnegan: Trillipses Designs; 1016 West Washington Street; South Bend, IN 46601-1435

Ms. Penny Finnegan: Meta Group; 380 Hurricane Lane, Suite 201; Williston, VT 05495-2070

Mr. Brent Fiore: Stanley Jones Corporation; P.O. Box 100963; Nashville, TN 37224-0963

Mr. Brian Firicano: The Gem Group; 9 International Way; Lawrence, MA 01843

Ms. Frances Fischer: First Energy; 253 White Pond Drive; Akron, OH 44320-1117

Mr. James Fischer: Data Systems; 842 Main Street; Baton Rouge, LA 70802-5528

Ms. Melinda K. Fischer: The Gap SDC; 100 Gap Boulevard; Gallatin, TN 37066-6000

Mr. Nathaniel Fischer: The Associates; 334 Boston Turnpike; Shrewsbury, MA 01545-3847

Mr. Wayne Fish: State of Illinois Department of Public Health; 535 West Jefferson Street; Springfield, IL 62702-5085

Mr. Campbell Fisher: Baker Electronics; 1734 Northgate Boulevard; Sarasota, FL 34234-2194

Mr. Daniel Fisher: Kasbar National Industry; 801 North James Campbell Boulevard; Columbia, TN 38401-2680

Mr. Derek Fisher: Cerner Corporation; 2800 Rockcreek Parkway; Kansas City, MO 64117-2521

Mr. John Fisher: Teledyne Brown Engineering; 300 Sparkman Drive NW; Huntsville, AL 35805-1912

Ms. LeeAnne Fisher: Macmillan Computer Publishing; 14084 Old Mill Circle; Carmel, IN 46032

Mr. Leon I. Fisher: Nationwide Global Holdings; 1 Nationwide Plaza; Columbus, OH 43215

Mr. Uwe Fisher: CISCO Systems; 7025 Kit Creek Drive; Research Triangle Park, NC 27709

Mr. Frederick D. Fitch: The Phat Group; P.O. Box 2533; Atlanta, GA 30301

Ms. Julia Fitzgerald: Educational Service Center; 1885 Lake Avenue; Elyria, OH 44035-2551

Mr. Michael Fitzgerald: PSW Technologies; 102 Shire Lane; Swedesboro, NJ 08085

Ms. Pattie Fitzgerald: Exigent International; 1225 Evans Road; Melbourne, FL 32904-2314

Mr. Shawn Flarity: Team Technologies; 1025 Technology Parkway; Cedar Falls, IA 50613-6951

Mr. Daniel W. Flaskey: Brookings Hospital; 300 22nd Avenue; Brookings, SD 57006-2474

Ms. Anita Fledderman: Sunman Telecommunications; P.O. Box 145; Sunman, IN 47041-0145

Mr. Stephen C. Fleeger: Lockheed Martin; 700 Robbins Street, Building 2B; Philadelphia, PA 19111-5002

Mr. Greg S. Flemal: United Audio Visuals, Inc.; South 81 West 19079 Apollo Drive; Muskego, WI 53150-9295

Ms. Vanamey Fleming: Network Data Services; 536 Grand Slam Drive; Evans, GA 30809-8014

Mr. Howard Flemming: Entertainment Electronics; 27350 Landon Place; Valencia, CA 91354-1903

Mr. Curtis Fletcher: Courts/County of Gadsden; 10 East Jefferson Street; Quincy, FL 32351-2429

Mr. John A. Fletcher: Health Care Financial Administration; 7500 Security Boulevard; Baltimore, MD 21244-1850

Mr. Michael Fletcher: Bax Global; 16808 Armstrong Avenue; Irvine, CA 92606-4936

Ms. Jean A. Fligor: First National Bank & Trust; 322 Main Street; Kokomo, IN 46901

Mr. Thad Flinck: Video Lottery Consultants; 23115 7th Avenue; Bozeman, MT 59715

Ms. Kathy Flodman: HM Electronics; 6675 Mesa Ridge Road; San Diego, CA 92121-3996

Mr. Gaston E. Flores: Seaboard Marine, Ltd.; 8050 Northwest 79th Avenue; Miami, FL 33166-2174

Mr. Louis Flores: ProComponents, Inc.; 300 Garden City Plaza; Garden City, NY 11530

Mr. Sean M. Flores: Amfels, Inc.; P.O. Box 3107; Brownsville, TX 78523-3107

Mr. Winston Florez: Mann Products, Inc.; 3202 Queens Boulevard; Long Island City, NY 11101-2332

Ms. Christina Flowers: Michigan Wheel Corporation; 1501 Buchanan Avenue SW; Grand Rapids, MI 49507-1697

Mr. Albert Foo: University of Missouri; 3212 Lemone Industrial Boulevard; Columbia, MO 65201

Mr. John Forbes: Ameritech; North 17 W24300 Riverwood Drive, Suite 144; Waukesha, WI 53188

Ms. Brenda Ford: St. John's Regional Health Systems; 1235 East Cherokee; Springfield, MO 65804

Mr. David G. Ford: Union Carbide Corporation; P.O. Box 186, BL 13; Port Lavaca, TX 77979-0186

Mr. Terry Ford: RWD Technologies, Inc.; 8805 Governors Hills Drive, Suite 330; Cincinnati, OH 45249-3312

Ms. Diana J. Foresto: The TM Group; 701 East Elm Street; Conshohocken, PA 19428

Ms. Jacquelyne Ml. Foroutan: Time Warner Telecommunications; 5700 South Quebec Street; Greenwood Village, CO 80111-2006

Ms. Catherine Forsman: Cforsman; 106 Cabrini Boulevard, #1A; New York, NY 10033

Mr. Jamie Forster: Compaq; 8 Cotton Road, NQO/P16; Nashua, NH 03063-1260

Ms. Lauren Forsyth: Common Cents Mortgage; 4543 South 700 East; Salt Lake City, UT 84107-4101

Dr. Rance Fortenberry Ph.D.: Hewlett Packard Lightwave Division; 1400 Fountain Grove Parkway; Santa Rosa, CA 95403-1799

Mr. Andrew Foster: Jayhawk Software; P.O. Box 826; Iola, KS 66749-0826

Mr. Royce Foster: Ivy Technical State College; 3208 Ross Road, #6299; Lafayette, IN 47905-5209

Mr. T. Joel Foster: Tile Center Inc.; 1331 Reynolds Street; Augusta, GA 30901-6091

Mr. Tim Foster: Northern Arizona University; P.O. Box 4131; Flagstaff, AZ 86011-0001

Mr. Samer Fouani: TCS; 5209 Curtis Street; Dearborn, MI 48126-2842

Ms. Joann Fournet: Havens Steel Company; 7219 East 17th Street; Kansas City, MO 64126-2890

Ms. Gina Fournier: LA Works; 5200 Irwindale Avenue; Baldwin Park, CA 91706-2097

Ms. Shauna Foust: Wyandotte High School; P. O. Box 360; Wyandotte, OK 74370

Mr. Steven Foust: USDA AMS Dairy Grading Branch; 800 Roosevelt Road, Suite A320; Glen Ellyn, IL 60137-5886

Mr. Matt Fowler: UUNet an MCI Worldcom Co.; 5000 Britton Road; Hilliard, OH 43026-9445

Sister Cynthia Fox: St. Agnes Hospital; 900 South Caton Avenue; Baltimore, MD 21229

Mr. David Fox: American Institutes Research; 3333 K Street NW; Washington, DC 20007-3500

Ms. Gisele S. Fox: Metamor Global Solutions; 1721 Hartley Drive; Algonquin, IL 60102-4373

Ms. Karen Fox: Vishay Intertechnologies; 1630 30th Street; Boulder, CO 80301-1014

Mr. James Frank: Kemske Computer; 509 Center Street; New Ulm, MN 56073-3101

Mr. Jeffrey Frank: Success Institute of Business; 10700 Northwest Freeway, Suite 350; Houston, TX 77092-7315

Ms. Claire L. Frankel: Inautix Technologies, Inc.; 137 East 36th Street, Apartment 17A; New York, NY 10016-3528

Mr. Dasha Franklin: Coram Healthcare; 2275 Half Day Road; Bannockburn, IL 60015-1217

Ms. Pamela Franklin: TCI; 20166 42nd Place; Denver, CO 80249

Mr. Warren E. Franklin Jr.: New York Technical College; 300 Jay Stret; Brooklyn, NY 11201

Mr. Steven M. Franz: IOS Technologies; 1937 East 2nd Street; Defiance, OH 43512

Mr. Mike Fraser: Pacific Bell; 1429 North Gower Street, Suite 100B; Los Angeles, CA 90028-8384

Mr. Jay G. Frater: Kohler Company; 4821 Windward Court, Apartment 14; Sheboygan, WI 53083-1862

Mr. Randy Fraysher: CSC-Integrated Business Services; 3190 Fairview Park Drive; Falls Church, VA 22042

Mr. Gary Frazier: Kansas City Missouri School District; 1215 East Truman Road; Kansas City, MO 64106-3152

Ms. Lisa Frazier: NNTC; 1090 Burns Road; Elko, NV 89801-3437

Ms. Prentice Frazier: Capital One Financial; 11011 West Broad Street; Glen Allen, VA 23060-5937

Mr. Terry Frazier: Arthur Andersen, L.L.P.; 120 East Baltimore Street, Floor 20; Baltimore, MD 21202-1674

Mr. Jerry E. Freck: Square D Company; P.O. Box 9247; Columbia, SC 29290-0247

Ms. Charlene Frederick: Dobson Cellular Systems; 626 West 18th Street; Merced, CA 95340-4708

Mr. Randy Frederick: Boeing; P.O. Box 3707, M.S. 7J-16; Seattle, WA 98124-2207

Mr. Alan Frederickson: MA Mortenson; 1875 Lawrence Street, Suite 600; Denver, CO 80202-1826

Ms. Susan Fredette: Access Medical; 10 Dubon Court, Suite 1; Farmingdale, NY 11735-1015

Mr. Jon M. Freeman: Philadelphia International Marketing, Inc.; 1100 East Hector Street, Suite 320; Conshohocken, PA 19428

Mr. Keith Freeman: Square D; 1415 Roselle Road; Palatine, IL 60067-7399

Mr. Michael Freeman: Analog Devices; 8041 Woburn Street; Wilmington, MA 01887-3462

Mr. Paul Freeman: University of Arkansas; P.O. Box 3468, School of Forest Resources; Monticello, AR 71656-3468

Mr. William T. Freeman: United States Army Corps of Engineers; 1645 South 101 Avenue; Tulsa, OK 74128

Mr. Bill Frerking: OSF Healthcare System; 800 Northeast Glen Oak Avenue; Peoria, IL 61603-3200

Mr. Pete P. Frey: American Family Insurance; 918 Golf Vu Drive; Fond du Lac, WI 54935

Mr. David Freytag: ITC Deltacom; 2200 Woodcrest Place, Suite 100; Birmingham, AL 35209

Dr. Jonathan D. Fridman Ph.D.: Volpe National Transportation Systems Center; 25 Christopher Lane; Sudbury, MA 01776-3109

Mr. Monte Fried: Peco II; P.O. Box 910; Galion, OH 44833-0910

Mr. Michael D. Friedberg: United States Army Reserve Command; 13818 Wood Breeze; San Antonio, TX 78217-1462

Mr. Gregory G. Friedmann: American Axle & Manufacturing, Inc.; 1840 Holbrook Avenue; Detroit, MI 48212-3442

Mr. Gene Frioli: Mental Health Centers of Central Illinois; 760 South Postville Drive; Lincoln, IL 62656

Mr. Poppy Friske: Reilly Mortgage Group; 2000 Corporate Ridge, Suite 925; McLean, VA 22102-7846

Mr. Darrin Friskney: Thomson Indiana; 1425 Chase Court; Carmel, IN 46302

Mr. Jon Fritts: Republic Financial Service; 2727 Turtle Creek Boulevard; Dallas, TX 75219-4897

Mr. Richard Froehle: Sikorsky Aircraft, Division of United Technologies Corporation; 6900 Main Street, #S209A; Stratford, CT 06614-1385

Mr. Russell Froemming: Douglas Machine; 8933 Pleasant Grove NW; Garfield, MN 56332-8119

Mr. David Frost: MELE Associates; 14660 Rothgeb Drive, #102; Rockville, MD 20850-5309

Mr. Eddie Frye: McMurray Fabrics, Inc.; 105 Vann Place; Aberdeen, NC 28315-0067

Ms. Laurinda Frye: Eckerd College; 4200 54th Avenue South; St. Petersburg, FL 33711-4700

Ms. Rita Fucetola : 28 Austin Street; Tinton Falls, NJ 07712-7758

Mr. Miguel A. Fuertes: ILM; P.O. Box 2459; San Rafael, CA 94912

Mr. Glenn Fueston: Washington/Baltimore Hidta; 7500 Greenway Center Drive, Suite 500; Greenbelt, MD 20770-3502

Mr. Fumio Fukunaga: Sumisho Nosan Kaisha Ltd.; 9f. Sumitomo Shoji Mitoshiro B 1, Kandamitoshirocho; Chiyoda-Ku, Japan 101-0053

Mr. Jerry Fulcher: Universal Leaf Tobacco Company; P.O. Box 25099; Richmond, VA 23260

Mr. Peter Fulton: Municipal Supply; 618 South Lincoln; Shelton, NE 68876

Mr. Chris Y.N. Fung: China Life Insurance Company, Ltd.; 313 Hennessy Road, 22/F Cli Bldgtr; Wanchai, Hong Kong

Mr. Chris Gabel: Jsp International; 273 Great Valley Parkway; Malvern, PA 19355-1308

Mr. Abdel Sameyi A. Gabr: St. Joseph's Hospital; 800 Main Street; Paterson, NJ 07503-2615

Ms. Sherry Gaden: Raytheon Systems; 2930 Sonoma Street; Torrance, CA 90503-6037

Mr. Kent Gaff: ARH; 1220 South Broadwsay; Lexington, KY 40504-2739

Mr. John Gafford Jr.: American Choral Directors Association; 501 Southwest 38th Street; Lawton, OK 73505

Mr. Charles Gahn: United States Army Corps of Engineer; 26 Federal Plaza, #1917; New York, NY 10278-0004

Mr. William Galasso: Cooper Electric Supply Company; 70 Apple Street; Tinton Falls, NJ 07724-2600

Mr. Rodel Galinera: Nextel Communications; 238 Afton Square, Apartment 203; Altamonte Springs, FL 32714

Ms. Susan Galipeau: Mercy Hospital; 485 West Market Street; Tiffin, OH 44883-2611

Mr. John Gallagher: Booz-Allen & Hamilton; 4975 La Cross Road, Suite 313; Charleston, SC 29406-6525

Mrs. Darla Gallant: States General Life Insurance Company; 115 West 7th Street, Suite 1205; Fort Worth, TX 76102-7033

Mr. Michael Gallegos: CSUMB; 100 Campus Center; Seaside, CA 93955-8000

Mr. Steve Galligher: Pease Windamatic System, Inc.; P.O. Box 10071; Fort Wayne, IN 46850

Mr. Troy Galloway: Raytheon Systems; 300 Science Park Road; State College, PA 16803-2214

Mr. Joe Gallucci: IDE; 150 Baker Avenue Extension; Concord, MA 01742-2126

Ms. Camille Gama: Boro Park Marketing and Manufacturing Company, Inc.; 821 Lochmoor Lane; Highland Village, TX 75077-3107

Mr. John Gambini: Dynamic Technologies, Inc.; 161 Heritage Lane; Exton, PA 19341-1614

Mr. Peter Gamble: Skylight Systems Inc.; 141 Greenwood Avenue; Wyncote, PA 19095-1325

Mr. Rick Gambriel: Cadmus Communications Corporation; 6620 West Broad Street; Richmond, VA 23230-1716

Mr. Milind C. Ganoo: Sedgwick James, Inc.; 1000 Ridgeway Loop Road; Memphis, TN 38120

Mr. Samuel Gaona: Center for Employment Training; 509 West Morrison Avenue; Santa Maria, CA 93458-6120

Mr. Robert Garcar: Alltel Information Services; 200 Highland Road; Twinsburg, OH 44087-2248

Mr. Hector A. Garcia: Global Resources, Inc.; 2610 Crow Canyon Road 300;

San Ramon, CA 94583
Mr. Miguel Garcia: Cable & Wireless OHNES; 5599 San Felipe; Houston, TX 77056
Mr. Oscar Garcia: Moore Stephents T.C.; 340 North Avenue East; Cranford, NJ 07016-2461
Mr. Rey Garcia: Costep; 1109 Nolana Street; McAllen, TX 78504-3768
Mr. Sam Garcia: Los Alamos National Laboratory; Ms B254; Los Alamos, NM 87545-0001
Mr. Stephen Garcila: Western Wireless; 7516 25th Avenue NE; Seattle, WA 98115-4608
Mr. Donald Gardner: Intermedia Communications; 3625 Queen Palm Drive; Tampa, FL 33619-1309
Mr. Albert Garduno: Cimex Mexicanos EWD; 1560 North Industrial Park Drive; Nogales, AZ 85621
Mr. Christopher P. Gariepy: United Space Alliance; P.O. Box 10065; Cocoa, FL 32927
Mr. Margaret Garmon: Gainesville College; P.O. Box 1358; Gainesville, GA 30503-1358
Mr. Michael Garner: AutoZone; 4400 Summer Avenue, Department 8126; Memphis, TN 38122-4037
Mr. Yves Garnier: Maison de France Television; 7 Esplanade Henri de France; Paris, France 75907
Mr. Jim Garrett: Cathedral of Praise; 5225 Alexis Road; Sylvania, OH 43560-2505
Mr. Lester J. Garrett: Data Management Group of Virginia; 677 Ellen Road; Newport News, VA 23608
Mr. Patrick Garrett: Pacificare Health Systems; 5995 Plaza Drive; Cypress, CA 90630-5028
Mrs. Lorna Garrido: Global Resources; 2610 Crow Canyon Road, Suite 300; San Ramon, CA 94583-1547
Mr. Chris D. Garvin: Bureau of Land Management; 4850 West Classic Drive; Meridian, ID 83642-5398
Ms. Rhonda Garvin: Central and South West Services; 2 West 2nd Street; Tulsa, OK 74103-3123
Mr. Joseph R. Gaudenti: Hoffman Video Systems; 1049 Flower Street; Glendale, CA 91201-3014
Ms. Francois Gauthier: Watch Mark Corporation; 248 118th Avenue SE, Apartment 38; Bellevue, WA 98005-3561
Mr. Bing H. Gaw: Grocers and Merch Insurance; 874 South Village Oaks Drive; Covina, CA 91724-3614
Mr. James Gay: Badgen Herald; 326 West Gorham Street; Madison, WI 53703
Mrs. Maxime Gedeon-Javier: Chase; 376 Sheridan Boulevard; Inwood, NY 11096-1202
Ms. Cindy Gehringer: Graybec Lime Inc.; P.O. Box 448; Bellefonte, PA 16823-0448
Mr. Gary Geiger: Compucom Systems; 768 Tyvola Road; Charlotte, NC 28217-3508
Mr. Curtis Gekle: Cognos Corporation; 250 West 34th Street; New York, NY 10119-0002
Mr. Jeff Gelzer: Aerospace Integration Corporation; 634 Anchors Street NW, Suite 202; Fort Walton Beach, FL 32548-3894
Ms. Teresa L. Gentrup: City of Danville; 17 West Main Street; Tilton, IL 61832
Mr. Brian Gentry: Horizon Internet Technology; 800 Main Street; Winfield, KS 67156-2859
Mr. Mark Georg: Computerland of Pittsburgh; 4726 High Point Drive; Gibsonia, PA 15044-7400
Ms. Cathey George: La Vega ISD; 3100 Bellmead Drive; Waco, TX 76705-3096
Mr. Peter Georgelas: Bridgewater State College; Maxwell Library Management; Bridgewater, MA 02325-0001
Ms. Sharyn Germata: Commerce Insurance; 211 Main Street; Webster, MA 01570-2273
Mr. Neal W. Gerrish: University of Pennsylvania; 1547 Buchert Road; Pottstown, PA 19464-2925
Mr. Marc Gerritt: International Paper Company; 2 Gateway Boulevard; East Granby, CT 06026-9799
Mr. Glenn Gersch: Naval Surface Warfare Center; 300 Highway 361; Crane, IN 47522-4000
Dr. Nahum Gershon Ph.D.: The Mitre Corporation; 1820 Dolley Madison Boulevard; McLean, VA 22102-3480
Mr. John Gerzsenyi: IBM; 9216 Miranda Drive; Raleigh, NC 27613
Mr. Steven Gettel: S3 Inc.; 2611 Heidi Loop; Flagstaff, AZ 86004
Mr. Franz Greg Getten: Prolyx LLC; 16 Corning Avenue #214; Milpitas, CA 95035
Mr. Ben Ghadimi: Applied Cardiac Systems; 22912 El Pacifico Drive; Laguna Hills, CA 92653-1378
Mr. Khalid M. Abdel Ghany: Cairo University Center for Advanced Software; 63 Manial Street; Cairo, Egypt 11451
Mr. Michel D Ghazi: Hewlett Packard Company; 3141 Fairview Park Drive, Suite 300; Falls Church, VA 22042
Mr. Asad Ghori: Windham School Ramsey 2; 1200 Fm 655 Road; Rosharon, TX 77583-8602
Mr. Subir Ghosh: S G Microwave Inc.; 1183 King Street East; Kitchener, Ontario, Canada N2G 2N3
Mr. Mohammed S. Ghouri: Bell Atlantic; 210 West 18th Street; New York, NY 10011
Mr. Daniel Giacomelli: CSC; 45017 Bennett Place; Holland, PA 18966-5556
Ms. Andrea G. Giantelli: Avon Products Inc.; Rye Plaza; Rye, NY 10581
Mr. Vincent Giasolli: Voraapps Consulting; 7939 South Gaylord Way; Littleton, CO 80122-3204
Mr. Geoffrey Gibbs: Data Connections Inc.; 1007 Norwalk Street; Greensboro, NC 27407-2061
Mr. Joe Gibson: Roberson Printing; 3010 Lausat Street; Metairie, LA 70001-5982
Mr. James Giese: IFT; 221 North La Salle Street; Chicago, IL 60601-1206
Mr. Robertas Gikas: HERO, Inc.; 736 Johnson Ferry Road, Suite C-200; Marietta, GA 30068
Mr. Mark Gilbert: Nycomed Amersham; 101 Carnegie Center; Princeton, NJ 08540-6231
Mr. Tim Gilbertson: Soft Serv Business Systems; 7040 Lakeland Avenue North; Minneapolis, MN 55428-5600
Mr. Jeff Gilchrist: Williams Communications Solutions; 500 Chastain Center Boulevard NW; Kennesaw, GA 30144-5562
Mr. Brian J. Gildea: IDX Systems Corporation; 169 Charles Bank Road; Newton, MA 02458
Mr. Ken Gill: Mogran, Lewis & Bockius, LLP; 1800 M Street NW; Washington, DC 20036-5802
Mr. Steven Gill: Fedex; 2600 Nonconnah Boulevard, Suite 191; Memphis, TN 38132-2122
Mr. Malcolm Gillespie: Digital Link; 10 Carlson Road; Rochester, NY 14610-1021
Mr. Chuck Gillmore: Delta Technology Incorporated; 720 Doug Davis Drive; Hapeville, GA 30354
Mr. Stephen W. Gilmer: SAIC; 8867 B Roll Roght Court; Columbia, MD 21045
Mr. Don Gilmore: McKibben Communications; 20640 Bahama Street; Chatsworth, CA 91311-6101
Mr. Jon Gilmore: Goldense Group Inc.; 6 Bigelow Street; Cambridge, MA 02139-2384
Mr. Ken Ginefra: MBC Group, Inc.; 156 Ramapo Valley Road; Mahwah, NJ 07430-1199
Mr. Ronald M. Ginsberg: Bristol-Myers Squibb; 1 Squibb Drive; New Brunswick, NJ 08901-1589
Mr. Timothy S. Giorgi: Optimum Solutions; 12090 Southeast Tawny Drive; Clackamas, OR 97015-8608
Mr. Bill Girsch: Collection Express Services; 3500 South Gessner Road; Houston, TX 77063-5128
Mr. Randy Giusto: International Data Corporation; 5 Speen Street; Framingham, MA 01701
Mr. Thomas Giventer: 119 Enfield Main Road; Ithaca, NY 14850-9367
Mr. Lee C. Glaeser: Spur Products Corporation; 9288 Emerald Street; Boise, ID 83704-9757
Mr. Richard Glass: San Joaquin Human Services; 102 South San Joaquin Street; Stockton, CA 95201-3006
Ms. Diane Glaze: MCV Physicians; 1415 Rhoadmiller Street; Richmond, VA 23220-1111
Mr. Donald Glenn: Neb Methodist Health System; 8511 West Dodge Road; Omaha, NE 68114-4108
Mr. Leonid Gleyzer: Apex Paper Box Company; 5601 Walworth Avenue; Cleveland, OH 44102-4492
Ms. Angie Glick: Eagle Soft A Patterson Company; 2202 Althoff Drive; Effingham, IL 62401-4604
Mr. Scott A. Glover: Universal Care; 415 South Prospect Avenue #106; Redondo Beach, CA 90277
Mr. Barry Glynn: Scoot (UK), Ltd.; Parkway Court; Oxford, England, United Kingdom OX4 2JY
Mr. James Gnacinski: Mannesmann Dematic Rapistan; 8600 Royal Lane, Suite 100; Irving, TX 75063
Mr. Paul Gobin: MCI Telecommunications; 1 International Drive, Floor 3; Rye Brook, NY 10573-1070
Mr. Chris E. Godfrey: Paxton Consolidated School District, #6; 308 North Elm Street; Paxton, NE 69155
Mr. Tom Godfrey: Jennifer Convertibles; 417 Crossways Park Drive; Woodbury, NY 11797
Mr. Tom Godon: Bollinger Insurance; 830 Morris Turnpike; Short Hills, NJ 07078
Mr. Tony C. Godwin: Greenville Utilities; P.O. Box 1847; Greenville, NC 27835-1847
Ms. Heidi L. Goerig: Adept, Inc.; 175 Crossing Boulevard; Framingham, MA 01702
Mr. Jonathan P. Golberg: North Carolina DENR/ITS; 1608 MSC; Raleigh, NC 27699-1608
Mr. Roxie Gold: Interpath Communications; P.O. Box 13961; Durham, NC 27709-3961
Mr. Michael Goldammer: Technology Management & Analysis Corporation; 2451 Crystal Drive, #1000; Arlington, VA 22202
Ms. Donna Goldberg: Central Arizona College; 8470 North Overfield Road; Coolidge, AZ 85228-9779
Mr. Jeff Golden: Richards-Zeta; 5979 Hollister Avenue; Santa Barbara, CA 93117
Mr. Jarrett Goldfedder: ETCI; 131 Gaither Drive, Suite F; Mount Laurel, NJ 08054
Ms. Angela Goldman: Stackig Advertising; 7680 Old Springhouse Road; Mc Lean, VA 22102-3475
Mr. Charles Goldman: Venture Capital; 380 Madison Avenue, Floor 12; New York, NY 10017-2513
Mr. Wayne Goldsmith: State of Louisiana; 1801 North 4th Street; Baton Rouge, LA 70802-5159
Mr. Ira J. Goldstein: BOCES/NERIC; 1031 Watervliet Shaker Road; Albany, NY 12205-2106
Mr. Jeff Goldstein: IDMS; 560 Broadhollow Road, Suite 109; Melville, NY 11747-3702
Mr. Gregory J. Gollinger: Westminster College; P.O. Box 677; New Wilmington, PA 16172
Mr. Gabriel Gomez: GST Telecom; 199 North Capitol Boulevard, Suite 302; Boise, ID 83702-5988
Mr. Gary A. Gomez: Flour Bluff Independent School District; 2505 Waldron Road; Corpus Christi, TX 78418-4798
Dr. Yifan Gong Ph.D.: Texas Instruments; 8330 LBJ Freeway; Dallas, TX 75243
Mr. Carlton P. Gonsalves: IFM Efector Inc.; 805 Springdale Drive; Exton, PA 19341-2874
Mr. Christopher M. Gonzalez: Tech Data; 202 2nd Avenue SE; Lutz, FL 33549-4319
Mr. Gonzalo Gonzalez: Government; 12071 Southwest 10th Street; Miami, FL 33184-2417
Mr. José L. Gonzalez: City of North Miami; 776 Northeast 125th Street; North Miami, FL 33161
Mr. Paul Gonzalez: Earthtech Inc.; 100 West Broadway, Suite 5000; Long Beach, CA 90802-4427
Mr. Clyde R. Gooden Jr.: Ketchum Directory Advertise; 7015 College Boulevard, Suite 700; Shawnee Mission, KS 66211-1535
Mr. William Goodsell: Superior National Insurance Group; 11150 Trinity River Drive; Rancho Cordova, CA 95670-2966
Mr. Melvin L. Goodwin: AT&T; 6 Wood Turtle Court; Franklin Park, NJ 08826-1810
Dr. Thomas J. Goodwin Ph.D.: Florida Hospital Home Care Services; 608 East Altamonte Drive, Suite 2200; Altamonte Springs, FL 32701-4821
Mr. Michael Goolsby: O'Sullivan Industries, Inc.; 1900 Gulf Street; Lamar, MO 64759-1899
Mr. Jack Goral: SPSS, Inc.; 10 Penny Royal Place; Woodridge, IL 60517-1724
Mr. Don Gordon: Jacobi Medical Center; 1400 Pelham Pkwy South; Bronx, NY 10461
Mr. Ralph Gorin: XKL, LLC; P.O. Box 2631; Redmond, WA 98073-2631
Ms. Donna J. Gorren: Florida Gift Fruit Shippers Association; 521 North Kirkman Road; Orlando, FL 32808
Ms. Mary Gosewehr: Nicholas Company; 700 North Water Street, Suite 1010; Milwaukee, WI 53202-4206
Ms. Kelly Gosh: Brilliance Corporation; P.O. Box 887; Grand Haven, MI 49417-0887
Mr. Robert D. Goshert: Superior Essex, Inc.; 8661 North 250 West; Columbia City, IN 46725
Mr. Roger C. Gough: MicroAge Computer Center; 314 Main Street; Murray, KY 42701-2151
Mr. Rob Gourley: Missouri State Water Patrol; 2728 Plaza Drive, Suite B0000; Jefferson City, MO 65109-1147
Mr. Mahendra Govada: Megasys Software Services; 1681 Old Henderson Road; Columbus, OH 43220
Mr. James Gowans: Smithsonian Institute Archives; 900 Jefferson Drive SW, #135; Washington, DC 20560-0004
Ms. Michelle Gowdy: Anthem Corporate Info Tech; 5587 West 73rd Street; Indianapolis, IN 46268-2162
Mr. Mukesh Goyal: ITDS; 128 Woodside Green, Apartment 1B; Stamford, CT 06905
Ms. Aiman H. Grace: Egyptian Cement; 6 Canal Street, Maadi; Cairo, Egypt 11431
Mr. John Graefe: Peco Energy Company; 2301 Market Street; Philadelphia, PA 19101
Ms. Carrie Graham: SAFECOL Insurance; 1527 South Eagle Ridge Drive; Renton, WA 98055-3549
Mr. Charles R. Graham: Medical Manager R&D, Inc.; 15151 Northwest 99th Street; Alachua, FL 32615-5738
Ms. Kelly Graham: Burch Munford Direct; 113 North Henry Street; Alexandria, VA 22314-2903
Mr. Randolph Graham Sr.: NRTC; 2121 Cooperative Way; Herndon, VA 20171-3081
Ms. Ruth Gramolini: Vermont Department of Texas; 109 State Street; Montpelier, VT 05609-0001
Mr. Sedrick Grandberry: United States Air Force; 5653 Luce Avenue; North Highlands, CA 95660-4635
Ms. Peggy Grant: Neverdahl-Loft & Associates; 4848 Valley Road; Lincoln, NE 68510-4962
Mr. Roger Grant: Lockheed Martin-ATM; 9221 Corporate Boulevard; Rockville, MD 20850-3248
Mr. Bruce Granville: Linc Systems; 5 High Bridge Road; Sandy Hook, CT 06482-1656
Mr. Edward Grasso: Spitzer Management Inc.; 150 East Bridge Street; Elyria, OH 44035-5219
Ms. Carol Gravel: Liberty Mutual Insurance; 225 Borthwick Avenue; Portsmouth, NH 03801
Ms. Janiss Graves: Jan Tek Services, Inc.; 14935 Clovercrest Drive SE; Huntsville, AL 35803-3913
Mr. Terry Graves: McCarthy Arch; P.O. Box 440; Tupelo, MS 38802-0440
Ms. Liz Gravette: Perot Systems Corporation; 5310 East 31st Street, Suite 600; Tulsa, OK 74135-5011
Mr. Robert Gravina: Mount Carmel High School; 9550 Carmel Mountain Road; San Diego, CA 92129-2799
Ms. Aimee Gray: Tri Vergent Communications; 120 East Calhoun Street; Anderson, SC 296215538
Mr. Albert L. Gray: Lake Washington Technical College; 11605, 132nd Avenue NE; Kirkland, WA 98034-8506
Mr. Chuck Gray: Software Specialist; 2010 Crow Canyon Place; San Ramon, CA 94583-1344
Mr. David J. Gray: ServiceMaster; 855 Ridge Lake Boulevard; Memphis, TN 38120
Mr. Eric Gray: Hughes Network Systems; 1605 Princess Street; Alexandria, VA 22314-2115
Mr. Hary Gray: The Boeing Company; 6209 Ridge Pond Road, Apartment B; Centreville, VA 20121-4094
Ms. Jamie Gray: Web Media Ventures, Inc.; 5307 East Mockingbird Lane; Dallas, TX 75206-5109
Mr. Jearl Edward Gray: Holloman Air Force Base; 531 Idaho Avenue Building 202; Holloman Air Force Base, NM 88330-8044
Mr. Nowick Gray: Cougar Webworks; P.O. Box 7; Argenta, British Columbia, Canada V0G 1B0
Mr. Tim Gray: Space Vector Corporation; 9223 Deering Avenue; Chatsworth, CA 91311-5804
Mr. Rick Gray-Lewis: Coleman Aerospace; 7675 Municipal Drive; Orlando, FL 32819
Mr. Craig Green: VNA Home Health Care; 50 Foden Road; South Portland, ME 04106-1709
Mr. Thomas Green: Anchor Bank; 2002 Oak Street; Myrtle Beach, SC 29577-3145
Ms. Yasmin Green: City of Flint Mayor's Office; 1101 South Saginaw Street; Flint, MI 48502-1416
Ms. Joycelyn Greenaway: Database Technologies; 4530 Blue Lake Drive; Boca Raton, FL 33431-4419
Ms. Janettarose L. Greene: Department of the Navy; 332 Ruscombe Avenue; Glenside, PA 19038-1613
Ms. Megan Greene: Acumen Consulting; 1919 Park Avenue; St. Louis, MO 63104-2536
Mr. Trevor G. Greenidge: Chase Manhattan Bank; 3512 Great Neck Road; Amityville, NY 11701-1922
Mr. Ron Greenspan: Cinci-

va Marketing-Media; 4601 Holly Road; Virginia Beach, VA 23451-2549
Mr. Randy Greenway: Bba Nonwovens; 840 Southeast Main Street; Simpsonville, SC 29681-7150
Mr. Benson Gregory: Mortenson Broadcasting; 3950 Lexington Road; Versailles, KY 40383-1742
Mr. Scott Gregory: Southwest Land Title; 1934 Pendleton, Suite 500; Garland, TX 75041
Mr. Garry E. Gregson: Utah Department of Insurance; 3110 State Office Building; Salt Lake City, UT 84114
Ms. Callie Gresham: Sprint PCS; 8001 College Boulevard, Suite 100; Overland Park, KS 66210-1800
Mr. Charlie Gresham: GTE-IBM Global Services; 325 James South McDonnell Boulevard; Hazelwood, MO 63042-2513
Ms. Melinda A. Gresham: United States Army CECOM; Myer Center, Room 3C-312; Fort Monmouth, NJ 07703
Mr. Daniel Grey: Genentech/Modis; 1422 Gibbons Drive; Alameda, CA 94501-4702
Mr. Gary Grice: Athens-Clarke County Unified Government; 325 East Washington Street, #370; Athens, GA 30601-4514
Ms. Salina Pleasant Grice: Bell Atlantic; 99 Shawan Road, Room 401; Cockeysville, MD 21030-1356
Mr. Ray Grier: Believe 2 Achieve; 402 Flatwood Curve; Wetumpka, AL 36092-8122
Ms. Monell Griffin: American National Insurance Company; 1718 West Lake Drive; Gladewater, TX 75647-3210
Mr. Neil Griffin: Bainbridge College; 2500 East Shotwell Streett; Bainbridge, GA 31717-8407
Mr. Robert T. Griffin: Parker Hannifin Corporation; 6035 Parkland Boulevard; Cleveland, OH 44124-4141
Mr. Victor Griffin: International Trading Bureau; 508 Auten Road, Apartment 4c; Somerville, NJ 08876-5057
Mr. James Griffith: Blue Cross Blue Shield of Florida; 4800 Deerwood Campus Parkway; Jacksonville, FL 32246-6498
Mr. Dennis Grimes: Teco Energy; P.O. Box 111; Tampa, FL 33601-0111
Mr. Paul Grindstaff Jr.: First St Bank; 201 East Columbia Street; Farmington, MO 63640-3187
Mr. Robert Grisby: Bank of America; 131 Trellis Place; Richardson, TX 75081-4768
Ms. Denise Grogen: Maestro Designs; 87 1/2 Murray; Binghamton, NY 13905
Mr. Paul Grojean : 2220 Dwight Way Apartment; Berkeley, CA 94704-4609
Mr. Clifford Gromley: Associated Press; 19 Commerce Court West; Cranbury, NJ 08512
Mr. J. M. Grooms: Air Vac Inc.; P.O. Box 528; Rochester, IN 46975-0528
Mr. Robert F. Gross: Allied Signal Technical Services; 401 Barberton Drive; Virginia Beach, VA 23451
Ms. Sarah E. Grotelueschen: Deloitt Consulting; 1901 Butterfield Road; Downers Grove, IL 60515
Mr. Cy Groves: Progress Telecom; 100 2nd Avenue, Suite 4005; St. Petersburg, FL 33701
Mr. M. Gruda : Harav Israel Porat 3, Ramat Three; Jerusalem, Israel 97298
Mr. Kent Grunden: Hoogwegt US, Inc.; P.O. Box 459; Libertyville, IL 60048-0459
Ms. Raquel Guardado: Southwestern Bell Telephone; 170 Easton Road; Dallas, TX 75202
Ms. Kimberly L. Gudmundson: Information Systems Engineering; 1331 Capitol Drive; Oconomowoc, WI 53066
Mr. Mark Guerfrieri: NCO TeleServices; 15 East Centre Street; Woodbury, NJ 08096-2400
Mr. Sergio P. Guerreiro: Lea & Elliott, Inc.; 14325 Willard Road, Suite 200; Chantilly, VA 20151
Dr. V. G. Guhan Ph.D.: Gartner Group; 56 Top Gallant Road; Stanford, CT 06904
Mr. Bud Gunn: GE Capital AFS; 540 West Northeast Highway; Barrington, IL 60010-3076
Mr. Gagan Gupta: LSI Logic Corporation; 440 Alegra Terrace; Milpitas, CA 95035
Mr. Sandeep Gupta: Sapient Corporation; 13403 Poplar Wods Court; Chantilly, VA 20151-2537
Mr. Sunil Gupta: Gupta Programming; 926 Tupelo Wood Court; Newbury Park, CA 91320-3650
Ms. Donna Gustafson: Campbell Ewald Advertising; 30400 Van Dyke Avenue, Floor 3; Warren, MI 48093-2368
Mr. Hjalmar Gutierrez: Cache, Inc.; 1460 Broadway, 15th Floor; New York, NY 10036
Ms. Helena Guzman: Tomato Works Art Studio; P.O. Box 88154; Indianapolis, IN 46208-0154
Mr. Dmitry Guzovsky: Visa International; 10461 Mill Run Circle; Owings Mills, MD 21117-5544
Ms. Ellen Ha: Network Associates; 3965 Freedom Circle; Santa Clara, CA 95054
Mr. Robert Haaga: Compuletter; 7545 North Natchez Avenue; Niles, IL 60714-3823
Ms. Christine Haas: SofTest; 19356 Lambeth Court; Riverside, CA 92508
Ms. Deanna Lyn Haas: Guide One Insurance; 1111 Ashworth Road; West Des Moines, IA 50265-3544
Ms. Lori L. Haas: Reed Smith Shaw & McClay,LLP; 1 Liberty Place, 1650 Market Street, 25th Floor; Philadelphia, PA 19103
Mr. Bob Hacker: Binney & Smith; 1100 Church Lane; Easton, PA 18044-0431
Mr. Stan Hackett: Southern Container Corp.; 100 Hawkes Street; Westbrook, ME 04092-4068
Mr. Richard Haddad: TALPX, Inc.; 303 West Madison Street, Floor 300; Chicago, IL 60606-3308
Ms. Kathy Haechten: Covantage; 9505 Arboretum Boulevard, Suite 300; Austin, TX 78759-7260
Mr. Chuck Hagan: Department of Social Services; 1701 High Street; Portsmouth, VA 23704-3103
Ms. Brandy J. Hageman: Extended Systems Inc.; 5777 North Meeker Avenue; Boise, ID 83713
Ms. Cathy Hagen: Midlands Technical College; P.O. Box 2408; Columbia, SC 29202-2408
Mrs. Maureen Hagen: Lexmark International; 6301 Northwest 5th Way; Fort Lauderdale, FL 33309-6131
Ms. Ronalee L. Haggard: Movo Media, Inc.; 6100 Wilshire Boulevard, Suite 1500; Los Angeles, CA 90048-5122
Mr. Pat Haggerty: Inacomp; 20715 Kelly Road; Eastpointe, MI 48021-3164
Dr. Nabeel F. Haidar: Lebanese American University; 13-5053; Beirut, Lebanon
Ms. Katherine Hainley: Sheetz, Inc.; 5700 6th Avenue; Altoona, PA 16602
Mr. Eve Halberg: Republic National Bank; 1 Hanson Place, Floor 10; Brooklyn, NY 11243-2907
Mr. Dirk L. Haldy: General Instrument Corporation; 2885 Breckinridge Boulevard, Suite 300; Duluth, GA 30096-7608
Mr. Kevin Hales: LIEN; 101 Wasatch Drive; Salt Lake City, UT 84112-8926
Ms. Kristen N. Haley: FamilyLife; 3900 Rodney Parham; Little Rock, AR 72211
Mr. Robert Haley: Hooper Holmes, Inc.; 112 Washington Street; Keene, NH 03431-3104
Mr. Andrew Hall: Crocodile Clips Ltd.; 11 Randalph Place; Edinburgh, United Kingdom EH3 7TA
Mr. Bill Hall: KOLO-TV; P.O. Box 10000; Reno, NV 89510-0005
Mr. Daniel Hall: Arthrex Inc.; 2885 Horseshoe Drive Court; Naples, FL 34104-6101
Mr. John Hall III: Epsilon Group; 104 Whitewood Road; Charlottesville, VA 22901-1662
Ms. Sheryl A. Hall: Washington State Department Retirement Systems; P.O. Box 48380; Olympia, WA 98504-8380
Ms. Jackie Halliday: Exa Corporation; 450 Bedford Street; Lexington, MA 02420-1520
Ms. Sandie Hallock: Santa Fe Community College; 3000 Northwest 83rd Street; Gainesville, FL 32606-6200
Ms. Lorie A. Halloran: CompUSA; 34 Saint Martin Drive; Marlborough, MA 01752-3021
Mr. Mark J. Halloran Jr.: PaylinX; 9666 Olive Boulevard; St. Louis, MO 63132
Mr. Daniel Halseth: Western Oregon University; P.O. Box 522; Monmouth, OR 97361-0522
Mr. John Halvorsen: Nortel Networks; 3500 Carling Avenue; Nepean, Ontario, Canada K2H 8E9
Mr. David Ham: EMAP Petersen, Inc.; 6420 Wilshire Boulevard; Los Angeles, CA 90048-5502
Mr. Jake Hamburger : 59 East 54th Street; New York, NY 10022-4211
Mr. Ken Hamilton: Community Care Network; 5251 Viewridge Court; San Diego, CA 92123-1646
Mr. Mark Hamilton: C.N. Hilton College; 4800 Calhoun; Houston, TX 77204-3902
Mr. Powell Hamilton: Price Waterhouse Coopers; 400 South Hope Street; Los Angeles, CA 90071
Ms. Deborah Hamlin: City of Perry; P.O. Box A; Perry, GA 31069-0019
Mr. Ryan Hammond: United States Air Force Pentagon Communications Agency; 1600 Air Force Pentagon; Washington, DC 20330-1600
Mr. Gary Hampson: Heska Corporation; 1825 Sharp Point Drive; Fort Collins, CO 80525-4401
Ms. Linda Hampton: Bureau of Workforce Initiatives; 30 East Broad Street, 31st Floor; Columbus, OH 43266-0423
Mr. Rick Hancock: Phobo.com, Inc.; 6711 Ritz Way; Beltsville, MD 20705-1384
Mr. S. Davis Hand: Americana Ships; 401 East Jackson Street, Suite 3300; Tampa, FL 33602-5233
Ms. Veronica Hand: Wicklow Excess Insurance; 351 California Street; San Francisco, CA 94104-2412
Mr. Tom F. Handyside Jr.: Emglo; 25 3rd Street; Houston, PA 15342-1404
Mr. Ray C. Haney: Sarasota Memorial Hospital; 1700 South Taniani Trail; Sarasota, FL 34239
Ms. Suzanne Haney: Bell Industries; 8615 West 46th Street; Indianapolis, IN 46234-9509
Mr. Dennis M. Hanks: Moose International; Route 31; Mooseheart, IL 60539
Mr. John Hanlin: J.M. Huber Corporation; 3150 Gardner Expressway; Quincy, IL 62301-9478
Mr. Troy Hannon: Hope Worldwide; 148 East Lancaster Avenue; Wayne, PA 19087-4103
Mr. David K. Hansen: Sentra Securities; 1600 Valley River Drive, Suite 102; Eugene, OR 97401
Mr. Brian Hanson: Culligan Soft Water Service Company; 6030 Culligan Way; Minnetonka, MN 55345-5993
Mr. Richard Hanson: Myron L Company; 6115 Corte Del Cedro; Carlsbad, CA 92009-1516
Mr. Jason Harbison: Freed Hardeman University; 158 East Main Street; Henderson, TN 38340-2398
Mr. Joe Harbuz: Galileo International; 1027 Jordan Court; Parker, CO 80134
Ms. Susan Hardek: New Millennium Group, Inc.; 1636 North Wells; Chicago, IL 60614
Mr. John Hardwick: South Callaway R-II Schools; 7615 State Road C; Fulton, MO 65251-6768
Mr. Scott E. Hardy: Allenbrook; 2 Meeting House Road; Scarborough, ME 04074-8225
Mr. Steven A. Hardy: Urban Future Organization; 29 Theobolds Road; London, England, United Kingdom WC1 65D
Ms. Tina M. Hardy: Genesee ISD; 2413 West Maple Avenue; Flint, MI 48507-3429
Ms. Linda J. Hares: Metropolitan Ministries; 2002 North Florida Avenue; Tampa, FL 33602-2204
Ms. Cherisa Hargrave: Work Advantage Board Administrative Office; 2601 Scott Avenue #400; Fort Worth, TX 76103
Mr. Arun Hariani: Northeast Georgia RDC; 305 Research Drive; Athens, GA 30605-2725
Mr. Ray Hariri: Densitron Corporation; 10430 Pioneer Boulevard, Suite 2; Santa Fe Springs, CA 90670-8245
Dr. Julie A. Y. Harkey Ph.D.: American Trans Air; P.O. Box 51609; Indianapolis, IN 46251-0609
Ms. Kasandra Harley: Brown Brothers Harriman & Company; 63 Wall Street, Floor 11; New York, NY 10005-3001
Mr. Jason Harman: APAC Customer Services; 11008 Worwick Boulevard; Newport News, VA 23601
Mr. David S. Harmer: ECC International; 100 Mansell Court, Suite 300; Roswell, GA 30076-4860
Mr. Mance Harmon: United States Air Force Academy; 2354 Fairchild Drive, Suite 6K41; USAF Academy, CO 80840-6299
Ms. Janet Harms: Alexandria City Public Schools; 5403 Kempsville Street; Springfield, VA 22151-3111
Ms. Charetta Harper: Spoon River College; 23235 North County Highway 22; Canton, IL 61520-9099
Ms. Paula Harper: Continental Stock; 2 Broadway, Floor 19; New York, NY 10004-2801
Mr. Keith Harr: Urm Stores Incorporated; 7511 North Freya Street; Spokane, WA 99217-8043
Mr. Rick Harradine: Tripp Lite; 1111 West 35th Street; Chicago, IL 60609-1404
Mr. Wayne D. Harrell: Corporation Counsel; 441 4th Street Northwest; Washington, DC 20016
Dr. Michael Harrington Ph.D.: The Mitre Corporation; 1613 Sereno Court; Vienna, VA 22182-1958
Ms. Carolyn Harris: Sharp Healthcare; 3554 Ruffin Road; San Diego, CA 92123-2596
Ms. Coretta Harris: TRW; One Space Park; Redondo Beach, CA 90278
Mr. Gregory Harris: Excite@Home; 555 Broadway Street; Redwood City, CA 94063-3122
Mr. Kenneth A. Harris: Specialized Computer Solutions; 5627 East Monlaco Road, Suite 101; Long Beach, CA 90808
Ms. Laurie Ann Harris: Pennsylvania National Bank; 52 South 4th Street; Hamburg, PA 19526-1202
Ms. Susan Harris: Wells Real Estate Funds; 3885 Holcomb Bridge Road; Norcross, GA 30092-2269
Mr. David Harrison: Glen Raven Mills; 1831 North Park Avenue; Burlington, NC 27217-1100
Mr. DuWayne D. Harrison: IBM; 27 Commerce Drive; Cranford, NJ 07016
Ms. Kitty Harrison: Strictly Business Computer; 611 3rd Avenue; Huntington, WV 25701-1308
Ms. Nancy S. Harrison: Greater Hazleton Health Alliance; 700 East Broad Street; Hazleton, PA 18201
Ms. Ruth Harrison: Reinsurance Group of America; 1370 Timberlake Manor Parkway; Chesterfield, MO 63017-6039
Mr. Peter John Harry: Telstra; 11/447 Lonsdale Street; Melbourne, Victoria, Australia 3000
Mr. Arthur J. Hart: Terra Industries, Inc.; 600 Fourth Street; Sioux City, IA 51101
Mr. Richard A. Hart: Dyno Nobel; 17562 Gum Road; Carthage, MO 64836
Ms. Beverly Hartis: Miravesque Spa and Salon; 2341 Russellville; Bowling Green, KY 42101
Mr. Ken Hartley: Pine Company; 10559 Jefferson Boulevard; Culver City, CA 90232-3513
Mr. David Hartmann: San Antonio Water System; P.O. Box 2449; San Antonio, TX 78298-2449
Mr. Rob Hartmann: Midsouth Extrusion Inc.; 2015 Jackson Street; Monroe, LA 71202-2533
Mr. D. Norman Hartnett: Threshold Enterprises; 23 Janis Way; Scotts Valley, CA 95066-3546
Mr. John Hartrick: GST Telecom; 4001 Main Street; Vancouver, WA 98663-1896
Ms. Darlyn Hartwig: Milwaukee Tool; P.O. Box 2039; Milwaukee, WI 53201-2039
Mr. Thomas Hartzell: Cooper Perskie Law Office; P.O. Box 748; Atlantic City, NJ 08404-0748
Mr. Dennis Harvey: TLC Management; 730 West 35th Street; Marion, IN 46953-4241
Ms. Holly Harvey: Pacificare Behavioral Health; 23046 Avenida de la Carlota, Suite 700; Laguna Hills, CA 92653-1536
Mr. Paul Harvey: Tactics Inc.; 2245 Bonnavit Court NE; Atlanta, GA 30345-4129
Mr. Siraj M. Hasan: Bear, Sterns and Company; 575 Lexington Avenue; New York, NY 10022
Mr. Craig Hass: Woodland Center; P.O. Box 787; Willmar, MN 56201-0787
Ms. Shelley Hasselbrink: WTC; 801 South Grand Avenue, Suite 700; Los Angeles, CA 90017-4635
Mr. Andrew Hatch: Monster.com; 5 Clock Tower Place; Maynard, MA 01754-2530
Mrs. Michaela S. Hatch-Drennon: US West; 931 14th Street, Room 520; Denver, CO 80202
Mr. Evan Hatchell: Citizens Utilities; 1300 South Yale Street; Flagstaff, AZ 86001-6328
Mr. Chris Hatcher: Associated Publishing Company; 1052 North 5th Street, Suite 102; Abilene, TX 79601-5144
Mr. Scott Hathaway: Attorneys Title Insurance Fund; 6545 Corporate Centre Boulevard; Orlando, FL 32822-3253
Mr. Kurt W. Hattendorf: Cooper Tire & Rubber Co.; 725 West 11th Street; Auburn, IN 46706-2022
Mr. Chris Haubner: Genencor International; 1870 Winton Road South; Rochester, NY 14618
Mr. Bob Haupt: Donnelley Marketing; 4001 Business Park Avenue; Marshfield, WI 54449
Mr. J. Chris Hausler: Proficient Solutions; 100 Citation Drive; Henrietta, NY 14467-9747
Ms. Brenda Hauther: Covington & Burling; 1201 Pennsylvania Avenue NW; Washington, DC 20004-2401
Mr. John A. Havens: McKesson HBOC; 1550 East Republic Road; Springfield, MO 65804-6530
Mr. Bryan Havenstein: Qualcomm, Inc.; 6150 Lookout Road; Boulder, CO 80301
Mr. Hollis M. Havers: Jitney

Jungle Stores of America; 3800 I 55 North; Jackson, MS 39211-6324
Ms. Gayle L. Hawes: McLeod USA Publishing; 2201 Willenborg Avenue; Effingham, IL 62401
Dr. David Hawkins Ph.D.: California Institute of Technology; 100 Leighton Lane, P.O. Box 968; Big Pine, CA 93513
Mr. Norman Hawkins: Ellwood Quality Steels; 700 Moravia Street; New Castle, PA 16101-3950
Ms. Connie Hawkinson: RTP Company; 580 East Front Street; Winona, MN 55987-4256
Mr. Joel Hawks: SunTrust Bank; 205 Beverly Road; Ashland, VA 23005-1805
Mr. Saleem Hayat: Service Merchandise; P.O. Box 24600; Nashville, TN 37202-4600
Mr. Billy E. Hayes: Williams; 2800 Post Oak Boulevard; Houston, TX 77056-6100
Mr. Howard Hayes: Loyola University Medical Center; 2160 South 1st Avenue; Maywood, IL 60153-5500
Ms. Lisa A. Hayes: Business Equipment Company; 7762 Reading Road; Cincinnati, OH 45237-2145
Mr. Daniel Haynes: Household International; 1441 Schilling Place; Salinas, CA 93901-4543
Mr. Matt Haynes: Deluxe Video Services Inc.; 555 Huehl Road; Northbrook, IL 60062-2336
Mr. John Hays: University of North Carolina at Pembroke; UCIS, P.O. Box 1510; Pembroke, NC 28372-1510
Ms. Alicia Hazel: Portland Clinic; 800 Southwest 13th Avenue; Portland, OR 97205-1999
Mr. Robert Hazelton: MTI; Page Industrial Park 229D; Poughkeepsie, NY 12603
Mrs. Patty Hazelwood: T.H. Wharton Power Plant Reliant Energy; P.O. 1700; Houston, TX 77251-1700
Dr. Shusheng He Ph.D.: Sharp Laboratories of America; 5700 Northwest Pacific Rim Boulevard; Camas, WA 98607
Mr. Donald Headrick: Alltel Mobile Communication; 1185 North St. Augustine Road; Valdosta, GA 31601-3533
Ms. Esther Heard: Leake & Watts Services, Incorporated; 463 Hawthorne Avenue; Yonkers, NY 10705
Ms. Joan Heath: Information Builders, Inc.; 440 East 88th Street, Apartment 2b; New York, NY 10028-1325
Dr. R. Heath Ph.D.: Allied Signal, Inc.; 101 Columbia Road; Morristown, NJ 07960-4658
Mr. Tom Heatherington: Webunet; P.O. Box 1142; Sherman, TX 75091
Mr. Douglas Heavner: Fuji Photo Film Inc.; P.O. Box 1306; Greenwood, SC 29645-1306
Mr. Wayne Hebert: Zeon Chemicals L.P.; 4100 Bells Lane; Louisville, KY 40211
Ms. Cathy Hebling: Metrocall; 251 South Reynolds Street M401; Alexandria, VA 22304
Dr. Anne Hedin Ph.D.: Platinum Technology; 1815 South Meyers Road; Oakbrook Ter, IL 60181-5225
Mr. Richard L. Hedrick: Interpath Laboratory; P.O. Box 1208; Pendleton, OR 97801-0780
Ms. Terry L. Hefner: Kool Tools; Rural Route 2, Box 86c; Killeen, TX 76542-9602
Dr. Steven R. Heidt: AT&T; 3405 West Drive, Martin Luther King Jr. Blvd.; Clearwater, FL 33607
Mr. Bruce Heimburger: Richland Company Public Library; 1431 Assembly, Suite # 1; Columbia, SC 29201-3101
Ms. Brandi Heinroth: Sweeny I.S.D.; 1310 North Elm Street; Sweeny, TX 77480-1399
Mr. Torsten Heinze: Cadre Computer Resources; 255 East Fifth Street; Cincinnati, OH 45202
Ms. Rebecca L. Heinzer: Chick-fil-A, Inc.; 3198-F Post Woods Drive; Atlanta, GA 30349-2998
Mr. John Heiser: National Park Service; 97 Taneytown Road; Gettysburg, PA 17325-2804
Mr. Jonas Hellgren : 503 Huron Avenue, #2; Cambridge, MA 02138-2168
Ms. Cheryl J. Helver: Digital Square; 705 Sinex Avenue; Pacific Grove, CA 93950
Ms. Debi Hembree: BMW Manufacturer; P.O. Box 11000; Spartanburg, SC 29304-4100
Mr. Scott Hemphill: Corporate Contractors; 2550 Corporate Place, Suite C111; Monterrey Park, CA 91754-7653
Mr. David Henderson: United States Air Force; 611 East Street; Travis Air Force Base, CA 94535
Mr. James Henderson: University of Oklahoma Engineering Computer Network; 865 Asp Avenue, Room 109; Norman, OK 73019-1029
Mr. Joe Henderson: ManagedComp; 28 Glenrose Road; Dorchester, MA 02124-2606
Ms. Kim Henderson: GSA; 18th & F Streets Northwest/ Room 5234; Washington, DC 20405
Mr. Scott Henderson: Polycon Industries; 65 Independence Place; Guelph, Ontario, Canada N1K 1H8
Mr. Mark Hendricks: Compaq Computer; 503 Hunters Creek Court; Allen, TX 75013-5485
Mr. Tom Hendricks: National Tech Team; 27345 West 11th Mile Road; Southfield, MI 48034
Mr. Jay Galvan Heneghan: New Orleans Net; 400 Poydras Street, Suite 2480; New Orleans, LA 70130-3218
Mr. James L. Henley: Davidson County Sheriff Office; 506 2nd Avenue North; Nashville, TN 37201
Mr. Lenny Hennig: Bergen County Sheriff's Department; 95 East Broadway; Hackensack, NJ 07601-6832
Mr. David J. Henninger: Standard & Poors; 55 Water Street; New York, NY 10041
Mr. Gregory Henriksen: Henriksen & Consultant; 212 Holly Ridge Lane; West Columbia, SC 29169-3726
Mr. Bill Henris: Brocton Central School; 138 West Main Street; Brocton, NY 14716-9749
Mr. Brian Henry: Valley Mental Health; 5965 South 900 East, Suite 330; Salt Lake City, UT 84221-1794
Ms. Diane Henry: Genoa Area Local School District; 303 West 4th Street; Genoa, OH 43430-1810
Mr. Mark S. Henry: Bell Atlantic; 2980 Fairview Park Drive; Falls Church, VA 22042
Mr. Philip Henry: Master Eagle Graphics; 40 West 25th Street; New York, NY 10010-2707
Mr. Rick Henry: County of Blair; 423 Allegheny Street; Hollidaysburg, PA 16648-2022
Mr. Steve Henry: Buy It Now Com; 8321 East 61st Street; Tulsa, OK 74133-1913
Mr. Allan Henshaw: The Minute Maid Company; 2000 Saint James Place; Houston, TX 77056-4123
Mr. Brad Hensley: Pepsi-Cola Bottlers; 1531 Monroe Avenue; Huntington, WV 25704-2335
Mr. Jim Hepfer: Northrop Grumman; P.O. Box 101, 18450 Showalter Road; Hagerstown, MD 21741-0101
Mr. Charles R. Herman: Sattel Global Networks, Inc.; 9172 Eton Avenue; Chatsworth, CA 91311-5805
Mr. Earl D. Herman: Southern Illinois University at Edwardsville; Campus Box 1068; Edwardsville, IL 62026
Mr. Michael Herman: Christianity Today, Inc.; 465 Gundersen Drive; Carol Stream, IL 60188-2498
Mrs. Scott Hermans: Oread, Inc.; 400 Farmington Avenue; Farmington, CT 06032
Ms. Mary Hernandez: Sabre; 4200 Buckingham Boulevard, MD 14194; Fort Worth, TX 76155-2618
Mr. Scott Herndon: ISS Security; 3507 Frontage Road, #200; Tampa, FL 33607
Mr. Kevin Herr: Sunbury Broadcasting Corporation; P.O. Box 1070; Sunbury, PA 17801-0870
Mr. Warren D. Herring: American Youth Foundation Miniwanca; 8845 West Garfield Road; Shelby, MI 49455
Mr. Richard J. Herro: Gulfport School District; P.O. Box 220; Gulfport, MS 39502-0220
Mr. Larry Herzog: University of North Dakota; 1951 28th Avenue South, Apartment 108; Grand Forks, ND 58201-6668
Mr. Ronald A. Heuring: Perry County Memorial Hospital; 434 North West Street; Perryville, MO 63775-1398
Ms. Lynne G. Hewett: Columbus County Hospital; 500 Jefferson Street; Whiteville, NC 28472-3634
Mr. Greg S. Heynssens : 333 East Butterfield Road, Floor 5; Lombard, IL 60148-5617
Ms. Paula W. Hickey: State University of New York College at Oneonta; Ravine Parkway; Oneonta, NY 13820
Mr. Steve Hickman: Symbiotics, Inc.; 2100 West Northwest Highway #1104; Grapevine, TX 76051-7808
Ms. Gloria Hicks: Tempe School District 3; 3205 South Rural Road; Tempe, AZ 85282-3853
Ms. Karen Hicks: Wella Corporation; 4650 Oakleys Lane; Richmond, VA 23231-2914
Mr. Ron Hicks: Hope Christian School; 3603 Cahaba Beach Road; Birmingham, AL 35242
Mr. Tiel Hicks: Spokane Teachers Credit Union; 1620 North Signal Drive; Liberty Lake, WA 99019
Mr. Frank Hidalgo Jr.: IBM Corporation; 1177 South Beltline Road; Coppell, TX 75019
Mr. Noor Hidayat: American Overseas Petro Lt.; 2925 Briarpark Drive; Houston, TX 77042-3720
Mrs. Melanie Higgins: American Lung Association of Oklahoma; 2805 East Skelly Drive, Suite 806; Tulsa, OK 74105-6267
Mr. Cameron Hight: CIBC World Markets; 230 East 30th Street, Apartment 13g; New York, NY 10016-8289
Mr. Samy Hilali: Seagate Technology, Inc.; 4574 Scotts Valley Drive; Scotts Valley, CA 95066-4517
Mr. Norman Hilario: West field Corporation, Inc.; 11601 Wilshire Boulevard, 12th Floor; Los Angeles, CA 90025-1748
Mr. Alston C. Hildreth Jr.: Wellman, Inc.; Rural Route 55, Box 455A; Fayetteville, NC 28301-8215
Mr. Mark S. Hiles : 1451 Tiverton Drive; Brandon, FL 33511-1814
Mr. David Hill: Citi; 12567 Summit Manor Drive, Apartment 404; Fairfax, VA 22033-5770
Mr. Henry Hill Ph.D.: Blinn College; P.O. Box 6030; Bryan, TX 77805
Mr. James R. Hill: Steris Corporation; 5960 Heisley Road; Mentor, OH 44060-1834
Mr. John Hill: Xerox Corporation; 262 Elmwood Terrace; Rochester, NY 14620-3706
Mr. Kenneth Hill: First Consulting Group; 1337 East Upsal Street; Philadelphia, PA 19150-2228
Ms. Lisa Harvey Hill: Cortez III NASA Glenn Research Center; 21000 Brookpark Road; Cleveland, OH 44135-3191
Mrs. Luvoise B. Hill: Greene County Board of Education; 301 Kingold Boulevard; Snow Hill, NC 28580-1305
Mr. Michael D. Hill: KPMG L.L.P.; 61 West Night Heron Place; The Woodlands, TX 77382-1035
Ms. Rachelle Hill: Southern Methodist University; P.O. Box 402, Office of Development; Dallas, TX 75221-0402
Mr. Stephan Hill: Times-Republican; P.O. Box 1300; Marshalltown, IA 50158-1300
Ms. Victoria Hill: St. Joseph Hospital; 5665 Peachtree Dunwoody Road Northeast; Atlanta, GA 30342-1764
Ms. Kim Hilliard: Kimtech Computer Services; 881 Homestead Drive; Ellabell, GA 31308-5545
Mr. Bruce Hillier: Reminger & Reminger Company Lpa; 113 St. Clair Avenue NE; Cleveland, OH 44114-1214
Dr. J. R. Hillman Ph.D.: Scottish Crop Research Institute; Invergowrie, Dundee; Angus, England, United Kingdom DD2 5DA
Mr. Wally Hinds: Adelphia Business Solutions; 5 West 3rd Street; Coudersport, PA 16915
Ms. Heather Hine: Kern District Marketing; 20300 Ventura Boulevard; Woodland Heights, CA 91364-2448
Mr. Anthony R. Hines: Standard Aero Alliance, Inc.; 1029 Ross Drive; Maryville, TN 37801
Mr. Jim Hinkle: Itic, Inc.; 999 18th Street, Suite 1999; Denver, CO 80202-2499
Mr. Shawn Hinkle: Spacenet, Inc.; 840 Franklin Court; Marietta, GA 30067
Mr. Harry Hinsey: US Carrier Telecom; 4931 Mercer University Drive, Suite C; Macon, GA 31210-6216
Dr. Bernard Hinton Ph.D.: Light Speed Fiberlink; 751 Rancheros Drive; San Marcos, CA 92069
Mr. Roger Hintz: Newell Rubbermaid, Inc.; 29 East Stephenson Street; Freeport, IL 61032-4251
Mr. Mike Hitchens: Innovative Controls; 1354 East Broadway; Toledo, OH 43605-3600
Dr. Gisli Hjalmtyssom Ph.D: AT&T Labs-Research; 61 Summit Avenue; Gillette, NJ 07933-2007
Mr. Robert Hlavecek: Macneal Health Network; 3249 Oak Park Avenue; Berwyn, IL 60402-3429
Mr. Cuong Hoang: The Orkand Corporation; 7799 Leesburg Pike #6085; Falls Church, VA 22043-2413
Mr. Jon B. Hobbs: Sales Support Service; 14950 F.A.A. Boulevard; Fort Worth, TX 76155
Mr. Dennis D. Hock: Detroit Edison Company; 70657 Lowe Plank Road; Richmond, MI 48062-5355
Mrs. Sharon Hockensmith: Systems Source; 130 East Chestnut Street; Hanover, PA 17331-2246
Mr. Umesh Hodeghatta: Tyro Submarine Systems, Ltd.; 250 Industrial Way West; Eatontown, NJ 07724
Ms. Carol L. Hodes: Pennsylvania State University; 1162 Smithfield Circle; State College, PA 16801-6423
Mr. Dave Hodge: Aetna US Healthcare; 1 Liberty Plaza; New York, NY 100061404
Ms. Kerilee Hodges: Rocky Mount Information Network; 2828 North Central Avenue, Suite 1000; Phoenix, AZ 85004-1027
Mr. Thomas Hodges: Emerald Solutions Inc.; 5902 Mount Eagle Drive; Alexandria, VA 22303-2513
Mr. Harold Hodnett: Star Systems, Inc.; 2600 Lake Lucien Drive, Suite 180; Maitland, FL 32751-7233
Ms. Danni Hodson: Edina Family Center; 5701 Normandale Road; Edina, MN 55424-2400
Ms. Sylvia Hoehns Wright: First Health Services; 4300 Cox Road; Glen Allen, VA 23060-3358
Mr. Gary W. Hoff: MCI World Com; 2424 Garden of the Gods Road; Colorado Springs, CO 80919-3190
Ms. Joanna Hoffler: System 42, Inc.; 11210 Old Baltimore Pike; Beltsville, MD 20705-2010
Mr. E. C. Hoffman: EDS; 600 Kellwood Parkway; Chesterfield, MO 63017
Mr. Kenneth A. Hoffman: Berrien County Court House; 811 Port Street; St. Joseph, MI 49085-1183
Dr. Thomas Hoffman Ph.D: Fraunhofer USA; 601 West 20th Street; Hialeah, FL 33010-2432
Mr. Fred M. Hoffmann: Greene Services; Route 1, Box 640; Spencer, IN 47460
Ms. Sally Hoffmaster: Avalon; 6300 Georgetown Pike, #F-220; McLean, VA 22101-2200
Ms. Dolores Hofmann : 36 Whitecliff Drive; Pittsford, NY 14534-2928
Mr. Rex Hogan: TRW; 12900 Federal Systems Park Drive; Fairfax, VA 22033-4421
Ms. Felicia T. Hogans: Telco Communications Group; 3900 Skyhawk Drive; Chantilly, VA 20151-3219
Mr. Darrell Hohlbein: Vickers, Inc.; 2425 West Michigan Avenue; Jackson, MI 49202-3964
Mr. Michael W. Hohner: Oracle Corporation; 618 Bedford Drive; Richardson, TX 75080
Mr. A. Holbert: Poseidon Systems; P.O. Box 11302; San Rafael, CA 94912-1302
Mr. Ross Holbrooks: Stanislans County; 948 11th Street. #34 North; Modesto, CA 95354-2308
Mrs. Lasona Holcomb: Floyd County Government; P.O. Box 946; Rome, GA 30162-0946
Mr. John M. Holdcraft: United States Air Force; 2515 Perimeter Place Drive; Nashville, TN 37214
Dr. Jolly Holden: Spacenet, Inc.; 840 Franklin Court SE; Marietta, GA 30067-8939
Mr. Michael Holdowsky: International Planning & Research; P.O. Box 1100, 10 Slalom Drive Eastman; Grantham, NH 03753-1100
Mr. Jack Holford: Corporate Systems; 13307 Bandera Drive; Amarillo, TX 79111-1416
Mr. Earl Holland: Montgogo, Limited; 2833 North 3rd Street; Phoenix, AZ 85004
Mr. William Holland: Stone & Webster Engineering; P.O. Box 2325; Boston, MA 02107-2325
Mr. David Hollins: United States Forest Service; 5500 Amelia Earhart Drive; Salt Lake City, UT 84116-3782
Mr. Jack Hollins: LSI Logic; 6010 Cottage Place; San Jose, CA 95123-5322
Ms. Lisa Carole Holloway: Swanson Services Corporation; 2113 63rd Avenue East; Bradenton, FL 34203-5000
Mr. Graeme Holman: RTM Star Center; 2 West Dixie Highway; Dania, FL 33004-4312
Ms. Traci A. Holman: United States Department of Agriculture - Natural Resources Conservation Service; 801 Broadway; Nashville, TN 37203-3816
Mr. Scott Holmes: FedEX; 30 Fed Ex Parkway Floor 1; Collierville, TN 38017-8711
Mr. John Holobetz: St. Clair Area School District; 227 South Mill Street; St.Clair, PA 17970-1338
Mr. Daniel L. Holt: RGI Computers, Inc.; 8362 Veterans Highway; Millersville, MD 21108-2565
Mr. John Holt: Shared Tech; 6402 West Ironwood; Glendale, AZ 35302
Mr. Mindi Holzschuh: San Jose Mercury News; Mercury Center, 750 Ridder Park Drive; San Jose, CA 95190
Mr. Don Homrich: Steelcase North America; P.O. Box 1967 CH-3W-04; Grand Rapids, MI 49501-1967
Mr. Donald Hood: CTA Acoustics, Inc.; P.O. Box

448; Corbin, KY 40702-0448

Mr. Ernie John Hopkins: COMPUSA; 826 South Wheatley; Ridgeland, MS 39157

Ms. Rebecca Hopkins: Wesley Business Forms; 1100 Old Beltway; Rural Hall, NC 27045-9537

Mr. Eugene Hoppa Jr.: EM & I, Inc.; 11404 Gate Hill Place, Unit P.; Reston, VA 20194-2044

Mr. Gregory Hopson: Gazette Technologies; P.O. Box 511; Cedar Rapids, IA 52406-0511

Mr. Tom Horley: Pennsylvania Governor's Office for Information Technology; One Technology Park Drive; Harrisburg, PA 17110

Mrs. Lee Ester Horn: Mississippi Valley State University; 14000 Highway 82 West; Itta Bena, MS 38941-1400

Mr. James Horne: Famu Fsu College of Engineering; 2525 Pottsdamer Street, #244; Tallahassee, FL 32310

Mr. Timothy E. Horoho: Independent Stationers I; 9900 Westpoint Drive, Suite 116; Indianapolis, IN 46256-3338

Mr. Benjamin Horowitz: EECS Department-Univeristy of California at Berkeley; Univeristy of California at Berkeley; Berkeley, CA 94720

Mrs. Blondell T. Horton: American Diabetes Association; 1660 Duke Street; Alexandria, VA 22314-3427

Mr. Ron Horton: Bell and Howell Phillipsbirg; Post Office Box 14986; Durham, NC 27709-4986

Mr. Paul Horvath: IBM; 1706 West Pearson Street; Chicago, IL 60622-5001

Ms. Elenora L. Hosburgh: REL Technology Services; 29-30 138th Street, Suite 3C; Flushing, NY 11354

Ms. Bertha Hoskins: University of Massachusetts; 100 William T. Morrissey Boulevard; Boston, MA 02125-3393

Mr. Dave Hosley: United Space Alliance; MSC USK 155; Kennedy Space Center, FL 32899-0001

Mr. Tingxiu Hou: Citation Corporation; 27730 Franklin Road; Southfield, MI 48034-2352

Mr. David Houser: Landline Communications; 40 Winding Hill Drive; Hockessin, DE 19707-2014

Mr. Lewis T. Houston: SETA; 6862 Elm Street; McLean, VA 22101

Mr. Kenneth L. Houtz: Choptank Electric Cooperative; P. O. Box 430; Denton, MD 21629

Mr. Bryce C. Hoverman: South Carolina Department of Consumer Affairs; P.O. Box 5757; Columbia, SC 29205

Mr. Allan Hovey: Union Pacific Railroad; 1416 Dodge Street; Omaha, NE 68179

Mr. Brian Howard: Abacus Software; 5370 52nd Street, SE; Grand Rapids, MI 49512-9766

Mr. Scott Howard: IBM Corporation; 32 Piper Lane; Levittown, NY 11756-3426

Mr. Steve Howard: Pearl River College; 402 South Strahan Street; Poplarville, MS 39470-2426

Ms. Wendy Howerton: Marriott Vacation Club International; 1200 Bartow Road, Suite 40; Lakeland, FL 33801-5907

Mr. Anthony D. Hoyle: Information Technology Consulting; 13554 Virginia Randolph Avenue, Apartment 403; Herndon, VA 20171-4427

Mr. Nebojssa Hrmic: Amazon.Com; 1629 Summit Avenue, Apartment 203; Seattle, WA 98122-2340

Mr. Michael Hsieh: Arx International; 2220 College Point Boulevard; Flushing, NY 11356-2534

Mr. Peter Hsieh: Linear Logic, Inc.; 14072 Firestone Boulevard; Santa Fe Springs, CA 90670-5809

Ms. Daisy Hsiung: SBC; 1010 Wilshire Boulevard, Suite 655; Los Angeles, CA 90017-2416

Mr. Donald Hsu: Dominican College; 470 Western Highway; Orangeburg, NY 10962-1295

Mr. Jimmy Hu: Illinois Power; 370 South Main Street; Decatur, IL 62523-1479

Mr. Ning Hua: C2 Multimedia, Inc.; 7700 Leesburg Pike, Suite 231; Falls Church, VA 22043

Mr. Gary Huang: Sprint Corporation; 7171 West 95th Street; Overland Park, KS 66212-2283

Dr. Paul Huang Ph.D.: United Defense; 4800 East River Road; Minneapolis, MN 55421-1498

Mr. Dave Hubbard: NCR; 870 Stovall Boulevard NE; Atlanta, GA 30342-3958

Mr. Fred Hubbard: Channelview Independant School District; 1100 Sheldon Road; Channelview, TX 77530-3518

Ms. Valerie Huber: South Pasadena High School; 1401 Fremont Avenue; South Pasadena, CA 91030-3809

Mr. Anthony T. Hucker: Gtech; 1632 Laporte Drive; Roseville, CA 95747

Mr. Brian Huddleson: Networx, Etc.; P.O. Box 1374; Galt, CA 95632-1374

Mr. James D. Hudspeth: B J Services, USA; 11211 FM 2920; Tomball, TX 77375-8927

Mr. Emmanuel Hue: Alcatel Its; 12030 Sunrise Valley Drive; Reston, VA 20191-3409

Mr. Dennis D. Huffman: Timken Research; 1835 Dueber Avenue SW; Canton, OH 44706-2798

Mr. Michael Hugel: Enable, Inc.; 11444 West Bernardo Court; San Diego, CA 92127

Mr. Brian Hughes: Idaho State University Computer Center; 890 South 5th Avenue MSC 8037; Pocatello, ID 83209-8037

Mr. David Hughes : 30 South Pearl Street; Albany, NY 12207

Mr. John Hughes: New Jersey Transit; 1 Pennsylvania Plaza East, Floor 6; Newark, NJ 07105-2245

Ms. Marilyn Hughes: Multnomah County; 4747 East Burnside Street; Portland, OR 97215-1144

Mr. Robert W. Hughes: Indiana Department of Correction; 411 Indianapolis Canal Walk; Indianapolis, IN 46202-3251

Mr. C. Humber: Inner City Broadcasting Corporation; 3 Park Avenue; New York, NY 10016-5902

Mr. Richard Humpherys: Stoner Associates; 9 Azalea Drive; Mount Holly Springs, PA 17065-1944

Dr. James T. Humphries Ph.D.: Hillsborough Community College; P.O. Box 31127; Tampa, FL 33631

Mr. Jesus Hung: INFOSAT; Parque Cristal; Caracas, Venezuela

Ms. Nancy A. Hunt: Southwest School Corporation; 820 North Section Street; Sullivan, IN 47882-1044

Mr. Timothy R. Hunt: Church of Jesus Christ of Latter Day Saints; 533 Valley Drive; Centerville, UT 84014-1059

Mr. Michael J. Hunter: OG&E Electric Services; 321 North Harvey Avenue; Oklahoma City, OK 73102-3449

Mr. Peter Hunzicker: Integrated Partnerships, Inc.; 10 West Market Street, Suite 2; Indianapolis, IN 46204-2954

Mr. Jim Hurd: HoosierNet, Inc.; 303 East Kirkwood Avenue; Bloomington, IN 47408

Mr. William Hurley: Gruntal And Company LLC; 1 Liberty Plaza Floor 13; New York, NY 10006-1404

Ms. Muriel Hurley-Carter: Hartford Hospital; P.O. Box 5037, 80 Seymour Street; Hartford, CT 06102-5037

Ms. Lynn Hurni: DCC; 5950 Hazeltine National Drive, Suite 410; Orlando, FL 32822-5003

Mr. Benjamin Hurst: City of Ocean City; 835 Central Avenue; Ocean City, NJ 08226

Mr. Thomas A. Husley : 218 Touchdown Drive; Irving, TX 75063-5383

Ms. Mary Huston: Norfolk Public Schools; 966 Bellmore Avenue; Norfolk, VA 23504-4199

Mr. Robert Huston: West Virginia State College; Campus Box 184, P.O. Box 1000; Institute, WV 25112-1000

Mr. Ed Hutchinson: MS. Carriers; 3171 Directors Row; Memphis, TN 38131-0400

Mr. Anthony Huynh: Los Angeles Police Department; 634 South Spring Street, Suite 500; Los Angeles, CA 91807

Mr. Phuoc-Long Huynh: C N T; 10651 Castine Avenue; Cupertino, CA 95014

Mr. Daniel J. Hyatt: Computing Solutions; 21372 Brookhurst, #418; Huntington Beach, CA 92646

Mr. Eric S. Hylick: FedEx; 1901 Summit Tower Boulevard, Suite 300; Orlando, FL 32810

Mr. Charles Hynson: Westat; 1650 Research Boulevard; Rockville, MD 20850-3195

Ms. Cheryl Hysinger: Maytag Appliance Sales Company; 240 Edwards Street; Cleveland, TN 37312

Mr. Tobias Iaconis: Jim Henson Productions; 5358 Melrose Avenue; Los Angeles, CA 90038-3147

Mr. Victor Iasprizza: Startcomm Corporation; 100 Biscayne Boulevard, Suite 402; Miami, FL 33132-2344

Ms. Flavia Ibanez: Pan American Life Insurance Company; 601 Poydras Street, Suite 1780; New Orleans, LA 70130

Ms. Jo A. Idoux: University of Texas Police Department; 1515 Holcombe Boulevard, #160; Houston, TX 77030-4009

Mr. Paul Iglesia: Adroit Systems, Inc.; 209 Madison Street, Suite 200; Alexandria, VA 22314-1764

Mr. Syed Asif Ijaz: Persistence Software Inc.; 3224 Ashley Way; Union City, CA 94587-4755

Ms. Shanmukha Immadi: New Millennium Technologies Inc.; 11675 West Bellfort, #1001; Houston, TX 77099

Mr. James William Ingalls: Willtronics Broadcasting; P.O. Box 100; French Lick, IN 47432-0100

Ms. Kristin Ingersoll: General DataComm; 1579 Straits Turnpike; Middlebury, CT 06762

Ms. Marcia Ingham: Ampc, Inc.; 2325 North Loop Drive; Ames, IA 50010-8281

Mr. Larry V. Ingle: EDS; 1401 East Hoffer Street; Kokomo, IN 46902-2426

Mr. Kenneth Ingram: Navis LLC; 155 Grand Avenue, Suite 610; Oakland, CA 94612-3747

Mr. Albert Internicola: Asti Technologies Development; 666 Marlisa Place; Victoria, British Columbia, Canada V9B 4Y8

Mr. Gregory L. Irvin: Barnes & Thornburg; 600 One Summit Square; Fort Wayne, IN 46802-3119

Ms. Jeanne Isberto: On Site Access; 680 5th Avenue; New York, NY 10019-5429

Mr. Antoine Ishak: Lester Electrical of Nebraska; 625 West A Street; Lincoln, NE 68522-1794

Ms. Judith H. Ishee: Defense Finance and Accounting Services; 250 Raby Avenue; Pensacola, FL 32509-5122

Mr. Khaled Ismail: Baytechs; 1782 Hurstwood Court; San Jose, CA 95121-1446

Mr. Mahdi Ismail: Complete Business Solutions Inc.; 172 East State Street #400; Columbus, OH 43215

Mr. Wan Israf: FRC Component Products; 1511 South Benjamin Avenue; Mason City, IA 50401-5607

Dr. Sergei Ivanov Ph.D.: Invention Machine; 200 Portland Street; Boston, MA 02114-1722

Mr. Alexander Ivanovic: Sescoi USA Inc.; 200 Town Center, Suite 1730; Southfield, MI 48075-1150

Mr. K. Iyer: Oracle Corporation; 3409 Grove Gate Court, Apartment 1723; Richmond, VA 23233-0229

Mr. Victor Izhak: New Horizons Computer Center; 1 Penn Plaza; New York, NY 10119-0002

Mr. Vincent Izzo: The Hartford; 200 Executive Boulevard 200-3; Southington, CT 06489-1096

Mr. David Jablonski: Boysville of Michigan; 8759 Clinton Macon Road; Clinton, MI 79236-9569

Mr. David Jackson: Chess; 4132 East 131st Drive; Thornton, CO 80241-2266

Mr. John R. Jackson: McCordick Clove & Safety Inc.; 75 Cowansview Road; Cambridge, Ontario, Canada N1R 7L2

Mr. John Jackson: University of Virginia; P.O. Box 555; Charlottesville, VA 22908-0001

Mr. Ross Jackson: Standard Forwarding Company Inc.; P.O. Box 129; East Moline, IL 61244-0129

Mr. Phillip Jacob: First Presbyterian Church; 408 Park Avenue; Dallas, TX 75201

Mr. Brian Jacobs: The Advisory Board Company; 600 New Hampshire Avenue Northwest, Suite 400; Washington, DC 20037-2403

Mr. Kurt Jacobs: Kemper Insurance Companies; 1 Kemper Drive, #K9; Long Grove, IL 60049-0002

Mr. Steven I. Jacobs: NCR Corporation; 1529 Brown Street EMD-5; Dayton, OH 45479

Ms. Tina M. Jacobs: Highland Management; 12 Alfred Street, Suite 307; Woburn, MA 01801

Mr. David B. Jake Jacobs-Pratt: Central Maine Technical College; 4 Private Acres Drive; Standish, ME 04084

Mr. Robert Jacobsen: Bell Atlantic; 80D Commerce Way; Totowa, NJ 07512-1154

Mr. Vijay Jadhwani: Tellabs; 1325 Ivy Lane, Apartment 103; Naperville, IL 60563-0473

Ms. Julie Jaehne: University of Houston; 9029 Kenilworth Street; Houston, TX 77024-3716

Mr. John Jaggers: Gilat Spacenet; 10819 Verde Vista Drive; Fairfax, VA 22030-4439

Mr. Thomas A. Jahrmann: Exel Logistics Americas; 1717 North Matzinger Road; Toledo, OH 43612-3841

Mr. Abhas Jain: Vital Processing Services; 8320 South Hardy Drive; Tempe, AZ 85284-2007

Mr. Rahul Jain: Interwave Communications; 656 Bair Island Road, Suite 108; Redwood City, CA 94063-2745

Mr. Sandeep Jain: Datamics Consultants, Inc.; 2400 Pleasant Hill Road, #215; Duluth, GA 30096

Mr. Sanjeev Jain: Thomas Jefferson University; 130 South 9th Street, Lobby 6; Philadelphia, PA 19107-5233

Mr. Seema Jain: Big Promotions, Inc.; 6825 Jimmy Carter Boulevard, #1303; Norcross, GA 30071

Mr. Vivek Jain: Lucent Technologies; Room E4D23, 283 King George Road; Warren, NJ 07059

Ms. Ann M. Jakits : 4100 Northwest 25th Way; Boca Raton, FL 33434-2535

Mr. Robert Jakobsze: Cendant Corporation; 900 Old Country Road; Garden City, NY 11530

Mr. Abdy Jalilvand: Rebis; 3000 Weslayan Street, Suite 260; Houston, TX 77027-5751

Mr. Tarek Jamal: INET; 1640 South Sepulveda Boulevard, Suite 320; Los Angeles, CA 90025-7510

Mr. Jermaine James: Illinois Department of Transportation; 310 South Michigan Avenue, Suite 1608; Chicago, IL 60604-4205

Ms. Susan James: Lawrence Berkeley National Laboratory; One Cyclotron Road; Berkeley, CA 94720

Mr. David Jamison: H&R Block; 4400 Main Street; Kansas City, MO 64111-1812

Ms. Janet M. Jamison: United States General Accounting Office; 5799 Broadmoor Street, Suite 600; Shawnee Mission, KS 66202-2482

Dr. Sudhakar Ratnakar Jamkhandi Ph.D.: Center for International Understanding at Bluefield State College; 219 Rock Street; Bluefield, WV 24701-2100

Mr. Steven Jancarek: Electronic Data Systems; 1700 Bayberry Court, Suite 2000; Richmond, VA 23226-3791

Ms. Sondra Janiro: Teledyne Metalworking Product; 1 Teledyne Place; La Vergne, TN 37086

Ms. Charity Janke: AT&T; 3210 Lake Emma Road; Lake Mary, FL 32746-3334

Mr. Jon Jankowiak: Best Buy; 21111 East 43rd Avenue; Denver, CO 80249-7055

Mr. Gerald Janssens: Siemens SA; 116 Chaussee de Charleroi; Brussels, Belgium 1060

Mr. Adam Japhet: Cnbc; 2200 Fletcher Avenue; Fort Lee, NJ 07024-5005

Mr. Rajesh Jaria: Motorola; 9134 North Lincoln Drive, Apartment 2F; Des Plaines, IL 60016-6953

Mr. Jeff Jarnigan: Labor Arbitration Institute; 205 Water Street South; Northfield, MN 55057-2043

Mr. Kent Jarrett: Jarrett Software; 1002 Arlene Court, Apartment 308; Bloomington, IL 61701-7161

Ms. Karen Jasinski: Town of Bellingham; 4 Mechanic Street; Bellingham, MA 02019-1634

Mr. Ajit Jayaswal: Saudi Arabian Airlines; CC992, 725 5th Avenue, Floor 18; New York, NY 10022-2519

Mr. Steven Jaynes: Comm Vault; 14753 Southwest Fern Street; Tigard, OR 97223

Mr. Charles Jeffers: Atlanta Convention Bureau; 233 Peachtree Street NE, Suite 100; Atlanta, GA 30303-1528

Mr. Mark Jeffers: Department of Transportation; 1811 South Rocky Mountain Drive; Tucson, AZ 85710

Mr. Harley Jeffrey: Control Southern, Inc.; 3850 Lakefield Drive; Suwanee, GA 30024-1241

Mr. Wayne Jenevein: United States Department of Housing and Urban Development; 501 Magazine Street, Floor 9; New Orleans, LA 70130-3319

Mr. Marlin Jenkins: Teligent Inc.; 2220 Holland Avenue, Floor 1; Bronx, NY 10467-9402

Ms. Marlyn Jensen: Portersville Christian School; P.O. Box 44; Portersville, PA 16051-0044

Dr. Jin-Ah Jeon Ph.D.: Utility Partners Inc.; 5241 West Spring Mountain; Las Vegas, NV 89150

Mr. Brent K. Jesiek: East Jordan Iron Works; P.O. Box 439; East Jordan, MI 49727-0439

Mr. Pat Jesten: Aztech Corporation; 4733 Bethesda Avenue; Bethesda, MD 20814-5228

Mr. David J. Jetmar: Snet/SBC; 530 Preston Avenue; Meriden, CT 06450-4893

Ms. Reba Jett: PageNet, Inc.; 422 Emerson, Suite 100; St. Louis, MO 63141

Mr. Clayton Jew: Keane Federal System; 14028 Crest Hill Lane; Silver Spring, MD 20905-4465

Mr. Steve Jex: International Paper; P.O. Box 311;

Natchez, MS 39121-0311
Ms. Joanne H. Jiadosz: City of Salem; One Salem Green; Salem, MA 01970
Mr. Parveen Jindal: Oracle Corporation; 737 East El Camino Real, Apartment 4418; Sunnyvale, CA 94087-2921
Mr. Chuck Joe: Mid America Computer Corporation; 111 Admiral Drive; Blair, NE 68008-2522
Mr. George John: Coler Memorial Hospital; 900 Main Street, Room 326; New York, NY 10044-0066
Mr. David Johnsen: PacifiCorp; 825 Northeast Multonomah Street, Suite 300; Portland, OR 97232-2157
Mr. Lee Johnsen: Equistar Chemicals; 11530 Northlake Drive; Cincinnati, OH 45150
Mr. Alan Johnson: Dynamic Metal Products; 967 Parker Street; Manchester, CT 06040-2297
Mr. Barry Johnson: Pcs Health Systems; 9501 East Shea Boulevard; Scottsdale, AZ 85260
Mr. Ben Johnson: SPX Corporation; 8001 Angling Road; Portage, MI 49024-7819
Ms. Carole Johnson: Technology Consulting Corporation; 926 Willard Drive, Suite 246; Green Bay, WI 54304-5071
Ms. Celine Johnson: 408th Signal Com; P.O. Box 25069; Fort Wainwright, AK 99703-0069
Mr. Chris Johnson: Florida Department of Law Enforcement; P.O. Box 1489; Tallahassee, FL 32302-1489
Mr. Craig M. Johnson: McLead, U.S.A.; 3809 South Western Avenue; Sioux Falls, SD 57105
Ms. Cynthia Johnson: Application Software Technologies, Inc.; 1410 West 2nd Street; Appleton, WI 54914-5062
Mr. Danette Johnson: Dentrix Dental Systems, Inc.; 732 East Utah Valley Drive, #500; American Fork, UT 84003-9773
Ms. Diane Johnson: University of Arkansas Medical Science; 4301 West Markham Street, #526; Little Rock, AR 72205-7101
Mr. Don Johnson: Universal Computer System Inc.; 6700 Hollister Street; Houston, TX 77040-5331
Mr. Doug Aubert Johnson: Math Soft Incorporated; 1700 Westlake Avenue North Suite 500; Seattle, WA 98109-3044
Mr. Duane Johnson: St. Cloud Public Utilities; 400 2nd Street South; St. Cloud, MN 56301-3622
Ms. Jacqueline Johnson: Cigna Healthcare; 480 Canyon Oaks Drive, #F; Oakland, CA 94605-3858
Mr. James Johnson: Westmont; 2525 Colonial Drive; Helena, MT 59601-4950
Mr. Jerald W. Johnson: University of California at Los Angelos Medical Center; 10880 Wilshire Boulevard, Suite 300; Los Angeles, CA 90024
Mr. Jim Johnson: Warner Publisher Services Inc.; 9210 King Palm Drive; Tampa, FL 33619-1328
Mr. Jim Johnson: Tennessee Technical University; P.O. Box 5071; Cookeville, TN 38505-0001
Mr. Lane K. Johnson: First National Mortgage Services Product World, Inc.; P.O. Box 9733; Longview, TX 75608-9733
Mr. Matthew K. Johnson: Real Time Enterprises; 26 Aberthaw Road; Rochester, NY 14610-2906
Mr. Maynard Johnson: Jackson & Blanc; 1970 Columbia Street; San Diego, CA 92101-2284
Ms. Melinda Johnson: EDS; 5400 Legacy Drive; Plano, TX 75024
Mr. Mike Johnson: Quantum Southwest Medical Management Inc.; 13750 San Pedro Avenue, Suite 330; San Antonio, TX 78232-4314
Ms. Rebecca W. Johnson: Boeing; 9566 Railroad Drive; El Paso, TX 79924-6318
Mr. Rick Johnson: United Central Industrial Supply; 1005 Glenway Avenue; Bristol, VA 24201-3473
Ms. Roberta Johnson: Lockesburg Public Schools; P.O. Box 188; De Queen, AR 71832-0188
Ms. Roxana H. Johnson: Hopkins Manufacturing Corporation; 428 Peyton Street; Emporia, KS 66801-3758
Mr. Russell Johnson: Naval Research Laboratory; 7017 Glenn Street; Metairie, LA 70003-4943
Mr. Scott Johnson: Caterpillar Inc.; 100 Northeast Adams Street; Peoria, IL 61629-0002
Ms. Sheila Johnson: Federal Data Corporation; 2201 C Street NW; Washington, DC 20520
Mr. Steven C. Johnson: Lake Region Healthcare Corporation; 712 South Cascade Street; Fergus Falls, MN 56537-2913
Mr. Tony Johnson: Promac, Inc.; 38 South Grove Avenue; Elgin, IL 60120-6404
Ms. Valerie Johnson: Systems & Computer Technology/City of Greenville; 206 South Main Street, Floor 3; Greenville, SC 29601-2897
Mr. Vickie Johnson: Raytheon Systems; 3925 North Mitthoeffer Road; Indianapolis, IN 46235-1866
Mr. Zacharay Johnson: IXL; 215 First Street; Cambridge, MA 02142
Mr. Glenn W. Johnston: Massachusetts Institute of Technology; 50 Memorial Drive; Cambridge, MA 02142-1347
Ms. Annette Jones: Arkansas Blue Cross Blue Shield; P.O. Box 8069; Little Rock, AR 72203-8069
Mr. Anthony Jones: Alabama State Employee Credit Union; 1000 Interstate Park Drive; Montgomery, AL 36109
Mr. Charles Jones: The Plain Dealer; 1694 Karg Drive; Akron, OH 44313-5502
Ms. Cheryl F. Jones: Verche Technologies, LLC; 1702 Spanish Bay Court; Mitchellville, MD 20721-3145
Mr. Chris Jones: Sola Optical USA, Inc.; 1500 Cader Lane; Petaluma, CA 94954-6908
Mr. Donald V. Jones: Honeywell IAC; 8770 West Glen; Houston, TX 77064
Mr. Ethan C. Jones: City of Fresno; 2600 Fresno; Fresno, CA 93721
Ms. Ina Jones: First Data; 6502 South Yale Avenue; Tulsa, OK 74136
Ms. Laura A. Jones: Cyborg Systems, Inc.; 2 North Riverside Plaza; Chicago, IL 60606-2600
Mr. Michael T. Jones: Lucent Technologies; 6200 East Broad Street; Columbus, OH 43213-1530
Mr. Nathaniel Jones: Harris County Department of Education; 6300 Irvington Boulevard; Houston, TX 77022-5799
Mr. Patrick Jones: Arch Communications Group; 11300 Cornell Park Drive; Cincinnati, OH 45242-1858
Mr. Peters P. Jones: Liberty Mutual Group; 225 Borthwick Avenue; Portsmouth, NH 03801-4199
Mr. Rodney B. Jones: Power Equipment Company; P.O. Box 2311; Knoxville, TN 37901
Ms. Sandra Jones: University of Alabama at Huntsville; 301 Sparkman; Huntsville, AL 35899-0001
Mr. Scott Jones: Intellimark; 5020 Richard Lane; Mechanicsburg, PA 17055-6906
Mr. Theodore E. Jones: Werner Company; 93 Werner Road; Greenville, PA 16125-9499
Mr. Glenn Jordan: Resources Trust; 8051 East Maplewood Avenue; Englewood, CO 80111-4757
Mr. Jason Jordan: Reynolds & Reynolds; 2525 Perimeter Place Drive, Suite 101; Nashville, TN 37214
Mr. Mark Jordan: City of Newport News; 2400 Washington Avenue, Department N; Newport News, VA 23607-4300
Ms. Mary Jordan: Art Plus Technology; 123 North Washington Street, Suite 401; Boston, MA 02114-2113
Mr. Jay Jorgensen: Matthew Bender & Company; 1275 Broadway; Albany, NY 12204-2694
Mr. Dominic Joseph: Millennium Pharma; 640 Memorial Drive; Cambridge, MA 02139
Mr. Parag Joshi: Verifone; 4988 Great America Parkway; Santa Clara, CA 95054-1200
Mr. Rameshwar Joshi: J&R Consulting; 100 Prospect Street, #302; Jersey City, NJ 07307
Mr. John Jude: Ameritech; 4715 Clayburn Drive East; Grove City, OH 43123-8899
Mr. Rolando Jumalon: Kweks Ent Inc; P.O. Box 9940; Tamuning, Guam 96931-5940
Mr. Eric Jungmann: Taymark; 4875 White Bear Parkway; White Bear Lake, MN 55110-3325
Mr. John Jurgensmeyer: Andersen Consulting; 406 Southwest Glendana Street; Lees Summit, MO 64081-3503
Mr. David P. Jurist: The Winfield Company; P.O. Box 101655; Denver, CO 80250-1655
Mr. Daniel J. Jutson Sr.: GTE Government Systems Corporation; Building 2-4953, Rae Lane; Fort Bragg, NC 28307
Mr. Alejandro Jáuregui: Parametric Technology; 128 Technology Drive; Waltham, MA 02453
Mr. Andre Kabel: Metis Associates; 1063 Morse Avenue, Apartment 21-302; Sunnyvale, CA 94089-1684
Ms. Laryssa Kachorowsky: Artemis Software Innovations, Inc.; 11241 North 37th Street; Phoenix, AZ 85028-2822
Mr. Ayam Kaddour: SR Telecom; 8150 Trans Canada Highway; St. Laurent, Quebec, Canada H4S 1M5
Mr. Sajid Kadri: Telesis Practice Services; 3430 Newburg Road; Louisville, KY 40218-2497
Ms. Cindy Kagels: Lockport Savings Bank; P.O. Box 514; Lockport, NY 14095-0514
Ms. Julie Kahl: Choice Products USA, Inc.; 3421 Traux Court; Eau Claire, WI 54703-6925
Mr. William Kahl: Mayfair Mills Inc.; P.O. Box 850; Arcadia, SC 29320
Mrs. Suzan Kaigle: BF Goodrich Aerospace; 100 Panton Road; Vergennes, VT 05491-1013
Mr. Michael Kalish: Holtz Rubenstein & Company, LLP; 125 Baylis Road, Suite 300; Melville, NY 17473823
Dr. Bernhard Kallup: Sedus Stoll, A.G.; Bruckenstrasse 15, Waldshut; Baden-Wurttemberg, Germany 79761
Mr. Gary R. Kalwaytis: Consultant Industries; 1121 Lees Crossing Court; Glen Allen, VA 23059-4543
Mr. Chakrapani Kamalanathan: Lockheed Martin; 1350 Arcadia Drive; Columbus, IN 47201
Mr. Charlie Kamer: Atlas Editors; 4343 Equity Drive; Columbus, OH 43228-3842
Mr. Arthur Kamesch: Aviation Challenge; 3600 B Street; Atwater, CA 95301-5109
Mr. Tim Kamps: Schwarz Pharmacy; 5600 West Country Line Road; Thiensville, WI 53092-4751
Mr. Lewis D. Kana: WelCom; 7768 Pine Center Drive; Houston, TX 77095-1637
Mr. Barry Kanig: Prudential Investment; 200 Wood Avenue; Souh Islien, NJ 07932-1597
Ms. Aline Kanjian: IHS Australia; 377 Sailorsbay Drive; Sydney, New South Wales, Australia
Mr. Renganathan Kannan: Guarantee Life Insurance; 9406 AC #5, Cunning Plaza; Omaha, NE
Mr. Chris Kanthan: Clarion; 1000 Escalon Avenue, D-2025; Sunnyvale, CA 94086
Mr. Kenneth G. Kantor: Browning Ferris Industries; 757 North Eldridge Parkway, #732; Houston, TX 77079-4435
Mr. Mike Kaplor: Dairyland Computers Consult; P.O. Box 156; Glenwood, MN 56334-0156
Mr. Paul J. Kapsar: United Community Hospital; 631 North Broad Street Extension; Grove City, PA 16127-9703
Ms. Beth Kar: Destination Marketing Group; P.O. Box 6427; Plymouth, MI 48170-8427
Mr. Hasan Karaburk: Truestar, Inc.; 9900 Main Street; Fairfax, VA 22031
Mr. Robb Karcsay: ICM Communications Inc.; 12300 Southeast Mallard Way, Suite 250; Milwaukee, OR 97222-4648
Mr. Alex Karetnikov: Cole Taylor Bank; 350 East Dundee Road; Wheeling, IL 60090
Ms. Marcia Karwowski: Keane; 6055 Rockside Woods Boulevard, Suite 300; Independence, OH 44131-2302
Mr. Steven E. Kaschimer: Gill Group, Inc.; 7330 North 16th Street, Suite A310; Phoenix, AZ 85020-5237
Mr. David J. Kasik: Boeing; 3903 219th Avenue SE; Issaquah, WA 98029-9282
Mr. Joseph C. Kasper: Common Wealth Communications; 256 North Sherman Street; Wilkes Barre, PA 18702-5316
Mr. Ara Kassabian: Techone, Inc.; 7677 Oakport Street; Oakland, CA 94621-1929
Mr. Amin Kassem: Arthur Andersen; 1 North State Street, #1519G; Chicago, IL 60602-3300
Mr. Angelo Kastroulis: ScholarAid.com; 11330-2 St. John's Industrial Parkway; Jacksonville, FL 32256
Dr. Kathryn S. Kaufmann Ph.D.: Office of Dr. Kathryn S. Kaufmann; 639 Geary Street; San Francisco, CA 94102-1668
Mr. Paul Kavanaugh: Santa Fe County Land Use Development; P.O. Box 276; Santa Fe, NM 87504-0276
Ms. Pamela Kay: Evit, Inc.; 12910 Culver Boulevard, Suite G; Marina Del Rey, CA 90066
Mr. Jack T. Kaye Jr.: The Ken Blanchard Companies; 125 State Place; Escondido, CA 92029-1398
Mr. Yin Kean: Metamor Technologies; 1 North Franklin Avenue; Chicago, IL 60606
Ms. Diane S. Keasler: University of South Alabama College of Nursing; 1504 Springhill Avenue; Mobile, AL 36604-3207
Mr. Eric Kedrowski: Wausau Financial Systems; 9 Indianhead Drive; Mosinee, WI 54455-9512
Mr. Jimmy Keeter: C&L Enterprises; 11180 Southwest 107th Street, Apartment 314; Miami, FL 33176
Ms. Heather C. Kehler: Entex Information Services; 6 International Drive; Port Chester, NY 10573-1058
Mr. Carvel C. Keiser II: Nova Care Employee Services; 2621 Van Buren Avenue; Norristown, PA 19403
Mr. C. J. Keist: Colorado State University; A212 B Engineering Building; Fort Collins, CO 80523-0001
Mr. Brian C. Keith: jeTech Data Systems; 5153 Camino Ruiz; Camarillo, CA 93012
Mrs. Carrie Keizer: Shriners Hospital For Children; 1900 Richmond Road; Lexington, KY 40502-1298
Ms. Lori Keller: PC Assistance; 430 Lawrence Bell Drive; Amherst, NY 14221-7085
Mr. Michael A. Keller: Cabletron Systems; 40 Lake Bellevue Drive, Suite 340; Bellevue, WA 98005-2480
Mr. Robert Keller: Presenting Solutions Inc.; 55 Santa Clara Avenue, Suite 150; Oakland, CA 94610-1375
Mr. Robert Keller: Anderson Financial Network; P.O. Box 3097, 404 Brock Drive; Bloomington, IL 61702-3097
Mr. Robert Keller: TASC; 12443 Research Parkway, Suite 202; Orlando, FL 32826-3252
Mr. Sean Keller: Highmark Blue Cross Blue Shield; 810 Parrish Street; Pittsburgh, PA 15220
Mr. Edward A. Kelley: World Trade Center/Seaport Hotel; One Seaport Lane; Boston, MA 02210
Mr. Jimmy L. Kelley: Ciba Vision Corporation; 11440 Johns Creek Parkway; Duluth, GA 30097-1556
Mr. Michael Kelley: Saddle Creek Corporation; 3010 Saddle Creek Road; Lakeland, FL 33801-9638
Mr. Sinoda R. Kelley: United States Postal Service; 23230 Geraldine Court; Hayward, CA 94541-3551
Mr. Thomas R. Kelley: Danville Public Schools; 31 Baltimore Avenue; Danville, VA 24541-4807
Mr. Clinton Kelly: Telstate International Corporation; P.O. Box 571; Big Bear Lake, CA 92315-0571
Mr. Dan Kelly: Nemschoff Chairs Inc.; P.O. Box 129; Sheboygan, WI 53082-0129
Mr. Eugene Kelly: Daniel Europe, Ltd.; Malton, Swinton Grange; North Yorkshire, England, United Kingdom YO17 0QR
Mr. Flynn Kelly: Hoffman Video Systems; 1049 Flower Street; Glendale, CA 91201-3014
Mr. John Kelly: United States Marine Corps; 4804 Quarters #B; Quantico, VA 22134-2207
Mrs. Suzanne Kelly: KeySpan Energy; 175 East Old Country Road; Hicksville, NY 11801
Ms. Theresa M. Kelly: Mass Mutual; 1295 State Street; Springfield, MA 01111-0002
Mr. Winston Kelly: V W Credit; 2333 Waukegan Road; Deerfield, IL 60015-5508
Ms. Anne Kelsey: Yale University; 175 Whitney Avenue; New Haven, CT 06511
Mr. Al Kemp: Ontario Power Technologies; 800 Kipling Avenue; Etobicoke, Ontario, Canada M8Z 6C4
Ms. Kristy Kendle: AIG; 17062 Sims Street, B; Huntington Beach, CA 92649-4352
Mr. Brian Kennedy: Digital Data; 62 Mayfield Avenue; Edison, NJ 08337-3821
Ms. Dawn Kennedy: M.A.M.G.; P.O. Box 3088; Santa Fe Springs, CA 90670-0088
Mr. Lamont E. Kennedy: Bureau of National Affairs; 1231 25th Street NW, Room 150; Washington, DC 20037-1157
Mr. Stan Kennedy: RSA Puget Sound; 467 West Street; Bremerton, WA 98314-5100
Mr. Willie J. Kennedy III: Cuero Independent School District; 405 Park Heights Drive; Cuero, TX 77954
Mr. Lee Kenneybrew: MCI Worldcom; 1902 South Union Avenue, #6; Tacoma, WA 98405
Ms. Deborah A. Kenny: Information Mapping, Inc.; 411 Waverley Oaks Road; Waltham, MA 01523
Mr. Derrick Kenny: Walls Communications, Inc.; 1025 Thomas Jefferson Street, Suite 502 East; Washington, DC 20007
Mr. Randi Kenny: UniDial

Communications; 4 Hutton Centre Drive, #150; Santa Ana, CA 92707
Mr. Sean E. Kent: Bell Oaks Company; 10 Glenlake Parkway, Suite 300; Atlanta, GA 30328
Mr. Bruce Kenworthy: Axint; 2000 Commonwealth Avenue; Auburndale, MA 02466-2004
Mr. Clark Kenyon: UTMC; 4350 Centennial Boulevard, #MS10; Colorado Springs, CO 80907-3778
Ms. Shauna Kenyon: St. John Hospital Medical Center; 22101 Moross Road; Detroit, MI 48236-2172
Mr. Jeff Kepler: Peoria Journal Star; 1 News Plaza; Peoria, IL 61643-0003
Mr. Mostafa Keraachi: Ziba Design; 2211 Southwest Park Place, Apartment 603; Portland, OR 97205-1153
Mr. Keith A. Kerlin: Commemorative Brands, Inc.; P.O. Box 149056; Austin, TX 78714-9056
Mr. Mike Kern: KCRA Television; 3 Television Circle; Sacramento, CA 95814-0750
Mr. Erik D. Kershaw: MRJ Inc.; 10393 Rapidan Lane; Manassas, VA 20109-6448
Ms. Val Keshishian: Spanning Tree Technology; 440 West Colorado Street, Suite 201; Glendale, CA 91204
Ms. Kari Keshkinen: Rule Company Inc.; P.O. Box 7072; Pasadena, CA 91109-7072
Ms. Mary Kessler: AgAmerica FCB, Western Farm Credit Bank; 3636 American River Drive; Sacramento, CA 95864-5901
Dr. Richard J. Kessler D.O.: ACLD; 807 South Oyster Bay Road; Bethpage, NY 11714-1000
Mr. Randy Ketner: Hauser, Inc.; 880 Hampshire Road, Suite A; Westlake Village, CA 91361-2820
Dr. Clifford R. Kettemborough Ed.D.: NASA-JPL; 6004 North Walnut Grove Avenue; San Gabriel, CA 91775-2530
Mr. Asghar Khan: Sap Public Sector & Education, Inc.; 1211 South Eads Street, Apartment 1101; Arlington, VA 22202-4705
Dr. Ghazanfar (Ali) Khan Ph.D.: TSG International; 8036 Pawnee Street, Apartment 202; Prairie Village, KS 66208-5144
Mr. Haiyan Khan: C.C. Industries; 222 North La Salle Street; Chicago, IL 60601-1003
Mr. Mohammed Khan: Union Computer Products; 22709 Armstrong Street; Riverview, MI 48192-8211
Mr. Waseem Khan: Electronic Data Systems; 35330 Drakeshire Place, Apartment 203; Farmington, MI 48335-3256
Mr. Harsch Khandelwal: Neotilt; 75 Westview Crest; Kitchener, Ontario, Canada N2N 2X7
Mr. Mazen Khanfak: Oracle; P.O. Box 6022; Winter Park, FL 32793-6022
Mr. Mark Khansary: Capital Group; 24500 Vista Lampara; Yorba Linda, CA 92887-4936
Ms. Jintendra Khare: New Media, Inc.; 12065 Edgewater Drive, Apartment 9; Cleveland, OH 44107-1717
Mr. Abdul Khatri: Winona Knitting Mills, Inc.; 902 East 2nd Street; Winona, MN 55987-4696
Ms. Monica Khurana: Hewlett Packard; 2380 Homestead Road, Apartment 9; Santa Clara, CA 95050-5562
Ms. Karen Kiefer: Schwartz Bros Insurance; 135 South La Salle Street, Suite 2035; Chicago, IL 60603-4471
Mr. Robert Kiefer Jr.: Kobrand Corporation; 134 East 40th Street; New York, NY 10016-1706
Mr. Robert Kiernan: Carnival Cruise Lines; 3655 Northwest 87th Avenue; Miami, FL 33178-2428
Mr. Gerald P. Kilcommins: CR Bard Irl Limited; Parkmore Industrial Estate; Galway, Ireland
Mr. Michael Kilduff: Fidelity Investments; 300 Puritan Way, #MM31; Marlborough, MA 01752-3078
Mr. Mark Killebrew: Orchard Foods Corporation; 11875 Silverdale Way NW; Silverdale, WA 98383-7807
Mr. Larry Killian: Times Printing Company, Inc.; 100 Industrial Drive; Random Lake, WI 53075-1636
Mr. Lonnie Wayne Killion: Directorate of Public Works and Logistics; 101 Fenton Circle; Fort Myer, VA 22211-1309
Mr. Wung Kim: M.C.P.D.; 5011 Continental Drive; Olney, MD 20832-2946
Dr. Young H. Kim Ph.D.: Handysoft Corporation; 5205 Leesburg Pike, Suite 1500; Falls Church, VA 22041-3895
Mr. Brian Kinahan: The Travelers; 49 Hickory Hill Road; Simsbury, CT 06070-2830
Mr. John Kinderkneckt: Network Management Group, Inc.; 324 East 4th Avenue; Hutchinson, KS 67501-6936
Mrs. Antoinette J. King: 19 Technology; 1819 Alvason Road; Cleveland, OH 44112
Mr. Corey King: Air Liquide; 12800 West Little York Road; Houston, TX 77041-4218
Mr. Franklin King: Amtrak; 10 G Street, NE; Washington, DC 20002
Mr. Hulas H. King: Unigraphics Solutions; 13736 Riverport Drive; Maryland Heights, MO 63043
Mr. Jonathan King: Usaopoly; 1190 Encinitas Boulevard; Encinitas, CA 92024-5334
Mr. Michael King : 555 South Emerald Loop; Cornelius, OR 97113-6614
Mr. Michael King: Omnimed Transcription; 6602 Grand Teton Plaza; Madison, WI 53719-1010
Ms. Sasha King: Idexx Informatics, Inc.; 2536 Alpine Road; Eau Claire, WI 54703-9560
Mr. Terry King: University of Louisville/Surgery Department; Hsc Campus 2nd Floor Acb; Louisville, KY 40292-0001
Mr. Ty King: Inuri/Eyecon; 4355 South Durango, #141; Las Vegas, NV 89117
Dr. Elnor Kinsella Ph.D.: Denison Memorial Library; 4200 East 9th Avenue; Denver, CO 80220-3706
Mr. Jon Kinsey: Kinsey Computer Systems; 13619 Lisbon Street NE; Paris, OH 44669-9723
Ms. Jonelle Kinsey: AT&T Broadband & Internet Services; 1717 East Buckeye Avenue; Spokane, WA 99207-4908
Mr. Randall Kinsey: Itron, Inc.; 2818 North Sullivan Road; Spokane, WA 99216-1897
Dr. Annette Kiper Ph.D.: Nextel Communication; 1750-112th Avenue, NE, #100; Bellevue, WA 98004-3752
Mr. Michael Kiralla: Recycled Wood Products; P.O. Box 3517; Montebello, CA 90640-8817
Mr. Jeff Kirby: Environmental Tests Systems; 23575 County Road 106; Elkhart, IN 46514-9787
Mr. Ernst W. Kirch: TASC; 4801 Stonecroft Boulevard; Chantilly, VA 20151
Mr. Matthew Kirk: Sync Consulting Group; 6565 Saylor Street; Canal Winchester, OH 43110
Mr. Richard Kirsch: Lens Express Inc.; 350 Southwest 12th Avenue; Deerfield Beach, FL 33442-3183
Dr. Thomas Kirsch Ph.D.: Analysts International; 4400 Memorial Drive, Apartment #1201; Houston, TX 77007
Mr. Paul Kiser: Trident Data Systems; 10455 White Granite Drive, Suite 400; Oakton, VA 22124-2764
Mr. Dmitry Kisselev: Swift Technologies; 10805 Copperwood Drive; Frisco, TX 75035-3973
Ms. Joy Kittan: 4C Solutions; 1201 7th Street; East Moline, IL 61244-1465
Mr. Thomas Klassen: Pacific Bell; 5546 Hillsdale Boulevard; Sacramento, CA 95842-3342
Mr. Matthew Klauber: Arcotoys; 80 Crossways Park Drive West; Woodbury, NY 11797-2019
Mr. Darren Klaum: Ppg Industries; 10800 South 13th Street; Oak Creek, WI 53154-6800
Ms. Elizabeth Kline: Insurer Physicians Services; 1035 Mumma Road; Wormleysburg, PA 17043-1147
Mr. Jon Kling: Anstr Pittsburgh; 248 National Drive; Pittsburgh, PA 15236-4437
Mr. Mike Klingler: Sunflower Datavision; 644 New Hampshire; Lawrence, KS 66044
Ms. Cristi Klingman: United States District Court of Northern Texas; 1100 Commerce Street, Suite 14a20; Dallas, TX 75242-1495
Mr. Helmut Klose: Infineon Technologies; 1580 Route 52 Zip 33F; Hopewell Junction, NY 12533
Mr. Christian Klotz: Icon Medialab; Rutschbahn 8; Hamburg, Germany 20146
Mr. John Klotz: Cytogen Corporation; 600 College Road East; Princeton, NJ 08540-6636
Mr. Alejandro M. Klurfan: DACG; 5847 San Felipe Street, Suite 3700; Houston, TX 77057-3011
Mr. Adam Knight: Citrix Systems, Inc.; 6400 Northwest 6th Way; Fort Lauderdale, FL 33309-6123
Mr. David F. Knight: HiServ NA, Inc.; 30 Independence Boulevard; Warren, NJ 07059
Ms. Karen Knight: Ibm Corporation; 44 South Broadway; White Plains, NY 10601-4425
Mr. Larry Knight: Quester Regional Services; P.O. Box 45360; Salt Lake City, UT 84145-0360
Mr. Brian L. Knotts: Triplett, Woolf, and Garretson; 2959 North Rock, Suite 300; Wichita, KS 67226-5100
Mr. Kevin Knowles: KCK Civil Engineering, Incorporated; 7806 South Aquarium Circle; Jacksonville, FL 32216
Mr. Darren Knox: Prime Bank; 6425 Rising Sun Avenue; Philadelphia, PA 19111-5299
Mr. Jeffrey Koch: NEC American, Inc.; 1525 West Walnut Hill Lane; Irving, TX 75038-3702
Ms. Kathryn M. Koch: New York City Police Department; 315 Hudson Street, 3rd Floor; New York, NY 10013-1009
Mr. Petra Koehler: Dresdner Bank Ag; Juergen-Ponto-Platz 1; Frankfurt, Germany
Mr. Marcus Koenig: Bell Atlantic; 7882 Butterfield Drive; Elkridge, MD 21075-6451
Mr. Mark A. Koenig: KPMG; 6 Grouse Path; Westport, CT 06880-1007
Mr. Arjun Kohli: C-Shell Inc.; 257 Lake Avenue; Metuchen, NJ 08840-2407
Ms. Jana Kohoutova: Schiller International University; 453 Edgewater Drive; Dunedin, FL 34698
Mr. Jeffrey Koke: SAIC; 22 Enterprise Parkway, Suite 200; Hampton, VA 23666-5844
Mr. Mike Kolasa: Houlihan Computer Solutions; 8725 Bollman Place, Suite 9; Savage, MD 20763-9751
Mr. Teofil Kolev: Adaptec, Inc.; 691 South Milpitas; Milpitas, CA 95055
Mr. Steve Koller: US West; 9394 West Dodge Road, Suite 300; Omaha, NE 68114-3319
Ms. Deborah Kolodji: Sonoma Systems; 4640 Admiralty Way, Suite 600; Marina Del Rey, CA 90292-6616
Mr. Sukumar Kommareddy: Valtronic USA, Inc.; 6168 Cochran Road; Solon, OH 44139-3313
Mr. Madan Kondayyagari: MCG; 9030 West 64th Place, Apartment 204; Merriam, KS 66202-4706
Mr. James Konugres: San Marcos Middle School; 650 West Mission Road; San Marcos, CA 92069-1599
Mr. Christopher P. Kopinski: Caterpillar; 100 Northeast Adams Street; Peoria, IL 61629-4330
Mr. Steve Koseter: Sprint Paranet; 635 Parma Way; Gardner, KS 66030-1294
Mr. Lisa A. Kositzky: Northern Michigan Bank; 723 Ludington Street; Escanaba, MI 49829-3802
Ms. Colette M. Kosmowski: Scott Shuptrine Furniture; 977 East 14 Mile Road; Troy, MI 48083-4519
Mr. Frank Kostelac: Nextlink; 2240 Corporate Circle; Henderson, NV 89014-6382
Mr. Jeff Koster: Greencastle Metal Works; P.O. Box 838; Chambersburg, PA 17201-0838
Dr. Andrew D. Kostic Ph.D.: IBM; 1580 State Route 52; Hopewell Junction, NY 12533-6526
Mr. Evangel P. Kostojohn: United States Department of Transportation; 55 Broadway; Cambridge, MA 0212-1093
Mr. Subhash Kothari: Reliant Tech, Inc.; 5 Warrenton Lane; Colts Neck, NJ 07722-1065
Mr. Gene Kouch: Supply Chian Services; 1 Becton Drive; Franklin Lakes, NJ 07417-1815
Mr. Frank Kratky: Goodwill Industries; 4140 Forest Park Avenue; St. Louis, MO 63108-2885
Mr. Richard Kratlian: Poly Medica Corporation; 11 State Street; Woburn, MA 01801-2050
Mr. Brian Krause: Wood County Telephone Company; P.O. Box 8045; Wisconsin Rapids, WI 54495-8045
Mr. David Krawcyzk: Rich Products Corporation; 1150 Niagara Street; Buffalo, NY 14213-1797
Mr. K. C. Krebs: ACS; 1130 Ridge Avenue, Apartment 312; Coraopolis, PA 15108-1980
Ms. Claudia Krepsky: Ann Marie Home; 722 Wilson Avenue; Sheboygan, WI 53081-6906
Mr. Mark R. Kretchmer: Cosentini Information Technology; 2 Penn Plaza , #3; New York, NY 10121-0001
Mr. Robert W. Kreuger Jr.: St. Paul Area Chamber of Commerce; 332 Minnesota Street, N-205; St. Paul, MN 55101
Mr. Steven H. Krikorian: Clarify; 3 Wallace Circle; Londonderry, NH 03053-2870
Mr. Manfred Krischek: Manesco Gmbh; Talstrasse 56A; Saarbruecken, Germany D-66119
Mr. Gopal Krishnaswamy: Renaissance Worldwide Inc.; 1700 Amelia Court Apartment 313; Plano, TX 75075-6115
Dr. Vasan Krishnaswamy Ph.D.: CAP Gemini America, LLC; 9401 Indian Creek Parkway, Suite 350; Overland Park, KS 66200
Dr. Adam Krob Ph.D.: Tulane University; 221 Richardson Building; New Orleans, LA 70118
Ms. Sue Kroupa: Catholic Diocese of Evansville; P. O. Box 4169; Evansville, IN 47724
Mr. Jimmy Krozel: Seagull Technology Inc; 16400 Lark Ave; Los Gatos, CA 95032
Ms. Cindy Krueger: Library of Michigan; P.O. Box 30007; Lansing, MI 48909-7507
Mr. Joseph Frank Krupa: Westinghouse Savannah River Company; 3 Kimberly Lane; North Augusta, SC 29860-9708
Ms. Melissa Krzemien: Comercia Bank; 3551 Hamlin Road; Auburn Hills, MI 48326-7301
Mr. Michael Kuchenberg: J.J. Plank Corporation; 728 Watermark G; Neenah, WI 54956
Mr. Bruce Kuczynski: Bracco Research, USA; 305 College Road East; Princeton, NJ 08540-6608
Mr. Chris Kufahl: Network Solutions; 5801 Packer Drive; Wausau, WI 54401-9325
Mr. Mike Kuglich: Carlo Givasi, Inc.; 750 Hastings Drive; Buffalo Grove, IL 60089
Mr. Rajeev Kulkarni: 3D Systems Inc.; 400 North Hollywood Way, Apartment 202; Burbank, CA 91505-4967
Mr. Anupam Kumar: Parsons Engineering Science, Inc.; 10521 Rosehave Street; Fairfax, VA 22030-2839
Mr. Deepak Kumar: Iris Software; 1021 Bluberry Court; Edison, NJ 08817
Mr. Hemanth D. Kumar: Arlington County Government; 2100 Clarendon Boulevard, Suite 612; Arlington, VA 22201-5445
Mr. Kiran Kumar: AT&TB; 481 Plainfield Road; Edison, NJ 08820-2630
Mr. Krishnaraj Kumar: Frontier Systems Inc.; 10 Parsonage Road, Suite 406; Edison, NJ 08837
Mr. Manoj Kumar: Mastech Corporation; 852 Kinwest Parkway Apartment 215; Irving, TX 75063-7402
Mr. Sundeep Kumar: Credit Suisse First Boston; 11 Madison Avenue; New York, NY 10010
Mr. Valsa Kumar: Sharjah National Travel & Tourist Agency; P.O. Box 17; Sharjah, United Arab Emirates
Mr. Victor Kumar: Worldtravel Partners; 6 West Druid Hills Drive; Atlanta, GA 30329
Mr. Vivek Kumar: Norlight Telecommunications; 275 North Corporate Drive; Brookfield, WI 53211
Mr. Darryl T. Kuniyuki: Mauna Loa Observatory; 123 West Kinai Place; Hilo, HI 96720-5695
Mr. Mike Kunkle: Jacob's Engineering; 7295 South Highway 94; St. Charles, MO 63301-2203
Ms. Susan Kunselman: Regency Lighting; 16665 Arminta Street; Van Nuys, CA 91406-1611
Ms. Mariette Kupecz: Ortho-McNeil Pharmaceutical; 1000 US Highway 202; Raritan, NJ 08869-1498
Mr. Doyle Kupper: Footwear Management Company; 2727 West 7th Street; Fort Worth, TX 76107-2218
Mr. Nick Kurinzi: Claims Investigation Agency; P.O. Box 20193; Tampa, FL 33622-0193
Ms. Carla Kurtz: Commercial Properties, Inc.; 1625 West University Drive; Tempe, AZ 85281-3268
Mr. Mark Kushelman Ph.D.: Oracle; 6025 Crocus Court; Alexandria, VA 22310-1640
Dr. James S. Kuwabara Ph.D.: United States Geological Survey; 345 Middlefield Road; Menlo Park, CA 94025-3561
Mr. Rob La Favor: American Academy of Neurology; 1080 Montreal Avenue; St. Paul, MN 55116-2311
Ms. Tracy La Mantia: Resumix; 84 Eagle Road; Worcester, MA 01605-3815
Ms. Paulette Labaton: RCS Computer; 10 East 39th Street; New York, NY 10016
Mr. Alex Labbate: Cisco Systems; 8600 Northwest 36th Street, Suite 401; Miami, FL 33166-6648
Mr. Steven E. Labkoff: Pfizer; 235 East 42nd Street; New York, NY 10017-5703
Mr. Rodney V. Lacey: TDS Telecom; P.O. Box 900; Centre, AL 35960
Mr. Sylvester Lada: Sol Manufacturing Technology; P.O. Box 607; Roseville, MI 48066-0067
Mr. Valdez Ladd: AT&T Global Solutions; 4625 Creekstone Drive, #3076; Durham, NC 27703-8448
Mr. Peter Ladefoged: Sonofon, Technical Department; Skelagervej 1; Aalborg, Denmark 9000

Mr. Yves S. Lafond: Inner City, Inc.; 120 Southampton Street; Boston, MA 02218

Mr. Gary Laguna: Lawrence Livermore National Laboratory; 7000 East Avenue, #L542; Livermore, CA 94550-9516

Mr. Niloy Laha: Transtech Inc.; 1333 Butterfield Road, Suite 555; Downers Grove, VA 60515-5610

Mr. Michael Lahickey: Online Information Bureau; 309 Talcottville Road; Vernon Rockville, CT 06066-4016

Ms. Leslie Lakatos: Lubrizol; 29400 Lakeland Boulevard, Suite 31B; Wickliffe, OH 44092-2298

Ms. Diana Lam: Charles Schwab; 1926 42nd Avenue; San Francisco, CA 94116-1021

Mr. Lan Lam: Shared Medical Systems; 1000 Broadway, Suite 450; Oakland, CA 94607-4039

Ms. Colleen Lamb: Torch Energy Advisors, Inc.; 1221 Lamar Street, Suite 1600; Houston, TX 77010-3039

Mr. Christopher Lambert: Canfor; 1823 Ingledew Street; Prince George, British Columbia, Canada V2L 1K9

Mr. Keith Lambert: Lambert Investments, Inc.; 2001 Wilshire Boulevard, Suite 505; Santa Monica, CA 90403-5640

Mr. Larry Lambert: Ericsson; 601 Brickell Key Drive; Miami, FL 33131-2662

Ms. Kim Lancaster: Nextel Communications; 201 State Route 17; Rutherford, NJ 07070-2574

Mr. Galen S. Landon: Nu Skin International Inc.; 75 West Center, Street; Provo, UT 84601-4432

Ms. Bobbie Landreth: Ferris State University; 330 Oak Street; Big Rapids, MI 49307

Dr. Eric L. Lang Ph.D.: Sociometrics Corporation; 170 State Street, Suite 260; Los Altos, CA 94022-2864

Mr. Jeff Langfeldt: Northwestern Travel Management; 7250 Metro Boulevard; Minneapolis, MN 55439-2128

Mr. Allen D. Lankford: En Point Technologies; 13601 Preston Road, Suite 1000-E; Dallas, TX 75240

Mr. C. Lanser: Microsoft Corporation; 13 West Main Street; Golden Bridge, NY 10526-1129

Mr. Sean Lanter: Connexions Engineering, Inc.; P.O. Box 3007; Woodinville, WA 98072-3007

Ms. Judy Lanum: Citgo Petroleum Corporation; P.O. Box 1562; Lake Charles, LA 70602-1562

Mr. Vincent Lanzillo: Securities Industry Automation Corporation; 2 Metrotech Center; Brooklyn, NY 11201

Ms. Jaymie L. Largent: Power Motive Corporation; 5000 Vasquez Boulevard; Denver, CO 80216-3089

Ms. Laura Larkin: City of Phoenix Prosecutors Office; 405 North 5th Street; Phoenix, AZ 85004

Mr. Ron Lasala: Pratt Whitney; P.O. Box 109615, MS 71201; West Palm Beach, FL 33410-9615

Mr. Bret M. Laskarzewski: The Document Company Xerox; 667 Bishops Lane; Webster, NY 14580-2456

Mr. Donald R. Laster Jr.: Dot4 Inc.; 6080 Jericho Turnpike, Suite 211; Commack, NY 11725

Mr. Richard Latayan: RR Donnelley & Sons; 41 Kensington Circle; Wheaton, IL 60187

Mr. Tak Man Lau: AXA; 30 Rockefeller Plaza, 20th Floor; New York, NY 10112

Mr. Russ Laughlin: ADT Security Services; 14200 East Exposition Avenue; Aurora, CO 80012-2540

Ms. Tammie Laughner: AGR International, Inc.; 615 Whitestown Road; Butler, PA 16001

Ms. Rebecca Lavalle: National Football League; 280 Park Avenue; New York, NY 10017-1216

Ms. Lynn Lavallee: La-Vigne, Inc.; 10 Coppage Drive; Worcester, MA 01603

Mr. Nick LaVecchia: Excel Communications, Inc.; 4550 Excel Parkway; Addison, TX 75001-5606

Mr. Timothy Lawless: University Southern Mississippi; P.O. Box 10002; Stennis Space Center, MS 39465-9462

Mr. Patrick E. Lawrence: Digital Microwave; 3325 South 116th Street; Seattle, WA 98168-1974

Mrs. Jo Ann Lawson: Henry County Public Schools, Fieldale Elementary School; P.O. Box 68; Fieldale, VA 24089

Ms. Elvira Laxamana: Ikon Office Solutions; 90 West Street; New York, NY 11209

Mr. Al Laylan: Best Power; 1204 Kilbourn; Tomah, WI 54660

Ms. Cindy Layman: Itawamba Community College; 2176 South Easton Boulevard; Tupelo, MS 38801-5981

Mr. Norman L. Layman: EDS; 3383 Tracy Drive; Sterling Heights, MI 48310-2574

Ms. Kola A. Layokun: Cellutech Communications, Inc.; 740 North Larch Avenue; Elm Hurst, IL 60126

Mr. Paul Lazarus: Louis Hornick Company, Inc.; 152 Broadway; Haverstraw, NY 10927

Mr. Shawn Le Mone: AS-CAP; 7920 West Sunset Boulevard, Floor 2; Los Angeles, CA 90046-3300

Ms. Kathleen Leach: NCI; 6116 Executive Boulevard, Room 501; Rockville, MD 20852-4920

Ms. Kimberly Leach: D.T.I. Technologies; 10 Commerce Park North; Bedford, NH 03110-6905

Mrs. Sarah Leach: Unisys; 8602 Kenilworth Drive; Springfield, VA 22151-1407

Mr. Patrick Leary: Eastman Kodak Company; 2662 Via Blanca; Carrollton, TX 75006-4654

Ms. Nataya Leavell: Automation Rental Inc.; 110 Southeast 6th Street; Fort Lauderdale, FL 33326

Mr. Dave Lebond: Aetna; 151 Farmington Avenue, MA34; Hartford, CT 06156

Mr. Claude Lebrun: Mita Copystar America, Inc.; 14800 Enterprise Drive, Apartment 26C; Dallas, TX 75234-3003

Mr. Brad Lechmaier: New Resources Corporation; 1000 North Water Street, Suite 950; Milwaukee, WI 53202-3197

Mr. Curt Lechner: Polygon.net; 14142 Denver West Parkway, Building 51; Golden, CO 80401-3115

Mr. Tysen G. Leckie: Meij-er, Inc.; 4894 Country Place North, Apartment D4; Allendale, MI 49401-9120

Mr. Richard L. Leclercq: Monmouth County Correctional Facility; 1 Waterworks Road; Freehold, NJ 07728

Mr. Craig S. Ledbetter: Per-Se Technologies; 268 West Hospitality Lane, Suite 300; San Bernardino, CA 92408-3241

Mr. Bert Ledford: United States Air Force; 104 Linden Court; Yorktown, VA 23693-5016

Mr. Jeong Lee: Spokane Regional Health District; 1101 West College Avenue; Spokane, WA 99201-2029

Mr. John Lee: Vital Care; 1367 West Main; Gaylord, MI 49735

Mr. Joseph S. Lee: University of Michigan; 201 East Hoover Avenue; Ann Arbor, MI 48104-3704

Mr. Kevin M. Lee: Computer Associates; 2000 Park Lane Drive; Pittsburgh, PA 15275

Mr. Mike Lee: IBM; 13800 Diplomat Drive; Dallas, TX 75234-8812

Ms. Mona Lee: Lockard and White, Inc.; 14511 Falling Creek Drive; Houston, TX 77014-1244

Mr. Pumjoo Lee: Hausmann McNally Sc; 633 West Wisconsin Avenue, Suite 2000; Milwaukee, WI 53203-1918

Mr. Robert Lee: Swiderski Electronics; 800 West Thorndale Avenue; Itasca, IL 60143-1356

Mr. William Lee: Cellit; 2246 Northwest 139th Avenue; Sunrise, FL 33323

Ms. Michelle Leeman: Clerary Group; 3275 West Hillsboro Boulevard, Suite 300; Deerfield Beach, FL 33442-9474

Mr. Don Legato: NUWAVE Technologies, Inc.; One Passaic Avenue; Fairfield, NJ 07004

Ms. Kiara Legner: Cunningham & Legner Ltd.; 1245 Executive Place; Geneva, IL 60134-2419

Mr. David Lehman: Elcotel Inc.; 6448 Parkland Drive; Sarasota, FL 34243-4038

Ms. Judith Lehman: Lehman Welding Service; 913 South Halliday Street; Anaheim, CA 92804-3874

Mr. Mark Lehr: Riverside College; 4800 Magnolia Avenue; Riverside, CA 92506

Mrs. Sheron H. Leigh-Thomas: National Rural Electric Cooperative Association; 89025 Madison Street; New Carrollton, MD 20784

Mr. Gregory Leites: Integral Smartware, Inc.; 454 Buckthorn Terrace; Buffalo Grove, IL 60089-1828

Mr. Petar Lemajic: Computer Associates International; 600 Superior Avenue East; Cleveland, OH 44114-2611

Mr. Russ T. Leming: Walt Disney Imagineering; 11151 Vanowen Street; North Hollywood, CA 91605-6316

Mr. Thomas Lenehan: Noville; 3 Empire Boulevard; South Hackensack, NJ 07606-1806

Mr. Gene Lenfest: Okeechobee County School Board; 925 Northwest 23rd Lane; Okeechobee, FL 34972-4320

Dr. Bennett Lentczner D.A.: Real Visions; 2030 Northeast 197th Terrace; North Miami Beach, FL 33179-3126

Mr. R. Titus Leo: Deloitte & Touche Consulting Group; Two Tower Center Boulevard; East Brunswick, NJ 08816

Mr. Oscar Leon: H.B. Fuller Latin America; P.O. Box 25216, Dept. Sjo 1455; Miami, FL 33102-5216

Mr. Darryl Leonard: Motorola; 1500 Gateway Boulevard; Boynton Beach, FL 33426-8292

Mr. Kevin M. Leonard: Blue Cross Blue Shield of Rhode Island; 444 Westminster Street, Department 1; Providence, RI 02903-3279

Mr. Michael F. Leonard: Morton Nippon Coatings; 2701 East 170th Street; Lansing, IL 60438-1107

Mr. William Leonard: MCI Metro; 8521 Leesburg Pike; Vienna, VA 22182-2411

Mr. Jim Leone: Chock Full O'Nuts; 520 Secaucus Road; Secaucus, NJ 07094-2502

Mr. Nick Leone: All Metro Health Care; 50 Broadway; Lynbrook, NY 11563-2519

Ms. Margaret Leong: Clarins, Ltd.; 95 How Ming Street, Unit K 12T; Kowloon, Hong Kong

Mr. Mark Leppert: USDA Gipsa; 10383 Northwest Executive Hills Boulevard; Kansas City, MO 64153-1394

Mr. Tom Lerch: Meltzr, Lippi, Gulostena, and Schlissel; 190 Willis Avenue; Mineola, NY 11501-2693

Ms. Crystal Lester: Valley Hospital Medical; 1798 North Garey Avenue; CA 91767-2918

Mr. Michael R. Leszcz: Internal Revenue Service; P.O. Box 2608; Washington, DC 20013-2608

Mr. Richard J. Leuenroth: Management Science Associates, Inc.; 6565 Penn Avenue; Pittsburgh, NY 15206

Mr. David P. Levan: Naval Med Info Management Center; 4105 Seaforth Road; Chesapeake, VA 23321-6002

Mr. Gary LeVan: Trex Medical; 103 Boulevard Drive; Danbury, CT 06810-7254

Ms. Angela Leverett: Georgia Southern University; P.O. Box 8104; Statesboro, GA 30460-1000

Ms. Laura Leverich: Seneca Data Distributors; 7401 Round Pond Road; North Syracuse, NY 13212

Mr. Terry Levins: Fendall; 5 East College Drive; Arlington Heights, IL 60004-1963

Mr. Louis J. Levner: CSTI; 8975 Guilford Road, Suite 100; Columbia, MD 21046-2390

Ms. Laurie Levy: West Teleservices; P.O. Box 40488; San Antonio, TX 78229-1488

Mr. Chad R. Lewandowski: Lockheed Martin; 988 County Highway 126; Amsterdam, NY 12010-6287

Mr. Kevin Lewellen: Louisville Gas & Electric Company; 820 West Broadway; Louisville, KY 40202

Mr. Brian Lewis: Systems and Computer Technology; 801 22nd Street NW; Washington, DC 20037-2515

Ms. Lenora Lewis: North County Transit District; 4961 Lassen Drive; Oceanside, CA 92056-5468

Ms. Lynn Lewis: A. Davis Grant & Company; 295 Pierson Avenue; Edison, NJ 08837-3118

Mr. Ralph Lewis: CTSI; 3950 Chambers Hill Road; Harrisburg, PA 17111-1508

Mr. S. Sheridan Lewis: S. Sheridan Lewis; 307 Boundary Avenue; Red Lion, PA 17356-2002

Ms. Trish Lewis: Office of Hearings & Appeals; 118 Broadway, Suite 400; Fargo, ND 58102-4974

Mr. Christopher Lezny: Nabisco, Inc.; 7 Campus Drive; Parsippany, NJ 07054

Mr. Andrew Li: Network Processors; P.O. Box 5606; Stanford, CA 94309-5606

Mr. Hao Li: RAINfinity; 139-74 Caltech; Pasadena, CA 91125

Ms. Loretta Li: Ascend Communications, Inc.; 1240 Harbor Bay Parkway; Alameda, CA 94502-6501

Dr. Tianzhu Li Ph.D.: Hyperion Associates, Inc.; 1127 International Parkway, #100; Fredericksburg, VA 22406-1142

Dr. Charlene Liang Ph.D.: Engage Technology; 100 Brickstone Square; Andover, MA 01810-1428

Mr. C. Liccardi: OC Pro components, Inc.; 300 Garden City Plaza; Garden City, NY 11530

Mr. Sam Seymour Lieberman: Omel Children's Home and Family Services; 4510 16th Avenue; Brooklyn, NY 11204

Ms. Christina Liebman: Research Systems, Inc.; 4990 Pearl East Circle; Boulder, CO 80301-2476

Ms. Sharon Liff: Computing Devices Canada; 3785 Richmond Road; Nepean, Ontario, Canada K2H 5B7

Ms. Melanie Lilla: Nelson, Mullins, Riley & Scarborough; 1330 Lady Street; Columbia, SC 29201-3300

Ms. Winny Lim: Chase Manhattan Corporation; 2 Chase Manhattan Plaza, 4th Floor; New York, NY 10081

Mr. Brett M. Limer: Sprint PCS; 6406 West 77th Terrace; Prairie Village, KS 66204-3153

Ms. Anna Tzy-in Lin: Chemical Computing Group; 1255 University Street, #1600; Montreal, Quebec, Canada H3B 3X3

Dr. Jerry J. Lin Ph.D.: DFW Technology; 3720 Cromwell Court; Plano, TX 75075

Mr. Julius J.Y. Lin: Millennia Vision Corporation; 444 Castrose, Suite 1101; Mountain View, CA 94041

Mr. Ping C. Lin: St. Josephs Hospital; 211 Lafayette Road, Apartment 325; Syracuse, NY 13205-2914

Ms. Susan Xiaoqin Lin: Columbia University; 1375 River Road, Apartment 4B; Edgewater, NJ 07020-1429

Mr. Ken Lind: Us Bor; 125 South State Street; Salt Lake City, UT 84138-1102

Mr. Tim Lindeborg: Printing & Graphics Services; The University of Montana; Missoula, MT 59812-0001

Mr. Kurtis A. Lindemann: Fisher College of Business, The Ohio State University; 2100 Neil Avenue; Columbus, OH 43210

Ms. Pat Linder: Bostwick Braun Company; P.O. Box 912, Computer Services; Toledo, OH 43697-0912

Mr. Darrell G. Lineberry: Renfro Corporation; 661 Linville Road; Mt. Airy, NC 27030-3101

Mr. Acree S. Link Jr.: MCI WorldCom; 49 Saybrooke Court; Newport News, VA 23606-1765

Mr. John Linkowsky: Firmenich; 250 Plainsboro Road; Plainsboro, NJ 08536-1999

Mr. Michael Linn: Memorial Medical Center; 2700 Napoleon Avenue; New Orleans, LA 70115-6996

Mr. Roger Linnenburger: Truly Nolen of America; P.O. Box 43550; Tucson, AZ 85733-3550

Mr. Andrey P. Lipavsky: Thrucomm Inc.; 6900 Fairfield Business Center Drive; Fairfield, OH 45014

Mr. Stefan Lipinski: ISI Systems Group; 175 West Jackson Boulevard; Chicago, IL 60604

Mr. John Lippiello: Aonix; 45 Lawrence Street; Wilmington, MA 01887-1927

Mr. Jerome Liscano: All-In-1; 327 West Broadway; Glendale, CA 91204-1301

Mr. Bruce Little: WebSite Designs; P.O. Box 4884; El Paso, TX 79914

Mr. Doug Littlejohn: FedEx; 2007 Corporate Avenue, Floor 2; Memphis, TN 38132-1702

Mr. Donald Livengood: COMPAQ Computer Corporation; 830 Forestwalk Drive; Suwanee, GA 30024-4243

Ms. Deborah Livingston: National Science Foundation; 4201 Wilson Boulevard, Room 205; Arlington, VA 22230-0002

Mr. Raymond L. Livingston: Teledyne Brown Engineering; 300 Sparkman Drive NW (MS 170); Huntsville, AL 35805-1994

Mr. Doron Livny: Omnitech; 550 Pinetown Road, Suite 206; Fort Washington, PA 19034-2607

Mr. Boris Livshits: Molloy Group, Inc.; 4 Century Drive; Potsippany, NJ 07407

Mr. Jason Liyanage: Moldex-Metric, Inc.; 10111 West Jefferson Boulevard; Culver City, CA 90232-3509

Mr. Denis Ljung: Fireman's Fund Insurance Company; 777 San Marin Drive; Novato, CA 94998-0001

Mr. Brad J. Lloyd: Rock Financial; 21562 Purlingbrook Road; Novi, MI 48375-5236

Ms. Terri Lloyd: Fairview Physicians Associates; 3400 West 66th Street #235; Edina, MN 55435

Mr. Calvin Lo: Pensare, Inc.; 5167 Manxwood Place; San Jose, CA 95111-1835

Ms. Sherry Lochard: Paragon Health Systems; 30 Merchant Street, Spc 2; Cincinnati, OH 45246-3750

Mr. Dean Lochkovic: Bell Industries; 5604 Fortune Circle S B; Indianapolis, IN 46241-5529

Mr. Randall A. Locke: Hardwick Clothes, Inc.; P.O. Box 2310; Cleveland, TN 37320-2310

Mr. Matthew Locker: Provoice; 189 Snake Den Road; Wanaque, NJ 07465-2502

Mr. Wilbur J. Lockett: Technipusa Corporation; 650 Cienega Avenue; San Dimas, CA 91773

Ms. Martha Lockwood: United States Air Force; 6000 Atlantic Drive; Cheyenne, WY 82001

Mr. Chuck Loehr: Kraft Foods, Inc.; P.O. Box 309; New Ulm, MN 56073-0309

Mr. Terje Loeland: Merkantildata; Olof Palmes Alle 44; Aarhus, Denmark

DK-8200
Dr. Edwin Lombridas Ph.D.: Guardian Life Insurance; Mail Stop H-19C, 7 Hanover Square; New York, NY 10004
Mrs. Amy Long: Info Systems; 49 Orourke Court; Newark, DE 19702-6846
Ms. Christy Long: Regions Bank; 60 Commerce Street , # Floor 12; Montgomery, AL 36104-3530
Mr. Randal L. Long: Tensor Information Systems; 5005 LBJ Freeway; Dallas, TX 75287
Mr. William A. Long: Insurdata, Inc.; 5215 North Oconnor Boulevard, Suite 800; Irving, TX 775039
Mr. Doug Longstreth: UUNET; 650 Town Center Drive, Suite 1300; Costa Mesa, CA 92626-7127
Mr. Richard Lopatdsky: Town of Southington; 93 Main Street, Floor 1; Southington, CT 06489-2504
Mr. Jacques Lopez: Alliance for Aging; 9500 South Dadeland Boulevard; Miami, FL 33156-2824
Mr. Roel Lopez: NPC; 29A Butterfield Trail Boulevard; El Paso, TX 79906-5249
Mr. Felix J. Lopez-Phillips: Geonex, Inc.; 8950 9th Street; St. Petersburg, FL 33702
Ms. Kaleigh W. LoPresti: Venture Sights; 7579 Southland Road; Mentor, OH 44060
Mr. Glen Lord: CompUSA; 158 Mansfield Boulevard North; Cherry Hill, NJ 08034-3609
Mr. Len Lorenz: New York; P.O. Box 7500 1 Broadway Center; Schenetady, NY 12301-7500
Ms. Anne Lorenzetti: Mt. Sinai New York University Health; 1 Gustave L Levy Place; New York, NY 10029-6500
Mr. Joe Loschiavo: Howzit Computer; 0077 Lewis Lane; Basalt, CO 81621-9389
Mr. Matthew Lotz: Eagle Soft; P.O. Box 1267; Effingham, IL 62401-1267
Mr. Shye L. Louis: Reach-out of St. Lawrence County, Inc.; P.O. Box 5051; Potsdam, NY 13676-2018
Mr. Chuck W. Lovelace III: City of St. Charles; 200 North Second Street; St. Charles, MO 63301
Mr. Roderick K. Lovely: Sea Consultants; 485 Massachusetts Avenue; Cambridge, MA 03304
Mr. Tim Lovestrand: First Call Resources Ltd.; 6909 Markwood Drive; Minneapolis, MN 55427-1535
Mr. James Lowery: United States Marine Corps; 6 Buchanan Drive; Havelock, NC 285323654
Mr. Dennis A. Lowrey: United States Army; 319 Lincoln Street, Apartment G; Santa Cruz, CA 95060-4371
Mr. Diarmuid Lowry: Bank of Ireland Asset Management (US), Ltd.; 20 Horseneck Lane; Greenwich, CT 06830
Mr. Ed Loyd: Aspect Telecommunications; 1730 Fox Drive; San Jose, CA 95131
Mr. Gary Loyd: Excel Specialty Products; 212 Mario Del Pero Street; Booneville, AR 72927-0200
Dr. Charles D. Lu Ph.D.: La County, Dmh.; 550 South Vermont Avenue, Floor 7; Los Angeles, CA 90020-1991
Mr. Xiaolin Lu: AT&T Labs, Research; 100 Schultz Drive, Room 4-236; Red Bank, NJ 07701-6750
Mr. Andrew Luca: Fidelity Investments; 30 Varnum Street; Arlington, MA 02474-8713
Ms. Kristine Luce: AC Software - Time Wizard; 2901 Riva Trace Parkway; Annapolis, MD 21401-7734
Ms. Cathy Lucid: Surf Soft; 820 Bay Avenue, Suite 101; Capitola, CA 95010-2134
Mr. Bob Luckey: Booz Allen & Hamilton; 225 West Wacker Drive; Chicago, IL 60606-1224
Mr. Erik Ludlow: Fargo Cass County Economic; 51 Broadway, Suite 400; Fargo, ND 58102-4933
Mr. Greg Luetkemeyer: Mercy Information Services; 5401 Ellsworth Road; Fort Smith, AR 72903-3219
Mr. Chris Luksha: Helmers Publishing, Inc.; P.O. Box 874; Peterborough, NH 03458-1291
Mr. Eric Lulkin: Nanosoft, L.L.C.; 190 Abbott Drive; Wheeling, IL 60090
Ms. Dina Lundy: Arizona State University; P.O. Box 870103; Tempe, AZ 852870103
Mr. Lan Ly: Merrill Lynch; 800 Scudders Mill Road, # Rd-2i; Plainsboro, NJ 08536-1698
Mr. Phil C. Ly: Nortel Networks; 102 Honeysuckle Lane; Cary, NC 27511
Mr. Jean-Claude G. Lyall: Watauga County Schools; P.O. Box 1790; Boone, NC 28607
Mr. Matthew J. Lydy: Glimcher Realty Trust; 20 South 3rd Street; Columbus, OH 43215-4206
Ms. Melita Lykiardopoulou: The Community College of Baltimore County; 7201 Rossville Boulevard; Essex, MD 21228
Mr. Carl Lyles: Medina Valley Independent School District; 8449 FM 471 South; Castroville, TX 78009-5309
Mr. Mike Lynch: Capital One; 4801 Cox Road; Glen Allen, VA 23060
Mr. Pamela J. Lynch: California Power Exchange; 1000 South Fremont Avenue; Alhambra, CA 91803-4737
Mr. Robert C. Lynch: Navasite, Inc.; 300 Federal Street; Andover, MA 01810-1038
Mr. Tony Lynch: United Stationers; 2064 Ginger Creek Drive; Palatine, IL 60074
Mr. John Lynes: Bombardier Capital; 8459 Firetower Road; Jacksonville, FL 32210
Mr. James Lynn: JR Lynn Consulting; 1122 North Wood Street; Chicago, IL 60622-3243
Mr. Robert K. Lynn: Smithline Beecham; P.O. Box 1539; King of Prussa, PA 19406-0939
Ms. Felina L. Lyons: Engineered Sintered Components; 250 Old Murdock Road; Troutman, NC 28166-9686
Mr. Michael Lyons: Land America Financial Group, Inc.; 275 West Hospitality Lane, Suite 200; San Bernardino, CA 92408-3239
Mr. Issa Mabrouk: Young Chemical; 6465 Eastland Road; Brookpark, OH 44142-1305
Mr. Johnny J. Mack: MemberWorks Inc.; 11165 Mill Valley Road; Omaha, NE 68154
Mr. Peter B. Mack: Fifth Third Bank; 38 Fountain Square Plaza; Cincinnati, OH 45202-3191
Mr. Colin Mackinnon: Microelectronic Packaging; 9577 Chesapeake Drive; San Diego, CA 92123-1304
Mr. Michael MacMillan: The News Journal Gannett; 1116 Linda Lane; Vineland, NJ 08360-5009
Mr. John S. MacNeill Jr., PELS: Johns S. MacNeill, Jr., P.C.; 74 N. West St.; Homer, NY 13077-1033
Mrs. Derborah Maddox: Piedmont Behavioral Healthcare; 245 Le Phillip Court; Concord, NC 28025-2900
Mr. James F. Maddox: Global Crossing; 24725 West 12 Mile Road, Suite 200; Southfield, MI 48034
Mr. Yacob Madha: Converge Global, Inc.; 233 Wilshire Boulevard , Suite 930; Santa Monica, CA 90401
Mr. Edwin Madonado: Gulf & Atlantic Maritime; 99 Wood Avenue South; Iselin, NJ 08830-2715
Mr. Kibwe Madyun: World Bank; 2503 Columbia Pike, Suite 149; Arlington, VA 22204-4442
Ms. Harumi Maede: Natural Energy, Inc.; 22796 Islamare Lane; Lake Forest, CA 92630-3634
Mr. Joshua Maeir: Yaskawa Electric America; 2121 Norman Drive West; Waukegan, IL 60085-6751
Mr. William Maetzold: Mrj; 10560 Arrowhead Drive; Fairfax, VA 22030-7305
Mr. Shiva Maganahalli: Escrow Inc.; 1730 South Amphdett Boulevard, #233; San Mateo, CA
Mr. Kevin Maggard: Oracle; 233 South Wacker Drive, Suite 4500; Chicago, IL 60606-6376
Mr. Joseph Maggiore: New York Life Insurance Company; 51 Madison Avenue; New York, NY 10010-1603
Ms. Ellen Magnis: Health IT; 9400 North Central Expressway, Suite 1215; Dallas, TX 75231-5045
Mr. Tom Mahaffey: META Group; 208 Harbor Drive, P.O. Box 120061; Stamford, CT 06912-6833
Mr. Yingsayam Mahapanyawongse: Machining Technologies; 4565 Imperial Drive, # A; Toledo, OH 43623-3331
Mr. Raju Maharjan: Department of Natural Resources; 402 West Washington Street, Room W255C; Indianapolis, IN 46204
Mr. Kevin Maher: Anaren Microwave Inc.; 6635 Kirkville Road; East Syracuse, NY 13057-9600
Ms. Susan Maher: Bellsouth; 600 19th Street N.; Birmingham, AL 35203-2210
Mr. Ahmed M. Mahmoud: Dell Computer Corporation; 10602 Showboat Cv; Austin, TX 78730-1442
Mr. Bilal Mahmud: Bell Atlantic; 9060 Town and Country Boulevard, Apartment D; Ellicott City, MD 21043-3211
Ms. Gina Homrock Mahn: James Builders; P.O. Box 22330; Akron, OH 44302-0330
Mr. Jeffrey E. Mahoney: Munice Power Products, Inc.; 201 East Jackson Street, Suite 500; Muncie, IN 47305-2838
Ms. Jessica Main: Questeq; 1150 Brodhead Road; Monaca, PA 15061
Mr. Micheal E. Mainguy: Maxim Group; 608 Finch Court; Walled Lake, MI 48390-3055
Ms. Linda Mainord: Memphis City Schools; 2597 Avery Avenue, Room 142; Memphis, TN 38112
Mr. Robert Majdak: Steelcase, Inc. Stow Davis; 67742 County Road 23; New Paris, IN 46553-9121
Mr. Dave Majewski: Compaq Computer Corporation; 20555 SH 249; Houston, TX 77070-2698
Mrs. Pamela W. Majors: Shorewood Packaging; #1 Shorewood Drive; Andalusia, AL 36420
Mr. Richard Makaras: Sprint Pcs; 4605 Duke Drive, Suite 200; Mason, OH 45040-9410
Mr. Sarbjot S. Makkar: Microstrategy, Inc.; 4915 King Solomon Drive; Annandale, VA 22003-4045
Mr. Paul Malandrinos: Mass Mutual; 1295 State Street, #J197; Springfield, MA 01111-0002
Mr. Jeffrey Malcolm: Andersen Consulting; 161 North Clark Street; Chicago, IL 60601-3200
Mr. J. R. Malena: Enterprise Development, Inc.; 11000 Cedar Avenue, Floor 4; Cleveland, OH 44106-3052
Mr. Tariq Malik: Wayne County; IT-Dept, 415 Clifford Street; Detroit, MI 48226-1596
Ms. Halina Malinowski: Bell Atlantic; 224 East 38th Street; New York, NY 10016
Ms. Jeanne Mallak: Delta College; F38; University Center, MI 48710-0001
Mr. Jeff Mallchok: Cotelligent; 11410 Northeast 122nd Way, Suite 300; Kirkland, WA 98034
Mr. Mike Mallett: Technicolor, Inc.; 3233 Mission Oaks Boulevard; Camarillo, CA 93012-5097
Ms. Monica Mallick: Oracle Corporation; 3061 La Selva Street, Apartment C209; San Mateo, CA 94403-2129
Mr. Thomas Maloney: Step Technology; 6915 Southwest Macadam Avenue, Suite 200; Portland, OR 97219-2364
Mr. Mark Maltz: Specialty Labs; 2211 Michigan Avenue; Santa Monica, CA 90404-3900
Mr. John Mamon: BMC Solutions, Inc.; 2140 Barrett Park Drive; Kennesaw, GA 30144
Ms. Tess Manalo: IDX; 1420 Harbor Bay Parkway; Alameda, CA 94502
Ms. Joan Manchester: Curry College Applied Computing and Technology; 1071 Blue Hill Avenue; Milton, GA 02186
Mr. Howard Mandelbaum: Wheatley Group, Ltd.; Stamford Harbor Park, 333 Cudlow Street; Stamford, CT 06902
Dr. Richard Mandelbaum Ph.D.: Applied Theory Corporation; 40 Cuttermill Road; Great Neck, NY 11021-3213
Mr. Phil Maness: Motorola SPS; 1240 East Lexington Avenue; El Cajon, CA 92019-2201
Mr. Nicholas Manfredi M.S.W.: West Anaheim Medical Center; 2483 Notre Dame Circle; Corona, CA 91719-3695
Mr. Robert Manfredonia: Winstar; 380 Lexington Avenue, Suite 503; New York, NY 10168-0002
Mr. Doug Manggrum: Coca Cola Enterprises; 3715 Northside Parkway; Atlanta, GA 30327
Ms. Shirin Mangold: Booz-Allen & Hamilton Inc.; 8283 Greensboro Drive; Mc Lean, VA 22102-3802
Mr. Derek Mangrum: Hope International University; 2500 Nutwood Avenue; Fullerton, CA 92831-3104
Mr. Geof Manley: Clackamas County; 121 Library Court; Oregon City, OR 97045
Mr. Bryce Mann: Federated Insurance; P.O. Box 328; Owatonna, MN 55060-0328
Mr. Edmundo Manrique: Andersen Consulting; 8750 Carr Loop; Arvada, CO 80005-1565
Ms. Janet P. Mansky: Credit Suisse First Boston Corporation; Eleven Madison Avenue; New York, NY 10010-3629
Mr. Sam F. Mansour: Ade Optical Systems; 9625 Southern Pines Boulevard; Charlotte, NC 28273-5558
Mr. Ashok Manthina: Oracle Corporation; 90 South Cascade; Colorado Springs, CO 80907
Mr. Steve Manuel: Baptist Spanish Publishing House; 7000 Alabama; El Paso, TX 79904
Mr. Vernon Scott Manwaring: Comcast Cablevision; 4350 Pell Drive; Sacramento, CA 95838-2531
Dr. Jianchang Mao Ph.D: IBM Almaden Research Center; 650 Harry Road; San Jose, CA 95120
Ms. Jeanne Marabello: United States Naval War College; 686 Cushing Road; Newport, RI 02841-1207
Mr. Bob Marages: VDO Control Systems Inc.; 150 Knotter Drive; Cheshire, CT 06410-1136
Mr. Jon Maran: Ikon Office Solutions; 17250 North Hartford Drive; Scottsdale, AZ 85255-5432
Ms. Susan Marcello: The Employment Guide; 310 Turner Industrial Way; Aston, PA 19014-3014
Ms. Jean Marcotte: Marketing Management Inc.; 4717 Fletcher Avenue; Fort Worth, TX 76107
Mr. Charles Marcum: Arch Communications; 1800 West Park Drive; Westboro, RI 01581
Mr. Jeffrey Marecic: EG & G, Inc.; 45 William Street; Wellesley, MA 02481-4004
Ms. Jennifer Marek: Dataworks International; 2938 Fernor Street, #W11; Allentown, PA 18103-7373
Ms. Megan Marek: Dataquest/Gartner Group; 251 River Oaks Parkway; San Jose, CA 95134
Mr. Ali Margello: Nextel Communications; 10224 Allinace Road; Cincinnati, OH 45242-4710
Mr. Rodney Margison: The Racing News; P.O. Box 1495; Nashville, IN 47448-1495
Mr. Gerard Mariani: NexData Solutions, Inc.; 2465 Central Avenue, Suite 100; Boulder, CO 80301-5728
Dr. Lyle Mark Ph.D.: McKesson HBOC; 141 Chase Creek Circle; Pelham, AL 35124-1780
Ms. Jenifer Markley: Brandywine Home Sales; 2623 McCormick Drive, Suite 102; Clearwater, FL 33759
Mr. Alan M. Marks: Roche Vitamins, Inc.; 45 Waterview Boulevard; Parsippany, NJ 07054
Mr. Dana M. Marks: Hewlett-Packard; 20397 Via Palamos; Cupertino, CA 95014-6331
Mr. Michael Marks: Raabe Corporation; P.O. Box 1090; Menomonee Falls, WI 53052-1090
Mr. Wendell Marks: Compact Air Products; 2424 Sandifer Boulevard; Westminster, SC 29693-3923
Mr. D. R. Marriott: Sharp & Howse Ltd.; 295-301 London Road; Headington, England, United Kingdom OX3 9HL
Mr. Lionel Marshall: MGM; 2500 Broadway; Santa Monica, CA 90404-3065
Mr. Michael S. Marshall: Watson Wyatt; 2556 Columbine Drive; Alpine, CA 91901-1305
Mr. Vincent T. Marshall: A++ Information Systems; 836 East Jefferson Avenue; Pomona, CA 91767
Mr. Rafael Marte: Smart Programming Inc.; 274 Madison Avenue; New York, NY 10016-0701
Mr. Aaron P. Martin: Data Systems International; 7541 Westgate Street; Shawnee Mission, KS 66216-3157
Ms. Angela Martin: Worthington Steel; 905 Dearborn Drive; Columbus, OH 43085-1543
Mr. Charles J. Martin Sr.: AAT Communications Corporation; 517 Route One South; Iselin, NJ 08830-3011
Ms. Cheryl Martin: CenturyTel; 27850 Harris Road/ P.O. Box 482; La Junta, CO 81050
Mr. D. Eric Martin: City of Alamogordo; 1376 East Ninth Street; Alamogordo, NM 88310
Mr. David K. Martin: Chamber of Commerce of Fargo Moorhead; P.O. Box 2443; Fargo, ND 58108-2443
Ms. Dianne Martin: Mountain Home Public School; 500 Bomber Boulevard; Mountain Home, AR 72653-4628
Mr. Doug Martin: Carilion Information Service; 37 Reserve Avenue SW; Roanoke, VA 24016-4916
Mr. K. Nous Martin: Peaksoft Mutinet Corporation; 1801 Roeder Avenue, #144; Bellingham, WA 98226
Mr. Luc Martin: Almerco Inc.; 8 1695 Rue Atmec; Gatineau, Quebec, Canada J8P 7G7
Mr. Pablo A. Martin: Visworld International; P.O. Box 402984; Miami, FL 33140-0984
Mr. Paul Martin: Pacific Bell; 2600 Camino Ramon, #25000q; San Ramon, CA 94583-5099
Mr. Pete Martin: Cross Country Printing; 80 Byrdland Drive; Greenville, SC 29607-2702
Mr. Daniel Martinez: Owens-Illinois; One Seagate; Toledo, OH 43604-1558
Mr. Joe G. Martinez: Bank One; 1700 Pacific Avenue; Dallas, TX 75201
Mr. John Martinez: El Paso

Energy; 750 Old Hickory Boulevard; Brentwood, TN 37027-4528
Mr. Ted Martinez: Nextlink Communication; 8871 Sandy Parkway; Sandy, UT 84070-6408
Ms. Leslie Martinich: Vignette; 901 South Mopac Expressway, Building III; Austin, TX 78746
Mr. Anthony Martino III: SuperStock, Inc.; 7660 Centurion Parkway; Jacksonville, FL 32256
Mr. Joe Martori: Trilogy Computer; 136 Briarwood; Irvine, CA 92604
Mr. Daniel Marty: ABSC D/692; 1204 Massillon Road; Akron, OH 44306-4186
Mr. Robert A. Marvin Jr.: New Technology Solutions Inc.; 170 Main Street, Suite 107; Tewksbury, MA 01876-1765
Ms. Leah Marz: Greer & Walker, Llp; 227 West Trade Street, Suite 1450; Charlotte, SC 28202
Mr. Steve Masey: Ameritech; 5 Laurel Valley Court; Lake in the Hill, IL 60102-5939
Mr. Ken Mason: PC Connections; 730 Milford Road; Merrimack, NH 03054-4631
Mr. Robert M. Mason: Choice Hotels International; 4225 East Windrose Drive; Phoenix, AZ 85032-7599
Ms. Tiffany L. Mason: Business Imaging Center; 1101 Arch Street; Philadelphia, PA 19107-2208
Mr. Dave Massen: Stony Brook University Hospital; 31 Research Way, Room 139; East Setauket, NY 11733-3454
Mr. Jerome H. Massey: Georgia Association of Realtors; 3200 Presidential Drive; Atlanta, GA 30340-3910
Mr. Thomas A. Massey: Twin Eagles GTC.G/GBCS; 11725 Twin Eagles Boulevard; Naples, FL 34120
Mr. Evans H. Massie: Virginia Department of Health Office; 1500 East Main Street; Richmond, VA 23219-3635
Mr. Lee Masters: BellSouth Telecommunications; 600 19th Street N, Floor 8; Birmingham, AL 35203-2210
Mr. Shehrever Masters: Professional Computer Development Corporation; 401 Tomahawk Drive; Maumee, OH 43537-1633
Mrs. Adria Maston: Lutheran Healthcare Network; 525 West Brown Road; Mesa, AZ 85201-3299
Ms. Eva Mata: Johnson Controls; 1320 Goodyear Drive; El Paso, TX 79936-6420
Mr. Michael J. Mateja: Technology Dot Com, Inc.; 975 East Nerge Road; Schaumburg, IL 60172
Mr. Byron D. Mathews: Bank of America; 233 South Wacker Drive, Suite 2800; Chicago, IL 60606-6314
Mr. Edward J. Mathews: Lereta Corporation; 1123 Park View Drive; Covina, CA 91724-3752
Mr. Arvind K. Mathur: Systems Plus, Inc.; 1370 Piccard Drive, Suite 270; Rockville, MD 20850-4326
Ms. Margaret Matthews: Fortis Benefits; 2323 Grand Boulevard, Floor 5; Kansas City, MO 64108-2670
Mr. Eugene Matusevich: AT&T; 399 Campus Drive; Somerset, NJ 08873-1178
Ms. Tina Mauersberger: Omnimed Transcription; 6602 Grand Teton Plaza; Madison, WI 53719-1010
Ms. Melissa Maul: Digital Xpress; 2550 University Avenue West, Suite 310S; St. Paul, MN 55114-1909
Mr. Chris Maxey: Lucent Technologies; 11107 Alcott, #A; Westminster, CO 80234
Mr. Chris Maxwell: Bell Atlantic, CCS; 801 Summit Run; Lewisville, TX 75077-2990
Ms. Julie May: Zena Comp Inc.; 17187 North Laurel Park Drive, Suite 351; Livonia, MI 48152-2600
Mr. Roger May: Flashnet Marketing; 21535 Cedar Cove Drive; Katy, TX 77450-5349
Dr. R. Edward Mayberry: AG Consulting's; 275 Battery Street, Fl5; San Francisco, CA 94111-3305
Mr. Kevin Mayeu: Electronic Data Systems; P.O. Box 20366; Rochester, NY 14602-0366
Mr. Bob Maynard: Lexmark International; 740 West New Circle Road; Lexington, KY 40511-1876
Mr. James Mays Jr.: Lancaster Health Alliance; 555 North Duke Street; Lancaster, CA 17604
Mr. Luis Maza: Golden Gate University; 536 Mission Street; San Francisco, CA 94105
Mr. Robert Mazzolin: Department of National Defense; 8464 Monarch Court; Annandale, VA 22003-1174
Mr. Michael McAfee: Fiberline; 111 Pacifica, Suite 120; Iruine, CA 92618
Ms. Robin McAhon: Westvaco Kraft Division; P.O. Box 118005; Charleston, SC 29423-8005
Ms. Janice McAllister: TVA; 1101 Market Street, SP 2D-C; Chattanooga, TN 37402-2881
Mr. Mike McBride: Data Processing; 1101 East River Road; Dixon, IL 61021-3252
Mr. Tim McCaffrey: G.& F. Graphics; 7045 Central Highway; Pennsauken, NJ 08109-4310
Mr. Jason McCall: IBM Global Services; 856 Southers Circle; Suwanee, GA 30024-1408
Mr. Dan McCart: Babbage's Etc.; 2250 William D Tate Avenue; Grapevine, TX 76051-3978
Mr. Bill McCaulley: Solutionvision.com; PO Box 550489; Fort Lauderdale, FL 33355-0489
Mr. Christopher A. McClain: Public Service Electrical & Gas - Nuclear; P.O. Box 236, N35; Hancocks Bridge, NJ 08038
Ms. Mary McCleaft: F. Schumacher & Co.; P.O. Box 6002; Newark, DE 19714-6002
Mr. Daniel McClelland: Westark College; 6010 Glenview Court; Fort Smith, AR 72916-8215
Mr. Sean D. McClelland: EIS Computers; 207 West Los Angeles Avenue, Suite 300; Moorpark, CA 93021
Mr. Keith McClure: Liberty Capital, Inc.; 106 Taylor Court, Apartment B; Hillsboro, OH 45133-1240
Mr. Scot McCombs: Jordan School District; 9361 South 300 East; Sandy, UT 84070-2998
Mr. Norman McConnell: Beatrice Board of Public Works; P.O. Box 279; Beatrice, NE 68310
Ms. Miriam McCoy: Employment & Human Services; 40 Douglas Drive; Martinez, CA 94553-4068
Mr. Randall McCoy: Lower Elwha Klallam Tribe; 2851 Lower Elwha Road; Port Angeles, WA 98363-8409
Ms. June McCracken: Asheville City Schools; 85 Mountain Street; Asheville, NC 28801-3854
Mr. John McCrickard: Wilton Corp; 300 South Hicks Road; Palatine, IL 60067-6900
Mr. Shawn McCullars: University of Chicago Hospitals; 5737 South Drexel Avenue; Chicago, IL 60637-1419
Ms. Melissa McCulloch-Souza: Integrated Technologies, Inc.; 20 Risho Avenue; East Providence, RI 02914-1297
Ms. Vickie McCullough: Palomar College; 1140 West Mission Road; San Marcos, CA 92069-1487
Mr. Shane McCutchen: Flagstar Bank; 32500 Cadillac Street; Farmington, MI 48336-4271
Ms. Linda McDaniel: Xenos Group; 3010 Lyndon B Johnson Fairway, Suite 301; Dallas, TX 75234
Mrs. Rosalie McDermid: St. Rose School; 727 25th Avenue; Longview, WA 98632-1856
Ms. Cathye McDonald: BellSouth; 365 Canal Street, Room 3050; New Orleans, LA 70130-1112
Mr. Greg McDonald: Camden Property Trust; Three Greenway Plaza, Suite 1300; Houston, TX 77046
Ms. Kathleen E. McDonald: CNA Insurance; CNA Plaza, 11 East; Chicago, IL 60604-4153
Mr. Kerry McDonald: Southwestern Bell Mobile; 1125 East Campbell Road; Richardson, TX 75081
Ms. Letta McDonald: Wickett & Craig of America, Inc.; 120 Cooper Road; Curwensville, PA 16833-1542
Ms. Pam McDonald: Hospital Communications Systems; 5809 Departure Drive, Suite 108; Raleigh, NC 27616-1858
Mrs. Betsy McDowell: Mount Taylor Enterprises; 60018 Cantina Acres; Grants, NM 87020-9644
Mr. John McDunn: TRW; 100 North Park Avenue, Floor 2; Helena, MT 59601-6287
Ms. Mona McFadden: I2 Technologies; 4487 McPherson Avenue, Unit A; St. Louis, MO 63108-2505
Ms. Patricia A. McFadden Sterr: Joliet Junior College; 1215 Houbolt Road; Joliet, IL 60431
Ms. Helen L. McFadin: Excel Telecommunications; 2364 Union Avenue; Alamogordo, NM 88310-3848
Mr. Donald McFarlane: Merrill Lynch; 400 College Road East; Princeton, NJ 08536
Mr. Larry McFeeters: Lockheed Martin; 26 West Martin Luther King Drive 406X; Cincinnati, OH 45268-0001
Mr. Tommy McGaughy: NCR Corporation; 1775 Corporate Drive, Suite 150; Norcross, GA 30093-2928
Mr. David McGeehan: Source W; 11 Stanwix Street; Pittsburgh, PA 15222-1312
Ms. Paula McGowan: Georgetown College; 400 East College Street; Georgetown, KY 40324-1628
Ms. Cathy McGrath: Ameritech; 240 North Meridian Street, Room 675; Indianapolis, IN 46204-1983
Mr. Joe McGrath: Angelo Patri School; 2225 Webster Avenue; Bronx, NY 10457-2439
Ms. Sharon McGrath: Cellular One; 2875 Union Road, Suite 35U; Buffalo, NY 14227-1491
Ms. Susan McGrath: Noblestar Systems; 505 Sansome Street; San Francisco, CA 94111-3106
Mr. Chris McIntyre: Midas Rex Pneumatic Tools Inc.; 3000 Race Street; Fort Worth, TX 76111-4116
Mr. David McIntyre: Communities Com; 10101 North De Anza Boulevard, Suite 100; Cupertino, CA 95014-2264
Mr. Grover L. McIntyre: Humana; 5401 West Kennedy Boulevard, Suite 200; Tampa, FL 33609-2448
Mr. Timothy McIvor: Omaha Public Power District; 444 South 16th Street; Omaha, NE 68102-2247
Mr. John F. McKay: Cooper Lighting; 400 Busse Road; Elk Grove Village, IL 60007-2100
Mr. Neill J. McKay: General Services Administration; Ruon 6600; Washington, DC 20407-0001
Ms. Casandra J. McKeaver: U.S.P.S.-O.I.G.; 4001 Sulgrave Drive; Alexandria, VA 22209-2020
Mr. Bob McKee: Pagemart; 3333 Lee Parkway; Dallas, TX 75219-5111
Ms. Theresa McKee: Georgia Pacific; 100 Wisconsin River Drive; Port Edwards, WI 54469-1492
Mr. John McKenna: Examiner Publications Limited; P.O. Box 21; Academy Street, Ireland Cork
Mr. John David McKenna: United Space Alliance; 2818 Pickett Drive; League City, TX 77573-4724
Ms. Cheryl R. McKnight: Cedar Hill Independent School District; 1601 West Pleasant Run Road; De Soto, TX 75115-2723
Mr. Sean McLafferty: Lear Corporation; P.O. Box 430; Elsie, MI 48831-0430
Mr. David McLaren: General Atomics; 3550 General Atomics Court; San Diego, CA 92121-1194
Ms. Sabrina McMahan: Norfolk Southern Corporation; 185 Spring Street SW, Box 152; Atlanta, GA 30303
Mr. Chris McMahon: Belleville Public Schools; 105 West A Street; Belleville, IL 62220-1326
Mr. T. Blane McMichen: Eli Lilly & Company; Lilly Corporate Center; Indianapolis, IN 46285-0002
Ms. Debi McMillan: Louisiana Department of Labor; P.O. Box 94094, Technical Support Room 302; Baton Rouge, LA 70804-9094
Mr. Rodney O. McPhearson: Complete Solutions; 3875 East 126th Street North; Skiatook, OK 74070-3308
Mr. Ronald D. McPherson: G&S Integration, Limited; 351 Executive Drive; Troy, MI 48083
Mr. John C. McQueen: TPM, Inc.; 12950 Millersburg Road, S.W.; Massillon, OH 44647-9717
Mr. Michael McSurley: Propper International; 700 Airport Road; Waverly, TN 37185-3047
Mr. Hugh D. McVicker: Indianapolis Public Housing; 5 Indiana Square; Indianapolis, IN 46204-2001
Mr. Brian McWhirter: Quality Communications, Inc.; 9931 Corporate Campus Drive; Louisville, KY 40223-4035
Mr. Norman McWilliams: Lockheed Martin; 3929 Calle Fortunada; San Diego, CA 92123-1828
Ms. Wendy Meade: Qualchoice of Virginia; 1807 Seminole Trail; Charlottesville, VA 22901-1129
Mr. Mark Meavers: IXOS Software, Inc.; 19 Campus Boulevard; Newtown Square, PA 19073
Mr. Doug Mecham: Sams Town; 5111 Boulder Highway; Las Vegas, NV 89122-6004
Mr. Richard Mecoy: Analysts International Corporation; 2365 Harrodsburg Road; Lexington, KY 40504-3373
Mr. Jose Medeiros: Intel Corporation; 1080 Noble Lane; San Jose, CA 95132-3127
Ms. Erica Meder: Sprint; 600 New Century Parkway; New Century, KS 66031-1101
Mr. Herb Meehan: Qualisoft; 452 Hudson Terrace; Englewood Cliffs, NJ 07632
Linda Meehan: University of Denver; 7150 Montview Boulevard; Denver, CO 80220-1866
Mr. Grady L. Meeks Jr.: The City of Daytona Beach; 301 South Ridgewood Drive; Daytona Beach, FL 32114-4976
Mr. Thomas Meeks: Crisp Hughes Evans Llp; 32 Orange Street; Asheville, NC 28801-2341
Ms. Andrea Meester: Gage Marketing Group; 5130 Industrial Street; Maple Plain, MN 55359-9673
Mr. J. F. Megee: Freudenberg NOK; 1700 Miller Avenue; Shelbyville, IN 46176-3114
Mr. Vikas Mehra: Oracle Corporation; 5621 Bethnalgreen Drive, Apartment D; Richmond, VA 23228-1859
Mr. Vivek Mehra: Cobalt Networks; 555 Ellis Avenue; Mountain View, CA 94043
Mr. Todd Meinerding: Ellcon-National, Inc.; 50 Beechtree Boulevard; Greenville, SC 29605
Mr. Jeremy Meissner: U.S. West Advanced Technologies; 4001 Discovery Drive; Boulder, CO 80303
Mr. Zaur Mekhtiev: Flynt Fabrics; 410 East Interstate Service Road; Graham, NC 27853
Mr. Derek L. Melber: Bartlett and Company; 4800 Main Street; Kansas City, MO 64112-2510
Mr. David Melchers: Kemper; 7 Falcon Ridge Court; Algonquin, IL 60102-1723
Mr. Marco A. Melendez: U.S. Army; 1124a Gilmore Drive; Key West, FL 33040-6743
Mr. Thor Melicher: Sarcom; 143C Dillmont Drive; Columbus, OH 43235
Mr. Christopher Mellillo: American Arium; 14281 Chambers Road; Tustin, CA 92780-6909
Mr. Michael M. Melliza: State of California Department of Consumer Affairs; 1823 14th Street; Sacramento, CA 95814-7119
Ms. Rosa Mello: KPMG; 594 South Beach Street; Fall River, MA 02724-2714
Mr. Matthew D. Melson: Medical Matrix, Inc.; 6421 Camp Bowie Boulevard, Suite 200; Fort Worth, TX 76116
Mr. John Mendonca: Motorola; 14700 Yora Drive; Austin, TX 78728-4307
Mr. Benjamin A. Mendoza: Optional Wireless Services; 1745 Parkland Way; San Diego, CA 92114-7820
Mr. Jason Lau Teck Meng: Scitex Digital Printing; 285B Toh Guan Road; Singapore, Singapore 11-106
Mr. Douglas W. Menkhaus: Xerox Corporation; 10560 Ashview Place, Suite 300; Cincinnati, OH 45242-3749
Mr. Sunil Menon: Sonus Networks; 5 Carlise Road; Westford, MA 01721
Mr. Charles J. Mercante: Zeneca; 1800 Concord Pike; Wilmington, DE 19850
Ms. Dawn Mercer: Toyota Motor Sales, USA, Incorporated; 16 Henderson Drive; West Caldwell, NJ 07006-6677
Mr. Joseph Mercer: Fleet Mortgage Corporation; 2210 Enterprise Drive; Florence, SC 29501-1109
Dr. Robert Merrill Ph.D.: Allied Signal; P.O. Box 31; Petersburg, VA 23804-0031
Mr. Brad Merritt: Stanley Recordings & Multimedia; 1717 Lincoln Boulevard; Venice, CA 90291
Mr. Trevor Merritt: First Federal Credit Union; 106 L Street, Suite F; Sacramento, CA 95814-3227
Mr. Larry Merritt-Gilbert: Maytag Corporation; 1801 Monmouth Boulevard; Galesburg, IL 61401
Mr. John Metcalf: Associated Oregon Industries; 1149 Court Street NE; Salem, OR 97301-4081
Mr. Jonathan Metcalf: A+ Computer Solutions; 1375 Sutter Street, Suite 322; San Francisco, CA 94109
Ms. Sallie G. Metzgar: United Way; 5 Hamptons Road; Norfolk, VA 23513
Mr. Steve Metzler: Information Services Washington Center; 232 West 25th Street; Erie, PA 16544-0002
Mr. Paul J. Meyer: EDS; 5400 Legacy Drive; Plano, TX 75024-3105
Mr. Scott Meyer: Eaglesoft; 2202 Althoff Drive; Effingham, IL 62401-4604
Mr. Robert Meyerink: Baxter Healthcare; P.O. Box 1390; Marion, NC 28752-1390
Mr. Brooke Meyers: Ottawa University; 2340 West Mission Lane; Phoenix, AZ 85021-2807
Ms. Ruth Meyers: Merchant Wholesale; 2517 Ellington Road; Quincy, IL 62301-8828
Dr. Yi Mi: DMr.Consulting Group, Inc.; 10900 Northeast 8th Street, Suite 1680; Bellevue, WA 98004
Mr. Joseph M. Miano: Information Management Services; 3826 East Watkins Street; Phoenix, AZ 85034-7265
Mr. Blake Michael: Samedan Oil Corporation; 110 West Broadway Street; Ardmore, OK 73401-6286

Ms. Stasha Michael: Airshow; 10801 120th Avenue NE; Kirkland, WA 98033-5024
Mr. Vijay Michael: Matrix Telecommunications, Inc.; 8721 Airport Freeway; Fort Worth, TX 76180
Mr. Byron B. Micke: American Electric Power; 5434-D Dunmere Lane; Dublin, OH 43017
Mr. Michael M. Mickelson: Western Wisconsin Technical College; 304 North 6th Street; LaCrosse, WI 54602
Mr. Mark Middleton: Tri County Council for Western Maryland; 111 South George Street; Cumberland, MD 21502-3087
Ms. Susan Midlarsky: Massachusetts Institute of Technology; 77 Massachusetts Avenue, #8-433; Cambridge, MA 02139-4301
Ms. Tammy Mihalski: 143 West Green Bay Street; Pulaski, WI 54162-9771
Mr. Marco Mijares: Voyager Technologies; 3305 Breckinridge Boulevard, Suite 115; Duluth, GA 30096-4932
Ms. Miljana G. Mijic: PNNL "Batelle"; 1511 Farrell Lane; Richland, WA 99352-2905
Mr. Philip J. Mikal: Harding Marketing Communications; 1288 Columbus Avenue, Box 210; San Francisco, CA 94133
Ms. Carrie Mikalauski: Petersen Health Care of Wisconsin, Inc.; P.O. Box 857; Rhinelander, WI 54501-0857
Ms. Sharon E. Mikesell: SMG Enterprises; 22336 Ponderosa Drive, P.O. Box 351; Twain Harte, CA 95383
Mr. Lee Milam: Computer Tech; 27118 North Creek Drive; Magnolia, TX 77354-4081
Ms. Lydia Milam: Bluefield State College; 219 Rock Street; Bluefield, WV 24701-2198
Mr. Brian Milby: Navy Supply Corps School; 1425 Prince Avenue; Athens, GA 30606-2271
Mr. Thomas Miliano: Pace University; 1 Pace Plaza,#407; New York, NY 10038-1598
Ms. Annie Milledge: PricewaterhouseCoopers LLP; 1155 Peachtree Street NE; Atlanta, GA 30309-7629
Mr. Allen W. Miller: Blair-Bedford County Computer; 300 Main Stret; Roaring Spring, PA 16673-1723
Mr. Ceasar Miller: Rockwell; 2150 Boggs Road; Duluth, GA 30096
Mr. Dennis Miller: Orion Scientific Systems, Inc.; 319 Washington Street, Suite 234; Johnstown, PA 15901
Ms. Desiree Miller: Ameritech Cellular; 1 Aviation Center; Rantoul, IL 6188663401
Mr. Gary Miller: Medtronic Inc.; 11367 Birch Pointe Drive; Whitehouse, OH 43571-9528
Mr. Gregory P. Miller: LSW Architects; 2300 Main Street; Vancouver, WA 98660-2671
Ms. Joyce Miller: Town of Vienna; 127 Center Street South; Vienna, VA 22180-5799
Mr. Lance A. Miller: Science Applications International Corporation; 5180 Parkstone Drive, Suite 100; Chantilly, VA 20151-3814
Mr. Larry Miller: Eagle Information Resources, Inc.; 3205 Quail Hill Drive; Midlothian, VA 23112-4429
Ms. Louise Miller: RESA IV and III; 404 Old Main Drive; Summersville, WV 26651-1360
Ms. Megan J. Miller: Santa Clara Convention Center; 5001 Great America Parkway; Santa Clara, CA 95054-1142
Mr. Michael A. Miller: Highwoods Properties, Inc.; 3100 Smoketree Court, Suite 600; Raleigh, NC 27604-1051
Mr. Nicholas A. Miller: Phoenix Software International; 5200 West Century Boulevard, #800; Los Angeles, CA 900455927
Mr. Paul Miller: Teleglobe; 11480 Commerce Park Drive; Reston, VA 20191
Mr. Raymond C. Miller: Lehigh Valley Hospital; 2024 Lehigh Street; Allentown, PA 18103-4734
Mr. Richard Miller: West Florida BOCES; 131 Drumlin Court; Newark, NY 14513-1863
Mr. Robin W. Miller: Lockheed Martin; 4005 Twilight Drive South; Fort Worth, TX 76116-7653
Ms. Shirley Miller: Lodge-Net Entertainment; 3900 West Innovation Street; Sioux Falls, SD 57107-7002
Mr. Steven Miller: UGI Utilities Inc.; 225 Morgantown Road; Reading, PA 19611-1949
Ms. Tammy F. Miller: GE Information Services; 100 Edison Park Drive; Gaithersburg, MD 22878
Mr. James Milo: Westdale Asset Management; 330 Commerce Street; Dallas, TX 75226-1632
Mr. Jim Milton: FERS; 401 North Michigan Avenue, Suite 2600; Chicago, IL 60611-4246
Mr. Nicola Minniti: BDO Siedman LLP; 330 Madison Avenue; New York, NY 10017-5001
Mr. Doug Minnix: Computer Aid Inc.; 897 Cold Spring Road Apartment 5; Allentown, PA 18103-6085
Mr. William S. Miracle: Roadmaster, Inc.; 5602 Northeast Skyport Way; Portland, OR 97218-1242
Ms. Debbie Miraglia: Semaphore, Inc.; 3 east 28th Street; New York, NY 10016-7408
Mr. Ted Miroulis: AT&T Local Services; 1 World Trade Center, Suite 5121; New York, NY 10048-5199
Mr. Brain B. Mischke: Noridian Mutual Insurance; 4510 13th Avenue SW; Fargo, ND 58121
Mr. Kunal Mishra: Bally Gaming & Systems; 6601 Bermuda Road; Las Vegas, NV 89119-3605
Ms. Shailendra Mishra: Oracle Corporation; 500 Okalle Parkway 40P970 Redwood Shores; Fremont, CA 94065
Dr. Harald Mispelkamp Ph.D: Doruier Gmbh/ Daimler Chrysler Areospece; Postfach 1420; Friedrichsh, Germany 7990
Mr. Rajesh K. Misra: IMI Systems, Inc.; 290 Broad Hollow Road; Melville, MA 11747
Mr. Lance Missry: N.P.D. Group; 900 West Shore Road; Port Washington, NY 11050-4624
Mr. Peter C. Misthos: Xpedite Systems, Inc./Premiere Tech; 1 Industrial Way West; Eatontown, NJ 07724
Ms. Joyce Mitamura: Inacom Corporation; 968 Waioli Street; Honolulu, HI 96825
Ms. Becky Mitchell: Meier Transmission, Ltd.; 1845 East 40th Street; Cleveland, OH 44103
Dr. Glenn E. Mitchell Ph.D.: .Com Consulting Group; 2114 Longview Drive; Tallahassee, FL 32303-7326
Ms. Shelley Mitchell: Nextel Communications; 2975 Breckinridge Boulevard; Duluth, GA 30096
Mr. Victor Mitchell: Sprint Blnoc; 9350 Metcalf; Overland Park, KS 6612
Mr. Scott Mizener: West Mifflin Area School District; 91 Commonwealth Avenue; West Mifflin, PA 15122-2396
Dr. Mark Moallemian Ph.D.: Michigan State University; 114 Computer Center; East Lansing, MI 48824-1042
Mr. Robert S. Moberly: McCammish Manufacturing; 148 Winn Avenue; Winchester, KY 40391
Mrs. Nina Mobilio: Shubert Organization; 330 West 42nd Street; New York, NY 10036
Mr. Esteban Mocagatta: C. I. T. E. F. A.; Zufriategui, 4380; Villa Martelli, Argentina 1603
Mr. Edward E. Mock: Quest Diagnostics; 2040 Concourse Drive; St. Louis, MO 63146-4119
Mr. Ashok Modi: Compudent Inc.; 9 Chase Drive; Morganville, NJ 07751-2102
Mr. Salil Mody: Sherpa Corporation; 40055 Eaton Street, Apartment 202; Canton, MI 48187
Mr. Kevin Moeggenberg: Macdonald Consulting Group; 15 Piedmont Center NE, Suite 1550; Atlanta, GA 30305-1557
Mr. Sepideh Moghadam: Bronner Slosberg Humphrey; 800 Boylston Street Prudential Tower 20th Floor; Boston, MA 02199
Mr. Mohammad Mohammad: Majestic Systems Integration; 321 Ella Street; Smryna, TN 37167-5561
Mr. Mushtaq Mohammed: Akili Systems Group; 2001 Bryan Street, #1500; Dallas, TX 75023-7539
Mr. Manas Mohanty: American Data Management; 1421 Southeast 23rd Street; Cape Coral, FL 33990-4631
Mr. J. G. Mohl: Pennsylvania State Police; 1800 Elmerton Avenue; Harrisburg, PA 17110-9758
Mr. Craig Mohler: GVG Technology/Trase Miller Solutions; 2211 Butterfield Road; Downers Grove, IL 60515-1157
Mr. Mike Mohr: Mckee Foods Corporation; P.O. Box 750; Collegedale, TN 37315-0750
Mr. Jerome P. Moisand: Unisphere; 31 Hawthorne Avenue; Arlington, MA 02476-7433
Mr. Willie L. Moise: Conagra, Inc.; P.O. Box 12372; Omaha, NE 68112-0372
Mr. Jose Molina: Capital One; 6008 Town North Country Boulevard; Tampa, FL 33615-3445
Ms. Wendy Mongaroo: Darjean Creations; 318 Edgeton Court; Houston, TX 77015-2102
Mr. Jeffrey Monnette: Pricewaterhouse Coopers; 10496 Langley Drive; Pinckney, MI 48169
Mr. Jonathan Montag: Fore Systems; 1000 Fore Drive; Warrendale, PA 15086-7502
Ms. Kristen Montan: IDEMA; 3255 Scott Boulevard, Suite 2-102; Santa Clara, CA 95054-3017
Mr. Paul Montecinos: Carolina Precast; P.O. Box 1061; Dunn, NC 28335-1061
Ms. Liana Montero: National Highway Institute; 1800 R Street NW, Apartment 904; Washington, DC 20009-1655
Ms. Autumn Montgomery: Computers 'n' Stuff; 610 Briar Hill Court; Riverdale, GA 30274-1560
Mr. Daniel Montgomery: INACOM; 5 Penn Plaza, 17th Floor; New York, NY 10001
Mr. Patrick Montgomery: Mohawk Industries, Inc; 243 Huffalcan Road; Rome, GA 30165
Mr. Raymond Montgomery: Inland Paperboard & Packaging; 4030 Vincennes Road; Indianapolis, IN 46268-3007
Dr. Ralph E. Montjo D.Sc.: Xerox Product Engineering; 225B Reeport Drive; Nogsles, AZ 86521
Mr. J. P. Montross: Standard & Poors; 343 Verplanck Avenue; Beacon, NY 12508-2821
Mr. Beau Moon: Software Spectrum; 2140 Merritt Drive; Garland, TX 75041-6184
Mr. Curtis H. Moon: Boystown USA; Boystown USA; Boystown, NE 68010
Ms. Linda Moon: Analytical Graphics, Incorporated; 325 Technology Drive; Malvern, PA 19355
Mr. Thomas Mooney: Reciprocal Inc.; 620 Main Street; Buffalo, NY 14202-1906
Mr. Calvin C. Moor: Ohio-American Water Company; 365 East Center Street; Marion, OH 43302
Mr. Chris B. Moore: Advanced System Designs; 1619 Fairwood Forest Drive; St. Peters, MO 63376
Mr. Douglas B. Moore: John Deere Community Credit Union; 1827 Ansborough Avenue; Waterloo, IA 50701-3629
Ms. Kay S. Moore: Employment Action Center Resource Inc.; 6715 Minnetonka Boulevard; Minneapolis, MN 55426
Mr. Michael D. Moore: Computer Stores Northwest; 230 Southwest 6th Street; Convallis, OR 97333
Ms. Randi Moore: Aptis; 8 Southwoods Boulevard; Albany, NY 12211-2351
Ms. Sherry Moore: Jay R Smith Manufacturing; P.O. Box 3237; Montgomery, AL 36109-0237
Ms. Sue Moore: Motorola, Inc.; 1701 Golf Road; Rolling Meadows, IL 60008-4227
Ms. Teri A. Moore: AT&T; 132 South Canyon Drive; Bolingbrook, IL 60490-1535
Mr. Miguel Morales: Document Technologies; 2265 West Desert Cove; Phoenix, AZ 85029-4912
Mr. Miguel Morales: Document Technologies; 2265 West Desert Cove; Phoenix, AZ 85029-4912
Ms. Kim Moran: National Pharmaceutical; 1894 Preston White Drive; Reston, VA 20191-5433
Mr. William J. Moran: MessageQuest; 1246 Ocean Reef Road; Wesley Chapel, FL 33543
Mr. David Moraniec: Maytag Corporation; 403 West 4th Street North; Newton, IA 50208-3034
Ms. Lori Morden: Hawaiian Cement; 1100 Alakea Street, Suite 2300; Honolulu, HI 96813-2841
Mr. Joe Moreland: Kansas Board of Emergency Medical Services; 109 Southwest 6th Avenue; Topeka, KS 66603-3826
Mr. Joseph A. Moreland: Hewlett Packard; 20 Perimeter Summit Boulevard; Atlanta, GA 30319
Mr. Ecleysis J. Moreno: Silo Technology; 1810 Lacombe Avenue, #1; Bronx, NY 10473
Mr. Juan Moreno: New Millennium Technology Consultant; 6820 Selfridge Street IJ; Flushing, NY 11375-5746
Mr. Richard Moreno: Ericsson; 730 International Parkway; Richardson, TX 75081-2893
Ms. Vivian D. Moreno: ACES; 55 Waugh Drive, Suite 1150; Houston, TX 77007
Ms. Angela Moretti: Nashville Convention Center; 601 Commerce Street; Nashville, TN 37203-3724
Ms. Donna Morgan: Bell South; 20341 Monteverdi Circle; Boca Raton, FL 33498-6784
Ms. Maren G. Morgan: City of Twinsburg; 10075 Ravenna Road; Twinsburg, OH 44087
Ms. Mary Morgan: Mcs Spectrum; 5540 Porter Road; Niagara Falls, NY 14304-1523
Mr. Raymond William Morgan: Compaq Computer Corporation; 791 Moody Street; Waltham, MA 02453-5007
Mr. Thomas Moriarty: Minutemen International; 101 Poplar Avenue; Elmhurst, IL 60126-3531
Mr. James E. Morin: RACO Manufacturing; 1400 62nd Street; Emeryville, CA 94608
Mr. Kenji Morishige: Kenjim, Inc.; 1359 Phelps Avenue, #10; San Jose, CA 95117
Mr. Thomas A. Moritz: New Boston Systems; 2488 Northlake Court NE; Atlanta, GA 30345-2226
Mr. Michael Morrell: Health Care Service Corp.; 300 East Randolph Street; Chicago, IL 60601
Ms. Cathy Morris: Page Digital; 6436 Racine Circle; Englewood, CO 80111-6465
Dr. Daniel P. Morris Ph.D.: International Business Machines Corporation; P.O. Box 218; Yorktown Heights, NY 10598-0218
Mr. G. Allen Morris: IX Labs; 31971 Pudding Creek Road; Fort Bragg, CA 95437-8105
Ms. Laura Morris: Enviroscan, Inc.; 1051 Columbia Avenue; Lancaster, PA 17603-3130
Ms. Terri Morris Williamson: Kemet Electronics; P.O. Box 5928, Mis; Greenville, SC 29606-5928
Ms. Ethel Morris-Shaw: JD Edwards; One Technology; Denver, CO 80237
Mr. Brian Morrison: National Account Systems; 34 West Colt Square Drive; Fayetteville, AR 72703-2888
Mr. Jeff Morrison: Equifax; 1525 Windward Concourse; Alpharetta, GA 30005-8884
Ms. Kelly Mortensen: Phoenix International; 1441 44th Street North; Fargo, ND 58102-2854
Mr. Andy Moshman: Patterson Kelley Company; 100 Burson Street; East Stroudsburg, PA 18301-2245
Mr. John T. Moss: Broward County; 540 Southeast 3rd Avenue; Fort Lauderdale, FL 33301
Ms. Loren L. Mossor: C-Soft, Inc.; 30 Sugarland Square Center; Sterling, VA 20164-1638
Ms. Eve Marie Motichka: Wiicomico County Board of Education; P.O. Box 1538; Salisbury, MD 21802-1538
Mr. John Motlagh: Sprint Paranet; 5601 Bridge Street, Floor 3; Fort Worth, TX 76112-2384
Mr. John H. Mott: General Cybernetics Operation; 1061 Milk Boulevard; Northport, AL 35476
Mr. Jerry Mounce: Packaging Service Company; 1904 Mykawa Road; Pearland, TX 77581-3210
Mrs. Victoria Mouroulis: Epicor Software; 195 Technology Drive; Irvine, CA 92618-2402
Ms. Velina Mouton: Little Rock School District; 810 West Markham Street; Little Rock, AR 72201-1306
Ms. Vickie Mouzon: La Salle University; Information Technology Department, 1900 West Olney Avenue; Philadelphia, PA 1941
Mr. Neysan Movaffagh: GCI; 2550 Denali Street, Suite 503; Anchorage, AK 99503-2751
Mrs. Kim C. Moynahan: G S E Lining Technology, Inc.; 19103 Gundle Road; Houston, TX 77073-3598
Mr. Mikesch Muecke: Iowa State University of Architecture; 156 Design; Ames, IA 50011-0001
Mr. Tom Muehleisen: Alltel Communications; 50 Executive Parkway; Hudson, OH 44236
Mr. Wolfgang Mueller: Infineon Technologies; 1580 Route 52 Zip 33F; Hopewell Junction, NY 12533
Mr. Ahmad Muhammad: Total Computer Solutions of Tennessee; 4119 Jackson Avenue; Memphis, TN 38128-6347
Mr. Ashish Mukherji: Esystems, Inc.; 343 West Passaic Avenue, A; Bloomfield, NJ 07003
Dr. Amit Mukhopadhyay Ph.D.: Lucent Technologies; 101 Crawfords Corner Road, Room 4K-467; Holmdel, NJ 07733
Mr. Preetish Mukundan: Warner Lambert Company; 776 Eves Drive; Hillsborough, NJ 08876
Mr. Patrick Muldoon: MIS System Consultants, Ltd.; 100 Maincentre, Suite 13; Northville, MI 48167-1594
Mr. John Mulkerin: Larscom Inc.; 1845 McCandless Drive; Milpitas, CA 95035-8046
Mr. James Mullaney: Administrative Office of the U.S. Courts; One Columbus Circle NE, Suite 3-280; Washington, DC 20754
Mr. Brian Muller: Hyatt Regency Beaver Creek; P.O.

Box 1595; Avon, CO 81620-1595

Mr. Joseph Mullican: Costello Strain and Company; 633 Chestnut Street, Suite 510; Chattanooga, TN 37450-0501

Mr. Daniel L. Mullikin: Emery World Wide; 2701 Northwest Vaughn Street; Portland, OR 97210-5311

Dr. James L. Mullins Ph.D.: Villanova University; 800 Lancaster Avenue; Villanova, PA 19085

Mr. Steve Mullins: New Horizons; 11 Concord Street; Concord, NH 03301-3604

Mr. Ricky Mumbru: Sterling Software; 5800 Tennyson Parkway, #MS 142; Plano, TX 75024

Mr. Dale Mumper: Entre Computer Center; 13400 Bishops Lane, Suite 270; Brookfield, WI 53005-6237

Mr. Kyung T. Mun: Pagemart Wireless; 3333 Lee Parkway, Suite 100; Dallas, TX 75219

Mr. Richard K. Munday: Integral Corporation; 1807 South Washington Street, Suite 110; Naperville, IL 60565

Mr. Paul Murkidjanian: Raytheon Company; 305 Mount Auburn Street; Watertown, MA 02472-1956

Ms. Anne Murphy: Cincinnati Bell Telephone; 201 East 4th Street; Cincinnati, OH 45202-4122

Ms. Anne-Marie Murphy: USDA National Finance Center; P.O. Box 60000; New Orleans, LA 70160

Mr. Robert Murphy: Keane Incorporated; 9800 Shelbyville Road; Louisville, KY 40222

Ms. Carmen Murray: MARTA; 3409 Tree Summit Parkway; Duluth, GA 30096

Mr. David Murrell: Xede Consulting Group; 21765 Outer Drive; Dearborn, MI 48124-3970

Mr. Christopher Murtland: Imij Corporation; 1428 Glade Street, Apartment 1; Winston Salem, NC 27101-2643

Mr. Kumar Murugaiyan: SKM, Inc.; 1227 Sanderson Lane; Allen, TX 75002-4469

Mr. Sabanayagam Murugiah: Oracle Corporation; P.O. Box 1512; Elmhurst, IL 60126-8512

Mr. Shakeel Mustafa: World Com; 15520 Tustin Village Way, Apartment 2; Tustin, CA 92780-4271

Mr. Bill Musty: Computer Connection; 48 Taft Avenue; White River Junction, VT 05001-1617

Mr. Jeffrey Myers: Cornerstone Career Learning Center; 159 4th Street SW; Huron, SD 57350-2406

Mr. Michael Myers: Bureau of Transportation Statistics; 1569 Colonial Terrace, Suite 268; Arlington, VA 72209

Mr. Nathan C. Myers: Whitko Middle School; 710 North State Road 5; Larwill, IN 46764-9776

Mr. Robert W. Myers: Quokka Sports; 525 Brannan Street; San Francisco, CA 94107

Mr. Scott Myklebust: Montgomery County; 301 North Thompson; Conroe, TX 77301

Ms. Barbara R. Myles: Boston Public Library; 700 Boylsten Street; Boston, MA 02116-2813

Mr. Dilip Nagaraja: Stonebridge Technologies; 14800 Landmark Boulevard; Dallas, TX 75240

Mr. John Nagel: GE Capital Fleet Services; 3 Capital Drive; Eden Prairie, MN 55344-3890

Mr. Mike Najarion: 15 Alan Avenue; Ridgewood, NJ 07452-2403

Ms. Julie Najjar: MCI World Com; 2400 North Glenville Drive; Richardson, TX 75082-4354

Mr. Aki Nakamura: Nomura Research Institute; 40 Wall Street, 34th Floor; New York, NY 10005

Mr. Andy Nallappan: Hewlett Packard; 41043 Pajaro Drive; Fremont, CA 94539-4433

Mr. Nalaka Nanayakkara: All State Communications; 8053 Deering Avenue; Canoga Park, CA 91304

Mr. David Nance: Williamsburg Community Hospital; 301 Monticello Avenue; Williamsburg, VA 23185-2882

Mr. Ravinder Nanda: Software Architects, Inc.; 1511 Northwest Shore Blvd., #970; Tampa, FL 33607

Mr. Hilario Y. Napoles: Timex Corporation; 2215 Crisp Drive; Little Rock, AR 72203

Mr. Keith A. Narr: Dayton Hudson Corporation; 6100 151st Lane NW; Ramsey, MN 55303-5637

Mr. Steve Narvaez: City Winter Park; 401 South Park Avenue; Winter Park, FL 32789-4386

Mr. Arshad Naseem: Made Corporation; 17 Captain Parker Arms, #15; Lexington, MA 02421

Mr. Tom Nataloni: Tenet Health care; 1500 Market Street, Floor 2401; Philadelphia, PA 19102-2100

Mr. Thomas Nather: Penske Logistics; 3750 Park East Drive; Beachwood, OH 44122-4308

Ms. Beverly Navarro: Pinkerton Computer Consultants Inc.; 104 Williams Avenue; Jersey City, NJ 07304-1129

Ms. Adriene Nazaretian: Yale University; Information Technology Services; P.O. Box 208089; New Haven, CT 06520-8089

Mr. Anthony C. Neading: Shaw Industrial, Inc.; P. O. Drawer 2128 MD 068-15; Dalton, GA 30722

Mrs. Rolanda E. Neal: Systems and Computer Technology; 9 Science Court; Columbia, SC 29203-9344

Mr. Mark Nebeker: Insatel; 2977 McFarlane Road; Coconut Grove, FL 33133

Mr. Mark Neckerman: City Of Columbia; 701 East Broadway; Columbia, MO 65201-4472

Mr. Eric J. Neef: Cap Gemini; 5613 Dtc Parkway, Suite 620; Englewood, CO 80111-3034

Mr. Anthony Negri: Psych Management, Inc.; P.O. Box 746; Farmington, CT 06034-0746

Mr. Greg Neimeth: South Western Bell Services; 10802 Executive Center Drive; Little Rock, AR 72211-4318

Mr. Roman Nektalov: National Media Technologies; 14418 73rd Avenue; Flushing, NY 11367-2413

Mr. John S. Nell: TIAA-CREF; 730 Third Avenue; New York, NY 10017-3206

Mr. Bruce Nelson: The Computer Store; 1200 Coolidge Avenue; Minot, ND 58701-7287

Dr. Burke Nelson Ph.D.: Logicon RDA; P.O. Box 9377; Albuquerque, NM 87119-9377

Mr. Dean Nelson: Optima Engineers and Constructors, Inc.; 744-4 Avenue SW, #700; Calgary, Alberta, Canada T2P 3T4

Mr. Jim Nelson: Vector Technologies, Inc.; 41 East Washington Street; Indianapolis, IN 46204-3517

Mr. Keith Nelson: Software Technologies Corporation; 404 East Huntington Drive; Monrovia, CA 91016-3633

Mr. Lanc M. Nelson: United States Air Force; 299 Carmel Avenue, Apartment K-75; Marina, CA 93933

Mr. Matthew A. Nelson: NCC Internet/Northwest Arkansas Networks; 2602 East Matthews; Jonesboro, AR 72401

Mr. Scott Nelson: 517 Abbott Street, Suite B; Salinas, CA 93901-4325

Mr. Shawn Nelson: Adelphia Business Solutions; 3050 Estate Drive; Oakdale, PA 15071-1081

Mr. Stephen Nelson: Sturdy Savings Bank; 9217 Third Avenue; Stone Harbor, NJ 08247

Mr. Tamra Nelson: Outagamie County; 410 South Walnut Street; Appleton, WI 54911-5936

Mr. T. Netherton: Lucent Technologies; 13225 North 26th Avenue; Phoenix, AZ 85029-1453

Mr. Chad L. Netwig: The Computer Guy Company; 23210 Cedar Creek Terrace; Moreno Valley, CA 92557

Mr. Ari Neugroschl: Schick Technologies Inc.; 3100 47th Avenue, Suite 5; Long Island City, NY 11101-3068

Mr. Christopher Neves: Trimat Software & Consulting; P.O. Box 31162; Tucson, AZ 85751-1162

Ms. Kelley Newell: Birch Telecom, Incorporated; 2020 Baltimore Avenue; Kansas City, MO 64108

Mr. Mark Newell: St. James Hospital; 1423 Chicago Road; Chicago Heights, IL 60411-3483

Ms. Toni Newkirk: Bell Atlantic; 2055 L Street NW, 7th Floor; Washington, DC 20036-4905

Ms. Janice Newlove: Lifescan; 1000 Gibraltar Drive; Milpitas, CA 95035-6312

Mr. Craig Newmaker: DSoft Technology, Inc.; 2510 Black Diamond Terrace; Colorado Springs, CO 80918-0537

Mr. Joshua Newman: Sharkbyte; 1141 Harriet Street; Palo Alto, CA 94301-3433

Mr. Chris Newton: AMR Research; 2 Oliver Street; Boston, MA 02109-4901

Mr. Sean Newton: Mid South Connections; 1770b Madison Street; Clarksville, TN 37043-4913

Mr. Dale Neyman: Nationwide Insurance Company; 800 Graves Mill Road; Lynchburg, VA 24502-4218

Ms. Alice Ng: Chase Manhattan Mortgage Corporation; 343 Thornall Street 8th Floor; Edison, NJ 08837

Mr. Ken Chung-Lai Ng: United Canada Network Solution; P.O. Box 47026; Scarborough, Ontario, Canada M1P 4Z7

Ms. Brittanie Ngo: Ingram Micro; 1038 South Rexford Lane; Anaheim, CA 92808-2334

Mr. Tang T. Ngo: Naval Research Lab; 4555 Overlook Avenue SW, Code 5595; Washington, DC 20375

Mr. Anh T. Nguyen: Maxim Integrated Products, Inc.; 120 San Gabriel; Sunnyvale, CA 94086

Mr. John Chung Nguyen: Calvert Hall College; 8102 Lasalle Road; Towson, MD 21286-8022

Mr. Michael Nguyen: Actel Corporation; 955 East Argues Avenue; Sunnyvale, CA 94086-4533

Mr. Minh Nguyen: IBM; 11303 Nutwood Cove, #9564; Austin, TX 78726-1300

Mr. Thuc D. Nguyen: A&T Systems, Inc.; 12520 Prosperity Drive, Suite 300; Silver Spring, MD 20904

Mr. Oleg Ni: Marshall Electronics; 5649 Mesmer Avenue; Culver City, CA 90230-6363

Mr. Dan K. Nichols: Computer Resource Management; P. O. Box 1766; Jefferson City, MO 65102-1766

Mr. Daniel Nichols: Channell Commercial Corporation; 26040 Ynez Road; Temecula, CA 92591-6033

Mr. Dan Nicholson: Computer Associates; 2400 Cabot Drive; Lisle, IL 60532-3621

Mr. Michael Nicholson: Mactac; 4560 Darrow Road; Stow, OH 44224-1898

Mr. Richard Nickelson: Pacific Telecommunications; 2454 South Beretania Street, Suite 302; Honolulu, HI 96826-1502

Mr. Gary Nickerson: Jmj Baking Corporation; 3811 23rd Street; Long Island City, NY 11101-3617

Ms. Carol Nicol: Kirkwood Community College; P.O. Box 2068; Cedar Rapids, IA 52406-2068

Mr. Joseph Nicol: Structured Management Systems; 7740 Shrader Road; Richmond, VA 23228-2500

Dr. Jerry Nieh Ph.D.: AEMP Company; 13312 Lakefront Drive; Earth City, MO 63045

Mr. Mark A. Niemi: R K N Technologies; 13664 Windmoor Drive; South Lyon, MI 48178-8147

Mr. Jim Nikonchik: American Management Systems; 12601 Fair Lakes Circle, 6th Floor; Fairfax, VA 22033-4902

Mr. Richard C. Nissel: West Virginia Treasurer's Office; 1900 Kanawha Boulevard East, Room EB-96; Charleston, WV 25305

Mr. Edward M. Nissen: 1284 Idylberry Rd.; San Rafael, CA 94903

Ms. Kathleen Nissley: Sterling Software; 10811 International Drive; Rancho Cordova, CA 95670

Mr. David Noble: Ray Morgan Company; 554 Rio Lindo Avenue; Chico, CA 95926-1876

Mr. William Noble: Raytheon; 2317 32nd Street; Santa Monica, CA 90405-2027

Mr. Claude Nogess: LHS Communications Systems, Inc.; 6 Condourse Parkway; Atlanta, GA 30328

Mr. Dave M. Nolan: University of Wisconsin; 1450 Linden Drive, #216; Madison, WI 53706-1562

Ms. Kathleen Nolan: Centenary College; 400 Jefferson Street; Hackettstown, NJ 07840-2100

Mr. Ken B. Noland: Loki Works; 245 4th Street ,#405; Bremerton, WA 98337

Ms. Sharon D. Nolen: AT&T; 15 West Sixth Street; Cincinnati, OH 45202

Mr. Marc Nolting: Anthem; 120 Monument Circle; Indianapolis, IN 46204-4906

Mr. Eric Norberg: Summit Technology Group; 2269 Sanford Road; Decatur, GA 30033-5524

Mr. John Norlander: Gateway Partners Inc.; 9255 Towne Centre Drive; San Diego, CA 92121-3033

Mr. Jeffery S. Norman: Kirkland & Ellis; 200 East Randolph Drive, Suite 5300; Chicago, IL 60657

Mr. Dan Norris: Celeritas Technologies; 7101 College Boulevard, 6th Floor; Overland Park, KS 66210-1823

Mr. Niles North H.S.: Niles North High School; 9800 Lawler Avenue; Skokie, IL 60077-1215

Mr. Kenny Norton: Dataforce Systems; 3200 Cobb Galleria Parkway, Suite 250; Atlanta, GA 30339-5942

Ms. Anne Marie Notarthomas: Rescue Mission; 120 Gifford Street; Syracuse, NY 13202-2341

Mr. Stephen R. Novak: Chubb Computer Services; 610 Herndon Parkway; Herndon, VA 20170-5478

Mr. Juan Novoa: SABRE, Inc.; 3013 Golden Gate Drive; Plano, TX 75025-4226

Ms. Kathleen Novosel: Gary T. Novosel & Associates; 10 King Street; Massena, NY 13662-2325

Mr. John Novotny: Circuit City Stores; 9954 Mayland Drive; Richmond, VA 23233

Mr. Ken Nowicki: Avnet Inc.; 2211 South 47th Street; Phoenix, AZ 85034-6403

Mr. James E. Nuckols: EDP Consultants; 3439 Shakertown Road; Dayton, OH 45430-1421

Mr. Singrung Numsangvanich: Lincoln University; 2293 Turk Boulevard, #1; San Francisco, CA 94118-4434

Ms. Melissa Nunley: Bluefield State College, Center for Economic Enhancement; 219 Rock Street; Bluefield, WV 24701-2198

Mr. Micheal Nunnally: Rheem Manufacturing Company; 559 Hollow Wood Road; Montgomery, AL 36109-3305

Dr. Hyacinth S. Nwana Ph.D.: BT PLC, UK; B61, 2/PP5 BT Laboratories, Martiesham Health; Ipswich, United Kingdom IP53B5

Mr. John Nyakoe Nyasani: Romac International, Inc.; 2630 Pleasant Avenue, Apartment 301; Minneapolis, MN 55408-1449

Mr. Erik Nyberg: Systems Integration, Incorporated; 3200 Haskell Avenue; Lawrence, KS 66046

Mr. William Boli Nyirenda: Ezugha, Musonda, and Company; Angoni House, Obote Avenue, P. O. Box 22144; Kitwe, Zambia

Mr. Charles O'Banion: Pittsburg State University; 702 Village Drive; Pittsburg, KS 66762-3540

Ms. Leona O'Brien: Data Communication Systems, Inc.; 135 Newbury Street; Framingham, MA 01701-4535

Mr. Neil William O'Connell: APL; 1703 Rosewood Lane; Chadds Ford, PA 19317-9709

Ms. Christine O'Connor: Electronic Data Systems; 50 Parker; Irvine, CA 92618-1604

Mr. Kevin O'Connor: Q Systems, Inc.; 5086 De Quincey Drive; Fairfax, VA 22032-2435

Ms. Peggy O'Connor: Ameritech Cellular; 777 Big Timber Road; Elgin, IL 60123

Mr. Dennis O'Donnell: CompuCorp; 13733 Southeast 272nd Street; Kent, WA 98042

Mr. Victor M. O'Ferrall: Cendant IT; 900 Old Country Road; Garden Cit, NY 11530-2128

Mr. Patrick O'Hagerty: Fleet Technology Solutions; 69 State Street; Albany, MA 12207

Ms. Nadine O'Halla: Artery & Hadden; 925 Euclid Avenue, Suite 1100; Cleveland, OH 44115-1475

Ms. Dolores O'Hara: Reliance Insurance Company; 3 Parkway; Philadelphia, PA 19102-1321

Mr. Stephen L. O'Hearn: Corbinian Technologies, Inc.; 12315 Manvel Lane; Bowie, MD 20715-2947

Mr. John O'Mara: Ryorson Tull; 600 Quail Ridge Drive; Westmont, IL 60559

Mr. Doug O'Neil: DataStudy, Inc.; 199 Cherry Hill Road; Parsippany, NJ 07054-1112

Mr. Sean O'Neill: Marsworks; P.O. Box 83001, Rpo Vista Centre; Ottawa, Ontario, Canada K1V 1A3

Mr. Roy Oakes: McHugh Software International;; 20700 Swenson Drive, Suite 400; Waukesha, WI 53186-0904

Mr. Farhang Obohhat: Multitasking Systems Inc.; 9037 Piney Grove Drive; Fairfax, VA 22031-2022

Mrs. Tracy Obrien: Konover & Associates Inc.; 2410 Albany Avenue; West Hartford, CT 06117-2514

Mrs. Jean Oby: Bridgestone Firestone; 6275 Eastland Road; Cleveland, OH 44142-1301

Mr. Michael J. Occhipinti: Saddleback Memorial Foundation; 24451 Health Center Drive; Laguna Hills, CA 92653-3689

Mr. Rob J. Oconnell: Toys R Us; 461 From Road; Paramus, NJ 07652-3526

Mr. Darryl Odom: EDS; 12369-D Sunrise Valley Drive; Reston, VA 20191-3415

Mr. John Oeffner: Missouri Division of Family Services; 615 East 13th Street, Room 407; Kansas City, MO 64106-2829

Ms. Brittany Ohman: Joshu D. Smith and Associates; 1380 Benton Street; Idaho Falls, ID 83401-4254

Mr. Hans Ohman: Nordstrom and Ohman, WCJ; P.O. Box 7581; Stockholm, Sweden 10393

Mr. Junko Ohmori: ESSEC Japan Representative Office; Sumitomo Fudesan, Kameido, Building 9F, 1-42-20; Kameido Kotoku, Japan 136

Mr. Tomoyuki Ohsawa: Sony Urban Entertainment, Inc.; 6-7-35 Kitashinagawa (Mz), Shinagawa-Ku; Japan 141

Mr. Bent Okhoun: Okholm Informatik A/S; Blokken 13; Birkeroed, Denmark 3460

Mr. Michael Okneski:

Computer Task Group; 737 Delaware Avenue; Buffalo, NY 14209
Mr. Scott Olafson: Minndata, Inc.; 250 3rd Street, P.O. Box 1069; Tracy, MN 56175-1069
Mr. Dwayne Oland: USAMISSA; 1422 Sulton Drive; Fort Detrick, MD 21702
Dr. Samuel Olanoff: Editscan & Samuel Olanoff's Desktop Publishing, Etc.; 79 East Piedmont Avenue; Port Orange, FL 32119-2433
Mr. Kenneth Olausson: The Interactive Institute; Box 24081; Stockholm, Sweden 10450
Ms. Mercedes Olejar: ModelWire, Inc.; 594 Broadway; New York, NY 10012
Mr. Robert Olfert: Service Master of Seattle; P.O. Box 670; Yelm, WA 98597-0670
Mr. Arturo J. Oliver: MicroStrategy; 8000 Towers Crescent Drive 1600; Vienna, VA 22182
Mr. Erik Olsen: Infoseek Corporation; 3809 Meridian Avenue North; Seattle, WA 98103-8344
Mr. Gary Olsen: Compaq Computer Corporation; 5555 Windward Parkway West; Alpharetta, GA 30004-3895
Mr. Kenneth R. Olsen: D & K Consulting; 2264 Alta Canyon Drive; Sandy, UT 84093
Mr. Wayne Olsen: Fluke Corporation; 13412 91st Place NE; Kirkland, WA 98034-1852
Mr. Gary Olson: H.B. Fuller Company; P.O. Box 64385; St. Paul, MN 55164-0385
Mr. Charles R. Olszewski: Rutgers University; 65 Davidson Road, #101; Piscataway, NJ 08854
Mr. Bob Omdahl: Great Plains Software; 1701 38th Street SW; Fargo, ND 58103
Mr. Olawace Omiteru: Geocon Technologies; 900 South Walden Way Unit 204; Aurora, CO 80017-3490
Mr. Yoshinori Ono: Sumitomo Yale Company, Ltd.; 2-75 Daitocho, Obu; Aichi, Japan 474-8555
Mr. Cornelis Oosterom: Fitch IBCA Inc.; One State Street Plaza; New York, NY 10004
Mr. Jonathan Openshaw: Avnet CMG; 14492 North 91st Street; Scottsdale, AZ 85260-7036
Mr. Joseph Openshaw: Meijer, Inc.; 2929 Walker Northwest; Grand Rapids, MI 49544
Mr. Paul A. Orme: Miami Valley Hospital; 1 Wyoming Street; Dayton, OH 45409
Ms. Erika Dawn Orrick: Fitch, Inc.; 4893 Stillbreeze Court; Columbus, OH 43230-5131
Mr. Stalin Alejandro Orta: Baan; CCCT 1ra. Etapa Piso 6 Of. 628 Chuao; Caracas, Venezuela 1062
Mr. Jeremy Ortego: Ville Platte Medical; 412 East Magnolia Street; Ville Platte, LA 70586-5534
Mr. Arthur J. Ortiz: New Horizons Computer Learning Center; 544-23rd Street; Rock Island, IL 61201
Dr. Johnny N. Ortiz Ph.D.: University of Missouri; 1300 North Bishop Avenue, Suite 1; Rolla, MO 65401-2163
Mr. Victor Ortiz: 3COM; 3800 Golf Road; Rolling Meadows, IL 60008-4022
Ms. Cindy L. Orwig: The Desk Top Shop, Inc.; P.O. Box 422061; Atlanta, GA 30342-9061
Mr. Anthony W. Orzechowski: PPG Industries; 440 College Park Drive; Monroeville, PA 15146
Mr. Mark Daniel Orzechowski: Cheektowaga Police; 3223 Union Road; Cheektowaga, NY 14227
Mr. Efosa Osayamwen: Cendant; 6000 Atrium Way; Mount Lauren, NJ 08054-3918
Mr. Andrew C. Osborn: Wells Fargo & Company; 201 North Sunrise Avenue; Roseville, CA 95661-2904
Ms. Lara Osteen: Bell South Mobility DCS; 317 Zimalcrest Drive; Columbia, SC 29210-6833
Mr. J.D. Ott: Sprint; 330 South Valley View Boulevard; Las Vegas, NV 89152-0002
Mr. Norbert Ott: Aucotec, Inc.; 750 East Lake Cook Road; Buffalo Grove, IL 60089-1816
Ms. Lisa Otts: Computer Sciences Corporation; 1919 Allen Parkway, Floor 1; Houston, TX 77019-2506
Mr. Mostafa Ouraie: Sina Group; 20430 Town Center Lane, Suite 5C; Cupertino, CA 95014-3207
Mr. Steve Ovadia: ACORD Corporation; 1 Blue Hill Plaza; Pearl River, NY 10965-3104
Mr. Darren Overfelt: Indiana University; 799 West Michigan Street, ET 012; Indianapolis, IN 46202-5132
Mr. James Overley: Wal-Mart; 66 North Yearling Road; Columbus, OH 43213
Mr. Edward Owen: Network Information Systems; 1518 North Atherton Street; State College, PA 16803-3041
Ms. Carolyn Owens: Indecon, Inc.; 4070 Fair Oaks Drive; Franklin, IN 46131-7420
Ms. Linda L. Owens: Perdue Farms; 2300 Industrial Drive; Monterey, TN 38574
Ms. Dana Oyler: Allwire, Inc.; P.O. Box 12602; Fresno, CA 93778-2602
Mr. Francesco Pablo Ozegna: Azienda Risorse Idriche di Napoli; Via Costantinopoli 98; Naples, Italy 80138
Mr. Dean Pacheco: DecisionOne; 20 Forbes Road; Northborough, MA 01532-2501
Mr. Victor Pacilio: Concept Consultants; 1243 Clearwater Drive; New Braunfels, TX 78130-3016
Mr. Kevin Packingham: Sprint PCS; 4900 Main Street, Floor 5; Kansas City, MO 64112-2630
Ms. Joy George Padamadan: NASD; 1390 Piccard Drive; Rockville, MD 20886
Mr. Rajesh Padmanabhan: CSC Consulting; 1 Newton Executive Park; Newton Lower Falls, MA 02462
Mr. Michael A. Paez: IBM Global Services; 1300 Kershaw Drive; Raleigh, NC 27609-5549
Ms. Heather Page: CRHC; 69 Loudon Road; Concord, NH 03301
Ms. Jianina Pagliarini: Digital Broadband; 76 Salina Street; Providence, RI 02908-2642
Mr. Frank C. Pagoria: PC Upgrades & More; P.O. Box 139; Aberdeen, KY 42201-0139
Mr. Allan Pahl: Connecting Point; P.O. Box 248; Green Bay, WI 54305-0248
Mr. Pavan Pai: Paragon Computer Professionals; 706B Village Drive South; North Brunswick, NJ 08902-2823
Mr. Sandhya Pai: University of Connecticut; 368 Fairfield Road, #41D; Storrs Manfield, CT 06269-2041
Mr. Soumendra Nath Paik: Oracle Corporation; 5210 Bullock Point, Apartment 207; Colorado Springs, CO 80919
Mr. Shawn Pala: Baldwin & Lyons; 1099 North Meridian Street; Indianapolis, IN 46204-1075
Mr. Vinoo Palayoor: Staples; 17 Liberty Street; Waltham, MA 02452
Ms. Jennifer Pallas: Aetna US Healthcare; 2636 Sir Thomas Way; Williamsburg, VA 23185-7945
Mr. Dale A. Palmer: Fountain Net Inc.; 312 West 8th Street; Kansas City, MO 64105-1513
Mr. Dale Palmer: Nortel Cala, Inc..; 1500 Concord Terrace; Fort Lauderdale, FL 33323-2808
Mr. Ronald Palmer: Bernstein, Shur, Sawyer; 100 Middle Street; Portland, ME 04104
Mr. Terry Palmer: Modtech Inc.; 2830 Barrett Avenue; Perris, CA 92572
Mr. Thaworn Panchasrirat: ColonialTax Compliance Company; 720 Meadow Walk Avenue; Lawrenceville, GA 30044-7555
Mr. Ho Yuen Pang: University of Arizona; 1230 East Speedway Boulevard, Ece Building; Tucson, AZ 85721
Mr. Bill Pantazopoulos: Mitotix Inc.; 1 Kendall Square, Suite 600; Cambridge, MA 02139-1562
Mr. Robert Panyi: Mellon Bank; Three Mellon Bank Center, AIM #153-1230; Pittsburgh, PA 15259
Mr. Patrick Panzenbock: Creative and Response Research; 500 North Michigan Avenue, Suite 1200; Chicago, IL 60611-3781
Mr. Carlos A. Panzica: Ryder Integrated Logistics; 21093 Escondido Way; Boca Raton, FL 33433
Mr. Jung Pao: New York City Board of Education; 5301 20th Avenue; Brooklyn, NY 11204
Mr. Dan Paramesh: Roper Scientific; 3660 Quakerbridge Road; Trenton, NJ 08619-1208
Ms. Julie Paratian: France Telecom Inc.; 1270 Avenue of the Americas, Suite 28; New York, NY 10020-1801
Mr. Paolo O. Parise: Featherlite Industries; 100 Englehard Drive; Aurora, Ontario, Canada L4G 3V2
Ms. Amy K. Parizo: Network Associates, Incorporated; 171 Northwest 152nd Avenue; Pembroke Pines, FL 33028
Mr. Greg Park: City of San Leandro; 835 East 14th Street; San Leandro, CA 94577
Mr. Brad Parker: Vyzynz International; 155 North 400 West Suite 125; Salt Lake City, UT 84103-1136
Mr. Braden Parker: Market Place Print; 600 Grant Street, Suite 4800; Pittsburgh, PA 15219-2801
Ms. Elma Parker: L V Stockard Middle School; 2300 South Ravinia Drive; Dallas, TX 75211-8914
Mr. Michael Parker: LTTB Inc.; 355 North Lantana Street, Suite 663; Camarillo, CA 93010-6038
Ms. Patricia D. Parker: Maryland Port Administration; 2310 Broening Highway; Baltimore, MD 21224-6639
Mr. Richard J. Parkington: Pricewaterhouse Coopers; 12902 Federal Systems Park Drive; Fairfax, VA 22033
Mr. William S. Parks Jr.: Citgo Petroleum Corporation; P.O. Box 3758; Tulsa, OK 74102
Mr. Joe Parlas: Global Knowledge; 17 Andrews Court; Parkton, MD 21120-9260
Mr. Nicholas J. Parrella: Picture Network International; 5200 Richardson Drive; Fairfax, VA 22032-3925
Mr. Keith Parris: Logicon Syscon; P.O. Box 1480, DSD Rural Route 206; Dahlgren, VA 22448-1480
Mr. Don Parrish-Bell: Visi-Com, Inc.; 10052 Mesa Ridge Court; San Diego, CA 92121-3984
Mr. Glen Parrott: Janus Capital Corporation; 100 Fillmore Street; Denver, CO 80206-4916
Mr. Jim Parsons: Aspen Technology; 1126 Lake Estates Drive; Sugar Land, TX 77478-5623
Ms. Kay Parsons: Carrollton Police Department; P.O. Box 1949; Carollton, GA 30117-7249
Ms. Mary Pascarella: Ambling Companies, Inc.; 348 Enterprise Drive; Valdosta, GA 31601-5169
Mr. Ismat A. Pasha: Teleglobe; 11480 Commerce Park Drive; Reston, VA 20171-4420
Ms. Sheri Pasqual: Axiss Advertising; 2100 Ponce De Leon Boulevard, Suite 1070; Coral Gables, FL 33134-5226
Mr. E. Pasternak: DMR Consulting Group; P.O. Box 154; Holmdel, NJ 07733-0154
Mr. Mark P. Patchett: Intertec Publishing; 9800 Metcalf Avenue; Overland Park, KS 66212-2286
Ms. Susan Pate: Century Tel; 100 Century Park Drive; Monroe, LA 71203-2042
Mr. Truptesh Patel: AT&T; 1A-38, 20 Independence Boulevard; Warren, NJ 07059
Mr. Viral Patel: Home Depot; 250 Summer Hill Circle; Stockbridge, GA 30281-6497
Mr. Yagnesh J. Patel: Call Sciences, Inc.; 98 Orion Road; Piscataway, NJ 08854-5423
Mr. David Patinella: Collective Intelligence; P.O. Box 617727; Chicago, IL 60661-7727
Mr. Asha Patki: Apex Business Systems, Inc.; 742 West Tierra Buena Lane; Phoenix, AZ 85023-4400
Mr. Mike Patnode: Spyrus; 667 Garland Terrace East; Sunnyvale, CA 94086-7928
Ms. Sharon L. Patterson-Betz: Clayton Public Schools; 300 West Chestnut Street; Clayton, NJ 08312-1700
Ms. Lisa Patton: Xerox Connect; 2950 North Loop West; Houston, TX 77092-8839
Ms. Susan Patton: Sprint; 2002 Edmund Holley Drive; Reston, VA 20191
Ms. Stephanie M. Patzius: Hollander Consulting, Inc.; 180 Weidman Road, Suite 117; Manchester, MO 63021
Mr. Jay G. Paulin: Bell Atlantic Direct Graphics; 2500 Monroe Boulevard; Norristown, PA 19403-2418
Mr. Michael S. Pavlik: Service Ware, Inc.; 333 Allegheny Avenue; Oakmont, PA 15139-2066
Mr. Sebastian Pawlowski: JMS Worldwide; 1200 South Washington Street, 428 East; Alexandria, VA 22314
Mr. Mike Payment: Johns Brothers, Inc.; 1384 Ingleside Road; Norfolk, VA 23502-1916
Mr. Bruce Payne: Northwest Analytical Inc.; 519 Southwest Avenue; Portland, OR 97205-3221
Ms. Debbie Payne: Pro-Business; 4125 Hopyard Road; Pleasanton, CA 94588-8534
Mr. Lee Payssa: Parfoam Products Inc.; 239 Van Rensselaer Street; Buffalo, NY 14210-1345
Mr. Thomas Pazel Sr.: Merck-Medco Managed Care, LLC; 100 Summit Avenue; Montvale, NJ 07662-3920
Mrs. Roni Peacock: Meadowbrook Insurance Group; 10985 Cody Street, Suite 135; Overland Park, KS 66210-1224
Mr. Kirk Pearson: Trim Systems, Inc.; 701 South Orchard Street; Seattle, WA 98108-3428
Mr. Douglas W. Peck: Braden River Middle School; 1711 91st Street NW; Brandenton, FL 34209-8143
Ms. Lindsay Pedder: Fluor Daniel Corporation; 1 Fluor Daniel Drive; Aliso Viejo, CA 92698-1000
Mr. Anthony Pedretti: Trans Union; 3726 South 58th Avenue; Cicero, IL 60804-4205
Mr. Jeff Peduto: Excel Partners; 1427 Girard Street; Mamaroneck, NY 10543-1310
Mr. Mark Peery: ESI - MicroVision; 7600 Quattro Drive; Chanhassen, MN 55317
Mr. Wayne Pehrson: Internet Computer, Inc.; 147 East 400 South; Blanding, UT 84511-3017
Ms. Sharon X. Pei: Tyco Electronics; 100 Chelmsford Street; Lowell, MA 01851
Mr. Richard Peirce: Vanderweil Engineers; 274 Summer Street; Boston, MA 02210-1106
Mr. Paul Peitzmeier: Vatterott College; 5898 North Main Street; Joplin, MO 64801-9611
Mr. Semih Pekol: Turk Ekonomi Bankasi A.S.; Medis-i Mebusan Cad. 35; Istanbul, Turkey 80040
Mr. Scott Pelham: GTE; 8400 Esters Boulevard, Suite 550; Irving, TX 75063-2231
Ms. Susan J. Pelski: Converse Network Systems; 300 Federal Street; Andover, MA 01810-1038
Mr. Ed Pena: GP Associates; PMB 111; Austin, TX 78727
Mr. Larry Pendarvis: First National Bank of Sharp; P.O. Box 8; Ash Flat, AR 72513-0008
Mr. Trevor Pendleton: Nova Southeastern University; 3100 Southwest 9th Avenue; Ft. Lauderdale, FL 33315-3025
Mr. Bo Peng: Lehman Brothers, Inc.; 3 World Financial Center, #9th; New York, NY 10285-0001
Mr. Robert Penn: Teledyne Electronic Technologies; 12964 Panama Street; Los Angeles, CA 90066-6599
Mr. Troy Penny: Johnson Controls, Inc.; 3655 North Point Parkway; Alpharetta, GA 30005-2025
Mr. Eric Penot: Sky Sites Inc.; 161 West 75th Street, Apartment 13E; New York, NY 10023
Mr. Erhardt Peper: West Heights Manufacturing; 1665 Highland Road West; Kitchener, Ontario, Canada N2N 3K5
Mr. Hugh Pepper: George C. Moore Company; P.O. Box 236; Edenton, NC 27932-0236
Ms. Karin Percario: Bourne, Noll & Kenyon; P.O. Box 690; Summit, NJ 07902-0690
Mr. Rukshan Perera: Philip Morris Latin America; 800 Westchester Avenue; Ryebrook, NY 10573
Mr. Alfredo M. Perez: Helen of Troy, LP; 6827 Market; El Paso, TX 79915
Mr. Anthony Perez: Cablevison/Optimum Online; 360 Crossways Park Drive; Woodbury, NY 11797-2050
Mrs. Colette Perez: Central Dupage Health System; 25 North Winfield Road; Winfield, IL 60190
Mr. Milton Perez: Chesebrough Ponds Manufacturing Company; P.O. Box 2005; Las Piedras, Puerto Rico 00771-2005
Mr. Oscar Perez: Attachmate Corporation; 1 Penn Plaza, Suite 2801; New York, NY 10119-2223
Mr. Rick Perez: EDS/ American Express Bank Account; 200 Vesey Street, 23rd Floor; New York, NY 10285-1000
Mr. James A. Pergulizzi: Autodesk, Inc.; 3900 Civic Center Drive; San Rafael, CA 94903
Mr. Christopher A. Perri: Eau Claire Press Company; 701 South Farwell Street; Eau Claire, WI 54701-3831
Ms. Denise M. Perrotta: Hill & Barlow P.C.; 257 Granite Street; Quincy, MA 02169
Ms. Kay Perry: Sprint; 330 South Valley View Boulevard; Las Vegas, NV 89107
Mr. Ken Perryman: Monroe County B.O.C.C.; 1200 Truman Avenue, Suite 211; Key West, FL 33043
Mr. Edward L. Persley: Greater Los Angeles VA Healthcare System; 11301 Wilshire Boulevard; Los Angeles, CA 90073
Mr. Steven J. Person: Lansing Police Department; 120 West Michigan Avenue; Lansing, MI 48933-1603
Mr. Yasir Pervaiz: Unistrut; 1140 West Thorndale Avenue; Itasca, IL 60143
Mr. Robert Pervin: Foldcraft Company; 615 Centennial Drive; Kenyon, MN 55946-1297
Mrs. Mandy Pet: Oracle Corporation; 9821 Broken Land Parkway; Columbia, MD 21046-1145
Ms. Janet Peterkin: Federal Bureau of Prisons; 320 1st Street NW; Washington, DC 20534-0002
Ms. Elaine Peters: New York State Veterans Home; 17850 Linden Boulevard; Jamaica, NY 11434-1467
Ms. Kelly L. Peters: Niemann Foods; P.O. Box C847; Quincy, IL 62306

Mr. David Peterson: Net Technologies Incorporated; 1721 North 4th Street; Bismark, ND 58501-1715

Mr. Derek Peterson: Portal Software, Inc.; 3574 Normandy Circle; Oceanside, CA 92056-4922

Mr. G. Craig Peterson: System Design & Installation Limited; 3117 Richmond Road; Staten Island, NY 10306

Mr. Jeff Peterson: Duke Energy Trading and Marketing; 4 Triad Center, #1000; Salt Lake City, UT 84098

Mr. Tony Peterson: Data Community Networks Inc.; 1304 North Clearview Avenue, Suite B; Tampa, FL 33607-4900

Ms. Dana Petrella: Sarcom-1016; 8337 Green Meadow Drive North; Lewis Center, OH 43035-9451

Mr. Richard J. Petrucci: Technistar Corporation; 1198 Boston Avenue; Longmont, CO 80501-5856

Mr. John Petrush: Sonoco Products Company; 1 North 2nd Street; Hartsville, SC 29550-3305

Mr. James Andrew Pettigrew III: United States Southern Command; 3511 Northwest 91st Avenue; Miami, FL 33172-1217

Ms. Loretta Pettis: California Commission on Aging; 1020 9th Street, #260; Sacramento, CA 95814-3515

Mr. Jason Pettway: Norfolk Southern Railroad; 99 Spring Street SW; Atlanta, GA 30303-3677

Mr. Roger Petty Jr.: Deere & Company; 3372 East Kimberly Road; Davenport, IA 52807

Mr. Brian G. Pettyjohn: Applied Card Systems; 800 Delaware Avenue; Wilmington, DE 19801

Mr. J. Peumans: Vlaamse Vervoermaatschappij De Lijn; Hendrik Consciencestraat 1; Mechelen, Belgium 2800

Mr. Leeon J. Pezok Sr.: Fleet CCS, LLC; 1195 York Road; Warminster, PA 18974-2009

Mr. Roy Pfleger: Allied Digital Technologies; 15 Gilpin Avenue; Hauppauge, NY 11788-4791

Ms. Lenora J. Phelps: Wickliff and Hall, P.C.; 1000 Louisiana Street, Suite #5400; Houston, TX 77002

Mr. George Philippakos: St. John's University; 29 Tudor Road; Hicksville, NY 11801-5329

Mr. Scott Phillips: Infoscape Inc.; 100 Broadway; San Francisco, CA 94111

Mr. Scott Phillips: Rollins Ranches; 2194 Country Walk; Snellville, GA 30039

Mr. Jason Piccola: Ketchum Directory Advertising; 6 PPG Place; Pittsburgh, PA 15222-5425

Mr. Victor Charles Picinich: Heald College; 1605 East March Lane; Stockton, CA 95210-6632

Ms. Lindsey M. Pickle Jr.: Oracle; 3718 Ramsey Drive; Marietta, GA 30062

Ms. Angela Pierce: MCI Worldcom; 500 Clinton Center Drive; Clinton, MS 39056-5654

Mr. Greg Pierce: Geographic Data Technology; 11 Lafayette Street; Lebanon, NH 03766-1445

Mrs. Marie Pierce: Trion Technologies; 739 Beta Business Mall; Mayfield Village, OH 44143

Mr. Sean Pierce: Aldine ISD; 17306 Chapel Pine Street; Spring, TX 77379-3890

Mr. Stephen T. Pierce: Bondnet Trading Systems, Inc.; 2 Pickwick Plaza; Greenwich, CT 06830-5530

Mr. Chris Pieron: Erisco, Inc.; 1085 Morris Avenue; Union, NJ 07083-7136

Mr. Armand R. Pilotte : 3123 Broadway Street, NE; Salem, OR 97303-5041

Mr. Michael L. Pinckert: Company; 20031 Pinehurst Bend Drive; Humble, TX 77346-1750

Ms. Dominic Pino: Hazleton Area School District; 1515 West 23rd Street; Hazleton, PA 18201-1699

Mr. John Pinola Jr.: Volcano Communications; P. O. Box 1070; Pine Grove, CA 95665-1070

Mr. Maurice Pinto: Federal Express Corporation; 323 Candia Avenue; Coral Gables, FL 33134

Mr. Stefan J. Pinto: Parallax Information Design; 1300 Rock Avenue, Suite L5; North Plainfield, NJ 07060-3531

Mr. Frank Piotrowski: City of Jersey City; 325 Palisade Avenue; Jersey City, NJ 07307-1714

Ms. Lisa Pison: YCEDC; 160 Roosevelt Avenue, Suite 300; York, PA 17404-3333

Mr. Anthony Pita: SSI Group, Inc.; 5118 North 56th Street, Suite 242; Tampa, FL 33610-5427

Mr. Charles Pitsch: Foamex International, Inc.; 3005 Commercial Road; Fort Wayne, IN 46809

Mr. Ed Pittarelli: Lucent Technologies; 283 King George Road; Warren, NJ 07059

Mr. Don Pizzi: Mark Adam Associates; 256 Canterbury Road; Westfield, NJ 07090-1905

Mr. Carlo Pizzini : Via Di Vittorio 10; Corsico, Italy 720609

Mr. John W. Plain: Buck Company, Inc.; 897 Lancaster Pike; Quarryville, PA 17566-9738

Ms. Linda Plante: Evans Police Department; 1100 37 Street; Evans, CO 80620-2036

Mr. Richard W. Platt Jr.: Triangle Auto Spring Company; P.O. Box 425; Du Bois, PA 15801-1015

Mr. David Plawsky: Forguson Consulting; 610 Boggan Pointe Court; Wildwood, MO 63011

Mr. Chris Pleasants: Addison Steel; 7351 Overland Road; Orlando, FL 32810-3409

Mr. James F. Plummer: Pharmacia & Upjohn; 1829 Nottingham Avenue; Kalamazoo, MI 49001

Mr. Albert J. Plunkett: Alltel; 3800 Rosemont Boulevard Apartment 113c; Akron, OH 44333-9249

Mr. David Podell: Lion Coffee; P.O. Box 11521; Honolulu, HI 96828-0521

Mr. Rex C. Poe III: Alaska Native Heritage Center; 8800 Heritage Center Drive; Anchorage, AK 99506-1655

Mr. Daniel J. Poett: Daughters Of Charity; 4600 Edmondson Road; St. Louis, MO 63145

Mr. Scott Poffenberger: Siemens Energy and Automation; 2037 Weems Road; Tucker, GA 30084

Mr. Yan S. Polevoy: Malcolm Pirnie; 218 Gainsborg Avenue; White Plains, NY 10604

Mr. Robert D. Policarpio: AXA Reinsurance; 17 State; New York City, NY 10004

Mr. Troy E. Polito: Equitable of Iowa Company; 909 Locust Street; Des Monies, IA 50309-2899

Dr. Guylaine M. Pollock Ph.D.: Sandia National Laboratories; M/S 0449, P.O. Box 5800; Albuquerque, NM 87185

Mr. Kevin T. Pollock : 11 West Spring Street; Freeport, IL 61032-4316

Mr. Nick Poltoranin: LTI Associates, Inc.; 614 Ocean View Avenue; Brooklyn, NY 11235-6314

Mr. J. Polydoropoulos: J. Polydoropoulous; 3 Athinaidos Str.; Athens, Greece 10563

Mr. Randall Pong: KHON TV-2; 88 Pi'ikoi Street; Honolulu, HI 96714

Ms. Peggy Pontier-Renery: MDL Information; 14600 Catalina Street; San Leandro, CA 94577-6608

Mr. Beki Pool: Texas Department of Human Services; P.O. Box 149030, Mail Code W 425; Austin, TX 7787149030

Mr. Bruce D. Poole: Answer Think Consulting Group; 101 Woods Lane; Landenberg, PA 19350-9109

Ms. Regina Pope: Wilmington Trust; 1100 North Market Street; Wilmington, DE 19890-0001

Mr. Rodney Popham: Goldston Engineering; 210 South Carancahua Street, Suite 20; Corpus Christi, TX 78401-3040

Mr. Howard Poppel: Interdata Systems; 26 Ayres Lane; Little Silver, NJ 07739-1201

Mr. Avery Porter: Lee County Division of Public Safety; 9061 Aster Road; Fort Meyers, FL 33912-5255

Ms. Dianne Porter: Teleprofessional Magazine; 501 Sycamore Street, Suite 120; Waterloo, IA 50703-4651

Mr. Duane Porter: Sprint; 2813 Northwest Westbrooke Circle; Blue Springs, MO 64015-7224

Mr. Ray Porter Jr.: Michael Saunders & Company; 1801 Main Street; Sarasota, FL 34236-5969

Ms. Teresa Porter: DPRC; 6530 South Yosemite Street, Suite 204; Englewood, CO 80111-5128

Mr. Oleg Portisky: Informatek, Inc.; 66 Redwood Drive; Newtown, PA 18940-9247

Ms. Kimberly H. Poston: Lucent Technologies; P.O. Box 20046; Greensboro, NC 27420-0046

Ms. Dana Potter: Karl Suss America, Inc.; P.O. Box 157; Waterbury Country, VA 05677-0157

Mr. Phillip Potter: Columbia/Hca Health care Corp.; 1 Park Plaza; Nashville, TN 37203-6527

Mr. Dewitt Potts: CSC Healthcare Systems; 800 North Pearl Street, Suite 1; Albany, NY 12204-1898

Ms. Michelle Freshly Potts: Interim Technology; 4890 West Kennedy Boulevard, Suite 255; Tampa, FL 33609

Ms. Anne Pouliot: Sarcom; 2617 Grissom Drive; Nashville, TN 37204-2820

Ms. Karen Poullard: City of Port Arthur; P.O. Box 1089; Port Arthur, TX 77641-1089

Ms. Gilda Pour: San Jose State University; P.O. Box 720926; San Jose, CA 95172

Mr. G. Kevin Powell: Anthem; 1099 North Meridian Street, Suite 110; Indianapolis, IN 46204-1075

Mrs. Trina Geneva Powers-Stevenson: BEI Consulting; P.O. Box 930444; Wixom, MI 48393

Mr. Kusnadi Pradinata: American Management System; 243 Rollins Avenue, Apartment 101; Rockville, MD 20852-4013

Ms. Partha Pramanik: Mindware Pertech, Inc.; 800 West Cummings Park, Suite 2500; Woburn, MA 01801

Ms. Anantha S. Prasad: Fedex; 90 Fedex Parkway, Building 90, 1st Floor; Collierville, TN 38017

Mr. Mike Pratt: Kennebec Savings Bank; 150 State Street; Augusta, ME 04330

Mr. Zach Pratt: Beta Shim Company; 11 Progress Drive; Shelton, CT 06484-6218

Mr. Krishnaswamy Prayaga: CBSI; 6102 Woodfield Drive SE, Apartment 4; Grand Rapids, MI 49548-8538

Mr. Sankar Prayaga: SCS, Inc.; 11 Reading Road #D; Edison, NJ 08817-6607

Mr. Mitchell C. Preble: Dead River Company; 55 Broadway; Bangor, ME 04401-5200

Mr. John L. Preher: JP Systems; 1011 Philadelphia Drive; Westerville, OH 43081-5400

Dr. Samuel S. Preisler Ph.D.: Albertson, Inc.; P.O. Box 20; Boise, ID 83726-0020

Ms. Pam Prescott: Choice Point, Inc.; 1000 Alderman Drive; Alpharetta, GA 30005

Ms. Ann Pride: TMP World Wide; 4701 West Schroeder Drive, Suite 100; Milwaukee, WI 53223-1473

Mr. Robert F. Primavera : 270 Union Street; Lynn, MA 01901-1318

Mr. Michael L. Primeau: Michael Primeau Electrical; 119 Pembroke Road; Concord, NH 03301-5707

Ms. Paula Prince: N.S.T.; P.O. Box 233; Atlanta, GA 30106

Mr. Michael Probansky: NCTC; 363 White House Way; Port Hueneme, CA 93043-4303

Mr. Carey Probst: Oracle Consulting Services; 4 Wheatstone Court; Saratoga Springs, NY 12866-5471

Mr. Charlie Prothero: IBM Global Services; 30 Scranton Office Park; Scranton, PA 18507-1755

Mr. Erik Przybla: Candle Corporation; 2425 Olympic Boulevard; Santa Monica, CA 90404-4030

Ms. Leah Przyborowski: Summit Service Corporation; 55 Challenger Road, Floor 5; Ridgefield Peak, NJ 07660-2109

Mr. Michael E. Puckett: Xylan Corp.; 26801 West Agoura Road; Calabass, CA 91301

Mr. Robert Puhalla: Advanced Computer Services of Nebraska; 707 West 1st Street; Grand Island, NE 68801

Ms. C. M. Pukalski : 5715 Charlestowne Drive; Baltimore, MD 21212-2416

Ms. Kim Pupke: C of C Foundation; 66 George Street; Charleston, SC 29424-1407

Ms. Gemeta Purifoy: Computer Emporium; 4026 Highway 24; Chidester, AR 71726-7902

Mr. Rajesh Puri: GTS; 13600 Valley Oak Circle; Rockville, MD 20850-3574

Mr. George Anna Purnell: South Moon Under; 8019 Coastal Highway; Ocean City, MD 21842-2895

Mr. Marek Purowski: Consulate General of Poland; 12400 Wilshire Boulevard, Suite 555; Los Angeles, CA 90025-1055

Dr. Jamie Waterman Purvis Ph.D.: CDC/ATSDR; 1600 Clifton Road NE; Atlanta, GA 30333

Mr. Richard E. Purvis: Lancaster Eagle-Gazette; P.O. Box 848, 138 West Chestnut Street; Lancaster, OH 43130-0848

Mr. Ravi Puthiyattil: CDI Info Services; 304 West North Street; Waukesha, WI 53188-7027

Ms. Lisa Putnam: MJM Investigations Inc.; 8001 Aerial Center Parkway, #300; Morrisville, NC 27560-8413

Dr. Zhongqiang Qian Ph.D.: Cellular One-SBC; 840 East State Parkway; Schaumberg, IL 60173

Ms. Joan Quenan: Shell Lake Schools; 402 Pine Ridge Drive; Shell Lake, WI 54871-8726

Mr. Dan Quinones: Maritz Information Resources; 1375 North Highway Drive; Fenton, MO 63026-1929

Mr. Michael D. Quinones: Boeing; 3855 Lakewood Boulevard; Long Beach, CA 90846

Dr. Riccardo Beckwith Quintana Ph.D.: Software Anance; Elderhays 2540 Chapel Valley Road; Madison, WI 537111

Mr. Rafael A. Quintero: City of Hollywood; P.O. Box 229045; Hollywood, FL 33022-9045

Mr. Gerald C. Quintiliani: Quincy Public Schools; 316 Hancock Street; Quincy, MA 02171-2292

Mr. Richard Raby: Healthlogic; 6185 Buford Highway; Norcross, GA 30043

Mr. Mario Radclife: Value Options; 444 North 44th Street, Suite 400; Phoenix, AZ 85008-7629

Mr. Bob Radcliffe: Kurt J. Lesker Company; 1515 Worthington Avenue; Clairton, PA 15025-2734

Mr. Dave Radcliffe: Cargas Systems, Inc.; 26 A East Roseville Road; Lancaster, PA 17601-3858

Mr. Mitch Radella: US Steel; 600 Grant Room 1786; Pittsburgh, PA 15219-2702

Mr. James Radtke: University of Wisconsin at River Falls; 410 South 3rd Street; River Falls, WI 54022-5013

Mr. Christopher Rae: iCAST.com; 8 Chestnut West, Apartment 1H; Randolph, WA 02368-2320

Mr. John Raeburn: United Airlines; 7401 Martin Luther King Boulevard; Denver, CO 80207-2406

Mr. Jess L. Ragaza: Internet Architecture, Inc.; 2829 Talladega Drive; Orlando, FL 32826

Mr. Jim Ragsdale: Comcast Cellular Communications; 480 East Swedesford Road; Wayne, PA 19087-1822

Mr. Rajesh Raheja: Oracle Consulting Service; 500 Oracle Parkway; Redwood City, CA 94065-1677

Mr. Syed Anies Rahman: MCI Worldcom, Inc.; 1175 Chapel Hills Drive; Colorado Springs, CO 80920

Mr. R. David Rahn: Zevnik Horton Guibord & Mc; 77 West Wacker Drive, Suite 3300; Chicago, IL 60601-1629

Ms. Sheri M. Rahn: Guarantee Trust Life Insurance; 1275 Milwaukee Avenue; Glenview, IL 60025-2463

Mr. Rangarajan Sundara Rajan: Mastech Corporation; 390 Hauser Boulevard, 1F; Los Angeles, CA 90036

Mr. Veettil Rajeev: New Bridge Networks, Inc.; 2517 Farmcrest Drive, Apartment 125; Herndon, VA 20171-3163

Mr. S. Rajender: Concepts In Computing; 777 East 5th Street; Brooklyn, NY 11218-5801

Mr. Vijay Ramanand: Interworld Corporation; 634 Sayre Drive; Princeton, NJ 08540-5832

Mr. Josefa Ramaroson: AT&T; 23 Terrance Terrance; Freehold, NJ 07728-1440

Mr. Guillermo E. Ramirez: Hewlett Packard; 5121 SW 154th Court; Miami, FL 33185-4421

Ms. Laura V. Ramirez-Degadillo: AT&T; 1301 Fannin, Suite 2420; Houston, TX 77002

Dr. Vasant C. Ramkumar Ph.D.: Mediaone Labs; 10355 Westmoor Drive; Westminster, CO 80021

Ms. Kathy Rampersad: Novasoft Information Technology; 505 Lawrence Square Boulevard South; Lawrenceville, NJ 08648-2675

Mr. Charlene Ramundo: Delta Dental; 1639 Route 10; Parsippany, NJ 07054-4506

Ms. Linda J. Randall : 591 Cedar Street; San Carlos, CA 94070-2131

Mr. Matthew Randall: Holy Cross Health System; 53680 Canvasback Trace; Granger, IN 46530

Ms. Mercedes Randall: Indiana University; 620 Union Drive, #618; Indianapolis, IN 46202-5130

Mr. Purna Rao: Massachusetts Department of Environmental Protection; 627 Main Street; Worcester, MA 01609-2022

Mr. Joseph Rapoport MA, MCP: Fulbright & Jaworski, LLP.; 1300 McKinney, Suite 5100; Houston, TX 77010

Mr. Gerald J. Ratchford: IBM; 1423 Sweet Gum Lane; Matthews, NC 28105-0880

Mr. Robin Ratchford: St. Mary's Hospital; 5801 Bremo Road; Richmond, VA 23226-1900

Mrs. Charlotte Ratliff: Torch Energy Advisors-Novistar; 1221 Lamar Street, Suite 1600; Houston, TX 77010

Ms. Deborah Ratliff: Hillman; 10590 Hamilton Avenue; Cincinnati, OH 45231-1457

Mr. Alain Ratour: Chambre de Commerce et D'Industrie; 8 Bd du Roi Rene BP 626; Angers Cedex, France 49006

Ms. Heather Rattana : 3100 Windy Hill Road SE;

Atlanta, GA 30339-5605
Mr. Josh Ratzlaff: Xon-Tech, Inc.; 6862 Hayvenhurst Avenue; Van Nuys, CA 91406-4717
Mr. Shailesh Raval: Avenir, Inc.; 73 Princeton Arms West; Cranbury, NJ 08512-1503
Dr. Gregg Ravenberg Ph.D.: Signature America.com; 6850 Peachtree-Dunwoody Road, 921; Atlanta, GA 30328
Ms. Karen Rawden: Sodus SCD; P.O. Box 220, Mill Street Extension; Sodus, NY 14551-0220
Ms. Diane Ray: Hanscom Air Force Base, United States Air Force; 50 Griffis Street; Bedford, MA 01731-1642
Mr. Larry A. Ray: JM Smucker Company; 1 Strawberry Lane; Orrville, OH 44667
Mr. Girija Rayasam: Blockbuster Entertainment Group; 1201 Elm Street; Dallas, TX 75270-2102
Ms. Jill Raymond: Adaptive Micro Systems; 7840 North 86th Street; Milwaukee, WI 53224-3418
Ms. Annette Bonano Raynor: XSI, Inc.; 24 Route 34, Suite 10; Colts Neck, NJ 07722
Mr. Dick Read: Digital Microwave NW; 3325 South 116th Street; Seattle, WA 98168-1974
Ms. George Reaves Jr.: Alief ISD; P.O. Box 68; Alief, TX 77411-0068
Mrs. Katherine Rebel CRS, CSTE: GTE Telecommunication Service, Inc.; P.O. Box 2924; Tampa, FL 33601-2924
Mr. David Redfearn: McKesson HBOC; 2312 West Allen Drive; Springfield, MO 65810
Mr. C. Reed: MallincKrodt, Inc.; P.O. Box 5840; St. Louis, MO 63134-0840
Mr. Christopher A. Reed: City of Lubbock; P.O. Box 2000; Lubbock, TX 79457
Mr. Jason Reed: Core Lab, Inc.; 6310 Rothway Street; Houston, TX 77040-5056
Ms. Krestine Reed: Z World Inc.; 2900 Spafford Street; Davis, CA 95616-6800
Mr. Aage Reerslev: Agens, AB; Box 300; Stockholm, Sweden 10125
Mr. Mike Reese: Booz-Allen & Hamilton, Inc.; 310 Locust Drive; Baltimore, MD 21228-5130
Ms. Susan Regnier: Purdue University Calumet; 9243 Cottage Grove Place; Highland, IN 46322-2820
Mr. Atid Rehman: Caere Corp.; 100 Cooper Court; Los Gatos, CA 95030
Ms. Kim Reid: Bellsouth Interconnection Services; 600 19th Street North, 9th Floor; Birmingham, AL 35203-2210
Mr. Richard Reif: McGraw Hill Companies; 1221 Avenue of The Americas; New York, NY 10020
Mr. Robert J. Reighard: Rockwell Collins; P.O. Box 833807; Richardson, TX 75083-3807
Mr. Alan Reighn: Progressive Software Computing, Inc.; Suite 201-B, Plaza Center, 3505 Silverside Road; Wilmington, DE 19810
Ms. Chrystal H. Reilly: Naval Sea Systems Command, SEA O.O.I.; 2531 Jefferson Davis Highway; Arlington, VA 22202-3903
Ms. Kristin Reimers: Computone Corporation; 1060 Windward Ridge Parkway; Alpharetta, GA 30005-3992
Mr. Jack M. Reinoehl: Norse; P.O. Box 1869; Columbus, OH 43216-1869
Mr. Andrew L. Reip: Healthplus; 250 South Linden Road; Flint, MI 48532-4199
Mr. Scott Reiser: Sandrik Tamrock; 345 Patton Drive SW; Atlanta, GA 30336-1817
Ms. Erica Reiss: The Northern Trust; 50 South La Salle Street, #M-12; Chicago, IL 60603-1006
Mr. Leslie H. Reisz: The Pep Boys, Manny Moe and Jack; 311 West Allegheny Avenue; Philadelphia, PA 19132
Mr. Robert Remillard: Worker's Credit Union; 815 Main Street, #900; Fitchburg, MA 01420-3171
Ms. Michelle Renee: David Star and Friend; 555 Sutter Suite 202; San Francisco, CA 94102
Mr. Greg Rennick: Wilmington Trust Co.; 1100 North Market Street; Wilmington, DE 19890-0001
Ms. Lori Reno: Diebold, Inc.; 2525 Perimeter Place Drive, Suite 116; Nashville, TN 37214-3674
Ms. Kelly Rensema: Detroit Tool Metal Products; P.O. Box 512; Lebanon, MO 65536-0512
Mrs. Jennifer L. Rentz: Bass, Inc.; 495 Byers Road; Miamisburg, OH 45342-3662
Mr. Armin Resch: Perot Systems Corporation; 8755 Southwestern Boulevard; Dallas, TX 75206-2718
Mr. David Resnick: Erisco Managed Care Technologies; 1085 Morris Avenue; Union, NJ 07083-7136
Mr. Donald James Rexrode: Leap IT.com; 509 South Exeter Street; Baltimore, MD 21202-1835
Mr. Rick Reyes: BMC, Inc.; 10415 Morado Circle; Austin, TX 78759-5638
Mr. Don W. Reynolds III: The Crouch Group; 300 A North Carroll Boulevard; Denton, TX 76201
Ms. Kim Reynolds: Q.C. Inc.; 1500 Huguenot Road; Midlothian, VA 23113-2478
Mr. Randy Reynolds: Deutsche Bank; 1 South Street; Baltimore, MD 21202-3298
Mr. Hassan Rezaei: Pb Farradyne, Inc.; One Penn Plaza; New York, NY 10119
Mr. Jeffrey A. Rhoads: USA Group; 11100 USA Parkway; Fishers, IN 46038
Mr. Kevin Ricci: The NLS Group; 9 Hillview Drive; North Providence, RI 02904
Ms. Lygeia Ricciardi: MaMaMedia, Inc.; 325 West 77th Street, Apartment 2D; New York, NY 10024
Mr. Kenneth E. Rich: RAHD Oncology Products; 2342 Charros Road; Sandy, UT 84092-4817
Mr. Carmeleete Richards: BCSP; 3485 Cassingham; Bexley, OH 43223
Mr. George Richards: AT&T; 40 Westminister Street; Providence, RI 02903-2525
Mr. M. Richards: Healthcare Service Company; 628 South Ash Street; Hobart, IN 46342-5008
Mr. Randall R. Richards: SAE International; 20828 Sequoia; Chillicothe, IL 61523
Mr. Bret Richardson: Jore Corporation; 45000 US Highway 93; Ronan, MT 59864-9678
Dr. Lloyd M. Richardson Ed.D.: Stratford College; 13576 Minnieville Road; Woodbridge, VA 22192
Mrs. Sheri Richardson: State of Georgia DOAS; 2267 Sparrow Ridge Drive Northeast; Marietta, GA 30066-2148
Mr. Gene Richer: Productivity Point International; 1789 Indian Wood Circle; Maumee, OH 43537-4096
Mr. Michael Richichi: Drew University; 36 Madison Avenue; Madison, NJ 07940-1434
Mr. Jerry Richman: IBM Global Services; 1300 South Clinton Street; Fort Wayne, IN 46802-3506
Mr. Todd J. Richter: Baystate Health Center; 3601 Main Street; Springfield, MA 01107
Mr. Nicholas A. Ridder: Oracle Corporation; P.O. Box 5486; Evanston, IL 60204-5486
Ms. Teresa Riffel: Cessna Aircraft Company; 5 Cessna Boulevard; Wichita, KS 67215
Ms. Dawn Riggs: Allied-Signal; 4060 East Bijou Street; Colorado Springs, CO 80909-6822
Mr. Lawrence M. Rigoni: Arthur Andersen; 14 Cour LaSalle; Palos Hills, IL 60465
Mr. Matt Riley: University of Redlands; 1200 East Colton Avenue; Redlands, CA 92374-3720
Mr. Guillermo Rios: Allegiance; 1 Butterfield Trail Boulevard; El Paso, TX 79906-4901
Mr. Jose O. Rios: Rug Doctor; 4701 Old Shepard Place; Plano, TX 75034
Dr. Gilberto J. Rios Sierra: Edif. Clinicas Medicas; 4 Avda. 15-73, ona 10; Guatemala City, Guatemala
Mr. Randal J. Ripps: Paragon Cable San Antonio Texas; 403 Urban Loop; San Antonio, TX 78207
Ms. Lisa Ritchie: Combe Incorporated; 1101 Westchester Avenue; Whit Plains, NY 10604-3597
Mr. Jeff Ritter: Randolph School; 1005 Drake Avenue SE; Huntsville, AL 35802-1099
Dr. Volker J. Ritz: Studiengesellschaft Für Eisenerz-Aufbereitung SGA; Grubenstr. 5; Lienburg-Othfresen, Germany D-38704
Mr. Jeffrey M. Rively: Clerk of the Board of Santa Clara; 70 West Hedding Street; San Jose, CA 95110-1705
Ms. Melissa Rivera: Salvation Army Social Services for Children; 132 West 14th Street; New York, NY 10011-7301
Mr. Ron Rivera: Prescription Solutions; 3515 Harbor Boulevard; Costa Mesa, CA 92626-1437
Ms. Melissa Rivera: Salvation Army Social Services for Children; 132 West 14th Street; New York, NY 10011-7301
Mr. Ron Rivera: Prescription Solutions; 3515 Harbor Boulevard; Costa Mesa, CA 92626-1437
Mr. Bob Roadcap: Berk Tek; 132 White Oak Road; New Holland, PA 17557-8303
Mr. Michelle Robbins: Ohio Valley Communications Center; P.O. Box 37; Evansville, IN 47701-0037
Mr. Raymond Robbins: United Health Care Companies; 770 Pelham Road; Greenville, SC 29615
Mr. Franklin D. Roberson: Department of Defense Navy; 9625 Moffett Avenue; Norfolk, VA 23511-2784
Mr. Brian Roberto: Metro Times; 733 Saint Antoine Street; Detroit, MI 48226-2936
Mr. David R. Roberts: CSC, Inc.; 431 East Locust Street; Bethlehem, PA 18018-2918
Mr. Phil Roberts: P R O; 5863 Blacksmith Drive; Raleigh, NC 276060-7700
Ms. Vicki Roberts: INTEL; 2802 Kelvin Avenue; Irvine, CA 92614-5826
Mr. Freddie André Robertson: United States Army; 2335 Rosehill Road; Fayetteville, NC 28301
Mr. Jon Robertson: New Horizons Computer Learning Center; 920 Hamshire Road, Suite S; Westlake Village, CA 91361-6076
Ms. Patricia A. Robertson: Marsh Company; 707 East B Street; Belleville, IL 62220
Mr. Dominique Robin: E Charge; 500 Union Street, #745; Seattle, WA 98115-7246
Ms. Daniela Robinson: Fidelity Investments; 2 Ash Lane; Merrimack, NH 03054-2309
Mr. Dwight Robinson: Qualcomm Inc.; 5775 Morehouse Drive; San Diego, CA 92121-1710
Mr. J. D. Robinson: Brett Martin, Ltd.; 24 Roughfort Road; Mallusk, United Kingdom BT3 4RB
Mr. Kit A. Robinson: Deloitte Consulting DRT Systems; 1633 Broadway, 35th Floor; New York, NJ 10019
Mr. Micheal J. Robinson: Computer Associates; 2827 South Smedley Street; Philadelphia, PA 19145-4823
Mr. Spencer M. Robinson : 131 Main Road; Gill, MA 01376-9715
Mr.Terrell Robinson: Sed International, Inc.; 4916 North Royal Atlanta Drive; Tucker, GA 30084-3031
Mr. Tod A. Robinson: Western Pioneer, Inc.; 4601 Shilshole Avenue NW; Seattle, WA 98107
Mr. Todd Rockey: Centillion Data Systems, Inc.; 333 North Alabama Street; Indianapolis, IN 46204-2151
Ms. Lynne E. Rockhold: Coleman Research Corporation; 806 10th Street; Idaho Falls, ID 83404-5065
Mr. Nathan Rockhold: Rocksolid Computing; 1104 North Cherry Street; Galesburg, IL 61401-2740
Ms. Deborah Rockwood: Lockheed Martin Canada; 3001 Solandt Road; Kanata, Ontario, Canada K2K 2M8
Ms. Patricia A. Rodarmel: Covance, Inc.; 202 West Providence Road; Primos, PA 19018-3828
Mr. Gary Roderick: Mountain Enterprises, Inc.; P.O. Box 190; Sheperdstown, WV 25443-0190
Dr. Mary Ann Rodgers Ph.D.: Riverside Publishing; 425 Spring Lake Drive; Itasca, IL 60143
Mr. Marlon Rodriguez: Henderson and Bodwell; 124 West Diversey; Elmhurst, IL 60126
Ms. April Edmonds Roe: Florida Department of Environmental Protection; 1413 Lola Drive; Tallahassee, FL 32301-6712
Ms. Lori Roe: Cape Helopen High School; 1250 Kings Highway; Lewes, DE 19958-1798
Mr. Ronald J. Roefaro: Appalachia Intermediate Unit 8; 580 Foot of Ten Road; Duncansville, PA 16635
Mr. Samuel Roeland: MC Maximum Capacity; 9920 Pacific Heights, Suite 5; San Diego, CA 92121-4334
Mr. Edward J. Rogers: ERS International; 6066 Johnston Drive; Oakland, CA 94611-3143
Mr. Michael Rogers: Logical Choice, Inc.; P.O. Box 144; Greencastle, IN 46135-0144
Mr. Robert B. Rogers: Ameritech; 1 Washington Boulevard, Room 1; Detroit, MI 48226-4420
Mr. Shaun Rogers: Cardinal Distribution; 11 Centennial Drive; Peabody, MA 01960-7901
Mr. Warren A. Rogers: Quabbin Wire & Cable Company; 10 Maple Street; Ware, MA 01082-1597
Mr. Richard Rohrer: Global One; 12490 Sunrise Valley Drive; Reston, VA 20196-0001
Mr. Patrick J. Rojo: GE Capital IT Solutions; 4474 Sigma Road; Dallas, TX 75244-4501
Mr. William Rolfe: Cahners Business Information; 8773 South Ridgeline Road; Highlands Ranch, CO 80126-2350
Mr. Felix Romeau: Computer Specialist, Incorporated; 209 Angelique Street; Weehawken, NJ 07087-5711
Mr. Kevin Romito: Leadership Dynamics Resources; 30572 Marbella Vista; San Juan Capistrano, CA 92675-1719
Dr. Ruowen Rong Ph.D.: GTE Labs Inc.; 40 Sylvan Road; Waltham, MA 02451
Mr. Ricky A. Roope: Lowe's Companies, Inc.; P.O. Box 111, 808 Highway 268 East; North Wilkesboro, NC 28659-8385
Ms. Jennifer Roos: Computer Network Technology; 6000 Nathan Lane North; Minneapolis, MN 55442
Ms. Gary Rose: Bexar County Information Services; 203 West Nueva, Suite 200; San Antonio, TX 78207-4507
Mr. Genelle Roselli: Adelphia; 830 Route 37 West; Toms River, NJ 08755-6408
Mr. Nicolas Roselli: Federal Aviation Administration; Atlantic City Airport; Atlantic City, NJ 08405
Mr. Ira Rosen: IDT; 225 Old New Brunswick Road; Piscataway, NJ 08854-3711
Ms. Charlotte Rosenstengel: Fulton State Hospital; 6000 East 5th Street; Fulton, MO 65251-1753
Mr. Chris Rosica: Rosica Mulhern & Associates; 11-13 Sunflower Avenue; Paramus, NJ 07652
Mr. John F. Rosnow: Damark International, Inc.; 7101 Winnetka Avenue, N.; Brooklyn Park, MN 55428-1619
Ms. Mary Ross: Service and Support; 109 East Church Street, Suite 230; Orlando, FL 32801
Mr. Thomas Ross: Highmark; 200 Corporate Center Drive; Camp Hill, PA 17011-1701
Mr. Mark A. Roth : 905 Elmhurst Drive; Papillion, NE 68046-6108
Mr. Dewey Rothering: Saks Incorporated; 4650 Shepherd Trail; Rockford, IL 61103
Ms. Karl Rothman: Ernest and Young LLP; 201 East 36th Street, Apartment 7d; New York, NY 10016-3608
Mr. Errol W. Rottman: DCV, Inc.; 115 Executive Drive; Highland, IL 62249
Mr. Brian J.O. Rourke: Dun & Bradstreet; 3 Sylvan Way; Parsippany, PA 07054-3805
Mr. Ed Rouse: Meers Engineering, Inc.; 2303 South Danville Drive; Abilene, TX 79605-6412
Mr. Gerry Rovelsky: Alltel Information Services; P.O. Box 1266; Twinsburg, OH 44087-9266
Ms. Leigh Rowan: Martin Yale Industries, Inc.; 251 Wedcor Avenue; Wabash, IN 46992-4201
Mr. Timothy Rowan: Multnomah County Health Department; 426 Southwest Stark Street, 7th Floor; Portland, OR 97204
Mr. Paul Rowell: City of Pascagoula; 603 Watts Avenue; Pascagoula, MS 39567-4220
Ms. Kelly Rowland: Caledonia Community Schools; 203 East Main Street; Caledonia, MI 49316-8905
Mr. Malcolm V. Rowland: Rockford Mutual Insurance Company; P. O. Box 5626; Rockford, IL 61125-0626
Ms. Gina Rowles: Ashland Distribution Company; P.O. Box 2219; Columbus, OH 43216-2219
Mr. Thomas Rowley: Knight Enterprises; 6056 Ulmerton Road; Clearwater, FL 33760
Mr. Mark Rubin: Directv; 2230 East Imperial Highway; El Segundo, CA 90245-3531
Mr. Marv Rubin: Remax Achievers; 5300 West Sahara ,#200; Las Vegas, NV 89146
Ms. Alison Ruble: Delta Dental of California; 11155 International Drive; Rancho Cordova, CA 95670
Mr. Jason Ruble: Somerset Independent Schools; 305 College Street; Somerset, KY 42501
Mr. Robert Rubow: AETN; P.O. Box 1250; Conway, AR 72033
Ms. Christy Rudolph: Trend Micro, Inc.; 10101 North De Anza Boulevard; Cupertino, CA 95014-2264
Mr. Brent Ruggles: Bisys Group, Incorporated; 2091 Springdale Road; Cherry Hill, NJ 08003
Mr. Eladio Ruiz de Molina: Consulting & Systems Integration, Inc.; 100 Corporate Parkway; Birmingham, AL 35242
Ms. Sharla Ruland: Excel Corporation; P.O. Box 579; Friona, TX 79035
Mrs. Lisa Rule: The Learning Company; 651 Boylston Street, 4th Floor; Boston, MA 02116-2804
Ms. Sharon T. Rule : 106 Apartment Lane; Jacksonville, NC 28546-8803
Mr. Ronald Rulli: Central Vermont Public Services; 77 Grove Street, # ISD; Rutland, VT 05701-3403
Mr. Paul S. Rumsey: Financial Network Investment Corporation; 2780 Skypark Drive, Suite 300; Torrance,

CA 90505

Mr. Ken K. Rundus: 7834 C F Hawn Freeway; Dallas, TX 75217-6508

Mr. Robert Ruocco: Healthfirst Inc.; 25 Broadway, Floor 9; New York, NY 10004-1010

Mr. Walter Ruppel: EDS; 7000 Chicago Road, Room A118; Warren, MI 48092-1663

Mr. Gregory W. Russell: S.C. Johnson & Son, Inc.; 1525 Howe Street; Racine, WI 53403-2236

Mr. Harold Russell: Software Spectrum, Inc.; 17935 Brent Drive; Dallas, TX 75287-5977

Ms. Kimberly K. Russell: NETech Corporation; 2591 44th Street; Grand Rapids, MI 49512

Mr. William M. Russell V: W.M. Russell Corporation; 17 North Johnson Street; Samson, AL 36477

Mr. Paul D. Rust: Strongwell; 3621 Industrial Park Drive; Lenoir City, TN 37771

Ms. W. Sydney Rust: IPI International, Inc.; P.O. Box 70; Elkton, MD 21922-0070

Mr. Barry Rutherford: US Office Products; 9600 Parksouth Court; Orlando, FL 32837-8366

Mr. Jack N. Rutherford: Oracle Advanced Programs Group; 706 Overlook Way; Winter Springs, FL 32708

Mr. Jim Ryan: Primeco Personal Communications; 9011 Areboretum Parkway; Richmond, VA 23236-3476

Mr. Patrick M. Ryan: TRW; 2021 Cunningham Drive; Hampton, VA 23666

Mr. Saqib Saadi: Fairview; P.O. Box 120988; Saint Paul, MN 55112-0028

Mr. Sunil Sabat: Callidus Software, Inc.; 160 West Santa Clara Street; San Jose, CA 95113

Mr. S. Neil Sabharwal: E-Force; 475 Whitney Drive; Rochester, MI 48307

Mr. Aaron Sables: Spirax Sarco Inc.; 1150 Northpoint Boulevard; Blythewood, SC 29016-8873

Mr. Santosh Saboo: Rapidigm; 3000 Swallow Hill Road, #445; Pittsburgh, PA 15220-1565

Mr. Harold Sage: Appleton City R II School; P.O. Box 126; Appleton City, MO 64724

Mr. Gurpreet S. Sagoo: TRW; 13708 Barksdale Drive; Herndon, VA 20171

Mr. Roberto Sahagun: Better Beverages, Ltd.; P.O. Box 346, 1415 U.S. Highway 90A East; Hallettsville, TX 77964-0346

Mr. Larry Saidman: Nordson Corporation; 2905 Pacific Drive; Norcross, GA 30071-1809

Mr. Maher Salah: University of Pennsylvania Health System; 346 East Lancaster Avenue, Apartment 308; Wynnewood, PA 19096-2227

Ms. Michelle Salgado: CS McKee; One Gateway Center; Pittsburgh, PA 15222

Mr. William Saliy: CIBC Oppenheimer; 425 Lexington Avenue; New York, NY 10017

Mr. Andy Salley: Sal Com Telecommunications; P.O. Box 542; Panacea, FL 32346-0542

Mr. Cam Salloum: Grange Mutual Casualty Company; 650 South Front Street, Floor 7; Columbus, OH 43206-1049

Mr. Leo Salvaggio: Unisys; 41100 Plymouth Road; Plymouth, MI 48170-1892

Mr. Thomas C. Salveta: Creative Solutions Group; 14700 East 11 Mile Road; Warren, MI 48089-1555

Mr. Doug Salvon: Motorola; 5555 North Beach Street, #7a; Fort Worth, TX 76137-2794

Mr. Quentin Samelson: Motorola A.I.E.G; 4000 Commercial Avenue; Northbrook, IL 60062

Mr. Max M. Samfield: Houston-Galveston Area Council; 3555 Timmons Lane, Suite 500; Houston, TX 77027

Mr. Richard Samson: Wiltel Data; 408 Saracino Drive; Maybrook, NY 12543-1130

Mr. Adam Samuelian: Personal Technical Research; 157 Lowell Avenue; Newtonville, MA 02460

Mr. John P. Samuelson: U.P.S. Army Corps of Engineers; 4820 University Square; Huntsville, AL 35816-1822

Mr. John Sanchez: Oneil Management Inc.; 8 Mason; Irvine, CA 92618-2705

Mr. Robert A. Sanchez: Federal Reserve Bank; 126 East Nueva; San Antonio, TX 78204-1020

Mr. Kevin A. Sanchez-Cherry: NASD, Inc.; 9513 Key West Avenue; Rockville, MD 20850

Mr. Eric Sanders: IBM; 1905 Calibre Vinings Way SE; Smyrna, GA 30080-6776

Mr. Fred Sanders: A&T Systems, Inc.; 12520 Prosperity Drive, Suite 300; Silver Spring, MD 20904-1664

Ms. Lenora Sanders: Carolina Power and Light Company; P.O. Box 1551; Raleigh, NC 27602-1551

Mr. Lyle R. Sanderson: Lason Inc.; 6560 Perham Drive; West Bloomfield, MI 48322-3821

Mr. Bennie Sandhofner: Meritcare Health System; 737 Broadway; Fargo, ND 58123-0001

Mr. Bradford J. Sandler: IBM; 103 Windwick Court; Raleigh, NC 27606-8440

Mr. Alberto Sandoval: International Systems & Software, Inc.; 200 East Big Beaver; Troy, MI 48083

Mr. Shane Sanford: Cullman Products; 1909 Beech Avenue SE; Cullman, AL 35055-5463

Ms. Jo Anne Sangregorio: Avon Products Inc.; 1 Avon Plaza; Rye, NY 10508-4005

Mr. Kannan Sankara: New Venture Gear; 294 Town Center Drive; Troy, MI 48084-1774

Mr. Phil Sansotta: Cougar Software Solutions; 7086 Harrison Street; Garden City, MI 48135-2261

Mr. Rick Sant'Angelo: Ikon Office Solutions-Technology Services; 3621 South Harber Boulevard #150; Santa Ana, CA 92704

Ms. Laura Santamaria: Household International; 1441 Schilling Place; Salinas, CA 93901-4543

Mr. Venkateshwar Santapur: BAL Association/Walt Disney World Information Services; 480 Sun Lake Circle, Apartment 212; Lake Mary, FL 32746-6162

Mr. Frank Santiago: Stonyfield Farm, Inc.; 10 Burton Drive; Londonderry, NH 03053-7436

Mr. Anthony F. Santora: Kean University; 1000 Morris Avenue; Union, NJ 07083-7133

Mr. Bill Sanzo: Eurotherm Gauging Systems Inc.; 900 Middlesex Turnpike; Billerica, MA 01821-3929

Dr. Demetrios Sapounas Ph.D.: NMP-AppNet; P.O. Box 424; Falls Church, VA 22040-0424

Mr. Sudesh Sapra: Computer Consulting Services; 31 Tyler Avenue, Apartment 3104; Iselin, NJ 08830-2967

Ms. Nahideh Sarrafieh: Infonet; 2100 East Grand Avenue; El Segundo, CA 90245-5024

Mr. Kirit Sarvaiya: Arthur Andersen, LLP; 1345 Avenue of the Americas; New York, NY 10105

Mr. Kevin M. Sass: Edwards O'Neill; 1029 32nd Avenue; Council Bluffs, IA 51503

Mr. Shawn R. Sasser: Blue Springs Ford; 3200 South Outer Road; Blue Springs, MO 64015-1797

Mr. Mike Satterfield: Lutheran Social Services; 647 West Virginia Street, Suite 300; Milwaukee, WI 53204

Mr. Alejo Saudcedo: Editoral El Sol; Washington 629 ote.; Monterrey, Mexico 64000

Mr. Inge Saunders: Ernst & Young, Llp.; 127 Morningside Drive; Battle Creek, MI 49015-4615

Mr. Byron Sauriol: Denon Digital Industries Inc.; 1380 Monticello Road; Madison, GA 30650-4663

Ms. Donna E. Sautter: Putnam Investments; 15 Ebbett Avenue; Quincy, MA 02170-3427

Ms. Ashish Saxena: Tata Consultancy Services; 123 South Front Street; Memphis, TN 38103-3618

Ms. Linda Scanlon: IBM; 8836 Hubbard Drive; Galloway, OH 43119

Mr. Lee Scarberry: Huddleston, Bolen, & Beatty; 611 3rd Avenue; Huntington, WV 25701

Mr. Leo Scarpelli: Followthrough Company; P.O. Box 2816; Olympia, WA 98507-2816

Mr. Anthony J. Scarpellini: Nantucket Cottage Hospital; 57 Prospect Street; Nantucket, MA 02554-2799

Mr. Eugene R. Schachte: Heinz USA; 1062 Progress Street; Pittsburgh, PA 15212-5990

Mr. Justin Schaef: Mid-Hudson Regional Information Center; 175 State Route 32 North; New Paltz, NY 12561-1029

Mr. John Schaffer: Magellan Software; 8717 Research Drive; Irvine, CA 92618

Mr. Robert M. Schaffer: United States Government; 162 1st Street; Port Hueneme, CA 93043

Mr. Shawn T. Schauble: Entex Info Systems; 44 Centergrove Road, F-11; Randolph, NJ 07869

Mr. Lawrence G. Schear: Lockheed Martin Corporation M&DS; P.O. Box 8045, M/S 10/2196; Philadelphia, PA 19101

Mr. Brett Schiftner: Lane Gorman Trubett; 2626 Howell Street, Suite 700; Dallas, TX 75204-4037

Ms. Nancy Schilling: Alban Tractor; 8531 Pulaski Highway; Baltimore, MD 21237-3092

Mr. Ryan Schilmoeller: Modis; 14922 Edna Street; Omaha, NE 68138

Mr. William Schirner: Ohio Department of Taxation; 1880 East Dublin Granville Road; Columbus, OH 43229-3523

Mr. Brian Schlagel: State of Wisconsin; P.O. Box 9; Winnebago, WI 54985-0009

Mr. Curtis Schlott: SAP America; 3823 North Pontiac Avenue; Chicago, IL 60634-1930

Mr. Dave L. Schmeltz: ITS Services/U.S. Customs; 1814 Price Lane; Bowie, MD 20716-1676

Ms. Elizabeth Schmidt: NDC Health Information Services; 501 West Walnut Street; Crown Point, IN 46307-3822

Mr. Mark D. Schmidt: SISU Medical System; 5 West 1st Street, Suite 200; Duluth, MN 55802

Mr. Peter Schmidt: Blue Cross Blue Shield; 225 North Michigan Avenue; Chicago, IL 60601-7601

Mr. Scott Schmidt: Minnesota Corn Processors; 3000 East 8th Street; Columbus, NE 68601

Ms. Shirley Schmidt: 3M; 3M Center Building, 225-3s-05; St. Paul, MN 55144-1000

Mr. William Schmidt: Wolverine Plating Corporation; 29456 Groesbeck Highway; Roseville, MI 48066-1969

Mr. Bernhard Schneider: AMIL International of Nevada; 9536 Wooden Pier Way; Las Vegas, NV 89117-0272

Ms. Kimberly Schneider: Future Force Technology and Training; 3414 Tyburn Tree Court; Herndon, VA 20171-4014

Mr. Mike Schnetzer: City of Bismarck; 221 North 5th Street; Bismarck, ND 58501-4079

Mr. Gregory Schnuck: Boehringer Ingelheim; P.O. Box 368; Ridgefield, CT 06877-0368

Mr. Michael Schoeny: Veterans Administration; 500 East Veterans Road; Tomah, WI 54660

Mr. Ben M. Schorr: Dam Key Leong Kupchak Hastert; 1600 Pauahi Tower, 1001 Bishop Street; Honolulu, HI 96813-3480

Mr. Michael R. Schrauth: Information Services; 2060 Craigshire Road; St. Louis, MO 63146-4010

Ms. Dianne Schreck: ACE Matrix Services; P.O. Box 32085; Cincinnati, OH 45232-0085

Ms. Melanie Schreiber: Brown Mackie College; 126 South Santa Fe Avenue; Salina, KS 67401-2810

Mr. John Schroeder: WSYX/WTTE-TV; 1261 Dublin Road; Columbus, OH 43215-7000

Ms. Nancy M. Schuessler: Covington & Burling; 417 East 89th Street, 1D; New York, NY 10128-6768

Mr. Bernie Schultz: Simplex Time Recorder Company; Simplex Plaza; Gardener, MA 01440-2216

Ms. Julie Schultz: Time Warner Cable; 3600 Sillect Avenue; Bakersfield, CA 93308-6328

Mr. Keith B. Schultz: Net Data Consulting Services, Incorporated; 511 Highway 98; Destin, FL 32541

Mr. Carol Schulz: Oracle Corporation; 6007 McNeely Way; Orangevale, CA 95662-4637

Ms. Angela Schumacher-Porras: Arma International; 4200 Somerset Drive, Suite 215; Prairie Village, KS 66208

Mr. Scott Schuman: Chaney Systems; 5100 South Calhoun Road; New Berlin, WI 53151-7902

Mr. Geoff Schunicht: Compaq Computer Corporation; 20555 SH 249; Houston, TX 77070

Mr. Steven Schurt: Aetna US Healthcare; 980 Jolly Road; Bluebell, PA 19422

Mr. Paul B. Schuster: Premiere; 2221 Rosecrans Avenue, Suite 126; El Segundo, CA 90245

Mr. Fleming Schutrumpf: Bold Tech Systems; 1675 Harimer Street, Suite 460; Denver, CO 80202

Mr. Thomas M. Schwartz: TRW Environmental Safety Systems; 2650 Park Tower Drive, #MS 734; Vienna, VA 22180-7300

Mr. Douglas Schwarz: State of Connecticut Workers Compensation; 21 Oak Street, 4th Floor; Hartford, CT 06106-8003

Mr. Steve Schwarz: Invesco Funds Group; 960 Fox Farm Road; Larkspur, CO 80118-7702

Mr. Mark B. Schweitzer: Computer Associates International; 2000 Park Lane Drive; Pittsburgh, PA 15275-1126

Mr. Greg Schweizer: Oregonian Publishing Company; 1320 Southwest Broadway; Portland, OR 97201-3499

Mr. David B. Schwemer: C.R. Bard, Inc.; 730 Central Avenue; New Providence, NJ 07974-1199

Mr. Jim Schwonek: Eaton Corporation; 34899 Curtis Boulevard; Eastlake, OH 44095-4015

Mrs. Marion Scoglio: Distributed Systems Service, Inc.; 3020 Penn Avenue; West Lawn, PA 19609-1421

Mr. Mike Scorzo: Kish Internet Delivery Systems (KIDS); 300 Heart Boulevard; Loves Park, IL 61111-7516

Mr. Craig Scott: Keiser College; 1800 West International Speedway; Daytona Beach, FL 32114-1233

Mr. James Scott: Lockheed Martin; 1433 Gordy Drive; San Jose, CA 95131-3301

Ms. Kathleen Scott: Brady Corporation-ISST Division; 6555 West Good Hope Road; Milwaukee, WI 53223

Ms. Maria Amparo Scott: Mitsubishi Caterpillar Forklift America; 2011 West Sam Houston Parkway North; Houston, TX 77043-2421

Mr. Mark D. Scott: Micro Endeavors Inc.; 8001 Lansdowne Avenue; Upper Darby, PA 19082-5407

Mr. Rich Scott: Korn Ferry International; 1800 Century Park East, Suite 900; Century City, CA 90067-1593

Ms. Tammy A. Scott: AAR Composites; 14201 Myerlake Circle; Clearwater, FL 33760

Ms. Stephanie Scungio: Pfizer, Incorporated; 194 Howard Street; New London, CT 06320

Mr. David E. Seabaugh: Virginia Medical Center; 1 Jefferson Barracks Road; St. Louis, MO 63125-4181

Mr. William Seat: The Computer Doctor; 201 South Main Avenue; Portales, NM 88130-6216

Mrs. Lisa Seaton: Analysts International; 2700 Gateway Centre Boulevard; Morrisville, NC 27560-9137

Mr. Joe Seay: United States Postal Service; 4924 Green Road; Raleigh, NC 27616-2832

Mr. Joe Secunda: Temple University; 1803 North Broad Street, 8th Floor, Carnell Hall; Philadelphia, PA 19122-6003

Mr. Neil Sederburg: American Lumber; 18 Sixth Avenue; Union City, PA 19438

Ms. Cindy Seiler: LG&E Energy Corporation; 220 West Main Street, Floor 8; Louisville, KY 40202-1395

Mr. Mark Seipler: Motorola, Inc.; 2324 Coneflower Lane; Algonquin, IL 60102-6620

Mr. Gregory Selverian: Biomatrix, Inc.; 60 Chelsea Drive; Saddle Brook, NJ 07663-4712

Mr. Mark S. Selvitelli: Project Resource Solutions; 10 Tower Office Park, Suite 412; Woburn, MA 01801-2120

Mr. Peter Sentz: Complete Data Solutions; 1125 West Center Street; Orem, UT 84057-5207

Mr. Alexandre Sequeira: Universo Virtual, LDA; Rua Serpa Pinto 2-4; Barreiro, Portugal

Mr. Melvin Antonio Sequera: Reckitt and Colman de Venezuela; Apdo 70149, Los Ruices; Caracas Miranda, Venezuela

Mr. Theodore Serbinski: United States Navy, Naval Sea Systems Command; 187 Harwill Drive; Stafford, VA 22554

Mr. Atul Sethi: Bell & Howell; 3791 South Alston Avenue; Durham, NC 27713-1803

Ms. Alethea Setser: Roanoke County Schools; 1816 Bloomfield Avenue; Roanoke, VA 24012-6762

Mr. Vittorio Severino: Hartford Life Company; 22 Gault Park Drive; Westport, CT 06880-2117

Mr. George W. Seward: Newport News Shipbuilding; 135 Wreck Shoal Drive; Newport News, VA 23606-1945

Mr. Justin Sewell: Management Trend Company; 14479 Pamlico Road, #1000; Apple Valley, CA 92307-5462

Mr. Philip Seyer: EDS; 651 Brannan Street; San Francisco, CA 94107

Mr. John Seymour: En Pointe Technologies; 1860 Embarcadero Road; Palo Alto, CA 94303-3335

Ms. Karyn Shaffener: Allentown Business School; 1501 Lehigh Street; Allentown, PA 18103-3880

Mr. David A. Shaffer MCSE: McLean Koehler Sparks & Hammond; 1122 Kenilworth Drive, Suite 500; Towson, MD 21204-2188

Mr. Anil Shah: Apna Consulting, Inc.; 1515 St. Julian Street; Suwanee, GA 30024-3684

Mr. Chirag V. Shah: The Designory, Inc.; 211 East Ocean Boulevard, Suite 100; Long Beach, CA 90802-4850

Mr. Jayesh Shah: Ficon Technology, Inc.; 1000 Route 9 North; Woodbridge, NJ 07095

Mr. Kamal Shah : 99 Rosewood Drive, Suite 140; Danvers, MA 01923-1300
Mr. Raj Shah: Lucent Technologies; 2600 Warrenville Road, ILI470, Room 42H14; Lisle, IL 60532
Mr. Sejal Shah: IBM Global Services; 22 Hopkins Drive; New Haven, NY 06512
Mr. Shailesh Shah: Brown Brothers Harriman Inc.; 24 Glynn Court; Parlin, NJ 08859-2501
Mr. Sunil Shah: Canon USA, Inc.; 1 Canon Plaza; Lake Success, NY 11042
Khurram Shahzad : 8549 Hawk Run Terrace; Montgomery Village, MD 20886-4374
Ms. Mary Shalow: Marshfield Clinic; 1000 North Oak Avenue; Marshfield, WI 54449
Mr. Brad Shambach: Altel; 3036 South 31st Street; Temple, TX 76502-1802
Mr. Stuart Shapiro: Savant Systems; 8615 Broadway, Apartment 14E; Elmhurst, NY 11373-5821
Mr. Kal GordoRenganathan Sharma : P.O. Box 6106, Room 303 ESB; Morgantown, WV 26506-6106
Mr. Roshan L. Sharma: Telecom Network Sc; 6050 Melody Lane, Apartment 238; Dallas, TX 75231-6724
Mr. David Sharp: General Instrument; 101 Tournament Drive; Horsham, PA 19044-3680
Ms. Sharon L. Sharp: Garvey School District; 2730 North Del Mar Avenue; Rosemead, CA 91770
Mrs. Aimee H. Shaw: Yellow Book USA; 1201 Main Street; Columbus, MS 39702
Ms. Alice Shaw: Virtual City Vision; 707 Greenwood Avenue; Fairhope, AL 35632-2832
Mr. Mark Shaw: South Dakota Network; 2900 West 10th Street; Sioux Falls, SD 57104-2543
Ms. Caitlin Shea: McDonald Bradley, Inc.; 8200 Greensboro Drive, Suite 805; McLean, VA 22102-3803
Mr. Thomas F. Shea: Home Town Health Network; 100 Lillian Gish Boulevard, Suite 301; Massillon, OH 44647
Mr. Raymond Sheedy: Allstate Insurance Company; 3100 Sanders Road, K5B; Northbrook, IL 60062
Ms. Gina Sheehan: Motorola Paging Division; 1500 Gateway Boulevard; Boynton Beach, FL 33426-8292
Mr. Christopher D. Sheets: ATO International, Inc.; 1206 Park Place Drive; Jonesboro, GA 30236
Mr. William W. Sheeve: Productivity Point International; 3555 Timmons; Houston, TX 77027
Mr. Yosef Sheinfil: Eliahu Industries; 867, 51st Street; Brooklyn, NY 11220-2907
Mr. Peter J. Shelfo Jr.: Electric Cities Of North Carolina Inc.; 1427 Meadowwood Boulevard; Raleigh, NC 27604-1532
Mr. John Shellshear: Powercerv Corporation; 400 North Ashley Drive, Suite 2700; Tampa, FL 33602-4324
Mr. Jay Shelton: Nextlink; 1000 Denny Way, Suite 200; Seattle, WA 98109-5397
Mr. Mike Shelton: Fidelity Investments; 100 Magellan Way; Covington, KY 41015-1999
Mr. Paul Shepherd: Lehman Brothers; 282 East Gun Hill Road, Apartment 5A; Bronx, NY 10467-2248
Mr. David Sheridan: Office of Academic Computing Service; University of Maryland College Park 221 Lefrak Hall; College Park, MD 20742-8231
Mrs. Jill Sherrill-Gary: Grand Haven Area Public School; 1415 South Beechtree Street; Grand Haven, MI 49417-2899
Mr. Keith Sherron: United States Customs; 1800 Paredes Line Road; Brownsville, TX 78521-1691
Mr. Brent G. Sherwood: Fred Meyer, Inc./Kroger Inc.; 7142 Southeast Cora Street; Portland, OR 97206-3461
Mr. Matt Sherwood: Honeywell Das; 9201 San Mateo Boulevard NE; Albuquerque, NM 87113-2227
Mr. Nicholas Sherwood: Coors Brewing Company; 6730 South Kilimanjaro Drive; Evergreen, CO 80439-5324
Mr. Yaw-Tyng Sheu: University of Denver; 2390 South York Street; Denver, CO 80210-5345
Ms. Yvonne L. Shevnin: Aardeus, Inc.; 351 Lowell Drive; Santa Clara, CA 95051-5816
Mr. James Shey: North High School; 2416 11th Avenue East; Saint Paul, MN 55109-2420
Mr. Lei Shi: E-Z Data, Inc.; 918 East Green Street; Pasadena, CA 91106
Mr. Barry Shields: NCR; Atlanta GA; 2940 Arden Ridge Court; Suwanee, GA 30024-3579
Mr. Dennis M. Shields: Welch Allyn, Inc.; 4341 State Street Road; Skan Falls, NY 13153-5301
Mr. Steven Shields: Texas School of Business; 105 East 14th Street; Houston, TX 77008-4228
Mr. Daniel Shih: Formosa USA; 20748 Nashville Street; Chatsworth, CA 91311
Mr. Henry Shih: City of Pleasanton; P.O. Box 520; Pleasanton, CA 94566-0802
Mr. Kirk D. Shimek: TRW; 5676 Industrial Park Road; Winona, MN 55987
Mr. Scott M. Shinners: Deloitte and Touche LLP; 180 North Stetson Avenue; Chicago, IL 60601-6710
Mr. Thomas M. Shinners: Capital Information Systems; 250 South Tejon Street; Englewood, CO 80110-1128
Mr. Chris Shinnick: City of Buffalo; 212 Central Avenue; Buffalo, MN 55313
Mr. Matt Shipley: Philadelphia Suburban Water; 1108 Westdale Place; Springfield, PA 18064-3940
Ms. Diane Shirah: Professional Convention Management; 100 Vestavia Parkway, Suite 220; Birmingham, AL 35216-3754
Mr. William C. Shires: First Data Systems, Inc.; 1187 Vultee Boulevard; Nashville, TN 37217
Mr. Tim Shirey C.N.A.: Alcatel USA; 1000 Coit Road; Plano, TX 75075-7838
Mr. John Shirk: Allied Telephone and Data Company; 7604 Babikow Road; Baltimore, MD 21237
Mr. Anunaya Shirvastava: Computech; 879 Century Drive #A208; Troy, MI 48083-1341
Mr. Jeffrey Shlosberg: Chase.com; 130 Belmont Drive; Somerset, NJ 08873-1201
Mr. Gary Shobe: Trinity Industries; 2525 North Stemmons Freeway; Dallas, TX 75207-2400
Mr. Dennis Shockko: Yankee Candle Company; P.O. Box 110; South Deerfield, MA 01373-0110
Mr. Michael A. Shoemaker: Wellspring FV Corporation; 336 College Avenue; Lancaster, PA 17603
Ms. Lawana Shook: Parents In Motion Inc.; 178 Mahaffey Street; Jefferson, GA 30549-1136
Mr. Brad Shorer: Sprint, PCS; 12500 Slater Lane; Overland Park, KS 66213-1774
Mr. Adam Short: Sigma Phi Epsilon; P. O. Box 1901; Richmond, VA 23218-1901
Mr. James A. Short: collegestudent.com, Inc.; 715 West 23rd Street, Suite M; Austin, TX 78705-5149
Mr. Rick Short: Scenic Earth Studios, Inc.; 6901 Northwest 14th Court; Plantation, FL 33313
Ms. Teresa L. Short: First Community Credit Union; 9100 Westview Drive; Houston, TX 77055-6420
Mr. Brett M. Shouse: United States West Long Distance; 1801 California Street, Suite 3100; Denver, CO 80202
Ms. Alicia C. Shows: Southwest Mississippi Community College; College Drive; Summit, MS 39666
Mr. Leonid Shraybman: UPS Information Systems; 2311 York Road; Lutherville, MD 21093-2215
Dr. Rajendra K. Shrivastava Ph.D.: SAIC; 3800 Watt Avenue, Suite 290; Sacramento, CA 95821
Mr. John R. Shriver: T.I.M.S., Inc.; 301 Alpha Park; Highland Heights, OH 44143
Mr. Vimal Shroff: Infoseric Comm; 2200 Waterview Parkway, Apartment 1615; Richardson, TX 75080
Mr. Jeff Shubert: Toyota Motor Sales USA; 19001 South Western Avenue #B2m7; Torrance, CA 90501-1106
Mr. Brian Shuhart: PISA; 1182 Kings Court; Greencastle, PA 17225
Ms. Lorna Shultis: Specsware; 5 Quail Run Road; Hopewell Junction, NY 12533
Mr. Paul Shunn: Broadreach Consulting; 4709 Tolley Court; Raleigh, NC 27616
Mr. Shawn C. Shutt Sr.: Memorial Hospital Union Company; 500 LonDon Avenue; Marysville, OH 43040
Mr. Jiatun Si: Karta Technology, Inc.; 1892 Grandstand Drive; San Antonio, TX 78238-4507
Mr. Randal L. Sibley: Aim Management, Inc.; 4319 Annawood Circle; Spring, TX 77388-5797
Mr. John J. Sidell: eSYNC International; 6629 West Central Avenue; Toledo, OH 43528
Mr. Thomas R. Sidlauskas: Spectrum Health; 100 Michigan Street NE; Grand Rapids, MI 49503
Ms. Debra Sieloff: Harris Corporation; 1025 West Nasa Boulevard, Mailstop 100-92; Melbourne, FL 32919
Mr. Rodger J. Sillars: Greater Cleveland Rta; 1167 Oxford Road; Cleveland, OH 44121
Mr. Pierre Simard: Scmreynolds; 101 Route Maritime; Baie Comeau, Quebec, Canada G4Z2L6
Mr. Kevin Simmers: Simplified Software, Inc.; P.O. Box 747; Chicago, IL 60690-0747
Mr. Ben Simmons: Custom Projects Inc.; 333 East Brooks Road; Memphis, TN 38109-2928
Mr. Brad Simmons: Applied PC Systems; 59 Interstate Drive; West Springfield, MA 01089-5100
Ms. Debbbie Simmons: Krasier Permenente; 6501 Loisdale Court; Springfield, VA 22150-1807
Mr. Ezell Simmons: Entergy; 425 West Capitol Avenue, #Tcby21; Little Rock, AR 72201
Mr. Mark Simmons: Semicoa; 333 McCormick Avenue; Costa Mesa, CA 92626-3479
Ms. Pam Simmons: Duke Engineering & Services; 400 South Tryon Street; Charlotte, NC 28285-0100
Mr. Scott W. Simmons: Crist Partners; 303 West Madison Street, Suite 2600; Chicago, IL 60606
Mr. Jimmy W. Simons: Community Care, Inc., Bluefield Health Systems; 210 Blana Street 3rd Floor; Bluefield, WV 24701
Mr. Robert Simpson: World Wide Web Shop, Inc.; P.O. Box 601; Lawrence, PA 15055-0601
Mr. William Simpson: IBM Global Services; 400 Clinton Square; Rochester, NY 14604-1728
Mr. Brian J. Singer: Dalco; 425 South Pioneer Boulevard; Springboro, OH 45066-3002
Mr. Gordon Singer: Focus Computer Center; 1328 45th Street; Brooklyn, NY 11219-2101
Mr. Ross A. Singer: APS/PVVGS; Mail Stop 7445/5801 South Wintersburg Road; Tonopah, AZ 85354-7529
Mr. Ashish Singh: BFL Software; 1335-B Lynnfield Road, #245; Memphis, TN 38119
Mr. Gurpreet Singh: SIS; 500 Northridge Road, Suite 500; Atlanta, GA 30350-3322
Mr. Inder Singh: The Culinary Institute of America; 433 Albany Post Road; Hyde Park, NY 12538-1501
Mr. Ninhi Singh: NIIT (USA), Inc.; 161 Rock Harbor Lane; Foster City, CA 94404
Ms. Nita Singh: ABC, Inc.; 7001 East Fish Lake Road; Maple Grove, MN 55311-2841
Mr. Randy Singh: ACE Technologies; 209 West Central Street, Suite 206; Natick, MA 01760-3716
Mrs. Ruby Singh: Vanguard Cellular; 3025 Pisgah Place, Apartment B; Greensboro, NC 27455-3272
Mr. Surinder Singh: TMI Communications; 1601 Telesat Court; Gloucester, Ontario, Canada K1B 5P4
Dr. Anoop Singhal Ph.D.: AT&T Labs; 200 South Laurel Avenue, Room D53B34; Middletown, NJ 07748-1998
Ms. Donna Singleton: Braxton County High School; 200 Jerry Burton Drive; Sutton, WV 26601
Mr. Patrick Sinnott: Dana Corporation; 4025 East San Angelo Avenue; Higley, AZ 85236-3331
Mr. Stephen Sirard: Next Level Communications; 6085 State Farm Drive; Rohnert Park, CA 94928
Mr. Vinai Sirkay: Sentient Networks, Inc.; 630 Alder Drive; Milpitas, CA 95035-7444
Mr. Preetam Sirur: Stanhope Network Services, Inc.; 14 Adams Court; East Brunswick, NJ 08816-4053
Ms. Cynthia Sisco: Liberty Mutual; 18 Pearl Street; Marblehead, MA 01945
Mr. Michael J. Sisneros: Business Systems Analysts and Designers; 5464 Alteza Drive; Colorado Springs, CO 80917-3802
Mr. Brian Sisson: Paradigm Application Solutions; 17210 Cambridge Grove Drive; Huntersville, NC 28078-5283
Mr. Daniel Sitler: P M I Food Equip Gro; 701 South Ridge Avenue; Troy, OH 45374-0001
Ms. Vicki Skaggs: Computer Sciences Corporation; 1520 Hughes Way; Long Beach, CA 90810
Mr. James M. Skains: Louisiana Technical College; 310 St. Charles Street; Houma, LA 70360
Mr. K. M. Skeaping: Scottish Homes, Edinburgh; Kinloch Rannoch, Bunrannoch House; Pitlochry, Scotland, United Kingdom PH16 5QB
Mr. Terry Skelley: SBIHS; 1622 12th Street; Charleston, IL 61920
Mr. Doyle Skipper: Fidelity Investments; 400 Las Colinas Boulevard East; Irving, TX 75039-5579
Mr. Mike Skivington: Salomon Smith Barney; 517a West Broadway; Long Beach, NY 11561-3027
Mr. William Skonsky: Fore Systems, Inc.; 421 Hoodridge Drive; Pittsburgh, PA 15234-1705
Mr. Tim Skrocki: Aspect Development; 1300 Charleston Road; Mountain View, CA 94043
Mr. Tim Slack: Bell South Telecommunications, Inc.; 365 Canal Street, Room 1010; New Orleans, LA 70130-1112
Mr. Stephen Slanovec: The Guardian Life Insurance Company; 3900 Burgess Place; Bethlehem, PA 18017-9097
Mr. Robert Slap: Levy Company; P.O. Box 540; Portage, IN 46368-0540
Dr. Roberta Bronson Slater Ph.D.: Cedar Crest College; 100 College Drive; Allentown, PA 18104-6196
Ms. Sharon Slaton: Unigraphics Solutions, Inc.; 9864 Clara Jean Street; Brighton, MI 48116-1947
Mr. Jim Sleeth: Salina Regional Health Center; 1213 Stack Avenue; Salina, KS 67401-3243
Ms. Danielle Slegus: The Timken Company; 1835 Dueber Avenue SW #BIC-18; Canton, OH 44706-0927
Ms. Marie Slominski: Daimler Chrysler; 25999 Lawrence Avenue; Center Line, MI 48015
Ms. Michelle Slominski: TMP Worldwide; 4124 South 88th Street; Greenfield, WI 53228
Mr. Roger Sluder: Advance Auto Parts; 5673 Airport Road NW; Roanoke, VA 24012
Mr. Lucas G. Slymen: Embee Technologies; 2158 South Hathaway Street; Santa Ana, CA 92705-5249
Mrs. Pamela Smallwood: Gaylord Entertainment; 1 Gaylord Drive; Nashville, TN 37214-1207
Mr. William Smart: New York Presbyterian Hospital; 333 East 38th Street; New York, NY 10016-2772
Mr. Pat A. Smereka: Polk; 10580 Boucher Street; Grosse Isle, MI 48138-2003
Mr. Ronald Smiley: Levi Ray & Shoup, Inc.; 2401 West Monroe Street; Springfield, IL 62704-1439
Mrs. A. Smith: Senior Central District 7; 66 Raymond Avenue; San Francisco, CA 94134
Mr. Al E. Smith: The First Bank of Brunswick; 3440 Cypress Mill Road; Brunswick, GA 31520-2856
Ms. Angela Smith: Quix Data (formerly Apex Solutions); 2000 Crow Canyon Place, Suite 185; San Ramon, CA 94583-1383
Mr. Anton Smith: Cyberstar; 1965 Charleston Road; Mountain View, CA 94043-1205
Mrs. Barbara Smith: Independent; 106 Central Park South Apartment 6g; New York, NY 10019-1569
Dr. Barton Smith Ph.D.: IBM Almaden Research Center; 650 Harry Road, Department NWE-B2; San Jose, CA 95120-6001
Mr. Bob Smith: CDSI/Consortium; 8205 Splashing Brook Court; Laurel, MD 20723-1055
Mr. Chad Smith: Champion Computer; 17361 Bendross Road; Jupiter, FL 33458-8974
Ms. Cheryl Smith: Thiokol Corporation; M/S N40, P.O. Box 707; Brigham City, UT 84302-0707
Ms. Cindy Smith: Danzas Corporation; 3650 131st Avenue SE; Bellevue, WA 98006-1334
Mr. Clarence R. Smith: Elkem Metal Company, L.P.; P.O. Box 613; Alloy, WV 25002
Mr. David E. Smith: Focus Direct; 9707 Broadway Drive; San Antonio, TX 78217-4903
Mr. Dudley Smith: University Air Care; 234 Goodman Street; Cincinnati, OH 45219
Mr. Frank Smith: Sierra Aluminum Company; 2345 Fleetwood Drive; Riverside, CA 92509-2426
Ms. Glenda Smith: District 4 Healthcare Services; 122 Gordon Commercial Drive; La Grange, GA 30240
Mr. Jay Smith: Cyberverse, Inc.; 2221 Rosecrans Avenue, Suite 130; El Segundo, CA 90245-4942
Ms. Jeanette Smith: Synergy 2000; 225 South Lake; Pasadena, CA 91101
Mr. Jeff Smith: Mvp Health Plan; 111 Liberty Street; Schenectady, NY 12305-1892
Mr. Jeffrey R. Smith: Nassau Broadcasting Partners; 619 Alexander Road , Floor 3; Princeton, NJ 08540-6003
Ms. Kay Smith: Reynolds & Reynolds; 11350 McCormick Road; Hunt Valley, MD 21031-1002

Ms. Kenitha Smith: Salvation Army Cleveland; 17625 Grovewood Avenue; Cleveland, OH 44119-3117
Mr. Kevin W. Smith: United States Army Reserve/Microsystems; 35 Hill Avenue; Mary Esther, FL 32569-1530
Ms. Khadija Smith: Florida Lottery; 250 Marriott Drive; Tallahassee, FL 32399-4000
Mr. Kurt Smith: Valassis Communications; 47585 Galleon Drive; Plymouth, MI 48170-2466
Ms. Leslie Smith: Rappahannock Community College; 52 Campus Drive; Warsaw, VA 22572-4272
Mr. Lester G. N. Smith: Chyron Corporation; 543 South Long Beach Avenue; Freeport, NY 11520-6109
Ms. Lylah Smith: Virginia Technical Computer Center; 1700 Pratt Drive; Blacksburg, VA 24060-6361
Mr. Mark Smith: Management Information Systems, Calvert County Government; 176 Main Street, Suite 102; Prince Frederick, MD 20678-3337
Ms. Meggan Smith: Forum Health Cardiovascular Nursing; 500 Gypsy Lane; Youngstown, OH 44504
Mr. Michael M. Smith: 75th Communications Squadron; 75CS/SCBE 5851 F Avenue; Hill Air Force Base, UT 84056-5713
Ms. Nora Smith: Virginia Western Community College; 1135 Lynchburg Turnpike; Salem, VA 24153-5316
Ms. Robin Smith: Dell Computer Corporation; 1 Dell Way; Round Rock, TX 78682-0001
Mr. Ross W. Smith: Bell Atlantic Mobile; 2155 Roper Road; Cumming, GA 30040-9144
Mr. Scott Smith: Emh Regional Medical Center; 630 East River Street; Elyria, OH 44035-5902
Ms. Sherry Smith: West Motor Freight; P.O. Box 587; Boyertown, PA 19512-0587
Mr. Stephen G. Smith: Information Builders Inc.; 328 Potomac Drive; Basking Ridge, NJ 07920-3124
Mr. Steve Smith: OES; 5520 Shelby Oaks Drive; Memphis, TN 38134-7315
Mr. Stuart Smith: Utah Department of Public Safety; 3888 West 5400 South; Salt Lake City, UT 84118
Mr. Terry L. Smith: Indian River County; 1840 25th Street; Vero Beach, FL 32960-3365
Ms. Tonya Smith: Premier Circuit Assembly; P.O. Box B, 5653 Macedonia Road; Spring Hope, NC 27882-9382
Mr. Walter G. Smith: Hartwick College; West Street; Oneonta, NY 13820
Ms. Wanda Smith: Oracle; 8622 Trumps Hill Road; Upper Marlboro, MD 20772-5051
Mr. William J. Smith: IBM; 914 Teresita Boulevard; San Francisco, CA 94127-2325
Mr. Terry Smyser: City of Indianapolis, Fleet Maintenance; 1651 West 30th Street; Indianapolis, IN 46208-4984
Mrs. Mary Ann Snider: Car Care Council; 42 Park Drive; Port Clinton, OH 43452-2074
Mr. Randy L. Snider: West Palm Beach VA Medical Center; 7305 North Military Trail; West Palm Beach, FL 33410-6415
Mr. Harvey Snodgrass: Union Carbide Corporation; P.O. Box 8361; South Charleston, WV 25303-0361
Mr. Dave W. Snyder: Bank of Lancaster County, N.A.; 1097 Commercial Avenue, P.O. Box 38; East Petersburg, PA 17520-0038
Mr. Viatcheslav Sobol: Clayton Group; 4 Corporate Drive; Shelton, CT 06440
Mr. Clive Soden: Symbol Technologies, Inc.; 340 Fischer Avenu; Costa Mesa, CA 92626-4523
Mr. Keith Soderberg: South Carolina Department of Natural Resources; P.O. Box 167; Columbia, SC 29202-0167
Mr. Alvin Soh: IPC Information Systems; 100 South Wacker Drive, Suite 1500; Chicago, IL 60606-4004
Mr. Ken Sohal: IBM; 4111 Northside Parkway; Atlanta, GA
Mr. Cecil W. Soileau: Brown Cunningham & Gannuch; 10012 Walden Drive; River Ridge, LA 70123-1548
Mr. James Soistmann: County of Morris; P.O. Box 900; Morristown, NJ 07963-0900
Mr. Piotr Sokolowski: Swak, Inc.; 3554 32nd Street; Astoria, NY 11106-2756
Mr. Craig Solinski: Citigroup; 1955 Erin Brooke Drive; Valrico, FL 33594-4012
Mr. Edward Sommers: Memorial Health Systems; 615 North Michigan Street; South Bend, IN 46601-1033
Mr. John A. Sonner: Plant; 76 Maple Street; Acton, MA 01720-3536
Mr. Bruce A. Sopher: NCR; 3325 Platt Springs Road; West Columbia, SC 29170
Mr. Mike Sorenson: Centry Constructors Engine; 375 Chipeta Way; Salt Lake City, UT 84108-1260
Mr. Anthony M. Sorrells: Ryobi North America; P.O. Box 35; Pickens, SC 29671-0035
Ms. Carolyn Yvette Soto: Sign of the Quill; 8000 Brompton Street; Springfield, VA 22152
Ms. Manny Soto: Soto and Gonzalez; 3850 SW 87; Miami, FL 33165
Mr. Mariano Soto: DeAngelo Exhaust; 3330 Southwest 2 Avenue; Fort Lauderdale, FL 33315
Mr. I. Philip Soucy: Soucy Louis Philip; 112 West Main Street; Fort Kent, ME 04743-1016
Mr. Gary C. Southern: General Motors Corporation; 1155 Brewery Park Boulevard; Detroit, MI 48207
Mr. Bruce Souza: U.S. Securities & Exchange Commission; 73 Tremont Street, Suite 600; Boston, MA 02108-3902
Mr. John A. Spadafora: Kenan/ Lucent Technologies; 5 Blossom Street; Arlington, MA 02474-2601
Mr. Thomas Sparks: International Benefit Services; 10805 Cobblestone Drive; Benbrook, TX 76126-4503
Mr. Wayne Speaks: United States Air Force; 7103-A McNickle Street; Oklahoma City, OK 73145-4515
Ms. Judy Spears: St. Johns Medical Center; 1923 South Utica Avenue; Tulsa, OK 74104-6520
Mr. Michael Speciner: Splash Technology; 900 Middlesex Turnpike, Building 8; Billerica, MA 01821
Mr. Bradley G. Spelman: Deutsche Bank; 300 South Grand Avenue, 41st Floor, Corporate Graphics Department; Los Angeles, CA 90071
Ms. Diane Spence: Smyth County Office Building; 121 Bagley Circle; Marion, VA 24354-3140
Mr. Henry C. Spencer: Macess Corporation; 402 Office Park Drive; Birmingham, AL 35223-2417
Mr. Isabella Noelani Spencer: Kaumana School; 1710 Kaumana Drive; Hilo, HI 96720
Mr. Mark L. Spencer: Computer Technology Associates, Inc.; 7150 Campus Drive, Suite 100; Colorado Springs, CO 80920-6592
Ms. Melinda Spencer: Bluestone Industries; 818 North Eisenhower Drive; Beckley, WV 25801-3112
Mr. Sherman Spencer: United States Army Aviation And Missiles; 1503 Sparkman Drive NW, Apartment 36; Huntsville, AL 35816-2639
Mr. Steve Sperber: Chase Bank; 270 Park Avenue, #27fl; New York, NY 10017-2014
Mr. Mark Spicer: Boone County; 2950 Washington Street; Burlington, KY 41005-8211
Ms. Caren Spiegel: Rapp Collins Worldwide; 11 Madison Avenue; New York, NY 10010-3629
Ms. Carla Spinelli: Nomadic Display; 7400 Fullerton Avenue; Springfield, VA 22153
Mr. Ralph P. Spinelli: Sytex, Inc.; 9891 Broken Land Parkway, Suite 304; Columbia, MD 21046
Mr. Philippe Spiteri: Insight Control Systems; 306 10th Avenue North; Safety Harbor, FL 34695-3416
Dr. Janet Spitz Ph.D.: College of Saint Rose; 432 Western Avenue; Albany, NY 12203
Ms. Sharon Spitzer: Illuminet; 7400 West 129th Street; Overland Park, KS 66213-2633
Mr. John Spivey: Litespec Optical Fiber Llc; P.O. Box 13667; Research Triangle Park, NC 27709-3667
Mr. Mike Spivey: Austin Energy; 721 Barton Springs; Austin, TX 78704-1194
Mr. Paul Spotts: Geisinger Medical; 100 Academy Lane; Danville, PA 17822
Mr. Martin Spratt: Sapient Corporation; 10 Exchange Place; Jersey City, NJ 07302-3901
Ms. Marcia D. Sprey: Bechtel; Washingtonian Boulevard; Rockville, MD 20850
Mr. Johnny Sprouse: ARS of Virginia; 4005 West Broad Street, Suite 100; Richmond, VA 23230
Mr. Mark Sprouse: Johnson Industries; 5944 Peachtree Corners E; Norcross, GA 30071-1336
Mr. James M. Spruill: Mighty Distributing System; 650 Engineering Drive; Norcross, GA 30092-2963
Mr. Gangoor C. Sridhara: Global Solutions, Inc.; 207A Lorren Drive, Suite 242; Freemont, CA 94536
Ms. Manjula Sriram: Metrix-Inc.; 157 Manchester Drive; Waukesha, WI 53188-4117
Mr. Jim St. Piere: National Institute of Standards & Technology; 100 Bureau Drive, Stop 8114; Gaithersburg, MD 20899-8114
Mr. John Staarmann: Team Labs; 6859 North Foothills Highway, D2000; Boulder, CO 80302
Ms. Terre M. Stack: Timberline Software; 15195 Northwest Greenbrier Parkway; Beaverton, OR 97006-5701
Mr. Neil Stackel: Bell Atlantic; 120 Hicksville Road; Massapequa, NY 11758-5898
Mr. Stepan Stadnyk: Genesys Telecomm Labs, Inc.; 1155 Market Street, Floor 6; San Francisco, CA 94103-1522
Mr. Ambrose M. Stafyleras: Federal Reserve Bank of New York; 95 Maiden Lane, 8th Floor; New York, NY 10038-4813
Ms. Pamela Stallard: Avionics Research Corporation Florida; 672 North Semoran Boulevard, Suite 101; Orlando, FL 32807-3367
Mr. Al Stamm: Application Objects, Inc.; 425 Walnut Street, Suite 2200; Cincinnati, OH 45202-3917
Ms. Joleen Stanczyk: Stanczyk Consulting; P.O. Box 211608; Denver, CO 80221-0380
Mr. Ricky Standley: CRI, The Resource Group; 2627 West Idaho; Boise, ID 83702
Ms. Jaton Stanford: ITT Technical Institute; 500 Riverhills Business Park; Birmingham, AL 35242-5039
Mr. Roger Stanford: City of Birmingham; 710 20th Street North; Birmingham, AL 35203-2216
Mr. Richard L. Stanich: Stanich Design and Associates, Inc.; 38025 2nd Street, Suite 103; Willoughby, OH 44094-6104
Mr. Ron H. Stanley: Varsity Computing, Inc.; 4920-B Corporate Drive; Huntsville, AL 35805
Mr. David G. Stanley-Brown: AT&T Global Wireless; 372 Holly Drive; Wyckoff, NJ 07481
Mr. Richard Stansfield: Raskas Foods; 165 North Meramec Avenue, Suite 300; Saint Louis, MO 63105-3772
Mr. Jamey Stanworth: NEXTLINK; 1660 Lincoln Street, Suite 2600; Denver, CO 80264
Mr. Lee Staples: Maine Medical Center; 420 Cumberland Avenue; Portland, ME 04101-2823
Mr. Jim Stapleton: AT&T; 55 Corporate Drive; Bridgewater, NJ 08807-1265
Ms. Lisa K. Stapleton: Global Technology Business Magazine; 1157 San Antonio Road; Mountain View, CA 94043
Mr. Lee H. Stapp: Marble Street Studio; 14312 Stalgren Court Northeast; Albuquerque, NM 87123-2209
Mr. David Stark: Centerior Energy Corporation; 205 West Saint Clair Avenue, Room C1e-291; Cleveland, OH 44113-1503
Mr. Paul Starkey: North Atlantic Energy; P.O. Box 300; Seabrook, NH 03874-0300
Mr. G. J. Stasyna: Toronto Police Department; 4620 Finch Avenue East; Scarborough, Ontario, Canada ON MIS 4G2
Mr. Chris Staszak: Sierra Com; 99 South Street; Hopkinton, MA 01748-2204
Mr. Steven J. Stauffacher: Cognos Corporation; 425 North Martingale Road, Suite 930; Schaumburg, IL 60173-2207
Mr. Ron Stead: Rich Products Manufacturing Corporation; 801 North Kent Street; Winchester, VA 22601-5415
Ms. Laurisa Stebbins: 229 Marion Street; East Boston, MA 02128-1725
Ms. Barbara Steele: Omni Point Communications; 95 Highland Avenue; Bethlehem, PA 18017-9424
Ms. Jennifer Steele: The Mentor Network; 313 Congress Street; Boston, MA 02210-1218
Ms. Mary Steele: Queen of the World School; 134 Queens Road; St. Marys, PA 15857-2199
Mr. Jason R. Stefanvich: United States Army; NCOIC Communications, 2156-A Hall Street; Wahiawa, HI 96786
Mr. John Steffy: Findlay Automotive Group, Inc.; 310 North Gibson Road; Henderson, NV 89014-6702
Mr. Michael Steich: McKessonHBOC Automated He; 700 Waterfront Drive; Pittsburgh, PA 15222
Ms. Jenny Stencel: Micromedex; 6200 South Syracuse Way, Suite 300; Englewood, CO 80111-4740
Mr. Scott Stenslien: Indus MIS; 340 South Oak Street; West Salem, WI 54669
Mr. Derek C. Stephens: IBM Corporation; 3525 San Patricio Drive; Plano, TX 75025-4427
Mr. Mike Stephens: Morris & Associates; P.O. Box 1046; Raleigh, NC 27602-1046
Mr. Ronee A. Stephens: Andersen Consulting; 1084 Old Saybrook Court; Stone Mountain, GA 30083-2666
Mr. Versie Stephenson: HOK, Incorporated; 323 West 8th Street, Suite 700; Kansas City, MO 64105
Mr. Michael Stern: Handey; 500 Campus Drive; Morganville, NJ 07751
Mr. Per Sterner: Sternal Consulting, Inc.; 9 Talcott Road; Rye Brook, NY 10573-1420
Mr. Joe Stevenson: Harris Stowe State College; 3026 Laclede Avenue; St. Louis, MO 63103-2199
Mr. Curtis Steward: Dakota Growers Pasta Company; One Pasta Avenue; Carrington, ND 58421
Ms. Sandy N. Steward: Anthem Alliance; 514 Butler Farm Road; Hampton, VA 23666-1500
Mr. Timothy Steward: Compuware Corporation; 19148 Votrobeck Drive; Detroit, MI 48219-2615
Mr. Andy Stewart: Texas Children's Hospital; 1102 Bates Avenue, Suite 650; Houston, TX 77030-2698
Mr. Leejay Stewart: Power Conversion Products; 115 Erick Street; Crystal Lake, IL 60014
Mr. Michael Stewart: Spokane County Independent School District; 2417 West Rosewood Avenue; Spokane, WA 99208-4450
Ms. Patricia L. Stewart: Mid-Hudson Regional Information Center; 175 State Route 32 North; New Platz, NY 12561-1029
Mr. Paul H. Stewart: Host Marriott Services Corporation; 6600 Rockledge Drive; Bethesda, MD 20817
Mr. Michael Stiber: University of Washington, Bothell; CSS Department, 22011-26th Avese; Bothell, WA 98021
Mr. Timm Stifter: Boca Lago Country Club; 8665 Juego Way; Baca Raton, FL 33433-2099
Mr. Kenneth Stigleman: Tarus Product Inc.; 38100 Commerce Drive; Sterling Heights, MI 48312-1006
Mr. Douglas A. Stine: Computer Science Corporation; 12 Turnburry Road; Washington, NJ 07882-1551
Ms. Liz Stinger: Mount Joy Career & Technology Center; 1730 Hans Herr Drive; Willow Street, PA 17584-9532
Mr. Donald M. Stitt: St. Thomas Church Fifth Avenue; 1 West 53rd Street; New York, NY 10019-5496
Mr. Hannemie Stitz: Public Relations Partners GmbH; Bleichstr., 5; Kronberg, Germany 61468
Mr. Jared Stivers: Vencor, Inc.; 2239 Boulevard Napoleon; Louisville, KY 40205-1846
Mr. Ian R. Stoba: Babcock And Brown, Inc.; 599 Lexington Avenue Floor 45; New York, NY 10022
Mr. Steven Stockman: GE Capital-Consumer Operations; 260 Long Ridge Road; Stamford, CT 06927-1600
Ms. Lavon Stough: Technomatix; 39810 Grand River Avenue; Novi, MI 48375-2138
Mr. Tom Strader: Carolina Computer Services; 480 Venture Court; Salisbury, NC 28147-6660
Mr. Barry Strain: First National Bank; 729 West 7th Avenue; Spearman, TX 79081-3407
Mr. Robert Stranathan: Unisys Corporation; 4618 West 5th Street; Santa Ana, CA 92703-3164
Mr. Nick Strange: Fidelity; 39 Redington Street; Swampscott, MA 01907-2003
Mr. Shaun D. Strauss: Crestone International; 14356 Sorrel Way; Eden Prairie, MN 55347-1615
Ms. Staci Strebeck: Mississippi Hospital Association; 6425 Lakeover Road; Jackson, MS 39213-8008
Mr. Randall Strey: Paragon Cable TV; 461 Strey Lane; Seguin, TX 78155-0707
Mr. Doug Striff: United States Air Force; 25th Street, Building 25702; Fort Gordon, GA 30905
Ms. Danielle Strom: The Computer Help Button, LLC.; 7252 South 37th Place; Franklin, WI 53132-9459
Mr. Richard Stroupe: Quality Systems Incorporated; 8201 Greensboro Drive; Mclean, VA 22102
Ms. Penny Struchtemeyer: City of Warrensburg; P.O. Box 1018; Warrensburg, MO 64093-1018
Mr. Rod G. Strumbel: Popp Telcom, Inc.; 620 Mendelssohn Avenue North; Golden Valley, MN 55427-4310
Mr. Audrey Stsudt: Benefit Planners; 194 South Main Street; Boerne, TX 78006-2399
Ms. Frances Stuart: Dynamic Computer Solutions;

1500 Grand Boulevard; Kansas City, MO 64108-1404
Ms. Renee Stubsten: ACS-Technology Solutions; 3030 LBJ Freeway Street; Dallas, TX 75234
Mr. Ron Studdard: AMS; 2827 Georgetown Drive, Apartment B; Hoover, AL 35216-5037
Mr. Ron Studer: Ernst & Young, LLP.; 250 East 5th Street; Cincinnati, OH 45202-4119
Mr. Mark Sturges: The Group; 1602 Rolling Hills Drive, Suite 104; Richmond, VA 23065
Mr. Paul J. Sturgis: A.B.W.E.; P.O. Box 8585; Harrisburg, PA 17105-8585
Mr. Mark Sturtevant: Rhi Consulting; 8600 Colfax Avenue South; Bloomington, MN 55420-2616
Mr. Andres Suarez: The Dow Chemical Company; Building 633; Midland, MI 48667-0001
Mr. Ravi Subbarayan: Comsat Satellite Services; 6560 Rock Springs Drive; Bethesda, MD 20817
Mr. Siva Subra: Computech Corp.; 610 Preston Drive, Apartment 315; Bolingbrook, IL 60440
Mr. Bhagya Subramanian: NERL/USEPA; 26 West MLK Drive; Cincinnati, OH 45268
Mr. Kulandaivelu Subramanian: Allied Informatics, Inc.; 45 Birchwood Road, Apartment 235; Randolph, MA 02368
Mr. Paul M. Suckow: Equiva Services LLC.; 12700 Northborough Drive; Houston, TX 77067-2508
Ms. Jeannie Suelke: Amplifier Research; 160 Schoolhouse Road; Souderton, PA 18964-2412
Mr. Dayle Suess: AG Edwards & Sons; 1 North Jefferson Avenue; St. Louis, MO 63103-2287
Mr. Jim Sughrve: C D I; 7640 Pelham Road; Greenville, SC 29615-5736
Dr. Ephraim Suhir Ph.D.: Bell Laboratories; 600 Mountain Avenue, Room 1D-443; Murray Hill, NJ 07974
Ms. Ann Sulkovsky: United States Coast Guard (G-SIA); 2100 2nd Street SW; Washington, DC 20593-0002
Mr. Jerry R. Sullenberger: On Point Training, Inc.; 621 North Broad Street; Cairo, GA 31728-1606
Ms. Roberta Sullivan: Walkway Technology Node, State University of New York at Buffalo; 212 Christopher Baldy Hall; Buffalo, NY 14260-0001
Ms. Carole Sumler: Cybertown, Inc.; 6252 Honolulu Avenue, Suite 100A; Glendale, CA 91214
Mr. Mitchell Summerlin: WABCO; 1040 Bennetts Bridge Road; Greer, SC 29651
Mr. Charles D. Sumner: Home Shopping Network; 10209 Newington Place; Tampa, FL 33626-1714
Ms. Jennifer Sumner: United States Air Force-21CS/SCXS; 175 East Stewart Avenue; Colorado Springs, CO 80914-1684
Mr. David Sumpter: Department of Defense; Naval Aviation Depot, 136 Terrapin Court; Newport, NC 28570-8635
Mr. Kumaran Sundaram: Kumara Systems, Incorporated; 19570 Crystal Rock Drive, Apartment 23; Germantown, MD 20874
Mr. Rahul Sundrani: Lante Corporation; 9027 Capitol Drive, #1B; Chicago, IL 60016
Ms. Ina M. Suprlock: Health Recovery; 1730 Blackwood Road; Guysville, OH 45735-9580
Mr. Jose Jorge Sus: Insumos Industrial; Gabriela Mistral 3876; Cap. Fed., Argentina 1419
Mr. Joe Sutphin: Belvac Production Machines; 237 Graves Mill Road; Lynchburg, VA 24502-4203
Mr. Donald J. Sutton: OTD, Inc.; 3885 South Decatur, Suite 2010; Las Vegas, NV 89103
Ms. Sherri Suzewitz: Archer Daniels Midland; 4666 East Faries Parkway; Decatur, IL 62526-5666
Mr. Bhaskar Swamy: Dell Computer Corporation; 1 Dell Way, MS-WC4/04; Round Rock, TX 78682-0001
Mr. Daniel P. Swanberg: United Technologies Corporation; 1805 Cedar Drive; New Brighton, MN 55112
Mr. Jeff Swanson: TAASC; 10042 South 94 East Avenue; Tulsa, OK 74133
Mr. Paul Swanson: Microsoft; 1 Microsoft Way; Redmond, WA 98052
Mr. Dan Sweeney: Adrian Correctional Facility; 2727 West Beecher Road; Adrian, MI 49221
Ms. Karen L. Sweeney: CTM Automated Systems; P.O. Box 1205; Sterling, VA 20167
Mr. Ted Sweeney: Motorola; 2116 East Mallory Street; Mesa, AZ 85213-1447
Mr. David Swift: Next Level Communications; 6112 Melrose Court; Fort Collins, CO 80525-5897
Mr. Jerry Swift: Evco Wholesale Food Corporation; 309 Merchant Street; Emporia, KS 66801-7207
Mr. Donald G. Swyers: Citigroup Travelers, Inc.; 36 Kencove Drive; East Hartford, CT 06118-3130
Mr. Keith Harley Sykora: Shady Oaks Nursery; P.O. Box 708; Waseca, MN 56093-0708
Mr. Darin W. Synhorst: Sykes; 1720 South Sykes Street; Bismarck, ND 58504
Mr. Michael J. Synovic: Siemens Building Technologies, Inc.; 1000 Deerfield Parkway; Buffalo Grove, IL 60089-4513
Ms. Joanne Szewc: Raymond James Consulting; 7406 Steeple Drive; San Antonio, TX 78256-1653
Mr. Mike Szymik: Harley Davidson; 10000 South Franklin Drive; Franklin, WI 53132-8665
Mr. Loan Ta: Worldspan; 2027 McLain Road NW; Acworth, GA 30101-4448
Mr. E. L. Tack: Iowa Interstate Railroad; 800 Webster Street; Iowa City, IA 52240-4806
Ms. Charolotta Taczalski: Computer Systems Builders; P.O. Box 15500, Panorama; Cape-Town, South Africa 7506
Mr. Jim Taglianetti: State of Hawaii Public Safety; 919 Ala Moana Boulevarde, Room 406; Honolulu, HI 96814-4920
Mr. Duncan Taitt: Sitech; 7901 4th Street North, Suite 200; St. Petersburg, FL 33702-4300
Mr. Naeem Taj: Charles River Association; 200 Clarendon Street, Suite T-33; Boston, MA 02116-5021
Mr. Hemant Takle: Oracle Corporation; 203 North La Salle Street, Suite 2000; Chicago, IL 60601-1220
Dr. Manorama Talaiver Ed.D.: Chesterfield County Public Schools; 990 Krause Road; Chesterfield, VA 23832-6535
Mr. Orrin P. Tallman: In-System Design; 12426 West Explorer Drive, Suite 100; Boise, ID 83713
Mr. Phil Talton: Telcor Communications; 3400 Rivergreen Court; Duluth, GA 30096-2519
Mr. Adriel Tam: GE Capital; Two Union Square; Seattle, WA 98101
Ms. Isabella Tam: Olsten Health Services; 5514 Northwest Foxhill Road; Kansas City, MO 64152-3428
Mr. Guillermo Tamariz: Njit; 63 Elizabeth Avenue; Kearny, NJ 07032-3228
Mr. Benson Tang: Deloitte Consulting; 50 Fremont Street, Floor 11; San Francisco, CA 94105-2230
Ms. Traci A. Tango: Telsource Corporation; 999 Riverview Drive; Totowa, NJ 07512-1165
Mr. Tom Tankelewicz: Dialog Corp.; 11000 Regency Parkway, Suite 10; Cary, NC 27511-8518
Mr. Stephen D. Tansey: LPS Industries; 1310 Baker Street; Hillside, NJ 07205
Mr. Yuming Tao Ph.D.: EMS Technologies, Incorporated; 21025 Trans Canada Highway; Ste Anne-de-Bellevue, Quebec, Canada G2E5W1
Mr. Gregg Taormina: Motorola; 600 North U.S. Highway 45; Libertyville, IL 60048
Mr. Joseph Tappeto: Bell Atlantic; 64 Taft Avenue; Lynbrook, NY 11563-1430
Mr. Jeffery H. Tarbox: Computer Science Corporation; 700 Washington Street; Bath, ME 04530-2574
Mr. Jamshid Tata: AVNET; 2211 South 47th Street; Phoenix, AZ 85034-6403
Mr. Srini Tatapudi: 4 Soft, Inc.; 38240 Remington Park; Farmington Hills, MI 48331-3776
Mr. Dana Tate: KPMG, LL.P; 1912 Sunnybrook Drive; Irving, TX 75061
Ms. Amy Tatge: Degroot Web; 2204 Timberloch Place, Suite 250; The Woodlands, TX 77380-1170
Mr. Michele Tavares: Beaver Brook Circuits; 10 Grassy Plain Street; Bethel, CT 06801
Mr. Hock T. Tay: Science Applications International, Corp.; 6725 Odyssey Drive; Huntsville, TX 35806
Ms. Bonita Taylor: Tech Ed Associates, Inc.; 119 Bamm Hollow Road; Middletown, NJ 07748-2901
Mr. Brian D. Taylor: Booz Allen & Hamilton Inc.; 8283 Greensboro Drive; McLean, VA 22102-3802
Ms. Carol A. Taylor: Bryan Independent School District; 101 North Texas Avenue; Bryan, TX 77803-5315
Mr. Chanse Taylor: WCG Media; 42 West 91st, 2A; New York, NY 10024
Mr. Dennis Taylor: FDI Information Resources LLC; 2020 North Central Avenue, Suite 250; Phoenix, AZ 85004-4503
Mr. Garrett Taylor: Sempra Energy Information Solutions; 9855 Scranton Road; San Diego, CA 92121-1765
Mr. J. C. Taylor: Jackson Hospital; 1725 Pine Street; Montgomery, AL 36106-1117
Mr. Joseph Taylor: Intelimail (A Division of Data Doc); 14601 West 99th Street; Lenexa, KS 66215-1106
Mr. Kevin Taylor: SBC Systems; 5403 Palace Drive; Richardson, TX 75082
Ms. Laura Taylor: Southwestern Oregon Community College; 1988 Newmark Avenue; Coos Bay, OR 97420-2911
Mr. Lester F. Taylor: Intermedia Communications, Inc.; 3625 Queen Palm Drive; Tampa, FL 33619-1309
Dr. Lynn Taylor Ph.D.: Bell South International; 200 Colonial Homes Drive NW, Suite PH8; Atlanta, GA 30309-1269
Ms. Ofelia Taylor: Alcoa Fujikura Limited; 12746 Cimarron Path, Suite 116; San Antonio, TX 78249-3420
Mr. Sean P. Taylor: Renaissance Worldwide; 1077 St. Augustine Place NE; Atlanta, GA 30306-4520
Mr. Stephen J. Taylor: Atlantic Engineering Services; 650 Smithfield Street, Suite 1200; Pittsburgh, PA 15222-3907
Mr. Steven M. Taylor Sr.: NASA Ames; 13994 La Honda Road; Woodside, CA 94062
Mr. Terry O. Taylor Jr.: HQ United States Air Force/REE; 1150 Air Force Pentagon; Washington, DC 20330-1150
Mr. Brad Teal: Bell South Entertainment; 412 Bay Point Way North; Jacksonville, FL 32259
Mr. D. Lim Teck Hiang: Freight Links Express Holding, Ltd.; 51 Penjuru Road, Suite 04-00; Singapore, Singapore 609143
Mr. Kevin D. Tedesco: The Times Leader; 15 North Main Street; Wilkes Barre, PA 18711-0250
Mr. Marcel Tedjasukmana: Ricardo Beverly Hills; 15915 Canary Street; La Mirada, CA 90638-5506
Dr. William Tee Ph.D.: Engineering Animation, Inc.; 14700 Northwest Greenbrier Parkway; Beaverton, OR 97006
Ms. Cherie K. Templeton: FMC Corporation; P.O. Box 872; Green River, WY 82935-5246
Ms. Caroline L. Terrell: QVC, Inc.; 1365 Enterprise Drive; West Chester, PA 19380-5967
Mr. David M. Terrigino: Lightnin; 3 Rolling Meadows Drive; Hilton, NY 14468-1059
Ms. Jennifer Terrill: XP Systems; 405 Science Drive; Moorpark, CA 93021-2093
Ms. Carol Terry: Miner & Miner; 1517 7th Street; Windsor, CO 80302-5912
Ms. Lois R. Testa: JBS Inc.; 2404 Mattis Avenue; Champaign, IL 61821
Mr. Ray Thomas Testa: CDC North American, Inc.; 9 West 57th Street, 43rd Floor; New York, NY 10019
Ms. Lisa Teuscher: Intouch Technology; 1383 Washington Street; Newton, MA 02465-2003
Mr. Robert Thacker Jr.: Orcom Solutions; 1001 Southwest Disk Drive; Bend, OR 97702-1998
Mr. Praful Thakkar: Eliassen Group, Inc.; 6 Kimball Court, Apartment G-7; Woborn, MA 01801
Mr. Manoj Thakur: Axiom, Inc.; 4000 Midlantic Drive; Mount Laurel, NJ 08054-1558
Mr. Malcolm Tham: Singapore Trade Development Board; Goethestrabe 5; Frankfurt, Germany 60313
Mr. Solomon Thangaraj: Norell Information Systems; 161 Evergreen Road, Apartment 6A; Edison, NJ 08837-2443
Mr. Sunil S. Thankamushy: Dreamworks Interactive; 640 North Sepulveda Boulevard; Los Angeles, CA 90049
Mr. Eric Thav: Citrix Systems, Inc.; 6400 Northwest 6th Way; Fort Lauderdale, FL 33309-6123
Mr. Trygve Thayer: Rexam Metallising, Inc.; 5705 Commerce Boulevard; Morristown, MN 37814-1049
Mr. Michael C. Theis: Computers Unlimited; 12 Dimmock Avenue; Newport News, VA 23601-2108
Mr. Roy Thelin: United States Air Force; P.O. Box 9179; Hurlburt Field, FL 32544
Mr. Claude Thibault: Martin International; 500 Pace Darmess, #2910; Montreal, Quebec, Canada H2Y 2W2
Ms. Judith Thibault-Forget: Simplex; 1 Simplex Plaza; Gardner, MA 01441-0001
Ms. Michelle Thilges: Cargill; 7650 Edinborough Way, Suite 600; Edina, MN 55435-5992
Mr. Jamie Thin: James Thin Ltd.; 53-59 South Bridge; , United Kingdom Ehl 1ys
Mr. Srividya Thirumalai: General Electric Information Services; 100 Edison Poule Drive, Mailstop M-L05; Gaithersburg, MD 20878
Mr. Brian R. Thomas: Bank One; 926 East McNair Drive; Tempe, AZ 85283
Mr. Dan G. Thomas: Cooper Lighting; 400 Busse Road; Elk Grove Village, IL 60007-2100
Mr. Greg Thomas: Fairfax County Government; 12000 Government Center Parkway, Suite 117; Fairfax, VA 22035-0001
Ms. Gwendolyn Thomas: Talus Solutions, Inc.; 380 Birchmere Close Southwest; Atlanta, GA 303331-8499
Mr. Jerry Thomas: Echo Management Group; 1700 Broadway, #800; Oakland, CA 94612-2116
Mrs. Jill Thomas: Jim Hubbard & Associates, Inc.; 100 Union Hill Drive; Birmingham, AL 35209
Mrs. Melanie T. Thomas: El Paso Independent School District; 120 North Stanton Street; El Paso, TX 79901-1442
Ms. Pam Thomas: Equitable of Iowa Companies; 909 Locust Street; Des Moines, IA 50309-2803
Ms. Tarquin C. Thomas: Barclays Global Investors; 45 Fremont Street; San Francisco, CA 94105-2204
Ms. Adaire Thompson: Flying Color Graphics; 1001 West North Street; Pontiac, IL 61764-1065
Ms. Betty Thompson: Wausau Financial Systems; 9 Indianhead Drive; Mosinee, WI 54455-9512
Mr. Greg Thompson: NCUBE; 110 Marsh Drive; Foster City, CA 94404-1184
Mr. Jeff M. Thompson: Pomeroy Computer Resources; 5209 Silverton Lane; Louisville, KY 40241-1793
Mr. Patrick Thompson: GTE Data Services; 1412 Lakehurst Way; Brandon, FL 33511-2319
Mr. Robert J. Thompson: Glen Raven Mills, Inc.; 1831 North Park Avenue; Burlington, NC 27217-1100
Mr. Robert Thompson: Bell Atlantic; 70401 Cradlerock Farm Court; Columbia, MD 21045-4436
Mr. Rodney Thompson: CAP Gemini America, LLC; 753 Deer Creek Road; O Fallon, IL 62269-4201
Mr. Ron D. Thompson: Discus; 1250 I Street, NW, Suite 400; Washington, DC 20005
Dr. Scott Thompson Ph.D.: Lockheed Martin; 4330 Bells Ferry Road NW; Kennesaw, GA 30144-1304
Ms. Shirley Thompson: Business Edge Solutions; 399 Thornall Street; Edison, NJ 08837
Ms. Stacey Thompson: Southwestern Bell; 12851 Manchester Road; St. Louis, MO 63131-1802
Ms. Theresa L. Thompson: Ebiz Webs.com; 1655 Clark Avenue, Unit 223; Long Beach, CA 90815-3808
Mr. Steven Jack Thoresen: Brunberg Thoresen Diaby and Associates; 5500 Wayzata Boulevard, Suite 910; Minneapolis, MN 55416-1248
Mr. Stephen J. Thorn: DST-Innovis CableData; 5272 Robert J. Mathews Parkway; El Dorado Hills, CA 95762-5705
Mr. Rusty Thornal: Nokia, Inc.; 6000 Connection Drive; Irving, TX 75039-2600
Mr. John Thornton: Kansas Department of Transportation; 217 Southeast 4th Street; Topeka, KS 66603-3504
Ms. Michelle M. Thornton-Frink: BellSouth; 21st Floor 675 West Peachtree Street; Atlanta, GA
Mr. Monte Thrash: The Eastman Group; 7421 Quorum Drive; Baton Rouge, LA 70817-5436
Ms. Deborah Thrasher: Baker College; 1050 West Bristol Road; Flint, MI 48507-5508
Mr. Ward Thrasher : 394 Westfield Avenue; Bridgeport, CT 06606-4132
Mr. David W. Throgmorton: Sterling Bank; 15000 Northwest Freeway, #FR; Houston, TX 77040-3299
Mr. Rohit Thukral: Netscape Communications; 17742 Southwest Janell Court; Beaverton, OR 97006-3776
Mr. Gopal Thyagarajan: America West Airlines; 1920 52nd Street University Drive; Tempe, AZ 85281
Mr. Nathan Tidwell: Southern Adventist University; P.O. Box 2218, D-214 Talge Hall; Collegedale, TN 37315-2218
Mr. Peter J. Tiernan: Lloyd

Lamont Design; 15208 Edicott Drive; Bowie, MD 20716-3201
Mr. David Tietjen: Pricewaterhouse Coopers; 5511 South Corning Avenue; Los Angeles, CA 90056-1302
Ms. Andie Tiffany: T. Chek Systems, LLC; 7525 Mitchell Road, Suite 200; Eden Prairie, MN 55344-1957
Mr. Robert Tiffany: Allied Signal; 4060 East Bijou Street; Colorado Springs, CO 80909-6822
Mr. I. Tilinin D.S.: D.W. Smith and Associates; 2929 Campus Drive, #200; San Mateo, CA 94403
Mr. John Tilley: HCW-L; 4010 Stone Way North, Suite 300; Seattle, WA 98103-8099
Mr. James Tillman: Sun Microsystems, Inc.; 7777 Gateway Boulevard; Newark, CA 94560
Mr. Michael J. Timlin: Ikos Systems, Inc.; 707 Salt Court; Redwood City, CA 94065-8430
Mr. Mark Timm: JC Penney, Inc.; 7001 Chateau Drive; Frisco, TX 75035-6193
Mr. Daniel Timmons: Sunpro, Inc.; 1 Orchardvale Road; Zillah, WA 98953-9021
Mr. Michael Tims: Concurrent Technologies Corporation; 100 CTC Drive; Johnstown, PA 15904-1935
Ms. Eoythrose Tincombe: Conrad's Inc.; P.O. Box 5650; Denver, CO 80217-5650
Ms. Janet Tinkler: Data Exchange, Incorporated; 6717 South Yale Avenue, Suite 205; Tulsa, OK 74136
Mr. Richard Tipton: Bank of the Sierra; 327 North Verdugo Drive; Porterville, CA 93257-1891
Ms. Sampath Tirumala: National Institutes of Health; NIDDK, Building 8; Bethesda, MD 20878
Mr. Thomas Tischler Jr.: TRW, Inc.; 7 Parkway Center, Suite 611; Pittsburgh, PA 15220
Ms. Rachel Titus: Two or More; P.O. Box 647013; Los Angeles, CA 90231
Mr. John E. Tkaczyk: Jersey City Police Department; 8 Erie Street; Jersey City, NJ 07302-2810
Mr. Cho W.S. To Ph.D.: University of Nebraska, Dept. of Mechanical Engineering; 104 North Walter Scott Engineering Center; Lincoln, NE 68588-0656
Ms. Caroline Tobey: NKI; 140 Old Orangeburg Road; Orangeburg, NY 10962-1157
Ms. Dianne Toledo: Turner Industries, Ltd.; P.O. Box 2750; Baton Rouge, LA 70821-2750
Mr. Jeff Tollison: Arkay Networking; 905 North Willow Avenue, Apartment D7; Cookeville, TN 38501
Mr. Vershun Tolliver: Hickory Specialties, Inc.; 783 Old Hickory Boulevard, #300; Brentwood, TN 37027-4508
Mr. Brian R. Tolloty: Gradall; 406 Mill Avenue SW; New Philadelphia, OH 44663
Ms. Jennifer Tomlin: Atlantic Gastroenterology; 3205 Fire Road, Suite 4; Egg Harbor Township, NJ 08234-5827
Mr. Chad A. Tompkins: Concert Management Service, Incorporated; 11921 Freedom Drive; Reston, VA 20190
Mr. James Tong: D2K Inc.; 226 Airport Parkway, Suite 638; San Jose, CA 95110-1029
Mr. Terry C. Toomey: Globix Corporation; 295 Lafayette Street, Floor 3; New York, NY 10012-2722
Mrs. Renee Topham: Air Dravlies Engineering Company; 4250 Pilot Drive; Memphis, TN 38118-6932
Ms. Kimberly D. Topps: Raytheon Systems Company; P.O. Box 832; Galena Park, TX 77547-0832
Mr. Mark G. Torres: Bellsouth Telecommunications; 3535 Colonnade Parkway, #S7H1; Birmingham, AL 35243-2346
Mr. Larry Torrez: Advance Telecom, Inc.; 2120 South Grape Street; Denver, CO 80222-5204
Ms. Valirie Touchette: Beaver Tales; 19 Louise Crescent; Embrun, Ontario, Canada K0A ZW0
Mr. Mobarak Toufic: Conexus; 68 Harvard Street; Brookline, MA 02445-7991
Ms. Karen Tovar: Auto-Power Corporation; 525 Technology Park; Lake Mary, FL 32746-7107
Ms. Diana Townsend: Garber Brothers; 35 West Crook Street; Brockton, MA 02302-3721
Mr. Robert Townsend: Thompson Greenspon A.; 3930 Walnut Street; Fairfax, VA 22030-4738
Ms. Denise Toy: CONECTIV; 6801 Black Horse Pike; Egg Harbor Township, NJ 98234-4131
Mr. Steven Toy: Andersen Consulting; 200 Galleria Officentre, Suite 300; Southfield, MI 48034-4707
Mr. John Tracy: SBC Communications, Incorporated; 175 East Houston Street; San Antonio, TX 78205-2233
Ms. Mary Beth Train: Passco Administive Services; 3305 Middlefield Road; Palo Alto, CA 94306-3049
Mr. Cong Tran: UMSCO; 1301 Broadway Boulevard NE; Albuquerque, NM 87102-1500
Mr. Thuong Tran: Teltech Resource Network; 560 Rolls Road; New Brighton, MN 55112-7627
Mr. Peter Trapasso: Sun Micro systems, Inca.; 655 Stockton Street, Apartment 207; San Francisco, CA 94108-2337
Mr. Dan Trautsch: Gensler; 308 Buchner Place; La Crosse, WI 54603-3149
Mr. Carlos Trenary: Vanderbilt University; P.O. Box 81B, Microcomputer Laboratory; Nashville, TN 37202-0081
Ms. Kim M. Trepanier: GTE Internetworking; 3 Van De Graaff Drive; Burlington, MA 01803-5148
Ms. Ira Trepper: Teale Data Center/State of California; 2005 Evergreen Street; Sacramento, CA 95815-3831
Mr. Eric C. Trevore: Bobrick Washroom Equipment; 11611 Hart Street; North Hollywood, CA 91605
Mr. Felipe Tribaldos: Lucent Technologies; 13630 Northwest 8th Street; Sunrise, FL 33325
Dr. Alan C. Tribble Ph.D.: Rockwell Collins; 1805 Agate Circle; Marion, IA 52302-5613
Mr. Jon Tribble: Oshkosh B'gosh; 112 Otter Avenue; OshKosh, WI 54903-0300
Mr. Hoa Trinh: Motorola; 2121 Palomer Airport Road; Carlsbad, CA 92009-1450
Ms. Jennifer Triplett: Parsons Brinckerhoff; 3200 Tower Oaks Boulevard; Rockville, MD 20852-4216
Mr. Stuart R. Triplett: Kaiser Permanente; 200 North Lewis Street; Orange, CA 92868-1538
Mr. Michael Trizna: IBM; 7277 Yola Lane; Manassas, VA 20111-4231
Mr. Joseph E. Trobaugh: Northwest Mortgage; 7485 New Horizon Way; Frederick, MD 21703-8388
Mr. Rony Troskey: APT; 704 Southview; Marshall, MN 56258
Mr. Douglas A. Troxell: Customer Development Corporation; 8600 North Industrial Road; Peoria, IL 61615-1504
Ms. Jerelyn Trumbo: Pharmacy Providers of Oklahoma; 45 Northeast 52nd Street; Oklahoma City, OK 73105-1825
Mr. Donald L. Trump: ARCH Paging of Florida; 158 Ridgewood Avenue; Holly Hill, FL 32117
Mr. Steven Tsang: EPRI; 639, 3rd Avenue; San Francisco, CA 94118-3906
Mr. Vim Gent Tseng: Durkopp Adler America; 3025 Northwoods Parkway; Norcross, GA 30071-1524
Mr. Charles Tsocanos: Westwood Regional Schools; 606 Apache Court; Mahwah, NJ 07430
Dr. Yweting Augustine Tsoi Ph.D.: Lucent Technologies; 20403, 600 Mountain Avenue; Murry Hill, NJ 07974
Mr. Greg Tsutaoka: Remedy Corporation; 4628 Melody Drive, Unit F.; Concord, CA 94521-5319
Mr. Yonggang Henry Tu: The Bank of New York; 385 Rifle Camp Road; West Paterson, NJ 07424
Mr. Michael S. Tucker: New Vision International; 1920 East Broadway Road; Tempe, AZ 85282-1702
Mr. Michael Tucker: Cocomp, Inc.; 2643 Midpoint Drive; Fort Collins, CO 80525-4428
Ms. Paige Tudas: CBSI; 896 West Nye Lane, Suite 101; Carson City, NV 89703-1567
Mr. Greg Tudor: Washington State Dnr; 3534 32nd Way NW; Olympia, WA 98502
Ms. Shelley E. Turley: Hechinger Home Quarters, HQ; 575 Lynhaven Parkway; Virginia Beach, VA 23452-7311
Ms. Cheryl Turner: First Clearing Corporation; 10750 Wheat First Drive; Glen Allen, VA 23060-9245
Mr. Douglass M. Turner: Hawker Powersource, Inc.; P.O. Box 808; Ooltewah, TN 37363
Mr. Eddie Turner: HiWAAY Information Services; P.O. Box 551; Huntsville, AL 35897-0001
Mr. James Turner: TRW; 2735 190th Street, Apartment 23; Redondo Beach, CA 90278-5442
Mr. Kevin B. Turner: University of Missouri; 11368 Fox Hall Lane; St. Louis, MO 63136-6121
Mr. Peter B. Turner: Golden Enterprises, Inc.; 4450 West Eau Gallie Boulevard; Melbourne, FL 32934-7213
Ms. Tammie Turner: S W Bell Telephone; 6000 Las Colinas Boulevard, Room 1460; Irving, TX 75039
Mr. Danny Tursky: Alltel Information Services; 4001 North Rodney Parham Road; Little Rock, AR 72212-2496
Mr. Dennis A. Twitchell: State of Illinois Department of Human Services; 100 South Grany Avenue East; Springfield, IL 62762
Ms. Kathy Tyler: Stap; 224 East Michigan Avenue; Kalamazoo, MI 49007-3910
Mr. Rick Tymer: Toyota Motor Sales; 19001 South Western Avenue; Torrance, CA 90509
Mr. Dan Uaje: Regional Transportation Authority; 181 West Madison Street; Chicago, IL 60602-4510
Mr. Louis Uetz: CBA Information Services; 111 Woodcrest Road, #R; Cherry Hill, NJ 08003-3620
Dr. Gang-Ryung Uh: Lucent Technologies; 1247 South Cedar Crest Boulevard, Room 55D; Allentown, PA 18103-6201
Ms. Nikol Uljaj: Bank of America Security; 9 West 57th Street; New York, NY 10019-2701
Mr. Steve Ulrich: VI-SI.Com; 3310 Fremont Avenue South, Apartment B2; Minneapolis, MN 55408-3567
Ms. Connie Unclebach: Genuine Parts Company; 2221 West Mockingbird Lane; Dallas, TX 75235-5420
Ms. Sarah Underdahl: Oneida Tribe of Indians; North 7210 Seminary Road; Oneida, WI 54155
Ms. Gail W. Upp: USC CNTV; 850 West 34th Street; Los Angeles, CA 90007-3501
Ms. Cathie C. Urban: Naval Station, United States Navy; 468 Brickby Road; Norfolk, VA 23505
Ms. Laura P. Urdiales: Savane International Corporation; 4171 North Mesa Street, Building D; El Paso, TX 79902-1444
Mr. Carlos Uribe: Paracelsus Healthcare Corp.; 2410 Tackaberry Street; Houston, TX 77009-7850
Ms. Doreen Urteaga: EDS; 17770 Cartwright Road; Irvine, CA 92614-5850
Mr. Raymond Ussery: Systems Technical Group; 2828 North Central Avenue, Suite 700; Phoenix, AZ 85004-1024
Mr. Darrin Uva: Young Minds, Inc.; 1906 Orangetree Lane, Suite 220; Redlands, CA 92374
Mr. Rick Vadgama: EMC Corporation; 206 State Street; Hopkinton, MA 01748
Mr. Bhanu Vadhera: Fleet Boston Financial; 1075 Main Street -WAL -90-03-03; Waltham, MA 02451
Mr. Ahoura Vahedi P.E.: Caltrans; 1120 North Street, MS20; Sacramento, CA 95814
Mr. Warren David Vail: A Vail Able Tech Inc.; 1462 Trestle Glen Road; Oakland, CA 94610-1850
Mr. J. A. Valancius: Continental Grain; 222 South Riverside Plaza, Suite 900; Chicago, IL 60606-3706
Ms. Mariam Valencia: NCR; 17095 Via Del Campo; San Diego, CA 92127-1711
Mrs. Martha Alicia Valencia BA: Roosevelt Cluster, #18, Los Angeles Unified School District; 456 South Mathews Street; Los Angeles, CA 90033-4326
Ms. Maria Valentino: Poughkeepsie Journal; 85 Civic Center Plaza; Poughkeepsie, NY 12601-2400
Mr. James T. Valles: Nissan North America; 106 Inverness Circle East; Englewood, CO 80112
Mr. A. J. Van De Kerk: Van Oord Acz Bv; P.O. Box 458; Gorinchem, Netherlands 4200 AL
Mr. Andrew Van Etten: Tax Management Inc.; 1250 23rd Street NW; Washington, DC 20037-1164
Mr. James Van Osdell: Vanley Systems Inc.; P.O. Box 2744; Mount Vernon, WA 98273-7744
Ms. Suzanne M. Van Spyk: OneSight, Inc.; 947 Marion Avenue; Highland Park, IL 60035-5127
Mr. Ray Van Wasshnova: Parke Davis; 2800 Plymouth Road; Ann Arbor, MI 48105
Mr. Kurt Van Zyl: Cypress Hotel Management Company; 805 Riverbend Boulevard; Longwood, FL 32779-2326
Mr. Robert Vance: Csti; 8975 Guilford Road, Suite 100; Columbia, MD 21046-2390
Ms. Terry Vande Kamp: Farm Bureau Financial Services; 5400 University Avenue #E2SW33; West Des Moines, IA 50266-5950
Mr. Dean VanderDoes: Premiere Conferencing; 2221 East Bijou Street, Suite 100; Colorado Springs, CO 80909-6001
Mr. Thomas D. Vanderzwaag: Harbor Distributing; 6000 Garden Grove Boulevard, Apartment 241; Westminster, CA 92683-1956
Mr. Peter Vanvleet: Roche Diagnostics; 7922 Wind Hill Drive; Indianapolis, IN 46256-1839
Mr. Robert J. Vargas: City of Evanston; 2100 Ridge Avenue; Evanston, IL 60201
Ms. Sheri Vargas: Sprint Corporation; 6500 Sprint Parkway; Overland Park, KS 66251
Mr. Cautam R. Varma: Metamor, USA; 4 Research Place, Suite 300; Rockville, VA 20850
Mr. Gary Varnadoe: West Hudson, Inc.; 5420 Lyndon B Johnson Freeway, Suite 1355; Dallas, TX 75240-6239
Mr. Mike John Vasconcelos: PeopleSoft; 4440 Rosewood Drive; Pleasanton, CA 94588
Mr. Jorge Vasconcelos-Santill n: National Autonomous University of Mexico; Diamante 77; Col. Estrella, Mexico 07810
Mr. Thomas Vashro: United Healthcare; P.O. Box 1459, Ms Mn010 W116; Minneapolis, MN 55440-1459
Mr. S. V. Vasudevan: Divi-Com; 1708 McCarthy Boulevard; Milpitas, CA 95035-7417
Mr. Prahalad Vasvdev: Design of Analog and Digital VLSI; 5 Downie Place; Austin, TX 78746
Mr. John P. Vaughn: RHI Consulting; 4481 Arden View Court; St. Paul, MN 55112-1944
Mr. Sidney L. Vaught: Advance Auto Parts, Inc.; 5673 Airport Road NW; Roanoke, VA 24012-1119
Mrs. Gail Vawter: Tech Software, Inc.; 12 Westerville Square, Suite 364; Westerville, OH 43081
Mr. Ronald Velez: Scarsdale Board of Education; 2 Brewster Road; Scarsdale, NY 10583-3050
Mr. Ben Velsher: Nortel Networks; 185 Corkstown Road; Nepean, Ontario, Canada K2H 8V4
Mr. Clay Velut: State Fund; 3031 North 2nd Street; Phoenix, AZ 85012
Mr. Satya Vempati: Andersen Consulting; Suite 2900, 500 Woodward Avenue; Detroit, MI 48226
Mr. Murali K. Vemulapalli: Persistence Software Inc.; 1235 Wildwood Avenue, Apartment 296; Sunnyvale, CA 94089-2720
Mr. Bob Venable: Blue Cross; 801 Pine Street; Chattanooga, TN 37402-2555
Mr. Randy Venenga: American Home Shield; 1524 US Highway 30 W.; Carroll, IA 514013305
Dr. Soma Venkat Ph.D.: Bell & Howell; 300 North Zeeb Road, Box 1; Ann Arbor, MI 48108
Dr. Narayana Venkateswaran Ph.D.: Peacock Laboratories, Inc.; 1901 South 54th Street; Philadelphia, PA 19143-5793
Mr. Sayibabu Ventarapragada: Manhattan Associates; 140 Spalding Trail NE; Atlanta, GA 30328-1070
Dr. Peter Veprek Ph.D.: Speech Technology Laboratory; 3888 State Street, Suite 202; Santa Barbara, CA 93105-3164
Mr. Greg F. Vera: Corpus Christi Army Depot; 308 Crecy Street Stop 6; Corpus Christi, TX 78419-5211
Mr. David Verdouw: Seeley Company; 444 South Flower Street, Suite 2200; Los Angeles, CA 90071-2923
Mr. Jason Verkaart: Spike Technologies; One Crestnut Street, Suite 305; Nashua, NH 03060
Dr. Dhirendra Verma Ph.D.: Daimlerchrysler AG; 14250 Plymouth Road; Detroit, MI 48348
Ms. Naresh Verma: Multi State Tax Commission; 444 North Capitol Street NW, Suite 425; Washington, DC 20001-1512
Dr. Silvia V. Veronese Ph.D.: Evans and Sutherland; 650 Komas Drive; Salt Lake City, UT 84102
Mr. Dennis Verrier: Plymouth Rock Assurance Corporation; 695 Atlantic Avenue; Boston, MA 02111-2623
Mr. Alex Vertlib: Galgon Industries Inc.; 37399 Centralmont Place; Fremont, CA 94536-6558
Dr. Rajendran K. Viayur Ph.D.: Oracle; 5909 Fondren Road, Apartment 401; Houston, TX 77036-2900
Mr. David Vielmetter: Clinical Micro Senors; 126 West Del Mar Boulevard; Pasadena, CA 91105
Ms. Damarie Viera: IT-HR, Inc.; 420 Lincoln Road, Suite 264; Miami Beach, FL 33139-3009
Dr. Joseph J. Vill護demoros Ph.D.: ITT Technical Institute; 801 Windsor Circle; Brandon, FL 33510-2926
Mr. Jun Villanueva: Options for Youth; 199 South Los Robles Avenue, Suite 700; Pasadena, CA 91101-2460
Mr. Oliver Villarreal: Edito-

ra El Sol; 2100 North Seymour Avenue; Laredo, TX 78040-6402
Mr. Jorge Villegas: University of Redlands; 1200 East Colton Avenue; Redlands, CA 92374-3755
Mr. Richard Vinger: Lands End; 1 Lands End Lane; Dodgeville, WI 53595-0001
Ms. Valerie Vinzant: Next Level Communications; 6085 State Farm Drive; Rohnert Park, CA 94928-2136
Mr. Joseph P. Violanti II: Say re Area School District; 333 West Lockhart Street; Sayre, PA 18840-1609
Mr. Brandon Visser: Tera Byte, Ltd.; 814 Ogden Avenue; Donners Grove, IL 60515
Mrs. Mary Visser: Southwestern University; P.O. Box 770, School of Fine Arts; Georgetown, TX 78627-0770
Mr. Jagannathan Viswanathan: KPMG; 3202 Callie Circle; College Station, TX 77845-5918
Mr. John P. Vitek: JPL; 320 North Halstead Street, #260; Pasadena, CA 91107
Mr. Salvatore Vittorio: AIAA Aerospace Access; 59 John Street, 7th Floor; New York, NY 10038-3709
Mr. Maximo A. Vizcaino: Young & Rubicam, Inc.; 285 Madison Avenue; New York, NY 10017
Mr. Brian Vocca: Catholic Health Initiative; 1149 Market Street; Tacoma, WA 98402-3515
Mr. Brad Voigt: Teleflex; 6980 Professional Parkway East; Sarasota, FL 34240-8414
Mr. John Vollick: Applied Theory Communications; 125 Elwood Davis Road; Syracuse, NY 13212-4311
Mr. Donald Vollmer: Oracle Corporation; 6501 East Belleview Avenue; Englewood, CO 80111-6028
Mr. Wilhelm Von Allworden: CASE Corporation; Berghaus Strasse; Neustadt, Germany 01844
Mr. Von Sleigher: Gulfstream Aerospace; 4817 Jennings Drive; Lewisville, TX 75056-1663
Mr. David A. Von Tress: JMV Services, Inc.; 16980 Dallas Parkway, Suite 203; Dallas, TX 75248
Mrs. Jacqueline L. Voorhees: Peoria Public Schools; 3202 North Wisconsin Avenue; Peoria, IL 61603
Mr. Hemant Vora: Maruti Associates; 9 Pebble Place; East Windsor, NJ 08520
Ms. Lisa Vuolo: Computer Horizons; 5455 Corporate Drive; Troy, MI 48098
Dr. Srinivas Vuppuluri Ph.D.: Caterpillar, Inc.; 3225 Dorchester Drive; Springfield, IL 62704
Dr. John Waclawsky Ph.D.: Cisco Systems; 6105 Spring Meadow Lane; Frederick, MD 21701-5819
Ms. Denise Waddle: Mediware Information Systems I; 11711 West 79th Street; Lenexa, KS 66214-1497
Mr. Bretton Wade: Microsoft; 2612 166th Avenue SE; Bellevue, WA 98008-5458
Mr. Tom Wade: Northside Integrated School District; 9527 Shining Elm; San Antonio, TX 78250
Mr. Chris Wagner: Computerland; 1221 North Atherton Street; State College, PA 16803-2984
Mr. Shawn D. Wagner: Principal Financial Group; 711 High Street; Des Moines, IA 50392
Ms. Tamatha Wagner: Bank of Atchison; 701 Kansas Avenue; Atchison, MS 66002-2451
Mr. Edwin Wai: Mid-America Consulting Group; 4010 Watson Plaza Drive, Suite 120; Lakewood, CA 90712-4035
Mr. David Wakefield: Sharp Manufacturing Company; Dep, 600; Memphis, TN 38193-0001
Ms. Suzanne Waker: Smartlink Computer Education Center; 175 Mansfield Avenue; Norton, MA 02766-0939
Mr. Gary R. Walden: Fortunoff; 70 Charles Lindbbergh Boulevard; Uniondale, NY 11553
Mr. Tim Walden : 530 Beacon Park West, Suite 701; Birmingham, AL 35209-3150
Ms. Elisa Waldman: Dream City Mall, Inc.; 3826 Raleigh Street; Charlotte, NC 28203-2043
Mr. Randall S. Waldman: Ichargeit; 17200 Mallet Hill Drive; Louisville, KY 40245
Mr. Wilson S. Waldrop: Symtx, Inc.; 4401 Friedrich, Lane Building 2, Suite 200; Austin, TX 78744
Mr. Pradeep K. Walia: Atlas Software Technologies Inc.; 4240 Greenburg Pike #101; Pittsburgh, PA 15221-4297
Ms. Barbara Brown Walker: National Business College; 811 Norwood Street; Lynchburg, VA 24504-1143
Ms. Cynthia Walker: Shaker Heights School District; 23773 Drake Road; Oakwood Village, OH 44146-6133
Mr. Don Walker: Booz-Allen & Hamilton; 1615 Murray Canyon Road, #220; San Diego, CA 92108
Mr. Harry Walker: Hollins University; P.O. Box 9658; Roanoke, VA 24020-1658
Mr. James Walker: Howard Systems International; Six Concourse Parkway, Suite 2140; Atlanta, GA 30328
Mr. Johnny Walker: UUNet; 757 Vista Drive; Columbus, OH 43230-5937
Ms. Mary Ann Walker: Marc Incorporated; 7850 North Belt Line Road; Irving, TX 75063-6098
Ms. Mary Carolyn Walker: Reflections In Silver; 22 Conway Drive; Mechanicsburg, PA 17055-6135
Ms. Nancy Catherine Walker: DBSI Computers LLC; 255 Route 12; Groton, CT 06340-3404
Ms. Pamela Walker: City of Morganton; P.O. Box 3448; Morganton, NC 28680-3448
Mr. Preston Walker: AFLAC; 917 Brown Avenue; Columbus, GA 31906-3627
Ms. Sherri Walker: Bell Atlantic; 400 Oxford Drive; Monroeville, PA 15146-2351
Mr. Stephen A. Walker: United Title Company; 514 Shatto Place, Floor 3; Los Angeles, CA 90020-1780
Mr. John Wall: Southwest Missouri State University; 901 South National Avenue; Springfield, MO 65804-0094
Mr. Bobby Wallace: Buffalo Rock; 34 West Oxmoore Road; Birmingham, AL 35209
Mr. Dan Wallace: Allied Signal; 532 Tyrella Avenue, Apt. 18; Mountain View, CA 94043-2150
Mr. J. Patrick Wallace: DST Systems, Inc.; 333 West 11th Street; Kansas City, MO 64105-1634
Mr. Roy V. Wallace Jr.: Space Imaging; 4300 Forbes Boulevard; Lanham, MD 20706-4383
Ms. Tamara Wallace: Findlay City Schools, Findlay High School; 1200 Broad Avenue; Findlay, OH 45840-2698
Mr. Paul Wallendal: Des Moines Public Schools; 2434 Southeast 5th Street; Des Moines, IA 50315-1708
Mr. Arlo D. Walljasper: Goodyear Tire & Rubber Company, Inc.; 400 North Goodyear Road; Mt. Pleasant, IA 52641
Ms. Darlene Walsh: W.W. Grainger, Inc.; 100 Grainger Parkway; Lake Forest, IL 60045-5201
Ms. Elizabeth A. Walsh: Sybase, Inc.; 561 Virginia Road, Building 4; Concord, MA 01742
Mr. Jacob H. Walsh: Portland General Electric; 121 Southwest Salmon Street, 3WTC-0505; Portland, OR 97204
Mr. Joseph Walsh: JGI; 201 West Passaic Street; Rochelle Park, NJ 07662-3100
Mr. Bill Walters: Scottish Rite Children; 975 Johnson Ferry Road NE, Suite 350; Atlanta, GA 30342-4735
Mr. Johnny J. J. Walters : 1108 Broadview Road; Fort Washington, MD 20744-3711
Mr. David Wanchalk: The Jay Group; 60 North Ronks Road; Ronks, PA 17572-9606
Mr. Larry J. Wandsnider: Navistar International; 100 Bishops Way; Brookfield, WI 53005-6205
Mr. Jean Wang: Bon Appetite Management Company; 100 Hamilton Avenue; Palo Alto, CA 94301
Dr. Weilin Wang Ph.D.: Nortel; 6741 Patrick Lane; Plano, TX 75024-6346
Mr. Dennis Ward: SAIC; 6011 East Bay Boulevard; Gulf Breeze, FL 32561-9726
Mr. Lane Ward: Ilumin Corporation; 1506 North Technology Way Building D30; Orem, UT 84097-2394
Ms. Linda S. Ward: Elliott Aviation; P.O. Box 100; Moline, IL 61266-0100
Ms. Susan Ward: Town of Apple Valley; P.O. Box 429; Apple Valley, CA 92307-0087
Mr. Jeff Ware: Great American Insurance; 49 East 4th Street, Suite 500; Cincinnati, OH 45202-3808
Mr. Robert J. Warja: Federal Reserve Bank; 230 South La Salle Street; Chicago, IL 60604-1413
Ms. Ann Warner: Andersen Corporation; 100, 4th Avenue North; Bayport, MN 55003-1096
Mr. Ben Warner: City of Fairfield; 5350 Pleasant Avenue; Fairfield, OH 45014-3567
Mr. John Warner: Atomic Energy of Canada; 2251 Speakman Drive; Mississauga, Ontario, Canada L5K 1B2
Mr. Steven Warner: Nyce Corporation; 606 Mountain View Avenue; Longmont, CO 80501
Mr. Richard Warrell: CADmatics; 2 Overlook Drive; Preston, CT 06365-8815
Mr. Darrin Warren: Trumbull County Services; 150 South Park Avenue; Warren, OH 44481
Mr. John R. Warrington: NZMP (North American); 3637 Westwind Boulevard; Santa Rosa, CA 95403
Mr. Andrew Warzecha: META Group; 1341 Ansley Court; Mundelein, IL 60060-2066
Ms. Nancy Waselich: CSC, Ltd.; 4000 Mahoning Avenue NW, #N; Warren, OH 44483-1924
Ms. Lisa Washington: EG&G; 900 Clopper Road, Suite 200; Gaithersburg, MD 20878-1360
Ms. Yolanda Washington: Time Warner Cable; 5450 Winchester Road; Memphis, TN 38115-4571
Mr. Yaser Wasim: Lucent; 2600 Warrenville Road, NSC-33E23; Lisle, IL 60553
Mr. Glen Waskiewicz: American Security Distribution; 4411 East La Palma Avenue; Anaheim, CA 92807-1803
Mr. D. David Waters: Optimum Solutions, Inc.; 210 25th Avenue North; Nashville, TN 37203-1606
Ms. Dianne Waterson: Seagate Technology; 1830 Lefthand Circle; Longmont, CO 80501-6720
Mr. Jeff Watkins: Check Into Cash Inc.; 224 North Ocoee Street, #550; Cleveland, TN 37311-5069
Mr. Don Watson: Flinn County Rural Electric Cooperative; P.O. Box 69; Marion, IA 52302-0069
Mr. Erick Watson: SLC Technologies, Inc.; 10704 Southwest 127th Court; Portland, OR 97223-1906
Dr. Dwight Watt Ed.D.: Athens Tech; 1317 Athens Highway; Elberton, GA 30635-4002
Mr. Bill Watts: Arapahoe County Government; 5334 South Prince Street; Littleton, CO 80120
Mr. Kenneth Watts: Commonwealth Industries, Inc.; 2922 Strawbridge Place; Owensboro, KY 42303-1658
Mr. Rick Watts: First Trust Corporation; 717 17th Street, Suite 2600; Denver, CO 80202-3326
Ms. Sarah C. Wayland: Entropic, Inc.; 400 North Capitol Street NW, Suite G100; Washington, DC 20001-1511
Dr. F. Stanford Wayne: Columbus State Community College; P.O. Box 307246; Gahanna, OH 43230-7246
Ms. Karen A. Webb: Center for Alternative Sentencing & Employment Services; 959 East 83rd Street; Brooklyn, NY 11236-3812
Mr. Lewis Polanco Webb: Elmburst College; 190 Prospect Avenue; Elmburst, IL 60126
Mr. Patrick R. Webb II: Puxis Corporation; 3750 Torry View Court; San Diego, PA 92130
Mr. D. Scott Weber: Teradyne Telecommunications Division; 2801 Canterbury Drive; Northbrook, IL 60062-6901
Mr. Dirk Weber: Spectrum 7 Inc.; 101 West Ohio Street, Suite 1540; Indianapolis, IN 46204-1997
Mr. Paul Weber: Deaconess Long Term Care; 8540 Blue Ridge Building; Kansas City, MO 64138
Mr. David H. Webster: Redback Networks; 1389 Moffett Park Drive; Sunnyvale, CA 94089-1134
Mr. Scott Webster: Progressive; 6300 Wilson Mills Road, #E42; Cleveland, OH 44143-2182
Mr. Karl Wee : 21 Mullholland Drive; Ipswich, MA 01938-2822
Ms. Christine Weekes: Integrated Data Solutions Inc.; 5951 Chicago Road; Warren, MI 48092-1606
Mr. Fred Weigel: Woodland Tractor & Equipment; 95 West Kentucky Avenue; Woodland, CA 95695-5800
Mr. Brendan Weir: IET Intelligent Electronics; 3425 South Bascom Avenue, Suite 230; Campbell, CA 95008-7300
Mr. Craig Weiss: University of Nebraska Department of Communication; Room 102c; Kearney, NE 68849-0001
Mr. Michael J. Weiss: Johns Hopkins University; 8719 Spring Brook Way; Odenton, MD 21113
Ms. Nina Weiss: ePresence; 12 Broad Street; Red Bank, NJ 07701-1938
Ms. Terri Weiss: Linens 'N Things; 6 Brighton Road; Clifton, NJ 07012-1647
Mr. Seth Weissbord: JCH Wire & Cable; 4527 Losee Road; North Las Vegas, NV 89031
Mr. Ilan Weitzer: Ford Motor Company; 15303 South Commerce Drive; Dearborn, MI 48120-1277
Mr. Donald Welker: Alltel Information Services; 2000 Highland Road; Twinsburg, OH 44087-2248
Mr. Donald D. Weller: Mitchell International; 18183 Sencillo Drive; San Diego, CA 92128-1324
Ms. Betty Wells: Harford; P.O. Box 150; Bel Air, MD 21014-0150
Mr. David Wells: Office of David Wells Independent Consulting; 621 Walnut Street; Iowa City, IA 52240-4641
Mr. James Wells Sr.: LMFS-Oswego; 1648 Rita Road; Vestal, NY 13850-3341
Ms. Karen L. Wells: Litton PRC; 6552 Redbud Place; McLean, VA 22102
Ms. Laura Wells: Arizona Department of Agriculture; 1688 West Adams Street; Phoenix, AZ 85007-2617
Mr. Paul Wells: On Command Corporation; 11401 Court House Road; Dinwiddie, VA 20109-2449
Mr. Rick Wells: Comp Tech Services; 498 Inman Avenue, Suite 203; Colonia, NJ 07067-1147
Mr. Brandon Welsh: Velcon Filters; 4525 Centennial Boulevard; Colorado Springs, CO 80919-3350
Mr. Daniel Welt: Coswelt Telecommunication, Inc.; 755 Rue Brunet; Saint Laurent, Quebec, Canada QC H4M 1Y4
Mr. Dennis M. Wenger: Hagen Systems; 6438 City West Parkway; Eden Prairie, MN 55344-7725
Mr. Gary M. Wenner: Aetna, Inc.; 151 Farmington Avenue; Hartford, CT 06156
Mr. Tom Wensmann: South Dakota Wheat Growers; 110 6th Avenue SE; Aberdeen, SD 57401-6024
Mr. Allen Wentland: Coach House Gifts; 707 5th Street; Ames, IA 50010-5900
Mr. Jonathan D. Werner: North America Telecommunications Corporation; 6580 Frankstown Avenue; Pittsburgh, PA 15206
Mr. Kristen D. Werner: County of Berks; 722 Franklin Street; West Reading, PA 19611
Mr. Bradley G. West: NIS/ Computer Solutions; 1518 North Atherton Street; State College, PA 16803-3041
Ms. Elizabeth West: Spector Group; 3111 New Hyde Park Road; New Hyde Park, NY 11042-1217
Mr. Travis West: RHI Consulting; 3801 Cypress; Woodward, OK 73801
Mr. Lance Westerlund: The Warner Group; 5950 Canoga Avenue, Suite 600; Woodland Hills, CA 91367
Mr. Larry J. Westfall: National City Corporation; 1726 Noe Bixby Road; Columbus, OH 43232
Mr. Mike R. Wetzel: Logos Communications, Inc.; 26100 1st Street; Westlake, OH 44145-1438
Mr. Charles Weyhmiller: Chase Manhattan Bank; 613 Harrison Avenue; Magnolia, NJ 08049-1514
Mr. Daniel Wheeler : 1 New York Plaza, Floor 31; New York, NY 10004-1901
Mr. Walter F. Whelan: IBM Global Services; 795 Top Notch Lane; Eureka, MO 63025-1045
Mr. Ike Whisenand: Yavapai College; 1100 East Sheldon Street; Prescott, AZ 86301-3297
Mr. Cliff Whisenhunt: Lockheed Martin; 498 Oak Road, #A39; Ocala, FL 34472-3099
Mr. Scott Whitacre: Pacific Bell; 2600 Camino Ramon, Room 4E450O; San Ramon, CA 94583-5099
Mr. Tyler Whitaker: Sento Corporation; 808 East Utah Valley Drive; American Fork, UT 84003-9773
Mr. Allen White: National Data Corporation; 6100 South Yale Avenue Suite 1900; Tulsa, OK 74136-1947
Ms. Anna White: Goliad Independent School District; P.O. Box 830, 210 West Oak Street; Goliad, TX 77963-0830
Mr. Sam White: High Plain Solutions; 2550 University Avenue West; Saint Paul, MN 55114-1052
Mr. Victor White: Ameritech; 613 North Union Avenue; Chicago, IL 60610-3968
Ms. Whitney J. White: Merrill Lynch; 130 West 74th Street, Apartment PHA; New York, NY 10023-2325
Ms. Heather White Fraccio: Top Echelon, Inc.; P.O. Box 21390; Canton, OH 44701-1390
Mr. R. Whitehead: Boeing Computer Service; 20911 6th Avenue South; Seatec, WA 98198-3270
Ms. Cassandra Whitlow: IBM Corporation; 2328 B. Shade Valley Road; Charlotte, NC 28205
Mr. Edward Whitten: San Diego County Treas-Tax; 1600 Pacific Highway, Suite 112; San Diego, CA 92101-2422
Ms. Jane Wiant: McDonald Observatory; P.O. Box 1337; Fort Davis, TX 79734-1337

Mr. O. Widigsson: Stora Enso, Oy.; S-791-80; Falun, Sweden
Mrs. Kay F. Wieder: Academy School District 20; 7610 North Union Boulevarde; Colorado Springs, CO 80920-3861
Mr. Everette H. Wieting : P.O. Box 316; Egg Harbor City, NJ 08215-0316
Mr. Michael Wiggin: Northeast Health Care Quality Foundation; 163 Brock Street; Rochester, NH 03867
Mr. Stan Wiggin: Pennzoil Company; 700 Milam Street; Houston, TX 77002-2806
Ms. Lynne M. Wiggins: GT Systems, Inc. - Adtranz, N.A.; 831 Lynda Lane; North Versailles, PA 15137
Ms. Melissa L. Wiggins: Frontier Communications; 3976 East River Drive; Green Bay, WI 54301-0910
Ms. Pam Wiginton: Guaranty National Bank; 100 East California Street; Gainesville, TX 76240-4002
Mr. Willy Wijaya: Environmental Enterprise Group, Inc.; 220 North Knoxville; Russellville, AR 72801
Ms. Marilyn Wilcke: Suffolk University; 8 Ashburton Place; Boston, MA 02108-2770
Mr. Doug Wilcox: Autoliv ASP; 3350 Airport Road; Ogden, UT 84405-1563
Mr. Gary Wildfang: Centurytel Inc.; 805 Broadway Street; Vancouver, WA 98660-3277
Mr. Dewayne Wilfong: Dallas Metrocare Services; 1380 River Bend Driver; Dallas, TX 75247-4914
Mr. Jay Wilkes: The Home Depot; 2455 Paces Ferry Road, SE #81; Atlanta, GA 30339-4024
Mr. Wendell Wilkins: Boeing; P.O. Box 21233; Orlando, FL 32815-0233
Mr. Shawn Wilkinson: Affordable Perfection; 3005 South Swope Drive; Independence, MO 64057-3368
Mr. Christopher Will: learnlots.com; 5875 Castle Creek Drive, Suite 495; Indianapolis, IN 46250
Mr. Dean B. Willard: On Line Financial Services, Inc.; 900 Commerce Drive; Oak Brook, IL 60523-1967
Mr. Jary Willard: CCAI; 6019 Robertdale Road; Oakwood Village, OH 44146-2553
Ms. Rudi Jo Willard: Indiana Department of Revenue; 100 North Senate Ave, Room N286; Indianapolis, IN 46204-2207
Ms. Karina Willes: Wellmark, Inc.; 636 Grand Avenue; Des Moines, IA 50309-2502
Mr. Steve Willey: Information Technology Genesis,LLC; P.O. Box 7804; Newark, DE 19714-7804
Ms. Tiffany William: Jefferson County Clerks Office; 527 West Jefferson Street; Louisville, KY 40202-2814
Mr. David R. Williams: Edwards, Inc.; 4119 Sheep Pasture Road; Spring Hope, NC 27882
Mr. Don Williams: Hutcheson Medical Center; 100 Gross Crescent Circle; Fort Oglethorpe, GA 30742-3669
Ms. Doris Williams: NCADD Work First New Jersey; 2333 Whitehorse Mercerville Lane; Hamilton, NJ 08609
Mr. Drew Williams: State of Alabama; 64 North Union Street; Montgomery, AL 36130-3020
Mr. Ed Williams: HQMTMC-DSC, Fort Eustis; 663 Sheppard Place; Fort Eustis, VA 23604-1626
Mr. Eric Williams: Michigan National Bank/National Australian Bank; 4300 West Saginaw Highway; Lansing, MI 48917-2191
Mr. Frederick Williams: F. Williams Group/MRI-Frisco; 5300 Town & Country Boulvard, Suite 160; Frisco, TX 75034
Mr. Gary M. Williams: NIOSH DSR; 1095 Willowdale Road; Morgantown, WV 26505-2888
Mr. George Williams: Earthlink Network; 3100 New York Drive; Pasadena, CA 91107-1501
Mr. George Williams: Gte Service Corporation; 600 Hidden Ridge; Irving, TX 75038-3809
Mr. Jeff Williams: Kellermeyer Building Services; 1575 Henthorne Drive; Maumee, OH 43537-1385
Mr. Jeffrey Williams: Interim Technology; 11801 Sunrise Valley Drive; Reston, MD 22091
Mr. Joe Williams: Tut Systems; 17 West 755 Buttefield Road; Oakbrook Terrace, IL 60181-4253
Mr. Justin Williams: Dot Printer; 315 East Bay Avenue, Apartment B; Newport Beach, CA 92661-1250
Mr. Keith Williams: Jh Networking; 1770 Kirby Parkway, Suite 427; Memphis, TN 38138-7408
Ms. Kenya Williams: Microsoft Corporation; 2803 Turnberry Drive, Apartment 1223; Arlington, TX 76006-2350
Mr. Lance Williams: Sprint; 2020 West 89th Street; Shawnee Mission, KS 66206-1946
Mr. Lawrence Williams: S H N Consulting Engineers; 812 West Wabash Avenue; Eureka, CA 95501-2138
Mr. Marc D. Williams: Oregon Department of Transportation; 955 Center Street NE, #461; Salem, OR 97310
Ms. Maxine Williams: Technocentric; P.O. Box 915139; Longwood, FL 32791-5139
Mr. Michael Williams: Kinkos, Inc.; 255 West Stanley Avenue; Ventura, CA 93002
Ms. Nancy A. Williams: GE Plastics; 1 Plastics Avenue; Pittsfield, MA 01201
Ms. Rebecca Williams: Kaiser Permanante; 2116 Santa Clara Avenue, Apartment L; Alameda, CA 94501-2885
Ms. Rosann Williams: Williams Consulting; 1001 West Park Boulevard, Apartment 205; Plano, TX 75075-2662
Ms. Sharon Williams: Emma L. Harrison; 409 Turner Street; Waco, TX 76704
Mr. Wade A. Williams: Omitech Robotics; 12017 Newport Drive; Brighton, CO 80601
Mrs. Lacretia M. Williams-Hall: Electronic Data Systems: Detroit Diesel Corporation; 13400 West Outer Drive; Redford, MI 48239
Mr. Ted Williamson: Onondaga County; 404 Malden Road; Syracuse, NY 13211-1211
Mr. Eric Glenn Willis : 1800 Prater Way Apartment Cl; Sparks, NV 89431-4374
Mr. Richard Willis Sr.: Oklahoma Office of State Finance; 2209 North Central Avenue; Oklahoma City, OK 73105-3293
Mr. Todd Willis: Cartel Marketing Inc.; 16501 Ventura Boulevard; Encino, CA 91436-2007
Mr. John J. Wills: Monadnock Family Services; 64 Main Street, Suite 301; Keene, NH 03431-3701
Mr. Olive Wilms: Crystal Factory; 8010 Beach Boulevard; Buena Park, CA 90620-3226
Ms. Bobbie Wilson: Pacific Bell; 21241 South Western Avenue; Torrance, CA 90501-2963
Mr. Charles A. Wilson: SMS; 51 Valley Stream Parkway; Malvern, PA 19355-1406
Ms. Cheryl Wilson: Vertronics Media; 118 Nicole Drive; Douglasville, GA 30134-4401
Mr. James Wilson: General Electric Information Services; 5112 Dudley Lane, Apartment 301; Bethesda, MD 20814-5481
Ms. Kathy Wilson: Quality Communications; Louisville Green; Louisville, KY 40601
Ms. Kelly Wilson: Davis Vision; 650 Franklin Street; Schenectady, NY 12306
Mr. Mark Wilson: The Dare Company; 8141 A White Street; Del Rio, TX 78840
Mr. Steve Wilson: Getronics WANG; 5100 East Virginia Beach Boulevard; Norfolk, VA 23502-3413
Mr. James Wimberley: St. Charles High School; 1200 Dunham Road; St. Charles, IL 60174-5728
Mr. James Winans: Frontier Insurance; P.O. Box 7000; Dublin, OH 43017-0701
Ms. Karen Wingfield: Hutchinson Community College; 1300 North Plum Street; Hutchinson, KS 67501-5831
Mr. Peter Winkler: Divers Alert Network; 6 West Colony Place; Durham, NC 27705-5588
Mr. Charles Winstead: Bridgestone Firestone, Inc.; P.O. Box 1139; Wilson, NC 27894-1139
Ms. Tracey Winters: Ecos Consulting (Aust) P/L; 7 Kulan Street; The Gap, Queensland, Australia 4061
Ms. Deanna Wise: St. Vincent Hospital; 9002 Purdue Road; Indianapolis, IN 46268
Ms. Kate Wise: JDS Systems, Inc.; 74831 Velie Drive, Suite 2; Palm Desert, CA 92260-1956
Mr. Winfred Wise: Bellsouth Information Systems; 4967 North Royal Atlanta Drive; Tucker, GA 30084-3083
Mr. Britt Wisenbaker: Arizona Western College; P.O. Box 929; Yuma, AZ 85366-0929
Mr. Robert Wisneski: City of Mesa; 59 East 1st Street; Mesa, AZ 85207
Ms. Tonya Wogomon: Lucent Technologies; 4006 Belt Line Road; Addison, TX 75001-4371
Mr. E. J. Wojtowicz: Citrix Systems; 6400 Northwest 6th Way; Fort Lauderdale, FL 33309-6123
Mr. Wesley Wolanski: Complete Business Solutions, Inc.; One Monarch Place, Suite 1230; Springfield, MA 01144
Mr. Robert C. Wolf: AccuDocs; 4537 112th Street; Urbandale, IA 50322
Mr. Kenneth R. Wolff: Electric Insurance; 152 Conant Street; Beverly, MA 01915-1692
Mr. Andreas Wolflig: Tiros Corporation; 9831 South 51st Street, D135; Phoenix, AZ 85044
Ms. Jillayn Wolleat: Bellsouth Long Distance; 28 Perimeter Center East; Atlanta, GA 30346-1905
Mr. Troy Woloshyn: Hinz Automation, Inc.; 204-801 Manning Road Northeast; Calgary, Alberta, Canada T2E 7M8
Ms. Margo A. Wolter: Cerika Corp; 13912 Northeast 20th Avenue, Suite 204; Vancouver, WA 98686-1465
Ms. Stephanie Wolters: Richmont; 1380 Pebble Hills Drive; Rockwall, TX 75087-2874
Mr. Raymond D. Wolverton Jr.: Cook County; 118 North Clark Street, Suite 230; Chicago, IL 60602-1307
Ms. Bo Yee B. Wong: Deluxe Payment Protection Systems; 19803 North Creek Parkway; Bothell, WA 98011-8214
Mr. Raphael S. C. Wong: Fordham University School of Law; 140 West 62nd Street; New York, NY 10023
Dr. T. Frank Wong Ph.D.: Telcordia; 16 Ross Hall Boulevard; Piscataway, NJ 08854
Ms. Amy Wood: Lucent Technologies; 2896 Landington Way; Duluth, GA 30096-6218
Mrs. Amy Wood: HomeRuns.Com, Inc.; 70 Inner Belt Road; Somerville, MA 02143
Mr. Charles M. Wood: CDC; Mail Stop F35; 4770 Buford Highway; Atlanta, GA 30341-3717
Mr. Chris Wood: Oklahoma Liquefied Gas; 1313 Highway 9 E; Seminole, OK 74868-3513
Mr. Christal D. Wood: Duplin Sampson Area Mental Health Department; P.O. Box 599; Kenansville, NC 28349
Ms. Lajuan Wood: Hyde Park Baptist School; 3901 Speedway; Austin, TX 78751
Mr. Michael J. Wood: Raytheon; 9625 Moffett Avenue; Norfolk, VA 23511-2784
Mr. Scott Wood: Broadlink Communications; 409 Mendolino Avenue; Santa Rosa, CA 45401
Ms. LaTamera Woodley: State of Tennessee Department of Human Services; 510 Heritage Drive, #85E; Madison, TN 37115-2600
Mr. Tim Woodruff: Rooney Engineering, Inc.; 12201 East Arapahoe Road; Englewood, CO 80112-6760
Mr. David E. Woods: VX2, Inc.; P.O. Box 123; Addison, IL 60101-0123
Mr. Steven T. Woods: IBM Corporation; 3355 Mainstay Place; Alpharetta, GA 30022-4495
Mr. Jim Woodward: Brookstore Company, Inc.; 17 Riverside Street; Nashua, NH 03062
Mr. John R. Woodward: Great Lakes Instruments Inc.; 9020 West Dean Road; Milwaukee, WI 53224-2853
Mr. Michael Woodward: Rosemount Analytical Inc.; 1201 North Main Street; Orrville, OH 44667-1016
Mr. Scott Woolcock: Texaco Exploration and Production; 4800 Fournace Place; Bellaire, TX 77401-2324
Mr. Frank Woolcott: Oracle Corporation; 1033 Northwest 80th Terrace; Plantation, FL 33322-5756
Mr. Micheal P. Workman: US West; 13981 West Cornell Avenue; Lakewood, CO 80228-5302
Mr. Mike Workman: Oracle; 6248 Winston Place West; Bealeton, VA 22712-9318
Ms. Linda Worthington: Newspaper Association of America; 1921 Gallows Road, Suite 600; Vienna, VA 22182
Mr. Joe Wortmann: ComFrame Software Corporation; 2158 Baneberry Drive; Birmingham, AL 35244-1400
Mr. Greham Worton: Petroleum Argus; #15-02 1 Scotts Road; Singapore, Singapore 228208
Ms. Sandy Wotring: Fenestrae; 6455 East Johns Xing, Suite 175; Duluth, GA 30097-1562
Mr. Terry Wozniak: Scitex Digital Printing, Inc.; 3000 Research Boulevard; Dayton, OH 45420-4003
Mr. Barnaby Wray: Zellweger Uster; 4201 Beechwood Road; Knoxville, TN 37920-6011
Mr. Brian Wright: Lending Tree; 10122 Glencrest Drive; Huntersville, NC 28078-5261
Mr. David Wright: Wrytha, Inc.; P.O. Box 1749; Mooresville, NC 28115
Mr. Harvey Wright: Latrobe Area Hospital; 121 West Second Avenue; Latrobe, PA 15650
Mr. Ian Wright: Experian; 945 East Paces Ferry; Atlanta, GA 30326-1125
Mr. Joseph Wright: COPART, Inc.; 5500 East 2nd Street; Benicia, CA 94510-1020
Mr. Robert Wright: Akron Beacon Journal; P.O. Box 640; Akron, OH 44309-0640
Mr. Joseph J. Wrzosek: 3M; 3M Center 224-4N-27; Saint Paul, MN 55144
Dr. Jin Zhong Wu Ph.D.: Applied Digital Technology; 3622 Northeast 4th Street; Gainesville, FL 32609
Mr. Liangfu Wu: Village of Downers Grove; 801 Burlington Avenue; Downers Grove, IL 60515-4776
Dr. Ying-Chieh Wu Ph.D.: Syncsort, Inc.; 50 Tice Boulevard; Woodcliff Lake, NJ 07675-7654
Mr. Thomas A. Wyskiel: Gartner Group, Inc.; 56 Top Gallant Road; Stamford, CT 06902-7700
Mr. Xiaoshi Xing: CIESIN, Columbia University; 61 Route 9 West; Palisades, NY 10964
Mr. Kai Xu: Lucent Technologies, Inc.; 1016 Deer Creek Drive; Plainsboro, NJ 08536-3252
Mr. Matthew Yach: Mankato City Telephone Company; P.O. Box 3248; Mankato, MN 56002-3248
Ms. Lori Yacisin: Forte Systems; 420 Lexington Avenue; New York, NY 10170-0002
Mr. Jim Yahazim: Digigami; 624 Broadway, Suite 200; San Diego, CA 92101-5407
Ms. Trish Yanagisako: Computer Sciences Corporation; P.O. Box 1681; M/S CS20A, CA
Mr. Keith E. Yanchek: Clinical Trial Services; 22661 Audubon Road; Audubon, PA 19403
Mr. Roberto Julio Yanez: Burchfield Ministries; P.O. Box 100; Columbus, TX 78934
Mr. Jisun Yang: United States West Communication Convoy; 930 15th Street #500; Denver, CO 80202-2934
Dr. Xingbo Yang Ph.D.: Speedfam-IDEC; 305 North 56th Street; Chandler, AZ 85226
Mr. Yaochou Angus Yang: IDT, Inc.; P.O. Box 641661; San Jose, CA 95164
Mr. Robin A. Yates: Net Unlimited, Inc.; 119 East Monmouth Street; Winston-Salem, NC 27127-3005
Ms. Gilchrista K. Yau: Federal Reserve Bank of Minneapolis; 90 Hennepin Avenue; Minneapolis, MN 55480-0291
Mr. Henry Ye: New York Business Systems; 1270 Broadway; New York, NY 10004
Mr. Michael Mingchueh Yeh: Allstate Insurance Company; 2844 Floral Drive #G2E; Northbrook, IL 60062
Mr. Nate Yelton: AIS Publications; P.O. Box 42603; Indianapolis, IN 46242-0603
Mr. Hiu K. Yeung: San Fernando Valley Community; 14535 Sherman Circle; Van Nuys, CA 91405-3087
Mr. Philip Yeung: AT&T; 137 Goldmeadow Drive; Cary, NC 27513-4928
Dr. Kevin Yick: DCH (U.S.A.); 1815 West Redondo Beach Boulevard; Gardena, CA 90247
Mr. Cem Yildirim: Cisco Systems; 5729 Fontanoso Way; San Jose, CA 95138
Mr. Brian R. Yniguez: HDC Corporation; 2109 O'Toole Avenue; San Jose, CA 95131
Mr. Frank Yonnett: Computer Systems Solutions; 33 Byers Road; Ottsville, PA 18942-9631
Mr. Chang-Hun Yoon: UUNET; 9411 Lee Highway, Apt. 1204; Fairfax, VA 22031
Mr. Ray York: Welco Lumber Company; 6615 172nd Street Northeast; Arlington, WA 98223-7745
Mr. Neil Yoshida: Hewlett Packard; 3000 Hanover Street; Palo Alto, CA 94304-1112
Mr. Dennis Young: General Manager; 1 Cobblestone Court; Laguna Niguel, CA 92677-5312
Mr. James Young: James Keay Young Consulting; 20115 Sweet Meadow Lane; Gaithersburg, MD 20882-1275
Mr. Kendrick Young: House Ear Institute; 1820 Garvey Avenue; Alhambra, CA 91803-4284
Mr. Kevin E. Young: Key Elements in Design; 1351 No. Curson Avenue, Suite 201; Los Angeles, CA 90046
Mr. Mark Young: Audio Visual Associates; 1 Stewart Court; Denville, NJ 07834-1028
Mr. Wilcox Young: Tri Valley Growers; 12667 Alcosta Boulevard; San Ra-

mon, CA 94583-4427

Mr. Carl Youngblood: Database Technologies, Inc.; 4530 Blue Lake Drive; Boca Raton, FL 33431-4419

Mr. J. Yurso: Q.E.D. Systems, Inc.; 4646 North Witchduck Road; Virginia Beach, VA 23455-6202

Mr. Robert Zacharski: Goldberg, Persky Et Al; 1030 Fifth Avenue; Pittsburgh, PA 15219-6219

Mr. Mark Zahringer: Hotoffice Technologies Inc.; 5201 Congress Avenue; Boca Raton, FL 33432

Ms. Melissa Zanardelli: Bayer Corporation; 100 Bayer Road; Pittsburgh, PA 15205-9741

Ms. Veronica Zanellato: Nervewire, Inc.; 200 Highland Avenue; Needham, MA 02494

Mr. Michael A. Zaneski: Info Trac; 875 Wells Road; Peconic, NY 11958-1732

Mr. Pete Zapulla: Empower Mediamarketing; 455 Delta Avenue; Cincinnati, OH 45226-1127

Mr. Vincent Zarcaro Jr.: Automatic Data Processing; 2106 Ridgeview Court; Parlin, NJ 08859-3132

Mr. Arash Zarei: Datacom; 1710 West Willow Street; Scott, LA 70583-5304

Ms. Natalia Zaretsky: Chase Manhattan Mortgage Company; 300 Tice Boulevard; Wood Cliff Lake, NJ 07675-8405

Mr. Dimitriy Zaslavskiy: Output Technologies; 14480 Sanford Avenue, Apartment 3K; Flushing, NY 11355-1615

Mr. Vyatcheslar Zayarny: Zacks Investment Research; 155 North Wacker Drive; Chicago, IL 60606

Mr. John Zbyszinski: Malco Technologies Inc.; 94 County Line Road; Colmar, PA 18915

Mr. Chaim Zeitz: PEI Partnership Architects; 257 Park Avenue South, Floor 19; New York, NY 10010-7304